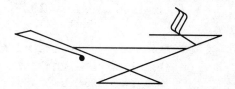

THE ENCYCLOPEDIA

AMERICANA

INTERNATIONAL EDITION

COMPLETE IN THIRTY VOLUMES   FIRST PUBLISHED IN 1829

AMERICANA CORPORATION   International Headquarters: Danbury, Connecticut 06816

Library of Congress Cataloging in Publication Data
Main entry under title:

THE ENCYCLOPEDIA AMERICANA.

Includes bibliographical references and index.
1. Encyclopedias and dictionaries.
AE5.E333   1978   031   77–24222
ISBN 0–7172–0109–0

	EARLY NORTH SEMITIC	PHOENICIAN	EARLY HEBREW (GEZER)	EARLY GREEK	CLASSICAL GREEK	ETRUSCAN		EARLY LATIN	CLASSICAL LATIN
						Early	Classical		
B	૭	⟨	૭	8	B	8		B	B

	CURSIVE MAJUSCULE (ROMAN)	CURSIVE MINUSCULE (ROMAN)	ANGLO-IRISH MAJUSCULE	CAROLINE MINUSCULE	VENETIAN MINUSCULE (ITALIC)	N. ITALIAN MINISCULE (ROMAN)
	ᗅ	ℬ	ხ	b	6	ხ

A.C. SYLVESTER, CAMBRIDGE, ENGLAND

DEVELOPMENT OF THE LETTER B is illustrated in the above chart, beginning with the early North Semitic letter. The evolution of the majuscule (capital) B is shown at top; that of the minuscule (lower-case) at bottom.

B, bē, is the second letter of the English alphabet and of nearly all ancient and modern alphabets. It first appeared about 1500 B.C. in the North Semitic alphabet (see ALPHABET) in the form of the modern capital B and became the prototype of the Greek, Etruscan, Latin, and modern European B. The Greek name *beta* was derived from the North Semitic *beth* and is the basis for the second portion of the word "alphabet." The North Semitic *beth* was derived from *bayith*, the word for "house," but contrary to what is commonly believed, the letter did not represent a house. It was simply a memory device used for teaching purposes.

The capital B exactly corresponds to the ancient Roman and Greek monumental and classical B, which was a symmetrical development of the North Semitic *beth*. The minuscule, or lower case, *b* in use today developed from the Roman cursive (handwritten) letter by eliminating the upper loop of the monumental B.

Pronunciation. The English letter *b* is pronounced by closing the lips and vibrating the vocal chords (as in *ball, brain, beat*) but its phonetic value may change in certain circumstances. When *b* follows *m* it may become mute, as in *dumb, lamb,* and *comb*. Generally speaking, *m* and *b* are closely related; both are bilabial (pronounced with both lips). Sometimes *b* occurs after *m* even though the root word has no *b*, as in the French *nombre* and English *number* from Latin *numerus*. It is also sometimes mute when it precedes *t*, as in *debt* and *subtle*.

In several languages the letter *b* exchanges phonetic value with *v, p, ph, f, m, w,* or *wh*. In the Greek alphabet of about 400 A.D. the phonetic value of *b* changed to that of *v*. As a result, when the Cyrillic alphabet was created in the 9th century, the letter *b* received the phonetic value of *v*, which it still has in Cyrillic alphabets such as Russian, Ukrainian, Serbian, and others. A new letter was then created for the sound of *b* and inserted into the alphabet.

The interchange of the phonetic values of *b, v, p, ph, f, m, w,* and *wh* is apparent when various Indo-European languages are compared. Latin *habere* (to have) and *caballus* (horse) became *avere* and *cavallo* in Italian. English *whale* and German *Wal* (fish) correspond to Latin *balaena*, Italian *balena*, and Greek *phalaina*. English *brother* and German *Bruder* correspond to Sanskrit *bhrâtr*, Greek *phrater*, and Latin *frater*. English *bear* (carry) corresponds to Sanskrit *bharami*, Old German *biru*, and Old Slavonic *bera*, as well as to Greek *pherein*, Latin *ferre*, and Italian *portare*. Latin *ruber* corresponds to English *red*, German *rot*, Sanskrit *rud-*hira, and Greek *eruthros*. Latin *tribus* (tribe) corresponds to the words for village in English (*thorp*), German (*Dorf*), and Gothic (*thaúrp*). And finally, German *heben* corresponds to English *heave*, Sanskrit *kampata*, Greek *kopē*, Latin *capere*, and Old High German *heffan*.

B as a Symbol. In musical notation, the English B (in France and Italy called *si*) represents the seventh note of the diatonic scale of C and was the first note in that scale to be modified by a semitone. In Germany, the English B flat is called B, while the English B is called H. The English B is also the keynote of the B major and B minor scales.

In chemistry, B is the sign of the element boron. In nautical charts, "b" designates blue water. In occult or cabalistic systems of interpretation, B has the numerical value of 2. Finally, B indicates that something is good but not first-rate, as a grade of B in school.

See also ALPHABET.

DAVID DIRINGER, *Author of "The Alphabet"*

Further Reading: See the bibliography for ALPHABET.

B MINOR MASS, a setting of the Latin text of the Mass, written for soloists, chorus, and orchestra, by Johann Sebastian Bach (q.v.). It is Bach's crowning masterpiece and one of the finest expressions of the religious spirit. The Mass is divided into 24 movements—6 arias, 3 duets, and 15 mighty choruses. Because of its huge dimensions, the Mass fits into neither the standard Protestant nor Roman Catholic services.

The first two sections of the B Minor Mass, the *Kyrie* and the *Gloria*, were written in 1733 to support Bach's application for the position of court composer to the elector of Saxony, Frederick Augustus II, who was a Roman Catholic. However, Bach was not appointed until 1736.

The *Kyrie* and *Gloria* were used in the Lutheran liturgy under the title *Missa* (Mass). Bach later expanded his *Missa* into a setting of the Roman Catholic Mass (albeit with certain Lutheran text differences) by writing new music and adapting movements from his earlier cantatas for the *Credo, Osanna, Benedictus, Agnus Dei,* and *Dona nobis pacem*. He also inserted a *Sanctus* he had written in 1724. The complete Mass was published in four sections, each with a separate title page. Bach probably did not intend the B Minor Mass to be performed in sequence as one work. Today when the entire mass is presented, it is often divided between afternoon and evening performances. It is an annual feature of the Bach Festival at Allentown, Pa.

CHARLES N. HENDERSON
Choirmaster, St. George's Church, New York

BA MAW (1897–   ), bä mô, was Burma's first prime minister. He held the office from 1937 to 1939, under a constitution granted by Britain in 1935, and was head of state in Japanese-occupied Burma during World War II.

Born in 1897 of Christian, Mon-Burman parentage, he was educated at St. Paul's mission school in Rangoon, attended Cambridge University, and earned a doctorate in law at the University of Bordeaux. A member of Burma's nationalist Swaraj party from the 1920's, he later joined a faction resisting British-sponsored constitutional reform. In the early 1930's he gained political notoriety through his courtroom defense of the jungle rebel Saya San.

After his term as premier, Ba Maw organized the Freedom Bloc in alliance with the Thakin nationalists to oppose Burma's participation with the Allies in World War II. Interned by the British in 1940, he was released by the Japanese in 1942 and placed in charge of their puppet government. From 1943 to 1945 he was officially Adipati (head of state) of "independent Burma." Following a brief exile in Japan after the war, he returned to Burma, shorn of political influence.

JOHN F. CADY, *Ohio University*

BAADE, bä′də, **Walter** (1893–1960), German-American astronomer, who established two general categories of stars and redetermined the size and age of the universe. He was the discoverer of the asteroids Icarus and Hidalgo. Baade was born in Schröttinghausen, Germany, on March 24, 1893, and received his Ph.D. from Göttingen University. In 1931, he went to Mount Wilson Observatory in California, remaining many years. He died in Göttingen on June 25, 1960.

In the 1940's, Baade began a detailed study of the great spiral galaxy in Andromeda. He found that its stars fell into two general categories: younger stars in the spiral arms, and older stars in the central regions. He called them Population I and Population II stars, respectively.

Certain variables–stars with periodic changes in brightness–had been used in determining distances to the galaxies. In 1952, however, Baade discovered a difference between Population I and II variables of the type being used. Resulting recalculations pushed the galaxies back to more than twice their previously supposed distances. Light takes time to travel, so the age of the universe was also doubled.

BAADER, bä′dər, **Franz Xavier von** (1765–1841), German Roman Catholic theologian and social philosopher. He was born in Munich on March 2, 1765, and studied medicine at Ingolstadt and Vienna. After receiving his medical degree in 1784, he assisted his father, who was court physician to the elector of Bavaria. In 1792 he decided to give up medicine and went to London to study mineralogy. During the four years he remained there he became acquainted with the English rationalist movement, including the empiricist philosophy of David Hume, which he found repellent. He turned then to the mystical works of St. Martin, Meister Eckhart, Jakob Böhme, and the Cabala.

On his return to Munich he was appointed consulting engineer for the Bavarian mines. At the same time he became deeply involved in a philosophical group that included Friedrich von Schelling. Schelling and Baader exerted a reciprocal influence on each other's development:

Baader introduced Schelling to the works of Böhme, and Schelling largely determined Baader's theological ideas. In 1826, Baader was appointed professor of philosophy and speculative theology at the University of Munich. In the same year a ministerial ruling prohibited laymen from teaching theology, and Baader resigned the position. He taught archaeology there until his death in Munich on May 23, 1841.

Baader's mystical philosophy, a reaction to the rationalism of 18th century thought as exemplified by Kant, was based on his conviction that, since Descartes, philosophy had progressively diverged from religion. He attempted to end this divergence by creating a theosophy founded on metaphysical principles and the divine truths revealed in the Old and New Testaments. Unfortunately, Baader did not succeed in creating a philosophical system. His works lack cohesion, and his terminology is obscure and equivocal, so that a synthesis of his ideas is difficult.

His social and political writings are, on the other hand, more clearly expressed. They represent a resolute opposition to the central-state theory. Baader visualized society as united by the universal application of the principle of love; an organic unity was to be achieved by the willing sacrifice of each part for the good of the whole. A society thus based on submission to an acknowledged authority would have as its natural center the universal church–the personification of faith and authority. Baader thus proposed an ideal Christian state, in opposition to the power society implicit in the central-state theory, which, he maintained, could lead only to inequity at home and war abroad. None of Baader's works have yet been translated into English. See also GERMANY–23. *Philosophy* (German Mysticism).

BAAL, bä′əl, is the title or name of certain deities found among Semitic peoples of antiquity. In the Semitic languages, *baal* means primarily "owner," "possessor," or "lord." As a common noun in Hebrew it could mean "husband," for the husband was possessor and lord of his wife. One could speak of the *baal* of a house, ox, or field. Elijah is called a *baal* of hair–a hairy man, or wearer of haircloth (II Kings 1:8). A *baal* of wrath was a man given to anger.

When applied to deities, *baal* was more a title, like the English "lord," than a personal name. The Akkadian form, *bel,* was used in Mesopotamia for the old Sumerian Enlil, god of the air, and later for Marduk, god of Babylon, and Asshur, god of Assyria.

Gods called Baal were found especially among the Canaanites–the people of Palestine and Syria in the 1000's B.C. and later of Phoenicia. They used the name Baal most often for one specific deity, the god of fertility and rain. Much information concerning this divinity comes from cuneiform texts of about 1400 B.C., found at Ras Shamra (ancient Ugarit) in Syria. There Baal was at first the title applied to Hadad, the ancient international storm-god, but Baal came to be used virtually as his name. In the Ugaritic pantheon he was the son of Dagan, god of grain. He was called Prince Lord of the Earth, the Rider of the Clouds, and Baal Zaphon (Lord of Mount Zaphon, a mountain usually covered with rain clouds).

Baal is one of the chief actors in the myths of Ugarit. In one of them he defeats Prince Sea, in a type of creation myth signifying the confinement of the primeval waters to their proper realm. In another myth Baal is the dying-and-rising god of fertility. He reigns in the season when the rains fall and the crops grow. When he dies each year, his place is taken by Mot, god of death and sterility, who represents the drought of summer. Baal's wife-sister, the virgin Anat, searches for him, and eventually he rises again from the netherworld. His rising represents the beginning of the autumnal rains.

In the Old Testament a few specific Baals are mentioned, such as Baal-berith (Lord of covenant), who had a temple at Shechem (Judges 8:33; 9:4), and Baal-zebub, the healing god of Ekron (II Kings 1:2ff.). In the period when the Hebrews were settling in Canaan, it is reported that they periodically forsook their god, Yahweh, to serve Baals (for example, Judges 2:11; 3:7; 8:33; 10:6, 10). These were probably local Canaanite deities adopted by the Hebrews. The name appears in Old Testament place-names, such as Mount Baal-hermon (Judges 3:3), Baal-tamar (Judges 20:33), and Baal-peor (Hosea 9:10). In such places there was doubtless a sanctuary for worship of the Baal who was considered the owner and lord of that place.

In the time of King Ahab, his wife Jezebel—a Phoenician princess—actively promoted the worship of her Baal, probably Melkart, god of Tyre. In the opinion of many scholars, Yahweh was sometimes called a baal, and features of Canaanite Baalistic theology and worship were adapted by the Israelites for their religion. The title baal for Yahweh is implied by certain Old Testament personal names, such as Eshbaal (man of Baal), son of Saul (1 Chronicles 8:33; 9:39), and Bealiah, which may mean "Yahweh is Baal" (I Chronicles 12:5). After full-fledged monotheism was reached, scribes frequently substituted bósheth (shame) for Baal; for example, Eshbaal appears (II Samuel 2:8) as Ishbósheth (man of shame). In New Testament times the name Baal-zebub became a synonym for Satan in the form Beelzebub, or Beelzebul (Matthew 10:25; 12:24, 27).

J. PHILIP HYATT, *Vanderbilt University*

BAAL SHEM TOV, bä'äl shäm tōv (c. 1700–1760), was a Jewish mystic who founded Hasidism. He was born *Israel ben Eliezer,* in Podolia, Russia, about 1700. A student of the Kabala (or Cabala), a body of mystical teachings, he early became known for miraculous cures, performed with the help of God's name. Like other such practitioners, he was popularly referred to as Baal Shem Tov (or Tob), "Master of the Good Name," or, by the initials of these words, as the *Besht.* From about 1740 until his death in 1760, he lived in Miedzboz, Podolia, attracting crowds of disciples by his teachings.

In contrast to traditional Judaism's stress on Talmudic learning, the Besht emphasized an emotional attachment to God. The way to God, he taught, was through fervent prayer, joyful observance of the commandments, and reliance on the Tzaddik, the saintly rabbi who mediates between God and the world. So strong was the appeal of these ideas that within a short time the Hasidic movement conquered a major part of East European Jewry. The Besht had added a new dimension to Jewish religious life. After his death he became a legendary figure. See also JEWISH HISTORY AND SOCIETY—9. *Hasidism.*

RAPHAEL PATAI, *Theodor Herzl Institute*

BAALBEK, bä'əl-bek, is a village in eastern Lebanon famous chiefly for the magnificent Roman temple ruins west of the village. Its Arabic name is *Baalabakk.* The village is attractively situated in an oasis high on the slopes of the Anti-Lebanon Mountains, about 53 miles (85 km) northeast of Beirut.

Baalbek's early history in obscure. It was a flourishing town of ancient Syria when the Greeks occupied it in 331 B.C. They renamed it

BAALBEK'S ROMAN RUINS, dating to the second century A.D., draw thousands of tourists each year.

J. ALLAN CASH FROM RAPHO GUILLUMETTE

THE TEMPLE OF BACCHUS is the best preserved of the Roman temples at Baalbek.

Heliopolis (City of the Sun). About the beginning of the 1st century A.D. the Romans colonized the town. In the course of the next three centuries they constructed on the nearby acropolis a monumental ensemble of two temples, two courtyards, and an enclosing wall built of gigantic stones.

The chief temple, which may have been started in Nero's reign (54–68 A.D.), was dedicated to Jupiter. It was surrounded by a portico of 54 columns. All that remains of the great temple are six of these columns. Each column is about 65 feet (20 meters) high. The other main temple, which was smaller, is the excellently preserved Temple of Bacchus, built about 100 A.D. A tiny round Temple of Venus near the acropolis dates from about 245 A.D. During the decline of paganism, in the 4th century, Emperor Theodosius built a Christian basilica (later destroyed during excavations) in the great court of the Temple of Jupiter.

BAB. See BABISM; BAHAI FAITH.

BAB BALLADS, bab bal'ədz, a collection of humorous and gently satiric verses by William S. Gilbert. He first published them in *Fun* in 1866–1871, using the pseudonym "Bab." They were issued in book form in two series—*Bab Ballads: Much Sound and Little Sense* (1869) and *More Bab Ballads* (1873). In their final editions the ballads also contain many of the songs from the librettos of the Gilbert and Sullivan operettas *Pinafore, The Gondoliers,* and *The Mikado.* About 170 titles are in the collection, which is also enlivened by Gilbert's humorous drawings.

In general the humor of the ballads lies in odd and nonsensical situations, enhanced by an unfailing wit and a buoyant mastery of rhyme and meter. Good examples of the nonsense ballads are *General John, Ferdinando and Elvira, Lorenzo de Lardi, Babette's Love,* and the celebrated *Yarn of the Nancy Bell.* Many of the ballads are also satirical in a mild and good-humored way. "His foe was folly and his weapon wit," reads the inscription on a memorial to Gilbert, and a large number of follies, affectations, and oddities current among his countrymen are handled in light nonsensical vein, but never with ridicule or indignation. Characteristic of

this group are *The Englishman, The Disagreeable Man, Bob Polter, The Aesthete, To the Terrestrial Globe,* and *Etiquette.* The mildly satirical turn is perhaps best illustrated in the well-known first lord's song from *Pinafore,* "When I was a lad I served a term." The satirical touch, as well as the purely humorous attitude, is in nearly all the poems.

BAB EL MANDEB, bab' el man'deb, is the strait between Arabia and the continent of Africa by which the Red Sea is connected with the Gulf of Aden and the Indian Ocean. It is 17 miles (27 km) wide, and is used by shipping between the Indian Ocean and the Suez Canal. The strait contains the bare, rocky island of Perim.

BABA YAGA, bä'bä yä'gä, in Slavonic mythology, is a thunder witch (the devil's grandmother). She is represented as a little, ugly, old woman with a monstrous nose, long teeth, and disheveled hair. She appears in Russian, Czech, and Polish folk tales as a cannibalistic demon who flies through the sky in an iron caldron and uses a broom to sweep her traces from the air.

BABBAGE, bab'ij, **Charles** (1792–1871), English mathematician, who built calculating machines whose design anticipated many features of modern electronic computers. In 1822, Babbage announced the construction of a small calculating machine that could perform intricate mathematical calculations correctly and rapidly. On the recommendation of the Royal Society he received financial backing from the government in 1823 to construct a larger machine (a difference engine).

Babbage abandoned this undertaking about 10 years later in order to build a more complicated device, which he called an analytical engine. This machine worked with punched cards, like the Jacquard loom. However, the government refused to support Babbage in this project, and the machine was never completed, although Babbage devoted 37 years and much of his personal fortune to perfecting it. Lady Lovelace, a daughter of Lord Byron, wrote a program for the analytical engine. See also COMPUTERS—4. *History.*

Babbage was born near Teignmouth, England, on Dec. 26, 1792. He graduated from Peterhouse College, Cambridge, in 1814 and was a professor of mathematics at Cambridge from 1828 to 1839. He died on Oct. 18, 1871. His works include *Table of Logarithms of the Natural Numbers from 1 to 108000* (1827), *On the Economy of Machinery and Manufactures* (1832), and *Passages from the Life of a Philosopher* (1864).

BABBITT, bab'ət, **Irving** (1865–1933), American educator and critic, who, as a classicist and humanist, upheld the traditions of Greek and Oriental thought against 19th and 20th century romanticism and naturalism. He was born at Dayton, Ohio, on Aug. 2, 1865. He graduated from Harvard in 1889 and then went to the Sorbonne in Paris (1891–1892), where he took up Oriental studies. In 1894, after returning to Harvard for further study, he began his long and brilliant career there as a teacher of French, becoming full professor in 1912. He died at Cambridge, Mass., on July 15, 1933.

Babbitt published editions of French authors, a translation of *The Dhammapada* (published posthumously, 1936), and a number of critical and philosophical works, including *Literature and* the American College (1908), *The New Laokoön* (1910), *The Masters of Modern French Criticism* (1912), *Rousseau and Romanticism* (1919), *Democracy and Leadership* (1924), and *On Being Creative and Other Essays* (1932). He also contributed to the symposium *Criticism in America, Its Function and Status* (1924). Two students greatly influenced by Babbitt's teaching were Norman Foerster and T.S. Eliot, although the latter maintained certain reservations.

In his last years Babbitt, together with his friend and fellow humanist Paul Elmer More, originated a controversial literary movement called New Humanism.

Further Reading: Levin, Harry T., *Irving Babbitt and the Teaching of Literature* (Cambridge, Mass., 1961); Manchester, Frederick, and Shepard, Odell, eds., *Irving Babbitt, Man and Teacher* (New York 1941).

BABBITT, bab'it, **Isaac** (1799–1862), American inventor. He was born in Taunton, Mass., on July 26, 1799. A goldsmith by trade, he became interested in the production of alloys, and in 1824 manufactured the first britannia ware to be produced in the United States. At the South Boston Iron Works, of which he became superintendent, he made the first brass cannon ever cast in the United States.

In 1839 he secured a patent for a journal box, suggesting that it be lined with an antifriction metal alloy that became known as Babbitt metal (see ANTIFRICTION METALS). For this important invention he was granted $20,000 by the United States Congress in 1842.

In association with a relative, Benjamin Talbot Babbitt (1809–1889), he later engaged in the manufacture of soap. He died in Somerville, Mass., on May 26, 1862.

BABBITT, bab'ət, is a novel by the American writer Sinclair Lewis (q.v.), published in 1922. It presents in great detail a representative cross section of the life of George Follansbee Babbitt, a prosperous real estate broker in the fictional city of Zenith in the Midwest. Several times in the course of the novel, Babbitt more or less consciously attempts to revolt from the limitations and deadening monotony of his domestic, business, and inner life, but each time finds himself unable to transcend permanently the pressures of his environment and his own poverty of intellect, imagination, and moral character.

Besides Babbitt, who is drawn sympathetically and with great effectivenes and verve, the important characters are his colorless wife, Myra; Paul Riesling, an artist by disposition turned businessman by necessity; Seneca Doane, a persuasive socialist lawyer; and Tanis Judique, an attractive, approachable widow, who surrounds herself with repellent pseudo-Bohemians. Babbitt's three children also figure prominently in the stresses of his family life.

Many critics regard *Babbitt* as the best of the Lewis novels, and there is evidence that the author himself ranked it high among his works. The book is both satirical and realistic, achieving a spirit of comic sadness. The novel has added the name of its hero to the American language, and the word "Babbitt" is included in standard dictionaries. To label someone a Babbitt is to stigmatize him as an obtuse and humorless philistine and a blatant optimist who uncritically and smugly accepts his own standards, however narrow, unenlightened, and unlovely they may be.

BABBITT METAL, bab'ət, is a group of white-colored tin alloys and lead alloys primarily used for machinery bearings. The original Babbitt metal, developed by Isaac Babbitt (q.v.) in 1839, was 88.9 percent tin, 7.4 percent antimony, and 3.7 percent copper. This tin alloy and other similar tin alloys have useful mechanical properties that provide superior performance in heavy service. Lead alloys, predominantly lead but also containing tin, antimony, or copper, are useful in light service. See also ANTIFRICTION METALS.

BABCOCK, bab'kok, **Orville E.** (1835–1884), American army officer. He was born in Franklin, Vt., on Dec. 25, 1835. After graduating from West Point in 1861, he served with distinction in the Civil War, becoming an aide-de-camp to Gen. Ulysses S. Grant in 1864 and a brigadier general of the Regular Army in 1865.

From 1869 to 1877, he was President Grant's private secretary and was also superintendent of buildings and grounds in Washington, D.C. At this time he became associated with a group of men who were defrauding the government of whisky revenues; he is known to have received costly presents from one leader of this group, which was known as the Whiskey Ring. He was indicted for "conspiracy to defraud" in 1875, but following Grant's deposition declaring that his secretary was innocent, Babcock was acquitted at a trial in 1876. He drowned in Mosquito Lagoon, Fla., on June 2, 1884.

BABCOCK, bab'kok, **Stephen Moulton** (1843–1931), American agricultural chemist. He was born in Bridgewater, N.Y., on Oct. 22, 1843. He graduated from Tufts College in 1866, studied chemistry at Cornell University, and received his Ph. D. from the University of Göttingen in 1879. Babcock was a chemist at the New York Agricultural Experiment Station in the 1880's. From 1887 to 1913 he was professor of agricultural chemistry at the University of Wisconsin and chief chemist, later assistant director, of the Wisconsin Agricultural Experiment Station.

In 1890, Babcock perfected a precise method for determining the butterfat content of milk. This test, known as the Babcock test, discouraged adulteration and thinning practices and stimulated the development of better dairy strains. He also invented an apparatus for determining the viscosity of liquids, and did pioneer work on metabolic water and in animal nutrition. He died in Madison, Wis., on July 2, 1931.

BABEL, bä'bəl, **Isaac Emanuilovich** (1894–1941), Russian short-story writer, who was one of the most popular literary figures in the USSR in the 1920's but later fell into official disfavor. He was born in Odessa, Russia, a son of a Jewish shopkeeper. He studied Hebrew, the Bible, and the Talmud at home, then attended a commercial school where he read the Russian classics and learned French. In 1915 he went to St. Petersburg (now Leningrad) to begin a writing career. Maxim Gorki published Babel's first stories in his literary and political magazine *Annals* in 1916 and then advised Babel to get more experience of the world before attempting further writing.

For seven years Babel led an adventurous life. He served in the Russian Imperial Army, the revolutionary forces in the civil war, and the secret police. Babel worked as a reporter and as a copy editor in a printing plant. His experiences as a soldier inspired the nightmarishly savage stories he began to publish in 1924. He also wrote ironically humorous stories of Jewish life in his native Odessa, using the colorful local dialect that is part Yiddish and part Ukrainian. The realism of his war stories was criticized as a defamation of the heroes of the Russian Revolution, and he fell victim to the Stalinist purges of the 1930's. In 1938 he was sent to a concentration camp in Siberia, where he died on March 17, 1941.

Babel wrote compact, tightly constructed stories with sharply developed plots building to highly dramatic climaxes. A careful workman, he wrote polished, rhythmic sentences and phrases. He excelled in the use of contrast, both in plot and language, inserting a sudden flash of poetry into a passage describing physical grotesqueness, or emphasizing intense physical agony by placing it in a commonplace setting. In his folk tales he was able to combine the bitterness characteristic of Jewish humor with the ludicrousness typical of Russian caricature.

He wrote *Odesskiye Rasskazy* (*Odessa Tales*) in 1923–1924. His first war stories appeared in a magazine in 1924 and were collected in the volume *Konarmiya* (1926; Eng. tr., *Red Cavalry*, 1929). He wrote two plays of Jewish life, *Zakat* (*Sunset*) in 1928 and *Mariya* in 1935, which were produced by the Moscow Art Theatre. His last work to appear in the USSR during his lifetime was a tribute to Maxim Gorki in 1938.

In 1957 a carefully censored edition of selections from Babel's works appeared in Moscow. In 1964 the official Soviet literary newspaper *Literaturnaya Gazeta* published some of his letters.

BABEL, Tower of, bā′bəl, in the Bible, a structure built by the descendents of Noah. As related in the Book of Genesis, they journeyed westward after the Flood and settled in the plain of Shinar (probably in the lower Euphrates valley). There they began to build themselves a city with walls and a high tower, in order that they might make themselves a name and not be scattered abroad over the earth. The Lord came to these people, who spoke a single language, and confounded their speech so that they could not understand one another. He also spread them over the face of the earth (Genesis 11:1–9).

This story combines three elements: (1) a primitive account of the origin of the different nations, (2) an explanation of their separate languages, and (3) a statement about the origin of sin in self-centered competition with God. This last element of the story sets forth the problem of man's alienation from men and God. A contrast is found in the New Testament account of Pentecost (Acts 2). On this occasion men were filled with the Holy Spirit and could speak to one another about the works of God.

The name Babel (Babylon) is Assyrian and means "gate of God." Ancient Babylon, partly situated in the plain of Shinar, was a cosmopolitan city of many languages, and the story may reflect an acquaintance with it. The name Babel in Genesis, however, has been connected through popular etymology with a Hebrew root *balal,* "to confuse." The tower described may have been the *ziggurat* of Babylon, a terraced pyramid.

BABES IN THE WOOD. See CHILDREN IN THE WOOD.

BABEUF, bȧ-bûf′, **François Noël** (1760–1797), French revolutionary who advocated a communist society. Also known as *Gracchus Babeuf,* he was born at St.-Quentin on Nov. 23, 1760, the son of a petty government official. His rural background, combined with his early employment as a researcher of feudal claims, convinced him of the need for more equal distribution of land in France.

During the turmoil of 1789, Babeuf committed himself to the revolution. He organized strikes and participated in attacks on government offices. Between 1789 and 1791 he was often imprisoned for ultrarevolutionary activities. Following the downfall of the monarchy in 1792, he was appointed a provincial administrator, first in the Somme region and then in the Montdidier district.

A charge of forgery against Babeuf forced him to give up this second position. He left for Paris, where after much hardship he secured a minor bureaucratic post. In 1794 he was acquitted of the forgery charge. In the same year Babeuf's hero, Robespierre, was toppled from power, and a reaction to the Terror set in.

As editor of the *Journal de la liberté de la presse* (later called *Le tribun du peuple*) in Paris at this time, Babeuf denounced the government that succeeded Robespierre's. Forced into hiding by his opponents, he continued his attacks until he was arrested in February 1795 and sent to prison in Arras.

Babeuf was released from prison late in 1795, went back to Paris, and was soon involved with the society of the Panthéon. This leftist society demanded more political and economic equality for the poor. When police spies infiltrated the movement, Babeuf was forced into hiding for a second time.

During the winter of 1796 opposition to the government increased because the value of paper money had fallen and the distribution of free food had ceased. Babeuf was asked to lead a group, called the Conspiracy of Equals, that would represent the Parisian lower classes. One of the conspirators was the Italian Buonarroti, who had been a supporter of Robespierre and who now looked on Babeuf as the new savior of the lower classes. Buonarroti's writings were later to bring Babeuf's views to the attention of 19th century revolutionists.

Babeuf and his fellow conspirators made elaborate plans for an uprising in the spring, hoping to receive support from discontented soldiers and police as well as the working class. Babeuf wanted to establish a communist society in which existing institutions would be eliminated and property would be communal. Spies had kept the government well informed of Babeuf's intentions, however, and as final preparations were being made, the leaders were arrested on May 10, 1796. After a prolonged trial, Babeuf was sentenced to death. He dramatically tried to commit suicide as the verdict was announced, but he lived to be guillotined the following day, May 28, 1797, at Vendôme.

Babeuf's program for achieving a communist society, known as *Babouvism,* attracted such later revolutionaries as Karl Marx and Lenin. His theories on class war and work—according to which everyone would contribute his labor for the good of all and take according to his needs— were developed in a more sophisticated fashion by later proponents of communism.

BABINGTON, bab'ing-tən, **Anthony** (1561–1586), English conspirator. He was born at Dethick, Derbyshire, England, in October 1561. He served for a time as page to Mary, Queen of Scots, then a prisoner in England. In 1580 he founded a society for the protection of Jesuit missionaries in England. With John Ballard, a Jesuit, and other Catholic emissaries, he formed, in 1586, a plot to murder Queen Elizabeth, rescue Mary, and reestablish the Catholic religion in England.

In working out the plot Babington behaved with indiscretion. He sent letters to Mary, and in reply the imprisoned queen approved of the plot. Sir Francis Walsingham, Elizabeth's secretary, had all the correspondence of the conspirators intercepted, copied, and sent on to their destinations. The conspirators were arrested and brought to trial, and Babington and six others were executed in London Sept. 20, 1586.

Babington's correspondence with Mary led directly to her execution in February 1587. The authenticity of a letter of Mary's to Babington (July 1586), approving Elizabeth's murder, has been questioned by Mary's apologists, and Walsingham has been accused of forging it. Babington considered it genuine; the day he died, he explained the code in which it was written.

BABIRUSA, bab-ərōō'sə, a wild swine native to northern Celebes and the surrounding islands in Indonesia. Also called the *Celebes pig deer*, it is found in the moist forests and along the shores of rivers and lakes. It is recognizable by its long upper tusks, which grow through the top of its muzzle (instead of from the side of the upper jaw) and curve backward. Its lower tusks grow from the sides of the lower jaw. It has an almost hairless, rough, and wrinkled skin that is usually brownish gray, but which is lighter on the underside of the animal. The babirusa is about 34 to 43 inches (86–109 cm) long and may weigh up to 198 pounds (90 kg).

A nocturnal herd animal, it feeds on berries, roots, and grubs. Reproduction takes place early in the year, a litter of two being produced after a 125 to 150-day gestation period. Although officially protected, it is killed for meat.

The babirusa belongs to the order Artiodactyla. There is one species, *Babirussa babirussa*.

Babirusa, the Celebes pig deer.

W. SUSCHITZKY

BABISM, bä'biz-əm, the doctrine of a religious sect founded in Persia by Mirza Ali Muhammad of Shiraz, known as the Bab. In accordance with a revelation that he experienced on May 23, 1844, he believed that he was the expected imam, long awaited by the Shiite Muslims as the herald of the manifestation of God's will. The Bab commanded the shah of Persia, his subjects, and even the kings and princes of the earth to follow him. The doctrines, ethical standards, social principles, and religious laws of the Babi revelation challenged the whole structure of the society in which it was born.

During the short ministry of the Bab (1844–1850), over 20,000 of his followers were put to death in Persia. Two sovereigns of the Kajar dynasty and their chief ministers, supported by the entire Shiite ecclesiastical hierarchy, attempted to stamp out the new revelation, concluding with the execution of the Bab himself in the public square at Tabriz.

Shortly after the announcement of his mission the Bab chose his first disciples, 18 in number, upon whom he bestowed the name Letters of the Living. Entrusting to each a specified task (recalling the words addressed by Jesus to his disciples), he sent them far and wide to the provinces of Persia to tell of the new revelation. None survived the frenzied persecution that grew as the full implications of the Bab's revelation became understood.

Contrary to expectation, the martyrdom of the Bab did not bring this new upsurge of religious conviction and consecration to an end. A few of his followers, known as Azelis, from their leader Subh-i-Ezal, attempted to continue the "Babi" movement. But the majority of those who had become imbued with the Bab's teachings and understood his reference to "He Whom God will make manifest" recognized Bahaullah, a devoted disciple of the Bab, as that manifestation. In 1863, as the 19-year cycle of Bab's pronouncement of his doctrine drew to a close, Bahaullah proclaimed his mission, and henceforth his followers became known as Bahais. Deriving their faith from the Bab's pronouncements, the Bahais affirm God's covenant with man and emphasize the unity of mankind. They urge the elimination of all forms of prejudice and superstition, and they believe that science and religion are not mutually exclusive.

The Bab and Bahaullah are considered by the Bahais to be the cofounders of their faith. See also BAHAI FAITH; BAHAULLAH.

The physical remains of the Bab were secretly buried and hidden in Persia for over 50 years. In 1909 they were transported to Palestine and placed in a shrine prepared by Abdul-Baha, son of Bahaullah, near Acre on Mount Carmel. Today the golden dome of the shrine of the Bab shines forth from the slopes of Mount Carmel and is used as a landmark for the ships entering the Bay of Acre.

Bibliography
Browne, Edward G., ed. and tr., *A Traveller's Narrative Written to Illustrate the Episode of the Bab*, reprint of vol. 2 of 1891 ed. (New York 1930).
Curzon, George N., *Persia and the Persian Question*, 2 vols. (London 1892).
Ives, H.C., *Portals to Freedom* (London 1962).
Nabil-i-Azam, *The Dawn-Breakers, Nabíl's Narrative of the Early Days of Bahá'í Revelation*, tr. by Shogi Effendi (New York 1932).
Shogi Effendi, *The Dispensation of Bahá'u'lláh* (New York 1934).
Younghusband, Sir Francis, *Modern Mystics* (New York 1935).

Gelada baboon, found in Ethiopia.

BABOON, ba-boon', is the common name for several types of mainly terrestrial African monkeys. They are characterized by their large size and distinctly doglike appearance. Their muzzles are elongated, with nostrils usually at the front rather than on the sides. Baboon cheek pouches are well developed for the temporary storage of food, and the males have enormous canine teeth, which may reach a length of two inches (5 cm) and are used in defense. The baboon's fore and hind limbs are nearly equal in length and strongly built, and the animal uses all four limbs in walking. The buttocks of baboons are covered with characteristic seat pads (ischial callosities), surrounded by large areas of naked skin, which may be brilliantly colored in some species.

Baboons are gregarious and have a well-defined social system. They travel in groups ranging from single families to large troops of 200 or more. The groups are under the leadership of a few old adult males. Baboons are aggressive and feed both on plants and on animals. They are active in the day, and at night they sleep in large trees or caves. Baboons breed throughout the year. One young is produced after a gestation period of six to seven months.

Types of Baboons. The baboons form a specialized group of the family Cercopithecidae, which comprises all the tailed monkeys of the Old World. There are about eight recognized species, which are placed in four genera. Specific differences are based chiefly on color, size, and length of tail, but there is some confusion about their nomenclature.

One of the best-known baboon forms is the chacma (*Chaeropithecus ursinus*), found in eastern and southern Africa. It ranges in height from 19 to 45 inches (48 to 114 cm) and may weigh 30 to 90 pounds (14 to 41 kg). Other species in the genus *Chaeropithecus* are the yellow baboon (*C. cynoephalus*), found in central and southern Africa; the smaller, reddish Guinea, or western, baboon (*C. papio*), found in western

and central Africa; and the Doguera baboon (*C. doguera*), found in the rocky open regions of Africa. Members of this genus have protruding muzzles and brown to yellow hair. They do not have the long manes common in other forms.

The baboon that is most interesting historically is the Arabian, or hamadryas (*Comopithecus hamadryas*), found in the hilly regions of Sudan, Ethiopia, and along the eastern border of the Red Sea in Arabia. This is the sacred baboon worshiped by the ancient Egyptians as the companion of Thoth, the god of wisdom magic, and letters. It is identified by the heavy mane of ashy gray hair that grows around the neck and shoulders of the older males.

Two west African baboons that are conspicuously different from others are the mandrills (*M. sphinx*) and drills (*M. leucophaeus*), in the genus *Mandrillus*. They have prominent, colored ridges along each side of their nasal bones, and their seat pads are reddish-purple. They also have a beard, crest, and mane of hair.

The gelada baboon (*Theropithecus gelada*) is found in the high mountainous regions of Ethiopia. It differs from the other genera in having its nostril openings on the sides of the nose rather than at the front. See also MONKEYS.
       JAMES HOWARD MCGREGOR, *Columbia University*

BABSON, bab'sən, **Roger Ward** (1875–1967), American statistician, economist, and business educator, who established advisory services for investors and pioneered in developing charts to forecast business trends. He was born in Gloucester, Mass., on July 6, 1875. He graduated from Massachusetts Institute of Technology in 1898 and gained early experience in the investment field in New York and Boston.

In 1904, at Wellesley, Mass., he founded the Babson Business Statistical Organization, which provided data on securities, together with interpretations, for banks and other investors. This led to development of *Babson's Reports,* consisting of information on when and what to buy and sell, and the Babson-Chart for business forecasting, developed from Sir Isaac Newton's law of action and reaction. Babson's interest in Newton led to his accumulation of the world's second-largest collection of Newtoniana.

In World War I, Babson served as director general of information and education under the U. S. secretary of labor. In 1919 he established a school, the Babson Institute of Business Administration, at Wellesley, Mass. With his wife, Grace, he founded Webber College, a similar school for women at Babson Park, Fla., and the Midwest Institute of Eureka, Kans. He published many books, including *Business Barometers and Investments* and *Business Fundamentals.* Babson died at Mountain Lake, Fla., on March 5, 1967.
       PAUL N. TAYLOR, *University of Connecticut*

BABUR, bä'bər, **Zahiruddin Mohammed** (1483–1530), the founder of the Mughul dynasty of India. The name, from a Mongol word meaning "tiger," also is spelled *Babar* or *Baber.* A Chugtai Turk, Babur was a descendant of Timur (*Tamerlane*) and Genghis (*Chingiz*) Khan. In 1493 he inherited the principality of Fergana in Turkestan from his father, Sheikh Omar Mirza. His ambition was to establish himself at Samarkand, the center of the Timurid renaissance in the 15th and 16th centuries. For brief periods in 1497, 1501, and 1511, Babur's forces occupied Samarkand but was driven off by the Uzbek Turks; he lost Fergana in 1503. Thereafter, until 1525, he maintained himself at Kabul, raiding from there both central Asia and northwestern India, though without success. At Kabul, he came under Safavid cultural influences and cultivated Persian tastes.

In 1526 he led his fifth raid against India. Success against Ibrahim Lodi at the battle of Panipat gave him control of Delhi and Agra. A year later at the battle of Khanwa he crushed the Rajput confederacy led by Rana Sangram Singh of Mewar. In May 1529 he completed his conquest of northern India by overcoming the Afghan rulers of Bihar and Bengal. He died on Dec. 26, 1530, at Agra, and was buried in Kabul.

Babur laid the foundation of Mughul rule in India, later consolidated by his grandson, Akbar (q.v.). He had ambivalent feelings toward India, which he considered was suffering from the triple curse of heat, dust, and strong winds; but having lost his ancestral base, Samarkand, he wanted to be compensated in India. He ordered a new capital to be laid out at Agra and imported Persian architects to design it. So strong was his love for natural beauty that wherever he went in India he set up gardens. A man of considerable literary ability, he left several poems in Turkish and Persian, a work on prosody, and the exquisite *Diaries* (*Babarnama*), which contain authentic accounts of Hindu customs and social institutions and Indian flora and fauna.

BRIJEN K. GUPTA, *Brooklyn College, New York*

BABYLON, bab'ə-lən, a city in ancient Mesopotamia, was located beside the Euphrates River about 55 miles (88 km) south of modern Baghdad and just north of modern Hilla in central Iraq. Probably in existence from the 3000's B.C., the small city-kingdom of Babylon first achieved significance as the headquarters of Semitic Amorite invaders. Under the sixth of the Amorite kings, Hammurabi, the old Babylonian empire reached its zenith, and Babylon as the capital became the most important commercial center of the Tigris-Euphrates Valley.

After the fall of the old Babylonian empire, a line of Kassite kings made Babylon their capital, and later it came under Assyrian rule. The Assyrian king Sennacherib completely destroyed Babylon in 689 B.C. But the town was rebuilt and soon became the capital of the Semitic Chaldeans who established the Chaldean or Neo-Babylonian empire, which reached its greatest magnificence under Nebuchadnezzar II. The "Hanging Gardens" and the Ishtar Gate date from this time. The city was taken by the Persians under Cyrus the Great in 539 B.C. Later Alexander the Great planned to make Babylon the capital of his eastern empire, but after his death Babylon gradually lost importance. Extensive, systematic archaeological excavations were not begun until the early years of the 20th century.

BABYLON, bab'ə-lən, a residential village in New York, is situated in Suffolk County on the south shore of Long Island, 37 miles (59.4 km) east of New York City. It is a fishing and boating center, and has a free public bathing beach. Belmont Lake State Park is just north of the village. The Robert Moses Causeway, a toll bridge to Captree State Park and to Robert Moses State Park on Fire Island, is two miles (3 km) east of Babylon. Government is by a mayor and council. Population: 12,897.

BABYLONIAN EMPIRE
▨ Babylonian Empire in 1686 B.C., at end of Hammurabi's reign

BABYLONIA, bab-ə-lō′nyə, was the name applied to southeastern Mesopotamia (now southern Iraq), between the Tigris and Euphrates rivers. It was bounded in ancient times by Elam on the east, the Persian Gulf on the southeast, the Arabian Desert on the south and west, and Assyria on the north. The name itself is quite late. In early times the region was called *Sumer* and *Akkad*, and under the Kassites, *Karduniash*. Among its chief cities were Babylon, Nippur, Erech (modern Warka), Larsa, Ur, Eridu, and Borsippa. Babylon became the political center of the land with the reign of Hammurabi (about 1700 B.C.).

The earliest settlements in Iraq—Hassuna, Samarra, and Tell Halaf in northern Mesopotamia —date from the Neolithic and Chalcolithic ages (before 3500 B.C.). The el-Obeid and Warka periods (about 3600–3000 B.C.) represent the beginning of settled culture in Babylonia proper, which had previously been marsh land. The earliest Babylonian inscriptions come from Erech and date before 3000 B.C. They are in a pictographic precursor of the cuneiform script that dominated Middle Eastern literary and commercial life for centuries.

Sequence of Control in Babylonia—Sumerians. A non-Semitic people, the Sumerians, controlled Babylonia until about 2300 B.C. Their civilization is now well known, especially from excavations at Ur, Nippur, and Lagash. Sumerian civilization was dominated by priests; at the head of the state was the *lugal* (literally "great man"), the representative of the gods. Sumerian religion was polytheistic. Probably each city-state originally had its own god, who was regarded as cosmic in power; but with the unification of the country, these tended to be fused into one, or to become mere aspects of one supreme deity. The Sumerians placed Anu, god of heaven, at the head of the pantheon, with Enlil, god of the storm, at his side. Enlil's shrine at Nippur was a center of cult in ancient Mesopotamia. Sumerian religious life centered about the ziggurats or staged templetowers.

A vast Sumerian literature is extant, much of which was reworked or echoed, not only in Babylonia and Assyria, but also in Hurrian and Hittite writings. Much of it is in epic form, but there are also hymns, incantations, lamentations, and proverbs. Many of the epics deal with the origins of the world. We find epic narratives of creation (expanded later in Babylonian into *Enuma elish*), episodes in the career of Gilgamesh (developed by the Babylonians into the Gilgamesh Epic), the narrative of the descent of Inanna (later Ishtar) to the Nether World, the story of the slaying of the Dragon (Babylonian *Tiamat*), and many others.

Akkad and Ur. From inscriptions found at Mari on the middle Euphrates and from other evidence, it is known that Semites had long been settled in Mesopotamia and that they finally gained the upper hand in the 24th century B.C. The dynasty of Akkad (about 2360–2180 B.C.), headed by Sargon, was the first Semitic empire in Mesopotamia, although Sumerian language, religion, and art lived on. Sargon and his successors ruled much of the Middle East, penetrating even into Anatolia. Under them the arts flourished.

The dynasty of Akkad collapsed about 2180 B.C. before the onslaughts of Guti barbarians from the Zagros Mountains. Then Sumerian culture enjoyed a renaissance, and the succeeding kings of the 3d dynasty of Ur (about 2060–1950 B.C.) ruled over an empire almost as great as that of the dynasty of Akkad. Ur-nammu, the first of the new kings, published the earliest law code yet recovered from Babylonia, dating before 2000 B.C.

Old Babylonian Period. After 1900 B.C. the Mesopotamian states gradually came under Amorite (West Semitic) influence. A number of independent Amorite states flourished in this period, including Larsa, Eshnunna, Mari, and Babylon. Wars and intrigues between them preceded the final victory of Hammurabi (1728–1686 or 1792–1750 B.C.), sixth king of Babylon's 1st dynasty, over Rimsin, king of Larsa, and other rivals.

Among the most noteworthy of Hammurabi's achievements was the promulgation of his famous law code. Moreover, a golden age of Babylonian science and scholarship was made possible in this period by the stability which Hammurabi's reign brought to Babylonia. In many fields, a standardization of learning, accepted in following centuries, is evident. Long lists of cuneiform signs and dictionaries of both Sumerian and Akkadian, the former still the language of learning, were compiled. Babylonian astronomers kept records of the movements of the planets and made lists of the stars and constellations. Besides astrology, other types of divination and magic were fostered and standardized. Solution of quadratic equations by Diophantine methods was developed. To the Babylonians are owed the 24-hour day and the system of counting 360 degrees in a circle.

Hittites, Hurrians, and Kassites. Decline was steady after Hammurabi's death. Finally the Hittite king, Mursil I, came from Anatolia and destroyed Babylon about 1530 B.C. The non-Semitic Hurrians (Biblical Horites) and their Indo-Aryan chieftains then established the kingdom of Mitanni in the north, while the non-Semitic Kassites overwhelmed the Amorite dynasty of Babylonia, founding a dynasty that lasted nearly 400 years.

Assyrian Empire. In the mid-14th century B.C., Assyria, profiting from the decline of Mitanni, rapidly came into prominence, and most of the subsequent history of Mesopotamia centers here in the northern Tigris Valley. Elam, Babylon's traditional foe, also became strong, and its kings repeatedly invaded Babylonia. Only one outstanding Babylonian king appears at this time, Nebuchadnezzar I, of the 2d dynasty of Isin, who came to the throne in the late 12th century; he defeated Elam and held Assyria at bay.

Assyrian power was in eclipse for 150 years (about 1075–925 B.C.), but Babylonia was unable to take advantage of this respite because of the infiltration of another wave of Semites, known as the Aramaeans. By the mid-11th century an Aramaean was on the Babylonian throne. Meanwhile, the related Chaldeans were pushing north from the shores of the Persian Gulf to settle in southern Babylonia about the start of the 10th century B.C., and by the 8th century their acculturation appears to have become complete.

Assyria began to rebuild her empire toward the end of the 10th century B.C. and for several centuries controlled Babylonian political life, dislodging the Chaldeans repeatedly. In the end, however, the Chaldeans won control of the land. As a rule, Assyrian kings treated Babylonia with great consideration, because of the latter's enormous religious and cultural prestige. In fact, the Assyrians absorbed Babylonian civilization almost completely. Most Assyrian kings were especially careful to respect the cult of Marduk (Biblical Merodach) at Babylon.

After defeating the Chaldean and Aramaean chiefs, Tiglath-pileser III of Assyria proclaimed himself king of Babylon (729 B.C.). During Sargon II's reign, Marduk-apal-iddina (the Biblical Merodach-baladan), a Chaldean prince, made himself king of Babylon, allied himself with Elam, and resisted Assyria for 12 years until 709. The strife between Babylonia and Assyria came to a climax a few years later; the city of Babylon was destroyed (689 B.C.), and the Marduk statue carried off to Assyria.

But Marduk was still destined to win. Esarhaddon again favored Babylonia, rebuilt the city, and restored its privileges. However, before his death, the empire was divided again, with Ashurbanipal ruling over Assyria, and his brother, Shamash-shum-ukin, over Babylonia—a condition which erupted into a ferocious civil war ending in the devastation of Babylon in 648. Upon Ashur-

"THE OLDEST WRITTEN POLITICAL HISTORY," compiled 4,500 years ago by a ruler of Lagash, is in Sumerian.

banipal's death, however, a Chaldean prince, Nabopolassar, gained control of Babylon, and allied himself with the Medes to the north; together they destroyed the Assyrian empire.

Neo-Babylonian Empire. For a time it appeared as if Babylonia had finally regained its ancient position in the Middle East. For three quarters of a century Babylon prospered, particularly under the famous Nebuchadnezzar II (604–562). This Neo-Babylonian empire was the greatest achievement, politically as well as culturally, of the Aramaean-Chaldean fusion in Babylonia.

Nebuchadnezzar's first great achievement was the victory at Carchemish on the upper Euphrates River in 605 B.C. over the Egyptian forces that had moved into the Middle East, ostensibly to aid the Assyrians. Thereafter, Babylonia held sway over all Syria and Palestine as far as the Egyptian border. Its troops also invaded Egypt and occupied Cilicia. However, Nebuchadnezzar is probably best known for his destruction of Judah and Jerusalem in 587 B.C. and the ensuing Babylonian Captivity of the Jews. Outside of this we know very little of his military activities, because, following the Babylonian tradition, he preferred to boast of his religious and architectural activity and to say nothing of his wars. He rebuilt the temple of Marduk in Babylon and constructed the "Hanging Gardens" (one of the Seven Wonders of the World). Also to be noted is the rapid development of Chaldean astronomy and astrology in this period.

But Babylon's days were numbered. The last king, Nabonidus, spent some eight years at Teima (Tema), an oasis in North Arabia, leaving his son Bel-shar-ushur (the Biblical Belshazzar) in active control.

Persians and Greeks. In 539 B.C. Babylon fell without a struggle to the Achaemenid Persian, Cyrus the Great. For a time it lived on, but after a final revolt in 514 against Darius the Great (521–485 B.C.), the city's walls were destroyed.

Babylon gradually declined in the Hellenistic period and was abandoned before the time of Christ. But the world still owes an enormous debt to the ancient civilization of Babylonia, which, through its influence upon Hebrew and Greek cultures, has contributed enormously to the civilization of the West.

Daily Life in Babylonia. The Babylonians were dependent on irrigation for agriculture, since winter rains in that region tend to be scanty and, when they do come, they pour down with destructive violence. Water for irrigation came from the Euphrates and Tigris rivers and the eastern tributaries of the Tigris. At a very early date—probably no later than the 5000's B.C.—the Babylonians began to build barrages across smaller streams, as well as deflector dams to catch flash floods. Before the dawn of written history they had developed an elaborate system of canals flanked by earthen dikes.

In Babylonian texts of all periods, much attention is paid to restoring canals that had fallen into disrepair. About 140 B.C. the irrigation system collapsed, probably because of the destructive Parthian conquest. The dikes that held back the waters of the Tigris and Euphrates were broken, and new riverbeds were formed; the modern courses of these rivers are almost entirely different from their ancient courses. Eventually the soil became saturated with mineral salts, and a crust of alkali formed over the surface, making agricultural use impossible.

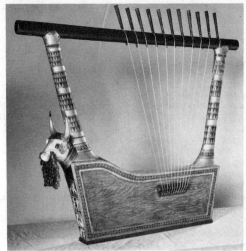

UNIVERSITY MUSEUM, PHILADELPHIA

SUMERIAN HARP, embellished with gold foil and lapis lazuli, was found during excavations at Ur.

The Babylonians depended heavily on agricultural staples such as barley and emmer for bread and sesame for oil. Dates took the place of most other fruit and sugar, and date palm logs were used in building. Onions, garlic, and marrows were common vegetables. Meat was an important part of the diet, and fowl and fish were eaten. Large and small cattle, goats, and sheep were raised for milk and flesh, hides, and wool, and donkeys were used for transport. Barley straw, sesame cakes, and other roughage were used as fodder.

Crafts were developed at an early stage, but the lack of raw materials, outside of agricultural products, made it necessary to import supplies from Anatolia, Syria, Iran, and Armenia. Agricultural surpluses provided a solid basis for trade, animal husbandry provided material for a flourishing textile industry, and imported raw materials made it possible to develop cabinet-making, gem-cutting, and metal-working industries. Since all articles of commerce had to be transported by donkey before the development of camel transport about the 12th century B.C., manufacturing was concentrated on luxury items.

In support of Babylonian economic life, great emphasis was laid on bookkeeping, which during the 3d dynasty of Ur (about 2000 B.C.) included a simple but adequate system of double-entry accounting. In fact, the practice of keeping accurate records is responsible for most of man's knowledge of the daily life of the Babylonians.

WILLIAM F. ALBRIGHT, *Johns Hopkins University*

Bibliography

Albright, William F., *From the Stone Age to Christianity* 2d ed. (Baltimore 1957).
Finegan, Jack, *Light from the Ancient Past* (Princeton 1949).
Frankfort, Henri, *Kingship and the Gods* (Chicago 1948).
Frankfort, Henri, *The Birth of Civilization in the Near East* (Bloomington, Ind., 1951).
Gadd, Cyril J., *History and Monuments of Ur* (London 1929).
Kramer, Samuel N., *Sumerian Mythology* (Philadelphia 1944).
Oppenheim, Adolf Leo, *Ancient Mesopotamia* (Chicago 1964).
Pritchard, James B., ed., *Ancient Near Eastern Texts Relating to the Old Testament*, 2d ed. (Princeton 1955).
Rogers, Robert W., *A History of Babylonia and Assyria* 5th ed. (New York 1925).
Saggs, Henry W.F., *Everyday Life in Babylonia and Assyria* (New York 1965).

BABYLONIAN CAPTIVITY, bab-ə-lō'nē-an kap-tiv'ə-tē, is the term commonly applied to the deportation to Babylonia of the Hebrews who were inhabitants of Judah (Judea) in the early part of the 6th century B.C. Traditionally, the Babylonian Exile, as it is also called, lasted 70 years. Various aspects of the Exile and Restoration are described in the Old Testament books of Jeremiah, Ezekiel, Daniel, Ezra, Nehemiah, II Kings, II Chronicles, and others.

The Babylonian king Nebuchadnezzar adopted the Assyrian policy of deporting conquered peoples in order to reduce local nationalism. He deported captives from Judah at least three times (Jeremiah 52:28–30). The first deportation (II Kings 24: 1–16) came in 598 B.C., following the Babylonian siege of Jerusalem, capital of Judah. The siege had been provoked by the rebellion of King Jehoiakim against his Babylonian overlords. Before the city surrendered, Jehoiachin ascended the throne of his father Jehoiakim and afterward was carried into captivity with many subjects. Traces of this period of the Exile remain in Babylonia, notably the cuneiform tablets found by German archaeologists, which list among the persons receiving rations "Yaukin, king of Judah" (Jehoiachin) and five royal princes, as well as other Jews.

The treachery of Zedekiah, set up as regent by Nebuchadnezzar, resulted in the complete destruction of Jerusalem in 587 B.C. and the deportation of all but the poorest inhabitants of Judah (II Kings 24:20–25:12). A third deportation followed in 582 B.C. All ancient towns of Judah that have been studied by archaeologists were destroyed at this time. Some were never rebuilt; others were rebuilt only after long intervals.

Conditions in Babylonia were at first very difficult for the Jews, but they gradually improved. As the exiles became more satisfied in their new surroundings, they began to lapse from their traditional religion, Yahwism. Yet there were some among them, like the prophet Ezekiel, who were faithful to their God and longed to return to their ancient homeland, dreaming of the restoration of their nation to the splendor of the Davidic and Solomonic kingdom.

In 538 B.C. the Persian king Cyrus issued an edict permitting the Jews to return to their homeland. Ancient accounts of this edict have been substantially confirmed by modern archaeological discoveries. However, the dangerous and expensive journey and the uncertainties of a troubled Palestine discouraged any wide response. The first group to return laid the foundations of a new temple, and under the leadership of Zerubbabel, grandson of Jehoiachin and governor of Judea, the second group completed the temple in 515 B.C. (Ezra 1–6). With the aid of Nehemiah, cupbearer to the Persian king Artaxerxes and later governor of Judea, the wall was rebuilt about 439 B.C. (Nehemiah 1–13). The mission to Palestine of Ezra, scribe and reformer (Ezra 7–10), who with Nehemiah dominates this period of Jewish history, seems to have been somewhat later. See also BIBLE: *Old Testament History;* EZEKIEL.

In Christian church history the term "Babylonish Captivity" has been applied to the period of papal residence at Avignon in southern France from 1309 to 1377.

W.F. ALBRIGHT
The Johns Hopkins University

BACĂU, bä-kŭ'oo, is an industrial city in northeastern Rumania. It is the capital of Bacău region in the former province of Moldavia. Situated on the Bistriţa River, near its confluence with the Siret, the city is also an important rail junction and communications and commercial center.

Bacău is in one of Rumania's largest oilproducing regions. The city markets and ships petroleum, and manufactures all kinds of oilfield equipment. Other manufactures include woolen and cotton textiles, blankets, leather goods, food products, hardware, clay products and pottery, glue, light machinery, and building materials. There are also woodworking, meatprocessing, and flour-milling plants. Large paper and pulp mills are near the city.

Bacău is believed to have been settled as early as the 400's A.D., but it did not become important until the 1900's when oil was discovered nearby. During World War I, the city was the headquarters of the Rumanian army. Before World War II, about half of the city's population were Jews. Most of them were executed or deported before 1944. Population: (1963) 65,763.

BACCHAE, The, bak'ē, a tragedy by Euripides posthumously produced in Athens by the author's son, probably in 405 B.C. With two other plays, the extant *Iphigenia at Aulis* and the lost *Alcmeon at Corinth,* it was awarded first prize in the drama contest. All three plays must have been written during the poet's retirement from Athens at the court of King Archelaus of Macedonia.

The Story. The plot of *The Bacchae* concerns the efforts of King Pentheus of Thebes to crush the worship of Dionysus (Bacchus), his own cousin. A Stranger (Dionysus) with a band of female Bacchanalians (Bacchae) invades Thebes. The Bacchae are peaceful, but if opposed, they are roused to ecstatic madness. Although he is warned by his grandfather Cadmus and by the prophet Tiresias that Dionysus must be acknowledged, Pentheus captures the Stranger. A mysterious earthquake frees him, however, and he hypnotically induces Pentheus to dress in female clothing and go into the woods to spy on the Bacchic band. A messenger narrates the sequel: Pentheus is detected and torn to pieces by the wild women, led by his own mother, Agave. Then Agave enters, carrying her son's head. As she gradually regains her senses, Dionysus, who had announced his coming triumph in the Prologue, appears without disguise and pronounces further penalties on the Theban royal house.

Interpretations. Interpretations of this macabre masterpiece differ sharply. Some critics consider it an object lesson against religion, or at least against orgiastic religion. Other critics contend that Euripides is urging recognition of the divine element in man.

A unique feature of the play is the presence of the god Dionysus, for although the Athenian dramatic festivals were held in honor of this god, very few tragic plots had any connection with him. Scholars assume that Euripides became interested in the cult of Dionysus because of his experience in Macedonia, a center of Dionysianism.

RICHMOND Y. HATHORN
Author of "Tragedy, Myth, and Mystery"

BACCHUS AND ARIADNE, by the 16th century Venetian master Tintoretto, shows one of the tales about Bacchus. Wearing vine leaves, he is about to wed Ariadne, while Venus gives a crown and ring to the bride.

BACCHANALIA, bak-ə-nãl′yə, were festivals in ancient Greece in honor of Bacchus (Dionysus). They were marked by much drinking and revelry and were often riotous and licentious. The celebrants, known as *Bacchantes*, originally were women but later men were included. They wore fawn skins, ivy on their heads, and carried *thyrsi* (staffs topped with pine cones).

Under the Romans the festivals became so dissolute that they were abolished by the Senate in 186 B.C., but they were reintroduced in the 1st century A.D. See also BACCHUS.

BACCHUS, bak′əs, in Greek and Roman mythology, the god of wine, known originally to the Greeks as *Dionysus* and later to the Romans as *Liber.* He was also the god of vegetation and of fertility, and in these offices he was worshiped perhaps as widely as Apollo. It was as the god of wine, however, that Bacchus was uniquely important, and in this capacity he represented at once the intoxicating and the beneficial influences of wine. Thus, his worship could lead to riotous revelry or debauchery (see BACCHANALIA), or it could encourage the promotion of civilization and culture. The festivals in his honor at Athens gave rise to the earliest Greek dramatic performances, so that Bacchus is regarded as the father of Greek drama.

Bacchus was the son of Zeus (Jupiter) and Semele, daughter of King Cadmus of Thebes, whom the god had courted in human form. Jealous of her husband Zeus' love for Semele, Hera (Juno) persuaded Semele to ask Zeus to appear before her in all his godly majesty. Zeus consented, and when he came before Semele amid thunder and lightning, she was burned to ashes. Bacchus, who was born prematurely, was saved by Zeus, who sewed him up in his thigh. A few months later, Bacchus had his second birth on Mount Nysa, once thought to have been in Thrace, but subsequently regarded as an imaginary place.

At Nysa, Bacchus was reared by nymphs, shepherds, and satyrs, and at some time in his development he learned the secrets of cultivating grapes and making wine. As a youth he was educated by Silenus, the oldest of the satyrs and the son of Pan, a wise, genial, old man given to bouts of drinking. In painting, Bacchus is often portrayed in the company of the satyrs, with Silenus at their head, who play the flute for his amusement and pour his wine.

On reaching manhood, Bacchus was rendered insane by Hera, who feared his newly discovered powers. Leaving Nysa, he traveled east and came to Phrygia, where the goddess Rhea cured him and taught him her religious rites. On the island of Naxos he met and married Ariadne, who had been deserted there by Theseus. Legend has it that Bacchus spent several years in India, where he taught the arts of cultivating grapes and making wine. On his return to Greece, he was accepted with enthusiasm, especially by women, and centers of his worship sprang up in Thrace, Thebes, Delphi, Athens, and in Asia Minor.

Like Apollo, Bacchus could be both a benevolent and a wrathful god—indulgent to those who accepted his rites or sought his counsel, vengeful to those who spurned him. For example, in Thebes, where his cousin Pentheus was king, the worship of Bacchus was forbidden at first. The women of Thebes, however, ignored the prohibition. During a celebration, Pentheus was torn to pieces by Agave, his mother, and Autonoë and Ino, his sisters, who in their frenzy had mistaken him for a wild boar.

In time the worship of Bacchus was regularized in Greece, and a cycle of festivals was held in his honor, beginning in December and ending in March. Essentially, these festivals had to do with the ritual of opening casks of new wine and were accompanied by general merriment and amnesty. Slaves and prisoners were set free, and the goods of debtors could not be seized. Drinking contests were held, and there were competitions in drama. In later times, when the worship of Bacchus was introduced into Rome, the festivals became so violent and licentious that in 186 B.C. they were outlawed by the Senate.

In his most typical representations, Bacchus was a youthful god—handsome, beardless, with long hair, and wearing vine leaves or ivy on his head. Many pictures show him riding on a panther or lion and carrying a *thyrsus* (a rod with a pine cone at the top). Sometimes he was depicted wearing the skin of a stag and with horns on his forehead.

BACCHYLIDES, bə-kil′i-dēz, a Greek poet of the early 5th century B.C., was an important younger rival of Pindar. Little is known about his life. He was born probably at Iulis, on the island of Ceos (now Kea). He was the nephew of Simonides, poet to Hiero I, tyrant of Syracuse. Bacchylides lived for a time at Hiero's court, and he also may have lived in Macedonia and Peloponnesus. He died probably at the time of the outbreak of the Peloponnesian War (431 B.C.).

Until 1896, Bacchylides was known only from fragments of his verse, but in that year Sir Frederic Kenyon discovered a well-preserved papyrus with a number of complete poems by Bacchylides. The papyrus, which Kenyon translated and published in 1897, contained 6 dithyrambs (poems usually in praise of Dionysus) and 13 epinicia (songs of triumph in war or games). The dithyrambs, which were in alphabetical order according to the first letters of their titles, tend to be simple ballads rather than extravagant, impassioned paeans to Dionysus. The epinicia, addressed to persons living in various parts of the Greek world—Athens, Thessaly, Macedonia, Syracuse—indicate that either the poet or his reputation had traveled far.

Bacchylides was a competent craftsman. His language is simple and clear, his style graceful and controlled, and his verses polished and elegant. But his ideas are commonplace, and his learning is often mere cataloging. The epithets he invented are unimaginative, and those he borrowed are not always apt. Nevertheless, he was among the last important lyric poets of the Periclean age.

BACCIO DELLA PORTA. See BARTOLOMMEO, FRA.

BACCIOCCHI, bät-chôk′kē, **Felice Pasquale** (1762–1841), French army officer. He was born in Corsica on May 18, 1762. An officer of good though impoverished family, in 1797 he married Maria Anna Elisa Bonaparte (1777–1820), oldest sister of Napoleon Bonaparte. Napoleon promoted him to general and made him a senator of France in 1804. He shared the fortunes of his wife, who was made Princess of Lucca and Piombino in 1805 and Grand Duchess of Tuscany in 1809. After Napoleon's fall, Bacciocchi and his wife lived on her estate near Trieste until her death. He died in Bologna on April 27, 1841.

BACH, bäкн, **Baron Alexander von** (1813–1893), Austrian government official. He was born in Loosdorf, Lower Austria, on Jan. 4, 1813. A lawyer and liberal, Bach was a leader of the March 1848 revolution in Vienna. Nevertheless, in October 1848 he accepted the post of minister of justice in the counter-revolutionary government led by Prince Felix von Schwarzenberg, and became minister of the interior in 1849.

The Schwarzenberg government was no less radical than the liberal regime that preceded it. As contemptuous of the old conservative aristocracy as it was hostile to the revolutionaries, its purpose was to suppress the traditional privileges of the various crown lands and to subject the entire Habsburg monarchy to an authoritarian, uniform, centralized, Germanizing bureaucratic administration. The support of the Catholic Church was sought, and, ironically, it was Bach, the one-time revolutionary, who negotiated a concordat with the Vatican in 1855.

After Schwarzenberg's death in 1852, Bach was the leading member of the ministry, and the experiment in centralization carried on until 1859 is usually identified as the "Bach system." The new regime, however, offended the national sensibilities of the non-German peoples of the monarchy. Hungary in particular, whose privileged status had been abolished in 1848, was restive and, it was feared, disloyal. The Austrian failure in the Italian war of 1859 and the danger of internal disintegration brought an end to the centralizing policies of Bach. He was dismissed, and a series of federal experiments was undertaken. Bach served as Austrian ambassador to the Vatican from 1859 to 1867. He died in Schönberg, Germany, on Nov. 12, 1893.

BACH, bäкн, **Carl Philipp Emanuel** (1714–1788), German musician and composer. He was born at Weimar on March 8, 1714. A precocious child, he was the second son of Johann Sebastian Bach, under whom he gained his early musical training. While still in his childhood, he composed a number of creditable keyboard pieces. In 1734 he began study at the University of Frankfurt, where he actively participated in the local musical life. In 1740, in Frankfurt, he became a member of the court orchestra of King Friedrich Wilhelm II of Prussia. In 1756, though still in the king's service, he went to Berlin, where he taught and established his reputation as a keyboard performer of the first rank. Quitting the king's service in 1767, he went to Hamburg, where he served as music director of several churches. He died in Hamburg on Dec. 15, 1788.

The music of Carl Philipp Emanuel Bach, unlike that of his father, places little emphasis on contrapuntal technique, relying instead on graceful melodic lines. He wrote numerous orchestral works, although, justifiably, he is best remembered for his keyboard compositions, which include nearly 70 sonatas. His church music includes four Easter cantatas, a *St. Matthew Passion*, a *St. Luke Passion*, and numerous motets and settings of psalms and litanies.

BACH, bäкн, **Johann Christian** (1735–1782), German composer and musician. He was born at Leipzig on Sept. 5, 1735, the youngest son of Johann Sebastian Bach, from whom he received his early musical training. After his father's death in 1750, he went to live in Berlin with his half-brother, Wilhelm Friedemann Bach. In 1756 he moved to Bologna, where he studied under Padre Martini and composed a considerable amount of church music. In 1760 he worked with the opera companies of Reggio, Parma, and Naples. He went to London two years later as the composer for the King's Theatre, and in 1763 his operas *Orione, ossia Diana vendicata* and *Zanaida* were successfully produced there. Bach remained musically active in England for the rest of his life, giving a full season of concerts each year. He died in London on Jan. 1, 1782.

Johann Christian Bach is best remembered as a composer of fine melodies and as a master of orchestration. He wrote innumerable songs for English, German, and Italian texts, as well as 49 symphonies, 13 overtures, and 37 clavier concertos. His chamber music includes a sextet for strings, winds, and pianoforte; 29 quartets for various instrumental combinations; 6 quintets for flute, oboe, and strings; and 38 sonatas for clavier and violin.

BETTMANN ARCHIVE

JOHANN SEBASTIAN BACH, the great German composer of the 18th century, from a portrait by Elias Hauss-mann, court painter at Dresden. *Right.* Bach's birthplace in Eisenach, East Germany, now used as a museum.

BACH, bäкн, **Johann Sebastian** (1685–1750), German musician and composer, whose many important works transcend the baroque era, to which they belong, and place their creator as one of the most important composers of all time. He is universally acknowledged to be the fore-most member of a family musical dynasty that spanned two centuries af Thuringian history.

Life. Bach was born at Eisenach on March 21, 1685. Orphaned at 10, he left Eisenach and went to Ohrdruf, the home of his oldest brother, Johann Christoph. He left there in 1700 to enroll in the Particularschule of St. Michael's Church in Lüneburg, where he stayed until 1702. Bach spent a few months in 1703 in the employ of the duke of Weimar before becoming organist of St. Boniface Church in Arnstadt, where he remained for four years. In 1708 he was organist at St. Blasius Church in Mühlhausen. From that year to 1717 he was variously employed by the duke of Saxe-Weimar as court organist, chamber musician, and concertmaster; then for six years he was kapellmeister (conductor of the court orchestra) for the duke of Cöthen. From 1723 until his death he resided in Leipzig as director of music and cantor of St. Thomas School, respon-sible to the town council for music in the main churches. His other titles were kapellmeister to the prince of Saxe-Weissenfels (1729) and royal Polish and electoral Saxon court composer (1736).

In 1707 he married his second cousin, Maria Barbara Bach; they had seven children, of whom three survived him, two becoming outstanding composers. His wife died in 1720, and in 1721 he married Anna Magdalena Wülcken, by whom he had 13 children. Six, including an important composer and a court musician, survived him.

He traveled often, though never far, usually to neighboring towns to test organs and to per-form on them. In his lifetime he was more fa-mous as an organist than as a composer. He knew the musical life of Dresden, and in 1747 visited Frederick the Great at Potsdam.

"I have had to be industrious," Bach used to say when asked how he acquired his skill in music. He was a hard worker, which is why much of his life seems uneventful. But he fol-lowed his aims tenaciously and fought interfer-ence. A probably legendary witness to this tenac-ity is the story of his Ohrdruf days when he copied secretly, by moonlight, music forbidden him by his brother. In Arnstadt he expressed his disgust at the incompetence of a certain bassoon player and so angered him that the two came to blows in the town marketplace. Bach was ad-monished that "man must live among *imperfecta.*" Half a year later he was reprimanded again for overstaying a leave of absence to visit the Lübeck organist, Dietrich Buxtehude, and also for con-fusing the congregation with his hymn accom-paniments. The accompaniments referred to may have been the setting of *To God Alone on High Be Glory* (vol. 40, p. 44, of the complete works), where the last two lines ("Now is great peace without ceasing, every feud has now an end") are set with a fierce array of diminished and minor chords as well as frightening modulations. The little piece is as biting an example of musical irony as can be imagined.

A year later Bach took a better position at Mühlhausen. But he was confronted there with a rector who belonged to the Pietist movement, a recent Lutheran offshoot that opposed elaborate church music. Before long, Bach seized a chance to move to safely orthodox Weimar. There began his shift of interest from the solitary organ bench to the instrumental-vocal ensemble into which his creative impulse was poured. The prospect of directing such musical forces took him to Cöthen, after he had been rejected for the cor-responding post at Weimar. The duke at first refused to accept his resignation and imprisoned him briefly "for too stubbornly forcing the issue of his dismissal," but finally let him go "with notice of his unfavorable discharge."

According to a letter written by Bach in 1730, his years at Cöthen were the happiest of his life. Yet three years before he left, he tried unsuccessfully for the post of organist in St. James Church, Hamburg. And in Leipzig his struggles with the authorities, who he said were "odd and little interested in music," became notorious. The authorities answered, saying, "not only did the Cantor do nothing, but he was not even willing to give an explanation of that fact . . . the Cantor was incorrigible."

Once cause underlying these disputes was the new Enlightenment, which had a center in Leipzig University. It was with the rationalist rector, Johann August Ernesti, that Bach in 1736 had his fiercest and most protracted quarrel. Their dispute had to do with a certain student's fitness to lead a choir. Ernesti had installed the boy in a morning church service, but Bach ejected him "with great commotion." Ernesti put him back for the afternoon service but again Bach forced him "out of the choir loft with much shouting and noise." As for another student who had obeyed Ernesti, Bach "sent him away from the table in the evening." To Ernesti himself Bach stated that "he would not budge in this matter, no matter what the cost." The affair dragged on for nearly two years, until apparently it was stopped by the intervention of the king of Saxony.

By 1739, Bach was tired of quarreling. When the question of his performing a passion on Good Friday came up, he remarked that "he did not care, for he got nothing out of it anyway, and it was only a burden." No further quarrels are known. But in 1749 the authorities arranged and attended a "trial performance (in Leipzig) for the future appointment as Cantor of St. Thomas's, in case the Kapellmeister and Cantor Mr. Sebastian Bach should die." When Bach's death did occur, at Leipzig on July 28, 1750, Burgomaster Stieglitz remarked: "The School needed a Cantor and not a Kapellmeister." With so little love did his associates take leave of him. One is reminded of the philosopher Wilhelm Dilthey's remark: "Seb. Bach was of a strong, self-willed race, and the conflicts with the authorities in which he was always finding himself lead one to suspect that this violent man was hard to live with."

Style. What was the ideal for which Bach fought so long and often so bitterly? As he put it, he could express himself "more in deed than in words" and so used few for the latter. But when asking the church at Mühlhausen for dismissal to accept the Weimar position, he spoke twice of his "goal,"—"a well-regulated church music to the Glory of God." The latter phrase occurred regularly in baroque definitions of music, and Bach echoed it again when he wrote: "The aim and final reason . . . of all music . . . should be none else but the Glory of God and the recreation of the mind." But with characteristic pugnacity he added: "Where this is not observed, there will be no real music but only a devilish hubbub."

It is misleading to interpret Bach's phrases "church music" and "Glory of God" in a narrow way. Bach was not a self-consciously pious man, and he used these words merely as a simple and general way of describing his musical style. The essence of Bach's style is his method of relating melody and harmony. Centuries of polyphony (music written as a combination of several simultaneous voices) converged on Bach. But during his time there arose a new system of key modulations, a so-called tonal harmony. Together with other developments, such as the instrumental concerto, the new tonal system forced the old polyphonic music into permanent eclipse and secured the dominance of the single melodic line with harmonic accompaniment. In this process Bach is a transitional figure. In his music the old style remains fully alive and the new style becomes equally vital. All his melodies exude the new harmonic thought, accounting for the textural intensity of his fugues. But it also follows that the harmonic notes that are needed to articulate each melody cannot always be supplied. This is the reason for the frequent dissonances that so mark his music. Dissonance is the price he pays for conceiving polyphony harmonically.

Since Bach was one of the discoveries of 19th century romanticism, it has often been claimed that his music is romantic, and many a melody may be cited to support this view. But infinitely expressive as his melodies may be, they are carried by rhythms, usually in the bass, that are wholly inflexible. The melody may be as anguished, as rhapsodic as the most extreme romantic gesture, but the rhythmic bass remains as unconcerned, as remote, as insistent as time itself.

A further tension in Bach is the matter of sonority. What was his ideal instrument? Was it the rigid, impersonal tone of the baroque organ that conjures up the sense of the eternal, or the warmer human sounds of voices and string and woodwind instruments? There is no final answer. Bach veers one way and then another. Many of his most affecting melodies are scored for organ; many of his starkest and grimmest compositions are given to voices and instruments.

The relationships in Bach's style between the various musical elements point not only in a generally religious but also in a specifically Christian direction. Such music was meant for the church, and its composer knew it.

Keyboard Music. Compared to Mozart or Schubert, Bach was slow in developing. He entered the musical world as an organist, and it was for the organ that his first major compositions were written. Intensive work at Weimar brought this branch of his art to a definite maturity. The main forms were: (1) the so-called "free" compositions, consisting of prelude, toccata, or fantasia, usually followed by a fugue, and (2) settings of chorale melodies. In all these compositions Bach built on the centuries-old traditions of German organ music, but in raising the chorale prelude to its highest level of expression, he began a trend that was directly against the spirit of his time. Few 18th century organ chorales of merit exist that are not from his pen. His works of this type may be classified as follows: (1) chorale variations; (2) chorale fughettas, or short fugues, usually on the first line of the chorale; and (3) the simple organ chorale (3a) where the complete melody occurs once. An important variant (3b) is the chorale fantasy, an enlarged form, where the lines of the chorale are separated by musical interludes. This part of Bach's work is represented most clearly in the unfinished collection of chorale preludes, mostly of type 3a, which he called the *Little Organ Book*. The manuscript is dated 1717, and he probably stopped work on it in Cöthen.

An equally large body of keyboard music without pedal part is now played on the piano, although it is not known for which instrument it was written originally. Bach's two most common string keyboard instruments were the harpsichord and clavichord, and his works as a whole show no clear indication of which instrument he had in mind. His favorite was said to have been the clavichord, which like the modern piano was sensitive to touch. In Cöthen he brought this branch of his music to full maturity in the preludes and fugues (in all the keys) of the *Well-Tempered Clavier* (part 1, 1722, sometimes wrongly called *Well-Tempered Clavichord;* no specific instrument is named in the title). The work reveals Bach's mastery of counterpoint and also shows evidence of the stimulus he received from the new tonal harmony and the remote keys recently made available through equal tempered tuning.

Instrumental Works. In the sonatas for flute, violin, and gamba with clavier, also composed at Cöthen, a certain dualism of style is apparent. The allegros are brilliant studies in fugal trio writing and lead directly to the six famous trio sonatas included in the organ works. The adagios are freer, deeper, and more mature in style. Unique landmarks in Bach's career are the solo violoncello suites and the solo violin suites and sonatas. As expressive as any composition ever written for one melodic line is the sarabande from the fifth cello suite. The solo violin works contain some of Bach's mightiest designs (such as the great fugues and the chaconne), perhaps because a satisfactory organ was not regularly accessible in Cöthen.

Cöthen is also the period of Bach's most famous orchestral works, including the Brandenburg concertos, where the baroque orchestral style achieves its most fascinating utterance. Records of the Cöthen court indicate that much of this music may have disappeared. At Cöthen, Bach's style ripened in almost every direction, and the great proportion of those works most often heard today were composed at that time.

Cantatas. The one branch of his music that was not yet mature proved to be his main extant work, the church music for voices and instruments. These pieces mark the realization of the goal announced at Mühlhausen in 1708 and are rightly associated with the Leipzig period. All told, there are about 200 cantatas (usually known by the numbers assigned them in the edition of his complete works) plus a few motets, passion settings, masses, and other music. Only five cantatas can be dated before 1714, and these works show the youthful Bach's dependence on the old German cantata style. The remainder reveal the influence of Italian opera, in their use of the madrigal form of the verse, the *da capo* aria, and recitative passages. The texts were prepared by contemporary authors, with occasional quotations from the Bible and Lutheran hymns. They illustrate the Bible readings of the traditional church year. Bach himself may have written a few of them. Over 20 Weimar cantatas are extant containing some of Bach's finest arias and showing his love for the solo obbligato instrument. About half of the more than 600 arias and duets, plus a few trios, use combinations of solo instruments without string orchestra.

But Bach was still searching for his final choral style. Cöthen gave him a chance to develop it. It is now certain that this non-Lutheran court did occasionally use concerted vocal music, and Bach wrote a number of cantatas there. As reconstructed by Friedrich Smend (*Bach in Köthen,* 1951), they show an increasing interplay of concerto orchestral elements with the chorus. Thus equipped, Bach launched himself on his Leipzig career of cantata composition.

The standard Bach cantata opens with a chorus, followed by perhaps four solo numbers, usually recitatives and arias, and closes with a simple chorale. The most important exception is the solo cantata, which dispenses with the opening chorus. A few other cantatas begin with an aria, with chorus following. Some choruses have contemporary texts, but most of those composed in 1723–1724 are set to Bible verses. Many cantatas use hymn stanzas, with the chorale tune confined to the choruses. Such verses, however, were ill-adapted for recitative or *da capo* aria settings. Thus, for his second series of cantatas, composed about 1735–1740 and all based on chorales. Bach had the texts for the middle movements paraphrased (or paraphrased them himself). The roughly three years of extant cantatas, plus the organ chorales in the third part of the *Clavier Übung* (published 1739) are Bach's reaffirmation of orthodox Lutheranism as opposed to the rationalist tendencies of his day.

This mighty union of art and religion is nowhere more graphically depicted than in Bach's longest work, the *St. Matthew Passion* (1729). In setting the Gospel narrative to music, a centuries-old tradition is perpetuated, while in adorning it with lyric meditation, Bach anticipates the religious spirit of the future. Hermann Abert called this work "a piece of religious folk art which the world has known only once before in similar fullness; in Greek tragedy. . . . So did Bach, without himself willing it, animate anew an ideal toward which the opera right down to Wagner strove in vain, because it was not able to create that which was most important in the classic tragedy, its religious foundation" (*Gesammelten Schriften,* 1929). Modern opera began with the purpose of recreating Greek tragedy. Yet Bach, who never wrote an opera, alone is credited with reaching the goal. The reasons why he never wrote in the operatic form become clear when we consider that the features of his mind and musical style inclined him toward religion. Still more important is the fact that his nature was lyric rather than dramatic. His work abounds in lyric contemplation of unexampled depth, power, poignancy, and intensity, which are always fused with the spirit of the eternal, and therefore are unsuitable for representing the more purely human emotions of the stage.

Bach celebrated the final maturing of his choral style with the B Minor Mass, consisting of two-thirds chorus and one-third arias and duets—no recitatives or chorales. It apparently was composed rather haphazardly, as indicated by the disproportionate size of the first Kyrie as well as by the arbitrary way in which Bach divided the Mass: "1. Missa [Kyrie and Gloria]. 2. Symbolum Nicenum [Credo]. 3. Sanctus. 4. Osanna, Benedictus, Agnus Dei, Dona nobis pacem." The Missa was sent to the king of Saxony in 1733 and the rest assembled about 1748.

As the amount of music he had written grew in volume, Bach often rearranged older compositions instead of composing new ones. He did this not only to save time but also in the interest of artistic perfection as well. His rule was not to arrange religious works for secular purposes, although he often turned secular works to religious uses. His material was the world of baroque music; his goal the service of the church. To this end everything in the former was to become subject to the latter, as can be seen, for example, in the final chorale cantata choruses. Above the highly contemporary elements of tonal harmony, of fugue, concerto, and thematic material of every kind there reigned the ancient, often modal chorale tune.

Last Works. In Bach's later years the rising spirit of modern scientific speculation seems to have inspired him to explore new musical mysteries in such works as the *Musical Offering,* memorializing the visit to Frederick the Great, and the unfinished *Art of Fugue.*

Considering how few of Bach's works were published during his life, it is remarkable how much influence he did exert. His numerous pupils kept alive the keyboard music. It profoundly influenced Mozart's work. Beethoven as a boy learned the *Well-Tempered Clavier* from his teacher, who had studied with one of Bach's pupils. Beethoven's pun on Bach's name is famous: "Not Bach (brook) but Meer (sea) should be his name." The romantic period provided a climate favorable to the reception of the church music, and on the 100th anniversary of Bach's death the Bach-Gesellschaft society was founded. In the following 50 years the society produced a virtually complete edition of his works. A new edition based on the latest research is now being published.

WILLIAM H. SCHEIDE, *Director, Bach Aria Group*

Bibliography
David, Hans T., and Mendel, Arthur, *The Bach Reader* (New York 1945).
Dickenson, A.E.F., *The Art of Bach* (London 1950).
Neumann, Werner, *Bach: A Pictorial Biography* (New York 1961).
Schweitzer, Albert, *J.S. Bach,* 2 vols., tr. by Ernest Newman (London 1923).
Spitta, Philipp, *Johann Sebastian Bach,* 3 vols., tr. by C. Bell and J.A. Fuller-Maitland (New York 1951).
Terry, Charles Sanford, *Bach: A Biography,* new ed. (Gloucester, Mass., 1964).

For Specialized Study
Bodky, Erwin, *The Interpretation of Bach's Keyboard Works* (Cambridge, Mass., 1960).
Boult, Adrian C., *The St. Matthew Passion: Its Preparation and Performance* (London 1949).
Hindemith, Paul, *J.S. Bach* (New York 1952).
Terry, Charles Sanford, *The Music of Bach: An Introduction* (London 1933).
Tovey, Donald F., *A Companion to "The Art of Fugue"* (New York 1931).

BACH, bäKH, **Wilhelm Friedemann** (1710–1784), German musician and composer, the eldest son of Johann Sebastian Bach. He was born at Weimar in November 1710. His early musical training was under the guidance of his father, who used such works as his own *Well-Tempered Clavier* to instruct Wilhelm. In 1733 the younger Bach was appointed organist at the Sophia Church in Dresden, a position that afforded him an opportunity to compose, teach, and study. In 1746 he left Dresden for the post of organist and music director at the Church of Our Lady in Halle. He remained there until 1764.

Despite his recognized musical talent, Wilhelm Friedemann Bach had a difficult disposition and many eccentricities, so that during the last 20 years of his life he was employed only irregularly and he lived in poverty and unhappiness. He died in Berlin on July 1, 1784.

The keyboard compositions of Wilhelm Friedemann Bach include seven chorale preludes and three fugues for the organ, as well as numerous fantasies, fugues, preludes, and sonatas for the clavier. His orchestral works include nine symphonies and several concertos for clavier and orchestra. His church music consists of 21 cantatas and a mass (*Deutsche Messe*).

BACH FESTIVAL, bäKH fes'tə-vəl, a music festival held annually since 1901 at Bethlehem, Pa. The festivals, presenting the greatest works of Johann Sebastian Bach, were begun by the Moravian Church of Bethlehem, which probably made the first use in the United States of trombones, flutes, and violas for church music. At the first festival, Bach's *Christmas Oratorio* was given in its entirety for the first time in the United States. The B Minor Mass is performed at each festival.

The Bach Festival choir has over 100 adult members; there also is a separate boys' chorus of about the same number. Since 1912, members of the Philadelphia Orchestra have helped make up the 60-piece festival orchestra. The festivals are held yearly for two days in May in the Packer Chapel of Lehigh University.

BACHARACH, bak'rak, **Burt** (1929–), American composer of popular music. He was born in Kansas City, Mo., on May 12, 1929, and grew up in the New York City area. His mother, a singer, insisted that he learn the piano. After playing at USO centers and Catskill Mountains hotels, he studied music at McGill University, the New School in New York, and Music Academy West in Santa Barbara, Calif. This was followed by two years of playing Army concerts and a period as accompanist for popular singers.

Bacharach also wrote songs, but not until he teamed with lyricist Hal David and pop singer Dionne Warwick did he achieve success. His music is lush, melodic, and soft, with rhythms based on Latin music and rock and with many time changes. *Don't Make Me Over* made the top ten in 1962, and *Raindrops Keep Fallin' on My Head* won an Academy Award in 1970. Bacharach wrote the scores for a number of films, including *A House Is Not a Home, What's New Pussycat?, Promise Her Anything,* and *Alfie,* and for the Broadway musical *Promises, Promises. The Bacharach-David Song Book* appeared in 1970.

BACHE, bäch, **Alexander Dallas** (1806–1867), American physicist, who was a founder of the first American magnetic observatory and of the National Academy of Sciences. A great-grandson of Benjamin Franklin, he was born in Philadelphia, Pa., on July 19, 1806. He was graduated first in his class at the U.S. Military Academy in 1825, served three years in the Army, then resigned to become professor of natural science and chemistry at the University of Pennsylvania. He was also in charge of research at the Franklin Institute in Philadelphia. Appointed the first president of Girard College in 1836, he spent two years studying school systems in Europe, and published *Education in Europe* (1839). He then returned to the United States and reorganized the public schools of Philadelphia during the period 1839–1842.

Having studied terrestrial magnetism since 1830, Bache established the first U.S. magnetic observatory in 1840 at Girard, and published *Observations at the Magnetic and Meteorological Observatory at the Girard College* (1840–47). Instruction at Girard could not commence until its buildings were complete, and this was not until 1848; so in 1843 Bache became superintendent of the U.S. Coast Survey. A regent of the Smithsonian Institution from 1846, he was also a founder and first president of the National Academy of Sciences. Bache died on Feb. 17, 1867.

BACHELLER, bach'ə-lər, **Irving Addison** (1859–1950), American journalist and novelist. He was born at Pierpont, N.Y., on Sept. 26, 1859. After graduating from St. Lawrence University in 1882, he went to New York City where he became a newspaper reporter. From 1883 to 1896 he pioneered the first syndicate service for newspapers. His service distributed feature stories, fiction, and gossip and household columns. From 1898 to 1900 he was on the editorial staff of the New York *World*. Bacheller died at White Plains, N.Y., on Feb. 24, 1950.

His first novel, *The Master of Silence,* was published in 1900. It was followed in the same year by *Eben Holden,* a humorous story of the upstate New York countryside in his boyhood. His other novels include *D'ri and I* (1901), *Vergilius* (1904), *Silas Strong* (1906), *The Master* (1910), *Charge It* (1912), *The Turning of Griggsby* (1913), *The Light in the Clearing* (1917), *The Prodigal Village* (1920), *In the Days of Poor Richard* (1922), *The Scudders* (1923), *Father Abraham* (1925), *Dawn—A Lost Romance of the Time of Christ* (1927), *A Candle in the Wilderness* (1930), *The Harvesting* (1934), *The Oxen of the Sun* (1935), and *The Winds of God* (1941). Autobiographical writings include *Opinions of a Cheerful Yankee* (1926), *Coming Up the Road* (1928), and *From Stores of Memory* (1938).

BACHELOR'S BUTTON. See CENTAUREA.

BACHELOR'S DEGREE. See DEGREE.

BACHOFEN, bäκн'ōfən, **Johann Jakob** (1815–1887), Swiss anthropologist and legal historian, who is best remembered for his studies of social institutions. In his most representative work, *Das Mutterrecht* (1861; *The Mother Right*), Bachofen posed the theory that modern social institutions derive chiefly from the matriarchy of earlier, more primitive, cultures. It was women, he argued, in their insistence upon monogamy and private ownership of property, who established the integrity of family life as it has been known in most of the civilized world. Bachofen's thesis had many advocates in the late 19th century, but now anthropologists reject his emphasis on matriarchy.

Bachofen was born in Basel, Switzerland, on Dec. 22, 1815. After studying law at Basel, Berlin, Oxford, Cambridge, and Paris, he returned to Basel, where he taught Roman law for several years. For most of the remainder of his life he served as judge of the criminal court at Basel, a post that allowed him time to devote to his ethnological and antiquarian studies. He died in Basel on Nov. 25, 1887.

BACHRACH, bak'rak, an American family of portrait photographers.

DAVID BACHRACH (1845–1921) was born in the Rhineland area of Germany. In 1850 he emigrated with his family to the United States, settling in Hartford, Conn. After moving to Baltimore in 1863, he opened his first photography studio there in 1868. Bachrach was among the pioneers in portrait photography, and with another photographer, Louis Levy, he received a patent on an early half-screen method for improving tone quality in photographic reproduction. He was also active in Baltimore politics and contributed articles to the Baltimore *Sun*.

LOUIS FABIAN BACHRACH (1881–1963), the elder son of David Bachrach, was born in Baltimore on July 16, 1881. He studied at the Maryland Institute of Design in Baltimore and at the Art Students League in New York City, and from 1900 to 1915 he was a photographer in his father's studios. He served as president of Bachrach, Inc., between 1915 and 1955 and as chairman of the board from 1955 until his death, in Boston, Mass., on July 24, 1963.

Louis Bachrach wrote extensively on photography and was widely recognized as a leading authority on the techniques of portraiture and lighting.

BRADFORD KEYSER BACHRACH (1910–), the elder son of Louis Fabian Bachrach, was born in Worcester, Mass., on Nov. 8, 1910. He graduated from Harvard University in 1933 and joined the family firm in the same year. He became president of Bachrach, Inc., in 1955. He was noted as a specialist in women's portrait photography.

LOUIS FABIAN BACHRACH, JR. (1917–), the younger son of Louis Fabian Bachrach, was born in Newton, Mass., on April 9, 1917. After graduating from Harvard University in 1939, he joined the family firm, where he became noted as a specialist in men's portrait photography. He also became active in a Boston banking firm.

BACICCIO (1639–1709), bä-chēt'chō, Italian painter, also called *Baciccia*. His real name was *Giovanni Battista Gaulli;* his nickname may have been a corruption of his middle name.

He was born in Genoa on May 8, 1639, and

BACICCIO'S MASTERPIECE, the baroque ceiling (1668–1683) of the Jesuit church of Il Gesù, Rome.

studied painting there, using as his models portraits by Rubens and Van Dyke. He went to Rome about 1660, came under the influence of Bernini, and began his career as a portrait painter. A youthful self-portrait (now in the Uffizi Gallery, Florence) dates from this period.

Sometime in the 1660's, Baciccio visited Parma, where he made brief studies of the dome paintings of Correggio. On his return to Rome he painted his most celebrated work, *The Adoration of the Name of Jesus* (1668–1683), on the ceiling of the church of Il Gesù, the mother church of the Jesuit order. The work is a striking example of illusionism, with hundreds of flying figures, both painted and in stucco, that seem to burst out of the frame of the ceiling, as clouds apparently carry saints, sinners, and devils down into the church. His effects are vastly more theatrical than those of his precedessors.

Baciccio's other church paintings include *The Glorification of the Franciscan Order* (1707), in the church of Santi Apostoli in Rome, and *The Virgin with the Child and Saint Anne*, in the church of San Francesco a Ripa in Rome. He also painted portraits of the seven popes from Alexander VII to Clement XI. He died in Rome on April 2, 1709.

Further Reading: Enggass, Robert, *The Painting of Baciccio* (University Park, Pa., 1964).

BACILLUS. See BACTERIA AND BACTERIOLOGY.

BACITRACIN, bas-ə-trā'sən, is a toxic antibiotic produced by the bacterium *Bacillus subtilis*. This organism was discovered in May 1943 by Balbina Johnson and Frank L. Meleney at the College of Physicians and Surgeons, Columbia University. It was isolated from the damaged tissue of an accident victim and was found to have a strong antagonistic action on other bacteria. Its active principle was demonstrated in a filtrate from the broth culture of the bacillus. Injections of the filtrate into test animals were effective against hemolytic (releasing hemoglobin from red blood cells) streptococcus. Furthermore, the filtrate was able to halt an inflammatory process in human beings when it was injected directly into the site of a hemolytic streptococcus infection.

The active principle of *Bacillus subtilis* was purified and concentrated, and this concentrate also was found to be nontoxic and effective when applied locally to human infections. However, certain toxic factors appeared in the commercial manufacture of bacitracin, and they have limited somewhat the use of this antibiotic.

The organisms that are chiefly susceptible to bacitracin treatment are the hemolytic and nonhemolytic streptococci, *Staphylococcus aureus*, pneumococcus, anaerobic cocci, and the organisms that produce gas gangrene and tetanus, as well as the spirochetes of syphilis. This bacterial spectrum is similar to that of penicillin, but there are many strains within these susceptible groups that are resistant to penicillin and susceptible to bacitracin. Furthermore, bacitracin is not inhibited by the organisms that produce penicillinase, an enzyme that inactivates penicillin. Bacitracin frequently is effective in the treatment of mixed infections when penicillin treatment has failed. Its chief usefulness at first was in local applications as a solution or ointment in the treatment of infections caused by organisms susceptible to it.

FRANK L. MELENEY, *Columbia University*

BACK, bak, **Sir George** (1796–1878), English explorer. He was born in Stockport, England, on Nov. 6, 1796. He entered the British navy as a midshipman in 1808, saw action in the Napoleonic wars, and in 1818 was a member of an expedition to Svalbard (Spitsbergen). He accompanied John (later Sir John) Franklin on an expedition along the northern coast of Canada, east of the Coppermine River in 1819–1822, and to the Mackenzie River in 1825–1827. In 1833 he led a party in search of Capt. (later Sir) John Ross, supposedly lost in the Arctic. He received word that Ross had returned to England, but remained to explore the Great Fish (now Back) River, in northern Canada, until 1835. In 1836–1837 he made his last trip to the Arctic, in command of the *Terror*, and was icebound for four months. Back was knighted in 1839 and became an admiral in 1857. He wrote *Narrative of the Arctic Land Expedition . . .* (1836) and *Narrative of an Expedition in H.M.S. Terror . . .* (1838). He died in London on June 23, 1878.

BACK RIVER, bak, is a stream in the Northwest Territories of Canada. Formerly called the *Great Fish River*, it is 605 miles (975 km) long. It rises in the District of Mackenzie and flows northeastward across the District of Keewatin, passing through Lakes Pelly, Garry, and Macdougall, and empties into Chantrey Inlet of the Arctic Ocean.

BACK TO METHUSELAH, mə-thoō'zə-lə, is a drama in five parts by George Bernard Shaw, published, together with an extended preface by the author, in 1921. Each of the five parts of the play is dramatically complete in itself and is assigned its own title, cast of characters, place, and time. The titles and times are: (1) *In the Beginning* (4004 B.C.); (2) *The Gospel of the Brothers Barnabas* (1920 A.D.); (3) *The Thing Happens* (2170 A.D.); (4) *Tragedy of an Elderly Gentleman* (3000 A.D.); (5) *As Far As Thought Can Reach* (31,920 A.D.).

Back to Methuselah, according to Shaw himself, is a parable of creative evolution, a theme that he first attempted on a much smaller scale in the Don Juan dream episode of *Man and Superman*. For his second attempt to present what for him was a religion, Shaw abandoned the legend of Don Juan and went back to the legend of the Garden of Eden, at the same time exploiting what he considered to be mankind's abiding interest in an indefinite prolongation of human existence beyond the allotted threescore years and ten. Behind a Shavian façade of witty paradox and satiric thrusts in all directions there is unfolded the central, dynamic conception of the eventual triumph of mind over matter via the slow and graduated transformations of evolution, seen as creatively purposeful (teleological) in the Bergsonian sense, rather than naturalistic (mechanical), as in the Darwinian sense.

To present the complete cycle of *Methuselah* is a formidable challenge to both producer and audience. It was first produced in 1922 by the Theatre Guild in New York City but proved too long and talky for American tastes and closed after nine weeks. The following year it was performed in England by the Birmingham Repertory Theatre. In 1957 a cast headed by Tyrone Power toured the United States with a greatly shortened version of the work.

BACKACHE, a pain in the back due to physical, pathological, or psychological causes. Most backaches arise from physical causes. The back is a complex of many muscles, ligaments, joints, and nerves that are in many ways only imperfectly adapted for man's upright posture. Thus the back is susceptible to ligament and muscle strains, muscle spasms, and problems affecting joints. Also, certain congenital defects of the spine may lead to pain in middle life because of prolonged physical stress.

Back pain may arise from several pathological conditions. Arthritis, especially the hypertrophic type in which there is overgrowth of cartilage and bone in the joints, is one example. Extrusion, or herniation, of a disk from its fibrocartilaginous envelope between two vertebrae may cause recurrent acute or chronic backache. Decalcification of the vertebrae in postmenopausal or elderly women also may lead to back pain and even spontaneous collapse of these bones. Prolonged severe backache is sometimes the result of cancer or abscess. Psychological disturbances also may result in chronic backache.

Diagnosis of the cause of backache requires a thorough general examination by a physician, and often X-rays and electronic diagnostic equipment are needed. Therapy depends on the cause. It may include bedrest on a hard mattress, braces or other supports, traction, surgery, or radiotherapy.

IRVING SOLOMON, M.D.
Mount Sinai School of Medicine, New York

BACKGAMMON, bak′gam-ən, is a game played by two persons with counters (also called "men" or "stones") on a double board. The throwing of dice determines the moves. The game is also called *trictrac.* One of its several variations, *acey deucey,* is popular in the armed services.

In backgammon, each player has 15 counters, two dice, and a dice cup. The board's two equal rectangles, the *inner table* and the *outer table,* are separated by a space called the *bar.* Twelve elongated triangles, or *points,* of alternating colors appear on each table. Each player sets up his 15 men as shown in the diagram. The white men move in the direction B1-B12-W12-W1, and the blacks in the opposite direction, until all 15 men are inside a player's own inner table. The first to *bear off* (remove) all his men from the board wins the game.

To begin play, players cast one dice for first move. The winner rolls his dice and moves one or more men the exact number of points on the dice. For example, if White rolls a 6 and a 3, he may move one man nine points (B1-B10) or one man 6 points (B12-W7) and one 3 (B12-W10). Players cast dice and move in turn, each using both of the numbers he rolls, if he can. If a double is rolled, the one number can be taken four times.

A man may not be moved to a point occupied, or *made,* by two or more adverse men. If a man moves to a point occupied by one adverse man, it is called a *blot.* The adverse man is placed *on the bar,* and its owner can reenter only by rolling the number of an exposed point on the adverse inner table. A player cannot make any other move while he has a man on the bar. With 15 men inside his inner table, a player begins to bear off. He may remove a man from an occupied point that corresponds to a number rolled. If the number is higher than any

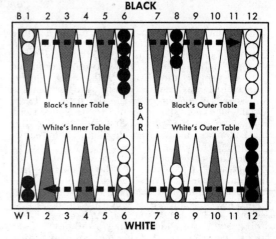

BACKGAMMON BOARD shows "men" on points for the start of the game. White moves in the direction shown by the arrows. Black moves in the opposite direction.

occupied point, he bears off the man on the next highest point.

FRANK K. PERKINS, *Boston "Herald"*

BACKHAUS, bäk′hous, **Wilhelm** (1884–1969), German pianist, who was noted for his interpretations of Beethoven and Brahms. He was born in Leipzig on March 26, 1884. In 1899, after studying at the Leipzig Conservatory, he went to Frankfurt, where he was a student of the pianist-composer Eugen d'Albert.

Backhaus made his debut as a soloist in Leipzig at the age of 15, and the following year appeared in London. He won the Rubinstein piano prize in Paris in 1905. After several successful appearances on the Continent, Backhaus toured the United States from 1912 to 1914, where he was enthusiastically hailed by critics, one of whom described him as "Liszt, Rubinstein, and Paderewski rolled into one." He also made tours of Europe, South America, Australia, and the Far East, and was well known as a recording artist. After World War II, he settled in Lugano, Switzerland. He died in Villach, Austria, on July 5, 1969.

Backhaus held teaching positions at conservatories in Manchester, England (1905–1907), and Sonderhausen, Germany (1907–1909), and at the Curtis Institute of Music, Philadelphia (1925).

BACKUS, bak′əs, **Isaac** (1724–1806), American clergyman. He was born on Jan. 20, 1724 in Norwich, Conn. A convert of the Great Awakening, Backus allied himself with the revivalists who separated from the Congregational Church to form new congregations. He was at first a Separatist minister, but in 1756 he helped establish the First Baptist Church in Middleborough, Mass., and he remained its pastor until his death on Nov. 20, 1806.

Backus was greatly influenced by the evangelistic preaching of George Whitefield and the theology of Jonathan Edwards. Elected to represent the Warren Association (the oldest cooperative organization among New England Baptists) in government affairs, he went before the First Continental Congress in 1774 to speak on behalf of liberty of conscience for dissenters. He wrote a history of New England and many other works. See also BAPTISTS; GREAT AWAKENING.

BACON, bā′kən, **Francis** (1561–1626), English statesman, scientist, and man of letters. He was born in London on Jan. 22, 1561. His father was Sir Nicholas Bacon, the witty and corpulent lord keeper of the Great Seal under Queen Elizabeth I; his mother, Lady Ann, a zealous and scholarly woman, was the sister of Lady Cecil, whose husband, soon to become Lord Burghley, was the queen's first minister and the most powerful man in the kingdom. The youngest of eight children, Francis Bacon was nurtured in the glittering precincts of the court and amid the greatest personages of the realm; he remained a courtier to the end of his life.

Bacon's childhood was passed at York House, the London residence of the lord keeper. At the age of 12 he entered Trinity College, Cambridge, with his elder brother, Anthony. (Late in life he declared that he had rebelled while at the university against the sterility of Aristotle's philosophy, but too much has been made of this recollection.) The precocious strength of his mind had, however, already impressed observers, and the queen herself delighted in questioning him and called him the "young lord keeper." In

FRANCIS BACON, a portrait from the studio of Paulus van Somer, in the National Portrait Gallery, London.

1576 he was admitted to the company of the lawyers of Gray's Inn, but he soon joined the suite of the English ambassador in Paris. During his sojourn in France he traveled widely and witnessed the bitter struggle between Roman Catholics and the reformers.

Career Under Queen Elizabeth. Bacon's prospects were changed by the sudden death of his father. Compelled to earn a living, he relinquished a diplomatic career for the law, and under the sanction of his uncle, Lord Burghley, he was admitted to the bar. However, further respectful appeals to Burghley for favor, prolonged over many years, were coldly received. Burghley was concerned with the advancement of his son, Robert Cecil, and suspected the vast intellectual designs of his nephew. (Bacon frankly exposed these suspicions later in a remarkable letter to his uncle.) Meanwhile in 1584, at the age of 23, he had taken a seat in

the House of Commons and quickly attained distinction in the debates and committees. In a *Letter of Advice to Queen Elizabeth* (1584 or 1585) he recommended measures for dealing with the Roman Catholics, and a few years later (1589) he put forward *An Advertisement touching the Controversies of the Church of England*, in which he impartially censured what he considered to be the harsh conservatism of the bishops and the bigotry of the Puritans. He was continually harassed by debts, and the revision of the clerkship of the Star Chamber, procured for him by Burghley in 1589, did nothing to relieve his anxiety, as the post did not become vacant for some 20 years.

Yet all the leisure hours he could snatch from the pursuit of public success he devoted to literature and philosophy; the main elements of his reform of knowledge were established in his mind with consuming strength by the time he was 32. His divided life, torn between ambition for office and the craving to achieve his immense program of intellectual reform, constitutes the tragedy of Bacon's career. At a later time he confessed to Sir Thomas Bodley that he knew himself by inward calling to be fitter to hold a book than to play a part. He wrote that he had led his life in civil causes, for which he was not very fit by nature and more unfit by the preoccupation of his mind with studies.

Despairing of the support of Burghley, he turned to a more flamboyant patron, Robert Devereux, earl of Essex, the queen's favorite. He devoted himself to the earl's affairs, and Essex repaid his assistance by pressing his claims on the queen for the office of attorney general. By ill fortune, Bacon had incurred the displeasure of Elizabeth in speeches in the House relating to the subsidies required for the defense against Spain. At length, after painful delay, the attorney generalship was given to Bacon's great rival Edward Coke. The rebuff deeply shook him, especially since at this period he was dangerously in debt and was once even arrested by a creditor. He was employed on much important business, including the examination of persons suspected of complicity in a plot to murder the queen; indeed, he frequently acted as a counsel at large to the sovereign.

In the meantime, he gradually became alienated from Essex, whose perilous courses he had foreseen; standing between the queen and the impetuous favorite, he was placed in a position of extreme delicacy. After the spectacular failure of Essex in Ireland in 1599, Bacon openly took part against him, and when the wild insurrection of the following year was suppressed, he appeared in court on the side of the prosecution at the earl's trial. His deadly cross-examination of the man who had been his friend and benefactor has been severely condemned. The report of the case, which he subsequently published in vindication of his conduct and in which he skillfully suppressed parts of the events, has, in the opinion of some writers, added to his perfidy. It must be recognized, however, that he had sought to moderate the queen's fury against Essex; and, in any case, as soon as the true character of the earl's designs was revealed, Bacon was forced to choose between his sovereign and a traitor.

Career Under James I. After the death of the queen in 1603, the fortunes of Bacon remained dubious for a period, although he hastened to pay court to the new king and the new men of power. He received, with many others, the honor of knighthood; he married Alice Barnham, the daughter of a rich alderman; and he performed his duties in Parliament and in the courts with distinction. He was prominent in the important issues of the time, but it was not until 1607 that the long-coveted position of solicitor general was granted him at the hands of James I. During the debates in 1607 on the union between England and Scotland he spoke with admirable foresight on the benefits of the union in opposition to the narrow prejudices of the Commons. He took a leading part in the gathering tension between Parliament and the crown. Robert Cecil, now earl of Salisbury and lord treasurer, proposed a bold scheme by which the king's government could meet its financial requirements. Under this plan the king would receive an immediate grant and a guaranteed annual income in return for the renunciation of certain unpopular feudal sources of revenue. After a series of exchanges between the king and the House of Commons in 1610, James rejected Cecil's advice and made demands so excessive that the Commons refused them with indignation. The king promptly dissolved Parliament. In these transactions Bacon attempted, in some ingenious speeches, to conciliate the House while defending the rights of the king.

He was soon engaged in further efforts to defend the royal prerogative against encroachment. He had argued in a paper published in 1606, *A View of the Differences in question betwixt the King's Bench and the Council in the Marches*, that the king held his prerogatives not from the law but immediately from God. And in private notes, named *Commentarius Solutus* (*Loose or Casual Commentary*), he candidly avowed his policy to exalt the king's "summary justice" in all circumstances. Bacon combined a sincere belief in the doctrine of the divine right of kings with a contempt for lawyers in politics. He offered the sinister counsel that the king should distract attention from internal dissension by foreign aggression.

In 1612, Salisbury died, and Bacon hastened to offer himself in his place. His anxiety to obtain promotion was rewarded in 1613 by the office of attorney general. Amid his manifold labors he found time to supervise the planning of the gardens at Gorhambury in Hertfordshire. His energy was unceasing. He was involved in great cases in the courts—in the examination, with torture, of Edmond Peacham (1615) for charges of treason, and in the prosecution of the earl of Somerset for the murder of Sir Thomas Overbury (1616). After the removal of Somerset he cultivated the acquaintance of the new favorite, George Villiers, later to be duke of Buckingham. The prolonged enmity between Bacon and Coke, who was now chief justice, culminated in 1616 over the question of the king's powers in the courts. Bacon naturally threw his weight in support of the royal prerogative, and at a dramatic meeting in the presence of James he secured the submission of Coke and the judges.

These services were not disregarded; he became a privy councilor in 1616, and in March 1617, to his intense gratification, he was appointed lord keeper. He made a triumphant entry into Westminster, clothed in purple and attended by a splendid cavalcade. For a time he was out of favor because of his opposition to the marriage of the daughter of the fallen Coke to the brother of Buckingham. He became reconciled with Buckingham and the king upon the receipt of a condescending letter from Buckingham, for which Bacon expressed profuse gratitude. In 1618 he was made lord chancellor, and shortly afterward he was created *Baron Verulam*. Among the notable legal activities of his chancellorship were the trials of the earl of Suffolk, the lord treasurer, for corruption (1619) and of Sir Henry Yelverton, the attorney general, for abuses of his office (1620). In January 1621, Bacon was raised to the dignity of *Viscount St. Alban*. The form *St. Albans* is found in some sources, but Bacon, in official documents, signed his name without the final "s." He loved magnificence and lived in princely style at York House and at Gorhambury.

Fall and Disgrace. Bacon had attained the pinnacle of his career when a terrible disaster fell on him, brought about by his political enemies. Beginning quietly with inquiries concerning abuses in the courts, charges against the lord chancellor multiplied, and a flood of accusations alleging bribery and perversion of justice accumulated. At first he treated the indictments lightly, but soon he was prostrate under the strain. The cases cited against him appear to be instances of carelessness rather than dishonesty, and, in receiving gifts from litigants, Bacon was yielding to the common practice. He clearly erred in accepting gifts while cases were pending, but there is no evidence that he put justice up for sale. He sent, however, a full confession and submission to the House of Lords and begged for mercy. Sentence was pronounced on May 3, 1621, by the chief justice in a crowded house: the Lord St. Alban was ordered to pay a fine of £40,000, to be imprisoned in the Tower, to be barred forever from public office, and to be forbidden to come within the vicinity of the court. The imprisonment and presently the fine were remitted. He retired to Gorhambury, where he lived in considerable state.

He devoted himself to literary and philosophical work, and the five years remaining to him saw the publication of the *History of Henry VII* (1622), the *De augmentis scientiarum* (1623, an expanded Latin translation of the *Advancement of Learning*), revisions of the *Essays*, and other important writings. He resisted Buckingham's efforts to purchase his old home, York House, but eventually consented in return for permission to enter London. In March 1626, intent on experiments relating to the preservation of flesh, he alighted from his coach, bought a fowl from a cottage, and stuffed it with snow. He contracted a chill and took refuge in the house of Lord Arundel (Thomas Howard, 14th earl of Arundel). There he died on April 9.

Bacon's personality has continued to fascinate and disconcert historians. In his political relations he often appears servile, ruthless, and unfaithful; yet on occasions he gave shrewd advice to James. His ideal of government was determined by the practice of Elizabethan monarchy. He desired a sovereign who would give ear to the counsels of experienced statesmen and heed the opinions of the popular assembly. But he was convinced that the king should preserve his independence and authority, for upon his prescience depended the safety and prosperity of the realm. In private life Bacon was genial and considerate, winning the admiration and affection of his friends.

Philosophical Doctrines. Bacon wrote more than 30 philosophical works, most of which are fragmentary and incomplete. They were taken up at intervals between sittings of Parliament and the courts and amid the incessant demands of the king's business. Under these conditions his achievement fell far short of the immense design he had envisaged in his youth. That design embraced a comprehensive reform of human knowledge and a searching denunciation of the prevailing purposes and methods of philosophy. The complete plan for the regeneration of knowledge is set forth in the introduction to the *Novum organum,* but most of Bacon's pieces cannot well be assigned to divisions of the system announced in this introduction. They are occupied with other topics, subsidiary to the main design; yet they contain much of Bacon's characteristic opinions.

These subsidiary works include the celebrated *Advancement of Learning* (1605), the only philosophical work published by him in English. It comprises two books, the first of which is an elaborate defense of learning against its detractors: divines, politicians, and learned men themselves. In passages of splendid eloquence he exposes "the errors and vanities which have intervened among the studies themselves of the learned," the preoccupation with literary style, the obsession with the degenerate Aristotelianism of the schools, and the credulous belief in magical science, astrology, and alchemy. He believes the greatest error to be the misplacing of the true end of knowledge, "the glory of the Creator and the relief of man's estate." In the second book Bacon surveys the intellectual world of the later 16th century, noticing deficiencies in various provinces. He treats in turn of history, poetry, and philosophy, and their numerous subdivisions.

Among many striking discussions, expressed in periods of intricate eloquence, two central doctrines are asserted. One is the new and original position assigned to metaphysics. The traditional metaphysics or first philosophy was concerned with the notion of being in general, analysis of which had yielded such all-pervading principles as matter—the indeterminate substratum of things—and forms, appropriate to each species of substance, which strive to organize and bring to actuality the indeterminate material element. Bacon rejects these venerable metaphysical agencies and boldly makes metaphysics the fundamental part of a materialist physics. He describes three levels of natural inquiry: (1) natural history, or the collection of scientific data; (2) physics, the investigation of particular natures and causes; and (3) metaphysics, the elucidation of the fundamental natures or forms of things from the conjunctions of which all things are composed, as the conjunctions of a few letters compose a language. Physics, accordingly, examines natural objects in a narrower context, metaphysics in a broader view; both consider the structures and processes of actual matter. The other notable doctrine proclaimed in the *Advancement of Learning* is the sharp separation of human truth from the dogmatic truths of revealed theology. He allows a limited function to reason in deriving consequences from the divine mysteries, but he asserts that the articles of religion are "placed and ex-

empted from examination of reason"; they are to be believed even when they appear contrary to our understanding. He holds that it is futile to seek knowledge in divinity or sacred theology in natural inquiry. The severance of knowledge from faith is a cardinal point of Bacon's outlook; it accords with his view that knowledge is limited to sensible material and finite things.

Besides the *Advancement of Learning,* a large number of works deal with topics more or less outside the *Instauratio magna* (*Great Instauration*), which was Bacon's grand project for the renovation of knowledge. Such are the early *Temporis partus masculus sive instauratio magna imperii humani in universum* (*Masculine or Generative Birth of Time,* first published in 1653), *Valerius Terminus of the Interpretation of Nature* (first published in 1734), *De interpretatione naturae prooemium* (*Preface to the Interpretation of Nature,* first published in 1653), *Cogitata et visa: de interpretatione naturae, sive de scientia operativa* (*Reflections and Views Concerning the Interpretation of Nature, or Concerning Applied Science,* first published in 1653), and *Descriptio globi intellectualis et thema coeli* (*Description of the Intellectual Globe and the Order of the Heavens,* first published in 1653). These fragments, unpublished during Bacon's lifetime, treat of the deficiencies of traditional learning and recommend a new method of investigation.

All these earlier ideas on the reform of knowledge are superseded by the complete design of the *Instauratio magna* as set forth in its preface, which was published together with the *Novum organum* in 1620. The grand program is to consist of six parts: (1) a review of the existing state of knowledge; (2) an account of the new logic of inquiry, based on induction, and an exposition of the prejudices that beset the mind in its search for truth; (3) a natural history, or collection of accurate data, embracing all the phenomena of nature; (4) illustrations of the application of the inductive method in selected fields; (5) provisional conclusions derived from the application of the method; and (6) a synthesis of knowledge constructed on the new method—"a task," Bacon confesses, "which lies beyond my powers and expectations." Of the vast scheme of the *Instauratio magna,* only a fragment, distributed through several works, was accomplished. The *De augmentis scientiarum* (1623), an expanded Latin version of the *Advancement of Learning,* is a hasty attempt to supply, late in the author's life, part one of the system. Part two, the most important section of the plan, is incompletely represented by the *Novum organum.* Various lists of topics for investigation are presented for part three, notably the *Parasceve ad historiam naturalem et experimentalem* (1620; *Preparative Study for a Natural and Experimental History*), and the *Historia naturalis et experimentalis ad condendam philosophiam* (1622; *Natural and Experimental History for the Foundation of Philosophy*). Among the subjects mentioned for investigation in this history are winds; density and rarity, or the contraction and expansion of matter in space; the phenomena of heaviness and lightness; and the natures of sulfur, mercury, and salt. Other incomplete pieces, such as Bacon's last work, *Sylva sylvarum,* published in 1627, may be allotted to part three of the *Instauratio magna.* Little remains of four and five and nothing of six.

Novum Organum. The title *Novum organum* is chosen in order to contrast the "new method of reasoning" with that of Aristotle's *Organon*. It contains two books. The first unfolds the celebrated account of idols, or false images, of the human mind that distort the judgment in its search for truth. Four classes of idols are described. The first, which he calls idols of the tribe, are errors native to human nature itself. They include the limitations of the senses and the corruption of the understanding by desire and comfortable prejudices. The second kind, idols of the cave, arise from the individual nature and education of the inquirer. Some men become preoccupied with certain ideas or methods and extend them unwarrantably in constructing systems. Bacon mentions Aristotle and his own contemporary William Gilbert as examples of this tendency. The third class of idols is the most troublesome. These are termed idols of the marketplace. They spring from misuses of language; for learned discussion is often occupied with words that refer to abstract concepts, which sometimes tend to become confused. The traditional physics contains many such terms. Finally, there are idols of the theater, the play books of philosophical systems such as those of Aristotle, of the alchemists, and of those who mix philosophy with theology.

Bacon rejected the old logic of Aristotle because of its concern with grammatical form. Where the aim of inquiry is discovery, the rational demonstration of deductive logic is useless. The new way of knowledge, expounded in the second book of the *Novum organum*, demands a logic that will be occupied with accurate observation and experiment in order to educe axioms from experience. His aim here is the discovery of form, and to this ancient notion he gives a novel turn. The forms become the fixed and essential laws of the operations of material bodies: "For when we speak of Forms we mean nothing more than those laws and determinations of pure actuality which order and constitute any simple nature, as heat, light, weight, in every kind of matter and subject that is susceptible of them. Thus the Form of Heat or the Form of Light is the same thing as the Law of Heat or the Law of Light." There are degrees of forms, from the restricted laws of specific inquiries to the fundamental laws and causes of all natural things. These fundamental forms are limited in number, and their conjunctions provide the ground plan of nature. Bacon's doctrine of forms envisages a mechanical and determinist naturalism that is logically connected with a program of profitable works. He constantly associates knowledge with practice: "human knowledge and human power meet in one," and "truth and utility are here the very same things, and works themselves are of greater value as pledges of truth than as contributing to the comfort of life." He points to the invention of printing, gunpowder, and the mariner's compass to show the bearing of knowledge on power, but he maintains that insight into the actual constitution of things by scientific methods must precede dominion over nature.

The new method of induction, by which the forms are to be brought to light, was to have included 11 processes, but Bacon describes no more than three of them. The first step is the "presentation of instances." In seeking the form of heat, the inquirer compiles first a wide variety of cases in which the phenomenon in question is present. A further table contains instances that resemble those in the first table, but in which the phenomenon of heat is absent. A third table accumulates instances in which the nature under investigation appears in different degrees, showing the increase or decrease of heat in various circumstances. Bacon gives many examples under the three tables, which correspond with John Stuart Mill's later methods of agreement, difference, and concomitant variations. From a scrutiny of these tables the investigator is able to eliminate certain irrelevant factors that bear on the nature of heat and to advance a tentative theory. This second step of inductive method is named the "first vintage," and the evidence points to the conclusion that heat is a species of motion. He now proceeds to the third stage of induction. This is a long series of tests, named "prerogative instances," designed to bring out more sharply the essential connections that are being sought. Some of these tests refine observation by means of instruments and devices; other tests provide aids to the understanding of the phenomena being observed; still others serve practical application. Many of these methods hint at procedures that later became important in scientific inquiry. At this point the account of the new inductive method breaks off; the further steps were never expounded.

Influence on Scientific Thought. When these incomplete proposals are compared with the procedure of the great scientists of the time, such as Galileo or William Harvey, their defects become apparent. Bacon pays insufficient regard to the way in which successful scientific investigation is guided by definite and limited questions and theories, and he fails to recognize the function of mathematics in physical science. He was out of touch with the advances in natural science and mathematics of the period and persisted in rejecting the Copernican theory. Sometimes he falls into animistic modes of thought. In *Sylva sylvarum* (*A Forest of Materials*) he amasses topics for investigation from the superstitions of ancient writers. Yet his vast influence on the scientific revolution of the 17th century cannot be challenged. His impressive statement of the need to contemplate "things as they are, without superstition or imposture, error or confusion," his concern with methods by which scientific evidence could be tested and enlarged; and his eloquent representations of science as the handmaid of technological progress gave a powerful impetus to the development of science in the 17th century. The *New Atlantis*, published posthumously in 1627, provided in its descriptions of the investigations of Salomon's House the model for the scientific societies that appeared in the latter part of the century, especially the Royal Society of London. Its members saluted Bacon as the founder of the "new philosophy," and in the history of modern thought he has been generally acclaimed as the prophet of the scientific outlook.

Literary Works. The most popular of all Bacon's writings was the *Essays or Counsels, Civil and Moral*. The first edition, comprising 10 essays, was published in 1597; a second edition, in which the original pieces were enlarged and 29 new essays added, appeared in 1612; a third revision, in which the number of essays was increased to 58, was published in 1625. The earlier set are written in a disjointed, aphoristic style; the later numbers are more continuous and richer in manner and allusion. These essays are full of practical wisdom, and disclose the author's penetrating, dry, and detached view of mankind. They also reveal further his social and political principles. Besides *The Historie of the Raigne of King Henry the Seventh* (1622), which has been described as the beginning of modern history in England, Bacon wrote fragments of further histories and began a dialogue, *An Advertisement Touching on Holy Warre* (1622). Among the compositions of his last years is the entertaining collection of witty stories named *Apophthegms New and Old* (1624–1625). His religious writings include *The Translation of Certaine Psalmes into English Verse* (1625). The collected works contain a number of his legal writings. See also ESSAYS OF BACON; NOVUM ORGANUM.

MEYRICK H. CARRÉ
Author of "Realists and Nominalists"

Bibliography

The Works of Francis Bacon was edited by James Spedding, Robert L. Ellis, and Douglas D. Heath, 14 vols. (London 1857–74); the last 7 vols. ed. by Spedding, have also been published separately as *Letters and Life.*
Anderson, Fulton H., *The Philosophy of Francis Bacon* (Chicago 1948).
Broad, C.D., *The Philosophy of Francis Bacon* (Cambridge, Eng., 1926).
Brown, Catherine D., *Francis Bacon* (Boston 1963).
Farrington, Benjamin, *Francis Bacon: Philosopher of Industrial Science* (New York 1949).
Green, A. Wigfall, *Sir Francis Bacon, His Life and Works* (Denver 1952).
Hall, A.R., *The Scientific Revolution 1500–1800*, 2d ed. (Boston 1956).
Jones, Richard F., *Ancients and Moderns* (St. Louis 1936).
Sorley, William R., *A History of English Philosophy* (New York 1921).
Sturt, Mary, *Francis Bacon* (London 1932).
Wallace, Karl R., *Francis Bacon on Communication and Rhetoric* (Chapel Hill, N.C., 1943).
Willey, Basil, *The Seventeenth Century Background* (New York 1942).

BACON, ba′kən, **Francis** (1909–   ), English painter, whose images of anguish and terror, painted in thin, rich colors, brought him to the top rank of English painters in the early 1950's. Bacon describes his work as "an attempt to make a certain type of feeling visual." His composition is usually a single figure, centrally placed in a dark or ominously lighted space. Most of his work is done in series, each series drawn from a single source of inspiration—often a photograph or another artist's painting.

Bacon was born in Dublin, Ireland, on Oct. 28, 1909, of English parents. As an artist he was entirely self-taught. He traveled in Germany and France before he settled in London in 1928 and began a brief, successful career as an interior decorator. He did not begin to paint until the early 1930's. The influence of Picasso, synthetic cubism, and surrealism is apparent in his early work. An early *Crucifixion* (1933) won favorable attention, but a full-time civil defense job in World War II kept him from painting much before 1944. That year he completed *Studies for Figures at the Base of a Crucifixion.*

Bacon's style reached maturity in the late 1940's and early 1950's. His best-known works of this period are the series of *Studies After Velázquez' Portrait of Pope Innocent X*, done between 1951 and 1953. They project a terrified—and terrifying—image of pomp and authority, with the pope's mouth open in a silent scream. The snarling dogs in a 1952 series

FRANCIS BACON, English painter of the bizarre.

project a similar feeling of being threatened and of threatening at the same time.

Bacon began to exhibit regularly at the Hanover Gallery in London in 1949. His work was first seen in the United States in 1953 and was featured at the Venice Biennale in 1954. During this period he began to spend his summers in the south of France. He traveled to South Africa by way of Egypt in 1950–1951, to Italy in 1954, and to Tangier in 1956.

In 1956 and 1957, Bacon painted a series that he called *Studies for a Portrait of Van Gogh*, based on Van Gogh's *The Painter on the Road to Tarascon.* These paintings show the lighter colors and heavier paint characteristic of Bacon's later work. His paintings of the 1960's (for example, *Study for a Portrait on a Folding Bed*, 1963) show a change of style toward greater distortion and abstraction in the figures.

Further Reading: Alley, Ronald, and Rothenstein, J., *Francis Bacon* (London 1964).

BACON, bā′kən, **Frank** (1864–1922), American playwright and actor. He was born in Marysville, Calif., on Jan. 16, 1864. After acting in various amateur productions, he joined the San Jose (Calif.) players in 1890, making his first appearance as Sample Switchell in *Ten Nights in a Barroom.* While with this company, he portrayed over 600 characters in various plays. After managing his own troupe in Portland (Oreg.) he played a long and successful season at the Alcazar Theatre in San Francisco, and in 1906, after the San Francisco earthquake, he moved his family to New York City.

He immediately appeared in a series of successful plays: *The Miracle Man, The Cinderella Man, Alabama,* and *Pudd'nhead Wilson.* On Aug. 26, 1918, he opened in the role of Bill Jones in *Lightnin',* written by him in collaboration with Winchell Smith. The play was immensely successful, running at the Gaiety Theatre in New York City for three years and a day, for a total of 1,291 performances. Bacon was playing the same role in Chicago when he died on Nov. 19, 1922.

His other plays include *Five O'Clock,* written with Freeman Tilden, and *Me and Grant,* written with James Montgomery.

BACON, bā'kən, **Henry** (1866–1924), American architect, who designed the Lincoln Memorial in Washington, D.C. He was born at Watseka, Ill., on Nov. 28, 1866. He attended the University of Illinois in 1888, and in 1889 he won the Rotch Traveling Scholarship, under which he spent two years studying in Europe. From 1888 to 1897, with the exception of 1890–1891, he was with the architectural firm of McKim, Mead, and White. In 1897 he formed the partnership of Brite and Bacon, and after 1902 he practiced alone.

A strict adherent to the classic Greek style of architecture, Bacon designed several important buildings, among them the public library in Paterson, N.J.; the Court of Four Seasons at the Panama-Pacific Exposition, San Francisco; and the Lincoln Memorial (q.v.) in Washington, D.C., dedicated in 1922. For the latter he received the gold medal of the American Institute of Architects in 1923. He collaborated with the sculptor Daniel Chester French, who executed the statue of Lincoln in the Lincoln Memorial, in over 50 memorials, and also did some work with Augustus Saint-Gaudens. Bacon died in New York City on Feb. 16, 1924.

BACON, bā'kən, **John** (1740–1799), English sculptor. He was born in London on Nov. 24, 1740. At the age of 14 he was apprenticed to a porcelain manufacturer. Later, he worked as a modeler of artificial stone. In 1768 he became a student in the Royal Academy Schools, and the next year he received from Sir Joshua Reynolds the first gold medal for sculpture given by the academy. The work for which he received the award was a bas-relief, *Aeneas Escaping From Troy.* The following year he was chosen as associate of the Royal Academy, and in 1778 he became a full member.

Bacon was much sought after for his monumental sculptures. His chief works are two groups for the interior of the Royal Academy; the statue of Judge William Blackstone for All Souls' College, Oxford; one of Henry VI for Eton College; the monument of William Pitt, earl of Chatham, in Westminster Abbey; and the statues of Dr. Samuel Johnson and the philanthropist John Howard in St. Paul's Cathedral. He died in London on Aug. 4, 1799.

John Bacon (1777–1859), his son, was also a sculptor. He completed his father's statue of William III in St. James's Square, London.

BACON, bā'kən, **Leonard** (1802–1881), American Congregational minister. He was born on Feb. 19, 1802, in Detroit, Mich., graduated from Yale in 1820, and studied theology at Andover Newton Theological Seminary in Andover, Mass. He became pastor of the First Church of New Haven, Conn., in 1825, and held the post until his death on Dec. 24, 1881, though he was not always active as its pastor. From 1866 until 1871 he was professor of revealed theology at Yale. He helped to found the New York *Independent* in 1847 and was one of its editors until 1863.

Bacon took an active interest in many causes. He worked in the temperance movement in the early part of the 19th century. In 1844 he expressed the conviction that a general conference ought to exist in which evangelical bodies might all be represented. He was one of the first persons to state such an opinion. His outspoken writings opposing slavery influenced Lincoln.

BACON, bā'kən, **Leonard** (1887–1954), American poet, who won the 1941 Pulitzer Prize in Poetry. He was born at Solvay, N.Y., on May 26, 1887. He graduated from Yale University in 1909, and while continuing graduate study there, he privately published his first volume of verse, *The Scrannel Pipe* (1909). In 1910 he began teaching English at the University of California, until 1923, when he left to devote full time to writing. He died at South Kingston, R.I., on Jan. 1, 1954.

Bacon wrote many volumes of witty and satiric verse dealing with contemporary social and political problems, including *Dream and Action* (1934) and the Pulitzer Prize-winning *Sunderland Capture and Other Poems* (1940).

BACON, Nathaniel. See BACON'S REBELLION.

BACON, bā'kən, **Sir Nicholas** (1509–1579), English government official, who was the father of Francis Bacon. He was born at Chislehurst, Kent, England. He was graduated from Corpus Christi College, Cambridge, in 1527, and was called to the bar in 1533. He received a large property from confiscated monastery lands and was appointed attorney to the Court of Wards and Liveries. Bacon stood in favor with Edward VI, and, although a Protestant, he was not prosecuted during the reign of Mary Tudor, but even retained his office. With the accession of Queen Elizabeth I in 1558 he was appointed lord keeper of the great seal.

The influence of Sir William Cecil (later Lord Burghley), his brother-in-law, undoubtedly aided Bacon's career, but his own astuteness made him a valued adviser to Queen Elizabeth. Mistrustful of Mary, Queen of Scots, he opposed her restoration to the throne. He died in London on Feb. 20, 1579.

BACON, bā'kən, **Peggy** (1895–   ), American artist and author. She was born in Ridgefield, Conn., on May 2, 1895. She studied in New York City, at the Art Students League under John Sloan, George Bellows, and Kenneth Hayes Miller, and at the School of Fine and Applied Arts. In 1920 she married Alexander Brook, the painter, whom she divorced in 1940. She is best known for her incisive, but good-humored, social satire, expressed in etchings and in verse. She also has been widely acclaimed for her perceptive eye concerning the ways of cats. She wrote and illustrated many children's books, among them *The Lion-Hearted Kitten and Other Stories* (1927), *The Good American Witch* (1957), and *The Oddity* (1962).

BACON, bā'kən, **Robert** (1860–1919), American banker and diplomat. He was born in Boston on July 5, 1860. Soon after graduating from Harvard in 1880 he entered the Boston banking house of Lee, Higginson, and Company, and from 1883 until 1894 he was a member of the firm of E. Rollins Morse and Brother. Thereafter he was a member of the New York banking house of J.P. Morgan and Company until 1903.

Long a keen student of foreign affairs, Bacon served as first assistant secretary of state under Elihu Root from 1905 until 1909. When Root entered the U.S. Senate in 1909, Bacon became secretary of state for a brief period. Before the end of 1909, President Taft appointed him ambassador to France, and he continued in this post until 1912. He urged United States entry into World War I. When this came about in 1917, he returned to France on the staff of Gen. John J. Pershing; the next year he served as head of the American military mission at British general headquarters. Bacon died in New York City on May 29, 1919. He was the author of *For Better Relations with Our Latin American Neighbors* (1915).

BACON, bā′kən, **Roger** (1214?–?1292), English philosopher and man of science, who helped lay the foundations of modern scientific thinking. He was aware of the interrelatedness of all the separate sciences and of the contributions that science makes to the understanding of reality. He explained the role of experience and experiment in confirming or refuting speculative hypotheses. He insisted on the practical value of scientific speculation and believed in the importance of an ethical system or moral philosophy to crown the whole edifice of scientific thought and to determine the uses to which scientific knowledge should be put.

Youth and Middle Years. There is little reliable information about his life except what may be gleaned incidentally from his writings. He was born in England, and his early studies were in the faculty of arts at the University of Oxford, where he also taught for some years. In the early 1240's he went to Paris, where he taught in the faculty of arts at the University of Paris. Bacon's method in his lectures and writings of these years is scholastic, and there is no evidence at this time of any special interest in science, nor is it likely that he ever attained sufficient competence in theology to become a doctor of theology. Indeed, in later life he objected to the prevailing method of studying theology by propounding theological questions and answering them. Instead, he believed in using the Scriptures to fortify faith.

After teaching for several years at Paris, he became acquainted with the pseudo-Aristotelian *Secretum secretorum,* which appears to have been instrumental in turning his attention to science. He was especially impressed with the aid that science might give to religion, and thereafter his major interests were scientific. Returning to England about 1250, he devoted himself to scientific study. He became acquainted with all the scientific knowledge of his day, carried out some experiments, and spent as much money as he could obtain from his family and other sources to acquire scientific books and materials. About 1252 he joined the Franciscan Order, but from the beginning he appears to have been unhappy in it, although for a time he was permitted to engage in his scientific speculations and carry out systematic observations, especially on the nature of light and such natural phenomena as the rainbow. Much of his best work was done in optics, where he had access to Muslim works on the subject.

In 1257 he was transferred to Paris, possibly because of personal and religious differences with his fellow friars and authorities within the order, but almost certainly not, as was once thought, by reason of his scientific studies. He regarded his transfer as a kind of imprisonment, although it did not prevent him from continuing his work, which included a treatise on the calendar.

"Opus Majus." About 1266, Bacon sent a message to the new pope, Clement IV, informing him of his project for a reform of Christian education through the use of science. The pope replied, expressing his interest, but told Bacon to proceed secretly because of the Franciscan rule against unauthorized writing.

At the time, Bacon was having difficulties in his Parisian convent, perhaps on account of his outspoken ways and irascible temperament and perhaps because of his general resentment at the restraints under which he was compelled to live. He lacked money and evidently did not have the support and encouragement of his order. Nevertheless he was able with great difficulty to prepare the *Opus majus,* which was intended to give some indication of the scope of his proposed work and which is filled with the moral fervor characteristic of most of Bacon's writings. It contains the short works that he had available and a number of other sections rather loosely tied together into what he calls a *persuasio,* a book intended to persuade the pope of the value of his investigations. In addition to the *Opus majus,* he sent the pope a shorter work, the *Opus minus,* which probably had been intended originally as a digest but had grown in the preparation to contain considerable new material. The pope died shortly afterward, and it is not known whether he ever read the works.

Later Years. Bacon probably returned to England soon after the death of his patron. He did not do much more writing, although a highly polemical work, dated 1272, directed against theologians and other opponents is extant, which may have produced difficulties for Bacon within his order. A late chronicle reveals that he was imprisoned for "suspected novelties" by the general of his order. But it is difficult to discover any such "novelties" in his work, which does not differ greatly from that of his time, except in its emphasis. The imprisonment, if it ever took place, was probably for reasons unconnected with his scientific work. He was in any case freed before his death. He left an uncompleted compendium of theology, which appears to be the effort of a tired old man and contains little that is original or interesting.

During his many years of scientific study, Bacon made it his business to discover all that could be known, and it seems clear that although he did some experimental work himself, his real claim to fame rests on his achievements as a scientific thinker and synthesist of other men's work. He has been variously credited with the discovery of gunpowder, eyeglasses, the telescope, and other important inventions. His works certainly describe these things, but he does not give himself credit for their invention, although he understood the principles on which they are based. His fame as a magician dates from later centuries, not his own. See also FRIAR BACON; OPUS MAJUS.

STEWART C. EASTON, *The City College, New York*

Bibliography

Full Text of the *Opus majus* was translated by Robert B. Burke, 2 vols. (Philadelphia 1928). Selections may be found in Richard McKeon, ed., *Selections from Medieval Philosophers* (New York 1928).

Crowley, Theodore, *Roger Bacon: The Problem of the Soul in His Philosophical Commentaries* (Louvain, Belgium, and Dublin, Ireland, 1950).

Easton, Stewart C., *Roger Bacon and His Search for a Universal Science* (New York 1952).

Fuller, B.A.G., *A History of Philosophy,* rev. ed. by Sterling M. McMurrin (New York 1955).

Knowles, David, *Saints and Scholars* (Cambridge, Eng., 1962).

Thorndike, Lynn, *History of Magic and Experimental Science,* vol. 2 (New York 1923).

BACON, bā′kən, is the flesh of a pig—usually the sides, belly, and back—which has been cured or preserved by salting or pickling, and afterward drying with or without wood smoke. By the old process of rubbing in the saline mixture, the curing occupied from three to four months. Modern methods used by the big meatpackers achieve the curing in 2 to 10 days by injecting or pumping pickle into the arteries of the meat. Bacon requires a good proportion of fat for the best flavor, and this makes it a food of high energy value.

In the United States the preferred bacon is the side or sometimes the belly; Canadian bacon comes from the loin; and European, especially British, is the Wiltshire side, which includes the ham and the shoulder.

BACON'S REBELLION, bā′kənz ri-bel′yən, was an uprising by settlers against the colonial government in 17th century Virginia. In spite of efforts to diversify the economy, Virginia during this period depended on one crop, tobacco. In the 1660's and 1670's tobacco prices were low, and Virginians were poor. One reason may have been the Navigation Acts of 1660 and 1663, which confined the tobacco trade to England, where heavy duties were collected upon importation. Only a part of these duties were rebated when tobacco was reshipped from England to the European market. In order to sell tobacco at all, merchants had to offer the planters low prices for it.

Grievances. The governor of Virginia, Sir William Berkeley, objected to the Navigation Acts, but his protests brought no relief. Berkeley had been a popular governor in Virginia from the time of his arrival in 1642. But in the 1660's his popularity was running out, and his closest followers were resented. While the rest of the people suffered, the governor's friends were able to stave off the effects of depression by obtaining favors from the government. The Governor's Council, which carried the most weight in all governmental decisions, enjoyed an exemption from taxation. The House of Burgesses, supposed to represent the people of every county, were allowed to sit without a new election from 1661 to 1676.

In 1675 resentment against the government was aggravated by an outbreak of Indian hostilities. The Indians living within the colony were few in number and broken in spirit, but the Susquehannocks on the border were more dangerous. In September 1675 a party of militia conducting a peace mission to the Susquehannocks slaughtered the chieftains who had come to negotiate with them. The Susquehannocks responded in January 1676 by killing 36 Virginians. Governor Berkeley, alarmed like other Virginians, proposed the erection of frontier forts, and new taxes were levied to construct them.

The Uprising. The combined danger of death and taxes provoked the Virginians to anger. Frontiersmen had little use for forts. They wanted action, and they wanted it fast and cheap. A self-appointed army gathered in Charles City County and asked Nathaniel Bacon (1647–1676) to lead them on a punitive expedition against the Indians. Bacon, a wealthy and well-educated young newcomer from England, was a member of the Governor's Council.

Bacon accepted, and after frightening away a settlement of tame Pamunkeys, he demanded a commission from the governor to conduct more expeditions. Berkeley declared him a rebel, and

called a new election of Burgesses to deal with the situation. Bacon, without a commission, visited the friendly Occaneechee Indians on the Carolina border. A quarrel broke out and he and his men killed most of the Occaneechee.

Upon returning from this campaign Bacon was elected to the new House of Burgesses and appeared at Jamestown in June 1676 to claim his seat and renew his demand for a commission. Berkeley had him arrested, but later pardoned him and restored him to the Council. The reconciliation was evidently not complete, for Bacon did not receive his commission. After a few days, he retreated to the upcountry, gathered forces, and returned to Jamestown. Berkeley, perhaps intimidated by the size of Bacon's following, gave him the commission to fight the Indians. But after Bacon departed, Berkeley again denounced him.

By this time, however, Bacon was more popular in Virginia than was Berkeley. The governor was obliged to flee to the Eastern Shore at the end of July. When he returned to Jamestown on September 8, Bacon drove him out again and burned the town on Sept. 19, 1676.

Bacon doubtless realized that Berkeley would receive assistance from England. Probably in order to present a united front to any royal investigation, Bacon imposed an oath of allegiance on the people of Virginia. While thus attempting to consolidate his position, he died of a fever on Oct. 26, 1676.

The rebellion continued under the command of Joseph Ingram, but Berkeley gained control of the rivers, and the rebels began to lose heart. By the end of the year Berkeley had restored his authority.

Aftermath. The governor exacted a ruthless revenge. When royal commissioners arrived in January and February 1677, they carried a royal proclamation of amnesty to all rebels except Bacon himself and an order for Berkeley's return to England.

Berkeley refused at first to issue the proclamation and, when he did, combined it with one of his own, excluding 18 persons from its benefits. He also refused to return to England until he had concluded business to his own satisfaction. When he departed on May 5, 1677, he had executed 23 men.

Berkeley died shortly after reaching England. The commissioners stayed on in Virginia, and peace was restored. In Berkeley's favor it must be said that no serious charges were proved against his regime and that he succeeded in overcoming the rebellion without assistance from England. He could not have done so without some measure of popular support. It must also be emphasized that Bacon's expeditions are not known to have killed any but friendly Indians.

On the other hand, the new House of Burgesses, sitting in June 1676, did enact a number of laws to reform such abuses as plural office-holding and favoritism in the government. Bacon has usually been given credit for these laws, but some of them appear to have been directed against him. All were repealed, but most were reenacted by the next assembly.

EDMUND S. MORGAN, *Yale University*

Further Reading: Andrews, Charles M., ed., *Narratives of the Insurrections, 1675–1690*, reprint (New York 1952); Middlekauff, Robert, *Bacon's Rebellion*, paperbound (New York 1964); Washburn, Wilcomb E., *The Governor and the Rebel* (Chapel Hill, N.C., 1957); Wertenbaker, Thomas J., *Torchbearer of the Revolution*, reprint (Magnolia, Mass., 1965).

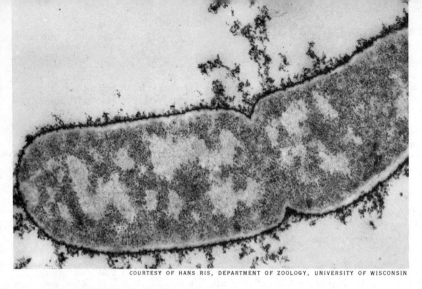

ESCHERICHIA COLI, a common bacterium found in the intestinal tract of man and higher animals, is shown during cell division. This picture, taken with an electron microscope, is magnified thousands of times.

COURTESY OF HANS RIS, DEPARTMENT OF ZOOLOGY, UNIVERSITY OF WISCONSIN

BACTERIA AND BACTERIOLOGY, bak-tir'ēə, bak-tir-ē-ol'ə-jē.

Bacteria are one-celled plants that sometimes are so small they must be viewed with an electron microscope. Some bacteria are free-living—they manufacture their own food. Others live on dead or decaying matter or as parasites on other living organisms. Still others cause disease. The science of bacteriology deals with the properties and activities of bacteria.

The bacteria constitute a useful and essential group in the biological community. Although some bacteria prey on higher forms of life, relatively few are pathogens (disease-causing organisms). Certain microorganisms spoil food and fiber, but most of these are subject to control. From the point of view of man these activities are "antisocial," but other organisms derive many benefits from the existence of bacteria. Life on earth depends on the activity of bacteria in mineralizing organic compounds and on their ability to capture the free nitrogen molecules in the air for use by plants. Also, bacteria are important industrially for the conversion of raw materials into useful products, such as the formation of organic chemicals, including antibiotics, and the manufacture of cheese.

1. Bacteriology As a Science

History. Bacteria were first described in 1676 by an amateur lens grinder named Anton van Leeuwenhoek of Delft, Holland. They received little attention for nearly 200 years until Louis Pasteur, a French chemist, became interested in the "diseases" of beer and wine. From his researches he concluded (1857) that such chemical compounds as lactic and butyric acids are produced by specific organisms. This significant concept was extended readily to the idea that a given disease may be caused by a specific microorganism. Robert Koch, a German physician, demonstrated this to be true (1876) for anthrax in cattle. He isolated the causative organism, *Bacillus anthracis*, from the blood of an infected animal and grew it in pure culture, which he then used to infect another animal. This demonstration, soon extended to other infectious diseases, marks the beginning of bacteriology as a branch of science. (See DISEASE, GERM THEORY OF.) Although bacteriology initially was concerned chiefly with pathogenic bacteria and the diseases they cause, such bacteria represent only a limited number of species. As the science developed, attention was directed toward organisms important in agriculture (soil and dairy bacteriology) and technology (fermentation and food). Recently, bacteriology has been recognized as an independent discipline, significant especially for its contributions in the field of molecular biology, without reference to its many important practical applications.

Relation to Other Organisms. The separation of all living things into two kingdoms—the animal and the vegetable—remained satisfactory until significant study of microorganisms began in the early part of the 19th century. As information developed, it became apparent that bacteria, molds, yeasts, algae, and protozoa could not categorically be classified as either plants or animals. For example, bacteria have rigid cell walls, as do plants, but some are motile and most use organic foods, as animals do; algae have chlorophyll, as do plants, but some are motile; yeasts have a rigid cell wall, but some share with animals the ability to make fats; and some protozoa and bacteria have chlorophyll. Ernst Haeckel solved this dilemma (1866) by proposing an additional kingdom, the Protista, to include protozoa, molds, yeasts, bacteria, and the simplest algae. This suggestion achieved little acceptance and today, as a result of work done primarily in the 19th century, protozoa are assigned to the animal kingdom, while bacteria, molds, yeasts, and algae are allocated to the vegetable kingdom. In recent years, viruses (the smallest known microorganisms) and the rickettsiae (intermediate in size between viruses and bacteria) have also been included in the plant category.

Classification. Bacteria are classified according to the following criteria: microscopic appearance and staining reaction; appearance of growth on the surface of solid media or in liquid media; physiological characteristics, including the effects of the bacteria upon the environment; the ability to produce disease; and, for some, serological reactions. The nomenclature of bacteria is binomial, using the genus and species names: for example, *Escherichia coli*. An International Code of Nomenclature of Bacteria and Viruses has been developed and adopted by the International Association of Microbiological Societies. It should be emphasized that this is an artificial

CONTENTS

Section	Page	Section	Page
1. Bacteriology as a Science	30	5. Ecology	35
2. Bacterial Anatomy	31	6. Bacteriophage and Bacteriogenetics	38
3. Bacterial Physiology	32	7. Bibliography	39
4. Technology	34		

classification and not a natural one such as is attempted for higher plants and animals. For efforts to classify bacteria there are few such guidelines of sexual reproduction or evolutionary development as are used for the higher forms. Sexual reproduction has been demonstrated in only a few bacteria; since bacteria have no parts that fossilize, little can be learned about their evolutionary development from paleontology. Thus, classification of bacteria is actually an arbitrary key to identification, such as that followed in *Bergey's Manual of Determinative Bacteriology*.

The bacteria have been assigned to the Protophyta, a special division of the vegetable kingdom that has three classes: Class I, Schizophyceae, the blue-green algae; Class II, Schizomycetes, the bacteria; and Class III, Microtatobiotes, including the rickettsiae and viruses.

The class Schizomycetes may be divided into 10 orders. The orders Eubacteriales and Pseudomonadales contain the largest number of species and include most of the bacteria important to man. These orders embrace the simplest rod, spiral, and spherical forms that most laymen would regard as bacteria. The order Actinomycetales embodies forms that have a moldlike appearance, with hyphae (thread-like extensions) and conidiospores (asexual spores), and are common in soil. Also included in this order are the microorganisms that cause tuberculosis, as well as many that produce antibiotics. The order Spirochaetales contains spiral-shaped forms that have flexible cell walls and resemble protozoa; important members of this order are those that produce syphilis and relapsing fever. The order Mycoplasmatales includes organisms that are highly pleomorphic—that is, they occur in more than one distinct form during their life cycles. The organisms are characterized by filaments that break up into coccoid (spherical) bodies. These cell bodies, which are soft and fragile, can cause disease; they are called pleuropneumonia-like organisms. In the order Chlamydobacteriales are found the iron bacteria, present in water, which deposit oxides or carbonates of iron in sheaths surrounding the cells. The order Hyphomicrobiales contains organisms that multiply by budding or by longitudinal fission and occur in aggregates that have a common stalk; these are also to be found in fresh water.

The order Caryophanales embraces very large bacteria (6 microns in diameter by 20 microns in length) that are found in the intestinal tracts of animals; in these larger cells a nucleus can be clearly discerned. The order Beggiatoales contains rod-shaped forms that move by a gliding motion, though they appear to lack flagella or other organs of locomotion; some contain granules of sulfur. The order Myxobacterales includes the flexible rods that produce slime; resting cells originate in fruiting bodies that are formed by the aggregation of a large number of vegetative cells.

2. Bacterial Anatomy

Methods of Investigation. Because of their microscopic size, cytological study of bacteria for many years was limited to application of staining methods to reveal size, shape, and such few specialized structures as flagella and spores. The predominant bacterial forms, ranging from 0.5 to 10 microns in length (1 micron = 0.001 millimeter), are spheres (cocci), rods (bacilli), and spirals (spirilla). The development of more

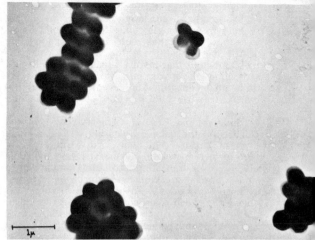

COCCUS, sphere-shaped bacteria, is one of the three basic cell shapes. *Staphylococcus aureus* is one type.

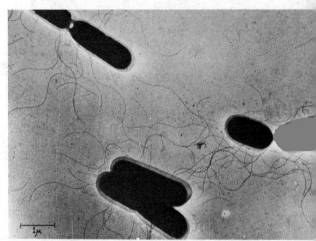

BACILLUS, rod-shaped bacteria, varies from species to species. *Clostridium tetani* cells are shown dividing.

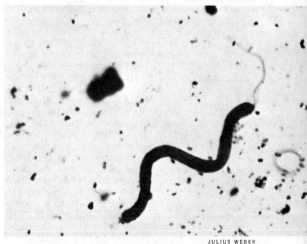

SPIRILLUM is the spiral bacterial shape. This organism, magnified hundreds of times, has a flagellum at one end.

powerful phase and electron microscopes and such specialized auxiliary techniques as slicing sections from a single cell with a delicate microtome have facilitated more intimate knowledge of the fine structure of the bacterial cell. Finally, methods that involve breaking the cells and separating the parts into various fractions by differential centrifugation reveal associations between structure and function at the molecular level.

Structure and Function. The typical bacterial cell has on the outside a coating termed a slime layer or capsule. In many, this structure is a high-molecular-weight polymer (a long molecule made up of repeating structural units) of a simple hexose sugar such as glucose (dextrans) or levulose (levans). In others, the structure is chemically much more complex, being formed of units of simple sugars (glucose, mannose, and galactose), derived sugars (amino sugars), and sugar acids (gluconic and glucuronic). Probably the cells of this type most widely studied are those associated with the pneumococci. The capsular material confers type specificity on the organism, which is to say that the type of pneumonia developing in the host depends on the molecular composition of the capsule. In *Bacillus anthracis* the capsule is a polymer of D-glutamic acid, the unnatural form of this amino acid.

In general, bacterial cell walls appear to be double- or triple-layered structures, each layer having a thickness of perhaps 0.002 to 0.003 micron. The chemical composition of the walls of "true" bacteria seems to be related to the gram-staining characteristics of the cell. The cell walls most studied are those of the gram-positive *Staphylococcus aureus.* (See GRAM, HANS CHRISTIAN JOACHIM.) They are a complex polymer of N-acetylglucosamine (the basic structural unit in chitin from insect exoskeletons), N-acetylglucosamine with a lactic acid molecule connected to it (muramic acid), and a small number of amino acids linked to the lactic acid molecule. Muramic acid—indeed, the entire polymer of the cell wall—is unique to bacterial cells; the antibiotic penicillin inhibits cell wall synthesis in gram-positive cells, whereas it does not interfere with growth of gram-negative bacteria, which contain very little of this unique polymer. The cell walls of gram-negative bacteria are more complex in that they contain true protein, polysaccharides, and lipid material.

Next to the cell wall lies a membrane composed of proteins and lipids. In addition to acting as part of the osmotic barrier between the external and internal environments of the cell, it contains many of the oxidation-reduction enzyme systems concerned with energy metabolism. In the cells of higher plants and animals, these systems are located in specialized structures called the mitochondria, scattered throughout the cytoplasm (defined as the material inside the cell membrane). Within the bacterial cytoplasm are the granules that act as reservoirs for food, pigments, and nucleic acids. Food can be stored both as carbohydrate polymers (such as starch and glycogen) and as true fats. It is noteworthy that, among the bacilli and some other species, the stored lipid is a simple polymer of beta-hydroxybutyric acid. The polymers of ribonucleic acid include a protein-synthesizing fraction analogous to the ribosomes found in cells of higher plants and animals.

Many bacteria possess one or more fine threadlike structures, called the flagella, which are used for locomotion. These are composed of a protein similar to myosin, the protein of muscle fiber.

Members of the Bacillaceae family of the order Eubacteriales, species of both aerobic *Bacillus* living only in the presence of oxygen and anaerobic *Clostridium* flourishing only in the absence of free oxygen, form endospores. These are highly refractile bodies that are extremely resistant to heat, to drying, and to many chemical agents. Their size, shape, and position within the mother cell are criteria employed for classification. Chemically, spores differ in several respects from vegetative cells, notably in having less water but more calcium. One compound, dipicolinic acid, is unique to spores, and it may account for from 10 to 15 percent of their dry weight. Endospores also contain fewer active enzymes than does the vegetative cell, but have dormant enzymes that can be detected only after activation by heat or chemical agents. This breaking of the dormancy is accompanied by intake of water; by increase in permeability; and by losses of refractility, heat resistance, and calcium dipicolinate. The spore coat breaks, and a new cell emerges. Since only one spore is formed per cell, this is not a method of reproduction, but a means of surviving adverse conditions.

3. Bacterial Physiology

Nutritional Types. Bacteria conveniently can be classified into three major groups according to the materials they employ as sources of energy: (1) chemoorganotrophs that use organic compounds; (2) photoautotrophs that utilize radiant energy; and (3) chemolithotrophs that oxidize inorganic molecules. The two last groups usually use carbon dioxide as the major source of carbon. In all groups, energy is obtained either aerobically, by employing molecular oxygen as the terminal electron acceptor, or anaerobically, in the absence of oxygen, by oxidation-reductions between organic compounds in the process known as fermentation. So-called facultative anaerobes can use either mechanism.

As do other forms of life, bacteria require water, minerals, vitamins, and sources of carbon and of nitrogen for growth. In culture these nutrients are conveniently provided for many species by a bouillon containing from 1 to 2 percent peptone, a hydrolyzed protein made from beef or casein; for colonial growth, a solidifying agent such as agar is added. For precise study of bacterial physiology, however, a synthetic medium made from known constituents is preferable.

Sources of Carbon and Nitrogen. The source of carbon in synthetic media is usually glucose, but other carbohydrates can be used, for example, in a diagnostic test. Sugar alcohols in the form of glycerol or mannitol are suitable for most species; others, such as the Bacillaceae, possess amylase that enables them to use starch. A few specialized forms have the enzyme systems necessary to break down cellulose, usually anaerobically and at temperatures greater than 45° C. Since few species form lipases, enzymes capable of hydrolyzing fats, generally they do not use fats as such. But many can utilize the salts of the lower fatty acids, especially acetic and butyric acids, as well as other organic acids, including the four carbon dicarboxylic acids, especially succinic and malic acids. Since nitrogen is required mainly for synthesis of cell protein, a mixture of amino acids is suitable. Some species, including many of the Bacillaceae, produce proteinases (enzymes that can digest protein), a faculty that allows them to use native protein as a source of these acids. Others utilize ammonia, urea, and nitrates, as do green plants, and a few can "fix" molecular nitrogen. See also section 5. *Ecology* (The Nitrogen Cycle).

Minerals and Growth Factors. Bacteria use the same types of mineral ions as do higher plants and for much the same purposes, but in relatively much smaller quantities; tap water will often meet their mineral needs. Mineral ions needed include such trace elements as molybdenum, manganese, and cobalt. Phosphates are frequently added to a medium, both as a source of phosphorus for synthesis of nucleic acids and to buffer the medium against excessive acidity through their capacity to neutralize acids.

The chief vitamin requirement is for the constituents of the B complex: riboflavin, thiamine, biotin, and pantothenic acid. Many organisms, including the Enterobacteriaceae that live in the intestinal tracts of man and animals, can synthesize their own vitamins; when the bacteria die, these are released to the host. Biological assay methods based on these requirements for specific vitamins or minerals by specific strains of bacteria have been developed. Furthermore, bacteria have been widely used to study the functions of these vitamins in metabolism as coenzymes required to maintain the activity of specific enzyme systems. Perhaps half of the vitamins in the B complex were originally discovered through studies of the nutritional needs of bacteria. See also VITAMINS.

When an animal cell anaerobically breaks down glucose sugar, it combines the glucose molecule with phosphates, and this phosphorylated sugar is split into two molecules of glyceraldehyde phosphate; this, in turn, is converted into lactic acid via pyruvic acid. Many bacteria use this Embden-Meyerhof-Parnas glycolytic pathway, named after the chief investigators of this process, but others have alternative pathways to pyruvic acid. For example, *Leuconostoc mesenteroides* successively converts hexose phosphate to phosphogluconic acid, to ribulose phosphate, to glyceraldehyde phosphate, and then to pyruvic acid. Regardless of the pathway, however, the liberated energy is stored in the phosphate portion of a molecule called adenosine triphosphate (ATP), where it can be drawn on for use when needed by converting ATP into the diphosphate (ADP). Species of the *Lactobacillus* and *Leuconostoc* form lactic acid, but the clostridium and the enterobacteria convert the pyruvate into various organic compounds, among which are the following: ethyl, isopropyl, and butyl alcohols; formic, acetic, propionic, butyric, and succinic acids; and acetone, acetoin, and 2,3-butylene glycol. Gases produced include carbon dioxide, hydrogen, and methane. The "will-o'-the-wisp" results when fermenting anaerobes in a marsh or bog form hydrogen and methane and these gases ignite.

Aerobically, the animal cell oxidizes lactic acid by returning it to pyruvic acid, which is oxidized to the acetyl group. The acetyl group, in turn, is condensed with a 4-carbon dicarboxylic (oxalacetic) acid to form a 6-carbon tricarboxylic (citric) acid. Citric acid goes through a series of reactions that eventually end with oxalacetic acid. The net result of this tricarboxylic acid (TCA) cycle is that a molecule of pyruvic acid is completely oxidized to carbon dioxide and water, with the liberated energy stored in the ATP-ADP reservoir. Many bacteria use the TCA cycle in oxidizing pyruvic acid, but others have developed alternative pathways.

The photoautotrophs belong to three families: Thiorhodaceae, the purple sulfur bacteria; Athiorhodaceae, the brown and purple nonsulfur bacteria; and Chlorobacteriaceae, the green sulfur bacteria. Their classification is based in part on the source of hydrogen used to reduce carbon dioxide. Photoautotrophs have a bacteriochlorophyll similar to that of green plants, but one that absorbs light of longer wavelengths. It is contained in structures called chromatophores and is completely obscured in the purple forms by pigments that color the cells yellow, brown, red, and purple. In contrast to the process in green plants, bacterial photosynthesis is obligately anaerobic.

Chemolithotrophic organisms include the following: *Hydrogenomonas*, the Knallgas bacterium, oxidizes hydrogen to water; *Nitrosomonas* and *Nitrobacter*, the nitrifiers, respectively oxidize ammonia to nitrite and nitrite to nitrate; *Thiobacillus* oxidizes sulfur or hydrogen sulfide to sulfate.

The Growth Curve. The energy liberated in the reactions described above is directed primarily toward biosynthesis of cell materials. Such growth is assayed by such methods as measuring turbidity or the amount of such formed products as carbon dioxide and lactic acid. These indirect methods are standardized against actual cell counts obtained by making suitable dilutions of the bacterial culture and plating (distributing) a measured quantity into an appropriate agar medium. After a period of incubation, colonies arising from the individual cells are readily counted.

If a suitable liquid medium is inoculated, little or no growth occurs for a period called the lag phase until the bacteria become adjusted to the new environment. This is followed by a period of accelerating growth that reaches its maximum in the log phase, during which growth is exponential. Soon the rate of multiplication decreases as cultural conditions become less favorable for maximum growth; exhaustion of nutrients, a deficient supply of oxygen, or an accumulation of toxic end product may be responsible. During the period of exponential growth many species have a generation time of from 10 to 60 minutes. This means that, with an initial inoculum of 100 cells per milliliter (ml) and a generation time of 20 minutes, the population might reach 100 billion cells/ml in 10 hours. Usually, however, maximum populations of 100 to 1,000 million/ml are the rule. The rate of death also increases and often becomes exponential, especially if the culture is exposed to factors deleterious either chemically or physically.

The death phase has been studied intensively because of man's desire to control the activities of microorganisms either to encourage or to inhibit growth. Except for the spores, which can be extremely resistant, bacteria are readily killed by heat. Another means of destruction is radiation by ultraviolet light. Often control is achieved by excluding contaminants through the use of cotton or sintered-glass filters. Chemicals used for inhibiting growth include sugar and salt for raising the osmotic pressure, as well as antiseptics and disinfectants. The latter exert their effect through destruction of the cell membrane, as by phenol or detergents; or by interference with the enzymes concerned either with an energy-liberating reaction, as by mercuric chloride, carbon monoxide, and cyanide, or with biosynthesis, as by sulfonamides and penicillin.

The rate and extent of bacterial growth are also markedly affected by factors in the environment other than food, water, and inhibiting substances. Two important ones are temperature and acidity. Most bacteria prefer a temperature range of from 25° to 37° C., but some species known as psychrophiles grow near the freezing point, while others known as thermophiles prefer temperatures as high as 60° to 70° C. The majority of bacteria prefer a neutral medium neither markedly acid nor alkaline, but the thiobacilli will develop in media with a pH near 0, roughly equivalent to that of 5 percent sulfuric acid.

4. Technology

Food Spoilage and Preservation. Consideration of the production and preservation of foods will illustrate the practical application of knowledge of the physiological properties of microorganisms. The type of decomposition that will occur in a food depends on its chemical composition, its environment, and the opportunity for contamination. Aerobically, molds are frequently the major decomposing agent, especially of cheese, the surfaces of meats, and acid fruits and vegetables. Yeasts bring about alcoholic fermentation in fruit juices and other sugar-containing liquids. Bacteria are more often concerned with changes in foods high in protein and starch, especially under anaerobic conditions and if the foods are neutral.

The three basic principles of food preservation are exclusion of microorganisms, inhibition of their growth, and their destruction. Examples of the first principle are to be seen in the natural protection afforded by the skins of fruits and the shells of eggs. Ordinarily, since it is not feasible to produce food under completely sterile conditions, this principle is used chiefly to keep down the "initial load." In the meat industry and in the production of milk for direct consumption or for conversion into dairy products, sanitation measures for reducing the initial load provide the key to successful preservation.

The second principle of inhibition of bacterial growth requires that the initial load be kept under population control. Effective physical methods include lowering the temperature, exemplified by chilling milk and the carcasses of butchered animals, and drying, as in the dehydration of fruits and vegetables. Such chemical agents as sugar and salt preserve by raising the osmotic pressure; at times, however, osmophiles will develop in brines, heavy sugar syrups, and honey. Other useful chemicals are organic acids, especially acetic acid in the form of vinegar, for pickling, and lactic acid, produced naturally in green plant tissue by members of the Lactobacillaceae to form sauerkraut, silage, and fermented pickles and olives. The addition of other preservative chemicals such as benzoate to soft drinks, propionate to control mold on bread, sulfite to dried fruits, and antibiotics to fish and poultry is regulated by law. See also FOOD—4. *Food Additives.*

An example of the third principle, destruction of bacteria, is the destruction of microorganisms by heat in pasteurization of milk and beverages and in the canning of foods. The technical problem is that of destroying all organisms that might cause trouble without lowering the quality of the product through excessive heating. In milk this is accomplished by exposing it to a temperature of 62.8° C for 30 minutes or to 71.6° C for 15 seconds. Pathogens are eliminated by this method, and the population of lactic acid bacteria is so reduced that souring will not occur for several days under proper refrigeration. In canning, heat treatment seeks to destroy even the spore formers, since many of these will develop under anaerobic conditions at room temperature. At times some spore formers, notably spore-forming thermophiles, will survive the processing and may cause such defects as flat souring through the formation of lactic acid by *Bacillus stearothermophilus;* so-called TA spoilage by acid and gas evolved by thermophilic anaerobic spore formers; and "stinker," hydrogen sulfide originating from *Clostridium nigrificans.* Finally, ultraviolet radiation is used to kill molds on the surfaces of meat, cheese, and bread. See also CHEESE AND CHEESE MAKING—*Pasteurization.*

Food Manufacture. Probably the most important food products dependent on microbial activity are the various types of cheese. Species of the Lactobacillaceae form lactic acid from the lactose of milk which, together with the added enzyme rennin, produces a curd of the casein (a milk protein). Much of the soluble material is then expressed as whey, a watery substance. After salting, the curd can be consumed directly (for example, as cottage cheese), but most cheeses require a period of curing or ripening during which the casein breaks down. The extent of this will depend on environmental factors that favor the development of certain types of curing agents present in the milk or added as a "starter." These factors include temperature used in manufacture and during curing; humidity; size of cheese; time; and amount of salt. Lactobacilli are largely responsible for ripening Cheddar cheese, but the Swiss type requires in addition an "eye former," which is a species of *Propionibacterium.* Brick and Limburger cheeses are cured by a mixture of proteolytic, aerobic, and facultative organisms growing as a "smear" on the surface. The mold, *Penicillium camemberti,* also is a surface-curing agent in Camembert cheese, but *P. roqueforti,* although aerobic, can grow through Roquefort, since holes are punched in the young cheese to let in air. See also CHEESE AND CHEESE MAKING.

Cultured buttermilk owes its distinctive flavor and aroma to bacteria. In its preparation, pasteurized skimmed milk is inoculated with acid-forming bacteria, which ferment lactose to lactic acid, and with aroma formers, which ferment citric acid to diacetyl and other aromatic compounds. Sometimes these bacteria are grown in cream before it is churned into butter.

Chemical Manufacture. One of the earliest uses of bacteria for a commercial process was the water-retting of flax (for linen) and hemp (for rope) by pectin-destroying clostridia such as *Clostridium felsineum* and *C. pectinovorum.* Today the important industry employing bacterial fermentation is devoted to the production of antibiotics, mostly by species of the higher bacteria belonging to the order Actinomycetales, especially those in the Streptomycetaceae family. (See ANTIBIOTICS; PENICILLIN; PLANTS AND PLANT SCIENCE—*14. Modern Medicinal Plants.*) A vitamin B_{12} preparation used in feeds is a by-product of the production of streptomycin, but it is also made commercially by a strain of *Propionibacterium freudenreichii.* Industrial lactic

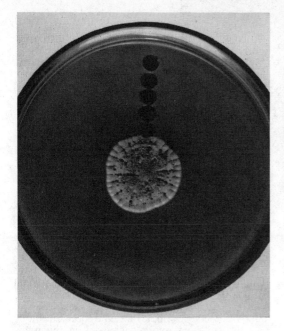

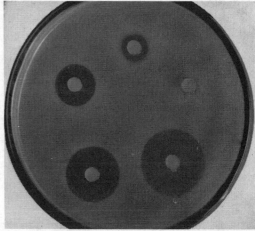

BACTERIA are the major source of antibiotics. In a test, plugs of agar (the culture medium) were removed from the six-day-old colony of *Penicillium notatum* (left) and tested for antibiotic activity against the *Staphylococcus* (right). Dark rings indicate antibiotic activity.

acid is made by the *Lactobacillus delbrueckii.*

Often overlooked among the commercial products formed by microorganisms are the enzyme preparations. Alpha-amylase from selected strains of *Bacillus subtilis* is used to hydrolyze starch to dextrin in making certain types of beer, in clarifying beer, and in desizing textiles. Also, *B. subtilis* forms a proteinase that is useful for desizing silk, removing proteins from hides in tanning, and reducing protein haze in beer. These two bacterial enzymes are especially useful, since they have a tolerance to heat higher than those from other sources.

5. Ecology

Of greater importance than the technical applications just discussed are the roles played by bacteria in their natural habitats: soil, water, and host plants and animals. In soil and water, bacteria are involved in what is called the cycle of the elements.

The Carbon Cycle. Green plants take simple compounds such as carbon dioxide, nitrates, and phosphates and build them into complex organic substances: carbohydrates, proteins, and fats. When the plant dies, these are returned to the soil; they can, of course, be consumed by animals and converted into tissue, but eventually most reach the soil or sea in the form of plant and animal remains or as manures and sewage. The organic substances must be mineralized before succeeding crops can reutilize the elements. The necessary decompositions carried out by fungi and bacteria may be either aerobic, in which case the end products are carbon dioxide and water, or anaerobic, in which event such fermentation products as organic acids may accumulate to be destroyed by aerobic microorganisms when oxygen becomes available. Such organic acids may cause a problem by "souring" the soil, but they can also help in solubilizing some soil minerals.

The Nitrogen Cycle. In the nitrogen cycle, proteins are first broken down to amino acids; the amino group is then liberated by conversion to ammonia. Aerobically, the filamentous fungi, ac-

tinomycetes, and species of *Bacillus* are largely concerned with such "ammonification," but anaerobically the clostridia and other bacterial species are the effective agents. The ammonia can be used as such by plants, but often it is converted into nitrite by the chemolithotroph *Nitrosomonas*, and the nitrite into nitrate by *Nitrobacter*. This completes the cycle, but along the way the nitrate may be used anaerobically by some bacteria as an electron acceptor in place of oxygen, liberating the nitrogen as the molecule to the vast reservoir in the atmosphere.

Eventually, all the nitrogen in the organic world would be unavailable as the inert molecule were it not for the existence of a compensatory process called nitrogen fixation. Hermann Hellriegel and Hermann Wilfarth discovered (1886) the most important type of fixation, which occurs through the association of leguminous plants with species of the root nodule bacterium *Rhizobium*. The bacterium invades the roots of legumes, causing formation of a nodule in which free nitrogen is converted into amino acids via ammonia. This process, called symbiotic nitrogen fixation, also occurs in several genera of nonlegumes (alder and bog myrtle, for instance); although here the associated endophyte (plant within a plant) has not been established, it is not *Rhizobium*. Asymbiotically, nitrogen is fixed both aerobically and anaerobically by several free-living forms, including species of *Azotobacter* and *Clostridium; Aerobacter aerogenes; Bacillus polymyxa;* representatives of all the photosynthetic bacteria; and blue-green algae.

It should be noted that not all of the organic matter returned to soil is mineralized immediately; a residue called humus gives soil desirable physical properties and helps to prevent leaching of soluble ions. This organic fraction decomposes slowly, finally releasing its mineral elements to the plant. In addition to participating in the carbon and nitrogen cycles, humus has numerous other functions. (See HUMUS.) The populations of the various species of soil microorganisms vary with the environment, which includes such physi-

ological factors as supply of food, oxygen, and water; temperature; and *p*H, or alkaline and acid reaction. (See Soil—*Soil Characteristics:* Acidity and Salts.) The farmer exerts some control over these factors and hence over the microorganism's activities through such cultural practices as plowing, draining, irrigating, and liming.

Sewage Disposal. Domestic and industrial sewage was once disposed of merely by running the waste into a body of water or onto vacant land. Today large communities seldom have or resort to such facilities. In their place the sanitary engineer has developed large disposal plants for handling an average of 150 gallons per day per inhabitant. In these plants the processes normally occurring in soil are carried out expeditiously in tanks.

In the Imhoff septic tank, anaerobic fermentations rapidly make soluble some of the organic matter colloidally suspended in the raw sewage flowing through the upper chamber; the remainder settles into a lower chamber for prolonged decomposition that eventually forms a humuslike material called sludge. The soluble material then is often sprayed onto a trickling filter in which a film of bacteria and protozoa on coarse rocks completes the oxidation.

Oxidation by similar groups of microorganisms is the initial step in the activated-sludge process. The raw sewage is inoculated with flocculent masses of microbial cells and protozoa and is vigorously aerated as it flows through tanks. In from five to eight hours most of the readily oxidizable organic matter has been oxidized, and the colloidal particles have flocculated to form more activated sludge. This readily settles out, and about one quarter is used for inoculum; the excess is dried for fertilizer or is further decomposed by slow fermentation in anaerobic gas holders. The gas formed—78 percent methane—can be used in gas engines to run the plant. See also Sanitary Engineering—*Sewage Treatment.*

Infectious Disease. In man and animal there is a range of association with bacteria all the way from the transient soil bacteria that may be present on the skin and mucous membranes, through those considered to be normal bacterial inhabitants, to the bacteria that produce infectious disease. The normal flora of the skin and mucous membrane include staphylococci, streptococci, lactobacilli, spirochetes, and *Corynebac-*

terium and *Neisseria* species. Among the normal flora of the intestinal tract are *Escherichia coli, Bacteriodes* and *Clostridium* species, lactobacilli, and streptococci. Both diet and oral antibiotic therapy can cause marked changes in the intestinal flora that may lead to disease in the host. Diet may also influence the growth and acid production of lactobacilli of the mouth, leading to dental caries. By contrast, under the usual conditions of host-bacteria interaction, some of the normal flora act to help the host. Examples of the latter activity are the synthesis of vitamins in the intestines by bacteria and the parallel synthesis of protein and vitamins in the rumen of cattle. The normal flora are usually considered to be nonpathogenic, but under unusual conditions they may produce disease. See also Parasites; Parasitic Diseases.

Host-Bacteria Relationships. A number of bacteria will produce disease when introduced into a susceptible host. The proof that bacteria can cause disease and subsequent investigation of their mode of action has led to the control of many bacterial diseases. If a bacterium is to cause disease. it must invade a susceptible host, grow, and produce damage.

In the late 19th century studies of *Bacillus anthracis,* it was first thought that bacteria caused disease by growing in great numbers and mechanically blocking blood circulation. Eventually it was discovered that some bacteria produce substances that cause damage to body areas distant from the original growth site. These substances, called toxins, are of two types. Exotoxins are soluble poisonous substances liberated from the bacteria during the period of growth; examples of these proteins are the diphtheria toxin of *Corynebacterium diphtheriae,* the tetanus toxin of *Clostridium tetani,* and the leukocytic toxin (involves leukocytes) and enterotoxin (responsible for gastrointestinal symptoms) of *Staphylococcus aureus.* The endotoxins of the gram-negative organisms—an example is *Salmonella typhosa*—are lipoprotein-polysaccharide complexes of the bacterial cell wall that are released only upon the cell's destruction. Each of the exotoxins has a specific pharmacological action (as, for example, the effect of diphtheria toxin on heart muscle), which accounts for some of the specific symptoms of diseases caused by bacteria that produce this type of toxin. By contrast, regardless of the species of gram-negative bacterium that produces them, all endotoxins (not soluble and only separable by disintegration of the cell body) exert approximately the same pharmacological action, manifested by fever and shock. See also TOXINS.

The host responds to invasion by a pathogenic bacterium in a variety of ways. First, there is an accumulation of white blood cells at the initial point of entry. These blood cells act as phagocytes to ingest and digest the bacteria. Blood and tissue fluids also accumulate at the site of infection, and the fluids usually contain such nonspecific substances as basic amino acids that may kill the bacteria. Later, blood fluids containing proteins called antibodies, which are specific for the particular bacterial species or its toxin, act in a variety of ways to kill or to inhibit the growth of the bacteria. If the bacteria are not eliminated by the actions cited, then metastasis (the spread of the infection to other parts of the host) may take place. If the body defenses can eliminate the pathogenic organism, the host recovers; if the bacterium is not eliminated, the host may die, or a chronic infection may follow. Alternatively, the host may recover clinically, but not bacteriologically, and thus may remain a "carrier." See also DISEASE, GERM THEORY OF; IMMUNITY.

Transmission of Infectious Agents. If a bacterium is to cause disease, it must be transmitted from the infected host or "healthy" carrier to the susceptible individual and must be able to survive this interhost period. The characteristics of transmission of certain pathogenic bacteria are a reflection of their ability to survive. Anthrax, a disease of cattle and sheep, is caused by a spore-forming bacterium, *Bacillus anthracis,* which in spore form can persist for many years in the soil. Thus, wherever anthrax has occurred, the disease agent always is present, and possibility of infection persists. Syphilis in man is caused

by a bacterium, *Treponema pallidum,* which can survive for only a few hours away from its host and thus generally must be transmitted directly from the infected host to the susceptible individual. Some bacteria are transmitted by insects and will live for long periods of time in these carriers.

The usual methods of transmission of pathogenic bacteria to a susceptible host are: (1) direct, as by sexual intercourse; (2) indirect, as by food, water, eating utensils, and air; and (3) by insect vectors. It is important to determine the exact method of transmission of each disease agent, for this information can be used to cut the line of transmission and thus control the spread of the disease. For example, the knowledge that *Salmonella typhosa,* the bacterium of typhoid fever, is spread by contaminated water has led to the development of sanitary engineering procedures that have tended to eliminate the disease. See also CONTAGION AND CONTAGIOUS DISEASES.

Diseases of Man. The importance of bacterial diseases is reflected, first, in the number of cases or of deaths resulting from a particular bacterium and, second, in the programs required to keep particular disease agents under control. In the United States, agents in the first category are *Staphylococcus aureus* (wound infections, pneumonia); *Streptococcus pyogenes* (septic sore throat, rheumatic fever); *Diplococcus pneumoniae* (pneumonia); *Mycobacterium tuberculosis* (tuberculosis); *Treponema pallidum* (syphilis); *Neisseria gonorrhoeae* (gonorrhea); and *Salmonella* species (food poisonings and enteric disease).

Bacterial agents important, not for the number of cases of disease or death, but from the standpoint of public health measures designed to keep them under control are *Salmonella typhosa* (typhoid fever); *Vibrio comma* (cholera); *Shi-*

BACTERIA are a major source of disease in man. Pneumococci (left) are among the pneumonia-causing bacteria; and streptococci (right) cause scarlet fever, tonsillitis, and other infections in man.

CHAS. PFIZER & CO., INC.

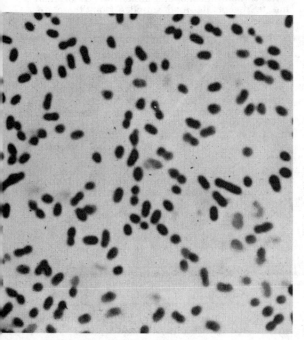
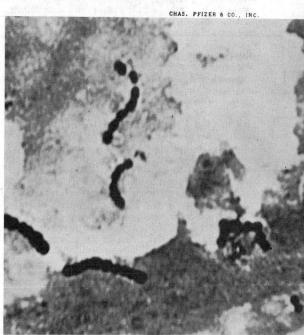

BACTERIA play an important role in the nitrogen-fixation process in plants. They cause the formation of nodules on the roots, and nitrogen is converted into amino acids in them. The plants at right were inoculated with root nodule bacteria; nodules formed. Those at left were not inoculated; no nodules formed.

COURTESY OF DR. J.C. BURTON, NITRAGIN COMPANY, MILWAUKEE, WIS.

gella dysenteriae (bacterial dysentery); Corynebacterium diphtheriae (diphtheria); and Pasteurella pestis (plague). In other areas, particularly in parts of Asia and Africa, bacterial agents of human disease—among them, typhoid fever, cholera, diphtheria, plague, and leprosy—are important both for the number of cases and deaths and also from the viewpoint of the development of programs of control by the World Health Organization of the United Nations and other public and private agencies. See also TROPICAL MEDICINE.

Diseases of Animals. Different species, as well as their geographical distribution, must be considered in the discussion of bacterial diseases of animals. From the standpoint of numbers of cases or deaths, some important agents are Staphylococcus aureus (mastitis in dairy cows and joint disease in poultry); Mycobacterium avium (tuberculosis in swine and poultry); Brucella suis (the cause of brucellosis or Traum's disease, resulting in abortion in swine); Mycoplasma (pleuropneumonia and other diseases in poultry, swine, sheep, and cattle); Leptospira species (leptospirosis in cattle, swine, and dogs); Pasteurella haemolytica (pneumonia in cattle and sheep); Salmonella species (abortion in mares and sheep and other disease in poultry and swine); Erysipelothrix rhusiopathiae (erysipelas in swine); and Escherichia coli (a major cause of death in newborn animals). Bacterial disease agents in animals that are important because of the effort devoted to control procedures are Mycobacterium bovis (tuberculosis in cattle and other animals); Brucella abortus (the cause of brucellosis or Bang's disease, resulting in abortion in cows); Bacillus anthracis (anthrax in cattle, sheep, and other animals); various Clostridium species (blackleg in cattle and other animals and overeating disease in lambs); and Salmonella gallinarum (bacillary white diarrhea in chickens). See also ANIMAL DISEASES.

Diseases of Plants. The major causes of infectious botanical diseases are molds (fungi, q.v.) and viruses. The fungus diseases number in the thousands. Bacterial diseases of plants are, by contrast, restricted to a few hundred, but they remain important, not only because they require the devotion of resources to control and eradicate, but because they regularly destroy sizable proportions of certain crops, force consequent and sudden reductions in the acreage devoted to production, and cause serious economic dislocations. Examples of important bacterial plant

pathogens and the diseases they cause are Erwinia amylovora (fireblight of apples and pears); E. carotovora (soft rot of vegetables); Agrobacterium tumefaciens (crown gall of fruits); and Streptomyces scabies (potato scab). See also PLANTS AND PLANT SCIENCE—5. Pathology.

Exobiology. Bacteria will undoubtedly play a role in the newly developing science of exobiology, the biology of space. If life is found elsewhere, it may well be that of all the organisms of this earth only bacteria could survive the extreme conditions characteristic of the planets nearest us. If we are to establish this, we must be certain that space vehicles sent out from earth do not contaminate the moon or planets. This requires the use of aseptic techniques in the manufacture and assembly of all components of space vehicles, techniques that must be more rigorous even than those used in the operating room. Microorganisms, including bacteria, also may be useful for manned space flight. It is possible to establish a complete cycle of matter by use of microorganisms in a closed system to eliminate carbon dioxide and other wastes of man and to regenerate food supplies from these excreta.

6. Bacteriophage and Bacteriogenetics

In the late 19th century filters that would retain bacteria were used to help prove that bacteria caused disease. If a fluid that contained an infectious agent lost its infectivity after passage through a filter, then it contained bacteria; if the fluid retained its infectivity, then the disease was caused by a "filterable virus," a term from the Latin meaning poison. Filterable viruses were found to be the agents of many infectious diseases (see VIRUS).

In the second decade of the 20th century, Frederick William Twort and Félix Hubert d'Hérelle discovered filterable agents that would lyse (burst) bacterial cells. These agents, named bacteriophage, were subsequently considered to be viruses that attack bacteria. Bacteriophages have been found for most bacteria. A phage is specific for a certain kind of bacterium and is named for the bacterium it will infect. Thus, a phage infecting the bacterium Escherichia coli is called a coliphage. Phages have a polyhedral head consisting of a protein shell containing nucleic acid and a hollow protein tube for a tail. Phages contain only one of the two kinds of nucleic acid; most phages contain deoxyribonu-

BACTERIOPHAGE VIRUSES, magnified thousands of times, have a polyhedral head and a protein tail.

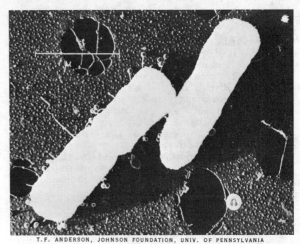

INFECTING PHAGE attach by their tails to the bacterial cell. A cell of *E. coli* is shown being attacked.

cleic acid (DNA), but a few contain ribonucleic acid.

Infection occurs when the phage attaches itself by its tail to the bacterial cell and injects the nucleic acid from the head through the hollow tail into the host cell. The phage nucleic acid changes the metabolism of the bacterial cell so that several hundred phage particles are produced, and the bacterial cell finally bursts, releasing the mature phage particles. This is called a lytic phage, and the phage particles are called vegetative phage. Such a phage, when introduced into growth of a bacterium on a solid medium, will cause clear areas to appear where the bacterial cells are lysed. These areas are called plaques. A temperate phage is one that infects a bacterial cell, and the phage DNA becomes part of the genetic mechanism of the cell and replicates at each cell division. This condition is termed lysogeny. The phage DNA is now called a prophage, and the bacterial cells are called lysogenic. The prophage may become active to form vegetative phage which is released by bursting of the bacterial cell.

Because of the ease with which bacteria can be grown and infected with phage, much basic information on the biology of the virus-host cell interaction has been developed with the phage-bacterial cell system. In the 1920's there was hope that phages which destroyed disease-producing bacteria could be used in treatment of disease. For example, it was thought that an individual with typhoid fever could be fed some phage that would destroy *Salmonella typhosa* and that the disease would be cured. Unfortunately, this did not prove to be true. Although phage has been tried in the treatment of a number of bacterial diseases, no serious consideration is now given to this method of therapy.

Cytological, biochemical, and genetic studies show that bacteria have a nucleus containing deoxyribonucleic acid (DNA) and that this DNA contains genetic information. (See GENES, NATURE AND ACTION OF.) Because bacteria ordinarily grow by vegetative reproduction (binary fission), change in the genetic material is usually the result of gene mutation. Markers that may be used in genetic studies with bacteria include antibiotic resistance, nutritional requirements, and sugar fermentation. Gene recombination between bacteria can occur by conjugation (brief cytoplasmic union) in which there are recognized donor and recipient cells. Transformation may take place when DNA from one cell is taken in by other cells, which then become genotypically (genetically) altered to express phenotypically (physically) a characteristic of the first cell type. Furthermore, genetic material from one bacterium may be introduced into another bacterial cell by a temperate bacteriophage, a bacteria-destroying agent, this process being known as transduction. Finally, a temperate bacteriophage may invade the genetic material of a bacterium and become a prophage, and this may be expressed phenotypically in the altered bacterium. This is known as lysogenic conversion.

PERRY W. WILSON and JOE B. WILSON
University of Wisconsin

7. Bibliography

Baldry, Peter E., *The Battle Against Bacteria* (London 1965).
Bulloch, William, *History of Bacteriology* (London 1938).
Clark, Paul F., *Pioneer Microbiologists of America* (Madison, Wis., 1961).
Doetsch, Raymond N., ed., *Microbiology: Historical Contributions from 1776 to 1908* (New Brunswick, N.J., 1960).
Lamanna, Carl, and Mallette, M. Frank, *Basic Bacteriology*, 2d ed. (Baltimore 1959).
Stanier, Roger Y., and others, *The Microbial World*, 2d ed. (Englewood Cliffs, N.J., 1963).

For Specialized Study
Alexander, Martin, *Introduction to Soil Microbiology* (New York 1961).
Braun, Werner, *Bacterial Genetics*, 2d ed. (Philadelphia 1965).
Breed, Robert S., and others, eds., *Bergey's Manual of Determinative Bacteriology*, 7th ed. (Baltimore 1957).
Dubos, René J., *Bacterial and Mycotic Infections of Man*, 3d ed. (Philadelphia 1958).
Foster, Edwin M., and others, *Dairy Microbiology* (Englewood Cliffs, N.J., 1957).
Frazier, William C., *Food Microbiology* (New York 1958).
Gunsalus, Irwin C., and Stanier, Roger Y., eds., *The Bacteria: A Treatise on Structure and Function*, 5 vols. (New York 1962–63).
Hagan, William A., and Bruner, Dorsey W., *The Infectious Diseases of Domestic Animals*, 4th ed. (Ithaca, N.Y., 1961).
Hayes, William, *The Genetics of Bacteria and Their Viruses* (New York 1964).
Maale, Ole, and Kjeldgaard, Niels O., *Control of Macromolecular Synthesis: A Study of DNA, RNA, and Protein Synthesis in Bacteria* (New York 1966).
Meynell, Geoffrey G., and Goodes, Harry, eds., *Microbial Reaction to Environment* (London 1961).
Meynell, Geoffrey G., and Meynell, Elinor, *Theory and Practice in Experimental Bacteriology* (London 1965).
Prescott, Samuel C., and Dunn, Cecil G., *Industrial Microbiology*, 3d ed. (New York 1959).
Topley, William W.C., and Wilson, Sir Graham S., *Principles of Bacteriology and Immunity*, 5th ed., 2 vols. (Baltimore 1964).

BACTERICIDE. See ANTISEPTICS; GERMICIDE.

BACTRIA, bak'trē-ə, was an ancient region, kingdom, and province in central Asia. It corresponded roughly to the area of modern Afghanistan between the Amu Darya River (earlier the Oxus River) on the north and the towering Hindu Kush range on the south.

About 1500 B.C., migrating Aryan tribes settled in this region and called it *Bakhdi,* describing it as the "Country of Lofty Banners." The inhabitants cultivated crops on the plains that sloped gently northward to the Oxus River. They worshiped Anahita, the goddess of waters. According to legend, Zoroaster, the prophet of the Zoroastrian religion, was born here, perhaps early in the 7th century B.C. By the middle of the 6th century B.C., the Persian Achaemenid empire, whose rulers were Zoroastrians, took over the region as a satrapy, which they called Bactria, and pushed its northern limits some distance beyond the Oxus River.

In 329 B.C., Alexander the Great led his army across the Hindu Kush into Bactria and took its main city, then called Zariaspa. At this time the name of the region appears to have been altered to *Bactra.* In about 250 B.C., Diodotus I, a Greek satrap of the Seleucid ruler Antiochus II, declared his independence and established the so-called Graeco-Bactrian kingdom, or Greek Bactria. Some 32 rulers of this line held the area between the Oxus River and the Hindu Kush until about 140 B.C., and pushed to the east across the Indus River. The capital of the kingdom remained at the earlier site, but it is not certain whether it was named Bactra.

Invading tribes brought about the downfall of the Graeco-Bactrian kingdom, and the region was subsequently held by minor dynasties until shortly after the middle of the 7th century A.D., when Arab armies, propagating the Muslim faith, entered the area and devastated the capital. Somewhat later it was rebuilt and, under the name Balkh, grew to be one of the largest and most flourishing cities of the Muslim world, acquiring the title "Mother of Cities." By the 9th century, the western half of the region had been absorbed into the neighboring province of Khorasan (Khurasan). In 1220, Balkh surrendered to the Mongol hordes of Genghis Khan, who then slaughtered all the inhabitants and burned the city. Just half a century later, Marco Polo passed through Balkh and described it as "a noble city and great," adding that it was strewn with the ruins of fine palaces and buildings of marble. Although the site was partially reoccupied, Balkh was eventually displaced as a regional center by the newer town of Mazar-i-Sharif, a few miles to the east. However, in the 18th and 19th centuries the area around the city was called the province of Balkh.

As the region expanded and contracted over the centuries, its limits were never precisely defined. Its ancient capital lay on the main caravan route across Asia, and its site covered an area at least seven miles in circumference, marked by the circuit of massive walls erected prior to the Mongol invasion. Excavations have failed to turn up objects of the period of Alexander the Great or of the Graeco-Bactrian kingdom. The remains of two great Buddhist stupas, or reliquary mounds, are visible, and there are two crumbling Muslim shrines of the 15th century.
DONALD N. WILBER, *Editor of "Afghanistan"*

BACTRIAN CAMEL. See CAMEL.

BAD GODESBERG. See GODESBERG.

BAD HOMBURG. See HOMBURG.

BAD LANDS. See BADLANDS.

BADAJOZ, bä-thä-hôth', a city in southwestern Spain, is the capital of Badajoz province. The province, 8,362 square miles (21,657 sq km) in area, is the largest province in Spain. Together with Cáceres, it forms the region traditionally known as Estremadura. Badajoz province is bordered by Cáceres and Toledo on the north, by Ciudad Real and Córdoba on the east, by Seville and Huelva on the south, and by Portugal on the west. The principal cities and towns, apart from the capital, are Mérida, Don Benito, Almendralejo, Villanueva de la Serena, Azuaga, and Jerez de los Caballeros.

The region is crossed by mountain ranges, and the slopes and valleys vary considerably in fertility and productivity. Nevertheless, Badajoz is predominantly agricultural and is among the leading provinces in the production of wheat, rice, barley, garbanzos, peas, cotton, grapes and wines, and olives and olive oil. The large amount of pastureland, especially in the eastern sector, makes the province the national leader in the production of livestock, especially sheep, swine, and mules. Minerals of varying commercial importance include antimony, zinc, lead, copper, nickel, iron, and coal.

The city of Badajoz, which is situated near the western limit of the province, is four miles (6.5 km) from the border of Portugal, on the railroad between Lisbon and Madrid. It is the principal market and commercial center for the province and handles much local and transit commerce with Portugal. Limited manufacturing yields diversified products such as wines, brandies, liquors, olive oil, wax, soap, flour, chocolates, and textiles.

The city, overlooking the Guadiana River, is ringed by walls and bastions that indicate the nature of its role in the history of Spain. Among the buildings of interest are several constructed in the 16th and 17th centuries, and the cathedral, which was begun in the 13th century under Alfonso X.

Badajoz was on the frontier between various tribes and kingdoms from pre-Roman times, and it had strategic military importance successively for the Romans, the Visigoths, and the Moors. The Moors held it until 1229 when Alfonso IX, king of León, incorporated it into Christian Spain. At various times in the 14th century it was part of neighboring Portugal but was finally established as a part of Estremadura in the kingdom of Castile and León. In the 17th and 18th centuries Portugal made repeated unsuccessful attempts to recapture Badajoz. In 1808 and 1809 the French troops occupying Spain in the War of Spanish Independence (the Peninsular War) attempted to take the city, but it did not fall into French hands until 1811. In 1812 allied troops of Spain, Britain, and Portugal, under the duke of Wellington, recaptured the city after a bloody battle.

Badajoz was one of the early strategic objectives of Francisco Franco during the Spanish Civil War. It fell to the Nationalist forces in August 1936. Population: (1960) of the city, 23,715.
M.M. LASLEY, *University of Florida*

BADAKHSHAN, bà-dàкн-shàn′, is a province of Afghanistan. It is situated in the extreme northeastern portion of the country and covers an area of about 16,000 square miles (41,440 sq km). On the north, Badakhshan is bounded by the Amu Darya River (the ancient Oxus), which forms the frontier between Afghanistan and the USSR; on the south, by the lofty mountain chain of the Hindu Kush, and on the west by the province of Kataghan (Qataghan). On the east the elevated Wakhan Corridor, a 200-mile (322-km) projection of the province reaches the western border of China.

With the exception of plains in the north which slope down to the Amu Darya River, the province is very mountainous, with many peaks exceeding 15,000 feet (4,572 meters) in height. The Kokcha River drains much of the region and empties into the Amu Darya. Only a few inches of precipitation fall annually, and cultivation is limited to land irrigated by dams on the Kokcha and small areas watered by natural springs and streams. Summers are cool and winters are very severe, with snow remaining on the higher peaks until midsummer.

A single motorable road runs from the west as far as Faizabad, the provincial capital, which is situated at an altitude of 4,000 feet (about 1,220 meters) on the edge of a plain where the Kokcha River emerges from the mountains. From Faizabad, a caravan trail leads about 30 miles (48 km) upstream to the village of Jurm at an elevation of 5,000 feet (about 1,520 meters). From Jurm, ancient trails wind eastward over the mountainous terrain of the Wakhan Corridor to China. There are few other villages of any size in the province.

Among the mineral resources of Badakhshan, the most famed are the lapis lazuli deposits, which have been worked for more than 3,000 years. Quantities of this semiprecious stone are exported to jewelers throughout the world. In ancient times, the province was renowned for its rubies. Emeralds and gold have also been mined.

Historically, Badakhshan has been important not only for its mineral wealth, but also because it is situated astride direct (though difficult) trade routes from Europe and the Middle East to China, and from central Asia to Pakistan and India. It was part of ancient Greek Bactria, and is associated with either occupation or transit by Alexander the Great, Tamerlane, and Marco Polo, and with frequent conflicts over control of trade in the Amu Darya River valley. After centuries as an international pawn, Badakhshan became, in 1859, an integral part of Afghanistan.

In spite of the isolation of. the region from roads and highways, many hunters move into the highest ranges in search of mountain goats and the famed Marco Polo wild sheep.

The inhabitants of Badakhshan are primarily Muslims of the orthodox Sunnite sect. Some are Tajiks (Tadzhiks) of Iranian stock who speak Persian, and others are Uzbeks who speak Uzbek, a Turkic language. In the 1950's and 1960's, Pushtu-speaking Pushtuns came into the province from southeastern Afghanistan to take advantage of the irrigation facilities along the lower reaches of the Kokcha River. Population: (1962) 400,000.

See also AFGHANISTAN; BACTRIA.

DONALD N. WILBER
Author of "Afghanistan: Its People,
Its Society, Its Culture"

BADEN, bä′dən, is a town in Austria, in Lower Austria province. Also called *Baden bei Wien,* it is a spa 15 miles (24 km) southwest of Vienna on the Schwechat River at the foot of the Wiener Wald. It has been a fashionable watering place since Roman times, when it was known as *Aquae Pannonicae.* There are beautiful villas, modern hotels, a summer theater, a museum, and several parks. It has architectural remains dating from the Roman settlement. Baden served as Soviet headquarters during the occupation of Austria (1945–1955). Population: (1961) 22,484.

BADEN, bä′dən, a former duchy, grand duchy, and state of Germany, is now a part of the state of Baden-Württemberg in West Germany. A historic and picturesque area, Baden forms the southwest corner of Germany. On the west, the Rhine River marks the boundary with France. The Danube has its headwaters in Baden.

In imperial times the Romans controlled the area, then inhabited by the Swabians. The weakening of Rome's authority was accelerated by attacks of the Alemanni tribe from the north, and by about 400 A.D. Roman control had ended. In ensuing years, dukes of Swabia and Alemannia had hegemony over the district. Members of the junior branch of the Zähringen family first called themselves margraves of Baden in the early 12th century.

In the 16th century the Reformation brought religious unrest and conflict that was to last for more than 100 years. At the death of Margrave Christopher I in 1527, the duchy was divided between his sons to form Baden-Durlach in the north and Baden-Baden in the south. Originally dynastic, the division soon came to reflect the religious dichotomy of the times, the northern part becoming Protestant and the southern part Catholic.

In the 17th century Baden became one of the principal battlegrounds of the Thirty Years' War. Areas changed hands and religions frequently, and religious change was usually enforced with the sword. The fury of the conflict turned wide areas into wastelands. It has been estimated that by 1653, Baden-Durlach had lost more than three quarters of its prewar population.

Disunion continued for many years, but the mid-18th century witnessed the advent of the remarkable Margrave Charles Frederick of Baden-Durlach, who was eventually to consolidate the area. Both able and lucky, he ruled for 65 years (1746–1811). In 1771 the Baden-Baden line of the family died out, so that Charles Frederick was able to reunite all of Baden. During the Napoleonic era he added the Rhenish Palatinate east of the Rhine and the region of Breisgau to his holdings. When he died in 1811, he left a politically cohesive, economically viable, and greatly enlarged duchy. In the political readjustments that followed the fall of Napoleon in 1815, Baden managed to retain its gains.

Baden joined the Prussian Zollverein, a customs union, in 1835, and its integration with the German empire followed in 1871. The last grand duke, Frederick II, was deposed by the revolution in 1918, and Baden joined the Weimar Republic, ending the 800-year Zähringen rule. With the advent of the National Socialist (Nazi) party in 1933, Baden became an administrative district of Germany. For the period after 1945, see BADEN-WÜRTTEMBERG.

A.G. STEER, JR., *Columbia University*

BADEN, bä′dən, a residential borough in southwestern Pennsylvania, is on the northeast bank of the Ohio River, about 22 miles (35 km) northwest of Pittsburgh. Most residents of Baden are employed in the steel mills and other industries of nearby Aliquippa and Ambridge, and of Pittsburgh. The Conway yard of the Pennsylvania Railroad is located at the northern limits of the borough.

Gen. Anthony Wayne fortified the site in 1792 and camped within what are now the borough limits. In the winter of 1792–1793, Wayne recruited and trained here the force with which he won the Battle of Fallen Timbers against the Indians in 1794. A historic Indian community called Logstown was situated within the present borough limits. Baden was permanently settled in 1819, surveyed as a village in 1838, and incorporated as a borough with burgess and council government in 1868. Population: 5,536.

HARVEY E. FAULK, *Gen. Anthony Wayne Chapter Sons of the American Revolution*

BADEN-BADEN, bä′dən bä′dən, is a city in West Germany, in the state of Baden-Württemberg. It is located 18 miles (29 km) southwest of Karlsruhe. The older part of the city is built on a spur of the Black Forest, overlooking the valley of the Oos River.

Baths built during the 3d century A.D. made the city famous as a watering place under its ancient name of *Aurelia Aquensis*. By the beginning of the 5th century the Romans had lost control of the area, and the city fell into ruins. In the 12th century, Baden-Baden revived after being made the seat of the margraves of Baden. The New Castle, standing on an isolated height above the town, was the residence of the rulers of Baden until 1918.

Since the early 19th century, saline and radioactive springs, reaching temperatures as high as 150° F (66° C), have helped to make the city a health resort. Many beautiful hotels, villas, walks, and parks have been built to attract visitors. In World War II the city served as a hospitalization area for German troops. After the war it was the headquarters of the French occupation forces. Population: (1961) 40,029.

BADEN-POWELL, bä-dən-pō′əl, **Robert Stephenson Smyth, 1ST BARON BADEN-POWELL OF GILWELL** (1857–1941), British army officer, who founded the Boy Scout and Girl Guide (Girl Scout) movement. He was born in London on Feb. 22, 1857. Educated at Charterhouse, he was commissioned in 1876 in the 13th Hussars, a cavalry regiment of which he eventually became honorary colonel. He served with his regiment in India, Afghanistan, and South Africa. Following other duties in Malta and West Africa, he saw action in the South African (Boer) War, during which he held Mafeking with a small force against Boer besiegers from Oct. 15, 1899, until relieved on May 17, 1900. He later organized the South African constabulary, which he headed as inspector general until 1903.

In training recruits for this force, Baden-Powell developed their self-reliance, resourcefulness, and courage, and following his return to Britain he was invited to develop a program for boys based on these principles. The movement which he then initiated developed in 1908 into the Boy Scouts, an organization that eventually spread throughout the world. He became lieutenant general in 1908 and was knighted in 1909. That year, with the assistance of his sister, Agnes Baden-Powell, he founded the Girl Guides (known later in the United States as the Girl Scouts). In 1910, King Edward VII persuaded him to retire from the army in order to devote himself exclusively to furthering the scout movement. A baronetcy was conferred upon him in 1922 and in 1929 he was created a peer, with the title of Baron Baden-Powell of Gilwell. He died in Nyeri, Kenya, on Jan. 8, 1941.

Baden-Powell's numerous books include: *Scouting for Boys* (1908); *My Adventures as a Spy* (1915); *The Wolf Cubs Handbook* (1916); *Girl Guiding* (1917); *Aids to Scoutmastership* (1920); *What Scouts Can Do* (1921); *Rovering to Success* (1922); *Scouting and Youth Movements* (1929); *Paddle Your Own Canoe* (1933); *Adventures and Accidents* (1934); *African Adventure* (1936); and *Birds and Beasts in Africa* (1938). He published his autobiography, *Lessons of a Lifetime*, in 1933.

See also BOY SCOUTS; GIRL SCOUTS AND GIRL GUIDES.

BADEN-WÜRTTEMBERG, bä′dən vür′təm-berкн, is a state of West Germany. Some of the most scenic and historic areas of Germany are in Baden-Württemberg. The state ranks second among the German states in the value of goods produced by its diversified industrial economy, which has steadily expanded since World War II. Metal products, machinery, and textiles are the leading industries. Included within the state's boundaries are the slopes of the northern Alps, the Black Forest, the northern portion of Lake Constance, and the historic upper reaches of the Rhine and Danube rivers.

After World War II, northern Baden was united with Württemberg to form the state of Württemberg-Baden as part of the United States occupation zone. The remainder of Baden, together with Württemberg-Hohenzollern, formed the French zone of occupation. After a plebiscite in December 1951, the states of Württemberg-Baden, Württemberg-Hohenzollern, and Baden united to form the state of Baden-Württemberg, with Stuttgart as the capital. The total area is 13,803 square miles (35,750 sq km). Population: (1961) 7,759,154. For history before 1945, see BADEN; WÜRTTEMBERG.

A.G. STEER, JR., *Columbia University*

BADGER, baj′ər, a stout, burrowing mammal closely related to skunks and weasels and native to various regions of the Northern Hemisphere. Badgers have short legs, elongated feet with powerful toes, and heavy claws for digging. Their large jaws have strong teeth that are used in defense. (Well-developed scent glands in the anal region are also used in defense.) The badger's hide is thick, but loose and flexible. It is covered with coarse fur, which usually is grizzled in brown or gray. Various markings about the face and on the upper side of the body identify the different species. Badgers are about 24 inches (61 cm) long and about 9 inches (23 cm) high at the shoulders. They weigh from 12 to 24 pounds (5.4 to 11 kg).

Badgers live in holes in the ground, in rocks, or in hollow trees or logs. Some forms dig extensive underground burrows, which may house several badgers. Badgers feed both on plants and on other animals. They are aggressive animals and are

American Badger (*Taxidea taxus*)

a white stripe from its nose to its shoulders and black patches on the face, chin, and throat.

The honey badger, or ratel (*Mellivora capensis*), is found in Senegal and in the northeastern region of Africa. The upper part of its body has gray to whitish fur, while the underparts are dark brown or black. Its hair is coarse, and its skin is very tough and thick, protecting it from the bites of insects and snakes that it feeds on. The honey badger attacks wild bees' nests in "partnership" with the honey guide bird (*Indicator indicator*), which leads the badger to the nests.

The other badger genera are found mostly in Asia. The Old World badger (*Meles meles*), whose range extends from Europe to southern China, is identified by the dark stripes bordered with white on each side of its face. A gregarious, nocturnal animal, it lives in huge underground burrows and feeds on insects and small rodents. The hog badger (*Arctonyx collaris*), found in southeastern Asia, has a pattern of white and black stripes on its head. It also has a long mobile snout that is used for digging. The stink, or skunk, badgers (*Mydaus javanensis* and *Suillotaxus marchei*), when provoked, emit an extremely offensive-smelling fluid from their scent glands. They are found on Sumatra, Java, and nearby islands. The ferret badgers (*Melogale personata*, *M. moschata*, and *M. orientalis*), found on the mainland and islands of southeastern Asia, have a black and white mask-shaped pattern on their faces. They are helpful in controlling insect pests.

savage when attacked. Badgers usually spend the colder weather in a winter sleep (not true hibernation because the body processes and temperature are not reduced).

The reproductive history of badgers is not well known, but in many species delayed implantation (sperm retained in the female reproductive tract until ovulation occurs at a later time) takes place. One to five young may be produced in a litter, although the usual number is two.

Types of Badgers. The badger belongs to the family Mustelidae in the order Carnivora. There are about seven genera. The American badger (*Taxidea taxus*) is found from southwestern Canada and the north central part of the United States south to central Mexico. It lives in deep burrows and feeds upon gophers, ground squirrels, and ground-nesting birds. It is identified by

BADLANDS, bad'landz, are regions of intricately rugged terrain, generally consisting of a series of steep slopes with small summits, separated by many closely spaced streams. The drainage pattern, which usually has been in existence for a long time, produces the extensive erosion that gives the landforms their ruggedness.

BADLANDS, with their rugged, eroded slopes, are preserved in Badlands National Monument in South Dakota.

The Big Badlands of South Dakota, east of the southern part of the Black Hills, are the most famous example of this kind of terrain in the United States. The term "badlands" was, in fact, first applied to this region by Indian hunting parties, and later by French-Canadian trappers, because of the difficulties they encountered in crossing the barren wastes. The region is an extensive peneplain, a land surface worn down nearly to a plain. The land is being actively dissected into valleys and ridges by stream erosion. However, the Big Badlands of South Dakota are by no means a monotonous, intricate succession of crests and valleys. Many flat tablelands remain in which stream erosion has not yet begun, although overgrazing or poor agricultural techniques on the flat areas facilitate erosion there as well.

Badlands of smaller area, or of less typical development, occur in other parts of the United States and Canada. Scattered areas are found in North and South Dakota, Wyoming, Colorado, Kansas, Nebraska, Arizona, and California; and in Canada, in the province of Alberta.

Formation. Badland formation depends on a combination of local conditions. The region must be well above the local base level—the lowest level to which streams can cut in that region—in order to allow the streams a relatively steep rate of descent. Easily eroded materials must also prevail, otherwise vegetation would cover the surface and hinder erosion. The materials must not be too soft, however, or the steep slopes produced would not persist. In the Big Badlands, the materials consist of poorly consolidated clays. Thin beds and isolated masses of sandstone prevail at intervals, leading to the formation of the fantastic features of the region.

Aridity or semiaridity also encourages natural badland formation, partly because it discourages vegetation growth and partly because the rainfall, although infrequent, occurs usually as a torrential shower. Light rains soften and round off the soil, but heavy downpours cut it down rapidly to form steep slopes.

Badland development frequently occurs in wind-deposited silt (loess). Such development may even occur in relatively humid areas, if the loessial material is of the right consistency. An illustration of this is to be found in the palisade formations of Council Bluffs, Iowa. A similar type of occurrence, on a much larger scale, is encountered in the loess regions of Shansi, China.

The occurrence of modified badlands, resulting from land exploitation or poor conservation practices, has become a not uncommon problem. One example is the badland area in the vicinity of Ducktown, Tenn. In this case, fumes from a copper smelter killed the vegetation, and the bared soil-and-rock mantle was eroded into badland forms.

Badlands National Monument. The Badlands National Monument was established in South Dakota in 1939 to preserve this weirdly beautiful region. The 40-mile (64-km) strip of White River badlands included in the monument covers an area of more than 170 square miles (440 sq km). A modern road passes through the monument. Park facilities include a museum, public campgrounds, and clearly marked nature trails. Rich fossil beds have also attracted paleontologists to the region. See also CONSERVATION; EROSION.

MALCOLM A. MURRAY, *Miami University, Ohio*

BADMINTON, băd′min-tən, is a court game that may be played indoors or outdoors. The equipment is extremely simple. A light racket, called a *battledore,* is used to drive a small hemispheric cork with a tail of 14 to 16 feathers (or a trailing "skirt" molded of a soft plastic material) over a high net. As the cork, known as a *shuttlecock, shuttle,* or *bird,* will not bounce, it must be hit while in the air. This keeps the players in almost perpetual action and provides continuous excitement. The tail slows the bird and keeps it from flying far beyond the ends of the court. The tail also causes the bird to take eccentric turns or to stop in midair and drop abruptly; therefore, speed and alertness are needed to play the game well.

The game has become a popular backyard sport and may be played and enjoyed by beginners and children and by players of various ages, degrees of skill, and experience. To avoid wind, championship competition is conducted indoors.

It is believed that badminton was played first in India, where it was called *poona.* British army officers brought it to England in the 1860's or early 1870's. The 8th duke of Beaufort introduced the game to English society in the early 1870's at his estate, called Badminton, in Gloucester. The game takes its modern name from his estate.

In 1887 the Bath Badminton Club in England codified the rules. Those regulations, with modifications, govern the game in all parts of the world today. Many leading players now come from India, Indonesia, Malaysia, Thailand, and the United States.

International Play. After the International Badminton Federation was formed in 1934, national championships were conducted in nine countries—Australia, Denmark, India, Malaya, Norway, Sweden, the United States, Mexico, and the Netherlands. By the mid-1960's, 40 countries had joined the federation.

International teams compete every three years for both the men's and the women's titles. Each country's team is composed of from four to six amateur players. Preliminary games are conducted in three zones: American, European, and Pacific. The team winning the interzone series challenges the previous winner of the trophy and plays in the holder's country. The men's trophy was donated in 1940 by George A. Thomas, president of the International Badminton Federation, but, because of World War II and its aftermath, matches for the trophy were not held until 1949. Malaya was the first country to win the Thomas Cup.

In 1956, Mrs. H.S. Uber, British badminton star, contributed a trophy for women's tournament play. The first Uber Cup competition was won in 1957 by the United States, which dominated play until 1966 when Japan won the cup.

Badminton in the United States. The first badminton club in the United States was organized in New York in 1878. The national championships, held annually since 1937 except in 1943–1946, are governed by the American Badminton Association.

Outstanding among American male competitors was David G. Freeman of Pasadena, Calif. Freeman began playing in national tournaments in 1939 at the age of 18 and remained unbeaten for the next 10 years. During that time he won six United States singles, five doubles, and three mixed-doubles titles and held off all foreign challengers in singles. He won the United States singles championship once again in 1953.

Other top United States players were Wynn Rogers of Arcadia, Calif., who took 10 doubles and eight mixed-doubles titles between 1948 and 1964, and Joseph Alston, of Pasadena, who won two singles, two mixed-doubles, and, paired with Rogers, seven doubles crowns between 1951 and 1964.

No badminton star, however, has matched the record of Mrs. Judith Devlin Hashman, a former Baltimore, Md., schoolteacher, who played world-class badminton between 1954 and her retirement in 1967. During these 13 years she won 32 U.S. championships—12 in singles, 12 in doubles (10 with her sister, Sue Devlin Peard), and 8 in mixed doubles—and 10 All-England (unofficial world championship) titles.

Rules. Badminton may be played by two or four persons. As in tennis, when two play, the game is called singles, and when four play, two to a side, it is called doubles.

The first serve of a game is from the right half court to the half diagonally opposite. If the receiving side commits a fault, the serving side gains a point and continues to serve. If the serving side commits a fault, no point is scored but, in singles, the serve shifts to the opposition. In doubles, a partner serves until his side commits a fault, then his teammate serves. There is one exception to this last rule: at the beginning of a doubles game, the serve shifts to the opposition as soon as the serving side commits a fault.

In both singles and doubles, the serve is made alternately from the right-half and left-half sides of the court, as in tennis. The players on the receiving side do not shift half courts between serves.

The players change court ends after each game. The winning side serves first. In doubles, either partner may serve first and either opponent may receive first. The winner of a match is the side that wins two games. If a third game must be played, the players change court ends when the score reaches 8 in a game of 15 points, or when the score reaches 6 in a game of 11 points.

Game score is 15 points in men's singles and all doubles, and 11 in women's singles. In 15-point games the side that reaches 13 points first has the option of extending the game to 18 points if the score becomes 13-all. If the game has not been set at 18 points, it may be set at 17 points when the score reaches 14-all. In women's singles, the game score may be set at 12 points if the score becomes 9- or 10-all.

A one-game match usually goes to 21 points. If tied at 19 points, it may be extended to 24; if tied at 20, it may be extended to 23 points. Extending a game often gives the receiver a chance to make a comeback and win.

The main faults are when the server strikes the shuttle while it is more than waist high or holds the racket head higher than his hand; when a player's foot touches a line during a stroke; or when the shuttle falls into the wrong court, lands short of the service line, drops outside the boundary lines, passes through or under the net, hits the roof or sidewalls of a court, or touches the person or clothing of a player.

Strokes. The basic strokes are the service, the clear, the smash, the drop shot, the forehand drive, and the backhand drive. The clear, drive,

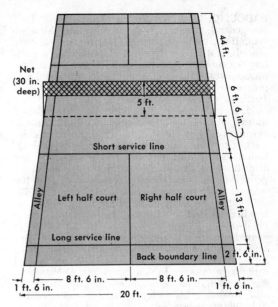

Official dimensions of a badminton court are shown in this diagram. The alleys along the sides are used only for doubles competition, increasing the width by three feet. Serving is done from the long service line in doubles play, from the back boundary line in singles.

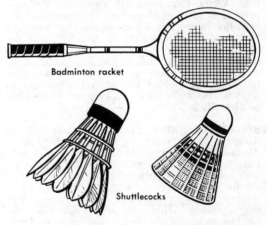

Badminton racket

Shuttlecocks

and drop may be used on service, since it is important to have a variety of serves. The clear is a shot deep into the opponent's court. A drive is a fast stroke in which the racket meets the bird at about the level of the hips and the swing continues with a follow-through motion. A drop shot is one in which the bird falls near the net, in the opponent's court. A smash is an overhead stroke which returns the bird at high speed. Much of the power in badminton comes from the snap of the wrist as the racket strikes the bird.

GEORGE McNICKLE, *New York "Times"*

Bibliography

American Association for Health, Physical Education, and Recreation, *Tennis-Badminton Guide* (Washington, current ed.).

American Badminton Association, *Official Handbook* (Waban, Mass., current ed.).

Davidson, Kenneth R., and Gustavson, L.R., *Winning Badminton* (New York 1964).

Davis, Patrick Ronald, *Badminton Complete* (New York 1967).

The Athletic Institute, *How to Improve Your Badminton* (Chicago, no date).

BADOGLIO, bä-dô′lyō, **Pietro** (1871–1956), Italian general. He was born at Grazzano Monferrato, Italy, on Sept. 28, 1871, attended military schools, and by his 20's had embarked on a military career. He served as a lieutenant in the unsuccessful Ethiopian campaign of 1896 and was promoted major after the Italo-Turkish War of 1912, in which Italy gained Libya.

During World War I, Badoglio distinguished himself at the Battle of Gorizia in 1916. In the closing weeks of the war, he was appointed chief adviser to Gen. Armando Diaz. Later he was selected as the Italian representative to sign the armistice that terminated hostilities. He became a general in 1919 and succeeded Diaz as chief of the general staff, serving in this capacity until 1921.

Sent to Brazil as ambassador in 1924, he was recalled in 1925 by Benito Mussolini to become chief of the general staff again. In the following year he achieved the rank of marshal. After serving as governor general of Libya from 1928, he returned to Italy in 1933 to head the general staff once more. In the invasion of Ethiopia (1935–1936), he commanded the Italian forces and, following his victory there, was created the duke of Addis Ababa.

Badoglio was still chief of the general staff when Italy entered World War II in 1940, but he was removed from the post in the same year after serious Italian reverses in Greece. In 1943, King Victor Emmanuel III appointed Badoglio premier to succeed Mussolini. He negotiated the armistice with the Allies—signed on Sept. 3, 1943—and later withdrew to Brindisi with the king. There they met violent opposition from some of the new Italian political parties. He resigned his premiership on June 5, 1944, after the king had yielded the royal prerogatives to his son. Badoglio died in Grazzano Monferrato on Oct. 31, 1956.

BADROULBOUDOUR, ba-drool′boo-door, was the daughter of the sultan of China in the tale of *Aladdin,* one of the stories in the *Arabian Nights' Entertainments.* She was married to Aladdin, who constructed a palace for her, but was taken off to Africa, together with the palace, by a sorcerer who got possession of the lamp with magic powers. Aladdin overtook them, killed the sorcerer, regained the lamp, and took his bride and her palace back to China. In some versions of the tale her name, meaning "moon of moons," is *Bedr el-Budur.* See also ALADDIN.

BAEDEKER, bā′də-kər, **Karl** (1801–1859), German publisher of travel guides. He was born in Germany, on Nov. 3, 1801, the son of a prominent bookseller. Baedeker established a printing plant in Coblenz in 1827. In 1839, under an arrangement with the London publishing house of John Murray, he brought out a small guidebook of the Rhine, Belgium, and the Netherlands. This was the precursor of a long line of guidebooks, all bearing his name, that covered most European countries and parts of North America and the Orient. The "Baedekers" were published in English, French, and German.

After Baedeker's death, in Coblenz on Oct. 4, 1859, the firm was headed by his son Fritz, who moved the business to Leipzig in 1872. Following World War II, the guidebooks were published in Hamburg. In 1950 the firm began publishing, in Stuttgart, a series of automobile touring guides.

BAEKELAND, bāk′land, **Leo Hendrik** (1863–1944), Belgian-American chemist and inventor. He was born in Ghent, Belgium, on Nov. 14, 1863. In 1882 he graduated from the University of Ghent, and in 1887 he was made laureate of the four Belgian universities. He taught chemistry at the University of Ghent from 1882 until 1889, when he went to the United States on a scholarship; remaining in that country, he subsequently became an American citizen.

In 1893 he founded at Yonkers, N.Y., the Nepera Chemical Company to manufacture Velox, a photographic paper of his invention that revolutionized the making of photographic prints. He also made numerous other contributions to photography, electric insulation, and electric and organic chemistry. After the Eastman Kodak Company acquired his holdings in 1899, he engaged in research engineering at his Yonkers laboratory. His best known invention was Bakelite, a chemical synthesis from carbolic acid and formaldehyde, used as a substitute for hard rubber and amber, and vital to the development of the plastics industry. He was president of the Bakelite Corporation from its establishment in 1910 until his retirement in 1939.

Baekeland was president of the American Chemical Society in 1924. He wrote effectively on the industrial aspects of chemistry and on patent reform. He died in Beacon, N.Y., on Feb. 23, 1944.

BAER, bâr, **George Frederick** (1842–1914), American lawyer and industrialist. He was born near Lavansville, Pa., on Sept. 26, 1842. After serving in the Civil War, he resumed his law studies at Franklin and Marshall College and was admitted to the bar in 1864. He later became legal adviser to J. Pierpont Morgan and in 1901 was elected president of the Philadelphia and Reading Coal and Iron Company. In 1902 he led the coal operators during a strike of anthracite miners. At one point in the dispute he asserted, "The rights and interests of the laboring man will be protected and cared for—not by the labor agitators, but by the Christian men to whom God in his infinite wisdom has given the control of the property interests of the country." Afterward he was often referred to as "Divine Right" Baer. He died in Philadelphia on April 26, 1914.

BAER, bâr, **Karl Ernst von** (1792–1876), German-Russian embryologist, who was one of the founders of modern embryology. Baer was the first to see and identify the female reproductive cell, or egg, in a mammal. Previously it had been thought that the Graafian follicle, a tiny fluid-filled sac in the mammalian ovary, was the egg; but Baer, in examining the follicle of a dog under a microscope, found that the egg itself was a much smaller structure attached to the inner wall of the follicle. This discovery made clear the similarity of mammalian eggs to the eggs of lower animals.

While examining the early growth of the egg, Baer found that the developing egg forms several distinct layers of cells. He named these layers "germ layers." He also saw these layers differentiate into the tissues of the various specialized organs of the developing embryo.

Baer also discovered similarities and differences among the embryos of various groups of animals and thus helped to establish comparative embryology. He found that vertebrates have a notochord (a rodlike cartilaginous structure in the back) in their early embryonic stages and that as they develop, the notochord is replaced by a spinal cord. The presence of the notochord in the embryos of vertebrates (including humans) shows their close relationship to some lower animals—primitive fishlike animals—that retain the notochord in adult life.

Baer's studies of vertebrate embryos also showed that some structures that differ greatly in mature animals (such as the wing of a bird and the arm of a man) develop from structures that are very similar in the embryonic stages of these animals. Darwin later used Baer's discoveries in comparative embryology to support his theory of evolution, although Baer himself did not accept Darwin's theory.

Baer was born in Piep, Estonia (now part of the USSR), on Feb. 29, 1792. He studied first in Estonia and later at Würzburg, Germany. In 1819 he became a professor of zoology at the University of Königsberg, where he did most of his important work. In 1834 he went to St. Petersburg (now Leningrad) to become librarian at the Academy of Sciences. He died in Dorpat, Estonia, on Nov. 28, 1876. Among his important works is *Development of the Fishes* (1835).

BAER, bâr, **Max** (1909–1959), American prizefighter, a colorful figure who held the world's heavyweight championship for one year in the mid-1930's.

Maximilian Adelbert Baer was born in Omaha, Nebr., on Feb. 11, 1909, and started boxing in 1929. After defeating leading contenders, including Max Schmeling, he met Primo Carnera of Italy in a title bout in New York on June 14, 1934. Baer floored the champion 11 times before the referee stopped the bout in the 11th round. He lost the title to James J. Braddock in a 15-round decision on June 13, 1935. He retired from the ring in 1941, the winner of 65 of his 79 professional bouts.

Called "Madcap Maxie" because of his playboy antics, Baer did bits in vaudeville and radio, and he played opposite Myrna Loy in the motion picture *The Prize-Fighter and the Lady* (1933). He died in Hollywood, Calif., on Nov. 21, 1959.

BILL BRADDOCK, *New York "Times"*

BAETICA, bē′ti-kə, was a Roman province of southern Spain. It occupied the western part of Andalusia. Baetica was famed for its fertility, wealth, and delightful climate. From the rich Baetis (Guadalquivir) Valley, grains, wines, oils, fish, meat, and minerals were exported to Rome. According to Pliny the Elder, the province had 175 towns, which were divided into four judicial circuits. The Vandals settled in Baetica for a time in the early 5th century A.D., and the region was the first part of Spain to be conquered and settled by the Moors in the 8th century.

BAEYER, bâ′yər, **Adolf von** (1835–1917), German chemist, who won the Nobel Prize in chemistry in 1905 "in recognition of his services in the development of organic chemistry and the chemical industry through his work on organic dyes and hydroaromatic combinations."

Baeyer was born in Berlin on Oct. 31, 1835. He studied chemistry at Heidelberg University with Robert Bunsen, who stressed the importance of physics in chemical training and research. Another one of his teachers was Friedrich August Kekulé, who first described the structure of benzene. At times, later in life, Baeyer discounted his formal education and claimed that he was really self-taught.

After receiving a doctor's degree from the University of Berlin in 1860, he became a chemistry teacher there. A few years later, he became head of the chemistry laboratory at the Berlin Gewerbeinstitut, a vocational school that grew into the Charlottenburg Institute of Technology. After the German repossession of Alsace, a new university was founded at Strasbourg, and Baeyer was appointed its professor of chemistry in 1872. In 1875 he moved to Munich, where he succeeded the leading organic chemist of the time, Justus von Liebig. The government built a new laboratory for Baeyer and gave him an official residence.

One of his first achievements was the preparation of barbituric acid, the base of many sleeping pills. He began his work with the dye indigo in 1865. By 1880 his patents for synthesizing indigo and other organic compounds were acquired by two large chemical and dye organizations, the Badische Anilin- und Soda-Fabrik and the Hoechst Farbwerke. Although his process for making synthetic indigo was not commercially feasible, he did accomplish much for the dye industry. He investigated phthaleins, which are triphenylmethane derivatives that are basically aniline dyes and hydroaromatic compounds. One of his students, Karl Graebe, synthesized alizarin, and this accomplishment was used industrially.

One of his many students and collaborators was the son of William Perkin, the English chemist who prepared the first synthetic dye. Baeyer and William Perkin, Jr., devised procedures for forming molecules that contain a ring of carbon atoms, and they established Baeyer's strain theory, which indicates why rings of 5 or 6 carbon atoms are the most common. Baeyer's students comprise a list of notables in organic chemistry in Germany during the early 20th century. They include Friedrich K.J. Thiele, F. Schlenk, Heinrich Otto Wieland, Kurt Meyer, Emil Fischer, and Otto Fischer.

Baeyer received numerous prizes and awards. In 1881 the Royal Society of London gave him the Davy Medal for his work on indigo. In 1905 his scientific papers were collected and published in two volumes. In the same year he was awarded the Nobel Prize in chemistry. Baeyer died at Starnberg on Aug. 20, 1917.

MORRIS GORAN, *Roosevelt University*

BÁEZ, bä′ās, **Buenaventura** (1810?–1884), Dominican dictator, who vied with Pedro Santana and others for control of the Dominican Republic. He was born of mulatto parentage at Azua, Santo Domingo, about 1810. He aided in establishing the republic and was chosen president in 1849. In 1853 he was banished by Santana, who then assumed the presidency. In 1856 Báez came into power for a second time but again deposed by Santana two years later. He returned to the presidency in 1865, holding the office at intervals until he was exiled in 1878.

In 1869, seeking insulation from Haitian interference in Dominican affairs, he negotiated treaties for the annexation of the Dominican Republic by the United States. Although President Grant favored the plan, the treaties failed of ratification in the U.S. Senate. Báez died in Puerto Rico on March 21, 1884.

BAEZ, bī-ez, **Joan** (1941–   ), American folk singer. She was born in New York City on Jan. 9, 1941. Her father was a Mexican-born physicist and educator, and when he was teaching at Harvard, folk-singer friends in Boston taught Joan to play the guitar and to sing a repertoire of folk songs, ballads, blues, and spirituals from all over the world. Her voice, though untrained, had a range of more than three octaves.

Miss Baez sang from time to time in Boston coffeehouses and then was invited to appear at the 1959 Newport music festival in Rhode Island. She sang there again in 1960 and that year made her first recording, an album labeled simply *Joan Baez*. It was an immediate best seller, and she subsequently became the most popular female folk singer in the United States.

BAFFIN, baf'ən, **William** (c. 1584–1622), English navigator, who was notable for his explorations of the Arctic region. The precise date and place of his birth are unknown. He was mate of a vessel that was dispatched in 1612 by a merchant of Hull, England, to the west coast of Greenland and reached the latitude of 67° north. In 1613 he entered the service of the Muscovy Company, an English enterprise, and for two years was chief pilot on fishing expeditions to Spitsbergen.

As chief pilot of the *Discovery* he embarked in 1615 on a voyage sponsored by the Muscovy Company to search for a northwest passage to the Orient. He passed through Hudson Strait and pushed northward but turned back when he sighted great landmasses ahead. On his return to England he declared his belief that Davis Strait was a more promising route, and in 1616 he took the *Discovery* up this strait and beyond to latitude 78° north. He discovered and named Smith Sound, Lancaster Sound, Jones Sound, and other geographical features and mapped them with reasonable accuracy. But he was convinced that no passage to the Orient could be found in the region and suggested to merchants in London that better fortune might attend a venture starting from Japan and sailing eastward.

He was then employed by the East India Company and from 1617 to 1621 was master of ships that surveyed the Red Sea and the Persian Gulf and visited India. In 1622 the East India Company agreed to help the shah of Persia in expelling the Portuguese from Hormuz, an island at the mouth of the Persian Gulf. In an attack of Jan. 23, 1622, on Qishm, an island near Hormuz, Baffin was mortally wounded.

Many of Baffin's observations in Arctic waters were of great value to later explorers. He was the first mariner to try to determine longitude by observations of the moon. Baffin Bay and Baffin Island were named for him.

BAFFIN BAY, baf'ən, lies between Greenland and the northeast coast of Canada. It is connected with the Atlantic Ocean to the south by Davis Strait and with the Arctic Ocean to the north and west by a series of sounds. It is about 700 miles (1,126 km) long and from 70 to 400 miles (112 to 644 km) wide. The depth of Baffin Bay ranges from 200 to 1,500 fathoms (366 to 2,744 meters).

The western shoreline includes Ellesmere, Devon, Bylot, and Baffin islands. Greenland forms the eastern shore, on which are Thule Air Base of the U.S. Air Force and the settlements of Thule, Kraulshavn, and Upernavik. The coasts are mountainous, barren, and indented by bays and fjords.

During most of the year the bay is covered by ice, which extends from shore to shore in winter. In the summer, navigable passages and occasional channels from shore to shore are formed as the ice softens. The Labrador Current passes through the bay, carrying icebergs to the south.

The first explorer to enter the bay was John Davis, an English navigator, in 1585. It was named for William Baffin, also an Englishman, who entered it in 1616 in search of a northwest passage to the Orient. The bay was an important sealing and whaling area in the 19th century.

BAFFIN ISLAND, baf'ən, the fifth-largest island in the world, is in the Canadian Arctic Archipelago, in Franklin District of the Northwest Territories. It is situated west of Baffin Bay and north of Hudson Strait and the mouth of Hudson Bay. Baffin Island is about 1,000 miles (1,600 km) long and up to 500 miles (800 km) wide. Its area is about 183,810 square miles (476,068 sq km).

There are mountains in the east, with glaciers and icecaps and some elevations over 8,000 feet (2,400 meters). The northern and southern parts are largely plateaus, while the west central coast around Foxe Basin is lowland. The island's coastline is broken by many bays and fjords, notably Cumberland Sound and Frobisher Bay in the south and Admiralty Inlet in the north.

Most of the inhabitants are Eskimo, whose principal occupations are hunting and fishing. Trade in furs is carried on, and there is some whaling. There are trading posts at Cape Dorset, Lake Harbour, Frobisher Bay, Pangnirtung, Clyde, Pond Inlet, and Arctic Bay, and airports at Frobisher Bay and Cape Dyer.

Martin Frobisher, the English mariner, explored the southern part of the island in 1576–1578. The island is named for William Baffin, also an Englishman, who visited the northern part in 1616. Population: 1,300.

BAGASSE, bə-gas', is the crushed, dry remains of sugarcane after it comes from the mill, where most of the juice has been extracted. It often is used as a fuel in the mills, as a source of cellulose (for papermaking), and as an ingredient in some animal feeds. The term is used for the dry remains of sugar beets.

BAGATELLE, bag-ə-tel', is a type of billiards (q.v.) that was popular in the 19th century. It employed nine balls and was played on a table that was semicircular at one end. In the bed of the table were 9 to 15 numbered holes or cups. After placing a ball on the table, a player stroked another ball with his cue, attempting to lodge either or both balls in the cups. After playing all of the balls in turn, the contestant tallied his score either by the number of cups filled or by the total point value of the cups filled. The game was popular because its added element of chance appealing to billiard players of little skill.

The name "bagatelle" was later extended to similar games played on tables of various shapes and using balls of various sizes and compositions. It was also applied to a children's game played on a tilted, nail-studded board onto which a ball was driven by a mechanical "cue" activated by a spring. This apparatus was a prototype of the modern pinball machine.

BAGATELLE, bag-ə-tel', is a musical term that is often applied by composers to their lightest and least consequential compositions. The word, in French, means "trifle." Bagatelles are often abbreviated piano pieces, but the name may be given to any short, unpretentious work and implies no specific structure or mode of organizing the musical material.

Among the major composers of bagatelles are François Couperin (*Les Bagatelles,* a harpsichord piece), Ludwig van Beethoven (Seven Bagatelles for piano, opus 33; and several later compositions), and Anton Dvořák (four pieces for harmonium, two violins, and cello, opus 47).

BAGEHOT, baj'ət, **Walter** (1826–1877), English economist, political theorist, and man of letters. He was born at Langport, Somerset, England, on Feb. 3, 1826. He was the son of Thomas Watson Bagehot, a partner in Stuckey's Bank in Somersetshire, and of Edith Stuckey, niece of the bank's founder. Walter Bagehot was educated at Bristol College and University College, London.

During a visit to Paris in 1851, the young man witnessed Louis Napoleon's coup d'état and established a literary reputation by contributing seven brilliant letters on the event to the *Inquirer,* a Unitarian journal. They shrewdly analyzed the French character and outraged readers by eulogizing the Roman Catholic Church, justifying Louis Napoleon's use of force, and maintaining that France was totally unfitted for parliamentary government.

In 1852 he abandoned the idea of practicing law and entered the family bank, thus acquiring a congenial occupation and leisure to write.

In the following years Bagehot published some of his finest literary and biographical essays on Oxford, Hartley Coleridge, Shakespeare (*Shakespeare—The Man*), Shelley, Edward Gibbon, Henry Peter Brougham, and Sir Robert Peel. The distinguishing feature of his literary criticism is his penetration behind the writing to the character of the writer himself, and his use of deduction to display the author's meaning and intention. He developed his theory of literature, that of types, in an essay: *Wordsworth, Tennyson and Browning; or Pure, Ornate and Grotesque Art in English Poetry* (1864).

In 1858, Bagehot married Eliza Wilson, eldest daughter of James Wilson, founder and editor of the *Economist* and financial secretary to the Treasury. The alliance launched him into the London social and political world, and in 1859 his pamphlet *Parliamentary Reform* made him a celebrity. In the same year he became director of the *Economist,* contributing two articles on economic and political subjects every year from 1859 to 1877. In 1861 he succeeded his friend Richard Hutton as editor, a post he held until his death, at Langport, on March 24, 1877.

In 1865 the first part of Bagehot's book *The English Constitution* appeared in the first number of the *Fortnightly Review.* It was published in volume form in 1867. The purpose of this, his greatest work, was to show how the constitution had developed since the first Reform Act (1832) and to examine its actual operation in the 1860's. Rejecting the traditional theory that the English Constitution guaranteed freedom by its separation of powers, he showed that its successful working depended on the fusion of the executive and legislative powers of the cabinet. For Blackstone's tripartite division, he substituted the dichotomy of the "dignified" and "efficient" parts of the constitution. The dignified parts—the monarchy and the House of Lords—"excite and preserve the reverence of the population"; the efficient parts—the cabinet and the House of Commons—are those by which it "works and rules." *The English Constitution* makes many references to the United States and is, in effect, a comparative study of the cabinet and presidential systems, with conclusions highly favorable to the former. President Woodrow Wilson was so impressed with his arguments that at one time he suggested introducing cabinet government into the United States.

In 1867, Bagehot published the first part of his second major work, *Physics and Politics,* again in the *Fortnightly,* a complete edition being brought out in 1872. It applies the Darwinian doctrine of natural selection to the growth and development of societies. In 1873 he published a third work, *Lombard Street,* a study of the London money market. His *Economic Studies,* intended to establish the aims and frontiers of economics as a science, was unfinished at his death and was published posthumously in 1880. Two works not formerly attributed to Bagehot but undoubtedly written by him are *Tennyson's Idylls,* which appeared in the *National Review* of October 1859, and *Festus,* in the *Prospective Review* of November 1847.

Walter Bagehot's extraordinary versatility makes him impossible to classify, and although it has commended him to the few, it partly explains his underestimation. Wit, humor, astringent observation, and a gift for aphorism and striking phrases have preserved the freshness of his writing. Consequently he is among the most readable of the great Victorians. The cool detachment of his mind makes him also a uniquely percipient critic of the age in which he lived.

NORMAN ST.JOHN-STEVAS
Author of "Walter Bagehot"

Further Reading: Barrington, Emilie I., ed., *The Collected Works of Walter Bagehot,* 9 vols. (New York 1915); Irvine, William, *Walter Bagehot* (New York 1939); St. John-Stevas, Norman, *Walter Bagehot* (Bloomington, Ind., 1959).

BAGGESEN, båg'e-sen, **Jens** (1764–1826), Danish poet and satirist. He was born in Korsør, Denmark, on Feb. 15, 1764, and attended the University of Copenhagen. In 1785 his *Comic Tales* in verse was a great success in the Danish capital, but four years later he left the city in disgust after the failure of his opera *Holge Danske.* He spent much of the next 17 years traveling in Europe. He lived in Copenhagen again from 1806 to 1820, and thereafter in Paris. His last years were blighted by personal tragedies, by imprisonment for debt, and, finally, by insanity. He died in Hamburg, Germany, on Oct. 3, 1826.

Baggesen's poetry was conservative and rigidly disciplined in form, but, at its best, highly imaginative and sensitive. A bitter critic of the romantics, he conducted a lengthy literary feud with the Danish poet and dramatist Adam Gottlob Oehlenschläger. Among Baggesen's best known works are *Labyrinthen* (1792–93), a satirical verse description of his early travels, and *Parthenais* (1803), an epic poem in German. He was especially gifted in the production of short poems and songs. One of his songs, *There Was a Time When I Was Very Little,* became a popular Danish classic.

BAGHDAD, bag'dad, is the capital and largest city of Iraq (formerly Mesopotamia), and the nation's most important trade, communications, and cultural center. It is located in the heart of the Middle East, in the historic Tigris-Euphrates valley, 430 miles (692 km) southwest of Teheran, Iran, and 500 miles (805 km) east of Beirut, Lebanon.

The Tigris River cuts through the center of Baghdad. The section on the east side of the river, called *al-Rusafah,* is the larger and older part. The western section of the city is called *al-Karkh.* Automobile and pedestrian and railway bridges connect the two sections of the city.

The Modern City. Until the 1920's, when modernization of the city began, Baghdad still had a medieval appearance. Since then, the city has been beautified by many improvements, including new streets and modern buildings. It has a railway station and an international airport. Much of the renovation was made possible by large oil royalties.

Baghdad has five historical museums and a museum of natural history. The Abbasid Palace Museum is a restored palace that dates back to the 1200's A.D. There are also fragmentary remains of several buildings from the city's golden age, the era of Abbasid rule.

There are two universities, the Al-Hikmah University of Baghdad, with about 400 students, and the University of Baghdad, with over 10,000 students. The University of Baghdad has 14 colleges, including schools of agriculture, arts, commerce, dentistry, education, engineering, law, medicine, pharmacy, sciences, and veterinary medicine. It also has affiliated institutes specializing in physical education, forestry, industrial engineering, public administration, languages, surveying, and natural history. In addition, the city has an Institute of Fine Arts.

The industrial center of Iraq, Baghdad has oil refineries, textile factories, gold and silver works, tanneries, and food-processing plants. Cloth, copper utensils, and felt are still manufactured by hand.

History. Baghdad was only a small village when the second Abbasid caliph, al-Mansur, decided to establish his capital there in 762 A.D. The city began to grow rapidly, mainly on the east side of the Tigris River. Within a few years of its establishment as the Abbasid capital, Baghdad had become one of the leading cultural and commercial centers of the civilized world. Situated in the Tigris-Euphrates valley, which had been the site of such great cities as Sumerian Kish, Semitic Babylon, and Persian Ctesiphon, Baghdad became the meeting place of international trade routes leading north to Mosul and Turkey, east to Persia and central Asia, south to the Persian Gulf, Arabia, and India, and west to Syria and the Mediterranean ports.

While serving as the seat of the Abbasid caliphs Harun ar-Rashid (reigned 786–809) and al-Mamun (reigned 813–833), the city enjoyed its golden age. Besides the caliphal court and the Arab aristocracy, it housed wealthy merchants, learned scholars, singers, musicians, and ballet dancers whose performances are colorfully depicted in *The Arabian Nights.* An especially significant institution was the "House of Wisdom," established by al-Mamun as an academy, a library, and a bureau of translation. During this period, some of the treasures of Persian, Greek, and Syriac literature were translated into Arabic. Previously, Arabic had been chiefly a language of religion and poetry. Shortly after this period, the caliphate moved its center temporarily to Samarra in the north.

In 1258 the last Abbasid caliph, al-Mustaasim was murdered and Baghdad was largely destroyed by Hulagu and his Mongol hordes. With the fall of the Abbasid caliphate, Baghdad entered its dark ages, a period that lasted from the mid-1200's well into the 1900's. Great damage was done to the entire irrigation system of the region by Hulagu, his successor Timur (Tamerlane), and other Mongol and Tatar invaders. As a result, all of the area around Baghdad was transformed from a flourishing agricultural land to a semibarren waste.

In the 1500's and early 1600's, Baghdad was a bone of contention between the Safavid Persians and the Ottoman Turks. In 1508, Shah Ismail of Persia occupied the city. Thirty years later the Ottoman sultan Suleiman the Magnificent took it from Persia. In 1621 the Persians again took Baghdad, but lost it 17 years later to the Ottoman Turks. From 1638 until World War I, the area that is now Iraq was part of the Ottoman empire, and Baghdad was a provincial capital.

After World War I, Iraq became a separate

BAGHDAD'S KAZIMAYN MOSQUE was begun by the Persian shah Ismail in the early 1500's. It was built to honor the seventh imam, from whom Ismail's dynasty, the Safavids, claimed descent.

IN BAGHDAD, pastel-colored houses line the banks of the Tigris River, which flows through the city.

country (under British mandate until 1930). In 1921, Faisal I was proclaimed king of Iraq, and he established Baghdad as the national capital. Population: (1964) 436,731.

PHILIP K. HITTI
Author of "History of the Arabs"

Bibliography

Alexander, Constance M., *Baghdad in Bygone Days* (London 1928).
Coke, Richard, *Baghdad: The City of Peace* (London 1927).
Dickson, Mora, *Baghdad and Beyond* (Chicago 1961).
Le Strange, Guy, *Baghdad During the Abbasid Caliphate* (London 1924).
Levy, Reuben, *A Baghdad Chronicle* (New York 1929).
Longrigg, Stephen H., *Four Centuries of Modern Iraq* (Oxford, Eng., 1925).

BAGHDAD PACT. See CENTRAL TREATY ORGANIZATION.

BAGHDAD RAILWAY, bag'dad, the name originally given to the trunk line connecting Constantinople (now Istanbul) with Baghdad. Until 1902, Britain, France, and Russia had been the powers with most influence in the Ottoman empire, but in that year the main part of the concession for building the railroad was granted to a German firm. This aroused the suspicions of France and Britain, who viewed the project as a threat to their prestige in the Middle East. Britain especially considered it a menace to its "imperial lifeline" to India. As German influence in Turkey increased, the Baghdad line became one of the complex contributing causes of World War I.

Financial, political, and technical difficulties delayed the building of the railroad during the prewar period, but with Turkey's entry into the war on the side of the Central Powers, construction began to be pushed. By 1918 the line was completed from the Bosporus to Nisibin (Nusaybin), leaving a gap of about 300 miles (485 km) on the way to Baghdad, from which 84 miles (135 km) of track had been laid. With the breakup of the Ottoman empire after the war, the meandering route of the line through the succession states of Syria and Iraq was taken over by the new governments. In time the line was completed to Baghdad. A later extension was built from Baghdad to Basra, near the Persian Gulf. The railroad now links the Bosporus with the Persian Gulf. The continuing development of air and other transportation, however, somewhat diminished the strategic importance of the line.

PHILIP K. HITTI, *Princeton University*

BAGLEY, bag'lē, **William Chandler** (1874–1946), American author and educator. He was born in Detroit, Mich., on March 15, 1874. He graduated from Michigan State College with the degree of B.S. in 1895 and received an M.S. at the University of Wisconsin in 1898 and a Ph.D. at Cornell University in 1900. After teaching in public and normal schools, he was professor of education at the University of Illinois from 1908 to 1917. From 1917 he was professor of education at Teachers College, Columbia University, where he retired as professor emeritus in 1940. He edited the *Journal* of the National Education Association from 1920 to 1925 and was president of the association's National Council of Education from 1931 to 1937. He also edited the periodical *School and Society* from 1939 to 1946.

In the 1930's Bagley became a leader of the essentialist school of educational philosophers, challenging theories advanced by proponents of progressive education. He joined another Columbia professor, Isaac L. Kandel, in attacking such progressive doctrines as stress on the felt needs of the child and rejection of traditional subject matter. Bagley and his school believed that education should preserve a body of essential knowledge.

He published more than 20 books, including

The Educative Process (1905), *Classroom Management* (1907), *Educational Values* (1911), *History of the American People* (with Charles A. Beard, 1918), *An Introduction to Teaching* (with J.A.H. Keith, 1924), *Determinism in Education* (1925), *Education and Emergent Man* (1934), *A Century of the Universal School* (1937), and *America Yesterday and Today* (with Beard and R.F. Nichols, 1938).

He was also editor of the *Journal* of the National Education Association from 1920 to 1925 and president of the National Council of Education from 1931 to 1937. From 1939 to 1946 he edited *School and Society*. He died in New York City on July 1, 1946.

BAGNOLD, bag'nəld, **Enid** (1889–   ), English novelist and playwright. She was born in Rochester, Kent, on Oct. 27, 1889, and attended schools in Switzerland and France. At the outbreak of World War I, she joined the British Voluntary Aid Detachment and was assigned to a hospital in London. *Diary Without Dates* (1917), her book about this experience, presented such a candid picture of rigid hospital discipline that she was removed from her post by irate military authorities. She then joined another voluntary unit and was sent to France as a driver for the French army in 1918.

In 1920 she married the head of the Reuters news agency, Sir Roderick Jones. Four years later she published anonymously the light novel *Serena Blandish: or, The Difficulty of Getting Married*, of which the American critic Joseph Wood Krutch wrote: "Whoever the author may be, he is one of the cleverest of contemporary writers." Other novels by her are *National Velvet* (1935) and *The Loved and Envied* (1951).

Enid Bagnold scored her great success as a playwright at the age of 66, when her drama *The Chalk Garden*, which had been refused by British producers, opened in New York City in 1955. The following year the work was performed in London. Her other plays include *Lottie Dundass* (1943), *Gertie* (1952), *The Last Joke* (1960), and *The Chinese Prime Minister* (1964).

BAGOT, bag'ət, **Sir Charles** (1781–1843), English diplomat and administrator. He was born at Blithfield House, Rugeley, Staffordshire, on Sept. 23, 1781. Educated at Rugby and at Christ Church, Oxford, he entered Parliament in 1807 and was appointed undersecretary of state for foreign affairs. He was minister to France in 1814, and from 1815 to 1820 served as minister to the United States.

In 1817 he negotiated with Richard Rush, acting secretary of state of the United States, an agreement that provided for demilitarizing the Great Lakes and set a precedent for the disarming of the entire U.S.-Canadian boundary. Bagot became ambassador to Russia in 1820, and ambassador to the Netherlands in 1824.

In 1841 he was appointed governor general of Canada, an office he held until his death in Kingston, Ontario, on May 18, 1843.

BAGOTVILLE, bag'ət-vil, is a town in Quebec, Canada, on Ha Ha Bay of the Saguenay River, 105 miles (168 km) north of Quebec city. Pulpwood is manufactured and exported. The town is the terminus of the Saguenay River steamship route. Population: 6,041.

BAGPIPE, bag'pīp, a family of musical wind instruments used in a number of European countries, particularly Scotland and Ireland. The instrument consists of a leather bag from which air is pressed into one or several pipes. The air may be supplied either by a tube blown by the player or by a bellows pressed by the player's arm. Mouth-blown bagpipes include the Scottish Highland bagpipe, the old Irish bagpipe, the Lowland bagpipe, the Breton *biniou*, the Italian *zampogna*, the French *cornemuse*, and the German *Dudelsack* or *Sackpfeife*. Among the bellows-blown bagpipes are the modern Irish bagpipe, the Spanish *gaita*, the French *musette*, and the Northumbrian bagpipe.

Mechanism. The Scottish Highland bagpipe has five tubes: a valved tube leading from the player's mouth to the bag; a pipe called a chanter, tuned to D, fitted with a double reed like that of an oboe, and pierced with eight

SCOTTISH BAGPIPE

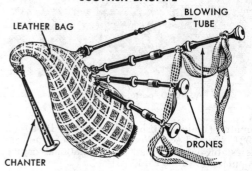

LEATHER BAG · BLOWING TUBE · DRONES · CHANTER

sounding holes for playing the melody; and three pipes called drones, which are fitted with single reeds like those of clarinets. Each drone produces a single note. Two of the drones are in unison with the chanter, and the third drone, which is the longest pipe, is pitched one octave lower. Formerly, however, the drones were sometimes tuned in fifths. Tuning is accomplished by lengthening or shortening the tubes. The compass of the Scottish Highland bagpipe is slightly more than an octave, ranging from G above middle C to A in the second octave above middle C.

The modern Irish bagpipe, which is blown by a bellows, has a two-octave chromatic scale. Besides the drones, there are three keys, called regulators, that are worked by the player's wrist. The drones are tuned in octaves, usually in A or in D.

The bagpipes of continental Europe are gen-

IRISH BAGPIPE

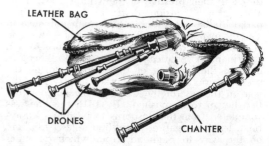

LEATHER BAG · DRONES · CHANTER

erally smaller than the great pipes of the British Isles. The *cornemuse* is primarily an instrument of the French peasantry and is often played in duet with the *vielle* (hurdy-gurdy). In Italy the *zampogna* is customarily played by traveling pipers during the Christmas season. The Spanish *gaita* has only one drone but is otherwise very much like the Scottish Highland bagpipe. It is usually adorned with heavy silk fringe and other eye-catching trim.

History. The bagpipe is of ancient origin. The Romans called it *tibia utricularis,* and it is said to have been played by Nero. It was played in many lands during the Middle Ages and is found in illustrations and sculptures of the period. The medieval bagpipe was called by several different names, including *symphonia, musa,* and *chevrette.* In England the instrument was common from Anglo-Saxon times and is referred to by Chaucer and Shakespeare. King Henry VIII is known to have owned at least one bagpipe in his large collection of musical instruments. It is not known when the bagpipe first found its way to Scotland, the country usually associated with the instrument, but by the 15th century it had become popular there. The oldest known extant bagpipe is in Edinburgh and dates from the early 15th century.

BAGRATION, bə-grə-tyē-ôn', **Prince Pyotr Ivanovich** (1765–1812), Russian general. He was born in Kizlyar, in the northern Caucasus. A member of a noble Georgian family, he entered the Russian army in 1782. He fought at the siege of Ochakov in 1788 and in Poland in 1792 and 1794. He served under Count Aleksandr Vasilievich Suvorov in Italy and Switzerland in 1799.

In 1805 he resisted a much larger French force at Oberhollabrunn (Hollabrunn) and commanded the vanguard of the Austrian Army at Austerlitz. His stubborn resistance at Eylau in 1807 made that battle exceptionally bloody. Bagration fought at Friedland in 1807. In the following year he made a daring march across the frozen Gulf of Finland, overrunning western Bothnia and the Åland Islands. In 1809–1810 he fought against the Turks, destroying a force sent to relieve Silistra. He was defeated by the French at Mogilev in 1812, but succeeded in withdrawing his forces to join the main Russian army. He was mortally wounded at the Battle of Borodino, near Moscow, on Sept. 7, 1812, and died on Sept. 24.

BAGUIO, bä'gyō, a city in the Philippines, is the summer capital of the country and houses the summer residence of the nation's president. About 125 miles (201 km) north of Manila, it is located in Benguet subprovince, in the southern part of Mountain province on the island of Luzon. Its pleasant location, about 5,000 feet (1,524 meters) above sea level, has made Baguio one of the most popular summer resorts in the Philippines. The city lies on a pine-covered plateau in an area of rugged mountains, waterfalls, and winding canyons. Temperatures there average between a high of 73° F (23° C) and a low of 59° F (15° C). It has a number of hotels and recreational facilities which cater to Filipinos attracted by the pleasant weather and picturesque scenery. Baguio, a gold mining center, is near some of the richest mines in the Philippines. The city's markets are renowned for the wood carvings and handicrafts of the Igorot aborigines.

Baguio was first visited by the Spaniards in 1829 but was of little importance until the 20th century. The modern city was planned in 1904 by an American architect, Daniel Hudson Burnham. The Japanese occupied Baguio in December 1941. After heavy fighting, it was captured by American forces on April 29, 1945. Population: (1960) 50,436.

BAGUIRMI, bə-gir'mē, was a sultanate of north central Africa, located southeast of Lake Chad and east of the Shari River. Incorporated into the French colonial system early in the 20th century, Baguirmi (also *Bagirmi* or *Baghirmi*) is now part of the republic of Chad. Among the chief towns are Fort-Lamy (capital of Chad) and Massénya.

The region is a steppelike plateau, semiarid but more fertile to the south. Millet, sesame, wild rice, cotton, and indigo are grown, cattle and ostriches are raised, honey is produced, and iron is mined. The Baguirmi are skilled in working metal and in weaving and dyeing textiles.

The Negro-Arab Baguirmi, coming from the east, conquered the native Fūlani and Arabs sometime before the 17th century. They were converted to Islam about 1600. For three centuries they warred against neighboring states, raiding south to the Ubangi River for slaves.

The country was explored in the early 1820's by the Englishman Dixon Denham, and in the 1850's and 1872 by the Germans Heinrich Barth and Gustav Nachtigal. In 1871 Baguirmi was overrun by the neighboring state of Wadai, and in 1890 by Rabah Zobeir, sultan of Bornu. The French, expanding in the area, defeated Rabah Zobeir at Kousseri (Fort-Foureau) in 1900. During the early 20th century French influence gradually replaced that of the Baguirmi sultan and the sultanate was eventually abolished.

BAGWORM, bag'wûrm, the larva of the bagworm moth. It is identified by its habit of constructing a baglike case of silk, interwoven with leaves and twigs, about its body. It sometimes is called the *basket worm.* The larva weaves its bag soon after hatching in the spring and carries it about until it is ready to enter the pupal stage of development. Then the larva attaches the bag to the twig of a tree and passes the pupa stage in the bag. The adult males emerge as winged adults with dark bodies and dark wings, which quickly become transparent. The wormlike adult females are wingless and legless. They remain in their bags and die soon after they mate and deposit eggs in the bags.

The bagworm belongs to the family Psychidae in the order Lepidoptera. Several hundred species are in the tropical and subtropical regions of the world, while others inhabit the temperate regions. A common species in the United States, the evergreen bagworm, *Thyridopteryx ephemeraeformis,* attacks red cedar and arbor vitae.

BAHADUR SHAH II, bä-hä'door shä, (1768?–1862), was the last ruler of the Mughul (Mogul) dynasty of India. His 20-year reign (1837–1857) was nominal only, actual power being held by the British East India Company. He fled during the Indian (Sepoy) Mutiny of 1857 but was captured. Tried for rebellion and found guilty in 1858, he was sentenced to life imprisonment in Rangoon, Burma, where he died on Nov. 7, 1862. See also SEPOY.

BAHAI HOUSE OF WORSHIP at Wilmette, Ill. Nine entrances symbolize the oneness of mankind and the unity of religion. This structure, begun in 1912, was formally dedicated in 1953.

BAHAI FAITH, bä-hä′ē, the religion founded by Mirza Husayn Ali, known as Bahaullah, during the middle of the 19th century in Persia. The essential tenets of the Bahai faith as revealed by Bahaullah are: the oneness of God is unknowable, but his will is expressed through Manifestations or the prophets; the spiritual oneness of the prophets; the progressive character of revelation; the unity of mankind; the equality of men and women; the essential harmony of science and religion; and the assurance of immortality for the human soul. Since its founder's time the faith has been carried by its members to more than 250 countries and territorial divisions throughout the world. In the United States, Bahais reside in some 1,500 cities and towns.

The coming of Bahaullah was heralded by Mirza Ali Muhammad of Shiraz, known to history as the Bab, who revealed his mission on May 23, 1844, and formulated the principles of the Bahai faith. His revelation had such a profound influence upon the people that the government officials and reactionary leaders of Islam were seriously disturbed and succeeded in bringing about his public execution at Tabriz, July 9, 1850. His remains are now interred on Mount Carmel in Israel.

In 1853 the same leaders seized Husayn Ali, member of a noble family and a follower of the Bab, immuring him in an underground prison in Teheran. There he became conscious of his station as the universal prophet foretold by the Bab. Banished to Baghdad, the prophet there attained such fame and influence through his spiritual knowledge and character that he and his followers were exiled to Constantinople in 1863. In that year, Husayn Ali announced his mission as the fulfillment of the prophecies of the Bab, and thereafter became known as Bahaullah, or "Splendor of God."

Bahaullah and his followers were sent to Adrianople (Edirne) and from there to the fortress-prison of Acre, Palestine, now the headquarters of the Bahai faith. He died in 1892, leaving a testament appointing his eldest son, Abbas Effendi, known as Abdul-Baha (the "Servant of Baha"), the sole interpreter of his message and the leader of the Bahais. Abdul-Baha, like his father, remained under surveillance by the state until the sultanate was overthrown by the Young Turks movement in 1908. In 1911 and 1913 he journeyed in Europe and in 1912 spent nearly nine months in the United States, where he addressed peace societies and other groups.

The eldest grandson of Abdul-Baha, Shogi Effendi, was named Guardian of the Faith (Walayi Amr Allah) in his grandfather's written testament. From 1921 until his death in 1957, Shogi Effendi applied, throughout the international Bahai community, provisions for an administrative order as outlined by Bahaullah. This order, with functions similar to those of the professional clergy in other religions, includes national and local elective assemblies as well as an international body, which will be elected in the future. Shogi Effendi also constructed the Shrine of the Bab on Mt. Carmel, established gardens around the Shrine of Bahaullah at Bahji, near Acre, and built the International Archives Building there to preserve the sacred relics and documents of the faith. As interpreter of the teachings, he clarified the relationship of the faith to current events and foretold future developments of human society, defined principles of the Bahai world order, and illumined the scope and purpose of the Bahai revelation. His English translations of selections from the holy writings of Bahaullah have been published throughout the West. In *God Passes By* (1944) he produced the authentic history of the first Bahai century, 1844 to 1944.

Bahais in the United States have completed the Bahai House of Worship at Wilmette, Ill., and have sent hundreds of pioneers to travel and teach in other countries. Over 80 local assemblies in the United States are legally incorporated. There are summer schools in Maine, Michigan, New Mexico, and California. In Canada the National Spiritual Assembly has its headquarters in Toronto, Ontario. The Bahai Publishing Trust, located in Wilmette, produces and distributes many of the writings of Bahaullah, Abdul-Baha, and Shogi Effendi, as well as books and pamphlets about the faith written by members of the Bahai community.

Since Shogi Effendi's death the international direction of Bahai affairs has been vested in a body of 9, elected by 27 Hands of the Faith, custodians appointed by Shogi Effendi in one of his last communications. See also ABDUL-BAHA; BABISM; BAHAULLAH.

Bibliography

Abdul-Baha, *Foundations of World Unity,* tr. by L.C. Barney (Wilmette, Ill., 1955).
Abdul-Baha, *Some Answered Questions,* tr. by L.C. Barney (Wilmette. Ill., 1937).
Bahaulla, *Book of Certitude,* tr. by Shogi Effendi (Wilmette, Ill., 1938).
Bahaulla, *Prayers and Meditations,* tr. by Shogi Effendi (Wilmette, Ill., 1954).
Shogi Effendi, *Bahá'í Administration* (Wilmette, Ill., 1945).
Shogi Effendi, *Message to the Bahá'í World* (Wilmette, Ill., 1958).
Shogi Effendi, *World Order of Bahá'u'lláh* (Wilmette, Ill., 1938).

BAHAMAS, Commonwealth of the, bə-häm'əz, an independent country composed of an archipelago of some 700 islands and 2,000 cays (keys), or islets, and innumerable reefs, scattered over 760 miles (1,223 km) of the Atlantic Ocean southeast of the United States. The archipelago extends from about 50 miles (80 km) east of the southern coast of Florida past the northern coast of Cuba to within 70 miles (112.6 km) of Haiti. It lies between latitudes 20° 50′ N and 27° 25′ N and longitudes 72° 37′ W and 80° 32′ W. Its total area is 5,380 square miles (13,-935 sq km). The commonwealth, known informally as the Bahamas, is a member of the Commonwealth of Nations. The easternmost islands, the Turks and Caicos Islands, though they are geographically part of the Bahamas, constitute a British colony, also part of the Commonwealth of Nations.

The population increased from 84,841 in 1953 to about 190,000 in 1972. Some 90% of the people are of African or of mixed Afro-European origin. Much of this population is concentrated on little New Providence Island where the capital, Nassau, is located.

Most of the islands are narrow and rocky with shallow soil. The climate is subtropical, averaging about 70° F from November to May and rarely above 90° in summer. Tropical and temperate zone forests grow side by side. Some original pine forests still exist on Abaco, Andros, and Grand Bahama. Most flowers and fruits are exotics, that is, not native to the islands. Tropical and subtropical plants flourish, including all kinds of citrus, bananas, pineapples, sapodillas, soursops, and many others. Birds include flamingos, hummingbirds, and green parrots, as well as many sea birds. There are almost no indigenous snakes or animals. Sea turtles are caught by commercial fishermen. The coral reefs, where myriads of jewel-like fish can be seen in an undersea world of strange beauty, are a celebrated attraction.

Economic Activity. The lovely beaches, famous sport fishing, and luxurious hotels attract many visitors, mainly from the United States. Tourists, exceeding half a million annually, greatly outnumber the residents. Bahamians depend economically upon the tourist industry and on international banking.

Next in economic importance are the earnings of some 3,800 farm laborers who work seasonally in the United States. There is not much agriculture in the Bahamas, except the growing of fruit and vegetables for local use, but some tomatoes are exported. Other exports include crayfish (rock lobsters), lumber, salt, sponges, shells, and handicraft ornaments of shells and straw.

The government's main source of revenue is customs duties, as there are no excise or income taxes. The currency was changed from the pound to the Bahamian dollar in May 1966. The new dollar was pegged at the value of seven shillings sterling, or slightly less than U.S. $1. Canadian and United States dollars are accepted almost everywhere. With the permission of the Bahamian government, development of a free port, where all goods may be imported without duty, was started in 1955 at Freeport on Grand Bahama by American and British capital.

Transportation and Communications. New Providence has a telephone system. Communication with the Out Islands (a designation including all the other islands) is by radiotelephone or telegraph. Nassau has the principal seaport and the

SYBIL SHELTON FROM MONKMEYER

BAY STREET, Nassau, shopping center of the Commonwealth of the Bahamas' capital, draws many tourists.

only international airport, but there are 15 landing fields in the Out Islands. Bahamas Airways, Ltd., provides an interisland service and uses amphibian aircraft to reach the islands that have no airstrip. In 1966 the Bahamas launched a local airline, International Air Bahamas.

Education, Religion, and Culture. Free elementary schools have existed since 1885. Attendance is compulsory for all between the ages of 6 and 14, although this is not completely enforceable in some of the Out Islands. Secondary education, free only to scholarship holders, is available at a government high school and at three grant-aided and three private denominational "colleges," all located in Nassau. More than 25,000 pupils attend primary schools and over 5,000 go to secondary schools.

STRAW MARKET in Nassau offers colorful hats, bags, and other handmade products for the tourist trade.

FRITZ HENLE FROM MONKMEYER

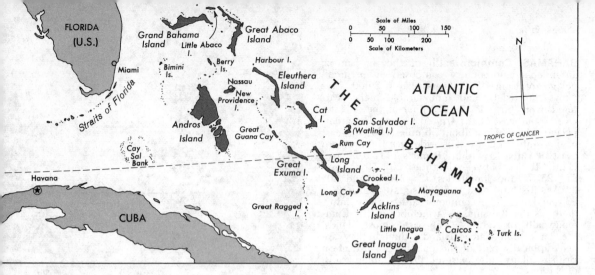

The Bahamas

The predominant religion is that of the Church of England; since 1861 a bishop of this church has been appointed to the see of Nassau. There is also a Roman Catholic bishop in Nassau, and some churches of other denominations.

The African Bahamians have kept alive some of their ancestral dances and music. A characteristic song is the goombay, sometimes narrative like the calypso but often a simple couplet sung to a complicated rhythm played on drums, maracas, and guitar. The fire dance with goombay music may be seen at its best in the Out Islands.

Government. The Bahamas, which became independent in 1973, had been a British colony governed as were many North American colonies in the 18th century. However, in 1962 both principal parties, the United Bahamian party and the Progress Liberal party, demanded responsible government in their election manifestos. In May 1963 a constitutional convention was held in London, and on Jan. 7, 1964, a new constitution came into force. This established a cabinet system with a premier and eight or more ministers chosen from the majority party in the House of Assembly to decide on policies. Until 1973 the Bahamas had complete internal self-government, but the British-appointed governor had final authority in foreign affairs, defense, and internal security, including police administration.

The constitution provides for a 38-member House of Assembly. Twenty-one seats are assigned to the Out Islands and 17 to New Providence. Its members are elected by universal adult suffrage.

The second chamber, the Senate, has 15 members. The Senate has only a limited suspensory veto over legislation.

History. According to tradition, Christopher Columbus discovered San Salvador (Watling Island) in 1492, but Spain made no use of the Bahamas except to enslave and deport the Arawak inhabitants. In 1647 the Eleutherian Adventurers' Company was formed in London to colonize the islands. The company brought out a few settlers, and others came from the Bermudas, but they had disorderly neighbors, the pirate crews who relaxed in the islands between raids on Caribbean shipping. In 1670, Charles II of England granted the Bahamas to six of the lords' proprietors of Carolina, but the governors they appointed were unable to control the pirates. A series of destructive Spanish attacks upon New Providence began in 1680, and

in 1703 the English settlement was almost wiped out by a combined French and Spanish force. For a time the islands were little more than land bases for the pirates, one of whom was the notorious Edward Teach, known as Blackbeard. In 1729 the crown assumed direct control to restore law and order. Finally this was achieved, and the pirates left or settled down to become respectable colonists. During the American War of Independence the Bahamas surrendered to Spain in 1782, but by the Treaty of Versailles in 1783 they were returned to Britain in exchange for eastern Florida. As a result, about 3,000 American loyalists, who had fled to Florida during the war, sailed to the Bahamas with their slaves. In 1787 the lords proprietors surrendered their rights to the crown. Slavery was abolished in 1834.

During the American Civil War, the Bahamas prospered because of the blockade-running trade between England and the Confederate ports. A similar feverish prosperity was enjoyed during the prohibition era (1920–1933); many rum-runners set up headquarters in the Bahamas, from which speedboats took their cargoes of contraband liquor to the Atlantic coast of the United States.

Under the destroyer-bases accord of 1940, a United States air base was established on Great Exuma Island. Many Royal Air Force flyers were trained at Nassau from 1942 to 1945, and the airport was heavily used by planes on the way from American factories to the fighting fronts.

On July 10, 1973, with Prince Charles representing Queen Elizabeth II, Britain ended 300 years of colonial rule, and the Bahamas became the Commonwealth's 33d independent member. The prime minister of the new nation, as he had been of the colony, was Lynden O. Pindling, who had led the drive for independence.

MORLEY AYEARST, *New York University*

Bibliography

Bell, Hugh M., *Bahamas: Isles of June* (New York 1934).
British Information Services, *Fact Sheets on the United Kingdom Dependencies: Bahamas* (New York, periodically).
Curry, Robert A., *Bahamian Lore* (Paris 1928).
Etheridge, Harry, comp., *Yachtsman's Guide to the Bahamas*, 4th ed. (Coral Gables, Fla., 1952).
Etienne Dupuch Jr. Publications, *Bahamas Handbook and Businessman's Annual* (Nassau, annually).
Haring, Clarence H., *Buccaneers of the West Indies in the 17th Century* (London 1910).
Schoepf, Johann D., *Travels in the Confederation, Seventeen Eighty-Three to Seventeen Eighty-Four*, tr. by A. J. Morrison (1911; reprint, New York 1968).

BAHARIYA, ba-rē′yä, is an oasis in the Libyan Desert of Egypt, about 200 miles (322 km) southwest of Alexandria. Lying in a basin surrounded by hills, its cultivated area of about 4 square miles (10 sq km) yields dates, olives, oranges, grapes, wheat, and rice. Population: (1960) 6,071.

BAHAULLAH (1817–1892), bä-hä-ōōl-lä′, was the founder of the Bahai faith. His original name was *Mirza Husayn Ali;* Bahaullah (or Baha Allah) is a Persian title, meaning "Splendor of God," that was bestowed upon him.

Born in Mazanderan, Persia, on Nov. 12, 1817, Bahaullah was among the followers of the Bab, who, on May 23, 1844, declared himself the herald of a manifestation of God. After the martyrdom of the Bab on July 9, 1850, Bahaullah became one of the most beloved and respected teachers of the Babi religion. This leadership exposed him to the displeasure of orthodox Islam in Persia, leading to persecution of the Babis and the imprisonment of Bahaullah. Unable to stop the spread of his teachings, the authorities were persuaded to exile him to Baghdad in 1853. Successive banishments took him from that city to Constantinople, Adrianople (Edirne), and finally to the prison city of Acre. Although suffering continuous exile or imprisonment from 1852 until his death on May 29, 1892, at Acre, Bahaullah proclaimed himself, in 1863, the one whom the Bab had heralded as "He Whom God will make manifest." He claimed to be the "Promised One of All Ages" and claimed as his mission the unification of all mankind.

His teachings declare the nature of religion to be progressive revelation. They also reaffirm the Covenant between God and man; emphasize the oneness of mankind; strongly urge the elimination of all forms of prejudice and superstition, whether national, cultural, racial, or religious; consider science and religion as complementary, not contradictory; and define the social and political bases of world peace.

Bahaullah was succeeded by his eldest son, Abdul-Baha (Abbas Effendi), who carried his father's teachings to Europe and the United States.

See also ABDUL-BAHA; BABISM; BAHAI FAITH.

Bibliography

Abdul-Baha, *The Promulgation of Universal Peace,* 2 vols. (Chicago 1921–25).
Abdul-Baha, *The Secret of Divine Civilization,* tr. by Marzieh Gail (Wilmette, Ill., 1957).
Bahaullah, *Epistle to the Son of the Wolf,* tr. by Shogi Effendi (Wilmette, Ill., 1941).
Esslemont, John E., *Bahá'u'lláh and the New Era,* rev. 2d ed. (London 1940).
Shogi Effendi, *God Passes By* (Wilmette, Ill., 1944).
Townshend, George, *Christ and Bahá'u'lláh* (London 1957).

BAHAWALPUR, bə-hä′wəl-pōōr, is one of 12 political divisions in West Pakistan province of Pakistan. Situated on the edge of the Thar Desert and bounded roughly by the Sutlej, Panjnad, and Indus rivers, Bahawalpur has an area of 17,508 square miles (45,346 sq km). The capital, Bahawalpur, is located near the Sutlej River. Wheat, dates, cotton, rice, and millet are raised, and handwoven textiles, pottery, and other handicrafts are manufactured.

A former princely state of the Punjab, Bahawalpur acceded to Pakistan in 1947 and was merged into West Pakistan in 1955. Population: (1961) 2,574,000.

CARL FRANK FROM PHOTO RESEARCHERS

BAHIA's capital, Salvador, is built on two levels. An elevator connects the busy port with the upper city.

BAHIA, bä-ē′ä, is a state in east central Brazil, extending approximately 500 miles (800 km) along the Atlantic Ocean. Its area is 216,185 square miles (559,919 sq km). The terrain is mountainous except for the tropical rain forest along the coast. The northern ranges of the Brazilian highlands (Planalto do Brasil) rise from the coastal plain and are divided in a north-south direction by the São Francisco River valley. In the highlands the tropical climate is dry, and severe droughts are not uncommon. The coast of Bahia is hot and humid.

Mineral resources in the mountains include gold, manganese, chromium, iron ore, nickel, petroleum, black industrial diamonds, and semiprecious stones. The highlands are cattle country and are Brazil's chief center for goat raising. Products from the interior include vegetable oils, carnauba wax from palm trees, and lumber. Extensive agricultural areas along the coast produce 90 percent of Brazil's cacao, as well as cotton, tobacco, coffee, castor beans, manioc, tropical fruits, and subsistence crops. Leading industries are sugar distilling, cotton milling, and the processing of cacao and tobacco.

Salvador, the capital of Bahia, is a seaport situated between the Atlantic Ocean and All Saints (Todos os Santos) Bay. It is the state's largest city and the fourth largest in Brazil. Other cities in order of importance are Feira de Santana, northwest of Salvador, and Itabuna, Ilhéus, and Jequié to the south.

The Portuguese discovered Brazil in 1500, and a governor for the Bahia area was named in 1549. Bahia became a province of the empire of Brazil in 1823 and a state of the republic of Brazil when the emperor was deposed in 1889. Population: (1960) 5,990,605.

BAHIA. See SALVADOR.

BAHÍA BLANCA, bä-ē′ä vläng′kä, is a city in eastern Argentina, in Buenos Aires province. It is on the Napostá Grande River near the head of Bahía Blanca (White Bay), about 350 miles (563 km) southwest of the city of Buenos Aires. It is the major port for shipping products of the grain and cattle regions of the southern pampas and is an important railroad center. The city's industries include dairying, flour milling, meat packing, tanning, wool processing, oil refining, and fisheries. The National University of the South is here.

The city originated as a fort built in 1828 to guard against a possible sea invasion by Brazil, then at war with Argentina. It was first named *Nueva Buenos Aires*. After 1838 it was settled largely by Italian immigrants. It developed rapidly after 1900 as the output of the pampas increased. Population: (1960) 150,354.

BAHR, bär, **Hermann** (1863–1934), Austrian critic, dramatist, and novelist. He was born at Linz, on July 19, 1863. A man of broad cultural sympathies, Bahr was European in his critical outlook rather than narrowly German, and he commanded a following in France as well as at home. He began as one of the *Jungwien* (Young Vienna), a group of writers that included Hugo von Hofmannsthal and Arthur Schnitzler. In 1906, he became manager of the Berlin Deutsches Theater. He died at Munich, Germany, on Jan. 15, 1934.

As a critic, Bahr anticipated the reaction against extreme naturalism in his *Studien zur Kritik der Moderne* (1890), and in *Die Überwindung des Naturalismus* (1891) he championed the new trend toward symbolism and neoromanticism. In his book *Expressionismus* (1918; Eng. tr., *Expressionism,* 1925), he analyzed the nature of the new literary style.

Of Bahr's nearly 80 plays, the one that is best remembered is *Das Konzert* (1909), which was translated into English in 1910. A sophisticated comedy about the matrimonial difficulties of a Viennese musician and his wife, it was highly successful in both Europe and the United States. In his novels, Bahr was a superb and witty narrator of the charm of old Vienna, giving most of his stories a theatrical background.

BAHR EL GHAZAL, ba′hər al go-zal′, is the main western affluent of the Nile River in northeastern Africa. It is formed by the joining of many rivers, of which the most important is the Jur, and its basin extends northwest of Darfur and southwest to the Congo watershed. Between the Jur and the Nile and parallel with them, several streams, including the Tonj, the Rohl, and the Deleb, flow north from the Congo-Nile watershed and join the Bahr el Ghazal. Lake No fills a depression about seven miles (11 km) long from west to east near the junction of the Bahr el Jebel with the Ghazal. The Bahr el Jebel, after passing through its eastern corner, is known as the Bahr el Abiad, or White Nile.

In the upper reaches the southern tributaries of the Ghazal cut deeply into the central African plateau. Through the huge swamp regions of the Nile it is next to impossible to trace the course of the various rivers. The distance from the junction of the Bahr el Arab with the Jur, above which point none of the many rivers is called Bahr el Ghazal, to the junction with the Nile at Lake No, is about 100 miles (160 km). Just above the Bahr el Arab confluence, the Jur broadens out to form Lake Ambadi, which is 10 miles long (16 km) and one mile (1.6 km) wide at low water and much larger in flood time. At first the Ghazal flows north, with lagoonlike expanses of great breadth but little depth. Turning northeast the channel grows narrower and deeper. Then the Ghazal turns east again and gets broader until it reaches Lake No. The rise of the river and the lower reaches of its main tributaries in flood time is only about three feet (1 meter), but this is enough to flood an enormous area.

In ancient times rumors of the existence of this river led some Greek geographers to imagine that the source of the Nile was to the west in the direction of Lake Chad. A map published in 1772 by the French cartographer Jean Baptiste d'Anville indicated fairly accurately, for the first time, the course of the Ghazal. Exploration of the river was undertaken after the ascent of the White Nile by the Egyptian expedition of 1839–1842. For a good part of the period between 1853 and 1865 the Welsh mining engineer John Petherick explored the region, giving particular attention to the main stream of the Ghazal and the Jur. In 1859, Giovanni Miani, a Venetian, explored the southern section of the basin and came out with reports of a large river (the Welle) flowing west beyond the Nile watershed. The Frenchman Guillaume Lejean surveyed the Ghazal in 1862 and published a map. Between 1869 and 1871, Georg Schweinfurth explored the southern district and discovered the Welle. Further exploration, for military purposes, was conducted in 1879–1881 by Romolo Gessi, the Italian governor of the province of Bahr el Ghazal. At about the same period Wilhelm Junker traversed the southern tributaries of the Ghazal. A French mission under Jean Baptiste Marchand made surveys of the southern tributaries and followed the Jur throughout its course.

The Ghazal is likely to become clogged by sudd—closely packed floating vegetation. In the time of the Mahdists (1882–1898) the river was almost completely blocked in this way. Early in the 20th century, British officers cleared the Bahr el Ghazal, the Jur, and other streams and thus established uninterrupted communication, in the flood season, between Khartoum and Wau, a distance of about 930 miles (1,497 km). The tributaries of the Ghazal flow through a vast area of marsh and swampland. Such great quantities of water are evaporated there that the Ghazal, draining a basin of some 200,000 square miles (518,000 sq km), contributes almost nothing to the volume of the White Nile.

BAHR YUSUF, ba′hər yōō′sŏŏf, is an artificial irrigation channel on the west bank of the Nile River, extending 150 miles from Asyut to El Faiyum, Egypt. Faiyum province owes its fertility to the waters of the canal. According to Coptic tradition, the canal was constructed during the administration of the Old Testament patriarch Joseph. The name, also spelled *Bahr Yusef,* means "Joseph's River."

BAHRAICH, bə-rīk′, is a town in north central India, near the Nepal border. It is the capital of Bahraich district in Uttar Pradesh state. The town is situated 65 miles (105 km) northeast of Lucknow on a tributary of the Gogra River. Bahraich began to flourish after a railroad reached it in the late 1800's. It is a trade center for grain, tobacco, oilseed, and timber. Its manufactures include cloth, fireworks, and processed sugar. The shrine of Masaud, an 11th century warrior and saint, attracts large crowds of Hindu and Muslim pilgrims. Population: (1961) 56,033.

BAHRAIN, bə-rān′, is an independent sheikhdom, formerly under British protection, consisting of several islands in the Persian Gulf. It is situated about 13 miles east of Saudi Arabia. Bahrain is a modest contributor to the world's supply of oil and was long a strategic British center in the Middle East. Population: (1971) 216,815.

Bahrain has an area of 231 square miles (598.2 sq km). Its principal island, also called Bahrain, is 30 miles (48 km) long and 12 (19.3 km) miles wide. The sheikhdom also contains the islands of Muharraq, Sitrah, Nabih Salih, Jida, and Umm Nassan; several uninhabited islands; and an extensive area of islets and shoals.

Manamah, the capital and principal city, with a population (1971) of 89,399, is at the northeast end of Bahrain Island. Made a free transit port in 1958, Manamah serves as headquarters for the fishing and pearling industries of Bahrain. There is a deepwater anchorage off the port, which is well equipped with lighterage facilities. Since 1962, Manamah has also had a deepwater pier that can accommodate six oceangoing vessels at once. While a protectorate, Bahrain was often used as a British air and naval base.

Muharraq, the second most important city, with a population (1971) of 37,732, is situated on Muharraq Island. The city is connected to Manamah by a 1½-mile (2.4 km) causeway, and is the site of Bahrain's international airport.

The name *Bahrain,* sometimes spelled *Bahrein,* is derived from an Arabic word meaning "two seas." It once was applied to the mainland of eastern Arabia as well as to the island of the present sheikhdom.

The People. The Bahrainis are mostly Arabs of various origins. The sheikhdom also has sizable communities of Indians, Pakistanis, Persians, Europeans, and Americans. About 95 percent of the people are Muslims. About half of the Muslims, including the ruling Khalifah family, belong to the Sunnite sect. The other half, mainly villagers, are members of the Shiite sect. The American Dutch Reformed Church established a mission in Bahrain in 1893 that now includes a hospital and primary school.

Economic Life. Oil, discovered in Bahrain in 1932 by the Standard Oil Company of California, provides about 70 percent of the sheikhdom's income. The original concession to prospect for oil on Bahrain Island was obtained by a British company in 1925. In 1927 the concession was passed to the Gulf Oil Company of the United States, which, in turn, sold it to the Standard Oil Company of California in 1928. In 1936 the ownership of Standard Oil's subsidiary, the Bahrain Petroleum Company (incorporated in Canada), was divided equally between Standard Oil and the Texas Company. In 1975, Bahrain obtained 60% controlling interest in the Bahrain Petroleum Company. Installations in Bahrain related to the oil industry include a modern refinery that produces about 11 million tons of oil a year, an excellent oil-shipping port off Sitrah Island, and community housing for American and British employees. Bahrain produces about 25 million barrels of crude oil per year. This oil, as well as crude oil piped in from Saudi Arabia, is refined in Bahrain for export.

Before the discovery of oil, pearling was the economic mainstay of Bahrain. The quality and the abundance of the pearls in Persian Gulf shoal waters are unsurpassed anywhere. The total annual production reached a value of $1,000,000

or higher during the early 1920's, but dropped to a quarter of that amount just before World War II. The pearl market declined partly because of the lack of an efficient marketing organization and partly because of a trend in buying habits away from genuine pearls. Other industries in the sheikhdom include boatbuilding, sailcloth making, and the manufacture of building materials, soft drinks, and reconstituted dairy products.

Approximately two thirds of Bahrain has no fresh water, and the limestone or sandy soil of the rest has never been adequate for farming. Rainfall is usually under five inches per year. Even the date crop is inferior in quality and must be supplemented by imports.

Government. Bahrain is ruled by an hereditary sheikh of the Khalifah family. The sheikh, who has considerable power, heads a council of administration composed of the heads of the governmental departments and members of the ruling family.

The four urban municipalities of Manamah, Muharraq, Hidd, and Rifaa, and the two rural municipalities of Sitrah and Jidd Hafs have separate administrative organizations for local affairs. Half the members of the local councils are nominated by the royal government, and the other half are elected.

History. The oldest remains of inhabitants of Bahrain lie in the extensive fields of burial mounds or tumuli, in the northern half of Bahrain Island. Archaeologists believe that the earliest of these mounds may date from 3000 B.C. Numbering perhaps 100,000 to 200,000, the mounds range in height from a few feet to 40 feet. They enclose stone crypts containing well-preserved skeletons, burial urns, and pottery.

Bahrain was known to the ancient Greeks and Romans as *Tylos. Awal* was also one of its early names. Some archaeologists have attempted to identify Bahrain with Dilmun, an ancient port described in Mesopotamian cuneiform records.

In the 4th century B.C., Bahrain was visited by a captain in Alexander the Great's navy. The

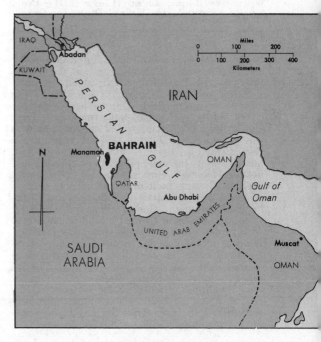

Greek geographer Strabo, late in the 1st century B.C., mentioned Tylos in relation to the ancient caravan port of Gerrha (possibly modern Uqair), on the Arabian coast. Pliny the Elder, writing in the 1st century A.D., reported that Bahrain was famous for its pearls.

Bahrain was occupied by the Portuguese from 1521 until 1602. Subsequently, it was largely under the control of Persia until 1783, when the Khalifah dynasty was established.

Bahrain made its first treaty of friendship with Britain in 1820. Britain sought to suppress piracy and the slave trade and to secure the safety of its vital sea route to the East. By later treaties, Britain gained control of Bahrain's foreign affairs and of the development of its natural resources. Britain has successfully withstood Iran's claim to Bahrain, which is based on the former Persian control of the islands.

With revenues from oil royalties after 1934, Bahrain made significant progress in many areas. Modern primary, secondary, and vocational schools were built. The country expanded its public health system and made headway against long-prevalent diseases. Numerous free, rural clinics were established in the islands, and a well-equipped state hospital was built in Manamah. The government established an electric light and power system and an agricultural experiment station. Bahrain's court system was adapted to the mixed character of its people.

Despite these and other advances, the Bahrainis continued to have little voice in their government. The reign of Sheikh Isa Ibn Salman Al Khalifah, who succeeded his father in 1961, was marked in its early stages by antigovernment riots. In 1970 a 12-member Council of State was created to direct internal and external affairs. Following the confirmation of Britain's decision to withdraw from the Persian Gulf by 1972, Bahrain made plans to enter a federation with Qatar and the Trucial States. In 1971, however, Bahrain changed its course and declared its independence. Population: (1969) 200,000.

Further Reading: Belgrave, James Hamed Dacre, *Welcome to Bahrain*, 2d ed. (London 1954); Caroe, Sir Olaf Kirkpatrick, *The Wells of Power; The Oilfields of Southwestern Asia* (New York 1951); Faroughy, Abbas, *The Bahrein Islands—750 to 1951* (New York 1951).

BAIAE, bā′yē, was a favorite bathing resort of the ancient Romans. It was located in Campania, Italy, on the Bay of Pozzuoli, about 10 miles (16 km) west of Naples, on the site of the modern village of *Baia*. Once a harbor for the Greek colony of Cumae, Baiae may have been named for Baios, a companion of Odysseus who was buried there. During the last years of the Roman republic, Baiae became a pleasure resort, famous for its thermal springs, mild climate, and beautiful location. Horace praised it in his poems. Wealthy Romans built luxurious villas there.

Until the 3d century A.D., Baiae was a favorite residence of the Roman emperors, who built villas and grandiose thermal establishments there with gardens, artificial pools, and other facilities. Remains of these baths, erroneously called temples, still exist, but they have been partly submerged in the bay by volcanic activity. The so-called temples of Diana, Venus, and Mercury were enormous circular halls surmounted by domes. Since the 1920's statuary that must have embellished the imperial villas has been recovered from the bay.

BAIE-COMEAU, bā′kô-mō′, a town in Quebec province, Canada, on the north shore of the St. Lawrence River, 273 miles (429 km) northeast of the city of Quebec. It is situated in a forested region, and the most important industry of Baie-Comeau is the manufacture of newsprint. Population: 12,109.

BAIE-SAINT-PAUL, bā saN pôl, is an industrial and resort town in Quebec, Canada, 57 miles (91.5 km) northeast of Quebec city. It is situated on the St. Lawrence River at the mouth of the De Gouffre River. Industries include sawmills, pulpwood mills, grist mills, a tannery, and a foundry. The town is noted for fox breeding. It is a gateway to the Laurentides National Park and to a fishing and hunting area. Baie-Saint-Paul was founded in 1681 and was incorporated as a village in 1893. Population: 4,163.

BAÏF, bà-ēf′, **Jean Antoine de** (1532–1589), French poet, who was a member of the "Pléiade," a group of seven Renaissance poets who abandoned medieval themes and forms in French poetry and took classical Latin and Greek poetry as their models. Baïf was born on Feb. 19, 1532, in Venice, where his father was French ambassador. After his family returned to Paris, he was tutored by the classical scholar Jean Dorat. A fellow student was Pierre de Ronsard, who later became leader of the Pléiade. Baïf then studied with Dorat at the Collège de Coqueret. In 1567, under the patronage of King Charles IX, he founded the Academy of Music and Poetry, which continued until 1584. He died in Paris on Sept. 9, 1589.

Baïf was the most erudite of the Pléiade poets. His best collection of verse, *Mimes, enseignements et proverbes* (1576), draws on topics from science, politics, and ethics. Another collection, *Le premier des météores* (1567), dedicated to Catherine de Médicis, was similarly inspired. Baïf's other poetry includes the volumes *Amours de Méline* (1552), *Amours de Francine* (1555), and *Passe-temps* (1573). He also wrote the comedies *Le brave ou Taillebras* (1567, adapted from a work by Plautus) and *L'eunuque* (1573, from a work by Terence).

BAIKAL, bī-kál′ **Lake,** largest freshwater lake in Asia and the deepest lake in the world. It is located in the USSR near the border with Mongolia. The large volume of this sickle-shaped lake has a moderating influence on the climate of the adjoining land, cooling it in summer and warming it in winter. The lake is frozen from late December to early May. The fauna of the lake consists largely of endemic species, including the Baikal hair seal and the viviparous Baikal oilfish (*Comephorus*).

The lake is fed by many rivers and drained by one, the swift Angara, the site of a vast hydroelectric project. The construction of a pulp and paper mill on the southern shore was denounced by Soviet scientists and writers in the mid-1960's because of pollution of the lake by the mill's waste products.

About 20 million years old, the lake is 395 miles (636 km) long and up to 49 miles (79 km) wide. Its greatest depth is 5,710 feet (1,741 meters). The lake level is 1,490 feet (454 meters) above sea level.

THEODORE SHABAD
Author of "Geography of the USSR"

BAIL, bāl, in law, is a term that has various meanings relating to the release of a prisoner from custody by giving security for his due appearance in court at a specified time. Bail may mean any or all of the following: (1) the act of procuring the release of one charged with an offense by becoming responsible, that is financially liable, for his appearing to answer the charge at the time appointed (bailing him out); (2) the delivery, or *bailment,* of a person to those who are giving surety for him; (3) those persons who agree to become security for (to "become bail" or "to go bail for") his appearing and submitting himself to the jurisdiction of the court; and (4) sometimes, the undertaking itself —that is, the *bail bond,* a legal liability for a money forfeit or damages, which is signed by other persons as sureties, against the event of the defendant's failing to appear. (There are several technically different bail procedures.)

The U.S. Constitution prohibits excessively high bail. Bail is fixed by the judge at the time of arraignment. If bail can be furnished in a sufficient amount, in a case where bail is allowable, it must be accepted by the court. Bail usually may be granted except in the case of murder.

In the 1960's the entire concept of bail came under searching review in the United States. The Bail Reform Act of 1966, which reformed federal bail procedures, provided for: (1) release of prisoners charged with noncapital federal offenses unless the judge found that the accused might flee; (2) release of prisoners charged with capital offenses or those convicted of an offense and awaiting sentence or the outcome of an appeal unless the judge found that the accused might flee or posed a threat to the community; (3) credit to be given toward sentence for time spent in jail awaiting trial.

BAILEY, bā′lē, **Ann** (1742–1825), American pioneer heroine. She was born in Liverpool, England. Immigrating to the American colonies at the age of 19, she lived the dangerous and difficult life of a pioneer on the western frontier of Virginia. After her first husband, Richard Trotter, was killed by Indians in 1774, she married John Bailey, a frontier leader.

When Indians besieged Fort Lee, Va., in 1791, she rode about 100 miles (161 km) through mountain wilderness to Fort Savannah (now Lewisburg, Ohio) and returned with sufficient gunpowder to enable the settlers to raise the siege. She died in Gallia County, Ohio, on Nov. 22, 1825.

BAILEY, bā′lē, **Francis** (c. 1735–1815), American publisher who, as an early government printer, published official copies of the *Declaration of Independence* and the *Articles of Confederation.* Other historic documents printed by Bailey included *The Constitutions of the Several Independent States of America* (1781) and a fourth edition of Thomas Paine's *Common Sense* (1776).

Bailey was born in Lancaster County, Pa. In 1771, after learning typesetting in Ephrata, Pa., he set up a small printing shop in Lancaster, Pa. He moved to Philadelphia in 1778. After 1781 he edited the *Freeman's Journal,* a political weekly whose contributors included the revolutionary poet Philip Freneau. Bailey built a large printing office in Sadsbury, Pa., in 1797. He died at his country residence, near Philadelphia.

BAILEY, bā′lē, **Gamaliel** (1807–1859), American abolitionist. He was born in Mount Holly, N.J., on Dec. 3, 1807. Graduated in 1827 from Jefferson Medical College in Philadelphia, he became editor of the *Methodist Protestant* in Baltimore in 1829. Two years later he moved to Cincinnati, where he began to practice medicine. He soon was converted to the abolitionist cause and, in 1836, with James G. Birney, he became editor of the Cincinnati *Philanthropist,* the first antislavery periodical in the West. Bailey assumed full ownership the following year. His office was attacked three times by mobs aroused by his denunciations of slavery, but he weathered the storm and in 1843 began publishing a daily paper called the *Herald.*

When the American and Foreign Anti-Slavery Society founded the weekly *National Era* in Washington, D.C., in 1847, Bailey was chosen editor in chief, a position he held for the rest of his life. This journal, with its wide circulation, became one of the most important organs of the abolitionist movement. It numbered among its contributors John Greenleaf Whittier, Theodore Parker, and Harriet Beecher Stowe, whose *Uncle Tom's Cabin* first appeared in the *National Era* in serial form in 1851–1852. Bailey died on June 5, 1859, while on a voyage to Europe.

BAILEY, bā′lē, **James Anthony** (1847–1906), American circus owner. He was born at Detroit, Mich., on July 4, 1847. Left an orphan at an early age, he first joined a circus troupe and then was a sutler's clerk during the Civil War.

After the war he returned to circus life. In 1872 he joined in organizing the Cooper & Bailey Circus, which toured the United States and South America and traveled as far as India and Australia. Bailey's show became the chief rival of Phineas T. Barnum's, and in 1881 the two organizations merged to form the famous Barnum & Bailey firm. Bailey was responsible for the Barnum & Bailey's purchase in 1882 of the giant elephant Jumbo from the Royal Zoological Society in Britain. After Barnum died in 1891, Bailey became sole owner of the firm. Shortly before his death he built a palatial home, in Mount Vernon, N.Y., which housed his notable art collection. He died at Mount Vernon on April 11, 1906.

BAILEY, bā′lē, **James Montgomery** (1841–1894), American humorist. He was born at Albany, N.Y., on Sept. 25, 1841. While working as a carpenter at Danbury, Conn., he wrote occasional pieces for newspapers. Later, while serving in the 17th Connecticut Regiment during the Civil War, he contributed humorous sketches of army life to a Danbury journal. In 1865, with Timothy Donovan, he purchased the Danbury *Times,* which he consolidated with the *Jeffersonian* in 1870 to form the weekly Danbury *News.* In 1878 he became sole owner and made it a daily.

Bailey soon gained a national reputation as "the Danbury *News* Man" for his popular humorous sketches of commonplace happenings, and his paper became known throughout the United States. Some literary historians refer to him as the first newspaper columnist. Among his works were *Life in Danbury* (1873), *They All Do It* (1877), *Mr. Phillips' Goneness* (1879), *The Danbury Boom* (1880), and *History of Danbury* (1896), completed by Susan B. Hill. He died at Danbury on March 4, 1894.

BAILEY, bā′lē, **Joseph Weldon** (1863–1929), American legislator. He was born in Crystal Springs, Miss., on Oct. 6, 1863. After completing his legal studies at the Lebanon School of Law in Tennessee, he moved to Gainesville, Texas, and was elected to the U.S. House of Representatives in 1890. He served five terms and acted as Democratic minority leader during the administration of President McKinley before entering the Senate in 1901.

In the Senate, Bailey advocated the free coinage of silver, sponsored the Hepburn Rate Bill of 1906 regulating railroad charges, and advocated the federal income tax and reorganization of the currency and banking system. Accused of accepting a bribe to secure a business permit for the Waters Pierce Oil Company, which had been expelled from Texas for violating antitrust laws, Bailey denied the charges and was reelected to the Senate in 1908. He resigned in 1913 in disagreement with President-elect Woodrow Wilson's program. He died in Sherman, Texas, on April 13, 1929.

BAILEY, bā′lē, **Liberty Hyde** (1858–1954), American horticulturist and botanist, whose most significant work was on North American sedges, New World palms, blackberries, and raspberries. He was born in South Haven, Mich., on March 15, 1858, the son of a farmer. He received much of his early training at home. In 1882 he graduated from Michigan State Agricultural College. After working as an assistant to Asa Gray at Harvard University in 1882–1883, Bailey organized a department of horticulture and landscape gardening at Michigan State in 1885—the first such college department in the United States. He served as professor in the department for three years, and afterward he became professor of horticulture at Cornell University. While at Cornell he introduced nature study and extension courses for farmers. In 1903 he was named dean and director of the College of Agriculture at Cornell. He retired in 1913 to write and work on his plant collection. He donated his library and botanical collection to Cornell, where the collection became known as the Liberty Hyde Bailey Hortorium. He died in Ithaca, New York, on Dec. 25, 1954.

In 1908 he served as chairman of Theodore Roosevelt's Commission on Country Life. He was chosen president of the American Association for the Advancement of Science in 1926 and was the first president of the American Society of Horticultural Science.

Bailey published approximately 50 books, including some general works, though most are of a technical nature. His technical writings include *Manual of Cultivated Plants* (rev. ed. 1949), a basic work in horticulture. He edited numerous reference works, notably *Cyclopedia of American Horticulture* (1900–02), *Standard Cyclopedia of Horticulture* (rev. ed. 1935), *Cyclopedia of American Agriculture* (1907–09), *Hortus* (1930), and *Hortus Second* (1941).

BAILEY, bā′lē, **Nathan** (died 1742), English lexicographer, who was the author of the best English dictionary before Dr. Samuel Johnson's. His first name also appears as *Nathaniel.* The first edition of Bailey's dictionary appeared in 1721 under the title *An Universal Etymological English Dictionary,* and it soon was republished in an enlarged form entitled *Dictionarium Britan-*

nicum (1730). Altogether some 30 editions of the work appeared up to 1802. Dr. Johnson made use of an interleaved copy of it when compiling his own dictionary.

Bailey also published a spelling book (1726), *All the Familiar Colloquies of Erasmus Translated* (1733), *The Antiquities of London and Westminster* (1726), and *Dictionarium Domesticum* (1736). He died at Stepney (now part of London) on June 27, 1742.

BAILEY, bā′lē, **Philip James** (1816–1902), English poet. He was born at Nottingham, England, on April 22, 1816. He was educated in Nottingham and at Glasgow University, and later he studied law at Lincoln's Inn in London. He was called to the bar in 1840 but never practiced. He died at Nottingham on Sept. 6, 1902.

Inspired by Goethe's *Faust,* Bailey spent three years on his own version of the legend. This poem, *Festus,* which was published in 1839, received an enthusiastic reception. Other volumes of Bailey's poetry included *The Angel World* (1850), *The Mystic* (1855), and *The Universal Hymn* (1867). In his later work, Bailey's youthful poetical freshness and concentration were often smothered under tedious verbosity and incoherency, typical failings of the "spasmodic" school of poetry in which critics have placed him.

BAILIFF, bā′ləf, a keeper or protector, a steward or agent; more commonly, a minor court official, deputy sheriff, or other ministerial official. Under the English common law, a "bailiff in husbandry" was one appointed by a private person to collect his rents and manage his estates. Similarly, a "bailiff of the manor" was a steward appointed by a lord as general superintendent of his manor.

In a related and broader usage, the term "bailiff" came to mean anyone to whom either real estate or personal property was entrusted, by either a public agency or a private individual, with the duty of collecting and accounting for the profits. For example, a committee or a guardian appointed by a court to manage and control the property of a mental incompetent is a bailiff of the court. In this sense, an attorney entrusted to collect money, a cotenant or tenant in common, or a receiver may also be designated as a bailiff. Some courts state that the technical distinction between a bailiff and a receiver is that the former is entitled to reasonable expenses, while the latter is not.

In addition to its rather obsolete meaning of custodian of property, bailiff refers to several categories of minor officials. It is in this latter sense that the term is most commonly used in modern law. Thus, a bailiff may be a specially appointed deputy of a sheriff or marshal, charged with the duty of guarding or protecting juries from improper communications and intrusions, or a deputy sheriff appointed at the request of a party to a lawsuit to serve or execute some writ or process of the court, or for some other special purpose.

RICHARD L. HIRSHBERG, *Attorney at Law*

BAILIWICK, bā′li-wik, the territory or jurisdiction of a sheriff or bailiff. In an exact sense, the term means the territory assigned to a sheriff or deputy for the service of process. In a broader sense, it denotes a county or other geographical area within which a particular official exercises authority.

BAILLET, bä-ye′, **Adrien** (1649–1706), French writer. He was born in Neuville, France, on June 13, 1649. He was ordained priest in 1675. His love for learning was so intense that, after discharging the duties of a parish priest for five years, he accepted the position of librarian to Guillaume de Lamoignon, president of the Parlement of Paris.

Baillet's first publication was entitled *Judgments of the Learned upon the Principal Works of Authors;* a book of criticisms, it taught better rules than it illustrated and brought on him the hatred of the Jesuits. His most important work was *The Life of Descartes* (1691). He also wrote *The Lives of the Saints* (1701) in which he critically treated the question of miracles. Baillet died in Paris on Jan. 21, 1706.

BAILLIE, bā′lē, **Joanna** (1762–1851), Scottish dramatist and poet. She was born in Bothwell, near Glasgow, on Sept. 11, 1762. In early life she moved to London, where in 1798 she published the first volume of her *Plays on the Passions,* in which she attempted to delineate the stronger passions by making each the subject of a tragedy and a comedy. This volume included *Basil,* a tragedy on love; *Trial,* a comedy on love; and *De Monfort,* a tragedy on hatred. The plays were not well suited for stage production, but they made her literary reputation. Her first volume was followed by a second in the same vein in 1802 and a third in 1812. Volumes of *Miscellaneous Plays* appeared in 1804 and 1836, and a complete edition of her dramatic works was published in 1850.

Several of her plays were produced on the stage. The tragedy *De Monfort* was presented by John Kemble in 1800, with Kemble and Sara Siddons in the leading roles; later, Edmund Kean portrayed the title role. A tragedy entitled *Family Legend* was produced in 1810 under the patronage of the playwright's friend, Sir Walter Scott, who greatly admired her writings. The language of her plays is simple and forceful, and she is particularly effective in her portraits of women. She died in London, England, on Feb. 23, 1851.

BAILLIE OF JERVISWOOD, bā′lē, jär′vis-wo͞od, **Robert** (died 1684), Scottish politician and conspirator, who died for the cause of Scottish nationalism and religious and civil liberty. He was a moderate in a strongly anti-Catholic Scottish Presbyterian church, but he was driven to extreme action by the high-handed interference in the Scottish church by the Anglican bishop, William Laud (q.v.).

Baillie was first marked as an opponent of the Anglican hierarchy in Scotland in 1676. To escape harassment he took a prominent part in 1683 in a plan for emigration to South Carolina. Nothing came of the plan however. Shortly thereafter he met with the duke of Monmouth, William Russell, and Algernon Sidney in London to devise ways to secure relief from the tyranny of civil and religious officials under Charles II. Falsely accused of conspiring against the life of Charles in the Rye House Plot and of conspiring to raise a rebellion, Baillie was arrested in London and imprisoned in Scotland. He was tried before the High Court of Justice at Edinburgh and condemned to death on insignificant evidence. He was hanged at Edinburgh on Dec. 24, 1684.

BAILLOT, bȧ-yō′, **Pierre Marie François de Sales** (1771–1842), French violinist. He was born in Passy (now part of Paris), France, on Oct. 1, 1771. The last of the classical Parisian school of violinists, Baillot was unexcelled as an interpreter of chamber music. From 1795 he was a professor of violin in the conservatory at Paris. He toured extensively in Russia, Belgium, Holland, and England. He composed numerous works for the violin, including nine concertos, and wrote several standard books on violin playing, including *L'art du violon* (1834). He died at Paris on Sept. 15, 1842.

BAILLY, bȧ-yē′, **Jean Sylvain** (1736–1793), French astronomer, legislator, and historian. He was born in Paris on Sept. 15, 1736. He studied painting but devoted himself to poetry and belles-lettres until he became acquainted with the astronomer Nicolas Lacaille. He then turned his attention to astronomy and calculated the orbit of the comet of 1759 (Halley's comet). He was admitted to the Academy of Sciences in 1763, to the French Academy in 1783, and to the Academy of Inscriptions in 1784, thus becoming one of the few to be a member of all three. In 1766 he published a treatise on Jupiter's satellites, and in 1771, a general treatise on the light of the satellites. Later he also wrote *Histoire de l'Astronomie* (5 vols., 1775–1787).

Bailly espoused the democratic cause in the French Revolution. He was elected from Paris, in 1789, as first deputy of the Third Estate, and was chosen president of the national assembly. In July 1789 he became mayor of Paris and discharged his duties, during 26 months of a most trying and dangerous period, with great firmness and wisdom. Losing his popularity by repressing rioting and by defending the queen, he gave up public life and lived in retirement until seized by the Jacobins and brought to Paris. He was condemned as a conspirator, and was executed in Paris on Nov. 12, 1793.

Several of his works were published after his death, among them *Essay on the Origin of Fables and Ancient Religions* (1799) and *Memoirs of an Eyewitness from April to October 1789* (1821–1822).

BAILMENT, bāl′mənt, in law, is the delivery of personal property by one person (the *bailor*) to another (the *bailee*) for a particular purpose. The legal concept of bailment may include, under appropriate circumstances, many different kinds of transactions, among them being deposit, storage, checking, rental, pledge, lending, and acquisition by finding. The relationship described by the term may be classified generally as contractual. Express agreements between the parties for the purpose of including every phase of this relationship are not essential, since many of the rights and duties arising from it are implied by law.

Bailment is characterized by a transfer of possession, as distinguished from a change in ownership. Another factor generally recognized as being essential to a bailment is the return, or other use as directed by the bailor, of the article bailed. Thus, sales and exchanges are, in most cases, readily distinguishable from bailment; although in some instances differentiation is difficult, such as conditional sales arrangements and rentals with options to buy.

Bailments are divided into various classes, primarily for the purpose of determining the rights and liabilities of the parties. There are three usual classifications: (1) bailments for the benefit of both parties; (2) bailments for the sole benefit of the bailor; and (3) bailments for the sole benefit of the bailee. In addition, there are numerous special types of bailment to which special rules apply, such as those resulting from the delivery of property to banks, innkeepers, warehousemen, and common carriers.

In a bailment for hire, which is typical of the bailment for mutual benefit (for example, an automobile rental), the law implies a warranty by the bailor that the bailed article is fit for its intended use. The bailor, therefore, is liable for any injuries caused by its unfitness for use at the time of delivery. Where the bailment is for the sole benefit of the bailee, however, the bailor is legally obliged only to disclose to the bailee such defects in the article as are actually known to him.

The care that must be taken of the property by the bailee varies according to the type of bailment in some jurisdictions. In those states which recognize various degrees of care, the bailee for his own sole benefit must exercise great care; for mutual benefit, ordinary care; and for the bailor's sole benefit, only slight care. The normal liability of a bailee may be reduced or extended by special contract. A bailment may be terminated by the agreement or conduct of the parties, destruction of the subject matter, completion of the purpose of the bailment, lapse of time in accordance with the terms of the bailment, or death of the bailor or bailee.

BAILY, bā'lē, **Edward Hodges** (1788–1867), English sculptor, who in 1840–1843 executed the 17-foot statue of Lord Nelson in Trafalgar Square, London. He was born at Bristol, England, on March 10, 1788. He early gained considerable success as a modeler in wax. He became a pupil of John Flaxman in 1807, and was elected a member of the Royal Academy in 1821. In addition to the Nelson monument, his principal works are *Eve at the Fountain* (1818), which established his reputation; portraits of Charles James Fox and Lord Mansfield in St. Stephen's Hall, Westminster; and the bas-reliefs on the south side of the Marble Arch in Hyde Park, London. He died in London on May 22, 1867.

BAILY, bā'lē, **Francis** (1774–1844), English astronomer. He was born at Newbury, Berkshire, April 28, 1774. Early in his life he traveled two years in America, the literary outcome of which was his curious *Journal of a Tour in Unsettled Parts of North America in 1796–1797*, published in 1856. In 1820 he became one of the founders of the Royal Astronomical Society, of which he was four times president, and in 1825 he retired from business to devote his attention entirely to astronomical work.

Baily improved the *Nautical Almanac*, helped revise several star catalogs, repeated the Cavendish experiment on the density of the earth, and investigated and described the phenomenon called Baily's Beads, first noticed in 1836. This is a phenomenon attending eclipses of the sun, whose unobscured edge appears discontinuous and broken immediately before and after the moment of complete obscuration. It is caused by the valleys and mountains on the edge of the disk of the moon. Bailey died in London on Aug. 30, 1844.

BAIN, bān, **Alexander** (1818–1903), Scottish psychologist and educator, who is probably best known for his scientific approach to the study of psychology. Unlike many earlier psychologists, he emphasized the close relationship between the functioning of the nervous system and various mental states. Bain was also known as a brilliant teacher, and he was influential in improving the standards of education in Scotland. He was especially interested in the teaching of grammar and composition.

Bain was born on June 11, 1818, in Aberdeen, Scotland. After attending Marischal College (later incorporated into the University of Aberdeen), he became a free-lance writer and assisted the English philosopher and economist John Stuart Mill in revising his book *A System of Logic* (1843). Bain then published two works of his own, *The Senses and the Intellect* (1855) and *The Emotions and the Will* (1859), both of which were highly esteemed by the American psychologist William James.

In 1860, Bain was appointed a professor of logic at the University of Aberdeen, and in 1872 he published *Mind and Body*. A few years later he became one of the founders of *Mind*, the first journal of psychology. It was first published in 1876, and Bain remained a major contributor until 1890. His other published works include two books on education: *Education as a Science* (1879) and *On Teaching English* (1887). He also wrote a biography of John Stuart Mill (1882) and many political and social pamphlets. Bain died in Aberdeen on Sept. 18, 1903. His *Autobiography* was published posthumously the following year.

Further Reading: Warren, Howard C., *A History of Association Psychology* (New York 1921).

BAINBRIDGE, bān'brij, **William** (1774–1833), American naval officer who held commands in the Tripolitan War and the War of 1812. He was born in Princeton, N.J., on May 7, 1774. Entering the merchant service at the age of 15, Bainbridge was made captain within four years. When the U.S. Navy was organized in 1798, he was given command of the schooner *Retaliation* and ordered to protect American shipping in the Caribbean Sea. He and his vessel were captured by two French frigates. Upon his release, Congress passed a law promising retaliation against the French for such acts.

Promoted to captain in the Navy in 1800, Bainbridge was given the frigate *George Washington* and ordered to take the dey of Algiers the tribute that the United States had agreed to pay in return for protection from piratical attacks. The dey humiliated Bainbridge and his government by forcing him to transport an Algerian mission to Constantinople.

During the Tripolitan War of 1801–1805, the United States took the first step toward ending the payment of tributes to North African governments. In 1803, Bainbridge, commanding the 44-gun frigate *Philadelphia*, was pursuing an enemy vessel into Tripoli harbor when he ran aground. He and 315 of his crew became captives of Tripoli until the war ended in 1805. A naval court absolved Bainbridge, and he was promoted commodore in 1808. During the War of 1812 he commanded the *Constitution* ("Old Ironsides") and captured the British frigate *Java* after a fierce battle off the coast of Brazil. He died in Philadelphia on July 27, 1833.

BAINBRIDGE, băn'brij, a city in Georgia and seat of Decatur County, is on the Flint River, 35 miles (56 km) northwest of Tallahassee, Fla. It is the trading center of an agricultural area producing peanuts, tobacco, livestock, truck crops, and timber. Diversified industries manufacture boxes, mobile homes, bottle-washing machines, automotive parts, aluminum windows, clothing, and fertilizer.

Bainbridge was Georgia's first inland port city for barge traffic to the Gulf of Mexico, via the Flint River, Lake Seminole, and the Apalachicola River.

During the Indian wars of 1817–1821 a fort was built on the present site of Bainbridge, and the settlement around it took the name of Fort Hughes. In 1829 the settlement received its charter and was given the name of Bainbridge. In the early 1900's a lumber boom brought prosperity and growth to the city. Bainbridge has a mayor-council and city manager form of government. Population: 10,887.

BAINES, bānz, **Edward** (1774–1848), English journalist. He was born at Walton-le-Dale, Lancashire, on Feb. 5, 1774. From printer's apprentice in nearby Preston and later in Leeds, he rose to become proprietor (1801) of the Leeds *Mercury*, which he made one of the leading provincial newspapers. A confidant and adviser of many parliamentary leaders, he succeeded Thomas Macaulay as a member of Parliament for Leeds in 1834. He remained in Parliament until 1841.

Baines, an independent liberal, advocated the separation of church and state and the reform of factory laws, and he opposed governmental interference in education. His son, Sir Edward Baines (1800–1890), shared his father's political views and followed a similar career.

The elder Baines, who died on Aug. 3, 1848, wrote *History of the Wars of the French Revolution from 1792 to 1815* (2 vols., 1818), which he later enlarged as *History of the Reign of George III* (4 vols., 1823).

BAINES, bānz, **Thomas** (1822–1875), English artist and explorer. He was born in King's Lynn, Norfolk. In 1842 he went to South Africa, and from there he accompanied the British army in the Kaffir War (1848–1851) as an artist. He went with Sir Augustus C. Gregory's safari to explore northwestern Australia (1855); with David Livingstone to the Zambezi River in southern Africa (1858); and with John Chapman's expedition to Victoria Falls, on the Zambezi (1861). In 1868 he headed an expedition to the gold fields of Tati, in Bechuanaland. Everywhere he made large numbers of sketches. His last journey was among the Kaffirs. He died in Durban, South Africa, on May 8, 1875.

A handsome folio of colored lithographs from his drawings of Victoria Falls was published in 1865. His writings include *Explorations in South-West Africa* (1864) and *The Gold Regions of South Eastern Africa* (1877).

BAINI, bä-ē'nĕ, **Giuseppe** (1775–1844), Italian musician. He was born in Rome on Oct. 21, 1775. He was associated with the papal choir at the Vatican from 1795 until his death, and became maestro di cappella there in 1818. Although very few of his compositions survive, he is known to have written a great many psalms, Masses, hymns, and motets. His masterpiece, *Miserere*

(1821) for 10 voices, was first sung in the Sistine Chapel during Holy Week in 1821; it is still occasionally sung there.

It was through historical research that Baini secured a prominent place in musical literature. He was a devotee of Palestrina and wrote an exhaustive biography of that composer—*Memorie storico-critiche della vita e delle opere di Giovanni Pierluigi da Palestrina* (2 vols., (1828). Baini died at Rome on May 21, 1844.

BAINVILLE, baɴ-vēl', **Jacques** (1879–1936), French historian. He was born in Vincennes, Feb. 9, 1879. A founding editor of the Catholic and ultraroyalist newspaper *Action française,* he became its foreign editor in 1906. An authority on Franco-German relations, Bainville wrote *Histoire des deux peuples* (1915), a study of German invasions of France. His *Conséquences politiques de la paix* (1920) was a reply to the British economist John Maynard Keynes. *Histoire de France* (1924) is his best-known work. He was elected to the French Academy in 1935. He died in Paris on Feb. 9, 1936.

BAIRAM, bī-räm', is the Turkish name for the two major Muslim festivals. The lesser Bairam, called *Id al-Fitr* in Arabic, concludes the fast of Ramadan. Ramadan occurs in the ninth month of the Muslim calendar year and is marked by fasting between sunrise and sunset. The fast is broken with the three-day feast of Bairam, during which presents are exchanged and visits are paid.

During the greater Bairam, called *Id al-Adha* in Arabic, an animal is sacrificed and consumed. This feast is observed at the time of the annual pilgrimage to Mecca.

BAIRD, bârd, **John Logie** (1888–1946), Scottish television pioneer. He was born in Helensburgh, Scotland, on Aug. 13, 1888. He attended the Royal Technical College and Glasgow University. From 1922 he devoted himself to experimenting in London with television, and two years later he completed his first workable apparatus.

His first public demonstration was given on Jan. 27, 1926, before a gathering at the Royal Institution, this marking the first time that true television, with gradations of light and shade, was demonstrated successfully. The first demonstration of transatlantic television came in February 1928, when the Baird Station in Coulson, Kent, transmitted a signal that was picked up and seen on a receiver in Hartsdale, N.Y. His system of television was adopted in 1929 by the German Post Office and the British Broadcasting Corporation; the latter, which became the first organization in the world to conduct a full scale television service, subsequently abandoned the Baird system in favor of that of Marconi.

In 1926 he had demonstrated his invention of the "noctovisor," for seeing in the dark and through fog by invisible infrared rays, and two years later he demonstrated television in natural colors; by 1939 he was demonstrating color television with an electronic apparatus, using the cathode ray tube—which he had adopted as the most successful method for providing a well-defined and brilliant picture. From 1941 he was consulting technical adviser to Cable and Wireless, Limited, working on the application of television methods to the transmission of facsimiles. He died at Bexhill, Sussex, England, on June 14, 1946.

BAIRD, bârd, **Spencer Fullerton** (1823–1887), American zoologist and naturalist. He was born in Reading, Pa., on Feb. 3, 1823, the son of a lawyer. He received his B.A. degree at Dickinson College in 1840 and his M.A. there in 1843. He was professor of natural history at Dickinson from 1846 to 1850. In 1850 he was named assistant secretary of the Smithsonian Institution in Washington, D.C., and he became its secretary in 1878. During his tenure there, the institution's collections of specimens in botany, zoology, and ethnology were increased greatly. In 1871, Baird was asked to head the new U.S. Commission of Fish and Fisheries, which he did until he died at Woods Hole, Mass., on Aug. 19, 1887.

Baird contributed to the sciences of ornithology and ichthyology. His detailed and accurate descriptions of many species of birds led to the formation of the "Baird school" of ornithology, which is dedicated to continuing the high standards of accuracy that Baird set. Under his direction American ichthyology also was expanded notably, and the marine laboratory at Woods Hole was developed. Among his more important works are *Catalogue of North American Birds* (1858); *Catalogue of North American Mammals* (1857); and, with Charles Girard, *North American Reptiles* (1853).

BAIRNSFATHER, bârnz'fä-thər, **Bruce** (1888–1959), English soldier and cartoonist. He was born at Murree, India (now in West Pakistan), on July 9, 1888. He was educated in England at the United Services College and served in the Warwickshire Militia (1911–1914). After World War I began, he served in France (1914–1916) with the Royal Warwickshire Regiment, and won promotion to captain in July 1915. Bairnsfather became famous for his humorous cartoons of life in the trenches, centering around the character of Old Bill. First published in the London *Bystander*, the cartoons later were collected in various volumes. His play *The Better 'Ole* (a title derived from the caption of his most noted cartoon) was produced at the end of the war.

In World War II, Bairnsfather was war cartoonist with the U.S. Army in Europe (1942–1944). His later publications include *Jeeps and Jests* (1943) and *No Kiddin'* (1945). He died at Norton, England, on Sept. 29, 1959.

BAIUS, ba'yəs, **Michael** (1513–1589), Flemish Roman Catholic theologian. He is also known as Michael de Bay or Michael Bajus. Born at Mélin-l'Évêque, Belgium, he was educated at Louvain University, where he held various administrative and teaching positions and in 1552 was awarded the chair of Holy Scripture. Baius deviated from the scholastic method of philosophy and based his teachings directly on the Bible and the writings of the fathers of the church, particularly St. Augustine. He thus formulated a systematic theology that is now known as *Baianism*.

Baius' views on the doctrines of grace, predestination, and free will caused much controversy, and in 1560 the faculty of the Sorbonne condemned 18 of his propositions as contrary to Catholic teaching. Nevertheless, in 1563 he was sent under the protection of Charles V of Spain to the Council of Trent. In 1567 some 79 statements from his works were condemned (without naming him as their author) by Pope Pius V in a bull that was reaffirmed by Gregory XIII in 1579. Baius maintained that he had not taught some of the condemned doctrines and that others had been presented incorrectly. Acknowledging that many could be construed as erroneous, he renounced these, disclaiming any intentional heresy.

Baius became dean of the faculty of Louvain in 1570 and chancellor of the university in 1575. Through one of his students he influenced the development of the 17th century doctrine known as Jansenism (see JANSENISM). His works were published more than a century after his death at Louvain on Sept. 16, 1589

BAJA CALIFORNIA. See LOWER CALIFORNIA.

BAJAZET. See BAYEZID.

BAJER, bī'ər, **Fredrik** (1837–1922), Danish crusader for world peace. He was born in Vester Egede, Denmark, on April 21, 1837. He was a member of the Folketing (legislature) from 1872 to 1895 and in 1882 founded the Danish Peace Society. He participated in the peace conference at Bern in 1884, as well as the First World Peace Congress in Paris in 1889. In Rome in 1891 he established the International Peace Bureau, of which he was president until 1907. Jointly with Klas P. Arnoldson, he won the Nobel Peace Prize for 1908. Among his works on neutrality is *The Scandinavian Neutrality System* (1906).

BAJI RAO II (died 1852), bä'jē rä'ŏŏ, peshwa (prince) of Maratha, was the last ruler (1795–1818) of the independent Maratha confederacy in west central India. He was compelled to seek British aid after being opposed by the Holkar Maratha dynasty and in 1802 signed the Treaty of Bassein with the British. He retained rule at Poona as a British subsidiary after the second Maratha War (1803–1805) in which the other houses of the dynasty were defeated. He was defeated by the British in the third Maratha War (1817–1818) and retired to Bithur.

BAKALEINIKOV, bak-ə-līn'ə-kôv, **Vladimir** (1885–1953), Russian violinist, conductor, and composer. He was born in Moscow, Russia, on Oct. 13, 1885. At the age of nine, for his skill as a violinist, he won a full scholarship at the Moscow Imperial Conservatory. From 1910 to 1920 he played the viola in the Grand Duke Mecklenburg String Quartet. In St. Petersburg (now Leningrad) he taught at the Imperial Conservatory in 1913–1920, and was conductor of the Musical Drama Theatre (1914–1916) and of the People's Theatre and the Preobrazhensky Orchestra (1916–1920). He returned to Moscow and taught at the conservatory (1920–1924) and was music director of the opera department of the Moscow Art Theatre (1920–1927).

In 1927, Bakaleinikov went to the United States and became chief violist and assistant conductor of the Cincinnati Symphony Orchestra. He held this position until 1938, when he became assistant conductor of the Pittsburgh Symphony Orchestra. He was made associate conductor in 1945 and musical adviser in 1948. He died at Pittsburgh, Pa., on Nov. 5, 1953.

Bakaleinikov's compositions include a concerto for the viola and two Oriental dances for orchestra. He was the author of *Elementary Rules of Conducting* (1937) and *Complete Course for the Viola* (1937–38).

BAKELITE, bāk′ə-līt, is a synthetic resin plastic invented by Leo Hendrik Baekeland, a Belgian-American chemist. Bakelite is formed by the combination of phenols and formaldehyde, which, under the influence of heat, becomes a hard, insoluble, and infusible substance resisting in a high degree chemical and mechanical agents. In its purest form it is a colorless or light golden-yellow mass resembling celluloid, but incombustible and harder.

Bakelite is used for making ornaments, beads, buttons, pen and pencil holders, umbrella handles, and pipe mouthpieces. See also PLASTICS–*The Synthetic Plastics* (Phenolic Resins).

BAKER, bā′kər, **Sir Benjamin** (1840–1907), English engineer. He was born at Keyford, Frome, Somerset, on March 31, 1840. Joining the staff of the English engineer Sir John Fowler in 1861, he became his partner in 1875. In 1877 he designed the special vessel that transported the obelisk known as Cleopatra's Needle from Egypt to London. The same year he became consulting engineer in the construction of the first Aswan dam. The American engineer J.B. Eads consulted him in connection with the design of the Eads Bridge across the Mississippi. On threatened inundation of the first tunnel construction under the Hudson River–the Hudson Tubes, begun in 1874 between Manhattan and Jersey City–he designed a pneumatic shield 2,000 feet (609 meters) in length which permitted successful tunneling operations during the period 1888–1891. In conjunction with Sir John Fowler he planned the Firth of Forth Bridge in Scotland. He was knighted in 1890 and died in Pangbourne, England, on May 19, 1907.

BAKER, bā′kər, **Frank** (1886–1963), American baseball player, known as "Home Run" Baker, who led the American League in home runs for three years in the "dead ball era" and was once rated the league's best third baseman.

John Franklin Baker was born in Trappe, Md., on March 13, 1886. A lefthanded batter, he was acquired by the Philadelphia Athletics in 1908. He became a part of Connie Mack's famous $100,000 infield that included John (Stuffy) McInnis at first, Eddie Collins at second, and Jack Barry at shortstop. His leading home run production in three years (1911–1913) was 9, 10, and 12. In 1914 he tied for home run honors with 8. However, he actually got his nickname for hitting two home runs in the 1911 World Series. After a disagreement with Mack, Baker was sold to the Yankees in 1916. Retiring after the 1922 season, he had a total of 93 home runs and a batting average of .307. He was voted into the Hall of Fame in 1955.

BILL BRADDOCK, *New York "Times"*

BAKER, bā′kər, **George Fisher** (1840–1931), American banker and philanthropist, who became a significant figure in American finance, holding directorships in 43 banks and corporations. He was born in Troy, N.Y., on March 27, 1840. Baker helped found the First National Bank of New York in 1863 and began work there as a teller. He rose to cashier in 1865, president in 1877, and chairman of the board in 1909. Early in the 20th century he was a director simultaneously in the U.S. Steel Corporation, American Telegraph and Telephone Company, and the New York Central Railroad.

He gave $6 million to Harvard University's Graduate School of Business Administration and presented Regnault's *Salomé* and other gifts to the Metropolitan Museum of Art. His benefactions also included large donations to the American Red Cross, Cornell University, and Dartmouth College. He died in New York City on May 2, 1931.

George Fisher Baker, Jr. (1878–1937), his only son, succeeded him as chairman of the board of the First National Bank. In 1930 he became a member of the American syndicate that built the yacht *Enterprise*, successful defender of the America's Cup against Britain's *Shamrock V.*

BAKER, bā′kər, **George Pierce** (1866–1935), American educator, who had a vital influence on theater education in the United States and especially on university courses in playwriting. He was born at Providence, R.I., on April 4, 1866. After graduating from Harvard in 1887, he taught there from 1888 to 1924–as full professor of English during the last 19 of these years.

At Harvard, Baker instituted a laboratory for instruction in dramatic composition, known as the "47 Workshop" because the course was listed in the college catalog as "English 47." Through Baker's initiative, Harvard became the first university in the United States to offer, as part of the regular academic curriculum, courses in the practical techniques of the theater. Some of the students in these special courses who became leading playwrights of the American theater included Philip Barry, S.N. Behrman, Sidney Howard, George Abbott, and, most important of all, Eugene O'Neill.

From 1925 until 1933, when he retired, Baker was a member of the Yale University faculty as chairman of the department of drama in the School of Fine Arts, professor of the history and technique of drama, and director of the university theater. He died at New York City on Jan. 6, 1935.

His published works include *The Principles of Argumentation* (1895), *The Development of Shakespeare as a Dramatist* (1907), and *Dramatic Technique* (1919). He also edited collections of plays.

BAKER, bā′kər, **Sir Herbert** (1862–1946), British architect. He was born in Cobham, Kent, on June 9, 1862. After studying architecture in England, he went to South Africa in 1892. He rebuilt Cecil Rhodes' mansion, Groote Schuur, near Cape Town, which subsequently became the official residence of the prime minister of the Union of South Africa. During his 20 years in Africa, he also designed the government buildings at Pretoria, South Africa; Rhodes' tomb in the Matopo Hills, Rhodesia; the Rhodes Memorial on Table Mountain, near Cape Town; and parts of the cathedrals at Cape Town, Pretoria, and Salisbury (Rhodesia).

From 1912, Baker worked in India and in London. He designed the secretariat and legislative buildings in New Delhi; his most important works in London were India House, Church House, and the Royal Empire Society building. He received a knighthood in 1926, and in 1930 he was made a knight commander of the Order of the Indian Empire. His writings included *Cecil Rhodes* (1934) and *Architecture and Personalities* (1944). He died in Cobham on Feb. 4, 1946.

BAKER, bă′kər, **Josephine** (1906–1975), American singer who lived most of her life in France, where she was acclaimed as the personification of "le jazz hot" of America. She was born in St. Louis, Mo., on June 3, 1906, and spent her childhood in the slums of that city. In her teens she joined the chorus of a traveling theatrical company and in 1923 appeared in the chorus of the Broadway musical *Shuffle Along.* She stayed in New York City for a short time, performing in theater and nightclub productions.

In 1925 she accepted a prominent dancing part in *La Revue Nègre*, an American show that was produced in Paris. Within a short time she joined the *Folies Bergère*, where she received star billing. She became a blues singer of international fame. During her last two years she enjoyed two triumphant appearances in New York.

Miss Baker, a Negro, aided the French underground in World War II and became a French citizen in 1937. In the 1950's she adopted a dozen orphans of various nationalities and lived with them in a château in southwestern France. She died in Paris on April 12, 1975.

BAKER, Howard Henry, Jr. (1925–   ), American political leader. He was born in Huntsville, Tenn., on Nov. 15, 1925, into a family active in law and politics. Both his father and his stepmother served in the U. S. House of Representatives. During World War II, Baker studied engineering under a Navy program and then served on a patrol torpedo boat.

After graduating from the University of Tennessee (LL. B., 1949), Baker practiced criminal and corporate law in Knoxville, Tenn. In 1964 he lost a contest for a U. S. Senate seat, but in 1966 he became the first popularly elected Republican senator from Tennessee. He was reelected in 1972.

Senator Baker's record was generally conservative. For years he supported U. S. policy in Vietnam, opposing attempts in the Senate to encroach on the president's management of the war, but in 1973 he voted to cut off funds for U. S. military action in Southeast Asia. He opposed busing schoolchildren to achieve racial balance, and he supported legislation to ensure clean air and water and to restrict strip mining of coal.

In 1973, as senior Republican on the Senate committee investigating the Watergate scandal, Baker became a national figure. He sought to establish the motives of the principals, and to determine whether President Nixon was involved. Baker was elected minority (Republican) leader of the Senate in 1977, an office once held by his father-in-law, Sen. Everett Dirksen (R-Ill.).

BAKER, Newton Diehl (1871–1937), American public official. He was born in Martinsburg, W. Va., on Dec. 3, 1871. After graduating from Johns Hopkins University and Washington and Lee Law School, he practiced law in Martinsburg.

Moving to Cleveland, Ohio, he became city solicitor under Mayor Tom Johnson. As mayor of Cleveland, Baker carried on Johnson's reform program for improving the city and fostering independence from state government.

At the 1912 Democratic national convention, Baker swung 19 Ohio votes to Woodrow Wilson for president. In 1916, Wilson named Baker secretary of war. World War I had begun in Europe. Baker, a pacifist, moved slowly to prepare the United States for war, and was severely criticized. But he was acting vigorously by the time the United States entered the war in 1917. He instituted and supervised a universal military draft law, raising 4 million men and sending half of them to France within 18 months. He held waste and corruption to a minimum and was an influential adviser to Wilson.

Resuming his law practice in Cleveland in 1921, Baker supported U. S. membership in the League of Nations. He served on the Permanent Court of Arbitration at The Hague, and he opposed the growth of federal power under President Franklin Roosevelt. Baker died in Shaker Heights, Ohio, on Dec. 25, 1937.

BAKER, bā′kər, **Ray Stannard** (1870–1946), American journalist and author. He was born in Lansing, Mich., on April 17, 1870. After graduating from Michigan State College in 1889 he studied law and literature at the University of Michigan. In 1892 he became a reporter on the Chicago *Record*. From 1899 until 1905 he was associate editor of *McClure's Magazine,* and from 1906 to 1915 he was one of the editors of the *American Magazine.* As a reform, muckraking writer, he turned out many articles on social and economic problems from a liberal standpoint. From 1899 until the 1940's he published books on various topics, including *Seen in Germany* (1901) and *The Spiritual Unrest* (1910). Under the pseudonym "David Grayson" he also wrote a number of popular books of essays, beginning with *Adventures in Contentment* (1907) and including *Adventures in Understanding* (1925).

In 1919, Baker served in Paris with the American Commission to Negotiate Peace as director of the press bureau. In this position he was closely associated with President Woodrow Wilson. In 1919 he published *What Wilson Did at Paris,* followed in 1922 by the 3-volume *Woodrow Wilson and World Settlement.* With William Edward Dodd, he edited the 6-volume *Public Papers of Woodrow Wilson* (1925–1926). Baker also wrote the monumental 8-volume biography, *Woodrow Wilson—Life and Letters* (1927–1939), winning the Pulitzer Prize in biography in 1940 for the last two volumes. Baker died in Amherst, Mass., on July 12, 1946. He wrote two autobiographies: *Native American* (1941) and *American Chronicle* (1945).

BAKER, bā′kər, **Sir Samuel White** (1821–1893), English explorer and author, who wrote about his experiences in Africa and Asia. He was born in London on June 8, 1821, and trained as an engineer. Baker went to Ceylon when he was 24, and in 1848 he established an agricultural settlement and sanatorium at Nuwara Eliya, about 6,200 feet (1,900 meters) above sea level. In 1859–1860 he supervised the construction of a railroad from the Danube River to the Black Sea.

A year later he embarked on the first of a series of explorations in Africa. Accompanied by his Hungarian-born wife, he spent a year exploring the tributaries of the Nile on the Ethiopian border of the Sudan, and then followed the great river southward. At Gondokoro, Sudan, in February 1863, he met John Hanning Speke and James Augustus Grant, who were returning down the river to Egypt after discovering the source of the Nile. Hearing from them of the supposed existence of another immense lake besides Lake Victoria, which Speke had discovered earlier, Baker determined to reach it. On March 14, 1864, he and his wife sighted the lake, which he called Albert Nyanza (Lake Albert). He found that the Nile actually flowed through the lake. The Bakers reached Khartoum in May 1865.

In October of the same year Baker arrived in England, where he received many distinctions and, in 1866, was knighted. In 1869 the khedive of Egypt engaged him to command, with the rank of pasha, a military expedition to the Upper Nile in order to suppress the slave trade and annex new territories for Egypt.

After Britain occupied Cyprus in 1879, Baker explored the island. In later years, he traveled in India, Ceylon, Syria, the United States, and Japan. He died near Newton Abbot in Devonshire, England, on Dec. 30, 1893.

His numerous books include *The Rifle and the Hound in Ceylon* (1854), *Eight Years' Wanderings in Ceylon* (1855), *The Albert Nyanza* (1866), *The Nile Tributaries of Abyssinia* (1867), *Cyprus as I Saw It in 1879* (1880), and *Wild Beasts and Their Ways* (1890).

BAKER, bā'kər, **Theodore** (1851–1934), American writer on music, whose compilation of biographies of musicians is a standard reference work. He was born in New York City on June 3, 1851. He studied music at the University of Leipzig, Germany, from which he received a Ph.D. degree in 1882. His doctoral thesis was the first study ever made of the music of a North American Indian tribe (the Seneca). He returned to the United States in 1891 to work for the music publishing firm G. Schirmer, Inc. as a literary editor and translator of German works on musical technique. After his retirement in 1926, he returned to Germany. He died in Dresden on Oct. 13, 1934.

Baker's most important work, *Baker's Biographical Dictionary of Musicians*, was first published in 1900. The book was revised, updated, and substantially enlarged by Alfred Remy in its third edition (1919) and by Nicolas Slonimsky in its fifth edition (1958). Baker's most popular work, *A Dictionary of Musical Terms*, went through 25 editions between 1895 and 1939. He also compiled *A Pronouncing Pocket Manual of Musical Terms* (1905) and *The Musician's Calendar and Birthday Book* (1915–17).

BAKER, bā'kər, **Valentine** (1827–1887), English soldier, who served in the British and Turkish armies and who commanded the Egyptian police. He was known as *Baker Pasha*.

Born in Enfield, England, on April 1, 1827, he was the brother of Sir Samuel White Baker, the explorer. He fought in the Kaffir War of 1852–1853 and in the Crimean War, and became colonel of the 10th Hussars. His career in the British army ended in 1875, when he was imprisoned for assaulting a woman.

In 1877 he entered the Turkish army. He distinguished himself in the Russo-Turkish War of 1877–1878, reaching the rank of lieutenant general, and in 1883 he was given command of the Egyptian police. With the outbreak of war in the Sudan he took command of a large Egyptian army, but it was utterly defeated at El Teb on Feb. 5, 1884, by the forces of Osman Digna. Baker made his escape and accompanied the British army that proved victorious in a second battle at El Teb. Baker continued to command the Egyptian police until his death at Tell el Kebir, Egypt, on Nov. 17, 1887.

BAKER, bā'kər, a city in Oregon, is the seat of Baker County, and is situated on the east fork of the Powder River, 77 miles (124 km) southeast of Pendleton. It is a trading and shipping center for livestock, lumber, and agricultural products. Working of the nearby gold and silver mines is now dependent on market prices. Recreational attractions in the area include fishing, hunting, camping, and skiing. Baker was settled in the early 1860's, after the discovery of gold in the vicinity. Government is by council-manager. Population: 9,354.

BAKER ISLAND, bā'kər, in the Pacific Ocean, is a non-self-governing territory of the United States. It is situated on the equator at longitude 176° 31' west, about 1,900 miles (3,060 km) southwest of Honolulu. Its area is 1 square mile (2.6 sq km). Guano deposits were worked by Americans from 1850 to 1890. The island, proclaimed a U.S. territory in 1936, has no inhabitants.

BAKER STREET IRREGULARS, an American literary club devoted to Arthur Conan Doyle's "Sherlock Holmes" stories and the writings about them. The organization was founded in New York City on June 5, 1934, and named for the group of street urchins used by Holmes to obtain information about the London underworld. It holds annual dinner meetings on Holmes' birthday (the first Friday after January 1). The club is affiliated with Sherlock Holmes societies in Britain, Canada, Denmark, and the Netherlands. It publishes the *Baker Street Journal,* a quarterly.

BAKER v. CARR, bā'kər, kär, is a historic American law case that had a profound effect on the apportionment of seats in state legislatures. The suit was brought to force the Tennessee legislature to reapportion itself as required by the state's constitution. The U.S. Supreme Court ruled on the case on March 26, 1962. The court's decision established for the first time that apportionment was subject to federal judicial scrutiny.

Prior to the *Baker* opinion, the interpretation of the 1946 case of *Colegrove* v. *Green* had been that apportionment was a "political thicket" into which the judiciary should not venture. Although changing that interpretation, the ruling in the *Baker* case stated only that federal courts possessed jurisdiction of the subject, that the citizens in Tennessee were entitled to relief, and that the federal district court in the state could settle the challenge to the apportionment statutes of Tennessee.

Using *Baker* as a precedent, other suits were begun, and in June 1964 the Supreme Court ruled on appeals from 15 states. In the major opinion of that group (*Reynolds* v. *Sims*), the court held that both houses of a state legislature must be apportioned substantially on the basis of population. Within two years, every state had taken some type of apportionment action.

The *Baker* decision resulted in a shift in political power within state legislatures from the rural to the urban-suburban areas of the states. The case is regarded as one of the most significant in the nation's history, and Chief Justice Earl Warren called it the most important case decided after he joined the court in 1953.

WILLIAM J.D. BOYD, *National Municipal League*

BAKER'S DOZEN, which means 13 for 12, is a phrase supposedly originating at a time when bakers were heavily fined or placed in a pillory for shortweighing. Consequently, bakers began adding an extra loaf, known as the "inbread" or "vantage loaf," to the dozen in order to protect themselves from penalties. Another explanation is that dealers who bought bread wholesale were privileged by law to receive an extra loaf as a bonus.

The custom survived in Britain until recent times and has been revived in America at Williamsburg, Va., which has been reconstructed along Colonial lines even to this small detail. The bake shop there still sells gingerbread by the "baker's dozen."

BAKERSFIELD, bā′kərz-fēld, is a city in south central California, the seat of Kern County. It is situated on the Kern River in the southern part of the San Joaquin Valley, 112 miles (180.2 km) north of Los Angeles. Bakersfield College, a two-year junior college, is located here.

The city is the center of a rich and varied region, in which oil fields and cultivated lands predominate. Ranches in the area produce cotton, alfalfa, and fruit.

Bakersfield's principal industries include an iron foundry and a steel fabricating plant. The city also manufactures cotton goods, bedding materials, electronic components, and cushions.

The city was founded in 1859 and incorporated in 1873. The discovery of oil in the Kern River fields in 1899 spurred the city's growth. Bakersfield adopted the council-manager plan of government in 1915. Population: 69,515.

BAKHCHISARAI, bäkн-chē-sä-rī′, is a historic town in the USSR, in the Crimean oblast of the Ukraine, 20 miles (32 km) southwest of Simferopol. From 1428 until 1783 it was the capital of the Tatar khans of the Crimea.

In the center of the town is the famous khan's palace, built in 1519. Damaged by fire in 1736, it was restored for Catherine the Great in 1787 by her minister Grigori Aleksandrovich Potemkin. Today the Suvorov museum occupies the khan's palace. There are also numerous tombs of the khans and magnificent fountains and mosques.

About two miles east of the town are the ruins of the Kirkor fortress (Qyrqier), which was once the home of the Crimean followers of the Karaite religion (see KARAISM). Population: (1959) 10,852.

BAKHTIARI, bäkн-tē-ä′rē, a loose confederation of tribes living in Iran. They herd their flocks in mountain country in southwestern Iran, moving great distances twice each year in search of grass for their sheep. The Bakhtiari country lies between the city of Isfahan on the east and the province of Khuzistan on the west. It is roughly coextensive with the oil-rich governorate of Bakhtiari.

The khans of these nomadic people frequently amass enough wealth to send their children to Europe to be educated. Soraya, the second wife of Shah Reza Pahlavi, was the daughter of a Bakhtiari khan.

Probably of Kurdish descent, the Bakhtiari moved to Iran from Syria in the 10th century. They belong to the Shiite branch of Islam and speak a language of Iranian origin. They number about 400,000.

BAKI (1526–1599), bä-kē′, was a Turkish poet. Born *Abdul-Mahmud* in Istanbul, he became a respected member of the legal profession, in which he reached the second-highest rank of judge to the army. Although serious and dignified as a judge, in private life Baki was a gay, witty man of the world who excelled in lyric poetry. He had the immense satisfaction of being acclaimed "King of the Poets" by his peers before his death in 1599.

His poems, characterized by a mastery of form, express the ephemeral nature of life. In them he advocates enjoyment of life's beauty while it lasts. Baki's masterpiece is the elegy to his patron, Suleiman the Magnificent.

J. STEWART-ROBINSON, *University of Michigan*

BAKING. See BREAD; CAKE AND PASTRY.

BAKING POWDER is a chemical preparation used in the place of yeast to give lightness to bread and similar foods. Yeast induces a kind of fermentation, accompanied by the generation of bubbles of the gas known to chemists as carbon dioxide; and it is the development of these bubbles within the dough that causes it to swell (or rise) and become light. When baking powder is used, the same gas is produced, but the gas is generated by direct chemical action instead of by fermentation.

Baking powder is a fine mixture of bicarbonate of soda with an acidic material and starch or flour. The acidic materials are (1) tartaric acid or its acid salts, (2) acid salts of phosphoric acid, (3) compounds of aluminum, or (4) any combination of the foregoing. So long as the powder is kept dry, its acidic and alkaline constituents do not combine with each other; but when moistened, combination takes place and carbon dioxide gas is set free.

Alum, formerly used in the lower-priced powders, has been entirely displaced by anhydrous sodium aluminum sulfate, sometimes erroneously called alum on the label. See also ALUM; CREAM OF TARTAR.

BAKST, bäkst, **Léon Nikolaevich** (1866–1924), Russian stage designer, whose sets and costumes for the Ballets Russes revolutionized stage design. He favored exotic oriental settings on which he could lavish his bold designs and sumptuous color.

Born *Léon Rosenberg*, in Grodno, Russia, he attended the Imperial Academy of Art of St. Petersburg (now Leningrad), and completed his studies in Paris. After returning to Russia in 1900 he painted, designed sets, and collaborated with Sergei Diaghilev (q.v.) on the journal *The World of Art*. In 1906 he went to Paris, and in 1909 he renewed his collaboration with Diaghilev, who was organizing the Ballets Russes there. Diaghilev commissioned Bakst to design sets and costumes for *Cléopâtre* (1909).

The success of his designs led to commissions for ballets that included *Schéhérazade* and *Carnaval* (1910); *Le spectre de la rose* and *Narcisse* (1911); *L'après-midi d'un faune, Thamar, Le dieu bleu,* and *Daphnis et Chloé* (1912); and *Les papillons* (1914). *La belle au bois dormant* (1921, *The Sleeping Beauty*) is generally considered his masterpiece. Bakst died in Paris on Dec. 27, 1924.

Further Reading: Levinson, André, *Léon Bakst, His Life and Art* (New York 1923).

BAKU, bə-kōō′ is the capital of the Azerbaidzhan republic in the USSR. It is a port on the Caspian Sea, on the south shore of the Apsheron Peninsula. Baku is one of the Soviet Union's leading oil-producing centers, with several refineries processing crude oil extracted both on the peninsula around Baku and from offshore deposits. Crude oil and refined products are shipped from Baku by rail, by Caspian Sea tankers, and by pipeline to Batumi on the Black Sea. The city also has machinery plants that produce equipment for the oil industry; chemical plants; and shipbuilding and repair yards.

Baku proper rises in the form of an amphitheater around Baku Bay, an anchorage sheltered against the strong northerly winds typical of this area. (The name "Baku" is believed to be derived from Persian words meaning "city of winds.") The Baku metropolitan area includes most of the Apsheron Peninsula and some of its hinterland, a total of 1,455 square miles (3,768 sq km). A small old city of winding narrow streets includes an 11th century mosque, a 15th century khan's palace, and the 90-foot (27.4-meter) Maiden's Tower, from which a khan's daughter threw herself, according to legend. In the new city are the Communist party and government buildings, and the university, conservatory, academy of sciences, and opera house. Baku's population includes Azerbaidzhanis (35 percent), Russians (35 percent), and Armenians (20 percent).

First mentioned in a 9th century chronicle, Baku flourished in the 15th and 16th centuries as a trading and craft center under the Shirvan shahs, a local independent dynasty, and under Persia's Safavid dynasty. Russia held the city briefly from 1723 to 1735 and took final possession from Persia in 1806. Commercial oil production began in the 1870's, and by the end of the 19th century Baku was one of the leading industrial centers of Russia. After the Bolshevik Revolution of 1917, the city was held by counterrevolutionaries before passing to Soviet control in April 1920. Since World War II its oil industry has been eclipsed by newly developed oilfields elsewhere in the Soviet Union. Population: (1965) of the city, 737,000; of metropolitan Baku, 1,147,000.

THEODORE SHABAD
Author of "Geography of the USSR"

BAKUNIN, bə-kōō′nyin, **Mikhail Aleksandrovich** (1814–1876), Russian anarchist and opponent of Karl Marx. He was born into an aristocratic family, near Tver (now Kalinin), on May 30, 1814. Educated in the St. Petersburg military school, Bakunin entered the army in 1832 but resigned his commission a few years later. From 1841 to 1843 he studied philosophy in Germany. But he finally abandoned formal philosophy and began to develop the idea that society as it was then known must be destroyed and replaced by a new society based on complete individual freedom. During the early 1840's, while active in various socialist and communist associations in western Europe, he met such influential thinkers as Pierre Proudhon and Karl Marx.

In 1847, when Bakunin refused an order by the czar to return to Russia, his property was confiscated. Later in the year, in Paris, he called for the unity of the Poles and Russians to overthrow the Russian government. As a result, the Russians demanded his expulsion from France.

Mikhail Bakunin

(1814–1876)

BETTMANN ARCHIVE

The call for Polish-Russian cooperation reflected Bakunin's early interest in pan-Slavism.

In 1848–1849, Bakunin was involved in revolutionary disturbances in several sections of Europe. Arrested in Dresden in 1849, he was sentenced to death for revolutionary activities but in 1851 was turned over to the Russians, who commuted the sentence to life imprisonment. He escaped from a prison in Siberia in 1861 and made his way to England.

After the Polish revolution failed in 1863, Bakunin concentrated on a program of universal anarchy. While in Italy in 1864, he organized the International Alliance of Social Democrats to be composed of several national units under an international body. About the same time Bakunin began to work with Marx's First International. Bakunin and Marx soon clashed over the methods to be used to achieve a new order, and Bakunin's group was expelled from the First International in 1872 for supporting a secret revolutionary organization within it.

During the next few years, although Bakunin remained relatively inactive, his ideas gained wider acceptance. His followers in Italy and Spain, as well as in Russia, were known as "Bakuninists." On July 1, 1876, Bakunin died in Bern, Switzerland. His book *God and State* was published posthumously.

Bakunin wanted complete freedom for the individual, while believing in the natural solidarity of men. After the 1840's he felt that his aims could be achieved only by the destruction of the social and political order. Although many subscribed to his theories, all of his attempts to effect a revolution failed.

BALAAM, bā′ləm, in the Old Testament, was a Syrian diviner who was hired by Balak, king of Moab, to curse the Israelites but was able only to pronounce a blessing upon them. The story is told in Numbers 22 to 24.

The Israelites, on their journey from Egypt to the land of Canaan, had arrived at the plains of Moab. The Moabites were overcome with fear of them. Their king Balak sent to Balaam, son of Beor, at Pethor on the Euphrates River in northern Syria, to come and curse the Israelites. Yahweh, the Israelite deity, was angry with Balaam for going, and three times the angel of Yahweh stood in the way of the ass on which Balaam was riding. The ass saw the angel, but Balaam did not, and three times he beat the ass. After the third time the ass spoke to Balaam, asking why he was being beaten. The eyes of Balaam were then opened, and he saw the angel. Yahweh permitted him to proceed, on condition that he speak only the word that Yahweh should bid him.

Arriving in Moab, Balaam could not curse the Israelites but could only bless them, because he spoke in Yahweh's name. He delivered four oracles depicting the prosperity and good fortune of Israel.

This story of Balaam is a good illustration of the power the ancient Semites attributed to blessings and curses and of the complete control of the deity over a diviner who spoke his word. It shows the belief of the Israelites that neither foreign king nor foreign diviner could frustrate the will of their God.

In Numbers 22 to 24, Balaam appears in a generally favorable light; but most later Biblical references to him are derogatory. He is said to have led the Israelites into the worship of Baal of Peor (Numbers 25:1–4; 31:16; Revelation 2:14), and he is used as an example of avarice (II Peter 2:15–16; Jude 11).

J. PHILIP HYATT, *Vanderbilt University*

BALABAC, bä-lä′bäk, is an island in the extreme southwestern Philippines. It lies southwest of Palawan Island, in Palawan province, and has an area of 125 square miles (324 sq km). Balabac Strait, 34 miles (65 km) wide, lies to the south of the island. Population: (1960) 4,591.

BALACHONG, bal′ə-chong, is an oriental condiment, composed of small fishes or shrimps, pounded up with salt and spices and then dried. It is also called *balachan.*

BALAKIREV, bə-lä′kyi-ryəf, **Mili Alekseyevich** (1837–1910), Russian composer, who was the founder and moving spirit of the "Mighty Five," a group of composers who attempted to establish a Russian national music. He was born at Nizhni Novgorod (now Gorki), Russia, on Jan. 2, 1837. He first studied music with his mother and later with Aleksandr Oulibichev, under whom he acquired a thorough knowledge of music history and learned orchestration. He made his debut as a pianist in 1856 in St. Petersburg (now Leningrad), playing a movement from his own First Piano Concerto.

In the 1860's he established himself in St. Petersburg as the leader of a group of young composers seeking a way to express musically the spirit of Russia. These composers, later known as the "Mighty Five," were Balakirev, Modest Moussorgsky, César Cui, Nikolai Rimsky-Korsakov, and Aleksandr Borodin. They studied Russian ecclesiastical melodies, folk songs and dances, and the Oriental influences in Russian art. In their compositions, they strove for novelty in harmonics and orchestration. The music of the Russians Mikhail Glinka and Aleksandr Dargomyzhsky influenced their development in one direction, and the music of more cosmopolitan composers, such as Hector Berlioz, Robert Schumann, and Franz Liszt, influenced it in another. See also RUSSIA—4. *Music.*

Balakirev was the soul of the movement and both the teacher and critic of his colleagues. Unfortunately, his own productivity suffered as a result. In addition to his work with the Five, he was a cofounder in 1862 of the Free School of Music in St. Petersburg. From 1869 to 1871

he conducted the concerts of the Imperial Russian Musical Society, and was director of the Imperial chapel from 1883 to 1894. He died at St. Petersburg on May 29, 1910.

Among Balakirev's most important compositions, many of which are based on Russian folk songs, are the symphonic poems *Russia* (1862) and *Tamara* (1882); *Islamey,* an Oriental fantasia for piano written in 1882; and piano arrangements of the works of Berlioz, Glinka, and others. He also wrote two symphonies, and at the time of his death, was at work on his Second Piano Concerto, which was completed by Sergei Liapunov.

BALAKLAVA, Battle of, bäl-ə-klav′ə, an engagement of the Crimean War. It was fought on Oct. 25, 1854, at the Russian village of Balaklava, in the Crimea, by British, French, and Turkish troops against the Russians. The village was the base of the allies' drive against Sevastopol, the chief fortress of the Crimea. The Russian army, commanded by Prince Aleksandr Sergeyevich Menshikov, tried unsuccessfully to break the allied defenses.

The battle is notable for the charge of 673 British light cavalrymen against massed Russian artillery, an assault that was immortalized by Alfred Lord Tennyson in his ballad *The Charge of the Light Brigade.* The charge was made on an ambiguous order from Lord Raglan, the British commander in chief, to Lord Lucan, commanding the cavalry. Misunderstanding the order, Lucan directed Lord Cardigan to lead the Light Brigade against a rank of Russian cannon at the head of a narrow valley. They broke through the line of guns and killed many gunners but were compelled to retreat. Of the 673 cavalrymen, only 195 answered at the next muster.

BALALAIKA, bal-ə-lī′kə, the national musical instrument of Russia, originating from the Tatar *domra.* A fretted instrument similar to a guitar, the balalaika is usually three-stringed, with a triangular sounding board and a finger board. Made in six sizes to form a complete family, the balalaika ranges in size from its counterpart, the traditional guitar, up to huge models resting on the floor. Almond-shaped holes on the surface of the sounding board, tending concentrically to form a star or a circle, resemble somewhat the S's on the sound box of the violin. Two strings are tuned in unison, usually at *e,* and the third string is tuned at *a.*

Balalaika

WALTER A. SCHWARZ

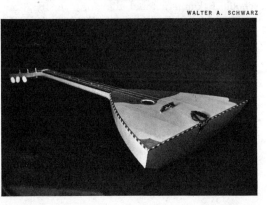

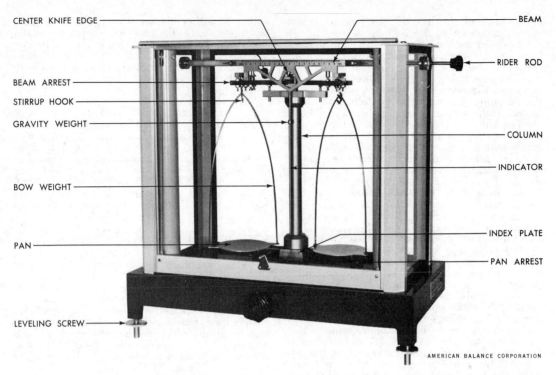

CENTER KNIFE EDGE

BEAM ARREST

STIRRUP HOOK

GRAVITY WEIGHT

BOW WEIGHT

PAN

LEVELING SCREW

BEAM

RIDER ROD

COLUMN

INDICATOR

INDEX PLATE

PAN ARREST

AMERICAN BALANCE CORPORATION

A BALANCE is a high-precision laboratory instrument.

BALANCE, an instrument for determining the weight or the mass of a physical body. (The word *balance* is derived from the Latin *bilanx*, which means "two pans.") Although the use of balances can be traced to ancient Egypt and Rome, precision measurements were attained only after knife-edges were used in constructing a balance. The Scottish chemist Joseph Black (1728–1799) has been given credit for the first use of such an instrument. His original balance is in the Royal Scottish Museum in Edinburgh. The best modern balances have an accuracy of better than one part in 100,000,000 when one-kilogram masses are compared.

Equal-Arm Balance. The type of balance most commonly used for precise scientific measurements is an equal-arm balance that has two pans suspended from a lightweight, rigid beam that is supported on a knife-edge fulcrum made of a hard material, such as boron carbide, steel, or agate. In principle, this type of balance is comparable to a seesaw.

Equal-arm balances used in scientific work are high-precision instruments. Because the balance responds to any external force that acts on the beam or the pans, care is taken to isolate the balance from external disturbances. The modern precision balance is enclosed in a glass case to avoid such disturbing factors as air currents and changes in humidity. The balance is set on a rigid supporting table to minimize the transmission of any vibrations that would upset its performance. The room in which the balance is used is kept under constant atmospheric conditions and is insulated. Sources of magnetic interference are kept away from the vicinity of the balance.

The balance case rests on adjustable legs so that the balance can be leveled. In addition, a spirit level or a plumb bob inside the case

helps in checking whether the balance is leveled.

An upright column is mounted on the floor of the balance case. This column supports the horizontal beam. A small plate of a special hard material is inlaid in the top of the column. A downward pointing knife-edge, which is rigidly attached to the center of the beam, rests on the plate. This central knife-edge serves as a fulcrum or pivot between the rigid upright column and the horizontal beam. The beam can move up and down like a seesaw, but only over small distances. There are also two upward pointing knife-edges that are rigidly attached to the ends of the beam. Each of these knife-edges supports a stirrup. The two pans are suspended from the two stirrups. A pointer is attached to the center of the beam. When the beam moves up and down, the pointer swings over a numbered scale, which is called an index plate.

Turning a control knob on the outside of the balance case raises the beam and the stirrups to an arrested position so that the three knife-edges are not supporting any loads. In this position the knife-edges are not damaged when the balance is being loaded and unloaded. After the balance is loaded, the control knob is turned to lower the beam onto the central knife-edge and lower the stirrups onto the two knife-edges

THE INDEX PLATE OF THE BALANCE

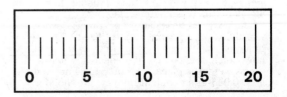

0   5   10   15   20

at the ends of the beam. This position is the operating position of the balance.

A second knob on the outside of the balance case controls the pan arrests, which are arms concealed under each pan. The pan arrests support the pans lightly to prevent them from moving when the beam and stirrups are lowered to the operating position. This control also is used to release the pan arrests just before a weighing.

The balance is ready for use if the pointer rests near the center division of the scale, the pan arrests just touch the pans when the beam is lowered, the mechanism for raising and lowering the beam and stirrups works smoothly, and the spirit level shows that the balance is level.

Operation of the Equal-Arm Balance. The first step in making measurements is to determine the equilibrium point of the balance. This point is determined before each series of weighings because the equilibrium point can be altered easily by factors such as changes in temperature and traces of dust. The equilibrium point is first found with the pans empty and the beam moving gently.

The equilibrium point is determined by calculating the arithmetic mean of the swings of the pointer. The swings of the pointer to the left and right are noted. For example, suppose that the swings to the right are 16.5 and 15.5 units from the zero mark, and the swings to the left are 3.0, 4.0, and 5.0 units from the zero mark. Then the average of the left swings is 4, and the average of the right swings is 16. In this case, the arithmetic mean is 10, and this point on the scale is the equilibrium point.

The material to be weighed is then placed on one pan, and weights are placed on the other pan until the same equilibrium point is obtained. The standard weights are handled with a forceps to keep them clean from extra material, such as grease from the fingertips. The first weight is chosen as the closest one for balancing the material to be weighed. This choice is tested by lowering the beam just long enough to determine in which direction the pointer first swings. If the weight is too heavy, the next lighter weight is used. If the weight is too light, additional weights are used. In scientific work, a set of weights usually includes weights of 1, 2, 3, 5, 10, 20, 30, 50, and 100 grams, as well as some fractional gram weights. The process of adding or subtracting weights and testing is repeated until the equilibrium point is obtained. The sum of the weights (standard masses) used to obtain equilibrium is equal to the unknown mass of the material.

Standard for Weights. Errors can be introduced by using weights that are not properly standardized. Weights that are made commercially are usually calibrated against the standard set by the International Bureau of Weights and Measures, which is located near Paris. The fundamental standard is a cylindrical object that has a mass defined as one kilogram. The cylinder is made of an alloy of platinum and iridium and is kept near Paris. Two accurate copies of this standard are kept in a vault at the National Bureau of Standards in Washington, D.C.

Accuracy in Weighing. For precise work the sensitivity of the balance is utilized. The sensitivity of the balance is expressed in terms of how much the pointer is deflected when a tiny excess weight is placed on one pan. For example, if a 0.005-gram weight moves the pointer 1.1

scale units, then the sensitivity is 0.0045 gram per scale unit. Because the sensitivity varies slightly with different loads, it should be determined under several different load conditions. The sensitivity is used in establishing the fourth decimal place of the value for the mass of the object.

For additional accuracy the weights and the object can be transposed from pan to pan to correct for any slight difference in the length of the balance arms. The object is first placed in the left pan, and the weights are placed on the right pan. After balancing, the values of the weights are added to a total, m_1. Then the object and the weights are interchanged and balanced again. The values of the weights are added to a total, m_2. The true mass, m, is found from the equation $m = \sqrt{m_1 m_2}$.

Types of Equal-Arm Balances. There are six types of equal-arm balances: rider, keyboard, chain, damped, constant load, and projection. The rider, keyboard, and chain types of balances eliminate the necessity for handling small pan weights. The damped, constant-load, and projection types provide other special advantages.

Physical Principles for Balances. All equal-arm balances measure mass rather than weight. The amount of material is the mass of an object, and it does not vary whether the object is deep in a mine, high on a mountain, on the moon, or far out in space. The weight of an object is the force of attraction between the object and the earth. The weight of an object varies with altitude and latitude.

At any specific location the mass and weight of an object are proportional. The relationship between the mass and weight of the object is given by the equation $w = mg$, where w is the local weight of the object, m is the mass of object, and g is the acceleration of the object due to gravity at that specific location.

All equal-arm balances are based on the principle of the lever, which has been known since antiquity. In equilibrium, the force on the unknown mass times its perpendicular distance to the fulcrum is equal to the force on the standard weights times their perpendicular distance to the fulcrum.

The operation of other kinds of balances depends on other principles. The operation of the spring balance is based on Hooke's law, which states that the stress in the spring is proportional to the strain. Spring balances were in use long before Robert Hooke published his law late in the 17th century. In the torsion balance, the amount of twisting of a wire or fiber is the principle on which measurements are based. Some microbalances, which are used to weigh fractional gram values, are torsion balances. The ultramicrobalance is used for weighing a few micrograms of a material. Quartz-fiber torsion ultramicrobalances were perfected early in the 20th century.

One early form of the balance had only one pan. This type of balance developed into the steelyard, which still is in use. See also WEIGHING MACHINES.

MORRIS GORAN, *Roosevelt University*

Further Reading: Ayres, Gilbert H., *Quantitative Chemical Analysis* (New York 1958); MacNevin, William M., *The Analytical Balance, Its Care and Use* (Sandusky, Ohio, 1951); Mellon, Melvin G., *Quantitative Analysis* (New York 1958); Pierce, W.C., Haenisch, E.L., and Sawyer, D.T., *Quantitative Analysis* (New York 1958).

BALANCE OF PAYMENTS,

the relationship between a nation's expenditures abroad and its income from other nations. What makes a balance of payments significant is that a nation, like an individual, must balance its receipts and expenditures, because it cannot continue indefinitely to lose gold or borrow from other countries.

The basic components of an international balance of payments—as exemplified by the U.S. balance of payments at the start of the 1960's—consist of the following items:

U.S. RECEIPTS FROM ABROAD, 1960
(in billions of dollars)

Export of goods	$19.4
Export of services	7.7
Repayment of U.S. government loans to other nations	0.6
Foreign investments in the U.S.	0.3
Total receipts	28.0

U.S. EXPENDITURES ABROAD, 1960

Import of goods	14.7
Import of services	6.4
Military expenditures	3.0
Foreign aid	3.3
Private investment	3.4
Transactions unaccounted for	1.0
Total expenditures	31.8

The $3.8 billion excess of expenditures over receipts (the deficit in the U.S. balance of payments) was covered by gold shipments abroad, amounting to $1.7 billion, and by an increase of $2.1 billion in U.S. debts to foreigners.

If a nation has a payments deficit, it must either increase its foreign earnings, by making its products more attractive, or it must restrict its people's spending abroad.

Increasing exports and decreasing imports can be achieved by these steps:

(1) Restricting the domestic economy, so that prices of goods produced fall and become cheaper abroad. At the same time, the people at home earn less and can buy less abroad.

(2) Devaluing the currency relative to other currencies, so that foreigners find the products of the exporting country cheaper in terms of their own money and thus more attractive. At the same time people in the country that has devalued its currency find imports more expensive and thus less attractive.

(3) Placing direct controls on spending for imports, or stimulating exports, or both. Exports may be stimulated by subsidies, tax rebates, and other direct incentives.

All three steps hurt the domestic economy, for they reduce the ability of the people to buy foreign goods and thus lessen the people's freedom of choice to buy from wherever they desire. But a nation living beyond its means must accept the impact of some restraint mechanism to bring its payments position back into balance.

The U.S. balance of payments is a special case. The United States in the 1960's was not spending more on foreign goods and services than it was earning abroad. Rather, its deficits arose from lending and investing abroad, plus foreign aid and military expenditures, in excess of what it earned from its balance of trade surplus (its excess of exports over imports). Thus the American payments problem resulted from the country's large amount of loans and aid abroad, rather than from living beyond its means. This problem was expected slowly to solve itself as U.S. investments abroad began to bring in more interest and dividend income.

PAUL S. NADLER, *New York University*

BALANCE OF POWER

in international relations is a condition of equilibrium among competing states designed to preserve peace by ensuring that no nation or bloc of nations achieves a dominant position over another. Such a balance is attained and maintained either by individual states increasing their own power or by states with mutual interests concluding a defensive alliance superior in power to that posed by the state or alliance commonly viewed as a threat.

The assumption underlying the concept of balance of power is that powerful states tend to expand until they are met by equal or superior power, and that in the absence of a legal system or a set of reciprocal restraints, competition among states can only be controlled by an equilibrium mechanism. In a world of many independent states, balance of power is an important regulatory principle. The term is used not only to describe the process by which power is checked, but also as a guide to foreign policy concerned with the maintenance of order.

The concept of balance of power is an ancient one. Kautilya, a minister of the ancient Indian Mauryan kingdom, is credited with having analyzed the workings of a balance of power system, the *mandala,* in the 4th century B.C. The Greek city-states also practiced the balancing of power. The term itself came into general use in Europe in the 16th century. Because of the near universality of its application, balance of power has been called a fundamental law of politics.

Maintaining the Balance. The fundamental problem of the balance of power principle lies in its inherent uncertainty. There is no precise way to determine a potential rival's power and intentions or to calculate the amount of power necessary to deter it. The competing sides are likely to strive for supremacy, rather than equality, as a precaution against defeat, thereby provoking ever higher levels of preparation for war. While a balance of power may curb major acts of aggression, it does not prevent violence and may even increase tensions.

At least three general strategies are commonly employed to maintain the balance: (1) deterrence based on a rival's vulnerability; (2) hegemony based on greater mobilization power; or (3) development of a coalition of states that possess superiority in the contested areas.

Deterrence is achieved when a nation convinces a potential aggressor that any attack on its territory would be prohibitively expensive, even though the aggression ultimately might be successful in military terms. Atomic weapons, for example, might deter an aggressor from conquering territory because the conquest might "cost" the aggressor state its major cities. Similarly, a small air force equipped with bombers might deter a larger state from invasion if the potential aggressor had vital centers vulnerable to attack.

A second possible strategy for maintaining a balance of power is based on a state of superior power committing its strength to the balance. Britain played the role of a superior power constantly committed to a European balance of power throughout much of the 19th century. Chancellor Otto von Bismarck's diplomacy in the 1870's and 1880's also was based on the conception of using superior power to consolidate the German states, without violating the equilibrium of the European community. In the same tradition, United States foreign policy since

World War II has been to "contain" Communist expansionism by means of a demonstrable military supremacy.

A third classic strategy in the maintenance of a balance of power is an alliance of states which, together, are superior to a potential aggressor, and in which member states pledge mutual defense. Such collective security is difficult to maintain because of its plural character and therefore is not always an effective instrument to thwart aggression. However, if the alliance is comprised of states roughly equal in power, it offers the flexibility and responsiveness necessary for mutual independence as well as mutual security against a potential enemy.

The Search for Political Order. The balancing of power attained its most elaborate development in Europe, beginning with the Italian city-state practice of the 16th century. It lasted until the "balance of terror" emerged from nuclear weapons technology in the mid-20th century.

From 1500 to the mid-1600's Italian practice of balancing for principle as well as expediency was adopted by major leaders in western Europe. After the Treaty of Westphalia (1648), there was a general recognition of the value of a balance of power in European international politics. While there were wars and political flux from the mid-17th century to the end of the 18th century, the system of international order through blocking coalitions survived. The Napoleonic revolution ended the 18th century system, but the Congress of Vienna (1815) and the subsequent concordance among the leading powers known as the Concert of Europe reestablished and strengthened a balancing system that lasted for almost a century, accompanied by a spirit of rationalism and peace. By the mid-1800's, the European system was no longer defined by a formal balance of power, but both Britain and Germany found it in their interest to cooperate in maintaining the balance. When Bismarck's diplomacy was overturned by Emperor William II in the 1890's, Britain and Germany became rivals, and the system's principal supports fell during the two world wars.

Challenges to the Balance. In Europe the balance of power has faced three major challenges: (1) uneasy relationships between great and small powers; (2) growth of extremely powerful states; and (3) ideological-nationalist expansion.

Historically, the balance of power mechanism ill-served small, defenseless states, the case of Poland's arbitrary partition by its powerful neighbors in 1772 being the most obvious. The Low Countries had a special relationship with Britain, and Switzerland, which was neutralized in 1815, was inaccessible to conquerors. Otherwise, lesser powers experienced little benefit from the balancing of power. In the periods after World War I and World War II, the weak states of eastern Europe encountered severe difficulties in preserving economic and political independence, and most of them were unable to maintain complete independence. In the contemporary world of more than 120 states, many of them exceedingly small, this weakness of the balance of power system of international order is greatly magnified.

The second major problem of the European balance of power was the differential effect of technological development. The location of iron and coal reserves in Germany and not in Italy made a major difference in power relationships. Slow industrialization weakened the position of France as compared with Britain and Germany. The Congress of Vienna and the Concert of Europe had differentiated between great and small powers, but the power differentials during the first half of the 19th century were not so great as they became about 1900. This posed a severe problem because much greater weights had to be balanced when the offensive power of attacking armies was increasing. After World War II, the United States and the Soviet Union confronted each other as superpowers with a near monopoly of force. Their military might was so formidable that the precarious equilibrium between them was viewed as a balance of terror.

A third major challenge to the balance of power in the history of Europe was the threat of ideology, both nationalist and Communist. Napoleon's vision of a French Europe and the Russian ambition of establishing Moscow as a second Rome and later as the capital of a socialist commonwealth upset European equilibrium. Ideology is not compatible with the flexibility necessary to support ever-changing alliances. Moreover, ideology and expansionism are threats to an international equilibrium based on national independence. The containment of Napoleon, the radical spirit of 1848, and the new nationalism before World War I all proved to be heavy burdens for a world primarily organized on the basis of the balance of power.

Balance of Terror and New Balance of Power. The development of nuclear weapons and nearly instantaneous delivery systems wrought a fundamental change in world politics. While nuclear weapons can inflict high levels of destruction, a nuclear war seems almost purposeless. The traditional aim of war was to bend an opponent into a new course of action or new relationship with the victor, and the balance of power required a minimum toleration of the right of different states to exist and compete in international politics. The power of nuclear arms makes possible the obliteration of rival states, but that is seldom the central purpose of war, and it is irrelevant to the balance of power. Two nuclear powers locked in war might cancel one another out, or one might win a Pyrrhic victory.

Winston Churchill suggested that the very nature of atomic weapons had produced a "balance of terror," a condition in which neither superpower dared convert its potential force into applied violence. Others, too, began to think of power as a deterrent to war; paradoxically, the instrument of immense destruction might hold the key to peace through a built-in inhibitive factor.

For the first ten years after World War II, during the tense stalemate of the cold war, it appeared that the structure of the world had changed radically—that the superpowers had divided up the world as Rome and Carthage had done in ancient times, and that the 19th century European balance of power was an anachronism. However, 15 years after World War II the bipolar world was in flux. In the 1950's the Soviet satellites and other Communist nations asserted their own interests, violently in the case of Hungary, Poland, and East Germany, and diplomatically in the case of Yugoslavia, Albania, and China. By 1960 the new nations of Africa and Asia were using the United Nations as a sounding board for a third bloc that called itself neutralist, and western Europe, having rebuilt its economy, was embarked on a plan of economic cooperation in which the United States was an outside power. Twenty years after World War II the process of national reassertion led to French-American rivalry and diminished the effectiveness of the North Atlantic Treaty Organization (NATO), which had supported joint military preparedness against Soviet expansion. Meanwhile, Chinese-Russian rivalry had become more strident. Thus, the middle-sized powers of the world enjoyed considerable latitude in foreign policy.

Throughout the world the superpowers have been stalemated in their ability to transform their nuclear force into effective international power. Historic rivalries have led to regional balances of power where the United States and the Soviet Union are only partners in rather than directors of foreign policy. The great powers continue to have influence, but primarily through wielding traditional instruments, such as aid and trade, rather than the threat of nuclear weapons.

The new structure of the international community has established a new kind of international equilibrium. The continuing threat of nuclear war increases the sensitivity of all governments to the dangers of violence in interstate relations. Although violence remains a fact of international life, it tends to take the form of indirect aggression, subversion, or guerrilla warfare. Like the 18th century, the mid-20th century is marked by deliberately limited conflict on the contested fringes of major powers. Regional alliances and joint forces are part of a revitalized balancing mechanism, which is possible because war between the nuclear powers would be without political purpose and because these great powers balance one another at a different level of world political competition.

WAYNE WILCOX, *Columbia University*

Bibliography

Claude, Inis L., Jr., *Power and International Relations* (New York 1962).
Dehio, Ludwig, *Precarious Balance: Four Centuries of the European Power Struggle* (New York 1962).
Gareau, Frederick H., ed., *Balance of Power and Nuclear Deterrence* (Boston 1962).
Gulick, Edward V., *Europe's Classical Balance of Power* (Ithaca, N.Y., 1955).
Morgenthau, Hans J., *Politics Among Nations*, 3d rev. ed. (New York 1960).
Seabury, Paul, ed., *Balance of Power* (San Francisco 1965).
Wright, Quincy, *A Study of War*, 2d ed. (Chicago 1965).

BALANCE OF TRADE. The annual statement of a nation's total international trading and financial transactions is known as its *balance of payments*. Among the most important components of this balance of payments are the exports and imports of goods and services. The difference between total exports and total imports in a given year is the nation's *balance of trade*. A nation may show either a positive or a negative net balance, depending on whether exports have exceeded imports during the year or imports have exceeded exports.

A great deal of economic theory and much economic policy have been based on the concept of the balance of trade. In the 17th and 18th centuries the mercantilist doctrine held that an export balance ought to be the goal of international trade. This position was held because international obligations then had to be paid in gold, silver, or some other universally accepted form of treasure. Because the sovereign and nation were considered to be identical, the increase of the wealth of the sovereign through an inflow of gold was thought to enrich the nation as well.

This philosophy is the source of the designation of an export balance as a "favorable" balance of trade.

The mercantilist position was vigorously attacked by Adam Smith in his *Wealth of Nations* (1776). In this important work Smith pointed out that a nation's wealth consists of the goods available for consumption and use by its residents, and not of treasure, which is itself only the means to obtain wealth. The classical school of economic thought which followed Smith argued that trade must result in a mutual advantage for both parties to the transaction, and that international trade based on specialization by each nation in the products that it could produce most efficiently would result in the greatest economic gain to all nations. This doctrine of comparative advantage led to the policy of international free trade which characterized classical and neoclassical economics.

The rejection of the mercantilist position has come to be accepted in orthodox economics, but the terms "favorable" and "unfavorable" balance of trade have persisted. The more generally accepted terms today for export and import balances are respectively "active" and "passive" balances.

A form of neomercantilism came into being in the early 1930's. This view conceded the validity of the orthodox position over the long run, but argued that the short-run problem of unemployment could be partially solved by an excess of exports over imports. The idea of "exporting unemployment" was one of the factors which led to the fierce international competition for markets that characterized the 1930's. This idea grew out of the fact that producing for export absorbs unemployed labor, while the goods produced are not placed on the domestic market to depress prices and profits still further.

That export balances are not necessarily favorable to the nation involved is witnessed by the experience of Ireland and India. Both nations exported large amounts of goods, the proceeds of which went to absentee landlords in England. England, on the other hand, was long able to maintain its high standard of living through an import surplus financed by international investment income. The loss of a major part of England's international investments as a result of World War II was in large measure responsible for that nation's economic plight after 1945.

The United States showed a passive balance of trade throughout most of its early history. There has been an export balance in every year since 1894. The passive balance of trade during the early period reflected the need of a new and growing nation for investment goods. After 1865 the export balance represented largely the repayment of international debt incurred during the earlier expansion. From 1918 on, the United States has been a creditor nation, but the active balance has persisted. In 1920, the United States had an active balance of trade of nearly $3 billion; after World War II, it was double that amount in some years.

U.S. BALANCE OF TRADE
(billions of dollars)

Year	Exports	Imports	Balance
1945	12.473	5.245	+7.228
1955	14.280	11.527	+2.753
1965	26.276	21.488	+4.788

Source: U.S. Department of Commerce

WILLIAM N. KINNARD, JR.
University of Connecticut

BALANCHINE, bal-ən-chēn', **George** (1904–   ), American choreographer, who became the dominant figure in American ballet in the 20th century and the leading choreographer of "objectified ballet," in which story is less important than patterns of movement.

Balanchine was born *Georgi M. Balanchivadze* in St. Petersburg (now Leningrad), Russia, on Jan. 9, 1904. In 1914 he entered the St. Petersburg Imperial Ballet School, from which he was graduated in 1921. He was touring Europe in 1924–1925 with a group of Soviet dancers when they were ordered back to the USSR. They refused to return, going instead to Paris. There, impresario Sergei Diaghilev of the Ballets Russes took Balanchivadze into his company as a dancer-choreographer and changed his name to Balanchine. He remained with the Ballets Russes until 1929, when the company broke up following Diaghilev's death.

Balanchine choreographed for several European companies, then went to the United States in 1933, establishing the School of American Ballet in 1934. In 1946, after staging dances for opera, films, and Broadway musicals, he became artistic director of the Ballet Society, which in 1948 became the New York City Ballet. As its artistic director and choreographer, he made the organization the leading American ballet company. He also continued to direct the School of American Ballet, thus providing the New York City Ballet and other groups with well-disciplined American-trained dancers. Typical Balanchine ballets are *Apollo* (1928), *Agon* (1957), *Electronics* (1961) and *Don Quixote* (1965).

Balanchine was married five times; each of his wives was a world-famous ballerina. He became a United States citizen in 1940.

Further Reading: Taper, Bernard, *Balanchine* (New York 1963).

BALANOGLOSSUS, bal-ə-nō-glös'əs, is a genus of wormlike marine animals found on the bottom of all seas except the Antarctic. Its long, slender cylindrical body, from 1 inch to over 2 yards (2.54 cm–2 meters) long according to species, is soft and fleshy and is divided into three regions—the proboscis, the collar, and the trunk. Each of the regions has a coelom (epithelium-lined body cavity). The proboscis tapers to a blunt point forward and swells out toward the base where it connects with the collar by a narrow neck. The collar is a cylinder about as long as it is wide and larger in diameter than either the proboscis or the trunk. The trunk is a long cylinder tapering from behind the collar to a slender "tail."

The mouth lies within the collar at the base of the proboscis. There is a double row of gill slits on the anterior portion of the dorsal surface of the trunk. A pair of genital ridges, sometimes forming winglike folds, extends along the trunk for a considerable distance behind the collar. Two rows of prominences, containing intestinal pouches, are found near the middle of the trunk.

As the annimal burrows, large quantities of sand and mud pass through the permanently open mouth. Small organisms and other organic matter are digested, and the sand is eliminated through the anus.

The sexes are separate, and, except in a single species, there is sexual reproduction, including a tornaria larva. The exception, *B. proliferans*, has an asexual phase with undeveloped

BALANOGLOSSUS, a wormlike marine animal, has characteristics similar to both vertebrates and echinoderms.

gonads. This phase with reproduction by transverse fission appears to alternate with the normal sexual phase. Also, there may be regeneration at the trunk, proboscis, and collar.

The genus *Balanoglossus* belongs to the class Enteropneusta (which contains the acorn or tongue worms) in the subphylum Hemichordata. The hemichordates are important phylogenetically because, although they are organized simply, they seem to be related to both the chordates and the echinoderms. They often are treated as chordates.

JOHN C. ARMSTRONG
The American Museum of Natural History

BALARD, bà-làr', **Antoine Jérôme** (1802–1876), French chemist. He was born in Montpellier, France, on Sept. 30, 1802. He was professor of chemistry, first at Montpellier and later at the Collège de France in Paris. He is most noteworthy for his discovery of bromine in 1826. He also discovered a process for extracting sulfate of sodium directly from seawater. Balard died in Paris on March 30, 1876.

BALATON, Lake, bo'lo-tōn, in western Hungary, 55 miles southwest of Budapest. It is called *Plattensee* in German. The largest lake in central Europe, Balaton has many resorts on its shores. The lake is constantly in a state of motion, sufficient to cause waves. Its waters are transparent and abound with fine fish, notably the *fogas*, a variety of perch that frequently weighs as much as 20 pounds. It has a delicious snow-white flesh.

The northern bank of Lake Balaton is bounded by vine-clad hills, and the southern bank is low. The hills of the Bakony Forest, in the background, drop abruptly to the lake.

The lake is 48 miles (77 km) long and has an average width of 8 miles (13 km). Its area is about 266 square miles (688 sq km), including the marshy shores. The average depth of the lake is approximately 10 feet (3 meters), although a depth of over 100 feet (30.5 meters) is found at one point.

It receives the waters of more than 30 small streams and mineral springs and is also fed by the Zala River, which enters the lake from the west. It discharges through the Kapos River and the Sió, which empties into the Sárviz, an affluent of the Danube.

BALBI, bäl′bē, **Gasparo,** Venetian merchant and traveler who lived in the 16th century. From 1579 to 1588 he traveled in Asia, seeking to discover the places of production and marketing of precious stones. His travels took him first to Aleppo, Syria, and from there down the Euphrates and Tigris rivers to the Persian Gulf; after reaching the Malabar Coast of India, he sailed finally for Pegu, in Burma, where he remained for two years.

Viaggio dell'Indie Orientali, published in 1590 after he returned to Venice, is an account of his explorations. He is on the whole very reliable in his accounts of what came under his own observation; but there was no limit to his credulity at secondhand.

BALBI, bäl-bē, is an active volcano in the Solomon Islands, in the South Pacific Ocean. It is situated on the northwestern part of Bougainville Island, in the Emperor Range. The volcano, 10,171 feet (3,100 meters) high, is the highest point on the island.

BALBO, bäl′bō, **Cesare, Count di Vinadio** (1789–1853), Italian statesman and author. He was born in the Piedmont city of Turin on Nov. 29, 1789. Balbo served in various capacities under Napoleon, whose government held Piedmont from 1797 to 1814. After the downfall of Napoleon and the reconstitution in 1815 of the kingdom of Sardinia (which included Sardinia, Piedmont, Savoy, Nice, and Liguria), he was secretary to the Sardinian ambassador in London until the Sardinian revolution began in 1821.

Because of his association with some of the leaders of the revolution, and also because of his attempts to persuade the regent of Sardinia, Charles Albert, to form a constitutional movement, Balbo fell into disfavor with the new Sardinian king, Charles Felix, who disavowed the regency in 1821.

For many years he devoted himself to literary pursuits. A biography of Dante appeared in 1839. His most famous book, *Speranze d'Italia* ("Hope of Italy"), was published in 1844, firmly establishing his reputation. In it he advocated the liberation of Italy, but by more moderate measures than those put forth by the revolutionary Mazzini. Balbo urged cooperation with the Italian princes and toleration of Austrian expansion in the Balkans to compensate that nation for its losses in Italy. The book aided the creation of a moderate nationalist party.

When Charles Albert, king of Sardinia since 1831, granted a constitution in 1848, Balbo became the first premier of a constitutional Sardinia. He resigned shortly afterwards, however, because of his alarm over agitation throughout Italy for further democratic reform. He died at Turin on June 3, 1853.

BALBO, bäl′bō, **Italo** (1896–1940), Italian aviator and politician. He was born near Ferrara, Italy, on June 6, 1896. During World War I he was an officer in the Alpine corps and, after the war, joined the Fascist movement. In 1922 he was a leader of one of the four Fascist columns whose march on Rome brought Benito Mussolini to power. He was appointed commander of the national militia in 1923.

As Italy's first minister of aviation (1929–1933), Balbo built up the Italian air force. He commanded transatlantic formation flights to Brazil in 1929 and to the United States in 1933, remarkable accomplishments for the time. Although he had begun to fall out of favor with Mussolini, Balbo was promoted to air marshal in 1933 and, in the same year, was made governor of Libya. It was there, at Tobruk on June 28, 1940, that he was killed in a plane crash during a British bombardment.

BALBOA, bal-bō′ə, **Vasco Núñez de** (1475–1519), Spanish explorer in America, who discovered the Pacific Ocean. He was born in Jerez de los Caballeros, Spain. At the age of 25 he went to America, joining the expedition of Rodrigo de Bastidas, with whom he explored part of the southwestern coast of the Caribbean Sea.

Settling in Hispaniola (Haiti), Balboa became a planter at Salvatierra but with such indifferent success that when he resolved to attach himself to Alonso de Ojeda's new colony on the mainland of South America, he found difficulty in escaping from his creditors. To elude their vigilance, he hid in a large cask, and was carried from his plantation to the landing and put on board one of Ojeda's vessels as a part of the cargo. It is probable that when he emerged from his place of concealment he would have been handed over to the authorities on shore if the expedition had not stood in need of every available fighting man.

Admitted to membership in Ojeda's colony as a common soldier, Balboa showed his talent for leadership when the undertaking seemed on the point of failure. He suggested transferring the colony to Darien (Panama) in 1510, describing the more favorable conditions there, as he had seen them on his previous voyage. His advice was taken, and the name Antigua (Santa María la Antigua del Darién) was given to the new settlement.

In 1513, Balboa received a letter from a commissioner whom he had sent to Spain, informing him that he might expect to be summoned to court to answer grave charges. These had been brought against him by the colony's earlier governor, whom Balboa had arrested and dispatched to Spain. Resolving to win back the royal favor by some striking service, he selected 190 men, the best of his soldiers, and with these and 1,000 native warriors and carriers, and a pack of bloodhounds, sailed from Antigua on Sept. 1, 1513. He followed the Darien coast westward until he reached a point opposite the Gulf of San Miguel, which extends far into the south coast from the Pacific, narrowing the isthmus to a width of about 50 miles. Information had been obtained from the Indians about the southern coast, the ocean that lay beyond, and the superior civilization of the Incas of Peru, whose country was to be reached by way of this ocean.

The march inland began September 6. Reaching an elevated plateau on the 24th, the Spaniards repulsed an attack by 1,000 Indians and found supplies in the village of Quarequá. The following day, Sept. 25, 1513, Balboa gained the summit of a mountain from which the waters of Mar del Sur (South Sea) were visible. The name "Pacific" was not applied to this ocean until seven years later, when it was bestowed by Magellan. On September 29, Balboa took formal possession of the "South Sea" by marching into the water and, in the names of the king and queen of Castile, claiming "these seas and lands."

Meanwhile, the warning that Balboa received from the Spanish court was justified in the event. He had already been superseded by Pedro Arias Dávila (or Arias de Ávila, usually called Pedrarias). Balboa's reward for his discovery was an empty title of Adelantado del Mar del Sur and the appointment as governor of Panama, Coyba, and the lands of the South Sea (the Pacific) which he had discovered; while on shore he was made the subordinate of Pedrarias, his rival and bitter enemy. Balboa led many successful expeditions, but these only aroused the jealousy and hatred of Pedrarias. The Spanish government tried in vain to mediate between them, and Balboa's marriage with the daughter of Pedrarias was arranged.

But a new dispute arose between the rivals. Balboa was induced to deliver himself up, was accused of rebellion, and, on the trumped-up evidence of a false friend, was convicted. In January 1519 he was beheaded in Acla, on the north coast of the isthmus.

Further Reading: Anderson, Charles L.G., *Life and Letters of Vasco Núñez de Balboa* (New York 1941).

BALBOA, bal-bō′ə, a town in the Panama Canal Zone, is at the Pacific Ocean end of the Panama Canal. It is the capital of Balboa district. The town's port, which is called La Boca, is a principal port of entry for the republic of Panama, although it is not under Panama's jurisdiction. Balboa is a terminus of the Panama Railway, which crosses the Isthmus of Panama to Colón. Balboa Heights, the administrative center of the Canal Zone, adjoins Balboa. Population: (1970 census, prelim.): 2,568.

BALBOA is the chief city of the Canal Zone. The U.S. Administration Building is shown in the center.

A. DEVANEY, INC.

BALBRIGGAN, bal-brig′ən, is a town in Ireland in Dublin County, 20 miles northeast of Dublin. It is an Irish Sea fishing port, a summer resort, and a textile manufacturing center. Balbriggan is noted for a knitted cotton fabric that is manufactured there and bears the town's name. Population: (1961) 2,943.

BALBUS, bal′bəs, **Lucius Cornelius,** Roman politician of the 1st century B.C. A native of Gades (Cádiz), Spain, he was made a Roman citizen by Pompey, under whom he fought in Spain against Quintus Sertorius. He went to Rome (72 B.C.) and became a friend of Julius Caesar, serving with him in Spain (61 B.C.) and Gaul (58 B.C.). Tried (56 B.C.) for improperly obtaining Roman citizenship, Balbus was acquitted through the defense put forward by Cicero, whose oration, *Pro Balbo*, was notable. Balbus sided with Caesar against Pompey and, after Caesar's death, with Octavian (later Emperor Augustus), who made Balbus Rome's first foreign-born consul.

He was sometimes surnamed *Maior,* distinguishing him from his nephew, *Lucius Cornelius Balbus* (*Minor*), who was awarded the honor of a triumph for a victory gained in Africa.

BALCH, bôlch, **Emily Greene** (1867–1961), American pacifist leader, who shared the Nobel peace prize in 1946 (with John R. Mott) for her work as a leader of world peace movements.

Emily Balch was born in Jamaica Plain, Mass., on Jan. 8, 1867. Following her graduation from Bryn Mawr College in 1889, she helped to found the Denison House Settlement in Boston and the Women's Trade Union League. She helped draft the first minimum wage bill put before a state legislature. In 1896 she joined the faculty of Wellesley College, where she taught economics and political science. During World War I she and Jane Addams formed a small group of pacifists that later became the Women's International League for Peace and Freedom. When she outspokenly opposed the entry of the United States into the war, Wellesley dismissed her as a professor. Miss Balch wrote extensively about the peace movement, in *Women at The Hague* (1915) and other books, and she held important posts in several pacifist organizations. She died in Cambridge, Mass., on Jan. 9, 1961.

BALCH SPRINGS, bôlch, is a city in northern Texas, in Dallas County, 10 miles (16 km) east of Dallas, of which it is a residential suburb. Aluminum castings are manufactured, and there is some cotton ginning. The city is a marketing center for the produce of truck farms to the east. It was incorporated in 1953. Government is by mayor and council. Population: 10,464.

BALCHEN, bal′kən, **Bernt** (1899–1973), Norwegian-American aviator, who piloted the first flight over the South Pole on Nov. 29, 1929. He was born on Oct. 23, 1899, at Tveit, Norway, and graduated from the Royal Aviation School in 1921. In 1925 he flew to the rescue of explorers Roald Amundsen and Lincoln Ellsworth, who had been forced down on Spitsbergen, Norway.

Balchen piloted Comdr. Richard E. Byrd's flight across the Atlantic in 1927 and was chief pilot for the Antarctic expeditions of Byrd in 1928–1930 and of Ellsworth in 1933–1935. Becoming a United States citizen in 1931, he was made a captain in the U.S. Air Force in 1941. In World War II he served in Greenland and in the Allied Transport Command, heading a secret air ferry supply service to the Norwegian and Danish underground fighters. Promoted colonel in 1946, he was assigned to USAF headquarters in 1951. He returned to civilian life in 1956, and died in Mount Kisco, N.Y., on Oct. 17, 1973.

BALCONES ESCARPMENT, bal-kō′nis is-kärp′-mənt, a long line of cliffs in south central Texas, forming a distinct boundary between the Edwards Plateau (a southeastern extension of the Great Plains) and the Gulf Coastal Plain. The escarpment, formed by faulting and erosion, extends from the Rio Grande near Del Rio eastward to the vicinity of San Antonio, then northeastward to the Colorado River near Austin and northward toward the Red River. From its highest section, about 1,000 feet (305 meters) in the Del Rio area, it slopes gradually to about 300 feet (90 meters) near Austin.

Viewed from the coastal plain, the escarpment appears as a range of rounded, wooded hills, facing south along the east-west extension and east along the remainder of its course. At places, the hills are said to have the appearance of balconies. The Spanish *balcones* may have come from this resemblance, although the exact origin of the name is uncertain. At the 31st parallel, north of Austin, the surface line of hills disappears and the subterranean fault line breaks into several roughly parallel lines.

BALCONY, The, bal′kə-nē, one of the most important plays of the "theater of the absurd" movement. It was written by the French playwright Jean Genet in 1959. It enjoyed a long and financially successful run in New York City, beginning early in 1960. A motion picture version of the play was released in 1963.

The play is set in a brothel that might be in any country at any period. At the brothel, customers play out their fantasies of power, assuming the costumes and roles of bishop, judge, or general. When the revolution raging outside the brothel kills the city's real authorities, their symbolic counterparts in the brothel continue their roles in a government that is no more corrupt or absurd than the government it replaces.

BALD CYPRESS. See CYPRESS.

BALD EAGLE. See EAGLE.

BALDACHIN, bôld′ə-kən, in church architecture, a canopy above an altar. The term is used interchangeably with ciborium, although their meanings vary slightly. Baldachin is derived from the Italian *Baldacco* (Baghdad), where a fine silk brocade was produced in the Middle Ages. Baldacco became synonymous with the cloth itself and later evolved into *baldacchino*, meaning a canopy of rich cloth. *Ciborium* comes from Latin and means cup- or goblet-shaped. In 4th century basilicas, many altars were surmounted by a column-supported cupola, to which the name "ciborium" was applied. Constantine the Great donated such a ciborium, the cupola of which was made of silver, to the basilica of St. John Lateran in Rome.

The altar coverings of the baroque period, frequently suspended from the ceiling or attached to the wall behind the altar, were called baldachins because they were ornamented with rich tapestry. Later, baldachins came to be constructed of various materials including marble and ivory. The Roman Catholic Church formerly required high altars to be covered by a baldachin or ciborium. The *Constitution on the Sacred Liturgy,* promulgated by Pope Paul VI in 1963, mentions such a structure as praiseworthy, but not essential.

BALDER, bôl′dər, in Scandinavian mythology, was the god of sunlight and the personification of brightness, beauty, and wisdom. His name is also spelled *Baldur* or *Baldr.* Of all the Aesir, the pantheon of gods in Asgard, he was the fairest, most amiable, and most beloved.

Balder was the son of Odin and the goddess Frigg. He had recurring dreams of doom, and to protect him his mother exacted from all creatures and inanimate things an oath not to harm him. She neglected, however, to require this of the mistletoe, for it seemed so harmless. Loki, the god of evil, by trickery learned from Frigg the secret of the mistletoe. He then made an arrow from this plant and induced Hoth, Balder's blind brother, to shoot it. With Loki's guidance, Hoth unwittingly killed Balder.

The gods mourned Balder's death and appealed to Hel, guardian of the region of the dead, to return Balder. She consented but required the unanimous approval of the gods. Loki refused, however, and Balder remained with the dead.

BALDNESS, bôld′nis, is a thinning or abnormal loss of hair of the scalp. It is known as *alopecia.* The condition commonly affects men and less frequently women. It may be permanent or temporary, partial or complete, slowly progressive or rapid.

Types and Causes. The most common type of baldness is male-pattern baldness. It may affect men from 18 to 50 years of age and is usually slowly progressive. The hair is lost on the frontal areas and on the crown of the scalp. In severe cases, known as "horseshoe baldness," the bald areas merge and almost the entire scalp becomes hairless. Male-pattern baldness is thought to be caused by a sex-limited dominant hereditary trait and by the male hormones.

An endocrine imbalance in either men or women can cause a loss of scalp hair. In male-pattern baldness, for example, the adrenal glands may produce too much androgen, resulting in the loss of scalp hair and an overabundance of

BRONZE BALDACHIN above the main altar at St. Peter's in Rome; designed by Bernini, it is 95 feet high.

LEONARD VON MATT, FROM RAPHO GUILLUMETTE.

body hair (hirsutism). A malfunction of other endocrine glands, such as the pituitary or thyroid, may also cause baldness.

Baldness in women may also be caused by other conditions. A temporary hormonal imbalance often present after pregnancy may cause some temporary loss of scalp hair, known as *postpartum alopecia.* An ovarian dysfunction (Stein-Levinthal syndrome) can also cause hirsutism or baldness. In addition, baldness in women may be caused or aggravated by "teasing" the hair, arranging it in ponytails, and by the use of hair straighteners, lacquers, and other products that tighten the scalp and damage the hair.

Baldness can occur rapidly in both sexes as a result of some serious illness such as typhoid fever, tuberculosis, syphilis, malaria, and other infectious diseases, and from the use of toxic chemicals such as heparin. This type of baldness, known as "toxic baldness," is usually temporary.

Baldness can also occur in patches. Such "spotty baldness," known as *alopecia areata,* is often found in children and young adults. The hair is lost in sharply defined patches, leaving the scalp smooth. The exact cause of this type of baldness, which often spreads rapidly, is unknown, but a nervous factor is thought to be responsible. Cortisone has been found to be an effective treatment.

Infections of the scalp (folliculitis) and the presence of excessive amounts of oil or of dandruff (seborrhea capitis) can contribute to baldness. Nervousness, tension, and strain can also affect normal hair growth.

Treatment. Male-pattern baldness, the most common type, is largely the result of heredity, advancing age, and normal male hormones secretion, and no treatment is really effective. However, if the baldness is premature or caused by some pathological condition, treatment may be available. If there is hormonal imbalance, the administration of the necessary hormones may correct the condition and prevent or slow down the hair loss. A diet low in chocolate, nuts, iodized salt, and shellfish may help eliminate excess oil and dandruff that contribute to baldness. Frequent shampooing and scalp massage are beneficial in maintaining the health of the scalp and hair. The use of hormonal (testosterone) lotions on the scalp may also be helpful. Ultraviolet and ultrasonic treatments are not effective, and many widely advertised commercial preparations and treatments are valueless.

IRWIN I. LUBOWE, M.D.
Metropolitan Hospital Center

BALDOMIR, bäl-dō-mēr', **Alfredo** (1884–1948), Uruguayan soldier and political leader. He was born at Montevideo on Aug. 27, 1884. A career officer in the army, he was placed in charge of military construction in 1931 and appointed minister of national defense in 1935.

Following elections controlled by the administration of his brother-in-law, President Gabriel Terra, General Baldomir was installed as president in 1938. In World War II, his support of the United States and Britain led him to impose strict controls on Axis sympathizers and to suspend the national congress in 1942. He provided the United States with air and naval bases in 1941, and at the end of his term helped to assure a pro-Allied succession. He retired in 1943. Baldomir died at Montevideo on Feb. 25, 1948.

BALDOVINETTI, bäl-dō-vē-nät'tē, **Alesso** (1425?–1499), Italian Renaissance painter, who was also an outstanding designer of mosaics, stained glass, wood inlay, and other decorative work. His name is also spelled *Balduinetti.*

Baldovinetti was born in Florence, probably on Oct. 14, 1425. He may have been apprenticed to Domenico Veneziano, whose influence is apparent in Baldovinetti's early works such as the Medici altarpiece and an *Annunciation,* both now in the Uffizi Gallery, Florence.

Baldovinetti painted a number of important frescoes for Florentine churches. However, his experiments with fresco media caused serious deterioration of these works, including a *Nativity* (1460–1462) in the Annunziata; an *Annunciation* (1466–1473) in San Miniato al Monte, and a series of scenes from the Old Testament (1466–1497) in Santa Trinità. Among his other surviving works are two Madonnas, one in the Louvre, Paris, and the other in the Uffizi.

Baldovinetti's decorative work includes a wood inlay panel for the New Sacristy of the cathedral in Florence—done while he was an assistant to Giuliano da Maiano; mosaic strips over Ghiberti's doors for the cathedral baptistery; and a stained glass window of St. Andrew over the altar of the Pazzi Chapel, Santa Croce, Florence. Baldovinetti died in his native Florence on Aug. 29, 1499.

Further Reading: Kennedy, Ruth W., *Alesso Baldovinetti* (New Haven, Conn., 1938).

BALDRIC, bôl'drik, a belt or sash worn over the right or left shoulder diagonally across the body. It is often highly decorated and enriched with gems, and is used not only to sustain a sword, dagger, or horn, but also for purposes of ornament and as a military or heraldic symbol. The fashion of wearing a baldric appears to have reached its height in the 15th century.

In the United States it now forms a part of the uniform of some fraternal organizations. It is still in use in European royal courts.

BALDUNG, bäl'dŏong, **Hans** (1484/1485–1545), German Renaissance painter, draftsman, and graphic artist, whose early Gothic style, influenced by Dürer, evolved into a powerful originality most evident in his allegorical and mythological fantasies. He is sometimes called *Hans Baldung-Grien* or *-Grün.*

Baldung was born at Weyersheim in Alsace, and probably served an apprenticeship under Dürer in Nuremberg between 1502 and 1507. In 1509 he settled in Strasbourg, where he married and remained for the rest of his life, except for trips to Freiburg where he executed a number of commissions. These included his masterpiece, the altarpiece for the cathedral, completed in 1516. Baldung died in Strasbourg in 1545.

Baldung's most original works are his mysterious allegorical paintings, which often contrast a sensuous female nude with a gruesome skeletal figure of Death. One of the most famous examples is *Death Kissing a Maiden* (1517). His religious paintings, besides the Freiburg altarpiece, include a *St. Sebastian* triptych (1507), two versions of *Lamentations* (1513, 1515), the *Baptism of Christ,* the *Rest on the Flight into Egypt,* three versions of the *Nativity,* and the *Adoration of the Magi* (1539). He also executed a large number of drawings, woodcuts, and etchings, and painted many portraits.

BALDWIN I (1171–?1205), bôl'dwən, was the first Latin emperor of Constantinople (empire of Romania). He was the son of Baldwin V, count of Hainaut. In 1195 he became count of Flanders (as *Baldwin IX*) and count of Hainaut (as *Baldwin VI*). He was a leader of the Fourth Crusade (1202–1204), and with the capture of Constantinople by the crusaders he was elected Latin emperor. He was crowned on May 9, 1204.

The area under his control included only the city, a small district around it, and some islands in the Aegean Sea. In a battle before Adrianople in 1205 he was defeated by the Greeks and Bulgarians; the latter captured him and held him until his death, probably in the same year.

BALDWIN II (1217–1273), bôl'dwən was the last Latin emperor of Constantinople (empire of Romania). He was the nephew of Baldwin I and the son of Peter of Courtenay. In 1228 he succeeded his brother, Robert of Courtenay, as emperor. John of Brienne ruled as regent until Baldwin reached his majority in 1237.

During Baldwin's reign the country was in desperate financial straits. In his search for aid, he sold holy relics to Saint Louis (Louis IX) of France. In 1261 he was driven from Constantinople by Michael VIII Palaeologus, ruler of the Eastern Roman Empire, and sought refuge in Italy. He disposed of his rights in 1267 to Charles I (Charles of Anjou), king of Naples. He died in 1273.

BALDWIN, bôl'dwən, the name of five kings of Jerusalem who were members of the family of the counts of Flanders.

BALDWIN I (1058–1118) was the brother of Godfrey of Bouillon, whom he accompanied on the First Crusade. He became ruler of Edessa (now Urfa) in 1098, and, following the death of his brother in 1100, king of Jerusalem. Despite Egyptian attacks, he extended the Latin kingdom by capturing Acre, Berytus (Beirut), and Sidon.

BALDWIN II (died 1131) succeeded his uncle, Baldwin I, as count of Edessa in 1100. Also known as *Baldwin de Burgh*, he became king of Jerusalem in 1118. While continuing his uncle's campaign against the Muslims, he was captured by them in 1123 and held until the next year. At Baldwin's death his son-in-law, Fulk V the Young, count of Anjou, was elected king.

BALDWIN III (1130?–1162), the son of Fulk V, followed his father to the throne in 1143. His mother, Melisinde, refused to surrender her position as regent until Baldwin campaigned against her in 1152. His 10 years of personal rule were occupied mainly with fighting the Muslims. Early in his reign the fall of Edessa to the Muslims provided the impetus for the Second Crusade (1147–1148). Baldwin was an able commander, but he had difficulty in maintaining his kingdom against larger Muslim forces. His brother, Amalric I, succeeded him as king.

BALDWIN IV (1160–1185) succeeded his father, Amalric I, as king in 1174. During much of his reign he had to combat attacks by Saladin, sultan of Egypt and Syria. He relinquished the crown to the infant Baldwin V in 1183.

BALDWIN V (1177–1186) was king in name only. His stepfather and first regent, Guy of Lusignan, disputed the rule of Jerusalem with Raymond of Tripoli. Raymond replaced the incompetent Guy as regent in 1184, but at Baldwin's death Guy was elected king.

BALDWIN, bôl'dwən, **Abraham** (1754–1807), American political leader. He was born in North Guilford, Conn., on Nov. 22, 1754. After graduating from Yale in 1772, he taught there and then served in the Revolution as a chaplain.

Moving to Georgia, he was admitted to the bar in 1784 and became a member of the state legislature in 1785. As an assemblyman, he wrote the charter of Franklin College (the oldest college of the University of Georgia); he was its president in 1786–1801.

Baldwin represented Georgia in the Continental Congress and in 1787 was a signer of the U.S. Constitution. He served in the U.S. House of Representatives (1789–1799) and Senate (1799–1807). He died in Washington, D.C., on March 4, 1807.

BALDWIN, bôl'dwən, **Henry** (1780–1844), American judge who was an associate justice of the U.S. Supreme Court. He was born in New Haven, Conn., on Jan. 14, 1780, and graduated from Yale in 1797. He was admitted to the bar in Pittsburgh and practiced law there and in Meadville, Pa. Baldwin represented Pennsylvania in the U.S. House of Representatives from 1817 to 1822.

A supporter of Andrew Jackson in the presidential campaign of 1828, he was named an associate justice of the Supreme Court in 1820. His record on the court lacked consistency. At first he adhered to the liberal tradition of John Marshall, but later abandoned this position, although he never became a strict constructionist. He died in Philadelphia on April 21, 1844.

BALDWIN, bôl'dwən, **James** (1924–   ), American writer, who won critical acclaim as a leading Negro novelist and essayist in the 1950's before becoming a major spokesman for his race in the civil rights movement of the 1960's. Baldwin was born in New York City on Aug. 2, 1924, the eldest of nine children of a Baptist preacher. He grew up in the Harlem slums. A sensitive child, he acutely felt what he called "the stigma of being a Negro." After graduating from high school, Baldwin worked at odd jobs to help support his brothers and sisters.

In his twenties, Baldwin received several writing fellowships that enabled him to satisfy his ambition to become an author. He published his first novel, *Go Tell It on the Mountain*, in 1953. He made a reputation as an original and provocative writer with two subsequent novels—*Giovanni's Room* (1958) and *Another Country* (1962)—and the essays in *Notes of a Native Son* (1955) and *Nobody Knows My Name* (1960).

Baldwin attracted attention with *The Fire Next Time* (1963), a revelation of the deep anguish of Negroes. The book became a best seller and catapulted him into the center of the civil rights turmoil. The next year his play *Blues for Mr. Charlie* opened on Broadway to generally favorable reviews. A collection of stories, *Going to Meet the Man*, appeared in 1965. In the same year *The Amen Corner*, a play written in 1953, was produced on Broadway.

In his writings and numerous public appearances, Baldwin portrayed the Negro as victimized by the "guilty imagination of the white people who invest him with their hates and longings." He wrote: "At the root of the American Negro problem is the necessity of the American white man to find a way of living with the Negro in order to be able to live with himself."

BALDWIN, bôl'dwən, **James Mark** (1861–1934), American psychologist. Born in Columbia, S.C., on Jan. 12, 1861, he graduated from Princeton University in 1884. While studying for a year in Germany, he developed an interest in psychology, but he began his career teaching German and French at Princeton in 1886. Baldwin was professor of philosophy at the University of Toronto from 1889 to 1903 and during this time brought out the *Handbook of Psychology* (2 vols., 1889–91). He returned to Princeton as professor of psychology in 1893. He was professor of philosophy and psychology at Johns Hopkins University from 1903 to 1909 and at the National University of Mexico from 1909 to 1913. He became noted for contributions in the fields of experimental, child, and social psychology. He ultimately settled in Europe, spending most of his time in Paris. From 1914 his work in psychology was subordinated to an interest in politics. He died in Paris on Nov. 8, 1934.

With James McKean Cattell, Baldwin founded the *Psychological Review* in 1894 and served as coeditor until 1909. His monumental achievement was the *Dictionary of Philosophy and Psychology*, which he edited from 1901 to 1906. Other works include *The Individual and Society* (1910) and *Genetic Theory of Reality* (1915).

BALDWIN, bôl'dwən, **Joseph Glover** (1815–1864), American lawyer and writer. He was born near Winchester, Va., in January 1815. While in his teens he studied law under his uncle's supervision. In 1836 he set out for Mississippi and Alabama to practice law; eight years later he served in the Alabama legislature. In 1854 he moved to California; and from 1858 to 1862 he was an associate justice of the state supreme court.

Baldwin wrote *The Flush Times of Alabama and Mississippi* (1853), an entertaining and popular volume, and *Party Leaders* (1855), a collection of serious studies of national political figures. He died on Sept. 30, 1864.

BALDWIN, bôl'dwən, **Matthias William** (1795–1866), American inventor and industrialist. He was born in Elizabethtown, N.J., on Nov. 10, 1795. He became a journeyman jeweler in 1818, and while so employed invented a simplified process of gold plating for which he secured a patent. In 1825 he settled in Philadelphia, where he became a toolmaker. He was the first man in the United States to manufacture bookbinders' tools and calico printers' rolls.

In 1827 he devised a method of printing calico by means of a 5-horsepower steam-driven stationary engine, and this worked so well that he was soon making others for use in factories. Then he was requested to make a diminutive steam locomotive along the lines of the steam engines which had then been recently constructed by George Stephenson in England. This model was shown in Peale's Museum, Philadelphia. It worked well, and in 1832 he built the locomotive *Old Ironsides* for the Philadelphia and Germantown Railway. This locomotive, the first to draw a train in the state of Pennsylvania, was capable of a speed of 30 miles (48 km) an hour, but was advertised to run only in fair weather.

Thereafter, Baldwin concentrated on the construction of locomotives, from 1854 in partnership with Matthew Baird. He formed the M.W. Baldwin Company, and from this developed the Baldwin Locomotive Works, which became the world's largest producer of its kind. It built more than 1,500 locomotives before his death.

Baldwin gave much support to the Franklin Institute and to religious and philanthropic activities, particularly those aiding Negroes. He died in Philadelphia on Sept. 7, 1866.

BALDWIN, bôl'dwən, **Robert** (1804–1858), Canadian political leader, who was the principal advocate of mid-19th century reforms to make the colonial government of Canada responsive to the will of Canadians.

He was born at York (later Toronto), Upper Canada, on May 12, 1804. He studied law, and in 1825 was admitted to the bar, practicing in York in partnership with his father, William Warren Baldwin (1775–1844), long prominent in political life. In 1829–1830 he represented York as a Liberal in the legislature of Upper Canada, and in 1836 Sir Francis Bond Head, the lieutenant governor, nominated him to a seat on the executive council. Within a few weeks he resigned to go to London to plead for a greater degree of self government, but on his return to Canada the next year he declined to support the insurrectionary movement led by William Lyon Mackenzie.

After the Act of Union of 1841 had again brought Upper and Lower Canada together, Baldwin became a member of the executive council under Lord Sydenham. In 1842 he and Louis Hyppolite Lafontaine jointly headed the first Canadian administration to accept "responsible government," a cabinet form of government representative of both French- and English-speaking Canadians. The joint premiers resigned the next year after a dispute with Sir Charles Theophilus Metcalfe, the governer general; but following elections in December 1847 at which the Liberals gained a majority, they formed the second Baldwin-Lafontaine ministry. This administration revised the judicial system, introduced a municipal system in Upper Canada, and freed the University of Toronto from sectarian control. The administration benefited French Canadians, who supported Baldwin. Because of party dissensions, Baldwin resigned in 1851. He died at Toronto on Dec. 9, 1858.

BALDWIN, bôl'dwən, **Roger Nash** (1884–   ), American reformer, a founder and leader of the American Civil Liberties Union (ACLU). Born in Wellesley, Mass., on Jan. 21, 1884, he graduated from Harvard in 1904 and earned a master's degree there in 1905. While teaching sociology in St. Louis, he became interested in social work and served as chief probation officer (1907–1910) and as secretary of the St. Louis Civic League (1910–1917). In 1917 he went to New York and became director of the American Union Against Militarism. He spent a year in prison as a conscientious objector.

Following his release, Baldwin became director of the newly established ACLU, an organization dedicated to the protection of freedom of inquiry and expression and to legal equality for all. During his long service with the ACLU (director, 1920–1950; national chairman, 1950–1955), Baldwin traveled, lectured, wrote numerous articles, and taught. He wrote *Juvenile Courts and Probation* (with Bernard Flexner, 1912) and *Liberty Under the Soviets* (1928). He edited *A New Slavery, Forced Labor* (1953).

BALDWIN, Stanley (1867–1947), British political leader who was prime minister of Great Britain for three times in the period between the world wars. When Britain was plunged into World War II after the failure of "appeasement," Baldwin's prewar leadership, especially in matters of foreign policy, aroused bitter historical controversy that tended to obscure his achievements. He was created *Earl Baldwin of Bewdley* on his retirement in 1937.

Baldwin was born at Bewdley, Worcestershire, on Aug. 3, 1867. After graduating from Harrow and Cambridge, he worked from 1888 to 1908 in his family's engineering firm. He ran unsuccessfully for Parliament in 1906. Two years later he succeeded his father as Conservative member for the Bewdley division of Worcestershire.

Baldwin's early career in the House of Commons was undistinguished, and he was 50 years old before he became a junior minister. Thereafter he rose rapidly, as financial secretary to the treasury in 1917–1921 and president of the Board of Trade in 1921–1922. In October 1922 he took the lead in persuading the Conservatives to abandon the coalition under Lloyd George and fight the ensuing election as an independent party. The party's triumph thrust him into prominence, and he was made chancellor of the exchequer in Andrew Bonar Law's cabinet.

In January 1923, Baldwin was sent to Washington to negotiate a settlement of war debts with the United States. He agreed to a costly settlement that Bonar Law was reluctant to support. But the cabinet insisted upon acceptance, and Baldwin's bargain was ratified.

Baldwin succeeded Bonar Law as prime minister in 1923 and almost immediately startled the country by opening up the question of a protective tariff to relieve unemployment. In this matter he has been accused of the political blunder of raising an issue on which his party was divided. In fact, his position succeeded in rallying the Conservatives who had remained attracted to Lloyd George. That the Conservatives lost the election of 1923 meant much less to Baldwin than that they were to be united in the future. When the election of 1923 offered the Labour party its first chance to form a government, Baldwin refused to block its way. He felt that Labour must be given "a fair chance" to learn the realities of governing.

Returning to office in 1924, Baldwin remained prime minister until 1929. His indolent and one-sided handling of the general strike of 1926 left a long-standing bitterness in British labor relations, but in general his second ministry was one of temperate and orderly progress. Pursuing a policy of "safety first," he tried no imaginative experiments; but over the years he came to symbolize for many of his countrymen the virtues of moderation, sanity, love of country, and, above all, trustworthiness. Behind his placid façade lay the qualities of an extremely able politician who often achieved his purpose by postponing decisions and stressing compromise. In the later 1920's these qualities helped to maintain stability in a rapidly changing Britain. In the 1930's they often proved wanting.

In May 1929 the electorate rejected "safety first," and a Labour ministry was returned. Despite violent press attacks on him, Baldwin retained his leadership of the Conservative party and in so doing, perhaps, helped keep its domestic policies moderate and flexible. When Labour's

BLACK STAR

STANLEY BALDWIN, prime minister of Britain, as he announced the abdication of King Edward VIII in 1936.

prime minister, Ramsay MacDonald, formed the national coalition cabinet of 1931, Baldwin accepted office as president of the council. Almost from the beginning, MacDonald was the prisoner of the Conservatives in the coalition. Nevertheless, Baldwin collaborated with MacDonald in overcoming Conservative resistance to the forward-looking Government of India Act.

Baldwin became prime minister for the third time in 1936. His last administration was dominated by foreign affairs which, unfortunately, never really engaged his interest. Like MacDonald, he underestimated Germany's growing air strength and failed to develop a sense of urgency about rearmament. Despite constant statements of support for the League of Nations, he appeared to abandon collective security. Critics of Neville Chamberlain's appeasement policy inevitably must find its beginnings in the earlier days of the national government under MacDonald and Baldwin.

Baldwin was much more successful in domestic affairs. By 1937, Britain was on the road to recovery, if not prosperity. Late in 1936, Baldwin maneuvered the abdication of King Edward VIII with extraordinary skill. What might have become a bitter and controversial constitutional crisis was transformed by his touch into a smooth triumph of good sense and good taste. On May 28, 1937, following the coronation of George VI, Baldwin retired. He was politically inactive from 1937 until his death, at Stourport-on-Severn, Worcestershire, on Dec. 13, 1947.

Stanley Baldwin (1952), the authorized biography by George Malcolm Young, caused a storm of protest. It was answered by Baldwin's son, Arthur W. Baldwin, in *My Father: The True Story* (1956) and by David Churchill Somervell in *Stanley Baldwin: An Examination of Some Features of Mr. G.M. Young's Biography* (1953).

HENRY R. WINKLER, *Rutgers University*

Further Reading: Mowat, Charles L., *Britain Between the Wars, 1918–1940* (Chicago 1955); Taylor, A.J.P., *English History, 1914–1945* (Oxford 1965).

BALDWIN, bôl′dwən, an unincorporated residential village in New York, is in Nassau County, on the south shore of Long Island, 28 miles (45 km) east of New York City. Its manufactured products include kitchen cabinets, knit goods, and venetian blinds. There are also boating and fishing industries.

The area was settled by Dutch colonists in the 1640's. The village was originally known as *Hick's Neck*. Baldwin is administered by Hempstead Township. Population: 34,525.

BALDWIN, bôl′dwən, a residential borough in southwestern Pennsylvania, is in Allegheny County, about 5 miles (8 km) southeast of downtown Pittsburgh, of which it is a suburb. It is separated from Pittsburgh by the Monongahela River. Baldwin's manufactures include primary metal products; electrical machinery, equipment, and supplies; and wood products. The Allegheny County airport is immediately southeast.

Baldwin was incorporated in 1950. Government is by council-manager. Population: 26,729.

BALDWIN COMPANY, bôl′dwən, an American piano manufacturing firm (in full, D.H. Baldwin Co.) whose instruments are used by such ensembles as the Boston Symphony and the Philadelphia Orchestra. Baldwin was the official piano of the Seattle World's Fair (1962) and New York World's Fair (1964–1965).

The company was founded in 1862 as D.H. Baldwin & Co. in Cincinnati, Ohio, by Dwight H. Baldwin, a piano teacher. At first it distributed the instruments of other firms, but it began manufacturing organs in 1889 and pianos in 1890. In 1901 it was incorporated as The Baldwin Co., with Lucien Wulsin, an early partner, as president. His grandson, Lucien Wulsin, Jr., became president in 1962. The present name of the firm was adopted in 1962.

BALDWIN PARK, bôl′dwən, is a city in southern California, in Los Angeles County, 18 miles (29 km) east of Los Angeles, of which it is a residential suburb. It is situated in an agricultural area of the San Gabriel Valley, where poultry, vegetables, berries, and citrus fruits are raised.

The city's manufactures include guided missile systems, aircraft component parts, screws,

tools, metal office furniture, concrete pipes, and clothing.

Baldwin Park developed around the Pacific Electric company station built in 1912. It was named for Elias Jackson (Lucky) Baldwin, who had operated the Santa Anita Rancho, a horse-breeding ranch, on the site. It was incorporated in 1956. Government is by council-manager. Population: 47,285.

BALDWINSVILLE, bôl′dwənz-vil, is a village in central New York, Onondaga County, 8 miles (13 km) northwest of Syracuse. It is situated on the Seneca River in an agricultural, dairying, and livestock-raising region. It has several flour mills and also manufactures various types of machinery.

Baldwinsville was settled in 1796 by veterans of the American Revolution, who received lands there as bonuses. The village was incorporated in 1847. Population: 6,298.

BALE, bāl, **John** (1495–1563), English author and clergyman. He was born at Cove, Suffolk, on Nov. 21, 1495. Reared as an English Catholic, he became a Protestant while studying at Cambridge University. He wrote religious plays concerned with corruptions in Catholicism and thus attracted the attention and protection of Thomas Cromwell, one of the ministers of Henry VIII. When Cromwell fell from power, Bale was forced to flee to Germany.

In 1547, at the accession of Edward VI, Bale returned to England, where he became bishop of the Irish see of Ossory in 1552. When Mary came to the throne in 1553, Bale again escaped abroad but returned when Elizabeth became queen in 1558. From 1560 until his death in November 1563, he was prebendary of Canterbury cathedral.

Because of his bitter and skillful pen he earned the sobriquets of "Bilious Bale" and "Foul-mouthed Bale." His writings include a history of English literature, *Illustrium Majoris Britanniae scriptorum summarium*, and *King John*, one of the first English historical plays.

BALEARIC ISLANDS, bal-ē-ar′ik, an archipelago in the Mediterranean Sea off the east coast of Spain, constituting the Spanish province of Baleares. The Balearics have an aggregate area of 1,935 square miles (5,012 sq km). The four largest islands, in order of size, are Majorca, Minorca, Ibiza, and Formentera. The capital is Palma (1960 population, 159,084), on the southwest coast of Majorca.

The climate of the islands, which are popular resorts, is fine but variable and the flora and fauna are similar to those of the nearest mainland. Fruit, wine, grain, and fish (anchovies and sardines) are the principal products. Typical manufactures are silver filigree work and majolica ware.

Colonized by the Phoenicians and Carthaginians, the islands were conquered by the Romans in 123 B.C., by the Vandals in 423 A.D., and by Moors in 798. They became a Moorish kingdom in 1009.

The kingdom was taken by James I of Aragon in 1229–1232 and united to Spain in 1349. It was ceded to Britain in 1713 but was finally regained by Spain in 1802. Population: (1960) 443,327.

BALEEN. See WHALE; WHALING.

BALEARIC ISLANDS' capital city of Palma has picturesque private homes crowding its rocky coastline.

DURVEE, FROM MONKMEYER

BALENCIAGA, bä-län-sē-ä'gä, **Cristóbal** (1895–1972), Spanish couturier in Paris, who became one of the most influential and sophisticated fashion designers of the 20th century. His fame rests on the strongly classical, sculptured, and simple character of his designs. The combination of Spanish solidity with French refinement and elegance makes his clothes timeless.

Influenced by his early environment, Balenciaga designed practical, comfortable clothes. Among his most noted contributions to fashions were the demi-fit suit; the short-front, long-back evening gown with flounced hem; and the controversial chemise style, which became a world-wide fashion in 1957.

Balenciaga was born in the Basque fishing village of Guetaria, in Guipúzcoa province, Spain, on the Bay of Biscay. His father owned a small fishing vessel; his mother was a seamstress. The young Balenciaga preferred sewing to sports. He made a dress for a marchioness, who encouraged him to study tailoring in nearby San Sebastian and in Madrid.

Balenciaga opened his first fashion house in 1916, in San Sebastian, and his second in 1932, in Madrid. In 1937 he began the Paris establishment that brought him world fame. He retired in 1968, emerging briefly only weeks before his death to design the wedding gown for the granddaughter of General Francisco Franco. Balenciaga died in Valencia on March 24, 1972.

ERMINA STIMSON, *"Women's Wear Daily"*

BALESTIER, bal-əs-tēr', **Charles Wolcott** (1861–1891), American journalist, author, and publisher. He was born in Rochester, N.Y., on Dec. 13, 1861, and was educated at Cornell University and the University of Virginia. He began writing at the age of 17 and in 1885 was appointed editor of *Tidbits,* which in 1886 became *Time,* a weekly humor magazine.

Balestier went to England in 1888 to acquire manuscripts for James G. Lovell, an American book publisher. In 1889 he became a partner in the publishing firm of Heinemann and Balestier of London and Leipzig. In 1892 his sister Caroline married Rudyard Kipling, one of the writers Balestier had procured for Lovell.

Balestier's books include *Life of James G. Blaine* (1884) and the novels *A Potent Philtre* (1884), *A Fair Device* (1884), and *A Victorious Defeat* (1886). *The Naulahka,* a story of an American in India, was written in collaboration with Kipling and published in 1892 after Balestier's death, in Dresden, Germany, on Dec. 6, 1891. Kipling dedicated his *Barrack-Room Ballads* (1892) to Balestier.

BALEWA, bä-le-wä', **Sir Abubakar Tafawa** (1912–1966), first prime minister of Nigeria. Born at Bauchi, in northern Nigeria, in December 1912, he was educated locally and became a teacher. In 1945 he spent a year at the London University Institute of Education. He was appointed to the Northern Region House of Assembly in 1947 and later served in the Nigerian Legislative Council. A moderate conservative, he defended northern interests and at the same time pressed for gradual progress in the north.

Balewa helped found the Northern People's Congress (NPC), which dominated the Northern Region, and he was elected on its ticket to the national House of Representatives. He served as minister of works from 1952 to 1954 and as min-

VOGUE PHOTOGRAPH © 1965 BY THE CONDÉ PUBLICATIONS INC.

BALENCIAGA, Spanish-born fashion designer, whose Paris salon has created notable trends in costume.

ister of transport from 1954 to 1957. As deputy leader of the NPC, the largest party in the House of Representatives, he became the country's first chief minister (later called prime minister) in 1957. He held this post continuously until the military coup of Jan. 15, 1966, when his government was overthrown and he was kidnapped from his home. His body was found January 21.

A man of great integrity, leading a government that was not noted for this virtue, Balewa never had a great personal following. He attempted to moderate divisions within the government but was helpless to prevent the drift and indecisiveness that came increasingly to mark Nigerian politics. Internationally he won respect and was awarded honors by many countries. He was one of the originators of the charter of the Organization of African Unity.

L. GRAY COWAN, *Columbia University*

BALFE, balf, **Michael William** (1808–1870), Irish composer and singer. He was born in Dublin, Ireland, on May 15, 1808, the son of a dancing master. He studied the violin and singing and in 1825 went to Italy for further study. There in 1826 he wrote his first important composition, the ballet *La Pérouse.* Two years later, in Paris, his singing came to the attention of Rossini, who gave him a three-year contract as leading baritone of the Théâtre Italien in Paris. Balfe's first complete opera, *I rivali di sè stesso,* was performed at Palermo, Sicily, in 1829.

In 1835, Balfe, by then a well-known melodist, returned to Britain and began his successful career as a composer of English opera. His first work there was *The Siege of Rochelle* (1835). He lived again in Paris from 1841 to 1843, when he returned to London to produce his most enduring opera, *The Bohemian Girl* (1843). His other important operas include *The Maid of Artois* (1836) and *The Rose of Castille* (1857). He died at Rowney Abbey, his estate in Hertfordshire, England, on Oct. 20, 1870. See also BOHEMIAN GIRL.

BALFOUR, bal'foŏr, **Arthur James** (1848–1930), British statesman and philosopher, who was prime minister of Britain and author of the Balfour Declaration favoring a Jewish national homeland in Palestine.

He was born into a family of highly educated aristocrats at Whitinghame (now Whittingehame), East Lothian, Scotland, on July 25, 1848. He was educated at Eton and Trinity College, Cambridge, and entered the House of Commons as a member from Hertford in 1874. From 1878 to 1880 he was private secretary to his uncle, Robert Gascoyne-Cecil, 3d marquess of Salisbury, at the Foreign Office. After the general elections of 1880, through which he retained his seat by only a small majority, he became active in the Conservative cause.

In the general elections of 1885, Balfour was returned for East Manchester, the constituency he represented until 1906. He became secretary of Scotland in 1886 and attained cabinet rank the following year. Becoming Irish chief secretary in 1887, he administered the repressive Irish Crimes Act with such vigor that he earned the epithet "bloody Balfour." He nevertheless succeeded in passing several ameliorative measures which later culminated in the Land Purchase Act of 1904. Succeeding William Henry Smith as first lord of the treasury and leader of the House of Commons in 1891, he led the opposition during the Liberal administration of 1892 and regained his former place in the government when the Unionist party returned in 1895.

On the resignation of his uncle, Lord Salisbury, in July 1902, Balfour succeeded him as prime minister, retaining this position until his resignation on Dec. 4, 1905. In the elections of 1906, his party collapsed, and he lost his seat for East Manchester. He was immediately returned for the City of London, however, and remained at the head of the opposition until 1911, when he relinquished his position to Andrew Bonar Law.

In June 1915, after a series of Allied disasters in World War I, Balfour was one of the "elder statesmen" invited to join the national ministry formed by Herbert Henry Asquith. In the redistribution of cabinet posts Balfour succeeded Winston Churchill as first lord of the admiralty. On the reorganization of the coalition cabinet in 1916, with Lloyd George as prime minister, Balfour was given the portfolio of minister of foreign affairs, and in April 1917, when the United States entered the war, he visited America as head of the British commission to the United States. In November of that year he issued the famous Balfour Declaration that promised a national homeland for Jews in Palestine, a project that he had long been interested in and that finally took shape at the Peace of Versailles. See also BALFOUR DECLARATION.

Balfour was the chief British representative to the League of Nations Assembly in 1920 and the Washington Naval Disarmament Conference in 1921–1922. Although he was remarkably alert until the end of his life, he resigned from the government in 1922. That year he was made Knight of the Garter and elevated to the peerage as *1st earl of Balfour and Viscount Traprain*. Recalled to government by Prime Minister Stanley Baldwin, Balfour served as lord president of the council from 1925 to 1929. He died at Fisher's Hill, near Woking, on March 19, 1930.

Balfour's earliest book, *A Defence of Phil-osophic Doubt*, appeared in 1879. In it he maintained that a dispassionate skepticism of science toward religion should produce a similar skepticism toward science itself. Amplifying his philosophic position throughout his life, he denied that he was undermining rational values with philosophic doubts, asserting that men, including philosophers, believe a great deal and that the task is to find the assumption on which "we may believe it most reasonably."

His works include *Essays and Addresses* (1893; new ed., enlarged, 1905), *The Foundations of Belief* (1895), *Insular Free Trade* (1903), *Criticism and Beauty* (Romanes Lecture, 1909), *Theism and Humanism,* his chief philosophical work (1915), *Essays, Speculative and Political* (1920), and *Theism and Thought* (1923).

Further Reading: Dugdale, B.E.C., *Arthur James Balfour,* 2 vol. (London 1936).

BALFOUR, Sir James (c. 1500–1583), Scottish judge and political intriguer, also called *Lord Pittendreich.* He was born in Fifeshire, Scotland, and was educated for the priesthood before entering law. In 1547 he was implicated in the plot to kill Cardinal Beaton and condemned to the galleys with John Knox and other Reformation leaders. Balfour secured his release by recanting in 1549. For ten years thereafter he supported the Catholic party of the dowager queen regent, Mary of Guise. He rejoined the reformers briefly in 1559 but shortly betrayed them.

Balfour ingratiated himself with Mary, Queen of Scots, after she assumed power in 1561. Mary appointed him privy councillor in 1565 and knighted him the next year. In 1567 he planned the murder of Mary's husband, Lord Darnley, but convinced Mary of his innocence and remained in her favor. Foreseeing Mary's downfall after her marriage to the earl of Bothwell two months after Darnley's death, Balfour changed sides again and betrayed Mary's military plans. In 1580 he furnished evidence of the earl of Morton's guilt in Darnley's murder. Balfour was exonerated and Morton executed.

BALFOUR DECLARATION, bal'foŏr dek-lə-rā'shən, an official statement issued on behalf of the British government in 1917, announcing its support in principle of a proposed home for the Jewish people in Palestine. It was drafted by British Foreign Minister Arthur J. Balfour in concert with prominent Zionist leaders and the British cabinet and was issued by Balfour in a communication to the 2d Baron Rothschild on Nov. 2, 1917. The declaration, which Zionists interpreted as a promise to make Palestine a Jewish state, was calculated to enlist Jewish support for the Allies in World War I. It was formally approved by representatives of the Allied governments at Versailles in 1919 and was the basis of the League of Nations mandate for Palestine.

The substance of the Balfour Declaration is contained in a single paragraph: "His Majesty's Government view with favour the establishment in Palestine of a national home for the Jewish people and will use their best endeavours to facilitate the achievement of this object. It being clearly understood that nothing shall be done which may prejudice the civil and religious rights of existing non-Jewish communities in Palestine, or the rights and political status enjoyed by Jews in any other country."

PADDY-RICE TERRACES in Bali. Cultivation of wet rice, or paddy rice, is the mainstay of the economy of the island.

BALI, bä′lē, a small island in Indonesia, is part of the Lesser Sunda (Nusa Tenggara) group, which extends from Bali eastward to Timor. Bali Strait, less than 2 miles (3 km) wide, separates Bali from the large island of Java to the west. Bali, in the midst of Muslim Indonesia, is famous for a Hindu culture whose rituals pervade every aspect of daily life and in which the arts (dance, painting, drama, temple-building) play a vigorous role.

Bali stretches about 90 miles (145 km) east and west, is about 55 miles (88 km) wide at its widest part, and has an area of 2,147 square miles (5,561 sq km). The largest city, Denpasar (1961 population, 56,000), in the south, is also the capital of Bali province, which includes, besides Bali, the small adjacent island of Nusa Penida. Other important towns are Singaradja (1961 population, 33,000), in the north, and its neighbor Buleleng, which, though small, is the principal port for the island. Bali's only commercial airport is Tuban, near Denpasar.

Land. Bali lies athwart one of the major volcanic arcs of Southeast Asia. A group of young volcanoes occupies much of the central part of the island and includes the mountains of Abang (7,059 feet; 2,152 meters), Tabanan (7,465 feet; 2,275 meters), and Agung (10,308 feet; 3,142 meters). The fertile alluvial plain of Denpasar extends south from the foot of the volcanoes and contains most of the cultivated area. Although most of Bali has year-round temperatures in the low 80's F (26° C–30° C), a fair amount of annual rainfalls, and luxuriant foliage and trees, droughts, especially in the north, can be both frequent and severe.

Economy. Bali's only important natural resource is arable land, and most Balinese are farmers. Rice occupies more than half the cultivated area, and rice culture is the island's leading industry. Paddy-rice terraces are a common sight along the edges of the uplands.

Bali is usually self-sufficient in food production. Maize, cassava, sweet potatoes, peanuts, soybeans, and fruits are grown to supplement the diet. Small plantings of coconuts, tobacco, tea, cacao, indigo, coffee, and rubber are cultivated to provide produce for the commercial market. A large number of cattle and pigs are raised in Bali, the pigs chiefly for Indonesia's non-Muslim, Chinese population.

There is some light manufacturing and food processing and a home handicraft industry using local bamboos and native textiles.

Religion and Culture. By the 10th century A.D. Bali's Hindu culture, which has many features of earlier animistic and ancestor-worship cults, was highly developed. Although an East Javan strain entered the culture with the Majapahit (Madjapahit) rulers in the late 13th century, Bali was never wholly Javanized but kept its own style of Hinduism. Indeed, the Majapahit rajas encouraged the native ritual arts.

The greater part of the cultural life of the Balinese centers on the villages. Community clubs, or *seka,* stage festivals in which all the villagers participate and in which music, drama, and dance are closely connected. The *gamelan,* an orchestra of gongs, keyed instruments, drums, and cymbals, accompanies the singing part of dramatic performances, and a variety of exotic instruments accompany such dances as the *legong* and the *bjauk* (performed by masked actors).

Balinese temples abound throughout the island—in family courtyards, villages, or rural settings (sacred slopes or lake shores). They

BALINESE TEMPLES. Eleven-roofed temples, at left, are dedicated to Hindu deity Shiva (Siva). At right, ornately carved temple gate at Ubud.

BALINESE DANCER being prepared for the *legong*, a traditional ceremonial dance performed by little girls.

DEANE DICKASON—EWING GALLOWAY, N.Y.

are frequently the focal points of the Balinese rituals. Both the styles of the shrines themselves and the traditional rites for which they provide the setting are expressive of the reverence, beauty, and dignity that are constantly present in Balinese life.

History. For centuries Bali's history has been closely linked with eastern Java, where most of Bali's population came from. Although remaining outside the control of the famous Srivijaya empire, which ruled much of Indonesia from the 7th to the 13th century A.D., Bali fell under the control of East Java about 1000 A.D. King Airlangga, who ruled over East Java in the mid-11th century, came originally from Bali. In the late 13th century, Bali came under the domination of the East Javanese Singosari-Majapahit empire. When the Majapahit rulers were overthrown by Muslims in the early 16th century, many Javanese priests, scholars, and artists took refuge in Bali, bringing with them their religion, philosophy, art, and skills. Bali has remained a repository of Majapahit religion and culture.

Although Bali was visited by the Dutch explorer Cornelis de Houtman in 1596, the island remained free of European incursions until the 1840's when the Dutch sent two expeditions against it. Although these met with fierce resistance, the Dutch took some land, and the island's local rulers made formal acknowledgment of Dutch suzerainty. It was the end of the 19th century, however, before the Dutch gained firm control of the north, and 1906 before they wrested the south from the native Hindu princes in a cruel massacre.

Bali was occupied by the Japanese during World War II, retaken by the Dutch in 1945, and later made a state of the new Republic of the United States of Indonesia. On Indonesia's reorganization in 1950 it was made a province. Population: (1961) of the province, 1,782,529.

FREDERICK L. WERNSTEDT
Pennsylvania State University

Further Reading: Belo, Jane, *Trance in Bali* (New York 1960); Covarrubias, Miguel, *Island of Bali* (New York 1950); Hiss, Philip H., *Bali* (New York 1941); McPhee, Colin, *A House in Bali* (London 1947).

BALIOL, bāl'yəl, an Anglo-Norman family that played an ill-starred part in the history of Scotland. The house was founded in England by the Norman baron *Guido* or *Guy de Baliol*, who is said to have landed with William the Conqueror in 1066. The name is also spelled *Balliol*.

JOHN DE BALIOL (d. 1269), the great-great-grandson of Guido, founded Balliol College, Ox-

ford, in 1263 by endowments of lands both before and after his death. He was one of the regents of Scotland during the minority of Alexander III. Removed from that office by the appointment of a new regency through the influence of Henry III, he gained the favor of Henry and sided with him in the Barons' War (1253–1265).

JOHN DE BALIOL (1249–1315), king of Scotland, third son of the preceding. When the Scottish throne became vacant in 1290 on the death of Margaret, the Maid of Norway, Baliol claimed the throne by virtue of his descent from David, earl of Huntington, brother of King William the Lion. Robert Bruce was his principal rival, but Edward I of England favored Baliol. Baliol recognized Edward as the overlord of Scotland and was crowned at Scone on Nov. 30, 1292. In 1295 he made an alliance with Philip IV of France, then at war with England. Baliol invaded Cumberland but was repelled and deposed by Edward in 1296. Exiled to his Norman estate in 1299, he died there in 1315.

EDWARD DE BALIOL (d. 1364), king of Scotland, was the eldest son of the preceding by his wife Isabel, daughter of the earl of Surrey. He was imprisoned and exiled with his father. In 1324 he returned to England as an aspirant to the Scottish throne on the invitation of Edward II. In 1332 he made a compact with Edward III of England, marched on Scotland, and defeated the Scottish nationalists under Archibald Douglas. On Sept. 24 he was crowned king of Scotland at Scone, acknowledging Edward III as his superior. In December he was defeated by Douglas at Annan but regained his kingdom after the defeat of the Scots at Halidon Hill. He was unseated again the next year but was restored by Edward III. Baliol became the English king's vassal and yielded all Lothian to him. In 1356 he ignobly surrendered all Scotland to Edward in return for a pension. He died childless near Doncaster, England, in 1364.

BALKAN ENTENTE, bôl'kən än-tänt', a political alliance of the 1930's among several Balkan states. It grew out of the *Balkan Conference*, an unofficial organization formed in October 1930, comprising Greece, Turkey, Yugoslavia, Rumania, Bulgaria, and Albania. Various problems in education, social welfare, trade, and the protection of minorities were jointly undertaken during the conference's three-year existence. But Bulgaria refused to agree to a pact of nonaggression or to a plan of mutual assistance. Bulgaria's refusal led to the formation of the Balkan Entente, which was essentially a mutual defense alliance against attack by another Balkan state.

The Pact of the Balkan Entente was signed at Athens on Feb. 9, 1934, by Greece, Turkey, Yugoslavia, and Rumania. The Pact was actually directed against Bulgarian aspirations to revise its boundaries. It sought to guarantee existing frontiers in the Balkans and to provide for consultation on common issues through a permanent council and an economic council. From its beginning, however, the entente was hampered by binding agreements of individual members with other nations, changes in government, and an increasing rapprochement by some members with the Axis powers. As German and Italian influence increased in southeastern Europe, the significance of the Balkan Entente declined. Its last communiqué was issued in February 1940.

PIX

THE BALKAN PENINSULA is characterized by mountainous terrain such as that which surrounds the village of Gjirokastrë in southern Albania. The name "Balkan" itself is derived from a Turkish word meaning mountain.

BALKANS, bôl′kənz, a group of nations of southeastern Europe, including Albania, Bulgaria, Greece, Rumania, and Yugoslavia. The name "Balkan" is derived from the Turkish word for "mountain." In the 19th century, when the term was first used, it usually designated the territory under the direct or indirect control of the Ottoman empire after the Treaty of Karlowitz (1699); it did not include the lands held by the Habsburg empire before 1918 that are now integral parts of Balkan states. Although European Turkey, including Istanbul (Constantinople), lies geographically within the confines of the Balkan Peninsula, it is now part of a non-Balkan state and generally is not considered part of the region. Hungary, despite its close links with the Balkans, is similarly considered a non-Balkan state.

Role in History. The Balkan Peninsula has played a major role in history. Its southern part was the center of the great ancient civilization of Greece. Later it formed part of the Roman empire. The Byzantine empire, which had its capital at Constantinople, dominated the southern section of the peninsula for more than 1,000 years. Although the subsequent 500 years of Ottoman control were a time of cultural, political, and economic stagnation for the Balkan peoples, the peninsula again became a center of political activity and diplomatic controversy in the 19th century. At that time the so-called Eastern Question, which involved, among other problems, the revolt of the Balkan Christians against Ottoman rule, was perhaps the single largest issue in European international relations. In the 20th century the five states have continued to occupy a central position in world political controversies.

The political history of the Balkan Peninsula has been affected by its geographic proximity to other great centers of civilization and by the configuration of the land, which offers easy access to foreign invaders and at the same time encourages division and diversity within the region. Outside interference and internal political conflict have thus been dominant characteristics of Balkan history. Situated at the crossroads of the Eastern Hemisphere, at a point where Asia, Europe, and Africa (through the eastern Mediterranean island chains) meet, the area has been subject to successive waves of invasion and to a wide variety of cultural influences. Roman, Venetian, Crusader, Tatar, Kuman, Turk, Magyar, and German, to mention only a few, all have left their mark on the land. Some of the conquests, for instance that of the Romans, were beneficial to the territory. The successive barbarian invasions from the north, however, were extremely detrimental, and the later years of Ottoman domination brought a long period of stagnation in the development of the Balkan peoples. Each conquest, however, has had a determining effect on all aspects of Balkan civilization and most especially on the ethnic composition of the population.

Internal Divisions. The frequent invasions of the Balkan Peninsula are largely responsible for the political divisions of the area and the variety of national characteristics among the people. Although the peninsula comprises an area of only about 295,000 square miles (764,000 sq km)—a little larger than the state of Texas—its peoples speak seven major languages (Albanian, Bulgarian, Greek, Rumanian, Serbo-Croatian, Slovene, and Macedonian) and are divided into three principal religions (Roman Catholic, Orthodox, and Muslim). The Orthodox churches themselves are organized on national lines.

Although the modern Balkan nations share certain traditions and general characteristics as a result of their similar histories, relations between the major political groups have been almost continually strained and competitive, even in the face of outside menace. The conflicts of modern times have their roots in the Middle Ages, when the early kingdoms of Serbia, Bulgaria, and Greek Byzantium fought over the lands composing present-day Macedonia. The subsequent period of Ottoman control, imposed largely because the Christian peoples failed to unite against a common foe, saw the Greeks struggling against Serbs and Bulgars over ecclesiastical administration and domination.

In the 19th century, national pressures, together with the conflicting interests of the great powers, who were intervening in Balkan politics, placed the peninsula in a state of almost continual turmoil. During a century (1815–1914) of relative peace in the rest of Europe, the Balkan Peninsula was the scene of warfare in 1821–1829, 1853–1856, 1875–1878, 1885, 1897, and 1912–1913. The unsettling effect of these contests was accentuated by frequent civil wars. The Balkans were again torn by war and invasion from 1914 to 1922 and from 1939, when Mussolini annexed Albania, to 1949, when the Greek civil war was brought to an end. The frequency and intensity of these conflicts have left a deep imprint on the outlook of the Balkan peoples, and they help to account for the low economic level of the area throughout most of its history.

The tendency of the Balkan nations to follow separate paths of national development continued into the years after World War II. After 1945, under strong outside influence, Albania, Bulgaria, Rumania, and Yugoslavia adopted socialist political systems closely modeled on the Soviet pattern. Subsequently, however, alterations were made in the relationships that had been established in the immediate postwar years. In 1948, in a sharp controversy with Soviet Premier Joseph Stalin, Yugoslav Premier Tito claimed his country's right to develop its own brand of socialism. In 1960, Albania broke with the Soviet Union, as it had broken previously with Yugoslavia, and thereafter sought closer relations with Communist China. By 1964, Rumania had asserted its independent position and its intention of determining its own economic policies. After a bitter civil war lasting from 1946 to 1949, Greece, with strong American military and economic assistance, remained linked with the West and retained its political and economic system. Bulgaria, in contrast to the other Balkan socialist states, maintained its close association with Moscow.

Outside influence and internal division have remained characteristic of Balkan political history in the present as in the past. The interrelations of the Balkan states have been largely determined in the postwar period by the internal political evolution of the individual states and by international events and the changing relations of the great powers—Communist China, the Soviet Union, and the United States.

1. The People

After both World War I and World War II there were great exchanges of population among the Balkan nations, so that today most of the states are relatively homogeneous in ethnic composition. The two important exceptions are the large Albanian populations in the Kosovo-Metohija area of Yugoslavia and the Hungarian minorities in Rumanian Transylvania. Although there are other minority groups, such as the Turks in Greek Thrace and the Hungarians in the Yugoslav Voivodina (Vojvodina), they are politically less significant.

Language and Religion. In addition to the three dominant religions, Roman Catholic, Orthodox, and Muslim, there are small groups of Protestants and Jews. Despite the length of the Ottoman occupation, very few inhabitants of the peninsula are of Turkish origin. It is believed that most of the present Muslims are the descendants of Christian converts.

With the exception of Yugoslavia, most of the Balkan states are organized on a national basis, with a centralized state administration and with a single language and religion predominating. Albania, with a population of 1,814,000, is the smallest Balkan nation, both in area and in population. The Albanian language is unrelated to that of any other Balkan people. The country's close association in the past with the Ottoman empire is shown in its religious composition. Approximately 70 percent of the Albanian people are Muslims, while about 20 percent are Orthodox and 10 percent are Catholic. Bulgaria, with a population of 8,144,000, is, in contrast, predominantly Orthodox, although it has a small Muslim minority. Its language is Slavic and close to Russian. Greece, with 8,510,000 inhabitants, is also Orthodox in religion. Its language is closely related to ancient Greek, which is evidence of the particularly long cultural heritage of the people. Rumania, the second largest of the Balkan countries, has a population of 18,297,000. Rumanian is a Romance language, but it has strong foreign elements. The principal religion is Orthodoxy, but there is a Catholic minority.

The most complex linguistic and religious structure is found in Yugoslavia. With a population of 19,511,000 people, it is the largest of the Balkan nations. Yugoslavia's ethnic problems are reflected in its federal administrative structure. Interwar and wartime conflicts between the peoples of Yugoslavia led to the organization of the state in 1945 on the basis of its six historic divisions—Slovenia, Croatia, Bosnia-Hercegovina, Serbia, Montenegro, and Macedonia. Slovenia, situated in the northwest of Yugoslavia, is predominantly Catholic in religion. Its people speak a language that is Slavic but that is not readily intelligible to the other peoples of Yugoslavia. Croatia, like Slovenia, is Catholic. Its language, Serbo-Croatian, is virtually identical to that spoken in Serbia, but it is written in the Roman rather than in the Cyrillic alphabet. Bosnia-Hercegovina, a transitional area between Serbia and Croatia, has a mixed religious composition of Orthodox and Catholics, and in contrast to the rest of Yugoslavia, it has a large Muslim minority (about 30 percent of the population). Serbo-Croatian is spoken in Bosnia-Hercegovina. Serbia, politically the most significant of the divisions, is Orthodox in religion, and the Serbo-Croatian language is used with the Cyrillic alphabet. Montenegro differs little from Serbia in religion or language. The sixth division, Macedonia, is Orthodox in religion. Its people speak Macedonian, which was recognized in Yugoslavia as a separate language only after World War II. It is similar to Bulgarian as well as to Serbo-Croatian.

Cultural Life. The rich and varied cultural heritage of the Balkan Peninsula is reflected in the life of its people and in the monuments of its past. The predominant influence in most of the area is that of the Ottoman occupation and the Byzantine-Orthodox cultural tradition that preceded it. This Eastern orientation is particularly characteristic of the lands that remained part of the Ottoman empire after the Treaty of Karlowitz (1699). In contrast, those lands—notably Slovenia, Croatia, and Transylvania—that fell under Austrian rule before this date have many similarities with the other areas that were part of the Habsburg monarchy (Austrian empire). The Dalmatian coast of Yugoslavia, long under the direct or indirect control of Venice, still shows the influence of the Venetian cultural tradition.

Turkish domination is reflected directly in Albania and Bosnia, both of which have large Muslim populations. Greek national feeling, even today, is strongly influenced by the traditions of ancient Greece and, even more significantly, by those of the Byzantine empire. The Roman past has a similar appeal to the Rumanians. In addition to these major trends, each Balkan people, indeed each individual area, has developed its own unique peasant culture, which is reflected in folksongs, costumes, village architecture, and painting.

Population Distribution. Until comparatively recent times the entire Balkan area was predominantly agricultural, and the vast majority of the population lived in small villages, in close societies with strong family ties. The emphasis on industrialization and modernization after World War II caused a revolution in the daily life of a large section of the population. The building of huge industrial complexes has created new population centers and has resulted in a large-scale movement from the villages to the cities. This change has been accelerated by the immense improvement in transportation and communication in all the states.

The Balkan Peninsula is thus undergoing a period of rapid change and development. The capital cities of the individual nations, all of which have experienced large increases in population since World War II, remain the centers of national life. The largest city on the peninsula is Istanbul, with 1,466,535 inhabitants; it is followed in size by Bucharest (1,236,065), Sofia (724,600), Athens (627,564), and Belgrade (585,234). Tiranë, the Albanian capital, has 140,300 people.

2. The Land and Natural Resources

The chief geographic feature of the Balkan Peninsula is its mountainous terrain. Dominated by the great Carpathian, Dinaric, Balkan, and Rhodope mountain chains, the area is relatively rich in forest and mineral resources, but it suffers from a lack of adequate agricultural land. The chief agricultural regions are Thessaly in Greece, the Maritsa Valley in Bulgaria, the Voivodina in Yugoslavia, and the Banat and Wallachia in Rumania.

The mountainous nature of the Balkan Peninsula and the lack of good agricultural land have had a decisive effect on the course of Balkan history and on the economic and social life of its inhabitants. The mountain chains divide the peninsula in a way that hinders internal communication, but that does not impede outside invasion.

Three great historic routes through the penin-

MAP BY DONALD T. PITCHER

The Balkan States

sula mark the paths of the conquerors of the past. The first runs from north of the Black Sea through Rumania, across the Balkan Mountains, to Istanbul (Constantinople). This was the gateway into the Balkans for the eastern invasions that occurred in the early years of Balkan history. In the 19th century the Russian armies followed this road in their campaigns against the Ottoman empire. The second route runs from Vienna to Belgrade, and then to Niš, where one branch turns toward Sofia and Istanbul, the other toward Thessalonike (Salonika) and Athens. This route is especially significant because it marks the main line of rail and road transportation in the Balkans today. The third road, the Roman Via Egnatia, was one of the major routes of the ancient world, but it has little significance today. It passes through Albania and northern Greece and runs to Istanbul. The Danube River has historically been the chief line of communication in the northern part of the peninsula.

Climate. The climate of the Balkan Peninsula is varied. Most of the region has a continental climate, characterized by cold winters and relatively even distribution of rainfall. These areas grow the standard grain crops of central Europe—wheat, rye, oats, corn, and flax. Cows and pigs are raised there. The coastal areas of the peninsula and the islands of the Aegean, Adriatic, and Ionian seas have a typically Mediterranean climate, with long, hot, dry summers and temperate winters. These lands produce olives, grapes, figs, and citrus fruits. Their principal livestock are sheep and goats.

3. The Economy

In modern times the economic life of the Balkan nations has been backward in comparison with the rest of Europe. The great differences in the standards of living and in the natural endowments of the different regions have been important aspects of Balkan economic life. In general, the areas formerly under Ottoman rule are less developed than those whose histories were more closely connected with the Habsburg monarchy. There is, for example, an obvious contrast in standards within Yugoslavia, where Slovenia and Croatia, formerly under Austrian rule, retain an advantage over the poorer regions of Bosnia-Hercegovina, Montenegro, and Macedonia, which were under Ottoman rule as late as the 19th century.

The 19th Century Background. One of the causes of the region's poverty is its political organization; the Balkan states individually are too small and do not possess the basic resources to be strong industrial nations. Other reasons for the area's relative backwardness are historic. All the modern Balkan states arrived late on the scene; they did not achieve real national independence until the 20th century. In the 19th century, nationalism led them to devote their efforts and resources to consolidating and extending their territory, so they concentrated on arms and armies, rather than on internal improvements.

At the end of the 19th century the Balkan states increased the exploitation of their mineral resources and initiated a degree of industrialization. This effort was accompanied by a high rate of foreign investment and by strong state direction. The trend continued until the outbreak of World War II, but comparatively little success was achieved. Despite their efforts, the Balkan states remained overwhelmingly agrarian.

Throughout the period before World War I, agriculture in the Balkans remained primitive, with poor methods of cultivation and low yields. Large estates were characteristic of Croatia, Rumania, and some parts of Greece, while small peasant holdings predominated in Serbia and Bulgaria. With the rise in population that occurred at this time and the consequent fragmentation of peasant holdings, the land problem became increasingly difficult. After World War I, redistribution plans were adopted, but the land problem remained acute. The peasant suffered from a growing birthrate, high taxation, low production, and a wide differential between agricultural and industrial prices.

Impact of Socialism. The period after World War II brought revolutionary economic changes with the introduction of socialist systems in four of the five Balkan states. The years immediately after the war were devoted to repairing war damage. Then the socialist governments embarked on a radically new course of economic development, with the abolition of private enterprise and concentration on rapid industrialization under strong state control and direction. Despite the fact that no Balkan state had a really adequate base for the system, the socialist governments developed their economies on the Soviet model. Each nation attempted to construct a balanced industrial complex. They first emphasized the development of heavy industry, with the result that production of consumer goods suffered by contrast.

Rumania and Yugoslavia have been the most successful in industrial development. The Rumanian economic growth rate has been the highest in the Balkans. Yugoslavia, despite repeated shortages and setbacks, has achieved a considerable increase in production.

In the postwar period all the Balkan states have made great advances in transportation and communications. The roads and railroads, although still inadequate, have been extended and improved. Most significant is the growth of air transport, which links previously remote and inaccessible regions with the major cities. The development of electrical power in all the nations has had an important effect on national economic life and on living standards.

With the chief effort directed toward industrial development, agriculture in the socialist states has suffered comparative neglect. Areas that formerly exported farm surpluses now have developed shortages. The new regimes first attempted to meet their agrarian problems with collectivization and an increased use of farm machinery. After repeated failures, Yugoslavia abandoned collectivization in 1953. Greece, the only nonsocialist state and still a predominantly agrarian country, has emphasized reclaiming and extending her agricultural lands. The effort was rewarded; in 1965, for the first time since World War II, Greece produced a surplus of grain.

The economic policies and external trade relations of the Balkan nations since World War II have been closely associated with their political evolution and with world events. Although in the immediate postwar period the Soviet Union gained a predominant influence in the socialist countries of Albania, Bulgaria, Rumania, and Yugoslavia, with the United States retaining influence in Greece and Turkey, this relationship soon underwent significant modifications. Yugoslavia in 1948, Albania in 1960, and Rumania in 1964 asserted their right to independent development in relation to the other socialist countries. These actions were accompanied by changes within the states and shifts in their external trade relations. After breaking with the Soviet Union, Yugoslavia accepted extensive aid from the United States and developed its trade with the West. Albania, in conflict with all the other Balkan states, tried to increase her trade with the West and with China.

4. History

The Balkan Peninsula has remains of human habitation dating back to approximately 6000 B.C. The area contained the center of ancient Greek civilization and was a part of the Roman empire. The Roman occupation left a particularly strong imprint on the culture and traditions of present-day Rumania, which in the 2d and 3d centuries A.D. comprised the Roman province of Dacia. Although the territory was subjected in later years to repeated invasions, Latin remained the base of the Rumanian language.

There were numerous barbarian invasions of the Balkan Peninsula, but that of the Slavs, which began in the 5th century and reached a peak in the 6th and 7th centuries, had the greatest effect on the subsequent ethnic composition of the area. Some Slavic tribes went as far south as the Peloponnesus (now part of Greece). The 7th century also witnessed the arrival of the Bulgars, a Turkic-speaking people, who subsequently were assimilated into the Slavic population.

Middle Ages. After the division of the Roman empire in 285 A.D. the greater part of the Balkan Peninsula fell to the Eastern Roman (Byzantine) empire. With its capital at Constantinople the Byzantine empire remained the most powerful military, political, and cultural force in the area for a thousand years. Its position of religious leadership was most important. After 1054, when the Christian churches of East and West split,

Constantinople became the center of the Orthodox world, and its influence extended not only over the Orthodox peoples of the Balkans but also over those in Russia.

This period, the Middle Ages of Balkan history, saw the formation, consolidation, and extension of Bulgarian and Serbian kingdoms. The first Bulgarian empire was founded by Simeon (893–927). After its destruction by the Byzantine empire, the second Bulgarian empire was founded in 1186 by the Asen brothers, with its center at Tirnovo. The Serbian kingdom was established by Stevan Nemanja (reigned 1168–1196), but its greatest ruler was Stevan Dušan (1331–1355). In 1204, another significant year in Balkan history, the Crusaders captured Constantinople, thus paving the way for the establishment of Frankish kingdoms in the southern part of the peninsula.

Ottoman Conquest. In the 14th century the Christian Balkan states, whose relations were characterized by intense and bitter rivalry, fell to the Muslim Turks. The Turks took Adrianople in 1365 and defeated the Serbian empire at the Battle of Kossovo in 1389. They then subdued Bulgaria and made vassal states of the Rumanian principalities of Wallachia and Moldavia. In 1453, Sultan Mehmed II (reigned 1451–1481) captured Constantinople. The height of Ottoman power was reached under Suleiman the Magnificent (reigned 1520–1566). During his reign the Turks took Belgrade (1521) and defeated Hungary at the Battle of Mohács (1526). The Ottoman armies were stopped only at Vienna in 1529.

For approximately 500 years Ottoman influence remained predominant in the Balkans. In that period the Christian communities were governed through their church organizations, because the Ottoman government recognized religious rather than national affiliation. Through the reign of Suleiman the Ottoman empire was an effective and viable political organization. Thereafter it began a long period of decline. As maladministration and corruption in the government increased, the position of the sultan's subjects deteriorated commensurately. The empire's internal weakness was reflected in its military position. After the failure of the second siege of Vienna (1683) the Ottoman armies were no longer a threat to the rest of Europe. In 1699, according to the terms of the Treaty of Karlowitz, the Ottoman empire was forced to surrender to Austria most of Hungary, Transylvania, Croatia, and Slavonia. Venice acquired Dalmatia and the Peloponnesus.

In the 18th century, Austria and Russia, usually acting together, won further victories in the Balkans. The provisions of the Treaty of Kuchuk Kainarji (1774) extended the Russian boundary to the Black Sea, and in subsequent years Russia used certain parts of the agreement to claim a special right to speak on behalf of the Balkan Christians. Russian rights were confirmed and extended by the treaties of Jassy (1792) and Bucharest (1812). At the Congress of Vienna (1815), Austria was awarded the former Venetian territory of Dalmatia.

Era of National Liberation. Although a spirit of national revival spread through the Balkans at the end of the 18th century, Balkan independence from Turkish rule was achieved only by slow stages throughout the 19th century. Because of the strategic significance of the peninsula, the "Eastern Question"—the problem of determining the political fate of the increasingly feeble Ottoman empire—became the chief issue in European international relations between 1815 and 1914.

The chief antagonists in the diplomatic conflict were Britain and Russia. Concerned with the preservation of its communications with the East and with India in particular, Britain feared that the collapse of the Ottoman empire would be followed by Russian domination of the area. Britain therefore tried to maintain Ottoman power but at the same time to secure reforms in the administration of the subject nationalities. Russia, on the other hand, was more willing to give direct help to the Balkan people, who were in the majority Orthodox and in part Slavic. Austria, apprehensive of a growth of Russian power, tended to take the British position. France, at odds with Britain over other Mediterranean issues, took a pragmatic approach, changing its position in every crisis to meet the demands of its own interests.

Despite the contradictory aims and policies of the great powers, the Albanians, Bulgarians, Greeks, Montenegrins, Rumanians, and Serbians were able to establish their independence by 1914.

Early 19th Century. The Serbian uprising against local Ottoman administration in 1804 began the age of national revolution in the Balkans. A second outbreak in 1815 gained Serbia the right to an autonomous administration.

In 1821 the Greeks revolted; their revolution and the problems associated with it dominated international relations in the 1820's. European intervention in the conflict ultimately led to the Battle of Navarino (1827), in which a combined British-French-Russian force sank the Turkish fleet.

In 1828 the Ottoman empire rashly declared war on Russia. The resultant Russo-Turkish War brought Russian armies again into the Balkans. In 1829 the defeated Ottoman empire was forced to sign the Treaty of Adrianople, which reaffirmed the autonomous rights of Serbia and Rumania, who were now put under Russian protection, and provided for the formation of a Greek state. Subsequently, in treaties signed in 1830 and 1832, Britain, Russia, and France, acting together, established an independent Greece, with extremely limited boundaries, and chose the Bavarian prince Otto (Othon) as its first ruler.

Later 19th Century. The Crimean War (1853–1856) led to further major changes. In the Treaty of Paris (1856) the Russian protectorate over Serbia and the Rumanian principalities was replaced by great power supervision. Russia also surrendered her claim to a special relationship with the Balkan Orthodox Christians. Because of subsequent differences between the powers, the Rumanian national movement then was able to make great progress. In 1859 the principalities of Wallachia and Moldavia both elected Alexander Cuza as their ruler, and in 1861 their administrative systems were amalgamated. A coup d'état in 1866 resulted in the replacement of Cuza with a foreign prince, Charles (Carol) of Hohenzollern.

In the following decade the Bulgarians inaugurated a successful revolt against Ottoman authority. After an uprising in Bosnia-Hercegovina (1875) and a Serbo-Montenegrin war against the Ottoman empire (1876), Russia once more intervened. The resultant Russo-Turkish War of 1877–1878 marked another Ottoman defeat. The

Treaty of San Stefano, signed at the end of the conflict, provided for the creation of a greater Bulgaria, including Macedonia. This agreement, in violation of previous pacts, aroused the fears of the other powers, who saw in the new Bulgaria a Russian satellite.

In the face of strong British and Austrian opposition, Russia accepted a revision of the Treaty of San Stefano at the Congress of Berlin (1878). Here greater Bulgaria was divided into three parts: Bulgaria, Eastern Rumelia, and Macedonia. Serbia and Montenegro both were given extensions of territory, and Serbia, Montenegro, and Rumania were granted full independence. Austria-Hungary was given the right to occupy Bosnia-Hercegovina.

Greece acquired Thessaly and Epirus in 1881. Rumania was recognized as a kingdom in 1881 and Serbia in 1882. Despite the provisions of the Treaty of Berlin, Bulgaria and Eastern Rumelia were united in 1885. In the major international crisis that resulted, the first Bulgarian ruler, Alexander of Battenberg, was forced to abdicate and was replaced by Ferdinand of Coburg.

After 1890 the two areas still under Ottoman rule that commanded international attention were Crete and Macedonia. At the end of a war between Greece and Turkey in 1897, accompanied by great power intervention, Crete was given a separate administration under the governorship of a Greek prince. The Macedonian problem, however, proved more difficult to settle.

Balkan Wars. In 1912, with Russian encouragement, Bulgaria, Greece, Montenegro, and Serbia formed the Balkan League, which started a war with the Ottoman empire. The First Balkan War, a victory for the Balkan allies, was followed by a quarrel over the division of Macedonian territories, and a new conflict followed. In the Second Balkan War, Greece, Serbia, Rumania, and Turkey were arrayed against Bulgaria. As a result of her defeat Bulgaria was virtually excluded from the partition of the remaining Turkish lands in Europe. The wars resulted in Greek annexation of Crete and the formation of Albania.

By 1913, Turkish control in the Balkans had been reduced to the area of Thrace immediately surrounding Constantinople. With the question of Turkish power in the Balkans settled, the major Balkan conflict remaining involved the relations of Austria-Hungary with her South Slav nationals and with the independent kingdom of Serbia. In 1908 the Habsburg monarchy changed its occupation of Bosnia-Hercegovina to complete annexation, thereby dealing a strong blow to Serbian hopes for eventual acquisition of the two provinces. The increasing tension between the monarchy and Serbia was paralleled within the empire by the increasing discontent of its Slavic peoples with their role in the state. The agitation surrounding these issues resulted in the assassination of Archduke Franz Ferdinand, the heir to the Habsburg throne, in Sarajevo, Bosnia, on June 28, 1914. Balkan national conflicts thus provided the incident that pulled all of Europe into World War I.

World War I and After. In World War I, Serbia, Rumania (in 1916), and Greece (in 1917) joined with France, Britain, and Russia; Turkey (in 1914) and Bulgaria (in 1915) aligned themselves with the Central Powers. Serbia was crushed by 1915, but in 1918 a major campaign beginning in Thessalonike resulted in victory for the Western allies and their supporters.

The war brought about three major changes in the political map of the Balkans. In 1918, Yugoslavia (called at first the Kingdom of the Serbs, Croats, and Slovenes) was formed from Serbia, Montenegro, and the Habsburg South Slav lands. Rumania completed the formation of her modern national state with the acquisition of Transylvania. Bulgaria lost to Greece her outlet on the Aegean Sea.

In general, the years between World War I and World War II were difficult for all the Balkan states. Greece underwent a major disaster in 1922, when after a defeat by nationalist Turkey, she was forced to accept the expulsion of 1,500,000 of her nationals from Anatolia. Bulgaria remained bitter and disillusioned after her defeat in two wars. Yugoslavia suffered from the inability of the Serbs and Croats to adjust their traditional rivalries within the new state. All the nations had internal economic difficulties and severe minority problems. The rise of fascist Italy and Nazi Germany in the 1930's brought the Balkan states face to face with an immediate threat in the international field. In 1939, Albania, unable to defend itself, was annexed by Italy.

World War II. In the first days of World War II the Balkan states were able to retain a precarious neutrality, but soon Bulgaria and Rumania were drawn into the German camp. Bulgarian forces cooperated in the occupation of Greece and Macedonia, and Rumanian armies fought alongside the Germans in Russia.

Actual conflict in the peninsula began in 1940 when Italy's dictator, Benito Mussolini, launched an invasion of Greece. The Italians' inability to carry through this campaign led to a German invasion of both Greece and Yugoslavia in 1941. The conditions of this conflict and the occupation that followed led to the creation of large guerrilla forces in both countries that were later of great political significance. After the defeat of Germany, Russian armies entered the Balkans, and by the conclusion of the war they were occupying Bulgaria and Rumania.

Postwar Conditions. The end of the war in 1945 introduced a period of revolutionary change. In Albania, Bulgaria, Rumania, and Yugoslavia, Communist regimes came to power—as they did in Czechoslovakia, East Germany, Hungary, and Poland. At first the Communist bloc states cooperated closely among themselves and with the Soviet Union. The Warsaw Pact, signed in 1955, joined all these states (except Yugoslavia) in a strong military alliance, the counterpart of the North Atlantic Treaty Organization (NATO). In Greece the prewar government returned to power, but only after a costly civil war (1946–1949) and with the help of extensive foreign aid from the United States. Greece and Turkey became partners in NATO. The postwar east-west division was thus reflected in the Balkans.

Although the Communist bloc countries, with similar political and economic institutions, were closely aligned at first, division among them and a renewed emphasis on national individuality increasingly characterized their postwar relations. The first major rift among these states was caused by Yugoslavia's actions at the time of the Tito-Stalin controversy of 1948. Expelled from the Communist camp, Yugoslavia turned to the West and received extensive economic and military assistance. Although relations between Yugoslavia and Russia improved after Stalin's death in

1953, Yugoslavia thereafter attempted to preserve a neutralist position in international affairs and, in her relations with other Communist states, to insist on following her own path toward socialism.

Albania, the second state to establish an independent position within the Communist bloc, first used the Tito-Stalin quarrel to throw off Yugoslav influence over her internal affairs. Subsequently Albania, through its strong support of Communist China in the latter's controversy with the Soviet Union over the issue of leadership of the world Communist movement, separated itself from the European Communist states and from Yugoslavia. The Albanian stand resulted in strong verbal attacks from the other Communist regimes and an economic boycott. In reply, Albania strengthened its ties with China and with some West European countries.

Rumania's move toward independence within the Communist world came later and was primarily caused by economic matters. In 1949 the Communist nations established the Council for Mutual Economic Assistance (COMECON) as the counterpart of the Marshall Plan. By 1960, COMECON had developed plans to coordinate the economies of its member states and to introduce a better division of labor among them. The states with developed industrial economies, such as East Germany and Czechoslovakia, were to retain their industrial specialization. Rumania, whose rate of industrial growth had increased greatly, nevertheless was cast primarily in the role of a supplier of raw materials. The Rumanian government strongly protested this plan, and in 1964 the Rumanian Communist party issued a strong declaration on the equality of all Communist parties. Rumania at the same time sought to strengthen its ties with the West and with China.

Of the Balkan Communist states, Bulgaria alone retained its original ties with the other nations of the Communist bloc and with the Soviet Union. In addition, relations with both Greece and Yugoslavia were improved considerably. In 1964, negotiations with Greece settled many of the problems outstanding between the two countries since World War I.

Although Greece has remained close to the Western powers, a serious weakness in the NATO defenses appeared in 1964 when Greece and Turkey hovered at the brink of war over the position of the Turkish minority on Cyprus. As a result of this crisis, the United Nations sent a force to keep peace on the island.

CHARLES JELAVICH
BARBARA JELAVICH
Indiana University

Bibliography
Dellin, L.A.D., ed., *Bulgaria* (New York 1957).
Forster, E.S., *A Short History of Modern Greece, 1821–1956*, 3d ed., revised by Douglas Dakin (London 1958).
Jelavich, Charles, and Jelavich, Barbara, *The Balkans* (Englewood Cliffs, N.J., 1965).
Jelavich, Charles, and Jelavich, Barbara, eds., *The Balkans in Transition: Essays in the Development of Balkan Life and Politics Since the Eighteenth Century* (Berkeley, Calif., 1963).
Roberts, Henry L., *Rumania: Political Problems of an Agrarian State* (New Haven 1951).
Stavrianos, L., *The Balkans since 1453* (New York 1958).
Tomasevich, Jozo, *Peasants, Politics, and Economic Change in Yugoslavia* (Stanford, Calif., 1955).
Warriner, Doreen, ed., *Contrasts in Emerging Societies: Readings in the Social and Economic History of South-Eastern Europe in the Nineteenth Century* (Bloomington, Ind., 1965).
Wolff, Robert Lee, *The Balkans in Our Time* (Cambridge, Mass., 1956).

BALKH, bälкн, a city in northern Afghanistan, was the capital of ancient Bactria. It was renowned as the "mother of cities" and the "city of high banners." Alexander the Great is believed to have founded a Greek colony at the site about 330 B.C., and the city, then known as *Bactra,* flourished as the capital of Graeco-Bactria. Later, Buddhist monasteries and stupas, or reliquary mounds, dotted the site.

Captured by Muslim armies at the end of the 7th century A.D., the city increased greatly in size and over several centuries was embellished with palaces and mosques. But early in the 13th century the Mongol hordes of Genghis Khan razed it to the ground. It never regained its former importance, but some resettlement after the Mongol destruction did take place. The ruined, tiled mausoleum of Khwaja Abu Nasr Mohammed Parsa was built about 1460. The new town of Balkh was incorporated into Afghanistan in 1850. Sections of the great walls of the ancient city remain, and limited excavations have brought to light objects of the early Muslim period. Nothing of earlier times has been found.

A few miles to the east of the site of Balkh is the modern city of Mazar-i-Sharif, which replaced the ancient city as the regional center. Mazar-i-Sharif means "noble tomb," and the Afghans believe the tomb is that of Ali Ibn Abi Talib, son-in-law of Mohammed the prophet. The tomb is part of a great shrine surrounded by a circular avenue. All the structures are sheathed in bright tiles in which blue-green predominates. See also BACTRIA.

DONALD N. WILBER, *Editor of "Afghanistan"*

BALKHASH, bäl-käsh', a city in the USSR, is located in Karaganda oblast in southeastern Kazakhstan, on the north shore of Lake Balkhash. The city was founded in 1928 as an industrial center and was named Balkhash in 1937, having first been called *Bertys* and later *Pribalkhash.* Balkhash is an important rail terminus and lake port. Truck farming is carried on in the region. However, Balkhash is important chiefly for the smelting of copper, which is brought from the Kounrad deposits, 12 miles (19 km) to the north. Population: (1959) 53,031.

BALKHASH, Lake, bäl-кнäsh', a body of water in southeastern Kazakhstan, Soviet Central Asia. With an area of about 6,671 square miles (17,-278 sq km) the lake is approximately 440 miles (708 km) long but only 15 to 55 miles (24 to 80 km) wide. It is shaped like a broad crescent, and is fed chiefly by the Ili River. The northern edge is well defined, but the southern shore is a labyrinth of islands, peninsulas, and strips of shallow water. Although it has no outlet, Lake Balkhash has a low salinity. Carp and perch are found in its shallow waters, and there are copper deposits on the northern shore.

BALL, bôl, **George Wildman** (1909–), American public official and diplomat, who was appointed U. S. ambassador to the United Nations in 1968. He was born in Des Moines, Iowa, on Dec. 21, 1909, and was educated at Northwestern University, where he received his law degree in 1933. For the next two years he was a government lawyer in Washington, D.C. After practicing tax law in Chicago (1935–1942), he returned to Washington as associate general counsel for the Lend-Lease Administration. Near the end of World War II he directed the U.S. Strategic Bombing Survey in London. As an international lawyer from 1946 to 1961, Ball represented the European Economic Community and worked in the European unification movement.

In January 1961, Ball headed a task force on trade and tariff policy for President-elect Kennedy. His tariff-cutting proposals became part of the Kennedy program, and he was named undersecretary of state for economic affairs in the new administration. On Nov. 26, 1961, Ball was made principal undersecretary with responsibility in the whole range of policy planning. He retired from the department in 1966, but served briefly in 1968 as ambassador to the United Nations. In 1969 he returned to his law practice.

BALL, bôl, **John** (d. 1381), English priest who with Wat Tyler was a leader of the Peasants' Revolt in 1381. Information on his life is incomplete, but he is believed to have been a priest at York and then at Colchester. He began to agitate for peasants' rights many years before the revolt. Some of his preaching—particularly his attacks on church ownership of property and on social inequality—resemble the doctrines of John Wycliffe. However, there is no evidence that Ball was a disciple of Wycliffe.

In 1366 the archbishop of Canterbury censured Ball and forbade the faithful to listen to his sermons. Later he was excommunicated and in 1376 an order for his arrest was issued. Ball was confined at various times, and was in prison when Tyler's revolt broke out in 1381. However, rebels from Kent freed him and he went with them to London, where he preached a sermon based on the famous couplet:

> When Adam delved and Eve span,
> Who was then the gentleman?

According to chroniclers of the revolt, Ball urged the people to kill the nobles and higher clergy.

After Tyler was killed and the revolt was crushed, Ball fled from London. He was captured, taken before King Richard II, condemned as a traitor, and executed at St. Albans. See also TYLER, WAT.

BALL, bôl, **Lucille** (1911–   ), American actress and television producer, who produced and starred in *I Love Lucy* and its successor, *The Lucy Show,* one of the most durable series on television. She was born in Jamestown, N.Y., on Aug. 6, 1911. Before her appearance on television in 1951 she was in some 55 films, beginning with a bit part in *Roman Scandals* (1934), usually as a wisecracking chorus girl. While working on *Too Many Girls* (1940), she met Desi Arnaz, a Cuban bandleader, whom she married in 1940. She subsequently appeared in such films as *DuBarry Was a Lady* (1943), *Best Foot Forward* (1943), *The Fuller Brush Girl* (1950), and *The Facts of Life* (1961).

In 1950 she and her husband formed a company—Desilu Productions—to produce filmed television shows. Their first production, telecast in October 1951, was *I Love Lucy,* starring themselves. Both the show and the production company were immediate successes, and both survived the couple's divorce in 1960. Arnaz, however, did not appear on the subsequent *Lucy Show.* Miss Ball won the 1956 Academy of Television Arts and Sciences "Emmy" award as the best actress in a comedy series in 1955.

BALL, bôl, **Thomas** (1819–1911), American sculptor, who was especially celebrated for his equestrian statue of George Washington in the Boston Public Garden. He was born in Charlestown, Mass., on June 3, 1819. His father's early death made it necessary for Ball to help support the family, and he was employed at the New England Museum in Boston as a boy-of-all-work. He then began to study painting and sculpture.

In 1854 he settled in Florence, Italy, where he remained until 1897 except for several years in the 1850's and 1860's when he worked in Boston on the statue of George Washington (unveiled in 1869). Daniel Chester French studied with Ball in Italy in 1876–1877. Ball published his autobiography, *My Threescore Years and Ten,* in 1891. He died in Montclair, N.J., on Dec. 11, 1911.

Ball's most important works, in addition to the equestrian Washington, include a life-size bust of Daniel Webster (1868), now in the Metropolitan Museum, New York City, and a statue of Edwin Forrest as Coriolanus (model completed in 1867), now in the Actor's Home, Philadelphia, Pa. The most important of his larger works are *Emancipation* (1875), a group with Lincoln and a kneeling slave, in Washington, D.C.; a statue of Daniel Webster (1876), in Central Park, New York City, based on the earlier bust; a statue of Josiah Quincy (1879), in Boston; and the Washington monument (1893), in Methuen, Mass.

BALL BEARINGS. See BEARINGS, ANTIFRICTION.

BALLA, bäl′lä, **Giacomo** (1871–1958), Italian painter, who was one of the founders and leading artists of the futurist school. He was born in Turin, Italy, on July 24, 1871. Except for a brief period of study in Paris, he was almost entirely self-taught. Settling in Rome in 1901, he began his career as a realistic painter, but he soon turned to symbolism and then to a form of neo-impressionism called "divisionism." With the Italian painters Umberto Boccioni, Carlo Carrà, Gino Severini, and Luigi Russolo, he signed the "Manifesto of the Futurist Painters" on Feb. 11, 1910. The painters of the futurist movement, which flourished only from 1910 to about 1916, attempted to represent objects, especially animals and machines, in motion. Balla exhibited with the futurists after 1912 and remained faithful to the movement long after its other adherents had deserted it. In the 1920's, however, he began to paint in other styles and by the 1930's had abandoned futurism for more traditionally representational painting. He died in Rome on March 6, 1958.

As a futurist, Balla was indebted to cubism (q.v.) for much of his style. His best futurist paintings are intensely dynamic and energetic. His subjects are frequently birds in flight, as in *Swifts: Paths of Movement* (1913), and automobiles in motion, as in *Speeding Automobile* (1912) and *Automobile Speed Plus Lights Plus Noises* (1913). Both Balla and Russolo tried to express body movements in many of their paintings. Balla's most notable attempts are *Dynamism of a Dog on a Leash* (1912) and *Rhythm of the Violinist* (1914). His important paintings in other styles include the socially conscious *The Sewer* (1902), from his realistic period, and *The Mad Woman* (1905), from his neoimpressionist period. See also FUTURISM.

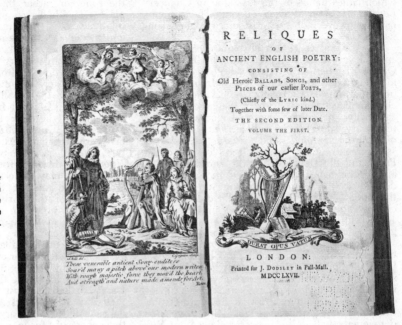

ENGLISH BALLADS were compiled by Thomas Percy in *Reliques of Ancient English Poetry*, first published in 1765 and reissued in 1767.

BALLAD, bal'əd, in literary usage, a simple narrative lyric of known or unknown origin that tells a story. In looser usage, nearly any type of lyric has been called a ballad, and certain musical compositions also are called ballads. Since the days of the romantic movement, with its enthusiastic medievalism, the traditional ballad orally handed on has found its way into the foreground of attention as a species of folk song. The human appeal of many such pieces, their charm of form and expression, and the fascinating mysteries of their origin have won them a place in poetical anthologies, both popular and scholarly, and made them the subject of much investigation. In many countries, notably England, Scotland, Denmark, and the United States, a large body of traditional material has become available. Ballads no doubt will always be composed and sung, although the influence of the phonograph, radio, and television and the lessening of old-time group singing have diminished the popularity of the older and more traditional ballads.

Nations vary in their preferred type of popular song. Denmark and the British Isles are peculiarly rich in ballads. A fine body of narrative song has been preserved from 16th century Denmark. The main body of extant English ballads dates from the late 15th century onward, the better pieces coming from the north of England rather than the south. France and Italy have relatively few traditional ballads. Story songs in these countries are overshadowed by pure lyrics, and in Germany, too, popular song is more lyrical than narrative. Spain is rich in romantic ballads, which are narrative and dramatic rather than lyrical. Ballads have also been gathered in abundance in Russia, the Balkans, Greece, and other countries.

Rise of Interest in Balladry. The English interest in ballads dates mainly from Bishop Thomas Percy's *Reliques of Ancient English Poetry* (q.v.), published in 1765 and reissued in 1767 and later, which included many traditional ballads. His texts are not strictly authentic. He added, subtracted, and altered, sometimes in a minor way, sometimes beyond recognition. The popularity of some of his pieces spread to Germany, inspiring Johann Gottfried von Herder (*Voices of the People*, 1778–1779); the brothers Grimm; Gottfried Bürger, the author of the celebrated ballad of the supernatural, *Lenore* (1773); and others. The English Romantics were much influenced by German ballad enthusiasm. Sir Walter Scott, a collector and imitator of old ballads, started his verse career by translating Bürger's ballad. Percy and Herd preceded him as collectors, and the "Great Collectors" Jamieson, Motherwell, Hogg, Buchan, and others followed him. Prominent among the American collectors was Francis James Child, who left us our most important body of English ballad texts. In Scandinavia, leading ballad collectors were Grundtvig and Olrik, who, with Child, studied the international relationship of ballads. Their pioneer activities have perhaps given disproportionate prominence to England and Scandinavia in the study of balladry.

The Word "Ballad." "Ballad" is a good name for the lyric species it identifies. The word derives from the late Latin and Italian *ballata* (from *ballare*, to dance). It has the same parentage as *ballade* and *ballet*. Partly because of this derivation, the assumption arose that the ballad, or lyrical narrative, developed from the dance. A popular view, long held, defined the ballad as a song originally created cooperatively in the dance improvisations of the common people and handed down in popular tradition. In reality, dance genesis has more immediate connection with other types of song than with the narrative. The name belongs historically to the courtly dance song, the *ballade* (q.v.), an intricate fixed form that arose in France and was popular in England in the late 14th and 15th centuries. An illustration is the ballade to which ladies dance in the Prologue to Chaucer's *Legend of Good Women* (q.v.). The common name, however, of the aristocratic dance song was *carole*.

For several centuries the name "ballad" was applied very loosely in England. In the time of Queen Elizabeth I it was given to lyrics of almost any type, love poems, short edifying poems, poems of satire or disparagement, religious and elegaic pieces, printed street ballads, and, occasionally, narrative pieces. Deloney, a contemporary, spoke of the ballads *The Fair Flower of Northumberland* and *Flodden Field* as "songs," and Sidney praised "the old song of the Percy and the Douglas." At the end of the 17th and beginning of the 18th century, ballad was defined as a "a common song sung up and down the street." The term "ballad" did not specifically apply to the story song until the later 18th century, taking its name, not from its genesis, but by borrowing and adoption.

Bishop Percy's *Reliques* made no distinction between narrative songs and pure lyrics. It was his contemporary Joseph Ritson (1783), foreshadowed by William Shenstone (1761), who first discriminated between "songs of sentiment, expression, or even description in contradistinction to mere narrative pieces which we now denominate ballads." He was followed by William Motherwell and Child, and modern usage continues the term in Ritson's specialized sense of short lyrical narratives adapted to singing or recital. Of the immense mass of lyrical poems those that tell a story are singled out as ballads. Sometimes the line between ballad and pure lyric is hard to draw. Ballads often lose their thread of story and become pure songs. But there is no body of evidence to support the conclusion that the reverse process ever takes place—that songs, however they originate, develop into ballads by an "epic process," as some assume.

France has no distinctive name for narrative songs, but groups both ballads and songs as *chansons populaires*. Similarly, the usual German name is *Volkslieder*, but for the narrative lyric, *ballade* is borrowed from the English. The Danish term for traditional ballad is *folkeviser*. The Spanish call them *romances* and call the ballad corpus *romancero*.

Origins and Antiquity. The concept that the ballad is something originally composed more or less spontaneously through the improvisation of dancing throngs of peasantry of common folk has long been adhered to and is still embedded in literary histories. Ballads were differentiated from other poetry as "springing mysteriously from the heart of the people." This belief had its origin in 18th century Germany, with Herder and the brothers Grimm as its apostles. In England it was upheld for a time by Andrew Lang. Its leading American adherents were F. B. Gummere, G. L. Kittredge, and others of the "Harvard school." Kittredge's fanciful picture of how *The Hangman's Tree* might have been composed cooperatively greatly influenced anthologists and teachers. The belief that ballads were cooperatively composed during the Middle Ages was held longer in America than in Germany or England.

Scholars also held for a time that the choral ballad, with the refrain as its germ, was the earliest poetic form of primitive people, that from the "ballad dance" came not only the dance but poetry and music as well. In reality

the song, or rather the songlet, deserves initial place. The ballad now seems to have been of relatively late appearance, definitely European and medieval. Rhyme appeared in the 11th century, and the ballad seems to have emerged about the 12th century, perhaps later. The 14th century "rhymes of Robin Hood and Randolph Earl of Chester," mentioned by Langland, quite possibly were not ballads but long narratives. "Rhyme" was a word frequently used in Middle English for these or for romances, as in the Prologue to *Cursor Mundi* (about 1300). The first certain ballad texts are from the 15th century, among them the very long *Geste of Robin Hood* (see ROBIN HOOD). There is a Danish ballad that may concern an event of the 12th century, and another that certainly concerns a happening of the early 13th, but the texts of these pieces are from later times. By the 16th century, ballads were abundant and were sung all over Europe. The majority of the fine English and Scottish ballads come from the 16th, 17th, and 18th centuries, and the events chronicled in many of the best of these occurred in the century in which they were composed. The Danish ballads, almost the only lyric species of their day in Denmark, were used in the courtly dances of 16th century knights and ladies. At the behest of Queen Sophia they were collected and presented to her, and they have ben preserved unimpaired. Ballads are still created in Europe and America, but for the most part they are of other than the old-time patterns and have less literary or folkloristic appeal.

There are many theories of ballad origins other than the one that takes them back to primitive times. We have seen that F. B. Gummere thought of the traditional ballads of England and Scotland as owing their origin to the "communal" improvisations of dancing groups of peasants. The English scholar W. P. Ker thought that the ballad emerged from the medieval *carole*, a secular dance song of spring and love. According to Chaucer's poetry and the romance of *Gawain and the Green Knight*, knights and ladies danced to carols. Later, "carol" came to mean a religious song of joy at Christmas and Easter or, generally, any song of joy or exultation. The "Harvard School" held that ballads developed from folk improvisations by an "epic process." W. J. Courthope believed in an opposite process, from length to brevity, rather than from brevity to elaboration. He thought that ballads were the relics of romances. It is more probable, however, that the romantic ballads he had in mind were independent creations on familiar earlier themes. C. H. Firth suggested that such ballads as those of the Percys, Stanleys, and Howards were made by the minstrels attached to these baronial houses to celebrate ancestral or contemporary adventures or events. It now seems that epic lays and romances existed before ballads and outlasted them as well as the *carole*. Ballads were utilized in the dance in such countries as Denmark and the Faeroe Islands, but not apparently in England, which was rich in other song material. However, there is absolutely no evidence to indicate that ballads were ever created in the dance improvisations of folk groups. Such creation is not only improbable on the basis of factual evidence, but hardly possible psychologically and mnemonically.

It is futile to linger over mysteries of origin

that might differentiate the ballad from other poetic species. The individual to create the first ballad was the person who thought of telling a story in verse directly to a gathering of people. It cannot be demonstrated that ballads originated in the same way. The large bodies of such songs now collected and available had multiple origins, like other folksongs. Ballads that deserve the name had authors and birthdates, although these were lost in oral transmission. Those coming down to us are from professional or semiprofessional hands. Medieval singers and reciters, histrioni, jongleurs, jugulares, and minstrels knew verse of many patterns, and some, by the 13th century, must have sung or recited ballads.

The authors of the extant English and Scottish ballads appear to have been minstrels, clerics, popular song composers, writers for court and stage entertainment, composers of journalistic broadsides, and individual folk or local poets. The earliest English texts associate themselves not with dancing but with religious edification, as in the ballads *Judas, St. Stephen,* and *Herod.* Various short recited tales or sung stories seem to have popularized religious material; minstrels sang religious matter in monasteries, as perhaps did friars, such as that in Chaucer's *Canterbury Tales,* who was a good singer.

The early Danish ballads are heroic. Improvisations are the shortest and most ephemeral of folksongs and are least likely to persist and find diffusion. Examples are lacking of such improvised songs developing into ballads. Nor is there much more accuracy in speaking of "communal re-creation" of ballads. In oral transmission the re-creation is by individual singers, not by a community. The same singer does not always sing the same words to the same tunes, nor do others of his region. Instead of communal texts, there are shifting texts in the mouths of many singers.

Kinds of Ballads. In literary usage it is convenient to distinguish several types of ballads: the traditional ballads orally handed on, the species that has attracted the greatest interest and discussion; the literary or "art" ballad, which may or may not imitate the popular ballad; and the broadside, or stall, ballad. In musical usage a ballad is a simple song, usually a solo but sometimes choral. It is often sentimental in character and is sung with a simple accompaniment. In the 19th century, instrumental ballads were composed by Chopin, Liszt, and Brahms for piano and orchestra. Some held that musical ballads should suggest a story, but this is no longer thought essential.

Traditional Ballads. Traditional ballads are those whose texts and tunes have been orally transmitted for a fairly long period of time, extending through at least several generations. The origin and authorship are forgotten. As a rule they tell their stories directly, addressing listeners rather than readers and employing plots rather than allusions. They have an epic element in that they are narrative and objective. Like lyric poetry, they are of song quality, and brevity is usual. The Robin Hood pieces from the late 15th century are quite long, however, as are the Spanish and Russian ballads. Ballads are dramatic in that they emphasize action and focus on situations or episodes. The story is unfolded in happenings and speech. Other dramatic or semidramatic elements include the use

of suspense and climax and the characteristic impersonality of the authorship.

In oral survival, circumstantial details may fade, while the basic situation remains. The personages are likely to be generalized or adapted. The type of reciter affects the handling of the material. Each singer may vary the texts, shorten them, or blend them with other pieces. However, no matter what kind of alterations occur in transmission, the main situation or episode usually persists. The critical moment or happening stands out.

Ballads, historical or otherwise, may or may not arise immediately out of the events they narrate. The date of composition may bear no relation to the theme, as is the case of Stephen Vincent Benét's *John Brown's Body* (q.v.), which does not date from Brown's own day. Insistence that the 14th and 15th centuries were the heyday of ballad composition is the reason why many ballads have been dated too early. Almost all literary anthologies, for example, group *Johnny Armstrong* and *Mary Hamilton* with pieces from the Chaucerian or post-Chaucerian period, although Johnny Armstrong was historically an outlaw of the early 16th century, and Mary Hamilton a lady-in-waiting of Mary Queen of Scots.

In the English and Danish ballads the leading characters are nobles, not royalty or peasants. In the foreground are heroes of adventures, fights, and forays. Among English traditional ballad themes may be found sacred legend and classical story (*St. Stephen and Herod* and *King Orpheo*); riddle ballads and wit contests (*Riddles Wisely Expounded*); chronicle ballads (*Otterbourne*); ballads of outlawry (*Robin Hood*), border raids (*Johnny Armstrong*), domestic tragedy (*Earl Brand*), and of the supernatural (*The Wife of Usher's Well*); love stories and romances (*Barbara Allen* and *Hind Horn*); and a few that are humorous. In the popular ballads of all countries may be found similarity of subjects, situations, handling, verbal repetition, stock formulas, and apparent anonymity of authorship. Different areas and different generations have their own preferences in themes and style, in song-modes, kinds of plot, characters, social environment. Underlying these elements is the perennial round of fundamental emotions—love, jealousy, ambition, and frustration—told with directness and simplicity.

Form. For some countries the ballad form is fixed; for other countries it is not. There is no standardized structure, as there is for sonnets and ballades. The characteristic English, Scandinavian, Czech, and Hungarian ballad form is stanzaic. Spanish ballads assonate rather than rhyme, with octosyllabic base and uniform meter and technique, but are not stanzaic. Estonian ballads are in rhymeless octosyllables, Ukrainian in unrhymed free verse. Balkan and Russian ballads are unrhymed and not strophic. Danish ballads are arranged in couplets or quatrains, as are most of the English, and the refrain is often present but not essential. It belongs more fundamentally to pure dance songs, movement songs, and game songs than to ballads. The refrains of English ballads are sometimes germane, sometimes meaningless, sometimes imported from other songs. They are less common in earlier texts than in late.

The English ballad measure derives, like the similar hymn measure, from the septenarius line of medieval Latin hymns (see HYMNS, LATIN). This line of 14 syllables, 7 feet, with rising or iambic metrical flow, first appears, with the addition of rhyme, in the *Poema Morale* (about 1170) and without rhyme in the *Ormulum* (about 1200). If printed in couplets, the rhyme comes at the end of the long lines (*aa*). If resolved into quatrains, the rhyme occurs at the end of the second and fourth lines (*abcb*), with four and three stresses and alternating eight and seven syllables. Occasionally ballad stanzas overflow into six lines or are doubled into eight, a variation imitated in Coleridge's *The Ancient Mariner*. Occasionally, too, there is inner rhyme. A frequent characteristic is the light final accentuation of words, a relic of archaic accent (forest', countrie') often spreading to native words of initial accent (ladie'). Other characteristics are frequent alliteration in minstrel style and use of stock formulas (red gold, brown brand, merry men). Although the ballad form, style, and structure vary from one country to another, fundamental resemblances can be found in the central situations, the episodic manner of narration, and the simplicity of language.

Music. Early collectors of traditional ballads gathered texts but not tunes, hardly realizing the importance of the latter. A pioneer collector of English national airs was William Chappell (1840), and another leading collector, for England and America, was Cecil J. Sharp. The melodies to which ballads are sung now attract the special interest of musicologists, and accurate phonograph recordings have been made. The music of folk tunes shifts even more than the texts, although it is the singing that keeps a ballad alive. Ordinarily the melody and the words of traditional songs are so associated in the minds of the singers that they have trouble remembering one without the other; yet the melody is not always sung the same by different singers. Knowing ballads by their stories, not their tunes, some singers care little about which airs they sing. Folk ballads are sung to some tune already in existence; hence, rather than always adhering to the traditional air, singers often adapt their words to a tune they know well. Exchanges of refrains, borrowings, crossings and blendings grow out of this confusion of tunes. The story, the central situation, and the characters have more stability than the music; chanted or recited ballads retain their integrity better. The difficulty, now greatly lessened, of recording the airs and the cost of printing them with the texts account for the absence of musical notations in some collections of today.

Broadsides. Broadside ballads, also called stall ballads, a semijournalistic creation of Elizabethan England, had their heyday in the 16th and the 17th centuries. They still occasionally appear for sale on thronged streets or street corners of large cities. Their name comes from the single broad sheet on which they were printed, which was often decorated with ornamentation or cuts, the latter not always appropriate. They were composed for the common people by professional rhymsters or hack poets to some popular tune and were sung by professional singers. This is the type of ballad mentioned by Shakespeare's Autolycus in *A Winter's Tale*. Broadside ballads were prompted by the growing popularity of the printing press and were the forerunners of modern journalism and news broadcasting. They dealt with historical events at home or abroad, social happenings, and stories of crime and disasters; some were sentimental pieces or love songs. Traditional songs were sometimes served up alongside the journalistic pieces. Usually the broadside versions are inferior to the older versions or the versions from the northern provinces. Broadside pieces, in general, have less quality and vigor and show a decline in the character of the topic. Poetical attractiveness is rare. The species is rather ephemeral. A few were collected in the publications of the Percy Society (1840–1853) and the Ballad Society (1868–1898). *The Roxburghe Ballads* (1871–1897) include only broadsides. The leading scholar in this field of balladry was Hyder E. Rollins of Harvard, editor of many volumes of broadsides dating from 1553 to 1693.

Literary and Imitative Ballads. Ballads of literary type, having fixed texts and coming from known poets, are to be distinguished from traditional ballads. Some imitate the latter; some do not. Sir Walter Scott not only collected ballads but also composed ballads and balladlike pieces, such as *The Eve of St. John* and *Jock O'Hazeldean*. His *Young Lochinvar* is not imitative. Wordsworth's *Lucy Gray* is in simple ballad form but without archaic touches. Coleridge's *The Ancient Mariner* is indebted to the older ballad style. So are Rossetti's *Stratton Water* and *The King's Tragedy*. Tennyson tried his hand at the archaic style in *The Sisters*. Browning's *Muckle Mouth Meg* is somewhat imitative; his *How They Brought the Good News from Ghent to Aix* and *Hervé Riel* are not. Swinburne was a fluent balladist in the archaic manner, as in *The Witch Mother* and *The Bride's Tragedy*. The best-known American ballads are Longfellow's *The Wreck of the Hesperus* and *The Skeleton in Armor*, the latter having an elaborate stanza form. Lanier's *The Revenge of Hamish* deserves a place among the finest American ballads.

Literally ballads are often called "art" ballads or ballads of "culture," as opposed to "folk ballads." This is a mistaken antithesis. It is hardly accurate to look on traditional ballads as a "singularly artless type." Even primitive poets have their fixed conventions, their own kind of art. So do songs of special groups, such as loggers, cowboys, or coal miners. Popular singers remain with the conventions of presentation they know, without thought of departure in their art patterns.

American Ballads. Until recently the ballads sung in the United States were brought there by immigrant groups, chiefly from the British Isles. French ballads circulate among those of French stock and language in Louisiana and Canada, and Mexican-Spanish ballads circulate in the Southwest. These have not found diffusion outside their own areas, nor have those of other language or racial groups in this country. Few indigenous ballads remain from colonial and provincial times, but a variety of pieces from both earlier and later periods, some of them ballads, are preserved in extant "songsters" and broadsides. These usually were sold along the streets or given circulation by wandering vendors. Still others found their way into newspapers.

An important source for collectors, other than print, is the manuscript, or "commonplace books", of favorite songs. These continued to be

THE BALLAD OF BABY DOE, Douglas Moore's opera of the American West, in its first New York performance, presented by the New York City Opera in 1958. Walter Cassel (center, in light jacket) plays the role of Horace.

NEW YORK CITY OPERA; PHOTO BY FRED FEHL

made into our own period, especially in regions where printed materials were scarce. Many songs in traditional currency were floated by the agency of professional singers, old-time entertainers of the stage and other itinerant groups; some perhaps were given impetus by such concert singers as the prima donna who sang *Andrew Martine* (the 16th century *Sir Andrew Barton*) in Boston about 1859. Of special interest are the many Old World ballads handed on in isolated communities free from outside influences. Because they were collected earlier, it seemed at first that the home of these pieces was chiefly the southern Appalachian Mountains and New England, but rich ballad collections have now been made from other areas, such as Missouri, Mississippi, Indiana, and Ohio.

Some leading American collectors of ballads are F. J. Child, who included some American variants in his monumental *English and Scottish Popular Ballads* (1882–1898); Cecil J. Sharp, Olive D. Cambell, and Maud Karpeles, who gathered texts and music from the Appalachian region; C. Alphonso Smith and A. K. Davis from Virginia; Phillips Barry from New England; and H. M. Belden from Missouri. More recently the ballads and songs of individual occupations or groups, such as loggers, coal miners, cowboys, and frontiersmen, have had much attention.

American ballads tell of criminals and outlaws (*Jesse James* and *Sam Bass*), the murderous lover (*Poor Lorella*), the reunion of parted lovers, the forsaken girl, harsh parents, local murders and disasters, and similar stories. The supernatural element in the foreground of European ballads faded in America. Other ballad types include deathbed confessions, songs of the railway and farm, and temperance and religious songs. Many American ballads have been modeled after Irish popular songs. American ballads are often adaptations of old literary pieces assimilated into popular verse.

Imported ballads are subject to adaptation in the New World. The locale changes, as does the status of character. For example, Lord Randal becomes Johnny Randall or Jimmy Randolph, no longer highborn. Archaic touches are lost, and there are the usual shiftings, omissions, insertions, crossings with other pieces, slips of memory, and abbreviations. In later songs there is less violence, fewer murders, and more humor. Some of the best-known indigenous American ballads are *Springfield Mountain*, *Frankie and Johnny*, *Casey Jones*, *John Henry*, and *Young Charlotte*. The latter, long thought to be by an unknown author, was found by Phillips Barry

to have been from the pen of the humorist Seba Smith (1792–1868).

Group singing, once a very popular form of entertainment for gatherings of students and others, declined somewhat with the widespread popularity of the radio and phonograph in the 20th century. Music was turned on rather than sung. But in the mid-20th century, balladry had a resurgence. Many singing groups emerged, particularly folk-singing groups among college students. These singers often sought out traditional ballads for their material. Such renewed interest has led to the production of new recordings of the conventional ballads and has greatly popularized folk and ballad concerts.

LOUISE POUND
Author of "American Ballads and Songs"

Songbooks

Belden, Henry M., *Ballads and Songs* (Columbia, Mo., 1940).

Eddy, Mary O., *Ballads and Songs from Ohio* (New York 1939).

Lomax, Alan, *Folk Songs of North America* (New York 1960).

Seeger, Pete, *American Favorite Ballads* (New York 1961).

Sharp, Cecil J., *English Folksongs from the Southern Appalachians*, rev. and ed. by Maud Karpeles (London 1932).

Wells, Evelyn K., *The Ballad Tree* (New York 1950).

White, Josh, *The Josh White Song Book* (New York 1963).

Bibliography

Entwhistle, William J., *European Balladry* (New York and London 1940).

Gerould, G.H., *The Ballad of Tradition* (New York 1932).

Hodgart, Matthew J.C., *The Ballads* (London 1950).

Hustvedt, Sigurd B., *Ballad Books and Ballad Men* (Cambridge, Mass., 1930).

Pound, Louise, *Poetic Origins and the Ballad* (New York 1921).

BALLAD OF BABY DOE, an opera written in 1955 by the American composer Douglas Moore, with a libretto by John LaTouche. The score, which makes abundant use of American folk music, is in the romantic tradition of Viennese light opera. The opera was commissioned by the Koussevitsky Foundation of the Library of Congress in honor of the bicentennial of Columbia University. It was first produced at the Central City (Colorado) Opera Festival on July 7, 1956.

The plot of *Baby Doe* is based on actual events that took place in Leadville, Colo., in the 1880's, and its characters are based on real people. Baby Doe (soprano), a miner's wife, leaves her husband for a rich mineowner, Horace Tabor (baritone), who is 30 years her senior. The scandal ruins Tabor, but the opera ends more or less happily when Baby Doe's love for him unexpectedly turns out to be deep and lasting.

103

BALLAD OF READING GAOL, bal'əd, red'ing jāl, a poem by Oscar Wilde (q.v.), first published in 1898. The poem, generally considered to be Wilde's best, was also the last literary work of his life. Unlike many of his earlier works that employed comic methods to expose the hypocrisy of society, *The Ballad of Reading Gaol* has a somber, mournful tone. Inspired by Wilde's own imprisonment from 1895 to 1897, it uses highly graphic descriptions of life in jail as a means of pleading for sympathy and understanding for men being destroyed by imprisonment.

Wilde depicts the criminal as a sufferer driven to his misdeed, and he condemns prison as a place where the world's evil is compounded rather than mitigated:

> The vilest deeds like poison weeds
> Bloom well in prison-air:
> It is only what is good in Man
> That wastes and withers there.

Although the poem occasionally resorts to rhetorical exhortation, its main strength lies in its vivid evocation of sorrow and its descriptions of despairing prisoners.

BALLAD OF THE SAD CAFÉ, a novel by the American writer Carson McCullers, first published in 1951 as the title piece of an omnibus volume of her works. It is the story of an aggregation of physical and emotional cripples, described with a sensitivity that is typical of all of Miss McCullers' work.

The Ballad of the Sad Café was adapted for the stage by Edward Albee and was produced on Broadway in 1963.

BALLAD OPERA, bal'əd op'rə, is a stage presentation, most popular in 18th century England, consisting of spoken dialogue complemented by songs borrowed from other sources. Ballad opera bears a close relationship to the *Singspiel* of Germany and the *opéra comique* of France, but these forms are artistically somewhat more ambitious than ballad opera.

Possibly the first, and certainly the most successful, ballad opera was John Gay's *The Beggar's Opera* (q.v.), first produced in London in 1728. *The Beggar's Opera*, like many works in this form that were to follow, was a parody on the pretentious conventions of much of the Italian opera that was being performed in London. A later ballad opera, *The Fashionable Lady* (1730) by James Ralph, even contained a blunt indictment of Italian opera, and one of its characters laughs at such operatic conventions as "squeaking recitatives . . . and trills of insignificant, outlandish vowels."

The music used in ballad opera sometimes originated from folk songs of the British Isles, but more often it was borrowed from songs that were popular at the time, including songs by Henry Purcell, George Frederick Handel, and Arcangelo Corelli. The words of the songs, however, were changed entirely to fit the needs of the performance. The initial popularity of ballad opera diminished considerably after 1735, although the form underwent a revival in the 1760's on the merit of new works written by Thomas Arne and Charles Dibdin.

The most notable ballad operas include *Love in a Riddle* (1729) by Colley Cibber, *The Village Opera* (1729) by Charles Johnson, and *An Old Man Taught Wisdom* (1735) by Henry Fielding.

BALLADE, bə-läd', a sophisticated poetic form that preceded the sonnet in popularity in France and England and was revived in the 19th century. The custom of distinguishing the highly polished *ballade* from the simpler *ballad* by spelling with the final *-e* became established in modern English usage.

In its Provençal beginnings, *balada* (from the Late Latin *ballare*, meaning "to dance") referred to any dance song. It was developed into an intricate fixed form by the French poets' guilds of the 13th century, and its structure was complete late in the 14th century with the addition of the *envoi* (envoy)—the peroration at the closing of a ballade addressed to a high member of the royal court, or to the poet's patron, and often beginning with the word "Prince."

Rules for the ballade form were first laid down in Jean Molinet's *L'art et la science de rhétorique* in 1493, but requirements have always been liberally interpreted. The standard features are three stanzas, a refrain, and an envoy. The refrain is repeated at the end of each stanza and at the end of the envoy. The poem generally employs only three or four rhymes, which recur in the same position in each stanza. No rhyme word is repeated, except in the refrain. Stanzas may vary in length, but the eight-line stanza is most common. A typical rhyme scheme is *ababbcbc*, with *bcbc* in the envoy.

The greatest master of the ballade was the 15th century French poet François Villon, one of the most romantic figures in literature. His most famous example, the *Ballade des dames du temps jadis*, was adapted into English in the 19th century by Dante Gabriel Rossetti as *The Ballad of Dead Ladies*. Also noteworthy among early French ballade writers were Guillaume de Machaut, Eustache Deschamps, Jean Froissart, and Alain Chartier—all preceding Villon—and Clément Marot in the 16th century.

The sonnet superseded the ballade in popularity in France in the 17th century, but the form was revived in the 19th century with the publication of Théodore de Banville's *Trente-six ballades joyeuses* (1875). The most famous of the later French ballades is that recited by Cyrano in Edmond Rostand's play *Cyrano de Bergerac* (1897). Cyrano defines the ballade structure and composes a ballade as he duels with the Vicomte de Valvert. As he completes the envoy, he pierces his antagonist, crying,

> I lunge! . . . I keep my word!
> At the last line, I hit!

The ballade, imported from France, first became popular in England in the late 14th century, when it was adopted by Geoffrey Chaucer and other poets. Among Chaucer's ballades are *Lack of Steadfastness, Ballade of Good Counsel,* and *Complaint to His Empty Purse,* which won him an annual grant from King Henry IV of England. John Gower (whose extant ballades are in French) and John Lydgate also wrote ballades at this time.

The form disappeared from English literature in the 16th century but was reintroduced in the late decades of the 19th century. After the publication of Andrew Lang's *Ballads and Lyrics of Old France* (1872), Henry Austin Dobson, Edmund Gosse, W.E. Henley, and Algernon Charles Swinburne started writing in the ballade form. Swinburne, in particular, handled the intricate form with ease, as in his *Ballad of Dreamland* (1876), part of which follows on the next page.

I hid my heart in a nest of roses,
    Out of the sun's way, hidden apart;
In a softer bed than the soft white snow's is,
    Under the roses I hid my heart.
Why should it sleep not? why should it start,
When never a leaf of the rose tree stirred?
    What made sleep flutter his wings and part?
Only the song of a secret bird.

· · ·

ENVOY

In the world of dreams I have chosen my part,
    To sleep for a season and hear no word
Of true love's truth or of light love's art,
    Only the song of a secret bird.

Swinburne also composed a sort of super-ballade, *In the Water*, with long lines of 20 syllables each in anapestic rhythm, stanzas of 10 lines, and an envoy of 5 lines, all composed in the same four rhymes.

The ballade form was first used in the United States in the 19th century. American writers of ballades include Thomas Bailey Aldrich, Henry Cuyler Bunner, and Brander Matthews.

Bibliography

Cohen, G., *La poésie française au Moyen Age* (Paris 1952).

Cohen, Helen L., *The Ballade* (New York 1915).

Cohen, Helen L., *Lyric Forms from France* (New York 1922).

Courthope, W.J., *A History of English Poetry* (New York 1962).

Graham, Victor, *Sixteenth Century French Poetry* (Toronto 1964).

Lote, G., *Histoire du vers français*, vol. 2, pp. 270–285 (Paris 1943).

Martin, Robert B., *Victorian Poetry* (New York 1963).

Raynaud, G., *Les cents ballades* (Paris 1905).

BALLANTYNE, bal'ən-tīn, **James** (1772–1833), Scottish printer, who published the works of Sir Walter Scott. Ballantyne was born in Kelso, where he was a boyhood friend of Scott. As a young man he edited and printed the Kelso *Mail*. In 1799 he printed *Apologies for Tales of Terror*, a small collection of Scott's ballads. Scott was so impressed with the quality of this printing that he commissioned Ballantyne to print a comprehensive collection of old Border ballads, *Minstrelsy of the Scottish Border* (1802).

At the end of 1802, with Scott's financial backing, Ballantyne founded in Edinburgh the Border Press (later called James Ballantyne & Co.), the firm that printed Scott's works. The company failed in 1826 but continued to operate under the creditors' trustees, with Ballantyne as its literary manager. Ballantyne died in Edinburgh on Jan. 17, 1833.

BALLANTYNE, bal'ən-tīn, **Robert Michael** (1825–1894), Scottish writer for boys. A nephew of the printer James Ballantyne, he was born in Edinburgh on April 24, 1825. Between the ages of 16 and 22 he was employed in Canada by the Hudson's Bay Company. He returned to Edinburgh in 1847, and for the next seven years worked for the publishing house of Constable and Company. In 1848 he wrote *Hudson's Bay, or, Life in the Wilds of North America*, and from 1856 he devoted himself to writing stories for boys. He died in Rome, Italy, on Feb. 8, 1894.

Ballantyne wrote more than 80 books. His first volumes dealt with life in Canada; his later works concerned adventure in Britain, Africa, and elsewhere. Among his most popular books were *The Young Fur Traders* (1856), *Ungava: A Tale of Eskimo Land* (1857), *The Coral Island* (1857), and *The Dog Crusoe* (1860). In 1893 he published *Personal Reminiscences of Book-Making*.

BALLARAT, bal'ə-rat, in Australia, is the third-largest city in the state of Victoria. It consists of three municipalities: Ballarat East, Ballarat West, and Sebastopol. Ballarat is an important railroad junction, situated about 65 miles (160 km) west-northwest of Melbourne, at an elevation of 1,416 feet (432 meters). Ballarat's temperate climate has helped to make the city a popular vacation resort.

The city owes its initial growth and prosperity to the discovery of gold in 1851. The alluvial goldfields in the surrounding area proved to be among the richest in the world, yielding some of the largest nuggets ever discovered. When the alluvial deposits became depleted, reef mining was begun; auriferous quartz was mined at depths of more than 2,500 feet (760 meters). Later, however, the annual output of gold was greatly reduced.

The city lies in the midst of a fertile agricultural district. It has many industries, including wool and flour milling, brewing, distilling, and the manufacture of iron and steel products. There are also railroad engineering works.

The Ballarat School of Mines, situated here, is associated with the University of Melbourne. Ballarat is the seat of Anglican and Roman Catholic bishoprics.

Ballarat was chartered as a town in 1855 and ranked as a city in 1875. Population: (1961) 41,037.

BALLAST, bal'əst, is heavy material placed in the bottom of a ship to steady it. Consisting of iron, stone, gravel, or water, it is used when there is not sufficient cargo or other weight carried to bring the ship to the proper trim for sailing or steaming. Most modern vessels are constructed with tanks which are filled with water to the weight of the ballast required. Too much ballast leads to stiffness, with heavy laboring and loss of speed; too little or too high ballast produces crankiness and a tendency to capsize. A merchant ship requires ballast when it is carrying no cargo. The ballast is sometimes shipped both for stability and to keep the propeller submerged.

The term is also applied to the sand placed in bags in the car of a balloon to steady it and to enable the aeronaut to lighten the balloon by throwing out part of the ballast; it also applies to the loose material used beneath and about the ties on a railroad in order to make the bed firm and enduring.

BALLENY ISLANDS, bal'ə-nē, five small volcanic islands and some islets lying across the Antarctic Circle south of New Zealand. They are included in the Ross Dependency, where jurisdiction has been claimed by New Zealand since 1923. The islands were discovered in 1839 by John Balleny, who was a British sealer. He was believed to be the first to discover land south of New Zealand.

The individual islands are named for partners in Enderby Brothers, a British mercantile firm that financed Balleny's expedition. (Enderby Brothers had begun sending ships into southern waters for seals as early as 1785.) Young Island is the largest and highest, rising to 12,000 feet. Others are Sturge, a cone-shaped island; Buckle, which was volcanically active in two places when Balleny sighted it; Borrodaile; and Row.

In 1948 a French polar expedition made cartographical studies of the Balleny Islands.

SWAN LAKE is a favorite classical ballet. Bolshoi production (above) stars Maya Plisetskaya and Nikolai Fadeyechev.

BALLET

BALLET, ba'lā, is a form of dance with unique traditions, techniques, methods or schools of training, and a style of movement that distinguish it from all other theatrical dance forms. The word "ballet" (from the Italian *ballare,* meaning "to dance") refers not only to a technique or style of movement but also to a company of ballet dancers and to the complete ballet production. The ballet production, hopefully a work of art, is traditionally defined as a synthesis of four arts—dancing, drama, music, and decor.

Classical Ballet. Classical ballet had its origins in the entertainments of the ducal courts of 15th century Italy, and it retains an elegance of style and deportment that can be traced back to this period when the dancers were kings, princes, and nobles. Balthasar de Beaujoyeulx was the choreographer of the first ballet to be called by that name. His *Ballet Comique de la Reine,* commissioned by Catherine de Médicis for the celebration of her sister's marriage, was performed in Paris in 1581. To Beaujoyeulx the art of ballet consisted of dancing bodies moving in geometric patterns to "the diverse harmonies of many instruments." This definition of ballet retains some validity, although the art has evolved into something more than, and something very different from, Beaujoyeulx's ballet.

The academic principles of classical ballet were firmly instituted when Louis XIV established the Royal Academy of Dancing in Paris in 1661. Since then, the elementary technical basis of ballet has been the five positions of the feet, with corresponding positions of the arms. Every classical ballet step or movement begins from one of these five positions and returns to one of them. However, classical ballet has since developed, expanded, and added to the five basic positions a large vocabulary of movements that are immediately recognizable to the trained eye of the dance student or the ballet follower. These steps and movements—arabesques, pirouettes, glissades, entrechats, and many others—were codified by a terminology in French that is still universally employed in the ballet schools and companies of every nation.

Dancing "on pointe," popularized by Maria Taglioni in *La Sylphide* in Paris in 1832, eventually became an integral part of classical ballet technique. Taglioni's great triumph in this role made dancing on the tips of the toes almost synonymous with ballet.

Classical ballet in its pure form reached its zenith in *The Sleeping Beauty,* first performed by the Imperial Mariinsky company of St. Petersberg (now Leningrad) in 1890. This production is a perfect example of the synthesis of dancing, drama, music, and decor. It combined the masterful choreography of Marius Petipa, a dazzling score by Tchaikovsky, a story beloved throughout the world, and elaborate scenery, costumes, and mechanical effects. There have since been many different productions of this work, and sections of it are performed by most ballet companies.

Petipa and the Imperial Mariinsky ballet company dominated ballet at the end of the 19th century. The influence of this company's classical style spread throughout the Western world in the 20th century, partly through the Ballets Russes de Sergei Diaghilev (q.v.), which, however, accented new ballet forms and stagings, and, after the Russian Revolution of 1917, through the influence of émigré teachers trained in Russia. Modern ballet in most Western countries has its origins in this Russian tradition.

Modern Ballet. The art of ballet today runs the gamut from pieces designed chiefly to display muscular prowess, through the most poetic expressions, to dance creations rooted in ideas and emotions. Modern ballet is characterized by greater freedom in all aspects of ballet production. Today's choreographer need not, if the nature of his musical accompaniment or his theme does not require it, feel bound to the traditional five positions of the feet. He may even choreograph an entire ballet without calling for the use of toe shoes by female members of the cast.

Today's ballet incorporates many modern dance principles into its choreographic fabric, and freely invented movement is used in some major modern ballet productions. But modern ballet differs from modern dance in its use of the fundamental movements of classical ballet, which remain firmly established and universally accepted. Although modern dance, like ballet, employs complex training methods based on body needs and the principles of movement, the choreographer of modern dance does not use a basic vocabulary of movements that are the same in the classroom as on stage. And unlike ballet, modern dance has no universally accepted terminology for its movements, because the choreographer of modern dance invents new movements for each new dance or gives new direction or sequence to previously used actions.

Modern ballet has also been freed from a rigid adherence to the traditional idea of ballet as a synthesis of four complementary arts. Some productions, such as Agnes de Mille's *Fall River Legend*, based on the Lizzie Bordon murder case, do combine dance, drama, music, and decor in almost equal quantities. But the abstract, nonnarrative ballets of George Balanchine are dance-music inventions in which the choreographer attempts to mirror in movement—classical, modern, or very avant-garde—the rhythms, forms, dynamic intensities, and moods of the music. Many Balanchine creations are done without formal decor, which is replaced by an unadorned backdrop and highly imaginative lighting designs. Practice clothes from the ballet classroom frequently are used instead of formal costumes.

In his *Concerto Barocco*, to music by Bach, Balanchine employs the classical ballet's traditional technique, including dancing "on pointe." He places these classical steps into new and fresh sequences, but the purity of classical dancing is accented. In his celebrated *Serenade*, to music of Tchaikovsky, Balanchine also finds basic material in classical technique, but he colors it with romantic overtones. There is no plot, but incident and situation are subtly indicated. When Balanchine choreographs to music of Anton von Webern in *Episodes*, or to the music of Charles Ives in *Ivesiana*, he makes radical departures from traditional ballet technique, because such contemporary music does not invite the same kinetic responses as the more traditional ballet scores. *Ivesiana*, for example, concludes with a section in which the entire company walks on its knees, almost aimlessly, in a very dim and somber light. In *Agon*, with its specially commissioned

WAYNE J. SHILKRET, NEW YORK

TWO GREAT CONTEMPORARY DANCERS: Margot Fonteyn and Rudolf Nureyev, in a scene from *Giselle*.

score by Balanchine's longtime associate, Igor Stravinsky, the choreographer juxtaposes and combines traditional and modern movements.

Another modern choreographer, Jerome Robbins, uses no "pointe" dancing, and indeed no steps immediately identifiable with classical ballet, in his widely hailed choreography for Stravinsky's *Les Noces*. Nevertheless, this creation represents the classical synthesis of dancing, drama, music, and decor. Much earlier, in his first ballet, the now-historic *Fancy Free*, Robbins combined ballet and jazz dancing, and none of the girls in the ballet wore toe shoes, or even soft ballet slippers. In his subsequent *Interplay*, he did incorporate dancing "on pointe," combining it with other classical techniques, jazz idioms, and freely invented movement.

National Contributions. Ballet is an international art form, not the product of one culture, as are ethnic dances. Many nations have contributed their own characteristics and training systems

TWO OF THE GREATEST DANCERS OF THE PAST: *(far left)* Vaslav Nijinsky (1890–1950) and *(left)* Anna Pavlova (1885–1931). In 1910 these stars danced briefly together under the leadership of Sergei Diaghilev—one of the great moments in the history of the classical ballet.

FRED FEHL

FRED FEHL

MODERN BALLET as used in the musical theater is exemplified by the athletic dancing in *West Side Story*.

INNOVATIONS IN BALLET were made by Agnes de Mille, who used American traditions, as in *Rodeo* (above).

without violating the traditional principles of ballet. Russian, English, Danish, French, and American companies have introduced national and regional themes as well as their own peculiar national flavor. In general it can be said that American ballet is athletic and expansive of movement, the Danish bouncy and ebullient, the British precise and elegantly lyrical, and the Russian dazzlingly flamboyant. Ballet styles vary even within one country; the Kirov Ballet of Leningrad (formerly the Imperial Mariinsky company) is aristocratic and suave, while the Bolshoi from Moscow has a circus-like flashiness.

American folk and jazz idioms have contributed to modern ballet, as in Agnes de Mille's *Rodeo* and Eugene Loring's *Billy the Kid*. The English-born choreographer Antony Tudor, working with American companies, introduced serious social and psychological themes in such ballets as *Pillar of Fire* and *Lilac Garden*.

Soviet ballet, on the other hand, includes popular divertissement programs such as *Spring Waters* and *The Doves*, which rely almost entirely on acrobatics for their effects. Their style is reminiscent of the acrobatic adagio teams of vaudeville. Soviet choreographer Igor Moiseyev draws heavily on elements of Russian folk dance, which he combines with classical steps and modern themes and movements in his ballets *Soccer Dance*, *The Partisans*, and *Sailor's Dance*.

National trends and styles frequently have a mutual influence in contemporary ballet. For example, in the early 1960's, American ballet began to be influenced by the brilliant virtuosity of the Bolshoi dancers. Russian dancing, in turn, was influenced by the freer modern choreography and other innovations of American ballet.

The great 18th century ballet master, Jean Georges Noverre, in his *Lettres sur la danse et sur les ballets* (1760), wrote: "Ballet is an art which does not admit to mediocrity, it exacts a perfection difficult to acquire." His words still apply to ballet today, although it remains an ever-changing art.

WALTER TERRY, *Author of "Ballet"*

GLOSSARY OF BALLET TERMS

Adagio.—Slow and sustained movements; also, the section of a pas de deux in which the ballerina, partnered by the danseur, displays her mastery of lyrical movement.

Allegro.—Fast movements.

Arabesque.—A position in which the dancer stands on one leg with the other leg extended in a straight line to the rear. The positions of the arms and the height of the raised leg may vary.

Attitude.—A position in which the dancer stands on one leg, the other leg raised behind the body with the knee bent. A similar position, but with the leg placed in front of the body, may also be called an attitude.

Ballerina.—The principal female dancer in a company. The term is misapplied when used to designate any female dancer. A large company may have two or more ballerinas, the chief one ranked as *prima ballerina*.

Ballon.—The resilience, lightness, or spring of a dancer in leaping or jumping movements.

Battement.—A kick, either high (grand battement) or low (petit battement), which may be executed in any direction.

Batterie.—Any action in which the legs beat together, usually when the dancer is in air.

Cabriole.—A batterie movement, usually for the male. One leg kicks high to the front or the back and is held in this extension until the supporting leg swiftly leaves the floor and meets the raised leg in a beat or in multiple beats.

Changement de Pieds.—A movement in which the dancer, starting in fifth position, jumps upward and returns to the floor in fifth position but with the position of the feet reversed. He might, for example, start with the right leg in front and conclude with the right leg in back.

Choreographer.—One who selects or invents the steps, movements, and patterns of a ballet. He must relate these motions to the music, the theme—abstract or dramatic—and the design of the production in order to make a ballet with form, sequence, and purpose.

Coda.—The last section of a pas de deux or of a full ballet.

Corps de Ballet.—The chorus of a ballet company; also called the *ensemble*.

Danseur Noble.—The male classical dancer, counterpart of the classical ballerina.

Demi-Pointe.—With the full weight of the body on the toes and the ball of the foot.

Développé.—The unfolding of the leg, accomplished by slowly bending and then straightening the knee as the leg is raised in an extension (to the front, side, or back) from the floor.

Divertissement.—A dance without plot, or that part of a dramatic ballet composed of a series of short dances without plot.

En Arrière.—To the back.

BALLET

Members of the New York City Ballet perform a sequence entitled "Rubies," from the ballet *The Jewels*. George Balanchine's choreography is to music by Igor Stravinsky, and Patricia Neary is the principal dancer.

A pas de deux from *Allegro Brillante* by George Balanchine, to music by Tchaikovsky, is performed by Patricia McBride and Anthony Blum of the New York City Ballet.

Patricia McBride and Edward Villella are the featured dancers in the New York City Ballet production of *Raymonda Variations*.

Dancers Marina Kondratieva and Maris Lieta of Moscow's Bolshoi Ballet execute a series of impressive leaps in *Spring Waters*, based on a song by Rachmaninoff. The Bolshoi production was choreographed by Asaf Messerer.

Tchaikovsky's *Sleeping Beauty*, a sumptuously mounted ballet based on the fable by Charles Perrault, is a specialty of London's Royal Ballet. The choreography is by Sir Frederick Ashton, and the soloist is Nadia Nerina.

LEADING AMERICAN CHOREOGRAPHERS Agnes De Mille *(left photo, center)*, at rehearsal, and George Balanchine *(right photo)* of the New York City Ballet. Dancer Maria Tallchief, prima ballerina, stands at Balanchine's left.

En Avant.—To the front.

En Dedans.—Inward, toward the body.

En Dehors.—Outward, away from the body.

Entrechat.—A jump directly upward, with the body maintaining a straight line and with multiple changes of positions of feet in air. An entrechat is an elaboration of the changement de pieds.

Five Positions of the Feet.—The five classical positions of the feet. Every ballet step or movement must begin with one of these positions and return to one of them. (See illustration.)

Fouetté.—A turn or spin on one leg, the body being propelled by a whipping motion of the free leg. It is usually performed by a female dancer.

Glissade.—A gliding step starting from fifth position, opening into second position, and closing in fifth. It may be held to the floor or used as a low leap.

Jeté.—A leap in which the dancer propels himself with a pushoff from one leg, covers space in air, and lands on the other leg.

Pas.—A step; also used to designate types of dances, as *pas seul* (solo) and *pas de deux* (dance for two).

Pas de Bourrée.—A traveling step in which the dancer may move in any direction on demi-pointe or on pointe. The calves are held as close together as possible while the dancer executes a series of swift miniature steps.

Pas de Chat.—A leap, starting from a plié in fifth position. The leading leg is drawn up with bent knee, followed almost immediately by the other leg. At the peak of the leap, both knees are bent outward to the side, and the toes are nearly touching. A *gargouillade* is the same movement, except that the leading leg does a rond de jamb en dehors and the following leg a rond de jamb en dedans while in air.

Pas de Deux.—A duet. A classical grand pas de deux consists of an entrée, adagio, two solos—one executed by the ballerina; the other done by the danseur—and a coda.

Pirouette.—A turn of the body done while standing on one leg, the other leg being held in any one of a number of traditional positions. A pirouette is done on demi-pointe by the male, on pointe by the female, dancer.

AMERICAN BALLET THEATRE'S *Fancy Free,* choreographed by Jerome Robbins to music by Leonard Bernstein.

109

Plié.—A bending of the knees with hips, legs, and feet turned outward.

Pointe.—The tip of the toe.

Port de Bras.—The positions and movements of the arms.

Relevé.—To rise onto pointe or demi-pointe.

Rond de Jambe.—A rotary movement of the leg. It can be done in a number of ways, such as on the floor with knee straight, or in air with a circular rotation of the knee from bent to straight.

Sauté.—A jump.

Terre-à-Terre.—Steps done on the ground.

Tour.—A turn. A pirouette is one kind of tour.

Tour en l'Air.—A turn done in air. The dancer springs upward from fifth position, makes one or more complete turns, and returns to the floor in fifth position.

Turnout.—The body positions of classical ballet in which the limbs are turned out from the hips at a 180° angle. Ballet beginners start with a less extreme turnout.

Tutu.—The fluffy skirt worn by the female dancer. In ballets of the romantic style, the tutu falls to below the calf. In the later, classical style ballet, it is short enough to reveal the legs completely.

Variation.—Usually a solo dance, or pas seul.

Bibliography

Ambrose, Kay, *Ballet-Lover's Companion* (New York 1949).

Bruhn, Erik, and Moore, Lillian, *Bournonville and Ballet Technique* (New York 1961).

Chujoy, Anatole, *The Dance Encyclopedia* (New York 1949).

Cohen, Selma Jeanne, and others, ed., *Dictionary of Modern Ballet* (New York 1959).

de Mille, Agnes, *To a Young Dancer* (Boston 1962).

Haskell, Arnold L., ed., *Ballet Annual* (New York 1947–   ).

Karsavina, Tamara, *Ballet Technique* (New York 1956).

Karsavina, Tamara, *Classical Ballet: The Flow of Movement* (New York 1963).

Kersley, Leo, and Sinclair, Janet, *A Dictionary of Ballet Terms*, 2d rev. ed. (London 1964).

Kirstein, Lincoln, *Classic Ballet* (New York 1952).

Lifar, Serge, *Ballet, Traditional to Modern* (London 1938).

Swinson, Cyril, ed., *Guidebook to the Ballet* (New York 1961).

Terry, Walter, *Ballet: A New Guide to the Liveliest Art* (New York 1959).

Verwer, Hans, *Guide to the Ballet* (New York 1963).

BALLETS RUSSES DE SERGEI DIAGHILEV, bȧ-lȧ′ rŭs, the ballet company that revitalized and revolutionized ballet in the early 20th century. The company was the creation of the brilliant Russian impresario Sergei Diaghilev (q.v.), who drew on the best talents of the time in music, stage design, choreography, and dance. He achieved a new synthesis of these arts, ending the total dominance of ballet by the prima ballerina and stimulating interest in ballet in Europe and the United States.

The first performance of the Ballets Russes, a sensational success, took place in Paris, on May 19, 1909. The first phase of the company's history, lasting until World War I, was dominated by the choreography of Michel Fokine, the sets and costumes of Léon Bakst and Alexandre Benois, and the dancing of Anna Pavlova and Vaslav Nijinsky. The music of Igor Stravinsky was heard in *The Firebird* (1910), *Petrouchka* (1911), and *Rite of Spring* (1913). Nijinsky's fame became legendary in *The Specter of the Rose* (1911) and *The Afternoon of a Faun* (1913).

The Ballets Russes entered a new phase around 1917, lasting until the company disbanded after Diaghilev's death in 1929. The ballets of this period featured the choreography of Léonide Massine and George Balanchine, stage designs by major French painters such as Matisse, Picasso, and Rouault, and new dancers such as Léonide Massine, Serge Lifar, and Alicia Markova. Strikingly modern innovations were introduced in ballets such as *Parade* (1917), with a scenario by Jean Cocteau, music by Erik Satie, and sets by Picasso.

BALLINGER, bal′in-jər, **Richard Achilles** (1858–1922), American lawyer and public official. He was born in Boonesboro (now part of Boone), Iowa, on July 9, 1858, and was graduated from Williams College in 1884. Admitted to the bar in 1886, he soon moved west and began to practice law in Port Townsend, Wash., in 1889. He was U.S. court commissioner in 1890–1892 and judge of the superior court of Jefferson County, Wash., in 1894–1897. In the latter year he moved his law practice to Seattle, and from 1904 to 1906 he was mayor of that city. During the next two years, he was commissioner of the General Land Office in Washington, D.C.

From 1909 to 1911, Ballinger was secretary of the interior in President William H. Taft's cabinet. He became the center of a controversy engendered when he discharged a subordinate who had accused him of impeding an investigation of coal-land claims in Alaska. Conservationists, led by the chief forester, Gifford Pinchot, attacked him. A congressional investigating committee exonerated Ballinger, but Taft's conservation policies came under fire, and the controversy was an issue of the presidential campaign in 1912. After resigning as secretary of the interior in 1911, he resumed the practice of law in Seattle, where he died on June 6, 1922.

BALLINGER, bal′in-jər, a city in south-central Texas, is the seat of Runnels County. It is on the Colorado River, 175 miles (282 km) southwest of Fort Worth. It is the commercial center of a rich farming district and ships cotton, wheat, cattle, and wool. Ballinger was incorporated in 1892 and has a council-manager government. Population: 4,203.

BALLISTA, bə-lis′tə, a military machine designed to throw projectiles of various types. It was used by armies from the time of the ancient Romans through the Middle Ages. Its propulsive power usually was generated by the torsion of ropes on a windlass. When the windlass was released, the projectile was thrown. The ballista was somewhat similar to a catapult, and later smaller models were like crossbows.

Some ballistas used by the Romans as heavy artillery weighed four tons and could hurl a 60-pound (27 kg) rock a quarter of a mile (0.4 km). Lighter ballistas discharged smaller missiles, such as flaming arrows.

BALLISTIC MISSILE. See GUIDED MISSILES.

BALLISTIC PENDULUM, bə-lis′tik pen′jə-ləm, a device that measures the velocity of a projectile. First used in the 1740's, it consists of a pendulum hung by wires that restrict its swing to one direction. The pendulum swings when a projectile is fired into a block at the lower part of the pendulum. The velocity of the projectile, which is caught in the block, can be determined from the equation: $wV = (W + w)v = (W + w)2\pi na$ (w is the weight of the bullet, V is the striking velocity of the bullet in feet per second, W is the weight of the block, n is the number of swings of the pendulum in one second, and a is the recoil distance in feet). The ballistic pendulum, which has been replaced by more modern instruments such as the chronograph, still is used in the physics laboratory to demonstrate the principle of the conservation of momentum.

JOHN D. BILLINGSLEY, *U.S. Military Academy*

BALLISTICS, bə-lis′tiks, is the science of the motion and general behavior of missiles, including projectiles, bombs, guided missiles, and rockets. A special branch of applied mechanics, it comprises *interior ballistics*—imparting energy to missiles; *exterior ballistics*—performance of missiles, both in the air and in space; and *terminal ballistics*—the effects of missiles at the target.

INTERIOR BALLISTICS

At the Battle of Crécy, in 1346, the English, by firing the first gun-launched projectiles (against the French), encountered interior ballistic problems that are still under investigation. Some of these problems are: how to give a projectile high speed without bursting the gun, how fast powder should burn, and how a gun can survive many firings without damage.

The projection of missiles at today's high velocities requires tremendous force. The source of this energy must be readily manufactured, easy to transport, and capable of being safely applied. Much of the information presented here on interior ballistics of guns is applicable also to rockets and recoilless weapons.

In a gun the important requirement is to impart to the projectile the highest possible velocity with the lowest possible peak pressure of gas. At the same time, consideration must be given to minimizing smoke, flash, and erosion of the gun barrel. These and other requirements must be met under battle conditions, where guns may undergo long periods of sustained firing in climates ranging from that of the hot, dusty desert of Africa to that of the wet, subzero Arctic.

The primary effort of interior ballistics is to study the effect of the propelling charge, during and after burning, upon the projectile. The ballistician seeks to coordinate the design of gun, propellant, and projectile. He seeks means by which pressures and velocities may be computed from the known characteristics of powders and projectiles. Progress in interior ballistics has, in general, followed the development of ballistic measuring instruments, of propellant powders, and of improved guns.

The first reasonably accurate ballistic measuring instrument, the ballistic pendulum (q.v.), was described by Benjamin Robins before the Royal Society of England in 1742. By 1791, Charles Hutton, of the Royal Military Academy in Woolwich, England, had developed a formula for the velocity of a spherical projectile.

Work by Gen. Thomas Jackson Rodman in the United States in 1857 led to improvements in the grain-form of powder and in the manufacture of guns. Rodman also devised a gauge for the direct measurement of the maximum pressures of powder gases in guns. Investigations by the British experimenters Capt. (later Sir) Andrew Noble and Sir Frederick Augustus Abel in 1874, were continued in France by Henri Resal and Émile Sarrau in deriving formulas connecting travel, velocity, and pressures in the barrel of a gun when black powder grains of the Rodman type were used. The development in France of the more efficient smokeless powders by Paul M.E. Vieille about 1884, however, made the existing formulas unsuitable. Col. Camille Le Duc (1856–1936), a French army artillerist, developed the formulas still used to determine powder pressure and projectile velocity when time or length of travel in the tube is known.

Action Inside the Gun. The modern cannon is essentially a heat engine. When the charge is ignited, gases are emitted from the surface of each grain of powder, and pressure builds. Resistance to initial motion of the projectile is great and is caused largely by inertia, friction, and the fact that the band of metal around the shell (called the rotating band) resists the cutting action of rifling in the gun barrel. The projectile normally does not begin to move until the pressure reaches about 6,000 pounds per square inch (4,218,600 kg/meter^2). Resistance to motion then decreases rapidly, and the projectile accelerates. As it moves, the volume of space behind it increases, and this decreases the pressure; however, the rate of burning of the charge continues to increase, because more powder surface is ignited. The net effect is a rapid increase in powder gas pressure up to the point of maximum pressure. This occurs at a short distance from the origin of rifling. Beyond that point, pressure drops and, at the muzzle, is about 10 to 30 percent of maximum pressure, depending upon weapon design. Muzzle pressure acts on the projectile for a slight distance beyond the muzzle, accelerating the projectile slightly, but unfortunately also causing it to yaw slightly.

For a given gun and projectile the following means of controlling the powder gas pressure and the velocity are available: (1) variation of chemical composition of the propellant; (2) variation of grain shape; (3) rate of ignition; and (4) variation of weight of charge.

EXTERIOR BALLISTICS

Exterior ballistics involves an extensive body of knowledge, including physics (particularly Newton's laws of motion); mechanics and the analysis of dynamic forces; aerodynamics and the complex forces of air; mathematics, including calculus; the principle of the gyroscope; and some meteorology. The ballistician seeks means of computing the trajectory of projectiles when their muzzle velocities, angles of departure, and air characteristics are known. From trajectory data he compiles selected information, which, with tabulated corrections for variations from standard conditions, are known as firing tables. See GUNNERY.

Early investigators assumed that air could offer little resistance to the passage of a projectile. In 1791, Hutton, using a ballistic pendulum, demonstrated that the projectile lost velocity quite rapidly in air over fairly flat trajectories and also that the rate of loss depended on the velocity. The French Gen. Isidore Didion, at Metz, continued and confirmed these findings in the 19th century.

In France, experiments on air resistance, using compressed air, gave promising results that led to the formation of a commission (at Gâvres), which published, in 1898, data comparing the air resistances of several projectile shapes. In Germany, Otto von Eberhard in 1912 determined and plotted the air resistances of various projectiles at different speeds. After World War I, exterior ballistics became increasingly important as the velocities of projectiles and therefore the ranges of weapons increased. Work in this field in the United States has been carried on largely at Aberdeen (Md.) Proving Ground.

Conditions of Flight. Unfortunately there is no fine line of demarcation between interior and

Figure 1. A projectile traveling faster than the speed of sound compresses air in its path, making shock waves.

exterior ballistics. As the projectile moves forward in the barrel, it pushes the air mass in front of it, causing the latter to emerge from the muzzle first. The internal air mass, now traveling at a high velocity, strikes the outside air, which is relatively at rest, and creates a shock wave that develops spherically. As the base of the projectile clears the muzzle, the main mass of propellant gas begins to pour out into the already turbulent air. Because of its small mass and the resistance to motion that it meets, the gas loses velocity very rapidly. Shortly thereafter the projectile overtakes and pierces the report wave (the wave that produces the noise of the exploding propellant). At this instant the projectile is accompanied by the head wave, or projectile shock wave.

A shock wave cannot form on the projectile unless the velocity of the projectile relative to the surrounding gaseous medium is equal to or exceeds the speed of sound. Since energy is required to establish and maintain a shock wave, the energy contained in a shock wave represents a loss of the kinetic energy of the projectile. With the hypersonic velocities of present and future projectiles and missiles, shock wave phenomena present tough problems.

Fig. 1 shows an experimental projectile moving at Mach 2.2 (Mach number is the ratio of the velocity of a projectile in air and the velocity of sound in air.) Shock waves form at the nose, the center, and at the edge of the base.

Gravity acts on a projectile, and after the projectile leaves the muzzle, this force begins to curve the trajectory of the projectile toward

the earth. A force called drag opposes forward motion. For a given projectile shape, the air forces acting on a projectile fired into the air are dependent on: (1) diameter and (2) velocity of the projectile; (3) density of the air; and (4) drag coefficient. The drag coefficient takes into account the factors not considered separately, such as projectile form, yaw, air viscosity, and Mach number.

Trajectory. The trajectory is the curve traced by the projectile in its flight (see Fig. 2). The factors that influence the trajectory of a specified short-range projectile are principally gravitation and the characteristics of the air through which it passes, but for long-range trajectories, additional factors must be considered, including the curvature of the earth and the variation of the gravitational field and atmospheric density with altitude.

If a projectile were launched at a given velocity and at a given angle, in a vacuum and in a steady gravitational field, the result would be a gradual slowing of the projectile until it reached the highest point of the trajectory, followed by an exactly equal acceleration to the point of fall. Such a trajectory would have the following characteristics: its shape would be that of a parabola; its highest point would be halfway between the gun and the point of fall; the angle of fall would be equal to the angle of elevation of the gun; the striking velocity would be equal to the initial velocity; and the maximum range would be from an angle of elevation of 45°. (This does not apply to self-propelled weapons.)

When the medium through which a projectile travels is air rather than a vacuum, however, the trajectory is influenced by air resistance in addition to gravity. The resulting retardation accounts for several effects. The velocity is now reduced by the air resistance, so that the final velocity will be less than the initial velocity. Therefore, since the projectile is traveling at a slower horizontal rate after it passes the highest point than it was traveling before it reached

Figure 2. Elements of the trajectory.

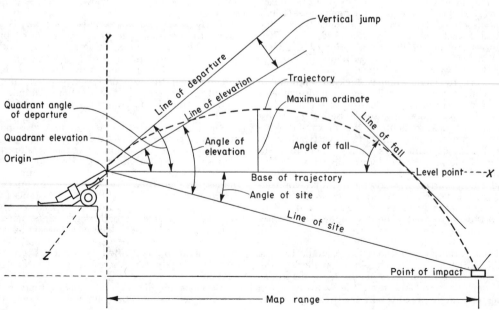

there, it will travel a shorter distance. This makes the descent shorter than the ascent and the corresponding angle of fall closer to the vertical than was the angle of departure from the gun.

Stabilization of Projectiles. Two methods are used to stabilize projectiles and obtain the desired type of flight: spin and fins. Most projectiles are stabilized by a spin imparted by the rifling inside the barrel of the weapon. The twist of the rifling determines the rate of spin of the projectile and is very important, since an overspun projectile fails to nose over in the descent, and an underspun one gyrates too much, creating excessive yaw. Fins control the flight of projectiles fired from some smoothbore weapons and are used on most aerial bombs.

Ballistic Coefficient. One of the most important factors in the calculation of a trajectory is the ballistic coefficient, derived from the weight and diameter of a projectile, and the projectile's streamlining as compared to that of an ideal projectile. In practice, it is determined by range firings. Trajectory is greatly affected by it—a projectile with a high ballistic coefficient travels many times farther than one with a low coefficient.

Bomb Ballistics. Prior to World War I it was impossible to drop missiles on an enemy at any great distance behind his front lines. This distance was limited to the range of artillery weapons. The use of aircraft vastly extended this range. World War I saw the development of bombing missiles—from steel darts, hand grenades, and converted artillery shells to the first aircraft bombs.

Initial attempts to control the flight of missiles involved the use of ropes trailing from bombs, and later, rigid tail-fin assemblies. During the years from World War I to World War II the technology of bombing progressed to the point where the average error did not exceed 240 to 300 feet (73–91 meters) when bombing from an altitude of 20,000 feet (6,100 meters). As each new bomber type attains greater altitude and speed than its predecessor, accurate placing of conventional bombs becomes more difficult. This has led to the development of bomber-launched rocket-bombs with their own propulsion and target-seeking devices.

Whereas a shell in an artillery trajectory generally rises and then falls, the bomb at release from a bomber begins its flight with the same forward speed as the aircraft, gradually losing this and gaining downward speed. The vertical velocity continues to accelerate until the bomb is falling at the limiting velocity, when retardation caused by air resistance is just sufficient to balance the accelerative force caused by gravity. The limiting velocity may be exceeded if the bomb is equipped with rocket propulsion; however, without it, bombs generally travel much more slowly than artillery projectiles—only very heavy bombs dropped from great altitudes reach the speed of sound.

Calculation of a bomb's trajectory depends, as with an artillery shell, on the bomb's ballistic coefficient, a figure relating the bomb's size, shape, performance in the air, and striking velocity with those of other bombs. For greater accuracy, separate ballistic coefficients are often used for the airplane's track over the ground and for the period of the bomb's fall. At impact the bomb will have lagged a considerable distance behind the aircraft, as shown in Fig. 3. This distance, known as the trail, is important in calculating trajectory and in the design of bombsights.

Since World War II, electronic computers have aided ballisticians in the computation of great numbers of trajectories and their compilation in ballistic tables. The tables furnish direct answers to many ballistic problems.

TERMINAL BALLISTICS

Terminal ballistics is concerned with the forces operating at the end of the projectile's trajectory, that is, at the target. In designing

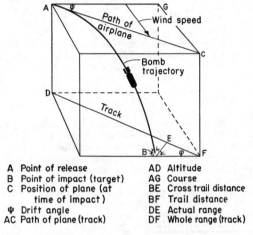

A Point of release	AD Altitude
B Point of impact (target)	AG Course
C Position of plane (at	BE Cross trail distance
time of impact)	BF Trail distance
Ψ Drift angle	DE Actual range
AC Path of plane (track)	DF Whole range (track)

Figure 3. A typical bombing problem.

weapons and ammunition, maximum desired terminal effect is the objective. A balance of many factors is essential. The most important of these are shape, weight, and material used in the projectile; type and weight of explosive charge; fuzing system; and terminal velocity.

The science of terminal ballistics has lagged behind the companion sciences of exterior and interior ballistics primarily because of difficulties in obtaining basic data for study. Rapid advances in radiography and high-speed photography have helped, but the problem of securing good data remains complex.

Means of Producing Damage. Whatever the type of weapon considered and whatever the nature of the target, damage can be produced by one or more of the physical phenomena associated with the impact of a missile, the detonation of an explosive, nuclear fission, or chemical or bacteriological action. These phenomena may be classified as follows:

(1) Fragmentation, or action of relatively small particles, usually from the case of a bomb, rocket, warhead, or shell.
(2) Impact, which pertains to the penetration or perforation of an object by a relatively large metallic body, such as an armor-piercing shot.
(3) Blast, release of energy in shock waves.
(4) Debris, set in motion at high velocities.
(5) Heat, in the flame front of the blast, or radiant heat.
(6) Fire, from the effects of an explosive or induced by special incendiary weapons.
(7) Chemical action, as by smoke or poison gas.
(8) Bacteriological action.
(9) Radioactivity.

Fragmentation. When a charge of high explosive detonates inside a closed metal container, the container is usually blown into pieces, called fragments. Capacity for damage depends on fragment size, velocity, and distribution. Terminal ballistic studies try to determine the laws and conditions governing the speed and distribution of fragments; the sizes and shapes that result from the bursting of different types of containers; and the influence of the explosive.

Upon detonation of the high explosive in a missile, the metal case expands very rapidly because of the internal pressure of the expanding products of the detonation. Fragmentation is not the only result—only 40 percent of the gas energy is absorbed in the fragmentation process. The balance of the energy produces a compressive wave in the air. The fragments are propelled at high velocity, and within a very short distance from the center of explosion, pass through the shock wave, which is retarded to a greater extent by the air. It is difficult to obtain ballistic data on individual fragments, but statistical analysis of the fragmentation of the whole container provides essential practical data. Ideal fragmentation missiles break into uniform fragments with size and velocity fulfilling predetermined requirements.

The fragments from a missile usually fly in a direction perpendicular to the surface of the casing. If the missile is detonated while in flight by fuze action, the side spray will have a slight forward thrust because of the forward velocity of the missile.

The damage produced by a fragment with a given velocity depends on the fragment's mass. Mass distribution of missile fragments is determined experimentally by means of static detonations in which the fragments, or a portion of them, are caught in sand pits and then recovered, sized, and weighed. In evaluating fragmentation effectiveness, the types of damage considered are casualties and normal perforation of mild steel of $\frac{1}{8}$-inch, $\frac{1}{4}$-inch, and $\frac{1}{2}$-inch (.3–1.3 cm) thickness. The determination of what will cause a casualty is called wound ballistics. It depends upon fragment mass, shape, and velocity at impact, along with target physiology.

Blast. When an explosive charge bursts in air, expanding gases, often referred to as the flame front, burst forth and compress the surrounding air, thus initiating a shock wave. The gases themselves have little inertia, cool rapidly, and will have lost most of their velocity at a distance of 40 to 50 times the diameter of the charge. The belt of compressed air in the shock wave has initially a high outward velocity, which it loses rapidly at first, finally approaching the velocity of sound, at which it may continue to move for some time. The shock wave, except for its intensity, has all the characteristics of a sound wave and travels through the surrounding air in the same manner; that is, without the transmitting medium moving with it. The shock wave is bounded by an extremely sharp front called the shock front, in which the pressure rises abruptly from atmospheric to a peak pressure—the positive, or pressure, phase—then declines to atmospheric pressure. The pressure continues to decline to subatmospheric pressure—the negative, or suction, phase—and then returns to normal. Two criteria must be satisfied in order to cause damage by blast: first, the peak pressure must exceed a certain value; and second, a certain minimum intensity of pressure must endure for a

sufficiently long period. For example, to collapse a 15-inch (38.1 cm) brick wall requires, in general, a minimum peak pressure of 3 to 4 pounds per square inch (.2–.3 kg/cm²) and a pressure of 2 pounds per square inch (.1 kg/cm²) for a period of 50/1000 to 60/1000 second. The nuclear bomb, producing long-lasting peak pressure over a wide area, required study of blast effects on all types of structures.

Hypervelocity Impact. At extreme impact-velocities the projectile makes a much wider and deeper crater in the target. This is called fluid impact, because at hypervelocity both projectile and target act like fluids. To obtain this effect, the trend is to higher muzzle velocities and lighter bullets for military small arms.

Defeat of Armor or Concrete. An important part of terminal ballistics concerns attack against concrete or armor by artillery. Of the three methods used, the first relies on kinetic energy for penetration, the second uses the shaped charge (also called the hollow-charge principle, or Munroe effect), and the third applies the Hopkins effect, in which the inner surface of the target is chipped, although the outer surface may not be penetrated.

The ability of a projectile to destroy a target depends in large part on the relation between the amount of protection possessed by the target and the power of the missile. At impact there is a contest between missile and target in which not only the target but also the missile may yield in varying degrees. The terminal ballistician provides ammunition and armor designers with data to maximize damage effectiveness on the one hand and to afford maximum protection against it on the other.

See also ARTILLERY; GUIDED MISSILES; GUNNERY; GUNS; PROJECTILES; ROCKETS; SMALL ARMS.

JOHN D. BILLINGSLEY, *Colonel, USA*
United States Military Academy

Further Reading: Association for Ballistic Missile Development, *Advances in Ballistic Missile and Space Technology* (New York 1959); Boughan, Rolla B., *Shotgun Ballistics for Hunters* (New York 1965); Dept. of Ordnance, U.S. Military Academy, *Ordnance Engineering*, Vol. I, *Ballistics* (West Point, N.Y., 1966); Whelen, Townsend, *Small Arms Design and Ballistics* (Harrisburg, Pa., 1955).

BALLIVIÁN, bä-yē-vyän', **José** (1804–1852), Bolivian soldier and president. He was born in La Paz, Bolivia, in May 1804. He fought in Upper Peru (now Bolivia) during the War of Independence. After the adoption of the Bolivian constitution in 1826, he took part in the internal struggle that ended two years later in the resignation of the country's first president, Antonio José de Sucre. When the next president, Andrés Santa Cruz, marched into Peru in 1835 to set up a protectorate over the country, Ballivián commanded a regiment. After the overthrow of Santa Cruz by a Chilean army in 1839, Ballivián challenged the rule of the new president, Gen. José Miguel Velasco, with whom he had previously been allied. He was forced into exile, but returned two years later, overthrew Velasco, and at the Battle of Ingaví (Nov. 20, 1841) defeated the Peruvians under Gen. Agustín Gamarra, and drove them out of Bolivia. Ballivián then became president, but was overthrown by revolution in 1848 and retired to Valparaíso, Chile. He died in Rio de Janeiro, Brazil, in 1852.

Adolfo Ballivián (1831–1874), the son of José Ballivián, was president of Bolivia in 1873–1874.

BALLOON, bə-lōōn', a lighter-than-air craft with no propelling system and no means of controlling horizontal flight. A balloon is an *aerostat*—an aircraft supported by the buoyancy of the atmosphere. It consists essentially of an impermeable bag filled with a lighter-than-air gas. The development of modern balloons for high-altitude and space applications, however, has led to many modifications in balloon design.

Balloon Structures. The ordinary sporting balloon is made of rubber or a synthetic fabric. The spherical bag has a tubular extension called a neck that is left open as a safety precaution after the bag is inflated. The bag is not fully inflated to begin with, so that on rising it will be filled out with the expanding gas. Increases in internal pressure due to further expansion of the gas are usually relieved by means of a valve operated by the balloonist.

The car or basket in which the balloonist rides is suspended beneath the bag by a network of cordage passing over the bag. Two controls over vertical flight are available: the valve for releasing gas, and the ballast (usually water or sand) that can be dropped to lighten the balloon. Gas and ballast are conserved as long as possible. The gas used is generally hot air or helium. Helium is preferred to the lighter gas, hydrogen, because helium does not burn, whereas hydrogen burns explosively. Helium lifts 92.64 percent as much weight as hydrogen can, and diffuses from the bag more slowly. If contaminated with air, helium can be purified cheaply. The purification of hydrogen is costly and hazardous.

Structural Changes. The basic balloon features of gas bag, valve, suspended basket, and ballast were all developed during the 18th century. Various modifications were made in following years. For example, a device called a "ripping panel" was introduced by a U.S. aeronaut, John Wise, in 1844, to empty the bag rapidly on landing, thus reducing the danger of bumping along the ground. In 1896 the German *Drachen* balloon was designed to overcome rotation by having an elongated form with a vertical lobe at the rear. The kite balloon, developed later in France, had three fins to give greater stability in flight.

Originally some cloth such as linen was used in making the gas bag. Natural and then synthetic rubber was later employed. More recently, polyethylene plastic demonstrated its superiority to rubber for high-altitude flights, and a polyester called Mylar has been developed that is about ten times stronger than polyethylene. Mylar absorbs less solar energy and is therefore less sensitive to temperature changes. Sometimes dacron threads are laminated to the Mylar for further strength.

Modern Balloon Designs. The special needs and problems encountered in dealing with high-altitude and space environments have required new concepts in balloon design. There are four types of specialized design in common use.

The *extensible balloon* is a closed vessel made of neoprene plastic. It carries scientific payloads to altitudes of 100,000 to 130,000 feet (30,000–39,000 meters). The balloon bursts on reaching these high altitudes, releasing its payload for return to earth by parachute.

The *zero-pressure balloon* is a vented and relatively inextensible balloon used mainly in scientific research. It is one of the largest types of balloon and can reach high altitudes with very heavy payloads. The vented balloon drops ballast at sunset to maintain its altitude.

The *superpressure balloon* is a closed vessel made of strong material in order to maintain a constant volume. The balloon has a global-range capability and floats at a constant altitude. It does not have to drop ballast to maintain altitude when it cools, because of its excess internal pressure. The balloon is developed in several different sizes, each of which is designed to carry scientific instruments to a specific altitude.

The *open-appendix, hot-air balloon* is basically the same as the ordinary sporting balloon. With the employment of stronger and reasonably light fabrics and of propane burners, however, it is finding considerable application as a tethered platform on which electromagnetic sensors can be operated free from ground disturbances.

Invention of Balloons. The ancient Greek legend of Icarus testifies to the antiquity of the human dream of soaring into the sky. Man's desire to conquer the air expressed itself in a search for both heavier- and lighter-than-air craft. At first, however, thought was channeled into heavier-than-air concepts, as there was no counterpart in nature for the development of lighter-than-air vehicles.

Early Design Concepts. The period of true scientific speculation about flight began with Leonardo da Vinci. In 1505 he worked out some rational principles of flight. His conceptions did not become known until 1797, but it was only a matter of time before other people began to reason scientifically about flight, once it was realized that air had weight and exerted pressure. In 1670 a Jesuit monk, Francesco de Lana, reasoned that "no air" is lighter than "some air." He conjectured that to remove the air from spherical metal containers would cause them to be buoyed upwards. This concept could not be achieved in de Lana's time, however, and men sought some easier way to obtain buoyancy.

Early in the 18th century Bartholomeu Lourenço de Gusmão of Portugal developed a

THE FIRST BALLOON to carry a live cargo—a sheep, a duck, and a rooster—made its ascent on Sept. 19, 1783.

small hot-air balloon. Later in that century a Dominican friar, Joseph Galien, theorized that air varies in density from sea level to high altitudes. He suggested that an airship could be built for travel in the denser atmospheric regions near the earth by capturing a large chunk of lighter air from higher altitudes and placing it in the craft.

First Balloon Flights. It was not until 1783, however, that the first large lighter-than-air craft was successfully flown, in France. Two brothers, Joseph Michel and Jacques Étienne Montgolfier, having carefully observed the behavior of smoke in chimneys, designed a test balloon that was made of silk and had an opening at the bottom. When burning paper was held near the opening the bag filled out with hot air and floated upward. The Montgolfiers tested progressively larger balloons until, on June 5, 1783, they publicly launched one that measured 23,430 cubic feet (703 cubic meters) and had a circumference of 105 feet (31.5 meters). The linen balloon rose 6,000 feet (1,800 meters) and traveled 7,660 feet (2,300 meters). This type of balloon soon came to be known as the *montgolfière.*

On Sept. 19, 1783, a larger *montgolfière* of linen and paper was filled with smoke. It ascended to about 1,500 feet (450 meters) and flew about 1.5 miles (2.4 km) in a public demonstration lasting 8 minutes. The balloon carried a sheep, a duck, and a rooster—the first airborne passengers. Two months later, on Nov. 21, 1783, the first manned flight took place. Jean François Pilâtre de Rozier, after several test flights in a captive balloon, finally made a free flight with his friend the Marquis François Laurent d'Arlandes in a *montgolfière* over Paris. The flight lasted more than 20 minutes and covered some 5 miles (8 km), attaining an altitude of about 3,000 feet (900 meters).

Hydrogen Balloons. The hydrogen balloon was developed almost simultaneously with the hot-air balloon. Jacques Alexandre César Charles, a

A MYLAR BALLOON is inflated for Project Star Gazer's two-man astronomical excursion to the upper atmosphere.

COURTESY OF USAF INFORMATION OFFICE

French physicist, with the help of the brothers Charles and M.N. Robert, stole the show from the Montgolfiers by constructing a spherical silk bag 13 feet (3.9 meters) in diameter and impregnated with rubber varnish. He inflated it with hydrogen and sent it aloft from the heart of Paris on Aug. 27, 1783. The balloon traveled 15 miles (2.4 km) in 45 minutes. It was destroyed by a group of terrified peasants when it landed.

On Dec. 1, 1783, an improved Robert balloon incorporating many of the features found in modern balloons was piloted by Professor Charles with one of the Robert brothers. The balloon was covered with a netting from which the car was suspended, and had a valve on top to permit the discharge of hydrogen at will. After two hours of flight the balloon descended to discharge Robert. Charles then ascended by himself for the second leg of the flight. Thus began a new era in practical aeronautics. The flight was discussed widely, and further flights and experiments were made in Europe and the United States during the 19th century.

Growth of Practical Ballooning. After the first balloon flights an era of practical ballooning began that yielded considerable aeronautical knowledge. Information was gained on air currents, temperature and pressure variations, and wind velocities in the atmosphere. The use of balloons in meteorological studies, for example, began almost contemporaneously with the first balloons. Ascents by the French physicist and chemist Joseph Gay-Lussac were recorded as reaching altitudes of 23,000 feet (4,600 meters) as early as 1804. These unequipped high-altitude ascents were dangerous, however, and unmanned balloons with automatic recording instruments were introduced later.

The first military application of balloons was made in 1793 by Jean Marie Contelle for the French army. His two 4-hour observation ascents were considered to have had military value in that they inflicted damage on enemy morale. The military use of balloons continued into the 20th century and through the two world wars. The uses included reconnaissance and propaganda-distributing flights, antiaircraft barrage balloons, and balloons used as high-altitude relay stations. More recently, balloons have been employed in the development of balloon-borne missile targets.

In the course of the 19th and early 20th centuries balloons also found many other areas of application, such as exploration, aerial photography, and the transportation of mail. They have been used by the lumber industry in lifting operations. And balloons continue to be used popularly in races and for demonstrations at fairs and other exhibitions.

Scientific Uses of Balloons. Balloons find their most important application in modern atmospheric research and the peaceful development of outer space. Research balloons have carried heavy scientific payloads to altitudes where they are above 99.8 percent of the earth's atmosphere. The payloads include such instruments as visible light, infrared, and X-ray telescopes; gas and isotope samplers and cosmic ray counters; and pressure and temperature sensors. Balloon-rocket combinations carry such payloads even higher, to altitudes of 300,000 feet (90,000 meters).

The National Aeronautics and Space Administration (NASA), together with the U.S. Navy and the National Science Foundation, carries out many scientific balloon programs in atmospheric re-

BALLOONING over the Alps is an annual international contest. Here a flight begins at Mürren, Switzerland, amid the striking beauty of the Bernese Alps. Participants in this event represented United States, Germany, England, France, Switzerland, Austria, and the Netherlands.

search. The programs are conducted through the National Center for Atmospheric Research. One such program is the Stratoscope series of balloons —astronomical observatories capable of obtaining high-resolution celestial photographs from altitudes above 15 miles (24 km). NASA's meteorological programs include the launching of specially instrumented weather balloons by rocket to about 200,000 feet (60,000 meters). Other special weather balloons are sent to heights of about 130,000 feet (39,000 meters). Radar is used to track the balloon payloads in order to determine the speed and direction of high-altitude winds. The Soviet Union also has an active aerospace balloon program and uses balloons for meteorological, industrial, and other scientific purposes as well.

Manned High-Altitude Flights. Men have risen to very high altitudes in modern balloons. The U.S. projects High-Dive and Man-High, for example, staged a series of bailouts from balloon gondolas at heights ranging up to 100,000 feet (30,000 meters) or more. Their purpose was to study high-altitude escape procedures. Project Strato-Lab, initiated in 1956, provides aeromedical data on its flight crews, who carry out geophysical and astrophysical observations as well. One such flight took place on May 4, 1961, when a balloon piloted by Comdr. Malcolm D. Ross rose to 113,500 feet (34,050 meters). The two-man crew rode in an open, cagelike gondola made of aluminum tubing. They were protected from the near-space environment at that altitude by pressure suits and by slightly modified household venetian blinds installed on the gondola.

Space Exploration. The first space balloon, Echo 1, was launched by NASA on Aug. 12, 1960. This spherical balloon, 100 feet (30 meters) wide, was inflated in space and went into a nearly circular orbit about 1,000 miles (1,600 km) above the earth. It had a skin of aluminum-coated Mylar. Two solar-powered radio beacons carried by Echo 1 assisted in locating and tracking a passive-relay communications satellite. A second Echo was launched in 1965. The project yielded data on the mechanism by which radiation and solar particles heat up the atmosphere.

Inflatable space equipment, stations, and vehicles were being developed in the 1960's. The structures are light and may be folded into small packages requiring relatively little lift to get them into orbit, where they can be inflated rapidly. Balloons may offer a new dimension in the exploration of other planets. They may be used to support measuring instruments set down on the planetary surfaces and to convey objects from one point to another, and may serve as shelters during manned landings.

EDWIN J. KIRSCHNER, *Transportation Consultant*

BALLOONING, bə-loon′ing, is a sport involving competition between manned balloons. Pilot excellence is judged by the best-conducted flight. Because wind alone determines the velocity and direction of a flight, a balloonist can seldom predict where his craft will land. But he must know the effects of air currents on height and direction and how to manipulate valves and ballast for ascents and descents.

Competitors participate in a variety of events, which include long-distance races, spot-landing matches, cross-country activity, and hare-and-hounds chases. In a long-distance race the winner's balloon is the one that travels the farthest and remains aloft the longest. In both spot-landing and cross-country matches, the pilot must take off and land within a specified time. In the former event, the one who lands closest to a designated point wins; in the latter, the one who goes the farthest is the winner. In hare-and-hounds racing, sports cars follow a balloon; the winner is the first driver to reach the landing spot.

Ballooning became an international sport in 1906 with the staging of the first James Gordon Bennett Trophy Race in France. This long-distance event took place nearly every year from 1906 to shortly before the beginning of World War II. In the 1950's, despite stringent air traffic controls and the high cost of the sport, enthusiasts from the many European balloon clubs revived free ballooning. Crews from several European nations and from the United States participated annually. Each year at Mürren, Switzerland, balloonists gathered to make the voyage over the Alps from Switzerland to Italy— a sporting event that began with Eduard Schweizer's flight over the Alps in 1910. The Fédération Aéronautique Internationale, in Paris, governs international meets.

In the United States, pilots must be licensed by the Federal Aviation Agency. The National Aeronautic Association (NAA) governs meets, and the Balloon Federation of America, a division of the NAA, coordinates local club activity. The Hot Air Balloon Club of America (Concord, Calif.) and the Balloon Club of America (Newtown, Pa.) are two prominent local clubs.

BALLOT, bal'ət, any object, now usually a sheet of paper, by which a secret vote is cast; hence also the act of voting, or the total number of votes cast at a given election. The word is derived from the Italian *ballotta,* meaning "little ball," this being the form in which the earliest secret votes were cast.

Ballots of this kind were used in ancient Athens in the people's courts and popular assemblies from the 5th century B.C.; they were also employed in popular assemblies and sometimes in the Senate in Rome. Commonly, balls of white or black were used to indicate a yes or no vote; sometimes the balls were dropped into different urns or boxes to express the voter's preference. In early colonial times in America, beans and corn were used on occasion as ballots. Some fraternal organizations still use white and black balls in voting on the admission of new members.

In democratic countries today, paper ballots are used in elections for public office to ensure the anonymity of the voter and thus achieve the maximum expression of the popular will. The paper ballot has been traced to a secret vote held in the Salem (Mass.) church in 1629, probably the first use of the ballot in America. Even the absentee ballot was allowed by an act of the Massachusetts colony in 1647, in the provision that freemen who remained at home could send their votes to the court of elections on open papers or papers folded once.

The use of paper ballots spread widely among the American colonies and later among the states until, by the Civil War, only Kentucky and Virginia were electing by voice vote. Kentucky, which had had the paper ballot from 1792 to 1799, was the last state to abandon voice voting. The legislature of the Northwest Territory enacted a law in 1800 that elections should be by ballot. A court case in Massachusetts, in 1829, decided that printed votes met the constitutional test of written votes. The party ticket, a strip issued for easy casting of a vote, came into use in the mid-19th century. To ensure secrecy, laws were enacted requiring clean, white paper for all party tickets. Various other regulations came in scattered states—dimensions, quality of paper used, and, in two states, the enclosure of the ballot in a sealed envelope.

Australian Ballot. Thirty years after the innovation in Australia of a secret, uniform ballot in 1858, the United States copied the idea. The characteristics associated with the Australian ballot are: uniformity, printing at public expense, secret voting, and official conduct of the election.

The English form of this ballot was simple—one office for which a few candidates were entered. But the adaptation of the Australian ballot by the United States quickly transformed it from such simplicity to several patterns of ballot, one of which was the party-column ballot which strikingly resembled the former party tickets consolidated on one sheet of paper.

For the general election this arrangement, known as the *Indiana ballot,* places all the candidates of a party in the same column, the order of the columns being determined either alphabetically, by the result of the vote in the preceding election, or in one-party states by common consent. Some states put an emblem over each column, so that the voter may more easily identify his column. About half of the states place a square or circle at the head of each column for a straight ticket mark and also the square beside the name of each candidate for a split ticket vote. Blank lines for each office and a blank column are put on the ballot for persons who wish to write in names of unlisted candidates.

The other arrangement, known as the *Massachusetts* ballot, groups the names of the candidates for each office—in some states with party label, in others without any party identification. The order of names for each office is decided by law, and may be determined by one of the following: (1) party vote in the preceding election, (2) alphabetical order, (3) drawing of lots, and (4) decision by the board of elections. Since the first position is the most desirable, many states require that the names be rotated or alternated in the various precincts. California allows the name of the incumbent to have first place.

For the general election more than half of the states use a consolidated or blanket ballot on which appear all candidates and proposals (initiated and referred measures). This ballot is usually white and of high quality paper. The size is often stated in the law; but usually the number of candidates and measures determines its size. The remaining states use separate ballots—a candidate ballot (or one for each level of government), one for proposals, and a nonpartisan ballot for a judicial or school election.

Some states, such as Vermont, designate a different color for each ballot, and a few even require that the box to receive each ballot be of matching color. When the certified form of the ballot has been set up, it is printed on inexpensive paper, conspicuously headed "Sample Ballot" or "Specimen Ballot," to be distributed and posted for educational purposes. Where the voting machine is used, the ballot label, or a reduced copy of it, is printed, bearing instructions for the voter.

A number of states require one or more election clerks to initial each ballot on the back before it is handed out. The clerk at the ballot box checks the folded ballot for the initials before the voter deposits it. More than half the states use a numbered perforated stub which is detached from the marked and folded ballot by the election judge. A few states use a double stub—the first half is torn off when the voter receives the ballot, the second before the folded ballot is deposited. Both stubs must bear the same number. The ballot remains secret; the stub(s) merely serve to ensure that the voter deposits only the official ballot which he received in the polling place. This device seeks to prevent "the Tasmanian dodge," by which a voter could deposit a ballot already marked for him and take away an official ballot to be marked for another voter. Fraudulent voting—repeating, ballot-box-stuffing, intimidation, and corrupt counting of ballots—are faults in election administration and not features of the ballot itself.

Primary Election Ballots. The primary is a party election to nominate candidates for the general election, although a special or a nonpartisan election may be held in conjunction with it. Subject to variations that are peculiar to the primary, the ballots are printed, distributed, and voted in the same manner as are general election ballots.

In the "open primary" (used in about ten states) the voter receives all the party tickets on one blanket ballot (for example, Minnesota), or on separate ballots clipped in one sheaf (Wisconsin), and he secretly votes the party ticket of his choice. In the "closed primary" the voter states

BALLOTS cast on paper, as in this improvised polling place in 1905, are gradually yielding to voting machines.

his party, or is registered as a member of a given party, and he votes only that particular ticket.

In any consideration of the primary, it may be noted that voters are free to express their preferences at the subsequent general election, regardless of their participation in the primary, unless the voter feels a moral constraint in relation to his own party. In some states the primary ballot carries a printed pledge that the voter will support the nominees of the primary, but there are varying interpretations of such pledges, both official and personal.

Some form of "run-off primary" is used in the Southern states. If a candidate in the primary has a majority, he is nominated; but if no one receives a majority, a second primary is held for the two leading candidates. This ensures a majority nomination unless there is a tie, in which case a state may authorize a third primary.

If the apparent result of a primary election is changed by the official count, ballots for the run-off primary may have to be rapidly changed. A write-in vote for a candidate declared eligible is occasionally necessary. Some sentiment has been expressed to lengthen the time between the two primaries to allow a satisfactory count and certification.

Voting Machine. Since the voting machine is merely a mechanical Australian ballot, its use is fully covered in the election laws of the states. The ballot label is arranged on some machines to present the party-column ballot with the straight ticket lever and a lever for a choice under each office (for example, in Rhode Island); and on other machines to present the office-group ballot, sometimes with a straight party lever also (as in Connecticut). There is provision for the write-in vote on the ballot label or on paper ballots placed within the curtain of the machine. The laws require a supply of paper ballots to be printed for use if a machine breaks down.

"Ballot title" is the term applied to the wording of a referred measure as it appears on the ballot label of the machine or on the paper ballot. Referendum and initiated measures commonly appear at the top of the ballot label for the voter's first consideration, although some machines are made for placing them at the right or bottom of the label. When a nonpartisan election is held in a primary or general election, as for judicial officers, the names of these candidates usually appear before the party candidates.

In addition to the well-established voting machine, another advanced type of ballot is the *automatic voting device.* This uses punch cards and electronic data processing. Each voter receives as many cards as the number of candidates

and questions requires. The cards are inserted in the device. To the right of each name (or of the "Yes" and "No" spaces for questions) the voter may punch in his choice. A card spoiled in the process of voting can be turned in for a new card. All completed cards are placed in an envelope and submitted to the election judges. The device can be carried in a briefcase, and the necessary number of devices can be furnished in each precinct.

This plan has been authorized in California, Georgia, and other states. It has the value of central counting as well as the relative economy of purchase and storage. The voting machine, with its accurate and speedy counting, is still widely used, and each year more cities and counties adopt it. Probably three fourths of all votes cast are recorded and counted mechanically or electronically.

Short Ballot. The November presidential election is actually the selection of presidential electors of the party obtaining the plurality vote in each state. The form of the ballot came to be an arrangement of names of party candidates for electors, with or without the names of candidates for president and vice president. This ballot was of quite large dimensions. Removal of the names of electoral candidates from the ballot was achieved in state after state throughout the first half of the 20th century so that more than half the states, electing about three fourths of the electoral college, use the presidential short ballot. The saving of space on the ballot has been considerable, and there is an economy of effort in casting and counting the ballot.

The presidential short ballot was suitable to the voting machine, and it was for the early machines that exceptions were first made to the listing of names of electoral college candidates. What came to be a short ballot for paper balloting was preceded by its application to the voting machine. The two movements, deleting electors from paper ballots and from the face of the machine, have continued simultaneously. The wording of the Illinois law is typical: "Placing a cross within the square before the bracket enclosing the names of President and Vice-President shall not be deemed as a direct vote for such candidates for President and Vice-President, but shall only be deemed to be a vote for the entire list of electors chosen by that political party or group so certified to the Secretary of State as herein provided."

Other arrangements found among the states for the presidential election are: (1) only the names of the presidential electors are on the ballot (Arkansas); (2) the names of the electors appear beneath the names of the presidential candidates, to be voted individually or as a group by a mark in the square beside the presidential names (Vermont); and (3) the names of electors are grouped beneath the presidential names with only one square to mark (Oregon).

In the United States the short ballot movement led to a reduction of elective officials, especially in relation to state administration. The result was an integration of authority around the governor, to whom various officials, formerly elected but now appointed, are responsible.

The movement served two significant purposes: (1) it brought about increased prestige and power for the governor, with an increased efficiency of administration, and (2) it gave the voter relatively few offices to vote for and a better notion of a unified, conspicuously responsible state government. In many counties the opportunity is still open for a short ballot, with similar emphasis on efficiency and responsibility in administration.

Legal Controls. Responsibility of those persons who handle ballots is very important. Not only must election officials observe the legal requirements of election administration, but other persons having some task related to ballot preparation and distribution are obliged to meet legal exactions. In Virginia, for example, the printer and each of his employees must take the following oath: "I . . . solemnly swear that I will print . . . ballots according to the instructions of the electoral board of the county of . . . ; that I will print, and permit to be printed, directly or indirectly, no more than the above number; that I will at once destroy all imperfect and perfect impressions other than those required to be delivered to the electoral board; that as soon as said number of ballots is printed I will distribute the type used. . . ."

Responsibility for both used and unused ballots continues after the election. When the ballots have been counted and properly certified by election boards, they are turned over to an officer for custody pending the possibility of a contest by a defeated candidate or group; then upon court order the ballots are subject to recount. If the election is not contested they are kept in the vaults of a county treasurer or by the central board for the legally required period (usually six months or one year) and then destroyed.

European Ballots. In Britain the ballot for election to the House of Commons carries one office, for which there are often not more than two candidates. Municipal elections carry a somewhat larger load, since council members (perhaps five) are the only persons to be elected. In "list" elections (on the Continent)—devised for emphasis on party lists of candidates—the representation in Parliament is chosen in multiple-member districts, thereby adding to the total number of names on the printed ballot. The choice for the voter relates to party and not at all, or perhaps only incidentally, to individual candidates.

Balloting in France and Germany is a much longer operation, though not at all to be compared with the labors of the American voter. The referendum vote is less used in European countries than in American states having the initiative and referendum. But the referendum is well known in Switzerland, and the expression of policy choice through a "plebiscite" is found in various other countries on the continent. In totalitarian nations elections receive a great deal of attention; but slates of candidates uniformly without opposition cannot in any way resemble electoral arrangements in democratic nations. See also ABSENTEE VOTING; ELECTION; INITIATIVE; PRIMARY ELECTIONS IN THE UNITED STATES; REFERENDUM; VOTING BEHAVIOR; VOTING MACHINE.

SPENCER D. ALBRIGHT
University of Richmond

Bibliography

Albright, Spencer D., *Ballot Analysis and Ballot Changes Since 1930*, Council of State Governments (Chicago 1940).
Albright, Spencer D., *The American Ballot*, American Council on Public Affairs (Washington 1942).
Childs, R.S., *Short-Ballot Principles* (New York 1911).
Council of State Governments, *Book of the States* (Chicago, biennially).
Evans, E.C., *History of the Australian Ballot* (Chicago 1917).
Harris, Joseph P., *Election Administration in the United States* (Washington 1934).
McKinley, A.E., *The Suffrage Franchise in the Thirteen English Colonies in America* (Philadelphia 1905).
Smith, Carl O., *A Book of Ballots* (Detroit 1938).
Wigmore, A.H., *The Australian Ballot System as Embodied in the Legislation of Various Countries* (Boston 1889).

BALLOU, bə-lōō′, **Hosea** (1771–1852), American Universalist clergyman, whose preaching and writings were responsible for an upsurge of liberal religious thought in New England. This upsurge greatly influenced the rise of Universalism, with its belief that salvation is universal because God is a loving father who will ultimately save all his children.

Ballou was born on April 30, 1771, in Richmond, N.H. He was baptized in 1789 as a Baptist, but was converted to Universalism that year. He began preaching in 1791, and became an itinerant preacher the following year. He spoke in a simple and often witty manner. In 1794 he was ordained a Universalist minister. After serving pastorates in Dana, Mass., Barnard, Vt., Portsmouth, N.H., and Salem, Mass., he was installed in 1817 as minister of the Second Universalist Society in Boston. This position he held until his death on June 7, 1852, in Boston.

Ballou was a prolific writer of pamphlets, discourses, poems, sermons, and letters. He founded and edited the *Universalist Magazine* (1819) and the *Universalist Expositor* (1830), the latter with his son. As a result of his work Universalism had an importance among humbler people that its sister denomination, Unitarianism, never had.

Further Reading: Cassara, Ernest, *Hosea Ballou* (Boston 1961).

BALLOU, ba-lōō′, **Maturin Murray** (1820–1895), American journalist, who helped found the Boston *Globe* in 1872 and was its first editor in chief. He was born in Boston, Mass., on April 14, 1820. Before his association with the *Globe*, he founded and edited one of the first American pictorial papers, *Gleason's Pictorial* (later called *Ballou's Pictorial*). In later life he toured extensively. He died on one of his journeys, on March 27, 1895, at Cairo, Egypt.

Ballou wrote a number of travel books, including *Due West* (1884), *Due South* (1885), and *Under the Southern Cross* (1888). His other works include *Biography of Hosea Ballou by his Youngest Son* (1853) and *History of Cuba* (1854). He also was the author of numerous adventure stories written under the pen name "Lieut. Murray," among them, *Red Rupert: The American Buccaneer* (1845).

BALLSTON SPA, bôlstən spä', a village in eastern New York, 25 miles (40 km) north of Albany, is the seat of Saratoga county. Situated in a dairy-farming and poultry-raising area, the village manufactures plastics, humidifiers, precision instruments, hosiery, yarn, cider, and vinegar. Its weekly newspaper, the *Journal,* was established in 1788.

Ballston Spa was founded about 1787 by the grandfather of Stephen A. Douglas and was named for the Rev. Eliphalet Ball, an early settler. The village was incorporated in 1807. In the early 1800's it developed as a fashionable health resort. After the Civil War, nearby Saratoga Springs offered greater attractions as a resort, and Ballston Spa turned more to industry. Population: 4,968.

BALLWIN, bôl'win, is a city in eastern Missouri, in St. Louis County. It is 18 miles (29 km) west of the center of St. Louis, of which it is a residential suburb. Its name derives from John Ball, owner of the land where the community was founded. The addition of "win" to the name was intended to express Ball's confidence in the community's future. Ballwin was incorporated as a village in 1950 and became a city in 1956. Government is by mayor and board of aldermen. Population: 10,656.

BALM, bäm, is an oily, aromatic, soothing substance. It is also the name of the plant yielding such a substance. The common balm is a fragrant seed plant that grows during all seasons of the year. Also known as *garden balm* or *lemon balm,* this plant is native to the Mediterranean region and to Asia but is widely grown in Europe, the United States, and other temperate areas. It is a branched, hairy plant, about 2 feet (60 cm) high. Its leaves, approximately 2 inches (5 cm) long, are oval and toothed. The irregular white or yellowish flowers are clustered in the angles formed by the leaves and the stems from which they arise. The inner floral envelope (corolla) is about ½ inch (12.7 mm) long and has 2 lips. The upper lip has 2 sharp projections; the lower lip has 3 lobes. The 4 stamens (pollen-bearing organs) are enclosed in the corolla.

Garden balm is valued because of the lemon-minty odor of the leaves and stems. It is used as a tea, as a seasoning for wines and liqueurs, as a perfume, and in the treatment of fevers. The scientific name for the common balm is *Melissa officinalis,* and it belongs to the mint family, Labiatae. Among other plants known as "balm" are: American bee balm (*Monarda didyma*), field balm (*Glecoma hederacea*), Moldavian balm (*Dracocephalum moldavica*), horse balm (*Collinsonia canadensis*), and Molucca balm (*Moluccella laevis*), also known as bells of Ireland or shell-flower. See also BALM OF GILEAD.

BALM OF GILEAD, bäm, gil'ē-əd, is an oily, resinous, aromatic substance secreted by some trees. The name is given also to several trees that yield the resin. Because of its fragrance, balm of Gilead is used in some perfumes. It is also famous for its supposed soothing and healing medicinal properties. The resinous substance, Canada balsam, obtained from the tree *Abies balsamea,* often is referred to as balm of Gilead. The balm mentioned in the Bible probably was obtained from the small evergreen tree *Balsamodendron gileadense* of the Middle East.

BALMACEDA, bäl-mä-sä'thä, **José Manuel** (1840–1891), president of Chile. He was born in the department of Melipilla, Chile, on July 19, 1840. Balmaceda was educated at the Seminario Conciliar in Santiago, but after accompanying Manuel Montt, the Chilean chief justice, on a diplomatic mission to Peru, he became interested in liberal politics and discontinued his preparation for the priesthood. He helped to establish the liberal journal *La Libertad* in 1866, and two years later joined in founding the Club de La Reforma, which organized the Liberal Democratic Party. He was elected to Congress in 1870, and served as a deputy for 15 years, becoming noted as an orator. Balmaceda was minister to Argentina (1878–1881), and successively minister of foreign affairs and minister of the interior under President Domingo Santa María (1881–1886). In the latter post he sponsored the establishment of civil marriages and civil registration of births and deaths.

Elected president of Chile in 1886, Balmaceda carried out large schemes of reform and democratization; public education was greatly extended, railroads were built, and other internal improvements were effected. However, many of these measures brought him into conflict with the clerical oligarchy, which not only largely ruled the state but also monopolized the offices; and when he attempted to prevent the ruin of his work by controlling the election of his successor, his opponents blocked the administration. Dissolving Congress, which had refused to approve measures for the collection of taxes, he made himself virtual dictator, and this involved the country in civil war.

The revolutionists, who had the support of the naval officers, commenced hostilities on Jan. 7, 1891, when they secured the nitrate provinces. Using nitrate revenues to purchase arms and ammunition, they utterly routed Balmaceda's forces in a decisive battle near Valparaíso on August 7. Balmaceda took refuge in the Argentine legation at Santiago, and there committed suicide on Sept. 19, 1891, rather than face a trial.

BALMAIN, bàl-maN', **Pierre** (1914–   ), French couturier. He was born at Saint-Jean-de-Maurienne on May 18, 1914. In 1932 he went to Paris to study architecture at the École des Beaux-Arts. Because of financial difficulties, however, he was forced to take part-time employment in 1934 at the fashion house of Captain Molyneux, where he soon became a full-time dress designer. His career was interrupted in 1939 by the outbreak of World War II, but after the German occupation of France in 1940 he returned to Paris and resumed fashion designing at the famous house of Lucien Lelong.

Balmain opened his own fashion house immediately following World War II, and his friends Gertrude Stein and Alice B. Toklas, the American expatriate literati, helped publicize his new business. In succeeding years the House of Balmain became a major influence in the world of dress design. With Christian Dior, Jacques Fath, and Balenciaga, Balmain was instrumental in launching the so-called "New Look" that swept the fashion world in the late 1940's. The "New Look" emphasized small waists and skirts with radically low hemlines. In 1951 the House of Balmain opened a branch in New York City that supplied fashions to shops in many of the major cities of the United States.

BALMER, bäl′mər, **Johann Jakob** (1825-1898), Swiss mathematician and physicist who, in 1885, found that the wavelengths of some spectral lines of hydrogen have a relationship that can be expressed by a mathematical formula. Balmer was born in Lausen, Switzerland, on May 1, 1825. He was a school teacher and university lecturer in Basel from 1865 to 1890. He died in Basel on March 12, 1898.

Balmer's formula, slightly modified by Johannes Robert Rydberg, can be written as

$$\frac{1}{\lambda_n} = R\left(\frac{1}{2^2} - \frac{1}{n^2}\right)$$

where λ is the hydrogen spectral-line wavelength, R is Rydberg's constant for hydrogen (109,678 cm⁻¹), and $n = 3, 4, 5$, and so on. Successively substituting the values for n in the formula yields a series of wavelengths, $\lambda_3, \lambda_4, \lambda_5$, and so on. This series, called the *Balmer series*, played an important role in Niels Bohr's theory of the hydrogen atom. See also ATOM; SPECTROSCOPY.

BALMERINO, Barons. See ELPHINSTONE, ARTHUR and JAMES.

BALMES, bäl′mäs, **Jaime Luciano** (1810–1848), Spanish philosopher and political writer. He was born at Catalonia, on Aug. 28, 1810. Educated at the University of Cervera, he was ordained a priest in 1833 and thereafter devoted himself tirelessly to the promotion of Thomistic philosophy and the reforms of Pope Pius IX. In the course of his short life, he edited three journals, two of which he also founded, and became the most important Spanish philosopher of his time. His works, conservative and scholarly, include *El protestantismo comparado con el catolicismo* (*Protestantism and Catholicism Compared*), published in 1842–1844. It was a Catholic answer to Guizot's *Histoire de la civilisation en Europe*. Balmes died at Vich, Spain, on July 9, 1848.

BALMONT, bäl′yə-mənt, **Konstantin Dmitriyevich** (1867–c. 1943), Russian poet, who was called the "Orpheus" of the symbolist movement in Russian poetry because of his highly musical verse. He was born in Gumnishchi, Russia (now in Vladimir oblast, USSR), on June 15, 1867. A sympathizer with the revolutionary movement in Russia, he was expelled from the gymnasium and then from the University of Moscow for leading student outbreaks. Later, however, he was allowed to continue his studies at the College of Law at Yaroslavl. Beginning in 1905, he spent about 10 years in worldwide travels. Returning to Russia, he supported the Russian Revolution of 1917. In 1918, after the Bolsheviks came to power, he settled in Paris, where he died during the German Occupation in World War II.

Balmont's earliest poetry, *Collection of Verses* (*Sbornik stikhotvoreni*, 1890), met with little success. However, he soon gained in popularity and between 1904 and 1910 was imitated by most of the young Russian poets. His best poems, written between 1894 and 1905, were published in the volumes *Under Northern Skies* (*Pod severnym nebom*, 1894), *Flaming Buildings* (*Goryashchiye zdaniya*, 1900), *Let Us Be Like the Sun* (*Budem kak solntse*, 1903), *Love Alone* (*Tolko lyubov*, 1903), and *The Liturgy of Beauty* (*Liturgiya krasoty*, 1905). He also translated the works of Shelley, Whitman, and Poe. See also RUSSIAN LANGUAGE AND CULTURAL LIFE–2. *Literature* (The Symbolist Movement).

BALMORAL CASTLE, bal-mor′əl, is a private residence of the sovereign of Great Britain, in Aberdeenshire, Scotland, 52 miles (84 km) west of Aberdeen. It is situated on the south bank of the Dee River. The site was purchased by Prince Albert, consort of Queen Victoria, in 1852. He built the castle of white granite in the Scottish baronial style. It was completed in 1855. It has a massive tower 80 feet (24 meters) high and many small turrets with pinnacles. Prince Albert bequeathed Balmoral to Queen Victoria, from whom it passed to her successors.

Abergeldie Castle, another royal residence, is 2½ miles (4 km) east of Balmoral.

BALNAVES, bal-nav′es, **Henry** (1512?–1579), Scottish judge and reformer. He was born at Kirkcaldy, Scotland. After studying at St. Andrews University and at Cologne, where he became a Protestant, he was appointed a lord of session by James V of Scotland in 1538. In 1543 he became secretary of state and helped negotiate the treaty of betrothal of Mary, Queen of Scots, to Edward VI of England. Later in the same year however, when the regent, the 2d earl of Arran, embraced the French and Roman Catholic causes, Balnaves was removed from office and imprisoned for his Protestantism and his English leanings.

Freed in 1544, Balnaves became an agent of the English following the seizure of St. Andrews Castle by the assassins of David Cardinal Beaton in 1546. After the castle was captured by the regent, Balnaves was imprisoned at Rouen, where he wrote a treatise on justification, *The Confession of Faith*, which was found after his death and published with a preface by John Knox in 1584. He returned to Scotland in 1557 and took part in the agitation for religious reform in 1559. In 1563 he was reinstated as a lord of session. Balnaves died in Edinburgh in 1579.

BALSA trees (*Ochroma lagopus*) of tropical America are the source of lightweight commercial timber. This picture shows a large balsa tree being cut in Ecuador.

BALSA-EDUCADOR LUMBER CORP.

BALSA, bôl′sə, is the name of a tropical American tree and of a wood derived from the tree. The tall, rapidly growing tree has alternate, simple, angular or 5- to 7-lobed leaves and conspicuous flowers at the tips of the branches; the 5 yellowish or brownish flower petals are 5 inches (12.5 cm) or more in length. The filaments of the numerous stamens are united into a tube. The seed capsule splits at maturity, exploding numerous seeds enveloped in brownish woolly hairs. Technically, the balsa tree is known as *Ochroma lagopus;* it belongs to the family Bombacaceae.

Balsa wood, which is almost white in color, is the lightest-weight commercially important timber. Although the specific gravity of the dry wood varies considerably, it is usually from 0.12 to 0.20. Balsa often is treated with hot paraffin solution, and because of its light weight, the waterproofed wood is used in life preservers, floats, and mine buoys. It also is used as insulation in refrigerators and as material for streamlining airplane parts, for building model airplanes, and for reducing sound in buildings.

EDWIN D. MATZKE, *Columbia University*

Garden balsam
(*Impatiens balsamina*)

T.H. EVERETT

BALSAM, bôl'səm, is a succulent annual herb native to tropical and subtropical Asia. It is commonly grown in summer in gardens and as a houseplant. Also known as *garden balsam,* this branched plant reaches several feet in height. Its leaves are long and toothed. Conspicuous flowers are found in the angles between the upper leaves and the stems from which they arise. They are variable in form but usually have three modified leaves (sepals) making up the outer floral envelope (calyx). One of the sepals is petal-like and prolonged into a spur. The flowers, one inch (2.54 cm) or more across, vary in color from pink or rose to yellow, white, or mottled. Cultivated forms of the balsam are often double, having more than the usual number of floral envelopes. There are five stamens (pollenbearing organs), and the ovary matures into a capsule that bursts suddenly, scattering the seeds. The scientific name for the balsam is *Impatiens balsamina,* and it belongs to the touchme-not family, Balsaminaceae.

EDWIN B. MATZKE, *Columbia University*

BALSAM, bôl'səm, is the name given to a considerable number of scented, resinous, and oily substances flowing from various plants. *Canada balsam* is obtained by making incisions into the bark of the balsam fir (*Abies balsamea*), a tree found in eastern North America, especially in the province of Quebec, Canada. The oil associated with the resin is removed by heating, and the resin is dissolved, commonly in xylol. This resin is used widely in mounting microscope preparations. *Oregon balsam* is similarly derived from the Douglas fir (*Pseudotsuga taxifolia*).

Balsam of Peru is a product of a tropical tree (*Myroxylon pereirae*), found from southern Mexico through Central America. Formerly the product was shipped from Peru to Spain—hence the name. In tapping the trees, portions of the outer bark are removed first; when the balsam no longer oozes out, further flow is induced by scorching. *Balsam of Tolu* is derived from a closely related species (*M. balsamum*) of South America, found particularly in Colombia and Venezuela. It has a higher resin content and is used in perfumes and cough mixtures.

EDWIN B. MATZKE, *Columbia University*

BALSAM APPLE, bôl'səm ap'əl, is the name given to several related vines in the gourd family, Cucurbitaceae. One common type, found in the temperate zone, is the wild cucumber (*Echinocystis lobata*) of eastern and central North America. It has oval, green, spiny fruits about 1½ to 2 inches (3.5 to 5 cm) long. Another type (*Momordica balsamina*), found in tropical regions, has ovoid orange fruits about 2 to 3 inches (5 to 8 cm) in length with toothlike protuberances. It is often planted as an ornamental climber.

Another related plant, the balsam pear (*M. charantia*), has large yellowish fruits; it is sometimes called a balsam apple. In dried form, it is used in curries. See also MOMORDICA.

EDWIN B. MATZKE, *Columbia University*

BALSAM FIR. See FIR.

BALTA, bäl'tə, **José** (1816–1872), Peruvian soldier and politician. Born at Lima, he became a colonel in the army and participated in an army revolt that overthrew the government of Juan Antonio Pezet in 1865. He became a minister under the new chief of state, Gen. Mariano Ignacio Prado, in November 1865. Balta organized an insurrection that ousted Prado in December 1867, and he himself succeeded to the presidency in April 1868. Balta's regime gave great impetus to public works, especially railroads, financed largely by the exploitation of guano. However, his administration left the country nearly bankrupt. He was assassinated at Lima in 1872.

BALTHASAR or **BALTHAZAR.** See WISE MEN FROM THE EAST.

BALTHUS, bäl-tüs' (1908–   ), French painter. Of Polish and Scottish ancestry, he was born *Balthasar Klossowski de Rola* in Paris on Feb. 29, 1908. When he was 11 years old he showed some of his sketches to Rainer Maria Rilke, the German poet and friend of his family, who was delighted enough to write accompanying texts for the drawings. Balthus was encouraged by his family to study painting, and his first showing was held in Paris in 1934. In 1961 he was appointed by his friend André Malraux, French minister of culture, to be director of the Villa Medici, a French government-controlled art academy in Rome.

Balthus, who may be loosely classified as a representational painter, claims his major influence to be the work of Gustave Courbet. His paintings are nearly photographic in detail, but possess a ghostly, dreamlike aura, reminiscent of the surrealist school. His works include the portraits *André Derain* (1936) and *Joan Miró and His Daughter Dolores* (1937), both in the Museum of Modern Art, New York City.

BALTIC LANGUAGES, bâl′tik lang′gwij-iz, a group of languages of which the most important are Lithuanian, Lettish (also known as Latvian), and the now extinct Old Prussian. The group forms a branch of the Indo-European language family. Other branches of the Indo-European family include Slavonic (or Slavic), Indo-Iranian, Greek, Italic, Germanic, Armenian, Albanian, Celtic, Hittite, and Tocharian. The common parent language reconstructed on the basis of a comparison of these languages is called Primitive Indo-European.

To simplify reference, the following abbreviations are used in this article: Li (Lithuanian), Le (Lettish), OP (Old Prussian), IE (Indo-European), and PIE (Primitive Indo-European).

In his book *Die Sprache der alten Preussen* (1845), Ferdinand Nesselmann first proposed the name "Baltic" because the speakers of these languages inhabit the region adjacent to the Baltic Sea. The term "Baltic" is to be preferred to the outdated "*Lettic*," "*Letto-Lithuanian*," or "*Lithuanian*" as a generic term for this language family. Another term, rarely used now, is "*Aistian*," introduced later in the 19th century by Kazimieras Jaunius and subsequently adopted by the Lithuanian linguist Kazimieras Būga. The term "*Aistian*" is taken from Tacitus' *Germania* (chapter 45), in which he mentions the Aistian peoples (*Aestiorum gentes*), but some scholars believe that the Aistians were of Germanic rather than Baltic stock.

It is customary to divide the Indo-European languages into two large groups, depending upon their treatment of the PIE consonants *k, *g, and *gh (an asterisk preceding a sound or word signifies that the element in question is postulated, but not attested by speech or documentary evidence). In the *centum* languages, these consonants are represented by velars, such as k and g, whereas in the *satem* group, native to Asia and eastern Europe, they have passed to hissing or hushing sibilants. Hissing sibilants are sounds like s and z, whereas hushing sibilants sound like the sh of *ship* (written as š in Li) or the s of *measure* (written as ž in Li). The terms *centum*, from Latin, and *satem*, from Avestan, an Indo-Iranian language, illustrate this difference in treatment. In the centum branch, evidencing an original k pronunciation of the initial consonant in the PIE word *kṃtom, "hundred," are Latin (Italic branch) *centum*, Greek (ἑ) *katón*, Gothic *hund* (in Germanic *k has passed to h), and English *hundred*. The sibilant pronunciation of the initial consonant in the word for "hundred" is characteristic of the satem branch, as in Old Church Slavonic (OCS) *sŭto*, Sanskrit *çatam*, Li *šimtas*, and Le *simts*. The Baltic languages, therefore, belong to the satem group.

Common Baltic. It is generally recognized that the Baltic languages are the most conservative of the living Indo-European languages. Contemporary Lithuanian retains features that had already been lost to Greek, Latin, and Sanskrit when they were first written. Thus, Li *sūnus*, "son," corresponds exactly to the Primitive Indo-European form that has been reconstructed for this word, whereas the other Indo-European languages have different forms, such as Old Attic Greek *huiús* and OCS *synŭ*.

The vocalic system of Common Baltic differs from Primitive Indo-European in showing the merger of PIE *ə, *o, and *a, the passage of *eu to au, and the shortening of the long diphthongs. Examples of the remarkable conservatism of the vocalic system can be multiplied easily: Li *aug-ti*, "to grow" (*-ti* is a typical Li infinitive ending), beside Latin *augeo*, "(I) increase"; and Li *medus*, "honey," beside ancient Greek *méthu*, "intoxicating drink."

The Common Baltic consonantal system is slightly less conservative than the vocalic system. Attention should be called to: (1) the merger of the voiced aspirate consonants with the simple voiced consonants (for example, the PIE voiced aspirate *dh*, reflected in Sanskrit *madhu*, "honey," and Greek *méthu*, is represented by a simple *d* in Li *medus*); (2) the process of satemization, such as the passage of PIE *k to š or s mentioned above; and (3) the creation of a series of palatalized consonants (see section on *Balto-Slavonic Unity*). Nevertheless, with the exception of these few changes, the Common Baltic consonantal system is very close to that of Primitive Indo-European.

A comparison of the Lithuanian noun declension with those of a few of the dead Indo-European languages shows the conservative nature of Lithuanian.

	LITHUANIAN	LATIN	SANSKRIT
Nominative	*vilkas* (wolf)	*lupus*	*vrkas*
Genitive	*vilko*	*lupī*	*vrkasya*
Dative	*vilkui*	*lupō*	*vrkāya*
Accusative	*vilką*	*lupum*	*vrkam*
Instrumental	*vilku*	....	*vrkeṇa*
Locative	*vilke*	....	*vrke*
Ablative	....	*lupō*	*vrkāt*
Vocative	*vilke*	*lupe*	*vrka*

The different endings do not correspond exactly, but Lithuanian has one less case than Sanskrit and one more than Latin.

On the other hand, the verbal system of Common Baltic has been completely revamped, and a single preterit (in *ā or *ē) has replaced the complicated tense structure of Primitive Indo-European. Likewise, the third person dual and plural endings have been lost and the etymological third person singular functions with plural and dual subjects, so that Li *veda* and Le *ved* can mean "he (or she) leads" or "they lead."

East Baltic. After splitting off from Primitive Indo-European, Common Baltic in turn subdivided into East Baltic (including Lithuanian, Lettish, and the extinct Curonian, Semigallian, and Selonian) and West Baltic.

The earliest printed book in Lithuanian is the translation of Martin Luther's *Small Catechism* by Martinas Mažvydas (Mosvidius), dating from 1547. The earliest Lettish texts date from 1585. In general, Lettish has a much less conservative aspect than Lithuanian. In Lettish, the sibilants š and ž have passed to s and z respectively (for example, Li *šimtas*, "hundred," but Le *simts*). Before *j* and front vowels, k and g have passed to c and dz respectively in Lettish (Li *geležis*, "iron," Le *dzelzs*). Tautosyllabic *an, en, in,* and *un* have passed to uo, ie, ī, and ū respectively in Lettish (Li *ranka*, "hand," Le *ruoka*). In final syllables, short a and e have been lost in Lettish but retained in Lithuanian (Li *vilkas*, Le *vilks*). In Lettish, the dative singular of certain categories of nouns has adopted the pronominal ending, as in *cilvēkam*, "(to the) man," with the dative singular ending *-am* from the pronoun *tam*, "(to) that." In final position, the diphthongs ai and ei have passed to Le i, and the diphthong au has passed to Le u: Li dative singular *rankai*, "(to the) hand," but Le *ruoki*; Li *darau*, "(I) do," but Le *daru*. In standard

Lettish, the etymological preterit in *-ē- has been replaced by the preterit in *-ā-: Li vedė, "(he) led," but Le veda. Lithuanian has a free stress as opposed to the fixed stress on the initial syllable of Lettish. This initial stress is sometimes ascribed to the influence of the neighboring Livonian and Estonian, which are both Finno-Ugrian languages.

Lettish is commonly divided into three major dialects: Tahmian; Central (the basis of the Lettish literary language); and High Lettish. Lithuanian has two major dialects: Low Lithuanian (also known as Žemaitish or Samogitian); and High Lithuanian (also known as Aukštaitish), which is the basis of the contemporary literary language.

The now extinct Curonian formed a bridge between Lithuanian and Lettish. At the beginning of the 13th century A.D., the Curonians occupied the area of western Latvia called Courland (or Kurland) and the Samogitian (or Žemaitish) regions and the Memel River area of Lithuania. The language died out about 1600, but a relic of the Curonian substratum is found in Lettish words in which the groups an, en, in, and un have been retained in tautosyllabic position instead of passing to uo, ie, ī, and ū. Le dzintars, "amber," (Li gintaras), shows the typical Lettish passage of g to dz before a front vowel and the typical Lithuanian retention of the etymological in.

West Baltic. The Prussian tribes, speakers of West Baltic, included Sudovian-Jatvingians, Skalvians, Galindians, Pomesanians, Pogesanians, and Samlandians. In the Old Prussian language, there are five documents: the Elbing German-Prussian Vocabulary (c. 1400), written in the Pomesanian dialect and containing 802 words; a 100-word vocabulary in Simon Grunau's Prussian Chronicle, written between 1517 and 1526; and three Lutheran catechisms, two of which date from 1545 and one of which dates from 1561.

In general, the Old Prussian catechisms are very slavish translations of the German originals, so it is not always clear to what extent these texts reflect the Old Prussian language. But insofar as it can be judged, West Baltic was even more conservative than East Baltic. For example, the diphthong ei is retained whereas in East Baltic it passed to ie under stress: Li Dievas, "God," Le Dievs, but OP Deiws. The neuter gender, which was lost in Lettish and Lithuanian, is represented in Old Prussian by such words as assaran, "lake," and panno, "fire." Common Baltic d and t (< *dj and *tj) have remained, whereas in High Lithuanian they have passed to dž and č and in Lettish to ž and š: OP median, "forest," but Li medžias and Le mežs. The vocabulary of Old Prussian contrasts with those of Lithuanian and Lettish: OP ains, "one," but Li vienas and Le viens; OP tirtis, "third," but Li trečias and Le treš; OP stas, "that," but Li and Le tas; OP aglo, "rain," but Li and Le lietus; OP assanis, "autumn," but Li ruduo and Le rudens. Old Prussian became extinct with the death of the last native speaker toward the end of the 17th century.

The Galindians and the Sudovians were mentioned by the Greek geographer Ptolemy (Claudius Ptolemaeus) around 150 A.D. The Russian Hypatian Chronicle mentions the Goljad' (probably the Galindians) in the 11th and 12th centuries around Gzhatsk and Mozhaisk in the easternmost portion of the Baltic area. Probably the word Galindian is derived from Baltic galas, "end," and denotes a people living in a border area. The Galindians and Sudovians were also classed as Prussians by Peter von Duisburg, who mentions them in his chronicle (1326).

Balto-Slavonic Unity. Probably the most disputed question in Baltic comparative linguistics is the degree and type of relationship of the Baltic and Slavonic languages. Views range from one extreme which holds that Baltic and Slavonic are to be considered separate branches of Indo-European to the opposite which maintains that the Baltic and Slavonic languages are to be grouped into a single Balto-Slavonic family. The 19th-century view of Balto-Slavonic unity was first questioned by Antoine Meillet (1866–1936) in his book Les Dialectes Indo-Européens (1908); he ascribed all of the common features of Baltic and Slavonic to parallel but autonomous development. After Meillet, many specialists in Baltic linguistics, such as Alfred Senn (1899–), Ernst Fraenkel (1881–1957), and Jānis Endzelīns (1873–1961), adopted the opinion that the similarities between the Baltic and Slavonic languages were either a result of the retention of the same characteristics from Primitive Indo-European or a consequence of similar innovations brought about during the period of contact after splitting off from Primitive Indo-European.

The question was raised again at the Fourth International Congress of Slavists in Moscow in 1958, when only the scholar Vytautas Mažiulis disputed the thesis of Balto-Slavonic unity. Unfortunately, the question had political overtones. In the interests of political unity, the Russians wished to emphasize the close relationships between the Baltic and Slavonic peoples in order to justify the Soviet Union's annexation of Lithuania and Latvia at the end of World War II. The linguistic question should, of course, be divorced from political considerations.

In studying the problem, one must decide which of the innovations and archaisms common to Baltic and Slavonic are trite (lacking in probative value) and which are important. A trite common innovation is the merger of PIE *a and *o into a single vowel (a in Baltic; o in Slavonic). This is characteristic of Germanic and certain other Indo-European languages as well as Baltic and Slavonic. A trite common archaism is the retention of the PIE word for "sister": OCS sestra and Li sesuo. This word is retained in other Indo-European languages, as in English sister, Sanskrit svasar-, and Latin soror. Features found only in Baltic and Slavonic, but in no other language family, are probably innovations rather than inheritances from PIE.

Numerous lexical items are common to Baltic and Slavonic alone, such as the following: Li ragas, "horn," and OCS rogŭ; Li ranka, "hand," and OCS roka; Li liepa, "linden tree," and Russian (Russ) lipa; and Li žvaigždė, "star," and Russ zvezda.

Among the common features of phonology are: (1) the identical reflex of the PIE sonants *r, l, m, and n in Baltic and Slavonic; commonly they are ir, il, im, and in and more rarely, and perhaps originally only after a velar stop, ur, ul, um, and un, as in the following: Li pirštas, "finger," and Proto-Slavonic *pirstŭ; and Li gurklys, "throat," and Proto-Slavonic *gŭrdlo; and (2) the creation of a series of palatalized consonants as a result of the simplification of the group consonant plus yod plus nonfront vowel, as in the case of PIE *tja passing to Common Baltic and Common Slavonic *ta.

Common morphological features include the following. (1) There are certain common patterns of stress in the noun declension: Li nominative singular (n.s.) barzdà, "beard," and žiemà, "winter," have the stress on the final syllable as in Russ n.s. borodá, "beard," and zimá, "winter," but Li accusative singular (a.s.) bar̃zdą and žiẽmą have the stress on the initial syllable as in Russ a.s. bórodu and zímu. (2) The dative plural ending is -mus, as in Old Li ragamus, "(to the) horns," and OCS rogomŭ (with loss of the final -s characteristic of Slavonic), but OP has a dative plural ending -mans, as in auschautenīkamans, "(to the) debtors." (3) Common to Baltic and Slavonic is the transfer of the PIE ablative case to the genitive function in certain classes of nouns, as in Li genitive singular (g.s.) vilko, "(of the) wolf," and Russ g.s. volka, both of which forms correspond phonologically to the Sanskrit ablative singular vrkāt, "(from the) wolf." But traces of the original g.s. ending in -s are to be found in OCS čiso, "(of) what," and OP Deiwas, "(of) God." There are many other common morphological features, but the divergences between the Baltic and Slavonic languages are also great.

The unbiased observer can only conclude that the question of Balto-Slavonic unity remains unsolved and will probably be so until the techniques of comparative linguistics have improved.

See also LANGUAGES OF THE WORLD.

WILLIAM R. SCHMALSTIEG
*Coauthor of "An Introduction
to Modern Lithuanian"*

Further Reading: Entwistle, William J., and Morison, Walter A., *Russian and the Slavonic Languages* (London 1949); Fraenkel, Ernst, *Die Baltischen Sprachen* (Heidelberg 1950); Gimbutas, Marija, *The Balts* (New York 1963); Senn, Alfred, *The Lithuanian Language, a Characterization* (Chicago 1942).

BALTIC SEA, bôl'tik, an arm of the Atlantic Ocean connected with the North Sea by the Kattegat and Skagerrak. It reaches far inland through the gulfs of Bothnia, Finland, and Riga, providing many lands of northern Europe with seacoast advantages. The surrounding countries are Denmark, Sweden, Finland, the Soviet Union (including the Russian SFSR and Estonia, Latvia, and Lithuania), Poland, and Germany. The sea has a total area of about 160,000 square miles (414,400 sq km).

Past the Skagerrak and Kattegat, the cluster of Danish islands, separated by narrow straits, shuts off the Baltic from the ebb and flow of oceanic tides. The sea has a low salt content (15 to 5 parts per thousand) because of the inflow of a number of rivers: the Neva, Narva, Western Dvina, and Neman from the east; the Vistula and Oder from the south; and the Dal, Angerman, Ume, and Torne from the west. Its low salinity facilitates freezing. The sea is deepest near the west coast (1,542 feet or 471 meters, south of Stockholm) and becomes shallow toward the east and south; its mean depth is 180 feet (55 meters). Shoals, sandbanks, and submerged rocks are numerous. Winds, often changing direction, and especially eastern gales, cause the water level to vary, at times considerably. Because of its storms, the Baltic is a treacherous sea for navigation.

The Baltic Sea has served as a crossroads of commercial routes since the 9th century. Raw materials flow from northeast to southwest, and manufactured goods take the opposite direction. The Kiel Canal provides a link with the North Sea, and the White Sea–Baltic Canal with the White Sea. Naval and military operations took place in the Baltic Sea during World War I (see WORLD WAR I–*The War at Sea*) and World War II. Following World War II, the only considerable naval force in the Baltic was that of the Soviet Union, based at Kronshtadt.

BALTIC STATES, bôl'tik. The Baltic states— Estonia, Latvia, and Lithuania—are republics of the USSR, situated on the east coast of the Baltic Sea south of the Gulf of Finland. The term "Baltic states" sometimes also includes Finland. The total area of Estonia, Latvia, and Lithuania is approximately 67,300 square miles (174,300 sq km) and supports a population of 6,257,000 (1963). Most of the people earn their living by farming. The chief crops are rye, oats, barley, potatoes, wheat, and flax. On less fertile soils dairying and poultry and stock raising are the chief occupations. Forestry is also important. The republics' industries produce steel and rolled metal, cement, fertilizers, and cotton fabrics.

Since the Middle Ages rival powers have battled for sovereignty over the Baltic states in order to dominate the ports and trade routes of the Baltic Sea. The Varangians (9th century), the Danes (11th century), the Germans (13th–14th centuries), the Poles (15th century), and the Swedes (17th century) in turn controlled the region. Russia took part of the area at the beginning of the 18th century and the rest of it before the end of the 18th century. Under Russian rule these lands formed the Baltic provinces.

In 1918, Estonia, Latvia, and Lithuania proclaimed their independence from Russia. They were forcibly annexed by the USSR in 1940, occupied by Germany during World War II (1941–1944), and retaken by the USSR in 1944–1945. After 1945 a state-controlled economy on Communist principles was introduced in each of the Baltic republics. See also ESTONIA; LATVIA; LITHUANIA.

NICOLAI RABENECK, *Linguist and Writer*

The Baltic States: Estonia, Latvia, Lithuania

George Calvert,
1st Baron Baltimore

(c.1580–1632)

BROWN BROS.

BALTIMORE, bôl′tə-mor, a barony held by members of the Calvert family, the English family that planned, founded, and were the proprietors of the province of Maryland. The family included George Calvert, its founder; five lineal descendants who inherited the title; and also the first governor of the colony.

GEORGE CALVERT, 1ST BARON BALTIMORE (c. 1580–1632), was born near or in Kipling, Yorkshire, England. He was the son of Leonard Calvert, a Yorkshire gentleman of Flemish extraction. In July 1594 he entered Trinity College, Oxford, taking the degree of bachelor of arts in 1597 and receiving the honorary master of arts degree in 1605. He followed his university career with a tour of the Continent, where he continued his study of French, Italian, and Spanish in preparation for a public life. About 1604–1605 he married Anne Mynne (d. 1622), of Hertfordshire, and from this union the succeeding barons of Baltimore were descended.

George Calvert began his public career about 1606. His ability brought him to the attention of Sir Robert Cecil, the chief secretary of state. Cecil, who needed linguists on his staff, made young Calvert one of his private secretaries. After Cecil died in 1612, Calvert continued in this position, assisting James I in his writings and taking over all the Spanish and Italian correspondence. In 1617, James knighted him in recognition of his public services, and in 1619 he was appointed a secretary of state.

A member of Parliament since 1609, he now held the trying and delicate position of intermediary between the king and the House of Commons, which James was attempting to dominate. By 1625 the rising tide of Puritanism in Parliament made it clear that that body intended to deprive Catholics of all state positions of trust. At this moment Sir George proclaimed his conversion to Catholicism. His resignation from public office led James to assert publicly his friendship for Calvert by giving him a barony in the Irish peerage, since Sir George held extensive estates in Ireland as well as in Yorkshire. He now assumed the title of Lord Baltimore, and shortly afterward retired from the court.

Lord Baltimore had been interested in American colonization for a number of years. He served as one of the councilors of the New England Company and had been a member of the Virginia Company. Later, when Virginia came under royal control, he was made a member of the Provincial Council. Such service gave him insight into all phases of colonization. In 1621 he established a small colony in Newfoundland. It was a heartbreaking failure, and after spending a winter in the bleak, cold region, he hastened to Virginia in 1629 with the plan of establishing a colony in that more favorable environment. The final selection fell to a tract of land in an unsettled region northeast of the Potomac. Charles I, who had ascended the throne in 1625, granted this territory to his friend Lord Baltimore in 1632. The colony became Maryland, named in honor of Queen Henrietta Maria, the wife of Charles I.

Calvert framed for his province a charter that is one of the most remarkable documents of its time. He wished, naturally, to establish a sanctuary for persecuted Catholics, but he wished also to conciliate warring Protestant and Catholic interests at home and to avoid the pitfalls encountered in Virginia and Plymouth. He modeled his charter on that of the medieval palatinate of Durham, giving the founders supreme power. Political enemies could find no fault in this English precedent. He likewise blocked criticism growing out of differences in religion by sidestepping that controversial issue. The charter makes no mention of a specific faith. Its broad statements were a guarantee of toleration for all Christian religions. George Calvert died in London on April 15, 1632, before the great seal was affixed to the document. The charter, dated June 20, 1632, was issued to his son Cecil.

CECIL (or CECILIUS) CALVERT, 2D BARON BALTIMORE (c. 1605–1675), was the son of George Calvert. Little of his early life is known except that he matriculated at Trinity College, Oxford, and that in 1628 he married Anne Arundell, daughter of Thomas Arundell, a Catholic peer. A reserved, practical man, he succeeded to his father's title at the age of 26 and inherited his

Cecil Calvert,
2d Baron Baltimore

(c.1605–1675)

BROWN BROS.

charter for Maryland. Beset by personal and political enemies and by conflicts arising from religious and state differences, Cecil Calvert was unable to leave England during the 43 years he was proprietor of Maryland. He delegated the direct administration of the colony to Leonard Calvert, a younger brother, whom he sent to Maryland in November 1633 with a group of settlers. The period encompassed by his proprietorship was marked by the establishment of basic policies regulating church and secular matters (in 1649 the Assembly passed the Act of Toleration, which guaranteed religious liberty to all who accepted the doctrine of the Trinity); by the attempt to make good his claims to all territory lying within the boundaries of his grant; and by trying, through conciliatory measures, to stem the force of the attacks made upon the colony by the growing power of Puritanism. (See section on *Leonard Calvert*.) He was the first to put into practice in the New World the principle of freedom of conscience. Cecil Calvert died on Nov. 30, 1675. His son Charles Calvert served as his last deputy governor in Maryland.

LEONARD CALVERT (1606–1647) was the younger brother of Cecil Calvert and first governor of Maryland. His administration began when he sailed from England with the *Ark* and the *Dove*, in November 1633, along with 20 gentlemen adventurers and about 200 artisans. Most of them were Protestants; others were Catholics. The colonists arrived in Maryland in March 1634, making their first permanent settlement on the 27th of that month at St. Marys. He established a governing body in the form of an assembly of freemen, with no religious restrictions on membership, and maintained rigid impartiality between Catholics and Protestants. Through the Assembly he carried out the proprietor's policy of compromise, and during his administration the Assembly was granted the right to initiate legislation. Although the proprietor retained the power of veto, this was a very important step toward self-government.

In defending the boundaries established by the charter, Leonard Calvert became embroiled in the Claiborne controversy. William Claiborne (q.v.), a Virginian who, prior to the settlement of Maryland, had established a trading post on Kent Island in Chesapeake Bay, refused to acknowledge the proprietorship of Cecil Calvert. This controversy continued intermittently for some 20 years. The civil war of 1642 in England, which resulted in the establishment of the Commonwealth under Oliver Cromwell, reverberated in the colony. Governor Calvert, aware of the seriousness of the situation, went to England to consult the lord proprietor. Both of them were anxious to maintain neutrality between Royalists and Roundheads. This, however, was impossible, for in Leonard's absence, Capt. Richard Ingle (q.v.), a trader and violent partisan of Parliament, stirred up trouble at St. Marys. The governor returned to Maryland just in time to meet the armed invasion of Ingle, allied with the opportunist Claiborne. They seized the government and instituted a dreary period of injustice known as the "plundering time." The governor fled to Virginia, where he was in hiding for nearly two years. In 1646 he returned to St. Marys and reestablished control over the colony. He died in Maryland on June 9, 1647.

CHARLES CALVERT, 3D BARON BALTIMORE (1637–1715), was born in England on Aug. 27, 1637. He was the son of Cecil Calvert, who sent him to Maryland in the capacity of governor in 1661. He inherited some of his father's steadiness and perpetuated his policy of religious toleration. Having succeeded to the title in 1675, he went to England a year later to settle controversial matters involving navigation on the Potomac and criticisms leveled at him by enemies who complained of laxity in matters of defense against the Indians and of moral degeneracy of the clergy. From 1679 to 1684 he governed the colony in person, during which time he was criticized for filling offices with relatives and coreligionists. He returned to England to defend his property rights against William Penn, and remained there the rest of his life. In 1689 a Protestant rebellion led by John Coode overthrew his government in Maryland, and in 1691 the crown withdrew his authority to govern the colony, although he retained his property rights. He petitioned the crown to restore his province in 1711, but was refused because of his Catholic faith. He died on Feb. 21, 1715.

BENEDICT LEONARD CALVERT, 4TH BARON BALTIMORE (1679–1715), was the son of the preceding. He embraced the Anglican faith in 1713, thus removing the barrier which had deprived the Baltimore family of proprietorship of Maryland. This change, probably one of policy, not conviction, alienated him from his father, but won him a pension from the crown. On succeeding to his father's title, he petitioned the king to restore to the family political control of Maryland, but he died on April 5, 1715, before action could be taken.

CHARLES CALVERT, 5TH BARON BALTIMORE (1699–1751), was born on Sept. 29, 1699. After the death in 1715 of Benedict Leonard Calvert, his father, he succeeded to the title, and the crown restored to the Calverts the full proprietary powers specified in the Maryland charter. An educated man, he was considered by his contemporaries to be honest and good-natured, but weak. He went to Maryland in 1732 in an attempt to settle with William Penn the dispute over the Maryland-Pennsylvania boundary line. His proprietorship was marked by the loss of 2.5 million acres of land to Pennsylvania, by the founding of the city of Baltimore, and by the settlement of Germans in the farm lands of the Monocacy area. He died on April 24, 1751.

FREDERICK CALVERT, 6TH BARON BALTIMORE (1731–1771), son of the preceding, was the last Lord Baltimore. He was selfish, degenerate, and mean. He considered Maryland only as a source of income and was indifferent to the interests of its people. He refused to contribute to their defense during the French and Indian Wars, largely because he did not want his estates to be taxed. He died in Naples on Sept. 14, 1771, without legitimate heirs, the title dying with him and the proprietorship falling to Henry Harford, a natural son.

See also MARYLAND—*History*.

HELEN G. HUTTENHAUER
Board of Education, Baltimore County, Md.

Bibliography

Browne, William Hand, *George Calvert and Cecilius Calvert, Barons Baltimore* (New York 1890).
Hall, Clayton C., *The Lords Baltimore and the Maryland Palatinate*, 2d ed. (Baltimore 1904).
Ives, Joseph M., *The Ark and the Dove: The Beginning of Civil and Religious Liberties in America* (New York 1936).
Maryland Historical Society, *The Calvert Papers*, Fund Publication Nos. 28, 34, 35 (Baltimore 1889–99).

BALTIMORE is one of the leading ports in the United States. The great facilities of its harbor have drawn to the city a diversity of industries.

M.E. WARREN, FROM CHAMBER OF COMMERCE OF METROPOLITAN BALTIMORE

BALTIMORE, bôl′ti-mōr, the largest city in Maryland, was the sixth most populous in the United States at the time of the 1960 census, and the center of the 12th most populous metropolitan area. Its vigorous economy is so balanced and diversified that no one industry has stamped its identity on the city. Situated in a "border" state, it shows some cultural aspects of both North and South, but possesses a character of its own.

Baltimore is one of the nation's major ports and this fact has been the most important determinant of Baltimore's past history and present position. It has attracted a variety of manufacturing plants which profit from tidewater delivery of bulk raw materials. The port is the most important reason for the existence of the huge rail complex centered on Baltimore, from which goods move by the shortest route from the Atlantic coast to the population centers in the Middle West.

Baltimore's past still colors it. Dockside streets carry names like Thames and Fleet and Shakespeare, which date back to the mid-18th century when this part of the city was laid out by a settler only one generation removed from England. Traffic doglegs around a monument erected in 1815 in honor of a battle in the War of 1812. Children play in Patterson Park, which was the gift of the father of Betsy Patterson Bonaparte, wife of Jerome Bonaparte, Napoleon's brother. Overlooking the inner harbor is Federal Hill, named on the occasion of a great civic celebration in honor of Maryland's ratification of the United States Constitution. Among the most sought-after residences in the city are rambling and solid but architecturally undistinguished houses in Roland Park, built in the early 1900's in the first completely planned residential community in the country.

Until the 1950's, Baltimore seemed in danger of living too completely in the past. It still cherished southern traditions ranging from beaten biscuit to segregation. The Baltimore and Ohio, Pennsylvania, and Western Maryland railroads, which had built the great port, continued to dominate it, to the detriment of the development of trucking facilities. The city, some felt smugly, had had its urban renewal when it rebuilt most of the downtown area after a great fire in 1904. And if it had typical city slums, it also had its landed gentry in the valleys north of the city. By mid-century, however, it was clear that the city would have to rejuvenate itself.

URBAN DEVELOPMENTS AND PROBLEMS

Like most of the great metropolitan cities of the East, Baltimore is trying to make a threefold adjustment to the last half of the 20th century. It must renew its central industrial and commercial core as well as its older housing; it must accommodate its traditional pattern of streets, transit system, economy, and even its cultural institutions to the new concentration of people and commerce on its periphery; and it must adjust to the large number of immigrants, colored and white, mostly from the South, who have arrived in the city since about 1940.

Urban Renewal. The adjustments have been begun. The most important force is the Baltimore Urban Renewal and Housing Agency. The overall program is distinguished particularly by its tremendous variety. The total urban renewal effort involves subsidized public housing, razing and replacement of slum neighborhoods and

---

INFORMATION HIGHLIGHTS

Location: On Patapsco River estuary (an arm of Chesapeake Bay), 40 miles (64 km) by road northeast of Washington, D.C.

Population: City—905,759, 6th largest in U.S.; Metropolitan Area—2,070,670, 12th largest in U.S. (includes Carroll, Howard, Anne Arundel, and Baltimore counties, and Baltimore city).

Area: 79 square miles (205 sq km) of land and 13 square miles (34 sq km) of water.

Elevation: Sea level to 445 feet (136 meters).

Climate: Temperature averages 76° F (24° C) in summer, 37.4° F (3° C) in winter; annual precipitation averages 42.5 inches (108 cm).

Government: Mayor and 21-member city council, all elected for 4-year terms.

central city office structures, provision of industrial parks, intensive health and building code enforcement in deteriorating neighborhoods, support of public institutions such as museums and universities, reclamation of the Inner Harbor which juts up into the city, and pioneer work in leasing existing buildings for public housing.

Charles Center. In the heart of the city, halfway between the financial-legal center and the concentration of retail stores, lies Charles Center. This project was conceived in 1958. In includes 33 acres of land on which an integrated complex of nine new high- and medium-rise office buildings, two apartment towers, a hotel, a theater, and a large retail store is scheduled for completion by the end of the 1960's. The first office building, designed by Mies van der Rohe, gave dramatic evidence of the community's financial as well as esthetic gain. Overall, Charles Center will have a final assessed valuation more than quadruple that of the original area, even though 30 percent of it is given over to parks, fountains, and other open space.

Rehabilitation. Techniques of rehabilitating existing housing have been tested in two disparate areas. In Harlem Park, some 2,000 properties occupied by predominantly low-income Negro families have been upgraded to standards above those required in the housing code. The block interiors have been cleared out and transformed into parks and play areas. On Bolton Hill, a section of formerly handsome town houses, most of the homes have been restored from apartment use to their previous elegance and charm.

Land Acquisitions. In support of public and quasi-public institutions the Urban Renewal and Housing Agency has been instrumental in acquiring and reselling land for the expansion of the University of Maryland graduate schools, Walters Art Gallery, Peabody Institute, the Johns Hopkins Medical Institutions, and various municipal office buildings and schools.

Inner Harbor Redevelopment. Most ambitious of the renewal programs is the 30-year, $260 million Inner Harbor redevelopment. Jutting into the central business district, the northernmost reaches of the huge port of Baltimore include rotting piers, deteriorated warehouses, an ob-

solete wholesale market area and a variety of small port-oriented businesses. Under the long-range transformation of the area, most of the existing structures will be razed. The remaining commercial port activity is being relocated in the middle and lower portions of the harbor. Utilizing the Inner Harbor as a unique central city asset will involve the construction of 55 acres (22 hectares) of parks, a small boat marina, almost 600,000 square feet (55,742 square meters) of space in new office buildings that will connect the harbor with Charles Center, a Port Authority Building offering an additional 300,000 square feet (27,871 square meters) to maritime businesses, a new home for the Maryland Academy of Sciences, and almost 3,000 intermediate and high-rise apartment units.

Closely related to the Inner Harbor project is the development of a new Municipal Plaza, centering on a mall stretching northward four blocks from the waterfront to the existing City Hall and municipal office buildings.

Housing. Two features have traditionally characterized housing in Baltimore city and even its suburbs. One is the reluctance of its citizenry to accept apartment living, and a complementary commitment to home ownership. The other is acceptance of the row house in a variety of forms. The row house combines economy of initial cost and upkeep with the advantages of a back and—in newer houses—a front yard, on which its owners often lavish great care. Even in the building boom since World War II, while much of the nation favored detached cottages, ranch houses, and split levels, a strong market remained in Baltimore for new blocks of row houses, usually of red brick with white trim.

As in all older cities, blight has been taking its toll, despite the efforts of urban renewal. A survey made in the mid 1960's showed evidences of major blight in almost 42 percent of the housing units and moderate blight in another 32 percent. Virtually all of the housing occupied by nonwhites falls in one of these categories.

An increasing expansion of the nonwhite population into the western, northwestern, and northeastern sections of the city has made more unblighted housing available to the Negro population. Urban renewal has made significant progress in razing and rebuilding in the worst slum areas, while rehabilitation and preventive programs have helped to check the spread of blight. An increasing degree of home ownership by the Negro population—approaching the 50 percent mark—may be a beneficial factor.

During the first two decades after World War II the city provided a significant amount of new housing on previously vacant land. Outside the city limits, the proliferation of new housing has proceeded at almost triple the city's rate.

Population Trends. Baltimore's population has followed the patterns of most other large cities. It rose steadily over the early years from 14,000 in 1790 to 212,000 in 1860. In the next 40 years it more than doubled to 509,000 in 1900 as the great waves of European immigrants rolled into —and through—the eastern cities. In the next 50 years the growth rate was somewhat less, but the population reached its peak of 949,000 in 1950. It declined to 939,000 in 1960 and to an estimated 918,000 in 1965. This was less than half the figure for the whole metropolitan area.

The decrease in the 1950's was due to the availability of new housing in the surrounding

ROW HOUSES are popular family homes in Baltimore. Many display red brick fronts and white marble steps.

suburban counties, particularly attractive to young, expanding families. As older housing in the city was abandoned in the flight to the suburbs, it was bought up by the Negro population, which had previously been tightly packed around the central core of the city and in certain sections of West and East Baltimore. The population trend seems likely to continue slightly downward as older housing is razed to make way for commercial and public uses (including expressways) and as overcrowding is relieved by migration to the suburbs and occupation of remaining housing at a lower density.

Ethnic Groups. Ethnically, about a quarter of the population of the metropolitan area is non-white—overwhelmingly Negro. Within the city limits the ratio is 40 percent and is growing.

Although descendants of German, Italian, Polish, and other national immigrant groups no longer cling so tenaciously together as they once did, clear distinctions remain. A central southeastern portion of the city is still known proudly to its inhabitants and other citizens as Little Italy. The residents of the northwestern section of Baltimore and its contiguous suburban area are predominantly Jewish. East central Baltimore and the suburbs in Baltimore County northeast of the city contain thousands of descendants of German, Polish, and Czech families.

Suburban Expansion. In the 1950's and the 1960's the exodus from the city to the suburbs was enormous. The surrounding counties burgeoned with developments of row houses, garden apartments, detached cottages, and handsome estates. In Baltimore County, surrounding the city to the west, north, and east, hundreds of thousands of new citizens demanded schools, police protection, and highways. The county groped toward urban adjustment with new zoning laws, water restrictions, a home-rule council, and higher taxes. Other counties adjusted more slowly.

Traffic Control. Traffic movement in metropolitan Baltimore is remarkably good, thanks to two factors. One is the typical urban highway system, which includes an outer beltway, a north-south expressway, and an east-west expressway to be completed in the 1970's. A cross-harbor tunnel carries most of the through traffic north and south. The second factor is a highly sophisticated, computerized traffic control system.

THE ECONOMY

The dominant feature of the city's—and even the state's—economy is the port of Baltimore. Over the years it has consistently handled the second or third greatest volume of foreign trade of any American port. Formed by the Patapsco River estuary, an arm of the Chesapeake Bay, the port of Baltimore can be reached from the Atlantic Ocean by the southern entrance to the bay or through the Chesapeake and Delaware Canal at the north end of the bay. The port has almost 200 berths, used each year by more than 5,000 ships, which pick up and discharge more than 44 million tons (nearly 40 million metric tons) of cargo.

The port's preeminence derives from three factors: an advantage of at least 150 miles over competing Atlantic ports in shipments to the midwestern market; a sheltered, easily accessible harbor reached by a 42-foot main channel from Chesapeake Bay; and a remarkably stable and efficient labor force, rated as "ideal" among Atlantic and Gulf ports in a federal survey.

M.E. WARREN, FROM PHOTO RESEARCHERS

SHIPYARDS AND STEEL MILLS are in the vast Bethlehem Steel Corporation complex at Sparrows Point. A ship (foreground) has just left the construction ways.

Baltimore has the world's largest coastal facilities for loading and discharging bulk commodities. Coal and coke, grain, steel products, animal feeds, and refined copper are loaded onto outgoing ships. Incoming vessels discharge vast tonnages of ore, petroleum, sugar, gypsum rock, sulfur, and molasses.

Since the establishment of the publicly financed Maryland Port Authority in 1956, a port previously dominated by railroads primarily interested in transshipping bulk cargo has moved vigorously into the development of its general cargo trade. The authority constructed its own 365-acre (148-hectare) marine terminal to handle a variety of specialized shipments. Within a few years more than 100,000 imported foreign cars were passing across its docks each year. The terminal also specializes in the handling of military equipment and containerized cargoes.

Manufacturing. The influence of the port on Baltimore's economy is all-pervasive. It accounts in great part for the presence of what is called the largest steel plant in the world, Bethlehem Steel Company's Sparrows Point complex. This completely integrated manufacturing facility, with a capacity of almost 10 million tons (9 million metric tons) of steel a year, is a maker of pipe, plate, sheet, and tin-mill products for both domestic and overseas consumption. Its annual payroll is the largest in the state. Bethlehem also operates a ship construction yard with nine ways and one of the most complete repair and conversion yards in the country.

Other companies whose manufacturing operations involve large quantities of bulk commodities—copper, steel, chemicals, and oil—cluster around the port.

This diversity has produced a balance of heavy and light industry, skilled and unskilled work opportunities. As a result, employment in the area is remarkably stable, and unemployment figures, particularly in times of recession, are almost uniformly below the national average—despite a fairly rapid rate of population growth among major metropolitan areas.

Research and Government Agencies. Metropolitan Baltimore's economy is varied further by two other elements. One is the concentration of research and development activity in the general Baltimore-Washington area, typified by the Johns Hopkins Applied Physics Laboratory, the God-

JOHNS HOPKINS UNIVERSITY has two sites in Baltimore. Gilman Hall (left) is prominent on the Homewood campus in the northern section of the city.

CULTURAL LIFE AND EDUCATION

The debate over whether Baltimore's culture is essentially northern or southern has never been resolved. Both influences continue. The Negro was an intimate part of life in Baltimore long before he appeared in numbers in northern, midwestern, and western cities during the great emigration from the South after World War II. So was the southern white, up from the Carolinas and Appalachia. But Baltimore has shared with the major cities of the north the flood of Germans, Poles, Italians, and other immigrants from Europe. If there is still in the South a more leisurely tempo of living, some of this is also visible in Baltimore. But the intensive industrialization and commercialization which came to the South relatively recently has long been part of Baltimore's history.

Foods. To some extent Baltimore is neither northern nor southern, but itself. Baltimoreans are fiercely loyal to their local foods and beers. Though others may eat oysters, crabs, shad, and rockfish, Baltimoreans claim a special dedication to seafood. Oysters remain in short supply because of long-term exploitation of Chesapeake Bay's resources—and traditional terrapin and beaten biscuits have become rarities—but the crab remains king. Heavily seasoned and steamed, the hard-shell Chesapeake Bay blue crab is a staple of taverns in all old Baltimore neighborhoods. The crab feast remains a certain drawing card for political rallies.

Sports. In sports, the first two decades of the second half of the century were marked by community dedication to the fortunes of the Colts of the National Football League and the Orioles of the American League in baseball and to increased activity at Pimlico race track in Baltimore city. Professional basketball and hockey have a smaller but faithful following.

In one sport Baltimore makes a unique contribution. It is the lacrosse capital of the world, where spring is announced by the sight of boys cradling and passing the ball as they stroll to school. In New England as in North Carolina it is a rare college lacrosse team that is not built on a nucleus of Baltimoreans.

Religion. Of residents of the Baltimore metropolitan area who profess a religion, some 25 percent are Roman Catholic, 15 percent Protestant, and 7 percent Jewish. Among the Protestants, Methodists predominate. There are smaller sects, and many persons have no church affiliations.

Education. The Baltimore public schools exhibit both the merits and defects of large urban educational systems. They have yet to find a way to deal effectively with culturally deprived students, although much progress has come with preschool classes, new teaching techniques, and specialized services. But the city offers good secondary education in many of its schools, notably at the Eastern and Western high schools for girls and Polytechnic and City for boys, all

dard Space Flight Center, and the National Institutes of Health. The other is a large concentration of Federal installations in the metropolitan Baltimore area. These include the national headquarters of the Social Security system, the middle-Atlantic regional customs headquarters, and the military installations at Fort Meade, the Army Proving Ground at Aberdeen, and the Army Intelligence Service Headquarters in Baltimore city.

Future Prospects. The future pattern of industrial and commercial growth seems unlikely to diverge greatly from the past. Large land areas are available in all the suburban counties. Utilities are adequate. With the tapping of the Susquehanna River, the water supply for all foreseeable needs is ensured until the turn of the century. Rail, water, and highway communications and plane operations out of Friendship Airport are capable of almost unlimited expansion. A variety of industry, commerce, and public activity seems likely to be attracted in the future.

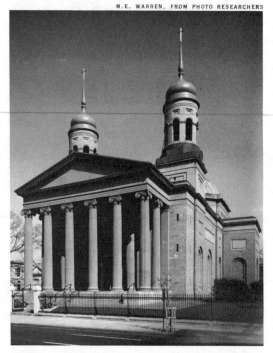

ROMAN CATHOLIC CATHEDRAL, the Basilica of the Assumption of the Blessed Virgin Mary (left), was designed by Benjamin H. Latrobe between 1805 and 1818.

WASHINGTON MONUMENT, in the center of Mount Vernon Place, was the earliest in the U.S. in honor of George Washington. The cornerstone was laid in 1815.

four of which are particularly oriented toward college preparatory work. Among the numerous private schools are Gilman, McDonogh (military), and St. Paul's for boys; Bryn Mawr, Roland Park Country, St. Timothy's, St. Paul's, and Garrison Forest for girls; and Friends School and Park School for both sexes.

In higher education, the preeminent institution is The Johns Hopkins University. The university proper is situated in the northern portion of the city on the Homewood campus, while the medical school and hospital and the school of public health occupy a huge complex of old and new buildings in the eastern part of the city. The University of Maryland's rapidly expanding graduate schools of medicine, law, nursing, dentistry, pharmacy, and social work occupy a large urban campus in the south central part of the city. Other colleges in the metropolitan area include Goucher and Notre Dame (for women), Morgan State, Loyola, Coppin, St. Mary's Seminary, and the University of Baltimore, as well as numerous junior colleges. The Maryland Institute College of Art attracts students of art and design from across the country and includes the famous Rinehart School of Sculpture. The Peabody Institute is the oldest privately endowed music school in the country.

Libraries. The Enoch Pratt Free Library is considered one of the nation's most dynamic public libraries and is studied by librarians throughout the nation and from many foreign countries. With a strong in-service training program, its staff has furnished the directors of such public library systems as those in Philadelphia, Kansas City, Los Angeles, and Richmond. The main library building includes Edgar Allan Poe and H.L. Mencken rooms. The Peabody Library, which has been merged with the Enoch Pratt public library, has a world-famous genealogy department.

Museums. The extraordinarily rich and varied collection of the Walters Art Gallery, housed in a Renaissance-style building, extends from Egyptian times to the 20th century and includes important groups of Roman sculpture, Etruscan, Byzantine, and Medieval art, manuscripts, Sèvres porcelains, Italian primitive paintings, and French painting of the 19th century. Other museums include the Baltimore Museum of Art, which holds, among a broad range of old masters and modern artists, the Cone collection of 19th and 20th century French art, with special emphasis upon Matisse and Picasso; and the municipal Peale Museum, founded by Rembrandt Peale and believed to be the oldest museum building in use today.

Communications. There are three area-wide daily newspapers. The Baltimore *News American* (evening and Sunday) is affiliated with the Hearst organization. The *Sunpapers* comprise *The Sun,* a morning paper that publishes a Sunday edition, and *The Evening Sun. The Sun* is internationally known, especially for its coverage of national affairs by its own bureau in Washington and of international affairs by its overseas bureaus. The *Sunpapers* and the *News American* each own a television station; Baltimore's third station is a member of the Westinghouse group. There are more than 20 AM or FM radio stations.

Places of Interest. Among the notable churches in Baltimore is the first Roman Catholic cathedral built in the United States, the Basilica of the Assumption of the Blessed Virgin Mary, designed by Benjamin H. Latrobe. The new Catholic Cathedral of Mary Our Queen was completed in 1959. Architecturally, it is described as a "modern expression" of "Gothic principles." Other places of worship include the Baltimore Hebrew Congregation Synagogue, a striking example of modern design, built in 1951; the First Unitarian Church, "the birthplace of Unitarianism in America," a Graeco-Roman edifice designed by Maximilian Godefroy; the Otterbein Church, the oldest (1785) in Baltimore; and Lovely Lane Church, with a museum of early Methodism.

The Washington Monument, whose cornerstone was laid in 1815, is the earliest in the country built in honor of George Washington. It is the centerpiece of Mount Vernon Place, whose four expanses of greenery and statuary form a striking formal square. Around Mount Vernon Place stand the Peabody Institute, the Mount Vernon Place Methodist Church, a number of magnificent old town houses, and the Walters Art Gallery.

Fort McHenry, besieged by the British in 1814, stands at the entrance to the Inner Harbor. While watching the siege from a ship in the harbor, Francis Scott Key wrote *The Star-*

Spangled Banner. The original manuscript of the poem may be seen in the Maryland Historical Society. Other places of patriotic interest are the Flag House, home of Mary Pickersgill, where the battle flag that flew over Fort McHenry was made; the *Constellation,* oldest ship in the United States Navy, launched in 1797, about a week before her more famous sister, the *Constitution;* and the Battle Monument, which honors the repulse of the British attack on the city in the War of 1812.

Other sights of note for tourists include the home and grave of Edgar Allan Poe; the Shot Tower, down whose 234-foot (71-meter) interior molten lead was dropped into a tank of water to form more than 12 million pounds (5.4 million kg) of shot a year; the home of Wallis Warfield, later the duchess of Windsor; a Lee-Jackson memorial, one of the few double equestrian statues in the United States; and the Transportation Museum, which has a unique display of full-size steam engines and other railroad relics.

GOVERNMENT

Both the city of Baltimore and its suburban counties have remarkably straightforward governmental structures, free of jurisdictional overlappings. Baltimore, an independent city which is not included in any county, is governed by a mayor and a 21-member City Council elected every four years. Traditionally the council is overwhelmingly Democratic and only occasionally is even one Republican elected to that body. Only one or two Negroes have sat in most councils. A redrawing of voting district lines in the mid-1960's may adjust the numerical imbalances.

Despite a three-to-one ratio of Democratic over Republican registration in the city, two Republicans have been elected mayor since 1927. One of these, Theodore Roosevelt McKeldin, served two terms as mayor, won election twice as governor and then was elected mayor again. What the city lacks in a genuine balance of parties is almost compensated by factional fighting among the Democrats, whose city primaries are crowded with dozens of competing names.

On the whole Baltimore has enjoyed good government in modern times. The kind of large-scale graft and corruption that occasionally has come to light in other large cities rarely occurs in Baltimore. While the city has managed to write a respectable record of municipal solvency, during the 1950's and 1960's it suffered an increasing strain in its dependence upon a rising property tax. It won authority from the state Legislature in the late 1960's to impose a temporary earnings tax on its own citizens and on suburban residents who work in the city.

Tentative steps toward some kind of limited metropolitan government are in prospect. In the suburban counties, two of the most populous have already adopted a mayor-city council form of government.

HISTORY

Baltimore was chartered as a "tobacco port" in 1729, and named after the Barons Baltimore who established the colony of Maryland in the early 17th century. The town soon found itself exporting more flour than tobacco. Gradually the merchants and maritime interests gained ascendancy and by the time of the American Revolution, Baltimore was a bustling port sending its ships not only to northern Europe but to the Mediterranean and Caribbean as well. For two months during the Revolutionary War, Congress, which had fled from Philadelphia in fear of the British, held sessions in Baltimore.

Early 19th Century. After the Revolution, the city boomed spectacularly and in 1797 it received from the Maryland General Assembly a city charter. Trade was enlivened by the growth of iron and copper industries. The speedy Baltimore clipper ships roamed the seas, taking advantage of Britain's preoccupation with wars in Europe. As a competitor on the sea lanes, Baltimore had a particular stake in the War of 1812, and its privateers were a source of especial annoyance to the British, who tried to capture the city. They were repulsed on land, at North Point, and Fort McHenry withstood the waterborne siege which was the occasion for Francis Scott Key's composition of *The Star-Spangled Banner*.

Later 19th Century. Industry and commerce prospered during the next 50 years. The first telegraph line in the United States was strung between Washington and Baltimore. The establishment of the Baltimore and Ohio Railroad opened the way for a massive interchange of goods and materials with the Middle West. Although Maryland did not secede from the Union during the Civil War, Baltimore was torn in its sentiments. Its emotional and commercial ties with the South were strong, but it was very much a border city in a border state. Federal troops occupied the city to keep order. Baltimore suffered with the devastated South during the postwar period and only gradually recovered from the disruption of every phase of its routine.

Disaster and Rebuilding. In the great fire that broke out on Feb. 7, 1904, no lives were lost although virtually all downtown was destroyed. But in rebuilding the city's center, its imaginative architects seized the opportunity to straighten and widen streets and to install modern paving, sewers, and water mains as well as to replace buildings. With the impact of World War I and increasing demand for ships and industrial products, the newly rebuilt city and its expanded port flourished. It became a center of heavy industry as well as of commerce and transportation.

After the Great Depression of the 1930's, World War II imposed both strains and challenges on the highly industrialized port city. Inhabitants of the mountains of Appalachia poured into the city to man the aircraft assembly lines at the Martin Company, the open hearths of the Bethlehem Steel works, and the sewing machines in the garment factories, and to weld and rivet in the huge yards turning out Liberty ships. Traditional old town houses were subdivided into apartments. The public transit system creaked under overloads of passengers. But by the mid-1950's the city had turned, with resourcefulness and enthusiasm, to the continuing task of self-renewal.

DUDLEY P. DIGGES, *The Evening Sun*

Bibliography
Baltimore Association of Commerce, *Metropolitan Baltimore—Its Supporting Economy* (Baltimore 1961).
Beirne, Francis F., *The Amiable Baltimoreans* (New York 1951).
Beirne, Francis F., *Baltimore, a Picture History, 1858–1958* (New York 1957).
Maryland State Planning Department, *Maryland County Economic Data Book* (Baltimore 1964).
Owens, Hamilton, *Baltimore on the Chesapeake* (New York 1941).
Semmes, Raphael, *Baltimore as Seen by Visitors, 1783–1860* (Baltimore 1953).

BALTIMORE & OHIO RAILROAD, bôl′tə-môr, ō-hī′ō, the first railway system in the United States, chartered on Feb. 28, 1827, and in continuous operation since Jan. 7, 1830. The B&O began its operational life hauling passengers in horse-drawn carriages fitted with flanged wheels; by the mid-1960's it had become primarily a freight railroad, drawing only 5 percent of its revenues from passenger trains.

Current Era. Principal lines extend 5,800 miles (9,333 km) from Philadelphia through Baltimore and Washington to Cumberland, Md., and from Cumberland by separate routes to Chicago (via Pittsburgh) and St. Louis. Entry to New York is obtained over tracks of the Reading Company (in which the B&O has a substantial interest) and the Central Railroad of New Jersey (which is controlled by the Reading). System headquarters are at Baltimore. In the mid-1960's the B&O had about 400 diesel locomotives, 400 passenger cars, and 69,000 freight cars.

The early 1960's were years of financial distress and physical deterioration for the B&O, and on Feb. 4, 1963, control of the nation's oldest railroad passed to its rich neighbor, the Chesapeake & Ohio Railway. Holding 90.7 percent of the B&O common stock and 90.6 percent of B&O preferred stock, the C&O made fresh capital available so that a vast modernization program could begin. By the end of 1965, the B&O was in a substantially improved position.

The B&O's cumbersome debt structure, still carrying some of the marks of the company's struggle to avoid bankruptcy during the depression years, prevented any immediate move on the part of the financially stronger C&O toward outright merger of the two railroads. However, a merger plan filed in 1965 by the C&O and the Norfolk & Western Railway, if consummated, would bring the B&O into a 26,000-mile (41,860-km) railway system, counterpoised against a second big system emerging in the East, the 23,000-mile (37,030-km) Pennsylvania-New York Central (whose merger was approved in 1966 by the Interstate Commerce Commission).

History. On Feb. 12, 1827, a group of Baltimore businessmen met at the home of George Brown, a banker, to consider means of recapturing western trade that was being diverted to northern cities by the recently opened Erie Canal. Impressed by the success of railways in Britain, the group decided that "rail roads" eventually would supersede canals, just as canals had superseded the turnpikes. Twelve days after the initial meeting, the Baltimore and Ohio Rail Road Company was granted a charter by the state of Maryland. The first stone was laid at Mount Clare, an estate on the outskirts of Baltimore, on July 4, 1828, the same day that the Chesapeake & Ohio Canal had its own ceremonial beginning in Georgetown (now part of Washington, D.C.). Charles Carroll turned the first spadeful of earth, commenting prophetically: "I consider this among the most important acts of my life, second only to my signing of the Declaration of Independence."

On Jan. 7, 1830, the railroad commenced operation, carrying passengers on excursion trips from the Baltimore Terminal on Pratt Street to Carrollton Viaduct, a stone-arch bridge then being built over Gwynn's Falls, west of Baltimore. On May 30, 1830, the railroad's first division, 13.5 miles (21.7 km) of track between Baltimore and Ellicott's Mills, was put into service. An

BALTIMORE AND OHIO RAILROAD

THE FIRST U.S.-BUILT LOCOMOTIVE, the Tom Thumb, operated on the B&O. In 1830, in a round trip between Baltimore and Ellicott's Mills, Md., it pushed a car containing 26 passengers and reached 18 mph (30 kph).

immediate success, the railroad grossed $20,000 in its first four months of operation. In August 1830 the B&O's first steam locomotive, the Tom Thumb, built by Peter Cooper of New York, was tested successfully. Subsequent studies determined that a steam locomotive could be operated for about $16 a day, in contrast to $33 for the same amount of work performed by horses.

The B&O's westward march was swift. Washington was reached on Aug. 25, 1835; Cumberland, Md., on Nov. 5, 1842; Wheeling, W.Va., on Dec. 25, 1852; and St. Louis in 1857.

The course of expansion was interrupted by the Civil War, in which the railroad played a distinguished role. Its right-of-way at Harpers Ferry was the scene of John Brown's raid in 1859, and two B&O employees were the first casualties in the skirmish. During the war years the railroad (whose strong ties with the North helped to keep Maryland in the Union) provided important security for Washington, serving as a route for the movement of reinforcements from the North and the West.

Despite great physical destruction suffered during the war, the B&O emerged strong and in an expansionist mood. Its tracks reached Chicago in 1874 and Philadelphia in 1886, and the physical profile, as it exists today, was substantially complete.

Often called "the railroad university of America," the B&O is the possessor of an impressive list of "firsts." B&O was the first railroad to publish a timetable (May 23, 1830); the first to use a baggage car (1834), dining or "refectory" cars (1843), and iron box cars (1844); the first to test an electrically operated locomotive (April 29, 1851), to operate an express company (Aug. 1, 1877), and to place an electric locomotive in regular service (June 27, 1895). It also was the first railroad to operate a streamlined passenger train (May 1900), an air-conditioned car (April 1930), and a completely air-conditioned train (May 1931).

LUTHER S. MILLER, *Editor of "Railway Age"*

BALTIMORE COUNTY, bâl-tə-mōr, in north central Maryland, nearly surrounds the city of Baltimore but does not include it within its limits. The county covers 610 square miles (1,579 sq km). It is bordered by Harford County on the east; Chesapeake Bay, Baltimore City, and Anne Arundel County on the south; Howard and Carroll counties on the west; and Pennsylvania on the north. The county seat is Towson, just north of the Baltimore city limits.

While much of the southern part of the county serves as a residential suburb of Baltimore, industry is a major and growing element in the county's life. What is said to be the largest steel-producing complex in the world is situated at Sparrows Point at Baltimore County's southeastern extremity. Nearby is an aerospace manufacturing plant that is a major contributor to the United States space program. Other areas of the county manufacture aluminum products, power tools, electronic equipment, and food products. The northern area is developing a network of landscaped industrial parks. Industry's contribution to the county's tax rolls is estimated to be approximately 25 percent.

The proximity and availability of transportation has contributed much to the county's growth and character. Three major railroads serve the area, and the county is crisscrossed with interstate and other highways. The county is readily accessible to seaborne traffic from Chesapeake Bay through the Dundalk Marine Terminal, located principally within the county.

The growth of residential housing in Baltimore County has paralleled that in other metropolitan areas. Until 1941 the county was primarily rural, with some suburban and industrial acreage on the fringes of Baltimore. Since that time, large tracts of land formerly used for farming have been developed into busy suburban communities. The Baltimore suburbanites and other new residents have transformed all but the northern third of the county, which remains primarily rural.

Baltimore County, which was established in 1650, has no incorporated towns or cities within its limits. All local governmental functions are supported by the county government under the provisions of a charter adopted in 1956. The legislative branch of the government is the 7-member county council; the executive functions are under the direction of a county executive. Both the council members and the executive are elected at large by the voters of the county to serve 4-year terms. Population: 621,077.

CHARLES W. ROBINSON
Baltimore County Public Library

BALTIMORE ORIOLE, bôl'tə-mōr ôr'ē-ōl, a songbird that breeds from Nova Scotia and southern Canada south to Georgia, Louisiana, and Texas, and inland to Montana and eastern Colorado. It winters from southern Mexico to Colombia. The male bird's head, neck, back, wings, and tail are black; its breast, rump, and outer tail feathers are orange; and there is a white bar on each wing. The female and the young are olive on the upper parts of the body and yellowish on the rump and underside; there are two white bars on each wing. The Baltimore oriole ranges in length from 7 to 8¼ inches (18 to 21 cm) and has a wingspread of 11¼ to 12¼ inches (28.5 to 32 cm).

The Baltimore oriole builds a long, slender

ARTHUR W. AMBLER FROM NATIONAL AUDUBON SOCIETY
Baltimore Oriole (*Icterus galbula*)

woven nest of weed stalks and strips of bark and strings. The nest is slung from the end twigs of a tall tree.

The scientific name of the Baltimore oriole is *Icterus galbula*. It belongs to the family Icteridae. (Old World orioles belong to the family Oriolidae.) The bird got its popular name because its colors are the same as those of the Baltimore family, founders of Maryland.

CHARLES VAURIE
American Museum of Natural History

BALTISTAN, bul-ti-stän', is a region in the Pakistani-occupied part of Kashmir. It is watered by the Indus River. Also called *Little Tibet*, it lies high in the Karakoram mountain range of the western Himalaya and contains several peaks over 25,000 feet (7,620 meters). The peak known as K², reaching an altitude of 28,250 feet (8,611 meters), is the highest mountain in the world after Mount Everest. Baltistan is largely inhabited by Baltis, Muslim tribes which are probably of Tibetan origin. Skardu, its principal town, is a trade center for nomadic shepherds.

BALTZER, bält'sər, **Johann Baptista** (1803–1871), German theologian. He was born at Andernach, Germany, on July 16, 1803. Ordained a priest in 1829, he became professor of theology at Breslau in 1830. He was an enthusiastic follower of Georg Hermes, who worked to effect a reconciliation of Roman Catholic teaching with the newer German philosophy. In 1839, Baltzer broke with Hermes and became a follower of Anton Günther, who held that the human spirit could penetrate the meaning and show the scientific truth of church dogmas, and also that decisions of the church about faith were conditional. When Günther came under the ban of the church, Baltzer submitted, but he became involved in other difficulties with church authorities and in 1862 was suspended from his position. He opposed the promulgation of the doctrine of papal infallibility and became an ardent promoter of the Old Catholic movement. He died at Bonn on Oct. 1, 1871.

BALTO-SLAVIC LANGUAGES. See BALTIC LANGUAGES.

BALUCHISTAN'S LARGEST CITY, Quetta, is situated in a mountainous district of Pakistan, in the northwestern part of the region. It is located on the trade route between Pakistan and Afghanistan.

BALUCHISTAN, bə-lōō-chə-stän′, is a region, formerly a province, of West Pakistan. It is bounded by Iran on the west, Afghanistan on the north, and the Arabian Sea on the south. The area of the region is about 134,640 square miles (348,718 sq km). Most of Baluchistan is now part of the division (administrative district) of Quetta. The capital of the division is Quetta, which, with a population of over 100,000, is the largest city in the region.

The People. Baluchistan is inhabited chiefly by the Baluchi tribes. These tribes are an intermixture of the Dravidian peoples that originally lived in this area and successive waves of Arab, Persian, and Scythian tribes that overran the region at various times throughout its history. The Baluchis generally live under ancient feudal rule, each tribe having a supreme chief. The Pathans, another Baluchistan tribe, are warlike, barbaric nomads that live in the northern hill country. The Pathans are of Afghan origin and are not so civilized as the Baluchis. Other large groups include the Bugti and the Marri tribes.

Baluchi, the language spoken by the majority of Baluchistan's people, is an Iranian dialect similar to some Afghan dialects. The language of the Brahuis, a large tribe of nomads, has puzzled ethnologists for years. It has a direct Dravidian root, and the Brahuis are thought to be the last remnant of pure Dravidian stock.

The Land. Baluchistan is rugged and mountainous, with some broad expanses of barren, sandy desert. The chief mountain ranges are the Sulaiman and the Kirthar, which meet at Bolan Pass, the principal gateway through the mountains from Hyderabad and Lahore to Quetta. The mountains are made up of compact limestone, enclosing marine shells and corals.

Baluchistan has a few fertile areas near the rivers, but the rest of the terrain is composed chiefly of deserts and arid stony plains, which receive less than 10 inches of rain a year.

Baluchistan's Arabian Sea coast is about 600 miles long. It is indented very little and has few good harbors. In the northeastern part of Baluchistan there are two large lakes, Hamun-i-Lora, which is fed by the Pishin Lora River, and Hamun-i-Mashkel, fed by the Mashkel River. In southern Baluchistan the Hingol, Dasht, and Purali rivers flow into the Arabian Sea.

The climate ranges from almost Arctic cold in the high mountains and in the north to subtropic heat in the south. Makran, in the south, is one of the hottest regions in the world.

The Economy. Baluchistan's economy is based chiefly on agriculture. Wheat, millet, barley, maize, rice, and potatoes are grown in the semiarid areas that can be irrigated. The fertile regions close to the rivers produce large quantities of grapes, apricots, peaches, apples, pears, and melons. Makran is famous for its dates.

Manufactures include rope, leather, coarse fabrics, food products, pottery, and farm tools.

Baluchistan has some mining, but most of the region's reserves of lead, iron, mineral salts, asbestos, and oil remain untapped. A small quantity of limestone is quarried in the mountainous regions, and gypsum is mined near Sibi. Coal is mined near Quetta and at Sharigh and Harnai in the Bolan Pass, and chromite is mined near Hindubagh.

Leading exports include mustard, dried fish, matting, and raw wool.

History. Archaeologists discovered that a rich culture flourished in Baluchistan about 3000 B.C. This culture was influenced by the thriving trade between the rich Indus valley region to the east and Persia to the west. Baluchistan was ruled by Arab tribes from the 7th century to the 10th century A.D., when it became a province of the Persian empire. Except for a brief period (1596–1638) when it was part of the Mughul (Mogul) empire, Baluchistan remained under Persian rule until the 1800's. The remoteness and inaccessibility of the region, however, afforded it a measure of independence. Its most illustrious ruler was Nasir Khan of Kalat (1739–1795), appointed ruler of Baluchistan by Nadir Shah of Persia.

In 1839, during the First Afghan War, British troops advanced through Baluchistan by way of the Bolan Pass and captured the town of Kalat. In 1854 a treaty was signed between the British government and Nasir Khan II. By its terms the khan received a yearly subsidy from the British government. British residents were appointed to the court of the khan, but Baluchistan retained independence for another 20 years.

In 1877, Quetta was occupied by British troops. In 1883, Baluchistan and the district of Bolan were ceded to the British by the khan, who received an annual quitrent in return. Finally, in 1891, Baluchistan became part of the British empire.

When Pakistan was created as an independent member of the British Commonwealth in 1947, Baluchistan was included in its area. It was formally admitted as a province in 1949. Under the 1956 constitution it lost its status as a province and became part of the division of Quetta, West Pakistan.

BALZAC, bál-zȧk', **Honoré de** (1799–1850), French novelist, whose name stands as a symbol of literary prowess and creativity. His major work, *La comédie humaine,* was composed mostly in the decade of the 1830's. It consists of nearly 100 completed novels and short stories, as well as some 50 other pieces that were left in a more or less unfinished state. Within this world of fiction over 2,000 characters circulate and often reappear. Yet these details, however impressive, do not tell the story of Balzac's herculean labors. It was not unusual for him to remain 24 hours at his desk and write out, at a forceful rate of speed, the entire first draft of a story. Nor, on the other hand, did he balk at 10 or 20 revisions of his manuscripts and galley proofs, thus incurring the ire of his publishers and printers. When this was done, there remained time for turning out a few dramas, elaborate pastiches of Rabelais, dozens upon dozens of magazine articles, and a huge correspondence; for living, if only intermittently, the life of a dandy and a man-about-town; for acting as his own promoter and commercial agent and launching upon extensive travels and ambitious business ventures; and last but not least, for playing hide-and-seek with his creditors. That he should have died from sheer exhaustion at the age of 51—he who considered himself and possibly was built to become a centenarian—comes as no surprise. During most of these 51 years, however, Balzac was an exceptional force of nature in a generation of supermen (Victor Hugo, Alexandre Dumas, and others) replete with energy and permeated with the Napoleonic complex.

The vision that crystallized into *La comédie humaine* did not, to be sure, spring from a sudden revelation. Balzac was not precocious in the manner of Victor Hugo, already an accomplished craftsman at the age of 17; nor did he develop as rapidly as Alfred de Vigny, whose entire philosophy of art and life asserts itself in his first book of poems. By contrast, Balzac's formative years bear witness to the slow, somewhat muddy development of his genius.

Early Years. His parentage was not overly distinguished. He was born at Tours on May 16, 1799. The aristocratic *de* before the surname Balzac (originally *Balssa*) occurs in a christening record of 1802, so that its arbitrary use must be credited—or debited—to the novelist's father, an aging and eccentric southerner born of peasant stock. The father, Bernard François Balzac (or Balssa) had risen to the middle class, migrated to Touraine in the course of an administrative career, and married a Parisian girl 31 years his junior. Honoré inherited from him such permanent traits as his robust constitution, his expansive nature, and perhaps even a number of theories or superstitions that his father was fond of expounding. However, it is clear that the mother exerted a closer and more lasting influence on the boy's life. Charming and vivacious when she chose to be but more often of a vexingly erratic and nagging disposition, Mme. Balzac, née Laure Sallambier, outlived her son and treated him, almost to the very last, as an immature little boy. He, on the other hand, accepted the maternal yoke with astonishing meekness, despite occasional fits of rebellion. The tangle of this relationship is evoked, at least indirectly, in the opening pages of *Le lys dans la vallée.* It should be said once and for all that many of Balzac's novels are semitransparent or transposed confessions from which there could be extracted a fairly accurate picture of his life and of his dreams.

His school days brought no outstanding promise of things to come. Both in the college of the Oratorians at Vendôme (1807–1813) and later in Paris, he proved an ordinary, though unruly, pupil. He earned among his schoolmates the reputation of an author, mostly by writing unmetrical Alexandrines, which testifies to his early literary ambition, although not necessarily to his early literary ability. He did sketch, however, a youthful essay entitled *Théorie de la volonté,* that became, despite its immaturity, one of the kernels of his future doctrine. Properly developed in later years, it was incorporated in *Louis Lambert,* another novel with strong autobiographic overtones, the hero of which lives a fictional counterpart of Balzac's childhood and early adolescence.

Balzac's debuts into the business world were not particularly auspicious. Two to three years in various law offices provided him with some local color, later to be used in *La comédie humaine,* but strengthened his conviction that he was not made for a legal career. In 1819, after a protracted struggle, he wrung from his father a meager allowance, valid for two years, and permission to try his hand at literature. The immediate result, bought at the cost of semistarvation, was a horrendous tragedy in verse, *Cromwell,* that had the whole family council shaking their heads dispiritedly. Long-range benefits accrued in *La peau de chagrin,* one of Balzac's most remarkable novels, which abounds in recollections of these wretched times. They were, in fact, so wretched, and so impaired was Honoré's health, that he won a new reprieve from his father and did not become a *notaire* after all.

First Novels. While writing *Cromwell,* he had embarked on his first novelistic venture. Modern scholarship unearthed (1936) the manuscript of *Sténie ou les erreurs philosophiques,* a fiction in epistolary form after the manner of Richardson and Rousseau. As incredibly dull as it is awkward, this attempt has the merit of seriousness and affords a better glimpse of the later Balzac, brimming over with metaphysical ideas, than do the potboilers that he published between 1821 and 1826 for purely utilitarian purposes. By that time the thought had taken hold of him that, in order to "make good" (the words are his), in order to conquer Paris by storm, as Eugène de Rastignac and Lucien de Rubempré will dream of doing in *La comédie humaine,* he must first of all acquire financial independence. Financial success, in turn, depended on his catering to public taste, however absurd and vulgar it might be. Thus, having entered a sort of literary factory, the guiding spirit of which was a 10th-rate author by the name of Le Poitevin de l'Egreville, Balzac produced, under various pseudonyms (Lord R'Hoone, Horace de Saint-Aubin, Viellerglé) and with several collaborators, lurid tales in the vein of Maturin, Ann Radcliffe, and "Monk" Lewis. The less said about these youthful works the better. It is possible, of course, to find in these stories, some of them four volumes long, part of the raw materials that were to enter into *La comédie humaine.* We may believe Balzac when he says that they taught him the tricks of his trade; but how conscious, purposeful, and well-directed this apprenticeship was is a question that should be left charitably unanswered.

One notch above Le Poitevin de l'Egreville

stood Horace Raisson, another expert in literary mass production, who in about 1824 launched on its sturdy career the genre known as "codes" or "physiologies." These satirical sketches, which purported to "codify" contemporary mores, appealed to Balzac's sense of observation and humor. Since 1822 he had been thoroughly conversant with Lavater's work on physiognomy, and he took delight in interpreting gestures, facial expressions, ways of speech, clothes, furniture, and so on as so many symbols of character. There is no way of knowing how many of the Raisson codes he helped in preparing, but at least 10 of them may be said to be unmistakably his in whole or in part (*Code des gens honnêtes*, 1825; *Code civil, manuel complet de la politesse*, 1825; *L'art de mettre sa cravate*, 1827; *L'art de payer ses dettes sans débourser un sou*, 1827; *Traité de la vie élégante*, undated, etc.). These light tidbits do not and cannot make any claims to psychological depth, but it is a fact that even the greater Balzac never stopped indulging them—*Physiologie de la toilette* (1830), *Physiologie du cigare* (1831), *Physiologie de l'employé* (1841), *Histoire et physiologie des boulevards de Paris* (1844), and so on—and that one at any rate, the *Physiologie du mariage*, begun in 1824, blossomed into a work of major proportions (1829).

Business Ventures. The means to the end— money as the key to freedom and glory—was slow in materializing, however. By 1825, Balzac sought to accelerate the pace and entered business, first as a publisher. Having edited Molière and La Fontaine, he was left with stacks of unsold copies and took the familiar course of expanding his commercial activities in order to remain solvent. He bought a printing house, only to sink deeper into debt. He then acquired the bankrupt stock of a type foundry and six months later, in 1828, was himself on the verge of bankruptcy. His mother, his relatives, and even his mistress, Mme. de Berny, made considerable sacrifices to appease his creditors; yet he remained saddled with a debt of over 90,000 francs, which handicapped and harassed him for the rest of his life. Fate had it that his masterpieces, instead of flowering in comfortable leisure as he had dreamed, would be born out of his torment. Some of them, such as *Illusions perdues* and, more notably still, *Grandeur et Décadence de César Birotteau*, were directly inspired by those trying days. Many of his major works were written under the yoke of financial necessity. All or nearly all evidence a preoccupation with money, which indeed burrowed at the very center of Balzac's life.

His moral and, more often, his material distress was relieved by the presence of Mme. de Berny, a lady of the old aristocracy, who was almost twice his age when they met in 1822. Her role in his early life resembles in several respects that of Mme. de Warens in the life of Jean-Jacques Rousseau. Unlike Rousseau, however, Balzac showed commendable tact and discretion in paying tribute to his beloved. She was a passionate and protective woman who divined and nurtured his genius and bore him a sympathy, a tenderness, an understanding, and an indulgence, too, that he had never known before and never knew again. She died in 1836, the very year when Balzac, then at the height of his creative power, dedicated to her the soft and lyrical prose of *Le lys dans la vallée*. Had it not been for her, the man whose words stirred countless feminine

CULVER PICTURES, INC.

HONORÉ DE BALZAC, from an old daguerreotype.

hearts would have proved a comparatively poor and unsuccessful lover in the realities of life. The plebeian Balzac set his sights—rather vaingloriously—on *grandes dames*, with results that were not altogether happy. The marquise de Castries had this modern Hercules sighing at her regal feet until he finally desisted and piled bitter scorn on her in *La duchesse de Langeais*. And given the character of Mme. Hanska, who became the model for Balzac's idolized and idealized "*étrangère*," it is the mootest of questions whether the remote control that she exerted on 18 years of his life may be called a boon or a disaster to him.

Balzac's Art. In 1828–1829, the period immediately following his commercial debacle, Balzac's literary talent came of age. Penniless, but as resilient and ebullient as ever, he accepted the hospitality of General de Pommereul, a friend of his family, at Fougères in Brittany. This was the country of hedgerows and bushes where part of the Chouan wars had been waged some 30 years before. While tramping the great woods or prodding old men's memories in search of local color, he was fired with the idea that a nearness to the pulsating life of people and things was really and truly the essence of the novelist's art. This seems like a fairly simple revelation, but it was an oblique one, since it did not result in Balzac's complete renunciation of ultraromantic trappings. What resulted was *Le dernier Chouan* (1829; later called *Les Chouans*), a narrative in the grand manner of Sir Walter Scott, with a suggestion of James Fenimore Cooper's *Last of the Mohicans*. The book, however, was genuinely "Balzacian," and the author knew it. For the first time, he felt no hesitancy in signing his name to a work that was his. In due time, *Le dernier Chouan* was deemed worthy of integration into *La comédie humaine* and became, chronologically, the cornerstone of the edifice.

The next step, a most logical one, consisted in turning from the past to the present, in applying to depictions of the contemporary stage the Scottian principle of historical accuracy. Balzac accomplished this aim in *Scènes de la vie privée*, a collection of six novelettes, published in 1830–32, two of which in retrospect seem to have set definite patterns for his future works. *Les dangers de l'inconduite* (subsequently, *Gobseck*) introduces the first of those few but outstanding Balzacian characters whose intuition, experience, and stamina give them mastery over their own souls and the souls of others. Gobseck the moneylender, Vautrin the archcriminal, and Benassis the good country doctor will be heroes and rulers in that particular sense and evoke their creator's undivided admiration as they rise to almost Napoleonic stature in their fields of endeavor. They are and must be exceptions, however. *Gloire et malheur* (better known as *La maison du chat-qui-pelote*) illustrates Balzac's prevailing rule, which is the subordination of most individuals to custom, atmosphere, and habitat. It is too little to say that in *Gloire et malheur* and the novels that followed it, Balzac concentrates on streets in the manner of a topographer, on dwellings and shops with the eye of an archaeologist, on rooms and furniture in the method of an antiquarian, and on clothes and personal mannerisms with the flair of a detective. His descriptions, however much they may tax a hasty reader's patience, are not mere inventories. They betray the author's creed that man is a product of circumstance and environment. The quaint house with the ancient tradesign (a cat playing with a ball of yarn) does not belong to M. Guillaume, the cloth merchant, as much as M. Guillaume, and his entire family, belong to the old quaint house. Breaking away from this kind of biological relationship entails the greatest of risks, as Augustine Guillaume finds out. In *La comédie humaine*, whoever steps out of character, whether through love, ambition, or daydreaming, is far more likely to fail than to succeed. Balzac's philosophy in this respect will become more and more that of a traditionalist, of an advocate of law and order who would entrust necessary changes to the slow processes of evolution. Politically a monarchist of the old school, socially a staunch believer in the steadying influence of the Roman Catholic Church, he will denounce, long before Paul Bourget and Maurice Barrès, the dangers of thoughtless "uprootings." *La comédie humaine* registers with alarm the first rumblings of the Industrial Revolution and is filled with forebodings of impending doom.

La peau de chagrin (1831), by far Balzac's greatest success to date, represents another step forward. In this fantastic tale, very much indebted to E.T.A. Hoffmann for its inspiration, the author does not abandon his newly found realistic vein but supplements it, so to speak, with a romantic one. What is then and will remain romantic in him is the urge to elaborate dogmatically, sometimes mystically, on the data of reality. Over and above his "scenes" of private, or political, or provincial, or Parisian life, each purporting to mirror things as they are and as they develop, such *études philosophiques* as *La peau de chagrin* will institute an inquiry into motivating causes. Why is it that the pulse of modern society has suddenly quickened? Why is it that this quickening, itself a tribute to human intelligence and resourcefulness, should, by some mysterious law of compensation, require a deadly expenditure of energy? To renounce action or to renounce a long life: such is the dilemma presented to the owner of the magic skin, essentially to Balzac himself, and if we are to believe him, to the new generations.

"La Comédie Humaine." The next revelation was truly decisive. By 1833, Balzac conceived the idea of linking together his hitherto disconnected novels, through the simple process of having certain characters reappear from work to work, at various stages of their careers, though remaining fundamentally the same men and women. The great impetus here was given by the famous scientific controversy (1830–1832) between Georges Cuvier and Étienne Geoffroy Saint-Hilaire, who held opposite views on the origins of species. "There is but one animal," Geoffroy Saint-Hilaire had stated; and Balzac followed him in his belief that this original animal had gone through multiple stages of differentiation and development, strengthening or gradually shedding some of his attributes under the influence of heredity and *milieu*. With this in mind, the novelist, already midway in the course of his life, set for himself the stupendous task of studying the social species—that is to say, the human animal in his basic unity and environmental differences—with the skill and thoroughness of a professional naturalist.

At about the same time, Balzac became addicted to occult theorizing and adopted the main tenets of Swedenborgian theosophy. The cosmos is one as it proceeds from the singleness of God, to which it will ultimately revert. Everything created is the product of an "ethereal substance," which we designate in turn by the names of electricity, heat, light, and so forth. Knowledge has for its precise object the understanding of the transformations and materializations of this substance without losing sight of its pristine identity. In the animal reign, for instance, it becomes psychic energy, or willpower (*volonté*), as Balzac puts it. Man has huge reserves of it, which he must cultivate lest he should tend toward the level of lower beasts. On the other hand, systematic attempts to develop his spiritual life, and correspondingly reduce his physical needs, may raise him to the status of an angel. Several of Balzac's major works present him in the garb of a visionary, intent on building up an all-embracing cosmic synthesis. These include *La peau de chagrin*, and the trilogy usually called *Le livre mystique* (*Louis Lambert*, 1832; *La recherche de l'absolu*, 1834; *Séraphita*, 1835), as well as numerous passages in *Le lys dans la vallée* (1836) and *Le cousin Pons* (1847). Modern scholarship, as a matter of fact, inclines to emphasize this aspect of his genius and contend that Balzac's universe, far from being a copy of our own, is the self-sufficient creation of a demiurge.

This immense undertaking had its Egeria in the person of Mme. Evelina Hanska. A lady of the old Polish nobility, she resided at the other end of Europe, on the Ukrainian estate of her aged and wealthy husband, Count Hanski. From 1832 to 1848 the story of the two lovers is that of their correspondence, broken only by a few occasional meetings. As told in Balzac's *Lettres à l'étrangère* (Mme. Hanska's replies have been destroyed), it is the story of a slave chained to his work, in desperate need of understanding and affection, and of a faraway princess who repaid him with intellectual sympathy but also with indecision, coldness, and jealousy. Partly through her fault, even the death of Count Hanski (1841) failed to reunite them. Yet Balzac persisted in his ambition to marry the woman who not only posed as a model for some of his feminine portraits (*Eugénie Grandet*, 1833; Mme. Hulot in *La cousine Bette*, 1847), but was also "the source of my efforts, the secret of my courage, the origin of my talents." Finally, in September 1848, an already ailing Balzac traveled to the Ukraine to meet and plead with her. They were married in March 1850. On the return journey, begun the same month, over wintry roads and in dreadful weather he was, to be sure, the proud husband of "one of the brightest, best born of ladies." But death was stalking him, and on Aug 17, 1850, he died in Paris.

But as early as 1842 the title *La comédie humaine* had been found. Fittingly, though perhaps not consciously, reminiscent of Dante, it crowned the first complete edition of Balzac's vast system of novels. The celebrated *Avant-propos* to that edition affirmed a singleness of purpose and composition that we now know had emerged slowly, darkly, and at times, painfully. But it had emerged. When Rodin carved the statue of Balzac, he chiseled a face at the top of a somewhat indeterminate form. This, in the words of Rainer Maria Rilke, was symbolic "of creation itself; of creation's pride, arrogance, ecstasy, intoxication. The head which was thrown back lived at the summit of this form like those spheres that dance on the spray of fountains. All heaviness had become light, rose and fell."

JEAN-ALBERT BÉDÉ, *Columbia University*

Bibliography

Balzac's *Oeuvres complètes* was edited by Marcel Bouteron and Henri Longnon, 40 vols. (Paris 1912–40); *La comédie humaine*, ed. by M. Bouteron, is available in 10 vols. (Paris 1935–37); English translations of *The Human Comedy* were edited by George Saintsbury, 4th ed., 36 vols. (New York 1929).
Bertault, Philippe, *Balzac and the Human Comedy* (New York 1963).
Billy, André, *Vie de Balzac*, 2 vols. (Paris 1944).
Bowen, Ray P., *Dramatic Construction of Balzac's Novels* (Eugene, Oreg., 1940).
Canfield, A.G., *The Reappearing Characters in Balzac's Comédie Humaine* (Chapel Hill, N.C., 1962).
George, Albert J., *Books by Balzac* (Syracuse, N.Y., 1960).
Hunt, Herbert J., *Honoré de Balzac* (New York 1957).
Maurois, André, *Prométhée, ou la vie de Balzac* (Paris 1966); Eng. tr. by Norman Denny, *Prometheus: The Life of Balzac* (New York 1966).
Oliver, E.J., *Balzac the European* (New York 1960).
Oliver, E.J., *Honoré de Balzac* (New York 1964).
Rogers, Samuel, *Balzac and the Novel* (Madison, Wis., 1953).
Royce, William H., *Balzac Bibliography*, 2 vols. (Chicago 1929–30).

BALZAC, bȧl-zak′, **Jean Louis Guez de** (1597–1654), French essayist and letter writer. He was born at Balzac, near Angoulême, France. In his youth he was secretary to Cardinal de La Valette in Rome. Returning to Paris, he devoted himself to literature, and during the administration of Cardinal Richelieu served as historiographer of France. Balzac, an influential member of the French Academy, was a leader of the literary and political salon that met at the Hôtel de Rambouillet. He died in Balzac on Feb. 18, 1654.

Balzac's influence on French prose ranks with that of François de Malherbe (q.v.) on French poetry: both introduced a new clarity and precision into the literature. Balzac's *Letters* (vol. 1, 1624; vol. 2, 1636) are the best example of his elaborate and formal style. His other works include *The Prince* (1631), a glorification of absolute monarchy; *The Christian Socrates* (1652); and the posthumous *Aristippus* (1658), a portrait of the ideal statesman.

HARRISON FORMAN, WORLD TRAVEL

BAMAKO'S PUBLIC BUILDINGS include the domed, rectangular structure housing Mali's National Assembly.

BAMAKO, bȧ-mȧ-kō′, is the capital of Mali, in West Africa. It is situated on the north bank of the Niger River in the southwestern part of Mali. Southwestward, the river is navigable from June to December as far as Kankan in Guinea; northeastward, it is open to Gao, Mali, by a canal around the rapids between Bamako and Koulikoro. A railroad connecting the city with Dakar, Senegal, 650 miles (1,050 km) to the west on the Atlantic Ocean, is the principal carrier of Mali's imports and exports. Although Bamako is principally an administrative city, it is also a trading center. From the north come salt and cattle; from the south, cola nuts; from the east, rice; and from the west, gold.

The city is built at the foot of an escarpment at a point where the valley of the Niger leads through to the valley of the Senegal. The site itself is impressive, and the city contains remarkable public gardens, a zoo, and a number of sumptuous modern public buildings. It has a university and several schools, including the National School of Administration, the School of Public Works, and a teachers training college. The former European section was constructed spaciously, mainly in neo-Sudanese style, while the African sections were laid out on rigidly rectangular lines. Although the city has ample room for expansion, building projects have failed to keep pace with population increase and unsanitary conditions have resulted.

The area around Bamako appears to have been occupied since prehistoric times. When the French arrived in 1883, they found a walled village with about 1,000 inhabitants. The French built a fort, and after a prolonged war against Samory (a Mandingo chief who had created a corps of warriors to fight the French), the town began to grow. In 1904 the railroad from Dakar reached Bamako, and four years later the town was made the administrative capital of the French colony of Haut-Sénégal-Niger (later French Sudan). The population, then about 6,000, grew slowly to 20,000 in 1931 and more rapidly in 1953. It was about 150,000 in 1966.

L. GRAY COWAN, *Columbia University*
Further Reading: Adloff, Richard, *West Africa; the French-speaking Nations Yesterday and Today* (New York 1964); Church, R.J. Harrison, *West Africa* (London 1963).

BAMBARA, bäm-bä'rə, an African tribe that inhabits the valley of the upper Niger River in Mali. Some Bambara are also found in Senegal and Guinea. They speak a dialect of Mande. From the middle 1500's until the 1800's, the Bambara formed two large states, one with its center at Ségou, now in Mali, the other extending from Bamako in Mali to Nioro in Senegal. In the 1800's these states were subject to the Tukulors. A treaty with the sultan of Ségou opened the country to French traders in the 1890's, and in 1904 it was included in the French colony of Upper Senegal-Niger, later known as French Sudan and now the independent republic of Mali.

BAMBERG, bam'berκн, is a city in West Germany, in the state of Bavaria. It is on the Regnitz River, 3 miles (5 km) above its junction with the Main River and 31 miles (50 km) north of Nürnberg. It is the northern terminus of the Ludwig Canal, connecting the Main and Danube rivers. Bamberg is a thriving industrial and commercial center, with cotton spinning, metal industries, and agricultural trade among its major activities.

A cathedral in late Romanesque and early Gothic styles, with four massive towers and two choirs, recalls the city's eminence during the Middle Ages. Construction of the cathedral began in 1004, and it was largely rebuilt in the 13th century. Besides a vast store of art treasures, it contains the tombs of Emperor Henry II and his wife, and Pope Clement II. Other historic buildings in Bamberg are the 12th century St. Michael's Church and two former bishops' palaces, the Renaissance Old Residence and the New Residence. The palaces are now museums.

Bamberg was first mentioned in historical records as a town, in 902. It was made the seat of a bishopric by Henry II in 1007 and remained the capital of a powerful ecclesiastical state until it was annexed by Bavaria in 1802. Population: (1961) 74,115.

(ABOVE) CARL FRANK, FROM PHOTO RESEARCHERS; (LEFT) ROCHE

BAMBOO grows mostly in tropical and semitropical areas. Black bamboo (left) is a small Asian species.

BAMBERGER, bäm'ber-gər, **Ludwig** (1823–1899), German economist and politician. He was born at Mainz, in the Rhenish Palatinate, on July 22, 1823. During the revolution of 1848–1849 he interrupted his studies and edited the liberal democratic newspaper *Mainzer Zeitung*. The failure of a republican uprising in the Palatinate forced him to flee, first to Switzerland and then to Paris, where from 1853 to 1866 he was in the banking business.

Although he had been condemned to death for his part in the revolution, Bamberger was able to return to Germany after an amnesty in 1866. He soon turned to politics and was a member of the Reichstag from 1871 to 1893. Until 1880 he supported the National Liberal party, specializing in economic policy and public finance. He promoted the adoption of the gold standard and was a leader in founding the Reichsbank.

Bamberger left the National Liberals in 1880 because he opposed Chancellor Otto von Bismarck's protectionist and colonial policies. After leaving the party, he became a leader of the Reichstag "Secessionists," who established the German Liberal party in 1884. He remained influential in the legislature until his retirement in 1893. He died in Berlin on March 14, 1899.

BAMBOCCIATA, bäm-bô-chē-ä'tä, a type of painting, often humorous or grotesque, depicting scenes from rustic life. The genre was especially popular in Rome and Flanders in the 17th century. The term comes from *il Bamboccio* (meaning "large, fat child" in Italian), the nickname of Pieter van Laar, a hunchback who was the originator and most important artist of the movement. The name was intended to describe what contemporary critics considered to be the moral deformity of van Laar's type of art. These critics, oriented toward classical idealism, denounced the "Bamboccianti" for painting such "filthy" things as baggy pants and beggars in rags. The Bamboccianti, who borrowed in part from the traditions of Domenico Feti (Fetti) and Jan Lys, included among their number Michelangelo Cerquozzi, Jan Miel, Michael Sweerts, and Thomas Wijck. The group had a major influence on the small-figure genre of the Dutch painters Adriaen van Ostade and Adriaen Brouwer.

BAMBOO, bam-boo', is the common name for a type of treelike grass found in the tropical regions of America and Asia. Like other grasses, bamboo grows in thick clumps, but like trees it often attains great height. Some species have been known to reach heights of 100 to 120 feet (30.5–36.5 meters), especially in the Asian monsoon forests. The flowers, which usually consist of six stamens and three scales, often bloom annually; in some species the flowers appear at intervals of as much as 60 years.

Although native to tropical regions, some bamboos have become adapted to temperate zones, and even to cold winters. In cultivating bamboo in northern climates, a mulch should be applied to conserve moisture and protect the plant against freezing.

Two types of bamboo are native to the United States: *Arundinaria macrosperma* and *A. tecta*. In the canebrakes of the South, bamboos are a common sight along river banks and in marshy areas as far north as Virginia. Many bamboos have been imported successfully and are grown in Florida, Louisiana, and southern California.

Because of its unusual characteristics, and also because of the great variations among its different species, bamboo has been used in a seemingly endless number of ways, ranging from food to heavy construction. The grain of the bamboo is consumed in many Asian countries, and the tender shoots either are eaten as a vegetable or are pickled and candied. Masses of silica, taken from the joints, have been used since ancient times as a medicine in the Orient, where it is called tabasheer. Large species, whose stems may be as large as 8 to 12 inches (20.5 to 30.5 cm) in diameter, supply timber for building houses and bridges. The stems may be used as planking and thatching material. Many types of receptacles (buckets and utensils) are made by retaining the partitions in the stem; the nodes may be reamed out to provide an open passage, as in pipes. Other uses include boat masts, fencing, papermaking, furniture, walking sticks, weaving, and wickerwork. Because of the lovely effect of their massed leaves and stems, bamboos have become popular as ornamental plantings.

Bamboo belongs to the tribe Bambuseae in the grass family, Gramineae. More than 200 species are known.

BAMBOUK, bam-book', is a region in West Africa, divided between Senegal and Mali. The name is also spelled *Bambuk*. The area, about 12,500 square miles (32,375 sq km), is bounded by the Falémé River on the west and the Senegal River on the east. Mandingo constitute the majority of the population. Most of them are Muslims.

The people of Bambouk earn their living chiefly by raising cattle and sheep, and by growing crops. The valleys and plains are extensively cultivated. The major crops are corn, cotton, millet, peanuts, rice, and sesame. Bambouk has rich deposits of gold and copper, and some iron, mercury, arsenic, and manganese are also found.

Once an independent state, Bambouk became a French protectorate in 1858. It was part of the French West African territories until 1960, when Senegal and Mali became independent.

BAMFORD, bam'fərd, **Samuel** (1788–1872), English author and social reformer. He was born at Middleton, Lancashire, England, on Feb. 28, 1788. A weaver by trade, he supported the movement to repeal the corn laws. After speaking at the parliamentary reform meeting in Manchester that ended in the "Peterloo Massacre" (1819), he was arrested on a charge of inciting to riot and imprisoned for a year.

Bamford wrote northern dialect verse in sympathy with industrial labor. His best prose work, *Passages in the Life of a Radical* (1840–44), portrays English industrial conditions in the early 1800's. He died at Harpurhey, Lancashire, on April 13, 1872.

BAMIAN, bäm-yän', is a valley in Afghanistan, 8,500 feet (2,591 meters) above sea level, in the Hindu Kush mountains, about 80 miles (129 km) northwest of Kabul. It is sometimes called *Qala Sarkari*. The valley is formed by the Bamian River, a tributary of the Amu Darya. Once an important center of Buddhist worship, the valley is lined with cave dwellings that Buddhist monks carved from the rock and painted by hand. Of particular interest are two colossal statues carved out of the valley rock and finished in fine plaster.

The larger of the two stands 175 feet (53 meters) high, and the smaller about 120 feet (37 meters). They were probably completed in the late 500's or early 600's A.D. An account of these monuments, and of the 10 or more Buddhist monasteries that occupied the caves, was written by Hsüan Tsang, a Chinese Buddhist traveler who visited Bamian about 630.

BAMPTON LECTURES, bamp'tən lek'chərz, a prominent series of "Divinity Lecture Sermons," established at Oxford University in 1780. Rev. John Bampton, Canon of Salisbury, endowed the series, specifying that it be given by Anglican scholars on an annual basis. Since 1895 the lectures have been presented biennially. Over the years a wide range of theological topics significant to the Church of England has been explored. The scholars who have contributed to the eminence of the series include R.D. Hampden, H.P. Liddon, Charles Gore, A.E. Rawlinson, and Kenneth Kirk. In 1954 a portion of the fund was allocated to the "Sarum Lectures," a series given by non-Anglican scholars. The first of these was delivered by the Congregationalist C.H. Dodd.

Mrs. Ada Byron Bampton Tremaine, a distant relative of the founder, endowed a general series of Bampton Lectures in the United States at Columbia University. E.L. Mascall held both lectureships, at Oxford (1956) and New York (1958).

EDWARD R. HARDY, *Berkeley Divinity School*

BAMPUR, bäm-poor', is a town in southeastern Iran, about 300 miles (480 km) southeast of Kerman. It is on the Bampur River, which flows westward into the Hamun-i-Jaz-Murian depression. It was once the capital of Persian Baluchistan and an important commercial center, but has declined since the early 1900's. Its chief landmark is a citadel that rises above the town. The fertile district around Bampur produces dates. Population: (1956) 1,585.

BAN, ban, in feudal times, a proclamation. The word derives from the Germanic verb *bannan*, meaning "to command." It still appears in the expression "banns of marriage."

In the Middle Ages, anyone who offended his king or lord could be proclaimed a traitor or criminal, and this proceeding was known as "placing under the ban." In modern times, the word is similarly used in such phrases as "under the ban of public opinion."

BAN, bän, was the title of the rulers of some of the medieval Slav states of the Balkan Peninsula. It was later adopted by the Magyars (Hungarians), who gave the title of ban to their governors of frontier regions, such as Croatia, Dalmatia, and Bosnia. In Yugoslavia the governors of provinces (*banovine*) were called bans until 1945, when Yugoslavia became a federal republic.

The word *ban* is derived from the ancient Slavic *pan*, meaning "head of a family." *Pan* is still used by the Czechs and Poles in the sense of "mister." The title *stepan*, meaning ban of bans, was used by the rulers of Moravia. From it came the proper name Stepan or Stefan (Stephen).

Banat, the Hungarian word for frontier province, now denotes a region of southeastern Europe that was divided between Rumania and Yugoslavia after World War I—the former Banat of Temešvar. See also BANAT.

BANANAS are grown commercially on large plantations in Central and South America and in the West Indies. Here a small tractor emerges from the plantation, hauling several carts laden with bananas on their way to market.

BANANA, bə-nan'ə, a perennial seed plant that produces an edible fruit, also called a banana. It is found in tropical regions.

Distribution. A native of the East Indies or Malay Archipelago, the banana was introduced early into the tropical regions surrounding the Caribbean Sea. The fruit now is grown in large quantities in Central America, some portions of South America, and the West Indies. These regions presently constitute the main producing centers for the American trade and a portion of the European trade. Large quantities of bananas are exported from Costa Rica, Guatemala, Honduras, Nicaragua, northern Panama, northern Colombia, from the island of Jamaica, and from Mexico. Exports from these countries to the United States amount to between 70 million and 80 million bunches annually. In addition, the banana grows abundantly in the Pacific islands, the Malay region, and the East Indies. It is also an important crop, especially in the dwarf species, in the Canary Islands.

Types. The banana tree belongs to the genus *Musa* and subgenus *Evmusa*. There are many different kinds of bananas, but five are of special importance. The common banana (*Musa sapientum*) includes the majority of the bananas grown in the Western Hemisphere. It is edible when raw. There are several varieties of this banana, including the Martinique, Jamaica, Gros Michel, and a red variety, the Baracoa. The Gros Michel type of *Musa sapientum* is the one found most commonly in American markets. It produces a firm and finely flavored fruit. The plantain (*Musa paradisiaca*) is another type of banana. Its greenish yellow fruit is edible when cooked. The scientific nomenclature is confused here, and many authorities consider the *sapientum* to be a variety of the species *paradisiaca*. These banana plants, which may grow to a height of 30 feet (9 meters), have long, wide leaves.

A third type of banana is the Chinese, or dwarf, banana (*Musa cavendishii*), found in the Canary Islands, Bermuda, and southern China. This banana plant usually attains a height of only 6 feet (1.8 meters) and its leaves are smaller than those of the common banana plant. It can be planted only 10 feet (3 meters) apart instead of the ordinary 15 to 20 feet (4.5 to 6 meters) apart. Two other types of bananas are note-

BANANA PLANTS in the first few weeks of development (*left*) are characterized by tiny green fruits, each tipped with a bright yellow blossom. When about four months old, the mature fruit is ready to be cut. After the plant has been notched near the top, the weight of the fruit causes the plant to bend, allowing workers to chop through the stem.

worthy. They are *Musa acuminata*, raised in the East Indies and Malay Archipelago, and the Abyssinian banana (*Musa ensete*), an inedible, ornamental species.

Cultivation. Bananas are cultivated on a large scale in all the countries mentioned. Differences in methods of cultivation depend on the soil and climatic conditions. Generally, bananas require deep, fertile, moist and well drained soil and protection from wind.

In Central America a new plantation is developed usually from virgin forest in a river valley or coastal plain. The undergrowth is cleared out. The trees are chopped down, and then fallen timber decomposes rapidly, adding to the humus content of the soil. Bits and portions of root stalk that are used as seed are then planted. In the course of a few months the young banana plants will be several feet high. Then the new growth of underbrush, grass, and weeds is cleared away. In about four months more the banana plants reach their full size. A mature plant is usually about 10 to 20 feet (3 to 6 meters) high. Continued occasional clearing is necessary to keep down the excess of wild growth.

The banana plant has an underground root stalk with buds, or eyes, that grow out and up, forming new aerial portions or suckers. Once the plantation is started, the continued development of these buds produces an oversupply of plants. The weaker and less desirable ones are pruned out. Eventually a large mat of plants develops where the small portion of root stalk was planted.

The banana plant does not possess a true stem above the ground. It has, rather, a pseudo-stem consisting of the basal portions of the leaf stalks, which overlap one another and are tightly pressed together. In this manner a trunk is formed that measures 8 to 15 inches (20 to 38 cm) in diameter at maturity.

When the plant is matured fully, a bud forms in the root stalk, grows up through the center of the mass of leaf stalks, and finally emerges from the center of the crown. This emergence is known as the shooting. The bud gradually unfolds, and a large number of clusters of flowers open up. Each of these clusters is protected in the bud by a thick, overlapping, modified leaf.

Only the upper clusters of flowers are fertilized and produce fruit; the lower ones wither and fall away. The number of clusters that develop fruit is variable, generally running from 6 to 15. Each cluster is known as a *hand*, and the individual fruits are known as *fingers*. When the fruit is approaching full development, it is cut from the plant; it is never allowed to ripen on the plant. After the bunch of fruit is removed, the plant that produced it is cut down to the ground. This is done because each plant produces only a single bunch. By proper selection and pruning of suckers, the cultivations are kept in almost continual production for years.

Throughout the cultivation process, care must be taken to prevent damage to the plant from low temperatures or from fungus infections.

The Fruit. The fruit is elongated and usually tapered at one end. Its soft, pulpy flesh is enclosed in a comparatively soft, usually yellow, rind. It has a very agreeable flavor and taste.

The banana is of considerable value as a food. It contains a large amount of starch and sugar. Analysis shows that bananas contain, on the average, 75.3 percent water, 1.3 percent protein, 0.6 percent fat, 22 percent carbohydrate, and 0.8 percent ash. This ash has been found to consist of a high percentage of alkaline salts. These constituents make bananas a very valuable food, especially as a source of quick energy. The banana yields about 460 calories per pound, approximately the same amount as corn and more than any other fresh fruit. The food value of bananas is about the same as the food value of potatoes. The banana is somewhat higher in fat content, lower in protein, and slightly higher in carbohydrate than the potato.

Bananas usually are eaten raw. They may also be baked or fried, and with some species, such as *Musa paradisiaca*, cooking is necessary.

Other Uses of the Plant. The fruit-producing banana tree contains a certain amount of fiber that might be used in the production of paper and twine, but this use has never been developed commercially. *Musa textilis* of the Philippines is the main source of the hemp for cordage. Also known as Manila hemp, this plant has thin leaf blades that are used for wrapping.

PROCESSING of banana fruit is carried out in large packing plants. The bunches are wrapped and loaded (*right*) for delivery to the packing plant. At the plant, they are washed, graded, weighed, and boxed (*below*).

BANANA OIL is a colorless oily liquid having the odor of bananas. It is made by the action of acetic acid on amyl alcohol. Often used as a solvent, it is a component in cellulose lacquers, adhesives, linoleum, and oilcloth.

Inhalation of banana oil causes a variety of medical effects, ranging from mild intoxication to seeing double, drowsiness, and unconsciousness; it is the ingredient in glues that affects "glue sniffers." Prolonged inhalation of banana oil may cause damage to the nose, respiratory organs, liver, and kidneys.

BANANA QUIT, bə-nan'ə ᴋwit, a small and familiar songbird of the West Indies. Also called *banana bird*, it is about 5 inches (12.5 cm) long and has a long curved beak. It is sooty black above and bright yellow below. Frequently there is a conspicuous white spot on the wing and a white streak through the eye. The bird is found throughout the West Indies (excepting Cuba), varying somewhat in color and size from island to island. Its voice is generally wheezy. It feeds on insects, the nectar of flowers, and ripe fruit.

The banana quit, *Coereba flaveola*, is a member of the honeycreeper family, Coerebidae.

CHARLES VAURIE
American Museum of Natural History

BANARAS. See VARANASI.

BANAS RIVER, bə-näs', a stream in Rajasthan, India. It rises in the Aravalli Hills and flows northeast for 120 miles (193 km), then southeast, entering the Chambal River 16 miles (26 km) north of Sheopur. Its total course is about 300 miles (483 km). There is good fishing for mahseer (*Barbus mosal*) in several places.

Another river of the same name also rises in the Aravalli Hills, but has a southwest course and disappears into the Rann of Kutch after about 180 miles (290 km).

BANAT, bə-nät', an agricultural region in the central Balkans that includes parts of western Rumania and northeastern Yugoslavia and a small portion of southern Hungary. *Banat* is a Serbo-Croation word meaning a frontier district governed by a *ban*, or governor. The Banat is bounded on the north by the Maros (Mureş) River, on the west by the Tisza (Tisa) River, on the southwest and south by the Danube, and on the east by Transylvania and Walachia. The southeast is mountainous, but most of the remainder is flat, well-watered, fertile country producing considerable amounts of wheat, barley, oats, and rye. Mineral deposits include coal, iron ore, zinc, and petroleum. The Banat's chief city is Timişoara (Temesvár) in Rumania.

Slavs began settling in the Banat in the 5th century and Magyars in the 9th. In the 13th century it became a frontier district of the kingdom of Hungary. Many Serbs settled there in the 15th century to escape the advancing Turks. In 1552 the region was conquered and converted into a province (*sanjak*) by the Turks. Recaptured by Prince Eugene of Savoy, the Banat was transferred by the Treaty of Passarowitz (1718) to Austria. Empress Maria Theresa put the district under civil government in 1751 and brought in thousands of German colonists. From 1779 until 1918, except for a brief period (1849–1860) as a section of the Austrian Vojvodina, the Banat was an integral part of the kingdom of Hungary.

When the Austro-Hungarian monarchy was dissolved after World War I, the Banat, under the terms of the Treaty of Trianon (1920), was divided between Rumania and Yugoslavia, except for the Szeged district, which remained in Hungary. On the eve of the partition, the Banat's population of 1,582,000 was about 40 percent Rumanian, 20 percent Serb, 23 percent German, and 14 percent Hungarian.

During World War II the German minority in the Yugoslavian Banat collaborated with the Nazis but fled before the advancing Soviet army. The frontiers of 1920 were reestablished at the end of the war.

DAVID MACKENZIE, *Wells College*

BANBURY, ban'bə-rē, is a municipal borough in England, in Oxfordshire, on the river Cherwell, 72 miles (116 km) northwest of London. Its name is familiar in the folk rhyme that begins "Ride a cockhorse to Banbury Cross." The rhyme probably dates from about 1500, when three crosses stood at crossroads in Banbury. All were destroyed by the Puritans. A cross was erected in 1858 on the site of one of them.

Banbury is a market town in an agricultural region and has been famous for centuries for Banbury tarts, a kind of pastry with currants. Population: (1961) 21,004.

BANCHIERI, bäng-kyâ'rē, **Adriano** (1568–1634), Italian musical theorist. He was born in Bologna on Sept. 3, 1568. Like Antonio Vivaldi, he was a musician-priest, serving in a Benedictine monastery near Bologna. He took an active part in the social life of the city, and he founded the Accademia de' Floridi in 1614. He died in Bologna in 1634.

Banchieri was a musical theorist of first rank. His most important work, *L'organo suonarino* (1605), established the earliest formal rules for figured-bass accompaniment. Banchieri also investigated the possibility of adapting madrigal music to drama.

A prolific composer of sacred and operatic music, and a famous organist, Banchieri was the first to use in print the marks *f* for *forte* (loud) and *p* for *piano* (soft), which appeared in a motet he published in 1613.

HUNGARY
Szeged
Arad
Maros (Mureş)
Transylvania
River
Tisza (Tisa)
Timişoara (Temesvar)
B a n a t
Danube R.
RUMANIA
YUGOSLAVIA
BELGRADE
Walachia
Danube R.
N
Scale of Miles
0　25　50　75
0　25　50　100
Scale of Kilometers

BANCO, bäng'kō, is a Late Latin word from which *bank* and *bankruptcy* are derived. Originally meaning "shelf" or "bench," the term became specialized in medieval Italy to designate the benches or tables on which money changers heaped coins to attract customers. In time the word was used to describe the business itself— Italian *banca*, French *banque*, and English *bank*. If customers became dissatisfied with a money changer, they might overturn his table. The term "bankruptcy" derives from this practice.

"Banco" later designated a unit of account in which banks in Venice, Genoa, Amsterdam, and Hamburg gave credit for deposits and kept their accounts. One of these, the Bank of Hamburg (1619–1873), received deposits of coins and bars of varying weights and fineness and gave credit in the "Mark banco," which was itself not coined but represented 8⅔ grams of fine silver. The Mark banco expedited commerce, for otherwise settlements would have required a multitude of coins of uncertain value.

BENJAMIN HAGGOTT BECKHART
Columbia University

BANCROFT, ban'krôft, **Anne** (1931–   ), American actress. She was born *Anne Marie Italiano*, in New York City, on Sept. 17, 1931. She began to appear in television dramas in the late 1940's. In 1951 she went to Hollywood, where for seven years she played a succession of vapid roles in about 15 films. While in Hollywood, she adopted her stage name.

In 1958 she began her stage career in *Two for the Seesaw*, a two-character play in which she portrayed a Jewish girl from the Bronx. For her performance she won the Antoinette Perry ("Tony") Award. In 1959 she opened in *The Miracle Worker*, a play about Annie Sullivan, Helen Keller's first teacher. For this role she received her second Tony award as well as the New York Drama Critics Circle Award. When she repeated the role on the screen, she won the 1963 Academy Award for "best actress."

Miss Bancroft also appeared on Broadway in *Mother Courage* (1963) and *The Devils* (1965). Her other films include *The Pumpkin Eater* (1964) and *The Slender Thread* (1965).

BANCROFT, ban'krôft, **Edward** (1744–1821), American scientist and secret agent. He was born in Westfield, Mass., on Jan. 9, 1744. He went to Dutch Guiana in 1763 and then moved to England, where he published *Natural History of Guiana* (1769). In London he gained the friendship of Benjamin Franklin, through whose influence he became a contributor to the *Monthly Review* on American topics.

After the outbreak of the American Revolution he went to Paris, where he entered the employ of Franklin and Silas Deane, the American commissioners to France. They sent him to England several times on secret service work, unaware that at the same time he was also in British pay as a spy upon the Americans. It is alleged that he informed the British of American plans for securing supplies from France and gave advance information of the 1778 treaty of alliance between France and the United States.

In 1785 the British assisted Bancroft in importing a type of oak bark used in calico printing. He wrote a series of publications on dyes that he discovered. He died in Margate, Kent, England, on Sept. 8, 1821.

George Bancroft

(1800–1891)

BETTMANN ARCHIVE

BANCROFT, ban'krôft, **George** (1800–1891), American historian and diplomat. He was born in Worcester, Mass., on Oct. 3, 1800. A precocious youngster, he graduated from Harvard in his 17th year. He went to Göttingen, Germany, for further study, taking a Ph.D. there in 1820. Two years later he returned to teach Greek at Harvard.

German example had suggested to him improvements in pedagogy, and Bancroft sought to reform teaching at Harvard. Disappointed at the opposition to his ideas, he joined Joseph G. Cogswell in opening a high school modeled on the German *Gymnasium*. Their Round Hill School at Northhampton, Mass., was a notable educational experiment during its 11 years (1823–1834). Bancroft pioneered in bringing German culture to the attention of Americans.

Government Service. Bancroft had become interested in politics, and he soon emerged as a spokesman for the Jacksonian Democrats. His service in this role won him an appointment as collector of the Port of Boston in 1837. Eight years later President Polk named him secretary of the navy, in which capacity he established the Naval Academy at Annapolis.

Bancroft next was sent as minister to England (1846–1849), where he accumulated a large collection of historical materials. As a Northern Democrat, with little influence in a party now dominated by Southerners, he was inactive politically for many years. In this interval Bancroft worked on his history and, during the Civil War, made speeches in behalf of the North.

In 1867, President Andrew Johnson named Bancroft minister to Berlin, where he remained for seven years. He had already gained international fame as a historian, and Bismarck's friendship gave him special distinction in Germany. When he returned to his native land, Bancroft was acclaimed the Nestor of American historians. His life spanned most of the century, ending in Washington, D.C., on Jan. 17, 1891.

The Historian. Bancroft's fame rests on his historical writings, not on his diplomacy. His *History of the United States from the Discovery of the American Continent* (10 vols.) was published between 1834 and 1874. It carried the story of the American colonies down to 1782. The narrative was continued to 1789 in his *History of the Formation of the Constitution of the United States of America* (2 vols., 1882).

Bancroft's theme was that "the spirit of the colonies demanded freedom from the beginning."

To support this thesis he distorted the relationship of the colonies to the mother country. He argued that the colonists were always right in their disputes with king and Parliament. Written in a time when nationalism was rife in the Western world, his history reflected the intense American nationalism of the 19th century.

Bancroft's work appeared at the precise moment when Americans craved a history to celebrate their great epic—the discovery and settlement of a new world and the creation of a new nation. Bancroft's history far surpassed all others in coverage and narrative power. His volumes quickly became the standard history of the United States, and their large sales made him wealthy. He wrote as a philosophic historian, with literary artistry and with a belief in progress. He celebrated the victory of liberty-loving peoples over authoritarianism. History, he felt, should instruct and entertain. God was manifest in the unfolding of history. The United States represented the goal to which all civilization should aspire.

Eventually, Bancroft's volumes came under severe criticism from the new school of "scientific historians." They criticized his excessive nationalism, his lack of objectivity, and his failure to see the complexity of issues. They also pointed out that his history was almost entirely a political and military narrative.

These criticisms were largely valid, yet Bancroft's work had great virtues. It brought American history out of its provincial setting into the world arena. He levied upon sources in Europe as well as in America. Though mistaken about the place of the colonies in the British empire, he communicated the fervor of Americans in the days when revolution swept the land. Often called the "Father of American History," he set a standard by which later historians measured their own achievements. As one historian expressed it, he could see farther "because he stood on Bancroft's shoulders."

MICHAEL KRAUS, *The City College, New York*

Further Reading: Howe, M.A, De Wolfe, *The Life and Letters of George Bancroft* (New York 1908); Nye, Russell B., *George Bancroft: Brahmin Rebel* (New York 1944).

BANCROFT, ban′krôft, **Hubert Howe** (1832–1918), American publisher and historian. He was born in Granville, Ohio, on May 5, 1832. He was employed in his brother-in-law's bookstore in Buffalo, N.Y., from 1848 until 1852, when he went to California. In San Francisco he established his own bookselling and publishing business. This venture prospered, and soon he was able to start gathering material on the West for a grand history of the region.

This monumental work in 39 volumes, known as the *West American Historical Series*, was published between 1875 and 1890 (it was reissued as *The Works of Hubert Howe Bancroft,* 1882–90). The first five volumes treat the "native races." The history proper comprises 28 volumes and covers the "Pacific states"—Central America, Mexico, and the Far West of the United States and Canada. The last six volumes are collections of miscellaneous essays. The series was issued under Bancroft's name, but he actually wrote only about four volumes. He edited the rest of the material—produced by an able staff.

Although criticized for his "history factory," Bancroft was soon credited with making a great contribution to American historiography. He amassed a collection of 60,000 historical volumes, manuscripts, and personal narratives, all of which he donated to the University of California in 1905. His broad approach to historical writing has rarely been equaled, and his histories were, in the main, reliable. He died at Walnut Creek, Calif., on March 2, 1918.

Further Reading: Caughey, John W., *Hubert Howe Bancroft: Historian of the West* (Berkeley, Calif., 1946).

BANCROFT, ban′krôft, **Richard** (1544–1610), archbishop of Canterbury and chief overseer of the translation into English of the Bible known as the "Authorized" or "King James" version. He was born at Farnworth in Lancashire, England. After graduating from Cambridge in 1570, he was ordained a priest and became chaplain to the bishop of Ely. In 1575 he became rector of Teversham in Cambridge, in 1584 rector of St. Andrew's, Holburn, London, and in 1585, treasurer of St. Paul's Cathedral in London. He was a vigorous and notable preacher. Bancroft staunchly upheld the necessity of properly consecrated bishops, against objections of the Puritans.

In 1597, Richard Bancroft became bishop of London, and because of the age and illness of John Whitgift, archbishop of Canterbury, he was virtual primate of the church and had the sole management of church affairs. He played an important role in the Hampton Court conference, convened by James I to hear Puritan objections to the Book of Common Prayer and to consider other religious questions. Here Bancroft defended the practices of confirmation, absolution, private baptism, and excommunication of lay persons. The conference was a victory for the opinions of Bancroft and the king. Its most lasting result was the king's appointment of a commission to produce a new translation of the Bible, much desired by the Puritans. This, the Authorized Version, was published in 1611.

In 1604, Bancroft was made archbishop of Canterbury. In this position, which he held until his death on Nov. 2, 1610, he continued his anti-Puritan activities, and also urged the consecration of Scottish bishops by the Church of England. This marked the beginning of the Episcopal Church of Scotland.

BANCROFT, ban′krôft, **Sir Squire** (1841–1926), English actor. He was born in London on May 4, 1841. His first stage appearance was in Birmingham in 1861. He then acted in Dublin and in leading provincial theaters in England before becoming leading man at the Prince of Wales's Theatre in London in 1865. At that time the Prince of Wales's Theatre was under the management of the actress Marie Effie Wilton, whom Bancroft married in 1867. With her, he was joint manager of the theater until 1879. From 1880 to 1885 they managed the Haymarket Theatre. Bancroft then limited his career to acting. He was knighted in 1897.

Bancroft wrote a volume of reminiscences, *Empty Chairs* (1925). With his wife, he also wrote *Mr. and Mrs. Bancroft, On and Off the Stage* (1888) and *The Bancrofts: Recollections of Sixty Years* (1909). He died in London on April 19, 1926.

Lady Marie Effie Wilton Bancroft (1839–1921), his wife, was popular for her portrayal of boys' roles and for her parts in comic extravaganzas. As a theater manager, she rehabilitated the Prince of Wales's Theatre.

BAND, a concerted group of musicians, comprising principally wind instrumentalists and usually some performers on percussion instruments. In earlier periods the term "band" was applied to many highly distinguished orchestral groups, such as The King's Private Band in 17th century England, consisting of 24 fiddlers in service to King Charles II.

The Ancient World. Thousands of years ago, when a procession of Egyptians marched toward the shrine of Serapis, the god of healing, musicians in the group probably played reed pipes, tambourines, and drums. The Bible mentions "an hundred and twenty priests sounding with trumpets." In ancient Israel no ceremonial meal was complete without its accompaniment of instrumental music, and victorious warriors were met at the city gates by "the band."

In Greece and Rome all triumphal processions were headed by trumpeters. The double-flute and cithera were favorite instruments among the people of Greece, and in Athens every boy was taught to play the lyre. In 570 B.C., Servius Tullius introduced bronze trumpets into the Roman army; these were without doubt the ancestors of the brass instruments of the present day. The Roman straight tuba, the cavalry trumpet, and *lituus*, and a short horn called the *buccina* became popular brass instruments in Rome. In the ancient world there were horns that only the priests were permitted to play. Our present-day band probably began its development only after the nobility lost its exclusive right to play drums and trumpets.

Development in Europe. In the 12th century A.D. the convention of musical notation was accepted; before then all music was played by ear. King Edward III of England (reigned 1327–1377) maintained a band composed chiefly of the wind instruments of that day.

During the next century the common people were first permitted to play trumpets, which before then had been reserved for the nobility. A great deal of experimentation took place during this period, and many new instruments made their debut, including the sackbut, which looked very much like the trombone of today, the rankett, the oliphant, the eunuch flute, trumpets with slides like trombones, and the zinke, an instrument made of leather-covered wood and having six finger holes.

In the 16th century, King Henry VIII of England had a band that was highly regarded in its time. Its instrumentation consisted of 14 trumpets, 10 trombones, 2 viols, 3 rebecs (forerunner of the violin), 1 bagpipe, 4 tambourines, and 4 drums. Henry VIII was himself an excellent musician, and during his reign many innovations in the instrumentation of the band took place; for example, the fife replaced the bagpipe as a favorite instrument. Tower trumpeters became bandmasters, and following the Reformation they were required to perform three times daily to call the people to prayer.

After the Thirty Years' War (1618–1648) another progressive step occurred in the evolution of the band. Before that time, military forces had been recruited at the beginning of each war and promptly disbanded when the war ended. However, standing armies were now created, and the stepping together of a large group of men in exact cadences and rhythm necessitated a new musical form. Thus the march was introduced as a popular type of band music.

RALPH CRANE, FROM BLACK STAR

HIGH SCHOOL BANDS, such as this one marching in New York, provide musical training for young people.

The bands of the British army date from the latter part of the 17th century. At the beginning of the 18th century their usual instrumentation consisted of two flutes, two oboes, two horns, one or two trumpets, two or three bassoons, and a bass trombone. Only a very few of the bands included drums. At the close of the 18th century the typical instrumentation of the French bands consisted of six clarinets, one flute, three bassoons, two horns, one trumpet, one serpent, and several drums.

Throughout the 17th and 18th centuries wind instruments continued to improve, although it was not until the early part of the 19th century that the various wind instruments were taken seriously by critical musicians. During this period more innovations and improvements continued to be made. For example, the trumpet was equipped with valves, and more exactness and precision was employed in the construction of wind instruments. With innovations and changes there came a great improvement in the standards of performance of the wind instrument musicians, resulting in better tone quality, improved intonation, and greater dexterity.

During the French Revolution the great opera houses and concert halls of France were forced to close. This resulted in a marked improvement in the wind bands of France, since most of the best instrumentalists became members of municipal bands throughout the country. Many outstanding concert bands were created in this way, and the band began to gain an important place in the musical world. The personnel of the average French band of this era consisted of approximately 70 musicians, and balance, effectiveness of instrumentation, and tonal color were carefully conceived. Many French composers wrote original band music, and on numerous occasions large band festivals were held. In 1802 the Garde Républicaine band was organized in France, and this ensemble quickly became one of the greatest bands in the world.

During the 19th century massed bands composed of hundreds of musicians became highly

CONCERT BAND of the University of Michigan, conducted by William D. Revelli.

popular. In 1838 a concert was presented in Berlin at which 1,200 musicians performed "en masse." The group was composed of 16 cavalry and 16 infantry bands, to which were added 200 drummers.

Development in the United States. As in the European countries, the band was born in the United States as a military organization, although on a less pretentious scale. In 1775 the Continental Congress authorized the etablishment of the Marine Corps, and a band of fifers and drummers was organized as a part of the unit. This marked the beginning of the United States Marine Band. During the Revolutionary War, fifes and drums were also used by the colonial armies, but with the end of the war, all of the military forces and their musicians were disbanded. In 1798, Congress reestablished the Marine Corps, which in turn reorganized a band of drums and fifes. In 1800, the year the band presented its first open-air concert in Washington, D.C., two oboes, two clarinets, two French-horns, one bassoon, and a bass drum were added to it. Since then the Marine Band has played for the inauguration of every American president.

In 1810 the Eleventh Militia Regiment organized the first authorized band in New York City, and by 1823 there were five bands in New York. All were composed of amateurs, performing without pay although serving with the militia. Later, a few "professional" bands were organized and vigorously competed for the various engagements formerly given to the militia bands. However, by the middle of the 19th century, little progress had been made in American bands, and they remained small in membership and poorly equipped.

The Modern Era. In 1874, Patrick Gilmore introduced a new era for bands and band music. The outstanding band conductor, organizer, and executive of his day, Gilmore possessed the ability to sell his band to the American public and quickly became the nation's most noted band conductor. His band was the largest, and the personnel and instrumentation the most highly developed, of its period. The success of the Gilmore Band had a national influence on both professional and amateur bands throughout the country.

Following Gilmore came John Philip Sousa, who was destined to become one of the most noted and beloved band conductors of all time. He was acclaimed throughout the world, first as conductor of the United States Marine Band (1880–1892), and later as conductor of his own band. The Sousa Band toured annually throughout the United States and in many foreign countries. Sousa was also a composer, and his marches have continued to be among the most popular ever written.

Among the more nationally prominent American bandmasters to follow Sousa were Arthur Pryor, Herbert Clarke, Thomas Preston Brooke, Frank Simon, and Edwin Franko Goldman, who was to succeed Sousa as the dean of American bandmasters. Also important are the seven military service bands, the members of which are trained at the Army, Navy, and Marine School of Music in Norfolk, Va.

School Bands. In the 20th century the band movement in the United States has been largely dominated by school and college bands. The most elaborate are the marching and symphonic bands; they contribute to making the American school band program the largest in the world.

WILLIAM D. REVELLI
Conductor, University of Michigan Bands

JOHN PHILIP SOUSA, one of the foremost American band conductors, with the U.S. Marine Band in 1893.

Bibliography
Atkins, H.E., *Treatise on the Military Band* (London 1931).
Giles, Ray, *Here Comes the Band* (New York 1936).
Goldman, Richard F., *The Concert Band* (New York 1946).
Graham, Alberta P., *Great Bands of America* (New York 1951).
Schwartz, H.W., *Bands of America* (New York 1957).

BAND SAWS are useful in cutting along curved lines.

BAND SAW, band sô, a power-driven tool for cutting wood and metals. Band saws are used mainly in sawmills and in cutting wood parts for furniture and metal parts for machinery.

The band saw has a thin, continuous ribbon of steel with teeth cut into one edge. The band of steel is mounted like a belt on two broad-faced wheels. The power-driven wheels cause the band to travel at rates ranging from 8,000 to 12,000 feet (2,400 to 3,600 meters) per minute. The lower speeds are used to cut hardwoods, and the higher speeds are used to cut softwoods.

In log mills, a band-saw blade usually is 49 feet (15 meters) long and 1 foot (0.3 meters) wide. The blade thickness is 14 gauge, the saw teeth are 0.75 inch (1.90 cm) long, and the distance between the teeth points is 1.75 inches (4.44 cm). For sawing very hard wood the teeth are shorter, the teeth points are spaced more closely, and the teeth have very little set.

For cutting white pine and similar softwoods, the recommended gauges, for all saw widths, are as follows: for bands up to 14 feet (4.27 meters) long, 22 gauge; for bands 15 to 17 feet (4.57 to 5.18 meters) long, 21 gauge; for bands 18 to 20 feet (6.59 to 6.10 meters) long, 20 gauge; for bands from 21 to 24 feet (6.40 to 7.32 meters) long, 19 gauge; and for bands 25 to 30 feet (7.62 to 9.14 meters) long, 18 gauge. For cutting hardwoods like oak and beech, the thickness of the blade should be increased by one gauge number, and the teeth points should be spaced more closely. For cutting metal, the thickness of the blade should be increased by three gauge numbers, the teeth points should be spaced 20 to the inch (8 to the centimeter), and the teeth should have little or no set.

For resawing, that is, sawing planks and boards into two or more thinner pieces, a thin saw is especially desirable to minimize waste. With the use of equipment such as automatic saw sharpeners, it has been found that thinner and thinner blades could be used. Saw blades as thin as 0.02 inch are used successfully.

The success of the band saw is due to the skill of the saw maker in turning out saw blades that retain a good cutting edge and are flexible enough to pass over the wheels without cracking. The usefulness of the saw also depends on the skill of the saw filer in fitting his saws.

BANDA, ban′də, **Hastings Kamuzu** (1902?–   ), leader of the Malawi independence movement and first prime minister and first president of Malawi. He was born in the Kasungu district of what was then the British protectorate of Nyasaland. He attended a mission school for several years and at the age of about 13 went to South Africa. There he worked as a clerk in the gold mines for eight years while continuing his education at night school. He then went to the United States to study to become a doctor. Banda graduated in 1928 from the Wilberforce Institute, a Negro secondary school in Ohio; attended the universities of Indiana and Chicago; and in 1937 received his medical degree from Meharry Medical School in Nashville, Tenn. He received further medical training in Scotland and in Liverpool, and in 1945 he set up practice in London.

Throughout this time, Banda kept up with affairs in Nyasaland, and after the Nyasaland African Congress was founded in 1944, he supported the party with funds and advice. He lobbied in London against the creation of a Central African Federation and continued to condemn the management after the federation was formed. He continued his campaign from the Gold Coast (now Ghana), and returned to Nyasaland in July 1958 as the leader of the nationalist movement.

In the following month he was elected president-general of the Nyasaland African Congress. He was arrested in March 1959 on a charge of planning to murder white settlers but was released in April 1960. As leader of the new Malawi Congress Party, he went to London to negotiate the political future of Nyasaland. In 1961 his party won an overwhelming victory in elections held under the new constitution. Banda became a member of the cabinet and in 1963, was named prime minister, a post he retained after Nyasaland gained independence as Malawi on July 6, 1964. When Malawi became a republic in 1966, he became its president.

L. GRAY COWAN, *Columbia University*

H.K. BANDA, first president of the Republic of Malawi.

BANDA ISLANDS, ban′də, an island group in Indonesia. Part of the southern Moluccas, the Banda Islands are in the Banda Sea, about 75 miles (121 km) south of Ceram. They cover an area of 17 square miles (44 km) and consist of three large islands—Great Banda (Lontar), Bandanaira, and Gunung Api—surrounded by seven smaller islands. All of them are of volcanic origin. The seat of administration is at Bandanaira, a seaport on Bandanaira island.

The rich soil of the islands is ideal for the cultivation of nutmegs, which are indigenous and constitute the principal export. Coconuts, fruits, and other spices also are grown. But it was nutmegs that brought the first Europeans to the islands. As part of the Spice Islands, the Banda Islands were a source of conflict between the Portuguese, Spanish, Dutch, and English in the 17th century.

The Dutch conquered the Banda Islands in 1621 and soon came into conflict with a small English settlement. The conflict finally led to the massacre of the English at Ambon (Amboina) in 1623. British forces occupied the Banda Islands from 1796 until 1800 and again during the Napoleonic Wars, restoring them to the Netherlands in 1814 under the terms of the Treaty of Paris.

In 1949 the islands became part of the Republic of Indonesia; they are administered as part of the province of Maluku (the Moluccas). Population: (1961) 13,686.

BANDA SEA, ban′də, a body of water in the Malay Archipelago. It is one of the seas that connect the Indian and Pacific oceans. The Banda Sea, some 600 miles (965 km) long and 300 miles (483 km) wide, is surrounded by islands of Indonesia. It is bounded on the north by the islands of Buru and Ceram; on the east by Kai and Aru; on the southeast by the Tanimbar group; on the southwest by Timor; and on the northwest by Celebes Island. The sea reaches its greatest depth, over 21,000 feet (6,401 meters), west of the Kai Islands.

BANDAGE, ban′dij, a wrapping, usually of gauze, muslin, or linen, used to hold sterile dressings in place and to support or immobilize certain parts of the body. Thin gauze of various widths is the most popular and useful material.

Types of Bandages. A *simple spiral* is one of the most elementary forms of bandage. In wrapping it, each turn of the bandage should overlap the previous one. The spiral is used to dress a body part that varies in width, such as the forearm.

The *circular turn* is similar to the simple spiral. The part to be bandaged simply is encircled by turns of the bandage. This type is limited to body parts that are of a uniform width, such as the neck.

One useful type is the *recurrent bandage,* in which the gauze is looped back and forth over the part to be dressed. The loops then must be secured by circular turns of the bandage. This type of bandage is suitable for bandaging the scalp and fingers, or the stump of an amputated limb.

Another important type is the *figure of eight.* In this type the bandage is carried back and forth in the form of a double spiral or figure of eight. It can be illustrated best by a bandage applied to the ankle. A few spirals are placed above the ankle for anchorage, and then the gauze is carried across the front of the ankle, around the foot from its outer surface to the arch, then across the front of the ankle again, completing the figure of eight. This type of bandage is suitable for most joints and sometimes is used to immobilize a fractured collarbone.

In applying a spiral bandage to an extremity, difficulty may arise because the limb tapers and gaps may occur in the bandage. In this case a *spiral reverse* must be used. In this bandage the usual spiral is not completed; instead the bandage is given a half-twist and then continued downward. The half-twist changes the direction of the spiral and so avoids a gap in the bandage. The reverse is repeated when needed.

Two other useful bandages are the *triangle* and the *cravat.* The triangle-shaped bandage is a versatile one that can be used for the hand, foot, head, chest, back, shoulder, hip, face, or back of head. Its application to the head is a good example. The base part of the triangle is placed at the forehead with the point of the triangle hanging down the back of the head. The two ends are carried around the head above the ears and crossed at the back of the head. The ends are carried back to the front and tied. The point at the back is tucked in.

When the triangular bandage is folded lengthwise, it forms a cravat. The width of this bandage is adjustable, and the bandage can be used for the head, ear, eye, neck, forearm, arm, leg, or thigh. The bandage simply is wrapped around the area to be covered and tied.

More specialized types include the *Velpeau* and the *scultetus* bandages. The Velpeau bandage immobilizes the arm against the front of the chest with the hand placed on the opposite shoulder. The bandaging involves a series of complicated turns, and although it formerly was used in the treatment of certain fractures, it is uncomfortable and has lost popularity. The scultetus bandage, or binder, consists of a rectangle of flannel applied to the patient's back with strips of flannel extending from either side. The strips are folded in succession across the abdomen and secured with safety pins, thus holding surgical dressings in place and giving support to the abdominal muscles.

Other Forms and Materials. In the therapy of varicose veins or a sprained ankle, the use of *elasticized bandage* gives needed support and helps reduce tissue congestion. It also is used postoperatively to prevent formation of clots in veins.

Ready-made bandages of various sizes are available. Adhesive plastic strips with a piece of gauze affixed to the center are popular and useful. Also available are *gauze squares,* which consist of many layers of folded sterile gauze. The squares are held in place by a bandage.

A *bandage compress* is a pad made of several thicknesses of sterile gauze sewed to the middle of a strip of gauze or muslin. They are used for any surface that they will cover.

In an emergency, when roller gauze is not available, bandages can be made from sheets of cotton or muslin. However, these bandages are not sterile.

IRVING SOLOMON, M.D.
Mount Sinai School of Medicine, New York

Further Reading: American National Red Cross, *First Aid Textbook* (Washington 1957).

COMMON TYPES OF BANDAGE

THE FIGURE OF EIGHT bandage, consisting of spiral loops, is used on limbs and at joints.

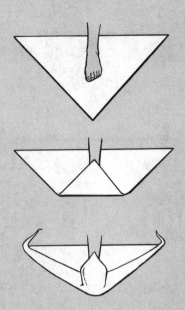

THE TRIANGULAR bandage is designed to cover such areas as the foot, hip, and back.

THE VELPEAU bandage immobilizes the arm for treatment of a fractured clavicle.

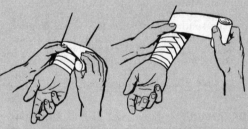

THE SPIRAL REVERSE bandage uses a "reverse" (left) to avoid bandage gaps.

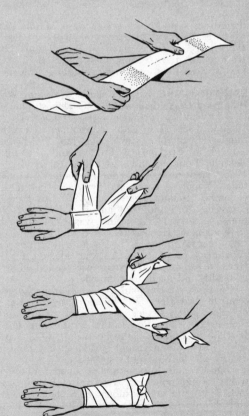

THE CRAVAT bandage, made from the triangular bandage, is used on the limbs.

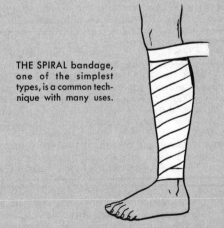

THE SPIRAL bandage, one of the simplest types, is a common technique with many uses.

BANDAI, bän-dī', a volcano in Japan, is on Honshu Island, in Fukushima prefecture, northeast of Wakamatsu and north of Lake Inawashiro. It reaches an elevation of 5,968 feet (1,819 meters). One of the volcano's four peaks was blown off in a violent eruption on July 15, 1888, which took 461 lives.

BANDANNA, ban-dan'ə, a large square of cotton or linen that has been treated in some parts of its surface by a substance that will resist dye. When the fabric is dyed, the undyed spots produce a pattern. It is used principally for scarfs, furniture coverings, and bunting.

The term bandanna was applied originally to yellow or red silk handkerchiefs, with white or yellow spots, that were made in India by a process called *bandhnu,* in which the areas to remain undyed were knotted tightly. Portuguese travelers brought the idea to Europe in the 16th century. In the 18th century bandannas became popular in England as neckcloths and handkerchiefs. In the United States they were worn as neckcloths by cowboys in the West.

BANDAR MAHARANI, bän'där mä-hä-rä'nē, is a seaport in Malaysia, on the Strait of Malacca. It is also called *Muar.* The seaport is located on the Malay Peninsula, at the mouth of the Muar River, in Johore state. The Muar district, of which it is the chief town, was a part of Malacca until 1877, when the British transferred it to Johore. The town was named for Maharani Abubakar, consort of a ruler of Johore. Population: (1970) 61,218.

BANDAR PENGGARAM, bän'där pəng-gä'räm, is a seaport in Malaysia, on the Strait of Malacca. It is also called *Batu Pahat.* The seaport is situated on the southwest coast of the Malay Peninsula, at the mouth of the small Batu Pahat River, in Johore state. Products of the surrounding area include rubber, coconuts, and fruit. There are iron and bauxite mines near Yong Peng, 14 miles (22 km) northeast of the city. Population: (1970) 53,291.

BANDARANAIKE, bän-drə-nī'ə-kə, **Sirimavo** (1916–   ), Sri Lankan political leader. She was born into the wealthy, aristocratic Ratwatte family, in Balangoda, Ceylon, on April 17, 1916. In 1940 she married Solomon W.R.D. Bandaranaike, who was then a state minister in Ceylon prior to independence and later became prime minister. Mrs. Bandaranaike was active in reform groups working for the education of women and family planning.

After her husband's assassination in 1959, she became a leader of his Sri Lanka Freedom party, a rural-based, Sinhalese nationalist party with socialist leanings. Elected president of the party in May 1960, she formed a no-contest pact with the Marxist parties for the July elections. Following her party's narrow victory, she became prime minister.

Her government continued policies similar to her husband's and faced similar difficulties. The United National party, which favored close Commonwealth relations, attacked her neutralist foreign policy; urban groups, including the Marxist parties, were alienated by her economic policies; and Tamil groups opposed her plan to make Sinhalese the national language. A military coup was put down early in 1962, but in the face of

Central Press

SIRIMAVO BANDARANAIKE of Ceylon was the first woman to become the prime minister of a modern nation.

dwindling support she resigned in March 1965. She was returned to power in 1970, but lost to the United National party, led by Junius Jayewardene, in the elections of July 21, 1977.

JAMES R. SHIRLEY, *Northern Illinois University*

BANDARANAIKE, bän-drə-nī'ə-kə, **Solomon West Ridgeway Dias** (1899–1959), Ceylonese political leader, who was prime minister of Ceylon from 1956 to 1959. Born into a prominent Christian family in Colombo, Ceylon, on Jan. 8, 1899, he studied in England at Oxford and the Inner Temple, London, and was called to the bar in 1925. Returning to Ceylon, he joined the National Congress party and won election to the Colombo Municipal council in 1927. In 1931 he converted to Buddhism, joined the United Nationalist party (UNP), and was elected to the state council. He was reelected in 1936 and became a state minister. In Ceylon's first independent election in 1948, he was elected to the House of Representatives and was named minister of health and local government.

In 1951, Bandaranaike resigned from the government and the UNP to form the Sri Lanka Freedom party. Reelected to the House of Representatives, he became leader of the opposition. In 1956 he organized the People's United Front, a four-party alliance, and became prime minister as a result of the Front's success.

Bandaranaike's government stood for a neutralist foreign policy, the removal of British bases in Ceylon, and establishment of Sinhalese as the official language. By 1959 his position was badly shaken by a split in the Front, economic problems, and language riots. He was shot by a traditionalist monk, and died at Colombo on Sept. 26, 1959.

JAMES R. SHIRLEY, *Northern Illinois University*

BANDELIER, ban-də-lēr', **Adolph Francis Alphonse** (1840–1914), Swiss-American archaeologist and historian, who was noted for studies of the Indians of the southwestern United States. Born in Bern, Switzerland, on Aug. 6, 1840, he moved to the United States in 1848 but returned to Bern to complete his education. From 1880 to 1889 he studied the Pueblo civilizations of the American Southwest, living among the Indians between 1880 and 1886. During the 1880's, he also did research on pre-Columbian cultures in Mexico and Central America. From 1892 to 1903 he investigated the Indians of Peru and Bolivia. He died in Spain on March 18, 1914.

The thoroughness of Bandelier's archaeological research represented a major advance over earlier historical studies. His *Final Report on Indians of the Southwestern United States* (1890–92) is a landmark in research. He wrote other histories and also incorporated the results of his research into the *Delight Makers* (1890), a novel about the Pueblo Indians. Bandelier National Monument in New Mexico was named for him.

BANDELLO, bän-del'lō, **Matteo** (c. 1480–1562), Italian writer, whose tales provided the themes for several English plays of the late 16th and early 17th centuries, including Shakespeare's *Romeo and Juliet* and *Twelfth Night,* Webster's *Duchess of Malfi,* and Beaumont and Fletcher's *Maid of the Mill.* Bandello's *novelle,* which also influenced Byron and Lope de Vega, are written in the style of Boccaccio but are characterized by an even greater bawdiness. Most are tales of trickery accompanied by some horrible vengeance. Three volumes of his *novelle* were published in 1554 and a posthumous volume in 1573. The tales were translated into French, and several appeared in English in William Painter's *Palace of Pleasure* (1566).

Bandello was born in Castelnuovo Scrivia, Piedmont. He was trained as a Dominican monk but spent much of his early career serving as an official of various Italian states. From 1515 to 1526 he lived in Mantua, where he was tutor to Lucrezia Gonzaga. In 1528 he became adviser to Cesare Fregoso, an Italian general in French service. In 1541 he moved to France, with Fregoso's widow as his protector. He was made bishop of Agen in France in 1550 but continued to write. He died in Agen on Sept. 13, 1562.

BANDICOOT, ban'di-kōōt, is the name applied to a family of marsupials found in Australia, Tasmania, New Guinea, and nearby islands and also to two genera of rodents found in India, southeast Asia, and the Middle East.

Found in open plains or forests, or in thick grass, the marsupial bandicoot has an elongated, pointed muzzle used for rooting in the soil. Its hind limbs are longer than the forelimbs, but it travels on all four limbs. The second and third digits of the hind limbs are fused, but the forelimbs have five fingers each, with sharp claws for digging. Its fur ranges from light gray through reddish-brown and brown to black in color and from very silky to stiff and spiny in texture. Its pouch opens downward and backward. Bandicoots range from 7 to 21 inches (174 to 550 mm) in length. They are mostly nocturnal animals. Some bandicoots burrow, while others dig trenches or build grass nests. Bandicoots belong to the family Peramelidae; there are 8 genera and about 19 species.

JOHN WARHAM

Brindled Bandicoot (*Isoodon torosus*).

The bandicoot rats (*Bandicota bengalensis* and *indica* and *Nesokia indica*) live in jungles, forests, and also commensally with man. Members of the Muridae family, they are pests to grain and root crops and to rubber plantations.

BANDIERA, bän'dyâ'rä, the family name of two brothers, *Attilio* and *Emilio,* who were active in the struggle for a united, independent Italy. Both were born in Venice: Attilio, on May 24, 1810, and Emilio, on June 20, 1819. They were the sons of an admiral in the Austrian navy, in which they served as lieutenants.

Inspired by the Italian patriot Giuseppe Mazzini, they laid plans in 1843 for an insurrection within the Austrian fleet. Their plans discovered, they fled to Corfu. In 1844 they landed in Calabria with 20 companions, believing that their appearance would signal a general insurrection. An accomplice betrayed them, and the party was captured by Neapolitan police. The brothers, along with seven of their comrades, were shot in Cosenza on July 25, 1844. Their execution was widely condemned, and many considered them martyrs to the cause of Italian independence.

BANDINELLI, bän-dē-nel'lē, **Bartolommeo** (1493–1560), Italian sculptor, who was a rival of Michelangelo for the favor of the Medici, rulers of Florence. His best work is a bas-relief of 88 apostles, prophets, and saints in the cathedral of Florence. He was also known as *Baccio Bandinelli.*

Bandinelli was born in Florence on Nov. 12, 1493. He studied sculpture under Gianfrancesco Rustici, but modeled his style after Michelangelo's. His most controversial work was the giant *Hercules and Cacus* (1534), which the Medici ordered as a companion piece to Michelangelo's *David* in the Piazza della Signoria in Florence. According to tradition, Bandinelli stole this commission from Michelangelo, with the result that more than 100 sonnets were written against the work by irate Florentines. Benvenuto Cellini, a rival of Bandinelli's, derided it in his autobiography: The head of Hercules "is so badly set upon the neck, with such poverty of art and so ill a grace, that nothing worse was ever seen. . . ." Bandinelli's other works in Florence include a copy of the *Laocoön* (now in the Uffizi Gallery), and an *Adam and Eve* (in the Bargello Palace). Bandinelli died in Florence on Feb. 7, 1560.

BANDJARMASIN, bän-jär-mä'sin, a city in Indonesia, is the capital of the province of South Kalimantan, on the island of Borneo. The chief seaport on Borneo's southeast coast, it is situated on a delta island at the junction of the Barito and the Martapura rivers, about 10 miles (16 km) from the Java Sea. Much of the city's transportation is by water. Because of the swampy terrain and the frequent inundation of the river banks, Bandjarmasin has been built largely on pilings or behind dikes. The city is a marketplace for products of the Barito Basin. Industries include diamond cutting, coal mining, sawmilling, and the manufacture of ovens. Bandjarmasin exports oil, timber, rattan, rubber, diamonds, coal, iron, and gold.

The Dutch founded a trading center at Bandjarmasin in 1606 and gradually established territorial control. They held the area until Indonesia achieved its independence in 1949, except for three periods of British control (1669–1707, 1795-1802, and 1811–1817) and the period of Japanese occupation during World War II. From 1950 to 1956 the city was the capital of the former vast province of Kalimantan, and since 1956 it has been the capital of South Kalimantan. Population: (1961) 212,683.

BANDUNG, bän'doong, the third-largest city of Indonesia, is located in the highlands of west central Java about 110 miles (180 km) southeast of Djakarta, the national capital. Besides being the capital of the province of West Java, Bandung is an important center of commerce, transportation, and education, and it is a much-frequented resort.

Bandung is situated on an alluvial terrace in the fertile Bandung basin at an elevation of 2,400 feet (730 meters) above sea level. The Tjikapundung River bisects the city. The high elevation creates a delightful springlike climate the year round. Temperatures vary little with the seasons, remaining usually in the low 70's° F (low 20's° C). Rainfall is quite heavy.

Bandung was founded along the banks of the Tjitarum River in the 17th century by the sultan of Cheribon. It was moved to its present location by the Dutch governor general Herman Willem Daendels early in the 19th century. At first a mere hill station and health resort, Bandung began to grow late in the 19th century with the arrival of the railroad and the development of rubber, tea, and cinchona (quinine) plantations in the Bandung basin and on the surrounding hills and mountains.

Agricultural products from the surrounding hinterland continue to be an important factor in the city's economy. Food-processing and canning establishments as well as tea and quinine factories are located in Bandung. The city also has become important as a center for the textile, ceramics, paper-manufacturing, chemical, rail repair, and consumer goods and services industries. Bandung is located at the center of an extensive road and rail network that connects it with all the major cities of Java. It is also served by commercial airlines.

Bandung is an attractive city of wide boulevards, numerous parks, and both European and traditional Javanese architecture. In the downtown section are imposing Western-style department stores, banks, hotels, and restaurants as well as a number of theaters, mosques, and churches. Bandung is a center of Sundanese culture, and performances of traditional music and the puppet theater are popular attractions. Several educational and research institutions are located in the city or nearby, notably Bandung Institute of Technology (part of the University of Indonesia), Bosscha Observatory, the Agricultural Research Institute, and the Pasteur Institute for serums and vaccines. There is also an excellent botanical garden, as well as a zoo, and a national archives center.

Several proposals have been made to move the capital of Indonesia to Bandung, but the only major national government office headquartered in the city by the mid-1960's was the mines department.

In April 1955 Bandung was the scene of the historic Asian-African Conference of prime ministers and deputies—the first large conclave of Asian and African leaders ever held. This meeting came to be referred to as the Bandung Conference (q.v.). Population: (1961) 972,566.

FREDERICK L. WERNSTEDT
Pennsylvania State University

BANDUNG CONFERENCE, bän'doong, an African-Asian congress held at Bandung, Indonesia, on April 18–24, 1955. Sponsored by Indonesia, Burma, Ceylon, India, and Pakistan, the conference was attended by delegates from 29 nations, representing more than half the world's population. It was intended to build closer relations between the African-Asian nations, to forge an African-Asian declaration of neutrality in the cold war (which was viewed by many delegates as a European struggle), and to speed the end of colonialism. Underlying the conference was the African-Asian reaction to centuries of European dominance, then drawing to a close.

The major debate over the issue of colonialism resulted in a declaration implying condemnation of the Soviet Union as well as the Western powers. Relations between Communist China and the other nations were strengthened by the moderation shown by Chinese Foreign Minister Chou En-lai, who refused to engage in controversy. He was applauded for his declaration of Chinese willingness to negotiate with the United States, an announcement that led to Sino-American talks at Warsaw.

The conference adopted a 10-point declaration on world peace and cooperation, incorporating the principles of the United Nations Charter and Indian Prime Minister Jawaharlal Nehru's five principles of peaceful coexistence. It also advocated universal UN membership and universal disarmament. Several trade, aid, and cultural agreements came out of the conference. For years thereafter, the so-called Bandung spirit of African-Asian neutralism and cooperation was hailed as its most important result.

JAMES R. SHIRLEY, *Northern Illinois University*

BANEBERRY, bān'ber-ē, is a genus of perennial herbs of the Northern Hemisphere, and also the acrid, poisonous berries produced by these herbs. These herbs thrive in woody and shaded areas. The leaves are composed of sharp-toothed leaflets. Small whitish flowers grow in terminal clusters and are followed by shiny, many-seeded berries. Baneberries belong to the genus *Actaea* of the crowfoot family, Ranunculaceae. There are several species, including the white baneberry (*A. pachpoda* or *A. alba*), the red baneberry (*A. rubra*), and the black baneberry (*A. spicata*).

BANÉR, ba�-năr', Johan (1596–1641), Swedish general and field marshal in the Thirty Years' War. His name is also spelled *Banner*. He was born in Djursholm, near Stockholm, on June 23, 1596. He held commands under King Gustavus Adolphus on campaigns in Poland and Russia, and then accompanied him to Germany in 1630.

After the king's death (1632), he was made chief commander of the Swedish army. He invaded Bohemia in 1634, but his victories were nullified by the disastrous defeat of the Protestant forces at Nördlingen. He later regained Swedish prestige by defeating the Saxons at Wittstock on Oct. 4, 1636. In 1639 he ravaged Saxony and defeated the imperial forces under Archduke Leopold William at Chemnitz. In 1641 he attempted to take Ratisbon (Regensburg) by surprise, but was forced to retreat to Halberstadt, where he died on May 10. Highly esteemed by Gustavus Adolphus, Banér was one of the Swedish king's ablest generals.

BANERJEA, ba̱'nôr-jē, Sir Surendranath (1848–1925), Indian political leader. He was born in Calcutta, India, on Nov. 10, 1848. Educated in Calcutta and London, he served for two years in the Indian civil service and subsequently founded a school in Calcutta which became Ripon College (1882). Thereafter he devoted his life to constitutional reforms that would increase Indian participation in government and Indian representation in the British Commonwealth. He edited the nationalist newspaper *Bengalee* and was one of the founders of the Indian National Congress, of which he served as president in 1895 and 1902. In 1919 he presided over the Moderate Conference at Bombay.

After leaving the nationalist congress because of its extremist position, he formed another liberal organization and was appointed minister in charge of local self-government and public health in Bengal. He was knighted in 1921, and his autobiography, *A Nation in the Making* (1925), was published shortly before he died in Barrackpore, India, on Aug. 6, 1925.

BAÑEZ, bä'nyäth, Domingo (1528–1604), Spanish theologian. His name is also spelled *Vañez*. Born at Medina del Campo on Feb. 24, 1528, he was educated at the University of Salamanca and later was a professor there. He entered the Dominican Order in 1547 and became the foremost exponent of a revival of Scholasticism in 16th century Spain. He is known for his debate with the Jesuit theologian Luis Molina concerning the problem of reconciling God's will with his gift of free will to man. Bañez died in Medina del Campo on Oct. 22, 1604.

BANFF, bamf, is a resort town in Alberta, Canada, near the border of British Columbia. It is situated in the Rocky Mountains, on the Bow River, 65 miles (105 km) west of Calgary.

Banff is an internationally known summer and winter resort, in the southern part of Banff National Park, of which it is the administrative headquarters and tourist center. Roads and horse and foot trails lead to scenic parts of the park. Hot sulphur springs are found at Sulphur Mountain nearby. The Banff School of Fine Arts, an extension of the University of Alberta, conducts summer courses. The Banff National Park Museum and the Luxton Museum, which is maintained by the Glenbow Foundation of Calgary, have Indian and natural history exhibits. Banff is on the Canadian Pacific Railroad and the Trans-Canada Highway. A landing field for light aircraft is near the town. Banff is unincorporated. Population: 3,532.

BANFF, bamf, is the name of a county and its county town in northeastern Scotland. Its area is 630 square miles (1,631 sq km). On the north it is bounded by the North Sea. Away from the coast the terrain is quite rugged. The highest mountain is Cairngorm (4,084 feet, or 1,245 meters). There are limestone, granite, marble, and slate quarries. Other minerals mined in the county are magnetite, chromite, asbestos, fluorite, and manganese.

Agriculture is economically important in the northern coastal areas, principally livestock and dairy farming. The chief crops are oats, barley, turnips, and potatoes. There is also much commercial fishing in the North Sea and for salmon in the rivers. Industries in the county include woolen mills, tanneries, boatyards, rope and sail works, breweries, and whisky distilleries.

There are numerous remains of prehistoric man in Banff County: stone axes, arrowheads, parts of stone circles, and urns. Later relics date from the early Celtic missionaries who brought Christianity to the northern Picts. Besides Banff, the county's principal towns are Buckie, Keith, and Macduff.

Banff, the county town, is on the North Sea at the mouth of the Deveron River, 40 miles (64 km) northwest of Aberdeen. Its industries include boatbuilding, rope- and sailmaking, tanning, and brewing. It exports grain, cattle, salmon, and herring. The traditional residence of Scottish kings, Banff was made a royal burgh in 1165. It is now governed by a provost and council. Population: (1971) of the county, 43,501; of the town, 3,775.

BANFF NATIONAL PARK is Canada's first national park, established in 1885 in southwestern Alberta on the British Columbia border. It covers 2,564 square miles (6,641 sq km) on the eastern side of the Rocky Mountains, and has some of the continent's most spectacular mountain scenery, with snow-capped peaks, glaciers and ice fields, lakes, alpine meadows, and hot springs. There are campgrounds and trailer lots for public camping. The town of Banff and Lake Louise are principal tourist centers. The Trans-Canada Highway passes through Banff and part of the park. Another highway connects Banff with Jasper National Park to the north.

BANG, bång, Bernhard Laurits Frederik (1848–1932), Danish veterinarian. He was born in Sorø, Denmark, on June 7, 1848. He was professor of pathology and therapy in the Royal Veterinary and Agricultural College, Copenhagen. He made extensive researches in veterinary science, especially in regard to contagious abortion and tuberculosis. In 1892 he originated his method of eradicating tuberculosis from dairy herds by isolating mildly affected animals and artificially feeding their calves with milk free from tubercle bacilli. The results were favorable.

In 1896, Bang discovered the cause of contagious abortion in cattle (Bang's disease) and afterward devoted much study to its treatment and the possibility of immunizing herds. He died in Copenhagen on June 22, 1932.

BANGALORE'S CHICKPET, a busy shopping street, is lined with Indian-style shops selling local wares.

BANG, bäng, **Herman Joachim** (1857–1912), Danish writer, who was noted for his sensitive tales of disillusionment. These impressionistic stories and novels of provincial life afford an intense insight into loneliness and frustration. His finest work was *Ved Vejen* (*By the Wayside*), a novella published in *Stille Existenser* (1886; *Silent Beings*).

Bang was born on the island of Als on April 20, 1857. He studied at the University of Copenhagen and later worked as an actor and as a journalist. He won attention with his autobiographical novel, *Haablöse Slægter* (1880; *Generations Without Hope*). His other novels include *Faedra* (1883), *Tine* (1889), *Ludvigsbakke* (1896; Eng. tr., *Ida Brandt*, 1928), *Det hvide Hus* (1898; *The White House*), and *De uden Fædreland* (1906; Eng. tr., *Denied a Country*, 1927). He also wrote verse, plays, and criticism. He died at Ogden, Utah, on Jan. 29, 1912, while on a world tour.

BANGALORE, bang'gǝ-lôr, is one of the major cities of southern India and the capital of Mysore state. It is situated midway across the Indian peninsula, 180 air miles (290 km) west of Madras, at an elevation of 3,113 feet (949 meters). The fifth-largest city in India, Bangalore has important military and industrial installations and is a transportation center.

The urban area consists of the (former British) military cantonment and civil administration station (one of the largest in India) and the city proper, which covers about 12 square miles (31 sq km). To the south lies Bangalore Fort, built prior to the founding of the city in the early 16th century and later rebuilt several times. In the northern part of the city is the Indian Institute of Science (founded 1911), devoted to chemistry, physics, and engineering. A healthy climate and a busy social life make Bangalore a favorite city of foreigners and Indians alike.

Bangalore is connected by the Southern Rail-

way with Madras city, Hyderabad and north India, Bombay, and the state of Kerala. It is also an important junction in the network of national highways.

Since the 1950's there has been a rapid growth in industry and commerce in Bangalore. There are government-owned factories making aircraft, telephones, machine tools, and electronics equipment. There are also public and privately owned factories producing soap, pharmaceuticals, tanned leather, glassware, procelain insulators, transformers, textiles, and cigarettes.

Bangalore was founded in 1537 and for long periods was ruled by the maharajas of Mysore. It was the scene of fighting in the Third Anglo-Mysore War (1789–1792), one of the conflicts between the British and Tipu Sultan, son of Hyder Ali, usurper of Mysore. Bangalore later became the headquarters of the British administration of Mysore (1831–1881). Population: (1961) 905,134.

JOEL M. ANDRESS
Central Washington State College

BANGE, bäNzh, **Charles Ragon de** (1833–1914), French artillery colonel. He was born in Balignicourt, France, on Oct. 17, 1833. In 1873, as director of the Paris arsenal's precision laboratory, he redesigned the light and heavy field pieces of the French army, which adopted his models in 1879. In the next decade he competed successfully against Germany's Krupp armaments firm to supply artillery for the Serbian government. Britain, Sweden, and Italy also adopted his guns.

Bange was the first to employ effectively the screw principle in the mechanism of the breechblock. His gas check, which prevents the escape of gases, is used in most large modern guns. He died at Le Chesnay, France, in 1914.

BANGGAI ARCHIPELAGO, bäng'gī är-kǝ-pel'ǝ-gō, a group of about 100 islands and inlets in Indonesia. The islands lie in the Molucca Sea off the east coast of Celebes, north of the entrance to the Gulf of Tolo. Their area is 1,222 square miles (3,165 sq km). The largest of the group (929 square miles or 2,406 sq km), is the only mountainous island. Next in size, and southeast of Peleng, is Banggai (112 square miles, 290 sq km), on which is situated the chief town of the archipelago, Banggai. The islands' forest products are ebony, resin, and rattan. The fisheries yield tortoise shell and trepang (edible sea cucumbers). Rice and sago palms are cultivated. Population: (1961) 144,747.

BANGKA, bang'kǝ, an island in Indonesia, is one of the major tin-producing areas in the world. It is located in the Java Sea off the southeast coast of Sumatra, from which it is separated by narrow Bangka Strait. The island, with an area of 4,611 square miles (11,943 km) is generally hilly with low, swampy coastal areas.

Bangka's economy is based mainly on the high-quality tin mines, which are owned by the Indonesian government. There are also deposits of iron, copper, manganese, lead, and gold.

The British took possession of Bangka in 1810 and two years later traded it to the Dutch in exchange for Cochin, India. The island was seized by Japan in 1942. At the end of World War II it was returned to the Dutch and has been part of the Republic of Indonesia since 1949. Population: (1961) 251,639.

BANGKOK'S SKYLINE, seen from across the Chao Phraya River, is graced by temple spires.

BANGKOK

BANGKOK, bang'kok, is the capital, largest city, and chief port of Thailand and one of the leading cities of Southeast Asia. The city, sometimes also called *Krung Thep,* is famous for its beautiful Buddhist temples and colorful Thai culture.

Bangkok is located in southern Thailand on one of the bends of the Chao Phraya (Menam) River, about 25 miles (40 km) upriver from the Gulf of Siam. Its temperatures are warm the year round, though there is a seasonal variation. The hot season, with temperatures averaging in the mid-80°'s F (around 30° C), extends from March through mid-May; the rainy season lasts from mid-May until October. The cool season, with average temperatures in the high 70°'s F (around 25° C), is from November through February. Rainfall is only 55 inches annually; nearly 90 percent of it comes during the rainy season. Droughts can be prolonged and severe. Bangkok's surrounding delta land, however, is extremely flat and subject to flooding during the rainy season.

History. The modern city of Bangkok was founded in 1782, when the ruler of Thailand, Chao Phraya Chakri (Chakkri), or Rama I (reigned 1782–1809), moved the capital from Thonburi, where it had been located since 1760, across the river to the east bank. By 1785 the Grand Palace and the first of the temples, the Wat Phra Keo (the Temple of the Emerald Buddha) had been constructed. This complex consisted of a walled compound, about one square mile (2.5 sq km) in area, containing, in addition to the palace and the temple, the royal chapel and several government buildings. As the city grew, official buildings were concentrated on the higher ground, while most of the population lived in wooden houses raised on stilts above the low-lying ground. A canal was constructed across the neck of land at the bend in the river, converting the old city into an island, outside of which permanent buildings and roads did not exist. All transportation was by boat along the many canals and river channels. The city itself was criss-crossed by canals, called *klongs,* most of which still exist. These canals have caused Bangkok to be called "the Venice of the Far East."

Much of the modernization of Bangkok, and of Thailand, occurred during the reign (1851–1868) of Mongkut, or Rama IV, who threw Bangkok open to foreign trade and recruited foreign experts to help modernize the government. His son Chulalongkorn, or Rama V (reigned 1868–1910), continued the modernization program, establishing increased trade relations and entering treaties of friendship with European nations. But neither Bangkok nor the country ever fell under the direct rule of any colonial power—which may account for the singular tolerance and kindliness the Thai people show to foreigners. Japanese military forces occupied Bangkok from 1941 to 1945, during World War II, when Thailand was allied with Japan.

Present-Day Bangkok. Bangkok's skyline, bristling with the flashing golden spires of the city's nearly 400 Buddhist temples, is occasionally blunted by the jutting, square-topped outline of a new multistory apartment block. But though the building boom, a phenomenon of the mid-1960's, has caused many of the older buildings of Bangkok to be displaced by Western-style concrete office buildings, apartment houses, hotels, and shopping centers, the glittering temples still give the city an exotic Oriental atmosphere. Among the better-known temples, besides the Temple of the Emerald Buddha, are Wat Arun (Temple of Dawn), Wat Benchamabopitr (Marble Temple), Wat Po (Temple of the Reclining Buddha), Wat Trimitr (Temple of the Golden Buddha), and Wat Rajabopitr (Temple of the Pearl Inlaid Doors).

In Bangkok, modern office buildings and stores are often found standing side by side with buildings of traditional Thai architecture. Many of the city's thoroughfares are broad and tree-lined; others are winding lanes, narrow and

THE FLOATING MARKET on Bangkok's crowded canals offers a wide variety of foods for sale from sampans.

GRAND PALACE COMPOUND in Bangkok contains the Temple of the Emerald Buddha, with gates guarded by mythological giants (*far left*), and the Chakri Building (*left*), once the residence of Thailand's monarchs.

crowded. Streets tend to conform more to the pattern of the river and canals than to a rectangular plan, and many of the principal roads have been built on filled-in canals. The river and canals are alive with boats of all descriptions. The famous Floating Market of Bangkok, a clamorous daily event, offers produce for sale from boats bobbing on the *klongs*.

Transportation. Bangkok is the hub of Thailand's transportation system. Above all, it is the premier port for Thailand and also for landlocked Laos. Until the 1950's oceangoing vessels had to anchor off the mouth of the Chao Phraya beyond a rivermouth sandbar and load and unload passengers and freight from lighters and barges. Now a modern port, Klong Toey, 5 miles (8 km) downstream from central Bangkok, provides wharfage for several oceangoing ships, and dredging operations have produced additional anchorage in midstream. About 85 percent of Thailand's foreign trade is handled through Klong Toey.

The Chao Phraya is navigable by steam launches for about 250 miles (400 km) during high-water season and for 120 miles (200 km) during low water. Regular riverboat services link Bangkok with all the main towns on the lower Chao Phraya, and thousands of miles of interlacing canals provide freight byways to most of the villages on the surrounding plain.

The State Railroad of Thailand operates a network of rail lines radiating from Bangkok and Thonburi in several directions: to northeastern Thailand and the Laotian border; eastward to the Cambodian border; into northern Thailand as far as Chiangmai; westward toward Burma; and southward through peninsular Thailand to the Malaysian border. Highways generally run parallel to the rail lines, but they are not very significant because very few of them are all-weather roads.

Don Muang Airport, 12 miles (20 km) from downtown Bangkok, is the hub of Thailand's domestic air system. It is also an important international air terminal and transfer point, and flights are available to all the major capitals of southern, southeastern, and eastern Asia.

Industry and Commerce. Most of Thailand's industrial and commercial activity centers on Bangkok. Rice milling and sawmilling are the leading industries, both in number of employees and number of factories. Other industries based on Thai products are sugar, paper, and textile milling; cigarette, match, and soap making; and distilling, tanning, metalworking, and food proc-

essing. Industrial concerns using imported materials include an oil refinery, a cement plant, shipyards, pharmaceutical companies, truck and automobile assembly plants, and electrical products plants.

In Bangkok are most of the nation's banks, including the government Bank of Thailand, and the branch offices of all the foreign financial institutions doing business in the country. The city is famous for a flourishing jewelry trade, dealing in silverware and bronzeware and also in star sapphires, zircons, emeralds, and rubies.

Culture. As the capital and only large city of the country, Bangkok is the seat of Thai cultural and governmental activities. Bangkok is the headquarters of SEATO (Southeast Asia Treaty Organization) and the regional center for many UN agencies, such as UNICEF, UNESCO, and the World Health Organization.

Situated on a beautiful campus in southeastern Bangkok is Chulalongkorn University (founded 1917). In the center of Bangkok is the larger Thammasat University (founded 1934). Other institutions of higher learning in Bangkok are the Medical Science, Agriculture, and Silpakorn (Fine Arts) universities.

The nation's twelve Thai-language newspapers are published in Bangkok, as are two newspapers in English (Bangkok *World* and Bangkok *Post*) and two in Chinese. The city has a number of theaters presenting Thai dancing and Thai plays and is the home of the National Museum, the National Library, Dusit Zoo, the National Stadium, and the Pasteur Institute for snake venoms. Dozens of hotels and Thai, Chinese, and European restaurants cater to tourists.

Population. Bangkok and the smaller city of Thonburi across the river constitute a single metropolitan area. This complex, known as Bangkok-Thonburi, has a population of more than 2 million. The population of Bangkok, according to the 1960 census, was 1,299,528, and that of Thonburi, 403,818.

Approximately 12 percent of the population of Bangkok was composed of alien Chinese at the time of the 1960 census, and many more were Chinese ethnically though Thai in nationality. There were several thousand Americans and Europeans in Bangkok, exclusive of United States military personnel.

FREDERICK L. WERNSTEDT
Pennsylvania State University

Further Reading: Hürlimann, Martin, *Bangkok* (New York 1963); Krull, Germaine, *Bangkok, Siam's City of Angels* (London 1964); MacDonald, Alexander, *Bangkok Editor* (New York 1949).

Pedicabs crowd the streets of the capital city, Dacca, where fuel is always in short supply, as in the rest of Bangladesh.

BANGLADESH, bäng-glä-desh', is a republic in South Asia. Between 1947 and 1971, when it gained its independence, Bangladesh formed the eastern part of Pakistan and was called East Pakistan. Before the partition of India into independent India and Pakistan in 1947, the area that now forms Bangladesh ("the land of Bengal") had been the eastern part of the Bengal province of the British Empire.

Bangladesh, a land of rivers, lies in the easternmost part of the Indian subcontinent. It is almost entirely surrounded by India, a condition that affects the foreign policy and economy of Bangladesh.

One of the most populous and poorest countries in the world, Bangladesh has about 80 million people living in an area slightly larger than the state of New York. Its population density, one of the highest in the world, ranges from 750 to 2,000 persons per square mile (290–770 per sq km). The population is expected to double by the end of the 20th century.

Most of the people live in rural areas. Only about 10% live in urban centers, the most important of which are Dacca, the capital of the new country, in central Bangladesh, and Chittagong, a major port city on the southeast coast.

Bangladesh has only a small agricultural surplus and limited manufacture with which to trade. Therefore commerce is insufficient to create the amount of capital needed to invest in power plants, in improvements in the transportation system, and in developing the other necessities of an industrial society.

Being primarily Muslim, the Bengalis of Bangladesh are separated by religion from the largely Hindu Bengalis of the Indian state of West Bengal. All of the Bengalis, however, share a common cultural heritage apart from religion, and all speak the same Bengali language, which has a rich literary tradition that is a thousand years old.

The country is a parliamentary democracy, secular in its intent, in contrast with the previous government of Pakistan, which has been characterized as a theocracy. The first government was formed by the Awami League, the party that played a primary role in the struggle for independence. Sheikh Mujibur Rahman, leader of the party, became the first prime minister.

The Land and Natural Resources. Bangladesh lies in the delta of several major rivers of the Indian subcontinent, primarily the Ganges (called the Padma in Bangladesh), the Brahmaputra, known as the Jamuna in its lower reaches, and the Meghna. They meet to form one river, which flows into the Bay of Bengal through a large delta formed by it. The tributaries of these and smaller rivers interlock, particularly in the monsoon season, making the central, western, and southern parts of the country a vast series of waterways surrounding low-lying, fertile land. Rainfall on the land itself is high, varying from 50 to 200 inches (1,270–5,080 mm) per year.

Because of the extensive waterways, transportation is primarily by boat. Craft ranging in size from small boats to large cargo and passenger steamers constantly ply the rivers.

The tropical climate and heavy rainfall ensure thick jungle vegetation, especially in the swamps, the Sundarbans, in the southern part of the delta. This country is plagued by almost annual cyclones, which bring great destruction and flooding, especially to the fishing villages and offshore islands. Such a storm in 1970 killed an estimated 500,000 people. Severe floods in 1974, the worst in 20 years, left 70% of the country flooded, 2,000 people dead, millions homeless, and widespread starvation.

INFORMATION HIGHLIGHTS

Official Name: The People's Republic of Bangladesh.
Head of State: President.
Head of Government: Prime Minister.
Legislature: Jatiyo Sangsad (National Parliament).
Area: 55,126 sq mi (142,776 sq km).
Boundaries: *West, north,* and *east,* India; *southeast,* Burma; *south,* Bay of Bengal.
Elevation: *Highest point,* Keokradong (4,034 feet, or 1,230 meters).
Population: 79,600,000 (1972 est.).
Capital: Dacca.
Major Languages: Bengali (official), English.
Major Religion: Islam.
Monetary Unit: Taka.
Weights and Measures: Metric System.
Flag: Red circle on a green field, with an outline of the country in gold within the red circle.
National Anthem: *Amar sonar bangla* ("My Golden Bengal").

Not all of Bangladesh is alluvial plain, however. Eastward from Chittagong, which before the destruction of the 1971 war boasted modern port facilities that could clear as many as 850 ships a year, the land rises abruptly into the Chittagong Hill Tracts. Here the jungles shelter tigers and elephants, though most of the latter have been trained as work animals. But in the hills, where land is cultivated, the primary crop is tea, rather than the rice and jute that are grown in the other agricultural regions of the country. The hill population is largely composed of colorful, non-Bengali tribes. Here too is the vast Karnaphuli Reservoir, a major source of hydroelectric power. The hills border the whole eastern part of the country.

Mineral resources, as far as is known, are almost nonexistent in this primarily alluvial land. Only three small pockets of natural gas and coal of a very low grade have been discovered.

Timber from deciduous and evergreen trees is plentiful in the southern jungles but not easily accessible. Moreover the wood is so hard as to be unusable. Consequently, sun-dried mud, bamboo, and thatch are the primary building materials in the rural areas.

In the forested areas are tigers and snakes of various kinds as well as spotted deer and wild fowl. The rivers are full of fish, a choice item in the Bengali diet.

The People. The great majority of the Bangladeshis speak Bengali, a language that forms the easternmost branch of the Indo-Aryan family. Some Bangladeshis speak Urdu, the primary language of what is now Pakistan. Urdu is written in a different script from Bengali. Others, in the hill areas of the east and north, speak languages mostly of the Tibeto-Burman family.

The Bengali speakers, most of whom are Muslims, share a physical and cultural heritage with their Hindu neighbors in West Bengal. They are generally smaller physically than most of the people of the subcontinent, tend to be dark in complexion, and have the reputation of being successful in such professional pursuits as law, medicine, politics, and the arts. Until the struggle that won independence for their country, they did not have a martial reputation. But their long and bitter struggle against a well-armed modern army produced a new military image.

The Hindus among the Bengali-speaking population, who share the physical and cultural characteristics of their Bengali-speaking Muslim brothers, are estimated to have numbered about 17 million after the vast exodus of Hindus to West Bengal in 1947. Many of these were among the 10 million people who fled to India before the Pakistan army in 1970 and 1971. Most of these returned to their homes in Bangladesh after independence, protected by the assurances of a secular government.

The only overt difference between Muslim and Hindu Bengalis is in the way the men and some women dress. Muslim men wear the *lungi*, a colorful garment resembling a sarong that is tied around the waist. The men often have beards in the Muslim style. The Hindus wear the *dhoti*, a white pleated garment brought between the legs and tied in front. Hindu women wear the sari, while in public many Muslim women wear the *burqa*, a black or white garment that covers the body from head to toe, with a veil for the eyes.

Hindu and Muslim Bengalis alike are justifiably proud of the long and rich cultural heritage they share. It has produced many poets, such as the brilliant Rabindranath Tagore.

The Urdu-speaking people of Bangladesh are mostly of the group loosely known as Biharis. Particularly during the partition in 1947, large groups of Muslims migrated to Bangladesh from the Indian state of Bihar. Other non-Bengali Muslims arrived to staff, manage, and operate the jute mills. There are also non-Bengali Muslim families who have lived in Bengal for generations and some even for centuries, tracing their ancestry not to Bengal but to the Islamic heartland to the west. These never absorbed Bengali culture. Some of this group were antagonistic to the freedom movement. But most of them chose to remain in Bangladesh after independence.

In the Chittagong Hill Tracts and farther to the north, in Sylhet, live approximately 300,000 tribal people, who speak a variety of languages some of which have never been studied. They differ radically in culture from both Hindus and Muslims. Some, such as the Chakma, are Buddhist in religion and live according to the tenets of that gentle faith. Others, such as the Lushai, Murung, and Kuki, practice primitive slash-and-burn agriculture and bride-capture.

BANGLADESH

0   100 Mi.

0   100 Km.

Water is sluiced into a rice field by means of a tin can maneuvered by ropes. Though rice is the chief food crop of Bangladesh, the country's output is not enough to feed the population.

Religion. Hinduism was the primary religious and cultural force in Bengal until the 12th century, when Islam began to assert itself. Conversions, probably largely voluntary, were made to Islam from among the Hindus. But there were also conversions made from Islam to the form of Hinduism called Vaishnavism.

Thus there are four types of Bengalis in what is now Bangladesh: (1) Muslims whose ancestors were converted from Hinduism; (2) Muslims descended from Muslim invaders from the west, who traced their lineage to the Islamic heartland in the Arabian peninsula; (3) Hindus; and (4) people neither wholly Hindu nor wholly Muslim. The last category is interestingly exemplified by the widespread syncretistic cults, such as that of Satya-pir (as it is known by Muslims) or Satya-narayana (as it is known by Hindus). Both communities engage in the rituals and festivals of their common deity.

Education. Despite the fact that Bangladesh is one of the world's poorest and most overpopulated countries, the Bengali penchant for intellectual activity expresses itself in the continuing value placed on education. There is no way of estimating the extent of elementary education. Most villages have local schools, perhaps an Islamic *madrassa* or even a traditional Sanskrit *tol*.

There are three great Western-style universities: Dacca, Rajshahi, and Chittagong. Many of the students and teachers at these universities were killed in the fight for independence. But education constitutes one of the ideals of Bangladesh. And, as in some parts of neighboring India, providing sufficient jobs for university graduates may become an acute problem.

The Economy. The economy of Bangladesh is almost entirely agricultural. The primary crops are rice, the major food staple; jute, the major export crop; fish, used both as food and as an export commodity to the Indian state of West Bengal; and tea, second to jute as a potential earner of foreign exchange. Other agricultural resources are scarce.

Some vegetables, fruits, and sugarcane are grown by peasants for home consumption, but, except for jute and tea, nothing is grown in commercial quantity. Thus Bangladesh has not been able to earn foreign exchange through exports, and it has been unable to import those essential commodities that are lacking in its own economy, including food grains, cotton for cloth, industrial raw materials, and consumer goods.

Rice. Rice occupies about 80% of the cultivated land and is grown in three separate crops. Summer rice (*aus*) is harvested in July or August, at which time autumn rice (*amon*) is planted while water from the monsoon rains is still plentiful. Winter rice (*boro*) is planted and harvested during the drier season of December through April. It is less plentiful, accounting for only 10% of the total rice production. In order to increase the size of the winter crop, high-yield strains had to be developed—as had been done in the research project at Comilla and the Rice Research Institute at Dacca—in addition to irrigation, so that the winter season could be used more efficiently.

Though rice is the most important food crop, the country's total output is not enough for the population. Furthermore, the output of most individual farms is barely sufficient to feed the farmer's family. The average farm is about 3 acres (1.2 hectares). The holdings are small, often scattered and inefficient. Many farmers have less than 3 acres, and their harvest may be no more than 2,000 pounds (900 km) per year, hardly enough for a family's needs. Although many farmers own their lands in this country of small farmers, about 20% in the period before independence were laborers who rented or sharecropped the lands owned by others.

Jute. Following the partition of India in 1947, much of the jute-processing equipment, being in and around the city of Calcutta, was left in India. Later, however, jute mills were constructed in East Pakistan. Until the war East Pakistan grew as much as 75% of the world's jute. During the period of the struggle for independence, many jute consumers who could no longer get jute from East Pakistan turned to newly developed synthetics. Therefore, when Bangladesh finally achieved independence, part of its all-important market for jute had disappeared.

Industry and Transportation. The only major commercial industry in Bangladesh is jute processing. The country is not well endowed with natural resources on which other industries can be built. Little coal or other mineral ore has been found. There is some potential for refining sugar and for the manufacture of paper and other wood-fiber products. But ways must be found to harvest and process the forests in the jungles of the south.

Another major obstacle to industrial development is the lack of an efficient transportation network. The railway system that the British developed was oriented primarily toward Calcutta. Roughly 75% of the villages of Bangladesh are more than 5 miles (8 km) from a paved road or a bus, rail, or steamer stop. In the war for independence, much of the transportation system—roads, bridges, vehicles—was destroyed. Chittagong's harbor was clogged with sunken ships.

Trade. In order to restore the transportation system and to develop industry, Bangladesh at the end of the war of independence found itself with massive needs that could be met only by imports or help from abroad. Most of the business in East Pakistan that had earned foreign exchange had been owned by West Pakistanis, whose profits benefited West rather than East Pakistan. During the war the West Pakistanis took their cash assets out of East Pakistan. So Bangladesh at the end of the war had little to export and was reported to have come out of the war with a mere $500,000 in foreign exchange.

Even though the market for jute declined during the war, Bangladesh still earns about 90% of its foreign currency from the sale of raw jute and manufactured jute. The market for its tea was West Pakistan, and after the war this was closed to Bangladesh. In the same period its textile industry was idled by the lack of cotton imports from Pakistan.

Bangladesh's natural trading partner is India. West Bengal needs cheaper fish, and Bangladesh needs the raw building materials, coke, iron, and cement that India could supply. India needs sugar, and Bangladesh needs railway cars.

One major resource of the country that has not been tapped to yield production for foreign trade is manpower. Advantage could be taken of this plentiful labor force to develop small industry, as in Hong Kong. In this way employment would increase and the export of the new industries' products would earn foreign exchange to finance essential imports.

History. Muslim rulers controlled Bengal from the 12th century until the British victory at the Battle of Plassey in 1757. After Britain won control of the area, it partitioned Bengal into Hindu and Muslim wings in 1905. The attempt was abortive, lasting only until 1912, and Bengal was to remain united until the eastern wing became East Pakistan in 1947.

The presence of the British had profound effects upon both Hindus and Muslims in Bengal. The British brought with them the English language and European-style education. The English language and Western literary forms and values are today inescapable parts of the intellectual life of the country. But from the communal point of view, the rift between Bengali Hindus and Muslims deepened. Many Hindus made rapid advances through the British commercial establishment, causing Muslims to feel disadvantaged.

In the partition of India in 1947 there was a massive movement of people. Hindus from the east went to India (though millions more chose to remain in East Pakistan), and millions of Muslims went to Pakistan. Much bloodshed accompanied these displacements, deeply scarring the feelings of the communities toward one another. Politically, a geographic monster was created that was doomed from the beginning. The nation of Pakistan had two wings that were totally unconnected, separated by India, and it was made up of two peoples of different languages and very different cultural traditions. The only common ground between the two wings of Pakistan was that of Islam, but even in this the Muslims of West Pakistan regarded the Islamic faith of many Bengalis as tainted with Hinduism. Thus the groundwork was laid in 1947 for the conflicts that led to the creation of Bangladesh.

Prelude to the War of Independence. As members of the state of Pakistan created in 1947, the Bengalis felt that they were being exploited culturally and economically. A people proud of their language and rich culture, the Bengalis resisted by force a West Pakistani attempt in 1954 to impose Urdu, the language of West Pakistan, upon them. Although they won their case, a strong element of suspicion toward West Pakistan arose. This was exacerbated by the fact that only 36% of the national budget was spent on East Pakistan, less than 20% of the country's foreign economic assistance was going to the east, less than 13% of the central government's employees were Bengalis, and less than 10% of the high-ranking army officers were from Bengal. Yet Bengal accounted for the majority of people in Pakistan and was the source of most of the country's foreign exchange. In addition, Bengalis saw themselves as providing a captive market for goods produced in West Pakistan, to the detriment of their own developing industry and handicraft.

Pro-Bengali forces began to coalesce under the leadership of Sheikh Mujibur Rahman in the mid-1960's. Despite Mujib's imprisonment for conspiracy in 1966, political agitation increased. When Yahya Khan, the commander in chief, became president of Pakistan in 1969, he allowed political parties to operate freely, withdrawing the case against Sheikh Mujib as a sign of his goodwill.

On Nov. 28, 1969, Yahya Khan announced a general election for members of a constituent assembly. In East Pakistan, Mujib and his party —the Awami League—campaigned on a platform

Sheikh Mujibur Rahman, founding father of his country, was killed in a military coup d'etat on Aug. 15, 1975.

UPI

of relative autonomy for East Pakistan within a confederation of the two wings of the country. This position was unacceptable to the politicians of the west. In December 1970 an election was held in which the Awami League won 167 of the eastern wing's 169 National Assembly seats, a majority of the 313-seat total.

Struggle for Independence. On March 1, 1971, the constituent assembly was postponed. This was interpreted in the east as a denial of majority right, and a general strike was called. The Pakistan army, consisting almost entirely of troops from the west, opened fire on the strikers on the same day, killing several. And on March 25, after several attempts at compromise had failed, Yahya ordered the army to act, declaring Bengal a "rebel" province.

From late March until the following December, the Bengalis fought a guerrilla war against the well-armed Pakistani army, which used terror tactics as the quickest way to bring the "rebels" under control. The lists of dead showed that the primary targets of the terror were members of the Awami League, students and teachers at the universities, Hindus, and professional men. As many as 10 million refugees fled to India.

In December 1971 fighting broke out on the Indo-Pakistan border in the west. The Indian army also invaded East Pakistan, and in two weeks had control of the country. The Bangladesh government-in-exile established itself in Dacca on Dec. 22, 1971. Efforts were increased to bring about the release of Sheikh Mujib, who had been imprisoned under sentence of death in West Pakistan since the preceding March. He was finally released in January 1972 and returned to Dacca to take over the leadership of the new nation. Confident that Sheikh Mujib would lead them out of economic and political trouble, the Bangladeshis gave an overwhelming vote to the Awami League in March 1973, and Sheikh Mujib continued as prime minister.

Early in 1975, Mujib amended the constitution to give himself more absolute executive authority. He adopted the title of president and banned all political parties except the Awami League.

The Great Powers' Reaction. The Bangladesh struggle was a focal point for the clarification of policy in South Asia by the Great Powers. The United States considered that it had an obligation to Pakistan, through the SEATO and CENTO pacts. Its policy was "tilted" in favor of Pakistan, and the United States labeled India as aggressor. The United States also dispatched the nuclear carrier *Enterprise* to the Bay of Bengal during the Indian invasion of the east. It was not until April 4, 1972, four months after independence and weeks after such nations as Britain and France had done so, that the United States extended diplomatic recognition to Bangladesh. Thereafter the United States became the largest foreign donor of aid to Bangladesh.

The only other strong backer of the Pakistan position was China. After the Chinese-Indian war of 1962, Pakistan had agreed to recognize Chinese territorial claims along the Tibetan border, and had been receiving aid in the form of small arms from China. To offset this alignment, the Soviet Union had been a major supplier of aircraft and arms to the Indian army—following the Indo-Pakistan war of 1965—as well as of economic aid of various kinds.

The War's Aftermath. It is hard to overestimate the damage done to the country during the struggle for independence. Sheikh Mujib declared that 3 million Bengalis died during the nine-month struggle, and over 1 million homes were destroyed. Many of the people killed were professionals—teachers, doctors, lawyers; many were trade specialists—skilled tea-plantation workers (many of whom were Hindus) and railway locomotive engineers. The tea plantations of Sylhet were ruined, and the jute mills were heavily damaged. Most of the jute-mill personnel, both management and labor, had been non-Bengali, and Bengalis now had to be trained to fill these vital roles.

Added to this vast physical destruction, including the great damage to the transportation system, was the social disruption of the country. Many of the 10 million refugees returned to find their homes in ruins.

In addition, the country was factionalized. Though much of the destruction had been the direct result of actions taken by the Pakistan army, many non-Bengalis in East Pakistan, the "Biharis," had played a role as a paramilitary force, working with the Pakistan army against the Bengalis. After the war many of the Biharis were placed in camps, and some were killed. The Biharis' future in Bangladesh remained uncertain until 1974 when Pakistan agreed to accept Bihari immigrants. In addition, in 1974, Pakistan granted diplomatic recognition to Bangladesh. In return, Bangladesh agreed not to try about 200 Pakistani prisoners of war.

On Aug. 15, 1975, President Mujib was killed in a coup d'etat by a small group of military officers. Khandaker Moshtaque Ahmed, former commerce minister, assumed the presidency. Early in November, an unsuccessful attempt to dismiss Maj. Gen. Zaiur Rahman as army chief of staff led to his assumption of control as "martial law administrator" and to his forcing Moshtaque Ahmed to yield the presidency to Abu Sadet Mohammed Sayem, chief justice of the Bangladesh Supreme Court. General Rahman remained in control, assisted by air force and army officers and an advisory council of six civilians. When, on April 21, 1977, President Sayem found it necessary to resign because of ill health, General Rahman succeeded him as president.

EDWARD C. DIMOCK, JR.*, *University of Chicago*

Bibliography

Ayoob, Mohammed, and Subrahmanyam, K., *The Liberation War* (S. Chand, New Delhi, 1972).

Chowdhury, Subrata Roy, *The Genesis of Bangladesh* (Asia Pub. 1972).

Gandhi, Indira, *India and Bangladesh* (Humanities Press 1972).

Kayastha, Ved P., *The Crisis on the Indian Subcontinent and the Birth of Bangladesh: A Selected Reading List* (Cornell Univ. Press 1972).

Nicholas, Marta, and Oldenburg, Philip, compilers, *Bangladesh: The Birth of a Nation*, general ed., Ward Morehouse (M. Seshachalam, Madras, 1972).

Sayeed, Khalid Bin, *The Political System of Pakistan* (Houghton 1967).

BANGOR, bang'gôr, a city in northeastern Maine, is the principal trading and commercial center for an area with a population of some 200,000. It is a port of entry, situated at the head of tidewater and of navigation on the Penobscot River, 128 miles (206 km) northeast of Portland. Shoes, pulp and paper, wood products, and textiles are manufactured here.

Bangor is the home of Husson College, a four-year business school, and of the Bangor Theological Seminary, a coeducational institution incorporated in 1814, which is affiliated with the United Church of Christ. The University of Maine has a campus in Orono, 8 miles (13 km) away. The community supports the Bangor Symphony Orchestra and is the home of the Northern Conservatory of Music. Bangor's public library, which has more than 400,000 volumes, is one of the largest in New England. Dow Air Force Base is on the edge of the city.

Indian gatherings were held on the site of Bangor. Its first white visitor was the French explorer Samuel de Champlain, who sailed up-river from the sea in 1604 to begin a period of French influence in the area. The first permanent settler, Jacob Buswell, arrived from Massachusetts in 1769. The town was first known as Kenduskeag (1776). It was incorporated as Bangor in 1791. It was a thriving seaport when the British occupied the town during the War of 1812. In the 19th century, Bangor was one of the leading lumber ports of the world, shipping lumber from the forests upstream. A busy ship-building industry arose in support of this commerce. Bangor was chartered as a city in 1834, and in 1931 it adopted the council-manager form of government. Population: 33,168.

ROBERT C. WOODWARD
Bangor Public Library

BANG'S DISEASE. See BRUCELLOSIS.

BANGUI, bäN-gē′, is the capital and largest city of the Central African Republic. It is situated near the geographical center of Africa, on the Ubangi (Oubangui) River, a tributary of the Congo. The city lies at the head of a stretch of waterway that is open half the year as far as Brazzaville, in the People's Republic of the Congo, 640 miles (1,030 km) south-southwest.

Bangui is a distribution and market center for a large agricultural district stretching as far north as neighboring Chad. Its river port handles most of the Central African Republic's foreign trade, major exports being cotton and coffee. Local industries include peanut and palm-oil processing mills, cotton gins, a textile mill, tanneries, a shoe factory, and a slaughterhouse.

The city consists of a spacious, formerly European center, surrounded by generally mud-built African sections. Its public electricity system, supplied by hydroelectric power, is the first in the nation. There is a jet airport.

Bangui's history began with a fort built on its site by the French in 1889 to act as a center for the pacification of the territory. The territory became known as Ubangi-Shari. A French military camp remained there for many years.

To meet administrative and military needs, the French brought in people from all over French Africa to join the existing small settlements of Mbaka, Ali, and Ndró peoples. Thus the ethnic composition became exceedingly diverse. The population, only a few hundred when the French had arrived, reached some 60,000 in 1948, and in the 1970's it approximated 150,000.

L. GRAY COWAN
State University of New York at Albany

BANISHMENT was the act of proclaiming a criminal to be an outlaw and sending him out of the country under penalties against return. In modern times the term has been superseded by "deportation" or "expulsion." See DEPORTATION; EXILE.

BANJO, ban′jō, a stringed musical instrument that was initially popularized by American Negroes. Various theories exist regarding the origin of the banjo, which in its primitive form was merely a gourd, hollowed out and strung. One theory, citing its similarity to the Senegambian *bania*, suggests that the forerunner of the banjo was introduced to the Negroes of western Africa by the Arabs. Another holds that the name is derived from the Italian *bandore* or *pandora*, a 16th century guitar.

Until the late 19th century, when the name "banjo" became fairly well established, the instrument was known by a variety of names. Thomas Jefferson, writing of the Negroes in his *Notes on Virginia* (1784), stated, "The instrument proper to them is the Banjar, which they brought hither from Africa. . . ." An 18th-century poem advised plantation owners:

> On festal days or when their work is done,
> Permit thy slaves to lead the choral dance
> To the wild banshaw's melancholy sound.

One of the earliest minstrel songs was entitled the *Banja Song* (about 1818); in 1848 this piece was included in the *Ethiopian Glee Book* as *Banga Trio for 3 Darkies*.

The banjo became a popular instrument for minstrel shows and later for Dixieland jazz, in which it is used both as a rhythm instrument and as a solo instrument. In the folk-music revival of the mid-20th century it was a featured instrument of hillbilly or bluegrass music.

The modern banjo is generally five-stringed, although six-, seven-, and even nine-stringed instruments exist. The tenor banjo, a four-stringed instrument similar in design to the five-stringed banjo, has gained in popularity.

The body of the banjo is round, like a tambourine, and is covered with vellum or parchment stretched to drumhead tension. The back is open. The strings pass from a tailpiece over a bridge on the drumhead and follow a long fretted neck to the tuning pegs. The player stops the strings with the fingers of his left hand, thus varying the pitch, and plucks with his right hand. Music for the banjo is written on the treble clef, an octave higher than its actual tones.

JOHN TASKER HOWARD
Author of "Our American Music"

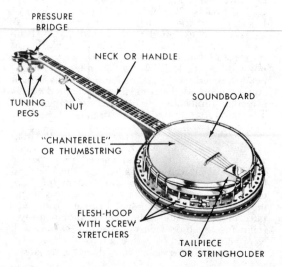

PRESSURE BRIDGE

NECK OR HANDLE

SOUNDBOARD

TUNING PEGS

NUT

"CHANTERELLE" OR THUMBSTRING

FLESH-HOOP WITH SCREW STRETCHERS

TAILPIECE OR STRINGHOLDER

BANJUL, bän-jŏŏl′, is the capital and chief port of The Gambia, the smallest nation in Africa. Until 1973 the city was known as Bathurst. It is on St. Mary's Island at the mouth of the Gambia River on Africa's west coast. The climate of the area is generally mild and pleasant, with a rainy season from June to October and a dry season from November to May.

Although the city is the seat of Anglican and Roman Catholic bishoprics, 90% of the population are Muslims. There are several hundred European residents. A government technical school provides training in carpentry and metalwork. A teachers training college is located in Yundum, 10 miles (16 km) southwest of Banjul.

The commercial activity of Banjul centers on the processing of peanuts. Peanuts are The Gambia's only important crop and the chief export shipped from Banjul's two deepwater wharves. Transportation to other parts of The Gambia is chiefly by the Gambia River and by a trunk road that joins the trans-Gambia highway. Yundum has an international airport.

Traders from the north and east are believed to have brought the Islamic religion to the Banjul area in the 12th century. Little else is known of the region's history until the mid-15th century when the Portuguese explored the Gambia River and began to trade in slaves and gold. Later, English and other traders rivaled them.

Gradually, the English gained control of the mouth of the river and in 1664 built Fort James on an island there. In 1816 a settlement was founded by British traders on St. Mary's Island and named for the 3d Earl Bathurst, who was then the British colonial secretary. Bathurst, with some surrounding land, was administered as the crown colony of Gambia from 1843 to 1866 and again from 1888 to 1965. Between these periods it was part of the British West African Settlements. When a British protectorate was established over other land along the Gambia River in 1889, Bathurst was made its capital.

In 1965 the colony and protectorate of Gambia became The Gambia, an independent nation, with Bathurst—now Banjul—as its capital. Population: (1971 est.) 36,570.

BANK OF AMERICA, a California banking institution with headquarters in San Francisco and about 900 branches throughout the state. It also has more than 40 overseas branches, of which about half are in Asia. It is the largest commercial bank in the United States and the largest nongovernment bank in the world.

With a capital investment of $150,000, the institution was founded in 1904 as the Bank of Italy by Amadeo Peter Giannini, a native Californian of Italian descent. Through a consolidation in 1930, the bank took its present formal name of Bank of America National Trust and Savings Association.

The Bank of America has initiated a number of special services. Its BankAmericard was started in 1958 as a statewide charge-account plan through which cardholders eventually became able to charge more than 150 kinds of goods and services. In 1965 the bank formed a credit subsidiary to spread its credit-card business across the nation by licensing other banks to issue the cards. The bank also operated a business services program of billing for doctors and was active in leasing. It began using computers in 1955 and became fully computerized in 1961.

BANK OF CANADA. See Banks and Banking—*Canada;* Canada—*Banking and Currency.*

BANK OF ENGLAND. See Banks and Banking—*Other Commonwealth Nations;* Great Britain and Northern Ireland—*Trade and Finance.*

BANK OF THE UNITED STATES, a banking corporation chartered by the federal government to serve as a central bank. The bank existed in two stages, known as the First Bank (1791–1811) and the Second Bank (1816–1836). Although the bank rendered important services to the economy, it became in its later years the focal point of a bitter political struggle that resulted in its eventual overthrow by President Andrew Jackson.

Hamilton's Proposal. The Constitution made no provision for the chartering of federal corporations, but this is what Alexander Hamilton proposed to Congress in his *Report on a National Bank,* Dec. 14, 1790. His plan involved the creation of a national bank that, while largely privately owned, would perform important public functions. Such a bank would act as the fiscal agency of the government and the principal depository of the Treasury, and would help to provide for the government's monetary requirements. It would lend to government. It would deal in foreign exchange. It would serve as a regulator of the country's money supply. At the same time, while directly aiding commerce and industry by its own loans, it would be a banker's bank—so that private state-chartered commercial banks could borrow from it.

Hamilton's bank was to be set up as follows. It would be chartered for 20 years and would have branches. It should not lend on land mortgages but on 60-day notes to the federal government, the states, and private individuals. It should be capitalized at $10 million, with the government subscribing to one fifth of the stock. Stock subscriptions were to be one fourth in specie (thus setting up the principle of a fractional reserve) and the rest in the government's new funded debt. Its board of directors was to be chosen by the stockholders, but no foreigners could serve on the board.

The bank was to deal only in bills of exchange, specie, and goods pledged for its loans, with 6 percent the maximum interest rate. It was to receive deposits and to issue bank notes, and these, on demand, were to be payable in specie. The notes were to be legal tender in all payments to the government. All debts of the bank, including notes but not deposits, could not exceed its capitalization.

First Bank. A bill along the lines indicated was passed in the Senate on Dec. 23, 1790, and in the House—after much debate on its constitutionality—on Feb. 8, 1791. President Washington signed the bill on Feb. 25, 1791.

The stock of the Bank of the United States was quickly subscribed and the bank began operations on Dec. 12, 1791. Its main office was set up in Philadelphia, and in time eight branches were created. This so-called First Bank was conservatively run, and it fulfilled brilliantly all of Hamilton's expectations. It handled the government's foreign-exchange operations; it was its depository, transferring public moneys from place to place; it helped importers pay their customs duties; and it assured the successful establishment of the United States Mint, toward this end

"KING ANDREW THE FIRST" is the caption for this contemporary cartoon attacking Jackson as an overbearing monarch. He holds his veto of Bank of the United States.

furnishing the bullion for the country's own coinage. It lent to the state banks and placed checks on their note circulation. As a private bank, it exercised restraint. It always paid handsome dividends.

When the charter expired in 1811, Madison was president. Like Jefferson's, his hostility to the bank had never ceased. Southern agrarians were of the same mind, and the bank's request for charter renewal was denied by Congress. The country had no controls over its monetary affairs from 1811 to 1816.

Second Bank. The turmoil in the country's finances as a result of the War of 1812—specie payments had been suspended and state banks were expanding their circulations recklessly—forced Congress' hand. The so-called Second Bank was set up by law on April 10, 1816. The provisions of its charter were similar to those of the First Bank with certain exceptions. The capitalization was to be $35 million, the government again furnishing one fifth. Five of the bank's 25 directors were to be appointed by the government. The immediate consequence of the bank's establishment was the resumption of specie payments on Feb. 20, 1817.

In its first seven years the Second Bank floundered and created hostility. In 1823, Nicholas Biddle, a wealthy Philadelphian and one of the government's five directors, became its president. Under Biddle, the Second Bank proceeded to deport itself like the central bank Hamilton had envisaged. He increased the number of branches to 29, and in several ways was able to regulate the country's money—and the ups and downs of its business. He was not averse, however, to using the bank for political purposes, and to Philadelphia's advantage, by imposing restraint on the government's own activities and by checking

overexpansion in banking in the Southwest and in New York State.

Biddle was a great banker, but his arrogance created too many enemies. Chief among these were President Jackson, the powerful Democratic party of New York State (controlled by Martin Van Buren), and the New York State bankers. Jackson, elected in 1828, was a hard-money man who was suspicious of all banks and paper money. To Jackson and the organized workingmen's parties, the bank was a monopoly, controlled by foreigners, and representing wealth.

Biddle's Whig friends in Congress introduced a bill on Jan. 9, 1832, for the bank's recharter. The existing charter was due to expire in 1836. Somewhat earlier, the Whigs had nominated Henry Clay for the presidency and voted to make the bank the issue of the campaign. The bill was passed on July 3. Jackson's quick temper was aroused. He vetoed the bill on July 10 in a message that denounced the bank as an agency of "the rich and the powerful" that was oppressing the poor. Congress did not override the veto, and the stage was set for the presidential contest. With the bank the primary issue, Clay was badly defeated in the 1832 election.

The bank might have been rechartered had it not been for Biddle's conduct. He antagonized the Treasury in his handling of foreign loans and in August 1833, to bring pressure to bear on the administration, he began to contract credit. Discounts and exchange handled by the bank fell by 20 percent, and state bank balances were sharply reduced. The country's economy—which Biddle had been insisting was his particular concern—began to suffer from a financial deflation.

Jackson's answer was to change his secretary of the treasury to one unfriendly to the bank (Roger B. Taney) and to order the withdrawal of the government deposits from the bank's branches. Biddle saw that he had lost, and he began to wind up the bank's affairs. The demise of the Second Bank in 1836 was both unfortunate and ironical. The expansion of state banking and note issue led to the sharp depression of 1837. Biddle converted the bank into a state institution with a Pennsylvania charter. It went bankrupt in 1841 as a result of his speculation in cotton.

The country was left without any regulator of its money supply and a period of "wildcat banking" ensued in the late 1840's and the 1850's. From 1837 to 1863, state banking alone remained in the field. In the latter year national banks were chartered. After the Civil War, the Treasury itself was forced to take on some of the functions of a central bank. It was not until 1914, with the establishment of the Federal Reserve System, that real central banking was finally achieved in the United States.

LOUIS M. HACKER
Columbia University

Bibliography

Catterall, Ralph C.H., *The Second Bank of the United States* (Chicago 1903).
Gouge, William M., *A Short History of Paper Money and Banking in the United States* (Philadelphia 1833; reprint, New York 1966).
Hacker, Louis M., *Triumph of American Capitalism* (New York 1940).
Hacker, Louis M., *Alexander Hamilton in the American Tradition* (New York 1957).
Hammond, Bray, *Banks and Politics in America* (Princeton, N.J., 1957).
Schlesinger, Arthur M., Jr., *The Age of Jackson* (Boston 1945).
Smith, Walter B., *Economic Aspects of the Second Bank of the United States* (Cambridge, Mass., 1953).

BANK SWALLOW, bangk swol'ō, a small swallow that breeds in summer in the Northern Hemisphere and returns in winter to South America, northern Africa, and some parts of Asia. It is known also as the *sand martin* or *sand swallow.* It has a gray-brown back and white breast, with a brown band extending across the upper breast.

Bank swallows arrive from their winter home in the early spring and spread northward as far as the borders of the Arctic Ocean. Many are seen in the United States, where groups nest along river banks or in piles of sand, clay, or gravel. To house their nests, the pairs of swallows bore tunnels very close to each other. These tunnels are usually about two or three feet (0.6 to 1 meter) deep, but they may be as much as six feet (2 meters) deep, or as little as one foot deep in difficult soils. The bank swallow's bill and feet are very weak, but pairs of birds working alternately excavate at a general rate of three to four inches (7.5 to 10 cm) a day. The inner part of the tunnel is furnished with a nest of dry grass and feathers. Three to six pure white eggs are laid in May or June. After the young no longer require brooding, the parents roost, as before nesting, in nearby marshes. The birds occupy the same bank year after year.

Bank swallows feed entirely on small insects, usually caught in the air. House sparrows sometimes occupy their burrows, and snakes, minks, weasels, and badgers have been known to enter or dig down and eat the young. Mites, lice, fleas, and fly larvae also bother them at times.

Bank swallows are in the swallow family, Hirundinidae. Their generic name is *Riparia riparia.*

CHARLES H. ROGERS
Museum of Zoology, Princeton University

Further Reading: Bent, Arthur C., *Life History of North American Flycatchers, Larks, Swallows, and Their Allies,* U.S. National Museum Bulletin 179 (Washington 1942); Peterson, Roger T., and others, *Field Guide to Birds of Britain and Europe,* 3d rev. ed. (Boston 1959).

BANKHEAD, bangk'hed, **John Hollis** (1872–1946), American politician. He was born in Moscow, Lamar County, Ala., on July 8, 1872. He was the son of John Hollis Bankhead (1842–1920), who served for 33 years in the U.S. House of Representatives and the Senate, and the brother of William Brockman Bankhead, speaker of the U.S. House of Representatives.

Educated at the University of Alabama and at Georgetown University Law School, John Bankhead started law practice in 1893 and formed a partnership with his brother in 1905 at Jasper Ala. In addition to his law practice he developed sizable business interests in coal and power. In 1903 he was elected to the Alabama legislature. He served in the U.S. Senate, as a Democrat, from 1931 until his death in Bethesda, Md., on June 12, 1946.

A leader of the Senate farm bloc, he supported most of the early New Deal measures and, with his brother, sponsored the Bankhead Cotton Control Act of 1934, repealed in 1936. In his final years he turned increasingly against some policies of Presidents Roosevelt and Truman.

BANKHEAD, bangk'hed, **Tallulah Brockman** (1903–1968), American actress, whose husky voice and flamboyant style made her one of the most colorful personalities of stage, screen, and broadcasting. She was born in Huntsville, Ala., on Jan. 31, 1903. Encouraged in her stage ambitions

HUGH M. HALLIDAY FROM NATIONAL AUDUBON SOCIETY

Bank Swallow (*Riparia riparia*)

by her father, William Brockman Bankhead (q.v.), she moved to New York City while still in her teens, and soon became part of the "Algonquin set," which met in the Hotel Algonquin and included such notables as Alexander Woollcott, Heywood Broun, and Dorothy Parker.

She made her New York stage debut in *Squab Farm* (1918), and gained stardom in 1923 in the London production of *The Dancers.* Her New York successes included *Dark Victory* (1934), *Rain* (1935), *The Little Foxes* (1939), *The Skin of Our Teeth* (1942), *A Streetcar Named Desire* (1956 revival) and *Eugenia* (1957).

She appeared in several films, including *Lifeboat* (1943). *Tallulah: My Autobiography* was published in 1952. Miss Bankhead died in New York City on Dec. 12, 1968.

BANKHEAD, bangk'hed, **William Brockman** (1874–1940), American political leader, who was speaker of the U.S. House of Representatives. He was born in Moscow, Lamar County, Ala., on April 12, 1874. His father, John Hollis Bankhead, and brother, John Hollis Bankhead II, were both U.S. senators. William was educated at the University of Alabama and Georgetown University Law School. Admitted to the bar in 1895, he practiced law briefly in Huntsville, Ala., before entering politics in 1900 as a state legislator. From 1910 to 1914 he was solicitor of the 14th Judicial Circuit of Alabama.

Elected to the U.S. Congress in 1916, Bankhead remained a representative from Alabama until his death. After years of relatively anonymous service, marked chiefly by his gift for dramatic oratory, he rose rapidly to national prominence during President Franklin D. Roosevelt's first term. He was elected chairman of the House Rules Committee in 1934, Democratic floor leader in 1935, and speaker in 1936; he held the latter office until his death at Bethesda, Md., on Sept. 15, 1940.

Bankhead was married twice and had two daughters, Evelyn and Tallulah, the actress.

BANKRUPTCY, bang′krəp-sē, in law, is regulated by statutes providing for the orderly adjustment of relationships between insolvent debtors and their creditors. The equitable distribution of available assets among creditors and the discharge from future liability of honest debtors are among the chief purposes of modern bankruptcy law. Both creditor and debtor interests are taken into account, to provide the creditor reasonable protection and to give the debtor in financial difficulties an opportunity to make a fresh start.

UNITED STATES

The Constitution gives Congress the power to establish "uniform Laws on the subject of Bankruptcies throughout the United States" (Art. I, Sect. 8, Cl. 4). The first bankruptcy act, passed by Congress in 1800, was patterned on the English laws and aimed primarily against fraudulent debtors. It was repealed in 1803, after which for nearly 40 years insolvent debtors were subject to state laws. The second federal law on bankruptcy was enacted in 1841, a consequence of the panic of 1837. An improvement on the first in providing for voluntary bankruptcy, it was repealed in 1843 when state insolvency laws again came into force. Economic difficulties during and subsequent to the Civil War, with attendant moratorium laws, caused the enactment by Congress of a third bankruptcy law in 1874; it was repealed in 1878.

The panic of 1893 and ensuing hard times were the background for the passage by Congress of the Bankruptcy Act of 1898. Although frequently amended, its main provisions are still in effect and it forms the basis of modern American bankruptcy law. Of the various amending acts, those of 1933, 1934, and 1935 attempted to help honest debtors to rehabilitate themselves, specifically the corporations which, due to depression conditions, were solvent but unable to meet maturing obligations.

The Chandler Act of June 22, 1938, has been called "the first thoroughgoing revision" of the American bankruptcy statutes in four decades. One of its provisions, designed to protect creditors from exploitation in the settlement of corporation bankruptcy cases, allows them to obtain free legal assistance from the Securities and Exchange Commission. In other bankruptcy proceedings it authorizes the court to have the bankrupt examined by a federal attorney and, if his findings so indicate, to oppose the bankrupt's petition. Important changes are made in corporate reorganization procedure and the Securities and Exchange Commission participates in most such proceedings. In sum, the later amendments to the 1898 act made important additions to the original provisions, notably in the fields of special relief for farmers and wage earners and in railroad and corporate reorganizations. Relatively minor amendments to the Bankruptcy Act were made in 1939 and frequently thereafter.

Concurrently with the gradual development of federal bankruptcy law, many states have enacted laws relating to bankruptcy and insolvency. However, when any conflict occurs federal law supersedes state law under the supremacy clause of the Constitution (Art. 6, Cl. 2).

Jurisdiction. Under the Bankruptcy Act, federal district courts exercise original jurisdiction in bankruptcy cases, with the courts of appeals and the U.S. Supreme Court acting successively on appeals. Most cases are handled wholly or in part by referees, who have powers equivalent to those of federal judges within this field. In the establishment of bankruptcy procedure, the general orders and forms promulgated by the Supreme Court have the force of law.

In addition to judges and referees, the administrative machinery of bankruptcy includes receivers or custodians, trustees, attorneys, and creditors' committees. A receiver may be appointed at any time after the filing of the petition in bankruptcy, which marks the beginning of the court's control over the assets of the debtor. It is the duty of the receiver to take possession of the debtor's property, in order to protect it and prevent loss, pending the qualification of a trustee. The trustee is an officer appointed by and directly representing the creditors. He obtains not only possession but also legal ownership of all assets of the bankrupt except those exempt under local law.

Types of Bankruptcy. The two main categories of proceedings available under the Bankruptcy Act are the "voluntary" petition, filed by the debtor himself, and the "involuntary" proceeding, filed against him by his creditors. Practically anyone with debts who has the legal capacity to make binding contracts may file a voluntary petition, regardless of his financial status.

Involuntary proceedings on the other hand can be filed only by three or more creditors, except where the total number of creditors is less than 12. The total of debts owed to unsecured creditors must be $1,000 or more. No person can be thrown into involuntary bankruptcy unless he is both insolvent in the bankruptcy sense and has committed an act of bankruptcy within four months prior to the filing of the petition against him. "Insolvent" and "act of bankruptcy" are technical terms, defined in the act.

"Insolvent" in the bankruptcy sense means not having enough property to pay one's debts. A similar term, "insolvent," in the equity sense, is significant in connection with other provisions of the act. The latter type of insolvency consists of inability to pay debts as they mature, regardless of the amount of assets and liabilities.

Any act of bankruptcy, plus insolvency in the bankruptcy sense, may serve as a basis for an involuntary petition. The acts of bankruptcy listed in the statute consist of the debtor's having: (1) disposed of or concealed, or permitted to be concealed or removed, any of his property with intent to delay or defraud his creditors; or (2) made or suffered a preferential transfer; or (3) while insolvent, allowed any creditor to obtain a lien on any of his property through legal proceedings or distraint, without having vacated or discharged such lien within a specified time; or (4) made a general assignment for the benefit of creditors; or (5) while insolvent, in either the bankruptcy or the equity sense, procured, permitted, or suffered, voluntarily or involuntarily, the appointment of a receiver or trustee to take charge of his property; or (6) admitted in writing his inability to pay his debts and his willingness to be adjudged a bankrupt.

Distribution of Property to Creditors. Once a bankruptcy proceeding has been started, by voluntary or involuntary petition, the property of the debtor (known as his estate) must be liquidated and the proceeds distributed in an orderly manner. The act expressly prescribes the priority which various kinds of unsecured debts shall have. Secured creditors are paid out of the proceeds of property on which they have valid liens, to the extent that such proceeds are sufficient. The rights of secured creditors in this respect are not affected by the priority rating of unsecured creditors.

In order to participate in the proceeds of a bankruptcy liquidation, an unsecured creditor must hold a claim which is "provable" under the express terms of the act. Typical examples of provable claims are open book accounts, promissory notes, and liabilities which have been reduced to judgment. Even a provable claim is not entitled to share automatically in the distribution of assets, but must be "allowed" by the court upon the fulfillment of certain requirements set out in the act, such as the filing of the claim within six months after the first date set for the first meeting of creditors.

The ownership of all property and assets of the debtor vests in the trustee as of the date of the commencement of the bankruptcy proceeding. Title to property which is exempt under the applicable state law or under nonbankruptcy federal law, however, is not vested in the trustee. Among typical state exemptions are homesteads, life insurance, tools of trade, and clothing. The estate of the bankrupt includes property acquired by inheritance within six months after bankruptcy.

Limitations on Debt Discharge. From the debtor's point of view, the primary object of the bankruptcy proceeding is to obtain a "discharge," the effect of which is to make certain debts unenforceable against him in the future. The discharge, if granted, is effective against all provable debts existing at the date of the filing of the petition, except as set forth in the act. Debts which are not provable cannot be discharged.

The categories of provable debts which are not affected by a discharge in bankruptcy are: (1) taxes; (2) liabilities for obtaining money or property by false pretenses or representations, for willful and malicious injuries to person or property, for alimony, for maintenance or support of wife or child, for seduction, for breach of promise accompanied by seduction, or for criminal conversation; (3) debts not scheduled in time for proof and allowance; (4) debts created by fraud, embezzlement, misappropriation or defalcation while acting as an officer or in any fiduciary capacity; (5) certain wages earned within three months prior to the commencement of the proceeding; and (6) certain debts due for moneys of an employee received or retained by an employer.

The statute provides various grounds for the denial of a discharge to a debtor. The grounds specified are that the bankrupt has: (1) committed an offense punishable by imprisonment, specified in Section 152 of the Federal Criminal Code; or (2) destroyed or failed to keep adequate books and records; or (3) obtained money or credit through a false written financial statement; or (4) fraudulently transferred property within one year of bankruptcy; or (5) obtained a discharge or composition settlement in a former proceeding within six years; or (6) refused to obey a lawful order or to answer a material question in a bankruptcy proceeding; or (7) failed satisfactorily to explain losses and deficiencies of assets.

RICHARD L. HIRSHBERG, *Attorney at Law*

BRITAIN AND THE COMMONWEALTH

Bankruptcy legislation in Britain may be said to begin with a statute of Henry VIII, passed in 1542, which was designed solely to afford relief to the creditors of fraudulent debtors. The first recognition of bankruptcy as distinguished from fraudulent debt appears in an act (1571) of Elizabeth I which provided for the sale for the benefit of his creditors of the goods of a trader who failed to meet his obligations. By acts passed in 1706 and 1712 bankrupts who had paid a dividend might, with the consent of their creditors, be discharged by the Court of Chancery, where bankruptcy jurisdiction lay until a special Court of Bankruptcy was created in 1831. By an act of 1849 composition by arrangement was made possible, and by 1861, the bankruptcy laws covered all insolvents.

Two important acts were passed in 1869, one remodeling the Bankruptcy Court and empowering the county courts to deal with local cases, and the other virtually abolishing imprisonment for debt. Severe punishment of fraudulent debtors was provided for by an act of 1883, which also empowered the Board of Trade to appoint official receivers. The bankruptcy laws were further modified in 1890 and 1913, and existing law is to be found mainly in the consolidating Bankruptcy Act, 1914, as amended by the Bankruptcy (Amendment) Act, 1926, together with the Bankruptcy Rules made under the 1914 act.

Jurisdiction in bankruptcy since the 1914 act lies in the High Court of Justice and such county courts as have not been excluded by order of the lord chancellor. The King's Bench division exercised this jurisdiction until 1921, when it was transferred to the Chancery division. General supervision of bankruptcy administration is the responsibility of the Board of Trade.

In general, any debtor may, in certain circumstances which are defined in the 1914 act, be made bankrupt in England and Wales. Any court having jurisdiction in bankruptcy cases in the district in which a debtor resides or carries on business may make a receiving order against him, either on his own petition, or on that of creditors whose claims amount to £50 or over, and the "acts of bankruptcy" on which the petition is to be founded are defined in the 1914 act. As soon as a receiving order is made, an official receiver is placed in charge of the debtor's property, and the debtor must submit a statement of his affairs to the official receiver. A meeting of creditors is then summoned by the official receiver to decide whether the court should be asked to adjudge the debtor bankrupt. Bankrupt estates are administered by trustees appointed by a majority in value of the creditors.

In Scotland, where bankruptcy was placed on a legal footing by an act of 1696, the estate of a debtor is realized and distributed among his creditors in a process of sequestration governed by the Bankruptcy (Scotland) Act of 1913. This process of sequestration is similar in most important ways to the English bankruptcy process.

Bankruptcy laws in the other Commonwealth countries closely follow the English Bankruptcy Acts. Much of the bankruptcy legislation of these countries is now embodied in consolidating acts, most of which were later amended.

In Australia, for example, a basic consolidating act was passed in 1924 (Act No. 37, 1924, now known as the Bankruptcy Act 1924–1960), while the Canadian parliament passed basic Bankruptcy Acts in 1919 and 1952. The basic New Zealand law is the consolidated Bankruptcy Act of 1908.

In India, also, English law has been the model for local legislation, and the Indian Provincial Insolvency Act, 1907 (which together with the Presidency Towns Insolvency Acts, 1909, formed the basis of the Indian code) has been used as a convenient bankruptcy law for application to colonial territories until they framed their own legislation.

RICHARD E. WEBB
British Information Services, New York

Bibliography
United States
Collier, William M., *Encyclopedia of Bankruptcy Law*, 14th ed., ed. by James W. Moore (Albany 1940 and supplements to date).
Nadler, Charles E., *The Law of Bankruptcy*, 2d ed., ed. by Saul L. and Myron J. Nadler (Atlanta 1965).
Zwanzig, William, *Bankruptcy Practice and Procedure*, 2d ed., ed. by Robert W. Newlon (Indianapolis 1954 and supplements to date).

Britain and the Commonwealth
Cruchley, Ivan, *A Handbook on Bankruptcy Law and Practice*, 2d ed. (London 1964).
Duncan, Lewis, and Honsberger, John D., Bankruptcy *in Canada*, 3d ed. (Toronto 1961).
Hajek, E.J., *Principles of Bankruptcy in Australia* (Brisbane 1962).
Sastry, L. Subrahmanya, *Provincial Insolvency Act with Rules*, 4th ed., by R.B. Seth (Allahabad, India, 1963).

BANKS, bangks, **Ernie** (1931–   ), American baseball player, who ranked as the greatest power hitter ever to play shortstop. He was the first player to receive the National League's Most Valuable Player award two years in a row (1958 and 1959).

Ernest Banks was born in Dallas, Texas, on Jan. 31, 1931. In 1950 he joined the Kansas City Monarchs of the Negro League. After two years in the U.S. Army, he was sold to the Chicago Cubs in September 1953, and he became the regular shortstop until he moved to first base in 1961.

A right-handed batter, the 6-foot 1-inch Banks won the National League home-run crown in 1958 with 47, a record for shortstops. He led the League again in 1960 with 41 and by 1965 had passed the 400 mark in home runs. He led both leagues in runs batted in with 129 in 1958 and 143 in 1959.

In the field, Banks set major league fielding records for shortstops by committing the fewest errors in a season (12) and compiling a .985 mark in 1959. He set another record by playing 424 consecutive games at the start of his career. Nicknamed Mr. Cub, he was selected for the All-Star squad six times as a shortstop and twice as a first baseman.

BILL BRADDOCK, *New York "Times"*

BANKS, bangks, **Sir Joseph** (1743–1820), English naturalist. He was born in London, on Feb. 13, 1743. On his initiative, as a student, lectures in botany were given at Oxford for the first time, and he was elected a member of the Royal Society at the age of 23. The same year (1776) he undertook an expedition to Newfoundland and Labrador, bringing back a rich collection of plants and insects. When Capt. James Cook embarked on his first voyage of discovery, which circled the globe (1768–1771), Banks accompanied him as a naturalist, fitting out the ship, the *Endeavour*, at his own expense.

As a result of his observations, the marsupial fauna of Australia were first made known to Western science; his notes on the expedition, however, were not published until 1900. Banks Peninsula, on South Island in New Zealand, was named after him by Cook, and through Banks' efforts the breadfruit tree was introduced into the West Indies.

In 1772 Banks explored Iceland and the Hebrides, discovering the great geysers in the former and making important observations on rock stratifications in the latter islands. He was elected president of the Royal Society in 1778, retaining that office until his death, and was made a baronet in 1781. He died at Isleworth, near London, on June 19, 1820. He left his library and celebrated botanical collection to the British Museum.

BANKS, bangks, **Nathaniel Prentiss** (1816–1894), American army officer, congressman, and governor. He was born in Waltham, Mass., on Jan. 30, 1816. Largely self-taught, he worked himself up from the position of bobbin boy in a cotton factory to the editorship of a weekly newspaper. He read law, was admitted to the bar, and soon became active in politics.

Banks was elected to the Massachusetts legislature in 1849 and served as speaker (1851–1852). In 1853 he presided at the state constitutional convention and the same year was elected to Congress as a Coalition Democrat (he subsequently was to represent four different party groupings in nine Congresses). After a bitter contest with William Aiken, a slaveholder of South Carolina, during which all legislative business was blocked, Banks was elected speaker of the House in 1856. None of his decisions while speaker was ever reversed by the House. He was Republican governor of Massachusetts from 1858 to 1861.

At the start of the Civil War, Banks was appointed major general of volunteers. He conducted operations in the Shenandoah Valley and directed the siege of Port Hudson. In 1864, much against his judgment, he was placed in command of the Red River expedition, which resulted in disaster for the Federal forces. Banks was widely censured for this failure and was relieved of his command. Years later, General Ulysses S. Grant vindicated him by placing the responsibility for the expedition on Bank's superiors. However, Banks could not be cleared of the charge of a lack of skill as a military tactician. After the war he again served in Congress (1865–1873, 1875–1879, 1889–1891).

Further Reading: Harrington, Fred, *Fighting Politician: Major General N.P. Banks* (Philadelphia 1948).

BANKS, bangks, **Thomas** (1735–1805), English sculptor. He was born in London on Dec. 29, 1735. He studied sculpture at the Royal Academy, London, and, from 1772 to 1779, on a scholarship in Rome. In 1785 he became a member of the Royal Academy. He died in London on Feb. 2, 1805.

Bank's first success was *The Death of Epaminondas* (1763), a bas-relief. His other works include *Cupid Catching a Butterfly* (1781), which was bought by Catherine the Great of Russia; the colossal *Achilles Enraged for the Loss of Briseis* (1784); and monuments in Westminster Abbey and St. Paul's Cathedral.

Further Reading: Bell, C.F., *Annals of Thomas Banks* (London 1938).

BANKS AND BANKING

MODERN BANKS, with spacious lobbies and open counters, provide a friendly atmosphere for their customers.

BANKS AND BANKING. Economic activity as it is known in the Western world could not survive without a continuing flow of money and credit. The economies of all market-oriented nations depend on the efficient operation of complex and delicately balanced systems of money and credit. Banks are an indispensable element in these systems. They provide the bulk of the money supply, as well as the primary means of facilitating the flow of credit.

1. Banks and Services

A bank is a business organization that receives and holds deposits of funds from others, makes loans or extends credit, and transfers funds by written order of depositors. The term is occasionally but inaccurately applied to commercial banks only, because of the peculiar types of services that commercial banks perform: they maintain and create demand deposits (checking accounts), which are part of a nation's money supply. (A bank creates a demand deposit when, for instance, it lends a customer $100 by crediting that sum of his checking account—the customer immediately has $100 to spend by writing a check.) The ability to maintain, create, or extinguish demand deposits is critical in the economic life of the nation.

Because the term "bank" denotes a variety of institutions of deposit, no distinction is made among categories in discussing banking services except to note when a particular activity or service is restricted to a particular type of institution. The facilities of banks are available to both individuals and businesses, whether they are depositors, borrowers, or general-service customers.

Services to Depositors. Individuals and businesses alike may maintain either demand deposits or time deposits.

Demand deposits represent deposits of funds (in commercial banks only) against which depositors may write checks or drafts. Checks are orders from the depositor to the bank to pay a specified sum to a designated recipient, or the bearer. Checking accounts offer depositors safety for their funds, as well as convenient transferability of deposits to pay for purchases or to satisfy

CONTENTS

Section	Page
1. Banks and Services	169
2. The Role of Credit	170
3. Origin and Development	172
BANKING IN THE UNITED STATES	
4. History of U.S. Banking	174
5. Commercial Banks	176
6. Trust Service	180
7. Clearinghouse Activities	181
8. Mutual Savings Banks	182
9. Federal Reserve System	183
OTHER FINANCIAL INSTITUTIONS AND ACTIVITIES	
10. Installment Lending	184
11. Mortgage Banking	185
12. Savings and Loan Associations	186
13. Investment Banking	187
14. Life Insurance and Pension Funds	188

Section	Page
15. Government Agencies	189
16. Bankers' Associations	191
BANKING OUTSIDE THE UNITED STATES	
17. Canada	192
18. Other Commonwealth Nations	192
19. Western Europe	193
20. Eastern Europe	194
21. South America	195
22. Africa	196
23. Asia	196
INTERNATIONAL BANKING	
24. Banking and World Trade	197
25. International Monetary Fund	198
26. Bank for International Settlements	199
27. World Bank	199
BANKING AS A CAREER	
28. Positions in Banking	201
BANKING TERMS	
29. Glossary	

debts. A checking account also gives the depositor receipts for his payments in the form of canceled checks. In addition to providing payment records to depositors, a checking account also gives them periodic (usually monthly) accounts of their financial balances. As the use of electronic accounting equipment expands, more banks furnish bill-paying services to their customers. Many offer credit-card plans whereby charges are automatically deducted from the purchasers' accounts.

Checking-account customers may be allowed overdrafts, which means that checks drawn in excess of the amount on deposit will be honored by the bank, rather than being refused payment or "bounced." Fees are assessed against the offender's account for this service. Commercial banks may regularly receive payroll checks directly, from large employers especially, and credit them to the accounts of individual employees. Individual depositors can arrange to have fixed sums transferred to savings accounts or to the purchase of U.S. savings bonds (under the payroll savings plan).

Commercial banks will certify checks drawn by depositors, which assures the payee that sufficient funds are on deposit and earmarked to cover the check. Similarly, banks will issue letters of credit to depositors for use during travel abroad.

For most services to demand depositors, commercial banks levy service charges on a "metered" or frequency basis. "Regular" checking accounts usually require a minimum balance against which service charges are measured. "Special" checking accounts, on the other hand, normally do not require a minimum balance; charges are based on so much per check, deposit, or other entry. Commercial banks in the United States are prohibited by law from paying interest on demand deposits.

Time deposits include savings deposits, savings accounts, share accounts—and even certificates of deposit. These normally pay interest based on the profitability of the savings institution. Interest is paid partly because the depositor gives up transferability of the funds (only the depositor may make withdrawals), and partly because the "bank" can invoke a waiting period before funds may be withdrawn. This period, varying with state or federal law, is commonly 30 days. Some time deposits, such as Christmas clubs and vacation clubs, are really a form of forced saving and do not pay interest.

Depository services are provided in several forms by banks and savings institutions. Deposits may be made in person during regular banking hours. In addition, "drive-in" and "walk-in" windows, open before or after regular hours, often offer convenient service to customers in such locations as shopping centers or transit terminals. Night depositories are particularly convenient and important to businessmen because they offer added protection for cash receipts. Deposits especially, but withdrawals as well, usually can be made by mail.

Services to Borrowers. Banks are in business to make money. They levy service charges and fees, but their primary source of income is interest charged on loans. This interest may be assessed at the end of specified periods ("straight interest") or it may be deducted from the principal sum at the outset ("discount"). The type of loan(s) that a specific kind of bank or financial institution may make depends on the law.

Commercial (demand deposit) departments of commercial banks typically concentrate on short-term (often self-liquidating) loans to businesses. They also make unsecured "signature" loans to individuals (with or without cosigners), as well as secured loans for the purchase and carrying of securities. These notes may have specified maturities or be payable on demand.

Savings institutions and commercial-bank savings departments make personal installment loans to finance the purchase of consumer durables, especially appliances and automobiles. Installment loans for other specific purposes such as "education loans" or "travel loans" are made for terms up to three years. Mortgage and property improvement loans are available from commercial-bank savings departments and all savings institutions.

Customers of commercial banks may often arrange lines of credit under which the bank will lend up to an agreed limit as the borrower requires. This has long been common for business purposes; it is now accepted for personal credit.

General Services. Although banks often give deposit customers preferential treatment in granting loans or providing other services, they also perform a wide range of services to the general public for a fee. In some few instances, the services are provided free. More often, certain services offered free to customers—especially depositors—involve a charge to the general public. Check-cashing and money-exchanging are examples.

Banks usually rent safe deposit boxes. They sell travelers checks or foreign exchange at a set rate. They also sell cashiers' checks.

Particularly for customers but also for others in some instances, banks will collect noncash items such as drafts, bills of exchange, or acceptances. With increased use of electronic data-processing equipment, banks prepare payrolls, handle accounting, and prepare and collect bills for local businesses. They will also verify credit on request.

Commercial banks in particular offer investment and business counseling. Bank trust departments will manage estates and investment portfolios, usually for ½ of 1 percent of the market value of the capital.

WILLIAM N. KINNARD, JR.
University of Connecticut

2. The Role of Credit

The banking business has been defined as dealing in money and instruments of credit. Credit is sometimes described merely as "a promise to pay money," or as "permission to use the capital of another person." Abstractly it is referred to as "the power which one person has to induce another to put economic goods at his disposal for a time on promise of future payment." The time element is often stressed as the essential feature of credit.

Commercial loans constitute a major outlet for bank credit. In the typical commercial credit operation, funds are advanced to manufacturers or merchants on their own promissory notes, or drafts drawn on customers are discounted. The bank thus substitutes its own credit for that of the borrower or his customers. The credit of the bank is transferable and is generally accepted as a means of payment. A bank loan is thus equivalent to transforming the credit of the borrower into money.

The extension of credit does not of itself imply an increase in wealth. But the process of gathering together the community's capital and putting it to use, which is effected largely through credit and credit instruments, has the net result of creating new wealth.

Credit and the Economy. The main function of credit is to facilitate the exchange of goods. Every extension of credit involves an advance of funds, goods, or services. Credit, like money, finds its main function in the field of production. Through its services in facilitating the exchange of goods, credit has helped make possible modern large-scale production and the widespread division of labor.

Credit renders still another important service: it promotes a fuller utilization of individual capacity and enterprise. Through credit advances, fixed forms of property may be converted into a purchasing medium. Also, capital temporarily advanced to others may be released in whole or in part. A merchant, for example, may be carrying many of his customers' purchases on open-book account. Pending the payment of these accounts, his resources are diminished and his activities curtailed. But if he can get credit, either from his suppliers or his bank, his tied-up capital is virtually released to him, and his productive operation is not restricted by lack of working capital. Quite frequently, credit puts capital into the hands of capable businessmen beyond the value of their individual possessions. Few businessmen could operate on a large scale if they had to depend on their own capital accumulation.

Classes of Credit. Credit may be classified under two general headings: (1) as to the recipient, and (2) as to time. Under the first heading, credit is either public or private.

Public credit is credit used by the people as a whole through their government—national, state, and local. It is evidenced by the issuance of interest-bearing bonds, notes, or bills, or by the issue of paper money.

Private credit is the credit used by industrial or mercantile concerns, by individuals, and by banks. It embraces all forms of credit that relate to private enterprise. A concern may issue bonds to assist in building a plant or to finance the carrying of current assets. A concern may give notes to a bank to provide funds with which to purchase goods, meet payrolls, or discount bills.

Bank credit relates to the credit which banks enjoy by reason of their capital structure and deposits as well as to the credit they obtain from other sources. A bank may obtain credit from its correspondent banks, from the central bank, from government agencies, or from the open market through the sale of acceptances.

Under the second—or time—heading, credit may be classified as to the length of time for which it is granted, which corresponds in general to the uses to which it is put. Accordingly the subdivisions are (1) investment (long-term, or fixed capital) credit; (2) commercial (short-term) credit; and (3) intermediate credit, covering borderline cases between the other two. Commercial credit may be further divided into producer and consumer credit.

Investment credit consists of funds borrowed for a long period of time. They are usually invested in fixed capital goods, such as railroads, land, buildings, and machinery. Long-term credit is usually obtained through the sale of bonds, mortgages, or debentures in the securities market.

Commercial credit is granted for only a short period. When used in the conversion of goods from the raw to the finished product, in the distribution of goods, or in the financing of service organizations, it is called *producer credit*. Generally speaking, credit so employed is kept as liquid as possible by investing it in current assets that in the normal course of business will be converted into cash and used to retire the obligation.

Consumer or installment credit, which is also classified as short-term credit, consists of credit obtained by individuals from merchants, commercial banks, loan companies, credit unions, finance companies, and other private lenders. Sometimes called retail credit, it is normally liquidated from earnings.

Intermediate credit comprises loans that are used jointly for short-term needs and for fixed

capital purposes such as plant improvements. The loans are generally of a long-term character, even though the funds may be partially invested in current assets that are constantly changing—from merchandise, to receivables, to cash.

Foundations of Credit. The granting of credit is based on the creditor's confidence in the debtor's willingness and ability to discharge his obligation in accordance with the terms of the agreement. The willingness of the debtor is entirely a matter of character and integrity. Ability to pay involves impersonal as well as personal factors. The personal factor may be described as the business capacity of the debtor. The impersonal factor is the marketability of the debtor's product. The primary factors of credit granting are the three *C's*: character, capacity, and capital. There is another important factor—conditions—which may be termed a fourth *C*. This has to do with conditions in the particular industry in which the company is engaged and also with general business conditions.

Character. This is the basic element in the extension of credit. While character does not of itself determine the amount of credit to be granted, it is a basic factor in both large and small grants of credit. The applicant's character as a moral risk is tested by his background, habits, associates, style of living, record for honest dealing, and reputation for paying bills—in fact everything that has a bearing on the applicant's willingness to discharge his obligation properly.

Capacity. A man may be honest in every sense of the word, but if he is deficient in ability or capacity, his desire to pay may be of no avail. The credit grantor takes into consideration the applicant's business experience, general education, inclination toward caution or the contrary, and his ability to operate his business profitably. The grantor determines whether the applicant has been tested for operating under adverse conditions, and whether he can make really advantageous use of the credit requested.

Capital. To meet the keen competition to which he is subjected, a businessman must have sufficient funds at his disposal. He must be able to equip his plant at least as adequately as his competitors. He must be prepared to meet any reasonable credit terms on a fully competitive basis. He must be able to discount his bills, and meet his payrolls. These are just a few of the things for which he will require sufficient permanent capital if he is to operate effectively.

In certain cases the credit applicant's capital, if inadequate, may be supplemented by outside capital, or collateral. Similarly, when capacity is not proved, collateral may be required. Endorsement by a responsible person, or a pledge of collateral by some outside source, may make it possible for a bank to grant credit.

Conditions. The alert credit grantor never overlooks general business conditions in the particular industry in which the applicant's company is engaged. The stage in the business cycle, and trends and developments in the local and surrounding areas are important factors to be considered. See also CREDIT, ECONOMIC; MONEY.

LOUIS J. ASTERITA
Insured Credit Services, Inc.

BANKING OPERATIONS in the 15th century are portrayed in this medieval miniature. The man at the right is depositing gold coins.

3. Origin and Development

Banking in the sense of money holding, money-lending, and money changing is as old as history. At least 5,000 years ago Sumerian and Babylonian priests were accepting deposits and making loans. Further refinements were slowly added, and by the early Christian era, private and public banks were accepting demand and time deposits, paying interest, making loans, and transferring funds by written order. However, they were not yet using paper money, checks, or fractional reserves.

Moneylending and Money Changing. With the decline in trade that followed the fall of Rome, banking practically disappeared from the Western world. It remained very much alive, however, in the Arabic countries and in China, where paper money and checks were already being used. When European trade again began to thrive in the 11th century, banking, aided by the knowledge reimported from the Middle and Far East, reawakened. Like capitalism, the modern commercial bank (a bank which accepts deposits, discounts loans, and creates money) had its roots in the Italian city-states of the Middle Ages and the Renaissance. It originated in the twin occupations of moneylending and money changing.

The religious orders and the Jews first made moneylending a thriving business. As early as the 10th century, monasteries that had accumulated a treasure from donations and rents were making loans to peasants, landowners, and the local nobility. Because these were consumption loans at very high interest rates (30 percent and often higher), they violated the church's rule against usury. This opened opportunities for the Jews, who were not bound by the Christian prohibition against interest-bearing loans. Aided by a knowledge of banking and some capital funds brought from the Middle East, the Jews, by the 11th century, were handling most of this essentially pawnbroking business.

Meanwhile, events in the monetary sphere brought back the ancient profession of money changing. During most of its history the medieval world suffered from a shortage of gold and silver and an oversupply of mints. Every major lord and some minor lords in Europe had the right to coin money. In an effort to increase their revenue, these masters of the mints kept reducing the silver content of their coins, and by the 11th century, Europe was overrun by a multiplicity of debased coins. Because the average citizen did not know the exact value of these moneys, he turned to the initiated for guidance. Soon money changers were going from fair to fair changing new coins for old, and domestic coins for foreign. In a short time, they extended their operations to include moneylending and the solicitation of interest-bearing deposits.

Broadening of Services. By the middle of the 12th century the Jews, who were the leading money changers and moneylenders, had begun to make business loans. They had become bankers instead of mere pawnbrokers. Because the business appeared to be lucrative, powerful rivals soon ended the Jewish hegemony. By the middle of the 13th century the Italians from Lombardy had taken over the leadership. They sometimes had the privilege of minting coins. They could solicit deposits, which the Jews were often prohibited from doing. They also managed to get around the church's edict against interest. They did not make loans and charge interest, but bought and sold bills of exchange payable in foreign currency. They were, therefore, merchants in banking who hoped by the difference in exchange to make a profit equal to the interest rate they would have charged for a loan. The bill of exchange was very old; it may have been used in Babylon, and a variant of it was used in Rome. The Genoese either developed it independently or brought it back from the East at about 1150, but it was not widely used until after 1350.

The Italians had another immense advantage: they were ideally situated to act as bankers to the church, the most important bank customer of the day. The church's Curia collected revenues all over the Christian world. At first the complications of collecting and changing money and converting payments in kind were handled by ecclesiastical officers. But by 1213 bankers from Siena were lending to German churchmen, and in 1233 they became fiscal agents for the papacy. This was a great windfall, for the deposits that were credited to Rome often remained with the same banker for many years.

Hazards for Banking Families. Banking was immensely profitable in the short run, but it was also a hazardous occupation, with ultimate disaster an odds-on chance. In 1298 the Bonsignori, the largest Siena banking house, failed and carried the whole city with it, but Florence was already waiting to pick up the pieces. By 1338, Florence had 80 important banking firms, of which the Bardi, the Peruzzi, and the Acciaiuoli were the most important. The Bardi, the largest, had 15 partners, and employed at least 100 clerks in branches that stretched from Cyprus to London. All three houses extended large credits to European sovereigns. For example, Edward III owed the Bardi the equivalent of $3.5 million in modern money. In the 1340's the "big three" collapsed when they could not collect the debts owed by Edward and by Robert of Naples.

Once again there were families eager and ready to fill the void left by wholesale bankruptcy. Of these, the Medici (1397-1494) were the most famous, although they were never as big as the Bardi or the Peruzzi.

By the time of the Medici, rivals were beginning to appear in other countries. In France the fabulous Jacques Coeur (1395–1456) is said to have amassed a fortune of $10 million before he went broke because his royal debtors defaulted. In the Low Countries, the Louchart and Cresping families did well. But the most successful of all the medieval bankers was the Fugger family of south Germany. They were the money power behind the house of Habsburg as well as the successors to the Medici as fiscal agents for the Curia. At one time the family is reputed to have been worth at least $50 million, but with the fall of the Holy Roman Empire, which they had done so much to maintain, the house disappeared from the business world.

Peculiarly enough, none of the great medieval banking families contributed any major innovations to finance, although Jakob Fugger was an extraordinary innovator in general business administration. Checks, which are really bills of exchange payable on demand, appeared as early as 1374, but they were not used on any broad scale until much later. Similarly, endorsements were used occasionally, but not commonly until after 1600. The innovations in banking during the time of the Medici came through the formation of the first public banks, the so-called exchange banks or transfer banks, the first of which was the Bank of Barcelona (1401). Similar to the modern clearinghouse these banks were created to eliminate abuses that had developed in money changing. Theoretically, an exchange bank could not make loans, but this edict was often violated. The Casa di San Giorgio in Genoa (1407) made short-term loans to the government. The Banco della Piazza di Rialto in Venice (1587) was very similar to a private bank. The Amsterdam Wisselbank (1609) made loans to the East India Company. The Bank of Hamburg (1619) had a twin that made loans on merchandise collateral.

Advances in the 17th Century. Banks of issue first appeared in the late 17th century. Johan Palmstruch, founder of the Bank of Stockholm, issued the first bank note in 1661, but the idea first became important in England after Charles I expropriated the private deposits in the mint in 1640. Depositors turned to the goldsmiths, who began to accept time and demand deposits, against which they issued drafts. Thus the check system appeared. The goldsmiths soon found they could issue more in drafts than they had in coin, and they began to use drafts instead of cash in making loans. They soon overextended

THE BETTMANN ARCHIVE

A 17TH CENTURY French banking office is depicted on the title page of a book on foreign exchange rates.

themselves, and when the government suspended in 1672, many goldsmiths could not meet their obligations. The trade fell into disrepute, but banking came back strongly with the creation of the Bank of England in 1694.

Banking in the 17th century became altogether different from that of the earlier years, and took the general shape of banking as it exists now. No matter how grandiose, banking in the 16th century had been a family matter in which immense unproductive credits were granted to economically inefficient kings and noblemen. But in the 17th century risks were more widely spread. Four things were especially important in the transformation: (1) the appearance of public banks of issue; (2) the opening of stock exchanges, which enabled bankers to float securities; (3) the introduction of systematic taxation, which made governments more responsible; and (4) the development—out of the wholesale, shipping, and commission business—of the modern merchant banker who discounted bills and dealt in government securities.

All these innovations appeared in their best light in Amsterdam, which after 1640 became the center of bullion and foreign exchange dealing.

One of the chief reasons for the formation of the Bank of England was the enviable record of the Bank of Amsterdam in making ample supplies of credit available at low interest rates.

HERMAN E. KROOSS, *New York University*
Author of "American Economic Development"

BANKING IN THE UNITED STATES

4. History of U.S. Banking

Colonial Period to 1863. Banking in the United States began in the 18th century when individuals, merchants, and colonial governments informally—but frequently—loaned money to one another. The first bank in the nation, the Bank of North America, organized in Philadelphia, was chartered by the Continental Congress in 1781 primarily to aid in financing the Revolutionary War. By 1790 the Bank of New York and the Bank of Massachusetts had received state charters. In this early period, both chartered banks and private banks financed trade with self-liquidating loans. Credit was extended to merchants to buy inventories which, when sold, provided funds to repay the loan. Loans were ordinarily made in currency—notes issued by the lending bank—because deposit money (checking accounts) had not yet become an acceptable medium of exchange.

Upon the urging of Alexander Hamilton, Congress in 1791 established the First Bank of the United States with a 20-year charter. It was a large bank by colonial standards and competed successfully with state banks in extending credit and issuing currency. Each year the First Bank issued $5 million in fully redeemable notes, which was 20 percent of all bank notes circulating. In addition, the First Bank performed central bank functions by serving as the fiscal agent for the U.S. Treasury and by exerting pressure on state banks to redeem their notes at full value. State bankers interpreted this action as unwarranted federal meddling and immediately began to undermine the Bank.

The First Bank was terminated in 1811 when, in spite of its functional success, Congress failed to renew its charter. Its dissolution complicated the financing of the War of 1812 and contributed to wartime inflation. Without competition from federal banks, the number of state banks grew with minimum regulation. Bank failures were common, and the public became skeptical of all bank notes.

In 1816 Congress recognized these problems and created the Second Bank of the United States. It was similar to the First Bank but had greater lending capacity. The Second Bank's history was brief and chaotic. Under the aggressive direction of the central banker, Nicholas Biddle, the Second Bank restored redemption values to bank notes and limited unnecessary credit expansion. Biddle's success antagonized state bankers and states' rights politicians. Andrew Jackson vigorously opposed the Second Bank as a federal encroachment on states' rights. As President he vetoed the charter extension and ended the life of the bank in 1836.

State banks dominated the industry until the Civil War. Following the pattern of legislation in New York, several states opened banking to anyone able to meet minimum standards. Bank performance in this period of free banking was less than satisfactory. States did not require banks to hold sufficient reserves to meet depositors' claims or to redeem notes. Bank failure was not unusual. In some areas, especially the West, free banking became "wildcat" banking. Wildcat banks were situated in remote places so that customers could not readily present bank notes for redemption. With each bank issuing its own notes, counterfeiters operated with incredible success. Despite these shortcomings, free bank financing contributed significantly to westward expansion.

Creation of National Bank System. Problems of financing the Civil War and uncontrolled free banking led Congress, in 1863, to pass the National Banking Act. The act provided for a system of national banks, established in local communities through the issuing of federal charters. The act also created a uniform national currency by limiting note issues of national banks and by requiring every national bank to redeem at full value bank notes issued by other national banks. National banks were also required to maintain adequate cash reserves to meet creditors' claims. Continuing stability was assured by creating the position of comptroller of currency. The comptroller regulated the type and amount of credit extended by national banks.

To expedite development of the national banking system, Congress levied a 10 percent tax on all new state bank note issues. The impact was immediate. By 1866 the number of nationally chartered banks increased to more than 1,600 and accounted for 75 percent of all bank deposits. Circulation of state bank notes declined and their replacement by national bank notes stabilized the value of currency. Public confidence in the national currency ended the threat of currency redemption panics. However, the act made no allowances for seasonal currency needs, nor did it provide a flexible lending mechanism. Its quantitative restrictions severely limited loans in the South, where credit was desperately needed to finance reconstruction. Limits on real estate lending prevented national banks from effectively supporting migration to the West. Finally, the act, by supporting decentralized unit banking, provided no unified system to channel excess bank funds in New England into the credit-starved South and West.

The banking industry began rapid expansion late in the 19th century. The number of banks increased from 2,000 in 1866 to 13,000 in 1900 and to 27,000 in 1913. The typical new bank was state chartered. It located in a small rural community and supplied credit to farmers. State bank expansion was facilitated by public acceptance of checking accounts, which reduced the discriminatory effect of the prohibitive tax on state bank notes. National banks grew more in size than in number. Numerically they became a smaller proportion of the banking industry while simultaneously increasing their share of all bank deposits. The largest of these banks, located in financial centers, supplied credit to an expanding industrial empire centered about railroads.

The initial stability imparted by the national banking system did not endure. Financial panics in 1893 and 1907 stimulated Congress to appoint a National Monetary Commission whose recommendations led to the Federal Reserve Act of 1913.

Creation of Federal Reserve. The Federal Reserve Act created a central banking system composed of 12 regional Reserve banks and member commercial banks. The Reserve banks were unified by a Board of Governors who determined policy for the system. The act required all na-

BARRED WINDOWS separated the tellers from the customers in the typical American bank of the early 20th century.

THE BETTMANN ARCHIVE

tional banks to become members and invited state banks to join, provided they met minimum requirements. Each member bank had to maintain reserves on deposit with its Federal Reserve bank. The reserve deposits were used to meet customer withdrawals and facilitated a national check-clearing and fund-transfer arrangement. The member bank could also borrow (discount) at its Federal Reserve bank whenever it needed currency or loanable funds. This discounting process added flexibility to the currency and credit-creating mechanism.

The initial task of the new Federal Reserve System was to help finance World War I. The act had given Reserve banks authority to purchase government securities. These security purchases, in turn, supplied commercial banks with loanable reserves which were used to acquire additional government obligations. The banking system bought $5.4 billion in government securities, contributing significantly to the success of the Liberty Loan drives. This wartime lending was accompanied by a continued rapid chartering of small state banks. By 1921, 31,000 banks operated in the United States—more than at any other time in history.

After 1921 the trend reversed and banking became concentrated in fewer firms. By 1929, 5,000 banks had suspended operations. Some in rural areas failed because agriculture was depressed. Others were absorbed by larger banks as competition became more intense. The remaining banks settled down to the "high finance of the Roaring Twenties." In this period banks provided 20 percent of all funds used for industrial expansion and also supplied loans to individuals to buy homes, automobiles, and securities. By the late 1920's security loans were disproportionately large in bank-loan portfolios because many banks had acceded to the demands of customers wishing to participate in the booming stock market.

The boom ended in October 1929, when the market crashed. Plummeting stock prices caused the failure of many banks that had overextended their credit facilities. The bank panic continued until March 1933, when President Franklin D. Roosevelt closed all banks for a four-day "bank holiday." Over 10,000 banks had failed in less than four years, and only 15,000 were sound enough to reopen after the holiday.

Restoration of Confidence. In 1933 the major task of banking was to restore confidence among the thousands of depositors who had lost money through bank failures. Congress initiated the restoration by creating the Federal Deposit Insurance Corporation in 1933. Federal insurance dispelled customers' fears of losing deposits and ended currency "runs" on insured banks. The following year Congress delegated control of stock-market credit to the Federal Reserve Board of Governors. The board specified the margin for security loans—the proportion of the purchase price that the borrower must supply in cash. The margin requirement prevented credit pyramiding which had contributed to the 1929 crash. Recovery came slowly, and banks extended a minimum of credit during the depression, although the federally created Reconstruction Finance Corporation stood ready to support substantial commercial bank lending.

The pace changed rapidly in the late 1930's as defense financing placed greater demands upon the banking system. During World War II commercial and Federal Reserve banks together purchased $100 billion in government securities —nearly half of all bonds sold. However, extensive bank lending contributed to inflationary pressures which necessitated restrictions on consumer and real estate credit. In the postwar period banks became the "department stores" of the financial industry as they supplied various types of credit to a diverse group of borrowers. By 1965 consumer credit had expanded to account for 17 percent of all commercial bank loans. Nonetheless, industrial credit dominated bank lending during the continuing prosperity of the mid-1960's.

The trend toward concentration in banking, begun in the 1920's, resumed after World War II. The number of banks diminished to less than 14,500 by 1965, causing deposits to become concentrated in large banks. However, the major cause for the increased domination of large banks was the liberalizing of state branch banking laws. Banking facilities usually were expanded by establishing branches of existing banks rather than by chartering a new bank as a separate unit. In addition, some unit banks were converted into branches by merging with other banks. Branches accounted for only 12 percent of all banking offices in 1929 and 28 percent in

1945. By 1965, 16,000 branches were operating, representing 53 percent of all banking offices. The nation's largest bank, the Bank of America, with headquarters in San Francisco, owes its size to its hundreds of branch offices.

The money and credit system is unlikely to change significantly in the near future. Its soundness was supported by the highly regarded Commission on Money and Credit of the Committee for Economic Development in 1961 when it recommended no fundamental changes in the banking structure.

See also BANK OF THE UNITED STATES; FEDERAL RESERVE SYSTEM; UNITED STATES—25. *Public Finance.*

THOMAS E. WENZLAU, *Lawrence University*

5. Commercial Banks

Commercial banking is a business, and commercial bankers are businessmen. Profits are the objective of commercial banking operations; bankers seek profits through lending and investing the funds placed at their disposal. These funds come in part from bank capital—money invested by the owners of the bank and reinvested profits from operations. The bank's deposits, however, constitute by far the most important source of funds for bank lending and investing.

Commercial banks are of singular importance in the United States. They are distinguishable from other financial institutions because they provide the principal type of money in use— *demand deposits.* Individuals, corporations, governments, and other organizations find it convenient to keep money balances as demand deposits with commercial banks. Such balances simply represent the obligation of the bank to pay the depositor on demand, in legal tender money, any sum up to the amount of his deposit balance. To the depositor, however, the most important consideration is that by writing checks he can transfer all or part of his balance to others to pay for purchases, satisfy debts, or for any other reason.

Commercial banks, however, do much more than receive deposits and pay checks written by their customers. Banks establish *primary demand deposit accounts* for customers bringing in cash —currency (including coin) and checks drawn on other banks. Banks also create *secondary demand deposit accounts* when they make loans. For example, a bank receiving a deposit of $100 in currency from a customer grants that depositing customer a credit on the bank's books against which he can draw checks up to $100 at any time. But a bank may also lend $100 to a borrowing customer, granting that customer a "created" credit against which he can draw checks up to $100 at any time. Each transaction results in increasing a demand deposit on the books of the bank. However, the first results from the physical transfer of money by the customer to the bank; the second deposit increase is created by the bank when it makes the loan.

This description of its functions provides a basis for defining a commercial bank: A commercial bank is a profit-seeking financial institution that receives and holds (primary) demand deposits, acquires earning assets through the process of lending and investing, and pays for these assets by creating additional (secondary) deposits.

The only aspect of this definition requiring further comment is the reference to commercial banks' receiving and holding demand deposits. Commercial banks also receive and hold *time deposits;* however, they are not unique in doing this. Other financial institutions do it also. Further, commercial banks provide a variety of other services, but none of these are provided only by commercial banks or are an essential part of the banking business. Receiving and holding demand deposits, however, is not only unique to commercial banking; it is its very essence, which consists of exchanging the bank's (created) demand deposit liabilities for earning assets (loans and investments). So generally acceptable have the demand liabilities of commercial banks become that they constitute money —a fact that vests these privately owned, profit-seeking financial institutions with a public purpose of tremendous significance.

Deposits. Deposits constitute the principal source of funds to individual commercial banks. Typically, they contribute over 90 percent of all the funds a bank has at its disposal. Deposits may be demand deposits, subject to withdrawal by check; or time deposits, withdrawable at specified future dates, after the lapse of a specified time, or upon 30 days' notice.

Demand Deposits. Three categories of demand deposits are usually segregated in banking statistics: (1) interbank demand deposits, (2) U.S. government demand deposits, and, (3) "other" demand deposits.

Interbank demand deposits are demand balances that some banks keep with other banks. Normally they amount to less than 10 percent of total commercial bank deposits, but they are significant for reasons other than as a source of bank funds. Because of a national pattern of a large number of banks spread unevenly over a wide geographic area, and in the absence of any central-banking arrangements in earlier years, an extensive network of "correspondent" relationships developed among U.S. banks to provide a connective tissue for the banking system. These relationships followed regional and national trade patterns. They arose in primary response to the need for a payments network—a system of relationships between banks through which checks could be cleared and collected.

Even after the Federal Reserve System was organized, the network of correspondent relationships persisted and continued to grow. Not all of the nation's commercial banks chose to become members of the Federal Reserve; to gain access to its nationwide check-clearing and collection facilities, such nonmember banks needed a correspondent relationship with a member bank. Also, the regional and national city-correspondent banks have over the years greatly expanded the range of their correspondent services to their country-bank customers, and the present broad range of services includes many that the central bank does not perform. Practically without exception, therefore, Federal Reserve member banks also find it desirable to maintain correspondent relationships with one or more other commercial banks.

U.S. government demand deposits are the Treasury's *tax and loan accounts* at commercial banks; they usually amount to less than 4 percent of total deposits. They are a special kind of demand deposit. The Treasury never draws checks on these deposit accounts. Instead, certain payments due the U.S. government may be credited to a bank's tax and loan account by the

AUTOMATION ASSURES both accuracy and speed as banks handle vast masses of data for their depositors, borrowers, and general-service customers.

FIRST NATIONAL CITY BANK, NEW YORK

bank, either for itself or for some of its customers. Examples are the proceeds of sales by the bank of U.S. government securities, social security tax and withheld income tax payments by employers, and periodic income tax payments of large corporations. Then, instead of writing checks, the Treasury periodically issues "calls" on its tax and loan accounts, instructing the commercial bank through the Federal Reserve banks to transfer portions of its balances to its general checking accounts at the Federal Reserve banks. This is one way the Treasury periodically replenishes its accounts at the Federal Reserve banks, on which all Treasury checks are drawn.

"Other" demand deposits include state and local government deposits and deposits of individuals, partnerships, and corporations, called "IPC deposits." Collectively, "other" demand deposits comprise almost 90 percent of total demand deposits and 65 percent of total deposits. Demand deposits of businesses constitute a small proportion of total checking accounts—about 10 percent—but amount to over half of total dollar balances in all privately owned checking accounts. Personal checking accounts constitute about 80 percent of total checking accounts but only 30 percent of total dollar balances in all privately owned checking accounts.

Time Deposits. Banks are prohibited by law from paying interest on demand deposits, but they pay interest on time deposits. The maximum rate of interest commercial banks are permitted to pay is set by the Board of Governors of the Federal Reserve System for member banks and the Federal Deposit Insurance Corporation for nonmember banks. No bank is required to pay the maximum rates, of course, and some do not.

There are three classes of time deposits: (1) savings deposits, (2) time certificates of deposit, and (3) time deposits, open account.

Savings deposits are held predominantly by individuals, although they may be held by nonprofit organizations. Savings accounts constitute the largest number of time accounts; the use of time certificates of deposit and time deposits, open account, is largely restricted to corporations and wealthy individuals. Ownership of a savings account is usually evidenced by a passbook. Banks may require at least 30 days' notice of withdrawal. As a practical matter, however, funds are available on demand upon presentation of the passbook.

Time certificates of deposit are deposits evidenced by a negotiable or nonnegotiable certificate providing for payment (1) on some date

not less than 30 days after the date of deposit, (2) after passage of a specified time, or (3) on at least 30 days' written notice, which must be given. Thus a time certificate represents a fixed-dollar deposit that may not be withdrawn until the certificate matures.

Time deposit, open account, is a deposit not classified as either of the first two types. A written contract prohibits withdrawal prior to the deposit's maturity date. The amount deposited in an open time deposit is not necessarily fixed. Periodic additions may be made, as in the case of Christmas club or vacation savings accounts.

Federal Deposit Insurance. The Banking Acts of 1933 and 1935 established a system of federal deposit insurance to protect depositors from loss due to bank failures. The acts created the Federal Deposit Insurance Corporation (FDIC), which insures up to $20,000 of each deposit account in an insured bank. This maximum of $20,000 applies to a depositor's account in one bank. By maintaining deposits in several banks, depositors may obtain $20,000 of insurance in several institutions. Because many accounts exceed $20,000, the FDIC insures only slightly over half the total dollar volume of deposits in insured banks. However, 98 percent of the insured accounts are fully covered.

All national banks and all state-chartered Federal Reserve member banks are required to belong to FDIC. Nonmember banks may join by meeting the FDIC's membership standards. The FDIC's insurance fund is accumulated through levying and investing annual assessments on insured banks. The amount of a bank's assessment is based on the total amount of its deposits.

When an insured bank fails, the insured portion of its deposits is immediately made available to depositors by the FDIC. Although the FDIC may pay off depositors in cash, usually new deposits are provided either in a new bank organized by the FDIC or in an existing bank that agrees to take the insolvent bank's sound assets and assume its liabilities.

Commercial Bank Credit. Bankers have a well-ordered system of priorities for use of bank funds. In order of priority, the uses to which bankers put the funds at their disposal are (1) liquidity reserves, (2) loans, and (3) investments for income.

Liquidity Reserves. These are not a major element in bank credit. Some liquidity reserves are held as currency and deposits with other banks. However, a portion is held as short-term, readily

177

marketable securities. But banks' lending and investing activities provide the major elements of bank credit.

Loans. Lending commands second priority in the use of bank funds, because bankers are businessmen and lending is the most profitable possible use of their funds. Ordinarily, lending is about twice as profitable as the next-best alternative, investments for income. Also, bankers regard lending as the most constructive use of funds, because to the highest degree it serves and benefits the banks' local communities.

Bank loans are divided into six categories, as follows:

Commercial and Agricultural Loans. Business loans consist mostly of loans to local borrowers and comprise about one third of all bank loans. They are either *short-term loans*, with initial maturities of under one year, or *term loans*, with maturities of one year and over. Typically, term-loan maturities fall within five years, although some few may run to eight or ten.

Short-term loans finance temporary needs for funds and are usually self-liquidating; that is, they generate their own repayment. (For example, loans to finance inventory buildups generate their own repayment through the subsequent sale of the merchandise.) Term loans finance fixed-asset acquisition or provide additional permanent working capital. They are repaid out of depreciation allowances and profits after taxes.

Farm loans closely parallel business loans, but aggregate much less in dollar volume, constituting only about 5 percent of all bank loans.

Loans for Purchasing and Carrying Securities. Such loans are made by most American commercial banks. Securities are pledged as collateral. The amount that may be lent is limited by Federal Reserve Regulation U (the "margin requirement") if the loan is used to purchase the securities pledged and if the pledged securities are listed on a national exchange (the New York or American Stock Exchange). Securities not listed on a national exchange are not subject to this regulation; a bank may lend any amount it chooses on them.

Loans to Financial Institutions. Included here are interbank loans—loans made by banks to other banks—and loans to nonbank financial institutions, such as savings and loan associations and finance companies. These are made to meet temporary liquidity needs of the financial community at both local and national levels. They indirectly finance mortgages, consumer loans, and securities purchases and help adjust commercial-bank reserve positions. Most are fully secured. Such loans represent about 6 to 7 percent of total bank loans.

Real Estate Loans. These are mortgage loans on predominantly urban residential properties, although commercial and farm mortgage loans are included. Real estate loans are an important current use of bank funds, adding up to about one fourth of all loans.

Other Loans to Individuals. Loans made to individuals to finance consumer expenditures make up about one fifth of commercial bank loans. Most such loans are installment credits. The rest are single-payment loans. These loans to individuals have grown spectacularly in dollar volume in recent years, largely because financing consumer expenditures is the most profitable use to which bank funds can be put.

Other Loans. This last and smallest loan category includes all loans not already classified above. Examples are loans to nonprofit organizations, and involuntary loans to depositors resulting from overdrafts. "Other loans" total only about 3 percent of all loans.

Investments. Funds remaining after liquidity needs have been met and the loan demand of a bank's local community has been satisfied are placed in investments for income. To some extent, the permanent investment portfolio can also benefit the community and the state in which the bank operates, because many banks hold in their portfolios municipal securities—debt obligations of state and local governments and their instrumentalities (school districts, fire districts, turnpike authorities, port authorities). Many state and local governments depend on the banks within their boundaries to make and support the market for their securities.

However, the bulk of bank investment portfolios ordinarily consists of intermediate- and longer-term U.S. government securities. Obligations of U.S. government agencies and instrumentalities, repayment of which is guaranteed by the U.S. Treasury, are also held by commercial banks, and sometimes corporate bonds are included in the portfolio as well.

Credit Expansion and Control. Through their lending and investing activities, commercial banks originate the bulk of the nation's money supply. This results from banks acquiring assets (loans and investments) and paying for them by creating liabilities (demand deposits). Commercial banks cannot generate money in unlimited amounts, however. Their ability to create demand deposits is limited by their holdings of "legal reserves," which they are required by law to maintain in amounts equal to specified percentages of their net demand and gross time deposits and in the form of currency on hand or deposits with Federal Reserve banks.

To be able to lend or invest, creating additional demand deposits in the process, a bank must first possess "excess reserves." Its total currency plus Federal Reserve balances must be greater than the legally required percentages of its deposits. A bank with excess reserves can only lend and invest until the amount of new demand deposits created approximates the original amount of excess reserves.

Also a bank's owners must supply an adequate amount of capital funds relative to total assets for the bank to be able to increase its volume of loans and certain types of investments. The principal function of bank capital is the protection of depositors from losses. Bank supervisory authorities consequently insist that banks maintain some minimum ratio of capital to "risk assets"—loans and certain securities which contain a possibility of loss to the bank. Banks failing to meet this minimum standard may be required either to obtain more capital or to curtail their lending.

The most important factor in bank credit expansion and control, however, is the Federal Reserve System's ability to influence the size of commercial bank reserves. The "Fed" also exercises direct controls (such as margin requirements) over certain types of bank lending, and from time to time acts through "moral suasion" to persuade bankers to do or not do certain things in the interest of the nation's economic health.

Service Functions. To gain primary deposits and borrowing customers, banks offer numerous services and inducements. The most useful service by far is providing checking (demand deposit) accounts. Making payments by check is extremely convenient to bank customers, eliminates the risk of losing cash, automatically provides receipts (the canceled checks) for payments made, and greatly simplifies personal bookkeeping.

Another valuable banking-service function is the collection of noncash items (such as drafts, notes, and bills of exchange) for individuals and businesses. Local items are collected through a clearinghouse and nonlocal items through the banking system's extensive network of correspondent relationships. Through correspondent relationships, funds may be transferred rapidly and easily anywhere in the country or the world.

Many banks also provide such additional services for business customers as preparing payrolls. They either put a cash payroll in envelopes or furnish special facilities for cashing payroll checks. With electronic computer facilities, the computation of each employee's weekly earnings with all applicable deductions can be performed easily. Bank computers are also used to keep the books of some business firms, and customer billing by banks for credit purchases from local businesses is becoming more common.

Most banks maintain safe-deposit facilities for the safekeeping of customers' valuables. In fact, the banking business had its origin in the provision of safekeeping services. The list of services rendered by banks now is almost endless, limited only by the imagination and capabilities of bank management. A few more may be mentioned: trust services, credit verification, check certification, purchase and sale of foreign exchange, and provision of advice and information to customers on a broad range of business and financial subjects, such as pension funds, domestic and foreign markets, and securities investment possibilities.

Multiple-Office Banking. Most commercial banks in the United States have only one office and are consequently called *unit banks*. The U.S. banking system can be characterized as a unit banking system, but it is not entirely unitary. There has recently been a substantial expansion in multiple-office banking, which may occur in any of three forms: *branch banking, group banking,* and *chain banking.* Branch banking involves the operation by a single bank of more than one banking office. Group banking occurs when a holding company controls the operations of two or more individual banks. Chain banking results when an individual, family, or some other close association of persons controls the operations of two or more banks. Branch and group banking have increased rapidly in importance in recent years, while the significance of chain banking has been declining.

Bank holding companies are corporations organized under the laws of some states to hold controlling stock interests in one or more commercial banks. A holding company is a less efficient substitute for bank branching, and few holding companies are found in states that have few or no restrictions on branching. Where bank holding companies exist, it is because they also have the advantage of being able to operate across state lines. Holding-company banks have about 8 percent of commercial bank deposits.

FIRST NATIONAL CITY BANK, NEW YORK

SAFE DEPOSIT box rental is among the many services that banks offer to the general public for fees.

Holding companies are regulated by the Federal Reserve Board under the Bank Holding Company acts of 1956 and 1966.

The branching ability of banks is determined by state law even for nationally chartered banks. A number of states permit statewide branching, others allow only city- or county-wide branching, and still others prohibit branches altogether.

Branch banking is a highly controversial issue. Vigorous opposition to branching comes from smaller country banks that fear competition from larger (branching) city banks. Opinion among city bankers is more evenly divided. Active support for branch banking comes from economists, bank supervisory officials, and, of course, branch bankers themselves. The debate revolves around service, competition, safety, and economic consequences. The opposing views may be summarized as follows.

The Case for Branch Banking. Many small banks cannot afford good management; in contrast, branch systems are able to employ competent, experienced personnel. A branch system is therefore better able to institute modern and efficient means of serving all depositors and borrowers.

Independent bankers who provide good service need not fear branch banking competition. A local bank always has a competitive advantage. But local communities are entitled to the benefits of (branch) banking competition and may suffer from local unit-banking monopoly.

Branch systems have greater financial resources, better management, and greater diversification of loans and deposits. Commercial bank branching operates on the principle that progress is achieved by replacing small and inefficient units with larger and more efficient ones.

DRIVE-IN WINDOWS make banking more convenient for motorists. More than 30,000 banking offices—over half of them branches—serve the American public.

The Case Against Branch Banking. Branch banking produces cogs, not bankers, its opponents contend. Restricted authority and subservience to a head office stultify initiative. A branch manager is a hired hand of a distant corporation, and does not have the same interest in the welfare of the local community as the officer of an independent local bank. As branch banking expands, unit banks tend to disappear, and the community is deprived of the benefits of banking competition.

Mere size is no guarantee of financial strength, and branch banks have failed. Moreover, a fundamental weakness of branch banking is its inherent tendency to promote expansion for its own sake rather than in response to any real need for more banking service.

Independent bankers have encouraged the growth of new local enterprise. Many a thriving corporation received its initial impetus from the financial aid of the local banker. And unit banking prevents centralization of credit power in the hand of monopolistic groups.

CLIFTON H. KREPS, JR.
University of North Carolina
Author, "Money, Banking, and Monetary Policy"

6. Trust Service

Fewer than 50 trust companies operating in the United States concentrate more or less exclusively on trust and agency activities. All other "trust companies" are either commercial banks —national banks or state-chartered commercial banks—that have been authorized to operate trust departments, or state-chartered trust companies that have been authorized to engage in commercial (and savings) banking. Although almost all state-chartered trust companies have commercial banking departments, a large majority of the nation's commercial banks, especially those in smaller cities and towns, do not have trust departments.

The trust institution plays a vital role in the American economic and social order. Serving both users and suppliers of capital, it has three broad economic functions: (1) it conserves wealth and private property by safekeeping accumulated capital and preventing its wasteful use; (2) it encourages the collective ownership of industry both by its handling of estates and by its services to corporations in connection with their securities issues; and (3) it helps stabilize investment and therefore stimulates enterprise by putting funds into productive uses.

Service to Individuals. Personal trust business includes performance of trust and agency functions for individuals. The trust functions include the settling of estates of deceased persons and the care and management of trusts created by either deceased or living persons.

An *executor* acts under the last will and testament of a deceased person; an *administrator* serves by appointment of the courts if the individual dies without leaving a will or naming an executor in his will. The duties of both are similar: to collect the assets of the estate, pay debts, taxes, and other charges, and distribute the balance. The duties of an executor are usually temporary; otherwise, if the will sets up a trust, it also names a *testamentary trustee*. Similar duties are performed by a *guardian* of the estate of a minor, whether appointed in the will or by the courts, and by a *conservator* of the estate of a legally incompetent person.

The most important *voluntary* or *living trusts* are retirement trusts, life insurance trusts, and pension trusts. Although the source of funds in each of these trusts differs, they share the common purpose of providing beneficiaries with

SWIFT COMMUNICATIONS are essential in modern banking operations. Here, closed-circuit television links two offices of one of the largest U.S. banks.

relief from problems of property management while at the same time sustaining the flow of income.

Oher types of personal trusts include *sheltering trusts,* set up, for example, by parents to ensure the support of their children; *spendthrift trusts,* to protect improvident beneficiaries from the consequences of their incompetence in money matters; and *charitable trusts,* for religious, educational, literary, or scientific purposes.

Most personal trusts call for active investment management by the trustee. *Legal trusts* restrict investments to those designated by state law, but *discretionary trusts* leave the manner in which the trust estate is to be invested to the judgment of the trustee. In any event, diligence and prudence are required of a trustee, and he may be surcharged by the courts for losses stemming from his deficiency in either respect while managing the assets entrusted to him.

Traditionally each trust was a separate unit with a separate portfolio; now, however, *common trust funds* are permitted. A number of small trusts may participate in both assets and income according to their relative sizes. The purpose of common trust funds is to achieve asset diversification, to facilitate efficiency in management, and to secure a higher yield on the investment of trust assets. Use of the device by the trust departments of national banks is regulated by Federal Reserve Regulation F, which recognizes three kinds of funds—for investment of small amounts, for general investment, and for mortgage investment. Common trust funds have become much more popular in recent years, and many commercial bank trust departments now use them to attract trust investment accounts formerly considered too small to handle economically.

Trust institutions offer various *agency services* to individuals. They act as agent for trustees and executors in handling the mechanical phases of their duties, as custodian in the physical care and handling of securities, and as *escrow agent,* safekeeping something of value that is to be delivered to another party upon the occurrence of some specified happening.

Services to Corporations. Trust departments, especially in larger financial centers, perform important trust and agency services for corporations. The principal corporate trust function is serving as trustee under an *indenture* or *mortgage* securing a bond issue. The trust department cooperates in drafting the indenture, or contract between the bond-issuing corporation and the bondholders. Then, during the life of the bonds, acting on behalf of the bondholders, the trust department monitors the issuer's performance, serves notice on the issuer of any breach of the indenture, and, if the defect in performance is not remedied, may institute legal or other action to protect the rights of the bondholders.

The agency functions that corporate trustees perform for business takes several principal forms. A *transfer agent* arranges and keeps records of ownership transfers of corporate stock. When stock is transferred through a sale between individuals, the agent issues new certificates and cancels the old ones. A *registrar* prevents overissue of shares by keeping a record of the issued and outstanding shares. The registrar's duty is primarily to the public; the transfer agent serves the corporation. For bonds, the trustee usually acts also as registrar, noting the holder's name and transfer date on the existing bond instead of countersigning a new certificate issued by the transfer agent.

A *fiscal agent* relieves a corporation of clerical work in keeping records and drawing checks. For example, trust companies and departments may act as agents for paying bond interest and the principal amounts of maturing obligations. They may also handle sinking funds when these exist behind bond and preferred-stock issues. They may act as dividend-paying agents, as depositaries, and as exchange agents, issuing new securities for old.

In some cases, a trust institution has been appointed receiver of a bankrupt business by the courts. In such an event, the institution may operate the business on a temporary basis, pending either reorganization or appointment of a trustee or liquidator.

CLIFTON H. KREPS, JR.
University of North Carolina

7. Clearinghouse Activities

A clearinghouse need be nothing more than a simple room or office where messengers from a community's banks may meet to transfer the checks that each bank wants to present to the others for payment. Actually, many clearinghouses have elaborate facilities maintained by associations of which the banks of the community are members. These clearinghouse associations often do more than merely providing clearing facilities. For example, some serve as trade associations for their member banks.

The physical exchange of checks among local banks is still the basis of the clearinghouse operation, but over the years provisions have been developed for the settlement of the net differences between the banks that arise from the clearing operation. In the United States, these net differences are characteristically settled by transfers on the books of a Federal Reserve bank or on the books of some common city-correspondent bank.

Clearing Process. The modern local clearing process may be simply illustrated. Assume that in the town of Anyplace, U.S.A., there are three banks—the Bank of Anyplace (Bank A), Businessmen's Bank and Trust Company (Bank B), and City State Bank (Bank C)—and that all three are members of the Anyplace Clearinghouse. Assume further that at the end of a day, each bank has cashed or had deposited with it checks on each other bank as follows:

Checks drawn on Bank	Checks held by Bank			Total drawn
	A	B	C	
A	–	$2,000	$4,000	$ 6,000
B	$3,000	–	5,000	8,000
C	1,000	7,000	–	8,000
Total held	$4,000	$9,000	$9,000	$22,000

On a bank-by-bank settlement basis, the following amounts are therefore owed and owing:

Bank A owes Bank C . . . . $ 3,000
    is owed by Bank B 1,000
    owes net . . . . $ 2,000

Bank B owes Bank A . . . . $ 1,000
    is owed by Bank C 2,000
    is due net . . . . $ 1,000

Bank C owes Bank B . . . . $ 2,000
    is owed by Bank A 3,000
    is due net . . . . $ 1,000

In the absence of a clearing arrangement, it would be necessary for Bank A to pay $3,000 to Bank C; for Bank B to pay $1,000 to Bank A; and for Bank C to pay $2,000 to Bank B. The same net result can be achieved through the clearinghouse, however, by settling only the *net clearing differences*, shown below:

	Bank A	Bank B	Bank C
Owed by clearinghouse	$4,000	$9,000	$9,000
Owes clearinghouse	6,000	8,000	8,000
Net (owed) or owing	($2,000)	$1,000	$1,000

These net differences will be completely settled if, on clearinghouse instruction, Bank A pays $1,000 each to Bank B and Bank C. These payments may be effected by reserve account transfers on the books of a Federal Reserve bank if all the banks involved are member banks, or if they are not members, by transfers of correspondent balances on the books of a common city-correspondent bank.

Advantages. In speed, ease, and convenience, the advantages to local banks of clearing locally drawn checks through a clearinghouse—rather than settling with each other on a bank-by-bank basis—are substantial even if only three banks are involved. The advantages grow rapidly larger as the number of local clearing banks increases. Consequently, clearinghouses are almost invariably found in all American cities served by three or more banks. They range in size up to the New York Clearinghouse, in which the exchanges exceed $1 trillion annually. Daily (and sometimes more frequent) clearing through these thousands of local clearinghouses is thus the characteristic mode of collection for local checks that are cashed at or deposited in a different local bank than the one on which they are drawn.

CLIFTON H. KREPS, JR.
University of North Carolina

8. Mutual Savings Banks

Mutual savings banks are the oldest specialized savings institutions in the United States and among the oldest in the world. The first modern mutual savings bank was founded in 1810 by the Rev. Henry Duncan at Ruthwell Parish in Dumfriesshire, Scotland. The first two mutual savings banks in the United States began operations only six years later, in 1816, in Boston and Philadelphia. Savings banks in the United States exist only in 18 states, Puerto Rico, and the Virgin Islands. They are solely state-chartered institutions.

Characteristics and Development. Savings banks are mutual institutions with no stockholders. They are managed by nonelected boards of trustees, directors, or managers, as they are variously called. Except for additions to protective reserves, all net earnings are distributed to depositors, who have the legal status of creditors. The mutual form of organization and the trustee system of management reflect the basic purpose and philanthropic origins of mutual savings banks, which were founded to promote thrift and financial security among the poor.

Savings deposits provide the major source of funds for mutual savings banks. In addition to the regular savings deposits that account for 99 percent of total deposit liabilities, savings banks offer a variety of special-purpose savings accounts. Deposits in savings banks are insured by the Federal Deposit Insurance Corporation and, in Massachusetts, by The Deposit Insurance Fund of the Mutual Savings Central Fund, Inc.

Long-term mortgage loans historically have provided the major investment outlet of mutual savings banks. After the enactment of legislation in the early 1950's permitting savings banks to invest in federally underwritten mortgages on properties beyond their own states, mutual savings banks sharply expanded their holdings of such loans. As a result, savings banks have become the nation's largest lenders on federally underwritten mortgages, and are important mortgage lenders in many states that do not have mutual savings banks. Mortgage loans represent more than three fourths of savings bank assets.

Savings banking spread rapidly in the northeastern United States after 1816, and the number of savings banks reached an all-time peak of 666 in 1875–1876. However, savings banks generally failed to follow the frontier westward, largely because economic and social conditions at first were more favorable to the formation of other types of institutions. The other institutions then became firmly entrenched as the new areas developed and as state financial legislation was codified. Largely because of mergers, the number of savings banks has declined to slightly more than 500. However, total assets and deposits of the industry, and the average size of individual institutions, have increased greatly. In 1966 mutual savings bank assets passed the $60 billion milestone.

Industry Structure. Four fifths of the mutual savings banks now in operation in the United States were in existence by 1875, mainly in the Northeast. The industry continues to be concentrated in the 11 New England and Middle Atlantic states, with fewer than 20 savings banks situated in other areas.

Mutual savings banks are an important factor in the savings account markets in all but a few of the 18 states that have mutual saving banks. In seven states, they hold more passbook savings than either commercial banks or savings and loan associations. The three leading savings bank states are New York, Massachusetts, and Connecticut, where almost three fourths of all mutual savings banks—with over four fifths of the industry's assets—are situated.

STATES LEADING IN MUTUAL SAVINGS BANKS ON SELECTED YEAR-END DATES

State	Number of banks			Assets (in billions)		
	1955	1960	1965	1955	1960	1965
New York	129	127	126	$18.321	$23.915	$33.758
Massachusetts	189	185	179	5.045	6.539	9.489
Connecticut	71	71	71	2.080	2.811	4.097
Pennsylvania	7	7	7	1.662	2.292	3.467
New Jersey	23	21	21	1.111	1.489	2.224
13 other states, Puerto Rico, and Virgin Islands	109	104	102	3.127	3.525	5.197
Total	528	515	506	$31.346	$40.571	$58.232

Sources: National Association of Mutual Savings Banks; Federal Deposit Insurance Corporation.

Limitations on Savings Banks. Mutual savings banks have achieved substantial growth despite their narrow geographic confinement and the effect of relatively more restrictive statutory and regulatory provisions than those governing national commercial banks and federal savings and loan associations. The organization of new savings banks has been impeded by stringent initial-capital requirements of the Federal Deposit Insurance Corporation and of the states, in contrast to much smaller requirements for new federal savings and loan associations. In addition, leading savings bank states, including New York and three of the next four largest, place maximum limits on the size of savings bank accounts. Laws of most savings bank states, moreover, do not provide for various types of "incentive" savings accounts, such as notice or bonus accounts. Provisions in 10 of the 18 savings bank states are narrowly restrictive on branching powers.

In most states, savings banks are restricted by law in their lending and investment programs to specific types of securities, mortgages, and other loans. Within statutory and supervisory limitations, all mutual savings bank states authorize investment in U.S. government securities, state and municipal obligations, railroad bonds, and conventional and federally underwritten real estate mortgage loans. Virtually all states also permit savings banks to invest in telephone and electric utility bonds and equipment obligations. A majority of states allow investment in nonbank corporate stock, commercial bank stock, Canadian bonds payable in U.S. dollars, real estate construction loans, acceptances and bills of exchange, and unsecured personal loans.

In contrast to commercial banks, mutual savings banks generally do not accept deposits from, or lend to, business organizations. Their ability to extend general-purpose unsecured personal loans to individuals is more limited, and savings banks in several states, including New York, are prohibited from making such loans.

Savings Bank Life Insurance. Mutual savings banks in New York, Massachusetts, and Connecticut sell low-cost savings bank life insurance. In the mid-1960's, savings bank life insurance was being offered "over-the-counter" by more than 300 mutual savings banks in these three states. There were more than 960,000 ordinary life insurance policies and group insurance certificates outstanding with a face value exceeding $2 billion.

SAUL B. KLAMAN
National Association of Mutual Savings Banks

9. Federal Reserve System

The Federal Reserve System was established in 1913 to act as the nation's central bank. Its objectives and activities have evolved over the years, as understanding about the role of monetary policy in a modern economy has developed. The fundamental purposes of the Federal Reserve coincide with the nation's general economic goals—the encouragement of economic growth, over-all price stability, full employment, and a reasonable balance in the country's transactions with foreign countries.

Thus, the activities of the Federal Reserve System are guided by how they can contribute to the attainment of these objectives; unlike commercial banks, the central bank does not operate to make a profit.

Structure. Membership in the Federal Reserve System is widespread. All national banks are required to belong, and other banks may join voluntarily. About 6,200 banks belong, and they hold about 85 percent of total commercial bank deposits in the country. Although banks pay a small amount on joining and receive a statutory dividend, they do not have voting rights as stockholders would have in a private corporation. Thus, banks do not control the policies of the system.

The Federal Reserve System is headed by a seven-man Board of Governors in Washington—appointed by the president of the United States with the consent of the Senate—and includes 12 regional Reserve banks located in the principal financial centers of the nation. (See FEDERAL RESERVE SYSTEM.) The policies of the Federal Reserve System affect the economy principally through their impact on the volume and cost of the reserves needed by its member banks. Because banks are required to hold a certain amount of reserves behind the deposits they obtain or create in the process of making loans, the Federal Reserve can affect the amount of money in the economy, the amount of credit advanced to businesses and consumers by the banking system, and the level of interest rates. But it must be recognized that Federal Reserve policy is only one of the means by which the nation's economic goals are influenced and is not necessarily the most powerful at all times and for all objectives.

How Credit and Money Are Regulated. The Federal Reserve uses mainly three interrelated instruments to regulate credit and money. One is the ability to vary *reserve requirements* behind demand and time deposits within the limits set by legislation. This authority is vested in the Board of Governors.

A second instrument is the ability to vary the interest rate charged by Federal Reserve banks on short-term loans of reserve funds to member banks. This interest rate is commonly called the *discount rate*. Each Reserve bank establishes its own discount rate, but the rate is subject to review and determination by the Board of Governors. At the time that the Federal Reserve System was established, it was thought that discount rates might frequently vary by regions, but with the further development of a national credit market, discount rates have tended to become uniform.

The third and most frequently used instrument of monetary control is called *open market operations*. By such operations the total amount of reserves available to banks can be either increased or decreased. When the Federal Reserve wishes to supply reserves to banks, it can do so by purchasing securities, principally short-term U.S. government securities, in the open market. The asset thereby acquired supports an equivalent increase in reserve balances of member banks, which are a liability of the Federal Reserve. Open market operations are under the control of the Federal Open Market Committee. This committee is composed of the seven members of the Board of Governors plus five Reserve bank presidents, including the president of the Federal Reserve Bank of New York and four others serving in rotation.

The Federal Reserve System has other functions besides those described above. Among them, the regulation of maximum interest rates member banks may pay on time and savings deposits has an important influence on credit and deposit flows. Other functions include operations in foreign exchange markets, regulation of stock market credit, consideration of bank mergers, and examination of banks.

STEPHEN H. AXILROD, *Federal Reserve System*

OTHER FINANCIAL INSTITUTIONS AND ACTIVITIES—U.S.

10. Installment Lending

In one short generation, consumer installment credit rocketed from $4.2 billion outstanding in 1946 to $72.6 billion in 1966. The importance of consumer installment credit to the development and growth of the U.S. economy becomes evident in the automotive industry, which is a bellwether of the economy: almost two thirds of all cars sold in the mid-1960's were financed through installment credit.

Commercial banks have played an increasingly important part in the phenomenal growth of this type of credit. Aggressive pursuit of the consumer's loan business made banking the major lender in the field in the mid-1960's with 43 percent of all consumer installment loans and 56 percent of the automobile loans.

Bank Loans. Bank installment-loan operations follow two distinct patterns—*indirect* (or *dealer-purchased*) *loans* and *direct loans*. In indirect loans, the bank does not deal directly with the borrower but purchases conditional sales contracts from retailers of goods or services.

In direct loans, the borrower makes application to the bank. Virtually all banks in the United States welcome the consumer-loan applicant. The purpose of the loan may be any of the things that people want money for. If the applicant is steadily employed and has a good moral background and a record of meeting his obligations satisfactorily, the loan probably will be granted.

In their search for more ways to serve more people better, banks have developed *credit cards* (sometimes called charge cards) and *revolving credit* (sometimes called check credit) as new instruments to supplement customary loan procedures. With a bank credit card the customer may buy merchandise from many retail outlets —assuming that the outlets are merchant members of the bank plan—and have the privilege of extended terms centered in one account rather than in many accounts. Bank credit-card plans generally offer the customer the option of payment in full without charge upon billing or of extending the payments over a term of months subject to a monthly service charge. A trend has developed toward credit-card plans that are statewide or nationwide in scope. Such companies as American Express, Carte Blanche,

and Diners' Club at first offered essentially noninstallment travel and entertainment credit, but in the mid-1960's they moved toward installment credit and offered participation to banks in national credit-card plans.

With revolving credit, the customer is provided with special checks and activates the loan by the issuance of a check. Charges accrue only when a check is written. The amount of the monthly payment is constant at perhaps 1/20th of the total credit line, although the total amount outstanding may fluctuate considerably. This loan service eliminates the necessity of trips to the bank and personal interviews each time additional funds are needed.

Other Lending Institutions. *Consumer finance companies*, sometimes called small loan companies or licensed lenders, operate under state small-loan statutes permitting rates from 3 to 3½ percent per month on the first $100 to $150 of loan balance. Because of the greater risk and the frequently small dollar amounts in loan applications, the permitted rate is not regarded as excessive.

Sales finance companies do not generally deal with the public except through their wholly owned consumer finance subsidiaries. Sales finance companies specialize in purchasing installment contracts from retailers of such products as automobiles, appliances, and furniture.

Credit unions, licensed under either federal or state statutes, are cooperative organizations. The nucleus is a common bond such as place of employment. The operation consists of the cooperative pooling of savings and the lending of the pooled savings to individual members. A loan applicant must be a member of the credit union. Credit unions hold 11 percent of all installment credit and their growth rate has been exceptional.

Lending powers of *mutual savings banks* are generally restricted to mortgage loans, but they are now also authorized to make loans for higher education. Lending powers of *savings and loan associations* also are generally restricted to mortgage loans, but they are permitted to make home-improvement loans.

Formerly a large factor in installment credit, *industrial banks* in many cases have converted to commercial banks. The leading industrial banks were the Morris Plan banks, which granted credit to wage earners on the basis of character. These banks came through the Great Depression of the early 1930's without a failure, and their success played a major role in the decision of commercial banks to become active in consumer loans.

Department store credit is limited to merchandise purchases in the individual store. In the 30-day charge version, department store credit is competitive with restaurant and travel-card services. In its extended version, it competes with bank credit cards and direct consumer lending.

Loan sources such as pawnbrokers, unlicensed lenders, or loan sharks generally are regarded only as last resorts. As a result of wider consumer education, their place in the installment credit economy is relatively insignificant.

FREDERICK K. GARDNER
American Bankers Association

INSTALLMENT CREDIT OUTSTANDING IN THE UNITED STATES
(billions of dollars)

COMMERCIAL BANKS	29.2
SALES FINANCE COMPANIES	16.1
CREDIT UNIONS	7.4
CONSUMER FINANCE COMPANIES	5.6
OTHER FINANCIAL INSTITUTIONS	1.9
RETAIL OUTLETS	8.1

Source: Federal Reserve Bulletin. 1966 data.

(billions of dollars)

CREDIT OUTSTANDING FOR AUTOMOBILES IN THE UNITED STATES
(5-year intervals)

Source: Statistical Abstract of the U.S.

2.1 — .46 — 6.1 — 13.5 — 17.7 — 28.8

1940 1945 1950 1955 1960 1965

11. Mortgage Banking

Among the countless financial transactions supporting the nation's economic activity, few are more complex or more important than real estate financing. Since the end of World War II, demands for mortgage funds have by far exceeded demands for other types of credit and for equity funds in the U.S. money and capital markets. And since the early 1960's, mortgage debt has exceeded the volume of federal debt and of any single category of private short-term or long-term debt.

Mortgage banking, therefore, ranks among the leading activities of financial institutions in the United States.

Nature of Real Estate Finance. A mortgage loan is evidence of debt secured by real property. It may be granted to finance land development, new construction, or purchase of a new or existing property or to refinance an existing mortgage. Mortgage debt is secured by a wide variety of properties, including (1) owner-oc-

cupied homes; (2) apartment houses; (3) commercial and industrial structures, such as stores, office buildings, warehouses, and plants; (4) religious, educational, hospital, and social and recreational-type buildings; and (5) farms. About three fourths of the nation's mortgage debt is on homes and apartments.

Residential mortgage debt is often classified in mortgage banking according to whether it is insured or guaranteed for lenders by agencies of the federal government, that is, the Federal Housing Administration (FHA) and Veterans Administration (VA). Loans not so insured are known as "conventional" loans. Nearly one third of the nation's residential mortgage debt is FHA-insured or VA-guaranteed.

Each mortgage loan contract carries a package of credit terms including interest rate, down-payment requirements, maturity, and amortization and prepayment provisions. Contract terms vary from loan to loan, reflecting differences in local mortgage-market conditions, practices of lenders, credit worthiness of the borrower, type and location of property used as collateral, and legal requirements governing real estate financing.

Almost universally, however, mortgage loans are amortized on a regular monthly basis over a long period—up to 30 years or more. This is in contrast with the 1920's and early 1930's when mortgage loans were seldom amortized and carried short maturities.

Institutions in the Mortgage Market. Savings and loan associations, mutual savings banks, life insurance companies, and commercial banks, the nation's main types of financial intermediaries, are the principal suppliers of mortgage credit. They hold nearly four fifths of the total mortgage debt outstanding.

Savings and loan associations are the most specialized in function, with well over four fifths of their assets in mortgages, primarily of the conventional home-loan type. Their tremendous postwar growth has permitted a rapid expansion in mortgage lending activity, and these associations now hold about one third of the nation's mortgage debt. Except in the New England and Middle Atlantic regions, they are the leading source of conventional home mortgage credit.

SHOPPING CENTERS often provide a convenient location for banks. This Bank of America branch is situated in Palo Alto, Calif.

Although confined largely to the northeastern section of the country, mutual savings banks provide mortgage credit to borrowers in all 50 states. They are the leading nationwide source of FHA-insured and VA-guaranteed mortgage credit, and a major source of conventional mortgage credit in their own local markets. Savings banks have expanded their mortgage holdings steadily in the postwar years to about three fourths of their total assets. They have stressed loans on owner-occupied homes but have channeled a significant volume of funds into multifamily and nonresidential loans as well. Of the nation's total mortgage debt, savings banks hold more than one eighth.

Life insurance companies, having broad alternative investment powers, are not as strongly oriented toward mortgage loans as are savings and loan associations and mutual savings banks. Mortgage loans account for about two fifths of the life insurance industry's assets. In general, life insurance companies do not have direct contact with home mortgage borrowers, but acquire their loans chiefly through mortgage correspondents throughout the nation. They invest in a wide variety of mortgage loans, residential and nonresidential, and hold over one sixth of the total outstanding mortgage debt.

Of all the main types of mortgage lenders, commercial banks have the smallest proportion of their assets in mortgage loans—a little over 10 percent. This reflects their basic orientation toward short-term business credits. At the same time, commercial banks are the most diversified type of mortgage lender, providing long-term, permanent mortgage loans; short-term construction credits; and inventory financing for other real estate mortgage lenders.

A variety of other investors also supply mortgage credit. They include (1) federal, state, and local government agencies; (2) pension funds; (3) fraternal orders; (4) fire and casualty insurance companies; (5) credit unions; (6) college endowment funds; (7) investment companies; and (8) mortgage companies.

Mortgage companies, commonly called "mortgage bankers," play a market role differing from that of other mortgage lenders. They do not acquire mortgage loans for their own accounts. Rather, they originate and service mortgages for the accounts of institutional investors, mainly life insurance companies and mutual savings banks.

Role of Government. The financing of real estate and construction is profoundly influenced by federal and state government actions. The supply and terms of mortgage credit are affected by actions of the Federal Reserve System and the Treasury Department in exercising their monetary and debt management responsibilities. More directly, other federal agencies have influenced and continue to influence the structure of mortgage markets. Through their mortgage insurance and guarantee programs, the FHA and VA have helped to standardize mortgage terms and improve property and borrower appraisal procedures. This has stimulated investor interest in mortgage loans, increased the mobility of mortgage funds, and made possible the development of a national mortgage market. The flow of funds into mortgage markets has also been encouraged by (1) the Federal Home Loan Bank System—the central credit facility for home mortgage institutions, primarily savings and loan associations—and (2) the Federal National Mortgage Association, which provides assistance to the secondary mortgage market by buying and selling FHA and VA mortgages.

SAUL B. KLAMAN
National Association of Mutual Savings Banks
Author of "Postwar Residential Mortgage Market"

12. Savings and Loan Associations

Third largest of U.S. financial systems (commercial banks and life insurance companies outrank them), savings and loan associations are the only financial institutions devoted almost wholly to thrift and home ownership. Savings and loan associations are the principal source of home financing and in the mid-1960's held about 44 percent of all mortgages on one- to four-family dwellings in the nation. Thus the associations contributed heavily to the fact that nearly two thirds of American families own their homes. According to their location in the United States, savings and loan associations are also called *building and loan associations, building associations, homestead associations, or cooperative banks.* By law the name *"savings and loan"* is required for all federally chartered associations, which represent more than half the assets of the business.

Origin and Development. The American savings and loan business began in 1831 in Frankford, Pa. (now in Philadelphia), with the founding of the Oxford Provident Building Association, which was patterned after the British building societies of the day. Most of the earlier associations were of the terminating type. Their sole purpose was to enable the members to buy homes. Each member deposited a monthly payment, and the institutions were so set up that this would provide a home for one member per month. The member who was granted a mortgage then paid monthly installments until his debt was satisfied. The terminating association stayed in business until all members had received funds to build homes of their own, and then it usually dissolved.

The terminating associations led to development, beginning in the 1850's, of serial associations. In these organizations members were admitted on a quarterly, semiannual, or annual basis, and the operation was much like that of a terminating association except that the organization was continuous. Many serial associations began to accept members who wanted to save but not necessarily to buy homes. Borrowers were charged interest on the loan; the savers were given back their contribution plus earning at the completion of their contract. This was the beginning of the savings and loan business as it is known today. The next step in the business was the organization of permanent associations. These institutions accepted members from day to day and paid earnings either in regular installments or at the members' option. They financed homes and charged interest in the same manner as is employed today.

In 1933, at the bottom of the Depression, Congress authorized the chartering, examination, and supervision by the federal government of federal savings and loan associations. These federally chartered savings and loan associations operate as mutual organizations, in which the depositors are owners. Like mutual savings banks, federal associations accept savings and investment funds, and, in turn, lend the funds in the form of mortgages. By law, a large proportion of loanable funds of associations are channeled into monthly amortized home mortgages (one- to four-family residences). Such loans must be made in most cases within a 100-mile radius of the association's principal office.

The remaining loans may be made on other types of improved real estate, especially apartments and also hotels, motels, churches, shopping centers, and industrial parks. Associations are authorized to invest in U.S. government bonds without limit. They may also make loans to finance college educations.

Most state-chartered associations operate on a similar basis.

Role in Economy. The volume of savings and loan business in the post-World War II period has reached unprecedented heights. In 1950 there were 1,526 federal associations and 4,466 state-chartered associations—a total of 5,992 institutions. Combined assets of the entire system were $16.7 billion. In 1965 there were 2,011 federal associations and 4,221 state-chartered institutions—a total of 6,232. Assets of the business in 1965 had risen to $129.4 billion.

Savings deposits in savings and loan associations amounted to $110.3 billion in 1965. This compared to $131 billion and $52.7 billion in commercial banks and mutual savings banks, respectively. All savings accounts in insured savings associations are insured up to $15,000 by the Federal Savings and Loan Insurance Corporation, an agency of the United States government, which is operated in the same manner as the Federal Deposit Insurance Corporation, the government agency which insures savings in commercial banks.

On the lending side of the savings and loan business, the record has been equally spectacular. In 1940, savings associations made 22.5 percent of the mortgages on basic one- to four-family dwellings; in 1965 their share of this market had risen to 44 percent, compared with about 14 percent each for commercial banks and mutual savings banks. Most mortgages made by savings and loan associations are of the conventional type—involving no government guarantees and made at the lender's own risk. In 1965, 96.8 percent of savings and loan mortgages were conventional.

See also SAVINGS AND LOAN ASSOCIATIONS.

NORMAN STRUNK
United States Savings and Loan League

13. Investment Banking

Investment banking is the process by which capital is raised to buy the buildings, machinery, and tools needed by modern industry. In essence, the investment banking mechanism simply channels the savings of thousands of individuals into corporate and public enterprises.

When business was conducted on a small scale, the cabinetmaker or blacksmith financed the purchase of his own tools through savings or from loans made by relatives or friends. As commercial and manufacturing enterprises grew in size, it became necessary to collect the savings of many people to provide the capital. Instead of continuing as individual proprietorships, the larger business entities were organized as corporations or joint trading companies, and shares of stock or bonds were issued to the investors who put up the money to finance them. The giant industrial enterprises of today represent colossal accumulations of such capital.

Management of New Issues. Investment banking in the United States is in the hands of hundreds of independent firms, of which about 150 are large enough to undertake the management of large new security issues. Investment banking firms buy large blocks of stocks or bonds from corporations needing additional capital and then endeavor to resell the securities to hundreds or even thousands of individual investors at a slightly higher price to compensate themselves for the services performed.

Investment banking houses are in the business of buying securities at wholesale from the issuing corporation and reselling them at retail. They should not be confused with commercial banks.

Before most individual investors will buy a security, they must be assured that there is a ready market for resale. Investment bankers consequently must assure the prospective purchaser of a continuing market for the securities they underwrite. Because of the similarity between selling new securities and buying and selling securities that are already outstanding, virtually all investment banking firms also engage in the general securities brokerage business, and many of them are members of the various stock exchanges.

An investment banking firm seldom undertakes the underwriting of a large issue of securities without outside help. If the issue is very large, no single investment banking firm is likely to have enough capital. But even where the capital is available, investment banking firms generally prefer not to tie up a large proportion of their funds in a single underwriting. The managing underwriter calls in other investment bankers and asks them to join together in a buying syndicate. Usually the managing firm undertakes the largest commitment. Buying syndicates range in size from 3 firms to 100 or more.

The sale of the new issue by members of the syndicate may be completed in a few days if the issue has been correctly priced and looks attractive to investors in relation to the current cost of other similar securities. However, if the issue has been priced too high or if the market takes a sudden downward trend, it may be difficult or even impossible for the underwriters to dispose of their securities at the proposed offering price. This element of risk is an important factor in determining the compensation demanded by the members of a buying syndicate. Firms in the selling group are penalized if they sell at less than the public offering price during the life of the agreement. However, if it is impossible to sell the new issue after extended effort, the agreement will be terminated and individual members of the buying group either can hold the unsold issue as an investment, or sell it for whatever price they can get in the open market.

Special Types of Securities. Municipal, railroad, and public utility bonds are generally purchased by competitive bidding. In arriving at a bidding price, a syndicate must estimate with a high degree of accuracy the price at which it believes it can resell the securities to the public or to large institutional buyers such as life insurance companies, banks, and trustees. At the same time, each bidding group must try to outguess its competitors. As many as six groups may bid for the new securities, and the bidding prices often are refined to the fourth decimal place.

All bids are opened at some fixed time and the securities are sold to the highest bidder.

Highly speculative enterprises are rarely underwritten by investment bankers. Instead, the corporation and the investment bankers usually enter into a "best efforts contract." The underwriter does not agree to buy securities from the corporation at a fixed price but rather agrees to sell as many securities as possible at some set price and turn over to the corporation the proceeds less an agreed-upon selling charge.

Investment Trusts. Investment trusts are companies that invest their funds in the securities of other companies. There are two types of investment trusts: *open-end funds*, or *mutual funds*, that constantly sell new shares to investors, and *closed-end funds* that on their original formation sell a fixed number of shares to investors. When an investor purchases a share of a mutual fund, a new share of stock is created. When he purchases a share of a closed-end fund, he must buy from a present holder.

The purpose of an investment trust is to provide the means for a person of small resources to gain the benefits of professional management and to spread his investment risk among a diversified list of concerns. A typical mutual fund may hold investments in 100 or more industrial, railroad, and public utility companies. A purchaser of a $50 share in an investment trust in effect will own a proportional fraction of the 100 or more securities held by the fund.

See also STOCK EXCHANGE.

LUTTRELL MACLIN
Paine, Webber, Jackson & Curtis

14. Life Insurance Companies and Pension Funds

The primary function of life insurance and pension funds is to provide financial security for households. In fulfilling this function, both have become important financial intermediaries that compete actively with banks and savings institutions for household savings. In turn, these intermediaries are equally important lenders in the capital market. Saving through life insurance and pension funds differs from other forms of household savings. Its contractual nature commits the household to periodic savings for an extended period of time.

These forms of savings grew rapidly during the 1950's, and by 1965 households owned $105 billion in life insurance reserves and $170 billion in pension funds.

Life Insurance. Household saving through life insurance occurs when households purchase straight life, limited-payment life, or endowment policies on a level-premium basis. Premiums in the early years of the policy exceed the insurance costs, and reserves accumulate; the reserves defray the higher costs in later years. The prepaid reserve constitutes a form of saving for the policyholder, accruing as a cash surrender value. When necessary, the policyholder may convert the surrender value into cash by canceling (surrendering) the policy or by borrowing from the insurance company. In addition to saving through insurance, households also save by purchasing annuities from life insurance companies. In the mid-1960's, households saved more than $4 billion annually through insurance companies.

Life insurance companies invest primarily in bonds and mortgages. After 1950, life companies gradually reduced their portfolio of government bonds in order to expand mortgage holdings. By The mid-1960's 45 percent of life insurance company assets was in bonds and 37 percent in mortgages. With over $55 billion invested in mortgages, life companies ranked second to savings and loan associations as a source of mortgage credit.

The shift of portfolio in favor of mortgages, along with generally rising interest rates, improved life insurance company investment earnings from 3.1 percent in 1950 to 4.5 percent in 1965. These higher earnings helped to finance benefit payments which exceeded $11 billion in 1965. Death payments to beneficiaries amounted to $4.5 billion, and policyholders' living benefits (dividends, surrendered cash value, annuities, and endowments) were $6.5 billion. As insurer, borrower, and lender, life insurance companies exert an increasing impact on personal and financial affairs.

Pension Funds. Saving through pension funds is much like purchasing an annuity for old age. Ordinarily both employee and employer contribute to the pension fund from which the employee will draw benefits. However, there is great diversity among pension programs. Pension funds may be publicly controlled by the federal government, as are OASDHI (Old Age, Survivors, Disability and Health Insurance), Civil Service Retirement and Disability Fund, and Railroad Retirement Fund, or by state and local governments as are public school teachers' retirement systems. Private pension funds may be controlled by life insurance companies, in which case they are called *insured pension plans*. Or private pension funds may be administered by the employer or specifically designated trustees, and are referred to as *uninsured pension funds*. Uninsured funds grew rapidly after the mid-1950's and by 1965 owned assets twice the size of those of insured programs.

Pension funds vary in the degree to which benefit rights are vested in the employee. Only in a fully vested pension do an employee's benefit rights become immediately and irrevocably his property and therefore capable of being carried to another job. Few plans other than OASDHI are immediately fully vested. More commonly, benefit rights are portable only after certain conditions—such as age and length of service—are met. Such deferred vesting characterizes the majority of pension programs. However, nonvested plans cover 40 percent of pension-eligible workers in private firms. To earn

SAVINGS OF INDIVIDUAL AMERICANS

LIFE INSURANCE
RESERVES
$110,400,000,000

COMMERCIAL BANKS
$100,420,000,000

SAVINGS AND LOAN
ASSOCIATIONS
$91,205,000,000

U.S. SAVINGS BONDS
$48,049,000,000

MUTUAL SAVINGS BANKS
$44,606,000,000

CREDIT UNIONS
$7,161,000,000

Source: *Statistical Abstract of the United States.* 1963 data.

pension benefits, these workers must be employed by the same firm until they retire. The absence of vesting greatly reduces labor mobility.

Pensions vary also in the manner of financing. Fully funded pension plans own sufficient assets to meet all future obligations to pensioners. In the few such plans in operation, benefits are paid entirely from assets accumulated in the participant's working life. More often benefits are paid partially from assets and partially from current contributions or, in nonfunded plans, entirely from current contributions on a pay-as-you-go basis.

Asset requirements for prudent funding depend directly upon the degree of vesting. The longer vesting is deferred, the less rigorous the funding requirements. Nonetheless, in practice many pension plans are inadequately funded, so that adverse economic conditions could force such plans to default on benefit payments to pensioners.

Growing at an annual rate of 15 percent during the 1950's and 1960's, pension funds channeled $12 billion annually into investment during the mid-1960's. Quantitatively, saving through pension funds is second only to savings accounts as a method for households to accumulate assets. Twenty-five percent of financial assets acquired by households in the mid-1960's was in pension fund reserves.

Household-owned pension fund reserves have certain limitations as a means of saving. (1) Pension fund assets are not available for current use by their owner as are most other forms of household saving; pension benefits are received only after the owner reaches a specified age. (2) Pension fund reserves are not legally owned by particular households until the pension is vested; thus many pension fund reserves represent potential rather than actual saving. (3) Inadequate funding jeopardizes the saving aspect of pension programs; pensioners cannot be certain they will receive all benefits.

Investment policies of pension funds depend upon the administering unit. Government pension funds are invested heavily in U.S. government securities and corporation bonds. Insured pension funds enter the capital market along with life insurance reserves and flow into bonds and mortgages. Private noninsured pension funds are less conservatively invested: 50 percent of their funds is invested in corporate stock and 40 percent is in corporate bonds. Pension funds supply more financing to American business than is supplied by any other financial intermediary.

Pension plan coverage is extensive. In 1965 over 90 percent of all employees were eligible for OASDHI benefits and 50 percent of employees in private enterprises had additional private pension coverage. Pension benefits totaled more than $26 billion and contributed 5 percent of personal income in the United States. Of the total benefits, $18 billion originated in OASDHI, and private plans paid more than $2.7 billion.

See also LIFE INSURANCE; PENSION or RETIREMENT SYSTEM; SOCIAL SECURITY.

THOMAS E. WENZLAU, *Lawrence University*

15. Government Agencies

One of the most significant developments in finance since the early 1930's has been the creation and expansion of U.S. government facilities for the guarantee of many kinds of loans granted by commercial banks and other financial institutions. These guarantees promote new business for the financial institutions by encouraging them to put funds into loans that otherwise would be unattractive.

Activities of various federal agencies include insuring and guaranteeing loans, participating in making loans, issuing commitments to participate, and taking over completely loans that financial institutions want to transfer. The range of these involvements extends from loan funds for student financial aid to loans to governments of underdeveloped nations. The most significant objective of federal credit programs is to make it possible for individuals and businesses to obtain loans from private financial institutions; only in a limited sense can federal credit agencies be considered as competitors of private institutions in lending. Instead, for the most part, the government agencies were established to ensure that certain classes of loans carrying above-average risks of nonpayment could nevertheless be placed in private loan portfolios.

Mortgage Insurance. Mortgage foreclosure rates rose so high during the Great Depression of 1929–1933 that mortgage lenders and borrowers alike sought temporary federal assistance. Some of the credit agencies and loan programs developed then were later abandoned; others were made permanent and expanded.

The Federal Home Loan Bank System was created in 1932 to provide a reservoir of credit for institutions holding mortgage loans on residential properties. It serves its members (savings and loan associations, mutual savings banks, and insurance companies) in much the same way the Federal Reserve System serves commercial banks. It permits them to expand their lending power by using some of their present resources as collateral for FHLB advances.

In the National Housing Act of 1934, Congress established the Federal Housing Administration, to lure private funds back into mortgages by providing government mortgage loan insurance. FHA-insured mortgages were designed to attract both borrowers and lenders: borrowers, by small down payments and loan maturities; lenders, by reduction of risk through loan insurance. The FHA itself provides no funds; instead, private lenders lend to private borrowers on terms qualifying for FHA insurance.

The Servicemen's Readjustment Act of 1944 provided for the guarantee by the Veterans Administration of private first and second mortgage loans made to veterans for the purchase of homes. The VA now guarantees only 60 percent of such loans up to a maximum of $7,500. But the VA also makes direct loans up to $10,000 to veterans failing to find private sources.

The Housing Act of 1938 provided for the establishment of the Federal National Mortgage Association, known as "Fannie Mae." It was financed with government funds and authorized to buy and sell FHA-insured and VA-guaranteed mortgages. Its purpose was to provide a secondary market in which approved mortgage loans could be sold. Under the Housing Act of 1954, Fannie Mae was rechartered and reorganized as a corporation privately owned by those who sell mortgages to it. It then undertook three functions: (1) continuing to provide a secondary market for federally underwritten mortgages; (2) furnishing special assistance for FHA- and VA-loan financing; and (3) liquidating the mortgages it had acquired under its original charter.

Business Financing. The effects of the Great Depression, the need to achieve high production during World War II, and the continuing under-capitalization problem of small business have all prompted Congress to legislate various programs to provide financial assistance to private business. The first of these was the Reconstruction Finance Corporation, initially created to provide aid to financial institutions and railroads. Its scope was later expanded to include other nonfinancial businesses. During World War II, its activities expanded further: it made loans to and bought securities from businesses engaged in war production; and it provided special assistance to small businesses. In 1945, it began to guarantee bank loans to businesses (up to 75 percent of loan authorizations) where such loans conformed to specified standards. The RFC's charter was finally allowed to lapse in 1954.

Its successor agency was the Small Business Administration, to which Congress assigned responsibility for helping small businesses (1) to gain access to adequate capital and credit; (2) to obtain a fair share of government contracts; (3) to obtain competent management, technical, and production counsel; and (4) to obtain disaster loans, which are also made to individuals. The SBA makes direct loans only when a borrower cannot obtain aid from private lenders. The maximum SBA loan or loan participation may not exceed $250,000 to any one borrower. The maximum maturity is set at 10 years. On the average, 60 percent of the business loans approved by the SBA have been participation loans with an average maturity range of from 5 to 10 years.

In 1934, Federal Reserve banks were authorized to provide financial assistance to firms that could not obtain needed funds from usual sources at reasonable terms; since 1941, however, few of these loans have been made. The Federal Reserve banks also administered the two Regulation V loan programs, one during World War II and the other during the Korean emergency. Various defense agencies guaranteed to private lenders the large volume of these loans to defense contractors. This program has not been active in recent years.

Besides its mortgage loan program, the Veterans Administration has authority to guarantee and insure loans to veterans for establishing or expanding a business. These loans are made by private lenders, who generally elect the insurance option, which insures the lender on up to 15 percent of the aggregate amount of eligible loans made.

Agricultural Agencies. Interest in improving farm credit sources in the United States dates back to 1912, when Congress appointed a commission to go to Europe and study farm credit institutions there. Since then, many public farm credit institutions have been established; however, most of these have been discontinued or merged with other organizations. There are now only four principal public agencies: the Commodity Credit Corporation, the Farmers Home Administration, the Rural Electrification Administration, and the Farm Credit Administration.

The Commodity Credit Corporation was organized in 1933 to engage in the purchase and sale of farm products and to make nonrecourse price-support loans secured by commodities. The CCC may either lend directly or guarantee loans made by commercial banks. Its purposes are twofold: (1) to support the prices of certain farm commodities, and (2) to promote more orderly marketing of farm products.

CCC price-support loans are unique. The borrowing farmer may or may not ever repay the loan, depending on what happens to the pledged commodity's market price after the loan is made. If the market price declines, the CCC routinely expects the farmer to default on the loan, and title to the pledged commodities passes to the CCC. Thus the farmer receives a stipulated floor price for his crop, in the form of the proceeds from the loan. If the market price rises, on the other hand, the farmer sells his crop, repays the loan, and retains the balance of the sale proceeds.

The Farmers Home Administration was established in 1946. It makes direct loans and also operates an insured-loan program. Both activities aim at developing and strengthening the family farm. Loans are also made to develop and operate farms whose owners are employed part-time in industry.

The Rural Electrification Administration, created in 1935, provides funds to finance the construction and operation of cooperatively owned electric facilities in rural areas. In the late 1940's its lending authority was expanded to include loans for rural telephone service.

The Farm Credit Administration was established in 1933. After six years of independent operation it was placed under the Department of Agriculture. In 1953, Congress reestablished the FCA as an independent agency under the executive branch of the federal government. It offers three major credit services to farmers: (1) the land bank service, (2) the short-term credit service, and (3) the cooperative bank service.

The land bank service comprises the 12 federal land banks and numerous federal land bank associations that make long-term farm mortgage loans and perform many services connected with farm real estate financing. The short-term credit service includes the 12 federal intermediate credit banks and numerous production credit associations. The intermediate credit banks extend credit to the production credit associations and other financing institutions that make short-term agricultural loans. The cooperative bank service encompasses 12 district banks for cooperatives and the central bank for cooperatives, all of which make loans to cooperative farm marketing associations.

The FCA was established to encourage eventual member-borrower ownership of local associations and district banks. Toward this end, the Farm Credit Acts have provided for the retirement of government capital so that each of these institutions some day will become wholly owned by its member-borrowers.

Other Agencies. There are other agencies which sponsor direct and guaranteed and insured loan programs covering a wide range of purposes. In the direct-loan group are the Urban Renewal Administration, loans for slum clearance and urban renewal projects; Community Facilities Association, construction loans to universities and colleges; Maritime Administration, loans for vessel construction; Office of Education, loan funds for student financial aid; and Export-Import Bank, the principal foreign-lending agency of the government.

In the loan-guarantee and insurance group are the Civil Aeronautics Board, which guarantees loans for aircraft purchases mainly by small airlines; Interstate Commerce Commission, which guarantees loans to railroads for certain purposes; and the Development Loan Fund, which guarantees loans to governments, organizations, and citizens of underdeveloped nations.

CLIFTON H. KREPS, JR.
University of North Carolina

16. Bankers' Associations

Bankers in the United States have developed a variety of national, state, and local associations. Besides providing education and information, the national associations engage in other activities common to trade organizations, including research on industry problems, maintenance of libraries relevant to the industry, and preparation of testimony on behalf of the industry for presentation to legislative bodies.

American Bankers Association. The ABA is the largest and oldest of the bankers associations. In the late 1960's membership was approximately 18,000 commercial and mutual savings banks. The vast majority of the members are commercial banks. Founded in 1875, the ABA has its headquarters in New York City, with a staff of 300, and also maintains a smaller office in Washington, D.C. The ABA issues many publications for information and education, including the monthly magazine *Banking*.

The ABA conducts two large educational operations, the Stonier Graduate School of Banking and the American Institute of Banking. The Stonier Graduate School of Banking is a summer resident school held at Rutgers University, New Brunswick, N. J., for bank officers. The sessions are supplemented by correspondence courses during the rest of the year. The work is designed to prepare students for bank management positions. The American Institute of Banking is a night school designed primarily to teach basic skills such as accounting and bank operations to bank employees at the nonofficer and junior-officer levels. The institute operates schools in principal U.S. cities, and writes and publishes textbooks for its courses. The ABA also publishes material for the education of the general public in banking.

National Association of Mutual Savings Banks. The NAMSB has a membership of approximately 500 banks, representing 99 percent of the total assets of the mutual savings bank industry. Founded in 1920, the association has its headquarters in New York City, where a staff of about 40 is located, and also maintains an office in Washington, D.C. The association publishes the *Savings Bank Journal* and the *National Fact Book*, containing a wealth of statistics on savings banks and related areas such as the mortgage market.

The association's Graduate School of Savings Banking and the Management Development Program are its two main educational activities. The Graduate School of Savings Banking is conducted at Brown University in the summer and is continued through correspondence courses. The school is restricted to young bank officers, and emphasis is placed on management decision-making in investments, marketing, and bank operations. The Management Development Program, held at Dartmouth College each summer, is designed for senior officers. Through study of liberal arts as well as technical subjects, the student seeks to understand better the changing economic and social environment in which he makes policy decisions.

United States Savings and Loan League. The largest of the savings and loan organizations, the league has a membership of about 4,700 and a staff of 140 employees. Its headquarters are in Chicago. The league publishes annually the *Savings and Loan Fact Book*, containing detailed statistics on the savings industry generally and the savings and loan business specifically. The league also publishes the *Savings and Loan News*, a monthly publication for members. The main educational activity of the league is the America Savings and Loan Institute, which holds classes in cities throughout the country to educate employees in fields related to the savings and loan business.

Mortgage Bankers Association. Founded as the Farm Mortgage Bankers Association in 1892, this organization became the Mortgage Bankers Association in 1926. Its headquarters are in Chicago. In the late 1960's it had over 2,000 members and a staff of about 30. About 60 percent of the members are mortgage loan correspondents (originators of mortgages in local areas). The other members are primarily commercial banks, mutual savings banks, and life insurance companies. The association publishes the monthly *Mortgage Broker*. Its primary educational activity, the School of Mortgage Banking, consists of three one-week summer sessions, and emphasizes the special problems of mortgage lending.

Independent Bankers Association. Founded in 1930, the Independent Bankers Association consists primarily of small, independent commercial banks. Its headquarters are in Sauk Centre, Minn. It has approximately 6,300 members and a staff of about 10 employees. The association publishes the monthly *Independent Banker*.

Other Associations. The National League of Insured Savings Associations, with about 500 members, has its headquarters in Washington, D.C. Virtually every state has a state bankers association; many states have a state savings and loan organization; and nine states have a mutual savings bank association. Almost every large city has a clearinghouse association that, besides clearing checks, engages in a certain amount of trade association activity. Many banks are members of research and trade groups, such as the National Bureau of Economic Research and the National Tax Foundation.

DAVID A. BOWERS, *Western Reserve University*

Bibliography

Banks and Banking in the United States

American Bankers Association, *Commercial Banking Industry* (Englewood, N.J., 1962).

Chandler, Lester V., *Economics of Money and Banking*, 4th ed. (New York 1964).

Hammond, Bray, *Banks and Politics in America from the Revolution to the Civil War* (Princeton, N.J., 1957).

Kent, Raymond P., *Money and Banking*, 4th ed. (New York 1961).

Kreps, Clifton H., Jr., *Money, Banking, and Monetary Policy* (New York 1962).

Klaman, Saul B., *The Postwar Residential Mortgage Market* (Princeton, N.J., 1961).

Maisel, Sherman J., *Financing Real Estate* (New York 1965).

National Association of Mutual Savings Banks, *Mutual Savings Banking: Basic Characteristics and Role in the National Economy* (Englewood Cliffs, N.J., 1962).

Robinson, Roland I., ed., *Financial Institutions*, 3d ed. (Homewood, Ill., 1960).

Sayers, Richard S., *Modern Banking*, 6th ed. (New York 1964).

Studenski, Paul, and Krooss, Herman E., *Financial History of the United States* (New York 1963).

Trescott, Paul B., *Financing American Enterprise* (New York 1963).

BANKING OUTSIDE THE UNITED STATES

17. Canada

The banking system of Canada consists of the Bank of Canada (the central bank), the chartered banks (commercial banks), loan and trust companies, various savings banks, credit unions, and small loan companies. The most important are the Bank of Canada and the chartered banks.

Bank of Canada. The Bank of Canada, with its head office in Ottawa, was founded in 1934 and nationalized in 1938. It is directed by statute to regulate credit and currency in the best interests of the nation's economic life. To accomplish this purpose the bank acts as fiscal agent of the Dominion and provincial governments; holds the deposited reserves of the chartered banks; has the sole right of note issue; manages the gold and foreign exchange reserves of Canada; may buy and sell securities issued by Canada or any of its provinces, by the United Kingdom, and by the United States; may extend loans and advances to the chartered banks or to the government of Canada or to any province; and may buy and sell securities, cable transfers, and bankers' acceptances.

The Bank of Canada implements its policies by changing rates of interest on loans; by altering the amount of deposited reserve which must be held by the chartered banks; by buying and selling securities (open-market operations) and, under the direction of the Dominion government, by changes in foreign exchange rates. Policy actions by the Bank of Canada enable it to influence economic conditions by bringing about changes in the money supply, by causing interest rates to rise and fall, and by making credit more or less available.

Commercial Banks. All commercial banks in Canada are chartered or incorporated under Dominion law. At one time there were many such institutions, but over the years by reason of failures, mergers, and amalgamations the number has been reduced to eight. Five of these have branches over the entire country, two operate principally in the province of Quebec, and one confines its activities to Montreal, Toronto, and Vancouver. Several have foreign branches. The chartered banks are Canada's largest financial institutions and have aggregate deposits of about $25 billion. With more than 5,000 branches (one banking office for every 3,500 persons), the chartered banks provide banking facilities for all parts of Canada, finance changing credit needs, and assist in developing new areas.

About 35 percent of their resources is represented by liquid assets—cash, Canadian government securities, and call loans. About the same percentage is represented by business loans, most of which are short-term and grow out of the need for working capital. Their remaining resources take the form of agricultural loans, consumer loans, mortgages, and loans to provinces and municipalities. Loans are well diversified industrially and geographically.

The Bank Act that governs the operations of the chartered banks was enacted by the Dominion government originally in 1871 and is revised about once a decade. The banks are subject to examination by the inspector general of banks, a Dominion official.

See also CANADA—*20. Banking and Currency.*

BENJAMIN HAGGOTT BECKHART
Columbia University

18. Other Commonwealth Nations

The banking systems of Commonwealth nations resemble the system in Britain. Each has a central bank, a few large commercial banks with many branches, and numerous specialized institutions.

Britain. The Bank of England, often called the mother of central banks, was founded in 1694 and nationalized in 1946. It acts as banker to the commercial banks, has the sole right of note issue, manages British gold and foreign exchange reserves, and serves as fiscal agent to the government. Since World War II it has endeavored—not always successfully—to safeguard the internal and external value of the currency. It does so by changing the rates of interest it charges on loans, by engaging in open-market operations, by imposing controls on consumer credit, by issuing lending directives to commercial banks, by control over the liquid assets of commercial banks, and by employment of moral suasion.

Nearly all of the banking business of England and Wales is in the hands of fewer than a dozen commercial banks (the joint stock banks). Their primary business is to receive, transfer, and pay out demand and time deposits, to deal in foreign exchange, and to finance credit needs. In financing credit needs, a borrower is permitted to overdraw his account by

A SKYSCRAPER BANK, the Canadian Imperial Bank of Commerce, is a prominent feature of Montreal's skyline.

GEORGE HUNTER

THE BANK OF ENGLAND is housed in this structure built in 1925—but its history goes back to 1694, when it was founded as a private firm. The bank was nationalized in 1946.

a stipulated amount and pay interest on the average amount of the overdraft.

Clustered about the Bank of England and the commercial banks are a host of specialized institutions: discount houses, which deal in short-term money market instruments; the accepting houses, which specialize in foreign trade finance; branches of overseas banks; issuing houses, which underwrite security issues; hire-purchase firms, which deal in installment credits; investment trusts; and many others. Together these specialized institutions comprise the London money market, which ranks next to the New York market in worldwide importance. See also GREAT BRITAIN AND NORTHERN IRELAND —7. *Finance* (Banking and Investment).

Australia. Branch banking has spread over the nation from such focal points as Sydney, Melbourne, and Adelaide. By amalgamations and failures, the number of commercial banks (trading banks) has been reduced to eight. One of these, the Commonwealth Trading Bank of Australia, is government owned and competes actively with the other commercial banks. The trading banks accept checking accounts, term deposits, and, by means of the overdraft, finance a great variety of credit needs, including in particular those arising from production of crops, wool, and meat. They have affiliated savings banks, which extend mortgage loans, and they own stock in finance companies, which finance consumer credit needs.

The Reserve Bank of Australia, the central bank, was established as a separate institution in 1959. It is owned by the commonwealth government, has its head office in Sydney, and has branches in Canberra and each state capital. It has a monopoly of the note issue, holds the reserves of and makes loans to the trading banks, issues lending directives to the banks, and manages the nation's foreign exchange reserves, which are located in London. In the postwar period it has been active in establishing a short-term money market.

Australia is well supplied with other types of financial institutions. They finance domestic capital needs and serve as a conduit for a large inflow of foreign capital. All have played an important role in the industrial development of the continent.

New Zealand. New Zealand is highly dependent on foreign trade. It exports meat, wool, and dairy products, and imports manufactures. The character of the economy as well as the existence of a welfare state has shaped the structure and operation of the banking system.

There are five trading banks (commercial banks), which maintain extensive networks of branches. The largest, the Bank of New Zealand, is government owned. Of the others, three are predominantly Australian banks and one has its head office in London. The banks receive demand and time deposits and, by means of the overdraft, finance their customers' credit needs, in which agriculture looms large.

The Reserve Bank of New Zealand, the central bank, is fully state owned and state controlled. In accord with government policy (it enjoys no autonomy), the Reserve Bank issues lending directives to the trading banks, manages the public debt, and operates overseas exchange controls. Its principal duty is to put into effect the government monetary policy as it is communicated from time to time by the minister of finance.

BENJAMIN HAGGOTT BECKHART
Columbia University

19. Western Europe

The banking systems of western European nations, derived from common origins and serving the needs of private enterprise, are similar in organization and functions. Each has a central bank that has the sole right of note issue, serves as fiscal agent of the government, holds gold and foreign exchange reserves, and, through its credit policies, helps to achieve the nation's economic objectives. Each has commercial banks that through networks of branches specialize in financing the credit needs of agriculture and business. In wartime they finance governmental needs, and they have begun to finance consumer credit requirements. Each banking system has a group of specialized institutions, established to finance investment, mortgage and small-business requirements.

France. The French banking system centers about the Bank of France, the central bank, founded in 1801 by Napoleon and nationalized in 1945. Commercial banks, called banks of deposit, finance the short- and medium-term credit needs of business. Four of the largest, operating in all parts of France, were nationalized at the end of World War II. The other commercial banks confine their operations to regions or localities.

The *banques d'affaires*—the investment banks —finance the long-term credit needs of business and have played an active role in the economic development of France. Other institutions include agricultural credit and mortgage banks, savings institutions, and cooperative banks.

Credit policy is formulated and harmonized by the National Credit Council, consisting of representatives of government and financial interests and implemented by the Bank of France. The French banking system tends to be somewhat more specialized than that of other continental systems. This characteristic has helped to promote French economic development. See also FRANCE—*Finance*.

West Germany. The Deutsche Bundesbank, the central bank, follows a conservative credit policy, as might be expected in a country that within a generation has twice witnessed the destruction of its currency. Its paramount duty is to safeguard the stability of the mark.

The commercial banking system consists of three extremely large institutions, plus many state, regional, and local banks; private banks confined to a few cities; and specialized institutions catering to the needs of particular industries. The relation between commercial banks and industry has always been close. Often banks have taken the initiative in organizing industries, in the initial financing of long-term credit needs, and in the underwriting and flotation of securities to repay the long-term bank loans. Credit cooperatives are numerous and extend loans to farmers, small businessmen, retail trade, and middle-class professions. Savings banks, many owned by local authorities, in recent years have competed actively with commercial banks in accepting demand deposits and in making loans to small business.

Despite the efforts of Allied military authorities to decentralize it, the banking system again resembles the prewar centralized system. In becoming centralized, it has been able to marshal the financial resources of Germany in economic reconstruction and in the defense of the currency. See GERMANY—*The Economy* (Banking and Public Finance).

Italy. Policies on the control of money, credit, and credit institutions are formulated in Italy by the Interministerial Committee for Credit and Savings. The members include the governor of the Bank of Italy and six cabinet members. The Interministerial Committee, in which the Bank of Italy plays the dominant role, has power to alter bank-reserve requirements, to regulate rates of interest charged on loans and paid on deposits, to approve the establishment of new banks and the merger of old, and to approve issues of shares and debentures. By restricting the amount it will lend to financial institutions, by open-market operations, and by issuing lending directives to the banking community, the Bank of Italy has exercised strict credit control in the postwar years.

The credit system of Italy includes not only commercial but also cooperative savings, and mortgage banks and institutions for agricultural

credit and for medium- and long-term industrial finance. Four of the largest commercial banks have nation-wide activities; others confine their operations to regions. The largest banks are owned directly or indirectly by the Italian government, principally as the result of salvage operations in the Great Depression. Public ownership has not lessened the extent or forms of competition nor destroyed the individual character of the separate banks.

Switzerland. The central bank, the Swiss National Bank, founded in 1907, is one of the youngest central banks in Europe. It is owned by the cantons, by the cantonal banks, by other banks, and by private holders. The liquidity of the Swiss economy, resulting from a continued influx of foreign funds, has caused the Swiss National Bank to rely on such measures as the sterilization of government funds and gentlemen's agreements with the banks in efforts to control credit. Sterilized government funds are funds that are withdrawn from circulation by being placed in blocked accounts with the central bank. The gentlemen's agreements often require commercial banks, as a means of restricting the inflow of foreign funds, to charge rather than to pay interest on deposits.

The Swiss banking system includes five large commercial banks, with branches throughout Switzerland; a number of cantonal banks; local banks; mortgage banks; and cooperative banks. Almost all cantonal banks are owned by the cantons in which they operate. They are really savings institutions, receiving time deposits, issuing debentures, and making mortgage loans. The local banks engage in a variety of operations. Some are essentially savings institutions, granting mortgage and installment credits; others extend business loans, deal in foreign exchange, and often specialize in business with particular countries. The private banks administer the funds of their wealthy clientele, participate in financing foreign trade, and cooperate in floating domestic and foreign capital issues. The credit institutions form a well-functioning financial system. Competition keeps interest rates low and sees to it that credit needs of the Swiss are fully met.

BENJAMIN HAGGOTT BECKHART
Columbia University

20. Eastern Europe

Monetary and banking systems in Communist nations render the same basic functions as in capitalist nations: the issuance of currency, the financing of short- and long-term credit needs, the transfer of funds, and the collection and investment of savings. Differences in banking result principally from differences in economic and political organization and structure.

Upon the introduction of communism in the USSR and eastern Europe, all credit institutions were nationalized. Central and commercial banking functions were concentrated in one huge institution, the state bank. Other credit functions having to do with the financing of agriculture, with investment operations, with foreign trade, and with the promotion of savings usually were delegated to specialized institutions.

The State Bank. The state bank in all Communist nations has close relationship with the ministry of finance, with other ministries that assist in formulating the over-all economic plan, and with the planning board. Its responsibilities are to meet currency needs, to meet the financing needs of the economic plan, to extend loans to factories and other economic entities, to make sure that the economic plan is being carried out, and to transfer funds. It accepts no deposits from individuals. Payments to and between individuals usually are made in currency.

Operations are highly centralized. Policies originate in the head office and are implemented by the branches, which in the USSR total about 5,000. Local offices issue currency and make loans in accordance with assigned quotas, report on deviations from the economic plan, and provide information to assist in preparing the plan. Information flows up and directives down.

Other Institutions. Specialized financing institutions are to be found in those areas requiring specialized skills. Thus investment banks, relying upon their staffs of engineers, disburse government funds under approved investment plans for building new plants and modernizing old ones. Although agricultural credits in the USSR are handled by the Gosbank—the state bank—agricultural banks still exist in some other Communist nations, chiefly for the financing of agricultural cooperatives. Foreign trade banks, where they exist, maintain branches abroad, handle relations with foreign banks, and provide foreign exchange facilities. They manage the gold and foreign exchange reserves of the country according to plan and exercise foreign exchange control. In the USSR, the Gosbank handles most of these functions.

Savings banks are the only institutions that establish accounts for individuals, enabling them to accumulate savings and providing them with checking facilities. Savings deposits pay interest and often carry lottery privileges. Savings banks invest their funds in government securities or make loans to individuals for the purchase of durable goods or cooperative apartments.

Two divergent tendencies developed in Communist banking in the 1960's. One was a tendency to merge specialized institutions with the state bank. The other tendency was to give managers of state bank branches somewhat greater leeway in making loans. The latter trend will become more important to the extent that factories produce goods in response to consumer demand.

BENJAMIN HAGGOTT BECKHART
Columbia University

21. South America

South American nations share many common characteristics that have shaped their monetary and banking systems. Average real incomes are low. Income distribution is uneven. Land ownership is heavily concentrated.

The tax system is inequitable. Savings are small. The propensity to consume is high. Governments overborrow at home and abroad. Inflation is endemic, although the symptoms may be suppressed by import and exchange controls. Currencies are periodically devalued. Resources are misused and misdirected, and economic development is stifled. The causes of inflation are government and private deficits, financed by increases in currency and bank credit. These factors are abetted by the cost-push resulting from the tying of wages to price indices.

Central, Foreign, and Local Banks. Each nation has a central bank or comparable institution whose main activity is to finance government

A. DEVANEY, INC.

PERU'S CENTRAL BANK is the impressive Banco Internacional del Peru, situated in Lima, the capital.

deficits and the borrowing needs of commercial banks that rise from private deficit financing. Occasional attempts to check inflation encounter strong political opposition and are usually short-lived.

Foreign commercial banks—British, German, French, Italian, United States, and Japanese—play an important role in the financing of foreign trade and the credit needs of their nationals. Indigenous commercial banks, state or privately owned, are the principal source of investment funds for local business enterprise. Businessmen do not wish to dilute equity by issuing stock. Inflation acts as a barrier to the sale of bonds. Commercial banks extend loans, nominally short but actually long, at interest rates that seem high until they are adjusted for price increases.

Savings, small but concentrated, are used mainly to buy lands or buildings (as an inflation hedge) or are placed with banks in foreign nations. Funds for domestic development, aside from those borrowed from commercial banks, are provided by the direct investment of foreign firms, by foreign governments, or by international lending institutions.

Other Institutions. To supplement the work of commercial banks, various types of financial intermediaries have been established, such as savings banks, development banks (the *financieras*), and capitalization companies. Capitalization companies are common in South America. They pay their policy holders a capital sum after a period of years against monthly premiums. The policies often contain lottery privileges. Some intermediaries are owned by commercial banks, some by private investors, and some by governments. They specialize in mortgage, mining, and industrial credits. They are relatively few in number, and many credit needs, particularly in agriculture, housing, and industrial finance, are not met. The establishment of additional financial intermediaries and their successful functioning awaits the elimination of inflation.

BENJAMIN HAGGOTT BECKHART
Columbia University

22. Africa

In South Africa and in the North African nations bordering the Mediterranean Sea, the banking systems are organized generally on the European model. The newer countries of tropical Africa, however, have monetary and banking systems that are shaped by certain common characteristics of their economies. Foreign trade makes up an important share of their total trade; their exports consist largely of raw materials; they are heavily dependent on foreign capital. Many Africans remain outside the money economy and are unfamiliar with financial institutions. Savings are small.

Banking began with British, Dutch, and French banks, established to finance export and import trade and the credit needs of their own nationals. With political independence the influence of foreign banks has tended to diminish and that of local institutions to increase. Central banks have superseded currency boards that issued local currency against foreign assets, usually pound sterling, and served as passive money changers. Central banks are status symbols of independence and help advise governments on financial matters, foster the growth of other financial institutions, and promote economic development.

Swings in exports cause sharp fluctuations in the deposits and cash reserves of the commercial banks. This makes them dependent on foreign money markets and causes them to concentrate on short-term loans. This tendency is reinforced by lack of bankable security (communal ownership eliminates land as collateral), by the financial weaknesses of one-man enterprises, by the lack of adequate accounting systems, by high working-capital requirements resulting from long delivery periods, and by attitudes of financial unreliability toward debt.

Conditions are changing. Industry is being diversified. Imports of capital are being encouraged. An entrepreneurial class is developing. The banking habit is growing. Native banks are being established and banks are extending branches from seaport towns to the interior.

There remain a number of credit gaps. Inadequate provision exists for medium- and long-term agricultural credit. Attempts are being made to solve the problem by the establishment of cooperative banks and land banks. Similarly, institutions are needed to finance the requirements of home construction and of small business.

BENJAMIN HAGGOTT BECKHART
Columbia University

23. Asia

Coins, paper money, credit instruments, and various types of credit institutions existed in Asia long before their establishment in Europe. European practices were not imported until the 19th century and were superimposed on indigenous arrangements.

India. The village moneylender continues to serve as the base of the credit structure. Next come the indigenous bankers who combine money-lending and trading. Modern commercial banking resulted from the establishment of exchange banks, mainly British, situated in the larger centers and concentrated on foreign trade finance.

Exclusively Indian commercial banks grew to prominence after World War I and experienced rapid growth after World War II. Unique among these is the government-owned State Bank of India, which has promoted agricultural and small business finance. It accounts for about one third of total commercial bank deposits. Specialized credit institutions include the important credit cooperatives, agricultural and land mortgage banks, and various investment banks that promote industrial development. The Reserve Bank of India, established in 1935 and nationalized in 1949, is the central bank. It has endeavored to promote the healthy development of the banking system, to strengthen the system of cooperative credit, and to develop medium- and long-term financing institutions.

Japan. Japan modeled its first banking law (1872) upon the National Banking Act of the United States. After a brief experimentation it was abandoned in favor of a central banking system. Commercial banks in their operations resemble the German system more than the American, in that they traditionally engage in financing investment credit needs. To do so they borrow heavily from the Bank of Japan— the central bank—and collect savings through their network of branches.

Supplementing the commercial banks are specialized institutions such as the Bank of Tokyo, which concentrates on foreign exchange operations, and the long-term credit banks, which issue debentures and finance plant and equipment expenditures of large business enterprises. Other specialized credit institutions cater to the borrowing needs of agriculture, or fisheries and forestry, and of small business, which has always played an important role in Japan.

The Bank of Japan has the sole right of note issue, handles treasury funds, serves as banker to other banks, and exercises credit control. It sets lending limits for each institution and provides guidance to commercial banks on their loan portfolios, business practices, and management. The Bank of Japan is under the close supervision of the government.

BENJAMIN HAGGOTT BECKHART
Columbia University

Bibliography
Banking Outside the United States

Auburn, Herbert W., *Comparative Banking* (London 1966).

Bank of England, *Quarterly Bulletin* (London, quarterly).

Bank of Japan, *Money and Banking in Japan* (Tokyo 1964).

Beckhart, Benjamin Haggott, ed., *Banking Systems* (New York 1954).

Crick, W.F., ed., *Commonwealth Banking Systems* (New York 1965).

Ellis, Howard S., ed., *Economic Development for Latin America* (London 1961).

Garry, George, *Money, Banking, and Credit in Eastern Europe* (New York 1966).

Marcus, Edward, and Marcus, Mildred, *Investment and Development Possibilities in Tropical Africa* (New York 1960).

Royal Commission on Banking and Finance, *Report of the Royal Commission* (Ottawa 1964).

Sayers, Richard S., ed., *Banking in Western Europe* (New York 1965).

24. Banking and World Trade

International banking encompasses a wide range of institutions, practices, and accumulated experience by which the world carries out financial transactions across national boundaries. Such institutions may be private, governmental, or international in character. Private institutions include commercial banks, foreign exchange traders, and investment banking houses. Governmental institutions are treasuries and central banks as well as long-term lending and aid-giving agencies. The international bodies most prominent in banking are the International Monetary Fund (IMF) and the International Bank for Reconstruction and Development (World Bank).

An international center is a place where domestic as well as international funds can float in and out freely, where funds can be held on deposit or invested, where funds can be borrowed to finance trade and investment, and where transactions can be conducted efficiently.

For a country to fulfill the role of international center, a fair degree of balance is required between payments abroad and receipts from abroad. The balance must be well enough adjusted over a period of time to preclude excessive deficits or surpluses and, consequently, excessive gains or losses of gold. The role of international center also requires a stable and sound currency, readily acceptable, voluntarily retained, and freely usable throughout the world. A century ago Walter Bagehot described the money, capital, and foreign exchange markets in England as "by far the greatest combination of economical power and economical delicacy that the world has ever seen."

In the 19th century, England was the banker to the world. Today, London remains an international money and capital market, but, because it restricts the rights of residents to purchase and hold foreign currencies, it is essentially an *entrepôt*—a center for handling the funds of third countries, using primarily "Eurodollars," as described below. Over the years since World War I, New York emerged as the prime financial center of the world. This was not the result of conscious decisions but the natural outcome of the growth of the U. S. economy, its savings, and its place in the world. During the late 1960's and early 1970's, the prolonged deficits in U. S. international payments, the controls imposed in the United States on flows of funds into other currencies, and the devaluation of the dollar in 1971 and its inconvertibility into gold and other international reserve assets adversely affected the dollar as the prime international currency and New York as the prime international center. Meanwhile, the swing of economic and monetary power back to Europe led to the establishment of a new international market spanning several European centers, linked through the "Eurodollar" and, one day perhaps, through a single European currency.

Role of Commercial Banks. International trade is kept moving through the financing provided by the great commercial banks of the world. The banks maintain a vast crisscrossing of branches and correspondent relationships with one another, linked by mail, teletypewriter, and telephone. They hold operating balances for businesses, traders, investors, and other banks. They are wholesale buyers and sellers of foreign exchange. They engage in foreign borrowing and lending. Much of this business is transacted in U. S. dollars. This is partly for convenience, but also because the dollar can be invested more readily or borrowed more expeditiously and in larger amounts than other currencies.

The growth of deposits and other short-term dollar assets held in the United States by other nations began from a very small base after World War II. Subsequently, however, the growth kept pace with the expansion of world trade and investment, particularly after the reestablishment in the late 1950's of a substantial degree of convertibility of currencies among the principal nations. Loans to foreigners by U. S. banks also rose greatly. Mostly, these credits are directly related to the financing of U. S. exports. Some represent the financing of commerce between third countries or of investment on an international scale by multinational organizations.

Outside the United States, since the mid-1950's, there has emerged a new international money market in "Eurodollars." These are U. S. dollars held on deposit in foreign banks or in foreign branches of U. S. banks—for example, in London. The banks in turn use the funds to meet temporary needs for additional liquidity or for relending. Banks in Europe have been particularly active in this field—hence the label "Eurodollar market." The label, however, is misleading since Eurodollars are not a special kind of dollar but differ from ordinary dollars only in respect to the channels through which they move. Furthermore, they are not confined to Europe but come from almost everywhere.

Role of Treasuries and Central Banks. While the commercial banks finance world trade, government treasuries and central banks typically engage in operations aimed at maintaining the foreign exchange value of their nation's currency. In the process, they buy and sell foreign exchange, mostly U. S. dollars. But this international "intervention" role is conditioned by the confidence of each government or central bank that the dollars they acquire would be accepted by the monetary authorities of other countries. For international banking rested importantly on the readiness of the United States to buy and sell gold freely in transactions with foreign monetary authorities for legitimate monetary purposes at a fixed price of $35 per fine ounce—convertibility suspended by President Nixon in August 1971. In March 1972 the dollar was devalued from $35 to $38 a fine ounce—by 7.89%—entailing an 8.57% increase in the U. S. monetary

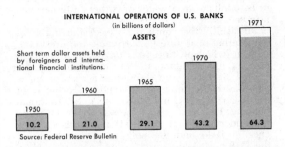

INTERNATIONAL OPERATIONS OF U.S. BANKS
(in billions of dollars)
ASSETS

Short term dollar assets held by foreigners and international financial institutions.

1950	1960	1965	1970	1971
10.2	21.0	29.1	43.2	64.3

Source: Federal Reserve Bulletin

gold price. The United States, however, gave no indication that it would convert, at the new price, dollars into gold or other international reserve assets.

Basically, the continued use of the dollar as an international reserve currency requires confidence, which in turn rests on reasonable price-cost stability at home and on acceptance by the United States of the discipline necessary for a currency with the international importance of the dollar. (See GOLD STANDARD.) International banking has also been shaped importantly by the undertakings at the Bretton Woods Conference in 1944 and the policies and practices of the IMF.

Other Instrumentalities. Other international banking instrumentalities are governmental long-term-lending and aid-giving institutions. In the United States, the Export-Import Bank of Washington, established in 1934, provides medium- or long-term credit to help finance U. S. foreign trade, thus supplementing and encouraging private lending. The proceeds of its loans are spent in the United States. The Export-Import Bank also guarantees loans made by U. S. commercial banks and issues export credit insurance policies. Its resources come mainly from income on its capital and from sales of certificates of participation in its loans. Because Export-Import Bank transactions are limited to loans repayable in dollars, the United States has evolved other forms of financial assistance, such as various aid programs, including loans by the Agency for International Development.

Among the international long-term lending agencies are, most prominently, the World Bank and its affiliates. Outside the World Bank group, there are five regional institutions—the Inter-American Development Bank (established in 1960), the African Development Bank (1965), the Asian Development Bank (1965), the European Investment Bank (1958), and the European Investment Fund (1958)—the last two being organs of the European Common Market.

Difficulties in Functioning. International banking as it has developed since World War II has served the world well, as evidenced by the remarkable expansion of world trade and investment. In the mid-1960's, however, difficulties appeared in the functioning of the international monetary system. Symptoms included the recurrent sterling crises and the prolonged deficits in the U. S. balance of payments. These were attributable to the U. S. government's defense and aid spending and private capital outlays as well as to the decline in its surplus on trade and services. A better balance in U. S. international payments in itself would strengthen, not weaken, the international monetary system. Nevertheless, it appeared prudent for the governments to review the working of the world monetary system and, if need be, make adequate provision for the future. Thus, in 1969, they established Special Drawing Rights (SDR's) and, in 1971, they provided greater flexibility in the exchange-rate pattern and announced their intention to work out fundamental reforms in the international monetary system.

At the same time, it became evident that such reforms as might be made would have to maintain monetary and fiscal discipline and support meaningful freedom of world trade and investment. The reforms also would have to help, not hinder, the pool of private international liquidity—private working balances and credit availabilities from private sources. It is this liquidity that does the vital job of lubricating the wheels of international commerce.

MIROSLAV A. KRIZ
First National City Bank, New York

25. International Monetary Fund

The IMF, created at the Bretton Woods Conference in 1944 and headquartered in Washington, D. C., has become an essential segment of international banking. The fund has almost 120 members, encompassing virtually all nations. The principal exceptions are Switzerland (which, however, cooperates in international monetary matters directly with other leading nations), the countries of eastern Europe, including the USSR, and the People's Republic of China.

Objectives. Under the IMF charter, the member governments have agreed on broad lines of international monetary policy—for the first time in history. They particularly aim at the establishment and maintenance of currency convertibility and the avoidance of competitive exchange depreciation. At the same time, they have provided the fund with a substantial pool of resources to help stabilize exchange rates by assisting countries over difficulties in their balances of payments.

An essential attribute of the fund is the principle that exchange rates are a matter of international concern. Each member undertakes:

(1) To establish an agreed par value for its currency in terms of gold—an obligation that, in December 1971, was qualified in that members could establish a "temporary" regime of "central rates" that could be changed without formal permission from the fund.

(2) To maintain buying and selling rates for exchange transactions in its currency within permissible margins—initially 1% on either side of parity, but widened to 2.25% in December 1971.

(3) To consult the fund on any change in the par value (except a once-and-for-all revision of not more than 10%). While helping to prevent competitive exchange depreciation, however, the fund has recognized that exchange rates should not become unalterably frozen to a point where they hinder trade and investment. In fact, many devaluations were made but relatively few upvaluations.

The fund's efforts to maintain reasonable currency stability and convertibility while reducing restrictions on payments are supported by the pool of resources with which it has been endowed. Each member is assigned a quota (determined by the size of its economy, foreign trade, and other factors). These quotas, following general increases in 1959, 1966, and 1970, totaled the equivalent of $29 billion in the early 1970's. Each member pays a subscription to the fund equivalent to its quota, normally 25% in gold and 75% in its currency. Voting power and eligibility to draw on the fund are linked to the size of the quota. The United States has a quota of $6.7 billion, the largest in the fund, and almost one fourth of the voting power.

Loans and Repayments. The IMF conducts operations only with the treasuries and central banks of its members. Whenever it makes a loan, it provides foreign currencies from its holdings to the borrower, and the borrower pays the fund the equivalent amount in its own currency. A loan—called a drawing—thus consists of a member's purchase of foreign currencies with its own currency. A repayment represents a member's repurchase of its own currency with gold or in a currency acceptable to the fund. Members are committed to maintain the gold value of their currencies held by the fund.

A country may draw virtually at will up to an amount equivalent to its gold subscription—the gold tranche or slice—plus such claims on the fund as it may have accumulated because of the fund's use of its currency to extend its loans to other members—the "super gold" tranche. Drawings exceeding these tranches—but not exceeding one half of the country's quota—are granted liberally (first "credit tranche"). For drawings of further amounts (in "higher tranches"), the fund expects substantial justification. These policies on drawings were supplemented in 1963 by compensatory financing arrangements designed to broaden the fund's balance-of-payments support to primary-producing nations that may suffer a temporary drop in export earnings as a result of price declines. For example, if coffee or cocoa prices fall and a producing country's income thus is cut sharply, it may borrow from the fund.

The currencies drawn are selected, following consultation, in the light of the balance-of-payments and reserve positions of members. Drawings are subject to charges, normally payable in gold. The fund generally enters into standby arrangements, giving a member the right to draw an agreed amount within an agreed period of time without further examination.

Members undertake repayments to the fund within a maximum of three to five years. Earlier repurchases are often made either voluntarily or according to a requirement that a member make a repurchase if its gold and foreign exchange reserves increase sufficiently. A member's repurchase obligation is reduced to the extent that other members draw its currency from the fund. In practice, the IMF has functioned as a revolving fund, and the currencies it has lent have been returned to the pool.

Increased Activities. Little use was made of the IMF from 1947, when it made its first transaction, to 1955. Beginning with 1956, IMF activities increased sharply, mainly because of large drawings by the United Kingdom to cope with various sterling crises, beginning in 1956.

As demands on the fund have increased, steps have been taken to strengthen its resources. Apart from three general quota increases, the fund has sold gold to its principal members to replenish its holdings of their currencies. In 1962 the fund entered into "general arrangements to borrow." In these, the leading nations agreed to lend it up to the equivalent of $6 billion (including $2 billion from the U. S.), if necessary, to forestall or cope with an impairment of the international monetary system. In each of the three years beginning with 1970, the IMF allocated to members Special Drawing Rights in a total amount equivalent to $9.5 billion. See GOLD STANDARD.

The IMF serves as a guardian of international reserves. Its resources, facilities, and procedures provide international liquidity for a rapidly expanding world trade and investment, and support the creditworthiness of nations.

MIROSLAV A. KRIZ
First National City Bank, New York

26. Bank for International Settlements

The Bank for International Settlements (BIS) was founded in 1930 to promote cooperation among central banks and facilitate international financial settlements. The idea took practical shape in the course of negotiations that led in 1929 to the Young Plan for adjustments in reparations owed by Germany after World War I. Bank headquarters are in Basel, Switzerland.

The evolution of the BIS has been one of adaptation to changing circumstances. In the early 1930's, the bank took an active part in attempts made to counteract the world's economic depression, including participation in emergency credits to Germany and several eastern European countries. These credits were fully repaid. During World War II, its activities were sharply curtailed. The Bretton Woods Conference in 1944 recommended the liquidation of the BIS. However, after the end of the war, when contacts were reestablished and the facts were seen in their true light, it was decided not to proceed with the resolution. Since the war, and especially beginning with 1961—the year of the first of the series of the Basel arrangements to support the pound sterling—the BIS has become the focal point of intercentral bank cooperation.

The setting for cooperation is the regular monthly meeting of the BIS board of governors. The United States has never taken membership in the BIS, but representatives of the Federal Reserve became regular participants in the 1960's. The board includes the governors of five founding central banks—Belgium, France, Germany, Italy, and the United Kingdom. These ex-officio members in turn have given directorships to the governors of the central banks of the Netherlands, Sweden, and Switzerland. Apart from these and other European countries, Australia, Canada, and Japan are also members. U. S. Federal Reserve representatives regularly attend the BIS board meetings.

When the BIS was being established, the central banks had the option of either subscribing to its shares or offering them for subscription to the public in their own markets. Most central banks chose to subscribe and now own three fourths of the shares. The remainder, mostly the shares of the U. S. issue, are owned privately, particularly in Europe. The rights of representation and voting are completely independent of ownership and are exercised by the central banks.

BIS resources consist primarily of deposits of central banks. They are used for loans to central banks and in gold transactions.

MIROSLAV A. KRIZ
First National City Bank, New York

27. World Bank

The World Bank—or, by its full title, the International Bank for Reconstruction and Development (IBRD)—was created in 1944 at the same time as the International Monetary Fund and has the same membership. The World Bank has its headquarters in Washington, D. C. It began operations in 1946, granting loans at "conventional" financial terms to member governments or, under government guarantees, to government agencies, development banks, or private undertakings. It has two offspring: the International Finance Corporation (IFC), founded in 1956 to provide funds, without government guarantees, for private projects in underdeveloped countries;

and the International Development Association (IDA), founded in 1960 to provide loans on "soft" financial terms.

Objectives. The main task of the World Bank is to provide finance for productive purposes out of its own capital, funds borrowed in capital markets, and retained earnings. Of the initial authorized capital, equivalent to $10 billion, 2% was paid in gold or U. S. dollars and may be used freely by the World Bank in any of its operations. Eighteen percent was paid in the national currencies of subscribing members but is available for lending only insofar as members deem it advisable to export capital and give their consent. The remaining 80%, not available for lending, is subject to call only when required to meet the World Bank's obligations for funds it has itself borrowed or guaranteed. The authorized capital was raised gradually to the equivalent of $27 billion in 1971. Cash payments were required only from new members. Voting power of the members is in proportion to their capital subscriptions.

The World Bank's capital structure provides in effect for a guarantee fund. Thus the capital structure greatly reinforces the security offered by the bank to private buyers of its bonds and, therefore, its borrowing power. The guarantees of the United States alone amount to $5.715 billion. Those of the United States, the United Kingdom, France, the Federal Republic of Germany, and Canada total over $10 billion—about double the World Bank's funded debt in the early 1970's. More than three fifths of the debt was owed to investors outside the United States.

Another source of funds for the World Bank is its own retained earnings. These are sizable, because the participating governments have asked for no dividends on their shares. During 1964–1971 the World Bank transferred $485 million of its earnings as grants to IDA.

In addition to these three basic sources of funds, the World Bank has obtained resources for lending by selling portions of loans to private investors and from repayments of principal on earlier loans.

Loans and Repayments. The World Bank extends credits to finance the foreign exchange costs of specific "infrastructure" projects—those that lay the groundwork for progress. In its first 25 years, about a third of the World Bank's lending was for development of electric power; another third for railways, roads, ports, pipelines, and other transportation; and the rest for agriculture, industry, and general development. Toward the end of this period, the bank placed growing emphasis on financing agricultural development and education.

Most of the loans have been made to less-developed countries. However, the bank has also lent to countries such as Australia, Italy, Japan, and Norway since 1950 and, prior to that, to a number of European countries to finance postwar reconstruction. The bank's largest borrower is Mexico, with India second, and Brazil third.

The World Bank's loans are medium- or long-term, averaging 20 years. They carried 7.25% interest in the early 1970's, as against 4.25% in the late 1940's. Prior to 1965, the rate was uniform for all borrowers at any given time. Thereafter, a higher rate—though in no case more than 1% above the standard rate—was applied on loans to countries able to cover the bulk of their external capital needs from market sources.

International Development Association. The World Bank's approach to lending has made a decisive contribution to world economic development. It has been widely felt, however, that development finance ought also to be supplied in ways that would not increase the burdens of foreign debt service carried by many of the less-developed nations. In 1960, therefore, the International Development Association (IDA) was brought into being to grant loans repayable over 50 years, free of interest and carrying only a 0.75% service charge. The IDA is separate from the World Bank financially but otherwise integrated with it. The IDA's special terms are granted in consideration of the borrower's balance-of-payments problems, but are not meant to subsidize individual projects. The World Bank applies the same technical and economic standards regardless of whether the money is provided from the IDA or from its own funds.

The IDA's lending terms preclude it from borrowing in capital markets and make it, therefore, entirely dependent on governments for funds. Initially, the IDA was endowed with funds of about $780 million in gold and convertible currencies supplied almost entirely by industrial countries. As most of these resources had been committed, a second round of contributions in 1966 provided the IDA with additional funds of $750 million in convertible currencies. The third replenishment in the amount of $2.4 billion was scheduled for 1971–1974. By 1971, IDA had extended credits to nations that totaled $3 billion.

International Finance Corporation. The IFC is designed to provide more specialized assistance to private industry than is possible through the World Bank. Apart from the capital subscribed by governments, the funds available to IFC come primarily from sales of investments and securities and from borrowings from the World Bank up to an amount equal to four times IFC's paid-in capital.

The task of the World Bank extends well beyond the lending in which it engages. The individual projects it finances must be related to the entire development effort of the borrowing nations. The World Bank thus has been deeply engaged in the art of economic development. Its accomplishments are indisputable, but, in a world short of capital and exposed to strong demands for investment, the difficulties are very real.

MIROSLAV A. KRIZ
First National City Bank, New York

Bibliography
International Banking

Annual Reports of the Bank for International Settlements (Basel, Switzerland); Export-Import Bank (Washington); International Bank for Reconstruction and Development (Washington); International Monetary Fund (Washington).

Coombs, Charles R., "Treasury and Federal Reserve Foreign Exchange Operations," in *Federal Reserve Bulletin* (Washington, beginning September 1962).

Holmes, Allan R., and Schott, Francis H., *The New York Foreign Exchange Market* (New York 1965).

Lary, Hal B., *Problems of the United States as World Trader and Banker* (New York 1963).

Princeton University, International Finance Section, *Essays in International Finance* (Princeton, N. J., occasional publications).

Reid, Escott, *The Future of the World Bank* (Washington 1965).

Roosa, Robert V., *Monetary Reform for the World Economy* (New York 1965).

Trued, Merlyn N., *United States Official Operations in the Foreign Exchange and Gold Markets* (Washington 1965).

BANKING AS A CAREER

28. Positions in Banking

Employees in a bank are divided into two categories—those who are officers and those who are not. In general, the officers have a degree of authority, depending on their rank, to commit the bank legally in business matters, one of the most important of which is the approval of loans. A person seeking a career in banking probably will not begin as an officer, unless he is an older person with business experience that the bank regards as valuable. However, if he is a college graduate, he can expect to become a junior officer within one to five years after employment, depending on his performance and the policies of his bank.

Bank Clerks and Tellers. Banks in the United States employ about 800,000 persons, and the ratio of nonofficers to officers is about 6 to 1. More than half of the jobs are held by women. Despite increased automation, the number of bank jobs has continued to increase each year.

Bank clerks make up the largest single group of employees. In addition to the obvious duties, some, such as interest-accrual bookkeepers or proof-machine operators, handle unusual jobs not found in other business offices. The second-largest employee group is made up of tellers, who receive and pay out money and record transactions. Because they deal with customers, tellers are selected in part for tact and courtesy.

Bank Officers. Titles of bank officers are important and meaningful but not necessarily standardized. In the typical arrangement, the lowest-ranking officer is called assistant cashier, followed in ascending order by cashier, assistant vice president, vice president, senior vice president, executive vice president (only one, usually), and on top the president, unless there is also a chairman of the board.

The level of responsibility of officers varies considerably from bank to bank. The work done by a senior employee in one bank may be done by a junior officer in another. Bank size is a primary factor in the responsibility that goes with a particular title, but even when two banks are virtually identical in size, the same title can represent quite different responsibilities. Bank managements hold differing philosophies as to the role of a bank officer. Sometimes the difference is due to dissimilarities in the kinds of business in which the banks are engaged. A bank heavy in "wholesale" banking has many large accounts requiring few officers, each of whom must have enough authority to commit the bank to large dollar obligations. In contrast, a bank with many small branches doing a great deal of "retail" or consumer lending and demand deposit business requires a great many officers to staff its branches and to approve many small loans. To indicate the range of responsibility that goes with a title, there is an old saying in the banking business, "Don't tell me what his title is— tell me his lending limit."

Specialization. As a person progresses in a banking career, he usually settles down to an area of specialization. The areas of specialization are many, but generally they may be grouped under the broad areas of banking service or bank operations, accounting, investments, and public relations and advertising. Within each of these areas there is sometimes a need for individuals with a high degree of specialization, especially in the very large banks. For example, automated accounting systems have created a great need for specialists in electronic data-processing equipment. Most large banks have technical specialists in the types of business to which they make a substantial dollar volume of loans. If a bank caters to the oil industry, there will be petroleum engineers on its staff. In agricultural areas, even small banks have experts in the appraisal of livestock and agricultural real estate. In savings banks and in savings and loan associations there are, of course, specialists in every phase of mortgage lending and property appraisal.

As a general rule banks prefer to bring their specialists up through their own ranks, but in periods of rapid expansion this is not always feasible. As a result, rapidly growing banks often employ specialists who have learned their specialty in an entirely different industry.

Education and Training. For beginning clerks and tellers, a high school education is adequate. With experience, clerks and tellers may advance to supervisory positions or even officer rank, particularly if they obtain additional education while employed.

A college education has become highly desirable and almost a prerequisite for a successful career as a bank officer—although many of the present officers of banks of substantial size have little or no formal education beyond the secondary school level. Banks prefer college graduates with degrees in economics or business administration, but liberal arts and other degrees are readily acceptable. The wide range of undergraduate specialization is acceptable because most banks recognize that a significant period of on-the-job training will be required.

The large metropolitan banks operate formal training programs during which the trainee rotates among the departments. His assignment at the end of the training period is determined by his desires, the bank's needs, and the bank management's evaluation of his aptitudes. Some larger banks have more than one training program, with specialized training for those going into such areas as foreign branches or the trust department. In smaller banks there usually is no formal program, but the new employee who indicates an interest in banking as a career will be assigned to work on problems in all departments and thereby gain diversity of experience.

Salaries. The beginner usually cannot command a high salary while he is in the process of training. After completing a formal training program (or, in the case of a small bank, gaining experience throughout the bank), he is in an excellent position to command a significantly higher salary. Typically, the first few years of employment are ones of rapidly increasing income for the successful trainee.

In most banks seniority counts for a great deal. In a sense there is a certain amount of "deferred compensation." The young officer who works hard may not be rewarded as rapidly as in some other industries, but his maximum income before retirement usually will be much higher than it would be in another industry where very high income is obtainable more quickly.

DAVID A. BOWERS, *Western Reserve University*

BANKING TERMS

29. Glossary

Acceptance—A draft or bill of exchange used in financing international and domestic trade in staple commodities. A trade acceptance is a draft drawn by the seller of goods on the buyer and "accepted" by the buyer. In a bank acceptance, banks substitute their own credit for their customers' credit and accept drafts drawn under letters of credit. Customers provide funds to pay acceptances at maturity. Bank acceptances are important instruments of short-term credit to provide funds pending completion of business transactions.

Accrued Interest—Interest owing but not yet paid. The term "accrued" may also be applied to dividends and other accumulations of funds due but not paid.

Amortization—The process of paying or reducing a debt by periodic payments sufficient to cover current interest and to extinguish part of the principal.

Appraisal—An estimate of value of property, especially real estate, to be offered as collateral for a loan.

Balance—(1) The amount standing to the credit of a depositor's account, representing the amount he is entitled to withdraw. (2) The difference between the total debits and credits, whether against or in favor of a bank, at the clearinghouse.

Bank Call—Demand made by supervisory authorities upon banks under their jurisdiction for the publication of statements of condition. Bank statements are usually published as of December 30 and June 30.

Bank Check—A check drawn by a bank on itself and signed by an authorized officer; also called treasurer's check, officer's check, or cashier's check.

Bank Draft—A check drawn by a bank against funds deposited to its account in another bank.

Bank Examiner—A person who, as the representative of a federal or state bank supervisory authority, examines a bank's financial condition, management, and policies.

Bank Note—A bank's promise to pay to bearer on demand, intended to be used as money—for example, a Federal Reserve note. Bank notes are often referred to as circulating notes, circulation, or currency.

Bank Statement—A statement of a customer's checking account, given him for his information. It shows all deposits recorded, checks paid, and charges made during a period, as well as the balance, and is accompanied by the customer's canceled checks.

Bearer—Holder or person in possession of money, or of a check, bill, note, or other instrument.

Beneficiary—(1) The person specified by a depositor in connection with an account in trust for another. (2) The person in whose favor a letter of credit is issued. (3) The person designated to receive the income or principal of a trust estate. (4) The person who is to receive the proceeds of, or benefits accruing under, an insurance policy or annuity.

Bond—An interest-bearing certificate of debt which promises under seal that the issuer (a government or a corporation) will pay a certain sum of money to the holder of the bond at a specified date. In effect it is a long-term loan by the bond-holder to the issuer. A bond differs from a promissory note in that it is issued as a part of a series of like tenure and amount and in most cases with a common security.

Bond of Indemnity—A written instrument under seal by which the signer, usually together with his surety or bondsman, guarantees to protect another against loss. It is sometimes required to protect the bank when the depositor asks that payment be stopped on a check or reports a lost passbook. Such an agreement without sureties is called an indemnity agreement.

Call Money—Money loaned by banks, usually to stock exchange brokers, for which demand may be made at any time.

Capital Funds—The total of the capital accounts of a bank, including total stated or par value of capital stock, surplus, undivided profits, and capital reserves.

Cash Items—Items, usually checks or coupons, that are accepted for tentative credit to a depositor's account, subject to reversal if the items are not paid.

Certificate of Deposit—A written acknowledgment by a bank of a deposit payable upon the return of the certificate on a specified date. The deposit is generally interest-bearing and the depositor may not withdraw it by check or prior to maturity.

Certification (Certified Check)—An assurance by a bank on which a check or draft is drawn that sufficient funds are on deposit to cover the check. The certification is stamped on the face of the instrument and signed by an authorized official of the drawee bank. On certification the bank charges the drawer's account and the instrument becomes the primary liability of the certifying bank.

Check—A draft drawn on a checking account payable on demand. It is, in general, a negotiable instrument.

Checking Account—A bank account against which checks may be drawn.

Clearing—Domestic clearing is the offsetting of bank counterclaims and the settlement of balances; it may be either local or nationwide. International clearing is the settlement of balances between countries through the medium of foreign exchange.

Clearinghouse—A place where representatives of the commercial banks in the same locality meet each day at an agreed time to exchange checks, drafts, and similar items drawn on each other and to settle the resulting balances.

Collateral—Specific property that a borrower pledges as security for repayment of a loan, agreeing that the lender shall have the right to sell the collateral if the borrower fails to repay the loan at maturity.

Collection Items—Items (drafts, notes, acceptances) received by a bank subject to collection before proceeds will be credited to depositors' accounts.

Comaker—A person who signs the note of another as an additional maker to strengthen the credit of the principal maker.

Commercial Paper—All classes of short-term negotiable instruments that arise out of commercial transactions as distinguished from speculative or personal transactions.

Compound Interest—Interest upon principal plus accrued interest.

Correspondent Bank—A bank that carries a deposit balance for a bank usually located in another city or engages in an exchange of services with it.

Countersign—To have another person sign what has already been signed in order to verify the authenticity of an instrument.

Credit—An advance of cash, merchandise, or other commodity in the present, in exchange for a promise to pay a definite sum at a future date, with interest if so agreed. Long-term credit is generally obtained by the sale of bonds or mortgages. Short-term credit is granted to a business to supply temporary commercial needs. Short-term credit granted to an individual for personal use is called consumer credit.

Currency—Technically, includes both paper money and metallic money (coin). Bankers generally use the term for paper money only.

Demand Deposit—Funds in a checking account subject to withdrawal on demand.

Demand Draft—A draft payable on presentation; also called sight draft.

Discount—Bank discount is interest paid at the beginning of a loan, based upon the sum to be repaid at maturity. True discount differs from bank discount in that interest is computed on the proceeds or amount borrowed.

Discount House—The name given to a banking corporation engaged in purchase and discount of trade and bank acceptances, bills of exchange, and other forms of commercial paper.

Dividends—In mutual savings banks and in savings and loan associations, a distribution to depositors of a specified percentage of net earnings.

Double-Name Paper—Notes, bills of exchange, and trade and bank acceptances with two signatures, each representing separate interests, responsible for payment. It is also known as two-name paper.

Draft—A written order signed by the drawer directing the drawee to pay a specified sum of money to, or on the order of, the payee.

Endorsement or Indorsement—The signature plus any other writing by which the endorser transfers his rights in an item to someone else. It is generally written on the back of the item. Technically the term is limited to an endorsement of negotiable paper.

Escrow—A written agreement, such as a deed or bond, entered into among three parties and deposited for safekeeping with the third party as custodian, to be delivered by the latter only upon the performance or fulfillment of some condition.

Exchange Charge—The term "exchange charge" has a variety of meanings. (1) A remittance charge that some banks deduct in paying checks drawn upon themselves when they are presented through the mails from out-of-town points. (2) A charge for drafts on other cities. (3) A charge that banks make for collecting out-of-town items, generally called a collection charge.

Exchanges—Items on banks in the local area presented for collection through the clearinghouse. Banks in a local area may exchange items directly instead of through a formal clearinghouse.

Federal Funds—Excess reserves of commercial banks on deposit at the Federal Reserve or with correspondent banks, which can be lent temporarily—overnight or for a few days—at the federal funds rate of interest, to banks with reserve deficiencies.

Fiduciary Service—A service performed by an individual or a corporation acting in a trust capacity. A banking institution authorized to do a trust business may perform fiduciary services, for example, by acting as executor or administrator of estates, guardian of minors, and trustee under wills.

Float—Items in transit by mail or otherwise that are not actually collected.

Foreclose—To deprive a mortgagor of his right to redeem the property mortgaged.

Guaranty—A written promise by one (the guarantor) to be liable for the debt of another (the principal debtor) if the principal debtor fails to perform his obligation and the guarantor is notified of that fact by the creditor.

Honor—To accept or pay an item when presented for acceptance or payment. (To refuse to accept or pay an item is to dishonor.)

Indirect Liability—A secondary or contingent liability assumed by the endorsement or guaranty of an obligation for which another party is primarily liable.

Interest—The sum paid for the use of money or credit.

Items—A flexible term, used in bank collections, that is broad enough to include instruments payable in money generally.

Joint Account—An account in the names of two or more persons. Often the funds may be withdrawn on the signature of one depositor.

Letter of Credit—An instrument issued by a commercial bank to an individual or corporation by which the bank substitutes its own credit for that of the individual or corporation. See also *Traveler's Letter of Credit.*

Loan—The letting out or renting of sums of money by a lender to a borrower, to be repaid.

Maker—The person who signs and delivers (executes) a note or other promise to pay. Sometimes the drawer of a check or draft is referred to as a maker.

Maturity—The due date of a mortgage, note, draft, acceptance, bond, or other instrument.

Money Order—A draft sold by a bank to a customer for a fee.

Mortgage—A method of pledging property for debt in which the lender may foreclose the security if the interest agreed upon is not maintained.

Negotiable Instrument—An unconditional written order or promise to pay money which can be transferred to a holder in due course, free from defenses between the original parties.

Nonpar Items—Items for which the payor bank will not remit to a collecting bank without deducting an exchange charge.

No Protest—A waiver of formal protest, which under the law includes the waiver of presentment and of notice of dishonor. It is usually evidenced by a stamp on the face of the item.

Open Market—A broad and freely competitive market in which participating or trading is not restricted to any group of persons, and on which the prices of commodities, securities, or money are determined. *Open-market operations* refer to Federal Reserve purchases and sales of U.S. government securities as part of credit and monetary stabilization policy.

Overdraft—(1) The amount owing to a bank by reason of paying an item or items drawn against insufficient funds. (2) Sometimes the term is used for an item drawn against insufficient funds whether or not paid by the bank.

Par Items—Items for which the payor bank will remit without charge.

Par Value—Of a bond, note, or other obligation for the payment of money, the amount agreed to be repaid, exclusive of interest.

Passbook—In general, a book supplied by a bank to a depositor for record purposes. A savings passbook contains a complete record of the customer's account, showing deposits and withdrawals as well as the interest credited at regular periods.

Postdated Check—A check dated ahead. It is not payable until the date specified. Thus a check issued July 1, dated July 15, is not payable until July 15.

Principal—The face amount or par value of a note or other evidence of debt. Also, the sum of money employed for profit or interest-bearing purposes.

Promissory Note—A written promise by the maker to pay a certain sum of money to the payee, or to his order, on demand or at a determinable future date.

Protest—A formal procedure necessary—unless waived—on dishonor of a negotiable check or draft which is: (1) not in fact drawn and payable within the state and (2) does not purport to be so drawn. Protest is permissible for other negotiable instruments to facilitate proof in a legal proceeding. It consists of a written certification, usually by a notary, that he has presented a negotiable instrument and that the instrument was dishonored by refusal to accept or to pay.

Raised Check—A check on which the amount has been fraudulently increased.

Rediscount—The process of discounting commercial paper a second time by one bank for another, or by a central bank for a member bank. The term applies almost solely to the discounting of paper by a Federal Reserve bank for a member bank. In substance, however, any note is rediscounted whenever an indorser negotiates it.

Reserves—Funds set aside by a bank to enable it to pay its depositors in cash on demand. Reserves may consist of cash on hand, demand deposits in other banks, and required deposits (legal reserves) with the Federal Reserve bank of its district.

Return Item—An item returned unpaid by a payor bank.

Safekeeping—The receipt by a bank of custody of property to be returned. It may be contrasted with safe deposit, where the property is placed in a safe deposit to which the renter, rather than the bank, has access.

Securities—That class of investments represented by engraved, printed, or written documents, evidencing ownership or creditorship in a corporation or other property. (Examples: stocks, mortgages, coupons.)

Service Charge—A fee charged to depositors for services rendered, usually in connection with checking accounts. The charge takes into consideration the maintenance costs, but also allows an earnings credit for the balance maintained in determining the charge to be made to the customer's account. Special bank service charges include charges for issuance of bank money orders and drafts, safekeeping of securities, excessive withdrawal activity in savings accounts, late note payments, and checks drawn against uncollected or insufficient funds.

Single-Name Paper—Notes that are the obligations of one party only—the maker. It is also known as straight paper. It represents loans without any other responsibility than that of the general credit of the maker. Although two or more names may appear on a note either as makers or indorsers, it is still single-name paper if the names represent identical interests.

Stop-Payment Order—An order or request by a depositor to his bank that it refuse payment of an item specified by him.

Surety Company—A company that insures against various types of losses, including fidelity of employees, of fiduciaries (such as executors, administrators, trustees, and guardians), and of public officers. A surety company executes bonds of many kinds, including bankers' blanket bonds, payment and performance bonds with respect to contracts, depository bonds, and bail bonds.

Survivorship Account—An account in the names of two persons which, on the death of one, belongs to the survivor. A survivorship account may be in the names of more than two persons, in which case the death of any one other than the last survivor terminates his interest. Usually items against the account may be drawn by any living depositor.

Teller's Check—A bank draft signed by a teller or tellers of the drawer bank. A teller's check may be used to pay withdrawal orders on savings accounts. They are sometimes sold by savings banks to customers for cash in lieu of money orders.

Time Deposit (Savings Deposit; Savings Account)—Deposits that may not be withdrawn by check and on which specified advance notice of intention of withdrawal may be required.

Transit Items—Cash items payable outside the city of the bank receiving them for credit to customers' accounts, and transmitted by mail or similar service by a collecting bank to a payor bank.

Transit Number—A number that indicates a bank and its location. The transit number in the American Bankers Association's system has two parts: the prefix, or number preceding the hyphen, designates the city or state in which the bank is located; the suffix, or number following the hyphen, indicates a particular bank. This number as a numerator is combined with a denominator, which is the check routing symbol.

Traveler's Check—A means by which a person may obtain money at banks or hotels while he is on a journey without carrying the usual means of identification. A traveler's check is sold by a bank or an express company and accepted by the drawee bank or express company, so that payment cannot be stopped. The buyer signs his name when he buys the check. He countersigns when he needs money; comparison of the signatures affords identification.

Traveler's Letter of Credit—A letter by a commercial bank, not to the seller, as in the case of a commercial letter of credit, but to a correspondent bank either in the same or in another country, authorizing the person named in the letter to draw drafts on the correspondent bank to the extent of the credit specified. Such person deposits with the issuing bank the total amount of the credit, plus the bank's charge for this service.

BANKS ISLAND, in the Arctic Ocean, is part of the Northwest Territories of Canada. The westernmost island in the District of Franklin, it is separated from Victoria Island by Prince of Wales Strait and from the mainland of Canada by Amundsen Gulf. Banks Island is 250 miles (402.3 km) long and covers approximately 26,000 square miles (67,340 sq km). The terrain is mainly a hilly plateau, with numerous lakes. Discovered by Sir Robert McClure in 1851, the island was thoroughly explored by Vilhjalmur Stefansson in 1914–1917.

BANNEKER, ban′ə-kər, **Benjamin** (1731–1806), American man of science and almanac maker, who participated in the survey of the Territory of Columbia (now District of Columbia). He was born a free Negro on Nov. 9, 1731, near Ellicott's Lower Mills (now Ellicott City) Md., the son of a freed Negro slave. His maternal grandparents were a freed Negro slave and a white English indentured servant. Banneker spent most of his life as a tobacco planter. Except for several winters of elementary schooling, he was entirely self-taught and demonstrated an instinctive skill with mathematics. In his early 20's he constructed a striking clock, carving each part from pieces of wood, without ever having seen one.

In 1789, George Ellicott, of the family that founded Ellicott's Lower Mills, lent Banneker several astronomical and mathematical texts and instruments. He studied and mastered them without guidance, and completed the ephemeris for an almanac for the year 1790. From February to April 1791, Banneker served as scientific assistant to Maj. Andrew Ellicott in making the survey of a 10-mile (16-km) square for the Territory of Columbia, in which the national capital was planned. During this period he came to the attention of Maryland and Pennsylvania abolitionist societies, which supported the publication of almanacs incorporating ephemerides he had compiled. The first almanac bearing his name and including his calculations was published for the year 1792. Five more issues followed before the series was discontinued. They were widely distributed, and more than 29 editions and printings of the six issues were published.

Due to poor health and his new scientific interests, Banneker abandoned tobacco farming in his later years and lived on income from the sale of parts of his 100-acre farm. He died on his farm on Oct. 9, 1806.

SILVIO A. BEDINI
Author of "The Life of Benjamin Banneker"

BANNING is a city in California, in Riverside County, 20 miles (32 km) northeast of the desert resort of Palm Springs. Situated at an altitude of 2,250 feet (686 meters) in scenic Gorgonia Pass, between the San Bernardino and San Jacinto mountains, it has long been known for its healthful climate. Its medical facilities include a modern community hospital, a clinic, and several convalescent homes. Banning's chief industries are the manufacture of garments and airplane parts. Some fruit is grown in the neighborhood. The Morongo Indian Reservation is located near the city.

Banning was founded in the early 1880's and was incorporated as a city in 1913. It has a council-manager form of government. Population: 12,034.

BANNISTER, ban′is-tər, **Sir Roger Gilbert** (1929–), English middle-distance and mile runner, who was the first to run a competitive mile in less than four minutes. His time of 3:59.4 was established at a dual meet in Oxford, England, on May 6, 1954. Aided by two teammates who set a planned pace, Bannister reached his goal with quarter-mile times of 57.5, 60.7, 62.3, and 58.9. Overcoming the psychological block of the "four-minute mile," he exceeded the previous world record of 4:01.4 set by Gunder Haegg of Sweden in 1945. John Landy of Australia broke Bannister's mark in July 1954, with 3:58.

Bannister was born in Harrow, England, on March 23, 1929. He received a B.A. from Oxford in 1950, graduated from St. Mary's Hospital Medical School in 1954, and received an M.D. degree at Oxford in 1963. He was knighted in January, 1975.

BILL BRADDOCK, *New York "Times"*

BANNOCKBURN, Battle of, ban′ək-bûrn, an engagement which resulted in Scottish independence from England. It was fought on June 23–24, 1314, about 2 miles (3 km) southeast of Stirling, Scotland. Robert Bruce, with an army of about 6,000 Scots, successfully withstood an attack by Edward II and 20,000 English troops.

The Scots were drawn up on the far side of Bannock Burn (stream) in a wooded area that prevented a surprise attack on their flank. The advancing English cavalry was crowded into a space too narrow for effective combat, and its supporting infantry was pinned behind it. At a critical point in the fighting, a reserve unit of the Scottish army attacked to force the English to retreat. The victory secured Scottish independence until the crowns of England and Scotland were united under James VI of Scotland in 1603.

BANNS, banz, are the announcement of an intention to marry, made in church at the principal weekly service. The object is to prevent an invalid marriage by enabling those knowing of an impediment to the marriage to reveal it.

In the Roman Catholic Church, banns are published in the parish church of each marriage partner for three Sundays preceding the ceremony. Banns are not required in mixed marriages. The obligation to reveal an impediment is binding in conscience on all Catholics.

Dispensation from the rule concerning banns is granted in time of war, during penitential seasons, or to avoid hardship to the contracting parties, as, for example, in a deathbed marriage. In such cases, the marriage partners must swear under oath that there is no impediment.

In the Anglican Church, requirements for the publishing of banns are set forth in the Book of Common Prayer. Parliament incorporated the rules in a marriage act of 1753 but limited them to Anglicans in Britain. Those settling overseas were free to accept or reject the rules.

Episcopal sanction of an intended marriage was begun in the 2d century to prevent illicit unions. After the 5th century, judgment was reserved to the pastor. In 1215 the 4th Lateran Council made the publication of banns a matter of church law, and the council of Trent ratified the law in its present form in the 16th century.

In the United States, only the Roman Catholic Church requires banns; publication is optional in the Episcopal and other churches. Canada accepts either banns or a license.

BANQUO, bang'kwō, a character in Shakespeare's *Macbeth,* was a fellow general with Macbeth in King Duncan's army. Macbeth ordered him slain when a prophecy foretold that Banquo's descendants would one day rule Scotland, thus, presumably, thwarting Macbeth's desire to seize and hold the throne. Banquo's ghost appears to Macbeth at a banquet and terrifies him into a public betrayal of his guilt.

Although Banquo is mentioned in Holinshed's *Chronicles* and in old Scottish genealogies, his historical existence is not firmly established.

BANTAM, bän-täm', is a region at the western end of the island of Java, in Indonesia. Now a part of West Java province, it was formerly a residency of the Netherlands East Indies, with Serang as its capital. The area is about 3,000 square miles (7,770 sq km). Bantam produces rice, tea, sugar, indigo, and coffee. Until 1683, when it first came under Dutch control, Bantam was the center of a Muslim sultanate which also controlled parts of Borneo and Sumatra. The town of Bantam, which was the capital of the Muslim sultanate and a flourishing Dutch port in the 1600's and 1700's, is now largely in ruins.

BANTAM. See CHICKEN.

BANTAM LAKE, ban'təm, in west central Connecticut, is the largest natural lake in the state. It is situated in Litchfield County, 30 miles (48 km) west of Hartford. It is 2.5 miles (4 km) long, and its area is 1,000 acres (405 hectares). Bantam Lake is a noted summer resort. The Bantam River enters the lake from the north and flows out to the northwest.

BANTAYAN ISLAND, bän-tä-yän', in the Philippines, is in Cebu province, 9 miles (14 km) west of the northern tip of Cebu Island. It is about 45 square miles in area (117 sq km). The island's chief crops are corn and coconuts. There is also some fishing. Population: (1960) 46,593. The municipality of Bantayan is situated on the southwest coast of the island.

BANTENG, bän'teng, a large wild ox, formerly found in Burma, Thailand, Indochina, the Malay Peninsula, and Java, but now extremely rare. A large bull, standing almost 5 feet (1.5 meters) at the shoulder, may have a head and body length of 6.5 feet (2 meters). Bantengs are usually blackish in color, with white feet and a white patch on the rump.

Bantengs are generally found in herds of 10 to 30, but solitary bulls, often larger than the average bull, are occasionally found. Bantengs prefer forested, hilly areas, but climatic conditions influence their choice of habitat. During the monsoon season the bantengs leave the lowlands and drift up into the hill forests, where they feed on tender new herbage. In the dry season they return to valleys and more open wooded areas, where they feed on grass. Shy and wary animals, the bantengs eat during the night and lie in dense thickets during the day. They mate during the dry season, and a single calf is born in late summer. The banteng (*Bos banteng*) belongs to the family Bovidae.

BANTING, ban'ting, **Sir Frederick Grant** (1891–1941), Canadian physician and cowinner of the 1923 Nobel Prize in physiology and medicine. Banting and his assistant, Charles H. Best, succeeded, in 1922, in extracting the hormone insulin from the pancreas, thus making it possible to prolong the lives of diabetes mellitus victims.

In diabetes mellitus, glucose accumulates in abnormally high quantities in the blood and appears in the urine. It causes weakness and other symptoms and usually leads to death if it is not treated. In 1890 an experiment by J. von Mehring and O. Minkowski showed that removal of the pancreas in experimental animals caused a form of diabetes. It was therefore believed that the pancreas produced a hormone that controlled the rate of glucose metabolism. The source of the hormone was suspected to be certain cells of the pancreas called the "islets of Langerhans." All efforts to isolate the hormone had failed, however, because when the pancreas was removed and ground up, its digestive enzymes broke down the insulin molecules.

Banting and Best, a medical student, tied off the pancreatic ducts of several dogs for a period of seven weeks. The pancreases shriveled up and became useless as digestive organs. The islets of Langerhans remained intact, however, and a solution was extracted from these cells. Injections of this extract into diabetic dogs (dogs whose pancreases had been removed) quickly restored the dogs to normal health. The insulin extract soon proved effective in treating diabetes mellitus in humans. Since then insulin injections have enabled millions of diabetics to lead relatively normal lives.

Banting and Best did their work on insulin in the laboratory of John J.R. Macleod, a professor of physiology at the University of Toronto. Although Macleod was away from the laboratory and did not participate in the work, the 1923 Nobel Prize in physiology and medicine was awarded jointly to Banting and Macleod "for their discovery of insulin." Banting was furious that Macleod, and not Best, had received a share of the award. He finally agreed to accept the prize but gave half his share of the money to Best. Macleod, in turn, gave his share to J.B. Collip, who had worked with him in purifying and standardizing insulin after Banting and Best had extracted it. Banting and Macleod were the first Canadians ever to be awarded the Nobel Prize.

NEW YORK ZOOLOGICAL SOCIETY

BANTENG cattle (*Bos banteng*), found in parts of Southeast Asia, now are scarce.

Life. Banting was born in Alliston, Ontario, Canada, on Nov. 14, 1891. He began studying for the ministry at the University of Toronto but then decided to study medicine and received his medical degree in 1916. He served as a medical officer during World War I and received the Military Cross for bravery in attending seriously injured men even after he had been wounded.

After the war he practiced medicine in London, Ontario, until May 1921, when he and Best began their work on insulin. In 1923 he was appointed head of the newly created Banting and Best department of medical research at the University of Toronto. In the same year the Canadian Parliament voted him an annuity, and in 1934 he was knighted.

Besides his work on insulin, Banting made important studies of the adrenal cortex and of cancer and silicosis. He died in an airplane crash in Newfoundland, while on a military medical mission, on Feb. 21, 1941.

BANTOCK, ban'tək, **Sir Granville** (1868–1946), English composer and conductor, who was influential in championing the works of younger English composers of the early 1900's. He was born in London on Aug. 7, 1868. In 1889 he became a scholarship student of composition at the Royal Academy of Music. He composed mostly program music on Oriental themes.

Bantock founded the *New Quarterly Musical Review* in 1893 and edited it for three years. During this time he also toured as a conductor of musical comedies. He became professor of music at the University of Birmingham in 1908 and was knighted in 1930. He died in London on Oct. 16, 1946.

BANTU, ban'tōō, is a group of closely related languages spoken in Africa south of an irregular linguistic boundary known as the Bantu line. From the southeastern corner of Nigeria on the Atlantic coast, this line runs roughly eastward, passing to the north of Lake Victoria; it then turns southward into Tanganyika and northeastward to the Indian Ocean on to the coast of Kenya. Most of the languages spoken in the vast area south of this boundary are classed as Bantu, a widely used word meaning "the people." The chief exceptions, besides English and Afrikaans, are the Click languages (notably Bushman and Hottentot) and Malgache.

The Bantu languages were formerly regarded as constituting a separate language family, but they have been shown to be related to the languages of West Africa, and are now classed as a part of one of the 15 subfamilies of a much larger Niger-Congo family. The many Bantu languages are distinct from one another and mutually unintelligible, despite their evident historical relationships.

The Bantu-speaking peoples vary considerably in physical type and culture, with marked differences in food, clothing, housing, arts and crafts, music, religion, social structure, and political organization. These differences are to be seen in comparing such groups as the Zulu and Swazi in southern Africa with the Kongo and Mbundu in Angola, the Mongo and Luba in the Congo region, or the Ganda and Nkole of Uganda, not to mention the Bantu-speaking Pygmies. The term "Bantu" is useful only for linguistic classification, not for distinguishing race or designating cultural features.

BANVARD, ban'värd, **John** (1815–1891), American artist and writer. He was born in New York City on Nov. 15, 1815, and moved to the West at the age of 15. In 1840 he traveled down the Mississippi River, making sketches for his most ambitious painting, *Panorama of the Mississippi.* This work, covering a half mile of canvas, was exhibited throughout the United States and England. Banvard's writings included two plays —*Amasis,* produced in Boston in 1864, and *Carrinia,* produced in New York in 1875. He died in Watertown, S. Dak., on May 16, 1891.

BANVILLE, bäN-vēl', **Théodore de** (1823–1891), French poet and story writer. He was born in Moulins on March 14, 1823. He first attracted notice as a poet with the publication of *Les cariatides* (1842) and *Les stalactites* (1846). However, his reputation was established with *Odes funambulesques* (1857), which won high praise from Victor Hugo. Banville spent most of his life in Paris, where he died on March 15, 1891.

Banville's poetry, which is notable for its delicate lyricism, was collected in volumes that include *Nouvelles odes funambulesques* (1869; reprinted in 1875 as *Occidentales*), *Idylles prussiennes* (1871), and *Trente-six ballades joyeuses* (1875). His prose writings include *Les saltimbanques* (1853) and *Esquisses parisiennes* (1859). He served as drama critic on Parisian newspapers and wrote verse dramas. A collected edition of his works, in eight volumes, was published between 1873 and 1878, and his memoirs appeared in 1883.

BANYAN, ban'yan, is a tree of the mulberry family. It is found in eastern India and as far south as Malaysia. It is an epiphyte (a plant that derives its moisture and nutrients from the air) and grows from seeds that germinate on branches of host trees, which soon die. Year by year, as the

JOHN H. GERARD

BANYAN tree (*below*) shows characteristic aerial root system. Inset (*right*) reveals two tiny figs growing on a branch.

JOHN R. BROWNLIE, FROM PHOTO RESEARCHERS

young banyan tree develops, it sends out aerial (prop) roots that eventually reach the ground and take hold to gain support and nourishment for the young tree. Trunks of more mature trees are composed of several aerial roots and new trunks constantly are formed in this way.

Banyans grow more in circumference than in height. Eventually, large arcades of aerial roots are formed, and the flat-topped crown of the tree may reach 1,500 feet (458 meters) in circumference. The banyan tree produces figs, which appear in pairs and are without stalks. These immature figs contain numerous small male and female flowers and minute fig insects, which pollinate the flowers. The figs ripen between February and May, becoming bright red, and are eaten by birds and bats.

Marketplaces frequently are located in the extensive sheltered area provided by a large arcade of banyan aerial roots. The strong aerial roots are used for tent poles and for cart yokes. The bark and hanging roots furnish a coarse fiber for rope making. Other parts of the tree also are used in various ways.

The botanical name for the banyan is *Ficus bengalensis;* the tree belongs to the mulberry family, Moraceae.

BAO DAI (1913–   ), bou dī, was emperor of Annam (now Vietnam) from 1932 to 1945 and emperor and chief of state of Vietnam from 1949 to 1955. Born *Prince Nguyen Vinh Thuy* on Oct. 22, 1913, the son of Emperor Khai-Din, he was the last member of the Nguyen dynasty founded by Emperor Gia Long in 1803. He was named heir apparent in 1922 and succeeded as titular ruler in 1926. He completed his education in Paris and ascended the throne in 1932.

Bao Dai submitted to French control of Annam before 1942 and to the Japanese occupation during World War II. He resigned as emperor in 1945 in the face of the Viet Minh Communists' domination of the nationalist cause. Courted by France to return as an alternative to the Viet Minh, he accepted the French offer in 1949, after extracting maximum political concessions, and was again proclaimed emperor. His government was recognized by the United States in 1950, but it failed to gain American support for genuine independence or to receive popular backing at home. Following the Indochinese War and the partition of Vietnam, Bao Dai accepted American-sponsored Ngo Dinh Diem as premier of South Vietnam in 1954, but he was ousted in a referendum that abolished the monarchy in 1955.

JOHN F. CADY, *Ohio University*

BAOBAB, bou'bab, a tree native to tropical Africa but cultivated in other tropical regions. The baobab is one of the largest trees in the world: it grows to a height of 40 to 60 feet (12 to 18 meters), its trunk sometimes measures 30 feet (9 meters) in diameter, and its branches spread 30 feet beyond the trunk. Growing singly or in small groups, this tree is common in dry coastal regions, savanna forests, and open country, and it is often found near villages. Its bark is smooth and grayish and has a characteristic purplish reflection. An unusual feature of this tree is that the leaves often appear after the flowers. The leaves are compound with leaflets up to five inches (12.7 cm) long; the flowers, which are six inches (15.2 cm) across,

ANNAN PHOTO FEATURES

THE BAOBAB TREE, native to Africa, bears a large, yellow fruit whose pulp and seeds have several uses.

are white and have purplish stamens (pollen bearing organs). The fruit, which hangs on long stalks, is oblong, woody, and may be from 6 to 12 inches (15 to 30 cm) long. It has yellowish woolly hairs on the outside and contains a pleasant-tasting, dry acid pulp (monkey bread) in which the seeds are embedded.

The pulp is used for a cooling drink, as an appetizer, for seasoning foods or curdling milk, as a coagulant of rubber, and as a fumigant for domestic animals. The young leaves are used as a vegetable. The pulp, seeds, and leaf powder have been used medicinally in the treatment of kidney troubles, dysentery, fevers, and earaches. Its bark has been used as a substitute for quinine. Even the tender roots of young baobabs are edible. Ground seeds or their ashes, rich in potash and phosphate, are used as fertilizers. The fruit and seeds may also be used for fertilizer and fuel and in soap or plaster. The bark of the baobab yields a very strong fiber used for cordage, packing material, packing paper, drinking vessels, and musical instruments. The wood, which is easily attacked by fungi, is light and spongy, and can best be used for wide canoes, floats for fishing nets, and other minor products. In the drier parts of Africa, the trunk may be hollowed out and used as a water reservoir or as a dwelling.

The botanical name for the baobab is *Adansonia digitata*, and the tree is a member of the family Bombacaceae. Among its host of popular names are monkey-bread tree, Ethiopian sour gourd, and cream of tartar tree. In India it is called the cork tree. In the United States, where it has been cultivated experimentally in southern Florida, it is known as the monkey tree.

THEODORE JUST, *Chicago Natural History Museum*

BAPTISM, bap′tiz-əm, is the application of water to a person as a sacrament or religious rite. Sacraments, as a rule, derive their outward form from common social acts but give to them a new spiritual significance. Thus the common meal of the group underlies the rite of sacrifice, and eventually that of the Eucharist; the anointing of the sick with oil underlies Holy Unction; the initiation of the individual into the group life of tribe or family, the naming of a child, and the rites of puberty or adulthood anticipate both baptism and confirmation.

So it is with baptism: rites of cleansing and purification are age-old, and are found in almost all the religions of mankind. This is especially true in the crises of birth, death, warfare, and contact with the dead or with spirits. In "primitive" religion, water was presumably thought of as alive, especially water which welled up out of the earth ("living water") and moved of its own accord in stream or river. Even lakes and seas, whose surfaces are in constant motion, were thought to be living. Hence it was natural to interpose the living force of water between the individual or group and the threat of defilement or danger or contact with destruction. In Greek religion there were many poetic survivals of this fancy, both in rite and in belief, from the living, divine, personified river Scamander in the *Iliad* to the oracular "singing water" of one of the latest poems in the *Greek Anthology*. In India the water of the "holy Ganges" was specially valued for cleansing; in Egypt, that of the Nile. In the cult of Isis, Nile water was carried in jars to such distant places as Rome, for use in lustral rites. The ancient Teutons and Celts practiced rites of cleansing and initiation long before Christian influences reached them. Among the Greeks and Romans the newborn child was bathed and named, and recognized by the father as his own. Among some peoples, baptism with blood, or with saliva, was practiced—always with emphasis on the initiation or admission of the child into the tribal or family group.

Origins of Christian Baptism. The Christian sacrament of baptism goes back to the very beginning of the Christian movement (Acts 2:37–42), and even earlier, when John the Baptist required his followers to immerse themselves in the river Jordan (Mark 1:4–5). The rite was ordinarily required of proselytes to Judaism: following circumcision, the converted Gentile immersed himself in water as a cleansing from the contaminations of idolatry, while two Jews stood outside the curtained enclosure and recited passages from the Torah (the Law or Pentateuch), which he was now binding himself to keep. What was distinctive of John's baptism was (1) his requirement of baptism on the part of all Jews, not only proselytes, and (2) its "eschatological" reference, as a symbol of repentance, turning from sin, and preparation for the coming Day of Judgment. Although Jesus himself was baptized, it is a question if he observed the rite in his own ministry (John 4:1–2); the dominical commandment is found only in Matthew 28:19–20, a post-resurrection saying.

Baptism in the early church probably included children (Corinthians 1:16), as did also Jewish baptism of Gentiles (Babylonian Talmud: *Yebamoth* 78A). The "baptism for the dead" (I Corinthians 15:29) was probably a kind of baptism by proxy (compare modern legal marriage by proxy), by which, it was hoped, the benefits of the sacrament might be conferred upon those who had died before the Gospel had reached them. It was a very extraordinary practice, and like other features peculiar to the church in Corinth, was not followed elsewhere. When the church spread to colder countries, baptism by pouring (or "affusion") became common, at least as an alternative mode of administration. By some groups baptism has been limited to adults. In the days of the martyrs a "baptism of desire" was recognized—when converts were unable actually to receive the rite of water baptism.

According to the New Testament, the benefits of baptism are the inauguration of the new life in Christ ("rebirth" or "regeneration") and the gift of the Holy Spirit (see John 3:3–8; Galatians 3:27). In later practice, in the West, the laying on of hands, which frequently accompanied baptism in the New Testament period, was separated from it, and became the rite of confirmation, usually administered at the beginning of adolescence and admitting the Christian child to the Holy Communion. In the East, confirmation follows at once in infant baptism. As a rule, adult baptism is followed everywhere by confirmation and first communion; and it is preceded, especially in the mission field, by a period of instruction and spiritual preparation for admission into the church. The usual formula is the one in Matthew 28:19, "in the name of the Father, and of the Son, and of the Holy Ghost." It has been argued that the usual New Testament formula was "in the name of Christ" (I Corinthians 6:11); but it is quite possible that this term meant only "as a Christian," and that the mystical sense of baptism "in" or "into" Christ came as a later interpretation. See also CONFIRMATION.

Modern Forms of Baptism. In the modern world various forms of baptism are observed. These include immersion (dipping or submerging the person in a pool or stream); pouring ("affusion," either from the bare hand or from a shell or saucer; the shell is usually a scallop shell or is shaped like one); and intinction (the minister moistens one finger and touches the candidate's head, usually his forehead). The use of flowers or other substitutes for water is not usually described as baptism. The Baptists, Jehovah's Witnesses, and some other groups practice mass baptism by immersion.

FREDERICK C. GRANT, *Union Theological Seminary*

Bibliography

Aquinas, St. Thomas, *Summa Theologica*, Eng. tr. by Dominican Fathers of the English Province (New York 1947).

Bowen, Clayton R., *Studies in the New Testament* (Chicago 1936).

Bultmann, Rudolf, *Theology of the New Testament*, vol. 1 (New York 1951).

Cullmann, Oscar, *Baptism in the New Testament* (Naperville, Ill., 1958).

Dunkerley, Roderick, *The Ministry and the Sacraments* (London 1937).

Flemington, W.F., *The New Testament Doctrine of Baptism* (New York 1949).

Gavin, Frank, *Jewish Antecedents of the Christian Sacraments* (New York 1928).

Grant, Frederick C., *Introduction to New Testament Thought* (Nashville, Tenn., 1950).

Hooker, Richard, *Ecclesiastical Polity*, rev. ed. by John S. Marshall, vol. 5 (Sewanee, Tenn., 1948).

Lampe, Geoffrey W.H., *The Seal of the Spirit* (London 1951).

Quick, Oliver C., *The Christian Sacraments* (London 1927).

Richardson, Alan, ed., *A Theological Word Book of the Bible* (New York 1950).

Stone, Darwell, *Holy Baptism* (London 1901).

THE BAPTISTERY at Pisa, Italy, is an example of the large, separate structures built for baptisms during the Middle Ages. This round, Romanesque building dates from the 12th to 14th century. Behind the baptistery are the cathedral and the bell tower—famous as the leaning tower.

BAPTISTA, bä-tēs′tä, **Mariano** (1832–1907), Bolivian publicist and political leader. He was born at Sucre and won distinction as a young man for courageous opposition to the dictatorship of Manuel Belzú. He went into exile in 1861 but returned to the political forum as a newspaper editor after Belzú's assassination in 1866. In 1873 he was appointed minister of the interior and of foreign relations.

Baptista was elected president of Bolivia in 1892 and served until 1896. He failed to secure a Pacific port through negotiations with Chile, but his administration fostered education and started the first topographical survey of Bolivia.

BAPTISTERY, bap′tə-strē, an area set aside for the purpose of adminstering the Christian sacrament of baptism. A river sufficed for this purpose in the apostolic age, but by the 3d century a special room or building separate from the church had developed. During the later Middle Ages, many churches had a baptismal font located in the nave, but in the 20th century there was a return to the use of a separate room or building.

BAPTISTS, bap′təsts, are a Protestant religious denomination that originated in the 17th century, as an offshoot of English Congregationalism, and formed part of the left wing of English Puritanism. The Baptists form the largest Protestant communion in the United States, and Baptist churches are found throughout the world.

DEVELOPMENT OF BAPTIST DOCTRINE

Early History. During the latter part of the 16th century, small groups of radical Puritans became impatient at the delay in reforming the English church. Adopting as their slogan, "Reformation without tarrying for any," they broke with the established church and formed churches of their own. Known as Separatists, they differed from their fellow Puritans only in their conception of church government, insisting that a true church is composed of believers only, and that each believer has an equal voice in deciding church affairs. This, they contended, was the New Testament pattern of the church and therefore the essential polity of any true church.

In 1606, John Smyth (or Smith), a former Anglican preacher in Lincoln, was serving as minister of a group of Separatists at Gainsborough, in Lincolnshire. Thomas Helwys, a noted Separatist, was active in this group. About 1608 religious persecution induced Smyth and Helwys to lead their congregation to asylum in the Netherlands. Some settled in Amsterdam, with Smyth as their minister. Another group settled for a time in Leiden, under their leader, the Puritan John Robinson, but eventually emigrated to America, and founded Plymouth Colony.

In Amsterdam, the Smyth company debated the meaning of membership in the Christian church, and the old question of baptism, long discussed by Separatists, was raised again. Smyth stated that according to Separatist belief, "the churches of the apostolic constitution consisted of saints only," and that baptism should therefore be reserved for those who could offer convincing proof of grace. This, he felt, was the true practice of New Testament churches, for he found no warrant in Scripture for infant baptism. Smyth's views on infant baptism were set forth in *The Character of the Beast,* a pamphlet issued in 1609. In that same year 36 adherents joined him in forming a new church on the principle of baptizing believers only. He baptized himself and others by applying water to the forehead.

The first schism in Baptist ranks occurred shortly after the formation of Smyth's church. When the existence in Amsterdam of the Mennonites, and Anabaptist group, was brought to his attention, Smyth began to question the propriety of baptizing himself and starting a new church. This procedure could be justified, he decided, only if no true church existed from which valid baptism could be secured. After some investigation, Smyth concluded that the Mennonites constituted a genuine church of God, and he recommended union with them. He was opposed by Thomas Helwys, who succeeded in rallying the support of some of the others. Helwys and his followers returned to London and established the first Baptist church in England. The group remaining in Amsterdam soon disbanded.

In England another schism occurred, this time between the General and the Particular

209

Baptists. Originally, Smyth and his followers had adopted the moderate Calvinism of Jacobus Arminius. (See ARMINIANISM; ARMINIUS, JACOBUS.) The churches influenced by those who returned from Amsterdam became known as General Baptist churches, because they believed in a general atonement for all. In 1638 a Baptist church was formed in London representing a more traditional Calvinism and adhering to a belief in a particular atonement, that is, atonement limited to the elect. A further division occurred in 1640, when some members of this church became convinced that baptism should be by immersion. See also BAPTISM.

The two decades from 1640 to 1660 constituted the great period of Baptist growth. In Cromwell's army, Baptist preachers found their great opportunity. Their converts rapidly multiplied around the campfires, and permanent Baptist communities arose along the line of march. After the Stuart Restoration in 1660, however, the Baptists paid a heavy toll for their ardor during the civil wars. Long imprisonment and heavy fines were the reward for their devotion to the cause of religious liberty. John Bunyan, a Baptist preacher, was confined for 12 years in Bedford jail for his refusal to stop preaching. He spent his time in prison writing many books; one of the most famous was *Grace Abounding to the Chief of Sinners* (1666).

The Revolution of 1688 freed the Baptists from the worst of their disabilities. However, their growth had been sufficiently checked, and it was not greatly advanced in England until the 19th century. The impetus for the revival was given by William Carey, who took the lead in organizing the English Baptist Missionary Society in 1792 and became its first missionary to India. This began the modern foreign missionary movement among English-speaking Christians.

Variations in Doctrine. Democracy breeds difference of opinion, and among Baptists the widest variety of opinion can be found. Consequently, it is possible to identify only the dominant traits.

On the whole, the Baptist Church has been characterized by an emphasis that has varied from a strong to a moderate Calvinism. Of the three most representative statements of faith, the London Confession (1689) and the Philadelphia Confession (1742) closely follow the Westminster Confession (1643) of the Presbyterians, while the New Hampshire Confession (1832) is less strongly Calvinistic. These confessions, however, have no special authority. Authoritative creeds are explicitly rejected by Baptists, and the Bible is the sole source of appeal in questions of faith.

By 1900 the older Calvinist tradition had largely disappeared, and in its place were three diverse currents—evangelicalism, modernism, and fundamentalism. Nineteenth century evangelicalism had become the dominant theological emphasis. Elaborated by the leaders of the Evangelical Revival in England, the later New England divines, and the revivalist clergyman Charles G. Finney, it was characterized as popular romanticism by the American historian Ralph Henry Gabriel. Modernism, which represented an adjustment to the new intellectual climate of the late 19th century, made major inroads among Baptists of England and the United States—particularly in the North—during the first decades of the 20th century, and the Baptists provided many outstanding leaders of the liberal movement.

As the 20th century advanced, a new emphasis, which identified itself as Fundamentalist, moved into a stronger position in the United States and the mission fields and displaced much of the older evangelicalism. This movement, which stressed the importance of correct doctrine, the verbal inspiration of the Bible, and belief in a second coming of Christ to establish a millennium of peace, engendered considerable controversy and produced several new divisions in the church.

Cardinal Principles. The real coherence and unity of the Baptists is found in six cardinal principles to which they all generally adhere:

(1) *The authority of the Bible as a sufficient guide to faith and practice.* Acknowledging no human founder, no human authority, and no human creed, Baptists seek to derive their doctrine and polity directly from the Scriptures. Creedal statements as authoritative tests of faith and fellowship have been consistently rejected by the major Baptist groups, since the Bible itself is regarded as possessing the only valid definitions.

(2) *Believer's baptism.* This is the most conspicuously distinctive principle of Baptists. As the movement developed, insistence on immersion as the apostolic form of the rite was added to the original belief. Since the 1900's, however, an increasing number of churches have adopted the practice of receiving members of churches of other denominations into associate or full membership without rebaptism.

(3) *Churches composed of believers only.* The Baptists hold strongly to the conception of the "gathered" or "voluntary" church, limited in membership to those who can give clear evidence of Christian conviction and experience.

(4) *The priesthood of believers.* By this principle Baptists understand not only that the individual Christian can rightfully serve as a minister to his fellows; they regard it as conferring upon each member of a church equal privileges and rights in determining the affairs of the church. In this democracy, the minister is called to his office by a vote of the congregation, and he is not regarded as having any special sacerdotal or ecclesiastical authority.

(5) *The autonomy of the local church.* Baptists affirm faith in the catholic church but most believe that its only visible expression is in local churches, formed according to the New Testament pattern and wholly independent of one another. The denominational organization includes associations, societies, and conventions, but these bodies are designed to serve specific purposes of common concern to the churches and do not possess any authority over the churches. The delegates or messengers sent to the meetings of these bodies represent only themselves and not the churches from which they come, since the churches cannot delegate their sovereign authority. The associations, conventions, and societies, therefore, are independent of the churches, define their own terms of membership, and do not need to submit their actions to the churches for ratification.

(6) *Separation of church and state.* From the time of Smyth, Baptists have contended that the "magistrate is not by virtue of his office to meddle with religion or matters of conscience, to force and compel men to this or that form

of religion or doctrine, but to leave Christian religion free to every man's conscience." In the United States the Baptists seized upon the Revolutionary War as an opportunity to establish this principle of complete religious freedom. Having set the example of religious freedom earlier in Rhode Island, the Baptists helped secure the same guarantees in the other states. They played an important role in securing the adoption of the "no religious test" clause in the federal Constitution as well as in securing the adoption of the First Amendment.

BAPTISTS IN THE UNITED STATES

In the American colonies, Baptist churches were mainly indigenous, the product of the same leftward movement among Puritans that was taking place in England. The first church was organized in Rhode Island in 1638, soon after that colony was founded by Roger Williams.

New England. Williams had adopted Congregationalist views soon after being ordained to the ministry of the Church of England. In 1631 he sailed for Massachusetts, where he was called to be minister of the Salem church. He soon became embroiled in controversy over the completeness of the separation of the Massachusetts churches from the Church of England, the authority of civil magistrates to punish other than civil offenses, and the validity of the title of the New England colonists to land taken from the Indians. In October 1635, Williams was sentenced to banishment from Massachusetts. To escape deportation, he fled, purchased land from the Narragansett Indians, and established the colony of Rhode Island in 1636.

The compact of the new community, which bound the settlers to obey laws duly enacted "only in civil things," was the initial expression of what became the American principle of separation of church and state. It is generally held that Roger Williams, convinced by Scripture that infant baptism was invalid, formed what is considered to be the first Baptist church in America. Some Baptist historians, however, dispute this claim and hold that the honor of founding the mother church in America belongs to John Clarke, a New Hampshire physician, who established a church at Newport at about the same time. This church soon became, if it was not from the first, a Baptist church.

In March 1639, Williams was baptized by Ezekiel Holliman. There has been some controversy as to how the baptism was administered. If it was by immersion, then immersion was practiced in America prior to its introduction among English Baptists. A letter from Williams to John Winthrop, years after the formation of the church, mentions the recent introduction of "a new baptism and the manner of dipping." In this same letter mention is made of a Mark Lucar, who was immersed in London in 1642 and came to America two years later. From this it is argued that immersion was introduced by this London Baptist. Williams continued the leftward pilgrimage that characterized the Puritan movement, and after a brief identification with the Baptists, he withdrew from the group and classified himself as a "Seeker" awaiting the reestablishment of the true church.

The colony at Newport became a center of Baptist activity. It was from Newport that Obadiah Holmes went to Lynn, Mass., in 1651 to hold a religious service. Apprehended by the

EWING GALLOWAY

THE FIRST BAPTIST MEETING HOUSE, now a landmark in Providence, R.I., was erected in 1775.

Massachusetts Bay authorities, he was sentenced to be "well whipped," and the sentence was carried out in the streets of Boston.

The Baptists, however, could not be permanently suppressed. In 1663 a company of Welsh Baptists settled at Swansea, Mass., and established a church. Two years later a Baptist church was formed in Boston. The first minister was imprisoned several times and treated with such severity that his health was impaired. When a meetinghouse was constructed in 1678, its doors were nailed shut by order of the General Court. The members of a church in Kittery, Me., then part of Massachusetts, were so harassed that they moved in a body to Charleston, S.C., and organized the first Baptist church in the South. Persecution did not abate until some toleration was granted by the charter of 1692.

The Philadelphia Association. The other great center of Baptist strength was the Philadelphia area, the first two churches being formed in 1688 at Pennepek, Pa., and at Middletown, N.J. Within the next decade, additional churches were organized, and in 1707 the Philadelphia Baptist Association was formed. This fraternal body had no legislative or judicial authority over the churches or ministers, but cared for their common interests and conducted missionary activities. Churches as distant as Virginia ultimately joined the association, but other associations were established when the churches became more numerous. In 1714 a number of General Baptists went to the American colonies. This group died out in the East but was later revived in the Midwest early in the 19th century.

The Great Awakening. Baptist growth was accelerated by the Great Awakening. Although the Baptists participated in the revival only in its final Southern phase, they reaped large numbers of recruits in New England from among the Separates who had been thrust out of the established churches by the antirevivalist majority. The increase in Massachusetts was more than tenfold during a 40-year period, and in the Southern colonies the rate of growth was even greater despite severe harassment in Virginia. The opening of the trans-Appalachian frontier offered the greatest opportunity, for the self-generating Baptist churches and farmer preachers were especially suited to the needs of the West. Their success in meeting the religious demands of the frontier made the Baptists one of the great American denominations. See also GREAT AWAKENING.

Moves Toward Unity. Denominational organization began in 1707 with the Philadelphia Baptist Association. It has been estimated that by 1800 there were at least 48 associations. The initial impetus for a national organization came from an interest in foreign missions.

Adoniram Judson and Luther Rice had been sent to India as the first missionaries of the newly organized American Board of Commissioners for Foreign Missions. During their journey they became convinced that only believers should be baptized, and when they reached Calcutta, they sought out English Baptist missionaries and were rebaptized. Rice returned to the United States to secure support for Judson from American Baptists. His efforts resulted in the formation of the General Missionary Convention of the Baptist Denomination in the United States for Foreign Missions. This body, formed in May 1814, soon became known as the Triennial Convention, because its meetings were held every three years. The American Baptist Publication Society was organized in 1824, the American Baptist Home Mission Society in 1832, and the American and Foreign Bible Society in 1837. These national societies became the bond of unity among the Baptist churches.

Divisions of the Church. The unity thus achieved was soon impaired. Opposition to Sunday Schools, to missionary and Bible societies, and to the Triennial Convention itself soon developed among Baptists who considered them unscriptural. An extreme Calvinism manifested itself among some of the frontier churches, resulting in the formation of the Primitive, or "Hard-Shell," Baptists. A larger secession, centering in Ohio and Kentucky, derived from the "Christian" movement of Alexander Campbell. In New England, the Christian movement of Abner Jones made similar inroads.

The major split, however, resulted from the controversy over slavery. During the decade prior to 1845, various compromises between pro- and antislavery parties were attempted unsuccessfully. In May 1845 a convention representing the Southern Baptist churches met at Augusta, Ga., and formed the Southern Baptist Convention. The Northern churches continued their common activities through the old societies, and in 1907 they were united by the establishment of the Northern Baptist Convention, in Washington, D.C. (now the American Baptist Convention), with Charles Evans Hughes as its first president.

The close of the Civil War gave immediate impetus to the formation of Negro Baptist churches. The first state convention of such churches took place in 1866 in North Carolina.

In 1880 the National Baptist Convention of America came into existence. In 1915, however, the convention split into two groups, the parent segment becoming the National Baptist Convention, U.S.A., Inc., and the smaller segment retaining the original name. The remarkable Baptist strength among Negroes resulted chiefly from the predominance of Baptists in the slave-holding states prior to the Civil War and from the ability of any small group to organize a church and ordain ministers on its own initiative.

Baptists have made notable contributions to education. Brown University was founded by Baptists in Rhode Island in 1764, and after the Revolutionary War Baptist educational institutions multiplied rapidly. The trans-Appalachian region produced the largest number, but not without opposition. Baptists from the South who settled in the new Western communities tended to be either indifferent or opposed to an educated ministry, and they especially distrusted missionaries from the East. Baptists from New England, however, inheriting the Congregationalist cultural tradition, established academies, colleges, and seminaries wherever they could. The culmination of the educational advance came in 1890 with the founding of the University of Chicago, intended to be a great national Baptist "super-university." Since the 1920's the ties of Baptist educational institutions with the denomination have become tenuous in the North and, to a lesser extent, in the South.

Membership. The Southern Baptist Convention is now the largest of the Baptist bodies in the United States. Its membership more than tripled during the first half of the 20th century, and by the mid-1960's it had more than 33,000 churches with a membership of about 10,600,000. The National Baptist Convention, U.S.A., Inc., is the second largest group, with a membership in the 1960's of over 5,500,000 in more than 26,000 churches. The third largest group is the National Baptist Convention of America with about 2,700,000 members in some 11,500 churches. The American Baptist Convention claims about 1,500,000 members in nearly 6,300 churches. Several groups of "national-origin" Baptists in the United States and Canada have their own organizations. The largest are the Swedish Baptist General Conference with about 87,000 members and the German North American Baptist General Conference with about 53,000 members.

There are also a number of smaller groups, maintaining separate organizations. Most of these date from the colonial or early frontier periods and represent isolated and dwindling communities. An extreme Calvinism is represented by the Primitive Baptists, organized in North Carolina in 1827 and claiming about 73,000 members in the mid-1960's, and the Two-Seed-in-the-Spirit Predestinarian Baptists, organized in Virginia about 1826. Among the Arminian groups are the General Six Principle Baptists, formed in Rhode Island in 1653, with about 125 members in the mid-1960's; the Free Will Baptists, formed in North Carolina in 1727, with about 172,000 members in the mid-1960's; the Separate Baptists in Christ, dating back to a North Carolina association of 1758 and claiming about 7,500 members in the mid-1960's; and the General Baptists—a later offshoot of the transplanted English General Baptists—organized in Indiana in 1823, having about 63,000 members in the mid-1960's.

Three moderately Calvinistic groups are products of the geographical isolation of the southern highlands. These are the Regular Baptists (a small group who remained apart from the union of Regular and Separate churches that took place in Virginia in 1787 and in Kentucky in 1801) with about 17,000 members; the United Baptists (a surviving fragment of the union of 1787 and 1801, perpetuating the name "United" in back-country districts after it had been dropped elsewhere) with about 63,000 members in the mid-1960's; and the Duck River (and Kindred) Associations of Baptists (organized in Tennessee in 1825) and having about 3,000 members. The Seventh Day Baptist General Conference, established in Rhode Island in 1671, and numbering about 6,000 in the mid-1960's, observe Saturday as the Sabbath.

Several groups have been organized since 1900 that represent a more rigidly defined type of orthodoxy. The one exception is the Christian Unity Baptist Association, with about 650 members, formed on the principle of open communion. The others are the American Baptist Association, with about 720,000 members, formed in 1905 mainly by churches in Oklahoma, Texas, and Arkansas; the General Association of Regular Baptist Churches, organized in the Midwest in the 1930's, with a current membership of about 155,000; and the Conservative Baptist Association of America, established in 1948, with a current membership of about 300,000.

BAPTISTS IN OTHER COUNTRIES

While Baptists have their greatest strength in the United States, where they numbered more than 25 million by the mid-1960's, there were about 4 million Baptists in other countries.

British Isles. The 19th century was the great era of English Baptists, whose spiritual life had been quickened by the awakening of missionary interest. It was a time of great preaching and overflowing congregations. Several of the preachers achieved an international reputation—most notably, Robert Hall, Charles Haddon Spurgeon, John Clifford, and Alexander Maclaren. Churches multiplied, membership increased rapidly, and the Baptists played no small part in creating the "nonconformist conscience," which at the end of the century was strong enough to make or break a prime minister.

In 1832 an instrument of denominational cohesion was forged with the formation of the Baptist Union. In 1891 the union was reorganized to include the General Baptists, who had led a separate existence for more than two centuries. The churches of Wales, Scotland, and Ireland were also brought into the new union. The first Baptist church in Wales had been organized in 1649 by John Myles, but the most influential of the early leaders was Vavasor Powell, a Welsh Baptist living in London, who established some 20 churches in the years after 1655. In Scotland the first Baptist church was formed in 1750, and the growth of the movement there was closely identified with the work of James and Robert Haldane. The movement in Ireland sprang from the activity of members of Cromwell's army.

From the earliest days, British Baptists have been divided on the question of communion with other churches. Closed communion—the restriction of the Lord's Supper to those who had been baptized as believers—was practiced by most of the early Particular churches and by some of the General churches. Most General Baptists and some Particular Baptists, on the other hand, favored open communion—an invitation to all Christians to participate in the Lord's Supper. A similar controversy has centered around open membership. From the beginning, some churches that practiced only believer's baptism admitted persons to membership who had not been so baptized. Since they believed that baptism was only a symbol, they would not make it a wall of division from those who could give proofs of grace. This was the practice of a number of Particular churches. By the 20th century most Baptist churches maintained open communion, and the open membership churches were increasing.

Since 1900, the number of Baptists in the British Isles has steadily declined. This has been true also of the membership of the Church of England and the other Free Churches. Baptists in the British Isles numbered about 295,000 in the mid-1960's.

Continental Europe. Baptists on the European continent have no connection with the Anabaptists of the Reformation but are the product of English and American Baptist influence. In France a church was formed in Paris in 1835, after three years of missionary work. From this center, other French Baptist communities arose, and by the mid-1960's there were about 3,300 members, a 100 percent increase over a 25-year period. In Germany a church was organized in 1834 at Hamburg by John Gerhardt Oncken, who had spent some years in England. He was baptized with six others by Barnas Sears, an American professor of theology who was studying in Germany. Oncken's church spurred Baptist growth, which maintained a steady pace. By the mid-1960's there were some 550 Baptist churches in Germany with 95,000 members.

The German Baptists established moderately successful missions in Austria, Bulgaria, Rumania, Switzerland, Belgium, the Netherlands, Denmark, Poland, and Russia. By the mid-1960's there were about 83,000 Baptists in Rumania, 22,000 in Poland, 19,000 in Hungary, 4,300 in Czechoslovakia, 9,300 in the Netherlands, and 3,700 in Yugoslavia. The greatest success of the German missions resulted from work among Russian prisoners during World War I, and the growth of Baptist churches in Russia during the years following was phenomenal. Conservative estimates placed the number of Baptists in the Soviet Union at more than 2 million in 1950, but by the mid-1960's membership was calculated at about 540,000.

Swedish Baptists owe their origin to two sailors, Gustav Schroeder, who was baptized in New York in 1844, and Frederick Nilsson, who was baptized by Oncken in 1847. The Swedes also sent missions to neighboring countries, principally Norway and Finland. By the mid-1960's 500 Swedish churches claimed a membership of more than 29,000. In Norway about 60 churches had a total membership of some 6,700. In Denmark more than 80 churches counted a total of 7,000 members, and in Finland nearly 50 churches had a total membership of about 3,000. Baptist missions have also been established in Spain and Italy by Baptists from the southern United States. In 1905 the Baptist World Alliance was formed in London to unite Baptists throughout the world. Periodic meetings of the Alliance maintain the continuity of the Baptist movement.

Canada. The Baptist churches of Canada were started by New England immigrants, by men influenced by the Great Awakening, and by Scottish immigrants who were converts of James and Robert Haldane. Until the mid-20th century Canadian Baptists were organized into three separate conventions—in the Maritime Provinces, in Ontario and Quebec, and in western Canada. Now linked in a loose confederation, they number more than 1,600 churches and 175,000 members.

Australasia. In Australia the first Baptist church was formed in Sydney in 1834, and the movement was extended from there to New Zealand and Tasmania. In the mid-1960's there were more than 720 churches in Australasia with a total membership of over 55,000.

Asia, Africa, and Latin America. Missionary work has been carried on by Baptists in almost every part of the world. Baptist communities in Asia now total more than 870,000 members, and those in Africa more than 1 million. Communities have been established in several Latin American countries, with a total membership of 265,-000, of which 230,000 are in Brazil.

WINTHROP S. HUDSON
Colgate-Rochester Divinity School

Bibliography
Boyd, Jesse L., *A History of Baptists in America* (New York 1957).
Maring, Norman H., and Hudson, W.S., *A Baptist Manual of Polity and Practice* (Valley Forge, Pa., 1963).
Rushbrooke, J.H., *The Baptist Movement on the Continent of Europe* (London 1923).
Sweet, William W., *Religion on the American Frontier*, vol. 1 (New York 1931).
Torbet, Robert, *History of the Baptists*, rev. ed (Valley Forge, Pa., 1963).
Underwood, A.C., *A History of the English Baptists*, rev. ed. (Greenwood, S.C., 1956).

BAR, bär, is a region of France that lies between Luxembourg, Lorraine, Franche-Comté, and Champagne. It is also known as *Barrois*. The region, situated between the Marne and Moselle rivers, is divided among the departments of Moselle, Meurthe-et-Moselle, and Meuse.

The principal city of Bar is Bar-le-Duc, an industrial center, with foundries, textile mills, and printing plants. Other cities in Bar are St.-Mihiel, Pont-à-Mousson, and Commercy.

When Julius Caesar conquered Gaul, Bar was inhabited by a people known as the *Leuci*. After over four centuries of Roman rule, Bar was conquered by the Franks. As part of the Carolingian empire, it became an administrative district known as a county. The counts achieved virtual independence in the 10th and 11th centuries. Frederick of Ardennes was named the first hereditary count of Bar by Emperor Otto the Great in 951.

The political fortunes of Bar changed abruptly under Count Henry III (reigned 1297–1302). When Henry fought for Edward I of England against Philip IV of France, his county was invaded by French forces, and he was imprisoned. He was freed on the condition that he take all of Bar lying on the left bank of the Moselle in fief from Philip IV. Henceforth this part of Bar remained firmly tied to France. The rest of the region recognized the authority of the Holy Roman Empire. Early in the 15th century both parts were united under the dukes of Lorraine, who remained in possession until 1737, when Lorraine was granted to King Stanislas of Poland. Upon his death in 1766, Lorraine and Bar returned to France.

BRYCE LYON, *Brown University*

BAR, bär, in law, a term used both in England and in the United States as a synonym for the legal profession. It arose in usage from the fact that a courtroom partition, usually a railing, separates the public from the judge, counsel, jury, and other principals in a trial. The term also applies to the area reserved to the principals.

In English superior courts, the king's counsel is admitted within the bar; other counselors sit or stand outside. The dock, or enclosed space, where accused persons stand or sit during their trial is also called the bar; hence the expression "prisoner at the bar." The term "bar" also refers to the railed-off space within the Houses of Lords and Commons.

BAR, bär, in music, a line drawn vertically across the staff, for the purpose of dividing a musical composition into equal measures of time. The term is very often improperly applied to the measures themselves.

The time assigned to the measure between two bars is either common or triple. Common time is equivalent to four quarter notes per measure, and triple time to three. The set of bars marking the end of a piece of music is called the double bar. Musical bars were first used about the mid-1400's. See also MEASURE.

BAR HARBOR, bär' här'bər, a township in eastern Maine, is one of the most famous resorts in the United States. It is situated on Mount Desert Island about 115 miles (185 km) northeast of Portland by air. The township includes the unincorporated community of Bar Harbor, which fronts on Frenchman Bay of the Atlantic Ocean. It is the headquarters and gateway of Acadia National Park, a region of rugged coastal and mountain scenery. Bar Harbor is a yachting, golf, and skiing center. A motor ferry runs to Yarmouth, Nova Scotia, Canada, in the summer. The Roscoe B. Jackson Memorial Laboratory for cancer and biological research is here. The museum of the Bar Harbor Historical Society and the Robert Abbe Museum of Stone Age Antiquities are attractions.

The first permanent English settlement was made in 1763. The town was incorporated in 1796 as *Eden;* it was renamed in 1918. Government is by town manager and council. Population: 3,716.

Mount Desert Island, Me., near the town of Bar Harbor.

JOHN J. SMITH

BAR-HEBRAEUS, bär-hē-brē′əs, **Gregorius** (1226–1286), Syrian scholar who was primate of the Jacobite church, a Christian sect with its headquarters in Syria. (See also JACOBITE CHURCH.) Bar Hebraeus or *Barhebraeus*, meaning "son of the Hebrew," is an abbreviated Latinized form of his Arabic name, *Abu'l-Faraj Ibn al-Ibri*. He was born at Malatya (now in Turkey). After studying medicine with his father, a Jewish physician who became a convert to Christianity, he became a monk at Antioch in 1243. Consecrated a Jacobite bishop in 1246, Bar-Hebraeus was raised to *Maphrian* (primate) of the East by the patriarch, Ignatius III, in 1264.

On the extensive travels this position required, Bar-Hebraeus collected materials for his diverse scholarly endeavors. These include: *Hewath Hekhmetha* (*Cream of Wisdom*), a work of encyclopedic scope that gives a solid accounting of the Arabian commentaries on the Aristotelian dialectic; *Chronicon syriacum*, a history of man from Adam to his own time; *Chronicon ecclesiasticum*, a history of the church; and *Ausar raze* (*Storehouse of Secrets*), a critical and doctrinal commentary on the Scriptures. He died at Maragha, Persia, on July 30, 1286.

BAR-JESUS. See ELYMAS.

BAR KOKHBA, bȧr kōKH′bä, "Son of the Star," was a Palestinian Jew who commanded a popular revolution against Rome in the 2d century A.D. He was born *Simeon Bar Kosiba* (or *Kosba*). He organized and led the revolt of 132 A.D. against Emperor Hadrian and won the support and admiration of the learned Rabbi Akiba, who acclaimed Bar Kokhba as the promised Messiah. (See AKIBA BEN JOSEPH.) Successful at first, Bar Kokhba liberated Jerusalem and, with Eleazar the Priest, established a revolutionary regime. For more than three years he defied Rome, but in 134–135, Roman legions led by Julius Severus forced him to withdraw to the stronghold of Betar. There, during a Roman onslaught, he was killed in 135.

Talmudic legend represents Bar Kokhba as a man of great strength, autocratic and irascible. Bar Kokhba's own letters, found at Wadi Murabaat in Jordan in 1952 and in the "Bar Kokhba" cave in Israel, near the Dead Sea, in 1960–1961, confirm this description by their harsh tone.

RAPHAEL PATAI, *Theodor Herzl Institute*

BAR-LE-DUC. See BAR.

BAR MITZVAH, bär-mitz′və, meaning "son of the commandment," is a Jewish religious ceremony that marks the entrance of boys of 13 years into the adult community. As adults, they are obligated to observe the precepts of the Torah (Law). The exact date at which the ceremony was introduced is unknown, but the ritual was definitely established by the 1200's.

At the ceremony, which takes place either on the Saturday following the 13th birthday (among the Ashkenazim) or on a weekday (in other communities), the boy is called on to read the weekly portion of the Pentateuch, the Five Books of Moses. A festive meal in the home of the boy's parents usually follows. Appropriate presents are given the boy by his parents and invited guests on this occasion.

Traditionally, the boy delivered a "bar mitzvah speech" at the feast, indicating his familiarity with the Bible and with Jewish religious lore. The father, who until the bar mitzvah was responsible for the boy's religious conduct, then recited a benediction, thanking God for having freed him from further responsibility.

In the United States, the bar mitzvah has become a great social occasion, second only to a wedding. Reform Judaism and, to a lesser extent, Conservative Judaism have introduced a parallel ceremony for girls, usually referred to as *bath* (or *bas*) *mitzvah*, meaning "daughter of the commandment."

RAPHAEL PATAI, *Theodor Herzl Institute*

BARA, bar′ə, **Theda** (1890–1955), American actress, who was the most celebrated "vamp" of silent films. She was born *Theodosia Goodman*, in Cincinnati, Ohio, on July 20, 1890. After her successful film debut as a sultry temptress in *A Fool There Was* (1915), her producers launched a publicity campaign that proclaimed her the daughter of a French artist and an Arabian princess; they claimed that her names were anagrams in which "Theda" was a rearrangement of the letters in "death" and "Bara" was "Arab" spelled backward. In fact, her first name was a contraction of Theodosia, and Bara was a family name.

From 1915 until her retirement in 1920 she appeared in about 40 films having such titles as *The Vampire* (the origin of "vamp"), *Cleopatra* (perhaps her most famous role), *Salome*, *The Vixen*, and *The She Devil*. She made her only stage appearance in *The Blue Flame* in 1920. She died in Los Angeles, on April 7, 1955.

BARABAS, bə-rab′əs, is the unsympathetic main character of Christopher Marlowe's tragedy, *The Jew of Malta*. He sets revenge above human feeling and dies cursing mankind.

BARABBAS, bə-rab′əs, in the New Testament, was the political prisoner released by Pontius Pilate in place of Jesus. All four gospels relate the incident (Matthew 27:15–26, Mark 15:7–15, Luke 23:13–25, John 18:28–40). It was the custom of the Roman government of Palestine to set free one prisoner at the Passover. Barabbas is said to have been a robber, a murderer, an insurrectionist, and a "notable" prisoner.

BARABBAS, bə-rab′əs, is a novel by the Nobel Prize-winning Swedish author Pär Lagerkvist, first published in 1949 and translated into English in 1951. Using the New Testament as its point of departure, *Barabbas* is the story of the condemned robber who was set free on the day of his intended crucifixion, with Jesus Christ taking his place on the cross.

The novel is essentially a depiction of Barabbas's struggle for faith. A hardened murderer and thief, he is strangely disturbed by a reproachful look from Christ's mother as he leaves the scene of the crucifixion. Now that he is free, Barabbas becomes a wanderer, increasingly confused by the events of his own life as well as by the new Christianity that is springing up around him. On the surface he appears to be a cynic and an opportunist, posing as a Christian when it suits his needs and renouncing Christianity when the occasion demands. However, a growing ambivalence begins to develop in his attitude toward the new religion, and when his wanderings finally bring him to Rome, he seeks out the apostle Peter and questions him about Christ. Eventually, Barabbas becomes so obsessed by Christianity that he mistakes the burning of a section of Rome for the return of Christ. Seizing a torch, he goes out into the streets, only to be arrested and imprisoned with the Christians, from whom he learns that it was not Christ but Caesar who had set Rome on fire.

Although he is now imprisoned with the Christians and is made to share their fate as a slave in the Roman mines, Barabbas remains irresolute in his attitude toward Christianity. During the mass executions of Christians, Barabbas is crucified with Peter. Before he dies, he makes an ambiguous statement that may be interpreted as an acceptance of Christianity.

BARABOO, bar′ə-boo, is a city in Wisconsin, the seat of Sauk County, 31 miles (50 km) northwest of Madison. It is the trading center of an agricultural area, and its industries include the processing of canned foods and manufacture of textiles.

Baraboo was winter headquarters for the Barnum and Bailey Circus from 1884 to 1938. It is now the home of the Circus World Museum, operated by the State Historical Society. John Ringling, a founder of Ringling Brothers' Circus (later merged with Barnum and Bailey), was born near Baraboo. The Sauk County Historical Society is located here.

Baraboo was first settled in 1840. It was incorporated as a village in 1867 and chartered as a city in 1882. The city has a mayor and council form of government. Population: 7,931.

BARACOA, bä-rä-kō′ä, is a seaport city on the northern coast of Cuba, near the eastern end of the island. It is in the province of Oriente, about 90 miles (145 km) northeast of Santiago. Baracoa is surrounded by mountains. A picturesque, anvil-shaped peak nearby is El Yunque de Baracoa, 1,932 feet (589 meters) high. The city has a landlocked harbor. Its industries include the manufacture of coconut oil and chocolate. Cacao, coconuts, and bananas are exported.

The first settlement of white men in Cuba was made at Baracoa by Diego Velásquez in 1512. Baracoa was the capital of Cuba from 1518 to 1522. Near the city, in 1895, Antonio Maceo and his followers began the struggle for Cuban independence. Population: (1953) 11,459.

BARAGUAY D'HILLIERS, bà-rà-gä′ dĕl-yä, **Count Achille** (1795–1878), marshal of France. The son of Louis Baraguay d'Hilliers, one of Napoleon's generals, he was born in Paris on Sept. 6, 1795. He took part in the French expedition to Algeria in 1830, and his success there gained him the confidence of the government, which created him a lieutenant general. In 1841 he was made governor general of Algeria. On the fall of Louis Philippe in the revolution of 1848, the provisional government appointed him to the command of the military division of Doubs. He replaced Nicolas Changarnier in the command of the army of Paris, and concurred in the accomplishment of Louis Napoleon's coup d'etat on Dec. 2, 1851.

In the war with Russia in 1854, Baraguay d'Hilliers was commander in chief of the Baltic expedition, and for his services received the dignity of marshal of France. Later he was nominated a senator. He took an active part in the campaign of 1859, when France joined with Sardinia to free Italy from Austrian domination.

He was governor of Paris in 1870. Baraguay d'Hilliers died at Amélie-les-Bains, France, on June 6, 1878.

BARAGUAY D'HILLIERS, bà-rà-gä′ dĕl-yä′, **Louis** (1764–1813), French general. He was born in Paris. Receiving an appointment in the army of Italy from Napoleon, he shared all the success of the campaign of 1796–1797 and was made general of a division and commandant of Venice in 1798. He accompanied the French expedition to Egypt, and afterward successively held appointments on the Rhine, in the Tirol, and in Catalonia. He fought brilliantly at Austerlitz and in Spain and commanded a division in the Russian campaign of 1812. During the retreat from Moscow he incurred the displeasure of Napoleon. He soon died in Berlin, on Jan. 6, 1813.

BARANOF ISLAND, bar′ə-nôf, is the most important island of the Alexander Archipelago, in southeastern Alaska. It is about 100 miles long and 25 miles broad (160 by 40 km). On its northwest coast is the town of Sitka. The island was named for the Russian trader Aleksandr Baranov, who took possession of it in 1799. Population: 7,400.

BARANOV, bə-rä′nôf, **Aleksandr Andreyevich** (1747–1819), Russian explorer and merchant. He was born in Kargopol, in northern European Russia. A merchant and manufacturer in Irkutsk, Siberia, in 1780, he became manager of the colony that had been founded in 1784 on Three Saints Bay, on Kodiak Island, Alaska. Soon after taking charge he transferred the trading post to St. Paul's Harbor, Kodiak, and established posts on the mainland coast in Cook Inlet and in Prince William Sound. At Vosressensky Harbor (now Resurrection Bay), in 1794 he built the first ship constructed on the northwest coast of America north of Vancouver Island.

In 1796, Baranov placed a colony at Yakutat Bay. On the organization of the Russian-American Company in 1799, he was chief manager, and his jurisdiction included all of Alaska and the Kuril Islands. In that year he established a post, Fort St. Michael, on the west side of Baranof Island, but it was destroyed by the Indians in 1802. In 1804 he drove the Indians from the site of the present Sitka. He built a fortified post there and named it New Archangel. The headquarters of the company were transferred there in 1808.

During Baranov's administration, the company maintained trading posts only in southern Alaska, from Sitka to Unalaska. It traded as far north as the Bristol Bay region and took seals on the Pribilof Islands, but had no settlements north of those places. In 1812, Baranov established a fortified post at Fort Ross, Calif., 60 miles northwest of the Golden Gate, and for several years maintained a station on the Farallon Islands, west of San Francisco.

Baranov entered into agreements with John Jacob Astor and later with the Hudson's Bay Company, and he extended the commerce of the Russian-American Company to the Spanish settlements in California, to Hawaii, and to China. His administration of company affairs ended in 1818, and in November of that year he sailed west for Europe. His ship was detained at Batavia (now Djakarta), Java, where Baranov fell ill of a fever. He died on April 28, 1819, a few days after leaving port.

BARANTE, bȧ-räNt', **Baron de** (1782–1866), French historian and public official. He was born *Guillaume Prosper Brugière,* in Riom, France, on June 10, 1782. He held various administrative posts and after 1815 served in the Chamber of Deputies. In 1819 he was made a peer. His principal work, *Histoire des ducs de Bourgogne* (1824), secured his election to the French Academy in 1828.

Between 1830 and 1840 he represented France at Turin and St. Petersburg; after the revolution of 1848 he devoted himself entirely to literary pursuits. He died at Barante, France, on Nov. 23, 1866. His grandson edited Barante's interesting *Souvenirs* (8 vols., 1890–1901).

BÁRÁNY, bä'rän-yə, **Robert** (1876–1936), Austro-Swedish physician, who made pioneering studies of the normal and pathological functioning of the balancing mechanism of the inner ear. He received the 1914 Nobel Prize in physiology and medicine "for his work on the physiology and pathology of the vestibular apparatus."

Contributions to Science. Bárány found that when he flushed a subject's ear with water that was above or below body temperature, dizziness and nystagmus (rapid rhythmical movements of the eyes) were produced. He concluded that these symptoms were the result of movement of the fluid in the semicircular canals of the ear, caused by a change in the fluid's specific gravity as it was warmed or cooled by the water. These effects did not appear in patients whose semicircular canals had been destroyed by illness.

Bárány also studied related effects with the cerebellum, the portion of the brain concerned with balance and coordination, which works closely with the inner ear's balancing mechanism. When patients whose ear had been flushed with cold water tried to point straight ahead with their eyes closed, they tended to point instead toward the side of the flushed ear. Bárány found that the same result occurred when certain parts of the cerebellum were detached by freezing or by changes caused by disease.

Using these experiments as a basis, Bárány devised simple ways to investigate both the semicircular canals and the cerebellum. These methods made it easier to diagnose various kinds of inflammations of the inner ear, making possible early surgical treatment when necessary. Bárány was also a pioneer in the treatment of otosclerosis, an important cause of deafness.

Life. Bárány was born in Vienna, Austria, on April 22, 1876. He attended the University of Vienna and received an M.D. degree in 1900. From 1903 to 1911 he worked under Adam Politzer at the latter's ear clinic in Vienna, and he became a lecturer on ear diseases at the University of Vienna in 1909.

During World War I, Bárány saw action as a physician and was taken prisoner by Russia. From 1917 he taught otology and headed the ear, nose, and throat clinic at the University of Uppsala, Sweden. In addition to the Nobel Prize, he was awarded the Guyot Prize of the University of Groningen in 1914 and the Swedish Medical Society Medal in 1925. Bárány died in Uppsala on April 8, 1936.

Bárány's works include *Physiology and Pathology of the Semicircular Canals* (1910), *Functional Testing of the Vestibular Apparatus* (1912), and *A New Method of Radical Operation for Chronic Ear Suppuration* (1922).

BARATARIA BAY, bar'ə-târ-ē-ə, is a body of water in Louisiana, about 40 miles (65 km) southeast of New Orleans. It extends north from the Gulf of Mexico, between the parishes of Jefferson and Plaquemines. The bay is about 15 miles long and 6 miles wide (24 by 10 km). It and the lagoons branching out of it were notorious in the years 1810–1814 as being both the headquarters and rendezvous of the celebrated Jean Lafitte and his buccaneers.

BARATIERI, bä-rä-tyä'rē, **Oreste** (1841–1901), Italian general, who was defeated by the Ethiopians at the Battle of Aduwa, one of the worst colonial disasters of the 19th century. He was born in Condino, Italy, on Nov. 13, 1841. He fought under Garibaldi in Sicily in 1860 and joined the regular army six years later.

In 1891 he was appointed governor of Eritrea, a new Italian colony on the Red Sea coast of Africa. Advancing with an army into the interior, he captured Kassala (now in Sudan) in 1894 and then invaded Ethiopia, defeating the prince of Tigre twice in January 1895. Opposed by 100,000 troops sent by King Menelek II of Ethiopia to repel the invaders, Baratieri was obliged to withdraw from Aduwa, the capital of Tigre. When the growing demoralization of his troops threatened to hamper his retreat, he determined to risk everything on a battle with the Ethiopians. Near Aduwa, on March 1, 1896, the vastly outnumbered Italians were routed with a loss of more than 7,000 men and all their artillery. Baratieri was court-martialed. Though absolved of criminal responsibility he was censured for his conduct of the campaign, and left the army. He died at Sterzing, Austria (now Vipiteno, Italy), on Aug. 8, 1901.

Baratieri published his *Memorie d'Africa 1892–1896* (1897) in defense of his handling of the Ethiopian campaign.

BARATYNSKY, ba-ra-tin'skû-i, **Yevgeni Abramovich** (1800–1844), Russian poet, who was a prominent member of the circle that surrounded the poet Alexander Pushkin. Baratynsky was born in Gut Vezhla, Tambov region, on Feb. 19, 1800. In 1820, after his expulsion in 1816 from the royal school at St. Petersburg (now Leningrad), he joined a Russian infantry regiment stationed in Finland, of which he became an officer. Retiring from military service in 1825, he traveled for two years through Germany, France, and Italy. In 1827 he settled near Moscow, where he joined the exclusive coterie of poets known as the "Pushkin pléiade," which included Nikolai Gnedich, Anton Delvig, Wilhelm Kuechelbecker, and Pyotr Aleksandrovich Pletnev. He died in Naples, Italy, on June 29, 1844.

Baratynsky's poetry placed him among the romanticists of Pushkin's group. His work is intellectual, concentrating on abstract subjects and influenced by the German romantic philosophers, particularly Schelling. Many of the poems are laments, and Pushkin called Baratynsky Russia's "first elegiac poet." The early poem *Eda* (1826), written while Baratynsky was still in Finland, is especially somber, but the tone runs through all of his best writing. Baratynsky wrote of his poetry: "My muse is no raving beauty, but one is struck by the uncommon expression of her face."

His poems include *Finland, The Last Death, On the Death of Goethe, The Ball, The Orgy,* and *The Gypsy Girl.*

BARBADOS, bär-bā′dōz, an island in the West Indies, is an independent member of the Commonwealth of Nations. Located in the Atlantic Ocean, about 100 miles (160.9 km) east of St. Vincent in the Windward Islands, at longitude 59°37′ W and latitude 13°4′ N, it is the easternmost of the Caribbean islands and lies south of the path usually taken by hurricanes. Roughly triangular in shape, the island is 21 miles (33.7 km) long and about 14 miles (22.52 km) at its widest point. It has an area of 166 square miles (430 sq km). Population: (1973 est.) 243,000.

Barbados' largest town is Bridgetown, the capital and chief port (1970 pop., 8,789). The center of Bridgetown is Trafalgar Square, with a Gothic cathedral and the parliament buildings. Speightstown is the only other sizable town on Barbados. Holetown was the site of the island's first settlement.

The People. In ancient times, Barbados was inhabited by Arawak and then by Carib Indians, but it was uninhabited when the first white settlers arrived from England in 1627. West African slaves were brought in during the 1600's and 1700's. About 75 percent of the people are Negroes, 20 percent are of mixed blood, and 5 percent are white. The language of the island is English, which all classes speak with a flat-voweled, lilting accent that differs from the speech of other West Indians.

Most Barbadians are Christians. The majority belong to the Church of England, but there are also some Protestants of other denominations and some Roman Catholics.

The population density is about 1,450 persons per square mile, one of the world's highest.

Geographical Features and Economic Life. The island is composed chiefly of coral, which accounts for the magnificent white sand beaches. Temperatures are equable because of the latitude, the ocean, and the trade winds that sweep unimpeded across the island from December to June. The temperature range is from 70° to 90° F, sometimes dropping into the 60's during the winter months. Rainfall averages 75 inches (191 cm) a year in the high central district and 50 inches (127 cm) in some coastal areas. Mount Hillaby (1,104 feet; 335.5 meters) is the highest point.

Although tamarinds, other fruit trees, ornamental palms, banyan trees, and other exotic plants are grown, almost half the total area of Barbados is devoted to the cultivation of sugarcane. The main industries are the manufacture of sugar and its byproducts, molasses and rum. Barbadian rum, lighter than the Jamaican type, is considered by many to be the best in the British West Indies. Most of the island's food is imported, but locally caught fish are plentiful. Barbadian cooks are expert in the preparation of the delicate and delicious flying fish. The sight of the flying-fish fleet putting out from Bathsheba harbor on the cliff-bound windward coast, or returning at sundown, each boat in turn racing through the reefs that guard the harbor, is an unforgettable spectacle.

Because of the need to import food and other goods of all kinds, there is a permanently adverse balance of trade, but this is partly offset by remittances from Barbadians abroad, interest on foreign investments, and tourist spending. Local currency is the Barbados dollar, comprising 100 cents.

Transportation and Communications. The island has about 700 miles (1126.5 km) of roads, most of them paved. Bridgetown is the center of a bus network serving much of the island. There are regularly scheduled steamship sailings to and from Britain, and several cruise ships stop at Bridgetown every winter. There is an airport at Seawell, 12 miles (19.3 km) from Bridgetown, that is used by a number of international airlines and by the interisland planes of British West Indian Airways. Other islands may also be reached by small cargo schooners. Cable and wireless services are available, and the island has a telephone system.

Tourism. Its pleasant, healthful winter climate, beautiful beaches, and clear blue water have made Barbados one of the most popular tourist resorts in the West Indies. There are many hotels, and beach cottages may be rented. There are no local handicrafts of much interest, but many visitors are attracted by the relatively low prices of imported British goods such as china and woolens. Barbados is a year-round resort, favored by British and Americans in the winter months and by Venezuelans in the summer.

Education. The island has free public elementary schools and secondary technical schools. Codrington College, now mainly a divinity school,

THE CAREENAGE, the old inner harbor of Bridgetown, shelters interisland ships and yachts. Across Trafalgar Square is the Parliament building (tower). Large ships tie up at the nearby Deep Water Harbour, built in 1961.

J. ALLAN CASH FROM RAPHO GUILLUMETTE

BARBADOS' ATLANTIC COAST, shown at Bathsheba, a beach resort, is cooled by northeast trade winds.

was founded in 1710. A technical institute was opened in 1955, and a branch of Jamaica's University of the West Indies opened in 1963.

Government. A British colony with full internal self-government since 1961, Barbados received its independence on November 30, 1966. As a Commonwealth country, it has a governor-general, appointed by the queen, who names the prime minister. He is always the leader of the majority party in the House of Assembly. The governor-general also names the leader of the opposition.

The assembly is elected by universal suffrage. It has 24 members and the senate has 21. Twelve senators are named by the prime minister, two by the leader of the opposition, and seven by the governor-general to speak for interests not represented otherwise. Policy decisions are made by the prime minister and his cabinet colleagues chosen by him, who are collectively responsible to parliament.

The constitution may be amended only by a two-thirds majority in each house. Laws concerning several other matters can be passed only by this special majority. To keep partisan influence out of administration, judicial, civil service, and police matters are handled by commissions composed of persons who are not in parliament, but who are picked by the prime minister after consultation with the leader of the opposition.

History. The name Barbados, which means "bearded," was probably conferred on the island by early Portuguese explorers because of the beardlike vines that they observed on its trees. In 1624, English sailors laid claim to the island in the name of King James I, and the king granted it to James Ley, who became 1st earl of Marlborough. Ley sponsored a colonizing venture by Sir William Courteen, who landed the first settlers at Hole Town (now Holetown) in 1627. An elected assembly began to meet in 1652. When sugar became Barbados' main commercial interest, the island was cut up into huge estates. The slaves were emancipated in 1834, but politics remained the concern of a small upper class.

It was not until the depression of the 1930's that the people began to demand political rights. Educated middle-class Negroes led the new movement. One of these, Sir Grantley Adams, founded the Barbados Labour Party in 1942 and became the island's first premier in 1954. He was also the first prime minister (1958–1962) of the West Indies federation (see WEST INDIES).

MORLEY AYEARST, *New York University*

Further Reading: Ayearst, Morley, *The British West Indies, the Search for Self-Government* (London and New York 1960); Parry, John H., and Sherlock, Philip M., *A Short History of the West Indies* (London 1956); *Report of Barbados*, with maps and bibliography (London, biennially).

SUGARCANE, Barbados' principal agricultural product, once was processed in this old mill (*left*), no longer used. Mature cane stalks (*right*) rise high above the harvesters.

BARBADOS CEDAR, bär-bā′dŏz sē′dər, a cedar, or juniper, tree found on Barbados island, Bermuda, and the Leeward Islands. It grows to a height of 50 feet (15 meters) and has spreading branches and light-green, sharp-pointed leaves. One of the most beautiful of the junipers, the Barbados cedar is often planted for decoration. The botanical name for the Barbados cedar is *Juniperus barbadensis.*

BARBADOS CHERRY, bär-bā′dŏz, a West Indian shrub or small tree that is classified as *Malpighia glabra* of the family Malpighiaceae. It has handsome crimson axillary flowers and is cultivated to some extent for its acid fruit, inferior to but resembling a cherry, which is used in jam and preserves. *M. urens* also bears an edible but smaller fruit, and is sometimes also called Barbados cherry.

BARBADOS GOOSEBERRY, bär-bā′dŏz gooz′-ber-ē, a shrubby slender cactus, native to tropical America. It bears lemon-yellow, smooth, edible egg-shaped fruits as large as olives. Now naturalized in peninsular Florida, it is widely used in greenhouses as a stock on which to graft other cactus species. The Barbados gooseberry, also called the blade apple and lemon vine, is classified botanically as *Pereskia aculeata.*

BARBARA, bär′bə-rə, **Saint,** a martyr venerated in the Greek and Roman Catholic churches. The many accounts of her martyrdom disagree as to her time (3d or 4th century) and place (Rome, Heliopolis, Antioch, Tuscany, or Nicomedia). The chroniclers agree on several details of her martyrdom, however. Her father Dioscuros, a rich non-Christian, had his beautiful daughter confined to a tower so that no man might see her. While he was absent on a journey, she ordered that a bathhouse being erected for her use should be altered to include three windows instead of two, as a symbol of the Trinity. On her father's return she acknowledged that she was a Christian. In a fury, he took her before the provincial prefect, who had her tortured and then condemned her to death by beheading. Her father carried out the sentence and was struck by lightning and consumed by fire. She was martyred at the same time as St. Juliana.

St. Barbara has been widely venerated since the 7th century. In art she is depicted standing by a tower with three windows. Because of the tower, she has come to be regarded as a patroness of architects and stonemasons. Because of a legend that she prayed fervently before her death, she is believed to be an intercessor for those about to die without the sacraments. She is also the patroness of armorers, gunsmiths, artillerymen, and miners. Because of doubt about the historical accuracy of the accounts of St. Barbara, her feast (Dec. 4) was removed from the universal liturgical calendar in 1969.

BARBARA ALLAN is a Scottish ballad, written by Allan Ramsay in 1724 and first printed in Thomas Percy's *Reliques of Ancient English Poetry* (1765). It tells of Barbara Allan, who rejects her lover and then mourns his death:

> O mither, mither, mak' my bed . . .
> Since my love died for me today,
> Ise die for him to-morrow.

Another ballad on the same theme, also in the *Reliques,* is entitled *Barbara Allen's Cruelty.*

BARBARA FRIETCHIE, bär′bə-rə frich′ē, is a ballad by John Greenleaf Whittier written in 1863. It relates a supposedly historical incident of the American Civil War, when the 95-year-old Barbara Fritchie hung out the Union flag at Frederick, Md., in defiance of Confederate troops commanded by Gen. Thomas Jonathan (Stonewall) Jackson. Its best-known lines are:

> "Shoot, if you must, this old gray head,
> But spare your country's flag," she said.

Her courage touched the general, who ordered his troops not to harm her.

BARBARI, bär′bä-rē, **Jacopo de'** (c. 1445–c. 1516), Italian painter and engraver, whose etchings influenced Albrecht Dürer, a contemporary. He was born in Venice and probably studied there under the Vivarini family of artists. From about 1500 he traveled extensively in Germany, where he was known as *Jakob Walch* and served as court painter to the elector of Saxony. After 1510 he lived in the Netherlands, where he was court painter to the regent, Margaret of Austria. He died in Brussels.

Barbari's work shows a blend of Venetian, German, and Dutch styles. His etchings include *Judith, Adoration of the Magi, Dying Cleopatra, Mars and Venus, Sacrifice to Priapus,* and six views of Venice. Among his paintings are two versions of Christ and two of the Holy Family.

BARBARIAN, bär-bâr′ē-ən, an uncivilized or uncultured person. The word comes from the Greek *barbaros* (strange, rude, ignorant), applied by the ancient Greeks to all foreigners who could not speak Greek. The Romans adopted the Greek word, and used it in its Latin form for all people not members of either Greek or Roman society. Other peoples have applied equivalent terms to any alien land, culture, or people that they believed to be inferior to their own.

BARBAROSSA, Holy Roman emperor. See FREDERICK I.

BARBAROSSA, bär-bə-ros′ə, is the name applied by Europeans to two Turkish corsairs of North Africa. Their father was Greek, and they were born probably at Mytilene on the island of Lesbos in the Aegean Islands.

BARBAROSSA I (died 1518) spent some years in the service of the Mamluk sultans of Egypt before going to Tunis and becoming a freebooter. His original name was *Horush* or *Arouj* or *Koruk.* With his brother Khizr he began the conquest of Algeria about 1514, sometimes aiding the local rulers against the Spaniards and sometimes turning against them for his own ends. He was killed by the Spaniards at Rio-Salado, Algeria, after attempting to seize Tlemcen.

BARBAROSSA II (died 1546) took command of his brother's possessions after the latter's death. His original name was *Khizr;* he was better known as *Khair ed-Din.* He became the North African deputy of Selim I, sultan of Turkey, and in 1533 was appointed admiral of the Turkish fleet by Suleiman I. The next year he seized Tunis but was driven out in 1535 by the forces of Emperor Charles V, commanded by Admiral Andrea Doria. In 1538, Barbarossa won a notable victory near Actium, defeating the emperor's forces. From 1541 until 1544 he controlled most of the Mediterranean. He died in Constantinople on July 5, 1546.

BARBARY, bär′bə-rē, is a general name for the coastal region of North Africa stretching from Egypt to the Atlantic Ocean north of the Sahara. It is inhabited mainly by Berbers.

Ancient Egypt and Libya. In ancient times the part of Africa known to the Europeans was made up of two divisions, Egypt and Libya, and the latter was subdivided into northern and southern Libya. Northern Libya comprised mainly what became known as the Barbary States. According to Herodotus, northern Libya was inhabited in his day by the indigenous race of Libyans, who were settled throughout the region, and by the foreign Phoenicians and Greeks, who settled at several points from Egypt to Carthage. Of the origin of the Libyans whom Herodotus called indigenous, there is no trace. According to Arabian tradition, the Libyans, who colonized the region, came from Yemen. The Phoenicians settled Carthage as early as the 9th century B.C. About 631 B.C. the Greeks founded a colony at Cyrene in Cyrenaica, just east of the bay of the Mediterranean called Syrtis Major (Gulf of Sidra). West of Carthage lay Numidia and Mauretania, extending to the Atlantic coast; east of Cyrene was Egypt.

Roman Domination. By the 6th century B.C. the powerful and rapidly expanding Carthaginians had colonies along the entire coast of North Africa west of Grecian Cyrene, and they controlled Sardinia and cities in Sicily. Carthage's expansion resulted in a series of wars with Rome. Known as the Punic Wars, they were fought over a period of 118 years, from 264 to 146 B.C. At the end of the Third Punic War (146) the Carthaginian power was extinguished, and Carthage itself was in ruins. The final subjugation of Numidia by the Romans was accomplished in the Jugurthine War (111–106 B.C.), and that of Mauretania in the reign of Claudius (42 A.D.). Thus the entire region of Barbary, once made up of independent native states and foreign colonies, came into the hands of Rome.

In the 5th century A.D. the Vandals, led by their king Genseric, advanced from Spain into Roman Africa. In 435 they founded a kingdom in Africa, with its capital at Carthage, that lasted 100 years. Then came the struggle under Emperor Justinian for the reestablishment of Roman supremacy. Belisarius, Justinian's able general, conquered the Vandal kingdom of North Africa and annexed it to the Byzantine empire (533–534). This relationship continued until the region was brought under Muslim domination in the 7th century. The Muslim Arabs overran Numidia and Mauretania to the Atlantic Ocean and early in the next century pushed across the Strait of Gibraltar in the conquest of Spain.

Muslim Africa. By about 800, with a weakening of the central government, Barbary split into several autonomous Muslim states. For eight centuries they were alternately tributary and independent, often fighting among themselves.

From the 16th to the 19th century the Barbary States—Tripolitania, Tunisia, Algeria, and usually also Morocco—were semi-independent states under Turkish suzerainty. The Barbary powers were notorious for large-scale piracy in the Mediterranean and even extended their raids into the Atlantic. Their corsairs (many of whom were Moors expelled from Spain and their descendants, while others were Turks) preyed on the shipping of the Christian nations and occasionally raided the coastal towns of Italy, France, and Spain. Captured vessels and cargoes were sold, and their passengers and crews held for ransom; the unransomed were sold as slaves.

Modern History. Several important punitive expeditions were undertaken against the Barbary States by the Christian powers, including those of Emperor Charles V in 1541 and the assaults of the French fleet under Adm. Abraham Duquesne (1682–1683). The United States was involved in two wars with the Barbary States—the Tripolitan War (1801–1805) and the war with Algiers (1815). An Anglo-Dutch fleet commanded by Lord Exmouth bombarded Algiers in 1816. The Barbary States, however, remained a pirate refuge until the French conquered Algiers in 1830. The French conquest broke the power of the Barbary States and ended the activities of the corsairs.

By 1912, Tunisia and Morocco also had come under French control. Tripolitania was transferred from Turkish to Italian sovereignty in 1911 and, with the annexed region of Cyrenaica, was given the ancient name of Libya. Libya became independent in 1951, Morocco and Tunisia in 1956, and Algeria in 1962.

BARBARY APE, bär′bə-rē āp, a tailless monkey found in northern Africa and on the Rock of Gibraltar. It is the only monkey now native to Europe. The Barbary ape may have a body and head length of 14.9 to 29.8 inches (382 to 764 mm) and a weight up to 28.6 pounds (13 kg). Its color ranges from olive to black but most commonly is a yellowish brown. The Barbary ape (*Macaca sylvanus*) belongs to the family Cercopithecidae.

Often found in troops, these strong brave apes are agile in trees and on the ground. They are also good swimmers. Mainly active during the day, they feed on a variety of plant and animal food. There is no definite breeding season for Barbary apes; occasionally two males may fight fiercely over a female. The young, usually born singly, are almost hairless and weigh approximately 15.8 ounces (453 g). They nurse for one year and mature in about four years. Their life span in captivity is 30 years or more.

Barbary ape (*Macaca sylvanus*)

BOMBARDMENT OF TRIPOLI by U.S. fleet in 1804, during the Barbary Wars, is depicted in this Currier lithograph.

THE GRANGER COLLECTION

BARBARY WARS, bär′bə-rē wôrz, a term applied in United States history to two wars waged with the Barbary States of North Africa: (1) the Tripolitan War of 1801–1805, and (2) the war with Algiers in 1815.

Causes. Prior to 1776, American ships in the Mediterranean trade, flying the British flag, enjoyed a measure of immunity from the depredations of the Barbary corsairs. This was because, in return for the tribute that Britain paid to the Barbary States, these states guaranteed colonial as well as home shipping from attack. By terms of the treaty of amity and commerce between the United States and France, signed on Feb. 6, 1778, France undertook to provide for the safety "of American vessels and effects against all violence, insults, attacks, or depredations, on the part of the said Princes and States of Barbary or their subjects."

After the American Revolution the United States was obliged to assume the protection of its own commerce, without French assistance. Congress in 1784 appropriated $80,000 as a first government tribute to the Barbary powers, thus following the example of the major European states in purchasing immunity and ransoming captives.

In July 1785 the Algerians captured two American vessels, and the dey of Algiers held their crews (21 men in all) for a ransom of $59,496, or more than $2,800 per man, although the latest French captives had been ransomed at about $500 each. Negotiations for the liberation of the American captives were protracted, and 11 of them died before the survivors were finally ransomed in 1795. Meanwhile, in 1787, Morocco signed a 50-year peace treaty with the United States, with no provision for tribute but with an understanding that some "presents" should be given the sultan. Morocco faithfully observed the terms of the pact except during a brief period in 1803.

In 1793 a squadron of Algerian vessels passed the Strait of Gibraltar into the Atlantic and captured 10 American merchantmen. Negotiations were begun, and two years later, on Sept. 5, 1795, a sorely humiliated U.S. Congress agreed to pay the dey of Algiers the equivalent of $992,463 for peace and the ransom of 115

sailors, including the survivors from among the 21 captives of a decade earlier. Part of the payment was a 36-gun frigate costing about $100,-000 and stores and ammunition of equal value. The United States further engaged to pay annual tribute of $21,600 in naval stores, $20,000 for recognition of a U.S. consul in Algiers, biennial presents of $17,000, and other regular and incidental blackmail. Four armed vessels were sent to Algiers in 1798 as arrears of payment.

This humiliating treaty was followed by others, equally humiliating, with Tripoli in November 1796 and with Tunis in 1799. But it should be remembered that all the chief maritime powers of Europe also paid for the protection of their merchantmen in Mediterranean waters. The 1790's were a period of great expansion of American shipbuilding and international trade. Both the government and the shipping interests believed that annual tributes would involve the country in less expense than a war.

In 1800, Capt. William Bainbridge, commanding the *George Washington,* brought the annual tribute to Algiers. The dey then ordered him to carry gifts to the sultan, which Bainbridge was forced to agree to, since his ship and American merchantmen in the harbor were at the dey's mercy. When Bainbridge arrived at Constantinople, however, he obtained from the sultan a decree protecting him from similar humiliations in future dealings with the Barbary powers.

Tripolitan War (1801–1805). The pasha of Tripoli early in 1801 decided that the treaty of 1796 with the United States was not sufficiently remunerative. He therefore demanded an immediate payment of $225,000 plus $25,000 annually. When this exaction was refused, he declared war on May 14, 1801. The United States thereupon dispatched a squadron commanded by Commodore Richard Dale to the Mediterranean. Dale blockaded Tripoli. This show of force persuaded Algiers and Tunis to abandon their plan of forming a war alliance with Tripoli, and they renewed their treaties with the United States.

The United States at first fought the Tripolitan War in a desultory fashion as Commodore Charles Morris succeeded Dale. But then Commodore Edward Preble headed the squadron (1803–1804). Preble forced Morocco, which had

222

joined Tripoli, to withdraw from the alliance and renew its treaty with the United States. He conducted a vigorous campaign, bombarding Tripoli five times. His successor, Commodore Samuel Barron, turned over the command to Commodore John Rodgers in the summer of 1805.

A combined land and sea operation finally turned the scales. Capt. William Eaton, who had been the U.S. consul at Tunis and had recently been appointed naval agent to the Barbary powers, marched a motley army of adventurers 500 miles (805 km) across the desert from Alexandria to Derna in Barca. After receiving supplies from the fleet, he stormed Derna on April 27, 1805, and with the aid of the fleet's guns repulsed an attempt to recapture it on May 13. The pasha of Tripoli, fearing an insurrection as well as further bombardments and an assault on his capital city, signed a peace treaty with the American plenipotentiary, Tobias Lear. Lear negotiated in haste, and the treaty, signed on June 4, 1805, committed the United States to a probably unnecessary payment of $60,000 ransom for prisoners.

War With Algiers (1815). Early in 1815, after the termination of the War of 1812, Commodores Bainbridge and Stephen Decatur were dispatched to suppress a new outbreak of piracy. Decatur captured the Algerian flagship *Mashuda* off Cape de Gat, Spain, on June 17, 1815, and entered the harbor of Algiers on June 28. On June 30 he forced the dey, on pain of destruction of his capital and capture of the rest of his fleet, to sign a treaty abandoning all tributes, surrendering all U.S. captives, and paying an indemnity. Decatur then proceeded to Tunis and Tripoli and exacted from their rulers similar treaties.

Decatur's expedition marked the end of Barbary attacks on United States ships. But the shipping of other countries was menaced by the Barbary pirates until 1830.

Bibliography
Allen, Gardner W., *Our Navy and the Barbary Corsairs* (Hamden, Conn., 1965).
Bailey, Thomas A., *A Diplomatic History of the American People*, 7th ed. (New York 1958).
Bemis, Samuel Flagg, *A Diplomatic History of the United States*, 5th ed. (New York 1965).
Broderick, A.H., *North Africa* (New York 1943).
Irwin, Ray W., *Diplomatic Relations of the United States with Barbary Powers, 1776–1816* (Chapel Hill, N.C., 1931).
Tucker, Glenn, *Dawn Like Thunder: The Barbary Wars and the Birth of the U.S. Navy* (Indianapolis 1966).

STEPHEN DECATUR, a naval hero of the Barbary Wars.

THE GRANGER COLLECTION

BARBAULD, bär′bōld, **Anna Letitia** (1743–1825), English poet, essayist, and editor. She was born *Anna Letitia Aikin* in Kibworth, Leicestershire, on June 20, 1743. In 1774 she married the Rev. Rochemont Barbauld. Her popular *Hymns in Prose for Children* (1781) was written for the pupils of the boarding school she and her husband established in Suffolk. She moved to Stoke Newington (now part of London) in 1802 and became a prominent member of London literary circles. In her most ambitious literary undertaking, she edited *British Novelists* (1810), a 50-volume set of English novels, for which she provided a critical essay and biographical notes. She died in Stoke Newington on March 9, 1825.

Anna Barbauld's earliest poetry was published in *Poems* (1773). In 1811 she published her longest poem, *Eighteen Hundred and Eleven*, a somber work on the future of Great Britain. Her other writing includes *Miscellaneous Pieces in Prose*, written with her brother, John Aikin. This volume contains two of her best essays, *Inconsistency in our Expectations* and *On Romances*. Dr. Samuel Johnson complimented the latter for its successful imitation of his style. Her collected works were published in two volumes by her niece, Lucy Aikin, in 1825.

Further Reading: Ritchie, Lady Thackeray, *Book of Sybils* (London 1883); Rodgers, Betsy, *Georgian Chronicle* (London 1958).

BARBEAU, bär-bō′, **Marius** (1883–1969), Canadian ethnologist, a leading authority in the folklore, arts and handicrafts, and Indians of Canada. Barbeau made the first detailed study of the civilization and dialects of the Tsimshian Indians of British Columbia. He wrote over 160 books and 500 articles and collected thousands of French-Canadian folksongs.

Charles Marius Barbeau was born on March 5, 1883, at Ste.-Marie-Beauce, Quebec, graduated from Laval University in 1907, and spent three years as a Rhodes scholar at Oxford. In 1911 he was appointed an ethnologist for the National Museum of Canada, at Ottawa, and served there for more than 50 years. He died in Ottawa on Feb. 27, 1969.

BARBÉ-MARBOIS, bàr-bā′ màr-bwä′, **Marquis François de** (1745–1837), French diplomat and government official. He was born at Metz on Jan. 3, 1745. After serving as a diplomat at several German courts, he was sent to the United States as the French consul general. From 1785 until his return to France in 1789 he served in Santo Domingo. During the French Revolution he was exiled to Guiana as a royalist (1797). He was recalled in 1800, however, and was made minister of the treasury in 1801.

In 1803 he skillfully negotiated the sale of Louisiana to the United States, obtaining a larger price than the French had anticipated. He entered the Senate in 1813 and the next year voted for the reestablishment of the Bourbon dynasty. He was well received by Louis XVIII and appointed a peer of France. When Napoleon returned to France from Elba, he ordered Barbé-Marbois to leave Paris. After the final defeat of Napoleon, Barbé-Marbois resumed his offices.

Following the revolution of July 1830 he again shifted his allegiance and showed the same fidelity to Louis Philippe that he had given to Napoleon and the Bourbons. He died in Paris on Jan. 14, 1837.

BARBEL, a freshwater fish of the carp family, derives its name from the beardlike filaments growing from its nose and mouth.

LAURENCE E. PERKINS

BARBED WIRE. The invention of wire fencing set with barbs at regular intervals was an important accessory to the westward movement in the United States in the late 19th century. Befor barbed wire was widely available, farmers lacked protection against untamed cattle, and ranchers were unable to safeguard property improvements or improved cattle breeds. Standard fencing materials of wood and stone were scarce on open prairies and plains. Then, in 1873, an Illinois farmer, Joseph Farwell Glidden, applied for a patent on a home-made barbed-wire fencing material that was practical and effective. This first commercially successful barbed-wire fencing became the basis of a flourishing new industry.

In the West, use of "bob wire" or the "devil's rope," as barbed wire was called, caused the natural hostility between cattlemen and farm settlers to flare into "fence wars," while in the East manufacturers became involved in litigation for control of various patents. Eventually, however, barbed wire was accepted as the answer to one of the most pressing needs of the times. It provided the protective boundaries without which the frontiers of settlement could not continue to advance.

Between 1873 and the end of the 19th century, aproximately 400 types of barbed wire were devised. Although many were successful, a few types dominated the industry until modern materials brought about changes both in domestic fencing and in wire used during the two world wars. In some regions today, smooth single-strand wire and woven-wire fences have replaced barbed wire; and in certain areas where livestock is not involved, fencing has been removed entirely.

HENRY D. McCALLUM
FRANCES T. McCALLUM
Authors of "The Wire That Fenced the West"

BARBEL, bär′bəl, is a genus of freshwater fish. It is distinguished by the small size of its dorsal and anal fins; by a strong spine replacing the second or third ray of the dorsal fin; and by four fleshy filaments (barbels) growing from the lips, two at the nose and one at each corner of the mouth, forming a kind of beard.

The barbel belongs to genus *Barbus* in the carp family, Cyprinidae. There are several species. A common one is the European barbel, *B. vulgaris*, which is found in the temperate zones of Europe. It averages 12 to 18 inches (30 to 45 cm) in length, but individual fish up to 3 feet (90 cm) in length and 15 to 18 pounds (6.8–8.2 kg) in weight have been found. It has a smooth, oblong head, with the upper jaw much longer than the lower. The dorsal spine, which is strong and serrated, often inflicts severe

wounds on fishermen and causes damage to their nets.

The barbel feeds on small fishes, aquatic insects, and worms that it obtains by boring with its barbels into the loose soil of river banks. Its flesh is very coarse and unpalatable, and the roe is dangerous to eat at spawning time.

Another species of barbel, which is found in the Nile region, has delicate, tasty flesh. When it is caught, the fisherman puts an iron through its jaw and fastens it by a short cord to the river bank, where it remains alive until needed.

BARBER, bär′bər, **Samuel** (1910–), American composer, who won two Pulitzer prizes in music and was commissioned to write the opera *Antony and Cleopatra* for the opening of the new Metropolitan Opera House in New York City in 1966.

The nephew of contralto Louise Homer, he was born in West Chester, Pa., on March 9, 1910. Barber is reported to have written his first composition, a piano piece called *Sadness*, when he was seven. At the age of 13 he enrolled at the Curtis Institute of Music in Philadelphia. While there, he wrote Serenade for String Quartet (1929); *Dover Beach* (1931), for baritone and string quartet; and Sonata for Violoncello and Piano (1932).

In 1933, Barber won the Bearns Prize from Columbia University for his overture to Richard Sheridan's play *School for Scandal*. In 1935 and 1936 he received Pulitzer traveling scholarships. As a fellow of the American Academy in Rome in 1936, he composed Symphony in One Movement (revised in 1943). While serving with the special forces of the U.S. Army Air Forces in 1944, he wrote *Symphony Dedicated to the Army Air Force* (revised in 1947). His major postwar compositions include the score for the Martha Graham ballet *The Cave of the Heart* (1946); Concerto for Violoncello and Orchestra, for which he won the New York Music Critics Circle Award in 1947; *Knoxville: Summer of 1915* (1947), for soprano and orchestra; and *Prayers of Kierkegaard* (1954), for soprano, chorus, and orchestra.

Barber won the Pulitzer Prize for music for his first opera, *Vanessa* (1958), with libretto by Gian Carlo Menotti, whom Barber knew from his student days at the Curtis Institute. New York *Times* critic Howard Taubman hailed the work as the best American opera ever presented at the Metropolitan Opera House. Barber's short stage piece, *A Hand of Bridge,* for four solo voices and chamber orchestra, for which Menotti also wrote the libretto, was presented at the Festival of Two Worlds in Spoleto, Italy, in 1959. Barber won a second Pulitzer Prize for his Concerto for Piano and Orchestra (1963).

224

BARBER, bär'bər, a person whose occupation is cutting and grooming hair, and shaving men's faces. The word "barber" derives from the Latin *barba,* meaning beard. Barbering has a long history, which for centuries was part of the history of medicine.

Ancient and Medieval Barbers. Barbering dates back to antiquity. Barbers are mentioned in Egyptian papyri, and in ancient Greece and Rome barbershops were favorite meeting places where men discussed the affairs of the day. In folklore, the barber has been represented as a talkative person, the retailer of news, gossip, and homely advice.

In early Christian monasteries barbers rendered the important services of cutting and shaving the hair of monks, who were required by ecclesiastical law to wear the tonsure. After a papal decree of 1163 had forbidden the clergy to shed blood, the practice of periodic bloodletting as a health measure was also given over to barbers. The monastery barber was called *Rasor et Minutor* (barber and remover of blood).

Barber Surgeons. Barbers figured importantly in the history of medicine, especially in the development of surgery as a recognized branch of medical practice. Most early physicians disdained surgery and gave over to barbers this and other ministrations such as bloodletting, cupping and leeching, treating wounds, and extracting teeth. In this they followed the dictates of the Arab physician Avicenna (980–1037), the leading medical authority of medieval times, and a staunch opponent of surgery.

Nevertheless, surgery gradually gained recognition and was admitted to the curriculum of many European universities. In an effort to distinguish between academic surgeons and barber-surgeons, the Collège de St. Côme, founded in Paris about 1210, identified the former as surgeons of the long robe and the latter as surgeons of the short robe. French barbers and surgeons were organized as a guild in 1361, and barber-surgeons were admitted to the faculty of the University of Paris in 1505. The father of modern surgery, Ambroise Paré (1510–1590), began his career as an itinerant barber-surgeon.

In England the barbers were chartered as a guild by Edward IV in 1462, and were merged with the guild of surgeons under a charter by Henry VIII in 1540. In practice, however, barbers who cut hair and gave shaves were forbidden to practice surgery. In France, a decree by Louis XV in 1743 prohibited barbers from practicing surgery, and in England in 1745 the surgeons were separated from the barbers by acts passed during the reign of George II. Their final separation came in 1800 with the founding of the Royal College of Surgeons during the reign of George III. From then on, barbers were specialists in haircutting, and not surgeons.

The traditional barber's pole of red and white stripes symbolizes the bloodletting and bandages formerly associated with barbers.

Modern Barbering. Today many barbershops offer additional services such as shampoos, scalp treatments, facial massages, manicures, and the fitting of hair pieces. In the United States barbers are usually trained in special schools and must pass examinations and be licensed by the states in which they work. In the mid-1960's there were 200,000 barbers in the United States, most of whom managed or were employed in small shops.

BARBER OF SEVILLE, bär'bər, sə-vil', is an *opera buffa* (comic opera) in two acts by Gioacchino Rossini (q.v.). The title in Italian is *Il barbiere di Siviglia.* The libretto, by Cesare Sterbini, is based on the play of the same name by the French dramatist Pierre Augustin Caron de Beaumarchais.

The Barber of Seville (originally titled *Almaviva, ossia l'inutile precauzione*) was first produced in Rome on Feb. 20, 1816, under the composer's direction. The opera, destined to be one of the most popular in the repertory, failed at first, possibly in part because of resentment over Rossini's daring in setting to music a libretto already used by Giovanni Paisiello. Soon, however, Rossini's *Barbiere* replaced Paisiello's in popular favor. Its present title was first used in 1816 in a production in Bologna.

Authorities differ as to the length of time in which the music was written. In any event, it was not more than three weeks, proving Rossini's immense facility of invention. It is said that when Donizetti was told that Rossini had written the music in 13 days, he replied: "It is quite possible; he has always been so lazy."

The *Barber* is full of irresistible verse, and the music is by turns piquant and graceful, rollicking and glittering. The story is a sort of prologue to that of Mozart's *Figaro,* but musically there is little in common between them. Rossini was concerned only with writing a comic opera that would amuse and charm the senses, and he succeeded to perfection. There are 20 distinct musical numbers connected by *recitativo secco,* or dry recitative, a style then common in Italian opera. The recitative approximates speech more nearly than song but is constantly about to break into music. Among the musical numbers the best known are Figaro's aria *Largo al factotum,* Rosina's cavatina *Una voce poco fa,* which has done service for most of the great prima donnas of the 19th century, and the "calumny" aria of Don Basilio. For the famous music lesson scene Rossini wrote a concerted number, but it has been lost—providentially, from the viewpoint of the prima donna, who has thus been able to introduce a showpiece of her own choice.

The *Barber* remains in the active repertory of most of the opera companies and bears well its century of life. The first performance in the United States took place in New York City in 1819, in an English translation, under the direction of Thomas Phillips; in 1825 it was produced in its Italian version by Manuel Garcia's Italian Opera Company. Adelina Patti was an unforgettable Rosina.

BARBERINI, bär-bā-rē'nē, an aristocratic Italian family which, by the end of the 15th century, had risen to great power and wealth in Florence through commerce. During the early part of the 16th century some members of the family settled in Rome. There they rapidly gained such influence that Maffeo Barberini (1568–1644) was elected pope in 1623 as Urban VIII. He carried nepotism so far that his three nephews became the most powerful figures of the papal court. The nephews were Taddeo (died 1647), commander of the papal forces; Antonio (1608–1671), cardinal and archbishop of Reims; and Francesco (1597–1679), cardinal and founder of the Barberini Library, one of the great libraries in Rome. The Barberini Palace, started by the architect Carlo Maderno under Urban VIII and later completed by Bernini, housed countless art treasures.

The principal opponents of the Barberini were the Farnese, dukes of Parma, with whom the papacy warred (1641–1644) for control of the duchy of Castro. Following the defeat of the papal forces and the death of Urban VIII, an investigation was conducted into the use of public funds by the Barberini. They took refuge in France but returned to Rome in 1652 when a pardon was granted by the new pope, Innocent X.

The male line of the Barberini became extinct in 1736, but the family riches and title passed through marriage to the Colonna family. The library remained in their possession until it was bought by Pope Leo XIII in 1902 and added to the Vatican Library.

BARBERRY, bär′ber-ē, is a genus of shrubs native to temperate climates. These shrubs generally have yellow wood, bark, and flowers, and sour berries. Their stamens (pollen-bearing organs) are sensitive and spring up when touched—an obvious aid in cross-pollination by insects. The common barberry (*Berberis vulgaris*) formerly was widely planted and now is found commonly along roadsides and hedgerows, and in open woods. It is a rather erect shrub about 2 to 10 feet (0.6 to 3.0 meters) tall, with gray branches. It has clusters of yellow flowers, which are succeeded by elongated, red fruit clusters that persist during the winter and even into the second summer. The shrub has three-pronged spines.

The common barberry has been uprooted in wheat-growing regions because it is an alternative host of the wheat rust (*Puccinia graminis*). Two other species are also hosts of this wheat rust: the American barberry (*B. canadensis*) and the Colorado barberry (*B. fendleri*).

The American barberry is native to dry woodlands and bluffs, from the mountains of Virginia and West Virginia to Georgia, and westward to

Barberry (*Berberis amurensis*)

ROCHE

southeastern Missouri. It has arching brown branches and ovoid berries. The Colorado barberry, similar to the American barberry, is native to the region from Colorado to New Mexico. The common barberry and the Japanese barberry (*B. Thunbergii*) are probably the commonest species in America. The Japanese barberry, however, is not widely naturalized, but is commonly planted for ornamentation. This species has single spines and brown branches. Its orange-red berries are borne singly and not in a long cluster.

The different species of barberry have several uses. The red, dark-blue, or black fruit of some species is used for making jellies having beautiful color and distinct flavor. The fruit of other species is used in dried form as raisins. In several species, the yellow roots and stems are used in dyeing and the bark in tanning. Many of the species, especially the Japanese barberry, are used for ornamental planting and hedges.

Technically, the barberry genus is called *Berberis*. It contains over 175 different species and belongs to the family Berberidaceae.

A plant, formerly classed as a barberry, is the Oregon Grape (*Mahonia aquifolium*). Its evergreen, spiny-margined leaves are arranged on each side of a common axis. Its fruit is blue-black and has a frosty coating that tends to rub off. This plant grows wild in Western North America, from British Columbia to Oregon.

ARTHUR H. GRAVES
Brooklyn Botanical Garden

BARBER'S ITCH, bär′bərz ich, is the name given to two different diseases of the skin. One of these diseases, *Tinea barbae*, is caused by a parasite, the fungus *Trichophyton*. It affects the hair follicles of the lower part of the face and neck and is a form of ringworm of the beard. The infection causes itching and scaly eruptions that secrete a thick mucus. It spreads out in a ring-like fashion. This disease is always contracted from another person or sometimes from lower animals. In its early stages it is readily curable, but in a chronic state it may be very difficult to treat successfully.

The other disease called "barber's itch" is not of a parasitic nature but is caused by a bacterial infection. It causes an inflammation of the hair follicles and the formation of pimples. These pimples are pierced by hair and may contain pus. Frequently running a chronic course, this disease affects the hairy parts of the face, especially the area of the upper lip and the upper portion of the face.

BARBERTON, bär′bər-tən, a city in Ohio, is situated in Summit County, 6 miles (9.5 km) southwest of Akron, of which it is a residential and industrial suburb. Barberton's diversified manufactures include rubber products, aluminum, chemicals, machinery, and boilers. The city is served by five railroads.

The city was named for Ohio Columbus Barber, president of the Diamond Match Company, who laid out the community in 1891 and moved the Akron plant of his company there. (The Diamond Match Company is no longer situated in Barberton). Barber, before his death in 1920, also invested millions of dollars in a huge experimental farm at Barberton.

The city was incorporated in 1892. Barberton has a mayor and council form of government. Population: 33,052.

BARBÈS, bàr-bes', **Armand** (1809–1870), French revolutionary. He was born at Pointe-à-Pitre, Guadeloupe, and was taken to France at an early age. In 1830 he went to Paris and soon became associated with Louis Auguste Blanqui, a socialist revolutionary. From the beginning of King Louis Philippe's reign in 1830 until the revolution of 1848, Barbès was constantly engaged in conspiracies against the government.

After an unsuccessful attempt to overthrow the government in May 1839, Barbès was condemned to death, but the sentence was commuted to life imprisonment. The revolution of 1848 restored him to liberty, but he immediately resumed his conspiracies. After the insurrection of May 1848, he was sentenced to prison. In 1854 he was again set at liberty and voluntarily exiled himself from France. He died at The Hague, Netherlands, on June 20, 1870.

BARBEY D' AUREVILLY, bàr-bā' dôr-vēyē', **Jules** (1808–1889), French writer whose ability as a critic won him the sobriquet "High Constable of Letters" from his contemporaries. He was born at St.-Sauveur-le-Vicomte, Manche, on Nov. 2, 1808. From 1833 he lived in Paris, where he served as literary and drama critic on several newspapers. He died in Paris on March 24, 1889.

His critical works, though vigorous and penetrating, are marred by a fiercely royalist and Catholic bias. They include *Les oeuvres et les hommes du XIXᵉ siècle* (26 vols., 1861–1909). His fiction includes the novels *L'ensorcelée* (1854) and *Le chevalier des touches* (1864) and a collection of short stories, *Les diaboliques* (1874).

BARBIER, bàr-byā', **Antoine Alexandre** (1765–1825), French bibliographer and librarian. He was born at Coulommiers on Jan. 11, 1765. In 1794 he went to Paris, where he became a member of the committee to collect works of literature and art that had been suppressed during the French Revolution. He was appointed keeper of the library of the Conseil d'État in 1798, and when the library was transported to Fontainebleau in 1807 he became librarian to Emperor Napoleon I. He later served as administrator of King Louis XVIII's private library. Barbier died in Paris on Dec. 5, 1825.

Barbier's most important bibliographic works are *Dictionnaire des ouvrages anonymes et pseudonymes*, 4 vols. (1806–09), and *Nouvelle bibliothèque d'un homme de goût* (1808–10). He also compiled the excellent *Catalogue de la bibliothèque du Conseil d'État* (1803).

BARBIERI, bär-byâ'rē, **Antonio Maria,** (1892–), first Uruguayan cardinal of the Roman Catholic Church. He was born on Oct. 28, 1892, at Montevideo, and entered the Capuchin Order at 21. He studied at Genoa and Rome, where he was ordained in December 1921. Ten years later he was appointed director of his order in Uruguay and Argentina. At this time he began radio broadcasts to teach doctrine to children and also initiated the Catholic Action movement. Appointed coadjutor archbishop of Montevideo in 1936, he founded the first major seminary in Uruguay and became actively engaged in improving his country's social conditions. He was elevated to cardinal in 1958 and led the Uruguayan delegation at Vatican Council II.

BARBIERI, Giovanni Francesco. See GUERCINO.

BARBIROLLI, bär-bi-rol'ē, **Sir John** (1899–1970), British conductor and cellist. He was born *Giovanni Battista Barbirolli* in London on Dec. 2, 1899, the son of Italian and French parents. He studied music in London, and at the age of 11 made his first appearance as a cellist with the Queen's Hall Orchestra. In 1925 he formed the Barbirolli Chamber Orchestra and conducted a series of concerts at the Chenil Galleries in Chelsea.

Subsequently he was conductor of the British National Opera Company (1926) and of the Scottish and Northern Philharmonic orchestras (1933–1937). In 1937 he succeeded Arturo Toscanini as conductor and music director of the New York Philharmonic Symphony Orchestra. He held this position until 1943, when he accepted the leadership of the Hallé Orchestra of Manchester, England, which he brought back to its former high repute. He made many appearances as guest conductor in England and on the Continent. From 1961 to 1967 he divided his time between conducting the Hallé Orchestra and leading the Houston (Texas) Symphony. Barbirolli was knighted in 1949. He died in London on July 29, 1970.

BARBITURATES, bär-bich'ə-rəts, are drugs that are used to induce sleep or sedation. Chemically, they are derivatives of malonylurea (barbituric acid), which is formed by combining malonic acid with urea. The first barbiturate used in medicine (barbital) was introduced in 1903. Since then, scores of different barbiturates have been made available for medical use.

Barbiturate Action. The basic actions of all barbiturates are similar. In full medical doses they induce sleep, and in lesser doses they tend to produce a degree of sedation and calming. Although small to moderate doses of barbiturates do not seem to have much effect on pain, doses that are large enough to cause the patient to lose consciousness also prevent the feeling of pain. In some patients, particularly the elderly, they may produce confusion.

Barbiturates also have an additive effect when taken with other sedative drugs, including alcohol, chloral hydrate, and tranquilizers. This combination may cause an unexpected loss of consciousness.

The exact mechanism and site of action of barbiturates are not known. Although considerable research has been focused on the ascending reticular formation of the brainstem, other parts of the brain also are affected.

Types of Barbiturates. Some barbiturates, such as phenobarbital (Luminal), are called long-acting because their effects last from 12 to 24 hours. Others, such as amobarbital (Amytal), are considered intermediate-acting; their effects last up to 10 or 12 hours. The most common short-acting barbiturates, pentobarbital (Nembutal) and secobarbital (Seconal), wear off in 3 to 8 hours. There also are ultrashort-acting barbiturates, such as thiopental sodium (Pentothal), which is given intravenously to begin anesthesia for surgery. After the patient has lost consciousness from the thiopental, the gaseous anesthetics are used to maintain anesthesia.

Most barbiturates are taken by mouth, but injectable preparations are available.

Uses of Barbiturates. Barbiturates are used in many conditions, including thyroid disease, coronary artery disease, heart failure, peptic ulcer, and high blood pressure, when it is helpful to slow down certain of the patient's body functions. Also, in certain types of epilepsy, small doses of barbiturates will prevent convulsions.

Barbiturates and Addiction. When taken as prescribed by a physician, barbiturates do not cause true addiction. In this respect they differ from narcotic drugs such as morphine and Demerol. Addiction to barbiturates occurs only when the user takes amounts substantially larger than those prescribed by physicians. Generally those who take excessive doses are persons with unstable personalities who obtain the drugs illegally.

Unfortunately, barbiturate addiction has become a major social problem. In some respects it is a more dangerous condition than morphine addiction, because barbiturate addiction causes greater deterioration of the mind and body of the addict. Accordingly, U.S. government regulations have been tightened to try to reduce barbiturate addiction. When taken in proper doses, however, and following a doctor's directions, barbiturates are among the safest drugs known.

SOLOMON GARB, M.D.
University of Missouri Medical School

BARBIZON PAINTERS, bär′bi-zon, a group of mid-19th century French artists, most of whom were landscapists. Some of the artists resided for a considerable time in Barbizon, on the edge of the forest of Fontainebleau, hence their name.

Barbizon painting usually connotes the type of landscape painting practiced in France from about 1835 until it was slowly replaced by impressionism. The common factor in the work of the Barbizon painters is a direct approach toward the natural scene, expressed in a style influenced by the Dutch masters of the 17th century and the newer discoveries of John Constable and the English school. At its best, the work of the Barbizon painters has a delightful freshness of coloring and effective spaciousness.

The most important Barbizon painters were Jean Baptiste Camille Corot (1796–1875), Théodore Rousseau (1812–1867), Charles François Daubigny (1815–1878), Jules Dupré (1811–1889), Narcisse Virgile Diaz de La Peña (1808–1876), and Henri Harpignies (1819–1916). Jean François Millet (1814–1875) and Constant Troyon (1810–1865) also are considered to be members of the group.

JOSEPH C. SLOANE, *University of North Carolina*

Further Reading: Herbert, Robert L., *Barbizon Revisited* (New York 1963).

BARBON, bär′bon, **Praisegod** (1596?–1679), English Puritan divine, whose simple-minded righteousness made him the object of Royalist contempt during the English Revolution. His name is also spelled *Barebone* or *Barebones*. His origins are obscure, but by 1630 he had become a prosperous London leather merchant and prominent Baptist street preacher. When the army under Oliver Cromwell expelled the members of the Long Parliament in 1653, Barbon was one of 140 clerics hastily summoned to sit in Parliament. Although Barbon evidently took no part in its debates, a variant of his name became the royalist label for the session (see BAREBONE'S PARLIAMENT).

Barbon vehemently opposed the restoration of the Stuarts and was imprisoned in the Tower of London for a year (1661–62) after the accession of Charles II. Thereafter he lived quietly in London until his death there in 1679.

BARBOSA, bər-bô′zə, **Ruy** (1849–1923), Brazilian government official. He was born in Salvador, Brazil, on Nov. 5, 1849. One of Brazil's greatest champions of freedom, he studied law at the University of São Paulo, led an antislavery campaign as editor of the *Diario da Bahia,* and in 1881 was elected to the imperial assembly. His opposition to slavery caused his defeat in the elections following the fall of Manuel Pinto de Sousa Dantas' government (1885). As minister of finance and justice after the revolution of 1889, he wrote the decrees establishing religious liberty, separation of church and state, and the federal republic, whose constitution (1891) was largely his work. He was a member of the Permanent Court of International Justice from 1921 until his death in Petrópolis, Brazil, on March 1, 1923.

BARBOUR, bär′bər, **James** (1775–1842), American public official. Elder brother of Philip Pendleton Barbour (q.v.), he was born in Barboursville, Va., on June 10, 1775. He represented Orange County in the Virginia House of Delegates (1798–1805, 1807–1812) and was governor of the state from 1812 to 1814. As U.S. Senator he took a strong states' rights position on such issues as the Missouri Compromise of 1820, although he was no extremist on the slavery issue.

A loyal supporter of President John Quincy Adams and his policies, Barbour was secretary of war (1825–1828) and U.S. minister to Great Britain (1828–1829). With the end of the Adams administration, Barbour lost his prominent place on the national political scene. He died near Gordonsville, Va., on June 7, 1842.

BARBOUR, bär′bər, **John** (1316?–1395), Scottish poet, who wrote the *Brus,* the national epic of Scotland. In 1355, Barbour became archdeacon of Aberdeen, where he died on March 13, 1395.

The *Brus,* completed about 1375, is a long narrative poem in octosyllabic couplets. It relates the life of Robert Bruce, from his accession to the throne of Scotland in 1306 to his death in 1329. Other works attributed to Barbour include the Scottish *Legends of the Saints,* the *Buik of Alexander,* and the *Ballet of the Nine Worthies.*

BARBOUR, bär′bər (1783–1841), **Philip Pendleton,** American political leader and Supreme Court justice, who was an early leader of the South's reaction against the growth of federal power.

Barbour was born in Orange County, Va., on May 25, 1783. After graduating from William and Mary College in 1799, he studied law and practiced in Virginia. He was a member of the Virginia legislature from 1812 to 1814, and a U.S. congressman from 1815 to 1825 and 1827 to 1830. He was speaker of the House between 1821 and 1823.

Barbour was an ardent states' rights supporter. He was one of the first to declare the right of a state to secede from the Union. He also advocated representation on the basis of property. As president of the Virginia constitutional convention in 1829–1830, he sided with the majority that opposed proportional representation for the settlers of western Virginia.

President Jackson appointed Barbour to the U.S. circuit court in 1830 and to the Supreme Court in 1836. He died at Washington, D.C., on Feb. 25, 1841.

BARBUDA, bär-boo′də, is one of the Leeward Islands of the West Indies. It is situated in the Caribbean Sea, about 25 miles (40 km) north of Antigua, and has an area of 62 square miles (161 sq km). Its only town is Codrington, named after the family that owned the island from 1691 until 1872.

Barbuda is well stocked with wild pigs and guinea fowl and is a popular area for sportsmen. Its principal crop is Sea Island cotton. The island is governed as a dependency of Antigua. Population: (1960) 1,162.

BARBUSSE, bȧr-büs′, **Henri** (1873–1935), French author. He was born in Asnières on May 17, 1873. After studying at the Collège Rollin in Paris, he wrote for the journals *Petit Parisien* and *Echo de Paris*. A volume of his verse, *Fleureuses* (1895), attracted the attention of the French writer Catulle Mendès, who took Barbusse as his protégé. Under the patronage of Mendès, Barbusse published two novels, *Les suppliants* (1903) and *L'enfer* (1908; Eng., tr., *The Inferno*, 1918).

Barbusse enlisted in the army early in World War I and received three citations for bravery before his discharge for illness. His reaction to his war experiences led him to become an intense pacifist, and in 1916 he wrote the powerful antiwar novel *Le feu, journal d'une escouade* (Eng. tr., *Under Fire*, 1917).

Barbusse joined the Communist party after the Russian Revolution of 1917 and for more than 15 years served as a correspondent for *L'humanité*, the French Communist newspaper. He also led in founding several organizations, including Clarté, which called for the abolition of national states; the Republican Association of Ex-Servicemen in France; and the World Congress Against War and Fascism. Barbusse's later writings, which were mostly propagandistic, include the novel *Clarté* (1919) and the political tracts *Les enchaînements* (1925), *Lénine* (1934), and *Staline* (1935). He died on Aug. 30, 1935, in Moscow, USSR, where he had gone as a delegate to a congress of the Communist International. See also UNDER FIRE.

BARCA, bär′kə, was a town in eastern Libya, 55 miles (88 km) east of Benghazi. It was founded by the Greeks about 570 B.C. and became an independent center of Hellenic culture. It survived capture and plunder by the Persians in 518 B.C. but declined under the Ptolemies of Egypt (323 B.C.–96 B.C.). In the following centuries it was a town of minor importance under Roman and, later, Byzantine rule.

After the Arab conquest in 642 A.D., Barca flourished once more as a trade center. The Banu Hilal and Banu Sulaym invasions of the 11th century ruined the town's prosperity, and Barca was eventually depopulated. A new town, *El Marj*, developed around a Turkish fortress built on the site of Barca in 1840.

Barca (Barqah) is also a name for the Libyan region better known as Cyrenaica, in which the town of Barca was situated. See CYRENAICA.

BARCAROLE, bär′kə-rōl, is a piece of music written in imitation of the boat songs sung by Venetian *barcaioli* (gondoliers). Its alternation of a strong and light beat in 6/8 time produces a rowing rhythm. A well-known song of this genre is the *Barcarole* from Jacques Offenbach's opera *The Tales of Hoffmann*.

BARCELONA, bär-sə-lō′nə, is the second-largest city in Spain, the former capital of the principality of Catalonia, and since 1833 the capital of Barcelona province. The leading industrial center and the most important port in Spain, it is on the Mediterranean Sea, 385 miles (619 km) northeast of Madrid. It has excellent road, rail, sea, and air communications. Barcelona is one of Spain's best-known cities, not only because of its considerable industry and material wealth but also because it is the leading cultural center in the Iberian Peninsula. Only in theater does it take second place to Madrid in the arts. Barcelona is also the center of the Spanish publishing world.

Setting and Plan of the City. Built on a wide plain between the Besós River to the north and the Llobregat River to the south, Barcelona stretches west from the sea to the hill of Tibidabo, from which there is a splendid view of the city. The plain is dotted with hills, among them the Taber, site of the cathedral, and Montjuich, crowned by a fort that has been made into a military museum.

Barcelona is divided into three well-defined sections. The first is the old medieval area of winding streets and ancient buildings, centered around the cathedral. It includes the sailors' quarter, called Barceloneta, made up of narrow, dark streets inhabited by seamen and artisans. The Ramblas, one of the most famous avenues in Europe, borders the southwest side of the old quarter. Once the bed of a stream, it is now a wide boulevard filled with open-air cafes, stalls selling birds and flowers, and shops of every description.

The second section consists of 19th and 20th century extensions of the city—wide, parallel avenues leading to the foothills. It is the fashionable residential district and contains the 100-year-old university and the more modern University City, restaurants, and night clubs. The most important streets are the Diagonal, which cuts across the avenues, and the Paseo de Gracia, the luxury shopping center of the city. The third section consists of old villages scattered over the plain. These are now absorbed into the city.

Points of Interest. One of the outstanding buildings in the old section is the imposing Gothic cathedral. The present church was begun in 1298, and its façade was built during the late 19th century. The Archivo de la Corona de Aragón contains a famous collection of documents of the kings of Aragón and records of the Generalidad (the Catalan parliament). There is a 14th century town hall and a 15th century Diputación (provincial building), the former meeting place of the Generalidad, which contains the Gothic Chapel of St. George, patron of Catalonia.

Of the many fine old churches the most important are San Pablo del Campo, Santa Ana, Santa María del Mar, and Belén. The huge Church of the Sagrada Familia, with its cluster of towers, is unfinished. Its controversial architect, Antonio Gaudí (1852–1926), also designed several other outstanding buildings in the city.

The city had already attained a wide reputation as a center of learning by the time the University of Barcelona was founded in 1430. After the capture of Barcelona by Philip V in 1714, the university was closed. It was reestablished in Cervera three years later and was returned to Barcelona in 1837. It is housed in buildings of various styles that were finished

BARCELONA'S "BARRIO CHINO," with its winding streets, preserves the medieval flavor of the old city.

in 1863. Even more than other Spanish universities, it has a politically alert student population that frequently resists the central authorities' demands. Barcelona also has a large technical training center and an industrial university.

The People. The Catalans are the most cosmopolitan of the Spaniards, yet they are fiercely proud of their race and language. Their chief characteristics are common sense and capacity for work. They are also great music lovers. The clavé Choir and the Lyceum Theater, where operas, ballets, and concerts are performed, are world famous. The typical folk dance is the ceremonious Sardana, and almost every Sunday morning groups of Catalans dance in public squares to the sweet, shrill music of the players.

The principal fiesta is held in September in honor of Our Lady of Ransom, patron saint of Barcelona. There is a wealth of attractions, ranging from bullfights to sporting events and from religious and civil ceremonies to art exhibits. Barcelona always has an abundance of regional food—principally paella, fish, and shellfish—which diners wash down with rich Alella, Priorato, or sparkling wines.

Industry and Commerce. Barcelona has always been Spain's chief manufacturing center, in part because of its relatively abundant electric power and the business acumen of its inhabitants. Before the Civil War of 1936–1939 the principal products were textiles, chemicals, machinery, and printing. Factories bombed during the Civil War were soon rebuilt, and others were established. Industry flourished even during the period 1946–1949, when General Franco's regime was not recognized abroad.

The relaxation of the rule requiring majority Spanish ownership in businesses brought in foreign capital and knowledge and led to a vast expansion in all fields of industry. Since 1950 the Pegaso and Seat automobile factories have been established in Barcelona. Processed food, optical and precision instruments, plastics, industrial machinery, and railroad equipment have been manufactured on an ever-increasing scale.

Although Spain is Barcelona's principal market, the city exports substantial quantities of potash, cement, chemicals, textiles, leather goods, machinery, and agricultural equipment. Its chief imports are petroleum products and raw materials. The large harbor has a floating drydock, shipyards, and a funicular railway.

History. The first settlement on the site of Barcelona was made by an Iberian tribe, at Laye on Montjuich, although tradition assigns the founding of the city to the Carthaginian Barca family, from whose name the city's ancient name of *Barcino* is derived. Roman conquest followed Carthaginian rule. Occupied by the Visigoths in 415 A.D., Barcelona became the capital of their realm. It was under Moorish domination from 713 and later formed part of the Spanish March under the French kings.

From the 9th to the 12th century, Barcelona took on new importance under the rule of independent counts. By the marriage in 1137 of Count Ramón Berenguer IV to Petronilla, queen of Aragón, it was united to Aragón. The city prospered under Aragón and soon became one of the most important commercial and naval ports of the Mediterranean. King James I of Aragón issued the first maritime code in 1259.

In 1640, Barcelona, with all Catalonia, withdrew its allegiance to Spain and offered it to France, only to submit again to the Spanish in 1652. In the War of the Spanish Succession the city sided with Archduke Charles of Austria, but Philip V of Spain captured it in 1714 after a long siege and abolished all of its ancient privileges. From 1808 to 1813, during the Napole-

SMALL FISHING BOATS and ocean-going vessels crowd the large harbor of Barcelona, the chief port in Spain.

THE CHURCH OF THE SA-
GRADA FAMILIA, built by the
controversial architect Antonio Gaudí, is one of the
city's most remarkable structures. It was never finished.

onic Wars, Barcelona was in French hands.

Barcelona supported the pretender to the throne during the Carlist Wars of the 19th century. There were revolts against the central government during the late 19th and early 20th century and the city was the center of anarchist and separatist movements. Its capture on Jan. 26, 1939, marked the virtual end of the Spanish Civil War. Population: (1960) 1,555,564.

J.P. FitzGibbon
Author of "Escollos del Inglés"

BARCELONA, bär-sä-lō'nä, a seaport in northern Venezuela, is 150 miles (240 km) east of Caracas. It is on the west bank of the Neveri River, 3 miles (5 km) from its mouth on the Caribbean Sea. It is the capital of the state of Anzoátegui and the trading and manufacturing center of a region that produces petroleum, coal, cotton, cattle, and cacao. Petroleum is a principal export. The city has sawmills, breweries, and bottling plants. Manufactures include furniture and leather goods. Population: (1961) 42,267.

BARCHESTER TOWERS, bär'chis-tər, is a novel by Anthony Trollope, published in 1857. It is the most widely known and the most charming of Trollope's "Barsetshire Chronicles," though perhaps not so powerful as *The Last Chronicle of Barset*. Exploiting the comedy of contemporary manners, Trollope seizes upon characteristic scenes and motifs of his age and interprets them in terms of a group of lively and ingratiating clerical characters. The result is social history and a species of realism which allows only such distortion as will forestall the ennui of complete literalness. The cathedral city of Barchester, as a geographical entity, has a form and substance given to only a few of the most vividly imagined places in the world of artistic illusion.

In the shadow of the cathedral towers we witness no Dickensian melodrama, and we hear only the distant buzz of Vanity Fair. Trollope chooses, rather, the very quiet and very simple narrative of the disposal of the wardenship of Hiram's Hospital, a charitable foundation supporting 12 old men. There is a struggle for the control of the diocese between Mrs. Proudie, the bishop's wife, and Mr. Slope, his chaplain, and there is a half-hearted attempt at a conventional Victorian love story; but such maneuvering adds up to very little action. So static a plot would not do for the great majority of 19th-century novelists.

One must go to Jane Austen to find a writer of similar spiritual and aesthetic purposes. But this apparently commonplace brew is seasoned with deliciously subtle humor and sly whimsicality. The style is perhaps more noteworthy for lucidity than for brilliance, but Trollope's commentary on men and manners is generally urbane, and the satire he presents often has an unexpected bite.

In large measure, however, *Barchester Towers* owes its continued popularity to its gallery of memorable characters. Chief among these is Mrs. Proudie, the sharp-tongued virago who rules the unhappy bishop with imperious grandeur. She is unforgettable, to be sure, but she is essentially Dickensian—an exaggeration, almost a caricature. This is not Trollope's usual way. More subtly conceived are the warden, kindly, unpresuming, selfless in his devotion to his holy trust; the bishop, devout and well meaning but subservient to his wife in spiritual as well as in temporal matters— a penetrating study in futility; and the archdeacon, Trollope's best character in the novel, worldly yet devout, hot tempered yet judicial, dignified yet gregarious.

Trollope's understanding of character and his skillful manipulation of engaging, though slender, plot materials make *Barchester Towers* a highly satisfying reading experience.

Bradford A. Booth
University of California
Editor of "Nineteenth-Century Fiction"

BARCLAY, bär′klē, **Alexander** (c. 1475–1552), Scottish poet and divine, whose fame rests on *The Shyp of Folys [Ship of Fools] of the Worlde* (1509). It is partly a translation, partly an imitation of Sebastian Brant's allegory *Das Narrenschiff* (1494). See BRANT, SEBASTIAN.

Barclay was educated at universities in England, France, and Italy. He took holy orders and was at various times a Benedictine monk at Ely; a Franciscan monk at Canterbury; a priest at the college of Ottery St. Mary, Devonshire; vicar of great Baddow in Essex; and rector of All Hallows, London. His *Eclogues* (1515–21) were adaptations from Aeneas Sylvius and Mantuan. He also translated Sallust's *Bellum Jugurthinum* in 1520. He died at Croydon on June 10, 1552.

BARCLAY, bär′klē, **John** (1582–1621), Scottish poet and satirist, who was the author of several political and religious satires in Latin. He was born at Pont-à-Mousson, France, the son of a Scottish professor of civil law and a French mother. He lived in London (1603–1616) and then in Rome, where he died on Aug. 15, 1621.

Barclay's *Euphormionis Lusinini Satyricon* (1603–07) is a satire against the Jesuits, written in the form of a semiautobiographical picaresque novel. It attracted the favorable attention of James I, to whom it was dedicated. His most widely known work is *Argenis*, a romance that is also a satirical allegory on contemporary political events in Europe. Translated into English by Ben Jonson in 1623, it achieved great popularity. Barclay's other works include *Icon Animorum* (1614) and several volumes of verse in Latin.

BARCLAY, bär′klē, **Robert** (1648–1690), Scottish Quaker, noted for his writings in behalf of his faith. He was born at Gordonstown, Murrayshire, Scotland, on Dec. 23, 1648. His family's lineage can be traced to the reign of David I of Scotland in the 12th century. His father, Col. David Barclay, sent him to Paris for a classical education at the Scots' College, where his uncle was rector. At the request of his dying mother, he returned to Scotland in 1664. A year later, following his father's example, he became a Quaker. He married Christian Mollinson, also a devoted Quaker, who bore him seven children.

Throughout his life Barclay exemplified the gentle ways of the Society of Friends. He suffered imprisonment for his beliefs, yet maintained a tolerant attitude toward others. On trips to Germany and Holland he helped to spread Quakerism and converted Elizabeth, princess palatine of the Rhine. He also defended and propagated Quaker ideals in a number of treatises: *Truth Cleared of Calumnies* (1670), *Catechism and Confession of Faith* (1673), *Theses Theologiae* (1675), *The Anarchy of Ranters* (1676), and *Universal Love* (1677). His most important work, *Apology* (1676), was dedicated to Charles II, and Barclay personally presented a copy to the king.

Esteemed at court, Barclay was able to advance the cause of religious freedom. In 1679, Charles II created Ury, Barclay's family estate, a free barony, thereby giving him legal and civil authority over it. James II appointed him nominal governor of the Quaker-held territory of East Jersey in America. Although Robert never traveled to the colony, his brother John established an estate there. Robert Barclay died at Ury on Oct. 3, 1690.

BARCLAY, bär′klē, **Robert Heriot** (1785–1837), British naval officer. Scottish-born, he served with Nelson at Trafalgar and lost an arm in the battle. Commanding the British flotilla on the Great Lakes in the War of 1812, he was defeated by Commodore Oliver Hazard Perry at the Battle of Lake Erie on Sept. 10, 1813. He was court-martialed for the loss of his fleet but was "fully and honorably acquitted."

BARCLAY DE TOLLY, bərk-lī′ də tô′lyē, **Prince Mikhail** (1761–1818), Russian field marshal. Of Scottish descent, he was born at Luhde-Grosshof in the Baltic province of Livonia, on Dec. 27, 1761. Entering the Russian army, he fought against the Turks (1788–1789), the Swedes (1790), and the Poles (1792–1794), and showed fine military qualities, which he also displayed against the French at the Battle of Pultusk (1806), where he held a command under Levin Bennigsen. With the rank of lieutenant general he fought against the Swedes in Finland in 1808, and two years later, although the Russians generally distrusted him because of his foreign origin, he was appointed minister of war by Emperor Alexander I.

When Napoleon invaded Russia in 1812, Barclay de Tolly was given command of the Russian armies, but because of inferior numbers he was compelled to retreat. His policy of continuous withdrawals aroused the impatience of the Russians, and after the French captured Smolensk, he was replaced as commander in chief by Mikhail Kutuzov. He commanded the right wing at the Battle of Borodino (where Kutuzov was defeated) and covered the Russian retreat.

In 1813 he took part in the campaign in Germany, and following the Battle of Bautzen, at which he again distinguished himself, he was reappointed to the chief command. After the Battle of Dresden he forced the surrender of Gen. Dominique René Vandamme, and he fought in the decisive Battle of Leipzig. On crossing the Rhine at the head of the Russian troops in 1814 he conciliated the French people by maintaining strict discipline among his troops. After the entry into Paris he was promoted to the rank of field marshal. In 1815 he was given command of an international corps in France and created prince. He died in Insterburg, East Prussia (now Chernyakhovsk, USSR), on May 26, 1818.

BARCROFT, bär′krôft, **Sir Joseph** (1872–1947), English physiologist. He was born on July 26, 1872. He received his education at King's College, Cambridge, and in 1896 received doctor's degrees in both medicine and science. A professor of physiology at Cambridge (1926–1937), he was an able researcher and lectured extensively in Britain and the United States. He was awarded the Copley Medal, the highest award the Royal Society can confer. He died at Cambridge, England, on March 21, 1947.

Barcroft is noted for his classical work on the transport of oxygen by hemoglobin, an iron-containing protein pigment found in the blood's red cells. He also did research on respiratory control mechanisms and on the nervous system. Barcroft often used himself as a subject for his physiological experiments. He served on the chemical warfare committee of the British War Office during World War II. His writings include *Respiratory Function of the Blood* (1914) and *The Brain and Its Environment* (1938).

BARD, bärd, **John** (1716–1799), American physician. He was born in Burlington, N.J., on Feb. 1, 1716. He was apprenticed to a surgeon in Philadelphia from 1731 to 1739, and practiced there until 1746, when he moved to New York City. When he left Philadelphia, his friend Benjamin Franklin wrote a song for him.

On Bard's recommendation, New York City acquired Bedloe's (now Liberty) Island in 1759 to isolate cases of infectious disease. With Peter Middleton, Bard introduced (1750) into the American colonies the practice of dissecting human bodies for medical instruction. He was the first physician to report (1760) a case of extrauterine fetus. Bard contributed papers on malignant pleurisy and yellow fever to the *American Medical and Philosophical Register*. He died at Hyde Park, N.Y., on March 30, 1799.

BARD, bärd, **Samuel** (1742–1821), American physician. He was born in Philadelphia on April 1, 1742. He studied at King's College (now Columbia University) and in Edinburgh, Scotland. He entered practice in New York City in 1765, an associate of his father, John Bard.

Through his efforts, a medical school was established in connection with King's College in 1768. He was appointed professor of the practice of medicine at the school and in 1792 became dean of the faculty. When the medical school was reorganized in 1811 as a separate institution called the College of Physicians and Surgeons, he was chosen its first president, an office he continued to fill until the close of his life. He was also one of the founders of the New York Hospital and the New York Dispensary. Bard's medical writings include *De Viribus Opii* (1765) and *A Manual of Midwifery* (1807). The latter became a standard textbook.

Giving up private practice when his father retired in 1798, Bard settled on a farm at Hyde Park, N.Y., where he raised Merino sheep. In 1811 he published *The Shepherd's Guide,* an excellent work on sheep breeding. He died at Hyde Park on May 24, 1821.

BARD, bärd, is the Celtic term for a professional poet and, since the 16th century, an English word designating any kind of poet. Greek writers referred to the *bardos* and Latin writers to the *bardus,* a hereditary singer of verse to harp accompaniment. Lucan, a Roman poet of the 1st century A.D., shows that "a singer [*cantor*] in Gaulish Celtic is called a *bardus,* who sings the praises of brave men and is a member of a bardic family [*gens bardi*]." The word "bard," with variations in spelling, appears in all Celtic languages whose writings survive. These languages are ancient Gaulish, Irish, Welsh, and Scottish Gaelic. There is evidence that it was also known in medieval Brittany and Cornwall.

British Isles. From the 12th to the 17th century, the bards of Ireland, Wales, and Scotland flourished in small schools that were like little universities. These bards were professional performers whose art was passed from generation to generation. Organized into highly trained groups, they had degrees conferred upon them, but only after many years of academic discipline in a highly complex art of versifying. Three orders of poetic artists were recognized in ancient Ireland: the *Fili,* or seer, the highest order of artists, who dealt with genealogies, tradition, and law; the *Druid,* or priest-magician; and the *Bard,*

whose main function was to recite the verse.

Bards, steeped in the literature and the history of their country, trained sons of aristocratic families in a strict poetic discipline. Surviving textbooks from Ireland show that the students spent whole days lying on their backs in the dark, composing set exercises in verse. Bardic verse is distinguished by its rigid conventions, including complex combinations of internal and end rhyme, alliteration in strictly traditional diction, and stanzas of 24 meters.

The bardic schools of Wales and Ireland decayed and became extinct by the 17th century. However, in the 18th century there was a renaissance of the Welsh literary language that led to a revival of bardic traditions, including the "Gorsedd Beirdd," or high court of bards. This, in turn, led in the 19th century to the establishment of annual "Eisteddfods," academic sessions for the guidance and encouragement of bardic poetry. At the Eisteddfods, competitions are held and ceremonial recognition is given to skillful bards. In the 20th century, the Eisteddfod has developed into an international art festival, including but not limiting itself to bardic lore. There has also been a vague but scarcely historical revival of bardic practices in connection with attempts to revive the Celtic Cornish language. Also, at Stonehenge a so-called "Druidical" ceremonial including these practices is held annually.

Scandinavia and Brittany. Direct bardic influence is seen in the elaborate and highly formalized verses of the Old Norse *Skáld* of the 10th to the 14th century. Their court style and elaborate metrical techniques parallel the Celtic and were influenced by Celtic contacts.

Bardic work survives in Brittany only indirectly, through medieval French versions of "Breton lays" that purport to be translations from Celtic originals. They consist of short tales of love and magic that were originally sung to harp accompaniment. Some bardic influences from Brittany reached the Provençal troubadours, and through them, the trouvères of northern France.

CHARLES L. WRENN, *Oxford University*

Further Reading: Bell, H.I., *The Development of Welsh Poetry* (London 1936); Corkery, Daniel, *The Fortunes of the Irish Language* (Dublin 1954); Curtis, Edmund, *History of Medieval Ireland* (Dublin 1938); Vigfusson, Gudbrand, and Powell, F.Y., eds. and trs., *Corpus Poeticum Boreale,* 2 vols. (New York 1964).

BARD COLLEGE, bärd, is a private coeducational liberal arts college at Annandale-on-Hudson, N.Y. The yearly student enrollment is more than 400, with about equal numbers of men and women.

Founded in 1860 as St. Stephen's College by John Bard, son of the noted physician Samuel Bard, the school was devoted primarily to training prospective ministers for the Protestant Episcopal Church until after World War I, when the curriculum and facilities were modernized. The college became affiliated with Columbia University in 1928. In 1934 its name was changed to Bard College, in honor of the founder. When Bard College became coeducational in 1944, it severed its connection with Columbia.

The 425-acre campus of Bard College overlooks the Hudson River, 100 miles north of New York City. Among the special collections at the school are historical documents on the mid-Hudson Valley and first editions of the works of Thomas Hardy, H.G. Wells, and Lord Dunsany.

BARDEEN, bär-dēn', **John** (1908–), American physicist, who was the first person to win two Nobel prizes in physics. He shared the 1956 Nobel Prize in physics with William Shockley and Walter H. Brattain "for their research on semiconductors and their discovery of the transistor effect," and he shared the 1972 Nobel Prize in physics with Leon N. Cooper and John Robert Schrieffer for developing in 1957 "a theory of superconductivity, which gave a complete theoretical explanation of the phenomenon." See also SUPERCONDUCTIVITY; TRANSISTOR.

Bardeen was born in Madison, Wis., on May 23, 1908. He received a B.S. in electrical engineering in 1928 from the University of Wisconsin where he continued doing graduate work in antenna radiation and geophysics. He followed his professor, L.J. Peters, to the Gulf Research Laboratories and there worked on the interpretation of magnetic and gravitational surveys.

In 1933, Bardeen went to Princeton University to do graduate work in mathematical physics. There he became a member of the now famous group of students that studied solid-state physics under professor E.P. Wigner in the mid-1930's. He completed his thesis (on the theory of the work function of metals) while a Junior Fellow of the Society of Fellows of Harvard University (1935–1938). He received a Ph.D. degree from Princeton in 1936. While at Harvard he worked with J.H. Van Vleck and P.W. Bridgman on cohesion and electrical conduction in metals. He was an assistant professor of physics at the University of Minnesota (1938–1941).

During World War II, Bardeen worked on the influence field of ships for application to underwater ordnance and minesweeping as principal physicist at the U.S. Naval Ordnance Laboratory. After the war he joined the solid-state research group at the Bell Telephone Laboratories where he contributed so essentially to the understanding of electrical phenomena in semiconductors. While he was there, he also started his work on superconductivity.

In 1951 he accepted a professorship in electrical engineering and physics at the University of Illinois, where with co-workers Cooper and Schrieffer he worked out the now famous "BCS" theory of superconductivity. Their method of theoretical attack had very significant applications to other physical problems such as elementary particle theory.

Bardeen has published many papers in scientific journals. Three should be mentioned, all published in *The Physical Review:* "Surface States and Rectification at a Metal Semiconductor Contact" (1947), "Physical Principles Involved in Transistor Action" (1949), and "Theory of Superconductivity" (1957). He has received many honors in addition to two Nobel prizes, including the Fritz London Award (1962). He is a member of the National Academy of Sciences, and has served on the U.S. President's Science Advisory Committee (1959–1962).

WALTER H. BRATTAIN
Nobel Prize Winner in Physics
Whitman College, Walla Walla, Wash.

Further Reading: Bardeen, John, and Brattain, Walter H., *Physical Principles Involved in Transistor Action,* Bell Telephone System Monograph B-1659 (New York 1959); Bardeen, John, *Understanding Superconductivity,* American Society for Testing and Materials (Philadelphia 1964); Brattain, Walter H., and Bardeen, John, "Surface Properties of Germanium," *Bell System Technical Journal,* vol. 32, no. 1 (New York 1953).

BARDESANES (c. 154–c. 222), bär-dē-sā'nēz, was a Syrian poet and theologian. He was born in Edessa (now Urfa, Turkey) and died in Armenia. He was one of the first converts to Christianity in Syria and one of the earliest to write in Syriac. His distinctive theological opinions are outlined in the *Ecclesiastical History* of Eusebius, who was bishop of Caesarea in the 4th century. Bardesanes considered the evil in the world to be only an accidental response of matter and absolved God from responsibility for it.

He is noted for the 150 hymns he and his son Harmonius composed. These were in use in the Syrian church until the 4th century, when St. Ephraem of Syria replaced them with his own. Though Bardesanes was an opponent of Gnosticism and a Christian missionary to Armenia, his writings also reflected a mystical astrology.

Bardesanes' followers constituted a distinct sect until the time of St. Ephraem but did not formally separate from the orthodox Christian church.

BARDI, bär'dē, a prominent merchant and banking family of Florence, whose business flourished from the mid-13th century to the mid-14th century. Partnership in the company was not restricted to members of the family, although they were the principal holders of the assets. Branches of the firm were established in the principal Italian cities, and also in England, France, and Flanders.

From 1303 the Bardi were in charge of apostolic finances, remitting to Rome the tithes collected by papal representatives in foreign countries. They lent important sums of money to the king of Naples, the king of England, and to other European rulers, in return for which they frequently were granted exclusive commercial privileges.

In time the Bardi acquired enormous land and business holdings, especially in Venice and Florence. (A main street in Florence still bears their name.) Their international financial position was sound enough to allow them to survive several financial crises that shook the position of their lesser rivals during the 1320's. However, difficulties with the kingdom of Naples, the republic of Venice, and especially the bankruptcy in 1345 of their chief debtor, Edward III of England, whose wars they had financed, led to their complete collapse. Although they later made a moderately successful recovery, they never regained their former position.

BARDI, bär'dē, **Giovanni,** COUNT OF VERNIO (1534–?1612), Italian scholar and music patron. He was born in Florence on Feb. 5, 1534, and belonged to a wealthy Guelph banking family. Bardi was an accomplished philologist, mathematician, philosopher, and poet. He gathered about him a group of musicians and poets who met at his house to discuss the music of ancient Greece. The Florentine Camerata, as the group was known, consisted of Jacopo Peri, Jacopo Corsi, Ottavio Rinuccini, Vincenzo Galilei, Giulio Caccini, Pietro Strozzi, and Bardi. The monodic lyric dramas they developed in imitation of Greek music drama were the first operas. Bardi wrote madrigals and composed librettos for two early operas, *L'amico fido* and *Il combattimento d'Apolline col serpente.* He moved to Rome in 1592 to act as chamberlain to Pope Clement VIII, and died there about 1612.

BARDOLF, bär'dolf, **Thomas** (1368–1408), English soldier. He was born at Birling, Sussex, England, on Dec. 22, 1368. The 5th Baron Bardolf, he became a friend of Sir Henry Percy, 1st earl of Northumberland, during Richard II's reign, and was implicated in Hotspur's rebellion against King Henry IV in 1403. Bardolf was restored to Henry's favor in 1404, but in 1405 he finally deserted the king in favor of Northumberland. Bardolf originated the treaty dividing England and Wales among Owen Glendower, Sir Edmund de Mortimer, and the earl of Northumberland. In 1406 he fled with Northumberland to Paris. Returning shortly to Scotland, he and Northumberland gathered an army, which in January 1408 crossed the Tweed River, in northern England, to face the forces of Henry IV. The following month they were decisively defeated at Bramham Moor, in Yorkshire. Northumberland was killed; Bardolf, mortally wounded, was captured. He died on Feb. 19, 1408.

Lord Bardolf (Bardolph) figures prominently in Shakespeare's *Henry IV*, part 2. The other Bardolph—the companion of Falstaff in the same play, in *Henry V*, and in *The Merry Wives of Windsor*—appears to be an imaginary figure.

BARDOLPH, bär'dolf, is a Shakespearean character who appears in *Henry IV*, Part 2, *Henry V*, and *The Merry Wives of Windsor* as a companion of the amiable rogue, Falstaff. He is purely fictitious, and should not be confused with the historical personage Lord Bardolf (Thomas Bardolf), who also appears in *Henry IV*, Part 2.

BARDOT, bär-dō', **Brigitte** (1934–), French motion picture actress who became an international sex symbol but also distinguished herself as a talented comedienne. She was born in Paris, the daughter of a prominent industrialist. At the age of seven, she began to study dancing, and at the age of 13 she won an award from the Paris Conservatory.

In 1950 she posed for the cover of the French fashion magazine *Elle*. Her photograph attracted the attention of film director Marc Allegret, and soon she was playing small roles in such films as *Le trou norman* and the American production *Helen of Troy*. Her first major role was in 1956 in *Et Dieu créa la femme* (*And God Created Woman*), which brought her worldwide fame. Later films include *La Parisienne, Babette Goes to War*, and *Viva Maria*.

BARDSTOWN, bardz'toun, a city in Kentucky and the seat of Nelson County, is 35 miles (56 km) southeast of Louisville. Established by act of the Virginia legislature in 1788, it is the second-oldest city in the state. The principal industry is distilling. Places of interest include a memorial to John Fitch, American inventor and a developer of the steamboat, who died here; St. Joseph's Cathedral, with paintings believed to have belonged to King Louis Philippe of France; nearby Federal Hill, a mansion said to have inspired Stephen Foster's song *My Old Kentucky Home;* and Abraham Lincoln National Historical Park, 27 miles (43 km) to the south. Bardstown has a mayor-and-council form of government. Population: 5,816.

BARDWAN. See Burdwan.

BAREBONE, Praisegod. See Barbon, Praisegod.

BAREBONE'S PARLIAMENT, bâr'bōnz, was a derisive term for the Little Parliament in England, summoned by Oliver Cromwell on July 4, 1653. The term was coined by the enemies of that assembly because one of its members was named Praisegod Barbon (q.v.) or Barebone.

After Cromwell dismissed the Rump Parliament on April 20, 1653, letters were sent out in his name and that of the Council of the Army to the Congregational churches in each county, inviting them to nominate fit persons, "faithful, fearing God, and hating covetousness," to serve in Parliament. These lists were duly sent in and were scrutinized by the army council, which excluded some names and added others. The Little Parliament thus constituted had 140 members— 129 from England, 6 from Ireland, and 5 from Scotland. Cromwell turned over his dictatorship to this "assembly of nominees." The Little Parliament began by abolishing the Court of Chancery and was proceeding to abolish tithes when, under pressure by the army, the majority resigned in a body. Cromwell dissolved Parliament on Dec. 12, 1653, and four days later assumed the title of lord protector of the commonwealth.

BAREILLY, bə-rā'lē, a city in northern India, is the capital of Rohilkhand division and of Bareilly district, in the state of Uttar Pradesh. It is situated 130 miles (209 km) east of Delhi, near the Ramganga River. Bareilly (or *Bareli*) is a railroad junction and a trading center for grain and sugarcane. Its industries include sugar and cotton processing, woodworking, and the manufacture of furniture, carpets, soap, and shellac. Northwest of the city, at Clutterbuckganj, are factories manufacturing bobbins, rosin, catechu, and matches. Bareilly College is affiliated with Agra University.

Founded in 1537, Bareilly passed to the British in 1801. During the Indian Mutiny it was recaptured by Sir Colin Campbell on May 7, 1858. Population: (1961) 254,409.

BARENTS, bà'rents, **Willem** (1550?–1597), Dutch navigator. He was born on the island of Terschelling in the Netherlands. Sponsored by Dutch commercial interests, Barents made three voyages in search of a northeast passage to Asia, during which he explored Novaya Zemlya in 1594–1595 and discovered Barents Island and Svalbard (Spitsbergen) in 1596. See also Polar Exploration, North.

In 1597, while attempting to return from his third voyage after a severe winter in the ice, he died, but his companions reached Kola in Lapland. Almost 300 years later, Barents' winter quarters were located, and some of the relics removed to the Hague.

Barents Island, in the Svalbard archipelago, and Barents Sea, north of Europe between Svalbard and Novaya Zemlya, were named after him.

BARENTS SEA, bar'ənts, part of the Arctic Ocean north of Norway and European Russia. It is bounded on the north by Svalbard and Franz Josef Land and on the east by Novaya Zemlya, which separates it from the Kara Sea. To the west it merges into the Norwegian Sea. The warm water of the North Atlantic Drift keeps the southwestern Barents Sea free of ice in winter. The sea is shallow and is good fishing ground. It was named for the Dutch navigator Willem Barents, who entered it in 1594.

BARÈRE DE VIEUZAC, bà-râr′ də vyu-zak′, **Bertrand** (1755–1841), French revolutionist. He was born at Tarbes on Sept. 10, 1755. A lawyer in Toulouse, he acted as a deputy in the National Assembly and was sent by the Hautes-Pyrénées department to the National Convention in 1792. He later edited the journal *Point du Jour* and attached himself to the "Mountain," the extreme left wing of the convention. His flowery and poetical oratory soon earned him the sobriquet, "the Anacreon of the Guillotine."

Barère was president of the convention when the sentence of death was passed on Louis XVI. He rejected other suggestions for punishing the king and gave his vote with these words: "The law is for death, and I am here only as the organ of the law."

Though a supporter of Robespierre, he deserted him before his downfall. Notwithstanding, Barère was impeached and sentenced to prison, but he escaped and became a secret agent of Napoleon. Elected a deputy during the Hundred Days, the brief period of Napoleon's return to power in 1815, he was banished after the second Bourbon restoration as a regicide. He then went to Brussels, where he devoted himself to literary work until an amnesty in 1830 permitted his return. He died at Tarbes on Sept. 10, 1841.

BARETTI, bä-rät′tē, **Giuseppe Marc'Antonio** (1719–1789), Italian writer and critic, who was a member of Samuel Johnson's circle in London. He was educated at Milan and Venice, and moved to England in 1751. His Italian-English dictionary, published in 1760, established his reputation. From 1763 to 1765 he was in Venice, where he edited the critical journal *Frusta Letteraria*, under the pseudonym Aristarco Scannabue. In 1766 he returned to London, where he died on May 5, 1789. Baretti's other works include *An Account of the Manners and Customs of Italy* (1768), *Journey from London to Genoa* (1770), and critical works on Italian literature.

BARGE, a square-ended, flat-bottomed boat used to transport bulk freight, chiefly on rivers and canals or in harbors. It may be towed by a tugboat or may be self-propelled by an engine or sails. On major rivers a number of barges are lashed together in a line to form a rigid unit (called a *tow*), which is pushed by a tugboat. Barges are in common use throughout the world.

Constructed of steel or wood, with protective bulkheads, barges are built in different models and sizes to meet the requirements of their cargo and the conditions of navigation which they will encounter. Typical barge cargoes are coal, steel, sand, gravel, and oil. A standard coal barge may be 175 feet (53 meters) long and 26 feet (7.6 meters) wide. It carries about 900 short tons (816 metric tons) of cargo. The heaviest barges are used in traffic along the seacoasts of the United States and on the Great Lakes.

Barges of great size are used to ferry railroad freight cars across water routes where no bridge or tunnel is available. Barges employed to load and unload large vessels that cannot berth at a pier are called *lighters*.

The term "barge" is applied also to a power-boat used by a naval flag officer, and to large pleasure boats, such as the college barges at Oxford University, England. In former times, elaborately furnished boats for members of a royal court were called barges.

BARGELLO, bär-jel′lō, the Italian national art museum in Florence. It was built between 1254 and 1346 as the official residence of the Florentine magistrate (Palazzo del Podestà). In the mid-19th century the building was restored and converted into a museum.

The Bargello is a three-story building dominated by a large tower and containing a central porticoed courtyard. It is especially important for its large collection of Florentine and Tuscan sculpture of the medieval and Renaissance periods. Included among its most famous works are a series of 14th century frescoes attributed to Giotto, as well as sculptures by Michelangelo, Donatello, Cellini, and Ghiberti.

BARHAM, bar′əm, **Richard Harris** (1788–1845), English writer, who was author of *The Ingoldsby Legends*, a series of tales in verse and prose. The tales, drawn from many literary sources, humorously reflect the taste and ideas of Victorian England. They were first published in *Bentley's Miscellany*, beginning in 1837, under the pseudonym *Thomas Ingoldsby*, and were collected in book form in 1840. Barham was also the author of two novels, *Baldwin* (1819) and *My Cousin Nicholas* (1834).

Barham was born in Canterbury on Dec. 6, 1788, and was ordained in the Anglican Church in 1813. He was appointed a minor canon of Saint Paul's Cathedral, London, in 1821. In 1824 he became a priest of ordinary of the Chapel Royal and the rector of a London parish. He died in London on June 17, 1845.

BARI, bä′rē, a city in southeastern Italy, is situated on the Adriatic Sea, 135 miles (209 km) east of Naples. It is the capital of the province of Bari in the region of Apulia. The old section of Bari is located on a peninsula that has a natural harbor on one side and an artificial harbor on the other. The more modern section, called the new town, developed inland as the city expanded.

In population, Bari ranks second to Naples among the cities on the Italian mainland south of Rome. It is also Italy's most important shipping point to ports in the Balkans and the eastern Mediterranean. An industrial and commercial center, Bari has flour mills, foundries, petroleum refineries, and steel works. Other factories in Bari produce furniture, machinery, textiles, glass, electrical apparatus, and soap. The town's

BARGES connected in a tow on the Mississippi River.

principal exports are wine, olive oil, grain, soap, and figs.

Each September, Bari is the site of the Fiera del Levante, an international trade fair. The Feast of Saint Nicholas, held annually on May 9 to honor the patron saint of the city, is one of the principal religious festivals in southern Italy. See also NICHOLAS, SAINT.

Almost all the buildings of interest are located in the old section of the city. The Church of St. Nicholas, begun in 1087, has an altar of silver and contains the relics of St. Nicholas. The cathedral, begun in 1034 and rebuilt in the 12th century, houses relics dating from the 11th century. A castle, built by Frederick II in 1233–1240, with ramparts added in the 16th century, is located in this section.

The main points of interest in the new town are the University of Bari, with over 20,000 students, and the provincial palace. The palace houses a fine collection of Italian paintings by such masters as Paolo Veronese, Giovanni Bellini, and Tintoretto.

History. Bari was probably founded by the Illyrians. Under the Roman Empire, it gained importance as a seaport and road junction. After the fall of the Western Roman Empire in the 5th century A.D., Bari's strategic importance made it a source of contention among the powers that vied for dominion over southern Italy.

Between the 7th and 11th centuries, control of Bari was contested primarily by the Byzantines and the Lombards. In the latter part of the 9th century, the city was the capital of the Byzantine governor of the surrounding region. In 1004, when the Saracens attempted to capture the city, the Venetians came to its rescue. In 1009, Bari became part of the Holy Roman Empire.

Robert Guiscard captured Bari for the Normans in 1071, and it served as a port of embarkation for the crusaders in the 11th and 12th centuries. It then declined in importance until the 13th century, when the Holy Roman emperor Frederick II refortified the city. It subsequently was held by various rulers, including the Angevin kings and the house of Sforza. After the death of Bona Sforza in 1557, it was united with the kingdom of the Two Sicilies, under Spanish kings.

Bari voted with the rest of the Two Sicilies to join in the unification of Italy in 1861. The city was an important Allied naval base during World War I, and was the embarkation point for Italian troops invading Albania in 1939. During World War II, Italian forces attacking Greece through Albania in 1940–1941 again used Bari as a port of embarkation. The city was occupied by the British in September 1943. Population: (1961) 312,023.

BARI, University of, bä′rē, a coeducational, government-supported institution of higher education in Bari, Italy. It was founded in 1924 with a faculty of medicine. There are now faculties of law, economics and commerce, pharmacy, agriculture, letters and philosophy, mathematics, science, engineering, veterinary medicine, and education, as well as an institute of Mediterranean studies. Although the university confers only doctoral degrees, enrollment neared 20,000 in the mid-1960's.

Seven libraries, each devoted to a particular discipline, have a total of approximately 200,000 volumes. On campus are museums of archaeology, anatomy, commercial products, and zoology.

BARILOCHE, bar-ə-lō′chē, is a resort town in western Argentina, in Río Negro province, 850 miles (1,367.5 km) southwest of Buenos Aires. Its official name is *San Carlos de Bariloche.* Situated on the south shore of Lake Nahuel Huapí in the Andes mountains, Bariloche is an all-year resort, with fishing and mountaineering in summer and skiing in winter. It is the gateway to the Nahuel Huapí national park. Bariloche is the terminus of a railroad from Buenos Aires and has highway connections.

The town was settled in 1905 by Swiss immigrants, and the architecture of its numerous chalets resembles that of a Swiss village. Population: (1960) 15,995.

BARING, bâr′ing, is the name of a family of English bankers and high public officials. The line began with John Baring, a Lutheran minister's son, who migrated from Germany to England in the early 18th century and became a cloth manufacturer. His sons Francis and John established the influential banking house of Baring Brothers in London. A number of the descendants of Francis achieved particular prominence. See biographies of important members of the family.

BARING, bâr′ing, **Alexander** (1774–1848), English banker and government official. He was born in London, on Oct. 27, 1774. The second son of Sir Francis Baring, he spent several years in the United States and Canada developing the financial operations of his father's banking house. After his father's death in 1810, he became the head of the house of Baring Brothers. He was a member of Parliament from 1806 to 1835. In Sir Robert Peel's first ministry, Baring was president of the Board of Trade and master of the mint from 1834 until 1835, when he was raised to the peerage as 1st Baron Ashburton.

Because of his knowledge of the United States, he was appointed special ambassador to that country in 1842 to negotiate the Maine–New Brunswick boundary question and other British–American disputes. He died at Longleat, England, on May 13, 1848. See also WEBSTER–ASHBURTON TREATY.

BARING, bâr′ing, **Edward Charles, 1ST BARON REVELSTOKE** (1828–1897), English financier. The third grandson of Sir Francis Baring, he became head of the financial house of Baring Brothers, which achieved its apex under his control. However, in the late 1880's, Baring Brothers had loaned a considerable sum of money to the Argentine government, and upon the latter's defaulting repayment, the house faced a financial crisis. It was saved from collapse by the Bank of England, which took over its liabilities and encouraged its reorganization as a limited company. The house has continued to play a prominent part in English financing.

Baring was raised to peerage in 1885, when his firm was at its height of financial power.

BARING, bâr′ing, **Evelyn** (1841–1917), British government official. He was born at Cromer Hall, Norfolk, on Feb. 26, 1841. Educated at military schools, he joined the Royal Artillery in 1858 and was stationed in the Ionian Islands. He went to Jamaica in 1864, visiting Gen. U.S. Grant at his Civil War battlefield headquarters on the way, and returned to England in 1867. In

1872 he went to India as private secretary to Lord Northbrook, returning to England in 1876. A year later he was sent to Egypt as British commissioner of the Egyptian public debt office. His report of Egypt's bankruptcy was responsible for Khedive Ismail Pasha's abdication in 1879. From 1880 to 1883 he was financial member of the council of the governor general of India. He returned to Egypt in 1883 as the British agent and consul general with plenipotentiary rank in the diplomatic service, a position he was to hold until his resignation in 1907. He was created baron (1892), viscount (1898), and 1st Earl Cromer (1901).

Baring made his record in Egypt, where he was the effective ruler at a time when Britain was occupying the country. On his arrival he found the country bankrupt and the people ground down by heavy taxation. He bolstered the country's credit, reduced taxation to a minimum, removed dishonest officials, abolished forced labor, built schools and hospitals, and introduced modern sanitation methods. He constructed the country's irrigation system, considered for years the model of the world. This greatly increased Egypt's prosperity by securing the farmers three crops a year. He saw to it that the small farmers received proportionately the same benefit as the owners of huge estates. He also reformed the Egyptian army, increased trade, and greatly extended railway, postal, and telegraph facilities. He checked the nationalist movement in Egypt by having Abbas II, who was sympathetic toward Great Britain, installed as khedive. In recognition for his services Parliament granted him $250,000 on his retirement in 1907.

Baring attended the House of Lords after his return to England, and wrote several articles on World War I. In 1916 he was appointed chairman of a commission to investigate the Dardanelles Campaign. He died in London on Jan. 29, 1917.

His publications include *Modern Egypt* (1908); *Political and Literary Essays* (1908–1913); *Ancient and Modern Imperialism* (1910); and a supplement (1915) to his *Modern Egypt*.

BARING, bâr'ing, **Sir Francis** (1740–1810), English banker, who, with his brother John, founded the London banking house of Baring Brothers. He was born at Larkbear, Devonshire, on April 18, 1740. He had a broad view of world affairs and was deeply concerned with the problems of India. His advice was frequently sought on Indian finance. He was a director of the East India Company from 1779 to 1792 and chairman of the company in 1792–1793. He was created a baronet for his services. He was a Whig member of the House of Commons intermittently from 1784 to 1806. At his death at Lee, Kent, on Sept. 11, 1810, his fortune was estimated at £7 million.

BARING, bâr'ing, **Sir Francis Thornhill** (1796–1866), English government official. He was born in Calcutta, India, on April 20, 1796. A grandson of Sir Francis Baring, he entered Parliament in 1826, serving without interruption until 1865. He became a member of the Cabinet in 1838, serving as chancellor of the exchequer until 1841, and as first lord of the admiralty from 1849 to 1852. The title Baron Northbrook was conferred upon him in the year of his death. He died at Stratton Park, England, on Sept. 6, 1866.

BARING, bâr'ing, **Maurice** (1874–1945), English journalist and writer, who achieved distinction as a poet, playwright, novelist, and critic. A great-grandson of the English banker, Sir Francis Baring, he was born in London on April 27, 1874. He was educated at Eton, in Germany and Italy, and at Cambridge University, and served in the British diplomatic service from 1893 to 1904, when he began a career in journalism. As correspondent for the London *Morning Post*, he was sent to Manchuria (1904), Russia (1905–1908), and Constantinople (1909). His trip to Russia and his interest in Russian literature inspired *A Year in Russia* (1907), *Russian Essays and Stories* (1909), *Landmarks in Russian Literature* (1910), and *An Outline of Russian Literature* (1914). In 1912 he covered the First Balkan War for the London *Times*. During World War I he served in the intelligence service of the Royal Flying Corps. An autobiography, *The Puppet Show of Memory*, was published in 1922. He died in Beauly, Scotland, Dec. 15, 1945.

Baring's novels include *Passing By* (1921), *A Triangle* (1923), *C* (1924), *Cat's Cradle* (1925), *Tinker's Leave* (1927), *Friday's Business* (1933), and *Darby and Joan* (1936). His volumes of verse include *Pastels* (1891), *Triolets* (1893), and *The Black Prince* (1903). Among his plays were *Gaston de Foix* (1903) and *Manfroy* (1920).

BARING, bâr'ing, **Thomas George** (1826–1904), English government official. He was born in London, on Jan. 22, 1826. The son of Sir Francis Thornhill Baring, 1st Baron Northbrook, he was educated at Christ Church, Oxford (B.A., 1846), and entered politics as a Liberal. He was a member of Parliament from 1857 to 1866, when he succeeded to his father's title, and in 1868 he was appointed undersecretary of war.

Four years later he became viceroy of India. His rule there was marked by a firm handling of finance and by a successful struggle against famine in Bengal. He dealt fairly with the differences between the Indians and the British residents, and he opposed the extension of British influence to Afghanistan. When he left India in 1876, he was created 1st earl of Northbrook in recognition of his work.

From 1880 to 1885 he served in William E. Gladstone's cabinet as first lord of the admiralty. He died at Stratton, Hampshire, England, on Nov. 15, 1904.

BARISAL, bu-ri-säl', a city in Bangladesh, is a busy river port in the Ganges delta, situated in former East Pakistan near the Tetulia mouth of the Ganges River, 70 miles (112 km) south of Dacca. Barisal has flour, rice, oilseed, and jute mills. It is the seat of nine colleges of the University of Dacca. The "Barisal guns," sounds resembling distant thunder or cannon heard from the direction of the sea, are an unexplained natural phenomenon, possibly of seismic origin. Population: (1961) 69,936.

BARISAN MOUNTAINS, bä-rē-sän', mountain chain in Indonesia, extending for about 1,000 miles (1,600 km) along the west coast of Sumatra. It consists mainly of two parallel ranges with a high, lake-studded valley between them. Many of the peaks in the chain are volcanic. The highest mountain is Kerintji, which reaches an altitude of 12,484 feet (3,805 meters).

BARITE, bâr'īt, is the most common barium-containing mineral. Its name comes from a Greek word meaning "heavy." The mineral is found in massive deposits and in veins, often associated with a wide variety of metal ores. It is also found in sandstones and igneous rocks, in stalactites, and as a replacement mineral in some fossils.

Crystals of barite are usually white or colorless, but colored varieties are also common. The flat, heavy, glassy crystals range from transparent to translucent. Fine crystal specimens are found near Baia Sprie, Rumania; Příbram, Czechoslovakia; Freiberg, East Germany; in Cumberland, England; and, in the United States, near Fort Wallace, N. Mex., and Sterling, Colo. The mineral occurs throughout the world. Massive deposits are mined in Arkansas, Missouri, and Nova Scotia.

Barite is the principal raw material for barium hydroxide, used in refining sugar. The mineral is used as a pigment in paint and as a filler in paper and cloth. Large amounts are employed in the petroleum industry for preparing a heavy drilling sludge. Some stalactitic varieties take a fine polish and are used ornamentally.

Composition: $BaSO_4$; specific gravity, 4.5; hardness, 3.0; crystal system, orthorhombic.

D. VINCENT MANSON
American Museum of Natural History

BARITO RIVER, bä-rē'tō, a stream in Indonesia. Located in southeastern Borneo, it rises in the Müller Mountains and flows generally southward for about 550 miles (885 km) to the Java Sea. Its lower course is a delta, which is flooded in the rainy season. The river is navigable for small steamers for nearly 250 miles (400 km). Near its mouth is the port of Bandjarmásin.

BARITONE, bar'ə-tōn, is a male singing voice between bass and tenor. The best tones are from A on the bass clef to F-sharp on the treble, but in French and Italian opera, baritones are frequently required to sing as high as A-flat. If the baritone voice approaches the bass in either quality or range, it is called *bass-baritone*.

The *baritone horn* is a saxhorn, one of the family of brass wind instruments invented in 1845 by Adolphe Sax of Belgium, for use chiefly in bands. The baritone horn has a semiconical bore and three valves; it is played with a cup mouthpiece. Its pitch is B-flat, the same as that of the trombone, and one octave below the pitch of cornets and trumpets.

The *baritone oboe*, also called the Heckelphone, was invented in 1905 by the German Wilhelm Heckel. It is similar to, and sometimes confused with, the baryton, a bass oboe of French descent.

As a stringed instrument, the *baritone* (also spelled *baryton* or *barytone*) is an obsolete member of the viola family, similar to a viola da gamba in tone. It was about the size of a modern cello, had six or seven gut strings that were played by a bow, and from 9 to 24 brass wire strings, passing under the neck of the instrument, that vibrated in sympathy with the gut strings. It was very popular in the 18th century for playing chamber music. Haydn composed extensively for it because his patron, Prince Esterházy, played the instrument. The baritone was also called the *viola paradon*, the *viola di bordone*, or the *viola di fagotto*.

See also MUSICAL INSTRUMENTS; VOICE.

BARIUM, bar'ē-əm, is a chemical element that occurs in the earth's crust. It is a member of the alkaline-earth family of elements, which includes beryllium, magnesium, calcium, strontium, and radium. All of these elements are in Group IIa of the periodic table. See also ALKALINE EARTH METALS.

The name "barium" is derived from the Greek word *barys* (heavy), which was used to name the mineral barite, also called heavy spar. The chemical symbol for barium is Ba. Sir Humphry Davy first isolated barium in 1808 by the electrolytic reduction of fused barium hydroxide.

Occurrence. Approximately 0.05 percent of the earth's crust consists of barium. The element is never found in the free, uncombined state because of its high reactivity. Instead, it is found mostly in the form of the minerals barite and witherite. Barite is barium sulfate ($BaSO_4$), and witherite is barium carbonate ($BaCO_3$). In addition, small quantities of barium compounds are found in most igneous rocks. Barite is found in large quantities in many parts of the United States, especially in Missouri. Depending on the type of impurities present, it is colored red, yellow, green, or gray. The most important deposit of witherite is in Cumberland, England.

Structure and Properties. The atomic number of barium is 56, indicating that the nucleus of the stable barium atom contains 56 protons. The nuclei of the naturally occurring, stable isotopes of barium also contain a varying number of neutrons, ranging from 74 to 82. The mass numbers of these isotopes are 130, 132, 134, 135, 136, 137, and 138. Barium-138 is the most abundant isotope. The atomic weight of a proportional mixture of these naturally occurring isotopes is 137.34, based on the scale in which the carbon-12 atom is assigned an atomic weight of 12.0000.

Barium, a typical metal, is silvery white, soft, and a good conductor of heat and electricity. It is relatively volatile and can be distilled easily. Barium crystallizes in a body-centered-cubic structure, has a melting point of 1,562° F (850° C), a boiling point of 2,984° F (1,640° C), and a specific gravity of 3.6 at 68° F (20° C).

Chemically, barium is similar to strontium and calcium. The electron configuration of the barium atom is: $1s^2$, $2s^22p^6$, $3s^23p^63d^{10}$, $4s^24p^64d^{10}$, $5s^25p^6$, $6s^2$. The two 6s electrons are the valence electrons, and hence barium is divalent. In chemical reactions, barium loses these valence electrons and forms the positive ion Ba^{+2}. The $+2$ state is the only known oxidation state of combined barium.

Reactivity. Because the free energy of formation of barium compounds is very high, barium is a very reactive element, and large amounts of heat are evolved when its compounds are formed. It is attacked by water, oxygen, nitrogen, hydrogen, ammonia, halogens, and sulfides. Barium also reacts with magnesium, lead, platinum, silicon, tin, zinc, aluminum, and mercury. Finely divided barium is so active that it is dangerous to handle in the presence of air or other oxidizing gases because it burns immediately. Thus, powdered barium must be stored in an atmosphere of dry, inert gas such as argon or helium. In view of its high reactivity, barium is considered to be a toxic substance.

Preparation and Use of Barium. Barium metal is manufactured by the King process, in which barium oxide is reduced by aluminum at 1,830° F (1,000° C) in a vacuum furnace at low pressure.

The reaction is:

$$6BaO + 2Al \rightleftarrows Ba_3Al_2O_6 + 3Ba.$$

The barium comes off as a vapor, which is condensed on cooler surfaces. Before removal from the condenser, the condensed barium liquid is cooled in an argon atmosphere to prevent reaction of the barium with air.

The most important use for barium is as a "getter" in radio vacuum tubes to remove residual traces of gases. When the evacuated tube is sealed, a pellet of the getter is vaporized electrically, and the barium vapor reacts with oxygen, nitrogen, and carbon dioxide. The excess barium vapor condenses on the inner walls of the radio tube.

Preparation and Use of Barium Compounds. The compounds of barium have greater commercial importance than the uncombined metal. The sulfate, carbonate, chloride, nitrate, oxide, hydroxide, and sulfide compounds are useful.

In the United States all the major barium salts are produced from barite by reduction of the insoluble barium sulfate with coal to form soluble barium sulfide:

$$BaSO_4 + 4C \rightarrow 4CO + BaS.$$

The barium sulfide, called black ash, is then converted to other major compounds by treatment with the proper reagent. The addition of sodium sulfate to black ash results in the precipitation of pure barium sulfate. The addition of zinc sulfate to black ash yields a mixture of barium sulfate and zinc sulfide called lithopone, a pigment with excellent covering power. Lithopone is not toxic and does not darken when exposed to hydrogen sulfide, as does white lead. Treatment of black ash with sodium carbonate results in barium carbonate, which can subsequently be converted to barium oxide and barium hydroxide by heating and addition of water. Treatment of black ash with hydrochloric acid produces barium chloride, which can subsequently be converted to barium nitrate by addition of sodium nitrate.

Soluble barium salts are very toxic because barium ions have an effect on the heart similar to that of digitalis. A fatal dose of barium chloride, for example, is 0.8 to 1.0 gram. Insoluble barium sulfate, however, can be used internally as an opaque contrast medium for X-ray diagnosis and fluoroscopy.

Other uses of barium sulfate are as a flux in glass manufacture to lower the melting point of oxide mixtures, as a filler in paints, as an inert white base in photographic paper, leather, and cloth, and as a remover of dirt and ground rock in treatment of oil wells.

Barium carbonate is used as a flux in ceramics, as an ingredient in the manufacture of fine glass and optical glass, and as a carbon carrier to case harden steels.

Barium chloride is used as a flux in the manufacture of magnesium metal, as a raw material in forming barium colors, and as a substance in heat-treating baths.

Barium oxide is used in the manufacture of lubricating-oil detergents. It is also used as a drying agent.

Barium hydroxide is useful as an additive, as a descumming agent in ceramic technology, and as an ingredient of barium greases.

The flame spectrum of a barium salt is yellowish green. Barium salts are often used for the color effect produced in pyrotechnic displays.

HERBERT LIEBESKIND
The Cooper Union, New York

BARK is the outer covering of a woody stem or root. Found on all such roots and stems more than one year old, bark never shows annual rings as the wood does. It is made up of all the tissues located outside the vascular cambium or formative layer of the plant stem. The term is not used in technical botanical literature because it lacks precise meaning.

Anatomy. As the tree grows older, the original layers on the outside of the cambium (epidermis, cortex, pericycle, and primary phloem) are gradually replaced by bark. The new bark is itself composed of two main layers: the inner secondary phloem and the outer periderm. The phloem consists of elements that are specialized for food conduction, which is the main function of this layer. The periderm, a three-layered tissue, is a protective tissue that functions in place of the epidermis or skin. It is composed of cells whose walls are waterproofed with a complex, fatty substance, called suberin, that is the basis of cork. The inner layer of periderm, called the phelloderm, consists of living cells that may participate in photosynthesis and food storage. The exchange of gases between the plant and the atmosphere is accomplished via small openings called lenticels. These lenticels are often characteristic for a species. As old bark is sloughed off, successive layers of periderm form new bark. See also PLANTS AND PLANT SCIENCE—2. *Anatomy* (Secondary Body).

Commercial Importance. Perhaps the most important commercial product derived from bark is the rubber manufactured from the latex produced by secretory tissues of *Hevea* and other plants. Another important product is cork; the cork that is used commercially is obtained by stripping the cork oak (*Quercus suber*), an evergreen, medium-sized tree found in Spain, Portugal, and elsewhere. (See also CORK.) The bark of chestnut, hemlock, oak, and other plants furnishes materials for tanning. Flax and hemp are two of the better known bast fibers (obtained from phloem); other fibers come from the ramie, jute, kenaf, paper mulberry, and other plants. Resins like kauri gum (from *Agathis*) and spruce gum (from *Picea*) also come from bark. Well-known drugs derived from bark include cascara and quinine. See CINCHONA BARK.

THEODOR JUST, *Chicago Natural History Museum*

CROSS SECTION OF BARK

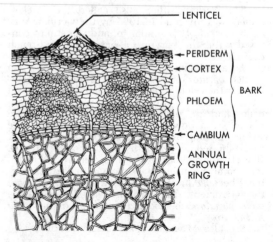

LENTICEL
PERIDERM
CORTEX
PHLOEM
BARK
CAMBIUM
ANNUAL GROWTH RING

BARK BEETLES, bärk bēt′əlz, are a group of insects that feed on the inner bark of trees. Bark beetles are small, usually less than one third of an inch (1 to 8 mm) in length and cylindrical in shape. They usually have a projection from the front of the fourth joint of the leg. Their antennae, divided into 11 or 12 segments, may have knoblike protuberances. These beetles are usually brown or black.

Bark beetles live beneath the bark of a tree. The adult bores into the tree and excavates a tunnel or gallery. In this "brood gallery" the adult female lays her eggs. When these eggs hatch, the larvae excavate tunnels away from the original "brood gallery." At the end of the tunnel, the larvae will become pupae and emerge through a hole the size of a bullet hole; for this reason these beetles often are called "shot-hole borers."

Sometimes they are called "engraver beetles" because the tunnels they excavate often form a characteristic design. Bark beetles cause millions of dollars of damage to forests each year. They kill many trees, especially evergreens, and also transmit some tree diseases.

Bark beetles belong to the family Scolytidae, which contains numerous genera, including *Ips* and *Dendroctonus*. The western pine beetle (*Dendroctonus brevicomis*) is representative. •

EDWARD O. ESSIG
University of California at Berkeley

BARK LOUSE, bärk lous, is the common name for several types of small insects that live on the bark of trees but are not true lice. Most of the common bark lice are in the order Psocoptera, family Psocidae. These insects, which have well-developed wings, occur on the bark or leaves of trees and shrubs, or sometimes under the bark. Scale insects and mealy bugs (order Homoptera, family Coccidae) also are called bark lice. The females, which are wingless, pierce the bark of trees with their long beaks and suck the sap. Coccid insects in large numbers may kill a tree. Aphids (q.v.) also are referred to as bark lice.

BARKAL JEBEL, bär′käl jeb′əl, an isolated sandstone hill in northern Sudan, near the Fourth Cataract of the Nile. The hill is 302 feet (92 meters) high, and is nearly perpendicular on all sides. At its foot are the ruins of the ancient Egyptian city of Napata.

BARKER, bär′kər, **George Granville** (1913–   ), English poet and novelist. He was born at Loughton, Essex, on Feb. 26, 1913. After leaving school at the age of 13, he spent the next several years doing manual labor. He wrote his first novel, *Alanna Autumnal*, when he was 18. It was published two years later, in 1933, the same year in which his *Thirty Preliminary Poems* appeared. His second book of verse, *Poems* (1935), was the first of his works to attract serious critical attention, and his *Sacred and Secular Elegies* (1943) and *Eros in Dogma* (1944) established him as one of the more important English poets of his day. His other books include *Collected Poems, 1930–55* (1957), *The View From the Blind I* (1962), and the novel *The Dead Seagull* (1950). Barker's novels were not generally well received. His poetry, however, was praised for its lyrical intensity, and his highly personal poetic voice has been called unusual in an age of socially orientated literature.

U. S. FOREST SERVICE

The adult Douglas fir beetle (*insert, above*) is a typical bark beetle, excavating "brood galleries" in which the female lays her eggs. Feeding larvae later excavate tunnels away from the galleries and emerge as pupae.

BARKER, Harley Granville. See GRANVILLE-BARKER, HARLEY GRANVILLE.

BARKER, bär′kər, **Jacob** (1779–1871), American financier. He was born at Swans Island, Me., on Dec. 17, 1799. He became a commission merchant in New York City and controlled a fleet of merchant vessels. During the War of 1812 he raised large sums for the government but suffered losses in ships and money.

In 1815, Barker founded the Exchange Bank in New York, which failed in 1819. When the Life & Fire Insurance Company, of which he was a director, failed in 1826, he was indicted for fraud. The indictment was quashed, and in 1834 he moved to New Orleans, La. He was admitted to the Louisiana bar and was prominent in New Orleans' business life, becoming president of the Bank of Commerce. He lost a large fortune during the Civil War. He died at Philadelphia, Pa., on Dec. 26, 1871.

BARKER, bär′kər, **Wharton** (1846–1921), American financier. He was born in Philadelphia on May 1, 1846. He graduated from the University of Pennsylvania in 1866 and entered the banking firm of Barker Brothers & Company, where he became special financial agent of the Russian government. Barker supervised the building of four cruisers for Russia and went to that country to advise on the development of coal and iron mining. He obtained valuable railroad and telegraph interests in China, but his concessions in that country were soon withdrawn.

In 1869 he founded a periodical called the *Penn Monthly*, devoted to political, economic, and social conditions. This was merged in 1880 into *The American*, a weekly, which was published until 1900. He proposed the names of James Garfield and Benjamin Harrison for the presidency and strenuously opposed a third term for Ulysses S. Grant. He was a Republican until 1896, when he joined the Populist party and soon gained prominence, becoming the "middle-of-the-road" Populists' candidate for the presidency in 1900.

A member of several learned societies, he traveled extensively in the United States, Europe, China, Japan, and South America. He was a leading advocate of a commercial union of all American nations and an opponent of all temporary arbitration treaties. He died in Philadelphia on April 8, 1921.

BARKHAUSEN EFFECT, bärk′hou-zən, the small, abrupt changes that occur in the internal magnetic field of a ferromagnetic sample being magnetized. Any large ferromagnetic sample, or core, has magnetic domains. Each domain is an individual magnet. When the sample is unmagnetized, the domains are small (a typical domain volume is about 10^{-3} cubic mm), and the direction of the magnetic field varies from domain to domain.

A ferromagnetic core is magnetized by establishing a current in a coil of insulated wire wrapped round the core. As magnetization proceeds, the domains undergo sudden increases in size, abruptly changing the internal magnetic field. The Barkhausen effect can be demonstrated by wrapping a second coil around the core and connecting this coil to an amplifier and a loudspeaker. As the core is magnetized, the loudspeaker emits distinct clicks that correspond to the abrupt changes.

SAMUEL OLANOFF, *Bard College*

BARKLA, bärk′lə, **Charles Glover** (1877–1944), English physicist who discovered the characteristic X-ray radiation of the elements in 1908. For this work, he was awarded the 1917 Nobel Prize in physics.

His research concerned the interactions between X-rays and matter. Roentgen had reported that as X-rays passed through air, a kind of secondary radiation was emitted in all directions. When Barkla examined this effect in detail, he found the secondary radiation was absorbed in the same way as the primary radiation, so he concluded that it was simply radiation scattered out of the primary beam of X-rays. Then he replaced the air by various gases and found that the intensity of the scattered radiation depended on the atomic weight of the gas. In his report of this discovery is the first suggestion of a relation between the number of electrons in the atom of an element and the position of the element in the periodic table, a relation of fundamental importance in physics.

He next found that X-rays scattered in a direction perpendicular to the primary beam were polarized. (Sunlight scattered by air is highly polarized in all directions perpendicular to a line from the observer to the sun.) This was evidence that X-rays were not particles like electrons but were transverse waves, in this respect being like visible light.

He discovered that when the scattering material was a chemical element, the scattered radiation also contained new rays peculiar to the element used. This new effect he called the "characteristic radiation" of the element. At that time he could not measure the wavelength of the new rays, but now they have been measured and the characteristic radiation is known to consist of a series of wavelengths, with a different series for each element. From these wavelength measurements the energies of the electrons closest to the nucleus can be calculated.

Barkla was born in Widnes, Lancashire, on June 7, 1877. He studied at University College in Liverpool, and at Trinity and King's Colleges of Cambridge University. His teaching and research were done at Liverpool University (1902–1909), at the University of London (1909–1913), and at the University of Edinburgh (1913–1944). He died in Edinburgh on Oct. 23, 1944.

ROBERT A. LUFBURROW, *St. Lawrence University*

BARKLEY, bär′kli, **Alben William** (1877–1956), American political leader, who was vice president of the United States (1949–1953). Barkley took a more active role in government than most vice presidents before him. His personal popularity lifted him still further from the traditional obscurity of his office. He was affectionately called "the Veep"—a nickname that clung to him even after he retired from office.

He was born in Graves County, Ky., on Nov. 24, 1877, the son of a poor tobacco farmer. Following graduation from Marvin College in Clinton, Ky., he studied law at Emory College, Oxford, Ga., and the University of Virginia. He practiced law in Paducah, Ky., from 1901 to 1905, when he became prosecuting attorney of McCracken County. He was judge of the McCracken County Court from 1909 to 1913.

Barkley was elected to the U.S. Congress as a Democrat from Kentucky's 1st district in 1912. He served seven terms before entering the U.S. Senate in 1927. During four consecutive terms as senator from Kentucky he became a national figure, first as a ranking minority leader and, for 10 years beginning in 1937, as majority leader. He was an influential spokesman for the legislative programs of Presidents Franklin D. Roosevelt and Harry S Truman. He was instrumental in guiding much of the New Deal legislation through the Senate, and he consistently supported Truman's Fair Deal program.

In 1948, Truman chose Barkley as his presidential running mate. Following their election, Truman determined not to repeat Roosevelt's practice of excluding the vice president from top-level meetings. He appointed Barkley to the National Security Council and consulted him on foreign and domestic issues. After leaving the vice presidency in January 1953, Barkley won back his old Senate seat in the 1954 elections. On April 30, 1956, he died suddenly while making a speech at Lexington, Va.

ALBEN W. BARKLEY, vice president of the United States in 1949–1953 under President Harry S Truman.

BARLAAM AND JOSAPHAT, bär'lā-əm, jos'ə-fat, was one of the most popular medieval religious romances, appearing in various languages. According to the narrative, Josaphat was the son of a king of India, who reared him in luxurious seclusion so that the prince might know nothing of human misery. Despite his father's efforts, the knowledge of sickness, poverty, and death could not be hidden from Josaphat, and he became oppressed by the mystery of existence. Barlaam, a Christian hermit, risked his life to find his way to Josaphat and converted him to Christianity. The prince then used his influence to promote his faith among his people. After making his kingdom very wealthy, he left it to spend the rest of his days as a hermit.

The narrative is substantially the story of Buddha. Even the phraseology of the Barlaam and Josaphat tale is at times almost a literal version of the Sanskrit *Lalita Vistara*. The name Josaphat, or Joasaph (Arabic *Yudasatf*), is a corrupt form of *Bodisat*, or *Bodisatva*, a common title for the Buddha in many stories of his birth. Likewise, "Barlaam" is related to *Bhagavan*, another of Buddha's titles.

The romance was evidently built on Buddhist sources. Its original authorship is uncertain, although it has been attributed to St. John of Damascus, a Greek theologian of the early 8th century. A Latin version was current in the Middle Ages. Three poetical French versions from the 13th century are also extant, and there are Italian, German, Spanish, Polish, and Czech versions derived from the Latin. There are also specimens in Icelandic, Swedish, Norwegian, and even in the Tagalog language of the Philippines. Boccaccio, Shakespeare, and others have drawn materials from the romance.

BARLACH, bär'laкн, **Ernst** (1870–1938), German sculptor and graphic artist, who was a pioneer in the expressionist movement. His wood or bronze figures, with strong planes and straight lines derived from cubism and Gothic art, convey powerful, often tragic, emotions. He also wrote several expressionist plays, including *Der tote Tag* (1912) and *Der arme Vetter* (1918).

Barlach was born in Wedel, Holstein, on Jan. 2, 1870. He studied art in Hamburg (1888–1891), in Dresden (1891–1895), and at the Académie Julian in Paris (1895–1896). A visit to Russia in 1906 awakened his sympathy with the sufferings of the common people, a theme that permeates all of his work. In 1908 he settled in Güstrow, in northern Germany.

During the 1920's Barlach did many of his most important works, including war memorials at Güstrow (1927) and Magdeburg (1930) and a series of figures for St. Catherine's church in Lübeck. The Nazi regime proscribed his work as "degenerate" and destroyed much of his sculpture. He died in Güstrow on Oct. 24, 1938.

BARLETTA, bär-lät'tä, is a seaport in Italy on the Adriatic Sea, in the region of Apulia, 34 miles (55 km) northwest of Bari. The city is a distribution point for the Adriatic coastal trade, transshipping such products as wine, grain, fish, olives, chemicals, and cement.

Chief points of interest include a Romanesque-Gothic cathedral (12th–15th centuries), a medieval castle, and a colossal bronze statue from ancient times believed to be of Valentinian I. Population: (1961) 67,419.

GRANT HEILMAN

BARLEY varieties commonly grown have either smooth-awned (*upper left*) or bearded (*lower left*) hulls.

BARLEY, bär'lē, is an annual cereal of the grass family. It matures in a relatively short period of time and therefore is adapted to growing in a wide variety of environments.

Types and Description. Barley is a cereal in the genus *Hordeum* of the grass family Gramineae. There are several species of *Hordeum*. Some of the wild species are weedlike and only slightly similar to cultivated barley in appearance. The cultivated species of barley are the common, six-rowed barley (*H. vulgare*) and the two-rowed barley (*H. distichon*). The small barley flowers (florets) occur in groups of three on alternate sides of the head (spike) of the plant. In common barley, all the florets are fertile and produce seeds, thus creating six rows of seeds along the spike. In two-rowed barley, the outer florets of each group of three are sterile. Therefore, only one row of seeds is left on each side of the spike. Each barley seed is enclosed in a strong outer covering (hull) which remains intact even during threshing. The naked barley seed within this hull is similar in shape to a kernel of wheat. The kernels of important varieties of barley are white or blue, but black-, red-, and purple-seeded varieties also exist.

Most barley varieties have a long beard (awn), which is part of the hull and extends for two or three inches (5 to 7.6 cm) beyond the kernel. The awn breaks away from the hull during threshing and remains with the chaff and stems. In the older varieties the awns have a row of sharp projections on two edges; these projections are a source of discomfort to persons working with the mature crop and can become lodged in the mouths of livestock that feed on barley straw. Research workers at agricultural experiment stations in the United States have imported a black-seeded, smooth-awned variety from Russia and a type of barley without awns (hooded) from Nepal. They have combined the favorable characteristics of these imported varieties with desirable characteristics of domestic ones and have developed

243

new and improved varieties. Some of these new smooth-awned varieties are called Glabron, Velvet, and Comfort. The hooded varieties are lower-yielding plants, but they are being grown increasingly.

The vegetative parts of the barley plant are very similar to those of wheat and oats. Barley may be distinguished by an ear-shaped appendage (auricle) at the base of the leaf. This auricle clasps about the stem and has pointed projections that overlap at the side opposite the leaf.

Sowing and Harvesting. Barley usually is sown by drills in rows six to eight inches (15 to 20 cm) apart at rates varying from 4 to 12 pecks (35 to 105 liters) per acre (0.405 hectares), depending on the variety and area. It grows well in a wide range of soil and rainfall. Harvesting in the United States is done mostly by combine harvesters and threshers.

Diseases. The chief diseases of barley are scab, smut, stripe, and rust. Scab (blight) makes the grain unsuitable for malting or for use as feed for hogs and horses. Smut in either of its two types—covered and loose—permits plant growth but prevents the production of whole kernels. Stripe kills or stunts the growing plants. Rust, also of two types—leaf and stem—impairs proper plant growth, resulting in shriveled kernels and reduced yield. The seed can be treated chemically to reduce the infection of scab, smut, and stripe, but the diseases have been avoided more effectively by the development of disease-resistant varieties of the barley.

Production. The Soviet Union is the leading producer of barley in the world; this leading position is a result of a sharp increase in production since the 1950's. The United States ranks second in production. The states that supply the greater part of the barley grown in the United States are North Dakota, California, Montana, Minnesota, Kansas, South Dakota, Colorado, Washington, Idaho, and Oregon.

Other countries that produce large amounts of barley are Britain, France, West Germany, Denmark, Canada, Turkey, India, Spain, East Germany, Czechoslovakia, Sweden, Poland, Morocco, Japan, and Australia. The average yield of barley per acre (0.405 hectares) is especially high in Denmark. The barley grown on Canadian soil comes mainly from the provinces of Saskatchewan, Alberta, Ontario, and Manitoba.

Uses. Barley is used mainly for feeding livestock. A large proportion, however, is made into malt, principally for beer. The relatively small amount that is milled for human food is called pot, or pearl, barley.

For malting, barley should be high in starch content and have a sufficient amount of diastase, an enzyme used in the conversion of starch to malt sugar. These characteristics are influenced by the growing conditions and the variety. Conversion to malt sugar requires germination, and malting barley must be sound and mature.

Feed barley is ground in feed mills and used chiefly on the farm where it is produced. Some high-yielding varieties suitable for food are not good malting varieties. For human food, barley of the larger, white-seeded, two-rowed varieties is "pearled" (hulls and outer layers of the kernels removed) or ground into flour.

Because of its early maturity, barley often is planted as a nurse or companion crop with small-seeded clovers and grasses. Some also is grown for winter pasture and hay.

Marketing. Marketing barley is helped in the United States by grades set up under the Grain Standards Act of 1916. Barley is graded under the broad classes "barley," "malting," "black," and "Western." Number 1 barley must weigh 47 pounds (21 kg) per bushel (35 liters).

History. Barley was one of the first cereals to be cultivated. It is believed to have originated in western Asia, where it served as a food for man and beast. It was used by the lake dwellers of Switzerland during the Stone Age. Charred remains of barley also have been found in tombs in Asia Minor dating from about 3500 B.C.

Until a few hundred years ago, barley was the chief grain for making bread in Europe. Then it was replaced gradually by wheat and rye. The earliest settlers brought barley to the North American continent. See also GRAINS.

W.A. DAVIDSON
U.S. Department of Agriculture

BARLEYCORN, bär'lē-kôrn, **Sir John,** a personification of the spirit of barley or malt liquor. It is used as a synonym for the liquor and, by extension, as a name for innkeepers. The name was derived from the title and main character of a humorous old English ballad. In the ballad, John Barleycorn's neighbors determine to have him killed. After each farcical attempt of the hired assassins to kill him, "John Barleycorn got up again And sore surprised them all." The assassins are finally forced to give up, in spite of John Barleycorn's good-natured attempts to cheer on his dispirited persecutors.

The name was used by Jack London for his autobiography, *John Barleycorn* (1913), an account of his "alcoholic memories."

BARLOW, bär'lō, **Arthur** (c. 1550–c. 1620), English navigator. In 1584, Barlow (or Barlowe) and Philip Amadas sailed from Plymouth, England, to select a location for the proposed colony of Sir Walter Raleigh. Arriving off the coast of North Carolina after a voyage of over two months, the two captains explored the island of Roanoke and returned to England in September of that year. Barlow's letter to Raleigh describing his voyage led to the latter's choice of Roanoke Island for his colony.

BARLOW, bär'lō, **Francis Channing** (1834–1896), American soldier and lawyer. He was born in Brooklyn, N.Y., on Oct. 19, 1834. A graduate of Harvard College (1855), Barlow practiced law in New York until the outbreak of the Civil War, when he enlisted as a private in the Union Army. He rose from the ranks to become a major general of volunteers in 1864. His military career, which included the command of a brigade at Gettysburg and heroic service at Spotsylvania during Grant's last campaign, has been commemorated by a monument on the battlefield of Gettysburg.

After the war, Barlow practiced law and entered politics, serving twice as secretary of state for New York (1865–1866 and 1869–1870). Appointed United States marshal for the southern district of New York in 1869, he was soon afterward put in command of the federal military, naval, and revenue forces for the New England and New York area. While attorney general of New York from 1871 to 1873, he started the prosecution of the notorious "Tweed Ring." He died in New York on Jan. 11, 1896.

BARLOW, bär′lō, **Joel** (1754–1812), American poet, political writer, and diplomat, who was one of the most influential American liberals of the years between the end of the American Revolution and the War of 1812.

Early Years. He was born in Redding, Conn., on March 24, 1754, the fourth son of Samuel and Esther (Hull) Barlow. His earliest extant poem, *The Prospect of Peace,* was read in pregraduation ceremonies at Yale College in 1778. After two years of graduate study he served until 1783 as an army chaplain. In 1781 he married Ruth Baldwin, sister of Senator Abraham Baldwin. Between 1783 and 1787 he lived in Hartford, Conn., where he became one of the Hartford Wits (q.v.) and contributed to their *Anarchiad,* a mock epic satirizing antifederalism. He also co-founded *The American Mercury* and revised Isaac Watts' *Congregational Book of Psalmody.* In 1786 he was admitted to the bar.

In 1787, Barlow completed eight years' work on *The Vision of Columbus,* a nine-book epic in which an angel exhibits America to its discoverer as the harbinger of universal peace and government by a world congress. Treating American history, republican philosophy, and social perfectibility in couplets studded with classical allusions, it was widely and uncritically acclaimed.

Europe. Barlow went to France in 1788. As European agent of the mismanaged Scioto Company, he netted nothing, but his own European business and property speculations made him wealthy. Two years in London (1790–1792) put him in touch with Thomas Paine, Joseph Priestley, and others who shared his increasing but moderate radicalism. The British government suppressed his *Advice to the Privileged Orders* (1792), attacking feudal property rights, monarchism, and the established church, and forced his return to France.

His *Letters to the National Convention of France* (1792), advising a refashioning of government after the American example, led the French to confer citizenship on him. A poem sent to London, *The Conspiracy of Kings* (1792), won both praise and condemnation in England. Homesickness was evident in his mock-pastoral poem *Hasty Pudding* (written 1793; published 1796), which, like his zestful and whimsical letters, surpasses his more pretentious works.

As American consul to Algiers in 1795–1796, Barlow negotiated peace with the Barbary powers and secured the release of several score enslaved seamen by borrowing their ransom money from the monarch who was demanding it. In Paris, in 1799, he addressed the American people, opposing war with France, advocating roads and canals, and calling for the substitution of moral for physical force in the art of government.

Return to America. In 1805, Barlow returned to the United States and aligned himself with the Jeffersonian Republicans. In 1807 he published *The Columbiad,* a revision of his early epic, *The Vision of Columbus.* It was well received only in circles where patriotism was more valued than poetry. An intimate of Presidents Thomas Jefferson and James Madison, Barlow felt hurt by the latter's failure to make him secretary of state.

Minister to France. Barlow ardently supported the Madison administration, however, and was sent to France in 1811 as American minister. Although Federalists called him "a complete Frenchman," his dread of Napoleon I made him averse to the impending war with England.

French negotiators described him as cold, reserved, and full of "American stubborness" in seeking indemnities for commercial spoliations during the Napoleonic wars. When Barlow showed the French foreign Office a private letter from Madison, dated Aug. 11, 1812, which threatened war with France as soon as peace should be made with England, he was requested to go to Napoleon's intended winter headquarters at Vilna (Vilnius), Russia, to complete a commercial treaty. Waiting there, he wrote his last and best poem, *Advice to a Raven in Russia December 1812,* which assailed Napoleon.

During the demoralized French retreat from Russia, the fleeing emperor passed him on the road to Warsaw. Accompanied by his secretary-nephew and a French official, Barlow headed toward Vienna in bitter cold. He died of pleuropneumonia on Dec. 26, 1812, in a peasant's cottage at Zarnowiec (near Cracow).

IRVING BRANT, *Author of "James Madison"*

Further Reading: Miller, Victor Clyde, *Joel Barlow: Revolutionist* (Hamburg 1932); Todd, Charles Burr, *Life and Letters of Joel Barlow . . . with Extracts from His Works . . .* (New York 1886); Woodress, James L., *Yankee's Odyssey: the Life of Joel Barlow* (Philadelphia 1958); Zunder, Theodore Albert, *The Early Days of Joel Barlow . . .* (New Haven 1934).

BARLOW, bär′lō, **Peter** (1776–1862), English mathematician and physicist, who wrote *A New Mathematical and Philosophical Dictionary* (1814) and *Essay on Magnetic Attractions* (1820). Barlow was born in Norwich, England, in October 1776. In 1823 he devised a star-shaped wheel suspended over a magnet. This device was a primitive motor that was similar to Faraday's disk generator. He also designed a negative lens, called a *Barlow lens,* for increasing the effective focal length—and hence the magnification—of a telescope. Barlow lenses are still widely used. Barlow died on March 1, 1862.

BARMECID, bär′mə-kid, the name of a politically powerful family in the early Abbasid court at Baghdad. Iranians from Balkh, the Barmecid (also transliterated *Barmakid*) family went to Iraq in the early 8th century and were converted to Islam. One of the family, Khalid, served the first and second Abbasid caliphs in high office. His son Yahya was appointed vizier (the chief officer of the administration) by the third Abbasid caliph, Harun ar-Rashid (reigned 786–809). Yahya's two sons al-Fadl and Jaafar were closely associated with him in this office for 17 years, and the three virtually ruled the empire during that period. Either tiring of their dominance or jealous of their power and wealth, Harun suddenly destroyed the family in 803, beheading Jaafar, committing Yahya, al-Fadl, and other Barmecids to jail, and seizing their property.

The Barmecids were responsible for introducing Persian influence into the Arab court. They lived on such a scale of luxury and bestowed gifts so lavishly that their name has lived to the present as a synonym for munificence. A Barmecid feast, meaning an imaginary banquet or make-believe entertainment, originates from an *Arabian Nights'* story in which a Barmecid puts before a beggar empty dishes, describing the merits of their nonexistent contents. Though starving, the beggar enters into the hosts's humor and is therefore rewarded not only with a dinner but also with a lucrative post.

PHILIP K. HITTI, *Princeton University*

GRANT HEILMAN

PREFABRICATED BARNS of many types, such as this dairy barn, have components of various materials.

BARN, a building used for housing farm animals or for storing farm products, feed, or equipment. The word derives from the Anglo-Saxon *berern,* derived in turn from *bere* (barley) and *ærn* (*close place*). The derivation of the word indicates its early use to denote a building for the storing of grain. During the early development of the United States a great majority of the people were engaged in agriculture as a means of self-support. Barns were used for the storage of grain produced and to furnish shelter for the few animals kept on the farm.

Since agriculture has now developed into an industry for production on a commercial basis, the meaning of the word "barn" has become much broader. In 1952 the Dairy Housing Terminology Committee of the American Society of Agricultural Engineers proposed that the society adopt the following terminology as an official recommendation: *Barn*—an enclosed covered building for the keeping of livestock and/or storage of dry roughages and bedding. It may include some but not necessarily all feed and bedding storages and feeding facilities for livestock. *Shed*—a simple structure for shelter of livestock, storage of feeds, or both, and open on one or more sides; it may be separate from or attached to another structure.

Types of Barns. In general usage the word "barn" is commonly prefixed by another word or term that indicates its specific use. Examples of such terms are: *dairy barn*—for the housing of dairy cattle; *beef barn*—for the housing of beef cattle; *sheep barn*—for the housing of sheep; *horse barn*—for the housing of horses; *swine barn* —for the housing of swine; *tobacco barn*—for the curing of tobacco; and *feeding barn*—for the feeding of animals and storage of the feed.

General Requirements. The development of agriculture on a commercial basis, with an all-year demand for agricultural products, has placed increased requirements on barns for the protection and handling of animals and products. Barns and other farm buildings today represent a sizable portion of the total investment in a farming enterprise. The major requirements of the modern barn are efficiency of operation, suitable sanitary conditions, conduciveness to maximum production of livestock, and over-all economy in both construction and operation.

Research work is constantly under way to determine specific environmental conditions within a barn that are necessary for maximum production from livestock and optimum keeping qualities of stored products. Once these requirements are known, the conditions can be attained by proper construction, adequate ventilation, and the use of heating or refrigeration as needed.

Materials of Construction. Wood and concrete have long been the two most important materials for barn construction. However, modern manufacturing techniques have produced numerous types of prefabricated structures that are used as barns. Such structures may utilize steel framing with coverings of galvanized sheet steel or aluminum and with or without built-in insulation. Such fabrication greatly reduces the cost of erection, and the metal construction is more fire resistant than wood. Concrete is still used for foundations for these buildings.

Planning Barns for Efficient Operation. Efficiency of operation within a barn entails many factors. For example, considerable labor can be saved by the use of mechanical equipment. Available equipment includes milking machines, cleaners for the handling of manure in the dairy barn, silo unloaders, feed carts, automatic waterers for livestock, and elevators for the handling of feed and other materials.

Considerable saving in labor can be realized even in those operations for which no mechanical equipment has been developed if proper attention is given to arrangement within the barn for maximum efficiency. Planning for efficient operation includes centralized operations or close arrangement of those operations that are similar in nature; circular travel or arrangement of work routes so that one operation is carried out in one direction and another operation is completed on the return trip; effective arrangement of equipment and space, including convenient working heights; bulk handling of feed and materials, which adapts the operation to mechanization; and eliminating or combining jobs, or postponing them until a more opportune time.

Barn Planning Assistance. There are numerous sources of technical assistance and advice available to a farmer to aid him in planning and constructing his barns. The Regional Plan Service developed by the United States Department of Agriculture in cooperation with the extension services of the various state colleges and universities makes available to the farmer detailed plans for the construction of almost any type of barn. Agricultural engineering departments in many colleges have published bulletins on the subject of barns, including information on general construction and recommendations for specific types, and some of these departments have extension personnel on their staffs who can furnish individual advice and assistance to a farmer. Many manufacturers also are prepared to furnish information to the farmer on barn construction.

HAROLD E. GRAY
Lord and Burnham Division, Burnham Corp.

Further Reading: Barre, Henry J., and Sammet, Loy L., *Farm Structures* (New York 1950); Carter, Deane G., and Foster, William A., *Farm Buildings,* rev. ed. (New York 1954); Teter, Norman C., and Giese, Henry, "New Barns for Old," *Yearbook of Agriculture 1960* (Washington 1961).

246

BARN OWL, bärn oul, a bird found in most parts of the United States; in the Canadian provinces of British Columbia, Ontario, and Manitoba; as far south as Argentina; and in Europe and Asia, except in the far north. Also known as the *monkey-faced owl* or *white owl,* it is recognized by its white or reddish heart-shaped facial disc, which gives it a monkeylike expression. Its upper parts are golden buff, finely mottled with gray, brown, and white; the underparts are white to deep buff and are spotted with black. The eyes are small and black, and the legs are long and covered with short feathers. The barn owl varies in length from 13 to 21 inches (33 to 53.3 cm) and has a wingspread up to 47 inches (119.3 cm).

Almost completely nocturnal, the barn owl nests in hollow trees, niches in cliffs or banks, or in barns and other buildings, usually in the spring. It seldom makes a nest, except possibly for a few twigs, and lays four to seven or more white eggs.

The barn owl is regarded as one of the most beneficial of birds to the agriculturist, since a large proportion of its food consists of rodents injurious to crops. It subsists on the cotton rat and mice in the Southern states, and on gophers, ground squirrels, and rabbits in the Western states, as well as on shrews, other birds, and large insects. It has several close relatives, of which one or two species of grass owl, widespread in the Old World, roost and nest on the ground.

The barn owl belongs to the order Strigiformes, which contains the owls, and the family Tytonidae. Its technical name is *Tyto alba.*

BARN SWALLOW, bärn swol′ō, the most familiar and widespread species of swallow. It is found throughout most of the Northern Hemisphere in summer, and in winter it migrates as far south as South Africa and southern South America. Its upper parts are a lustrous steel-blue, and the forehead, chin, and throat are a dull chestnut, bounded by a collar of steel-blue. In American barn swallows the collar marking is broken and the lower breast and abdomen are of a salmon shade, while in European varieties the collar is complete and the lower parts vary from the chestnut tone of the throat to white. The barn swallow is readily distinguished from the nearly square-tailed cliff swallow by its deeply forked tail. The barn swallow is from 5¾ to 7¾ inches (14.6 to 19.6 cm) long and has a wingspread of 12½ to 13½ inches (31.7 to 34.2 cm).

The barn swallow builds an open nest of mud pellets mixed with straw and lined with feathers inside a barn or other building, usually on a rafter. The eggs, ordinarily numbering four to six, are white, marked with brown or purple; usually two broods are reared each season. House sparrows are sometimes destructive to the nest and its contents.

Barn swallows are remarkably powerful and swift flyers, and are extremely graceful in flight. They often are seen fluttering and darting about in search of flying insects; and by killing great numbers of pests and injurious insects, they perform a service to man and domestic animals. Several closely related species are found in Europe.

The barn swallow belongs to the order Passeriformes and the family Hirundinidae. There are two species: *Hirundo rustica* and *H. erythrogaster.*

BARNABAS, bär′nə-bəs, **Saint,** apostle and companion of St. Paul in the 1st century. Barnabas was the surname given to *Joses,* or *Joseph,* and is translated as "son of consolation" or "of exhortation" or "of prophecy."

Life. Barnabas was a Levite, a native of Cyprus, who contributed to the sharing of property in the early Jerusalem church (Acts 4:36–37) and sponsored Paul, the former persecutor (9:26–27). Barnabas was sent from Jerusalem to investigate conditions in the church of Antioch (11:19–24); from there he went on to Tarsus, and brought Paul back to Antioch (11:25–30). A year later the church sent the two missionaries out on their first extended journey through Cyprus, southern Asia Minor, and back again (Acts 13–14). It was probably soon after their return that the conflict with the "Judaizers" over the requirement of circumcision arose, and Paul and Barnabas presented their case at Jerusalem (Acts 15; Galatians 2). Upon the proposal to revisit the mission field in Asia Minor, Barnabas wished to take along his nephew, John Mark, but Paul objected, as Mark had abandoned the first mission and gone home (Acts 13:13). Accordingly, Barnabas and Mark set out for Cyprus, while Paul went overland to Galatia.

After that time the life of Barnabas is veiled in obscurity. Paul mentions him in I Corinthians 9:6, but they probably never worked together again. Legend relates that Barnabas preached in Rome, and became the first bishop of Milan; perhaps somewhat more probable is the statement that he was martyred in Cyprus. His feast day is June 11.

Writings Attributed to Barnabas. A number of works have been attributed to St. Barnabas: the Acts of Barnabas, the Epistle of Barnabas, and the Gospel of Barnabas. In addition, Tertullian attributed to him the Epistle to the Hebrews, but this is more a guess than a tradition.

The Acts of Barnabas are apocryphal and late—probably 5th century or later. They recount the journeys and martyrdom of the apostle.

The Epistle of Barnabas is one of the New Testament Apocrypha, found in Codex Sinaiticus (see BIBLE—*The Text of the New Testament*) and in a codex discovered at Constantinople in 1875 by Archbishop Bryennios. There are also eight defective manuscripts and a Latin version of chapters 1–17 found in one manuscript. Some scholars think the Latin version represents the original epistle (written in Greek c. 130 A.D.) before the "Two Ways" or "Teaching of the Apostles" (chapters 18–21) had been added. It was quoted as Scripture by Clement of Alexandria, and is an important document of the period when the church was facing the problem of interpreting the Jewish Scriptures, and when Marcion and Justin took opposite views, the one rejecting the Old Testament, the other retaining it. The author of the Epistle, probably an Alexandrian, offered a mediating view, namely, that the Old Testament was true, but not literally —its real meaning was to be discovered only by allegorical interpretation (see EXEGESIS). For example, the number 318, of the men in Abraham's household (Genesis 14:14), written TIH in Greek, meant the cross (T = 300) of Jesus (IH = 18); and he adds (Epistle of Barnabas 9:9): "No one has learned a more excellent lesson from me, but I know you are worthy of it." The Old Testament laws were also allegorically interpreted, much as Philo had found deeper ethical or philosophical meanings in them, though he refused to abandon the literal meaning or the divine requirement of their observance. The six days of creation in Genesis 1 were interpreted to mean that the world is to last 6,000 years until Christ returns and holds the Last Judgment; for "a day is with the Lord as a thousand years" (compare Psalm 90:4).

There was also a Gospel of Barnabas, referred to by several ancient authors, especially in the "Decree of Gelasius" (c. 500 A.D.); but there is no means of knowing what its contents or character were. However, there is in existence a long Italian manuscript under this title, written from the Muslim standpoint and containing a strong element of Gnosticism. It was edited in 1907 by Lonsdale and Laura (M. Roberts) Ragg, who held it to be the work of an apostate from Christianity, sometime between the 13th and 16th century. Like most of the patristic and medieval apocrypha, the work is highly imaginative, a work of fiction rather than of historical tradition, but it has a strongly marked ethical emphasis.

FREDERICK C. GRANT
Union Theological Seminary

Bibliography

Dibelius, Martin, *A Fresh Approach to the New Testament and Early Christian Literature* (New York 1936).

Filson, Floyd V., *New Testament History* (Philadelphia 1964).

Grant, Robert M., ed., *Apostolic Fathers*, vol. 3 (Camden, N.J., 1965).

Hastings, James, *Dictionary of the Bible*, rev. ed. (New York 1927).

James, Montague R., tr., *The Apocryphal New Testament* (Oxford 1924).

Weiss, Johannes, *Earliest Christianity*, 2 vols., ed. by Frederick C. Grant (Magnolia, Mass., 1959).

BARNABY RUDGE, bär'nə-bē ruj, is a novel by Charles Dickens (q.v.), first published in 1841. It was the first of Dickens' two historical novels. (The second was *Tale of Two Cities*.) *Barnaby Rudge* is built around the anti-Roman Catholic riots and the destruction of Newgate prison that occurred in London in 1780. It includes the historical personage and fanatic Lord George Gordon (q.v.) as one of its characters. The irresistible surge of the riot—provoked by both the unscrupulous and the deluded—its climax in the storming and destruction of the prison, and its effect on Barnaby Rudge stand out vividly from the intricate action of the novel.

Using the theme of public violence as a background for his story, Dickens develops a multiplicity of plots that include the mysterious murder of a wealthy gentleman, Reuben Haredale, and the difficulties of Haredale's daughter Emma and her suitor Edward Chester, whose plans for marriage are opposed by their elders. In spite of the book's title, Barnaby Rudge, a feebleminded young man who assumes a passive role in the novel's action, is not among the most important characters. However, Barnaby's father, Haredale's former servant, who is falsely believed to be dead, is finally apprehended as Haredale's murderer and pays with his life for his crime.

As in many of Dickens' novels, the most memorable characters in *Barnaby Rudge* are minor ones. They include Dolly Varden, the coquettish daughter of the locksmith Gabriel Varden; Miss Miggs, the Vardens' treacherous servant; Simon Tappertit, Varden's apprentice; and Willet, the host of the Maypole Inn. Grip, Barnaby's pet raven, also figures in the novel.

BARNACLE, bär'ni-kəl, a group of sessile marine animals that grow on rocks, wharves, floats, ships, whales, turtles, and almost any other surface covered by water. Like lobsters and crabs, barnacles are classified as crustaceans. Because of peculiarities in their structure and life cycle, however, these unusual animals were for many centuries a puzzle to biologists. Some thought they were unusual clams, some thought they resembled plants, and still others guessed that they were created by spontaneous generation from the feathers of sea birds.

Barnacles are a nuisance to boat and ship owners because they retard the passage of vessels through the water and because they tend to speed rusting and corrosion of metal hulls unless removed regularly.

Structure. Barnacles vary considerably in size. Some adults are only ⅛ to ¼ inch (0.3 to 0.6 cm) in diameter, and some are as long as 6 inches (15 cm). The skeleton of the barnacle

BARNACLES, members of the class Crustacea, are found along the shore. Common types are leaf barnacles (*left*), on high tide rocks; goose neck barnacles (*center*), found in the Bay of Fundy; and acorn barnacles (*right*).

consists of hardened calcified plates that protect the soft body parts within. These calcified portions usually are supported by a stalk of some type.

Barnacles commonly seen along the seashore are generally of two types—*acorn barnacles* and *gooseneck barnacles*. Most acorn barnacles have shells composed of six plates, whereas the shells of gooseneck barnacles have five plates and are attached by a leathery stalk of variable length. Many barnacles have a movable covering known as the operculum, which is divided into two parts. When the animal feeds, the two parts of the operculum are separated, and the appendages of the animal are extended to catch food. The operculum also acts as a protective device because it can be closed to seal off the soft parts of the animal completely from enemies and from exposure to fresh water.

Reproduction. In general appearance the barnacle shows little resemblance to other crustaceans; however, its relationship to other crustaceans has been determined by similarities in their methods of reproduction. Also, barnacles and other crustaceans pass through the same stages of development.

Barnacles carry on sexual reproduction, although they are hermaphroditic. Each barnacle is equipped with a specialized extensible appendage, or cirrus, several inches long, by which it passes sperm to other barnacles within reach. Cross-fertilization is facilitated, and the eggs hatch as nauplius larvae—free-swimming stages completely independent of parental care, in the life cycle of many crustacea. The larvae stay within the mantle cavity of the parent barnacle for only a short time.

After several molts, the nauplius metamorphoses into a cypris larva. This is a two-shelled stage that swims with a butterfly-like movement. The cypris larva then attaches itself to a rock or some other substrate by means of a cement produced from glands at the base of its front pair of antennae. Next it passes through a pupal stage and metamorphoses into a small version of the sessile adult form. At this time it secretes around itself a shell of calcium carbonate plates, which protect its soft internal parts.

Feeding. Barnacles feed only when they are submerged in water. They catch food primarily by extending their featherlike cirri through the operculum opening. The cirri are homologous to the jointed appendages or legs of other crustaceans such as crabs, lobsters, and crayfish.

The cirri sweep through the water collecting food particles such as microscopic algae, eggs of other animals, microscopic animals, and detritus. After sweeping the water several times, the cirri are brought into contact with the mouth parts, which scrape the collected food into the mouth. The food then is swallowed and passed through the digestive tract. Throughout the feeding process the animal is lying on its back.

Classification. Barnacles are of the class Crustacea, subclass Cirripedia. Typical species belong to the order Thoracica. Most are either stalked or peduncled (gooseneck barnacles) and belong to the family Lepadidae, or sessile (acorn shell barnacles), belonging to the family Balanidae. The other principal orders are the burrowing barnacles (Acrothoracica) and parasitic barnacles (Rhizocephala).

DAVID A. OTTO
Stephens College

ALLAN D. CRUICKSHANK FROM NATIONAL AUDUBON SOCIETY

Barnacle goose (*Branta leucopsis*)

BARNACLE GOOSE, bär′nə-kəl goōs, a medium-sized goose identified by its extensively white face and its lavender-gray mantle barred with black and white. Its only known breeding places are northeastern Greenland, Svalbard (Spitsbergen), and Novaya Zemlya. It is a common winter visitor to Europe as far south as northern France, and nests in colonies on ledges of cliffs and infrequently on low islands. The nest is a hollow, used annually and lined with down; three to six gray-white eggs are laid.

The barnacle goose, also known as the *white-cheeked goose*, belongs to the family Anatidae. Its species is *Branta leucopsis*.

Medieval European peasants believed that the barnacle goose was born from the stalked barnacles adhering to driftwood or to the branches of trees that reach down into the sea at high tide. Circumstantial accounts of the birth of the young, whose tiny wings (the waving filaments of the feeding barnacles) protruded from the shells from which they were supposed to escape, found their way into the literature of the time. Actually the "goose" barnacles were named after the bird, as their supposed parent, and not the bird after the crustacean.

BARNARD, bär′nərd, **Chester Irving** (1886–1961), American corporation executive, who was president of the United Service Organizations (USO) in World War II and president of the Rockefeller Foundation from 1952 to 1954.

Barnard was born in Malden, Mass., on Nov. 7, 1886, and attended Harvard. Barnard spent his entire business career with the American Telephone and Telegraph Company, and in 1927 became the first president of New Jersey Bell Telephone Company, a subsidiary. He received the Presidential Medal of Merit for directing the USO from 1942 to 1945, when the organization provided recreational facilities for U.S. servicemen around the world. Barnard was coauthor of the State Department's postwar report on international control of atomic energy, which became the basis for U.S. policy, and was chairman of the National Science Foundation from 1952 to 1954. He wrote *Functions of the Executive* (1938) and *Organization and Management* (1948). He died in New York City on June 7, 1961.

BARNARD, bär'nərd, **Edward Emerson** (1857–1923), American astronomer, who is known for his achievements in astrophotography. Barnard was born in Nashville, Tenn., on Dec. 16, 1857. The boy received little formal schooling but studied photography while working in a Nashville studio. Eventually he became interested in astronomy, and his discovery of a comet in 1881 was the first of 16 such discoveries. In 1887, Barnard was graduated from Vanderbilt University, where he had been in charge of the observatory, and was appointed assistant astronomer at Lick Observatory in California.

While at Lick (1887–1895), Barnard discovered Jupiter's 5th satellite and the nebulous ring around Nova Aurigae (1892) and began an important series of photographs of the Milky Way. From 1895 until his death in Williams Bay, Wis., on Feb. 6, 1923, he was professor of practical astronomy at the University of Chicago and astronomer at Yerkes Observatory in Wisconsin. There he studied globular clusters and novae and determined that the dark regions in the Milky Way are not gaps among the stars but are caused by dark clouds of obscuring gases, or nebulae. In 1916 he discovered Barnard's Star, a faint nearby star whose movement through the sky—about 10.3 seconds of arc per year—is the greatest of any star known.

BARNARD, bär'nərd, **Frederick Augustus Porter** (1809–1889), American educator. He was born at Sheffield, Mass., on May 5, 1809. After studying at Yale College, he served as a tutor in mathematics there and later as a teacher in the Hartford (Conn.) Grammar School, the Ameri-

can Asylum for the Deaf and Dumb (1831–1832), and the New York Institute for the Deaf and Dumb (1832–1837). In 1838 he moved to the University of Alabama, where he taught mathematics, natural philosophy, chemistry, natural history, and English literature. In 1847 he married Margaret McMurray. In 1854 he was ordained into the Protestant Episcopal Church, and in the same year he went to the University of Mississippi. There he served as professor of mathematics and astronomy until he became chancellor of the university in 1858.

On the outbreak of the Civil War, Barnard found his sympathies lay with the Union, and he resigned and returned to the North. He headed the map and chart department of the U.S. Coast Survey in Washington, D.C., until 1864. In that year he became the 10th president of Columbia College in New York City. He held this position until his death, which occurred in New York on April 27, 1889.

Columbia developed rapidly during his tenure as president. Enrollment grew from 150 to 1,500. Barnard instituted elective courses and provisions for graduate study and research. He enlarged the curriculum, established the School of Mines, and, in 1883, inaugurated college instruction for women. Because of his efforts on behalf of women's education, Barnard College was named in his honor.

Barnard contributed to many fields. He wrote more than 60 books and pamphlets on arithmetic, grammar, science, and education. His annual reports to the Board of Trustees of Columbia are valuable discussions of problems in higher education. Many of his letters were concerned with college administration. There are collections of his letters in the Library of Congress and the library of Columbia University. He also edited Johnson's *Universal Cyclopaedia* and served as president of the American Association for the Advancement of Science.

RICHARD E. GROSS, *Stanford University*

GEORGE GREY BARNARD'S *Struggle of the Two Natures in Man,* in the Metropolitan Museum, New York City.

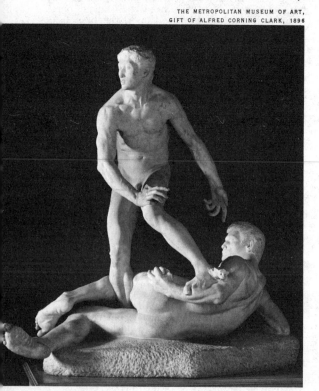

BARNARD, bär'nərd, **George Grey** (1863–1938), American sculptor. He was born in Bellefonte, Pa., on May 24, 1863, and studied at the Art Institute of Chicago and the École des Beaux-Arts, Paris. His *Struggle of the Two Natures in Man* caused a sensation at the Paris Salon of 1894 and established his reputation. This work is now in the Metropolitan Museum of Art, New York City.

Barnard taught at the Art Students League of New York from 1900 to 1904. From 1902 to 1912 he worked on one of his major commissions, the 31 allegorical figures representing "Broken Laws" and "Laws We Keep," in the state capitol at Harrisburg, Pa. Another major work was the large statue of Lincoln (1917), in Lytle Park, Cincinnati, Ohio. The statue's rugged surface and the slouching stance of its subject caused a popular outcry at the time. Barnard's last endeavor was his plan for a "Rainbow Arch," a structure that was to stand 100 feet high on the New York City shore of the Hudson River. He died on April 24, 1938.

Barnard's collection of Gothic art was bought by John D. Rockefeller, Jr., in 1925 and presented to the Metropolitan Museum of Art. It is now in the Cloisters, a branch of the museum, in Washington Heights, New York City. Barnard's work is in the Barnard Museum, Madison, Ind., and in the Swarthmore College collection.

BARNARD, bär'nərd, **Henry** (1811–1900), American educator. He was born at Hartford, Conn., on Jan. 24, 1811. After graduating from Yale College in 1830, Barnard taught at an academy in Pennsylvania, then studied law, and was admitted to the bar in Connecticut in 1835. He was elected for three successive terms to the Connecticut legislature, and in 1838 he framed the bill for a State Board of School Commissioners. He subsequently was appointed secretary of the board.

His efforts to improve schools in Connecticut paralleled the work of Horace Mann in Massachusetts. Since Barnard's proposals meant increased taxes, he aroused the opposition of conservatives and those opposed to the idea of free public elementary schools in the state. His first annual report dwelt on the need for free high schools open to all classes of society.

In 1845, Barnard became secretary of the newly established board of education in Rhode Island. He returned to Connecticut in 1849 as superintendent of common schools. From 1850 to 1854 he was principal of the state normal school in New Britain. He later served as chancellor of the University of Wisconsin (1858–1860) and as president of St. John's College, Annapolis, Md. (1866–1867).

As early as 1837, Barnard had proposed that the federal government collect and publish educational statistics. In 1867 he gained the opportunity to build such a national service when he was appointed first United States commissioner of education. As commissioner (until 1870) Barnard was only partially successful. He did not understand Washington politics and wanted the Bureau of Education to extend its activities beyond the scope intended by Congress.

Barnard was a highly productive writer and editor. He founded and edited the *Connecticut Common School Journal* and the *Journal of the Rhode Island Institute of Instruction*. In 1855 he began publishing his encyclopedic *American Journal of Education*. This work ran to 32 volumes, which appeared at irregular intervals until 1882. A number of sections of the Journal were later republished as the *Library of Education*. His educational writings were the first to have truly national circulation and impact, and they made a significant contribution to the development of professional education in America. Barnard died at Hartford on July 5, 1900.

RICHARD E. GROSS, *Stanford University*

BARNARD, bär'nərd, **John Gross** (1815–1882), American military engineer, who made major contributions to harbor improvement in the United States. He was born at Sheffield, Mass., on May 19, 1815. He graduated from West Point in 1833 and joined the Army engineers. Barnard's assignments included the construction of the Delaware breakwater and a study of the problems of navigating the mouth of the Mississippi River. His recommendation that parallel jetties be built to channel the river flow set a long-lasting pattern of construction.

At the outbreak of the Civil War Barnard was put in charge of the defenses of Washington, D.C., and supervised the construction of an elaborate system of forts. He was chief engineer on the staff of Gen. George B. McClellan in the Peninsular Campaign of 1862 and on Grant's staff in Virginia in 1864. He died in Detroit on May 14, 1882.

BARNARD COLLEGE is the undergraduate college for women of Columbia University, located in New York City. The affiliated women's college was named for President Frederick A.P. Barnard of Columbia College. Chartered in 1889 it began instruction in the fall of that year.

Under an agreement made in 1900, the president of Columbia was made ex officio president of Barnard and Barnard's internal administration was conducted by a dean. This plan was superseded by a new agreement in July 1952, whereby the chief administrative officer of Barnard became its president, retaining, however, the title and rank of a dean in the university. Columbia's president was made an ex officio trustee of Barnard. The separate financial organization of Barnard was maintained.

Barnard professors are nominated by the president of the college and appointed by the Barnard Board of Trustees. Their appointment is also approved by Columbia University's Board of Trustees, and they rank as professors of the university. Barnard offers a four-year liberal arts course. Graduates of Barnard receive the bachelor of arts degree from the university. Enrollment grew from 14 in 1889 to 1,500 in the mid-1960's. See also COLUMBIA UNIVERSITY.

BARNARDO, bär-när'dō, **Thomas John** (1845–1905), British philanthropist, who founded a series of refuges for destitute children known as Dr. Barnardo's Homes. He was born in Dublin, Ireland, on July 4, 1845. While still a youth, he became an active Protestant missionary worker. In 1866 he went to London to become a medical missionary, but he set aside his plans for service overseas to work among London slum children. In 1867 he founded the East End Juvenile Mission in London. Three years later he opened a boys' home at Stepney Causeway and, in 1876, a girls' village in Essex.

Barnardo sent a group of boys to Canada in 1882 for rehabilitation, and subsequently other groups were sent overseas. He enlisted the aid of wealthy children in his cause by organizing a Young Helper's League in 1891. To insure the continuance of his work, his homes were incorporated in 1899 as The National Incorporated Association for the Reclamation of Destitute Waif Children. Barnardo died at Surbiton, Surrey, England, on Sept. 19, 1905.

Further Reading: Williams, Arthur E., *Barnardo of Stepney*, 2d ed. (London 1954); Wymer, Norman D., *Dr. Barnardo* (London 1962).

BARNAUL, bər-nə-ōōl', is an industrial city in the USSR, in southwestern Siberia, 120 miles (193 km) southeast of Novosibirsk. It is the capital of Altai krai in the Russian republic. Barnaul is an important junction on the Turkestan-Siberian and South Siberian railroads. It is also a river port at the junction of the Ob and Barnaulka rivers.

Situated near the industrial region of the Kuznetsk Basin, Barnaul is one of the busiest industrial centers of Siberia. Its textile industry, among the most important in the Soviet Union, was greatly expanded with the addition of new cotton mills in the 1960's. Besides cotton and woolen textiles, the city's chief manufactures are boilers, machine tools, and leather. The city is situated in a mining area that produces coal and gold, silver, iron, copper, lead, and zinc ores, some of which are refined in Barnaul.

Barnaul was founded in 1738 as a silver mining center. After the emancipation of the serfs in 1861, the silver industry, based entirely on slave labor, gradually declined. The completion of the Turksib railroad in the 1930's connected the city with the most important cotton-growing areas of Soviet Central Asia and provided the basis for development of the textile industry and for the renewed growth of the city. Population: (1963) 357,000.

BARNAVE, bàr-nàv', **Antoine Pierre Joseph Marie** (1761–1793), French political leader. He was born in Grenoble, France, on Oct. 22, 1761. Elected deputy from Dauphiné to the States-General in 1789, he formed with Alexandre Lameth and Adrien Duport a revolutionary extremist group known as the "triumvirate," and was active in a club which came to be known as the Jacobins. He also served as president of the Constituent Assembly from October 1790 to its dissolution, and won fame for his oratory there.

His association with Marie Antoinette, while bringing Louis XVI and the royal family back to Paris in 1791 from Varennes, where they had been caught while trying to flee the country, caused him to modify his revolutionary views and to favor the establishment of a constitutional monarchy. Denounced by the revolutionary government in 1792 for his supposed royalist sympathies, and for allegedly plotting counterrevolutionary schemes, he was condemned and was guillotined at Paris on Nov. 29, 1793.

BARNBURNERS, bärn'bûr-nərz, was the nickname for the progressive faction of the Democratic party of New York from about 1843 to 1852, the opposing faction being known as "Hunkers." At first the factions split over such local issues as further expenditures for canals and the chartering of state banks, which the Barnburners opposed. Later, on national issues, the division was on the slavery question; the Barnburners opposed the extension of slavery and constituted the Van Buren, or Free-Soil, wing (see FREE-SOIL PARTY). In state politics, they stood for the "Albany Regency," as against the Polk "machine," which the new administration was trying to build up in New York, and which favored the extension of slavery into the territories. The nickname given them by their opponents derives from the story of the man who burned down his barn to free it from rats.

BARNBY, bärn'bē, **Sir Joseph** (1838–1896), English conductor, organist, and composer, who wrote the popular song *Sweet and Low.* He was born in York on Aug. 12, 1838, and as a child sang in the choir at York Minster. He served as organist at St. Andrew's in London from 1863 to 1871, as precentor and choirmaster at St. Anne's from 1871 to 1886, and as precentor and director of musical instruction at Eton College from 1875 to 1892. He became head of the Guildhall School of Music in London in 1892 and was knighted that year. He died in London on Jan. 28, 1896.

An outstanding conductor, Barnby introduced Dvořák's *Stabat Mater* in London in 1883 and, in a concert version, Wagner's *Parsifal* in 1884. He wrote more than 250 hymn-tunes, of which the best known are *Now the Day is Over* and *O Perfect Love.* He also composed the oratorio *Rebekah,* church services, and anthems, including *King All Glorious.*

BARNEGAT BAY, bär'ni-gat, is on the east coast of New Jersey. It is separated from the Atlantic Ocean by the peninsula of Island Beach and by Long Beach Island. Barnegat Inlet, between the peninsula and the island, connects the bay and the ocean. The bay, about 25 miles (40 km) long and popular for fishing and boating, is part of the small-craft inland waterway that runs along the Atlantic coast.

BARNES, bärnz, **Albert Coombs** (1872–1951), American drug manufacturer who assembled a multimillion-dollar collection of modern art. He was born in Philadelphia, Pa., on Jan. 2, 1872. In 1892 he received an M.D. degree from the University of Pennsylvania, and in 1901 created the antiseptic Argyrol. Barnes set up a company to manufacture and market the product in 1902, and within five years was a millionaire.

Early in the 1900's, Barnes began collecting works of art in Europe, and by 1913 he was devoting all of his time to this avocation. He was among the first collectors to recognize the value of contemporary French paintings and made some incredible purchases. He bought his first Picasso for $20 and his first Matisse for $50. Besides his fine collection of impressionist and cubist works, he also bought paintings by old masters and works of primitive art. By the early 1920's his collection was valued at $20 million.

In 1922, Barnes set up the Barnes Foundation (q.v.) at Merion, Pa., to house his collection and to provide education in art appreciation. He also gave frequent lectures and conducted art tours of Europe for the most promising students. In 1926 the philosopher John Dewy participated in such a tour, and later dedicated his work on aesthetics, *Art as Experience* (1934), to Barnes.

Barnes was the author of several works on art, including *Art in Painting* (1926) and, in collaboration with Violette de Mazia, the foundation's educational director, *The Art of Cézanne* (1939). He died near Phoenixville, Pa., on July 24, 1951.

BARNES, bärnz, **Barnabe** (c. 1569–1609), English poet. He was born in Yorkshire. In 1586 he enrolled in Brasenose College, Oxford, and in 1591 joined the forces of the earl of Essex on an expedition to Normandy. In 1593, after returning to England, he became involved in an exchange of insults with the satirist Thomas Nashe. Barnes published the caustic sonnet *Nashe, or the Confuting Gentleman,* and Nashe responded in kind with a tract accusing Barnes of cowardice and foppery, and claiming that the poet was "laughed out [of the royal court] by the noblemen and ladies." Barnes died in St. Mary-le-Bow, Durham, in December 1609.

Literary evaluations of Barnes' work are mixed. His images were clever and his language vigorous, but he used to a fault the artificial conceits of his age and had a fondness for what one critic called "obscure indecency." His best works are the madrigals contained in an early collection of love poems, *Parthenophil and Parthenophe* (1593). A second volume of verse, *A Divine Century of Spiritual Sonnets* (1595), containing religious poems, is generally considered inferior to the first. Barnes also wrote an antipapal tragedy, *The Devil's Charter,* based on the life of Pope Alexander VI. The play was performed before King James I by Shakespeare's company in 1607.

BARNES, bärnz, **Harry Elmer** (1889–1968), American historian and sociologist. He was born at Auburn, N.Y., on June 15, 1889, and was educated at Syracuse and Columbia universities. He taught at several colleges, lectured, wrote newspaper editorials, and served as a government consultant. Credited with "encyclopedic" knowledge, Barnes often stirred controversy. He blamed the Allies for starting World War I and called for a new concept of God. Barnes died at Malibu, Calif., on Aug. 25, 1968.

His writings cover history, sociology, and penology. Among them are *Society in Transition* (1939, rev. 1952); *Contemporary Social Theory*, with Howard Becker (1940); *An Intellectual and Cultural History of the Western World* (1941, rev. 1965); *New Horizons in Criminology*, with N.K. Teeters (1943, 3d ed. 1959); *Prisons in Wartime* (1944); *Historical Sociology* (1948); and *History of Historical Writing* (1962).

BARNES, bärnz, **Julius Howland** (1873–1959), American wheat dealer and government official. He was born in Little Rock, Ark., on Feb. 2, 1873. He became a wheat dealer in Duluth, Minn., where he joined a brokerage firm of which he became a partner. The Barnes-Ames Company acquired world-wide interests in wheat. Barnes served with the U.S. Food Administration from 1917 to 1919 and was U.S. wheat director in 1919 and 1920, sending large shipments of grain reserves to European countries devastated by World War I.

Barnes was president of the U.S. Chamber of Commerce from 1921 to 1924 and chairman of the board from 1929 to 1931. He was a champion of private enterprise against government controls. He died in Duluth on April 17, 1959.

BARNES, bärnz, **Margaret Ayer** (1886–1967), American novelist. Born *Margaret Ayer* in Chicago on April 8, 1886, she graduated from Bryn Mawr College in 1907, and in 1910 married Cecil Barnes, a Chicago lawyer. She died in Cambridge, Mass., on Oct. 25, 1967.

Her writing career began in 1928 with the publication of *Prevailing Winds*, a collection of short stories. In 1930 she wrote the Pulitzer Prize novel *Years of Grace*, which traced the life of a Chicago matron from the "era of respectability" before World War I into the jazz age. She also wrote the two novels *Edna, His Wife* (1935) and *Wisdom's Gate* (1938), and was co-author, with Edward Sheldon, of the plays *Jennie* (1929) and *Dishonored Lady* (1930).

BARNES, bärnz, **Robert** (1495–1540), English martyr, who was among the first Roman Catholics in Britain converted to Lutheranism. Born at Lynn, Norfolk, he joined the Austin friars at Cambridge and studied at Louvain in Belgium. Under the influence of Thomas Bilney he became a member of the proto-Protestant "modernists" of Cambridge who met to discuss Luther's views. In 1526, after preaching a scathing attack on the worldliness of the clergy, he was examined by Cardinal Wolsey. Threatened with burning, Barnes recanted his Lutheran beliefs. He was put under house arrest but in 1528 escaped to Wittenberg where he lodged with Martin Luther. When Henry VIII found that he needed Protestant assistance in his dispute with the papacy, the king recalled Barnes to England in 1531. In 1539, Barnes acted as negotiator for the king's disastrous marriage to Anne of Cleves. The fall of Henry's minister, Thomas Cromwell, in 1540 and the concurrent Catholic reaction led to Barnes' condemnation as a relapsed heretic by an act of attainder. Without benefit of a trial, he was burned at the stake at Smithfield on July 30, 1540.

BARNES, bärnz, **William** (1801?–1886), English philologist and poet, who wrote dialect verse that places him among the best of the English pastoral poets. The son of a farmer, he was born at Rushay, Dorsetshire, and was baptized on March 20, 1801. He became a schoolmaster and in 1835 established his own school at Dorchester. In 1847 he took religious orders and in 1862 became rector of Winterborne Came, where he died on Oct. 7, 1886.

Barnes' poetry, found in *Poems of Rural Life in the Dorset Dialect* (collected edition, 1879) and *Poems of Rural Life in Common English* (1868), avoids the stylistic mannerism of Robert Burns in favor of simple praise of rustic life.

As a philologist, Barnes attempted to purify the English language of words derived from Latin roots. He published *Outline of English Speech-Craft* (1878) and *A Grammar and Glossary of the Dorset Dialect* (1864).

BARNES FOUNDATION, bärnz, an art school and museum located in Merion, Pa. It was established in 1922 by Dr. Albert C. Barnes (q.v.) to house his multimillion-dollar art collection, and to provide free instruction in art appreciation to deserving students. The foundation's collection is especially noted for its early modern paintings, including 200 works by Renoir, 100 by Cézanne, 75 by Matisse, and 35 by Picasso. The foundation also possesses a number of works of the old masters, and a fine collection of primitive art.

The museum of the Barnes Foundation was closed to the public during Dr. Barnes' lifetime. After his death in 1951, the foundation's trustees became involved in litigation over whether to open the collection to the public. At the end of 1960, an agreement was reached with the attorney general of Pennsylvania to permit public visiting on a restricted basis.

BARNESVILLE, bärnz'vil, a city in Georgia, is the seat of Lamar County. It is situated 30 miles (48 km) northwest of Macon. Its chief industries are cotton milling, pecan processing, and furniture making. Gordon Military College, a two-year junior college with an advanced ROTC program, is located here. Gideon Barnes founded the community in 1826. Barnesville has a mayor and council form of government. Population: 4,935.

BARNET, bär'net, is a borough of Greater London, England, 12 miles (19 km) north of the center of London. It is principally a residential section. The borough includes the former urban district of Barnet, which was in Hertfordshire until the political reorganization of Greater London by an act of Parliament in 1963.

The Battle of Barnet, a decisive engagement in the Wars of the Roses, was fought in this area on April 14, 1471. The Yorkist army of King Edward IV defeated the Lancastrian forces and killed Richard Neville, earl of Warwick. An obelisk marks the spot where he fell. Population: (1964) 318,000.

BARNETT, bär′net, **John** (1802–1890), English singer and composer, who wrote the first modern English opera, *Mountain Sylph*. He was born in Bedford on July 15, 1802, and began his career as a singer. He later composed many songs, collected in *Lyrical Illustrations of the Modern Poets* (1834). He also taught singing at Cheltenham and published several books, including *Systems and Singing Masters* (1842) and *School for the Voice* (1844).

Mountain Sylph was first produced in London in 1834. Barnett's later operas include *Fair Rosamond* (1837) and *Farinelli* (1839). He died near Cheltenham on April 16 or 17, 1890.

John Francis Barnett (1837–1916), his nephew, was a pianist and composer, whose best-known work is the oratorio *The Raising of Lazarus*, first produced at Hereford in 1876. He was born in London on Oct. 16, 1837, and died there on Nov. 24, 1916. He wrote many choral cantatas, including *The Ancient Mariner* (1867) and *Eve of St. Agnes* (1913).

BARNETT, bär′net, **Samuel Augustus** (1844–1913), English clergyman and social reformer. He was born at Bristol, England, on Feb. 8, 1844, and was educated at Oxford University. In 1867 he became curate of St. Mary's, London, and in 1873 vicar of St. Jude's, Whitechapel, in the slums of East London. He and his wife, whom he married in 1873, devoted their lives to improving life in the poor sections of the city.

Besides writing on slum clearance and on pension systems, and raising funds to provide country holidays for children, Barnett began art exhibitions in 1881. These resulted in the building of Whitechapel Art Gallery. His most significant achievement was in the direction of reformed and improved education and in bringing university men to the cities to live and work there for urban improvement. As a result of this "university settlement" plan, Toynbee Hall was founded in 1884, with Barnett as its first warden. He was canon and subdean of Westminster from 1906 until his death at Hove, Sussex, on June 17, 1913.

His most important writings are *Practicable Socialism* (1888), *Religion and Progress* (1907), *Religion and Politics* (1911), *Worship and Work* (1913), and *Vision and Service* (1917).

Henrietta Octavia Weston Barnett (1851–1936), his wife, shared in her husband's many activities and collaborated in his writings. In 1903 she formed the Hampstead Garden Suburb Trust, a pioneer garden housing project, with homes for members of every income group. Mrs. Barnett wrote her husband's biography, *Canon Barnett* (1918).

BARNEY, bär′nē, **Joshua** (1759–1818), American naval officer. He was born in Baltimore, Md., on July 6, 1759. He went to sea in 1771 and, after the outbreak of the American Revolution, distinguished himself during the capture of New Providence in the Bahamas. Later, while serving aboard armed sloops and armed merchantmen, Barney was captured three times. Twice he was exchanged; the third time he escaped from Mill Prison near Plymouth, England, and made his way to France in 1781. In April 1782, aboard the *Hyder-Ally*, he captured the British ship *General Monk* off Cape May, N.J.

Because the American navy had been disbanded at the end of the war, Barney went to France in 1794 and later served in the French navy (1796–1802) as captain and *chef de division* (commodore). Upon the outbreak of the War of 1812, he owned and commanded privateers until July 1814, when he was called to assist in the defense of Washington, D.C. His force of 500 sailors, supporting the American militia at Bladensburg, Md., in the engagement of August 24 which preceded the burning of the capital, repulsed two British attacks and was the last unit to fall back. Barney was wounded and captured. He died in Pittsburgh, Pa., on Dec. 1, 1818.

BARNFIELD, bärn′fēld, **Richard** (1574–1627), English poet. He was born in Norbury, Shropshire, and was educated at Brasenose College, Oxford. His lyrics *As It Fell Upon a Day* and *If Music and Sweet Poetry Agree* were included in the *Passionate Pilgrim* (1599), and for that reason were long attributed to Shakespeare. (See PASSIONATE PILGRIM.) Besides these lyrics, Barnfield's work includes *The Affectionate Shepherd* (1594), *Cynthia, with Certain Sonnets* (1595), and *The Encomion of Lady Pecunia* (1598).

BARNHART, bärn′härt, **Clarence Lewis** (1900–), American lexicographer and editor. He was born near Plattsburg, Mo., on Dec. 30, 1900. After briefly attending Transylvania College in Lexington, Ky., he went to the University of Chicago, where he received the bachelor of philosophy degree in 1930 and pursued graduate study in philology between 1934 and 1937.

While still an undergraduate he began working for the Chicago publishing firm of Scott, Foresman and Company, where he met the educational psychologist Edward L. Thorndike. The association between the two men produced several notable school dictionaries, including the *Thorndike Century Junior Dictionary* (1935) and the *Thorndike Century Senior Dictionary* (1941). Barnhart's later projects included editing the *American College Dictionary* (1947), the *Thorndike-Barnhart Comprehensive Desk Dictionary* (1951), and the *New Century Cyclopedia of Names* (1954).

BARNSTABLE, bärn′stə-bəl, a town in southeastern Massachusetts, on Cape Cod, about 70 miles (103 km) southeast of Boston. It is the seat of Barnstable County. The town includes the villages of Cummaquid and West Barnstable, on the north shore of Cape Cod; and Hyannis, Hyannis Port, Craigville, Centerville, Osterville, Wianno, Oyster Harbors, Marstons Mills, and Cotuit, on the south shore.

Industries include fishing, oyster culture, and cranberry raising and canning. There is a commercial airport at Hyannis. Among noteworthy old buildings in Barnstable is the Sturgis Library, part of which was built by John Lothropp, who was the town's first minister from 1639 to 1653. President John F. Kennedy had a summer home at Hyannis Port. The town attracts many summer visitors.

Barnstable was settled in 1637 and incorporated in 1639. By the time of the Revolution it had a prosperous coastal shipping trade, and from 1800 to 1860 vessels from Barnstable voyaged to world ports. Government is by an elected board of selectmen. Population: 19,842.

BARNSTORMING. See AEROBATICS.

BARNUM, bär'nəm, Phineas Taylor

P.T. BARNUM (below), American showman. Poster (left), with Barnum and partner J.A. Bailey, advertises their circus, begun in 1881.

Truly Yours, P.T. Barnum

ELIZABETH STERLING SEELEY, P.T. BARNUM MUSEUM

BARNUM, bär'nəm, **Phineas Taylor** (1810–1891), American showman, who, with Yankee wit, shrewdness, and imagination, transformed the amusement business. He lifted the circus from a rather drab affair peopled with seedy mountebanks to the "Greatest Show on Earth." And he was one of the first entrepreneurs, in or out of show business, to realize the value of publicity.

P.T. Barnum was born in Bethel, Conn., on July 5, 1810. He moved to New York City in 1834, and sold hats and caps on commission, ran a boardinghouse, and worked in a grocery store. In the latter job, opportunity, in the person of ancient Joice Heth, knocked at his door. Joice Heth was a Negro woman believed to be 161 years old and said to have been George Washington's nurse. Taken in by the tale, the 25-year-old Barnum quit the grocery and, with savings and borrowed money, purchased the old woman and embarked on a career that was to make him the world's greatest showman.

Barnum's early years in show business were devoted to freaks and oddities more bizarre than authentic. After Joice Heth, who was later exposed as a fraud, came the Feejee Mermaid, which was a female monkey torso joined to a large stuffed fish tail, and other fakes. Subsequently he exploited more legitimate oddities such as midgets, a bearded lady, a tattooed man, and Chang and Eng, the Siamese twins. To house and exploit his odd characters, Barnum acquired a run-down museum at Broadway and Ann Street, New York City, in 1841. This building became Barnum's American Museum, one of New York's leading centers of entertainment.

Tom Thumb. In 1842, Barnum discovered a 5-year-old midget named Charles Stratton (q.v.) in Bridgeport, Conn. Barnum took him to New York, taught him to dance, sing, and tell topical jokes, outfitted him with several uniforms, and introduced him to the world as General Tom Thumb. The sprightly midget was an instant success. Barnum exhibited him in New England and as far south as Washington, D.C.

In 1844, Barnum took his young star to England, where he became the darling of the British aristocracy and a sensation in the London press. By royal invitation Barnum and his small protégé called at Buckingham Palace. There, before Queen Victoria, Tom Thumb danced a hornpipe and gave his imitation of Napoleon.

Jenny Lind. From the profits of Tom Thumb's successful tours of Europe and the United States, Barnum built Iranistan, a $150,000 Oriental palace, at Bridgeport. He sent an agent to Europe to sign for an American tour the newest musical sensation, Jenny Lind, the "Swedish Nightingale." The cautious soprano required the showman to deposit $187,500 in a London bank to guarantee the contract, a condition that forced Barnum to mortgage Iranistan, the museum, and other property, and to borrow from his friends.

Barnum's inspired promotion and shrewd management (and Jenny Lind's golden voice) made the tour a triumphant success. She opened at Castle Garden in New York City on Sept. 11, 1850, and gave 95 concerts in 19 cities. In addition to critical acclaim, the tour reaped gross receipts of $712,161.34, of which Barnum's share, before expenses, was $535,486.25.

Bankruptcy and Recovery. In 1855, Barnum invested heavily in a Connecticut clock company. The company soon failed, and Barnum, committed for more than $500,000, went bankrupt. At 46, ridiculed in the press for his foolhardy business venture and deeply in debt, Barnum started afresh. With Tom Thumb and a newly discovered child prodigy, 9-year-old Cordelia Howard, who played Little Eva in the Howard family production of *Uncle Tom's Cabin*, he sailed for England early in 1857. Again the British gave the showman and his troupe a warm welcome. They toured the British Isles and Europe with such success that Barnum was able to pay back thousands of dollars of his debt.

New Ventures. Barnum discovered that he had become a celebrity in his own right and that people were as eager to see him as to gape at his freaks. To capitalize on this interest he took to the lecture platform. Occasionally, in earlier years, he had talked before church groups on temperance and morality. For his London debut in 1858 he chose as his topic *The Art of Money-Getting*. Thousands flocked to hear him, and a London publisher offered him $6,000 for the right to print his lecture as a booklet.

Returning to the United States, his burden of debt reduced, Barnum repurchased and refurbished his American Museum, recovered much of his East Bridgeport property, lectured, and planned new enterprises. He exhibited white whales captured off Nova Scotia, a hippopotamus, a band of Indian chiefs, and two new midgets, Commodore Nutt and Lavinia Warren. The romance of dainty Lavinia and Tom Thumb, and their marriage on Feb. 10, 1863, caused a sensation that brought thousands of people to the museum. Barnum offered the undersized couple $15,000 if they would postpone their wedding one month so that he might more fully exploit the romance, but the midgets refused, saying, "No, not for $50,000!"

The Circus. In 1870, Barnum joined William C. Coup, an experienced circus manager, in organizing a great traveling show—museum, menagerie, caravan, and hippodrome, plus Dan Costello's circus of acrobats, tightrope walkers, and clowns. After opening in Brooklyn on April 10, 1871, the "Great Travelling World's Fair" went on the road with 500 men, 200 horses, and a caravan of floats and wagons. Barnum plastered the countryside with posters. The culminating phase of the great showman's career had begun.

When Barnum lent his name to another circus enterprise, he and Costello quarreled, and the partnership ended. Then, in 1881, Barnum joined forces with the International Allied Shows, whose managerial genius was James Anthony Bailey (q.v.). Together they created "The Barnum and Bailey Greatest Show on Earth."

The crowning achievement of the new partnership was the acquisition from the London Zoo of Jumbo, reputed to be the world's largest elephant. After the deal had been closed, Queen Victoria, the prince of Wales, John Ruskin, and the *Times* of London all demanded that the contract be broken. The London press stormed and protested as Jumbo was led to the docks to be shipped to the United States. By the time he joined the circus in 1882, Jumbo was an international *cause célèbre*. Barnum estimated that the big elephant, which had cost $30,000 to purchase and transport to the United States, brought $336,000 into the box office in six weeks.

Other Activities. Barnum was elected to the Connecticut legislature in 1865 and in his one term led a successful fight against the railroad lobby. In 1875–1876 he served as mayor of Bridgeport. Barnum's first wife died in 1873, and in 1874 he married an English girl 40 years his junior. He died in Bridgeport on April 7, 1891.
EMMET CROZIER, *Author of "Yankee Reporters"*

Further Reading: Barnum, Phineas T., *Struggles and Triumphs, or the Life of P.T. Barnum Written by Himself* (New York 1855); Root, Harvey W., *The Unknown Barnum* (New York 1927); Wallace, Irving, *The Fabulous Showman* (New York 1959); Werner, Morris, *Barnum* (New York 1923).

BAROCCI, bä-rôt'chē, **Federigo** (1528?–1612), Italian painter, whose mature work foreshadowed the baroque style. His name is sometimes spelled *Baroccio.* He was born in Urbino, where he studied with Battista Franco. About 1548 he visited Rome and came under the influence of Raphael, Correggio, and other masters. He spent most of his life in Urbino, and many of his works, including a *St. Sebastian* (1557) in the cathedral, are located there. After returning to Rome in 1560, he worked on a series of frescoes (1561–1563) for the casino of Pope Pius IV in the Vatican gardens. His health failed and, convinced that he had been poisoned by jealous rivals, he went back to Urbino, where he died.

Among Barocci's major works are the *Madonna del Popolo* (1579, Uffizi Gallery, Florence); *The Burning of Troy* (1598, Borghese Gallery, Rome); *The Crucifixion* (1595, cathedral at Genoa); *The Last Supper* (1592–99, Santa Maria sopra Minerva, Rome); and *The Visitation* and *The Presentation* (1594, Chiesa Nuova, Rome). Barocci was also a portraitist and engraver.

BARODA, bə-rōd′ə, is a city in Gujarat state, India, and was the capital of the former princely state of Baroda. It is situated on the Viswamitri River between Bombay and Ahmadabad. Baroda is a well-planned city with wide thoroughfares and handsome public buildings and parks. A palace dating back to 1721 still stands in the city. The Museum and Picture Gallery, established in 1894, contains a large selection of Indian medieval paintings and sculptures. Baroda's educational facilities include a university (founded in 1949) and a medical college.

Located in a fertile agricultural region, the city is an important marketing center for cotton, tobacco, and millet. It has large cotton mills and manufactures hand-loomed cloth interwoven with silver. It also produces chemicals, woolens, and machinery. Baroda is also an important rail center.

The princely state of Baroda, with its capital at the city of Baroda, was established upon the breaking up of the Mughul (Mogul) empire in the 18th century. The state signed a treaty of alliance with the British in 1805 and was brought under the control of Britain in 1817. Sayaji Rao III, ruler of Baroda from 1875 to 1939, was one of India's most enlightened rulers. He gave the state an enviable reputation for progressive administration and educational advancement. Baroda became part of the Indian Union on Aug. 15, 1947, was merged with Bombay state the following year, and in 1960 was made part of the newly formed state of Gujarat. Population: (1961) 295,144.

BAROJA Y NESSI, bä-rô′hä ē nes′sē, **Pío** (1872–1956), Spanish novelist, who was a leading writer in the literary renaissance in Spain during the early decades of the 20th century. He was born in the Basque town of San Sebastián on Dec. 28, 1872. He received a medical degree in Madrid in 1893 and practiced for a few years in the Basque provinces. In 1900, after returning to Madrid, he published a collection of literary sketches, *Vidas sombrías,* and thereafter devoted himself entirely to writing. He was elected to the Spanish Academy in 1935. In 1936, at the outbreak of the Spanish Civil War, he fled to France, where he lived for a number of years. He published his multivolume memoirs, beginning in 1944, under the title *Desde la última vuelta del camino: El escritor según los críticos.* He died in Madrid on Oct. 30, 1956.

Baroja's work, though vigorous and peppered with a wry humor, is strongly pessimistic in tone. His heroes are generally underdogs—vagabonds or picaresque rogues—who rebel against convention but ultimately come up against the fact of their own lack of willpower and purpose. Baroja's plots, although loosely constructed, are filled with action. His language, sparse and simple, has an underlying lyrical strain that becomes particularly apparent in his descriptions of nature.

Baroja's best works are either those that describe the underworld of Madrid, such as the trilogy *La lucha por la vida* (1904; Eng. tr., *The Struggle for Existence,* 1922–24), or those that describe Basque life, such as the trilogy *Tierra vasca* (1900–09). His most ambitious undertaking was the 22-novel cycle *Memorias de un hombre de acción* (1913–35), which describes the life of a political adventurer of 19th century Spain.

BAROMETER

BAROMETER, bə-rom′ə-tər, an instrument for measuring the pressure of the atmosphere. Since atmospheric pressure decreases with altitude above sea level, a barometer can also be used to measure altitude. Barometers are of two general types: *mercury* and *aneroid*. In the mercury barometer, pressure is measured by the height of a column of mercury supported by the atmosphere, whereas in the aneroid the pressure is measured by a metallic diaphragm.

Mercury Barometer. The history of the mercury barometer involves many scientists and experimenters. The Italian mathematician Evangelista Torricelli demonstrated the principle of the barometer in 1643. A few years later Blaise Pascal in France contributed confirming experiments, and Florin Périer carried a barometer up a mountain to demonstrate the decrease of pressure with altitude. Other contributors were René Descartes and Robert Boyle. The word "barometer" was first used by Boyle in about 1663.

If a glass tube about 3 feet (1 meter) long with one end closed is filled with mercury and then inverted in a container of mercury without allowing air to enter the tube, a simple mercury barometer is produced. The weight of the atmosphere pressing down on the open surface of the mercury in the container balances the weight of the mercury column in the tube. If the air pressure increases, the level of the mercury in the container will drop slightly while the level in the tube will rise appreciably.

There are two types of mercury barometers: fixed cistern and adjustable cistern. In the former the container, or cistern, is fixed in relation to the glass tube. The mercury level in the cistern rises and falls slightly with changing atmospheric pressure, so that the height of the column in the tube is measured from a changing reference point in the cistern. In the adjustable cistern type, the mercury level in the cistern is adjusted by varying the volume of the cistern. As a result, measurement of the height of the column in the tube always starts from a constant reference point built into the top of the cistern.

The mercury column is about 30 inches (76

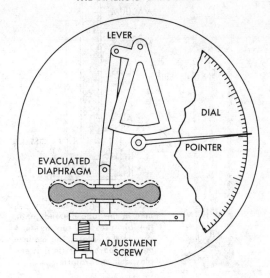

THE ANEROID BAROMETER

An aneroid (liquidless) barometer senses air pressure with an evacuated diaphragm, but its readings are shown (*below*) in inches or centimeters of mercury.

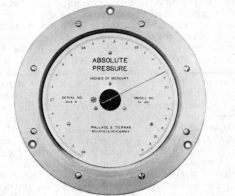

WALLACE & TIERNAN INC.

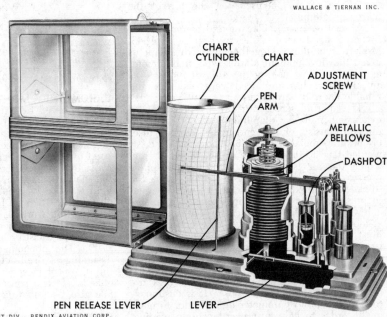

THE BAROGRAPH

Barographs record barometric readings and are commonly of aneroid design. The instrument at right has a metallic bellows as its evacuated diaphragm. The bellows is sufficiently powerful to move a pen that records air pressure changes on a chart affixed to a rotating cylinder.

FRIEZ INSTRUMENT DIV., BENDIX AVIATION CORP.

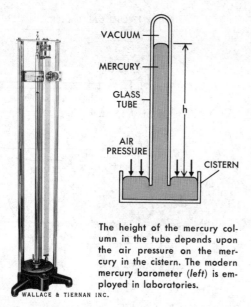

VACUUM

MERCURY

GLASS
TUBE

h

AIR
PRESSURE

CISTERN

The height of the mercury column in the tube depends upon
the air pressure on the mercury in the cistern. The modern
mercury barometer (left) is employed in laboratories.

WALLACE & TIERNAN INC.

cm) high at sea level, making for a usable-sized instrument. A water barometer would be about 34 feet (102 meters) high. The low vapor pressure of mercury is also important, since any residual vapor in the vacuum above the liquid in the tube detracts from the accuracy of measurement. Since the density of mercury varies with temperature, and the materials used in the barometer's structure expand and contract with temperature, corrections must be made for variations from the temperature at which the barometer has been standardized. A mercury barometer has a thermometer mounted on it for this purpose. The barometer is also equipped with a vernier scale to facilitate accurate reading. It is usually housed in a protective case, and must hang vertically. Further refinements for precise work involve correcting the readings for the local value of gravity, which varies slightly with both latitude and altitude, and correcting for the convex shape of the meniscus on the top of the mercury column.

Aneroid Barometer. The aneroid barometer was invented by Lucien Vidie in France in 1843. Modern metallurgy, together with the impetus given the development of this type of barometer as a result of its use by the aircraft industry as an altimeter, has produced very accurate and reliable aneroid barometers.

The aneroid senses pressure by means of an evacuated metallic diaphragm. A typical diaphragm consists of two corrugated cupped discs of flexible metal. The discs are soldered or welded face to face to form a thin chamber from which the air is removed. As the atmosphere presses on the exterior of the diaphragm, the thickness of the diaphragm changes with changes in pressure. The variation in thickness is small—a few thousandths of an inch, or centimeter, for a moderate pressure change—and consequently must be amplified by a lever mechanism to be read easily. A hairspring is mounted on the pointer shaft (see diagram) to eliminate backlash from the mechanism, which must be as friction-free as possible. Jeweled bearings are often employed for the purpose. It is customary to tap an aneroid barometer lightly prior to reading in order to help ensure an accurate reading.

Aneroid barometers vary in size from about 2 to 8 inches (5–20 cm) in diameter, and are very portable. They range widely in quality, from simple units for amateur use to highly precise instruments for professional work.

Three major sources of errors in aneroid barometers are temperature, position, and drift. Temperature affects the elastic properties of metals and the lengths of links and levers. Temperature compensation is obtained by using various combinations of special alloys having suitable thermal properties, and by leaving a small amount of air inside the diaphragm. To prevent position errors, an aneroid barometer must always be used in one position, or else have a well-balanced mechanism. Elastic metals under constant pressure tend to change with age, with the result that the indication of the aneroid barometer may gradually shift from its correct value. Consequently, the barometer should be checked periodically in order to maintain accuracy.

Barograph. A barograph is a recording barometer. Barographs using a mercury column have been developed, but barographs commonly employ the aneroid principle, in the form of a metallic bellows or a stack of diaphragms. The basic mechanism is larger than that of the aneroid barometer, and is sufficiently powerful to operate a pen. The pen draws a line indicating pressure on a chart, which is driven by a clock mechanism usually located in the chart cylinder.

The barograph thus furnishes a permanent record in the form of a graph of pressure plotted against time. This makes it easy to evaluate the trend of the pressure changes, which is often of great significance. A barograph is sensitive to being jarred, and a liquid-filled device called a dashpot is frequently employed to prevent oscillations of the pen from extraneous causes.

Pressure Units. The expression of atmospheric pressure in inches or centimeters of mercury developed naturally from the mercury barometer and is still in common use. The *millibar*, a true unit of pressure, is employed in scientific work. Standard pressure at sea level is 29.92 inches (76 cm) of mercury, or 1,013.2 millibars.

L.E. Wood, *The Bendix Corporation*

Further Reading: Middleton, W.E. Knowles, *The History of the Barometer* (Baltimore 1964); Middleton, W.E. Knowles, and Spilhaus, Athelstan F., *Meteorological Instruments* (Toronto 1953); United States Weather Bureau, *The Aneroid Barometer* (Washington 1957); United States Weather Bureau, *Mercury Barometers and Manometers* (Washington 1960).

BAROMETRIC LIGHT, bar-ə-meˈtrik līt, is the light observed in a tube containing mercury and a rarefied gas when the tube is agitated. The glow is produced by an electric discharge through the gas, a difference in electric charge having been built up between the mercury and the tube walls by the agitation of the tube. The color of the glow depends on the nature of the gas. The light is called barometric light because it was first observed in 1675 by Jean Picard, a French astronomer, while working with a mercury barometer. It was further studied by Francis Hauksbee, an English physicist, who reported on his work in 1709. The phenomenon has been used in the designing of "self-acting" Geissler tubes. These tubes, useful in spectroscopy, ordinarily have an outside electric source for producing discharge. See also GEISSLER TUBES.

BAROMETZ. See CIBOTIUM.

BARON, bȧ rôɴ', **Michel** (1653–1729), French actor, who played leading roles in the newly formed Comédie-Française. He was born *Michel Boyron,* in Paris, on Oct. 8, 1653. Baron made his debut in Molière's company in 1670. Three years later he joined the troupe of the Hôtel de Bourgogne, which merged with Molière's company in 1680 to form the Comédie-Française. Through his work in the Comédie-Française, Baron became noted as both a farceur and a tragedian. At the height of his career, in 1691, he retired for no apparent reason. Thereafter he performed only occasionally at the royal court and at private presentations, until 1720, when he rejoined the Comédie-Française as its leading actor. He died in Paris on Dec. 3, 1729.

BARON, bar'ən, is the lowest rank in the British peerage. The title is acquired by royal decree or inheritance. The title is also carried elsewhere in Europe by persons dignified by past and surviving monarchies and, in the case of France, by the republican government.

In the feudal system of the Middle Ages, baron was the term applied to any immediate tenant by his superior. Since some barons were vassals of kings and greater lords and others were vassals of lesser lords, they were early divided into greater barons and lesser barons.

The title, as a mark of special rank, was introduced into England by William the Conqueror to signify an immediate vassal of the crown, who had a seat and a vote in the royal court tribunals and, subsequently, in the House of Peers. In the early Anglo-Norman period, barons emerged as the second rank of nobility, inferior only to earls. Later, dukes, marquises, and viscounts were created and set above the barons.

A baron of the United Kingdom has the title of "right honorable lord" and should be addressed as "my lord" or "your lordship." In letters, a baron is always addressed as "Lord," while other peers are called by their actual titles. A baron's wife also is entitled to be called "right honorable" and may be addressed as "madam" or "your ladyship."

In old records the citizens of London and members of the House of Commons elected by the Cinque Ports were called barons, but the title was honorary and not hereditary. Until the passage of the Judicial Act of 1873, certain judges in England and Ireland also were called barons.

In Germany, the ancient barons of the Holy Roman Empire were the immediate vassals of the emperor and, therefore, very important. These ancient feudal lords eventually were dignified with ranks of count or prince, and the title of baron became synonymous with *Freiherr,* a comparatively inferior rank of the nobility.

BARONET, bar'ə-nət, is the lowest hereditary titled order in Britain. Baronets, unlike barons, are commoners. The order was instituted by James I on May 22, 1611. A baronet ranks below a baron but has precedence over all knights except knights of the garter.

Like knights, baronets are addressed by having Sir (or Lady) prefixed to their given names. Baronets are created by letters patent under the great seal, and the honor is generally conferred to the grantee and his legitimate male heirs, though sometimes it is transferred to a collateral line and even to female heirs.

The order was founded nominally to assist in settling Englishmen and Scots in Ulster. The primary reason for creating the order was to raise money for the king: each baronet, on receiving the honor, was obliged to pay into the treasury a sum of more than £1,000. The first person to be created baronet was Sir Nicholas Bacon of Redgrave, whose successors in the title hold the rank of premier baronet of England.

In 1622 there were 200 baronets in England, this being the number to which the order was originally limited. Meanwhile, in 1619, James created a baronetage of Ireland with a prescribed limit of 100 titles. Qualifications were similar to those for English baronetcies. Charles I set up an order of baronets of Scotland and Nova Scotia in 1625 in accordance with the intention of his father, James I. Candidates were required to invest in land in Nova Scotia. The number was fixed at 150, and in ten years 107 were created. The creation of new Scottish and English titles ceased in 1707, after the Act of Union; thereafter baronets of Great Britain were created. Following the union of Great Britain and Ireland in 1801, no new baronets other than baronets of the United Kingdom were created.

BARONIUS, bə-rō'nē-əs, **Caesar** (1538–1607), Italian historian and cardinal who is called the "father of ecclesiastical history." Born at Sora (Latium) on Oct. 31, 1538, *Cesare Baronio* (he later Latinized his name) studied law at Naples and, after 1557, at Rome. There he met St. Philip Neri, whose order he joined in 1564. At St. Philip's suggestion Baronius undertook the immense project of compiling a history of the church (*Annales ecclesiastici,* 1588–1607) to refute the Protestant *Magdeburg Centuries,* which disputed the soundness of Roman Catholic doctrine. In 1586 he published a new chronicle of martyrs (*Martyrologium Romanum*).

Baronius was named cardinal in 1596, and in 1597 he was appointed Vatican librarian by Pope Clement VIII. After Clement's death Baronius was nearly elected pope but failed of election because of Spanish opposition. He had angered the Spaniards by contesting their claim to Sicily.

After Baronius' death at Rome on June 30, 1607, his *Annals* were continued by others. Because of Baronius' deficiency in Greek and Hebrew, his work became a target for attacks by scholars like Isaac Casaubon. It remains nonetheless a pioneering work in ecclesiastical history.

BARONS' WAR, bar'ənz, the name given to the English civil war of 1263–1267. The war was provoked by the costly and inept rule of King Henry III. In 1258 a powerful group of disenchanted barons forced Henry to accept the Provisions of Oxford, a document providing for baronial control of the king's power. Henry unilaterally annulled the Provisions in 1261, and in 1263 hostilities began between the barons, led by Simon de Montfort (q.v.), and the royalists. Simon's forces swept the south of England in the summer of 1263, captured the king, and ruled most of England for the next two years. Opposition from the papacy and exiles in France, as well as some serious defections among his supporters, led to Simon's defeat and death at the Battle of Evesham on Aug. 4, 1265. Without Simon the baronial faction disintegrated. The dispute was settled tentatively in the Dictum of Kenilworth (1266) and finally in the Statute of Marlborough (1267).

BAROQUE ART AND ARCHITECTURE, bə-rōk', is one of the major historical developments in Western art. Like other great styles, the baroque first found expression in architecture and spread from there to painting and sculpture and eventually even to music. It flourished from the latter half of the 16th century to the beginning of the 18th century, with its high-water mark probably being the decade from 1630 to 1640. In the past, some interpreters, especially in England and France, were inclined to consider the baroque as a mere perversion of the Renaissance style. This view, however, is now outdated, and in recent years there has been a widespread revival of interest in the baroque.

Characteristics and Origin. The richness and variety of baroque forms make it difficult to characterize the style. All artistic styles contain certain contradictions, but the baroque is particularly full of them. The word "baroque," of uncertain origin, was first used in the 17th century as a term of abuse to describe art that did not meet the "classical" rational standards. Some scholars believe the term "baroque" is derived from the Portuguese *barroco* (an irregularly shaped pearl), and indeed the essence of the baroque style is best described in a single word: irregular.

The baroque, aptly called the art of the impossible, is characterized by movement. To some critics its main features are its ebullience, its ornateness, its somber pomp; to others, its dynamic character, its predilection for curves, its avoidance of clear outline and distinct contrast, its preoccupation with expressing states of mind, feelings, moods. The last characteristic—a concern with the inner life—caused distinctive national and regional differences in the forms of the baroque, of which the Italian, Spanish, French, German, and Austrian are particularly noteworthy.

All baroque art was polarized around a set of feelings that had a common field of movement, intensity, tension, and force. Hence, the baroque found its richest expression in the castle and the opera, two artistic forms in which many arts have to be worked into a harmonious whole.

Historically, the baroque style began with the Jesuit mother church, Il Gesù, in Rome, designed by Giacomo da Vignola in 1568. But this remarkable creation might have remained an isolated instance had it not expressed some generally felt need of the time. Some have argued that the baroque was the style of the Catholic Counter Reformation, others that it was related to monarchical absolutism. But baroque works were created where neither of these factors existed, indicating that a more general kind of feeling must have been the basis of the style. If it is true, as one interpreter has put it, that "baroque means the unthinkable," then we can understand why baroque artists sought to accomplish the impossible task of expressing the contradictory forces and feelings of the time—materialism and spiritualism, radical naturalism and extreme formalism, the most terrifying realism and the most precious illusionism. An increasing excitement over the potentialities of man, engendered by the rise of modern science and the emergence of the modern state, gripped the artist in the baroque age. The power of man, as well as his impotence, were more intensely felt than ever before. Thomas Hobbes, the English philosopher, made what may be the age's most revealing statement: "So that in the first place, I put for a general inclination of all mankind, a perpetuall and restlesse desire of Power, after Power, that ceaseth only in Death."

The baroque was one of the most productive periods in the arts, literature, and music. The sense of limitless power, checked by an overwhelming sense of cosmic relationships, produced a style that startles by its contrasts yet exhibits a singular and distinctive character.

Baroque Architecture and Sculpture. Rome, with Il Gesù, was the birthplace of baroque architecture. The beginning of the style also can be seen in some of the late work of Michelangelo. Il Gesù, a curious combination of medieval and Renaissance features, combines the longitudinal Gothic tradition with an emphasis on the central portion of the building that is characteristic of the Renaissance. The free-floating effect of the cupola, expressive of a longing for the infinite, has been described as a "movement of physical nature toward spiritual goals." Il Gesù heralded the baroque feeling for the fluidity of space, a feeling that ultimately found expression in such baroque features as richly ornamented façades, magnificently sweeping staircases, and ornament-

BAROQUE STYLE began with Il Gesù, the Jesuit mother church in Rome, designed by Giacomo da Vignola in 1568.

al gardens that, unlike the center-related Renaissance gardens, served as the setting and a foreground for a distant view from the great castles built during the period.

Baroque architecture and sculpture go hand in hand. Many artists, such as Lorenzo Bernini, were masters of both. The dynamic effects of baroque architecture were aided by the fullest possible use of decorative sculptural detail. At the same time, the architecture, whether of a church or a castle, became ever more crucial to the plastic creations of sculpture. As baroque art spread and unfolded, its full flowering after 1600 studded Europe with castles, churches, bridges, fountains, theaters, villas, statues, and a vast variety of furniture and bric-a-brac that embellished the homes of the aristocracy and of wealthy merchants and businessmen. Rome, Vienna, Munich, Madrid, Warsaw, and Prague are among the great showplaces of the baroque style. The finest work belongs largely to the "high baroque," from 1600 to 1660.

Among the greatest and most fascinating figures of the baroque period was Lorenzo Bernini, the greatest Italian architect and sculptor after Michelangelo. He was born in 1598 and died in 1680, having produced magnificent buildings and art works in unbelievable profusion. He was the daring genius who fully grasped and molded the spirit of his age. Next to him, Francesco Borromini (1599–1667) and Guarino Guarini (1624–1683) were preeminent among Italians.

Among the French, François Mansart (1598–1666) maintained strongly classicist reservations in the face of the baroque movement. Claude Perrault (1613–1688) was outstanding as the builder of the Louvre; his design won over Bernini's more forcefully baroque proposal.

Spain produced no architect equal in distinction to these, although the Escorial (1563–1584), designed by Juan de Toledo and Juan de Herrera, is a powerful monument of the early baroque. More important than the architects of Spain proper were those of the Low Countries, especially Jacques Franquart (1577–1651) in the Spanish Netherlands and Jacob van Campen

(1595–1657) and Pieter Post (1600–1669) in the independent Netherlands. From these centers and from Italy a number of minor architects went to the many courts of Germany, Austria, and the eastern monarchies, especially Poland and Russia. In these countries during the early 18th century, a second period of baroque architecture, tending toward rococo forms, produced some of the finest baroque churches and castles. The greatest names are Fischer von Erlach (1656–1723), the brothers Asam (Cosmas Damian, 1686–1739, and Egid Quirin, 1692–1750), and Balthasar Neumann (1687–1753). The episcopal palace at Würzburg, the Hofburg and other castles in Vienna, and the churches of Salzburg are among the best-known works of the period. Prague, Krakow, and Warsaw also are studded with magnificent late baroque works.

In England, always somewhat apart from the rest of Europe in its architectural development, the dominant architect of the high baroque was Inigo Jones (1572–1651). Inspired by the great Renaissance artist Andrea Palladio, Jones created a number of masterpieces in the "classicist" tradition, especially the castles at Greenwich and Wilton. Christopher Wren (1632–1723), active in rebuilding London after the fire of 1666, was more directly baroque in style.

Baroque Painting. In painting, the baroque period reveled in the effects of light and shadow, employing many-hued grays, browns, and greens, rather than clear colors. It explored the subtleties of individuality in portraying landscapes and the human face. Among its distinctive traits were the gradual elimination of distinct outlines and the use of quantities of pigment heavy enough to make the brushstrokes visible.

Except for England and Germany, all the great European nations produced marvelous painters during the baroque period. At the beginning we again find the Italians in the lead. Guido Reni (1575–1642), who produced the famous *Aurora*, and Pietro da Cortona (1596–1669), creator of the frescoes in the Palazzo Barberini in Rome, gave us some of the most jubilant baroque pictures.

BAROQUE ORNAMENTATION is exemplified by the ornate staircase of the Residenz (1737–1750) in Würzburg, Germany, by the architect Balthasar Neumann.

Spain produced Diego de Silva y Velázquez (1599–1660), one of the greatest painters of all time. His work was thoroughly baroque, evolving from a relatively rigid style toward a much looser and more dashing treatment. The *Surrender of Breda* (1635) and his many portraits reveal his masterly psychological insight.

The Dutch painter Peter Paul Rubens (1577–1640) was closely allied with the baroque painters of Italy and Spain. He painted with a verve and a sense for the glittering beauty of colored surface that makes him unique in the history of Western painting. Rubens undertook to dissolve the fixed and isolated figures of Renaissance painting. Pathos and sensuality were combined to fill his paintings with dynamism, life, and a kind of cosmic unity in every part.

France also produced a remarkable group of baroque painters, more restrained than the Italians but equally dramatic, especially Nicolas Poussin (1593–1665) and Claude Gellée, called Lorrain (1600–1682). They both spent most of their lives in Rome, but their work displays a typically French refinement. Poussin's efforts were directed toward portraying dramatic scenes of great commotion, such as the *Bacchanal* (after 1630) and the *Rape of the Sabine Women* (1637–1639). Lorrain was the lyrical master of luminous scenes of quiescent mood, the incomparable master of sunsets casting a golden sheen on the waters of quiet harbors. Other artists of the

French classicist baroque were Eustache Le Sueur (1616–1655), Charles Le Brun (1619–1690), and Philippe de Champaigne (1602–1674), whose work appears more academic but is truly baroque in conception.

Baroque Painting in the Netherlands. No other nation in Europe could rival the Netherlands in the rich variety of baroque painting. The incredible welter of brilliant talent produced there was the culmination and fulfillment of baroque painting. Among the outstanding painters were Rembrandt Harmensz van Rijn (1606–1669), Anthony van Dyck (1599–1641), Frans Hals (1580?–1666), Adriaen van Ostade (1610–1685), Jan van Goyen (1596–1656), Meindert Hobbema (1638–1709), Jacob van Ruisdael (1628?–1682), Jan Vermeer (1632–1675), Jan Steen (1626–1679), and Philips Wouverman (1619–1668).

All the baroque painters of the Netherlands are overshadowed, however, by Rembrandt. In his work, baroque art and painting achieved universal significance. Such masterpieces as *The Night Watch* (1641)—sometimes called the greatest baroque painting—and *The Anatomy Lesson of Dr. Tulp* (1632) struck out against all idealizing. With startling realism, Rembrandt depicted the human body and face without regard to age and beauty, eventually achieving a new spirituality by investing all that is human with an inner life. His expressive handling of light and dark and his baroque efforts at unity and universality were unique. Color and light, surface and space were used to render visible the hidden meaning of nature and man. His life became tragic as his willful disregard of all conventions, and his uncompromising insistence on what he saw as the truth, alienated even his most devoted patrons.

His famous *Portrait of an Old Lady* (1639) is completely indifferent to the conventions, seeking only to capture the quintessence of a human being. His numerous self-portraits, of such rich variety and at times of such pathetic sorrow, have been the source of ever-renewed wonder and admiration. A final and perhaps ultimate combination of all Rembrandt's originality was revealed in *The Return of the Prodigal Son* (1668–1669). Rembrandt's intense religious feeling, beautifully conveyed in his sketches and etchings of the life of Christ, was here given its highest expression. In this painting, as in the greatest music of Johann Sebastian Bach, the ultimate spirit of the baroque was achieved.

CARL JOACHIM FRIEDRICH
Author of "The Age of the Baroque"

Bibliography

Bazin, Germain, *Baroque and Rococo Art* (New York 1964).
Burckhardt, Jacob, *Recollections of Rubens* (New York 1950).
Fokker, T.H., *Roman Baroque Art: The History of a Style* (London 1938).
Friedell, Egon, *Baroque and Rococo* (New York 1931).
Friedrich, Carl J., *The Age of the Baroque 1610–1660* (New York 1952).
Friedrich, Carl J., and Blitzer, Charles, *The Age of Power* (Ithaca, N.Y., 1957).
Hempel, Eberhard, *Baroque Art and Architecture in Central Europe* (Baltimore, Md., 1965).
Huyghe, René, ed., *Larousse Encyclopedia of Renaissance and Baroque Art* (New York 1964).
Sitwell, Sacheverell, *Southern Baroque Art* (London 1931).
Sypher, Wylie, *Four Stages in Renaissance Style* (Garden City, N.Y., 1955).
Tapie, Victor L., *The Age of Grandeur* (London 1960).
Willey, Basil, *The Seventeenth Century Background* (London 1934).

BAROQUE MUSIC, bə-rōk', is music of the period beginning about 1600 with the reforms of Claudio Monteverdi and culminating in the 18th century in the works of Johann Sebastian Bach and George Frideric Handel.

Italy. In the Baroque period, Italy, the "cradle of the baroque," was not a nation, so its musical culture should be considered regionally, or locally. In the north, particularly in Florence, monodic music drama began as a belated realization of the Renaissance ideal for restoring ancient Attic music and drama. Inspired by the Greek scholar Girolamo Mei (1519–1594) and led by the lutanist-composer Vincenzo Galilei (about 1520–1591), the Florentine *camerata* abandoned polyphonic traditions for dramatic musical forms conducive to unimpeded verbal communication, accompanied by melodic and harmonic settings.

Claudio Monteverdi (1567–1643), the first great master of this "new music," established its representative style. *Basso continuo* provided the harmonic foundation and *stile rappresentativo* the expressive content for his 16 pioneering works in music drama. Monteverdi continued the practices of both the old and new styles in his church music, and his *Vespers* (1610) also utilizes the multiple chorus techniques of Giovanni Gabrieli (1555–1612) and others in Venice.

The work of Pier Francesco Cavalli (1602–1676) and Pietro (Marc' Antonio) Cesti (1623–1669) led to the Italian high baroque operas of Alessandro Stradella (1642–1682), Alessandro Scarlatti (1660–1725), and Giovanni Pergolesi (1710–1736). The latter's *opera buffa, La serva padrona,* prefigured the achievements of Gluck and Mozart in dramatic musical characterization and motivic synthesis.

A magnificent instrumental tradition also developed in northern Italy. At Bologna, composers such as Maurizio Cazzati (about 1620–1677), Giovanni Battista Vitali (died 1692), and Pietro degli Antonii (1648–1720), built upon the rather primitive beginnings of earlier masters, Giovanni Battista Fontana (died 1631) and Biagio Marini (1597–1665), to prepare the way for the epochal *concerti, concerti grossi, sinfonie,* and sonatas of Arcangelo Corelli (1653–1713), Giuseppe Torelli (1658–1709), Antonio Vivaldi (about 1675–1741) and Giuseppe Tartini (1692–1770).

In Rome, baroque chamber music and opera were overshadowed by sacred dramatic works, a musical phase of the Counter Reformation. Monodic cantatas and motets appeared in Lodovico Viadana's *Concerti ecclesiastici* (1602) and Paolo Quagliati's *Affetti amorosi spirituali* (1617). At the same time Roman musicians began those traditions that led to the "colossal baroque" of Gregorio Allegri (1582–1652) and Orazio Benevoli (1605–1672) and to the Roman operas of Domenico Mazzochi (1592–1665) and Luigi Rossi (1598–1653). Meanwhile, Girolamo Frescobaldi (1583–1643) created a new dramatic style in the toccatas and ricercares of the Roman organ school.

France. Drama also underlay the musical baroque in France, where innovations stemmed from the *ballet de cour,* a fusion of poetry, music, and dance. French opera, at first modeled after the Italian, came into its own early in the reign of Louis XIV. The chief figure was Jean-Baptiste Lully (1632–1687), who composed some 30 ballets and 20 operas. French cantatas and oratorios developed by Jean de Cambefort (1605–1661) and Marc-Antoine Charpentier

(1634–1704), the supreme sacred composer of the French baroque, were strongly influenced by Italian models. The last master of the French baroque was Jean Philippe Rameau (1683–1764).

Important instrumental composers of the French baroque include the lutanist Denis Gaultier (about 1600–1672) and the great masters of the keyboard, Jacques Chambonnières (1602–1672), the Couperins (Louis, 1626–1661, and François le Grand, 1668–1733), and Rameau.

Germany. Naturalized Italian forms, styles, and techniques also began the baroque in Germany, as may be seen in the works of Hans Leo Hassler (1564–1612), Michael Praetorius (1571–1621), Johann Hermann Schein (1586–1630), Johann Jakob Froberger (1616–1667), and Heinrich Schütz (1585–1672). Schütz was a student of Giovanni Gabrieli and later of Monteverdi, and his sacred choral music bears traces of the influence of both. However, these early elements were transformed in his later highly personal, expressive style.

Northern German music, influenced by Schütz through his pupil Matthias Wechmann (1619–1674), developed first in such small centers as Lübeck, where Franz Tunder (1614–1667) and his son-in-law Dietrich Buxtehude (1673–1707), made important contributions to the development of organ repertory, chorales, and cantatas. They also contributed to the organization of church and community musical life that paved the way for the achievements of J.S. Bach (1685–1750), whose organ music, cantatas, motets, oratorios, and Passions mark the culmination of the German baroque. Bach's chamber music was rivaled by that of George Frideric Handel (1685–1759) and Georg Philipp Telemann (1681–1767).

Italianate opera also took root in Germany, especially at Hamburg, where Johann Sigismund Kusser (1660–1727) and Reinhard Keiser (1674–1739) established the chief operatic center in northern Europe. Handel joined them and produced his first two operas there in 1705.

England. After four years of work in the musical centers of Italy (1706–1710), Handel went to London, where he composed, performed, and produced stage works for the rest of his life. There he wrote some five dozen superb stage works and formulated the English oratorio, which, until recently, overshadowed all his other works.

Handel adopted as his own the legacy of the great native tradition that had flourished during the brief lifetime of Henry Purcell (1659–1695). Purcell completed the post-Cromwellian restoration of English music, begun by Pelham Humfrey (1647–1674), Matthew Locke (about 1630–1677), and John Blow (1649–1708), and infused new vitality into it through adaptation of French and Italian musical achievements. In his exquisite songs and profound chamber works, and especially in his dramatic compositions—notably *Dido and Aeneas*—he fulfilled the musical ideals of the early baroque and briefly restored to England the musical vitality of Elizabethan times.

Spain. Spanish baroque music, built on the work of the 16th-century composers Antonio de Cabezón and Diego Ortiz, culminated in a brilliant school of keyboard composers begun by the Italian-born Domenico Scarlatti (1685–1757).

FRANKLIN B. ZIMMERMAN, *Dartmouth College*

Further Reading: Bukofzer, Manfred F., *Music in the Baroque Era* (New York 1947); Donington, Robert, *The Interpretation of Early Music* (London 1963); Rowen, Ruth Halle, *Early Chamber Music* (New York 1949).

BAROTSELAND, bə-rot′sē-land, is a province and protectorate of southwestern Zambia, in south central Africa. It has an area of 44,920 square miles (116,343 sq km). The capital is Mongu. Barotseland, which is drained by the Zambezi River, is largely a grass-covered plain and is noted for its big-game hunting.

The Barotse, who inhabit the region, were conquered by the Kalolo from Basutoland (now Lesotho) in the early 1800's but later revolted and restored their own rule. They still enjoy a degree of internal autonomy, originally granted them by the British in 1900. They raise livestock and grain. Population: (1964) 378,600.

BARQUISIMETO, bär-kē-sē-mä′tō, is a city in Venezuela, 170 miles (275 km) southwest of Caracas. It is situated on a high plain, on the Barquisimeto River, and is the capital of the state of Lara. The city is well built, with wide streets and excellent transportation facilities; among its prominent buildings are the government palace, barracks, market, and cathedral. It is the commercial center for a fertile agricultural district—coffee, cacao, sugar, copper, and cattle being the principal articles of trade.

Founded by the Spanish in 1552, the city was first called New Segovia. It was rebuilt after being severely damaged by an earthquake in 1812 and by fighting during the War of Independence (1813–1823). Population: (1961) 199,691.

BARR, bär, **Alfred Hamilton, Jr.** (1902–   ), American museum official and art historian, who was the first director of the Museum of Modern Art in New York City. He was born in Detroit, Mich., on Jan. 28, 1902. He received his B.A. (1922) and M.A. (1923) from Princeton University. After brief periods of teaching at Vassar College and Princeton, he became professor of fine arts at Wellesley College in 1926 and inaugurated there the first American college course devoted exclusively to modern art. In 1946 he took a doctorate at Harvard.

Barr was appointed director of the newly founded Museum of Modern Art in New York City in 1929. In the 14 years he served as director he helped expand the traditional concept of the art museum to include not only the fine arts but architecture, industrial design, and motion pictures as well. In 1943 he resigned as director and became head of research in painting and sculpture at the museum. Three years later he was named director of collections.

Barr published several books on art, including *What Is Modern Painting?* (1943), *Picasso: Fifty Years of His Art* (1946), and *Matisse: His Art and His Public* (1951).

BARR, bär, **Amelia Edith** (1831–1919), American author. She was born *Amelia Edith Huddleston* in Ulverston, Lancashire, England, on March 29, 1831. She was educated in Glasgow and married Robert Barr, a clergyman, in 1850. They moved to Texas in 1854. After her husband and three sons died of yellow fever in 1867, she went to New York City and wrote for the publications of the well-known preacher Henry Ward Beecher.

Her first successful novel, *Jan Vedder's Wife* (1885), was followed by about 75 others, including *The Maid of Maiden Lane* (1900) and *The Strawberry Handkerchief* (1908). Her autobiography, *All The Days of My Life*, appeared in 1913. She died in New York on March 10, 1919.

BARR, bär, **Stringfellow** (1897–   ), American educator and author. He was born *Frank Stringfellow Barr,* in Suffolk, Va., on Jan. 15, 1897, and graduated from the University of Virginia in 1916. A Rhodes scholar, he studied in Europe before returning to the University of Virginia in 1924 to teach modern European history. He edited the *Virginia Quarterly Review* there from 1930 to 1934. In 1937 he became president of St. John's College in Maryland, where he inaugurated a controversial liberal arts program in which the student spends four years studying great books. An effort to counteract specialization on the undergraduate level, this program has been followed in part by other universities.

He left St. John's in 1946, and from 1955 to 1964 taught humanities at Rutgers University. Active in world government organizations after 1940, he was president of the Foundation for World Government from 1948 to 1958. His works include *Citizens of the World* (1952); *Purely Academic* (1958), a satire on American education; and *The Three Worlds of Man* (1962).

BARRA, bar′ə, an island in Scotland, is one of the Outer Hebrides. It lies 5 miles (8 km) south of South Uist Island, from which it is separated by the Sound of Barra. Rocky and much indented, the island is 8 miles long and 2 to 5 miles wide (13 km by 3–8 km), and it has an altitude of 1,260 feet (384 meters) at its highest point. It is composed mainly of Archaean gneiss, with shell sand and grass covering areas in the western and northern parts. The chief town, Castlebay, is the center of the island's fishing industry.

Situated on a rock in Castlebay's harbor are ruins (partly restored) of the castle of Kisamul, formerly the seat of the Clan Macneil. Elsewhere on the island are remains of ancient chapels, stone circles, and Norse duns (hill forts).

Barra (or Barra Islands) is also the name of the parish comprising this island and a group of smaller ones nearby, including Berneray (the southern point of which is called Barra Head), Mingulay, Sandray, and Vatersay. The parish is administratively part of Inverness County. Population: (1961) 1,467.

BARRACK-ROOM BALLADS, bar′ək-rōōm bal′ədz, a collection of poems by Rudyard Kipling, published in *Ballads and Barrack-Room Ballads* (1892). The 21 Barrack-Room Ballads were written in the cockney dialect with the exception of *Gentlemen-Rankers* and the final poem, *L'Envoi.* They deal in general with the experiences and sentiments of the British common soldier in various parts of the empire, the chief spokesman being Tommy Atkins. Full of soldiers' slang and mixed with foreign expressions, the ballads are strongly rhythmical, with catchy refrains that have had wide popularity in the English-speaking world. Several of them have been set to music; the best known, perhaps, is *Mandalay.* Kipling's subject matter ranges from the humorous portrayal of "a first-class fighting man" in *Fuzzy Wuzzy* to the grim tragedy of a military hanging in *Danny Deever.*

The narrative ballads that constitute the first section of *Ballads and Barrack-Room Ballads* are written in conventional English and take their subjects chiefly from foreign legends and sea tales. They include the popular *The Ballad of East and West* and the poet's strong expression of imperial sentiment, *The English Flag.*

BARRACKPUR, bur′ək-poŏr, is a city in West Bengal, India, 15 miles (24 km) north of Calcutta, on the Hooghly River. Its industries include the processing of rice and jute, lumber milling, and the manufacture of hosiery.

Barrackpur probably received its name in 1772 when British troops were first barracked there. It was the scene of an Indian troop mutiny in 1824 during the first Burmese War and of a preliminary outbreak of the general Indian Mutiny in 1857. During World War II, Barrackpur became the main United States air base for the district and served as a terminus for the Air Transport Command. Population: (1961) 63,778.

BARRACUDA, bar-ə-koō′də, the fishes of the family Sphyraenidae, composed of the various species of a single genus, *Sphyraena*. The barracudas are swift, slender, blue and silvery, saltwater fishes. They are recognized by their long, pike-like bodies, two dorsal fins, pointed heads, and long jaws armed with large, dangerous-looking teeth.

The larger species, such as the great barracuda, are solitary, but some of the small species school. The usual sizes caught range from 3 to 50 pounds (1.3 to 22.7 kg), depending on species and age. The accepted anglers' record catch, however, weighed 103¼ pounds (47 kg) and was 5½ feet (1.7 meters) long.

The flesh of young barracuda is considered a delicacy. At a weight of some 3 pounds (1.3 kg), however, the barracuda changes its diet from smaller fishes to one that includes some of the puffers (Tetraodontidae), which have poisonous body parts. This poison is believed to be the cause of illness reported by some persons who have eaten barracuda.

Barracuda are found both offshore and close inshore in tropical waters, but some species run into colder waters. Barracudas are known to make direct attacks on bathers, and their easily recognizable bite is deep and serious.

For an inclusive account of this fish, see *Systematics and Life History of the Great Barracuda, Sphyraena barracuda* by Donald P. de Sylva (1963).

CHRISTOPHER COATES
The New York Aquarium

Barracuda

ROBERT HERMES, FROM NATIONAL AUDUBON SOCIETY

BARRAGE, bə-räzh, a barrier of fire, usually laid down by artillery. An *antiaircraft barrage,* sometimes called a *predicted barrage,* is a concentration of antiaircraft fire shot into the air where enemy aircraft are expected to fly. An antiaircraft barrage by guns surrounding a defended target is called a *box barrage.* A *normal* or *standing barrage* is a prearranged barrier of fire designed to protect friendly troops and installations by impeding enemy movement. An artillery barrage that precedes attacking infantry or armored troops at a predetermined rate to protect them and facilitate their advance is called a *rolling* or *creeping barrage.* A system of balloons supporting wires and nets as protection against air attacks is called a *balloon barrage.*

JOHN D. BILLINGSLEY, *Colonel, USA*
United States Military Academy

BARRANQUILLA, bär-räng-kē′yä, a city in Colombia, on the west bank of the Magdalena River, 10 miles (16 km) from its mouth. It is Colombia's largest port on the Caribbean Sea and has the country's leading airport. Surrounded by a rich agricultural region, Barranquilla is the seat of Atlántico department, and a center for industry and commerce. Near the city's Terminal Maritima is the Commercial Zone, which allows the unrestricted import of foreign raw materials for local processing. Natural gas is piped 140 miles (230 km) to the city from the Cicuco field.

Barranquilla's manufactures include aluminum products, synthetic fibers, plywood and wallboard, metal containers, vegetable oils and margarine, soap, and perfumes. There are also canneries, flour mills, and a petrochemical plant. At the center of the city is the Plaza Bolívar, which has many fine buildings, including the government palace and an ornate Gothic cathedral. Barranquilla's residential suburb, El Prado, was developed by an American engineer in 1919 on a meadow (*prado*) overlooking the city.

After its founding—reputedly by a group of cowboys in 1721—Barranquilla developed slowly until the mid-19th century, when steamboats began navigating the Magdalena River. However, sandbars at the river mouth prevented the city from becoming a seaport until they were dredged in the mid-1930's. Barranquilla has two universities, Universidad del Atlántico (1941) and Universidad Seccional del Atlántico (1956). Population: (1964) 493,034.

BARRAS, bå-ràs′, **Viscount Paul François Jean Nicolas de** (1755–1829), French revolutionist. He was born at Fox-Amphoux on June 30, 1775, a member of a noble family from Provence. Barras began his career as an officer in the French campaign against the English in India in 1776. He resigned from the army a few years later and quickly squandered his fortune.

With the outbreak of the French Revolution in 1789, he took part in the storming of the Bastille and in the attacks on the Tuileries, and he represented the department of Var in the National Assembly. Elected to the National Convention in 1792, he voted for the death of Louis XVI and played a part in the downfall of the Girondists. In 1794 he was commander of the troops that arrested Robespierre. In the following year he was elected president of the National Convention, which, on his advice, entrusted Napoleon Bonaparte with the suppression of the royalist uprising in Paris.

From 1795–1799, Barras was one of the five executives of the Directory and exerted an enormous influence on French policy. His prestige was maintained to some extent by the victories of Napoleon, whose marriage to Josephine de Beauharnais, one of Barras' ex-mistresses, Barras helped to arrange. He assisted in putting Napoleon in command of the Italian army and backed his coup d'état of the 18th Brumaire (Nov. 9, 1799).

Napoleon, however, distrusted Barras, who was forced to retire to his country estate. Napoleon exiled him to Italy in 1810 and then interned him at Montpellier. After his retirement, Barras lived on the vast fortune he had amassed as a member of the Directory. Although Barras had often been suspected of royalist sympathies during the Revolution, he was unable to gain favor with Louis XVIII after Louis' accession to the throne in 1814; but since Barras did not support Napoleon during the Hundred Days in 1815, he was allowed to remain in France. He died at Chaillot on Jan. 29, 1829. Barras' *Mémoires* describe political life during the Directory.

BARRATRY, băr′á-trẽ, *in maritime law,* is an offense committed by the master of a vessel or his sailors, by which the goods committed to their charge are unlawfully damaged or lost. In cases arising from fraud or other illegal acts, or negligence so gross as to evidence fraud, insurance against the shipowner's loss is effective. A mutiny in which a ship's officers are deprived of command is a form of barratry.

In criminal law, barratry is the offense of repeatedly exciting or stirring up groundless lawsuits or quarrels. An indictment for this offense must charge the offender with being a common barrator and the proof must show at least three instances of offending. It must be distinguished from *maintenance*—the officious intermeddling with suits that do not concern the party, by lending personal or other assistance; and on the other hand from *champerty*—an illegal bargain made between one of the parties to a suit and a third party whereby it is agreed that the latter shall share in the proceeds of the action in return for financial support of its pursuit.

BARRATT, bar′ət, **Sir Arthur Sheridan** (1891–   ), British air marshal. He was born in Peshawar, India (now in Pakistan), on Feb. 25, 1891. He was educated for the army at the Royal Military College in Woolwich and entered the Royal Flying Corps in 1914. He saw action in France during World War I, becoming wing commander and lieutenant colonel by the war's end, and in 1919 he went over to the newly formed Royal Air Force. He became senior instructor at the staff college in Andover and in 1932 became senior air officer at the Indian headquarters.

From 1936 to 1939 he was commandant of the RAF Staff College in Andover. After the outbreak of World War II, he became the commanding officer of the British air forces in France. In 1940 he was promoted to air marshal and knighted, and in November he was made head of the Army Co-operation Command, one of the first combined commands of the war. From 1943 until 1945 he was commander in chief of the RAF Technical Training Command, and he served from 1945 to 1947 as inspector general of the RAF, retiring in the latter year. He was promoted to air chief marshal in 1946.

BARRAULT, bȧ-rō′, **Jean-Louis** (1910–   ), French actor and director. He was born in Vésinet on Sept. 8, 1910. After studying with the mime Étienne Ducreux and with Charles Dullin of the Théâtre de l'Atelier in Paris, he made his debut as a director in 1935. His first production, *Autour d'une mère,* was an adaptation, half in pantomime, of William Faulkner's novel *As I Lay Dying.* In 1940, Barrault joined the Comédie-Française as actor and director.

With his wife, the French actress Madeleine Renaud, Barrault formed a repertory company in 1947 at the Théâtre Marigny in Paris. Until 1956 he directed and acted there in his own productions of such works as *Hamlet* (in André Gide's translation), Marivaux's *Les fausses confidences,* and Molière's *Amphitryon.* In 1958 he was appointed a director of the Théâtre du Palais-Royal and in 1959 he became director of the Théâtre de France.

Barrault's most famous film role was his portrayal of the 19th century mime, Jean-Baptiste Deburau, in *Les enfants du paradis* (1944; U.S. release, *Children of Paradise,* 1946). Among his other films were *La symphonie fantastique* (1941) and *D'homme à hommes* (1948). Barrault also wrote works on the theater, including *Réflexions sur le théâtre* (1949; Eng. tr., *Reflections on the Theatre,* 1951) and *Nouvelles réflexions sur le théâtre* (1959; Eng. tr., *The Theatre of Jean-Louis Barrault,* 1961).

BARRÉ, ba-rā′, **Isaac** (1726–1802), British officer. He was born in Dublin of French parentage. He was wounded at the Battle of Quebec, where he was beside James Wolfe when the British commander fell. Barré is represented in Benjamin West's painting *The Death of Wolfe.*

Barré entered Parliament in 1761 and served in cabinets under the 3d earl of Bute, William Pitt, the marquis of Rockingham, and the 2d earl of Shelburne. In Pitt's second administration he exposed the corruptions of the ministry. Barré was a strong opponent of the ministry of Lord North and opposed the taxation of America.

The towns of Barre, Mass., and Wilkes-Barre, Pa., were named in his honor. He died in London on July 20, 1802.

BARRE, bar′ē, is an industrial city in Vermont, situated in Washington County, 7 miles (11 km) southeast of Montpelier. Barre is said to be the largest granite center in the world and is sometimes known as the Granite City. The quarries are of interest to tourists. Another attraction is a famous granite statue of the Scottish poet Robert Burns, which is noted as an exceptional piece of sculpture. The city manufactures machines and tools, and it is a center for winter sports, hunting, and fishing. Berlin airport, 4 miles (6½ km) from Barre, supplies commercial air service.

Barre was settled about 1788 and was organized as a town in 1793. The quarrying and cutting of granite began in Barre shortly after the War of 1812, when returning soldiers opened the first quarry on Cobble Hill. This stone was used in the 1830's in the construction of the state capitol in Montpelier. When the Vermont Central Railroad reached Barre in 1875, an influx of skilled stonecutters and quarrymen began that multiplied the population in the next 20 years. Barre became a city in 1894. Government is by mayor, council, and city manager. Population: 10,209.

BARREL is a unit of measure for liquids and dry commodities. In liquid measure in the United States, one barrel generally is equivalent to 31.5 gallons. In Great Britain and Canada, one barrel is equivalent to 36 imperial gallons. In dry measure in the United States, one barrel generally is equivalent to 105 dry quarts. Barrel measures for certain liquids and dry commodities may be different from these values. See also WEIGHTS AND MEASURES.

BARREL ORGAN, a mechanical musical instrument used by street musicians. A somewhat larger version was used in many English churches during the 18th and 19th centuries. All barrel organs operate according to the same principle: a barrel, upon which a series of pins is arranged, is revolved either by hand or by a mechanical device. The revolving pins act as levers to operate a series of small organ pipes, which produce the desired music. The barrels are changeable, each containing a different hymn or song. Barrel organs were often preferred to standard organs by English clergymen, and it has been claimed that English church music declined in quality during the 18th and 19th centuries for this reason.

BARREN GROUND is a novel by the American author Ellen Glasgow. Published in 1925 and generally considered her finest novel, *Barren Ground* was one of the first realistic novels of life in the Southern United States. Miss Glasgow said of the book, which presents a psychologically accurate portrait of its main character, Dorinda Oakley, that "all minor themes, episodes, and impressions are blended with the one dominant meaning that character is fate."

The harsh farm country of Virginia provides a symbolic setting for the novel, which takes place about 1900 and portrays the life of Dorinda Oakley, daughter of a poor white farmer in Virginia. She falls in love with Jason Greylock, a young physician from an old wealthy family. They plan to marry, but Jason succumbs to social pressure to marry a girl from a more respectable family. Desperate, Dorinda flees to New York City, where she works for two years, until the death of her father takes her back home. After seeing Jason Greylock retreating into chronic alcoholism, she gradually regains her integrity and self-respect by making the "barren ground" of the family farm productive again.

BARRÈS, bà-res', **Maurice** (1862–1923), French author and politician, known for his fierce nationalism and belief in the importance of regional ties. He was born *Auguste Maurice Barrès* at Charmes-sur-Moselle, Lorraine, on Sept. 22, 1862. After studying at the lycée of Nancy, he went to Paris where, in 1885, he attracted the attention of literary circles with a pamphlet, *Huit jours chez M. Renan,* satirizing the French man of letters Ernest Renan. Barrès' first novel, *Sous l'oeil des barbares,* was published in 1888. In 1906 he was admitted to membership in the French Academy.

Barrès became a member of the violently anti-German Boulangist movement in the late 1880's, and from 1889 to 1893 he served as a Boulangist representative in the French Chamber of Deputies. In 1894 he founded *La Cocarde,* the newspaper of the Nationalists, a chauvinistic, militaristic party of which the Boulangists became adherents at the turn of the century. Barrès was reelected to parliament in 1906 and served there until the end of his life as the intellectual spokesman for the Nationalist movement. During World War I, he wrote daily articles for the journal *L'écho de Paris,* which were later compiled into *La chronique de la grande guerre* (1920–24). He died at Neuilly-sur-Seine, near Paris, on Dec. 5, 1923. His journals were published posthumously under the title *Mes cahiers* (14 vols., 1930–56).

A master of lyric prose, Barrès cultivated a refined, delicate style. Without sacrificing his literary integrity to his convictions, he used most of his novels as vehicles for his ideas. His first trilogy, *Le culte du moi,* published between 1888 and 1891, revolves around the theme of self-development. It initiated a "culte du moi" among the young people of Paris, who attempted, in the words of one of Barrès' characters, "to feel as much as possible while analyzing oneself as much as possible." The theme of regionalism, which is central to much of Barrès' fiction, appears first in the trilogy *Le roman de l'énergie nationale* (1897–1903). *Les déracinés* (1897), the most important book of the trilogy and one of the most influential novels of modern French literature, tells the story of seven provincials from Lorraine who failed in life because they had been uprooted (*déraciné*) from their native traditions by their education. Another novel, *Colette Baudoche* (1909), describes the relationship between the people of Lorraine and the Germans who annexed the province.

Barrès' other fiction includes *La colline inspirée* (1913), a mystical novel containing some of his most beautiful writing, and *Un jardin sur l'Oronte* (1922). He also wrote descriptions of travel in Greece, *Le voyage de Sparte* (1905), and in Spain, *Greco, ou le secret de Tolède* (1912), and a book of essays, *Le mystère en pleine lumière,* published posthumously in 1924.

BARRETT, bar'et, **John** (1866–1938), American diplomat, who was for 13 years head of the Pan American Union. He was born at Grafton, Vt., on Nov. 28, 1866. He was educated at Worcester Academy and Vanderbilt University and was graduated from Dartmouth College in 1889. Thereafter he moved to the Pacific coast and worked for several newspapers. While assistant editor of the Portland (Ore.) *Evening Telegram,* he supported Grover Cleveland in the presidential election of 1892. Two years later Cleveland appointed him minister to Siam. He served in that position from 1894 to 1898, resigning his diplomatic post to become a correspondent in Cuba during the Spanish-American War. He advocated a strong United States policy in the Far East.

After serving as special commissioner for the United States in Asia and Europe and as delegate to the second Pan American Congress in Mexico, Barrett was appointed minister to Argentina in 1903. He was minister to Panama in 1904 and to Colombia in 1905–1906. In January 1907 he became director general of the International Bureau of American Republics, which in 1910 was renamed the Pan American Union. He held this office until his retirement in September 1920. Barrett's dedication to closer inter-American relations won him friends and honors throughout the hemisphere. After 18 years of self-imposed retirement in his native Vermont, he died at Bellows Falls on Oct. 17, 1938. He was the author of several books on Latin America.

BARRETT, bar'et, **Lawrence** (1838–1891), American actor who specialized in Shakespearean roles and was associated with Edwin Booth. He was born in Paterson, N.J., on April 4, 1838. He made his stage debut in 1853 in *The French Spy*. During the Civil War he served as a captain in the infantry. After the war he toured widely as an actor, becoming very popular, especially in the Shakespearean roles of Hamlet, Shylock, and Cassius. The latter was his most famous role, which he often played opposite Booth's Brutus. He also played Othello to Booth's Iago. In 1887, Barrett and Booth began a regular association in Shakespearean plays. This partnership lasted until Barrett's death, in New York City on March 20, 1891.

Barrett wrote biographies of the actors Edwin Forrest (1881), Edwin Booth (1886), and Charlotte Cushman (1889).

BARRETTS OF WIMPOLE STREET, bar'ets, wim'pōl, a play in four acts by the English playwright Rudolf Besier (1878–1942). It was first performed at the Malvern (England) Festival in August 1930. The plot centers on the romance of the 19th century English poets Elizabeth Barrett and Robert Browning, and on her struggle to escape the household of her domineering father.

After its premiere the play had a successful run of nearly a year and a half in London, with a cast headed by Cedric Hardwicke as Mr. Barrett. It opened in New York City at the Empire Theatre on Feb. 9, 1931, with Katharine Cornell as Elizabeth and Brian Aherne as Browning. One of Katharine Cornell's greatest successes, *The Barretts of Wimpole Street* ran for 370 performances in New York City, then had a very successful road tour. It has been revived frequently, notably for a tour of U.S. military fronts during World War II.

BARRIE, bar'ē, **Sir James Matthew** (1860–1937), Scottish novelist and playwright, whose most lasting claim to fame is the play *Peter Pan, the Boy Who Wouldn't Grow Up*. The play, first acted on Dec. 27, 1904, in London, where its revival is an annual event, has remained a favorite with both children and adults. In the United States the play was made into a successful musical in 1954, and the musical was later presented on television.

In a sense, Barrie himself would never grow up, and his character had a strong (or weak) element of childlikeness. Whether this is to be admired as the ability to cling to the grace and freshness of childhood, or deplored as infantilism, it was his preeminent and most characteristic quality. It runs like a silver thread (or a baby ribbon) through the texture of nearly all his novels and plays; and it is the soft streak that attracts his devotees and repels only those who insist on putting away childish things as soon as childhood has ended. For Barrie, childhood ended only with his death at the age of 77.

Life. Barrie was born in Kirriemuir, Forfarshire (now Angus), Scotland, on May 9, 1860, the 9th of 10 children of a handloom weaver. Barrie's background was not so much one of poverty as of hard work, burning ambition, and the Scottish zeal for education. His father was determined to give his children every opportunity that he himself had been denied, and all had good brains. One son, intended for the ministry, was drowned while skating at the age of 14. His

Sir James M. Barrie

(1860–1937)

THE GRANGER COLLECTION

death profoundly affected his younger brother James' character, both directly and through its effect on their mother, Margaret Ogilvy, for James was her chief comforter until her own death 28 years later.

At 13, Barrie went to school at Dumfries in southwest Scotland. There he learned to love the theater, acting in amateur theatricals and haunting the town's old playhouse, for which Robert Burns had written one or two prologues. Its walls still stand. From Dumfries Academy, Barrie went to Edinburgh University, taking his M.A. degree in 1882. He then went to work as a journalist, and for nearly two years wrote daily editorials for a Nottingham paper.

Barrie married in 1894, but the marriage was dissolved in 1909. A lonely man, short of stature, he seemed to go out of his way to gain sympathy for his solitariness and shortness. Bernard Shaw, describing Thomas Hardy's funeral in Westminster Abbey in 1928, said that John Galsworthy and himself, as pallbearers, made no effort to conceal their imposing height. "But," he added, "Barrie, realizing that he could not stand up to us, made his effect by miraculously managing to look exactly three inches high."

For all his shyness, or pretense of shyness, Barrie could be an inspired speaker, and his St. Andrews University address on courage (1919) is among the best speeches of the 20th century. Lady Cynthia Asquith, his private secretary for many years, reports in her excellent, intimate, and appreciative *Portrait of Barrie* (1954) that "his speeches were carefully written to sound impromptu, and to be *acted*."

Barrie was made a baronet in 1913. From 1919 to 1922 he was lord rector of St. Andrews University, and in 1922 he was appointed to the Order of Merit, chiefly because of his services to the British theater. From 1930 he served as the chancellor of Edinburgh University. He died in London on June 19, 1937.

Books. Barrie's last published work, *The Greenwood Hat* (1937), is a collection of his earlier articles, with a valuable and revealing comment after each; the whole amounts to an unorthodox autobiography, packed with charm. The book is an excellent instance of Barrie's very Scottish avoidance of waste, for these early pieces had already been expanded into his first published books. *Auld Licht Idylls* (1888) did not pretend to be anything more than a series of sketches, in his native Kirriemuir and other local dialects, that had appeared in a weekly paper. Less episodic but with the same origin was the novel *A Window in Thrums* (1889), which immediately caught and held the public fancy. Barrie wrote *The Little Minister*, a highly sentimental novel, in 1891, and in 1897 he turned it into one of his first successful plays (under the same title). *When a Man's Single* (1894) and *Sentimental Tommy* (1896) are both novels about a little boy in Thrums (Kirriemuir) who became a more or less successful writer. Another novel of fantasy, *The Little White Bird* (1902), foreshadowed the children's play *Peter Pan* and was the first of several whimsical little novels about the eternal boy, Peter, and his "little mother," Wendy.

Plays. In the London theater, Barrie's successful *The Little Minister* was followed by his charming *Quality Street* (1902); both plays were introduced to American audiences by Maude Adams, who was the first to play the title role in *Peter Pan*. Then came the ingenious and witty *The Admirable Crichton* (1902). He reverted to Scottish life and character in the masterly *What Every Woman Knows* (1903). Then, a year later, came *Peter Pan*.

In 1917, Barrie wrote the haunting and haunted *Dear Brutus* and, in 1920, *Mary Rose*, which takes its heroine into the Hebrides and quite magically loses her there. As late as 1936, for the Austrian actress Elisabeth Bergner, he wrote his final play, *The Boy David*, which reads far better than it acts. The same may be said of many of Barrie's plays, for their elaborate, extended, and often distinctly poetic stage directions are frequently more rewarding and evocative than their dialogue.

Evaluation. Barrie was always something of a little boy, quite often lacking in self-criticism. Even in *Peter Pan*, an accepted masterpiece, he can make the most uncritical child in the audience wince when he reveals his theory about the source of fairies: "When the first baby laughed for the first time, his laugh broke into a million pieces, and they all went skipping about. That was the origin of fairies." Against these occasional embarrassments can be set the countless felicities of the best of the adult plays and of his short last novel, the macabre *Farewell, Miss Julie Logan* (1931).

But Barrie is a difficult writer to assess. Even his severest critics, who try to dismiss his lifework as a morass of sentimentality, have to admit that the morass has its will o' the wisps; its darting streaks of indisputable magic. Nor can any responsible critic deny that the best of Barrie's plays are the work of a formidable creator of character, or that they reveal an uncanny command of theatrical effect. After World War II, Barrie generally fell out of favor, but probably only temporarily, for the best of his writing, especially in the plays as published, is too vivid and imaginative to perish. He had no rivals, and has had no followers. Barrie was unique, inimitable.

ALAN DENT, *Author of "Mrs. Patrick Campbell"*

Further Reading: Asquith, Cynthia, *Portrait of Barrie* (London 1954); Darlington, William A., *J.M. Barrie* (London 1938); Green, Roger L., *J.M. Barrie* (New York 1961); Mackail, Denis G., *Barrie: The Story of J.M.B.* (New York 1941).

BARRIE, bar′ē, is a city in Ontario, Canada. It is situated at the head of Kempenfelt Bay, on Lake Simcoe, 50 miles (80 km) north of Toronto. Barrie's industries include tanneries, machine shops, a brewery, a flour mill, a creamery, a meat-packing plant, a planing mill, and tent and tarpaulin, shoe, and cosmetics factories. The city obtains cheap hydroelectric power from the Severn River. Barrie is situated in a productive farming and dairying district and is a popular summer resort. Camp Borden, a large training base of the Canadian army and air force, is just outside the city limits of Barrie. Population: 27,-676.

BARRIER REEF, bar′ē-ər rēf, a rocky ridge, built up by coral or other organic material, that emerges from the sea roughly parallel to a coastline and separated from it by a lagoon. Although more or less continuous, the reef usually is pierced by channels, which provide access to the lagoon. It develops through upward growth of organic matter along with changes in water level. The most remarkable example is the 1,250-mile (2,012-km) Great Barrier Reef off the northeast coast of Australia. See also CORAL.

BARRING OUT, bär′ing, a practice once common in some English schools, where the boys barred the doors of the school and defied the masters from the windows a few days before vacation. It was understood that the pupils could dictate terms as to holidays for the ensuing year if they could prevent the masters from entering for three successive days. The origin of the practice is not known.

The custom was also observed in America. It forms the basis for one incident in *The Hoosier Schoolmaster* (1871) by Edward Eggleston.

BARRINGTON, bar′ing-tən, is a residential city in northeastern Illinois. It is situated in Cook and Lake counties, 32 miles (51 km) northwest of Chicago. There is a coffee and tea processing plant, and tableware is manufactured.

Barrington was incorporated in 1865. Government is by council-manager. Population: 7,701.

BARRINGTON, bar′ing-tən, is a residential borough in southwestern New Jersey, in Camden County, 6 miles (9.6 km) southwest of Camden. It was settled about 1890 and incorporated in 1917. Population: 8,409.

BARRIOS, bär′ryōs, **Justo Rufino** (1835–1885), Guatemalan soldier and political leader. His determination to unite the states of Central America in a political union ended in failure and resulted in his death.

He was born at San Lorenzo, Guatemala, on July 17, 1835, the son of Gerardo Barrios, a liberal revolutionist executed by the Conservatives in El Salvador. Justo Rufino studied law but was prevented, during the intensely anti-Liberal dictatorship of Rafael Carrera, from succeeding in his profession. He joined the Liberal revolutionists led by Miguel García Granados. After Carrera's death in 1865, Liberal fortunes rose. When the Conservative president, Vicente Cerna, was deposed in 1871, Barrios assumed command of the army and became the virtual dictator of the country. He ruled as president from 1873 until his death.

After securing the loyalty of the army, Barrios undertook broad, liberal reforms. During his administration the country's first railroad was built, roads were improved, and agriculture was diversified. Large landholdings were broken up. Barrios expelled the Jesuits and members of the church hierarchy.

Barrios repeatedly interfered in the affairs of El Salvador and Honduras in an effort to bring their Liberal forces to power. In 1876, at Barrios' suggestion, a conference of representatives of all the Central American states was held at Guatemala City to plan a political union. It and succeeding efforts were disrupted by rebellions in several of the states. Barrios was killed while leading an army into Chalchuapa, El Salvador, on April 2, 1885.

BARRISTER, bar′ə-stər, in England and Wales, a counsel (lawyer) permitted to try cases in superior courts. The legal profession in England and Wales is divided into two branches: *barristers* and *solicitors.* The legal professions in Scotland and Northern Ireland are separate, but similar. The Scottish equivalent of barrister is *advocate.*

In England and Wales there are about 2,000 barristers, all of whom have the right to appear in any court in those countries, from the House of Lords (the ultimate appellate court), the Court of Appeal, the High Court, and the superior criminal courts to the small local tribunals. Generally speaking, a barrister is employed in substantial civil actions, divorces, or major crimes, which can be tried in superior courts only. His services may be retained only through the agency of a solicitor.

The main role of barristers—except for a few specialists—is to prepare formal pleadings and to present and argue cases in court. The barrister works in conjunction with a litigant's solicitor, who carries out the necessary pretrial investigation and case preparation. Members of the English bar (barristers) practice from the Temple or Lincoln's Inn in London and belong to one of four ancient Inns of Court—Lincoln's Inn, Gray's Inn, and the Inner and Middle Temples.

Solicitors are by far the more numerous branch of the legal profession in England and Wales. There were about 21,500 in the mid-1960's. They advise clients on everyday business, family, and property problems. The solicitor may conduct lawsuits in the lower courts only, ranging from minor criminal prosecutions and matrimonial disputes in local magistrates' courts to lesser civil actions in the county courts. The solicitors' profession is regulated by the Law Society, which is responsible for discipline and the conduct of special qualifying examinations.

In the United States, the practical distinction between barristers and solicitors does not exist. A lawyer may advise clients and conduct lawsuits for them, or engage in any of the other branches of law.

JOHN MICHAEL WRIGHT
Lincoln's Inn, London, Barrister at Law

BARRON, bar′ən, **Clarence Walker** (1855–1928), American newspaper publisher, who pioneered the development of economic journalism. His leading contribution was insistence that his publications, primarily *The Wall Street Journal,* go beyond the earlier practice of providing only bare statistics and formal statements. He sought the facts back of the figures or statement, seeking to explain them intelligibly to nonexpert readers.

He was born in Boston on July 2, 1855, and was for 11 years a reporter on the Boston *Transcript.* In 1887 he founded the Boston News Bureau to specialize in business news; with its success he acquired Dow Jones & Company in 1901 from its founder, Charles Dow. By the time of Barron's death, Dow Jones' main publication, *The Wall Street Journal,* had grown from a small, local paper to one of national circulation publishing on both coasts. He also founded, in 1921, *Barron's* magazine as a national financial weekly.

Barron was a portly, gregarious, hard-driving man. His two volumes of *They Told Barron,* recording conversations with famous men of his day, are rich source materials on the history of that era. His other books include *War Finance* and *Twenty-Eight Essays on the Federal Reserve Act.* He died at Battle Creek, Mich., on Oct. 2, 1928.

VERMONT ROYSTER, *"The Wall Street Journal"*

BARRON, bar′ən, **James** (1768–1851), American naval officer, who was the central figure in a famous controversy in the United States Navy early in the 19th century. He was commissioned a lieutenant in the Navy in 1798, and in 1807 he was named to command the *Chesapeake,* with the rank of commodore.

On June 22, 1807, when the United States and Britain were at peace, the *Chesapeake* was halted off Cape Henry, Va., by the British frigate *Leopard. The Leopard's* captain demanded that Barron surrender four seamen who allegedly were deserters from the British navy. Barron refused, and the *Leopard* opened fire. The *Chesapeake,* which had just left port for a long voyage, was unready for action. Barron fired one gun and then surrendered his ship. It had suffered great damage. Three men had been killed and 20 wounded, including Barron. The alleged deserters were removed by the British, and the *Chesapeake* was allowed to limp back to port.

Barron was tried by court-martial. He was acquitted of cowardice but was convicted of neglecting to have his ship cleared for action and was suspended for five years without pay. Restored to duty in 1813, he was denied a sea command and became convinced that several naval officers were conspiring against him. His enmity centered on Commodore Stephen Decatur, a hero of the Navy, who had sat on the court-martial. In 1820, Barron challenged Decatur to a duel and killed him. Barron remained on "waiting orders" for the rest of his life. He died at Norfolk, Va., on April 21, 1851.

BARROS ARANA, bär′rōs ä-rä-nä, **Diego** (1830–1907), Chilean historian. He was born at Santiago on Aug. 16, 1830. Obliged by ill health to give up legal studies, he devoted himself to historical and literary pursuits.

The favor with which his historical sketch of the campaigns of 1818–1821 was received encouraged Barros Arana to begin the extensive *History of Chilean Independence* (1854–57).

His other major works are *Vida y viaje de don Hernando de Magallanes* (1864); *Historia de la guerra del Pacífico* (1881); and his monumental *Historia general de Chile,* 15 vols. (1884–97). He died at Santiago on Nov. 4, 1907.

BARROSO, bər-rō′zōō, **Gustavo** (1888–1959), Brazilian writer and lawyer. He was born at Fortaleza, Brazil, on Dec. 29, 1888. Educated for the law at Fortaleza and Rio de Janeiro, he edited the *Jornal do Ceará* (1908–1909) and the *Jornal do Commercio* (1911–1913). He served as secretary of the Brazilian delegation at the Versailles Peace Conference in 1919, after World War I. He was director of the Brazilian Museum of National History from 1922 to 1959.

Barroso wrote fiction, history, and political tracts. His works include *Terra de sol* (1912), *Heróis e bandidos* (1917), *Luz e pó* (1932), *A viagem submarina* (1934), *Historia secreta do Brasil*, 2 vols. (1936, 1937), *Reflexões dum bode* (1937), and *Coração de menino* (1939). He died at Rio de Janeiro on Dec. 3, 1959.

BARROW, bar′ō, **Henry** (c. 1550–1593), English church reformer, who was one of the founders of Congregationalism. His name is also spelled *Barrowe*. After graduating from Cambridge, he led a frivolous life at court, but about 1581, as a result of a sermon he heard and after a period of study and retreat, he became a strict Puritan. He was much influenced by the reformer Robert Browne, and the two established congregations independent of the Church of England. Barrow held that the abolition of the established church was necessary to the true practice of Christianity, and both he and Browne believed that the church had the right and duty to carry out needed reforms without awaiting parliamentary permission.

Because Barrow was a sincere and eloquent speaker, his presence at secret meetings of Separatists in London made him a dangerous person in the eyes of state and church. To both these authorities, loyalty to the established church was a matter of national security. Lack of loyalty was considered possible treason. Imprisoned in 1586 for his Separatist activities, Barrow was tried and sentenced with John Greenwood, another radical reformer, and the two were hanged on April 6, 1593.

BARROW, bar′ō, **Isaac** (1630–1677), English mathematician and theologian, who was Isaac Newton's teacher and friend at Cambridge University. Barrow was born in London in 1630. His early education was at the Charterhouse and at a school in Feldsted, where he began to show talents signaling his future great reputation. He entered Trinity College, Cambridge, in 1643, and he was chosen a scholar in 1647. At first he studied anatomy, botany, and chemistry and aimed to be a member of the medical profession. However, he changed his mind and shifted to the study of divinity, mathematics, and astronomy. In 1653 he received an M.A. degree from Oxford.

Barrow made an extensive tour of the Continent in 1655–1659. During this period his first work, an edition of Euclid's *Elements*, was published at Cambridge. Shortly after his return to England, he was ordained.

In 1660 he became a professor of Greek at Cambridge, and two years later he became a professor of geometry. The Royal Society elected him a member as its first choice after incorporation. In the same year, he was appointed the first Lucasian professor of mathematics at Cambridge.

This appointment proved to be a critical one because Barrow's mathematical and theological ideas influenced his pupil Newton. Barrow gave lectures on his own methods for analyzing tangents and finding areas, and Newton attended these lectures. Thus, Barrow's considerable mathematical talents were a basis for Newton's development of the calculus.

In 1669, because of his convictions as to his religious duty, Barrow determined to give up mathematics and adhere exclusively to divinity. Accordingly, after publishing his *Lectiones opticae*, he resigned his chair to Newton.

In 1673, King Charles II nominated Barrow to the membership of Trinity College. In 1675 he was chosen vice chancellor of Cambridge University. He died in London on May 4, 1677.

Barrow's other works include *Euclidis data* (1657); *Archimedis opera* (1675); and *Lectiones geometricae* (1676). All of his works in English are theological; the most important one is *Treatise on the Pope's Supremacy* (1680). See also NEWTON, SIR ISAAC.

Further Reading: Burtt, Edwin A., *Metaphysical Foundations of Modern Physical Science* (New York 1952); Osmond, Percy H., *Isaac Barrow, His Life and Times* (London 1944).

BARROW, bar′ō, **Sir John** (1764–1848), English traveler and admiralty official. He was born near Ulverston, Lancashire, England, on June 19, 1764. As secretary to a diplomat, he traveled in China and South Africa before being appointed second secretary of the admiralty in 1804. He held this place for 40 years except for a brief interlude.

Arctic exploration was one of his interests, and he encouraged and assisted many explorers. Barrow Strait in the Arctic and Point Barrow, Alaska, were named for him. He was the chief founder of the Royal Geographical Society and was knighted in 1835. He died in London on Nov. 23, 1848.

BARROW, bar′ō, a village in Alaska, is the most northern community in the United States and the largest Eskimo village in the world. It is situated 9 miles (14 km) southwest of Point Barrow. Population: 2,104.

The principal occupation of its people is whaling. Barrow has modern shops, cafés, theaters, schools, a hospital, and a church. The houses, most of them built since World War II, are made of lumber and plywood and are heated by natural gas piped in from a nearby well. The United States Navy operates the Arctic Research Laboratory near the village.

Barrow was a tiny hamlet until the 1930's, when many Eskimos flocked there to draw federal aid and remained. In 1942 the Navy made Barrow the base for oil explorations in the inland Naval Petroleum Reserve No. 4. The Navy employed many Eskimos, who used their wages to build new houses or to improve others. Considering that the Eskimos might lose their native skills, the Navy allowed the exploration crews to continue whaling part-time. When their naval employment was over, they were able to resume their former occupation.

EDWARD L. KEITHAHN
Alaska Historical Library and Museum, Juneau

BARROW, Point, bar′ō, a promontory in Alaska. The northernmost point in the United States, it is near latitude 71°25′ north, longitude 156°20′ west. Point Barrow is a low sandspit 4 miles (6.4 km) long. It was discovered in September 1826 by Captain Frederic William Beechey of the British navy, who named it in honor of Sir John Barrow, a patron of Arctic exploration.

BARROW, bar'ō, in archaeology, is the term used in England to denote an artificial mound of earth built over a burial place. In Scotland, Ireland, and Wales, such a construction, when made of stones, is called a *cairn*. American usage, since the first discoveries of Indian barrows, has preferred the term *burial mound*.

Barrows were erected throughout the Western world from the Stone Age until some time after the introduction of Christianity. Stone Age barrows were usually long and used for multiple burials, while those of the Bronze Age tended to be round and used for single burials. Persons accorded this honor were usually chiefs or others of high standing. Their bodies, along with weapons, ornaments, and other cherished possessions, were usually placed in stone vaults, which were then covered with earth.

The barrows of England are among the largest in the world. One, at Silbury Hill in Wiltshire, is about 170 feet (51.8 meters) high and covers about 5 acres (2 hectares) of ground. Another is the Sutton Hoo Ship Burial, discovered in 1939. In this mound an early Anglo-Saxon king (c. about 650–660 A.D.) was buried with his treasures in a ship about 80 feet (23.3 meters) long.

BARROW-IN-FURNESS, bar'ō, fûr'nəs, is a seaport and industrial center in Lancashire, England, on the southwest coast of Furness Peninsula, 50 miles (80 km) northwest of Liverpool. It includes within its limits the island of Walney.

In the mid-1800's, Barrow was a fishing village of 300 inhabitants. Its later phenomenal growth resulted from the mining of hematite iron ore in the district, and the building of a railroad spur to the city. Barrow imports lumber from northern Europe and from Canada, cattle from Belfast, Northern Ireland, and preserved food from the United States. Large quantities of iron ore and pig iron are shipped from the port. Passenger traffic is heavy between Barrow, the Isle of Man, and Belfast.

Barrow is also a major shipbuilding and engineering center. It has large iron foundries and steel works, and manufactures rolling stock, chemicals, and armaments. There are also flour mills, paper mills, and salt works. Smaller industries produce rope, sails, and bricks.

The city, which has the status of a county borough, is laid out in a well-defined rectangular plan. It has a college, free public libraries, and a workmen's institute. A substantial residential suburb, Vicarstown, has grown up on the east coast of Walney. Near Barrow are the ruins of Furness Abbey, a Benedictine monastery, founded in 1127. Population: (1961) 64,927.

BARRUNDIA, bär-rōōn'dyä, **José Francisco** (1784–1854), Central American statesman, who was an ardent advocate of Central American confederation. He was born in Guatemala in 1784. In 1813, during the struggle against Spanish rule, Barrundia was sentenced to death for treason. He escaped and became leader of the Revolutionary party in 1819. In 1823–1824 he was a member of the constitutional convention of Central America that established the confederation under a liberal constitution. He was president of the Central American federation in 1829–1830. The federation collapsed in 1838 but, when it was revived briefly in 1851–1852, he was again president.

He went to the United States in 1854, as minister from Honduras, to propose the annexation of that territory to the United States. Before anything was accomplished, he died suddenly at New York City on Aug. 4, 1854.

BARRY, bar'ē, **Sir Charles** (1795–1860), English architect who designed the Houses of Parliament in Westminster, London. He was born in London on May 23, 1795, and as a youth was apprenticed to a company of surveyors. He showed an early talent for drawing, and many of his works were exhibited at the Royal Academy. In 1817 he took the few hundred pounds that constituted his inheritance and set out on three years of travel through Italy, Greece, and the Middle East, studying and sketching the buildings that interested him. He returned to London in 1820, where his drawings quickly attracted the attention of England's leading architects.

Barry settled in London and began practicing architecture. His early designs included the plans for St. Peter's church in Brighton (1823), the Royal Institute of Fine Arts in Manchester (1824), and the Travelers' Club in London (1829–1831). His designs for King Edward's School in Birmingham (1833–1836) marked his first important use of the Perpendicular style, a Gothic form characterized by a preponderance of vertical straight lines. Many critics consider the Reform Club in London (1837) to be Barry's best work. Built in the style of an Italian palace, it contains a covered inner courtyard that serves as a grand-scale drawing room.

In 1835 a competition was held for the design of buildings to replace the Houses of Parliament, which had been destroyed by fire a year earlier. Barry was awarded the commission, and in 1837 he began the construction of the new Houses of Parliament. This project became his main preoccupation for the rest of his life. Though the design of this structure is highly complex, Barry achieved an appearance of relative simplicity by successfully employing the Perpendicular style that he had used earlier in King Edward's School. The building was formally opened in 1852, but was not completed until several years after Barry's death, in London, on May 12, 1860. His son, Edward Middleton Barry (1830–1880), supervised its completion.

Barry, who became a member of the Royal Academy of Arts in 1841 and was knighted in 1852, was an eclectic architect whose early work was of either Gothic or classic design according to the dictates of expediency and circumstance; however, his later works showed a marked tendency toward the Gothic. Towers and domes usually ornament his skylines, and those that adorn the Houses of Parliament are generally considered to be among the finest in the world.

BARRY, bar'ē, **Elizabeth** (1658–1713), English actress, who was the first woman to achieve prominence on the English stage. She was known especially as a tragedienne and for many years played opposite Thomas Betterton. Elizabeth Barry never married, but she became the protégée and mistress of the earl of Rochester, and the playwright Thomas Otway fell hopelessly in love with her. She appeared in more than 100 roles, including those of Monimia in Otway's *The Orphan* and Belvidera in his *Venice Preserved*. She retired in 1710, and died in Acton on Nov. 7, 1713.

BARRY, bar'ē, **John** (1745–1803), American naval officer, who is regarded as one of the most skillful and daring American commanders in the Revolutionary War. He was born in Tacumshane, Ireland, went to sea as a youth, and became a shipmaster in Philadelphia. At the outbreak of the Revolution he was one of the first captains commissioned by the Continental Congress.

Commanding the brig *Lexington*, he captured the British sloop *Edward* off Chesapeake Bay on April 7, 1776. This was the first capture in action of a British vessel by a commissioned American warship. Later that year Barry led a notable raid by four small boats on British craft in the Delaware River near Philadelphia, seizing a quantity of supplies. He served briefly in the American Army, leading a volunteer company of artillery at the Battle of Trenton on Dec. 26, 1776. From 1780 to the end of the war he commanded the frigate *Alliance*, engaging in several actions. His fight with the British *Sybil* on March 10, 1783, was the last sea action of the war.

When the United States Navy was reorganized, Barry was named senior captain and in 1794 was placed in command of the new frigate *United States*. During the naval war with France (1798–1800) Barry's command included all American warships in the West Indies. He took seven prizes. Under his command the *United States* carried to France the commissioners who negotiated the end of the war. When Barry died in Philadelphia on Sept. 13, 1803, he stood at the head of the officers' list in the Navy.

BARRY, bar'ē, **Philip** (1896–1949), American-dramatist, who wrote a number of successful drawing-room comedies. He was born in Rochester, N.Y., on June 18, 1896. After graduating from Yale University in 1919, he studied from 1919 to 1922 at George Pierce Baker's 47 Dramatic Workshop at Harvard University. In 1922, Barry's play *You and I* won the Harvard Prize and was produced professionally in New York.

Barry made his reputation primarily with popular comedies, including *Holiday* (1929), *Tomorrow and Tomorrow* (1931), and *The Animal Kingdom* (1932). His greatest success was *The Philadelphia Story* (1939), a comedy of manners that was made into a very popular motion picture in 1940. Among his later comedies was *Foolish Notion* (1944).

Barry's serious dramas, although they received some critical acclaim, were not very successful. They include *John* (1927), an experimental play based on the life of John the Baptist, and *Hotel Universe* (1930), a psychological study of several troubled characters. His most successful serious works were *Here Come the Clowns* (1938) and *Liberty Jones* (1940). The first, an allegory of the conflict between good and evil, was based on Barry's novel *War in Heaven* (1938). The second, also an allegory, was inspired by the outbreak of World War II. Barry died in New York City on Dec. 3, 1949.

BARRY, bar'ē, **Spranger** (1719–1777), Irish actor, who was the great rival of the English actor David Garrick. He was born in Dublin on Nov. 20, 1719. He made his debut in *Othello* at the Smock Alley Theatre in Dublin in 1744. In 1746 he was engaged to play alternately with Garrick in *Hamlet* and *Macbeth* at the Drury Lane Theatre, London. Garrick and Barry played together as Jaffier and Pierre in Thomas Otway's *Venice Preserved,* as Chamont and Castalio in Otway's *The Orphan,* and as Lothario and Horatio in Nicholas Rowe's *The Fair Penitent.*

In 1750, Barry went to Covent Garden, where he played Romeo, Lear, and Richard III while Garrick was appearing in these roles at the Drury Lane. Barry was generally conceded to be one of the great stage lovers of his time, superior even to Garrick in Romeo's love scenes. From 1754 to 1758 he tried unsuccessfully to found a theater in Dublin. He returned to London and played at the Haymarket Theatre until 1766, when Garrick engaged him to play again at the Drury Lane. In 1768, Barry married Ann Street Dancer (1734–1801), an outstanding comedienne, who also played tragedy. They acted together at the Drury Lane and Covent Garden until his death, in London, on Jan. 10, 1777.

BARRY, bar'ē, **William Taylor** (1784–1835), American public official. Born in Lunenburg, Va., on Feb. 15, 1784, he practiced law in Lexington, Ky., and in 1806 was elected to the Kentucky House of Representatives. From 1814 to 1816 he was a U.S. senator and from 1817 to 1821 a state senator. A staunch supporter of Andrew Jackson in the 1828 presidential campaign, Barry served in Jackson's cabinet as postmaster general from 1829. Congressional investigations into his administration of the department exonerated him of various charges, but he resigned in 1835. Appointed minister to Spain, he died while on his way there, in England, on Aug. 30, 1835.

BARRY LYNDON, bar'ē lin'dən, is a novel by the English writer William Makepeace Thackeray (q.v.). It was first published serially in *Fraser's Magazine* in 1844 as *The Luck of Barry Lyndon, a Romance of the Last Century, by Fitzboodle.* When it was published in book form in 1856, Thackeray changed the title to *The Memoirs of Barry Lyndon, Esq., by Himself.* A comparatively short novel, *Barry Lyndon* is generally considered by critics to be one of the best of Thackeray's works although it has never had a large audience.

Thackeray intended the novel as a satire on the practice of giving heroic stature to villainous characters, as in Fielding's *Jonathan Wild* (1743) and Bulwer-Lytton's *Paul Clifford* (1830) and *Eugene Aram* (1832). The hero of *Barry Lyndon,* however, has redeeming qualities, such as frankness and courage, which weaken the satire but strengthen the reader's interest in the hero.

The story is told in the first person by Barry Redmond, son of a widow whose relatives have cheated her of her wealth. He falls in love with his cousin Nora, duels with her fiancé, and is forced to flee to Dublin. There he joins the British army but later deserts to the Prussians. At the end of the Seven Years' War, he is sent by Frederick the Great to spy on a man believed to be an Austrian agent. The man turns out to be Barry's uncle, Barry of Ballybarry, a gambler living in Dresden. Barry deserts the Prussian service to join his uncle. He learns to gamble and eventually wins a large fortune. Determined to raise his social position, he begins a relentless pursuit of Lady Honoria Lyndon, whom he finally bullies into marrying him. He takes her name, mistreats her and her son, and squanders her fortune. Her relatives finally succeed in having him thrown into prison, where he dies.

THE BARRYMORES, John, Ethel, and Lionel—three of the great stage and screen stars of the 20th century.

BROWN BROTHERS

BARRYMORE, bar'i-môr, is the name of an outstanding American theatrical dynasty that has popularly been called "the royal family of the American stage." The name "Barrymore" is a stage name only, for the *Blythe* family, and was never adopted legally.

MAURICE BARRYMORE (1847–1905) was born *Herbert Blythe* at Agra, India. The son of an English surveyor in the East India Company, he was sent to England to study law at Oxford University. He developed an interest in boxing and won an amateur boxing championship and the Queensberry Cup in 1872. The same year he began his stage career, making his first appearance in a London revival of *London Assurance* and adopting the stage name of Barrymore. He made his American debut in 1875 in a Boston production, *Under the Gaslight*, and subsequently performed in New York City, where he was highly praised for his Shakespearean roles.

In 1876 he married the actress Georgianna Drew, and in 1878–1879 he toured several states in a road company with his wife and his brother-in-law John Drew. His best-known theatrical alliance was with Mme Helena Modjeska, for whom he wrote the play *Nadjeska*, produced in 1884. He performed frequently in Europe, and in England he was welcomed into the brilliant society of the day. His wife died in 1893, and in the following year he married Mary Floyd. In 1901 he suffered a mental breakdown. He spent his remaining years in a sanitarium at Amityville, N.Y., where he died on March 26, 1905.

GEORGIANNA EMMA DREW BARRYMORE (1856–1893), Maurice Barrymore's wife, was born in Philadelphia, Pa. The daughter of actors John and Louisa Lane Drew, she began her stage career under her mother's direction in 1872, making her first appearance in *The Ladies' Battle*, at Philadelphia's Arch Street Theatre, which her parents owned. She married Maurice Barrymore on Dec. 31, 1876. They had three children, Lionel, Ethel, and John, all of whom became major figures in the American theater. Highlights of her career included roles in *As You Like It, Divorce,* and *The School for Scandal.* She died at Santa Barbara, Calif., on July 2, 1893.

LIONEL BARRYMORE (1878–1954) was born *Lionel Blythe* in Philadelphia on April 28, 1878, the eldest child of Maurice and Georgianna Barrymore. His first stage performance was in an 1893 production of *The Rivals,* in which his grandmother, Louisa Lane Drew, appeared as Mrs. Malaprop. Although as a child he wished to be a painter, family tradition kept him on stage. His outstanding talent was first recognized in 1898, when he appeared as an organ grinder in *The Mummy and the Hummingbird* with his uncle John Drew. Among his outstanding stage performances were those in *Peter Ibbetson* (1917), *The Jest* (1919), and *Macbeth* (1921).

He made his motion picture debut opposite Mary Pickford in the silent film *The New York Hat* (1915), but his great film successes were in sound pictures. His performance in *A Free Soul* (1931) won him an Academy Award. Among his other notable films were *Arsene Lupin* (1931) and *Grand Hotel* (1932), both with his brother John; *Rasputin and the Empress* (1933), with John and with their sister Ethel; and *Treasure Island* (1934). On radio he was known for his annual interpretation of Ebenezer Scrooge in Charles Dickens' *A Christmas Carol,* first performed in 1934.

Crippled in his later years by several hip fractures, Barrymore remained active on the stage and in films, performing from a wheelchair. Also a talented writer, he was the author of a successful novel, *Mr. Cantonwine: A Moral Tale* (1953). He died at Los Angeles, Calif., on Nov. 15, 1954.

ETHEL BARRYMORE (1879–1959) was born *Ethel Blythe* in Philadelphia on Aug. 15, 1879, daughter of Maurice and Georgianna Barrymore.

GEORGIANNA DREW BARRYMORE, herself a famous actress, with her children, Ethel, Lionel, and John.

BROWN BROTHERS

She made her professional stage debut in New York City in 1896 in *Rosemary*, with her uncle John Drew. In 1901 she starred in the New York production *Captain Jinks of the Horse Marines*, for which she was acclaimed the outstanding young actress in the United States. Highly successful stage performances followed in *A Doll's House* (1905), *Alice-Sit-by-the-Fire* (1906), *The Silver Box* (1907), *Cousin Kate* (1912), *Déclassé* (1919), and *The Second Mrs. Tanqueray* (1924). Between 1922 and 1926 she distinguished herself in Shakespearean roles.

In 1928, Miss Barrymore celebrated the opening of the Ethel Barrymore Theater in New York City by appearing in *The Kingdom of God*. Her later stage successes included the highly praised *The Corn Is Green* (1940) and *Embezzled Heaven* (1944). She also gave outstanding performances in several motion pictures, most notably *None But the Lonely Heart* (1944). She died in Los Angeles, Calif., on June 18, 1959.

JOHN BARRYMORE (1882–1942) was born *John Sidney Blythe* in Philadelphia on Feb. 15, 1882, the youngest child of Maurice and Georgianna Barrymore. He worked briefly as an illustrator for two New York City newspapers before turning to a career in the theater. He made his theatrical debut in 1903 in a Chicago production, *Magda*. He performed in New York City in *The Dictator* (1905) and toured with that play in the United States, England, and Australia. His first important dramatic role was in John Galsworthy's *Justice* (1910), and he later costarred with his brother Lionel in *Peter Ibbetson* and *The Jest*.

In his early years Barrymore distinguished himself as an interpreter of Shakespeare. His first major Shakespearean performance was in 1920, when he played the title role in *Richard III*. In 1922, as Hamlet, he was acclaimed the greatest Shakespearean actor of the day.

Barrymore left the legitimate stage after 1923 and went into motion pictures, returning to the theater only once, in an inferior play, *My Dear Children* (1939). His early film successes included *Dr. Jekyll and Mr. Hyde*, *Beau Brummell*, *The Sea Beast*, and *Don Juan*. Later pictures of some merit included *Moby Dick*, *Grand Hotel*, *Twentieth Century*, and *Romeo and Juliet*. John Barrymore became a popular radio actor during the last years of his life. His autobiography, *Confessions of an Actor*, was published in 1926.

Barrymore was married to Katherine Corri Harris, Michael Strange, and Dolores Costello. He died in Los Angeles on May 29, 1942.

DIANA BARRYMORE (1921–1960) was born *Diana Blythe* in New York City on March 3, 1921, the daughter of John Barrymore and his second wife. Her Broadway debut in 1939 in *The Romantic Mr. Dickens* was followed by performances in such plays as *The Eagle Squadron* (1942) and *The Ivory Branch* (1955). She also acted in several films, including *Ladies Courageous* (1945). Her autobiography, *Too Much, Too Soon* (1957), recounts her struggles with alcoholism. She died in New York City on Jan. 25, 1960.

JOHN BARRYMORE, JR. (1932–   ) was born *John Blythe, Jr.*, at Beverly Hills, Calif., on June 4, 1932, the son of John Barrymore and his third wife. He made his motion picture debut in *The Sundowners* (1950) and later appeared in numerous films, including *While the City Sleeps* (1956) and *Big Night* (1960).

BARSTOW, bär'stō, a city in southeastern California, is in San Bernardino County, about 90 miles (145 km) northeast of Los Angeles. It is a center for a large desert region that is dotted with ranches and mines. Barstow is an important railroad division point, and the diesel maintenance shops of the Atchison, Topeka and Santa Fe Railway are here. A U.S. Marine Corps depot and the Goldstone tracking station are nearby. The ghost town of Calico, where silver was mined in the early 1880's, is near the city. Barstow was an early mining and frontier town. It was named in 1886 for William Barstow Strong, president of the Santa Fe Railroad, and incorporated in 1947. Government is by mayor and council. Population: 17,442.

BARSUMAS (c. 420–c. 490), bär-sōō'məs, was a Syrian monk, who, as bishop of Nisibis (now Nasaybin, Turkey), vigorously supported Nestorianism. This doctrine upheld two natures in the Incarnate Christ (see NESTORIANISM). Adherents of the doctrine were condemned at the Latrocinium Council (439), but the decrees of this body overruled by the Council of Chalcedon (451). Barsumas became bishop of Nisibis sometime after 457. He was welcomed at the royal court in Persia and is regarded as the leader of Nestorianism there. He often advanced his beliefs by force. A theological school established by him in Nisibis became highly influential. He was also called *Barsuma* or *Bar Soma*.

BART, bär, Jean (1650–1702), French seaman. He was born in Dunkerque (Dunkirk), on Oct. 21, 1650. He entered the Dutch navy but on the outbreak of war between France and the Netherlands in 1672 he entered the service of France, commanding a privateer. He soon distinguished himself and, becoming known to Louis XIV, was commissioned to cruise in the Mediterranean. He was appointed a captain in 1686 and commander of a squadron in 1697.

In 1692, Bart broke through the blockade of Dunkerque by the English and Dutch fleets, destroying many merchantmen and finally landing near Newcastle, England, where he destroyed 200 houses, and returned with a large booty. The following year under Tourville he helped to defeat the Anglo-Dutch fleet, his single ship the *Glorieux* destroying six of the enemy. He died in Dunkerque on April 27, 1702. A bronze statue of Bart by David d'Angers, erected by public subscription, was unveiled in the city of his birth in 1845.

BARTAS, bär-tàs', Seigneur du (1544–1590), French author and diplomat who is best known for his epic poem *La semaine*. The work is an account of the creation, and probably influenced John Milton's *Paradise Lost*.

He was born *Guillaume de Salluste*, at Monfort, the son of a prosperous Huguenot family. His first extant poetic effort was *Judith*, which was followed in 1578 by *La semaine*. Parts of *La semaine* were first translated into English by Sir Philip Sidney. Joshua Sylvester translated his entire works into English as *Du Bartas his Devine Weekes and Workes* (1608). In 1587, Bartas traveled in Scotland and England as a diplomat for Henry of Navarre (later Henry IV of France). A second biblical epic poem, *La seconde semaine*, remained unfinished at the time of his death, in Paris in July 1590.

BARTER is the exchange of goods or services without the use of money. The earliest trade, before the invention of money, took the form of barter. Among nonliterate peoples in many parts of the world, barter is still widely practiced; however, the use of money in the form of national currencies has everywhere tended to replace ancient barter customs.

Early Trading. Barter was the earliest basis for the development of markets, where the concept of "fair value" or "equivalent value" emerged even without a standardized medium of exchange. Such concepts as "value" and "price" generally developed in the process of bargaining or haggling, a way of arriving at a fair price by consensus. A man wishing to exchange a surplus of potatoes by barter must find someone who, first, needs his potatoes, and, second, has something to exchange that the seller needs. A man wishing to acquire potatoes must find someone who has potatoes to dispose of and wishes to acquire something the would-be buyer has available. Then the two men must bargain to decide how many potatoes will be exchanged for the other commodity.

Anthropologists have found more examples of barter between tribes and communities than within such groups. This is most likely explained by the fact that internal exchanges often represent social and ceremonial gift-giving, whereas intergroup barter is a means of meeting economic needs. Tribal peoples, like nation-states, are seldom economically self-sufficient and must find ways of complementing what they themselves are able to produce.

Silent Trade. The most striking type of barter is the so-called "silent trade," in which no direct contact occurs between the parties to the exchange. One group leaves trade items at a designated place. Members of the second group come later and if they find the items desirable, leave goods of their own in place of those they take. Such barter has occurred between groups that have hostile relations or no relations at all with each other, and between people of mutually unintelligible languages.

Examples of silent trade were reported by ancient and medieval historians such as Herodotus and Ibn Battuta. Modern anthropologists have observed silent trade among tribes of California Indians, Pygmies and Bantus in the Congo, natives of New Guinea, and others. These examples show how the need to trade overrides what might appear to be insurmountable difficulties.

Trading Chains. Intertribal trade frequently involves the development of trade partnerships, some of which form chains passing through many groups and across hundreds of miles. Examples of this sort of barter have been found among Australian tribes in modern times: stone axes from southern sources are known to have been distributed in this manner to northern tribes. Such trading chains probably also explain why such items as barracuda jaws from the Gulf of Mexico and mica from the Rocky Mountains are found among the archaeological remains of the prehistoric Hopewell peoples of Ohio.

Even in industrialized societies, some bartering still goes on. In the United States, for example, "swapping" through the medium of newspaper columns is barter in pure form. See also MONEY; TRADE.

ERIKA BOURGUIGNON
The Ohio State University

BARTERED BRIDE, The, a comic opera in three acts by the Czech composer Bedřich Smetana, with a libretto by Karel Sabina. The Czech title is *Prodaná Nevěstá.* The opera was first produced in Prague, at the Provisional National Theater, on May 30, 1866. Its American premiere was in Chicago, at the Haymarket Theater, on Aug. 20, 1893. In Great Britain and the United States, the opera is usually given in German as *Die verkaufte Braut.* Smetana, who is often considered the founder of modern Czech music, said that he wrote the opera to prove that he could compose in the Czech style after critics complained that his first opera, *The Brandenburgers in Bohemia,* was too Wagnerian.

The plot of *The Bartered Bride* deals with the prematrimonial problems of Marie, whose parents have arranged for her marriage to Wenzel, the son of the rich peasant Micha. However, Marie is in love with Hans, a boy of unknown ancestry. The marriage broker Kezal bribes Hans to give up Marie, and Hans, taking the money offered, agrees, but with the stipulation that Marie should be given in marriage to a son of Micha. Marie then spitefully agrees to marry Wenzel. At the wedding, however, Hans is recognized by Micha as his son by a previous marriage and, therefore, by the terms of the agreement is entitled to Marie's hand. The opera ends with Marie and Hans receiving their parents' blessings.

BARTH, bärt, **Heinrich** (1821–1865), a German explorer and geographer, who wrote extensively of his discoveries in Africa and the Mediterranean region. He was born in Hamburg on Feb. 16, 1821, and in 1845 began his first exploration of the countries bordering on the Mediterranean Sea. Returning to Germany in 1847, he wrote an account of his travels under the title *Wanderungen durch die Küstenländer des Mittelmeers* (1849; *Journeys Through the Border Lands of the Mediterranean*).

Barth was next invited by the British government to accompany an expedition to central Africa. He spent five years on the expedition and traveled almost 12,000 miles (19,312 km) through the interior of Africa. The result of these travels was published in a book entitled *Travels and Discoveries in North and Central Africa* (1857–58). Barth died in Berlin on Nov. 25, 1865.

BARTH, bärth, **John** (1930–), American novelist. He was born in Cambridge, Md., on May 27, 1930. His early interest was in jazz, and he studied orchestration briefly at the Juilliard School of Music in New York City before going to Johns Hopkins University in Baltimore, where he received his B.A. and M.A. degrees. Barth taught English at Pennsylvania State University and at the State University of New York in Buffalo. His novels include *The Floating Opera* (1956), *The End of the Road* (1958), *The Sot-Weed Factor* (1960), and *Giles Goat-Boy* (1966).

Barth's fiction relies heavily on a combination of humor and surrealistic fantasy in order to express serious themes, and he has readily acknowledged his debt to James Joyce and Franz Kafka. *Giles Goat-Boy* is generally considered to be his most important novel. It is, according to the author, a simile turned into a metaphor, its locale being "a university that *is* the world—not one that is just *like* the world."

BARTH, bärt, **Karl** (1886–1968), Swiss theologian. He was born in Basel on May 10, 1886, and studied at Bern, Berlin, Tübingen, and Marburg. In 1909 he became an assistant pastor in Geneva, and in 1911 he was appointed pastor at Safenwill in Aargau. Here he heard the thunder of artillery at the south end of the western front throughout World War I, and this experience gave Barth an impression of the collapse of civilization that never left him. After the war he was professor successively at Göttingen (from 1921), Münster (from 1925), and Bonn (from 1930). In 1935, because of his opposition to the Nazi government, he returned to Switzerland to teach at Basel, where he died on Dec. 9, 1968.

Widely popular as a teacher, and author of many books on theology, Barth became one of the most influential forces in modern religious thought. His theological position changed more than once, a fact that attracts rather than repels the "existential" thinkers of today, for Barth's theology is addressed to the problems of today. His *Epistle to the Romans* (1919) is a proclamation of a new and independent approach to all Christian teaching. But even this was revised in 1922 and repeatedly thereafter. *The Word of God and Theology* (1924) is a more popular exposition of the principle of modern scriptural interpretation, still in strict continuity with the fundamental doctrines of Reformed theology. *Christian Doctrine* (1927) and *I Believe* (that is, the Creed, 1935) set forth his views more systematically. Thus far, Barth's aim was criticism and correction of current theology—"to add a pinch of spice" and emphasize revelation. But in 1932 he began an immense undertaking in systematic, exegetical, and apologetic theology. By the mid 1960's it included thirteen double volumes.

A Theology of Crisis. Barth's combination of free Biblical criticism and exegesis with a commanding allegiance to "orthodox" or "neoorthodox" theology attracted students in all Christian churches, and beyond. He early broke with the scholars who dominated German theology in the opening decades of the 20th century, giants like Adolf Harnack and Wilhelm Herrmann. Their "liberal" theology seemed far too academic for a world at war or crushed by its aftermath.

What Barth sought to articulate was a "theology of (or for) crisis." For multitudes the world over, the horrors of war were a denial not only of God but of a rational theology in explanation of God's ways. The whole traditional theodicy embedded in patristic, Scholastic, and Reformation theology, and in popular modern thought, had collapsed under the unbearable burden of a total denial of God and of our understanding of Him. God is still "the unknown God." Revelation is not arrived at as the end of a historical or philosophical process but is really superhistorical. History is only a parable projecting or pointing to the true reality. Christianity is centered in Christ, the supernatural divine being, not in the historical Jesus. The Fall was not an event in history but a superhistorical reality, which can be discovered and attested or experienced today. Hence every moment of human existence calls for decision—not to create an ideal state, the Kingdom of God, but to add to the glory of God. No one can be sure of salvation, but one may hope for it by the mercy of God.

Central Position of Christology. Barth rejects the whole traditional Western and especially Roman scheme of "natural theology." "Barthianism" is

Karl Barth

(Swiss theologian)

MAX EHLERT, FROM CAMERA PRESS-PIX INC.

not opposed to philosophy as set forth by the great teachers, Plato and Kant, but supplements it. The contradictions of philosophy are met by the strategy of modern "dialectic"—not Plato's, but the dialectic of the no-man's-land of today, where opposing truths and insights are in conflict, and the only possible reconciliation is to acknowledge that "we see in part." This is not God's fault, nor a sad defect in the divine revelation, but is due to human inability to see both sides of a subject—or object—at one time. Such "dialectic" is inevitable in this present world and for such limited observers and interpreters as we are. But "the foundation of God stands sure," and the real ground of our hope is not rational coherence but the assurance given in revelation.

On the basis of this view of Christian theology, the centrality of Christology (the doctrine of Christ) is obvious, since revelation is completed and perfected in Christ. This is not the traditional or classical Christian view, which makes God central and the Incarnation of His Son the mode or act of God in dealing with the universe, with human sin, and with the final consummation of creation. The Scholastic debates over the necessity of the Incarnation with or without man's sin lose their significance today; the finality of Christ all but sweeps aside the doctrine of God the Creator, Redeemer, and Sanctifier—though Barth does not reject the Trinitarian doctrine. But the more recent varieties of popular apologetics reflect the inescapable implications of Barth's doctrine of "the unknown God," the "wholly Other," and his rejection of human efforts at progress or self-salvation.

FREDERICK C. GRANT
Union Theological Seminary

Bibliography

Bouillard, Henri, *Karl Barth* (Paris 1957).

Casalis, Georges, *Portrait of Karl Barth,* tr. by R.M. Brown (Garden City, N.Y., 1963).

Clark, Gordon H., *Karl Barth's Theological Method* (Philadelphia 1963).

Hamer, Jerome, *Karl Barth,* tr. by D.M. Maruca (Westminster, Md., 1964).

Kung, Hans, *Justification: The Doctrine of Karl Barth and a Catholic Reflection,* tr. by Thomas Collins (New York 1964).

Parker, Thomas H.L., ed., *Essays on Christology for Karl Barth* (London 1956).

Pauck, Wilhelm, *Karl Barth, Prophet of a New Christianity?* (New York 1931).

Van Til, Cornelius, *Christianity and Barthianism* (Philadelphia 1962).

BARTHÉ, bär-tā', **Richmond** (1901–), American Negro sculptor, whose best-known works are portrait studies of eminent Negroes. He executed (1945) the bust of Booker T. Washington for the Hall of Fame at New York University and the statues of Toussaint L'Ouverture and Général Dessalines, commissioned by the Haitian government in 1952. Barthé was born in Bay St. Louis, Miss., on Jan. 28, 1901. He studied painting at the Chicago Art Institute from 1924 to 1928 and then turned to sculpture. Among his many honors and prizes are a Julius Rosenwald fellowship (1931–1932) and a Guggenheim fellowship (1940–1941).

BARTHÉLEMY, bär-tāl-mē', **Marquis François de** (1747–1830), French diplomat. He was born in Aubagne, France, on Oct. 20, 1747, and was brought up by his uncle, Jean Jacques Barthélemy, the author of *Anacharsis*. The duke of Choiseul established him in diplomacy. In 1795 he successively negotiated with Prussia, Spain, and the Elector of Hesse the Peace of Basel, the first treaties concluded by France after the abolition of the monarchy in 1792. This settlement, which was favorable to France, won him an enviable reputation, and he was elected a member of the Directory in 1797.

After the coup d'état of the 18th Fructidor (Sept. 4, 1797), he was removed from the government, arrested, and transported with Charles Pichegru and Jean Pierre Ramel to French Guiana. But Barthélemy escaped to the United States and made his way to England. Following the overthrow of the Directory and the establishment of the Consulate, Napoleon, who was first consul, recalled Barthélemy and made him a senator. On the establishment of the empire, he received the title of count and showed great devotion to Napoleon during the course of his prosperity. But as soon as misfortune threatened Napoleon, Barthélemy sided at once with the emperor's enemies. He was made minister of state and a marquis by Louis XVIII. He died in Paris on April 3, 1830.

BARTHÉLEMY, bär-tāl-mē', **Jean Jacques** (1716–1795), French archaeologist. He was born at Cassis on Jan. 20, 1716. He prepared for religious orders but left the church when he found that he lacked a religious vocation. He then went to Paris, where he became interested in the study of classical Greece and Rome.

In 1747 he was named a member of the Academy of Inscriptions. About this time he became acquainted with the future duke de Choiseul, who invited Barthélemy to accompany him when he was appointed ambassador to Rome in 1754. Three years of study in Italy gave Barthélemy a good archaeological background.

Although he wrote technical books on archaeology, his most influential work was *Travels of the Younger Anarcharsis in Greece* (1788), an account of the government, customs, and buildings of Greece in the 4th century B.C. as they might have appeared to a traveler at that time. Barthélemy's work was one of the most widely read books in 19th century France, was translated into many languages, and helped stimulate interest in the classical period. In 1789 he received a place in the Académie Française. He was arrested in 1793 on a charge of aristocratic leanings but was soon released. He died in Paris on April 30, 1795.

BARTHÉLEMY SAINT-HILAIRE, bär-tāl-mē' saN-tē-lâr', **Jules** (1805–1895), French politician and scholar. He was born in Paris on Aug. 19, 1805. After an early career as a journalist and government official, he taught philosophy at the Collège de France. In the revolution of 1848 he was elected to the constituent assembly. After the coup d'etat of December 1852, he retired until his election to the legislature in 1869. In 1880 he became minister of foreign affairs in the cabinet of Jules Ferry, but he retired from public life the next year to devote his time to scholarly work. He completed his French translation of Aristotle in 1892. He died in Paris on Nov. 24, 1895.

BARTHOLDI, bär-tôl-dē', **Frédéric Auguste** (1834–1904), French sculptor, who created the statue *Liberty Enlightening the World*, popularly known as the *Statue of Liberty*. Bartholdi conceived the idea and initiated the project in 1874, after a visit to the United States. The statue, given to the United States by France, was dedicated in 1886. See STATUE OF LIBERTY.

Bartholdi was born in Colmar, Alsace, on April 2, 1834. He began his career as a student of painting but later turned to sculpture. In 1880 he completed the gigantic sculpture *Lion of Belfort*, carved in the red-rock hill that towers above Belfort, France. The statue commemorates the city's defense against the Prussians in the Franco-Prussian War of 1870–1871.

Bartholdi's many other monumental sculptures include statues of *Lafayette* and *George Washington*, in the Place des États-Unis in Paris; *Lafayette Arriving in America* (1873), in Union Square, New York City; the *Bartholdi Fountain* (1875), in the Botanical Gardens, Washington, D.C.; and *Switzerland Assuaging the Sorrows of Strasbourg in 1870* (1895), in Basel, Switzerland. He died in Paris, on Oct. 4, 1904.

BARTHOLIN, bär-tōo'lin, **Thomas** (1616–1680), Danish scholar and physician. He was born in Copenhagen, Denmark, on Oct. 20, 1616, the son of Kaspar Bartholin, a distinguished Danish scholar and physician. Thomas Bartholin was professor of anatomy at the University of Copenhagen from 1648 until 1661; later, he returned to the university as librarian. Bartholin did extensive work on the lymphatic system and in 1652 published *De lacteis thoracicis*, confirming the existence of a thoracic duct (a main trunk of the lymphatic system) in man. He also revised his father's *Institutiones anatomicae*. He died in Hagestedgaard, Denmark, Dec. 4, 1680.

Erasmus Bartholin (1625–1698), a physician, was the brother of Thomas Bartholin. He earned his doctor's degree in medicine at the University of Padua in Italy, and, returning to Denmark, was appointed professor of mathematics and medicine at the University of Copenhagen. In 1669 he observed that a single ray of light passing through a transparent crystal, called Iceland spar, refracted in two different angles. Knowledge of this phenomenon of double refraction aided in the study of polarized light.

Kaspar Bartholin (1655–1738), an anatomist, was the son of Thomas Bartholin. Educated at the University of Copenhagen, he was professor of anatomy there until 1701. He is credited with the discovery of the larger accessory duct of the sublingual salivary gland and of Bartholin's vaginal glands.

BARTHOLIN'S GLANDS, bär-tō'linz, are two small mucous glands situated one on either side of the vaginal opening. In the presence of disease they are subject to inflammation, known in medical circles as bartholinitis. They are named after their discoverer, the Danish anatomist Kaspar Bartholin (1655–1738).

BARTHOLOMAE, bär-tō-lō-mä', **Christian** (1855–1925), German philologist and linguist, who wrote several important treatises on the Indo-European language family. He was an advocate of the neogrammarian theory of linguistics, which holds that as a language evolves its phonetic changes follow consistent patterns.

Bartholomae was born at Forst ober Limmersdorf, near Bayreuth, on Jan. 21, 1855. He studied philology and philosophy at the universities of Munich, Leipzig, and Erlangen. From 1874 to 1879 he studied comparative philology and oriental languages at Leipzig, which was the center of neogrammarian scholarship. Thereafter he taught at the universities of Halle, Münster, and Giessen, and from 1909 to 1924 he was professor of Sanskrit and Indo-Germanic philology at the University of Heidelberg. He died on the island of Langeoog, in the North Sea, on Aug. 27, 1925.

His studies in Indo-European languages include *Das altiranische Verbum* (1878), *Arische Forschungen* (1882–87), and *Handbuch der altiranische Dialekte* (1883).

BARTHOLOMAEUS ANGLICUS, bär-thol-ə-mē'əs ang'glikəs, was an English encyclopedist of the 13th century. The English form of his name is *Bartholomew the Englishman*. He was a Franciscan monk, and he has been confused with the English Franciscan Bartholomaeus de Glanville. There is no longer doubt, however, that Bartholomaeus Anglicus was the author of the first important medieval encyclopedia, *De proprietatibus rerum* (*On the Properties of Things*).

After serving as a professor at the University of Paris, he traveled to Magdeburg in 1231 and there compiled the encyclopedia. It included all the scientific knowledge that his age had recently gleaned from Latin translations of Greek, Arabian, and Jewish naturalists and medical scholars. Bartholomaeus quoted Aristotle, Hippocrates, and less famous writers. He also described such creatures as griffins and sweet-throated swans, producing an extraordinary mixture of fact and fable. Despite its shortcomings, his highly popular and widely circulated work, which was translated into several languages, helped to stimulate scientific inquiry.

BARTHOLOMÉ, bär-tô-lô-mä', **Paul Albert** (1848–1928), French sculptor of the academic school, who is best known for his "classical" funeral monuments featuring grieving nudes. He was born at Thiverval on Aug. 29, 1848, and studied painting in Geneva and Paris. He first turned to sculpture in 1886, after the death of his wife, and his first work was a memorial to her, erected in the cemetery of Bouillant. His second major piece of sculpture, usually considered his masterpiece, is the *Monument to the Dead*, which represents humanity in mourning. The model was exhibited in 1895, and a large limestone version was erected in 1899 at the entrance to Père Lachaise Cemetery, Paris.

Bartholomé became a champion of the academic or "classical" French style, which at that time was especially opposed to the ruggedly unconventional new style introduced by Auguste Rodin. Among Bartholomé's works in Paris are the bronze *Weeping Child*, in the Luxembourg Palace; the monument *Paris 1914–1918*, at the Place du Carrousel near the Louvre; and a monument to Jean-Jacques Rousseau, at the Panthéon. Bartholomé died in Paris on Oct. 31, 1928.

BARTHOLOMEW, bär-thol'ə'mū, **Saint,** one of the 12 apostles of Christ. He is mentioned in the New Testament Gospels of Matthew, Mark, and Luke. The name "Bartholomew" is not the saint's given name but is derived from his father's name "Tholmai" plus "bar," meaning (in Hebrew) "son of." There are many indications that the Nathanael of St. John's Gospel and Bartholomew are the same person. His full name, therefore, would be Nathanael Bar Tholmai.

Tradition relates that Bartholomew preached the gospel in India and afterward traveled to Greater Armenia. There he converted many to Christianity and, according to the Roman martyrology, "was flayed alive by the barbarians, and by command of King Astyages fulfilled his martyrdom by beheading." Because of this legend, St. Bartholomew is often represented in art, as in the *Last Judgment* of Michelangelo, as flayed and holding his own skin in his hands. His feast day is August 24.

BARTHOLOMEW, bär-thol'ə'mū, **John** (1831–1893), Scottish map maker. He was born in Edinburgh and, as a young man, joined his father's firm of map engravers and publishers there. One of his notable publishing achievements was a series of maps of Great Britain, reduced from the maps by the government ordnance survey. Bartholomew's maps were drawn to the scale of ½ inch or ¼ inch to the mile.

BARTHOLOMEW, bär-thol'ə'mū, **John George** (1860–1920), Scottish map maker. He was born in Edinburgh on March 22, 1860, the son of the map maker John Bartholomew. After 1889 he directed the family firm. His maps, especially in his atlases of Scotland and of England and Wales, presented a large amount of geographical and statistical information. He made many technical improvements in the drawing and printing of maps. The most important of these was his refinement of the use of layering (graded shading or coloring to indicate contours). He died at Cintra, Portugal, on April 13, 1920.

BARTHOLOMEW FAIR, bär-thol'ə-mū fâr, is the last of the great comedies of Ben Jonson. It was written for Lady Elizabeth's Company and was first presented on Oct. 31, 1614, at the Hope Theatre, London, used for both plays and bear-baiting.

Evidently with the Hope's somewhat rowdy audience in mind, Jonson in this play abandoned his usual stinging satire in favor of farcical situations, vigorous dialogue, and boisterous laughter. As he says in his "Induction," the play is "merry and . . . full of noise." It lacks a continuous story but presents a series of brilliantly etched characters who haunt Bartholomew Fair, which was held annually at Smithfield, London, from 1135 to 1855. In the toyseller, Lantern Leatherhead, Jonson may have been ridiculing the architect Inigo Jones. Other characters in the play include "a strutting Horsecourser," "a fine oyly Pig-woman with her Tapster," "a wise Justice of Peace meditant," "a civill Cut-purse serchant," "and as fresh an Hypocrite, as ever was broach'd, rampant." The hypocrite is Zeal-of-the-Land Busy, a Puritan whose attempts to stifle pleasure draw the playwright's scorn.

John Aubrey says that the satire on the Puritans derived from a royal suggestion. Whether or not this claim is accurate, the play was presented at Whitehall the day after its initial performance "and then dedicated to King James." As Puritanism gained strength in England, the popularity of *Bartholomew Fair* declined. After the Restoration, however, Charles II is known to have enjoyed the play's ridicule of his political opponents. Because of the topicality of its subject matter, the play is seldom revived.

BARTHOU, bàr-tōō′, **Jean Louis** (1862–1934), French statesman. He was born at Oloron-Ste.-Marie on Aug. 25, 1862. In 1884, after attending the University of Bordeaux, he began practicing law but soon entered politics and was elected to parliament in 1889. From 1894 until his death he served as a cabinet minister.

On March 22, 1913, Barthou became prime minister. During his premiership, which lasted until December 1913, the period of compulsory military service was lengthened from two to three years. After the conclusion of World War I, he represented France in many important international conferences. As president of the Reparations Commission in 1922 he evolved a method for determining Germany's capacity to pay reparations that later materialized in the Dawes Plan.

When Gaston Doumergue became prime minister in 1934, Barthou was named minister of foreign affairs. As part of his plan to contain possible Germany aggression, Barthou sought to strengthen France's relations with Russia, England, and the Danubian states. After a tour by Barthou of eastern Europe, Alexander I of Yugoslavia was invited to Paris to discuss Franco-Yugoslav relations. Barthou and the king were assassinated on Oct. 9, 1934, in Marseille.

Barthou was elected a member of the French Academy in 1918. His principal published work was a biography of Mirabeau.

BARTLEBY THE SCRIVENER, bàr′təl-bē, skriv′-nər, is a short story by Herman Melville (q.v.), first published in *Putnam's Magazine* in 1853. It is a surrealistic tale that mixes elements of the bizarre with a touch of grim comedy in a manner similar to that which was to be employed later by such writers as Franz Kafka.

The story is told in the first person by a New York City lawyer who employs young Bartleby as a minor clerk in his office. Bartleby, who gradually decides that his tasks are of too menial a nature for his efforts, finally refuses to do any work at all. He remains at his place, however, gazing blankly at the wall in front of him. After he has been dismissed from his job he refuses to leave, preferring to remain staring at the wall. The distraught lawyer is finally forced to move his business to a new location, and Bartleby is taken to prison. There he is visited by the lawyer who feels vaguely responsible for his former clerk's predicament and secures special privileges for him. Bartleby, who by now refuses even food, eventually dies.

BARTLESVILLE, bär′təlz-vil, is a city in northeastern Oklahoma, on the Caney River, 50 miles (80 km) by road north of Tulsa. It is the seat of Washington County. The city is at the center of the older section of the Mid-Continent oilfield, where Oklahoma's first commercial oil well was completed in 1897. Two of the major oil- and gas-producing companies in the United States have headquarters in Bartlesville, and there is a federal petroleum experiment station in the city. Industries include pump manufacturing, zinc smelting, and the manufacture of plastics and inorganic fertilizers. Bartlesville is the home of Central Pilgrim College and contains the 19-story Price Tower, designed by Frank Lloyd Wright. The community was founded in 1877 and was incorporated in 1897. It adopted city-manager government in 1927. Population: 29,683.

BARTLETT, bärt′lət, **John** (1820–1905), American author and publisher, who compiled the famous *Familiar Quotations* (1855) that, in its numerous editions, has remained the standard reference work in its field. He was born in Plymouth, Mass., on June 14, 1820, and began his career in 1836 as a clerk in a Cambridge, Mass., book-store, which he bought in 1849. He joined the Boston publishing company of Little, Brown in 1865, and became a senior partner in 1878. Bartlett also compiled a *Complete Concordance to Shakespeare's Dramatic Works and Poems* (1894). He died in Cambridge on Dec. 3, 1905.

BARTLETT, bärt′let, **John Russell** (1805–1886), American historian and bibliographer. He was born in Providence, R.I., on Oct. 23, 1805. From 1836 to 1850 he was a partner in the New York City book publishing house of Bartlett and Welford. His *Dictionary of Americanisms* (1850) enjoyed wide popularity. After acting in 1850–1853 as a commissioner to fix the boundary between the United States and Mexico, he published *A Personal Narrative of Explorations and Incidents in Texas, New Mexico, California, Sonora, and Chihuahua* (2 vols., 1854). From 1855 to 1872 he was secretary of state of Rhode Island. He edited *Index to the Acts of the General Assembly of Rhode Island, 1758–1862* (1863). He died in Providence on May 28, 1886.

BARTLETT, bärt′lət, **Joseph** (1762–1827), American lawyer, legislator, and author. He was born in Plymouth, Mass., on June 10, 1762. After graduating (1782) from Harvard, he went to Salem to study law and also opened a school there. Soon abandoning these pursuits, he went to London and embarked on an adventurous life, which landed him in debtor's prison. A play he wrote in prison—which he claimed was the first American play performed on the English stage—brought him the money to pay his debts. He then returned to Boston to study.

Bartlett began his legal career in Woburn, Mass. Later he moved to Cambridge, which he represented (1798–1801) in the state legislature. He was an ardent democrat and disciple of Thomas Paine, and his political writings reveal a gift for pungent satire. In 1810 he published a volume of original aphorisms. His best-known work is the satiric poem *The New Vicar of Bray* (1823). Noted for his eccentricities, he once painted his house black and called it "The Coffin." He died in Boston on Oct. 20, 1827.

BARTLETT, bart'lət, **Josiah** (1729–1795), American patriot. He was born in Amesbury, Mass., on Nov. 21, 1729. He began the practice of medicine in 1750, at Kingston, N.H., and established a reputation during a sore throat epidemic in 1754 by his original treatment with cinchona. He received appointments from the royal governor, John Wentworth, but lost them in 1775 for supporting the colonists' cause.

Chosen a delegate to the Continental Congress, he was the first who voted for the Declaration of Independence, his name being first called as representative of the most northerly colony. In 1778 he also had the honor of being the first delegate to vote for the Articles of Confederation.

He was appointed chief justice of the New Hampshire court of common pleas in 1779 and chief justice of the state superior court in 1788. He was an active member of the state convention called to ratify the federal Constitution in 1788. In 1790 he was elected chief executive of New Hampshire and in 1793 was elected governor under the newly amended state constitution. He retired in 1794 and died in Kingston, N.H., on May 19, 1795.

BARTLETT, bärt'lət, **Paul Wayland** (1865–1925), American sculptor, whose best-known works are monumental portrait studies, including the equestrian statue of Lafayette that was presented to France by the schoolchildren of the United States in 1908 and stands in the court of the Louvre.

Bartlett was born in New Haven, Conn., on Jan. 24, 1865, and studied at the École des Beaux-Arts in Paris. *Bear Tamer,* now in the Metropolitan Museum of Art, New York City, won a medal at the Paris Salon of 1887. His most important works in the United States are statues of Columbus and Michelangelo in the Library of Congress in Washington and the six colossal figures over the entrance of the New York Public Library. Bartlett became director of sculpture at the Glasgow (Scotland) School of Art in 1913. He died in Paris, France, on Sept. 20, 1925.

BARTLETT, bärt'let, **Robert Abram** (1875–1946), British-American explorer. He was born in Brigus, Newfoundland, on Aug. 15, 1875. He began his explorations with Robert E. Peary in 1897 and commanded Peary's expedition ship, the *Roosevelt,* in 1905–1909. On the Canadian Government Arctic Expedition of 1913–1914, he commanded the *Karluk,* which was crushed by the ice. Bartlett reached Wrangel Island, Siberia, with 17 others, and later secured a rescue party. He brought 13 survivors to Nome (Alaska) in September 1915.

Bartlett was in charge of the Arctic expeditions which combined hunting, hydrography expeditions, and student settlement cruises from 1926. From 1942 to 1945, under contract to the United States Navy and Army, he made a series of voyages exploring for war bases in the Arctic. He died in New York City on April 28, 1946.

BARTLETT TROUGH, bärt'lət trôf, is a trench in the floor of the Caribbean Sea south of Cuba. It extends in an east-west direction nearly to the Cayman Islands. Its greatest depth is about 22,800 feet (6,950 meters). Bartlett Trough is the deepest basin in the Caribbean. It is sometimes called *Bartlett Deep* or *Cayman Deep.*

Béla Bartók
(1881–1945)

CULVER PICTURES

BARTÓK, bär'tôk, **Béla** (1881–1945), Hungarian composer, who was a major figure in modern music, ranking with Stravinsky and Schönberg. However, because he steadfastly refused to teach composition (in the belief that it would adversely affect his own composing), Bartók left no artistic progeny, as Schönberg did. And his music, while equal to Stravinsky's, is less easy to assimilate. Nevertheless, many of Bartók's structural concepts were later transformed by others, and almost every important composer since his time felt, in some sense, Bartók's influence.

Bartók was also a virtuoso pianist and had a distinguished career as a concert artist. From 1907 to 1934 he was the foremost teacher of piano at the Budapest Academy of Music.

Life. Béla Bartók was born in Nagyszentmiklós, Hungary (now Sînnicolau Mare, Rumania), on March 25, 1881. He received his first piano lessons from his mother, who taught school in order to support Béla and his sister after their father's death in 1889. From 1899 to 1903 he studied at the Academy of Music in Budapest, where his talents as a pianist were quickly recognized.

In 1905, Bartók began the lifelong involvement with folk music that eventually gave him an international reputation as a scholar. This interest in folk music took him on field trips to all parts of Hungary, as well as to Rumania, North Africa, Turkey, and other countries.

The political upheaval that culminated in World War II ultimately took Bartók to the United States, where he settled in 1940. There, in addition to the money he earned from his appearances as a piano recitalist, he received several commissions for new compositions, a stipend from Columbia University to transcribe and prepare for publication a collection of Serbo-Croatian folk songs, and some financial assistance from the American Society of Composers, Authors, and Publishers (ASCAP). This assistance enabled him to subsist and to receive medical care, but he lived in severe poverty in the United States, and his health, which had always been poor, deteriorated completely. He died in New York City on Sept. 26, 1945.

Works. Bartók published approximately 100 works, of which many are part of the standard concert repertoire. His first major composition, the *Kossuth Symphony* (1904), brought him considerable public attention, partly because it took certain liberties with the Austrian national anthem. Even in his earliest compositions, he began to experiment with new harmonic and rhythmic techniques. His first work to employ these new procedures exclusively was Fourteen Bagatelles for Piano (Opus 6, 1907). This relatively simple early work shares the essential characteristics of later and more complex compositions, such as the Sonata for Two Pianos and Percussion (1937). In both pieces, the influence of folk music is evident in the embellishing figures, the juxtaposition of variable tempos, and the fixed, repetitive, rhythmic patterns.

Bartók's six string quartets span the period from 1910 to 1939. They are regarded as among the finest quartets in the literature and are often compared with the late Beethoven quartets. Bartók's two violin sonatas (1921 and 1922) are difficult to play and elusive in structure. The Sonata for Two Pianos and Percussion (1937), a strong and complex piece, is seldom heard, but Contrasts for Violin, Clarinet, and Piano (1938) is frequently performed.

Major works requiring larger groups of performers include the two violin concertos (1908 and 1938), the two piano concertos (1926 and 1931), Music for Strings, Percussion, and Celesta (1936), and Concerto for Orchestra (1943). Bartók did not finish two other large compositions—a third piano concerto and a concerto for violin and orchestra, but they were completed by the Hungarian-American composer Tibor Serly and published in 1945.

Bartók wrote three stage works: a one-act opera, *Bluebeard's Castle* (1911), and two ballets, *The Wooden Prince* (1916) and *The Wonderful Mandarin* (1919). He also composed two important sets of pieces that are widely used by students: 44 Duos for Violin (1931) and a piano work, *Mikrokosmos* (1926–1939).

Characteristics. Folk music research had a profound effect on Bartók's compositions. From folk music he inferred principles of musical organization that led to the discovery of his most characteristic melodic and harmonic styles. As he wrote in his autobiography, it also enabled him to gain complete and unrestricted control over each tone in the chromatic system of 12 tones.

Bartók achieved his intricate counterpoints by making the melody in one part of a composition imitate the melody in another part, often at dissonant intervals. He exploited rhythmic techniques, such as the use of nonmetrical patterns, extended syncopation, percussive chords at irregular intervals within a measure, and even the combination of several different and complex rhythms simultaneously. But the use of such structural techniques only partially characterizes Bartók's music and distinguishes it from the work of his contemporaries. His special inventiveness in the manipulation of instruments to obtain new sounds was equally remarkable.

ALLEN FORTE
Author of "Contemporary Tone-Structures"

Bibliography

Austin, William, *Music in the 20th Century* (New York 1966).
Bartók, Béla, *Hungarian Folk Music*, tr. by Michel D. Calvocoressi (New York 1931).
Bartók, Béla, and Lord, Albert B., eds., *Serbo-Croatian Folk Songs* (New York 1951).
Bator, Victor, *The Béla Bartók Archives: History and Catalogue* (New York 1963).
Fassett, Agatha, *The Naked Face of Genius* (Boston 1958).
Stevens, Halsey, *The Life and Music of Béla Bartók*, rev. ed. (New York 1964).
Szabolcsi, Bence, *Béla Bartók; His Life in Pictures*, tr. by Sára Karig and Lili Halápy (New York 1965).

BARTOLINI, bär-tō-lē'nē, **Lorenzo** (1777–1850), Italian sculptor, whose neoclassical works were popular during the Napoleonic era. He was born in Savignano on Jan. 6, 1777, and studied in Paris with François Frédéric Lemot. Bartolini's commissions included a large portrait bust of Napoleon I, now in Bastia, Corsica, and a bas-relief for the Vendôme Column in Paris. In 1808, Bartolini founded a school of sculpture in Carrara, Italy. After 1814 he lived in Florence, where he did a monument to Gen. Nikolai Demidov. Bartolini made many neoclassical portrait busts. He died in Florence on Jan. 20, 1850.

BARTOLOMMEO, bär-tō-lôm-mä'ō, **Fra** (1475–1517), Italian painter, who was one of the leading masters of the High Renaissance style in Florence. The monumentality of his paintings is achieved through simplification of form and clarity of color. He was especially known for his masterly painting of drapery. His full name was *Bartolommeo di Pagolo del Fattorino*, and he is sometimes called *Baccio della Porta*.

Bartolommeo was born in Florence on March 28, 1475. He studied with Piero di Cosimo and in the workshop of Cosimo Rosselli, where he met Mariotto Albertinelli, a painter who became a frequent collaborator in his work. Bartolommeo also studied the works of Leonardo and Michelangelo, whose influence is apparent in such early works as the fresco *Last Judgment* (1499–1501, Museo di San Marco, Florence). After the death of Girolamo Savonarola, of whom he was an admirer and follower, Bartolommeo took holy orders in 1501 and joined the Dominican monastery of San Marco. He did not paint for four years. In 1506, Raphael visited Florence and gave Bartolommeo instruction in perspective, receiving in return lessons in coloring and painting drapery.

After a visit to Venice in 1508, Bartolommeo returned to Florence and opened a workshop, with Albertinelli as his chief assistant. They provided many of the most important altarpieces for Florentine churches during the next decade. Among Bartolommeo's major works are the *Vision of St. Bernard* (1504–1507, Accademia, Florence); *God the Father with St. Catherine of Siena and the Magdalene* (Museo, Lucca), two panels of the *Marriage of St. Catherine* (1511, Louvre, Paris; 1512, Pitti Palace, Florence), *Madonna della Misericordia* (1515, Lucca), *Pietà* (1515–1517, Pitti), and *Salvator Mundi* (1516, Pitti). Among the paintings on which Albertinelli assisted Bartolommeo are the *Assumption of the Virgin* (1507–1508, Staatliche Museen, Berlin), *Madonna with Saints* (1509, Museo di San Marco, Florence), and the altarpiece for Cardinal Carondelet (1511–1512, Besançon Cathedral, France).

In 1515, Bartolommeo visited Rome, where he painted two panels, *St. Peter* and *St. Paul*, in the Vatican. He again met Raphael and saw the later works of Michelangelo and Leonardo, which impressed him profoundly. In his mature works Bartolommeo introduced innovations that eventually became an accepted part of 16th-century painting style. These include the use of generalized draperies, rather than contemporary costumes, for religious figures and the use of generalized settings with a minimum of picturesque detail. After about 1514, Bartolommeo's leadership among Florentine painters was challenged by Andrea del Sarto, and his workshop declined after his death, in Florence, on Oct. 31, 1517.

BARTOLOZZI, bär-tō-lôt'tsē, **Francesco** (1727–1815), Italian engraver. He was born in Florence, the son of a goldsmith. He studied at the Florentine Academy, where he excelled in drawing. Turning later to engraving, he studied under Joseph Wagner in Venice. He became active in Venice and in Rome, engraving copies of the works of 17th century master painters.

In 1764, at the invitation of the librarian to King George III, he went to London, where he became engraver to the king. He lived in England for nearly 40 years, in close association with his friend Giovanni Cipriani, and produced numerous engraved copies of the works of such artists as Holbein, Gainsborough, Reynolds, Cosway, and Fra Angelico. In 1802, after accepting a commission to make an engraved portrait of the regent of Portugal, he went to Lisbon, where he became director of the Royal Academy. He died in Lisbon on March 7, 1815.

Bartolozzi exerted a strong influence on French and English engravers of his time, who adopted his use of the stipple, or "red chalk," method. This technique makes it possible to produce varying shades of black and gray, thereby allowing the engraver to achieve a complete range of tones.

Bartolozzi produced more than 700 engravings, prized for their delicacy of execution and accuracy of design. His more notable copies of masterworks include *Death of Lord Chatham,* after John Singleton Copley; *Virgin and Child,* after Carlo Dolci; *Clyte,* after Annibale Carracci; *Venus, Cupid, and a Satyr,* after Luca Giordano; and *St. Jerome,* after Correggio.

BARTOLUS, bär'tō-ləs (1314–1357), Italian legal scholar, who helped revive the historical method in law instruction. He was born at Sassoferrato in 1314. After receiving his LL.D. degree at Bologna, he became professor at Pisa and later at Perugia. He published several works based on studies of the common law and ancient authorities. The most important are *On Procedure, On Evidence,* and *Commentary on the Code of Justinian.* Bartolus, or *Bartolo,* died at Perugia.

BARTON, bär'tən, **Bruce** (1886–1967), American advertising executive and writer. He was born in Robbins, Tenn., on Aug. 5, 1886. After graduating from Amherst College in 1907, he worked briefly in a railroad camp in Montana before taking an editorial job on the *Home Herald,* a magazine published in Chicago. In 1912 he became assistant sales manager for the publishers P.F. Collier and Son in New York City, and it was for this firm that he wrote his first advertising copy.

In 1919, with Roy Durstine and Alex Osborn, he founded an advertising agency, which merged in 1928 with the George Batten Company to become Batten, Barton, Durstine and Osborn, Inc., with Barton as chairman. BBDO (as the firm was familiarly known) quickly became one of the most influential advertising agencies in the world, and much credit for its growth goes to Barton. He created the character Betty Crocker for General Mills and was instrumental in projecting a favorable public image of the United States Steel Corporation. Barton also wrote numerous books, including the best-selling *The Man Nobody Knows* (1925), a popularized treatment of the life of Christ. He died in New York City on July 5, 1967.

Clara Barton

(1821–1912)

BARTON, bär'tən, **Clara** (1821–1912), American humanitarian, who organized the American Red Cross. She was successively a school teacher, clerk, battlefield heroine, lecturer, and relief organizer.

Clarissa Harlowe Barton was born in North Oxford, Mass., on Dec. 25, 1821. Forced to give up her teaching career because of a throat ailment, she worked in the Patent Office in Washington, D.C., from 1854 to 1861. Distressed at the lack of supplies and "comforts" for the wounded in the Civil War, she began, without official organization or affiliation, to minister to casualties on battle sites in Virginia. Soon known as the "Angel of the Battlefield," she divided her time between caring for the wounded and cooking pies and puddings for them. Eventually she was accredited as superintendent of nurses with the Army of the James.

In 1865, at Miss Barton's urging, President Lincoln authorized her to gather records on missing Union soldiers. Thousands of the dead were thus identified, particularly many victims of the notorious Andersonville Prison in Georgia. While combining this work with lecturing, Miss Barton became nationally famous, but in 1869 her health broke and she went to Europe to recuperate.

In Geneva, Miss Barton first heard of the International Red Cross, established in 1864 at the instigation of Jean Henri Dunant. Enrolling as a volunteer to help civilian victims of the Franco-Prussian War, she visited Paris and other cities, remaining abroad until 1873.

After resettling in Washington as a lecturer, Miss Barton was invited by Red Cross authorities in 1877 to work for affiliation of an American society with Geneva. The American group she formed was incorporated as the American Association of the Red Cross in 1881, and in 1882 the U.S. Senate voted adherence to the Geneva Convention of 1864 that established Red Cross principles in international law. Miss Barton assumed the presidency of the American Red Cross.

Aided by a few devoted assistants, but with no formal organization, she introduced to the Red Cross program relief for victims of major disasters, issued appeals for help, and personally led many relief expeditions into regions devastated by forest fires, floods, and hurricanes. In 1898, at the age of 77, she outfitted a ship to take relief supplies to the Cuban insurgents; but with the outbreak of the Spanish-American War she diverted the ship to aid the American forces and ran the operation from a Cuban beachhead.

By 1900, growing criticism of Miss Barton's type of personal leadership brought about reincorporation of the American Red Cross by Congress. The new charter required the rendering of an annual financial report. Although controversy over Miss Barton's methods of control continued, she remained as president until 1904, when she resigned, and the society was reorganized.

With the pains of the early Red Cross long since forgotten, and no evidence ever bringing to question Clara Barton's character, her name rests securely among the great and imaginative pioneers in philanthropic accomplishments.

Her publications include *A Story of the Red Cross* (1904) and *Story of My Childhood* (1907). See also RED CROSS.

CHARLES HURD, *Author of "The Compact History of the American Red Cross"*

Further Reading: Ross, Ishbel, *Angel of the Battlefield* (New York 1956); Williams, Blanche C., *Clara Barton* (Philadelphia 1941).

BARTON, Sir Edmund (1849–1920), Australian prime minister and judge. He was born in Sydney, on Jan. 18, 1849. Educated at the University of Sydney, he was a member of the New South Wales legislature in 1879–1887 and 1891–1894. Following the death of Sir Henry Parkes, Barton was a leader of the movement for Australian federation and in 1900 headed the delegation to London for the passage of the Commonwealth Constitution bill in Parliament. On December 31 of that year he became Australia's first prime minister. He resigned in 1903 and became a justice of the Australian High Court. He died at Medlow on Jan. 7, 1920.

BARTON, Elizabeth (c. 1506–1534), Englishwoman, who figured in a political and religious controversy during the reign of Henry VIII. She was born at Aldington, Kent, and became a servant in Canterbury. Prone to hysterical, perhaps epileptic, seizures during which she uttered religious revelations and prophecies, she became famous when some of these came true. The "Maid of Kent," as she came to be called, attracted the attention of William Warham, archbishop of Canterbury, and he ordered an investigation of the case. Meanwhile, Henry VIII delegated Thomas More to make inquiries. More found her utterances nothing but "what a right simple woman might speak of her own wit."

Edward Bocking, Canterbury's investigator, apparently exploited her for his own political ends. She became a nun at his suggestion, and it is believed that he prompted her political prophecies. She admonished Henry VIII that if he married Anne Boleyn, he would die within six months; following his marriage she warned him that he would be disavowed by his subjects. Henry considered this warning treason, and he had Elizabeth arrested and examined before the Star Chamber. The chamber produced a confession that she had feigned the trances. She was condemned, without benefit of trial, and was hanged at Tyburn, on April 21, 1534. Bocking and four others also were executed.

The validity of documents attesting to her confession has been questioned. Without any trial records to examine, it is impossible to judge whether she was a conspirator, a saint, or a woman with a mental illness. Some authorities believe she was a simple, deluded, and much exploited victim of political intrigue.

BARTONVILLE is a village in north central Illinois, in Peoria County, just southwest of the city of Peoria. Its industrial and business districts border the west bank of the Illinois River, and the residential section lies on a bluff to the west. Major industries are steel and wire production and related metal manufacturing. Machinery, lumber, and livestock feeds also are produced. Peoria State Hospital is in Bartonville. The village was incorporated in 1903 and was named for William C.H. Barton, former owner of the site. Government is by trustees. Population: 7,221.

N. DUTTON, *Peoria Public Library*

BARTOW, bär'tō, a city in central Florida and the seat of Polk County, is situated 38 miles (61.1 km) east of Tampa. It is in a region that raises cattle, grows citrus fruits, and produces phosphate rock. Lake Hancock, a popular recreation center, is nearby. The community was settled in 1851 and named in 1867 after Francis Bartow, a Confederate general. It was incorporated in 1893 and is governed by a council and manager. Population: 12,891.

BARTRAM, John (1699–1777), American botanist, who was described as the "greatest natural botanist in the world" by Linnaeus and is frequently called the "father of American botany." He was born near Darby, Pa., on March 23, 1699. As a young farm boy, he became interested in botany and tried to read, even in Latin, all the available books on the subject. He founded a botanical garden at Kingsessing, Pa., and began there what were probably the first experiments in hybridization. Not especially interested in the details of classification, Bartram was above all a lover of living things. Though his main interest was always botany, he also gave some attention to zoology and geology. He traveled extensively in the eastern United States and in 1751 published a report of its inhabitants, climate, soil, and other conditions. He was in constant correspondence with European botanists and sent them American plant specimens. He died on Sept. 22, 1777, at Kingessing, Pa. A genus of mosses, *Bartramia*, is named for him.

William Bartram (1739–1823), his son, was a traveler and naturalist. He was born in Kingsessing, Pa., on Feb. 9, 1739. He traveled in the southeastern United States and in 1791 published a fascinating book describing his findings. The book is believed to have influenced Wordsworth and Coleridge. William Bartram also corresponded with European naturalists. After his father's death, he and his brother, John, managed the Kingsessing Gardens. He died at Kingsessing on July 22, 1823.

BARTSCH, bärch, **Johann Adam Bernhard von** (1757–1821), Austrian writer on art and engraver, who produced the authoritative critical catalogue of engravers, *Le Peintre-Graveur* (21 vols., 1803–21). The book includes descriptions and evaluations of all principal European engravers up to the 19th century.

Bartsch was born in Vienna on Aug. 17, 1757. At the age of 16 he did a series of engravings of gold and silver medals that were issued during the reign of Maria Theresa. He also produced more than 500 etchings. In 1781 he was appointed keeper of the prints of the royal collection. Bartsch died in Vienna on Aug. 21, 1821.

BARUCH, bə-rōōk', **Bernard Mannes** (1870–1965), American financier, philanthropist, and public official. As a public official, a self-made multimillionaire, and adviser to several presidents, Baruch reflected the temper of the American scene for half a century. A sounding board and spokesman for unformulated public opinion, Baruch, the legendary "park bench statesman," often put into words what the average American thought and felt but did not have the opportunity to say. He was, by turns, a Wall Street tycoon, a Wilsonian idealist, a reluctant New Dealer, and an Eisenhower Democrat. A man whose fame and influence were considerable, Baruch, in his determination to remain behind the scenes and avoid political risks, also forfeited many of the rewards of public service.

Entering public life in 1916 during the administration of President Wilson, Baruch mobilized American industry in World War I as chairman of the War Industries Board. His last major national service was in 1946 when President Truman named him to present to the United Nations the U.S. plan for atomic energy control.

Early Life. Baruch was born in Camden, S.C., on Aug. 19, 1870. He was the second son of Dr. Simon Baruch, a surgeon born in Posen, East Prussia, who had served with the Confederate forces under Gen. Robert E. Lee, and of Belle (Wolfe) Baruch, of Winnsboro, S.C., whose American heritage reached back to colonial days. The family moved to New York in 1881, and Baruch graduated from the City College of New York in 1889. In 1897 he married Annie Griffen, who died in 1938. They had three children.

Baruch started out in Wall Street as a runner earning $3 a week. He had amassed his first million dollars by the time he was 30, and by his mid-30's he had $1 million for every year of his age. He was a member of the legendary "Waldorf crowd," a group of financiers who frequented a bar in the old Waldorf-Astoria Hotel in New York City. Trained in speculation by such masters as Thomas Fortune Ryan and James R. Keene, Baruch took part in the development of vast industrial complexes.

Adviser to Wilson. A Democrat, Baruch attracted the attention of his fellow Southerner, President Wilson. In 1916, Wilson appointed Baruch (whom he nicknamed Dr. Facts) to the Advisory Commission of the Council of National Defense and made him chairman of the Commission on Raw Materials, Minerals, and Metals. Later, Wilson put him in charge of all Allied purchasing. In March 1918, the president appointed him chairman of the War Industries Board. Baruch later rejected Wilson's offer to make him secretary of the treasury, although he accompanied the president to the Paris Peace Conference. As an economic adviser to the Peace Commission, a member of the Supreme Economic Council, and an American delegate dealing with economics and reparations clauses of the peace treaty, Baruch sat in at secret meetings of the Big Four—Orlando, Wilson, Lloyd George, and Clemenceau.

Later Government Service. Baruch had a few official responsibilities in the 1920's. Presidents Coolidge and Hoover used him to help get support from reluctant Southern Democrats for Republican programs. In the 1930's he turned down President Franklin D. Roosevelt's offer of an ambassadorship. He also rejected the job of war mobilization director in 1943. However,

BERNARD BARUCH was an "adviser to presidents."

after James F. Byrnes accepted the latter post, Baruch assisted him and also headed special fact-finding commissions for the president.

Celebrated Friendships. An intriguing mixture of sophistication and guilelessness, of Southern charm and American bluntness, Baruch enjoyed friendships that included Francis Cardinal Spellman and showman Billy Rose and that bridged the years from "Diamond Jim" Brady to President John F. Kennedy. He was a lifelong friend of Sir Winston Churchill, whom he first met at the Paris Peace Conference in 1919. As prime minister, Churchill stayed at Baruch's New York home during a visit to the United States in 1953.

Brauch once quipped, "I like anyone who's at the top of his profession"; yet his gift for friendship also embraced the humble. No one valued his public image more than Baruch, but he declined a medal for his public services on the grounds that his advice was so seldom taken.

Last Years. His later career was climaxed by his appointment as U.S. delegate to the UN Atomic Energy Commission, before which he flung down the simple challenge: "We are here to choose between the quick and the dead." Although it was vetoed by the Soviet Union, the Baruch plan for the control of atomic energy remained the official U.S. policy until the USSR developed its own atomic bomb.

Baruch was a talented amateur boxer in his youth and an avid hunter and swimmer into his 90's. He always maintained that old age was 15 years older than he was. He died in New York City on June 20, 1965, leaving the bulk of his great fortune to his alma mater, the City College of New York, and for medical research.

Baruch was the author of *The Making of the Reparation and Economic Sections of the Treaty* (1920), *American Industry in the War* (1941), *A Philosophy for Our Time* (1954), *Baruch: My Own Story* (1957), and *Baruch: The Public Years* (1960).

MARGARET COIT, *Fairleigh Dickinson University*

Further Reading: Coit, Margaret L., *Mr. Baruch* (Boston 1957); Field, Carter, *Bernard Baruch, Park Bench Statesman* (New York 1944); Rosenbloom, Morris V. *Peace Through Strength: Bernard Baruch and a Blueprint for Security* (New York 1953); White, William L., *Bernard Baruch, Portrait of a Citizen* (New York 1950).

BARUCH, bâr′ək, **Books of,** three prophetic documents attributed to Baruch, the son of Neriah and disciple of the Hebrew prophet Jeremiah. He wrote the discourses of Jeremiah at the prophet's dictation and in 605 B.C. read them to the people in the temple court and to the officers of the king (Jeremiah 36). He accompanied Jeremiah to Egypt after the fall of Jerusalem. Three books remain under his name.

Baruch (or I Baruch) is counted as apocryphal by Protestants and Jews but is included in the Roman Catholic Bible. It is made up of four different compositions, probably by four different authors: a historical introduction and a confession of sin (1:1–3:8); praise of wisdom, identified with the law (3:9–4:4); lamentation and comfort (4:5–5:9); an epistle to the exiles (6:1–72). None of the work can be ascribed either to Baruch or to Jeremiah. The first three parts may come from the 2d and 1st centuries B.C.; the fourth part, from 323–100 B.C. The book is a valuable witness of Jewish beliefs among the communities of the Dispersion. The themes of national guilt, of the perfection of the law, and of the hope of the restoration of the glory of Jerusalem are prominent. The part (3:37) in which wisdom is said to appear on earth and to mingle with men is thought by many to be a Christian interpolation, but it may be a personification of the law (compare Ecclesiasticus 24:7–11). The book was probably written in Hebrew and has survived in a Greek translation; some scholars think that the third part was written in Greek.

The Syriac Apocalypse of Baruch (II Baruch) was written in Hebrew but survives only in a Syriac translation of a lost Greek version of the original. It was compiled about 130 A.D. from materials composed about 50–100 A.D. It sets forth and defends the beliefs of Pharisaic Judaism of the New Testament period and has points of contact with IV Esdras; in spite of this, it was widely circulated in the early Christian church. Of special interest is the treatment of Adam's sin and the Fall, with its assertion that "each man is his own Adam," its complacency in the law, and its insistence on justification through the works of the law. The book also exhibits some curious parallels with the New Testament.

The Greek Apocalypse of Baruch (III Baruch) was discovered at the end of the 19th century. It was written in Hebrew and is preserved in a Greek translation. It is probably to be dated early in the 2d century A.D. Its Jewish ideas have been affected by Hellenistic and Oriental mythology. Like other apocalyptic books, it exhibits the belief in the seven heavens and contains a complex angelology. A Christian editor has interpolated the work in an attempt to make the book an appeal to Jews to embrace Christianity. See also APOCALYPTIC LITERATURE; BIBLE—1. *Canon of the Old Testament.*

JOHN L. MCKENZIE, S.J., *West Baden College*

BARY, Heinrich Anton de. See DE BARY, HEINRICH ANTON.

BARYE, bà-rē′, **Antoine Louis** (1796–1875), French sculptor, who was noted for his animal figures. He was born in Paris on Sept. 24, 1796, the son of a goldsmith. He was a student of the sculptor François Joseph Bosio and also studied with the painter Antoine Jean Gros, who had a great influence on his art.

After working as a goldsmith from 1823 to 1828, Barye began to achieve artistic success in the Paris salons of the early 1830's, making especially favorable impressions with his *Tiger Devouring a Crocodile* (1831) and *Lion Crushing a Serpent* (1833). However, many of his works, including the admirable *Lion in Repose* (1836), were rejected by later salons. It was not until the exhibition of his powerful *Centaur and Lapith* in 1850 that Bayre achieved national prestige. In 1854 he was appointed professor of drawing at the Louvre, and in 1855 he was made a chevalier of the Legion of Honor. In spite of his success, however, he was dogged by poverty for most of his life. He died in Paris on June 25, 1875.

Barye's smaller pieces, which were designed to be reproduced in bronze, have great charm; his larger works are executed in a strong, realistic, and frequently dramatic style. Many of his major works, such as *Theseus and the Minotaur, Jaguar Devouring a Hare,* and *Jaguar and Gavial,* are in the Louvre in Paris. The Metropolitan Museum in New York City has several important pieces, including *Group Symbolizing Force* and *Group Symbolizing War.* The Brooklyn Museum also has a good selection of his sculpture, including *Ethiopian Gazelle, Ape Riding a Gnu, Fawn Reclining,* and *African Elephant.*

BARYON, bar′ē-on, any of a number of relatively massive subatomic particles. The word "baryon" comes from the Greek word meaning "heavy." Specifically, a baryon is any particle with an atomic mass number, or baryon number, equal to 1. In addition, there are antiparticles corresponding to all baryons and these antibaryons have mass numbers equal to −1. The other two general types of subatomic particles are mesons and leptons, all of whose mass numbers equal zero.

Baryons include the familiar protons and neutrons, which are the chief components of the nucleus of the atom. In addition to these particles, which are collectively called nucleons (N), baryons also include five other classes of particles heavier than the nucleons. These heavier particles, called hyperons, are denoted by the Greek letters lambda (Λ), sigma (Σ), delta (Δ), xi (Ξ), and omega (Ω).

A great deal of current research in physics have been involved with the problem of the subatomic particles, particularly the baryons. An explanation for their great number and diversity, as well as an understanding of the symmetry and conservation laws describing their behavior, has still to be worked out to physicists' satisfaction.

BARZANI, bär-zä′nē, **Mustafa al-** (1904–　　　　), Kurdish nationalist leader in Iraq. He was born in the Kurdish village of Barzan, northern Iraq, and while still an infant was imprisoned with his mother following a revolt led by his brother. By the early 1930's, Mustafa was the recognized leader of the Barzani tribe. After a period of seclusion in southern Iraq and then in Iraqi Kurdistan, he returned to Barzan in 1943 and led an uprising against the central government. He was forced to withdraw to Iran in 1945, when he became premier of the short-lived, Soviet-sponsored Kurdish republic. In 1947 he went to the Soviet Union, returning to Iraq in 1958.

In the 1960's, Barzani and his Kurdish forces were in almost continuous revolt against the Iraqi government. They sought self-government and certain minority rights for the Kurdish people.

BARZUN, bär′zən, **Jacques** (1907–   ), American historian, educator, and author. Born in Créteil, France, on Nov. 30, 1907, he moved to the United States in 1919 and graduated from Columbia University in 1927. That year he was made a lecturer in history at Columbia. He became a United States citizen in 1933. Appointed a professor in 1945, he was dean of the Columbia graduate faculties from 1955 to 1958, when he became dean of faculties and provost of the university. At Columbia he helped organize a two-year course of reading and discussion of great books to advance his view that undergraduate education should involve a broad study of the liberal arts rather than specialization.

Barzun wrote on many aspects of art and intellectual life, including music. Among his books are *The Teacher in America* (1945), *Berlioz and the Romantic Century* (1950), *Music in American Life* (1956), *The Energies of Art* (1956), *The House of Intellect* (1959), *Classic, Romantic, and Modern* (1961), and *Science: The Glorious Entertainment* (1964). He also edited the letters of Lord Byron, Hector Berlioz, and John Chapman. In *The House of Intellect*, his most controversial work, Barzun attacked the American educational system for producing pseudo-intellectuals who are "captivated by art, overawed by science, and seduced by philanthropy." In *Science*, he discussed the domination of thought by science.

BAS-RELIEF, bä-ri-lēf′, is a form of sculpture in which raised and modelled parts project from a flat background. Specifically, bas-relief, also called *low-relief*, refers to relief sculpture in which the modelled surface is only slightly raised. In this sense it is distinguished from middle- and high-relief. But the term "bas-relief" is sometimes used in a general sense for all sculptured reliefs, as distinguished from free-standing sculpture in-the-round. Relief sculpture has proved to be especially adaptable for ornamental purposes in architecture, and for use as subordinate decoration in large sculptural works.

Early History. Bas-relief sculpture can be traced to the beginning of artistic representation. Even the prehistoric cave paintings at Altamira, Spain, were applied to raised areas on the cave walls, creating a form of low-relief. The walls of Egyptian tombs were often decorated with very low relief, or with a variant form called intaglio relief, in which the figures are cut into the stone, making the background a raised surface. Relief sculpture was also important in Mesopotamian cultures, which produced the splendid 9th century B.C. Assyrian reliefs now in the British museum, London. Excavations at the site of Persepolis indicate that the use of reliefs remained a strong tradition in ancient Persia.

Greece and Rome. The ancient Greeks were the first to realize the full potential of relief decoration in architecture. The reliefs from the metopes of the Greek temple at Selinunte in Sicily, from the temple of Zeus at Olympia, and above all, those from the Parthenon at Athens, are among the highest expressions of classical art. The Parthenon metopes are carved in relatively high relief, but the reliefs on the frieze below are bas-relief. Later Greek art produced the beautiful "Ludovisi throne" and the dynamic Hellenistic reliefs of the Pergamon altar.

In Roman art, reliefs were used to decorate triumphal arches and columns throughout the

BAS-RELIEF, *Centaurs and Lapiths,* was part of sculpture decoration on the Parthenon in Athens, Greece.

empire. Sarcophagi, too, were heavily decorated, usually in very high relief.

Early Christian and Medieval. Early Christian art continued many of the traditions and conventions of Roman art, including the use of relief decoration. Miniature ivory relief carvings are among the most exquisite works of Byzantine craftsmen. In medieval times, relief sculpture again became an important part of architectural decoration. This was particularly true in the Romanesque era of the 11th and 12th centuries, which evolved a regular plan for the decoration of great churches such as those at Moissac and at Vézelay, both in France. A low-relief representation of the Last Judgment on the tympanum of the central portal usually dominated the façade. Romanesque relief sculpture was often very flat, stylized and expressive, with the suggestion of strong movement. Later Gothic sculpture was more naturalistic and usually in higher relief.

Renaissance. Bronze church doors decorated in bas-relief were a medieval tradition that was continued in the early 15th century by Lorenzo Ghiberti in his two great sets of doors for the cathedral baptistery in Florence. At about the same time a monumental bas-relief figure style was originated by Jacopo della Quercia on the portal of San Petronio in Bologna. Among the other great Renaissance artists who worked in bas-relief were Donatello, the artists of the della Robbia family, and Desiderio da Settignano. Renaissance relief sculpture culminated in Michelangelo's early *Madonna of the Steps* and *Battle with the Centaurs.*

Post-Renaissance. After the Renaissance, bas-relief ceased to be a major sculptural form, although it still was used for occasional masterpieces such as Alessandro Algardi's baroque relief of St. Leo and Attila in St. Peter's, Rome. Neoclassical artists of the 19th century, including the Danish artist Bertel Thorwaldsen and his American follower Horatio Greenough, brought about a brief revival of the form. The 20th century Italian sculptor Giacomo Manzù produced major works in bas-relief, especially his bronze doors for St. Peter's, Rome, and for Salzburg Cathedral, Austria.

WILLIAM GERDTS, *University of Maryland*

BAS-RHIN, bä- raɴ′, is a department in eastern France, in Alsace. The Rhine River separates it from Germany on the east. It is a rich agricultural area that produces cereals, hops, sugar beets, and fruit. There are oil wells in the north. Automobiles and machinery are the most important manufactures. Bas-Rhin has an area of 1,848 square miles (4,886 sq km). Strasbourg is the capital city. Population: (1962) 770,150.

BASAITI, bä-sä-ē′tē, **Marco** (c. 1470–c. 1530), Italian painter. He was born in Friuli, probably of Albanian or Dalmatian parentage. The earliest recorded date of his life is 1503, when he was a pupil of Alvise Vivarini in Venice. Although little is known of his life, he apparently was most active as a painter in Venice.

Basaiti's work shows unmistakable influences of Giovanni Bellini, and of Bellini's pupil Giorgione. Although Basaiti's paintings display very little originality, they are rich in color and precise in detail. He was a prolific artist, and his paintings are to be found in galleries and museums throughout the world. His notable works include *The Calling of the Sons of Zebedee*, in the Museo Correr, Venice; a *Madonna*, in the National Gallery, London; and *Portrait of a Young Man* and *Virgin and Child*, in the National Gallery, Washington, D.C.

BASAL METABOLISM, bā′səl mə-tab′ə-liz-əm, is the rate of heat production by the body when it is fasting and at complete rest. By eliminating the variables produced by digestive processes and voluntary movement, it provides a standard measure of the speed at which the chemical reactions of the body proceed. It is fairly constant in value for a given individual and is an important medical indicator of general physiological function.

Measurement of basal metabolism, or more precisely of the *basal metabolic rate* (BMR), can be made directly by calorimetry, but this method is too complex and expensive for most purposes. More commonly, the BMR is computed from measurements of the patient's oxygen consumption, because body heat production is roughly proportional to oxygen consumption. The latter is measured by the *Benedict-Roth apparatus*. The value obtained can then be used to determine the BMR from a standard table or chart that takes into account age, sex, body surface area, and other facts. The BMR often is expressed on a scale where zero represents normal and ± 15 percent are the acceptable limits of variation. There are, however, wide variations.

Classically, the BMR test has been used to diagnose thyroid disease, since the thyroid gland is an important regulator of metabolism. In hyperthyroid cases, the BMR may be more than 50 percent above normal, while in hypothyroidism it may be almost 40 percent below normal. Many other factors can have marked effects on the BMR, and the test is not conclusive.

Today, there are better tests of thyroid function. An abnormal BMR is suggestive evidence of many disorders, although other criteria are necessary for diagnosis.

IRVING SOLOMON, M.D.
Mount Sinai School of Medicine, New York

BASALT, bə-sôlt′, is a class of igneous rock that is formed by volcanic action. Basalts are the most abundant of the volcanic rocks. They are especially plentiful in those regions that have undergone volcanic disturbance within geologically recent times. Most present-day volcanoes erupt basaltic material.

Basalts consist essentially of calcium-sodium feldspar and usually contain the silicate mineral augite. Iron ores such as magnetite and ilmenite are accessory mineral constituents.

There are several varieties of basalt. Most contain olivine, an iron-magnesium silicate, and those containing notable quantities of this miner-

BASALT'S tendency to assume a columnar structure is clearly visible in the formation known as the Giant's Causeway, on the coast of Northern Ireland. Throughout the ages, erosion has emphasized the unusual appearance of this volcanic basaltic formation.

al are known as olivine basalts. More rarely, basalts contain such minerals as brown hornblende, quartz, brown biotite, and leucite.

In texture, basalts vary from finely crystalline masses to coarsely crystalline material. The normal type of basalt is a fine-grained, black rock in which olivine is the only mineral that can be recognized without the use of a microscope. Denser varieties of basalt may contain more or less glass, which has been formed by the rapid cooling of the original molten lava.

Basalts are found as extensive lava flows in many areas around the world. In the United States the most noted occurrence is in the region of the Columbia and Snake rivers. Basalt tends to assume a columnar structure, which often lends a striking note to scenery. The most noted of these formations is the famous Giant's Causeway on the north coast of Ireland.

See also ROCKS—*Igneous Rocks;* VOLCANO.

BASANAVICIUS, bä-sä-nä'vi-cho͞os, **Jonas** (1851–1927), Lithuanian cultural and political leader. He was born near Vilkaviškis, Lithuania, on Nov. 11, 1851. After studying medicine at the University of Moscow, he worked as a hospital director in Bulgaria and then became active in the movement for Lithuanian independence from Russia. In 1883 he founded the periodical *Aušra* (Dawn) to promote the cause of freedom and a cultural rebirth in his country. *Aušra* was published in Germany and smuggled across the border into Lithuania. Basanavičius issued the historic memorandum of November 1905 demanding Lithuanian autonomy and was president of the revolutionary National Diet that assembled in Vilnyus in December. Although this attempt to gain self-government failed, Lithuania gained its independence in February 1918, and Basanavičius was one of the signers of the proclamation of independence. He also played a leading part in forming the cultural institutions of the new state. He died at Vilnyus on Feb. 16, 1927.

BASCOM, bas'kəm, **Florence** (1862–1945), American geologist. She was born in Williamstown, Mass., on July 14, 1862. Taking her Ph.D. at Johns Hopkins in 1893, she was the first woman to receive that degree from any American university. In 1895 she joined the faculty of Bryn Mawr College, where she was full professor of geology from 1906 to 1928. She was with the U.S. Geological Survey (1896–1936). She died in Williamstown on June 18, 1945.

BASCOM, bas'kəm, **Henry Bidleman** (1796–1850), American Methodist leader. He was born in Hancock, N.Y., on May 27, 1796. He was licensed as a Methodist preacher when he was only 17, and became a frontier circuit rider. He was chaplain of the U.S. Congress from 1824 to 1826 and president of Madison College, in Uniontown, Pa., from 1827 to 1829. He taught moral science at Augusta College in Kentucky from 1832 to 1842 and then was president of Transylvania University at Lexington until 1849.

When the Methodists split over the slavery issue, Bascom sided with the South; in 1846 he became the first editor of the *Southern Methodist Quarterly Review*. He was elected a bishop of the Methodist Episcopal Church, South, shortly before his death in Louisville on Sept. 8, 1850. His books include *Methodism and Slavery* (1847). He was famous for the eloquence of his sermons.

BASCOM, bas'kəm, **John** (1827–1911), American educator and philosopher. Born in Genoa, N.Y., on May 1, 1827, he graduated from Williams College in 1849 and from Andover Theological Seminary in 1855. That year he became professor of rhetoric at Williams, where he introduced a study of aesthetics into the curriculum. In 1874 he became president of the University of Wisconsin. Then a small school with a limited program, Wisconsin greatly increased its academic stature under Bascom's administration. Bascom resigned from the University in 1887 following a dispute with the governing board. He returned to Williams as a lecturer in sociology and served as professor of political science there from 1891 to 1901.

Bascom wrote extensively on philosophical questions, expounding a liberal rational theology. His works include *Aesthetics* (1862), *Philosophy of Rhetoric* (1866), *Ethics* (1879), *The New Theology* (1891), *Evolution and Religion* (1897), and the posthumously published autobiography *Things Learned by Living* (1913).

BASE, as traditionally defined in chemistry, any chemical compound that tastes bitter, feels soapy, neutralizes acids, turns the dye litmus blue, and turns the dye phenolphthalein pink when the compound is in a water solution. The hydroxides of alkali metals, such as potassium hydroxide (KOH) and sodium hydroxide ($NaOH$), and the hydroxides of alkaline earth metals, such as calcium hydroxide, $Ca(OH)_2$, and magnesium hydroxide, $Mg(OH)_2$, are strong bases because they break up completely into hydroxide ions and metal ions when in a water solution. The term *alkali* often is used to denote bases that are strong. A weak base, such as ammonium hydroxide (NH_4OH), does not completely break up into ions when in solution.

Svante Arrhenius (1859–1927) defined a base as any compound that yields the hydroxide ion $(OH)^-$ when in a water solution. A more modern definition of a base is that it is any molecule or part of any molecule that accepts hydrogen ions. By this definition, compounds that yield the hydroxide ion are bases because the hydroxide ion readily accepts a hydrogen ion (proton). But this definition also includes many other substances as bases. For example, sodium carbonate (Na_2CO_3), calcium oxide (CaO), and ammonia (NH_3), and the chloride ion (Cl^-) are bases because they accept hydrogen ions when in solution. Water (H_2O) breaks up into equal concentrations of $(H{\cdot}H_2O)^+$ and $(OH)^-$ ions.

Thus, water acts as both an acid and a base because the $(H{\cdot}H_2O)^+$ ions (hydronium ions) donate hydrogen ions, and the $(OH)^-$ ions accept hydrogen ions.

In the chemistry of organic compounds, the term "base" refers to amines and alkaloids. Generally, organic compounds are weak bases.

See also ACID.

MORRIS GORAN, *Roosevelt University*

BASE, in geometry, is the side of a polygon that is chosen as the bottom side on which the figure stands. The height of the polygon is given by a line that is perpendicular to the base. In the case of solid figures, forms other than a straight line are the base. For example, in a right circular cone and a right circular cylinder, the base is a circle. A pyramid has a base that is a polygon, usually a square. See also TRIANGLE.

BASEBALL

BASEBALL, bās'bôl, is a game between two teams of nine players each, played on a field with bat and ball, and refereed by one or more umpires. Beloved by millions of Americans, it is generally regarded as their national game. Though a growing minority now questions its claim to that distinction, it is hard to dispute baseball's preeminent position among American sports when one considers its deep roots in American life, its great appeal to the young, and the tremendous popular interest that develops each year in the major league pennant races and the world series.

Unlike certain other sports (soccer, basketball, track), baseball does not have a worldwide following. Outside the United States it is played chiefly in Latin America, Canada, and Japan. The game became very popular in Japan during the American occupation after World War II.

The following section describes the rules of baseball as it is played professionally in the United States:

HOW BASEBALL IS PLAYED

The Players. The nine-man team is made up of a pitcher and catcher (together called the battery); a first, second, and third baseman, and a shortstop (infielders); and a left, center, and right fielder (outfielders). A professional baseball squad also includes substitutes, coaches, and a manager, who directs the team. Players may be shifted from one position to another during the game. Managers are permitted to substitute players freely, but a player yielding to a substitute is not permitted to reenter the game. Major league squads are limited (from a period 30 days after the start of the season to September 1) to 25 active players.

Equipment and Uniforms. All players on a team wear uniforms identical in color, trim, and style. The uniform usually consists of knee stockings, knickers, and a half-sleeved flannel shirt, under which a long-sleeved jersey is worn. The shirt usually displays the name of the team and a number to identify the player. A visored cap, often with team initials, completes the uniform. Players wear spiked oxford-style shoes.

The regulation baseball is a sphere formed by winding yarn around a core of cork and rubber; its cover consists of two stripes of tightly stitched white horsehide. The ball must weigh not less than 5 or more than 5¼ ounces and must measure not less than 9 or more than 9¼ inches in circumference. The bat, a smooth round stick generally made of ash, can be no more than 2¾ inches in diameter at its thickest point and no more than 42 inches in length.

Each of the infielders (excepting the first baseman), each outfielder, and the pitcher wears on one hand a flexible leather finger glove with some padding. The catcher uses a heavily padded glove with a cleft between the thumb and index finger, and wears a chest protector, shin guards, and a wire mask to protect his face. The first baseman uses a glove which is smaller and more flexible than that used by the catcher. When at bat, the player usually wears a plastic helmet as a skull protector.

The Playing Field. Much of the play of the game takes place within a square called the infield or diamond. The sides of this square measure 90 feet and its four corners constitute four bases, the most important of which is the home base, called home plate. First base is diagonally to the right and third base diagonally to the left of home plate. The distance between home plate and second base, and between first base and third base is 127 feet, 3⅜ inches. White lines (called the foul lines) run from home plate past first and third base to the grandstands or outfield fences. All of the territory within the 90° angle formed by the foul lines is called fair territory; that outside is considered foul territory. (See diagram of the baseball field.)

Home plate, 17 inches long and 12 inches wide, is marked by a five-sided slab of whitened rubber at ground level. At each of the other three bases are white canvas bags, 15 inches square and not less than 3 inches nor more than 4 inches thick. The bags are tied down by straps, and are located entirely within fair territory. The pitcher's rubber is a slab 2 feet long and 6 inches wide, situated 60 feet 6 inches from home plate in the direction of second base. It is located on the pitcher's mound, also called the "hill"; this is a circular mound with gradual slopes, which rises to a height of 15 inches above the base lines and home plate at the point of its greatest elevation.

Beyond the infield are the wide ranges of the outfield, which vary in area in different ball parks (although there has been a recent tendency to standardize playing fields). Under present rules, the minimum distance from home plate to an outfield grandstand or fence at the foul lines is 250 feet. However, since 1958 no professional club has been permitted to build a new field that does not have a minimum distance of 325 feet at the foul lines and 400 feet in center field.

General Principles of the Game. The object of baseball is the scoring of more runs than the opposition, and the zest of the game and all of its strategy hinges on the continuous struggle between the offense (the team at bat), which attempts to score, and the defense (the team in the field), which attempts to prevent such scoring. Initially, and throughout much of the game, the struggle is centered in the contest between the pitcher and the batter. As the pitcher throws (pitches) the ball to the catcher behind the plate, the batter attempts to judge whether the pitch is in the strike zone (see *Balls and Strikes*, below) and, if it is, to hit it out of reach of the defensive players in the field. Members of the offensive team come to bat one at a time, each attempting to reach base safely, that is, without being put out (see *Put-outs*, below). When a batter reaches base, he becomes a runner, and it becomes the task of the succeeding batter to advance him to the next base. Only one runner may occupy a base at any one time. A run is scored when a member of the team at bat, having advanced around the diamond counterclockwise, touching first, second, and third base in succession, completes the circuit and touches home plate. Three put-outs (that is, the retirement of three players) retires the side, whereupon the team which has been defending comes to bat and its opponents take the field.

Each team's time at bat constitutes a half-inning, an inning being that portion of the game in which both teams take one turn at bat. The standard game consists of 9 innings. The visit-

REGULATION BASEBALL DIAMOND, showing the official measurements of the field and all players in their usual positions, is illustrated below. At lower left is a detailed layout of the batter's and the catcher's boxes.

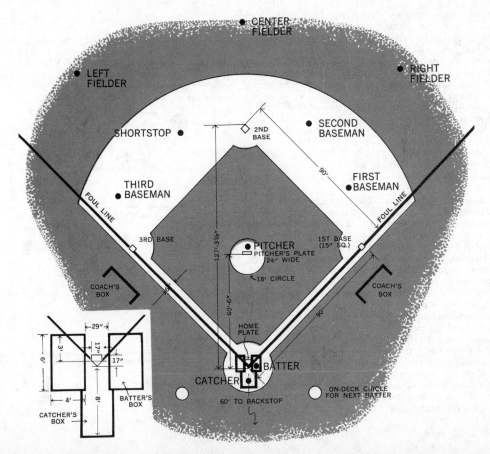

ing team bats first, and if the home team is ahead after 8½ innings, the game ends. In the event that the score is tied after 9 innings, the game continues until the tie is broken, unless darkness or other conditions prevent further play. When a game is terminated by rain, failure of lighting, or some other factor which in the judgment of the umpire interferes with the play, 5 innings constitute a legal game (4½ innings if the home team is ahead).

The Start of the Game. Before the game begins, each team presents to the umpire in chief its starting lineup or batting order, the order in which the players will bat. As play is about to start, the home team players take their positions on the playing field. The pitcher takes his place on the mound; the catcher stands in a prescribed catcher's box (a rectangular area marked out behind home plate); and the other players move to the best strategic positions to cope with a ball hit in fair territory by the batter. Infielders rarely "hug" their bases, standing 5 to 20 feet from the bags, and the shortstop generally plays far back ("deep") in the infield between second and third base. The game begins when the umpire calls "Play ball."

Balls and Strikes. The batsman or batter stands in either of two 4-foot by 6-foot batter's boxes marked out on either side of home plate (for the convenience of right-handed or left-handed hitters). The pitcher directly faces the batter in one of two legal pitching positions—the windup or the set. His purpose is to throw the ball in the strike zone, the space directly over the plate and between the batter's shoulders and his knees as he takes a natural stance. A pitch within this area, if it is not hit by the batter, is called a strike. A strike is also a legal pitch that is struck at by the batter and missed; or which is hit into foul territory, when the batter has less than two strikes against him; or which is nicked (or tipped) by the bat and is held by the catcher; or which touches a batter while he swings at the ball. Three strikes constitute a put-out (in this instance called a strike-out), and the man thus retired is succeeded at the plate by the next player in the batting order.

Any pitch outside of the strike zone is called a ball if not struck at by the batter. Four balls, called a base on balls (also called a walk or a pass), permit the batter to go to first base. The batter also reaches first base if hit by a pitched ball which he has tried to avoid, or if the catcher or any other fielder interferes with his batting swing.

Base Hits and Errors. The primary aim of the batter is to get a base hit, that is, to hit the ball anywhere in fair territory and reach as many bases as he possibly can without being put out. A hit is called a single, when the batter stops at first base; a double, when the batter safely reaches second base; a triple, when he reaches third base; and a home run (or homer), when he makes a complete circuit of the bases and touches home plate. The great majority of home runs occur when the ball is hit on the fly (in the air without touching the ground) over an outfield barrier in fair territory. When a ball bounces over the barrier the batter is usually required to stop at second base (a "ground rules" double).

A batter may also reach base safely on an error. An error occurs when, in the opinion of the official scorer (see below), a fielder mishandles the ball.

FIRST BASEMAN, stretching to reach a wide throw, pulls his foot off base as the runner beats out the hit.

FIELDING AND CATCHING

Shown here are techniques used in catching thrown balls at the bases, executing a double play, and handling a grounder, pitch, and fly.

TO CATCH a low throw to first base, the baseman reaches into the diamond, glove on the ground and opposite his front foot.

MOST GROUNDERS are fielded with the legs about in normal walking position, weight on the balls of the feet and knees and hips bent. The ball is caught opposite the front foot, with thumbs out and fingers down. The weight transfers to the rear foot, and then the front foot steps in the direction of the throw as it is made.

THE CATCHER, in an exciting play at home plate, fails to make the put-out as the runner slides under the tag.

THIRD BASEMAN, in perfect position for a tag play, waits for the base runner to slide directly into the ball.

SHORTSTOP, in one motion, leaps over the runner he has just retired and fires to first for the double play.

PITCHING TARGET is made by the catcher's hands and body. To present a low target (*left*), he squats, hands with thumbs together and fingers up. Pitcher aims for the glove. If pitcher prefers a body target (*right*), catcher spreads his hands, thumbs out and fingers down.

LOW PITCH is handled as the catcher drops to the ground on one or both knees to block the ball. He catches it with arms slightly extended, glove on the ground.

RIGHT FIELDER, with arm fully extended, makes a leaping catch to snare a ball headed for the stands.

AN OUTFIELDER must learn to judge the flight of a fly ball and get under it fast. He keeps the ball in front of him. When running back for a long fly, he turns his head once or twice to spot the ball.

Bunts. In some situations, the batter may attempt to bunt, that is, instead of swinging at the ball he may attempt to block it with his bat and thus tap it onto the infield. While this usually results in the retirement of the batter, it also usually serves to advance a runner; when both of these circumstances obtain, the play is called a sacrifice. Some fleet-footed batters occasionally bunt to reach first base safely, especially when the infielders are playing deep.

Put-outs. The aim of the team in the field is to make three put-outs (or outs) and thus to retire the team at bat. The defensive players may make put-outs in a number of ways: by catching a ball hit by the batter in either fair or foul territory before it touches the ground (called a fly ball or a fly); fielding a grounder (that is, catching a ball bouncing on the ground in fair territory) and relaying the ball to a defensive player at first base before the batter reaches that base; by tagging a runner between bases; or, in certain circumstances, when there is a runner on base, by throwing the ball to the succeeding base before the runner reaches it. This last is called a force-out and is possible only when a runner is forced to advance by one base to prevent a put-out from being made, as when the runner is on first base and the batter hits a grounder.

Three strikes also constitute an out (see above, *Balls and Strikes*), provided the catcher does not drop the third strike. In the event that a third strike is dropped, the out can be secured only if the batter is tagged before he can run to first base or the ball is thrown to first base before he can reach the bag.

Outs are also made: when a batter against whom there are two strikes bunts foul; when, with two or three runners on base and less than two outs, the batter hits an infield fly; when the batter attempts to hit a third strike and the ball touches him; when, in the umpire's judgment, a spectator's interference clearly prevents a fielder from catching a fly ball; or when a runner is hit by a batted ball.

Double and Triple Plays. It is often possible to retire two men on one play, as when, with a runner on first base, the batter hits a grounder to the second baseman. The latter may step on second base, "forcing" the runner (putting him out on a force play, see above), and then relay the ball to the first baseman, who may touch first base, retiring the batter before he can reach the bag. This is called a double play and can occur only if less than two men are out before the play begins. Another type of double play may result when, for instance, an infielder catches a hard-hit ball (a line drive) before it touches the ground, automatically retiring the batter, and steps on the base behind a runner, "doubling off" the runner. This possibility arises from a rule which forbids a runner to advance to the next base before a fly ball is caught and which therefore makes it mandatory for him to "tag up," that is, to touch his base after the catch is made. Since runners normally take a "lead" (move several steps toward the next base before the pitch is thrown) in order to take full advantage of a hit, or to be in a position to steal (see next section), or to protect themselves against a force play, they are occasionally unable to return to their base and are doubled off.

Triple plays, or three outs on one play, are rare, but, through various combinations of the circumstances described above, they can and do occur. A triple play is possible only when there are no outs and two or more runners are on base.

Baseball Strategy. The strategy followed by each team during the course of a game is determined by the manager, aided by the coaches. The manager decides which players are to play, when substitutions are to be made, where the players should play, how batters should be pitched to, and, often, whether a batter should swing or not swing at a particular pitch. The catcher is expected to know the weaknesses of opposition hitters and, before each pitch, to "call" for a certain kind of pitch by means of a hidden signal to the pitcher, and the pitcher is permitted to request a different call from the catcher by shaking his head negatively, but both men often operate under strict instructions from the manager.

When there is a runner on second or third base and first base is unoccupied, the manager may order his pitcher to deliver an intentional base on balls to a dangerous hitter to set up the possibility of a double play, or in order to have his pitcher face a weaker hitter; such a decision may often hinge on a consideration of the right-handed pitcher's slight advantage over a right-handed batter as against a left-handed batter, a fact borne out by voluminous statistics.

Much of baseball's strategy has to do with the running game, that is, the tactics resorted to by men on base in their efforts to advance and score. The team at bat stations coaches in foul territory behind first and third bases to coach the runners. The third base coach has the responsibility of deciding whether a runner speeding toward third base can reasonably be expected to score before the ball is relayed to home plate, and he must signal the runner accordingly.

The stolen base is an important part of the running game. A runner is permitted to attempt to steal a base, that is, advance to the next base, while the pitcher is in the process of delivering a pitch to the batter. (If the batter hits a foul ball, the runner is not allowed to advance, and if he hits a fly or line drive which is caught in either foul or fair territory, the runner must tag up, as described in the section above.) Chances of success in the base-stealing maneuver depend on several variables, including among others, the element of surprise, the runner's speed, and the catcher's ability to throw accurately to the fielder who moves over to defend the base (and who, in order to retire the runner, must actually tag him with the ball before he reaches the bag). The manager often reserves to himself the decision as to whether the steal attempt is to be made, especially when a double steal is involved (that is, when two runners simultaneously attempt to advance by means of stolen bases).

The hit-and-run play is almost invariably undertaken only on the manager's initiative and requires prearrangement with the batter and the runner, who are usually informed that they are to attempt the play, by means of secret signals relayed to them by one of the coaches. In the typical hit-and-run play, a runner at first base begins to steal as the ball is pitched, drawing the second baseman toward second base to defend against the steal. The batter, knowing that this will happen, attempts to hit the ball through the wide gap created in the right side of the infield when the second baseman leaves his normal fielding position. The success of the play usually results in advancing the runner to third base and putting another runner on first base.

WIDE WORLD

TED WILLIAMS, one of the greatest hitters, shows perfect balance at the end of a powerful swing.

BATTING

Keys to good hitting, in addition to courage and determination, include a relaxed position in the batter's box, an ability to follow the entire flight of the pitched ball, a fast and level swing of the bat, and strong wrists. It is important that the weight, length, and balance of the bat suit the physical characteristics of the batter.

SACRIFICE BUNT is executed to advance a base runner at the expense of the batter. In this bunt, the batter either pivots toward the pitcher or shifts his feet and faces the pitcher, allowing the ball to meet the bat which he holds stationary at impact.

GOOD BATTING FORM demands that the entire body be poised for utmost ease and effect. Awaiting the pitch, the batter keeps his weight on the balls of his feet, with hips, shoulders, and eyes level, and bat high. On the approach of the pitch, he whips his bat into the ball with loose arm action and snaps his wrists. He keeps his two hands on the bat during the entire swing.

The art of moving runners around the bases by means of the stolen base, the sacrifice bunt (see *Bunts*, above), and the hit-and-run play, has been called "inside baseball." Such great teams as the Baltimore Orioles (1894–1896) and the Chicago Cubs (1906–1910) were most adept exponents of inside baseball, and John McGraw (q.v.), who managed the New York Giants from 1902, was extremely successful with this strategy for over a quarter of a century. However, with the steady advance of home run hitting since the early 1920's, inside baseball has largely given way to what has been facetiously termed "outside baseball." While there were 358 home runs hit in the major leagues in 1910, there were 2,688 in 1965. This development has been variously ascribed to a "livelier" ball, to changes in the design of the bat, or to the increasing average size and strength of ballplayers, but whatever the reason, most managers today prefer to play for a block of runs from a home run, rather than for the single run. Such teams as the Los Angeles Dodgers, however, continued to play the old style of baseball in the 1960's.

Hitting and Pitching. Willie Keeler is credited with developing hitting into a science. He described his technique as follows: "I hit 'em where they ain't." The earmarks of the great hitters have included keen eyesight, good physical development, powerful wrists, and an intuitive knowledge of the pitcher's strong and weak points.

If there is a science of hitting, as demonstrated by such outstanding practitioners as Keeler, Ty Cobb, Rogers Hornsby, Ted Williams, and Stan Musial, there is also a science of pitching. A strong, wiry, durable arm which enables a pitcher to throw the ball with exceptional speed is a great advantage, and such Hall of Fame pitchers as Rube Waddell and Walter Johnson have won baseball immortality largely on their ability to "throw the ball past the hitters." But pitchers without such natural gifts must resort to every wile of their craft, and even fast-ball pitchers find that a variety of deliveries increases their effectiveness. Since a pitcher often loses his speed as he ages, many pitchers noted initially for their fast balls (Bob Feller, Warren Spahn, Robin Roberts) have extended their careers to the two-decade mark and beyond by mastering the subtler aspects of the science, most importantly, the ability to control sharply breaking pitches.

In addition to the standard deliveries—the fast ball, curve, and change of pace (slow ball) —modern pitchers have developed such pitches as the knuckler (pitched off the knuckles), screw ball, fork ball, slider, palm ball, and a so-called "junk ball" (a slowly revolving ball thrown at various speeds). Many of these present-day pitches were termed drops, outcurves, incurves, and slow balls by earlier generations. The famed "fadeaway" of Christy Mathewson, who pitched between 1900 and 1916, is the present-day screw ball, a ball which, when thrown by a right-handed pitcher, breaks in toward a right-handed batsman instead of curving away from him as does the standard curve ball.

KEEPING YOUR OWN SCORE CARD

Keeping a score card while watching a ball game enables the spectator to review every play that has taken place during the game. This simple and effective record reveals at a glance almost any statistic, such as strike-outs, consecutive put-outs, or individual performances. The columns at the right show totals for the day: AB—times at bat; R—runs scored; H—base hits; PO—putouts; A—assists; and E—errors.

BRUINS	1	2	3	4	5	6	7	8	9	10	AB	R	H	PO	A	E
JONES, 2B	0/6		0/7		1-3			=	6-3		5	0	1	2	3	0
WILSON, CF	1-3			= / ⊖ −		K		0/3			4	1	1	4	0	0
WOOD, RF	−			− =		0/8		0/7			4	0	2	2	0	0
SMITH, LF	5-3				−	0/7		K			4	0	1	4	0	0
BROWN, 1B		1-3		K			⊜		⊖ BB		3	2	1	8	1	0
CHARLES, 3B		0/8		K			S −		−		4	0	2	1	4	0
FOX, C		0/9		K			4-3		K		4	0	0	2	5	0
OWENS, SS			6-3		6-3		1-3		K		4	0	0	4	3	0
FLYNN, P			5-3		K		0-8		−		4	0	1	0	2	0
HITS / RUNS	1 / 0	0 / 0	0 / 0	0 / 0	3 / 1	0 / 0	0 / 0	2 / 1	1 / 0	2 / 1	36	3	9	27	18	0

NUMBER PLAYERS AS FOLLOWS:

PITCHER 1	SECOND BASEMAN 4	LEFT FIELDER 7
CATCHER 2	THIRD BASEMAN 5	CENTER FIELDER 8
FIRST BASEMAN 3	SHORTSTOP 6	RIGHT FIELDER 9

SYMBOLS FOR PLAYS

Single —	Reached Base on Error ....E	Stolen Base ....S	Struck Out ....K
Double =	Fielder's Choice ....FC	Sacrifice Hit ....SH	Base on Balls ....BB
Triple ≡	Hit by Pitcher ....HP	Passed Ball ....PB	Forced Out ....FO
Home Run ≣	Wild Pitch ....WP	Balk ....BK	

```
WP     S

(PB)   E-4
```

SCORING BLOCK, left, is from score card above. Code numbers and symbols are used to record a runner's progress on bases. Home plate is represented by the lower left corner of the block. Counterclockwise, the lower right corner is first base; upper right is second; and upper left, third. In this example batter reached first because of an error (signified by letter E) on the part of the opposing second baseman (player's code number 4). Runner then stole second base (S), went to third on a wild pitch (WP), and got home on a passed ball (PB). Circling symbols at home plate pinpoints all scoring plays.

Yet pitchers must also live with the human frailty of the men that support them in the field. A perfectly executed pitch may be negated when an infielder fumbles a simple grounder, or when a pair of outfielders, each expecting the other to catch a high fly ball, let the ball drop between them. Errors of commission and omission are important factors in baseball, and crucial errors and mental lapses have lost league championships and world series.

Umpires. The game is supervised by umpires, who are in full charge of the game and are responsible for its conduct according to the rules. The umpire's decisions on all matters requiring judgment are final. Only reasonable doubt as to his interpretation of the rules can be appealed. Some decisions are made by the umpire only after direct protest by the offended team. For example, a runner is declared out for failing to touch a bag, and a batter is declared out for batting out of turn, only after the defending team has appealed to the umpire by means of an "appeal play."

In the major and minor leagues, umpires are appointed by the league presidents; for world series and all-star games, they are appointed by the commissioner of baseball (see the section *Organized Baseball*, below). The number of um-

pires assigned to a game varies. In the major leagues, there are four, with the umpire behind the plate designated as the umpire in chief. The latter is also the sole judge of whether a pitch not struck at by the batter is a ball or a strike, and must make each "call" without a moment's hesitation. For the World Series and the All-Star games, there are six umpires. In minor league play, there are usually two umpires, one behind the plate and one on the bases.

Umpires are dressed in dark blue uniforms, of which they sometimes remove the coat. They wear shin guards and steel protectors for their shoes. The plate umpire wears, in addition, a chest protector and face mask.

Official Scorers. Baseball is a game whose avid followers demand accurate and detailed statistics. The man appointed by the league president to tabulate every play made in a game is called the official scorer. Picked from among the newspaper reporters, the official scorer has the sole authority to make "scoring" decisions requiring judgment, such as a decision as to whether a fielder who fails to hold a sharply hit ball and complete the put-out is to be charged with an error. Many fans enjoy keeping an "official" score. An explanation of how this is done accompanies the score card illustrated above.

PITCHING

Pitchers use either an overhand or a sidearm delivery. They can throw fast balls, curve balls, or slow balls from one of the two basic motions. In addition, by gripping the ball in several different ways, they are able to develop their assortment of pitches to the highest degree of effectiveness.

UPI

SANDY KOUFAX of Los Angeles displays the form that made him strikeout king of baseball.

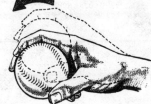

PITCHING GRIPS vary with individuals. Two pitchers seldom hold a ball in exactly the same way in delivering any given pitch. In general, however, these variations develop from a few basic grips as shown in these illustrations.

FAST BALL (*left*) is gripped firmly, fingertips on the seam. It is thrown with a downward wrist snap. Spin and hop can be imparted to the ball as it rolls off the ends of the first and second fingers.

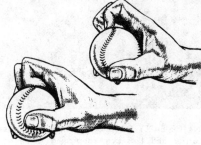

CURVE BALL is held with a loose wrist and tighter finger grip than a fast ball. A downward snap and outward twist releases the ball along the side of the first finger, imparting a curving spin.

CHANGE OF PACE (slow ball) is held as for fast ball or curve and thrown with the same motion, minus the arm twist. First two fingers are raised on release to make the ball "float," not spin.

KNUCKLEBALL (*above*), effective for its unpredictable path, is gripped across the seams with knuckles or fingertips. Ball is thrown with stiff wrist, no snap or spin.

PITCHING TECHNIQUES involve the windup, the delivery, and the follow-through (shown in this sequence of drawings). One purpose of the windup is to produce a smooth and natural delivery of the pitch. This helps to ensure control, the most important element in the art of pitching. In his follow-through after delivery, the pitcher should be facing the plate squarely, in order to be in position to field any ball hit at or near him.

RIGHTHANDED PITCHER's position on the mound is shown in the above diagrams. The pitcher begins the delivery with both feet on the rubber, the left foot slightly behind the right (1). The windup position permits the pitcher one step backward on his left foot, before stepping forward with this foot during the delivery (2). After releasing the ball, the momentum of the follow-through will carry him another step forward (3).

IN THE EARLY DAYS of baseball, the batters used long, slender bats and the fielders wore no gloves. This 1866 Currier and Ives print depicts a game at Philadelphia between the Brooklyn Atlantics and the Athletics.

THE HISTORY OF BASEBALL

Origin and Early History. Legend holds that baseball was invented in Cooperstown, N.Y., in 1839 by Abner Doubleday (q.v.). On Dec. 30, 1907, a special committee, consisting of prominent baseball executives and including two United States senators, confirmed Cooperstown as the game's birthplace and Doubleday as its originator.

But baseball historians today place little credence in the Cooperstown-Doubleday story, and feel that the Special Baseball Commission of 1906–1907 did an incompetent job. Various investigators have shown that the term "baseball" was used approximately a century before 1839. For example, a description of a game called "base-ball" appeared in the *Little Pretty Pocket-Book,* a popular children's book published in 1744. A game similar to the one supposedly invented by Doubleday was described in *The Boy's Own Book* by William Clarke, a volume published in London in 1829, and in *The Book of Sports,* written by Robin Carver and published in Boston in 1834.

During the controversy over the origin of baseball in the early 1900's, Henry Chadwick (q.v.), maintained that American baseball was merely a glorified version of the British game of rounders, which was, in turn, an offshoot of cricket. Today Chadwick's thesis is generally accepted by students of baseball. Though baseball grew up in the United States and has many American embellishments, it unquestionably is an adaptation of a game which had been played for centuries, in which a batsman hit a thrown ball and ran around one or more bases which might be rocks, stakes, posts, inverted milking stools, or canvas bags.

The game of rounders was brought to the United States from England in the 18th century. It was not standardized, having many variations and names. It was called round ball, goal ball, post ball, town ball, and baseball. Fields could be of any size, and there was no set number of players. When three or more boys played the game, it became known as one old cat, two old cat, or three old cat, depending on the number of bases in addition to home base.

The American now given credit for playing the largest part in the evolution of modern baseball is Alexander J. Cartwright (q.v.), who in 1845 drew up a set of rules having much in common with the present-day game. He drew a diagram of a ball field with 90-foot base lines and had the batter stand at home plate instead of in a separate batter's box some distance from the plate. His rules prohibited the retirement of a runner by "plugging"—hitting him with a thrown ball when off base. The rules nevertheless differed in many respects from those of modern baseball. For example, balls caught on a first bounce constituted an out; pitchers were restricted to throwing the ball underhanded; runs were called aces; and the winner was the first team scoring 21 aces.

Cartwright was a member of the New York Knickerbocker Base Ball Club, and his rules were primarily for the use of this club. But other clubs in New York and elsewhere quickly adopted them. It is evident that other teams were playing a good brand of ball, for in the first baseball game on record, played in Elysian Fields, Hoboken, N.J., on June 19, 1846, a team called the New Yorks, playing under Cartwright's rules on a diamond of his specifications, defeated the Knickerbockers (23 to 1 in four innings).

Early baseball was played by young men of means and social position. (Much the same was true, at the time, of cricket in England.) However, baseball had a general appeal and, in the 1850's, artisans, tradesmen, and shipwrights formed teams and challenged the socialites. The first convention of baseball clubs was held in New York in May 1857, to straighten out differences between what had become known as the New York game and the Massachusetts game, and, on March 10, 1858, the National Association of Baseball Players was organized. These meetings changed the scoring unit from aces to runs, and gave victory to the team ahead after nine innings. The game was still basically amateur, although there had been, at times, some passing of money under the table to induce strong-playing "amateurs" to join certain clubs. In 1864, Alfred J. Reach became the first avowed pro.

During the Civil War, baseball was played extensively behind the lines. Many boys from farms, factories, and countinghouses, who received their first introduction to the game, were later to carry it back to their communities. After the war the game spread like wildfire. In 1869 the Red Stockings of Cincinnati, Ohio, became the first all-professional team. The club, organized by Harry Wright, had an annual payroll of about $9,300. The team played the entire 1869 season without defeat (56 victories and 1 tie) and stretched its winning streak to 79 in 1870 before losing to the Brooklyn Atlantics.

The first professional baseball league, the National Association of Professional Base-Ball Players, was formed on March 4, 1871, and lasted five seasons, the Boston club winning the championship four times. It became a rowdy league. There was open gambling on games, liquor selling in parks, bribery, and other chicanery.

The National League. Out of this mess, in 1876, was created the National League of Professional Baseball Clubs, which took in most of the National Association teams, but which sought to rid baseball of gambling, drunkenness, and rowdyism. Its constitution provided that a club forfeit its franchise if it sold alcoholic beverages or played Sunday baseball. The National League began life with eight charter members: Boston, Philadelphia, New York, Hartford, Chicago, Cincinnati, St. Louis, and Louisville.

By 1882, when the American Association became a rival to the National League, there had been some shifts in membership. The two leagues drew up a national agreement, a loose pact covering player and territory rights and relations with minor leagues. Following player disputes in 1891, four clubs then in the American Association—St. Louis, Louisville, Baltimore, and Washington—merged with the National League in 1892, to form a new 12-club league called the National League and Association. It was St. Louis' third appearance in the league; the Missouri city was represented in 1876–1877 and 1885–1886. In the 19th century, National League franchises also were held, at various times, by clubs in Providence; Indianapolis; Milwaukee; Buffalo; Troy, N.Y.; Syracuse; Cleveland; Worcester, Mass.; Kansas City, Mo.; Pittsburgh; and Brooklyn.

The 12-club league lasted from 1892 until 1899, when it was reduced to eight teams by dropping Cleveland, Baltimore, Washington, and Louisville. The National League then unquestionably ran the baseball world.

CHRONOLOGY

Some of the outstanding events in the history of major league baseball follow. Asterisk (*) indicates a modern (since 1901) major league record.

1904 Jack Chesbro (N.Y. Yankees) wins 41 games*.

1905 Christy Mathewson (N.Y. Giants) pitches 3 world series shutouts*; Mordecai Brown (Chicago Cubs) is first to pitch 4 straight shutouts in regular season play.

1906 Chicago Cubs, with their Tinker to Evers to Chance double-play combination, dominate the National League. Chicago American League "Hitless Wonders" win the pennant and world series.

1908 Fred Merkle forgets to touch second base, forcing the Giants into a play-off in which they lose the pennant to the Chicago Cubs.

1910 Philadelphia Athletics, with the "$100,000 infield," begin their domination of the American League.

1911 Cy Young retires, after winning 511 games*.

1912 Rube Marquard (N.Y. Giants) wins 19 consecutive games*.

1914 Boston's "Miracle Team" wins the National League pennant after being in the cellar on July 4.

1915 Ty Cobb (Detroit Tigers) steals 96 bases in a 154-game season*.

1916 New York Giants win 26 straight games*.

1919 Branch Rickey originates the farm system for the training of big league ballplayers.

1920 Ray Chapman (Cleveland Indians) is killed by a bean ball (only such fatality in major league history). Spitball is outlawed. Dodgers and Braves play a 26-inning*, 1–1 tie game.

1921 New York Yankees, under Miller Huggins, begin a winning record of 6 pennants in 8 years.

1924 Rogers Hornsby (St. Louis Cardinals) bats .424*.

1925 Pitcher is allowed to use resin bag.

1927 Babe Ruth (N.Y. Yankees) hits 60 homers in a 154-game season*.

1928 Ty Cobb retires with a lifetime batting average of .367* and a career total of 4,191 hits*.

1934 The colorful "Gas House Gang" (St. Louis Cardinals) wins the National League pennant and the world series. In the all-star game, Carl Hubbell (N.Y. Giants) strikes out in succession Babe Ruth, Lou Gehrig, Jimmy Foxx, Al Simmons, and Joe Cronin, considered one of baseball's outstanding pitching achievements.

1935 Night baseball is introduced in Cincinnati.

1936 New York Yankees, under Joe McCarthy, begin their domination of the American League.

1938 Johnny Vander Meer (Cincinnati Reds) pitches 2 consecutive no-hit games*.

1939 Lou Gehrig (N.Y. Yankees) benches himself after playing in 2,130 consecutive games*.

1941 Joe DiMaggio (N.Y. Yankees) hits safely in 56 consecutive games*.

1947 Jackie Robinson, first Negro to play in the modern major leagues, joins the Brooklyn Dodgers.

1949 New York Yankees, under Casey Stengel, open an era in which they win 10 American League pennants in 12 years and 5 consecutive world series*.

1951 Bobby Thompson hits a ninth-inning home run to win the National League pennant for the New York Giants in the deciding game of a play-off with the Brooklyn Dodgers.

1956 Don Larsen (N.Y. Yankees) pitches a perfect game in the world series*.

1961 Roger Maris (N.Y. Yankees) hits 61 homers* in a 162-game season.

1962 Maury Wills (L.A. Dodgers) steals 104 bases in a 162-game season. Stan Musial (St. Louis Cardinals) surpasses Ty Cobb's career record of 5,863 total bases, advancing the mark to 6,134* before retiring in 1963.

1965 Sandy Koufax (L.A. Dodgers) pitches a no-hitter against Chicago on Sept. 9, to become the first man to pitch four no-hitters in his career*.

1966 Willie Mays (S.F. Giants) breaks the National League lifetime home run record of 511 set by Mel Ott (N.Y. Giants) in 1946.

1968 Don Drysdale (L.A. Dodgers) sets a major league record by pitching 58⅔ consecutive scoreless innings* and six consecutive shutouts.

1969 Major Leagues expand to 24 cities, including Montreal, the first one outside the United States.

1973 Nolan Ryan (California Angels) sets a new major league season strikeout record with 383*.

1974 Henry Aaron (Atlanta Braves) breaks Babe Ruth's major league home-run record, hitting his 715th home run on April 8, in Atlanta, off Al Downing (Los Angeles Dodgers). Lou Brock (St. Louis Cardinals) steals 118 bases* in a 162-game season. Frank Robinson is named first black manager of a major league team (Cleveland Indians).

HOUSTON ASTRODOME, the first domed professional baseball park, is the home of the National League Astros. The structure provides seating for 46,000.

UPI

The American League. The reduction by the National League gave Byron Bancroft Johnson, president of the Western League, the opportunity to establish a second major league, the American League. The move to put second clubs in Philadelphia and Boston and to take up vacated territory in Baltimore and Washington set off a bitter baseball war in 1901–1902, in which the American League raided the National League for many of its top stars. It began in 1901 with clubs in the four eastern cities listed above and with western clubs in Chicago, Cleveland, Detroit, and Milwaukee. In 1902, the Milwaukee club was shifted to St. Louis, and in 1903 the Baltimore club was moved to New York.

The American League emerged victorious in the struggle, and when a peace pact was drawn up in Cincinnati in January 1903, the two leagues established the National Commission. This body was made up of the two major league presidents and headed by a chairman.

The establishment of the American League and the rivalry between the two leagues was to increase popular interest in the game greatly and to give it its most famous and distinctive annual event, the climactic world series.

Expansion of Major Leagues. From 1903 to 1952, big league baseball was caught in a log jam, with two clubs each in New York, Boston, Philadelphia, Chicago, and St. Louis; single National League clubs in Brooklyn, Pittsburgh, and Cincinnati; and single American League clubs in Cleveland, Detroit, and Washington. The log jam was broken in the early spring of 1953, when the Boston Braves organization of the National League abruptly moved its franchise to Milwaukee. In the American League, the St. Louis Browns shifted to Baltimore and became known as the Orioles in 1954, and, in 1955, the Philadelphia Athletics went to Kansas City. The most spectacular moves followed the close of the 1957 season, when two historic National League clubs, the New York Giants and Brooklyn Dodgers, made hops to San Francisco and Los Angeles. In 1966, after only 13 seasons in Milwaukee, the Braves moved to Atlanta.

In 1961, the American League expanded to 10 clubs. A new club called the Senators was installed in Washington, D.C., to replace the old team of that name, which moved to Minneapolis St. Paul and became known as the Minnesota

Twins, and another new team, called the Angels, was created in Los Angeles. The next year the National League also increased to 10 clubs, adding the New York Mets and the Houston Colt .45's (later renamed the Astros). In 1968 the Kansas City franchise moved to Oakland. By 1969 each league had increased to 12 teams, the American League adding expansion teams in Kansas City and Seattle, and the National League installing new teams in Montreal and San Diego. Later, the Washington franchise moved to Arlington, Texas, and the Seattle team went to Milwaukee. Each league thus had two 6-team, east-west divisions:

American League		National League	
East	West	East	West
New York	Chicago	New York	Atlanta
Boston	Minnesota	Philadelphia	Cincinnati
Baltimore	Kansas City	Pittsburgh	Houston
Cleveland	California	Montreal	Los Angeles
Detroit	Oakland	Chicago	San Diego
Milwaukee	Texas	St. Louis	San Francisco

The teams now play a 162-game schedule; division playoffs determine World Series participants.

The World Series. The game's great autumn extravaganza, the World Series, dates from 1903, although a postseason series was played in 1882 and from 1884 to 1891 by the pennant winners of the National League and the American Association. No series was played in 1904, but in 1905, the National Commission took charge of the World Series and made it an annual event. Many features of the 1905 series, such as winning 4 games out of 7 and awarding 60% of the receipts of the first 4 games to the players, remain in effect. From 1919 to 1921 the champion was required to win 5 games out of 9.

All-Star Game. All-star games, contests between two teams picked from top stars of each league, have been played since 1933, when Arch Ward, Chicago *Tribune* sports editor, introduced the idea as a Chicago World's Fair feature. The idea immediately caught favor; the two major leagues scheduled an all-star game every year thereafter, except in 1945. Two games were played each year in 1959–1962. Beginning in 1963, the leagues returned to a schedule of one game a year. Squads were first picked by a poll of fans. They were later chosen by vote of players, managers, and coaches. In 1970, voting for All-Star players was restored to the fans.

MAJOR LEAGUE CHAMPIONS

(For year 1969 and later: E = Eastern Division; W = Western Division)

	National League	Won	Lost	Percentage	American League	Won	Lost	Percentage
1901	Pittsburgh Pirates	90	49	.647	Chicago White Sox	83	53	.610
1902	Pittsburgh Pirates	103	36	.741	Philadelphia Athletics	83	53	.610
1903	Pittsburgh Pirates	91	49	.650	Boston Red Sox*	91	47	.659
1904	New York Giants	106	47	.693	Boston Red Sox	95	59	.617
1905	New York Giants*	105	48	.686	Philadelphia Athletics	92	56	.622
1906	Chicago Cubs	116	36	.763	Chicago White Sox*	93	58	.616
1907	Chicago Cubs*	107	45	.704	Detroit Tigers	92	58	.613
1908	Chicago Cubs†*	99	55	.643	Detroit Tigers	90	63	.588
1909	Pittsburgh Pirates*	110	42	.724	Detroit Tigers	98	54	.645
1910	Chicago Cubs	104	50	.675	Philadelphia Athletics*	102	48	.680
1911	New York Giants	99	54	.647	Philadelphia Athletics*	101	50	.669
1912	New York Giants	103	48	.682	Boston Red Sox*	105	47	.691
1913	New York Giants	101	51	.664	Philadelphia Athletics*	96	57	.627
1914	Boston Braves*	94	59	.614	Philadelphia Athletics	99	53	.651
1915	Philadelphia Phillies	90	62	.592	Boston Red Sox*	101	50	.669
1916	Brooklyn Dodgers	94	60	.610	Boston Red Sox*	91	63	.591
1917	New York Giants	98	56	.636	Chicago White Sox*	100	54	.649
1918	Chicago Cubs	84	45	.651	Boston Red Sox*	75	51	.595
1919	Cincinnati Reds*	96	44	.686	Chicago White Sox	88	52	.629
1920	Brooklyn Dodgers	93	61	.604	Cleveland Indians*	98	56	.636
1921	New York Giants*	94	59	.614	New York Yankees	98	55	.641
1922	New York Giants*	93	61	.604	New York Yankees	94	60	.610
1923	New York Giants	95	58	.621	New York Yankees*	98	54	.645
1924	New York Giants	93	60	.608	Washington Senators*	92	62	.597
1925	Pittsburgh Pirates*	95	58	.621	Washington Senators	96	55	.636
1926	St. Louis Cardinals*	89	65	.578	New York Yankees	91	63	.591
1927	Pittsburgh Pirates	94	60	.610	New York Yankees*	110	44	.714
1928	St. Louis Cardinals	95	59	.617	New York Yankees*	101	53	.656
1929	Chicago Cubs	98	54	.645	Philadelphia Athletics*	104	46	.693
1930	St. Louis Cardinals	92	62	.597	Philadelphia Athletics*	102	52	.662
1931	St. Louis Cardinals*	101	53	.656	Philadelphia Athletics	107	45	.704
1932	Chicago Cubs	90	64	.584	New York Yankees*	107	47	.695
1933	New York Giants*	91	61	.599	Washington Senators	99	53	.651
1934	St. Louis Cardinals*	95	58	.621	Detroit Tigers	101	53	.656
1935	Chicago Cubs	100	54	.649	Detroit Tigers*	93	58	.616
1936	New York Giants	92	62	.597	New York Yankees*	102	51	.667
1937	New York Giants	95	57	.625	New York Yankees*	102	52	.662
1938	Chicago Cubs	89	63	.586	New York Yankees*	99	53	.651
1939	Cincinnati Reds	97	57	.630	New York Yankees*	106	45	.702
1940	Cincinnati Reds*	100	53	.654	Detroit Tigers	90	64	.584
1941	Brooklyn Dodgers	100	54	.649	New York Yankees*	101	53	.656
1942	St. Louis Cardinals*	106	48	.688	New York Yankees	103	51	.669
1943	St. Louis Cardinals	105	49	.682	New York Yankees*	98	56	.636
1944	St. Louis Cardinals*	105	49	.682	St. Louis Browns	89	65	.578
1945	Chicago Cubs	98	56	.636	Detroit Tigers*	88	65	.575
1946	St. Louis Cardinals†*	98	58	.628	Boston Red Sox	104	50	.675
1947	Brooklyn Dodgers	94	60	.610	New York Yankees*	97	57	.630
1948	Boston Braves	91	62	.595	Cleveland Indians†*	97	58	.626
1949	Brooklyn Dodgers	97	57	.630	New York Yankees*	97	57	.630
1950	Philadelphia Phillies	91	63	.591	New York Yankees*	98	56	.636
1951	New York Giants†	98	59	.624	New York Yankees*	98	56	.636
1952	Brooklyn Dodgers	96	57	.627	New York Yankees*	95	59	.617
1953	Brooklyn Dodgers	105	49	.682	New York Yankees*	99	52	.656
1954	New York Giants*	97	57	.630	Cleveland Indians	111	43	.721
1955	Brooklyn Dodgers*	98	55	.641	New York Yankees	96	58	.623
1956	Brooklyn Dodgers	93	61	.604	New York Yankees*	97	57	.630
1957	Milwaukee Braves*	95	59	.617	New York Yankees	98	56	.636
1958	Milwaukee Braves	92	62	.597	New York Yankees*	92	62	.597
1959	Los Angeles Dodgers†*	88	68	.564	Chicago White Sox	94	60	.610
1960	Pittsburgh Pirates*	93	61	.604	New York Yankees	97	57	.630
1961	Cincinnati Reds	95	59	.617	New York Yankees*	109	53	.673
1962	San Francisco Giants†	103	62	.624	New York Yankees*	96	66	.593
1963	Los Angeles Dodgers*	99	63	.611	New York Yankees	104	57	.646
1964	St. Louis Cardinals*	93	69	.574	New York Yankees	99	63	.611
1965	Los Angeles Dodgers*	97	65	.599	Minnesota Twins	102	60	.630
1966	Los Angeles Dodgers	95	67	.586	Baltimore Orioles*	97	63	.606
1967	St. Louis Cardinals*	101	60	.627	Boston Red Sox	92	70	.568
1968	St. Louis Cardinals	97	65	.599	Detroit Tigers*	103	59	.636
1969	New York Mets*† (E)	100	62	.617	Baltimore Orioles† (E)	109	53	.673
	Atlanta Braves (W)	93	69	.574	Minnesota Twins (W)	97	65	.599
1970	Cincinnati Reds† (W)	102	60	.630	Baltimore Orioles*† (E)	108	54	.667
	Pittsburgh Pirates (E)	89	73	.549	Minnesota Twins (W)	98	64	.605
1971	Pittsburgh Pirates*† (E)	97	65	.599	Baltimore Orioles† (E)	101	57	.639
	San Francisco Giants (W)	90	72	.556	Oakland A's (W)	101	60	.627
1972	Cincinnati Reds† (W)	95	59	.617	Oakland A's*† (W)	93	62	.600
	Pittsburgh Pirates (E)	96	59	.619	Detroit Tigers (E)	86	70	.551
1973	New York Mets† (E)	82	79	.509	Oakland A's*† (W)	94	68	.580
	Cincinnati Reds (W)	99	63	.611	Baltimore Orioles (E)	97	65	.599
1974	L.A. Dodgers† (W)	102	60	.630	Oakland A's*† (W)	90	72	.556
	Pittsburgh Pirates (E)	88	74	.543	Baltimore Orioles (E)	91	71	.562
1975	Cincinnati Reds*† (W)	108	54	.667	Boston Red Sox† (E)	95	65	.594
	Pittsburgh Pirates (E)	92	69	.571	Oakland A's (W)	98	64	.605
1976	Cincinnati Reds*† (W)	102	60	.630	New York Yankees† (E)	97	62	.610
	Philadelphia Phillies (E)	101	61	.623	Kansas City Royals (W)	90	72	.556
1977	L.A. Dodgers† (W)	98	64	.605	New York Yankees*† (E)	100	62	.617
	Philadelphia Phillies (E)	100	61	.623	Kansas City Royals (W)	102	60	.630

* Won World Series. † Won pennant in postseason playoffs.

GREAT NAMES IN BASEBALL

Baseball has produced giants in all departments since the National Association was born in 1871. Pictured here are a few outstanding stars—great pitchers and hitters, renowned managers, and famous record-breakers and record-holders.

WALTER JOHNSON (*far left*), the Washington Senators' immortal righthander, with Ty Cobb of the Detroit Tigers, major league baseball's finest hitter. Christy Mathewson (*left*), ace pitcher of the New York Giants. Babe Ruth (*above*), New York Yankees' home run king.

HONUS WAGNER led National League hitters for eight years.

GROVER CLEVELAND ALEXANDER won 373 games for the Phils, Cubs, and Cards.

ROGERS HORNSBY batted .424 in 1924, the highest mark ever reached.

MANAGERS John McGraw (*left*) and Connie Mack meet at 1911 World Series.

FOUR SLUGGERS in the Yankees 1936 World Series lineup: (*from left*) Bill Dickey, Lou Gehrig, Joe DiMaggio, and Tony Lazzeri.

WIDE WORLD

STAN MUSIAL (*above*) of St. Louis holds more batting records than any other National Leaguer. (*Right*) Cleveland's fireballing Bob Feller.

WIDE WORLD

WIDE WORLD

WARREN SPAHN (*left*) won 327 games in 18 seasons, mostly with the Boston and Milwaukee Braves. Brooklyn Dodger star Jackie Robinson (*above*) broke color barrier in 1947.

CASEY STENGEL, one of baseball's most colorful personalities, was player, coach, and manager in a 55-year career.

MICKEY MANTLE (*left*), Yankees' star outfielder. Roger Maris (*center*), whose 61 home runs in 1961 were the most ever hit in one season. Willie Mays (*right*) hit 660 home runs in his 22-year career.

(CENTER) AUTHENTICATED NEWS; (OTHERS) WIDE WORLD

NATIONAL BASEBALL HALL OF FAME AND MUSEUM

The National Baseball Hall of Fame and Museum is situated at Cooperstown, N. Y.

NATIONAL BASEBALL HALL OF FAME MEMBERS

Elected by Committee on Veterans

1937
Morgan G. Bulkeley
Byron B. Johnson
John J. McGraw
Cornelius McGillicuddy
(Connie Mack)
George Wright

1938
Alexander J. Cartwright, Jr.
Henry Chadwick

1939
Adrian C. Anson
Charles A. Comiskey
William A. Cummings
William B. Ewing
Charles Radbourne
Albert G. Spalding

1944
Kenesaw M. Landis

1945
Roger P. Bresnahan
Dennis Brouthers
Frederick C. Clarke
James J. Collins
Edward J. Delahanty
Hugh Duffy

Hugh A. Jennings
Michael J. Kelly
James H. O'Rourke
Wilbert Robinson

1946
Jesse C. Burkett
Frank L. Chance
John D. Chesbro
John J. Evers
Clark C. Griffith
Thomas F. McCarthy
Joseph J. McGinnity
Edward S. Plank
Joseph B. Tinker
George E. Waddell
Edward A. Walsh

1949
Mordecai P. Brown
Charles A. Nichols

1953
Edward G. Barrow
Charles A. Bender
Thomas H. Connolly
William J. Klem
Roderick J. Wallace
William H. Wright

1955
J. Franklin Baker
Raymond W. Schalk

1957
Samuel E. Crawford
Joseph V. McCarthy

1959
Zachariah D. Wheat

1961
Max G. Carey
William R. Hamilton

1962
William B. McKechnie
Edd J. Roush

1963
John J. Clarkson
Elmer H. Flick
Edgar C. Rice
Eppa Rixey

1964
Urban C. Faber
Burleigh A. Grimes
Miller J. Huggins
Timothy J. Keefe
Henry E. Manush
John M. Ward

1965
James F. Galvin

1966
Charles Dillon Stengel

1967
Wesley Branch Rickey
Lloyd James Waner

1968
Hazen S. Cuyler
Leon Allen Goslin

1969
Stanley A. Coveleski
Waite Charles Hoyt

1970
Earle Combs
Ford C. Frick
Jesse Haines

1971
Dave Bancroft
Jake Beckley
Chick Hafey
Harry Hooper
Joe Kelley
Rube Marquard
George M. Weiss

1972
Lefty Gomez
Will Harridge
Ross Youngs

1973
Billy Evans
George Kelly
Mickey Welch

1974
Jim Bottomley
Jocko Conlon
Sam Thompson

1975
Earl Averill
Bucky Harris
Billy Herman

1976
Roger Connor
Cal Hubbard
Fred Lindstrom

1977
Amos Rusie

Elected by Baseball Writers' Association of America

1936
Tyrus R. Cobb
Walter P. Johnson
Christopher Mathewson
George H. Ruth
John P. Wagner

1937
Napoleon Lajoie
Tristram E. Speaker
Denton T. Young

1938
Grover C. Alexander

1939
Edward T. Collins
Henry L. Gehrig
William H. Keeler
George H. Sisler

1942
Rogers Hornsby

1947
Gordon S. Cochrane
Frank F. Frisch
Robert M. Grove
Carl O. Hubbell

1948
Herbert J. Pennock
Harold J. Traynor

1949
Charles L. Gehringer

1951
James E. Foxx
Melvin T. Ott

1952
Harry E. Heilmann
Paul G. Waner

1953
Jay Hanna Dean
Aloysius H. Simmons

1954
William M. Dickey
Walter J. Maranville
William H. Terry

1955
Joseph P. DiMaggio
Charles L. Hartnett
Theodore A. Lyons
Arthur C. Vance

1956
Joseph E. Cronin
Henry B. Greenberg

1962
Robert W. Feller
Jack R. Robinson

1964
Lucius Appling

1966
Theodore S. Williams

1967
Charles H. Ruffing

1968
Joseph M. Medwick

1969
Roy Campanella
Stanley F. Musial

1970
Louis Boudreau

1972
Yogi Berra
Sandy Koufax
Early Wynn

1973
Roberto Clemente
Warren Spahn

1974
Whitey Ford
Mickey Mantle

1975
Ralph Kiner

1976
Bob Lemon
Robin Roberts

1977
Ernie Banks
Al Lopez
Joe Sewell

Elected by Committee on Negro Baseball Leagues

1971
Satchel Paige

1972
Josh Gibson
Buck Leonard

1973
Monte Irvin

1974
James Bell

1975
William (Judy) Johnson

1976
Oscar Charleston

1977
Martin Dihigo
John Henry (Pop)
Lloyd

The Hall of Fame. Cooperstown, N.Y., has become the home of baseball's national shrine—the National Baseball Hall of Fame and Museum. It was dedicated on June 12, 1939.

By the 1960's, more than 100 of baseball's leading players had been elected to the Hall of Fame. According to the rules, candidates are chosen "on the basis of playing ability, integrity, sportsmanship, character, and their contribution to the team on which they played and to baseball in general."

Modern-day players are chosen by secret ballot of members of 10 years' standing in the Baseball Writers' Association of America. Earlier stars (and leading baseball figures not famous as active players) are selected by a special 12-man Committee on Veterans, appointed by the directors of the Hall of Fame.

In the first ballot by the baseball writers in 1936, a mighty quintet—Ty Cobb, Babe Ruth, Honus Wagner, Walter Johnson, and Christy Mathewson—were swept in. By 1939, 21 others, including Connie Mack, John McGraw, Napoleon Lajoie, Tris Speaker, Denton (Cy) Young, Grover Cleveland Alexander, Eddie Collins, Lou Gehrig, Willie Keeler, and George Sisler, had joined the original quintet.

In addition to the bronze plaques to baseball's immortals in the Hall of Fame, the Cooperstown Museum has the most complete existing collection of the game's memorabilia.

Organized Baseball. The head of professional or organized baseball is the commissioner, who is empowered to take action against anything that may be considered detrimental to the game. The commissioner also acts as the final court of appeal. He is assisted by an executive council, consisting of the two major league presidents, one club owner and one player representative from each major league, and the president of the National Association of Professional Baseball Leagues (the association of minor leagues). Player representatives have voice only in player-management relations, and the National Association representative takes part only in major-minor league matters.

The administration of organized baseball by a commissioner arose as a result of the White Sox scandal of 1919, in which eight players of the Chicago White Sox baseball team were indicted for accepting bribes to affect the outcome of the World Series. To restore public confidence in the game, the post of commissioner was created and offered to Judge Kenesaw Mountain Landis, who served from 1921 to 1944. Subsequent commissioners, elected for 7-year terms by major league owners, were A. B. Chandler (1945–1951), Ford C. Frick (1951–1965), William D. Eckert (1965–1969), and Bowie Kuhn (1969–   ).

Each of the major leagues is administered by a president. Recent presidents of the American League have been Ernest S. Barnard (1927–1931), William Harridge (1931–1958), and Joseph J. Cronin (1959–   ). National League presidents were John A. Heydler (1919–1934), Ford C. Frick (1934–1951), Warren C. Giles (1951–1969), and Charles Feeney (1969–   ).

Reserve Clause. Organized baseball, which controls a player from the time that he signs his first contract until the time that he gets an unconditional release, has frequently been criticized and termed a monopoly. Its reserve clause and blacklist especially have been subject to attack. Yet, its friends contend that baseball needs this system to prevent gravitation of the top stars to the few very wealthy clubs, with a consequent diminution of competition, followed by a loss of popularity and the ultimate impoverishment of the professional structure. The system has had the sanction of the highest courts. In 1922, with Oliver Wendell Holmes reading the decision, the Supreme Court found among other things that baseball was "a peculiar business," that the games were played by personal effort and did not constitute a commodity and that, therefore, no antitrust law was violated.

In 1953, the Supreme Court again ruled that organized baseball is a sport rather than interstate commerce within the meaning of federal antitrust laws. When, however, the Supreme Court ruled in 1957 that professional football was subject to antitrust laws, the effect was to give organized baseball a preferential position not enjoyed by other sports. There were extensive Congressional hearings in 1957 and 1958, and baseball was included in a sports control bill passed by the House of Representatives, which was, however, shelved as a result of an adverse committee vote in the Senate.

Minor Leagues. The minor leagues, former feeders of major league talent, have fallen on difficult days. As late as 1949, there were 59 flourishing minor leagues. By the 1960's, the number had faded to fewer than 20 leagues, and most of these were struggling for survival. Reasons for the collapse of much of the minor league structure include the growth of television (not only the telecasts of major league games but TV entertainment per se), competition from other sports, dissatisfaction with minor status, and use of the minors almost solely for the training of major league "farmhands" (option players). The prevailing present practice is to sign youthful free agents and to place them in existing minor leagues under option. The independent minor league operator, a man with no major league attachments, has become extinct. In the 1960's, the minor league structure was being substantially revised to assure the survival of this very important branch of baseball.

Semipro and Amateur Baseball. Hundreds of thousands of people play baseball in semipro (semiprofessional) leagues, and millions of boys participate in amateur leagues. The National Baseball Congress, founded in 1935, sponsors a national championship in August at Wichita, Kans. Thousands of teams engage in district, state, and regional tournaments in order to qualify for that event and share in the prize money. Independent promotors and industrial companies also sponsor many teams and leagues.

In addition to the amateur baseball which is played in many colleges and high schools, many leagues are sponsored by the American Legion, Little League, "Pony" League, Babe Ruth League, Colt League, Veterans of Foreign Wars, National Amateur Baseball Federation, and others. World series are generally held each year by most of the leagues.

Baseball in Other Countries. In some parts of the world (Japan, the Dominican Republic, Panama, Venezuela, and Puerto Rico), baseball is even more firmly established as the national sport than it is in the United States. Brought to Japan by missionaries in the late 19th century, it had such a large following there by 1931 that a visiting team of American big league stars drew 450,000 people in 17 games. Japan now has two strong professional leagues, the Pacific and Central leagues, whose champions annually play their own version of the world series. Baseball is Japan's leading college sport, centering around the Six-University League of the Tokyo area. The game is also played extensively in Mexico, with three strong leagues affiliated with minor leagues north of the border. Cubans played baseball long before the Spanish-American War, and their country has sent many star players to the American professional diamond.

While baseball took an early hold in Japan, Canada, and Latin America, it has never become a truly international sport such as soccer, basketball, boxing, or horse racing. It was introduced at the 1936 Berlin Olympics, but failed to take hold as a quadrennial event. Baseball missionaries led by Albert G. Spalding tried to take the game to England and Ireland as early as 1874, but Britons were nonreceptive. Today a few leagues function in Australia and England, and baseball has made some headway in Italy.

FREDERICK G. LIEB
Author of "The Story of the World Series"

Bibliography

Allen, Ethan N., *Baseball Play and Strategy* (New York 1959).
Allen, Lee, *The National League Story* (New York 1961); id., *The American League Story* (New York 1962).
Anderson, Clary, *The Young Sportsman's Guide to Baseball* (New York 1963).
Baseball Register (St. Louis, annually)
Crosetti, Frank, *Secrets of Baserunning and Infield Play* (New York 1966)
Danzig, Allison, and Reichler, Joe, *The History of Baseball, Its Great Players, Teams and Managers* (Englewood Cliffs, N.J. 1959).
Einstein, Charles, ed., *The Fireside Book of Baseball* (New York 1956); id., *The Second Fireside Book of Baseball* (New York 1958)
Lieb, Frederick G., *The Story of the World Series*, rev. ed. (New York 1965).
McConnell, Mickey, *How to Play Little League Baseball* (New York 1960).
Official Baseball Guide (St. Louis, annually)
Official NCAA Baseball Guide (New York, annually)
Olan, Ben, *Big-time Baseball* (New York 1965).
Reichler, Joe, *Encyclopedia of Baseball*, 2d ed. (New York 1964).
Rickey, Branch, and Riger, Robert, *The American Diamond* (New York 1965)
Turkin, Hy, and Thompson, S.C., *Official Encyclopedia of Baseball*, 3d ed. (New York 1963).
Watts, Llewellyn, III, *Fine Art of Baseball: A Complete Guide to Strategy, Skills, and System* (Englewood Cliffs, N.J., 1964).

GLOSSARY OF BASEBALL TERMS

The following are terms used in baseball that have not been defined in the text:

Assist—A throw or deflection by a fielder that aids in making a put-out.

Bag—First, second, or third base. Also called sack or cushion. The terms two-bagger, three-bagger, and four-bagger refer, respectively, to a double, triple, and home run (also called a four-sacker).

Balk—An illegal act by a pitcher with one or more runners on base, permitting each to advance one base.

Bases loaded—A runner at each base.

Batting average—Though often called a percentage, it is actually a fraction carried to the third decimal point and represents the number of hits divided by a batter's number of "official at bats"; the latter excludes walks, sacrifices, hit batsmen, and catcher's interferences, but includes the times that the batter reached base on errors.

Bean ball—A ball pitched at a batter's head in order to drive him back from the plate; the pitch is illegal, but premeditation is difficult to prove.

Blank—To pitch any number of innings or a full game without permitting a run.

Bleachers—The cheapest seats, usually beyond the outfield's boundaries, in the sun, but now covered in some ball parks.

Blooper—A softly hit ball that drops or dribbles safely for a hit.

Bobble—To fail to hold on to a fielded ball. Also called fumble or muff.

Bonus player—An amateur player who is given more than the minimum established by the commissioner's office for signing a professional contract.

Book—(1) The records of baseball; hence, any unusual play is "one for the book." (2) The store of knowledge about a player's weaknesses and strengths. (3) The standard unwritten rules of strategy that are ordinarily followed in any given situation.

Bullpen—A special area where relief pitchers warm up during the game.

Bush league or bush—(1) A minor or semipro league. (2) By extension, conduct below major league standards of dignity or quality.

Called game—A game in which, for any reason, the umpire terminates play.

Cellar—Last place in the league standing.

Cheap or Chinese homer—A pop fly that just falls into the grandstands near a short foul line for a home run.

Choke—(1) To hold the bat well up on the handle. (2) To be too nervous or frightened to cope with a difficult situation.

Circuit clout—A home run.

Cleanup hitter—The fourth man in the batting order.

Clothesline—A line drive to the outfield, usually a single, which travels "straight as a clothesline," no more than 10 to 15 feet above the ground.

Clutch hitter—A batter with a reputation for delivering a hit with runners on base, or at a crucial point of the game.

Crowding the plate—Standing in a crouch position as close to home plate as the boundaries of the batter's box permit.

Dead ball—A ball that is out of play because of a legally created suspension of play.

Double header—Two ball games, played consecutively on a single day, for which only one admission is charged.

DP—A double play.

Drag bunt—A ball bunted by a batter who has started to run while in the act of reaching for the ball with the bat.

Dugout—The seating facilities (usually below the level of the playing field) reserved for players, substitutes, manager, and coaches. Only men in uniform may sit in the dugout. Also called the bench.

Duster—An inside pitch thrown at the batter, forcing him to throw himself on the ground (in the dust) to prevent being hit.

Earned run average—An earned run is a run scored without the aid of an error or passed ball. A pitcher's earned run average represents the average number of runs legitimately scored off his deliveries per full nine-inning game (27 outs); the figure is usually carried to two decimal points.

Fan—(1) A spectator at a ball game. (2) An intense devotee of the sport. (3) To strike out.

Fielder's choice—The decision of a fielder, when a ball is hit, to retire a runner instead of throwing to first base to retire the batter.

First division—The top half of the league standing.

Flag—The pennant, symbol of league championship.

Forfeited game—A game declared ended by the umpire for illegal acts on the part of one team, such as the obvious employment of stalling tactics, or failure to remove an ejected player. The game is officially scored 9 to 0. A game may also be forfeited to a visiting team because of the unruly behavior of hometown fans.

Full count—Three balls and two strikes on the batter.

Fungo—A fly ball hit to a fielder during fielding practice with a light bat called a fungo stick.

Gopher ball—Any pitch which is hit for a homer.

Grand slam—A home run with bases loaded.

Grandstander—A player who is conscious of impressing the fans; one who makes easy chances look difficult.

Grapefruit league—Informal league of major league teams in spring training in Florida. Teams training in Arizona belong to the Cactus league.

Hitting the dirt—(1) Quick action by the batter in throwing himself on the ground to avoid being hit by a close pitch, or duster. (2) Sliding into a base.

Hot corner—Third base.

Keystone—Second base.

Knocked out of the box—Said of a pitcher when he has been forced to retire from the game under a rain of hits.

Leadoff man—(1) First man in the batting order. (2) First hitter in any half-inning.

Liner—A line drive.

Live ball—A ball which is in play.

KORAKUEN STADIUM in Tokyo is one of the more than 20 large stadiums located in Japan. In no country except the United States does the game enjoy such a devoted following.

No-hitter—A game in which the pitcher does not yield a single hit.

On deck—Said of the player who follows the man at bat; he normally waits in a large, white circle near the batter's box.

Passed ball—A pitch that goes past the catcher, allowing a runner to advance; it differs from a wild pitch in that the official scorer rules that the catcher should have stopped it.

Perfect game—A no-hitter in which no opponent reaches base, 27 men being retired in order.

Pick-off—A throw by a pitcher or a catcher to a fielder, catching a runner off base.

Pinch hitter—A substitute sent in to bat for the scheduled batter. A pinch runner is a substitute sent in to run for a batter who has reached base.

Pitchout—A pitch deliberately thrown wide of the plate, so that the catcher is in a better position for a pick-off throw.

Pop fly or pop-up—A short, high, easily handled fly ball, usually over the infield.

Pull hitter—A hitter who normally hits "ahead" of the ball; that is, a left-handed batter who usually hits the ball to right field, or a right-handed batter who usually hits the ball to left field.

Quick return—An illegal pitch, hurried, with the obvious intent to catch the batter off balance.

Rabbit ball—Extremely lively ball, which, it is said, jumps like a rabbit.

Rally—Combination of hits, bases on balls, or opponents' errors which produces several runs.

RBI—Run batted in. A batter is credited with an RBI when he bats in a run with a hit (including himself on a home run), an infield out, a sacrifice fly, a bunt, or when he gets a base on balls with the bases loaded.

Relief pitcher—A pitcher who has been substituted for another pitcher in a game, or one who is normally used to relieve other pitchers rather than to start ball games.

Rhubarb—Noisy, turbulent argument between players, or between players and umpires.

Riding the bench—(1) The yelling of taunting, derisive remarks at rival players or at the umpires from a seat in the dugout; also called bench jockeying. (2) Said of a player who has not played for a long time.

Rookie—(1) Young player trying for a big league berth. (2) Any player playing his first year in the major leagues.

Round tripper—A home run.

Rundown—The act of running down and tagging out a runner who has been trapped between bases.

Sacrifice fly—A long fly ball, fair or foul, permitting a runner on third to score after the catch.

Second division—The lower half of the league standing.

Seventh inning stretch—A tradition which dictates that the fans rise to their feet in the seventh inning when their favorite team comes to bat, supposedly to bring it luck.

Shake off—Negative motion of the pitcher's head, indicating to the catcher that the pitcher prefers to throw a different pitch than that signaled for by the catcher.

Shoestring catch—A ball caught at the height of the outfielder's shoe tops, often made possible by a lunge or dive at the last moment.

Shutout—A game in which the losing team does not score a single run. Also called a whitewash.

Slide—The forward thrust of a runner who throws himself to the ground either feet first or head first to reach base ahead of a throw.

Slugger—A heavy hitter, one that produces home runs and extra-base hits.

Southpaw—A left-handed pitcher.

Spitball or spitter—The pitching of a ball which has been moistened with saliva so that it will curve or break more sharply; such a pitch is now illegal.

Spray hitter—A player who can hit the ball to any part of the field.

Squeeze play—An attempt to score a runner from third by means of a bunt. In the suicide squeeze, the runner starts for home on the pitch; in a safety squeeze, he waits until the batter has bunted.

Streak—A succession of victories, hits, brilliant catches, or whatever. A losing streak (for a team or a player) is often called a slump.

Stuff—Amount of spin, curve, and break a pitcher can apply to the ball.

Switch hitter—A batter who can bat from either side of the plate.

Taking a pitch—Not swinging at a pitch, even if it is in the strike zone.

Texas leaguer—A short fly ball that falls between the infield and the outfield for a hit.

Tie game—A game that ends without either team winning. Such a game must be replayed.

Trapped ball—A batted ball that the defensive player takes on a short, first hop, often pretending that he has caught the ball before it touched the ground.

Triple Crown—Distinction won by a batter who, at the end of the year, leads his league in batting average, RBI's, and home runs.

Waivers—Except for certain optionable players, a major league club must obtain waivers from the clubs in its league, and then from the clubs in the other major league, before it can send a player to the minor leagues or give him an unconditional release. A club refusing to waive claim may obtain the player at a fixed price.

Warm-up—Physical activity readying a player for service in a game, applied especially to a pitcher, who normally executes several warm-up pitches to loosen his arm muscles.

Waste pitch—A pitch deliberately thrown outside of the strike zone to a batter against whom there are two strikes and no balls, in the hope that he will misjudge it and strike out.

Wild pitch—A pitch that is too high, or low, or wide for the catcher to handle, thus allowing a runner to advance.

Windup—Movements of a pitcher before he releases the ball, whereby he attempts to get the maximum speed, stuff, and body follow-through behind his pitch. Used when it is not necessary to hold a runner on base.

BASEDOW, bä′zə-dō, **Johann Bernhard** (1723–1790), German educational reformer and author. He was born at Hamburg, Germany, on Sept. 11, 1723. He attended the *gymnasium* at Hamburg and studied philosophy and theology at the University of Leipzig. He became a professor of moral philosophy at the academy in Sorø, Denmark, in 1753 but was forced to resign in 1761 because of his nonconformist religious views and the jealousy of other instructors. Later he taught at a *gymnasium* in Germany.

Basedow's great book, *Das Elementarwerk,* was published in four volumes in 1774. It outlined a complete system of elementary education. In the same year he opened a school in Dessau called the *Philanthropinum.* This school was intended to embody his progressive educational ideas, which he hoped would be the basis for a new national system throughout Germany. Wealthy parents paid double tuition so that funds were available for scholarships for the poor. The school offered an eclectic program. Innovations included individualized attention, group work, student aides, a summer camp, student government, correlated studies, instruction in current events, and sex education.

Basedow lacked administrative ability, and he was forced to give up direction of his school some years before it closed in 1793. He and his teachers, however, wrote important educational treatises, and institutions similar to his school developed throughout Germany and Switzerland. Basedow evolved practical ways to attain the aims of many great educators who preceded him, such as John Comenius and Jean Jacques Rousseau. He was the greatest of the 18th century German school reformers.

RICHARD E. GROSS, *Stanford University*

BASEL, bä′zəl, a canton in northern Switzerland, is bordered by France on the northwest and Germany on the northeast. It also borders on the Swiss cantons of Bern, Solothurn, and Aargau. It is known as *Bâle* in French and is sometimes called *Basle* in English. The total area is 179 square miles (463 sq km). Much of its territory is wooded and of rugged topography. Its orchards are famous throughout Switzerland.

There are several major machinery and chemical plants, woolen mills, and watchmaking factories. Heavy industry and commerce are concentrated in the city of Basel, although there are some hydroelectric plants on the Rhine.

As a result of a bloody struggle between the rural districts and the urban trade guilds in the early 1830's, the canton was divided in 1833 into two half-cantons, each with its own constitution and laws. Basel-Stadt (14 square miles; 36 sq km) has its capital at Basel. Basel-Land (165 square miles; 427 sq km) has its capital at Liestal. Population: (1960) Basel-Stadt, 225,588; Basel-Land, 148,282.

GEORGE KISH
University of Michigan

BASEL, bä′zəl, a city in Switzerland, is on the Rhine River at the mouth of the Birs and Wiese rivers. Its name in French is *Bâle;* it is sometimes called *Basle* in English. It is 55 miles (88.5 km) west of Zurich, at an elevation of 918 feet (280 meters). Basel is Switzerland's second-largest city, its most important port, and one of its leading industrial centers. It is the capital of and virtually coextensive with the half-canton of Basel-Stadt.

Although the original settlement was located on a low spur overlooking the Rhine River, Basel consists today of two distinct parts separated by the river: Greater Basel (Gross Basel), on the left or southwestern bank; and Lesser Basel (Klein Basel), on the right or northeastern bank. The left bank is the business and administrative center of the city. The majority of its educational institutions and residential sections are also located here. The right bank is the industrial area and includes the port installations.

Economy. Basel's principal industries trace their origins back to the Reformation, when the city became a center of refuge for Protestants from all over western Europe. Its textile industries first became prominent in the 16th century and continue to be the second-largest industry today. The principal industry is chemicals and pharmaceuticals. The leading pharmaceutical company, CIBA (Chemische Industrien Basel), is a worldwide concern.

In addition to industry, Basel is important as a transportation and financial center. Bordering on Germany to the north and France to the west, the city is situated at the head of navigation of the Rhine River. It is the home port of the Swiss river fleet, consisting of more than 400 vessels, with a tonnage of 376,000 tons. The city is also one of the most important railway centers of western Europe and is often called the "golden door" to Switzerland. The airport at Blotzheim, France, five miles (8 km) to the northwest, serves Basel. The Bank for International Settlements has been located in Basel since 1930.

Culture. The city's intellectual life has long been of great importance to Switzerland. The first Swiss university was founded in Basel in 1460 by Pope Pius II, and a number of major European figures have lived here. These included the humanist Desiderius Erasmus, the Renaissance painters Konrad Witz and Hans Holbein the Younger, and the 19th century philosopher Friedrich Nietzsche. Basel's native sons include the painter Arnold Böcklin, the historian Jakob Burckhardt, the Bernoulli family of scientists, and the poet Johann Peter Hebel.

The core of the city is the low spur over the Rhine, where the cathedral (consecrated 1019) is located. The 16th century Rathaus and the Spalen-Tor, a town gate, as well as a number of attractive fountains, are noteworthy. The most scenic part of the city is along the Rhine, where hotels, restaurants, cafes, and promenades attract both residents and tourists.

History. The origins of Basel go back to an early Celtic settlement. The first mention of the town, as *Basilia,* occurred in 374 A.D., when Roman Emperor Valentinian I visited it. The early history of the city is bound up with the flowering of the bishopric, which moved to Basel in the 7th century following the destruction of Augusta Raurica (modern Augst).

From 1096 to 1501, when it joined the Swiss Confederation, Basel was a free city of the Holy Roman Empire. From 1431 to 1449 it was the scene of a famous church council (see BASEL, COUNCIL OF). The city was won by the Protestants in 1529, during the Reformation. Population: (1960) 206,746.

GEORGE KISH, *University of Michigan*

BASEL, Confession of, bä′zəl, a Protestant statement of doctrine elaborated by Oswald Myconius from a shorter version (1531) by Johannes Oecolampadius and adopted in Basel, Switzerland, in 1534. Simple and comparatively moderate, it represents a position intermediate between the positions of Martin Luther and Ulrich Zwingli.

The First Helvetic Confession (1536) is sometimes called the Second Confession of Basel. Resulting from an ecumenical effort of the Swiss Reformed churches, the Second Confession gained national authority in Switzerland and in 1549 was recast by John Calvin and Heinrich Bullinger into the Consensus of Zurich (*Consensus Tigurinus*). It thus marked the initial Swiss departure from Zwinglian to Calvinist theology.

BASEL, Council of, bä′zəl, a council of the Roman Catholic Church held in Basel and Lausanne, Switzerland, from 1431 to 1449. The council was called by Pope Martin V, in accordance with the decision taken at the Council of Constance to convene church councils periodically. In 1423, Martin V called a council at Pavia but it was transferred to Siena because of an outbreak of plague. Although this council accomplished little, before it was dissolved (1424) it set Basel as the place of its next meeting.

The Council of Basel opened in 1431 under the presidency of Giuliano Cardinal Cesarini. External and internal problems pressed the church: the Turks were threatening the Eastern Empire and indeed the whole of Christendom; the heresies of John Wycliffe and Jan Hus still disturbed England and Bohemia; the papal demands for fees and taxes were considered exorbitant; the standards of the clergy were low; and many thought that the church needed reform in its "head and members."

No sooner had the council opened than Pope Eugene IV, successor to Martin V, ordered it to dissolve (December 1431), fearing that he might not be able to control it. The council refused to dissolve, declaring on Feb. 15, 1432, that it was a continuation of the Council of Constance and therefore ecumenical, properly representing the church; deriving its authority entirely from God, it could be dissolved only by its own free will.

The work of the assembly began slowly, and effective legislation became almost impossible because of mutual distrust between pope and council. On frequent occasions the council invited the pope to come to Basel. After many refusals, the council declared him contumacious on Feb. 19, 1433. With no alternative, Eugene IV expressly recognized the council on August 1 and on December 15 withdrew his earlier manifestos against it. Meanwhile, the authority of the council was augmented by its successful negotiations with the Hussites, resulting in the Compact of Prague (Nov. 30, 1433), which granted the Bohemians certain doctrinal concessions.

Disciplinary reform of the church was begun by the council in January 1435, with decrees against clerical concubinage and abuse of excommunication and interdict. It also ordered the discontinuance of annates and other papal taxes. Eugene IV saw clearly that the legislation was directed against the papacy and that compromise was impossible. After the council once more declared him contumacious on Oct. 1, 1437, Eugene issued a call for removal of the council to Ferrara, Italy.

This move split the Council of Basel. Cardinal Cesarini and others followed the pope's lead, but remaining at Basel were such leaders as the militant reformer Louis Cardinal Allemand, Enea Silvio de' Piccolomini (later Pope Pius II), and Nicholas of Cusa. Under the leadership of Allemand, the council at Basel agreed that Eugene IV must be replaced and declared (1) that a general council is superior to a pope, (2) that it cannot be dissolved by a pope, and (3) that anyone who disputes these propositions is a heretic. Accordingly, Eugene IV was suspended on Jan. 24, 1438, and deposed on June 25. On Oct. 30, 1439, the council elected Amadeus, ex-duke of Savoy, to the papal throne. Taking the name Felix V, he was generally considered an antipope, although parts of Europe recognized him until 1449. Confusion and dispute spread through the church, and a lack of confidence in the monarchial government of the church made its appearance, especially in France and Germany.

In 1438, at the Synod of Bourges, the decrees of the Council of Basel were incorporated into the laws of France through the adoption of the Pragmatic Sanction of Bourges (see GALLICANISM). But, one by one, the countries submitted to Eugene IV. Following the German declaration of loyalty early in 1447, the council voted on June 25, 1448, to move to Lausanne. At the urging of the king of France, Felix resigned, and the council dissolved itself on April 25, 1449, after recognizing Nicholas V, who had been elected on the death of Eugene in 1447. Although overtly defeated, the principle of conciliarism continued to be held by many leaders of the church.

RAYMOND W. ALBRIGHT
Episcopal Theological School, Cambridge, Mass.

Further Reading: Haller, J., and others, eds., *Concilium Basiliense: Studien und Quellen zur Geschichte des Konzils von Basel,* 8 vols. (Basel 1896–1936); Hughes, Philip, *Church in Crisis: A History of the General Councils* (Garden City, N.Y., 1961); Küng, Hans, *Structures of the Church* (Camden, N.J., 1963).

BASEL, University of, bä′zəl, a public coeducational institution of higher education in Basel, Switzerland. Established by Pope Pius II through a papal bull of Nov. 12, 1459, and opened on April 4, 1460, it is the country's oldest university. Early in its history it became a leading center of humanism, chiefly through its association with the noted printers Johann Froben (1460?–1527) and Hans Amerbach (1444–?1513) and with the renowned humanist scholar Desiderius Erasmus (1469–1536).

The victory of the Reformation in Switzerland caused many teachers and students to leave the university, and for a time it was feared that it would have to close. However, it was reorganized in 1532 under authority of the canton of Basel and became a stronghold of Protestant theology. In 1818 it was again reorganized by the canton and began receiving financial support from public funds. The school has always drawn outstanding scholars to its faculty, including Johannes Oecolampadius, a contemporary of Erasmus; the Bernoulli family of scientists; Friedrich Nietzsche and Jakob Burckhardt in the 19th century; and Karl Barth and Karl Jaspers in the 20th.

Basel confers only doctoral degrees in its five faculties: theology, law, philosophy and history, philosophy and natural science, and medicine. German is the language of instruction. Enrollment exceeds 3,000 students.

BASENJI, bə-sen′jĕ, an African breed of hound dog that rarely barks. Weighing about 20 to 25 pounds (9 to 11 kg), it usually has chestnut-brown hair, a curly tail, and straight legs. Its forehead is deeply wrinkled.

BASHAHR, bush′ər, was a princely state of India, known also as *Bussahir,* the capital of which was Kampur. One of the Punjab hill states, it was situated on the southwestern slope of the Himalaya and was crossed from east to west by the Sutlej River. Its area of 3,651 square miles (9,456 sq km) was incorporated in the new state of Himachal Pradesh (now a territory) in 1948. The former ruling family and the upper classes in the southern part of Bashahr are Rajputs. The area has valuable forest resources.

BASHAN, bā′shən, in the Old Testament, was a rich, grain-producing plateau east of the Sea of Galilee in what is now southwestern Syria. From here caravans went into Galilee. To the Israelites the name "Bashan" suggested mountains, magnificent oaks, lions, sheep, and enormous cattle. The "fat bulls of Bashan" (Psalm 22:12) are famous. Bashan was at one time ruled by King Og, said to be a giant, who was destroyed by Moses (Numbers 21:33-35). The region was taken over by the Israelite half-tribe of Manasseh during Israel's conquest of Canaan. At this time, Bashan included 60 walled cities (I Kings 4:13). Among them were Bosra Edrei, Kenath, and Golan. Some of these early cities have been excavated by 20th century archaeologists. During the reign of Solomon, taxes had to be paid on the wealth acquired from grain in this region. By the 10th century B.C. most of Bashan was under Aramaean control.

Part of Bashan was included in the kingdom of the later Maccabees (1st century B.C.), and all of it was included in that of Herod the Great (reigned 37–4 B.C.). The tetrarchy of his son Philip (reigned 4 B.C.–34 A.D.) comprised the districts of Trachonitis (the ancient Argob), Gaulanitis (Golan), Auranitis (Hauran), and Batanaea (Bashan proper), as well as Ituraea.

BASHKIR AUTONOMOUS SOVIET SOCIALIST REPUBLIC, bəsh-kēr′, a political subdivision of the Russian republic of the USSR. It is also known as *Bashkiria.* The Bashkir republic covers an area of 55,443 square miles (143,597 sq km) in eastern European Russia, in the western foothills of the Ural Mountains. It is bounded on the east by the Chelyabinsk oblast, on the south and southwest by the Orenburg oblast, on the west by the Tatar autonomous republic, on the northwest by the Udmurt autonomous republic, and on the north by the Perm and Sverdlovsk oblasts. The republic consists of the forested foothills of the Ural Mountains and a plateau extending southwest of them. The forelands are mostly open steppe, with fertile meadowlands in the valleys. Bashkiria is watered by several rivers, including the Belaya and its principal tributary, the Ufa, both of which are navigable in their lower reaches. Besides Ufa, the capital, the chief towns are Sterlitamak, Oktyabrski, Salavat, and Beloretsk.

Economy. The republic has valuable forest and mineral resources, the most important of which is oil. Bashkiria is the most important oil-refining area in the entire country. The chemical industry has also developed rapidly. Minerals produced include iron, manganese, copper, lead, bauxite, and gold. There are metal refineries, paper mills, food processing establishments, and factories manufacturing a wide variety of products, including steel, machinery, building materials, textiles, and leather goods. In the highlands the timber and stock raising industries are important. Grain, potatoes, vegetables, sugar beets, and hemp are the chief agricultural products.

People and History. The Bashkirs, a Turkic Muslim people speaking a Turko-Tatar language, were originally a nomadic pastoral group. They first appeared in recorded history in the 10th century. In the 13th century they came under the control of the Tatars of the Golden Horde and then of the emergent Kazan khanate. Following the conquest of the Kazan khanate by Ivan IV (the Terrible) in 1552, Bashkiria came under Russian rule. The Russians, however, in order to establish their hegemony, were obliged to resort to severe measures to suppress many uprisings.

After 1574, when they established Ufa, the Russians extended their colonization efforts in the area, often in the face of resistance. Mining operations were commenced in the 18th century, providing additional stimulus to Russian settlement. With the subsequent growth of industry, especially under the Soviet regime, the Russians became the majority element in the republic's population. Like the other formerly nomadic peoples of Bashkiria, the Bashkirs now live in settled communities; they comprise about a fourth of the population. The rest of the non-Russian people in the Bashkir republic are mainly Turko-Tatars.

In 1918, Bashkiria was the scene of heavy fighting between the Bolshevik and White Russian armies. In February 1919 the territory was won by the Bolsheviks, and in March 1919 the Bashkir Autonomous Soviet Socialist Republic—one of the first such administrative entities in the country—was formed. Since World War II industrial expansion and technical training, along with general education, have been stressed in Bashkiria. Population: (1965) 3,696,000.

BASHKIRTSEFF, bəsh-kyēr′tsəf, **Marie** (1859–1884), Russian diarist and painter, who is best known for her autobiographical *Journal,* published posthumously in Paris in 1887 and first translated into English in 1890. She was born *Maria Konstantinovna Bashkirtseva,* near Poltava, Ukraine, on Jan. 24, 1859. From 1877, after vocal training in Italy, she studied painting in Paris, where she was a pupil of Robert-Fleury and Jules Bastien-Lepage. She died of tuberculosis, in Paris on Oct. 31, 1884.

She began her *Journal,* which seems to have been written with ultimate publication in mind, on Aug. 6, 1872, when she was 13 years old, and continued it until the time of her death. Like Jean Jacques Rousseau's *Confessions,* the *Journal* claimed to be an absolutely candid expression of personal experience. However, the manuscript was severely bowdlerized by her mother before its publication, and no complete edition was ever published. Doris Langley Moore's *Marie and the Duke of H* (1966) sheds light on many previously unknown details concerning the *Journal.* Marie Bashkirtseff's *Letters,* consisting of her correspondence with Guy de Maupassant, was published in 1891.

BASIC ENGLISH, bā'sik ing'glish, is the product of a new kind of functional thinking about language that shows how we may improve and reshape our linguistic instruments. It is not an invented language but a system of 850 English words, setting up restrictions of its own within accepted English usage, to be used for certain defined purposes. The system was originated and developed between 1925 and 1932 by the English scholar C.K. Ogden, who was director of the Orthological Institute and editor of the International Library of Psychology, Philosophy and Scientific Method.

Purposes and Character. The primary object of Basic English is to provide an international secondary language for general and technical communication. Its qualifications for this purpose are that it is an undistorted form of what is practically a world language, and that it is simple enough to be quickly and easily learned, yet sufficiently flexible to be adequate for conveying information and expressing ideas. Its systematic character and selectivity make it also an effective introduction to English for the foreign learner, while the principles underlying the limitation of its vocabulary fit it for use as an antidote to confused thinking and verbal abuses by the English-speaking peoples themselves. By implication it is not intended as a substitute for any language or as a literary medium, or for any purposes to which the persuasive and evocative uses of language are appropriate.

Ogden was indebted to Jeremy Bentham, who studied the question of an international language and invented the word *international*, for some of the fundamental ideas on which the system is based. Particularly valuable were Bentham's investigation of linguistic fictions, his analysis of emotive language, and his penetrating observations on the verb.

After the threefold elimination of words which are emotive rather than referential, of literary and stylistic nuance words, and of words used in special contexts not normally coming within the scope of general discourse, it was clear that the vocabulary of the system could be reduced to less than 1,000 words. A first tentative selection of 850 words was revised in the course of an extensive survey of definitions, aided by a specially prepared radial chart of definition routes applying principles set out by Ogden and I.A. Richards in *The Meaning of Meaning* (1923). The value of each word had to be tested by its capacity for combining with the other words and fitting usefully into the system. *Sort* displaced *kind*, for example, to avoid an unnecessary homophone and because its range of sense could be extended by adding *-er, -ing,* and *-ed*. With the exception of names of common objects, all words for which concise definitions could be given with the Basic vocabulary were excluded from the Basic list. Its resources were then further tested by the translation of a wide variety of material from ordinary English.

Although the Basic list contains no words that are not in common use, its composition was not influenced by word counts. It includes many words that are not among the first 4,000 of Edward L. Thorndike's frequency list, and one (*reaction*) which is in the ninth thousand. The most remarkable economy effected in the Basic vocabulary is the analytic reduction of the verbs to 16 simple operators (*come, get, give, go, keep, let, make, put, seem, take, be, do, have, say, see, send*) and 2 auxiliaries (*may, will*), by relying on combinations formed by these operators with prepositions (*go in* for *enter*), with adjectives (*get ready* for *prepare*), with nouns (*give pain* for *hurt*), and so on. By this means the foreign learner is spared the irregularities of most of the strong verbs and made familiar with an essential feature of colloquial English.

Vocabulary and Structure. The vocabulary of Basic English consists of 600 nouns (200 of which are names of readily pictured objects), 150 adjectives (50 of which have the mnemonic advantage of being opposites of other words in the list), and 100 structural words, including operators, pronouns, and others. This list is reinforced by 50 nouns that have acquired wide international intelligibility (for example, *hotel* and *radio*) and certain systematic additions that do not rank as learning items in the full sense: namely, the numerals, the calendar, and the names of weights and measures and currency. Such are the resources that suffice for ordinary communication. They are not adequate, obviously, for communicating at the levels with which specialists are concerned, and for this purpose supplementary lists of technical terms have to be provided. Thus there are 100 general science words and 50 words for each of the principal sciences, as shown in *Basic for Science* (1944). The Bible has been translated (*The Basic Bible,* 1950) with the help of 100 words for verse reading and 50 special Bible words.

Except for the omission of *shall* and *should* (which are seldom used as grammar prescribes) and of the obsolescent subjunctive mood, the structural pattern of Basic conforms to that of ordinary English, being only more restricted. The operators and pronouns are conjugated in the normal way. Basic also uses the regular and irregular plural forms, the ordinary degrees of comparison, and the possessive *'s*. In accordance with English usage, the *-er, -ing,* and *-ed* endings may be added to 300 of the nouns, and adverbs may be formed from adjectives with *-ly*. By the exclusion of other terminations many troublesome anomalies for the learner are avoided. Further recommendations restrict the senses of the Basic words and limit their idiomatic use at two levels, the first related strictly to the learner's needs, the second providing some necessary latitude for the English writer. These rulings, which are essential to an understanding of the system, are found in *The Basic Words* (1947) and *The ABC of Basic English* (1944).

Translation into Basic English from full English, or from any other unrestricted language, is of a vertical kind—that is, it involves restatement at a simpler level. It is seldom possible to produce a word-for-word parallel. Words, and sometimes whole sentences, cannot be treated as isolated units of sense. They must be carefully examined in their context, and the whole thought fully grasped. Often the form of the statement must be completely reorganized, and in the process ambiguities may become apparent and have to be resolved. For an English-speaking person the main effort required in learning Basic English is to become proficient in this analytic technique, which makes the translator independent of ready-made synonyms. It is a salutary discipline which promotes the habit of reading for sense and develops interpretative powers.

A comparison of the last clause of the Basic English version of the Atlantic Charter with the

THINGS
400 General

ACCOUNT	COMMITTEE	EDUCATION	HUMOUR	METAL	POWDER	SENSE	SYSTEM	
ACT	COMPANY	EFFECT	ICE	MIDDLE	POWER	SERVANT	TALK	
ADDITION	COMPARISON	END	IDEA	MILK	PRICE	SEX	TASTE	
ADJUSTMENT	COMPETITION	ERROR	IMPULSE	MIND	PRINT	SHADE	TAX	
ADVERTISEMENT	CONDITION	EVENT	INCREASE	MINE	PROCESS	SHAKE	TEACHING	
AGREEMENT	CONNECTION	EXAMPLE	INDUSTRY	MINUTE	PRODUCE	SHAME	TENDENCY	
AIR	CONTROL	EXCHANGE	INK	MIST	PROFIT	SHOCK	TEST	
AMOUNT	COOK	EXISTENCE	INSECT	MONEY	PROPERTY	SIDE	THEORY	
AMUSEMENT	COOPER	EXPANSION	INSTRUMENT	MONTH	PROSE	SIGN	THING	
ANIMAL	COPY	EXPERIENCE	INSURANCE	MORNING	PROTEST	SILK	THOUGHT	
ANSWER	CORK	EXPERT	INTEREST	MOTHER	PULL	SILVER	THUNDER	
APPARATUS	COTTON	FACT	INVENTION	MOTION	PUNISHMENT	SISTER	TIME	
APPROVAL	COUGH	FALL	IRON	MOUNTAIN	PURPOSE	SIZE	TIN	
ARGUMENT	COUNTRY	FAMILY	JELLY	MOVE	PUSH	SKY	TOP	
ART	COVER	FATHER	JOIN	MUSIC	QUALITY	SLEEP	TOUCH	
ATTACK	CRACK	FEAR	JOURNEY	NAME	QUESTION	SLIP	TRADE	
ATTEMPT	CREDIT	FEELING	JUDGE	NATION	RAIN	SLOPE	TRANSPORT	
ATTENTION	CRIME	FICTION	JUMP	NEED	RANGE	SMASH	TRICK	
ATTRACTION	CRUSH	FIELD	KICK	NEWS	RATE	SMELL	TROUBLE	
AUTHORITY	CRY	FIGHT	KISS	NIGHT	RAY	SMILE	TURN	
BACK	CURRENT	FIRE	KNOWLEDGE	NOISE	REACTION	SMOKE	TWIST	
BALANCE	CURVE	FLAME	LAND	NOTE	READING	SNEEZE	UNIT	
BASE	DAMAGE	FLIGHT	LANGUAGE	NUMBER	REASON	SNOW	USE	
BEHAVIOUR	DANGER	FLOWER	LAUGH	OBSERVATION	RECORD	SOAP	VALUE	
BELIEF	DAUGHTER	FOLD	LAW	OFFER	REGRET	SOCIETY	VERSE	
BIRTH	DAY	FOOD	LEAD	OIL	RELATION	SON	VESSEL	
BIT	DEATH	FORCE	LEARNING	OPERATION	RELIGION	SONG	VIEW	
BITE	DEBT	FORM	LEATHER	OPINION	REPRESENTATIVE	SORT	VOICE	
BLOOD	DECISION	FRIEND	LETTER	ORDER	REQUEST	SOUND	WALK	
BLOW	DEGREE	FRONT	LEVEL	ORGANIZATION	RESPECT	SOUP	WAR	
BODY	DESIGN	FRUIT	LIFT	ORNAMENT	REST	SPACE	WASH	
BRASS	DESIRE	GLASS	LIGHT	OWNER	REWARD	STAGE	WASTE	
BREAD	DESTRUCTION	GOLD	LIMIT	PAGE	RHYTHM	START	WATER	
BREATH	DETAIL	GOVERNMENT	LINEN	PAIN	RICE	STATEMENT	WAVE	
BROTHER	DEVELOPMENT	GRAIN	LIQUID	PAINT	RIVER	STEAM	WAX	
BUILDING	DIGESTION	GRASS	LIST	PAPER	ROAD	STEEL	WAY	
BURN	DIRECTION	GRIP	LOOK	PART	ROLL	STEP	WEATHER	
BURST	DISCOVERY	GROUP	LOSS	PASTE	ROOM	STITCH	WEEK	
BUSINESS	DISCUSSION	GROWTH	LOVE	PAYMENT	RUB	STONE	WEIGH	
BUTTER	DISEASE	GUIDE	MACHINE	PEACE	RULE	STOP	WIND	
CANVAS	DISGUST	HARBOUR	MAN	PERSON	RUN	STORY	WINE	
CARE	DISTANCE	HARMONY	MANAGER	PLACE	SALT	STRETCH	WINTER	
CAUSE	DISTRIBUTION	HATE	MARK	PLANT	SAND	STRUCTURE	WOMAN	
CHALK	DIVISION	HEARING	MARKET	PLAY	SCALE	SUBSTANCE	WOOD	
CHANCE	DOUBT	HEAT	MASS	PLEASURE	SCIENCE	SUGAR	WOOL	
CHANGE	DRINK	HELP	MEAL	POINT	SEA	SUGGESTION	WORD	
CLOTH	DRIVING	HISTORY	MEASURE	POISON	SEAT	SUMMER	WORK	
COAL	DUST	HOLE	MEAT	POLISH	SECRETARY	SUPPORT	WOUND	
COLOUR	EARTH	HOPE	MEETING	PORTER	SELECTION	SURPRISE	WRITING	
COMFORT	EDGE	HOUR	MEMORY	POSITION	SELF	SWIM	YEAR	

original illustrates some of the means by which simplification is achieved:

> *Eighth* [from the original] it is their belief that all the nations of the earth, for material reasons no less than because it is right and good, will, in the end, give up the use of force. Because war will come again if countries which are, or may be, ready to make attacks on others go on using land, sea, or air power, it is their belief that it is necessary to take away all arms from them till a wider system of keeping the general peace, more solid in structure, comes into being. They will further give their help and support to all other possible steps which may make the crushing weight of arms less for peace-loving nations.

> *Eighth* [in Basic] they believe all of the nations of the world, for realistic as well as spiritual reasons, must come to the abandonment of the use of force. Since no future peace can be maintained if land, sea or air armaments continue to be employed by nations which threaten, or may threaten, aggression outside of their frontiers, they believe, pending the establishment of a wider and permanent system of general security, that the disarmament of such nations is essential. They will likewise aid and encourage all other practicable measures which will lighten for peace-loving peoples the crushing burden of armaments.

Development and Uses. Basic English has never been exploited on purely commercial lines. In spite of severely limited finances, its practitioners retained the scholarly direction that gave full scope to experiment and research, and Basic English made rapid international progress in the 1930's. It soon attracted the attention of educators and administrators in many parts of the world, and it established itself with great promise in countries with different educational outlooks,

as, for example, in China, India, and Greece.

This international development was interrupted by the war, but Winston Churchill's address at Harvard University on Sept. 6, 1943, revealed that he had not overlooked the relevance of Basic to postwar planning and reconstruction. Subsequently the system received a measure of British governmental support and some temporary financial assistance, but this was insufficient to enable it to be promoted on a scale that would relieve it of the need for endowment. As a result, the early postwar history of Basic English was one of developing potentialities rather than of fulfilling them. Nevertheless, Basic provided the means of teaching the elements of English to some hundreds of thousands of emigrants to Commonwealth countries. A request for Basic textbooks by the Indian army and the use of Basic by NATO in the preliminary training of French air crews were possible indications of further developments, for the problems of communication posed by the growth of international agencies and the world's increasing technological interdependence are of a kind which Basic is peculiarly fitted to solve. A further impetus was given to the study of English by the national emergence of the Eastern peoples and their reliance on technical assistance from the West. In countries such as India, Ceylon, Indonesia, Burma, Japan, and the Philippines, dissatisfaction with the old methods of teaching English, whose strong literary bias is quite un-

THINGS
200 Pictured

ANGLE	COAT	KNEE	SCREW
ANT	COLLAR	KNIFE	SEED
APPLE	COMB	KNOT	SHEEP
ARCH	CORD	LEAF	SHELF
ARM	COW	LEG	SHIP
ARMY	CUP	LIBRARY	SHIRT
BABY	CURTAIN	LINE	SHOE
BAG	CUSHION	LIP	SKIN
BALL	DOG	LOCK	SKIRT
BAND	DOOR	MAP	SNAKE
BASIN	DRAIN	MATCH	SOCK
BASKET	DRAWER	MONKEY	SPADE
BATH	DRESS	MOON	SPONGE
BED	DROP	MOUTH	SPOON
BEE	EAR	MUSCLE	SPRING
BELL	EGG	NAIL	SQUARE
BERRY	ENGINE	NECK	STAMP
BIRD	EYE	NEEDLE	STAR
BLADE	FACE	NERVE	STATION
BOARD	FARM	NET	STEM
BOAT	FEATHER	NOSE	STICK
BONE	FINGER	NUT	STOCKING
BOOK	FISH	OFFICE	STOMACH
BOOT	FLAG	ORANGE	STORE
BOTTLE	FLOOR	OVEN	STREET
BOX	FLY	PARCEL	SUN
BOY	FOOT	PEN	TABLE
BRAIN	FORK	PENCIL	TAIL
BRAKE	FOWL	PICTURE	THREAD
BRANCH	FRAME	PIG	THROAT
BRICK	GARDEN	PIN	THUMB
BRIDGE	GIRL	PIPE	TICKET
BRUSH	GLOVE	PLANE	TOE
BUCKET	GOAT	PLATE	TONGUE
BULB	GUN	PLOUGH	TOOTH
BUTTON	HAIR	POCKET	TOWN
CAKE	HAMMER	POT	TRAIN
CAMERA	HAND	POTATO	TRAY
CARD	HAT	PRISON	TREE
CARRIAGE	HEAD	PUMP	TROUSERS
CART	HEART	RAIL	UMBRELLA
CAT	HOOK	RAT	WALL
CHAIN	HORN	RECEIPT	WATCH
CHEESE	HORSE	RING	WHEEL
CHEST	HOSPITAL	ROD	WHIP
CHIN	HOUSE	ROOF	WHISTLE
CHURCH	ISLAND	ROOT	WINDOW
CIRCLE	JEWEL	SAIL	WING
CLOCK	KETTLE	SCHOOL	WIRE
CLOUD	KEY	SCISSORS	WORM

QUALITIES
100 General — 50 Opposites

ABLE	MATERIAL	AWAKE
ACID	MEDICAL	BAD
ANGRY	MILITARY	BENT
AUTOMATIC	NATURAL	BITTER
BEAUTIFUL	NECESSARY	BLUE
BLACK	NEW	CERTAIN
BOILING	NORMAL	COLD
BRIGHT	OPEN	COMPLETE
BROKEN	PARALLEL	CRUEL
BROWN	PAST	DARK
CHEAP	PHYSICAL	DEAD
CHEMICAL	POLITICAL	DEAR
CHIEF	POOR	DELICATE
CLEAN	POSSIBLE	DIFFERENT
CLEAR	PRESENT	DIRTY
COMMON	PRIVATE	DRY
COMPLEX	PROBABLE	FALSE
CONSCIOUS	QUICK	FEEBLE
CUT	QUIET	FEMALE
DEEP	READY	FOOLISH
DEPENDENT	RED	FUTURE
EARLY	REGULAR	GREEN
ELASTIC	RESPONSIBLE	ILL
ELECTRIC	RIGHT	LAST
EQUAL	ROUND	LATE
FAT	SAME	LEFT
FERTILE	SECOND	LOOSE
FIRST	SEPARATE	LOUD
FIXED	SERIOUS	LOW
FLAT	SHARP	MIXED
FREE	SMOOTH	NARROW
FREQUENT	STICKY	OLD
FULL	STIFF	OPPOSITE
GENERAL	STRAIGHT	PUBLIC
GOOD	STRONG	ROUGH
GREAT	SUDDEN	SAD
GREY	SWEET	SAFE
HANGING	TALL	SECRET
HAPPY	THICK	SHORT
HARD	TIGHT	SHUT
HEALTHY	TIRED	SIMPLE
HIGH	TRUE	SLOW
HOLLOW	VIOLENT	SMALL
IMPORTANT	WAITING	SOFT
KIND	WARM	SOLID
LIKE	WET	SPECIAL
LIVING	WIDE	STRANGE
LONG	WISE	THIN
MALE	YELLOW	WHITE
MARRIED	YOUNG	WRONG

100 Operations, etc.

COME	TO	WHY
GET	UNDER	AGAIN
GIVE	UP	EVER
GO	WITH	FAR
KEEP	AS	FORWARD
LET	FOR	HERE
MAKE	OF	NEAR
PUT	TILL	NOW
SEEM	THAN	OUT
TAKE	A	STILL
BE	THE	THEN
DO	ALL	THERE
HAVE	ANY	TOGETHER
SAY	EVERY	WELL
SEE	NO	ALMOST
SEND	OTHER	ENOUGH
MAY	SOME	EVEN
WILL	SUCH	LITTLE
ABOUT	THAT	MUCH
ACROSS	THIS	NOT
AFTER	I	ONLY
AGAINST	HE	QUITE
AMONG	YOU	SO
AT	WHO	VERY
BEFORE	AND	TOMORROW
BETWEEN	BECAUSE	YESTERDAY
BY	BUT	NORTH
DOWN	OR	SOUTH
FROM	IF	EAST
IN	THOUGH	WEST
OFF	WHILE	PLEASE
ON	HOW	YES
OVER	WHEN	
THROUGH	WHERE	

Addition of "s" to things when there is more than one
Endings in "er," "ing," "ed" form 300 names of things
"ly" forms from qualities
Degree with "more" and "most"
Questions by change of order, and "do"
Form-changes in names of acts, and "that," "this," "I," "he," "you," "who," as in normal English
Measures, Numbers, Days, Months, and the International Words in English Form
Courtesy, The Orthological Institute.

---

suited to contemporary needs, led teachers to examine Basic and press for its introduction in the schools.

Although Basic English is not just an English course, or even a method, but a language in itself, it is associated with certain teaching principles which are essential for its easy assimilation. These concern the proper grading of the material presented to the learner—the relating of expanded senses to root meanings, the logical building up of constructions, and so on. These teaching principles are developed most fully in *The Basic Teacher* (see *Bibliography*), a textbook for European adults. They have been applied to the preparation of an introductory oral course commissioned for use in Gambia, where children are taught English in the schools before they are fully literate. Teaching aids of many kinds have also been developed, including a set of wall pictures embodying new techniques of visual presentation. The teaching principles first developed in connection with Basic English have profoundly influenced studies on the teaching of English as a foreign language by focusing attention on vocabulary control and scientific grading. Whether the diffusion of these Basic teaching concepts would prepare the way for the wider diffusion of the system itself remained to be seen, but improved methods of teaching are not a substitute, and no alternative to Basic English had appeared by the mid-1960's.

L.W. LOCKHART, *The Orthological Institute*

Bibliography
Lockhart, L.W., *The Basic Teacher* (London 1950).
Ogden, C.K., *The System of Basic English* (New York 1934).
Ogden, C.K., *The ABC of Basic English* (London 1944).
Ogden, C.K., *Basic English* (London 1944).
Ogden, C.K., *Basic for Science* (London 1944).
Ogden, C.K., *The Basic Words* (London 1947).
Ogden, C.K., ed., *General Basic English Dictionary* (London 1940).
Richards, I.A., *Basic English and Its Uses* (New York 1943).

BASIE, bā′sē, **Count** (1904–   ), American jazz musician. He was born *William Basie* in Red Bank, N.J., on Aug. 21, 1904. He learned jazz piano technique from "Fats" Waller and got his first band job in Kansas City, Mo., in 1928 with Walter Page's "Blue Devils." In 1929 he joined the Benny Moten band and became its leader after Moten's death in 1935. Soon afterward the group broadcast nightly over a local radio station, whose announcer dubbed Basie "Count."

About 1936, Basie increased the number of musicians in his group from 9 to 14, which was standard "big band" size. After playing for a time in Chicago, the band made its first recording in 1937 and had a very successful debut in New York City in 1938.

Basie's band was known for its strong rhythm section and for a succession of fine soloists, such as vocalist Jimmy Rushing and trombonist J.J. Johnson. Basie wrote many of the band's most popular numbers, including *One O'Clock Jump* and *One, Two, Three O'Lairy*.

BASIL, baz′əl, **Saint** (c. 329–379), one of the Fathers of the Catholic Church. Basil is often called *St. Basil the Great.* He was one of ten children of an extraordinary Christian family. His parents (Basil the Elder and Emmelia), grandmother (Macrina the Elder), sister (Macrina the Younger), and two brothers (Gregory of Nyssa and Peter of Sebaste) are all recognized as saints. Born at Caesarea (now Kayseri, Turkey), the capital of Cappadocia, he studied there and at Constantinople. Around 351 he went to Athens where his lifelong friend, St. Gregory of Nazianzus, was already a student. After a brilliant academic career, Basil returned to Caesarea to teach rhetoric. Two years later, he fulfilled a long-held ambition: he resigned his position, received baptism, and traveled through Egypt, Palestine, Syria, and Mesopotamia to observe the life of the monks there.

The Rules of St. Basil. On his return, he sold his possessions and went into seclusion near Annesi on the Iris River in Pontus. Others joined him there to share a life of prayer, study, mortification, and manual labor. Basil recorded the principles for the monastic life in the widely known *Short Rules* and discussed practical application of these principles in the *Long Rules.* These works, arranged in question and answer form, are not *a rule* in the meaning given this term in the West. The *Rules* center on the Scriptures as the norm of all monastic doctrine and practices. Basil emphasized the social character of religious perfection and insisted that love of God and neighbor was most nobly expressed in the common life of prayer and work. He advocated the primacy of the vow of chastity, complete renunciation of individual proprietary rights, unwavering obedience, and moderation in austerities.

Although Basil remained at his Pontic retreat for only five years, his *Rules* had far-reaching effects. St. Benedict, the father of Western monasticism, became acquainted with the *Rules* through a Latin translation. Thus Western monasticism was, to some degree, shaped by Basil's thinking. To the present, the monks of the Eastern Orthodox churches and some monks of the Catholic Byzantine rite follow St. Basil's *Rules.*

Defender of Orthodoxy. Around 364, Eusebius, archbishop of Caesarea, persuaded Basil to be ordained. In 370, Basil succeeded Eusebius as metropolitan of Cappadocia. In this office he won the esteem of his flock and founded hospitals, homes for the poor, and hospices for travelers. He also won lasting fame by combating Arianism. In the struggle against Arianism (q.v.) he wrote *Against Eunomius* and *On the Holy Spirit,* defending the orthodox view on the consubstantiality of the Son and the Holy Spirit, and he courageously resisted the threats of the emperor Valens.

Broken by his labors, Basil died on Jan. 1, 379. His feast is celebrated on January 1 by the Eastern Church and on the anniversary of his consecration, June 14, by the Latin Church.

Writings. Basil's masterpiece, the *Hexaemeron,* is a series of nine homilies on the six days of creation. It exerted great influence in the West, particularly on St. Ambrose. *Homilies on Psalms,* a book of 23 sermons, is correctly attributed to Basil, but *Commentary on Isaias,* another book of homilies, is no longer considered his. An educational treatise, *Address to Young Men,* presents Basil's view that pagan literature could be profitably read if the writer's teachings were good

and noble. *The Morals,* a collection of 80 rules to guide all Christians to perfection, together with two treatises, *On the Judgment of God* and *On the Faith,* form a compendium of ascetical theology. His 365 *Letters,* two thirds belonging to the period when he was a bishop, are of particular value as primary sources on the civil, political, social, cultural, and religious conditions of the times. Universal tradition in the Eastern Churches attributes to Basil the so-called *Liturgy of St. Basil.*

HERMIGILD DRESSLER, O.F.M.
The Catholic University of America

Further Reading: Basil, St., *Ascetical Works,* tr. by M. Monica Wagner (New York 1950); Clarke, William, *St. Basil the Great* (New York 1913); Gibson, Arthur, *St. Basil's Liturgical Authorship* (Washington 1966); Murphy, Sister Mary Gertrude, *St. Basil and Monasticism* (Washington 1930).

BASIL I (c. 812–886), baz′əl, was Byzantine emperor from 867 to 886. Since he was born in Macedonia, he came to be known as *Basil the Macedonian.* A member of a humble Armenian family, he made his way to Constantinople about 840 and subsequently became an officer of the court of Michael III. Basil was appointed high chamberlain about 856 and advanced rapidly in the emperor's favor. In 865 he murdered his chief rival, Caesar Bardas, and was made joint ruler with Michael in 866. Michael had made himself hated by his cruelty and debauchery, and in 867 Basil headed a conspiracy against him. Michael was murdered, and Basil usurped the throne, founding the Macedonian dynasty.

Basil proved to be an able and just emperor who paid equal attention to internal administration and foreign relations. He reformed the imperial finances and began an important recodification of Byzantine laws. In 867, Basil deprived Photius of the see of Constantinople and restored St. Ignatius, but on the death of the latter (877) he recalled Photius. Basil's armies fought in southern Italy and extended the frontiers of the empire in Asia Minor, while his fleets were successful in the Adriatic and Ionian seas. He died in a hunting accident on Aug. 29, 886.

BASIL II (958?–1025), baz′əl, was one of the most prominent of the Byzantine emperors. The son of Romanus II, he was crowned when he was two but did not exercise power until 976. The early years of his actual reign were troubled by two formidable rebellions led by Bardas Skleros and Bardas Phocas, scions of the two most powerful families in Byzantium. Basil survived to become one of the most vigorous emperors Byzantium ever had and to lead the empire to the apogee of its political and military power.

Basil broke down the last resistance of Islam in the east, laid the foundations for the annexation of Armenia, broadened the possessions of the empire in southern Italy, and, in what was no doubt his greatest military triumph, destroyed the Bulgarian kingdom by 1018. So cruel were his wars against the Bulgars that he became known as *Bulgaroctonus* (Bulgar Slayer). Basil also negotiated the conversion of Vladimir of Russia to Greek Christianity, thereby extending the cultural influence of the empire to Russia. At his death Byzantium had become the greatest power in the Christian and Muslim worlds.

PETER CHARANIS, *Rutgers, the State University*

Further Reading: Ostrogorsky, George, *History of the Byzantine State* (New Brunswick, N.J., 1957).

Purple
basil

ROCHE

BASIL, baz'əl, any of several aromatic seed plants. These plants, native to tropical Africa, Asia, and the Pacific Islands, may be either annual or perennial. They are used as ornamentation, and their leaves are used as a seasoning in foods. The basils belong to the genus *Ocimum* of the mint family, Labiatae. The common or sweet basil (*O. basilicum*) usually grows about one foot (30 cm) high. It has oval-shaped leaves and white, bluish, or purplish flowers. There are several other species, including the bush or dwarf basil (*O. minimum*), the tree basil (*O. suave*), and the East Indies basil (*O. gratissimum*).

BASILAN ISLAND, bä-sē'län, is in the Philippines, in Zamboanga del Sur province. It is situated southwest of Mindanao Island, from which it is separated by Basilan Strait, 10 miles (16 km) wide. Basilan Island is 35 miles long and 22 miles wide (56 by 35 km) and covers an area of 495 square miles (1,282 sq km). The terrain is largely mountainous, rising to a height of 3,317 feet (1,011 meters) and much of the land is covered with virgin forests of valuable woods. The soil is rich and produces a variety of crops, including coconuts, rice, corn, and rubber. Isabela, on Basilan Strait, is the chief port.

The name *Basilan Islands* is used for Basilan and a group of about 50 adjacent islets. The total area is 530 square miles (1,373 sq km). Formerly part of Zamboanga City municipality, the islands were formed into Basilan City municipality after World War II. Population: (1960) 155,712.

BASILICA, bə-sil'ı-kə, is the name given to historic and privileged Roman Catholic churches, chiefly in Rome. In its original Greek use, the word "basilica" meant the house or the court in which the king-archon dispensed justice in Athens. After it had become the distinctive name for a stoa or portico, the word was adopted by the Romans, who, as early as the 2d century B.C., brought it into more common usage for their courts of justice and places of commerce.

Roman Basilicas. The typical Roman basilica, as described by the Augustan architect Vitruvius, had a rectangular plan and was either enclosed by a wall or surrounded by a peristyle. Two or more rows of columns divided the interior lengthwise into aisles, the central one being of greater width and sometimes open to the sky, as in the ancient Greek temple. Sometimes the basilica also had galleries over the side aisles. When the central portion was roofed, its supporting walls were carried up above the side aisles, thus providing a space for windows, or a clerestory (clearstory), to illuminate the spacious interior. At the far end of the building, opposite the main entrance, a raised platform provided space for the seats of the Roman judge and his assistants, or served as a religious shrine. This was called the tribune and was backed by a semicircular apse covered with a semispherical dome.

Examples of Roman imperial basilicas are the ruins of the Basilica Aemilia and the Basilica Julia in the Roman Forum. The latter was begun in 46 B.C. by Julius Ceasar, who named it in honor of his daughter Julia, and was completed by authorization of Augustus Caesar before 14 A.D. It served for both religious and civic functions throughout the imperial period. The Basilica of Constantine, overlooking the Forum, was begun in 308 by Maxentius and completed by Constantine in the 4th century. It represents the fully developed groined-vaulted structure with double axes.

Christian Basilicas. After the Edict of Milan in 313 gave imperial sanction to Christianity, Constantine encouraged the building of churches. The early Christians either appropriated pagan basilicas for their worship or built new edifices according to the old models, and so "basilica" became the usual name for a Roman church.

The Christian high altar replaced the table or shrine for pagan sacrifice or the chair of the Roman praetor in the center of the apse, where the encircling exedra (benches with high solid backs) served as a seat for the clergy. The cathedra, or throne of the bishop, was originally

Floor plan for the basilica of San Clemente, Rome

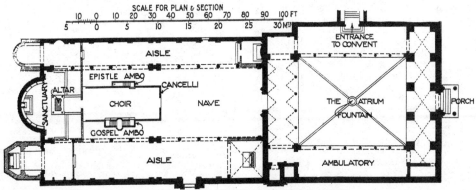

SCALE FOR PLAN & SECTION

ENTRANCE TO CONVENT

AISLE

EPISTLE AMBO · CANCELLI

SANCTUARY · ALTAR · CHOIR · NAVE · THE ATRIUM FOUNTAIN · PORCH

GOSPEL AMBO

AISLE · AMBULATORY

BASILICA of Sant'Apollinare in Classe, Ravenna, Italy, consecrated in 549. Marble columns separate the nave from the side aisles. In the apse a colorful Byzantine mosaic allegorically depicts the Transfiguration of Christ.

in the center of the exedra, but soon was moved to the side of the altar. Care was taken so that the altar was east of the congregation—toward the holy city of Jerusalem. These ritual areas were given prominence by being elevated upon the tribunal platform, now called the bema, and separated from the nave by a triumphal arch effect. Beneath the raised area an underchapel or crypt served as an especially safe and sacred burial place. In front of the bema, pulpits or ambos were placed on either side. A baldachin or ciborium over the altar served as a focal point. The need for more space for the increasing number of clergy participating in the service led to the extension of the bema on either side. This developed into transepts and gave the symbolic cruciform plan of later medieval churches. The space in front of the altar sometimes was called the presbytery, and the area at the sides of the bema or down in the center of the nave was occupied by the choir (*schola cantorum*). Eventually all the space reserved for clergy and choir and separated by a screen (*cancellus*) became known as the chancel.

At the western entrance of most early Christian basilicas there was a forecourt called the atrium. This adaptation from the Roman house probably served as the initial congregating place for many Christian groups. The pool (*impluvium*), another feature borrowed from domestic architecture, served as the baptismal font and its sheltering arcades, or peristyle, were popular places for memorial tablets and tombs. The side of the atrium adjoining the main body of the church became the entrance vestibule, called the pronaos or narthex, a place originally appropriated to penitents. Only after baptism were the worshipers welcomed into the nave (Latin *navis*), the "ship" in which the faithful worshiped so as to be borne safely over the sea of life into the haven of eternity.

Famous examples of early Christian basilicas in Rome are San Giovanni in Laterano (begun 324;

rebuilt 904–911, 1308–1314, 1362–1378; altered and modernized 1650?–?1655), San Paolo fuori le Mura (founded 386; rebuilt 1823), Santa Maria Maggiore (built 352–355; altered 432–440; altered and restored 1288–1292), San Pietro in Vincoli (built 442; rebuilt c. 560 and c. 775), San Clemente, (begun before 392; rebuilt 1108; frequently restored), and San Pietro (St. Peter's) in Vaticano (consecrated 326; reconstructed 1425–1455 and 1506–1626).

The three- or five-aisled basilican plans were retained with slight modifications to suit climatic and material requirements throughout the long medieval period of great church building. The Romanesque architects developed the vaulting and, as at Pisa, used a dome over the intersection of the nave and transept and designed pronounced transepts with apsidal terminations. Multiple chapels and pilgrim processions led to the continuation of the side aisles around the high altar and chancel in an ambulatory, from which additional chapels opened. The combination of ambulatory and radiating chapels formed the chevet choir, a notable feature of the eastern end of Gothic cathedrals in France—a logical derivative of the early classical basilica.

RALPH FANNING, *Ohio State University*

Bibliography

Anderson, William J., and Spiers, R.P., *The Architecture of Ancient Rome*, rev. by *Thomas Ashby* (New York 1927).
Conant, Kenneth J., *Carolingian and Romanesque Architecture 800–1200* (Baltimore 1959).
Frothingham, Arthur L., *The Monuments of Christian Rome from Constantine to the Renaissance* (New York 1908).
Krautheimer, Richard, *Early Christian and Byzantine Architecture* (Baltimore 1965).
Lethaby, William R., *Medieval Art* (New York 1913).
Lowrie, Walter, *Monuments of the Early Church* (New York 1901).
Morey, Charles R., *Early Christian Art* (Princeton, N.J., 1942).
Morey, Charles R., *Christian Art* (New York 1935).
Porter, Arthur K., *Medieval Architecture*, 2 vols. (New York 1909).
Rivoira, Giovanni T., *Roman Architecture* (New York and London 1925).

BASILICATA, bä-zē-lē-kä′tä, is a region of southern Italy, part of ancient Lucania, comprising the provinces of Matera and Potenza. It has an area of 3,856 square miles (9,988 sq km). Potenza is the capital. The western part is crossed by the Apennines, rising to 7,375 feet (2,250 meters) in Monte Pollino on the Calabrian border and sloping eastward into a hilly region and southward to the low marshy coast along the Gulf of Taranto. A short strip of rocky coast along the Tyrrhenian Sea also belongs to Basilicata. The chief rivers, all flowing into the Gulf of Taranto, are the Bradano, the Basento, and the Sinni. Earthquakes and floods are frequent.

There are extensive forests and pastures on which sheep, goats, and cattle are raised. The shepherds still preserve their hierarchic organizations and ancient traditions. Corn, maize, olive oil, wine, and fruit are the chief products. Citrus fruits grow only near the coast.

The isolation in which are area has remained for centuries has hindered progress. Cultural and economic standards are extremely low, and communications are poor. Industries, except for some local handicrafts, are practically nonexistent. Basilicata is sparsely populated. Extreme poverty and disease have driven many of the people, who are of mixed Italic, Lombard, Greek, Arabian, Norman, and Albanian descent, to emigrate; the exodus was particularly heavy between 1880 and 1914. Malaria is a scourge along both the coast and the lower valleys. Reclamation works and improvement of sanitation are under way. Following World War II, important land reforms were introduced.

The coast of ancient Lucania was colonized by the Greeks in the 7th century B.C.: Metapontum, Heraclea, and Siri were prosperous towns of Magna Graecia. After the Pyrrhic and Punic wars the area declined. Malaria, silting, and pirate raids drove the people inland. After the fall of Rome, Lucania was occupied by Byzantines, Goths, and Lombards; the name "Basilicata" is derived from the Greek (Byzantine) word *basilikos*, meaning "royal official." The region rose to importance briefly in the 11th century when Melfi, in the northwest part of the area, was the capital of the Norman duchy of Apulia. But after its inclusion in the kingdom of Naples in the 13th century, the region continued to decay. Population: (1961) 644,297.

BASILIDES (died 140), bas-ə-lī′dēz, was a Gnostic philosopher who founded the heretical sect called the *Basilidians*. Probably born in Syria and educated at Antioch, he taught at Alexandria during the reign of Roman Emperor Hadrian (117–138). He wrote *Exegetica*, a 24-volume commentary on the Gospels, which is now lost. Since few of his other works survive, the primary sources for his views are the works of his contemporaries—Irenaeus, Hippolytus, Clement of Alexandria, and Origen. They disagree so widely that a reconstruction of his philosophy is impossible. Scholars differ about the origins of his teachings. Some find its roots in Greek philosophy, others in Oriental religion. However, he is generally considered one of the foremost exponents of Gnostic doctrine (see GNOSTICISM).

Basilides' son Isidorus was his most famous follower. After the death of Basilides, his followers' views altered; the sect spread westward but was little known after the 4th century.

BASILISCUS (died 478), bas-ə-lis′kəs, usurped the throne of the Byzantine empire in 475–476. He was a brother of Verina, wife of Emperor Leo I. Through his sister's influence he was appointed commander of the great expedition fitted out by Leo in 468 to attack Genseric, king of the Vandals, at Carthage in North Africa. The vast fleet reached Africa safely, but it was soon destroyed or dispersed by Genseric through the incapacity or treachery of Basiliscus. Basiliscus escaped and returned to Constantinople, where he was pardoned through his sister's intercession. Emperor Leo died in 474, and his son-in-law Zeno and Zeno's child Leo II became coemperors. When the child died in 475, Zeno temporarily lost the throne to Basiliscus. Unable to secure his position, Basiliscus was in turn overthrown in 476 and imprisoned by the restored Zeno. Basiliscus died two years later in Cucusus, Cappadocia, in Asia Minor.

BASILISK, bas′ə-lisk, a group of lizards found throughout the American tropics, from Jalisco and Veracruz in Mexico, southward to Columbia and Ecuador. A conspicuous crest extends from the back of the head of the adult male and there is a high crest down the center of the back. A similar but smaller crest is present on the tail of some males. Some basilisks attain a total length exceeding 30 inches (75 cm).

In many parts of their range, particularly on the dry Pacific slopes of Mexico and Central America, basilisks are usually found near water, which they enter for food and protection. They frequently run across the surface of the water by raising their forelimbs and paddling so rapidly with their hind limbs that they appear not to break the surface film of the water. If they are interrupted, they sink and resort to swimming. Despite their bizarre and often fierce appearance, they are quite harmless and timid, usually fleeing to the water when an intruder approaches. When found away from water, they often escape to trees and climb to considerable heights.

The basilisks belong to the genus *Basiliscus*, which belongs to the family Iguanidae. In Mexico, basilisks are known as *paso-ríos* or "river-crossers." They are also called *Jesús Cristo* or "Jesus Christ lizards" because of their ability to run on the surface of the water.

The name "basilisk" was used in ancient times to describe a fiendish-looking mythological monster with malignant powers. It was said to exist in inaccessible regions, such as the African desert or the Swiss Alps.

Basilisk (*Laemanctus*, native to British Honduras).

BASIN, bȧ-zᴀɴ, **Thomas** (1412–1491), French archbishop and historian. He was born at Caudebec, France, in 1412. He taught canon law at Caen until he became bishop of Lisieux in 1447. As bishop he negotiated the surrender of Caen by the English to Charles VII of France, whose trusted adviser he soon became. After Louis XI came to the throne, Basin lost favor and was compelled to flee.

His most important historical work is an account of the reigns of Charles VII and Louis XI, although his judgment of the latter is marred by his personal dislike for the king. He died at Utrecht, the Netherlands, in 1491.

BASIN, bā'sən, a considerable area of the earth's surface which is depressed below the level of the surrounding terrain. Basins may be caused by vertical movements of the global crust, by upswellings of molten magma often accompanied by volcanic action, or by prolonged erosion.

Relatively small basins, such as those in which London and Paris are located, were the result of a synclinal rearrangement of rock strata sloping toward a common center. More extensive basins are often delimited by the upsurge of loftier elevations round about, which tend to provide natural watersheds; hence they may embrace a considerable drainage area. This is particularly true of large lakes or marginal seas which include not only the water-filled depression but also adjacent territory drained by such streams as may flow into them.

Basins may be arid or even desert, like the Great Basin which occupies much territory in several western states of the United States and in Mexico. Similar dry basins are found elsewhere, notably in Australia, Africa, and central Asia; some are without access to the sea.

River basins are usually the result of erosion: they tend to deepen and broaden as rains wash away the soil and currents eat ever deeper into underlying rock strata. River erosion has also excavated many lake basins, while others were gouged out by glacial action during the Ice Age. See also Lake; Valleys.

BASIN AND RANGE PROVINCE, a geologic province of the United States. It occupies all of Nevada and large areas of Utah, Arizona, California, New Mexico, and southwestern Texas, and it extends into northwestern Mexico. It is bounded on the north by the Columbia River plateau, on the east by the Wasatch Mountains of central Utah and by the Colorado plateau, and on the west by the Sierra Nevada range.

The province is a semidesert region characterized by a large number of parallel mountain ranges separated by sediment-filled basins, or valleys. This topography results from block-faulting—the displacement of large blocks of crustal rock along steep normal faults (see Fault). The faulting has been taking place in the region ever since the Miocene epoch (beginning about 25 million years ago). The faults have a generally north-south orientation, so that the mountains and valleys are similarly oriented.

Death Valley, California, is the deepest of the basins in the province. It contains the lowest point in the United States, 276 feet (84 meters) below sea level. Other basins may be as high as 6,000 feet (1,800 meters) above sea level; the mountains on the average rise about 4,000 feet (1,200 meters) above the basins.

Most of the basins have no drainage outlets. Therefore, sediments and salts dissolved in rainwater tend to accumulate in them. Thus, some of the basins are occupied by salt flats (the Bonneville, Utah, salt flats of automobile racing fame are an example) and by playa lakes—shallow, ephemeral bodies of evaporating water. Great Salt Lake in Utah is one of several large saline lakes that are remnants of much larger fresh-water lakes formed about 20 thousand years ago during the glacial Pleistocene epoch. Because a climate change resulted in relatively low rainfall and high evaporation, the ancient lakes shrank to their present dimension over the last 10 thousand years.

W.E. Yasso, *Teachers College*
Columbia University
C.G. Tillman, *Virginia Polytechnic Institute*

BASKERVILLE, bas'kər-vil, **John** (1706–1775), English printer, whose Baskerville type inspired the standard modern type style. He was born at Wolverley, Worcestershire, on Jan. 28, 1706. As a young man he taught penmanship and bookkeeping, and from 1740 to 1749 he manufactured lacquerware in Birmingham. He became interested in printing around 1750 and spent the next few years perfecting the materials of his craft. He invented his own elegant type faces, a fine ink, and a parchmentlike paper.

In 1757, Baskerville brought out a quarto edition of the works of Virgil, which English essayist Thomas Macaulay later pronounced "the first of those magnificent editions that went forth to astonish all the librarians of Europe." In 1758, Baskerville was appointed an official printer of Cambridge University. He died in Birmingham on Jan. 8, 1775.

After his death his wife continued to operate her husband's plant until 1777, when the Baskerville fonts were sold to the French author Caron de Beaumarchais, who used them to print a 70-volume edition of the works of Voltaire.

Though greatly admired by a small group of connoisseurs, Baskerville's editions were not generally appreciated in his lifetime. Within the next 50 years, however, they became internationally renowned and inspired the typographical innovations of Giambattista Bodoni in Italy and the Didot family in France. Baskerville's publications, many of which are in the British Museum, London, include *The Book of Common Prayer* (1760), the Bible (1763), *Aesop's Fables* (1761), and a dictionary (1765), as well as editions of the works of Milton (1758), Addison (1761), Congreve (1761), and Horace (1770). See also Printing.

John Baskerville

(1706–1775)

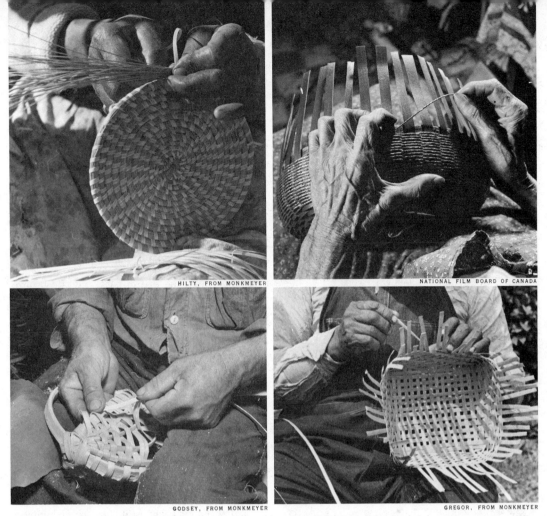

BASKETMAKING uses various techniques and materials. (*Top left*) Coiled basket of grass bound into strips. (*Top right*) Twine interwoven onto splints. (*Lower left*) Weaving white oak splints. (*Lower right*) Lighter splints.

BASKET, a receptacle of coiled or interwoven strands of flexible material such as osier (willow) twigs, rushes, or strips of wood, bamboo, or rattan. The word derives from the Latin *bascauda* (dishpan), which is thought to be etymologically rooted in the Celtic *basc* (bracelet). The connection probably stems from the manner of making certain bracelets by coiling or interweaving strands of material.

Basketry, the art of working such strands into various shapes and designs, includes the making of mats, hats, coffins, fans, cradles, sandals, and even boats, as well as baskets. It is one of the most ancient crafts and is closely related to weaving. Basketmaking, one of the earliest forms of basketry, was already well developed in the Neolithic Age, the period of transition from nomadic hunting societies to settled agricultural civilizations. The basket's function as a vessel for holding, storing, and carrying various commodities gave it major importance in early agricultural societies. Basketmaking therefore developed in widely separated areas. Gathering and carrying seeds, fruit, roots, or other items were frequently woman's activities in primitive society; so women often made baskets.

Techniques. Coiling and weaving are the two basic techniques in basketmaking. *Coiling* was perhaps the earliest technique developed and is considered the most important. This method has carried over from prehistoric times. Coiled baskets have no explicit relation to woven products. They are made of a foundation, or core, of various plant materials and a wrapping or sewing strip. The foundation is coiled spirally in the desired shape, and the coils are bound together by the sewing strip. The foundation can be colored, and the sewing can form patterns.

The coiling technique is widespread. Important early examples come from Egypt. In North America, some of the finest specimens have been produced by Indians in the western United States, especially the Pomo tribes of northern California, who embellish their baskets with brightly colored feathers or beads. Coiling was also used in making the foundation for bowl-shaped *quaffas*, the Mesopotamian boats.

Of the varieties of weaving, the most elemental is the simple *checkerboard weave*. This involves interweaving two sets of strands at right angles, after the pattern of warp and weft. From this technique derives the characterization of basketry as the mother of all loom work. The entire basket may be constructed in this fashion, but often only the bottom is made this way, while the sides are formed by a latticework or other weave. A very close checkerboard weave is frequently employed in Ecuador in making "Panama" hats. Other types of weaving involve complex methods that produce intricate patterns.

EGYPTIAN BASKET, nearly 3,500 years old, was found in a tomb. Such ancient baskets are rarely discovered.

Twining is one of the most common varieties of weaving and is sometimes considered a separate basic technique. Twining involves twisting together two flexible strands, which act as wefts, around a series of parallel warp rods. Twining was used with great effect by the Tlingit Indians of British Columbia and by tribes in the northwestern United States. Another weaving variant is *twilling.* The weft strands are manipulated over the warp materials to produce a diagonal effect. Elaborate examples come from the Malay Archipelago. Older specimens of twilled baskets were unearthed from pre-Columbian sites in Peru.

These basic techniques have remained virtually unchanged. More specialized and complex patterns developed as basketmaking became a decorative as well as a practical art. The inherently simple basket form, determined by its practical purpose, has kept basketmaking essentially a hand industry. On the other hand, textile weaving, to which basketry had early technical affinities, is no longer basically a handcraft. Machine production was made necessary by the increased diversity of textile styles and usage.

History. The organic materials used in basketry are subject to rapid decay; hence archaeologists have difficulty establishing a history of baskets. Dry sands, however, are excellent preservatives, and coiled and twined basketry dating from between 9000 and 7000 B.C. has been unearthed in Nevada and Utah. This testifies to the existence of basketry well before Neolithic times. Elsewhere, some of the richest yields are from Jarmo in Iraq and the Faiyum in Egypt. The objects from Jarmo are mud impressions of basketry, dated from 5270 to 4630 B.C. From the Faiyum, actual coiled baskets have been uncovered. Later Egyptian burial sites indicate that palm became the most common basketry material.

Pottery is in a direct line of descent from this Neolithic basketry. Many baskets were lined with mud or other clay material to make them impervious to liquids. The basket often decayed, but the hardened clay remained. Thus basketry led to some of the earliest pottery forms. Basketry impressions have been left on pottery from a late Neolithic Chinese culture of about 3000 B.C. There are also many Biblical references to baskets used for ceremonial as well as mundane purposes.

The earliest European evidence of basketry comes from Swiss lake villages dated about 2500 B.C. Here twined and net work predominated. Several basketry impressions were left on later Neolithic pottery found in the Balkans. Examples from an Early Bronze Age culture (about 2000 B.C.) come from the British Isles, and late Bronze Age basketry has been found near Zürich, Switzerland. Baskets were used in ancient Greece in religious rites and for fishing, and the Roman poets Juvenal and Martial refer to British baskets as rare and exotic items.

The ancient Basket Maker peoples of the southwestern United States have been given this name because of their great skill in the art. Their successors, ancestors of the Pueblo Indians, continued the tradition until about 1300 A.D. Some of the finest later basketry comes from Indian sites of western North America, as well as from Asia. Examples from American Indian burial sites show tribal legends and religious symbols coiled or woven in a variety of techniques. Many baskets buried with the dead were deliberately broken or "killed" to ensure their passage into the land of the dead with the spirit of the departed human.

Today baskets are still primary containers for carrying and storing materials, particularly in many parts of Africa, Asia, and Latin America. In the industrialized countries, machine-made containers have tended to supplant baskets in workaday use. However, basketmaking is still practiced as an art form and a hobby.

Further Reading: Albion, Leonard, *Basic Basketry* (London 1961); Bobart, Henry H., *Basketwork Through the Ages* (London 1936); Crowfoot, Grace M., "Textiles, Basketry, and Mats," in *A History of Technology,* ed. by Charles Singer, vol. 1 (New York 1954); Evans, Glen, and Campbell, T.N., *Indian Baskets* (Austin 1952).

INDIA: An example of a mud-plastered woven basket.

JAMAICA: An openwork basket used to carry produce.

BASKETBALL

BILL MARK

BASKETBALL, bas′kit-bôl, is the most widely played and watched team game in the world. It is also the newest of the major team games. Unlike games that evolved slowly through various forms before they acquired accepted playing rules, basketball was invented for a specific purpose at a specific time and place. In December 1891, in Springfield, Mass., the two-team court game was created by James Naismith, a 30-year-old instructor in physical education at the International Young Men's Christian Association Training School, now Springfield College.

Naismith's original assignment from Luther H. Gulick, his superior at Springfield, was to develop some form of athletic activity that could be used indoors during winter months in a northern climate. Baseball, football (both soccer and the American variety then developing), and many other outdoor games were well established and popular with participants and spectators. But between the end of the football season in autumn and the beginning of baseball the next spring, calisthenics and gymnastics were the only activities that indoor facilities permitted, especially in New England. These activities offered nothing as attractive as the exertion, competitive fire, scoring, and strategy of the outdoor team games.

Naismith, therefore, simply took a standard soccer ball, hung a peach basket at either end of his small gymnasium, divided his 18-man class into two nine-man teams, and made the object of the game an elementary one: to throw the ball into one basket while preventing the other side from throwing it into the other basket. Running with the ball was forbidden. In the 1897–1898 season, five-man teams became standard.

Essentially basketball is the same game today as it was in the beginning. It is now played in every section of the world, both by women and by men, in schools, colleges, and clubs, and at national and international levels. It has also become a major professional sport in the United States. No accurate statistics on players and spectators are available, but attendance at formally organized games in the United States alone exceeds 100 million each year. The Olympic Games program has included basketball since 1936. In addition, all the countries of Europe and the Americas and many nations in both Asia and Africa take part in various other international competitions.

HOW BASKETBALL IS PLAYED

The nature of basketball is the key to its popularity. The game requires equipment that is relatively simple and usually available: a flat rectangular playing surface (indoors or outdoors), two baskets, one ball, a timing device, and suitable shoes for the players. It calls for five-man teams, a manageable number, but it can be played happily for practice or recreation with any number down to "one-on-one." It can be as rough, physically, as the participants want to make it, although in theory basketball is not a contact game. It calls into play standard athletic skills—speed afoot, alert reflexes, quick thinking, marksmanship, and strength. Yet basketball does not demand extremely specialized functions by certain members of the team at the expense of other functions (as does the function of a pitcher in baseball, a goalie in hockey, or a quarterback in football). And its continuous action, with

321

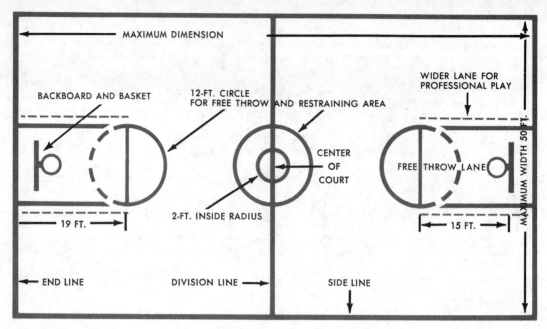

REGULATION BASKETBALL COURT and floor markings for college and amateur games in the United States are shown in this diagram. The free throw lane used by professionals (indicated by broken lines) is 18 feet wide.

frequent scoring, appeals to both player and spectator. Regardless of the score, every player is constantly engaged, and except in time-outs, spectators always have something to watch.

The rules of basketball are not completely standardized. U.S. college teams, international amateur groups (including the Olympic Committee), and U.S. professionals differ. Rule changes are made almost every year. For example, in 1971, the rules for women's basketball were changed to make them similar to those for men.

The fundamental rules, however, are universal. Almost all variations deal with two basic problems: determining the proper degree of penalty for a foul, and finding some means of counteracting the advantage held by an exceptionally tall player.

Scoring. A *basket* or *field goal* counts two points. A *free throw* or *foul shot* is worth one point. Both are made by throwing the ball into the hoop from above: for a basket, from any point on the floor against the efforts of defenders; for a foul shot, from the free throw line without interference.

The Ball. A basketball is spherical, 30 inches in circumference, and weighs from 20 to 22 ounces. Its cover may be of leather or of comparable synthetic material, usually orange or brown in color. It is inflated to a degree that enables it to bounce back about 50 inches when dropped onto a solid wooden floor from a height of 72 inches.

The Court. The recommended dimensions of the playing site (known as a *court*) are 94 feet long and 50 feet wide. However, courts down to two thirds of each of these dimensions have been accepted and used successfully. At the midpoint of each end of the court, a *basket* is suspended so that its rim is 10 feet above floor level and about 4 feet in from a point above the end line of the court called the *base line* or *end line*.

The basket itself is a metal ring, commonly called the *hoop*, 18 inches in diameter, with its plane parallel to the floor. It is attached to a *backboard*, a surface of glass or wood hung perpendicular to the floor. The backboard is usually rectangular, 6 feet wide and 4 feet high, but a smaller fan-shaped board also is used. The basket ring is attached to the backboard so that the back of the hoop is 6 inches from the surface of the board and about 12 inches above the lower edge of the board. Suspended from the hoop is a funnel-shaped net of cord. The net slows down the ball as it passes through the basket, making its passage more visible.

The playing area is divided in half by a center line midway between the baskets. At the middle of this line are two concentric circles, 2 feet and 6 feet in diameter. This is where the *center jump* takes place at the start of the game and at certain other times.

The most important floor markings are in front of each basket. Parallel to the backboard, and 15 feet from it, is the *free throw line*, also called the *foul line*, from which a player makes his free throws after he has been fouled. This line lies within a circle 12 feet in diameter, which is used as a restraining line when *jump balls* (similar to the center jump) must be held in that half of the court.

From the ends of the foul line to the base line run two lines that form the *free throw lane*, or *foul lane*. In U.S. college and amateur games, this lane is 12 feet wide, so that the pattern, when viewed from above, resembles an archway. (Formerly, when the lane was only 6 feet wide, the foul circle at its top made the figure look like a *keyhole*.) The professionals use a lane 18 feet wide, forming a rectangular restricted area wider than the actual free throw line (see diagram). In international play the foul lane is 17 feet wide at the base line, and therefore its lines slant outward from the 12-foot-wide free throw line.

The inside of this foul lane area, whatever its size, is a restricted zone. No offensive player may remain in it for longer than three seconds at a time. The purpose of this *three-second rule* is to prevent the tallest player, or best jumper, from taking up a dominating position close to the basket. In practice, the three-second restriction simply means that players must keep moving through this zone, and must make their *shots* (at the basket) and *passes* (to teammates) while on the run.

The entire back half of the court—that is, the half farther from the basket under attack—becomes a restricted area 10 seconds after a team gains possession of the ball. This rule prevents the offensive team from stalling or eluding the defense by withholding the ball from the offensive area.

Time. The team that scores more points in a stipulated time wins the game. American high schools and women play a 32-minute game divided into 8-minute quarters. Men's college teams play two 20-minute halves. Professionals use a 48-minute game, divided into 12-minute quarters. If the score is tied when the regulation time ends, *overtime periods,* usually of five minutes' duration, are played until a decision is reached. As many as six extra periods have been required to determine the winner in major professional and college competition.

Officials. Two officials, equipped with whistles, control play. One is the *referee,* who has superior authority in case of dispute. The other is the *umpire.* In practice their duties are indistinguishable. Both move all around the court, calling infractions, putting the ball in play, ruling on the legality of scoring and substitutions, and enforcing discipline. Usually, one official works from a position under the basket being attacked, while the other is at mid-court; when the action shifts to the other end, they switch assignments.

An *official scorekeeper* and a *timer* sit at a table alongside the court. The timer operates the clock according to the rules governing when time in "in" (ball in play) and when it is not.

The Teams. A basketball team is composed of five players. The *center, left forward,* and *right forward* are referred to as front court players, and the *left guard* and *right guard* as back court players. Their functions are much less differentiated than the functions of players in other popular team sports. All five have equal rights and restrictions under the rules, and they may range all over the floor, taking part in all offensive and defensive maneuvers. There are, of course, tactical specializations; but because the necessary teamwork requires very close cooperation, duties are remarkably interchangeable.

Each team has a *coach,* who sits on the bench with the substitutes and directs play. He chooses the starting lineup, makes substitutions, gives all basic strategic orders, and trains the players between games.

Substitution of players is allowed whenever play comes to a halt. There is no restriction as to the number of times a player may leave and re-enter the game (unless he has fouled out).

Restrictions. Essentially, the only purpose of the game is to put the ball through the basket. All the restrictive rules are aimed at coping with the physical difficulties arising when players move at high speed in a relatively small enclosed place.

One set of restrictions deals with the mobility of player and ball. The player may not run with the ball in his possession. He may pass the ball to a teammate, shoot it at the basket, or move it around the court himself by using the *dribble.* A dribble consists of bouncing the ball continuously with one hand, while running, walking, or standing. Once a player stops dribbling, he may not start again; he must pass the ball or shoot it. If he breaks this rule, he is called for a *traveling* violation. Infractions that do not involve physical contact, such as traveling or remaining too long

---

OFFENSIVE MANEUVERS

The ball may be advanced by dribbling (bouncing it on the court with one hand in uninterrupted motion) or by passing (throwing to a teammate). Faking consists of feints that deceive an opponent. A pivot is a whirling movement.

DRIBBLING

PASSING

FAKING

PIVOTING

SHOOTING

A set shot is made from a stationary position. A jump shot is thrown at the top of a vertical jump. A hook shot is released over the shoulder. In a one-hand push shot, the ball rests on one hand and is pushed off with the other.

TWO-HAND SET SHOT

JUMP SHOT

HOOK SHOT

ONE-HAND PUSH SHOT

in the three-second zone, are called *violations,* and are punished by awarding possession of the ball to the other team.

A second set of restrictions deals with physical contact. Infractions that involve physical contact are termed *personal fouls,* or simply *fouls,* or sometimes *personals.* Since the basket is 10 feet above the floor and the playing area is confined, interference with the offensive players has to be restricted, or it would keep them indefinitely from scoring. Therefore, in general, no physical contact is allowed as a deliberate means of defense. The defender may not push, pull, trip, tackle, or in any other physical manner interfere with his opponent; in return, offensive players may not use body blocks or similar maneuvers to aid their teammates.

A player who is fouled is awarded one or more free throws. The player who committed the infraction is charged with a personal foul. When a player has been charged with the maximum number of personals allowed (five in high school, college, and amateur play, six among professionals), he must leave the game permanently. This disqualification of players is the most effective deterrent to fouling.

Other Rules. When the ball goes out of bounds, possession of it is considered lost by the team that last touched it in bounds, and the ball is awarded to the other team. When a ball rolls or bounces free within bounds, it is a free ball, and body contact is allowed between players in the act of pursuing it.

When there is a *held ball* (that is, when players from opposing teams are each firmly holding it) or some other indeterminate situation (such as an out-of-bounds play where both teams touched the ball simultaneously as it left the court), a *jump ball* is required. The referee tosses the ball straight up between two opposing players, who try to tap it to a teammate and are forbidden to catch it or to interfere with each other.

When a score is made, the team scored upon puts the ball in play from out-of-bounds under the basket in which the points were scored. This applies to a free throw as well as a basket, provided the free throw is the last of any series of free throws awarded on one play. When a shot at the basket fails to go in, the *rebound* is in play and may be recovered by either team.

The above rules, with only minor variations, apply to all levels of basketball. In the treatment of free throws, however, there are important differences, and it is here that rule makers in all organizations have tinkered endlessly with the rules, changing the pattern from year to year.

Closely related, and even more important, is the time limit for shooting. Here, too, no uniformity has been achieved. In U.S. professional play a *24-second rule* decrees that a team must make a try for a basket (defined as a shot that touches rim or backboard) within 24 seconds after gaining possession of the ball. If it does not, a violation is called, and the other team gains possession. In international amateur play a similar limitation applies, but for a period of 30 seconds. U.S. colleges and high schools, however, have resisted this attempt to prevent *freezing the ball* and have no such time limit on shooting. The freezing tactic is most often used by a team having a narrow lead with only a few minutes left in the game.

Generally, the penalty for fouling a man in the act of shooting is two free throws, and for any other foul one free throw. There are a number of variations, however, as follows:

In professional and international play, a personal foul by an offensive player is penalized by loss of possession but no free throw, although the foul does count toward disqualification for the man who committed it. In college games, an offensive foul is punished by a free throw.

In international play, if a man is fouled while shooting and makes the basket anyway, the basket counts; the defender is charged with a foul, but there is no free throw. If the fouled player's basket attempt misses, he gets two free throws. In professional and college basketball, however, the older method is in force: a basket made while the shooter is being fouled counts, and the shooter gets one free throw in addition, making possible a *three-point play.*

In one way or another, all current styles penalize a team for excessive fouling in any half (or quarter), regardless of how many fouls any one player may have committed. In professional basketball, the extra penalty is that the other team gets an additional chance to make the ordinary number of free throws: that is, two chances to make one, or three chances to make two. The penalty is imposed after a team makes six fouls in one quarter. In college, after six fouls in a half, a team enters a "one-and-one" situation. If the penalized team commits another foul that normally calls for one free throw, the offended player gets an extra shot, for an extra point, if he makes the first one.

The Sequence of Play. The game begins with a *center jump*—a jump ball held in the center circle, with the referee tossing up the ball. The team that gains possession works for a basket until it either makes one, is fouled, or loses the ball out of bounds or on a violation. Then the other team follows the same procedure. Time is "out" during all free throws, or when there is any abnormal delay caused, for example, by an injury or by retrieving a ball from far out of bounds. Teams may call a limited number of *time-outs* during a game for strategic reasons or to rest.

Techniques. The essence of basketball, an offense-oriented game, is shooting skill. Until recent years, the basic styles of shooting were a *lay-up* and a *set-shot.* In the lay-up, which is still basic, the player gets the ball near the basket and, while he is still on the run, curls it up and in, using the backboard as a carom surface. In a set shot, the shooter may use one or two hands, and he faces the basket with his feet firmly planted.

Centers have developed a *pivot* shot, which begins while the player has his back to the basket. This shot may be a sweeping one-handed *hook,* effective because the shooter's body keeps the defender away from the ball, or a little *spin,* gotten off while the player is in mid-air.

By far the most common shots in the modern game, however, are *jump shots* and *running one-handers.* The jump shot is exactly that: the shooter jumps straight up and releases the ball with one or two hands at the instant that he is at the top of his jump—out of reach of the defender, who can seldom make his counterjump soon enough. The running one-handers are less planned and fit well into a wide-open, fast-break offense. Equally important, but not equally enjoyable for most players, are the *ball-handling* skills—the arts of dribbling, passing, and other play involved in delivering the ball to an unguarded teammate. In an era of great shooting prowess, these skills have been relatively neglected in the United States, especially by exceptionally tall players. But teams in other countries, where tallness is not so common and where experience is more limited, stress these fundamentals to a greater degree.

Defense may consist of individual guarding or team patterns. Individual *man-to-man defense* is both a basic style of play and the name of a team strategy in which each player is assigned to cover one opponent wherever he goes on the floor. This is the prevailing form of team defense. Also used extensively is some form of the *zone defense*, in which a player is given a specific area of the floor to guard and picks up any opposing player coming through it.

Offensive styles fall into two basic types. A *running game* (or *fast break*) depends primarily on getting a rebound at the defensive basket and swiftly moving the ball to the offensive basket before the opposition can recover its own proper defensive positions. In contrast, a *set pattern* develops at a fairly deliberate pace, and players move through one or a combination of prearranged patterns to create an opening for the shooter.

For the individual player, either quickness or size is essential. All the basic offensive maneuvers involve the ability to *fake*—that is, by some gesture, to fool the defender into committing himself in one direction while the offensive player moves in another and thus gains the one-step advantage that makes him free to shoot, pass, or receive a pass. The defender, in turn, must have the reflexes to recover from such fakes without losing his man. In both instances, the essentials are quickness of foot, hand, eye, and thought—agility as distinct from mere running speed.

Physical height, which involves also *effective height*, is of basic importance. The ability to jump can make a six-footer's effective height equal to that of a man a few inches taller who cannot jump as high or time his leap as well. Over an extended period, height determines the number of times a team will have possession of the ball, because capturing rebounds of missed shots is the primary method of getting possession. Offensively, a taller player is closer to the basket and has an easier shot. Defensively, he can block more shots near the basket (although interfering with the ball above the rim, known as *goaltending*, is forbidden) and can force the shooter to use an unnatural trajectory.

In theory, any position on the floor belongs to the man who occupies it first, and he must be given a reasonable amount of room in which to move. The responsibility for causing illegal body contact lies with the man who moves into a rival's clearly established path or position. After physical contact occurs, the referee must decide the *blocking*-or-*charging* issue: Did the offensive man *charge* into the defensive man, or did the defensive man *block* the offensive man's legitimate path of advance? It is strictly the referee's judgment that determines who fouled whom; a play may look different from a different angle, and the spectators are rarely impartial. For these reasons, there is more criticism of refereeing in basketball than in other mass spectator sports.

Ultimately, there is only one way to guard against a good shooter: to stay close, harry him, and prevent him from getting set for the kind of shot he likes at the spot he likes to take it. On the offensive, the best help a player can give a teammate is to *set a pick*—that is, get a position on the floor that will block off a defensive man without committing a foul.

HISTORY OF BASKETBALL

When James Naismith (who later became a doctor of medicine) and Luther H. Gulick developed basketball in 1891, they had in mind nothing more than promoting healthful recreation. With bewildering speed, however, basketball spread beyond their expectations or control. Within a year, it was being played with great enthusiasm on both coasts of the United States and in Canada, Naismith's homeland. Within 15 years, the game was known in places as far away as Japan, China, France, England, Germany, and sections of the Middle East, and had been demonstrated at the 1904 Olympic Games in St. Louis.

The Early Years. The first source of the game's growth was the YMCA. During the Christmas vacation in 1891, members of Naismith's original class in the International YMCA Training School at Springfield, Mass., took the new game to California, North Carolina, Canada, and elsewhere. Naismith published the first set of rules in the Jan. 15, 1892 issue of the *Triangle*, the Springfield YMCA school paper, and by 1897 a translation had been published in France. Branches of the YMCA throughout the Northeastern states adopted the game. In the New York City area, the game took root particularly well. By 1893 there was a championship tournament for the Metropolitan area, won by Brooklyn Central YMCA.

With modifications of the rules, the game also became immediately popular with women, particularly in colleges. An intercollegiate game was played by girls' teams representing California and Stanford in 1896—almost a year before the first generally recognized men's intercollegiate game between Yale and Pennsylvania on March 20, 1897. (Yale won that game at New Haven, 32–10.) The first official rules for women were adopted in 1899 at Springfield, Mass.

At first, college boys generally looked down on the game, partly because its popularity among women and its restrictions on rough play made it seem effeminate. But within a few years, boys who learned to play it in YMCA classes as teenagers became college students, and they retained their fondness for the game. Moreover, the players managed to make basketball rough enough to be considered manly. In 1909, President Charles W. Eliot of Harvard called basketball "more brutal than football"—although he admitted that he had never seen it played.

By 1901 basketball had grown too large for the YMCA to administer. With Gulick as chairman, a basketball rules committee was formed by the Amateur Athletic Union. Ever since then, the AAU has been in charge of amateur and industrial team basketball in the United States.

In April 1905 the colleges organized their own rules committee. They have controlled their own game since that time.

Professional teams emerged during the 1890's. In many instances, YMCA branches had dropped basketball after it became too competitive for their purposes, so the former YMCA teams began charging admission to meet rental expenses. Once

THE INVENTOR OF BASKETBALL, James Naismith (in suit), poses with history's first basketball team at the International YMCA Training School, Springfield, Mass.

in the ticket-selling business, the teams needed better players and winning records to attract crowds, and the paying of players was the final step toward professionalism.

Growth in the United States. For about 30 years after 1905, college teams dominated basketball, but competition was conducted essentially on a regional rather than national basis. Although many teams made intersectional trips during Christmas vacations, formal championships were restricted to sectional conferences and leagues. Playing styles and rules interpretations differed from section to section, making officiating more difficult. Even games that aroused great public interest in their localities were played in armories or gymnasiums with relatively small seating capacities.

But in 1934, Ned Irish, a New York sportswriter, arranged to stage college doubleheaders in Madison Square Garden, then the country's largest and most glamorous sports arena. The program was a great success, and made regular intersectional competition both feasible and desirable. Within a few years, large arenas in Boston, Philadelphia, Buffalo, Cleveland, and Chicago were part of an informal circuit for college teams. And the financial success of the arenas stimulated colleges to construct field houses with

A TRIUMPHANT DANCE STEP by Goose Tatum typifies the crowd-pleasing tactics of the Harlem Globetrotters.

capacities of 15,000 spectators. The abolition in 1937 of the center jump after each score made the game much faster and enhanced its spectator appeal. This coincided with the growth of the big arenas and intersectional play.

In 1938 the first major intercollegiate championship tournament—sponsored by the Metropolitan Basketball Writers Association and called the National Invitation Tournament, or NIT—was held at Madison Square Garden and won by Temple. The next year, the National Collegiate Athletic Association (NCAA) followed suit with its own tournament. Since World War II, the NCAA tourney has surpassed the NIT in importance, but both continue to thrive. The NCAA also conducts a small-college championship, while other smaller schools take part in an older National Association of Intercollegiate Athletics (NAIA) tournament.

The College Scandals. By 1950, college basketball was challenging football and baseball in public interest. Then scandal struck in 1951. Many games in Madison Square Garden and elsewhere had been "fixed"; that is, players had been bribed by gamblers to limit the "point spread," or margin of victory. During the next 10 years, three separate waves of scandals and resulting convictions implicated more than 100 players from more than 40 colleges in every section of the country. The biggest shock came early. Star players from City College in New York, the only team ever to win both the NIT and NCAA tournaments in the same season (1950), were found to have accepted bribes in the 1950 and 1951 seasons.

Basketball is particularly vulnerable to this sort of crime because of the nature of the game, the gambling practices surrounding it, and the high-pressure recruitment of college players that obviously produces profits for someone. In betting on basketball, the gambler gives or takes points, so that he can win a bet if his team loses the game by fewer than the designated number of points. Many college players were bribed to "shave" points—that is, not to lose the game, but to keep the winning margin within stipulated bounds. Players could easily manipulate a game without detection because the natural incidence of scoring and of errors in basketball is so high. Since the scandals, college basketball has been generally confined to campus arenas, but its popularity has not suffered. The scandals did, however, give the professional game its big chance.

Success of the Professionals. No stable professional league was established through the 1920's and 1930's, although barnstorming was profitable. In 1946–1947 the arenas that did so well with college basketball started their own professional league, the Basketball Association of America. The new league offered college-style play and recent college stars. In 1949 it merged with an older Midwestern circuit, the National Basketball League, and became the National Basketball Association (NBA).

The pro game, considered less reputable than college play in earlier periods, moved to the center of the basketball stage after the collegiate scandals. More of the great college players turned pro. By the 1960's, the NBA stretched from coast to coast, its star players earned up to $100,000 a year, and its annual attendance exceeded 2,500,000.

Other Countries. Meanwhile, basketball spread to other countries. The game's popularity was stimulated by American servicemen overseas during both world wars, particularly the second one. Since World War II, many instructional and exhibition tours sponsored by the U.S. State Department have helped the game to grow. In many countries—particularly in Russia, France, and Brazil—proficiency has developed to the point where U.S. teams can be successfully challenged.

FAMOUS PERSONS IN BASKETBALL

As the father of basketball, Naismith won a place in the Basketball Hall of Fame established in Springfield, Mass., in 1959. (See also NAISMITH, JAMES.) Gulick's early and continuing interest as rule maker and administrator won him also a charter membership in the game's Hall of Fame. Others included in the first set of electees to the Hall of Fame were: Ralph Morgan of Pennsylvania, the motivating force behind the first collegiate organization; Oswald Tower, outstanding interpreter of the rules; and John Schommer, early player and official.

The Original Celtics. During the 1920's, the Original Celtics, a professional team from New York City, reigned as the most famous basketball organization. Too strong to operate as a unit in any stable league, the Celtics made their reputation mainly by touring the country and proving all but invincible against local talent. Key players were Nat Holman, Joe Lapchick, Dutch Dehnert, Johnny Beckman, Chris Leonard, Pete Barry, Dave Banks, and George Haggerty. In honor of these early Celtics, Walter Brown, owner of the Boston team in the Basketball Association of America, chose the name "Celtics" for his team.

Outstanding Coaches. College teams began hiring professional coaches in the early 1900's, and these men developed the fundamentals of strategy and the techniques of play and conditioning. Because coaches tend to be judged by the won-lost records of their teams, however, their success depends more on recruiting ability than on teaching ability. During the 1930's, the coaches that emerged with the biggest reputations were Holman, at City College in New York; Lapchick, at St. John's in Brooklyn; Clair Bee, at Long Island University; Phog Allen, at Kansas; Hank Iba, at Oklahoma A & M; Adolph Rupp, at Kentucky; Ed Diddle, at Western Kentucky; and John Bunn, at Springfield.

The Great Players. The most publicized individual college player up to his time was Hank Luisetti of Stanford, who played in 1936–1938. He popularized the running one-hander, a shot that attracted attention in the East when Stanford made a trip to New York's Madison Square Garden and other Eastern arenas during the 1936 Christmas holidays. Stanford's wide-open style, coinciding with the end of the center jump, did as much as any single event to raise basketball to a new level of spectator appeal, and Luisetti, a truly great player, symbolized the new game.

From that time on, the spotlight has been on scorers, and the scorers usually have been giants. George Mikan, a 6-foot 10-inch center with broad shoulders, sharp elbows, plenty of weight, and the competitive urge to match, led De Paul to basketball fame in the mid-1940's. At the same time, Bob Kurland, taller but less agile than Mikan, was the foundation of Oklahoma A & M's deliberate style, stressing ball possession and careful shooting. Mikan went on to become the dominant player among the professionals, while Kurland chose AAU competition (with the Phillips Oilers) and achieved Olympic triumphs.

After World War II, a new breed of basketball player appeared. Men whose height ranged from 6 feet 4 inches to 6-11 developed agility, quickness, and fine skills previously possessed only by smaller players. From this point on, almost every college star went on to become a professional star. The three most important players in the postwar era were Bob Cousy, Bill Russell, and Wilt Chamberlain.

Cousy, a 6-footer, was a spectacular ballhandler, perfecting a behind-the-back dribble and dazzling hook passes. In contrast to the giants, he was a "small man" with whom the average spectator identified more closely.

But Cousy could not bring the Boston Celtics to championship stature until he was joined in 1956 by Russell. A 6-foot 9-inch center with remarkable reflexes, jumping ability, and basketball sense, Russell revolutionized basketball for top-level competitors. His defensive skill was so great that he became, in effect, a legal goalie. He could move fast enough to block attempts at lay-ups as they left the shooter's hands,

TWO OF THE GREATEST PROFESSIONALS display their scoring styles: (*Left*) George Mikan of Minneapolis registers a goal against the Fort Wayne Pistons. (*Right*) Cincinnati's Oscar Robertson tallies against New York.

SOME COMMON BASKETBALL TERMS

Assist.—A pass or hand-off directly resulting in a basket by a teammate.

Backboard.—The surface of wood or glass to which the basket is affixed, used to carom shots into the basket.

Back Court.—The half of the court away from the basket under attack; the two guards are called *back court men*.

Basket.—(1) The iron hoop through which goals are scored; (2) a field goal, worth two points.

Blocking.—A foul by a defensive player who blocks the legal path of an offensive player; the opposite of *Charging*.

Center Jump.—The method of putting the ball into play at the beginning of each period by having the referee toss up the ball between the rival centers.

Charging.—A foul by an offensive player who charges into a defensive player who has legal position; the opposite of *Blocking*.

Dribble.—Continuous bouncing of the ball, the only legal means of moving with the ball.

Fast Break.—A style of offense in which a team attempts to race to the offensive basket before the defense can get set.

Field Goal.—A basket scored from the floor; it counts two points.

Free Throw.—An unobstructed shot from the foul line, worth one point, awarded as a penalty for a foul by the opposing team.

Free Throw Lane.—The area on the floor bounded by the free throw line, the end line under the basket, and two connecting lines forming a 12-foot lane; also called *foul lane*.

Free Throw Line.—A line, 15 feet from the basket, behind which the shooter must stand in attempting a free throw; also called *foul line*.

Front Court.—The half of the court in which a basket is under attack.

Goal-Tending.—Illegal interference with a shot above the rim of the basket.

Hand-off.—Handing the ball to a teammate (instead of passing it).

Hook Shot.—A sweeping, one-handed field goal attempt, with the shooter's back at least partially to the basket.

Hoop.—(1) the rim of the basket; (2) synonym for basket in the sense of a score.

Jump Ball.—A means of putting the ball into play by having an official toss it upward between two players.

Jump Shot.—A field goal attempt in which the ball is released at the top of a vertical jump.

Lay-up.—A shot from alongside the basket, using the backboard as a guide.

Man-to-Man Defense.—A style of team defense in which each player is assigned one specific opponent to guard anywhere on the court.

Offensive Foul.—A personal foul committed by a member of the offensive team, usually not involving a free throw as part of the penalty.

Palming.—An illegal means of carrying the ball along while dribbling.

Personal Foul.—Any of a variety of body-contact fouls; five (or, in professional ball, six) personals disqualify the player who commits them.

Pick.—A legal method of providing shooting room for a teammate, by taking a position that "picks off" or blocks a defensive man.

Pivot.—A position taken by a player with his back to the basket, at the head of or alongside the free throw lane, from which he can spin and shoot or hand off to teammates moving past him toward the basket; also, the floor area where pivot play is feasible.

Post.—A synonym for pivot. "High post" means farther from the basket, "low post" closer.

Press.—A style of defense in which offensive players are closely guarded and harried. (A "full-court press" is applied all over the floor; a "half-court press" only after the ball is brought across the mid-court line.)

Rebound.—A shot that caroms off the basket or backboard and remains in play, to be recovered by either team.

Set Shot.—A field goal attempt, with one or both hands, from a stationary position, usually relatively far from the basket.

Slough.—A style of team defense in which players guarding men on the perimeter of the attacking formation "slough off" to help guard the pivot area or other special threat.

Switch.—A defensive technique in which players who have man-to-man assignments switch responsibilities with each other as their offensive men cross paths.

Technical Foul.—A foul imposed for misbehavior or for some technical rule infraction. The penalty is a free throw plus possession of the ball for the offended team.

Ten-Second Rule.—The requirement that a team bring the ball across the mid-court line within 10 seconds after gaining possession.

Three-Pointer.—A field goal made by a man who is fouled in the act of shooting, plus the free throw that he makes. But in the professional ABA, a field goal from beyond 25 feet counts three points.

Three-Second Rule.—The restriction against offensive players taking up set positions within the free throw lane for more than 3 seconds.

Traveling.—Illegally moving the ball by violating the dribbling rules.

Twenty-Four-Second Rule.—In the professional NBA, the requirement that a team make a field goal attempt within 24 seconds after gaining possession of the ball; in international amateur competition, the limit is 30 seconds.

Violation.—Any infraction not classified as a foul. The penalty is loss of possession of the ball.

Zone.—A style of team defense in which each player is assigned to guard a designated floor area, rather than a specific opponent.

NATIONAL BASKETBALL ASSOCIATION PLAY-OFF CHAMPIONS

Year	Champion	Year	Champion	Year	Champion
1951	Rochester	1960	Boston	1969	Boston
1952	Minneapolis	1961	Boston	1970	New York
1953	Minneapolis	1962	Boston	1971	Milwaukee
1954	Minneapolis	1963	Boston	1972	Los Angeles
1955	Syracuse	1964	Boston	1973	New York
1956	Philadelphia	1965	Boston	1974	Boston
1957	Boston	1966	Boston	1975	Golden State
1958	St. Louis	1967	Philadelphia	1976	Boston
1959	Boston	1968	Boston	1977	Portland

AMERICAN BASKETBALL ASSOCIATION PLAY-OFF CHAMPIONS

Year	Champion	Year	Champion	Year	Champion
1968	Pittsburgh	1971	Utah	1974	New York
1969	Oakland	1972	Indiana	1975	Kentucky
1970	Indiana	1973	Indiana	1976	New York

U. S. COLLEGE BASKETBALL CHAMPIONS

Year	NCAA	NIT	Year	NCAA	NIT
1939	Oregon	Long Island U.	1959	California	St. John's
1940	Indiana	Colorado	1960	Ohio State	Bradley
1941	Wisconsin	Long Island U.	1961	Cincinnati	Providence
1942	Stanford	West Virginia	1962	Cincinnati	Dayton
1943	Wyoming	St. John's	1963	Loyola (Chicago)	Providence
1944	Utah	St. John's	1964	UCLA	Bradley
1945	Oklahoma A & M	De Paul	1965	UCLA	St. John's
1946	Oklahoma A & M	Kentucky	1966	Texas Western	Brigham Young
1947	Holy Cross	Utah	1967	UCLA	Southern Illinois
1948	Kentucky	St. Louis	1968	UCLA	Dayton
1949	Kentucky	San Francisco	1969	UCLA	Temple
1950	City College, N. Y.	City College, N. Y.	1970	UCLA	Marquette
1951	Kentucky	Brigham Young	1971	UCLA	North Carolina
1952	Kansas	La Salle	1972	UCLA	Maryland
1953	Indiana	Seton Hall	1973	UCLA	Virginia Tech
1954	La Salle	Holy Cross	1974	North Carolina State	Purdue
1955	San Francisco	Duquesne	1975	UCLA	Princeton
1956	San Francisco	Louisville	1976	Indiana	Kentucky
1957	North Carolina	Bradley	1977	Marquette	St. Bonaventure
1958	Kentucky	Xavier (Ohio)			

JACK ZEHRT, F.P.G.

(*ABOVE*) A BALLETLIKE ENCOUNTER pits defender Bob Pettit of the St. Louis Hawks against Bill Russell, who led Boston to several titles.

(*LEFT*) The Celtics' Bob Cousy, a spectacular ballhandler, sights a gap in the Los Angeles Lakers' defense and dribbles toward the basket to score. (*Right*) Seven-foot-tall Wilt Chamberlain adds to his effective height with jump shot.

UPI

KEN REGAN, BIRNBACK

thus making the traditional objective of the offense—the area right under the basket—a danger zone instead of an advantage. Since Russell could also control most of the rebounds, he was able to initiate fast breaks, directed by Cousy, who could make the unerring pass up court after getting the ball from Russell. To some extent, all big men emulated Russell's techniques, but none were so effective. Even after Cousy retired in 1963, Russell kept Boston rolling to more league championships than any other team had ever won. In 1966, upon the retirement of Arnold (Red) Auerbach as Celtics coach, Russell was appointed to succeed him. He thus became the first Negro to serve as head coach of a major athletic team in the United States.

Chamberlain was the biggest man ever to play top-level basketball. Standing 7 feet tall and weighing 250 pounds, he had the speed and coordination to be an outstanding runner and shotputter in college. Entering the NBA in 1960, he shattered many scoring records. One season he averaged 50 points a game; once he scored 100 in a single game. But Chamberlain never had Russell's supporting cast or Russell's defensive skills, and he was usually considered second to Russell in total value. He and Russell were by far the highest paid basketball stars, commanding annual salaries estimated at around $100,000. Other pros who rank among the greatest players of all time are Oscar Robertson, Elgin Baylor, Bob Pettit, Dolph Schayes, Jerry West, and Joe Fulks.

The 1964–1965 season produced one of the most remarkable college players of all, Bill Bradley of Princeton. A great shooter, 6 feet 5 inches tall, and master of all the moves, he led Princeton to within two games of the NCAA title against much stronger teams. A Rhodes scholar, he studied at Oxford and then signed a $500,000 four-year contract with the New York Knickerbockers.

BASKETBALL TODAY

In the U.S. basketball world, the professional league now has clear title to top rank. The National Basketball Association, operating since 1949, is firmly established financially and in the public mind. Because of basketball's peculiar history and development, especially the advent of the tall men who were also accomplished athletes, the pro league can make the unchallenged statement that it is playing the game at a higher level of proficiency than any other group of teams ever has, anywhere, any time. The Boston Celtics, led by Auerbach until his retirement as coach in 1966, and depending primarily on Russell's skill, gathered a long string of championships in the 1950's and 1960's to establish itself as probably the best basketball team ever.

A second league, the American Basketball Association, began its first season in 1967. Following the 1975–1976 season, during which the number of ABA teams dwindled from ten to six, the league merged with the NBA to form a 22-team circuit—18 from the NBA and four from the ABA. Surviving ABA teams were the New York Nets, Indiana Pacers, Denver Nuggets, and San Antonio Spurs. They joined NBA clubs operating in Boston, New York, Philadelphia, Buffalo, Washington, Atlanta, Cleveland, Houston, Milwaukee, Chicago, Phoenix, Detroit, Kansas City, Los Angeles, Seattle, Portland, New Orleans, and Oakland (Golden State).

Financial Aspects. Until the late 1960's, built-in limitations kept pro basketball from reaching a status comparable to baseball or football in the spectator-sport complex of American life. Outdoor stadia that accommodate 50,000 to 100,000 customers for a sufficiently attractive baseball or football event made possible a scale of operation that indoor basketball could not achieve. How-

CHRONOLOGY

December 1891—James Naismith invented basketball at International YMCA Training School in Springfield, Mass.

March 1897—First intercollegiate game: Yale 32, Pennsylvania 10.

1897–98—Five-man teams established.

1904—Basketball demonstrated at Olympic Games.

1907–08—Five-minute overtime periods to break ties adopted.

1908–09—Personal foul limit introduced; five fouls put player out of game.

1910–11—Personal foul limit cut to four.

1913—National AAU championships established on annual basis.

1932–33—Three-second and 10-second rules adopted to combat stalling.

1934–35—Madison Square Garden doubleheaders began.

1936—Basketball became a regular Olympic event.

1937–38—Center jump after scores abolished.

1938—First National Invitation Tournament.

1939—First NCAA tournament.

1944–45—Personal foul limit raised to five; all restrictions on substitutions removed.

1946–47—Basketball Association of America (professional) established.

1949–50—Merger of BAA with National Basketball League created National Basketball Association.

1950—City College, New York, won both NIT and NCAA tournaments.

1951—College basketball's first major "fix" scandal became public.

1952–53—First version of "one-and-one" free throw rule used by colleges.

1954–55—Pros adopted 24-second rule.

1955–56—Free throw lane doubled in width to 12 feet.

1967—American Basketball Association (professional) established.

1972—United States lost first Olympic basketball game, and gold medal, to the Soviet Union.

1976—National Basketball Association and American Basketball Association merged to form 22-team league.

ever, with interest in pro basketball increasing, the birth of the ABA, and NBA expansion, the picture changed considerably.

Consequently, the value of the professional basketball franchise has grown rapidly. A franchise in baseball or football is worth about $10 million. When the Boston Celtics were sold in 1965, the price was $3 million; nine years later, the Detroit Pistons were sold for $8.1 million. In total yearly attendance, professional baseball runs to about 30 million; football to 15 million; basketball to 11 million. For the player, the average annual salary is about $40,000 in baseball, $32,000 in football, and $85,000 in basketball. Partly because of the high salaries, a majority of pro basketball teams were losing money in the mid-1970's.

Widespread Participation. In every gym in the United States, men and boys play basketball informally. Countless garage doors or backyard fences have baskets attached. Playground basketball is a summerlong activity for neighborhood children. Of all the team games, basketball is the most practical and rewarding for a casual player in an informal setting.

At U.S. schools of every level, basketball is a primary varsity sport and the most popular intramural sport. For thousands of U.S. high schools and for many colleges, it is the rallying point for student loyalty. At these institutions, where varsity football has proved, or would prove, too expensive, varsity basketball fills the bill perfectly. A few students can fill out a squad, travel is easy and inexpensive, equipment is not elaborate, and games can be played two or three times a week.

Noncollegiate amateur teams are usually sponsored by business firms. The best known of these operate on a level that is professional, except that the players are employed by the firm and not paid for playing basketball. The annual AAU tournament has been dominated by such teams, including the Phillips 66ers, Peoria Caterpillars, Wichita Vickers, and Denver Truckers.

Tournaments. Big-time college basketball continues to thrive in the United States, and more large field houses constantly are being built. The National Collegiate Athletic Association tournament now embraces 32 teams; the National Invitation Tournament has 16. Dozens of holiday tournaments give a championship flavor to the early part of the season. High school championship tournaments are conducted in most states. In some states, a school competes in one of several tournaments, depending on the size of its enrollment; in other states, all schools compete in one tournament. These tournaments may require the playing of hundreds of games over a period of several weeks.

International Competition. The AAU is also the main force in selecting America's Olympic squads, and this is usually done by holding a special try-out tournament in Olympic years. The U.S. squad is composed of several members of the winning team, plus outstanding players from other teams in the tournament. Similar, but less elaborate, procedures are used for choosing U.S. teams that take part in the quadrennial Pan-American Games, world championship (amateur) tournaments, and various other international matches. See also OLYMPIC GAMES.

Basketball for Women. Rules, skills, and strategies for women's basketball are similar to those for the men's game. As of 1971, rules of the Division of Girls' and Women's Sports (DGWS)—AAU Joint Rules Committee provide for a five-player game with eight-minute quarters. Two forwards, two guards, and a center function in offensive and defensive roles. This formation requires each player to perform fundamental offensive and defensive skills and encourages the development of a more completely skilled player. An added feature of the game requires a team to shoot for its basket within 30 seconds after gaining possession of the ball. Women's competition has increased so that high schools, colleges, and independent teams may now compete on local, state, or national levels under their respective governing bodies.

The Globetrotters. The famous Harlem Globetrotters do not fit into any of the standard categories. This all-Negro unit, built into a worldwide success by Abe Saperstein, is a professional team but not a member of any league. The team's trademark is highly skilled clowning; the Globetrotters, who play good basketball even though they emphasize comedy, have performed their amusing routines in many countries.

LEONARD KOPPETT, *New York "Times"*

Bibliography

Auerbach, Arnold, *Basketball* (New York 1961).

Bee, Clair F., and Norton, Ken, *Basketball Fundamentals and Techniques* (New York 1959).

Bell, Mary M., *Women's Basketball* (Dubuque, Iowa, 1964).

Bunn, John W., *Basketball Techniques and Team Play* (Englewood Cliffs, N.J., 1964).

Naismith, James, *Basketball, Its Origin and Development* (New York 1941).

Newell, Pete, and Bennington, John, *Basketball Methods* (New York 1962).

Wooden, John R., *Practical Modern Basketball* (New York 1966).

BASKIN, bas'kən, **Leonard** (1922–   ), American sculptor and graphic artist, who, in an era dominated by abstract expressionism, never abandoned his belief in the importance of man as a central subject of art. He has said, "The human figure is the image of all men and of one man. It contains all and can express all." His work expresses not only the nobility of man but his corruption and despair as well. Some critics see a mystical quality in Baskin's work, especially in his use of birds, either alone or combined with figures.

Baskin was born in New Brunswick, N.J., on April 15, 1922, and studied art at New York University (1941) and at Yale (1941–1943) before serving as a Navy pilot during World War II. In 1949 he received his B.A. from the New School for Social Research in New York City and then studied for two years in Paris and Florence. After 1953 he taught at Smith College, where he founded the Gehenna Press, which printed limited editions of rare books.

Graphics, particularly woodcuts and etchings, brought Baskin his earliest fame and won him a Guggenheim Fellowship in 1953. A major achievement was his illustrations for Richmond Lattimore's translation of Homer's *Illiad* (1962).

In 1953, Baskin had his first one-man show in New York City. His sculpture was included in the New Images of Man exhibition at the Museum of Modern Art in New York in 1959, and an exhibition of his work was seen in major European cities in 1961. His sculpture includes *Man with a Dead Bird* (1954), *Poet Laureate* (1955), *The Great Dead Man* (1956), *Seated Man with Owl* (1959), *Oppressed Man* (1960), and *Seated Woman* (1961).

BASLE. See BASEL.

BASOCHE, bà-zôsh', in France, a type of guild made up of clerks specializing in law. When the word *basoche* (or *bazoche*) first appeared in the Middle Ages, it denoted a guild of clerks that provided legal representatives known as *procureurs*. Such a guild existed in France at least as early as the 12th century. Clerks who were skilled in law offered their services either as representatives in the law courts or as advocates, and they organized into *basoches* in the towns where the principal courts were held. Like the craft and merchant guilds, the *basoches* established standards of excellence, set fees, and initiated necessary regulations.

As the law became more complicated, the *basoche* was broken down into separate groups of clerks, each specializing in different aspects of the law. During the early 14th century the advocates and the representatives formed separate bodies. Only clerks who limited their work to clerical tasks remained members of the *basoche*. Generally, they worked for the advocates and representatives and aspired to become one of the latter. Although the *basoche* ceased to be an important legal guild in the 14th century, many of its prerogatives and traditions continued. In the 18th century its members were still permitted to plead certain cases. The guild continued to be called the "kingdom of the *basoche*," and a "king" was elected annually, up to the end of the 1600's. In Paris the clerks of the Palais de Justice publicly gave literary and satirical performances and presented morality plays.

BRYCE LYON, *Brown University*

BASOV, bä'sôf, **Nikolai Gennadiyevich** (1922–   ), Russian nuclear physicist who helped to establish the principles of the maser. He was born near Voronezh, USSR, on Dec. 14, 1922. After serving in the Soviet army during World War II, he went to the Moscow Institute of Physical Engineering and graduated in 1950. He then went to the Lebedev Physical Institute in Moscow, where he took his doctoral degree in 1956.

Basov's doctoral dissertation, a refinement of theoretical and experimental ideas concerning masers (an acronym for *m*icrowave *a*mplification by *s*timulated *e*mission of *r*adiation), eventually led to his receiving the Nobel prize in physics in 1964, together with the American C.H. Townes and A.M. Prochorov, Basov's colleague at the Lebedev Institute. Masers are highly sensitive resonance devices that handle electromagnetic radiation with much greater fidelity than conventional devices. Their operation depends on the fact that when electrons fall toward the nucleus, the atom emits radiation energy at a characteristic frequency.

Basov also studied lasers, which are masers capable of amplifying light and producing light beams of intense strength. Masers and lasers have been used in radio astronomy, radar, satellite communication, and other fields.

Basov is a corresponding member of the Soviet Academy of Science and a recipient of the Lenin Prize (1959). He is a member of the Communist party, a professor at the Moscow Institute of Physical Engineering, and an assistant director of the Lebedev Physical Institute. See also LASER; MASER.

L.L. LAUDAN, *University College, London*

BASQUES, basks, a people whose homeland is on the southeast coast of the Bay of Biscay and in the adjoining mountains of the Pyrenees. Politically their homeland is divided between France and Spain. Of the historical Basque provinces, three—Labourd, Basse-Navarre, and Soule—are on the French side of the border. Called the *Pays Basque* (Basque Country), they now make up the greater part of the department of Basses-Pyrénées. The four Spanish provinces are Navarre, Álava, Vizcaya, and Guipúzcoa.

The Basque language is spoken by about 100,000 people in the French provinces and by more than 500,000 in Spain. Many thousands of Basques have emigrated to South America and the United States, usually to sheep-raising country since the Basques are accomplished herders. It is estimated that there are about 60,000 Basques living in the western United States, including original immigrants and their descendants.

Land and Economy. Sheep and cows are raised in the mountainous parts of the French Basque country. In the more humid lowlands, cereals, corn, fruit trees, and grapes are grown. Industry centers on Bayonne and tourism on Biarritz and Hendaye. On the Spanish side, the northern slopes of the mountains are heavily settled with herders and farmers, though the forests and the ruggedness of the land, cut by deep valleys, restrict the expansion of farm acreage. Chestnut and walnut groves, vineyards, meadows, and orchards alternate with fields of corn, rye, potatoes, flax, and hemp. Deep-sea fishing is an important industry. The area around Bilbao is the center of Spain's iron-mining district. Many of the waterfalls are harnessed to power various industries.

BASQUES have fished the Bay of Biscay for centuries. These fishermen are tending their nets at the Spanish coastal resort of Lequeitio.

Ethnology and Language. The origin of the Basques and of their language is a matter of surmise and scholarly dispute. One school considers the language a survival of a tongue spoken on the Iberian peninsula in pre-Roman days. Another school relates it to the languages of the Caucasus, theorizing that groups migrated from the Caucasus to the Iberian peninsula in about 2000 B.C.

The language is agglutinative and has no apparent affinity with other European languages. It is represented by several dialects. The French group of dialects are Labourdin, Lower Navarrese, and Souletin; the Spanish are Guipúzcoan, Upper Navarrese, and Biscayan.

The name Basque is not a native term but a French derivation from Latin *Vascones.* The Spanish name, *Vascongados,* evidences a similar derivation. In their own tongue the Basques call themselves *Eskualdunak* (those who speak the *Eskuara*) and their country *Eskual-Herria.*

Basque Characteristics. The pride and independent spirit of the Basques is proverbial, as is their obstinacy. The typical Basque lives in a small village or in a lonely farmhouse. Inured from childhood to the rugged life of a fisherman, farmer, or lonely herder, he is naturally bold and energetic. Basques sailed with Magellan and served under the conquistadors in Latin America. In the 16th century they were the first Europeans to exploit the whale fisheries of the Bay of Biscay, and in the same century they pioneered the cod fisheries of the Newfoundland Banks with the Bretons.

A deeply religious and conservative people, they have retained certain religious practices from medieval times that have long since fallen out of use elsewhere. For the Basques, the feast of Corpus Christi, instituted in the 13th century, is still the "New Feast." Despite their strong religious faith (Ignatius Loyola and Francis Xavier were Basques), they have always maintained freedom from ecclesiastical domination. Thus, in Spain they would not allow the bishops to appoint their priests, and attempts of ecclesiasts to interfere with their traditional games and dances were fiercely resisted.

The small beret, or *boina,* and rope-soled shoes (*alpargatas*) are typical of Basque dress. The iron *makhila,* carried by a thong, is used both as a walking stick and as a weapon. Native games include the fast-moving *pelota* and the *passolaris,* a weight-lifting sport. Basque dances, such as the *espatadantzaris,* or sword dance, are vigorous and colorful.

History. It is fairly well established that during the 5th century the Basques were driven into their mountain fastnesses by invading Visigoths. It was the Basques who in 778 ambushed the rear guard of Charlemagne's army at Roncesvalles during its retreat from Muslim forces. The battle at Roncesvalles was later immortalized in the epic *La chanson de Roland.* By 920 the territories that the Basques occupied were included in the kingdom of Navarre, and so, ultimately, the greater part came under the rule of Spain.

The Basques, however, maintained their special assemblies and their *fueros,* or local rights. French sovereigns down to the Revolution and Spanish sovereigns to the mid-19th century observed these rights, acknowledging the Basques as quasi-independent. The fueros guaranteed to the Basques the right to elect their own officials, to refuse military service except in wars of national defense, and to fight only under their own officers when national defense was involved. When the Spanish Cortes in 1832 abolished the fueros, the loss of these rights stirred the Basques to such violent resistance that the government restored them.

Devoted followers of Don Carlos, the conservative pretender to the Spanish throne, the Basques fought for the Carlist cause in the rebellions against the government in the 1830's and in the 1870's. The crushing of the second rebellion in 1876 resulted in the final abolition of the fueros, although the Basques did manage to retain some of their traditional privileges.

On the outbreak of the Spanish Civil War in 1936, they attempted to maintain a neutral position by organizing an autonomous government at Guernica. But in 1937, Gen. Franco's armies crushed this separatist movement.

In the 1960's both the local clergy and the workers in the industrial centers publicly opposed the government in several instances. The clergy protested against government censorship and criticized the methods of the police. Strikes for better pay and housing were almost as frequent in the city of Bilbao as in the mining centers of the Asturias.

Further Reading: Aldecoa, Ignacio, *The Basque Country,* tr. by Doireann MacDermott (New York 1963); Gallop, Rodney, *Book of the Basques* (New York 1930); Tovar, Antonio, *Basque Language,* tr. by Herbert P. Houghton (Philadelphia 1957).

BASRA, bäs'rä, is Iraq's principal port and third-largest city, as well as the capital of the province of Basra. It is situated on the Shatt al-Arab (a river formed by the junction of the Tigris and Euphrates), about 75 miles (120 km) from the Persian Gulf and 280 miles (450 km) southeast of Baghdad. It has a hot and humid climate.

Located at the southern terminus of the railroad from Baghdad, and connected with the Persian Gulf by a channel (which must be dredged continually) at the mouth of the Shatt al-Arab, Basra exports most of Iraq's products. The oil industry and exports of dates account for a large part of its revenues. The oil is pumped through pipelines to the Persian Gulf town of Fao, where it is loaded on tankers.

The dates are grown in the large date gardens that lie outside the city. Basra is in the middle of a fertile agricultural region that grows rice, corn, millet, barley, and wheat.

History. The city was originally founded by the caliph Umar I in 638 A.D. at a site eight miles distant from the present city. Today the village of az-Zubayr stands on the site of the old city. Basra flourished as a commercial and cultural center under the Abbasid dynasty (750–1258), although the neighboring city of Baghdad tended to overshadow it. The city was established on its present site after it had been all but destroyed by the Mongols in the 13th century.

From 1508 to 1534, it was held by the Persian shah Ismail. Later in the century it became part of the Ottoman empire. In the 17th century it was opened to English, Portuguese, and Dutch traders, and its commercial importance was revived. During the 18th and 19th centuries, Basra was the chief city of southern Iraq and the country's only port. It remained a primitive city until after the great plague of 1831, when it began to modernize, although the process was slow.

The English occupied the city in World War I, used it as a supply base, and greatly improved the harbor. Throughout World War I and the subsequent period (1920–1932) under a British mandate, the city's prosperity greatly increased. In World War II, the Allies routed supplies to the Russians through Basra. Population: (1970 est.) 370,900.

BASS, bas, **Sam** (1851–1878), American desperado. He was born near Bedford, Ind., on July 21, 1851. Orphaned at an early age, he lived with an uncle and later left for Texas, arriving in 1870. After working as cowboy and a teamster, he took up horse racing. In 1876 he rode with a cattle herd to Nebraska and went on to Deadwood, Dakota Territory, a center of gold-mining operations. To recoup gambling losses, he and others robbed stagecoaches, but with little success.

In 1877, Bass was one of six men, led by Joel Collins, who held up a Union Pacific train at Big Springs, Neb., taking $60,000 in gold coins from the express car and money and jewelry from passengers. Back in Texas, Bass formed and led a new outlaw band. Early in 1878 he robbed four trains near Dallas, without taking much loot. Chased by Texas Rangers and local posses, he was betrayed by an associate and wounded in a street battle at Round Rock, Texas. He died two days later, on July 21, 1878.

WAYNE GARD, *Author of "Sam Bass"*

MARINELAND OF FLORIDA

Black sea bass

E.P. HADDON, U.S. FISH AND WILDLIFE SERVICE

Largemouthed black bass

BASS, bas, is the name given to more than a dozen North American species of spiny-rayed food and game fishes of both fresh and salt waters. It includes members of at least six different fish families.

True Sea Bass. Most of the species called "bass" belong to the family Serranidae. An important saltwater representative of this family is the striped bass (*Roccus saxatilus*) of the Atlantic and Pacific coasts of North America. It is a highly prized food and game fish.

A native of the East Coast of North America, from the Gulf of St. Lawrence to Florida, the striped bass exists in at least three population units in the Atlantic Ocean. The largest population is found in the waters of the Middle Atlantic Bight (North Carolina to Massachusetts). Of this population unit, 90 percent originate from spawning in the fresh waters of rivers that run into Chesapeake Bay. The newly hatched young quickly descend to salt water. At two years of age some, but only a minor proportion, migrate in the spring to various points along the Middle Atlantic coast. These, together with older and larger migrating fish, make up the seasonal supplies of striped bass in the Middle Atlantic coastal states.

Fall migration begins in September or October, and the fish return to a wintering area that extends from central New Jersey to North Carolina. Striped bass of this population often reach large sizes: fish weighing 20 to 30 pounds (9 to 13.5 kg) are captured frequently, and specimens of 40 pounds (18 kg) are not unusual. Fish over 100 pounds (45 kg) have been captured, but the size usually taken is between 2 and 10 pounds (1 and 4.5 kg).

Striped bass of the St. Lawrence population have a much slower rate of growth.

In 1879, striped bass were introduced successfully into the waters of San Francisco Bay when a few hundred small striped bass were shipped across the continent by train from New Jersey. Twenty years later, 1,234,000 fish were caught in California waters, and the species has since spread along the Pacific coast.

Striped bass are taken by angling from beaches, jetties, and piers, or from small craft operating in bays or close to ocean beaches. Trolling or casting metal jigs, plugs, spoons, and feathered or haired lures are the preferred means, although such bait as shedder crabs, clams, squid, and worms often is employed.

Other saltwater species of the family Serranidae include the common black sea bass (*Centropristes striatus*) of the United States Atlantic coast; and the kelp bass (*Paralabrax clathratus*), the sand bass (*P. nebulifer*), and the spotted sand bass (*P. maculato-fasciatus*)—all of the Pacific coast.

The family Serranidae also includes several freshwater species. One of these is the white or silver bass (*lepibema chrysops*). This fish prefers still waters, and has a strong tendency to form schools. It is found in the upper Mississippi River system, the Great Lakes drainage basin, and the east central longitudes of the United States. In weight it seldom exceeds 3 pounds (1.3 kg). The white bass is caught by angling in lakes and rivers and can be taken on both live bait and artificial lures.

Another freshwater species is the yellow bass (*Morone interrupta*) found in the east central longitudes of the United States. It bears some resemblance to the striped bass with its black, longitudinal lines. The lines of the yellow bass are, however, broken. Its size range is similar to that of the white bass. The gamy and culinary qualities of the yellow bass are highly valued.

Sunfish. The name "bass" also is given to some members of the sunfish family, Centrarchidae. The sunfishes are an exclusively North American freshwater family. One of the sunfishes known as "bass" is the largemouthed black bass (*Micropterus salmoides*). Known also as "Oswego," "largemouth," "green trout," and "straw bass," it occurred originally from southern Canada (Ontario and Quebec), the Great Lakes drainage, and the Mississippi Valley to northeastern Mexico and Florida and north to North Carolina along the coastal plain. It has been introduced into other parts of North America and elsewhere. Largemouths often attain a weight of 6 pounds (2.7 kg) or more in the northern part of their range and over 9 pounds (4 kg) in the southern portion. This bass prefers warm, weedy, mud-bottomed lakes, ponds, and sluggish streams, and it frequents backwaters and bayous. A popular game fish, it is taken on both bait and artificial lures and is particularly susceptible to surface lures used in the late evening or at night.

Another of the sunfishes known as "bass" is the smallmouthed bass (*Micropterus dolomieu*). It is known also as "smallmouth," "blackback," and "bronzeback." This bass occurred originally from Minnesota to Quebec (and in the Nipigon River) and south to Alabama and Oklahoma, but it has been introduced into other parts of North America, and into Britain and Europe. It can be distinguished readily from the largemouth by its jaw, which does not extend back beyond the eye, and by its finer scales—14 to 18 rows on the cheek. In addition, the smallmouth seldom exceeds a weight of five pounds (2.2 kg). It prefers cool lakes and rivers with extensive bottom areas of rocks and gravel; it also occurs in streams, where it is apt to be stunted.

The smallmouth, often found in schools on shoal areas, feeds extensively on crayfish and other bottom invertebrates. One of the gamest of fishes, the smallmouth can be taken on a variety of baits and "artificials," including worms, leeches, crayfish, frogs, hellgrammites, minnows, streamers, "bass bugs," spinners, and plugs.

Three other members of the sunfish family are called "bass." They are: the spotted bass (*Micropterus pseudoplites*), known also as "Kentucky bass" and "Ozark bass"; the rock bass (*Ambloplites rupestris*); and the calico bass (*Pomoxis nigro-maculatus*), known also as "black crappie" and "strawberry bass."

Other Bass. Although the families Serranidae and Centrarchidae contain most of the species called "bass," some other families are referred to by this name. These are the Sciaenidae, Xenichthyidae, Scorpaenidae, and Scorpidae.

JAMES WESTMAN, *Rutgers University*

BASS, bās, is a musical term with several meanings. It comes from the Italian word *basso,* meaning "deep" or "low."

(1) Bass is the lowest male voice, with a normal range from E or F above middle C, to E two octaves below middle C.

(2) The bass is the lowest of the parts in a musical composition. In the 18th and early 19th centuries the terms *figured bass, thorough bass,* or *basso continuo* were used for a method of notation whereby the bass notes, together with symbols denoting the intervals and chords to be played above them, were all that were given to indicate the accompaniment of a composition.

(3) A bass is a musical instrument—the largest and lowest-toned member of the violin family. It is also called a *double bass.* The term also denotes the lowest member, in range, of other families of instruments, such as a bass clarinet. (See also BASS VIOL.)

BASS ISLANDS, bas, in western Lake Erie, about 55 miles (89 km) west of Cleveland. They are part of Ottawa County, Ohio. The group, named for the abundance of bass in the surrounding waters, includes North Bass, Middle Bass, and South Bass. South Bass, about 3½ miles (5.5 km) long, is the largest island. The islands are summer resorts and are noted for grape culture and wine making. The principal villages are Isle St. George, on North Bass; Middle Bass, on Middle Bass; and Put-in-Bay, on South Bass.

The Battle of Lake Erie in the War of 1812 was fought off Put-in-Bay on Sept. 10, 1813. Commodore Oliver Hazard Perry defeated a British fleet there, enabling the Americans to control Lake Erie and invade Canada. The Perry Memorial, a monument 352 feet (107 meters) high, is near the harbor of Put-in-Bay village. It was dedicated in 1913, the centennial of the battle.

BASS ROCK, bas, in southeast Scotland, is a traprock island at the mouth of the Firth of Forth, 4 miles (6.4 km) northeast of North Berwick. It is sometimes called *The Bass.* Circular in shape, it is about a mile in circumference, and it is 350 feet high. The island is inaccessible except for a shelving point at the southeast. Flocks of seabirds, especially gannets, nest on the island. A lighthouse was built on the summit in 1902. Halfway up one side are the ruins of a chapel, once the hermitage of St. Baldred, and on the summit are the remains of a castle.

At one time the island belonged to a family named Lauder, whose chief was called Lauder of the Bass. It was purchased by the English government in 1671 and the castle was converted into a state prison. The last band of Jacobins who held out against King William III of England took refuge on the island and were forced to surrender only because they were threatened by starvation.

BASS STRAIT, bas, is a shallow body of water between the coast of Victoria on the Australian mainland and the island of Tasmania. It merges with the Indian Ocean on the west and the Tasman Sea of the Pacific Ocean on the east. The strait is about 200 miles (322 km) in length and ranges from 80 to 150 miles (129 to 241 km) in width; the average depth is 230 feet (70 meters). Among the islands it contains are King Island, the Hunter islands, and the Furneaux group. Bass Strait was named for the British navigator George Bass, who discovered it in 1798.

BASS VIOL, bās vī′əl, a stringed instrument, often called viola da gamba (q.v.), although this is properly the name for the whole viol family. The bass viol was widely used in the 16th and 17th centuries, primarily for solo work. It was about the size of a violoncello but had a longer neck (about 30 inches, or 76 cm, from the nut to the bridge). Usually it had six strings, although a few continental varieties had seven. The bow was held underhand as for the double bass.

Today, the term "bass viol" is often applied erroneously to the double bass.

BASS VIOL, built by Giovanni Battista Ciciliano in Venice about 1550.

BASSANIO, bə-sa′nē-ō, a character in *The Merchant of Venice* by William Shakespeare. Bassanio is the lover of Portia, a rich heiress. In order to win Portia's hand, Bassanio must choose correctly among three caskets—gold, silver, and lead. Unlike Portia's earlier suitors, who, blinded by greed, chose the gold and silver caskets, Bassanio refuses to be swayed by external appearances. He selects the lead casket and marries Portia.

BASSANO, bäs-sä′nō, a family of Italian painters of the 16th century, who were members of the Venetian school of painting. They were the descendants of Francesco da Ponte, a provincial painter of no great merit. He was active in Bassano from about 1500 to 1540.

JACOPO (or GIACOMO) DA PONTE, called BASSANO (1517/1518–1592), a son of Francesco, was the outstanding painter of the family and one of the great Venetian painters of the 16th century. He was born in Bassano and studied in Venice with Bonifazio di Pitati, a follower of Titian.

BASS ROCK, Scotland, looms behind the ruined walls of Tantallon Castle, which was built in the 14th century.

Although the works of Jacopo Bassano show successive waves of influence—Titian, Parmigianino, Tintoretto—they have an originality that evolved into a personal, richly colored, mannerist style. He is one of the first genre painters, showing a preference for religious subjects that would allow him to include animals, farmhouses, and natural landscape. Ultimately he produced completely secular, genre works such as *Rural Scene* (about 1565–1570; von Thyssen Collection, Lugano, Switzerland).

Jacopo's many important works include a *Crucifixion* (1561–1563; Pinacoteca, Treviso, Italy), *Adoration of the Shepherds* (1568; Galleria Nazionale, Rome), *Adoration of the Magi* (Galleria Borghese, Rome), *Annunciation to the Shepherds* (National Gallery of Art, Washington, D.C.), *Descent of the Holy Ghost* (Museo Civico, Bassano), and *Acteon and the Nymphs* (Art Institute of Chicago).

Jacopo worked in Bassano during intermittent periods throughout his life and died there on Feb. 13, 1592. He also established a workshop in Venice, where three of his sons assisted him.

FRANCESCO BASSANO (1549–1592) was Jacopo's eldest son. He assisted his father in many of his late paintings and, after 1578, headed the workshop in Venice. His large, crowded compositions were in great demand during his lifetime but are now considered too closely imitative of his father's style. Among his major works are the *Martyrdom of St. Catherine* (Pitti Palace, Florence), *Circumcision* (1577; Museo Civico, Bassano), and *The Preaching of the Baptist* (about 1570; San Giacomo dall'Orio, Venice). Francesco committed suicide in 1592.

LEANDRO BASSANO (1557–1623) headed the workshop after his brother's death. His work depends heavily on ideas formulated by his father and brother, though his portraits have a realism associated with north European art. They include *Sculptor* and *A Boy and His Tutor*, both at Hampton Court, England.

GEROLAMO BASSANO (1566–1621) assisted his brothers in the Venice workshop after 1581. His work, in close imitation of his father's style, is characterized by a very free brushstroke. A major work is the *Virgin and Child in Glory with Saints Justina, Barbara, and Mark*, in the Church of San Giovanni Battista, Bassano.

BASSANO DEL GRAPPA, bäs-sä'nō däl gräp'pä, is a town in Italy, in Vicenza Province, 37 miles (60 km) northwest of Venice. Beautifully situated on the left bank of the Brenta River at the foot of Monte Grappa, Bassano has a pleasant appearance, with narrow arcaded streets, many ancient houses with painted facades, and villas with beautiful gardens. A colonnaded wooden covered bridge spanning the Brenta is celebrated in Italian war songs. First mentioned in 1209, the bridge was often destroyed in floods and wars but was always rebuilt according to the original plan. The municipal museum contains paintings by the da Ponte family, who were called "Bassano" in honor of their birthplace. Other landmarks are the Gothic Church of San Francesco and a 10th century cathedral.

Bassano was long under the sway of the lords of Milan, Padua, and Verona. Included in the republic of Venice from 1402 to 1797, it had flourishing wool and silk industries and a thriving trade. In 1796, Napoleon defeated the Austrians near Bassano. Monte Grappa was the scene of bloody battles in World War I. The town suffered some bomb damage during World War II. Population: (1970 est.) 31,000.

BASSE-TERRE, bäs-târ, is the capital of Guadeloupe, an overseas department of France in the West Indies. The city is a seaport on the southwest coast of Basse-Terre Island. On the island is Grande Soufrière, a volcano 4,869 feet (1,484 meters) in height. Since the anchorage at Basse-Terre is unsheltered and exposed to a constant swell, most of the external trade of Guadeloupe is conducted through the port of Pointe-à-Pitre, on the neighboring island of Grande Terre. Basse-Terre was founded in 1643. Population: (1967) 15,690.

BASSEIN, bə-sān', a city in Burma, is the capital of a district of the same name and of the Irrawaddy Division. It is situated on the east bank of the Bassein River, one of the tributaries of the Irrawaddy, 90 miles (145 km) west of Rangoon. The city is in the center of a large rice-growing region. Considerable quantities of rice are exported by means of the Bassein River, which is navigable to ocean-going vessels. The city is connected with Rangoon by a railroad. Population: (1953) 77,905.

BASSEIN, bə-sān', is a port on the Arabian Sea in Maharashtra state, India. It is situated 25 miles (40 km) north of Bombay, at the southern end of the small island of Bassein. The port was seized in 1536 by the Portuguese, who developed it into a wealthy city of over 60,000 inhabitants. The Marathas captured Bassein in 1739, but thereafter wars and plagues caused its prosperity to decline. A Maratha-British treaty was signed in Bassein in 1802. Population: (1961) 22,598.

BASSELIN, bás-laɴ', **Olivier** (c. 1350–c. 1419), French songwriter. He is also known as *Olivier Bachelin.* He was born in Vire, Normandy, and may have been a cloth presser by trade. Basselin was one of the Compagnons du Vau de Vire (Companions of the Vire Valley), a group of provincial poets who wrote drinking and love songs. The generic name of their songs is *vaux de vire,* which is probably the source of the word *vaudeville.*

An anthology of *vaux de vire* that appeared in the early 17th century was at one time ascribed to Basselin but is now believed to be the work of Jean le Houx, a 16th century lawyer of the Vire region. Basselin was the subject of a 15th century Norman dirge that suggests he was killed in the wars between the French and King Henry V of England.

BASSERMANN, bäs'ər-män, **Albert** (1867–1952), German actor, who was one of the outstanding interpreters of Ibsen in Germany. Bassermann was born on Sept. 7, 1867, in Mannheim, where he made his theatrical debut at the age of 19. In 1899 he joined Otto Brahm, whose company, the Freie Buhne ("Free Stage"), furthered the work of such playwrights as Ibsen, Strindberg, and Schiller. He later worked with Max Reinhardt at the Deutsches Theater in Berlin.

Bassermann left Germany when the Nazis rose to power. He lived chiefly in Hollywood, where he appeared in character roles in many films, including *Dr. Ehrlich's Magic Bullet* (1940), *Foreign Correspondent* (1940), and *The Moon and Sixpence* (1942). He also played in the British film *The Red Shoes* (1948). In 1944 he made his debut on the English-speaking stage in the Broadway production of *Embezzled Heaven.* He returned to Europe after World War II. He died in Zürich, Switzerland, on May 15, 1952.

Basset hound

WALTER CHANDOHA

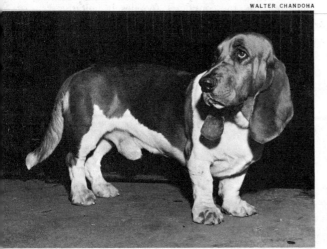

BASSET HOUND, bas'it, a dog with many houndlike characteristics. It is low, from 11 to 15 inches (27 to 38 cm) high from the shoulder, with a long, bulky body. The legs are short, terminating in massive paws. In a type popular in America, the front legs are crooked at the knee. The head of a basset hound is massive, with a long nose and long, soft, and pendulous ears. Its coat is smooth, fine, and glossy, and usually is black, white, or tan. Weight ranges from 25 to 45 pounds (11 to 20 kg). Various types of basset hounds can be distinguished by the differences in head and eye shape and size.

The basset hound, which probably originated in France, is a docile and loyal hunting dog. A steady and accurate trailer with a well-developed scenting ability, it is used for hunting foxes, rabbits, and pheasants. It also is popular as a pet. See also Dog.

BASSETERRE, bas-târ′, in the West Indies, is the capital of St. Kitts (St. Christopher) Island and the chief town of the British Colony of St. Kitts-Nevis-Anguilla in the Leeward Islands. It is about 375 miles (603 km) east of Puerto Rico. Basseterre is a seaport on the southwest coast of St. Kitts at the edge of the Basseterre valley, which raises sugar, Sea Island cotton, and tobacco. Population: 15,579.

BASSETT, bas′et, **John Spencer** (1867–1928), American historian and editor. He was born in Tarboro, N.C., on Sept. 10, 1867. He graduated in 1888 from Trinity College (now Duke University), where he taught before completing requirements at Johns Hopkins for his Ph.D. in 1894. He returned to Trinity as a professor and established himself as one of the South's ablest historians. He encouraged the collection of materials on Southern history and edited the *South Atlantic Quarterly.* In 1906 he accepted an appointment at Smith College.

Bassett's distinction as a historian of the South rests on numerous publications, including an edition of *The Writings of Colonel William Byrd of Westover in Virginia* (1901). He won a national reputation with his volume *The Federalist System 1789–1801* (1906) in the American Nation Series. He then prepared the *Life of Andrew Jackson* (2 vols., 1911). This scholarly biography was followed by the 6-volume *Correspondence of Andrew Jackson* (1926–35). He died at Washington, D.C., on Jan. 27, 1928.

MICHAEL KRAUS, *The City College, New York*

BASSETT, bas′et, **Richard** (1745–1815), American public official and signer of the Constitution. He was born in Cecil County, Md., on April 2, 1745. Though by birth a Marylander, Bassett spent most of his life in Delaware. During the Revolution he was captain of a troop of Dover light horse. In the decade 1776–1786 he served in both branches of the Delaware legislature and was a member of the state constitutional convention. He was a delegate to the federal Constitutional Convention, and played a leading part in securing Delaware's ratification of the Constitution.

Bassett was a U.S. senator for the term 1789–1793, and for the succeeding six years was chief justice of the state court of common pleas. He was governor of Delaware from 1799 to 1801, when President Adams appointed him a judge of the U.S. circuit court. Bassett was a public servant of superior capacity and efficiency. An ardent Methodist, he was a lifelong friend of Francis Asbury, first bishop of the Methodist Episcopal Church in the United States. He died at Bohemia Manor, Md., on Sept. 15, 1815.

BASSOMPIERRE, bå-sôn-pyâr′, **François de** (1579–1646), French military leader, who was involved in court intrigues in the early 17th century. A nobleman, he was born at the Château d'Haroué in Lorraine on April 12, 1579. Bassompierre fought in various campaigns for King Henry IV. He was named a marshal of France in recognition of valorous service rendered during the Huguenot revolt of 1621–1622. In 1628 he fought for the king at the siege of La Rochelle. Soon thereafter he was entrusted with various diplomatic missions, none especially successful.

Bassompierre was involved in the unsuccess-ful plot of 1630 to overthrow Richelieu. He was imprisoned in the Bastille from 1631 until Richelieu's death in 1643. Bassompierre died at Provins on Oct. 12, 1646. His *Mémoires* are a valuable source for the history of his time.

BRYCE LYON, *Brown University*

BASSOON, bə-sōon, a wind instrument in the double-reed or oboe family that is prominent in the modern orchestra as the chief bass woodwind. It is also called *fagott.* When played fast and staccato, the bassoon can produce comical sounds, and it is sometimes referred to as the clown of the orchestra. Beethoven used it in his Sixth (*Pastoral*) Symphony to depict the gyrations of a drunken village musician.

Bassoon

The earliest type of bassoon, a connected pair of tubes bored in a single wooden shaft, was developed in Italy in the 16th century. It quickly gained popularity, and in the 17th century it became one of the first woodwinds to be included in the orchestra. It evolved into its present form in France between 1750 and 1850.

The modern bassoon is formed of an eight-foot conical tube, doubled on itself, with a curved mouthpiece projecting at a right angle. The instrument has 22 regular keys and additional trill keys, and a range of over three octaves, from the third B flat below middle C to the second E flat above middle C. A variation of the bassoon is the larger double bassoon or contrabassoon, which is pitched about an octave lower.

BASSWOOD, bas′wood, is the name of several related trees found in the temperate regions of the Northern Hemisphere as far south as Mexico in North America and as far south as central China in Asia. They are also known as *lindens.* These ornamental trees are grown for their beau-

U.S. FOREST SERVICE

American basswood (*tilia americana*). Inset at right shows detail of the flower.

JOHN J. SMITH

tiful foliage and fragrant flowers. The leaves are heart-shaped and sharp-toothed. The small whitish flowers, which grow in drooping clusters, are fragrant and yield nectar. The fruit of the basswood is spherical, dry, and woody. The wood, soft and light-colored, is often used for the interior of houses and for wood carving. The tough inner bark of the tree is used in mats and cords.

The basswood belongs to the genus *Tilia*, which contains about 25 species and many hybrids. *T. americana, T. neglecta,* and *T. heterophylla* are three common species found in the United States. The white or silver linden (*T. tomentosa*), a species poisonous to bees, is found in eastern Europe and Asia Minor.

BAST, båst, in Egyptian mythology, was a goddess of life and fruitfulness. Represented with the head of a cat or lioness, she held a high place in the city of Bubastis, similar to that held by Neit in Saïs. In ancient times, nearly a million Egyptians made pilgrimages to her shrine each year. She is often depicted with a sistrum in one hand, a shield in the other, and with a basket over one arm. When shown with a cat's head the goddess was usually given the name *Pasht.*

BAST, bast, is the fibers of the thin layer of tissue outside the cambium, or formative, layer of most plants. Also known as *bass,* it popularly refers to the inner bark of some shrubs and trees. In technical botanical literature, the term *bast* largely has been discarded because it lacks accurate meaning. It has been replaced by such terms as *phloem, pericycle,* and *cortex.*

Bast varies in form, length, density, stiffness, and strength. Some fibers, like flax, are soft and flexible; others, like hemp, are strong. Bast is used as cloth in China and Polynesia; in ancient times it was used as writing paper.

BASTARD, bas'tərd, an illegitimate child; that is, a person begotten and born out of wedlock. A child conceived before marriage and born in wedlock is legitimate, as is a child conceived during marriage but born after divorce, death, or other termination of the relationship. A child conceived and born while the mother is lawfully married is a bastard if the mother's husband is not the father. Under the early common law of England it was virtually impossible, except in rare instances of the husband's absence "beyond the four seas," to establish the illegitimacy of a child born to a married woman. Although this rule has been modified in all jurisdictions, the law still strongly favors legitimacy. Under modern law, the presumption of legitimacy can be rebutted by a showing of the husband's impotency, his absence during all the time when conception could possibly have occurred, or his presence only under circumstances clearly precluding sexual intercourse.

Contrary to the early common law of England, modern statutes provide that under some circumstances the status of a bastard may be changed to that of a lawfully born child by a process known as "legitimation." In many states a child born of a legally void marriage may thus be made legitimate. Similarly, many statutes provide for the legitimation of bastards by the subsequent marriage of their parents or by the acknowledgement of the father. Legitimation generally gives the child the same legal rights and duties as a child born in lawful wedlock.

Unless otherwise provided by statute, the right to the custody of a bastard belongs to the mother, and she likewise is responsible for its care and support. The father's right to care and custody of the child, although subordinate to the mother's, is superior to that of other persons, such as relatives of the mother. The rights of the mother or father may be forfeited by abandonment of the child or by other improper conduct. Where the custody of an illegitimate child is disputed, the question may be presented for the decision of a court, which will give primary regard to the benefit and welfare of the child rather than to the rights of the claimants in making its determination. Such factors as the moral fitness and financial ability of the claimant as well as the preference of the child itself are weighed by the court.

Although the father has no duty in common law to support a bastard, such an obligation may be imposed by statute or assumed voluntarily through legitimation, adoption, or contract. Most jurisdictions now have statutes providing for judicial proceedings to compel the father of an illegitimate child to contribute to its support, such "filiation" or "bastardy" proceedings usually being initiated by complaint of the mother. Most states consider a bastardy action as being civil in nature, since its object is to establish paternity and to secure the maintenance and support of the child; but in a minority of jurisdictions the suit is deemed criminal because the statute also provides a punishment for the father. The amount of a judgment awarded in bastardy proceedings is largely within the discretion of the court, which takes into account the financial situation of the defendant and the needs of the child measured in relation to the social and financial status of the parties.

Under early common law a bastard could not inherit, was not entitled to a name, and could have no heirs except direct descendants. These legal disabilities have been substantially removed by statute. In most states illegitimate children now have at least a limited right to inherit property as well as to receive gifts made by will or during the lifetime of the donor.

RICHARD L. HIRSHBERG, *Attorney at Law*

BASTIA, bäs-tē'ä, is the chief city of the French island of Corsica. It is located on Corsica's northeastern coast, about 65 miles (105 km) northeast of the capital, Ajaccio. Farther northeast, about 80 miles (129 km) across the Tyrrhenian Sea, is the Italian port of Leghorn (Livorno).

Bastia is the most populous city and the commercial center of Corsica. It exports wine, citrus fruit, olive oil, liqueurs, and cork, and manufactures cigarettes, cutlery, and briar pipes. There are anchovy and coral fisheries. The city, which extends along the sea and climbs the surrounding hills, reveals strong Italian influences. The older, more picturesque sections are in the southern part of the city around the old harbor, which is dominated by a 16th–17th century citadel. It replaced a 14th century Genoese bastion whose walls and massive tower still stand. The modern city and port are to the north.

Bastia was a small fishing village in 1380 when the Genoese started the construction of fortifications on the hill to the south. Its name is derived from *bastiglia,* the Italian word for bastion. It became the seat of the Genoese governors and eventually acquired commercial and political importance, reaching the height of its prosperity in the 1600's. In 1764 the French general Marbeuf conquered the island, which has since remained in French hands. Population: (1962) 49,929.

BASTIAN, bäs'tē-än, **Adolf** (1826–1905), German anthropologist, who was a founder of modern enthnology. A worldwide traveler, tireless researcher, and prolific writer, he advanced the theory that all peoples, regardless of their culture, have the same psychic disposition. According to this theory, the cultural traits, beliefs, folklore, and myths of different ethnic groups are essentially alike; they differ only in form, a function of geographical environment.

Bastian was born in Bremen, Germany, on June 26, 1826. After taking a medical degree at the University of Prague (1850), he spent several years traveling around the world as a ship's doctor and collecting data in support of his theory of psychic unity. He was professor of ethnology and head of the ethnological museum at the University of Berlin. He was also a founder and editor of the *Journal of Ethnology* of the Berlin Anthropological Society. He died in Port of Spain, Trinidad, on Feb. 3, 1905.

BASTIAT, bás-tyá', **Frédéric** (1801–1850), French economist and social philosopher, who advocated free trade and attacked socialism. He was born at Mugron, France, on June 29, 1801. After working in an uncle's countinghouse in Bayonne, he engaged in farming and served as a justice of the peace. Bastiat first gained wide recognition in 1844 with the publication of an article opposing protectionism. For the next six years, until his death, he wrote vigorously on controversial economic issues and became a world figure as an economist. His works included the series *Economic Sophisms* and the pamphlet *Petition of the Left Hand Against the Right.*

Bastiat helped create the first French freetrade association, in Bordeaux in 1846. He served as a deputy in the Constituent Assembly and the Legislative Assembly in the revolutionary years of 1848 and 1849 and issued pamphlets against socialism during that time. In 1850 he published *Harmonies of Political Economy,* based on the premise that economic interests, if left alone, would tend to work for the common good. He died in Rome on Dec. 24, 1850.

BASTIEN-LEPAGE, bás-tyaɴ' lə-pàzh', **Jules** (1848–1884), French painter, whose outdoor scenes were widely imitated by French and English artists of his times. He was born in Damvillers on Nov. 1, 1848. In 1867 he moved to Paris, where he studied at the École des Beaux-Arts under Alexandre Cabanel. He early attracted notice with his impressionist paintings, beginning with *Spring Song,* which was exhibited in 1874. He died in Paris on Dec. 10, 1884.

Bastien-Lepage's most important works include *The Haymakers* (1878) and *Joan of Arc Listening to the Voices* (1880), both of which helped to establish his reputation as an "open-air" painter. He was also noted for his portraits, especially those of Sarah Bernhardt (1879) and the Prince of Wales (1880).

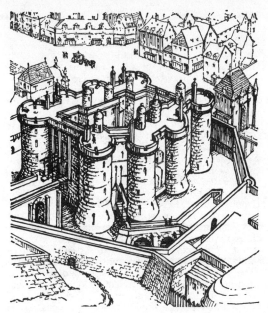

THE BASTILLE, symbol of the French monarch's arbitrary power, was seized by a Paris mob on July 14, 1789.

BASTILLE, ba-stēl', was a state prison and citadel in the eastern part of Paris. It was originally built to protect the palace of King Charles V during the Hundred Years' War with England. The capture of the Bastille on July 14, 1789, marked the shift in France from a parliamentary revolution to a popular revolution. The word "bastille," not capitalized, means any armory or fortified building, usually at the entrance to a city.

The Bastille was begun under the direction of Hugues Aubriot in 1370. Built as a giant rectangle, the building was composed of eight large towers about 75 feet (23 meters) high, connected by walls of the same height. The fortress was further protected by a wide moat. Until the middle of the 17th century, the Bastille was used for military purposes. In 1652, during the Fronde (q.v.), the duchess de Montpensier, called *La Grande Mademoiselle,* used the cannon of the Bastille to cover the retreat of the prince de Condé from Paris.

Beginning with the ministry of Cardinal Richelieu in the 1620's, the fortress was also used as a state prison. Many were held prisoner there without trial for indefinite periods by *lettres de cachet,* which were legal orders signed by the king and countersigned by a government minister. Through rumor and the writings of pamphleteers, the public came to think of the Bastille as a prison whose dungeons were packed with state prisoners. Alexandre Dumas' *The Man in the Iron Mask* is a popular story of imprisonment in the Bastille.

In time the Bastille was also used to detain people whose liberty was embarrassing to their noble families or to important government officials. In 1784 the use of the *lettres de cachet* was curtailed, and the demolition of the outmoded citadel was proposed. For the next few years the lettres were used only for serious offenses, and imprisonment was limited to two or three years. Among the famous prisoners held in the Bastille was the writer Voltaire.

Although the number of prisoners in the Bastille declined after 1784, it continued to be associated with tyrannical rule. On July 14, 1789, during the turmoil of the early days of the French Revolution, a mob formed around the Bastille and asked the commander of the small garrison in the fortress, the marquis De Launay, to surrender arms and munitions. When he refused, the mob proceeded from the outer court to the inner court. Although the crowd had no weapons with which to storm the towers, the panic-stricken guards opened fire, killing many.

When army officers in the crowd brought some small cannon to the Bastille, De Launay capitulated, after being promised safety for himself and his men. As the garrison emerged from the Bastille, several of its members, including De Launay, were seized by the excited rioters and murdered. Only seven prisoners were found in the dungeons when the Bastille was captured. Destruction of the fortress began immediately and was completed within a few months. The key to the Bastille was presented by the marquis de Lafayette to George Washington and is still at Mount Vernon. The Place de la Bastille covers part of the former location of the prison. A column in the middle of the square, the July Column, commemorates those killed in the July Revolution of 1830.

The actual fall of the Bastille was not an important military event in the Revolution. Its significance lay in the symbolic value that the capture came to have. To many, the fall of the Bastille indicated that the king had lost control of Paris. The day was soon saluted as marking the triumph of popular insurrection over the arbitrary power of the crown. In 1880, July 14th, also known as Bastille Day, was chosen as the French national holiday.

BASTOGNE, bȧ-stôn′yȧ, is a town in Belgium, in the province of Luxembourg, about 45 miles (72 km) south of Liège. It is located on the Wiltz River, in the Forest of Ardennes. Bastogne is a rail and road junction and the market town for a farming region. Population: (1961) 6,161.

In World War II, Bastogne was the site of a key engagement during the Battle of the Bulge (1944–1945). The Germans, who had surrounded the town, called upon the American defenders to surrender. The U.S. commander, Brig. Gen. Anthony C. McAuliffe replied, "Nuts!" Later the town was relieved by American armored forces. See WORLD WAR II—5. *Recovery of France and Advance into Germany.*

BASTROP, bas′trȧp, is an industrial town in northeastern Louisiana, 165 miles (26.5 km) north of Baton Rouge. It is the seat of Morehouse Parish (county). It has abundant deposits of natural gas, and its industries include the production of kraft and other papers, turned wood products, lumber, printing inks, varnish, carbon, and other chemical products. Agriculture in the surrounding region is devoted to truck farming and raising cotton, peaches, rice, and cattle. The town is served by a municipal airport. Chemin-à-Haut State Park is nearby.

Bastrop was founded about 1845 and its population increased after the discovery of natural gas in the area in 1916. Government is by mayor and council. Population: 14,713.

BASUTOLAND, bȧ-sōōt′ō-land, was a British territory in southern Africa. It achieved independence in 1966. See LESOTHO.

BAT, any of a group of small flying mammals. They are found in the temperate and tropical regions of both hemispheres and are the only mammals that fly.

Bats range in length from ¾ inch to 15 inches (1.9 cm to 37.5 cm) and have a wing spread of up to five feet (1.5 meters). They have fur that may be white, red, brown, gray, or black. Bats usually live in caves, crevices, buildings, or tree cavities. During the colder weather, some species either hibernate or migrate.

Anatomy. The wings of bats are their most characteristic structures. They are formed by an extension of the skin of the back and belly. The two layers of skin are stretched between the elongated bones of the arms and hand and extend along the side of the body to the lower legs and then, in most forms, from the tip of a cartilaginous spur on the foot to the tail. There is no flesh between the membranes of the wings but only connective tissue containing the blood vessels and nerve fibers.

The forelimbs of bats have the same number of bones as those of other mammals, but they are greatly elongated, especially the bones of the fingers. The thumb digit is comparatively small and lies at right angles to the other finger bones. It is equipped with a claw and is used in clinging to support.

The legs are small in relation to the forelimbs and are rotated outward so that the knees bend backward. This leg position is thought to be related to the method by which bats hang by their hind legs when not flying. The toes are equipped with sharp, curved claws. In flying, the arms and legs move in unison.

The tail in many bats has no membranes. It is variable in length, but never prehensile or bushy. A number of species have no tail. The remainder of the bat skeleton is modified for flight by being rigid and lightweight.

Sensory Apparatus. Many bats have grotesquely shaped leafy membranous appendages hanging from nostrils and ears. Although not present in the larger, fruit-eating bats, these appendages, or nose leaves, are common in small, insect-eating, nocturnal bats. There is also a small lobe, called the tragus, at the base of each ear opening.

The tragus and the nose leaves are believed to be the sensory apparatus of the bat, used for orientation in the dark. The process is called echolocation and is based on a sonar principle. The bat emits supersonic sounds through its nose or mouth. The sounds are reflected as echoes from nearby objects and are picked up by the sensitive sensory apparatus. Thus the bat can ascertain the position, for example, of the walls and stalactites in a cave or the position of furniture in a dark room, and avoid those objects. (In addition to their supersonic voices, bats also have voices for expressing emotion and communicating.)

All bats can see, but in most species the eyes are small, concealed by fur, and useless in the dark. Some bats, notably members of the flying fox family, have large prominent eyes that readily reflect light at night.

Reproduction. Bats generally have one young per year. Only the red and hoary bats have two, three, or even four young at a time. In nonhibernating bats, breeding and ovulation are in the spring. In hibernating forms, breeding is in the fall, and the sperm are retained in the female tract until spring, when ovulation occurs.

Types of Bats. Bats belong to the order Chirop-

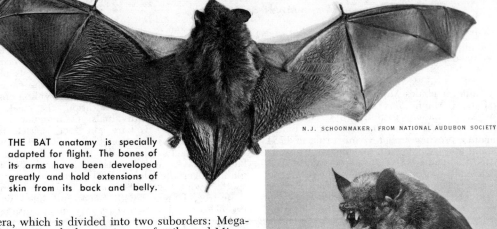

THE BAT anatomy is specially adapted for flight. The bones of its arms have been developed greatly and hold extensions of skin from its back and belly.

tera, which is divided into two suborders: Megachiroptera, which contains one family, and Microchiroptera, which contains 16 families. There are 178 genera.

The Megachiroptera are the fruit-eating bats found in the Old World tropics. Their large size (wingspread about five feet, or 1.5 meters), reddish fur, and foxlike heads have given them the name of flying foxes. Their chief distinguishing feature is that their molar teeth have no cusps but instead are marked with a longitudinal furrow. These bats spend the day in large groups, or "camps," suspended from the branches of large trees or in caverns.

The Microchiropetera generally are smaller than the Megachiroptera and have molar teeth with sharp cusps adapted to cutting and crushing insects, their main source of food. This group includes all the ordinary bats found in North America and Europe.

Among the most striking and widespread of the North American bats is the hoary bat (*Lasiurus cinerea*) of the northeastern United States. About 5½ inches (13¾ cm) long, it has silvery frosting on its yellowish-to-mahogany brown hair. It is found in wooded regions and migrates to the south for winter. The red bat (*Lasiurus borealis*), about 4½ inches (11¼ cm) long, is common in the Allegheny mountain region. Brick red to rusty red in color, it spends the day hanging from a bush or small tree. It also migrates southward.

The "common" bat, a small brown bat often seen around homes and gardens, belongs either to the genus *Eptesicus* or to the genus *Myotis*. *Eptesicus* remains in the same area all year and hibernates in hollow trees, caves, or buildings during the cold weather. It emerges at night in warm weather to seek its insect prey in farmyards and gardens.

Other types of bats feed on the pollen and nectar of flowers. Their long, pointed heads and long tongues are adapted to this method of feeding. They are found in the tropics and semitropics. Still others are carnivorous and feed on small mammals, birds, lizards, frogs, and fish.

The South American vampire bats (*Desmodus*) feed exclusively on blood from small wounds that they make in other animals by a single bite. Their large canine and upper incisor teeth are razor-sharp and modified for this purpose, and their esophagus is so narrow that it will admit only liquid food. They have a wingspan of about 8 inches (20 cm) and normally hide in caves. The vampire bats often are confused, through exaggerated descriptions, with the much larger flying foxes, which are not blood-eating forms. Vampire bats often carry disease-causing viruses, especially those causing rabies,

Common brown bat (*Eptesicus*)

and transmit them when they bite their victims.

See also Acoustics; Flying Fox; Leaf-Nosed Bat; Vampire Bat.

GEORGE H.H. TATE
American Museum of Natural History

Bibliography

Allen, Glover M., *Bats* (Cambridge, Mass., 1939).
Griffin, Donald R., *Listening in the Dark: The Acoustic Orientation of Bats and Men* (New Haven 1958).
Griffin, Donald R., *Echoes of Bats and Men* (New York 1959).
Peterson, Russell F., *Silently, By Night* (New York 1964).
Ripper, Charles L., *Bats* (New York 1954).
Walker, Ernest P., *Mammals of the World* vol. 1, pp. 182–392 (Baltimore 1964).

Fruit bats (*Pteropus giganteus*)

BATAAN, bə-tän', is a province and peninsula in the Philippine Islands, on the island of Luzon. The peninsula is 30 miles long and 15 miles wide (48 by 24 km) and has an area of 517 square miles (1,339 sq km). It is traversed by the volcanic Zambales Mountains, and marks the separation of Manila Bay from the China Sea. Northwest of Bataan is Subic Bay, and west, across Manila Bay, is the city of Manila. Bataan was made a province under Spanish rule in 1754. Its capital and chief town is Balanga.

After the United States entered World War II, Bataan Peninsula was the scene of bitter fighting between American-Filipino forces under Gen. Douglas MacArthur (later under Maj. Gen. Jonathan M. Wainwright) and the invading Japanese. On April 9, 1942, Bataan's defenders surrendered, but a small force remained on Corregidor, an island off the south tip of the peninsula, and continued to fight until May 6.

About 37,000 U.S. and Filipino soldiers were captured on Bataan. Thousands of them died during a 70-mile "death march" from Mariveles, at the tip of the peninsula, to a concentration camp at San Fernando. Bataan was retaken by U.S. forces under General MacArthur in February 1945. The battlefields of Bataan and Corregidor are national shrines. Population: (1960) 145,323. See also CORREGIDOR.

BATAILLE, bà-tä'yə, **Félix Henry** (1872–1922), French playwright. He was born in Nîmes on April 4, 1872. He entered the École des Beaux-Arts to study painting in 1890, but soon turned to writing. His first play, *La belle au bois dormant* (1894), lacked maturity of style, but his next effort, a volume of verse entitled *La chambre blanche* (1895), showed considerable talent. After the success of his second play, *La lépreuse*, in 1896, Bataille became a playwright exclusively. He died in Rueil, near Paris, on March 2, 1922.

In his earlier plays, Bataille, who was essentially a romantic, tended to disregard the social problems that were the concern of most contemporary playwrights and wrote about the effect of sexual passion on men's lives. His more popular plays on this subject include *Maman Colibri* (1904), *La marche nuptiale* (1905), *La femme nue* (1908), *Le scandale* (1909), and *La vierge folle* (1910). Bataille's later plays, which mark his evolution toward a theater of ideas, include *L'amazone* (1916), *L'animateur* (1920), and *La chair humaine* (1922). A collection of his complete works for the theater was published in seven volumes (1922–27).

BATAK, bä'täk, a Malay people living in north-central Sumatra in Indonesia. Thought to be indigenous to the island, they were probably forced inland to the mountainous Lake Toba region by invaders from the Malay Peninsula. The Batak, numbering about 1,500,000, are divided into five tribes—the Toba, Mandailing, Karo, Pakpak, and Timur. An agricultural people, they cultivate rice on hillside terraces. Many dwell in large tribal houses where members of an entire clan live together. Their wooden houses are ornamented with carvings, often of a bull's head to ward off evil spirits. Their language includes many Sanskrit terms. Formerly cannibalist and animistic, many were converted to Christianity or Islam in the late 19th and early 20th centuries.

BATALEUR, ba-tə-lûr', a small, long-winged, voluminously crested African eagle, also called *bateleur*. Its scientific name, *Terathopius ecaudatus*, refers to the unusual shortness of its tail. It has the handsomest plumage of all the eagles, presenting bold contrasts of black, white, gray, and bronzy brown. In addition, the back is maroon in some individuals, cream-colored in others. The face is bare; the feet, scarlet; the bill, yellow; and the tip of the bill and claws, black. It feeds on carrion and small animals, largely snakes and lizards, which it hunts by gliding over the plains. It lays one almost unspotted white egg. Its small, untidy nest, high in a tree, is made with twigs and lined with green leaves. For two years the young are mostly brown in color.

BATALHA, bə-tä'lyə, is a commune in Leiria district, Portugal. It is on the Lena River, 6 miles (10 km) south of the city of Leiria. Batalha is known chiefly for a Dominican monastery and for the church of Santa Maria da Vitória. These structures, outstanding examples of Spanish Gothic architecture, are now a national museum.

The monastery, the church, and an octagonal chapel were begun in 1388 by King John I of Portugal to fulfill a vow he made before his victory in 1385 over King John I of Castile. The original architect of the buildings was Afonso Domingues. Additions were made up to 1438. The church contains the tombs of John I, of several later kings of the house of Aviz, and of Prince Henry the Navigator. Population: (1960) 7,053.

BATAN ISLANDS, bä-tän', an island group in the Philippines, comprising Batanes province. The archipelago, covering an area of 76 square miles (197 sq km), consists of three principal islands —Itbayat, Batan, Sabtang—and 11 islets. Situated in Luzon Strait about 190 miles (306 km) north of Luzon, the island group constitutes the smallest and northernmost province of the Philippines. Formerly known as the Bashi Islands, it is separated from Formosa, to the north, by Bashi Channel, and from the Babuyan Islands, to the south, by Balintang Channel. Basco, located on the northwestern coast of Batan Island, is the largest town of the group (population, 804) and the capital of the province. Batan, the most important island, covers an area of 27 square miles (70 sq km) and is the site of an extinct volcano. The largest island of the group is Itbayat, with an area of 33 square miles (85 sq km). Rice and corn are grown on the islands, and coal is mined. Population: (1960) 10,309.

BATANGAS, bə-tang'gas, a municipality in the Philippines, is an important seaport and the capital of Batangas province. Located in southwestern Luzon opposite the island of Mindoro, it is near the mouth of the Calumpan River on the northeast coast of Batangas Bay. The city is about 58 miles (93 km) south of Manila, with which it is connected by good roads and coastal shipping. Batangas, lying in a fertile agricultural area, is a trade center and port for sugarcane, corn, and coconuts. During World War II, Japanese troops occupied the city on Dec. 24, 1941, and Allied troops landed there in early 1945. Population: (1960) city, 14,182; municipality, 82,627.

BATAVI, bə-tā′vī, an ancient Germanic people who inhabited part of the present-day Netherlands, particularly an area formed by a branch of the Rhine that empties into the sea near Leiden and by the estuaries of the Waal and the Meuse (Maas) rivers. Their territories at times extended much beyond this area.

Their bravery was commended by the Roman historian Tacitus. About 15 B.C., when the Roman general Germanicus was about to invade Germany from the sea, he made their shores the rendezvous of his fleet. Subjected to the Romans, they served them with such courage and fidelity that they were given the title of friends and brethren of Rome. They were exempted from Roman tributes and taxes and were permitted to choose their leaders from their own people. Their cavalry was particularly excellent.

During the reign of Vespasian, the Batavi revolted in 69–70 A.D. under the command of Civilis and extorted favorable terms of peace from the Romans. They were brought under Roman rule again by the emperors Trajan and Hadrian in the 2d century. At the end of the 3d century the Salian Franks took their lands and the Batavi were gradually assimilated.

BATAVIA, bə-tā′vē-ə, is an industrial city in northeastern Illinois. It is situated in Kane County, on the Fox River, 35 miles (56 km) west of Chicago. There are iron and brass foundries, and farm machinery, electric switches, television tubes, and pharmaceuticals are manufactured. Limestone deposits are nearby.

Settled in 1833, Batavia was incorporated as a city in 1891. Government is by mayor and council. Population: 8,994.

BATAVIA, bə-tā′vē-ə, a city in New York, is the seat of Genesee County. It is situated 33 miles (53 km) southwest of Rochester and 36 miles (57 km) northeast of Buffalo. Its diversified industries include the manufacture of television sets, transformers, heavy and light machinery, machine parts, mobile homes, fiberglass boats, women's shoes, men's shirts, processed foods, candy, and champagne. Among its educational institutions is a state school for the blind. There is also a Veterans Administration facility. The Batavia Downs racetrack has harness racing.

Batavia was the center of the Holland Land Purchase, the large western New York tract acquired in 1793–1797 by Dutch capitalists. The town was laid out in 1801 and named after the Batavian Republic, as the Netherlands was then called. The Holland Purchase Historical Society now occupies the office built in 1815 by Joseph Ellicot, surveyor and agent for the Holland Land Company. Another interesting old building is the Genesee County Courthouse, built of limestone in 1841 in the Greek Revival style. William Morgan, noted opponent of the Masonic Fraternity, was a resident of Batavia until his mysterious disappearance in 1826.

Batavia was incorporated in 1826 and became a city in 1914. In 1958, city-manager government was instituted. Population: 17,338.

BATAVIAN REPUBLIC, bə-tā′vē-ən, a republic formed in the Netherlands on May 16, 1795. It existed until the establishment of the kingdom of Holland under Louis Bonaparte on June 8, 1806. Officially independent, the Batavian Republic actually functioned under the aegis of a French army of 25,000, which had invaded the country in 1795 and occupied Amsterdam. In the absence of Prince William V of Orange, who had fled to England, the opposition party of the Patriots established the republic, which was acknowledged by the powers of Europe for the next 10 years. It was named for *Batavia,* an ancient land bordering the North Sea near the mouth of the Rhine, inhabited by the Batavi, a Germanic people.

The National Assembly of the republic was established in The Hague. Sweeping reforms were effected, including abolition of the nobility's privileges, nationalization of the affluent East India Company, and adoption of a constitution modeled after the French. Napoleon Bonaparte, however, rang the republic's death knell in 1805 when he appointed a head of state and grand pensionary, in preparation for his brother Louis' enthronement the next year.

BATES, bāts, **Barnabas** (1775–1853), American clergyman and postal official, who promoted the introduction of cheap postage in the United States. He was born in Edmonton, England, but was brought to the United States as a child. He became a Baptist preacher in Rhode Island and was, for a time, port collector of Bristol.

During Andrew Jackson's administration he was assistant postmaster under Samuel Gouveneur, postmaster of New York, and at one period acted as postmaster. Influenced by Sir Roland Hill's pamphlet on penny postage (1837) and Hill's invention of the adhesive postage stamp, Bates investigated the subject of cheap postage for years. He wrote, published pamphlets, and lectured throughout the United States, finally helping to win a material reduction in the rates of land postage. He was working to obtain a corresponding reform in ocean postage at the time of his death in Boston, Mass., on Oct. 11, 1853.

BATES, bāts, **Edward** (1793–1869), American lawyer and political leader, who served as attorney general in President Lincoln's first cabinet. Bates was born in Goochland County, Va., on Sept. 4, 1793, the youngest of 12 children of an influential Virginia farmer. He completed his formal education at Charlotte Hall Academy in St. Mary's County, Md. After brief service in a Virginia militia unit during the War of 1812, he moved to the Missouri Territory. He read law in an office at St. Louis and in 1816 began a successful practice there.

In 1826, Bates was elected to the U.S. Congress as a Whig. He was defeated by a Democrat after one term and never again served in elective office outside Missouri. His reputation as a border-state moderate, however, recommended him in the 1850's to politicians seeking a compromise between North and South. After 1856, Bates gravitated to the Republican party, whose national convention of 1860 gave him 48 first-ballot votes for the presidential nomination.

Following Lincoln's nomination and election, Bates was appointed attorney general. His appointment was intended in part to win Southern support for the new administration. During the Civil War he became increasingly critical of the government's policies. His influence rapidly waned, and he retired in November 1864.

Bates, who married in 1823, had 17 children. He died at St. Louis on March 25, 1869.

BATES, bāts, Katharine Lee (1859–1929), American author, editor, and educator, who wrote the words of the well-known patriotic hymn *America the Beautiful*. She was born in Falmouth, Mass., on Aug. 12, 1859. In 1880 she graduated from Wellesley College where she subsequently taught English. She died in Wellesley, Mass., on March 28, 1929.

Miss Bates wrote several volumes of poetry, including *America the Beautiful* (1911), and *The Pilgrim Ship* (1926). She also wrote travel books (*Spanish Highways and Byways*, 1900, and *From Gretna Green to Land's End*, 1907) and scholarly studies (*The English Religious Drama*, 1893, and *History of American Literature*, 1898).

BATES, bāts, Sanford (1884–1972), American penologist. He was born in Boston, Mass., on July 17, 1884. As commissioner of the Massachusetts Department of Correction from 1919 to 1929, he revised the state's parole system and initiated prison industries and university extension courses for prisoners. In 1930, and again from 1933 to 1937, he directed the U.S. Bureau of Prisons. He was parole commissioner of New York (1940–1945) and commissioner of institutions and agencies in New Jersey (1945–1954). Bates also served as a delegate to international conferences on penology. His *Prison and Beyond* (1936) stresses the need for rehabilitation. He died in Trenton, N.J., on Sept. 8, 1972.

BATES COLLEGE is a small, private, coeducational, nonsectarian liberal arts college in Lewiston, Me. It was established in 1855 by Free Will Baptists as Maine State Seminary, a secondary school. The charter was amended to provide collegiate status in 1862, and a second charter revision in 1864 gave full collegiate accreditation and changed the name to Bates College. It was the first New England college to admit women students.

Bates offers a full liberal arts curriculum. A core program, called the Bates Plan, requires all students to take a 47-semester-hour group of courses covering social and natural sciences, philosophy and religion, English composition and literature, psychology, and a sequence called "cultural heritage." The college also offers a five-year cooperative engineering program with Rensselaer Polytechnic Institute, New York University, and Massachusetts Institute of Technology; a junior year abroad; and a citizenship laboratory. The Bates debating teams have participated in international competition since 1921. The library has a special collection on the Free Will Baptists.

CHARLES FRANKLIN PHILLIPS
Bates College

BATESON, bāt'sən, William (1861–1926), English biologist, who is often called the "father of genetics." While still a student, Bateson recognized that the wormlike creature, *Balanoglossus*, then classified as an echinoderm, possessed a primitive notochord and was actually a chordate. This was the first clue that chordates (including man and other vertebrates) had evolved from a primitive kind of echinoderm.

Bateson was an enthusiastic supporter of Mendel's findings and did much to spread the ideas of the new science of "genetics" (a name he coined). Through his experiments, however, Bateson discovered that Mendel's laws of segregation and random assortment do not always hold. He found that some genes remain linked in parental combinations as they are passed to offspring. He also found that one gene may influence the action or manifestation of another gene. Bateson also studied the hereditary nature of such diseases as hemophilia, albinism, and color blindness. He coined several technical terms, including "homozygote" and "heterozygote," now in standard use in genetics.

Bateson was born in Whitby, England, on Aug. 8, 1861. He studied zoology at St. John's, Cambridge, and began his experimental work there. He was elected to a chair of biology at Cambridge University in 1908 and was appointed director of the John Innes Horticultural Institution at Merton Park, Surrey, England, in 1910. He died in Merton, England, on Feb. 8, 1926. Bateson's writings include *Mendel's Principles of Heredity—a Defence* (1902).

BATESVILLE, bāts'vil, an industrial and commercial city in northern Arkansas, is the seat of Independence County. It is situated on the White River, 100 miles (160 km) northeast of Little Rock. Rich deposits of marble are located near the city, and quarrying is the leading industry. Marble, lime, grain, cotton, livestock, and lumber are shipped. Batesville is the site of Arkansas College, founded in 1872, and of the University of Arkansas livestock and forestry experiment station. Government is by mayor and council. Population: 7,209.

BATFISH, bat'fish, is the common name for several related groups of fishes found in tropical waters, often at considerable depths. These fish, which seldom exceed 12 inches (30 cm) in length, are peculiarly shaped. They are flattened out from back to belly, and the pectoral fins extend at angles from either side of the head. The gill openings are small and are found behind the pectoral fins. With its specialized fins, the batfish can "walk" along the bottom of the sea, moving alternate pelvic and pectoral fins together. The batfish is also known to angle for prey. A short stem, usually hidden in the head of the fish, may be extended, affixed with bait, and used to lure prey.

The name "batfish" is applied to several related groups of the order Pediculati ("little feet"), family Ogcocephalidae.

BATH, 1st Earl of. See PULTENEY, WILLIAM.

BATES COLLEGE CHAPEL dominates the spacious campus. One of the men's dormitories is in the background.

MAINE DEPARTMENT OF ECONOMIC DEVELOPMENT

EWING GALLOWAY   BRITISH TRAVEL ASSOCIATION

BATH, England, has many interesting structures, such as the Roman bath (left) and the covered Pulteney Bridge.

BATH, bath, a city in England, is the only county borough in Somerset. It is famous for its hot springs and fine architecture. Bath is situated in a hilly curving valley of the Avon River, 100 miles (160 km) west of London. It has long been a fashionable health resort. Its three mineral springs yield 500,000 gallons (about 2 million liters) of water a day at a temperature of 120° F (49° C). The baths and drinking water have been found helpful in the treatment of rheumatism, arthritis, and gout.

According to legend, the waters of Bath healed the ailing son of a British king in the year 800 B.C. The Romans, soon after they invaded Britain in 43 A.D., recognized the unusual qualities of the springs. They named their settlement here *Aquae Sulis* ("Waters of Sul") after the Celtic sun goddess Sul, whom they associated with their deity Minerva. The baths they built are the finest Roman remains in Britain.

Bath became fashionable in the early 18th century when the celebrated Richard ("Beau") Nash became its social arbiter. Several of its handsome Georgian buildings—dating from the middle and later years of the century—were designed by John Wood, Sr., and John Wood, Jr. The father designed the buildings known as Queen Square and the Circus, and the son designed Royal Crescent and the Assembly Rooms. Among other beautiful buildings in Bath is the Abbey Church, a fine example of the Late Perpendicular Gothic style.

Visitors to Bath may see the homes of many famous residents of the city, including those of Admiral Nelson, William Pitt, Thomas Gainsborough, Jane Austen, and Charles Dickens. There have been many literary references to the city, beginning with Chaucer's *Wife of Bath*. Bath suffered severely from World War II air raids, but most of the old buildings have been restored. The Assembly Rooms now house the Museum of Costume that covers the history of 300 years. The Bath Festival, every June, offers music, drama, and sports. Population: 80,901.

BATH, bath, a city in Maine, is the seat of Sagadahoc County and is situated near the mouth of the Kennebec River and the Atlantic Ocean, 28 miles (45 km) northeast of Portland. Once a famous shipbuilding center, it is now a summer resort and has diversified light industries. Some are associated with shipbuilding, including the manufacture of windlasses, deck machinery,

and nautical lights. There are also a bottling works, a fish cannery, and a shirt factory.

The *Virginia,* said to be the first vessel built (1607) in America, came from the yards at nearby Popham. During the early 19th century many clipper ships were built in the Bath shipyards. After the Civil War the Bath Iron Works became famous for its square-rigged ships and other naval and commercial vessels. The battleship *Georgia* was built in these yards, as were some cruisers and lighthouse tenders. Among the better known yachts and sailboats built here were J.P. Morgan's yacht *Corsair* and the 1937 America's Cup winner *Ranger.* The Bath shipyards were active during both world wars.

The Davenport Memorial Building in Bath has many maritime exhibits, including old ship paintings and models of sailing vessels. The bell in its tower was cast in 1805 at the Paul Revere foundry. Bath was incorporated as a town in 1781, and as a city in 1847. It has a manager-council form of government. Population: 9,679.

BATH, bath, an industrial village in southern New York, is the seat of Steuben County. It is situated on the Cohocton River, 30 miles (48 km) northwest of Elmira. Bath is the center of the Steuben County potato industry. Manufactured products include ladders, bus bodies, and corrugated pipe. The Westinghouse Corporation has an electronics branch just outside the village. Bath is the site of a U.S. Veterans Administration hospital. Founded in 1793, Bath was incorporated in 1816. Government is by mayor and council. Population: 6,053.

BATH, Most Honourable Order of the. See DECORATIONS AND ORDERS—*Great Britain.*

BATHOLITH, bath'ə-lith, a large intrusive mass of igneous rock that has melted its way up across the enclosing rock beds. A batholith is irregular in shape. It extends downward to unknown depths and upward to some distance below the earth's surface.

Batholiths differ from *laccoliths* in being intruded across the beds, rather than between them. They are usually many miles in extent, and often form the cores of mountain ranges, as in the case of the Sierra Nevada of the western United States. Bodies of the same form, but smaller, are often called *stocks* or *bosses.* See also ROCKS—*Igneous Rocks.*

BÁTHORY, bä′tō-ri, a noble Hungarian family, originating in the 13th century. Five members of the family, whose name is also spelled *Báthori* and *Batory,* were princes of Transylvania, and one became a renowned king of Poland.

STEPHEN BÁTHORY (1533–1586) was prince of Transylvania and king of Poland. He spent his early years at the Habsburg court and later entered the army of the king of Hungary, John Sigismund Zápolyai. Stephen so distinguished himself in Hungary that he was elected Zápolyai's successor as prince of Transylvania in 1571.

Stephen became involved with Poland when the last of the Jagellon dynasty died in 1572 and Poland instituted an elective monarchy. After the first elected king, Henry of Valois, left Poland to become Henry III of France in 1574, a dispute arose over the election of a new king. Emperor Maximilian II was proposed by the Habsburg party and was elected by the Polish Senate in 1575. But the nobles wanted to avoid Habsburg domination and chose Stephen, who quickly accepted the offer and left his brother Christopher as prince of Transylvania. In accordance with one of the nobles' conditions, Stephen married Ann, sister of the last Jagellon, immediately following his coronation at Kraków early in 1576.

All of Poland was under Stephen's control within a few months, except for Danzig, which was not pacified until 1577. With the aid of his extremely capable prime minister, Jan Zamoyski, the new king then turned his attention to Russia, which had occupied Livonia, an area along the Baltic Sea. In a war lasting until 1582, Stephen defeated the forces of Ivan the Terrible several times and forced Ivan to agree to an unfavorable peace that gave Livonia and other areas to Poland and denied Russia access to the Baltic.

Confronted by two great powers, the Ottoman empire on the south and the Habsburgs on the west, Stephen allied Poland with the Ottoman Turks to escape domination by Austria. Although the alliance with the Muslims alarmed the papacy, Stephen was pro-Catholic. He allowed the Jesuits to bring the Counter Reformation to Poland, but he also insisted on toleration for the Protestants, in order to avoid religious wars. Stephen's alliance with the Muslims was strictly one of convenience, and he was planning a united Christian effort against them when he died at Grodno, Lithuania, on Dec. 12, 1586.

Stephen Báthory is remembered as one of Poland's greatest kings. Besides his wide-ranging foreign policy, he was active in internal reforms. He reorganized the military forces, providing the basis for the first regular standing army, and revised the judicial system, making progress toward a uniform code of laws.

SIGISMUND BÁTHORY (1572–1613) was the son of Stephen's brother Christopher. He was crowned prince of Transylvania in 1581 but was controlled by a regency until 1588. After he assumed power, he reversed the traditional Transylvanian policy of accommodation with the Turks and by so doing aroused discontent in Transylvania.

The turning point in his career came in 1599 when he voluntarily resigned his dominions to Emperor Rudolf II in order to enter a monastery. The next year he had a change of heart and tried to regain his throne with Turkish help. Defeated by his former vassal, Michael the Brave, in 1600 and 1601, Sigismund retired to Prague, where he died on March 27, 1613.

BATHS AND BATHING. Baths are the receptacles, rooms, or buildings designed for bathing, the process of washing or soaking oneself. Throughout history baths have varied in size and elaborateness, from the private tub to the public swimming pool, according to the purpose of the bather. Three different purposes, discernible at an early stage of history, remain today. These are general well-being, ceremonial purification, and cleanliness.

The idea of bathing for general well-being was known to the ancient Greeks of Homer's time. In Greece and Rome, warm baths were extensively used for relaxation and pleasure. Among the Romans, and later the Turks, bathing places became social and recreational centers. Bathing was also favored as a means for treating diseases. The modern custom of "taking a cure" at a spa can be traced back to an early belief in the medicinal qualities of mineral springs.

Bathing for ceremonial purification is also an ancient custom. Very early records of such ceremonial cleansing came from Egypt, where bathing was regarded as primarily a religious rite. The Mosaic code of the Hebrews required ritual washing, and this code influenced the Muslims. Among the Hindus, bathing has always been looked on as an essentially religious duty. The Hindus bathed for ritual purposes whereas the Greeks bathed for comfort.

Some authorities have speculated that the use of water for ritual purification grew out of the custom of washing for simple cleanliness, but it is difficult to determine which custom came first. It may be noted that at various times in history people have washed for ceremonial purposes or bathed for social and curative reasons even though they had very little concern for hygiene. In fact, the idea of washing to remove harmful bacteria from the skin could not have been conceived until after the germ theory of disease had been accepted. Not until modern times did cleanliness, for the sake of hygiene and appearance, become the unquestionably primary motive for bathing.

Ancient Civilizations. The public baths of Mohenjo-Daro, in the Indus Valley, and the palace baths at Knossos, on Crete, are the earliest known to man.

Built by a highly civilized people, Mohenjo-Daro is estimated to be about 5,000 years old. One of its greatest features was a public bath about 24 by 40 feet (7.3 by 12.2 meters). In addition, an elaborate drainage system enabled most houses to have at least one bathroom, with horizontal drains usually of brick, and terra cotta pipes fitted with spigot and faucet joints and protected by brickwork or by the walls.

The Minoan palace at Knossos included a sophisticated drainage plan with bathrooms, foot baths, and tubs, believed to date from between 2000 and 1800 B.C. The drains were made of stone, and vertical pipes, interlocked and cemented at the joints, may have been used for an upward flow of water. A modern looking bathtub (dating from between 1700 and 1400 B.C.) found in the queen's apartments is evidence that the structure of the tub, deriving as it does from its function, has remained relatively constant through history. There are, in fact, almost no examples in history of a "primitive" tub.

The bathing habits of the Egyptians are known from their early writings. Priests washed themselves four times a day in cold water. A small bathroom found in the city of Akhenaton

BATHS OF CARACALLA, built in Rome in 216 A.D., are now ruins where operas are held out-of-doors.

at Tell el 'Amarna suggests that about 1350 B.C. something akin to the provisions on Crete existed for the Egyptian aristocracy. The ancient Sumerians had bathing facilities in buildings at Kish, near Babylon. They built vertical drains leading from rooms believed to have been bathrooms, and constructed a large swimming pool.

Mosaic law, devised for the wandering Jews after their sojourn in Egypt, insisted on a high standard of cleanliness and made frequent references to ablutions as a form of religious rite. The *mikhvah*, or ritual bath for women, is still performed as part of this tradition. It has been contended that Moses and other ancient lawgivers who gave instruction about washing deliberately provided a religious sanction to encourage practical cleanliness. During the reigns of David and Solomon, after the Jews had become city dwellers in Palestine, they constructed great waterworks.

Among the ancient Greeks, bathing was part of a restorative process, as evidenced in Homer's description of the bathing of Odysseus in the palace of Circe. Homeric heroes are represented as bathing in a tub, following what became a typically Western custom, as contrasted with the Oriental custom of a tubless bath in which water was poured over the bather from a jug. The Greek tubs are usually described as made of polished stone, marble, or wood, but Homer expressed special admiration for the silver tub

brought by Menelaus from Egypt. Water for bathing was heated in cauldrons set on tripods.

The Scythians, a nomadic tribe of the Ukraine region, described by the Greek historian Herodotus in the 5th century B.C., are considered among the first inventors of the vapor, or steam, bath. The bath that they devised consisted of a felt tent hung over a tripod, in which water and hempseed were thrown over red-hot stones to produce a vapor. The medicine bath of the North American Indian was a similar type of steam bath.

Both the Russian vapor bath and the Finnish sauna bath are said to derive from this ancient Scythian steam bath. The Russians and Finns use large bathing houses. The bathers beat themselves with birch twigs to stimulate circulation and clean the skin. Both the sauna and the Russian vapor bath are usually followed by a plunge in a cold stream or snow.

Classical Greece and the Roman Empire. The Greek attitude toward bathing varied according to their general views on bodily comfort. At the time of the Persian Wars (499–479 B.C.) the Athenians and the Spartans, nurtured in a school that condemned everything suggestive of self-indulgence, made use of a form of cold-water bathing in which the water was poured over the bather. The warm baths in tubs enjoyed by the earlier Homeric heroes had been superseded temporarily by this early form of shower bath.

PLAN of the Baths of Caracalla, which could serve 1,600 bathers at once. Air circulated through wall vents heated the baths.

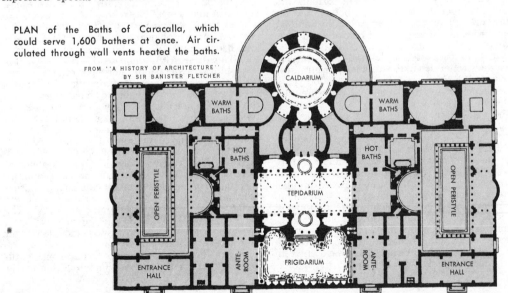

TILED CALDARIUM (hot room), in an ancient Roman bath at Chedworth, a villa in Gloucestershire, England.

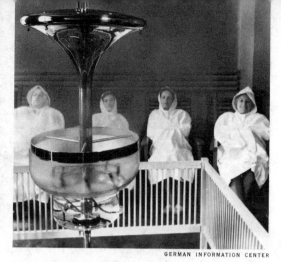

BAD SALZUFLEN, West German spa noted for thermal brines, here reduced to a mist inhaled by the patients.

Later in the 5th century B.C., public baths were constructed in Athens despite protests from those who upheld austerity. These baths rapidly became popular, and by the time of Socrates the public bath was a meeting place for Athenian society. Bathing became an integral part of Greek life and was depicted by Greek artists in many vase paintings.

The first Greek public baths contained cold-water pools or cold-shower facilities for use after wrestling or gymnastic exercises. Later Greeks introduced warm baths, but unlike the Romans they took these after initial cold baths. Ultimately, the Athenian government built and controlled public baths, with separate facilities for women, but these never matched the architectural achievements of the Romans.

The ancient Romans, like the Greeks, were at first distrustful of too much bathing. Public baths of a sort existed in Rome from the end of the 4th century B.C., but only cold water was used. As the empire grew, public taste demanded more and more luxury. By the 4th century A.D. there were nearly a thousand baths of various sizes at Rome and many others were found in the provinces.

The Stabian baths at Pompeii, one of the oldest Roman baths extant, was originally built in the 2d century B.C. In distant Britain the Romans constructed a great public bath in the 1st century A.D. around the Aquae Sulis, the mineral springs, from which the present city of Bath took its name. Remains of the Roman bathing establishment were discovered in the mid-18th century. Today, hot water from the mineral springs still runs through a Roman conduit about 2,000 years old. Remains of a large Roman bath were discovered in 1964 in London.

The elaboration of the sweat bath was the outstanding feature of the Roman system. The steps involved in the Roman bathing procedure have been determined, although the order in which these steps were taken is unclear. It is thought that the bather first exercised and then disrobed. Anointed with oil, he passed through the tepidarium (warm room), the caldarium (hot room), and the laconicum (steam room), the most intense of the sweating stages: Sweat and oil were pressed from the body with a strigil, a grooved metal scraper that had been introduced by the Greeks. The bather may then have entered the frigidarium (cold bath). Finally, the bather

anointed himself with oil again, and the bathing process was complete.

Water for baths in the city of Rome was supplied by aqueducts from the Alban Hills, constructed before the advent of the public baths. Further supplies were necessitated by an increasing demand as baths multiplied in Rome.

The social model for the baths was derived from Greek practice, but Roman love of luxury in the days of the empire required the inclusion of gardens, a stadium, shops, and exedrae (open courtyards for poetry readings or lectures). In time, however, the exedrae lost their select character as the baths became a pleasure available to many. The initial purpose of bathing to develop a sound mind in a healthy body was subordinated as the baths became more and more great social centers.

The most elaborate baths were the imperial thermae. The first of this type was built on the Campus Martius by Agrippa, the Roman statesman and general who was the son-in-law of Emperor Augustus. The general architectural plan of the imperial thermae—an open garden with bath chambers either in the center or at the rear, and surrounding smaller club rooms—was followed throughout the empire, though on a lesser scale than in Rome.

The baths of Caracalla and Diocletian were of colossal dimensions, and their extensive ruins are among the most famous. The Baths of Caracalla covered an area of nearly 28 acres (11 hectares) and had a capacity of 1,600 bathers. Sculpture found in these baths indicate the richness of the furnishings. Operas are now performed in the well-preserved remains of Caracalla. The Baths of Diocletian are thought to have been twice the size of Caracalla, accommodating some 3,200 bathers, with a swimming bath about 290 feet (88.4 meters) long and a theater. The tepidarium of these baths was reconstructed by Michelangelo to form the Church of Santa Maria degli Angeli. The Romans developed a system of buttressing, cross-vaulting on interior columns, and galleried windows, to provide roofs, ventilation, and light for the enormous rooms. These architectural feats inspired later builders. The old Pennsylvania Railroad Station in New York, torn down in the 1960's, was modeled after the Baths of Caracalla.

From the many references to baths and bathing in the works of such Roman historians as

Seneca and Pliny the Younger, it is known that men and women bathed separately, at different times or in different establishments. The practice of mixed bathing developed later and was condemned by the Roman emperors Hadrian and Marcus Aurelius, and in the Eastern Roman empire by Justinian I, the lawgiver.

The Christian Attitude. The early Christian church did not evolve any code regarding cleanliness. In this, Christianity was almost unique among the great religions of the world. Baths were used by Christians in the days of the Roman empire, but with certain limitations: Christians were forbidden to bathe with Jews and, in some cases, with the excommunicated. The great Roman baths, however, encouraged practices repugnant to Christian thought. Perfumes and cosmetics, regularly sold in the Roman baths, were regarded as symbols of moral decay. Early Christians who had suffered persecution condemned the extravagance of the thermae. Like the Semites, Christians abhorred the nudity common to the Graeco-Roman tradition.

To some extent the problem for the Christian church was solved by barbarian invasions, which left Roman aqueducts and the principal baths unusable. Meanwhile, a cult of asceticism arose among Christians to counteract the cult of well-being. Some Christians regarded being dirty as a suitable means of mortifying the flesh and a proper penance for sin. This attitude persisted into the Middle Ages. In the 11th century it was considered a creditable act of renunciation that Adalbert, archbishop of Hamburg and Bremen, abstained from bathing. Asceticism was carried to such extremes in certain areas that church leaders were forced to rebuke those preachers who forbade bathing altogether. A more moderate Christian view seems to have prevailed later in the Middle Ages.

Medieval kings and nobles followed the moderate course and occasionally bathed. Charlemagne, for example, made use of the sulfur springs near his residence at Aachen (Aix-la-Chapelle), where the Romans had constructed baths in the 1st century A.D. In England, King John bathed three times a year, before major church festivals.

The famous medical treatise *Regimen Sanitatis Salernitanum,* variously dated from the 11th to 13th century, suggested occasional bathing as a requisite for good health, but the general populace had little opportunity to wash. The few existing baths usually provided facilities resembling the modern tub, although large pools occasionally served a more social purpose. Hot water was not used to any great extent, falling under the general Christian condemnation of self-indulgence. The celebrated 13th century Welsh physician, Rhiwallon of Myddvai, Carmarthenshire, recommended cold water bathing in the summer for health. An exception to these generalizations was the practice in certain monasteries where sweat baths were built for use of the monks. These were especially favored in France under the Merovingian and Carolingian dynasties. The Roman system of bathing was also preserved in the Byzantine empire.

In the later Middle Ages, public baths were found on the European continent, but some antipathy to bathing remained. In the 13th century epic, *Parsival,* the young knight is offered a bath with maidens in attendance—a practice traceable to the customs of Greece. Parsival, however, a model of Christian virtue, dismissed his attendants before taking his bath. Nonetheless, by the 15th century, European public baths had become notorious for promiscuous mixed bathing. Condemned by monks as hotbeds of vice, these establishments generally comprised large swimming pools, where music, food, and wine were favored accompaniments to bathing. Woodcuts of the period depict these public baths.

The Impact of Islam. Christianity had inherited the Jewish attitude toward nudity, while rejecting the Judaic idea of ceremonial cleanliness. Islam, the new religion of the 7th century, drew from both Jewish and Christian sources. In its views on cleanliness, Islamic civilization was influenced chiefly by Judaism, but ceremonial purification was originally accompanied by a strain of Christian puritanism that ruled out the luxuries of the Roman world as forms of sin and self-indulgence. Later, this strict code was softened by contact with the conquered provinces of Rome. However, insistence on ceremonial cleanliness remains to this day a characteristic of Muslims.

In the Middle Ages the Moorish rulers of Spain constructed numerous and elegant baths. In Córdoba alone there were hundreds of public baths, and many individual dwellings had private bathrooms. Water from the mountains supplied

SPRUDELHOF, or bubbling mineral springs, at Bad Nauheim, in West Germany. Noted for its cardiac cures, Bad Nauheim is also a center for medical research.

FAMILY BATH on Hokkaido Island, in northern Japan, combines comfort and beauty.

LOUIS RENAULT FROM PHOTO RESEARCHERS

FAMILY BATH on Hokkaido Island, in northern Japan, combines comfort and beauty.

these facilities. In the time of Charlemagne, Muslims were considered to be the cleanest people of the world. In later centuries, returning Crusaders introduced into Europe the Turkish bath, an Ottoman version of the Roman bath. Even in the 14th century, however, the contrast between the cleanliness of the Muslims and the dirtiness of the Franks was widely apparent.

After Spain was reconquered from the Moors, the Moorish baths were destroyed and the Moors were forbidden to bathe. Public baths remained in use, however, in the Christian state of Aragon.

The Muslim cult of the bath developed with the same internal contention observed in the Christian world. Muslim purists protested against practices that went far beyond the basic requirements of cleanliness. The Islamic hammam, or public bath, the Oriental version of the Roman thermae, evolved into a decadent institution. Bodily exercise and intellectual stimulation were replaced by indolent relaxation.

The hammam consisted of a large central chamber surrounded by smaller chambers with mosaics and marble-lined inner walls. A dome with small round glazed openings for light covered the central chamber which heated by steam from a central jet of water. The outer rooms were used for relaxation and refreshments.

The combination of Islamic laws on personal hygiene and Islamic bathing practice helped to achieve for the East a higher standard of cleanliness than medieval Christendom attained.

Europe After the Middle Ages. The cultural revolution of the Renaissance left the problems of dirt and disease almost untouched. From the end of the Middle Ages until the mid-19th century, the growth of towns and cities accentuated these problems. Even the meager standards of hygiene maintained during the Middle Ages declined after the 15th century. This decline has been attributed, in part, to the Reformation and the Counter-Reformation. Puritanical tendencies noted in the early Christian tradition became more marked as rigid ethical standards found harsher expression among Catholics and Protestants. This reaction was not altogether unwarranted so far as bathing customs were concerned. The word "stew," originally meaning bathhouse, had come to signify a brothel.

For a number of reasons, Europeans used perfumes and cosmetics as a substitute for bathing

for over two centuries. In a very few houses domestic baths were found, but these were exceptional and not frequently used. Elizabeth I of England, however, bathed once a month "whether she required it or not."

Most doctors, as well as church authorities, frowned on bathing. However, the therapeutic value of bathing was sometimes supported by physicians. In the 18th century, mineral springs were exploited for their curative properties, although European standards of cleanliness were at their nadir.

Public swimming pools were thought to contribute to the spread of disease. Numerous epidemics and the absence of any disinfection system in public baths substantiated this belief. There is, however, no evidence that epidemics encouraged a higher standard of domestic cleanliness in Europe until the 19th century.

European colonists took their attitudes on bathing to America. The old laws of Pennsylvania, Virginia, and Ohio give examples of legislative attempts to restrict or forbid bathing. Benjamin Franklin, who took a bath regularly, is considered a pioneer of American bathing.

As in the time of the Crusades, it was the influence of the East that changed Western habits. Englishmen who had long resided in India and Turkey in the 18th and 19th centuries returned with the habit of daily bathing. David Urquhart, whose life in the East had convinced him of the value of the Turkish steam bath, introduced it into London in 1862 The Turkish bath became an institution in the West.

Effects of the Industrial Revolution. The "sanitarian movement," made possible and inevitable by the Industrial Revolution, was another influence brought to bear on the bathing practices of the peoples of Western nations. At the start of the Industrial Revolution, there was an almost total absence of plumbing. The growth of overcrowded slums around city factories increased the problems of dirt and disease. Edwin Chadwick and other early pioneers of social reform in England were ridiculed when they first made proposals for improvement. Adverse medical opinion was reversed only after cholera first struck London in 1832.

Large-scale efforts to deal with the problem of personal cleanliness were made in Britain, Germany, and America from the mid-19th century onward. A public baths and wash houses act was passed in 1846 in England, and other measures followed. The British became pioneers in plumbing. The same industrial conditions that had produced slums and disease proved capable of providing physical remedies. Public and private groups began to build public bathhouses for those without private facilities. These bath houses were set up on Western models, distinct from the classical and Turkish forms. They were designed simply as places where people could get clean, and initially they consisted of individual bathrooms with plumbing controlled from a central place. Shower baths and swimming pools were added as athletic activities increased.

More elaborate establishments, built on the Roman model, were constructed around mineral springs. Medicinal baths at mineral springs have existed in nearly all countries since Roman times. Some of the best known are at Baden-Baden, Germany; Carlsbad (Karlovy Vary), Czechoslovakia; Vichy and Aix-les-Bains, France; Bath and Harrogate, England; and Spa, Belgium. In addition, there are many medicinal baths in the Far East, especially in Japan where bathing, often associated with massage, has always been popular. In the United States, notable medicinal baths include those at White Sulphur Springs, W.Va.; Hot Springs, Ark.; Warm Springs, Ga.; and Saratoga Springs, N.Y.

In the Victorian era the bathroom gradually evolved as a separate unit in the house. Some houses had independent heating arrangements in the bathroom for tub and shower baths, while others used circulating hot water systems. The Victorian tub was frequently a hooded affair, usually made of wood, copper, or iron. Bathroom fixtures were often disguised out of a desire for modesty. The tub, for example, might have a cover resembling a sofa or chaise longue. Home bathroom facilities gradually became common in western Europe, Canada, and the United States. The White House in Washington, D.C., however, did not have a bathtub until 1851, and a generation later a bathroom in the house was still a mark of the wealthy classes.

In the 20th century, American technology led the way in developing private bathing facilities for the majority of people. Nevertheless, a Cornell University study made in the mid-1960's found the American bathroom "minimal in terms of contemporary knowledge, technology, values, and attitudes." European countries tended to follow the pattern of the United States, and the private bathroom was common enough so that it was no longer a status symbol. In the developing nations, however, a home bathroom remained a luxury.

REGINALD REYNOLDS
Author of "Cleanliness and Godliness"
Revised by the Editors

Bibliography

American Public Health Association, *Swimming Pools and Other Public Bathing Places* (New York 1957).

Ashe, Geoffrey, *Tale of a Tub* (New York 1950).

Carcopino, Jerome, *Daily Life in Ancient Rome,* ed. by H.T. Rovell, tr. by E.O. Lorimer (New Haven 1940).

Kira, Alexander, *The Bathroom: Criteria for Design* (Ithaca, N.Y., 1966).

Mullett, Charles F., *Public Baths and Health in England, 16th–18th Centuries* (Baltimore 1946).

Reynolds, Reginald, *Cleanliness and Godliness* (New York 1946).

Scott, George R., *The Story of Baths and Bathing* (London 1939).

Viherjuuri, H.J., *Sauna, the Finnish Bath* (Helsinki 1960).

Wright, Lawrence, *Clean and Decent* (New York 1960).

BATHSHEBA, bath-shē'bə, in the Old Testament, was the wife of Uriah the Hittite, one of King David's warriors. While Uriah was campaigning against the Ammonites, David saw Bathsheba bathing. Impressed by her beauty, he seduced her, and she conceived a child. In order to make Bathsheba his wife, David successfully plotted to have Uriah killed in battle. He repented of this deed after hearing the prophet Nathan's parable of the ewe lamb (Psalm 51). David and Bathsheba were punished by the death of their first son. They had a second child Solomon, for whom Bathsheba secured the right to succeed to the throne of Judah and Israel. The story is in II Samuel 11, 12 and I Kings 1, 2.

BATHURST, bath'ûrst, a family of English officials whose ancestors settled in Sussex before the Norman conquest. Leading members were:

ALLEN BATHURST, 1ST EARL BATHURST (1684–1775), was born in London on Nov. 16, 1684. He was a member of Parliament representing Cirencester from 1705 until he was created Baron Bathurst in 1712. As a member of the House of Lords he opposed Sir Robert Walpole and, on the latter's resignation as prime minister in 1742, Bathurst was made a privy councillor. He was elevated to earldom in 1772 and died near Cirencester, on Sept. 16, 1775.

HENRY, 2D EARL BATHURST (1714–1794), was the eldest surviving son of Allen Bathurst. He was born on May 2, 1714. He represented Cirencester in Parliament from 1735 to 1754, when he was appointed judge of the common pleas. In 1771 he became lord chancellor and was made Baron Apsley. In 1779 he became a member of the ministry as lord president of the council. He died at Oakley Grove, near Cirencester, on Aug. 6, 1794.

HENRY, 3D EARL BATHURST (1762–1834), was the elder son of the second earl. He was born on May 22, 1762. He was a member of Parliament from Cirencester from 1783 to 1794, when he succeeded his father to the earldom. Because of his close friendship with William Pitt the Younger, he held many public offices. He was lord of the admiralty (1783–1789), lord of the board of control (1793–1802). He later was foreign secretary, colonial secretary, and lord president of the council. He died on July 27, 1834.

BATHURST, bath'ûrst, in Australia, is a city in New South Wales, on the Macquarie River, about 100 miles (161 km) northwest of Sidney. It is a trade and processing center for the sheep-grazing and fruit-growing industries of the surrounding plains region, and a tourist center noted for trout fishing. Gold and other metals are mined nearby. The site was settled in 1815, and the town was developed after gold was discovered in 1851. Population: (1971) 17,169.

BATHURST, bath'ûrst, was the name, until 1973 when it was changed to Banjul, of the capital and chief port of The Gambia. It is on St. Mary's Island at the mouth of the Gambia River. The climate of the area is mild and pleasant, with a rainy season from June to October and a dry season from November to May.

Although the city is the seat of Anglican and Roman Catholic bishoprics, 90 percent of the population are Muslims. There are about 500 European residents. A government technical school provides training in carpentry and metalwork.

A teachers training college is located in Yundum, 10 miles southwest of Bathurst.

The commercial activity of Bathurst centers around the processing of peanuts. Peanuts are The Gambia's only important crop and the chief export shipped from Bathurst's two deep-water wharves. Transportation to other parts of The Gambia is chiefly by the Gambia River and by a trunk road that joins the trans-Gambia highway. Yundum has an international airport.

Traders from the north and east are believed to have brought the Islamic religion to the Bathurst area in the 12th century. Little else is known of the region's history until the mid-15th century when the Portuguese explored the Gambia River and began to trade in slaves and gold. They were later rivaled by English, Dutch, and French traders.

Gradually, the English gained control of the mouth of the river and in 1664 built Fort James on an island there. In 1816 a settlement was founded by British traders on St. Mary's Island and named for the 3d Earl Bathurst, who was then the British colonial secretary. Bathurst, with some surrounding land, was administered as the crown colony of Gambia from 1843 to 1866 and again from 1888 to 1965. Between these periods it was part of the British West African Settlements. When a British protectorate was established over other land along the Gambia River in 1889, Bathurst was made its capital.

In 1965, the colony and protectorate of Gambia became The Gambia, an independent nation, with Bathurst as its capital. Population: (1964) 28,896.

BATHURST, bath′ûrst, a fishing port and resort city in Northeastern New Brunswick, Canada, is the seat of Gloucester County. It is situated 122 miles (180 km) northeast of Fredericton, on Nipisiguit Bay, an arm of Chaleur Bay, which is an inlet of the Gulf of St. Lawrence. Its fisheries produce salmon, cod, smelt, mackerel, and lobster. The town has lumber mills, pulp and newsprint mills, machine works, and a thermal-electric power station. Nearby are abundant lead, zinc, copper, and pyrite deposits, and there are extensive mining and smelting operations. Bathurst is a popular summer resort. Founded in 1818 as *St. Peters,* it was renamed Bathurst in 1826 and incorporated in 1912. Population: 16,674.

BATHURST INLET, bath′ûrst, is an arm of Coronation Gulf, on the Arctic coast of Canada, in Mackenzie District of the Northwest Territories. It is about 300 miles (480 km) north of Great Slave Lake.

BATHURST ISLAND, bath′ûrst, Australia, is in the Timor Sea, off the northern coast of the continent. It lies just west of Melville Island, and is part of Northern Territory. Bathurst is an aboriginal reservation.

BATHURST ISLAND, bath′ûrst, in the Arctic Ocean, is one of the Parry Islands in the Northwest Territories of Canada. It was discovered in 1819 by Sir William Edward Parry. The Parry Islands form part of the archipelago known since 1954 as the Queen Elizabeth Islands.

BATHYCLES, bath′ə-klēz, was a Greek sculptor of the 6th century B.C. He lived in Magnesia, Thessaly. About 550 B.C. he built a colossal throne for the statue of Apollo at Amyclae, near Sparta. Of his work, only fragments have been recovered, but it is described in great detail in Pausanias' *Description of Greece.*

BATHYSCAPHE, bath′ə-skāf, a type of underwater vessel that is used in deep-sea exploration. It was invented by the Swiss physicist Auguste Piccard and made its first, unmanned dive in 1948. Essentially an underwater balloon, it consists of a small spherical cabin, or gondola, suspended from a larger, buoyant hull.

The hull is divided into gasoline-filled compartments. Through regulation of their contents and the use of ballast, the vessel can be made to rise or sink. Motor-driven propellers give the vessel limited mobility underwater, but it has to be towed to its place of operation. There are lights on the hull for illuminating the black ocean depths. The gondola is pressurized and can hold two or three passengers. Within it are operating controls and scientific instruments.

The bathyscaphe was the first type of craft capable of controlled descent to the deepest ocean bottom. On Jan. 23, 1960, the bathyscaphe *Trieste I* reached a depth of 35,800 feet (10,920 meters) off the coast of Guam. Aboard the vessel during the descent were Piccard's son Jacques and Lt. Don Walsh, USN.

See also DEEP-SEA EXPLORATION.

THE BATHYSCAPHE *Trieste I* (left) made a historic descent of 35,800 feet near Guam in 1960. In 1963, the improved *Trieste II* (right) was used to find and photograph the remains of the sunken U.S. submarine *Thresher.*

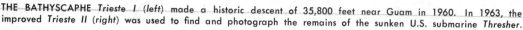

OFFICIAL U.S. NAVY PHOTOGRAPH   OFFICIAL U.S. NAVY PHOTOGRAPH

FIRST BATHYSPHERE, with designer Otis Barton (*right*), who made descents in it with William Beebe (*left*).

MODERN BATHYSPHERE used by the famous undersea explorer Jacques-Yves Cousteau undergoes trials in France.

BATHYSPHERE, bath′ə-sfēr, a device used for deep-sea exploration. The bathysphere is a hollow steel ball, more or less spherical, that typically can hold two passengers. It is lowered from a ship by means of heavy cables. The pressurized sphere has thick fused-quartz windows and is equipped with powerful lights. The men aboard are unable to move the bathysphere horizontally. Furthermore, should the cables break, the men would be unable to return to the surface.

The bathysphere made exploration of the very deep ocean possible for the first time. The first bathysphere was built in 1930 and was used by the American naturalist William Beebe off the coast of Bermuda for the study of deep-sea animal life. During one of his descents in 1934, Beebe reached a depth greater than 3,000 feet (915 meters), a record for the bathysphere.

See also Deep-Sea Exploration.

BATIK, bə-tēk′, is a method of adding design to fabric by means of wax applications. It is used chiefly on cotton and silk fabrics but can also be applied to velvet, wool, and leather. In the traditional method the artist draws his design with pencil or charcoal on the cloth, then traces liquid wax along the outline with an instrument called a *tjanting*. When the wax is dry and stiff, the fabric is dipped in dye. The ornamented portions of the cloth, protected by the wax, "resist" the dye, and stand out against the colored background when the wax is removed by boiling the material.

Batik, also spelled *battik,* means literally "wax painting" in Malayan. It was first practiced by the ancient Egyptians but reached its highest development in Java, where it has been used since the 7th century A.D. The process is also used in other parts of Indonesia, as well as in China and India. Batik was introduced into Europe by Dutch traders in the 17th century.

Most designs of Oriental batik are traditional (some date back as far as the 11th century) and have nature subjects. In Java the color of a batik garment indicates the region where it originated.

BATISTA, bä-tēs′tä, **Fulgencio** (1901–1973), Cuban soldier and political leader, who was virtual dictator of Cuba for most of the period from 1933 to 1959.

Fulgencio Batista y Zaldívar was born at Banes, Oriente province, Cuba, on Jan. 16, 1901.

His family were impoverished farmers. Joining the army as a recruit in 1921, he studied stenography and became a sergeant in 1928. Batista took part in the overthrow of the Gerardo Machado dictatorship in August 1933 and, with a group of other sergeants, seized control of the government on September 4. Promoted to colonel (later major general) and commander in chief of the army before the end of the year, he exercised virtually dictatorial powers and in 1940 was elected president.

Barred by law from succeeding himself, Batista left office in 1944, traveled widely, and lived for a time in Florida, where he settled a fortune on his divorced wife. After his return to Cuba, he was elected senator (1948) and on March 10, 1952, staged a second coup, regaining control of the government. He was reelected president without opposition on Nov. 1, 1954.

During his first term as president, Batista promoted mass education and public health, encouraged independent economic development, and improved the conditions of labor. Administrative procedures were simplified, and graft was reduced. In the 1950's, however, the corruption of his regime and its brutal terror against political opponents turned the people against him. A rebel group led by Fidel Castro began a guerrilla campaign in 1956 and launched a successful offensive late in 1958. On Jan. 1, 1959, Batista resigned as president and fled the country with his family and many of his followers to asylum in the Dominican Republic. Later he settled in Estoril, near Lisbon, Portugal. He died in Marbella, Spain, on Aug. 6, 1973.

See also Cuba—*History.*

FULGENCIO BATISTA, Cuban dictator, shown at the height of his power, was forced out of the presidency by Fidel Castro in 1959.

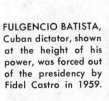

BATISTE, bə-tēst′, is a fine, white compact fabric, originally woven from linen fibers, but now also from cotton, rayon, silk, or wool fibers. It is distinguished by its delicate, firm, and uniform threads. The name derives from Jean Baptiste de Cambrai, a 13th century weaver in Cambrai, France, who is said to have made the first fabric of this type.

BATJAN, bä′chän, an island in Indonesia, is one of the North Moluccas. It is situated in the Molucca Sea southwest of Halmahera, and has an area of 913 square miles (1,365 sq km). Batjan is about 50 miles long and 25 miles wide (80 by 40 km) and is mountainous. Timber, spices, copra, and resin are the major products. Labuha, on the west coast, is the chief port. The island was visited by the Portuguese in 1558, and became a Dutch settlement in 1609. In World War II it was an important Japanese naval base. Since 1950 it has been part of Maluka province.

BATLLE BERRES, bät′yä ber′əs, **Luis** (1897–1964), Uruguayan journalist and political leader. He was born in Montevideo on Nov. 26, 1897. Both his grandfather, Lorenzo Batlle (1812–1872), and uncle, José Batlle y Ordóñez, were presidents of Uruguay. Luis was educated at the University of Montevideo. He inherited control of the newspaper *El Día,* through which he promoted the liberal views that his family had long supported. He served in the Congress from 1923 to 1933, and was president of that body from 1943 to 1945. He was elected vice president of Uruguay in 1947 and succeeded to the presidency on the death of Tomás Berreta in August of that year, serving until 1950. From 1954 to 1956 he was president of the council that, by constitutional amendment in 1951, replaced the executive. He died at Montevideo on July 15, 1964.

BATLLE Y ORDÓÑEZ, bät′yä ē ôr-thō′nyäs, **José** (1856–1929), president of Uruguay. He was born in Montevideo, Uruguay, on May 21, 1856. The son of Lorenzo Batlle (president of Uruguay, 1868–1872), he studied law in Montevideo but interrupted his education to go to Paris, where he pursued his interest in ideas of liberal government. Upon his return to Montevideo, he founded

El Día (1886), which became Uruguay's leading newspaper.

Entering active politics in 1887, Batlle y Ordóñez reformed the Colorado party, which he made an instrument of liberal progressivism, and after serving as a member of the lower house and the Senate, he was elected to the presidency in 1903. When his term expired in 1907, he went to Switzerland, and returned to Uruguay imbued with new ideas for improvements in government and social conditions.

Elected to the presidency for a second term (1911–1915), he brought sweeping changes to the country; his administration is credited with bringing stability to Uruguay for the first time since its independence in 1830 and with innovating most of the social welfare practices which stamped it as one of the most progressive countries in South America. Outstanding among his achievements were an improved educational system, social security and labor benefits, and the creation of state corporations to operate banking, transportation, and some industries, when private capital proved ineffective. He died in Montevideo, on Oct. 20, 1929.

BATON, bə-ton′, a short stick or wand used by the conductor of an orchestra to direct the musicians. It was widely adopted in the early 19th century to enable musicians to see the conductor's movements after orchestras became too large to be guided solely by his hands. The baton is usually made of light wood and varies in length from 15 to 28 inches (38 to 71 cm). It is held in the right hand. At first it was used only to mark time, with the left hand indicating volume and expressive nuances. However, the Hungarian conductor Arthur Nikisch (1855–1922) and later conductors enlarged the role of the baton to express musical subtleties as well as the musical beat.

"Baton" also refers to the short staff or truncheon used as an official badge of office—as a field marshal's baton—and to the round staff, weighted on one end by a ball, which is twirled by drum majors and others who lead marching bands. In athletics, the baton is the wooden cylinder passed from one runner to the next in relay races. In heraldry, the baton is a narrow diagonal band that appears on a coat of arms.

THE BATON ROUGE skyline is marked by the tower of the state capitol rising over the Louisiana State Library.

BATON ROUGE, bat′ən rōōzh′, a city in Louisiana, is the capital of the state and the seat of East Baton Rouge Parish (county). It is situated on the east bank of the Mississippi River, 72 miles (116 km) northwest of New Orleans. The city acquired a cosmopolitan character during the 18th century when it was ruled successively by the French, British, and Spaniards. In the 19th century it gained added distinction by becoming capital of the state and seat of Louisiana State University.

Industries. Baton Rouge is the industrial center of a great petroleum and petrochemical complex. One of the world's biggest and most diversified oil refineries is situated there. The petrochemical industries are the city's largest employers. Essential to this giant complex are the natural resources in or near the city. These include petroleum, natural gas, sulfur, salt, and more than 300 billion gallons (1,136 billion liters) of fresh water supplied daily by the Mississippi River. Many plans for industrial expansion are based on this great natural wealth. Rubber and plastics also are manufactured in or near Baton Rouge, as are scientific instruments, concrete products, tile, and wood, paper, and food products.

Port. The port of Baton Rouge, a relative newcomer among important United States ports, is equipped to handle both ocean-going vessels and river barges. It is a major interchange point for Mississippi barges, and its water-borne freight each year amounts to more than 30 million tons. As the farthest inland deepwater port on the Gulf of Mexico, it is the most distant point on the Mississippi reached by ocean-going ships. The river is about half a mile (0.8 km) wide here, and the channel is 35 feet (10.6 meters) deep. The Port Allen lock on the Gulf Intracoastal Waterway from Florida to Texas is adjacent to the port. Baton Rouge is also served by railroads and three airlines.

Educational Institutions. Louisiana State University was moved to Baton Rouge in 1869, and its present campus was begun in 1923. A major project for its Nuclear Science Center is a $1.5 million nuclear reactor. Southern University, another state institution, was moved to Baton Rouge from New Orleans in 1914. Other institutions include state schools for the deaf and blind, and state and parish libraries.

Capitol Buildings. Among the most interesting buildings in the city are the two state capitols. The present capitol is a 34-story building constructed in 1931 and set in a well-landscaped park. The old capitol, built in 1882, was modeled on a previous building, which dated from 1847–1850 and was burned during the Civil War.

History and Government. The words *baton rouge* mean "red stick" or "post" in French. One legend traces the name to a big cypress tree, largely denuded, growing on the site when it was discovered by the French. Another legend has it that a red stick was placed there by Indians to mark a boundary line between two Indian hunting grounds.

French explorers visited Louisiana in the late 17th century, and there is known to have been a settlement at Baton Rouge as early as 1719. By the Treaty of Paris (1763), France ceded to Britain territory that included Baton Rouge. This region was conquered by the Spanish in 1779, during the American Revolution. In 1800 they returned it to France, but Spain claimed the territory again when the United States made the Louisiana Purchase from France in 1803. American residents of the territory rebelled against the Spanish in 1810, and in 1812 Louisiana was admitted to the Union. Baton Rouge was incorporated in 1817 and became the state's capital in 1849. During most of the Civil War, it was occupied by federal troops, and the state government did not return until 1882.

Baton Rouge is governed in a unique manner. A consolidated city-parish (county) government became effective on Jan. 1, 1949. The legislative branch consists of two councils, a city council and a parish council. The first is composed of seven councilmen elected at large from the city of Baton Rouge. The parish council includes these seven plus three rural members elected from two rural wards. An executive officer called a mayor-president is elected for a four-year term. As chief administrator of the city and parish, he prepares budgets for both and presides at meetings of both councils. Population: 165,963.

WILLIAM W. SHAW, *Tulane University*

BATONI, bä-tō′nē, **Pompeo Girolamo** (1708–1787), Italian painter, who was both a fashionable portrait painter and a painter of altarpieces and scenes from mythology. His name also is spelled *Battoni*. He was born in Lucca on Jan. 25, 1708. In 1728 he went to Rome to study the works of Raphael, whose influence is especially apparent in Batoni's altarpieces. He died in Rome on Feb. 4, 1787.

As Batoni developed his skill in painting, he abandoned the cluttered style of the late baroque period in favor of a cleaner neoclassical style. He is credited with helping to rescue Italian painting from the exaggerated mannerisms of 17th century rococo art by employing the discipline of classical art. He intended his masterpiece of church art, *The Fall of Simon Magus* (1760), to be placed in St. Peter's, but it was installed in the Roman church of Santa Maria degli Angeli. Among his mythological paintings are *The Marriage of Cupid and Psyche* (1756) and *The Education of Achilles* (1760).

Batoni's portraits, of popes, emperors, and important visitors to Rome, usually show their subjects in settings of classical antiquity, such as the Colosseum. They include portraits of the exiled Stuarts and of Englishmen taking the Grand Tour. Although Sir Joshua Reynolds professed to have a poor opinion of Batoni's work, perhaps because Batoni was a rival for commissions from English gentlemen, his portraits show evidence of Batoni's influence.

BATTALION, bə-tal′yən, is the basic maneuver unit in the armies of most countries. Depending on mission and armament, a battalion contains from 500 to 1,000 men, usually commanded by a lieutenant colonel. Armed principally with individual weapons, the infantry battalion is the basic combat element of an army; but there are other types of combat battalions as well, such as artillery, armor, airborne and mechanized infantry, aviation, and combat engineers. Noncombatant battalions perform support functions, such as medical, ordnance, signal, and supply.

During World War II and the Korean War the U.S. Army normally had three infantry battalions to a regiment and nine to a division, and this remains the practice of the U.S. Marine Corps. Armored divisions usually had three tank and three infantry battalions.

Since 1963 the practice in the U.S. Army, as in most Western armies, has been to set no fixed number of battalions per division but to use battalions (usually about 10) as "building blocks" to create divisions tailored to mission and environment. A division heavy in tank battalions is an armored division, but the ratio might be changed to a preponderance of infantry battalions should the division move to a region unsuitable for armor. Various combinations of battalions thus can be used to create infantry, armored, mechanized infantry, airborne, and airmobile divisions. Battalions usually contain a headquarters company, a heavy weapons company, and three rifle companies, augmented often by other attached units.

In mechanized cavalry units, the term *squadron* is equivalent to battalion, as it is, in general, in naval and aerial units. The U.S. Navy and Air Force do have construction battalions; those in the Navy are known as Seabees.

CHARLES B. MacDONALD
Historian, Department of the Army

BATTAMBANG, bat'əm-bang, is the second-largest city of Cambodia and the capital of Battambang province. The city is situated on the Battambang River, 160 miles (257.5 km) northwest of Phnom Penh. The market center for a fertile rice-growing region, Battambang also has fish packing, cigarette manufacturing, and textile industries. The city has ruins of the Khmer empire dating from the 10th century. Population: (1962) 38,846.

BATTANI, al- (c. 858–929), bat-tä'nē, one of the most important astronomers of medieval Islam. He was called *Albategni* or *Albatenius* by medieval Latin writers. He was born at or near Harran, in upper Mesopotamia, of a Sabian family, although he himself was a Muslim. Most of his life was spent at Raqqa on the Euphrates, where he devoted himself to astronomical observations. His most important work, the *Zij* (astronomical tables), was translated into Latin in the 12th century and into Spanish in the 13th. It greatly influenced the development of astronomy in Europe. Against Ptolemy's opinion, al-Battani demonstrated the mobility of the solar apogee and proved the variation of the apparent angular diameter of the sun. He determined the obliquity of the ecliptic with remarkable accuracy and corrected the Ptolemaic value for the precession of the equinoxes.

A.I. SABRA, *University of London*

BATTELLE MEMORIAL INSTITUTE, ba-tel', the world's largest nonprofit scientific institute. It operates four major research complexes—at its headquarters in Columbus, Ohio; in Richland, Wash. (in what was formerly an Atomic Energy Commission laboratory); in Geneva, Switzerland; and in Frankfurt, West Germany. It employs more than 5,000 scientists, engineers, economists, and supporting personnel to conduct research in science, technology, and economics under contracts with public agencies and private firms. Battelle developed xerography with the Xerox Corporation, pioneered in peaceful uses of nuclear energy, and helped develop titanium for the aerospace industry. Gordon Battelle, member of a Columbus industrial family, set up the institute under terms of his will.

BATTENBERG, bat'ən-bûrg, **Prince Henry Maurice of** (1858–1896), British soldier, who was born in Milan, Italy, on Oct. 5, 1858. He was the third son of Prince Alexander of Hesse, and in 1885 married Princess Beatrice of England, the youngest daughter of Queen Victoria. He joined the British expedition of 1895 in the Ashanti War and died at sea on Jan. 20, 1896, of a fever contracted during his military service.

His youngest son, *Prince Maurice of Battenberg,* died of wounds received in action during World War I. Prince Henry Maurice's daughter, *Princess Victoria,* married King Alfonso XIII of Spain in 1906. In 1917 the eldest son, *Prince Alexander,* changed his title to marquess of Carisbrooke.

BATTENBERG, bat'ən-bûrg, **Prince Louis Alexander** (1854–1921), British admiral. He was born in Gratz (now Graz), Austria, on May 24, 1854. He was the eldest son of Prince Alexander of Hesse, and in 1884 he married the eldest daughter of the Princess Alice Maud Mary, Grand Duchess of Hesse-Darmstadt and second daughter of Queen Victoria. Becoming a naturalized British subject in 1868, he entered the navy and rose rapidly. He was director of naval intelligence in 1902–1905 and was appointed first sea lord of the Admiralty in 1912. Following the outbreak of World War I and a campaign in the British press against resident aliens from enemy countries, he resigned his office on Oct. 29, 1914. In accepting his resignation, the first civil lord of the Admiralty, Winston Churchill, paid a high tribute to the provision he had made for the immediate concentration of the Grand Fleet at the opening of the war. In 1917 he and the members of his family resident in England relinquished their German titles and Anglicized "Battenberg" into the surname "Mountbatten." Louis Alexander was then created marquess of Milford Haven. He died in London on Sept. 11, 1921.

BATTENBERG, bat'ən-bûrg, is a title of nobility taken from the name of a village near Marburg, West Germany. A family of counts held the title until it died out about 1314. In 1851, upon the morganatic marriage of Prince Alexander of Hesse-Darmstadt to Julia Teresa, countess von Haucke, the latter received the title of countess of Battenberg. The countess and her children were raised to the rank of princes and princesses in 1858. Their descendants retained the title until World War I, when those living in England anglicized it to Mountbatten.

BATTERING RAM, the earliest, simplest, and, until the development of heavy artillery in the 1300's, most effective device for destroying stone walls and the ordinary defenses of fortified towns. The primitive ram was a huge beam of seasoned and tough wood, hoisted on the shoulders of men. Running with it at full speed against a wall, gate, or palisade, they did what damage they could with one charge after another. Ancient armies used two different kinds of battering ram —one type was suspended and swinging, like a pendulum, and the other moved on rollers.

The swinging ram resembled a ship's mast and was suspended horizontally at its center of gravity by means of chains or cords, from a movable frame. Waxed cord was bound around the beam at short intervals, and cords at the back end were pulled in unison to cause the pendulum motion.

The rolling ram was much the same in its general construction, except that instead of a pendulum motion, it was given only a simple to-and-fro motion, produced by men pulling on cords passing over pulleys. The rolling ram seems to have been first used at the siege of Byzantium in 196 A.D. These rams often were extremely heavy. In Roman literature, Appian writes that at the siege of Carthage he saw two rams so colossal that 100 men worked each;

Battering ram (from a drawing made about 1605).

Vitruvius affirms that the beam was often from 100 to 120 feet (30–36 meters) in length; and Justus Lipsius describes some as 180 feet long and 2 feet 4 inches in diameter (54.9 by 0.7 meters), with an iron head weighing at least a ton and a half, and a total weight of more than 45,000 pounds (20,385 kg).

The efficacy of the ram depended almost entirely upon the proper timing of its intervals of oscillation. At first it would produce no obvious effect upon the wall; but repeated blows soon caused a barely perceptible tremor in the wall, then more extensive vibrations. The attackers adjusted the oscillations of the ram to that of the wall, until finally the wall gave way.

BATTERSEA, bat′ər-sē, former metropolitan borough of London, England, 3 miles (5 km) southwest of Charing Cross, on the south bank of the Thames River, opposite Chelsea. It is a workers' residential district and has a large electric power station. The London Government Act of 1963 divided Greater London into new administrative districts, and Battersea became a part of the borough of Wandsworth.

BATTERSON, bat′ər-sən, **James Goodwin** (1823–1901), American business executive. He was born in Bloomfield, Conn., on Feb. 23, 1823. He was educated in public schools at Litchfield, Conn., and in 1845 became a dealer in granite and marble. His business grew into one of the most extensive of its kind in the United States. He supplied stone for the state capitol building in Hartford and important office buildings in New York City. He devised many improvements for the building-stone industry, including machinery for polishing granite. In 1863 he founded the Travelers' Insurance Company. He was its president until his death in Hartford, Conn., on Sept. 18, 1901.

BATTERY, bat′ə-rē, the basic army artillery unit, averaging 120 men and 5 officers, using two or more heavy weapons of one type. The unit compares with a *company* in the infantry and a *troop* in armored or air cavalry. Artillery of the U.S. Army's standard division consists of: (1) a headquarters battery, (2) a composite battalion made up of a headquarters battery, three 155-mm howitzer batteries of six guns each, a rocket battery with two launchers, and a service battery; and (3) three battalions, each comprising a headquarters battery, three 105-mm howitzer batteries with six guns each, and a service battery. In the airmobile division, which travels in its own aircraft, the composite battalion is replaced by an aviation battery and three aerial rocket artillery batteries. Missile launchers, machine guns, and searchlights also are grouped in batteries. A naval battery is two or more guns or weapon launchers operated as a unit.

BATTERY, bat′ə-rē, is a term in common law meaning the application of force to the person of another without his consent. It becomes a criminal offense if it is willful and intentional. Even if the force is mere carelessness, it may be considered a trespass to the person and answerable in damages. A battery is excusable if committed in defense of self, wife, husband, child, parent, master, servant, or guest, or in defense of one's property, or to retake personal property from a wrongdoer. See ASSAULT.

BATTERY, Electric, bat′ə-rē. Electric batteries consist of electrochemical cells in which chemical energy is converted to electrical energy. Each cell has a negative electrode, a positive electrode, an electrolytic solution, and electrode separators, placed in a suitable container.

The negative electrode is in a reduced state while the positive electrode is in an oxidized state. When the cell is operating, the negative electrode becomes oxidized, and the positive electrode becomes reduced. The negative electrode yields electrons to an external circuit, and the positive electrode accepts electrons from this circuit. Thus the electrons flow from the negative electrode to the positive electrode—a direction contrary to what is conventionally known as the "direction of the current." Current is carried through the battery by ions of the electrolytic solution. Usually, each electrode is made by joining a number of plates in parallel. The electrical capacity is proportional to the number of plates.

There are two general types of electric cells: *primary* and *secondary*. In primary cells chemical energy is converted to electrical energy, and the process cannot be efficiently reversed. In secondary cells interconversion of chemical and electrical energies can be achieved in repeated cycles. Because of this reversibility, secondary batteries are also called *storage batteries*.

There are four types of primary cells: wet, dry, reserve, and fuel. Wet types contain a mobile (liquid) electrolyte. Although wet types previously were used extensively, they have been largely superseded by other types or other energy sources. Wet types have high capacity and low self-discharge rates. They are suited for long service when low currents are needed; for example, for railway signals and marine beacons.

Dry primary batteries are nonspillable and nonrefillable. The electrolyte usually is immobile (contained in an absorbent material). Because of this immobility, ion migration is slower in dry cells than in wet cells. Dry cells, therefore, sustain lower currents than wet cells. Because dry cells are nonspillable, they can be used on the person; for example, in hearing aids.

Reserve cells are activated immediately before use. Many materials that cannot be used in wet or dry cells because of their high reactivity can be used as components of reserve cells. Because reserve cells are inert until activated, they have a much longer storage life than all other types, except for fuel cells. They can be activated by gas, water, heat, or an electrolyte. However, once they are activated, they must be used at once.

Fuel cells have electrode materials that are added continuously during cell operation. Oxygen is invariably added at one electrode, and the fuel (hydrogen, hydrocarbons) at the other electrode. Fuel cells can operate longer than other cells because the electrode materials are replenished as they are consumed. Fuel cells also can be modified so that the electrolyte can be replaced at intervals during operation.

There are two general types of secondary cells: acid and alkaline. The lead-acid cell is the sole acid type. Nickel-iron, nickel-cadmium, zinc-silver, and cadmium-silver cells are alkaline types.

Historical Development. The first cells were wet primary cells made by Alessandro Volta in 1796. They consisted of tin or zinc and copper

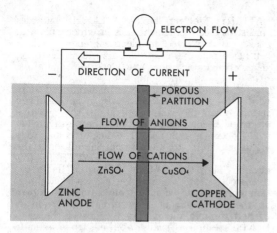

ELECTRON FLOW

DIRECTION OF CURRENT

− +

POROUS PARTITION

FLOW OF ANIONS

FLOW OF CATIONS

ZnSO₄ CuSO₄

ZINC ANODE

COPPER CATHODE

THE DANIELL CELL has a zinc anode in a zinc sulfate electrolyte and a copper cathode in a copper sulfate electrolyte. In the electrolytic solutions, ions are the current carriers. In the external circuit, electrons are the current carriers. The electron-flow direction is opposite to the conventional current direction.

or silver separated by pasteboard or hide soaked in water, vinegar, or salt solution. Other scientists made Volta cells in various designs. One of special interest was introduced by William Wollaston in 1816. Copper plates, doubled around zinc plates with a space between the plates, were submerged in dilute acid when the battery was in use and were withdrawn when it was not in use. This battery was a precursor of modern reserve cells.

In 1836, John F. Daniell introduced another modification that avoided the disadvantages of polarization and corrosion exhibited by Volta cells. Daniell immersed a zinc electrode in a solution of zinc sulfate (acidified with sulfuric acid) and a copper electrode in a solution of copper sulfate. He then placed a porous earthenware diaphragm between the electrodes. The Daniell cell voltage was 1.06 to 1.09 volts. In a modified form, called the gravity cell, the less dense zinc-sulfate solution was placed over the more dense copper-sulfate solution. The gravity cell had a longer life than the unmodified cell because there was less diffusion of the electrolyte.

In 1839, Sir William R. Grove invented two cells of special significance. His first cell was made with zinc and platinum electrodes placed in dilute sulfuric acid and strong nitric acid, respectively. The acids were separated by a porous diaphragm. This cell had nearly double the voltage of the Daniell cell. His second cell, a one-fluid type, was a forerunner of modern fuel cells. He electrolyzed a sulfuric acid solution between platinum electrodes and collected the resultant hydrogen and oxygen gases in tubes placed over the electrodes. At the end of the electrolysis the electrodes were half submerged in the acid. Grove obtained a voltage of 1.1 volts, which depended on the hydrogen and oxygen adsorbed on the electrodes. The cell had little capacity, however, because its electrode area was limited. (Modern fuel cells use highly porous electrodes for efficient gas adsorption.) Grove's gas cell is a secondary cell because it can be recharged.

Other primary cells were proposed in the 1800's by Robert Bunsen (1841), Georges Le-clanché (1866), Latimer Clark (1874), Felix La-lande and Georges Chaperon (1883), Hermann Aron (1886), and Edward Weston (1893). Bunsen used chromic acid in place of Grove's nitric acid. Leclanché used zinc negatives (negative plates) and manganese dioxide and carbon positives (positive plates) in ammonium chloride solutions. His cell was the forerunner of the familiar dry cell. Clark used electrodes of zinc and mercury–mercurous sulfate in zinc sulfate solutions. Weston replaced the zinc and zinc sulfate by cadmium and cadmium sulfate. The Clark and Weston cells did not sustain appreciable currents but exhibited constant voltages for long periods; thus they have found wide use as voltage standards. Lalande and Chaperon used electrodes of zinc and copper oxide in potassium hydroxide. Aron replaced the copper oxide with mercury oxide. Aron's cell was the forerunner of the mercury dry cell developed by Samuel Ruben in World War II.

Although Grove's gas cell was the first secondary cell, the first practical one was developed by Gaston Planté in 1859. It consisted of two lead sheets separated by rubber strips and immersed in sulfuric acid. On being charged, the surface of one sheet became spongy lead and the other became lead dioxide. Camille Faure in 1881 patented a process for increasing the surface area by pasting grids with lead oxides that were subsequently converted either to spongy lead or to lead dioxide. At the turn of the century, Waldemar Jungner and Thomas Edison independently developed alkaline storage batteries. Jungner developed the nickel-cadmium type, and Edison developed the nickel-iron battery.

Reserve cells were developed during World War II because conventional types of batteries could not be adapted readily to the stringent requirements of modern warfare. Later interest in fuel cells arose because the rapid advances in postwar technology created a need for new power sources.

Wet Primary Cells. The wet primary cells now in use are the caustic soda (or Lalande), air, and LeCarbone cells. Standard cells (for measurements) are not used as a source of electric power and, therefore, are not considered here.

Caustic Soda Cells. A caustic soda cell has flat zinc negatives, flat copper oxide positives, a sodium hydroxide solution, a glass jar container, and a porcelain lid that supports the electrodes on a single rack. A thin layer of oil over the solution protects it from atmospheric carbon dioxide. These cells are made in various sizes and have rated capacities ranging from 75 to 1,000 ampere-hours. The cells have voltages of only 0.6 volt, but they give long service, and they deliver about 14 watt-hours per pound or 0.7 watt-hour per cubic inch. Caustic soda cells are used chiefly in rural areas to activate railroad signals.

Air and LeCarbone Cells. The air cell is similar to the caustic soda cell, except that a depolarizer of atmospheric oxygen is used. The oxygen in the air is adsorbed on a water-repellent, activated-porous-carbon electrode. The air cell has an operating voltage of 1.1 to 1.2 volts and sustains current densities of 0.03 ampere per square inch of the carbon electrode or 2 amperes per square inch when the electrode is in a pure oxygen atmosphere. Some LeCarbone cells differ from air cells only in minor structural details; others use electrodes of manganese dioxide in activated carbon submerged in ammonium chloride solutions. Both air and LeCarbone cells are used in radios and for railroad signal service.

Dry Primary Cells. Dry primary cells made in appreciable quantities are the Leclanché, alkaline manganese dioxide, and mercury cells. Silver chloride and silver oxide cells are made in lesser amounts. Other types of dry cells are manufactured only in limited quantities.

Leclanché Dry Cells. Leclanché cells are produced in various sizes and shapes. The cylindrical type is packaged as a unit cell; a well-known example is the flashlight battery (commonly called a battery even though it has only one cell). The flat types are used only in cell assemblies. A Leclanché cell has zinc negatives, an ammonium chloride electrolyte, and positives of finely divided carbon and manganese dioxide packed around a carbon-rod terminal. The unlike electrodes are separated by moistened paper, starch-flour gel, or some other porous nonconductor. Generally, the nonconductor contains zinc and mercuric chlorides. Mercuric chloride is used to amalgamate the zinc in order to increase the storage life.

When the cell is made in cylindrical form, the zinc usually serves both as the negative electrode and as the container. Duplex electrodes are used in flat cells. A flat zinc sheet, covered on one side by a coating of granular carbon mixed with a plastic binder, is adjacent to a molded cake of manganese dioxide, carbon, and ammonium chloride. The bare side of the zinc, which serves as the negative for one cell, is separated from the cake by moistened paper or some other porous nonconductor.

The reaction at the negative electrode is:
$$Zn + 2\ OH^- \rightarrow ZnO + H_2O + 2\varepsilon,$$
where ε denotes the electron and OH^- denotes the hydroxyl ion, which comes from the ionization of water:
$$H_2O \rightleftharpoons H^+ + OH^-.$$
The reaction at the positive electrode, if the discharge rate is slow, is:
$$2\ MnO_2 + 2\ H^+ + 2\varepsilon \rightarrow Mn_2O_3 \cdot H_2O.$$
This reaction is followed by
$$Mn_2O_3 \cdot H_2O + ZnO \rightarrow ZnO \cdot Mn_2O_3 + H_2O.$$
If the discharge rate is high, the reaction at the positive is:
$$2\ MnO_2 + 2\ NH_4^+ + 2\varepsilon \rightarrow Mn_2O_3 \cdot H_2O + NH_3.$$
The ammonium ion (NH_4^+) comes from the ionization of the ammonium chloride. In each case the cell reaction is the sum of the reactions at the two electrodes. The nominal open-circuit voltage of a Leclanché cell is 1.54 volts.

The output of Leclanché cells is linearly dependent on cell weight and volume for low currents but is nearly independent of weight and volume for high currents. Leclanché cells provide almost 45 watt-hours per pound if the currents are low and intermittent.

Conventional dry cells become inoperative at 0° F (−18° C) because the electrolyte freezes. Special types that use lithium chloride or calcium and zinc chlorides will operate at temperatures as low as −40° F (−40° C).

Alkaline Dry Cells. Alkaline dry cells are similar to Leclanché dry cells, except that potassium hydroxide is used as the electrolyte. They sustain higher discharge rates than Leclanché cells and, therefore, are sometimes called high-rate cells. In some alkaline cells mercury oxide is mixed with the manganese dioxide.

Mercury Dry Cells. Mercury dry cells are alkaline cells that use potassium hydroxide saturated with zinc oxide as the electrolyte and zinc and mercury oxide as the electrodes. The reaction at the negative electrode is:
$$Zn + 2\ OH^- \rightarrow ZnO + H_2O + 2\varepsilon.$$
The reaction at the positive electrode is:
$$HgO + H_2O + 2\varepsilon \rightarrow Hg + 2\ OH^-.$$
The cell reaction is the sum of the reactions at the two electrodes. This sum shows that the cell reaction is independent of the electrolyte concentration. The OH^- comes from the ionization of potassium hydroxide:
$$KOH \rightarrow K^+ + OH^-.$$
Mercury dry cells have flatter voltage curves on discharge than Leclanché cells. The working voltage under moderate loads is 1.30 volts. On low drains the mercury cell provides 53 watt-hours per pound.

Mercury cells are made in various forms. They are used in portable radios, hearing aids, and various appliances.

Silver-Chloride Dry Cells. Silver-chloride cells are made in designs similar to cylindrical Leclanché or mercury cells. A depolarizer of silver chloride is fused on a silver-wire positive, or a powdered form is placed on a sheet-silver positive. A zinc negative is used. Sodium, zinc, or ammonium chloride is generally used for the electrolyte. This cell, which has a voltage of 1.03 to 1.06 volts and is little affected by temperature, is suitable only for low current drains.

Silver-oxide dry cells, which are similar to mercury cells, are used in hearing aids.

Reserve Cells. The common reserve cells are activated by gas, water, heat or an electrolyte.

Gas-Activated Cells. A common gas-activated cell is the chlorine cell. Chlorine gas, supplied by tank or other source, is adsorbed on water-repellent, activated carbon. Chlorine positives

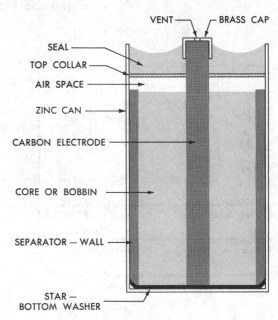

VENT — BRASS CAP

SEAL

TOP COLLAR

AIR SPACE

ZINC CAN

CARBON ELECTRODE

CORE OR BOBBIN

SEPARATOR — WALL

STAR — BOTTOM WASHER

THE CYLINDRICAL LECLANCHÉ DRY CELL is the familiar flashlight battery. Zinc can is both negative electrode and container. Bobbin is a mix of ammonium chloride, carbon and manganese dioxide. Ammonium chloride is the electrolyte. Carbon, manganese dioxide, and carbon rod together form the positive electrode.

OPERATION OF
A LEAD-ACID STORAGE BATTERY

A – FULLY CHARGED

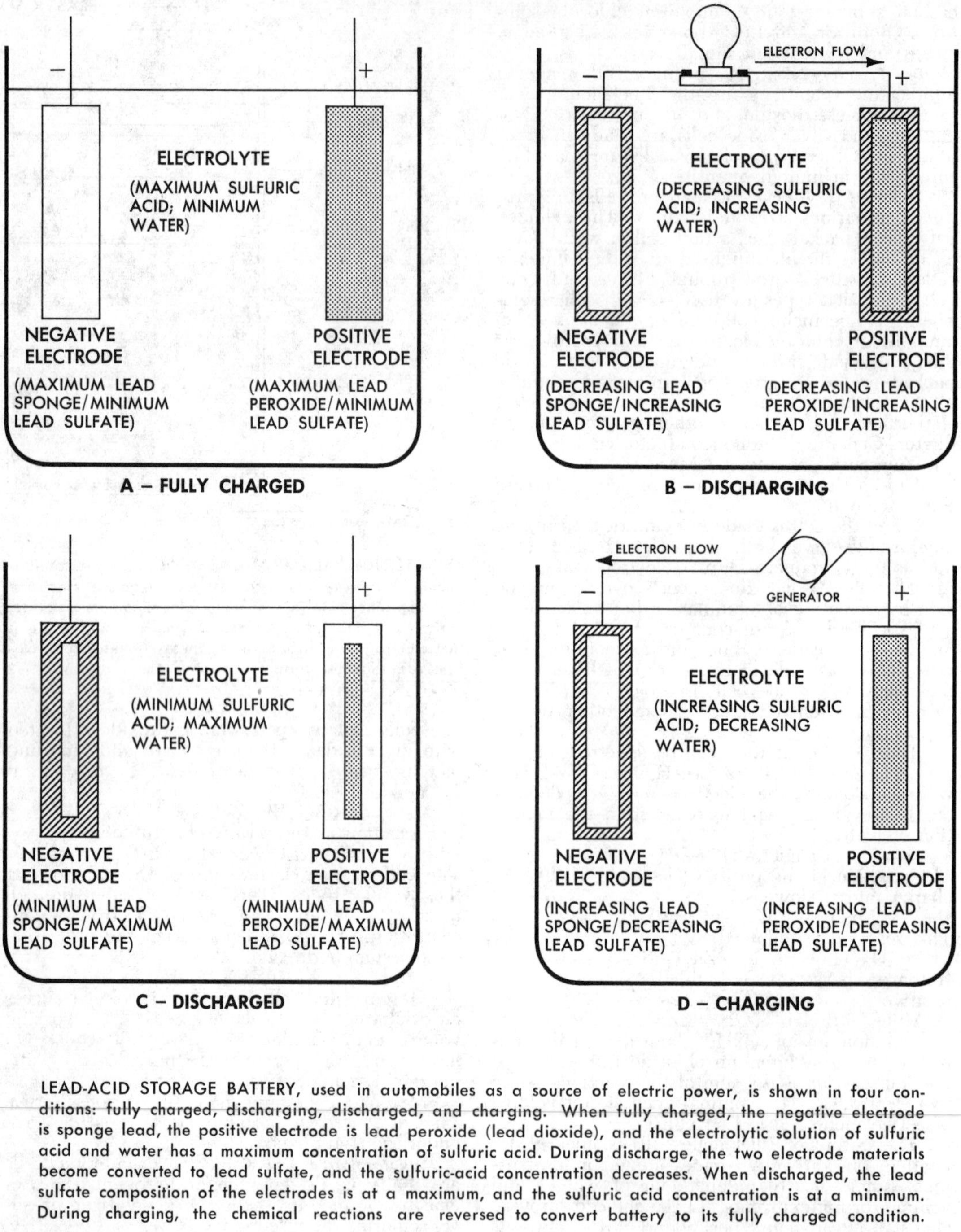

ELECTROLYTE

(MAXIMUM SULFURIC ACID; MINIMUM WATER)

NEGATIVE ELECTRODE

(MAXIMUM LEAD SPONGE/MINIMUM LEAD SULFATE)

POSITIVE ELECTRODE

(MAXIMUM LEAD PEROXIDE/MINIMUM LEAD SULFATE)

B – DISCHARGING

ELECTRON FLOW

ELECTROLYTE

(DECREASING SULFURIC ACID; INCREASING WATER)

NEGATIVE ELECTRODE

(DECREASING LEAD SPONGE/INCREASING LEAD SULFATE)

POSITIVE ELECTRODE

(DECREASING LEAD PEROXIDE/INCREASING LEAD SULFATE)

C – DISCHARGED

ELECTROLYTE

(MINIMUM SULFURIC ACID; MAXIMUM WATER)

NEGATIVE ELECTRODE

(MINIMUM LEAD SPONGE/MAXIMUM LEAD SULFATE)

POSITIVE ELECTRODE

(MINIMUM LEAD PEROXIDE/MAXIMUM LEAD SULFATE)

D – CHARGING

ELECTRON FLOW

GENERATOR

ELECTROLYTE

(INCREASING SULFURIC ACID; DECREASING WATER)

NEGATIVE ELECTRODE

(INCREASING LEAD SPONGE/DECREASING LEAD SULFATE)

POSITIVE ELECTRODE

(INCREASING LEAD PEROXIDE/DECREASING LEAD SULFATE)

LEAD-ACID STORAGE BATTERY, used in automobiles as a source of electric power, is shown in four conditions: fully charged, discharging, discharged, and charging. When fully charged, the negative electrode is sponge lead, the positive electrode is lead peroxide (lead dioxide), and the electrolytic solution of sulfuric acid and water has a maximum concentration of sulfuric acid. During discharge, the two electrode materials become converted to lead sulfate, and the sulfuric-acid concentration decreases. When discharged, the lead sulfate composition of the electrodes is at a maximum, and the sulfuric acid concentration is at a minimum. During charging, the chemical reactions are reversed to convert battery to its fully charged condition.

are used with zinc negatives in zinc-chloride solutions. The chlorine cell has an open-circuit voltage of 2.05 volts under a chlorine pressure of one atmosphere. The chlorine cell type may also be operated at high pressures, utilizing liquid chlorine. Under chlorine-gas pressure of 90 psi, this cell can sustain 0.8 to 0.9 ampere per square inch of chlorine electrode surface area.

Water-Activated Cells. Water-activated cells utilize magnesium negatives and either silver chloride or cuprous chloride positives. They are activated by being dipped in seawater. They will also operate, but less efficiently, in distilled or tap water. After activation they show a delay time in attaining maximum voltage. The delay time depends on the current drain; 20 to 40 minutes are required if the current is 1.3 to 1.5 amperes per cubic inch. Water-activated cells are used mostly in marine and meteorological applications.

Heat-Activated Cells. In heat-activated cells (called thermal cells), the electrolyte is a solid before activation. Upon heat activation the electrolyte melts, ions migrate to the electrodes, and the cell operates. A typical thermal cell has calcium negatives, silver positives, and an electrolyte that is a eutectic mixture of lithium chloride, potassium chloride, and some potassium chromate. A thermal cell has an exceedingly long storage life in the unactivated state. At 752° F (401° C), the typical thermal cell yields about 20 watt-hours per pound or 0.12 watt-hour per cubic inch.

Electrolyte-Activated Cells. Electrolyte-activated cells, which can have almost any electrode materials, are activated by various electrolytes. For example, lead and lead-dioxide electrodes are activated by sulfuric, perchloric, fluoboric, or fluosilicic acid electrolytes. Zinc and silver-oxide electrodes are activated by potassium hydroxide. Electrolyte-activated cells are used almost exclusively in military equipment.

Fuel Cells. Many electrode-electrolyte combinations have been studied in designing fuel cells. The Bacon cell is the most advanced type of fuel cell. It has hydrogen negatives, oxygen positives, and an electrolyte that is a potassium hydroxide solution. Under pressure, both gases are supplied continuously to the surfaces of highly porous nickel plates. The cell operates at 464° F (240° C) at a pressure of 53 atmospheres, has voltages of 0.6 to 0.9 volt (depending on the load), and can provide 10 kilowatts per cubic foot. It can also be operated at a temperature of 120° F to 140° F (49° C to 60° C) by using air at a pressure of one atmosphere, but the output then is only 300 watts per cubic foot. These cells can operate continuously for several days before the electrolyte needs replacement. See also FUEL CELL.

Secondary Batteries. Each of the five types of secondary batteries has favorable characteristics for a particular application. Lead-acid batteries are economical and desirable when it is necessary to know the state of charge at any instant. Nickel-iron batteries are preferable when ruggedness is of prime importance. Nickel-cadmium batteries are useful when a minimum of gassing is essential. Zinc-silver batteries serve best when high discharge rates are prerequisites and charge retention is less important. Zinc-cadmium batteries provide both high discharge rates and good charge retention.

Lead-Acid Batteries. Lead-acid batteries are manufactured in various designs to suit different applications, such as aircraft, automotive, material handling, marine, standby, or low-discharge service. A lead-acid cell consists of lead negatives; lead-dioxide positives; a sulfuric acid electrolyte; separators of rubber, wood, fiber glass, or plastic; a container of hard rubber, glass, plastic, ceramic, or composition material; a cover; vents; a sealing compound; and terminals. The negative plates of a cell are joined in parallel, as are the positive plates. The plates may be pure lead (Planté construction) or made with lead-antimony (6 to 13 percent) or lead-calcium (less than 0.1 percent) grids and lead-oxide pastes. The lead-antimony alloy is used in batteries that are operated periodically. The lead-calcium alloy is used in standby batteries. Planté plates are made from pure lead sheets. The surface area is increased either by chemical etching or by a formation process in which the plates are repeatedly charged and discharged. In this process one electrode becomes covered with spongy lead and the other with lead dioxide; the spongy lead and lead dioxide are called active materials. In making pasted plates, a paste of litharge, red lead, and sulfuric acid is applied to a grid, where

it sets like cement. The plate is then formed to negatives or positives by electrolysis in sulfuric acid.

Various acid concentrations are used, depending on the intended use of the battery. For automotive and marine service the specific gravity for a fully charged battery is 1.260 to 1.280. The use of a higher specific gravity leads to higher outputs per unit volume. A higher specific gravity, 1.300, can be used in low-discharge batteries because they are made with pure lead plates that show less local action (or corrosion) than alloy plates.

During discharge the active material of the negatives and the positives is converted to lead sulfate. The sulfate ion $(SO_4^=)$ comes from the ionization of the sulfuric acid (H_2SO_4):

$$H_2SO_4 \rightarrow 2\,H^+ + SO_4^=.$$

The reaction at the negative electrode is:

$$Pb + SO_4^= \underset{\text{charge}}{\overset{\text{discharge}}{\rightleftharpoons}} PbSO_4 + 2\varepsilon.$$

The reaction at the positive electrode is:

$$PbO_2 + 4\,H^+ + SO_4^= + 2\varepsilon \underset{\text{charge}}{\overset{\text{discharge}}{\rightleftharpoons}} PbSO_4 + 2\,H_2O.$$

The cell reaction is the sum of the two reactions. Sulfuric acid is consumed during discharge, and the specific gravity of the solution decreases. On

LEAD-ACID STORAGE BATTERY, shown in a cutaway view. Positive plate is lead dioxide. Plate separator is made of wood or fiber glass. Negative plate is lead. Vent releases gases. Two terminals are for external connections. Sealed cover protects battery, and rubber container encases assembly. Chamber is for sediment.

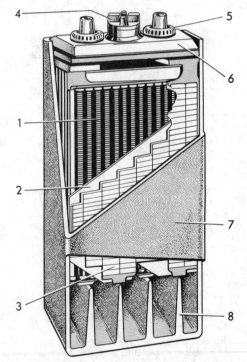

1 POSITIVE PLATE	5 TERMINAL
2 PLATE SEPARATOR	6 SEALED COVER
3 NEGATIVE PLATE	7 JAR OR CONTAINER
4 VENT	8 SEDIMENT CHAMBER

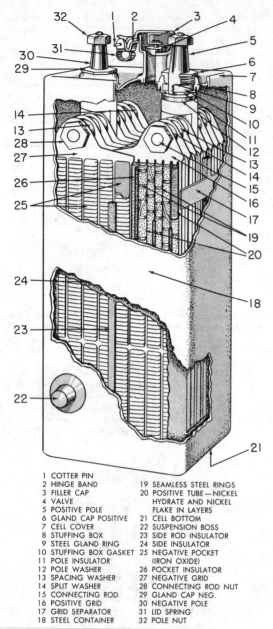

1 COTTER PIN
2 HINGE BAND
3 FILLER CAP
4 VALVE
5 POSITIVE POLE
6 GLAND CAP POSITIVE
7 CELL COVER
8 STUFFING BOX
9 STEEL GLAND RING
10 STUFFING BOX GASKET
11 POLE INSULATOR
12 POLE WASHER
13 SPACING WASHER
14 SPLIT WASHER
15 CONNECTING ROD
16 POSITIVE GRID
17 GRID SEPARATOR
18 STEEL CONTAINER

19 SEAMLESS STEEL RINGS
20 POSITIVE TUBE—NICKEL
   HYDRATE AND NICKEL
   FLAKE IN LAYERS
21 CELL BOTTOM
22 SUSPENSION BOSS
23 SIDE ROD INSULATOR
24 SIDE INSULATOR
25 NEGATIVE POCKET
   (IRON OXIDE)
26 POCKET INSULATOR
27 NEGATIVE GRID
28 CONNECTING ROD NUT
29 GLAND CAP NEG.
30 NEGATIVE POLE
31 LID SPRING
32 POLE NUT

NICKEL-IRON ALKALINE BATTERY of the Edison type, shown in a cutaway view. Major components include positive pole (5), positive grid (16), positive nickel-plated tubes (20), negative pockets filled with ferrous oxide (25), negative grid (27), negative pole (30), special venting valve (4), and container (18).

charge, the opposite is the case. At 80 percent of full charge appreciable gassing starts and continues simultaneously with the final charging of the plates. This gassing comes from the electrolysis of the water in the acid.

Fully charged batteries have voltages of 2.09 to 2.15 volts, depending on the acid concentration at full charge. In use the voltage decreases slowly to about 1.75 volts. Thereafter, it decreases rapidly. On the average, lead-acid batteries yield 10.5 watt-hours per pound or about 1 watt-hour per cubic inch. They function well

until the temperature drops below 0° F (−18° C); then the batteries accept a recharge inefficiently.

Nickel-Iron Batteries. A nickel-iron battery has iron negatives, nickel-oxide positives, an electrolyte that is a 21 percent solution of potassium hydroxide and contains some lithium hydroxide, a suitable container, covers, vents, and terminals. Special vents allow the escape of gas but prevent the intake of air, thereby avoiding electrolyte contamination by atmospheric carbon dioxide. The negatives are made of small nickel-plated steel boxes or pockets with perforated sides. These boxes are fastened to a nickel-plated steel grid, which has a series of vertical openings to accommodate the boxes. The boxes are filled with finely divided iron that has been partially oxidized to ferrous oxide. A little mercury is added to increase plate conductivity. The positives consist of a series of perforated nickel-plated tubes containing a mixture of nickel oxide and flake nickel. The tubes are supported in a nickel-plated steel grid.

The reaction at the negative electrode is:

$$Fe + 2\,OH^- \xrightleftharpoons[charge]{discharge} FeO + H_2O + 2\varepsilon.$$

The reaction at the positive electrode is:

$$NiO_2 + H_2O + 2\varepsilon \xrightleftharpoons[charge]{discharge} NiO + 2\,OH^-.$$

The cell reaction is the sum of the two reactions and is independent of the electrolyte concentration. Accordingly, the state of charge cannot be determined by measuring the specific gravity of the solution because it is the same for a fully charged or a fully discharged battery.

Nickel-iron batteries, on the average, yield 12 watt-hours per pound. Their working voltage decreases at a very slow rate from about 1.30 volts to 1.00 volt. Thereafter, it decreases rapidly. Nickel-iron batteries are used in material handling, railway lighting, telephone exchanges, and other applications.

Nickel-Cadmium Batteries. There are two types of nickel-cadmium batteries. One type has pocket-tubular plates similar to those in nickel-iron batteries. The other type has sintered plates. The reactions at the electrodes are the same as those given for the nickel-iron battery except that cadmium replaces iron in the first equation. Sintered plates and pocket-tubular plates give comparable results except at high discharge rates, where the former show superiority because of their high porosity.

These batteries are also made with the electrolyte largely confined in the separators. These types can be hermetically sealed for use in power-driven toothbrushes and screwdrivers.

Nickel-cadmium cells have open-circuit voltages of 1.33 to 1.34 volts, have flat discharge curves, and yield, on the average, 12 watt-hours per pound. They are used in aircraft, railroad lighting, and in other applications.

Zinc-Silver and Cadmium-Silver Batteries. Zinc-silver and cadmium-silver batteries have zinc or cadmium negatives (in sheet or pasted form), pasted silver-oxide positives on silver- or nickel-plated copper screen, and an electrolyte that is a 20 to 40 percent potassium hydroxide solution. The separators are made of cellulosic or similar material. The batteries have suitable containers, covers, vents, and terminals. Silver oxide exists in two forms. It exists as the univalent silver oxide, Ag_2O, and divalent silver oxide, AgO. With zinc negatives the Ag_2O provides 1.59 volts, and the AgO provides 1.82 volts. With cadmium negatives the Ag_2O provides 1.16 volts and the AgO provides 1.38 volts. For zinc-silver cells the electrode reactions are:

$$Zn + 4\,OH^- \xrightleftharpoons[\text{charge}]{\text{discharge}} ZnO_2^= + 2\,H_2O + 2\,\varepsilon,$$

$$2\,AgO + H_2O + 2\,\varepsilon \xrightleftharpoons[\text{charge}]{\text{discharge}} Ag_2O + 2\,OH^-,$$

$$Ag_2O + H_2O + \varepsilon \xrightleftharpoons[\text{charge}]{\text{discharge}} 2\,Ag + 2\,OH^-.$$

The cell reaction is the sum of the zinc reaction and one of the silver-oxide reactions, depending on which silver oxide is present.

The reaction at the cadmium negative electrode is:

$$Cd + 2\,OH^- \xrightleftharpoons[\text{charge}]{\text{discharge}} Cd(OH)_2 + 2\,\varepsilon.$$

This reaction can be used with either silver-oxide reaction to give the cell reactions for the cadmium-silver cell.

Zinc-silver batteries generally provide 35 watt-hours per pound. The cadmium-silver type provides somewhat less. These outputs exceed those of other secondary batteries by a factor of nearly three. Because of the high discharge characteristics of these batteries, they are used extensively in military applications. Dry types of zinc-silver cells are used in hearing aids.

Solar and Nuclear Batteries. Solar and nuclear batteries are not electrochemical, and probably should not be called batteries in the true sense. Nevertheless, it has become common practice to do so. Solar cells are photovoltaic cells that operate with an efficiency of nearly 15 percent. Common types use p-n silicon junctions. When light strikes a solar cell, electrons flow from the n-type material (containing excess electrons) to the p-type material (with a deficiency of electrons) and thence to an external circuit. Under full sunlight a voltage of 0.6 volt is produced at the p-n junction. Under load the maximum voltage is 0.45 volt, and currents of nearly 40 milliamperes per square centimeter of surface area are obtained.

Nuclear batteries convert radioactive energy into electrical energy. Their operation is based on the fact that particles or rays are ejected from the atomic nucleus. In the strontium-90 battery, the emitter is strontium-90 embedded in gold foil, and the collector is an aluminum rod. A plastic is used to absorb slow-moving electrons that are reflected from the collector. The voltage across the small electrodes may reach 10,000 volts. Cells that are 1 inch (2.54 cm) high, $\frac{3}{8}$ inch (0.95 cm) in diameter, 5 ounces (140 grams) in weight, and contain 2 millicuries of strontium-90 provide a maximum current of only 50 micromicroamperes. They are expensive. Nuclear batteries can provide only extremely low currents, but they can operate at extremely low temperatures where other batteries fail.

WALTER J. HAMER, *National Bureau of Standards*

Bibliography
Hamer, Walter J., "New Dry Cells," *Product Engineering*, Vol. 21, No. 3 (New York 1950).
Hamer, Walter J., "Modern Batteries," IRE *Transactions*, Vol. CP-4, No. 3 (New York 1957).
Vinal, George W., *Primary Batteries* (New York 1950).
Vinal, George W., *Storage Batteries* (New York 1955).

BATTERY, The, bat'ə-rē, a park in New York City, at the southern tip of Manhattan Island, covering 22 acres (9 hectares). Its official name is Battery Park but it is commonly called the Battery after harbor defenses that stood here at various times. A waterfront promenade gives a fine view of the harbor. Boats from the Battery carry visitors to the Statue of Liberty on Liberty Island. The walls of Castle Clinton stand in the park. This structure was completed as a fort in 1811 and later was used as an amusement center, an immigrant station, and the New York Aquarium. The aquarium was relocated in 1941, and the building was abandoned for a time. It has since been designated the Castle Clinton National Monument.

BATTICALOA, bət-i-kə-lō'ə, is a seaport in Ceylon. The capital of the Eastern province, it is located on an island in a lagoon on the east coast of the country and is connected with the Ceylonese mainland by a bridge and causeway. Batticaloa is a railroad terminus and has a sheltered harbor frequented by coastal shipping vessels. The city is in an extremely hot region, but the warm weather is beneficial for growing rice and coconut. Fishing is also an important industry. The phenomenon of the "singing fish"—sounds emanating from the lagoon at night—has not been clearly explained, although it is believed that the musical sounds come from a type of shellfish.

The Portuguese settled here early in the 17th century but were displaced soon after by the Dutch, who in 1682 built a fort whose ruins remain. The city was ceded to the British in 1796. In World War II it was an Allied naval base. Population: (1963) 22,957.

BATTISHILL, bat'ə-shəl, **Jonathan** (1738–1801), English organist and composer. He was born in London in May 1738. In the early 1760's he was named harpsichordist at Covent Garden Theatre. After 1764 he was organist of various London churches and devoted much of his time to writing church music. Battishill composed the opera *Almena* (1764), with Michael Arne, and the pantomine *The Rites of Hecate* (1763). He died at Islington on Dec. 10, 1801.

BATTLE is a town in England, in East Sussex, 6 miles (9.5 km) northwest of Hastings. It is near the site of the Battle of Hastings (Oct. 14, 1066), in which Duke William of Normandy defeated the Saxons led by King Harold and established his conquest of England. The early name of the place was *Senlac;* it was renamed after William's victory. The battle was fought on Senlac Hill, southeast of the present town.

To commemorate his victory, William built Battle Abbey on the spot where King Harold was killed. The abbey was consecrated in 1094, and for centuries its Benedictine monks received many privileges from the English kings. After the Reformation the abbey was suppressed, and the property was presented by King Henry VIII to Sir Anthony Browne, who made it his home. Little remains of the original buildings, but there are remnants of later construction, including the abbot's lodge and a 14th century gatehouse in the English Decorated style.

A list supposedly containing the names of the Norman nobles who fought under William at Hastings was preserved at Battle Abbey and was known as *Battle Abbey Roll.* The list survives only in several 16th century versions, which may be copies of a 14th century compilation. The surviving copies contain some spurious entries. Many of the families listed were not established in England until several centuries after 1066. It is believed that the list was not drawn up until the 14th century and included names of some who were then supposed to have accompanied William and perhaps names of others whose descendants wished to claim that distinction.

BATTLE, an encounter between organized military forces engaged in a determined effort to defeat each other by the application of military power. The forces engaged may be land, sea, or air forces, which may act singly or in combination. In modern times air forces play an important role in land and sea battles.

Battles may be classified, generally, as *defensive, offensive,* or *offensive-defensive* (sometimes called *active defense*). The classification of a given battle depends on the point of view. In a battle in which one side seeks only to prevent its own destruction by the attack of its opponent, the battle is a defensive battle as far as the defender is concerned and an offensive battle from the viewpoint of the attacker.

Defensive Tactics. In a land battle, forces on the defensive are able to take shelter and to construct fortifications, so that an attacking force, which must expose itself in advancing to attack, suffers greater losses at first than the defending force. However, if the attack is successful, the defender's losses mount rapidly, and in the end usually exceed those of the attacker. In air and sea battles the defender lacks the advantage of natural protection. Although air or naval forces may have the mission of defending an area and so may be said to be on the defensive, they would invite disaster if they confined their efforts to self-protection. Therefore, in air and naval battles each side usually operates offensively.

A land force employing purely defensive measures can hope only to force the attacker to exhaust himself. A decisive victory through this means has rarely, if ever, been attained. Competent military forces assume the defensive only through necessity or in furtherance of an action elsewhere. An initial inferiority may require assumption of the defensive to ward off an opponent until sufficient strength can be mustered to attack. Or a force may take up the defensive as part of a larger plan in which its function is to engage a portion of the enemy forces or to protect the flank and rear of a friendly force which seeks to gain a decision elsewhere.

Offensive-Defensive Tactics. In an offensive-defensive battle the defender disposes his forces so as to entice the attacker into a situation in which the attacker himself becomes disadvantageously exposed to attack. Then the defender turns to the offensive. If the ruse succeeds, a great victory may be gained. But if the attacker does not adopt the line of action expected, the defender is in a critical situation, for he has surrendered the initiative to the attacker and must conform to his maneuvers. The defender's dispositions, planned as a trap, may not be capable of modification in time to meet the course adopted by the attacker.

When two hostile marching forces meet, the action is termed a *meeting engagement.* Being on the march, neither side is favorably disposed for battle. Each commander hastens to bring his forces forward to strike in force before his opponent does. The result is usually a progressive reinforcement of the battlefront in which one side is finally forced on the defensive, and the battle becomes a normal battle.

In the early days of warfare, when battles were fought between closely formed groups armed with hand weapons, the side with the greater number of men usually emerged victorious. The progressive introduction of new weapons of war has reduced the influence of preponderance in numbers. The relative strength of opposing force in battle is now measured in terms of *combat power,* which is over-all evaluation of those human and material elements employed in warfare.

Types of Defense. A land force on the defensive may employ one of two principal types of defensive—*defense of a position* or *delaying action.* In the former the defender intends to fight to a decision on a previously prepared position; in the latter he plans to fight on one position, inflicting maximum loss on the attacker but withdrawing to another position as the attacker closes in on the position. This procedure is repeated on the second position and may be continued on successive positions.

In the defense of a position the defender may adopt a *cordon defense* or a *defense in depth.* In a cordon defense the defender places the preponderance of his force along the battle line. The disadvantage of this form of defense is that if the attacker breaks through the battle line, there is little behind this line to resist him, and he is in a favorable position to gain a victory. In a defense in depth the defender disposes his forces in several lines, lightly along the forward line and with groups held in reserve behind locations which favor the attacker. Thus, if an attacker should break through a section of the forward line, he will be engaged by other lines while reserves are moved quickly to the troubled area to repel the attacker.

Offensive Tactics. Two forms of attack are generally available to the attacker, a *penetration* or an *envelopment.* In a penetration the attacker attempts to pierce a selected portion of the defender's line and to attack the separated portions in flank and rear. This is the most costly form of attack because it is directed against the prepared defenses of the defender. It is generally used only when the flanks of the position are strong and no choice is offered. An envelopment seeks to avoid the prepared defenses of the enemy and to attack him on the flank or rear. An attempt to envelop one flank is termed a *single envelopment;* both flanks a *double envelopment.* If the enveloping force is airborne, the maneuver is termed a *vertical envelopment;* if seaborne, it is called an *amphibious envelopment.*

In an attack, the attacker seeks to apply a preponderance of force against a selected area where terrain or enemy dispositions favor success. This is termed the *main attack.* In addition, in order to deceive the defender as to the place where the main attack will occur and to prevent movement of defending forces from other parts of the front to the main attack area, the attacker may launch one or more attacks with lesser forces at other parts of the line. These attacks are *secondary* or *subsidiary* attacks.

See also STRATEGY; TACTICS.

VINCENT JOSEPH ESPOSITO
United States Military Academy

BATTLE ABOVE THE CLOUDS, the popular name given to the fight for Lookout Mountain in the Battle of Chattanooga, during the American Civil War. It was fought on Nov. 24, 1863. Union troops, led by Gen. Joseph Hooker, successfully attacked the Confederate position on the summit of Lookout Mountain. Since the mountain overlooked the Tennessee River and the railroad, its capture opened a direct route for passage of Union forces. See CHATTANOOGA CAMPAIGN.

BATTLE-AX, an ax designed as a weapon of war. Fighting axes with horn, stone, or bronze heads and wooden shafts were widely used in the Late Stone Age and Early Bronze Age. Anthropologists have given the name "battle-ax warriors" to peoples that swept into Europe from Asia between 2300 and 1900 B.C. Bronze axes were known to the ancient Greeks; Homer tells of their use in the Trojan War. Axes became still more effective as men learned to make iron weapons. The iron ax was one of the favorite weapons of the Germanic tribes that fought the Romans during the declining years of the empire.

The battle-ax reached its highest development in the Middle Ages. The broad-bladed ax was one of the standard weapons of the Saxon armies in England, and the Bayeux Tapestry shows axmen fighting at Hastings. Mounted warriors tended to prefer the sword as a hand weapon, but the ax continued in use. For example, at Bannockburn in 1314, King Robert Bruce of Scotland killed an English champion with one blow of his ax.

Some medieval battle-axes had a single blade, often with a spike or knob opposite the cutting edge. Double-bladed axes were also made. Handles varied in length from about the length of a modern hatchet to four feet or more. The halberd, used by foot soldiers in the late Middle Ages, was a combination of ax, pike, and hook on a shaft about six feet long.

BATTLE CREEK is an industrial city of south central Michigan, in Calhoun County. It is situated at the junction of Battle Creek and the Kalamazoo River. It has diversified manufactures but is best known for the production of cereal foods. Other manufactures include trucks, automotive valves, packaging machinery, boxboard and cartons, screw machine parts, and welded wire and steel products. The U.S. Defense Logistics Services Center in Battle Creek is the federal government's central cataloging agency.

The Symphony Orchestra, Civic Theatre, Community Chorus, and Civic Art Center are sponsored by the Battle Creek United Arts Council. Other educational and cultural facilities include Kellogg Community College; the Kingman Memorial Museum, devoted to natural history and situated in the Leila Arboretum; the Kellogg Auditorium; and Willard Public Library.

The battle that gave the creek its name was only a skirmish between surveyors and a few Indians on the banks of the stream in 1825. In 1833, Battle Creek was adopted as the name for a settlement that had originated two years earlier. Chartered as a village in 1850, Battle Creek was incorporated as a city in 1859. Before the Civil War, Battle Creek was an important stop on the "underground railroad," the route by which slaves escaped from the South. Sojourner Truth, an ex-slave who did much to help her people, came to Battle Creek in 1858;

her grave is in Oak Hill Cemetery.

The cereal industry developed from the semi-religious emphasis on health foods in the 19th century. The Seventh-day Adventists ran a medical boarding house that grew into the famous Battle Creek Sanitarium under the direction of Dr. John Harvey Kellogg. To vary the vegetarian diets of his patients, Dr. Kellogg invented some 80 grain and nut-food products, including peanut butter and flaked breakfast foods. His younger brother, W.K. Kellogg, and C.W. Post took the idea of these products and developed them for worldwide sale. The Seventh-day Adventists still operate the sanitarium here.

Battle Creek adopted the city manager form of government in 1960. Population: 38,931.

HELEN L. WARNER, *Willard Public Library*

BATTLE CRY OF FREEDOM, a patriotic song of the North during the American Civil War. It contains the line, "We'll rally round the flag, boys!" Both words and music were written by George Frederick Root in 1861. Shortly after it was written, the song was sung at a rally in Chicago by two popular singers of the day, Frank and Jules Lombard. By the end of the rendition thousands of listeners had joined in singing the refrain. The Hutchinson family, a traveling troupe of singers, then added the song to their repertory. It became a favorite marching song of the Union Army. The same composer wrote *Tramp, Tramp, Tramp, the Boys Are Marching*, which attained a similar success.

BATTLE HYMN OF THE REPUBLIC, a popular patriotic song written during the American Civil War by Julia Ward Howe (q.v.), and sung to the tune of *John Brown's Body*. Julia Howe wrote the words in December 1861 while she was visiting Union troops under Gen. George B. McClellan near Washington, D.C. It was published in the February 1862 edition of the *Atlantic Monthly* magazine and immediately became widely popular, especially with partisans of the Union cause. It was largely on the strength of this work that Mrs. Howe became the first woman to be elected to the American Academy of Arts and Letters. The text of the song follows.

Mine eyes have seen the glory of the coming of the Lord;
He is trampling out the vintage where the grapes of wrath are stored;
He hath loosed the fateful lightning of His terrible swift sword;
His truth is marching on.

I have seen Him in the watch-fires of a hundred circling camps;
They have builded Him an altar in the evening dews and damps;
I can read His righteous sentence by the dim and flaring lamps;
His day is marching on.

I have read a fiery gospel, writ in burnished rows of steel:
"As ye deal with my contemners, so with you my grace shall deal;
Let the Hero, born of woman, crush the serpent with his heel,
Since God is marching on."

He has sounded forth the trumpet that shall never call retreat;
He is sifting out the hearts of men before His judgment seat;
Oh, be swift, my soul, to answer Him! be jubilant, my feet!
Our God is marching on.

In the beauty of the lilies Christ was born across the sea,
With a glory in His bosom that transfigures you and me;
As He died to make men holy, let us die to make men free,
While God is marching on.

BATTLE OF ALCAZAR, bat'əl, äl-kä'thär, a play in verse by George Peele. It was first acted in 1589 and published in 1594. It is based on the actual events of Aug. 4, 1578, at Alcázar (now Alcázarquivir), Morocco. Muly Mahamet, a usurper, having just lost the kingdom of Morocco to Abdelmelec, the rightful king, offers to cede the country to King Sebastian of Portugal if Sebastian helps him overthrow Abdelmelec. Sebastian agrees, and in the ensuing battle of Alcázar all three are killed. The character Stukely, who accompanies Sebastian and also is killed, is based on Thomas Stucley, an English adventurer.

The Battle of Alcazar, though its structure is chaotic and its style pretentious, was apparently very popular in its day. Shakespeare may have been indebted to it for his characterization of Aaron, the Moor, in *Titus Andronicus* (1593).

BATTLE OF MALDON, bat'əl, mâl'dən, is a 325-line fragment of an Old English poem that commemorates a battle between the Danes and the English in the 10th century. Although written some three centuries later than *Beowulf*, it resembles that poem in technique and vigor.

The poem describes a battle that took place in 991. It probably was written contemporaneously with the event. A large Viking expedition that had plundered Ipswich had sailed down the English coast to Essex, landing near Maldon, at the mouth of the Blackwater River. It was met there by an English military force led by the ealdorman Byrhtnoth. *Battle of Maldon* describes step by step the course of the struggle that ensued. In the first part of the poem the English have the upper hand; then, a mistake in judgment allows the Danes to cross the river, and the battle hangs in the balance. Two events occur at this point in the poem that determine the battle's outcome. Byrhtnoth is felled by a poisoned arrow, and the coward Godric flees on the slain man's horse. Others follow him, thinking their leader is retreating, leaving a hopeless few to continue the battle. Over a third of the poem is devoted to this last heroic struggle. Especially effective are the lines spoken by the thane who dies fighting beside Byrhtnoth's body.

> My life has been long. Leave I will not,
> but beside my lord I will sink to earth,
> I am minded to die by the man so dear.

The manuscript in which the fragment was found was badly burned in a fire in 1731, but the lines had been copied and published at Oxford in 1726. Translations into modern English appear in *Ten Old English Poems* (1941).

BATTLE OF THE BOOKS, The. See TALE OF A TUB.

BATTLE OF THE FROGS AND MICE, The, an ancient Greek mock epic written in hexameters. Its Greek title is *Batrachomyomachia*. It was formerly attributed to Homer, but modern critics ascribe it to Pigres. Only 316 lines of the epic are extant.

BATTLESHIP. See WARSHIPS—*The Development of Modern Warships.*

BATU KHAN (died 1255), bä'tōō KHän, was a Mongolian overlord of Russia and founder of the Golden Horde, to which many Russian princes were to pay tribute for 250 years. The second son of Juchi and grandson of Genghis Khan, Batu participated in all the major military campaigns of the nomadic Tatar Mongols, which were undertaken to carry out the decision made by the rulers of Mongolia in 1229 to conquer the lands north of the Caspian and Black seas. As a result of two campaigns (1236–1238, 1239–1243), he became suzerain of the area between the Danube on the west and the Irtysh river in Kazakhstan. Batu delivered the coup de grace to the Kievan Russian state, which had been declining since 1132. Having wiped out most of the urban centers of Russia (including Ryazan in 1237, Vladimir in 1238, and Kiev in 1240) and enslaved 10 percent of the Russian population, he permanently destroyed Russia's urban democratic tradition and severely damaged the crafts. Most of the Russian countryside reverted to a natural economy.

In 1243, Batu established the Golden Horde at Sarai on the lower Volga. Much of Russia was subject to the Golden Horde only in political matters and was forced to pay tribute to it. Batu did not administer most of Russia himself but ruled it through Russian princes of the house of Rurik, dating from the 9th century. He devoted much effort to reviving trade in the Volga region. Batu supported the revolution of 1250 in the Mongol empire, during which Mongka (Mangu) of the Tului family became great khan.

RICHARD HELLIE, *University of Chicago*

BATUMI, bä'tōō-mē, a city in the USSR, is the capital of the Adzhar autonomous republic in Georgia. One of the best ports on the Black Sea, it is the terminus of a railroad and pipelines from the petroleum center of Baku, by way of Tbilisi. The chief local industry is oil refining, and from the port goes much of the oil exported by Russia. The climate is hot and wet. Palms, oranges, and lemons are plentiful in the surrounding area, and there are extensive tea plantations.

Batumi, called *Batum* until 1936, was taken from Turkey at the Treaty of Berlin in 1878 and annexed to Russia. Under the treaty Batumi became a free port, but in 1886 Russia abrogated the pact and made the port into a naval base. During World War I, Russia was obliged by the Treaty of Brest Litovsk (March 1918), to evacuate the province of Batum. A Turkish force occupied the city in April, and a British force took over in December after the collapse of Turkey. By a treaty signed in 1921, Turkey restored Batumi to Russia. The port was a major Axis objective in World War II, but the German thrust into the Caucasus failed to reach it. Population: (1970) 101,000.

BAUCIS AND PHILEMON, bô'sis, fil'ē-mən, in Greek legend, a woman and her husband who lived in Phrygia. Despite old age and poverty, they were devoted to each other. When Zeus (Jupiter) and Hermes (Mercury), disguised as mortals, sought hospitality in Phrygia, they were refused by all except Baucis and Philemon. Declaring Phrygia to be a sinful city, the gods destroyed it by flood. Only Baucis and Philemon were saved, and on the site of their cottage a temple arose. The couple were permitted to remain as priests. At their death, Baucis and Philemon were turned into a linden and an oak, forever united as a reward for their faithfulness.

BAUDELAIRE, bō-dlâr', **Charles** (1821–1867), French poet, who was a precursor of the symbolist movement and by the early 20th century had become the most influential of all modern poets. He is best known for his collection, *Les fleurs du mal* (1857).

During his lifetime Baudelaire was condemned as the morbid and decadent author of immoral verse, and only after his death was his poetry granted its present standing. In the last decade of the 19th century, symbolist poets of several countries proclaimed themselves his disciples. Today, far from appearing to be an eccentric and satanic enemy of divine and human laws, Baudelaire is regarded by many as, in the words of T.S. Eliot, "a classicist born out of his due time and a Christian born out of his due time."

The greatness of Baudelaire's poetry stems from its joining of the most diverse qualities, both romantic and classical. It expresses a hypersensibility that is both delicate and profound, and it explores the world of sensations, even those that verge on the morbid and macabre. Baudelaire is also the poet of strangeness, ugliness, fear, and systematic self-destruction. And he was, along with Victor Hugo, one of the first to define the poet's task as an analytical exploration of modern life as lived in large cities.

But Baudelaire added to these romantic elements other qualities that may be described as classical. He considered art the outcome of lucid and patient calculation and refused to worship instinct and inspiration. He stressed composition or, as he called it, the "architecture" of both individual poems and of whole volumes. His form is never loose, commonplace, or facile, but instead is remarkable for its density and for the sumptuous force of its images. In an apt definition of the artist, Baudelaire characterized his own aim in poetry: "I wish to illuminate things with my spirit and to project its reflection upon other spirits."

Youth. Baudelaire was born in Paris on April 9, 1821. His father, an elderly man who was fond of painting, died in 1827. Although Charles could hardly remember his father, he never forgave his young mother for remarrying the year after his father's death.

Baudelaire's relationship with his mother was strangely complex: he loved her tenderly, needed her long after he had grown into a man and a Bohemian poet, and wrote her some of the most pathetic letters ever sent by a poet to his mother —letters begging for both money and understanding. He was hurt by her occasional neglect when, busy with her social life after her second marriage, she entrusted her son to a maid, Mariette, of whom the child became very fond.

Baudelaire's stepfather, Major Aupick, was highly esteemed as an officer in the French army, and for his charm and social poise. He soon became a general, then served as ambassador to Constantinople and later to Madrid. But Baudelaire, considering himself another Hamlet, never developed much admiration for his stepfather.

In his youth Baudelaire was a successful student at the lycée of Lyon and then at Louis-le-Grand in Paris. But he soon dissipated much of the money he had inherited from his father and ran heavily into debts that pursued him all his life. He indulged in a gay and debauched life in the Latin Quarter, and it was probably during this period that he contracted the venereal disease that hastened his decrepitude and death. He

THE GRANGER COLLECTION

Charles Baudelaire (1821–1867)

took a mulatto woman as his mistress—the "black Venus," Jeanne Duval, whom he both loved and despised. Many of his tenderest love poems (*Le balcon, Harmonie du soir,* and *La chevelure*) are addressed to her, as are some of his fiercer poems alluding to her luxuriousness.

Middle Period. In 1841, Baudelaire's stepfather, attempting to tear him away from his dissipated life, packed him off on a ship bound for India. In response to Baudelaire's vehement protests, the captain let him off the ship at the Cape of Good Hope or at Bourbon Island (now Réunion), near Madagascar. He returned to Paris, bringing back a rich supply of exotic visions and dreams of more colorful lands, which later were conjured up longingly and vividly in his verse.

Baudelaire would not reform his life, nor give up his Bohemian friends and mulatto mistress. His few other love affairs were neither prolonged nor successful. Two other women inspired about a dozen poems each. They were Mme. Sabatier, a rather sensuous and corpulent woman whom Baudelaire abruptly renounced after a single night, and a blond actress, Marie Daubrun, who preferred another poet, Théodore de Banville, to Baudelaire. To the actress he addressed the melancholy *Chant d'automne* and the celebrated musical piece *L'invitation au voyage*. Baudelaire, the greatest love poet in the French language, preferred to dream about love and to idealize women from a distance. His love poetry, except for two or three pieces, is surprisingly pure, even the notorious (though very austere and moral) poems on Lesbian love, *Femmes damnées*.

It is probable that a dozen or more of the finest pieces in *Les fleurs du mal* were composed as early as 1842–1843. A few pieces appeared in little-read magazines, but Baudelaire would not rush into print too early. He chose to mature slowly and to wait for the great prestige of his predecessors, the romantic poets, to decline.

However, he began to be known as an extraordinarily discerning art critic and as a fastidious translator of Edgar Allan Poe. Inspired by his admiration of Honoré de Balzac, he also tried his hand at the short story and the personal novel. But Baudelaire was not endowed with the ability to imagine a plot or to compose a long piece either in prose or poetry. His early tales,

Le jeune enchanteur (1846) and *La fanfarlo* (1847), are closer to Théophile Gautier's graceful fantasies than to Balzac's visionary and philosophical stories. A short fragment, *Du vin et du haschisch* (1851), is far more revealing of Baudelaire's persistent obsession—how to increase one's individuality and multiply the self. It later supplemented an important volume titled *Les paradis artificiels* (1860), which also included a translation from De Quincey's *Confessions of an Opium-Eater*. In all that Baudelaire wrote, the same urge recurs: to plunge deeper into evil and into the lower depths of the self—to the realm of the erotic, the satanic, and the irrational. He hoped by these means to extend his knowledge of human nature and to rise above it, becoming more than a man. The title, *Les fleurs du mal* (*Flowers of Evil*), symbolizes his endeavor to pluck new, undreamed-of flowers and to extract a new perfume from their languid and putrescent strangeness.

Baudelaire's art criticism appeared in the form of reviews of the annual art exhibitions, or "salons," of 1845, 1846, and 1859. The second of these contains the often-quoted definition of romanticism, a movement of which Baudelaire always spoke with respect. His goal was to pour into his verse the very best of the legacy of romanticism, and to purify that romanticism through classical restraint, and clarity of form.

His contemporaries failed to perceive the greatness of Baudelaire's poetry when, in 1857, at age 36, he published his one collection of verse, *Les fleurs du mal*. As a serious artist and as a moralist in his attitude toward evil, he was deeply hurt when he was called into court and fined for offenses to public morals. Six of the poems (the *"pièces condamnées"*) had to be excised from French editions. They did not appear in the enlarged edition that was published in 1861, which, however, included a new section titled *Tableaux parisiens*.

Last Years. Baudelaire lived 10 more years after the publication of the first edition of *Les fleurs du mal*. He worked in a relatively new genre, the poem in prose. These pieces appeared in a posthumously published volume, *Le spleen de Paris* (1869). His last years were lived in wretchedness; he sank more and more heavily into debt and was weakened by disease. Finally, afflicted with general paralysis and aphasia, he died miserably in Paris on Aug. 31, 1867.

HENRI PEYRE, *Yale University*

Bibliography
Eliot, Thomas Stearns, *Selected Essays* (New York 1932).
Peyre, Henri, ed., *Baudelaire, a Collection of Critical Essays* (Englewood Cliffs, N.J., 1962).
Peyre, Henri, *Connaissance de Baudelaire* (Paris 1951).
Sartre, Jean-Paul, *Baudelaire* (New York 1950).

BAUDISSIN, bou'di-sin, **Count Wolf Heinrich von** (1789–1878), German translator. He was born in Copenhagen, Denmark, on Jan. 20, 1789. He was a courier in the Danish diplomatic service from 1810 to 1814.

In 1827 he settled in Dresden, Germany, where he collaborated with Ludwig Tieck and August W. von Schlegel on a noted German translation of Shakespeare's plays. Baudissin also translated into German the works of François Coppée, Carlo Goldoni, and Molière. His translation of English plays, *Ben Jonson und seine Schule* (*Ben Jonson and His School*), was published in two volumes in 1865–67. He died in Dresden on April 4, 1878.

BAUDOUIN I (1930–   ), bō-dwaN', king of the Belgians, who replaced his father, King Leopold, after the latter's abdication. He was born in the palace of Laeken near Brussels on Sept. 7, 1930, and was christened *Baudouin Albert Charles Leopold Axel Marie Gustave*, duke of Hainaut and prince of Belgium. On the death of his grandfather, King Albert I, in 1934, he became duke of Brabant, the customary title of the Belgian crown prince. In the following year his mother, the popular Queen Astrid, was killed in an automobile accident in Switzerland.

The young prince's private schooling was interrupted by the Nazi invasion of 1940, and he was sent to France and to Portugal. He returned in the same year to Belgium, following its surrender to Germany, but he was held virtually a prisoner by the Germans. Later, he was moved to Germany and Austria, when he was liberated by the U.S. Seventh Army in May 1945.

Baudouin continued his education in Switzerland while his father, King Leopold, who had been exiled for his alleged pro-Nazi sympathies during the war, remained abroad. Prince Charles, younger brother of the king, had been selected as regent by the Belgian parliament in 1944. In March 1950, 58 percent of those voting in a referendum approved an end to Leopold's exile, and the king returned to Brussels on July 22, 1950. Immediately, the country was torn by civil strife of such intensity that Leopold was forced to agree to the transfer of royal powers to Baudouin and to the accession of the prince on his 21st birthday. By special parliamentary action, Baudouin became prince royal—with the constitutional powers of king—on Aug. 11, 1950. Leopold signed the act of abdication on July 16, 1951, and on the following day Baudouin formally acceded to the throne.

Baudouin was in Léopoldville when the Belgian Congo's independence was proclaimed on June 30, 1960. In 1960 he married a Spanish noblewoman, Fabiola de Mora y Aragón.

BAUDOUIN I of Belgium and Queen Fabiola, whom he married on Dec. 15, 1960, attend a banquet in Brussels.

BAUDOUIN DE COURTENAY, bō-dwaɴ' də kōōrt-nä', **Jan Ignace** (1845–1929), Polish linguist and teacher, who was a pioneer in structural linguistics. He was born in Radzymin, near Warsaw, on March 13, 1845. After studying at the universities of Warsaw, Prague, and Jena, he received a Ph.D. degree from the University of Leipzig in 1870. He began his long teaching career in 1871 when he was appointed to the faculty of the University of Kazan, Russia. He subsequently taught at several universities of eastern Europe and was on the faculty of the University of Warsaw from the end of World War I until his death, in Warsaw, on Nov. 3, 1929.

By treating the sounds of language as structural entities, Baudouin de Courtenay anticipated the basic concepts of modern structural linguistics. In 1895 he published his chief work, *Versuch einer Theorie phonetischer Alternationen* (*Essay on a Theory of Phonetic Alternations*).

BAUDRY, bō-drē', **Paul Jacques Aimé** (1828–1886), French painter. He was born in Bourbon-Vendée (now La Roche-sur-Yon) on Nov. 7, 1828. After studying painting under Michel Drolling in Paris, he went to Rome, where he was influenced by the school of Correggio.

Baudry was responsible for the decorations of many Parisian buildings. His best-known commission was the lobby of the Paris Opera, on which he worked 10 years. He also did the ceiling murals of the Palace of Justice. Among his paintings are *Le supplice de la vestale* (1857) at the Lille museum and *Charlotte Corday qui vient d'assassiner Marat* (1861) at the museum of Nantes. He died in Paris on Jan. 17, 1886.

BAUER, bou'ər, **Bruno** (1809–1882), German philosopher and historian of the rational school. He was born in Eisenberg, Germany, on Sept. 6, 1809. Bauer was a leader of the Young Hegelians, who interpreted Hegel's philosophy as being antithetical to Christianity, and thus influenced Marxist thought. He denied both the divinity and the historical validity of Jesus and characterized the gospels as myth. In 1834 he began lecturing in theology at Berlin, but his license was revoked in 1842 as a result of the publication of two works detailing his criticism of the Gospels. He moved to Rixdorf, where he remained until his death on April 15, 1882.

Bauer wrote important works demonstrating his heroic concept of history, according to which change comes about through the ideas of great men. Among these books were a comprehensive study of 18th century thought and a history of Germany and the French Revolution under Napoleon.

BAUER, Georg. See Agricola, Georgius.

BAUER, bou'ər, **Otto** (1882–1938), Austrian Socialist, who was perhaps the leading Austro-German Socialist theorist associated with the non-Communist Socialist left. He was born in Vienna on Sept. 5, 1882. He took his doctorate in law and political science at the University of Vienna in 1906 and became secretary of the parliamentary club of the Social Democrats in 1907.

His two most important Socialist theoretical works are *Die Nationalitätenfrage und die Sozialdemokratie* (1907) and *Die österreichische Revolution* (1923). The latter considers the Austrian socialists in the revolution of 1918 as a third force between capitalism and communism.

In 1918–1919, Bauer was secretary for foreign affairs in the first cabinet of the new Austrian republic. After his resignation in 1919, he concentrated on shaping the international and domestic policies of his party. For the greater part of his political life he led the Socialists as an opposition party to conservative governments. Forced to seek refuge abroad after the failure of the Socialist workers' revolt in 1934, he died in exile in Paris on July 4, 1938.

Robert A. Kann, *Rutgers University*

BAUGH, bô, **Sammy** (1914–   ), American football player, who was one of the greatest forward passers in the history of the game.

Samuel Adrian Baugh was born in Temple, Texas, on March 17, 1914. He attended Texas Christian University and in 1935 and 1936 made the All-America squad as quarterback. After graduation from college in 1937 he joined the Washington Redskins, whom he led to the Eastern Division title five times between 1937 and 1945 and to the National Football League championship in 1937 and 1942. Rated one of the most accurate passers in the game, Baugh usually threw hard "bullet" passes but could vary them according to the ability of his receiver. Playing tailback in the single wing and quarterback in the "T" formation, he was also an adequate runner and expert punter.

Nicknamed Slingin' Sam, Baugh's individual feats in 16 seasons as a professional player filled the record books. He held career records for most passes completed (1,709), most yards gained on passes (22,085), most touchdown passes (187), and best punting average (44.9 yards for 300 punts). He also set records for most yards gained passing in one season (2,938 in 1947) and in one game (446 in 1948). In the 1945 season his passing efficiency reached a high of 70.3 percent.

Baugh retired from pro football to his ranch in Rotan, Texas, in 1953. He coached the Hardin-Simmons University football team from 1955 to 1959, the New York Titans of the American Football League in 1960 and 1961, and the Houston Oilers of the same league in 1964.

Bill Braddock
New York "Times"

Sammy Baugh

UPI

BAUHAUS, bou′hous, a famous school of design in Germany that was the center of European avant-garde art in the 1920's and early 1930's. The school successfully combined in its teachings the principles of art and 20th century technology, and its influence is felt in such diverse forms as glass and steel office buildings, modern typography, and tableware.

The Bauhaus was founded at Weimar in 1919, as a state school of the arts, by the brilliant German architect Walter Gropius, who continued as its director throughout most of its existence. In 1925, after hostility to the school's "radical" ideas arose in Weimar, the institution moved to Dessau, which offered it support. The Dessau buildings, especially those designed by Gropius, exemplified one of the school's primary aims: the unification of all the creative arts in architecture. The buildings were functional, with a clean, pleasing line, and were divided into different units of studios and workshops, offices and classrooms, and dormitories. Many of the workrooms were designed to blend into one another by the removal of sliding walls.

Led by such teachers as the architects Gropius and Mies van der Rohe (Gropius' successor), the painters Paul Klee and Vasily Kandinsky, and the architect-designer Marcel Breuer, Bauhaus pupils undertook the study of mechanical crafts, aesthetic values, varied art forms, functional materials, and even sociology and accounting. All of these were considered necessary for the integration of artistic invention with mass-production techniques.

With the advent of Hitler's dictatorship and the degeneration of culture in Germany, the Bauhaus closed in 1933. However, its basic ideas, which had been promulgated by such distinguished "Friends of the Bauhaus" as Albert Einstein and Le Corbusier, continued to spread. Both directors of the school went to the United States—Gropius to teach at Harvard, and Mies to teach at the architectural school of the Illinois Institute of Technology. Bauhaus designer László Moholy-Nagy founded the New Bauhaus in Chicago, which grew into the successful Chicago Institute of Design. Other Bauhaus artists who went to the United States include Marcel Breuer, Josef and Ann Albers, and Alexander Schawinsky.

BAUHINIA, bō-in′ē-ə, is a genus of tropical trees, shrubs, and climbers. The members of this genus have broad leaves and long leafstalks. The flowers are showy, and white to purple.

The genus *Bauhinia* belongs to the family Leguminosae. There are approximately 180 different species included in the genus. An Indian species (*B. variegata*) is a showy ornamental known in the United States as the orchid tree. Also named mountain ebony because of its dark wood, it is used in tanning, dyeing, and in medicine. In southern Florida and southern California about 15 species, including *B. monandra*, *B. purpurea*, and *B. variegata*, are popular as ornamentals. Only a few species succeed in greenhouses because of the difficulty of maintaining a dry enough atmosphere without injury to the plants. *B. natalensis*, *B. variegata*, and the climber *B. corymbosa* are probably the most successful greenhouse species. Some species, like the maloo climber (*B. vahlii*), are used for making rope. The genus is named after Jean and Gaspard Bauhin, 16th century Swiss botanists.

GEORGE H. LAWRENCE, *Cornell University*

BAULE, bōl, **La,** a town in France in Loire-Atlantique department, on the Bay of Biscay. Sometimes called *La Baule-sur-Mer*, it is 8 miles (13 km) west of Saint Nazaire.

La Baule is one of the most popular French seaside resorts, with a 5-mile (8-km) semicircular beach. Along the beachfront are hotels, villas, and a wide promenade. The town, founded in 1879, lies among pine trees originally planted to moor the shifting sands of the beach. Population: (1962) commune, 13,225.

BAUM, bäm, **Lyman Frank** (1856–1919), American author and playwright, who is best known for his fantasies for children, especially the Wizard of Oz stories. He was born at Chittenango, N.Y., on May 15, 1856. He began his writing career in 1880 as a South Dakota newspaperman, and in 1899 published his first book, *Father Goose: His Book*, which became a best seller. Baum next wrote his most famous book, *The Wonderful Wizard of Oz*, which was published in 1900 and produced as a play, with immense success, in 1902. It was filmed in 1938.

With his almost instant riches, Baum moved to Pasadena, Calif., and there produced books at a prodigious rate, none of them of lasting value but all very popular in their time. Under the pen name "Floyd Akers" he published six books for boys, and as "Edith Van Dyne" he wrote 24 books for girls. As "Schuyler Staunton" he wrote *The Fate of the Clown* (1905) and *Daughter of Destiny* (1906), two serious novels. He also wrote 13 other tales of Oz. The best among them are *The Woggle-Bug Book* (1905), *The Emerald City of Oz* (1909), *Tik-Tok Man of Oz* (1914), and *The Scarecrow of Oz* (1915). Baum died in Hollywood, Calif., on May 6, 1919.

L. FRANK BAUM'S children's book *The Wonderful Wizard of Oz* was illustrated by W.W. Denslow.

BAUM, boum, **Vicki** (1888–1960), Austro-American novelist and playwright. She was born in Vienna on Jan. 24, 1888, and studied at the Vienna Conservatory of Music. She became harpist of an orchestra in Darmstadt, Germany, and in 1916 married Richard Lert, its conductor. In 1926 she was employed as a magazine editor at the Ullstein publishing house in Germany. The firm published her first stories and novels.

When her play *Grand Hotel* opened in New York City in 1931, she and her family went to the United States. In 1932 she moved to Los Angeles, where she worked on motion picture scripts. She became an American citizen in 1938, and died in Hollywood, Calif., on Aug. 29, 1960.

Vicki Baum's novels include *Shanghai* (1939), *Hotel Berlin* (1943), *Headless Angel* (1948), and *Theme for Ballet* (1958).

BAUMANN, bou'män, **Oskar** (1864–1899), Austrian traveler and explorer, who made many geographical discoveries in Africa. He was born in Vienna on June 25, 1864. In 1885 he served as geographer on a Congo River expedition that reached Stanley Falls. The following year he explored the island of Fernando Po in the Gulf of Guinea, and the results of his explorations were published in *Fernando Po und die Bube* (1888). With Hans Mayer in 1888, he explored the highlands of Usambara in Tanganyika (then German East Africa), and from 1890 to 1895 he explored the unknown reaches of German East Africa. He is credited with discovering the source of the great Kagera River, which is the chief tributary of Lake Victoria. From 1896 to 1897 he studied archaeological remains on the island of Zanzibar. Baumann died in Vienna on Oct. 12, 1899. His other writings include *Usambara* (1891) and *Der Sansibar-Archipel* (1896–99).

BAUMÉ, bō-mā', **Antoine** (1728–1804), French chemist who invented a hydrometer and devised the Baumé scale for hydrometer readings. Baumé was born in Senlis, France, on Feb. 26, 1728. He became a professor of chemistry at the Collège de Pharmacie in Paris about 1752. His *Éléments de pharmacie* was published in 1762. Baumé died in Charenton le Pont on Oct. 15, 1804.

The Baumé hydrometer and the Baumé scale are used in measuring liquids lighter than water and liquids heavier than water. A hydrometer for measuring liquids lighter than water is calibrated in degrees Baumé (°B). In this case, readings increase as the specific gravity decreases. In a hydrometer for measuring liquids heavier than water, readings increase as the specific gravity increases. Baumé hydrometers are used in the chemical and petroleum industries.

BAUMEISTER, bou'mīs-tər, **Willi** (1889–1955), German artist. He was born on Jan. 22, 1889, in Stuttgart and studied art under Adolph Hoelzel at the Stuttgart Academy. In 1928, Baumeister was appointed professor at the Frankfurt School of Fine Arts. He was dismissed by the Nazis in 1933 as a "degenerate" artist, and all his paintings were withdrawn from German museums and galleries. He continued painting, in secret, until the end of World War II. From 1946 until his death he taught at the Stuttgart Academy. He died in Stuttgart on Aug. 31, 1955.

In Baumeister's early works, such as *Gouache* (1923), figures and forms are rigid and geometrical. The forms of his later works are more fluid and often, as in the *African Histories* series (1942), surrealistic. His paintings include *Figures with Black Oval* (1935), *Vital Landscape* (1947), *Hommage à Jérôme Bosch* (1953), and *Bluxao* (1955). He is the author of *Das Unbekannte in der Kunst* (1947; *The Unknown in Art*).

BAUMGARTEN, boum'gär'tən, **Alexander Gottlieb** (1714–1762), German philosopher. A follower of the rationalist philosopher Christian von Wolff (q.v.), he was the founder of aesthetic philosophy in Germany. He was born in Berlin on July 17, 1714, and studied at the University of Halle, where he became a professor in 1737. In 1740 he was appointed professor of philosophy at Frankfurt an der Oder. He died at Frankfurt on May 26, 1762.

Baumgarten coined the term *aesthetics* (*aesthetica*) in his *Meditationes philosophicae de nonnullis ad poema pertinentibus* (1735; Eng. tr., *Reflections on Poetry*, 1954). He developed his theory of aesthetics, which he defined as the science of the beautiful, in *Aesthetica acromatica* (1750–58).

BAUR, bour, **Ferdinand Christian** (1792–1860), German theologian and Biblical critic. He was born at Schmiden, near Stuttgart, on June 21, 1792, the son of the pastor at Schmiden. After preparatory studies in the seminary at Blaubeuren he went to the University of Tübingen in 1809. In 1817 he became professor at Blaubeuren and while holding this position published his first important work, *Symbolik und Mythologie* (1824–25; *Symbolism and Mythology*). In 1826 he was called to Tübingen as professor in the evangelical faculty of the university. Baur retained this position until his death at Tübingen in Dec. 2, 1860.

Baur was the founder of the so-called Tübingen school of theology. His first work had shown the influence of Friedrich Schleiermacher and Friedrich von Schelling. However, he soon adopted the philosophy of history of Georg Wilhelm Friedrich Hegel and applied it to the development of Christianity. The Hegelian concept of the course of history finds a clear expression in *Das Christentum und die christliche Kirche der drei ersten Jahrhunderte* (1853; *Christianity and the Christian Church of the First Three Centuries*). Jewish (Petrine) Christianity was what Hegel called the thesis; Gentile (Pauline) Christianity, the antithesis; and ancient Catholicism, the synthesis. In *Die Christuspartei in der korinthischen Gemeinde* (1831; *The Christ-Party in the Corinthian Church*), Baur maintained that St. Paul, as the leader of the Gentile Christians, was in conflict with the Petrinists. Further developing this view in *Paulus, der Apostel Jesu Christi* (1845; *Paul, the Apostle of Jesus Christ*), he accepted as genuine only those writings attributed to Paul that show clear signs of this conflict. Thus, Baur considered the epistles to the Corinthians, Galatians, and Romans (except the last two chapters) to be authentic. The writers of other epistles attributed to Paul and of the Acts of the Apostles, in Baur's judgment, were Paulinists of the 2d century who wanted to reconcile their views with those of the Petrinists.

In *Kritische Untersuchungen über die kanonischen Evangelien* (1847; *Critical Inquiries concerning the Canonic Gospels*) Baur held that the Gospels are dependent on an earlier account

(Urevangelium); that of Matthew is Petrine and closest to the original, while Luke's is later and Paulinist. Mark's is still later, and John's is idealistic, laying no claim to historical truth; in both, Baur finds traces of a reconciliation.

Baur's revolutionary and controversial works were accompanied by others more purely theological and historical in character. These include *Der Gegensatz des Katholizismus und Protestantismus* (1834; *The Contrast Between Catholicism and Protestantism*); *Die christliche Lehre von der Versöhnung* (1838; *The Christian Doctrine of Reconciliation*); *Die christliche Lehre von der Dreieinigkeit und Menschwerdung Gottes* (1841–43; *The Christian Doctrine of the Trinity and Incarnation*); *Lehrbuch der christlichen Dogmengeschichte* (1847; *Compendium of the History of Christian Dogma*); and his monumental *Kirchengeschichte* (1853–63; *History of the Church*).

The Tübingen school, prominent in the 1840's, declined thereafter. One of Baur's pupils, Albrecht Ritschl, abandoned the Tübingen position and founded another school of theology.

BAUSCH, boush, a family of American optical manufacturers. *John Jacob Bausch* (1830–1926), who was born at Süssen, Württemberg, Germany, emigrated to the United States in 1849 and settled at Rochester, N.Y., where in 1853 he and Henry Lomb founded the Bausch & Lomb Optical Company. Two Bausch sons, *Edward* (1854–1944) and *William* (1861–1944), became officers of the company. Edward worked with Thomas A. Edison on the Kinetoscope and with George Eastman on photographic devices. He wrote *Manipulation of the Microscope* and perfected an assembly-line technique for making inexpensive microscopes.

In 1915, when World War I curtailed imports of European (mostly German) optical glass, William Bausch developed a new production method and uncovered American sources of raw materials. As a result, about 65 percent of the U.S. government's wartime requirements for optical glass were produced by the company.

In 1960 the company changed its name to Bausch & Lomb Incorporated. Its products include optical scientific and electronic instruments, lenses, frames, and other ophthalmic products. It has affiliated and subsidiary companies in Canada and nine other countries.

BAUTZEN, bou'tsan, is a city in East Germany in the former state of Saxony. It overlooks the Spree River, 32 miles (51 km) northeast of Dresden, and is a manufacturing center. The chief products are textiles, machinery, chemicals, and aluminum and iron goods. The old town is encircled by ancient walls that have been converted into promenades. The 13th century cathedral of St. Peter has been used since 1524 for both Protestant and Roman Catholic services.

Originally the Slav fortress of *Budissin*, Bautzen was absorbed by the Germans during the early 11th century. Bohemia, Bradenburg, Meissen, and Poland contested the town's possession until 1320, when it passed to Bohemia. Napoleon defeated the allied armies of Russia and Prussia at Bautzen on May 20–21, 1813. However, the failure of French General Ney to press the attack allowed Emperor Alexander I of Russia and General Blücher of Prussia and their forces to retreat safely. Population: (1962) 42,281.

BAUX, bō, **Les,** a village in southern France in Bouches-du-Rhône department, 6 miles (10 km) northeast of Arles. Set on a rocky hilltop, the village castle was first used as a refuge from Muslim invaders in the 8th century. The lords of Les Baux held extensive lands in Provence and Dauphiné during the Middle Ages. After the ruling family died out in 1426, the town lost its importance and was merged with Provence. Only ruins remain of the castle, which was demolished in 1632 by Louis XIII because it was a stronghold of opponents of the crown.

Bauxite, the main source of aluminum, was discovered at Les Baux in 1821 and later was named after the town. Population: (1962) 87.

BAUXITE, bôks'ĭt, is the principal ore of the metal aluminum, and is an important source of alum as well. It has several other uses, including oil filtration and the making of abrasives, refractories, aluminum salts, and bauxite brick. The name "bauxite" derives from Les Baux (near Arles), France, where the substance was first found in 1821.

Bauxite is a claylike material. It consists of a mixture of more or less hydrated (water-containing) aluminum oxides, including such minerals as gibbsite, boehmite, and disaspore. Bauxite itself is no longer considered a distinct type of mineral, but the term is still useful in describing the mixture, particularly as the minerals of which it is composed are difficult to distinguish visually.

The material generally occurs in large earthy masses or claylike deposits, commonly in the form of small round grains up to one fourth inch (one half cm) in diameter. The material has a dull luster and its color may range from dirty white to dark brown. Bauxite usually contains some amount of iron, in the form of the mineral limonite, but its color is no sure criterion of the iron content. Thus, a white variety containing 3.7 percent iron oxide is known, but a strongly red variety contains about the same amount, while a yellow variety consists of nearly 14.4 percent iron oxide.

Bauxite results primarily from the weathering of aluminum-bearing silicate rocks or clay-bearing limestones, especially where the weathering takes place under tropical conditions of contrasting wet and dry seasons. Deposits of the substance are found in many parts of the world, including the United States, France, Hungary, Yugoslavia, the USSR, India, Jamaica, Guyana, and Brazil. A fine grade of bauxite occurs at Irish Hill (near Larne), in County Antrim, Ireland. The finest grade there is almost free from iron, containing as little of that metal as good china clay.

In the United States, where domestic production accounts for about half the total amount consumed, bauxite is found in considerable quantities in Saline and Pulaski counties, Arkansas, and in a deposit extending eastward from Calhoun County, Alabama, into Georgia. It is thought that in the latter location the bauxite may have been deposited by hot springs. The American deposits of bauxite are well suited to the production of aluminum, as ore in quantity can be had there that contains as little as 1 percent iron oxide and 3 percent silica.

General formula: Al_2O_3 plus Al and H_2O; hardness, 1 to 3; specific gravity, 2.0 to 2.5; crystal system, amorphous.

See also ALUMINUM.

BAVARIA'S NEUSCHWANSTEIN CASTLE in the mountains southwest of Munich. It was built for Ludwig II.

BAVARIA, bə-vâr′ē-ə, is the largest of the federated states of West Germany. Called *Bayern* in German, this primarily agricultural region lies in the southeastern corner of West Germany. Bavaria's great beauty, its extensive forests, and its impressive mountain country have made it a great tourist center.

Bavaria has an area of 27,239 square miles (70,549 sq km) and a population of over 9,500,-000. It is bounded on the north by East Germany, on the west by the West German states of Hesse and Baden-Württemberg, on the south by Austria, and on the east by Czechoslovakia. Bavaria is divided into seven areas (Upper Palatinate; Upper, Middle, and Lower Franconia; Swabia; and Upper and Lower Bavaria). Each area has a distinct historical development and each was formerly a part of the old duchy of Bavaria.

The People. Over 70 percent of the Bavarians are Roman Catholic, and the remainder are mostly Protestant. The Catholic dioceses include the two archbishoprics of Munich (German: München) and Bamberg and five bishoprics. The Protestants live mainly in the northwest.

The Bavarians are less formal than the Prussians to the north, and their dialects are softer than those of Prussia. That they are a people of high cultural attainment is evidenced by Bavaria's fine museums and music and theater festivals.

Bavarians are intensely loyal to their state. Until Hitler forced its integration into Germany in the 1930's, Bavaria had maintained a distinct identity from the rest of the country. The Wittelsbach dynasty's rule of over 700 years had given Bavaria a cohesiveness that other sections of Germany lacked. Though Bavaria today is united with the other states of West Germany, the Bavarians have retained many of their special characteristics and customs.

Land and Natural Resources. Bavaria reflects in general the main physical features of southern Germany, with minor ranges of mountains and wide plains. Hilly rather than mountainous, the country is distinguished by great natural beauty. A third of the land is covered by forests.

Bavaria belongs to the Rhine and Danube river basins. On its course toward the Rhine, the Main River crosses northern Bavaria from east to west. With its tributaries, the Main waters nearly one third of Bavaria. The other two thirds of the state is fed by the Danube River, which flows northeast to Regensburg and then southeast toward Austria, receiving tributaries such as the Iller, Lech, Isar, and Inn rivers. The Danube enters Bavaria near Ulm and covers some 270 miles (435 km) before it passes into Austria at Passau. The river is navigable upstream for large ships only as far as Regensburg. The Ludwig Canal connects the Regnitz River, a tributary of the Main, with the Altmühl River, a tributary of the Danube, thus linking the two Bavarian river systems.

In the extreme south of Bavaria, along the Austrian border, are the Bavarian Alps, which are heavily forested up to elevations of over 5,000 feet (1,500 meters). The Zugspitze (9,721 feet; 2,963 meters) in the Bavarian Alps is Germany's highest mountain. There are three low areas in the Bavarian Alps: the upper Iller River valley, the basin of the Amper River, and the low-lying area near Berchtesgaden.

As a result of glacial action, the land just north of the Alps is a jumble of low, grassy hills. Nearer the Danube River the land is more rolling and easily cultivated. The valleys of the Danube's tributaries are the most fertile parts of southern Bavaria.

Between the Danube and the Main rivers, to the east of Nuremberg (German: Nürnberg), is the Franconian Jura, an extension of the Jura mountains of France. There is a plateau west of Nuremberg, about 1,500 feet (450 meters) high, which runs from north to south. Eastern Bavaria

BAVARIAN FARMERS harvest hay in the fields outside the small village of Ofterschwang in the mountains along the Austrian border.

near the Czechoslovakian border is a mountainous area that is the most deserted region of Germany, with heavy rainfall and large fir forests. The middle section of the Main Valley has the mildest climate and some of the best farmland in Germany. West of this fertile area, is the Spessart, a thickly wooded plateau.

Bavaria has poor natural resources. There are few minerals, except for salt near Berchtesgaden and Bad Reichenhall, minor deposits of lignite on the northern slopes of the Bavarian Alps, and crystalline graphite in the Bavarian Forest near Passau. There is only a small amount of iron ore, but there is an ample supply of wood in the forests.

Economy. Although there has been a steady decline in farming, agriculture remains the basis of the economy. About a third of the population obtains its livelihood from small farms. The main crops are rye—replaced by wheat in some of the warmer sections—potatoes, and hops. Cattle, pigs, and some sheep are raised.

Bavaria's extensive forests are of substantial economic importance. The cut timber is used for building materials and also in the manufacture of paper. For centuries the readily available lumber has been fashioned by Bavarian craftsmen into folk art products and architectural embellishments and into commercially significant products such as furniture and violin cases.

Industrial progress, slow in the 19th century, was accelerated in the 20th century by the development of hydroelectric power. Though tradition has favored light industry, increasing attention has been given to the development of heavy industries. The principal light industries are textiles, paper, glass and porcelain, and pencils and toys. Bavarian beer, known throughout the world, is brewed mainly in and around Munich, Nuremberg, and Kulmbach. Rosenthal china is also well known. Modern heavy industry, concentrated in the larger cities, includes the manufacture of light motors and ball bearings, precision tools, automobiles, and agricultural machinery.

The economy was stimulated after World War II by the immigration of over two million refugees to Bavaria from Silesia, East Prussia, and other Communist-dominated areas. The influx of these nonagricultural people into a hitherto predominantly peasant population led to serious social problems. There was much suffering among the refugees until commerce and industry were developed that could make use of their skills.

Tourism is an important element of the Bavarian economy. Colorful local costumes and dances, such as the *Schuhplattler,* or clog dance, performed by the Bavarian peasants, attract many visitors. The area's social life, especially in the festive *Fasching* carnival period immediately preceding Lent, is also well known. Tourists from foreign countries are attracted by the scenic landscape, particularly in the Alpine areas. Bad Kissingen, Bismarck's favorite holiday spa, draws many tourists each year. Brine from the salt mines near Bad Reichenhall is piped in for the use of patients. Garmisch-Partenkirchen is a world-famous center for winter sports.

Cultural Life. Although it is a comparatively small state, Bavaria has made significant cultural contributions. There are highly regarded universities at Munich (moved from Landshut in 1826), Würzburg, and Erlangen, as well as a technical school and an academy of art and music in Munich and a school for economics in Nuremberg. The university of Munich has had a long line of great teachers, including the physicist Wilhelm Roentgen and the philosopher Friedrich von Schelling.

Albrecht Dürer, a native of Nuremberg, established an important school of painting in the 16th century. The painters Hans Holbein the Elder and his son, Holbein the Younger, were both born in Augsburg. The 19th century painter Franz von Lenbach was also a Bavarian.

Cultural activities are centered mainly in Munich, the third-largest German city after Berlin and Hamburg. Munich has important art museums and galleries, libraries, symphony orchestras, and baroque churches. The Glyptothek houses a fine collection of ancient and modern sculpture. One of Europe's greatest galleries is the Alte Pinakothek, which has noted collections of Rubens and Dürer. Tourists are attracted to Munich by the Alter Hof, the first ducal residence of the Wittelsbach dynasty. In the countryside are elaborate castles built between 1869 and 1886 by the eccentric King Louis (Ludwig) II. One of the most outstanding is the magnificent Neuschwanstein Castle, overlooking a lake southwest of Munich.

Among the best-known cultural centers is Bayreuth, 40 miles (64 km) northeast of Nuremberg. Here Richard Wagner, the great German composer, settled in 1872. In 1876 an opera house, designed by the composer, was completed, and Bayreuth became the center of productions of Wagner's operas. The tradition has continued to the present under his grandsons, with modernistic settings in place of the old formalized stage designs.

Government. The government of Bavaria is in general similar to that of the other states in West Germany. The Bavarian constitution, adopted on Dec. 2, 1946, provides for a democratic, constitutional state within the federal republic. The executive officer is a minister-president, elected by the Parliament, or Diet, for a term of four years. The Diet is popularly elected and consists of the Landtag, or lower house, and the Senat, an advisory body. Bavaria is the only state that has a Senat, a group of experts who represent various economic and social interests.

The minister-president, with the approval of the Landtag, appoints and dismisses all state ministers and state secretaries. He has a cabinet composed of ministers of the interior, justice, education, finance, industry, agriculture, and work. The Constitutional Court decides on the constitutionality of all legislation and handles accusations against governmental ministers or Landtag deputies. The highest regular judicial bodies are the courts of appeal in Munich, Bamberg, and Nuremberg. Below them are state and other lesser courts.

The two major political parties are the Christian Social Union and the Social Democratic party. Each is supported by aproximately one third of the electorate. The two groups remained in an uneasy alliance until 1954, when a coalition government excluding the Christian Social Union was formed. In 1957 the Christian Social Union regained its position as the leading political party. In the 1960's there was a slight growth of the right-wing National Democratic party of Germany (NPD).

History. The original inhabitants of Bavaria were probably Celtic in origin. In about 15 B.C., during the reign of the Roman emperor Augustus, the Celts were conquered by the Romans, and their land became a Roman province. At the end of the 5th century A.D. the Roman legions, pressed by the Germanic tribes, retreated from the area and left the Romanized population to fend for itself. The land was then invaded from the east valley of the Danube by Germanic tribes, including the *Baiuwarii*. These tribes were the ancestors of the Bavarians.

Middle Ages to 1500. In the early Middle Ages quarrelsome tribal dukes fought for control of the area. About 555, Bavaria came under the rule of Garibald I of the Agilolfing family. Until the early 8th century the dukes repulsed the Slavs on the east, while gradually freeing themselves from domination by the Franks on the west. During the reigns of the Frankish kings Charles Martel and Pepin the Short, however, Bavaria became subject to the Franks. When Tassilo III became duke in the mid-8th

MEDIEVAL FORTRESS in Nuremberg rises above the former home (on left) of the artist Albrecht Dürer.

century, he tried to free the Bavarians from Frankish control, but he was defeated in 787 by Charlemagne. The duchy was later incorporated into the Carolingian empire. By the Treaty of Verdun in 843, which divided the Carolingian empire among Charlemagne's three grandsons, Bavaria, along with other German areas, was given to Louis II the German. During this period Bavaria was being Christianized by Irish and Scottish missionaries from Burgundy.

In the 10th century Bavaria became part of the Holy Roman Empire, while retaining its own dukes. In 1180 the duchy came under the control of Count Otto VI, a member of the Wittelsbach family, who became Duke Otto I of Bavaria. This was the beginning of the Wittelsbach dynasty that ruled Bavaria until 1918. The Wittelsbachs, controlling land on the plain between the Lech, Danube, and Inn rivers, managed to retain an independent Bavaria despite the many divisions in the family and despite attempted inroads by neighboring feudal magnates. By the end of the 14th century there were four Bavarian duchies, each ruled by a branch of the Wittelsbachs.

The Unified Duchy, 1545–1806. From the end of the 14th century until 1545 branches of the Wittelsbach family struggled for control of Bavaria. An important step in consolidation was the establishment of the principle of primogeniture by Duke Albert IV the Wise in 1506. Albert's son William IV finally united the duchy in 1545.

Although they were an important force in southern Germany, the Wittelsbachs were never successful in their ambition to make Bavaria a great power. Situated in the heart of Europe, the duchy was surrounded by powerful neighbors who hemmed it in and reduced its role in power politics to a secondary one. Since it did not have protective geographical frontiers, Bavaria was repeatedly devastated in a series of wars during the 17th and 18th centuries. The Thirty Years' War, the War of the Spanish Succession, and the

War of the Austrian Succession all brought foreign troops into Bavaria.

In 1777 the succession went to Charles Theodore, the Elector Palatine, thereby joining the Palatinate to Bavaria. In the War of the Bavarian Succession (1778–1779), Frederick II the Great of Prussia prevented a large part of Bavaria from being incorporated into Austria.

During the French Revolution and the Napoleonic era, Bavaria oscillated between a pro- and an anti-French position. In 1793 it joined the first anti-French coalition. Two years later a French army invaded Bavaria and advanced as far as Munich, where liberals greeted it enthusiastically. In 1799, Bavaria was occupied by Austria, then preparing for war against France. Under the ministry of Montgelas, Bavaria joined the second anti-French coalition (1799–1800). Bavaria was defeated by the French and lost the Palatinate by the Treaty of Lunéville in 1801.

Bavaria reversed its traditional anti-French policy in 1803 and fought against the third anti-French coalition. By the Treaty of Pressburg (1805), Bavaria was rewarded for its support with additional territory. The treaty also raised Bavaria from a duchy to the status of a kingdom. Elector Maximilian IV Joseph became King Maximilian I.

Kingdom of Bavaria, 1806–1871. Encouraged by this territorial award, Bavaria continued to take part in Napoleon's campaigns and to increase its holdings. In 1813, Bavaria again reversed its role vis-à-vis France and joined the coalition of German princes against Napoleon. It was an advantageous switch, for it strengthened Bavaria's position at the Congress of Vienna in 1815. With lands acquired at the Congress, Bavaria emerged as the third-strongest German state after Austria and Prussia. The leader of the minor German States, it acted as a buffer to preserve the uneasy balance between Austria and Prussia.

Maximilian's son, Louis (German: Ludwig) I, succeeded his father in 1825. He began his reign in a liberal spirit, but the outbreak of the Revolution of 1830 in France frightened him into reaction. He instituted reactionary policies and persecuted the Protestants. His infatuation with a dancer, Lola Montez, united all political parties against him. This opposition forced Louis to abdicate on March 20, 1848, at the beginning of the Revolution of 1848.

Maximilian II, who succeeded Louis, was faced with the task of maintaining Bavaria's integrity against encroachment by either Austria or Prussia. In 1850 he concluded a pact with Saxony, Hannover, and Württemberg as a counterweight to Austrian and Prussian power. In the balance-of-power politics, Maximilian generally supported Austria against Prussia.

Louis II, who succeeded his father in 1864, at first continued his father's pro-Austrian policy, allying Bavaria with Austria in the Austro-Prussian War in 1866. After Prussia's victory, Bavaria, in line with Bismark's conciliatory attitude toward Germans, had to cede only two small districts to Prussia and pay a modest indemnity. Bismarck's shrewd policy paid dividends when Bavaria switched its allegiance to Prussia. In the Franco-Prussian War, Bavarian troops fought against France.

Absorption into the German State. In January 1871, Bavaria became part of the Second German Empire. It received a greater measure of independence than any other state in the Second Reich, retaining a separate army, diplomatic service, and postal and railway systems.

At this time Louis II, already showing signs of insanity, began to retreat into a private dream world. He drained the treasury by building one elaborate castle after another. On June 7, 1886, after Louis had been proclaimed insane, his uncle Luitpold was named regent. A few days later Louis II committed suicide. Luitpold continued as regent during the reign of Louis II's brother, Otto I, who was also declared insane. Luitpold's son, Louis III, ruled first as regent in 1912, and from 1913 to 1918 as king.

Revolution broke out in Munich on Germany's defeat in World War I. Kurt Eisner, an Independent Socialist and a journalist, seized control of the government, declared the Wittelsbach dynasty deposed, and proclaimed himself head of a Bavarian republic. Eisner was assassinated in February 1919, and in the ensuing chaos revolutionary workers' and soldiers' councils began a Red terror, followed by a short-lived Bolshevik government (April 4–May 1, 1919). After units of the Reich army loyal to the Weimar Republic recaptured Munich, an equally bloody White terror was directed against the Communists.

Under a constitution proclaimed on Aug. 14, 1919, Bavaria became a state in the Weimar Republic. Bavaria still retained her old sense of particularism, and relations with Berlin were strained. In the post-World War I period, Bavaria became a center of nationalist and monarchist reaction. Adolf Hitler's National Socialist German Workers' party (NSDAP) originated in Munich, and the city became the center of the Nazi movement. In Munich, Hitler led his abortive Beer Hall Putsch, an important milestone in the rise of national socialism.

When Hitler assumed power in 1933, he finally destroyed Bavaria's traditional semiautonomy by abolishing local government and placing the state under the rule of a Nazi governor. From this time until the collapse of Germany in 1945, Bavaria remained the stronghold of nazism. Hitler built a vast administrative complex for the Nazi party in Munich. His notorious racial laws of Sept. 15, 1935, were named the Nuremberg Laws. Because it had been a center of nazism, Nuremberg was chosen as the site for the war crimes trials that convicted many Nazis following World War II.

A new Bavarian constitution was promulgated on Jan. 12, 1946. On May 23, 1949, Bavaria joined the ten other states of West Germany to form the Federal Republic of Germany. Bavaria has shared in West Germany's general prosperity since World War II. Politically, Bavaria is oriented toward the West, although there has been a slight growth in right-wing nationalist sentiment. Population: (1961) 9,515,479.

LOUIS L. SNYDER
The City University of New York

Bibliography

Almond, G.A., ed., *The Struggle for Democracy in Germany* (Chapel Hill, N.C., 1949).
Busch, Harald, and Breidenstein, H., *Beautiful Bavaria* (London 1956).
Holborn, Hajo, *History of Modern Germany*, vol. 1 (New York 1959).

For Specialized Study

Channon, Henry, *The Ludwigs of Bavaria* (New York 1933).
Dittmar, William Robert, *The Government of the State of Bavaria* (New York 1934).
Hubensteiner, Benno, *Bayerische Geschichte, Staat und Volk, Kunst und Kultur* (Munich 1955).

BAWEAN, bä'vä-än, is an island in Indonesia, in the Java Sea between Java and Borneo. It is situated some 100 miles (160 km) north of Surabaja, Java. The island, with an area of 77 square miles (199 sq km), is volcanic in origin and the soil is fertile. The capital and chief port is Sangkapura. Population: (1957) 47,589.

BAX, baks, **Sir Arnold Edward Trevor** (1883–1953), English composer. He was born in London on Nov. 8, 1883. He entered the Royal Academy of Music in 1900, studying piano with Tobias Matthay and composition with Frederick Corder. Having a sufficient income to meet his needs, he devoted his life exclusively to composition, reading, and travel. Bax was knighted in 1937, but he never held an official appointment until 1942, when King George VI named him adviser on music to the royal household ("master of the King's Musick"). Sir Arnold retained that post under Queen Elizabeth II. He died at Cork, Ireland, on Oct. 3, 1953.

Bax's Irish background is reflected in his many songs set to poems by writers that included William Butler Yeats and John Millington Synge, as well as in such instrumental works as *Moy Mell* (1917) and the *Irish Elegy* (1917), which was scored for English horn, harp, and strings. The lyrical second subjects in his sonata-form movements are also generally considered to be colored by a Celtic spirit.

His large output includes practically every musical genre with the exception of opera. He wrote seven symphonies, a violin concerto, a cello concerto, *Phantasy* for viola and orchestra, *Symphonic Variations* for piano and orchestra, and music for ballet. His symphonic poems include *In the Faery Hills* (1909), *The Garden of Fand* (1916), *Tintagel* (1917), *November Woods* (1917), and *The Happy Forest* (1922). His smaller works include many songs, four piano sonatas, and numerous compositions for chamber ensembles.

A volume of reminiscences, *Farewell, My Youth,* was published in 1943.

BAX, baks, **Ernest Belfort** (1854–1926), English socialist and philosopher. He was born in Leamington, Warwickshire, on July 23, 1854. He was privately educated and went to Germany to study music. There he became interested in philosophy.

He was a correspondent for English newspapers on the Continent from 1880 to 1881, but returned to England where he became active in socialist groups, especially the Democratic Federation, a workingmen's group, in which he was associated with William Morris. Later, a dissident faction of the federation, including Morris and Bax, left it to form the Socialist League (1885) for which Bax edited the weekly *Commonweal.* As the league veered toward anarchism, however, he resigned to join the Social Democratic Federation, for which he edited *Justice.* He died in London on Nov. 26, 1926.

Bax wrote *Socialism: Its Growth and Outcome* (1894) with Morris, and an autobiography (1918). His historical works include *Jean-Paul Marat* (1878) and *The French Revolution* (1890); his philosophical works include *The Problem of Reality* (1907), *Problems of Men, Mind and Morals* (1912), and *The Real, Rational and Alogical* (1920).

BAXTER, baks'tər, **John Babington Macaulay** (1868–1946), Canadian judge and statesman. He was born in St. John, New Brunswick, on Feb. 16, 1868. He was educated in the public schools of St. John, studied law, and was admitted to the bar in 1891. After serving as alderman of St. John, he was a member of the provincial Parliament from 1911 to 1921. During that period he became attorney general (1914–1917), and leader of the Conservative opposition (1921).

Elected to the federal House of Commons in 1921, Baxter resigned four years later and returned to New Brunswick politics. He was premier of the province from 1925 to 1931, when he was appointed to the Supreme Court of New Brunswick. Baxter was chief justice of the Supreme Court from 1935 until his death in St. John, on Dec. 27, 1946.

BAXTER, baks'tər, **Richard** (1615–1691), English clergyman who was active during the period of Oliver Cromwell, Charles II, and James II. Noted for saintliness and learning, he endeavored to liberalize the Church of England, so that it might conform to his understanding of the principles of the Scriptures, and also to keep the Puritans in the church. He disapproved of the English form of episcopacy—the institution of bishops—and he once declined to become bishop of Hereford when the diocese was offered him. However, he was only a moderate Nonconformist. It was his simple but forthrightly expressed conviction that the forms of church government must be subservient to the true purposes of the Christian religion.

Born on Nov. 13, 1615, at Rowton in Shropshire, he was ordained priest in the Church of England in 1638 but refused to take the oath of approval of the doctrine and discipline of the Church of England, known as the "et cetera" oath. Nevertheless, he became curate in the parish of Kidderminster, near Birmingham, in 1640 and remained there, except for a break during the Civil War, until 1660. He was a resourceful pastor, and his ministry uplifted the morality of the town. He also formed an association of the local clergy of all denominations so that they could better perform their duties.

During the Civil War he sided with Parliament and became a chaplain in Cromwell's army. Later, however, he manifested open disapproval of Cromwell's regime and urged nonresistance to the Scottish troops that Charles II brought with him into England.

At the Restoration, Baxter was made a royal chaplain by Charles II. He settled in London, where he became known as a great preacher. He worked earnestly—notably at the Savoy Conference, convened in 1661 to reform the liturgy—to keep the Nonconformists in the Church of England.

In 1685 he was arrested for his views and tried for sedition. The judge, Sir George Jeffreys, would not hear Baxter or his counsel, and Baxter was convicted on very shaky grounds and imprisoned for 18 months. After his release he continued to preach. He was also a productive writer, his most popular works being *The Saints' Everlasting Rest* (1650) and *Call to the Unconverted* (1657). He died in London on Dec. 8, 1691. His funeral was attended by both Anglicans and Dissenters.

Further Reading: Martin, Hugh, *Puritanism and Richard Baxter* (Toronto 1954).

BAXTER SPRINGS, baks'tər, a city in Kansas, is situated in Cherokee County, 150 miles (241 km) south of Kansas City, in the southeast corner of the state. It is a lead- and zinc-mining center and manufactures mining supplies.

Baxter Springs was named for a settler who built a sawmill here near mineral springs in 1847. It was incorporated in 1868. In Baxter Springs National Cemetery are buried the victims of a raid on the town by Confederate guerrillas under William Clarke Quantrill in 1863. In the late 1860's, cattle driven over trails from Texas were loaded onto railroad cars at Baxter Springs. Population: 4,489.

BAY, bā, several small trees and shrubs with stiff leaves and small berries. An important representative is the sweet bay (*Laurus nobilis*). Widely cultivated for ornamentation in the United States and Europe, this tree is a popular tub plant used in open-air restaurants and esplanades because of its ability to withstand neglect, abuse, and shearing. It has stiff, dull green leaves that are used to flavor some culinary dishes. Its sweet, fragrant, cherrylike, purple fruits are edible. The sweet bay is the laurel of poets and was the tree used in the crowning of heroes in ancient times. The bay laurel (*Prunus laurocerasus*), perhaps better known as the cherry laurel, is also widely used as a decorative plant. The loblolly bay (*Gordonia lasianthus*), the white bay (*Magnolia glauca*), and the red bay (*Persea borbonia*) are other well-known examples and are native to the southeastern United States. The name "rose bay" is given to various rhododendrons, oleanders, and to some types of fireweed. Bay rum is not made from a bay tree, but from the West Indian bayberry (*Pimenta racemosa*).

BAY, bā, an inlet of a body of water, such as a sea or a lake, that extends into the land. A bay usually is smaller than a gulf, and its widest part usually is at its mouth, but the rules for applying the name are not rigid. Hudson Bay, Canada, is much larger than many gulfs and is widest in the middle. Baffin Bay, in the Canadian Arctic region, is merely a broad portion of a series of straits. The Bay of Bengal, east of India, is widest at the mouth but is larger than some gulfs.

BAY, Laguna de, vä'ē, the largest lake in the Philippines. It is in Luzon Island, about 8 miles (13 km) southeast of Manila. The crescent-shaped lake is about 32 miles (51 km) long and covers an area of 344 square miles (891 sq km). It empties into Manila Bay by way of the Pasig River to the northwest.

BAY CITY, bā, is an industrial center and port of entry in eastern Michigan. The city is the seat of Bay County. It is situated on Saginaw Bay, an arm of Lake Huron, at the mouth of the Saginaw River, about 108 miles (174 km) northwest of Detroit. The river channel has been deepened and is navigable by large vessels. Since the opening of the St. Lawrence Seaway (1959), providing a route to the Atlantic Ocean, at least 100 foreign-flag vessels enter the port each year.

Bay City's industries include shipbuilding, beet sugar refining, and the manufacturing of automobile parts, power shovels and hoists, electrical and welding machinery, woodworking machinery, and magnesium castings. The city was once known as the Lumber Queen of the World. In the early 1880's more than 100 sawmills were in operation in the Saginaw Bay region, but as the great pine tracts of northern Michigan were stripped, the mills gradually gave way to diversified industry.

Bay City is also the principal market center for the state's richest farmlands, which produce sugar beets, potatoes, and dairy products.

A short distance north of Bay City and bordering on Saginaw Bay is Bay City State Park, with facilities accommodating hundreds of thousands of visitors each year for swimming, boating, camping, and fishing. Close by is Wenonah Park, another recreation area for vacationers. Directly west of the city is Chippewa River State Forest; to the northwest, the large Ogemaw State Forest. The latter is a game refuge, where wild animals are seen in their natural habitat.

The first white settler came to the site of the present city in 1831. He had been sent to teach farming to the Indians, in fulfillment of a treaty pledge given the Chippewas in 1819, as part of their price for ceding territory to the United States. In 1859 several of the small settlements that had flourished along the Saginaw River since the 1830's were consolidated and incorporated as a village. The city was chartered in 1865. West Bay City, directly across the river, was annexed to Bay City in 1905. The city is governed by a manager and a commission. Population: 49,449.

BAY CITY, bā, an industrial center and port in southeastern Texas, is the seat of Matagorda County. The city is situated on the east bank of the Colorado River, 70 miles (113 km) southwest of Galveston and about 20 miles (32 km) north of the Gulf of Matagorda.

Bay City is the shipping and industrial center for an agricultural area in which the principal products are cattle, poultry, rice, cotton, pecans, and figs. Water for the irrigation of the rice fields comes from the Colorado River. The region also has extensive sulfur mines and oil fields. Industries include meat-packing, the manufacture of petrochemicals, oil refining, welding, sheet-metal working, and rice milling.

Incorporated in 1902, Bay City has a mayor-council form of government. Population: 11,733.

BAY LAGOON. See BAY, LAGUNA DE.

BAY MINETTE, bā mi-net', is a city in Alabama, 22 miles (35 km) northeast of Mobile. It is the seat of Baldwin County. The city is an agricultural trading center, and its principal industries are forest products, furniture, fabricated metal, and clothing. Bay Minette State Junior College is situated here. The region is noted for hunting and fishing. Mobile Bay, opening into the Gulf of Mexico, is only 20 miles (32 km) distant. The city is governed by a mayor and council. Population: 6,727.

BAY OF PIGS, a bay on the south coast of Cuba, about 97 miles (156 km) southeast of Havana. It is called *Bahía de Cochinos* in Spanish. On April 17, 1961, it was the scene of an armed invasion by 1,300 Cuban refugees trained in Central America under the direction of the United States Central Intelligence Agency and transported in American merchant vessels escorted by U.S. destroyers. However, air cover by

U.S. planes was forbidden by President Kennedy at the last minute.

The invasion attempt proved a complete failure. The 1,300 men landed at Playa Girón on the west coast of the bay and tried to make their way inland through the swamps of the Peninsula de Zapata. To oppose them, the Cuban Communist leader Fidel Castro rallied a large force of militiamen and soldiers. When the fighting ended on April 19, 90 of the invaders had been killed. The rest were taken prisoner.

BAY PSALM BOOK, the name generally applied to the first book printed in the British colonies of North America. The Puritan ministers Richard Mather, John Eliot, and Thomas Weld (or Welde) undertook a new translation of the Psalms in 1636. They wanted to produce a work that adhered more closely to the original Biblical texts than the King James Version had succeeded in doing. At the same time, they planned to render the Psalms into verse suitable for singing at the prayer meetings of the Massachusetts Bay Colony. Mather phrased their aim as "Conscience rather than elegance, fidelity rather than poetry." The result, a rustic and rather undistinguished work of 148 pages, bore the title *The Whole Booke of Psalmes Faithfully Translated into English Metre.* It was printed at Cambridge in 1640 by Stephen Day (Daye). His handpress had already produced the pamphlet *An Almanack, Calculated for New England,* as well as the broadside *Freeman's Oath* in 1639.

Although the Bay Psalm Book is neither a unique literary work nor a singular printing achievement, the value of the 11 surviving copies of the 1,700 originally printed is immense. In 1947 one copy of the Bay Psalm Book was sold in New York City for $151,000.

The question of which book was the first printed in the New World, however, is still problematic. Some maintain it was *Escala espiritual para llegar al cielo,* a translation of the *Scala Paradisi* (*Ladder to Paradise*) of St. John Climacus, believed to have been printed in Mexico City in 1535. No copy of this work, however, is known to exist. Its printing has been attributed both to Juan Pablos (Giovanni Paoli), an Italian from Brescia, and to the Spanish-born Esteban Martín. The religious manual *Doctrina breve muy provechosa de las cosas que pertenecen a la fé católica y a nuestra cristianidad* (Mexico City 1544), by Bishop Juan de Zumárraga, is believed to be the earliest American book of which a copy remains.

Further Reading: Haraszti, Zoltan, *The Enigma of the Bay Psalm Book* (Chicago 1957).

BAY RUM is a fragrant cosmetic liquid prepared from alcohol (originally from rum) and the oil of the West Indian bayberry (*Pimenta recemosa*), which is related to the allspice or pimento tree (*P. officinalis*). An oil extracted from orange peel is usually added.

BAY SAINT LOUIS is a resort city on the Gulf coast of Mississippi, 15 miles (24 km) southwest of Gulfport. It is situated on Mississippi Sound at the entrance to St. Louis Bay. It is the seat of Hancock County. The National Aeronautics and Space Administration's Mississippi Test Facility (part of the Marshall Space Flight Center) is situated here. The city's main industry is lumber milling.

Bay Saint Louis, originally known as Shieldsborough, was incorporated in 1854. Government is by commission. Population: 6,752.

BAY SHORE is an unincorporated residential village in southeastern New York, in the town of Islip, in Suffolk County. It is situated on the southern shore of western Long Island, on Great South Bay, 40 miles (64 km) east of New York City.

Bay Shore was developed mainly after 1840 and was a dairying and truck farming center. Its more recent development has been as a resort. It has some light industry, including the manufacture of clothing, machinery, and awnings. Its waterfront supports a large marina, and fishing and boating attract many visitors. Bay Shore is the northern terminal for ferries to communities on western Fire Island. Population: 11,119.

BAY VILLAGE is a suburban residential city in Ohio, in Cuyahoga County, on Lake Erie, 12 miles (19 km) west of Cleveland's Public Square. Its name sometimes is shortened to *Bay.* There are a number of wildlife preserves in the vicinity. Cahoon Park is a 116-acre recreational area within the city. Adjacent to Bay Village is Huntington Park, which includes the Lake Erie Junior Nature and Science Center. Other nearby places of interest are the Bradley Road and Rocky River Reservations of Metropolitan Park and Clague Park in Westlake.

The area was settled in 1810 by the Cahoon family of Vermont. Bay Village was a part of Dover Township until it was incorporated separately in 1901. Population: 18,163.

HELEN M. CASEY
Cuyahoga County Public Library

BAY PSALM BOOK of 1640 has this title page.

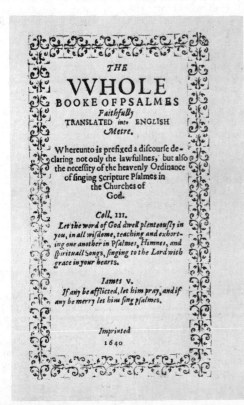

THE
VVHOLE
BOOKE OF PSALMES
Faithfully
TRANSLATED *into* ENGLISH
Metre.

Whereunto is prefixed a difcourfe declaring not only the lawfullnes, but alfo the neceffity of the heavenly Ordinance of finging Scripture Pfalmes in the Churches of God.

Coll. III.

Let the word of God dwell plenteoufly in you, in all wifdome, teaching and exhorting one another in Pfalmes, Himnes, and fpirituall Songs, finging to the Lord with grace in your hearts.

Iames V.

If any be afflicted, let him pray, and if any be merry let him fing pfalmes.

Imprinted
1640

BAYA, bī′ya, the sparrowlike weaverbird (*Ploceus philippinus*), which the people of India and the East Indies often keep about their houses, not only in cages, but as a free pet trained to do a variety of tricks. The bird is even able to learn how to find small articles and to carry notes to designated places. It is also called *baya weaver*.

BAYAMO, bä-yä′mō, is a town in eastern Cuba, in Oriente province. It is situated north of the Sierra Maestra on the Río Bayamo, a tributary of the Cauto, Cuba's longest river, and is 60 miles (96 km) northwest of Santiago. It is a commercial center that handles sugar, rice, and coffee grown nearby. The city has a large condensed milk plant.

Bayamo was founded in 1513. It is regarded as a patriotic shrine by Cubans. The Ten Years' War (1868–1878) and the revolt of 1895 began here. At Bayamo, Lt. Andrew S. Rowan met the revolutionary leader Calixto García Íñiguez early in 1898 with a message from President William McKinley inquiring whether García would cooperate with United States forces. The incident was embellished by Elbert Hubbard in his essay *A Message to Garcia*. Population: (1953) 20,178.

BAYAMÓN, bä-yä-môn′, is an industrial town in northern Puerto Rico, 10 miles (16 km) southwest of San Juan. It has sugar mills, canneries, a brewery, tobacco factories, iron foundries, an oil refinery, brick works, and ice works. Fruit and sugarcane are grown in the vicinity. Nearby are the ruins of Caparra, the earliest Spanish settlement in Puerto Rico, said to have been founded by Ponce de León in 1509. It was abandoned in 1521. Population: 15,109.

BAYAR, bī-är′, **Mahmud Celâl** (1883–   ), third president of Turkey. He was born in Umurbey, a village in Bursa province, on May 15, 1883. His father was headmaster of a local school. After elementary and secondary instruction in the village schools, Bayar completed his education at the University of Istanbul, aided by an uncle who stimulated the young man's liberal principles and hatred of the despotic rule of Sultan Abdul-Hamid II. In 1905 he began to earn his living as a clerk in a Bursa bank. Participating enthusiastically in the activities of the Young Turks (a group of intellectuals opposed to the sultan), he joined the Committee of Union and Progress in 1907 and, a year later, became its principal representative at Bursa. He then became executive secretary of the party organization at İzmir.

During the dismemberment of Turkey at the end of World War I, Bayar, who had been a member of parliament at Istanbul, fled to Ankara. In 1919 he prepared the resistance against the Greeks in the İzmir region and was a commander of militia forces when the Greek Army advanced in Anatolia. He also helped to organize the National Assembly, becoming minister of national economy in 1921.

Recognizing his abilities as organizer and director, President Atatürk gave Bayar the task of establishing the Turkish Affairs Bank (Türkiye İş Bankası) and in 1932 again made him minister of economy. Appointed prime minister in 1937, he resigned that office shortly after Atatürk's death (Nov. 10, 1938) and İsmet İnönü's succession to the presidency.

Convinced that democratic freedom and economic progress could only be achieved by adopting the competitive party system of Western countries, Bayar in the fall of 1945 resigned the vice presidency of the nation's sole political group, the Republican People's Party. On Jan. 7, 1946, with three assembly colleagues, Bayar founded the Democratic party. At the national elections of May 14, 1950, his party gained a sweeping victory over the İnönü government, and on May 22 the National Assembly elected him president. Bayar was reelected on May 14, 1954, and again on Nov. 1, 1957. Under Bayar, Turkey played an important role in the Middle East Treaty Organization (renamed the Central Treaty Organization in 1959) and strengthened its ties with the United States.

Bayar was ousted by the military coup of May 27, 1960, led by Gen. Cemal Gürsel. Along with other former leaders of the Democratic party regime, Bayar was imprisoned and tried by a special court on charges of having violated the constitution and on other charges. After a trial lasting several months, Bayar and other former high officials were found guilty, and Bayar was sentenced to death. The sentence of the former president, however, was commuted to life imprisonment on Sept. 16, 1961.

Bayar was provisionally released for reasons of health on March 22, 1963, but his release was revoked six days later, following massive demonstrations in his behalf. On Nov. 7, 1964, he was again released, and in July 1966 he was pardoned, although his political rights were not restored.

BAYARD, bī′ərd, a family of American public officials and lawyers, identified for over two centuries with the Middle Atlantic region from New York to Maryland. They were descended from a family of French Huguenot refugees, whose patriarch was a Paris theological professor who fled to Holland about 1580 to escape persecution. His son Samuel became a wealthy Amsterdam merchant and married Anna, the accomplished, energetic, and capable sister of Peter Stuyvesant. Stuyvesant himself had married Samuel's equally accomplished sister Judith. Samuel died in Holland, and his widow, with her three sons, accompanied her brother to New Amsterdam in 1647.

NICHOLAS BAYARD (1644–1707), son of Samuel and Anna Bayard, was born in Alphen, Holland, and became associated with his uncle, Peter Stuyvesant, in public office in the province of New Netherland. After the English conquest of what then became New York (1664), he was provincial secretary. A member of the governor's council, he became mayor of New York in 1685.

Bayard had to flee for his life to Albany when Jacob Leisler usurped government power in New York following Gov. Edmund Andros' overthrow. Discovered in Albany, Bayard was imprisoned by Leisler, but he was made councillor again on Leisler's downfall. In 1699 the new governor, the earl of Bellamont, accused Bayard of complicity in protecting pirates. Later he was charged with advocating sedition, mutiny, and Jacobitism and was condemned to death for high treason. Upon investigation of his case, he was released and restored to his honors and possessions by an order in council. He died in New York in 1707.

JOHN BUBENHEIM BAYARD (1738–1807), great-grandnephew of Nicholas, was born at Bohemia Manor, Md., on Aug. 11, 1738. He became a prominent Philadelphia merchant and a member of the Sons of Liberty and later of the Pennsylvania Provincial Convention of 1774.

During the Revolution, he volunteered for service with the Continental Army and was commended by General Washington for his gallantry at the battle of Princeton. He was a member of the Pennsylvania board of war and speaker of the assembly in 1777 and 1778.

Bayard furnished arms to Congress and fitted out one of the earliest efficient privateeers. In 1785 he was elected to the Continental Congress from Pennsylvania. He moved in 1788 to New Brunswick, N.J., where he served in various civil and political positions until his death there on Jan. 7, 1807.

JAMES ASHETON BAYARD (1767–1815), nephew of the preceding, was born in Philadelphia on July 28, 1767, and was adopted by his uncle after his father's death in 1770. He graduated from Princeton in 1784, studied law, and settled in Wilmington, Del.

In 1796, Bayard was elected to Congress as a Federalist. A noted constitutional lawyer, he became the leader of the party in the House of Representatives. In 1800, when the presidential election resulted in a deadlock between Thomas Jefferson and Aaron Burr, both Republicans, and the election was thrown into the House, Bayard succeeded in withdrawing sufficient Federalist votes from Burr to permit Jefferson's election.

President John Adams, toward the end of his term, appointed Bayard minister to France, but he declined. Bayard served in the House until 1803. The following year he was elected to the Senate from Delaware, and he held the seat until 1813. During the War of 1812 he was made peace commissioner (1813) by President James Madison and was one of those who concluded the Treaty of Ghent on Dec. 24, 1814. Subsequently he declined appointment as minister to Russia. He died in Wilmington on Aug. 6, 1815.

JAMES ASHETON BAYARD (1799–1880), son of the preceding, was born in Wilmington, Del., on Nov. 15, 1799. He became a lawyer of high rank in Wilmington and was United States district attorney for Delaware from 1838 to 1843. He served in the U.S. Senate from 1851 to 1864. Although first elected as a Democrat, he joined the Republicans with the approach of the Civil War. Bayard protested the test oath of loyalty to the Constitution for federal officeholders, and after the Senate passed the measure, he resigned his seat (1864). His successor, George R. Riddle, died in 1867, and Bayard was returned to the Senate to fill out his own unexpired term, to March 1869. Eventually he went back to the Democratic party. His son, Thomas F. Bayard, a Democrat, was chosen to succeed him in the Senate. The elder Bayard then returned to his law practice in Wilmington, where he died on June 13, 1880.

RICHARD HENRY BAYARD (1796–1868), brother of the preceding, was born in Wilmington, Del., on Sept. 26, 1796, and graduated from Princeton College in 1814. He began to study law, served briefly in the War of 1812, and upon his return resumed his law studies and was admitted to the bar in 1818. He became very popular both socially and professionally in Wilmington.

Bayard was defeated in the 1828 election for a seat in the House of Representatives, but in 1832 he was elected first mayor of Wilmington under its new charter. In 1836 he was elected as a Whig to the U.S. Senate but resigned in 1839, after the Whig party gained control of the Delaware Senate, to become chief justice of the state. In 1841 he again became a member of the U.S. Senate, filling the vacancy he had left; he served until 1845 and then returned to private law practice. From 1850 to 1853 he was chargé d'affaires in Belgium, but upon his return to the United States he retired from government service. Bayard died in Philadelphia on March 4, 1868.

THOMAS FRANCIS BAYARD (1828–1898), son of the younger James Asheton Bayard, was born in Wilmington, Del., on Oct. 29, 1828. He embarked on a business career and was placed in a New York mercantile firm, his elder brother being marked to carry on the family tradition of public service. The latter, however, died in 1848, and Thomas returned to Wilmington, studied law with his father, and was admitted to the bar in 1851. He was appointed United States district attorney in 1853 but resigned the next year. He moved to Philadelphia and practiced law, then returned to Wilmington in 1858.

Elected to the U.S. Senate as a Democrat to succeed his father, he took his seat in 1869, and served by successive reelections until 1885. One of the leading Democratic figures in the Senate, he was its president pro tempore in 1881. He was mentioned prominently as a candidate for the presidency before the Democratic national conventions of 1880 and 1884 but was never nominated.

In 1885, Bayard was appointed secretary of state in the cabinet of President Cleveland. As secretary until 1889, he faced such vexatious questions as the Bering Sea and North Atlantic fisheries disputes. He was U.S. ambassador to Britain (1893–1897) during Cleveland's second term, the first American granted ambassadorial rank anywhere. He died in Dedham, Mass., on Sept. 28, 1898.

THOMAS FRANCIS BAYARD (1868–1942), son of the preceding, was born in Wilmington, Del., on June 4, 1868, and graduated from Yale University (B.A., 1890). He then studied law until 1893, when he was admitted to the Delaware bar. He moved to New York City and in 1897 received an appointment as assistant corporation counsel. Returning to Wilmington in 1901, he served as chairman of the Democratic state committee (1906–1916) and as city solicitor of Wilmington (1917–1919). He was elected as a Democrat to the U.S. Senate from Delaware in 1922, serving in that capacity until 1929. He died in Wilmington on July 12, 1942.

BAYARD, bà-yàr′, **Seigneur de** (c. 1473–1524), French soldier, whose name has become a synonym for the perfect knight. Because of his courage, his almost incredible feats of arms, his loyalty to his king, and his piety and generosity, he became known as *le bon chevalier* and later as *le chevalier sans peur et sans reproche.* He has often been regarded incorrectly as epitomizing medieval chivalry at its height. However, he lived not in the Middle Ages but in the Renaissance, and his behavior was not typical of most warriors in a period when the values associated with medieval chivalry were rapidly disintegrating.

He was born *Pierre Terrail* at the Château Bayard, near Grenoble, and came to the attention of King Charles VIII of France early in his youth. He joined the royal entourage and distinguished himself during the famous Italian expedition of Charles VIII in 1494. Henceforth his name was associated with most of the glorious French feats of arms in the early 16th century. At the bridge of Garigliano in Italy, Bayard is reported to have held 200 Spaniards at bay. This exploit caused Pope Julius II to attempt to entice Bayard into the papal bodyguard. When the French were defeated in 1513 by the English at the Battle of Guinegate (known as the Battle of the Spurs), Bayard, reluctant to give up his sword to an armed man, continued fighting, but finally offered it to an unarmed English soldier. King Henry VIII of England was so impressed by Bayard's bravery that he released him without ransom. The young Francis I esteemed Bayard so highly that the king received knighthood from his loyal warrior.

One of Bayard's most celebrated military achievements took place at Mézières in 1521. Besieged by the army of Emperor Charles V, which numbered at least 30,000, and holding a place considered indefensible, Bayard and 1,000 men resisted for six weeks and compelled the imperial army to withdraw. This stroke saved central France from invasion and pillage and enabled Francis I to recruit an army with which to drive the enemy from France. For this exploit Bayard was hailed as the savior of his country, made a knight of the elite order of St. Michael, and given the command of 100 men-at-arms, an honor normally bestowed only upon princes of the royal family.

Bayard met his death on the field of battle. In 1523 he and Admiral Bonnivet led a French force into Italy. Bonnivet was wounded in an engagement at Robecco, and the French were forced to retreat. Taking sole command, Bayard directed the retreat and fought to protect the army's rear columns. While so engaged at a passage near the Sesia River, he was mortally wounded by the ball of an arquebus. He died on April 30, 1524, in the hands of the Spanish, who so admired him that they returned his body to the French for decent burial.

In addition to his qualities as a noble warrior, Bayard should be remembered for the professional way in which he conducted campaigns. He was invariably well informed about the strength and position of the enemy, he knew the value of continual reconnaissance, and he relied upon an efficient espionage system. Admirable for his heroic qualities, Bayard was at the same time shrewd and realistic in battle.

BRYCE LYON, *Brown University*

BAYBARS I (1233?–1277), bī-bars', was a slave army officer who rose to become the fourth Mamluk sultan of Egypt (1260–1277) and the first great builder of the Mamluk empire of Egypt and Syria. He reorganized the administrative and military machinery of the Mamluk state. He reaffirmed the Mamluk attachment to Muslim orthodoxy by transferring the Abbasid caliphate, symbol of Muslim unity and orthodoxy, to Cairo from Baghdad; by winning suzerainty over the holy places of Mecca and Medina; and by supporting the orthodox religious community.

Baybars' reign was occupied with almost incessant warfare to incorporate greater Syria into the Mamluk empire. Independent local rulers were displaced, and heretical Ismaili communities were rooted out. The Mongols were defeated in 1260 at Ayn Jalut in Palestine, and Syria was defended against renewed incursions. He eventually secured Syria against political and religious enemies of Mamluk rule and of Muslim orthodox society. Baybars died in Damascus in 1277.

Baybars also relentlessly whittled away the remaining Crusader principalities. Between 1265 and 1271 he captured many of the coastal towns, including Caesarea, Jaffa, and Arsuf. In 1268 he seized Antioch, which had been in Christian hands since 1099. Baybars also raided Cilician Armenia in 1275, beginning a century-long effort to incorporate that province into the Mamluk domains.

IRA LAPIDUS
University of California, Berkeley

BAYBERRY, bā′ber-ē, a West Indian tree and a North American shrub. The tree, *Pimenta acris,* is closely related to the allspice tree. Known also as the *Jamaica bayberry* and the *bay rum tree,* it is small and aromatic, with white flowers and large leathery leaves. The dried leaves are the source of a yellow aromatic oil called bay oil or oil of myrica, used in perfumes. The shrub, *Myrica pensylvanica,* has stiff whitish-gray branches and deciduous, dark green, oval-shaped leaves. It is a member of the wax myrtle family and is found along the eastern coastal plain of North America.

The name "bayberry" also is given to the small fruits of these species and of bay and wax myrtle trees.

Bayberry

(*Myrica pensylvanica*)

ROCHE

BAYEUX, bȧ-yü′, a town in France, is situated on the Aure River in Calvados department, about 17 miles (27 km) northwest of Caen. Its chief industries are dairy products and canned beef, but lace and porcelain also are manufactured. The most impressive building is the Cathedral of Notre Dame, built during the 12th–15th centuries in Norman Gothic style. Its most striking features are the portal and three towers; the center tower, 240 feet high (73 meters), is in flamboyant Gothic style. The famous Bayeux Tapestry, which depicts the Norman conquest of England, is in the Museum of Queen Matilda.

Called *Augustodurum* by the Romans, Bayeux was made a bishopric in the 4th century. In 1106 it was pillaged by Henry I of England. During the Hundred Years' War, the town was twice captured by the English, and during the French religious wars of the 16th century it changed hands several times. Bayeux was the first French town to be liberated by American forces during World War II. Population: (1962) 9,335.

BAYEUX TAPESTRY, an embroidery measuring 231 feet, is displayed at Museum of Queen Matilda, Bayeux, France. The tapestry, recounting the Norman conquest of England, is a major source of information on the Middle Ages.

BAYEUX TAPESTRY, bà-yü′ tap′ə-strē, a medieval embroidery in outline stitch, rope stitch, and laid work, made of wool on linen, 231 feet (70.4 meters) long and 19½ inches (49.5 cm) wide. It is preserved in the Museum of Queen Matilda at Bayeux in Normandy, France.

The embroidery is not a tapestry in any sense of the word, but this misleading name is now too firmly attached to be changed. The embroidery represents the Norman Conquest of England in 1066, with the events leading up to it, in a series of scenes of the utmost vivacity; a running inscription in Latin tells the story.

The tapestry, recorded in an inventory of Bayeux Cathedral in 1476, came to the attention of the learned world early in the 18th century. There has been much controversy as to when and where it was made and for whom, but there is now general agreement that it was commissioned by Odo, bishop of Bayeux, William the Conqueror's half brother, who figures prominently in the narrative, and that it was made before 1083. There is less certainty about the nationality of the designer—English scholars usually claim him as a Saxon; French scholars, as a Norman. The tradition that the work was carried out by William's wife, Matilda, and her ladies is not supported by any evidence.

The embroidery is unique, though similar hangings are known from written descriptions to have existed; its importance, both as a work of art and as a document, is hard to overestimate. No other textile is an original source for political historians, and few provide such an amount of information for students of armor, fortifications, ships, costume, architecture, and even astronomy (the tapestry includes a representation of Halley's comet of April 24–30, 1066). Minute details, such as the distinction between the English and the Norman fashions of cutting men's hair and trimming horses' manes, are so consistent and, where they can be checked against written sources, found to be so accurate, that there is complete confidence in the embroidery as a record of life and manners during the 11th century.

More than 120 books and articles have been written about the Bayeux Tapestry. A. Levé's *La tapisserie de la reine Mathilde* (Paris 1919) states the French position; Eric Maclagan's *The Bayeux Tapestry* (London 1945) gives an admirable summary from the English point of view. The most comprehensive work on the subject is *The Bayeux Tapestry* (New York 1957), edited by Frank Stenton and others. The best illustrations, including color reproductions of details, are in André Lejard's *La tapisserie de Bayeux* (Paris 1946).

EDITH A. STANDEN
Metropolitan Museum of Art

PANEL FROM THE BAYEUX TAPESTRY shows the Norman invaders battling the English defenders in 1066. An inscription in Latin that describes the events pictured is embroidered throughout the entire length of the tapestry.

BAYEZID I (1354–1403), bī-yə-zēd', was an Ottoman sultan. His name is also transliterated as *Bayazid* and *Bajazet*. The son of Sultan Murad I, he served as governor in Anatolia, where his ardor as a soldier won him the sobriquet "the Thunderbolt." He came to the throne in June 1389.

Early in his reign, Bayezid successfully dealt with revolts in western Anatolia and the Balkans. Alarmed by the expansion of his European dominions, Hungary and Venice organized a new "crusade." This ended with a resounding victory for Bayezid at Nicopolis in September 1396. Late in 1399, Timur (Tamerlane) appeared in Anatolia, claimed suzerainty over the area, and gave refuge to the local rulers expelled by Bayezid. The almost inevitable clash between the two Turkish leaders occurred at Ankara in July 1402. Bayezid was defeated and captured, and he died in captivity in March 1403. The budding Ottoman empire, first centralized by Bayezid, went through a period of internecine warfare until the interregnum was ended by Mehmed I in 1413.

J. STEWART-ROBINSON
University of Michigan

BAYEZID II (1448?–1512), bī-yə-zēd', an Ottoman sultan, was the son of Sultan Mehmed II. He fought his younger brother Jem for the throne, which he mounted in June 1481. He brought Hercegovina under Ottoman control (1483) and extended his frontiers to the Dniester River (1484), thereby securing the overland route to the Crimea, which was ruled by his vassals, the Tatar khans.

A war against Venice (1499–1503) resulted in important territorial gains in the Peloponnesus of Greece and along the Adriatic coast. His military activities in the east (1485–1491), however, failed to dislodge the Mamluks from southern Anatolia. In the first decade of the 16th century he was unable to deal effectively with the threatening Safavids from Persia because of his conflict with his son Selim, who finally deposed him in April 1512. Bayezid died at Demitoka the following month, leaving his successor a more mobile army, which would occupy the rest of the Middle East, and a greatly strengthened fleet, with which to rule the Mediterranean for the remainder of the century.

J. STEWART-ROBINSON
University of Michigan

BAYLE, bȧl, **Pierre** (1647–1706), French philosopher, who had a great influence on the *philosophes* and encyclopedists of the 1700's.

The son of a Calvinist minister, he was born at Carla-le-Comte (now Carla-Bayle), in Ariège, on Nov. 18, 1647. He studied at the College of Puy-Laurens and at the Jesuit University of Toulouse, where he was converted to Roman Catholicism in 1669. About a year and a half later he apostatized, bringing upon himself the censure of excommunication. He lived in Geneva, Switzerland, for a time, but in 1675 returned to France, where he was appointed professor of philosophy at the Calvinist Academy of Sedan.

When Louis XIV suppressed the academy in 1681, Bayle left France for Holland. That same year he was appointed to the chair of philosophy at the University of Rotterdam. He taught there until 1693, when authorities removed him from his professorship for his political and religious views. Bayle died in Rotterdam on Dec. 28, 1706.

Thought. Throughout his writings, Bayle displayed a gift for clear, animated presentation of matters of intellectual controversy. He was an extreme freethinker for his day, although later ages have found him somewhat guarded in his manner of exposition. He did not hesitate to subject any question of belief to the scrutiny of reason. Both his rationalism and the irony in which he clothed it were adopted by the *philosophes* of the 18th century, who incorporated into their works, including the *Encyclopédie*, many of Bayle's arguments against orthodoxy.

Bayle made the first and most forthright statement of his beliefs in the speculative work *Pensées diverses sur la comète* (1682). This introduced many of his later themes—the condemnation of superstition, the belief that morality may exist independently of religion, the mistrust of tradition and authority, and the strong affirmation of the principle of tolerance. This last doctrine was strongly reiterated in his *Commentaire philosophique sur le compelle intrare* (1686), for which he was denounced by both the Catholic and Protestant clergy.

Dictionnaire. Bayle's greatest work was the *Dictionnaire historique et critique* (4 folio vols., 1685–97; Eng. tr., *Historical and Critical Dictionary*, 1964). In orthodox dictionary fashion, the work lists important figures of classical and sacred history. However, Bayle's *Dictionnaire* was unique in appending to each article a learned note, often longer than the article itself, which comments on the absurd or conflicting aspects of the tradition cited. Disguising its arguments in irony, understatement, and slyly humorous barbs, the *Dictionnaire* exposed the ways in which fiction had been mixed with and even replaced fact in the body of accepted belief.

When the book was attacked by the Protestant theologian Pierre Jurieu and by a Protestant consistory, Bayle promised to remove several "offensive" items. However, finding the times ripe for his rationalist views, he left the work, with the exception of a few trifles, unaltered. The most complete edition of the *Dictionnaire* appeared in 1730, and an 18-volume edition was published in 1820.

Further Reading: Robinson, Howard, *Bayle, the Sceptic* (New York 1931); Sandberg, Karl C., *At the Crossroads of Faith and Reason* (Tucson, Ariz., 1966).

BAYLIS, bā'lis, **Lilian** (1874–1937), English theatrical manager. She was born in London on May 9, 1874. She toured England and South Africa as a concert violinist and returned to London in 1898 to become assistant manager under her aunt, Emma Cons, of the Royal Victoria Theatre, popularly known as the "Old Vic," a music and lecture hall for workers. After her aunt's death in 1912, she became manager of the theater, transforming it into a theater for opera and, only incidentally, drama.

After Shakespearean drama took over as the Old Vic's staple offering, Miss Baylis purchased the derelict Sadler's Wells Theatre in London and turned it into a celebrated showcase for the production of opera and ballet. For ballet mistress she hired Ninette de Valois, who developed the Sadler's Wells ballet company (later the Royal Ballet) into one of the world's leading dance ensembles. Meanwhile, the Old Vic had become internationally preeminent for its Shakespearean productions. Lilian Baylis died in London on Nov. 25, 1937.

BAYLISS, bā′lis, **Sir William Maddock,** (1860–1924), English physiologist. He was born in Wolverhampton, England, on May 2, 1860. He began to study medicine at University College, London, in 1881, but four years later gave up the idea of a career as a medical practitioner and went to Wadham College, Oxford, to study physiology. In 1888 he returned to University College as a teacher of physiology, and remained on the faculty there for the rest of his life, being awarded a professorship in 1912.

From 1891, in collaboration with Ernest Henry Starling, Bayliss carried out researches of far-reaching importance, including studies of the innervation of the intestine and of the electromotive phenomena attendant upon heart action. His major achievement was the discovery of the hormone secretin, produced by the intestinal glands and carried by the blood to the pancreas, where it stimulates the flow of pancreatic juice. During World War I, Bayliss introduced the use of saline injections in the treatment of surgical shock, saving many lives. He published *The Nature of Enzyme Action* (1908); *Principles of General Physiology* (1915), a highly original textbook which quickly won international recognition; and *The Vaso-motor System* (1923). He was knighted in 1922. Bayliss died in London on Aug. 27, 1924.

BAYLOR, bā′lər, **Elgin** (1934–   ), American basketball player, who became one of the leading scorers and finest all-around players in the National Basketball Association (NBA). He was born in Washington, D.C., on Sept. 16, 1934. An outstanding forward at Spingarn High School in Washington, he won All-America rating while at Seattle University in 1958. He joined the Minneapolis (later Los Angeles) Lakers that year, and at the end of his first season he was named Rookie of the Year.

Baylor, a Negro, attained personal high-scoring marks of 71 points in a league game in 1960 and of 61 points in a playoff game in 1962. Although slowed by service in the U.S. Army in 1961–1962 and by a knee injury in 1965, the 6-foot 5-inch Baylor ranked among the league's leading all-time scorers.

BILL BRADDOCK, *New York "Times"*

BAYLOR, bā′lər, **Robert Emmet Bledsoe** (1793?–1873), American judge and Baptist leader for whom Baylor University was named. Born in Kentucky on May 10, 1791 or 1793, he served in the War of 1812 and later was admitted to the Kentucky bar. In 1820 he moved to Alabama, where he was elected to Congress for one term in 1829. He settled in Texas in 1839. Two years later he was appointed an associate justice of the Texas supreme court. He played a prominent part in drafting the state constitution, and after Texas entered the Union in 1845 he was appointed a United States district judge— a position he held until 1861.

Baylor had joined the Baptist church in Alabama, and he continued to preach in Texas, conducting services wherever his court was in session. He served as moderator of the Texas Baptist Union Association and as president of the Baptist State Convention. As president of the Texas Baptist education society he was influential in establishing the Baptist college that later became Baylor University. He died in Washington County, Texas, on Dec. 30, 1873.

BAYLOR UNIVERSITY, bā′lər, is a private, co-educational institution, with campuses at Waco, Dallas, and Houston, Texas, operated by the Baptist General Convention of Texas. It was chartered in 1845 by the Texas Baptist Educational Society, in what was then the Republic of Texas, and named for Robert E.B. Baylor. Originally it was located at Independence, Texas, but it was moved to Waco in 1886 and consolidated with Waco University under control of the Baptist General Convention.

Baylor's college of arts and sciences, its schools of business, education, law, music, and nursing, and its graduate school are at the Waco campus; the college of dentistry, the graduate research institute, and the medical center are at Dallas; and the college of medicine is at Houston. An honors program is offered for outstanding students, and there is a master's program for military personnel from Fort Sam Houston in clinical medicine and hospital administration.

The Waco campus has a museum devoted to Texas plant and animal life, and the library of 340,000 volumes contains an outstanding collection of memorabilia on the English poet Robert Browning. The research institute, at Dallas, is noted for its work on hematology. Total university enrollment, which stood at 2,400 in 1940, increased to 6,500 by the mid-1960's.

BAYNE, bān, **Stephen Fielding** (1908–   ) American Episcopal clergyman. He was born in New York City on May 21, 1908. After serving as chaplain of Columbia University (1942–1947), he was bishop of Olympia, Wash. (1947–1959).

In 1960 the archbishop of Canterbury made him executive officer of the Anglican Communion (churches in communion with the Church of England). In this post Bayne helped formulate "Mutual Responsibility and Interdependence," a major statement on Anglican missionary activity and ecumenical relations. In 1963 he became first vice president of the executive council of the Episcopal Church and director of its overseas department.

BAYONET, bā′ə-net, is a weapon of the dagger type made to fit on the muzzle of a rifle. The name probably derives from the French city of Bayonne, home of Maréchal de Puységur, who is said to have invented the bayonet about 1640. There is evidence, however, that it had previously been adapted to the harquebus and other early firearms. With the invention of such weapons it was a logical step to affix a metal lance to the firearm.

The bayonet used by Puységur's troops when they took Ypres for King Louis XIV in 1647 was a steel dagger with a cross guard and wooden haft or grip that was tapered to fit into musket muzzles of various calibers. This plug-type bayonet was often too loose or tight, and prevented firing of the musket.

A bayonet attached to the muzzle by two loose-fitting rings appeared in the late 1600's, and this was supplanted by the closer-fitting socket-bayonet, adopted between 1697 and 1703 by the English, German, and French. Not until 1800, however, were the socket locks secured by means of locking springs.

In the course of their development, bayonets have varied greatly in length and shape. The regulation bayonet of United States troops in the late 1960's was 8 inches (20.3 cm) long.

BAYONNE, bȧ-yôn', is a city in France, in Basses-Pyrénées department, 55 miles (88 km) northwest of Pau. It is located at the confluence of the Nive and Adour rivers, about 4 miles (6.4 km) from the Bay of Biscay. Large vessels can enter the harbor despite a hazardous shifting sandbar. The rivers divide the city into three parts: Great Bayonne, on the left bank of the Nive; Little Bayonne, between the rivers; and St. Esprit, on the right bank of the Adour.

A citadel, built by the Marquis de Vauban (1633–1707), commands the harbor and the city. The cathedral is a beautiful building dating from 1213, with two towers added during a 19th century restoration. The arsenal, the mint, and the Basque museum are among other places of interest. Industries in the city include shipbuilding, distilling, textiles, chocolate, and resins. Among its exports are the famous Bayonne hams.

In the 3d century A.D. the Roman town built on this site was known as *Lapurdum*. In 1199 it passed into English hands and was not retaken by the French until 1451. At a meeting in Bayonne in 1808, Emperor Napoleon I forced King Ferdinand VII of Spain to abdicate his throne, and Ferdinand's father, Charles IV, to renounce his claim to the throne, paving the way for the assumption of the Spanish crown by Napoleon's brother, Joseph Bonaparte. Population: (1962) 30,865.

BAYONNE, bȧ-ōn', is an industrial city in northeastern New Jersey, in Hudson County, about 8 miles (13 km) southwest of the southern tip of Manhattan Island. It is on a peninsula with water frontage on New York Bay to the east, Newark Bay to the west, and the Kill van Kull to the south. The 1,652-foot (503.5-meter) span of the Bayonne Bridge connects Bayonne with Staten Island over the Kill van Kull.

The city formerly was a major center for petroleum refining. Its later development has been in light industry. Bayonne produces chemicals, electrical equipment, heating apparatus, metal products, petroleum products, pharmaceuticals, vegetable oil products, and wearing apparel. Its extensive docks serve as a coal distributing point for the New York metropolitan area. The U.S. Naval Supply Center and a Military Ocean Terminal are in the city.

The site of Bayonne was visited by Henry Hudson in 1609 and called Konstable's Hoek (Gunner's Point), later Constable Hook. It was settled by the Dutch and English in 1656. In its earlier days the area was largely residential. It had a powder plant during the War of 1812, but its history as an industrial center dates from the establishment of its first oil refinery in 1875. During World War I more than 700 submarine chasers were completed at Bayonne shipyards. The city was a shipping and embarkation center during World War II.

Bayonne was incorporated as a city in 1869, including the villages of Salterville, Bergen Neck, and Centerville. Since 1962 it has been governed by a mayor and council. Population: 72,743.

BAYOU, bī'ōō, a sluggish body of water that forms an arm of a larger body, such as a lake or a river. The term is a rendering by the French in Louisiana of the Choctaw Indian word *bayuk*, meaning "river" or "creek." The word is common in Louisiana and Mississippi; the latter is called the Bayou State.

MONKMEYER

BAYREUTH'S FESTSPIELHAUS is a world-famous theater devoted to performances of operas by Wagner.

BAYREUTH, bī-roit', is a city in West Germany in the northeast part of the state of Bavaria, known for its festivals of Wagner operas. It is on the Red Main River, 41 miles (66 km) northeast of Nuremberg. The main industries of the city are machinery manufacturing, textiles, chemicals, paper, musical instruments, and brewing.

The principal buildings are the old palace, the new palace with park and garden, the 18th century opera house, and the Wagnerian Festspielhaus, designed by Richard Wagner. The Festspielhaus, built by the architect Gottfried Semper, was specifically designed for the production of Wagner's operas. Among the interesting private residences rebuilt since World War II are the Villa Wahnfried, the former home of Wagner, who is buried on its grounds, and the house of the author Jean Paul Richter. In the city cemetery are the graves of Richter and the composer Franz Liszt.

The town is particularly known as the mecca of Wagnerites. In 1872, with funds collected partly from patrons and partly from Wagnerian societies, the erection of a theater for the production of Wagner's works was begun. This Festspielhaus was opened in 1876 with a grand performance of *Der Ring des Nibelungen,* and since then music lovers have been attracted to Bayreuth from all over the world. The theater was closed during World War I, but was revived and continued during World War II until 1945. Annual performances were resumed in 1951 under the artistic leadership of Wagner's grandsons, Wolfgang and Wieland.

Founded in 1194 under Bishop Otto II of Bamberg, Bayreuth fell to the burgrave of Nuremberg in 1248. From 1248 until 1806 it was under the control of one or another of the branches of the Hohenzollern family. It passed to the margraves of Brandenburg-Kulmbach in 1603, Prussia in 1791, and Napoleon in 1806. After it was ceded to Bavaria in 1810, it remained in the hands of the Wittelsbach dynasty until World War I. Population: (1961) 61,835.

BAYTOWN, bā′toun, is an industrial city in eastern Texas, situated in Harris County, on Galveston Bay, about 22 miles (35.3 km) east-southeast of Houston. It has oil refineries and manufactures petrochemical products.

The first white settlement was made in Baytown in 1853. Incorporation in 1948 resulted from consolidation of Goose Creek (incorporated 1918), Pelly (incorporated 1922), and Baytown. Government is by mayor and council. Population: 43,980.

BAZAINE, bà-zân′, **Achille** (1811–1888), French general, who surrendered the French army in the Franco-Prussian war. He was born at Versailles on Feb. 13, 1811, and joined the army in 1831. After fighting in Algeria, Spain, and in the Crimean War, he accompanied the French expeditionary force to Mexico in 1862 and soon was named its commander. He was made a marshal of France in 1864. He returned to France after participating in an abortive plot to overthrow Emperor Maximilian of Mexico.

Bazaine was a popular hero in France. After the first French defeats in the Franco-Prussian War in 1870, Napoleon III named him commander in chief of the army. After several engagements in which he displayed an excess of caution, Bazaine withdrew his army of 180,000 men into the fortress of Metz. He surrendered on Oct. 28, 1870, after a seven-week siege. For this action, he was condemned to death by a court martial in 1873, but the sentence was commuted to 20 years' imprisonment on the island of Sainte-Marguerite. Bazaine escaped from the island in 1874 and lived in exile. He died at Madrid on Sept. 28, 1888.

BAZARD, bà-zàr′, **Saint-Amand** (1791–1832), French socialist. He was born in Paris on Sept. 19, 1791. A fiery revolutionary, he was opposed to the Bourbon restoration after Napoleon's overthrow in 1815. He helped found the secret French Carbonari movement, was arrested, and escaped. He then threw himself ardently into the socialist, Saint-Simonian schemes for the reorganization of society. After Saint-Simon's death in 1825, he and Barthélemy Prosper Enfantin became the leaders of the Saint-Simonian school. He also collaborated in the journal *Le producteur,* in which he used as early as 1825 the term "social science."

Bazard published a series of his lectures in the *Exposition de la doctrine de Saint-Simon* (1828–1830), a work to which Enfantin also contributed. It is in this work that the phrase "exploitation of man by man" first appears. Representing a rational and serious element among the Saint-Simonians, he withdrew in 1831 after violent conflict with Enfantin over the issue of feminism. Although he is credited with formulating, rather than inventing, many of the principal socialist ideas of the day, his influence on Karl Marx and John Stuart Mill is recognized. During a heated discussion with Enfantin, Bazard collapsed and died on July 29, 1832, at Courtry.

ANNE S. TILLETT, *Wake Forest College*

BAZIGARS, bä-zə-gärz′, a nomadic tribe in India, living chiefly in the state of Punjab. Usually Muslims, they earn their living as performers. Both men and women are skillful jugglers, acrobats, and tumblers. Their name comes from a Persian word meaning "who does the play."

BAZIN, bà-zaN′, **Germain** (1901–   ), French art historian and curator of the Louvre Museum in Paris. He was born in Suresnes, a suburb of Paris, on Sept. 24, 1901. After studying art history at the University of Paris and at the École du Louvre, he took a job in 1928 in the department of drawings at the museum of the École des Beaux-Arts in Paris.

In 1937, Bazin was appointed curator of paintings and drawing at the Louvre. After an interlude as director of the periodical *L'amour de l'art,* he returned to the Louvre in 1951 as chief curator. His books on art that have been translated into English include *The Louvre* (1957), *A Concise History of Art* (1958), and *The Loom of Art* (1962).

BAZIN, bà-zaN′, **René François Nicolas Marie** (1853–1932), French novelist. Born in Angers, France, on Dec. 26, 1853, he was educated in Angers and studied law at the University of Paris. Adopting a literary career, he became one of the most popular French novelists of his day. He was elected to the French Academy in 1903. His best novels, *La terre qui meurt* (1899), *Les Oberlé* (1901), and *Le blé qui lève* (1907), are studies of provincial life. He died in Paris on July 20, 1932.

U.S. ARMY

BAZOOKA, a rocket launcher, is aimed by one bazookaman and loaded by another in the Korean War.

BAZOOKA, bə-zōō′kə, a shoulder weapon that enables an infantryman to damage a tank. The U.S. Army officially named the weapon *Launcher, Rocket,* but soldiers nicknamed it *bazooka* because of its resemblance to a unique musical instrument of the American comedian Bob Burns.

The bazooka is a light, two-part, smoothbore tube, open at both ends, with stock, handgrips, and trigger. A man rests it on his shoulder, aims it, and fires; another man loads. There is no recoil since the backblast exists from the rear of the tube. The bazooka was first used in 1943 against German tanks in North Africa. It fired a rocket of 2.36-inch (5.99-cm) diameter, weighing 3.3 pounds (1.5 kg). This model was superseded in 1950 by the 3.5-inch (8.9-cm) bazooka, firing an 8.5-pound (3.9-kg) rocket from a 13-pound (5.9-kg) tube. Although slow and of short range (1,300 feet or 396 meters), the rocket's shaped charge blasts a hole through the strongest armor. Rocket-launching tubes on aircraft are also called bazookas.

BAZZI, Giovanni Antonio de'. See SODOMA, IL.

BDELLIUM, del′ē-əm, is an aromatic gum found in various countries. It resembles myrrh in its appearance and is often fraudulently substituted for it. Bdellium is obtained from the trees *Commiphora mokul* and *C. agallocha*. It has a sweet smell but bitter taste, softens readily between the fingers in front of a fire, and dissolves partially in alcohol and still more in water. A variety of bdellium produced by the West African tree *C. africana* is used in plasters.

The bdellium mentioned in Scripture—in Hebrew *bedolach*—is rendered in Greek, in Genesis 2:12, as *anthrax* (literally, "burning coal"), while in Numbers 11:7 it is translated *krystallos*—rock crystal. Some writers, following the Greek translations, make it a mineral (ruby, garnet, or red sapphire), as are the gold and onyx stone with which it is associated in Genesis 2:12.

BEA, bā′ə, **Augustin** (1881–1968), German cardinal and theologian of the Roman Catholic Church. He was born at Riedbachringen, Baden, Germany, on May 28, 1881. After two years at the University of Freiburg he entered the Society of Jesus at Blynbeek, in the Netherlands, in 1902. He was ordained in 1912, and continued his studies in advanced theology at Valkenburg and Berlin. In 1924 he began his long teaching career at the Biblical Institute in Rome. During this time he exerted increasing influence within the leadership of the church, first as adviser to Pope Pius XI and later as confessor and adviser to Pius XII.

John XXIII elevated Bea to cardinal in 1959 and, a year later, appointed him to head the new Secretariat for Promoting Christian Unity—a cause Cardinal Bea had long advanced. He used the two years preceding the opening of the Second Vatican Council to assess the thinking of many Protestant and Orthodox leaders. At the Council he became one of the leading liberal spokesmen. Two of Cardinal Bea's works have been translated into English: *Study of the Synoptic Gospels* (1965) and *Unity in Freedom* (1964). He died in Rome on Nov. 16, 1968.

BEACH, bēch, **Alfred Ely** (1826–1896), American publisher and inventor, who was co-owner of the *Scientific American,* and who invented a method for building tunnels. Beach was born in Springfield, Mass., on Sept. 1, 1826. His father was Moses Yale Beach, and his brother was Moses Sperry Beach. After Alfred Beach received an education at Monson Academy in Monson, Mass., he became associated with his father in publishing the New York *Sun*. In 1846 he formed a partnership with Orson D. Munn and purchased the *Scientific American*. In 1847 he invented a typewriter for the blind; it printed raised letters on a strip of paper.

In 1867 he constructed an eight-foot-diameter, 100-foot-long tube through which passengers were carried back and forth in a car. This car, which fit tightly in the tube, was driven by air pressure produced by a rotating fan. Beach also devised a pneumatic tube for conveying letters from a street letter-box to the postoffice.

One important invention was a shield for tunneling under streets and rivers. The so-called Beach shield, developed in 1868, was a large cylindrical form; the front circular edge was sharp, and the rear edge had a thin iron hood. The cylinder was propelled slowly forward through the earth by several hydraulic rams. After the shield was forced forward, a new section of tunnel was constructed in the thin hood at the rear of the cylinder. Using his shield, Beach constructed a tunnel in New York City in 1869. In 1870, a car was driven back and forth on tracks in the tunnel by means of pneumatic power. This event inaugurated underground transit in New York.

From 1872 to 1876, Beach edited *Science Record,* an annual publication of the *Scientific American,* and in 1876 he originated the *Scientific American Supplement*. He also was instrumental in beginning the publication of the *Scientific American Builders' Monthly*.

Beach obtained patents on a typewriter (1847), a typewriter for the blind (1857), a cable railway (1864), pneumatic tubes for mail and passengers (1865), and his tunneling shield. He died on Jan. 1, 1896.

BEACH, bēch, **Amy Marcy** (1867–1944), American pianist and composer. She was born *Amy Marcy Cheney* in Henniker, N.H., on Sept. 5, 1867. She studied piano with Ernst Perabo and Carl Baermann, and made her professional debut in Boston in 1883. The following year she was a soloist with the Boston Symphony Orchestra. She married Dr. Henry H.A. Beach, a Boston surgeon, in 1885.

After her marriage she retired for a time from the concert stage and devoted herself to composing. In 1892 she was commissioned to write a *Festival Jubilate* for the opening of the World's Columbian Exposition in Chicago. Her other works include a chorale composed for the Omaha Exposition in 1898, a mass in E-flat (1892), and *Gaelic Symphony* (1896).

Following her husband's death in 1910, she returned to performing. She toured Europe for four years, playing her own compositions under the professional name *Mrs. H.H.A. Beach*. She died in New York City on Dec. 27, 1944.

BEACH, bēch, **Frederick Converse** (1848–1918), American editor and publisher, who was editor in chief of the *Encyclopedia Americana* from 1902 until 1918. He was born in Brooklyn, N.Y., on March 27, 1848, the son of Alfred Ely Beach, publisher of the *Scientific American*. The younger Beach graduated from the Sheffield Scientific School of Yale University in 1868.

In 1866, as a result of his interest in photography, Beach suggested to the U.S. commissioner of patents the practicability of using the photolithographic process to reproduce diagrams for patent specifications. This plan was later adopted. After graduating from Yale, Beach worked in Washington as a solicitor for a company owned by his father that gave advice on patents. Going to New York City, he became assistant superintendent of construction for a tunnel under Broadway. In 1877 he joined the staff of the *Scientific American,* and in 1896 he became a director of the corporation—a post he held after he became editor of the *Encyclopedia Americana*.

Throughout his life Beach retained his interest in photography, conducting extensive experiments and writing widely on the subject. In 1884 he founded the New York Society of Amateur Photographers, now the Camera Club of New York, and in 1889 he helped found the magazine *American Amateur Photographer* (later *American Photography*). He died at Stratford, Conn., on June 18, 1918.

BEACH, bēch, **Moses Sperry** (1822–1892), American editor and inventor. He was born in Springfield, Mass., on Oct. 5, 1882, the son of Moses Yale Beach, who in 1838 became proprietor of the New York *Sun*. In 1845, after a brief connection with the Boston *Daily Times*, Beach joined his father on the *Sun*. He became sole owner of the newspaper in 1851. Under his management, the *Sun* catered to a popular readership, providing condensed news coverage, jokes, and fiction by best-selling authors.

Beach retired in 1868, selling the *Sun* to Charles A. Dana. Beach was one of the party of tourists, including Mark Twain, that toured Europe and Palestine aboard the *Quaker City* in 1867. Their experiences are recounted in Twain's book *Innocents Abroad.* Beach died in Peekskill, N.Y. on July 25, 1892.

A technician as well as an editor, Beach made several contributions to the mechanics of newspaper production, including a device for feeding paper to the presses from a roll. He was also the first newspaper publisher to print on both sides of the sheet at the same time.

BEACH, bēch, **Moses Yale** (1800–1868), American newspaper publisher, under whose management the New York *Sun* became the city's most popular newspaper. He was born in Wallingford, Conn., on Jan. 15, 1800. He spent his early career in Springfield, Mass., where he invented and promoted such devices as a gunpowder engine and a rag-cutting machine. In 1834 he moved to New York City to become production manager of the *Sun*, which was owned by his brother-in-law, Benjamin H. Day.

In 1838, Beach bought out Day's interest and became the paper's publisher. Under his leadership, the *Sun's* circulation rose from 30,000 to 50,000. In 1848, Beach began publishing the *American Sun*, a weekly edition of the paper for distribution abroad. Later that year he turned the *Sun* over to his sons, Moses Sperry Beach and Alfred Ely Beach. He died in Wallingford, Conn., on July 17, 1868.

BEACH, bēch, **Rex Ellingwood** (1877–1949), American novelist, who was best known for his adventure stories about Alaska. He was born in Atwood, Mich., on Sept. 1, 1877. In 1900 he left Kent College of Law to join the gold rush to Alaska, where he spent most of the next five years. In 1905 he sold his first story, *The Colonel and the Horse Thief*, to *McClure's Magazine*, a leading periodical of the day, to which he became a regular contributor. In 1906 he published the best-selling novel *The Spoilers*.

Beach's later works included *The Barrier* (1907), *The Silver Horde* (1909), *Heart of the Sunset* (1915), *The Crimson Gardenia* (1916),

Laughing Bill Hyde (1917), *The Winds of Chance* (1918), *Flowing Gold* (1922), *Son of the Gods* (1929), *Men of the Outer Islands* (1932), and *The World in His Arms* (1946).

Many of Beach's novels were made into films. His psychological novel *Woman in Ambush*, which was unfinished at the time of his death, had been sold to Hollywood for $100,000—the highest price ever offered up to that time for an unpublished manuscript. Beach died in Sebring, Fla., on Dec. 7, 1949.

BEACH, bēch, **Sylvia Woodbridge** (1887–1962), American publisher in France, who produced the first edition of James Joyce's *Ulysses*. She was born in Baltimore and was educated in Switzerland, Germany, and France. Between 1919 and 1941 she operated Shakespeare and Company in Paris, a combination bookshop and avant-garde publishing house. A friend of many writers, most notably James Joyce, she accepted his novel *Ulysses* in 1922, after it had been rejected by several publishers because of its alleged pornographic passages. The book later was hailed as a literary masterpiece and was published by major companies in the United States, England, Germany, and France. Copies of the original Shakespeare and Company edition became highly valued as collectors' items. Miss Beach's autobiography, *Shakespeare and Company*, was published in 1959. She died in Paris on Oct. 4, 1962.

BEACH, bēch, a deposit of sediment found along lake and ocean shorelines. The sediment movement forming the beach is induced by waves. A typical beach may extend landward from a water depth of about 30 feet (9 meters) to the limit of wave attack during storms. Because storm tide levels are often up to a few yards above normal high tide, storm waves may produce erosion and deposit sediment hundreds of yards landward.

A beach may be divided into a *backshore zone* extending landward of high-tide level, a general concave *foreshore zone* between low-tide and high-tide level, and an *offshore zone* lying seaward of low-tide level.

The gently landward-sloping backshore may have one or more terraces called *berms*. A berm is a sand ridge built to the limit of wave swash at high tide. As the beach grows seaward during late spring and summer, the previous winter's berm may be left stranded on the backshore. The gentle seaward slope and smooth bottom of many beaches allows wading for hundreds of yards from shore at low tide. The offshore zone may also contain submarine troughs and bars.

W.E. YASSO, *Teachers College*
Columbia University
C.G. TILLMAN, *Virginia Polytechnic Institute*

IDEALIZED CROSS-SECTION OF A TYPICAL SAND BEACH

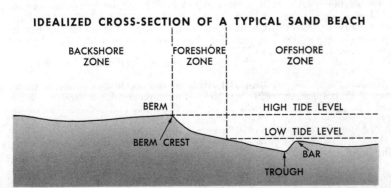

BACKSHORE ZONE   FORESHORE ZONE   OFFSHORE ZONE

BERM

BERM CREST

HIGH TIDE LEVEL

LOW TIDE LEVEL

BAR

TROUGH

BEACHES are deposits of sediment formed by waves along lake and ocean shorelines. A wide foreshore terrace is a feature of many sandy beaches.

BEACH FLEA, any of numerous 10-legged crustaceans that swarm on beaches around the world. In spite of its name, it is not a flea. The beach flea normally has 6 distinct thoracic segments that bear leglike appendages and make up most of the total body length. The abdominal segments are fused, and there is no hard dorsal plate covering the body. The first antennae of the beach flea is noticeably shorter than the second. The last three pairs of legs are short and stiff. The beach flea moves with leaping, flealike motions.

Beach fleas are scavengers. They are frequently found under stones and in decaying vegetation.

Beach fleas comprise many species in the genus *Orchestia*, family Orchestiidae. They are arthropods, but, unlike true fleas, they are not insects.

BEACH FLY. See AMPHIPODS.

BEACH PEA. See LATHYRUS.

BEACH PLANTS are plants that live on shores, particularly on seashores or nearby dunes and marshy strips. They usually are characterized by fleshiness, leatheriness, downiness, or dense hairiness. These features, which resemble those of plants living in other salty and arid localities, result from adaptation to desert conditions. These are necessary since beach sands are very hot, receive practically no water from either the sea or the land, and are unable to conserve rainwater.

Some common beach plants are the seaside goldenrod (*Solidago*), the salt marsh and smooth aster (*Aster*), certain huge tropical morning glories (*Ipomoea*), the marsh rosemary (*Limonium*), and the yellow sand verbena (*Abronia*). These plants are oily and juicy because they store water with little evaporation under the arid conditions of their habitat.

Many important characteristics of other beach plants also enable them to obtain and conserve moisture. One of these adaptations is a reduction of surface areas so that there is less area from which moisture evaporates. The marsh samphire (*Salicornia*) has a reduced surface area because of its cylindrical shape and scalelike leaves. The bases of the leaves of the saltwort (*Salsola*) also are cylindrical and are armed with stout prickles that discourage animals from feeding on them. Many fleshy beach plants contain salts that retain water. Others, like some tamarisks, give off salts. During the day, these salts form a crust over the openings (stomata) in the leaf surface, preventing evaporation; at night the salts attract the dew and moisture in the air.

The hairiness of some beach plants is another adaptation for conserving water. Plants with such leathery and hairy foliage are the bearberry (*Arctostaphylos*), the bayberry (*Myrica*), and the beach plum (*Prunus*). The pale, hairy undersurface of the beach plum's leaves is especially effective in keeping rising moisture from flooding the stomata. Other hairy beach plants are the marshmallow (*Althaea*), the clotbur (*Xanthium*), and many of the salt marsh plants.

Some beach plants are useful in preventing the shifting of sands and dunes. The most important of these are the coarse grasses—marram (*Ammophila*) and sea lyme (*Elymus*)—whose tough, long roots interweave through the sand to form a mat that holds the sand in place.

JOHN J. SMITH

Dusty miller (*Artemisia stelleriana*) is found on beaches.

BEACHWOOD is a residential city in northeastern Ohio, in Cuyahoga County, 14 miles (22 km) east of Cleveland. It has a 200-acre Commerce Park for business and light industry. Places of interest include a historic cemetery containing graves of Revolutionary and Civil War veterans. The first settlement was made by colonists from the Isle of Man. Beachwood was incorporated as a village in 1915 and received a city charter in 1927. Government is by mayor and council. Population: 9,631.

LEWIS C. NAYLOR, *Cuyahoga County Library*

BEACHY HEAD is a promontory, in England, on the coast of Sussex, about three miles (5 km) southwest of Eastbourne. It is 532 feet (162 meters) high. Situated at the eastern end of the English Channel, its lighthouse marks an important landfall for mariners entering or leaving the Strait of Dover. Off Beachy Head, on June 30, 1690, an Anglo-Dutch fleet of 56 warships, under Lord Torrington, was defeated by a French fleet of 68 warships, under Comte de Tourville. Beachy Head is a popular resort for tourists visiting Sussex Downs.

BEACON is a city in southern New York, in Dutchess County. It is on the east bank of the Hudson River, opposite the city of Newburgh, about 60 miles (96 km) north of New York City. The Newburgh-Beacon Bridge spans the river. Directly behind the city rises Mount Beacon, 1,540 feet (469 meters) high. An inclined railway ascends to the summit. Dutchess County airport is 10 miles (17 km) northeast of Beacon. The city's industries include the manufacture of women's apparel, bleaching and dyeing, and metal anodizing.

Beacon was named for the beacon fires lighted in the area as signals by patriots during the Revolutionary War. The Mme. Brett Homestead (1709) is one of the oldest houses in Dutchess County. Beacon, incorporated in 1913, has a commission form of government. Population: 13,255.

HELEN E. MONSON, *Newburgh Free Library*

BEACON HILL, in Boston, Mass., is one of three hills on the original peninsula of Boston. It is north of Boston Common and received its name from the fact that the public beacon was fixed on its summit in early Colonial times. The streets on the sides of the hill are lined with handsome, old, red-brick houses.

BEACONSFIELD, bē′kənz-fēld, **1st Earl of** (1804–1881), British statesman and writer, better known as *Benjamin Disraeli*. Disraeli, who was prime minister of Britain in 1868 and 1874–1880, was the architect of the modern Conservative party and one of the most brilliant parliamentarians in the history of the House of Commons.

Disraeli was born in London on Dec. 12, 1804. His grandfather, Benjamin D'Israeli, emigrated to London in 1748 from a colony of Spanish Jews living near Venice; he prospered as a trader and stockbroker and married Sarah Shiprut, who was related to the prominent Portuguese Jewish family of Villareal. Their only son, Isaac D'Israeli, became a respected man of letters in London. He married Maria Basevi, a descendant of Italian Jews. They had a daughter and subsequently four sons, the eldest of whom was Benjamin. In 1817, Isaac D'Israeli abandoned Judaism and in the same year his daughter and three surviving sons were baptized in the Anglican Church. Benjamin was educated at private schools at Blackheath and Epping Forest. He did not attend a university.

Early Career. When he was 17, Disraeli was apprenticed to a firm of London solicitors to study law. Although his name was entered on the roll at Lincoln's Inn three years later, he never practiced law. From 1824 to 1826 he engaged in stock market and publishing ventures that proved disastrous and left him with debts he was unable or unwilling to pay.

Embittered but still full of confidence, he announced his intention to become a writer. Isaac D'Israeli's position gave Benjamin an easy entrance to literary society, and the young man's style in dress and manner assured him attention there. Benjamin played the dandy. He was variously regarded as brilliant, clever, impudent, and vulgar.

His first novel, *Vivian Grey*, appeared anonymously in two volumes in 1826 and 1827. Its crude but lively satire of the activities of well-known contemporaries attracted considerable attention. Its author's identity was soon disclosed, and the harsh ripostes directed at him contributed to the anxieties that brought on a nervous collapse in 1828. Disraeli retired to his father's house in Buckinghamshire and avoided the spotlight entirely for the next three years. During that time he published an inferior novel, *The Young Duke* (1830). Following a 16-month trip to the Mediterranean in 1830–1831, he returned to Buckinghamshire and shortly announced his candidacy for Parliament as a Conservative from High Wycombe.

Entry into Politics. Between 1832 and 1835, Disraeli offered himself as a candidate three times at High Wycombe and once at Taunton and lost all four elections. He bided his time but did a prodigious amount of writing, including numerous bombastic political pamphlets and the novels *Contarini Fleming* (1832) and *Alroy* (1833). Thereafter he published *Vindication of the English Constitution* (1835), an analysis of English history in which he first expressed his theory of popular Toryism as an alliance of the crown, the church, and the people against the Whig oligarchy. He wrote several other political works, mostly pamphlets, and two more novels: *Henrietta Temple* (1836), a love story based on his own liaison with Henrietta, the wife of Sir Francis Sykes; and *Venetia* (1837).

Election to Parliament. In 1837, King William

CULVER PICTURES, INC.

BENJAMIN DISRAELI, 1st Earl of Beaconsfield, from a photograph taken during his second administration.

IV died. The accession of Victoria and the consequent formation of a new Parliament afforded Disraeli his long-awaited opportunity. The borough of Maidstone returned two members to Parliament, one of whom, Wyndham Lewis, held an assured seat. Through the influence of important friends, Disraeli was invited to enter the bitter contest for the other seat. During the ensuing campaign his character was attacked on fair and specious grounds. His unpaid debts, his racial origins, his open liaison with Mrs. Sykes, and his fierce, often wounding speeches in the past were used against him. But he pressed his campaign and won the seat.

His maiden speech in the House of Commons on Dec. 7, 1837, was a disaster. The speech itself was overwrought, and the speaker was, in the opinion of most members, overdressed. The combination of his ringlets and ruffles and the extravagance of his oratorical style produced shouts of derision from opponents and, before the speech was finished, general laughter in the house. Shouting to be heard, Disraeli concluded the debacle with the defiant prophecy: "I will sit down now, but the time will come when you will hear me." Chastened by the experience, he gradually moderated his style.

Within a year, Wyndham Lewis, his conservative colleague from Maidstone, died, and on Aug. 28, 1839, Disraeli married Lewis' widow. She brought him wealth, which he was never able to acquire in his own right, and the semblance of a social position. Although the marriage was contracted largely for practical reasons —his wife was 12 years his senior—they became an extremely devoted couple. Years later she declared: "Dizzy married me for my money, but if he had the chance again he would marry me for love."

QUEEN VICTORIA, in *Punch* cartoon, raises Disraeli to peerage after he added "Empress of India" to her title.

Rebellious Tory. After his marriage Disraeli resolved to establish a firmer political position for himself. His idealized vision of a common cause between the Tory monarchy and the workingman led him into sympathy with Chartism, the first great political movement of the British working class. His skeptical view of the Reform Law of 1832 placed principal blame for the miseries of labor on the Whigs, but the pragmatism of the Tories led by Sir Robert Peel also clashed with his own ideas. When Peel rather curtly declined Disraeli's irregular request to be included in the Tory ministry formed in 1841, Disraeli resolved to loosen his ties with the party leadership and veered toward more outspoken support of workmen's grievances.

Disraeli's sympathy with the industrial poor was undoubtedly sincere. In an effort to present his view of what he saw as a conspiracy against them, he wrote two of his most persuasive novels: *Coningsby* (1844) and *Sybil, or the Two Nations* (1845). *Coningsby* is a portrayal of the Young England movement that arose within Tory ranks in the 1840's and looked to Disraeli for leadership. The novel's effect was sensational. Its idealized view of conservatism's role in regenerating England gave Disraeli the instrument he needed to split the Tory party and eventually erect a new Conservative party.

The opportunity presented itself in 1845, when Peel, in response to a new famine in Ireland, came out in support of repealing the corn laws—protective tariffs on foreign grain that favored landowners and burdened poor consumers. In doing so, Peel reversed a long-standing policy of the party. Disraeli and other protectionists rebelled. The repeal bill passed, with the support of the Whigs, but the rebels brought down the government in June 1846.

Party Leader. The split and partial disintegration of the old Tory party inaugurated a long period of political confusion in which neither of the traditional parties had a clear majority. During the Whig administration (1846–1852) of Lord Russell, Disraeli advanced to the leadership of the Conservatives in Commons, but with the Peelites in active opposition to the party majority the prospect of a Conservative government seemed distant. Disraeli realized that the party's stand on protectionism was unpopular, but his recent attacks on Peel prevented him from reversing his position.

After Russell's government fell in 1852, Disraeli became chancellor of the exchequer in the minority government of the earl of Derby. Later in the year Derby's government fell, and the Conservatives returned to the opposition for six more years, during most of which a coalition of small parties ruled. In 1858 a setback for the emerging Liberal party permitted the Conservatives, still led by Derby, to form another short-lived government. Disraeli seized the opportunity the following year to introduce a moderate bill dealing with long-overdue electoral reform. The measure was defeated, and the Conservatives returned to the opposition for seven more years.

Already approaching 60 and his party's leader in Commons for more than a decade, Disraeli saw his chances slipping away. He was doubly cheated by the long survival of Derby. In 1866, when the Conservatives installed a third minority government, an aged and ailing Derby again became prime minister, and Disraeli was again his chancellor of the exchequer.

First Prime Ministry. Disraeli was determined that credit for electoral reform should go to the Conservatives. He introduced a bill in the House of Commons that became law in 1867, but the Liberals, whose majority in the House had attached important amendments to the bill, got most of the credit. In February 1868, Derby retired and Disraeli became prime minister. John Bright, a prominent Liberal, described the event as "a great triumph of intellect and courage and patience and unscrupulousness employed in the service of a party full of prejudices and selfishness and wanting in brains."

Disraeli remained prime minister only until November, for the first general elections based on the new reform law returned the Liberals to power. Their commanding new leader was William Ewart Gladstone, whose personal vendetta with Disraeli helped finally to polarize two modern parties in Britain. Before Disraeli left office, Queen Victoria, whose fondness for him became legend, offered him a peerage. At his request, the title was conferred on his wife so that he might remain in Commons.

Opposition. During the first few years of Gladstone's administration Disraeli luxuriated in the comparative ease of opposition. For the first time in more than 20 years he wrote a novel, *Lothair* (1870), a gaudy romance that did nothing to enhance his prestige. Restive party members questioned his leadership. Nothing seemed to erode the popularity of the Liberals.

But after 1870, Disraeli concentrated on party organization, and the fortunes of the Conservatives began gradually to rise. Liberal defeats in by-elections signaled discontent with Gladstone's concessions to Irish nationalism and with his accommodation to emerging Prussian and Russian power in Europe. Disraeli sensed the feeling of the country and shrewdly appealed to its damaged pride. On March 11, 1873, the Conservatives narrowly defeated a Liberal bill to create an Irish university for Catholics. Gladstone resigned and suggested that Disraeli form a minority government. Disraeli shrewdly refused, and Gladstone, whose popularity was rapidly declining, was forced to return. His mandate was exhausted. In January 1874 he dissolved Parliament, and in February the Conservatives won a majority of 83 seats—their first majority in a general election since 1841.

Second Prime Ministry. Disraeli, for the first time, formed a new government. He was nearly 70 and had led his party in Commons longer than any man in the history of the House. Tragically he had had to wait too long. Age and intermittent illness, and loneliness after his wife's death in 1872, denied him the vigor that he could have brought to the office earlier.

Disraeli formed a distinguished and able cabinet and set about redeeming his campaign promises to act on social welfare problems. In addition to landmark legislation on urban renewal and workers' housing, his administration enacted a trade union act more favorable to the unions than earlier acts, a drug act, and the comprehensive Public Health Act of 1875, which codified numerous existing laws on health and sanitation. These and other laws filled important gaps in welfare legislation left by the Liberals.

In foreign affairs, which dominated the later years of his administration, Disraeli devoted his efforts to bolstering Britain's declining prestige overseas. In 1875, acting entirely on his own initiative and against the advice of his foreign minister, he arranged government purchase of a substantial interest in the Suez Canal Company from the khedive of Egypt. Although not a controlling interest, it enhanced Britain's imperial power, secured the nation lower canal rates, and led to eventual British control of the waterway. Disraeli's secret canal transaction was both a diplomatic and political coup.

In 1877, the year after Disraeli obtained from Parliament the addition of "Empress of India" to Queen Victoria's titles, she created him earl of Beaconsfield. In 1878, Beaconsfield successfully checked Russian imperialism in Turkey and the Balkans. Using the threat of intervention and exercising masterly control of the European delegates called at his urging to the Congress of Berlin in 1878, he engineered a revision, extremely favorable to Britain, of the treaty ending the Russo-Turkish War.

Disraeli's prestige was never higher, but he was rapidly failing in health. Against his wishes, he remained in office, but renewed problems at home and abroad brought defeat to his party in the general election of April 1880. He retired from politics to finish *Endymion*, his last novel. He died at his London house on April 19, 1881.

·Bibliography

The complete fiction of Disraeli is collected in *Novels and Tales by the Earl of Beaconsfield*, 11 vols. (London 1881); several of the novels are available individually in later editions. A comprehensive selection of his correspondence is contained in *Lord Beaconsfield's Letters, 1830–1852*, ed. by R. Disraeli, 2d ed. (London 1928).

Graubard, Stephen R., *Burke, Disraeli, and Churchill: The Politics of Perseverence* (Cambridge, Mass., 1961).

Jerman, B.R., *The Young Disraeli* (Princeton, N.J., 1960).

Maurois, André, *Disraeli* (New York 1942).

Monypenny, William F., and Buckle, G.E., *The Life of Benjamin Disraeli*, rev. ed., 2 vols. (New York 1929).

BEACONSFIELD, bē′kɔnz-fēld, is a residential city in southern Quebec province, Canada, on Montreal Island, 15 miles (24 km) southwest of Montreal. It is situated on the shore of Lake St. Louis, an expansion of the St. Lawrence River, west of Pointe-Claire. The surrounding area formerly had apple orchards and vegetable farms, but the expansion of Montreal since the early 1900's has made the town a residential suburb. Beaconsfield was originally a part of Pointe-Claire, which was founded in 1713. It is named for the 1st earl of Beaconsfield (Benjamin Disraeli). Beaconsfield was incorporated in 1910. Population: 19,389.

BEADLE, bē′dəl, **George Wells** (1903–   ), American biologist, who pioneered in the field of chemical genetics and, with Edward L. Tatum and Joshua Lederberg, won the 1958 Nobel Prize for medicine and physiology. Beadle and Tatum were cited for "their discovery that genes act by regulating specific chemical processes."

Contributions to Science. Beadle began his genetic studies with his Ph.D. research, involving the study of chromosome behavior and cell division. He continued these studies afterward, but with an organism that was better known genetically—the fruit fly, *Drosophila melanogaster*.

Having mastered the genetic intricacies of chromosome behavior in *Drosophila*, he collaborated with Boris Ephrussi in developing an organ transplantation technique in the fruit fly. From this work they discovered that certain genes in *Drosophila* chromosomes were responsible for different biochemical steps in the synthesis of the eye color pigments in the fly; at least two of the steps were arranged in sequential fashion.

It was Beadle's work with E.L. Tatum, however, that led to the award of the Nobel Prize. Realizing the limitations of *Drosophila* as a biochemical organism, Beadle turned to the bread mold, *Neurospora*. Experiments with X-ray and ultraviolet mutations of particular genes enabled Beadle and Tatum to develop the following fundamental concepts in genetics. They found that all biochemical reactions in all organisms are controlled in a stepwise fashion by genes, with each gene controlling a particular step in the reaction. These reactions are catalyzed by enzymes (organic catalysts), and each gene is responsible for the synthesis of a given enzyme. Alteration in a gene, known as a mutation, will result in alteration of the enzyme, and this in turn results in a blocking of the biochemical reaction or synthesis catalyzed by the enzyme.

Life. Beadle was born on a farm near Wahoo, Nebr., on Oct. 22, 1903. He received his B.S. and M.S. degrees from the University of Nebraska and his Ph.D. from Cornell in 1931. For the next five years he was in the biology department at the California Institute of Technology as a National Research Council fellow and an instructor. In 1937, Beadle moved to Stanford University, where he began his successful collaboration with E.L. Tatum. He was professor of biology and chairman of the biological division at Cal Tech from 1947 through 1961. In 1961 he became chancellor of the University of Chicago.

Beadle received many awards, including the Albert Einstein Commemorative Award in 1958. He served as president of the Genetics Society of America and of the American Association for the Advancement of Science.

WILLIAM M. HEXTER, *Amherst College*

CEREMONIAL BEADS strung in many colors decorate a Masai girl of southern Kenya.

RAPHO GUILLUMETTE

BEADS, bēdz, are small objects of varying shape that are pierced and strung together as necklaces, bracelets, belts, headbands, and the like. From prehistoric times, beads have also been attached to clothing or to various parts of the face such as the ears and nose.

Beads are made of many materials, most commonly glass, metal, stone, coral, amber, gems, shell, and wood. Magical properties have been ascribed to many of these materials through the ages, and archaeologists believe that early kinds of beads were worn as amulets or talismans for religious or ceremonial reasons, with ornamentation as only a secondary purpose. Beads also came to be used in trade; hence beads found in archaeological sites are important indicators of ancient trade routes.

The English word "bead" is derived from Middle English *bede*, meaning "prayer." The name was first transferred to strung objects used in prayer, such as rosaries (prayer beads), and then to other kinds of strung objects.

Early Makers of Beads. No date for the first manufacture of beads can be given with certainty, but shell bead necklaces from the Old Stone Age have been found. Greater quantities and more varieties of beads have been found dating from around 4000 B.C., or toward the latter part of the New Stone Age. Beads made of translucent calcite in a segmented, or ribbed, shape have been found at Tell Arpachiyah in Mesopotamia and attributed to the early Halaf period of about 4000 B.C. Other early examples come from predynastic Egyptian sites. These beads were made of stone and of blue faience, a glazed earthenware formed of a sand core of quartz grains cemented together and glazed over with copper salts or manganese. This sand-core technique was later adapted for pottery making. Segmented beads of faience have been discovered in Egyptian graves of about 2800–2600 B.C.

Beads similar to the Egyptian type were unearthed from Bronze Age sites in Britain; they may have been carried to Britain by traders from Crete and Mycenae. A Bronze Age necklace of tin, faience, and amber beads found in Holland is considered evidence that a trade route from the Baltic to England, with amber going in one direction and tin in the other, passed through Holland. Ostrich-eggshell beads from Africa have been unearthed in Nineveh, Greece, and Rome.

Varieties of Beads. Glass is known to have been used for beaded collars and breastplates from the end of the Old Kingdom period in Egypt, and glass beads were common during part of the 18th dynasty. Glass beads found at Tell el Amarna, Egypt, dated about 1370 B.C. (18th dynasty), correspond to tubular, segmented beads found at Knossos, dated about 1600 B.C., and to beads found in European Bronze Age sites.

A popular type of glass bead was the "eye" bead, made of opaque glass with circles or rods of different-colored glass (the "eyes") pressed into the surface. Notable in Etruscan times were glass "button" beads, made of halves of different-colored buttons cemented together. The bore and the thread passed through the cement, and only rarely through the glass. Glass beads were very widely used and, in certain eras, are the only evidence of the use of glass in ancient times. In Italy the manufacture of glass beads on the island of Murano, near Venice, began in the 13th century and became a profitable industry.

In some African tribes, beads were long used in social customs, especially courtship. Love letters in beadwork were common, the pattern and color indicating the meaning. American Indian tribes recorded legends in beadwork, using codes and patterns that were handed down through generations. The American Indians also used strands or belts of beads, called wampum, for barter or as money. The practice was adopted by European traders and colonists, who spread various types of wampum over the continent.

In the modern world, beads are used mainly for decoration. The decorative bead industry reached a peak during the Victorian era. Heavily beaded fashions went out of style in the early 20th century but had a new vogue in fashions in the 1920's and again in the 1960's. Beadwork and bead collection continue as hobbies.

BEAGLE, bē'gəl, a hunting dog, the smallest of the trailing hounds. Compact and shortlegged, the beagle is usually 13 to 16 inches (33 to 40 cm) in height. It has a slightly domed head and a strong, clean neck. Its long ears are set close to the head, and its large hazel or brown eyes are wide apart. Beagles have sloping shoulders, a broad chest, straight front legs, and hard feet. They have a keener scenting ability than

Beagle

EVELYN M. SHAFER

foxhounds, a species they resemble. These characteristics help make beagles excellent and persistent trailers.

The beagle's coat is hard and close. The coloration may be solid or spotted; black, white, and tan are the most common colors. There are both rough- and smooth-haired varieties; the common American beagle is smooth-haired. Beagles are intelligent, companionable, and cheerful. They have melodious voices and are sometimes called "buglers."

First used in England for hunting hares, beagles are now popular sporting hounds both in the United States and in England. Their origin is uncertain, but they were known in Great Britain as early as the 16th century. At one time a diminutive breed—no larger than a well-grown kitten—was popular. See also DOG.

BEAGLE, The, bē′gəl, a 10-gun brig of the British Navy which sailed from Devonport, England, on Dec. 27, 1831, to circumnavigate the world, and arrived home on Oct. 2, 1836. The ship was on a surveying expedition and had for its naturalist Charles Darwin who, in his autobiography, said: "The voyage of the Beagle has been by far the most important event in my life."

BEAL, bēl, **Gifford Reynolds** (1879–1956), American artist, who was known for his marine and figure paintings. He was born on Jan. 24, 1879, in New York City, where he studied art under William M. Chase, Frank DuMond, and Henry Ranger. He became a member of the National Academy of Design in 1914 and served as president of the Art Students' League of New York from 1914 to 1929. He died on Feb. 5, 1956 in New York City.

Beal's paintings, including *Mayfair* (1913), *Equestrian* (1933), *Portrait of Paul Manship* (1946), and *Mending the Nets off Straitsmouth* (1951), are in the Art Institute of Chicago, the Metropolitan Museum of Art in New York City, and other American museums. He also painted a mural for the Department of Interior building in Washington, D.C.

BEAL-MALTBIE SHELL MUSEUM, bēl môlt′bē, a museum at Rollins College, Winter Park, Fla., devoted exclusively to shells. Its collection of more than 70,000 specimens from all the oceans and continents of the world was assembled over a period of 50 years by James Hartley Beal. In 1940, when the collection was given to Rollins, B.L. Maltbie erected a building to house it on the campus.

The collection includes shells of both aquatic and nonaquatic animals. It contains a unique shell of a 700-pound clam and numerous specimens only slightly larger than grains of sand.

BEALE, bēl, **Dorothea** (1831–1906), English pioneer in higher education for women. She was born in London on March 21, 1831, and studied at the newly opened Queen's College for Ladies, where she later became head teacher. In 1858 she was appointed principal of the first English proprietary girls' school, Ladies' College, Cheltenham, which had been founded in 1854. She devoted her life to building up the school. When she became principal, the enrollment was 69; by 1912 it had risen to 1,000.

Miss Beale also promoted higher education for women. She helped to found two teacher training colleges for women—St. Hilda's College, Cheltenham (1885), and St. Hilda's, Oxford (1906). She died at Cheltenham on Nov. 9, 1906.

BEALE, bēl, **Edward Fitzgerald** (1822–1893), American frontier courier and government surveyor. He was born in Washington, D.C., on Feb. 4, 1822. He graduated from the U.S. Naval Academy in 1842, but served only a few months at sea. Attached to the army in the Mexican War, he distinguished himself for daring as a courier behind enemy lines.

After the war, Beale resigned from the Navy and remained in the Far West as a government courier. He is credited with having brought to the east the first authentic news of the discovery of gold in California (1848). Until the end of the Civil War he surveyed California and Nevada for the U.S. Government and laid out overland trails. After the war he retired to a large ranch that he acquired near Bakersfield, Calif. He was U.S. minister to Austria in 1876. He died in Washington, D.C., on April 22, 1893.

BEAME, Abraham David (1906–   ), American public official. He was born in London, England, on March 20, 1906, the son of Polish-Jewish parents. Beame was taken to the United States and grew up in New York City. He worked hard from an early age, and in 1928 graduated with honors in accounting from City College. Settling in Brooklyn, he worked as an accountant and taught accounting for two decades.

Beame became active in Democratic politics and served as assistant director of the city's bureau of the budget and as budget director. In 1961 he was elected city controller. In 1965 he won the Democratic nomination for mayor but lost to John Lindsay, then a Republican. He recaptured the controllership in the 1969 election, and in 1973 won the mayor's office, running as an experienced administrator and money manager. These qualities were quickly tested as the city in 1975 slipped perilously close to default on its loans. The national recession, high interest rates, a shrinking tax base, and generous settlements with civil service unions were adverse factors. New York state created two agencies to help put the city's finances in order, and Beame's powers were diminished. The federal government helped with a guarantee of city loans.

BEAN, bēn, **Roy** (c. 1825–1903), American frontier justice of the peace. He was born in Mason County, Ky. After work as a teamster, trader, and saloonkeeper in the Southwest, he settled in San Antonio, Texas. Early in 1882 he moved to the desolate lower Pecos River and set up a saloon to serve workmen building the Southern Pacific Railroad. Soon he was appointed justice of the peace, a post to which he later was elected. His crude saloon in Vinegaroon (later renamed Langtry), Texas, became his courtroom, and the bearded Bean became known as the "law west of the Pecos." He was noted for his humor and his informal but often shrewd decisions. In 1898 he staged on a Rio Grande sandbar the Fitzsimmons-Maher heavyweight championship fight that Texas had banned. He died in Langtry on March 16, 1903.

WAYNE GARD, *Author of "Frontier Justice"*

Further Reading: Sonnichsen, C.L., *Roy Bean* (New York 1943).

COMMERCIAL BEAN SPECIES include the lima bean (*at left*) and the kidney bean (*at right*).

GRANT HEILMAN PHOTOS

BEAN is the common name for several leguminous plants and their seeds. Originally the name was applied to the seed of the broad bean (*Vicia faba*), or the plant that bears it. However, the word now is used in a much wider sense, without specific scientific delimitations.

Kidney Bean. The best known bean plant of the New World is the common or kidney bean (*Phaseolus vulgaris*). An annual, it is either erect and bushy or twining, with leaves usually composed of three pointed leaflets with smooth borders. The flowers, which are about half an inch (1.27 cm) long, are white, yellowish, or purplish. The petals are developed into a standard (an upper, broad, erect petal), two wings, and a keel. Nine of the stamens are fused and one is free. The ovary develops into the pod, which may be six inches (15.24 cm) or more in length. The pod contains the seeds, which are white, brown, reddish, bluish to black, or variegated. Each seed consists of a coat, or integument. A scar or hilum, by which the seed was attached to the pod, and a minute opening, or micropyle, are on the coat. Inside the coat are two large cotyledons in which food is stored; a hypocotyl, or root; and a plumule, or bud.

According to American horticulturist Liberty H. Bailey there are some 200 types and 400 to 500 named commercial varieties of the common bean, *P. vulgaris;* other estimates are as high as 1,000 varieties. Almost all field beans, which are grown commercially for their seeds, are of the "bush" form; these include the navy or pea bean and the various kinds of kidney beans. Garden beans, of which the unripe pods with their developing seeds are gathered for human consumption, are of both "bush" and "pole" forms. String and stringless beans, wax beans, and the "butter" beans of the northern states are in this group. Michigan, California, Idaho, New York, Colorado, and New Mexico are important in the production of field beans. Garden beans are grown widely east of the Mississippi, especially in Michigan, the seaboard states, and California. More than half of the white pea beans grown in the United States come from Michigan.

Field beans do not make heavy demands upon the soil; for garden beans, especially those of the "pole" type, richer soil is necessary. As in other legumes, the roots contain bacteria that fix atmospheric nitrogen, which ultimately is converted into nitrates. After the danger of frost is past, the seeds are planted in warm soil. Harvesting the garden beans at regular intervals favors their continued bearing. In addition to their use as human food, the poorer qualities of beans are fed to livestock and the plants are used for forage. They rank high as a cheap source of protein and calories.

Other Types. The lima bean (*Phaseolus limensis*) and the sieva bean and dwarf lima (*P. lunatus*) are native to tropical America. The lima bean, sometimes called the "aristocrat of the bean family," is a perennial, but it is cultivated as an annual. It requires high temperature and humidity and fertile soil, and is grown in California and the Eastern and Gulf states. It has broad flat pods and seeds and a sweet flavor due to its cane sugar content. The lima beans of the southern United States are called "butter" beans. They take a relatively long time to mature and are subject to many of the same diseases as the common bean, such as anthracnose, rust, and common blight.

The broad bean (*Vicia faba*), the original bean of the Old World, also is called the horse, Scotch, or Windsor bean. It probably is native to Africa and southwestern Asia, but it is grown extensively in England and continental Europe. It has large white flowers marked with purplish blue. The broad bean is used as human food and for forage. In North America it is raised to some extent in Canada, Washington, Oregon, and California. Since it does not do well in high summer temperatures it is not known generally in most parts of the United States.

The scarlet runner (*Phaseolus coccineus*), American in origin, is a perennial that is treated as an annual. In the United States it is grown as an ornamental plant for its bright red flowers, but in England, continental Europe, and Mexico some varieties are used for food. Tepary beans (*P. acutifolius* var. *latifolius*), native to the southwestern United States and cultivated in arid regions, have small, varicolored seeds that serve as food. The mung, golden, or green gram (*P. aureus*) of Asia is consumed widely there; related to this variety is the urd or black gram (*P. mungo*). The adzuki bean (*P. angularis*) of Asia is important in China and Japan, while the soybean (*Glycine max*) is of tremendous significance there and in the United States. Other genera include the velvet bean (*Stizolobium*) of the Orient, grown in the New World as a forage crop and as an ornamental; the jack bean (*Canavalia ensiformis*) of the West Indies, used as animal food and for human consumption; the hyacinth bean or lablab (*Dolichos lablab*), widely raised for food, and also in some varieties as an ornamental; and the asparagus bean (*Vigna sesquipedalis*), cultivated to some extent for food and forage, but also for the novelty of its narrow pods, which are a foot (30.5 cm) or more long. Other plants, sometimes called beans and related to the above, are the vigorous kudzu vine (*Pueraria Thunbergiana*); the ancient and orientally important cowpea (*Vigna sinensis*); and the sweet pod of the carob (*Ceratonia siliqua*).

In the moist woodlands of eastern North America there are 3 genera and half a dozen species of native wild beans—*Apios*, with 5 to 7 leaflets, and *Strophostyles* and *Phaseolus polystachios* with 3-foliate leaves.

Other plants and plant parts are sometimes called "beans," although they are not related to the above genera. These include the castor bean, in the spurge family; the coffee bean, which is the seed of the coffee tree; the sacred bean, seed of the East Indian lotus (*Nelumbo nucifera*); the Indian bean, a name applied to the catalpa (*Catalpa bignonioides*) and to its elongated capsule. Also included is the Mexican jumping bean, the seeds of several plants in the spurge family, especially *Sebastiania* and *Sapium*, which are inhabited by the larva of a moth, whose gyrations cause the seed to "jump."

Diseases and Pests of Beans. Beans are hosts to a multitude of diseases and pests. Anthracnose, caused by *Colletotrichum lindemuthianum*, one of the sac fungi, has done extensive damage not only throughout most of North America—reaching even into Alaska—but in South America, Europe, India, and Japan as well; it attained epidemic proportions in Italy in 1891 and in Germany in 1915 and 1916. This disease produces dark brown cankers on the seeds, leaves, stems, and pods. Control measures include the planting of "clean"—disease-free—seeds, which can be produced in Colorado and in certain other Rocky Mountain and Far Western states, the development of resistant strains, and crop rotation.

Bean rust, caused by the fungus *Uromyces phaseoli typica* and first described in Germany in 1795, has since been reported from every continent. Rust-colored pustules, especially on the leaves and pods, result from the production of the spores, which are largely wind disseminated. Remedies include the application of sulfur dust or sprays at frequent intervals, starting when the plants are small and continuing until the flowers begin to appear. The use of strains of beans resistant to the rust is also effective, but is complicated by the presence of numerous physiological races of the fungus, to which the host plants are resistant in varying degrees.

Common blight is a bacterial infection caused by *Xanthomonas phaseoli*. It is especially abundant in the eastern part of the United States, and it is present also in Europe, Asia, Australia, and Africa. Moist spots are produced on the leaves and pods, and these develop reddish brown margins. The bacteria are transmitted by the seeds, by insects, and by wind-blown rain. Control consists in planting disease-free seeds, which are produced in some parts of western United States, in practicing crop rotation, and in using resistant varieties of beans.

Beans are subject to various virus diseases, such as the bean mosaic. The leaves become mottled and malformed, often yellowish, and the pods may be poorly developed. The virus is transmitted by insects, infected seeds, and perhaps by pollen. Resistant varieties are available.

Destructive insect pests include the Mexican bean beetle, which devours the under portions of the leaves, removing the soft parts so that vein skeletons remain; it is controlled by dusts and sprays. Stored beans also are attacked by the bean weevil, which eats holes in the seeds; this pest can be checked by fumigation or by low-temperature treatment.

Classification. Most of the bean plants are classified in the pea or pulse family, the Leguminosae. Some botanists designate part of this family as the bean family, Fabaceae. Also, there are some "bean" plants and their seeds, like the castor bean, that are not in the family and have only a superficial resemblance to it.

EDWIN B. MATZKE, *Columbia University*

Bibliography
Allard, H.A., and Zaumeyer, W.J., *Responses of Beans (Phaseolus) and Other Legumes to Length of Day,* U.S. Department of Agriculture Technical Bulletin 867 (1944).
Harter, L.L., and Zaumeyer, W.J., *A Monographic Study of Bean Diseases and Methods for Their Control,* U.S. Department of Agriculture Technical Bulletin 863 (Washington 1944).
Norman, Arthur G., ed., *Soybean* (New York 1963).
Thompson, Homer C., and Kelly, William, *Vegetable Crops* (New York 1957).
Walker, John C., *Diseases of Vegetable Crops* (New York 1952).

BEAN GOOSE, a Eurasian wild goose. Classified as *Anser arvensis*, it is distinguished from the greylag goose (*A. anser*), ancestor of the domestic goose, by its comparatively small bill, which is orange-yellow and black, whereas that of the greylag is bright orange with no black and with whitish nail. The bean goose is the brownest of the gray geese. At least one subspecies has a pink and black bill and pink feet.

The bean goose breeds chiefly within the Arctic Circle. It migrates to Great Britain, Mediterranean countries, and eastern Japan. It generally feeds at marshes and lakes and prefers to roost inland. The bean goose receives its name because of its fondness for field beans.

BEAN WEEVIL, bēn wē'vəl, a type of beetle that deposits its eggs in the pods of beans. It is found in all parts of the world. Like all beetles, it has an anterior pair of wings that are hardened to protect the posterior functional wings. The bean weevil is a short, stout insect, usually not more than 0.2 inch (5 mm) long. Its body is narrowed in the head region, and the head curves downward to form a snout. The mouthparts of the bean weevil are well developed. The antennae have slightly toothed terminal enlargements. The color is commonly a tawny gray with several inconspicuous lighter spots and about eight blackish spots on each wing cover.

The bean weevil, unlike many of its relatives, may produce more than one generation per year. The female lays her eggs on the pods of beans in the field or on the pods of dried beans. The larvae bore into the seeds, where pupation takes place. The adult emerges through a little hole in the skin of the bean. The life cycle may take from 3 weeks to 3 months, depending on temperature and other environmental conditions.

The bean weevil causes serious damage to stored beans. Infested beans should not be used for seed, but they may be heated to kill the larvae and then used in animal food. The bean weevil belongs to the genus *Acanthoscelides*, family Lariidae.

POLAR BEARS live in the vicinity of the North Pole. They lead a nomadic life, frequently on ice floes in the ocean.

BEAR, a family of large, heavy, meat-eating mammals. Bears are found throughout all of the Northern Hemisphere and in some parts of the tropics, but not in Africa or Australasia.

In their structure and dentition, bears are related most closely to the dog family. They have a large body and head with short, but strong, limbs and short tails. The jaws are extended and powerful, while the teeth are large and well adapted for crushing food. The eyes and ears are small, and their eyesight and hearing are not as good as their sense of smell. The limbs have long and powerful claws that are used for tearing and digging, as well as for fighting and killing animals for food. The whole sole of the bear's foot rests upon the ground, and the bear leaves a footprint resembling that of a man. The bear's coat of fur is long and shaggy and usually is a shade of brown, black, or white.

Bears are rather slow and clumsy when they move; yet almost all bears, except the heaviest, climb trees, and all are agile in climbing over rocks and ice. When enraged or frightened, they can cover ground at great speed. Most bears are wanderers and, in tropical and temperate regions are active in the evening and at night.

Bears are omnivorous and feed on plants, insects, fish, and some larger animals. Some may raid herds of swine and cattle and flocks of sheep. Some bears, such as the Alaskan brown bear, or Kodiak, live almost entirely on fish. Bears also eat ants, honey-making bees, and wasps. They dig up anthills and overturn rotting logs and stumps to find ants, and they search out bee honeycombs and tear them to pieces for the honey. They also eat succulent leaves and herbs, roots, fruit, and sweet acorns and berries.

Bears generally live alone except during the mating and breeding season. They live in caves, crevices among the rocks, hollow logs, or dense thickets. One genus is aquatic. During the winter, bears stay in a deep winter sleep, which is similar to hibernation except that their body temperature is not reduced and their bodily functions continue. One litter of one to four young is born each year (usually after hibernation) after a gestation period of six to nine months. The young remain with the mother until they are fully grown. Their life span is 15 to 30 years when wild; one animal in captivity reached an age of 47 years.

If cornered or attacked, bears are among the most dangerous animals that man can encounter. They usually attack by striking with their paws and then tearing with their teeth. They can be tamed easily, however, and remain docile.

Bears belong to the family Ursidae of the order Carnivora. They comprise seven genera.

Polar Bear. The most northern in distribution of the bears is the polar or ice bear (*Thalarctos maritimus*). Its elongated body, long pointed head, relatively slender limbs, large hairy-soled feet, and cream-white coat are its distinguishing characteristics. It ranges in length from 7 to 8 feet (2.2 to 2.5 meters), and large specimens may reach 9 feet (2.7 meters). Its average weight is about 900 pounds (410 kg).

Polar bears are numerous around the North Pole. They wander great distances away from the coasts on the ice, sometimes swimming many miles. Often they winter on the ice floes and

THE BROWN BEAR of Alaska is the largest member of the genus *Ursus,* and is the largest living carnivore.

Spectacled bear (*Tremarctos ornatus*)

Himalayan black bear (*Selenarctos thibetanus*)

sometimes bear their young there. Polar bears live mainly off seals, young walrus, and fish, which they scoop out of the surf and from the coastal rivers where they come to breed. In the summer, they eat other types of food, including marine grass and shore herbage. The polar bear is hunted by the Eskimo for its fur and fat.

Brown and Grizzly Bears. These bears are found in the western part of North America and in parts of Europe and Asia. Originally regarded as several species, they now are classified into one species, *Ursus arctos*, because of their marked similarities.

The Alaskan brown bear (also called Kodiak or Kadiak) is the largest living carnivore. Found on Kodiak Island in Alaska and on the neighboring mainland, it reaches 9 feet (2.8 meters) in length and 1,700 pounds (780 kg) in weight. It is dark brown or grizzled, and it feeds on both plants and animals.

The grizzly bear originally was found from the Black Hills and Badlands of the Dakotas westward to the Pacific coast and from Mexico to northern Alaska. At present, it is found in the wild parts of Alaska and Canada and under protection in Yellowstone and Glacier national parks.

Its size varies, but a length of 8 feet (2.5 meters) and a weight of 790 pounds (360 kg) are average. Color also varies, from reddish brown to gray and even black. The grizzly bear is a massive animal with a broad, squarish head and muscular body. Because of its large size, it does not climb trees, but it is agile in moving about rough mountains or in dense forests.

The common brown bear of Europe and Asia is about 8 feet (2.4 meters) long and usually is yellowish brown, reddish, brown, or black. It is found in the more mountainous parts of Europe, Russia, Asia Minor, and throughout Asia north of the Himalaya. This is the bear most often seen in European menageries, where it breeds readily, and it can be led about by bear tamers and taught dancing tricks.

American Black Bears. This group of bears (*Euarctos americanus*) is widespread in forested regions of North America south to Mexico. It usually is black, although it may be brown, reddish, yellowish, or cream-colored. It ranges in length from 5 to 6 feet (1.5 to 1.8 meters) and normally weighs from 265 to 330 pounds (120 to 150 kg).

Black bears climb trees easily and wander extensively. They feed on both animal and plant life, and occasionally they raid livestock. They are timid and secretive and rarely are dangerous unless wounded or cornered. They often are captured and tamed.

Spectacled Bears. The only bear found in South America and the only bear that reaches the Southern Hemisphere, the spectacled bear (*Tremarctos ornatus*) is found in the mountains from Colombia to Chile. It is a small black species ranging in height from 5 to 6 feet (1.5 to 1.8 meters); it may weigh up to 300 pounds (140 kg). The species is identified by whitish spectaclelike rings around its eyes. Little is known about its habits, and it appears to subsist mainly on fruits and nuts.

Asiatic Black Bear. This species (*Selenarctos thibetanus*) is found in the forests and bushy areas of southern and eastern Asia. Somewhat smaller than the American black bear, it ranges in height from 4 to 5 feet (1.3 to 1.6 meters) and weighs up to 265 pounds (120 kg). It is black with a light-colored crescent-shaped mark on its chest. The hair on its neck is usually long, giving it a sort of ruff. An aggressive bear, it kills sheep, goats, and cattle. It also lives on fruits and nuts.

Malayan Sun Bears. The smallest of the bears, the sun bear (*Helarctos malayanus*) is found in the forests of the Malay Peninsula and islands east to Borneo. Its coat is short and fine, and the color is black with a white or orange crescent marking on the breast. Its lips and tongue are long and flexible. It ranges in height from 3.5

AMERICAN BLACK BEARS, familiar sights in some national parks, have been put under protection in the United States and Canada in order to increase their numbers.

to 4.5 feet (1.1 to 1.4 meters) and from 60 to 145 pounds (27 to 65 kg). The sun bear is an agile climber and especially likes to rob bees' nests for honey. Small animals and fruit form the rest of its diet.

Sloth, or Indian, Bears. A large animal that lives in the jungles of India and Ceylon, this species (*Melursus ursinus*) is black with unusually shaggy hair and a yellowish crescent on its chest. It has an elongated mobile snout and a very long tongue used for sucking up insects.

This species ranges from 4.5 to 6 feet (1.4 to 1.8 meters) in height and from 120 to 300 pounds (54.5 to 136 kg) in weight. It is regarded as one of the most dangerous carnivores of the Indian forests, yet it often is tamed by Hindu jugglers, who call it "aswail."

Cave Bears. Fossil bears, commonly called cave bears, have been found in Quaternary rocks (1,000,000 years old) of many caves in Europe and North and South America. Some are closely related to or identical with living species. Others, such as the California and South American cave

bears, are referred to as a distinct genus, *Arctotherium*, which may be related to the spectacled bear.

In the Tertiary rocks (70,000,000 to 1,000,000 years old) of the New and Old World, remains have been found of a series of animals (*Hemicyon, Agriotherium,* and others) that appear to connect the bears with primitive examples of the dog family, Canidae. This may indicate that bears are an offshoot of the dog family.

KARL F. KOOPMAN
The American Museum of Natural History

Bibliography

Allen, Glover M., *Extinct and Vanishing Mammals of the Western Hemisphere* (New York 1942).
Harper, Francis, *Extinct and Vanishing Mammals of the Old World* (New York 1945).
Hibben, Frank C., *Hunting American Bears* (New York 1950).
Seton, Ernest T., *Lives of Game Animals,* vol. 2 (New York 1925–28).
Storer, Tracy I., and Tevis, Lloyd P., *California Grizzly* (Berkeley, Calif., 1955).
Walker, Ernest R., and others, *Mammals of the World* (Baltimore 1964).
Wright, W.H., *The Grizzly Bear* (New York 1909).

GRIZZLY BEARS, found in the wild only in parts of Canada and Alaska, formerly were common in the western half of North America. They grow up to nine feet long and weigh about 900 pounds.

BEAR, The, a short story by the American writer William Faulkner, published in *Go Down, Moses, and Other Stories* (1942). *The Bear* is one of the most celebrated, and possibly the finest, of Faulkner's short stories. It is also one of the longest and most obscure.

On a realistic level, *The Bear* tells simply of a bear hunt, but on a symbolic level it is the story of a young man's initiation into manhood. The dramatic impact of the story is enhanced by violent racial hatred between whites and Negroes.

BEAR FLAG REVOLT, a rising of American settlers in the Sacramento Valley of California, then under Mexican rule, in 1846. In May, fearing expulsion from the province, the settlers appealed to the American soldier and explorer John C. Frémont, who was encamped at Marysville Buttes in the valley. Frémont encouraged the settlers' defiance as what he called the "first steps in the conquest of California." Early in June the first local act of war occurred—the seizure of a herd of Mexican government horses. On June 14 the Americans captured Sonoma and proclaimed the "Republic of California," its flag a grizzly bear facing a red star.

Meanwhile, the Mexican War had begun in May, and when U.S. forces occupied California, the U.S. flag supplanted the "Bear Flag" on July 10. The present state flag of California is modeled on the "Bear Flag."

BEAR MOUNTAIN STATE PARK, New York, is on the west side of the Hudson River, 40 miles (64 km) north of New York City. It is part of Palisades Interstate Park. Its area is 5,051 acres (2,045 hectares). There are individual camping sites, picnic grounds, fields for various sports, a lake for boating, and hiking trails. Bear Mountain (1,314 feet or 430.5 meters high), for which the park is named, is ascended by a motor road. Bear Mountain Bridge, a highway toll bridge, crosses the Hudson to the base of Anthony's Nose, a spectacular promontory. The park is one of the state's most popular recreation centers.

BEAR RIVER, a stream about 350 miles (560 km) long in Utah, Wyoming, and Idaho. Rising in the Uinta Mountains of Utah, it first takes a northwesterly and then a southeasterly course, forming nearly an inverted letter V. More than half the entire length is in Idaho. It empties into Great Salt Lake, 13 miles (18 km) west of Brigham City. Its valley is about 6,000 feet (1,830 meters) above sea level. The river is used to irrigate 50,000 acres (20,235 hectares) in Utah and Idaho.

There is a United States migratory waterfowl refuge of 64,000 acres (25,901 hectares) at the mouth of the river.

BEARBAITING, bâr′bā-ting, is the practice of setting dogs on a chained bear for the amusement of spectators. It was popular in England from the 11th century and had become a nationwide sport by the 16th century, when Henry VIII created an office of Master of the Royal Game of Bears and Mastiff Dogs. The entertainment was finally abolished in 1853.

The gory contests were held in "bear gardens" in London and at public squares in the villages, where they were features of church festivals and celebrations. Dogs were specially bred for bearbaiting. Usually four mastiffs were loosed on the bear, which, fastened to a long chain, and often with his teeth ground down, fended off the attackers with his huge paws. Fresh mastiffs replaced wounded or discouraged dogs. Several bears were baited at each session, and some valiant ones were spared to battle again and thus become popular attractions.

A companion sport was called *bullbaiting*. Like the bear, the bull was tethered in midring, but the bull fought the dogs singly. The dog's task was to seize the bull by the muzzle ("to pin the bull," as it was called), but frequently the dog was tossed on the bull's horns.

The spectacles of bearbaiting and bullbaiting concluded when the bear or the bull, worn out from the ordeal, collapsed on the ground.

BILL BRADDOCK, *New York "Times"*

BEAR MOUNTAIN (foreground) commands a magnificent view of the Hudson River and the Hudson Highlands.

N.Y. STATE DEPARTMENT OF COMMERCE

JOHN J. SMITH

Bearberry, or hog cranberry (*Arctostaphylos uva-ursi*).

BEARBERRY, bâr'ber-ē, any of several plants of the genus *Arctostaphylos*, found mostly in north and Central America, but also in northern Europe and Asia. These hardy, trailing, evergreen shrubs are grown for ornament and as a cover for sandy banks and rocky slopes. They have small flowers in terminal clusters and red or brown fruits. There are several species. The common bearberry is *A. uva-ursi*. It has white flowers tinged with red and shiny red berries.

"Bearberry" is used sometimes to refer to a deciduous shrub of the southern United States— *Ilex decidua*, which has green flowers.

BEARD, bērd, **Charles Austin** (1874–1948), American historian, political scientist, and municipal reformer. He was born near Spiceland, Ind., on Nov. 27, 1874. He graduated from DePauw University in 1898 and soon left for Oxford, England. There he helped establish Labour (later called Ruskin) College in 1899. Returning to the United States, he took his Ph.D. at Columbia University in 1904, joining its faculty that year.

In 1917, Beard resigned from Columbia in protest against the dismissal of two colleagues opposed to United States entry into World War I. In 1918 he helped organize the New School for Social Research in New York City. He was adviser to the Institute of Municipal Research in Tokyo in 1922 but returned to Columbia in 1939 and went to Johns Hopkins the next year.

Textbooks on European history by Beard, in collaboration with James Harvey Robinson, expanded the horizon of students usually limited to histories of politics and wars. Later, Beard burst upon the national scene with *An Economic Interpretation of the Constitution* (1913). It harmonized with the spirit of progressivism then flourishing, but it was flayed by conservatives. In 1915 he published *Economic Origins of Jeffersonian Democracy*, reaffirming the thesis that economic factors were of the utmost importance in framing the Constitution and forming political parties. *The Rise of American Civilization*, with his wife, Mary Beard, as coauthor, appeared in 1927. Less insistent on an economic interpretation, it was a sweeping view of American history, and it captivated scholars and laymen alike. *America in Midpassage* (1939) dealt with the 1920's and 1930's. *The American Spirit* (1942) analyzed the nature of civilization in America.

In the 1930's and 1940's, Beard supported New Deal domestic policies but opposed Frank-

lin D. Roosevelt's foreign policy. In books and articles he attacked the administration and, in effect, argued that Roosevelt had forced Japan to war upon the United States.

Beard's influence, once great among scholars, waned even before his death in New Haven, Conn., on Sept. 1, 1948. But he did succeed in challenging historians to reexamine old assumptions. Though criticism of his scholarship mounted, a host of people remembered his gadfly quality and his passion for academic freedom. Beard championed relativism in history, asserting that a historian's conviction about the movement of history "is a subjective decision, not a purely objective discovery."

Mary Ritter Beard (1876–1958), his wife, was born in Indianapolis, Ind., and graduated from DePauw University in 1897. They were married in 1900 and over the years collaborated on a number of important historical studies. On her own she published several books, most notably those concerning the labor movement and women's role in society. Her biography of her husband, *The Making of Charles A. Beard*, appeared in 1955.

MICHAEL KRAUS, *The City College, New York*

Charles A. Beard

(1874–1948)

CULVER PICTURES, INC.

Mary Beard

(1876–1958)

WIDE WORLD

BEARD, bērd, **Daniel Carter** (1850–1941), American artist, author, and Boy Scout leader. He was born at Cincinnati, Ohio, on June 21, 1850, the son of the artist James Henry Beard. He was educated at Covington, Ky., and studied at the Art Students League in New York City from 1880 to 1884. By 1900 he had achieved a national reputation as an author and artist. His best-known work, *American Boys' Handy Book*, appeared in 1882. Beard also wrote and illustrated articles for several magazines, was an illustrator for Mark Twain's books, and wrote over 20 books, mostly for boys. As an instructor at the Women's School of Applied Design (1893–1900), he inaugurated what was said to be the world's first organized class in animal drawing. He died at Suffern, N.Y., on June 11, 1941.

In 1905, while he was editor of *Recreation*

DANIEL BEARD, leader of the Boy Scouts.

magazine, Beard established "The Boy Pioneers, Sons of Daniel Boone," a recreational society with clubs organized as "forts" throughout the country. In 1910 he merged the society with the nascent Boy Scouts of America, and he served as national scout commissioner until his death. Known to millions of American scouts as "Dan Beard" or "Uncle Dan," he received the only golden eagle badge ever awarded. Mount Beard, a peak in Alaska, was named in his honor.

BEARD, bērd, **Thomas Francis** (1842–1905), American cartoonist and lecturer, who was noted for his "chalk-talk" lectures, in which he com-

bined witty dialogue with blackboard illustrations. During the 1870's and 1880's his "chalk talks" were a popular feature of the summer cultural center at Chautauqua, N.Y.

Known professionally as *Frank Beard,* he was born in Cincinnati, Ohio, on Feb. 6, 1842. During the Civil War he was a cartoonist for *Harper's Weekly.* From 1881 to 1884 he was professor of aesthetics at Syracuse University, and in 1884 he became chief cartoonist of *Judge,* a humor magazine. After 1890 he was an editor of the religious magazine *Ram's Horn.* He died in Chicago on Sept. 28, 1905.

BEARD, a growth of hair on the sides of the face or on the lower lip and chin, as distinct from a mustache, which is hair on the upper lip. The term "whiskers" commonly suggests the hairs of a long beard. Throughout history the wearing or nonwearing of beards has been determined largely by religious customs or secular fashion.

Early Customs. The ancient Egyptians shaved their faces for religious reasons. On the other hand, among the Jews, adult men were required to wear full beards, which they were forbidden to trim in the manner of neighboring tribes. To this day men of the ultraorthodox sect of Hasidic Jews wear long uncut beards. Mohammed ordained the wearing of a beard to set his followers apart from shaven idolaters, but they were required to clip their beards to distinguish themselves from the full-bearded Jews. In later times the Sikhs of the Punjab regarded the full beard, rolled up and pinned under the chin, as a mark of manliness.

The ancient Greeks wore beards. The great Homeric heroes were described as bearded, and Greek philosophers were distinguished by their

BEARDS have been worn from ancient to modern times and have gone through many changes in style, from neatly cut and closely trimmed to flowing and full. The beard is often associated with authority, as in the cases of the Assyrian king (*top row, left*) King Henry VIII (*top, third from left*), and Emperor Franz Joseph (*bottom left*). Beards have been worn by scholars since Sophocles (*top, second from left*) and shown in art, as by Van Dyck (*top, right*).

Assyrian, 800's B.C.   Greek, 400's B.C.   English, 16th century   Spanish, 17th century

Austrian, 19th century   Mutton chops, 19th century   American, 1860 style   Full beard, 19th century

long flowing beards. In Greek the word *pōgōno-trophos* signifies a bearded man or a philosopher. Among the Greeks the custom of shaving is attributed to Alexander the Great, who is said to have ordered his soldiers to shave so that they could not be grasped by the beard in combat.

The early Romans wore their beards uncut until about 300 B.C., when barbers were introduced. The first Roman known to have shaved every day was the great general Scipio Africanus (237–183 B.C.), and shaving soon became a regular practice. For a time Roman young men dedicated the cuttings from their first shaves to the goddess Fortuna, who in this connection was known as Fortuna Barbata. In time of mourning the Romans let their beards grow, whereas the Greeks cut their beards.

The Roman custom of shaving influenced the Roman Catholic practice of having the clergy beardless and clean-shaven. In the 16th and 17th centuries the wearing of beards was revived among popes, cardinals, and priests, and such famous men as Cardinal Richelieu were bearded. Later Roman Catholic practice eliminated the wearing of beards, except in the case of the Franciscans and other monastics. In the Greek and other Eastern churches the priests have always been bearded. At the time of the Great Schism the Eastern clergy considered shaving, as practiced by the Western clergy, to be a serious defect.

Like most Teutonic peoples the Saxons originally were bearded. After the Norman Conquest, under the influence of the custom of the clergy in northern France, the practice of shaving was introduced among the laity in England. Efforts to revive the custom of wearing beards during the reign of Henry I were vigorously suppressed by the clergy. Nevertheless, beards returned to popularity in the reign of Edward III (1312–1377) and were fashionable during the reigns of Francis I of France (1494–1547) and Henry VIII of England (1491–1547), who themselves wore full beards. By the 18th century, beards had gone through successive periods of favor and disfavor. Under Peter the Great a tax was levied on the wearing of beards in Russia.

The 19th and 20th Centuries. The return of the beard in the early 19th century was at first associated with revolutionary politics and Bohemian ways of life. Bearded men were stigmatized as radicals or social outcasts, and in the eastern United States beards were regarded unfavorably. By mid-century, however, whiskers had become a mark of Western pioneers and prospectors, and many well-known writers, scholars, and medical practitioners wore beards. Thus the beard gained respectability again. Significantly, Abraham Lincoln was the first president to wear a beard. No signer of the Declaration of Independence or of the Constitution wore a beard or even a mustache. During the Civil War beards were worn both by Union and by Confederate generals, many of whom had entered the war clean-shaven.

In the first half of the 20th century, beards went out of style in Western countries, particularly the United States. Ragged whiskers became a cartoonist's symbol for Bolsheviks and anarchists. Certain famous men who still wore beards —Sigmund Freud and Bernard Shaw, for example —stood out by contrast with the clean-shaven majority. After World War II, beards gained in favor among artists and writers; they also became a trademark of the young men called "beatniks."

BEARDSLEY woodcut for *Salomé*.

BEARD MOSS. See USNEA.

BEARDSLEY, birdz'lē, **Aubrey Vincent** (1872–1898), English illustrator, who was a leading exponent of Art Nouveau (q.v.). Combining a love of decorative pattern with a bent toward the grotesque, Beardsley's style emphasized the cruel, the macabre, and the erotic in his subjects. He contrasted large areas of black or white with long, sinuous tendrils of line. In his own time, his work was often criticized for being gloomy, unwholesome, and too sensual.

Beardsley was born in Brighton on Aug. 21, 1872. In 1888 he took a position in an architect's office in London. Encouraged by the painter Sir Edward Burne-Jones, he studied at the Westminster School of Art. His style was influenced by Japanese prints, Greek vase painting, and the works of Whistler and Toulouse-Lautrec.

Beardsley's mature work, done between 1892 and his death in Menton, France, on March 16, 1898, consists of black and white drawings, except for some designs for book covers and posters. His first important work was 350 illustrations for an edition of Malory's *Morte Darthur* (1893–94). His style reached full maturity in his drawings for Oscar Wilde's *Salomé* (1894). He became art editor of the *Yellow Book* in 1894 and later of *Savoy*, two of the leading contemporary literary publications in England. He also illustrated Pope's *Rape of the Lock* (1896) and Jonson's *Volpone* (1898). Beardsley's elegant, often erotic fiction was collected in *Under the Hill* (1904).

WILLIAM GERDTS, *University of Maryland*

Further Reading: Gallatin, A.E., *Aubrey Beardsley: A Catalogue of Drawings and Bibliography* (New York 1945); Symons, Arthur, *Aubrey Beardsley* (London 1949); Walker, R.A., *The Best of Beardsley* (New York 1948).

BEARDSTOWN is a city in western Illinois, in Cass county. It is situated on the Illinois River, 45 miles (72 km) northwest of Springfield. There are railroad shops, flour and feed mills, and glove factories. The surrounding farmlands produce melons for the city markets. The city was named for Thomas Beard, who settled here in 1819. Beardstown was the site of the Duff Armstrong murder trial (1858), in which Abraham Lincoln won an acquittal for the defendant. Government is by mayor and council. Population: 6,222.

BEARINGS, bâr′ingz, are machine elements that reduce the friction between moving parts of a machine. The major classes of bearings are rolling contact bearings and sliding bearings. Rolling contact bearings, often inappropriately called antifriction bearings, include ball and roller bearings. Sliding bearings include journal (or radial), thrust, and guide bearings.

Examples of each type are found in automobiles. The crankshaft utilizes journal bearings, and the wheels are supported with tapered roller bearings. Each type of bearing is selected because of its suitability in a particular application. Bearing design and analysis are closely related to past experience with successful installations. However, the principal equation that relates the variables governing the operation of sliding bearings was first established by Osborne Reynolds (1886), who used data from the experimental work of Beauchamp Tower (1883, 1885).

Bearing Structure and Characteristics. In principle, bearings are simple structures. A journal bearing, for example, is composed of the journal (a shaft that rotates or oscillates), the bearing, and the housing surrounding the bearing. The journal and the bearing are separated from each other by a very small clearance in which there is a lubricant. The function of the lubricant is to keep the two surfaces apart in order to minimize wear, reduce friction, and transfer the heat caused by the relative motion of the journal and the bearing.

In a journal bearing, except for start-up, there is no metal-to-metal contact because the journal is supported by a film of lubricant. In rolling contact bearings also, actual contact is prevented by the hydrodynamic effect of the lubricant, except when at rest.

In a rolling contact bearing the major parts are the inner and outer rings, the ball or roller cage, and the balls or rollers. Ball and roller bearings, though similar in many respects, differ in that ball bearings theoretically have point contact between mating elements, whereas roller bearings have line contact.

One of the significant reasons for the use of rolling contact bearings in various machines is that the starting friction is not much greater than the operating friction, and there is considerably less starting friction than for any type of sliding bearing where metal-to-metal contact may exist in the initial stages of start-up. For rolling contact bearings the coefficient of friction has little variation with speed and load. This characteristic makes it desirable to use rolling contact bearings when the operation of a machine element, such as the wheel on a car or a turbine on an aircraft jet engine, is started and stopped often. Other characteristics of rolling bearings are: they can carry both axial and radial loads; they need very little maintenance or lubrication if properly installed; they usually have a higher noise level and cost than comparable journal bearings; they have a limited but statistically predictable operational life; they take less axial but more radial room than journal bearings; they can be readily installed to meet very critical dimensional requirements; and they can carry heavy momentary overloads without failure.

Rolling Contact Bearings. Ball and roller bearings are manufactured in standard types and sizes that are listed in manufacturers' handbooks, along with other recommended technical information. The manufacturing industries that supply ball and roller bearings have provided for dimensional interchangeability between bearings of their own and competitors' manufacture. However, functional interchangeability depends on many other variables that have not yet been standardized. Ball and roller bearings are manufactured to high standards of precision and to closely controlled material and heat-treat specifications. A high degree of surface finish is required on both the rolling part and the race to avoid premature failure of the bearing caused by surface fatigue.

Types of Ball Bearings. Many types of rolling bearings are manufactured. However, some of the principal ones can be classified according to a few basic designs. The deep-groove ball bearing, probably the most widely used, is one in which the balls are assembled by placing the inner and outer rings in contact and then placing as many balls as possible in the grooves. The rings are then centered, and the balls are kept in position by a cage (also called a separator or retainer). This type of bearing is capable of supporting combined high radial and thrust loads, but it is not self-aligning. Accurate alignment between shaft and housing is needed.

In contrast to the deep-groove ball bearing is the filling-slot ball bearing, which has a slot or notches in a race to permit the inclusion of more balls. When completely assembled, this type of bearing has a high radial load capacity but a very limited thrust capacity.

Angular-contact ball bearings are designed to take radial and thrust loads where the thrust component may be large. This type of bearing is often preloaded, that is, an initial axial load that is independent of the working load is placed on the bearing. In this manner a virtually constant alignment of parts is maintained.

A double-row ball bearing actually is two single-row, angular-contact bearings that are built as a unit. Each ring has two grooves. The two rows of balls give the bearing a rated capacity slightly less than that of two single-row bearings. These bearings usually are installed with a known amount of preload to minimize deflection under a combined radial and thrust load. Although two single-row bearings could normally accomplish the same job, the use of a double-row bearing will usually require fewer parts and less space.

Other types of ball bearings are modifications of the previously mentioned types. These types include self-aligning radial and thrust

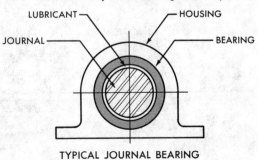

JOURNAL BEARING, widely used in machines, carries loads transmitted by the rotating shaft (journal).

TYPICAL JOURNAL BEARING

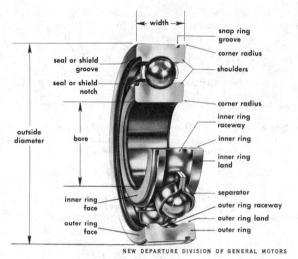

BEARING NOMENCLATURE for a typical ball bearing assembly. The balls are placed between two rings.

bearings, which are used when compensation for shaft misalignment or deflection is needed, and thrust bearings, which are used when the load is completely axial rather than radial.

Types of Roller Bearings. Many varieties of roller bearings are available commercially. They are usually classified by the design of the rollers and raceways.

Predominant among roller bearings is the cylindrical roller bearing. As contrasted to a similar size of ball bearing, a cylindrical roller bearing will carry a greater radial load because the contact is along a line rather than at a point. Its principal disadvantage is the requirement that the geometry of the raceways and rollers be almost perfect. Even the slightest misalignment will cause the rollers to skew and increase the frictional loss. Hence, the retainer usually is very heavy. Cylindrical roller bearings are not usually designed to take thrust load.

Helical rollers are made by winding rectangular materials into rollers. They are hardened and then ground to size. Because of their inherent flexibility, they are used when alignment poses a problem.

The spherical roller bearing normally is a two-row, self-aligning bearing in which the races are ground so as to give point contact on the outer race and line contact on the inner race. The rollers are ground smaller at the outer end than at the inner end so that a component of the applied load forces them against the center flanges of the inner ring. By this technique, skewing is eliminated, and the retainers are able to space rather than guide the rollers. Both axial and thrust loads are supported.

The tapered roller bearing is used to support both thrust and radial loads. It is constructed with its rolling elements as truncated cones.

Most roller bearings have roller diameters about equal to their length. Needle bearings, however, have rollers that are 8 to 12 times as long as their diameter. This type of bearing is very useful where radial space is limited. Needle bearings are not true roller bearings because at times they function with the needles stationary and thus exhibit the characteristics of plain journal bearings. One example of a needle bearing installation is its use in the universal joint of an automobile.

Selection, Lubrication, Materials. There is no precise way to calculate the life of ball or roller bearings. Hence, statistical methods of analysis are used. Commercially identical bearings may have a life range as great as 50 to 1. Generally, ratings are on a basis that 90 percent of a statistical sample of bearings under a given load will survive a specified life, such as 1,000,000 revolutions. When selecting a bearing for a particular application, it is necessary to consult manufacturers' data books.

The proper lubrication of all types of ball and roller bearings is essential to avoid premature failure. The lubricant must minimize the damage from the metal-to-metal sliding contact that inevitably occurs, help to prevent the entry of foreign matter into the bearing, protect the bearing surfaces from the atmosphere, and dissipate the heat so that the bearing may be kept at a safe operating temperature.

BALL BEARING inner ring has an accurately ground raceway (groove) to hold balls and the separator.

BALLS in bearing are kept evenly spaced by a separator. Two halves of separator close to hold balls.

BALL BEARING outer ring has a raceway to hold balls and separator between inner and outer rings.

BALL AND ROLLER BEARING INFORMATION CENTER

The most common lubricants are greases and mineral oils. Greases are used only for low or medium speeds. At high speeds too much lubrication should be guarded against because excessive churning of the oil will cause overheating. Consequently, high-speed bearings often use an atomized air-oil mist for lubrication. Manufacturers commonly provide prelubricated bearings with integral seals that are expected to last for the life of the bearing. Prelubrication is an advantage where maintenance is difficult.

One of the most widely used materials for the rolling contact bearings is an SAE 52100 alloy steel that contains 1 percent carbon and 1.5 percent chromium. The balls and rings normally are hardened to Rockwell C 58 to C 65 to give good wear characteristics and retain a very smooth surface finish when ground.

For special situations, nonferrous metals occasionally are used. There is a very limited use of plastic ball bearings, such as nylon and Teflon bearings. For high-temperature work, glass and pyroceram show promise.

Applications for Rolling Contact Bearings. Applications for ball and roller bearings are commonplace. Airplanes, trains, automobiles, machine tools, precision instruments, household appliances, and turbines could not operate efficiently without them. In fact, the ball-point pen is a ball bearing with excess lubricant, the ink. It is hard to conceive of any type of machine without thinking about rolling contact bearings. A challenging application is the use of bearings in space vehicles where usual lubrication methods cannot be used. Although ball bearings usually are associated with rotary-motion applications, axial-motion applications also are quite common. Ball nut and screw combinations are typical.

Sliding Bearings. Sliding bearings, sometimes classified as radial, thrust, and guide in accordance with their functional use, are simple and satisfactory answers to many bearing problems. In principle, they can operate whenever there is a lubricant between two surfaces that have relative motion in such a way as to wedge the lubricant against the surface. This wedge then forms a pressure pattern that will support a load. A water skier who is supported by the pressure of the water against the inclined moving skis is a practical example of this principle.

Of all of the sliding types of bearings the radial bearing—generally called a plain journal or sleeve bearing—is the most common. It is called a full journal bearing if it has 360-degree contact with its mating shaft. It is called a partial journal bearing if it has less than 360-degree contact. Perhaps the most common example of a use for the plain journal bearing is the automobile crankshaft and connecting rod assembly. Thrust bearings have their principal load along the axis of the shaft. The supporting of the vertical shaft of a waterwheel in a large hydroelectric plant is an example of an application. Guide bearings are utilized, for example, for the translational motion of the table of a machine tool moving on its way.

Sliding Bearing Friction and Lubrication. When two dry surfaces slide against each other when held together by a load, the force necessary to cause them to move is called the dry friction force. Its value depends on the nature of the materials and their surfaces. The dry friction force is considerably greater than the force that is required to move the same two surfaces when they are completely separated by a lubricant. This condition is called thick-film, hydrodynamic, complete, or perfect lubrication. Thin-film lubrication, which exists when the extremes of the two previous cases are not met, is called imperfect, partial, or boundary lubrication.

All three conditions exist in most journal bearing operations. Dry friction exists at start-up, thin-film lubrication takes place just after start-up and when the relative velocity is low, and thick-film lubrication takes place during normal operations.

For the conditions of dry friction and extreme thin-film lubrication the properties of the bearing and journal materials are of great importance. When the two surfaces make contact, there may be a welding of the surfaces. If welding occurs, material is torn from the bearing surfaces. Studies have shown that welding caused by surface-to-surface contact is minimized when the materials of the two surfaces differ.

For the condition of thick-film lubrication the friction force that resists the motion of the parts is independent of the nature of the mating

ROLLING CONTACT BEARINGS include ball and roller bearings. Angular-contact ball bearing (A) takes large radial and thrust loads. Double-row ball bearing (B) saves space and parts. Self-aligning ball bearing (C) compensates for shaft misalignment. Needle bearing (D) is useful when radial space is limited. Tapered roller bearing (E), which resembles cylindrical roller bearing, supports radial and thrust loads.

Angular-contact

Double-row   Self-aligning   Needle   Tapered

(A, B) NEW DEPARTURE DIV., GENERAL MOTORS; (C) FAFNIR BEARING CO.; (D) TORRINGTON CO.; (E) TIMKEN BEARING CO.

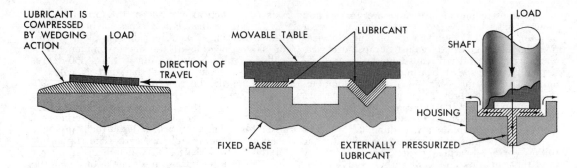

SLIDING BEARING PRINCIPLE   SLIDER GUIDE BEARING   HYDROSTATIC THRUST BEARING

SLIDING AND HYDROSTATIC THRUST BEARINGS. Sliding bearing depends on wedging action of lubricant compressed between two surfaces. Wedge provides support for load (*left*). This bearing is used in machine tools where movable table rides on lubricant (*center*). In hydrostatic thrust bearing, pressurized lubricant supports shaft (*right*).

surfaces and is directly dependent on the viscosity of the lubricant. Generally, a higher viscosity oil will have a greater load-carrying capacity but a higher friction force. Viscosity, which really is a measure of the rate of shear of the fluid film, changes with temperature. It usually is desirable to have a higher viscosity oil for operating conditions rather than starting conditions because friction causes heating of the oil and decreases the load-carrying capacity. However, a low-viscosity oil is desirable for starting conditions when the load normally is smaller but the coefficient of friction is higher. Oil companies recognize this problem. They provide dual-viscosity lubricating oils, such as SAE 10–30, which has low viscosity characteristics for cold-weather starting and high viscosity characteristics for operation at normal temperatures.

Sliding Bearing Design. Many factors are involved in bearing design. However, experience has shown that it is desirable to have a $\frac{ZN}{p}$ value as close to the minimum friction or thin-film lubrication point as is consistent with design requirements. Z is the absolute viscosity of the lubricant in centipoises; N is the journal speed in revolutions per minute; and p is the pressure in pounds per square inch of projected area. Too low a $\frac{ZN}{p}$ value will cause failure because of surface-to-surface contact. Too high a value will cause undue heating because of high friction.

Full journal bearings require a small shaft-to-journal clearance in which the lubricant pressure builds up because of the wedging action while the shaft is rotating. This clearance is about 0.001 inch (0.025 mm) per inch of journal diameter.

The bearing housing, usually a symmetrical design, should support the entire bearing sleeve. The sleeve finish should be as good as commercial practice can provide. Generally, the journals are hardened and ground. Bearing temperatures usually are limited by a lubricant temperature of about 160° F (71° C).

Bearing materials for sliding bearings include tin- and lead-base babbitts, copper alloys, silver-plate alloys, cast iron, aluminum, rubber, wood, and plastics, such as phenolic, Teflon, and nylon. If little or no maintenance for a machine can be expected, lubricant-impregnated bearings are used. Sintered powder-metallurgy products and plastics commonly are used for such bearings.

In sliding bearings the relative motion of the journal and the bearing usually is sufficient to generate oil-film pressure to support the load. However, under conditions of starting, stopping, low velocity, or very high load, the oil-film pressure may not be sufficient. If the load at starting conditions is high, then undue wear of the bearings will occur, and failure might result. Rolling mills, turbogenerators, and radar antenna mounts are examples of applications where the load at starting is high.

Hydrostatic Bearings. To overcome the problem of high starting load, a lubricant is introduced at a point in the bearing opposite the load. The lubricant, usually oil, is introduced under high pressure. With correct pressure and quantity of lubricant, the shaft will be supported by a lubricant film regardless of its rotation. This technique reduces the friction drag to a minimal value. Bearings operated in this manner are called externally pressurized bearings. They also are known as bearings with hydrostatic lubrication, and sometimes they are called contactless bearings. Radial, thrust, and sliding contact bearings, with oil, water, air, or other gases as the lubricants, use this principle.

Various machines, such as dental drills, grinders, and centrifuges, use air as a lubricant. Air-lubricated machines have been reported to operate at speeds greater than 200,000 rpm, and a speed of more than 1 million rpm has been reported for a laboratory test.

DONALD N. ZWIEP
Worcester Polytechnic Institute

Bibliography

Carmichael, Colin, ed., "The Bearing Book," *Machine Design*, vol. 35, no. 14 (Cleveland 1961).
Faires, Virgil M., *Design of Machine Elements* (New York 1965).
Fuller, Dudley D., *Theory and Practice of Lubrication for Engineers* (New York 1956).
General Motors, *New Departure Ball Bearing General Catalog* (Sandusky, Ohio; issued periodically).
Gross, W.A., *Gas Film Lubrication* (New York 1962).
Morton, H.T., *Anti-Friction Bearings* (Ann Arbor, Mich.; issued periodically).
Radzimovsky, E.I., *Lubrication of Bearings* (New York 1959).
Texaco, Inc., *Lubrication* (New York; issued periodically).
Timken Roller Bearing Co., *Timken Engineering Journal* (Canton, Ohio; issued periodically).
Torrington Company, *Torrington Bearing Catalog*.

BÉARN, bā-är′, is an area of southwestern France that is bordered by Spain on the south and by the Bay of Biscay on the west. Now a part of the department of Basses-Pyrénées, it was a frontier province for centuries.

The name Béarn is derived from the name of the town known to the Romans as Beneharnum. The early history of Béarn is obscure, but in the 6th century, after Roman rule had ended, it was conquered by the Gascons. In the early 9th century, Béarn became a viscounty; the viscounts came to hold it in fief from the dukes of Aquitaine.

In the 11th century the viscounts broke their feudal ties and became independent rulers. In order to retain their precarious independence, they played off the French and English kings against each other, shifting sides to suit their political objectives. Between 1229 and 1290 the viscount Gaston VII did this with consummate skill. Because Gaston had only daughters to succeed him, Béarn went to the family of Foix at his death. Later the Bourbon family acquired Béarn before they acceded to the French throne. Finally in the 17th century Béarn became a part of the royal domain.

The peculiar legal and institutional developments of medieval Béarn are important aspects of its history. Beginning in the 11th century the people of Béarn acquired special customs called *fors,* which specifically defined their rights and the powers of the viscounts. During the 12th century it became customary for the viscounts to consult the clergy, nobles, and bourgeoisie of the towns when taxes were levied. Eventually the three estates won considerable political and fiscal power, and a system of representation was devised for the assemblies that the viscounts convened to deal with political, financial, and legal matters.

BRYCE LYON, *Brown University*

BEAS RIVER, bē′äs, in northern India, is one of the five great rivers of the Punjab. It forms part of the Indus River system. Also spelled *Bias,* the river was known as the *Hyphasis* in ancient times.

The Beas rises in the Punjab Himalaya near Rohtang Pass at an altitude of 13,000 feet (3,-962 meters). It flows through the Kulu valley of northeast Punjab and crosses Himachal Pradesh into northwestern Punjab. There it passes through the Siwakli Range and joins the Sutlej River near the Pakistan border. The Beas has a total length of 285 miles (460 km).

BEAT GENERATION, bēt jen-ə-rā′shən, a term that became widely current in the mid-1950's in the United States to denote men and women in their teens and early twenties who affected an alienation (also referred to as disengagement and disaffiliation) from general society. Their activities were marked by an experimental quest for new ways of living and a rejection of conventional values. Their attitudes were reflected from the beginning in poetry, and later in prose forms, the theater, and motion pictures, as well as in painting, sculpture, and other nonverbal arts.

Writing. Beat poetry exhibits a high degree of improvisation, "cut-up" effects, a juxtaposition of seemingly unrelated images, and an erotic orientation. Following in the tradition of *vers libre* and tending to blur the line between poetry and prose, the beat writers early acknowledged the influence of Walt Whitman, James Joyce, Gertrude Stein, Ezra Pound, William Carlos Williams, Ar-thur Rimbaud, Federico García Lorca, Bertolt Brecht, Pablo Neruda, and Jean Genet. They counted Kenneth Rexroth, Kenneth Patchen, and Henry Miller among their immediate precursors. Characteristic of beat prose was the disappearance of the "story line."

The first to achieve prominence in the poetry and prose of the beat mystique were Jack Kerouac, Allen Ginsberg, William Burroughs, and Lawrence Ferlinghetti. By the early 1960's, Michael McClure, Jack Spicer, and Philip Whalen were attracting an audience; by the mid-1960's the older and already influential but little read works of Charles Olson, Robert Duncan, and Gary Snyder were receiving recognition.

In form and style, beat writings range from the oral "breath-length" line and free form improvisation to a highly controlled prosody, but nearly all beat writers followed Pound ("Make it new"), Williams ("The prosody of English does not apply to American"), and Charles Olson ("the HEAD, by way of the EAR to the SYLLABLE/the HEART by way of the BREATH, to the LINE").

Other Fields. In the mid-1960's the beat, by way of pop art, op art, and camp, proliferated into the plastic arts and, by way of the "happening" or "total theater," into the theater. It invaded art films and music—from jazz to folk, to folk-rock, and to protest songs. In all the arts a reintegration was stressed, especially in California (North Beach in San Francisco and Venice "West" in Los Angeles), where poetry and jazz became a popular art form in coffee shops.

Beats involved themselves in the civil rights and peace movements and in campus anti-"multiversity" and free speech demonstrations. Their activities, which were regarded by some as signs of regeneration, were deplored by others under the blanket epithet "beatnik."

LAWRENCE LIPTON
Author of "The Holy Barbarians"

Further Reading: Allen, Donald M., ed., *The New American Poetry* (New York 1960); Lipton, Lawrence, *The Holy Barbarians* (New York 1962); Lipton, Lawrence, *The Erotic Revolution* (Los Angeles 1965); Parkinson, Thomas, ed., *A Casebook on the Beat* (New York 1961).

BEATIFIC VISION, bē-ə-tif′ik, the complete human felicity or well-being accorded the just after death. A most intimate union with God, it involves the consummation of a life of religious faith and love on earth. In a supremely free and gracious act of creative love, the Triune God gives Himself to man, introducing the latter, despite his finitude and past offenses, into a real fellowship with Divine Persons.

This doctrine expresses a belief held in common, despite questioning at times, by most Christians; namely, that man's religious life gravitates ultimately toward an even greater, more perfect union with God than the one established by faith and love before death. This union, which the Greek Fathers expressed as man's deification through Christ and His gifts, is a complex New Testament reality: the final perfection of man's divine sonship or assimilation to God (I John 3:1-3); the expected passage from obscure faith to sight (I Corinthians 13:8-13); and the ultimate achievement of God's kingdom, reserved for those who have served their neighbor on earth and, possibly without realizing it, have thus ministered to Christ in His brethren (Matthew 25:31-46). The term in question recalls the transition of Christian theology from a predominantly Semitic thought-form to one that was Hellenistic and later Scholastic. Hence the union with God is described in terms of knowledge, though admittedly affective.

CARL J. PETER
The Catholic University of America

BEATIFICATION, bē-at-ə-fə-kā′shən, in the Roman Catholic Church, is an act by which the pope declares a person beatified, or blessed, after his death. It is sometimes the first step to canonization, or the raising of a person to sainthood.

Beatification has its origin in the Catholic doctrine of the veneration, invocation, and intercession of the saints. In the earlier periods of the history of the church the devotion to saints was first local and then was passed from one church to another by authority of the bishops. Two classes of persons were thus honored: martyrs and confessors. The first constituted those who had sacrificed their lives for the faith, while the second comprised those who had lived long lives of self-denial and Christian virtue. Toward the close of the 11th century the pope found it necessary to restrict the power of the bishops in decreeing who should be held up for public venerations and ordered that such honors should not be accorded until they had been approved by a council of the church. This practice was initiated by Urban II. In 1634, Urban VIII published a bull that reserved to the Holy See the sole right of beatification. The declaration by Pope Alexander VII in 1661 that St. Francis de Sales was a "beatus" is considered the first formal beatification according to the new rules.

Beatification differs from canonization in that it constitutes only a permission to venerate a certain person, with restrictions to certain places and to certain liturgical exercises. Outside the boundaries of the places designated it is unlawful to pay reverence to the person beatified or to celebrate Mass with prayers referring to him, unless special permission, called an *indult*, has been granted. Canonization is universal and also implies a precept.

Beatification is often a protracted process. The case is presented to the tribunal in Rome by an official known as a *postulator*. The postulator chooses a *vice postulator*, whose function is to promote judicial inquiries outside Rome. The inquiries are instituted under the supervision of the local bishops. When completed, the results of these inquiries are sent to the Congregation of Rites in Rome. The documents are then translated into Italian, and a public copy is made. After this an *advocate of the cause* is appointed to prepare a brief for the candidate, and a *promoter of the faith* (sometimes incorrectly called the "devil's advocate") is appointed to prepare a brief against the cause. There must be evidence of virtue to a heroic degree during life and of the performance of at least two miracles at the intercession of the person in question. Finally, the pope issues a decree, and the solemn beatification takes place in the Vatican.

BEATITUDES, bē-at′ə-tōōdz, the "blessings" pronounced by Jesus upon those worthy of admission to the Kingdom of God. The general theme is "Happy are the righteous." These blessings are found in simple form in Luke 6:20–23, where they are followed by contrasting woes, and in an expanded form, possibly arranged for liturgical use, in Matthew 5:3–10. The Beatitudes are expressed in a literary form common in the Bible and in ancient Jewish literature (for example, Psalm 1:1 and Luke 10:23). The usual form of such maxims is "Blessed are those who please God or lead exemplary lives."

The first Beatitude in Matthew in the Revised Standard Version is: "Blessed are the poor in spirit, for theirs is the kingdom of heaven." The "poor in spirit" are not the "spiritless" or "dispirited," but those who recognize their limited spiritual resources and achievements: the opposite is pride and self-satisfaction. The "sorrowful" and the "meek" are thought to be the poor, who suffer in this world but look for satisfaction to the coming reign of God. So also the "hungry" and "thirsty," who in Matthew are qualified as thirsting "for righteousness." In Luke the Beatitudes promise blessings on those who are actually poor in this world's goods and the woes condemn the rich; but Matthew's version safeguards the strictly religious interpretation, reading poor "in spirit," hunger "for righteousness," pure "in heart," and persecuted "for righteousness' sake."

FREDERICK C. GRANT
Union Theological Seminary

BEATLES, bē′təlz, an English popular-musical quartet whose novel singing style, long hair, and unconventional mode of dress made them favorites of teenagers in the 1960's. The group included *John Lennon, Ringo (Richard) Starr, Paul McCartney,* and *George Harrison,* all of whom were born in the early 1940's.

Organized in 1958, the Beatles first played in "cellar clubs" in Liverpool. In 1962 they obtained television bookings and recording contracts; their success was instantaneous and enormous. Lennon and McCartney wrote most of the Beatles' songs, including *She Loves You (Yeah, Yeah, Yeah), I Want to Hold Your Hand,* and *We All Live in a Yellow Submarine.* The Beatles' films include *A Hard Day's Night* (1964) and *Help!* (1965).

BEATON, bē′tən, **Cecil** (1904–   ), British photographer and designer. He is best known for his portrait photographs of celebrities and his designs of scenery and costumes for ballet, opera, and many theatrical productions in London and New York.

Beaton was born in London on Jan. 14, 1904. His parents were well-to-do, conventional, and in no way professionally connected with the arts. At Harrow and Cambridge, Beaton became interested in painting. He left Cambridge in 1925 without a degree and went to work in the London office of his father, a timber merchant. In his free time he designed stage settings that he hoped to sell, and took up photography. Edith Sitwell and her brothers were among his first camera subjects.

In 1930, Beaton published *The Book of Beauty,* the first of many collections of his photographs, and also signed a contract with *Vogue* magazine. In 1935 he created his first scenery and costumes on contract, for the London ballet production *Follow the Sun.* Thereafter his elegant period settings graced such stage productions as *Lady Windermere's Fan* (1947) and *Quadrille* (1954). He designed the costumes for both the stage and film versions of *My Fair Lady* and sets for the Metropolitan Opera and the Comédie Française.

BEATON, bēt'ən, **David** (1494–1546), Scottish churchman and chancellor. His family name is also spelled *Bethune*. He was the nephew of the archbishop of St. Andrews, *James Beaton* (1470?–1539), who, as chancellor (1513–1526), primate of Scotland (1522–1539), and one of the regents during the minority of James V, had promoted the Scottish alliance with France and opposed the pro-English party. The suppression of the preachers of the Reformation, who were supported from England by Henry VIII, and a French marriage for the young king were inevitable corollaries of James Beaton's policy, later continued by his nephew James Beaton (1517–1603).

David Beaton was educated at St. Andrews, Glasgow, and Paris, and in 1519 he was appointed resident for Scotland at the French court. He was given the abbacy of Arbroath, Scotland, in 1523 and in 1528 became lord privy seal. Later he took part in the negotiations for the successive marriages of James V to Madeleine of France and to Mary of Guise. He was made bishop of Mirepoix, France, in 1537. The next year he was created a cardinal by Pope Paul III, and in 1539 he succeeded his uncle as primate of Scotland and archbishop of St. Andrews, where he inherited his uncle's impregnable castle.

On the death of James V in 1542, Beaton produced an alleged will of the king nominating Beaton and three others as regents for the infant Mary Stuart (Mary, queen of Scots). This "will" was set aside by the estates (general assembly), and James Hamilton, 2d earl of Arran, was named governor. Beaton, briefly imprisoned but soon released, put himself at the head of a powerful faction opposed to the English alliance and the marriage of Mary Stuart to Edward, the son of Henry VIII, which Arran had negotiated in July 1543. In the same month, by a bold stroke, Beaton's party carried the infant queen and her mother, Mary of Guise, from surveillance at Linlithgow to freedom at Stirling Castle. In September, Arran repudiated the English treaties and went over to the anti-Reformation party. This move brought on a war with England.

Cardinal Beaton, who became chancellor in 1543, was now at the height of his power. In 1546, however, George Wishart, one of the most eloquent of the Reformation preachers, was executed as a heretic at the instance of Beaton, and on May 29, 1546, Beaton himself was murdered in his castle, in revenge.

BEATRICE, bä-ə-trē'chä, is the name given by Dante Alighieri to the woman who inspired his poetic genius. She is the object of his great love in the *Vita nuova*, and in the *Paradiso* section of the *Divine Comedy* she leads him through the spheres of heaven to a vision of God. Beatrice probably met Dante only once or twice, first when she was eight and he was nine years old. She undoubtedly was not aware of her significance for him.

Her real name was *Bice Portinari*. (Dante called her "Beatrice" to signify her beatitude.) She was born in 1266, and sometime before 1287 married Simone dei Bardi. She died in Florence on June 8, 1290.

BEATRICE, bē-at'ris, a city in southeastern Nebraska, is the seat of Gage County. It is situated on the Big Blue River, 35 miles (56 km) south of Lincoln. Grain and livestock are raised in the surrounding region. Beatrice has large flour mills and manufactures farm machinery, irrigation equipment, windmills, gasoline engines, hardware, electric metering equipment, and voting machines. Four miles (6 km) northwest of Beatrice one of the first homesteads under the national Homestead Act of 1862 was claimed by Daniel Freeman, a Union soldier in the Civil War. The Homestead National Monument was established in 1939 at the site. Beatrice was incorporated as a city in 1873. Government is by commission. Population: 12,389.

BEATRIX (1938–   ), bä'ə-triks, princess of the Netherlands. She was born at Soestdijk Palace on Jan. 31, 1938, the first child of Queen Juliana and Prince Bernhard. Beatrix became heir presumptive to the throne in 1948 following her mother's accession. Her marriage, on March 10, 1966, to Claus-Georg von Amsberg, a German nobleman, aroused much controversy because of his brief service in the German army in the latter part of World War II.

BEATTIE, bē'tē, **James** (1735–1803), Scottish poet and essayist. He was born in Laurencekirk, Kincardine, on Oct. 25, 1735. He studied at Marischal College in Aberdeen, where in 1760 he was appointed professor of moral philosophy and logic. His poetry began to appear in *Scots* magazine, and he published two volumes of verse, *Original Poems and Translations* (1761) and *Judgment of Paris* (1765). These books attracted little attention. However, his later poetic work, *The Minstrel* (1771–74), was very well received and was said to have influenced a number of the romantic poets, particularly Lord Byron. Beattie was a frequent visitor to London, and became a member of the circle of Dr. Samuel Johnson and Sir Joshua Reynolds, who painted his portrait. He died in Aberdeen on Aug. 18, 1803. His complete poetic works were published posthumously in 1866.

The philosophical work that gained Beattie his greatest contemporary fame was *The Essay on the Nature and Immutability of Truth* (1770), a treatise intended as a refutation of the skeptical philosophy of David Hume. Hume took little notice of the work, and it is considered insignificant in the history of philosophy. However, it achieved great popular success at the time of its publication (King George III was one of its admirers) and within four years had been issued in five large editions. Beattie's other philosophical works include *Dissertations, Moral and Critical* (1783) and *Evidences of the Christian Religion* (1786).

BEATTY, bēt'ē, **David** (1871–1936), British admiral, who fought important naval battles in World War I and was commander in chief of the British fleet in the latter part of the war. In recognition of his services he was created *1st earl of the North Sea and of Brooksby* in 1919.

Beatty was born at Stapeley, near Nantwich, Cheshire, on Jan. 17, 1871. He joined the navy as a midshipman at the age of 13. In 1896 and 1898, as a lieutenant in command of a small squadron of gunboats on the Nile, he gave decisive bombardment support to the army operating along the river against rebellious Sudanese tribesmen. In the Boxer Rebellion in China in 1899–1900 he rendered such distinguished service that he was promoted to captain at the age of 29.

In January 1910 he was made a rear admiral, the youngest to hold the rank in more than 100 years. He was flag secretary to Winston Churchill, first lord of the admiralty, in 1912, and the next year he was appointed commander of the battle cruiser squadron.

On the outbreak of World War I, Beatty favored aggressive action. He led a sweep into the Heligoland Bight off the German coast on Aug. 28, 1914, sinking three German cruisers. On Jan. 24, 1915, commanding five battle cruisers and a light cruiser squadron, he encountered three German battle cruisers and an armored cruiser off the Dogger Bank in the North Sea. The armored cruiser was sunk, and the other German vessels were damaged, but a confusion in the British signals permitted them to escape.

Beatty played a prominent part in the Battle of Jutland on May 31, 1916, the war's only meeting between the bulk of the British and German fleets. His battle cruisers and four battleships scouted south through the North Sea about 70 miles (112 km) ahead of the British Grand Fleet led by Adm. Sir John Jellicoe. The British knew that the German fleet was at sea. Beatty engaged the German battle cruisers, and after heavy fighting in which two of his ships were sunk he turned north to lead the Germans toward Jellicoe. The general engagement that followed was indecisive.

Beatty commanded the British fleet from 1916 to 1919 with the acting rank of admiral. He received the surrender of the German fleet in November 1918. He was promoted to admiral and then to admiral of the fleet in 1919, and he was first sea lord of the admiralty from 1919 to 1927. He labored to keep the navy in a strong position in the disarmament moves that followed the war. He died in London on March 11, 1936.

BEATTY, bē'tē, **Sir Edward Wentworth** (1877–1943), Canadian railway executive. He was born in Thorold, Ontario, on Oct. 16, 1877. Educated at the University of Toronto, he was called to the bar in 1901, and in that year joined the legal department of the Canadian Pacific Railway. In 1918 he became president, and in 1924 chairman and president of the Canadian Pacific system. He was affiliated also with nearly a score of Canada's leading transportation enterprises and was a director of many concerns, including the Bank of Montreal, the Waldorf-Astoria Hotel Company of New York, and the Sun Life Assurance Company.

One of Beatty's interests was McGill University, of which he was chancellor from 1921. He was also chairman of the Rhodes Scholarship Selection Committee for Quebec and president of the National Committee for Mental Hygiene. He was created a knight in 1935. He died in Montreal on March 23, 1943.

BEAU BRUMMEL. See BRUMMEL, GEORGE BRYAN.

BEAUCE, bōs, is a fertile limestone region in France, southwest of Paris between the Seine and the upper Loir rivers. Its area extends into the departments of Loir-et-Cher and Eure-et-Loir. The flat, dry, and treeless land is occupied mostly by large farms. Because of its extensive wheat fields, it is sometimes called the "granary of France." Sugar beets and potatoes also are important crops. The commercial center for the region is Chartres.

BEAUFORT, bō'fərt, is the name of a noble family in England, descended from the union of John of Gaunt, duke of Lancaster (of Beaufort castle in Anjou, France) and Catherine, the widow of Sir Hugh Swynford. The four illegitimate children from this union, later legitimated by Parliament, were: *John Beaufort* (1373?–1410), earl of Somerset and marquess of Dorset, who assisted Richard II against the lords appellants in 1397 and became admiral of the fleet; *Henry Beaufort* (q.v.); *Thomas Beaufort* (d. 1427), duke of Exeter, who was fleet commander, chancellor, and member of the council under Gloucester's protectorate; and *Joan Beaufort* (d. 1440), the wife of Ralph Neville, first earl of Westmorland.

The children of John Beaufort were *Joan* (or *Jane*) *Beaufort* (d. 1445), the wife of James I of Scotland; *John Beaufort* (1403–1444), 1st duke of Somerset, commander of Henry V's army in France and the father of Margaret Beaufort (q.v.); and *Edmund Beaufort* (d. 1455), earl of Dorset, who with his brother, recaptured Harfleur in 1440.

BEAUFORT, bō'fôr', **Duke de** (1616–1669), French nobleman, who was prominent in the first years of the civil war of the Fronde. He was born *François de Vendôme* in Paris on Jan. 16, 1616. He conspired with Cinq-Mars against Cardinal Richelieu in 1642 and was forced to flee from France until the cardinal's death later in the year. After the accession of Louis XIV in 1643, he became a favorite of the queen regent, but he soon began to intrigue against Cardinal Mazarin, Richelieu's successor, who had Beaufort arrested in 1643.

In May 1648 he escaped from Vincennes and by January 1649 he had become one of the leaders of the Fronde, a shifting alliance of nobles and bourgeois that sought to check the growing power of the crown. His opposition to the royal forces blockading Paris made him a hero of the city's common people, who called him *le roi des halles* (king of the markets). After the return of Louis XIV to Paris in 1652, however, Beaufort transferred his allegiance to the crown. An admiral in the French navy, he was killed in a battle in Crete on June 25, 1669.

BEAUFORT, bō'fərt, **Henry** (1377?–1447), English prelate and statesman. He was born at Beaufort Castle, Anjou, France, the second son of John of Gaunt and Catherine Swynford. His ambitions were both political and ecclesiastical. He became chancellor of Oxford in 1397 and bishop of Lincoln in 1398.

As half-brother of King Henry IV, Beaufort exercised great power after Henry's accession in 1399. He was chancellor of England in 1403–1405, 1413–1417, and 1424–1426. Both Henry IV and Henry V borrowed so heavily from Beaufort that for a time the chancellor had a stranglehold on royal finances. He exercised his consequent political power wisely as a member of the "peace party," the faction in England seeking accords with France. Beaufort became bishop of Winchester in 1404 and a cardinal in 1417. After the accession of Henry VI in 1422, his conflicting obligations to church and state aroused the hostility of Humphrey, duke of Gloucester. Beaufort, however, retained vast political power until his retirement from politics in 1443. He died at Winchester on April 11, 1447.

BEAUFORT, bō'fərt, **Margaret,** COUNTESS OF RICHMOND AND DERBY (1443–1509), English noblewoman, who was the daughter of John Beaufort, 1st duke of Somerset. The heiress of John of Gaunt, she was married three times. Her first husband was Edmund Tudor, earl of Richmond. Their son Henry Tudor, earl of Richmond, became King Henry VII of England. Margaret's second and third husbands were Henry Stafford, son of the duke of Buckingham, and Lord Stanley, a minister of Edward IV.

Margaret Beaufort is remembered as *Lady Margaret,* the patron of education, who endowed divinity professorships at Oxford and Cambridge universities, and who supported the early English printers William Caxton and Wynkyn de Worde.

BEAUFORT, bō'fərt, is a seaport town in South Carolina, about 70 miles (113 km) by road southwest of Charleston. The seat of Beaufort County, it is situated on Port Royal Island, on the Intracoastal Waterway, and has a deep natural harbor.

Beaufort is a winter resort with a year-round tourist business. Its most important industries are shrimp and oyster fishing, and truck farming. It has a U.S. naval hospital. There is a U.S. Marine Corps training station on nearby Parris Island. Points of interest include Beaufort Arsenal, built in 1795, and a national cemetery.

The area where Beaufort now stands was visited in 1521 by Spaniards, who named the harbor "Punta de Santa Elena." The town was laid out in 1711, and was the site of a British post during the Revolutionary War. It was incorporated in 1803. Government is by city manager. Population: 6,298.

BEAUFORT SCALE, bō'fərt, is a scale of comparative wind velocities. It was first developed in 1805 by an English commander (later admiral), Sir Francis Beaufort, for describing the force of a wind on the sails of a "well-conditioned man-of-war." Modified and standardized so as to apply to winds on land as well as at sea, the Beaufort scale is now in worldwide use by meteorologists as a simple means of referring to wind velocity.

THE MODERN BEAUFORT SCALE

Beaufort Number	Speed (miles per hour)	Speed (kilometers per hour)	Description
0	less than 1	less than 2	calm
1	1 to 3	2 to 5	light air
2	4 to 7	6 to 11	light breeze
3	8 to 12	12 to 19	gentle breeze
4	13 to 18	20 to 29	moderate breeze
5	19 to 24	30 to 39	fresh breeze
6	25 to 31	40 to 50	strong breeze
7	32 to 38	51 to 61	moderate gale
8	39 to 46	62 to 74	fresh gale
9	47 to 54	75 to 87	strong gale
10	55 to 63	88 to 101	whole gale
11	64 to 75	102 to 120	storm
12	above 75	above 120	hurricane

BEAUFORT SEA, bō'fərt, the part of the Arctic Ocean that lies north of Alaska and the coast of northwest Canada and west of Banks Island in the Arctic Archipelago. Its maximum depth is more than 10,000 feet (3,000 meters). The sea has no islands. It was explored by Vilhjalmur Stefansson, who crossed the ice in its southern section to Banks Island in 1915, and it was subsequently investigated by scientists based on drifting ice stations.

BEAUGENCY, bō-zhän-sē', is a town in France, in Loiret department, 15 miles (24 km) southwest of Orléans, on the Loire River. It is a mattress manufacturing center and also produces sparkling wines. It was formerly surrounded by a wall, parts of which still stand. The rectangular keep of the castle, known as the Tower of Caesar, dates from the 11th century. The churches of Notre Dame and St. Étienne are Romanesque. The house of the Knights Templar with its Romanesque façade can still be seen.

In 1152 a church council meeting at Beaugency annulled the marriage of Louis VII of France and Eleanor of Aquitaine. When the future King Henry II of England married Eleanor, he acquired her extensive holdings and therefore controlled more territory in France than his nominal suzerain, Louis VII. Joan of Arc defeated the English at Beaugency in 1429 before raising the siege of Orléans. The town was burned and sacked by the Huguenots in 1567. In 1870, the French general Antoine Chanzy was defeated by the Germans near Beaugency. Population: (1962) 3,919.

BEAUHARNAIS, bō-ȧr-ne', **Viscount Alexandre de** (1760–1794), French soldier. He was born on the West Indian island of Martinique in 1760, the son of the governor. He served with distinction as a major under Count de Rochambeau during the American Revolution. In 1779 he married Joséphine Tacher de la Pagerie, later the Empress Joséphine, and had two children by her, Eugène and Hortense, whom Napoleon I adopted when he subsequently married their mother.

At the outbreak of the French Revolution in 1789, Beauharnais was chosen a member of the National Assembly and was for a time its president. He was made general of the army of the Rhine in 1792 and shortly thereafter was offered the position of minister of war, which he refused. In 1793 he was obliged to retire because of the decree against officers of noble birth. Falsely accused of conspiring in the surrender of Mainz to Prussian and Austrian forces in 1793, he was convicted and guillotined on July 23, 1794.

BEAUHARNAIS, bō-ȧr-ne', **Eugène de** (1781–1824), French general and statesman, who was the stepson of the emperor Napoleon I. He was born in Paris on Sept. 3, 1781. His father, Alexandre, Viscount de Beauharnais, was executed in 1794. Two years later his mother, Joséphine Tacher de la Pagerie, married Napoleon.

Beauharnais accompanied Napoleon on his military campaigns in Italy and Egypt and was promoted to general. He was made a prince of France and viceroy of Italy in 1805. He married Princess Amelia Augusta of Bavaria in 1806. For nine years he governed Italy, administering the Napoleonic laws and expanding the economy by developing public works. He raised an army that fought for Napoleon in Austria and Spain. He led a corps in Napoleon's invasion of Russia in 1812 and commanded the army in the last stages of the retreat after Napoleon had fled.

When Napoleon was overthrown in 1814, Beauharnais retired to the court of his father-in-law, King Maximilian I, in Munich, Bavaria. He was made duke of Leuchtenberg and prince of Eichstadt. He died in Munich on Feb. 21, 1824.

His sister, *Hortense de Beauharnais,* was the wife of Louis Bonaparte, Napoleon's brother, who was made king of Holland.

BEAUHARNAIS, bō-ȧr-nā, **Hortense de** (1783–1837), French noblewoman who was the wife of Louis Bonaparte and queen of Holland. She was born in Paris on April 10, 1783, the daughter of Alexandre de Beauharnais and of Josephine, later the wife of Napoleon Bonaparte.

After Napoleon married Josephine in 1796, Hortense became closely associated with the Bonaparte family and followed Napoleon's wishes in marrying his brother Louis in 1802. She became queen of Holland in 1806 when Napoleon placed Louis on the Dutch throne. Louis gave up the crown in 1810 after a dispute with Napoleon over the Dutch economy. Although Hortense's marriage had been unhappy from the beginning and had been the cause of much friction between Napoleon and Louis, she had remained with Louis at Napoleon's request. In 1810 the emperor allowed Louis and Hortense to separate.

While she was the wife of Louis, Hortense gave birth to three sons, but a lover, rather than Louis, was suspected of fathering the third, the future Napoleon III. In 1811 she had a fourth son, the future duke of Morny, by the Count of Flahaut. Hortense remained loyal to Napoleon after her separation, and her support of the former emperor during the Hundred Days in 1815 led to her exile from France after Napoleon's final defeat. After traveling in Germany and Italy, Hortense bought the château of Arenenberg in the Swiss canton of Thurgau, where she died on Oct. 3, 1837.

BEAUHARNOIS, bō-ȧr-nwä', an industrial city in Quebec, Canada, is the seat of Beauharnois County. It is situated 20 miles (32 km) southwest of Montreal on the south shore of Lake St. Louis. Beauharnois is the site of one of the world's largest hydroelectric power developments. Industries include the manufacture of chemicals, paper, and steel and aluminum alloys. It was founded in 1819 and was incorporated as a town in 1863. Population: 8,121.

BEAUJOLAIS, bō-zhô-lā', is a former province of France on the west bank of the Saône River, north of Lyon. Situated in the department of Rhône, it is considered to be part of the region of Burgundy and is known for the excellence of its red wine, Beaujolais.

The province developed from the feudal lordship formed in the 10th century around the small village of Beaujeu. Although the lordship of Beaujeu never became a feudal state, its lords played a prominent role in the history of the duchy of Burgundy. Guichard of Beaujeu, who died in 1216, was a trusted servant of King Philip Augustus of France. Guichard's successor, Humbert, fought against the Albigensian heretics and won a constableship. Throughout the 14th century the lords of Beaujeu remained devoted to the French kings. Edward of Beaujeu, a marshal of France, fought at the Battle of Crécy. When his son died without heirs in 1374, Beaujeu passed to a cousin, Edward of Beaujeu, who in 1400 yielded all his lands in the Beaujolais to the duke of Bourbon. The dukes of Bourbon held them until the early 16th century when they passed to Louise of Savoy, the mother of King Francis I. In 1531 these lands became part of the royal domain, but in 1560 the Bourbons regained them. Eventually they went to the house of Orléans.

BRYCE LYON, *Brown University*

Pierre
Beaumarchais

(1732–1799)

CULVER PICTURES

BEAUMARCHAIS, bō-mär-shā', **Pierre Augustin Caron de** (1732–1799), French dramatist and adventurer, who is remembered chiefly for his two comic masterpieces *The Barber of Seville* and *The Marriage of Figaro*. Beaumarchais was first a man of affairs who made and lost several fortunes, and only second a man of letters.

Early Years. He was born in Paris on Jan. 24, 1732, the son of a watchmaker, André Caron. He married a wealthy customer of his father's shop, Madeleine Francquet, one of whose estates, called Beaumarchais, provided him with a new last name. His wife soon died, and Beaumarchais, an accomplished harpist, went to Versailles and became music teacher to the daughters of Louis XV. Beaumarchais' extraordinary business sense and unscrupulous audacity impressed the great financier Joseph Duverney, who entrusted him with large sums of money and sent him on missions to England and to Spain, where he tried unsuccessfully to secure a monopoly of the slave trade in the Spanish colonies. Through his dealings with Duverney, Beaumarchais made a fortune that he used to purchase a brevet of nobility.

In 1767, Beaumarchais published his first play, *Eugénie,* with an introduction that is a critical manifesto in defense of sentimental bourgeois drama stressing pity for the misfortunes of virtuous and modest people. He called for an end to the use of classical models in tragedy, which are founded on terror and primarily involve princes and nobles. But virtuous didacticism hardly suited Beaumarchais' temperament, and neither *Eugénie* nor his next play, *Les deux amis* (1770), is now staged.

Middle Life. Meanwhile, he married another wealthy widow, who also died soon after the wedding. He easily charmed women and utilized them in dubious business dealings that eventually resulted in his being briefly imprisoned. His first taste of literary fame followed the publication of his four caustic *Mémoires* (1773–74), in which he defended his position in a complicated lawsuit resulting from speculations undertaken with a partner whom he survived. The *Mémoires*, full of wit, irony, and satirical brilliance, won the public to his side, although he lost the suit.

In 1775, Beaumarchais' comedy, *The Barber of Seville,* took Paris by storm. The central character, Figaro, appeared to contemporaries as the symbol of the intelligent man of the lower classes in revolt against political despotism and social inequality. The play was the basis of operas by Paisiello and Rossini.

In spite of the political overtones in Beaumarchais' writings, Louis XVI protected him and used him as a secret agent to Austria. Beaumarchais also was largely responsible for the king's decision to intervene on the side of the American colonies in their struggle for independence from Britain. He personally organized a fleet to carry weapons and equipment to the colonies, enlisted volunteers, and advanced enormous sums of money, which the American government only partially repaid to his estate in 1835. It is said that no European did as much as Beaumarchais for American independence.

Later Years. In 1778, Beaumarchais finished his masterpiece, *The Marriage of Figaro,* a sequel to *The Barber of Seville.* When, in 1783, he finally received the king's permission to have the play performed, it was a great success. Its irreverent treatment of the privileged classes, however, brought Beaumarchais another brief prison sentence. The theme, taken from earlier plays about husbands deceived by clever wives, was treated with witty originality. The dialogue and Figaro's famous monologue are dazzling. The play inspired Mozart's *Le nozze di Figaro.*

At the outbreak of the French Revolution in 1789, Beaumarchais was engaged in editing a monumental 70-volume edition of Voltaire's works (1784–90), which was a financial disaster. He also lost money in 1792 in attempting to sell muskets, imported from Holland, to the revolutionary armies. For a while he was classed as an émigré, and his property in Paris was confiscated, but it was later returned to him. He died in relative poverty, in Paris on May 18, 1799.

See also BARBER OF SEVILLE; MARRIAGE OF FIGARO.

HENRI PEYRE, *Yale University*

Bibliography
Cox, Cynthia, *The Real Figaro* (New York 1963).
Kite, Elizabeth, *Beaumarchais and the War of American Independence,* 2 vols. (Boston 1918).
Lemaître, Georges, *Beaumarchais* (New York 1949).
Meyer, Jean, *Le mariage de Figaro* (Paris 1953).
Pomeau, René, *Beaumarchais, l'homme et l'oeuvre* (Paris 1956).
Ratermanis, J.B., and Irwin, W.R., *The Comic Style of Beaumarchais* (Seattle, Wash., 1961).

BEAUMONT, Francis. See BEAUMONT AND FLETCHER.

BEAUMONT, bō'mont, **William** (1785–1853), American surgeon. He was born in Lebanon, Conn., on Nov. 21, 1785. In 1822, while serving in the U.S. Army, he treated a young patient, Alexis St. Martin, for a gunshot wound in his left side. Although St. Martin eventually regained his health, an opening, 2.5 inches (6.3 cm) in circumference, remained and exposed his stomach. From 1825 to 1833, Beaumont performed a series of experiments on St. Martin's stomach. The opening provided him with a unique opportunity to study stomach functions, and Beaumont proved the presence and active function of the gastric juices in the stomach. In 1833 he published his findings in *Experiments and Observations on the Gastric Juice and the Physiology of Digestion.* His experimental evidence and conclusions contributed much to the knowledge of human physiology and are still valuable. Beaumont died in St. Louis, Mo., on April 25, 1853.

BEAUMONT, bō'mont, an industrial city and inland port in southeastern Texas, is situated on the Neches River, about 25 miles (40 km) from the Gulf of Mexico and 85 miles (137 km) east of Houston. The city is the seat of Jefferson County.

A deepwater channel connects Beaumont with the Intracoastal Waterway and the Gulf of Mexico, making available water transportation to coastal and inland ports of the United States as well as to foreign ports. Major highways and railroads converge on the city, and there is an airport (shared with Port Arthur) equipped to handle the largest jets. All these facilities make Beaumont a major trade and distribution center for the many large industries of the area.

Beaumont is the largest city in the Beaumont-Port Arthur metropolitan area. It is a center for petroleum refining, the manufacture of chemicals, rubber, and oil field equipment, metal-fabrication plants, machine shops that serve the large refineries and factories, and shipbuilding. Large mills process the rice grown in surrounding areas, especially Jefferson County, which is the leading rice-producing county in the state. Cattle ranks second to rice as an agricultural product. Nearby supplies of timber furnish raw materials for plywood, pulp, paper, and other wood products. The greatest growth in industry since 1960 has been in chemical and rubber manufacturing and sulfur mining.

The major institution of higher education is Lamar State College of Technology, a coeducational college specializing in engineering but offering degrees in many other fields. Beaumont has both a city and a county library, an art museum, a symphony orchestra, a civic opera group, an interfaith choral society, and a community theater. A special group, called the Melody Maids, travels widely for USO (United Service Organization) performances.

Recreation is provided by more than 20 city parks, which contain swimming and wading pools, an 18-hole golf course, and bridle paths with horses available for nominal fees. The Neches River Festival in April, a horse show in May, a rodeo in June, and the South Texas State Fair in October are the leading annual events.

The town of Beaumont was laid out about 1835 on the banks of the Neches River, where a settlement had been growing for about a decade. In 1838, Beaumont became the seat of Jefferson County. Lumbering developed as the principal industry of the town, and the surrounding farmlands produced rice, cotton, sugarcane, and cattle. Beaumont remained primarily a trading center and a market for rice, cattle, and timber products until 1901. On January 10 of that year the Anthony F. Lucas gusher, the first well in Spindletop Oil Field, blew in. This event marked the beginning of the Texas oil industry and of Beaumont's growth as an industrial city.

The name of the city is of uncertain origin. It may honor a person or a pioneer family named Beaumont, or the French words *beau mont* ("beautiful hill") may have been chosen to describe the area immediately to the south that became the Spindletop Oil Field.

Beaumont was incorporated in 1881. It has had a council-manager form of government since 1947, when the present charter was adopted. Population: 115,919.

LOUISE LOOMIS
Beaumont Library Commission

BEAUMONT AND FLETCHER, bō'mont, flech'ər, English poets and dramatists of the early 17th century, were the most famous collaborators in the history of English literature. Contemporaries of Shakespeare, they were ranked above him by the Jacobeans.

FRANCIS BEAUMONT (1584–1616) was born at Grace-Dieu, Leicestershire. He entered Broadgates Hall of Oxford University in 1597 but left the university two years later when his father, a judge of the common pleas, died. In 1600 Beaumont enrolled in the Inner Temple to study law, but he never became a lawyer. Instead, he established himself among the brilliant coterie at London's Mermaid Tavern, becoming a good friend of Ben Jonson, Michael Drayton, and later of John Fletcher. He was married about the year 1613, and died at the age of 31, on March 6, 1616. He was buried in the Poets' Corner of Westminster Abbey.

JOHN FLETCHER (1579–1625) was born at Rye, Sussex, in December 1579. In 1591 he entered Benet (Corpus Christi) College, Cambridge, of which his father, Dr. Richard Fletcher, had at one time been president. Dr. Fletcher, who became bishop of London in 1594, died heavily in debt in 1596, leaving only his books to his sons. For several years after this time, Fletcher lived near the Globe Theatre in London with Beaumont, his friend and coworker. He later became associated with the playwright Philip Massinger. Fletcher died of the plague on Aug. 29, 1625, and was buried at St. Saviour's Church, Southwark, London.

WORKS OF BEAUMONT AND FLETCHER

Although the biographical details of the friendship and collaboration of Beaumont and Fletcher are uncertain, it seems probable that Fletcher began writing plays for the London theaters as early as 1604–1605, and that his friendship with Beaumont was established by 1607. In that year both Beaumont and Fletcher prefixed commendatory verses to Jonson's *Volpone*, and *The Woman Hater*, probably written by Beaumont alone, was published. In 1612, in the address to the reader prefixed to the *White Devil*, John Webster praises "the no less worthy composures of the both worthily excellent Master Beaumont and Master Fletcher," ranking them on equal terms with such scholars and experienced dramatists as Chapman and Jonson, and apparently above Shakespeare, Dekker, and Heywood. Before 1612 the reputation of Beaumont and Fletcher as dramatists was well established. By 1612 the work of their collaboration appears to have been completed, since there is no direct evidence that Beaumont wrote anything for the public stage after that date. Their collaboration, therefore, comprises only some half dozen years.

Early Collaboration. During this time the dramatists apparently lived as brothers, sharing everything in common; and so intimate was their association as writers that it is only recently that criticism has been able to separate their respective shares in the authorship of the plays with any degree of probability. Fletcher's energies seem to have been devoted exclusively to the theater; but Beaumont wrote verses to the countess of Rutland and elegies on the Lady Markham, Lady Penelope Clifton, and the countess of Rutland, as well as a wedding masque in 1613, performed with great splendor by the gentlemen of the Inner Temple and Gray's Inn.

The long poem *Salmacis and Hermaphroditus* (1602) may have been written by him; it is so assigned in the entry of 1639 in the *Stationer's Register*. Eight plays may be assigned to the period before 1612 with considerable certainty, each being the result of collaboration except where the contrary is indicated: *Philaster; The Coxcomb; The Maid's Tragedy; Cupid's Revenge; A King and No King; The Woman Hater* (probably by Beaumont alone); *The Knight of the Burning Pestle* (Beaumont); *The Faithful Shepherdess* (Fletcher). Eight other plays may be assigned before 1612 with more or less probability: *The Woman's Prize* (Fletcher); *Wit at Several Weapons* (first version); *Love's Cure; Thierry and Theodoret; Monsieur Thomas* (Fletcher); *Four Plays in One* (possibly in collaboration with Nathan Field); *The Scornful Lady; The Captain.*

The brief period of their collaboration came at the climax of the astonishingly rapid and varied development of the Elizabethan drama. During this time the greatest plays of Jonson and Shakespeare were written. But a growing critical consciousness among the dramatists themselves and increasing patronage from the court seemed to promise a future for the drama even greater in achievement than its past. Beaumont and Fletcher, gentlemen by birth and breeding and attached to the court rather than to the people, naturally joined with Jonson in viewing the plays of their predecessors with critical, though doubtlessly appreciative, minds, and in seeking for a more cultivated audience and a more critical art. The attitude of these three men toward the drama that preceded their own is indicated by the fact that they abandoned several kinds of plays that had long been popular but were now subject to attacks by Jonson. Beaumont and Fletcher in their collaboration made no use of the historical matter of the chronicles or of the methods or spectacles of the chronicle play; nor did they use the theme of blood vengeance, which had been popularized by Kyd in *The Spanish Tragedy*, transformed by Shakespeare into *Hamlet*, and was still the prevailing type of tragedy. Some of their earlier plays were experiments that further attest to their reforming attitude. Beaumont's *The Woman Hater* was a comedy in Jonson's manner; and his *Knight of the Burning Pestle*, written under the inspiration of *Don Quixote*, was a burlesque on contemporary plays of adventure. Fletcher's *Faithful Shepherdess* was an attempt to replace the abortive pastorals of earlier playwrights with a genuine and elaborate pastoral tragicomedy modeled on Guarini's *Il pastor fido*. These plays won critical praise, but even the manifest genius of the last two works failed to avert the disapproval of a public unused to such innovations in drama.

Public Acceptance. The later plays, though hardly less novel in character, and displaying fully the authors' gifts of invention and language, did succeed in captivating the public. These successes, the result of constant attention to theatrical effectiveness, fell into two distinct classes, the comedies and the heroic romances. Both were immediately popular and exerted a large influence on the later history of the drama.

The comedy of Beaumont and Fletcher has its affinities with the drama that preceded it; but it is a distinct departure from Jonson's comedy of "humours," and it marks a line of development that was to lead to the plays of the Restoration later in the 17th century. Fortified by a lively plot, abounding in surprises, this form of comedy combines in a love story the manners of the day, the excitements of romance, an overflowing wit, and an absence of morals. Its full development belongs to Fletcher's later years; *The Scornful Lady* is perhaps the best representative of the collaboration.

The romances, sometimes tragic and sometimes tragicomic, also mark important innovations. The dramatic period immediately preceding theirs had been distinguished by Shakespeare's tragedies, the prevalence of realistic comedy, and the absence of sentimental or romantic comedy or tragicomedy. The return to romance seems to have been heralded by *Philaster,* and resulted in six plays that form the most distinctive product of the collaboration. Other plays of the collaboration and many written later by Fletcher might be grouped with these; but the six plays, *Four Plays in One, Thierry and Theodoret, Philaster, The Maid's Tragedy, Cupid's Revenge, A King and No King,* serve to define the type, and resemble one another so closely in material, construction, characterization, and style that a single analysis will serve for all.

Dramatic Style. Their plots usually are original and are ingenious complications of suspense and surprise. Like most of the earlier tragedies, they deal with royal or noble persons, foreign localities, and the plots and passions that convulse kingdoms; but there are no battles or processions and the action is confined mainly to the rooms of the palace or an adjoining forest. A theme of gross sensual passion usually is juxtaposed with one of idyllic sentiment, and a great variety of incidents are supplied to keep interest at fever heat. A girl disguised as a page is stabbed by the man she loves; a woman accused of adultery defies her accusers; the hero is saved from a tyrant's wrath by a timely insurrection—such idyllic or melodramatic material as this is constructed skillfully into a number of telling theatrical situations, leading through a series of surprises to startling climaxes or catastrophes. In ingenuity of structure even more than in choice of material, the romances marked a departure from preceding plays. The dramatis personae are well suited to their impossible and romantic situations, and are usually of certain types—the sentimental or violent hero; his faithful friend, a blunt outspoken soldier; the sentimental heroine, often disguised as a page in order to save the hero; the evil woman who makes the most of the trouble; and the poltroon, usually a comic personage. With the addition of a king, some persons of the court, and some from the lower ranks, the cast is complete. Even at their best, such plays afford little that is valuable in the revelation of character or the criticism of life; yet the masterpieces of the class, *Philaster* and *The Maid's Tragedy,* approach the quality of Shakespeare because of the skill of their invention and the felicities and vigor of their poetry.

Both the romances and the comedies delighted their contemporaries, and the young authors were quickly established among the poets of the highest rank in critical and popular estimation. There is evidence that their heroic plays prompted Shakespeare's change from tragedy to romance and that *Philaster* led almost directly to *Cymbeline.* Certainly their comedies and romances were much imitated by dramatists of the next 30 years. The dramatists' freedom in versification, their emphasis on stage situation rather than interpretation of character, their amoral attitude, and their fondness for the abnormal and sensational all contributed to an era of decadence in the English theater. However, many worthy qualities in the drama of the 17th century may be traced to the initiative of Beaumont and Fletcher, and their plays remained the favorites of the theater during the Restoration. By the beginning of the 18th century, pseudoclassicism brought them into disrepute with critics, and a chastened stage condemned their immorality. Beaumont and Fletcher never have recovered their favored position on the stage, but the numerous editions of their plays testify to continued interest in them.

Fletcher's Later Works. After 1612, Fletcher continued for 13 years to write plays with unabated energy, displaying even greater versatility of invention and wit than when writing with Beaumont, but becoming more addicted to his mannerisms and more careless of moral decency. About 1613 he seems to have collaborated with Shakespeare on *Henry VIII* and *The Two Noble Kinsmen,* and the association with the great master inspired some of his finest passages. It is certain that he collaborated frequently with various authors, especially with Massinger. *The Queen of Corinth, The Double Marriage, The Laws of Candy, The False One, The Prophetess,* and *The Spanish Curate,* which are some of the plays most certainly to be ascribed to this partnership, are most typical of the two authors.

Fletcher, however, did not require collaboration for stimulus. In *Bonduca* he produced one of the most vivid of historical tragedies; and in a series of romances and comedies, of which *The Little French Lawyer, The Chances, The Wild Goose Chase, The Loyal Subject,* and *The Lover's Progress* are among the best, he gave continued evidence of his extraordinary fertility both as a playwright and as a poet.

Most of the characteristics of these later plays may, however, be traced to the period of Fletcher's collaboration with Beaumont. Though modern criticism has denied to the latter a share in the majority of the plays long published under his name, it is difficult to separate the sentiments and opinions of the two friends or to divide their contribution to the development of the drama.

ASHLEY H. THORNDIKE, *Author of "The Influence of Beaumont and Fletcher on Shakespeare"*

Bibliography

Texts of the works of Beaumont and Fletcher are published in Alexander Dyce's standard edition, *The Works of Beaumont and Fletcher,* 11 vols. (London 1843–46; 2d ed., 2 vols., 1852); M.C. Bradbrook, ed., *Selected Plays of Beaumont and Fletcher* (New York 1929); J. St. Loe Strachey, *Beaumont and Fletcher,* 2 vols. (New York 1949–50); and Alfred Royney Waller and Arnold Glover, *The Works of Francis Beaumont and John Fletcher,* 10 vols. (Cambridge, Mass., 1905–10).

Appleton, William W., *Beaumont and Fletcher, a Critical Study* (New York 1955).

Bertram, Paul D., *Shakespeare and the Two Noble Kinsmen* (New Brunswick, N.J., 1965).

Danby, John F., *Poets on Fortune's Hill* (New York 1952).

Macaulay, George Campbell, *Francis Beaumont, a Critical Study* (London 1883).

Maxwell, Baldwin, *Studies in Beaumont and Fletcher and Massinger* (Chapel Hill, N.C., 1939).

Oliphant, Ernest Henry Clark, *Plays of Beaumont and Fletcher* (New Haven 1927).

Thorndike, Ashley H., *The Influence of Beaumont and Fletcher on Shakespeare* (Worcester, Mass., 1901).

Waith, E.M., *Pattern of Tragicomedy in Beaumont and Fletcher* (New Haven 1952).

Wallis, Laurence Bergmann, *Fletcher, Beaumont and Company* (New York 1947).

BEAUNE, bōn, is a town in France in Côte-d'Or department, 23 miles (37 km) southwest of Dijon. The plan of the town is circular, and walls that have been converted into a promenade surround the town. Among the architectural attractions is the 12th century church of Notre Dame. The most famous building is the hospital, the Hôtel-Dieu, founded for the poor in 1443. The entire cost of the hospital is met by the income from vineyards donated by benefactors to the Hospices de Beaune. The wines sold through the Hospices are among the most famous of Burgundy. The town is the center of the Burgundian wine trade and is noted for its own wines. Manufactures include textiles, cutlery, and leather.

Under the Romans, Beaune was a prosperous livestock and wine-producing center. In the 13th and 14th centuries it flourished under the dukes of Burgundy. Louis XI conquered the area and made Beaune part of the royal domain in 1478. When the revocation of the Edict of Nantes in 1685 forced many Huguenot craftsmen to leave, the town's prosperity declined for many years. Population: (1962) 14,695.

BEAUPORT, bō-pôr', is a suburban residential city in southern Quebec, on the St. Lawrence River, 5 miles (8 km) northeast of Quebec City. Industries include saw and grist mills, cement and brick works, and quarries. L'École Apostolique du Sacré-Coeur, a Roman Catholic college, is situated there. Beauport, settled in 1634, is one of the oldest communities in Canada. Population: 14,681.

BEAUPRÉ, bō-prā', a town in southern Quebec, is situated on the St. Lawrence River, 28 miles (45 km) northeast of Quebec City. Its industries include a distillery, a pulp and paper mill, and a thermal-electric power station. Farming and dairying are carried on in the surrounding area.

The site was settled about 1660. Beaupré was formerly part of Ste. Anne de Beaupré, 3 miles (5 km) to the southwest. It became a separate municipality in 1927 and was incorporated in 1953. Population: 2,862.

BEAUREGARD, bō'rə-gärd, **Pierre Gustave Toutant** (1818–1893), American Confederate general, who directed the bombardment of Fort Sumter in the harbor of Charleston, S.C., that began the Civil War. He was born in New Orleans, La., on May 28, 1818. Beauregard graduated from West Point in 1838 and served with distinction in the Mexican War of 1846–1848. He was named superintendent of West Point in 1860 but was removed after serving only five days because he declared that his loyalty would be to Louisiana if the state seceded from the Union. Beauregard resigned from the United States Army on Feb. 20, 1861, and was appointed a brigadier general in the Confederate army, assigned to Charleston.

On orders from the Confederate government Beauregard demanded the surrender of Fort Sumter. When it was refused, he opened a bombardment that brought the capitulation of the fort on April 12, 1861. As field commander under Gen. Joseph E. Johnston, he was largely responsible for the Confederate victory at the First Battle of Bull Run on July 21, 1861. When Gen. Albert Sidney Johnston was killed in the Battle of Shiloh on April 6, 1862, Beauregard succeeded to his command. However, Union reinforcements turned his apparent victory into defeat, and he retreated to Corinth, Miss. From September 1862 until April 1864 he defended Charleston against a Union siege. In the spring of 1864 he blocked Union Gen. Benjamin F. Butler's move up the James River to Richmond, Va., and that summer he held Petersburg, Va., against Grant until Lee's army arrived. He was with Gen. Joseph E. Johnston in North Carolina when the war ended.

After the War, Beauregard was a railroad president and director of the Louisiana state lottery. He refused invitations to command the armies of Rumania and of the khedive of Egypt. He died at New Orleans on Feb. 20, 1893.

BEAUTIFUL AND DAMNED, a novel by F. Scott Fitzgerald, published in 1922. Set in the United States in the "jazz age" after World War I, the novel shows how the wealthy youth of the period were "damned" by their money and frivolity.

At the beginning of the novel its hero, Anthony Patch, is confidently awaiting the death of his multimillionaire grandfather and the legacy that he expects from him. Meanwhile, Anthony and Gloria Gilbert, a beautiful society girl, embark on a jazz-age marriage centered on parties, money, and drinking. A rift develops between them, and their life becomes even more frantic.

Because of his extravagances, Anthony is disinherited shortly before his grandfather's death. He contests the will in a long court battle but loses all his money and self-respect in the interim. By the time he wins the case, he has become an alcoholic, is despised by his wife, and has had a nervous breakdown.

BEAUTY. See AESTHETICS; ART.

BEAUTY AND THE BEAST, a story common to the folklore of many peoples, has as its theme the marriage of a human being and an animal. Typically, the beast is a man who by a curse has been transformed into an animal and can be restored to human form only by a woman's love.

In a French version of the story, Beauty is the youngest of several children of a merchant who has lost his fortune. Whereas the others bemoan their reduced circumstances, Beauty accepts her lot with grace. Before leaving on a trip in the hope of regaining his wealth, the merchant asks his children what gifts they would like him to bring. All request finery except Beauty, who simply wishes for his safe return and asks for a rose. The merchant fails in his venture, and on his way home stops at a beautiful estate to pick a rose. The Beast appears, entertains the merchant, but threatens him with death unless one of his daughters will come to live on the estate. Beauty volunteers to do so and, after living for some time with the Beast, discovers his innate goodness and falls in love with him. On the day of their wedding, the Beast is transformed into the handsome prince he used to be.

The best-known version of *Beauty and the Beast* is Andrew Lang's translation of the original French story *La Belle et la Bête,* published in 1757 by Jeanne-Marie Leprince de Beaumont.

BEAUTY CARE. See COSMETICS; HAIRDRESSING; MAKEUP.

BEAUVAIS, bō-vā', a city in France, is the capital of Oise department. It is 42 miles (68 km) northwest of Paris, in the former province of Île de France, and lies in a fertile valley of the Thérain River. The famous Gobelin tapestries were once manufactured in the city; however, the factory was destroyed during World War II. Pharmaceuticals, building materials, and machinery are the main industries.

The most notable building is the unfinished cathedral of St. Pierre, consisting of the choir and transept. It has the highest stone vault in the world (157 feet; 48 meters) and beautiful stained-glass windows. The choir was started in 1247, but collapsed twice before additional supports enabled it to be completed.

As *Caesaromagus* and later as *Bellovacum*, Beauvais was a Roman town. It was the capital of a countship by the 9th century and was subsequently under the rule of its bishops. In 1472 the town successfully resisted an attack by Burgundians under Charles the Bold. The exploits of the attack's heroine, Jeanne Hachette, are marked by an annual celebration. During World War II the city was badly damaged, but it was rebuilt according to its original plan. Population: (1962) 33,559.

BEAUVAIS TAPESTRY. See TAPESTRY—*European Tapestry* (17th Century).

BEAUVOIR, bō-vwȧr', **Simone de** (1908–   ), French writer, whose works reflect the existentialist movement in modern France. She was born in Paris on Jan. 9, 1908. She studied at the Sorbonne, where she received a degree in philosophy in 1929. From 1931 she taught philosophy at several women's colleges, but in 1943 she left teaching to devote her life to writing. Her novels include *L'invitée* (1943; Eng. tr., *She Came to Stay,* 1949) and *Le sang des autres* (1945; Eng. tr., *The Blood of Others,* 1948). Her philosophical works include *Pour une morale de l'ambiguité* (1947; Eng. tr., *The Ethics of Ambiguity,* 1948) and *Le deuxième sexe* (1949; Eng. tr., *The Second Sex,* 1953). Three autobiographical volumes have appeared in English translation under the titles *Memoirs of a Dutiful Daughter* (1959), *The Prime of Life* (1962), and *Force of Circumstance* (1965).

During the early 1940's Simone de Beauvoir and the writer Jean-Paul Sartre presided over informal philosophical discussions in various left-bank cafés in Paris. In these discussions was born their special form of existentalism, an atheistic humanism that sees man as the creator of his own moral values in the absence of a meaningful, theologically orientated body of absolute moral law. Implicit in this concept of personal morality is the importance attached to a highly developed sense of personal responsibility, an idea that is central to Simone de Beauvoir's novels. Her novels dramatize her ethical theories and complement her philosophical essays. In this respect her work is similar to that of Sartre and Albert Camus.

See also EXISTENTIALISM.

BEAUX, bō, **Cecilia** (1863–1942), American portrait painter. She was born in Philadelphia, where she studied with William Sartain. She later studied at the Académie Julian and the Lazar School in Paris.

Highly regarded by her contemporaries, her paintings have been compared with those of John Singer Sargent. Her most outstanding works were portraits of women and children, including *Mother and Daughter, A New England Woman, Girl with the Cat, Portrait of Mrs. Dupont,* and *Sita and Sarita.* She also painted portraits of such notable personages as Theodore Roosevelt and Georges Clemenceau. In 1926 she won the Gold Medal of the American Academy of Arts and Letters. Her many other awards included the Gold Medal of the Philadelphia Art Club, the National Academy of Design Dodge Prize, the Carnegie Institute gold and bronze medals, and the Temple Gold Medal of the Pennsylvania Academy of Fine Arts. Her paintings are exhibited at the Metropolitan Museum of Art, New York City; the Corcoran Gallery, Washington, D.C.; the Uffizi Gallery, Florence, Italy; and the Luxembourg Palace, Paris.

Her autobiography, *Background with Figures,* was published in 1930. She died at Gloucester, Mass., on Sept. 17, 1942.

BEAUX-ARTS, L'Académie des. See INSTITUT DE FRANCE.

BEAUX' STRATAGEM, bōz' strat'ə-jəm, the last and best-known comedy by George Farquhar, produced in 1707. The play has an atmosphere of reality and genuine merriment that sets it apart from the typical comedy of manners of the time.

Two impoverished gentlemen-adventurers, Aimwell and Archer, impersonate Aimwell's wealthy older brother and his servant as part of a plan to rehabilitate their fortunes. The plot is involved, but the play ends, fortunately for Aimwell, with the death of the elder brother and the accession of Aimwell to his title and fortune. Lady Bountiful, whose name has become a synonym for a charitable woman, and the butler Scrub, who is the go-between for the various sets of lovers, are the play's best-delineated characters.

BEAVEN, bē'vən, **Robert** (1836–1920), Canadian political leader. He was born at Leigh, Staffordshire, England, on Jan. 28, 1836, and moved to Canada with his parents in 1843. He was educated at the College of Upper Canada, Toronto, and in 1858 moved to the territory of British Columbia. After British Columbia joined the Dominion in 1871, he represented the capital city of Victoria in the provincial legislature from 1871 to 1894.

Beaven was provincial minister of finance and agriculture from 1878 to 1882, and prime minister of the province in 1882–1883. He led the Conservative opposition from 1883 to 1894, and was mayor of Victoria in 1892, 1893, and 1896. After failing to form a ministry in 1898, he retired from politics. He died at Victoria, B.C., on Sept. 19, 1920.

BEAVER, bē'vər, a residential borough in western Pennsylvania, is the seat of Beaver County. It is situated on the Ohio River in an industrial region, and is 35 miles (56 km) northwest of Pittsburgh. Fort McIntosh, the first U.S. military post north of the Ohio River, was erected here in 1778 as a base for operations against the British and their Indian allies. The town was laid out in lots in 1792 and was incorporated in 1802. Population: 6,100.

KARL H. MASLOWSKI, FROM NATIONAL AUDUBON SOCIETY

Beaver (*Castor canadensis*)

BEAVER, a large aquatic rodent of the Northern Hemisphere. Beavers are recognized by their adaptation to an aquatic life. They have large, fully webbed hind feet, which are used for swimming, and an extraordinary tail, which is very broad and covered with scaly skin. The fur, usually brownish, is exceedingly close and fine, and when freed from the long hairs that are scattered through it and overlie the undercoat, forms one of the most valuable commercial furs. A large beaver is about 2.5 feet (76 cm) in length from the base of the tail to the end of the nose, with a tail about 1.5 feet (45.7 cm) long. It weighs 60 to 70 pounds (27 to 31 kg). Its flesh is edible.

Originally beavers were widespread throughout Europe and northern Asia, but they became extinct in the British Isles in the 12th century. In continental Europe they remain only in a few of the wilder streams of Norway, Poland, and Russia, and in some of the tributaries of the Rhône and the Elbe, where they are protected. In some cases, colonies of captives have reestablished themselves under protection. The beaver still exists in Siberia and Mongolia.

When North America was first entered by Europeans, the beaver inhabited almost all the woodland streams of the continent, from the Arctic Circle down to northern Mexico. Its temperament and manner of life made it an easy prey and prevented it from adapting itself to changed conditions. It rapidly disappeared, therefore, wherever civilization progressed or trapping was carried on systematically. Beavers now are rarely found south of the rivers that flow into Hudson Bay, except in the Rocky Mountains, Sierra Nevada, and Coast Ranges, and in a few remote and scattered places, like the forests of Maine and the Lake Superior region, where they are more or less protected by law. A few survive, nevertheless, in the wilder ranges of the southern Appalachians and along the borders of Mexico. In some places, chiefly in the northeastern United States, the beaver has been reintroduced for its value in water conservation.

Reproduction. The beaver, especially the female, is generally monogamous. Mating occurs in January and February of the second mating season after birth. A pungent secretion, called castoreum, found in glandular pouches of the abdomen, is thought to attract the sexes to each other. The litter, normally of two to four, is born in April or May. The young remain with the family until maturity is reached in two or three years.

Natural History. The beaver's main food is the bark of hardwood trees, such as maple, linden, birch, and poplar. The animals never eat the bark of coniferous trees, and thus are not found living in forests composed entirely of conifers or in a treeless country. They are gregarious and dwell in colonies, which in favorable circumstances may persist for centuries.

The colonies are usually along a sluggish stream in the woods, preferably where the ground is low and level. There the beavers dig a burrow in the bank with an entrance below the surface of the water and a tunnel leading upward into the earth above the high water level. This part of the stream bank is enlarged into a chamber with a bedding of grass or leaves.

In order to maintain a supply of water that will hide the entrance of the burrow and allow for food storage, the beavers build a dam

BEAVER LODGES are shelters made of mud and sticks. They may reach 6 feet in height and 40 feet in diameter.

LEONARD LEE RUE, FROM NATIONAL AUDUBON SOCIETY

BEAVERS can fell trees of as much as eighteen inches in diameter by gnawing with their sharp lower teeth.

ALLAN D. CRUICKSHANK, FROM NATIONAL AUDUBON SOCIETY

across the stream at a place below their settlement. They choose a place in the stream where the water is not more than 2½ feet (76 cm) deep and the bottom is firm. Beginning in the center of the channel, they place a number of long sticks parallel to the current and hold them down by piling mud and stones on them. Then extensions are built to each shore.

The poles used in building the dam are cut with the beavers' very large and strong front teeth. Their teeth are faced with a hard yellow enamel; the back part of the teeth, however, is made of a softer material, which wears away more rapidly with use. This wear leaves the tooth with a sharp, chisel-like edge. The beavers gnaw around the stem of a tree until it falls; they are able to cut down trees as much as 42 inches (107 cm) in diameter.

As the beavers increase in number, and the young ones grow up, they settle in the immediate neighborhood, and after a few years a considerable colony may arise. During all this time, work progresses on the dam, each beaver gathering driftwood, branches, logs, stones, mud, pieces of sod, and anything else available, and working it into the structure of the dam. The result is a tangled heap, having a long slope and a comparatively tight surface on the upper side, which may hold back a large pond, but has many channels running through it.

Meanwhile each family of beavers has erected a conical house or lodge for itself on the bank of the pond or on some islet adjacent to one of the channels. The interior of the house may be a room six or seven feet (1.8 to 2.1 meters) wide. It has no opening to the outside air, but is entered from beneath the water by two channels, one of which is the usual entrance, while the other forms a means of escape in case of attack by a mink or other aquatic predator. These houses are even more solidly constructed than is the dam, and when frozen in winter are so strong that nothing less than a bear is able to break into them. The houses are largest and strongest in cold northern regions.

During the summer beavers go ashore and feed on the roots and stems of aquatic plants, and obtain bark for food, some of which is stored for the winter. They do this by felling large trees near the water's edge, cutting them up into portions they can handle, and placing them near their houses. In winter, they eat the bark; in spring, they use the sticks for continuing their work on the dam.

When the beavers exhaust the supply of nearby trees, they excavate canals that gradually are extended farther into the woods, enabling them to reach more fresh trees. In some of the swampy forests of the upper Mississippi valley these canals have been known to extend several hundred feet, and in such places colonies of beavers have existed for more than 200 years. Channels are kept free from weeds and at a proper depth, for the most important function of the dam is to maintain the proper level of water in the canals. Beaver dams are valuable for maintaining a steady supply of water during dry summers to localities below the dam, as well as for holding back spring floods.

The American beaver seems to have carried its architectural work to a higher degree of perfection than the European beaver usually does. There are few records of such elaborate structures having been made in central Europe, and

the beavers now inhabiting the streams of Germany and France make few attempts at either dams or houses, but usually live in bank burrows. Beavers thrive in confinement, and colonies exist in the zoological gardens of several large cities.

Beavers (*Castor fiber*) are the sole living representatives of the family Castoridae. Most naturalists, however, maintain that the American beaver is specifically different from that of the Old World and therefore is entitled to its specific name of *Castor canadensis*.

Fossil beavers have been found far back into the Tertiary period (the past 70 million years). Small-sized species with some distinctive peculiarities occur in rocks of the Oligocene epoch (40 to 32 million years ago) in the western United States. A huge beaver (*Trogonotherium*) lived in Eurasia in the Pliocene and Pleistocene epochs (the past 10 million years) and an even larger form (*Castoroides*) occurred in the Pleistocene of North America.

KARL F. KOOPMAN
American Museum of Natural History

Bibliography
Morgan, Lewis H., *The American Beaver and His Works* (Philadelphia 1868).
Rounds, Glen, *Beaver Business: An Almanac* (Englewood Cliffs, N.J., 1960).
Rue, Leonard L., III, *World of the Beaver* (Philadelphia 1964).
Vevers, Geoffrey M., *The Life Story of the Beaver* (New York 1946).
Warren, Edward R., *The Beaver, Its Work and Its Ways* (Baltimore 1927).

BEAVER DAM, bē′vər, an industrial and commercial city in southeastern Wisconsin, in Dodge County. It is situated on Beaver Dam Creek, at the outlet of Beaver Dam Lake, 40 miles (64 km) northeast of Madison. The city is a trading center for an agricultural and dairying district. Its principal industries are the canning of peas, corn, and beans and the manufacture of stoves, shoes, cement blocks, metal products, and cheese. Places of interest include the county historical museum and Wayland Academy. The town was settled in 1841 and incorporated as a city in 1856. It took its name from dams built by beavers in the vicinity. Government is by mayor and council. Population: 14,265.

BEAVER FALLS, bē′vər, is an industrial city in western Pennsylvania, in Beaver County, 30 miles (48 km) northwest of Pittsburgh. It is situated on the Beaver River, 4 miles (6 km) from its junction with the Ohio River. The surrounding area produces coal, natural gas, oil, limestone, clay, silica, and building stone. It is an important steel center and is known as the home of the cold-drawn steel industry. Its manufactures include steel castings, miscellaneous metal products, clay refractories, vitreous china, mineral wool, and plastics. Beaver Falls is the seat of Geneva College, a coeducational institution. The site of Beaver Falls was purchased in 1792 by General Daniel Brodhead, and in 1806 the town was platted. In 1859 the Harmony Society, a communal group, purchased nearly the entire site at a sheriff's sale for $34,500. Additional land was added later. Originally called Brighton, after a city in England, the community was later renamed for the falls in the Beaver River. Beaver Falls was incorporated as a borough in 1868 and received a city charter in 1930. Government is by mayor and council. Population: 14,375.

BEAVER ISLAND, in Michigan, is the largest island of the Beaver Archipelago in northern Lake Michigan. It is 13 miles (21 km) long and 3 to 6 miles (4.8 to 9.7 km) wide. It is situated in Charlevoix County and is connected by air and ferry service with Charlevoix on the mainland, 25 miles (40 km) away. Fishing and hunting make the island a popular resort, but the permanent population is very small. St. James (population, 34), at the northern tip of the island, is the only village in the archipelago.

From 1847 to 1856 the island was the site of a Mormon colony founded by James Jesse Strang. Crowned king in 1850, Strang reigned supreme in both spiritual and temporal affairs until his assassination by rebellious followers. Throughout its existence the colony had been a source of antagonism to neighboring non-Mormons. After Strang's death, an expedition of mainlanders dispersed the population. Some 2,600 Mormons were expelled from Michigan.

BEAVERBROOK, bĕ′vər-brŏok, **1st Baron** (1879–1964), British financier, newspaper proprietor, and cabinet minister. He was born *William Maxwell Aitken,* in Maple, Ontario, Canada, on May 25, 1879. He grew up in Newcastle, New Brunswick; and went to work at 16, engaging in investment banking at Halifax, Nova Scotia. He became a multimillionaire before he was 30.

In 1907, Aitken married Gladys Drury, a member of a prominent Nova Scotia family. In 1910 they moved to London, and in the same year he was elected to Parliament as a Conservative from Ashton-under-Lyne. He attached himself to another Canadian, Andrew Bonar Law, and was largely instrumental in engineering Bonar Law's rise to Tory leadership in 1911.

World War I gave Aitken's talents as political manipulator fullest scope. In intervals between assignments as a war correspondent in France, he played a large role in arranging David Lloyd George's accession to the British prime ministry in 1916. Aitken was raised to the peerage as Lord Beaverbrook in 1917 and joined the cabinet as minister of information in 1918.

During the war, probably in 1916, Beaverbrook had acquired control of the London *Daily Express.* In 1918 he founded the *Sunday Express* and in 1923 acquired the London *Evening Standard.* Although he was a tireless propagandist, he anchored his papers to entertainment value.

In the interwar years, Beaverbrook's two principal press campaigns were his "Empire free trade crusade," in which he ran renegade Conservatives for Parliament against official Conservatives, and his championship of Edward VIII in the abdication crisis of 1936. In both efforts he was defeated by Stanley Baldwin, the Conservative premier. The Beaverbrook papers' influence waned, but their circulation expanded. By 1936 the *Express* could claim the "world's largest daily net sale." Circulation reached 3 million in 1940 and 4 million in 1950.

As World War II approached Beaverbrook's press continued to assert, "There will be no war," but when Winston Churchill came to power in 1940 he called Beaverbrook to office as minister of aircraft production. Beaverbrook's courage and unorthodoxy worked miracles and provided the planes that won the Battle of Britain. As minister of supply in 1941–1942, he visited Washington and Moscow, coordinating Allied production. In February 1942 cabinet

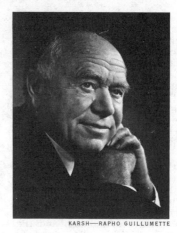

Lord Beaverbrook

(1879–1964)

KARSH—RAPHO GUILLUMETTE

tensions created by his capriciousness led to his resignation. Back in office from 1943 to 1945 as lord privy seal, he acted as troubleshooter and odd-job man for Churchill. The unsuccessful Conservative election tactics in 1945 seem to have been largely inspired by Beaverbrook.

Beaverbrook's political career ended there. He remained in active control of his newspapers, however, and was a keen if mercurial political propagandist to the end. In his last years he was a benefactor and chancellor of the University of New Brunswick. His first wife died in 1927; in 1963 he married Marcia Dunn, the widow of Sir James Dunn. Beaverbrook died in Surrey on June 9, 1964.

Beaverbrook wrote several books on politics and personalities, including *Success* (1921), *Politicians and the Press* (1926), *Politicians and the War* (1928), *Men and Power, 1917–1921* (1956), *The Decline and Fall of Lloyd George* (1963), and *The Abdication of King Edward VIII* (published in 1966, after his death).

H.G. NICHOLAS, *Oxford University*

Further Reading: Wood, Alan, *The True History of Lord Beaverbrook* (London 1965).

BEAVERTON is a city in northwestern Oregon, in Washington County. It is primarily a residential suburb of Portland, which is 6 miles (10 km) to the northeast. The manufacture of oscilloscopes is one of the city's light industries. Beaverton was founded in 1868 and incorporated in 1898. Government is by council-manager. Population: 18,577.

BEAZLEY, bēz′lē, **Sir Charles Raymond** (1868–1955), English historian and geographer. He was born at Blackheath, England on April 3, 1868. After graduating from Oxford in 1889, he studied and taught history and geography there and at the University of Birmingham. His history of medieval travels and geography, *The Dawn of Modern Geography* (3 vols., 1897–1906), remains one of the most readable and reliable studies in its field. It provides extensive treatment of Viking expeditions to North America.

Beazley is also the author of *James of Aragon* (1890); *Henry the Navigator* (1895); *John and Sebastian Cabot* (1898); *Elizabethan Seamen* (1907); *Notebook of Mediaeval History* (1917); *Nineteenth Century Europe* (1922); and *The Road to Ruin in Europe* (1932). He was knighted in 1931. He died at Birmingham, England, on Feb. 1, 1955.

BEBEL, bä′bəl, **August** (1840–1913), German socialist leader. He was born in Deutz, near Cologne, on Feb. 22, 1840. The son of a Prussian noncommissioned officer, Bebel was orphaned at an early age and grew up in poverty. After minimal formal schooling, he was apprenticed to a wood turner. His travels as a journeyman took him to Leipzig, at that time the center of the German workers' movement. There in 1861 he joined the Arbeiterverein, whose purpose was to bring education to the working class.

His views on political matters assumed their final form after Wilhelm Liebknecht introduced him to Marxism in 1864. In 1869 in Eisenach he helped found the German Social Democratic party (SPD), and his belief in the efficacy of the trades union movement in advancing the aims of Marxist socialism became the theoretical basis of the party.

Until his death Bebel remained his party's unchallenged leader. His contribution to German socialism before World War I was immense. After Bismarck's Anti-Socialist Laws had sent the party into exile (1878–1890), Bebel kept its ranks organized and increased its membership. When the party was again allowed to operate it became the strongest in Germany, and only the discriminatory electoral system kept it from being the strongest in the Reichstag (parliament).

In the Reichstag, to which he belonged almost continuously from 1871 until his death, Bebel was one of the sharpest critics of Bismarck's policies. He was a superb and impassioned speaker, and his writings exerted far-reaching influence. The very popular *Die Frau und der Sozialismus* (1883; *Women and Socialism*) grew out of his concern for women's emancipation, of which he was an early proponent.

Influence on His Party. Always a firm believer in the Marxist principle of class war, Bebel was convinced of the historical inevitability of socialism. Like Engels, he thought that socialism would soon inherit the earth and that the date for this event could be determined with mathematical exactitude. So under his guidance the SPD confined itself to parliamentary opposition and refused to collaborate in the conduct of government. The party preferred to distance itself from bourgeois parties and await the socialist revolution.

In historical perspective, Bebel's career is both paradoxical and tragic. It is paradoxical because, although Bebel insisted on the party's quiescence in anticipation of the appointed hour of its historical mission, his revolutionary rhetoric produced in the minds of the conservative classes the impression that the SPD was a fiery and irresponsible band of adventurers that must be opposed forcefully. The consequences of this misinterpretation of the SPD are still felt today. The tragedy of his career is that, in insisting that the party maintain its distance from government affairs, Bebel made it impossible for his constituents, a large bloc of society, to identify themselves with the life of the nation. Moreover, the SPD's refusal to involve itself in the administration of government left it without any practical political experience when it acceded to power in 1918.

Bebel died in Passug, Switzerland, on Aug. 13, 1913. His autobiography is titled *Aus meinem Leben* (3 vols., 1910–14; abridged Eng. tr., *My Life,* 1912).

C.M. KIMMICH, *Columbia University*

BEC, bek, is a Benedictine abbey at Bec-Hellouin in Normandy, France. Founded by Hellouin in 1034, the abbey gained eminence under two great priors, Anselm and his successor Lanfranc. Both, while at Bec, wrote works championing the orthodox position on theological controversies of the 11th century. During the 12th century Bec became famous throughout Europe because of the scholars who were trained there, including the future Pope Alexander II.

The abbey was sacked by the English during the Hundred Years' War, rebuilt, sacked again by the Calvinists in 1563, and again rebuilt. It fell into ruins after the French Revolution, but was restored after World War II. See also ANSELM, SAINT; LANFRANC.

BECCAFICO, bek-a-fē′kō, a small olive-brown garden warbler (*Sylvia hortensis*), called in England "petty-chaps." It has the habit of pecking holes in the rind of ripening figs and other fruits in search of small insects, hence its name (Italian for "fig pecker"). The damage done to the fruit is very slight.

These birds were eaten with much delight by the ancient Romans, and are still in high favor on Greek, French, and Italian tables, especially in Venice. An annual feast made on beccaficos is called the Beccaficata. The name "beccafico" is also used in continental Europe, rather indiscriminately, for different kinds of sylvan warblers when fat and in condition for the table.

BECCAFUMI, bäk-kä-fōō′mē, **Domenico** (1486–1551), Italian painter. He was born *Domenico di Pace,* near Siena. While working as a shepherd boy, he amused himself by drawing figures in the sand. He attracted the attention of a wealthy man, who discerned his genius and sent him to Siena to study drawing. He took the name "Beccafumi" from this benefactor. He is also known as *Il Mecherino.*

In Siena, Beccafumi saw, admired, and tried to imitate the paintings of Perugino, but having heard much of Raphael and Michelangelo, he obtained money from his patron to travel to Rome. After studying the masterpieces in the Vatican, he returned to Siena and enriched its buildings with many frescoes. He drew and colored well, possessed strong inventive powers, was thoroughly acquainted with perspective, and excelled in foreshortening. However, he was not free from mannerism, and his heads are, in general, deficient in both dignity and beauty. His paintings include *St. Catherine Receiving the Stigmata; Madonna and Child;* and *Marriage of St. Catherine.* Beccafumi died at Siena, where he was buried in the cathedral.

BECCARIA, bäk-kä-rē′ä, **Cesare** (1738–1794), Italian philosopher, criminologist, and economist, whose pioneering analysis of penal laws stimulated major changes in European criminal codes. The son of the Marchese Beccaria Bonesana, he was born in Milan on March 15, 1738, and inherited his father's title.

Beccaria studied jurisprudence at the university in Pavia. He was greatly influenced by the social theories of Jean Jacques Rousseau, and he sought to apply them to contemporary social and philosophical problems. In 1764 he published *Dei delitti e delle pene* (*Essay on Crimes and Punishments*). In this work, Beccaria advocated the abolition of torture and the death penalty, preventive rather than punitive justice, and public rather than secret prosecution. He advanced a program of universal education to inform the public about legal penalties for crimes—knowledge he believed would deter criminals. The impact of his treatise was reflected in the works of reformers in Italy, England, and Austria. Beccaria's thinking influenced the drafting of the French civil code and the Russian court reform of 1864, and many modern penal codes have their origin in his work.

Although he is regarded chiefly as an outstanding criminologist, Beccaria was also a noted economist. In 1768 he was appointed professor of political economy at the university in Milan. In his lectures he espoused a liberal economics that in some measure anticipated Adam Smith's *Wealth of Nations* (1776), and he advocated a theory of the relation between production and population that was similar to and in advance of Thomas Malthus' political economics. His lectures were published posthumously as *Elementi di economia pubblica* (1804). Many of Beccaria's ideas were developed in *Il Caffè*, a periodical he helped found and edit.

Beccaria was known for his philosophical grammar and theory of style, *Ricerche intorno alla natura dello stile* (1770). He was also a magistrate and a counselor of state. He died in Milan on Nov. 28, 1794.

BÊCHE-DE-MER. See TREPANG.

BECHER, bĕkH′ər, **Johann Joachim** (1635–1682), German physician, chemist, and economist, He was born in Speyer, Germany, on May 6, 1635. After serving as professor of medicine and court physician at Mainz from 1660 to 1666, Becher became a leading economic adviser to Emperor Leopold I in Vienna. He advocated strong government regulation of trade, production, and finance and the building of a Rhine-Danube canal to open trade with the Low Countries. He also tried to transmute the sands of the Danube into gold. Later, in England, where he fled after losing favor in Vienna, he wrote a number of works on chemistry.

In *Physica subterranea* (1669), an attempt to relate physics and chemistry, Becher proposed the idea that inorganic bodies are composed of three constituents: the vitrifiable, or glassy; the volatile, or combustible; and the mercurial, or fiery. This theory was developed further by his pupil Georg Ernst Stahl, who went on to explain combustion by the phlogiston theory (q.v.). Becher is believed to have died in London in October 1682.

BECHET, be-shā′, **Sidney** (?1897–1959), American jazz musician. He was born at New Orleans, La., on May 14, probably in 1897. One of the first jazz musicians to use the soprano saxophone as his primary instrument, Bechet, a Negro, developed an individual style marked by a soaring intensity. In 1928 he joined Noble Sissle's band in France. Following his popular jazz recording of *Summertime* (1938), he appeared frequently as the leader of small jazz groups in night clubs and at concerts in the United States. In 1946 he appeared on Broadway in *Hear That Trumpet*.

About 1950, Bechet settled permanently in France, where he died, at Garches, on May 14, 1959. His autobiography, *Treat It Gentle*, was published posthumously in 1960.

BECHSTEIN, bĕkH′shtīn, **Carl** (1826–1900), German piano manufacturer. He was born at Gotha on June 1, 1826. His full name was *Friedrich Wilhelm Carl Bechstein*. After serving his apprenticeship in piano factories in Berlin, Paris, and London, he opened his own shop in Berlin in 1853. The firm prospered and opened branches in Paris, St. Petersburg, and London. A year after Bechstein's death in Berlin on March 6, 1900, the company opened a concert hall (later Wigmore Hall) in London. The firm's foreign branches were closed during World War I. The London branch reopened in 1924 and in 1931 became the firm of Bechstein Piano Co., Ltd.

BECHUANALAND, bech-wän′ə-land, was a British territory in southern Africa. It achieved independence in 1966. See BOTSWANA.

BECK, bek, **Sir Adam** (1857–1925), Canadian public official. He was born in Baden, Ontario, on June 20, 1857. He represented London, Ontario, as a Conservative in the Legislative Assembly of the province (1902–1919, 1923–1925) and served without portfolio in the provincial ministry (1905–1914, 1923–1925). Beck introduced legislation for the establishment of the Hydro-Electric Power Commission of Ontario. As chairman of the commission from its inception in 1906 until his death, he played a major part in the development of Niagara Falls as a source of power. He was knighted in 1914 and died in London, Ontario, on Aug. 15, 1925.

BECK, bek, **David** (1894–　　　), American labor leader, who was president of the Teamsters Union from 1952 to 1957. He was born in Stockton, Calif., on June 16, 1894. Beck was long the leading U.S. exponent of "business unionism"—the idea that unions are simply another form of business. He was the most prominent labor leader to support Dwight D. Eisenhower's election campaigns, and he was a regent of the University of Washington. However, in 1957 a U.S. Senate committee, with Senator John L. McClellan as chairman, contended that Beck had misappropriated hundreds of thousands of dollars of union funds and had accepted "loans" from an employer. The Teamsters were expelled from the AFL-CIO in 1957, and Beck was sentenced to prison in 1958 on charges of larceny.

HUGH G. CLELAND
State University of New York at Stony Brook

BECK, bek, **James Montgomery** (1861–1936), American public official. Born in Philadelphia, Pa., on July 9, 1861, he graduated from Moravian College, Bethlehem, Pa., in 1880. He was United States attorney for eastern Pennsylvania (1896–1900), assistant attorney general of the United States (1900–1903), and then a leading corporation lawyer in New York City. From the outset of World War I he was an outspoken supporter of the Allies; he was also a leading critic of President Wilson's war policies. Beck was U.S. solicitor general from 1921 to 1925. A conservative Republican, he was a congressman from Philadelphia from 1927 to 1934, when he resigned in opposition to the New Deal policies of Franklin D. Roosevelt. Beck's books include *The Evidence in the Case* (1914), an argument for the Allies in World War I, and *The Constitution of the United States* (1923). He died in Washington, D.C., on April 12, 1936.

BECK, bek, **Józef** (1894–1944), Polish statesman. He was born in Warsaw on Oct. 4, 1894.
At the outbreak of World War I he served as a
cavalry officer against the Allies. Later he transferred to the Polish Legion, organized by Józef
Piłsudski, which supported the Allies in the closing stages of the conflict. In 1922–1923, he was
Poland's military attaché at Paris.

After Piłsudski became dictator in 1926, Beck
became closely identified with his regime. Appointed minister of foreign affairs in 1932, he
succeeded in negotiating nonaggression pacts
with Germany and Russia and alliances with
France and Rumania. His refusal to yield Danzig to Germany in 1939 was one excuse Hitler
used for the Nazi invasion of Poland. When
Germany and Russia overran Poland, he fled to
Rumania, dying near Bucharest on June 6, 1944.

BECKER, bek'ər, **Carl Lotus** (1873–1945), American historian. He was born in Lincoln Township, Iowa, on Sept. 7, 1873. He received
bachelor's and doctor's degrees from the University of Wisconsin in 1896 and 1907 and
taught at several universities, including Dartmouth and Kansas, before going to Cornell in
1917. There he taught for 28 years, until his
death in Ithaca, N.Y., on April 10, 1945.

At Wisconsin, Becker studied under Frederick Jackson Turner. At Columbia, where he
was a graduate fellow in 1898–1899, James
Harvey Robinson and Charles A. Beard were his
chief mentors. They emphasized the development of ideas, and Beard and Becker became
the leaders of the relativist school of historians
in the United States.

Becker had a superior literary gift. The
American and French Revolutions had a powerful hold on his imagination. Two of his most
important books were *The Declaration of Independence* (1922) and *The Heavenly City of
the Eighteenth Century Philosophers* (1932).
His textbook *Modern History* (1931) was widely
used in American schools. In his books he defended the liberal tradition of Western civilization against antidemocratic theories.

MICHAEL KRAUS, *The City College, New York*

Further Reading: Smith, Charlotte Watkins, *Carl
Becker: On History and the Climate of Opinion* (Ithaca,
N.Y., 1956).

BECKER, bek'ər, **John Joseph** (1886–1961),
American composer. He was born at Henderson,
Ky., on Jan. 22, 1886. He studied music under
Wilhelm Middelschulte and Alexander von
Fielitz and graduated from the Wisconsin Conservatory of Music in Milwaukee. Becker spent
much of his life teaching in midwestern universities and colleges, including Notre Dame. He
also served as associate editor for the publication *New Music* and contributed widely to other
music periodicals. He died at Wilmette, Ill., on
Jan. 21, 1961.

Becker's compositions were written in a struc-
turally bold, ultramodern manner, employing
highly complex harmonic and contrapuntal
schemes. Stylistically his works are often classified with those of Charles Ives, Carl Ruggles,
and Wallingford Riegger; but they are seldom
played today. Becker's numerous compositions
include seven symphonies; several concertos;
mixed works for chorus, orchestra, and soloists;
overtures; ballets; incidental music for stage performances; and solos for piano and organ.

BECKET, bek'ət, **Saint Thomas à** (1118?–1170),
English prelate and martyr. In 1162, Henry II
of England gave the post of archbishop of Canterbury to his friend and chancellor Thomas à
Becket. The king expected him to help subordinate the power of the church to the throne. Instead, Becket steadfastly defended ecclesiastical
privileges. The antagonism between these two
strong-willed men intensified, until Becket was
murdered by royal courtiers in 1170. He was
canonized two years later, and his shrine became
the most venerated in England. After eight centuries, the story of his martyrdom continues to
be retold in major works of literature.

Early Career. Contrary to a long-standing tradition, Becket was of Norman rather than Anglo-
Saxon descent. Born in London, the son of a
French-born merchant of that city, he was educated by the canons of Merton in Surrey and in
schools in London and Paris. By 1143, he had
been admitted to the service of Theobald, archbishop of Canterbury, who allowed him to study
canon law in Italy and France.

In 1152, Becket, acting as Theobald's agent,
secured the papal letters necessary to prevent the
English king, Stephen, from crowning his son
Eustace successor to the throne. This service
won the esteem not only of the archbishop, but
also of Henry of Anjou, who in 1154 became
Henry II, the first Plantagenet king of England.
In the same year, Theobald made Becket archdeacon of Canterbury, and in 1155 the king appointed him high chancellor and preceptor to
his young son, Prince Henry.

Chancellor. Becket at this time acted the complete courtier, conforming in most respects to
the whim of the king. As Henry's closest companion, he held splendid receptions and courted
popular applause. In 1158 he visited Paris to negotiate a marriage between Prince Henry and the
eldest daughter of King Louis VII of France.
The opulence of his manner, dress, and entourage
greatly impressed the French, and he returned
to England with the young princess in hand. In
1159 he accompanied King Henry on a campaign
against Toulouse, leading a large body of knights
into battle and defeating a well-known French
knight in single combat.

He had been chancellor for about six years
when his patron, Theobald, died in 1161. Becket,
busy in France, returned in May 1162 with
Prince Henry, whose right to succeed to the English throne had been recognized by the great
barons through Becket's efforts. King Henry
then made the mistake of raising his friend to
the vacant primacy on the assumption that Becket
would support him in curtailing church power.
Becket is said to have accepted his promotion as
archbishop of Canterbury with reluctance and to
have foreseen a change in the king's attitude
toward him, from love to hatred.

Archbishop. Becket was consecrated archbishop
in June 1162. Immediately, he assumed an
austerity of conduct appropriate to the course he
chose to follow.

In May 1163 he attended a general council at
Tours called by Pope Alexander III. There,
Becket formally charged that the laity had in-
fringed on the rights and immunities of the
church. On his return to England, he also acted
in the spirit of this complaint by prosecuting
and excommunicating several nobles and others
who held lands claimed by the church. At a
council in July 1163, he successfully opposed

the king on a point regarding taxation—the first case of this kind recorded in England.

Henry, an able and politic monarch, desired to abolish certain privileges of the clergy that exempted them from the jurisdiction of the civil courts, and to institute a measure of royal control over the decisions of ecclesiastical courts. After arguing violently against these measures, Becket acquiesced (December 1163). The king then summoned a convocation or parliament at Clarendon in January 1164, to embody his proposals in documents bearing the seal of the archbishop. Becket was induced to give his verbal assent. After the celebrated documents known as the Constitutions of Clarendon had been drawn up, however, he refused to affix his signature on the ground that they violated canon law. See CLARENDON, CONSTITUTIONS OF.

Exile. Finding himself now very much in the king's disfavor, Becket attempted twice to leave England but was twice intercepted. Henry undertook, without success, to bend the archbishop to his will by supporting several suits against him. One suit claimed money lent to Becket during his chancellorship, and another claimed the proceeds of benefices that he had held vacant while chancellor. Continuing his refusal to submit to the king, Becket was nearly condemned as a traitor by Henry's council. He was saved because certain bishops hostile to him wanted to secure his prior dismissal by the pope.

In this desperate situation, Becket made his escape to Flanders (November 1164), met the pope at Sens in France, and offered to resign the archbishopric. The offer was refused, and Becket took up residence at the Cistercian abbey of Pontigny in Burgundy. From there he sent (1166) expostulatory letters to the king, excommunicating seven of his councilors and threatening to excommunicate the king as well. Henry was so exasperated that he obliged the Cistercians to send Becket away from the abbey. On the recommendation of King Louis, Becket moved to the abbey of Ste. Colombe at Sens, where he spent another four years in exile.

By the end of 1169 negotiations for a reconciliation between Henry and Becket were well advanced, but they soon received a setback. At the insistence of the king, Prince Henry was crowned (June 14, 1170) as his successor by Roger, archbishop of York. Such coronations had been the prerogative of the archbishop of Canterbury. Incensed, the pope proceeded to suspend York and the other bishops participating in the coronation.

In spite of this, an understanding was reached by King Henry and Becket in the fall of 1170. Becket, now supposedly restored to his see with all of its former privileges, returned to England and made a triumphal entry into Canterbury in early December. He was met, however, by officers of the king, who demanded immediate absolution of the suspended bishops. Becket refused, arguing that the pope alone had the authority to absolve the bishops. The clerics immediately appealed to Henry, then in Normandy. The king is said to have uttered a bitter complaint that none of his followers would rid him of an insolent prelate who caused him perpetual vexation.

Martyrdom. Shortly after the bishops' appeal, four of the king's barons, Reginald Fitzurse, William de Tracy, Hugh de Morville, and Richard le Breton, whose motives are still conjectural, went to Canterbury, where, on Dec. 29, 1170, they formally commanded the archbishop to restore the suspended bishops. He again refused. On the evening of the same day, they placed soldiers in the courtyard and, armed with swords, entered the cathedral, where they found the archbishop at vespers. Advancing toward him, they threatened him with death if he continued to disobey the orders of Henry. Becket, according to most accounts, pronounced himself willing to die for the rights of his church and added the threat of a curse upon the barons if they should harm any of "his people." The confederates attempted to drag him from the church, but not being able to do so, killed him on the spot with repeated blows on the head from their swords. The site of the murder is thought to be the steps leading from the cathedral's nave to its choir.

The body was buried in the crypt on the following day, and the grave almost at once became a place of pilgrimage and a scene of reported miracles. As a penance, the assassins were forced to do 14 years' service in the Holy Land. Henry, though he denied ordering the murder and probably did not desire it, allowed himself to be scourged at the martyr's tomb in 1174.

Thomas à Becket was in his early fifties when he died; he was canonized on Feb. 21, 1173 (his feast day is December 29). A tall slender man of aristocratic bearing and vigorous intellect, he was a great favorite with the English commoners, whose desire for his elevation to sainthood may have been responsible for his canonization so soon after his death. In the reign of Henry III, his body was taken up and placed in a magnificent shrine erected by Archbishop Stephen Langton. The continued popularity of pilgrimages to St. Thomas' tomb some 200 years after his murder is attested to in Geoffrey Chaucer's *Canterbury Tales*.

In 1538, Henry VIII was involved in his own struggle with church authority and was particularly hostile to the continued veneration of Becket. The king had the shrine destroyed, and possibly he had the bones of the martyr burned. By royal command, the names of many churches and hospitals were also changed from St. Thomas the Martyr to St. Thomas the Apostle.

Becket and his martyrdom have been the subject of several notable plays—Tennyson's *Becket* (1879); T.S. Eliot's *Murder in the Cathedral* (1935) and Jean Anouilh's *Becket* (1960), both of which were also filmed; and Christopher Fry's *Curtmantle* (1961)—as well as many biographical novels.

Bibliography
Borenius, Tancred, *St. Thomas Becket in Art* (London 1932).
Brooke, Zachary N., *The English Church and the Papacy from the Conquest to the Reign of John* (New York 1931).
Compton, Piers, *Turbulent Priest* (Toronto 1957).
Dark, Sidney, *St. Thomas of Canterbury* (New York 1927).
Duggan, Alfred, *My Life for My Sheep* (New York 1955).
Garnier de Pont-Sainte-Maxence, *La vie de St. Thomas le martyr* (New York 1923).
Hutton, William H., *Thomas Becket* (London 1900).
Knowles, David, *Archbishop Thomas Becket* (New York 1949).
Knowles, David, *Episcopal Colleagues of Archbishop Thomas Becket* (New York 1951).
Morris, John, *The Life of St. Thomas Becket*, 2d ed. (London 1885).
Mydans, Shelley, *Thomas* (New York 1965).
Ross Williamson, Hugh, *Arrow and the Sword; an Essay in Detection*, 2d ed. (London 1955).
Speaight, Robert, *St. Thomas of Canterbury* (New York 1938).
Ward, Henry S., *The Canterbury Pilgrimages* (London 1904).

BECKET, bek'ət, **Welton David** (1902–1969), American architect, who designed the Music Center for the Performing Arts in the Los Angeles (Calif.) cultural center. He was born in Seattle, Wash., on Aug. 8, 1902. After graduating from the University of Washington with a B.A. in architecture in 1927, he studied for a year in France. In 1932 he became a partner in the architectural firm of Plummer, Wurdeman, and Becket, and in 1949 established his own company, Welton Becket and Associates. Becket became a member of the American Institute of Architects (AIA) in 1941 and a fellow of the AIA in 1952.

Becket designed a wide variety of structures, from simple retail stores to gigantic office buildings and employed almost every type of building material in them. He designed a hotel in Melbourne, Australia; a bank in São Paulo, Brazil; and the American embassy in Warsaw, Poland. Most of his work, however, is on the West Coast of the United States. His most notable structure is the Los Angeles Music Center for the Performing Arts, which opened in December 1964, the first of several planned buildings for the city's cultural center. In 1965 he received a contract to design the John F. Kennedy Civic, Cultural, and Educational Center, to be built at Mitchel Field, Long Island, N.Y. Becket died in Los Angeles on Jan. 17, 1969.

BECKETT, bek'it, **Samuel** (1906–   ), Irish writer. He was born in Dublin on April 13 (Good Friday), 1906. A novelist and playwright living in Paris and writing both in French and in English, Samuel Barclay Beckett gave the theater of the 1950's the unforgettable *Waiting for Godot.* In a long series of strange works, he spun fable after fable of persons trapped by perfectly logical, demoralizing absurdity.

Life. He studied modern languages at Trinity College, Dublin, graduating in 1927. He then spent two years (1928–1930) teaching English at the École Normale Supérieure in Paris. After returning to Trinity College for a year of graduate work in 1931, he taught French there in 1931–1932. He spent the next few years wandering in London and through France and Germany, contributing stories and poems to avant-garde periodicals, before settling in Paris in 1937.

Early in World War II, during the German occupation of France, the Gestapo discovered Beckett's activities in connection with the French resistance movement, and he was compelled to flee to the unoccupied zone about 1942. He found sanctuary at Roussillon in the Vaucluse department. After the war he returned to Paris and began writing in earnest. Although *Waiting for Godot* brought him international fame after 1952, as translations and productions of the play proliferated throughout the world, he continued to lead an utterly secluded life. He was awarded the 1969 Nobel Prize in literature.

Writings. Beckett's first novel, *Murphy* (1938), contains all the elements of his later work: the normal, busy world; someone who cannot come to terms with it; and a language whose low-keyed precision is disturbed by nothing it undertakes to describe, however grotesque or ridiculous. In Beckett's next novel, *Watt* (1942–1944), the language remains explicit though the situations become increasingly strange. In the trilogy *Molloy, Malone Dies,* and *The Unnameable* (1947–1949), the reader is plunged into the mysterious

world where Beckett appears most at home.

In Beckett's world, the reader is clearly told everything except the things he is used to knowing. Thus, in the play *Waiting for Godot,* which was written in 1948 and published in French in 1952 and in English in 1953, it is clear that two tramps are waiting for Godot, that they return to their rendezvous night after night, that they fill up time with games and dialogues, and that Godot may make an immense difference to their lives. But who Godot may be and what difference he will make is never indicated. Beckett denies that Godot is a symbol for God and that any general scheme of systematic meanings underlies the work. Its mysteriousness is the deliberate instrument of the play's disturbing power.

The play *Endgame* (1958), possibly Beckett's most remarkable single work, appears to be about the end of humanity. The novel *How It Is* (1964) presents a life shaped by mysterious encounters amid darkness and mud. Yet these bleak, enigmatic works are unsettlingly funny. Their precision of style and extravagance of conception are hallmarks of a first-class comic writer.

HUGH KENNER
Author of "Samuel Beckett, A Critical Study"

Further Reading: Fletcher, John, *The Novels of Samuel Beckett* (New York 1964); Kenner, Hugh, *Samuel Beckett, A Critical Study* (New York 1961); id., *Flaubert, Joyce and Beckett, the Stoic Comedians* (Boston 1963); Tindall, William York, *Samuel Beckett* (New York 1964).

BECKFORD, bek'fərd, **William** (1759–1844), English writer, whose most famous work is the wildly imaginative "Oriental" romance *Vathek.* Written in French when its author was in his early 20's, *Vathek* was first published anonymously, in an English translation, in 1786. Beckford also wrote *Modern Novel Writing, or The Elegant Enthusiast* (1796) and *Azemia* (1797), both of which are burlesques of the popular romantic novels of the period.

Beckford was born at Fonthill, Wiltshire, on Sept. 29, 1759. When he was 10 years old, he inherited a large fortune from his father, who had been lord mayor of London. While in his early twenties, Beckford traveled on the Continent. From his experiences abroad he wrote a number of unusual travel journals and letters that were published originally as *Dreams, Waking Thoughts, and Incidents* (1783) and were republished with omissions and additions as *Italy, with Sketches of Spain and Portugal* (1834). Although he had little interest in politics, Beckford was a member of the House of Commons from 1784 to 1794 and from 1806 to 1820.

In 1796, Beckford began to build a splendid edifice on his estate of Fonthill, where he gathered together his library and his collection of art. Having largely depleted his fortune by 1822, he sold Fonthill and settled at Bath, where he died on May 2, 1844.

BECKLEY, bek'lē, is an industrial city in West Virginia, 55 miles (88 km) southeast of Charleston. Situated in a coal mining region, it is surrounded by small mining communities, scenic recreation areas, and fertile valleys. Its manufactures include mining equipment, electronic devices, processed foods, and lumber. The city is the home of Beckley College. Beckley became the seat of Raleigh County in 1850, a decade after the community was founded. It has a mayor-council government. Population: 19,884.

BECKMANN, bek'män, **Max** (1884–1950), German expressionist painter. He was born in Leipzig, Germany, on Feb. 12, 1884. Like the earlier artists James Ensor and Edvard Munch, Beckmann painted penetrating and sometimes mysterious statements on the condition of man. Throughout his long career, he expressed psychological insight with increasing monumentality and symbolic invention. His work culminated in nine great triptychs, created in the last 18 years of his life.

Beckmann received a traditional education in art at the Weimar academy, which he attended from 1900 to 1903. After a year of study in Paris (1903–1904), he settled in Berlin, where he exhibited with the Berlin Secession group. In 1906 he married Minna Tube, a fellow art student from his Weimar days. In 1913, in Berlin, he exhibited a series of epic canvases, including the *Destruction of Messina* (1909) and the *Sinking of the Titanic* (1912). The German impressionist Lovis Corinth influenced Beckmann's early style. Beckmann also admired Rembrandt, Goya, Delacroix, and Munch.

Beckmann joined the German army medical corps when World War I began in 1914. In 1915, after serving in East Prussia and Flanders, he was discharged because of ill health and settled in Frankfurt.

The terrible experiences he suffered in World War I deeply affected his work. His style began to show the expressive distortion of medieval painting, as well as his own innovations in design. His paintings in the early 1920's were savage statements on the hopelessness of life. His drypoint etchings and lithographs reveal the same powerfully symbolic personal style that is found in his paintings.

In 1925, Beckmann divorced his first wife and married Mathilde von Kaulbach, called "Quappi." She appears in many of his later paintings. Also in 1925, Beckmann exhibited with the Neue Sachlichkeit (New Objectivity) group, and began teaching at the Frankfurt Art Academy.

Beckmann finished the first of his monumental triptychs in 1933, the year the Nazis came to power in Germany. After they dismissed him from his post at the Frankfurt academy, he moved to Berlin. In 1937, however, after ten of his works were included in a Nazi exhibition of "degenerate art," he went to the Netherlands.

His ten years in Amsterdam, from 1937 to 1947, were very productive in spite of the hardships he suffered during the German occupation of the Netherlands in World War II. French painting had begun to influence him about 1930, bringing fuller forms, richer colors, and an interest in purely formal subjects, such as still lifes and landscapes. Among Beckmann's most important works of the World War II period are *Odysseus and Calypso* (1943) and the triptychs *The Actors* (1942) and *Blindman's Buff* (1945).

In 1947 Beckmann and his wife emigrated to the United States. He taught at Washington University in St. Louis, Mo., until 1949, when he began teaching at the Brooklyn Museum in New York. He completed his triptych *The Argonauts* just before his death in New York City on Dec. 27, 1950.

PERRY T. RATHBONE, *Museum of Fine Arts, Boston*

Further Reading: Kaiser, Hanns, *Max Beckmann* (Berlin 1913); Rathbone, Perry T., ed., *Max Beckmann* (St. Louis 1948); Reifenberg, B., and Hausenstein, W., *Max Beckmann* (Munich 1949); Selz, Peter, *Max Beckmann* (New York 1964).

BECKNELL, bek'nəl, **William** (c. 1790–c. 1832), American explorer and trader, often called "the father of the Santa Fe Trail." Although probably born in Kentucky, he was living in Missouri when he established his reputation as a trader.

In 1821, Becknell was on a trading expedition near the border of New Mexico, which was then part of Mexico and, under Spanish rule, had been closed to American traders. Hearing that Mexico had just become independent, Becknell hastened to Santa Fe, the capital of New Mexico, with packhorses carrying goods to be sold. The financial success of this expedition encouraged him to organize another in 1822. This time he set out from Franklin, Mo., with three wagonloads of goods and 21 men. But instead of traveling to the upper waters of the Arkansas River and then south to Santa Fe, he took a shorter route through the Cimarron valley, where the party suffered severely from heat and thirst. Of his life after the successful conclusion of this trip, little is known.

The significance of the 1822 expedition to Santa Fe was twofold: it pioneered a route that was used by later traders in the lucrative Santa Fe trade; and it proved the feasibility of crossing the plains in wagons.

BECKWOURTH, bek'wûrth, **James Pierson,** (1798–1867?), American Negro frontiersman and Indian scout. He was born on April 26, 1798, in Virginia, but spent his adult life in the Far West. In the 1820's he was a member of expeditions led by the fur trader William H. Ashley. He lived with Crow Indians for a half-dozen years and later (1844) joined the forces of Stephen W. Kearny in California. After the Mexican War he lived in California, Missouri, and Colorado. Finally, after taking part in the Cheyenne War of 1864, he settled near Denver, where he died, possibly in 1867.

Beckwourth (or, sometimes, *Beckwith*) discovered the pass named for him in the Sierra Nevada of California. He is also credited with being a founder of Pueblo, Colo. His autobiography, *The Life and Adventures of James P. Beckwourth*, was edited by T. D. Bonner and published in 1856; it was reissued in 1931.

BÉCQUER, be'ker, **Gustavo Adolfo** (1836–1870), Spanish lyric poet. He was born in Seville on Feb. 17, 1836, the son of a well-known painter, José Domínguez Bécquer. When he was 10 years old, his father died, and he was left in the care of a guardian, who later deserted him. At the age of 18 he went to Madrid, where he earned a precarious living for 15 years as a free-lance journalist and a translator. For a short period, from 1864 to 1868, he worked as a government censor. He died in Madrid, on Dec. 22, 1870.

The main themes of Bécquer's poetry are the romantic ones of longing and frustration. His language is simple and restrained, characteristically transmitting emotion through understatement. Bécquer's outstanding works include the poems *Volverán las oscuras golondrinas, Cerraron sus ojos, Olas gigantes que os rompéis bramando,* and *Cuando me lo contaron sentí el frío;* and the volume of verse *Rimas* (1860). His popular prose tales, which show the influence of Poe and E.T.A. Hoffmann, were published as *Leyendas españolas* (1860–64). His collected works appeared in 1885 and an English translation of his stories and poems in 1936.

BECQUEREL, be-krel', **Antoine Henri** (1852–1908), French physicist, who discovered radioactivity in 1896. For this achievement he was awarded the 1903 Nobel Prize in physics jointly with Pierre and Marie Curie.

Experiments. Becquerel's discovery, which marks the beginning of modern nuclear physics, was stimulated by Wilhelm Roentgen's discovery of X-rays in November 1895. When Becquerel heard of Roentgen's discovery of X-rays, a penetrating radiation coming from a fluorescent spot on a cathode-ray tube, he thought that other materials might also emit such rays while fluorescing or phosphorescing. To test this idea, he wrapped a photographic plate in black paper to protect it from light, placed a crystal of phosphorescent material (which by chance contained some uranium) on the wrapped plate, and caused the crystal to phosphoresce by placing the wrapped plate and the crystal in sunlight. If this phosphorescing crystal emitted penetrating rays, they would pass through the paper and expose the plate. When developed, the plate would show a silhouette of the crystal. When such a silhouette appeared, Becquerel concluded that his hypothesis was confirmed and that the crystal had emitted X-rays as it phosphoresced.

Shortly thereafter, however, when a similar experiment was frustrated by cloudy weather, Becquerel returned a wrapped plate and a crystal to a dark drawer. However, because the phosphorescence of this type of crystal lasted no more than $\frac{1}{100}$ second after it was removed from light, Becquerel did not expect penetrating radiation from the crystal to affect this plate. Yet, rather than risk failure in case it had been exposed to diffuse light, he prepared a new plate when he continued his investigation. Then, for some reason, he developed the old plate along with the new one and, to his surprise, found silhouettes of great intensity on the old plate. This crystal had emitted its penetrating rays in the dark, so it was clear that this radiation was not connected with the phosphorescence of the crystal as he had assumed. Once this misconception was corrected, Becquerel was able to determine that the source of the penetrating radiation was the uranium in the crystal. It was later shown that the penetrating radiation discovered by Becquerel consists of alpha particles, beta particles, and gamma rays rather than X-rays. (See also ALPHA PARTICLES; BETA RAY; GAMMA RAY.)

Life. Becquerel was born in Paris on Dec. 15, 1852. He was the son of Alexandre Edmond Becquerel and grandson of Antoine César Becquerel, also physicists. He entered the École Polytechnique in 1872 and the École des Ponts et Chaussées in 1874. In 1875 he was appointed lecturer at the École Polytechnique. He became an assistant at the Musée d'Histoire Naturelle under his father in 1878 and later became professor of physics there in the chair previously held by his father and his grandfather. In 1888 he received the degree of doctor of science, and the following year he was admitted to the Académie des Sciences. He became a professor of physics at the École Polytechnique in 1895. He died at Le Croisic, Brittany, on Aug. 25, 1908.

Becquerel's research included studies of the absorption of light in crystals, the rotation of polarized light in a magnetic field, and phosphorescence.

See also RADIOACTIVITY.

ROBERT A. LUFBURROW, *St. Lawrence University*

BED, an article of furniture on or in which a person may rest or sleep. It originally developed as a luxury of the upper classes in ancient civilizations.

The Ancient World. In ancient Egypt, beds were used only by the more privileged classes. The common people slept on the ground with a wooden "pillow" of a type still used in many parts of the world. Among the treasures excavated from the tomb of Tutankhamen was a bed of carved ebony and chased gold, one of several Egyptian beds discovered in those excavations. All of them had foot panels, and some had "heads" that represented animals. The ruling classes of Assyria and Babylonia sometimes used beds of bronze studded with gems. Although the frequent references to beds in the Old Testament show that beds were common, the iron bed on which Og, king of Bashan, was supposed to have slept was clearly an object of wonder.

In Greece an early legend refers to the bed as "the ill-famed contrivance of Procrustes." Early Greek beds were of wood ("turned on a lathe" is an expression used by Homer to describe them), with thongs to support the body. Greek habits were simple in regard to beds, as in other respects, until the conquests of Alexander the Great led to an infusion of Persian luxury. In the time of Xenophon the Persian kings had been accustomed to increase the resilience of their soft beds by placing the feet of the bedsteads on carpets. Alexander usually held court while sitting on a golden couch.

Graeco-Roman custom made much of the couch. Even the heroes of Homer and the fathers of the Roman Republic, whose wooden beds were notably hard and austere, reclined on couches for meals. Beds were of various types, from the built-in shelf of the poorer Romans to the multiple beds (made for as many as six persons) that were used at luxurious banquets in the time of the emperors. Materials varied from wood or masonry to precious metal. Separate rooms for married couples were customarily found in upper-class Roman households—a practice not revived until modern times—although the double bed (lectus genialis) also was found in Roman homes.

The Middle Ages. With the breakdown of the Roman empire, the bed, as known to the ancients, practically disappeared. It was at about the time of Charlemagne (742?–814) that the bed returned, together with many other comforts of the ancient world. Throughout the Middle Ages in Europe, beds were used only in the houses of the aristocracy and the rising middle class—a condition that still exists in some Asian countries.

Early medieval art shows beds that rise steeply from the foot to the head. They were built into the thickness of the wall or stood on bedsteads of various materials, including bronze and sometimes even silver. From the 13th century on they were generally made of wood. The bed at this time became horizontal once more, and soon afterward the "tester," a canopy generally suspended from the ceiling, made its appearance above the bed.

Toward the end of the Middle Ages, beds reached vast proportions, the most famous example being the Great Bed of Ware, which was about 12 feet (3.6 meters) square and stood 7½ feet (2.3 meters) from the ground. Shakespeare refers to it in *Twelfth Night;* Ben Jonson, in *Epicoene;* and Farquhar, in *The Recruiting Officer.*

The 16th Century. By the time of Queen Elizabeth the importance of beds was beginning to rival, and was soon to surpass, anything known in the empires of antiquity. The value of a bed is indicated by Shakespeare's will, in which he left his wife his "second best bed."

The function of the bed as a place of honor spread rapidly in France during and after the 16th century, and notable persons, including kings and their mistresses, were displayed to the public, after death, on a *lit d'honneur*. Great ladies seized upon every possible pretext to hold court on a *lit de parade*, and in his old age Cardinal Richelieu even traveled in a bed so large that walls had to be broken down to admit him. A royal bed in France was the object of such great veneration that by the 17th century it was entitled to receive genuflections even when unoccupied. Louis XIV considered beds so important that he possessed 413 of them.

Expanding Use. William Harrison's *Description of England* (1577) mentions among the changes of the 16th century the emergence of the bed as a common article of furniture. The bed, he wrote, was replacing the straw pallet ("and a good round log under their heads") that was in customary use by an earlier generation. By the 18th century the bed, as such, was democratized in western Europe. But although lavish expenditure on beds and bedding remained a favorite form of extravagance among those who had wealth to display, the standard of comfort was not very high in any class. Fleas and even bedbugs, for which no effective remedy had yet been found, were casually mentioned as inevitable pests. The feather beds in use were unwholesome. A guest at an inn might be expected to share a bed with at least one complete stranger, since beds, though large, were in short supply.

In eastern Europe there was no appreciable advance in sleeping comfort. A Russian household provided only the floor to sleep on. Special braziers or other heating devices placed under beds have long been known in many parts of the world.

Colonial America. The first American settlers brought with them the habits, and often the beds, of contemporary Europe. There was probably little imitation of the extravagance then practiced by wealthy Europeans. The heavy "four-posters" commonly used in Jacobean England were found to be unsuited to the simple habits of colonists struggling for existence; and after an initial time lag, certain tendencies toward simplification appeared in American furniture.

The "press bed" (a bed set within a cupboard with doors), already in use in Europe, was the first of many lighter styles to be developed in America. "Field beds," with a canopy carried on an arched frame, were lighter beds typical of American styles in the mid-18th century. There was a period, in the reign of Napoleon I, when increased commerce with Europe brought a temporary outside influence to bear on American designs, but by 1840 a purely American style had emerged once more in the form of the graceful "sleigh bed," without posts but with curved boards at each end.

An early extravagance that later disappeared was the lofty structure achieved by piling up layers of feather beds, so that bed steps were necessary for the ascent. During these years pioneer women made the "crazy quilts" that became a typically American contribution to the ornamental aspect of the bed.

Later Beds. In Europe, too, beds of a lighter design began to take the place of the Jacobean fourposter of the 17th century. They came first in France and then in England. Curtains remained but were confined to the head of the bed, below the canopy, which was attached to the bedposts. With various modifications, as for instance in the overstrained ingenuity of later British designers, the general pattern remained unaltered until the mid-19th century, when the effect of the Industrial Revolution on public taste was seen in the emergence of bedsteads made of cast iron or brass. Wooden bedsteads, temporarily discredited by a belief that they harbored bugs, returned to favor in the 1920's.

At about the same time, a new divan type of bed became popular. It was built low and without any framework for the long-abandoned curtains. In keeping with the general trend in 20th century furniture, it was smaller and simpler than any of its modern precedecessors. In the United States it was called a "Hollywood bed" and consisted simply of an innerspring mattress resting on a box spring and supported by low legs or an adjustable metal frame; a headboard was sometimes attached. Also, "twin beds" began to displace the double bed that, in varying forms, had survived for centuries.

Other 20th century developments include the introduction of the "sofa bed"—an upholstered sofa that contains a mechanism for converting it into a bed—especially popular in small apartments where the living room also serves as the bedroom; the "rollaway bed," a type of cot that folds for storage and has wheels for "rolling it away" when not wanted; "bunk beds," built in tiers, with one sleeping place above the other, and used chiefly in children's rooms; and the "hospital bed," having a metal frame in three sections, any section of which can be raised and lowered.

REGINALD REYNOLDS, *Author of "Beds"*

Bibliography
Carcopino, Jérome, *Daily Life in Ancient Rome* (New Haven, Conn., 1940).
Carter, Howard, and Mace, Arthur C., *The Tomb of Tut-Ankh-Amen* (London 1923).
Gray, Cecil, and Gray, Mary, *The Bed* (London 1946).
Hayward, Charles H., *English Period Furniture* (Philadelphia 1949).
Holloway, Edward S., *American Furniture and Decoration* (Philadelphia 1928).
Reynolds, Reginald, *Beds* (New York 1951).
Viollet-le-Duc, Eugène, *Dictionaire raisonné du mobilier français* (Paris 1869–75).

BÉDARD, bā-dàr′, **Pierre Stanislas** (1762–1829), Canadian legislator and judge. He was born in Charlesbourg, Quebec, on Nov. 13, 1762. He was educated at Quebec Seminary and in 1790 was called to the bar of Lower Canada. Bédard was elected to the Legislative Assembly of Lower Canada in 1792, there becoming the leader of the French Canadian party. He was one of the founders of *Le Canadien,* established in 1806 as the organ of French Canadian nationalism. Upon the seizure of that paper by the governor, Sir James Craig, in 1810, Bédard was imprisoned, but was subsequently released without trial. In 1812 he left the legislature to become a judge. He died in Trois Rivières on April 26, 1829.

Elzéar Bédard (1799–1849), his son, was elected to the Legislative Assembly of Lower Canada in 1832. He was a judge of the court of the King's Bench (1836–1838; 1841–1849).

Common bedbug (*Cimex lectularius*)

BEDBUG, any of several wingless, bloodsucking bugs that feed on the blood of mammals. They are found throughout the world. Bedbugs are about ¼ inch (6 mm) long and are oval in shape. They are flat and completely wingless. A rusty brownish color is usual, but the young may be yellowish with a darker band across the middle. The bugs have a very unpleasant odor, especially when crushed. They are only moderately prolific; the female lays from 100 to 250 eggs at a time. The young require from two to seven months to mature, depending on temperature and the availability of food. Full-grown individuals can live without food for a long time.

All bedbugs are nocturnal. During the day they hide under mattress "buttons," in cracks in beds or floors, or under wallpaper. At night they come out and suck the blood of humans. They are not important carriers of disease. The bite of a bedbug usually produces only slight irritation, but it may cause large welts or even systemic poisoning in some people if the bites are numerous. Bedbugs also attack laboratory animals, such as rats, mice, monkeys, and rabbits.

Bedbugs belong to the family Cimicidae. The common bedbug (*Cimex lectularius*), which has almost a worldwide distribution, may be picked up in hotels, theaters, subways, or infested homes. Cleanliness of the premises does not prevent its appearance. The tropical bedbug (*C. rotundatus*), which is seldom found in temperate regions, is more nearly round than the common bedbug, but it has similar habits. The only other bedbug that commonly attacks man is the poultry bug (*Haematosiphon inodorus*), which is a serious pest of poultry in Mexico, New Mexico, and Texas.

Bedbugs have a few enemies, including cockroaches. Another enemy is the bedbug hunter (*Reduvius personatus*), which may also bite humans, especially around the mouth; for this reason it is sometimes called the "kissing bug."

The control of bedbugs was formerly difficult. More recently, DDT, chlordane, dieldrin, and lindane have provided sure and long-lasting control.

CHARLES HOWARD CURRAN
American Museum of Natural History

BEDDING, in geology, is the characteristic division of sedimentary rock into beds—also known as layers or strata—of varying color, texture, hardness, and chemical composition. Some beds are only a fraction of an inch, or centimeter, thick; others may be several feet, or meters, thick. The line of transition from one bed of rock to another is called a *bedding plane*.

Sedimentary rock is built up over long periods of time through the transporting and depositing of rock material by water and wind. Bedding results from variations in the materials being deposited in the region involved, as a result of changes in climatic or surface conditions. The change in chemical composition may be slight, but the resulting changes in texture or color can be striking. A gradation of structure within an individual bed, as from coarse- to fine-grained material, is known as *graded bedding*.

See also ROCKS—*Sedimentary Rocks*.

BEDDOES, bed′ōz, **Thomas** (1760–1808), English physician and scientific writer. He was born at Shiffnal, Shropshire, on April 13, 1760. He attended Oxford University and became a doctor of medicine in 1786. In 1793 he published *Observations on the Nature of Demonstrative Evidence*, a mathematical treatise; and the *History of Isaac Jenkins*, a work illustrating the evils of drink. Beddoes initiated the idea for a "pneumatic institution" for the cure of diseases by the inhalation of gases. The institution, with Humphry Davy as supervisor, was established in 1798, but it ceased to function shortly after Beddoes' death, at Clifton on Dec. 24, 1808.

BEDE, bēd, **Saint** (673–735), English historian and scholar. His name is also spelled *Beda* or *Bæda,* and he is known as "the Venerable Bede." He was born in 673 in what was later the territory of the twin monasteries of Wearmouth and Jarrow, in Northumbria. From the age of seven he was brought up under the care of Benedict Biscop, abbot of Wearmouth and one of the leading scholars of the time, who, together with Ceolfrith, abbot of Jarrow, directed his education. The remainder of his life appears to have been spent in the Benedictine monastery of Wearmouth and Jarrow.

Bede was ordained deacon at the age of 18 and priest at 29. He never held positions of greater dignity, and his title of "venerable" is merely a traditional term of respect. He declined the office of abbot on the grounds that it would have interfered with his chosen work of "learning, teaching, and writing."

Largely as a result of his labors, Northumbria became one of the great centers of learning in Europe. He himself taught Latin, Greek, Hebrew, astronomy, mathematics, grammar, rhetoric, and music—in short, all the subjects that were necessary for the service of the church: languages for the study of the Scriptures, astronomy and mathematics for determining the date of Easter, rhetoric for preaching and instruction, and music for the church services. He is reported to have taught with a vivacity and charm that endeared him greatly to his pupils. Besides the normal monastic duties and his teaching, Bede wrote voluminously.

Bede died in 735 at Jarrow, Durham, where he was buried; but in the 11th century his bones were placed in St. Cuthbert's coffin at Durham. At the translation of St. Cuthbert in 1104, Bede's bones were lodged in a casket of silver and gold in Durham Cathedral. This casket was rifled in 1541, and the bones disappeared. Bede was canonized and made a doctor of the church in 1899. May 27 is his feast day.

Writings. Bede's most important work is his *Historia ecclesiastica gentis Anglorum*, or *Ecclesiastical History of the English People*, completed in 731 and revised shortly after. It is a primary source for the early history of the Anglo-Saxons. Bede gathered much material from the kings and ecclesiastics of the Anglo-Saxon kingdoms and from the papal archives in Rome. The *Historia* is primarily an account of the conversion of the Anglo-Saxons and a history of the church, but it contains much political history. Our knowledge of the period would be almost a blank without it, although it is likely that its existence was responsible for the disappearance of other works that covered the same or similar ground. As a historical document it has very great value, but comparison with other sources suggests we should not place absolute reliance on its interpretation of events.

The *Historia* is remarkable for the way in which Bede wove the various strands of local accounts into a coherent and logical fabric. It is no longer a chronicle, but history in the strictest sense. It records various miracles, but it is no uncritical compilation of legends. It contains some of the most famous incidents of early English history—for example, the story of Caedmon, of St. Gregory and the English slaves at Rome, of the conversion of Northumbria, and of the conclusion of the Synod of Whitby in favor of the Roman usage. Bede's Latin style here, as elsewhere, is workmanlike and lucid, in striking contrast to the almost grotesque Latin of certain of his contemporaries, such as Aldhelm.

The *Historia* is preserved in some 160 manuscripts, a remarkable tribute to its popularity and influence, but four manuscripts of the 8th century are of the greatest value. These comprise: the Moore manuscript (M), in Cambridge University Library; the Leningrad manuscript (L), which was overlooked by Charles Plummer in his edition; and two manuscripts in the British Museum—Cotton Tiberius A xiv (B) and Cotton Tiberius C ii (C). A fifth manuscript from Fulda containing Books 4 and 5 is preserved at Kassel, Germany. The *Historia* was translated into Old English under the direction of King Alfred in the late 9th century as part of his work of making important books available in the vernacular. It was also used as a source for the earlier entries in the *Anglo-Saxon Chronicle*.

Bede's other important historical work is the *Historia abbatum*, or *History of the Abbots of Wearmouth*, written after 716 and based on an earlier work. In *De natura rerum*, Bede set forth the principles of physical science then known.

To a summary of the chief events of the *Historia*, Bede added a brief autobiography in which he records over 30 books that he had written. These include homilies; textbooks of grammar, science, and chronology; commentaries on the Scriptures; and historical works. All were in Latin. He also wrote Latin verse, and one chapter in his *Historia ecclesiastica* is a hymn in verse to St. Æthelthryth.

Of his works in the vernacular we have evidence in the account of his last hours written by his pupil, Cuthbert. He was dictating a translation of the Gospel of St. John on his deathbed and completed it shortly before he died. It is lost, but we possess a poem of five lines in Old English composed on the same occasion. His reputation as a mathematician was very great, and for five centuries after his death his works were regularly used and copied. The current system of chronology based on the Incarnation was adopted in England through his example.

Learning and Views. Bede's intellectual circle included Acca, bishop of Hexham, who commissioned several of his works and to whom several are dedicated. He was also in correspondence with Albin of Kent; Cyniberct, bishop of Lindsey; Daniel, bishop of Worcester; Abbot Esi of East Anglia; Nothhelm, priest of London; Tatwine (a Mercian), archbishop of Canterbury; and Tobias, bishop of Rochester. Bede's learning was largely in the Scriptures and the fathers, but he was well acquainted with such pagan authors as Virgil and the younger Pliny. He was aware of the importance of textual criticism in the study of the Scriptures, and one of the manuscripts he used was identified as the Codex Laudianus, now in the Bodleian Library, Oxford.

Bede's religious views were strictly orthodox, and much of his work is devoted to the refutation of heresies. For no doubt similar reasons, the dispute about the date of Easter looms unusually large in the *Historia ecclesiastica*, and it is of interest that the Alfredian translation discarded much of this. Bede's method of scriptural exposition is frequently allegorical, and he sees in the events of the Old Testament a prefiguration of events in the New. The abiding impression that his writings leave is of a simple, natural piety allied to a sober judgment.

Editions. Bede's works are collected in Jacques Paul Migne's *Patrologia Latina*, vols. 90–95 (1850) and in *Venerabilis Bedae opera omnia*, edited by John A. Giles (12 vols., 1843–44). The canon is examined in Charles W. Jones's *Bedae Pseudepigrapha* (1939). The standard edition of the *Historia ecclesiastica* is in *Venerabilis Baedae opera historica*, edited by Charles Plummer (2 vols., 1896). This contains much valuable material, but its chronology needs to be corrected, and it takes no account of the Leningrad manuscript, which is of great importance textually. This manuscript is discussed in Olof S. Anderson's *Old English Material in the Leningrad Manuscript of Bede's Historia Ecclesiastica* (1941); a facsimile of the manuscript was published in 1953 by Olof S. Arngart.

The Old English translation was edited by Jakob Schipper as vol. 4 of Richard P. Wül[c]ker's *Bibliothek der Angelsächsischen Prosa* (1899) and by Thomas Miller in *The Old English Version of Bede's Ecclesiastical History*, vols. 95–96 (1890–91; reprinted 1959). *Baedae opera historica*, edited by J.E. King (2 vols., 1930), has an English translation based on the Elizabethan version of Thomas Stapleton.

J.L.N. O'LOUGHLIN
Coeditor of "Odhams Dictionary of the English Language"

Bibliography
Hunt, William, *History of the English Church* (London 1907).
Jones, Charles W., *Saints' Lives and Chronicles in Early England* (Ithaca, N.Y., 1947).
Stenton, Sir Frank M., *Anglo-Saxon England*, 2d ed. (Oxford 1947).
Thompson, A. Hamilton, ed., *Bede: His Life, Times, and Writings* (Oxford 1935).
Whitelock, Dorothy H., *The Beginnings of English Society* (Harmondsworth, Eng., 1952).

BEDEN. See IBEX.

BEDFORD, bed'fərd, **Gunning** (1747–1812), American lawyer and public official. Born in Philadelphia, Pa., he was graduated from the College of New Jersey (Princeton) in 1771 and settled in Delaware as a lawyer.

Bedford was a member of the Continental Congress in 1783–1786, and of the Annapolis Convention of 1786. In the following year he was a delegate to the federal Constitutional Convention, in which he was notable as a determined, occasionally intemperate opponent of a strong central government and a champion of the rights of the smaller states. He signed the Constitution as "Gunning Bedford Jun" (Junior) to distinguish himself from his cousin, Gunning Bedford (1742–1797). In 1789, President Washington appointed him United States district judge for Delaware. He held this office until his death in Wilmington, Del., on March 30, 1812.

BEDFORD, bed'fərd, **Gunning S.** (1806–1870), American physician. He was a nephew of Gunning Bedford, a framer of the Constitution and United States judge for the district of Delaware. Gunning S. Bedford was born in Baltimore and was graduated in 1825 from Mount Saint Mary's College, Emmetsburg, Md. He took his degree in medicine at Rutgers in 1829. He spent the next three years studying abroad, and in 1833 he became professor of obstetrics at Charleston Medical College. Gunning went from there to the New College foundation, in Albany, N. Y.

In 1836 he moved to New York City, and in 1840 founded the University Medical College, in connection with which he established the first free obstetrical clinic in America. His *Clinical Lectures on the Diseases of Women and Children* (1855), and *Principles and Practice of Obstetrics* (4th ed., 1868) were much used as texts. He died in New York on Sept. 5, 1870.

BEDFORD, bed'fərd, is a municipal borough in England. It is the county town of Bedfordshire and is situated on the Ouse River, 50 miles (80 km) northwest of London. A residential and marketing town for the surrounding agricultural area, Bedford is noted for its educational institutions, chiefly those controlled by the Harpur trust. The trust was founded by Sir William Harpur, a native of Bedford, who was lord mayor of London in 1561, and who left lands now of great value in the heart of London. Bedford School, one of the largest preparatory schools in England, was founded in 1552 and endowed by Harpur in 1561. Harpur is buried in Bedford, in St. Paul's Church, which is built in the Decorated and Perpendicular styles.

John Bunyan was born at Elstow, a nearby village, and the Bunyan Meeting (1850), a chapel, now stands in Bedford on the site of the barn in which Bunyan preached. Many of his personal relics are preserved in the Bunyan Museum. Bunyan was imprisoned in the Bedford jail in 1660–1672, and again for six months in 1675–1676, during which time he wrote part of *Pilgrim's Progress.*

Bedford is mentioned in the *Anglo-Saxon Chronicle,* in which, as *Bedican-fortha,* it was the scene of a defeat of the Britons by the Saxons under Cuthwulf in 571. The town was burned by the Danes in 1010. Bedford was one of the earliest centers of English lace manufacture, originally introduced by Huguenots from France. Modern manufactures are farm implements, machinery, bricks, electrical equipment, and ale. Population: (1961) 63,334.

BEDFORD, bed'fərd, a city in Indiana, is the seat of Lawrence County. It is situated 20 miles (32 km) south of Bloomington, in the heart of the Indiana limestone district, which has great quarries and stone mills. Its industrial products are aluminum, cranes, saws, refrigerators, furniture, and clothing.

In or near the city are a Carnegie library, a museum operated by the Lawrence County Historical Society, a high school, three large city-owned parks with swimming and golfing facilities, an experimental farm owned by Purdue University, a state fish hatchery, and a state park. Bedford was incorporated as a village in 1825, and as a city in 1889. It has a mayor and council form of government. Population: 13,087.

BEDFORD, bed'fərd, a town in Massachusetts, in Middlesex County, is a residential suburb 15 miles (25 km) northwest of Boston. There are several electronics and systems research firms in Bedford, as well as Laurence G. Hanscom Field and a Veterans Administration hospital. Bedford was settled in 1642. The Bedford flag, which the town owns, was carried in the Battle of Concord (1775). Government is by a board of selectmen. Population: 13,513.

BEDFORD, bed'fərd, a city in Ohio, in Cuyahoga County, is a residential suburb of Cleveland, which is 11 miles (17 km) to the northwest. Bedford manufactures office furniture, rubber goods, chinaware, machine tools, distilled liquors, aircraft parts, dog food, and concrete blocks. It was settled about 1813 on the site of a Moravian settlement established in 1786. Bedford has a council-manager government. Population: 17,552.

BEDFORD, bed'fərd, a city in northeastern Texas, in Tarrant county, is about 12 miles (19 km) northeast of the center of Fort Worth and about 20 miles (32 km) west of the center of Dallas. The region between the two large cities, known as the Mid-Cities area, has developed rapidly. The Dallas-Fort Worth Regional Airport, which is expected to become one of the largest in the world, is about 5 miles (8 km) east of Bedford. A residential city, Bedford's population in 1950 was 175. In the 1960 census, the figure was 2,706. Through the 1960's, and as the 1970's began, the rate of growth continued high as new areas were opened to homes. Population: 10,049.

BEDFORD HEIGHTS, bed'fərd hīts, is a residential city of northeastern Ohio, in Cuyahoga County. It is situated about 10 miles (16 km) southeast of Cleveland, of which it is a suburb. The site was first settled about 1810. Bedford Heights, incorporated in 1951, is governed by a mayor and council. Population: 13,063.

BEDFORDSHIRE, bed'fərd-shēr, is a county in England, in the south Midlands, bounded north by Northamptonshire and Huntingdonshire, east by Cambridgeshire, southeast by Hertfordshire, and west by Buckinghamshire. It is the fourth-smallest English county, with an area of 473 square miles (1,225.5 sq km). It lies mainly in the basin of the river Ouse, which enters the county from the west and flows northeastward in a winding course. The generally level land rises to a spur of the Chiltern Hills in the south.

Bedfordshire is basically an agricultural county despite its increasing industrialization and the growth of its population. Truck gardens producing vegetables for the London market predominate in the eastern section of the county. Other sections are devoted to grain farming (chiefly wheat) and dairying.

The largest industrial centers are Luton, Bedford (the county seat), and Dunstable. Their manufactures include automobiles, farm machinery, electrical equipment, and hats. Other industries are the brickworks south of Bedford—which make use of local clay deposits—and sand and limestone quarries. Lace making and plaiting straw for hats were notable among cottage industries of earlier times. The lace industry, which no longer exists, was developed under Flemish and Huguenot craftsmen who migrated to England following religious persecutions on the Continent in the 16th and 17th centuries. Luton, where straw plaiting began in the early 1600's, is still a center of the hat industry.

Bedfordshire has some prehistoric remains as well as evidences of Roman occupation. The Roman road known as Watling Street crossed the county. Later antiquities include the remains of an Augustinian priory, incorporated in the Church of St. Peter and St. Paul at Dunstable; the church at Elstow, near Bedford; and the Saxon church tower at Clapham.

Bedfordshire is first mentioned in historical records in 1016, when it was devastated by the Danish king Canute II. During the reign of Charles I (1625–1649) it was a stronghold of the Parliamentary party in its struggle against the king. Chiefly because of the Flemish and Huguenot immigrations it was also a center of religious dissent. John Bunyan was born at Elstow in 1628. Population: (1961) 380,837.

BÉDIER, bā-dyā′, **Charles Marie Joseph** (1864–1938), French scholar of medieval French literature. He was a pioneer in modern methods of textual criticism and advanced a widely accepted theory of the origin of the chanson de geste.

Bédier was born on Jan. 28, 1864, in Paris, and studied there at the Collège de France under Gaston Paris. He taught Romance philology at the universities of Fribourg and Paris, and in 1903, after the death of Gaston Paris, replaced his former teacher at the Collège de France. Bédier died at Le Grand-Serre, Drôme, on Aug. 30, 1938.

Bédier's most important publication was the 4-volume *Légendes épiques de la France* (1908–21), in which he advanced the theory that the chansons de geste were the work of individual authors who developed them from tales they encountered at monasteries along the pilgrim routes of 11th century France. This theory, deduced from internal evidence in extant manuscripts, replaced earlier, more speculative theories that explained the chansons as folk poems evolved from camp songs or Merovingian epics.

Bédier's other publications include *Les fabliaux* (1893), a modern version of *Tristan et Iseult* (1900), a critical edition of *Chanson de Roland* (1921), and, with Paul Hazard, *Histoire de la littérature française* (2 vols., 1923–24), one of the best modern histories of French literature.

BEDIVERE, bed′ə-vēr, **Sir,** in Arthurian legend, one of King Arthur's most trusted knights. It was Sir Bedivere who cast the sword Excalibur into the lake and carried the dying Arthur to the vessel in which he was borne away to Avalon.

BEDLAM, bed′ləm, is the popular name of a hospital for the insane, originally called Saint Mary of Bethlehem and located in London. Bedlam is a corruption of "Bethlehem." Because of its associations, the name became a common word meaning "uproar."

Saint Mary of Bethlehem was a church priory founded in 1247 but used as early as 1402 as a hospital for the insane. In 1815 the hospital was moved to Lambeth, then a suburb of London, and in 1930 to the vicinity of Croydon. Now a part of the national health service and called Bethlehem Royal Hospital, it is still popularly referred to as Bedlam.

BEDLINGTON TERRIER, a small terrier with a thick, crispy coat and a deep, rounded head, giving it a lamblike appearance. The breed was named in the 1820's for the coal mining town of Bedlington, England. However, its origins are uncertain, and it was previously known by other names, including Rothbury terrier. The miners valued the Bedlington terrier's gameness and used the breed for retrieving, ratting, and poaching.

The Bedlington terrier may be either blue or liver, blue being the more popular color. Blue-coated dogs, which are born black, have black noses and dark eyes. Liver-coated dogs, which are born dark liver, have brown noses and hazel eyes. The preferred height for males is 16½ inches (42 cm), and for females, 15½ inches (39 cm). The preferred weight is between 17 and 22 pounds (7.7–10 kg).

ANNA NEARY, *Bedlington Terrier Club of America*

BEDLOE'S ISLAND, bed′lōz, the former name of Liberty Island in New York harbor, on which the Statue of Liberty is situated. It became a national monument in 1937 and was renamed Liberty Island in 1956. See STATUE OF LIBERTY.

Bedlington terrier

EVELYN M. SHAFER

BEDOUIN, bed'ə-wən, a desert and steppe dweller of the Middle East and North Africa. The word is a French transliteration of the Arabic *badawiyin,* which literally means, from its root, "people who become visible" (as in an open area). Now in numerical and economic decline, the few million who remain still follow regular routes in their wanderings. Bedouins are Arab and Muslim, but the bedouin nomads of North Africa, mainly Berbers by origin, differ from those of the eastern Arab world.

Historically the bedouins have been important in the armies that conquered new lands for Islam—as exemplars of such Arab-Muslim values as courage, generosity, and cunning; as stockbreeders; and as guides and raiders along the caravan routes. Although their mode of life is an adaptation to the harsh environment of the desert and steppe, they have always had close relations with agricultural villages and towns. These relations have been mainly economic, for the bedouins have sought to retain their independence by avoiding the controls of urban authorities and central governments.

With the rise of national states in the area inhabited by the bedouins and with the introduction of technological advances, the economic position and political autonomy of the bedouins have declined. Most of the countries in which they live now have a policy of settling them on the land or even in the cities. Many of them find employment in the oil industry and as policemen and soldiers.

Bedouin social organization has been simple, compared with that of settled peoples; but it has had, nevertheless, a structure of families, clans, and tribes. Differences in status have been based on mobile wealth, military prowess, nobility of ancestry, and certain virtues. Tribes perform most of the social functions performed in other societies by governments. The tribes, moreover, are related to one another in various sorts of alliances, and some are considered noble and others dependent.

Although bedouins as a group value independence highly, as individuals they are highly dependent on the group. The family, clan, and tribe assume responsibility for the individual and in turn exact conformity from him. Virtue consists in doing as one's elders do rather than in striking new paths. Women are often freer among bedouins than in the lower levels of the village and city population, but the harsh environment and close social organization permit the bedouin—man or woman—little more than a primitive physical freedom. Bedouin societies respect religion, although few of them are reported to be very faithful in its practice. To flourish, Islam requires the adjunct of learning and learned men, neither of which nomadic life encourages.

MORROE BERGER, *Princeton University*

BEDSTRAW, bed'strô, a genus of about 220 annual or perennial herbs with four-angled stems. They belong to the family Rubiaceae. Most of the bedstraws grow in temperate climates in the Northern Hemisphere. They are often attractive for their regular whorls of leaves and their panicles of profuse white, yellow, green, or purple blossoms, which in some species are used by florists to add lightness to bouquets of heavy flowers and to cover rockeries. The two species most cultivated for this purpose are *Galium*

FRITZ HENLE, FROM MONKMEYER

THE BEDOUIN has for centuries wandered over the deserts and steppes of North Africa and the Middle East.

mollugo and *G. boreale.* The former is sometimes called baby's breath, a common name more frequently applied to the perennial herb *Gypsophila paniculata.*

Yellow bedstraw (*G. verum*), a species with yellow flowers, yields a yellow dye when boiled in alum solutions, and its roots yield a red dye. The plant is also used in curdling milk. This species, together with *G. trifidum* and *G. boreale,* redden the bones and milk of animals that eat them in quantity. Goose grass or cleavers (*G. aparine*), a troublesome weed common to Europe, Asia, and America, yields a seed sometimes used as a substitute for coffee. It is noted for its hooked prickles. In China, *G. tuberosum* is cultivated for its farinaceous tubers.

BED-WETTING is the inability of a person, usually a child, to control the discharge of urine at night. The inability to control the bladder is known as *enuresis,* and when it occurs only during the day it is called *diurnal enuresis.*

There are many causes of bed-wetting. The most common are psychological disturbances. Other causes are malformations of the genitourinary tract, neurological disorders, and diseases that cause one to drink excessive amounts of fluids. Such diseases include diabetes mellitus and diabetes insipidus.

When psychological factors are the cause, psychological therapy is generally recommended. Usually the disturbance is severe enough to cause other problems, even though the enuresis may clear up spontaneously.

Malformations of the genitourinary tract should be corrected early, not only to control the enuresis but also because if they are not treated they may, over a period of years, lead to eventual destruction of the kidneys. A large number of these malformations can be corrected surgically. When bed-wetting is caused by a neurological disorder, treatment is more difficult and may not be effective. When caused by excessive intake of fluids, it may be controlled by drugs.

LOUIS J. VORHAUS, M.D.
Cornell University Medical College

HONEYBEES are typical social bees that live in colonies. Their hairy bodies enable them to collect pollen.

BEE

BEE is a general term applied to various flying insects but technically reserved for certain members of the insect order Hymenoptera. This is a group that also includes wasps, hornets, ants, sawflies, and others.

There are many kinds of bees, but all of them are classified under the superfamily Apoidea. Some bees are wasplike, but they may be distinguished from wasps by their branched body hairs, especially on the top of the thorax. Also, the first tarsal segment (foot segment) of each hind leg in bees is greatly enlarged and covered with hairs that form a brush or pollen basket used for collecting and carrying flower pollen. Bumblebees and honeybees have very hairy bodies that aid them in gathering grains of pollen from the flowers.

Bees, as do all other Hymenoptera, have four steps or stages in their life cycles. These are: egg, larva (grub), pupa (inactive stage), and the adult, or winged, insect. Insects having all four of these stages are said to have complete life histories.

Different kinds of bees vary greatly in their habits. They are identified as either *social* or *solitary*. Many of them, such as the bumblebees and honeybees, live in colonies consisting of a queen, or egg-laying female, many workers, and some drones (males). These are called social bees. Other bees, such as leaf-cutter bees, are solitary or nonsocial in habit. Each female builds her nest and stocks it with food for her young, but she has no workers to aid her. Thus, each nest is an individual project, and there is no social organization.

Social Bees. The true social bees belong to the Apidae, a family that includes the honeybees and bumblebees. The honeybee (*Apis mellifera*) may be used as an example of a typical social bee.

Anatomy of the Honeybee. Like all insects, the honeybee has a body that is divided into three parts: head, thorax, and abdomen. The head contains most of the sensory apparatus, including the antennae, or feelers. The eyes are of two types. On the sides of the head are the large compound eyes made up of many individual eyes, or ommatidia. Each of these is connected to the brain by an individual nerve fiber and probably sees but a small portion of the visual field. Vision of this type is known as mosaic vision. Three simple eyes, or ocelli, are located on the top of the head. These eyes probably are of little use except for distinguishing between different intensities of light. In general, it is believed that bees, like most other insects, are near-sighted, but their eyes are capable of perceiving motion. Unlike human eyes, bees' eyes are sensitive to ultraviolet light rays and also can distinguish polarized light.

The jaws, or mandibles, and other mouthparts of the honeybee, as well as the pharynx (first part of the digestive canal), also are attached to the head.

The midsection, or thorax, is more or less boxlike in form. Two pairs of wings and three pairs of legs are attached to it. The two pairs of wings are hinged to the top of the thorax. Their attachment is flexible and their movement is brought about by a very complex system of thoracic muscles. Some of these muscles are attached directly to the roof of the thorax and the wings are raised when these muscles contract. Other muscles, which cause the wings to beat downward by an indirect effect, extend horizontally through the thorax and cause wing movement by changing the shape of the thorax. In flight, a bee's wings not only move up and down but also forward and backward. Strangely, when the wing is beating downward its movement is not only downward but forward as well. The combined effect of these wing movements is that the tips of the wings follow figure-eight paths. In the case of bees and most other insects, the wings on each side move in unison; that is, they beat downward or upward together. The bee's hind wings are anchored to the fore wings by a series of small hooks along their front edges. As compared to an airplane, a bee's flight is very efficient, and it can take off and fly with very heavy loads in proportion to the small size of its wings.

Each of the six legs of a honeybee is made up of two short basal segments, the coxa and the trochanter. Connected to the trochanter is a long segment, the femur. Beyond this is the tibia, which has five short foot joints or tarsi attached at its end. On the last tarsal joint are two claws, between which is the adhesive organ that enables the bee to cling to smooth surfaces.

The legs of the honeybee are especially fitted to aid it in carrying out its various duties. Located on the tibia of the fore legs is an eye brush used for brushing pollen and dust from the eyes. At the base of the first tarsal joint is a notch set with hairs and a flat spur attached to the tibia that is used to clean the sensitive antennae. The only special tool on the middle legs is a slender spine arising from the tibia and used to remove scales of wax from the abdomen. The tibia of the hind legs is enlarged and flattened, and its outside surface is fringed by long hairs forming a basket called the corbicula. As the bees visit one flower after another, their bodies become dusted with large amounts of pollen, which periodically is combed off into the baskets.

The hind portion of the bee's body is the abdomen, which is made up of ten segments, each overlapping the one just behind it. Mirrors, or wax plates, where scales of wax are formed are located on the bottom, or ventral, plates of the last four abdominal segments. The wax used for comb construction is produced from honey by young bees when they are about 17 days of age. It is secreted slowly in small scales that are removed by the bee with specialized spines on its legs and transferred to its jaws where they are chewed into the necessary shape for building the comb.

At the rear of the abdomen is the sting and its surrounding organs. A bee's sting actually is a modified ovipositor, or egg-laying apparatus, and is much more complicated than might be imagined at first. The spearlike sting is made up of three pieces which surround a central canal. Connected to the base of the sting are two poison sacs. Also there are two sensitive, fingerlike projections that tell the bee when the tip of her abdomen is in contact with the object she wishes to sting. In the act of stinging, the spearlike sting is thrust outward and muscular poison sacs in the abdomen force the poison into the wound. However, once the barbed sting is inserted into the object, it cannot be extracted easily. When the bee flies away, her sting and its attached organs are pulled from her body, and she eventually dies.

As is the case with all insects, bees have hard exoskeletons; that is, their skeletons are hard, protective shells on the outside of their bodies. Muscles are anchored to the inner surfaces of the exoskeleton, and the various body organs are well protected.

The digestive system of the bee extends from the mouth to an opening at the posterior end of the body. The esophagus leads from the mouth, or pharynx, through the thorax and into the abdomen where it connects with the honey stomach, or crop. When collecting nectar from flowers, nectar is stored in this honey stomach for transport back to the hive. At the rear of the honey stomach is a valve that prevents stored nectar from passing on into the rear portion of the digestive system, except for the small amount needed by the bee to sustain life. Beyond this valve is the stomach, or ventriculus, which is quite large and is bent into a U-shaped loop. Its walls are muscular and contain glands that secrete digestive enzymes. It is in this portion of the bee's digestive system that food materials

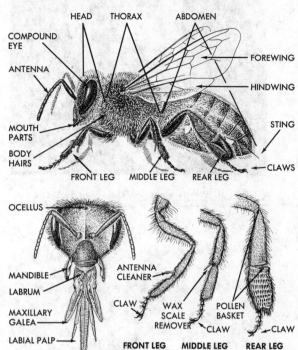

ANATOMY OF THE BEE

HEAD · THORAX · ABDOMEN
COMPOUND EYE
ANTENNA
FOREWING
HINDWING
MOUTH PARTS
BODY HAIRS
STING
CLAWS
FRONT LEG · MIDDLE LEG · REAR LEG

OCELLUS
MANDIBLE
LABRUM
MAXILLARY GALEA
LABIAL PALP
LABIAL LIGULA
ANTENNA CLEANER
CLAW
WAX SCALE REMOVER
POLLEN BASKET
CLAW
CLAW
FRONT LEG · MIDDLE LEG · REAR LEG
MOUTH PARTS

are absorbed into the blood. Excretory organs (Malpighian tubules), which correspond roughly in function to kidneys, are attached at the posterior end of the ventriculus. They are hollow, threadlike tubes and number about a hundred. Beyond this point, waste materials from the digestive system enter the coiled, small intestine, then are emptied into the large intestine and, eventually, into the rectum before being voided.

Bees, like other insects, have what is termed an "open circulatory system." That is, blood passes forward to the head through a tubelike "heart," which has valvular openings, or ostia, located at several points along its length. The blood is moved forward by muscular contraction of the heart tube. The blood flows backward from the head to the body organs and bathes them with nutrient materials. There are, however, membranes that direct the blood as it flows backward so that it reaches all places where it is needed.

Unlike the blood of warm-blooded animals, insect blood does not contain red coloring matter (hemoglobin); thus it is not important in the transportation of oxygen. In insects, air is carried directly to the organs and tissues through a system of fine tubes called the tracheal system. The external openings of the tracheal system are located along the sides of the body and are called spiracles. In the bee there are a number of large thin-walled air sacs connected to the tracheal system. These give buoyancy to the insect by lessening its weight without decreasing its size, and they also increase the efficiency of the bee's respiratory system.

As in higher animals, a bee's sensory and muscular systems are connected to each other by a complex nervous system. All of the activities

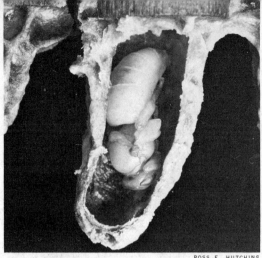

A NEW QUEEN develops in this queen cell. Fed on royal jelly, she will be a sexually functional bee.

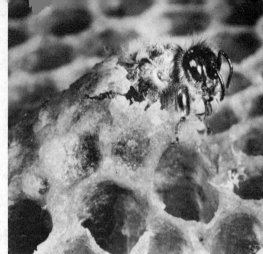

THE QUEEN EMERGES from her cell. Her main purpose in the hive is to lay eggs to produce new workers.

TWO QUEENS fight to the death for control of the hive. Only one queen bee can remain in the hive.

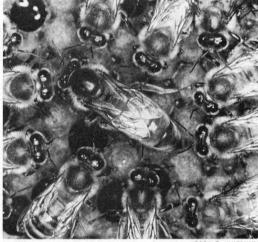

THE QUEEN, surrounded by workers, passes out "queen substance," which prevents development of other queens.

of the bee—feeding, flight, walking, and other functions—are controlled by the nervous system. It consists of an enlarged nerve center, the brain, located in the head, and a nerve cord extending backward to the rear portion of the abdomen. Enlarged nerve centers or ganglia are located at various points along this nerve cord (two in the thorax and four in the abdomen). Small, branching nerves extend from each ganglion and connect with the various body parts. Unlike the nerve cord of higher animals, the bee's nerve cord extends along the floor of the body (ventrally) instead of along the back (dorsally). The worker bee has the largest brain since it carries out most of the complex activities of the colony, such as caring for young, harvesting food, cooling the hive, and other duties.

Life in the Honeybee Hive. Honeybees are social insects, and their colonies are made up of a queen, several thousand workers, and, usually, a few drones (males). Both the queen and the workers are females, but only the queen is sexually perfect and able to mate and lay eggs that will develop into queens and workers. Under certain conditions, workers may lay eggs, but these produce only males since the workers have

not mated. (Drones arise from nonfertilized eggs.)

The wax cells built by bees for their hives are of two kinds: smaller cells used for rearing workers and for storing honey and pollen; and larger cells for rearing drones. As the queen goes from one cell to another laying eggs, she apparently can control whether or not the eggs are fertilized. She lays only fertilized eggs in worker cells and nonfertilized eggs in drone cells.

These eggs hatch into grublike larvae, which are fed and cared for by workers or unmated females. When the larvae are fully grown and ready to transform into the pupal stage, the wax cells are sealed or capped by the worker bees. Within this cell the larval tissues slowly transform into adult organs and, in time, the winged adults emerge.

At certain seasons, or when living conditions within the hive become crowded, the bees begin building special queen cells, preparatory to swarming. These cells are vertical instead of horizontal, and they have openings at the bottom. In each of these cells the queen deposits a fertilized egg that is identical to the eggs laid

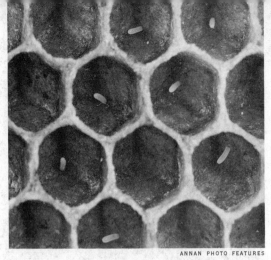

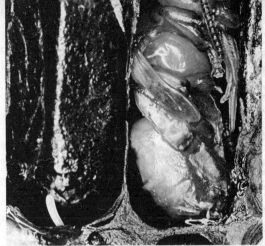

WORKERS will develop from these eggs. All bee eggs are alike; caste is determined by cell shape and food.

A WORKER PUPA is almost ready to hatch. The worker caste is not sexually perfect and is unable to lay eggs.

WORKERS do all the work of the hive. There may be 60,000 of them, and their duties depend on their ages.

WORKERS 17 to 21 days old must guard the hive so that bees from other hives do not enter and steal honey.

in the worker cells. When the eggs in the queen cells hatch, the larvae are no different from the worker larvae. However, they are fed continually on a special food called royal jelly, a substance secreted by the worker bees. This material is highly nutritious and causes the larvae to develop completely and thus into functional queens.

The eggs that are laid in worker cells hatch into larvae. Except for the first day or two, they are fed on a mixture of pollen and honey, and these larvae mature into workers that are not sexually perfect. As their name implies, worker bees do all the work of the hive.

In an average hive there are from 30,000 to 60,000 worker bees and, in general, their duties correspond to their ages. During the first two days of adulthood, workers spend their time cleaning the hive. On the third day they are promoted to the feeding of the older larvae, a duty which they continue until the fifth day when they are promoted to the feeding of the younger larvae. (The feeding of the larvae requires a great deal of time since each larva must be fed about 1,300 times each day or about 10,-000 times during its development.) At about ten days of age, the worker bees change their duties;

for about a week, they receive the food brought in by the field bees and place it in the cells for storage. Then they begin making short exploratory flights away from the hive to familiarize themselves with the territory where they will go later to gather pollen, nectar, and propolis. (Propolis is a resin, known also as "bee glue," obtained from trees and used to seal openings to make the hive watertight and for other purposes.)

On their 17th day, the workers assume the duty of guarding the hive entrance until their 21st day. Then they become full-fledged field bees whose duty consists of gathering food. This will be their work for the rest of their lives. As older bees, however, they eventually may become scouts who go out and seek new sources of pollen and nectar and report this information back to the other field bees.

The Honey Dances of the Bees. The method used by scout bees to inform their sisters about the location of flowers is the so-called "honey dance." When the scout bees return to the hive, they perform circular dances or tail-wagging movements on the comb. Until recently it was believed that these dances merely indicated that

A HONEY DANCE is performed by a scout bee (arrow). Direction and distance to the pollen source are indicated.

THESE WORKERS are beating their wings to circulate air in order to evaporate water from the honey.

the scouts had found nectar or pollen and that the other workers should go out and seek it. But Karl von Frisch of Germany discovered that these honey dances, which he called the *Schwanzeltänze*, actually were an amazing charade that the scouts used to convey precise information to their sisters about the direction and the distance to the location of a new food source.

The form of the dance, which varies, indicates the distance and the direction. For example, if the flowers are more than 100 yards (91.4 meters) away, the dance is in the form of a figure-eight. When the nectar source is closer than about 10 yards (9.14 meters), the dance has a circular form. It takes on a sickle-shape as the distance of the nectar source increases, eventually becoming the typical figure-eight dance. If the distance is beyond 100 yards, the speed of the promenades indicates distance—the slower the runs, the greater the distance. Bees from different localities of the world have different "dialects" in their dances. For example, von Frisch found that bees from Austria used the round dance to indicate distances up to 275 feet (84.1 meters), as contrasted with 120 feet (36.5 meters) for Italian bees. (Differences in the "dialects" of other species of honeybees in India also have been discovered.) As the scout makes her tail-wagging run or promenade across the "waist" of the figure-eight she is indicating the direction of the flower source with respect to the sun. However, we must remember that the dance is performed on the vertical comb in the dark hive. Within the hive the promenade indicating the sun's direction is made with respect to gravity. Thus if the sun is directly overhead she makes her promenade straight up on the comb, but if the sun is to the right she makes her promenade at the proper angle to the right to indicate the sun's location. Since the hive is dark, the bees apparently are able to follow the actions of the dancing bees with their sensitive antennae, but some authorities believe that sound plays a part in communication. Thus the "dance" gives the bees in the hive all the information they need to fly out and find the flowers. The scout also gives them samples of the nectar so that the bees know what kind of flowers to look for and also so that they can sample the quality of the nectar that the scout has found.

The Queen's Influence. The queen honeybee does not "rule" her subjects in the sense that a human queen does, yet she has a profound influence on the lives of all the bees in the hive. Her basic duty is egg-laying, and she lays from 1,500 to 2,000 eggs a day during summer. In addition, she continually secretes a glandular material called "queen substance." This substance, now called a pheromone, or the "social" hormone, is passed on from worker to worker by mouth so that every worker receives a sample. This substance has a controlling effect on almost every facet of the bees' lives. It inhibits the development of the worker bees' reproductive glands so that additional queens do not develop. However, when the queen becomes old and her secretion of queen substance slows down, or when she dies, the decrease or absence of queen substance allows the workers' reproductive glands to develop and soon some of them begin laying eggs. But since these workers have not mated, all their eggs develop into drones (males). The queen's importance in the hive is shown by the fact that if the queen is killed or removed from the hive, the entire hive will become disturbed within a short time and the bees will not work properly. They quickly become aware of the loss of their queen because the supply of queen substance has stopped.

Colony Reproduction. As contrasted to the honeybee colony, a hornet or bumblebee colony exists only for one summer. With the arrival of autumn, all the inhabitants die except for the young mated queens who hibernate in sheltered places. They establish new colonies in the spring. A honeybee colony, however, exists for many years. Honeybees are able to survive the cold of winter by forming themselves into a compact ball or cluster; their body temperature is regulated by their muscular activity.

The honeybees' natural method of colony reproduction is by swarming, which usually occurs in spring but may occur later if conditions in the hive become too crowded. The first step in swarm production is the creating of new queens. Queen cells are built and the queen lays an egg in each. The larvae that hatch are fed entirely upon royal jelly secreted by the workers so they will develop into queens. When the first adult queen emerges from her cell she immediately de-

BEES

PLATE 1

SOME COMMON KINDS OF BEES

Honeybee

Leaf-cutter bee

Alkali bee

Bumblebee

(Above) Parasitic bee

(Below) Large carpenter bee

Euglossa bee

(10) storing honey

(15) bee moth larvae feeding on comb

(3) queen laying eggs

(12) storing pollen

(4) feeding larvae

(5) sealing brood cells

(7) cleaning empty brood cells

(6) workers emerging

(6) drones emerging

(1) queen emerging from brood cell

(9) hive bees receiving nectar from foragers

(2) queens fighting

ACTIVITIES INSIDE A HONEYBEE HIVE

This illustration is a composite of the many activities that go on inside a hive. *Life Cycle:* The colony's largest member is the queen, who, after emerging (1) and perhaps killing a rival queen (2), deposits her eggs in empty brood cells (3). The larvae that hatch are fed by workers (4), who also cap the cells before the larvae pupate (5). Later, the adults emerge (6) and the cells are cleaned (7) before new eggs are

(11) capping honey cells

(8) scout performing honey dance

(16) building new comb cells

(14) ejecting drones

(13) fanning and guarding the hive entrance

laid. **Gathering and Storing Food:** The location of a new food source is indicated to foragers by a scout bee performing a "honey dance" (8). When foragers return from the field they transfer their nectar to hive bees (9), who convert it into honey and store it in cells (10) that are then capped (11). Pollen is stored by the field bees themselves (12). **Other Activities:** Workers at the entrance ventilate the hive by fanning their wings (13) and others eject drones that are no longer needed (14). Bee moth larvae are hive parasites that feed on the wax comb (15), but new comb cells are quickly built (16).

ILLUSTRATION BY ARABELLE WHEATLEY

PLATE 4

ACTIVITIES OUTSIDE THE NEST

(Left) Eucerine bees, like many other solitary bees, spend the night clinging to a leaf or stem by their mouthparts. Sometimes, they come back to the same plant night after night.

EDWARD S. ROSS

(Below) Burrowing bees, as well as many other types of bees, are covered with feathery hairs that are well adapted for collecting pollen. The pollen, together with some flower nectar, is then placed inside individual nest, or brood, cells where it later serves as food for the young larvae.

(Below) A leaf-cutter bee uses its scissorlike mouthparts for cutting off a strip of leaf. The rolled-up leaf strip will then be used for lining the leaf-cutter's underground nest.

EDWARD S. ROSS

ALEXANDER B. KLOTS

WALTER DAWN

(Right) A honeybee that has been sucking nectar from a zinnia pauses for a few moments to clean off its mouthparts.

SWARMING starts a new colony. The swarm settles on a tree limb, and scouts find a place for a new nest.

BEE CHAIN is formed as workers take honey from the old hive and make wax from it to build the new comb.

stroys all the other queen cells, thus eliminating competition.

Meanwhile, the old queen has left the hive along with several thousand workers and a few drones. This swarm usually settles on some near-by tree limb where it forms a tight cluster. Scout bees then fly away seeking suitable locations for the new nest. These scouts return one by one and perform charadelike dances similar to those used to indicate the location of flowers. These dances go on for some time, and the scouts that have found the best locations dance the most enthusiastically. Eventually, a site is decided upon, and the swarm flies to it and establishes a new colony.

Before leaving the parent hive, the workers composing the swarm fill themselves with honey so that they can secrete wax to build the new hive. The cells that they build are very remarkable containers. It has been determined that these hexagonal cells will hold the largest amount of honey for the smallest amount of wax used. One pound (0.5 kg) of wax will build 35,000 cells in which about 22 pounds (9.9 kg) of honey can be stored. It is estimated that bees must consume about eight pounds (3.6 kg) of honey to produce one pound of wax.

Varieties of Honeybees. The scientific name of the honeybee, *Apis mellifera*, is quite appropriate since *Apis* means "honey maker" while *mellifera* means "honey carrier." There are several varieties or races of these honeybees found originally in various countries. One of these, the Cyprian honeybee from the island of Cyprus, is considered by some authorities to be the mother race of all the yellow varieties; however, the golden Italians are the chief ones used at present by most beekeepers. Italian queens are very prolific and the workers are relatively gentle. These bees are characterized by the golden coloration of the first three or four segments of the abdomen.

Black varieties of the honeybees, originally from Holland and Germany, have been introduced into the United States but no longer are favored by beekeepers. They have several redeeming characteristics but are ill-tempered and not so easy to manage as are the golden Italian bees. In addition to black bees from Holland and Germany, there are black varieties originat-

ing in Africa, Britain, and other places. Another variety of bees sometimes favored by beekeepers is the Carniolan, a large silver-gray bee from the Alps. These are believed by some to be more gentle in disposition than most other honeybees and to reproduce abundantly. On the other hand, they form swarms excessively and so are not suitable in apiaries or bee yards that are not closely watched. Some American beekeepers have had excellent results with crosses between these bees and other varieties.

The honeybee varieties discussed above belong to the *mellifera* group, but there are several other species of the genus *Apis*. One of these (*Apis indica*) is found in India while another, smaller species (*Apis florea*) is found in the East Indies.

Bumblebees. In general, the structure and habits of bumblebees are quite similar to those of the honeybees. Some authorities classify them in the same family, the Apidae, while others place them in a separate family, the Bombidae.

Bumblebees are large or medium-sized social bees with hairy bodies conspicuously marked with yellow and black or, sometimes, red or white. They are common insects that live in family colonies consisting of a queen and many workers. Bumblebees are found in most parts of the world and usually nest in cavities in the ground, such as old mouse or bird nests.

In temperate climates, only the mated queens survive the winter. When spring arrives the queens select nesting sites and build wax cells in which the young are reared. During this period of nest-establishment, the queen assumes all the labor of gathering pollen and nectar, building cells, and feeding the young. During periods of cool damp weather she broods the young with heat from her own body. In order that she may have a store of food for her developing young, she constructs a wax "honey pot," which she fills with nectar gathered from flowers.

After her first larvae have transformed into pupae and have emerged from their cells as adult workers, they carry on the field work of gathering food. From then on the queen remains in the nest. By summer's end, the bumblebee colony may consist of several hundred individuals, but with the coming of cold weather all of the workers die. Only the recently emerged and

BROOD CELLS, built on the ground, are bumblebees' nests. Like the honeybee, the bumblebee is a social bee.

BUMBLEBEES have yellow and black hairy bodies. The long mouth parts enable them to pollinate red clover.

mated queens survive the winter by hibernating in protected places. In spring the queens emerge from hibernation and search for places to establish nests. It is a common sight in the spring to see bumblebee queens flying about near the ground investigating every hole or cavity which might serve as a nesting place.

While most bumblebees are very industrious insects, like their relatives the honeybees, there are certain kinds (*Psithyrus*) that are social parasites in other bumblebee nests. These bees have no worker caste and the queen is unable to found her own colony. She invades a bumblebee nest and lays her eggs there; the young are reared by the unsuspecting host workers. The parasitic queen has no pollen-collecting baskets on her hind legs, since this duty is carried out by the workers of the bumblebee colony she invades.

There are several different kinds of *Psithyrus* bees, each with somewhat different habits. Some *Psithyrus* queens kill the rightful queen, but other kinds live in harmony with her. However, the *Psithyrus* queen often devours the bumblebee young.

Nonsocial Bees. The nonsocial bees vary in behavior but none of them is a truly social insect. Some, such as the carpenter bees, remain together for a time, indicating perhaps the beginning of the colonial or social way of life.

Generally the females of nonsocial bees build their own nests and stock them with food for the young; then they depart to build other nests. Thus, the nonsocial larvae receive no individual care. There is no worker caste as in the social bees. Many kinds of nonsocial bees have nesting habits quite similar to such wasps as the thread-waisted (*Sphex*) wasp. Unlike the wasps, however, the nonsocial bees do not stock their nests with paralyzed prey as food for their young; they store only pollen and nectar collected from flowers.

The most common nonsocial bees belong to the following families:

Family Andrenidae: Burrowing Bees. A large family that occurs throughout the world, these bees are medium-sized and usually are black, marked with yellow or red. Some kinds resemble honeybees. Sometimes, large numbers of these bees nest close together and so are considered to be colonial in habits. The females excavate ground tunnels, which are filled with pollen and nectar

for the young. In some cases the nests are excavated in open, sandy areas, while in other cases they are in clay banks along streams. In building the tunnels, the main shaft usually is constructed vertically and has lateral chambers extending out at right angles. The young are reared in the lateral chambers. Winter is spent in these underground tunnels in either the adult or pupal stage, depending on the species.

Family Halicidae: Mining Bees. These are small or medium-sized bees that often are black with metallic hues. Many kinds have red or yellow markings. The females have well-developed equipment for collecting pollen and, like the burrowing bees, they excavate their nests in the ground and stock them with pollen and nectar gathered from flowers. Some kinds, such as *Halictus*, have more or less social habits. Several females may cooperate in excavating a burrow, with each female making side galleries and cells in which she rears her young. A few of the mining bees are wasplike and live as social parasites in the nests of other halictid bees.

The beginnings of social habits are found in the habits of some of the mining bees. For example, the female of one kind (*Halictus quadricinctus*) builds a crude comb consisting of about 20 cells in her underground nest and stocks the cells with food. She then guards the chamber until the young transform into the adult stage. Other kinds of female mining bees spend the winter together in the underground nests and, with the arrival of spring, set about housecleaning. However, a fight eventually takes place among these females and the losers leave to build their own nests. The first young emerge from their cells in June, but these young do not mate. Their status may be compared to that of worker honeybees since they do a large part of the work in the nest. The females that mature late in summer mate and survive the winter. In these respects, habits of these mining bees are rather similar to those of bumblebees.

Family Anthophoridae: Mining Bees. These are medium-sized bees of variable color, often yellowish, brown, metallic gold, or coppery. Some kinds are black. Pollen baskets or pollen-collecting hairs are present on the hind legs of some.

These mining bees usually nest in large colonies in clay or sandy banks. Often their cells are lined with clay in order to hold the mixture of pollen and honey with which they are stocked.

Some kinds construct clay entrances to their burrows in the form of elbows. While most kinds nest in the earth, a few nest in rotten wood.

These bees have a number of enemies. One is the wingless female of a blister beetle (*Hornia*), which lays her eggs in the bees' nest. When the eggs hatch, the larval beetles attach themselves to the adult bees. The beetles feed on the stored food when the adult bees build new nests.

Family Megachilidae: Leaf-Cutter Bees. These are stout-bodied bees of moderate size. A few are parasitic. Some kinds excavate tunnels in the earth while others cut tunnels in wood. Still others make nests in hollow twigs or in almost any elongated cavity. There are many different kinds of leaf-cutter bees, and they occur in almost all parts of the world. Their habits are diverse. In the case of *Megachile*, burrows are made in rotten wood, hollow plant stems, or in the earth. These tunnels, which may be several inches long, are lined with oval sections cut from plant leaves or petals and are partitioned off into cells by means of circular leaf sections. About a dozen cells may be built. They are stocked with a mixture of pollen and nectar, and an egg is laid in each one.

Leaf-cutter bees transport pollen by means of brushes on the underside of their abdomen rather than on their hind legs. They use their scissor-like jaws to cut out the round and oval leaf-sections; and the leaf sections are held horizontally in their legs beneath their bodies as they fly back to the nests.

Other kinds of Megachilidae, instead of using leaf-sections, line their nests with thistledown, cotton, or other plant fibers. A few kinds construct clay cells.

Family Xylocopidae: Large Carpenter Bees. These are large, heavy-bodied bees that resemble bumblebees. Usually they are black or blue-black in color, and their legs are stout and hairy but have no special baskets for collecting pollen. They are solitary in habit and construct their nests in cavities that they cut in solid wood or in the stems of plants. Each kind is more or less specific in its choice of woods. The large carpenter bee (*Xylocopa*) excavates its nest in solid pine or other soft wood timbers such as rafters. These tunnels are about the size of a dime in cross section, and penetrate into the wood for an inch or so, then follow the grain for nearly a foot. The arduous work of cutting these tunnels is done with the bee's sharp jaws and requires considerable time.

Once the tunnel is completed, the female collects pollen and nectar and stocks a cell at the far end. An egg is then laid, and the cell is sealed off with wood chips cemented together. A number of additional cells are constructed similarly, and when the eggs hatch, the young feed upon the store of food. Eventually these larvae all pupate and then transform into adults. As might be expected, the bee in the distal cell matures first and cannot escape because of the presence of the other cells. Thus, it must wait until the other bees, one by one, become adults. Then the female leads them out of the tunnel on their first flight. This, perhaps, may be another indication of the beginning of the social habit. However, in some species the first bees to become adults simply break out of their cells and scramble over those still in the process of maturing.

CARPENTER BEES build their nests in cavities that they cut in timbers or plant stems. They are nonsocial.

It is logical that a tunnel excavated in solid wood should be used again, and this is what occurs. Usually, one of the daughter bees uses the parent tunnel to rear her own young. Male carpenter bees take no part in the work of nest construction but often may be seen buzzing about places where the females are at work. Sometimes, carpenter bees become so abundant that their tunneling activities in house timbers do considerable damage.

Since the nesting tunnels constructed by carpenter bees are relatively secure from enemy intrusion, it is not surprising that other insects often take advantage of them. One of these insects is a large black and white wasp (*Monobia quadridens*) that constructs clay partitions in old carpenter bee tunnels and stocks them, one by one, with paralyzed cutworms.

There are about 350 different species of large carpenter bees in the world, most of which occur in the tropics. In the United States, *Xylocopa virginica* is the most abundant kind. In Burma, there is a beautiful reddish and golden carpenter bee (*X. rufescens*), which is nocturnal in habits.

Family Ceratinidae: Small Carpenter Bees. These bees are much smaller than the Xylocopidae, but their habits are quite similar. Instead of excavating their tunnels in solid wood, however, they nest in the hollow stems of reeds or small twigs.

Economic Importance of Bees. Bees are of great importance to human beings for a number of reasons. Not only do honeybees produce honey and wax, but they also aid the farmer and fruit-grower by pollinating crops and fruit trees. Most flowers are dependent upon bees of one kind or another for carrying pollen from the anthers (male part) of one flower to the stigmas (female part) of other flowers. If these flowers are on separate plants, the process is called cross-pollination and usually results in better seed. Pollination of a flower by its own pollen is called self-pollination. Some flowers, however, cannot be pollinated by pollen from the same flower, or from the same plant or tree. Thus the purpose of colorful flowers is largely to attract bees for their aid in carrying pollen.

Many fruit trees will not produce fruit abundantly unless bees are present to pollinate them. Examples are almond, apple, cherry, pear, plum, and peach trees. Among the many seed crops that require the presence of bees are alfalfa,

POLLEN and nectar are collected by the workers, to be used both for food and for making honey and wax.

POLLEN is gathered on hairs along the bee's hind legs. Any grains on their bodies are combed onto their legs.

A POLLEN BASKET filled with pollen is shown here. When the baskets are full, the bee returns to the hive.

HONEY is made from nectar that is stored in the bee's crop. Here a bee (*right*) extrudes honey from its crop.

clover, pumpkin, sunflower, sweet clover, and vetch. Some flowers cannot be pollinated except by bumblebees, which have long tongues. The best example of this is red clover. When red clover was first planted in New Zealand it did not produce seed. Then it was discovered that there were no bumblebees in that country, and they had to be imported from England so that the red clover could produce seed.

Considerable research has been carried out to determine the number of bees needed to pollinate a given number of fruit trees or a certain number of acres of crops. It is estimated that from two to three hives are needed per acre of alfalfa for proper seed production. About two colonies of bees are needed for each acre of Ladino, alsike, and white Dutch clovers. Some beekeepers rent colonies of bees to orchards and farmers for their services in pollination.

Honeybees and bumblebees are not the only bees useful in pollination. Almost all of the pollen and nectar-collecting bees are helpful in this respect. In some areas, burrowing (andrenid) bees are important pollinators of field crops. These bees, however, favor plants of the mustard, daisy, rose, and legume families. Mining (halictid and anthophorid) bees also are important as pollinators.

Honey produced by honeybees has been considered a delicious food for thousands of years, and the honeybee is among the most ancient of domestic animals. It was known in ancient Egypt as early as 3500 B.C., and the delicious honey it produced was man's first source of sweets. Honey is manufactured by bees from flower nectar by the process of concentration and partial digestion. It contains about 25 percent water and 8 percent sucrose (cane) sugar. Other sugars such as fructose and glucose are also present. It also contains several enzymes that digest carbohydrates. Honey also contains certain vitamins. Thus, in addition to being a delicious food, honey may also be considered an important dietary addition.

In addition to honey, bees also produce wax, which they use in building combs. Beeswax has many commercial uses such as in the manufacturing of polishes, candles, crayons, and cosmetics. The greatest use for beeswax, at present, is in the cosmetic industry, which uses more than 1 million pounds (454,000 kg) annually. Another important use of beeswax is in the manufacture of sheets of artificial foundation used in beehives. Bees use these foundations to build cells for honey storage and for rearing their young.

ROSS E. HUTCHINS
Mississippi State University

Bibliography

Crompton, John, *Hive of Bees* (New York 1958).
Frisch, Karl von, *Dancing Bees* (New York 1961).
Grout, Roy A., *Hive and the Honey Bee* (Hamilton, Ill., 1963).
Hoyt, Murray, *World of Bees* (New York 1965).
Lindauer, Martin, *Communication Among Social Bees* (Cambridge, Mass., 1961).
Ribbands, C. Ronald, *Behavior and Social Life of Honeybees* (New York 1953).
Sakagami, Shoichi, and Michener, Charles, *Nest Architecture of the Sweat Bees (Halictinae)* (Lawrence, Kansas, 1962).
Snodgrass, R.E., *Anatomy of the Honeybee* (Ithaca, N.Y., 1956).

BEE KEEPING, is the maintenance of bee colonies for the commercial production of honey and other bee products and for use in cross-pollination of crops. According to the U.S. Department of Agriculture, over 260,000,000 pounds (118,-040,000 kg) of honey are produced annually by the bee keeping industry in the United States. However, the honeybees' chief value lies in their ability to pollinate over 60 agricultural crops, and thus increase the production of fruit and seed. Bees are responsible for 80 to 85 percent of all crop pollination performed by insects in the United States. With the increased use of insecticides and more intensive cultivation of the land, many wild insects have been destroyed, leaving the important task of pollination more and more to the honeybee.

There are several species of bees, but the most important, from a commercial standpoint, is *Apis mellifera.* This species comprises the black bee of the United States; the Italian bee from the southern part of Italy; the Syrian bee of Palestine; the Cyprian, from the island of Cyprus; the Carniolan, from Austria; and the Caucasian from the Caucasus Mountains. The most important of all these varieties is the Italian bee, which is the most industrious and the gentlest. The Italian bees, together with the dark Caucasian bees are used most extensively in the United States—in fact, throughout much of the world.

Types of Hive Bees. There are three kinds of bees in the hive: the workers, or undeveloped females; the queen, a fully developed female; and the drone, or male bee. The queen lays all the eggs of the hive and may lay as many as 2,000 in a day. There may be from 10,000 to 100,000 bees in a single colony. The drones are incapable of gathering honey, and they exist only to fertilize the young queens. The workers gather all the honey and pollen, fill all the combs, and rear the young bees. As soon as the mating season is over, the drones starve to death.

How to Handle Bees. There is a general impression that ordinary honeybees are vicious and will attack any one who comes near their hives. This is a misconception. Under certain conditions, when their habits are known, they will permit one to open their hives apart, remove their honeycombs, and not even sting the intruder. But an inexperienced or awkward person may irritate them.

A method used to bring them into a state of subjection is to blow smoke into the entrance and over the combs. If a person's motions about the hive are careful and deliberate, the bees will not attack. Smoke, when intelligently used, disarms opposition and puts the bees into a quiet state.

The bee smoker used for this purpose is a small bellows attached to a cylindrical stove having a nozzle from which the smoke is blown. Besides the bee smoker, the beekeeper generally uses a bee veil made of wire cloth. Gloves are sometimes used by timid persons or beginners, but all work with the bees usually is performed with bare hands. Stings are, of course, received occasionally, but beyond a sharp, momentary pain, no permanent effect will be felt after the first season, for the beekeeper very soon becomes immune so that no swelling takes place.

Marketable Products of the Hive. Beeswax, comb, and extracted honey are products produced in the hive and sold commercially. Beeswax, which is secreted by the bees and used in building their combs, is an important commercial product and commands a good price in the United States. Three to five million pounds are produced there annually. This wax is used for polishes, for liturgical candles, and in cosmetics. Beeswax is harvested by melting old or damaged honeycombs and the cappings taken off in extracting. A common method of rendering the wax is to melt the combs in a glass-covered pan heated by the sun. Various devices are on the market, but if much wax is produced, it is advisable that the bee keeper make a careful study of the methods of wax extraction.

Comb Honey Production. Comb honey usually is produced in little square boxes. Several million of these are made and used in the United States annually. Extracted honey is in the liquid form. It is thrown from the combs by means of centrifugal force in a honey extractor.

Honey in the comb cannot be adulterated or manufactured. Bee keepers use a commercial product known as "comb foundation," which is sheeted wax embossed on both sides with indentations having the exact shape and form of the bottom of the cells of honeycomb. It is put into the hive where the bees draw it out into comb. But this is as far as the skill of man can go, and there is no such thing as artificial comb honey.

Producing comb honey requires considerable skill. Hives and supers are arranged so that the little boxes containing sheets of comb foundation are accessible to the bees and so that they can build the foundation into comb, fill the cells with honey, and seal them over. When the bees are at work in the fields and the combs are beginning to whiten and to be filled with honey in what is called the brood nest, the honey boxes are put in the upper part of the hive. These are allowed to remain on during the height of the honey flow until they are filled and capped over. Then they are removed, and others are put in their place.

Extracted Honey Production. The business of producing extracted (or liquid) honey requires

BEE KEEPERS generally use wooden box hives such as these for housing their honey-producing apiaries.

ANNAN PHOTO FEATURES

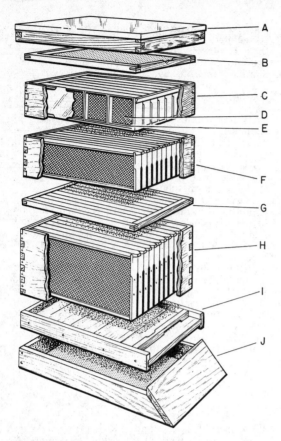

take up new quarters and start housekeeping anew. The young bees, together with those unhatched, with a young queen, are left to take care of the old hive.

In ordinary practice it is a custom for the bee keeper to rehive the swarm by taking the bees as soon as they cluster and putting them into another hive. Some beekeepers clip the old queen's wings, preventing her flight with the swarm. However, later the swarm will leave with the new queen, so unless some further swarm preventive is used clipping only delays the swarm.

Prevention of Swarming. When a colony is allowed to swarm, the population loss hampers its ability to produce honey; therefore every effort should be made to overcome this impulse. Since crowded, overheated hives are conducive to swarming, this tendency is overcome by providing adequate ventilation and additional room in the hive. Another preventative against swarming is frequent examination of the hive during the swarming season for the purpose of cutting out queen cells. Also, requeening with young queens early in the season generally prevents swarming.

Robbing. There are certain times during the season when no nectar is secreted by the flowers. During such periods the bees will rob each other if they can. When sweets can be obtained in considerable quantity from a weak colony unable to defend itself, the bees are apt to become furious. There is a rush and when the sweets suddenly are cut off, the bees are inclined to be cross and to sting. The wise and careful beekeeper will see to it that the entrances of his weak colonies are made smaller so that the sentinels or guards can protect themselves from intrusion from other bees.

Feeding. When bees are short of honey, sugar sirup may be substituted. This is fed to the bees in an inverted can with a few small holes punched in the lid. This is placed on top of the colony and enclosed in the upper story of the beehive. However, it is always better to give bees combs of honey or a whole hive body of combs containing honey. Sugar sirup—two

SMOKE is used to subdue bees for handling. The apparatus is a smoke pot containing smouldering wood chips.

BEE HIVE for comb honey: A—metal-clad cover; B—inner cover; C—section super, for comb honey; D—thin super, beeswax comb foundation; E—comb section box; F—shallow super, for honey storage; G—excluder, to keep queen in brood nest; H—deep super, for brood nest or honey surplus; I—bottom board; J—hive stand.

almost the same intelligent care and attention. Instead of section boxes, however, an extra set of combs is put in the upper story of the hive. The combs also are placed above the lower or brood part of the hive. When these are filled with honey and capped over, they are taken from the hive and the bees are removed from the combs so they can be transported to the extracting house and extracted. The thin film of wax covering the cells of the comb is shaved off with a knife specially designed for the purpose. After the combs are uncapped, they are put in the honey extractor and revolved at a high rate of speed. The honey flies out of the comb by centrifugal force against the sides of the extractor. Then the combs are reversed, and the other surfaces are emptied. Finally, the combs are returned to the hive to be filled again by the bees.

Swarming. At the beginning of or during the honey flow, when the colony has reached a high state of prosperity and the combs are being filled with honey, a swarm may come forth between the hours of 9 A.M. and 3 P.M. Half of the bees, including the queen, are likely to come out of the hive. The bees hover about for 15 or 20 minutes, and then cluster on some bush or tree. They will wait here for two or three hours, or perhaps overnight. Then they will fly into some hollow tree or cave where they will

A HIVE COMB is shown being held out. The honeybees cap each comb cell with wax after it is filled with honey.

WORKER BEES cover this hive frame. Most of the honey cells are capped, and the comb is ready for extraction.

parts sugar, one part water—is not a natural food and should be used only when no sweet is available from the field.

Wintering. At the beginning of winter each colony should have a minimum of 60 lbs. (27 kg) of stored honey and preferably more. The hive entrances should be reduced to prevent small predators, such as mice, from getting into the hive. In some very cold northern regions, bee-keepers pack their hives with insulation to conserve the consumption of honey.

Diseases of Brood. There are two diseases that attack the brood of honeybees: American and European foul brood. The American foul brood is the more serious, and there is no cure. The bee keeper who finds it in his hives should burn the combs, bees and all, and scorch out the interior of the hive with a blowtorch. Terramycin and sulfathiazole also are used as a preventative and control. European foul brood can be cured by building up the colony's strength by requeening with a good strain of Italian bees known to be resistant to the disease, so that the vigor of the colony will be increased rapidly. Combs having foul brood scales should be melted and rendered for wax, and new foundations should be put in the frames.

Enemies of Bees. A number of insects, birds, and mammals must be classed as enemies of bees, but of these the larger wax moth, the lesser wax moth, and ants are the only ones of importance. Moth larvae often destroy combs. To prevent this the combs are fumigated with paradichlorobenzene or ethylene dibromide in tiers of hives or in tight rooms. In warm climates ants are a serious pest. The usual method of keeping them out is to put the hive on a stand and to rest the legs of the hive in vessels containing oil or creosote.

E.R. ROOT, *A.I. Root Company*

Bibliography

Dadant, Camille P., *First Lessons in Beekeeping* (Hamilton, Ill., 1960).
Deans, Alexander S.C., *Beekeeping Techniques* (Edinburgh 1963).
Laidlaw, Harry Hyde, and Eckert, John Edward, *Queen Rearing*, 2d ed. (Berkeley 1962).
Phillips, Everett F., *Beekeeping* (New York 1960).
Root, Amos Ives, *ABC and XYZ of Bee Culture*, 3d ed. (Medina, Ind., 1966).
Smith, Francis Godfrey, *Beekeeping in the Tropics* (Dorchester, Engl., 1960).

EXTRACTOR machines remove the honey from the combs. The combs then are reinstalled within the hive.

BEEBE, bē'bē, **Charles William** (1877–1962), American scientist, explorer, and author. He was born in Brooklyn, N.Y., on July 29, 1877. He was graduated from Columbia University in 1898, and from 1899 he was associated with the New York Zoological Society as curator of ornithology and director of the Department of Tropical Research. He made the collection of living birds at the New York Zoological Gardens (Bronx Zoo) one of the world's finest.

Beebe led over 60 scientific expeditions to all parts of the world. In 1934, while conducting a series of investigations of deep-sea creatures in Bermuda waters, he and Otis Barton descended 3,028 feet (923 meters)—a record at that time— in an iron ball called a bathysphere (q.v.).

As a writer of natural history, Beebe had few peers. His books on birds, fishes, and insects are full of charm and fascinating observations, and they often became best sellers. The best known include *Galapagos, World's End* (1923); *Jungle Days* (1925); *Beneath Tropic Seas* (1928); *Half Mile Down* (1934); *High Jungle* (1949); *Unseen Life of New York* (1953); and *Adventuring with Beebe* (1955). Beebe died near Arima, Trinidad, on June 4, 1962.

BEECH, a large hardwood tree found in the temperate regions of the Northern Hemisphere. It often grows more than 80 feet (24 meters) high, with a trunk over 3½ feet (1 meter) in diameter. It has smooth gray bark, dark green foliage, and sweet-flavored, edible nuts. The wood is reddish brown, solid, finely grained, and brittle. The roots, which extend for a considerable distance, lie near the surface of the soil and partly above it.

Beech trees normally live about 250 years and rarely produce fruit before they are 50 years old. They thrive on a soil mixture of limestone, clay, silt, and sand, but grow poorly in damp areas.

The beeches make up the genus *Fagus*, which has several species. Two important species are the common or European beech (*F. sylvatica*) and the American beech (*F. grandifolia*). The European beech has shiny, dark green leaves, which may turn a reddish brown in the autumn, but often persist throughout the winter. The American beech has pale green, slightly longer leaves, which turn yellow in the autumn before they fall. The leaves of the American beech are more coarsely toothed and contain more veins. Both species yield sweet, edible nuts.

The copper purple beech (*F. sylvatica atropunicea*) has purple leaves. A variety of the European beech, it is common in America. *F. betuloides,* found in Tierra del Fuego off the southern coast of South America, has evergreen foliage and is a striking feature of the winter landscape. The wood of this species is used in making floors and roofs. *F. sieboldii* is an ornamental beech found in Japan.

The blue or water beech (*Carpinus americana*) is not a member of the beech family (*Fagaceae*), but is a Hornbeam (q.v.).

Beech trees have several uses and furnish many products. Their colorful bark and foliage make them attractive ornamental plantings. Young beeches are useful as hedges because their branches will coalesce if tied together. Beechwood makes an excellent fuel. It is also used in dams and water mills because it is remarkably long-lasting when immersed in water. This resistance to water is especially true of the European beechwood, which is used in making wooden shoes (*sabots*) in France. The bark of a beech tree is sometimes used in tanning. Creosote, an oil used as a wood preservative, is obtained from beech trees.

BEECH GROVE is a city in central Indiana, in Marion County, 7 miles (11 km) southeast of Indianapolis, of which it is a residential suburb. It is situated in a farming region that raises cattle and produces grain and fruit. Railroad shops are the largest industry here. Manufactures include electrical equipment, machine-tool parts, and clothing. Beech-Bank, the home of Sarah T. Bolton (1814–1893), pioneer Indiana poet, is preserved here. Settled in 1902, Beech Grove was incorporated in 1906 and named for the beech trees on the site. Government is by mayor-council. Population: 13,468.

BEECHAM, bē'chəm, **Sir Thomas** (1879–1961), English orchestra conductor, who founded the Royal Philharmonic Orchestra. He was born *Godfrey Thomas Beecham* in St. Helens, Lancashire, on April 28, 1879, the son of a wealthy manufacturer. Beecham attended Rossall School and Wadham College, Oxford, where he received some musical training under the organist John Varley Roberts. He also studied music with Charles Wood and Moritz Moszkowski in the early 1900's. However, he was largely self-taught musically.

In 1905, Beecham made his first concert appearance in London, as conductor of the Queen's Hall Orchestra. A year later he founded the New Symphony Orchestra and in 1908 established the Beecham Symphony. In 1910 he presented the first of a long series of opera seasons in London's Covent Garden, and three years later he helped to bring Russian ballet and opera to London. He was knighted in 1916.

Beecham was the founder of the London Symphony in 1932 and the Royal Philharmonic in 1947. He also was a frequent conductor in the United

THE AMERICAN MUSEUM OF NATURAL HISTORY

THE AMERICAN BEECH (*Fagus grandifolia*) produces edible nuts (*left*) after reaching maturity.

GOTTSCHO-SCHLEISNER, INC.

States. He led the Seattle Symphony in 1941 and 1942, the orchestra of the Metropolitan Opera, New York City, in 1942–1944, and the Houston Orchestra in the late 1950's. He died in London on March 8, 1961.

Beecham was a legend in his time, as much for his unpredictable personality and fiery temperament as for his musical genius. He did much to popularize opera in Britain and was especially instrumental in promoting the music of the English composer Frederick Delius, beginning with his presentation of Delius' opera, *Village Romeo and Juliet*, in 1910. Beecham also favored the music of the 18th century, particularly that of Mozart, and he arranged several orchestral suites from 18th century works, including *The Great Elopement* (1945), a ballet suite from the music of Handel. Beecham was the author of a witty autobiography, *A Mingled Chime* (1943).

Further Reading: Reid, Charles, *Thomas Beecham* (New York 1962).

BEECHER, bē′chər, an American family that made important contributions to the religious and cultural life of the United States in the 19th century. The first Beechers to go to America arrived in Boston in 1637 with a group of Puritans who founded New Haven the following year. Succeeding generations of Beecher men, who were renowned for their great physical strength, worked principally as farmers and blacksmiths.

The family was brought to national prominence by *Lyman Beecher* (1775–1863), who had learned blacksmithing from his father and grandfather before entering Yale College. Lyman Beecher became one of the greatest American preachers of his time and was also longtime president of the Lane Theological Seminary in Cincinnati.

The Beecher tradition was one of large families—and also often of several marriages: Lyman Beecher's father married five times and had 12 children. Lyman's first wife was Roxana Foote, a millworker of Guilford, Conn. She was the mother of nine of his 13 children, including all (except Thomas Kinnicut Beecher) who later became well known. This shy and sensitive woman died in 1816; in 1817, Lyman Beecher married Harriet Porter, an aristocratic woman from Portland, Me., and they had four children. When she died in Boston in 1835, Beecher married Mrs. Lydia Beals Jackson of Boston; they had no children.

Lyman Beecher had a robust but volatile nature. His children absorbed his Calvinist teachings from their earliest years, yet none of them accepted religion in later life without serious questioning and soul-searching. Four sons followed in their father's footsteps to achieve national reputations as clergymen and educators: *Edward Beecher* (1803–1895), *Henry Ward Beecher* (1813–1887), *Charles Beecher* (1815–1900), and *Thomas Kinnicut Beecher* (1824–1900). Henry Ward Beecher, the most celebrated of the brothers, was a popular preacher and lecturer as well as a prolific author. His books include *The Life of Jesus the Christ* (1871) and *Evolution and Religion* (1885). He married only once but was the father of 10 children.

One of Lyman Beecher's five daughters, *Harriet Elizabeth Beecher Stowe* (1811–1896), who had become aware of the evils of slavery during the family's residence in Cincinnati, was the author of *Uncle Tom's Cabin*. Although she wrote many other books, none of them enjoyed anything like the enormous popularity of this famous antislavery novel.

Another of the daughters, Lyman's first-born child, *Catharine Esther Beecher* (1800–1878), also exemplified the family's involvement in public issues and social improvement. She was a pioneer in the education of women.

See also separate articles on these prominent members of the Beecher family.

Further Reading: Stowe, Lyman Beecher, *Saints, Sinners and Beechers* (Indianapolis 1934).

BEECHER, bē′chər, **Catharine Esther** (1800–1878), American educator, whose life interest was the improvement of education for women. She was the eldest of 13 children of Lyman Beecher. When she was 16, her mother died, and Catharine helped raise a family that included several noted members.

She was born at East Hampton, Long Island, N.Y., on Sept. 6, 1800, and moved with her family to Litchfield, Conn., in 1810. After the death of her fiancé in 1823, Miss Beecher—who never married—established a young ladies' school in Hartford, Conn. She started a similar school in Cincinnati, Ohio, when she moved there with her father in 1832. Returning east in 1837, she worked to improve women's education, particularly in the "western" states, and helped found several "female colleges." She was, however, strongly opposed to the woman suffrage movement. Miss Beecher died at Elmira, N.Y., on May 12, 1878.

BEECHER, bē′chər, **Charles** (1815–1900), American Congregationalist minister and educator. He was born in Litchfield, Conn., on Oct. 7, 1815. After graduating from Bowdoin College in 1834, he studied for the ministry under his father, Lyman Beecher, in Cincinnati, Ohio. He was pastor of Congregational churches in Fort Wayne, Ind. (from 1844), Newark, N.J. (from 1851), and Georgetown, Mass. (from 1857). Beecher, who wrote two books on spiritualism, was convicted of heresy in 1863 for believing in the preexistence of souls. The action was later rescinded. In 1864 he served in the Massachusetts legislature and from 1871 to 1873 was Florida state school superintendent. He died in Georgetown on April 21, 1900.

BEECHER, bē′chər, **Edward** (1803–1895), American clergyman and educator, who was active in the antislavery movement. He was born at East Hampton, Long Island, N.Y., on Aug. 27, 1803, the son of Lyman Beecher, and graduated from Yale College in 1822. From 1826 to 1830 he was pastor of the Park Street Church, Boston, Mass.

Named first president of Illinois College, at Jacksonville, Ill., in 1830, Beecher helped organize the first statewide antislavery society in Illinois. In 1838 he wrote his *Narrative of the Alton Riots*, an account of the mobs that attacked the Alton, Ill., printing plant of his friend Elijah P. Lovejoy, a noted abolitionist, and killed Lovejoy. Beecher became pastor of the Salem Street Church, Boston, in 1844 and of the First Congregational Church of Galesburg, Ill., in 1855. In 1871 he retired to Brooklyn, N.Y., where his brother Henry Ward Beecher was a famous clergyman. He died there on July 28, 1895.

Henry Ward Beecher (1813–1887), American clergyman.

BEECHER, bē′chər, **Henry Ward** (1813–1887), American clergyman, who was one of the most colorful and influential religious figures of the 19th century in the United States. He was the brother of Harriet Beecher Stowe, who wrote the famous antislavery novel *Uncle Tom's Cabin* (1851). For nearly 40 years, until the day of his death, Beecher was pastor of Plymouth Church (Congregational) in Brooklyn, N.Y. Each week he addressed congregations of 2,000 to 3,000 persons. They came to hear Beecher comment on current events and needed social reforms, as well as on church doctrine. His national popularity was only slightly diminished by a public scandal in his 61st year.

If Beecher was a dominant influence in the life of 19th century America, he also mirrored its changing character. He was born on June 24, 1813, in Litchfield, Conn., the son of Lyman Beecher, a Calvinist preacher. Beecher's upbringing was strict, in the Puritan style of colonial America. But during his 20's and 30's he lived and preached in lusty frontier communities of the Middle West.

In those years Beecher was slow to take a stand on slavery, the burning issue of the day. He was rarely, in fact, a leader or original thinker. But he was a brilliant exponent of the consensus, and of his own convictions once he had arrived at them. When civil war threatened, Beecher came out firmly against slavery and was an articulate supporter of Abraham Lincoln for president. His liberalism increased with the years, and he was one of the few clergymen to favor Charles Darwin's theory of evolution. He was also a warm advocate of woman suffrage. In 1884, Beecher broke with the Republican party, of which he had long been an influential member, to join the Mugwumps, or independent Republicans, in support of Grover Cleveland.

Education and First Pastorates. In his youth Beecher was a poor student and was sent to several New England schools before matriculating at Amherst College. After graduating in 1834, he decided to follow in his father's footsteps, although he had felt no call to become a preacher. His father was then the first president of the Lane Theological Seminary in Cincinnati, Ohio. While a student there, the young Beecher experienced a revelation. Walking in the woods

one morning, he felt that God loves man "in his sins" in order to help him out of them.

Beecher accepted his first pastorate in Lawrenceburg, Ind., in 1837, and that summer he married Eunice White Bullard, a Massachusetts girl to whom he had become engaged while at Amherst. The first of their 10 children was born in Lawrenceburg. Beecher became pastor of the Second Presbyterian Church of Indianapolis, Ind., in 1839 and remained there for eight years. He was much in demand for revival services and began to write for the newspapers. He was acquiring a national reputation.

Beecher in Brooklyn. In 1847 he refused calls to two well-known Boston churches and accepted the pastorate of Plymouth Church, a small Congregational church in Brooklyn, N.Y. When this church burned down in 1849, a much larger one, with a semicircular auditorium, was built to accommodate the many people who were already coming to hear him. Beecher preferred to speak from a platform, rather than from a pulpit, and never wrote out his sermons.

About this time, Harriet Beecher Stowe wrote of her brother: "He has had the misfortune of a popularity which is perfectly phenomenal." Beecher's overflowing vitality was his principal characteristic. He was robust of body, with a leonine head, long hair, and flashing blue-gray eyes. His oratory was rich in symbolism and imagery. At heart, Beecher was a poet. He loved nature and people, was always informal in dress and manner, and rather disorganized in his conduct of church and personal affairs. He preached not hellfire and damnation, but love.

Beecher became a contributor to the *Independent*, a weekly periodical in New York, and was named its editor in 1861. Its managing editor was Theodore Tilton, 22 years younger than Beecher but a devoted admirer. In fact, Beecher had officiated at the wedding of Theodore and Elizabeth Tilton in 1855 and had become a family friend. When Beecher went to England in 1863 to plead the cause of antislavery, Tilton succeeded him as editor of the *Independent*.

In the summer of 1870, Mrs. Tilton told her husband she had committed adultery with Beecher. She later retracted her confession, at the prompting of Beecher, but the story got out and was published. Beecher publicly denied the rumors in 1873. The following year Tilton published a statement charging Beecher with gross immorality. A committee of six from Plymouth Church investigated and cleared the pastor of the charges. In 1874, Tilton filed a complaint against Beecher for adultery and asked $100,000 damages. The six-month trial in 1875 received nationwide publicity and resulted in a hung jury. The jury's vote was said to have been nine to three in favor of Beecher. A council of Congregational churches also cleared him.

Beecher was the author of several books that were popular in the 19th century: *Seven Lectures to Young Men* (1844); *Norwood, or Village Life in New England* (1867), a novel; and *The Life of Jesus the Christ*, of which the first volume appeared in 1871 and another posthumously. He died in Brooklyn on March 8, 1887. See also BEECHER (family).

Further Reading: Hibben, Paxton, *Henry Ward Beecher* (New York 1927); Rourke, Constance M., *Trumpets of Jubilee* (New York 1963); Shaplen, Robert, *Free Love and Heavenly Sinners* (New York 1964); Stowe, Lyman Beecher, *Saints, Sinners, and Beechers* (Indianapolis 1934).

BEECHER, bē′chər, **Lyman** (1775–1863), American clergyman and educator, who was an important figure in the religious life of the United States in the first half of the 19th century. Several of his children also achieved national prominence (see BEECHER, family). Lyman Beecher was born on Oct. 12, 1775 in New Haven, Conn., the son and grandson of blacksmiths. When he was 18, he entered Yale College. After graduation, he remained to study for the ministry under Timothy Dwight, president of Yale and a leader of what was called the New England theology.

Beecher became pastor of the Presbyterian church at East Hampton, Long Island, N.Y., in 1799 and within 10 years had attracted much favorable attention, particularly for a sermon attacking dueling. In 1810 he was called to a Congregationalist parish in Litchfield, Conn., which was then one of the cultural centers of New England.

As an advocate of the new school of Calvinism, Beecher took a liberal view of the doctrine of predestination, and he preached his more hopeful faith with revivalist vigor. Conducting two services on Sunday and other meetings elsewhere during the week, he acquired a large and devoted following. He turned to the evils of intemperance in 1825 and delivered six successive sermons on the subject that were published and widely read in the United States and Britain.

In 1826, Beecher was invited to become pastor of a new church on Hanover Street in Boston, Mass. Congregationalist churchmen there were troubled by the defection, in 1813, of a large number of their churches to Unitarianism. They hoped Beecher, in the pulpit of a new church, could help recover their lost congregations. So successful were Beecher's evangelical methods, in fact, that he was soon being compared with Jonathan Edwards, who had led the "Great Awakening" in New England in the 1740's. Unfortunately, some of Beecher's vehement sermons aimed at Roman Catholicism were indirectly responsible for the sacking of an Ursuline convent by a Boston mob in 1831.

The next year Beecher was chosen to become the first president of the new Lane Theological Seminary and pastor of the Second Presbyterian Church in Cincinnati, Ohio. He welcomed the opportunity to exert a strong religious influence in the frontier communities of the developing West. During his 18 years with the seminary, several of his sons received their religious training there. His daughter Harriet married Calvin E. Stowe, a seminary teacher. She later became famous as Harriet Beecher Stowe, author of *Uncle Tom's Cabin* (1851). She based her famous antislavery novel on information she acquired while living in Cincinnati.

Presbyterians of the "old school" bitterly attacked Beecher for his moderate Calvinism and, in 1835, charged him with heresy. The case was in the church courts and councils for three years before it was finally withdrawn. The seminary suffered, too, because against Beecher's wishes the trustees forbade the students to discuss the slavery issue. He eventually secured the cancellation of this rule, but in the meantime the seminary had lost much of its enrollment. In 1850, Beecher retired and went to Brooklyn, N.Y., to live with his son Henry Ward Beecher, who was becoming famous as the pastor of Plymouth Church. Lyman Beecher died in Brooklyn on Jan. 10, 1863.

BEECHER, bē′chər, **Thomas Kinnicut** (1824–1900), American clergyman, who for 46 years was pastor and pastor emeritus of the Independent Congregational Church of Elmira, N.Y. He was born on Feb. 10, 1824, in Litchfield, Conn., the son of Lyman Beecher, noted Presbyterian clergyman. In 1843, Thomas graduated from Illinois College, where his half-brother, Edward, was president. He studied for the ministry under his father in Cincinnati, Ohio, but taught school before being ordained in 1851. Beecher accepted the Elmira pastorate in 1854 and during his long residence there became a popular figure. He served briefly as a Union chaplain in the Civil War. Beecher died in Elmira on March 14, 1900.

BEECHER'S BIBLES was a term applied to the Sharps rifles distributed among Northern emigrants to the Kansas Territory in the late 1850's. As the controversy on the slavery issue grew before the outbreak of the Civil War, proslavery Missourians attempted to prevent the flow of antislavery Northerners into the West, thereby arousing the Eastern abolitionists. A meeting was held in New Haven, Conn., in March 1856, for the purpose of equipping a company of free-state emigrants to Kansas. Henry Ward Beecher, an outspoken opponent of slavery, stated at the meeting that a Sharps rifle (one of the earliest successful breech-loading guns) was a greater argument than a Bible for the persuasion of slaveholders. Thus these rifles came to be known as "Beecher's Bibles."

BEECHEY, bē′chē, **Frederick William** (1796–1856), English rear admiral and geographer. He was born in London on Feb. 17, 1796. A son of Sir William Beechey, the painter, he entered the navy at the age of 10. In 1818 he accompanied Lieutenant (afterward Sir John) Franklin on an expedition to discover the Northwest Passage, a voyage that he described in his *Voyage of Discovery towards the North Pole, performed in His Majesty's ships Dorothea and Trent, under the command of Captain David Buchan* (1843). The next year he took part in a similar enterprise with Capt. William E. Parry.

From 1821 to 1822, Beechey, with his brother, William E. Beechey, was assigned the task of surveying the north coast of Africa in the sloop *Adventure*, commanded by Capt. William Henry Smyth. The brothers collaborated on an account of these years, published in 1828. During the years from 1825 to 1828, Frederick Beechey commanded the *Blossom* on another Arctic expedition, by way of the Pacific and Bering Strait. After this trip he published his *Narrative of a Voyage to the Pacific and Beering's Strait . . .* (1831); subsequently (1839), others published a botanical and zoological description of the regions visited on the voyage. Beechey died in London on Nov. 29, 1856.

BEECHEY, bē′chē, **Sir William** (1753–1839), English portrait painter. He was born at Burford, Oxfordshire, on Dec. 12, 1753. After a brief start in a business career, he determined to make painting his profession and in 1772 became a student at the Royal Academy. He adopted the technique of Sir Joshua Reynolds and eventually became portrait painter to Queen Charlotte. A large equestrian painting, *George III and the Prince of Wales Reviewing Troops*, was instrumental in gaining him a knighthood and election to the Royal Academy in 1798. His reputation was now assured, and a constant flow of commissions kept him busy for the rest of his life. He died at Hempstead on Jan. 28, 1839. Two of his portraits, *Portrait of a Lady* and *Frederick Augustus, Duke of York and Albany*, are in the Metropolitan Museum of Art in New York City. Two highly regarded landscape pen sketches are in the British Museum in London.

BEEF. See MEAT.

BEEFEATER. See YEOMEN OF THE GUARD.

BEEFWOOD is the popular name for several species of trees that yield a hard wood, also called beefwood. They are native to Australia and are found also in California and Florida. The trees, which may be 30 to 70 feet (9 to 21 meters) tall or more, have drooping, largely leafless branches. The closely grained wood has a reddish color and is used in cabinet and ornamental work. Beefwood trees belong to the genus *Casuarina*.

BEELZEBUB, bē-el′zə-bub, is the name given in the New Testament, to the "prince of devils," or Satan (Matthew 12:24, Mark 3:22, Luke 11:15). The name may be derived from *Baalzebub* (meaning "lord of the flies"), a god of the Ekronites in Philistia, who is mentioned in the Old Testament (II Kings 1). It may also be a variant of *Beelzebul* (meaning "lord of filth"). This form of the name is offered in the Greek text of the Gospels and is preferred in the Revised Standard Version of the Bible.

In Milton's *Paradise Lost*, Beelzebub is the name of the fallen angel ranking second to Satan in importance.

BEER, George Louis (1872–1920), American historian. He was born on Staten Island, N.Y., on July 26, 1872, and received his B.A. (1892) and M.A. (1893) degrees from Columbia. Beer's major contributions to historical literature were in the area of English colonial policy, especially its economic aspects. His viewpoint was free from patriotic bias and he stressed the view that the colonists were participants in the mercantilist system rather than victims of a tyrannical motherland. He wrote *British Colonial Policy, 1754–1765* (1907), *Origins of the British Colonial System, 1578–1660* (1908), and *The Old Colonial System, 1660–1754* (2 vols., 1912). He died in New York City on March 15, 1920.

BEER, Thomas (1889–1940), American essayist, biographer, and novelist. He was born in Council Bluffs, Iowa, on Nov. 22, 1889, and spent his childhood in Ohio and New York State. He graduated from Yale University in 1911 and from Columbia University Law School in 1913. He turned to writing after serving in the U.S. Army in France during World War I.

Beer's first novel, *The Fair Rewards* (1922), was followed by the highly praised biography *Stephen Crane* (1923). In 1926 he published *The Mauve Decade*, a social history of the 1890's that is considered to be his most important book. His other works include *The Road to Heaven* (1928), a novel, *Hanna* (1929), a biography of the politician Marcus A. Hanna; and *Mrs. Egg and Other Barbarians* (1933), Beer died in Yonkers, N.Y., on April 18, 1940.

BEER is the general name for all beverages resulting from the fermentation of a malt and cereal brew, including malt liquor, ale, stout, porter, and bock beer, as well as the beverage known simply as "beer." All are brewed from the same ingredients: starchy cereal grains (principally malted barley), water, hops, and yeast. In remote areas, such as the Australian back country, some South Sea islands, central Africa, and isolated parts of South America, "beers" are brewed from corn or millet, the most readily available grains. Such "beers" are made in the primitive fashion that these people have employed for generations.

Brewing of Beer. Commercial beers are made by a process that is basically the same throughout the civilized world. The malt is ground to a coarse grist, is weighed, and is placed in a mash tub, or mash tun, and then water is added. The prepared cereal mash usually is cooked to liquefy the starch and then is added to the malt fraction. The malt's enzymes convert the starch into fermentable sugars—maltose and dextrin. The resultant liquid, called wort, is filtered through a mash filter, or lauter tub. It then flows into the brewing kettle where hops are added, and the mixture is boiled for several hours. After the brewing operation the hop wort is filtered through a°hop separator, or hop jack. The filtered liquid is pumped through a wort cooler and flows into a fermenting vat where pure-culture yeast is added for fermentation.

In making beer, 7 to 11 days are required for the conversion of all the fermentable sugars into alcohol and carbonic acid gas (CO_2). Beer uses a "bottom-fermentation" yeast strain, and the temperature of the mass is kept between 38° and 48° F (3.3°–9° C). For ale a "top-fermentation" yeast strain is used, and the temperature varies from 50° to 70° F (10°–21° C). Five to six days is sufficient time to complete an ale fermentation. In all cases the carbonic acid gas produced by fermentation is collected, compressed, and stored, to be returned later to the beer.

The freshly brewed beer, to which a small portion of unfermented wort is added to ferment slowly at a low temperature, is then stored in tanks; that is, lagered (from the German word *lagern*, "to store"). The beer is kept at a temperature of 33°–34° F (0.5°–1.1° C) for several months to permit mellowing and sedimentation. When it is ready for packaging, it is filtered under pressure at the low lager temperature. The precise amount of carbonic acid gas desired is returned to the brew, and the beer is packaged in bottles, cans, or barrels.

Barreled, or draft, beer, intended for quick consumption, is marketed without further processing. Most bottled or canned beer, intended for shelf storage up to four months (cans) or six months (bottles), is pasteurized to prevent further fermentation.

United States beers vary in alcoholic content from 3.6 percent to 4.9 percent by weight, while the special beer marketed as "malt liquor" varies from 4.08 percent to 6.3 percent by weight. Ales average about 4.2 percent by weight.

The caloric values of beers and ales vary in accordance with the alcohol, protein, and carbohydrate content of the individual brand. The average United States beer has some 12½ to 13⅓ calories per ounce. Bock beer, malt liquor, ale, stout, and porter are fuller bodied and have higher caloric values.

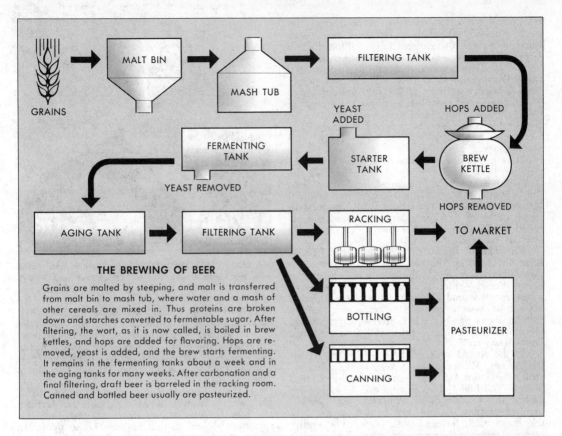

THE BREWING OF BEER

Grains are malted by steeping, and malt is transferred from malt bin to mash tub, where water and a mash of other cereals are mixed in. Thus proteins are broken down and starches converted to fermentable sugar. After filtering, the wort, as it is now called, is boiled in brew kettles, and hops are added for flavoring. Hops are removed, yeast is added, and the brew starts fermenting. It remains in the fermenting tanks about a week and in the aging tanks for many weeks. After carbonation and a final filtering, draft beer is barreled in the racking room. Canned and bottled beer usually are pasteurized.

Types of Beers. In the United States the name "beer" is generally given to a bright, pale golden, light-flavored, light-bodied, crisply fresh beverage that is drunk chilled, somewhere between 44° and 48° F (6.6° and 9° C).

Bock beer is a special, full-bodied brew, somewhat darker and sweeter than regular beer. It is brewed in winter for use in the spring. Bock Beer Day, the day on which it is first sold, is planned to herald the arrival of spring. The bock beer season lasts about six weeks.

Malt liquor is a special kind of beer that varies considerably among brands. Some malt liquors are quite pale; others are rather dark. Some are quite hoppy; others are only mildly so. Their essential characteristic is a higher alcoholic content than in other beers.

Lager is generally understood to be a light, bright, sparkling beer, but today all malt beverages in the United States are lagered.

Pilsner is a term often seen on beer labels around the world. The original and true Pilsner beer is the Pilsner Urquell, which has been brewed at Plzeň in Bohemia, Czechoslovakia, for some 800 years, and has never been equaled.

Ale is an aromatic, golden, fuller-bodied, and bitterer malt beverage with a slightly higher alcoholic content than beer. All ales are top-fermentation brews.

Stout is a darker ale with a maltier flavor. It is sweeter than ale and has a strong hop character.

Porter is a still darker, fuller-bodied ale yielding a rich, creamy foam. Strongly roasted malt is used to give a richer body. It is sweeter and less hoppy than regular ale.

Sake, a Japanese brew made from rice, is given a high alcoholic content by refermentation.

The difference between light- and dark-colored beers stems from the amount of kilning or roasting of the barley malt. The more it is roasted, the darker it becomes and the greater is the caramelization of its sugars. Thus, the darker the brew, the sweeter it will be.

The basic difference between draft beer and beer packaged in a bottle or can has been that draft beer is not pasteurized. Packaged beer is usually pasteurized to prevent refermentation in the container. However, the use of microporous materials that filter out all the yeast cells now permits unpasteurized beer to be bottled and canned. The filtered beer is safe to store and retains its fresh-brewed character and flavor.

Virtually all types of beers and ales are brewed in the United States. The bulk of consumption is, and no doubt will continue to be, of the light-colored, light-bodied style. The outstanding characteristic of United States beer is its lightness, a quality Americans favor.

U.S. Production and Consumption. The United States is the world's largest producer of malt beverages, turning out annually over 100 million barrels, each containing 31 gallons (117 liters). Of this total, 82 percent is packaged in bottles and cans and 18 percent in barrels for draft service. However, the United States is only 10th in per capita consumption, with 16 gallons (60 liters) per person per year. Belgium, West Germany, Australia, New Zealand, Britain, Austria, Denmark, Switzerland, and Canada, in the order listed, have a higher per capita rate than the United States.

Excluding shipments to the armed forces abroad, the United States exports only a tiny fraction of the malt beverages it produces. Exports equal 400,000 cases of 24 twelve-ounce containers, or 900,000 gallons (3.4 million liters). United States imports of malt beverages have increased and continue to increase at a substantial rate. During the 1956–1965 decade they nearly tripled, reaching about 20,700,000 gallons (over 78 million liters)—still less than 1 percent of total U.S. consumption. Principal exporters to the United States are, in order of volume, West Germany, Canada, Netherlands, Norway, and Denmark.

Beers of Europe and the Americas. The most popular beers of Germany, Denmark, and the Netherlands are the pale-colored, light brews, like the Bohemian Pilsner Urquell—for which no equal has yet been found. Dark beer is also popular in some parts of Europe. Munich, Germany, is noted for its darker, richer beers that are more strongly flavored with hops.

The classic brews of England and Ireland have always been the ales and stout. These are generally darker and fuller than the European beers. Porter—which is short for "porter's beer," a beverage favored by the porters of the London market halls—is a richer kind of stout. British poets of every age—Chaucer, Shakespeare, Milton, Housman—have sung the praises of their country's "nut-brown ale."

In the Americas, Canada has been noted for its fine ale. Mexico makes a very light, pale beer which has also become popular in the United States. The beers of Argentina and Uruguay are among the best in South America. By government regulation, the brewers there must use only the finest malt, flavored with hops. The spring water in these two countries is of excellent quality for the brewing of beer.

Storing and Serving Beer. Since beer is affected by light, bottled beer should be stored in a dark place and, like canned beer, should be kept cool. Beer should be served at a temperature of about 45° F (7° C) and ale at 50° F (10° C). Beer glasses should be cleaned and rinsed carefully. Soap or soapy water should not be used. Any soapy film on the inside of the glass will break down the "head," or collar of foam, on top of the beer. Beer should be poured straight into the glass. Tilting the glass so the beer pours down the side reduces the collar on the beer.

History. Records have shown that man has brewed malt beverages for centuries. Archaeologists have found hieroglyphic accounts of how to brew beer. They also have found jugs that were used for beer more than 5,000 years ago. Chemical analysis of the jugs has uncovered the barley and the yeast cells by which the beer was produced. During the pharaonic period in Egypt the arts of brewing beer and baking bread were prerogatives of the temple priests. The Greeks learned brewing from the Egyptians, and malt beverages have been produced continuously in Europe ever since.

HAROLD J. GROSSMAN
Author of "Grossman's Guide
to Wines, Spirits and Beers"

Bibliography
Baron, Stanley W., *Brewed in America* (Boston 1962).
Grossman, Harold J., *Grossman's Guide to Wines, Spirits and Beers*, rev. ed. (New York 1964).
United States Brewers Association, *United States Brewers Almanac* (New York 1965).
United States Brewers Foundation, *A Beer Dispensing Handbook* (New York 1952).
Weeks, Morris, Jr., *Beer and Brewing in America* (New York 1949).

CULVER PICTURES, INC.

SIR MAX BEERBOHM, the English writer and artist, who was best known for his caricatures and essays.

BEERBOHM, bĕr'bōm, **Sir Max** (1872–1956), English author, whose ability to mimic the styles of well-known writers made him one of the most devastating parodists of the early 20th century. Wit, essayist, artist, and dandy, Beerbohm personified the "man about town" in the London of 1900.

He was born in London on Aug. 24, 1872, and was educated at Merton College, Oxford. He first became known through early satirical essays published in the famous *Yellow Book*. In 1898 he succeeded George Bernard Shaw as drama critic of the *Saturday Review*. In 1910 he married the American actress Florence Kahn, and they settled in Rapallo, Italy. Beerbohm was knighted in 1939. He died at Rapallo on May 20, 1956.

Beerbohm wrote one novel, *Zuleika Dobson* (1911), a burlesque of student life at Oxford. *A Christmas Garland* (1912) consists of parodies of Thomas Hardy, Joseph Conrad, and other contemporary writers. His other books, mainly collections of short pieces from periodicals, include *The Happy Hypocrite* (1897), *More* (1899), *Yet Again* (1907), *And Even Now* (1920), *A Variety of Things* (1928), *Mainly on the Air* (1946), and *Around Theatres* (1953).

Beerbohm was also a noted caricaturist, and his insight into human nature is seen clearly in his incisive drawings of famous people. His books of caricatures include *Caricatures of Twenty-Five Gentlemen* (1896), *Poet's Corner* (1904), *Rossetti and His Circle* (1922), and *Observations* (1925).

Further Reading: Behrman, Samuel N., *Portrait of Max* (New York 1960); Cecil, David, *Max* (Boston 1965); Moers, Ellen, *The Dandy: Brummell to Beerbohm* (New York 1960).

BEER-HOFMANN, Richard (1866–1945), Austrian poet and dramatist. He was born in Vienna on July 11, 1866. He graduated from the University of Vienna with a doctorate in jurisprudence, but turned to writing and in 1893 published his first book, *Novellen*, two short tales. With Hofmannsthal and Schnitzler he was a leader of the neoromantic school of Austrian writers. His most celebrated poem, *Schlaflied für Miriam* (Eng. tr., *Lullaby for Miriam*, 1941), appeared in 1898. He adapted his first play, *Der Graf von Charolais* (1904; *The Count of Charolais*), from *The Fatal Dowry* (1632) by Massinger and Field. He planned a trilogy of plays on the Biblical David, but completed only *Jaâkobs Traum* (1918; Eng. tr., *Jacob's Dream*, 1946) and *Der junge David* (1933; The Young David). A Jew, Beer-Hofmann left Austria when the Nazis took over in 1938. He settled in the United States and died in New York City on Sept. 26, 1945.

BEERNAERT, bār'nȧrt, **Auguste Marie François** (1829–1912), Belgian statesman. He was born in Ostend, Belgium, on July 26, 1829. He began his political career as minister of public works from 1873 to 1878. In 1884 he became a member of the cabinet as minister of agriculture and industry. He was president of the council and minister of finance from 1884 to 1894 and president of the chamber of deputies from 1895 to 1900. As leader of the Catholic party, he generally supported King Leopold II, but broke with him over the annexation of the Congo.

Beernaert was a prominent member of the international peace conferences of 1899 and 1907. In 1909 he was a joint recipient of the Nobel Peace Prize. Beernaert died at Lucerne, Switzerland, on Oct. 6, 1912.

BEERS, bẽrz, **Clifford Whittingham** (1876–1943), American humanitarian who pioneered in the mental hygiene movement. He was born in New Haven, Conn., on March 30, 1876, and was educated at Yale University. In 1900 he began suffering from mental illness, and during a three-year period he was confined in several institutions. He found that patients were neglected and abused rather than helped, and after his recovery he began a campaign to increase public understanding of mental illness and to improve methods of treatment. His autobiography, *A Mind That Found Itself* (1908) helped achieve his aim.

In 1908, Beers formed the Connecticut Society for Mental Hygiene, the first organization of its kind in the United States. In the following year he founded and became secretary of the National Commission for Mental Hygiene. He organized the American Foundation for Mental Hygiene in 1928 and was its secretary until his death.

Beers' influence spread outside the United States. He helped Clarence M. Hincks found the Canadian National Committee for Mental Hygiene in 1918, and with Hincks established the International Committee for Mental Hygiene in 1920. Beers organized the first International Congress on Mental Hygiene in 1930. He died in Providence, R.I., on July 9, 1943.

BEERSHEBA, bēr-shē'bə, a city in Israel, is the capital of the Negev, or Southern Region. It is situated about 55 miles (89 km) south of Tel Aviv. Beersheba is the industrial, commercial, and transportation center of the Negev, a semi-desert expanse comprising a little more than half of Israel's land area.

Beersheba has been dramatically transformed since the founding of Israel. From a desert outpost it became a bustling city with new schools, hospitals, housing, and industrial and commercial establishments, encircled by a green belt of trees and farm crops. Beersheba is the seat of the Institute for Arid Zone Research, which has contributed significantly to the reclamation of the Negev. The population of Beersheba grew from 8,300 in 1950 to an estimated 65,200 in 1965. It is designated a center for the settlement of immigrants.

Like virtually all the Negev, Beersheba was neglected for centuries, until it was refounded by the Turks about 1900. In World War I the British in a surprise attack captured Beersheba intact on Oct. 31, 1917. Under a League of Nations mandate, approved in 1922, the British controlled Palestine, including Beersheba, until the United Nations partitioned the area in 1947. The Arabs seized control of the town and held it until it was captured by the Israelis on Oct. 21, 1948.

In Biblical times, Beersheba was Palestine's southernmost city, as Dan was its northernmost, giving rise to the expression "from Dan to Beersheba" as a measure of the full extent of the country. Beersheba was noted for its wells, and the name has been interpreted to mean "well of the seven" or "well of the oath," in allusion to compacts made at various times by Abraham and Isaac with Abimelech, king of Gerar (Genesis 21:25–31; 26:32–33).

The city was an important religious sanctuary from very early times. Jacob, on his way to Egypt, stopped at Beersheba to consult its oracle (Genesis 46:1–5). Joel and Abijah, sons of the prophet Samuel, were prophets in Beersheba (I Samuel 8:2). After Elijah slew the prophets of Baal and incurred the wrath of Jezebel, he fled and took refuge near Beersheba (I Kings 19:1–3).

BEERY, bēr'ē, **Wallace** (1886–1949), American film actor. He was born in Kansas City, Mo., on April 1, 1886. He ran away from home as a boy, joined a circus, and became a highly skilled elephant trainer. Later he went on the musical comedy stage with his brother Noah, and finally into silent films. He made his first film in Chicago in 1913, playing the comedy role of a Swedish maid. About two years later he went to Hollywood, where his first featured role was in *Behind the Door* (1917). In the early 1930's he starred with Marie Dressler in a series of films—including *Min and Bill* and *Tugboat Annie* —that brought him his greatest fame. In all he made over 250 films.

In 1931, Beery won an Academy Award for his performance in *The Champ,* and in 1934 he received a gold medal at the International Motion Picture Exposition (Venice, Italy) for *Viva Villa!* He died in Beverly Hills, Calif., on April 15, 1949.

BEESWAX, bēz'waks, is a solid, fatty substance secreted by bees. It is a complex mixture of fatty acids and esters. Its natural color varies from a dull yellowish white to brown. It may be bleached chemically or by exposure to sunlight. Its melting point is 143° to 151° F (62° to 66° C).

Beeswax is produced by bees in the form of thin scales given off from glands on the under (ventral) side of the abdomen. The bees use the wax to build honeycombs in which they store food and raise their young. The wax may be obtained commercially by melting the honeycombs with boiling water and then straining and cooling the wax.

Beeswax is used in candles, polishes, adhesives, cosmetics, and leather dressings. It is also used in encaustic painting and as a modeling wax.

Common beet
(*Beta vulgaris*)

BEET, a plant with several cultivated varieties used as food for humans or livestock. The name "beet" also is given to the large roots of these plants, especially of the red garden beet and the sugar beet.

The common beet (*Beta vulgaris*) is an annual, biennial, or perennial plant whose roots are fleshy and often thick. The leaves are fleshy, and green, dark red, or yellow in color. They have slender stems and oval or pointed blades. One stem or more rise out of each root, then branch out to form a pyramid shape. The flowers, in clusters of three or more, dry to form the hard seedball that is characteristic of the beet.

Wild Beet. A wild beet (*B. maritima*) is believed to be the original form from which the specialized types were derived. It is found on the seacoast along the Mediterranean from Asia Minor to Spain and along the Atlantic coast of Europe north to Norway. It has annual, biennial, and perennial varieties. The wild beet and its closely allied species (*B. patula, B. atriplicifolia,* and *B. macrocarpa*) intercross readily with the cultivated beets.

Red Garden Beet. This vegetable characteristically has small red-purple tops and turnip-shaped roots. Departures from these characteristics, especially light-red, yellow, or white color and zoned flesh, are indications of outcrossing (mating of different strains). Popular varieties for the garden are Detroit Dark Red (a favorite in canning), Egyptian, and Eclipse.

The red garden beet is grown commonly in home and market gardens. It does well on loams (a mixture of clay, silt, and sand), but like all other members of the species it has wide adaptability to soil types. Soil fertilization procedures must be adapted to the particular area, but special attention should be given to the boron content of the soil, since the beet is very sensitive to boron deficiency. Without adequate boron in the soil, some leaves turn black and become deformed, cankers form on the roots, and black blemishes develop in the flesh.

Seed may be sown early in spring, since the beet is frost-hardy except for a very brief period when the first leaves are being drawn out of the soil. The rows are spaced 15 to 18 inches (38 to 46 cm) or more apart, depending on whether culture is manual or mechanized. In ordinary garden culture, the plants are thinned an inch or two (2.5 to 5 cm) apart in the row. Successive pullings of plants, as they reach a size of 1 or 2 inches in diameter, provide additional thinnings. Varieties such as Winter Keeper may be planted in midsummer or late summer to provide roots for winter storage.

Mangel-Wurzel. This variety of beet is characterized by its large size and the tendency of its roots to extend above the surface of the soil. It has red, yellow, or orange-colored flesh, but it is never purple in the standard varieties. Mammoth Long Red, Golden Tankard, and Giant Half Sugar are common varieties in the United States, but in Europe many other types are grown.

In the United States, mangels commonly are used to add moisture to the feed rather than as a main livestock feed, as in Europe. Culture of mangel-wurzels therefore is limited in the United States to small acreages. The crop is grown with wide spacing so that large-sized roots are formed. Sometimes the roots are dug during fall and early winter, but they should be harvested and stored before severe frosts injure the crowns.

Sugar Beet. This form of the common beet is characterized by parsnip-shaped roots whose crowns project slightly above the ground. The roots are white-fleshed, and the skin color is white or creamy white. The leaves are green, but the stems and leaf blades may show a pink or red color because of a pigment (anthocyanin) in the skin.

Swiss Chard. In this variety of the common beet, the roots are small and branched. Also known as the spinach beet or, in Britain, the silver beet, this plant has abundant, large leaves. The leaf blades are long and curled, and their stems are broad and thick. The leaves are used like spinach, and the stems like asparagus. The plant is an abundant yielder. Common varieties are Lucullus, Fordhook Giant, and Rhubarb.

Use and Food Value. Beet tops are rich in vitamins and high in calcium and iron. The tops of red garden beets and the foliage of Swiss chard, used as greens, are excellent sources of vitamin A and B_2 (riboflavin) and are a good source of vitamin B_1. Small beets are an excellent green-leaf vegetable.

Mangel-wurzels are grown chiefly as feed for cattle and poultry. Though they contain sufficient sugar and carbohydrates, livestock raisers usually supplement mangel-wurzel feed with food concentrates to provide additional nutrients.

The sugar beet excels the mangel-wurzel in food value for livestock, chiefly because of its higher sugar content. Sugar beets are grown sometimes for stock feed, especially in areas that are not easily accessible to a sugar factory.

Sugar is extracted from beets by treatment with hot water. As a by-product of this procedure, beet pulp is obtained from the remaining small, shredded portions (cossettes) of the beet. These cossettes are known as "wet pulp," since they have a 90 percent water content. They may be run through rolls to remove some of the water and are then called "pressed pulp." This pulp can be used as feed.

Classification. The beet belongs to the genus *Beta* in the goosefoot family, Chenopodiaceae. GEORGE H. COONS, *U.S. Department of Agriculture*

BEET SUGAR. See SUGAR GROWING AND SUGAR MAKING.

BEETHOVEN, bā'tō-vən, **Ludwig van** (1770–1827), German composer, who brought about gigantic alterations in the nature and techniques of music—an achievement matched by few other artists. He found music a rococo-dramatic art, the orchestra a relatively small ensemble, and the piano a newly established successor to the harpsichord. By his aggressive, iconoclastic, even egotistic nature, and by his huge ability to manipulate and balance musical ideas and forces, Beethoven marked his later creations with his own stormy, tender, lyrical, and intellectual character. By employing textless music to communicate philosophical ideas and to serve as autobiography, he pushed music far along the road toward 19th century romanticism and bequeathed to his successors the portrait of the great creator as culture hero. He expanded the size of the orchestra and the possible length of orchestral compositions, preparing the way for Schubert, Berlioz, Richard Wagner, Johannes Brahms, Gustav Mahler, Anton Bruckner, and Richard Strauss. He went far toward establishing the piano as the foremost musical instrument. Not a great craftsman when handling the human voice, Beethoven excelled in all other branches of music. The taste of the 20th century inclines to call Bach, Mozart, and Beethoven the greatest of all musical creators.

BEETHOVEN, from Gustav Jaeger's portrait (c. 1840).

Early Years. Beethoven was born at Bonn, probably on Dec. 16, 1770, and was baptized on December 17. Of Flemish-German descent, he was the second of seven children of Johann van Beethoven, who sang tenor in the chorus of the elector of Cologne. Ludwig's mother was Maria Magdalena Laym (née Kewerich). The boy demonstrated musical talent as early as his sixth year, and his father tried to develop him into a child prodigy like Wolfgang Amadeus Mozart. At 10, Ludwig was sent to study with Christian Gottlob Neefe, the elector's court organist. Neefe nourished him on Johann Sebastian Bach's *Well-Tempered Clavier* and wrote in 1783: "If he goes on as he has started, he will certainly become a second Mozart."

In 1784, Beethoven was appointed assistant court organist to Elector Maximilian Franz, an enlightened young ruler. Beethoven visited Vienna for the first time in the spring of 1787, meeting Mozart, who was too much involved in the composition of *Don Giovanni* to do much more than listen to his playing and praise him. Beethoven was summoned back to Bonn by the illness of his mother, who died a few weeks later. His father had become a drunkard, and the family would have been poverty-stricken but for the help offered Ludwig by his friends.

In November 1789, Beethoven persuaded the elector to make him legal head of his family and to pay him half of Johann's salary. In this way he succeeded in bringing some order into his home. The young man's compositions began to circulate in manuscript. The great Joseph Haydn, visiting Bonn in July 1792, examined a cantata that the 21-year-old Beethoven submitted to him, and encouraged him to continue composing. Beethoven's noble patrons persuaded the elector to finance a trip to Vienna and probable lessons with Haydn. Just ahead of the troops of revolutionary France, Beethoven left Bonn in November 1792, never to return, and installed himself at Vienna.

Vienna. Johann van Beethoven died in December 1792, and for a time the moneys arriving in Vienna from Bonn were often interrupted. Haydn gave Beethoven some lessons for almost nothing, even inviting the young man to join him on his second visit to England. Beethoven, armed with introductions from his Bonn patrons, was soon taken up by several wealthy Viennese families. He attracted pupils, became renowned for his astonishing ability to improvise at the keyboard, and generally began to savor life fully for the first time. Continuing to study and to compose, he was soon widely famous as a virtuoso pianist.

At this period Beethoven traveled extensively in Austria, Bohemia, Germany, and Hungary, winning particular success in Prague. In 1798 he began to suffer from incipient deafness, the resulting shock apparently being directly related to the increased power, even ferocity, of his compositions of the time, including the *Pathétique Sonata,* Opus 13, for piano. On April 2, 1800, he gave his own first public concert, which included pieces by Haydn and Mozart as well as his own septet for wind instruments and strings and his C Major (First) Symphony. The symphony shocked many Viennese, who were more favorably disposed toward the music Beethoven wrote for the ballet *Die Geschöpfe des Prometheus* (*The Creations of Prometheus*). He himself became extremely displeased with his creative efforts and in 1802 said: "I am discontented with my works up to now; from here on I shall take a new path." On Oct. 10, 1802, he dated at the village of Heiligenstadt the overwhelming document known as the *Heiligenstadt Testament.*

The testament is a nearly incoherent outpouring of grief and rage against the senseless cruelties of life. Part of Beethoven's tragic intensity was the result of his increasing deafness, part resulted from his continued treatment for a physical condition that was very probably syphilitic. He became more and more an irascible, imperious, difficult, antisocial man. Though increasingly isolated inside himself, he fell in love numerous times, frequently with young girls of noble birth who were clearly beyond his reach. A document almost as shattering as the *Heiligenstadt Testament* is the so-called "Letter to the Immortal Beloved," an unsent outpouring of passionate yearning for a girl who cannot be identified. Beethoven never married.

Middle Period. Beethoven's personal eccentricities, his proud boorishness, and even his lack of personal cleanliness were accepted as the marks of the genius he was. A short, muscular, stocky man, he had a bush of wild hair and fierce, piercing black eyes in a notably ruddy face. His upper-class friends suffered at his hands but stubbornly remained faithful to him. They supported him by providing comfortable lodgings, by giving him money, and by patronizing his concerts and publications. On April 5, 1803, for example, his Second (D Major) Symphony and his Third (C Minor) Piano Concerto were first heard at a public concert. By 1804 he was composing such of his great piano sonatas as the *Waldstein* (Opus 53) and the *Appassionata* (Opus 57), and probably had embarked on his only opera, *Fidelio*. The opera was delayed, finally being performed on Nov. 20, 1805, when Vienna was under French occupation. It was given three times and was a failure. Beethoven's friends persuaded him to revise it and to reduce its three acts to two. It was restaged on March 29, 1806, with more promise of success, but Beethoven quarreled with the impresario, and it was withdrawn after two performances. More than eight years later he again revised it; it was then produced with enormous success on May 23, 1814, and was chosen to open the Hofoper's 1815 season. (See also FIDELIO.)

Meanwhile, by 1805, Beethoven had begun to sketch his Fifth (C Minor) Symphony, his

Fourth (G Major) Piano Concerto, and the first of his *Rasoumovsky* (*Razumovski*) string quartets. In 1806, in the midst of the Napoleonic disorders, he composed his only violin concerto, first heard on December 23 of that year. While Beethoven worked on the concerto, his desk was littered with advanced sketches of his Fourth, Fifth, and Sixth symphonies. The Fourth (B Major) was first heard in the spring of 1807; the Fifth (C Minor) and Sixth (*Pastoral*, F Major) were played at a concert on Dec. 22, 1808, which included half a dozen others of his works (the premières of the *Choral Fantasy* and the Fourth Piano Concerto).

On completing his Third (*Eroica*) Symphony, in E Flat, in 1804 (see EROICA SYMPHONY), Beethoven had inscribed it to Napoleon, thinking of him as a democratic liberator; this inscription he later angrily struck out. Nevertheless, he seriously considered, as late as 1808–1809, an offer from Jérôme Bonaparte, king of Westphalia, to become his *Kapellmeister* at Kassel. Hearing of this, three of Beethoven's Viennese patrons, including the young Archduke Rudolf, joined to offer him a yearly income, and he decided not to emigrate. Although after Haydn's death on May 31, 1809, Beethoven was unquestionably the most famous of living musicians, the years from 1809 to 1813 appear to have been relatively inactive for him. He was by then almost totally deaf, but as one of the world's most famous men he led a very active social life. In 1811 he encountered Johann Nepomuk Maelzel, inventor of the metronome, with whom he formed a close, if passing, friendship. In 1812, visiting fashionable Teplitz (Teplice), he met Johann Wolfgang von Goethe, who said of him: "His talent amazed me; unfortunately, he is an utterly untamed personality,

---

BEETHOVEN'S WORKS

Symphonies and Other Works for Orchestra: Nine symphonies—No. 1, C Major, Opus 21 (1795–1800); No. 2, D Major, Opus 36 (1802); No. 3, *Eroica*, E Flat Major, Opus 55 (1802–1804); No. 4, B Flat Major, Opus 60 (1806); No. 5, C Minor, Opus 67 (?–1807); No. 6, *Pastoral*, F Major, Opus 68 (1807–1808); No. 7, A Major, Opus 92 (?–1812); No. 8, F Major, Opus 93 (?–1812); No. 9, *Choral*, D Minor, Opus 125 (1817–1823); *Coriolan Overture*, Opus 62 (1807); *Wellington's Victory*, Opus 91 (1813); overture, *The Consecration of the House*, Opus 124 (1822); pieces listed in section *Music for the Stage*.

Concertos: Five piano concertos—No. 1, C Major, Opus 15 (1797); No. 2, B Flat Major, Opus 19 (1794); No. 3, C Minor, Opus 37 (1800); No. 4, G Major, Opus 58 (?1805); No. 5, *Emperor*, E Flat Major, Opus 73 (1809); Violin Concerto, D Major, Opus 61 (1806); two romances for violin and orchestra—G Major, Opus 40 (1803); F Major, Opus 50 (?1802); Concerto for Piano, Violin, and Violoncello, C Major, Opus 56 (?–1804).

Music for the Stage: Opera, *Fidelio*, Opus 72 (1803–1805; rev. 1806, 1814); four overtures for *Fidelio*— *Leonore* Nos. 1, 2, and 3 and *Fidelio*; incidental music to the following—Goethe's *Egmont*, Opus 84, overture and other music (1810); August von Kotzebue's *Ruins of Athens*, Opus 113, overture and other music (1811); Kotzebue's *King Stephen*, Opus 117, overture and other music (1811–1812); ballet, *The Creations of Prometheus*, Opus 43, overture and other music (1800).

Music for Voices with Orchestra: *Missa solemnis*, D Major, Opus 123 (1818–1823); Fantasy, C Minor, for piano, chorus, and orchestra, Opus 80 (1808); oratorio, *Christ on the Mount of Olives*, Opus 85 (?–1800); Mass, C Major, Opus 86 (1807); scene and aria, *Ah, perfido!*, for soprano and orchestra, Opus 65 (1796); songs with piano accompaniment and 149 folk songs arranged for solo, duet, and sometimes chorus with accompaniment of piano, violin, and violoncello. The most familiar songs are *Adelaïde*, Opus 46 (?1797); the cycle *An die ferne Geliebte*, Opus 98 (1816); and *In questa tomba oscura*, no opus number (1807).

Chamber Music: String quartets—six quartets, Opus 18 (?–1801); three quartets, *Rasoumovsky*, Opus 59 (?–1806); quartet, *The Harp*, E Flat Major, Opus 74 (?–1809); quartet, *Serioso*, F Minor, Opus 95 (?–1810); quartet, E Flat Major, Opus 127 (?–1824); quartet, B Flat Major, Opus 130 (1825; new finale, 1826); *Grosse Fuge*, B Flat Major, Opus 133 (original finale of Opus 130); quartet, C Sharp Minor, Opus 131 (?–1826); quartet, A Minor, Opus 132 (?–1825); quartet, F Major, Opus 135 (1826); ten violin sonatas (1798–1812); five violoncello sonatas (1796–1815); six trios for piano, violin, and violoncello (1795–1811), the last (B Flat Major, Opus 97) being the renowned *Archduke Trio*; duos, trios, quartets, a quintet, sextets, a septet, and octets for varying combinations.

Music for Piano Solo: Sonatas—No. 1, F Minor, No. 2, A Major, No. 3, C Major, Opus 2 (?–1796); No. 4, E Flat Major, Opus 7 (?–1797); No. 5, C Minor, No. 6, F Major, No. 7, D Major, Opus 10 (?–1798); No. 8, *Pathétique*, C Minor, Opus 13 (?–1799); No. 9, E Major, No. 10, G Major, Opus 14 (?–1799); No. 11, B Flat Major, Opus 22 (?–1802); No. 12, A Flat Major, Opus 26 (1801); No. 13, E Flat Major, No. 14, *Moonlight*, C Sharp Minor, Opus 27 (?–1801); No. 15, *Pastoral*, D Major, Opus 28 (1801); No. 16, G Major, No. 17, D Minor, No. 18, E Flat Major, Opus 31 (?1802); No. 19, G Minor, No. 20, G Major, Opus 49 (?–1805); No. 21, *Waldstein*, C Major, Opus 53 (1804); No. 22, F Major, Opus 54 (1804); No. 23, *Appassionata*, F Minor, Opus 57 (1804?–1806); No. 24, F Sharp Major, Opus 78 (1809); No. 25, *Sonatine*, G Major, Opus 79 (?–1810); No. 26, *Les adieux*, E Flat Major, Opus 81A (1809); No. 27, E Minor, Opus 90 (?–1814); No. 28, A Major, Opus 101 (1815–?1816); No. 29, *Hammerklavier*, B Flat Major, Opus 106 (1818–1819); No. 30, E Major, Opus 109 (?–1820); No. 31, A Flat Major, Opus 110 (?–1821); No. 32, C Minor, Opus 111 (?–1822); three sonatas without opus number; variations—numerous sets, including the *Prometheus* (*Eroica*), Opus 35 (1802); the *Diabelli Variations*, Opus 120 (1821?–1823); and the 32 Variations, C Minor, no opus number (1806–1807); numerous other brief piano pieces; works for the piano four hands.

not altogether wrong in holding the world to be detestable, but not making it any more enjoyable either for himself or for others by his attitude." During this year Beethoven completed his Seventh (A Major) and Eighth (F Major) symphonies.

In May 1813, hearing of the duke of Wellington's victory over Joseph Bonaparte's troops at Vitoria, Spain, Beethoven agreed to compose for the panharmonicon, a music-playing machine invented by Maelzel, a piece to be played in England. *Wellington's Victory* is orotund trash, yet Beethoven astonishingly orchestrated it for performance in Vienna, where its success was stupendous. Almost unnoticed in the din of its first performance on Dec. 8, 1813, was the première of Beethoven's Seventh Symphony. The Eighth Symphony was first heard on Feb. 27, 1814.

When the Congress of Vienna convened on Nov. 1, 1814, to rearrange the world disordered by Napoleon, Beethoven was the object of keen interest to the visiting sovereigns and their entourages. The Austrian government lent him the two halls of the Redoutensaal for a series of concerts, and he personally invited the sovereigns, Charles-Maurice de Talleyrand-Périgord, and other visiting dignitaries. The first concert attracted 6,000 people, and the series earned Beethoven a large sum of money. The year 1815 found him in comfortable circumstances, although his deafness had forced him to give up ensemble playing and to carry on all conversations by means of pencil and paper. In November his brother Karl died, leaving a widow, whom Beethoven detested, and a nine-year-old son, Karl, of whom he was coguardian with the widow. This boy was to be the cause of much unhappiness and ill-advised behavior on his uncle's part. In Nov. 16, 1815, Beethoven was awarded the freedom of the city of Vienna, thus becoming tax exempt. The death of his patron Prince Lobkowitz in 1816, however, reduced his income, and for the first time in years he was pressed for money.

Last Works. Between 1817 and 1823, Beethoven completed the last 5 of his 32 piano sonatas. In 1818 he began a mass intended for use at the installation of his friend Archduke Rudolf as archbishop of Olmütz (Olomouc). He did not complete it until Feb. 27, 1823; the *Missa solemnis* was first sung at a private performance in St. Petersburg on April 6, 1824. As early as 1812, Beethoven had planned a symphony in D minor. He worked at it desultorily until 1823, when he seriously set to work to complete it. He decided to make its last movement a choral setting of Friedrich von Schiller's *Ode to Joy* and pronounced the Ninth Symphony complete on Sept. 5, 1823. He had accepted £50 from the Philharmonic Society of London in return for a promise that it would receive his new symphony in manuscript. But he had also promised the première to Berlin and had dedicated the symphony to the king of Prussia. When his Viennese patrons insisted that it be heard in Vienna first, he yielded, salving his conscience by sending the actual autograph score to London. The first hearing of the Ninth Symphony occurred in Vienna on May 7, 1824. When the audience broke into frantic applause, the deaf Beethoven was unaware of the enthusiasm until someone turned him around so that he could see the demonstration.

From 1824 to 1826, Beethoven completed the five string quartets (Opus 127, 130, 131, 132, and 135) that many critics regard as the towering peak of his achievement. He also began to sketch a tenth symphony. He was increasingly ill during this period and worried unceasingly over the wastrel his nephew Karl had become. The boy's attempted suicide in the summer of 1826 further unnerved him. After a senseless and futile visit to the country in an attempt to persuade his prosperous brother Johann to name young Karl as his heir, Beethoven furiously rushed back to Vienna in an open carriage, arriving on December 2 and taking to his bed with a high fever. After his 56th birthday (Dec. 16, 1826) he also quarreled with his nephew, who shortly joined his regiment and never saw his famous uncle again. Johann van Beethoven and his wife arrived to take care of the invalid. Franz Schubert visited him. When a set of George Frideric Handel's works arrived from London, Beethoven looked through it and said: "Handel is the greatest of us all." During February 1827 he was five times tapped for dropsy. He was given the last sacrament on March 24. Two days later Vienna was beset by a late afternoon storm. The dying man opened his eyes, shook his fist at the sky, and died; it was March 26, 1827. His funeral three days later was an impressive public event watched by more than 20,000 people in the streets and by another multitude at the cemetery. For it was the funeral of one of the two or three most famous men in the world

CREATIVE PERIODS

Custom long has divided Beethoven's numerous works into three periods. These inexact, overlapping categories represent actual changes in style. The first period shows Beethoven as the direct heir and imitator of Haydn and Mozart. Opening about 1800, the second period, far more idiosyncratic, includes the majority of his most popular works: symphonies Nos. 2 to 8 inclusive, *Fidelio*, the last three piano concertos, the violin concerto, the *Leonore*, *Egmont*, and *Coriolan* overtures, the *Rasoumovsky* string quartets, other chamber music, and 14 of the piano sonatas. The third of the Beethoven periods, one of distillation and summation, encompasses the Ninth Symphony, the five final string quartets, and the *Missa solemnis*. Critics still discuss whether or not Beethoven's deafness influenced the special character of his later works.

HERBERT WEINSTOCK, *Author of "Men of Music"*

Bibliography

Anderson, Emily, ed., *The Letters of Beethoven*, 3 vols. (London and New York 1961).
Bekker, Paul, *Beethoven*, tr. by M.M. Bozman (London 1925).
Burk, John N., *The Life and Works of Beethoven* (New York 1943).
Grove, George, *Beethoven and His Nine Symphonies*, 3d ed. (London 1898).
Hamburger, Michael, ed. and tr., *Beethoven: Letters, Journals and Conversations* (New York 1952).
Newman, Ernest, *The Unconscious Beethoven* (London and New York 1927).
Rolland, Romain, *Beethoven the Creator*, tr. by Ernest Newman (New York 1929).
Scott, Marion M., *Beethoven* (London 1934).
Sterba, Editha, and Sterba, Richard, *Beethoven and His Nephew* (New York 1954).
Sullivan, John W.N., *Beethoven: His Spiritual Development* (New York 1960).
Thayer, Alexander W., *The Life of Beethoven*, tr. by Henry E. Krehbiel, 3 vols. (New York 1921); rev. ed. by Elliot Forbes, 2 vols. (Princeton, N.J., 1964).
Tovey, Sir Donald F., *Beethoven* (New York 1945).
Wagner, Richard, *Beethoven* (Leipzig 1870).

BEETLE, an order of insects that are differentiated from other insects by having thickened or leather-like front wings, or elytra, which are not used in flight. In most families the elytra are heavy, forming a shield under which the membranous hind wings are folded; in some families they are leathery in texture. The elytra usually cover the abdomen or all but its terminal segment, but are sometimes shortened and cover only the basal segments. In determining families, genera, and species, wing characteristics such as venation (arrangement of veins) and the creases caused by folding are major factors.

Description. Beetles range in length from approximately 0.01 inch to more than 8 inches (0.254 mm to 20.3 cm); the smallest ones are the fungus beetles and the longest are the long-horned beetles. The shape of beetles is extremely variable. They may be large or small; sturdy or delicate; and long and slender or nearly circular. Some have deep, fairly narrow bodies; others are flattened and almost paper thin.

The head is freely movable but sometimes almost entirely hidden by the thorax. The mouth parts may be located on the underside or at the front of the head, depending upon the feeding habits. In the predaceous forms the mouth is always at the front and usually fitted for grasping and holding prey. The eyes are round or oval and are divided or partly divided; they have large or small facets, which are of different sizes; sometimes the facets are absent. Those beetles

without eyes generally are cave dwellers. The thorax is usually narrower in front, and often has various modifications. A hard plate or scale on the thorax, called the scutellum, is present in most groups. The legs are usually strong. In some cases they are long and slender and adapted for rapid running, as in the tiger beetle; in others, they are very short so that they may be drawn closely under the body as in the lady beetle and leaf beetle; in still others, they are adapted for swimming, digging, or grasping prey. The abdomen normally is composed of ten segments, but the first usually is not visibly separated from the second. The terminal segment frequently is exposed and may, at times, function as an ovipositor (egg-layer). Sexual dimorphism (male and female differing in form) is not uncommon.

The larvae are usually larger or longer than the adult beetles. There are two general types of larvae: the scarabaeid type, which is soft-shelled, robust, rounded, short or elongated, and often crescent shaped, and normally lives in concealment; and the carabid type, which is flattened and elongated, with well-developed legs, antennae, and other appendages, and is active and usually free-living.

Classification. Beetles belong to the order Coleoptera, which contains more than a quarter of a million described species, or about 40 percent of the known insect species. About 26,000 of these species are found in the United States. Within the order Coleoptera are three suborders and some 20 superfamilies, containing a total of more than 150 families.

There are three suborders, Adephaga, Polyphaga, and Rhynchophora. These are differentiated as follows: The Adephaga have threadlike and usually tapering antennae and five-segmented tarsi (end portion of leg). The first visible side body wall plate is divided into two parts by the third pair of coxae (basal leg segment). The Polyphaga have variously constructed antennae and from three to five tarsal segments. The first visible abdominal body wall plate is almost always completely visible. The Rhynchophora, or weevils, are identified by the prolongation of the head into a beak and by elbowed antennae, of which the first segment is longer than the others and the terminal segments are usually conspicuously enlarged.

Beetle Suborder: ADEPHAGA

Water beetle

ROSS E. HUTCHINS

Tiger beetles

ROSS E. HUTCHINS

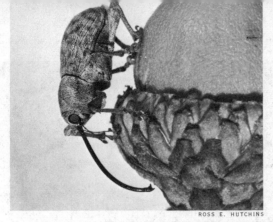

ROSS E. HUTCHINS

Acorn weevil

Beetle Suborder: RHYNCHOPHORA

JOHN R. CLAWSON, FROM NATIONAL AUDUBON SOCIETY

Snout beetle

ROSS E. HUTCHINS

Cotton boll weevil

Adephaga. Among the most important families of the Adephaga, which includes the predaceous, or carnivorous forms, are the Carabidae, or ground beetles, of which more than 22,000 kinds are known. They are predaceous in both the adult and larval stages, and run about freely in pursuit of other insects and small animals. Most of them live on the ground, but several kinds climb trees in search of prey. The smallest is a blind ant-like species from Australia, *Illaphanus stephensi,* which is one twenty-fifth of an inch (1 mm) long. The largest North American species is *Calosoma scrutator,* a tree climber that hides in the ground during the day and searches for caterpillars at night. Other species of *Calosoma* have similar habits and are important in the control of cankerworms, gypsy moths, and other caterpillars. A few species are attracted to light in large numbers and may become temporary house pests.

The tiger beetles, or Cicindelidae, are generally long-legged and brightly colored. The adults are tireless hunters, dashing quickly over the ground and taking flight at the slightest provocation. Some nocturnal species are wingless, with the elytra fused over the back, and a few kinds are tree climbers. The larvae live in tunnels in the soil near water, where they lie in wait for crawling insects. A hook on their backs provides an anchor to hold them fast in their tunnels.

The Dytiscidae, or predaceous diving beetles, are aquatic in both the adult and larval stages and feed upon other insects and small aquatic life, including small fishes. The legs of the adults are fringed with hairs for swimming, and they store air under their wing covers before they enter the water so they can remain there for long periods. Most species are attracted to light. Some of the large Adephaga are used for food in the Orient.

Polyphaga. Among the Polyphaga the large family of Hydrophilidae (water scavenger beetles) contains species of diverse forms and habits. These differ from the dytiscids in having clubbed antennae. Almost all are aquatic, but a few are semiaquatic or terrestrial. The turnip mud beetle, *Helophorus rufipes,* feeds on the roots and leaves of young turnips.

Most of the Silphidae, the carrion or scavenger beetles, feed on carrion, and many of them bury small animals. A few species of *Silpha* are destructive to plants.

The Staphylinidae, or rove beetles, are characterized by having wing covers less than half as long as the abdomen. The more than 20,000 species have varied habits, some living on animal matter, others on plants, and some being cannibalistic. One large American species, *Greophilus maxillosus,* will attack live earthworms. More than 300 small species live in the nests of ants. Many of the male and female fireflies (Lampyridae) have luminous organs in the adult stage and some of the larvae are also luminous.

The click beetles (Elateridae) have an extension on the anterior part of the thorax that fits

461

ELSIE M. RODGERS, FROM NATIONAL AUDUBON SOCIETY

Horned beetles

LYNWOOD M. CHACE, FROM NATIONAL AUDUBON SOCIETY

Colorado potato beetle

LYNWOOD M. CHACE, FROM NATIONAL AUDUBON SOCIETY

Longhorn beetle

LYNWOOD M. CHACE, FROM NATIONAL AUDUBON SOCIETY

Japanese beetle

MASLOWSKI & GOODPASTER, FROM NATIONAL AUDUBON SOCIETY

Unicorn beetle

ROSS E. HUTCHINS

June beetle

ROSS E. HUTCHINS

Eyed click beetle

ROSS E. HUTCHINS

Lightning bug

ROSS E. HUTCHINS

Ladybird beetle

JACK DERMID, FROM NATIONAL AUDUBON SOCIETY

Stag beetle

ROSS E. HUTCHINS

May beetle

ROSS E. HUTCHINS

Hickory twig girdler

DON WOOLRIDGE, FROM NATIONAL AUDUBON SOCIETY

Wood borer

into a groove on the middle part of the thorax. When lying on their backs, they can snap this extension and thus throw themselves into the air. They are long slender beetles and many are pests. Some tropical forms, genus *Pyrophorus*, have luminous spots on the thorax.

The metallic wood borers (Buprestidae) have serrate (tooth-edged) antennae, and their larvae, which are flatheaded borers, mine in leaves, tunnel in wood, and infest dead and dying wood. Several are harmful to trees and shrubs. The ladybirds, or lady beetles (Coccinellidae), are predaceous and beneficial, but a few, such as the Mexican bean beetle, are serious pests.

The Scarabaeidae (June beetles, scarabs, dung beetles, cockchafers, and others) are one of the largest and best known families. Their antennae have several leaflike segments at the tips and their mouth parts are normal. The larvae of all are crescent-shaped and they are generally known as white grubs. Except for the dung feeders, which include the famous Egyptian scarab, the adults and larvae have different feeding habits, the larvae feeding upon the roots of plants, the adults upon the foliage. The Japanese beetle, or *Popillia japonica*, is an example of this type. In some forms the thorax of the male bears one or more long horns, or the head may form a single horn. Some authorities now divide the Scarabaeidae into 11 distinct families.

The longhorned beetles (Cerambycidae) have long antennae, four segmented tarsi, and usually a slender form. The larvae are round-headed wood borers and many of them are serious pests, although the majority live in dead or dying timber. They vary in length from about one fourth of an inch to 8 inches (6.4 mm to 20.3 cm), and are found in all parts of the world.

The leaf beetles (Chrysomelidae) feed on living plants. The tarsi have four segments; the antennae are rather slender, and the shape is varied. The family includes the flea beetles, the goldbugs, the potato beetles, and a number of other pests.

Rhynchophora. The suborder Rhynchophora comprises nearly 45,000 species distributed among five families. The largest family, Curculionidae, contains about 40,000 of them. These are characterized by small mouth parts situated on a beak of various lengths. The antennae are elbowed, have an elongated first segment, and end in a club. This family contains many pests of cultivated and forest crops, including the clover leaf weevil and the alfalfa weevil, belonging to the genus *Hypera*. The genus *Anthonomus* includes such serious pests as the apple blossom weevil (*A. pomorum*), the cotton boll weevil (*A. grandis*), the pepper weevil (*A. Eugenii*), and the strawberry weevil (*A. signatus*). *Conotrachelus nenuphar* is the plum curculio, which attacks the fruit of plums, apples, peaches, apricots, and pears. The poplar and willow borer, *Cryptorhynchus lapathi*, often kills trees by its attacks on the trunks. The white fringed weevils, belonging to the genus *Pantomorus*, of which several species have been introduced into the southern United States from Argentina, are both wingless and parthenogenetic (that is, the eggs develop without male fertilization), no males being known. The granary weevil (*Sitophilus granarius*) and the rice weevil (*S. oryzae*) attack various cereals and hard cooked foods made from cereals. They occur in most parts of the world. The larvae are curved, without distinct legs.

The Brentidae are long and narrow, often with very long snouts. They are tropical wood borers and are peculiar in that many of them are gregarious, specimens of two generations often living together. A few forms are predaceous.

The Scolytidae, or bark beetles, differ from the others in having leaflike plates on the end segments of the antennae and a short beak. They are small beetles, usually under one third of an inch (8.3 mm) long and dull-colored. The larvae live under bark of dead or living trees and bore into living or dead wood. A large number of the approximately 2,000 species are pests whose depredations in the United States cause a loss of more than $100,000,000 annually. They not only attack trees directly but transmit diseases from one tree to another.

Beneficial Beetles. In contrast to the large number of pest beetles, a few beetles are beneficial. The ladybirds play an important part in keeping pests under control by feeding on plant lice, scale insects, white flies, and other small insects. The Adephaga are almost all predators, only a few being parasitic. Certain larvae, particularly the large plump ones, are used as food by natives in many parts of the world. Dried and powdered beetles of the family Meloidae have been used for centuries as an aphrodisiac, diuretic (increases the flow of urine), and vesicator (induces blistering). Cantharidin, which produces a blistering effect on the skin, is obtained chiefly from the Spanish fly, *Lytta* (*Cantharis*) *vesicatoria*.

CHARLES HOWARD CURRAN
University of Florida

Further Reading: Dillon, Elizabeth S., and Dillon, Lawrence S., *Manual of Common Beetles of Eastern North America* (New York 1961); Fox, Richard M., and Fox, J.W., *Introduction to Comparative Entomology* (New York 1964); Kissinger, David G., *Curculionidae of North America North of Mexico: A Key to the Genera* (South Lancaster, Mass., 1964).

BEETS, bāts, **Nikolaas** (1814–1903), Dutch writer and clergyman. He was born in Haarlem on Sept. 13, 1814. He studied theology at Leiden and, after his ordination in 1839, held pastorates at Heemstede (1840–1854) and Utrecht (1854–1874). From 1874 to 1884 he taught theology at the University of Utrecht. He was also known as *Hildebrand*.

A strong vein of romantic melancholy runs through Beets' early works, such as the poems *José* (1834) and *Guy de Vlaming* (1837). This mood, which may have been the result of his having translated several of Byron's poems into Dutch about that time, vanishes in his masterpiece, *Camera Obscura* (1839-51). A prose work consisting of tales and sketches of life and scenery in the Netherlands, *Camera Obscura* displays Beets' keen observation and delicate sense of humor. Some of his later pieces show a deep religious feeling. Beets died in Utrecht on March 13, 1903.

BEEVILLE, bē'vil, a city in Texas, is the seat of Bee County. It is situated 80 miles (130 km) southeast of San Antonio. In earlier days, cattle and cotton were its chief products, and Beeville was a typical cow town. Although it is still an agricultural center, oil has become its economic mainstay. Beeville's principal manufactures are oilfield equipment, packaged frozen meats, leather goods, sheet-metal roofing, soft drinks, and brooms. The city has a council-manager form of government. Population: 13,506.

BEFANA, bä-fä'nə, the good but ugly old hag who, Italian children believe, distributes sweets to the good and coal to the naughty on Epiphany eve (January 5). According to the legend she protested that she had too much housework to do and therefore could not join the three kings in their search for the Christ Child. Hence she must seek him out among all the children of the world between the first and sixth day of every new year. Although "Befana" is said to be a corruption of the Italian *Epifania,* parts of her legend are of pre-Christian origin.

BEFFROY DE REIGNY, be-frwä' də rä-nyē', **Louis Abel** (1757–1811), French author and composer. He was born in Laon on Nov. 6, 1757.

In his periodicals *Les lunes* (1785–1787) and *Courrier des planètes* (1788–1792) he established his reputation as a writer on eccentric and bizarre subjects. He also wrote dramatic farces, including *Nicodème dans la lune* (1790), and *Nicodème aux enfers* (1791), both of which he later rewrote as operas. His *Dictionnaire néologique des hommes et des choses de la Révolution,* published between 1795 and 1800, was suppressed by Napoleon in 1802.

Beffroy de Reigny wrote under the pseudonym *Cousin Jacques.* He died in Paris on Dec. 17, 1811.

BEG. See BEY.

BEGAS, bä'gäs, a family of German artists of the 19th century.

KARL BEGAS (1794–1854), a painter, was born at Heinsberg, near Aachen, on Sept. 30, 1794. His early work attracted the attention of Frederick William III of Prussia, who helped to sponsor his studies in Paris and in Italy. Begas taught for many years at the Royal Academy in Berlin. He painted genre, historical, and religious subjects, and portraits of eminent contemporaries. He died in Berlin on Nov. 23, 1854.

OSKAR BEGAS (1828–1883), Karl's eldest son, was also a painter. He was born in Berlin on July 31, 1828. He studied with his father and in Italy, where he painted a large *Deposition from the Cross* for the Michaeliskirche in Berlin, a work that won him admission to the Prussian Academy. Like his father, he specialized in historical paintings and portraits. He painted some of the murals in the Berlin Rathaus (1870). He died in Berlin on Nov. 16, 1883.

REINHOLD BEGAS (1831–1911), another son of Karl, was a sculptor who became the most famous member of the family. He was born in Berlin on July 15, 1831. The leading German sculptor of his time, Begas was a follower of the naturalistic school that sprang up in Berlin as a reaction to the neoclassical style of the late 18th century. He studied at the Berlin Academy and in Rome, where he was strongly influenced by the realism of baroque art.

Most of Begas' important works were official commissions. They include the group *Borussia* at the Berlin stock exchange; the monument to Frederick William III in Cologne; the Schiller monument in Berlin; the sarcophagus of Frederick II at Potsdam; the fountain of Neptune in the Schlossplatz in Berlin; and monumental portraits of William I and of Bismarck for the Reichstag in Berlin. He also executed many portrait busts of members of the Hohenzollern family and other well-known persons of the

time. He died in Berlin on Aug. 3, 1911.

KARL BEGAS (1845–1916), another son of the elder Karl, was a sculptor. He was born in Berlin on Nov. 23, 1845. He studied sculpture under his brother Reinhold and then in Rome. His most important pieces of sculpture are the Franco-Prussian War memorial at Kassel and the *Boar Hunt* in the Berlin Tiergarten. He died in Köthen on Feb. 20, 1916.

Further Reading: Meyer, A.G., *Reinhold Begas* (Berlin 1901).

BEGGAR ON HORSEBACK is a musical comedy, with book and lyrics by George S. Kaufman and Marc Connelly and music by Deems Taylor, first produced in 1924.

It is the story of Neil McRae, a composer, who is in love with Cynthia Mason but is compelled by poverty to seek to marry into the rich and vulgar Cady family. Before his marriage he falls asleep and dreams of his unhappy future life with the Cadys. In the dream, which is enacted onstage, Neil is employed in his father-in-law's widget factory, miserable and unable to do creative work. His frustration drives him to murder the entire Cady family, and he is brought to trial in a court where the resurrected Mr. Cady acts as his judge. Neil's defense consists of an elaborate pantomime entitled *A Kiss in Xanadu,* which fails to convince the jury that he should be allowed to go free. He is sentenced to hard labor in the Cady Consolidated Art Factory, where he is forced to spend the rest of his life writing bad music. Awakened from his dream, Neil is released from his engagement by his fiancée and returns to Cynthia.

BEGGAR TICK. See BUR-MARIGOLD.

BEGGAR'S OPERA, a musical play by John Gay, first performed in London on Jan. 29, 1728. The play satirized the habits of polite London society and the corrupt politics of the day. The characters are thieves and bandits, who represent lords and high officials. Songs for *The Beggar's Opera* were arranged from popular airs by John C. Pepusch, who also wrote the play's overture. Gay's language is often coarse, but the opera, in expurgated form, is still frequently performed and was made into a movie in 1953.

The Beggar's Opera relates the adventures of Captain Macheath, the leader of a band of robbers and a very popular man with the ladies. He is secretly married to Polly Peachum, the daughter of the patron of the gang. Upon learning of the marriage, Peachum has Macheath arrested and confined at Newgate prison, where he is confronted by Lucy, daughter of the jailer Lockit. She also loves Macheath and promises to help him escape. In return for this favor she receives from him the promise of an immediate marriage. Polly visits her husband in prison and remains faithful to him in spite of his disowning her in Lucy's presence. Lucy helps Macheath to escape, but he is soon recaptured. Although both Lucy and Polly beg their fathers to spare him, their efforts are to no avail; and Macheath reflects that while rich men escape the gallows, poor men must hang. He becomes resigned to his impending death, but the mob, feeling that the poor should be entitled to their vices as well as the rich, raises a clamor for his release. Charges are dropped, and Macheath, now free, returns to his faithful Polly.

BEGONIA TYPES: *Begonia semperflorens, B. rex* (Rex begonia), and *B. boliviensis* hybrid (tuberous begonia).

The Beggar's Opera served as the basis for *Die Dreigroschenoper* (1928), a German musical satire written by Bertolt Brecht, with music by Kurt Weill. A pro-socialist parable, *Die Dreigroschenoper* was well received in pre-Nazi Berlin. During the 1950's it was translated into English by Marc Blitzstein as *The Threepenny Opera,* and ran long and successful engagements in New York City and London. The Brecht play retains virtually all of the characters, situations, and social overtones of *The Beggar's Opera,* differing from Gay's comedy primarily in details of dialogue and in its use of Weill's original musical score.

BEGGARWEED. See Tick Trefoil.

BEGGIATOA, bə-jat′ə-wə, is a genus of bacteria that consist of unattached filaments moving in a wavy pattern. Known as sulfur bacteria, they derive their energy from the oxidation of sulfur. They are found in sulfur waters, in swamps, in sea water, and wherever sulfur and hydrogen sulfide are present. Their presence in large quantities indicates that the water is contaminated.

BEGHARDS. See Beguines.

BÉGIN, bā-zhaN′, **Louis Nazaire** (1840–1925), Canadian cardinal and archbishop of Quebec. He was born on Jan. 10, 1840, in Lévis, Quebec. He graduated from the seminary in Quebec and in Rome, where he was ordained in 1865. Returning to Canada, he was professor of theology at Laval University from 1868 to 1884, when he became principal of the Laval Normal School. In 1888 he was appointed bishop of Chicoutimi. In 1891 he became coadjutor to Cardinal Taschereau, whom he succeeded as archbishop of Quebec in 1898. He was made a cardinal in 1914.

As archbishop, Bégin was instrumental in organizing the Catholic social action group in Quebec, and under his direction new parishes were added to the archdiocese. His writings include works on papal infallibility, the rule of faith, and veneration of the saints. He died in Quebec on July 19, 1925.

BEGONIA, bi-gōn′yə, a large genus of plants native to tropical and subtropical regions (except Australia). They are cultivated frequently in hothouses and conservatories for their foliage and showy blooms.

Begonias are fleshy herbs. Some have short, congested stem parts, while others have creeping or thick underground stems (rhizomes); a few are climbers. The large, angular leaves of the begonia plant occur at varying heights along the stem. The flowers, found in branched clusters, are of two types: staminate (male) and pistillate (female). The staminate has four parts to the floral envelope and numerous stamens (pollen-bearing organs). The pistillate has five parts to the floral envelope and numerous minute seeds. The color of the flowers varies from white to all shades of red, purple, and yellow. The fact that most of the flowers have either stamens or pistils, but not both (that is, they are imperfect flowers), suggests that they are pollinated by insects. Nectaries and scent, however, are usually missing. Experimental evidence indicates that well-nourished plants produce a higher proportion of pistillate flowers.

There are approximately 800 species of begonia and numerous hybrids and varieties. An important species in the *Begonia rex,* native to Assam, a state in northeastern India on the edge of the Himalayas. This species and its many varieties are prized for their large, decorative leaves, which often are blotched, streaked, or mottled with red, purple, white, or silver. It is the principal parent of numerous ornamental-foliaged begonias. Rex begonias are propagated by planting stem or leaf cuttings on or in damp sand. Another important species is *B. semperflorens,* the parent species of most begonias sold by florists. Native to Brazil, this species grows about one foot (0.3 meter) high, has shiny green or red leaves, and abundant showy flowers. The wax begonia is a popular, cultivated, fibrous-rooted begonia derived from it. An important South American species, *B. boliviensis,* is used in making many hybrids with large, striking flowers. The most popular begonia is the attractive *B. gloire de Lorraine,* a hybrid with numerous flowers.

Edwin B. Matzke, *Columbia University*

BEGUINES, bă′gēnz, in the Roman Catholic Church, laywomen who have renounced the world in order to devote themselves to prayer and good works. This movement originated in the Netherlands during the early 12th century at the time of the Crusades, when thousands of men were going to recapture the Holy Land. Some of the solitary women left behind filled their days by ministering to the sick and poor. Eventually many of them moved into adjacent houses, thus forming communities called Beguinages. Unlike nuns, the Beguines (or *Beguinae*) took no vows and were self-supporting. Since they retained their material goods, many of the wealthy Beguines lived with retinues of servants. At the end of the century the movement had gained such popularity that not a single Dutch commune was without a Beguinage.

The Beguines inspired men to follow their pious example. These laymen, called Beghards, organized communities somewhat like those of the Beguines. The men professed no vows and were loosely organized, but they lived under one roof and were supported by a common purse. Whereas many of the Beguines were of the nobility, the Beghards were invariably of humble origin. They were dyers, weavers, fullers, and other tradesmen who supported their communities by these endeavors.

In the mid-13th century some of the Beguine and Beghard communities lapsed into heretical practices. Their members subscribed to mystical pantheism or indulged in self-torture. The Council of Vienne (1312) suppressed both the Beghards and the Beguines, but Eugenius IV reinstated the Beguines in 1430. The Beguinage of Notre Dame in Ghent, Belgium, is the most notable of the few surviving.

BEGUM, bē′gəm, is a Muslim title of honor equivalent to princess. A feminine form corresponding to *beg,* or *bey,* it is used mostly in India and Pakistan.

BEHAIM, bă′hīm, **Martin** (1436 or 1459–1507), German geographer. He was born at Nuremberg, Bavaria. He engaged in commerce and traveled about Europe to promote Flemish trading interests. He was also a student of mathematics and nautical science. About 1480 he was in Portugal, which at that time was a center of exploration of the Atlantic Ocean. He claimed to have sailed in the fleet of the Portuguese explorer Diogo Cam in his second voyage along the coast of Africa in 1485–1486. He was said to have been knighted by King John II of Portugal when he returned from this voyage.

Later he returned to Nuremberg, where in 1492 he constructed a terrestrial globe, which is still preserved there. This work shows the influence of the ancient geographer Ptolemy but attempts to incorporate some contemporary knowledge of geography. Since the globe was made in the year of Christopher Columbus' first voyage to the New World, it displays no detail of lands beyond the Atlantic. Behaim is known to have tried to adapt the astrolabe, an instrument devised by the ancient Greeks to observe the heavenly bodies, to the determination of latitude. Some older Spanish historians have asserted that he gave Columbus valuable advice. However, no association of the two men has been established, but they probably were in Portugal at the same time. Behaim died in Lisbon on Aug. 8, 1507.

BEHAM, bă′häm, the name of two German artists of the 16th century. The brothers, Hans and Barthel Beham, were members of the "Little Masters" school of engravers, as the followers of Albrecht Dürer were called.

HANS SEBALD BEHAM (c. 1500–1550) was born in Nuremberg, Bavaria. In 1525 he and his brother were expelled from their native city for political agitation. After wandering for six years, Hans settled in Frankfurt, where he remained for the rest of his life. He died in Frankfurt on Nov. 22, 1550.

Hans Beham was one of the most industrious engravers of his day. The catalog of his works lists 1,074 woodcuts, 252 copper engravings, and 18 etchings. His woodcuts, mostly large and designed for mural decoration, include *Military Pageant in Munich, Farmers' Dances, Marching Soldiers,* and *Fountain of Youth.* He also did several illustrations for books of the Old Testament and miniatures for the prayer books of Cardinal Albert of Brandenburg that are now at the Château of Aschaffenburg and the library of Kassel in Germany. Among Hans' other works are four tabletop paintings of the life of David and the etching *Virgin and Child.*

BARTHEL BEHAM (c. 1502–c. 1540) also was born in Nuremberg. After being banished from that city with his brother he settled in Munich in 1527 and became attached to the court of Duke William IV of Bavaria as official painter. Much of Barthel's work shows the influence of Italian art, and it is likely that he made a trip to Italy in the 1520's. He died on a visit to Rome around 1540.

Barthel was a painter as well as an engraver. His masterpiece was the religious painting *The Testing of the True Cross* (1530), now at the Alte Pinakothek in Munich. His portraits include those of Count Palatine Otto Heinrich and Chancellor Leonhard von Eck. Among his engravings are the miniatures *Cleopatra* and *Judith.*

BEHAN, bē′han, **Brendan** (1923–1964), Irish playwright. He was born in Dublin on Feb. 9, 1923, and was educated in the Roman Catholic schools there until he was expelled in 1936. He joined the IRA (Irish Republican Army) as a messenger boy and in 1939 was sent to England to help blow up a battleship in Liverpool harbor. Before he could accomplish his mission he was arrested for possessing explosives and sent to a Borstal (reform school). Released in 1942, he returned to Ireland but was arrested and imprisoned several more times for IRA activities before he was forced to leave the country and go to France in 1952. He died in Dublin on March 20, 1964.

Behan's prison experiences formed the basis for his first play, *The Quare Fellow* (1956; a "quare fellow" is what prisoners call a condemned man). This rather somber play had an off-Broadway production in New York in 1958. *Borstal Boy* (1958) is an uninhibited account of Behan's life in the Liverpool reform school. His play *The Hostage* (1958), a rollicking farce about a British soldier in Ireland who is kept prisoner in a brothel, was presented in London in 1958 and in New York in 1960. *Brendan Behan's Island: An Irish Sketchbook* (1962) is part travel book, part joke book. It also contains two short stories and an early play.

BEHAR. See BIHAR.

BEHAVIORISM, bi-hā′vyə-riz-əm, is a school of psychology that developed around the time of World War I and has influenced most psychological study since that time, particularly in the United States. Proponents of this school insisted that psychologists study behavior that could be observed objectively—muscle reactions, for example—rather than states of mind or feelings. The background for the development of behaviorism can be found in earlier views of what behavior is and how it can be studied.

Views of Behavior. As employed in psychology the term "behavior" seldom carries the popular meaning of good or bad deportment toward others but almost exclusively denotes the actions and reactions of an organism toward its environment. This adjustmental viewpoint owes much to Herbert Spencer and the other English biological psychologists such as Charles Darwin and Lloyd Morgan. Spencer defined living as the continuous adjusting of internal relations to external relations, and held that the function of the psychic aspect of the organism was that of helping the organism to adapt to its environmental conditions. These generalities led to more attention from others to particular mental processes and their role in the living animal's survival—a biological type of emphasis in the study of psychology that became well established as a British tradition. This emphasis profoundly affected American thought as well, taking explicit shape in the school of "functional psychology." One's emotions, his sensory keenness, his thought powers, his ability to form new habits, and his memory all came to be viewed as means whereby he can more accurately meet and deal with the exigencies of life.

A different view, of a more atomistic nature, was taken by zoologists such as Jacques Loeb. They formally broke down the behavior of an organism into its component reflexes and then sought the specific physical-chemical details of the surroundings that evoked those reflexes. This was a completely deterministic system of explanation on a local-action level. Meanwhile, a broader conception was held by others such as Herbert S. Jennings, who noted the exploratory character of much of the animal's movements.

Ivan P. Pavlov (1849–1936). His experiments influenced the behaviorist school.

CULVER PICTURES

They emphasized the spontaneous, trial-and-error, and adaptive character of animal behavior. This was an organismic viewpoint.

Watson and Behaviorism. Behaviorism became an active school of American psychological thought with lectures by John B. Watson in 1912, followed by journal articles describing his researches on infants and on lower animals and eventually by his systematic textbooks. Behaviorism started as a protest against the assumption that the proper data of psychology are mentalistic data, that the primary as well as the ultimate interest is in states of mind, experienced awareness, and feelings.

In the orthodox psychological tradition, the study of consciousness had been held to be the final justification of more objective studies. Wilhelm Wundt, for instance, had encouraged the study of reaction-time measurement in his laboratory, but only as a procedure by which the reaction consciousness could be set up, to some extent controlled, and thereby studied in its typical forms. The laboratory instrumentation was merely to aid in getting one's experiences under observation. Similarly, problems of sight, hearing, and the other senses had taken the form not of

TASS: SOVFOTO

BEHAVIORISM in America owed much to the objective psychology of the Russians Vladimir Bekhterev and Ivan Pavlov. The latter is shown here in his laboratory, watching an experimental study.

determining what things in the world man is sensitive and therefore reactive to, for the sake of this knowledge on its own account, but of determining what and how many kinds of sights and heard-sounds and tastes he could have.

The behaviorists made a double-barreled attack on this way of thinking. First, they argued that mental states are intangible and evanescent; one cannot hold them fixed for examination. They are far from being suitable objects of a natural science; they are survivals of the medieval soul-concept. This unreliability of subjective data became the more obvious when it was borne in mind that all scientific findings must be verifiable by other investigators. It seemed obvious that what one person may report as to how he senses, feels, and thinks cannot be directly checked by anyone else.

The second part of the behaviorists' argument was their most effective contention. They pointed out that when psychologists study such subjects as young children or psychotic and neurotic adults, and such things as conditions of mental efficiency, learning processes, advertising and selling, intelligence, personality, and social interrelations, they are not particularly interested in what the human beings under their study are experiencing. Psychologists are concerned with their actions and general modes of behavior. Those who study children find it impractical or impossible to get even indirect evidence of their states of mind. If the psychologist is interested in children's fears, for example, he does not set about trying to collect the children's descriptions of how they feel when afraid, but makes surveys of the situations which do or do not excite visible fears in them. Most of the habits a person acquires he picks up unconsciously; most of his memorizing is a drilling in verbal acts; and in any case, the final test and evidence of his having learned anything lie not in any mental panorama but in his ability to reproduce habit or memorized word. Intelligence, again, is not something to be found on one's mental scene but is a characterization of the ways he is able to go about dealing with problems that confront him. It is measured with objective methods. When studying a man's personality—even one's own—the psychologist does not take as his data the man's feelings or thoughts or other inner experiences. Instead, he collects observations and opinions from other people about how the man comports himself when he meets obstructions in his path. Indeed, the typical human being is a notoriously unreliable judge of his own motives and abilities.

The Program of Behaviorism. Behaviorism was not merely a protest but also offered a positive program. Put your human being under objective observation, it was said, just as you would any animal. Control the environmental setting, apply your carefully chosen and measured stimulations, then note precisely the responses that appear. Carried through, such a program offered the prospect of a knowledge of the why's of human conduct that would satisfy nearly all the practical or even theoretical interests of the human mind. The teacher, the lawyer, the clergyman, the salesman, the politician, and the moralist could ask no more.

The contrasts between the subjectivistic approach and the objective approach of the behaviorist is well illustrated in the handling of sensory problems. The question "What are the different

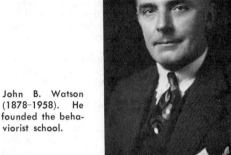

John B. Watson (1878-1958). He founded the behaviorist school.

kinds of colors that I can experience?" may be restated as, "To what wave frequencies can I (or he, or it) react differentially?" Thus stated, it is a question that all competent investigators could answer unequivocally and in a way that could be checked. Further, perception is restated as one's way of reacting to stimulations in learned ways. And here a clear contrast of approach is shown. What used to be defined introspectively as "a number of sensory impressions supplemented by imagery" or as "the consciousness of particular material things present to the senses" is by the behaviorist defined as "reacting to one or several stimuli not as single stimuli but as cues to further dealings with the whole object." For example, when a child perceives an orange, what was introspectively described as the child's experience of a yellow color of certain dimensions supplemented by imagined tastes, odors, and touches, became objectively described as the child's behavior toward the visual stimulus in a manner involving many previously learned responses appropriate to dealing with the object. Or consider how a person recognizes the direction from which a sound is coming. He is unable to find in his conscious experience differences or qualities in the hearing that serve to direct his judgment. However, by employing instruments another person is able to detect differences in wave intensity, frequency, timbre, or phase, and these are found to be the influencing factors.

Other psychological topics and their behaviorist restatement may be mentioned. Emotion is a matter of muscular and glandular involvements in activity. Memory is ability to recall to use. Personality is the totality of one's habits and abilities, especially as they determine his reactions toward other persons. Even imagination and thinking—though undoubtedly not easily redescribed—are rated by their output and expression in conduct, and are assumed to be nascent kinds of vocal or gestural or other symbolic reactions.

More closely viewed, the behaviorist program involved teasing out the smallest units of stimulus-response relationships (reflexes), noting how they may be altered (by conditioning), and then noting how they operate in larger and larger patterns, both native (instincts, emotions) and acquired (habits). The viewpoint was atomistic in its logical character. It was illustrated in an extreme degree by studies of the white rat; the rat's ability to run through a maze was described as patterns of flexor and extensor reflex muscular thrusts of its legs appearing in a definite learned sequence. Later it came to be recognized that such descriptions are too piecemeal, and furthermore attribute an inflexible character to the learned performance, which turns out actually to be variable and adjustable: however skillfully the rat runs the maze, it never runs it in precisely the same sequence of movements on two separate trials.

Influence of Bekhterev and Pavlov. The American program of behaviorism was blood brother, or better still, a child, of Russian objective psychology. Watson undoubtedly took his cue from the work of Vladimir M. Bekhterev who had already been elaborating a reflexology of man in his "objective psychology." Bekhterev, simultaneously with Ivan P. Pavlov, but independently, had been experimentally analyzing the processes involved in the forming of new "associative" or (to use Pavlov's term) "conditioned" reflexes. Pavlov had found that after a dog had been frequently presented with the ticking of a metronome just before being given meat powder to evoke saliva flow, the dog would eventually come to salivate after the metronome sound alone. A conditioned reflex had been established. Critical variations on the experiment established conditioning as not a matter of "association of ideas" but as a phenomenon operating on a more fundamental biological level. Its value for the unraveling of many nonrational learned responses, inexplicable likes and dislikes, phobias, and manias was soon apparent. The avidity with which psychologists seized upon it as a key to all learning, even as the prototype of all learning, is understandable. Later investigations were delightful in their clarity and their precision, but they exhibited conditioning as a truly complex set of phenomena. Pavlov's disciples seem to have oversimplified Pavlov's own interpretations of his experiments.

Influence of Behaviorism. This oversimplification followed naturally from the atomistic structuring of early behaviorist theory in America. But eventually this onesidedness was corrected by a "molar" behaviorism enunciated particularly by Edward Chace Tolman, in which the behavior of "organisms-as-wholes" was established as the proper subject matter of psychology. Here the impact of another line of contemporary emphasis, that of the "organismic" interpretation, is easily discerned. The swing of the pendulum back from the atomistic viewpoint to that of the organism-as-a-whole, or personality-as-a-whole, was not a swing away from behaviorism in its broader meaning: it was a change of emphasis within behaviorism. Similarly, the later students of behavior do not follow early behaviorists in refusing to have any commerce with purposes or goals or ends, but recognize that much behavior cannot be properly understood except in terms of motivation toward goals. Still they show no less insistence upon objectivity of approach.

There are some popular confusions regarding behaviorism. The behaviorist has been damned as a determinist and a mechanist. Yet he is no more so than the introspectionist, for the latter also sets up as his scientific objective the precise determining of antecedents and consequents. The behaviorist is too often assumed to be a strict environmentalist and to minimize the importance of heredity. However, this attitude is true only of Watson's writings; it does not follow logically from the behaviorist approach, nor is it found in other behaviorists' writings.

The behaviorist mission has served to remind the student of human nature that "mind-gazing" is not all, or even the major part, of the approach. For man is not merely a possessor and observer of mental states; he is an active and reactive organism in innumerable relationships with other organisms. See also PSYCHOLOGY.

JOHN FREDERICK DASHIELL
Author "Fundamentals of Objective Psychology"

Bibliography
Boring, Edward G., *History of Experimental Psychology,* 2d ed. (New York 1950).
Dashiell, John F., *Fundamentals of Objective Psychology* (Boston 1928); revised as *Fundamentals of General Psychology,* 3d ed. (Boston 1949).
Tolman, Edward C., *Purposive Behavior in Animals and Men* (New York 1932).
Wann, T.W., ed., *Behaviorism and Phenomenology* (Chicago 1964).
Watson, John B., *Psychology from the Standpoint of a Behaviorist,* 2d ed. (Philadelphia 1924).
Woodworth, Robert S., and Sheehan, M.R., *Contemporary Schools of Psychology,* rev. ed. (New York 1948).

BEHISTUN INSCRIPTIONS, bā-his-tōōn', cuneiform texts on a cliff near the Iranian village of Behistun (or Bisitun or Bisutun), 20 miles (32 km) east of Kermanshah. High on this cliff is carved a bas-relief showing Darius I, king of Persia, accompanied by two warriors, his foot on a prostrate man, nine captives chained by the neck before him, and above the whole a mythological figure.

Three cuneiform inscriptions—in Old Persian, Babylonian, and Elamite—recount how the monarch, after the suicide of Cambyses, gained power over the rebels and pacified his empire. The English Orientalist Sir Henry Rawlinson first scaled the cliff in 1835 and began to copy and decipher the inscriptions. By 1850 he had largely completed the decipherment of the Old Persian text and, with the help of other scholars, of the Babylonian. The Elamite legend was identified and the text definitively established in the course of the first half of the 20th century by American and British scholars. It was Rawlinson's study of the Behistun inscriptions, however, that provided a vital key to the deciphering of all cuneiform writing.

BEHN, bān, **Aphra** (1640?–1689), English playwright, who was the first Englishwoman to earn her living as a professional writer. The date and place of her birth remain obscure. Some authorities speculate that her father was James Johnson, a barber of Canterbury; others that she was the daughter of John and Amy Amis of Wye, Kent. It is certain that as a child, Aphra (also spelled Afra and Ayfara) went with relatives to Surinam (Dutch Guiana), then an English possession, and that, on her return to England about 1658, she married a London merchant named Behn. Her husband died in 1666, leaving her penniless. She sought favor at the court of Charles II and became an English secret agent in the Netherlands during the Second Dutch War (1665–1667), adopting the code name *Astraea,* which later became her nickname in literary circles. She was not paid by the English government for her services in the Netherlands, and on her return to England she was forced to serve a term in debtors' prison. Around 1670 she wrote her first play, *The Forc'd Marriage,* which was a popular success in London in 1671. From that time on she earned her living as a playwright, leading a Bohemian existence, and becoming, in the words of English critic Edmund Gosse, "the George Sand of the Restoration." She died in London on April 16, 1689, and was buried in Westminister Abbey.

Aphra Behn's plays, laced with wit, were as ribald as those of any male writer of the Restoration. They were very popular but not of high literary quality. Her most successful plays include the comedies *The Rover* (in two parts, 1677–1681), *The Roundheads* (1682), *The City Heiress* (1682), and *Sir Patient Fancy* (1678), with a plot taken from Molière's *Le malade imaginaire*, and a tragicomedy, *The Widow Ranter*, posthumously published in 1690. Her novel *Oroonoko, or the Royal Slave* (1688), which tells of a slave revolt led by a native prince of Surinam, foreshadows some of the work of Daniel Defoe. Mrs. Behn also wrote the volume of poetry *Love Letters to a Gentleman*, which was published posthumously in 1696. Many editions of her works appeared in the 18th century. A 20th century edition, prepared by Montague Summers, was published in 1915.

Further Reading: Sackville-West, Victoria M., *Aphra Behn* (New York 1928).

BEHRENS, bā'rəns, **Peter** (1868–1940), German architect, who was one of the outstanding early modern designers of industrial buildings. His innovations influenced the younger architects Le Corbusier, Ludwig Mies van der Rohe, and Walter Gropius, all of whom worked in Behrens' office early in their careers.

Behrens was born in Hamburg on April 14, 1868, and studied art, but not architecture, at Karlsruhe. Art nouveau influenced his early painting and book designs; it also influenced his first architectural venture, his own home in the artists' colony at Darmstadt (1900). From 1903 to 1907 he was director of the School of Applied Arts in Düsseldorf. Much of his early architecture, such as the Schröder house (1908–1909) and the Cuno house (1909–1910), both near Hagen, and the German embassy in Leningrad (1911–1912), is a blend of modern simplicity and romantic neoclassicism.

In 1909, Behrens was appointed architect for the German General Electric Company (A.E.G.), a position that inspired his most creative work. For the A.E.G. complex in Berlin he designed a turbine factory (1909), a high-tension and small-motors factories (both 1910), and a large-machine assembly hall (1911–1912). The turbine factory and the hall introduced a new concept of functional simplicity in the use of materials.

From 1922 to 1927, Behrens was professor of architecture at the Vienna Academy. He designed low-cost housing for workers in Vienna (1924–1925) and in Stuttgart (1927). His work of the early 1920's, such as the I.G. Farben works at Höchst (1920–1924), shows the influence of expressionist ideas. Later work, such as New Ways house in Northampton, England (1925–1926), was influenced by the international style in architecture. He died in Berlin on Feb. 27, 1940.

BEHRING, bā'ring, **Emil Adolph von** (1854–1917), German bacteriologist, who was the winner of the first Nobel Prize in physiology and medicine. Behring was one of the founders of immunology and, more specifically, of serum therapy. He discovered and was the first to use antitoxins against diphtheria and tetanus.

In 1884, Friedrich Löffler discovered the bacillus that causes diphtheria and also showed that some animals have a natural immunity against diphtheria. In 1888, Pierre Roux and Alexandre Yersin showed that the diphtheria bacillus produces a toxin, or poisonous substance. The tetanus bacillus was also found to produce a toxin.

Behring believed that if these toxins could be neutralized in the bodies of infected persons, much of the damage done by the germs could be avoided. In 1890 he found that by injecting dead or weakened diphtheria germs (toxins) into guinea pigs in a series of increasingly strong doses, he was able to produce in them a degree of immunity to the disease. He demonstrated that this was due to the appearance in the animal's blood serum of a chemical that neutralized the diphtheria toxin. Behring introduced the term "antitoxin" to describe this chemical.

The same results were achieved with tetanus germs. A surplus of the tetanus antitoxin was produced in the blood of experimental animals. Behring and a coworker, Shibasaburo Kitasato, injected some of the serum that contained the tetanus antitoxin into other animals and found that it produced in them a strong immunity against tetanus. Behring returned to his experiments with diphtheria germs, followed similar procedures, and achieved similar results.

Serum that contained diphtheria antitoxin was tested on humans; the first case was a child in Berlin in 1891. The antidiphtheria serum was found effective in producing immunity to the disease even after the disease had set in. In the case of tetanus, antitoxin serum was found effective only if given in advance or immediately after the victim became infected; it was not effective if given after the disease had set in.

Later, Behring was the first to administer a toxin-antitoxin mixture. The antitoxin part provides immediate passive immunity, while the toxin part stimulates the body to produce its own antitoxins, thus developing active and long-lasting immunity.

Diphtheria antitoxin was first marketed in 1892. Its use soon became widespread, and it produced a rapid and marked decrease in the mortality rates of diphtheria victims. Since then, diphtheria, which was once a dreaded childhood disease, has been brought under control.

The 1901 Nobel Prize in physiology and medicine was given to Behring "for his work on serum therapy, especially its application against diphtheria, by which he has opened a new road in the domain of medical science. . . ." Behring's discoveries led other scientists to seek antitoxins for a number of other diseases. Behring himself later produced a vaccine to immunize cattle against tuberculosis.

Life. Emil Adolph von Behring was born in Hansdorf, Germany, on March 15, 1854. He studied medicine in Berlin and entered the army medical corps as a surgeon in 1880. In 1889 he began to work as an assistant at Robert Koch's Institute for Infectious Diseases in Berlin, where he did the work that won him the Nobel Prize. He became a professor at the University of Halle in 1894, and in 1895 was appointed director of the Institute of Hygiene in Marburg. He died at Marburg on March 31, 1917. His writings include *Blood Serum Therapy* (1892), *Introduction to the Science of Control of Infectious Diseases* (1912), and books on diphtheria and tetanus.

S.N. Behrman

BEHRMAN, bâr'mən, **S.N.** (1893–1973), American dramatist, whose comedies of manners were a feature of many New York theater seasons during the 1930's and 1940's. He was born *Samuel Nathaniel Behrman* in Worcester, Mass., on June 9, 1893. After attending Clark University, he graduated in 1916 from Harvard, where he studied in George Pierce Baker's famous playwriting course, the "47 Workshop." In the early 1920's Behrman supported himself by writing articles for the *New Republic*, the *New Yorker*, and other magazines and by working as a press agent.

Behrman's career as a successful playwright began in 1927 with the New York Theatre Guild presentation of his comedy *The Second Man*, starring Alfred Lunt and Lynn Fontanne. Critics heralded the "emergence of a mature comedy talent," and Behrman immediately started on his second play, *Serena Blandish* (1928), based on the novel of the same name by the British author Enid Bagnold, which satirized society life in London. In a more serious vein, *Meteor* (1929), again starring Lunt and Fontanne, pictured a fanatically egotistical Wall Street tycoon. Behrman next wrote the play *Brief Moment* (1931), which caused a minor sensation by featuring critic Alexander Woollcott in the role of an obese hedonist.

Influenced by the turmoil of the 1930's, Behrman attempted to probe political and social problems in such dramas as *Rain from Heaven* (1934), dealing with fascism, and *End of Summer* (1936), concerning inherited wealth. Negative critical reaction to these plays led him to write the autobiographical drama *No Time for Comedy* (1939), about a playwright torn between his talent for comedy and his concern for human suffering.

Behrman's later plays include *The Pirate* (1942); *Fanny* (1954), written in collaboration with Josh Logan; and *Lord Pengo* (1962). He also wrote scenarios for such films as *Queen Christina* (1933) and *A Tale of Two Cities* (1935). His books include biographies of art dealer Joseph Duveen (*Duveen*, 1952) and of critic Max Beerbohm (*Portrait of Max*, 1960) and his autobiography, *People in a Diary: A Memoir* (1972). He died in New York City Sept. 9, 1973.

BEIDERBECKE, bī'dər-bek, **Bix** (1903–1931), American jazz musician. He was born *Leon Bismarck Beiderbecke*, in Davenport, Iowa, on March 10, 1903. He taught himself to play the cornet and the piano and was influenced by recordings of jazz music by New Orleans "Dixieland" bands and soloists. By 1923 his individual style of playing the cornet, characterized by brilliance of phrasing, clarity of tone, and richness of invention, had won him a reputation among other jazz musicians and a small coterie of fans. As a composer—chiefly of piano music—he adapted the harmonic ideas of Debussy.

Beiderbecke's sensitive nature and artistic ambition made him ill-suited for playing in large commercial dance orchestras, the only way a jazz musician in the 1920's could earn a living. As a result, he grew restless, began to drink heavily, changed jobs frequently, and went through long periods of illness caused by alcohol and malnutrition. He died on Aug. 7, 1931.

After his death, Beiderbecke acquired the status of a legend. Jazz enthusiasts sought out his recordings, which in 1953 were collected into three long-playing albums by Columbia Records under the title *The Bix Beiderbecke Story*. Dorothy Baker's novel *Young Man with a Horn* (1938) was inspired by, but not based on, his life.

BEILBY, bēl'bē, **Sir George Thomas** (1850–1924), Scottish industrial chemist, who devised improved chemical processes for industry. He was born in Edinburgh, Scotland, on Nov. 17, 1850. After graduating from Edinburgh University, he went into industry and developed a process for increasing the recovery of ammonia and paraffin from shale oil. He also invented a method for manufacturing alkaline cyanides.

Beilby studied Great Britain's coal economy and sought ways to prevent smoke. During World War I, as director of the Fuel Research Board, he was concerned with finding ways to produce oil from coal. In his book *Aggregation and Flow of Solids* (1921) he presented ideas on the flow of solids and their hardening under cold-working.

Beilby was elected a fellow of the Royal Society in 1906. He was a president of the Institute of Chemistry (1909–1912) and of the Institute of Metals (1916–1918). In 1912 he was a member of the royal commission on fuels and engines for the navy. He also served as chairman of the Royal Technical College in Glascow. Beilby was knighted in 1916. He died in London on Aug. 1, 1924.

BEILSTEIN, bīl'shtīn, **Friedrich Konrad** (1838–1906), Russian chemist who compiled the first standard handbook of organic compounds. This *Handbuch der organischen Chemie*, classifying and describing all known organic compounds, was published in 1883. Commonly known as *Beilstein*, it has since been expanded to many volumes.

Beilstein was born in St. Petersburg (now Leningrad), Russia, on Feb. 18, 1838. He was educated at Heidelberg and Göttingen universities in Germany. In 1860, at Göttingen, he became assistant to Friedrich Wöhler, the first chemist to synthesize an organic compound. Beilstein returned to Russia in 1866 to be professor of chemistry at St. Petersburg's Institute of Technology. He died in St. Petersburg on Oct. 18, 1906.

BEING AND NOTHINGNESS is a philosophical treatise by the French existentialist philosopher Jean-Paul Sartre (q.v.). Called *L'être et le néant* in French, the work was first published in 1943 (Eng. tr., 1956).

Sartre differentiates between three types of existence: first, Being In-Itself, the inert, homogeneous mass of what is, apart from human consciousness; second, Being For-Itself, or consciousness, the active, creative principle; and third, the forms into which the mind orders its perceptions. It is consciousness, itself impersonal, that creates the illusion of personal selves, and of distinct objects in an ordered world. To accept as true the natural attitude that the world and self exist independently of consciousness is to live in bad faith. To live in good faith, man must have the courage to face what lies beyond the self.

God is nonexistent in Sartre's philosophy. Though man strives with passion to lose himself in the infinite, "the idea of God is contradictory, and we lose ourselves in vain." However, the absence of God gives man freedom. There are no fixed laws of morality, because there is no transcendent being to decree them. Man must make his own choices. An "authentic" choice, made in good faith, involves acceptance of responsibility for one's own actions and responsibility for others.

Sartre is pessimistic about man's accepting the second responsibility. All human relationships, according to his philosophy, are based on conflict and hatred derived from the reluctance of each self to be merely an object of someone else's world. This point of Sartre's treatise is most succinctly expressed in his play *No Exit* (1944): "Hell is—other people."

BEING AND TIME is a work by the German philosopher Martin Heidegger that greatly influenced existentialist writers, particularly Sartre. Titled *Sein und Zeit*, it was first published in 1927 (Eng. tr., 1962). The book, planned as a total investigation of Being, was never completed, but Heidegger wrote other works expounding and elucidating its tenets. Although Heidegger was a strong proponent of the idea that language is not necessarily sufficient to convey complicated meanings, especially those concerned with truth and reality, he was disturbed by the great controversy over the interpretation of his treatise. He claimed that few students grasped its meaning, and it is likely that he chose not to complete his magnum opus because of the possibility of further misinterpretation.

Being and Time deals with the problem of human existence. Man, according to Heidegger, comes from nothing and inevitably must return to nothing. Plunged into a sea of brute facts, which have no intrinsic significance, man projects meaning into the world by transforming these facts—the "that-which-is"—into tools for his purposes. He is then confronted with a choice: he may either bury himself in the world of his making or he may face the true fact of his existence—his death and the return to nothingness. To live truly as a man, he must make a resolute choice to face the "nothing" and live with the dread that this choice entails. For it is as "nothing" that Being as such (as distinguished from the "that which is") is revealed to man. Heidegger claims that only by contemplating and living with the fact of death and nothingness can man pay proper homage to the sustaining cause of his existence.

BEINUM, bān'əm, **Eduard van** (1900–1959), Dutch conductor. He was born in Arnhem, Netherlands, on Sept. 3, 1900, into a family of musicians. After early musical training at home, he enrolled in 1918 in the Conservatory of Music in Amsterdam, where he studied the piano. He began his career as a pianist but gradually gave up the piano for conducting. After several years conducting choirs and small orchestras, he was made conductor of the Haarlem Orchestra in 1927.

He began his association with Amsterdam's Concertgebouw in 1931, as an assistant conductor under Willem Mengelberg. From 1938 he was associate conductor, and from 1945 (when Mengelberg retired) until 1956 he was chief conductor and musical director. Beinum specialized in interpreting Anton Bruckner's works and introduced to Dutch audiences the works of many modern composers.

Beinum made his American debut in 1954 as conductor of the Philadelphia Orchestra. Later that year he returned to the United States on a good will tour with the Concertgebouw. From 1956 he conducted the Los Angeles Philharmonic. He died in Amsterdam on April 13, 1959.

BEIRA, bā'ē-rə, is a port city in Mozambique, an overseas province of Portugal. One of the busiest ports on the East African coast, Beira is on the Mozambique Channel of the Indian Ocean, at the mouth of the Pungwe River. The city is the capital of Manica e Sofala district.

The city's harbor, airport, and rail connections make it the gateway to Rhodesia, Zambia, and Malawi. Oil was piped from the city to the Rhodesian refinery at Umtali except when the British blockade of Rhodesia in 1966 cut off oil shipments to Beira. Business activity in Beira is conducted mainly by the city's 16,000 Europeans and Asians. Industries include sugar refining, grain milling, and the manufacture of insulated cable, cigarettes, nails, and paint.

Beira was founded in 1891 as the headquarters of the Mozambique trading company of Portugal. The Portuguese government took over city administration in 1942. Population: (1960) 59,329.

BEIRUT, bā-rōōt', is the capital of the Republic of Lebanon and the chief port on the eastern shore of the Mediterranean Sea. Long a center of east-west trade, Beirut is also one of the major cultural, commercial, and banking centers of the Middle East. The city's name is *Beyrouth* in French and *Bayrut* in Arabic.

The population of Beirut is about two-thirds Christian and one-third Muslim. Arabic is the principal language, but French and English are widely used in the business center of the city.

Shipping is the major industry in Beirut. The city's protected harbor can accommodate large oceangoing vessels. There is a free zone for handling transit goods. Airlines operating from Beirut's international airport link the city with most of the countries of the world and are a stimulus to Beirut's growing tourist trade. The city has some small industries, including the manufacture of textiles, air-conditioning and heating equipment, soap, tiles, and beverages.

Beirut has four universities: the American University, noted for its medical school; the Lebanese University; the French University of St. Joseph; and the Arab University, a branch of Alexandria University. There is a music academy,

J. ALLAN CASH, FROM RAPHO GUILLUMETTE

BEIRUT is located on the shore of the Mediterranean below the Lebanon Mountains. Much of the city was destroyed in 1975–1976 during Lebanon's civil war.

a fine arts academy, the Ecole Supérieure des Lettres, and the Centre d'Études Mathématiques.

The ancient city, *Berytus* (from the Phoenician word for "wells"), is mentioned in Egyptian annals of the 1400's B.C. It played no important historical role, however, until it was made a Roman colony by Emperor Augustus about 15 B.C. He named it Julia Augusta Felix Berytus, for his daughter.

In the 200's A.D., Berytus was the site of a school of Roman law that developed into one of the most renowned law schools in the Roman empire. The works of two of its professors, Aemilius Papinianus (died 212) and Domitius Ulpianus (died 228), contributed importantly to the Justinian Code when it was compiled 300 years later. The city's contribution to the code prompted Emperor Justinian I to call Berytus "the mother and nurse of the law." When the city was destroyed by earthquake in 551, the school was demolished, and the town did not recover its former splendor until the 20th century.

The Arabs took possession of Beirut in 635 and held it until the advent of the Crusaders. Baldwin I included it in his Latin kingdom in 1100. Saladin, sultan of Egypt and Syria, recaptured it in 1187. The Ottoman Turks wrested it from the Mamluks in 1516. Except for a short period in the 1600's when it was held by the Druse prince Fakhr al-Din, Beirut remained a part of the Ottoman empire until the end of World War I. Immediately after the war the French took over Lebanon under a League of Nations mandate and chose Beirut as the capital. Parts of the city were destroyed in the war between Christian and Muslim-Palestinian forces in 1975–1976. Population (1970): 474,870.

PHILIP K. HITTI, *Author of "Lebanon in History" and "History of the Arabs"*

BEISSEL, bī′səl, **Johann Conrad** (1690–1768), German-American religious leader who established a monastic community of Seventh Day Baptists at Ephrata, Pa. He was born in Eberbach, Germany, and as a boy was apprenticed to a baker who taught him to play the violin. By the time he was 30, Beissel had adopted ascetic religious views for which he was forced to leave Germany. He emigrated to America in 1720 and settled in Germantown, Pa., where he was baptized a Dunker. He became the leader of a Dunker congregation, which eventually split with him over his pietistic doctrines of celibacy and observance of Saturday as the Sabbath. In 1732 he established the Solitary Brethren of the Community of Seventh Day Baptists at Ephrata.

A self-sufficient colony, the Solitary Brethren practiced Beissel's social and religious theories in a communal, celibate society that sought to recapture the spirituality of primitive Christianity. The community was noted for having one of the earliest and most famous printing presses in colonial America. *The Martyrs' Mirror,* the story of the persecution of the Mennonites in Europe, was an outstanding printing achievement by the Ephrata press. The colony was also known for its choral singing, hymns, and sacred scores. Among the most notable, written completely or in large part by Beissel himself, were *Turtle Dove* and *Paradisaical Wonder Music.* Though a novice musician, he greatly influenced American hymnology by his unique system of harmony and musical notation. He died in Ephrata on July 6, 1768. His colony declined after the Revolutionary War, although its influence lasted into the 19th century.

BEJAIA. See BOUGIE.

BÉJART, bā-zhar′, a family of French actors in Molière's troupe.

MADELEINE BÉJART (1618–1672) was an established actress and head of a family troupe when Molière (q.v.) fell in love with her and therefore decided to become an actor. In 1644 they formed a company called L'Illustre Théâtre that failed initially in Paris but triumphed in the provinces and finally returned to Paris in 1658. Madeleine shared Molière's despairs and triumphs and stayed with him until her death in 1672, a year before his. She took an active part in the administration of the theater and created the roles of the principal soubrettes in his plays—notably Dorine in *Tartuffe* and Frosine in *L'avare.*

ARMANDE BÉJART (1642?–1700) was Molière's wife. The circumstances of her birth are not known, but she was registered officially as the sister of Madeleine, who raised her. However, the fact that Madeleine gave birth to a child who reportedly did not survive aroused suspicions that Armande was really this child and even that Molière was her father. She made her debut as Élise in *La critique de l'école des femmes* and created the roles of Elmire in *Tartuffe,* Henriette in *Les femmes savantes,* and Célimène in *Le misanthrope.* Although her marriage to Molière was unhappy, she bore him three children and kept his theatrical company going for nearly 30 years after his death.

JOSEPH BÉJART (1616?–1659), Madeleine's older brother, was a member of Molière's company from its inception. A popular actor despite a stammer, he created the roles of Lélie in *L'étourdi* and Eraste in *Le dépit amoureux.*

LOUIS BÉJART (1630–1678), Madeleine's younger brother, joined the Molière troupe in 1653 and remained with it until he was forced to retire in 1670 because of lameness. He created roles in nearly all of Molière's plays, and Molière wrote the part of La Flèche, a cripple, in *L'avare* for him.

GENEVIÈVE HERVÉ (1622?–1675), Madeleine's sister, appears to have performed mostly in tragedies presented by the company. The name Hervé was her mother's maiden name.

BEJEL, bej'əl, is a chronic infectious disease found chiefly in the Arabian Peninsula and elsewhere in the Middle East. Very similar to yaws (q.v.), the disease causes lesions on the skin and bones. The initial lesions often appear near the lips and in the mouth. Following a pattern similar to yaws and syphilis, bejel proceeds to affect the genitalia and anal region. Bone lesions also occur in both the early and later stages of the disease. In untreated cases, skin lesions and rubbery tumors may involve the palate and nasal membranes.

Bejel is not a venereal disease, but it is caused by a microorganism that is very closely related to the spirochete (*Treponema pallidum*) that causes syphilis. The infection usually is acquired by children and subsequently transmitted to the adults of the family. Up to 90 percent of a village may be affected with the disease. Bejel is an important cause of chronic illness in the Middle East. Treatment with penicillin has proved effective in controlling the disease.

BEKE, bēk, **Charles Tilstone** (1800–1874), British geographer, who made contributions to Biblical history and philology. He was born in London on Oct. 10, 1800, and received a business education. He began his business career in 1820 but became interested in law, which he studied at Lincoln's Inn. In 1834 he published his first important book, *Origines Biblicae, or Researches in Primeval History,* in which he attempted to reconstruct history on the principles of the science of geology. For this work he was awarded a Ph.D. by the University of Tübingen in Germany.

In 1840, Beke made his first journey to Ethiopia (Abyssinia). He mapped thousands of miles of that country and collected vocabularies of the languages and dialects spoken there. Returning to London in 1843, he was awarded the gold medals of the Royal Geographical societies of London and Paris. The results of his discoveries were published in *Abyssinia* (1945). Beke then resumed his business career and made several unsuccessful efforts to establish commercial relations with Ethiopia.

In 1861–1862 he traveled with his wife in Syria, Palestine, and Egypt. When several British subjects were imprisoned by King Theodore of Ethiopia in 1864, Beke went to that country to attempt to secure their release. He was temporarily successful, but the captives were soon imprisoned again and during the subsequent British military action in Ethiopia, Beke's knowledge of the country was of great value to the British forces.

In 1873 he journeyed to the Middle East on an unsuccessful quest to locate Mount Sinai, which he believed was to the east of the Gulf of Aqaba. Beke died in Bromley, Kent, on July 31, 1874.

BÉKÉSY, bā'kā-sē, **Georg von** (1899–1972), Hungarian-American physicist, who was awarded the 1961 Nobel Prize in medicine and physiology for his findings concerning the stimulation of the cochlea of the ear.

Békésy, one of the foremost investigators in the field of sensory physiology, contributed in a fundamental way to the understanding of the ear and of sensory reception in general. He brought together and developed methods and techniques from physics, physiology, and psychology and applied himself to the basic questions of how sense organs and their nerve connections give information about external objects. His observations encompassed nearly every aspect of hearing and profoundly influenced the theory of hearing.

Békésy was born in Budapest, Hungary, on June 3, 1899. After receiving his early education in several countries, he obtained a Ph.D. in physics at the University of Budapest in 1923. Soon afterward he joined the scientific staff of the Hungarian telephone system and later was appointed professor of experimental physics at the University of Budapest.

While working for the telephone system, he investigated the causes of failure in telephone communications. These problems led him to study the anatomy and physiology of the ear. His consideration of the movements of cochlear structures resulted in the development of a working model of the cochlea. To gain an understanding of the relations between the mechanics of the ear and auditory experiences, he entered into a long series of psychological and psychophysical studies, in which he dealt with such problems as the nature of beats and combination tones and the effects of rapid changes in sounds on their subjective quality.

Békésy left Hungary in 1946 and went to the Karolinska Institut in Sweden, where he studied the disturbances of hearing caused by ear diseases. He also designed a new type of audiometer in which the patient himself carries out most of the testing procedure.

In 1947, Békésy went to the United States and joined the staff of the Psycho-Acoustic Laboratory at Harvard University. There he constructed a model of the cochlea that uses the skin of a person's arm as a receptive surface. This model strikingly exhibits the role of the nervous system in sensory perception and discrimination.

Békésy also carried out a series of experiments on the electrophysiology of the ear and discovered the direct potentials that are present in the cochlea. He extended his studies to other senses, including taste and skin sensitivity and the perception of vibrations by the skin. This work, considered as a whole, gives a unified picture of the nature of sensory and nervous processes in producing our perceptions of the external world. In 1966, Békésy became research director of the Laboratory of Sensory Sciences at the University of Hawaii. He died in Honolulu on June 13, 1972.

Békésy wrote more than a hundred articles on hearing, vibratory sensitivity, and other subjects. Most of his papers on the ear, written from 1928 to 1958 in three different languages, were collected and translated into English in the book *Experiments in Hearing* (1960). Later articles were published in the *Journal of the Acoustical Society of America* and other acoustical and psychological journals.

ERNEST GLEN WEVER, *Princeton University*

BEKHTEREV, byăkн'tyi-ryəf, **Vladimir Mikhailovich** (1857–1927), Russian neuropathologist, who did extensive work on the human brain. Bekhterev was born in Viatka province in Russia on Jan. 20, 1857. He studied in St. Petersburg (now Leningrad) and later in Leipzig and Paris. While professor of psychiatry at the Military Medical Academy in St. Petersburg, he founded a psychoneurological institution (later known as the Psychoneurological Academy). He died in Moscow on Dec. 24, 1927.

Bekhterev studied the localization of functions in the brain and described the fiber layers in parts of the brain. He also studied human reflexes, applying some of the information Pavlov had obtained in his work on dogs. He founded the periodical *Nevrologicheski Vestnik*. His books include *The Nerve Currents in the Brain and Spinal Cord* (1882) and *The Functions of the Nervous Centers* (1909).

BEL AIR, bel-âr', a town in Maryland, is the seat of Harford County and is situated 25 miles (40 km) by road northeast of Baltimore. The town is the trading center of a rich farming area. Prior to 1787, Bel Air was farmland known as "Aquilla Scott's Old Fields." By enactment of 1787, citizens of the county were given the privilege of holding an election to select the site of the courthouse and prison. Bel Air was chosen. The courthouse contains portraits of celebrated citizens, among them Governor William Paca and actor Edwin Booth.

The town was incorporated in 1874 and rechartered in 1941. It has a commission form of government. Population: 6,307.

BEL AND THE DRAGON is one of several additions to the Old Testament Book of Daniel. It is found in the Greek version but is not in the Hebrew Bible. It belongs to the Apocrypha or deuterocanonical books added to the Old Testament.

The purpose of this fantastic story is to unmask the deceptions of idolatry. In the first part, Daniel proves to the king of Babylon, a devout worshiper of Bel (that is, Marduk, chief god of Babylon), that the store of food in the temple of the idol is not for the use of the deity but for the priests and their families, who steal it at night. In the second part, Daniel destroys a dragon worshiped by the Babylonians by feeding it pitch, fat, and hair, whereupon it bursts open. In punishment for his destruction of the beast, Daniel is thrown into a lion's den, where the prophet Habakkuk takes care of him.

The book probably was written in the 2d or 1st century B.C., as part of the literary propaganda of Jews in Egypt against the folly and stupidity of idol worship in the surrounding pagan world. It scarcely matches the literary excellence of most of the Apocrypha, and its context is completely improbable.

FREDERICK C. GRANT
Union Theological Seminary

BÉLA III (died 1196), bā'lo, was a member of the Árpád dynasty of Hungarian kings. The son of Géza II, he was educated at Constantinople while a hostage of the Eastern emperor. In 1173, Emperor Manuel I Comnenus put Béla on the throne of Hungary in the hope that Hungary would be dependent on the Eastern empire. Although he remained friendly with the East, Béla increased Hungary's ties with western Europe. When refused permission by the church to marry a relative of Manuel I, Béla married Marguerite, the sister of Philip Augustus of France.

Béla's primary objective was to regain Dalmatia, a region along the eastern coast of the Adriatic Sea, which had come under the control of Venice after his father's death. Two wars with Venice (1180–1188 and 1190–1191), however, proved only partially successful. Béla was aiding Emperor Isaac II Angelus against the Bulgarians when he died in 1196.

BÉLA IV (1206–1270), bā'lo, was the last strong ruler in the Árpád dynasty of Hungarian kings. Soon after he ascended the throne in 1235, Béla faced the Mongol invasion that affected the entire course of his long reign. Under Batu Khan the Mongols began their invasion of the West through Russia in 1237. Béla saw the threat to his kingdom and to Christendom in general, but his appeals for help to the pope and the emperor were not successful.

In 1241 the Mongols entered Hungary. Béla tried to unite the nobility, but they suspected him of trying to curb their independence and did not respond. With his own forces Béla met the Mongols at Mohi on the Sajó River on April 11, 1241, and was disastrously defeated. He was forced to flee to Dalmatia while the Mongols continued ravaging the country. Fortunately for Hungary, Batu Khan withdrew the next year to take part in the election of a new Mongol leader.

Béla returned to Hungary in 1242 and spent the rest of his reign restoring order and recovering territory that had been annexed by Frederick, Duke of Austria, during his absence. In 1246 he defeated and killed Frederick. Béla's reorganization of the Hungarian state was so successful that Hungary was able to repulse a Mongol advance in 1261. From 1265 to 1270 he was at war with Ottokar (Otakar) II of Bohemia over the possession of Styria, a region now in Austria. Ottokar gained control of Styria after Béla's death on May 3, 1270.

BELAFONTE, bel-ə-fon'tā, **Harry** (1927–   ), American singer and actor. He was born in New York City on March 1, 1927. He moved with his family to Jamaica, in the West Indies, in 1935, and returned with them to New York City in 1940. He began his career singing popular songs in nightclubs. In 1950 he started to investigate folk music and soon became known for his interpretations of West Indian and other folksongs. In 1953 he was given a role in the Broadway review *John Murray Anderson's Almanac*, for which he won the 1954 "Tony" (Antoinette Perry) award for the best featured act in a musical. He also appeared on Broadway in *3 for Tonight* (1955). Otto Preminger engaged him to play Joe (Don José) in the film adaptation of *Carmen Jones* (1955), although another singing voice was used on the sound track. His other films include *Island in the Sun* (1957) and *Odds Against Tomorrow* (1959).

Much of Belafonte's fame was the result of his success as a recording artist, especially with such folksongs as *Day-O, Matilda,* and *Venezuela,* calypso songs, and his many albums. He frequently appeared on television and won a 1960 Academy of Television Arts and Sciences "Emmy" award for *Tonight with Belafonte* (1959). A Negro, Belafonte championed civil rights.

BELAIN, bə-laN′, **Pierre,** SIEUR D′ESNAMBUC (1570?–1636), French privateer. He was born in Dieppe, France. About 1625 he sailed from Dieppe in a brigantine for the West Indies. He landed on the island of Saint Kitts with a party of English colonists, with whom he divided the island; until his death he held the French half of the island with extraordinary tenacity. In 1635 he took possession of Martinique and Guadeloupe in the name of the king of France. He died on Saint Kitts in December 1636.

BELALCÁZAR, bä-läl-kä′thär, **Sebastián de** (1495?–1551), Spanish conqueror of Ecuador. His name is also spelled *Benalcázar*. He was born *Sebastián Moyano* at Belalcázar, Córdoba, Spain. Enlisting at Seville for colonial service in Darién (Central America), he participated in the conquest of Nicaragua in 1520. He left Panama City in 1530 as an aide to Francisco Pizarro on the expedition to conquer Peru. The year after the conquest, in 1533, Belalcázar led an army to the northern Inca capital of Quito, where he defeated the forces of the Inca chieftain, Rumiñahui. He advanced farther north into Popayán (now in Colombia) and founded the city of Guayaquil before returning to Quito. As governor of Popayán from 1538 to 1550, he ruled with cruel and unscrupulous efficiency. Recalled to Spain to answer charges of political murder, he died on the way, at Cartagena (Colombia).

BÉLAND, bā-laN′, **Henri Séverin** (1869–1935), Canadian public official. He was born in Louiseville, Quebec, on Oct. 11, 1869. After receiving his medical degree (1893) from Laval University he practiced in Beauce county, which he represented as a Liberal in the Quebec legislature from 1897 to 1901. From 1902 until 1925 he sat in the Canadian House of Commons, serving as minister of public health and of soldiers′ civil reestablishment from 1921 to 1925. He was appointed to the Senate in 1925. He died in Eastview, Ontario, on April 22, 1935. Taken prisoner by the Germans in World War I, while serving with the Belgian hospital corps, Béland recounted his experiences in *My Three Years in a German Prison* (1919).

BELANEY, bə-lā′nē, **George Stansfeld** (1888–1938), Canadian naturalist and writer, known as *Grey Owl*. The identity of his parents, his birthplace, and even his first name (*Archie,* according to some sources) are uncertain. He claimed to have been born in Mexico of an Apache Indian mother, but Canadian sources indicate that he was born in Hastings, England.

Belaney arrived in Canada in 1903 and became a trapper, guide, and forest ranger. After serving in World War I with the Canadian Expeditionary Force, he identified himself as half-Indian, was adopted by the Ojibways, and took the name of Grey Owl (Indian *Wa-Sha-Quon-Asin,* meaning "he who walks by night"). In 1925 he married an Iroquois woman named Anahareo. He devoted the rest of his life to the conservation of wildlife and to writing.

Grey Owl was a popular lecturer, especially in England, where he was received at court. His books include *Men of the Last Frontier* (1931), *Pilgrims of the Wild* (1934), *The Adventures of Sajo and Her Beaver People* (1935), and *Tales of an Empty Cabin* (1936). He died at Prince Albert, Saskatchewan, on April 13, 1938.

BELASCO, bə-las′kō, **David** (1853–1931), American theatrical producer and playwright. He was born in San Francisco on July 25, 1853. In 1858 his family moved to Victoria, British Columbia, where, at the age of 11, Belasco played a role in Charles Kean′s production of *Richard III*. After the Civil War the Belasco family returned to San Francisco, and David joined a theatrical touring company that barnstormed through California. Between 1874 and 1880 he held several managerial positions in San Francisco theaters. In 1880 he took the production *Hearts of Oak* to New York City, where it failed. Two years later he again went to New York and joined the Madison Square Theatre, for which he wrote a number of plays and was an assistant producer. He left the Madison Square Theatre in 1886 and for several years collaborated with other writers on such plays as *Lord Chumley* (1887), and *The Heart of Maryland* (1895).

In 1900, Belasco was coauthor (with John Luther Long) and producer of the highly successful *Madame Butterfly,* a work that later became famous as the basis of Giacomo Puccini′s opera of the same name. Other Belasco successes included *The Girl of the Golden West* (1905; also adapted by Puccini), *The Return of Peter Grimm* (1911), and *Laugh, Clown, Laugh* (1923). Belasco opened two theaters bearing his name in New York City, and one of the houses is still in operation.

When Broadway underwent numerous transformations after World War I, including a stronger emphasis on serious drama, Belasco failed to keep pace, and his reputation declined. He died in New York City on May 4, 1931.

Belasco′s most important contribution to the theater was his pioneering of many highly effective stage devices, including extensive and imaginative lighting and the use of realistic props and sets. Having little interest in the literary aspect of drama, he relied on notable and popular stars for his success. Many famous actors and actresses appeared in his productions, including David Warfield, Leonore Ulric, and Katharine Cornell. He was noted for his many flamboyant personal affectations.

BELAÚNDE TERRY, bā-lä-ōōn′dä ter′ē, **Fernando** (1912–   ), Peruvian political leader and architect. He was born in Lima, Peru, on Oct. 7, 1912. After studying in Peru and France, he completed architectural studies at the University of Texas in 1935. He then returned to Lima and soon won a reputation as a leading architect.

Belaúnde′s active interest in urban planning led him into politics. He was elected to the Chamber of Deputies in 1945 and waged a battle for low-cost public housing. In 1956 he organized the left-of-center Popular Action party and was its presidential candidate that year. He was defeated then and again in 1962, but overwhelming popular support enabled him to win a six-year presidential term in June 1963. As president, he launched a social reform program designed mainly to benefit the poor. He was deposed by an army coup in October 1968 and went into exile.

BELCH, belch, **Sir Toby,** a character in Shakespeare′s *Twelfth Night*. A roistering humorous knight, he is uncle to Olivia and boon companion to Sir Andrew Aguecheek. He aids in the discomfiture of Malvolio.

BELCHER, bel′chər, **Jonathan** (1682–1757), American colonial governor. He was born in Cambridge, Mass., on Jan. 8, 1682. After graduating from Harvard in 1699 he traveled in Europe and then became a prosperous merchant in Boston. In 1718 he was elected to the Massachusetts Council, and he served eight terms.

Belcher was commissioned governor of Massachusetts and New Hampshire in 1730. Although disposed toward compromise, the American-born royal governor had stormy relations with the colonists. Issues in dispute included control of such natural resources as timber and the contested Massachusetts-New Hampshire boundary. Political enemies took their grievances to England, and Belcher lost his posts in 1741.

Belcher himself then went to England and reestablished his standing with the British government. From 1747 until his death he was governor of New Jersey. In this post he was generally successful, despite serious riots by landseekers protesting the proprietors' grants. Belcher enlarged the charter of the College of New Jersey (Princeton), to which he gave his valuable library. He died in Elizabeth, N.J., on Aug. 31, 1757.

BELCHERTOWN, bel′char-toun, in Massachusetts, is a town in Hampshire County, situated 20 miles (32 km) by road northeast of Springfield. It is a dairy-farming and apple-growing center. At Belchertown is Stone House Museum, of interest for its early collection of farm machinery and spinning wheels. The community dates from 1761. Population: 5,936.

BELCOURT, bel-cōōr′, **Napoléon Antoine** (1860–1932), Canadian public official. He was born in Toronto on Sept. 15, 1860, and received a law degree from Laval University in 1882. In that year he was admitted to the bar of the province of Quebec and in 1884 to the Ontário bar.

A leading lawyer, he represented Ottawa as a Liberal in the Canadian House of Commons from 1896 until 1907, serving as speaker in 1904–1906. He was in the Senate from 1907 until his death. As owner and editor of *Le Temps* of Ottawa, Belcourt wrote extensively on social, legal, and educational subjects. He strongly supported the use of the French language in the French separate schools of Ontario. Belcourt died at Blue Sea Lake, Quebec, on Aug. 7, 1932.

BELDING, bel′ding, is a city in south central Michigan, in Ionia County, 25 miles (40 km) east of Grand Rapids. It is in a farming and orchard region. Its industries include foundries and the manufacture of refrigerators, plastics, and children's clothing. Government is by mayor and council. Population: 5,121.

BELÉM, bə-lãn′, a city in northern Brazil, is the major receiving and distributing center for the entire Amazon valley. It is the capital of the state of Pará and is known also as *Pará*. The city is situated on the Pará River, a tributary of the Amazon River, 90 miles (145 km) from the Atlantic Ocean.

Most of the city's commerce is moved by water, but there is a railroad to Bragança, 144 miles (231.6 km) on the coast to the east, as well as airline connections. A highway, 1,470 miles (2,356 km) long, to Brasília, the capital of Brazil, was opened in 1960.

The city has sawmills, shipyards, brick and tile factories, and machine works. Its exports include rubber, jute, timber, Brazil nuts, pepper, vegetable gums, rice, and maize.

Goeldi Natural History Museum in Belém houses displays of the ethnology and archaeology of the Amazon region. The governor's palace, built in 1762, is a fine example of Portuguese colonial architecture. Belém's University of Pará was founded in 1957. The city was founded in 1615. Population: (1960): 380,667.

BELEMNOID, bel′əm-noid, any of a small group of largely extinct, invertebrate, squidlike aquatic animals belonging to the phylum Mollusca and having arms (cephalopodia), with suckers, extending from the region of the head. They appeared suddenly in the Triassic period (200 million to 165 million years ago), reached their peak in the middle of the Mesozoic period (about 135 million years ago), and then began to die out. The belemnoids comprise two groups: the belemnites and *Spirula*.

The belemnites are extinct. Their fossils are cone-shaped cavities in which the remains of an internal shell may be found. The young belemnites are believed to have secreted a shell that gradually became internal.

Spirula is the only living representative of the belemnoids. It is a small cephalopod with a many-chambered shell coiled in a flat spiral. It is found in tropical seas.

BELEN, bə-len′, is a town in west central New Mexico, in Valencia County. It is situated on the Rio Grande, 30 miles (48 km) south of Albuquerque. Belen is a railroad division point and commercial center in a region that raises alfalfa, cereals, wool, fruit, and vegetables. The first settlement was in 1741, when the population consisted of Spaniards and Indians. Incorporated in 1918, Belen is governed by a mayor and council. Population: 4,823.

BELESME, be-lãm′, **Robert of,** EARL OF SHREWSBURY, Anglo-Norman nobleman of the 11th–12th century. He is also known as *Robert of Bellême*. In •1077 he supported the rebellion of Robert (later duke of Normandy) against the latter's father, William I the Conqueror; and in 1088 he sided with Robert in the insurrection against William II Rufus. Subsequently he served under William II in the invasion of Normandy, and in 1098 succeeded to the earldom of Shrewsbury. For his part in the unsuccessful revolt against Henry I in 1102 he was banished from England; he found refuge in Normandy. He returned to England in 1112 as ambassador of Louis VI, king of France, but he was seized, tried for former crimes, and imprisoned for life.

BELFAST, bel′fast, a city in eastern Maine and the seat of Waldo County, is a seaport on Penobscot Bay, 30 miles (48 km) southwest of Bangor. It is the trading center for an area which raises potatoes, corn, and poultry. Leading industrial products of the city are leatherboard, clothing, and shoes. Belfast has a good harbor, and is a popular tourist center.

The first settlers, in 1769, were Scotch-Irish. The town was incorporated in 1773, and in the 1790's became a shipbuilding center. Belfast obtained a city charter in 1853, and has a city-manager form of government. Population: 5,957.

BELFAST: (*Left*) A residential street slopes toward the shipyards in the background. Shipbuilding is a major industry in the city. (*Right*) Statue of Queen Victoria is a landmark in front of the City Hall in Donegal Square.

BELFAST, bel'fast, is the capital of Northern Ireland and one of the chief ports of the British Isles. It is situated on the river Lagan at the head of Belfast Lough, 103 miles (166 km) north of Dublin, astride the boundary of counties Antrim and Down. In addition to its importance as a seaport, it is a major industrial and commercial center.

The linen industry was the chief single cause of Belfast's growth. Fostered by Huguenot refugees beginning with the close of the 17th century, linen manufacture expanded enormously in the 19th century, spurred by the introduction of power machinery, which had been employed earlier in Belfast in the cotton industry. The cotton industry had died out in the city because of raw-material restrictions imposed by the American Civil War. In time Belfast became the world center of the linen industry. In more recent years, linen has been partly supplanted by a thriving industry in synthetic fabrics.

Shipbuilding on a large scale came with the harbor improvements that followed commercial expansion. The shipyard of Harland and Wolff grew into the largest in the world, winning renown for its huge ocean liners. Belfast also has the world's largest ropeworks. Other industries include aircraft manufacture, machinery, oil refining, furniture, aerated waters, distilling, the processing of foodstuffs, and tobacco products. The city is also a commercial and transport center for Northern Ireland's considerable industry in farm produce and cattle.

Belfast is handsomely situated between hills and the sea. The city is of relatively modern growth. Most of its center is Victorian in style. There are many fine public parks. It has a university and other institutions for higher education and professional training, a museum and art gallery, and many libraries. Transportation is provided from two airports, three railway stations, and the large harbor, from which ships sail to several English and Scottish ports.

Belfast has four parliamentary divisions, each sending one member to the United Kingdom House of Commons, and it is represented by 16 members in the Northern Ireland Parliament. Municipal affairs are under a lord mayor and corporation. The city has the status of a county borough. With an area of only 28 square miles (72.5 sq km), Belfast overflows its boundaries into a number of suburban towns, principally Stormont, where the government buildings are located, and Sydenham.

History. The city's name, referring to its location, comes from the Gaelic *beol feirste*, meaning "the ford at the sand bank." A castle, the first of several, was built by John de Courcy in 1177 to command the ford. In 1611, Lord Deputy Sir Arthur Chichester, the Devon administrator, having received a grant of land here in 1604, built a castle and a little town which was given a charter in 1613 and representation in the Irish Parliament. The first British settlers in Belfast included Devon folk, Scots, and some Manxmen. The town remained small until the end of the 18th century (its population in 1782 was only 13,105), but from then on it grew rapidly with the Industrial Revolution.

In the late 19th century, Belfast became the chief center of a vigorous political movement to preserve the union with Great Britain. When the Government of Ireland Act was passed in 1920, it became the seat of government of Northern Ireland. Population: (1971) 360,150.

For recent events, see NORTHERN IRELAND.

HUGH SHEARMAN
Author of "Ulster" and "Modern Ireland"

QUEEN'S UNIVERSITY in Belfast was founded as Queen's College in 1845. It received a university charter in 1908.

BELFAST, Queen's University of, bel'fast, is a government-supported coeducational institution in Belfast, Northern Ireland. It was established as Queen's College by royal charter in 1845 and opened for instruction in 1849. A year later it joined with colleges at Galway and Cork as Queen's University. It became a constituent of the Royal University of Ireland in 1879 and retained this status until 1908, when it was established as Queen's University of Belfast. Colleges associated with Queen's are Edgehill Theological College, the Municipal College of Technology, and Presbyterian College, all of Belfast, and Magee University College, Londonderry.

Queen's offers a well-rounded curriculum of studies at the university level and special programs in Celtic studies. The university library houses 330,000 volumes, and there are museums of archaeology, natural history, and medicine. Enrollment approximates 3,300.

BELFORT, bel-fôr', a town, in northeastern France, is the capital of the Territory of Belfort department. It is an industrial and transportation center on the Savoureuse River, 25 miles (40 km) southwest of Mulhouse. Belfort has industrial plants producing locomotives, engineering equipment, smokestacks, cable, pipe, and cotton textiles. It is also a marketing center for the cereals, grains, and wines that are produced in the surrounding region.

The town dominates the historically strategic Belfort Gap, a pass between the Vosges and Jura mountains that gives access from the Rhine Valley to the Paris Basin. Belfort was ceded to France by Austria in 1648 and, because of its strategic position, was heavily fortified (by the marquis de Vauban) beginning in 1686. In the Franco-Prussian War, it was besieged by the Prussians on Nov. 3, 1870. Its gallant defenders resisted for 108 days before yielding on orders of the French government. *The Lion of Belfort,* carved in rock at the foot of the town's castle by Frédéric Auguste Bartholdi, commemorates the epic siege. Population: (1962) 47,576.

BELFORT, Territory of, bel-fôr', is a department of France, 235 square miles (610 sq km) in area. Situated between the Vosges and Jura mountains, it is bounded by the departments of Haut-Rhin, Haute-Saône, and Doubs, and by Switzerland. The town of Belfort is the capital and principal city. Belfort was the only part of Alsace not ceded to Germany in 1871, and it remained a separate department when Alsace was returned to France after World War I. Population: (1962) 109,371.

BELGAE, bel'jē, a warlike people of ancient times who lived principally in northeastern Gaul and southern Britain. They were grouped into loosely associated, independent tribes. Settling early in the Rhine Valley, they adopted German customs and claimed German blood and fighting skill, but their language, names, and appearance were Celtic. Probably they were wholly Celtic.

By the 2d century B.C. the Germans had driven the Belgae into the lands between the Rhine, the Seine, and the Marne. From there some Belgae crossed the Channel about 75 B.C. and dominated southeastern Britain.

The Belgae developed cattle raising and agriculture and had metal coinage. Normally, tribal kings ruled the noblemen, freemen, and serfs, Their religion was polytheistic, but probably not Druid. They lived in fortified woodland cities.

Julius Caesar called them the least Romanized of the Gauls and the fiercest fighters, praising their cavalry. Despite tribal hostilities, the Belgae led Gallic opposition to German and Roman conquests; the Belgae alone successfully opposed the invasion of Gaul by the Cimbri and Teutoni. Caesar fought from 57 to 50 B.C. to subdue them. After the Roman conquest of Gaul, the Belgae again fled to Britain, settling in the southwest. They remained the most subborn opponents of Rome's conquest of Britain.

War casualties and slavery decimated the hardfighting Belgae. Gradually they suffered political and cultural oblivion as they were assimilated into the Roman empire.

ELEANOR HUZAR, *Michigan State University*

BELGAUM, bel-goum', a city in Mysore state, southwestern India, is the capital of the district of Belgaum. Situated on the Deccan Plateau some 250 miles (400 km) southeast of Bombay, the city is about 2,500 feet (762 meters) above sea level. It is a trading center for rice, ghee, and timber, and is well known for its weaving industry. Furniture, matches, chemicals, and cameras are manufactured. The city's six colleges are affiliated with Karnatak University. Belgaum was known in ancient times as *Venugrama.* It has a large fort, built in the 16th century which is now in ruins; the fort was captured by the British in 1818. Two Jain temples still stand in the city. Population: (1961) 127,-885.

Belgaum District, covering an area of 5,163 square miles (13,372 sq km), is drained by the Kistna and Ghatprabha rivers. Cotton, millet, rice, tobacco, and wheat are the most important crops grown in the district. Its chief towns and trading centers, in addition to Belgaum, include Athni, Gokak, and Nipani. Belgaum district was part of the state of Bombay until 1956, when it was incorporated into Mysore state. Population: (1961) 357,469.

BELGIAN CONGO, bel'jən kong'gō, a former Belgian colony in equatorial Africa. An independent state since 1960, it is officially known as the *Democratic Republic of Congo,* but frequently is referred to as *the Congo.* (See CONGO, DEMOCRATIC REPUBLIC OF.)

BELGIOIOSO, bāl-jō-yō'sō, **Princess di** (1808–1871), Italian patriot and writer. She was born into the distinguished Trivulzio family in Milan on June 28, 1808, and was given the name Cristina. At 16 she married Prince di Belgioioso d'Este. Exiled by the Austrian government in Milan in 1830, she settled in Paris, where she established a great salon frequented by the most prominent writers and musicians of the day. She wrote tirelessly in the cause of Italian freedom. She returned to Italy during the revolution of 1848 and equipped several hundred volunteers for Charles Albert of Sardinia in his struggle against the Austrians. Exiled again in 1849, she later returned to Italy, where she founded the political journal *L'Italie* in Milan. She died in that city on July 15, 1871.

Her writings include *Histoire de la maison de Savoie* (1860) and *Réflexions sur l'état actuel de l'Italie et sur son avenir* (1869).

GEORGIA ENGELHARD, MONKMEYER

Belgium preserves the charm of the past in towns such as Bruges, the Venice of the North.

CONTENTS

Section	Page	Section	Page
1. The People	482	7. Culture	495
2. Land and Natural		Painting	496
Resources	484	Sculpture and	
3. Economy	485	Architecture	496
4. Education	487	Music	496
5. Government	488	Literature	497
6. History	488		

BELGIUM, bel'jəm, is a constitutional monarchy in western Europe. An independent nation since 1830, it combines a highly developed modern economy with a great cultural tradition. A visitor to Brussels, the capital, or to the port of Antwerp is impressed with the country's prosperity and economic vitality as a key member of the European Economic Community (Common Market). On the other hand, in few regions of Europe do the beauty and mystery of the Middle Ages come more alive than in the Belgian cities of Ghent and Bruges.

Belgium's history is a microcosm of the history of Europe. The country has been alternately the marketplace and the battlefield of the Continent. Despite its small size, it has experienced the religious and nationality divisions that have racked so many European countries. Its location on main war and trade routes involved it in the dynastic struggles of Burgundians and Habsburgs, Bourbons and Bonapartes.

The jealousies of the great powers allowed the Belgian revolt from the United Netherlands to succeed in 1830, but those jealousies also threatened the nation's continuing existence. Belgium was spared during the Franco-Prussian War of 1870, but its permanently guaranteed neutrality was violated by Germany in 1914. Recovery from World War I and from the havoc

Belgium's Coat of Arms

wreaked by the persistent depression of the 1930's was barely accomplished by 1940, when Hitler launched his blitzkrieg through the country, which had just readopted a policy of neutrality.

These experiences have confirmed the Belgians' belief in the necessity of European cooperation. Enthusiasm for integration has been further stimulated by distrust of Communist expansion and by a desire to be part of a larger entity giving Belgium increased leverage and importance in dealing with its North Atlantic Treaty allies in economic and defense matters. Belgium's pride in serving as tutor to the Congo was wounded by the breakaway of the colony in 1960, but the subsequent economic crisis was successfully weathered.

Proximity to the mouths of the Rhine and Meuse rivers and to London and Paris has made Belgium a natural trading center. Long a chief agricultural region of Europe, it was the first of the Continental nations to become highly in-

BRUSSELS' ATOMIUM (in the distance beyond the park) is a permanent symbol of the 1958 Brussel's World's Fair.

dustrialized; despite the ravages of two foreign occupations in the 20th century, it has continued to be a leading exporter of manufactured goods. Since World War II many foreign corporations have established factories and financial centers there.

Belgium's contributions to the advancement of civilization have been far out of proportion to the size of the country. Over the ages Belgium has maintained a rich culture and a high level of prosperity. Paradoxically, this has in part been the result of the country's linguistic division and geographical location, which in other ways have caused so much difficulty. The strongly Roman Catholic Flemings of the northern and western regions have contributed much by their industry and by the artistry of their painters, weavers, and builders. The French-speaking Walloons, who are concentrated in the southeast, led the state in its formative years and have made French culture part of the Belgian heritage.

INFORMATION HIGHLIGHTS

Official Name: Royaume de Belgique; Koninkrijk België.

Head of State: King of the Belgians.

Head of Government: Prime minister.

Legislature: Chambers of Parliament.

Area: 11,779 sq mi (30,507 sq km) in Belgium proper; 2.7 sq mi (7 sq km) in enclave of Baarle-Hertog.

Boundaries: *North,* North Sea and the Netherlands; *east,* the Netherlands and Germany; *southeast,* Luxembourg; *south and southwest,* France.

Elevations: Highest point—Botrange, 2,277 feet (695 meters); lowest point—the polders, a few feet below sea level.

Population: 9,428,000 (1964).

Capital: Brussels (Bruxelles; Brussel).

Major Languages: Flemish, French, and German. Flemish and French are official languages of the national administration.

Major Religious Groups: Roman Catholics; Protestants.

Monetary Unit: Belgian franc (100 centimes).

Weights and Measures: Metric system.

Flag: Three vertical stripes—black, yellow, and red.

National Anthem: *La Brabançonne (Après des siècles d'esclavage).*

---

1. The People

The population of Belgium can be broadly divided into three linguistic groups. A majority are Flemings of Germanic stock who speak a dialect similar to Dutch. The Walloons, of Celtic antecedents, originally spoke dialects that differed markedly from Parisian French. These dialects have now nearly disappeared and have been replaced by a slightly Belgicized version of French, although in the countryside near Mons (Bergen) and Liège (Luik) they still may be heard occasionally. The German-speaking population of Belgium numbers less than 90,000 persons, yet because it is concentrated about Eupen and Malmédy and near the border with Luxembourg, it has been able to win language rights in those areas.

The Linguistic Boundary. The origin of the division of Belgium between Walloon and Fleming is lost in the shadows of the early Middle Ages. Between the 3d and 6th centuries the Salian Franks moved across the Rhine and established their control over the area presently between Boulogne in France, Cologne in West Germany, and the Netherlands' Inland Sea. South of a line that could be drawn from Boulogne to Maastricht in the Netherlands, the Roman influence, first introduced by Julius Caesar, was dominant; and although the Franks eventually conquered Gaul, the populace had become so Latinized that its language was never replaced by the Germanic speech of the Franks. North of the line, the Franks established themselves so thoroughly that their language became that of the people.

The linguistic boundary has remained distinct, with only slight modification, for 1,400 years. Along the Atlantic coast it has moved north to coincide with the Franco-Belgian border. In the interior the line has shifted south, and in the 20th century this shift has been accelerated by the superiority of the Flemish birthrate over that of the French-speaking populace.

The location of the boundary is now established by law. On one side of the legal dividing line all public signs and most advertising are in Flemish; a few yards down the road they are in French. Only in the national capital, Brussels, 20 miles within the Flemish zone, does the law require all official signs and publications to be in both languages. It was estimated that following the revision of the linguistic frontier on Sept. 1, 1963, the Flemish zone had 55.3 percent of the population, and the Walloon, bilingual, and German regions had 32.9, 11.2, and 0.6 percent respectively.

The leading Flemish cities are the medieval trading towns of Ghent (Gent, Gand) and Bruges (Brugge), along with the port of Antwerp (Antwerpen, Anvers). The chief centers of Wallonia are the fortified cities of Namur and Liège.

Bilingualism is frequently found in Belgium, particularly among the Flemings, who until recently have found it necessary to learn French to get ahead. The revolution of 1830 was dominated, as was the government for the ensuing 90 years, by the upper bourgeoisie, which was primarily Walloon. French was therefore the language of administration, of the parliamentary chambers, of the courts, and of military command. Only after expansion of the franchise and the stimulation of the Flemish movement by German occupation authorities during World War I

BELGIUM

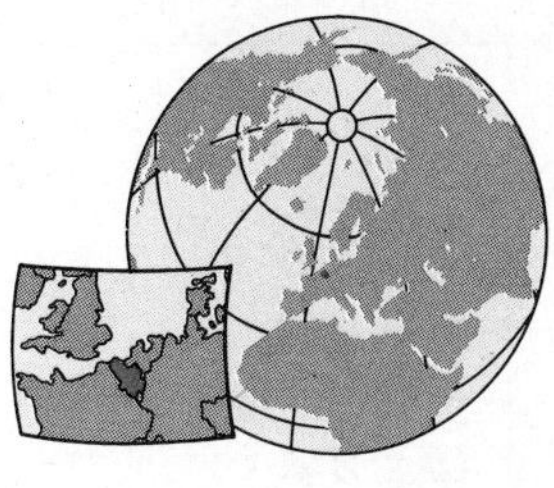

AGRICULTURE, INDUSTRY and RESOURCES

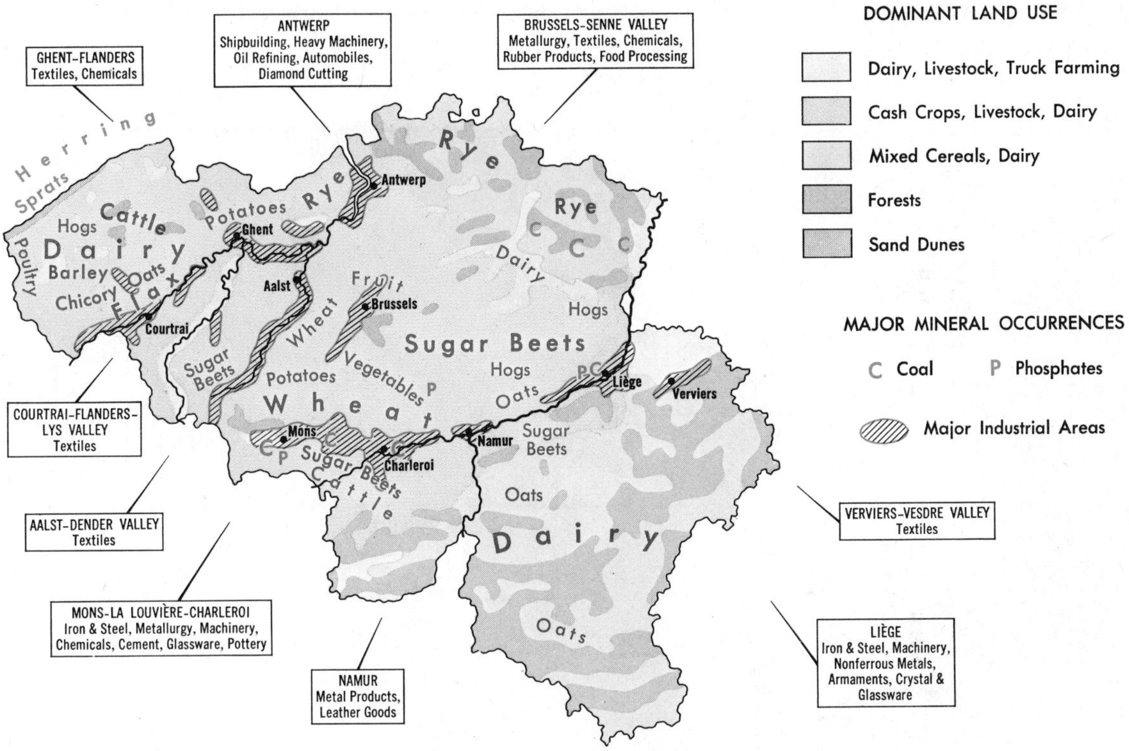
GHENT-FLANDERS
Textiles, Chemicals
ANTWERP
Shipbuilding, Heavy Machinery, Oil Refining, Automobiles, Diamond Cutting
BRUSSELS-SENNE VALLEY
Metallurgy, Textiles, Chemicals, Rubber Products, Food Processing
COURTRAI-FLANDERS-LYS VALLEY
Textiles
AALST-DENDER VALLEY
Textiles
MONS-LA LOUVIÈRE-CHARLEROI
Iron & Steel, Metallurgy, Machinery, Chemicals, Cement, Glassware, Pottery
NAMUR
Metal Products, Leather Goods
VERVIERS-VESDRE VALLEY
Textiles
LIÈGE
Iron & Steel, Machinery, Nonferrous Metals, Armaments, Crystal & Glassware
Herring
Sprats
Cattle
Hogs
Dairy
Poultry
Barley
Oats
Chicory
Flax
Potatoes
Rye
Antwerp
Ghent
Aalst
Courtrai
Brussels
Fruit
Wheat
Sugar Beets
Vegetables
Hogs
Oats
Liège
Verviers
Mons
Charleroi
Namur
Cattle
Dairy
DOMINANT LAND USE
Dairy, Livestock, Truck Farming
Cash Crops, Livestock, Dairy
Mixed Cereals, Dairy
Forests
Sand Dunes
MAJOR MINERAL OCCURRENCES
C Coal
P Phosphates
Major Industrial Areas

TOPOGRAPHY

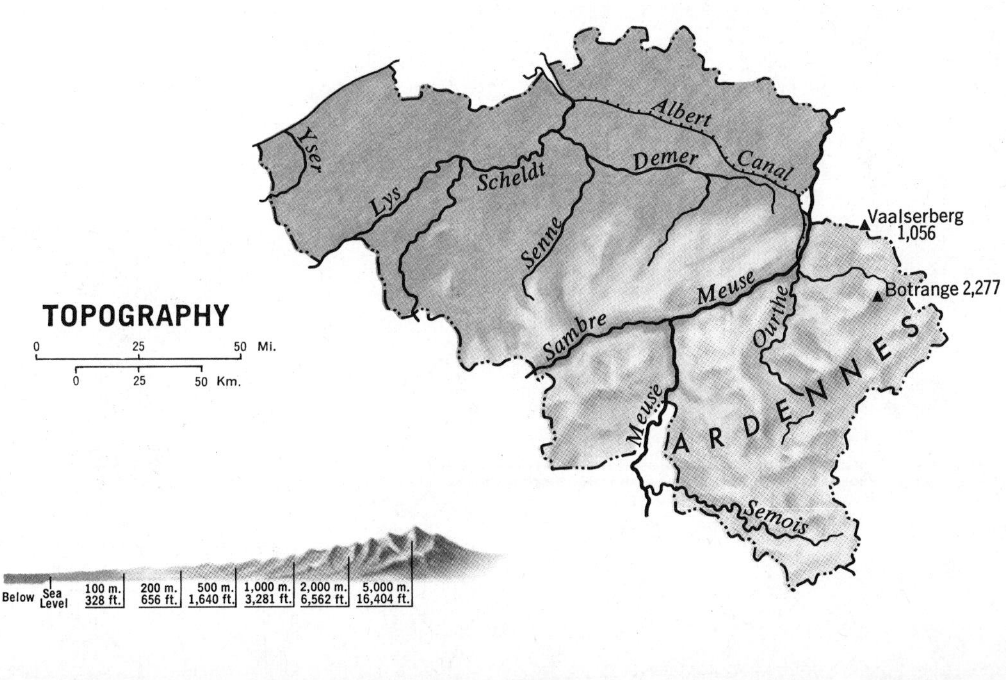
0 25 50 Mi.
0 25 50 Km.
Yser
Lys
Scheldt
Senne
Albert Canal
Demer
Sambre
Meuse
Ourthe
Semois
ARDENNES
Vaalserberg 1,056
Botrange 2,277
Below Sea Level
100 m. 328 ft.
200 m. 656 ft.
500 m. 1,640 ft.
1,000 m. 3,281 ft.
2,000 m. 6,562 ft.
5,000 m. 16,404 ft.

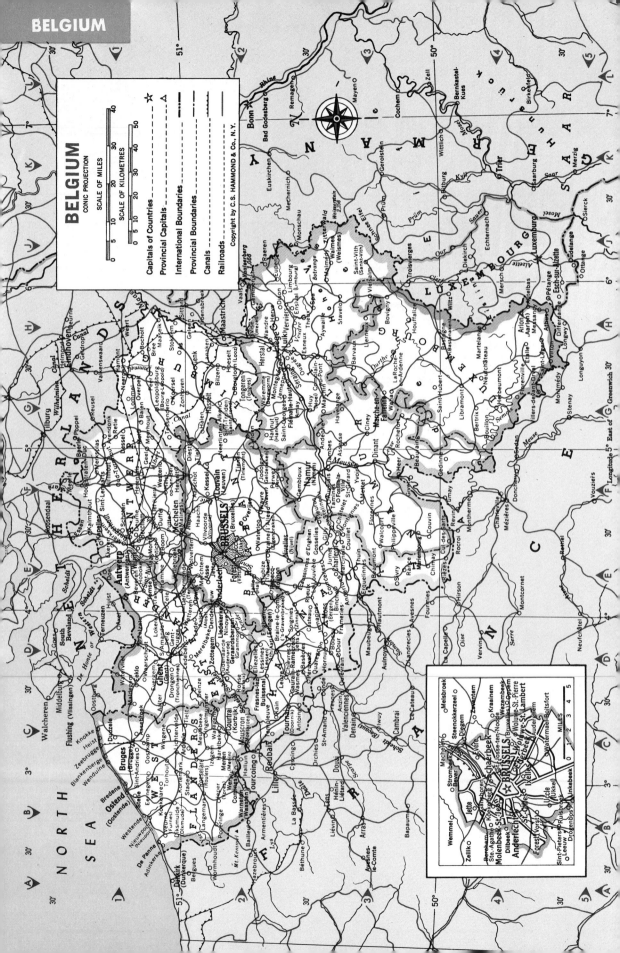

BELGIUM

Total Population, 9,556,380

PROVINCES

Antwerp, 1,506,627 F 1
Brabant, 2,130,276 E 2
East Flanders, 1,301,073 D 2
Hainault, 1,331,953 D 2
Liège, 1,017,875 H 2
Limburg, 631,326 G 2
Luxembourg, 220,315 G 4
Namur, 380,265 F 3
West Flanders, 1,036,670 B 1

CITIES and TOWNS†

Aalst, 45,900 D 2
Aalter, 8,569 C 1
Aarlen (Arlon), 14,191 H 4
Aarschot, 12,329 F 2
Aat (Ath), 10,094 D 2
Adinkerke, 2,713 A 1
Alken, 8,054 G 2
Alost (Aalst), 45,900 D 2
Amay, 7,561 G 2
Andenne, 8,068 G 3
Anderlecht, 102,189 B 4
Anderlues, 12,930 E 3
Antoing, 3,435 C 2
Antwerp (Antwerpen), 241,154 E 1
Ardooie, 7,163 C 2
Arendonk, 9,516 G 1
Arlon, 14,191 H 4
As, 4,087 H 1
Asse, 12,631 E 2
Assebroek, 15,195 C 1
Assesse, 1,138 G 3
Ath, 11,094 D 2
Athus, 7,185 H 4
Audenarde (Oudenaarde), 21,980 D 2
Auderghem, 37,782 C 4
Autelbas, 1,606 H 4
Auvelais, 8,412 F 3
Aywaille, 3,813 H 3
Baerle-Duc, 2,171 F 1
Balen, 14,719 G 1
Barvaux, 1,727 H 3
Basècles, 4,245 D 2
Bastogne (Bastenaken), 6,476 H 4
Beaumont, 1,762 E 3
Beauraing, 2,703 F 3
Berchem, 49,880 F 1
Berchem-Sainte-Agathe, 17,689 B 4
Bergen (Mons), 27,042 D 3
Bertrix, 4,481 G 4
Beveren, 15,359 E 1
Bilzen, 7,000 G 2
Binche, 10,340 E 3
Blankenberge, 10,400 C 1
Bocholt, 5,582 H 1
Boom, 17,280 E 1
Borgerhout, 50,226 E 1
Borgloon, 3,543 G 2
Borgworm (Waremme), 7,623 G 2
Bouillon, 3,089 G 4
Bourg-Léopold (Leopoldsburg), 9,621 G 1
Boussu, 11,626 D 3
Bovigny, 1,015 H 3
Braine-l'Alleud, 16,028 E 2
Braine-le-Comte, 11,343 D 2
Bredene, 9,381 B 1
Bree, 10,462 H 1
Bruges (Brugge), 52,249 C 1
Brussels (capital), 1,074,586 C 4
Bruxelles (Brussels) (cap.), 1,074,586 C 4
Casteau, 1,900 D 3
Charleroi, 24,895 E 3
Châtelet, 15,314 F 3
Châtelineau, 20,293 F 3
Chièvres, 3,154 D 2
Chimay, 3,309 E 3
Ciney, 7,431 G 3
Comblain-au-Pont, 3,538 G 3
Comines, 8,219 B 2
Couillet, 15,055 E 3
Courcelles, 17,157 E 3
Courtrai, 45,310 C 2
Couvin, 4,192 F 3
Cul-des-Sarts, 993 E 4
Deinze, 6,214 D 2
Denderleeuw, 9,699 E 2
Dendermonde, 9,683 E 1
De Panne, 6,792 B 1
Dessel, 7,170 G 1
Deurne, 75,819 F 1
Diegem, 4,760 C 4
Diest, 9,587 F 2
Diksmuide, 6,557 B 1
Dilbeek, 13,620 B 4
Dinant, 9,700 F 3
Dison, 8,809 H 2
Dixmude (Diksmuide), 6,557 B 1
Doel, 1,395 E 1
Doornik (Tournai), 33,309 C 2
Dour, 10,407 D 3
Drogenbos, 4,648 B 5
Drongen, 8,312 D 1
Dudzele, 2,112 C 1
Duffel, 13,560 F 1
Ecaussinnes d'Enghien, 6,696 E 3
Edingen (Enghien), 4,279 D 2
Eeklo, 19,007 D 1
Eernegem, 5,865 B 1
Eigenbrakel (Braine-l'Alleud), 16,028 E 2
Ekeren, 24,535 E 1
Ellezelles, 3,676 D 2
Enghien, 4,279 D 2
Ensival, 5,515 H 2
Erquelinnes, 4,812 E 3
Esneux, 5,923 H 2
Essen, 10,515 E 1
Étalle, 1,179 H 4
Etterbeek, 52,299 C 4
Eupen, 14,856 J 2
Evere, 22,289 C 4
Evergem, 12,329 D 1
Flémalle-Haute, 7,800 G 2
Fleurus, 8,475 F 3
Florennes, 4,070 F 3
Florenville, 2,526 G 4
Forest, 55,799 B 4
Fosse, 3,887 F 3
Frameries, 11,624 D 3
Frasnes-lez-Buissenal, 2,672 D 2
Furnes (Veurne), 7,475 B 1
Ganshoren, 19,154 B 4
Gaurain-Ramecroix, 3,599 D 2
Gedinne, 1,021 F 4
Geel, 28,484 F 1
Geldenaken (Jodoigne), 4,194 F 2
Gembloux, 11,030 F 3
Gemmenich, 2,608 H 2
Genk, 55,596 H 2
Gent (Ghent), 157,048 D 1
Gentbrugge, 22,986 D 1
Geraardsbergen, 9,201 D 2
Ghent, 157,048 D 1
Gilly, 24,155 E 3
Gosselies, 10,970 E 3
Grammont (Geraardsbergen), 9,201 D 2
Haacht, 4,372 F 2
Hal (Halle), 20,071 E 2
Halen, 5,321 G 2
Halle, 20,071 E 2
Hamme, 17,083 E 1
Hamont, 6,626 H 1
Hannut (Hannuit), 3,069 G 2
Harelbeke, 17,981 C 2
Hasselt, 38,773 G 2
Havelange, 1,495 G 3
Heer, 578 F 3
Heist, 9,289 C 1
Heist-op-den-Berg, 13,206 F 1
Herbeumont, 590 G 4
Herentals, 18,377 F 1
Herselt, 7,318 F 1
Herstal, 29,602 H 2
Herve, 4,357 H 2
Hoboken, 31,815 E 1
Hoei (Huy) 13,398 G 3
Hoeselt, 5,570 H 2
Hoogstraten, 4,376 F 1
Hornu, 10,905 D 3
Houffalize, 1,297 H 3
Huy, 13,398 G 3
Ieper, 18,461 B 2
Ingelmunster, 9,973 C 2
Ixelles, 92,532 C 4
Izegem, 22,729 C 2
Jambes, 14,924 F 3
Jemappes, 12,906 D 3
Jemeppe, 12,232 G 2
Jette, 37,354 B 4
Jodoigne, 4,194 F 2
Jumet, 28,811 E 3
Kain, 4,900 C 2
Kalmthout, 12,122 F 1
Kapellen, 12,297 E 1
Kessel-Lo, 21,351 F 2
Knokke, 14,268 C 1
Koekelare, 6,423 B 1
Koekelberg, 17,348 B 3
Koersel, 10,756 G 1
Kontich, 13,193 E 1
Kortemark, 5,839 C 1
Kortrijk (Courtrai), 45,310 C 2
Kraainem, 10,560 C 4
La Louvière, 23,447 E 3
Lanaken, 8,216 H 2
Landen, 5,247 G 2
Langemark, 4,787 B 2
La Roche-en-Ardenne, 1,894 G 3
Lede, 10,229 D 2
Ledeberg, 11,056 D 2
Lens, 1,790 D 2
Leopoldsburg, 9,621 G 1
Lessines (Lessen), 9,047 D 2
Leuven (Louvain), 32,125 F 2
Leuze, 7,128 D 2
Libramont, 2,774 G 4
Lichtervelde, 7,372 C 1
Liedekerke, 10,273 D 2
Liège, 153,134 H 2
Lier, 28,557 F 1
Lierneux, 2,847 H 2
Lierre (Lier), 28,557 F 1
Limbourg (Limburg), 3,973 J 2
Linkebeek, 4,096 B 5
Lokeren, 26,654 D 1
Lommel, 20,567 G 1
Looz (Borgloon), 3,543 G 2
Louvain, 32,125 F 2
Luik (Liège), 153,134 H 2
Maaseik, 8,383 H 1
Machelen, 7,331 C 4
Maldegem, 14,182 C 1
Malines (Mechelen), 65,728 F 1
Malmédy, 6,482 J 3
Marche-en-Famenne, 4,423 G 3
Marchin, 4,361 G 3
Marcinelle, 25,992 E 3
Marienbourg, 1,776 E 3
Martelange, 1,594 H 4
Mechelen, 65,728 F 1
Meerhout, 8,359 G 1
Meerle, 2,809 F 1
Melsbroek, 2,034 C 4
Menen (Menin), 22,458 C 2
Merchtem, 8,722 E 2
Merelbeke, 13,755 D 2
Merksem, 39,011 E 1
Merksplas, 4,950 F 1
Messancy, 3,064 H 4
Mettet, 3,366 F 3
Meulebeke, 10,619 C 2
Moeskroen (Mouscron), 37,624 C 2
Mol, 27,320 G 1
Molenbeek-Saint-Jean, 67,271 B 4
Mons, 27,042 D 3
Montegnée, 11,882 G 2
Montignies-sur-Sambre, 24,048 F 3
Mortsel, 27,999 E 1
Mouscron, 37,624 C 2
Namur (Namen), 32,621 F 3
Neerlinter, 1,431 G 2
Neerpelt, 8,273 G 1
Neufchâteau, 2,739 G 4
Nieuwpoort (Nieuport), 7,165 B 1
Nijvel (Nivelles), 15,384 E 2
Ninove, 12,087 D 2
Nivelles, 15,384 E 2
Oostende (Ostend), 57,749 B 1
Oostkamp, 8,560 C 1
Ophoven, 2,487 H 1
Opwijk, 9,622 E 2
Ostend, 57,749 B 1
Oudenaarde, 21,980 D 2
Oud-Turnhout, 8,219 F 1
Ougrée, 21,152 H 2
Overijse, 14,119 F 2
Overpelt, 10,002 G 1
Peer, 5,882 G 1
Péruwelz, 7,814 D 3
Perwez (Perwijs), 2,858 F 2
Philippeville, 1,822 E 3
Poperinge, 12,619 B 2
Poppel, 2,246 G 1
Putte, 6,856 F 1
Quaregnon, 18,289 D 3
Quiévrain, 5,685 D 3
Raeren, 3,490 J 2
Rance, 1,443 E 3
Rebecq-Rognon, 3,831 E 2
Renaix (Ronse), 25,371 D 2
Retie, 6,339 G 1
Rièzes, 307 E 4
Rochefort, 4,242 G 3
Roeselare, 40,077 C 2
Roeulx, 2,605 E 3
Ronse, 25,371 D 2
Roulers (Roeselare), 40,077 C 2
Ruisbroek, 5,685 B 5
Saint-Georges, 6,085 G 2
Saint-Gérard, 1,626 F 3
Saint-Gilles, 57,238 B 4
Saint-Hubert, 3,104 G 3
Saint-Josse-ten-Noode, 24,335 C 4
Saint-Léger, 1,600 H 4
Saint-Trond (Sint-Truiden), 21,131 G 2
Saint-Vith (Sankt-Vith), 2,935 J 3
Schaerbeek, 122,329 C 4
Schoten, 28,543 F 1
Seraing, 40,937 G 2
's Gravenbrakel (Braine-le-Comte), 11,343 D 2
Sint-Amandsberg, 24,778 D 1
Sint-Andries, 15,062 C 1
Sint-Lenaarts, 4,464 F 1
Sint-Niklaas, 48,851 E 1
Sint-Pieters-Leeuw, 15,978 B 5
Sint-Truiden, 21,131 G 2
Sivry, 1,384 E 3
Soignies, 11,320 D 2
Spa, 9,683 H 3
Staden, 5,581 B 2
Stavelot, 4,661 H 3
Steenokkerzeel, 3,877 C 4
Stene, 9,304 B 1
Stokkem, 3,380 H 1
Strombeek-Bever, 10,027 C 4
Tamines, 8,139 F 3
Tamise (Temse), 14,559 E 1
Templeuve, 3,737 C 2
Temse, 14,559 E 1
Termonde (Dendermonde), 9,683 E 1
Tessenderlo, 10,665 G 1
Theux, 5,491 H 3
Thuin, 5,877 E 3
Tielt, Brabant, 3,813 F 2
Tielt, West Flanders, 13,887 C 2
Tienen (Tirlemont), 22,660 F 2
Tongeren (Tongres), 16,880 G 2
Torhout, 14,301 C 1
Tournai, 33,309 C 2
Tronchiennes (Drongen), 8,312 D 1
Tubize (Tubeke), 10,269 E 2
Turnhout, 37,828 F 1
Uccle (Ukkel), 76,579 B 4
Verviers, 35,730 H 2
Veurne, 7,475 B 1
Vielsalm, 3,702 H 3
Villers-devant-Orval, 777 G 4
Vilvoorde (Vilvorde), 34,040 F 2
Virton, 3,956 H 4
Visé, 6,595 H 2
Vorst (Forest), 55,799 B 4
Waarschoot, 7,852 D 1
Waasten (Warneton), 3,215 B 2
Waha, 2,664 G 3
Waimes, 2,787 J 3
Walcourt, 2,077 E 3
Wandre, 6,833 H 2
Waregem, 16,928 C 2
Waremme, 7,623 G 2
Warneton, 3,215 B 2
Wasmes, 13,933 D 2
Waterloo, 14,615 E 2
Watermael-Boitsfort, 24,730 C 4
Watervliet, 1,812 D 1
Wavre (Waver), 11,007 F 2
Weismes (Waimes), 2,787 J 3
Wemmel, 11,404 B 4
Wenduine, 1,756 C 1
Wervik, 12,728 B 2
Westende, 2,746 B 1
Westerlo, 7,630 F 1
Wetteren, 20,775 D 2
Wezembeek-Oppem, 10,536 D 4
Wezet (Visé), 6,595 H 2
Willebroek, 15,650 E 1
Wilrijk, 42,109 E 1
Wingene, 7,178 C 1
Woluwe-Saint-Lambert, 44,102 C 4
Woluwe-Saint-Pierre, 37,314 C 4
Wolvertem, 5,326 E 2
Ypres (Ieper), 18,461 B 2
Yvoir, 2,837 F 3
Zaventem, 9,941 C 4
Zeebrugge C 1
Zele, 18,386 E 1
Zellik, 5,165 B 4
Zelzate, 11,751 D 1
Zinnik (Soignies), 11,320 D 2
Zonhoven, 12,910 G 1
Zottegem, 6,905 D 2

OTHER FEATURES

Albert (canal) F 1
Ardennes (forest) F 4
Botrange (mt.) J 3
Dender (river) D 2
Deûle (river) B 2
Dommel (river) H 1
Dyle (river) F 2
Hohe Venn (plat.) H 3
Lesse (river) F 3
Lys (river) B 2
Mark (river) F 1
Meuse (river) F 3
Nethe (river) F 1
North (sea) B 1
Ourthe (river) H 3
Rupel (river) F 2
Sambre (river) D 3
Schelde (Scheldt) (river) C 2
Scheldt (river) C 2
Schnee Eifel (plat.) J 3
Semois (river) G 4
Senne (river) E 2
Vaalserberg (mt.) J 2
Vesdre (river) H 2
Weisserstein (mt.) J 3
Yser (river) B 2
Zitterwald (plat.) J 3

*City and suburbs. †All figures are those of communes.

All figures—1967 off. est.

THE MEUSE RIVER, which here flows past the old citadel in Dinant, is bordered in its upper reaches by many châteaus.

were the Flemings organized and angry enough to demand and obtain concessions. Each alteration of the boundary following a census now leads to controversy in local villages and in the national chambers. The desire of many to serve under military leaders who speak their own language and to fight for soil that is Flemish or Walloon, rather than Belgian, is an indication of how detrimental the issue is to national harmony.

Although the class distinctions that were so marked in the 18th and 19th centuries are less distinct in the 20th, Walloons still hold a preponderant number of the higher positions in the economy and in government. However, the Flemings are winning increased opportunities, and the Flemish movement is gaining in leadership and momentum. Of course, all Walloons are not businessmen or government officials; the majority are farmers, miners, and laborers. The top financial and governmental circle, which includes both Flemings and Walloons, is small, and certain families have been consistently represented in it for nearly a century.

Religion. Both Flemings and Walloons are Roman Catholic, but with markedly different attitudes. Many Walloons give Roman doctrine a liberal interpretation and are not strict in their attendance at Mass. In the Flemish areas of Belgium the churches are crowded, Roman doctrine is strictly adhered to and seldom questioned, and the local clergy have considerable influence within their parishes. On a higher level the archbishop of Mechelin (Malines) enjoys universal respect and is one of the national leaders.

Religious liberty is well established, and the state pays a portion of the salaries of the Roman Catholic, Protestant, Anglican, and Jewish clergy. The Protestant denominations in Belgium are not strong, although they have grown since World War II.

Population Changes. The birthrate among the devoutly Roman Catholic Flemings exceeds that of the Walloons. The over-all rate of national population increase fell from 1.03 percent per year in 1900 to 0.84 percent in 1930 and after 1958 to 0.5 percent or less. The crude rate of births in 1963 was 17.1 per 1,000, while that of deaths was 12.6.

By the census of 1961 the population totaled 9,189,741 persons, approximately 2,500,000 more than in 1900. Belgium is one of the most heavily inhabited countries of Europe, with an estimated population density in 1963 of 304 persons per square kilometer, as compared to 87, 244, and 356 respectively for France, West Germany, and the Netherlands. As a result of losses during the war, women outnumbered men in the 1960's

by approximately 200,000, but births of males were exceeding those of females.

Ways of Life. Many Flemings prefer—or have become accustomed to—a simpler form of life, with a plainer diet and more rough-hewn ways, than the Walloons. Yet while certain distinctions may be drawn between the ways of life of the Fleming and Walloon, the similarities are more important. All relish the innumerable village fairs and the traditional festivals, such as the Mardi Gras held at Binche. The cinema and sports, particularly soccer and bicycle racing, are followed closely, and most Belgians participate fully in what has jokingly been called the national pastime—drinking the many varieties of beer brewed in their country.

The Belgian standard of living is one of the highest in Europe, per capita income is high and increasing, and a large part of the economy is directed toward production for the consumer market. Housing is less crowded than in most of Europe. The pace of life in the cities is hectic, yet the Belgians know how to relax, and they do so at sidewalk cafés and at the restaurants known throughout Europe for the preparation of the Belgians' favorite dishes: mussels, deep-fried potatoes, oysters, endive, and Flemish *waterzoei* (chicken). Household camping along the Meuse and in the Ardennes has become popular.

Although modern informality is making inroads among the student generations, the tradition of the tight family circle and formal relations with others is maintained. The home is still the focus of life. Regionalism is strong, and while they may visit the capital on occasion, many Belgians prefer not to wander far from their place of birth.

2. Land and Natural Resources

In geographical rather than linguistic terms, Belgium is divided into three main areas: Lower Belgium in the west; the central plain; and the Ardennes tableland in the southeast.

Lower Belgium is a flat region bordered by the Netherlands and by the North Sea for approximately 40 miles (64 km). The province of West Flanders in Lower Belgium encompasses 193 square miles (500 sq km) of polders, rich lands reclaimed from the ocean. The Campine (Kempenland) to the north and east has a sandy and less fertile soil; beneath the surface, however, lie important coal deposits. Anthracite coal is Belgium's only major mineral resource; some income is also gained from kaolin, lime, and iron ore.

The central and most populous area of Belgium is a gently undulating plain cut by numerous valleys. It is a fertile region that until recently has also been Belgium's chief source of coal. The veins in the Borinage zone near Mons have now begun to run out and become uneconomical to mine, resulting in unemployment there and in the nearby metallurgical center of Charleroi, where the ore deposits are also nearing exhaustion. While the Lys (Leie) and the all-important Scheldt (Schelde, Escaut) rivers are assets to the northwest section of Belgium, the center of the country possesses no large natural waterways.

The Ardennes tableland is separated from the central plain by the Sambre and Meuse (Maas) rivers. The gently rolling Herve plateau near Liège and Huy, which has been so accommodating to invading armies, is fertile, but the coal mines near Liège are suffering the same fate as those of the Borinage. To the south the plateau gives way first to the Famenne depression of woods and meadows and then to markedly higher and more rugged terrain, with the limestone cliffs and wooded hills of the Ardennes providing scenery but little opportunity for cultivation.

Although forests cover only 18 percent of the total area of Belgium, approximately 70 percent of the three eastern provinces is wooded, making possible a moderate lumbering industry. The Ardennes is the least settled region of Belgium, and pursuit of the wild boar, which lives in its thickets, is considered high sport.

The area of the Ardennes does not provide sufficiently difficult terrain to block invasion. Belgium's lack of a natural border on all sides but the northwest has had a tragic effect on its history. The highest point in the Ardennes, the Botrange, reaches 2,277 feet (695 meters) above sea level. Most of the region is considerably lower, however.

Belgium deserves the appellation "low country," as the average altitude of the country is 526 feet (160 meters), and the entire northern third is only 60 feet (18 meters) above sea level on the average.

Climate. The sea determines Belgium's climate. Warmed by its influence, which is all the more beneficial thanks to the proximity of the Gulf Stream, Belgium is spared the rigors of the winters that might be expected at 51° north latitude. Some snow falls during the coldest months, but the accumulation is negligible except in the east, where temperatures are a bit lower than at Brussels. The capital experiences a mean temperature of 65° F (18° C) in the summer and 37° (3° C) in winter. As these figures show, Belgium's climate, like its geography, is not one of extremes; temperature variations are moderate, the summers are generally cool, and humidity is constantly present. Rainfall is plentiful (30 to 40 inches, or 76 to 102 cm, per year), even during the fall, the most pleasant season of the year. Precipitation is frequent, coming usually in showers and drizzles, although heavy storms do occur.

3. Economy

The economy of modern Belgium has profited from the country's location near the heart of western Europe's industrial region. Full advantage could not be taken of this situation, however, until the formation of the Benelux economic union at the end of World War II, the European Coal and Steel Community in 1951, and the European Economic Community in 1957.

World War II and Its Aftereffects. The rapidity of the German advance through Belgium in 1940 meant that surprisingly little of its industry was destroyed at that time. Belgium was exploited during the war, and many of its factories deteriorated. The greatest devastation occurred during the Allied advance of 1944. The liberation of the city of Antwerp several weeks before Rotterdam benefited Belgium, as Antwerp was made a chief port of entry for Allied shipping to the Continent. While Belgium's position in the early postwar years was superior to its neighbors', a decade later some of Belgium's antiquated factories and mines were to suffer from the competition of new plants constructed elsewhere.

The 1950's proved disappointing, and a marked recession was experienced in 1958 and 1959. The over-all picture was brightened, however, by the introduction of considerable foreign capital and the construction of a wide variety of modern industries, particularly in the northern regions of the country. An austerity program was necessitated by the breakaway of the Congo colony in 1960 and the subsequent chaos there. Losses were limited reasonably well, and many of the corporations active in the Congo were able to reach profitable arrangements with the new government.

In the 1960's production and exports, long hindered by European tariffs, increased steadily in an atmosphere of confidence. Between 1956 and 1964 the national income expanded by more than 50 percent. To maintain this growth rate and the level of exports, an economic development plan was worked out in close cooperation with private sectors of the economy and approved by Parliament in 1963. A dip in the growth rate at the beginning of 1966 stimulated new legislation designed to attract foreign capital. The 1966 laws made credit easier and provided tax abatements to new industries.

Industry. The largest portion of Belgium's gross national product flows from its industries. The manufacturing industries make the most significant contribution; in the early 1960's it was approximately four times that made by the construction or transportation industries. The role of utilities and mining is a good deal less. The growth of industrial production after World War II was healthy. In the period from 1958 to 1965 it increased by 48 percent, mainly in construction, electricity, and manufacturing.

Much of Belgium's manufacturing is devoted to the processing of imported raw materials. Hence the significance of the European Common Market for Belgium's economic growth. As most of Belgium's ore deposits have been exhausted, its steel industry is dependent on supplies from France, Luxembourg, and Sweden. The sheet and plate metal, industrial steel, and wire produced are used extensively in Belgium's well-established metalworking industry, the most famous plant of which is probably the locomotive- and rail-producing Cockerill works. Processing of imported nonferrous metals, with the exception of copper and to a certain extent zinc, is not undertaken on a large scale. A different example of processing is the assembly of imported automobile parts.

The textile industry is also dependent on sizable imports. Foreign competition has now forced the Belgians to concentrate on highly finished products. The greatest growth has been in the areas of synthetic and jute fiber textiles and in the manufacture of carpets, nearly 90 percent of which are for export. Linen made from flax grown in the region of Kortrijk (Courtrai) is still highly prized, but quality lace manufacture is declining as younger generations fail to learn the difficult art of its hand weaving.

Belgian glass, much of it produced in the region of Liège, continues to be admired throughout Europe. Increasing attention is being given the production of chemicals, and centers for this purpose have grown up near Antwerp and also about Mons, helping to relieve the unemployment of the Borinage region. The diamond-cutting industry at Antwerp, which draws much of its supply from the Congo, makes Belgium the world's leading exporter of industrial diamonds. Its breweries make Belgium a leading beer producer, particularly of specialty beers that are mostly consumed locally. The extensive consumer service industry, supported by affluent upper and middle classes, ranks next to manufacturing and commerce as the greatest contributor to the gross national product. Mention should also be made of some of the products of Belgium's small but nevertheless noted industries: leatherwork, bookbinding, cement, technical glass, and sporting arms.

Much of Belgium's industry is controlled by six huge trusts. The most important of these is the Société Générale, which was founded in 1822 and which in 1965 owned about 35 percent of the electricity, 40 percent of the coal, 50 percent of the steel, and 65 percent of the nonferrous metal industries in the country. The Groupe Solvay controls chemical manufacture, and Brufina Confinindus has wide holdings in coal, steel, heavy engineering, and electricity. Empain is important in tramways and electrical equipment, as are the Groupe Coppée in coal and steel and the Banque Lambert in petroleum.

The government interferes infrequently with business and has traditionally been sensitive to business interests. The only major instance of subsidization is the mining industry. Following World War II the government did all it could to rehabilitate the coal mining industry, the only extractive industry of size in Belgium. A record output was achieved in 1953, and extensive modernization continued, but thereafter production declined. The depth and thinness of the already heavily exploited veins and the faulted structure of the strata have made operation of many Borinage mines uneconomical. Further development of the Campine fields is expected to compensate for the Borinage decline. A new source of power is nuclear energy. In 1953 a study center was opened at Mol that conducted important research in the application of nuclear power to industrial uses.

Agriculture. Agriculture no longer plays as great a role in the economy as it once did. It nevertheless is extremely important, for what food is not raised within the populous country must be imported, to the detriment of the balance of payments. The amount of land devoted to agriculture has decreased slightly since World War II, yet it continues to meet about 80 percent of the nation's needs. Production has been aided by the trend to larger units in the 1950's and 1960's; many farms are still less than 12 acres in size. Strip farming and intensive cultivation, the result of centuries of land division among families, are still predominant in Belgian farming. The use of modern techniques and fertilizers is spreading.

Livestock raising on the pastures of the Campine and Ardennes is the leading agricultural activity, making Belgium nearly self-sufficient in most beef and pork products. Wheat, barley, and oats are grown extensively, yet Belgium must still import grains. Much land, especially in the eastern and central zones, is devoted to potatoes and to the cultivation of fodder and sugar beets. The latter two crops are large and make a significant contribution to the overall agricultural economy. Flax continues to be grown in Flanders, and some experimentation is being done with tobacco. Belgium is noted for greenhouse grapes, endive, and for the quality hops that make its beers so outstanding.

Labor. Only about 6 percent of the population is employed in agriculture, and there has been a continuing slow decrease in the number of farmers. Increments in the labor supply have generally occurred in the manufacturing industries. Most farmers own their own land. Many

BELGIUM is one of the most important flax fiber producers in the world. Flax is grown primarily in the region of Kortrijk (Courtrai). Below, flax is gathered into shocks for curing (*left*) and processed by "scutching" (*right*).

TOM HOLLYMAN, FROM PHOTO RESEARCHERS

ANTWERP, which lies 50 miles upstream from the sea on the Scheldt River, is one of the world's busiest ports.

find it necessary to supplement the income gained from their small acreage by taking part-time jobs in the towns.

In the economic expansion of the first half of the 1960's, employment in manufacturing went up approximately 12 percent, and over-all unemployment dropped in the same period from 6.3 percent to 2.5 percent. Laborers from abroad, especially Italy, have been attracted by these conditions, yet unemployment has continued to exist in the Borinage and West Flanders.

Commerce and Finance. By the mid-1960's, while approximately 40 percent of Belgium's total production was for export, over 70 percent of its industrial output was for that purpose. The leading customers of the Belgium-Luxembourg Economic Union (BLEU) have for some years been the Netherlands and West Germany, while BLEU's leading suppliers have been France and Germany. Over half of BLEU's trade is now with countries of the European Economic Community, and this percentage is increasing. Principal imports are textiles, transport equipment, nonelectric machinery, petroleum products, chemicals, iron ore, steel, and copper. Much of these are processed and in turn exported, especially the iron, steel, copper, and textiles.

Brussels is a key financial center of Europe. The bank of issue is the National Bank of Belgium, a joint-stock institution in which the government has held half the shares since 1948.

Transportation. Income is also gained from Belgium's transportation facilities. Antwerp, located 50 miles (80 km) up the Scheldt from the sea, is so heavily used for the entry and exit of goods from the Continent that it is one of the world's leading ports. Other ports are Zeebrugge, Brussels, and Ostend. The Société Nationale des Chemins de Fer Belges, which operates the rail system, is government-controlled with some private participation. Although the rail system is the densest in Europe and successfully handles a high-volume freight and passenger service, as much or more freight is transported on the inland waterway system. The complex system of canals serves nearly all the country. Chief among the waterways are the Ghent-Terneuzen Canal; the Roupel Canal, linking Brussels to the sea; and the famous Albert Canal, between Antwerp and Liège.

Sabena, the semiprivate airline controlled by the government, has a monopoly on air transportation in Belgium. It has international airports at Brussels and Deurne, near Antwerp.

4. Education

Belgium's educational system is highly developed despite the ill effects of two major controversies. The oldest of these concerns the role of the church and religious education in the training of youth. In 1945 great efforts were made to end the century-old "school war." The Socialists and Catholics, who made up the two largest parties, were aware that their differences on this and on other issues were dividing the country seriously. Agreement was therefore reached on a far-ranging bill that was made into law in 1959. It acknowledges the right of each school-administering authority—national government, commune, or church—to devise its own curriculum as long as it meets the minimal requirements of the ministry of education. Political propaganda is barred from the classroom, and proselytizing for state or church schools is banned.

The 1959 law established that it is the national government's responsibility to see that satisfactory schools of all kinds are within reach of all children. Attendance from the age of 6 to 14 has been compulsory since 1914. Salaries, pensions, benefits, and all tax-supported subsidies generally must be the same for all schools. One exception concerns construction of new buildings. The national government constructs its own schools. Provinces and towns may receive state subsidies of 60 percent of the cost of new buildings. Church school construction is not subsidized, however, on the theory that salaries paid to the teaching nuns and monks do not go to them personally but to their religious orders, which may use the funds for capital construction. No subsidies are given to Jewish or Protestant institutions.

The second controversy affecting the schools concerns the language of instruction. The Flemings early resented the fact that instruction was solely in French, and Flemish schools were gradually established in Flemish-speaking regions in the 19th century. A law of 1932 states that instruction in the schools should be given in the language of the region in which the school is located. The other national language is to be the first modern foreign language taken up for study.

The linguistic status of the Belgian universities is hotly debated. Flemish demonstrations forced the conversion of the University of Ghent into a Flemish-language institution in 1930. Many courses are given in Flemish at the University of

Louvain, but riots and petitions in the early 1960's did not persuade church authorities to abolish the French section of the university.

Of the four Belgian universities, all of which are known for their high quality, those at Ghent and Liège are state-controlled. The University of Louvain, founded in 1426, is Roman Catholic and by far the largest. Its world-famous library was burned during the invasions of 1914 and 1940, but it remains one of the great libraries of Europe, especially for medieval materials. The Free University of Brussels was founded by the Liberals in 1834 as a counter to Louvain.

Higher liberal arts education is still primarily for the upper and middle classes. For others there are seven commercial colleges, a polytechnical institution, and several agricultural schools, as well as specialized institutions of higher learning. Brussels, Liège, Ghent, Antwerp, and Mons each possesses a royal academy of fine arts and a royal conservatory. There are numerous other schools of music and design and about 165 normal schools.

5. Government

The government of modern Belgium, established by the Constitution of 1831, is a hereditary constitutional monarchy, which, though thoroughly democratic and representative, has traditionally allowed the sovereign much latitude in action. Succession is by the rule of male primogeniture; if there is no male heir, the reigning king designates his successor with Parliament's approval.

A traditional concern of the monarchy is defense, for the king is commander in chief of the armed forces. The king declares war, signs treaties, and makes peace, but only with the approval of Parliament. He can also confer titles and grant pardons. Any act of the king must be countersigned by a minister to have validity.

Legislature. The Parliament, with which the monarch shares legislative power, consists of a Senate and a Chamber of Representatives. Sessions begin each November and are held for at least 40 days. The king, who appoints and dismisses his ministers, may also call and dissolve extraordinary sessions of Parliament. Such dissolution, however, must be followed by new elections within 40 days and a sitting of the new Parliament within two months. The powers of Senate and Chamber are equal; bills may be introduced in either and must receive approval of both before going to the king for signature.

According to the constitutional revision of 1921, some senators are elected directly and others indirectly, and all sit for four years. In the mid-1960's the Senate had 175 members. Those elected directly equal half the number of members of the lower chamber. Each of the nine provincial councils also elects senators, at the ratio of one for every 200,000 inhabitants; with each province sending at least three. In the mid-1960's there were 46 provincial senators. A third category of senators, numbering half those sent by the provinces, is chosen by the Senate itself, an arrangement that assures influential or aging leaders a seat despite the fickleness of the electorate. All senatorial elections, whether direct or indirect, are by the method of proportional representation, as are those for the Chamber of Representatives. Voting is compulsory for citizens over 21 years of age who meet a residential requirement of six months.

Representatives are elected directly from local districts for terms of four years. Their number is determined by the population, and each seat must represent at least 40,000 citizens. According to a law of 1949, the current size of the chamber is 212 deputies. Unlike the senators, who must be 40 years of age, deputies may be as young as 25.

Political Parties. Proportional representation has not led to the widespread multiplication of parties that it has produced in other countries, although there are splinter groupings. In the 19th century the traditional parties were the Catholics and the Liberals. With the rise of the Socialist party in the 20th century the Liberals have experienced the same fate as the Liberals in Britain. Squeezed between the left and the right, they have lost electors to both sides and have found it difficult to establish a meaningful middle-ground position. By clinging to policies of former years, particularly their opposition to welfare projects and state aid for church schools, they had become one of the most conservative groupings in post-World War II Belgium. In an effort to obtain a new image and regain popularity, a program more relevant to current problems was devised in 1961, and the party was renamed the Party of Freedom and Progress. A similar step had already been taken by the Catholics, who assumed the name Christian Social party after the war.

Since 1945 the Christian Socialists have generally won a plurality of votes, but often they have been required to make concessions to the Socialists or to form coalition governments with them. The Liberals have sought to win enough seats to control the balance of power.

Minor political groupings range from the Communists on the left to a strange cluster of semifascist groupings on the right. Only a few Communist deputies are elected, and while rightist groups have held demonstrations, they lack sufficient votes to place their members in Parliament.

The linguistic division has led to the creation of Flemish and Walloon wings within the major parties. It has also stimulated the growth of specifically linguistic parties. The Walloons have been slow to form their own groupings, but recently there have appeared organizations determined to protect the rights of Wallonia and the French language. Flemish parties have existed for some time, gaining their main impetus from the formation of the Front party among soldiers during World War I.

6. History

The struggle for unity in domestic matters and independence in international affairs is the theme that runs through Belgian history. As natural as these goals might be, their achievement has been delayed for centuries by internal divisions, particularly those of religion and language, and by the territories' location in a coveted area surrounded by aggressive powers.

The first successful attempt to unify the region following the breakup of the Carolingian empire in the 9th century was made by the dukes of Burgundy. In 1384, Philip the Bold became count of Flanders, since his wife, Marguerite de Male, had inherited the territories from her father. By the reign (1419–1467) of Philip the Good all the principalities in the Lowlands had been brought under the control of the house of Burgundy. These territories extended well beyond the regions that constitute the major areas of present-day Belgium (Liège was still an independent bishopric, however). They also included French Artois, the left bank of the Rhine in the east, and Zeeland, Holland, Gelderland, and other lands to the north that now form the Netherlands. The history of Belgium is therefore synonymous with the history of the Lowlands in their entirety until the Dutch revolt and separation at the end of the 16th and beginning of the 17th century.

Burgundian Rule. Establishing cohesiveness among the regions and towns long accustomed to autonomy was a difficult task. Philip the Good tactfully balanced the influence of the communes, the clergy, and the nobility, yet he did not hesitate to use force against such adamantly independent towns as Bruges and Ghent.

Although Philip's moderate success in bringing some unity to the government can be partly attributed to his energy and skill, equal credit must be given the temper of the times. Belgium had been torn by warfare for decades, and even the people of the great communes were wearying of the strife involved in defending municipal autonomy and supremacy over neighboring areas. The rural populations were tired of domination by the towns and were therefore sympathetic to Philip's cause. More important, changes were occurring in the region's economy. Trade had now so developed that municipalities were bound together by common interests perhaps stronger than were realized at the time. Rapidly growing towns, such as Brussels and Antwerp, which drew their livelihood primarily from trade rather than manufacture, were willing enough to support the duke.

While commercial centers grew, many of the formerly independent wool-cloth-weaving localities, such as Ypres and Ghent, declined. During the 15th century, English cloth production increased at such a rate that soon Flemish towns began to suffer from the reduction of the supply of English raw wool and the competition of imported English finished goods. New avenues had to be explored, and it was at this time that the Belgian linen industry received its initial development. The great city of Bruges nevertheless experienced an irremedial setback as the silting up of the river Zwijn closed the nearby port of Damme. Fate was more kind to Antwerp, as a series of inundations widened and deepened the Scheldt, opening the channel to the ocean.

The desire of the dukes to maintain the independence of their holdings led them through a devious course during the latter part of the Hundred Years' War. At first they sided with England and then with France. But the basic principle of their policy, the maintenance of a balance of power that would prevent either France or England from establishing undue influence over the Lowlands, remained constant.

In 1477, Philip's son, Charles the Bold, was slain at the siege of Nancy, and the holdings of Burgundy, now including the prince-bishopric of Liège, which Charles had ruthlessly subdued, passed to his daughter Mary. Threatened by resurgent particularism within Belgium and by French invasion, Mary strengthened her position by marrying Archduke Maximilian, the future emperor of the Holy Roman Empire. This step, while preventing the disintegration of the Burgundian holdings, endangered Belgium's inde-

DURBUY hugs the banks of the Ourthe River. A tiny town today, its palace bears witness to its former importance.

pendence by tying the country for over two centuries to the great Habsburg domain.

Charles V and the Pragmatic Sanction. Until the close of the reign of Maximilian's successor, Charles V, the situation was not serious. Charles and his governors-general were solicitous of the welfare of the provinces both because they were the richest portion of the realm and because of emotional ties. The activities of the Burgundian dukes had briefly separated the fate of the Lowlands from that of Germany. A continuing separation was now assured by Charles, who, uncertain that his son would succeed him as emperor, wished to make the Lowlands part of the Habsburg patrimony. In the Transaction of Augsburg of 1548 he forced the governing body of the empire, the Diet, to acknowledge the "circle of Burgundy" as an entity and to admit that, although the circle was to pay the empire a small sum, it was to be a virtually independent state, free of imperial jurisdiction and laws. The Pragmatic Sanction of 1549 solidified the Transaction by unifying the succession rights of the provinces and declaring that the 17 provinces were inseparable.

Charles V's reign was a happy epoch for Belgium as trade and culture thrived. But, ironically, this very period of unity and relative autonomy contained the seeds of destruction of those treasured goals. Despite the emperor's vigorous efforts to repress the Protestant heresy, the followers of Calvin became increasingly numerous, particularly in the northern provinces. The religious strife was aggravated by the passage of the Spanish throne—and thus control of the Netherlands—to Charles' son Philip II in 1556. Unlike his father, the new monarch did not hold much sympathy for the attitudes and wishes of the inhabitants of the Lowlands or know their tongues. The Belgians found themselves subject to rule not from Brussels but from Madrid by a foreigner rather than by a "national" sovereign.

Philip's policies quickly assured his unpopularity in the Lowlands. He did not hesitate to require the rich provinces to bear the brunt of the costs of his war with Henry II of France. The garrisoning of Spanish troops on the populace aroused much opposition; so too did Philip's economic policy, with its 10-percent turnover tax. The nobles were angered by the creation of a secret *consulta* that superseded the council of state in advising the governor, Marguerite of Parma. The clergy resented the appointment of Philip's agent, Bishop Granvella of Arras, to the influential archbishopric of Malines. Catholics and Protestants alike feared a rigorous application of the anti-Calvinist laws and the establishment of the Inquisition.

Revolt. In 1566 approximately 2,000 Protestant and Catholic leaders joined in the Compromise of Nobles, petitioning that Marguerite administer the religious laws moderately, avoid any inquisition, and summon the States General to consider new rules regarding heretics. Because of a derogatory remark made about the simple dress of the 300 who presented the petition or perhaps because of their motto, "Faithful to the king to beggary," the nobles acquired the party name of *gueux,* or beggars. The unity of their party was ruptured, however, by an outbreak among the lower classes, which led to the sacking of many churches.

Disturbed by the excesses of the iconoclasts, many moderate Catholic leaders rallied to the support of Marguerite, while William of Nassau, prince of Orange, and his Calvinist followers drifted further from allegiance to the throne. Within a short time it was clear that the nobles had lost control and that in the place of a united national movement separate Protestant and Catholic parties were appearing.

The year 1567 witnessed the beginning of civil warfare that eventually resulted in the division of the Lowlands into two states. The dissolution of the Compromise of the Nobles played into the hands of Philip, who sent the duke of Alva to punish the rebels. His persecution of the signers of the Compromise, including the moderates, was organized by the council of Troubles, soon termed the "Council of Blood." The execution of the counts of Egmont and Hoorn brought widespread protest and provided the opposition with martyrs.

Thousands joined the standard of William the Silent, who first retreated to the north, where his greatest support lay, and then fled the country. Marguerite herself resigned her position. Although Alva did establish his control throughout the Low Countries, bands of rebels continued their opposition. Following five years of repression and inordinate taxation, the seizure of the port of Brill by "water beggars" stimulated new revolt, concentrated in the northern provinces. Its success was such that, in 1573, Alva requested his own recall.

The more moderate policies of Alva's successor, Luis de Requeséns, only partially meliorated the situation, and the violent sack of Antwerp by Spanish troops shortly after Requeséns' death (1576) led to a realliance of Protestant and Catholic groupings. By the Pacification of Ghent of 1576 all 17 provinces united to drive the Spaniards from the lowlands. Roman Catholicism was recognized as the dominant religion of the country, and toleration was established everywhere but in Holland and Zeeland, which were to be Protestant.

Division of the Lowlands. Although the intent was that disputes would be resolved and former animosities forgotten, feelings were too deep. Both groups violated the terms of the Pacification, and the leadership of William was not strong enough to curb the extremists of either faction and win the support of his critics. An organization of Catholic "Malcontents" soon appeared, around which Alexander Farnese, who became governor in 1578, skillfully built his strength in the southern provinces.

In January 1579 the Confederation of Arras was formed by several southern Catholic provinces. Later that month the breach was made definitive by the Union of Utrecht, in which the seven northern provinces (Holland, Zeeland, Utrecht, Gelderland, Friesland, Overijssel, and Groningen) bound themselves to act together in external matters. Southerners and northerners alike claimed to be acting in the name of unity. The true nature of the situation was finally acknowledged by the Utrecht group when in 1581 it announced its independence of Spain and awarded the hereditary *staathaldership* to William of Orange.

The division of the Low Countries was unfortunate from many points of view and originally undesired even by those who achieved the break. All the inhabitants were caught between traditional respect for legitimacy and the desire to be independent of Spanish domination. The strongest call was for unity, but the firm entrenchment of Spanish troops in the south, if not in the north, implied that unity would have to be established within rather than outside the Spanish empire. The unenlightened policies of Philip, however, had already provoked two attempts at the latter course, which had failed because of distrust among the religious groupings.

William and Farnese would have welcomed unity, but they and more particularly their supporters each demanded it be on their own terms. Without compromise far greater than either religious faction would admit and in the absence of total military victory, separation was the only possible outcome. It was not a lack of patriotism but rather a more positive respect for the Roman faith and a fear of Calvinist extremism that led the southern provinces, or Belgium proper, reluctantly to continue to accept Spanish rule. Even this might not have been the case except for the shrewd conciliatory measures of Farnese, who finally gave the Catholic and Spanish cause a leadership that matched and perhaps excelled that provided the Calvinists by William.

Under Farnese's generalship the Spanish reasserted their authority over Ghent, Brussels, and Antwerp, in each instance allowing Protestants to migrate north. The fall of Antwerp brought English aid to the Republic of the United Provinces, and the defeat of the Spanish Armada in 1588 caused an abatement of Spanish efforts to reconquer the North, as Farnese was forced to turn his attention to battles in France.

The Twelve Years' Truce. In 1609 a 12-year truce halted completely the strife with the Protestant provinces. The pause was needed in Belgium. Long ravaged by war, with its major cities subjected to siege on several occasions and forced to pay heavy taxes and to support Spanish soldiery, it had seen its traditional prosperity decline sharply.

No region suffered more severely than that of Antwerp. The fortunes of war had delivered the port to Spain but had granted control of the mouth of the Scheldt to the United Provinces. The Dutch promptly closed the river, thus cutting off Belgian trade to the benefit of Amsterdam.

With the exception of the brief span from 1815 to 1830, free access to Antwerp has remained a difficult issue in Belgo-Dutch relations.

Despite this and other hindrances, the economy of Belgium slowly revived. In cultural matters the Catholic Counter Reformation was everywhere triumphant. The intellectual freedom of previous years was forgotten, as humanism retreated and Jesuit methods and views monopolized education and set the moral standard for the country. As most Protestants had by now moved north, stress was placed less on combating heresy than on revitalizing the Roman faith.

Border Adjustments. The hope that peace would be permanently restored was disappointed. At the close of the truce the Spanish resumed the war against the United Provinces, which were by now strengthened by the commercial successes of Holland. Equally disappointing was the death without heir in 1633 of Isabella, daughter of Philip II, who had in 1598 been appointed ruler of the Belgians to satisfy their longing for a national sovereign. The provinces therefore reverted to the Spanish king, Philip IV, and became involved in the confusing latter phases of the Thirty Years' War. Caught between the United Provinces and France, the Belgians fought for the Spanish, from whom they expected more autonomy.

The Treaty of Westphalia (1648) officially acknowledged the division of the 17 provinces and left Belgium in Spanish control. Philip IV continued to resist the annexationist aspirations of Louis XIV, but by the Treaty of the Pyrenees (1659) he was forced to surrender to France much of Artois and 11 strategic cities in the Belgian provinces. Dunkirk went to England. Louis XIV continued his depredations, and the southern border of Belgium was adjusted to his advantage by the treaties of Aix-la-Chapelle (1668) and Nijmegen (1678) and the Truce of Regensburg (1684). The War of the League of Augsburg led to the burning of the center of Brussels, as Belgium served as a main battleground for the great powers. The Treaty of Ryswick (1697) brought peace, minor readjustments in favor of Spain, and a seeming check to French expansion.

The respite was brief, for in 1702 the War of the Spanish Succession again brought French invasion as Louis XIV tried to seize the Lowlands in the name of his son. At first the English sided against the French, but when Charles III of Spain became emperor, the English switched their allegiance in order to preserve a balance of power. The result was the Treaty of Utretcht (1713). The regions of Tournai, Furnes, and Ypres were restored to the Belgian provinces, which as a whole were awarded to the Austrian Hapsburgs as compensation for loss of the Spanish throne. Far more damaging to the autonomy and unity of the southern Lowlands was the Barrier Treaty, concluded the following year by Austria and the United Provinces, which granted Dutch control of several strongholds from Termonde to Namur as a barrier against future French aggression. Having served as a battleground for dynastic and power struggles for centuries, Belgium now became the officially acknowledged buffer intended to protect other nations from the sufferings of war with which the "cockpit of Europe" was so familiar.

Austrian Rule. With the Scheldt still closed, the economy of the Austrian Netherlands, as this area was now called, languished. Austrian rule, although it took little pains to consult the people, was for the most part benevolent. The enlightened policies and obvious concern of Maria Theresa were appreciated, but the reign of Joseph II proved turbulent. By 1780 the populace had partially forgotten the hardships that had made the generations of the first part of the century willing to settle for the end of strife at the expense of unity and autonomy. Moreover, the economic difficulties caused by the decline of Antwerp could not help but nourish discontent. The spark that provoked revolution was the headlong and dictatorial manner in which Joseph II, unlike his prudent mother, pursued the most radical of the reforms of the Enlightenment.

Certain of his measures irritated the populace by their encroachments on what remained of Belgian autonomy and by their lack of understanding of Belgian mores and traditions. Decrees curbing the influence of the church, authorizing liberty of worship, mixed marriages, and the suppression of monasteries, convents, and episcopal seminaries were unwelcome in a land that had become a stronghold of the Counter Reformation. The bruising of religious sensibilities was matched in the political sphere by a sweeping reorganization of administrative and court structures.

Outraged by these infringements on privileges that had been maintained through decades of foreign rule, many Catholics, led by Henri Charles van der Noot, rose in opposition. They were joined by others, chief among whom was Jean François Vonck, who were inspired by the current unrest in France. The alliance was uneasy, for, although both groups opposed Joseph's rule, they did so for very different reasons.

Brabançonne Revolution and French Occupation. News of the fall of the Bastille in Paris in 1789 stimulated the revolutionaries, as did the encouragement van der Noot received from the Dutch and Prussians. Half-hearted Austrian military efforts, hindered by the defection of Walloon troops, failed to stem the uprising. By December of 1789 the Brabançonne Revolution was triumphant.

Far from being radical, the movement was aristocratic and conservative. The confederative constitution adopted on July 11, 1790, contained no declaration of the rights of man, protected the church, and preserved the rights of the individual provinces. Objects of persecution, many Vonckists fled to France. The rift between the noble and clerical supporters of the old ways and the bourgeois advocates of *liberté, égalité, fraternité* rapidly widened. The ideological quarrel, joined with the regionalism that has always been close to the surface in Belgium, forbade a military effort sufficient to prevent the troops of Leopold II (who succeeded Joseph in February 1790) from retaking the provinces that summer.

Aristocratic revolution from within failed, but radical change was soon brought from without. French victory over the Austrians at Jemappes (Nov. 6, 1792) first opened the provinces to the troops of the French republic. Forced by Austria to withdraw in 1793, they returned two years later, adding to the provinces Flemish Zeeland, thus opening the Scheldt and other former Dutch territories about Maastricht and Venlo (Treaty of The Hague, May 1795). On Oct. 1, 1795, the Belgian provinces were divided into nine departments and officially annexed to France.

Although many of the bourgeoisie originally welcomed the French "liberation," they came to resent inordinate taxation to finance French wars, the secularist spirit of the French Revolution, limitations placed on the use of the Flemish language, and French centralization, the latter of which was so contrary to both Belgian particularism and independence. Napoleon's peace with Rome, symbolized by the Concordat of 1801, eased the religious issue. Heavy taxation continued, but modest prosperity was reborn with the increase of activity at Antwerp and the growth of textile manufacturing at Ghent.

Only in the last of Napoleon's campaigns were the Low Countries again ravaged by war. Indicative of Belgium's still-important location for the military affairs of the Continent, however, was Napoleon's final defeat at Waterloo, only a few miles south of Brussels.

The United Netherlands. Deliverance from the French yoke did not bring independence, for, to the surprise of the Belgians, the regions of St.-Vith, Eupen, and Malmédy were given to Prussia, and the provinces themselves were awarded to William of Holland. Austria, exhausted by the war and more interested in protecting itself to the south than in struggling with the rebellious Belgians, parted with the provinces in return for compensation in Italy. Britain was desirous that Antwerp, the pistol Napoleon had "pointed at the breast of England," not be in the control of any great power, and all the members of the victorious coalition wished to prevent France from expanding again. The powers meeting at the Congress of Vienna in 1815 therefore resurrected the concept of a buffer state. It was inconceivable that two separate small states could halt France, and it was decided to reconstitute the Netherlands by uniting Belgium and the United Provinces.

The venture of the United Netherlands proved an unhappy one. Although the agricultural and industrial economy of Belgium complemented the commercial economy of the Dutch and although Antwerp and Ghent again prospered, old divisive factors—especially those of language and religion—continued to operate. William I, ruler of the United Netherlands, tended to treat the Belgians as second-class citizens of annexed territories rather than as equal partners within the union. In signing the Treaty of Eight Articles with the powers, the king had promised to grant Belgium full equality, political liberty, and freedom of religion, but his actions frequently violated that treaty in spirit if not in letter.

To avoid a long constitutional struggle, William decided to add a few amendments to the Fundamental Law, adopted in the North in 1813, and to persuade the Belgians to accept the amended law as their own. The amendment required by the Treaty of Eight Articles establishing freedom of religion was ferociously attacked by the Belgian clergy, who wished to prevent any inroads by Calvinism. Belgian liberals criticized the proposed constitution because it granted Belgium only half the seats in the two-chamber States General, although the Belgian population outnumbered the Dutch by approximately 3,400,000 to 2,000,000. On the other hand, although the Dutch national debt was almost 2 billion florins compared to Belgium's 30 million, the Belgians were required to assume the burden of half the combined liabilities of the new state. Unwilling to make concessions on these and other points and supported by the powers on the religious issue, William forced the Fundamental Law on the Belgians.

The French-oriented liberal middle class was further irritated by new taxes, William's commercial policies, exclusion of Belgians from top posts, and the ruling that all civil servants in the Flemish region use Dutch. Conservative Catholic opposition increased as William tried to remove the schools from Roman Catholic control. The king thus achieved what most men thought impossible—an alliance between Belgian liberals and Catholics.

Belgian Revolution. The universal disapproval that met the government's repression of the liberal journalist Louis de Potter led to the formation of the Union of Opposition in 1828. But although anti-Dutch sentiment increased, it was not until news of the July Revolution of 1830 in Paris reached Brussels that an uprising appeared likely. On August 25 disturbances were sparked by a performance of the inspiringly patriotic opera by Auber, *La muette de Portici.*

William at first dealt with the revolt gently, sending the popular Prince of Orange to Brussels. Although the prince himself entered the city, barricades and the attitude of the crowds persuaded him not to bring in his troops. Following his return to The Hague, the moderate Committee of Public Safety was formed. Radical elements from Wallonia and France, however, continued to drift into Brussels, and on September 20 the Hôtel de Ville was stormed and the committee disbanded.

This action provoked a show of force from William. After three days of heavy fighting in the park before the Brussels palace, the Dutch were forced to withdraw on September 27. Two days before, the revolutionaries had formed a provisional government that cut across all party lines. On October 4 that government proclaimed the nation's independence, and a month later an elected national congress met to draft a constitution and choose a head of state.

Although the northerners were still capable of asserting military authority over the south, they were held in check by interested foreign powers, particularly France and Britain. The British maneuvered to prevent any Dutch action that might stimulate intervention by the new French regime of Louis Philippe. The result of British diplomacy was an ambassadorial conference, which, under the leadership of Lord Palmerston, served as midwife to the birth of a fully independent Belgium. For although the delegates believed, when the London Conference first convened, that their main task would be to modify the government of the Low Countries and uphold William's sovereignty, by December 2, rival ambitions and fear that any other solution, such as partition, would bring general war had required them to recognize the principle of Belgian independence.

The Constitution. Important in this development were the speed and thoroughness with which the Belgians defined their break with the Dutch. The provisional government proclaimed a full gamut of liberties and abolished the state police and the secrecy of public accounts and judicial proceedings even before the national congress met. Election to the congress was by direct ballot, and the franchise was expanded. The constitution created by the congress confirmed these steps and was notably democratic, although the franchise, liberal for the times, was awarded only to men of property, thus assuring the rule of the middle class.

A key issue involved the form of government. The establishment of a republic might bring foreign intervention, and as its proponents were in a minority, a constitutional monarchy was decided upon. The powers were shocked by a declaration that excluded all members of the house of Nassau from Belgium, thus preventing the election of the prince of Orange. When the congress had the audacity to elect the duke of Nemours, second son of Louis Philippe, several powers protested what they considered the passing of Belgium to France. The French king was forced to decline the throne for his son.

The Belgians elected Leopold of Saxe-Coburg monarch on June 4, 1831. The widower of British Crown Princess Charlotte, he was acceptable to the British; when he indicated willingness to marry into the family of Louis Philippe, French objections were withdrawn.

Boundary Settlements. Leopold's election did much to further Belgium's negotiations with the powers. According to the Bases of Separation established by the London Conference in January 1831, Belgium would accept the boundary of 1790 as its border with the northern provinces. This stimulated the greatest opposition, and the congress rejected the January arrangement. After much negotiation, Leopold persuaded the London Conference to adopt a program of 18 articles more favorable to Belgium, which left certain territorial matters to further discussion.

This arrangement was not pleasing to the Dutch. On August 4, scarcely two weeks after Leopold had entered Belgium, they launched a vigorous attack. Overwhelmed in the Ten Days Campaign, Belgium appealed to the French, whose troops forced the Dutch to withdraw. The demonstrable inability of the new country to defend itself weakened its case, and the result was a new set of 24 articles proclaimed by the London Conference. These were more favorable to the Dutch than the previous set, but they awarded to Belgium the Walloon section of Luxembourg—about 60 percent of the duchy. Convinced that further resistance to the London Conference might provoke partition, Belgium signed the accord on Nov. 15, 1831.

It was not until 1839 that the Dutch king acquiesced. The treaty signed by the powers in April of that year, confirming the modified terms of the 24 articles and establishing Belgium as a legitimate member of the European polity, was later to become famous as the "scrap of paper" that the German chancellor von Bethmann-Hollweg denounced in 1914 at the outbreak of World War I. The object of his scorn was the clause guaranteeing the permanent neutrality of the Belgian state. Designed to prevent Belgium from becoming the pawn of any great power, the clause was unique in European diplomatic history up to that time and was to be the dominating influence on the small country's foreign policy for the next 80 years.

Economic and Political Development. After independence the economic basis of the country shifted from agriculture to industry, towns became cities, and foodstuffs were replaced by manufactured goods as Belgium's main export. With access to the sea assured by treaty, Antwerp grew steadily, becoming one of Europe's busiest ports.

Political issues lay dormant for several years after the revolution as the Belgians closed ranks behind the king they revered for his strong leadership. It is significant that in 1848, when much of Europe was experiencing rebellion, no indigenous revolt occurred in Belgium. This demon-

BETTMANN ARCHIVE

GERMAN TROOPS paraded through the streets of Brussels only 17 days after invading Belgium in World War I.

strated the success of the 1830 revolution, the democratic nature of the new constitution, which had already turned the governing of the country over to the middle classes, and the economic prosperity of the state.

The union of parties that had made possible the revolution did disintegrate in 1847, as some of the old differences regarding the role of the church in the state were revived. The Liberals called for the laicization of instruction and at times demanded a complete secularization of the schools. The Catholic party opposed this view and usually proved more conservative. An important exception to the latter pattern was expansion of the franchise. The Liberals, who believed that the government should be in the hands of propertied men, were reluctant to expand the electorate. The Catholics, who had considerable support among laboring and agricultural groups, took a broader view. Until 1884 the Liberals maintained their dominance, but in that year opposition to their policy favoring secular public schools brought the Catholics to power. The latter remained in tenuous control until they succeeded in 1893 in establishing universal male suffrage combined with a system of plural voting. From then until the outbreak of World War I the Catholics kept firm hold on the cabinet.

Colonization. Many parliamentarians questioned the economic advantages of colonization and feared the dangers of competing with the great powers. Leopold II, who had acceded to the throne in 1865, desired a greater arena for his activities than tiny Belgium afforded. Therefore he undertook his quest for adventure and riches on his own in the Congo. When the Congo Free State was established in 1885, it had no official connection with Belgium save for its ruler. Nevertheless, in the eyes of Europe and the United States the Congo state was viewed as a Belgian affair, and the Brussels politicians soon found their country sharply criticized because of Leopold's colonial policies. With the view of curbing Leopold's actions and mollifying their accusers, the chambers in 1907 forced the monarch to approve Belgian annexation of the colony, almost 80 times the size of the mother country.

World War I. Belgium's vulnerable position in Europe, the obvious coveting of its colony by the

BRUSSELS, which succumbed to Hitler's blitzkrieg in 1940, was freed by Belgian and British troops on Sept. 3, 1944.

great powers, and the mixture of coolness and excessive friendliness emanating from both the Entente Cordiale (Britain, France, and Russia) and the Triple Alliance (Germany, Austria-Hungary, and Italy) led its politicians to take precautionary measures. On his deathbed in 1909, Leopold II signed Belgium's first compulsory military service law.

Despite military preparations, Belgian troops were unable to check the sudden German attack launched on Aug. 4, 1914. King Albert I, nephew and successor of Leopold II, appealed to the guarantors of the treaty of 1839. British and French aid was neither prompt enough nor sufficient in quantity to rescue Belgium immediately; all but a thin coastal strip fell to the invader.

The country suffered throughout the war, as its factories, mines, and agriculture were utilized by the occupation troops and systematically despoiled to the advantage of factories and mines in Germany. The lot of the population would have been worse were it not for the Commission for Relief in Belgium, established by the American Herbert Hoover, which shipped over 5 million metric tons of supplies into the occupied regions.

Interwar Period. Because of the declarations of the Entente during the war and their own heroic resistance, the Belgians expected generous treatment at the peace conference. Although the areas of St.-Vith, Eupen, Malmédy, and Moresnet were given them and Britain yielded to pressure and allowed the former German territories of Ruanda-Urundi in Africa to pass under Belgian protectorship, the Belgians were bitter over the denial of their aspiration for Flemish Zeeland and the duchy of Luxembourg. Disappointed also by what they considered an inadequate share of reparations and slighting treatment by the Big Four (Britain, the United States, France, and Italy), the Belgians adopted a policy of activism. Since permanent neutrality had been discredited, a military accord was reached with France. Vigorous efforts were undertaken to collect reparations due from Germany, culminating in the 1923–1925 Franco-Belgian occupation of the Ruhr Valley in Germany. Attempts to obtain a bilateral treaty with Britain failed, but the conclusion of the Locarno accords in 1925 gave Belgium what it desired: the guarantee of French and British aid in the event of future German aggression.

As serious as were Belgium's external problems following the war, the domestic ones were more so. There was economic unrest, and the monopoly of the nation's government by the middle classes was now challenged by the Socialists. Although the Belgian Labor party had been building since 1885, it had never controlled a cabinet post until the war, when a national union cabinet was formed. The impact of the war and of the Russian revolution, and the leadership of Émile Vandervelde now made the Labor party a factor to be considered. Plural voting was abolished in favor of simple universal male suffrage in 1919, and thenceforth Socialists were frequently members of the government.

More dangerous to the unity of the country was the unrest in Flanders. The German occupation authorities during World War I had nurtured Flemish nationalism. After the war the Flemings became increasingly convinced that they were being relegated to second-class citizenship. They clamored for equality for their language and conversion of the University at Ghent from a French- to a Flemish-speaking institution. King Albert recognized the need for concessions and supervised their implementation. Peace was restored until the middle of the 1930's, when controversy broke out over a proposed military bill. Sufferings caused by the depression earlier in the decade still lingered. Various disgruntled splinter parties were appearing, the most notable of which was the Fascist Rexist party, led by Léon Degrelle. Each of the three major parties was torn by divisive Flemish and Walloon factions, and when the government proposed a military bill sorely needed to meet the threat posed by Hitler, the defection of the Flemish deputies in 1936 brought legislative progress to a standstill.

A prime goal of the Flemings was abrogation of the secret military accord with France, which they viewed as a symbol of Walloon domination. Many Belgians of both extractions feared the accord would force them into war at a Parisian whim, and the government had been attempting for several years to negotiate the accord's termination. Leopold III, who had come to the throne in 1934, saw the need for some gesture to reestablish unity within his country and called for a foreign policy that would be "exclusively Belgian." The military accord was soon renounced, and Belgium returned to the neutrality that it earlier had so eagerly abandoned.

World War II. The failure of the powers to stem Mussolini in Ethiopia, Hitler's rearmament, and the remilitarization of the Rhineland had done much to persuade Belgium that neutrality might be the best method of avoiding Hitler's aggression. Extensive military preparations were of no avail, however, against the blitzkrieg Hitler launched on May 10, 1940. The surrender of the Belgian army 18 days later was criticized by the Allies, but there was little else the Belgians could do.

The Nazi occupation was brutal. Resistance leaders were dealt with summarily, and many Jews lost their lives. King Leopold, with the intention of meliorating the occupation by judicious representations and more importantly of providing a focal point for national unity, declined his ministers' urging to go into exile and remained at his palace at Laeken. Throughout the war controversy swirled about this decision. A particularly sharp break developed between the king and Paul Henri Spaak, the Socialist leader, who challenged both the constitutionality and the propriety of the king's actions during the war.

Postwar Issues. Peace in 1945 brought an end to only the military conflict. Within Belgium severe hostilities developed between the Walloons and the Flemings, some of whom had not disguised their collaboration with the German invaders. Punishment of the few did not meet the larger issue, which was further complicated by the royal question. The Flemings supported Léopold strongly, while many Walloons demanded his abdication. After a voluntary exile and a plebiscite and parliamentary vote in his favor in 1950, the king was nevertheless forced in the following year to turn his powers over to his son Baudouin in the face of unrelenting Socialist demonstrations that threatened to tear the nation asunder.

Other issues were resolved more amicably, as the franchise was extended to women in 1948 and the Socialists and Catholics reached agreement in 1958 regarding the percentage of the costs of church schools that could be supported by national taxes. Many of the lingering animosities of the royal issue were forgotten in the crisis connected with the establishment of Congolese independence in 1960. The colony's demand for separation caught Belgian leaders by surprise, and indeed in terms of economic, educational, and political preparation the colony was far from ready to operate on its own. Nevertheless, in order to avoid a problem similar to that Algeria had recently posed to France, a hasty turnover of government to the Congolese was permitted. The subsequent chaos in the Congo was compounded by the tenacity with which certain Belgian financial and industrial organizations, such as the Société Générale and the Union Minière du Haut-Katanga tried to maintain a controlling interest in Katanga and other regions. It is true that their actions at first upheld rather than disrupted order, but the companies soon came in conflict with the central Congolese government and the United Nations.

The intervention of the United Nations shocked all levels of the Belgian population, and the hitherto warm appreciation of the international organization of which Belgium was a charter member cooled. The austerity program instituted by the government to compensate for the economic loss caused by the separation of the colony was only partially successful. The winter of 1960–1961 witnessed severe Socialist-led strikes and demonstrations, which centered in Liège.

The economic condition of Belgium greatly improved in the early 1960's. Belgium's increasing prosperity was in part attributable to the Belgium-Netherlands-Luxembourg (Benelux) economic union, created after the war, and more importantly to the European Common Market, of which Brussels became the chief financial and negotiating center. Led by Spaak, the Belgians became important members of the North Atlantic Treaty Organization (NATO). In 1967 the Supreme Headquarters of the military arm of NATO was transferred from Rocquencourt, France, to Casteau, in southwestern Belgium.

But the linguistic controversy continued to rage. Frequent modifications of the linguistic boundary in favor of the growing number of Flemings did not satisfy their demands and stimulated fears among Walloons. Administrative autonomy was increasingly established for the two regions of Belgium.

The **CHÂTEAU DE LAERNE**, like others near Ghent, recalls the prosperity of Flanders under Burgundian rule.

Thus, despite centuries of warfare and endless attempts to reach compromise on religious, political, and ethnic matters, the Belgians found themselves in the latter half of the 20th century prosperous and independent—indeed more free of foreign tutelage than ever before—but still searching for the long-desired goal of unity.

JONATHAN E. HELMREICH, *Allegheny College*

7. Culture

The Flemish, of Germanic blood, and the Walloons, with Latin ties, have been less at odds in cultural endeavors than the linguistic situation would seem to indicate. They both look back on a common inheritance from the Flemish masters in the plastic arts. Their painters share a love of color and of the picturesque. Many writers of Flemish background used French as their medium with superb results. Flemish (which is a dialect of Dutch that differs from Dutch no more than American differs from English), on the other hand, is now experiencing a dynamic literary expansion in Belgium.

Belgium's artistic output has coincided with the years of its greatest economic expansion, for example, the Burgundian period. The 15th century was especially rich in painting, music, architecture, and literature. By the end of the 17th century, artistic production was nearly at a standstill. After 1830, with Belgian independence, a rebirth of the arts began and gathered momentum toward the close of the century. The 20th century has witnessed ever-increasing cultural activity.

It is somewhat difficult to define "Belgian art." This is not only because Paris and other foreign capitals have long attracted Belgian artists but also because independent Belgium dates only from 1830. The linguistic division also introduces an element of confusion. Thus, some of the artists discussed below might also be called, for example, "Dutch writers" or "French composers." All of them, however, either were born within the boundaries of present-day Belgium or made important contributions there.

PAINTING

The term "Flemish painting" is applied not only to Flanders but also to neighboring countries and provinces. Few Flemish paintings predate the 15th century, although a painters' guild had existed in Ghent since 1331. The great period of Flemish painting occurred between the 15th and 17th centuries. Craftsmen, illuminators and designers of tapestries, jewelers, lacemakers, and wrought-iron craftsmen also flourished during the same period.

The Flemish primitive painters, the most famous of whom are probably the van Eyck brothers, were inspired by the Gothic sculptors and manuscript illuminators, such as Pol de Limbourg (Book of Hours of the Duke de Berry). Jan van Eyck's best-known work is the *Adoration of the Mystic Lamb* altarpiece in Ghent, completed in 1432. His art is characterized by realistic detail and brilliant coloring. His oil-painting technique dominated Europe over the succeeding century. The other leading 15th-century painters of Belgium also followed in his path: the Master of Flémalle; Roger van der Weyden (or Rogier de la Pasture); Dirk Bouts, easily recognized for his elongated and rigid figures; Hugo van der Goes, a very original artist whose types are distinctive; and Hans Memling, who, though born in Mainz, settled in Bruges, where he came under the influence of van der Weyden. Gerard David was influenced by Memling and by the Italian school, which also influenced Memling. The effect of the Italian Renaissance shows clearly in the paintings of Quentin Massys (Matsys). He gave considerable importance to landscape, an emphasis that was to continue with Joachim Patinir.

The traditions of the Flemish school were carried on into the 16th century in spite of the considerable concessions made to the Italians. Pieter Brueghel the Elder, who was not generally appreciated in his time, was an exception to the general rule of Italianization. His profoundly original works are full of intense animation.

In the 17th century Peter Paul Rubens and his baroque school evaded a direct Italian influence. He painted religious and pagan scenes as well as landscapes and portraits. A student of Rubens, Anthony Van Dyck, lived for a while in England. He was a technician especially known for his portraits. Another student, Jacob Jordaens, was an outstanding colorist. Rubens was followed by other, less imposing artists, including David Teniers, Adriaen Brouwer, and the animal specialist Frans Snyders.

The 18th century showed little interest in painting. Romanticism in the 19th century was represented by Gustav Wappers, Louis Gallait, and Hendrik Seys. An impressionist school produced Rik Wouters, who was also a sculptor.

In the 20th century, James Ensor, the father of Flemish expressionism, was very influential with his experimental forms. Prominent also were Théo van Rysselberghe and the expressionists Constant Permeke, Gustave van de Woestijne, Fritz van den Berghe, Gustave de Smet, Floris Jespers, and Jean Brusselmans.

The surrealists René Magritte and Paul Delvaux enjoy international renown. The generation of painters of the 1920's included Jozef Vinck, Julien Creytens, Jacques Maes, and Henri Wolvens. During the mid-century period, such painters as Rik Slabbinck, Jan Cox, Marc Mendelson, G. Bertrand, and Luc Peire appeared. In the 1960's the abstract painters Octave Landuyt, Jan Burssens, Maurice Wijkaert, and Serge van der Camp typified the continual vigorous movement in Belgian painting. See also FLEMISH PAINTING.

SCULPTURE AND ARCHITECTURE

Claus Sluter and Claus van de Werve were the outstanding sculptors of the 14th century, but they did their work in Burgundy under Philip the Bold and Philip the Good. A period of Italian influence followed, but it did not dominate certain 17th century sculptors who were influenced by the Rubens school of painting: Lucas Fayd'herbe, Jean Delcour, François Duquesnoy, and Arnold Quellyn.

In the 19th century the realist movement produced Constantin Meunier, painter turned sculptor at the end of the century, who specialized in genre subjects. Later prominent sculptors included Georges Minne, Victor Rousseau, Henri Puvrez, and Charles Leplae. Jozef Cantré, Robert Massart, and Oscar Jespers were influential Belgian sculptors in the mid-20th century.

The new generation of abstract sculptors includes Rik Poot, Roel D'Haese, Jan Dries, Marcel Arnould, and Roger Bonduel.

The oldest Belgian churches belong to the Romanesque period (900–1150). Of these the most remarkable examples are St. Quentin at Tournai and St. Vincent at Soignies. Most of the architectural vestiges of the Middle Ages remaining today are from the subsequent Gothic period. Damage in both world wars was considerable, but many cities, jewels of architecture, were spared. The Grand'Place of Brussels, the cities of Bruges and Ghent, and the many monuments of Antwerp and Liège are all architectural marvels surviving from other ages.

Cornelis de Vriendt was the master of the 16th century Flemish Renaissance style who designed, notably, the Antwerp town hall. Early in the 20th century Victor Horta and Henry van de Velde, leader of the art nouveau movement in architecture, were especially important.

MUSIC

While Flanders produced the most outstanding works of painting, it was Walloon territory, Hainaut and Liège, that produced the musical genius of the country. The musical contribution of Belgium to European culture is less well known than its painting but no less remarkable. The art of modern music was born on what is now Belgian soil. Colomban, abbott of St.-Trond (Sint-Truiden), is often credited with one of the oldest pieces of music known, the *Complainte pour la mort de Charlemagne* (9th century). Other Belgian composers of the period were trained in St.-Trond at the cathedral school.

Later centers of musical training were located at Tournai, under Hucbald, and at Liège, under Jean Ciconia, Arnold de Lantins, and Jean Brassart. By 1450, Guillaume Dufay had made the region of Hainaut the center, if not the birthplace, of polyphonic music. Gilles Binchois (15th century), one of the earliest experimenters with counterpoint, helped to liberate music from primitive harmony with its sterile abstractions. Henceforth, voices in concert would interweave their melodic curves, supporting each other, parting and rejoining. Jean Ockeghem (d'Okeghem) developed the supple and complicated interplay of voices much as his contemporary Jean Lemaire de Belges was to do in the field of poetry.

GHENT is architecturally harmonious, although diverse styles from different periods stand side by side in this historic capital of Flanders.

HENRI CARTIER-BRESSON, FROM MAGNUM

By the end of the 15th century this school was exerting great influence in Europe. Josquin Desprez (Deprés) perfected and liberated it even more with his great imagination and invention. Josquin was praised for his charming and natural style by Martin Luther and Lorenzo the Magnificent, ruler of Florence. Josquin caused an awakening of music in Italy as well as at the French court of Louis XII. A 16th century Fleming, Adrian Willaert, also a follower of Josquin, was called to Venice, where he directed music at the chapel of St. Mark, to be succeeded in turn by another Fleming, Cipriano da Rore, the "divine Cipriano."

From Mons came the universal musical soul of Roland de Lassus, whose chansons, madrigals, and sacred music embody the spirit of the 16th century. Like many other great Belgian artists, he spent much of his life abroad, mostly in France.

A new focus of musical production radiated from Liège during the 17th century with Henri du Mont, who rivaled Jean Baptiste Lully as chapelmaster of Louis XIV. Jean Noël Hamal was an 18th century popularizer of music, utilizing Walloon patois in his operas. He was a predecessor of the better-known André Grétry. The operas of Grétry, who came from Liège, evolve from French patriotic themes. Grétry was one of the official cantors of the French Revolution (*Chant du 14 juillet*).

The 19th century opened with the musically erudite works of François Joseph Fétis, organist of Mons, and of François Auguste Gevaert, who reorganized the conservatory of Brussels. Schools of music were also founded at Ghent and Antwerp. A Flemish movement in music was begun by Pierre Benoit, inspired by renewed interest in Flemish literature. The group used folkloric themes as well as subjects from the 16th century paintings.

Walloon tendencies in music during the 19th century closely parallel the French, producing an art of sentiment or psychology, sometimes animated by popular themes. The Liège master César Franck, in turn, was influential in French circles. He contributed simple and profound feeling and sublime phrases. He was followed by his student Guillaume Lekeu.

Jean Absil is the best known of 20th century Belgian composers. Marcel Quinet is noted for his great sensitivity. Since 1939, the foundation of the Queen Elisabeth Musical Chapel has provided an opportunity for the most gifted artists to perfect their talents.

LITERATURE

Because of the linguistic division of the country, Belgium has always possessed two literatures, French and Flemish. The matter is further complicated by the fact that Flemings have, at times, written their works in French.

The European spirit of Belgian letters results from the country's position as a crossroads of Europe constantly enriched by ideas from neighboring countries. In an area not unfamiliar with invasion, Belgian authors show the influence of English, German, and especially French literature. There is, nonetheless, no lack of originality in Belgian letters. The Flemish taste for color and mystery has produced important drama, fiction, and poetry. The literature of this meeting ground of Germanic and Romance civilizations must be considered under its two divisions, French and Flemish.

French Literature in Belgium to the 20th Century. The oldest French literary texts were written on Belgian soil. The *Cantilène de Ste. Eulalie* (9th century) is believed to have come from Hainaut. *La vie de St. Alexis* exists in a Walloon text older than any French version. The oldest farce, *Le garçon et l'aveugle*, comes from Tournai. There exist moral and mystery plays from 13th century Liège. It was probably a trouvère from Hainaut who wrote *Aucassin et Nicolette*. The *Roman de Renart* was inspired by a Flemish work written by a Ghent cleric, Maître Nivard. Chrétien de Troyes wrote his *Perceval*, or *Conte del Graal*, for Philip of Alsace, count of Flanders. Adenet le Roi, trouvère of Duke Henry III of Brabant, composed the *Berthe aux Grands Pieds*.

A 14th century chronicler, Jean d'Outremeuse, wrote the first adventure novel, the *Voyages de Sir John Mandeville*. The Liège area was the homeland of the chroniclers Jacques de Henricourt and Jehan le Bel. Some of the later chroniclers, notably Jean Froissart, Georges Chastellain, and Philippe de Commines (Commynes), were also "Belgian."

Jean Lemaire de Belges wrote the *Concorde des deux langages* for Louis XII of France. His poetic rhetoric was very important in French letters during the 16th century. During the same period, Marnix van Sint Aldegonde, the "Rabelais of the North," wrote in French and Flemish.

A long period of literary blight was interrupted only near the end of the 18th century when Charles Joseph, prince of Ligne, produced his 33-volume *Mélanges militaires, littéraires et sentimentaires,* a monument to the Old Regime.

The romantic revolution and Belgian independence coincided (1830). Belgian letters from 1830 to 1880 generally took the path of utilitarian rather than of artistic aesthetics. At least one poet of the period, André van Hasselt, deserves mention. Illustrative of the national awareness is the great novel of the epoch, *La légende d'-Ulenspiegel et de Lamme Goedzak en pays de Flandre et d'ailleurs*, written by Charles de Coster and published in 1867. This "epic of the Flemish people" is written in archaic language. Its hero, Till Eulenspiegel (Tyll Ulenspiegel) typifies the spirit of Flanders during the fight against the Spanish—ribaldry, a love of liberty, and a disdain for bigotry. Lamme, Till's partner, represents the love for maternal things, and Nele, his fiancée, represents the heart of the country.

More than 25 literary reviews and papers appeared between 1814 and 1884. The country underwent a great awakening of letters under the patronage of the bourgeoisie. The leaders of the generation of 1880 were Octave Pirmez, a writer of classic prose, and, especially, Max Waller, who founded the review *La Jeune Belgique*. The period of utilitarian art had ended. The Parnassians and Symbolists united, and the group had for its motto "Be Ourselves." Around Max Waller were Iwan Gilkin and Albert Giraud, both poets. They were later joined by Émile Verhaeren, Valère Gille, Georges Eekhoud, Georges Rodenbach, Maurice Maeterlinck, Charles Van Lerberghe, Grégoire Le Roy, and Max Elskamp.

The naturalistic novels of Camille Lemonnier shocked Belgian critics with their violence. He later became more poetic and with his colorful style and vehement lyricism produced some of his best works. Georges Eekhoud described the effects of industrialization on the Antwerp area in the bitter novel *La nouvelle Carthage* (1888).

Maurice Maeterlinck, a symbolist poet of great feeling, was also a dramatist of considerable influence on the theater of the West. His most important plays, *La princesse Maleine, Pelléas et Mélisande*, and *L'oiseau bleu* (*The Blue Bird*), won him the Nobel Prize in 1911. He was also a prolific writer of essays.

Apart from the Jeune Belgique group there existed several Walloon regionalist novelists, such as Hubert Krains, Edmond Glesener, and Jean Tousseul. The poetic works of the end of the 19th century have generally survived better than the drama, essays, or novels.

French Literature in Belgium in the 20th Century.

The best poet at the turn of the century was Émile Verhaeren. Influenced by Walt Whitman, his Symbolist writings bore a social message. He introduced Flemish characteristics into French poetry. Another poet, Odilon Jean Périer, showed great promise, but he met an untimely death at the age of 21 in 1928. A veteran of World War I, Maurice Gauchez wrote novels on his wartime experiences and also poetry. The most original poet of the post-World War I period was Marcel Thiry, who combined war experiences with a taste for the exotic. Certain poetesses also merit mention: Lucienne Desnoues, Anne-Marie Kegels, and Renée Brock. At mid-century the most important name in poetry was Henri Michaux, a surrealist specializing in black humor.

Poets of the postwar period include Robert Goffin, Armand Bernier, Liliane Wouters, Gérard Prevot, Jean Tordeur, and Arthur Haulot.

The novel at mid-century was represented by Georges Virrès, André Baillon, and especially Charles Plisnier, Franz Hellens, and Georges Simenon. Plisnier was the first foreigner to win the Goncourt Prize in France. He represented a restoration of traditional poetic values. Franz Hellens, a doctor and a symbolist poet, is best known for his novels about the mysteries of Flanders. Georges Simenon, from Liège, began writing detective stories in 1930. The "Maigret" series is justly famous for this prolific author's penetrating psychology. His novels were not limited to one genre, as is witnessed by *Le train* (1961), a work dealing with the psychology of war refugees.

Marie Gevers was a realist novelist who described the land and people of the Antwerp area. Another feminine novelist deserving mention is Maud Frère. Françoise Mallet-Joris, winner of the Prix Fémina in 1965, is a technician of psychological realism. Her best-known work is *Le rempart des béguines* (1951). Other mid-century novelists include Alexis Curvers, Stanislas d'Otremont, Daniel Gillès, and Francis Walder, winner of the Goncourt Prize in 1958.

Modern Belgian drama in French is represented by Fernand Crommelynck, whose *Cocu magnifique* (1921) won him fame on the Parisian stage. Michel de Ghelderode showed both expressionist and mystic influence in his plays, which include *Hop Signor, Escurial*, and *Pantagleise*. In the 1960's José André Lacour and Georges Sion showed great promise.

Flemish Literature in Belgium to the 20th Century.

It was in Flanders that the literature of the Dutch language was born and flourished during the Middle Ages. The great works of the early period include the *Sint Servatius Legende* (about 1170), written by the Limburger Heinrich von Veldeke, and *Beatrijs*, a legend concerning the nun Beatrice who returned to secular life and whose place in the convent was kept by the Virgin herself. Maître Nivard of Ghent wrote a satirical animal epic, *Ysengrimus*, predecessor of the Renard series. A related work, the *Reinaert* of Maître Willem, is also an animal epic, a parody of the heroics of aristocratic literature. This type of parody was to be adapted by most of the great cultures of Europe.

In about 1250, Jacob van Maerlant began his didactic verse work, the *Spieghel historiael* (*The Mirror of History*), which was to earn him the title of "father of Dutch poetry." There exist also dramatized poems, such as *Esmoreit, Lancelot*, and *Floriant*, but the greatest and the most influential work was the symbolic *Elkerlijk* (*Everyman*), which gave birth to English and German versions of the Everyman theme.

Two mystic writers stand out during the Middle Ages: Jan van Ruysbroeck (the Admirable), a monk who lived in the forest of Groenendael and who wrote long discourses on the way to grace, and the nun Hadewijch, who wrote poetry.

Chambers of rhetoric were established in Flanders during the 15th century. These were literary groups in which the local bourgeoisie participated. The introduction of printing in 1413 by Thierry Maertens at Alost led to a number of printing establishments springing up at Louvain, Bruges, and Brussels, not to mention the famous shop of Christophe Plantin at Antwerp.

The Reformation brought several writers to the fore. Marnix van Sint Aldegonde wrote his bitter attack on the church: *Den biëncorf der H. Roomsche Kercke* (1569; *The Bee Hive of the Holy Romish Church*). Others, including Anna

Bijns and Cornelius Crul, supported the Catholic cause. The political and religious struggles leading to the separation of the southern Netherlands from the north at the end of the 16th century produced an intellectual apathy in the country, and Flemish literature disappeared until the 19th century.

The wave of nationalism released by the independence of the country in 1830 stimulated the exploitation of historic themes. The first great Flemish novel of the century, *De leeuw van Vlaenderen* (*The Lion of Flanders*) was written by Hendrik Conscience and published in 1838. This opened the way for a flood of other novels, among them the works of the realist novelist Virginie Loveling. The first daily newspaper in Flemish dates from this period. In poetry Albrecht Rodenbach typified romantic nationalism. From the utilitarian art of the historical novel the Flemings moved to the novel of idealized contemporary customs and from there, eventually, to the art-for-art's-sake ideals of the generation of 1880.

Guido Gezelle was the greatest Flemish poet of the 19th century. A priest with a Gothic spirit, he rose to great heights of lyricism in his poems about the ceremonies of the church and about the Flemish countryside. Also a linguist, he translated Longfellow's *Hiawatha* into Flemish (1886).

Flemish Literature in Belgium in the 20th Century. In the 1890's the new writers rallied around the liberal review *Van nu en straks* (*Today and Tomorrow*). The leader of the movement was August Vermeylen, an internationalist, author of *De wandelende Jood* (1906; *The Wandering Jew*). Naturalist writers included Cyriel Buysse and Herman Teirlinck, whose *Het ivoren aapje* (1909; *The Ivory Monkey*) demonstrates his powers in the domain of the psychological novel. There was also Stijn Streuvels, a nephew of Gezelle, an epic novelist whose love of his native soil and its inhabitants is demonstrated in *Werkmenschen* (1927; *Workmen*). The great lyric poet Karel van de Woestijne concentrated on self-analysis. He was a true humanist and a great poet, possessing great metaphysical depth.

A true flowering of letters had taken place in Flanders before World War I. The war brought on a search for new experience and greater interest in lyricism, in the interior life, and in the community of men. The review *Ruimte* (*Space*) represented those who espoused their new ways of thinking. Flemish expressionism, a representative of European avant-garde letters, exalted the instincts and espoused *élan vital* (vital force). It revolted against intellectualism and against society itself. Its language was sober, governed by the idea. The poets of the movement include Paul van Ostayen, who wrote *Bezette stad* (1921; *The Occupied City*), Wies Moens, Gaston Burssens, and Jan-Albert Goris (pseud. Marnix Gijsen), whose masterpiece is *Het boek van Joachim van Babylon* (1948).

A traditionalist school continued to find its values in rural society. Among its writers were Felix Timmermans, espousing a pantheistic joy of life (*Boerenpsalm*, 1935; *Farmer's Song*), Ernest Claes, and Maurits Sabbe.

Several powerful novelists carried on the humanist tradition: Maurice Roelants (*Komen en gaan*, 1927; *Come and Go*), who utilized the style of the French analytic novel; Gerard Walschap (*De verloren zoon*), whose vitalist novel

showed the influence of the Spanish Miguel de Unamuno's tragic sentiment of existence; and Willem Elsschot (*Het dwaallicht,* 1946), who was a predecessor of later experimental novelists. The writers of the post-World War II period included the esoteric Raymond Brulez and the sensitive poet Maurice Gilliams. Certain writers of the prewar era, especially Teirlinck and Gijsen, were still active.

At mid-century among the most important writers was Johan Daisne, a prolific novelist whose "magic realism" was based on the tension between the worlds of dream and reality. Hubert Lampo (*Terugkeer naar Atlantis*, 1953; *Return to Atlantis*) wrote novels touching on the supernatural. A social novelist, Piet van Aken (*Klinkaart*, 1954) was influenced by American novelists. He was the student of Filip de Pillecyn, who excelled in depicting the interior life. Louis Paul Boon was inspired by historical subjects in his novels of social protest. His style is brutal; he favors the malcontent in society, protests against the decline of man, and calls for revolt. *De bende van Jan de Lichte* (1957; *The Band of John the Light*) is an interpretation for modern times of the life of a Flemish bandit.

An experimentalist difficult to classify, Hugo Claus has an international reputation. He is a realist in sexual description and is hostile to established order. His best novel, *De verwondering* (1948; *The Surprise*), deals with the resurrection of fascism. His theatrical work began in 1953 with *Een bruid in de morgen* (*A Bride in the Morning*).

Other contemporary experimentalist writers include Paul De Wispelaere, Yvo Michiels, the poet Paul Snoek, and Jan Walravens. The cold-war generation of Belgian writers is characterized by synthesis, search, and doubt—somewhat analogous to the Lost Generation of the 1920's. In Flanders it has shown extreme variety and richness.

ROBERT A. MEININGER, *University of Nebraska*

Bibliography

Arango, E. Ramón, *Leopold III and the Belgian Royal Question* (Baltimore 1961).
Cammaerts, Émile, *A History of Belgium from the Roman Invasion to the Present Day* (New York 1921).
Clough, Shepard B., *A History of the Flemish Movement in Belgium* (New York 1930).
Gerson, Horst, and Kuile, E.H. ter, *Art and Architecture in Belgium, 1600 to 1800* (Baltimore 1960).
Goris, Jan-Albert, *Belgian Letters* (New York 1946).
Goris, Jan-Albert, ed., *Belgium* (Berkeley, Calif., 1945).
Hymans, Louis, *Histoire parlementaire de la Belgique de 1830 à 1890,* 8 vols. (Brussels 1877–1901).
Institut Royal des Relations Internationales, Brussels, *La Belgique et les Nations Unies* (New York 1958).
Kalken, Frans van, *Histoire de la Belgique et de son expansion coloniale* (Brussels 1954).
Kuyck, Hugo van, *Modern Belgian Architecture,* 3d ed. (New York 1955).
Lilar, Suzanne, *The Belgian Theater Since 1890,* 2d ed. (New York 1957).
Mallinson, Vernon, *Modern Belgian Literature,* 2d ed. (New York 1966).
Mallinson, Vernon, *Power and Politics in Belgian Education 1815 to 1961* (London 1963).
Miller, Jane K., *Belgian Foreign Policy Between Two Wars 1919–1940* (New York 1951).
Pirenne, Henri, *Belgian Democracy: Its Early History* (Manchester 1915).
Pirenne, Henri, *Histoire de Belgique des origines à nos jours,* rev. ed., 4 vols. (Brussels 1948–52).
Reed, T.H., *Government and Politics of Belgium* (New York 1924).
Rooses, Max, *Art in Flanders* (New York 1914).
Scheinert, David, *Écrivains belges devant la réalité* (Brussels 1964).
Weisgerber, Jean, *Formes et domaines du roman flamand 1921–1960* (Brussels 1963).
Zuylen, Pierre van, *Les mains libres: Politique extérieure de la Belgique 1914–1940* (Brussels 1950).

BELGRADE'S new residential quarter, constructed after World War II, lies on the western, or left, bank of the Sava River.

BELGRADE, bel'grăd, is the capital and largest city of Yugoslavia. It is also the capital of Serbia, one of Yugoslavia's constituent republics. The Serbian name for the city is *Beograd,* meaning "White Castle" or "White City."

Situated at the confluence of the Sava and Danube rivers, the city is an active port, as well as a rail and air center. It lies athwart the main rail route between western Europe, Greece, and Asia Minor. It has plants manufacturing machinery, tools, electric equipment, textiles, shoes, and paper. There are also plants for processing agricultural products.

Places of Interest. An open space called the Terazije forms the traffic center of the city. It is bordered by hotels and the Albanija, a large office building. The university, the national museum, the Orthodox cathedral, and the ancient Kalemegdan fortress lie to the north and northwest of the Terazije. To the south of it, on a main boulevard called the Bulevar Revolucije, stand the administrative offices of the Central Committee of the Communist party, the 20th-century building used as a parliament building until World War II, and opposite this building, the former royal palace, now used for public receptions. The new parliament buildings and the president's office are located across the Sava to the west in the suburb of Novi Beograd.

The Kalemegdan fortress, which crowns a limestone promontory above the confluence of the two rivers, is bounded on its south side by a park. In 1928 the famous Yugoslav sculptor Ivan Meštrović designed the monument that stands near the fortress. It is topped by a 14-foot (4-meter) bronze figure, the *Messenger of Victory.* A public garden occupies part of the Kalemegdan fortress, and beyond the great Zindan gate there is a zoo. The lower fortress, partially destroyed in World War II, the 18th century Prince Eugene gate, and an octagonal tower overlook the rivers to the north and west.

The university, founded in 1863, is situated on Students' Square, halfway between the fortress and the Terazije. Just north of the Terazije is the Trg Republike (Square of the Republic), in the center of which is a statue of Prince Michael Obrenović (1825–1868), who helped liberate the Balkans from the Turks. The national museum, forming one side of this square, contains artifacts dating back to prehistoric times as well as an impressive collection of paintings and sculpture.

The only mosque that remains of the 20 that once stood in Belgrade is the 16th century Barjak mosque ("Flag" mosque), built by Suleiman the Magnificent. Just south of the Kalemegdan fortress is an Orthodox cathedral, built between 1837 and 1845.

History. The Romans built two forts, Taurunum and Singidunum, at the junction of the Sava and Danube rivers, a position previously fortified by the Celts. The Huns destroyed both Roman forts in the 4th century, and the remaining defenses were razed by the Goths early in the 5th century. The site was not refortified until the Bulgars seized it in the 9th century, naming it *Beligrad.*

During the next six centuries Belgrade was ruled at various times by Hungary, Byzantium, and toward the end of this period by Serbia. The Turks made their first attempts to take it in the 15th century, but it did not fall to them until 1521. Austria captured the city three times from the Turks between 1688 and 1789 but in each instance held it only briefly. The Serbian leader Karageorge (George Petrović) entered Belgrade in 1807, but the Turks succeeded in expelling him. Belgrade remained under Turkish control until 1867, when the Serbs drove out the Turkish garrison and made it their capital.

During World War I, Austria-Hungary held the city from 1915 until the end of the war, when it became the capital of the newly created kingdom of Serbs, Croats, and Slovenes (Yugoslavia). The Nazis invaded Yugoslavia in 1941 and bombed the city. It was retaken by Russian troops and Yugoslav guerrillas in 1944, and in 1945 it once more became Yugoslavia's capital. Population: (1971) of city and environs, 1,204,271.

BELGRADE LAKES, bel'grăd, a group of lakes in southern Maine, in Kennebec county, 15 miles (24 km) north of Augusta. The larger lakes are Long Pond, Great Pond, and Messalonskee Lake. The smaller lakes are East, North, Ellis, and McGrath ponds. The Belgrade Lakes, which are connected by streams, form the center of a resort region noted for fishing, boating, and swimming. The town of Belgrade is headquarters for the resort area, which also includes the villages of Belgrade Lakes and North Belgrade.

BELGRANO, bel-grä'nō, **Manuel** (1770–1820), Argentine patriot and general, who was born in Buenos Aires, on June 3, 1770. After studying law in Spain at Valladolid and Madrid, he returned to Buenos Aires in 1793. As a captain of the city militia, he helped to defeat the British invasion of 1806–1807. At the start of Argentina's war of independence against Spain, he commanded an abortive expedition to Parguay in 1810–1811, and in the following year led a force into the Banda Oriental (now Uruguay). In Argentina, his gaucho cavalry severely defeated Gen. Pío Tristán's royalists at Tucumán on Sept. 24, 1812, and at Salta on Feb. 20, 1813.

Belgrano then invaded Upper Peru (now Bolivia), but lost the Battle of Vilcapugio (Oct. 1, 1813), and his army was nearly destroyed at Ayohuma (Nov. 26, 1813). Retreating with the remnants of his forces to Argentine territory, he was replaced by José de San Martín.

In 1815, Belgrano went to Europe with Bernardino Rivadavia on an unsuccessful diplomatic mission. Returning to Buenos Aires early in 1816, he was given command of the army in Peru. For three years he engaged the Spanish forces in Chile and Peru with varying success. In 1819 he was recalled to Argentina to suppress a revolt at Santa Fe. He died in Buenos Aires on June 20, 1820. An equestrian statue of Belgrano adorns the Plaza de Mayo in Buenos Aires.

BELIEF is a commitment, either intellectual or emotional, or both, to something such as a proposition, a position, a procedure, or a person. In the scale of attitudes it is located above surmise or conjecture and below knowledge. On a scale in which the number 1 represents absolute certainty, belief ranges from a subjective probability of over ½ to the level of great confidence, just short of 1. Belief is one of the key concepts in the borderland between philosophy and psychology and has frequently been grossly oversimplified by leaders of reform movements in both fields, such as introspectionists, behaviorists, idealists, and empiricists.

The concept of belief has aroused particular interest because it has seemed possible to analyze the concept of knowledge in terms of belief. For example, knowledge has been defined as justified true belief—a definition that has been proved faulty. Another interesting aspect of belief is its close connection with religious or political partisanship. In this role, belief is sometimes defined as synonymous with faith and sometimes as a weaker version of faith. From this definition it has been argued that belief is immune from any need for a rational basis. It is true that belief can be well founded without being founded on any process of rational inference, this is a different point. Individual perceptions provide immediate knowledge without any intervening process of inference, and long experience may train our perception (or intuition) until it is entirely rational to rely on it. But this does not show that untested intuition is of any value in achieving real knowledge, however strong a belief it may engender. Reason is the only safe path to knowledge or sound belief, although it is not a guaranteed route. The mystic's slogan "I believe because it is absurd" may be honest, but it is not logical.

Although it can generally be said that a person believes what he knows to be true, the category of absolutely certain knowledge has been held to constitute a special case. It would seem odd to say that we "believe" that men usually have a head, or that $1 + 1 = 2$, or that we are awake as we read this. But this is presumably because we feel that the term "belief," as opposed to knowledge, involves too little commitment to the certainty of what is believed. We can say "I believe this, but it may not be true"; on the other hand we cannot say "I know this, but it may not be true."

In the realm of psychology, belief has great effects on our bodies as well as on our minds. It is the power behind the placebo effect, faith-healing, and other forms of psychosomatic therapy. It is also a factor in the success of heroes and great leaders of men. We do not have immediate voluntary control over our beliefs, but many people unconsciously adjust their beliefs to their convenience—whether personal convenience, as in blind loyalty, or social convenience, as in antiliberalism. Extreme forms of rationalization illustrate the control of belief over reason. Recent research, supplementing the historic psycho-analytical hypotheses of Freud, has begun to illuminate the effect on belief of such nonrational mechanisms as subliminal advertising, hypnosis, cognitive consonance, brainwashing, psychedelic drugs such as LSD and mescaline, and suggestibility phenomena in general.

MICHAEL SCRIVEN, *Indiana University*
Author of "Primary Philosophy"

BELINSKY, byi-lyĕn'skĕ, **Vissarion Grigorievich** (1811–1848), Russian literary critic who championed the "natural school" of writers that included Nikolai Gogol, Alexander Pushkin, and Mikhail Lermontov. He evaluated literature by its social significance and by the accuracy of its reflection of reality. An ardent liberal for most of his life, Belinsky exerted an immense influence on Russian intellectuals generally, and especially on Dostoyevsky and other realistic writers of the 19th century.

Belinsky was born in Sveaborg, Finland (then part of Russia), on June 13, 1811. He was expelled from Moscow University in 1832 for writing a play that attacked the institution of serfdom. His *Literary Reveries* (1834), an essay on Russian literature in which he reflected the romantic nationalism of Friedrich von Schelling, established his reputation. In 1838 and 1839 he edited the *Observer* in Moscow, but in the latter year he moved to St. Petersburg. Belinsky's mature work, defending sociological realism in literature, was influenced by the ideas of Ludwig Feuerbach and the French humanitarian socialists.

In 1847 he wrote a famous letter to Gogol denouncing the defense of church and state authority in Gogol's *Selected Passages from Correspondence with My Friends* (1847). Belinsky died in St. Petersburg on June 7, 1848.

BELISARIUS (505?–565 A.D.), bel-ə-sâr'ē-əs, was perhaps the greatest general of the Byzantine empire. He was born at Germane, Illyria (in present-day Yugoslavia). Having served in the imperial bodyguard, he was made a general in 529 by the emperor Justinian I (reigned 527–565) and placed in command of the Byzantine army, then engaged in a war with Persia. At Daras in 530 his outnumbered troops triumphed over the Persians, but at Callinicum, Syria, in the following year, his forces were beaten in the only battle that Belisarius was destined to lose. Though not in disfavor, he was then recalled to Constantinople, and there, in 532, he suppressed the Nika Revolt, which would have cost Justinian his throne.

During 533–534, Belisarius, with only 16,000 men, reconquered from the Vandals most of North Africa west of Egypt, accomplishing this in two victories. He captured the Vandal king, Gelimer, and enormous treasure besides. His triumph in Constantinople was the first held there and the first conferred on any Roman subject since the reign of Tiberius (14–37 A. D.). A medal was struck in his honor, and he was named consul in 535.

Emboldened to regain other lost provinces, Justinian moved to take Italy from the Ostrogoths and placed 8,000 men under Belisarius for this task. In 535 Belisarius recovered Sicily, and in 536 all Italy south of Rome fell to him. He entered Rome in December 536, withstanding the enemy's siege until it was raised in March 538. Continuing northward, Belisarius captured Ravenna in 540 and then returned to Constantinople with booty and the captive king and queen of the Ostrogoths. But he was accorded a cool reception by Justinian, who transferred him to the eastern front in order to meet the renewed menace from Persia. By 542, Belisarius had repulsed the Persians.

Meanwhile, the Ostrogoths had reconquered much of Italy, and, in 544, Belisarius was again shifted to the Italian peninsula. This time, because of inadequate forces, few reinforcements, and the paltry funds available to pay his troops, his progress was slow. Discouraged, he at last requested recall in 548, leaving the partial recovery of Italy to others. After his return to Constantinople he lived in retirement for a decade, emerging to repel Bulgar raiders in 559.

Belisarius was accused of conspiring against Justinian in 563 but was absolved by the emperor. He died on March 13, 565, probably in Constantinople.

There are stories that tell of the general's final disgrace and poverty, of his blinding and imprisonment by Justinian, and of his last days as a beggar on the Constantinople streets. Historians contemporary with Belisarius, however, are silent about these stories, and most modern scholars stigmatize them as inventions by later romancers.

P. R. COLEMAN-NORTON, *Princeton University*

BELIVEAU, be-lē-vō', **Jean** (1931–   ), Canadian hockey player, who was the highest scoring center in the history of the National Hockey League when he retired in 1971 after 18 years with the Montreal Canadiens. His total of 507 goals ranked fourth among all players, and he stood second in career points with 1,219. He was elected to the hockey hall of fame in 1972.

Beliveau was born in Trois Rivières, Quebec, on Aug. 31, 1931. A record-breaking "amateur" (he was salaried) with the Quebec Aces, the 6-foot 3-inch center joined the Canadiens in 1953. Netting a record 47 goals for a center, and with 41 assists, he led the league in scoring in the 1955–1956 season with 88 points. In the Stanley Cup playoffs that season, he equaled Maurice Richard's record of 12 goals. Beliveau was chosen All-Star center ten times and voted the Hart Trophy as the most valuable player twice.

BILL BRADDOCK, *New York "Times"*

BELIZE, bə-lēz', is a British colony on the Caribbean shore of Central America. Formerly known as British Honduras, it officially adopted the name Belize in June 1973. It is bounded on the north by Yucatán, Mexico, and on the west and south by Guatemala. It has a population (1971 est.) of 124,000 and an area of 8,867 square miles (22,965 sq km).

The most probable derivation of the name Belize is from the French word *balise,* meaning "beacon." It is also possible that it derives from the mispronunciation of the name of a Scottish pirate, Peter Wallace (or Wallis), or from a Mayan Indian root.

Most of the people of Belize live on or near the coast. More than one fourth of the population reside in the city of Belize, the colony's largest city, onetime capital, and its principal port. Historically, the colony's commercial and political center, Belize City suffered major hurricane damage in 1931 and in 1961. This led to the building of a new, inland capital, Belmopan, 50 miles (80 km) southwest of Belize City. Government offices began moving to the new city in 1970, and it became the official capital of the colony in 1972.

The People. The population of Belize is made up of several different cultural communities. The largest group is the Creoles (Belizeans of African descent), some black, some mixed, who speak an English Creole dialect closely related to that of Jamaica. Indeed, various aspects of Creole culture in Belize can be identified with the culture of the British West Indies. The Creole community traces its ancestry to the slaves brought to Belize by the English in the 17th and 18th centuries. Though they were converted to Protestantism during the period of slavery, the Creoles are now largely Roman Catholic.

The next largest cultural community is composed of Spanish-speaking peoples, mostly Maya Indians. Small groups of Maya in southern and central Belize migrated from Guatemala. Much larger groups in the North, near the Hondo River, came from Mexican Yucatán.

Of the smaller groups, one of the most distinctive is the Black Carib, derived principally from unions between Carib Indians and Africans. Post–World War II arrivals include Mennonites from Mexico and Canada, who form an industrious group.

The Land. Traditional lumbering activities have resulted in extensive deforestation, and much of the landscape might be described as pine-

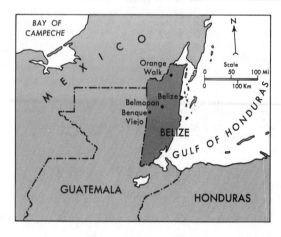

BAY OF CAMPECHE

MEXICO

Orange Walk

Belmopan
Benque Viejo
Belize

BELIZE

GUATEMALA

GULF OF HONDURAS

HONDURAS

Scale
0   50   100 Mi
0   100 Km

N

palm savanna. Many rivers cross the colony, draining both the Petén hinterland of Guatemala, which lies landlocked to the west, and the Maya Mountains in southern Belize where the maximum elevation, in the Cockscomb range, is less than 3,700 feet (1,100 meters). Some areas have fertile soils, others have been leached by rainfall, and still others are virtually useless because of swamps or mountains.

The many cays, or islets, along the coast are related to an extensive reef system, and clear water usually prevails, making the area attractive for commercial and sport fishing.

The Economy. Belize was once one of the major producers of logwood (*Haematoxylon campechianum*), an extremely important source of dyestuff until modern chemical dyes were developed, and of mahogany, the "noble wood" long basic to ship construction and fine furniture. New market conditions and a history of uncontrolled forest exploitation make the prospects of the forest industry inadequate to the economic needs of the country. Fortunately, a high potential for agriculture and fishing has been demonstrated. Citrus fruit, bananas, and some sugarcane are grown for export, and maize, rice, and beans are major subsistence crops.

A hopeful sign for the underpopulated colony was the organization in the 1960's of Belize Sugar Industries, Ltd., a firm that planned to produce cane sugar by automated means.

Districts and Towns. Belize is divided into six political districts: Belize, Corozal, Orange Walk, Toledo, Stann Creek, and Cayo. With the exception of Toledo, each has as its headquarters a town of the same name. Except for Belize, district populations are small. There are perhaps a hundred small villages that tend to cluster near the headquarters towns. Benque Viejo, a border town in Cayo district, is important as the gateway to Guatemala.

Government. Under the constitution that went into effect in 1964, the British governor remained in charge of foreign affairs, defense, and the civil service. However, the right to make internal policy was transferred to a cabinet appointed by the premier (the leader of the majority party). The constitution provided for a bicameral legislature. The Senate's eight members were appointed by the governor upon the advice of the premier, the opposition, and others. The House of Representatives had 18 elective members, eight representing heavily populated Belize district and two representing each of the other five districts. The cabinet and premier were made strictly responsible to the legislature, which could remove them through votes of no confidence.

History. European settlement of British Honduras began in the 17th century with the economic activities of English seamen in the western Caribbean. Yucatán and the Bay of Honduras were favorite haunts of the buccaneers who preyed on Spanish shipping bound to or from Mexico and the Isthmus of Panama. By the mid-1600's, estuaries along the shore of what is now known as Belize were occupied intermittently by English seamen.

Gradually a settlement at the mouth of the Belize River became most significant, producing logwood, an extraordinarily profitable commodity in Europe. Spain consistently opposed such activities by non-Spanish entrepreneurs. The British were driven out a number of times but always returned. By 1770, mahogany export had become more important than logwood, and African slaves brought in for woodcutting exceeded the white population in number. Driven out one last time (1779–1783), the British returned with the limited protection of the Anglo-Spanish treaties of 1783 and 1786, which allowed British exploitation of the forests. Though usually under the eye of a British superintendent from Jamaica, after 1786 the settlement at Belize essentially governed itself through public meetings and elected magistrates, who had both executive and judicial functions. In the early 19th century, merchant traders in Belize took advantage of Spain's troubles to trade very profitably with Mexico and Central America.

In 1862, British Honduras was finally declared a colony, with a lieutenant governor subordinate to the governor of Jamaica. By this time the area had fallen into an economic depression, which was to continue to the end of the 19th century. A legislative assembly established in 1853 was abolished at its own request in 1871, and British Honduras thus became a crown colony, forfeiting internal autonomy. In 1884 it separated politically from Jamaica, and the lieutenant governor was raised to governor.

Though British Honduras experienced a decade of relative prosperity before World War I, its economy remained undeveloped in the 20th century. Serious developmental efforts began only after the hurricane of 1931.

Major constitutional reforms, looking to the goal of independence, began to be instituted in 1954. The constitution of 1964, which granted internal autonomy, was widely felt to presage the granting of independence to the colony by Britain. In 1972 tensions were renewed between Belize and its neighbor Guatemala, which, for many years has claimed the colony as an inheritance from Spain.

WAYNE M. CLEGERN
Colorado State University

BELIZE CITY, bə-lēz′, is a city in the British colony of Belize (formerly British Honduras). The colony's former capital, it is its chief port. It is situated on the Caribbean Sea at the mouth of the Belize River, about 860 miles (1,384 km) south of New Orleans. The town extends along both sides of the river.

Belize City is a trading center for lumber, chicle, coconuts, rice, and citrus fruits. Among its industries are sawmilling and rice hulling. An airport, Stanley Field, supplies commercial service overseas and within Belize.

Tradition says that a Scottish pirate, Peter Wallace, founded a settlement near the present site in 1603. However, the town apparently dates from a settlement that he made in 1638. After the British capture of Jamaica in 1655, the early settlers were joined by disbanded soldiers. Spain, regarding the British as intruders in the area, launched frequent attacks against the settlement. The British gradually established themselves, nonetheless, and British Honduras was declared a British colony in 1862.

Often struck by severe hurricanes, the city was nearly destroyed in 1931 and in 1961. After the 1961 hurricane, a new capital, Belmopan, was built 50 miles (80 km) southwest of Belize City. It became the official capital in 1972. See also BELIZE.

RICHARD WEBB
Formerly, British Information Services, New York

BELL, Alexander Graham (1847–1922), Scottish-American scientist, who invented the telephone. Bell was born in Edinburgh, Scotland, on March 3, 1847. Until the age of ten, he was taught at home by his mother, Eliza Grace Symonds Bell, an accomplished portrait painter and musician. After graduating from the Edinburgh Royal High School he went to London for over a year with his grandfather, Alexander Bell, who was widely known as a lecturer and speech teacher. From him young Bell gained seriousness of purpose and a zeal for studying and teaching the mechanics of speech and sound. At the age of 16 he became a student teacher in Elgin, Scotland, but returned home for a year at Edinburgh University before continuing his teaching in Elgin and then in Bath, England. In 1867 he became an assistant to his father, Alexander Melville Bell, who originated the phonetic "visible speech" system for teaching the deaf and who had moved to London in 1865 to continue the grandfather's work.

From 1868 to 1870 young Bell was a partner in his father's practice in London. During his father's absence on a lecture tour in America, he carried on the full program of teaching deaf-born children to speak and of giving speech lessons at various schools. In addition, he found time to take university lecture courses in several subjects, including anatomy and physiology. About this time his brothers—one older, one younger—died of tuberculosis, and his own health was impaired by his heavy schedule. The bereaved father gave up London practice and lectureships and moved the family to Canada in August 1870. Living in the country near Brantford, Ontario, young Bell soon regained vigorous health.

In April 1871, at 24, the young man began teaching "visible speech" to instructors of the deaf in and near Boston. The following year he opened a special class of vocal physiology in Boston, and from 1873 to 1877 he was professor of vocal physiology at Boston University. In this period he met Gardiner Greene Hubbard, a wealthy lawyer whose daughter Mabel had been made deaf by scarlet fever at the age of four. Mabel became Bell's pupil, and the two fell in love. She inspired him through years of exhausting, extra-hours' work on several inventions—a period climaxed by the American telephone patent granted him March 7, 1876, and their marriage the following year.

Inventions. Bell's early experiments and inventions based on his expert knowledge of sound led inevitably to his telephone achievement. As a boy he had constructed a speaking automaton using rubber, cotton, and bellows to simulate the human organs of speech, and had manipulated his pet Skye terrier's throat to turn cooperative growls into words. Later, he obtained a human ear from a medical school and made a workable phonautograph by attaching a thin straw to the ear drum so that it would trace vocal sound patterns on smoked glass. In 1874 he was granted patents on a multiple, or harmonic, telegraph for sending two or more messages simultaneously over the same wire. If this brilliant invention had been immediately successful, Bell might not have driven himself through months of experimentation to the hot June day in 1875 when he accidentally produced electric speech for a split second. The accident completed his telephone concept: that the varying sound of the human voice can be made to vary the intensity of a cur-

THE BETTMANN ARCHIVE

Alexander Graham Bell (1847–1922)

rent of electricity, which varying current can in turn be reproduced as speech.

The newly patented telephone was a late and obscure entry at the Centennial Exposition in Philadelphia in June 1876. In dramatic, last-minute consideration by the judges it won a gold medal award and the accompanying public acclaim. Two months later the first long-distance voice message traveled eight miles over telegraph wires from Paris to Brantford, Ontario, and before the end of the year the "long distance" had been increased to 143 miles. The 29-year-old inventor had reached the threshold of the first financial independence he had known.

In 1880, following 18 months abroad, Bell patented his photophone, in which selenium crystals and thin mirrors enabled him to apply his telephone principle in transmitting words on a beam of light. He thus achieved the first wireless transmission of speech. Though limited to a short distance, the device embodied principles linking it to the development of many later marvels of science, including the photoelectric cell and the transistor. That same year France awarded its Volta Prize to Bell for his invention of the telephone, and a few months later made him an officer in the French Legion of Honor. Bell used the award money to establish the Volta Laboratory in Washington, D. C. He and his Volta associates produced and patented the graphophone and wax recording cylinders, commercially successful improvements on Thomas A. Edison's first phonograph and cylinders of metal foil. They also experimented with flat disc records. When the graphophone patents were later sold, Bell gave his entire $200,000 share for perpetuation of the Volta Bureau, which he had formed for all conceivable kinds of research on deafness.

President James A. Garfield's assassination and lingering death, July-September 1881, stimulated Bell's development of two telephonic devices for locating metallic masses in the human body. One was used widely before the advent of the X-ray method.

Bell became a citizen of the United States and a resident of Washington, D. C., in 1882. In 1885 he took his family on vacation to the Bras d'Or Lakes of Nova Scotia's Cape Breton Island. Returning there a year later, they selected the verdant headland on Baddeck Bay that became the inventor's spring-to-autumn retreat for 35 years. There his laboratory turned out hydrofoil speedboats, seawater converting units, complicated electrical equipment, and several early devices that anticipated and later ones that implemented aerial locomotion by man. His man-carrying kites employed tetrahedral design for strength and lift. His three-bladed propellers set in metal rings and launched vertically presaged the helicopter rotor. Some of these he powered mechanically, others by rockets at the blade ends, still others by feeding alcohol vapor through tubes to the blade tips to create jet thrust—a half century before the jet age. Glenn H. Curtiss was one of Bell's young associates in his Aerial Experiment Association early in the 20th century.

Having learned at some cost the importance of documenting his ideas, Bell described his Baddeck researches at length in notebooks with simple but dynamic sketches. These records have become a fascinating part of the collection of Bell models, inventions, photographs, and memorabilia on view in the Alexander Graham Bell Museum built by the Canadian government at Baddeck and officially opened on Aug. 18, 1956.

Societies and Honors. Bell was a founding member of the National Geographic Society in 1888 and its president from 1898 to 1903. He initiated plans for popularizing geography that were successfully carried out and amplified by his son-in-law Gilbert Grosvenor and his grandson Melville Bell Grosvenor. In 1898, Bell was appointed a regent of the Smithsonian Institution and became a prime mover in bringing the remains of founder James Smithson from Genoa, Italy, to Washington for burial in 1904.

The range of Bell's practical and scientific experimentation seemed inexhaustible. In his study in his Washington home near the White House, he arranged a special air-cooling system for hot days. He also directed experiments in sheep breeding for many years, developing a multinippled strain that produced twin or triplet lambs in more than half of the births. He served Clarke School for the Deaf at Northampton, Mass., for 51 years as teacher, consultant, researcher, and president of the board. Brantford, Canada, commemorated his work on speech transmission while he was resident there with a massive granite and bronze memorial (1917).

His native city of Edinburgh elected him an honorary burgess and guild brother in 1920. Among organizations awarding medals to Bell were the Society of Arts, London; the Franklin Institute, Philadelphia; the Royal Cornwall Polytechnic Society; the American Institute of Electrical Engineers; and the French International Exposition of 1878. He died in Baddeck, Nova Scotia, on Aug. 2, 1922.

See also TELEPHONE—*Development of Telephone Technology.*

MELVILLE BELL GROSVENOR
National Geographic Society

Further Reading: Burlingame, Roger, *Out of Silence into Sound* (Macmillan, N. Y., 1964); Costain, Thomas B., *Chord of Steel* (Doubleday 1960); Mackenzie, Catherine Dunlop, *Alexander Graham Bell* (Houghton 1928); Stevenson, Orlando J., *Talking Wire: The Story of Alexander Graham Bell* (Messner 1947).

BELL, Alexander Melville (1819–1905), Scottish-American educator. He was born in Edinburgh on March 1, 1819. He studied at the University of Edinburgh under his father, an authority on phonetics and speech, and served as a lecturer in elocution there from 1843 to 1865. He then taught at the University of London until he moved to Canada in 1870 to be a lecturer in philology at Queen's College, Kingston, Ontario.

In 1881, Bell moved to Washington, D. C., where he pioneered in using his "visible speech" method for the education of deaf mutes. His system proved successful in teaching the deaf and dumb to speak. It included the development of graphic diagrams, which were symbolic alphabetical characters representing the positions and motions of the vocal organs. Bell, who became an American citizen in 1897, won a reputation as an authority on phonetics, elocution, and stenography. He died in Washington on Aug. 7, 1905. He was the father of Alexander Graham Bell, the inventor of the telephone.

RICHARD E. GROSS, *Stanford University*

BELL, Andrew (1753–1832), Scottish educator and clergyman. He was born at St. Andrews on March 27, 1753, and was educated at St. Andrews University. He moved to Virginia as a tutor in a planter's family in 1774. He returned to Britain in 1781 and was subsequently ordained in the Church of England. In 1787 he went to India as an army chaplain, and in 1789 he was appointed superintendent of a school for orphaned children of European soldiers, established by the East India Company at Madras.

Unable to find qualified teachers, Bell was forced to conduct his school with the help of student aides. He first taught older and more able students a set of basic lessons. These students then taught the same material to the other pupils. The lessons were planned so that essentials were presented as clearly as possible. While the system was mechanical and uncreative, it did provide a way in which large numbers of children could be taught economically.

In 1797, Bell returned to England for reasons of health. He then published a pamphlet on his method of "mutual tuition." Entitled *An Experiment in Education Made at the Male Asylum of Madras*, it gained wide circulation in Britain. Meanwhile, his ideas were spread, in a modified form, by Joseph Lancaster, who had founded a society to promote similar schools along nonsectarian lines. Ultimately, Lancaster's name became more famous than Bell's in connection with what came to be called monitorial schools, especially as they were popularized in the United States in the early 1800's. See MONITORIAL SYSTEM.

In 1807 the Church of England decided to institute schools on Bell's pattern, and he was called from his rector's work in Dorset to organize the system. In 1811 he became superintendent of the new National Society for Promoting the Education of the Poor in the Practices of the Established Church. Charity schools for this purpose spread throughout the country.

In 1819, Bell was made a prebendary of Westminster. During his later years he wrote several treatises on education, and gave his fortune for educational purposes. He died at Cheltenham on Jan. 27, 1832, and was buried in Westminster Abbey.

RICHARD E. GROSS, *Stanford University*

BELL, Bert (1894–1959), American football commissioner, who was largely responsible for the growth of professional football.

DeBenneville Bell was born in Philadelphia, Pa., on Feb. 25, 1894. He played quarterback at the University of Pennsylvania in 1916 and 1917, and was team captain in 1919 after military service in France. From 1920 to 1931, he served successively as backfield coach at his alma mater and Temple University. He was co-owner of the Philadelphia Eagles (1933–1945) and then of the Pittsburgh Steelers in the struggling years of the professional game.

Elected National Football League commissioner in 1946, Bell increased the authority of his office, forged a cohesive league, and arranged a merger with the All America Conference. He effected a highly successful television broadcast of league games. He was a charter member of the National Professional Football Hall of Fame. Bell died of a heart attack on Oct. 11, 1959, while attending a league game in Philadelphia.

BILL BRADDOCK, *New York "Times"*

BELL, Sir Charles (1774–1842), Scottish anatomist and surgeon, noted for his work on the nervous system. He was born in Edinburgh and was educated at the University of Edinburgh. In 1807 he discovered that the anterior spinal nerve roots are motor in function, while the posterior spinal nerve roots are sensory (Bell's Law). This discovery, substantiated by François Magendie (q.v.), was an important contribution to an understanding of the nervous system. Bell also did work on respiratory and facial nerves. Later, he taught at several English hospitals and colleges. Honored by the Royal Society and knighted, he returned to Scotland and served as professor of surgery at the University of Edinburgh from 1836 to 1842. He died near Worcester, England, on April 28, 1842.

Bell's writings include *Anatomy of Expression* (1806), *System of Comparative Surgery* (1807), *Anatomy of the Brain* (1811), and the *Nervous System of the Human Body* (1830).

BELL, Clive (1881–1964), English art critic. He was born in East Shefford, Berkshire, on Sept. 16, 1881, and was educated at Cambridge, where, according to Desmond MacCarthy, "he seemed to live, half with the rich sporting-set, and half with the intellectuals." In his 20's he was associated with the writers and artists known popularly as the "Bloomsbury group," a coterie of friends rather than a formal artistic movement. The group included E.M. Forster, Lytton Strachey, John Maynard Keynes, Duncan Grant, and Vanessa and Virginia Stephen, daughters of Sir Leslie Stephen. Bell married Vanessa, a gifted painter, in 1907. His sister-in-law became the well-known writer Virginia Woolf. Bell died in London on Sept. 18, 1964.

Bell attained fame when his *Art* (1914), with its battle cry of "significant form," was published. In *Since Cézanne* (1922) he argued the case for the modern "isms," discarding subject matter and realism as relevant criteria in judging works of art. These books were of the utmost historical importance in gaining acceptance for modern ·art.

Bell's other publications include *Landmarks in Nineteenth-Century Painting* (1927) and *An Account of French Painting* (1931). *Old Friends,* his reminiscences, was published in 1956.

BELL, Eric Temple (1883–1960), Scottish-American mathematician and author, noted for his books popularizing mathematics and its history. His best-known works are *Men of Mathematics* (1937); *The Magic of Numbers* (1946); and *Mathematics, Queen and Servant of Science* (1951). Bell also wrote two standard textbooks, *Algebraic Arithmetic* (1927) and *The Development of Mathematics* (1940). Under the name of *John Taine* he wrote science-fiction novels, including *The Crystal Horde* (1952).

Bell was born in Aberdeen, Scotland, on Feb. 7, 1883. He emigrated to the United States in 1902, graduated from Stanford University in 1904, and took a Ph.D. in mathematics at Columbia in 1912. He taught mathematics at the University of Washington (1921–1926) and at the California Institute of Technology (1926–1960). He died in Watsonville, Calif., on Dec. 20, 1960.

BELL, Gertrude Margaret Lowthian (1868–1926), English traveler, archaeologist, and government official. She was born in Durham County, England, on July 14, 1868. After completing her education at Oxford Unviersity in 1888, she began a series of travels which included a voyage around the world, long visits in Rumania and Iran, and several seasons of mountain climbing in the Alps, where she set a number of records. Her strong enthusiasm for the Middle East determined the course of her life. She learned Persian, and in 1899 spent a winter in Jerusalem studying Arabic. Her courage and daring were demonstrated on extensive Middle Eastern travels, some of which are recorded in her *Safar Nameh* (1894; reprinted as *Persian Pictures,* 1928) and *Amurath to Amurath* (1911). Her description of Syria, *The Desert and the Sown* (1907), is considered one of the finest works in its field. On architecture she wrote *The Thousand and One Churches* (1909), in collaboration with W.M. Ramsay, and *The Palace and Mosque of Ukhaidir* (1914).

During World War I, Gertrude Bell offered her services to the British government and was assigned in 1915 to the Arab Intelligence Bureau, where her knowledge of Middle Eastern geography, languages, and personalities was of immense value. Personally esteemed by many Arab leaders, she was especially useful in liaison work between them and the British. She went to Baghdad in 1917 as adviser to the British civil administrator of the Mesopotamian region (Iraq) and retained that position after the war. Believing strongly in political independence for the Arabs, she was influential in establishing the modern state of Iraq and in placing Faisal I on the throne in 1921. The rest of her life was devoted to the foundation and direction of the national archaeological museum in Baghdad. She died in Baghdad on July 11/12, 1926.

Further Reading: Bell, Lady Florence, ed., *The Letters of Gertrude Bell,* 2 vols. (London 1927); Bodley, Ronald, and Hearst, Lorna, *Gertrude Bell* (New York 1940).

BELL, Henry (1767–1830), Scottish engineer. He was born at Torphichen Mill, Linlithgowshire, Scotland. Apprenticed in the millwright's trade, he worked in London under the engineer John Rennie. He returned to Scotland in 1790 and eventually settled in Hellensburgh on the Firth of Clyde, where he worked as an engineer and carried out his own mechanical projects.

In January 1812, Bell put his first practical

steamboat, the *Comet*, into service between Glasgow and Greenock. A ship of about 30 tons, it was driven by a three-horsepower engine and reached a speed of seven miles ((11 km) per hour. Since Robert Fulton had realized a similar project with the *Clermont* in the United States as early as 1807, Bell's ship was not the first to be powered by steam; however, he is credited with the introduction of steam river navigation in Europe. Bell derived little profit from his achievement, but the trustees of the river Clyde awarded him a pension in his old age. He died in Helensburgh on Nov. 14, 1830.

BELL, bel, **Henry Haywood** (1808–1868), American naval officer. He was born in North Carolina, on April 13, 1808. Appointed a midshipman in the United States Navy in 1823, he later served on the *Grampus* (1828–1829), which was engaged in clearing the Cuban coast of pirates.

Although he was a Southerner, he remained loyal to the Union during the Civil War, and in 1862 he was appointed fleet captain in the West Gulf Squadron under David Farragut. In April of that year he commanded one of the three naval divisions that captured New Orleans. He took command of the East India Squadron with the rank of commodore in 1865 and was made rear admiral the following year. On Jan. 11, 1868, after he had resigned his command, he was drowned when his barge capsized in the Yodo River near Osaka, Japan.

BELL, bel, **John** (1797–1869), American lawyer and legislator. He was born near Nashville, Tenn., on Feb. 15, 1797. After graduating in 1814, at the age of 17, from Cumberland College (now George Peabody College for Teachers), he practiced law in Franklin, Tenn., and then in Nashville, where he became a leading lawyer. In 1827 he began his 14-year tenure in the U.S. House of Representatives. At first, Bell was a Jacksonian Democrat, but he broke with Jackson during the controversy over the Bank of the United States and eventually consolidated his position as leader of the Whigs in Tennessee. He was speaker of the House in 1834. In 1841, Bell became secretary of war in the cabinet of President William Henry Harrison. He held this post for only a few months, resigning after Harrison's death when the new president, John Tyler, withdrew from the Whig party.

From 1847 to 1859, during the growing sectional strife over the slavery issue, Bell was a U.S. senator from Tennessee. Consistently conservative, he supported slavery but placed national unity first and rejected the views of both Northern and Southern extremists. He affirmed the right of Congress to prohibit slavery in the territories and opposed the Kansas-Nebraska Bill (1854), predicting the violence that passage of the bill actually brought.

With the demise of the Whig party, Bell ran for president in 1860 as the candidate of the Constitutional Union party, but he carried only his own state of Tennessee and two other border states. Early in President Lincoln's administration, Bell tried to effect a compromise to save the Union, but after Fort Sumter was fired upon, he advised his state to resist a Northern invasion. He took no active part in the Civil War. Bell died in Stewart County, Tenn. on Sept. 10, 1869.

Further Reading: Parks, Joseph H., *John Bell of Tennessee* (Baton Rouge, La., 1950).

BELL, bel, **John** (1691–1780), Scottish traveler. He was born in Antermony, Stirlingshire, and obtained a medical education. He went to St. Petersburg (now Leningrad) in 1714, entered the service of Czar Peter I, and was sent as medical attendant on an embassy to Persia.

On his return to the Russian capital in 1718 he obtained an appointment on another embassy to China. He returned to Russia in 1722, again visited Persia, and in 1737 went to Constantinople on his final mission for Russia. In about 1746 he went back to Scotland with his Russian wife. He died in Antermony on July 1, 1780. Bell wrote *Travels from St. Petersburg in Russia to Various Parts of Asia* (2 vols., 1763).

BELL, bel, **John Joy** (1871–1934), Scottish novelist. He was born in Glasgow on May 7, 1871, and was educated at Glasgow University. His first novel, *The Noah's Ark,* was published in 1898. In 1902 he achieved success with *Wee Macgreegor,* the first of three highly popular novels featuring the colorful character Macgreegor. This series, which also includes *Wee Macgreegor Again* (1904) and *Wee Macgreegor Enlists* (1915), consists of episodic sketches of humble Scottish life and makes extensive use of the broad Glasgow dialect. Bell died in Aberdeen on Nov. 14, 1934.

Bell's other works include *Mistress M'Leerie* (1903), *Pennycook's Boy* (1905), *Oh Christina* (1909), *Clyde Songs* (1911), *Courtin' Christina* (1913), *A Kingdom of Dreams* (1914), *Johnny Pryde* (1918), *Secret Cards* (1922), *The Invisible Net* (1924), *Mr. Craw* (1924), *Exit Mrs. M'Leerie* (1927), and *Laird of Glenlaggan* (1931).

BELL, bel, **Marie** (1900–   ), French actress and theater manager. She was born in Bordeaux on Dec. 23, 1900. Her real name was *Marie de Bellon.* She studied at the drama conservatories of Bordeaux and Paris and won a first prize in acting at the latter.

In 1921 she joined the Comédie Française, and with that company she played many of the young heroines of the French classic repertoire. Her most notable triumphs were in Racine's *Phèdre* and *Bérénice,* Molière's *Le misanthrope,* Henri Becque's *Les corbeaux,* Rostand's *Cyrano de Bergerac,* and Hugo's *Ruy Blas.* One of her most celebrated performances was in an abridged version of Claudel's *Le soulier de satin* in 1943.

Mme. Bell left the Comédie Française to form the Compagnie de Marie Bell in 1953. In 1955, as a guest with Jean-Louis Barrault's company, she was hailed for her magisterial Clytemnestra in the *Oresteia.* With her own company she played in *La bonne soupe* (1958), *Le balcon* (1960), and *La voleuse de Londres* (1960). She appeared with her company in New York in 1963 in performances of *Phèdre* and *Bérénice.*

Mme. Bell also played in more than 30 motion pictures. These included two classic films of the 1930's— *Le grand jeu* (1934) and *Carnet de bal* (1937).

BELL, bel, is a residential and industrial city in southwestern California, in Los Angeles County. It is situated 6 miles (9.6 km) south of downtown Los Angeles. Bell has iron and steel plants, and manufactures automobile and aircraft parts. Incorporated in 1927, Bell is governed by a city manager. Population: 21,836.

J. ALLAN CASH, FROM RAPHO GUILLUMETTE

BELLS of West and East: (l.) bells in the Church of the Nativity, Bethlehem, Palestine; (r.) a religious bell in China.

EWING GALLOWAY

BELL, a hollow, cup-shaped object of resonant material that rings when struck at the lip. The word "bell" is derived from Anglo-Saxon *bellan,* meaning "to bellow." The word in other languages is *cloche* (French), *Glocke* (German), *klok* (Dutch), *cloc* (Old Irish), and *clocca* (Middle Latin). The English cognate of these words is *clock,* a timepiece that rings the hour. The science and art of bells and bell ringing is *campanology,* a word derived from Italian *campana,* meaning "bell."

The form of the musical bell of today was established in Western Europe around 1400. It is suspended from a yoke by a crown attached to the head; its shoulders are quite square; and its graceful inward curving waist ends at a counter curve called the sound bow, where the clapper strikes just above the mouth.

Origin and Development. The history of the ringing bell begins with the Bronze Age. Staves, dishes, pots of hammered metal and cast bronze all have a certain ring, and it may easily be conceived that the more or less resonant tone of such vessels was known and utilized as a form of amusement and as a signal.

Primitive ringing objects appeared some time before this. Extremely small, not much more than mere rattles, they were fashioned from hammered plate and strung together on the same thong to hit upon each other when shaken. When the rattle was fashioned with an open mouth and made to sound by a pebble attached to the inside, the bell originated.

Bells divide themselves into two distinct types: the Occidental and the Oriental. The Oriental bell has the shape of an elongated pot or barrel with walls of approximately the same

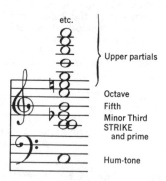

Tonal series of a perfectly tuned carillon bell.

thickness throughout. Suspended from a wooden truss at the entrance to a temple, it is struck on the outside by a wooden mallet.

The bell's development in the West is based on the form of a cup, such as a Roman "tintinnabulum," a hemispherical gong with a loop at the top through which the finger could be inserted and sounded by a clapper hung on the inside. Many such bells have been found throughout southern and western Europe, dating from the early Christian era. During the Middle Ages the Irish monks, introducing Christianity to all Europe, used hammered iron bells at consecration of the Mass and as a warning in case of fire, flood, or invasion. These iron-plate bells, 8 to 12 inches (20–30 cm) high and riveted together at the corners, are common to the civilized Western world of that time.

Around the 9th century a collar near the lip of the bronze bell was added to protect it against cracking under the blow of the clapper, or when set down after ringing. From the addition of the collar developed the sound bow, to which the Western bell owes its tone. As the early communities expanded, signals were needed which carried farther, and bells became increasingly larger. The loop at the top was fashioned into a rudimentary crown by which thongs or primitive iron fastenings secured it to a wooden stock. The early bells were rung by hand by being

A carillon bell, showing shape and location of overtones.

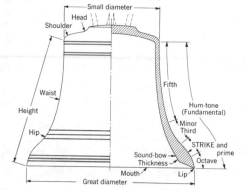

rocked to and fro, and no matter what their weight, the latter motion has sounded them since they have hung in towers.

During the early Middle Ages bells were convex and long-waisted, but in the 13th century they made a definite break with all primitive forms. The waist became concave and approached the form known so well today. The reinforced lip grew into a definite bulge, later developing into the sound bow, that part which produces the main tone of the bell. During the Middle Ages there were also series of small bells, today known as "hand bells," hung from a common staff and played by one or two hammers.

In Flanders, Holland, and some parts of Switzerland and Germany, bells were cast with purity of tone in mind, and as early as the 15th century bells of excellent tonal quality were being made. In Flanders at this time the complex tonal pattern of a bell was understood, and if a bell did not produce an acceptable tone when cast, tuning was attempted by removing metal from the inside.

To announce the presence of someone at the gate, to inform the populace of the passing hours, to warn in times of danger, to call together to worship or govern, to mark a birth or a death, to celebrate victory or mourn defeat—these are but a few of the many uses found for bells.

Design and Construction. Formerly made by rule of thumb, today a perfect bell is the result of many sciences and crafts. The diameter is calculated according to the note it must sound; this measurement governs the shoulder width, the height and thickness. Both outer and inner profiles are designed, cut out of sheet metal and fastened to a "strickleboard." The resulting template, mounted to turn about a vertical axis, will generate the shape of the bell. An inner mold, or "core," is built of brick, covered with clay and shaped by the template. The outer mold, or "cope," is fashioned by first making a "dummy" bell in clay, the size of the one to be cast, and covering it with a thin coat of beeswax. Ornamentations and inscriptions of wax are now added and the waxen bell is covered with thin coats of a mixture of clay, egg-white, and dung, carefully applied with a camel's-hair brush. Gradually the mold is built up of ever-thickening applications of clay. A fire bakes the clay and melts the wax in an operation called the "lost-wax" process. The cope is lifted off the dummy, placed over the core and sealed tight. The space between them receives the molten bell metal, an alloy of four parts copper to one part tin. When the casting has cooled, the mold is removed, and the bell is cleaned and prepared for tuning.

As in all musical sound, the tone of a bell is composed of many overtones. Nature gave the string, the pipe, and the reed a harmonic series of tones: the fundamental, octave, fifth, double octave, major and minor thirds (for a full discussion of harmonics see HARMONICS; HARMONIC ANAYLISIS). Pianos and organs are tuned by pitching only the fundamental; all other tones fall into place. This is not true of a bell. Man had first to develop a form that would embrace a pleasing series of overtones, then tune each to correct pitch before the bell could be considered true. The partials of a tuned bell are the fundamental or hum tone; the strike tone an octave above the fundamental; the minor third, fifth, and octave above the strike tone; a major third, fifth, and another octave; and so on. It is the

EWING GALLOWAY

WORLD'S LARGEST BELL, the Czar Kolokol in the Kremlin, Moscow, weighs over 220 tons.

minor third that distinguishes the bell from all other musical instruments, and gives it its plaintiveness and its appeal.

Famous Bells. Certainly the largest bell is the Czar Kolokol in the Kremlin in Moscow. Cast in 1733, it is 272 inches (690.9 cm) across the mouth, and weighs 443,772 pounds (201,472.5 kg). When first rung it was broken due to a fault in the casting and its tone has never been heard. The Bell of Mingoon in Burma weighs 201,600 pounds (91,526.4 kg) and measures 203 inches (515.6 cm) in diameter. A second bell in Moscow, cast in 1819, weighs 127,350 pounds (57,816.9 kg). The heaviest tuned bell in the world, the St. Peter Bell in Cologne Cathedral, a low C, weighs 25 tons (22.7 metric tons). The Bourdon of the Rockefeller Carillon in Riverside Church, New York City, cast in 1930, weighs 18½ tons (16.8 metric tons). The Wanamaker Bell of the John Wanamaker store, Philadelphia, Pa., rings a low D; it was cast in 1926 and weighs 38,640 pounds (17,542.6 kg). London's "Great Paul" in the Cathedral of St. Paul weighs 37,483 pounds (17,017.2 kg).

Other famous bells include Big Ben in the Clock Tower of the British Houses of Parliament, Westminster, London, and the great bell of the Cathedral of Notre Dame, Paris. The great bells of the cathedral of York, England; of St. Peter's in Vatican City; and the bell known as "Great Tom," in Christ Church College, Oxford University, Oxford, England, have all played their part in history and literature.

Modern Uses. Because of their greater carrying power, whistles and sirens have superseded bells in some civic functions. Clocks, nevertheless, still strike the hour, and church bells still ring for service. The use of the bell as a signal has never been far removed from its use as a musical instrument. Today, more than ever before, bells must be pleasing musically, and it is in their use in chimes and carillons that they have found their highest expression.

See also CHIMES AND CARILLONS; GLOCKENSPIEL; RESONANCE.

ARTHUR L. BIGELOW, *Princeton University*

Bibliography
Coleman, Satis N., *Bells, Their History, Legends, Making, and Uses* (Chicago 1928).
Morris, Ernest, *Bells of All Nations* (London 1951).
Raven, John J., *The Bells of England* (London 1906).
Tyack, George S., *A Book About Bells* (London 1898).

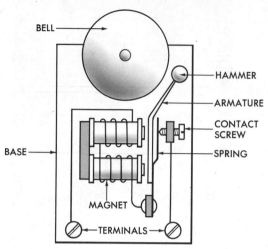

BELL

HAMMER

ARMATURE

CONTACT SCREW

SPRING

BASE

MAGNET

TERMINALS

THE ELECTRIC BELL is a common device for making an audible signal. The hammer repeatedly strikes the gong and moves away as the circuit is opened and closed.

BELL, Electric, a common device that is used for audible signaling. Examples of applications are doorbells, burglar alarms, and fire alarms.

The electric bell operates when an electrical circuit is completed—for example, by pushing a button. Current then flows to an electromagnet, causing it to produce a magnetic field. The electromagnet attracts an iron or steel arm that is attached to a flat spring at one fixed end and to a small hammer at the free end. As the arm moves toward the electromagnet, the hammer hits against a gong to cause a sound. However, this movement of the arm also opens the circuit, causing a loss of the magnetic field. Therefore, the electromagnet no longer attracts the arm. The spring then moves the arm back to its initial, closed-circuit position. The electromagnet is energized again, and the sequence of events is repeated so long as the pushbutton is depressed.

The power for a doorbell is obtained from a transformer that reduces the house line voltage from 120 volts a-c to 6 or 8 volts a-c. In other applications, such as alarm systems, 1.5- or 6-volt batteries are used as the power source.
MARVIN BIERMAN, *RCA Institutes Inc.*

BELL, BOOK, AND CANDLE, elements in the ritual of excommunication used in the medieval Roman Catholic Church. The bishop read the decree from the book of episcopal ritual; lighted candles were thrown down, symbolizing a fall from grace; and a bell was tolled.

BELL GARDENS, an urban community in California, is a suburb of Los Angeles in an industrial and residential district of Los Angeles County, 8 miles (13 km) southeast of the Los Angeles civic center. The community lies in the triangle formed by the confluence of the Los Angeles River and the Rio Hondo Channel. The Long Beach Freeway parallels the river on the community's western border. Bell Gardens adjoins the city of Bell on the west and Downey on the southeast. This area southeast of Los Angeles has developed rapidly since World War II with the manufacture of automotive and aircraft parts. The community of Bell Gardens is unincorporated. Population: 29,308.

BELL ROCK is a sunken reef of sandstone in the North Sea, off the east coast of Scotland. It also is known as the *Inchcape* (or *Inch Cape*) *Rock*. It lies opposite the Firth of Tay about 12 miles (19 km) southeast of Arbroath. The reef is about 700 yards (640 meters) long. At certain tides much of it is uncovered and is dangerous to navigation. Many vessels have been wrecked on it. A lighthouse was built on the reef in 1807–1812 by Robert Stevenson, father of novelist Robert Louis Stevenson.

According to legend, an abbot of Arbroath fixed a bell to the reef. The sound of the bell, as it swung with the tide, warned mariners of the danger. A pirate cut the bell from the rock, and on a later voyage his ship was wrecked there. Robert Southey based his ballad *The Inch Cape Rock* on this legend.

BELL TELEPHONE LABORATORIES is one of the largest research organizations in the United States, established in 1925 as a subsidiary of American Telephone and Telegraph Company. About one third of its employees are trained scientists or engineers. Its chief mission is to carry on research and development for the Bell System in 17 centers situated in 9 states. Ten branches are also maintained for liaison with Western Electric, equipment maker for the Bell System. Bell men also carry on testing projects for the U.S. Department of Defense at White Sands Missile Range, N. Mex., and on Kwajalein atoll in the Pacific.

Bell Laboratories has pioneered in many discoveries, including the Bell solar battery, power source for earth satellites; laser beams; two-way transoceanic radiotelephone; coaxial cables; microwave radio relay systems; transoceanic telephone cable; and direct distance dialing. Telstar, the communications satellite, was a Bell achievement. In the 1960's, Bell worked with laser beams to study the nature of the moon's surface; produced two-color pictures by "capturing" light waves on a special photographic plate, thus foreshadowing lensless photography; and advanced transmission speed experimentally by sending in 15 minutes the information in a 10,000-volume library. Bell scientists have received many honors, including two Nobel prizes.
COURTNEY ROBERT HALL
Author, "History of American Industrial Science"

BELLA VISTA, bel´ə vis´tə, a resort in northwest Arkansas, is situated in the scenic Ozarks of Benton County. Besides facilities for water sports, the chief attractions are a natural spring and a large cavern.

BELLADONNA, bel-ə-don´ə, is a perennial poisonous disagreeable-smelling herb, also known as *deadly nightshade.* It is native to southern Europe and India but now is grown extensively throughout the world. Belladonna is an erect herb, normally about 3 feet (1 meter) high. It has oval-shaped, pointed leaves that may be from 3 to 6 inches (7 to 15 cm) long and reddish or purplish bell-shaped flowers. It also has shiny black, sweetish, poisonous berries. The plant contains a red sap. Belladonna (*Atropa belladonna*) is a member of the nightshade family, Solanaceae.

Belladonna has several uses in medicine. The red sap enlarges the pupils of the eye and is used frequently by oculists. An important antispasmodic pain-relieving drug, atropine, is obtained from the roots and leaves of the plant.

The name "belladonna" means "beautiful woman." This name was probably given to the plant because of the use of the red belladonna sap as a cosmetic to enlarge the pupils of the eye and give the eyes a bright and glistening appearance.

BELLADONNA LILY. See AMARYLLIDACEAE.

BELLAIRE, bə-lâr', a city in eastern Ohio, is in Belmont County, on the Ohio River, 26 miles (42 km) south of Steubenville. A bridge crosses the river to West Virginia. Bellaire is in a region that is rich in coal, clay, and limestone. There are dairy, truck, and poultry farms outside the city. Bellaire produces glass and caskets.

Bellaire was settled in the 1790's and platted in 1836. It was incorporated as a village in 1858 and chartered as a city in 1874. It has a mayor-council government. Population: 9,655.

BELLAIRE, bə-lâr', is a city in eastern Texas, in Harris County, 8 miles (13 km) southwest of Houston, of which it is a residential suburb. There are oil research establishments here. Government is by council and city manager. Population: 19,009.

BELLAMONT, bel'əmont, **1st Earl of** (1636–1701), British colonial administrator in America. His name is also spelled *Bellomont*. Born *Richard Coote*, he was the son of an Irish peer, but he sat in the English Parliament from 1688 to 1695 after his marriage to a landed Englishwoman. He supported the accession of William III and was rewarded with an Irish earldom in 1689.

For his integrity more than for his gifts, Lord Bellamont was appointed governor of New York, Massachusetts, and New Hampshire in 1697, with instructions to suppress the illegal trade and piracy rampant in those colonies. He arrived in New York in May 1699 and, during his brief administration, succeeded in reimposing a semblance of law and order in mercantile affairs. However, his choice of Captain Kidd as his principal weapon against piracy proved a mistake (see KIDD, WILLIAM). Bellamont also farsightedly encouraged development of better relations with the Indians. He died in New York City on March 5, 1701.

BELLAMY, bel'ə-mē, **Edward** (1850–1898), American author. He was born in Chicopee Falls, Mass., on March 26, 1850. He traveled abroad in 1868, spending most of his time in urban slum areas of Germany, where he was deeply impressed by what he described later as "the extent and consequences of Man's inhumanity to man." He returned to the United States after a year and studied law. Although he received his law degree, he chose a career in journalism, working briefly for the New York *Evening Post*, then returning to Massachusetts, where he became editor of the Springfield *Union*. In 1880 he and his brother Charles founded the Springfield *Daily News*. In that year he also published his first novel, *Dr. Heidenhoff's Process*. His second novel, *Mrs. Ludington's Sister* (1884), was a romance about psychic phenomena.

In 1888, Bellamy published his most important novel, *Looking Backward*. This work, reflecting his strongly socialistic opinions, attempted to offer a solution for the problems of

Edward Bellamy

(1850–1898)

BROWN BROTHERS

political and social inequality. The wide interest that the novel generated resulted in the establishment of numerous "Bellamy clubs," organized to discuss the social implications of Bellamy's thought. Perhaps the most interesting thing about *Looking Backward* for the 20th century reader is its predictions of such inventions as radio, motion pictures, and television. Though the book was condemned by many of Bellamy's contemporaries, it was praised by William Dean Howells as "intensely democratic."

In 1891, Bellamy founded the *New Nation*, a short-lived magazine that served as an organ for his social and political views. In 1891 he published his last novel, *Equality*, a highly polemical work that had little success. He died at Chicopee Falls on May 28, 1898.

Bibliography

Aaron, Daniel, "Edward Bellamy: Village Utopian" in *Men of Good Hope: A Story of American Progressives* (New York 1951).

Bowman, Sylvia E., *Year 2000: A Critical Biography of Edward Bellamy* (New York 1958).

Bowman, Sylvia E., and others, *Edward Bellamy Abroad: An American Prophet's Influence* (New York 1962).

Morgan, Arthur E., *The Philosophy of Edward Bellamy* (New York 1945).

Taylor, Walter F., "Edward Bellamy" in *The Economic Novel in America* (Chapel Hill, N.C., 1942).

BELLARMINE, bel'är-mĭn, **Saint Robert** (1542–1621), cardinal and doctor of the Roman Catholic Church. Born *Roberto Francesco Romulus Bellarmino* on Oct. 4, 1542, at Montepulciano, Italy, he was a nephew of Pope Marcellus II. He entered the Society of Jesus in 1560, and was ordained in 1570. At this time he was appointed the first Jesuit professor of philosophy at the University of Louvain (now in Belgium). His lectures on the *Summa* of St. Thomas Aquinas were effective, though disguised, refutations of Baius' popular but heretical teachings on grace. (See BAIUS, MICHAEL.)

In 1576, Bellarmine was awarded the newly created Chair of Controversial Theology at the University of Rome, and in 1590 he became director of the Roman College. There he encountered the young Aloysius Gonzaga, whose cause for canonization he later championed. Elevated to cardinal by Pope Clement VIII in 1598, Bellarmine was, except for two years as archbishop of Capua, unusually active in the affairs of the Holy See. He died in Rome, pauperized by his own zealous charity, on Sept. 17, 1621. He was canonized in 1930, and declared a doctor of the church in 1931. His feast is May 13.

Bellarmine's writings demonstrate a knowledge, not only of Catholic dogma, but of Protestant theology. His incisive four-volume *Disputations on the Controversies of the Christian Faith* systematized the controversies on dogma of his time. This work was such an effective argument against the Protestant *Magdeburg Centuries* that several universities established chairs precisely for the purpose of attacking the *Disputations.*

Bellarmine also served on the committee to revise the Sistine Vulgate Bible, and wrote the preface. On a commission from Clement VIII, he prepared two catechisms that are still in use. In 1610 he published *Of Papal Power* as a reply to Richard Barclay's tract *Of the King and Royal Power,* which upheld the divine right of kings. Bellarmine not only denied the theory of divine right, but also declared that secular power can be bestowed by the people alone. This theory implied that papal authority was restricted. Pope Sixtus V rejoined by placing the book on the Index and the French Parlement publicly burned the work.

Bellarmine's writings are so numerous that a reprinting of his works, compiled (1870–74), by J. Fèvre required 12 volumes (*Opera omnia ex editione Veneta,* New York 1965).

BELLAY, be-lā′, **Joachim du** (c. 1522–1560), French poet, called the "French Ovid" and "prince of the sonnet." He was born of a noble family in Liré, France. A scholar well acquainted with the Latin poets, he joined Pierre de Ronsard, Jean Dorat, Étienne Jodelle, Remi Belleau, and Jean Antoine de Baïf in forming the Pléiade, a society dedicated to the elevation of the French language to the level of the classical tongues. Bellay's first contribution to the group was *Défense et illustration de la langue française* (1549). He served as secretary to his cousin, Jean Cardinal du Bellay, and in 1553 accompanied him to Rome. The trip served as inspiration for two collections of verse, *Les antiquités de Rome* (1558) and *Les regrets* (1559). Bellay's verse is strongly personal, often reflecting an attitude of melancholy. He died in Bordeaux.

BELLBIRD, a loud-voiced white bird (*Procnias nivea*) found in northern South America. The bird has a bell-like voice that makes it conspicuous in the tropical forests. It has white plumage and a black fleshy outgrowth from the region of the head. The female is smaller than the male and has some protective green coloring. The name "bellbird" is sometimes given also to other birds with bell-like voices and to some Australian and New Zealand honey-eating birds.

BELLE DAME SANS MERCI, bel dàm säN mer-sē′, a ballad written by John Keats (q.v.) in 1819 and first published in 1820. The poem is a dreamlike evocation of a *femme fatale,* who, after enticing a knight with her charms, disappears mysteriously while the knight lies asleep dreaming of death. The knight awakens to find himself alone "On the cold hill's side." The work, though open to many interpretations, is probably an autobiographical allusion to Keats' hopeless love for Fanny Brawne.

BELLE FOURCHE, bel fŏ̄orsh, a city in western South Dakota, at the northern edge of the Black Hills, is the seat of Butte County. It is situated at the junction of the Belle Fourche and Redwater rivers, 50 miles (80 km) northwest of Rapid City. The geographical center of the United States (including Alaska and Hawaii) is about 25 miles (40 km) to the north. Sheep and cattle are raised in the region, and Belle Fourche has wool markets and stockyards. It mines bentonite and manufactures bricks. Belle Fourche Reservoir, nearby, supplies water to the surrounding valleys. Since 1918 the Black Hills Roundup has been an annual event. Belle Fourche was founded in 1890 and incorporated as a city in 1903. Population: 4,236.

BELLE GLADE, bel glăd, is an industrial and commercial city in southeastern Florida, in Palm Beach county. It is on Lake Okeechobee, 75 miles (120 km) northwest of Miami. Situated in a rich truck-garden area, it is a center for the shipment of winter vegetables to northern markets. The surrounding country also produces large quantities of sugarcane, and cattle raising is becoming an important industry. Belle Glade's manufactured products include fertilizers, cattle feed, crates, and wooden boxes. There is excellent fishing in Lake Okeechobee, and there is good hunting in the vicinity.

The first permanent settlers arrived in 1912. In 1928, the year Belle Glade was incorporated, the town was devastated by a hurricane, and hundreds of its inhabitants were killed. The city has since grown considerably. Government is by council and manager. Population: 15,949.

BELLE-ÎLE, be-lēl′, a French island off the southern coast of Brittany, is in the Bay of Biscay, 8 miles (13 km) southwest of the Quiberon Peninsula. It is part of Morbihan department. *Belle-Île-en-Mer,* as it is sometimes called, has an area of 32 square miles (83 sq km). Le Palais, a fortified port, is the principal town. Fishing and farming are the main occupations, along with tourism in summer. Population: (1962) 4,647.

BELLE-ISLE, be-lēl′, **Duke de** (1684–1761), French army officer and government official. He was born *Charles Louis Auguste Fouquet* at Villefranche-de-Rouergue, France on Sept. 22, 1684. He was a grandson of the French superintendent of finance Nicolas Fouquet. After entering the army, he distinguished himself during the War of the Spanish Succession (1701–1714). He also fought in the Spanish War of 1718–1719, and in the War of the Polish Succession (1733–1735). In 1736, Louis XV appointed him governor of Metz and olso promoted him to marshal of France.

He was given command of the French armies at the outset of the War of the Austrian Succession (1740–1748). He took Prague by assault and, when forced to withdraw from Eger when Prussia made a separate peace, he carried out the retreat with remarkable skill. From 1746 to 1748 he was in command of the French troops who repelled the invasion of southern France by forces of Maria Teresa. In 1748 he was created duke and a peer of France.

As minister of war from 1757 to 1760 (during the Seven Years' War), Belle-Isle introduced many reforms in army administration. He died at Versailles on Jan. 26, 1761.

BELLE ISLE, Strait of, bel-īl′, a narrow channel separating Newfoundland and Labrador. It is about 35 miles (56 km) long and 10 to 15 miles (16 to 24 km) wide. The Strait of Belle Isle is the more northerly of two channels connecting the Gulf of St. Lawrence with the Atlantic Ocean. It affords the most direct route for shipping from Europe to the St. Lawrence, but is often choked with ice in winter and spring.

At the Atlantic entrance to the strait is the island of Belle Isle, which has an area of 15 square miles (39 sq km). There is a lighthouse at the southern end of the entrance.

BELLEAU, be-lō′, **Remi** (1528–1577), French poet, who was one of the Pléiade, a group of seven poets led by Pierre de Ronsard. His first name is also spelled *Rémy.*

Belleau was born in Nogent-le-Rotrou. He served as a soldier and then as tutor at the court of Lorraine. His descriptive and pastoral sonnets, odes, eclogues, and hymns were published in three collections: *Petites inventions* (1556), which includes his most famous lyric *Avril; Bergerie* (1565 and 1572), his most notable work; and *Amour et nouveaux échanges de pierres précieuses* (1576). He also translated classical works and wrote the comedy *La reconnue* (1577). He died in Paris on March 6, 1577.

BELLEAU WOOD, bel′ō, a small forest near Château Thierry, France, was the scene of the second battle between American and German forces in World War I. Five German divisions were attacked by the 4th Marine Brigade on June 6, 1918, and again on June 9, and the woods were taken after approximately three weeks of bitter fighting.

The American forces lost 285 officers and 7,585 men killed, wounded, or missing, and they captured 24 guns and 1,654 prisoners.

The battlefield was dedicated in 1923 as a permanent memorial to the American officers and men who lost their lives there. Subsequently the French government changed the name of the wood to Bois de la Brigade Marine.

BELLEFONTAINE, bel-foun′tən, is an industrial and agricultural city of west central Ohio, and the seat of Logan County. It is situated about 56 miles (90 km) northwest of Columbus. Just east of the city is Campbell Hill, the highest point in the state, 1,550 feet (472 meters) high. Indian Lake, a summer resort, is 12 miles (19 km) northwest of the city.

The chief industries of Bellefontaine are manufacturing, printing, and dairying. Leading manufactured products are electric motors and circuit breakers, aluminum extrusions, sleeve bearings, power tools, and food. Corn, wheat, soybeans, cattle, and hogs are raised in the area.

Originally the site of a Shawnee Indian village, it was occupied by white pioneers in 1818. Bellefontaine, named for the many springs in the vicinity, was incorporated in 1835. The first concrete street in the United States was laid here in 1891. Government is by mayor and council. Population: 11,255.

BELLEROPHON, bə-ler′ə-fon, in Greek legend, was the son of Glaucus, king of Corinth, and the grandson of Sisyphus. Originally named *Hipponous,* he became known as Bellerophon, meaning "killer of Belleros," for having accidentally killed a relative, perhaps a brother, of that name. He fled to Argos, where Anteia, the wife of King Proetus, fell in love with him. When he spurned her, she accused him of trying to seduce her. Because Bellerophon was a guest in his court, Proetus would not kill him. Instead, he sent Bellerophon to Iobates, king of Lycia, bearing a sealed letter demanding his execution. Iobates sent Bellerophon to destroy the firebreathing dragon Chimera. On his way, with the aid of Athena (Minerva), Bellerophon captured and tamed the winged horse Pegasus, and by riding above the dragon he was able to kill it with bow and arrows.

Sent again into danger by Iobates, Bellerophon defeated the Solymi and Amazons. He was accepted by Iobates, whose daughter he married. Given an exalted position, Bellerophon grew overly proud, and in attempting to ride Pegasus to Olympus, he was made to fall to earth. Crippled and blind, he spent the rest of his days as a pathetic wanderer and misanthrope.

BELLEVILLE, bel′vil, an industrial and mining city in southwestern Illinois, is the seat of St. Clair County. It is situated 14 miles (22.5 km) southeast of East St. Louis, in a coal-mining region. The chief manufactures are stoves and allied products, stencil machines, and beer. Other products include boilers, industrial furnaces, brick, caskets, and clothing.

Belleville Junior College is situated in the city. The National Shrine of Our Lady of the Snows, visited by more than a million pilgrims each year, is 5 miles (8 km) to the northeast. Scott Air Force Base, the home of the Military Air Transport Service and the Air Force Communications Service, is 6 miles (9.6 km) east.

Belleville was platted about 1814 and incorporated in 1819. The discovery of coal in the vicinity in 1828 attracted a host of German immigrants, and the city was nicknamed "Dutch Town." Neighborhood customs still reflect the early German influence. Belleville has a mayor-council government. Population: 41,699.

BELLEVILLE, bel′vil, is an industrial city in northeastern New Jersey, in Essex County. It is situated on the Passaic River 4 miles (6.4 km) north of Newark. Manufactures include wire products, leather goods, machinery, fire extinguishing equipment, water purifiers, electrical equipment, tools, and toiletries. Notable among the city's old buildings is the Reformed Dutch Church, built in 1725.

Belleville was settled by the Dutch about 1680 and was commonly called the "Second River Section" of Newark until it was separated from the city in 1839. The first low-pressure steam engine built in the United States, designed by John Stevens, was constructed in Belleville. It was used in 1798 to power an experimental steamboat on the Passaic River. Incorporated in 1910, the city has a council-manager form of government. Population: 34,643.

BELLEVILLE, bel′vil, is an industrial city in southeastern Ontario, Canada, and is the seat of Hastings County. It is situated at the mouth of the Moira River, on the north shore of the Bay of Quinte of Lake Ontario, 110 miles (176 km) southwest of Ottawa. Its manufactures include mining and papermaking machinery, boilers, foundry products, cement products, planing mill products, cheese, plywood, jewelry, paints, and electric welding apparatus. Belleville is also the center of a productive agricultural area.

The city is the site of Albert College, a co-educational boarding school affiliated with the University of Toronto and Victoria University. The Hastings County Museum and the Ontario School for the Deaf are situated in Belleville. The community was founded as Meyer's Creek in 1790. Its name was changed to Belleville when it was platted in 1816. It was incorporated as a city in 1877. Population: 35,128.

BELLEVUE, bel'vū, a village in eastern Nebraska is in Sarpy County, on the Missouri River, about 10 miles (16 km) south of Omaha. Founded as a fur-trading and riverboat post in 1823, it is the oldest permanent settlement in the state. Baptist missionaries arrived here in 1833, and Presbyterians built a mission in 1848. Bellevue was the capital of Nebraska Territory in 1854. It was incorporated in 1855 and was the county seat until 1875. Nearby is Offutt Air Force Base, headquarters of the Strategic Air Command. Government is by mayor and council. Population: 19,449.

BELLEVUE, bel'vū, a borough in western Pennsylvania, in Allegheny County, is a residential suburb of Pittsburgh. It is 10 miles (16 km) northwest of Pittsburgh, on the Ohio River.

In the Bayne Memorial Park is an ancient elm, the "Lone Sentinel," said to be 350 years old; the specimen is carefully preserved. Bellevue was settled in 1802 and incorporated as a borough in 1867. Government is by mayor and council. Population: 11,586.

BELLEVUE, bel'vū, a city in western Washington, is in King County. It is situated on the eastern shore of Lake Washington, 2 miles (3 km) east of Seattle, of which it is a residential suburb. Bellevue manufactures electrical and electronic components, control systems, and prefabricated homes; other industries include printing, binding, and engraving.

Bellevue was settled in the 1880's. The completion of the Floating Bridge across Lake Washington in 1941, providing easy access to Seattle, stimulated the community's growth. A second bridge across the lake, the Evergreen Point Floating Bridge, was completed in 1963. The city has a council-manager form of government. Population: 61,102.

BELLFLOWER, bel'flou-ər, is a city in southwestern California, in Los Angeles County. It is situated 14 miles (22 km) southeast of downtown Los Angeles. Bellflower is the retail center of a region in which poultry and dairy cattle are raised. Products of its industries include grains and feeds, machine tools, boilers, automatic screw machine parts, steel pipe, and plastic aprons.

The first settlers of the site of Bellflower were Dutch farmers. The community was established in 1906. It was named *Somerset* when the post office was created in 1909, but the post office department rejected the name because it duplicated the names of other post offices. The new name was derived from an orchard of bellflower apples on the ranch where the town was laid out. Bellflower was incorporated as a city in 1957. Government is by council-manager. Population: 51,454.

Bellflower (*Campanula latifolia*)

BELLFLOWER is a popular name given to many species of herbs prized for their brightly colored, often bell-shaped, flowers. These small herbs of the genus *Campanula* are found throughout the Northern Hemisphere, from lowlands to mountains. The flowers may be white, yellow, blue, or purple. The different species range in height from 2 or 3 inches (5–7.5 cm) to the unusually tall, 6-foot (1.8-meter) *C. americana*, an annual found in shady areas in eastern regions of North America.

Bellflowers are popular pot plants and often are found in flower and rock gardens; the hardy east European tussock bellflower (*C. carpatica*) is an especially good rock garden plant. The perennial *C. latifolia*, a rather tall plant with large, toothed leaves and large, purplish blue flowers, is an important species that has many varieties. Another favorite is the strong, stiff willow bell flower (*C. persicifolia*). Other noteworthy species include the Canterbury bellflower (*C. medium*), the chimney bellflower (*C. pyramidalis*), and the harebell or bluebell of Scotland (*C. rotundifolia*). The roots and leaves of one species—the rampion (*C. rapunculus*)—sometimes are used in salads.

BELLI, bel'lē, **Giuseppe Gioacchino** (1791–1863), Italian poet, who was one of the first realists in Italian literature. His most famous works are sonnets that present a lively picture of the life and language of the common people of Rome during the early 19th century.

Belli was born in Rome on Sept. 10, 1791. His marriage to a rich widow in 1816 made it possible for him to devote most of his time to poetry. He held several minor offices in the papal government, and died in Rome on Dec. 21, 1863.

Belli's more than 2,000 sonnets were written between 1830 and 1839. These vivid, irreverent poems express a satirical distrust of convention, papal rule, the bureaucracy of government, and the ritualism of the church. Belli later repented the poems' irreverence, and tried to prevent their further circulation, but they were published posthumously by his son in 1865. Shortly before his death, Belli published a beautiful translation of the Latin Breviary into Italian.

BELLIGERENCY, bə-lij′ə-rən-sē. In the legal sense, belligerency means war, or a situation of conflict by armed force in which all the participants are legally equal in respect to the hostilities. This implies that all belligerents are bound to observe the laws of war, are free to exercise war powers, and are entitled to expect from other states observance of the law of neutrality. While properly applied to international hostilities of this type, the term is more commonly applied to such hostilities arising from civil strife. Belligerency is to be distinguished from piracy and brigandage, from insurgency, and from aggression. The initiators of these types of hostility are not regarded as legally equal to the national or international forces engaged in their suppression.

See also BLOCKADE; INSURRECTION; INTERNATIONAL LAW; NEUTRALITY; PRIVATEER; WAR; WAR, LAWS OF.

BELLIGERENT, bə-lij′ə-rənt, a nation or a large section of a nation engaged in carrying on war. On the outbreak of war between sovereign powers the rights and duties of the warring nations in regard both to each other and to neutral powers are clearly defined by international law. The first general stipulation is that neutral powers must be formally notified of the existence of a state of war. International law and custom demand that noncombatants be protected and that barbarous weapons or methods be avoided.

An insurgent state cannot claim the recognition of belligerency from a neutral state as a matter of right. The grant of belligerent rights to insurgents imposes certain obligations on them, such as the observance of the rules of international law both in regard to their opponents and to neutrals. Its advantages lie in the moral support gained from recognition by neutrals, giving it the right to negotiate loans and placing its commanders and their troops under the protection of the laws of war.

BELLINGHAM, bel′ing-əm, **Richard** (c. 1592–1672), colonial governor of Massachusetts. He was born in Boston, Lincolnshire, England. One of the patentees of the Massachusetts Bay Company charter, he emigrated to Boston in 1634. The following year he was elected deputy governor of the colony (a post he also held in 1640, 1653, and from 1655 to 1665).

In 1641, Bellingham was elected governor over his adversary John · Winthrop. His tenure was marked by disputes with other officials, notably over his irregular, self-performed second marriage. Prosecuted for this act, he refused to leave the bench to stand trial and thus escaped punishment. He was governor again in 1654 and from 1665 until his death. During the latter period he successfully defended the authority of the colonial charter against a royal commission sent from England. Bellingham died in Massachusetts on Dec. 7, 1672. His will, leaving a large estate for the eventual use of the clergy, was the subject of litigation for more than a century.

BELLINGHAM, bel′ing-ham, a town in eastern Massachusetts, is in Norfolk County, 28 miles (45 km) southwest of Boston. It is situated in an agricultural region. The town was named for Richard Bellingham, colonial governor of Massachusetts in the mid-17th century. The town was settled about 1713 and incorporated in 1719. Population: 13,967.

BELLINGHAM, bel′ing-əm, a city in northwestern Washington, is the seat of Whatcom County. It is a port of entry situated on Bellingham Bay of Puget Sound, 80 miles (129 km) north of Seattle and 18 miles (29 km) south of the Canadian border. It has one of the largest natural harbors in the area, with dockage facilities accommodating the largest vessels.

Bellingham is in an agricultural region where dairying, poultry raising, truck farming, and fruit growing are important commercial activities. The city's principal manufactures include lumber and wood products, paper and pulp, and processed foods. Fishing is an important industry, and the city is a supply point for salmon canneries.

Bellingham is the site of Western Washington State College, one of the state's largest educational institutions. The home of George Edward Pickett, Confederate general in the American Civil War, is maintained in Bellingham as a memorial. Pickett was commandant of Fort Bellingham in the 1850's, during a time of tension between Great Britain and the United States over possession of the San Juan Islands at the northern end of Puget Sound.

To the east of the city is Mount Baker, a popular skiing and summer recreational area. A nearby feature is the Peace Arch at Blaine on the Canadian border, commemorating more than a century and a half of peace between Canada and the United States.

The first settlement on the site of the present city was made in 1852 by Henry Roeder, who built a sawmill on what is now Whatcom Creek. Bellingham was formed in 1903 through the union of four separate towns in the area. The city government is headed by a mayor and council. Population: 39,375.

BELLINGSHAUSEN, bel′ingz-hou-zən, **Fabian Gottlieb von** (1778–1852), Russian naval officer and Antarctic explorer. He was born on the island of Saaremaa, in Estonia, on Sept. 9, 1778. Graduating from the Russian naval academy at Kronshtadt, he became an officer in 1797. In 1819 he was assigned by Emperor Alexander I to the command of two ships for the purpose of conducting an exploring expedition into the southern polar regions. He succeeded in penetrating the Antarctic Circle to latitude 70° S, discovering and naming Alexander I Island and Peter I Island. The expedition returned to Kronshtadt on Aug. 5, 1821.

Seven years later Bellingshausen so distinguished himself in the naval operations against the Turks at Varna, Bulgaria, that he was made a vice admiral and was given command of the Russian Baltic fleet. Later he became military governor of Kronshtadt. A narrative of his polar explorations was published in St. Petersburg in 1831 and was translated into English for the Hakluyt Society as *Voyage of Captain Bellingshausen to the Antarctic Seas, 1819–1821* (1945). He died at Kronshtadt on Jan. 13, 1852.

BELLINGSHAUSEN SEA, bel′ingz-hou-zən, in Antarctica, a part of the South Pacific Ocean, extending westward from Alexander Island, at the base of the Antarctic Peninsula, to Thurston Peninsula. It was named for Adm. Fabian Gottlieb von Bellingshausen, a Russian explorer, who in 1821 discovered Alexander I Island and Peter I Island; the latter is in the middle of the sea.

GIOVANNI BELLINI'S masterpiece, *Allegory of Purgatory* (about 1480), in the Uffizi Gallery, Florence.

BELLINI, bä-lē′nē, a family of Italian painters of the early Renaissance, including Jacopo Bellini (c. 1400–c. 1470) and his sons Gentile (c. 1429–1507) and Giovanni (c. 1430–1516). The turning point from the late Gothic to the Renaissance style in Venetian painting can be seen in comparing the work of Jacopo with the paintings of his sons. Giovanni Bellini was the greatest painter of the three and, indeed, the greatest Venetian painter of the 15th century. In his warm, rich color and facile handling of oil paint the Venetian style of the Renaissance first reached maturity.

JACOPO BELLINI was born in Venice about 1400, and died there in 1470 or 1471. He studied under Gentile da Fabriano and may have worked with him in Florence from 1423 to 1425. He was also influenced by Francesco Squarcione, a Paduan painter whose adopted son and greatest pupil, Andrea Mantegna, married Bellini's daughter in 1453.

Jacopo's work is known chiefly through two of his sketchbooks, one in the British Museum, London, and the other in the Louvre, Paris. The drawings in the earlier sketchbook, in London, are unmistakably Gothic in style. The sketchbook in the Louvre, however, shows an incipient interest in such typically Renaissance subjects as perspective, landscape, and classical antiquity.

Almost all of Jacopo's paintings have been destroyed or lost. Only four signed paintings survive: a *Christ on the Cross*, in the museum at Verona, and three paintings of the *Virgin and Child*—one in the Tadini Gallery, Lovere, Italy, another in the Venice Academy, and the third in the Brera Gallery, Milan. The Byzantine influence, which was very strong in pre-Renaissance Venice, is apparent in the half-length, frontal pose of the Madonna in these paintings. Most of the unsigned paintings attributed to Jacopo are also portraits of the Virgin and Child. A fresco that he painted for the cathedral at Verona was destroyed in the 18th century.

GENTILE BELLINI, the elder son of Jacopo, was born in Venice, probably in 1429. He studied painting under his father and collaborated with him and his brother Giovanni on a series of 18 paintings representing the life of the Virgin. Although subsequently overshadowed by his brother, Gentile was a worthy Venetian painter, particularly in the fields of narrative painting and portraits. Among his earliest signed works are a portrait of the poet Lorenzo Giustiniani (1465) at the Venice Academy and the organ shutters (1466) for St. Mark's Cathedral in Venice. The quality of stiffness in these works is reminiscent of the painting of the Paduan school, particularly as exemplified by Squarcione.

In 1474, Gentile was commissioned to restore the paintings and the decorations in the palace of the doge at Venice. During the next few years his reputation as a portrait painter grew, and he was chosen to go to the court of the Turkish sultan, Mohammed II, at Constantinople (now Istanbul), when that ruler requested the Venetians to lend him a good artist. During his stay in Constantinople (1479–1480), Gentile painted several pictures of Mohammed and was well rewarded. Works surviving from his stay in Constantinople include an attributed portrait of the sultan, now at the National Gallery, London.

During Gentile's visit to Turkey, his brother Giovanni occupied his post at the doge's palace, and when Gentile returned to Venice, the two brothers painted in the palace a brilliant series of frescoes depicting the conflict (1159–1176) between Pope Alexander III and Emperor Frederick I Barbarossa. This work was completely destroyed by fire in 1577.

Among the most remarkable of Gentile's surviving works are the *Procession of the Relic of the Cross in the Piazza of San Marco* (1496) and *The Miracle of the True Cross* (1501), both at Venice Academy, and *St. Mark Preaching in Alexandria*, at the Brera Gallery in Milan. *St. Mark Preaching* was commissioned in 1505, and scholars feel that its richer, warmer quality, as compared with that of the other two works, must be credited to Giovanni, who completed the work after Gentile's death in Venice, in February 1507. The intricacy of the architecture and the accuracy of the perspective in the backgrounds of these paintings suggest the influence of Jacopo, whose sketchbooks show his interest in architecture. But Gentile, the painter of portraits, emerges in the work done on the processions and crowds thronging the streets and squares. Many carefully painted likenesses of Gentile's fellow citizens are in the panorama; some critics have suggested that one of Bellini's purposes in doing these paintings was to show certain Venetians of the day in the streets of their city. Although Gentile skillfully arranged crowds in his paintings, his inclusion of formal portraits in a scenic canvas gives an over-all impression of stiffness.

GIOVANNI BELLINI, born in Venice about 1430, was probably an illegitimate son of Jacopo. In addition to being the most important Venetian painter of the 15th century, he was a master of two famous pupils, Il Giorgione and Titian. Giovanni Bellini was the first to realize fully the warmth and the modulation that can be achieved in oil painting and that later became so distinguishing a mark of the Venetian school. He also gave a new importance to landscape in his paintings and was the first to master the rich, glowing color that came to characterize the Venetian school of the Renaissance. Unlike later Venetian painters, most of his works were of religious subjects.

He was an assistant in his father's studio until he was about 30 years old. The painting of his earliest period shows the influence of his brother-in-law, Andrea Mantegna, a leader of the Paduan school of painting until his departure for Mantua about 1460. Characteristic of the Paduan school was a severity and stiffness that is especially noticeable in the hard, straight lines of fabrics and draperies. A typical work by Giovanni in this tradition is the *Agony in the Garden,* in the National Gallery, London, probably done in 1464. The painting of the sunrise in the background foreshadows this artist's later skill with light effects. The *Pietà,* at Rimini, painted about 1470, is less harsh. Both pictures show great depth of religious feeling.

From about 1470, Giovanni's style became more independent, and he gradually developed the warm color and light that came to be associated with Venetian art. The great *Coronation of the Virgin,* at Pesaro, done in the 1470's, shows him in almost full possession of his personal style, as does *The Transfiguration,* in the National Museum, Naples.

Sometime during the decade 1470–1480, Giovanni learned the process of oil painting, his work until this time having been done in tempera. The oil medium was peculiarly suited to the talents of Giovanni and later Venetian painters. Fresco and tempera, with their tendency toward severity, were well adapted to the draughtsmen of Florence, but the warmth of light and color that could be achieved in oils was of the greatest value to the sumptuous art of Venice. The Venetian spirit and sense of beauty and color are apparent in Giovanni's celebrated *Allegory of Purgatory,* painted sometime during the 1480's and now in the Uffizi Gallery, Florence. The painting may have been inspired by Guillaume de Digulleville's poem *Le*

GENTILE BELLINI is believed to be the painter of this portrait of Mohammed II, sultan of Turkey, in National Gallery collection, London.

ALINARI; ART REFERENCE BUREAU

pèlerinage de l'âme (The Pilgrimage of the Soul), written in 1355. In the *Allegory,* Giovanni Bellini brought the painting of landscape and atmospheric effects to unprecedented heights. Other paintings of the artist's middle period are such important works as the altarpieces of San Giobbe, of San Zaccharia, and of San Francesco della Vigna, all in Venice, and the altarpiece of Santa Corona at Vicenza.

From 1488 to 1505, Giovanni was constantly engaged on decorations and restorations in the ducal palace at Venice, all later destroyed by fire. He was appointed state painter to the republic of Venice on Feb. 26, 1483. In this capacity he executed, about 1500–1505, the portrait of Doge Leonardo Loredano that is now

GIOVANNI BELLINI'S *Virgin with Child and Saints,* in the church of San Zaccheria, Venice, Italy.

ANDERSON, ROME; ART REFERENCE BUREAU

in the National Gallery, London. The last picture by Giovanni to which a date can be assigned with certainty is the altarpiece (1513) of the church of San Giovanni Crisostomo in Venice. He died in November 1516.

There are many extant paintings attributed with near certainty to Giovanni Bellini. Many of these are in the Venice Academy. Other important works are in the Louvre, Paris; the National Gallery, London; the National Gallery, Washington, D.C.; and the Metropolitan Museum and the Frick Collection, New York City.

Bibliography

Berenson, Bernard, *Italian Pictures of the Renaissance: The Venetian School* (New York 1957).
Berenson, Bernard, *Venetian Painting in America* (New York 1916).
Fry, Roger, *Giovanni Bellini* (London 1899).
Goloubew, V., *Les dessins de Jacopo Bellini* (Brussels 1912).
Hendy, Philip, and Goldscheider, Ludwig, *Giovanni Bellini* (New York 1945).
Tietze, Hans, and Tietze-Conrat, E., *The Drawings of the Venetian Painters in the 15th and 16th Centuries* (New York 1944).
Vasari, Giorgio, *Lives of the Most Eminent Painters, Sculptors and Architects*, tr. by Gaston de Vere (London 1912–15).
Walker, John, *Bellini and Titian at Ferrara* (London 1956).
Wind, Edgar, *Bellini's Feast of the Gods: A Study in Venetian Humanism* (Cambridge, Mass., 1948).

BELLINI, bāl-lē′nē, **Lorenzo** (1643–1704), Italian surgeon. He was born in Florence on Sept. 3, 1643. In 1663 he became professor of anatomy at Pisa. Later he became physician to the grand duke of Tuscany and senior consulting physician to Pope Clement XI. He was the first to observe and comment on the action of the nerves on the muscles. The uriniferous ducts of the kidneys, now known as Bellini's tubes, were named after him. His principal work is *Exercitatio anatomica de structura et usu renum* (1662). He died in Florence on Jan. 8, 1704.

BELLINI, bāl-lē′nē, **Vincenzo** (1801–1835), Italian opera composer who, as a representative of the *bel canto* school, wrote operas celebrated for their lyrical beauty and dazzling vocal embellishments. His music was popular throughout most of the 19th century, but then went into an eclipse. It won renewed respect with the revival of interest in *bel canto* in the mid-20th century. *Norma* (q.v.) is his most popular opera.

Early Career. Bellini was born at Catania, Sicily, on Nov. 1, 1801. He studied at the Naples Conservatory under the composer Nicola Zingarelli. His first opera, *Adelson e Salvini* (1825), was performed at the conservatory and brought him to the attention of the influential impresario Domenico Barbaja. Through Barbaja, Bellini was commissioned to write *Bianca e Fernando* (1826; revised 1828) for the San Carlo opera company in Naples, and *Il pirata* (1827) for La Scala in Milan. *Il pirata*, which gives a glimpse of his later melodic style, was followed by *La straniera* (1829), an indifferent success, and by *Zaira* (1829), a fiasco. Bellini salvaged some of the music from *Zaira* for his next work, *I Capuletti ed i Montecchi* (1830), an opera based on *Romeo and Juliet*. Unfortunately, the opera's tragic realism is marred by the fact that Bellini wrote the role of the hero for a mezzo-soprano.

The Great Operas. Bellini's most important creative period began in 1831 with *La sonnambula*. Then came *Norma* (1831), which most

OPERA NEWS

VINCENZO BELLINI, Italian opera composer, from a portrait that hangs in the museum of La Scala, Milan.

critics agree is his greatest opera. Not only is it rich in spectacular melodies, it is also infused with a dramatic energy only rarely achieved by its composer. Such moments as Norma's prayer (*Casta diva*), the ferocious battle chorus, and the moving final scene must be included among Bellini's finest. *Beatrice di Tenda* (1833) shows some falling off, but in his last opera, *I puritani* (1835), he was again at the top of his form. He died at Puteaux, France, on Sept. 24, 1835.

Style. While Bellini cannot be thought of as an innovator in music, his individual melodic style is highly personal. Probably the greatest single influence on his style was the tenor Giovanni Battista Rubini, who possessed extraordinary breath control, an extensive vocal range, and a highly cultivated technique. It was for such voices as Rubini's that Bellini's *bel canto* melodies were written. At the time Bellini was writing *Il pirata* (which, like *I puritani*, was tailored to Rubini's voice), Rubini worked closely with the composer, teaching him how to write effectively for well-trained voices.

For a composer of his period, Bellini wrote surprisingly few operas, and, perhaps unsure of his technique, he wrote slowly. He was usually an unenterprising harmonist and a weak orchestrator, and his vocal ensembles often contain only one strong part. Nevertheless, he was able to write beautiful melodies, such as *Ah! non credea* from *La sonnambula*, which, in spite of their apparent simplicity, are musically and dramatically expressive.

Influence. Bellini's influence as a composer is most clearly seen in the piano music of Frédéric Chopin. The long-flowing, intricate melodies of Chopin, with their long suspensions, find their antecedents in Bellini's arias. Other echoes of the Bellini idiom, so congenial to the spirit of the Romantic Age, are found in the music of such diverse composers as Giuseppe Verdi, Franz Liszt, and Richard Wagner.

WILLIAM ASHBROOK, *Author of "Donizetti"*

BELLMAN, bel'màn, **Carl Michael** (1740–1795), Swedish poet. He was born in Stockholm on Feb. 4, 1740. He grew up in a deeply religious home, and the first proofs he gave of his poetic talents were pious effusions. However, he was soon attracted to the pleasure-seeking life of a group of young men in Stockholm, and these figures became the subject of his poetry.

Bellman's wit and gaiety soon spread his name throughout Sweden, attracting the attention of King Gustavus III, who gave him an appointment in 1776 that enabled him to devote the rest of his life to writing poetry. His odes, adapted from Swedish peasant songs, were truly national, with love and drinking as their most common themes. The most famous of these works are two collections of dithyrambic odes, *Fredmans epistlar* (1790) and *Fredmans sånger* (1791), both intimate descriptions of quixotic roués in and about the cafés of Stockholm.

Bellman died in Stockholm on Feb. 11, 1795. Much of his work was published posthumously.

BELLMAWR, bel-mär', is a borough in southwestern New Jersey, in Camden County. It is situated 5 miles (8 km) south of Camden. The community occupies the site of the old Bell Farm, which was long known for breeding draft horses. Originally named Heddings (for a church built there in 1865), Bellmawr acquired its present name when a post office was established. The borough was incorporated in 1926, and has a mayor-council government. Population: 15,618.

BELLMEAD, bel'mēd, is an industrial town in central Texas, in McLennan County, adjoining Waco, and 83 miles (133 km) south of Dallas. Its chief industries include a bomb casing plant and railroad maintenance shops. The surrounding area is noted for cotton and dairy farming. The James Connally Technical Institute, a branch of Texas Agriculture and Mechanical University, founded in 1965, is situated northeast of the city limits, on the former site of the James Connally Air Force Base. Bellmead was established in 1924. Its population numbered 450 in 1940. Government is by city manager and council. Population: 7,698.

DAVID EARL HOLT
Waco-McLennan County Library

BELLMORE, bel'môr, an urban community in New York, is in Nassau County, about 25 miles (40 km) southeast of Times Square, New York City. It is situated on East Bay on the south shore of Long Island. Bellmore is connected with Jones Beach State Park by a 6-mile (9-km) causeway, which is part of the Wantagh State Parkway. It has some diversified light industry manufacturing boats, sportswear, and scientific instruments. Bellmore is unincorporated. Population: 18,431.

BELLO, bä'yō, **Andrés** (1781–1865), South American scholar, author, poet, and political leader. He was born in Caracas, Venezuela, on Nov. 29, 1781. He received a classical education in Caracas and tutored the youthful Simón Bolívar there. From 1810 to 1829, Bello was a diplomatic representative in London for Venezuela, Colombia, and Chile, successively. In 1829 he accepted an appointment as Chile's minister of foreign affairs. He settled at Santiago and in the 1830's served in the national congress.

Bello was the guiding spirit and first rector of the University of Chile, founded in 1842, and the principal instigator of dramatic secondary school reform. Working on a commission from the government from 1835 to 1855, he drafted a civil code that became the model for codes adopted in Chile, Colombia, and Ecuador.

Between diplomatic missions for the government, he wrote books on international law, philosophy, geography, sociology, literary criticism, and philology. His Spanish grammar (1847) remains an authoritative work throughout Spanish America. His poetry, gathered in the *Silvas americanas,* is read in all Spanish-language countries. Bello died at Santiago, Chile, on Oct. 15, 1865. See SILVAS AMERICANAS.

BELLOC, bel'ək, **Hilaire** (1870–1953), British Roman Catholic writer, who was a master of English prose, a fierce, brilliant satirist, a gallant political figure, and a consummate fashioner of light verse, limericks, and children's poems. He is probably best remembered as one of the two doughty paladins (the other was G.K. Chesterton) who reintegrated Roman Catholicism in Britain with European Roman Catholicism, and who inaugurated the Roman Catholic literary renaissance in Britain.

Life. Joseph Hilaire Pierre Belloc was born in Paris on July 27, 1870, of a French father and an English mother. He was educated at the Oratory school, Edgbaston, England, and at 17 went to work on a Sussex farm. He then traveled for a time in the United States, after which, as a French citizen, he did his two years' military service in the French army. He went to Balliol College, Oxford, when he was 22; there he was awarded the major history prize, became president of the Oxford Union, and took first class honors.

On June 16, 1896, Belloc married an American girl, Elodie Hogan, in California. In 1897 and 1898 he lectured in the United States. In 1900 he first met Chesterton, his junior by four years, saying "Chesterton, you write very well." In 1901, Belloc hiked from Toul in the north of France to Rome, and the resulting *The Path to Rome* (1902) is perhaps his best-known travel book. He became a citizen of Great Britain in 1902.

In 1906, in spite of the anti-Roman Catholic prejudice that was then prevalent in Britain, Belloc was elected to Parliament from Salford in the Liberal landslide. He found some Liberal leaders antipathetic, and his own overt anti-Semitism limited his value as a hardworking young politician. In the 1910 election he squeaked in by 314 votes, but resigned his seat later that year before the new election held after the death of King Edward VII.

In 1912, Belloc helped launch and coedited *The Eye-Witness,* a political weekly. That same year he traveled to Moscow, which was then several days' journey from London, to view (for only six hours) the setting of Napoleon's retreat, about which he later wrote. In 1937 he was visiting professor of history at Fordham University in New York City. He died in Guildford, England, on July 16, 1953.

Writings. In addition to pamphlets, translations, magazine articles, reviews, and numerous other short pieces, Belloc wrote well over a hundred books. In November 1896 he published *The Bad Child's Book of Beasts,* a volume of nonsense verse that sold out its first printing within four days. He wrote several biographies, including *Danton* (1899), *Robespierre* (1901), *Marie Antoinette* (1909), and *Napoleon* (1932). His first politically oriented book was *Lambkin's Remains* (1912), and his most prophetic was *The Servile State* (1912), an attack on both capitalistic industrialism and socialistic utopianism.

Belloc's Roman Catholicism showed most clearly in his books on religion—*Europe and the Faith* (1920) and *The Great Heresies* (1938). But his religious outlook was most militant in his 4-volume *History of England* (1925–32), which he wrote to correct what he considered the overly Protestant view of history.

ANNE FREMANTLE
Author of "This Little Band of Prophets"

Further Reading: Jebb, Eleanor, and Jebb, Reginald, *Belloc, the Man* (Westminster, Md., 1957); Speaight, Robert, *The Life of Hilaire Belloc* (New York 1957).

BELLOC, Marie Adelaide. See LOWNDES, MARIE ADELAIDE BELLOC.

BELLONA, bə-lō′nə, in Roman mythology, was the goddess of war. She was known also as *Duellona*, and the Greeks called her *Enyo*. Bellona was Mars' chief associate, perhaps his sister, wife, or daughter. She prepared his war chariot and drove his horses in battle. She is typically depicted with disheveled hair and carrying a shield and lance.

The Romans erected a temple in her honor on the Campus Martius, near the Flaminian Circus, outside the walls of Rome. The Senate convened at the temple to receive foreign ambassadors or to welcome victorious Roman generals, and the Romans declared war by hurling a spear over one of its pillars. Bellona's priests, known as *bellonarii*, practiced the ritual of inflicting wounds on themselves and offering their blood to the goddess.

Some authorities believe that Bellona may have been an Asian goddess of war, worshiped in Cappadocia and Phrygia, and introduced to Rome by the dictator Sulla.

BELLOT, be-lō′, **Joseph René** (1826–1853), French naval officer and explorer, who was lost on an expedition to the Arctic region. He was born at Rochefort on March 18, 1826. He entered the naval academy at Brest at the age of 16 and two years later became a midshipman. For bravery in an expedition against Madagascar in 1845 he was created a chevalier of the Legion of Honor, although he was not yet 20 years old.

In June 1851 he volunteered for an expedition being sent by Lady Franklin to search for her husband, Sir John Franklin, an English explorer, whose two vessels had been missing in the Arctic since 1845. During this expedition Bellot, with a sledge party, reached the narrow strait between Boothia Peninsula and Somerset Island, Canada, that has been named Bellot Strait in his honor. The party found no trace of Franklin.

In June 1853 he joined another expedition to carry dispatches to Sir Edward Belcher, commanding the *Assistance*, which was in the Arctic searching for Franklin. When the vessel reached the vicinity where Belcher was supposed to be, Bellot volunteered to carry the dispatches over the ice. He set out with four sailors, but the party was separated in a gale on August 18, and Bellot and two others drifted away on a small ice floe. He was never seen again.

BELLOT STRAIT, be-lō′, is the passage on the northern coast of Canada, separating Somerset Island from the Boothia Peninsula and connecting Prince Regent Inlet with Franklin Strait. Its eastern entrance was discovered in 1852 by Joseph René Bellot, and the passage was first explored by Sir Francis Leopold McClintock.

The strait is about 20 miles (32 km) long and approximately one mile (1½ km) wide at its narrowest part; granite shores rise in places to some 1,500 feet (460 meters). The strait is very windy and has permanent currents and flood tides, which come from the west.

BELLOTTO, bäl-lôt′tō, **Bernardo** (1720–1780), Italian painter of city scenes, who was the nephew and follower of Canaletto (q.v.). Until recent years, many of Bellotto's best early works were attributed to his uncle, whose name he often added to his own signature. Modern scholars now rank Bellotto as an important and original painter in his own right.

Bellotto was born in Venice on Jan. 30, 1720, and studied with Canaletto, his mother's brother. His early works include views of Venice, Turin, Florence, and Rome, as well as *capricci* (imaginary landscapes). From 1747 to 1767, Bellotto lived in Dresden as court painter to Augustus II, elector of Saxony. After 1767 he lived in Warsaw, Poland, under the patronage of King Stanislas II. The series of paintings that he did of Warsaw are usually considered his most important and original works. Bellotto died in Warsaw on Nov. 17, 1780.

BELLOW, bel′ō, **Saul** (1915–   ), American writer, who won distinction as one of the finest stylists, most intelligent craftsmen, and ablest storytellers of his generation. Many of his novels, especially *Herzog* (1964), deal with Jewish life in contemporary America, and most of his books reveal a lively sense of humor. For his "human understanding and subtle analysis of contemporary culture" he was awarded the Nobel Prize in literature for 1976.

Life. Bellow was born in Lachine, Quebec, on July 10, 1915. In 1924 his family moved to Chicago, Ill., and Bellow entered the University of Chicago in 1933. He later transferred to North-

PICTORIAL PARADE

Saul Bellow

GEORGE BELLOWS' painting *Stag at Sharkey's* is among the American artist's best-known paintings.

western University, from which he graduated with honors in 1937. He taught four years at the Pestalozzi-Froebel Teachers College in Chicago, and in 1943 joined the editorial department of the *Encyclopædia Britannica,* where he worked on Mortimer Adler's "Great Books" project.

Bellow served briefly in the merchant marine in World War II. He taught English at the University of Minnesota from 1946 to 1948 and then was awarded a Guggenheim Fellowship, which he used in 1948 and 1949 to write in Paris and Rome. In the 1950's he taught at Princeton University and at Bard College. He received a second Guggenheim Fellowship in 1955 and a Ford Foundation grant in 1959–1960. In 1961 he taught at the University of Puerto Rico and in 1962 was appointed professor at the University of Chicago.

Writings. In his novels and plays, Bellow shows his concern for the individual in an indifferent society. His special literary quality results from a combination of skill at characterization and the ability to create in the reader a sense of delight in the movement of the narrative.

Out of Bellow's experience in the merchant marine came his first novel, *Dangling Man* (1944), a study of a noncombatant in wartime. In 1953 he published *The Adventures of Augie March,* for which he won the 1954 National Book Award. *Henderson the Rain King* (1959) is a comic treatment of a serious subject—the pathos of human suffering.

In 1964 he wrote his most successful novel, *Herzog,* a chronicle of a contemporary Jewish Everyman. It won the 1965 National Book Award. A full-length play, *The Last Analysis* (1964), failed on Broadway. A bill of three one-act plays, with the omnibus title *Under the Weather,* was produced in London in 1966. Later appeared *Mosby's Memoirs* (1968), *Mr. Sammler's Planet* (1969), and *Humboldt's Gift* (1975). The latter won the 1976 Pulitzer Prize for novels.

BELLOWS, bel'ōz, **George Wesley** (1882–1925), American painter, whose strong, simple compositions made him one of the most popular American realists of the early 20th century. A younger follower of "The Eight," Bellows did city scenes, portrayals of sports events, landscapes, and por-

traits that have a stylistic freedom reflecting a great natural technical facility. His powerful black and white lithographs helped to bring about a revival of interest in that art form in the United States.

Bellows was born in Columbus, Ohio, on Aug. 12, 1882. After graduating from Ohio State University in 1903, he went to New York City and studied with Robert Henri, a leader of the American realists who called themselves "The Eight." Bellows was also strongly influenced by the painter Jay Hambridge, developer of "dynamic symmetry," a system of mathematical principles derived from an analysis of Greek and Egyptian art. He utilized Hambridge's system in developing the powerful spatial clarity of his own work.

Bellows' rise to fame was rapid. He established his own studio in New York City in 1906, and three years later, at the age of 27, became the youngest man to be elected an associate of the National Academy of Design. Among his important paintings of this period are *Forty-two Kids* (1907), *Rain on the River* (1908), *Up the Hudson* (1908), and *Polo Game at Lakewood, N.J.* (1910). He began to teach at the Art Students League in 1910 and helped to organize the famous Armory Show (q.v.) of 1913.

Bellows never visited Europe and resided all of his life in New York City. During the summer, however, he painted landscapes while on trips to Monhegan and Ogunquit, Me.; Newport, R.I.; Carmel, Calif.; Santa Fe, N.Mex.; and Woodstock, N.Y. Among the products of these trips are *The Red Vine* (1916), *The Sand Team* (1917), and *Fishermen's Huts* (1918).

But Bellows' name is usually associated with scenes of city life, such as *Men of the Docks* (1912), *The Cliff Dwellers* (1913), and *River Front* (1925). He loved sports, especially boxing, which is the subject of several of his best-known paintings, including *Stag at Sharkey's* (1907), *Dempsey Through the Ropes* (1924), and *Ringside Seats* (1925). He also drew on these subjects for the lithographs that increasingly absorbed his interest after 1916. Bellows died in New York City on Jan. 8, 1925.

Further Reading: Eggers, George W., *George Bellows* (New York 1931); Morgan, Charles H., *George Bellows* (New York 1965).

BELLUNO, bāl-loo'nō, a city in Italy, is the capital of Belluno province, in the Veneto (Venetia) region, 50 miles (80 km) north of Venice. It stands on a ridge in the foothills of the eastern Alps, on the Piave River. Because it is near the mountain resorts of the Dolomites, Belluno is a popular tourist center. Its manufactures include electrical goods, liquor, soap, and furniture.

In parts of the old city squares and streets are flanked by arcades and old Gothic and Renaissance houses. The cathedral, built in the 16th century, and later restored, has a tall bell tower and contains paintings of the Venetian school. The Renaissance Palazzo dei Rettori (1491) was the residence of the Venetian governors. The municipal tower, the Palace of the Jurists (housing the municipal museum), and the Gothic church of Santo Stefano are other notable landmarks.

A Roman settlement, Belluno gained some importance under the Lombards and was later the seat of a Frankish county. In the 10th century it was ruled by its counts-bishops, who extended their power over the countryside. The free commune of Belluno, established in the 12th century, was torn by factional struggles and fought against neighboring Treviso. During the 13th and 14th centuries, Belluno passed under a succession of foreign lords; then, in 1404, it voluntarily declared its allegiance to the republic of Venice, under whose peaceful rule it remained until 1797. Austrian domination followed, lasting until 1866, when Belluno became part of the kingdom (now republic) of Italy. Population: (1961) 15,400.

BELLUSCHI, bel-oos'kē, **Pietro** (1899–   ), American architect and educator. He was born in Ancona, Italy, on Aug. 18, 1899. After receiving a doctorate in civil engineering at the University of Rome in 1922, he went to the United States and attended Cornell University, where he took a second civil engineering degree in 1924. In 1925 he joined the architectural firm of A.E. Doyle & Associates, in Portland, Oreg., as a draftsman and designer and became a partner in 1932. He established his own architectural firm in 1943, practicing first in Portland, Oreg., and later in Boston, Mass. He was dean and professor of architecture and planning at the Massachusetts Institute of Technology from 1951 to 1965. He also served as architectural consultant to the U.S. Air Force in the design of the Air Academy (1959) at Colorado Springs, Colo., and to Princeton University beginning in 1966. Belluschi became an American citizen in 1929.

Belluschi's notable commissions include the Equitable Building (1948) in Portland, Oreg., and the Juilliard School of Music for the Lincoln Center for the Performing Arts in New York City.

BELLWOOD is a residential and manufacturing village in northeastern Illinois, in Cook county, 15 miles (24 km) west of downtown Chicago. Its industrial products include electrical components, ink, hardware, iron castings, and lift trucks. Founded as an agricultural community after the Civil War, the village was originally registered as Bellewood, and was incorporated under its present name in 1900. The population has increased considerably since 1950. Government is by mayor and board of trustees. Population: 22,096.

JOANNE KLENE, *Bellwood Public Library*

Bellwort (*Uvularia sessifolia*)

BELLWORT, bel'wûrt, is the common name of the five species of plants of the genus *Uvularia* of the lily family, Liliaceae. Bellworts are found in thickets, woods, and clearings from New Brunswick and southern Manitoba to Florida and Louisiana. Their name comes from the fancied resemblance of the nodding lilylike flowers to bells.

The flowers, ¾ to 2 inches long (1.9 to 2.5 cm), are spring blooming, 6 parted, and yellowish, yellowish white, or greenish yellow. The erect stem commonly forks above the middle, and its lower part usually bears a few sheathlike structures. The leaves have parallel veins, are alternate, and are stalkless. In *U. perfoliata* and *U. grandiflora* the leaves are perfoliate—the stem appears to pass through the leaf blade.

JOHN W. THIERET
Chicago Natural History Museum

BELMAR, bel'mär, is a resort borough in eastern New Jersey, in Monmouth county. It is situated on the Atlantic Ocean, at the mouth of the Shark River, 3 miles (5 km) south of Asbury Park. Fishing and boating attract many visitors, and there is a marina. Government is by mayor and commissioners. Population: 5,782.

GRACE T. ROPER, *Belmar Free Public Library*

BELMONT, bel'mont, an American family prominent in banking, the arts, and politics in the 19th and 20th centuries. Two of its leading members were August and Perry Belmont.

AUGUST BELMONT (1816–1890) was born at Alzey, Hesse, Germany, on Dec. 2, 1816. Son of a wealthy landowner, he entered the employ (without pay) of the Rothschild banking house in Frankfurt am Main at the age of 14. His talent for finance quickly won him advancement. At the age of 21 he was sent to Havana to take charge of the Rothschilds' interests there, but he soon was transferred to New York, where he established his own firm (Augustus Belmont & Company). Using his agency for the Rothschilds as his principal capital and taking advantage of the financial crisis of 1837, he prospered immediately, and in a few years his company was one of the leading American financial institutions.

In 1844, Austria appointed him consul in the United States, but he resigned in 1850 in protest against Austria's treatment of the Hungarian revolutionaries. Long active in the Democratic party, he was appointed by President Franklin Pierce as U.S. ambassador to the Netherlands (1853–1857). During the Civil War he made good use of his connections with European banking circles, visiting the Continent in 1861 and 1863 to argue the Union cause. He was noted as an art collector and was for many years president of the American Jockey Club. He died in New York City on Nov. 24, 1890.

PERRY BELMONT (1850–1947), son of the preceding, was born in New York City on Dec. 28, 1850. He attended Harvard College and Columbia Law School. In 1881 he was elected to the House of Representatives from New York. In Congress he prepared reports on the proposed canal across Nicaragua and on the sugar industry in Hawaii. His resolution designed to bring peace between Chile and Peru led to a congressional investigation of the South American policy of Secretary of State James G. Blaine. In 1885 he became chairman of the House Committee on Foreign Affairs. Defeated for reelection in 1888, he was appointed minister to Spain (1888–1889) by President Cleveland. He died at Newport, R.I., on May 25, 1947. Belmont wrote a number of books on American history and politics, including *Political Equality: Toleration from Roger Williams to Thomas Jefferson* (1927) and *An American Democrat* (1940).

AUGUST BELMONT (1853–1924), another son of the elder August Belmont, was born in New York City on Feb. 15, 1853. Graduated from Harvard in 1874, he entered his father's banking firm, assuming control on the latter's death in 1890. Under his management, August Belmont & Company continued to exert the large influence in United States financial and railroad affairs that it gained under its founder. In 1900 he organized the Rapid Transit Subway Construction Company to build the rapid transit system in New York City. Like his father, he was active in the national councils of the Democratic party. He died in New York City on Dec. 10, 1924.

ELEANOR BELMONT (1879–   ), wife of the preceding, was born Eleanor Robson at Wigan, Lancashire, England. She made her stage debut at the California Theatre in San Francisco. In 1910, after successes in New York in such plays as *Merely Mary Ann* (1903), *She Stoops to Conquer* (1905), and *The Dawn of Tomorrow* (1908), she was married to Belmont and retired from the theater. Thereafter she devoted much of her time to social and philanthropic work and especially to the Metropolitan Opera Association. She was the first woman on its board of directors, which she joined in 1933. In 1935 she founded the Metropolitan Opera Guild. A book of her memoirs, *Fabric of Memory*, was published in 1957.

BELMONT, bel'mont, is a residential city in western California, in San Mateo County. It is situated on San Mateo Peninsula, between the Pacific Ocean and San Francisco Bay, 19 miles (30 km) southeast of San Francisco. Belmont's manufactures include electrical equipment, gunsights, aluminum alloy forgings, building materials, textiles, chemicals, paints, and enamels. The College of Notre Dame (for women) is situated in Belmont. A landmark among the city's buildings is Ralston Hall, an 80-room Victorian mansion built by William Chapman Ralston, a 19th century financier. Incorporated in 1926, Belmont has a mayor and council. Population: 23,667.

BELMONT, bel'mont, is a residential town in Massachusetts. It is situated in Middlesex County, seven miles (11 km) northwest of Boston. First settled about 1630, it was incorporated in 1859. It was formed from parts of Watertown, Waltham, and Arlington.

Principally an agricultural community, Belmont began to develop as a residential suburb about 1910. In 1926 the town government was changed from an unlimited form to a limited form of town meeting. Population: 28,285.

BELMONTE, bel-mōn'tā, Juan (1892–1962), Spanish matador, who is considered the founder of modern bullfighting. *Juan Belmonte y García* was born in Seville on April 14, 1892, and began performing there in 1910. After his success in Seville, he and Juan Gómez Ortega ("Joselito") launched what came to be regarded as the "golden age of bullfighting" at Barcelona in March 1914. They fought together until Joselito was gored to death on May 16, 1920, in a one-man corrida.

Belmonte, small and bandy-legged, could not maneuver his feet quickly, and he changed the style by fighting closer to the bull. He was grazed by the beast's horns and tossed many times as he wrapped the bull around his waist with passes. In 1919 he set a record by appearing in 109 corridas. When he retired in 1935, the "King of the Matadors" had been gored some 50 times in killing over 1,650 bulls. He died near Seville on April 2, 1962, a millionaire.

BILL BRADDOCK, *New York "Times"*

BELMOPAN, bel-mō'pän, became the capital of British Honduras in August 1970. The city, whose construction was begun in 1964, is situated on a plain near the Belize River, about 50 miles (80 km) inland from the Caribbean coast. It is named for a tribe of Indians reputed to have gallantly opposed Spanish conquest of the region.

The building of Belmopan was undertaken after the devastation of the traditional capital, Belize (or Belize City), by the hurricane of Oct. 31, 1961, one of many storms to have swept that seaport. As the transfer of government took place, British Honduras anticipated achieving independence as a nation to be called Belize.

BELO HORIZONTE, bâ-lô-rē-zōnn'tĕ, is a city in eastern Brazil, 220 miles (354 km) northwest of Rio de Janeiro. It is the capital of the state of Minas Gerais. Founded in 1897, it was the first planned city in South America, patterned after Washington, D.C. It is situated in a valley and is known for its cool, dry, healthful climate.

Belo Horizonte is the economic, cultural, and political center of Minas Gerais. It processes products of Brazil's chief mineral region, where manganese, high-grade iron ore, gold, and precious stones are mined. It also manufactures steel, iron, seamless tubes, textiles, cement, and electric rolling stock. Diamond cutting is an important craft. The city is the hub of rail and highway networks. The highway from Brasília to Rio de Janeiro passes through Belo Horizonte, and there is a highway connection to São Paulo. An air shuttle system operates to Rio de Janeiro.

Belo Horizonte is noted for its modern architecture in public and commercial buildings and in private homes. The suburb of Pampulha has been developed as a recreation area, with an artificial lake and several clubs. In Pampulha also is the Chapel of São Francisco, designed by Oscar Niemeyer and decorated by Cândido Portinari. The chapel was unconsecrated for many years because the bishop objected to its radical style. The University of Minas Gerais and the Catholic University of Minas Gerais are in Belo Horizonte. Population: (1960 census) 693,328; (1966 est.) 1,015,000.

GREGORY RABASSA, *Columbia University*

BELOEIL, bə-lû′yə, is a town in Quebec, Canada, in Verchères County. It lies along the Richelieu River, 19 miles (30.5 km) east of Montreal, of which it is a suburb. It is situated in the old seigniory of Beloeil, established in 1694. Beloeil's principal products are agricultural chemicals and explosives. Population: 12,274.

BELOIT, bə-loit′, is an industrial city in southeastern Wisconsin, in Rock County. It lies at the juncture of Rock River and Turtle Creek, 70 miles (112.5 km) by road southwest of Milwaukee. Its manufactures include papermaking machinery, diesel engines, electric motors and generators, pumps, and shoes.

In 1824 a trading post was established here for trade with the Winnebago Indians, and in 1837 the first permanent settlers arrived from New England. It was incorporated as a village in 1846 and received a city charter in 1859. Since 1929 it has had a city manager government. Beloit is the site of Beloit College and the birthplace of Roy Chapman Andrews, noted explorer. Its former names include Turtle, Blodgett's Settlement, and New Albany. Population: 35,729.

FRANCES CLARK, *Beloit Public Library*

BELOIT COLLEGE, bə-loit′, is a private, coeducational, liberal arts institution in Beloit, Wis. It is affiliated with the Congregational and Presbyterian churches but has been nonsectarian since its inception. The college was chartered in 1846, and instruction began in 1847.

Beloit grants bachelor's and master's degrees in 33 departments. Studies are also offered in interdisciplinary fields of concentration such as American studies, Russian studies, and comparative literature. Preprofessional programs include medicine, law, dentistry, engineering, and business administration. The college has an honors program for superior students, and provision is made for overseas study.

A library of 180,000 volumes includes collections on Russian literature, drama, the Wilson and Franklin D. Roosevelt eras, and the American Indian. Other facilities include the Logan Museum of Anthropology and the Theodore Lyman Wright Art Center. Enrollment rose from 600 in 1940 to about 1,200 in the mid-1960's. The campus is the site of a number of 15th century Indian mounds.

MILLER UPTON, *President, Beloit College*

BELON, bə-lôn′, **Pierre** (1517–1564), French naturalist and traveler. He was born in the Sarthe region of France. Belon was one of the first to recognize similarities in vertebrate skeletons. He also wrote noteworthy treatises on trees, herbs, birds, and fish and accounts of his travels in Asia Minor, Egypt, and Arabia. His other writings include *Histoire naturelle des étranges poissons marines* (1551) and *L'histoire de la nature des oyseaux* (1555).

BELORUSSIAN SOVIET SOCIALIST REPUBLIC, bye-lə-rush′ən, is one of the 15 union republics that make up the USSR. It is also known as *Belorussia, Byelorussia,* or *White Russia*. Its area of 80,154 square miles (207,600 sq km) is bounded by Poland on the west, the Lithuanian and Latvian republics of the USSR on the north, the Russian republic on the east, and the Ukrainian republic on the south. Belorussia is a member of the United Nations, where it enjoys the same legal status as the Soviet Union, a privilege shared by only one other constituent republic of the USSR, the Ukrainian republic.

Land and Climate. Most of Belorussia is a large plain, slightly elevated in the north and sloping downward to the east and south. Much of the land is still covered by forest, and lumbering is an important industry. Numerous streams flow into the Berezina and Pripyat (Pripet) rivers, which are tributaries of the Dnieper (Dnepr) River, and into the upper courses of the Western Dvina and Niemen rivers. The basins of the Dnieper and the Western Dvina are joined by a system of canals that provides waterways of limited capacity from the Baltic to the Black seas. The southern lowlands, or Polesie, which are virtually coextensive with the Pripyat (Pripet) Marshes, turn into a sea every spring, isolating some of the towns for weeks at a time.

The climate is continental, with temperatures averaging about 20° F in winter and 70° F in summer. Rainfall averages from 20 to 25 inches (50.8 to 63.5 centimeters) a year.

People. Ethnically the Belorussian people are an eastern division of the Slavs. They are believed to be direct descendants of the primary Slavic tribes—Krivichi, Radzimichi, Dregovichi, and Viatichi—that settled in the area during the first centuries A.D. They have all been called "Russians" since the foundation of the Kievan Russian state in the 9th century.

Belorussia's estimated population in 1965 was 8,570,000. This figure was still about 2 million short of the prewar level. The total is made up of Belorussians (81.1 percent), Russians (8.2 percent), Poles (6.7 percent), Jews (1.9 percent), Ukrainians (1.7 percent), and others (0.4 percent). Although most of the people still live in rural areas and earn a living from the land, the recent emphasis on industrialization has caused an enormous migration to the cities. The urban population increased from 14.4 percent before World War I to 40 percent in the mid-1960's.

Chief cities, in the 1965 population, are Minsk (707,000), the capital; Gomel (216,000); Vitebsk (187,000); Mogilev (156,000); Bobruisk (115,000); and Grodna (99,000).

Language. The Belorussian language, so named to distinguish it from the Russian and Polish spoken by the educated classes, was originally the vernacular of the illiterate peasantry. The name of the dialect, Belorussian, was accepted by the people, and it became the symbol of national self-determination when the concept of a separate linguistic community developed toward the end of the 19th century.

Regional dialects of Belorussian developed as they were influenced by the proximity of the dialect groups to Russia, Poland, or the Ukraine. No attempts to unify and organize the idiom were made until the first Belorussian grammar appeared in 1918. Modern Belorussian, as it has been organized since that time, is still largely an artificial product confined to literature, and

BELORUSSIA'S GOVERN-MENT HOUSE, where the chief governing bodies of the republic meet, is in Minsk.

the regional dialects remain the spoken language. Phonetically the vernacular differs from Russian in several ways. In morphology and syntax the language preserves many features of Old Russian and Church Slavonic. The vocabulary is full of archaic words and words derived from Polish and Lithuanian.

Culture. The Belorussian cultural heritage, consisting chiefly of folklore, is one of the richest in eastern Europe. The most notable modern writers are Janka Kupala (1882–1942) and Jakub Kolas (1882–1958). The Belorussian Academy of Sciences, founded in 1928, has its headquarters in Minsk. The republic has some 7,000 libraries, with about 40 million books, pamphlets, and periodicals. The great majority of books published in Belorussia are in Russian rather than Belorussian, although both languages have equal legal status. Of 1,946 books and pamphlets published in 1964, only 341 were in Belorussian.

Economy. Belorussia is not rich in natural resources, and the land is not well suited to agriculture. Extensive drainage programs have increased the arable area by 40 percent since 1940. The chief crops are potatoes, fodder, flax, and hemp. In the more elevated sections of central Belorussia, wheat, rye, and barley are grown. Cattle, pigs, sheep, and goats are raised, as well as some poultry.

Belorussia's chief industrial products are peat, steel, fertilizers, cement, pulp, textiles, shoes, trucks, and tractors.

The republic's network of railroads, totaling 3,335 miles (5,367 km), and highways, totaling 8,450 miles (13,647 km), has remained virtually the same since 1955.

History and Government. The name *White Russia* first appeared in the 1300's to describe the Russian lands that paid no tribute to either the Tatars in the East or the Lithuanian lords in the West. Eventually the country was incorporated into the Russian Lithuanian state united with Poland under a common monarch, Jagello (reigned 1386–1434). In the late 1700's the land was made part of the Russian empire and was known as the "northwestern provinces."

Belorussia proclaimed its independence of Russia on March 25, 1918, under the Austro-German military occupation. This period of illusory statehood, however, ended with the defeat of the Central Powers in World War I. In December 1918 the Poles occupied the western part of the country, and the Russians took over the eastern part. On Jan. 1, 1919, the two Belorussian provinces east of the Polish frontier were organized as the first Belorussian Soviet Socialist Republic.

Hostilities between the two occupying forces, Poland and Russia, ended two years later in the formal partition of Belorussia between the two countries (Treaty of Riga, 1921). The Russians organized their half as the second Belorussian Soviet Socialist Republic, which was recognized by the neighboring states. On Dec. 30, 1922, it entered into a formal union with the Russian, Ukrainian, and Transcaucasian Soviet Socialist republics.

By 1940, with territorial concessions granted by Moscow (1924–1926) and with the addition of Western (Polish) Belorussia to the Belorussian republic at the beginning of World War II, the republic had grown to four times its original size. In June 1941 it was invaded by the Germans and remained under their occupation for three years. A Nazi puppet government tried to restore the "national image" of Belorussia by remodeling or destroying everything the Soviets had built. Their work was in turn undone by Russian guerrilla forces and then by Soviet armies as they drove the Germans west. By the end of World War II, Belorussian losses were estimated at several million human lives. After World War II the Belorussian Soviet Socialist Republic was restored on the basis of its 1937 constitution, as amended in 1939 and 1944.

NICHOLAS P. VAKAR, *Ohio State University*

Further Reading: Vakar, Nicholas, *Belorussia: The Making of a Nation* (Cambridge, Mass. 1956); id., *Bibliographical Guide to Belorussia* (Cambridge, Mass., 1956).

BELOVO, bye'lə-və, is a city in the USSR, in Kemerovo oblast in the Russian republic. It is situated on the Bachat River, 60 miles (96 km) equidistant by rail from Kemerovo and Novo-kuznetsk (formerly Stalinsk). A fast-growing city in the Kuznetsk Basin, Belovo is a coal-mining center with engineering industries and metallurgical plants that process zinc and lead ores. Its radio and cinema industries are also important. Population: (1962) 118,000.

W.A. DOUGLAS JACKSON
University of Washington

BELPRE, bel'prē, is a residential city in south-eastern Ohio, in Washington County. It is situated on the Ohio River, 12 miles (19 km) south-west of Marietta. It has aluminum and synthetic rubber factories.

Settled about 1790, it originally was called Belle Prairie. It was the site of the first public library in the Northwest Territory. In the river opposite Belpre is Blennerhassett Island, which was the home of Harman Blennerhassett, a co-conspirator with Aaron Burr. The city is governed by a mayor and council. Population: 7,189.

BERNICE HAYES
Washington County Public Library

BELSEN, bel'zən, was a notorious concentration camp in Hitler's Germany. It was situated in the village of Belsen (population, 1961, 166), now in the West German state of Lower Saxony. Like others of its kind, the camp contained a large proportion of Jewish prisoners, many of whom were murdered. When the survivors—over 50,000 sick and starving—were liberated by the British army on April 15, 1945, 10,000 unburied corpses were found. Soon afterward some 13,000 others died from malnutrition, disease, and the effects of torture. On Dec. 13, 1945, 11 persons convicted of atrocities at the Belsen and Auschwitz camps were hanged at Hameln.

BELSHAZZAR, bel-shaz'ər, was the son of Nabonidus, king of Babylonia, in the 6th century B.C. Belshazzar ruled as regent about 550–539. According to the Book of Daniel (5 to 8), his rule was lax and dissolute. During a last orgiastic feast (539) there appeared on a wall an inscription in Aramaic (the "handwriting on the wall"), which only Daniel could decipher. That night Babylon was invaded by Cyrus the Great of Persia, and Belshazzar was slain. In the Bible (Daniel 5) Belshazzar is identified as the son of Nebuchadnezzar, but cuneiform inscriptions indicate that Nabonidus was his father. For discussion of the handwriting on the wall, see MENE, MENE, TEKEL, UPHARSIN.

BELSHAZZAR'S FEAST, bel-shaz'ərz fēst, as described in the Bible (Daniel 5), is the subject of several important works of art. Handel based his oratorio *Belshazzar* (1745) on the story, and Sir William Walton used a text by Sir Osbert Sitwell for his cantata *Belshazzar's Feast* (1931).

In literature the Belshazzar theme is treated in Lord Byron's poem *Vision of Belshazzar* (1815) and in Robert Landor's poem *The Impious Feast* (1828). It is the subject of plays—one in Hannah More's *Sacred Dramas* (1782), and *Belshazzar* (1822), by Henry Hart Milman.

In painting, Washington Allston began his pictorial interpretation of Belshazzar's Feast in 1817 but did not complete it.

BELT CONVEYOR. See CONVEYOR—*Belt Conveyor.*

BELT DRIVE. See POWER—8. *Transmission of Other Forms of Power* (Mechanical Power Transmission); PULLEY.

BELTON, bel'tən, is a city in northwestern South Carolina, in Anderson County, 30 miles (48.2 km) by road south of Greenville. The manufacture of textiles and clothing are the principal industries.

Named after John Belton O'Neall, a judge and railroad developer, Belton was incorporated in 1855. It has a mayor-council form of government. Population: 5,257.

BELTON, bel'tən, is a city in central Texas, 58 miles (93 km) north of Austin. It is the seat of Bell County. Its chief industries are the manufacture of rock-wool insulation, furniture, and farm implements and the production of sand and gravel. Mary Hardin-Baylor College for women is in Belton. Belton Dam and Reservoir are 3 miles (5 km) to the north.

The community was organized in 1850 and was called Nolanville. Its name was changed in 1851 to Belton, possibly in honor of Peter Bell, governor of Texas. Belton was incorporated in 1884 and has a council-manager form of government. Population: 8,696.

LENA ARMSTRONG, *Belton Carnegie Library*

BELTRAFFIO, bäl-träf'fyō, **Giovanni Antonio** (1467–1516), Italian painter. His name is also spelled *Boltraffio.* He was born in Milan, of a noble family (somewhat unusual for an artist of the period). He appears to have studied with various teachers before becoming a disciple of Leonardo da Vinci, and he undoubtedly formed his style to a point just short of servile imitation of Leonardo. Beltraffio's paintings lack power, but some, chiefly his madonnas, exude a pallid variety of Leonardesque charm.

Beltraffio is also known as a portraitist. He tried fresco, but the example surviving in the churches of San Maurizio (Milan) and San Onofrio (Rome) do not reveal a deep understanding of the medium. Much of his work is in public and private collections in Milan. The *Madonna of the Casio Family,* one of his best works, is in the Louvre in Paris. Beltraffio died in Milan on June 15, 1516.

BELTRAMI, bäl-trä'mē, **Eugenio** (1835–1900), Italian mathematician. He was born in Cremona on Nov. 16, 1835. His mathematical talents were apparent when he was very young, and he developed them to the full. At the age of 27, he became a professor of analytical geometry at the University of Bologna. From then until his death, he occupied posts in the finest Italian universities, including Pisa, Rome, and Pavia.

Beltrami's work ranged over the entire field of pure and applied mathematics. He is best known for his work on theories of surfaces and space of constant curvature. He also devised the first models of non-Euclidean geometry. His collected papers, *Opere matematiche* (1902–20), contain articles on subjects as diverse as the theory of fluid flow and electromagnetism. Beltrami was named president of the Accademia dei Lincei in 1898, and he became a senator in 1899. He died in Rome on Feb. 18, 1900.

L. PEARCE WILLIAMS, *Cornell University*

THE BELUGA, or white whale, commonly is found in the Arctic Ocean and surrounding waters. It is one of the few whales able to swim backward. This pair of belugas is at the New York Aquarium.

BELUGA, bə-lōō′gə, a small dolphin which is also known as the *white whale*. It is commonly found in the Arctic Ocean and in some northern rivers. Occasionally it is found as far south as Japan and Ireland. Belugas are caught in fairly large numbers and serve many uses. The blubber furnishes oil, and the hide provides leather for boots and shoelaces. The flesh is used for food.

The beluga has an extremely flexible body for a whale; the narwhal is the only other whale that has the ability to bend its neck. The male beluga may grow to 15 feet (4.5 meters), but the female rarely exceeds 8 feet (2.5 meters). The weight of the animal ranges from 500 to 1,500 pounds (225 to 675 kg). The beluga takes on its characteristic white color at about 5 years of age. It has 32 to 40 peg-shaped teeth.

Belugas are often found in groups (pods) of several hundred individuals of all ages and sizes. They can swim at the rate of 15 miles per hour (24 kilometers per hour) at the surface and can at times be seen swimming backward by sculling with their tails. The basic diet of belugas consists of fish (such as flounder and halibut), squid, and crustaceans. They are bottom feeders and are the prey of killer whales.

Belugas are sometimes called "sea canaries" because they make a variety of audible sounds, from a harsh creaking to a shrill whistle. They also make some supersonic sounds.

Reproduction. Beluga females are sexually mature when they are about 5 years of age. The gestation period is 14 months. The calf, about 5 feet (1.5 meters) long and dark grayish at birth, grows quickly for the first few years and becomes lighter in color.

Classification. The beluga (*Delphinapterus leucas*) and narwhal make up the family Monodontidae in the order Cetacea, a group of aquatic mammals that includes porpoises as well as whales. See also WHALE.

BELUGA, bə-lōō′gə, a large sturgeon found in the Caspian, Black, Azov, and Adriatic seas. Its maximum size is usually given as 26.24 feet (8 meters) with a weight of 2,865 pounds (1,300 kg).

The beluga is of great commercial importance. The eggs are used for caviar, the internal organs (except the kidneys) for other food, the air bladder for glue and isinglass, and the skin for ladies' shoes. The scientific name for the beluga is *Acipenser huso*. See also STURGEON.

BELVIDERE, bel′və-dēr, a city in Illinois, is the seat of Boone County. It is located on the Kishwaukee River, 14 miles (22.5 km) east of Rockford. It is an industrialized community in a dairy-farming area. The Chrysler Corporation's passenger car assembly plant, built in the mid-1960's on 531 acres that were annexed to the city, is designed for operation with up to 5,000 employees. Among Belvidere's other industries are manufactures of casket trimmings, commercial scales, and women's corsets.

The city was laid out in 1836 and was a stop on the Chicago-Galena stage route. Incorporated in 1847 and again in 1857, it has a mayor-council form of government. Population: 14,061.

BESSIE SULLIVAN, *Ida Public Library, Belvidere*

BELY, byä′lē, **Andrei** (1880–1934), Russian poet and novelist. He was born *Boris N. Bugayev* in Moscow on Oct. 26, 1880. He studied at the University of Moscow, and from about 1903 associated himself with the symbolist writers, publishing under the pen name "Andrei Bely." His volumes of poetry included *Gold in Azure* (1904), *The Urn* (1909), and *Ashes* (1909). He also wrote the novels *The Silver Dove* (1910) and *Petersburg* (1916), as well as numerous critical essays and three volumes of memoirs. He died in Moscow on Jan. 7, 1934.

Bely's novels, often compared with those of James Joyce, contain a mixture of fantasy, realism, symbolism, and philosophy. Critic Marc Slonim has called *Petersburg* "one of the most important Russian novels of the 20th century." The Soviet government called Bely's work reactionary, although he declared himself a Marxist during the last years of his life.

BELZONI, bäl-tsō′nē, **Giovanni Battista** (1778–1823), Italian explorer and archaeologist. He was born in Padua, Italy, on Nov. 15, 1778. A giant of a man, six feet seven inches tall, he made a precarious living for more than a decade by performing feats of strength at circuses and fairs in England (1803–1812) and in Spain, Portugal, and Malta.

From 1815 to 1819, Belzoni lived in Egypt, where he obtained a commission to collect Egyptian antiquities for the British Museum. In 1816 he removed the colossal bust of Rameses II (a sculpture now called *The Young Memnon*) from the Valley of the Kings and had it transported from Thebes to the British Museum.

In 1817 he opened the great temple at Abu Simbel and a number of royal tombs, including that of Seti I in Thebes. Still referred to as "Belzoni's Tomb," it contained the magnificent alabaster sarcophagus now in the British Museum. A year later he discovered the entrance to the pyramid of Chephren (Khafre) at Giza, the second-largest burial monument in the world. Exploring the coasts of the Red Sea, he discovered the emerald mines of Zubara and correctly identified the ruins of the ancient city of Berenice. Belzoni's account of his investigations, *Narrative of the Operations and Recent Discoveries in the Pyramids, Temples, Tombs, and Excavations in Egypt and Nubia,* was published in London in 1820. He died in Gwato, Nigeria, on Dec. 3, 1823.

BELZÚ, bel-sōō', **Manuel Isidoro** (1808–1865), Bolivian soldier and political leader. Born at La Paz, Bolivia, into a Creole family, he received no formal education before entering the army as a youth. He rose to the rank of general, and in 1848 he overthrew the government, and occupied the presidency until 1855.

His administration was tyrannical; he jailed, murdered, or banished his political enemies and made a mockery of Congress. In the name of socialism, he restored to the Indians their communal lands and reestablished the provincial governments, but his incitement of the Indians led to murder and pillage. In 1856 he resigned and went to live abroad. Belzú seized the presidency again in 1865 but was assassinated at La Paz before the end of the year.

BEM, bem, **Józef** (1794–1850), Polish general. Born in Tarnów, Poland, on March 14, 1794—the year before the final partition of Poland by Prussia, Austria, and Russia—he was a leading representative of a generation which saw its life's goal in restoring Polish independence.

Bem was the son of a lawyer who was ennobled in 1803. He was educated in Kraków and at Warsaw's school of artillery and engineering. A lieutenant of horse artillery in the army of the Grand Duchy of Warsaw, he fought the Russians in Napoleon's 1812 campaign. In 1815 he joined the army of the semiautonomous Congress Kingdom of Poland, but in 1822 was demoted and imprisoned for participating in secret patriotic societies. Although the sentence was commuted, his advancement was blocked and he left the army in 1826.

During the Polish insurrection against Russia (1830–1831), his outstanding ability as an artillery commander and his conspicuous fearlessness earned him swift advancement to the rank of brigadier general. After the defeat of the insurrection, Bem took a leading part in fostering the "great emigration" of Polish war veterans to France. In 1833 he tried in vain to form a Polish legion in Portugal. His book, *On the Polish National Insurrection,* was published in 1846–1848.

Bem was engaged in the political agitation that preceded the wave of national revolutionary movements of 1848, and commanded Vienna's rebels in their defense against the imperial Austrian army. Appointed by Lajos Kossuth to command the Hungarian army in Transylvania, Bem freed that province in a brilliant winter campaign (1848–1849) against superior Austrian and Russian forces. In the last days of the Hungarian war

of independence, Bem was appointed commander in chief, but he could not prevent defeat in the summer of 1849.

Expecting a Turko-Russian war, Bem became a Muslim and joined the Turkish army under the name of Murad Pasha (Amurat Pasha). He died shortly, in Aleppo, Syria, on Dec. 10, 1850.

JAN LIBRACH
Author of "The Rise of the Soviet Empire"

BEMBA, bem'bə, a Bantu people of the central African plateau, inhabiting a wide area in northeastern Zambia. Variations of the name include *Awemba, Babemba,* and *Wemba.*

The Bemba number about 150,000. An agricultural people, they practice shifting cultivation, raising cereals and starchy vegetables for their own subsistence, and supplement their diet by hunting. They have no cash crops, little livestock, and few crafts; they generally lack material possessions. Their matrilineal settlements, led by hereditary headmen, are organized into districts of several villages under paramount chiefs. Numerous Bemba men left their native villages to work in the copper mines of southern Africa.

BEMBO, bem'bō, **Pietro** (1470–1547), Italian cardinal and writer. He was born in Venice on May 20, 1470. Bembo, who was of a noble family, was educated at Florence, Venice, Padua, and Messina, completed his philosophical studies at Ferrara, and entered the church. From 1506 to 1512 he lived at the courts of Ferrara and Urbino and then followed Giuliano de' Medici, the duke of Nemours, to Rome, where he became secretary to Giuliano's brother, Pope Leo X.

When Leo died in 1521, Bembo, with his Roman mistress Morosina, who bore him three children, retired to Padua to study and to write. In 1529 he accepted the post of historian of the Venetian Republic and in the following year became librarian of St. Mark's. Morosina died in 1535, and in 1539, Pope Paul III made Bembo a cardinal. A short time later, he became a priest. He then gave up his classical studies and devoted himself to the writings of the church fathers and to the Scriptures. He was given the bishopric of Gubbio in 1541 and the rich see of Bergamo in 1544. He died at Rome on Jan. 18, 1547.

Bembo represented well the spirit of the Italian Renaissance. He was an elegant humanist without being particularly original, and intellectually he was as much interested in early Italian culture as he was in the classics. His first noteworthy work was *Asolani* (1505; *People of Asolo*), dialogues on platonic love dedicated to Lucrezia Borgia, whom he had courted. *Prose della volgar lingua* (*Discussions of the Italian Language*), which appeared in 1525, was his most important work. It was the first Italian grammar, as well as a passionate defense of the Italian language as being equal to Latin. He argued that the Tuscan dialect of Italian could become a refined language of literature. Four volumes of Bembo's works published in Venice in 1729 also included love poems, Latin odes, and a lengthy history of Venice.

Bembo's contributions to Italian linguistics, long neglected or misunderstood, are considered significant by modern critics. His Italian grammar was a quest for harmony more than for rigid rules.

BEMELMANS, bem′əl-mənz, **Ludwig** (1898–1962), Austrian-American painter and writer. He was born in Meran, Austria (now Merano, Italy) on April 27, 1898. He went to the United States at the age of 16 and worked as a busboy in New York City before being naturalized and joining the army in 1918. After the war he returned to New York as a waiter at the Ritz Hotel and later became manager of a new restaurant, Hapsburg House, which he embellished with his sketches.

In 1934, Bemelmans wrote and illustrated his first children's book, *Hansi,* but his first important success came with *Madeline* (1939), a beguiling account of a little girl in Paris. Four more *Madeline* books followed, all marked by a blend of sophistication and innocence that has appealed to readers of all ages. Bemelmans' writings for adults include the novels *Now I Lay Me Down to Sleep* (1943), *Dirty Eddie* (1947), *Are You Hungry Are You Cold* (1960), and *The Street Where the Heart Lies,* published posthumously in 1963. Although these works are mainly satirical, any intended trenchancy in them gives way inevitably to the author's natural ebullience and good humor. His short stories, essays, and sketches appeared in leading magazines, and his paintings have been shown in major galleries. He died at New York City on Oct. 1, 1962.

BEMENT, bē′ment, **Clarence Sweet** (1843–1923), American collector. He was born in Mishawaka, Ind., on April 11, 1843. The son of a manufacturer and inventor of machine tools, he was a businessman who devoted much of his leisure time to a mineral collection that eventually become one of the foremost in the world. In 1900 it was purchased by J. Pierpont Morgan for the American Museum of Natural History in New York City. The mineral bementite is named after him.

Another major interest was his rare book collection, a portion of which was bought by Harry Elkins Widener and formed the nucleus of the Widener Library at Harvard. Bement was also associated with A.S.W. Rosenbach in the book-dealing firm of Rosenbach and Company. Later he became interested in numismatics and established one of the finest coin collections in America. He died in Philadelphia on Jan. 27, 1923.

BEMIDJI, bə-mij′ē, a city in northern Minnesota, is situated on Bemidji Lake, 140 miles (225 km) northwest of Duluth. It is the seat of Beltrami County and the center of a resort area noted for its excellent hunting and fishing. There are also industries manufacturing woolens, plywood and hardboard, and cement. Bemidji was originally an important lumber center. An 18-foot (5-meter) statue of Paul Bunyan, mythical lumberman-hero, and Babe, his blue ox, stands on the shore of Lake Bemidji. Named for a Chippewa chief, Bemidji was settled about 1892 and incorporated as a village in 1896 and as a city in 1905. It is the home of Bemidji State College. Government is by city manager. Population: 11,490.

LILA BRUUN, *Bemidji Public Library*

BEMIS, bē′mis, **Samuel Flagg** (1891–1973), American historian. Born in Worcester, Mass., on Oct. 20, 1891, he graduated from Clark University in 1912 and received a Ph.D. from Harvard in 1916. He taught at Whitman College, George Washington University, and elsewhere before settling at Yale in 1935 as professor of diplomatic history. In 1961 he was president of the American Historical Association.

From the beginning of his career, Bemis made American diplomatic history his specialty. His *Jay's Treaty: A Study in Commerce and Diplomacy* (1924) won a $3,000 prize offered by the Knights of Columbus. A companion piece, *Pinckney's Treaty* (1926), was awarded the 1927 Pulitzer Prize for history. In 1935, Bemis brought out *The Diplomacy of the American Revolution* and in 1936 the *Diplomatic History of the United States,* a widely used introduction to this field. He was editor and part author of *The American Secretaries of State and Their Diplomacy* (10 vols., 1927–29), to which more volumes were added subsequently. With Grace Gardner Griffin, he compiled *Guide to the Diplomatic History of the United States* (1935).

Bemis' most distinguished work was a 2-volume study of John Quincy Adams. The first volume, *John Quincy Adams and the Foundations of American Foreign Policy* (1949), won the Pulitzer Prize for biography in 1950. The second volume, *John Quincy Adams and the Union,* appeared in 1956. The emphasis in this work is on the diplomatic achievements of Adams, whom Bemis called one of the ablest men of his time. Bemis retired from Yale in 1960. He died in Bridgeport, Conn., on Sept. 26, 1973.

MICHAEL KRAUS, *The City College, New York*
Author of "The Writing of American History"

BEN BELLA, ben bel′ə, **Mohammed** (1919–   ), Algerian independence leader and first president of the Republic of Algeria. He was born in Marnia, in western Algeria, on Dec. 25, 1919, and attended school in Tlemcen. During World War II he joined the French army and fought in Italy, receiving several decorations for bravery. Rapidly disenchanted with the failure of the French to extend Muslim rights in Algeria after the war, he decided that armed rebellion would be necessary to achieve Algeria's independence.

When the French cracked down on extreme nationalists in Algeria, Ben Bella escaped to Cairo. He was one of the nine founders of the Revolutionary Committee of Unity and Action (CRUA), which organized the war of independence that started on Nov. 1, 1954. He became arms procurer for the National Liberation Front (successor to the CRUA) and in 1956 was arrested by the French and imprisoned in France. While in prison, Ben Bella was named deputy premier by the provisional government of the Algerian republic at its creation in 1958. He was released following the cease-fire agreement signed in March 1962 and returned to Algeria.

In alliance with the army under Houari Boumedienne, Ben Bella seized control of Algiers and became prime minister of the new republic. He enunciated a policy of Algerian socialism and instituted sweeping reforms. In a referendum held in 1963 he was elected president of Algeria. He was overthrown by a coup on June 19, 1965.

L. GRAY COWAN, *Columbia University*

BEN DAY PROCESS. See DAY, BENJAMIN; PHOTOENGRAVING—*The Ben Day Shading Process.*

BEN-EZRA. See IBN EZRA, ABRAHAM BEN MEIR.

BEN-GABIROL. See IBN GABIROL, SOLOMON BEN JUDAH.

BEN-GURION, ben gŏŏr-yôn', **David** (1886–1973), first prime minister of Israel, who may be called the father of his country. A flamboyant socialist politician, creative statesman, indefatigable orator, and amateur philosopher, he held the premiership, with a two-year voluntary interruption (1953–1955), for a dozen years. In that period he durably shaped the society and the domestic politics of Israel and its international role.

Career to 1948. Born *David Green* (or *Gryn*) on Oct. 16, 1886, in the Polish city of Płońsk (then part of czarist Russia), he settled at the age of 20 in Palestine, then a neglected corner of the decaying Ottoman (Turkish) empire, and became a leader of the nascent Zionist socialist movement. Exiled in 1915 on suspicion of favoring the Allied cause, he traveled to the United States to help found Hechalutz (or He-Haluz) organization for the training of prospective socialist emigrants to Palestine. He also joined, and assisted in raising recruits for, the Jewish Legion, which was attached in 1917–1918 to the British forces that fought against the Turks in Palestine and the other Ottoman Asian provinces.

Soon after the Palestine mandate was assigned to Britain in 1920, the Histadrut, or General Organization of Jewish Labor in Palestine, came into being. The Histadrut grew into the country's most powerful nongovernmental body, furnishing Ben-Gurion, its secretary-general from 1921 to 1935, with his principal source of influence in the affairs of the Palestinian Jewish community. He gradually converted this influence into political power. Late in 1930 he masterminded the fusion of the two largest socialist parties into the united Mapai, or Palestine Workers Party. In 1935 he rose to the chairmanship of the World Zionist Organization and of the Jewish Agency for Palestine, the guardians of the Jewish National Home. He clung to the two posts until the expiration of the mandate in 1948, and thus presided over the Jewish quasi-government in the critical years of preparation for independence.

In World War II, Ben-Gurion remained the inflexible foe of British policy on Palestine, formulated in the White Paper of 1939, which restricted Jewish immigration and settlement at the time when the Nazis were pursuing their program of exterminating the Jews. He urged his fellow Jews to continue fighting the "White Paper as if there were no war, and the war as if there were no White Paper." The British policy outlasted the war, and Jewish resistance to Britain was intensified, developing by 1946 into a struggle for independence. In the crucial months that followed, Ben-Gurion provided the leadership that by May 1948 transformed the mandate into the sovereign state of Israel.

Prime Minister. Ben-Gurion contrived the system of coalition rule under which Mapai, though a minority party, dominated successive governments. As the recurrent prime minister he invariably retained for himself the defense portfolio. From the outset he recognized that Israel's survival in the hostile Arab environment dictated achieving a favorable military balance.

Ben-Gurion's inflexibility, which in Israel's formative years proved a mighty asset, became in the state's adolescence a mighty liability—a divisive rather than a unifying force. He finally released the political controls in his 77th year, in 1963; by then, a whole generation of aspiring politicians had been bypassed. His political star

David Ben-Gurion, Israeli statesman.

began to pale even before he left the helm, but he was never voted out of office. He stepped down twice of his own accord (1953 and 1963). He staged one comeback in 1955 (to plan and direct Israel's preemptive strike against Egypt in Sinai a year later) but was defeated in a second attempt in 1965, when he separated from Mapai to form his own socialist party, Rafi. He died in Tel Aviv on Dec. 1, 1973.

J.C. HUREWITZ, *Columbia University*

Further Reading: Edelman, Maurice, *David: the Story of Ben Gurion* (New York 1965).

BEN-HUR, ben hur, subtitled *A Tale of the Christ*, is a novel by Lew Wallace (q.v.), first published in 1880 and reissued in many editions. It became one of the best-selling books in American publishing history, selling more than 2.5 million copies in the United States alone.

The action takes place at the beginning of the Christian era, mainly in Jerusalem. John the Baptist and Jesus appear in the story, which is, however, principally concerned with the adventures of Judah Ben-Hur, his mother, and his sister, and the conversion of the hero to the Christian faith. Falsely accused by his boyhood friend Messala of attempting to assassinate the Roman governor of Judea, Ben-Hur is sentenced for life in the Roman galleys. His mother and his sister are imprisoned in a dungeon and there contract leprosy. Ben-Hur escapes from the galleys and saves the life of a powerful Roman, who adopts him and brings him to Rome. Although he has gained freedom and wealth, Ben-Hur returns to Jerusalem, where, in the novel's best-known episode, he exacts his revenge on Messala in a chariot race. He is later reunited with his mother and sister, whom Jesus miraculously cures.

Ben-Hur has been presented many times on the stage and has served as the basis of two spectacularly successful films (1926 and 1959).

BEN NEVIS, ben nĕ'vis, is the highest mountain in Great Britain. It is situated in Inverness County, Scotland, 5 miles (8 km) southeast of Fort William. It reaches an altitude of 4,406 feet (1,343 meters), with a precipice of 1,450 feet (442 meters) on the northeast side. Ben Nevis is of volcanic origin.

BEN-ZVI, ben-tsvē', **Yizhaq** (1884–1963), second president of Israel, who was one of the country's founding fathers. He was born *Isaac Shimshelivitz* on Nov. 24, 1884, in Poltava in the Ukraine. An ardent Zionist, he settled in Ottoman (Turkish) Palestine at the age of 23 and began the study of law in 1912 at the University of Istanbul. After the Ottoman empire entered World War I on the German side, Ben-Zvi became an enemy alien, was exiled from Palestine, and eventually found his way to the United States, where he helped recruit the Jewish Legion. As a legionnaire he belonged to a volunteer unit of the British army and participated in the capture of Palestine.

While living under Ottoman rule, Ben-Zvi had already begun to play a principal role in fashioning the antecedents to those agencies of the Jewish community of Palestine that eventually became central to Jewish sovereignty—self-governing institutions, defense forces, and organized labor. Under the British mandate that immediately followed World War I, Ben-Zvi served on the municipal council of Jerusalem and on the Va'ad Leumi, or National Council, of Palestine's Jewish community, becoming its chairman in 1931 and its president in 1944. As the elected leader of the Palestine Jewish community, he helped shape that community's contribution to the Allied effort in World War II and to the postwar struggle for independence.

Ben-Zvi was one of the signers of Israel's declaration of independence on May 14, 1948, and he sat in the first Kneset (unicameral legislature) as a representative of Mapai, the moderate socialist labor party that dominated Israel's coalition cabinets. On the death in 1952 of Israel's first president, Chaim Weizmann, the Kneset elected Ben-Zvi to that honorific office.

Ben-Zvi was a writer rather than an orator and a political mediator rather than a political actor, and he exerted a calming influence on the public. His equable personality won him support among all parties. As a result, he was twice reelected head of state. His knowledge of Arabic and Turkish enabled him to study the history of the Jews in Muslim lands, on which he wrote several monographs. Ben-Zvi died in office on April 23, 1963.

J.C. HUREWITZ, *Columbia University*

BENALCÁZAR, Sebastián de. See BELALCÁZAR, SEBASTIÁN DE.

BENARES, bi-nä'res, was a princely state in northern India. Created out of the family domains of the maharaja of Benares in 1911, it was the last of the princely states to be organized. It consisted of two sections lying along the Ganges River and had an area of 866 square miles (2,243 sq km). The capital was Ramnagar. On Oct. 15, 1949, Benares was merged with the state of Uttar Pradesh.

BENARES, city, India. See VARANASI.

BENAVENTE Y MARTÍNEZ, bä-nä-vän'tā ē märtē'näth, **Jacinto** (1866–1954), Spanish dramatist, who received the Nobel Prize for literature in 1922. He was born in Madrid on Aug. 12, 1866, and went to the University of Madrid, where he began to study law before turning to literature. His first significant publication was *Versos* (1893), which was followed by essays, sketches,

and contributions to journals. His first play, *El nido ajeno* (*Another's Nest*), was produced in 1894.

In 1896 the production of Benavente's *Gente conocida* (*People You Know*) established his reputation as a playwright. This was followed in 1898 by *La comida de las fieras* (*The Feast of Wild Animals*), a satire directed against the highest social classes of Madrid.

Benavente's other plays include *La gobernadora* (1901; Eng. tr., *The Governor's Wife*), *La noche del sábado* (1903; Eng. tr., *Saturday Night*, 1918), *Rosas de otoño* (1905; Eng. tr., *Autumnal Roses*, 1919), *Los malhechores del bien* (1905; Eng. tr., *The Evil Doers of Good*, 1917), *La princesa Bebé* (1906), *Los intereses creados* (1907; Eng. tr., *The Bonds of Interest*, 1917), *La malquerida* (1913; Eng. tr., *The Passion Flower*, 1920), *Pepa Doncel* (1928), and *La infanzona* (1945; *The Noblewoman*). Benavente became a member of the Spanish Academy in 1913. He died in Madrid on July 14, 1954.

Los intereses creados and *La malquerida* are generally considered to be Benavente's best works. *Los intereses creados* resembles a puppet play and utilizes the conventions of the *commedia dell'arte*. *La malquerida* draws from classical mythology to present a treatment of the Hippolytus-Phaedra theme. In 1920 this play was presented in its English translation on Broadway and was enthusiastically received. It was later made into a successful movie.

Critics have attacked Benavente's plays for their lack of depth and for their excessive cleverness and sophistication. However, his drama bears the mark of master craftsmanship and contains sparkling and plausible dialogue, as well as penetrating observation of character. His best works consistently show a genuine understanding of human frailty.

Bibliography

Texts of Benavente's works have been published as *Obras completas*, 4th ed., 11 vols. (Madrid 1958); John G. Underhill translated many of the plays into English, 4 vols. (New York 1917–24).
Onís, Federico de, *Jacinto Benavente* (New York 1923).
Perez de Ayala, Ramón, *Las máscaras* (Madrid 1924).
Starkie, Walter F., *Jacinto Benavente* (New York 1924).

BENAVIDES, bä-nä-vē'thäs, **Óscar Raimundo** (1876–1945), Peruvian soldier and political leader. He was born in Lima on March 15, 1876, and studied at military schools in Peru and France before accepting a commission in the Peruvian army. He became chief of staff of the Peruvian army in 1913 and headed the military junta that overthrew President Guillermo Billinghurst in 1914. He immediately became chief of the governing junta and was provisional president for a short time in 1915. Subsequently, for nearly two decades, he was either in exile or filling diplomatic posts.

When a crisis developed over Peru's seizure of Leticia, Colombia's outlet to the Amazon, Benavides was recalled and made minister of defense in 1933. Following the assassination of President Luis Sánchez Cerro in the same year, congress elected him president. His administration was marked by advances in social welfare, settlement of the Colombian dispute, and strong opposition to the leftist Aprista movement. Faced with an Aprista victory in the 1936 presidential election, Benavides voided the election results and ruled until 1939 as a virtual dictator. He was ambassador to Spain (1940) and to Argentina (1941). He died in Lima on July 2, 1945.

536   BENBOW–BENDA

BENBOW, ben′bō, **John** (1653–1702), English admiral. He ran away to sea and served in the navy and the merchant marine before being commissioned as a lieutenant in 1689. Within a few months he was promoted captain and commanded vessels in operations against the French in the English Channel. He also participated in attacks on the French ports of Saint-Malo and Dunkirk. As a rear admiral in 1696 he was ordered to pursue the French commander Jean Bart, but was unable to bring him to action. He led an expedition against pirates in the West Indies in 1698.

In 1702, Benbow was again sent to the West Indies, as vice admiral in command of a fleet to fight the French. On August 19 his seven ships encountered nine French vessels off Santa Marta, Colombia. The fleets engaged in intermittent battle for five days. On August 24, Benbow's right leg was broken by an enemy shot. After the wound had been attended to, he was brought to his quarter deck. The captains of his other ships suddenly appeared on board to demand that the action be ended. Benbow yielded to their judgment and took the fleet to Jamaica, where he ordered a court martial to be convened. As a result of the court's findings, two captains were shot, a third was dismissed from the navy, and two others were suspended from duty.

Benbow died at Port Royal on Nov. 4, 1702, before the sentences were carried out. Some writers have contended that the irresolution of his captains in the battle was due to Benbow's failings.

BENCH, the place where a judge sits in court, hence the judge or judges of a court. As a collective term, "the bench" is commonly used to designate the judiciary as a whole, as distinguished from counselors and attorneys at law, who are referred to as "the bar." The term may also refer to a particular class of judges, or the judges comprising a particular court, as in the phrases "the high bench," used to describe the justices of the U.S. Supreme Court or other high court, and "the full bench," denoting all of the judges of a specific court. It is sometimes used in the description of particular courts, such as the King's or the Queen's Bench (a former court of record in England). In English ecclesiastical law, the word "bench" may also refer to the aggregate body of bishops.

BENCH WARRANT, a writ or process issued by a presiding judge or by a court, for the attachment or arrest of a person. Commonly employed to compel attendance in cases of contempt committed outside the courtroom, or to bring an accused into court after indictment, the bench warrant may also be used under some circumstances to require the appearance of a witness, to produce an escaped prisoner, to bring a convict confined in a penitentiary to trial in another case, and for similar purposes.

BENCHLEY, bench′lē, **Robert** (1889–1945), American humorist. He was born in Worcester, Mass., on Sept. 15, 1889, and was educated at Phillips Exeter Academy and Harvard University. At Harvard he showed an early talent for humor as editor of the *Lampoon.* As a writer he became famous for his inspired nonsense, in short pieces published in newspapers and in such magazines as the *New Yorker.*

In 1923, Benchley made his first stage appearance, which was highly successful, doing a monologue entitled *The Treasurer's Report, and Other Aspects of Community Singing.* From 1929 he acted in a series of movie shorts and theatrical revues. His specialty was portraying a confused and ordinary little man who laughed at his own misfortunes. Among the best of his films was *How to Sleep,* which won an Academy Award as the best film short of 1936. From 1937 he was a popular master of ceremonies on radio broadcasts. He died in New York City on Nov. 21, 1945.

Benchley's books include *Of All Things* (1921), *Love Conquers All* (1922), *The Early Worm* (1927), *From Bed to Worse; or, Comforting Thoughts About the Bison* (1934), *My Ten Years in a Quandary and How They Grew* (1936), *Inside Benchley* (1942), and *One Minute, Please* (1945).

Nathaniel Benchley (1915–   ), his son, was a novelist and short-story writer. He was born in Newton, Mass., on Nov. 13, 1915, and graduated from Harvard University in 1938. He worked for the New York *Herald Tribune* and *Newsweek* magazine before devoting himself entirely to free-lance writing. His short stories appeared in numerous magazines, and a novel, *Side Street,* was published in 1950.

BEND is a city in central Oregon, 95 miles (153 km) east of Eugene. It is the seat of Deschutes County. Its major industries are sawmilling and agriculture, and it is an outdoor-recreation center for both summer and winter sports. Called "Farewell Bend" when the site was a pioneer river crossing, it was named Bend in 1900. Incorporated in 1904, Bend has a council-manager government. Population: 13,710.

BENDA, ben′dä, a family of Czech musicians, who were prominent in Germany in the 18th century.

FRANTIŠEK (FRANZ) BENDA (1709–1786) was a gifted violinist. He studied violin with his father Jan Jiří (Hans Georg) Benda, a weaver and amateur musician of Alt-Benatek, Bohemia. In 1742, František was appointed to the court orchestra of Frederick the Great of Prussia, and the family moved to Potsdam. He served Frederick for 40 years as violinist, concertmaster, and composer, and accompanied the king, himself a gifted flutist and composer, in thousands of performances. Benda composed symphonies, concertos, trio sonatas, and sonatas, which still are performed occasionally.

JIŘÍ ANTONIN (GEORG) BENDA (1722–1795), younger brother of František, was an inventive composer. After the family moved to Potsdam, he was appointed court *Kappelmeister* at Gotha, where he composed music dramas, church music, symphonies, concertos, and sonatas. As the first composer to develop *Singspiele* (spoken lines in music-drama), he exerted an important influence on later musicians, particularly Mozart.

FRIEDRICH WILHELM HEINRICH BENDA (1745–1814), eldest son of František, was a violinist. As a court musician at Potsdam he composed three operas and a few instrumental works.

FRIEDRICH LUDWIG BENDA (1746–1792), eldest son of Jiří Antonin, was a composer of operas, church music, and numerous instrumental works. From 1780 until his death he was, in turn, director of the Hamburg opera, court musician at Schwerin, and concert director at Königsberg.

BENDA, baN-dá', **Julien** (1867–1956), French critic and novelist. He was born in Paris on Dec. 26, 1867, and graduated from the University of Paris in 1894. His first major work, *Mon premier testament*, appeared in 1910, followed by his first novel, *L'ordination*, in 1912.

Benda was a leader of the antiromantic movement in French criticism, and in *Le Bergsonisme, ou une philosophie de la mobilité* (1912) and *Sur le succès du Bergsonisme* (1917), he opposed the philosophical ideas of Henri Bergson. One of his most successful works is *La trahison des clercs* (1927), in which he contends that it is moral treason to permit political considerations to warp intellectual judgment. (*La trahison* was published in English translation in Britain as *The Great Betrayal,* and in the United States as *The Treason of the Intellectuals,* both in 1928.) His rationalism influenced such writers as T.S. Eliot and D.B. Wyndham Lewis. Benda died in Fontenay-aux-Roses on June 7, 1956.

BENDA, ben'də, **Wladyslaw Theodor** (1873–1948), Polish-American painter and illustrator. He was born in Poznán, Poland, on Jan. 15, 1873. He studied at the Kraków Academy of Art prior to 1899, when he settled in the United States, becoming a citizen in 1911. He made many strikingly original illustrations for books and for such periodicals as the *Century Magazine, Scribner's, Cosmopolitan, McClure's,* and *Collier's.* For use in the theater he created a new type of mask known as the Benda mask. He died in Newark, N.J., on Nov. 30, 1948.

BENDER, ben'der, **Chief** (1883–1954), American baseball player, who was elected to the National Baseball Hall of Fame in 1953 for his pitching feats with the Philadelphia Athletics. A Chippewa Indian, *Charles Albert Bender* was born in Brainerd, Minn., on May 5, 1883, and attended the Carlisle (Pa.) Indian School and Dickinson College. From 1903 to 1914 he won 193 regular season games and 6 World Series games for the A's. With Baltimore (Federal League) in 1915 and Philadelphia (National League) in 1916–1917, he raised his total major league victories to 212 against 128 losses. Bender coached at the U.S. Naval Academy in 1924–1928. He died in Philadelphia on May 22, 1954.

BILL BRADDOCK, *New York "Times"*

BENDIGO, ben'di-gō, a city in Australia, is an important gold mining center. Formerly known as Sandhurst, the city is located in the center of Victoria state, 80 miles (129 km) northwest of Melbourne. It was founded in 1851, when gold was discovered in the surrounding area. From a mining settlement it expanded rapidly, becoming a city in 1871. Bendigo is now a busy manufacturing city and rail center. Its products include wine and beer, woolen textiles, leather goods, and pottery. Population: (1961) 30,195.

BENDIX, ben'diks, **Vincent** (1882–1945), American engineer, inventor, and industrialist. He is known especially for his work in developing improved automobile components and for his pioneering activities in the aviation industry.

Bendix was born in Moline, Ill., on Aug. 12, 1882. At the age of 16 he went to New York City and studied mechanics and engineering. Within a decade he had organized his own automobile production company, and by the age of 30 he had developed the Bendix drive for automobiles. This drive made practical for the first time the use of self-starters in automobiles. In the same period the brake company that he organized began the first mass production of four-wheel brakes. Other products associated with Bendix are generators, magnetos, a radio-direction-finding apparatus for oceangoing vessels, an automatic home washer, and landing gears for airplanes.

In 1929, Bendix combined several companies to form the Bendix Aviation Corporation. Under his direction it became a manufacturing concern of world importance. Besides aviation, marine, and automobile equipment, the corporation manufactured a variety of radio and radar devices. Bendix also showed his interest in aviation by founding the Bendix Transcontinental Air Race (1931), for which he donated the Bendix trophy.

Bendix resigned as board chairman of the aviation company in 1942 to form Bendix Helicopters, Inc. He planned to develop a four-passenger helicopter for mass production, but his death in New York City on March 27, 1945, came before he could achieve this aim.

BENDS, bendz, is an illness in which gas bubbles are present in body tissues. The bubbles press on tissues and obstruct blood vessels, causing pain or damage to vital organs. Also known as *decompression sickness, caisson disease,* and *aeroembolism,* the disease results from exposure to rapidly decreasing atmospheric pressure. Its most frequent victims are tunnel workers and deep-sea divers, who must surface after prolonged periods of breathing compressed air, and flyers of unpressurized aircraft that ascend higher than 25,000 feet (7,500 meters).

The cause of bends can be explained by simple physical principles. Since a caisson worker breathes air at high pressure (one atmosphere for each 33 feet, or 10 meters, of descent below sea level), additional nitrogen is forced into solution in his body, especially in fatty tissue. If he remains for several hours and then ascends to sea level too quickly, the extra nitrogen bubbles out of solution. Nitrogen is less diffusible than carbon dioxide and oxygen; thus the body is not able to equilibrate rapidly its nitrogen content with that of the air outside. The result is bends.

The symptoms of decompression sickness have been given rather colorful names. The "bends" is the severe pain in muscles and joints that contorts the limbs, while the "chokes" describes a difficulty in breathing and a constricted feeling in the chest. Sometimes there is a loss of equilibrium, called the "staggers." Involvement of the brain and spinal cord can result in paralysis or even death. Extreme fatigue, skin rashes, and itching also are common symptoms.

Most symptoms are reversible if treatment is begun very early. The patient first is "recompressed"—returned to high atmospheric pressure—in a device designed for the purpose. He then is slowly "decompressed"—brought to sea-level air pressure. Preventive measures include replacing nitrogen in the compressed air with the more easily diffusible helium; controlling the rate of decompression as a caisson ascends; and excluding obese and other vulnerable individuals from such work.

IRVING SOLOMON, M.D.
Mount Sinai School of Medicine, New York

BENEDEK, ba'nə-dek, **Ludwig August von** (1804–1881), Austrian military officer. He was born in Sopron, Hungary, on July 14, 1804. He joined the army as an ensign in 1822. By 1846 he was a colonel, and he won recognition in suppressing an insurrection in Galicia. He fought against the Italians in 1847–1848, and against the Hungarian patriots in 1849. He distinguished himself at the Battle of Solferino in 1859.

Benedek was military governor of Hungary in 1860, and soon after was made commander in chief of the Austrian Army in Venetia and the Alpine provinces. In the war with Prussia in 1866 he commanded the Austrians until after his defeat at Sadowa, when he was superseded. He died in Graz, Austria, on April 27, 1881.

BENEDETTI, bā-nā-dāt'tē, **Count Vincent** (1817–1900), French diplomat known for his role in the outbreak of the Franco-Prussian War. He was born in Bastia, Corsica, on April 29, 1817. Educated as a lawyer, he entered the diplomatic service in 1840 and held posts in Cairo, Palermo, and Constantinople. In 1861 he was appointed ambassador to Italy, and in 1864 to Prussia.

In 1870 great excitement was aroused throughout Europe when Chancellor Bismarck caused the publication of a draft in Benedetti's handwriting of a secret treaty between France and Prussia, in which the latter agreed to French occupation of part of Belgium. The document's authenticity was not denied, and other European powers condemned France for its expansionism.

At the same time Benedetti was under orders to request that King William of Prussia confirm the withdrawal of Prince Leopold of Hohenzollern-Sigmaringen as a candidate for the crown of Spain. Through the Ems Dispatch (q.v.), which was released to the press, Bismarck announced King William's refusal to accept the French demand. The refusal greatly offended France and was made a pretext for declaring war on Prussia within a few days.

Benedetti's diplomatic career ended with the war. He withdrew from public life to practice law in Corsica. In 1871 he published a pamphlet charging Bismarck with the whole responsibility of the secret treaty, to which the latter made a vigorous reply. Benedetti was the author of *Ma mission en Prusse* (1871), and *Essais diplomatiques* (Eng. tr., *Studies in Diplomacy*, 1896). He died in Paris on March 28, 1900.

BENEDETTO DA MAIANO (1442–1497), bā-nā-det'tō dä mä-yä'nō, Italian sculptor and architect, whose pulpit for the Church of Santa Croce in Florence is the finest example of marble pictorial relief in Italian sculpture. His real name was *Benedetto di Leonardo*. He was born in Maiano, near Florence, in 1442. By 1474 he was established in Florence and was already renowned for his graceful, yet strong, carving. His most celebrated work—the pulpit for Santa Croce (1472–1475)—combines sculpture and architecture, with carvings depicting scenes from the life of St. Francis.

The influential Strozzi family of Florence employed Benedetto to design the work on which his reputation as an architect rests—the Strozzi palace in Florence. This work, begun in 1489, was completed after his death. In 1490 he did a portrait bust of Filippo Strozzi the Elder, and in 1491 he designed Filippo's tomb. Benedetto died in Florence on May 24 or 27, 1497.

BENEDICT, ben'ə-dikt, **Saint** (c. 480–547), the father of Western monasticism. He is often called *St. Benedict of Nursia*. He was born at Nursia, near Spoleto, Italy. His family were undoubtedly gentry of sufficient means to educate him in the classics at Rome. The sole primary source on Benedict's life, the *Dialogues* of St. Gregory the Great, reports that he was appalled by the immorality of Rome and retired to the mountain wilderness of the Abruzzi. Settling eventually at Subiaco, he lived in the caves, aided only by Romanus, a neighboring monk, who brought him food and gave him monk's robes to wear. A community of hermits at Vicovaro, attracted by Benedict's piety, invited him to be their superior. However, Benedict's conviction that a superior must be a lawgiver, as well as a spiritual father, created conflict, and he returned to Subiaco.

At Subiaco, Benedict enjoyed neither solitude nor anonymity. Disciples flocked to him, and again he assumed the role of superior. He organized 12 monasteries, each with 12 monks under a superior. Benedict remained abbot of Subiaco until the enmity of a local priest forced him to leave with a small band of disciples. On the mountain of Cassino, around the year 520, Benedict established the monastery that became the mother foundation of one of the most influential religious organizations in the world (see BENEDICTINES). At Monte Cassino he composed the rule that eventually replaced the Eastern and Celtic rules throughout Europe and became the basic guide for Western monastic life. Renowned for his many miracles and the gift of prophecy, St. Benedict predicted the day and hour of his death. On that day—March 21, 547—he was carried to the church at Cassino, where he received communion and died. His feast is kept on March 21.

T. MICHAEL HALL, O.S.B.
The Catholic University of America

BENEDICT I (died 579), ben'ə-dikt, pope from 575 to 579. During the Lombard invasion of Italy, he showed generosity to the starving people. He died on July 30, 579, as the Lombards were besieging his native Rome.

BENEDICT II, ben'ə-dikt, **Saint** (died 685), pope in 684–685. A Roman, he was trained for an ecclesiastical career. He distinguished himself in service to Popes Agatho and Leo II and was elected pope after Leo's death in 683. During his 11-month reign he secured Emperor Constantine IV's agreement to abolish the requirement of imperial confirmation of a pope-elect; strove to reconcile Marcarius, leader of the Monothelites, to the church (see MONOTHELITES); and upheld the claims of St. Wilfrid of York (see WILFRID, SAINT). He died in 685 on May 8, the day celebrated as his feast.

BENEDICT III (died 858), ben'ə-dikt, pope from 855 to 858. Treachery delayed his accession to the papacy. Envoys dispatched to obtain ratification of his election from emperors Lothair and Louis II substituted the name of Cardinal Anastasius. The emperors unwittingly confirmed Anastasius pope, but the people of Rome rebelled and forced Benedict's reinstatement. Benedict restored Rome, which had been devastated by the Saracens in 846. Pope Benedict died on April 7, 858.

BENEDICT IV (died 903), ben′ə-dikt, pope from 900 to 903. Of noble Roman birth, he was acclaimed by contemporaries for his generosity and zeal for the public good. He crowned Emperor Louis III the Blind and granted special privileges to the great German monastery at Fulda.

BENEDICT V (died 965), ben′ə-dikt, pope in 964–965. Elected after the death of John XII, he incurred the wrath of Emperor Otto I, who had selected Leo VIII as pope. Otto marched on Rome, restored Leo, and took Benedict to Germany. Acknowledged as pope by some German clergy, Benedict died in the custody of the archbishop of Hamburg-Bremen on July 4, 965.

BENEDICT VI (died 974), ben′ə-dikt, pope in 973–974. He was elected in 972 to succeed John XIII, but his consecration was delayed. A faction of Roman nobles, led by Crescentius, brother of John XIII, seized power, imprisoned Benedict, and in August 974 strangled him and placed on the throne the antipope Boniface VII.

BENEDICT VII (died 983), ben′ə-dikt, pope from 974 to 983. He was bishop of Sutri before he was elected pope through the influence of Emperor Otto II. He succeeded the antipope Boniface VII, who was forced to leave Rome by the imperial envoy, Count Sicco. During his peaceful nine-year reign, Benedict reasserted the position of the papacy, advanced monasticism, and checked simony. He died in his native Rome in October 983.

BENEDICT VIII (died 1024), ben′ə-dikt, pope from 1012 to 1024. At this period whichever faction dominated Rome also controlled the papacy. Thus, the powerful Alban dukes of the house of Tusculo obtained the papacy for three of their own. Benedict VIII, a layman and son of Gregorio Tusculo, was the first of the Tusculum popes. An effective ruler, he made an alliance with the Normans to defeat the Saracens, crowned Henry II emperor at St. Peter's in 1014, and obtained from Henry confirmation of the Holy See's right to the donations of Charlemagne and Otto. He also reduced the privileges of the nobility who had taken over ecclesiastical estates. A progressive as well as strong pontiff, Benedict supported the monastic reforms advocated by the Abbey of Cluny, suppressed clerical immorality, and officially added the Nicene creed to the Roman rite. He was succeeded by his brother, John XIX.

BENEDICT IX (c. 1011–1055), ben′ə-dikt, pope from 1032 to 1044. A count of Tusculum and nephew of popes Benedict VIII and John XIX, he was little more than 20 years old when elected pope. His dissolute life gave factions hostile to his family an excuse to overthrow him and install the antipope Sylvester III in March 1045. By May, Benedict had expelled the usurper, but he soon resigned in favor of his godfather Giovanni Graziano (see GREGORY VI). Regretting this, Benedict attempted to regain the papacy, but Emperor Henry III intervened. The Synod of Sutri (1046) rejected all three claimants and named Clement II pope. On the death of the latter, Benedict tried for the last time to obtain the chair but was defeated. He retired to a monastery at Grottaferrata.

BENEDICT X, ben′ə-dikt, antipope in 1058–1059. His original name was *Giovanni Mincio.* He was a cardinal when he was named pope by a faction of Roman nobles who opposed the reformers led by Hildebrand (later Gregory VII). The reformers, supported by Empress Agnes, elected Nicholas II pope. Benedict was deposed and was imprisoned in Rome, where he died around 1080. See also GREGORY VII.

BENEDICT XI, ben′ə-dikt, **Blessed** (1240–1304), pope in 1303–1304. Born *Niccolò Boccasini,* at Treviso, Italy, he entered the Dominican order and became master general in 1276. Elevated to cardinal in 1298, he served Pope Boniface VIII in several capacities, chiefly as peacemaker to King Philip IV of France. Relations between Boniface and France finally crumbled completely when Sciarra Colonna, an Italian nobleman, and Guillaume de Nogaret, one of Philip's ministers, attempted to seize Boniface at Anagni. The pope was rescued by the people but died a month later and was succeeded by Benedict.

The new pope established peaceful relations with France by removing papal censure but excommunicated Guillaume de Nogaret and Sciarra Colonna. Benedict died suddenly at Perugia on July 7, 1304. It is believed that Guillaume de Nogaret poisoned him. Clement XII beatified Benedict XI in 1773.

BENEDICT XII (1285–1342), ben′ə-dikt, pope from 1334 to 1342. Born *Jacques Fornier,* Saverdum (Foix), France, he became a Cistercian monk and a master at the University of Paris. A distinguished theologian, he was made bishop of Pamier and Mirepoix successively and in 1327 was elevated to cardinal. At this period the pope was residing at Avignon, in France, but there was pressure for a return to Rome. Benedict was elected pope in 1334 as a compromise candidate by cardinals wishing to remain at Avignon. He surprised the curia by implementing reforms within a month of his accession. He ordered all clergy at Avignon who had benefices elsewhere to return to their duties, reorganized the papal offices to prevent bribery, and vowed to return to Rome. Realizing that Italy's chaotic condition precluded this, he undertook the construction of the papal palace (Palais-Vieux) at Avignon.

This austere and zealous man's attempts to reform religious orders and to intervene in politics were ineffectual because of the papacy's lack of prestige. Although Petrarch and others maligned Benedict, his integrity and his honest desire to purify the church are historically evident. He died at Avignon on April 24, 1342.

BENEDICT XIII (c. 1329–1423), ben′ə-dikt, antipope from 1394 to 1423. He was born *Pedro de Luna* of a noble family of Aragon. His virtuous life, learning, industry, and diplomatic skill attracted the attention of Gregory XI, who made him a cardinal in 1375. He took part in the election of Pope Urban VI but later shifted his allegiance to the antipope, Clement VII, at Avignon. Elected to succeed Clement in 1394, he pledged to end the Great Schism of the West. However, he obstinately resisted every attempt to end the split in the papacy. Deposed by the Council of Constance in 1417, he fled to Spain. He continued to claim the papacy until his death on May 23, 1423.

BENEDICT XIII (1649–1730), ben'ə-dikt, pope from 1724 to 1730. He was born *Pietro Francesco Orsini*, of the archducal Orsini-Gravina family, on Feb. 2, 1649, at Gravina, Italy. Despite family protest, he became a Dominican friar and was advanced to cardinal in 1672. In four conclaves called to elect popes he was one of the *zelanti*, a group of cardinals who agreed to consider only the spiritual qualifications of a candidate. He accepted his own election to the papacy only in obedience to his Dominican superior.

As pope, he left political decisions to his advisers and thus was led into blunders in dealings with the kings of Savoy, Naples, Portugal, and France. He directed his energies to renewing spirituality in the church. By demanding universal and unqualified adherence to Clement XI's bull *Unigenitus*, a condemnation of Jansenism, he virtually destroyed this heresy. Many of his efforts at reform were vitiated by the unscrupulous Cardinal Coscia. Benedict trusted him with ecclesiastical government and remained ignorant of his venality. After Benedict's death on Feb. 23, 1730, Cardinal Coscia was imprisoned by the Romans.

BENEDICT XIV, ben'ə-dikt, antipope, who claimed rule from about 1425 to 1430. He was elected on the authority of only one cardinal after the death of the antipope Benedict XIII. Little more is known of his life.

BENEDICT XIV (1675–1758), ben'ə-dikt, pope from 1740 to 1758. Of a distinguished Bolognese family, he was born *Prospero Lambertini* on March 31, 1675. Educated at Rome, his exceptional gifts were detected early, and immediately after his ordination he was appointed to the Roman curia. He advanced rapidly, acquiring an almost legendary reputation for learning, hard work, and sound judgment. He became titular bishop of Theodosia (1725), archbishop of Ancona (1727), cardinal (1728), and archbishop of Bologna (1731). He participated in the conclave of 1740, which, because of rivalries of the Catholic political powers, lasted for over six months. Finally, on the 255th ballot, Lambertini was proclaimed pope (August 17). His election was well received everywhere, by Catholics and non-Catholics, especially in scholarly and literary circles.

The low prestige of the Holy See at the time of Benedict's accession made it necessary for him to adopt a defensive policy on every side. Inflexible in matters of principle, the realistic Benedict was nevertheless anxious for compromise and conciliation in political matters. His willingness to go to the limit of possible concession has been criticized as occasionally excessive. In the Spanish Concordat he ceded control of 12,000 benefices to the crown, retaining only 52 for the Holy See. Similar concessions to the kingdoms of Naples, Sardinia, and Portugal greatly increased state control of the clergy. His long reign encompassed the War of the Austrian Succession and the first part of the Seven Years' War—both of which involved him in difficulties with the courts of Berlin and Vienna.

If his political policies were perhaps too yielding, Benedict governed the church with wisdom and firmness. He clarified obscure laws through his numerous bulls and encyclicals, ruled on the vexing question of mixed marriages, and revised the Roman Martyrology (see MARTYROLOGY). During his pontificate two new religious orders, the Passionists (1741) and the Redemptorists (1749), were recognized. He settled the controversies over the Chinese and Malabar rites and defended the Brazilian Indians against the Portuguese colonists.

Because of Benedict's exceptional combination of gifts, he enjoyed widespread popularity. Surrounded by scholars and literary men, he encouraged learning in every field. He was the first pope praised by Protestant writers, and Voltaire even dedicated his tragedy *Mahomet* to Benedict. But his greatest claim to immortality rests on his many writings. His masterly study (1738) of the process of beatification and canonization of saints alone secures his reputation as a scholar. He was as famous for his wit and irrepressible humor as for his astonishing industry. He was a vigilant protector of Rome's ruins, established the Capitoline museum, and expanded the Vatican library. His own splendid library was given to the University of Bologna after his death at Rome on May 3, 1758.

MSGR. FLORENCE D. COHALAN
Cathedral College, New York

Further Reading: Pastor, Ludwig von, *History of the Popes* (St. Louis 1961).

BENEDICT XV (1854–1922), ben'ə-dikt, pope from 1914 to 1922. He was born *Giacomo della Chiesa*, at Genoa, on Nov. 21, 1854, of a noble family. He studied law at Genoa and then began ecclesiastical studies at Rome. After his ordination in 1878, he attended the church's foreign service school, Accademia dei Nobili Ecclesiastici, entered the diplomatic corps, and served as secretary to Marino Cardinal Rampollo during his four-year nunciature to Spain. When Rampollo was appointed papal secretary of state, della Chiesa returned to Rome. In 1907 he was appointed archbishop of Bologna and in May 1914 was elevated to cardinal. Only four months later the College of Cardinals, recognizing the need for a highly trained diplomat to guide the church in wartime, elected him pope.

World War I and its aftermath overshadowed his pontificate and absorbed most of his energy. From the beginning, Benedict XV held tenaciously to a three-point policy: to maintain the strictest neutrality, but to condemn immoral acts of either side; to do everything possible to end the war and establish a just peace; and to give maximum assistance to war victims, especially

THE BETTMANN ARCHIVE

**Pope Benedict XV
(1854–1922)**

prisoners, regardless of their creed or nationality. His proposals for a just peace, outlined in his peace note *Dès le début* (Aug. 1, 1917), foreshadowed Wilson's Fourteen Points. Though rejected by both sides, Benedict's proposals could have led to a negotiated peace in time to avert the Bolshevik Revolution and the financial exhaustion of the Western powers.

Excluded, at Italy's instigation, from the Versailles Conference, the pope nevertheless improved his relations with Italy without any formal change in the position of the Vatican or the Italian government (see CHURCH STATES). He relaxed the ban on Catholic sovereigns' visits to the king of Italy and approved the founding of the Popular party in Italy by Don Luigi Sturzo. During his reign, embassies accredited to the Vatican increased notably, and diplomatic relations with France and Portugal, severed by his predecessor, were reinstated.

Not neglectful of the inner life of the church, Benedict promulgated the Code of Canon Law begun by Pius X and wrote *Maximum illud,* the encyclical that is the charter of modern missionary work. He established the Oriental Congregation, the Oriental Institute, and the Congregation of Seminaries and Universities. He died after a brief illness on Jan. 22, 1922.

MSGR. FLORENCE D. COHALAN
Cathedral College, New York

Further Reading: Peters, Bruce, *The Life of Benedict XV* (Milwaukee 1959).

BENEDICT, ben'ə-dikt, **Sir Julius** (1804–1885), German-English conductor and composer. He was born in Stuttgart on Nov. 27, 1804. In 1821 he studied in Dresden under Carl Maria von Weber, and two years later he became the conductor for a theater in Vienna. He went to England in 1835, and in following years he was a conductor at the Norwich festival, as well as an opera conductor in London. He was knighted in 1871. He died in London on June 5, 1885.

Benedict's first opera, *Giacinta ed Ernesto* (1829), was a failure. However, his later operas, including *The Gypsy's Warning* (1838), *The Bride of Venice* (1843), *The Crusaders* (1846), *The Lily of Killarney* (1862), and *The Bride of Song* (1864) met with more success. He also wrote the cantatas *Undine* (1860), *Saint Cecilia* (1866), and *Graziella* (1882), and the oratorio *Saint Peter* (1870).

BENEDICT, ben'ə-dikt, **Ruth Fulton** (1887–1948), American anthropologist, whose studies of primitive societies lent support to the doctrine of cultural relativity. According to this doctrine, every human culture, primitive or advanced, has a set of values that distinguishes it from others. Accordingly, what is considered true, good, or right in one may not be so regarded in another. In her now classic *Patterns of Culture* (1934), Mrs. Benedict analyzed the basic structure and character of three primitive societies: the Zuñi Indians of New Mexico—peaceful, traditional, and cooperative; the Dobuans of New Guinea—hostile, treacherous, and paranoid; and the Kwakiutl Indians of Vancouver and British Columbia—competitive and status-seeking. She observed that the specific traits of each of the three primitive societies were variously repeated among so-called advanced cultures.

Mrs. Benedict was born Ruth Fulton in New York City on June 5, 1887. She studied at Vassar

College and Columbia University and became a professor of anthropology at Columbia. Her other studies include *Zuñi Mythology* (1935), *Race: Science and Politics* (1940), and *The Chrysanthemum and the Sword: Patterns of Japanese Culture* (1946). She died in New York City on Sept. 17, 1948.

BENEDICT BISCOP, ben'ə-dikt bis'kəp, **Saint** (c. 628–690), English abbot, scholar, patron of learning, and builder of monasteries. His contributions to the development of the English church were invaluable. He made five trips to Rome and brought back manuscripts, sacred relics, and art treasures, in addition to the Roman liturgical chant. From France he introduced the practice of building churches of stone and the art of making window glass. As abbot of the Benedictine monasteries at Wearmouth and Jarrow, he trained many of the foremost scholars of his time, notably the Venerable Bede, who had been entrusted to his care as a child.

St. Benedict Biscop, whose original name was *Biscop Baducing*, was born of a noble family in Northumbria, England, and lived until the age of 25 at the court of the Northumbrian king Oswy. After his second trip to Rome, he joined the Benedictine order at Lérins, France, and shortly afterward became abbot of St. Peter and St. Paul (later St. Augustine's) in Canterbury. He founded the monastery at Wearmouth in 674 and that at Jarrow in 682. His feast day is January 12.

BENEDICT OF ANIANE, ben'ə-dikt, a-nyàn', **Saint** (c. 751–821), French monastic reformer. He was born near Dijon and trained for knighthood at the court of Pepin the Short. After serving Charlemagne in the Lombard campaign (773), he decided to forsake courtly life.

At Aniane, his family estate, he founded a monastery based on the rule of St. Benedict of Nursia. It was soon adopted as a model for monastic reform by Louis I (the Pious), who wished to unite all the monasteries in the empire under one rule. Benedict wrote two guides for monastic life (*Code of Rules* and *Concord of Rules*), which Louis promulgated at the Synod of Aachen (817) as binding for all abbeys. Benedict's reforms prepared the way for the monasteries of the 10th century to flourish as great centers of learning. Benedict died at Inge in 821. His feast day is February 11.

BENEDICTINE, ben-ə-dik'tēn, is a strong, brandy-colored liqueur made in France. It is probably the oldest liqueur still made and is generally considered one of the finest. Its recipe is a secret, but it contains 28 different herbs and other flavorings, including honey and China tea. It was first made by the Benedictine monk Dom Bernardo Vincelli and was produced at his abbey until the French Revolution. At that time the abbey was destroyed, and the recipe was lost for nearly 100 years. It was rediscovered by Alexandre Legrand in a collection of old papers.

Today, Benedictine is made at the site of the original abbey. It is no longer produced by the religious order, but is made by a private corporation according to the original, still-secret recipe. The liqueur is aged for four years before it is bottled. Each bottle bears the initials "D.O.M." for *Deo optimo maximo,* meaning "To God, most great and good."

BENEDICTINE MONKS walk across the sands to Mont-Saint-Michel to commemorate the founding of this great abbey, which stands on an islet in Normandy, France.

BENEDICTINES, ben-ə-dik'tēnz, are priests, nuns, and lay brothers of the Roman Catholic Church who follow the rule of St. Benedict of Nursia (see BENEDICT, SAINT). The Benedictines are recognized both in canon law and in fact as the chief of the Roman Catholic religious orders. In the strictest sense, however, they do not constitute an order, for they are not organized under one centralized authority. Rather, each Benedictine monastery is autonomous.

Rule of St. Benedict. The pattern of Benedictine life is set by the rule that St. Benedict composed for his monks at Monte Cassino in 520. This rule has long endured because Benedict, unlike many earlier monastic legislators, established a practical rather than an austere monastic life. He intended his rule for "beginners" and made it moderate enough so that both the weak and the strong could seek God within the confines of monastic legislation. An observant and sympathetic student of human nature, Benedict did not wish to create a regimen of such rigidity that some, because of human weakness, would abandon their vocations.

Prayer, study, meals, manual labor, and other exercises necessary for a well-regulated community are carefully integrated into the rule. The rule requires that the official public prayer of the Roman Catholic Church, the Divine Office, be recited daily and that contemplative prayer and meditation also be included in the daily routine. The rule also provides that an abbot be elected from the membership, usually for life tenure. He acts as father, lawgiver, teacher, and guide to the community, and each monk professes a solemn vow of obedience to him. Benedictine monks also make the vow of perpetual stability in the monastery of their profession and the vow of "conversion of life." The latter vow, in accordance with Benedict's emphasis on the virtue of humility, requires the monks to strive constantly toward God and to abandon self-seeking. Perpetual chastity and the renunciation of private property are also promised.

History of the Benedictines. The original monastery that Benedict founded at Monte Cassino was abandoned in 575 when the Lombards devastated the area. The monks established a new community in Rome under the patronage of Pope St. Gregory the Great, who probably also gave the rule to the monastery he founded in his own home on the Caelian Hill in Rome. In 596, Pope St. Gregory sent a group of Benedictine monks, led by St. Augustine of Canterbury, to evangelize Britain. Eventually they established the first known Benedictine house outside Italy. With papal support the Benedictine rule spread rapidly throughout Europe. By 600 there were Benedictine monasteries in France, the first of which was Altupa in the diocese of Albi; by the 8th century houses in Germany had adopted the rule. Soon Benedictine monasteries extended from Spain in the west to Hungary in the east and from the Mediterranean north to Scandinavia and even to Iceland. It is estimated that by the 12th century there were in Europe at least 3,000 Benedictine monasteries of monks or nuns.

Part of this phenomenal growth can be traced to the great Burgundian Abbey of Cluny, founded by William of Aquitaine in 910. The early abbots of Cluny introduced needed reforms in monastic discipline and founded daughter houses throughout Europe. These houses and their dependencies came to form a great reform federation under the overall direction of the abbot of Cluny. Although these monasteries were primarily concerned with prayer and contemplation and with agriculture and other manual work, many of the abbeys became centers of learning. The monks preserved much of the literary heritage of the classical age and the theological writings of the early church fathers. They also acted as chroniclers and established schools for boys. To a large extent it was through them that the Scholastic tradition was perpetuated.

During the 11th century other monastic federations, which observed stricter interpretations of the rule of St. Benedict than the so-called "Black" Benedictines, were founded. The Carthusians (founded by St. Bruno at Chartreuse, France, in 1084) and the Camaldolese (founded by St. Romuald at Camaldoli, Italy, in 1012) were two such communities that wished to follow the stricter eremetical life. The Cistercians, or "White" monks, were founded by St. Robert of Molesme and St. Stephen Harding at Citeaux, France, in 1098 for the purpose of following the strict and literal observance of the rule and thus restoring the primitive Benedictine life. The Cistercians later divided into the "Common" observance and the "More Strict" observance, or, as the latter are called, the Trappists.

Benedictine life suffered a decline at the end of the Middle Ages. The Protestant Reformation ended the flourishing Benedictine family in England as well as in northern and eastern Europe. Benedictinism revived in France and Germany in the 17th century, however, and several reformed congregations were established. The congregation of St.-Maur in France, the most outstanding of these, was founded in 1618. The Maurists made great contributions to scholarship and research. Although Benedictinism again declined in the 18th century, in the 19th century its monks returned to England, and branches were established in North and South America as well as in the mission areas of Asia and Africa. In the 1960's Benedictine houses were found on every continent—a total of about 225 monasteries and 12,000 monks.

Several congregations are represented in the United States. The American-Cassinese Congregation, founded at St. Vincent Archabbey in Latrobe, Pa., by monks from Metten, Germany, has 20 member abbeys. The Swiss-American

Congregation, founded in 1854 by monks from Einsiedeln, established its original abbey at St. Meinrad, Ind., and added 16 others within 100 years. The English congregation is represented by three American monasteries. In all, there were 41 houses in the United States in the 1960's.

Benedictines regard their chief work as prayer and the performance of the church's sacred liturgy. The abbeys, however, have undertaken various labors compatible with community life and essentially of contemplative orientation. In the United States, as in other countries, education has been the major external work of the Benedictines: many of the houses conduct both colleges and secondary schools. Pastoral work has also been a significant contribution of the American Benedictines. Benedictines have been active in liturgical renewal and in reviving interest in medieval church music.

Organizational Structure. Since the Middle Ages, Benedictine monks in each monastery have been divided into so-called "choir monks" and "lay brothers." Under this system the choir monks, who normally became priests, recited the full Divine Office in choir, while the lay brothers did the bulk of the manual work. In the 20th century there has been a strong movement away from this distinction. The essential monastic vocation, as distinct from the priesthood, has been reemphasized in an attempt to recover the simplicity of the original Benedictine monasteries. In the early days, priests were few, and a single class of monks shared the common life of prayer and work, having little contact with the world.

Beyond the antonomous abbey structure, modern Benedictine monasteries are grouped into congregations along national lines. The abbots of the member abbeys meet regularly in general chapters to discuss common problems and adopt certain common rules, and they appoint one of their number to act as president of the whole congregation. The president, however, has only limited supervisory authority over the houses. The national congregations, in turn, are united in the Confederation of Black Monks of Saint Benedict, which is headed by an abbot primate.

Benedictine Nuns. The communities of women who follow the rule of St. Benedict lead a life parallel to that of the monks. Benedictine nuns existed at least during the Carolingian period and perhaps earlier; some claim that St. Scholastica, St. Benedict's twin sister, was the original Benedictine nun. In the 1960's there were 27 abbeys and priories of nuns in Europe. In the majority, the nuns are strictly cloistered; they lead a contemplative life and engage in scholarly endeavors or practice arts and crafts.

In the United States there were some 8,000 sisters from 43 mother-houses in the 1960's. These sisters follow an active life, without rules of enclosure. Many of the American communities conduct colleges and secondary schools for girls. They also maintain missions throughout the country to staff parochial schools.

T. MICHAEL HALL, O.S.B.
The Catholic University of America

Further Reading: Chapman, John, O.S.B., *Saint Benedict and the Sixth Century* (New York 1929); Delatte, Paul, O.S.B., *The Rule of St. Benedict, a Commentary* (London 1921); Hilpisch, Stephan, O.S.B., *Benedictinism Through Changing Centuries* (Collegeville, Minn., 1958); Knowles, David, O.S.B., *The Benedictines* (New York 1930).

BENEDICTION. See BLESSING.

BENEDIKTSSON, ben'e-dikts-sôn, **Einar** (1864–1940), Icelandic poet. He was born near Reykjavík on Oct. 31, 1864. He took a law degree at Copenhagen, Denmark, in 1892, and then returned to Iceland, where he edited and published a political journal from 1896 to 1898. Through both his journalistic activities and his poetry, he played a prominent part in Icelandic political life. He published several volumes of poetry between 1897 and 1930. (Selections from these volumes were translated into English by Frederic T. Wood and published as *Harp of the North* in 1956.) His poetry, neoromantic in its philosophic idealism, is written in an elevated, occasionally ornate style. It greatly influenced his younger contemporaries in Iceland.

Benediktsson was a conservative with respect to Icelandic language and literature, urging the Icelandic people to preserve their cultural heritage. But he was also a social and political progressive, and he exhorted his compatriots to promote industrialization by developing Iceland's natural resources. He died in Iceland on Jan. 14, 1940.

BENEFICE, ben'ə-fəs, a revenue-producing endowment that is permanently attached to a church office. The churchman who is appointed to such an office becomes the legal recipient of all the accrued revenues in exchange for performing the required ecclesiastical functions.

The system originated in the 6th century as a result of several factors. In the early Christian church the local clergy transmitted their congregations' donations to the bishop, who, in turn, distributed and administered the funds. In 321, Constantine decreed that the Christian church could receive any gift or grant—a privilege unparalleled in history. Consequently, the church became the holder of vast estates. At the same time, the church experienced a tremendous expansion in both membership and geographical extent. This growth in wealth and size produced administrative problems. To meet them, the church imitated the custom practiced by kings and lords of awarding lands to valiant warriors or political supporters (see INVESTITURE). Church lands, called benefices, were permanently awarded to a clergyman by a bishop. The priest could then use the money for his personal and administrative expenses for the rest of his life.

During the Middle Ages the system was greatly abused both by greedy clerics and by temporal rulers who frequently asserted a right to the revenues from unclaimed benefices. Pope Gregory VII (Hildebrand) made great strides in reforming the system, but as late as the 18th century Spain and Portugal clashed with the papacy over the allotment of benefices (see BENEDICT XIV). Few benefices exist in the United States, but the tradition is continued in Europe in both the Roman Catholic and Anglican churches.

The Second Vatican Council decreed that the system be abandoned or at least reformed in the Roman Catholic Church. The Council recommended that a common fund for the support of priests and diocesan works be instituted. Ideally, the fund should be administered by a board of financial experts headed by the local bishop. The Council reiterated the church's long-held teaching that where the beneficiary system continues, the rights to revenues should be considered secondary to the ecclesiastical office itself.

BENEFIT OF CLERGY, in English history, was the privilege, originally extended only to the clergy, of exemption from prosecution in the secular courts. The practice was established in the 12th century. Accused clerics were arraigned in the secular courts and, at their request before or after trial, were turned over to the church for trial by the more lenient ecclesiastical courts. By the 14th century, exemption from trial by secular courts was usually extended to anyone who could read, whether or not he was a cleric. However, an increasing number of grave offenses were being tried "without benefit of clergy." By the 15th century the general rule was modified to permit exercise of the privilege only once. After the Reformation the benefit was extended to some persons who could not read, and, in 1707, removal of the reading qualification made the benefit universal.

Since 1576, however, it had had no actual connection with the church. In that year Parliament made it a right to discharge on the first offense, at the discretion of the court, after a year's imprisonment. The survival of benefit of clergy served to moderate the severity of archaic criminal laws. The benefit was abolished in 1827.

BENELLI, bā-nel′lē, **Sem** (1877–1949), Italian playwright, who was a leading figure in the Italian theater of the 20th century. Many critics have ranked his works just below those of Luigi Pirandello. Benelli, who was born at Prato on Aug. 10, 1877, wrote 30 dramas and comedies, including *La tignola* (1908), *La maschera di Bruto* (1908), *La cena delle beffe* (1909), and *L'amore dei tre re* (1910). He died at Zoagli, near Genoa, on Dec. 18, 1949.

L'amore dei tre re provided the libretto for an opera of the same name, composed by Italo Montemezzi and first produced at La Scala in Milan in 1913. Benelli's most popular drama was *La cena delle beffe*, which was produced successfully in the United States in 1919 as *The Jest*, with John and Lionel Barrymore in the leading roles. In 1924, *La cena delle beffe* was made into an opera by Umberto Giordano.

BENELUX, ben′e-luks. This acronym for Belgium, the Netherlands, and Luxembourg refers to a customs union agreement between these states, signed in London on Sept. 5, 1944. The term is also frequently applied to the three countries themselves when considered collectively.

The agreement, as revised by the Hague Protocol of March 14, 1947, went into operation early in 1948. Customs duties were to be abolished within the union, and a common tariff was to be applied to imports from outside. The Benelux tariffs were halfway between those of the Belgium-Luxembourg tariff union of 1921 and the lower Netherlands rates. As the former Dutch free list was reduced, the effect of Benelux was to raise tariffs against outside countries. Within the union, quotas, licenses, subsidies, and safeguards against over-rapid removal of duties remained until 1950, when they were largely removed in accordance with the liberalizing policy of the European Payments Union.

The experience of Benelux manifests the difficulties in establishing free trade among countries which have had different tariff policies, but it was hoped this experience would be useful in developing more extensive customs unions in Europe, particularly a union of Benelux with France and Italy to be known as Fritalux. The formation of the European Coal and Steel Community (ECSC) in 1952, among six European states (Benelux, France, Italy, and West Germany), gave promise of an even wider union, realized to some extent in 1958 in the European Economic Community (EEC) among these states. EEC is sometimes known as the European Common Market, or "Little Europe".

Aiming at eventual economic integration, the Benelux countries formed a 50-year Benelux Economic Union in 1958. It provided for free movement of persons, goods, and capital among the three countries.

QUINCY WRIGHT, *University of Virginia*

BENEŠ, be′nesh, **Eduard** (1884–1948), president of Czechoslovakia. He was born at Kožlany, Bohemia (now in Czechoslovakia) on May 28, 1884, the son of a farmer. After receiving his education at Charles University (Prague), the Sorbonne, and Dijon, he taught political science at the Prague Academy of Commerce before World War I. After the war he lectured on sociology for many years at Charles University. During World War I, Beneš (in Paris) and Tomáš Garrigue Masaryk (in London) worked together for an independent Czechoslovakia. In 1918, When the Czechoslovak Republic was formed, Beneš became minister of foreign affairs, a post he held until 1935. He was also prime minister (1921–1922) and a delegate to the Council of the League of Nations (1923-1927).

Beneš succeeded Masaryk as president of Czechoslovakia in 1935, but resigned in 1938 after the Munich Pact had sanctioned the surrender of the Sudeten area to Germany. He then went into exile in the United States and Britain. In 1939 he became leader of the Czechoslovak National Committee in London that set up the government in exile, and was recognized by Britain and the United States as rightful president of the country. In December 1943 he went to Moscow to conclude a Soviet-Czechoslovak treaty of alliance, and after Germany's defeat he returned to Prague to resume the task of establishing his country's independence.

In 1946 the Constituent Assembly elected

Eduard Beneš, Czechoslovak statesman (1884–1948).

Beneš president to serve until a new constitution could be drafted. The Communist leader Klement Gottwald was named premier in the all-party government, and the country remained under an uneasy coalition through 1947. Beneš, while he based his foreign policy on the country's alliance with Russia, sought to maintain friendly relations with the West and to make Czechoslovakia a "bridge between East and West." But the Communists asserted their power more and more truculently, and 12 non-Communist ministers resigned in protest in February 1948. Beneš refused to accept their resignations, but a few days later, following a Communist coup, he yielded to avert civil war. He resigned on June 7 rather than sign the new Communist constitution. Soon afterward, on Sept. 3, 1948, he died from a paralytic stroke at Sezimovo Ústí.

Many of Beneš' important articles and addresses have been collected by Karel Hudec in *Edvard Beneš in His Own Words* (1944). Among his other works are *My War Memoirs* (tr. by Paul Selver, 1928); *Democracy Today and Tomorrow* (1939); and *Memoirs* (tr. by Godfrey Lias, 1954).

Further Reading: *Grabités,* Pierre, *Beneš, Statesman of Central Europe* (New York 1936); Mackenzie, Compton, *Dr. Beneš* (London 1946).

BENÉT, bə-nā', **Stephen Vincent** (1898–1943), American poet and author. He was born in Bethlehem, Pa., on July 22, 1898, the younger brother of William Rose Benét. Stephen graduated from Yale in 1919. As an undergraduate he had published two books of verse: *Five Men and Pompey,* a group of six dramatic monologues; and *Young Adventure.* In the summer of 1921 he wrote his first novel, *The Beginning of Wisdom,* and that autumn accepted a fellowship at the Sorbonne in Paris. Upon his return to the United States in 1923 he published *King David, The Ballad of William Sycamore, 1790–1880,* and *Jean Huguenot,* a novel. *Tiger Joy* (1925) contained an octave of sonnets called *The Golden Corpse* and the ballad *Mountain Whippoorwill.*

In 1926, Benét returned to France for two years, where he worked on *John Brown's Body* (1928). This poem about the Civil War, which won the Pulitzer Prize in 1929, is one of the few lengthy narratives to achieve permanence in American poetry. It is distinguished both by a remarkable command of history and by cunning variations of prosody and rhythm, a particular "tune" being associated with each of the main characters or each section of the warring states.

In 1933, Benét and his wife Rosemary Carr Benét wrote *A Book of Americans,* a group of verses about famous personalities in the country's history. In 1936, Benét published *The Burning City,* best remembered for the dramatic poem *Litany for Dictatorships.* The following year he presented a radio broadcast of his one-act play *The Headless Horseman,* with music by Douglas Moore. *Thirteen O'Clock* (1937), a collection of his best short stories, included *The Devil and Daniel Webster,* which was later made into a play, an opera with music by Douglas Moore, and a motion picture entitled *All That Money Can Buy. The Devil and Daniel Webster* has by common consent become a permanent, if minor, classic. Subsequent volumes of Benét's work were more uneven in quality. An important activity of his later life was the rejuvenation of the American Academy of Arts and Letters, of which

he had been elected a member; in the opinion of the younger generation, this had become too much of a gentleman's club.

Benét died in New York City on March 13, 1943. In 1944 he was posthumously awarded the Pulitzer Prize for his volume of verse *Western Star,* and the same year saw the publication of *America,* a brief history written for the U.S. Office of War Information for distribution abroad.

See also DEVIL AND DANIEL WEBSTER; JOHN BROWN'S BODY.

HOWARD MUMFORD JONES
Author of "The Theory of American Literature"

Further Reading: Fenton, Charles A., *Stephen Vincent Benét* (New Haven 1958).

BENÉT, bə-nā', **William Rose** (1886–1950), American poet and critic. He was born in Brooklyn, N.Y., on Feb. 2, 1886. He graduated from Yale in 1907, held several positions in the publishing field, and in 1920 became associate editor of the *Literary Review* of the New York *Post.* Four years later he resigned to become a founder of the *Saturday Review of Literature,* which later became the *Saturday Review.*

Benét's poetry, which is characterized by its variety of form and subject, includes the volumes *Merchants from Cathay* (1913), *The Falconer of God* (1914), *The Great White Wall* (1916), *The Burglar of the Zodiac* (1918), *Perpetual Light* (1919), *Sagacity* (1929), *Day of Deliverance* (1944), and *Timothy's Angels* (1947). An autobiographical poem, *The Dust Which Is God,* won the Pulitzer Prize for 1942. In addition, Benét wrote a novel, *First Person Singular* (1922), and a verse novel, *Rip Tide* (1932), as well as many critical pieces. In 1932 he collected the poetical work of his second wife, Elinor Wylie, into a single volume, and in 1938, coedited the *Oxford Anthology of American Literature.* He died in New York City on May 4, 1950.

Though in a sense overshadowed by his brother Stephen Vincent Benét, he was a perceptive critic, poet, and novelist in his own right.

HOWARD MUMFORD JONES
Author of "The Theory of American Literature"

BENEVENTO, bā-nā-ven'tō, an Italian city in the region of Campania, is the capital of Benevento province. Benevento, 38 miles (62 km) northeast of Naples, is situated on a hill in a picturesque mountain amphitheater formed by the confluence of the Sabato and Calore rivers. It has small industries, including distilling. The town has been an archbishopric since the 900's.

There are monuments of Roman, medieval, and Renaissance times, including the well-preserved Arch of Trajan (114); the remains of a Roman theater; the 8th-century polygonal Church of Santa Sofia (later rebuilt); the 13th-century Romanesque cathedral, severely damaged in World War II; and a 14th-century castle.

Originally a Samnite settlement, it came under Roman rule in the 3d century B.C. and was an important center on the Appian Way. Once *Maleventum,* its name was changed to *Beneventum.* The town was the seat of a powerful Lombard duchy from the 6th century to the 11th, and then was under papal rule until 1860, except for periods of foreign occupation. Benevento was the site of the battle (1266) in which Manfred, king of Sicily, was killed and his forces were defeated by Charles of Anjou. Population: (1961) 41,467.

BENEVOLENCE, bə-nev′ə-ləns, in English history, a forced contribution, in the guise of a gift, levied by kings on their wealthier subjects without sanction of Parliament. Edward IV, on pretext of an imminent war with France, summoned the principal London merchants in 1474 and requested of each an outright gift or "benevolence." Before this, in similar circumstances, a king at least would have pretended the levy was a loan. This first benevolence marked a stage in the growth of royal despotism and the corresponding weakening of the powers of the House of Commons. However, when Richard III succeeded in 1483 and sought to use this instrument that had enriched his late brother, Parliament in 1484 abolished benevolences, calling them "new and unlawful inventions."

Despite the parliamentary prohibition, during Henry VIII's reign Thomas Cardinal Wolsey extended the practice of benevolences on behalf of his sovereign. The city of London was assessed £20,000 in 1522, and its wealthier citizens were forced to give the cardinal an account of the value of their estates. Wolsey again applied the system in 1525, and royal commissions in every county demanded a tenth of the annual income from the laity and a fourth from the clergy. So violent was the opposition to these demands that Wolsey was forced to retract them.

In 1614, James I, through the Royal Council, demanded benevolences from rich landowners, but in three years he could raise only £60,000. In 1628 the Petition of Right again declared benevolences illegal unless exacted with the consent of Parliament. Finally, the Bill of Rights (1689) put an end to them in any form.

BÉNÉZET, bā-nā-ze′, **Saint** (1165?–?1184), a French saint who reputedly directed the building of the famous Pont d'Avignon across the Rhône. It is said that Bénézet as a young boy was tending his sheep when he was divinely inspired to journey to Avignon to build the bridge. He convinced Avignon's bishop of his sincerity and supervised the building of the stone bridge from 1177 until his death about 1184. He died before the bridge was completed and was buried in a chapel built on the structure. Much of the bridge has since been washed away, but its remains are now a pilgrimage site. St. Bénézet is reputed to have founded the now extinct order called the Bridge Building Brotherhood. His feast day is April 14.

BENEZET, ben-ə-zet′, **Anthony** (1713–1784), American educator and philanthropist, who was an ardent Quaker abolitionist. Born into a Huguenot family in St.-Quentin, France, on Jan. 31, 1713, he moved to America in 1731. After some years in business in Philadelphia, he turned to teaching, first in the Germantown Academy and then in a Friends' school in Philadelphia. Interested in women's education, he conducted a school for girls from 1755 to 1766. He campaigned vigorously to abolish Negro slavery; his most significant work was *A Caution and Warning to Great Britain and the Colonies on the Calamitous State of the Enslaved Negroes* (1766). He instituted a night school for Negroes and left funds in his will for the establishment of a general school for Negro education. He also aided French refugees from Acadia and advanced the cause of the American Indian. Benezet died in Philadelphia on May 3, 1784.

BENGAL, ben-gôl′, is a region in the eastern part of the Indian subcontinent, on the Bay of Bengal, divided between India and Bangladesh. Its area is 89,046 square miles (230,629 sq km).

History. Located on the outer fringe of early Aryan India, and at the edge of later Muslim India as well, Bengal has been a culturally unified region since the first centuries of the Christian era. Written records in the Bengali language go back perhaps to the 9th or 10th century A. D. Bengal was a political entity for the first time from the 8th through the 12th century, under the Buddhist Pala kings. At its height, under Emperor Devapala (reigned 810?–?850 A. D.), the Pala empire included all of what is now known as Bengal, as well as most of Assam, Irissa, and Bihar, and farther west to Varanasi.

In the late 11th century the Hindu Sena dynasty began to rise from the remnants of the Pala empire and gradually gained control of a unified Bengal. About 1200, however, Lakshmana Sena (reigned 1179?–c. 1200) withdrew to what is now Bangladesh (East Bengal) under pressure from the advancing Muslim armies of Muhammad Bhaktyar (Bakhtiyar Khalji).

Muslim domination of Bengal lasted until the defeat of the Muslim ruler Siraj-ud-Daula (Surajah Dowlah) by Robert Clive at the Battle of Plassey in 1757. Many of the Bengali Muslim rulers cultivated the language and literature of Bengal in their courts. They were patrons of some of the most famous poets, both Hindu and Muslim, during a high point of Bengali literary development from the 15th to the 17th century. A large number of conversions of Hindus and Buddhists to Islam, however, especially in eastern Bengal, established a religious division of Bengal which twice became a political reality. The first such division into separate territories, in 1905, ended in 1912; the second was in 1947.

The Battle of Plassey marked the beginnings of British rule in India and Bengal continued as a part of British India until 1947, when India and Pakistan became independent states. With its majority of Muslim inhabitants, East Bengal, along with the major portion of the former Assam district of Sylhet, became the province of East Pakistan in Pakistan, and West Bengal became a state of India. In 1971, East Pakistan gained its independence under the name Bangladesh. Despite its political division, however, Bengal has retained a cultural and linguistic unity.

WEST BENGAL

One of the states of the Republic of India, West Bengal is bordered on the east by Bangladesh and Assam; on the north by Bhutan and Sikkim; on the west by Nepal, Bihar, and Orissa; and on the south by Orissa and the Bay of Bengal. It is 33,920 square miles (87,853 sq km) in area, with a population (1971) of 44,312,011. The average population density is about 1,306 per square mile (504 per sq km). Although the majority of the inhabitants live in villages, there are numerous cities with a population of 100,000 or more. Of these, Calcutta, the capital, is by far the most important, being the major center of industry and the focus of intellectual and business life. As a port, it is the largest terminal in southern Asia. The Calcutta urban complex has a population of 7,031,382.

Kharagpur is a great rail center. Among the historic towns are Nabadwip, long the center of intellectual and religious life in Bengal; Murshid-abad, the center of Muslim power in the region; and Darjeeling, famous as a resort and summer capital of Bengal.

The People. The people of West Bengal are over 78 percent Hindu and about 20 percent Muslim, with fractional percentages of Christians, Buddhists, Sikhs, Jains, Parsis (Zoroastrians), Jews, and others, including tribals (mostly Munda-speaking Santals concentrated in the northwest and southwest). Social divisions, as in other parts of India, are along caste as well as religious lines. Traditional, but hardly accurate, is the division into Brahmans (traditionally priests and scholars) and 36 other castes (endogamous and sometimes occupational groupings). Another traditional classification is into four groups: Brahmans, Kshatriyas, Vaisyas, and Sudras. Sudras are classified as "clean" (whom Brahmans can serve as priests) and "unclean." There are in addition the untouchables, who are entirely beyond the caste system. As in other parts of India, there is caste mobility, the Kshatriyas, for example, originally scribes, claiming the status of nobility. Caste and religious-sectarian lines are often coterminous, as with the Vaishnavas, who are both a sect and a caste. Bengali Brahmans frequently eat fish, and some will eat meat, dietary habits frowned upon by Brahmans in other parts of India. Muslims are also divided into castelike groups, to some extent occupationally, to some extent according to claim of ancestry; chief among these groups are the sayyids, Pathans, and shaykhs.

The Land. Lying at the head of the Bay of Bengal, West Bengal includes the deltaic regions of the great river systems of the Ganges, Padma, Brahmaputra, Meghna, and Jamuna. Tributaries of these systems wander through the plains, making the whole area a river complex. The extreme flatness of the land in the plain and the loose alluvial soil make possible widespread floods in the monsoon season, and changes in river courses have had a profound effect on the social and economic history of the region. The extremely low-lying delta proper merges in the north into the foothills of the Himalaya. In the west the land rises more slowly into the plateau region of the neighboring state of Bihar.

EWING GALLOWAY

WEST BENGAL, India, predominately an agricultural state, uses bullocks as the principal beast of burden.

With such variation in altitude, the climate in West Bengal varies considerably. In a single district in the sub-Himalayan region, where the land rises from 300 feet to 10,000 feet (91 to 3,048 meters) above sea level in a short span, annual rainfall varies from 86 inches (218 cm) in one place to 210 inches (533 cm) in another. There is also wide temperature variation in the sub-Himalayan region, the mean maximum in January varying from 47° F (8° C) in the mountains to 74° F (23° C) in the lower hills, and in May from 66° F (19° C) in the mountains to 89° F (32° C) in the hills. In the deltaic plain the climate is uniformly damp and hot, with the mean maximum temperature at Calcutta 80° F (27° C) in the cool season (November to February) and 97° F (36° C) in the hot season (April to June). The monsoon rains last from late May or early June until September, with the temperature gradually cooling during this period.

Natural Resources and Industry. The potential of natural resources in West Bengal has been lessened severely by the denudation of the once-great forests of the delta and foothills. Forest types vary widely with height above sea level. In the mountains of the northwest (10,000 to 12,000 feet; 3,048 to 3,658 meters), the forests are Himalayan fir and juniper; at lower levels, oak, chestnut, maple, and elder predominate; in the lowest-lying plains, forests are mainly of fig, bamboo, reedy grasses, cane, and water plants growing in the *bil* (a swamp or backwater filled with water left by the rains or floods). Important forest products include timber (especially teak), reeds for mats, dyes, rubber, and medicinal roots. Because of deforestation, wildlife is now abundant only in the government forest sanctuaries, as at Darjeeling. In this and other forest areas of the north, tigers, panthers, elephants, rhinoceroses, and bears can be found. Monkeys, hares, and jackals abound throughout the area, and there are some tigers and panthers in the Sundarbans area near the river mouths.

In this country of many rivers, fishing is a principal occupation, and numerous varieties of fish are found. Near the Bay of Bengal, saltwater shellfish, especially shrimps and prawns, are an important source of food and income.

Mineral deposits remain largely untapped.

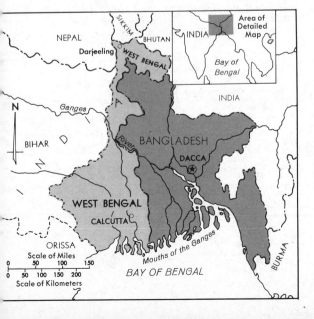

547

Great seams of high-quality coal as well as fine deposits of iron and manganese and some aluminum are found in the west near the Bihar border, though the main deposits are in Bihar. Limestone is also plentiful in this area. Coal, clay, limestone, iron, manganese, and aluminum deposits in the area around Asansol, together with the development of rail centers and electric power, have made this one of the great centers of Indian industry. West Bengal employs 17 percent of all manufacturing workers. The other major industrial center in West Bengal is the belt on both sides of the Hooghly River near Calcutta. Rural or cottage industries include cotton and silk weaving, leatherworking, and the manufacture of brass and bell-metal products, ceramics, and various art products.

Though industry is prominent in the economy of West Bengal, agriculture is the major occupation. The primary crops are rice and jute, though most of the jute-raising land went to Pakistan in the partition. *Aman* (winter rice) uses about four fifths of the cropped land in most areas; *boro* and *aus* (early rice crops), as well as pulses and cash crops of sugarcane and oilseed, are also important, as are market vegetables and fruits, cereal grains, tobacco, and tea.

Education. Bengalis long have had a reputation for intellectual and political leadership in India. West Bengal has a literacy rate of about 33 percent (43 percent for males and 22 percent for females). Calcutta University, founded in 1857, with colleges throughout the state is one of the largest universities in the world.

Government. West Bengal has a governor appointed by the president of India; a cabinet responsible to the legislature; and two legislative houses. The lower house, the Legislative Assembly, is directly elected by universal adult suffrage. The upper house, the Legislative Council, is appointed by the chief minister and the cabinet.

BANGLADESH

Bangladesh, formerly East Pakistan, is coterminous with East Bengal except for the addition of part of Sylhet, from Assam. The country borders on West Bengal, Assam, and Meghalaya to the north; Assam, Tripura, Mizoram, and Burma to the east; the Bay of Bengal to the south; and West Bengal to the west.

Bangladesh has an area of 55,126 square miles (142,776 sq km) and a population (1974) of 71,316,517. Its major cities are the capital, Dacca (1973 estimated population, 1,132,373), on the Burhi Ganga River; the important seaport Chittagong (492,153); and Khulna (467,891).

The population is almost entirely rural and is predominantly Muslim, though there are some Hindus and some tribal peoples. The population of the Chittagong Hill Tracts is 90 percent tribal. Except in the hills, population density is high, averaging 1,294 per square mile (499 per sq km) for the whole country.

The Land. As in West Bengal, the river systems are the most significant geographical and economic features of the country. The five major river systems, with their source in the Himalaya, make their way back and forth across the great deltaic plain. The constant changes of river courses and the resulting transition of certain areas from active to moribund delta have played an important role in all phases of the country's life. In most places the deltaic plain is barely 30 feet (9 meters) above sea level, and the northern part of the delta is dotted with swamps and *bil,* for the most part dry in the hot season. There are no important hill or mountain ranges in Bangladesh, the Chittagong Hills in the southeast and extensions of the Assamese foothills in Sylhet for the most part being well under 2,000 feet (610 meters) in altitude. The highest peak in the country (Keokradong) is 4,034 feet (1,230 meters) high.

There is little variation in climate, the temperature ranging from an April maximum of 91° to 96° F (33° to 35.6° C) in the plain to a January minimum of about 50° F (10° C) in the hills. There is high rainfall in the monsoon season (June to September), nowhere less than 60 inches (152 cm) and in the southeast as much as 150 to 200 inches (381 to 508 cm).

Resources and Industry. Except that jute is more important, crops are approximately the same as in West Bengal, including rice, cereals, sugarcane, cotton, and, in the Sylhet District, some tea. Rice, either *aman* or *aus,* is grown on 62 percent of the land. Grazing lands are poor, though cattle are kept for milk products as well as for hides and skins, which constitute an export commodity.

Forests make up about 16 percent of the area of Bangladesh, mostly in the south and southeast, though there is a major forest preserve in the central area. Types of forest range from tropical evergreens to the cane, bamboo, and grass forests of the low-lying plain. Chief forest products are teakwood, a fine quality of which grows in the Chittagong Hills; sundari wood (*Heritiera minor* or *H. fomes*) from the Sundarbans areas near the river mouths, used as lumber for boats and houses; and the soft wood from *gewa* (*Excoecaria agallocha*), used for boxes and matchsticks.

The production of the fine muslin of Dacca, once famous in the courts of Europe and throughout the world, has fallen off rapidly since the early 19th century. Some cotton and silk weaving is still done on a small scale, though tea factories and some jute mills and presses are the only real industries to be found in the country. While most of the jute-growing area of Bengal is found here, the jute-processing plants are mostly in West Bengal, and the resultant economic situation severely taxes both parts of Bengal. There is little mining. The Karnaphuli project, in the southeastern part of Bangladesh, produces approximately 160,000 kilowatts of hydroelectric power. See also BANGLADESH.

EDWARD C. DIMOCK, JR.*, *University of Chicago*

Bibliography

Ahmad, Nafis, *An Economic Geography of East Pakistan* (London and New York 1958).

Bose, Nemal Sadhan, *The Indian Awakening and Bengal* (Calcutta 1960).

Chattopadhyay, Gouranga Ranjana, *A Village in West Bengal* (Calcutta 1964).

Das Gupta, Yogendra Natha, *Bengal in the Sixteenth Century* (Calcutta 1914).

Dutt, Romesh Chunder, *Cultural Heritage of Bengal,* 2d ed. (Calcutta 1962).

Gopal, Ram, *How the British Occupied Bengal* (New York 1964).

Majumdar, Ramesh Chandra, and Sarkar, Sir Jadunath, eds., *The History of Bengal,* 2 vols. (Dacca 1943–47).

Rahim, Muhammad Abdur, *Social and Cultural History of Bengal* (Karachi 1963).

Raychaudhuri, Tapankumar, *Bengal Under Akbar and Jahangir* (Calcutta 1953).

Sarkar, Sir Jadunath, ed., *The Nawabs of Bengal* (Calcutta 1952).

Sinha, Narendra Krishna, *The Economic History of Bengal from Plassey to the Permanent Settlement* (Calcutta 1961–62).

BENGAL, Bay of, ben-gôl′, a northeastern arm of the Indian Ocean. Ceylon and India lie on its western shore, India and East Pakistan are on its northern coast, and Burma is situated to its northeast. On the southeast, the Andaman and Nicobar Islands (a territory of India) separate it from the Andaman Sea. The Indian Ocean opens to the south. Roughly triangular in shape, the bay is about 1,000 miles (1,609 km) wide at its broadest point.

The Ganges and Brahmaputra rivers empty into the Bay of Bengal in the north; on the west, the bay receives the principal rivers of peninsular India: the Mahanadi, Godavari, Krishna, and Kaveri. All of these rivers have deltas. There are no natural harbors on the western coast, but artificial ports have been built at Madras and Visakhapatnam in India. The other principal seaports are Trincomalee (Ceylon), Calcutta (India), Chittagong (Pakistan), and Akyab (Burma). The surface currents of the bay are greatly affected by the monsoons—the northeast monsoon in the winter and the southwest monsoon in the summer.

BENGALI LANGUAGE AND LITERATURE, bengôl′ē, the most important of the easternmost group of languages (including also Bihari, Assamese, and Oriya) in the Indo-Aryan subfamily of Indo-European. It is a descendant of Old Indo-Aryan (represented in our records by Sanskrit) through the Prakrit or Middle Indo-Aryan dialect called Magadhi.

Among the some 70 million speakers of Bengali found chiefly in the state of West Bengal in India and in East Pakistan, there are many dialects. The modern standard colloquial is the dialect spoken by the educated classes of Calcutta; and on it the modern literary standard is based. This same area, the western part of the Ganges delta,, has been important politically and culturally throughout the whole life of Bengali as a language, and its dialects were basic to the older literary style as well. The Bengali alphabet is a local variety of the Devanagari alphabet commonly used throughout northern India, but its forms are so divergent that it must be learned as a separate system of writing.

Early Literature. Bengali literature in its early period had subject matter and techniques that continued the traditions of Sanskrit, Prakrit, and other Indian vernacular literatures in their early stages. Lyric poetry expressed devotion toward the popular gods of Hinduism, especially Krishna and other forms of Vishnu; the epic and purana tales of ancient India were retold in popular verse. Literary prose rarely occurred except in descriptive passages mingled with the narrative verses. From the period prior to 1200 A.D. little remains except for a few songs belonging to a Tantric Buddhist sect.

The flourishing period of the early literature is marked by adaptations in Bengali of the Ramayama by Krittivasa (14th century), of the Mahabharata by Sanjaya (14th century) and Kasiram (17th century), and of the Bhagavata Purana by Maladhar Vasu (15th century). Lyrics were written in honor of Krishna and Radha by Candidas (15th century), in honor of the goddess Candi by Mukundaram (1589 A.D.), and in honor of Durga by Ram Prasad (18th century). A slightly new genre, that of poetical biography, was developed by followers of the great Vaishnava religious teacher Caitanya (1486–1534); many of them, beginning with his disciple Govinda, wrote of the master's life. This early, traditional period with its adaptations, lyrics, and poetical biographies continued to the end of the 18th century.

Western Influence. The impact of Western, especially English, life and literature in the 19th century had a great secularizing and fructifying influence on Bengali literature. This happened earlier and with profounder effect in Bengal than elsewhere in India, and modern Bengali literature has led the way for the whole of India.

The currents of social reform that produced a reintegration of Bengali intellectual life were best represented in the works of Ram Mohan Roy (1772–1833). He couched his ideas in Bengali prose, which was evolved from the language of the earlier poetry with the addition of innumerable Sanskrit words to its vocabulary. Many writers of social and political essays, of philosophical, historical, and other learned works, used this style. The drama was revived and refurbished with a social and satirical content in this style until the middle of the 19th century. Even novels were written in this style of language, except that the colloquial came to be used more and more in conversational passages.

Modern Style. After the middle of the 19th century serious writers gradually abandoned the old archaic style, employing for literature the spoken language in the form used by the educated in Calcutta. This modern style has not entirely won out over its older rival, but it has invaded all the genres of literature, including even poetry, and well-informed Bengalis predict that the old style soon will disappear.

Among the great names of recent Bengali literature are the novelist Bankim Chandra Chatterji (1838–1894), whose social and historical novels inaugurated modern Indian fiction; Michael Madhusadana Dutt (1824–1873), a poet and dramatist of high rank who pioneered the new Bengali poetry and drama; the scholar and novelist Romesh Chandra Dutt (1848–1909); and many successors in writings on religion and morality.

The greatest figure is Sir Rabindranath Tagore (1861–1941). His poetry, dramas, and novels gained him much renown in Bengal, and the publication in English translation of his volume of poems entitled *Gitanjali* (Handful of Songs) in 1912 won him the Nobel Prize for literature in 1913. Though he spoke as a thorough son of India, he nevertheless spoke for humanity also, and his own English translations of many of his works, even if they did not always do justice to his Bengali style and his subject matter, won him a worldwide audience. See also INDIA —*Languages.*

MURRAY B. EMENEAU
University of California, Berkeley

Bibliography

Anderson, James Drummond, *A Manual of Bengali Literature* (New York 1962).
Chatterji, Suniti Kumar, *The Origin and Development of the Bengali Language,* 2 vols. (Calcutta 1926).
Dabbs, Jack A., *Spoken Bengali: Dialects of East Bengal* (College Station, Texas, 1965).
Ghosh, Jyotish, *Bengali Literature* (Oxford 1948).
Guha-Thakurta, Prabhucharan, *The Bengali Drama* (London 1930).
Sen, Dinesh Chandra, *History of Bengali Language and Literature* (Calcutta 1911).
Sen, Priyaranjan, *Western Influence in Bengali Literature* (Calcutta 1932).
Sen, Sukumar, *History of Bengali Literature* (New Delhi 1960).

BENGHAZI, ben-gäz′ē, is the second-largest city and one of the two capitals of Libya. It is situated in Cyrenaica on the Gulf of Sidra, some 400 miles (644 km) east of Tripoli. Although a new administrative capital was begun at Beida (Baida) in 1961, Benghazi and Tripoli remain the official capitals.

Benghazi is a commercial center for the surrounding agricultural area. As the leading port of Cyrenaica, its economic life was transformed with the discovery of oil in the 1950's. The city became the main importation center for equipment needed in the petroleum industry, and its harbor has been greatly improved. Today Benghazi is the site of many foreign economic and diplomatic missions, and a number of oil companies have established branch offices in the city. Construction has become one of the most important industries in the city as new offices and dwellings are built for the rapidly increasing population. The University of Libya was founded in the city in 1955.

Benghazi stands on the site of ancient *Hesperides,* founded by the Greeks in the 6th century B.C. Later, when the city was under Egyptian rule its name was changed to *Berenice* by Ptolemy III in honor of his wife. The area was subsequently conquered by the Romans, Vandals, Byzantines, Arabs, and Turks. In the 17th century the Turks, who ruled from the 16th century to 1911, built a fort on the coast, near the tomb of the holy man Sidi Ibn Ghazi, after whom Benghazi was named. For more than two centuries, Benghazi remained a small town, inhabited by a few traders and protected by the Turkish garrison. The Turkish rulers made a few improvements in the late 19th century. Then, in the 1930's, the Italians, intent on colonizing Cyrenaica with Italian peasants, decided to use Benghazi as an administrative center. The city became a road and rail hub, and an airport was built nearby at Benina. Benghazi suffered great devastation in World War II, but it has since been rebuilt. Population: (1964) 90,860.

L. GRAY COWAN, *Columbia University*

BENI HASAN, ba′nē ha′san, is a village in Egypt, remarkable for the ancient rock tombs in the area. Known also as *Beni Hasan el Shuruq,* the village is on the east bank of the Nile River, about 140 miles (225 km) south of Cairo. Some 39 tombs are cut in the calcareous stone of the mountain. Sepulchers of the monarchs who ruled the district about 2000 B.C., they exhibit interesting paintings and hieroglyphics. The paintings portray incidents and customs in the life of ancient Egypt, and the inscriptions are of value for the light they throw upon the history of the 12th dynasty.

BENI ISRAEL, be′nē iz′rē-əl, a sect in India, whose religion is a modified form of Judaism. The members of the sect live chiefly in Bombay and in the coastal cities of southwestern India. Their name, which is also spelled *Bene Israel,* means "sons of Israel" in Hebrew. They are thought by some to be a remnant of the Ten Lost Tribes of Israel although this view is not supported by tradition. Several thousand in number, they closely resemble the Jews of Arabia.

The Beni Israel abstain from the flesh of unclean animals, strictly observe the Sabbath, and perform the rite of circumcision. They also observe several of the religious customs common among their neighbors, the Hindus. Their language is Marathi, but some also speak Hebrew. Little is known of the time of their settlement in India, but it is certain that they had been there for many centuries when, in 900 A.D., according to tradition, the reformer David Rahabi introduced them to many ceremonies of Judaism. Their communities are governed by the *Mukadam,* or head man, and their religious chiefs are called *cadi.*

BENI SUEF, ba′nē soo-wāf′, is a city in Egypt, the capital of a province of the same name. Situated on the west bank of the Nile River, the city is connected by railroad with Cairo, 68 miles (109 km) to the northeast. Beni Suef is the trading center for cotton, cereals, and sugarcane grown in the fertile surrounding area, and it maintains cotton and sugar mills. Population: (1960) 78,829.

BENICIA, bə-nē′shə, is a city in California, in Solano County, 22 miles (35 km) northeast of San Francisco. It is situated on the north shore of Carquinez Strait, which connects Suisun Bay with San Pablo Bay, the northern arm of San Francisco Bay. Benicia is a seaport and has a 2,400-foot (730-meter) wharf to accommodate oceangoing vessels. An industrial park was developed on the site of the United States Arsenal (established 1851) when the arsenal was deactivated in 1964. The park contains 2,400 acres (1,000 hectares) and is occupied by various industries, including a large oil company. A bridge across Carquinez Strait connects Benicia with Martinez, Berkeley, and Oakland.

Gen. Mariano Vallejo, last Mexican governor of California, deeded the land for Benicia to Dr. Robert Semple, and the town was laid out in 1847. Benicia was one of Mrs. Vallejo's given names. The city was incorporated in 1850 and served as the capital of California for 13 months (1853–1854). The old brick capitol building is now a state historical museum. Benicia has a council-manager government. Population: 8,783.

BENIN

INFORMATION HIGHLIGHTS

Official Name: People's Republic of Benin (prior to 1975, the Republic of Dahomey).

Head of State: President.

Head of Government: President.

Area: 43,483 square miles (112,622 sq km).

Boundaries: *North,* Upper Volta and Niger; *east,* Nigeria; *west,* Togo.

Population: (1974 est.) 3,029,000.

Capital: Porto-Novo (pop., 1972 est.) 84,000.

Major Languages: French (official); Fon, Yoruba, Fulani, and other tribal languages.

Major Religions: Animism, Christianity, and Islam.

Monetary Unit: CFA franc.

Weights and Measures: Metric system.

Flag: Green rectangle with a red five-pointed star in the upper hoist corner.

National Anthem: *L'Aube Nouvelle (The New Dawn.)*

A village in Benin, with many of its homes built on stilts, is typical of the densely populated lagoon region.

MARC AND EVELYNE BERNHEIM, FROM RAPHO GUILLUMETTE

BENIN, be-nēn' (officially PEOPLE'S REPUBLIC OF BENIN), is an independent country of West Africa. Once an important African kingdom, and more recently part of French West Africa, it achieved independence on Aug. 1, 1960. Formerly called Dahomey, the People's Republic of Benin came into being on Nov. 30, 1975.

The People. Benin's total population (1974), 3,029,000, is a mosaic of people from different tribes. The principal ethnic groups are the Fon (800,000), Aja (250,000), and Yoruba (170,-000), who inhabit the southern third of the country; the Bariba (175,000), who are strongest in the center of the country, around the region of Parakou; and the Somba (90,000), Peul (68,000), and Dendi (40,000), who inhabit the northern reaches of the country. The vast majority of these people are subsistence farmers who grow maize, millet, manioc, and plantains. The Peul are herders and the Yoruba are engaged mainly in petty commerce.

Benin's population includes about 5,000 Europeans, mostly French, and about 2,000 persons of Syrian and Lebanese origin.

The country's population is very unevenly distributed. In the north there are a sparse 55 persons per square mile (21 per sq km), whereas in parts of the south the population density reaches 650 persons per square mile (250 per sq km). Fully one half of the people live on the 15% of the land that is situated between the Atlantic Ocean and the town of Abomey.

The population is growing at the rate of 2.9% annually. About 88% of the people live in rural areas. Cotonou, with a population (1972 est.) of 175,000, is the largest city and principal port. It was designated the new capital after independence, but the transfer was not completed because of the country's unstable political situation. Benin's other principal cities are Porto-Novo, the capital (population, 1972 est., 84,000); Abomey, the former royal capital (1970 est., 42,000); Ouidah, the old slave port (20,000); and Parakou, an important rail terminal in the center of the country (16,000).

The overwhelming majority of the people (65%) are animists, 15% are Christians, and 13% are Muslims. French is the nation's official language and the medium of instruction in its schools. Some 31% of the primary school age children are attending school. In the early 1970's there were about 186,000 pupils enrolled in primary schools, over 27,000 students in secondary schools, and some 2,000 in various technical schools. The University of Benin, founded in 1970, has over 1,000 students. Hundreds of other students study abroad, primarily at the University of Dakar in Senegal or in France.

The Land and Natural Resources. Benin, located on the Atlantic Ocean, has an area of 43,483 square miles (112,622 sq km). The country is divided into five natural zones or regions with an extraordinary diversity in topography.

Topography. The southernmost part of the country, parallel to the coast, is a sandbar broken

550a

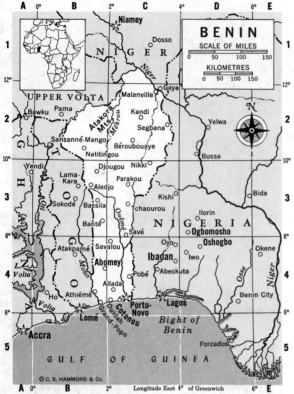

BENIN MAP INDEX

Total Population: 3,029,000

Area: 43,483 square miles (112,622 sq km)

CITIES AND TOWNS

Abomey, 29,000	B 4
Aledjo	B 3
Allada, 2,284	C 4
Athiémé, 1,782	B 4
Banté, 1,052	B 3
Bassile, 3,200	B 3
Béroubouaye	C 2
Cotonou, 175,000	C 4
Djougou, 7,000	B 3
Grand-Popo, 2,545	B 4
Kandi, 5,100	C 2
Malanville, 1,900	C 2
Natitingou, 2,260	B 2
Nikki	C 3
Ouidah, 20,000	C 4
Parakou, 15,000	C 3
Pobé, 6,962	C 4

Porto-Novo (cap.), 84,000	C 4
Savalou, 5,000	B 4
Savé, 6,262	C 3
Segbana, 1,224	C 2
Tchaourou, 2,300	C 3

PHYSICAL FEATURES

Atakora (mts.)	B 2
Benin, Bight of (bay)	C 5
Guinea (gulf)	C 5
Mékrou (river)	C 2
Mono (river)	B 4
Niger (river)	C 1
Ouémé (river)	C 3

Total pop.—1974 est.; Porto-Novo and Cotonou—1972 est.; other pops.—1961 off. est.

the Togolese border it is about 32 inches (813 mm) a year, whereas at Cotonou it reaches 41 inches (1,041 mm) annually. North at Savalou the climate becomes tropical rather than equatorial, and the temperature is generally a few degrees lower. The rainy season lasts from March to July.

Natural Resources. The country's greatest natural asset is the fertile stretch of land that extends from the Atlantic coast northward to the region of Savalou. The great plantations of oil palms, Benin's most important crop, are concentrated here.

Benin has few mineral resources. Iron ore has been found in the Atakora Mountains, but its remoteness from the rail terminus at Parakou has severely limited its exploitation. Some gold is mined at Natitingou, in the northwestern part of the country, and phosphates are mined in the region of Pobé in the southeastern part; however, neither of these minerals has contributed substantially to the development of the nation's economy. Oil was discovered off the coast of Benin in 1968, but it has not been ascertained whether the oil reserves are of sufficient size to be commercially exploitable.

The Economy. The economy of Benin suffers from the traditional malaises of many former colonial territories of Africa. The country has an agricultural economy, poor transportation, and is overdependent on foreign aid. Efforts to improve the economic situation have been hampered by the country's lack of both natural and financial resources.

Agriculture. Agriculture is the mainstay of the country's economy, providing 95% of its gross national product. Benin's agriculture, however, is excessively dependent on a single crop—palm oil. Some 3,000 square miles (7,700 sq km) in the south are devoted entirely to its production.

Palm oil accounts for some 74% of the total tonnage and 67% of the total value of the country's exports. Other crops of lesser importance such as coconuts, cotton, and groundnuts (peanuts) are also grown in sufficient quantity to permit some exports, though they are mostly consumed within the country itself.

Transportation. Another major problem standing in the way of the nation's economic development is the weakness of its transportation system. Benin has only one railroad, the Benin-Niger line, which runs from Cotonou on the coast to Parakou, an inland city about 272 miles (438

by a series of lagoons that continue into Togo in the west and Nigeria in the east. Fishing and the cultivation of coconut palms are the principal means of subsistence in this region. The Terre de Barre (Earth of Clay) region is situated north of the coastal lagoons and is bisected by the Ouémé and Cuffo rivers. The land here becomes undulating and rises to 300 feet (90 meters) above sea level. Between the towns of Allada and Abomey lies a vast marshland known as the Lama Depression, which extends eastward to the Nigerian border. Small portions of the original rain forest that once covered this region remain, but most of it is now densely planted with oil palms. The country's most fertile land is located here.

The Plateau region stretches north of Abomey to the foothills of the Atakora Mountains in the northwestern part of the country. This area is also heavily planted with oil palms, although oranges and bananas are important secondary crops. The Niger plains area extends south of the Niger River and west of the Nigerian frontier. Some cotton, millet, and guinea corn are grown here, but except for the areas bordering the banks of the Niger River, the soil is extremely poor. The Atakora Mountains region in the northwestern part of the country touches the border with Upper Volta and then stretches southwesterly into Togo. Rainfall is heaviest here, reaching 50 inches (1,270 mm) annually. The important Quémé River, which traverses the country from north to south, has its source in these mountains.

Climate. Benin has two rather distinct climatic zones. In the southern part the climate is hot and humid, with temperatures fairly constant at between 75° and 80°F (23°–25°C). Rainfall varies significantly in this coastal region. At km) to the north. This railroad has two spur lines, one running east and north 68 miles (108 km) from Cotonou to Pobé via Porto-Novo, and another running westward from Pahou to Seboroué, a distance of 21 miles (34 km). Any goods destined for points north of Parakou must travel either by road or by air, which greatly increases transport costs.

The country's road system consists of 3,800 miles (6,100 km) of routes, only 400 miles (640 km) of which are paved. Cotonou has functioned as a deepwater port only since 1965. Since it serves not only Benin but Niger as well, the port will probably prosper in the years ahead. Its prosperity will depend to a great extent on whether Benin and the *Nigériens* realize their plan of extending the present railroad northward beyond Parakou to Niamey, the capital of Niger.

Foreign Aid and Investment. One further weakness of Benin's economy is its overdependence on external aid. After achieving independence in 1960, the country had an unfavorable balance of trade. Imports were valued at more than twice the value of exports. Without the annual subsidy of $5 millon given by France, the country would have suffered bankruptcy.

Like the other former French colonies in Subsaharan Africa, Benin is associated with the European Common Market. However, the political instability that reigned in the country from 1963 frightened off potential investors. Such investments as were made thereafter were relatively modest. They included a fertilizer plant, foodprocessing concerns, and a match factory.

History. Dahomey, now called Benin, took its name from an ancient kingdom whose origin goes back at least to the 15th century. At that time the southern part of the country was inhabited primarily by the Aja people, ethnically and linguistically related to the populous Yoruba tribe in western Nigeria. The Aja founded a kingdom whose capital, Allada, still exists. As a result of disputes among members of the ruling family, however, two of its royal princes left and founded chiefdoms of their own, one at Porto-Novo and the other at Abomey. Although these chiefdoms subsequently prospered, they continued to maintain at least a nominal allegiance to the older kingdom of Allada until the 16th century.

The Slave Coast. The Portuguese, followed by other Europeans, started to come to the region in search of slaves for the New World in the latter part of the 16th century. So great was the abundance of the human cargo provided by Dahomey that the region soon came to be known as the "Slave Coast." Intertribal warfare—already great before the arrival of the Europeans—grew in intensity as Dahomeans vied with one another to seize as many captives as possible for sale into slavery. The kings of Porto-Novo, Ouidah, and other coastal settlements competed fiercely to attract European traders to their shores, for the goods brought by the Europeans and the sums they spent for slaves added greatly to the local kings' coffers. To facilitate this trade the kings allowed the Europeans first to build trading "factories" and later to erect forts to protect them. In so doing, the local rulers laid the basis for their own subsequent conquest.

Kingdom of Dahomey. By 1625, under the reign of King Dako, the chiefdom of Abomey had grown into the kingdom of Dahomey. Dako's successors further enlarged the realm by conquering most of the neighboring lands, including Allada. But Ouidah and Porto-Novo, the two most important slave ports on the coast, continued to oppose Dahomey and to maintain their independence as separate kingdoms.

Ouidah was attacked, devastated, and then incorporated into the kingdom of Dahomey under the reign of King Agadja in 1727. However, the powerful Yoruba state of Oyo conquered Dahomey in 1738 and for the next century exacted annual tribute from it. To make matters worse, from 1767 onward, a severe economic depression afflicted Dahomey because of a decline in the number of slave ships calling at Dahomean ports. The Dahomean economy had by this time come to depend almost entirely on the slave trade; with the trade's decline, serious dislocations began to occur throughout the kingdom. Economic uncertainty soon led to political instability, and Dahomey was beset with internal dissension for the next 30 years.

A turning point was reached with the accession of King Ghézo to the throne in 1818. A man of extraordinary ability, Ghézo set about to reassert the royal power and to end the dissension that had so weakened Dahomey. He organized a powerful army, which included among its ranks a corps of women warriors. His reign, which lasted for 40 years, restored internal order, threw off the Oyo yoke, and made Dahomey one of the most powerful kingdoms in West Africa.

Under Ghézo's leadership the slave trade, which for a century had been the basis of Dahomey's economy, was pursued with renewed vigor. However, the outlawing of the trade by the British in 1807 greatly diminished the visits of slave ships. Realizing that these external forces, which had such serious repercussions on his nation's well-being, were beyond his control, Ghézo concluded that the slave trade alone was insufficient to guarantee the prosperity of his kingdom. Accordingly, he ordered that coconut and oil palms be planted along the coastal areas and that manioc be cultivated throughout the country. These preliminary steps were to have profound implications for the subsequent development of the country, for they laid the basis of Dahomey's modern economy.

Ghézo's successor, King Glélé, who reigned from 1858 until 1889, carried out his ancestors' traditions of military combat. During his reign Porto-Novo was incorporated into the realm. Glélé also established diplomatic relations with the Portuguese, British, Dutch, and French. But relations with the Europeans often turned hostile, and it was not long before Glélé found himself at odds with the French. His successor, King Béhanzin, attacked the French at Ouidah but was repelled. In November 1892 the French marched on the capital of Abomey, only to find that Béhanzin had ordered the city to be burned before he fled. However, he was captured and banished to Martinique in 1894. Thereafter, the old kingdom passed entirely into French hands.

French Colony. Dahomey had assumed its present form by 1901. Three years later it was incorporated into the newly organized Federation of French West Africa. Sporadic uprisings against French rule continued until 1918, but in every case they were put down.

After World War II, France enacted a number of reforms that granted citizenship to Africans, accorded Africans the right to form political parties, and allowed the overseas territories to

COURTHOUSE in Cotonou, largest city of Benin. Cotonou was to have replaced Porto-Novo as the capital after independence, but the transfer was not completed.

MARC AND EVELYNE BERNHEIM FROM RAPHO GUILLLUMETTE

send deputies to the French National Assembly. Three political leaders emerged who were to dominate Dahomean politics in the following decades: Sourou Migan Apithy, whose stronghold was in the southeastern part of the country in and around Porto-Novo; Justin Ahomadegbe, whose support came mainly from the towns associated with the old kingdom of Dahomey (Abomey, Ouidah, and Cotonou); and Hubert Maga, whose support came mainly from the region north of Parakou.

In the French referendum of Sept. 28, 1958, Dahomey overwhelmingly approved the Constitution of the Fifth French Republic and the decision of the Dahomean leaders to join the new French Community. In 1959, Dahomey joined Upper Volta, Niger, and the Ivory Coast in forming the Council of the Entente.

Independence. Dahomey achieved full independence on Aug. 1, 1960. Late in 1960, Hubert Maga's Rassemblement Démocratique Dahoméen (RDD) party joined forces with Sourou Migan Apithy's Parti Républicain du Dahomey (PRD) to form the Parti Dahoméen de l'Unité (PDU). In the elections held on Dec. 11, 1960, the PDU won a smashing victory over the opposition Union Démocratique Dahoméene (UDD), led by Justin Ahomadegbe. Hubert Maga became the new republic's first president.

During Maga's tenure in office an elaborate new capital was built at Cotonou to replace the old colonial capital at Porto-Novo. The cost of the new capital, and the return of thousands of Dahomean administrators from other newly independent neighboring states, vastly increased government expenditures. In order to relieve the deficit in the national budget, President Maga was forced to resort to a number of harsh austerity measures, including a 25% reduction in salaries of all workers in the government and private sectors. These measures immediately provoked a conflict between the government and labor unions and, later, between President Maga and Apithy. The ensuing stalemate was ended by a military coup d'etat that was led by the commander of the army, Col. Christophe Soglo, in October 1963.

Three months later, Colonel Soglo restored the government to civilian rule. Apithy was named president of the republic, and Ahomadegbe was named prime minister. Personal quarrels between Apithy and Ahomadegbe, however, impelled Colonel Soglo to intercede once again in December 1965. This time Soglo (now a general) became head of state and government.

General Soglo temporarily ended the quarreling among the nation's politicians through the simple expedient of exiling them. However, he was unable to solve Dahomey's serious economic problems, and in December 1967 he was overthrown and replaced by Lt. Col. Alphonse Alley. During his brief tenure, Alley drafted a new constitution, which was approved in March 1968. It called for a unicameral legislature and a president elected by universal suffrage for a five-year term.

The election of May 1968 was voided by the military junta when the exiled leaders—Maga, Apithy, and Ahomadegbe—were not allowed to return, and most of the electorate stayed away from the polls. In July 1968, Emile Derlin Zinsou, former foreign minister under General Soglo, was installed as president by the junta. However, on Dec. 10, 1969, Zinsou was removed by the army, and the three exiled political leaders were allowed to return. In April 1970 a Presidential Commission was established, providing for a rotation of the presidency every two years among the three leaders. Maga was chosen to be president until 1972, to be succeeded by Ahomadegbe, who in turn would be succeeded by Apithy.

On Oct. 26, 1972, President Ahomadegbe was ousted by the army, which named an 11-man military government with Maj. Mathieu Kerekou as head of state. Dahomey thus had had 11 changes of government, including five successful military coups, since gaining independence in 1960. A definite leftist trend ensued, and on Nov. 30, 1974, Kerekou proclaimed Dahomey a "Marxist-Leninist scientific socialist" state with a ruling six-member Politburo and a 70-member National Revolutionary Council (membership half military, half civilian) headed by Kerekou.

On the first anniversary of this proclamation, Nov. 30, 1975, Kerekou announced that the country had changed its name to the People's Republic of Benin.

VICTOR D. DU BOIS[*]
American Universities Field Staff

Further Reading: Akinjogbin, I. A., *Dahomey and Its Neighbors* (London 1967); Argyle, William J., *Fon of Dahomey* (New York 1966); Herskovits, Melville J., *Dahomey, an Ancient West African Kingdom*, 2 vols. (Evanston, Ill., 1967); Thompson, Virginia, "Dahomey," in *Five African States*, ed. by Gwendolen M. Carter (Ithaca, N. Y., 1963).

BENIN, Bight of, bə-nin′, bīt, a large bay in the northern section of the Gulf of Guinea. Located off the west coast of Africa, it extends from the Niger River delta westward to Cape Saint Paul, a shoreline distance of some 500 miles (800 km). It forms the southern boundary of Togo, Dahomey, and part of Nigeria, an area formerly known as the Slave Coast because its ports were a center of the slave trade. The main ports today are Lomé (the capital of Togo), Cotonou (in Dahomey), and Lagos (the capital of Nigeria).

The bight, which receives the Benin River, acquired its name from the kingdom of Benin (see BENIN CITY). The Forcados River flows into the bight and forms the principal water route between the Atlantic and the Niger above the delta.

BENIN, People's Republic of. See DAHOMEY.

BENIN CITY, bə-nin′, in southern Nigeria, is the capital of the Mid-West region. It is situated in the tropical rain forest area, on a branch of the Benin River, 150 miles (241 km) east of Lagos. Yams are the principal crop of the countryside, but cacao, cassava, plantains, and other crops are also grown. Kola trees and oil and coconut palms are grown, and rubber is collected. Coal and lignite are mined nearby. The city has rubber-processing facilities and sawmills. Its handicraft industries include brassworking and woodcarving.

From the 13th to the 18th century, Benin city was the center of the kingdom of Benin, one of the most highly organized states of West Africa. At its peak the city had a population of over 80,000 and was known for the magnificence of its art. When the Portuguese first came in the late 15th century, they found a prosperous city-state, surrounded by a wall and a moat, and producing naturalistic bronze and brass works of art. Within the city, crafts were organized along guild lines, with guilds of blacksmiths, brass-smiths, carvers of wood and ivory, and leather-workers.

Local tradition says that the people of Benin came from the north and that the first *oba* (king) came from Ife about the 12th century. The ruler of Benin was a sacred figure, and elaborate ceremonies surrounded his person and movements. After the arrival of the Portuguese, Benin became the main center for trade between the Europeans and the Africans farther inland. Slaves, pepper, blue cotton cloth, and coral beads were exported. The state grew rich on this trade and was able to buy firearms with which it raided neighboring areas for slaves—as far as Lagos in the west and Bonny in the east. But war and slave-raiding devastated and depopulated the countryside, and as the supply of slaves fell off, so did the wealth of the city. By the 19th century the kingdom was in full decline, and when the British arrived in 1897, it was to find only the remnant of a once great civilization.

Archaeological discoveries in the 20th century brought to light the great art of Benin. This art, whose surviving masterpieces are principally in brass, is characterized by the variety of its forms and its realism. The works include statues, reliefs, ornaments, doors, and pillars. It is probable that the art forms in some way derived from the much older Nok culture of central Nigeria. Population: (1953) 53,753.

L. GRAY COWAN, *Columbia University*

BENÍTEZ, bä-nē′tās, **Jaime** (1908–   ), Puerto Rican educator and legal scholar, and the first president of the University of Puerto Rico. He was born in Vieques on Oct. 29, 1908. He became university chancellor in 1942. In 1966 the chancellorship was replaced by the office of president, to which Benítez was appointed. During his tenure as chancellor, enrollment grew from 5,000 to 26,000. He viewed the university solely as a "house of studies" and worked to broaden its curriculum. In 1951 he headed the committee on the Bill of Rights at the Puerto Rican constitutional convention.

A proponent of strong U.S.-Puerto Rican ties, he wrote several books, including *The United States, Cuba, and Latin America* (1961).

BENITO CERENO, bä-nē′tō sā-rā′nō, is a short story by Herman Melville (q.v.), first published in *The Piazza Tales* in 1856. It is based on a chapter in *Voyages and Travels* (1817) by Amasa Delano, a Massachusetts sea captain. The story concerns the mutiny of a cargo of Negro slaves on board a Spanish merchant ship commanded by Benito Cereno, a young Spanish captain. The American poet Robert Lowell adapted the story into a one-act play.

BENJAMIN, ben′jə-mən, was the name of a person and a tribe in the Old Testament. The man named Benjamin was the 12th and youngest son of Jacob (Genesis 35:16–18). Named Ben-oni ("son of my sorrow") by his mother, Rachel, who died at his birth, he was called Benjamin ("son of my right hand") by his father. Benjamin was especially dear to Jacob because Rachel had been the wife he loved best, and he thought her only other son, Joseph, was dead (Genesis 37). Benjamin was later used by Joseph to gain the upper hand over their half-brothers, who had sold Joseph into slavery, and finally to reunite the family and bring it to Egypt.

The story of Benjamin is part of the history of the tribe of Benjamin. The territory of the tribe seems to have lain west of the Jordan River and north of Jerusalem, between the regions held by Judah and Ephraim, and it included the cities of Bethel, Jericho, Gibeon, Mizpah, and Ramah (Joshua 18:21ff). The boundary between Judah and Benjamin apparently went through Jerusalem (Judges 1:21). Benjamin was a very warlike tribe (Judges 4 to 5, 19 to 21). When the Israelite nation divided after the death of Solomon, Benjamin, with Judah, formed the southern kingdom. The best-known members of the tribe of Benjamin were Saul, who was Israel's first king, and St. Paul.

BENJAMIN, ben′jə-mən, **Asher** (1773–1845), American architect and author. He was born in Greenfield, Mass., on June 15, 1773. Little is known of his life except that he followed his profession as architect and builder in Massachusetts and Vermont. He waged a sustained campaign to popularize architecture in America, and he wrote the first American books on architecture. Benjamin has been credited with designing the Old South Congregational Meeting House in Windsor, Vt.; the West Church, Boston, Mass.; and the First Congregational Church, Bennington, Vt.

His books include *The Country Builder's Assistant* (1797) and *The Rudiments of Architecture* (1814). He died in Springfield, Mass., on July 26, 1845.

BENJAMIN, ben′jə-mən, **Judah Philip** (1811–1884), American lawyer and public official. Of Jewish ancestry, he was born on St. Thomas, then part of the British West Indies, on Aug. 6, 1811. When he was a boy, he and his parents settled in Charleston, S.C. After attending Yale, he went to New Orleans and studied law. He was admitted to the bar there in 1832, soon rising to prominence in his profession. With Thomas Slidell he published in 1834 a valuable digest of Louisiana appeal cases. This work and his brief in the case of the brig *Creole*, which reviewed the status of slavery (see CREOLE CASE), established his reputation nationally and brought him wealth. He also operated a large sugar plantation and was an active railroad promoter.

Entering politics in the early 1840's, Benjamin was elected to the U.S. Senate as a Whig in 1852 and reelected as a Democrat in 1858. He was an early champion of secession, and after Louisiana seceded in 1861, he left the Senate. Shortly before the outbreak of the Civil War his friend Jefferson Davis, president of the Confederacy, appointed him attorney general and, a few months later, secretary of war.

Widely and probably unjustly criticized for confederate military losses in 1862, the increasingly unpopular Benjamin was steadfastly supported by Davis. Becoming secretary of state early in 1862, Benjamin worked energetically but in vain during the remainder of the war to obtain foreign recognition of the Confederacy. Early in 1865 he proposed that slaves willing to fight for the South be freed. After the Confederacy collapsed in 1865, he fled to England.

There Benjamin began the study of law and was admitted to the bar in 1866 under a special ruling, after only a few months of study. He developed a highly successful and lucrative practice, being named queen's counsel officially in 1869. His *Treatise on the Law of Sale of Personal Property* (1868) won immediate recognition as a legal classic. He died in Paris on May 6, 1884.

Further Reading: Meade, Robert D., *Judah P. Benjamin* (New York 1943).

BENJAMIN, ben′jə-mən, **Park** (1849–1922), American lawyer and writer. He was born in New York City on May 11, 1849. A graduate of the U.S. Naval Academy in 1867, he served on Admiral Farragut's flagship but resigned from the service in 1869. He graduated from the Albany Law School the following year and practiced law in New York City as a patent expert.

Benjamin edited the journal *Scientific American* (1872–1878) and *Appleton's Cyclopaedia of Applied Mechanics* (1881–1892). He wrote *Shakings: Etchings from the Naval Academy* (1867), *Wrinkles and Recipes* (1875), *The Age of Electricity* (1886), and *The United States Naval Academy* (1900). He presented a valuable collection of books (chiefly scientific) that he amassed with E.J. Berwind and R.M. Thompson to the U.S. Naval Academy. He died in Stamford, Conn., on Aug. 21, 1922.

BENJAMIN OF TUDELA, ben′jə-mən, too̅-thä′lä, (died 1173), Spanish traveler and rabbi, whose discoveries provide important information on the history of the Jews in the 12th century. He was born in Tudela, in the province of Navarre, Spain. From 1159 until 1173 he traveled from Saragossa, through France, Italy, Greece, Palestine, and Persia (Iran), and reached the western border of China; he returned by way of Arabia, Egypt, Sicily, and Spain. As the first European traveler to penetrate far into Asia, he brought back a great amount of useful information on the people and geography of the East.

His *Itinerary*, compiled from his notes, was first published in Hebrew at Constantinople (now Istanbul), in 1543. It was translated into Latin by Arias Montanus in 1575, and later into Dutch, German, French, and English.

BENN, ben, **Gottfried** (1886–1956), German expressionist poet and writer, whose harshly cruel observations of life and death influenced the group of disillusioned German writers after World War II. Benn was born in Mansfeld, West Prussia, on May 2, 1886. He was raised in a Protestant parsonage but underwent an early conversion to atheism and nihilism under the influence of the writings of Nietzsche.

The study and practice of medicine (he was a skin surgeon by profession) influenced Benn's writing from the beginning. He adapted the clinical language of medical literature to a mordant literary style of his own. Physical injuries and diseases dominate as symbols of social putrefaction in the most important collections of his poems—*Morgue* (1912), *Fleisch* (1916), and *Schutt* (1924). In addition to what is called his "dissectional lyric poetry," Benn wrote influential criticism. He died in Berlin on July 7, 1956.

BENNET, Henry. See ARLINGTON, EARL OF.

BENNETT, ben′ət, a family of American actors, of whom the best known were the sisters Constance and Joan.

RICHARD BENNETT (1872–1944), an actor and manager, was born in Cass County, Ind., on May 21, 1872. From 1896 to 1908 he was associated with the Charles Frohman theatrical enterprises as a producer. He formed his own company in 1913 to produce Eugène Brieux's controversial play *Damaged Goods* (*Les avariés*), in which he also starred, and in 1915 he produced Brieux's *Maternity*. Bennett's most notable stage roles were in *They Knew What They Wanted* (1924), *The Barker* (1927), and *The Royal Family* (1927). He appeared in the films *Arrowsmith* (1931) and *The Magnificent Ambersons* (1942). Bennett died in Los Angeles, Calif., on Oct. 22, 1944.

CONSTANCE BENNETT (1905–1965), Richard's daughter, was born in New York City on Oct. 22, 1905. After making her film debut in *Cytherea* (1924), she appeared in scores of films, including the very successful *Topper* (1937), with Cary Grant. Making her stage debut in *Easy Virtue* (1940), she later produced films and radio shows. She also operated her own cosmetics business and designed Constance Bennett Originals for a Cincinnati dress company. Miss Bennett died at Fort Dix, N.J., on July 24, 1965.

JOAN BENNETT (1910–   ), another daughter, was born in Palisades, N.J., on Feb. 27, 1910. She made her stage debut in *Jarnegan* (1928), with her father. Her career in movies spanned more than 25 years, taking her from ingenue roles in such films as *Bulldog Drummond* (1929) and *Little Women* (1933) to character parts in *Father of the Bride* (1950) and *We're No Angels* (1955). She returned to the stage in 1938 in a revival of *Stage Door*.

Arnold Bennett

(1867–1931)

BENNETT, ben′ət, **Arnold** (1867–1931), English novelist and playwright, who is best known as the author of *The Old Wives' Tale* (1908) and other novels about the "Five Towns," an imaginary manufacturing district in west central England. In these books Bennett subjected the dull and commonplace lives of the lower-middle-class inhabitants of the region to close scrutiny, painting them with sympathy, warmth, and humor.

Life. *Enoch Arnold Bennett* was born near Hanley, Staffordshire, on May 27, 1867, the son of a solicitor. He attended Newcastle Middle School and in 1885 began working as an unpaid clerk in his father's office, preparing to study law at the University of London. In 1888 he took a job as a clerk in a solicitor's office in London. Then, abandoning the law, he decided to make writing his profession and in 1893 became assistant editor of a fashionable weekly magazine, *Woman,* for which, in addition to book reviews and dramatic criticism, he wrote beauty hints and an advice-to-the-lovelorn column.

The publication of Bennett's short story *A Letter Home,* in the July 1895 issue of the *Yellow Book* magazine, confirmed him in his decision to make writing his career. He became editor of *Woman* in 1896 and two years later published his first novel, *A Man from the North.* In 1900 he resigned from the magazine, moved to Fontainebleau, France, and settled down to writing about a half million words a year. He married a Frenchwoman, Marie Marguerite Soulié, in 1907. Bennett and his wife lived in France until 1912 and in London until their separation in 1921. In 1922 he met and fell in love with an English actress, Dorothy Cheston, by whom, although they never married, he had a daughter in 1926. He died in London on March 27, 1931.

Writings. A prolific and versatile craftsman, Bennett wrote more than 30 novels, several volumes of short stories, and 13 plays. He was known as a skillful, though run-of-the-mill, writer until 1901, when the appearance of *The Old Wives' Tale* established him as one of the outstanding English novelists of his time. *The Old Wives' Tale,* regarded as a classic of English realism, ranks among the best English novels of the 20th century. It is set in the pottery manufacturing region of Staffordshire, where Bennett was born—the "Five Towns" of several of his works, including the Clayhanger trilogy (*Clayhanger,* 1910; *Hilda Lessways,* 1911; and *These Twain,* 1916). The quality of Bennett's work began to fall off when he abandoned this background, although *Riceyman Steps* (1923), *Elsie and the Child* (1925), and *Lord Raingo* (1926) are superior novels.

Most of Bennett's plays suffer from having no strong central ideas. They entertain for an evening but are quickly forgotten. The best known of them are *Milestones* (1912), which he wrote in collaboration with Edward Knoblock, and *The Great Adventure* (1913), which he adapted from his own novel *Buried Alive* (1908). *Buried Alive* was also filmed as *Holy Matrimony* (1943).

BENNETT, ben′ət, **Floyd** (1890–1928), American aviator. He was born in Warrensburg, N.Y., on Oct. 25, 1890. As a boy he attended the public schools and worked on a farm. Later he attended an automobile school in Schenectady, N.Y., and worked in a garage. In 1917 he enlisted in the United States Navy and served at the Hampton Roads and Pensacola naval aviation bases.

In 1921, when Commander Richard E. Byrd accompanied the MacMillan Expedition into the Arctic, Bennett was one of the naval aviators selected to accompany him. On this trip he proved his great ability as a pilot. When Commander Byrd organized his North Pole Expedition, he selected Bennett as his pilot; in 1927 when Commander Byrd was preparing for his transatlantic flight, he again chose Bennett as his pilot, but an injury received in a test flight prevented Bennett's accompanying Byrd on that trip. In 1928 Byrd appointed him as his second in command, and turned over to him the work of assembling the transportation equipment. He was considered indispensable by Byrd, and was consulted on all matters.

On a rescue mission to Greenly Island in the Saint Lawrence River, Bennett fell ill. He was taken to Quebec with pneumonia and died there on April 25, 1928. For his part in the North Pole flight, he was awarded a medal by the National Geographic Society, and the Congressional Medal of Honor.

BENNETT, ben′ət, **Hugh Hammond** (1881–1960), American soil scientist and government official, who has been called the "father of soil conservation" in the United States. He was born on April 15, 1881, near Wadesboro, N.C. After graduating from North Carolina University in 1903, he joined the U.S. Department of Agriculture as a soil scientist. Bennett conducted several large-scale soil surveys in the Panama Canal Zone (1909), Alaska (1914), and Cuba (1925–1932). He headed the Agriculture Department's soil erosion and moisture conservation bureau from 1928 to 1933.

Soil Erosion, a National Menace, which Bennett published in 1928, highlighted a problem that was to become acute in the United States during the depression years that followed. From 1933 to 1935 he successfully directed the U.S. Department of the Interior's struggle to control the "dust bowl" drought that developed on the Great Plains of the United States. In 1935 the Agriculture Department established its Soil Conservation Service, and Bennett was its director until he retired in 1952. He died in Burlington, N.C., on July 7, 1960.

BENNETT, ben'ət, **James Gordon** (1795–1872), American newspaper publisher and editor, who founded the New York *Herald* and made it the most powerful voice in American journalism in its day.

He was born in Keith, Banffshire, Scotland, in 1795. His parents were Roman Catholics, and young Bennett began to study for the priesthood. However, he left the seminary in 1819 and went to the United States. He worked as a proofreader and as a book salesman in Boston, performed minor newspaper chores in New York City and Charleston, S.C., and in 1827 became a Washington correspondent for the New York *Enquirer*. For four years he reported congressional proceedings and wrote lively, barbed comments on the Washington scene, meanwhile gaining insight into American politics.

In 1834, after unsuccessful attempts in 1832 and 1833 to establish a newspaper, he rented a cellar at 20 Wall Street in New York City; his only office equipment was a plank laid across two flour barrels that served as a desk and counter. He engaged two Ann Street printers to set his type, and on May 6, 1835, with $500 capital, he launched his penny daily, the New York *Herald*. Bennett was editor, reporter, proofreader, ad-taker, folder, and cashier—"one poor man in a cellar against the world."

Bennett was the first to print accounts of stock market transactions, and his "money" article became a daily feature of the *Herald*. He covered single-handed the great fire of December 1835 in New York City, writing a graphic account of it for his four-page paper. In 1836 he became financially independent as the result of an advertising contract with a patent medicine manufacturer, and a short time later he quit the cellar, hired a managing editor, and moved to the corner of Fulton and Nassau streets.

During the Mexican War in 1846, Bennett arranged weekly overland express service to carry the war news to New York City. To get news from Europe ahead of his competitors, he maintained fast dispatch boats off Sandy Hook, N.J. After meeting incoming ships 50 to 100 miles at sea, these boats would speed up New York Harbor with fresh news for the *Herald*. During the Civil War he employed 63 war correspondents and spent $525,000 to gather war news.

Even after he could well afford a large staff, Bennett continued to do much of the work on the *Herald*. Usually he rose at daybreak and wrote editorials, short fillers, and miscellany before breakfast. From 9 A.M. to 1 P.M. he read newspapers, talked to callers, and edited copy, often writing a column of news as well. In the afternoon he went to Wall Street for financial items, read proofs, took advertisements, and kept his books. He died in New York City, on June 1, 1872.

JAMES GORDON BENNETT (1841–1918), his son, was also a newspaper editor and publisher. He was born in New York City on May 10, 1841. He assumed control of the New York *Herald* just before his father's death and continued the policies of the elder Bennett. He also established an afternoon paper, the *Telegram*, and founded the English-language Paris *Herald* for Americans traveling abroad. In 1871 he commissioned Henry M. Stanley to search Africa for the missing missionary Dr. David Livingstone. Bennett died in Beaulieu, France, on May 14, 1918.

EMMET CROZIER, *Author of "Yankee Reporters"*

BENNETT, ben'ət, **John Coleman** (1902–   ), American clergyman and theologian. He was born in Kingston, Ontario, Canada, on July 22, 1902. He studied at Williams College, at Oxford University, and at Union Theological Seminary. In 1939 he was ordained a Congregational minister. In 1943 he became professor of social ethics at Union Theological Seminary, and in 1964 president of the seminary. He served on committees of the World Council of Churches, and was vice chairman of the Liberal party in New York State.

His writings include *The Christian as Citizen* (1955) and *Christians and the State* (1958). He was editor of *Nuclear Weapons and the Conflict of Conscience* (1962) and coeditor of *Christianity and Crisis*, a periodical.

BENNETT, ben'ət, **Richard Bedford** (1870–1947), Canadian political leader, who was prime minister during the Depression of the 1930's. He was born on July 3, 1870, in Hopewell, New Brunswick. As a young man he moved to Calgary, Alberta, where he built up a successful law practice and, through judicious investments and a valuable inheritance, became one of Canada's wealthiest men. He took an active part in the political life of western Canada and was first elected to the House of Commons in 1911.

In 1927, Bennett succeeded Arthur Meighen as national leader of the Conservative party. Three years later, riding the wave of antigovernment sentiment brought on by the depression, Bennett led his party to victory over Prime Minister Mackenzie King's Liberals. In spite of his efforts during the next five years, however, Bennett's administration became increasingly unpopular, and it was soundly defeated in the general election of 1935. Bennett retained the leadership of the party until 1938, when he retired from politics. He moved to England in 1939 and was elevated to the House of Lords with the title of *Viscount Bennett* in 1941. He died at his estate in Mickleham, Surrey, on June 26, 1947.

Although Bennett succeeded in preserving the integrity of Canada's financial structure during extremely difficult years, his name has come to be indelibly linked with the hardships and adversity of the Great Depression. In spite of extravagant promises made during the election

R.B. Bennett, prime minister of Canada, 1930–1935.

campaign of 1930, his administration failed to bring any real measure of relief to unemployed industrial workers and drought-stricken farmers. He was unable in 1930 to foresee the magnitude of the Depression. Consequently his antidepression policies, based as they were on the principles of pre-Keynesian economics, were almost certainly doomed to failure. It is unfortunate that four arduous years passed before he was convinced that a new approach was necessary.

Finally, in late 1934, Bennett was persuaded that the time had come to establish the Conservative party as the party of reform. A so-called "New Deal" was hurriedly fashioned, and an attempt was made to foster in Canada the spirit of recovery that President Franklin D. Roosevelt's New Deal was beginning to stimulate in the United States. The program envisaged a partial abandonment of laissez-faire and increased government participation in welfare and labor matters. Unfortunately, after the program had been launched, the prime minister could not convince the most influential members of his party that such a course was wise. As a result of dissension within the party and inadequate organization, the New Deal failed to capture the imagination of the Canadian people.

In addition, Bennett's failure to give prudent and forceful leadership to the New Deal program earned him a reputation for insincerity and political opportunism. This judgment should be tempered by consideration of such progressive legislation as his government's minimum wage and workmen's compensation acts and also by the fact that Bennett was persuaded to accept the principle of the New Deal seemingly out of fear of anarchy. He feared that the responsibility for implementing reform would fall into the hands of incapable and immoderate men after another general election.

MICHAEL SWIFT
Public Archives of Canada

Further Reading: Beaverbrook, Lord, *Friends* (London 1959); Watkins, Ernest, *R.B. Bennett* (Toronto 1963).

BENNETT, ben'ət, **Robert Russell** (1894–   ), American composer, conductor, and arranger. He was born in Kansas City, Mo., on June 15, 1894. From 1909 to 1913 he studied harmony with Carl Busch, conductor of the Kansas City Symphony. In the early 1920's Bennett began working in New York City as an orchestrator of musical comedy scores. Later he studied with Nadia Boulanger in Paris, and in 1927 and 1928 held Guggenheim fellowships that permitted him to devote time to composing. His orchestral works include *Sights and Sounds* (1929), *Abraham Lincoln Symphony* (1929), *Concerto Grosso* (1932), and his most popular composition, the symphony *The Four Freedoms* (1943), inspired by Norman Rockwell's series of paintings.

After 1935, Bennett spent much of his time in Hollywood, arranging, composing, and conducting music for such films as *Show Boat* (1936), *The Hunchback of Notre Dame* (1939), and *Rebecca* (1940). Returning to the Broadway stage in the 1940's, he reorchestrated Bizet's music for *Carmen Jones* (1943) and orchestrated the scores for almost all of the Rodgers and Hammerstein musicals, including *Oklahoma!* (1943), *South Pacific* (1950), and *The Sound of Music* (1959). He also orchestrated Lerner and Loewe's *My Fair Lady* (1956) and *Camelot* (1960).

BENNETT, ben'ət, **William Andrew Cecil** (1900–   ), Canadian public official. He was born in Albert County, N.B., on Sept. 6, 1900. After service in the Flying Corps in World War I he settled in British Columbia and developed a chain of hardware stores. His public career began in 1941 when he was elected to the provincial legislature as a Conservative. In 1951 he broke with the coalition government and joined the Social Credit party. Following the election of 1952, Bennett was invited to form a minority government, thus becoming the first Social Credit premier of British Columbia. His party received a majority in the 1953 election and retained power in the elections of 1956, 1960, 1963, and 1966 but was defeated in 1972.

BENNETT, ben'ət, **Sir William Sterndale** (1816–1875), English pianist and composer. He was born in Sheffield on April 13, 1816. He studied at the Royal Academy of Music in London from 1826 to 1836. Afterward, on the advice of his friend Felix Mendelssohn, he studied in 1836–1837 at Leipzig, then one of the main musical centers in Germany. His performances and compositions were highly regarded by the younger German musicians, especially Robert Schumann.

In England, Bennett was one of the founders of the Bach Society in 1849, and in 1856 he became conductor of the Philharmonic Society. He was appointed professor of music at Cambridge University in 1856 and principal of the Royal Academy of Music in 1868, and was knighted in 1871. He died in London on Feb. 1, 1875.

As a composer, Bennett is best known for the overtures *Parisina* (1834) and *The Naiads* (1837) and the cantatas *The May Queen* (1858) and *The Woman of Samaria* (1867). He also wrote chamber music and several concertos for piano and orchestra.

BENNETTSVILLE, ben'ets-vil, is a city in northeastern South Carolina and the seat of Marlboro County, located 125 miles (201 km) north of Charleston. The surrounding region produces corn, peaches, tobacco, and cotton. Bennettsville has yarn and tire fabric mills, a lumber yard, a kitchen cabinet factory, and an electric equipment plant. Government is by mayor and council. Population: 7,468.

BENNIGSEN, ben'iKH-sen, **Count Levin August Theophil** (1745–1826), Russian general. He was born in Brunswick, Germany, on Feb. 10, 1745, and entered the Russian army at an early age. In 1806 he was appointed to command the Russian force that went to the aid of the Prussians against Napoleon. He fought in the battles of Pultusk (1806) and Eylau (1807). After the Peace of Tilsit he retired to his estates for several years.

During Napoleon's invasion of Russia in 1812, Bennigsen commanded the Russian center at the Battle of Borodino. Before the French retreat began, he defeated Joachim Murat at Maloyaroslavets in October 1812. He retired from the army because of differences with the commander in chief, Mikhail Kutuzov, but after the latter's death he became commander of the Russian army of reserve, which in 1813 he led into Saxony. He took part in the Battle of Leipzig that year and was created a count by Emperor Alexander on the field. Bennigsen died in Hannover, Germany, on Dec. 3, 1826.

BENNINGTON, ben'ing-tən, is a town in southwestern Vermont. It lies just west of the Green Mountains, about 150 miles (240 km) northwest of Boston, Mass. The town, the seat of Bennington County, is legally a "half-shire" town: its county court is shared with another county. The town comprises the villages of Bennington, Old Bennington, and North Bennington.

Bennington lies in an agricultural area. Its major manufactures include batteries, lubricating equipment, electronic capacitors, lithographic products, furniture, brushes, plastics, knitted wear, and paper products. Tourism is economically important, and the town is a ski center. Bennington College for women is in the village of Bennington.

First settled in 1761, the town was named for Benning Wentworth, the first royal governor of New Hampshire (1741–1767). Chartered in 1749, it was one of Wentworth's township grants that were claimed by New York and defended by Ethan Allen and the Green Mountain Boys. Catamount Tavern, their headquarters in 1770, is preserved in Old Bennington. At North Bennington is a 302-foot (92-meter) granite monument commemorating the victory of the Americans over the British in the Battle of Bennington, Aug. 16, 1777. Bennington was incorporated as a village in 1849. Government is by town and village meetings. Population: town, 14,586; village, 7,950.

BENNINGTON COLLEGE, ben'ing-tən, is a private liberal arts institution for women, in Bennington, Vt. It was chartered in 1925 as an independent four-year college embodying a "thoroughgoing experiment in higher education along modern lines," and classes began in September 1932.

There are no prescribed courses of study. Students, guided by faculty counseling, elect an individual program of study arranged to suit their capabilities and interests, and all students receive weekly counseling or tutoring throughout their college careers. Bennington's school year is divided into three terms, consisting of two 14-week resident terms and one 9-week work period of vocational or educational value in schools, government or social agencies, hospitals, laboratories, museums, or offices. Studies are offered in dance, drama, literature and language, music, science and mathematics, social sciences, and visual arts. Regular workshops are held in music, drama, and dance. Bennington's Crossett Library houses about 45,000 volumes and has an extensive collection of records, tapes, and microfilm.

The student body, which numbered 280 in 1940, increased to 370 by the mid-1960's. Some male students are admitted to the music, drama, and dance departments.

BENNY, ben'ē, **Jack** (1894–1974), American comedian. He was born *Benjamin Kubelsky* in Chicago, Ill., on Feb. 14. At the age of 17 he entered vaudeville in Waukegan, using the violin, which he had studied seriously, as a comic stage property. After serving in the Navy in World War I, he resumed his vaudeville career in the 1920's and entered motion pictures in 1929, eventually starring in more than a dozen films.

Jack Benny's radio program was first broadcast in 1932 and continued, with few changes in format, for over 20 years, winning for Benny a number of citations as the nation's favorite comedian.

In 1950 he began appearing on television, with a weekly show in 1960–1965. He portrayed himself as a vain miser, quite the opposite of his true character. He was married to Mary Livingstone (Sadie Marks) in 1927. He died in Beverly Hills, Calif., on Dec. 26, 1974.

BENOIS, bə-nwa', **Alexandre** (1870–1960), Russian-born French artist and art historian. He was born in St. Petersburg (now Leningrad) on May 4, 1870. With Sergei Diaghilev and Léon Bakst of the Ballets Russes he helped establish Russian ballet in western Europe. As an artist he is known chiefly for the scenery he designed and painted for Igor Stravinsky's ballet *Petrouchka* (1911), for which he also provided the story outline.

Benois served briefly as curator of paintings at the Hermitage museum in Leningrad and wrote several books on the history of Russian art. He died in Paris on Feb. 9, 1960.

BENOIT, bə-nwa', **Pierre Léonard Léopold** (1834–1901), Belgian composer. He also used the first name *Peter*. He was born at Harelbeke, Belgium, on Aug. 17, 1834. The principal leader of the Flemish national movement in music, Benoit composed operas, oratorios, cantatas, and a religious tetralogy.

From 1867 he directed the Fleming School of Music (later the Royal Flemish Conservatory) at Antwerp. He died at Antwerp on March 8, 1901.

BENOÎT DE SAINTE-MAURE, bə-nwa' də sant-môr', French poet and chronicler of the later 12th century A.D. His name is also spelled *Sainte-More*. He wrote the *Roman de Troie* about 1160 and dedicated it to Eleanor of Aquitaine, wife of Henry II of England. A Norman-French romance in some 30,000 verses, the *Roman* recounts the story of the siege of Troy. Benoît also wrote the 42,000-verse *Chronique des ducs de Normandie* for Henry II about 1170–1175.

BENONI, bə-nō'nī, a city in the Republic of South Africa, is an important gold mining center. Located in southern Transvaal province, 16 miles (26 km) east of Johannesburg, the city is 5,419 feet (1,652 meters) above sea level.

Benoni is one of the cities along the great gold-bearing reefs of the Witwatersrand, that came into existence in the late 19th century and continued to prosper because of the extraordinary richness of its mines. Benoni is now heavily industrialized, with iron and brass foundries and electrical equipment works. Population: (1960) 122,502.

BENSENVILLE, ben'sən-vil, is an industrial and residential village in northeastern Illinois, in Du Page county, 18 miles (29 km) northwest of Chicago. It has a number of industries, including railroad shops and the manufacture of dresses and fluid control machinery. The village is served by nearby O'Hare Airport.

The site of Bensenville was purchased in 1872, and the village was incorporated in 1873. Settlement of the area had begun some 50 years earlier. The village is named for Bensen, Germany. It has a village government, with a president of the board and a village clerk. Population: 12,833.

DOROTHEA F. SCHMIT
Bensenville Community Public Library

BENSON, ben'sən, **Arthur Christopher** (1862–1925), English writer. He was born in Crowthorne, England, on April 24, 1862, the second son of Edward White Benson (q.v.). Educated at Eton and King's College, Cambridge, he was a master at Eton from 1885 to 1903 and a fellow of Magdalene College, Cambridge, from 1904 to 1915, when he became master of the college. He died in London on June 17, 1925.

His first book, *Memoirs of Arthur Hamilton* (1886), was published under the pseudonym "Christopher Carr." Among his writings are lives of his father, his brother Robert, Tennyson, and Ruskin. Other books include *From a College Window* (1906), *Beside Still Waters* (1907), and *Memories and Friends* (1924).

BENSON, ben'sən, **Edward Frederic** (1867–1940), English author. He was born in Crowthorne, England, on July 24, 1867, the third son of Edward White Benson (q.v.). After graduating from King's College, Cambridge, he did archaeological work in Athens (1892–1895) and Egypt (1895). Benson became famous in 1893 for his satirical novel *Dodo*, to which he wrote several sequels. He also produced novels of school and university life, such as *The Babe, B.A.* (1897) and *Colin II* (1925), and tales of the supernatural, including *The Luck of the Vails* (1901). Among his books combining personal reminiscence and social history are *As We Were* (1930), *As We Are* (1932), and *Final Edition* (1940). He died in London on Feb. 29, 1940.

BENSON, ben'sən, **Edward White** (1829–1896), English clergyman, who was archbishop of Canterbury from 1883 to 1896. He was born into a prominent Birmingham family on July 14, 1829, and graduated from Trinity College, Cambridge, in 1852. In 1859 he became headmaster of the new Wellington College. Appointed the first bishop of Truro in 1877, he was largely responsible for building the cathedral there.

In 1883, Benson became archbishop of Canterbury. His achievements as head of the Church of England included expansion of missions and improvement of relations with other churches. In 1890 he rendered judgment on charges that Edward King, bishop of Lincoln, was using a ritual close to that of Roman Catholicism. This decision, known as the "Lincoln Judgement," generally supported the bishop and helped end a controversy over ritual. Benson died at Hawarden on Oct. 11, 1896.

BENSON, ben'sən, **Egbert** (1746–1833), American Revolutionary patriot and lawyer. He was born in New York City on June 21, 1746, graduated from King's College (now Columbia) in 1765, and was admitted to the New York bar.

When the Revolution began, he helped to organize New York state's government and was its attorney general (1777–1787). He served in the Continental Congress in 1781–1784 and later worked for New York ratification of the Constitution. As a representative in the 1st and 2d U.S. Congresses (1789–1793) he was an ardent supporter of the administration. Benson, who had a high reputation as a legal scholar, then became a justice of the New York supreme court. After 1801, except for brief service in Congress in 1813, he held no public office. He died in Jamaica, N.Y., on Aug. 24, 1833. Benson was a founder of the New York Historical Society.

BENSON, ben'sən, **Ezra Taft** (1899–   ), American public official. He was born in Whitney, Idaho, on Aug. 4, 1899. He graduated as bachelor of science in 1926 from Brigham Young University, in Provo, Utah, and as master of science in agricultural economics from Iowa State College in 1927. He then continued with work he had begun in 1923, managing a farm in Whitney.

From 1929 to 1938, Benson was connected with the University of Idaho's extension service, beginning as county agricultural agent in Preston and becoming in 1930 head of the service's agricultural economics and marketing department. In 1930 he helped organize the Idaho Cooperative Council, serving from 1933 to 1938 as its secretary. From 1939 to 1944 he was executive secretary to the National Council of Farmer Cooperatives. He was a member of the board of trustees of the American Institute of Cooperatives from 1943 and its chairman in 1952. An active Mormon, he became a member of the Quorum of Twelve Apostles in 1943.

In 1953, President Eisenhower appointed Benson secretary of agriculture. The secretary sought to reduce the federal government's role in agriculture and to modify existing price-support policies. Congress adopted his program of flexible price supports for basic farm commodities in 1954, but two years later restored some rigid supports. His measures, which failed to stimulate farm prices, aroused bitter controversy, and he was blamed by many fellow Republicans for election reverses in the farm states. Benson and Postmaster General Arthur E. Summerfield were the only cabinet officers to serve through the eight years of the Eisenhower administration.

BENSON, ben'sən, **Frank Weston** (1862–1951), American painter and etcher. He was born in Salem, Mass., on March 24, 1862. After studying at the Museum of Fine Arts, Boston (1880–1883), and at the Académie Julian in Paris (1883–1885), he was a teacher of painting and drawing at the Museum of Fine Arts in Boston from 1889.

In 1912, as a hobby, Benson began etching, mostly wildfowl. In 1915 an exhibit of his works established his fame in that field. He won many honors, including the Clark Prize of the National Academy of Design (1891) and the Logan Prize of the Chicago Society of Etchers (1918). He was a member of the National Academy and the American Academy of Arts and Letters. His works include, besides many paintings, a set of seven murals for the Library of Congress. He died in Salem on Nov. 14, 1951.

BENSON, ben'sən, **William Shepherd** (1855–1932), American admiral. He was born in Bibb County, Ga., on Sept. 25, 1855. Graduated from the U.S. Naval Academy in 1877, he rose from ensign to rear admiral. In 1915 he was named chief of naval operations, a newly created office. In 1916 he was promoted admiral.

Benson was appointed by President Wilson to serve on the American War Commission, set up to unify Allied plans during World War I. The work of the group led to the creation of the Interallied Naval Council. In 1918, Benson was the American naval representative in the drafting of the naval terms of the armistice.

In 1920, he was appointed chairman of the United States Shipping Board and trustee of the Emergency Fleet Corporation. He retained his association with the shipping board for 28 years, during which time he emphasized the importance of an adequate navy and merchant marine. He died in Washington, D.C., on May 20, 1932.

Benson revised Adm. Stephen B. Luce's *Text-Book of Seamanship* in 1898, and wrote *The Merchant Marine* (1923).

BENT, bent, **Charles** (1799–1847), American fur trader and territorial governor. He was born in Charleston, Va. (now W.Va.), on Nov. 11, 1799. After trapping and trading in the region of the upper Missouri River, he and his brother William and Ceran St. Vrain established themselves, under the firm name of Bent, St. Vrain & Company, in the Indian trade in the valley of the upper Arkansas River. At first they built a rude stockade between the present towns of Pueblo and Canon City, Colo., but subsequently they began the erection of a permanent structure which was known as Bent's Fort (q.v.).

Charles Bent married and settled at Taos, N. Mex., though still retaining his interest in the trading firm at Bent's Fort. After the occupation of Santa Fe by American forces under the command of Gen. Stephen W. Kearney in 1846, Charles Bent was appointed civil governor of the territory of New Mexico. He was killed at Taos, N.Mex., on Jan. 19, 1847, during an insurrection of Mexicans and Indians.

BENT, bent, **Silas** (1820–1887), American naval officer. He was born in St. Louis, Mo., on Oct. 10, 1820. He entered the Navy in 1836, served in the Seminole War, and was with Commander James Glynn and Commodore Matthew C. Perry on several cruises to Japan. He was on the brig *Preble* under Glynn at Nagasaki, Japan, in 1849, when Glynn procured the release of 18 American seamen who had been held prisoners. Bent piloted the U.S. fleet into Naha, Okinawa, and was U.S. commissioner in the negotiations for a treaty with the Okinawa regent, Prince Sho Jun. He resigned his commission as flag lieutenant in 1861. He died on Shelter Island, N.Y., on Aug. 26, 1887.

Bent was especially active in survey work. On Perry's Japan expedition he had charge of the hydrographic survey, and his excellent work became the basis of the surveys undertaken later by the Japanese government. His most important work was to delineate and describe scientifically the Kuroshio, or Black Tide, the great northward-flowing stream of the Pacific, corresponding to the Atlantic Gulf Stream.

BENT, bent, **William** (1809–1869), American fur trader and pioneer. He was born in St. Louis, Mo., on May 23, 1809. A trapper and trader on the upper Missouri, he joined his brothers Charles, Robert, and George and Ceran St. Vrain in organizing and establishing the business of Bent, St. Vrain & Company in the valley of the upper Arkansas. The permanent trading post of this firm, known as Bent's Fort, was mainly developed by Charles Bent, but William was subsequently its manager. During the quarter century following its completion in 1834 it became one of the focal places in the history of the surrounding region.

In 1835, William Bent married Owl Woman, a daughter of White Thunder. Gaining great influence among the Indians, he continued to manage the trading at Bent's Fort after the death of his brothers and the retirement of St. Vrain. In 1849, declining the government's low offer to buy the fort, he destroyed most of it. He later built another trading post downstream, and in 1859 he leased it to the government and turned to ranching.

Known as the first permanent white settler of Colorado, Bent served a brief term as a government Indian agent. He died near Las Animas, Colo., on May 19, 1869. Bent County, Colo., was named in his honor.

BENT GRASS commonly is grown for forage and turf. The Redtop variety (*Agrostis alba*) is shown here.

USDA

BENT GRASS is a genus of grasses, many of which are important as forage and turf. Usually perennial, bent grasses are found all over the world in temperate and cold regions. They often have erect or creeping stems, numerous narrow leaves, and small flowers. They require a somewhat acid soil and large quantities of water, and these grasses are subject to some serious fungus diseases.

The bent grasses belong to the genus *Agrostis*, family Gramineae; there are approximately 100 species. The most common species is Colonial or Rhode Island bent grass (*A. tenuis*), native to Europe but widely naturalized in the United States. Often used for pasture and lawns, especially in cool, moist climates, this species has narrow leaves and purplish satiny flowers. It has several varieties, including Astoria, Prince Edward Island, and New Zealand bent grass.

Another important species is Redtop, or Fiorin (*A. alba*), originally found in Europe but now widely grown for forage purposes in northeastern North America. It has a strong, creeping stem, coarse foliage, and large, loosely branched flower clusters. A slender, finely branched species, brown bent, or velvet bent (*A. canina*), is used frequently for lawns, especially on golf courses. Another noteworthy species is cloudgrass (*A. nebulosa*), cultivated in Spain and used in dry bouquets.

BENT TWIG, The, a novel written in 1915 by the American author Dorothy Canfield Fisher. *The Bent Twig* is set in a Midwestern university town. It concerns Sylvia Marshall, a child of genial, easygoing parents, who is slighted when she enters college because the town's more conventional people hold her family in contempt and regard the Marshall home as a rendezvous for the college freaks. Sylvia, after an unfortunate affair with a playboy, falls in love with a serious-minded man and settles down.

BENTHAM, ben'thəm, **Jeremy** (1748–1832), English philosopher, reformer, and founder of utilitarianism—the first systematic effort to describe and evaluate all human acts, institutions, and laws in terms of immediate sensible pleasures and pains. He might well be called "the Luther of the legal world," for in late 18th century England, the ancient, corrupt, and unreformed legal system was venerated as a national religion; and he not only dared to challenge it but created a whole new structure of law, attracted an army of disciples, and ultimately inspired a thorough reformation.

Life. Bentham was born in London on Feb. 15, 1748, where he lived all his life and where he died, on June 16, 1832. A child prodigy who read Latin at the age of 3, he was only 12 when his proud father enrolled him at Oxford, and 16 when he graduated. His placid, secluded, bachelor's life was largely an adventure of the mind. Freed from the necessity of earning a living by a small inheritance from his mother's estate and then by a much larger one left by his father in 1792, he dedicated his life to his one great passion: the radical critique and reconstruction of every English institution—economic, moral, religious, educational, political, and legal.

His only major leap into practical affairs left him poorer, sadder, and more radical than ever. Sickened by the callous and brutal treatment then given to prisoners, he borrowed his brother Sam's design for a "Panopticon," a model prison arranged like a wheel with central management at the hub. In 1794, Bentham signed a contract with the British government to build and run such a prison, but the plan was buried under the pressures of the French Wars.

Bentham helped found the first utilitarian journal, the *Westminster Review*, in 1823 and also helped found University College, London, in 1826. He left his body for dissection, and his skeleton, neatly dressed in his own suit, still sits upright at University College.

Writings. Perhaps no great thinker is so difficult to study as Bentham, for he was driven so relentlessly by his vision that he continually ran from one subject to another, never finishing, never revising, and casually entrusting his piles of manuscripts to any willing disciple. In the 1770's he proclaimed his lifelong ambition, to draw an exhaustive map of all thought and action, laid out on utilitarian lines. His method was always the same: first, a description and critical analysis of what is, and then a minutely detailed reconstruction, in theory and practice alike, of what ought to be.

Only his first two books, *A Fragment on Government* (1776) and *An Introduction to the Principles of Morals and Legislation* (1781), are commonly known and available, and both are mere fragments of his vast enterprise. Perhaps his two masterpieces, magisterial and exhaustive syntheses of his system of thought, are *The Rationale of Judicial Evidence*, edited by John Stuart Mill in 1825, and the two-volume *Constitutional Code*, written about 1830.

Thought. Bentham's orthodox, ambitious father had taught him to worship the law and had intended him to be one of the law's high priests. But the adolescent boy, fresh out of Oxford in 1764 and studying law at Lincoln's Inn, Westminster, saw with growing horror what seemed to him the moral and intellectual debasement and the lies, hypocrisies, greed, venality, corruption,

COPYRIGHT BY NATIONAL PORTRAIT GALLERY, LONDON

JEREMY BENTHAM (1748–1832), English philosopher and reformer, from a painting by H.W. Pickersgill.

and fraud practiced in the courts. Far from being the sanctified temples of justice and wisdom he had been trained to revere, they were, he found, sinkholes of suffering and degradation, where money determined everything—justice and injustice, sanctity and criminality, alike. Nine tenths of the people were literally outlawed because they were unable to pay the minimum initial fees that every lawsuit cost. Thus, wealth was virtue; poverty was vice.

Turning from the practice of law to philosophical study and scientific experiment, he found what he sought—better standards of value, security, method, justice, and social progress. Eventually he saw the law as analogous to medicine, with its own language and psychology; or, in his words, a "metaphysics" and the "axioms of mental pathology" defined and determined by the amount of pleasure and pain they produce.

Utilitarianism. Bentham's system of utilitarianism, in all its bewildering, fragmentary, labyrinthine mass and its range of subjects and styles was intended not as a fixed mechanical science but as a merely probable art-and-science, a social medicine that the legislator might use to oversee the health of the body politic. From the scientist Joseph Priestley, Bentham borrowed the phrase "the greatest happiness of the greatest number" and extended it as the measure of value of all human action. Bentham attempted to create a complete structure of law, a set of blueprints for the national social good. Government, he declared, should try to increase the four subordinate ends of utility—security, subsistence, abundance, and equality—and then try to achieve the crowning abstraction and end, the normative "greatest happiness of the greatest number."

Bentham presented the propositions of this logic in codes of procedure and evidence in civil and penal law and in constitutional and international law. He called these codes the "adjective and substantive" branches of direct law and thought of them as products of physical, legal, and religious sanctions. But his vision went further: he hoped to see men freed from force and punishment and more widely guided by moral sanctions alone. He hoped that in time the silken threads of indirect, preventive legislation would silently do everything, and the clanking, primitive chains of direct law would be broken forever.

Bentham was born a century and a half too soon. He conceived a Utopian welfare state, more radical, comprehensive, and visionary than any created even in the 20th century. When 20th century urban planners spoke, as Walter Gropius did, of "the scope of total architecture," they tended to limit themselves to buildings and landscapes. Bentham's blueprints were truly total; above all he was interested in improving and planning the style and quality of life lived in and around those buildings. In his plans for "Panopticon Hill Villages," which he designed in 1797 as refuges for every suffering and helpless social cripple—the orphan, the widow, the unemployed and his family, the aged, and the criminal—he drew up detailed schemes for experimental animal- and plant-breeding centers, medical laboratories, portable houses, music schools, unemployment exchanges, sex education and experimental early marriage centers, and centers for professional training in several skills (because he assumed what time-and-motion studies later proved, that mechanical repetition is intolerably boring and degrading).

Victorian Benthamism. Bentham's ambition was truly gigantic. But in the wake of the Industrial Revolution, as the already smug atmosphere of George III's England swelled into Victorian complacency and pride, the visionary, creative side of his work was smothered and sank unread and unknown. The Victorians remade him in their own image, and thus he survived: a rigid, simpleminded reductionist; an unfeeling philistine; a cold, calculating mechanical rationalist.

Bentham's philosophical system was satirized in Dickens' *Hard Times* by Mr. Gradgrind's cry for "Facts, facts, facts." Bentham's ideas were held responsible for the much hated poorhouses built under the 1834 Poor Laws, often so barbarous that many suffering wretches preferred to die untended in alleys and fields. In this shape the 20th century received him, and if it detested his ideas, it celebrated their power. It generally acknowledged the triumph of Utilitarianism as the theology of Victorian England. In this warped form, perhaps it was.

See also UTILITARIANISM; HEDONISM.

MARY PETER MACK
Author, "Jeremy Bentham: An Odyssey of Ideas"

Bibliography

Davidson, William L., *Political Thought in England: Utilitarians From Bentham to Mill* (New York 1915).
Halévy, Élie, *Growth of Philosophic Radicalism* (Boston 1955).
Leavis, Frank R., *Mill on Bentham and Coleridge* (New York 1950).
MacCunn, John, *Six Radical Thinkers* (New York 1964).
Mack, Mary P., *Jeremy Bentham: An Odyssey of Ideas* (New York 1963).
Mill, John Stuart, *Utilitarianism, On Liberty, Essay on Bentham*, ed. by Mary Warnock (Cleveland 1962).

BENTHOS, ben'thos, the animals and plants living in, on, or immediately above the sea bottom and directly dependent on it. The benthos is distinguished from the plants and animals living in the pelagic zone—at the surface or in mid-water between surface and bottom. Starfish, shells, eels, and flounders belong to the benthos, and so do most members of the codfish family that feed off the bottom though they swim above it.

Benthos can also be used in a more restricted sense only for the plants and animals that grow on, rest upon, or burrow in the bottom. Under this definition, the members of the codfish family fall into the category of *benthonic nekton* (freeswimming forms) because they feed on the bottom as distinct from the mackerel of the pelagic nekton. See also MARINE BIOLOGY.

BENTINCK, ben'tingk, **Lord George** (1802–1848), British political leader. He was born *William George Frederic Cavendish Bentinck* at Welbeck Abbey, Nottinghamshire, on Feb. 27, 1802. A son of the 4th duke of Portland, he was best known throughout most of his life as a horse-racing enthusiast. After a brief career in the army he became private secretary to his uncle, George Canning, then foreign secretary.

Bentinck entered Parliament as a Whig in 1828 and voted with the majority of his party for the Catholic Emancipation bill of 1829, and the Reform Law of 1832. In 1834, however, he left the Whigs and for more than 10 years was a follower of Sir Robert Peel, the Tory leader and prime minister. He strongly opposed repeal of the Corn Laws in 1845, broke with Peel on that account, and assumed the leadership of the opposition Tories. His support of a measure qualifying Jews for Parliament in 1847 forced him to resign his leadership. He died suddenly at Welbeck Abbey on Sept. 21, 1848.

BENTINCK, ben'tingk, **Lord William Cavendish** (1774–1839), British soldier and colonial administrator. He was born on Sept. 14, 1774. His father, the 3d duke of Portland, was twice prime minister of Britain. William entered the army at the age of 17 and served in Flanders, Italy, and Spain during the Napoleonic Wars. He was appointed governor of Madras in 1803 but was recalled three years later after a mutiny of Indian troops at Vellore. From 1810 to 1814 he was Britain's envoy and military commander in the Kingdom of the Two Sicilies but was recalled again for his seemingly whimsical decree of a republican constitution for the kingdom.

In 1827, when his brother-in-law, George Canning, was prime minister, Bentinck was appointed governor of Bengal, the largest administrative area in India. His administration inaugurated a far-reaching policy of Westernizing India. He introduced English as the language of higher education and administration, abolished the practice of suttee, and initiated a policy of noninterference in the affairs of native princes. From 1833 to 1835 he was the first governor general of all India. He declined a peerage after his return to England in 1835 ("lord" was a courtesy title) and entered the House of Commons the next year. Bentinck died in Paris on June 17, 1839.

BENTINCK, ben'tingk, **William Henry Cavendish,** 3D DUKE OF PORTLAND (1738–1809), British prime minister. Born in Oxford on April 14, 1738, he succeeded his father to the dukedom in 1762. He began his political career by joining the Whig forces of the marquis of Rockingham, and was a member of Rockingham's first cabinet (1765–1766). In 1782 he was appointed lord lieutenant of Ireland.

A Whig coalition swept him into power as prime minister in 1783, but he held the office for only nine months. Afterward, as a leader of the opposition to William Pitt, his successor, he was outshone by the more spectacular talents of Fox and Burke. They induced him to join a Whig alliance with Pitt to contain the French Revolution, and Bentinck was home secretary from 1794 to 1801. He became prime minister again in 1807, though he was old and unequal to the task. He resigned shortly before his death at Bulstrode, Buckinghamshire, on Oct. 30, 1809.

BENTIVOGLIO, ben-tē-vô′lyō, an Italian family that ruled Bologna during the second half of the 15th century. Aided by Gian Galeazzo Visconti, tyrant of Milan, Giovanni I Bentivoglio in 1401 triumphed over the other leading Bolognese families who fought for mastery of the city. The Visconti overthrew and killed him in 1402. His son Anton, after several attempts to seize Bologna, was received in triumph by the populace in 1435, only to be killed by the papal legate in the same year. Anton's son Annibale declared himself first citizen of Bologna and drove out the Visconti. In 1445 he too met a violent death, at the hands of a rival family. The Bolognese accepted another of Giovanni's grandsons, Sante, as their ruler in 1446.

Sante began a renovation of the city, which was continued by Giovanni II, son of Annibale, after Sante's death in 1462. Giovanni established a brilliant court, frequented by many of the greatest artists of the day. He embellished Bologna with new streets, squares, and churches and built the Bentivoglio palace. He also fostered industry and trade. He strengthened his position by allying himself with the Sforza of Milan, the Medici of Florence, and other powerful lords of Italy. When the French crushed his allies at the turn of the century, Giovanni was unable to resist papal attacks on Bologna, and in 1506 Pope Julius II seized it. Giovanni fled with his family and died in Milan in 1508. Several times his sons tried to recapture Bologna, but the people rejected them and destroyed Giovanni's palace. The Bentivoglio family took up residence in Ferrara and later produced several noted prelates.

BENTLEY, bent′lē, **Eric Russell** (1916–   ), American theater critic and director, whose scholarly yet lively analyses of theater for the *New Republic* (1952–1956) and other publications made him one of the most respected theater critics in the English-speaking world. He is also known as the principal sponsor of the plays of Bertolt Brecht in the United States.

Bentley was born in Bolton, Lancashire, England, on Sept. 14, 1916. He studied at the Bolton School, at Oxford (B.A., 1938; B. Litt., 1939), and at Yale (Ph.D., 1941). Bentley taught at Black Mountain College (1942–1944) and at the University of Minnesota (1944–1948), where his books *The Playwright as Thinker* (1946) and *Bernard Shaw* (1947) were written.

Guggenheim and Rockefeller Foundation grants enabled Bentley to travel in Europe from 1948 to 1951. His experiences as a member of the audience and as guest director in Dublin, Zürich, and Padua are recorded in *In Search of Theater* (1953). Articles he wrote as critic for the *New Republic* were collected in *The Dramatic Event* (1954) and *What Is Theater?* (1956). He has also been the principal American translator of Brecht's plays. Bentley became Brander Matthews professor of dramatic literature at Columbia University in 1953.

BENTLEY, bent′lē, **John Francis** (1839–1902), English church architect, who designed Westminster Cathedral, London. He was born in Doncaster on Jan. 30, 1839. Bentley worked for a short time with a firm of builders before starting his own architectural practice in 1862. That same year he joined the Roman Catholic Church, for which he executed most of his works. In

1898, Bentley visited the United States, where he worked on the plans for a Roman Catholic cathedral in Brooklyn, N. Y. He died in Clapham (now part of London) on March 2, 1902.

Bentley's most famous work, the Roman Catholic cathedral at Westminster (1894–1903), is a vast Byzantine structure for which he designed everything from the foundation to the most minute decorative feature. His other works include the convent of the Franciscan nuns at Bockingbridge, Essex, and the fine Neo-Gothic church of the Holy Rood at Watford.

BENTLEY, bent′lē, **Phyllis** (1894–   ), English novelist. She was born in Halifax, England, on Nov. 19, 1894. She taught in a boys' grammar school during World War I and later engaged in library work before devoting full time to writing. Her first novel was *Environment,* a semiautobiographical work published in 1922.

Phyllis Bentley's fiction is traditional rather than experimental in style. Her best-known novels are family sagas set in her native Yorkshire. These include *Cat-in-the-Manger* (1923), *Inheritance* (1932), *A Modern Tragedy* (1934), *Sleep in Peace* (1938), *The Rise of Henry Morcar* (1946), *The House of Moreys* (1953), and *A Man of His Time* (1966). She also wrote historical fiction, including *Freedom Farewell!* (1936), a treatment of the decline of republican ideals in ancient Rome.

Miss Bentley lectured in England and the United States on literary topics and wrote several literary studies, including *Some Observations on the Art of Narrative* (1946), *The Brontës* (1947), and *The Young Brontës* (1960). Her autobiography, *O Dreams, O Destinations,* was published in 1962.

BENTLEY, bent′lē, **Richard** (1662–1742), English classical scholar. He was born at Oulton, Yorkshire, on Jan. 27, 1662. Bentley received his A.B. from St. John's College, Cambridge, at 18 and earned master degrees from both Cambridge (1684) and Oxford (1691). His brilliance was early acknowledged, and in 1692 he was selected to deliver the first Boyle lecture at Oxford. He took the occasion to attack the views of Hobbes in *Confutation of Atheism,* thus precipitating the first of many controversies in which he became involved. His skirmish with William Temple has been immortalized in Alexander Pope's scathing poem, *The Dunciad.* Pope notwithstanding, Bentley's *Dissertation on the Letters of Phalaris* (1699) had proved that Temple's attribution of certain letters to a 5th century B.C. Sicilian tyrant, Phalaris, was wrong because the letters were of a much later period.

Bentley, meanwhile, had served as keeper of the royal library and chaplain-in-ordinary to King William II. In 1699 he was appointed headmaster of Trinity College, Cambridge, where his despotic rule and haughty manner caused the masters to rebel. Bentley ignored them, as well as Jonathan Swift's satire of him in *Battle of the Books,* and continued his careful work. His editions of Terence, Cicero, Phaedrus, Manilius, Lucian, and Horace were landmarks of classical scholarship. Only his edition of Milton's *Paradise Lost* failed to win praise.

Bentley was respected and acclaimed by members of his generation as a genius of textual criticism. Subsequent generations acknowledge him to be the founder of historical philology.

BENTON, ben'tən, **James Gilchrist** (1820–1881), American soldier and inventor. He was born in Lebanon, N.H., on Sept. 15, 1820. He graduated from West Point in 1842 and served in the Army ordnance department throughout his life. He was in command of the Washington Arsenal and was principal assistant to the chief of ordnance during the Civil War, at the close of which he was transferred to the Springfield (Mass.) Arsenal. He was twice brevetted for bravery.

Benton devoted himself especially to the improvement of firearms. The various models of the Springfield rifle, known as the models of 1866, 1868, 1873, and 1879, were made under his direction. He refused to patent any of them because he believed that the government, having educated him, had every right to benefit from his time and talents. He died in Springfield, Mass., on Aug. 23, 1881.

BENTON, ben'tən, **Thomas Hart** (1782–1858), American legislator, who was a leading U.S. senator and a national figure in the Jacksonian era. He was born near Hillsboro, N.C., on March 14, 1782. In 1801, ten years after his father's death, Mrs. Benton moved her family to the Cumberland River Valley of Tennessee. Young Thomas helped farm the land, taught school, and studied law.

Early Career. In 1806, Benton was licensed to practice law in Tennessee and he became state senator in 1809. During the War of 1812, he was made lieutenant colonel, and he served on the staff of Gen. Andrew Jackson. A close association with Jackson was shattered in 1813 when personal animosities, growing out of Jackson's role as a second for his friend William Carroll in a duel with Benton's brother Jesse, erupted into a street brawl in Nashville. Conflict with the popular general lessened Benton's opportunities in Tennessee. He moved to St. Louis in 1815.

Benton made immediate connections with the established leadership of St. Louis, especially the Spanish land claimants and the big fur traders. Becoming editor of the St. Louis *Enquirer* in 1818, he made that newspaper into an effective organ to advance his aspirations in politics—a field much more attractive to him than law. With the backing of conservative, established interests, he was elected U.S. senator from the new state of Missouri in 1820.

Political Views. By 1824, Benton had started to anchor his political support in the rising tide of popular democracy. Ignoring past differences, he supported Jackson over John Quincy Adams for the presidency that year. He rapidly became the leading politician in Missouri and a nationally recognized advocate of the two major principles upon which the mass strength of the Jacksonian movement was based: (1) greater popular democracy and (2) greater equality of social and economic opportunity. Enunciating a faith in the people to govern themselves and in the wisdom of their final decision, he ridiculed any suggestion to "refine" the popular will.

As a constant champion of cheap land, Benton helped provide a greater opportunity for many persons to become more useful and productive citizens. He considered the chartering of companies with exclusive or extraordinary privileges as creating inequalities. The Bank of the United States, with its power to issue notes, was his biggest specific target, and he was the Senate leader in the successful fight against rechartering the bank. Opposing the deposit of treasury funds in selected state "pet banks," he supported the independent treasury plan adopted in 1846 to separate government from banking. In Missouri, Benton led the successful effort to keep banking and note issue under strict control. His demand for hard money earned him the title of "Old Bullion."

A dramatic spokesman for westward expansion, Benton voiced a "manifest destiny" for the American people. He was not, however, an imperialist. He rejected unilateral annexation of Mexican territory, and he supported President Polk's withdrawal from the demand for an Oregon boundary of 54° 40'.

A supporter of bona fide national internal improvements, especially for the West, Benton sought to guard against the encroachment of national power operating within a state. Although he respected the rights of the states, he never supported the doctrine of nullification.

Benton was alarmed by the connection of the slavery question to the annexation of Texas (1845), which he opposed until it could be accomplished by agreement with Mexico. But when war came with Mexico in 1846, he gave the conflict his full support. His defense of the right of Congress to legislate on slavery in the territories widened the breach between him and the proslavery forces. As the sectional dispute intensified over the extension of slavery, Benton came to see the Southern leadership as posing the greatest threat to the Union.

Later Years. Benton's program and philosophy appealed to the agrarian nature of early Missouri. But the growing commercial interests of the state, with their need for banks, credit, and currency, came to oppose him. At the same time, his opposition to the Southern demand for a constitutional guarantee for the extension of slavery lost him party support. Rising politicians, eager to challenge his power, were able to bring about his downfall over these issues. Finally defeated for reelection to the Senate in 1850, Benton served one term in the House of Representatives (1853–1855), and in 1856 he ran unsuccessfully for the governorship of Missouri.

In his later years, Benton wrote his *Thirty Years' View* (2 vols., 1854–56), a massive commentary on national politics: an *Abridgment of the Debates of Congress, 1789–1856* (16 vols., 1857–61); and *Historical and Legal Examination* (1857), an elaborate criticism of the Supreme Court's decision in the Dred Scott case. He died in Washington, D.C., on April 10, 1858.

Benton's personality was an important factor contributing to his political success—and then to his defeat. He developed around his name and person an image of the leader who fought those powers that would allegedly hold the common people and the West in secondary positions. But in his later years in the Senate he became increasingly arbitrary and vindictive, and honest differences of opinion brought such harsh reaction that men were driven from him.

PERRY G. McCANDLESS
Central Missouri State College

Bibliography

Chambers, William Nisbet, *Old Bullion Benton: Senator from the New West* (Boston 1956).

Roosevelt, Theodore, *Thomas Hart Benton* (Boston 1887).

Smith, Elbert B., *Magnificent Missourian: The Life of Thomas Hart Benton* (Philadelphia 1958).

BETTMANN ARCHIVE

THOMAS HART BENTON, painter of American life. His *Wreck of the Old 97* (right), completed in 1944, was based on an old American ballad.

WIDE WORLD

BENTON, ben'tən, **Thomas Hart** (1889–1975), American painter, who was one of the leading artists of the American "regionalist" movement that flourished in the 1930's. The most vociferous champion of this movement, which also included Grant Wood and John Steuart Curry, Benton stated in 1932 that "no American art can come to those who do not live an American life, who do not have an American psychology, and who cannot find in America justification of their lives." The subjects of his best-known works are American mountaineers, dust farmers, Negro cotton pickers, revivalists, and other characters from small town and rural life in the South and the Midwest. Nevertheless, his approach was not a completely naturalistic one, for Benton's art also displays an interest in the grotesque and in caricature, together with a somewhat abstract rhythmic pattern that reveals his early interest in the more avant-garde movements of that time.

Benton was born in Neosho, Mo., on April 15, 1889, the son of Congressman Maecenas E. Benton and the grandnephew of Senator Thomas Hart Benton. He studied at the Art Institute of Chicago in 1906–1907 and in Paris from 1908 to 1911. In Paris he was enrolled for a time at the Académie Julian, and became a friend of Stanton Macdonald-Wright, who was then developing synchronism, a nearly abstract modernist style.

Benton returned to the United States in 1912 and settled in New York City. In the Forum Exhibition of 1916 he exhibited *Figure Organization No. 3*, a compromise between the modernism he had learned in Paris and a new, more realistic strain.

Benton served as an architectural draftsman in the Navy during World War I, an experience that profoundly affected his tendencies toward naturalism. After the war he repudiated modernism entirely and began to make periodic trips through the South and Midwest, studying and painting subjects typical of those regions. From 1926 to 1935, Benton taught at the Art Students League in New York City. During this period he painted some of his best-known works, including *Boomtown* (1927), *Louisiana Rice Fields* (1928), *Cotton Pickers* (1932), and *Homestead* (1934).

During the 1930's Benton became one of the most active muralists in the United States. Among his important murals are those in the New School for Social Research, New York City (1930); the original Whitney Museum of American Art, New York City (1932); the statehouse in Jefferson City, Mo. (1935), and the Harry S Truman Library, Independence, Mo. (1959). From 1935, Benton lived in Kansas City, Mo., where he died on Jan. 19, 1975. His autobiography, *An Artist in America*, was published in 1937 (rev. ed., 1951).

WILLIAM GERDTS, *University of Maryland*

BENTON, ben'tən, **William Burnett** (1900–1973), American advertising executive, publisher, and public official. He was born on April 1, 1900, in Minneapolis, Minn. In 1921 he graduated from Yale and went to work as a salesman for the National Cash Register Company in New York City. Between 1922 and his retirement from business in 1936 he made a fortune in advertising—principally in the agency of Benton and Bowles, which he founded with Chester Bowles in 1929. The University of Chicago retained him as a public relations consultant in 1936 and as a vice president from 1937 to 1945. When the university acquired the *Encyclopædia Britannica* in 1943, Benton provided the operating capital in exchange for two thirds of the common stock. He became board chairman of Encyclopædia Britannica, Inc., and its affiliates.

As U. S. assistant secretary of state for public affairs from 1945 to 1947, Benton helped organize the nation's overseas information service. A Democrat, he was appointed to the U. S. Senate from Connecticut by Gov. Chester Bowles in 1949 and was elected to serve two years of an unexpired term in 1950. He was defeated for reelection in 1952. Benton is the author of *This is the Challenge* (1958), a report on Soviet education, and *The Voice of Latin America* (1961). He died in New York City on March 18, 1973.

BENTON, ben'tən, is an industrial city in central Arkansas, the seat of Saline County, 18 miles (29 km) southwest of Little Rock. Benton's industries include aluminum mining and refining, and the production of furniture, plywood, steel, and electronic appliances. Government is by mayor and council. Population: 16,499.

BENTON, ben'tən, is a city in southern Illinois, about 130 miles (208 km) by air southeast of Springfield. It is the seat of Franklin County. Farm supplies, parking meters, and dresses are manufactured in the city. Gen. John A. Logan, Union soldier in the Civil War and Republican candidate for vice president in 1884, lived here. Benton was incorporated in 1841. Government is by commission. Population: 6,833.

BENTON HARBOR, ben'tən här'bər, is an industrial and commercial city in southwestern Michigan, in Berrien County. It is situated on Lake Michigan, at the mouth of the St. Joseph River, 187 miles (300 km) west of Detroit. The city is a trading center for an area that produces lumber, grain, and fruits. Its industrial activities include research and engineering and the production of auto accessories, steel castings, heavy equipment, canned goods, machine products, record changers, and plastics. Mineral springs with medicinal properties are found in and near the city. Ross Field, a nearby airport, provides commercial air service. The House of David, a religious sect, established a colony at Benton Harbor in 1903.

Benton Harbor was settled about 1840. It was incorporated as a village in 1866 and as a city in 1891. Government is by city manager. Population: 16,481.

BENTONITE, ben'tən-īt, is an aluminum silicate material composed of several clay minerals, mainly montmorillonite. It is named for Fort Benton, Wyo., where it was first found. When wet, bentonite swells to several times its original size and forms a gel-like suspension. This characteristic makes it useful as a filler in oilfield drilling muds and in molding sands. It is also used in ceramics for decolorizing oil. Beds of bentonite occur in western North America and many other parts of the world.

BENT'S FORT, bents, was a great trading post of the American West. A fortified, castlelike adobe landmark on the Arkansas River in what is now southeastern Colorado, it stood on the main Santa Fe Trail but was bypassed by the Cimarron Cutoff. It was built in 1833–1834 by Charles and William Bent and Ceran St. Vrain, partners in Bent, St. Vrain & Company, to replace a log stockade on another site.

The fort, at first called *Fort William* by some, faced east toward approaching caravans. It measured 137 by 178 feet (42 by 54 meters), with walls 14 feet (4 meters) high and 3 feet (1 meter) thick. The fort could garrison 200 men; the walled corral in the back held 300 animals. The owners, who were hospitable to travelers, dealt in furs brought in by Indians and by white traders, including Kit Carson. They sent vast quantities of buffalo robes, beaver pelts, and other furs to St. Louis by wagon train. William Bent, who married into the Cheyenne tribe, helped to keep peace with the Indians. He refused a government offer to buy the fort and blew up most of it in 1849. He later built a new one 38 miles (61 km) downstream.

WAYNE GARD, *Author of "The Great Buffalo Hunt"*

Further Reading: Lavender, David, *Bent's Fort* (Garden City, N.Y., 1954).

BENUE RIVER, bān'wā, in West Africa, the chief tributary of the Niger. It is also known as the *Binue* or *Bénoué*. It rises in the Adamawa Mountains of Cameroon and flows 870 miles (1,400 km) until it enters the Niger. Together with the Niger, it forms the only navigable route to the far interior of Africa.

The Benue flows first in a northerly direction and receives the Mayo-Kebbi River, which joins the Benue with the Logone during high water, thus connecting the Niger and Chad systems. Garoua, an important shipping port in the center of a cotton- and peanut-growing area, is situated at this confluence. From this point to the Niger the Benue is navigable throughout the year by small vessels drawing no more than five feet (1.5 meters). The Benue then flows west into Nigeria to the town of Yola, where it becomes navigable by larger vessels for the remaining 500 miles (804 km) of its course. Flowing southwest across eastern and south central Nigeria, the Benue passes the towns of Ibi and Makurdi and joins the Niger opposite Lokoja. The Benue receives the Gongola and Faro rivers from the north and the Donga and Katsima Ala rivers from the south. During the year the water level of the river varies as much as 75 feet (23 meters) between its highest level, which occurs in August-September, and its lowest level in March-April.

The German explorer Heinrich Barth discovered the Benue in 1851. Its valley was first explored three years later by a British expedition under William Balfour Baikie, which sailed about 400 miles (640 km) up the river in a small steamer called the *Pleiad*. His explorations showed that a large, fertile, and populous region of Africa, previously little known, was accessible by means of a navigable river.

BENVENUTO CELLINI, bĕn-vā-nōō'tō chä-lē'nē, an opera in three acts by Hector Berlioz (q.v.), first performed at the Opéra in Paris on Sept. 10, 1838. The libretto, by Léon de Wailly and Auguste Barbier, is based on the autobiography of the Italian Renaissance artist and adventurer Benvenuto Cellini (q.v.). Set in Rome in 1532, the plot tells of Cellini's rivalry with Fieramosca, sculptor to the pope, for the hand of Teresa, daughter of the papal treasurer, and for the commission to complete the bronze *Perseus*. Although the opera has never been a public favorite, the overture is among Berlioz' best-known works.

BENVOLIO, ben-vō'lē-ō, a character in Shakespeare's *Romeo and Juliet,* is a friend and cousin of Romeo. His account of the deaths of Mercutio and Tybalt saves Romeo from execution.

BENZ, bents, **Karl** (1844–1929), German engineer and inventor, who pioneered in the development of the automobile. Benz was born in Karlsruhe, Germany, on Nov. 25, 1844. His father, a locomotive engineer, died when Karl was two years old. He studied at the Technical University at Karlsruhe, and, in 1871, established a small workshop at Mannheim. In 1877 he began to design and develop a two-stroke engine. By 1885 he had a thriving business producing gasoline engines, and in 1886 built the first gasoline-powered motorcar.

On Jan. 29, 1886, Benz received a patent for the "Patent Motor Car," which he drove around Mannheim in July of that year. This car had a gasoline engine, a water cooling system, electric ignition, and a differential gear. It could reach a speed of 9.3 mph.

By 1900 his company had become the largest automobile manufacturer in Europe. Benz retired from management of the company in 1903. The Benz Company merged with the Daimler Company in 1926 to form Daimler-Benz AG, the maker of Mercedes-Benz automobiles. Benz died in Ladenberg, Germany, on April 4, 1929.

MARCUS CLARY
Daimler-Benz of North America Inc.

BENZALDEHYDE, ben-zal′də-hīd, is the simplest member of the group of aromatic aldehydes. Its formula is C_6H_5CHO. It can be obtained from bitter almonds, but it is produced synthetically for industrial and commercial uses.

Benzaldehyde is formed by the decomposition of amygdalin, a constituent of bitter almond, when the kernels of bitter almond are crushed and allowed to stand in water. Benzaldehyde is produced synthetically by the hydrolysis of benzl chloride:

$$C_6H_5CHCl_2 + H_2O \rightarrow C_6H_5CHO + 2HCl$$

Another method is to use toluene, oxygen, and a metal-oxide catalyst:

$$C_6H_5CH_3 + O_2 \xrightarrow{\text{Catalyst}} C_6H_5CHO + H_2O$$

Benzaldehyde is a colorless, volatile liquid. It boils at 354° F (179° C). Its index of refraction is 1.546. It has an odor that is similar to the bitter-almond odor.

Benzaldehyde is an important dye intermediate in the manufacture of triphenylmethane and acridine dyes. It is used in the synthesis of numerous organic compounds, such as benzoic acid, cinnamic aldehyde, perfumes, flavoring agents, and photographic chemicals. See also ALDEHYDE.

BENZEDRINE. See AMPHETAMINE.

BENZENE, ben′zēn, is the simplest member of a class of organic compounds called aromatic hydrocarbons or arenes. It is a colorless, flammable liquid that boils at 176.2° F (80.1 C) and melts at 41.9° F (5.5° C). Its molecular formula is C_6H_6. Benzene is useful industrially, and its structure is important in chemical studies.

Benzene was first discovered in illuminating-gas systems that used a gas obtained from the thermal decomposition of whale oil. The gas was delivered under pressure to households in London. In 1825, Michael Faraday isolated a substance from the oily condensate deposited from the gas. He called this substance "bacarburet of hydrogen." About eight years later other investigators obtained the same substance by the distillation of benzoic acid with lime. In 1845, A.W. Hofmann used coal tar to obtain the same substance, which he called benzene.

The structure of the benzene molecule was deduced by Friedrich August Kekulé in 1865. Benzene is a regular, planar hexagon of carbon atoms with sides 1.397 A in length. Each carbon atom has one hydrogen atom attached to it.

Reactivity. The study of how the structure of benzene influences its chemical reactivity has been of major importance in developing the theory of organic chemistry. Benzene does not undergo the addition reactions that might be expected of a molecule with such a low ratio of hydrogen atoms to carbon atoms. The typical reaction involving benzene is a substitution reaction, wherein an attacking group displaces one of the hydrogen atoms and becomes attached to a carbon atom in the benzene ring. The explanation of this behavior lies in the fact that six of the electrons of benzene are delocalized over the six carbon atoms of the ring rather than being associated with particular atoms. This delocalization results in a stabilization of the molecule and a concomitant modification of its chemical and physical properties.

The benzene substitution reactions are important because a very large number of aromatic

ALTERNATIVE STRUCTURES OF THE BENZENE MOLECULE

compounds are formed by such reactions.

Production. Before World War II the important sources of benzene were the tar products that are formed when coal is heated at high temperatures in the absence of air. During World War II the demand for benzene and related aromatic hydrocarbons (toluene and the xylenes) increased so markedly that other sources had to be found. More than 75 percent of the benzene now produced in the United States is derived from petroleum. The principal process is the dealkylation of toluene ($C_6H_5CH_3$) or of petroleum containing toluene. This process involves the use of hydrogen, high temperatures and pressures, and a catalyst. In a second method, petroleum stocks rich in naphthenes are dehydrogenated at high temperatures and pressures.

Uses. The principal industrial use of benzene is as the starting material for the synthesis of styrene and phenol (which are used to make plastics), of nylon components, and of synthetic detergents. Much benzene is used in aviation gasoline. See also AROMATIC COMPOUNDS.

ALVIN I. KOSAK, *New York University*

BENZIDINE, ben′zə-dēn, is an organic chemical compound that is used in manufacturing dyes, drugs, and perfumes. Its formula is $NH_2C_6H_4C_6H_4NH_2$.

Benzidine is produced by reducing nitrobenzene ($C_6H_5NO_2$) to hydrazobenzene ($C_6H_5NHNHC_6H_5$) and then treating the hydrazobenzene with an acid. Benzidine melts at 262° F (128° C) and boils at about 752° F (400° C).

Benzidine yellow, Congo red G, and Hessian brown BB are typical dyes made by using benzidine as an intermediate. It also is used in the laboratory to stain specimens for microscopic examination. Benzidine hydrochloride is particularly valuable in the detection of blood stains.

BENZINE, ben′zēn, is a highly volatile and inflammable mixture of aliphatic hydrocarbons derived from petroleum. The name is confusing because it resembles so closely in spelling and pronunciation the term "benzene," which is a single substance with the formula C_6H_6. Another term for benzine is *petroleum ether,* which is also misleading since there is no ether present in it. A better name is *cleaners' naphtha,* and a standard material of this type is the Stoddard solvent.

Because of many fatal accidents, volatile hydrocarbons have been largely replaced in household use by such substances as carbon tetrachloride, which can be used to extinguish fires.

When used commercially, light, volatile, inflammable liquids, whose vapors form explosive mixtures with air, are carefully enclosed in special equipment with adequate ventilation and protection against being ignited.

BENZOIC ACID, ben-zo′ik as′əd, is the prototype of a family of aromatic organic acids that includes toluic acid, chlorobenzoic acid, bromobenzoic acid, nitrobenzoic acid, and salicylic acid. It is a white solid with the formula $C_6H_5CO_2H$. It melts at 252° F (122° C), boils at 480° F (249° C), and sublimes at 212° F (100° C). The acid is slightly soluble in cold water, but it is readily soluble in hot water.

Benzoic acid was first obtained in 1560 from the distillation of gum benzoin (frankincense of Java), which contains the acid in amounts of 10 to 20 percent by weight. However, the composition of the acid was not determined until 1832, when it was established by Justus von Liebig and Friedrich Wöhler. Benzoic acid occurs in the free state and in the form of its ester derivatives in resins, balsams, and various plants, including most berries.

Preparation. Almost all the commercially available benzoic acid is manufactured. The major process involves the liquid-phase oxidation of toluene, $C_6H_5CH_3$, by air in the presence of cobalt naphthenate or copper magnesium benzoate. The catalytic decarboxylation of phthalic anhydride, $C_6H_4(CO)_2O$, is another important source, as is the hydrolysis of benzotrichloride, $C_6H_5CCl_3$.

The more important laboratory syntheses of benzoic acid and substituted benzoic acids are the carbonation of Grignard reagents or aryllithiums ($ArMgX + CO_2 \rightarrow ArCO_2MgX \rightarrow ArCO_2H$, where Ar is an aryl and X is a halogen), the hydrolysis of aryl nitriles under either acidic or basic conditions ($ArCN + H_2O \rightarrow ArCO_2H$), the oxidation of alkyl side chains with strong oxidizing reagents such as dichromate or permanganate ($ArCH_3 + KMnO_4 \rightarrow ArCO_2H$), and the hypohalite oxidation of aceto compounds ($ArCOCH_3 + OX^- \rightarrow ArCO_2^- \rightarrow ArCO_2H$).

Reactions. Typical reactions of benzoic acid and related acids include ester ($ArCO_2R$) formation, which usually takes place readily on refluxing with an alcohol in the presence of an acidic catalyst; the production of the acid chloride ($ArCOCl$) by treatment with thionyl chloride or phosphorus pentachloride; decarboxylation, which takes place when the acid is heated with soda lime or copper powder; and reduction to the corresponding alcohol by using lithium aluminum hydride or diborane.

Uses. The two largest uses of benzoic acid are in the preparation of its salt, sodium benzoate, and of synthetic plastics. Other uses are in dyeing calico and curing tobacco. It also is used as a reference standard in analytical chemistry.

Benzoic acid is widely used as a food preservative because it inhibits bacterial growth in acidic foods. The free acid is only slightly soluble in water, and therefore it is used in the form of the soluble sodium benzoate. The acid and its salt are almost tasteless and relatively nontoxic. After ingestion it is combined in the body with the amino acid glycine to form hippuric acid, which is excreted in the urine. This detoxication mechanism is used by most vertebrates.

Benzoic acid can be safely applied to the skin in high concentration. In the form of Whitfield's ointment, it is used to treat fungus infections such as ringworm. This ointment also contains salicylic acid.

ALVIN I. KOSAK, *New York University*

BENZOIN, ben′zō-in, is an aromatic compound that is used extensively as an antiseptic. Its formula is $C_6H_5CHOHCOC_6H_5$. Benzoin is prepared by treating benzaldehyde (C_6H_5CHO) with a catalyst, such as a hot alcoholic solution of potassium cyanide. Benzoin is formed on cooling, and is separated from other materials by filtration. The compound forms colorless, six-sided crystals. Its melting point is 279° F (137° C), and it is soluble in hot alcohol.

BENZOIN GUM, ben′zō-in, is a reddish brown resin that exudes from the styrax tree (*Styrax benzoin*), which grows in Sumatra, Java, and other parts of the East. It is a mixture of various resinous substances, together with free benzoic acid. Cinnamic acid is also present in the free state in many cases, but it is absent from the Siamese gum.

Benzoin gum has a pleasant odor when burned, and for that reason has been much used for incense and in making pastilles. It has mild antiseptic properties, and preparations of it are used as a dressing for wounds, and in the manufacture of court-plaster. Benzoin is readily soluble in alcohol, and when the tincture so formed is dropped into water it forms a white milky fluid, which is used in France as a cosmetic under the name *lait virginal*. This tincture is also added to water, and steam inhalations from the mixture are prescribed as treatment for asthma, chronic catarrh, and other respiratory congestions.

The gum is obtained from the styrax tree by making incisions in the bark, through which the resin oozes. It is allowed to harden by exposure to the air before removal. The best gum is obtained during the first three years of the tree's life, though a good quality may be had for seven or eight years subsequently.

BENZOL, ben′zōl, is the preferred name in Germany for benzene (q.v.), while in English-speaking countries it generally means incompletely refined benzene; a mixture, more than half benzene, containing small amounts of other aromatic hydrocarbons, such as thiophene, sulfur compounds, paraffins, naphthalene, and phenols.

Benzol is a source of solvents, dry-cleaning fluids, dyes, drugs, mothproofing substances, waterproofing agents, and other coal-tar products.

BENZOPHENONE, ben-zō-fē′nōn, is a chemical compound used as a fixative for heavy synthetic perfumes and for perfumed soaps. It is also used in manufacturing insecticides, antihistamines, and sleep-inducing drugs.

Benzophenone is synthesized from benzene and either benzoyl chloride or carbon tetrachloride, in the form of white prisms smelling of rose or geranium. Also called *diphenyl ketone* and *benzoylbenzene*, it has the formula $(C_6H_5)_2CO$.

BENZPYRENE, benz-pī′rēn, is a coal-tar chemical compound composed of benzene and methanol. It is believed to be a principal cause of lung cancer. Benzpyrene is known to cause cancer in animal tissues if it remains long in contact. Incomplete combustion in the burning of a cigarette leaves a tar residue containing benzpyrene, and although it has not been proved that this causes human lung cancer, experiments with dogs that were subjected to cigarette smoke showed cancerous development in their bronchial tubes.

Incomplete combustion of petroleum fuels in automobile and other internal combustion engines expels benzpyrene and other pollutants into the air, and this is believed to be a major reason for the higher incidence of lung cancer among urban than rural populations.

In its dry form, benzpyrene consists of yellowish crystalline needles and plates. It is chemically described as a hydrocyclic aromatic hydrocarbon, with the formula $C_{20}H_{12}$.

BEOTHUK INDIANS, bā′ə-thŏŏk, a tribe of North American Indians who lived in northern Newfoundland. They are believed to have been the first inhabitants of that island. They were known as the "Red Indians" for their custom of painting their bodies, clothing, and possessions with red ocher. The Beothuk lived in large huts covered with bark or skins. Their canoes were so built that the gunwale curved sharply upward in the middle as well as on the ends.

After many years of depredations by French settlers and by the Micmac Indians of Nova Scotia, the numbers of the Beothuk were greatly reduced. A series of famines further depleted their population, and many survivors were assimilated into other tribes. Although the British in 1810 passed laws to protect the Beothuk, these Indians rapidly lost their tribal identity, and within approximately two decades they were virtually extinct.

BEOWULF, bā′ə-wŏŏlf, is the longest (3,182 lines) and greatest poem extant in Old English, the language of the English nation prior to the Norman Conquest. *Beowulf* has been preserved in one manuscript (Cotton Vitellius A XV, in the British Museum), written about the year 1000. It was damaged, though not disastrously, in the fire that ravaged the Cottonian collection in 1731. The two best guesses as to the place and date of *Beowulf's* composition would be Northumbria during the "Age of Bede" (about 720–750) or Mercia during the reign of Offa II (757–796).

The Story of Beowulf. The poem opens by recounting the career of Scyld Scefing, a hero-king sent by God to the leaderless Danes. After Scyld's death the Danes prosper under his descendants, especially Hrothgar, who builds them a great hall, Heorot. Heorot is soon invaded by Grendel, a half-human monster, one of Cain's kin and hated by God. The Danes are helpless against Grendel's attacks until Beowulf, a young warrior of the Geats, arrives to aid them. He engages Grendel in fierce hand-to-hand combat within Heorot and destroys the monster by tearing off his arm. The Danes rejoice, but soon Grendel's mother comes to avenge her son. Beowulf and Hrothgar follow her to her lair, an eerie and hideous swamp-lake. Beowulf dives into the water and fights another furious battle with Grendel's mother in her "anti-hall" at the bottom of the lake. Beowulf's weapons fail him, but God aids him, and he kills the monster with an old sword he finds in the hall. Returning with Grendel's head to Hrothgar, Beowulf is lavishly rewarded and soon leaves for his own land, where he tells his adventures to his uncle, King Hygelac.

At this point the poet passes over 50 years to the time when Beowulf, in old age, is himself king of the Geats. The hero fights his last battle against a dragon, the guardian of a cursed treasure, who has been provoked by a chance violation of his hoard. The old king tries to fight the dragon alone, as he did Grendel, but the creature's fiery breath destroys the weapons and armor Beowulf has chosen, and he can defeat the dragon only with the aid of his young relative, Wiglaf, after all his other retainers have run away. The dragon dies but mortally wounds Beowulf, and the old king expires, gazing on the treasure. His death signals the decline of the Geats, who are surrounded by enemies made in campaigns described allusively throughout the last part of the poem. The poem ends on a note of double mourning, for Beowulf and for his nation.

Literary Origins. There is no specific literary source for *Beowulf.* Many of its characters and digressions belong to the corpus of Germanic tradition that was preserved through the oral heroic poetry of the aristocratic minstrels and was first written down, and then composed in writing, during the Old English period. That some of this material is based on historical fact is attested to by documentary evidence of the period. For example, Hygelac, king of the Geats and Beowulf's uncle, is mentioned by Gregory of Tours (537–593) in his *History of the Franks.* However, the central episodes of *Beowulf*—the hero's three great battles with monsters—are related to folklore rather than history, and one can distinguish similarities between *Beowulf's* adventures and those in the widely disseminated "Bear's Son" tale. There may have been a character named Beowulf who performed similar deeds in an earlier heroic poem, but this is doubtful, as the *Beowulf* poet seems deliberately to have chosen adventures involving his hero not with other heroic figures but with nonhuman creatures of symbolic import.

Analysis. Of Beowulf's author we know nothing, and we can only guess about the poem's originality. The form of Old English poetry is so conventional that distinctions between original and reworked material cannot safely be made. A sample (lines 4–11) of the traditional Germanic alliterative verse in which *Beowulf* is composed follows:

Oft Scyld Scefing sceaþena þreatum
monegum mægþum meodosetla ofteah;
egsode eorl[as], syððan ærest wear
feascæft funden; heþæs frofre gebad:
weox under wolcnum, weorðmyndum þah,
oðþæt him æghwylc þara ymbsittendra
ofer hron-rade hyran scolde,
gomban gyldan— þæt wæs god cyning.

In modern English this reads:

Often Scyld Scefing deprived many nations, many enemy armies, of their mead benches, and became a terror among noble warriors, after first being discovered destitute. He was compensated for this beginning: he grew up and achieved great glory, until everyone in neighboring lands across the sea had to obey him and pay tribute—that was a great king!

The half-lines into which each line is divided are linked across the break (caesura) by alliteration of the stressed syllables (marked in the first two lines). Several conventional half-lines, which appear elsewhere in Old English poetry, are underlined. The poetic diction is heavily metaphorical: note the expressions "took away mead benches," meaning "defeated," and *hron-rade* ("whale-road") for "sea."

The structure of *Beowulf* is both tripartite (the three fights) and bipartite (the rise of the young hero versus the fall of the old king). Any point in the poem may therefore be seen from a double perspective: either as part of the inevitable decline and self-destruction of the noble and steadfast hero (and heroic ideal), or as a moment in life to which there exists an ironically parallel yet contrasting moment in the other half of the poem. The use made of the latter perspective is especially striking. For example, treasure is a symbol of triumphant civilization in the first part, while in the second part it becomes the cursed dragon-infested hoard, a symbol of fate and of the transitory nature of doomed civilization.

A similar principle of double perspective underlies *Beowulf*'s Christian elements. In fighting Grendel, Beowulf is not only the death-defying Germanic hero but also God's instrument in His age-old battle against evil (Cain's kin). As God's agent, Beowulf purges heroic society (Heorot) of an evil principle (Grendel) that has come to dwell in it at its moment of apparent triumph (the building of Heorot) and against which it is powerless. Yet in fighting the dragon, Beowulf is fighting fate itself, a hostile, non-Christian fate that broods over civilization cursing ignorant man to final destruction. The world of *Beowulf* is thus ambiguous in its ultimate meaning; and given this uncontrollable ambiguity, Beowulf's heroism must be appreciated as an intrinsically noble response to life, rather than as a wise or even a successful one.

ROBERT W. HANNING, *Columbia University*

Bibliography
Beowulf was edited by F. Klaeber, 3d ed. (Boston 1950). A translation into modern English by John R. Clark Hall was revised by C.L. Wrenn (New York and London 1954).
Brodeur, Arthur G., *The Art of Beowulf* (Berkeley, Calif., 1959).
Chambers, Raymond W., ed., *Beowulf: An Introduction*, 3d rev. ed. by C.L. Wrenn (New York and London 1959).
Lawrence, William W., *Beowulf and the Epic Tradition* (Cambridge, Mass., 1928).
Nicholson, Lewis E., *An Anthology of Beowulf Criticism* (South Bend, Ind., 1963).
Pope, J.R., *The Rhythm of Beowulf* (New Haven, Conn., 1942).
Sisam, Kenneth, *The Structure of Beowulf* (New York and London 1965).
Whitelock, Dorothy, *The Audience of Beowulf* (New York and London 1951).

BEPPO, bep'pō, is a satirical poem on Venetian life by George Gordon, Lord Byron (q.v.), published in 1818. Beppo (his name is a nickname for Giuseppe), the husband of an attractive Italian woman, returns home in the garb of a Turk after a long absence. At a carnival he encounters his wife and her lover, who do not recognize him. Mock heroics that travesty tragic love stories are developed before Beppo reveals his identity. The couple are then reconciled over cups of coffee.

The poem was Byron's first exercise in the mock heroic style popular in Italy. It foreshadowed his more ambitious *Don Juan*, which he began the year he completed *Beppo*. The story of Beppo is told in 99 stanzas of facetious, slightly naughty, wandering narrative.

BEPPU, bep'ōō, is a resort city and seaport in southern Japan. It is situated in Oita prefecture, on the northeast coast of Kyushu, on Beppu Bay, part of the Inland Sea. It has famous hot alkaline springs. Population: (1960) 107,734.

BÉRANGER, bā-rän-zhā', **Pierre Jean de** (1780–1857), French poet and songwriter, who was regarded in his lifetime as France's national poet. His verses, often set to old tunes, are simply worded, neatly phrased, and highly rhythmic, but they have not sustained the high reputation they had in the poet's lifetime.

Béranger was born in Paris on Aug. 19, 1780, of humble parents (he added the "de" to his name in adulthood). In 1789 an aunt took him from his parents, who had neglected him, and brought him up in Péronne, in Picardy. At 14 he was apprenticed to a printer.

In 1804, Lucien Bonaparte, Napoleon's brother, saw several of Béranger's lyrics. He liked them and bestowed a small pension on the poet, adding a professional sinecure in 1809 that enabled Béranger to devote most of his time to writing. His first published collection of verses was *Chansons morales et autres* (1815), which contained his already famous and most enduring satire, *Le roi d'Yvetot,* a gentle mockery of Napoleon.

Béranger's next collection, *Chansons,* 2ème *recueil* (1821), aroused both the wrath of the restored Bourbon monarchy and the adulation of French republicans. He was fined 500 francs and sentenced to three months in prison, where he began the collection *Chansons nouvelles* (1825). *Chansons inédites* (1828), in turn, brought him a nine-month prison term and a 10,000-franc fine. Béranger became the national hero of the republicans, who paid the fine by public subscription.

After publication of *Chansons nouvelles et dernières* in 1833, Béranger lived in retirement. He lampooned the Second Empire, which he regarded as a betrayal of republican ideals, and declined all honors that Napoleon III eagerly proffered. He died in Paris on July 16, 1857.

BERBERA, bûr'bər-ə, is a town in Somalia and the country's second-largest port. It is situated on the coast of the Gulf of Aden, 150 miles (240 km) directly south of Aden and 140 miles (225 km) southeast of Djibouti. It has a small but well-protected harbor with a daily unloading capacity of 200 tons (180 metric tons). Passengers must be taken ashore by small boats. There is a European quarter with stone houses and warehouses and a native quarter laid out with broad streets but consisting chiefly of huts or sheds.

The port's commerce is chiefly with Aden. Principal exports are cattle, sheep and camels, skins and hides, ghee, and gums, such as frankincense and myrrh. Cloth, dates, sugar, and rice are imported. During the hot season about half the inhabitants move to the highlands in the interior to escape the torrid southwest monsoon winds. Population: (1964) 50,000.

BERBERINE, bûr'bər-ēn, is an alkaloid obtained from the roots of the barberry and other plants. Berberine was discovered in 1837. It is used in medicine as a tonic.

Berberine, which has the formula $C_{20}H_{19}NO_5$, is a member of the isoquinoline group of alkaloids. It forms yellow, needle-shaped crystals. Its melting point is 293° F (145° C). Berberine is soluble in water at ordinary temperatures, moderately soluble in alcohol, and slightly soluble in chloroform. Berberine phosphate and berberine sulphate also are used for medicinal purposes. See also ALKALOIDS.

BERBERS, bûr′bərz, are a people of North Africa who speak the Berber language, a subfamily of the Hamitic linguistic group. Numbering over 5 million, they form the basis of the population of Morocco, Algeria, Tunisia, and, to a lesser extent, Libya, parts of northern Mauritania, northern Mali, and northern Niger.

A Caucasian people, the Berbers are related in physical type to the Mediterranean subgroup of southern Europe. But they have been deeply affected by the peoples who conquered the area in which they now live, especially by the Arabs, and today they are mostly Muslims, and much of their culture is Arabized. It is believed that the Berber-speaking peoples came originally from the eastern Mediterranean area before 2000 B.C. They moved across North Africa and went as far as the Canary Islands, where a Berber language, Guanche, was spoken when the Spanish landed in the 15th century A.D.

Today the Berbers are found chiefly in the mountainous regions and desert of North Africa. The main groups are the *Riffians* (in the mountainous Riff area of northern Morocco), the *Beraber* (in the mountains south of Fez), the *Shluh* (in the southwestern Atlas), the *Kabyles* (in the mountains between Algiers and Constantine), and the *Shawia* (in the Aurès mountains of eastern Algeria). Other groups, including the *Tuareg*, are scattered over the Sahara in oases as far east as Siwa in Egypt.

The Berber language may be divided into three broad groups: Masmuda, Sanhaja, and Zenata. However, there are several hundred dialects, some of which are not mutually intelligible. There is in fact no evidence of a common feeling of unity among those who speak Berber.

Way of Life. Almost all of the Berber-speaking people are Muslims, although there are a number of Jewish Berbers in Morocco. Among Muslim Berbers many pre-Islamic religious elements survive, including allegiance to local saints, holy places, and ceremonies, such as the ceremony conducted to obtain rain. Women enjoy a greater degree of freedom than among the Arabs. The Berbers of Mzab practice a very puritanical form of Islam.

Berber society is extremely fragmented. The basic unit is the family. Several families form a clan (about 100 persons), and several clans a community. The largest unit is the tribe, which may have a common place of pilgrimage or a regular common market but is loosely united except in time of war. Authority is usually extremely dispersed. Community affairs are governed by an assembly (*jemaa*) of all adult males. Generally, Koranic law has replaced tribal custom, and since the countries of North Africa achieved independence the assimilation of Berbers into their national societies has been hastened. The basis of their economy is subsistence agriculture, with wheat and barley the staple crops. Animal husbandry is also important, and many Berbers live a nomadic life with their sheep, goats, and cattle during the summer.

Culturally, the Berbers have been dominated by the invaders, although Berber rugs, blankets, and pottery still have characteristic geometric patterns. There are no national epics, but wandering poet-singers transmit some form of common culture. Poetry is usually put to music and is generally ritual in nature.

History. The Carthaginians, Romans, Vandals, Byzantines, Arabs, Turks, Spaniards, and French have at various times in the past conquered all or part of the Berber country. But the Arabs, who conquered the area beginning in the 7th century, left the deepest imprint. Over the centuries, Berbers have frequently rebelled against invaders. The widespread Donatist heresy of the 4th century reflected Berber opposition to the Romans, and it was centuries before the last Christian Berber groups adopted Islam. But these revolts were not "national" movements. The Berbers have never reacted as a group, and even the states they have created adopted an official language other than Berber.

Two Berber dynasties—the Almoravid (11th century) and the Almohad (12th century)— preaching reformed religious doctrines, established temporary supremacy in North Africa. But these dynasties lasted only a few decades, and their official language was Arabic. Individual Berbers who acquired more than local fame also spoke languages other than Berber. The best known of them were the Roman author Apuleius, the Roman emperor Septimius Severus, and St. Augustine, whose mother was a Berber. The mountaineer and oasis Berbers often managed to elude real control by coastal states, but they were never able to unite.

L. GRAY COWAN
Columbia University

BERCEO, ber-thä′ō, **Gonzalo de** (c. 1198–c. 1265), Spanish poet, who was one of the earliest to write in the vernacular Castilian dialect and one of the first poets to be identified by name in Spanish literature. He was born in Berceo, near Calahorra, Logroño, and served as a secular priest of the monastery of San Millán de la Cogolla.

All of Berceo's known works are on religious themes, such as *La vida de Santo Domingo de Silos* and *Los milagros de Nuestra Señora.* He was one of the first poets to use *cuaderna vía*, a verse form with stanzas of four 14-syllable lines and a single rhyme for each stanza.

BERCEUSE, ber-sûz′, is a French word meaning literally "lullaby" or "cradlesong." By extension, the term is used to denote a musical composition, usually instrumental and in 6/8 time, with a rocking accompaniment. The most familiar berceuse is Chopin's Opus 57, for piano. The same form in German music is called *Wiegenlied.*

BERCHEM, ber′kнəm, **Nicolaes Pietersz** (1620–1683), Dutch painter. His family name is also spelled *Berghem.* He was born in Haarlem on Oct. 10, 1620. He studied landscape painting with Jan van Goyen and Jan Baptist Weenix, and his work reflects the former's naturalism and the latter's romanticism. He later spent several years in Rome, where he received further training in drawing, color, and perspective. He lived most of his life in Amsterdam, and his paintings achieved wide popularity there. Berchem died in Amsterdam on Feb. 18, 1683.

Most of Berchem's paintings are landscapes with Italian themes. These works are characterized by warm colors and skillful use of perspective. His canvases include *Italian Landscape* and *Allegory of the Growth of Amsterdam,* both of which are in the Rijksmuseum in Amsterdam; *The Ford,* in the Albertina Museum, Vienna; and *Landscape and Cattle,* in the Museum of Fine Arts, Richmond, Va.

BERCHET, bär-shā', **Giovanni** (1783–1851), Italian poet and patriot, who was a pioneer of the romantic movement in Italian literature. He was born in Milan on Dec. 23, 1783. His strong sentiments against Austrian rule in Lombardy become well known through his contributions to the patriotic journal *Il conciliatore*, and in 1821, warned of impending political arrest, Berchet fled to London. In 1829 he moved to Belgium, where he continued to write patriotic poems. He returned to Italy in 1846 and was briefly a member of the Piedmontese parliament. He died in Turin on Dec. 23, 1851.

In 1816, Berchet published *Lettera semiseria di Grisostomo*, which has been called the manifesto of the Italian romantic movement. In it he urged that poetry appeal to the emotions and concern itself with everyday experience and popular traditions. Among his works are several ballads (including *I profughi di Parga*), which he called *romanze*, and a long poem, *Le fantasie*, about a patriot's dreams in exile.

BERCHTESGADEN, berкн-təs-gä′dən, is a town in West Germany in the state of Bavaria, 10 miles (16 km) south of Salzburg, Austria. Situated in the Bavarian Alps at an altitude of about 1,880 feet (575 meters), it is a popular summer resort and winter sports center. It has an abbey with 12th century Romanesque transepts.

The town was known by the 12th century for its Augustinian abbey, which was granted a salt monopoly by the Holy Roman Empire. An independent ecclesiastical state was administered by the abbey until 1803.

Adolf Hitler built his villa, the Berghof, in Berchtesgaden. The villa had an elevator to take him to his mountaintop retreat, the *Adlerhorst* (Eagle's Nest). It was here in 1938 that he forced Chancellor Kurt von Schuschnigg to accept Nazi domination of Austria. Later in the year Hitler met English Prime Minister Chamberlain in the town and obtained his agreement to German annexation of the Sudetenland. Population: (1961) 4,795.

BERCHTOLD VON UND ZU UNGARSCHITZ, berкн′tōlt, ŏŏng′gär-shits, **Count Leopold** (1863–1942), Austro-Hungarian diplomat. He was born in Vienna on April 18, 1863, the scion of one of the aristocratic families of the Habsburg empire. He entered the Austrian diplomatic service in 1894. He held positions in the Austrian embassies in Paris and London and then succeeded Count von Aehrenthal as ambassador to Russia in 1907. In 1911 he left Russia, and in February 1912 he became Austro-Hungarian minister of foreign affairs. Following his resignation in January 1915, he accepted a position at court. After the dissolution of the Habsburg empire at the end of World War I, he withdrew from public affairs and lived on his estates. He died near Sopron, Hungary, on Nov. 21, 1942.

Berchtold held his positions of high responsibility in critical times. He was undoubtedly a dedicated public servant. As ambassador to Russia, he played a part in the Bosnian annexation crisis of 1908–1909. Justified criticism concerning Austria's all-too-risky policy at that time should be leveled primarily against Berchtold's then superior, Foreign Minister Aerenthal. On the other hand, Austria's refusal in 1913 to allow Serbia an access to the Mediterranean Sea after the Balkan Wars was very largely due to the management of diplomatic affairs by Berchtold. His intransigence in this and other respects undoubtedly aggravated, but did not create, the Balkan crisis. The ultimatum presented to Serbia in July 1914 after the assassination of the Austrian heir apparent, Archduke Francis Ferdinand, ignited the crisis that led to World War I.

Whether a more skillful and courageous statesman in Berchtold's position could have prevented general war is not certain. It is certain that the unacceptable demands of the Austrian ultimatum to Serbia, approved by Berchtold, facilitated the war's outbreak. Unable to come to an understanding with Italy about its role in the war, Berchtold resigned as foreign minister in January 1915. It is part of the tragedy of the Habsburg empire that the thoroughly mediocre Berchtold directed its foreign affairs in such times of crisis.

ROBERT A. KANN, *Rutgers University*

BERCOVICI, bûr-kō-vē′sē, **Konrad** (1882–1961), American novelist and short-story writer. He was born in Brăila, Rumania, on June 22, 1882. He spent much of his youth among gypsies, whom he describes with intimate understanding in novels and short stories. He went to the United States in 1904 and, after holding a number of odd jobs, worked for the New York *World* (1917–1920) and *Evening Post* (1920–1921).

In 1917 he published his first book, *Crimes of Charity*. His short stories and novels of gypsy life include *Murdo* (1921), *Iliana* (1924) *Singing Winds* (1926), and *Peasants* (1928). Other works include the play *Costa's Daughter* (published 1924); the descriptive *Around the World in New York* (1924); the novels *The Marriage Guest* (1925) and *The Volga Boatman* (1926); *Alexander: a Romantic Biography* (1928); travel books, including *The Incredible Balkans* (1932); and fictional biographies of Moses (*Exodus*, 1947) and the French poet Arthur Rimbaud (*Savage Prodigal*, 1948). *It's the Gypsy in Me* (1941) is an autobiography. He died in New York City on Dec. 27, 1961.

BERDICHEV, byer-dyē′chəf, a city in the USSR, is in the western Ukraine, about 115 miles (185 km) southwest of Kiev. It is situated in Zhitomir oblast. A railway junction, Berdichev lies in the center of an agricultural area that is noted for its sugar beets. Besides processed foods, the city manufactures leather, clothing, chemicals, and machinery.

Berdichev was founded in the 14th century. In 1546 it fell to Lithuania in the treaty of demarcation between the Poles and Lithuanians, and came under the rule of both countries when Poland and Lithuania united in 1569. In 1793 it passed into Russian hands. Often called "The Jerusalem of Volhynia" (see VOLHYNIA), Berdichev became the center of the Jewish Hassidic movement, and in the 19th century it was the chief commercial town in the western Ukraine. In 1863 it had a population of over 53,000, which reached 75,000 by World War I. In 1939, the population was about 66,000. During World War II, the city was overrun and occupied by the Germans from 1941 to 1944. Berdichev has undergone extensive reconstruction. Its ancient Carmelite monastery has been converted by the Communist government into a state museum. Population: (1961) 53,206.

W.A. DOUGLAS JACKSON, *University of Washington*

BERDYAEV, byər-dyȧ'yəf, **Nikolai Aleksandrovich** (1874–1948), Russian religious philosopher. He was born of noble parents, in Kiev, on March 6, 1874. During his university years he was attracted to Marxism, but he soon abandoned this ideology, turning to Christianity, largely as interpreted by Dostoyevsky. From 1904 to 1914 he played an influential part in the important religious and cultural revival that was taking place in Russia. In 1922, after the overthrow of the czar, he was expelled from the Soviet Union, having fallen into disfavor with the leaders of the revolution. He settled in Paris, where he founded a religious philosophical academy and published numerous works that gained him increasing recognition as a religious philosopher. The most important of his works translated into English are *Freedom and the Spirit* (1935), *The Meaning of History* (1936), *The Destiny of Man* (1937), *Dream and Reality: An Essay in Autobiography* (1950), and *The Beginning and the End* (1952). Berdyaev died at Clamart, France, on March 23, 1948.

Berdyaev's basic concept—that a person as a spiritual entity is the highest value—placed him in direct opposition to the philosophies, economic systems, and scientific views that reduce man to a body-mind organism and thus degrade and depersonalize him. Philosophically, he classed himself as an existentialist, although he derived his insights from Dostoyevsky rather than from Kierkegaard or Heidegger. He regarded existence, spirit, and freedom as primary, and being, matter, and determinism as secondary. Holding that being denotes matter, while existence connotes spirit, he made a sharp distinction between a man who lives on the natural, psychosomatic level and a man who attains a spiritual mastery over the natural. He called the former an individual; the latter, a person. He asserted that "Man ought to be free, he dare not be a slave. . . . Such is the will of God." He protested against "objectification," by which a spiritual entity is converted into a mere object. According to his belief, this is done in social life whenever man is used as a means to any end lower than himself. Rather, man should be recognized as an end in himself. Berdyaev's sociology and philosophy of history argue that no real progress can be made by economic, political, or cultural means alone unless the human agents are first transformed spiritually. These means would then be used for the common good rather than for destructive ends.

MATTHEW SPINKA
The Hartford Seminary Foundation

BEREA, bə-rē'ə, is a city in northeastern Ohio, in Cuyahoga County, 15 miles (24 km) southwest of Cleveland. Its principal manufactures are metal, plastic, and paper products, and it is the packing and shipping center for the vegetable-growing area to the west. Baldwin-Wallace College, known for its music department and annual Bach Festival, is here. The Cleveland Municipal Airport is 3 miles (4.8 km) away. Settled in 1809 and incorporated in 1836, Berea is governed by a mayor and council. Population: 22,396.

BEREA COLLEGE, bə-rē'ə, is a coeducational nonsectarian institution in Berea, Ky., founded in 1855 by Kentucky leaders of the antislavery movement. It was incorporated in 1859, but the articles of incorporation were not recorded until 1866 because of the Civil War. College-level instruction began in 1869.

Berea's primary aim is to provide education and opportunities for self-support to promising students of limited means from the mountain region of the South. About 90 percent of the student body comes from the Southern Appalachian region, which includes areas of Alabama, Georgia, Kentucky, North Carolina, South Carolina, Tennessee, Virginia, and West Virginia. The basic liberal arts program is supplemented by departments of agriculture, education, and library science, and by programs leading to degrees in nursing and industrial arts. All students are required to spend a minimum of 10 hours a week in gainful employment.

The college library includes special collections of 18th-century English literature; literature, ballads, and histories of the mountain area; and Lincoln memorabilia and other Civil War era documents. Enrollment in the mid-1960's totaled 1,350 students.

BEREANS, bə-rē'ənz, an extinct sect of Calvinist dissenters from the Church of Scotland. The sect was founded in 1773 by John Barclay, a Scottish clergyman, and its adherents were sometimes called *Barclayites*. The Bereans took their name from the Bereans mentioned in Acts 17:10–13. They professed to follow this ancient example in building their system of faith and practice on Scripture alone, without regard to human authority. With the majority of Christians, the Bereans held the doctrine of the Trinity as a fundamental article of belief. They differed, however, on other points, particularly the nature of revelation. They held that the existence of God cannot be proved from experience or observation; therefore Scripture must be accepted on faith "illuminated by the Holy Ghost."

BERELSON, ber'əl-sən, **Bernard** (1912–   ), American sociologist and educator. He was born in Spokane, Wash., on June 2, 1912. He worked for the Federal Communications Commission during World War II. Later he taught library science and was dean of the graduate library school at the University of Chicago. His survey of graduate study was reported in *Graduate Education in the United States* (1960). In 1960–1961 he headed Columbia University's Bureau of Applied Social Research, and from 1962 to 1963 he directed the communications research program of the Population Council. Berelson was editor of *Education for Librarianship* (1949) and coauthor of *The People's Choice* (1944) and *Reader in Communications and Public Opinion* (1950).

BERENGAR, ber'ən-gär, was the name of two kings of medieval Italy. In Italian the name is *Berengario* and in Latin *Berengarius*.

BERENGAR I (died 924) was a son of the duke of Friuli by a daughter of Emperor Louis I the Pious. Elected king of Italy in 888, he lost his crown the next year to Guy of Spoleto, and until 896 his power was confined to northeastern Italy. In 896 Berengar agreed to partition Italy with Lambert, Guy's son, and he regained the throne on Lambert's death in 898. Berengar's position was threatened by the Italian nobles, who invited Louis III (later called the Blind) of Provence to invade Italy. Berengar repulsed Louis in 902 and again in 905, when he blinded him before sending him back to Provence.

In 915, as a reward for helping repel the Muslims who had been devastating southern Italy, Berengar was crowned emperor by Pope John X. However, Berengar found himself unable to assert his claim to the imperial authority because of the greater power of the kings of Germany. In Italy, Berengar was opposed by powerful nobles, who hoped to increase their own power by starting disputes for control of the crown of Italy. As part of this policy, the nobles encouraged King Rudolf II of Burgundy to usurp Berengar's title.

When Rudolf invaded Italy in 922, Berengar's weakness in Italy forced him to call in Hungarians as allies. Berengar was defeated by Rudolf Firenzuola, near Florence, in 923 and had to take refuge in Verona. He was assassinated in Verona in 924.

BERENGAR II (died 966) was the grandson of Berengar I. As count of Ivrea, he was the most powerful opponent of Hugh of Provence, king of Italy. Forced to flee from Italy in 942, Berengar was aided by Otto I, king of Germany, who wished to increase his influence in Italy, in exchange for an acknowledgment of Otto as his suzerain. Berengar collected a force in Germany and invaded Italy in 945. Hugh abdicated in favor of his son Lothair II, who reigned nominally until his death in 950. Actual power during his reign was held by Berengar.

Berengar succeeded Lothair as king of Italy in 950 and imprisoned Lothair's widow, Adelaide, because he feared that she would become a rallying point of his rivals. In 951 she sought the aid of Otto, who came to Italy and married her. Otto returned to Germany and left troops to pursue Berengar. Two years later Otto became reconciled with Berengar. Berengar, however, continued to strengthen his own position at the expense of Otto's authority. By 961 Berengar was at war with the pope, who asked Otto's aid. Otto invaded Italy, deposed Berengar, and kept him in prison in Bamberg, Germany, until Berengar's death in 966.

BERENGARIA, ber-ən-gär'ē-ə, queen consort of Richard I of England. The daughter of King Sancho VI of Navarre, she married Richard on May 12, 1191, at Limassol, Cyprus, during the Third Crusade. She accompanied the king to Acre, Palestine, where she stayed while he fought the Saracens. From 1192 to 1194, while Richard was imprisoned in Germany, she lived in Poitou, France. She became estranged from Richard soon after his release and seems never to have joined him again. In 1230 she founded a Cistercian monastery called Pietas Dei at Espau, near Le Mans, France. She died soon afterward and was buried there.

BÉRENGER OF TOURS (c. 1000–1088), bā-rän-zhā', toor, French logician and theologian. He is also known as *Berengarius* or *Berengar*. He studied with Fulbert at the cathedral school of Chartres and in 1031 became director of St. Martin's School at Tours. About 1040 he was appointed archdeacon of Angiers, but he remained at Tours. Bérenger helped to develop and, through his teaching, to spread the new study of dialectics. But in applying dialectical reasoning to the mystery of the Eucharist, he turned away from orthodox Christian beliefs and came into conflict with church authority.

Bérenger maintained that it was unreasonable to believe in the real presence of Christ in the material elements of bread and wine at the Mass. His denial of this belief (which later became the doctrine of transubstantiation) incited Lanfranc of Bec to clarify and defend the orthodox position. In *De corpore et sanguine Domini* (*The Body and Blood of Christ*) Lanfranc, the leading theologian of the times, refuted Bérenger's belief that the bread and wine were merely symbols or memorial signs of the body and blood of Christ. Bérenger wrote Lanfranc in 1050, further expounding his own position. When Lanfranc read this letter to the Council of Rome, Bérenger was excommunicated. The controversy continued for years. Bérenger recanted at councils in 1050, 1054, and 1078.

Bérenger's questioning of belief in the real presence, however, spurred the church to begin a clarification of transubstantiation at the Council of Rome in 1079. Bérenger died, reconciled with the church, in 1088.

See also TRANSUBSTANTIATION.

BERENGUER Y FUSTÉ, bā-reng-ger' e fōos-tä', **Damaso** (1873–1953), premier of Spain from January 1930 to February 1931. He was born in Cuba on Aug. 4, 1873. Berenguer attended military schools and rose rapidly in the military ranks. He was appointed secretary of war in 1918 and served for the next three years as high commissioner in Morocco. As a result of his refusal to lead an inadequate force against Riff tribesmen, he was court-martialed and demoted, but in 1924 his sentence was commuted and he became chief of the royal guard.

In January 1930, following dictator Primo de Rivera's resignation, Berenguer became premier. When he attempted to restore the constitution of 1876 instead of drafting a new one limiting the king's powers, riots and disorder resulted. Martial law was declared in December 1930, but the riots and demonstrations broke out anew in January 1931. In February Berenguer issued an election decree for a constitutent Cortes. When the riots continued, King Alfonso XIII canceled the elections. The resulting furor brought about Berenguer's resignation, the voluntary exile of the king, and the establishment of the Spanish republic in April 1931.

Berenguer offered his services to the new government but instead was imprisoned for his actions against the rioters. In 1953, however, the Spanish supreme court absolved him of blame. He died in Madrid on May 19, 1953.

BERENICE, ber-ə-nī'sē, was the name of several Egyptian princesses:

BERENICE I (c. 340–281 B.C.) married Philippus, a Macedonian. Their son, Magas, became king of Cyrene. After the death of her husband she went to Egypt with her aunt Eurydice, who married Ptolemy I. About 317 B.C., Berenice became the mistress of Ptolemy I and then succeeded Eurydice as his wife. She was the mother of Ptolemy II.

BERENICE (c. 280–246 B.C.), the daughter of Ptolemy II and Arsinoë I, married the Seleucid king Antiochus II, who had divorced Laodice in order to marry her. Laodice took revenge by murdering Antiochus, Berenice, and their son.

BERENICE II (c. 273–221 B.C.), the daughter of King Magas of Cyrene, married Ptolemy III, thereby uniting Cyrene and Egypt. When her husband went off to war in Syria, she dedicated her beautiful hair to Venus so that he might return safely. When the hair disappeared from the temple, the astronomer Conon of Samos declared that the gods had transferred it to the heavens as a constellation. From this legend came the name of the northern constellation, Coma Berenices. Following her husband's death, Berenice II became co-ruler of Egypt with her son, Ptolemy IV, who had Berenice put to death in 221 B.C.

BERENICE (born c. 28 A.D.), ber-ə-nī′sē, Judean princess. Her name is also spelled *Bernice*. She was the eldest daughter of Herod Agrippa I, king of Judea. Married first to Marcus, son of Alexander, head magistrate of the Jews in Alexandria, she later married her uncle, Herod of Chalcis. After his death in 48 A.D., she lived with her brother, Herod Agrippa II. Their relationship was reputedly incestuous, and to quiet scandal, she married Polemon II, king of Olba in Cilicia. She soon deserted Polemon and returned to her brother. She was with Agrippa at Caesarea when St. Paul was taken before the king for a hearing (Acts 25:13 to 26:32). Unable to halt the Jewish revolt of 66 A.D., she and her brother were forced to flee to the Romans.

Titus, son of the Roman emperor Vespasian, made Berenice his mistress during his stay in Judea. She followed him to Rome, where popular opinion caused him to send her away. She tried unsuccessfully to renew their relationship when Titus became emperor in 79, and she died sometime later. The love of Titus and Berenice is the subject of Racine's drama *Bérénice* (1670).

BERENICE, ber-ə-nī′sē, was a city of ancient Egypt, on the Red Sea, 155 miles (250 km) east of Aswan. It was founded by Ptolemy II in the 3d century B.C. and named in honor of his mother. Ptolemy built a road across the desert connecting Berenice with Coptos, on the Nile. Berenice became the chief port for Egyptian trade with Arabia and India in the 1st and 2d centuries. A.D.

The Italian archaeologist Giovanni Battista Belzoni, exploring the Red Sea coast between 1815 and 1819, found the remains of temple decorations and other ruins, which he identified as part of Berenice.

BÉRÉNICE, bā-rā-nēs′, is a tragedy by Jean Baptiste Racine (q.v.), first produced in 1670. The play concerns the clash between love and obligation, and is notable for its insight into human reactions to crisis. It was a rival production to Pierre Corneille's *Tite et Bérénice*, which is based on the same theme. Racine's work is generally considered the superior of the two.

When the play opens, Titus, newly crowned emperor of Rome, is soon to marry Bérénice, queen of Palestine. However, the emperor learns that the Romans will not tolerate his marriage to a foreigner. He is torn between his great love for Bérénice and his duty to the state, but he finally decides to order Bérénice to leave Rome.

Titus sends his friend, Antiochus, to carry out the command, but Bérénice indignantly refuses to accept her dismissal by anyone but Titus himself. When the emperor himself prevails upon her, she accedes with dignity and resignation. In the climax to this moving scene, Bérénice bids Titus a final farewell and resolves to love no one after him.

BERENSON, ber′ən-sən, **Bernard** (1865–1959), American art critic, who was one of the world's foremost authorities on Renaissance art. Born *Bernhard Berenson* in Vilna, Lithuania, on June 26, 1865, he moved with his family to the United States when he was 10. He graduated from Harvard College in 1887, after which Mrs. Jack (Isabella Stewart) Gardner, who early sensed his artistic acumen, sponsored him on a series of European "art-seeing" tours. For about a decade, beginning in 1894, he spent almost $3 million on art for Mrs. Gardner, thus forming the nucleus of her Fenway Court Collection in Boston.

From 1900, when he married Mary Logan Smith Costelloe, a sister of the essayist-scholar Logan Pearsall Smith, Berenson made his permanent home at I Tatti, an 18th century villa at Settignano, near Florence, Italy. I Tatti was the perfect setting for a scholar and urbane, sometimes acerb man of the world with an abiding curiosity and passion for conversation. There he entertained guests and collected art objects and a vast library on art. During World War II, Berenson, a Jewish convert to the Roman Catholic Church, was forced to take refuge at times to escape persecution by the Fascists. He died at Settignano on Oct. 6, 1959. At his death he left

Bernard Berenson

(1865–1959)

WIDE WORLD

his villa and its collections to Harvard as an art-research center.

Berenson made a handsome income advising art collectors and dealers, particularly the English dealer Joseph Duveen, with whom he worked for 30 years. The method Berenson followed to establish the authorship and authenticity of paintings was to discover what characteristic each artist had that was not shared by any other. Although he sometimes arrived at conclusions that were later successfully challenged, even by himself, he corrected so many erroneous attributions of paintings that the opinion of "B.B." was sought on almost every major transaction and collection involving works of the Italian Renaissance. Later in life Berenson spoke of regretting the time he had squandered on giving critical advice that could have been used in broadening his experience and learning.

Berenson's reputation as a critic and scholar was established by three books published early in his career: *Venetian Painters of the Renaissance* (1894), *Florentine Painters of the Renaissance* (1896), and *Central Italian Painters of the Renaissance* (1897). These, with *North Italian Painters of the Renaissance* (1907), were revised and gathered together in *The Italian Painters of the Renaissance* (1930), probably the most influential handbook on Italian Renaissance painting produced in the 20th century. An indispensable guide to his methodology was the series *The Study and Criticism of Italian Art* (3 vols., 1901, 1902, 1916). In 1932 he published *Italian Pictures of the Renaissance*, which listed the principal artists and their works, along with an index of locations. In 1938 he brought out the 3-volume *Drawings of the Florentine Painters*. His other books include *Aesthetics and History* (1948), *Sketch for a Self-Portrait* (1949), and *Rumor and Reflection* (1952). His final work, *The Passionate Sightseer: From the Diaries of Bernard Berenson, 1947–1956*, was published posthumously in 1960.

BERESFORD, ber′iz-fərd, **Charles William de la Poer** (1846–1919), British admiral, who was a controversial figure because of his criticism of British naval policy. After more than 40 years of service in the navy and in Parliament, he was created *Baron Beresford* in 1916.

Beresford was born at Philipstown, King's County, Ireland, on Feb. 10, 1846, and entered the British navy in 1875. He won regular promotion, and during the Egyptian crisis of 1882 he commanded a gunboat at the bombardment of Alexandria. When the city was occupied by the British, he was named chief of police. He was on the staff of Lord Garnet Wolseley in the expedition for the relief of British forces in Khartoum in 1884–1885 and commanded the naval brigade at the Battle of Abu Klea.

When Beresford returned to England, he was appointed fourth naval lord of the admiralty, but he resigned after two years of policy disagreements with his superiors. His outspoken opposition to naval leaders also involved him in controversy on later command assignments in the English Channel and the Mediterranean Sea. But he was made a full admiral in 1906 and appointed to command the Channel fleet. Here his disapproval of the reorganization of the naval forces caused him to be ordered ashore in 1909, and to be retired in 1911. Beresford served several terms in Parliament between 1874 and 1916; in his later years he was known as "M.P. for the navy." He died at Langwell, Caithness, Scotland, on Sept. 6, 1919.

BERESFORD, ber′iz-fərd, **William Carr** (1768–1854), British general. For his services during the Napoleonic Wars he was created *Baron Beresford* in 1814 and *Viscount Beresford* in 1823. He was born on Oct. 2, 1768. He entered the British army in 1785 and served in Nova Scotia, Corsica, and the West Indies. He commanded a brigade in Egypt (1801–1803) and in the capture of the Cape of Good Hope in 1806. Later that year he led a small force that captured Buenos Aires from the Spanish, but he was unable to hold the city and was defeated and imprisoned for six months. He escaped to England and served in Portugal (1807) under Wellington.

Beresford was detached from British service in 1809 at the request of the Portuguese government to reorganize the Portuguese army. He fulfilled this assignment so well that Wellington used Portuguese troops to fight along with the British in Spain. Beresford rejoined the British army in 1811 with a command in southern Portugal and in Spain. Although his troops won several victories, his generalship was questioned, particularly in the Battle of Albuera, where one of his subordinates saved the day. He rendered notable service in the fighting in France in 1813, especially at the Battle of Toulouse. After 1819 he sat in the House of Lords, where he was a strong conservative supporter of Wellington. He was master general of the ordnance in 1828–1830. He died at Bedgebury, Kent, on Jan. 8, 1854.

BEREZINA RIVER, bye-ryā′zyi-nə, one of the largest tributaries of the Dnieper River in Belorussia. It flows south between Minsk and the Dnieper, joining the latter 16 miles (26 km) above the city of Rechitsa. The Berezina is about 365 miles (587 km) long and is navigable for 310 miles (499 km). It runs through a wooded, swampy valley, has low banks, and freezes each winter from December through March.

The largest cities on the banks of the Berezina are Borisov and Bobruisk. Its largest tributary is the Svisloch. The Berezina is the biggest timber-floating river in Belorussia, carrying more logs than even the Dnieper. In czarist times the northern part of the Berezina was linked with the Western Dvina River by a chain of canals and small rivers called the Berezina water system. Although this system still exists, its waterways have fallen into disrepair and now are not open to through traffic.

The Berezina River is famous in history as the scene of one of Napoleon's greatest defeats. In their 1812 retreat from Moscow, Napoleon's forces were surrounded on all sides by Russian armies and were nearly trapped on the east bank of the Berezina. The main bridge at Borisov had been burned by the Russians, who also held the city. Needing to cross the Berezina at all costs, Napoleon attempted a ruse. He hired local guides to find a ford south of the city, knowing that they would tell the Russian troops of his apparent intention to cross there. Meanwhile, the French army actually tried to cross the river two miles north of Borisov. There on November 26 the French built two bridges with great difficulty, because both riverbanks were wide swamps covered, like the river, with ice too thin to support troops. After a few French units had crossed, Russian armies attacked on the east bank from both north and south. Napoleon's army panicked and rushed onto the bridges as a disorganized horde. Many Frenchmen were pushed from the bridges to their death in the river, while others drowned trying to cross the river ice. By the end of the battle, November 29, Napoleon had lost half his army.

ELLSWORTH RAYMOND, *New York University*

BEREZNIKI, bye-ryez-nyi-kē, a city in the USSR, is one of Russia's leading chemical centers. It is located on the western slopes of the Ural Mountains in Perm oblast of the Russian republic. Situated on the Kama River in an area rich in deposits of common salt, potash, and magnesium salts, Berezniki produces nitrogen fertilizer, aniline dyes, potash, magnesium, titanium, synthetic ammonia, soda ash, and chlorine. The city, about 15 miles (24 km) south of the historic salt-mining center of Solikamsk, is entirely a product of the Soviet period. It was built in the early 1930's on the site of salterns dating from the 16th and 17th centuries. Population: (1965) 132,000.

THEODORE SHABAD
Author of "Geography of the USSR"

BERG, berкн, **Alban** (1885–1935), Austrian atonal composer, who wrote *Wozzeck* (q.v.), one of the most celebrated operas of the 20th century. Berg evolved an individual style that combined traditionally romantic lyricism with the dissonant harshness of contemporary harmonics.

He was born in Vienna on Feb. 9, 1885, into a moderately wealthy family. He was musically self-taught until he was 19, when he met Arnold Schönberg, who had the greatest influence on his work and with whom he studied from 1904 to 1908. In 1913, in Vienna, Schönberg conducted the premiere performance of Berg's first orchestral work, the *Altenberg Songs*. The audience was so incensed by this avant-garde (but not atonal) work that they rioted and the concert had to be cut short.

Berg served in the Austrian army in World War I but found time between 1917 and 1921 to write most of his masterpiece, the opera *Wozzeck*, which he based on a play by Georg Büchner. Although fragments of the opera were performed in 1924, the entire opera did not have its premiere until Dec. 14, 1925, at the Berlin State Opera. *Wozzeck*, an immediate and sensational success, made Berg famous overnight.

Berg found the material for his second opera in Lulu, a demoniacally erotic character in two plays by Frank Wedekind. Berg began work on *Lulu*, his only 12-tone opera, in 1928. By 1934 he had completed the vocal parts, but he was still working on the orchestration when he died in Vienna on Dec. 24, 1935. The opera was first presented, just as he left it, in Zürich, Switzerland, on June 2, 1937.

Berg's most important instrumental work is probably his concerto for violin and orchestra. Written in 1934, it had been commissioned by the American violinist Louis Krasner, who gave it its first performance on April 19, 1936, in Barcelona, Spain. Among Berg's other important works are a piano sonata (1908); a string quartet (1910); four pieces for clarinet and piano (1913); three pieces for orchestra (1914); *Chamber Concerto* (1925), for violin, piano, and 13 wind instruments; *Lyric Suite* (1926), for string quartet; and *Der Wein* (1929), a concert aria for soprano and orchestra, set to three poems by Baudelaire. He wrote several art songs and *An das Frankfurter Opernhaus*, a canon for four voices, composed in 1930 for the 50th anniversary of the opera house at Frankfurt am Main.

BERG, bûrg, **Gertrude** (1899–1966), American actress and author. She was born *Gertrude Edelstein* in New York City, on Oct. 3, 1899, and in 1918 was married to Lewis Berg. She began writing the popular radio series *The Rise of the Goldbergs* in 1929. The program, starring Mrs. Berg as Molly Goldberg, an amiable Bronx housewife who spoke a Yiddish-English dialect liberally sprinkled with malapropisms, was on the air for most of the next 20 years. Mrs. Berg took the Goldbergs to Broadway in 1948 in the show *Me and Molly*. A year later she inaugurated the television series *The Goldbergs* and in 1951 was coauthor and star of the motion picture *Molly*.

Mrs. Berg's performance on Broadway in the comedy *A Majority of One* (1959) won her the Antoinette Perry (Tony) Award. Her autobiography, *Molly and Me: Memoirs of Gertrude Berg*, was published in 1961. She died in New York City on Sept. 14, 1966.

BERG, bûrg, **Patty** (1918–   ), American golfer. In over 30 years of competition, she won 83 tournaments (40 as an amateur) and held nearly every women's championship.

Born in Minneapolis, Minn., on Feb. 13, 1918, *Patricia Jane Berg* won her first golf title (the Minneapolis City championship) at the age of 16. A surprising runner-up in the women's national amateur matches in 1935 and again in 1937, she won the title in 1938 while a student at the University of Minnesota. She played on the Curtis Cup team in 1936 and 1938.

Miss Berg turned professional in 1940. After serving in the Marine Corps Women's Reserve, she won the first U.S. Women's Open in 1946. She won the Titleholders Tournament (Augusta, Ga.) and Western Open seven times each and was awarded the Vare Trophy for the lowest average score three times. The only honor to elude her was the Ladies Professional Golfers' Association title, for which she was a runner-up twice. She is a member of the LPGA Hall of Fame.

BILL BRADDOCK
New York "Times"

BERG, berкн, is a hilly region in West Germany, on the right bank of the Rhine River, between the Ruhr and Sieg rivers. Once a duchy, it is now in the administrative districts of Cologne and Düsseldorf. It is noted for its high-grade iron and for textile manufacturing.

The counts of Berg were established in the area by the middle of the 11th century. As they increased their territory, the counts became influential in the archbishopric of Cologne. The Berg line died out with the murder of Englebert, archbishop of Cologne, in the 13th century, and the countship went by marriage to the house of Limburg. In 1348, Berg passed to the Jülich family, which received the ducal title in 1380. The succession failed again in 1609, and the counts palatine of Neuburg gained control of the area in 1610. Napoleon revived the title in 1806 and conferred it, with enlarged territory, on his brother-in-law, Joachim Murat. In 1815 the Congress of Vienna gave Berg to Prussia.

BERGAMA, ber-gä-mä′, is a town in western Turkey in the valley of the Bakir River, about 58 miles (93 km) north of İzmir. Bergama is noted for the manufacture of morocco leather. There is also trade in wool, tobacco, and grains.

Bergama occupies the site of the ancient city of *Pergamum* (q.v.) and contains numerous remains attesting to its ancient magnificence. In the center of the town are the remnants of a large Roman basilica, a Byzantine church now converted into a mosque, and a curious double tunnel, 200 yards long, through which the Bakir River runs. East of the town is a steep hill topped by the remains of a Roman palace. West of the town are the ruins of an ancient amphitheater, which was so constructed that its arena could be flooded with water for nautical sports. Population: (1965) 24,113.

BERGAMO, ber′gä-mō, a city in Italy, is the capital of Bergamo province, in Lombardy region. It is situated in the area between the rivers Brembo and Serio, 30 miles (48 km) northeast of Milan. The city is divided into two distinct sections—the old upper city, or *Bergamo Alta*, situated on hills and reached by a cable

ARTHUR W. AMBLER FROM NATIONAL AUDUBON SOCIETY
Wild bergamot (Monarda fistulosa)

BERGAMOT, bûr′gə-mot, a citrus shrub or small tree that is cultivated in Italy and other parts of southern Europe for its green, bitter volatile oil. This product, known as oil or essence of bergamot, is expressed or distilled from the highly aromatic rind of the pear-shaped fruit and is used in perfumery. The common name *bergamot* comes from two Turkish words meaning "prince's pear." The scientific name is *Citrus bergamia.*

The common name is also applied, mainly in Europe, to many varieties of pears, and in both Europe and America to several mints, notably *Mentha aquatica, Monarda didyma,* and *Monarda fistulosa.*

BERGEN, bur′gən, **Edgar John** (1903–   ), American comedian, who became a major radio star during the 1930's. An expert ventriloquist, Bergen shared his fame with his wooden dummies, Charlie McCarthy and Mortimer Snerd.

Bergen was born in Chicago, Ill., on Feb. 16, 1903. His real family name was *Bergren.* He developed his natural ability in ventriloquism while still in grade school, and in high school he created his first dummy, Charlie McCarthy, who was modeled after a tough Irish newsboy. The Bergen-McCarthy act helped to finance Bergen's premedical studies at Northwestern University, but he left college in 1926 to play the vaudeville circuit, and later in nightclubs and Broadway shows. In 1927 he toured Europe.

On Dec. 17, 1936, Bergen and McCarthy made their first radio appearance on the Rudy Vallee show. He was an instant success, and in 1937 he received a contract for a show of his own. He remained one of the top 10 radio comedians for more than 10 years. During World War II, Bergen frequently entertained American troops abroad. He also appeared in many motion pictures and on television. Bergen's daughter Candace made her debut as a screen actress in *The Group* in 1965.

BERGEN, bər′gən, is the chief shipping center of Norway. It is the capital of the county of Hordaland and also constitutes a separate county in itself. For many centuries Bergen was Norway's leading city, until it was surpassed by Oslo, 190 miles (306 km) to the east. A railroad connects the two cities.

Bergen is on the west coast of Norway and is situated on and about a promontory between two small inlets, one of which forms the harbor. The tongue of land between the harbor (Vågen) and the other inlet (Pudde Fjord) forms an elevated ridge topped by the old fort Fredriksberg. The harbor is sheltered, backed by ridges rising from 800 to 1,600 feet (244–488 meters), and is protected on the northeastern side by two fortresses, Sverresborg and Bergenhus. The latter served as the palace of Norwegian kings during the Middle Ages. There are several squares and marketplaces in the city, the largest being the fish market along the waterfront. The climate is mild and very humid; precipitation averages 89 inches (226 cm) a year.

Industries. Bergen is the great fish market of Norway, and its principal trade is the export of stockfish (dried fish), fish oils, herring, and fish roe. There is also extensive shipbuilding.

Other leading industries include distilling, flour and textile milling, iron founding, and the manufacture of porcelains, tobacco products,

tramway, and the lower city, or *Bergamo Bassa.* Bergamo Alta, with its hilly streets, old buildings, and lofty ramparts—now transformed into promenades—has a picturesque medieval appearance. The more extensive new section in the plain is modern in atmosphere. Bergamo is an industrial and trading center and manufactures textiles, pipes, and steel.

The city has an academy of painting and sculpture with a fine collection of Italian masters. There are also several museums and a theater. Buildings of interest include a cathedral dating from 1483; several old churches, notably Santa Maria Maggiore, dating from 1137; the Colleoni Chapel (1476), with several sculptures executed by Giovanni Antonio Amadeo; and the octagonal Baptistery (1340).

The people of Bergamo and its surroundings have a legendary reputation for their jollity, and, accordingly, the comic characters in Italian masked comedies are always Bergamascos. Among the distinguished native sons of Bergamo are the 15th century soldier of fortune Bartolomeo Colleoni and the 19th century composer Gaetano Donizetti. Pope John XXIII (reigned 1958–1963) first served as a priest in Bergamo.

History. *Bergomum,* as the town was called in ancient times, was settled by the Gauls and became a municipium of Rome during Caesar's time. It was sacked by Attila and later became a Lombard duchy. The city fell to Milan in 1264 and from 1296 to 1428 was in the hands of the powerful Visconti family of Milan. During the Renaissance, Bergamo was a celebrated center for musicians and composers. The city was ruled by the Venetian Republic from 1428 until it fell to Napoleon in 1796 and became part of the Cisalpine Republic in 1797. In 1815 it was transferred to the Austrians, who held it until 1859. The city furnished large numbers of men in 1860 to the forces of the nationalist hero Giuseppe Garibaldi. In World War II, Bergamo was taken by Allied forces in April 1945. Population: (1961) 110,065.

leather goods, soaps, furniture, glassware, paper, electric appliances, pianos, and rope. The chief imports are coal, grain, salt, woolens, cotton, machinery, and sugar.

Cultural Life. During the 19th century Bergen was the cultural center of Norway. Groups of young writers, dramatists, and poets congregated in the city. Edvard Grieg and Ole Bull were born here, and Henrik Ibsen lived here for a time. The city contains one of Norway's two universities, the University of Bergen, opened in 1948, and has various other schools of higher education, including an academy of music, a commercial college, a marine academy, and a geographical institute. Bergen's National Theater, founded in 1850, is one of the oldest in Norway. A meteorological institute, with an observatory, is located in the city, and there are several museums, including a fishery museum, and a museum of natural history, as well as art galleries.

Buildings. There are several old and beautifully designed buildings in Bergen, the most prominent of which are the fortress Bergenhus, the Rosencrantz Tower (1562), and the Haakonshallen, a great feasting hall of the Vikings, built in the 13th century. There are several churches of interest, notable among them being the Mariakyrkan (Church of St. Mary), a Romanesque building of the 13th century.

History. Founded as *Bjorgvin* by King Olaf Kyrre (Olaf III) in 1070–1075, Bergen quickly became the foremost city in Norway. It remained for many years the residence of Norwegian kings and was a center of monastic activity and building. It soon attracted the attention of German merchants, who in the 13th and 14th centuries managed to secure trade monopolies there. With the formation of the Hanseatic League about 1350, Bergen became one of its four principal foreign ports and was placed under rigid trading controls, which lasted until 1560. The town was sacked in 1395 by pirates, and during the tumultuous riots of the Reformation nearly all of the monasteries and churches were destroyed. The town was occupied by the Germans in 1940 and was held by them until the end of World War II. It suffered during the war from heavy Allied bombing. Population: (1960) 115,689.

BERGEN OP ZOOM, ber'ĸʜən ôp zōm, is a town in the Netherlands, in the province of North Brabant. It is located on the delta of the Scheldt River where the Zoom enters it, 20 miles (32 km) northwest of Antwerp, Belgium. An industrial and trading town, it has fisheries, distilleries, potash and sugar refineries, iron foundries, and ceramic factories. Large quantities of oysters and anchovies are exported.

Bergen was formerly a strong fortress, as the surrounding morasses made it almost inaccessible to an assailing force. During the war of liberation against Spain in the 16th and 17th centuries it was a strategic point, successfully resisting the attacks of Alessandro Farnese, duke of Parma, in 1581 and 1588 and of Ambrogio di Spinola in 1622. New fortifications were built by Baron Menno van Coehoorn later in the 17th century. Bergen was taken by the French in 1747 after a siege of nearly three months. In 1795 the French under Charles Pichegru again gained possession of it. It was unsuccessfully besieged by the British under Sir Thomas Graham in 1813. Population: (1960) 33,190.

BERGENFIELD, bûr'gən-fēld, is a residential borough in northeastern New Jersey, in Bergen County, 15 miles (24 km) east of Paterson. Pharmaceuticals and clothing are the most important of its several light industries. The Old South Church, built in 1799, is noteworthy. Government is by mayor and council. Population: 33,131.

BERGER, Hans. See ELECTROENCEPHALOGRAPH.

BERGER, bûr'gər, **Victor Louis** (1860–1929), American Socialist leader and editor. One of the most prominent Socialists in the United States during the formative years of socialism in the early 1900's, Berger was the first Socialist elected to the U.S. Congress.

Berger was born in Nieder-Rehbach, Austria-Hungary, on Feb. 28, 1860, and was educated in Vienna and Budapest. He emigrated to the United States in 1878, eventually settling in Milwaukee, Wis., where he taught school and became active in various Socialist groups. He was editor of the daily *Wisconsin Vorwärts* (1892–1898) and the weekly *Social Democratic Herald* (1901–1911), as well as its successor, the daily Milwaukee *Leader* (1911–1929)—all Socialist papers.

After a split with the Socialist Labor party, Berger and Eugene V. Debs founded the Social Democratic party, which in 1901 merged with a dissident group of the parent party to form the Socialist party.

In 1910, Berger was elected to the House of Representatives. In Congress he was an early proponent of the eight-hour day, child labor laws, old-age pensions, and federal relief for farmers. Berger failed to be reelected in 1912 and 1914. He was elected again in 1918 but was refused admission to Congress because of his antiwar stand during World War I. He was tried for sedition, found guilty, and sentenced to 20 years' imprisonment. Released on appeal to higher courts, he was reelected in 1919 to fill his own vacant seat but again was refused admission. In 1921 the U.S. Supreme Court reversed his conviction. Berger was then elected to Congress in 1922 and this time was admitted, serving three successive terms. He died in Milwaukee on Aug. 7, 1929.

Berger steadfastly supported his party's ideals despite persecution. He stressed the importance of social reforms as the means of achieving a socialist society. He rejected extremism and violence, advocating peaceful transition through the ballot. His editorials and congressional speeches are collected in *Voice and Pen* (1929).

BERGERAC, Cyrano de. See CYRANO DE BERGERAC.

BERGERAC, ber-zhə-ràk', is a town in southwestern France. It is situated in Dordogne department, on the Dordogne River, 50 miles (80 km) east of Bordeaux. It contains a large neo-Gothic church, dating from 1856.

Industries in Bergerac include brewing, flour milling, paper manufacture, tanning, weaving, hatmaking, and the manufacture of hosiery. The town trades in brandy, fish, and wine.

Bergerac has given its name to a wine, sometimes called *petit champagne*, made from grapes cultivated on the banks of the Dordogne. Population: (1962) 20,972.

BERGH, bûrg, **Henry** (1811–1888), founder of the American Society for the Prevention of Cruelty to Animals (ASPCA). He was born in New York City on Aug. 29, 1811. He studied at Columbia College and, with his brother Edwin, managed the shipyard of their father, Christian Bergh, until after the latter's death in 1843. Inheriting a fortune, he traveled in Europe and the East for several years. Appointed secretary of legation at St. Petersburg (now Leningrad), Russia, in 1863, he resigned in 1864 because his wife could not endure the cold climate.

Horrified at the cruelty to animals he observed in Russia, and stimulated by his acquaintance with the Earl of Harrowby, president of the Royal Society for the Prevention of Cruelty to Animals, Bergh returned to New York after the Civil War and in 1866 obtained a state charter for the ASPCA. As its president he devoted the rest of his life to organizing branch societies and securing laws against cruelty to animals. In 1875, with Elbridge T. Gerry and others, he also founded the Society for the Prevention of Cruelty to Children. He died in New York City on March 12, 1888.

BERGHEM, Nikolaas. See BERCHEM, NICOLAES PIETERSZ.

BERGIUS, ber'gē-ŏŏs, **Friedrich Karl Rudolph** (1884–1949), German chemist and Nobel Prize winner, who first used high pressures to change coal dust into oil. Bergius was born in Goldschmieden, Germany, on Oct. 11, 1884. His father was the president of a chemical factory. Bergius studied at the universities of Breslau, Leipzig, and Berlin, as well as at the Karlsruhe and Hanover institutes of technology. At Karlsruhe, he came under the tutelage of Fritz Haber, who had perfected a high-pressure procedure for the synthesis of ammonia. This was the first practical use of high pressure in chemical reactions.

In 1909, Bergius became a lecturer at the Hanover Institute of Technology. He also founded a private research laboratory in Hanover where he continued to study the influence of high pressure on chemical reactions. His book, *The Use of High Pressure in Chemical Reactions,* was published in 1913. He developed a method for producing oil from coal by the action of hydrogen on coal at high temperature and pressure. The product was capable of being refined in the usual way into gasoline, tar, and light oils with a low boiling point. After about 12 years of additional research and the expenditure of much money, the process became an economical one, and large factories for the Bergius reactions were built within Germany.

The patents were purchased by the I.G. Farbenindustrie and the Standard Oil Company of New Jersey. In 1913 the first patents relating to the action of hydrogen on coal were issued to Bergius while he was still working at the Hanover Institute of Technology. His later experiments were done at the Goldschmidt laboratories in Essen, and then at Mannheim-Rheinau in a specially built plant.

In 1931, Bergius was awarded a Nobel Prize in chemistry for his contributions to the invention and development of high-pressure procedures in chemistry. Bergius shared the chemistry prize with Carl Bosch, who made Haber's high-pressure nitrogen-fixation process an industrial suc-

cess. While developing his process for getting oil from coal, Bergius also arrived at a theory of how nature changed plants into coal.

Before World War II, Bergius worked on the production of synthetic food, notably the problem of converting wood into sugar. By 1933 he had succeeded in treating sawdust with hydrochloric acid and removing the acid by using a hot mineral-oil treatment. The product had a limited use as fodder for cattle. During the war, Germany used the Bergius coal-into-oil process much more extensively than the synthetic food process. In 1946, Bergius announced a method for preparing synthetic meat from wood.

Bergius left Germany after the war and lived in Austria, Spain, and Argentina. In Argentina, he was a technical adviser to the combustibles division of the ministry of industries. He died in Buenos Aires on March 30, 1949.

MORRIS GORAN, *Roosevelt University*

BERGMAN, bar'yə-màn, **Hjalmar** (1883–1931), Swedish novelist and playwright. He was born in Örebro, Sweden, on Sept. 19, 1883. His full name was *Hjalmar Fredrik Elgérus Bergman.* He studied at the University of Uppsala and in Italy, where he spent a number of years.

Attracted by the theater, he began his literary career as a dramatist and wrote several highly successful plays, including *Marionettspel* (1917), *Herr Sleeman kommer* (1917), and *Swedenhielms* (1925). He is best known, however, for his brilliant novels and short stories, many of which are psychological studies of life in a small town. Among them are *Markurells i Wadköping* (1919; Eng. tr., *God's Orchid,* 1924), *Farmor och Vår Herre* (1921; Eng. tr., *Thy Rod and Thy Staff,* 1937), and *Chefen fru Ingeborg* (1924; Eng. tr., *The Head of the Firm,* 1936). Bergman died in Berlin, Germany, on Jan. 1, 1931.

BERGMAN, bar'yə-màn, **Ingmar** (1918–   ), Swedish motion picture producer and stage director. He was born *Ernst Ingmar Bergman,* in Uppsala, on July 14, 1918. In 1937 he entered the University of Stockholm, where he ran a youth club theater. He was appointed an assistant director at the Swedish Royal Opera House in the early 1940's, and during the next several years he directed productions at the municipal theaters of Hälsingborg, Göteborg, and Malmö. In 1959 he became the youngest director ever appointed at Stockholm's Royal Dramatic Theater, which he headed from 1963 to 1966.

Ingmar Bergman

While successfully pursuing his career as a stage director, Bergman became internationally famous as the producer of a series of searching, provocative motion pictures. His motion picture career began in 1944 with the production, in Sweden, of his film script *Torment*, which won the Grand Prix du Cinéma at the international festival in Cannes, France, in 1946. Between 1947 and 1952, using a troupe of prominent actors borrowed from the Swedish stage, he directed the films *Crisis, Seaport, Three Strange Loves,* and *Monica*. His first comedy, *Waiting Women,* which he both wrote and directed, was produced in 1952. Thereafter he wrote and directed almost all his motion pictures.

In 1956, Bergman produced what many critics consider to be his masterpiece, *The Seventh Seal,* a stark, allegorical tale set in the Middle Ages. The hero, a returned Crusader, is involved throughout the film in a grim chess game with the figure of Death in an attempt to ward off his fate (probably death from the plague) long enough to perform "one single meaningful action." The film won an award at Cannes in 1957.

The starkness of the *Seventh Seal* contrasts sharply with the humanity of Bergman's *Wild Strawberries,* released in 1957, which concerns the attempt of an honored but selfish old man to recapture his long-buried feelings of love and tenderness. Bergman's other films include *Smiles of a Summer Night* (1955), *The Magician* (1958), *The Virgin Spring* (1959), *Through a Glass Darkly* (1961), *The Silence* (1963), *Persona* (1966), and *Cries and Whispers* (1972).

BERGMAN, bûrg'mən, **Ingrid** (1915–   ), Swedish actress, best known for her leading roles in Hollywood films. She was born in Stockholm on Aug. 29, 1915. After attending the High School for Girls, she studied at the school of the Royal Dramatic Theater in Stockholm in 1933–1934.

Ingrid Bergman's motion picture career began with a small part in the Swedish film *Munkbrogeven* in 1935. She quickly rose to stardom in Sweden. After she played the leading role in the Swedish film *Intermezzo* (1937), the American producer David O. Selznick signed her for an American version of the film, produced in 1939. During the next several years she starred in such Hollywood classics as *Casablanca* (1942); *Gaslight* (1944), for which she won an Academy Award; and *Spellbound* (1945).

In 1949, Miss Bergman went to Italy to appear in *Stromboli,* a film directed by Roberto Rossellini. A year later she divorced her husband, Dr. Peter Lindström, whom she had married in 1937, and married Rossellini. The circumstances of her second marriage created a furor in the United States, and for a time she did not appear in American movies. (Her second marriage was dissolved in 1958, when she married the Swedish impresario Lars Schmidt.) Under Rossellini's direction she made a series of not-too-successful films in the early 1950's. She resumed her Hollywood career in 1957 with *Anastasia,* for which she won an Academy Award and a New York Film Critics Award. Other films included *Indiscreet* (1958), *Goodbye Again* (1961), *The Yellow Rolls-Royce* (1965), and *Murder on the Orient Express* (1974), for which she won an Academy Award as best supporting actress.

Miss Bergman also appeared in several stage successes in the United States: *Liliom* (1940),

INGMAR BERGMAN'S *Seventh Seal* had Bengt Ekerot (left) as Death and Max von Sydow as a knight.

Anna Christie (1941), and *Joan of Lorraine* (1946). In London, in 1971, she starred in Bernard Shaw's *Captain Brassbound's Conversion.*

BERGMAN, bar'yə-mån, **Torbern Olof** (1735–1784), Swedish analytical chemist and mineralogist. He was born in Katrineberg, Sweden, on March 20, 1735. He was educated at the University of Uppsala, where he became a doctor of philosophy and instructor in physics in 1758. In 1761 he was made adjunct professor of mathematics and in 1767 professor of chemistry.

Bergman conducted many experiments on the chemical characteristics of metals. His work on nickel and bismuth was particularly valuable. He published a classification of minerals in which the chief divisions were based on their chemical characteristics and the subdivisions on their external forms. He also investigated the geometrical relations between different crystals of the same substance. In *Elective Attractions,* an essay published in 1775, he advanced a theory of chemical affinity. He died at Medevi, Sweden, on July 8, 1784.

INGRID BERGMAN (right), with Helen Hayes, plays an award-winning role in the motion picture *Anastasia.*

BERGSON, berg-sôn', **Henri** (1859–1941), French philosopher and winner of the Nobel Prize for literature in 1927, who was one of the most influential thinkers of the 20th century. His books, written with a rare combination of lucidity and suggestive power, aroused widespread discussion and controversy both in Europe and in the United States. Responses to Bergson's philosophy ranged from severe attacks by Bertrand Russell and George Santayana to enthusiastic acclaim by William James, who found in Bergson an ally in his attack on "intellectualism." Bergson's ideas also had great effect on a variety of philosophical, political, and literary movements.

Life. Henri Bergson was born in Paris on Oct. 18, 1859. As a student in the Lycée Condorcet he was deeply interested in both classical and scientific studies; and at the École Normale Supérieure he excelled in mathematics and wrote a distinguished essay on a problem in Pascal's geometry. Then, greatly influenced by the writings of John Stuart Mill and Herbert Spencer, he devoted himself to research in philosophy of science and became highly skeptical of the value of metaphysics. When, however, he reached the conclusion that "duration" and "freedom" have no place in the scientific picture of the world, he decided to explore these concepts as a speculative philosopher. After his appointment to the professorship of philosophy at the Collège de France in 1900, he developed and expounded his views in numerous writings and in lectures.

After World War I, Bergson turned from his scholarly work to devote himself to politics and international affairs and headed diplomatic missions to Spain and to the United States. Near the end of his life, he became interested in the relationship between his philosophical views and religious problems, and it is thought that he was converted to Roman Catholicism. Because of his Jewish origin, however, he refused to make his beliefs public during the German occupation of France during World War II and he declined exemption from the Nazi "Jewish laws." He died in Paris on Jan. 4, 1941.

Works. Bergson's principal works are *Essai sur les données immédiates de la conscience* (1889; Eng. tr., *Time and Free Will*, 1910), *Matière et mémoire* (1896; tr., *Matter and Memory*, 1911), *Introduction à la métaphysique* (1903; tr., *Introduction to Metaphysics*, 1912), *L'évolution créatrice* (1907; tr., *Creative Evolution*, 1911), and *Les deux sources de la morale et de la religion* (1932; tr., *Two Sources of Morality and Religion*, 1935).

He also wrote *Le rire* (1900; tr., *Laughter*, 1911), *La perception du changement* (1911; tr., *The Perception of Change*, 1911), *L'énergie spirituelle* (1919; tr., *Mind Energy*, 1920), *Durée et simultanéité* (1922), and *La pensée et le mouvant* (1934; tr., *Creative Mind*, 1946).

Bergson's Philosophy. The root belief of Bergson's philosophy—what he would have referred to as his fundamental "intuition"—is that ultimate reality is a vital impulse (*élan vital*). The nature of the *élan vital* can be grasped only by a mind capable of transcending the limits of intellect.

The Essence of Reality. Bergson worked against the dominantly intellectualist grain of the French philosophical tradition, which tended to conceive of reality as a logical or geometric structure, and took as a model of adequate understanding the reasoning of the logician and scientist. Contrary to these conceptions, Bergson held that reality has no fixed structure, that change is of its essence, and that it cannot be adequately known by reason. Whereas science can offer us useful generalizations concerning the nature of the physical world, only a philosophy based on the "immediate data of consciousness" can attain absolute knowledge of the nature of real time, change, creation, and human freedom.

Such views placed Bergson in square opposition to the French positivist movement still in ascendancy during the early part of the 20th century. Yet rather than ignore the findings of science, Bergson interpreted scientifically observed phenomena as evidence for the existence of metaphysical realities. From his early investigations in psychology, for example, he arrived at the view that whereas the functions of movement, sensation, perception, and recollection are dependent on the brain, this was not the case with "pure memory." The latter he conceived of as a spiritual reservoir of images of the past, from which normally only those relevant to present action are drawn. In place of a Cartesian dualism of matter and mind he thus proposed a dualism of (1) "matter," an aggregate of images surrounding the body, defined as a "center of action"; and (2) "pure memory," a source of images that present themselves in abnormal states in the form of fantasies and in moments of creative endeavor as insights unavailable to perception or conscious recall.

Creative Evolution. Later, in his theory of "creative evolution" based on biological investigation, Bergson replaced this dualism of matter and memory with the conception of a single spiritual force, the *élan vital*, which finds both a source of resistance and a medium for creation in "matter," itself the result of the "running down" of this vital energy.

Bergson's theory of "creative evolution" presents, in addition to his metaphysical views, a kind of natural history of human understanding. Denying the adequacy of a mechanistic theory of evolution to explain the persistence of forms throughout variations, he proposed in its place the view that an initial creative force releases its energy in divergent directions, producing the "torpor" of plant life, the "instinct" of the arthropods, and the "intelligence" of the vertebrates. He defined "instinct" as the power of acting directly and unreflectively on objects, as the wasp does in building its nest. This type of action differs from the intelligent behavior of the human architect or surgeon in that the instinctive animal cannot devise instruments to achieve its ends. Such fashioning of the means to achieve practical ends is the characteristic action of intellect. This intellect, however, can attain its practical goals only by concentrating on those aspects of things that are related to their use. Thus man, in using his intellect, ignores the unique, everchanging qualities of things and observes only their general and unvarying characteristics. His intellect treats all objects as if they were spatial things, composed of parts; for only by thus "spatializing" them can it gain practical control over them.

Intuition. By abstracting himself from these practical limitations of intellect, however, man can develop a power that he rarely uses since he is primarily a doer and not a knower: that of "real intuition," the highest product of the evolution of understanding. This faculty is analogous to instinct in its directness of grasp, but it is different in that it is self-conscious and free. Its development requires an effort, since it entails a reversal of the normally practical tendency of the human mind. But unless this effort is made, men will be limited to a superficial, intellectual view of the nature of things, unable to grasp the inner nature of events, which discloses itself only to intuition.

The Limitations of Intellect. Thus Bergson stressed the pragmatic function of intellect and declared that the conceptualizations of science and common sense are by their very nature unable to deal with the real qualities of things. Things in our external and internal environment are constantly in a state of change, although the intellect conceives of them, for practical purposes, as if they were unchanging. For example, a desk used for writing may undergo many changes of appearance; yet so long as it continues to serve the practical function designated by the concept "desk," it will be considered as the "same desk." Moreover, our inner experience —if we attend to it directly—is one of constant variation in quality and intensity; but rarely do we have any use for the perception of these subtle modifications. We conceive of ourselves as composed of distinct, spatialized states of consciousness, externally related one to the other, and we lose sight of the fact that each so-called "state" is really an intellectual abstraction from the vital flow of experience, each present moment of which is tinged with the past and is constantly qualifying the future.

The "concrete objects" dealt with by the scientist are thus in reality only abstract schematizations of real events; and whereas these concepts may be derived from intuitions, intuitions cannot be derived from them. Interested primarily in action and in prediction for the sake of control, the intellect interprets all things as signs of the uses to which they can be put. And more often than not it confuses the signs with that of which they are signs: hence the illusion of concreteness. As Bergson put it, the intellect is content with the convenient labels it puts on things and forgets that the label conceals rather than reveals the full nature of that to which it is attached.

Duration. Real events that can be experienced only by "that intellectual sympathy which is intuition" are moments of real time, or duration. To give us some sense of this *durée réelle*, Bergson resorted to image after image, among them "a spectrum of a thousand shades, with imperceptible gradations leading from one shade to another." He described it as having the form our psychological experience takes when we experience each moment of that experience as endlessly in process and flowing from the past into the future.

The nature of duration is perhaps best understood, however, by contrasting it with physical time, which is a conception devised by the physicist as a means of measuring the passage of events. Since only homogeneous units can be measured, the physicist disregards the individual, unique qualities of moments, that is, the qualities they have as a result of occurring before or after other moments. He disregards the felt differences between time suffered and time enjoyed, as well as the cumulative nature of the temporal process. In real, or psychic, duration,

moments interpenetrate and are internally related. In the physical formulation of time this fact of inner relation is concealed by the symbolic representation of each moment in a temporal series as distinct from, or as "taking place" before or after, other moments. Physical time, in a word, is a construction of the intellect, which confuses it with space. Intuition alone can make us aware of the nature of real duration.

This real duration, as intuitively known, or as "lived," is not only an unceasing, everchanging flow of events: it is also a creative force. Events in real time are not merely the products of past events; they contain an element of novelty as a result of being rich with their past. Just as the character of each note of a melody depends on the notes that precede it, and just as the melody itself is something more than the sum of its notes, so events in duration possess novel characteristics by virtue of their being the products of qualitative changes that occur in real time. This factor of novelty or creativity is ignored, Bergson believed, by both mechanistic and finalistic conceptions of reality. The former conceives of reality as a ready-made, "block universe" in which spontaneous, novel events cannot occur; the latter conceives of it on the model of a preformed pattern, in which novel occurrences cannot take place, because determination is derived from the end to be achieved.

Ethical Freedom. This conception of a real duration, in which novel, creative events can occur, forms the metaphysical foundation of Bergson's theory of ethical freedom. Arguing against both the British associationists and French positivists, Bergson contended that their belief that free, spontaneous action is impossible stems from their intellectualized conception of human personality and their mechanistic view of the process of events.

The determinist holds that in any situation where a final decision between alternatives is made, the final choice is determined by psychological and social conditions. The determinist concludes that given sufficient information about these conditions, such choices are predictable. This mode of interpretation, Bergson held, is applicable to decisions only after they have been made and does not deal with the process of decision in the making. The determinist views the situation conceptually, in terms of states of consciousness determining one another, and is unaware of the internal experience of deciding, which can be grasped only by intellectual sympathy.

Viewed intuitively, the situation is felt as one of tension and release, of weighing alternatives against one another, of resisting the pressure to act in one way rather than another. And the unpredictable, free act is, precisely, one that is performed by the inner self's acting against the pressures of the past in the form of habit and convention. To the psychological and sociological determinist such acts are inconceivable since they seem to defy the laws of causality. Such laws, however, while applicable to physical events and to the behavior of human beings when they act—as they ordinarily do—mechanically, do not apply to the free acts of the inner psychic life. Since the source of such acts is the fundamental self, which changes constantly, no laws of uniform behavior can be applied.

Most acts are admittedly not free: men do live ordinarily as conventional, predictable beings. The issue of freedom arises, however, when there is a conflict between such habitual action and the impulse to express one's individual nature and convictions. When, for example, a man is faced with the problem of adhering to a principle to which he is inwardly dedicated, at the price of pain or even destruction, he has a choice between the paths of convenience and freedom. That he can or did act freely in such a situation he can never demonstrate to himself or to others; for demonstrations must be conducted in deterministic terms. He must, rather, from his inner resources *create* the free act, which, after it is performed, may be called a determined act by those who interpret it from without. Yet the free agent himself, or one able to intuit this act, will realize that its free quality lay in the fact that the impetus for the final decision came not from the superficial, but from the fundamental self.

Morality and Religion. This theme of contrast between the intuitive and the intellectual, the habitual and the spontaneous, appears in Bergson's late writings in the form of a duality between the static and dynamic forms of morality and religion. Whereas static morality has its roots in a "closed society" and is nothing but a mechanical response to the pressure of custom, dynamic morality is derived from an "open society" in which the insights of the saint, prophet, and hero replace the tenets of social obligation. And over against static religion with its devitalized rituals and institutions there is the dynamic experience of religion which penetrates to the center of reality and discovers there a divine source of vitality and freedom.

Art. Finally, it should be mentioned that the conception of art as a product of creative action and as a source of intuitive knowledge figures prominently in Bergson's philosophy. On this subject he did not—except in the last pages of *Laughter*—write systematically; but illustrations drawn from the field of art abound in his writings.

It is evident that he conceived of the function of the artist and of the intuitive metaphysician as similar when he said, "The intention of life, the simple movement that runs through the lines, escapes our ordinary vision. This intention is just what the artist tries to regain, by placing himself within the object by a kind of sympathy, in breaking down, by an effort of intuition, the barrier that space erects between him and his model." The painter, for example, can pierce through the veil of conventional views and grasp the evanescent "inner qualities" of landscapes or of human beings. The comic playwright reveals the absurdities of living when it is made a matter of routine and convention, while the tragic dramatist discloses those facets of personality hidden beneath the cloak of habit. And finally, in his view, the musical composer can grasp intuitively the "laws of the life of feeling" and give us an intimation of the nature of the *élan vital* itself. See also CREATIVE EVOLUTION.

ARTHUR SZATHMARY, *Princeton University*

Bibliography

Carr, H.W., *Henri Bergson* (London 1912).
Chevalier, Jacques, *Henri Bergson* (New York 1928).
Höffding, Harald, *Lectures on Bergson* (New York 1914).
Lindsay, Alexander D., *The Philosophy of Bergson* (New York 1911).
Stephen, Karin, *The Misuse of Mind: A Study of Bergson's Attack on Intellectualism* (New York 1922).
Stewart, J.M., *A Critical Exposition of Bergson's Philosophy* (London 1911).

BERIA, byä′ri-yə, **Lavrenti Pavlovich** (1899–1953), Soviet political leader and official in the secret police during the Stalin era. He was born in Merkheuli, Georgia, on March 29, 1899. Educated as an architectural engineer, he joined the Bolshevik (Communist) party in 1917. From 1921 to 1930 he was a member of the Soviet secret police in the Caucasus, rising to command of the police in the entire area. From 1931 to 1938, Beria was an official of the Communist party in the Georgian and Caucasian regions. He became a member of the central committee of the Communist party in 1934.

One of the most faithful of Joseph Stalin's followers, Beria glorified Stalin's early career in *On the History of the Bolshevik Organization in Transcaucasia* (1935). In 1938, Stalin appointed him head of the ministry of internal affairs, which had charge of the secret police. Beria replaced Nikolai Yezhov. This shift in police officials coincided with the end of the purges of Communist party officials during the 1930's. Because of Stalin's reliance on the secret police, Beria's influence constantly grew. In 1939 he became a member of the politburo of the Communist party and in 1941 a deputy premier of the Soviet Union.

After Russia entered World War II, Beria became a member of the war cabinet and was given charge of ammunition production as well as of the police. When the war ended, he remained in command of police and intelligence activities. When the politburo was reorganized as the presidium in 1952, Beria retained his membership. After the death of Stalin in March 1953 he was made first deputy premier, a member of the presidium of the Council of Ministers, and minister of internal affairs.

Immediately after Stalin's death Beria's power was thought to be exceeded only by that of Georgi Malenkov. In July 1953, however, there was an official announcement of Beria's expulsion from the Communist party and the Soviet government. A month later it was announced that Beria would be charged with treason. He was accused of trying to seize total power in Russia, of being a foreign spy, and of attempting to bring capitalism to Russia. Rumors that he had been able to escape from Russia proved false. Beria was brought to trial in December 1953. After a six-day trial he was executed on Dec. 23, 1953, presumably in Moscow.

BERIBERI, ber′ē-ber′ē, is a disease caused by a deficiency of vitamin B_1, or thiamine, in the diet. Although some thiamine may be synthesized by bacteria living in the intestines, they cannot produce it in quantities large enough to meet the body's needs. Beriberi can be prevented only by eating foods containing the vitamin. These foods include whole grain products, such as whole wheat bread and unhusked rice, nuts, milk, pork, chicken, and legumes, such as peas. Sometimes a person whose diet includes raw fish may develop the disease even though he eats some thiamine-rich foods. This is because raw fish contains an enzyme, called thiaminase, that inactivates thiamine.

Prevalence. Beriberi is most common in the countries of the Far East, where husked, or polished, rice makes up a large part of the average diet. Uncooked fish is also widely eaten in many of these countries. In other parts of the world, beriberi occurs mostly in alcoholics, whose diets often do not include thiamine-containing foods. Sometimes beriberi occurs in pregnant women, whose supply of thiamine is depleted by the developing embryo.

Types. There are three major forms of beriberi: wet, dry, and infantile. *Wet beriberi* is an acute disease that causes heart failure, anemia, and edema (an accumulation of body fluids that results in swelling). *Dry beriberi* is a chronic disease generally characterized by neuritis (inflammation of the nerves), causing numbness and tingling in the hands and feet and sometimes producing a burning sensation in the soles of the feet. Eventually paralysis may occur, with a wasting away of the muscles of the arms and legs.

Infantile beriberi occurs in infants who are nursed by mothers afflicted with beriberi. This form of the disease occurs within the first year of life, usually between the first and fourth month, and is generally characterized by rapid heartbeat, vomiting, and convulsions. Unless the infant is treated immediately, he may die within a few days after the onset of symptoms.

Treatment. All three forms of beriberi are treated by the administration of thiamine, either orally or through injections. In the wet and infantile forms, the patient may show signs of improvement within a few hours after receiving the vitamin. For dry beriberi, treatment takes longer, depending on how severely the nerves have been damaged.

History. The earliest written record of beriberi was found in an ancient Chinese medical book dated about 2700 B.C. It was not until the late 1800's, however, that the cause of the disease was suspected. In 1897, while working at a hospital for beriberi patients in Java, the Dutch physician Christiaan Eijkman noticed that laboratory chickens that were fed polished rice left over by patients soon developed a disease similar to beriberi. In studying this disease, Eijkman found that the chickens could be cured by feeding them rice that had not been husked. Unfortunately, however, Eijkman's findings were published only in Dutch and were not generally known for some years.

During the early 1900's, an outbreak of beriberi among plantation workers in Malaya posed a serious threat to the area's rubber production. Two British scientists, Henry Fraser and Ambrose Stanton, were sent to Malaya in 1909 to investigate the disease. Through their studies, which were similar to Eijkman's, they discovered that beriberi is caused by a deficiency of a certain substance in the diet. In later years, as more vitamins were isolated and studied, this substance was found to be the B vitamin thiamine.

Further Reading: Goldblith, S.A., and Joslyn, M.A., *Milestones in Nutrition* (Westport, Conn., 1964); Williams, Robert R., *Toward the Conquest of Beriberi* (Cambridge, Mass., 1961).

BERING, bā′rĕng, **Vitus** (1680–1741), Danish navigator in the service of Russia. He was born at Horsens, Jutland, Denmark. He entered the Russian navy in 1704 and served in the war against Sweden. In 1725, Czar Peter I sent him to explore the northeastern coast of Asia. He crossed Siberia to Kamchatka, where he built several vessels. In 1728 he traversed the strait between Siberia and Alaska that bears his name, and discovered Big and Little Diomede Islands in the strait and St. Lawrence Island in the Bering Sea.

A similar exploring commission was given to him by Empress Anna in 1730, but it was not until 1740 that he reached Kamchatka again. He founded the town of Petropavlovsk-Kamchatski there and from this base sailed on June 4, 1741, with two ships, the *St. Peter* and the *St. Paul.* The vessels became separated, and Bering continued in the *St. Peter* to the southern coast of Alaska, sailing past Kodiak Island and sighting Mount St. Elias. On the return voyage, the *St. Peter* was wrecked on an island in the Komandors group off Kamchatka, and Bering died on the island (later named Bering Island) on Dec. 19, 1741.

BERING SEA, bēr′ing, a northern extension of the Pacific Ocean, connected by Bering Strait with the Chukchi Sea of the Arctic Ocean. It is bounded on the west by Siberia and the Kamchatka Peninsula, in Asia; on the east by Alaska; and on the south by the Aleutian Islands. The sea extends 930 miles (1,500 km) from north to south and 1,240 miles (2,000 km) from east to west, and has an area of more than 875,000 sq mi (2,266,250 sq km). Its largest gulfs are the Gulf of Anadyr on the west and Norton Sound and Bristol Bay on the east. The major islands are Nunivak, St. Lawrence, St. Matthew, the Pribilofs, and the Komandors (or Commanders). In the north and east the sea is relatively shallow. The greatest depths, about 13,500 feet (4,115 meters), occur at the western end of the Aleutians.

In winter, pack ice occurs as far south as St. Matthew Island and along the Alaskan coast into Bristol Bay. The northern part of the sea is closed to navigation from late October to late June. Good weather is rare. Moderate to strong gales with rain and snow are common during fall and winter. Fog is prevalent during spring, summer, and early fall. The chief resources are fish, taken in quantity along the Alaskan coast, and the fur-seal herds of the Pribilof Islands. The sea was named for Vitus Bering (q.v.).

BERING SEA navigation is impeded by ice. Here, a U.S. Coast Guard icebreaker makes a passage.

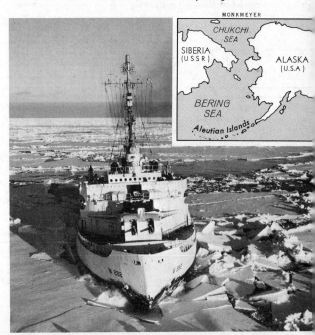

BERING SEA CONTROVERSY, an international dispute over the territorial status of the Bering Sea, chiefly between the United States and Britain. In 1867 the Russians ceded the Pribilof Islands in the Bering Sea, along with Alaska, to the United States. These islands had long been the summer breeding grounds of a valuable seal herd that migrated south in the winter. By acquiring the Pribilofs, the United States gained control of fur-sealing operations on the islands and three miles at sea, and it restricted the killing to male seals. As sealing became more profitable, however, pelagic, or open-sea, sealing was increasingly practiced in the Bering Sea by several nations, notably Canada. This involved the indiscriminate slaughtering of females and thus threatened the herd with extinction.

The Alaska Commercial Company, which had the United States sealing monopoly, objected to this practice, and in 1886 the United States seized and condemned three Canadian pelagic sealers. Britain protested, and when several more vessels were subsequently seized, the question became a matter of serious diplomacy. In 1889, Congress proclaimed U.S. control over the Bering Sea, in effect declaring it a *mare clausum* (closed sea). Britain objected to this as contrary to established international law, and the matter was referred to an international court of arbitration. In 1893 this tribunal decided against the United States: the Bering Sea was held to be part of the high seas and damages were to be assessed against the United States for the seized vessels. This specific aspect of the Anglo-American controversy was settled in 1898 when Congress appropriated $473,151 to pay for the seized Canadian ships.

Although the 1893 arbitration decision contained certain restrictions on pelagic sealing, these restrictions proved ineffective, and the problem of preserving the fast-dwindling seal herd was unresolved. Finally, in 1911, the North Pacific Sealing Convention was signed by Britain, Russia, Japan, and the United States. This accord forbade pelagic sealing completely, and the United States, having jurisdiction over land-sealing in the Pribilofs, agreed to pay Japan and Britain an annual percentage of the proceeds from its sealing activities. Under strict supervision the seal herd was built up again.

BERING STRAIT, bĕr'ing, is a passage between Alaska and Siberia connecting the Chukchi Sea of the Arctic Ocean and the Bering Sea, an arm of the Pacific Ocean. Between Cape Prince of Wales, on the Seward Peninsula of Alaska, and Cape Dezhnev, on the Chukchi Peninsula of Siberia, the strait is 55 miles (88 km) across—the narrowest distance between the continents of North America and Asia. In the middle, and separated by the International Date Line, lie the Diomede Islands, less than 3 miles (5 km) apart: the larger, Big Diomede (Ratmanov) Island, belongs to Russia, and the smaller, Little Diomede Island, belongs to the United States. With Fairway Rock, lying to the south in American waters, these islands are the remains of a land bridge that once connected the two continents.

The strait has a maximum depth of 170 feet (52 meters) and is frozen over between October and June. It was discovered by the Russian navigator Semen Dezhnev in 1648 and was later named for Vitus Bering, who, on St. Diomede's Day, Aug. 16, 1728, discovered islands there.

BERKELEY, bärk'lē, **George** (1685–1753), Irish philosopher and bishop, who opposed the philosophic views of John Locke (q.v.). Berkeley was born near Kilkenny, Ireland, on March 12, 1685. Though Anglican in religion and of English stock, he always regarded himself as a true Irishman. In 1699 he entered Trinity College, Dublin, where he took his degree in 1704. He was ordained a deacon in 1709 and was married in 1728.

Berkeley remained connected with Trinity until 1724, when he became dean of Derry. At Derry he had for the first time sufficient means to set on foot a strange project that he had long contemplated. He planned to establish a college in the Bermudas for the education and religious enlightenment of American Indians. A college so placed in those days could hardly have succeeded; however, he obtained a royal charter and a promise from Parliament of £20,000, and in 1728 he set out for America. He went first to Rhode Island to wait for his money to be paid; but Sir Robert Walpole, who distrusted his plan, permitted and perhaps encouraged delay, and the scheme was finally abandoned in 1731.

GEORGE BERKELEY, the 18th century Irish philosopher, from a portrait painted by J. Simbert, dated 1725.

For the last 20 years of his life, Berkeley was bishop of Cloyne, near Cork, in which period he wrote on the religious and economic problems of Ireland, besides discharging his episcopal duties. He died on Jan. 14, 1753, while on a brief visit to Oxford, England, where his son George was entering Christ Church College.

Writings. The works on which Berkeley's fame rests were produced while he was very young. In his subtle *Essay Towards a New Theory of Vision* (1709) he deliberately stopped short of his ultimate conclusions, apparently with the idea that his novel opinions should be presented only by stages to the public. His greatest work, the *Treatise Concerning the Principles of Human Knowledge*, was published in 1710, and in 1713 he aimed at a wider audience by presenting the same doctrine in more elegant and popular form in the *Three Dialogues Between Hylas and Philonous*. Important among his later writings are *De motu* (1721), a Latin essay on the philosophy of science; *Alciphron, or the Minute Philosopher* (1732), a long dialogue mainly directed against the Deists; and *The Analyst* (1734), an acute criticism of some logical difficulties in the work of Sir Isaac Newton. His last substantial book, *Siris* (1744), the ponderous and even rambling style of which is startlingly unlike the grace and clarity of his early writings, presents no actual change of doctrine, but puts a new and significant emphasis on the strong metaphysical strain in his thinking.

Philosophy. The perennial interest of Berkeley's philosophy is the result of his unusually diverse gifts. He had an acute critical intellect, which he usually employed in the defense of common-sense opinions, and a high talent for bold and speculative metaphysics. His position can best be seen by contrasting it with John Locke's, whose *Essay Concerning Human Understanding* (1690) Berkeley had carefully studied as a student. Locke was the apostle of the great scientific achievements of the 17th century and was himself a friend of its leading scientists. He presented the universe as a material system in which "bodies," corpuscular in structure, act mechanically, by "impulse," on each other and on the human senses. Their action on the human nervous system causes "ideas" to occur in the mind, and these ideas are the sole objects of which man has direct awareness. The ideas of "primary qualities" faithfully represent the actual character of material things, but ideas of "secondary qualities" do not. It is "by mistake," Locke argued, that men "attribute reality" to color, sound, taste, and smell. He held that, besides matter, "immaterial substances" exist; but he confessed that he could find no way of proving this, and indeed did not wholly reject the idea that consciousness might be merely a property of matter. Against all this Berkeley reacted vigorously. He held that the scientific world view was radically incoherent and that it encouraged atheism and therefore vice; he accused it of absurd deviation from common sense; and, finally, he felt it to be simply repulsive. Accordingly, he set before himself the twin aims of defending common sense against its scientific detractors and of undermining the supposed metaphysical foundations of science. He believed that these aims were not inconsistent and perhaps hardly realized that they were distinct.

The essence of his procedure was simple. Taking over from Locke himself the axiom that "ideas" are the only objects of direct awareness, he pointed out that, if so, there could be no warrant for belief in "matter," in a world of "external objects" conceived to be distinct from and independent of our ideas. If we are aware of nothing but ideas, on what basis could we assert the existence of anything else? Locke's view implies that we cannot be directly aware of the most ordinary objects; hence ordinary objects are unlike what they appear to be, and we cannot know at all what they are really like, or even that they exist. But if we hold, Berkeley argued, that ordinary objects simply are "collections of ideas," then we can hold that we are indeed directly aware of them and can and do know what they really are. They are just as they appear to us to be. But—and the metaphysical strain enters at this point—if objects are collections of "ideas," they can exist only "in a mind"; their *esse* is *percipi*. But this, Berkeley held, is no real paradox. For the mind of God is present always and everywhere; all ideas are always in the mind of God, and it is by direct communion with His mind that human beings are supplied with the ideas that make up their experience. It is literally true that "in Him we live, and move, and have our being." Thus, the reality of the everyday world is secured by being made directly dependent upon the mind of God; and the notion of "matter," the foundation of the scientific world view, is simply rejected.

This conclusion, of course, forced upon Berkeley the problem of the true status of science. He held that the current physical theories could not be literally true, for he denied the existence of what they purported to deal with. At first he was inclined to hold that much should be rejected as mere confused nonsense; but in *De motu* and later writings he developed a pragmatic view of science as a useful "fiction," a body of suppositions, mathematically convenient, but to be sharply distinguished from statements of actual fact. This view, which was unique and boldly original in his day, became increasingly current as difficulties in the literal interpretation of physical theory became more prominent. The idea is independent of, though certainly convenient for, Berkeleian metaphysics, and has commended itself to many who would regard Berkeley's general position as untenable.

G.J. WARNOCK, *Author of "Berkeley"*

Bibliography
Berkeley's Works were edited by Arthur A. Luce and Thomas E. Jessop, 6 vols. (New York 1950).
Armstrong, David M., *Berkeley's Theory of Vision* (New York and London 1960).
Johnston, George A., *The Development of Berkeley's Philosophy* (New York 1924).
Luce, Arthur A., *The Life of George Berkeley* (New York 1949).

BERKELEY, bärk'lē, **John, 1ST BARON BERKELEY OF STRATTON,** English army officer and colonial proprietor of the 17th century. He commanded Royalist forces in Devonshire and Cornwall during the first phase of the English Civil War and in 1648 joined the court in exile in Paris as manager of the household of the duke of York (later James II). In 1658 he became a peer, and after the Restoration he received various offices.

Berkeley was one of the eight original proprietors of the Carolina colony (1663), and in 1664 he and Sir George Carteret were granted proprietary rights over New Jersey by the duke of York. Berkeley never visited the colonies, and in 1674 he sold his share of New Jersey to the Quakers for £1,000. He died on Aug. 26, 1678.

BERKELEY, bärk-lē, **Miles Joseph** (1803–1889), English botanist. He was born at Biggin Hall, near Oundle, Northamptonshire, on April 1, 1803. Educated at Christ Church, Oxford, he was ordained, became curate at Margate (Kent) and Market Harborough (Leicestershire), and subsequently was made vicar of Sibbertoft (Leicestershire).

Berkeley became a leading British authority on fungi and plant pathology and was especially well known for achievements in mycology. About 6,000 species of fungi were identified by him. Among his most important works was the section on fungi contributed to Smith's *English Flora* (1836). His *Introduction to Cryptogamic Botany* (1857) and *Outlines of British Fungology* (1860) were also important. He assembled an herbarium of more than 9,000 species, now at the botanical Kew gardens and regarded as one of the most noteworthy in the world. Berkeley died at Sibbertoft on July 30, 1889.

BERKELEY, bärk′lē, **Sir William** (1606–1677), American colonial governor. He was born at Bruton, Somersetshire, England. His father and brother were both interested in colonial settlements. Graduating from Oxford in 1629, he traveled on the continent for a year, and returned to a career as courtier, playwright, and merchant capitalist. In 1632 he was given a commission empowering him to trade with Canada (then claimed by England), and he seems to have invested in voyages there. He was knighted in 1639. In 1641, Berkeley was appointed governor of Virginia, where he arrived the following year. The governor soon made himself popular. He sought to advance the economic welfare of the colony by introducing the cultivation of a variety of new products, especially silk, which he hoped would displace the exclusive reliance of the colony on tobacco growing. After the Indian massacre of 1644, he led the settlers in an Indian war that ended in the capture of the chieftain Opechancano and subdued Indian power in Virginia for 30 years. In relations with England he sought greater freedom of trade for the colony.

After the execution of Charles I in 1649, Berkeley led the Virginians in defying Parliament but capitulated when a parliamentary commission, sent in 1652 to subdue the colony, offered favorable terms. In 1659, with the Restoration imminent, the Virginians asked Berkeley to resume the government. He did so provisionally. The next year Charles II recommissioned him as royal governor, and he remained in office until 1677.

Berkeley's second administration saw the development of the "Greenspring Faction," a group of favorites named after the governor's plantation near Jamestown. Berkeley's favors to this group in the way of land grants and political offices helped to develop hostility against him. Since tobacco prices were low in the 1660's and 1670's, most Virginians were suffering economic distress. This situation heightened their resentment against governmental officers and specifically against the members of the governor's council, who were exempt by law from taxation.

Grievances against the faction might have found a means of redress through the colony's representative assembly, the House of Burgesses. But Berkeley kept the same burgesses in office from 1661 to 1676 by failing to hold a new election. The burgesses became subservient to the faction and ceased to be truly representative.

When a new outbreak of Indian attacks occurred in 1676, Berkeley proposed to erect a series of forts. The people, disgusted with the taxes that these forts would require, undertook a quicker and cheaper method of dealing with the Indians. Under the leadership of a young newcomer, Nathaniel Bacon, a group of settlers undertook a punitive expedition without authorization of the government. Bacon, returning, demanded that the governor commission him to carry on further expeditions.

Berkeley's response was to declare Bacon a rebel. At the same time he issued writs for a new election of burgesses. When the election was held, Bacon won a seat from Henrico County and appeared at Jamestown in June 1676 with 600 of his followers. Berkeley pardoned him, and in the face of this show of force gave him the commission he asked for.

A month later, after Bacon had departed, Berkeley again denounced him as a rebel. But when the rebel turned his attention from the Indians to the governor, Berkeley was obliged to flee. Fortunately for Berkeley, Bacon died of a fever on Oct. 26, 1676. In the ensuing months Berkeley gradually regained control. By the time an investigating commission arrived from England early in 1677, the rebellion was over.

Berkeley exacted a harsh revenge. In spite of a royal proclamation of amnesty and in spite of orders to return to England, he remained in Virginia until May 5, 1677 and secured the execution of a total of 23 rebel leaders. Within a few weeks of his arrival in England, Berkeley died at Twickenham, Middlesex, on June 9, 1677.

Although Berkeley's reputation has suffered from his vindictiveness in crushing Bacon's Rebellion, the investigating commission found no serious complaints against his conduct of the government before the rebellion began.

Berkeley was the author of a play, *The Lost Lady* (1638), and of *A Discourse and View of Virginia* (1663).

E.S. Morgan, *Yale University*
Further Reading: Washburn, Wilcomb, *The Governor and the Rebel* (Chapel Hill, N.C., 1957).

BERKELEY, bûrk′lē, a city in California, is in Alameda County, on the east shore of San Francisco Bay, 8 miles (13 km) east of San Francisco. It is the seat of the main campus of the University of California, one of the largest educational institutions in the world. Berkeley has been called the "City of Homes," and about 60 percent of its dwellings are single-family units. But lack of land has brought the construction of high-rise apartment buildings.

The city rises from the bay to an elevation of 1,320 feet (402 meters) in the Berkeley Hills section to the east, which is mostly residential. The "flat" section of the city, near the shore, is industrial, with manufactures of soap, toiletries, drugs, bakery products, printing inks, and structural aluminum.

Berkeley enjoys a temperate climate the year round. The mean average yearly temperature is 57.1° F (14° C), snow is rare, and the average annual rainfall is 22.12 inches (56.1 cm). Most of the rain falls from November to March.

The University of California has eight other campuses in the state, but it originated in Berkeley in 1864 as the College of California. The Lawrence Radiation Laboratory, where the first fully working model of the cyclotron was built in 1931, is an important scientific adjunct to the university. The university library contains more than 3 million volumes.

Much of the city's character is determined by the thousands of students and hundreds of faculty members at the university. Students demanding "free speech" in university affairs and advocating student participation in such causes as civil rights and the antiwar movement have been spectacularly active on the Berkeley campus.

Other educational facilities in Berkeley include the California School for the Blind and Deaf, a business college, and six theological schools.

Berkeley has had a city manager since 1923. There is also a mayor and city council. The Berkeley police department has won a number of national awards for efficiency. Members of the force are required to have had at least two years of college education. Berkeley sponsors a mental health program and a family planning clinic.

BERKELEY'S skyline is marked by the Sather Tower, a landmark at the University of California.

Another municipal program, "Workreation," which is designed to provide meaningful summer employment and recreation for young people, has been in operation since 1952 and has gained international recognition.

History. The region now occupied by Berkeley was probably first reached by Europeans in 1772, when a 16-man expedition led by Lt. Pedro Fages and Father Juan Crespi, a Franciscan priest, traveled north along the east shore of San Francisco Bay. In 1820 the Spanish governor of California granted the land to Luis María Peralta, who in 1840 gave to his son José Domingo Peralta the tract that now includes Berkeley. A group of San Francisco businessmen bought José Peralta's holdings in 1853, gradually reselling the land for homesteads and farms. During the gold rush period in the early 1850's, large sections of Berkeley were occupied by squatters.

In 1864 the College of California moved from Oakland to a site at the foot of the Berkeley Hills. The college trustees named the town Berkeley in honor of the 18th century philosopher George Berkeley, bishop of Cloyne, Ireland. In 1867, Berkeley was selected as the site for the California School for the Blind and Deaf. The following year the legislature decided to establish a state university at Berkeley. When its newly constructed buildings were ready for occupancy in 1873, the university also took over the campus of the College of California.

In 1878, Berkeley became an incorporated town, and in 1895 a new town charter was adopted. The community expanded as improvements in transportation in the late 19th century —a shoreline railroad and trolley lines—made it more accessible. The disastrous earthquake and fire in San Francisco in 1906 drove many people to the cities across San Francisco Bay, and Berkeley's population rose rapidly—from 13,214 in 1900 to 40,434 in 1910. The city operated under the commission form of government from 1909 to 1923, when the council-manager type was adopted. A fire swept a large part of the northern section of the city in 1923. Nearly 600 buildings were destroyed, and 4,000 people were left homeless. Recovery was rapid, however, and Berkeley continued to grow. By 1940 the population was double that of 1910, and further increases during the years of World War II brought it over the 100,000 mark. Population: 116,716.

FRANK J. DEMPSEY, *Berkeley Public Library*

BERKELEY, bûrk'lē, an unincorporated village in northeastern Illinois, is in Cook County, west of Chicago, near the Du Page County line. Berkeley has railroad shops and yards, but it is chiefly a residential suburb of Chicago. Population: (1960 census) 5,792; (1964 special census) 6,152.

BERKELEY, bûrk'lē, a suburban city in Missouri, is in St. Louis County, 12 miles (19 km) northwest of St. Louis. It is a rapidly developing community, with three parks and a number of general businesses. The Lambert-St. Louis Municipal Airport and McDonnell Aircraft Corporation are situated nearby. An attempt by Berkeley to annex the area containing these facilities was voided by a circuit court in 1960. Berkeley was incorporated in 1937. Population: 19,743.

BERKELEY SPRINGS, bûrk'lē, a town in West Virginia, is a health resort and the seat of Morgan County. It is situated near the Potomac River, about 100 miles (160 km) northwest of Washington. It is famous for its warm mineral springs with supposed curative properties. The colonial owner of the site, Lord Fairfax, gave the springs to the people of Virginia in 1756. The town was founded in 1776 as *Bath* (still the official name, although the name of the post office is Berkeley Springs), and the springs were reserved in a park. Besides resort facilities, the town has canneries and other small industries. Berkeley Springs Sanitarium (state-owned) and Morgan County War Memorial Hospital are here. Population: 944.

BERKELIUM, bûr'klē-əm, is a man-made chemical element that exists only in radioactive forms prepared by nuclear reaction. Its symbol is Bk, and its atomic number is 97. Berkelium is similar to the rare-earth elements (atomic numbers 57-72) in its properties; its oxidation states are like those of cerium, and its relationship to its neighbors is comparable to the corresponding relationship of its homologue, terbium (atomic number 65).

Berkelium was discovered by S.G. Thompson, A. Ghiorso, and G.T. Seaborg in December 1949 at the Lawrence Radiation Laboratory of the University of California at Berkeley. It was named after the city of Berkeley.

Properties. It is meaningless to speak of the atomic weight of berkelium, since atomic weight is defined in terms of naturally occurring isotopes.

About 10 isotopes are known, with masses ranging from 243 to 250 and with half-lives ranging from about 4 hours to about 1,500 years. The most common isotope is ^{249}Bk (half-life about 1 year), but it is difficult and expensive to prepare even in moderate amounts.

Most of the chemical properties of berkelium can be understood by comparison with the properties of the rare-earth elements. The elements in the region of berkelium are often called the second rare-earth or actinide series. The relative changes in atomic radii between the adjacent members of the two series are quite similar. The tripositive oxidation state is the typical oxidation (valence) state and the most stable one under ordinary conditions for both series of elements. Bk^{+3}, like the rare earths, forms water-soluble nitrates, chlorides, and sulfates.

Production. Berkelium is produced by three types of nuclear reactions: charged-particle bombardments; irradiations with neutrons (slow time scale) in high-flux nuclear reactors, followed by beta decay; and irradiations with neutrons (fast time scale) in a thermonuclear device.

STANLEY G. THOMPSON
Lawrence Radiation Laboratory

BERKLEY, bûrk'lē, is a residential city in southeastern Michigan. It is situated 10 miles (16 km) northwest of Detroit and forms part of the suburban area of Greater Detroit. Berkley was incorporated as a village in 1925 and as a city in 1932. It is governed by a mayor and council. Population: 22,618.

BERKMAN, bûrk'mən, **Alexander** (1870–1936), Russian-American anarchist and author. He was born on Nov. 21, 1870, in Vilnyus, Lithuania, which was part of Russia. By 1887, when he emigrated to New York City, he had been influenced by Russian nihilists. He soon became involved with radical labor groups in New York, and was associated with Johann Most and, especially, Emma Goldman, leading anarchists. Berkman gained notoriety in 1892 at the time of the Homestead strike when he attempted to assassinate steel magnate Henry C. Frick. For this he served 14 years of a 22-year prison sentence. With Emma Goldman he opposed conscription during World War I. Both were arrested in 1917 for obstructing the draft and, after serving two years in prison, were deported to Russia. Disenchanted with the Bolshevik regime, Berkman left in 1922, spending his remaining years in Germany and then in France. He died a suicide in Nice on June 28, 1936. His books include *Prison Memoirs of an Anarchist* (1912) and *The Bolshevik Myth* (1925).

BERKSHIRE, bärk'shir, is a county in southern England. Its greater part is situated in the basin of the Thames River, west of London. The Thames forms its northern boundary. Dairy farming is important, and the famous Berkshire hogs are raised in the county. Industries include the manufacture of agricultural implements, carpets, and biscuits, and boat-building.

The county town is Reading. There are major nuclear research centers at Harwell and Aldermaston. The Royal Military Academy is at Sandhurst. Ascot Heath, near Ascot, is a famous racecourse. Among the county's archaeological features is the figure of a horse, 374 feet (114 meters) long, cut at an unknown date in the side of a chalk hill in the Valley of the White Horse. Berkshire's area is 725 square miles (1,878 sq km). Population: (1961) 504,154.

BERKSHIRE FESTIVAL, bûrk'shēr fes'tə-vəl, a summer music festival held annually at Tanglewood, an estate in Lenox, Mass. Staffed by the Boston Symphony Orchestra, with visiting performing artists, it is the outstanding American institution of its kind.

It was originated in 1934 by Henry K. Hadley, who conducted three concerts at each of the first two seasons. In 1936 the sponsors invited the Boston Symphony Orchestra and its conductor Serge Koussevitsky to perform. Since then, this orchestra has performed, and its incumbent conductor has directed the festival.

In 1937, Mrs. Gorham Brooks of Brookline, Mass., donated her Tanglewood estate to the festival. In 1938 the tent used for performances was replaced by an open-sided steel "shed," designed by Eero Saarinen to seat 6,000 persons. A theater–concert hall and chamber-music hall, with 1,200 and 500 seats respectively, were subsequently built. Annual patronage exceeds 200,000. The Berkshire Music Center, established in 1940, provides training and performing opportunities for advanced students in instrumental work, conducting, opera, and composing.

BERKSHIRE HILLS, bûrk'shēr, the highlands of western Massachuetts, in Berkshire County. They are part of the Appalachian system and consist of ranges running north and south from the Vermont border to the Connecticut border. The name is sometimes restricted to the Taconic Mountains in the west, along the New York border, but often is used to include the Hoosac Range east of the Hoosic River and the ridges east of the Housatonic River. The average elevation is 1,500 to 2,300 feet (455 to 700 meters). The highest peak is Mount Greylock (3,505 feet, or 1,068 meters), which is also the highest point in Massachusetts. The hills, which are wooded and have many lakes and streams, are an all-year resort area. Lenox, Stockbridge, and Great Barrington are important centers.

BERLAGE, ber'lä-gə, **Hendrik Petrus** (1856–1934), Dutch architect and city planner, whose buildings, together with those of Frank Lloyd Wright, inaugurated the purist movement called functionalism.

Berlage was born at Amsterdam on Feb. 21, 1856. He received his architectural training in Amsterdam and Zürich and later settled at The Hague. At the Hague, after a short period of conformity, he became a leader of functionalism, which arose as a reaction against the eclectic neo-Gothic style of P.J.H. Cuypers. The construction in Amsterdam, in 1897–1903, of Berlage's bourse (stock exchange), with its solid wall of brick decorated with natural stone, marks the beginning of a new architectural movement in the Netherlands that had international influence.

Characteristics of Berlage's work were his extensive use of brick as a building material, simplicity and severity of line, and an honest construction derived from the use to which the building was to be put—without style imitation. His interests also extended to furniture and glass. In his later years he was adviser on city planning to The Hague, Amsterdam, and Rotterdam. He died at The Hague on Aug. 12, 1934.

BERLE, bûr′lē, **Adolf Augustus, Jr.** (1895–1971), American lawyer, teacher, economist, diplomat, and public official. He was born in Boston, Mass., on Jan. 29, 1895. He graduated from Harvard with honors in history when he was 18, received an M.A. the next year, and at 21 became the youngest graduate in the history of Harvard Law School. Soon after, he embarked on a highly successful career as a corporation lawyer in New York and, beginning in 1927, also taught corporation law at Columbia Law School.

Berle entered public affairs in 1933 as an economic expert in Franklin D. Roosevelt's original "brain trust." From 1934 to 1937 he worked simultaneously as a planner for the federal government and the city of New York. He laid the groundwork for the Securities and Exchange Act and for the reorganization of New York City's government under Fiorello La Guardia. As U.S. assistant secretary of state for Latin American affairs from 1938 to 1944 he implemented the "good neighbor" policy and promoted postwar agreements for collective security. In 1945–1946 he was ambassador to Brazil. He was President Kennedy's special adviser on Latin America. Berle died in New York City on Feb. 17, 1971.

Of Berle's books, *The Modern Corporation and Private Property* (1932), written with Gardiner C. Means, was the most influential.

BERLICHINGEN, ber′likн-ing-ən, **Götz von** (1480–1562), German knight. His given name also appears as *Gottfried*. He was born at Jagsthausen, in Württemberg. In 1498 he fought for Emperor Maximilian I in Burgundy and about 1500 formed an independent force of men. He lost his right hand in 1504 at the siege of Landshut and in its place wore an iron one. He was known thereafter as *Götz of the Iron Hand*. Constantly engaged in quarrels with his neighbors, he was twice put under the ban of the empire for disregarding the edict against private warfare.

After the outbreak of the Peasants' Revolt in 1525, he was forced by the rebels to lead them, but in 1526 the empire acquitted him of guilt for his part in the revolt. He was imprisoned by the Swabian League (1528–1530) when a promise of safe conduct was broken. In 1542 he took part in the Hungarian crusade against the Turks, and in 1544 he fought for the emperor against France. He died near Mosbach on July 23, 1562. Berlichingen wrote an autobiography that presents an entertaining picture of 16th-century Germany. The autobiography was the source of Goethe's tragedy *Götz von Berlichingen*.

BERLIN, bûr′lin′, **Irving** (1888–   ), American popular-song writer. He had no formal musical education, but his inexhaustible melodic inventiveness produced successful songs for over half a century. Some of the most enduring of his approximately 800 songs came from his scores for musical shows.

He was born *Isadore Baline* in Russia on May 11, 1888. He went with his family to the United States when he was five and lived in a poor neighborhood on New York City's Lower East Side. While in his teens, Berlin sang for small change in saloons along the Bowery and worked as a singing waiter in Mike Salter's Café. His first published work was the lyrics for *Marie from Sunny Italy* (1907). In 1909 he became staff lyricist for Ted Snyder's music company, and the next year he appeared in vaudeville and

in the musical *Up and Down Broadway*.

The most successful song hit of Berlin's early career was *Alexander's Ragtime Band* (1911), which popularized ragtime throughout the United States. The first musical for which he wrote the complete score and lyrics was *Watch Your Step* (1914). As a sergeant in the infantry during World War I, he organized, wrote, and starred in *Yip-Yip Yaphank* (1918). The following year he founded the firm of Irving Berlin, Inc., to publish his music.

On Jan. 4, 1926, Berlin, a Jew, married Ellin Mackay, daughter of Clarence H. Mackay, a leading Roman Catholic layman and president of Postal Telegraph. Mackay at first opposed the marriage on both social and religious grounds, and the wedding was one of the most publicized events of the 1920's.

Berlin wrote scores for many Broadway musicals during the next 40 years. His World War II armed services show, *This Is the Army* (1942), won him the U.S. government's Medal for Merit in 1945. His greatest theatrical success came the next year with *Annie Get Your Gun*. This was revived in 1966 with Ethel Merman, the original Annie, and the addition of a new song. Other hit musicals included *As Thousands Cheer* (1933), *Louisiana Purchase* (1940), and *Call Me Madam* (1950). He also wrote scores for films, and a number of his Broadway shows were filmed.

Berlin gave a new direction to the popular song—away from set formulas and toward greater freshness and originality. Many of his best compositions, such as *Always* and *All Alone*, are simple melodies of tender sentiment. Some of his most memorable are rousing songs like *God Bless America*. One showstopper, *There's No Business Like Show Business*, became virtually the battle hymn of the American theater.

BERLIN, bûr-lin′, **Sir Isaiah** (1909–   ), English social historian and philosopher. He was born in Riga, Latvia, on June 6, 1909. When he was 11 years old, he emigrated with his parents to England. He won a scholarship to Oxford University, where he received a B.A. degree in 1931 and an M.A. degree in 1935. He taught at Oxford from 1932, and in 1957 received the chair of Chichele professor of social and political theory. In 1966 he joined the faculty of the City University of New York as professor of humanities.

The problem of individual free will is a major concern in much of Berlin's writing. *Historical Inevitability* (1955), although not denying the validity of determinism, holds that determinist reasoning is irrelevant to the study of history. *Two Concepts of Liberty* (1958), which has been compared with the work of John Stuart Mill on the subject, clarifies Berlin's argument for the existence of "limited" free will. Berlin's other books include *Karl Marx; His Life and Environment* (1939) and *The Age of Enlightenment* (1956).

BERLIN, bûr′lin, a residential town in central Connecticut, is in Hartford County, 10 miles (16 km) southwest of Hartford. It includes the villages of East Berlin and Kensington. Plastics, lacquers, tools, zippers, and structural steel are manufactured. The first tinware in America was made here about 1740. Simeon North, an early pistol maker, and Emma Hart Willard, educator, were born here. Population: 14,149.

BERLIN

GEDÄCHTNISKIRCHE stands as a reminder of wartime destruction amid the modern buildings of West Berlin.

GERMAN INFORMATION CENTER

BERLIN, bər-lin', is the German city that was the capital successively of Brandenburg, of Prussia, and of a unified Germany. Berlin fell victim to the devastation of World War II and to subsequent disagreement among the victorious Allies. The war left Berlin—like Germany as a whole—divided. Only the eastern part of the City was able to maintain the normal functions of a capital, in relation to the contiguous territory of East Germany (German Democratic Republic); and even it suffered limitations imposed by residual Allied rights over the city and its approaches. West Berlin became a political exclave of West Germany (Federal Republic of Germany), to be approached only across 100 miles (160 km) of East German territory. Although the West German president has an official residence at Schloss Bellevue in West Berlin, and although in spite of East German protests both houses of the West German Parliament hold occasional sessions there, the western part of the city has had to see its effective capital functions transferred to Bonn.

A Divided City. The 29-mile (46-km) line separating the two parts of the city allowed relatively free movement until August 1961, when construction by the East Germans of the heavily guarded Berlin Wall restricted crossing to a few closely controlled points. The best known of these is the entry point for foreigners in the once-busy Friedrichstrasse, known as "Checkpoint Charlie." Normal movement for West Berliners across the 72-mile (115-km) boundary with East Germany had already been banned in 1952; from 1961, with rare exceptions, West and East Berliners were forbidden to meet each other.

At this stage the subway system was split, and the surface rail system, while run by the East Germans, was divided into two so far as the passengers were concerned. West Berlin has extended its subway system outward and has added north-south and east-west links which avoid East Berlin. A very few international expresses still run through both sections of the city, stopping at the Zoo station in West Berlin and at the Friedrichstrasse entry station and the East station in East Berlin. East German internal services are led tediously around the periphery of West Berlin; the old terminal stations on lines that pass through West Berlin are abandoned. The Berlin highway ring is well clear of the city, but much East German waterway traffic is obliged to pass through West Berlin, while West Berlin receives two fifths of its supplies, mostly heavy commodities like coal, by water through East Germany.

Rail traffic between West Germany and West Berlin is restricted to four routes across East Germany; the limitations of rail traffic are reflected in the fact that only just over a fifth of of West Berlin's supplies arrives in this way, less than half the quantity carried by trucks on the four permitted main roads, notably the highways from Hanover and Munich. Air transport along the three air corridors from West Germany is much favored for passengers and even for the more valuable freight, since it is free from East German control. Indeed, only the airlift to the three small West Berlin airfields at Tempelhof, Tegel, and Gatow kept West Berlin supplied with the basic necessities of life during 11 months of total blockade in 1948–1949. East Germany, with none of West Berlin's acute space restrictions, has been able to establish a large international airport at Schönefeld, just beyond the city limits.

Physical and Climatic Setting. Berlin stands on a plain of sandy glacial outwash covered by pine forest, and cut by a broad southeast-northwest depression within which flows the river Spree. On the eastern fringe of the city, in the neighborhood of Köpenick, and along the north-south course of the Havel through Spandau, glacial action has left behind chains of lakes that are today the favorite sailing and bathing places of the Berliners. In these same areas heavily forested glacial moraines provide the highest natural elevations in the city (the Müggelberge, 377 feet, or 115 meters), although these are exceeded by the 394-foot (120-meter) Teufelsberg, a hill of rubble from the bombed city that West Berlin has landscaped and equipped with ski jumps and other recreational features. Forests and lakes account for about a fifth of the land area of Berlin, and provide valuable excursion spots, especially for the West Berliners, who are penned into their "island" city. The Berlin climate is also claimed as a natural advantage: on the uninterrupted plains of Brandenburg there is a rapid interchange of maritime air from the North Sea and Baltic with continental air from farther east. The alternation is said to be particularly stimulating to intellectual activity. Berlin has an average temperature in January of 31° F (−0.7° C), in July of 66° F (18.7° C); its annual average rainfall is 23 inches (587 mm).

THE PEOPLE

The original 13th century German settlers of Berlin appear to have come from the area surrounding the Harz Mountains, from the lower Rhine, and even from Flanders. The subsequent rise of the city involved continual immigration from all parts of Germany and even from beyond. The 17th century saw the arrival of French Huguenot (Protestant) refugees, who formed a distinct and privileged community and contributed significantly to the expansion of manufacturing and commerce. The 19th and early 20th centuries brought massive immigration, especially from northern and eastern Germany. In its 74 years as the capital of a united country, Berlin was a magnet for men of talent and enterprise from all over Germany; hence, understandably, Berliners are characteristically restless and less tolerant of authority than most other Germans. These characteristics were perhaps manifested to their greatest, even excessive, extent in the period 1918–1933. Brilliant achievements in the theater (Max Reinhardt, Bertolt Brecht, and Erwin Piscator), music (Paul Hindemith), expressionist painting (Emil Nolde and Karl Hofer), architecture (Hans Poelzig, Max Taut, and Eric Mendelsohn), and science (Max Planck, Albert Einstein, Max von Laue, and Otto Hahn), coincided with inflation, unemployment, and street fighting between left- and right-wing extremists.

Many of the artistic and intellectual leaders emigrated after the Nazi seizure of power in 1933; but even so, Hitler was never at ease with the cosmopolitan and irreverent Berliners. The abortive July 1944 plot against Hitler was directed in part by Berliners. Berliners continued to demonstrate their independence in the first and only postwar free election for the entire city in 1946, as well as in the West Berlin blockade and the unsuccessful East Berlin revolt of 1953 against the East German government.

In 1939, Berlin had a population of 4.3 million, which by the end of World War II had sunk to 2.8 million. Postwar recovery brought the population to 3.2 million by 1946; thereafter the total did not greatly change, in marked contrast to all the other great urban centers of Europe. Because of the worsening political situation after the war, many of the younger and more active elements of the Berlin population did not return. The invigorating flow of new immigrants largely ceased, and the city was left with an ever-increasing proportion of the older age groups, especially women. In West Berlin there are 133 women to every 100 men (in West Germany as a whole, 110 to 100); 15% of the male population and 24% of the larger female population are over 65 (West Germany, 10% and 14%). One consequence of this age structure is that deaths markedly exceed births, and in the absence of renewed immigration West Berlin's population seems condemned to drift downward. The aging of the population will also have adverse economic effects through the shrinking of the work force and greater demands for pensions and social services.

The position in East Berlin is broadly similar; during the period of massive refugee movements out of East Berlin the population drifted gently downward; but there was a slight recovery after the building of the Berlin Wall in 1961. East Berlin's population structure is marginally more favorable than that of West Berlin, reflecting its more active connection with its hinterland. There are 127 women to every 100 men (East Germany, 119 to 100); 12% of the male population and 20% of the female population are over the age of 65 (East Germany, 13% and 17%).

DESCRIPTION OF WEST BERLIN

Bombing and subsequent ground fighting in World War II destroyed 40% of Berlin's residential capacity. Damage was particularly concentrated in and around the central administrative and business district, where at the end of the war 10 square miles (25 sq km) lay in ruins, forming a "dead heart" of the city. The boundary between East and West Berlin runs through this devastated area, leaving most of the historic center of the city as a peninsula of the eastern sector. Postwar rebuilding has had to adapt itself to the new situation, and both parts of Berlin have tended to turn their backs on the dividing line. Whereas East Berlin was in some measure able to re-create the historic center, West Berlin has created new administrative and cultural facilities dispersed throughout the city, although with a distinct central business district around the Kaiser Wilhelm Memorial Church.

The Central Area: South and West. West Berlin contains only the fringe of the historic central area. South of the foreigners' crossing point into East Berlin through the Berlin Wall (Checkpoint Charlie), the Friedrichstrasse, once the principal north-south traffic artery of Berlin, runs almost unused through the ruins of what was once a busy commercial and press quarter. The area is too remote from the new centers of West Berlin to attract much rebuilding. The position is similar at the Potsdamer Platz, at the southwest corner of the central area. Once this was the heart of the Berlin "West End," surrounded by department stores and fashionable restaurants,

with the greatest traffic density in continental Europe. Today it is dead and weed-grown, crossed by the blank face of the Berlin Wall. As an act of faith in the ultiimate reunification of the city, West Berlin is developing the area near the Potsdamer Platz as a new cultural center, with a concert hall, a national library, and a group of museums in which pictures, sculpture, and objects of art that have been dispersed throughout West Berlin will be progressively gathered together.

The Tiergarten. Unter den Linden, the major east-west axis of central Berlin, is barred by the wall at the Brandenburg Gate. Its western continuation through the Tiergarten is now known as the Street of June 17, in memory of those who fell in the 1953 East German rebellion; on its axis, a mile (1½ km) west of the Gate, is the Siegessäule (Victory Column), commemorating the Prussian military campaigns of 1864, 1866, and 1870–1871. The Tiergarten, once a swampy area along the course of the Spree, was later successively a hunting ground and a royal park. Such trees as survived World War II mostly disappeared into the stoves of freezing Berliners in the winter of 1945–1946, but the Tiergarten is now again a peaceful island of wood and water in the midst of the city.

Isolated by the Tiergarten from the main centers of West Berlin is the Reichstag (Parliament) building, burned in mysterious circumstances at the time of the Nazi seizure of power in 1933. Nearby is the similarly isolated Kongresshalle (Congress Hall), a gift of the United States to the 1957 Berlin International Building Exhibition. A further product of the exhibition is the rebuilt Hansa district, north of the Tiergarten, which contains buildings by such internationally famous architects as Alvar Aalto, Walter Gropius, and Oscar Niemeyer. The southern fringe of the Tiergarten was the favored district for embassies and legations before the war; these have not been replaced because of Berlin's loss of its functions as a capital city. In part this area is becoming a specialized quarter for hotels, which range from a Hilton to student hostels.

The Inner Suburban Ring. Except for the Tiergarten, the central area of the city is surrounded by a belt of dense urban development, typically consisting of 5-story apartment houses. The outer edge of this belt is marked approximately by the S-Bahn ring railroad and in West Berlin by the new ring highway. Even before 1939, department stores were spreading westward from central Berlin toward the Zoo (in the western end of the Tiergarten) and the Kaiser Wilhelm Memorial Church, and the same district had emerged as the main entertainment center. These trends have been accentuated by the division of Berlin. The ruined tower of the otherwise rebuilt Memorial Church now serves to remind passersby of wartime destruction. Around it cluster shops, restraurants, and movie houses, topped by soaring office towers; the district is a blaze of colored lights at night. Leading westward, the Kurfürstendamm, lined with sidewalk cafés, is now Berlin's main shopping street.

The middle-class inner suburbs southwest of the center of the city have taken over West Berlin's administrative functions, which were dispersed from the historic Town Hall in the eastern sector. The seat of the mayor, senate, and assembly is at the Town Hall on John-F.-Kennedy Platz in the Schöneberg district. In its tower hangs the "Freiheitsglocke," a copy of the Liberty Bell, paid for by the subscriptions of 17 million citizens of the United States and presented to the city in 1950. Other sections of the city administration and the important Berlin offices of the federal government are in the district of Wilmersdorf.

After crossing the Tiergarten, the main east-west axis of Berlin (here called the Bismarckstrasse) bisects the greatly expanded facilities of the Technical University and enters the enormous expanse of the Ernst-Reuter-Platz, surrounded by another group of new office towers. A memorial in the form of a 26-foot (8-meter) bronze sculpture of a flame commemorates Ernst Reuter, the mayor who led and inspired West Berlin in the difficult postwar years. Slightly further out, the restored Charlottenburg Palace, built between 1695 and 1790, is perhaps the finest surviving monument in Berlin to the building activities of the Prussian royal house. Today it houses another group of the Berlin museums, with important sections devoted to objects of art and to prehistory. The most popular exhibit is un-

BRANDENBURG GATE, built in 1791, stands in what is now the eastern sector of Berlin. A portion of the Berlin Wall can be seen in front of the gate, and in the foreground is a sign that reads: "Warning! You are now leaving West Berlin."

ACHTUNG!
Sie verlassen jetzt
WEST-BERLIN

doubtedly the head of Queen Nefertiti, perhaps the finest and most lifelike portrait in all Egyptian art.

North and south of the traditional center, the inner suburbs in areas like Wedding, Moabit, Kreuzberg, and Neukölln are predominantly working class in character. Here are the Mietskasernen ("rent barracks"), 5-story apartment houses that not only line the roads but fill the interiors of the blocks with a maze of dismal courts. The courts shelter hundreds of small and medium-sized factories of such industries as clothing, electronics, and printing. Wartime bombing provided the opportunity for some rebuilding and for the provision of much-needed open space, but hundreds of thousands of these dwellings remained substandard.

The Outer Suburbs. Beyond the S-Bahn ring railroad and the new ring motorway, development is more open in character. The larger industries of Berlin moved to this area in search of land for expansion; the greatest concentration is along the railway and the navigable Spree River running west to Spandau. Here, for example, is the Siemens electrical power plant; its associated workers' settlement, built by Gropius and others in 1928–1931, won international acclaim as a model of its kind. In the same area and dating from the same period are the radio center and several permanent exhibition halls. Hitler added the stadium and other sports facilities for the 1936 Olympic Games.

Throughout the outer suburban belt, formerly sleepy village streets have been transformed into busy shopping centers for the satellite residential areas that were merged in 1920 to form the present city of Berlin. The interwar years in particular saw the development of villa suburbs with tree-lined streets, like Dahlem. Dahlem has one of the world's finest museums for the ethnography and art of non-Western peoples. In a research institute in Dahlem, in 1938, Otto Hahn and Fritz Strassmann produced the first fission of the uranium atom. In 1948 this institute's buildings offered shelter to the students and teachers who migrated from the Humboldt University in East Berlin to establish the Free University of Berlin.

The outer districts of West Berlin still contain a surprising amount of open land, which since World War II has enabled the city to house thousands of families from the congested central districts. One of the most striking of the new developments is Buckow-Rudow, a "new town" for 50,000 people in the extreme southeast angle of West Berlin; it is linked to the city by an extension of the subway. The western limits of Berlin run along a belt of glacial hills, lakes and forests that is followed by the north-south course of the Havel. This magnificent recreation area is an invaluable antidote to the claustrophobic nature of life in West Berlin. On an island where the route to the west crosses the Havel lies the district of Spandau. In the Middle Ages, Spandau was a trading town. Older than Berlin itself, Spandau was absorbed by Berlin in 1920.

DESCRIPTION OF EAST BERLIN

The Historic Center. The medieval nucleus of Berlin consisted of two towns: Berlin north of the Spree and Kölln on an island to the south. During the 17th and 18th centuries Berlin, as the capital of Brandenburg and later as the capital of the kingdom of Prussia, expanded westward. New quarters were laid out on the axis of Unter den Linden, which at its western end passed through the triumphal arch of the Brandenburg Gate and into the Tiergarten. Today the blocked western end, dominated by the ornately gloomy Soviet Embassy, has little life.

Eastward along Unter den Linden, newly built restaurants and cafés, and the strolling passersby beneath replanted linden trees, give a much livelier air. At the eastern end, beyond the Humboldt University, a group of splendidly restored palaces around the Opera House gives some idea of the architectural quality of royal building in the capital; they are now mostly used by the university. There too is K. F. Schinkel's classically perfect Neue Wache (Guardhouse) of 1816–1818, now a monument to "Victims of Fascism and Militarism," and the earlier, baroque Zeughaus (Armory), now a historical museum. The principal group of museums is on the "Museum Island" across the southern branch of the Spree. The museums have lost some of their original contents, since those works that escaped wartime destruction by evacuation to the West have been retained in West Berlin. Great riches nevertheless remain, notably in the Pergamum Museum, which houses one of the world's great collections of classical art, dominated by the great Altar of Pergamum from the Greek colony in Asia Minor.

South of Unter den Linden, the former government quarter on Otto-Grotewohl-Strasse (formerly the Wilhelmstrasse) suffers from its isolation on the sector boundary, and has been little rebuilt. Hitler's Chancellery has been completely removed, and the ruins of the bunker in which he met his end lie buried beneath a deserted grass-grown mound. The center of government in East Berlin has tended to migrate back to the sites of medieval Berlin and Kölln, where the wartime ruins have given way to a spectacular rebuilding project. The ruins of the royal palace have been swept away to form the Marx-Engels-Platz, a great square that is the scene of many political demonstrations. It is overlooked on three sides by new government buildings; one of them—the official seat of the State Council—has built into it the balcony from which the revolutionary Karl Liebknecht proclaimed Germany a republic in 1918. The fourth side of the square is dominated by the battered hulk of the Berlin Cathedral, which was never the most highly esteemed of the city's buildings.

Beyond the complex of buildings about the Marx-Engels-Platz, a further great open space has been created stretching as far as the Alexanderplatz—clear across what had been the center of medieval Berlin. Overlooking this great square is the 19th century red-brick Berlin Rathaus (City Hall), the center of East Berlin's administration, as well as new shops and restaurants. Two buildings spring from the central open space: the Marienkirche, the oldest surviving church of Berlin, and the 1,180-foot (360-meter) television tower, which dominates not only East Berlin but the whole city. The area of central redevelopment terminates at the Alexanderplatz, East Berlin's major traffic node and a center of department stores and hotels. Running eastward from the modern center, rebuilding of very different type stretches along the former Stalinallee, now Karl-Marx-Allee and Frankfurter Allee. Built in the 1950's in the then-fashionable Moscow style as a narrow corridor of heavily ornate apartment buildings with shops beneath, the Stalinallee was more suited to political processions than to the age of the automobile.

East Berlin Suburbs. The crowded 19th century apartment buildings of East Berlin's inner suburbs suffered severely from bombing. Many were later cleared and replaced by groups of workers' apartments. Beyond, in the outer suburban belt, the mixture is much as in West Berlin. Industry clusters on the radiating water and rail routes, especially along the Spree southeast of the city's center. The suburban housing developments are more exclusively working-class than in West Berlin, but there are a few groups of villas for political and intellectual leaders, notably at Pankow. For Western visitors the best-known monument in this zone is the colossal Soviet war memorial in Treptow, built partly of colored marble from Hitler's Chancellery. Since the original Berlin Zoo is in West Berlin, East Berlin created a particularly fine one at Friedrichsfelde. The animals are grouped in natural geographical associations, and roam as freely as possible.

On the southeast fringe of the city a belt of glacial hills, forest, and lakes, (especially the Müggelsee) is a favorite excursion area for East Berliners, corresponding to the Havel lakes in West Berlin. Here too the formerly independent town of Köpenick, on an island at the confluence of the Dahme with the Spree, mirrors Spandau in the west. Unlike the West Berliners, the East Berliners can travel for recreation outside the city limits; likewise, facilities that are inappropriate within an urban area, like the airport, can spill over into the open country beyond.

ECONOMY

Until 1945, Berlin's economy was based on the city's role as the capital of a unified Germany and of Prussia, its largest state. Besides those employed in administration, a large portion of the working population served in banking, commerce, transportation, and communication, fields all closely related to Berlin's function as a capital city. In addition, Berlin was a major industrial region in its own right, depending not on any local raw materials but on the skill and enterprise of its inhabitants, on its own large internal market, and on good communications with all parts of Germany. Major industries included electrical equipment (half of Germany's total output), machine tools and other machinery, printing and publishing, fine chemicals, and clothing (particularly the fashion trade), together with the food and drink industries normal in great cities.

West Berlin. Wartime destruction and postwar division greatly altered the economic situation. In West Berlin the functions of a capital were lost, although well over half the employed popu-

CHARLOTTENBURG PALACE, now a public museum, houses collections from many periods of European art.

BERLINERS stand on a rubble pile near Tempelhof to watch a transport land during the 1948–1949 Berlin airlift.

lation is still in administration, commerce, transportation, and services. Great efforts have been made to build up West Berlin as a tourist and conference center; nevertheless, its ultimate self-sufficiency can only come through industrial development, which is being supported by massive assistance from the West German government and other Western sources.

Nearly all the materials required by West Berlin's industry must come from West Germany, which also purchases four fifths of its output. Most of the remainder is exported to Western countries—sales to East Germany and the Communist bloc are small. High-value products that can absorb the cost of transport have an obvious advantage. Not surprisingly, the manufacture of electrical equipment still is the most important industry, accounting for over a quarter of West Berlin's total output by value and over a third of its industrial employment, although West Berlin has lost its former predominance in this area because of the establishment of many new plants in West Germany.

Nearly as important by value of output are the food, drink, and tobacco industries, which serve chiefly the Berlin market, but which have been stimulated by federal tax concessions on spirits and tobacco processed in Berlin. Machine building, fine chemicals, and clothing all retain their importance for West Berlin's economy, but they have not been able to regain their prewar share of the West German market. Nevertheless, the growth rate of West Berlin's industry in the 1950's and 1960's was not very different from that of the Federal Republic as a whole. There is anxiety, however, over the aging and declining labor force, over the lack of investment in new plants, and over the tendency of firms to move their head offices and their technologically most advanced facilities to the west.

East Berlin. East Berlin still continues to function as a capital, so it is not surprising to find that nearly half of its active population is in administration, commerce, and the service industries, and that these sectors are steadily increasing in importance. About 30% of the active population is in industry, which has a branch structure broadly similar to that of West Berlin. Once more the electrical and electronics branches dominate, and East Berlin is by far the most important center of these industries in East Germany. Also important are machine tools, precision instruments, fine chemicals, photographic materials, and clothing. The importance of printing and publishing reflects the concentration of East Germany's considerable information services in the political capital. Because of the labor shortage and the lack of industrial land in East Berlin, it is official policy to concentrate on high-value, capital-intensive products that do not require massive supplies of raw materials.

GOVERNMENT

Berlin as we know it today was formed territorially in 1920, when the city of Berlin as it then stood was united with seven hitherto independent towns and a large number of rural communities to form a new unit of 340 square miles (882 sq km) in area. The enlarged Berlin was divided administratively into 20 districts (*Bezirke*), which still provide the lower tier of administration in both sectors of the city today. City administration was vested in the Berlin assembly and the Magistrat, a city cabinet or administrative board. The postwar division of the city gave 12 districts to the Western powers and 8, including the Central District, to the Soviet Union.

West Berlin. Although Berlin is normally described as the capital of Germany, it has effectively lost that function as regards West Germany. West Berlin, according to the city constitution of 1950, is in practice a constituent state (Land) of the Federal Republic, though it has simultaneously the administrative powers appropriate to a city. The residual Four Power occupation status prevents complete assimilation of Berlin into the Federal Republic of Germany. Berlin's representatives in the Federal Parliament in Bonn do not vote, while federal legislation is not valid in West Berlin until formally adopted by the city.

West Berlin is ruled by a freely elected Abgeordnetenhaus (House of Representatives), which in turn elects the Regierender Bürger-meister (chief mayor) and the senate. The members of the senate are in charge of the various branches of the city administration. Each district has its own elected assembly, district mayor, and district administration. Although the districts have populations as great as major cities in West Germany, their powers are distinctly less, since in a continuous urban area like West Berlin control over such functions as police, traffic control, economic development, and city planning must obviously be retained at the center.

East Berlin. East Berlin is the capital of the German Democratic Republic (East Germany), established in 1949. In practice the status of the city government resembles that of the districts (*Bezirke*) into which East Germany was divided in 1952. Certain differences have arisen —partly from the special needs of administering a completely urbanized area, partly from lingering remnants of Four Power status. For example, the East Berlin representatives to the East German Parliament (Volkskammer) are indirectly elected by the East Berlin Stadtverordnetenversammlung (assembly). Election to the assembly is by single list. The assembly elects the Magistrat, an inner cabinet, which is presided over by the Oberbürgermeister.

Under the system of "democratic centralism," the Magistrat must act under the guidance and control of the central government; on the other hand, great emphasis is placed on participation in local government by the citizens, who act through special commissions. The political organs of the East Berlin Districts (Stadtbezirke) repeat this pattern at the next lower level. At all levels of administration, parallel organs of the Socialist Unity (Communist) party stimulate and control the activities of the elected members and officials.

HISTORY

Organized human occupation of the Berlin region can be traced back at least as far as the reindeer hunters at the close of the Ice Age (about 9000 B.C.), but agriculture began only after 3000 B.C. with immigrants who possessed Neolithic techniques. The Iron Age saw the arrival of Germanic tribes, but after 650 A.D. these were replaced by Slavs, whose activities centered in the valleys and the waterways. The Slavs of the Spree Valley had their fortified centers at Köpenick, which thus greatly antedates Berlin itself in development. The main center of the Havel Slavs was Brandenburg, but they also occupied the crossing point at Spandau. Spandau acquired greater importance in the course of the medieval German advance east of the Elbe, when for a time, from about 1160, it appears to have been a frontier fortress and trading post. It developed into a town earlier than Berlin, and remained an important trading center until the close of the Middle Ages.

Unlike the Slavs, the Germans did not cling to the waterways, but spread into the low sandy plateaus between the rivers, establishing their villages wherever the land was good enough. At this time a crossing of the Spree for a south-north land route became necessary. At the heart of what is now Berlin the Spree Valley was relatively narrow and was uncomplicated by the lakes that lie to the east and west, and here the twin settlements of Berlin and Kölln grew, apparently from the close of the 12th century. The first documentary reference to Kölln on its island in the Spree dates from 1237; Berlin proper was first mentioned in 1244. An agreement of 1307 confirmed the merger of the two towns for purposes such as defense and trade. Formal union came in 1432. The twin towns prospered through trade, notably in the grain and timber of the Mark Brandenburg. In the confusion of late medieval times the towns were able to achieve substantial freedom from outside control.

Berlin and Brandenburg. A new era began in 1415 with the investiture of the Hohenzollern Frederick I as elector of the Mark Brandenburg. As elsewhere in Germany in this period, a process of territorial consolidation under the princes led to attacks on the freedoms of the towns. Berlin was not exempt from this movement. Dissension among the citizens gave Frederick II the chance to intervene, and his success in establishing control over Berlin was symbolized in 1443 by the palace he began to build on the Kölln island, astride the wall that hitherto had defended the liberties of the inhabitants.

The Protestant Reformation spread rapidly among the people of Brandenburg and Berlin, and after careful consideration of the political and economic advantages involved, it was duly accepted by Elector Joachim II in 1539. Later the adoption of Calvinism by Elector John Sigismund in 1613 led to divisions both in the ruling house and among the people. These dissensions were soon swallowed up in the greater disaster of the Thirty Years' War. Berlin was not involved in actual military operations, but the material demands of a succession of occupying armies, the interruption of trade, and the visitations of pestilence were a heavy burden, and population declined sharply.

Berlin and Prussia. After the Thirty Years' War, Berlin took on the characteristic aspect of a princely capital. At first the medieval walls were replaced by an elaborate ring of fortifications with 13 great bastions. The city could not long be confined within these narrow limits, however, and from the end of the 17th century the electors (kings of Prussia from 1701) created a new, aristocratic Berlin to the west, lying north and more particularly south of the grand triumphal axis of Unter den Linden. Most of the surviving historic buildings of central Berlin date from this period. Frederick the Great (reigned 1740–1786) had particularly sweeping plans for the creation of great buildings and dramatic vistas. Unfortunately his prolonged involvement in war curtailed his building operations, although it did raise Berlin to a new status among the European capitals.

Berlin as an electoral and later a royal capital was almost completely dependent on the palace—politically, economically, and socially. Court officials of all kinds and officers of the garrison became the leading element in the population. The demands of the court and of the new standing army for clothing and weapons stimulated manufacturing, in which religious refugees from France, Switzerland, and the Palatinate were prominent. Royal support fostered learning and the arts: the Academy of Sciences was founded in 1700 under the influence of Leibniz, the University in 1810 through the efforts of Wilhelm von Humboldt.

The last two decades of the 18th century were a period of peace and prosperity for Berlin, in which the atmosphere of the Enlightenment

EAST BERLIN nursery-school children take the air on Karl-Marx-Allee, a spacious thoroughfare that was formerly called Stalinallee.

flourished. The ideas of the French revolutionaries were eagerly received, but the city's later occupation by Napoleonic troops was a severe check to its development. However, this occupation brought forth as a reaction a great wave of romantic nationalism and a demand for liberty. These were submerged by a restoration of conservatism after 1815. Much the same was true of the Berlin uprising in 1848; the vacillating Frederick William IV was forced to honor the dead of the uprising before the Berlin Palace, and a Prussian National Assembly met for a time; but there was no lasting effect. Not liberalism but nationalism was to be the dominant force in Germany; as Prussia unified more and more of the country, so Berlin became ever more important, until in 1871 it became the heart of the German Empire. Between 1870 and 1914 the city's population rose from 826,000 to over 2 million, and Berlin became the largest single industrial town of Germany.

1918–1945. At the end of World War I, the monarchy was dissolved in a left-wing revolution, which ushered in a period of prolonged political instability; the shooting of the Communist leaders Karl Liebknecht and Rosa Luxemburg in the Tiergarten in 1919 was not the last instance of political murder in the city. Unemployment reached 235,000 in the 1923 inflation and exceeded 600,000 after the world economic crisis of 1929. In such conditions the streets of the working-class quarters of Berlin were the scene of bitter fighting between extremists of left and right, both sides happy to see the destruction of the social democratic and liberal supporters of the Weimar Republic's democracy. The Nazis (National Socialists) never obtained a majority of votes in Berlin, but they were nevertheless able to seize power in 1933. Left-wing leaders were quickly killed or imprisoned, and many of the intellectual and artistic leaders of the brilliant 1920's emigrated. On "Kristallnacht" (Nov. 9–10, 1938) the burning of synagogues, the plundering of shops, and attacks on individuals heralded the destruction of Berlin's Jewish community.

Berlin had to pay a bitter price for National Socialism. Air bombardment in World War II destroyed 20% of all buildings and damaged a further 50%. For two terrible weeks at the end of April 1945 the last reserves of old men and boys defended the city in fruitless street fighting.

Hitler killed himself in his shelter just before the German troops capitulated on May 2.

The Division of the City. In the postwar period Berlin continued to be the victim of wider political developments. The city was divided into 4 sectors of occupation, reflecting the division of Germany as a whole. At first there was a central administration from the Berlin City Hall in the Soviet sector, but the Soviet-backed scheme for a union between the Social Democratic and Communist parties was rejected in the Western sectors. The new Socialist Unity party was in fact decisively defeated in the only free postwar elections for the whole city, after which relations between the Soviet authorities and the elected city administration deteriorated steadily.

Meanwhile discord among the occupying powers was also increasing in Germany as a whole. The decision to adopt the new West German currency for West Berlin was the signal for the imposition of a Communist blockade of Berlin on June 24, 1948; it lasted 11 months. Simultaneously, Communist demonstrators drove out the elected members of the city assembly, and over the next few months the various branches of the city administration were divided between east and west. The success of the Berlin Airlift in frustrating the blockade, and the extraordinary tenacity of the population, allowed West Berlin to remain independent, but it was progressively sealed off from East Germany. A moment of great danger came with the abortive East Berlin rebellion in 1953, but the Western powers prevented any action that might have extended the struggle. The same attitude was taken to the building of the Berlin Wall, which finally sealed off West Berlin in 1963. Clearly the Western powers were prepared to strive to maintain West Berlin's independence, but not to allow it to become the occasion of conflict that might lead to a general war. Berlin appeared to be condemned to indefinite division.

Population: of West Berlin (1967 est.) 2,-173,000; of East Berlin (1966 est.) 1,079,000.

T. H. ELKINS
University of Sussex, England

Further Reading: Plischke, Elmer, *Government and Politics of Contemporary Berlin* (New York 1963); Pounds, Norman J. G., *Divided Germany and Berlin* (Princeton 1962); Smith, Jean Edward, *The Defense of Berlin* (Baltimore 1963); Windsor, Philip, *City on Leave: A History of Berlin 1945–1962* (New York 1963).

BERLIN, bûr′lin, is an industrial city in northern New Hampshire, at the northern edge of the White Mountains. It is situated on the Androscoggin River, 115 miles (185 km) north of Concord. The city is surrounded by forests and has a plentiful supply of water power. Its leading industry is paper and wood pulp. Other products are cotton, rubber goods, and artificial leather. Berlin is a center for skiing, and a winter carnival is held each year.

The city's site was settled in 1821, largely by French Canadians and Norwegians, as a logging camp called *Maynesborough.* The name *Berlin* was adopted when the town was chartered in 1829; the city was incorporated in 1897. Government is by city manager. Population: 15,256.

BERLIN, ber′lin, is a city in east central Wisconsin, in Green Lake and Waushara counties, 96 miles (155 km) northwest of Milwaukee. It is situated in an agricultural and dairying region. Among Berlin's industrial products are leather goods and furs, metal products, and machinery. The first settlement was made in 1846, and the city was incorporated in 1857. Berlin is governed by a mayor and council. Population: 5,338.

BERLIN, Free University of, a coeducational institution in West Berlin, Germany. It was founded in 1948 to accommodate those faculty members and students of Frederick William University who had been cut off from their studies when the Russians closed the eastern sector of Berlin, in which the parent university was located. (See BERLIN, HUMBOLDT UNIVERSITY OF.) The Free University is supported financially by the city and federal governments.

Medicine has the largest faculty; next is that of philosophy, which includes theology, liberal arts, music, drama, and education. Others are mathematics and natural science, economics and social science, veterinary medicine, and law. There are also several institutes. The university and institute libraries house 835,000 volumes. In the mid-1960's there were 13,000 students, including 700 from foreign countries.

BERLIN, Humboldt University of, coeducational institution in East Berlin, Germany, supported by the East German government. Before the division of Berlin into eastern and western sectors following World War II, the university was known as *Frederick William University of Berlin.* When the city was divided, the main university buildings fell within the Russian zone of occupation, and it now serves East Germany. It was renamed Humboldt University in 1948 in honor of Wilhelm von Humboldt, Prussian minister of education when the university was established. Members of the faculty and student body in West Berlin joined the Free University of Berlin, opened in 1948 in the American sector (see BERLIN, FREE UNIVERSITY OF).

Frederick William University was founded in 1809 and opened in 1810. It soon began to build a worldwide reputation for the quality of its teaching and the excellence of its faculty. Before it was 10 years old, it had such teachers as Barthold Georg Niebuhr, August Böckh, August Immanuel Bekker, and Georg Wilhelm Friedrich Hegel. Later, Leopold von Ranke, Johann Gustav Droysen, Hermann von Helmholtz, Jacob and Wilhelm Grimm, Karl Richard Lepsius, Karl Ritter, Rudolf von Gneist, Friedrich Karl von Savigny, Rudolf Virchow, and other scholars added to its reputation.

A second generation of scholars included such men as Robert Koch, Emil Du Bois-Reymond, Heinrich von Sybel, Ernst Curtius, Theodor Mommsen, Ulrich von Wilamowitz-Moellendorff, Wilhelm Dilthey, Adolf von Harnack, Ernst Troeltsch, Hans Lietzmann, Gustav Adolf Deissmann, Walther Hermann Nernst, and many others. There were departments of theology, philosophy, law, mathematics, medicine, natural science and other sciences, with 895 professors and teachers and approximately 12,000 students in 1939. The university also included postgraduate schools, institutes of physics, medical clinics, museums, and the observatory in Babelsberg. Unique and famous was the scientific organization of the Kaiser Wilhelm Gesellschaft, whose celebrated Institute of Physics was directed by Albert Einstein from 1914 to 1933.

The university was supported by the state, under control of the minister of education. Men and women of all nationalities were admitted. The university library consisted of over 679,000 volumes together with a very large number of theses and other papers. The chief library facilities for students, however, were in the Prussian State Library, immediately in front of the university library. The state library contained 2,400,000 volumes, 64,000 manuscripts, and 250,000 musical works.

The university was closed during World War II and was reopened in 1946. As presently constituted, Humboldt's faculties reflect the ideology of East Germany. They comprise philosophy (which encompasses the liberal arts), mathematics and natural science, law, economics, education, theology, medicine, veterinary medicine, agriculture and horticulture, forestry, pre-university studies for workers and peasants, social science, modern languages, and Marxism-Leninism. There are also 200 institutes, clinics, and divisions. Library facilities include over 1,700,000 volumes, and there are museums of mineralogy and petrography, geology and palentology, and zoology. In the 1960's student enrollment totaled about 12,000.

BERLIN AIRLIFT, an air supply operation mounted by the United States, Britain, and France in 1948–1949 to counter a Soviet blockade of the western sector of Berlin.

After World War II, Berlin was an island city in the Russian zone of occupied Germany. A four-power agreement guaranteed access to it from the three western Allied zones of Germany, including use of three, 20-mile-wide air corridors. Early in 1948, however, the Soviet Union began hampering surface traffic to the western sectors of Berlin. A complete shutdown of roads, rails, and waterways occurred on June 22, 1948.

The United States reacted swiftly. On June 26, the U.S. Air Force was directed to use all available C-47 transports to airlift 80 tons of food and medicine to West Berlin from Wiesbaden. The airlift soon was designated the Combined Airlift Task Force, known as "Operation Vittles" to Americans and "Operation Plainfare" to the British. French forces provided some ground support and other aid.

Additional aircraft were sent from the United States. By mid-July some 150 aircraft were flying a daily total of 1,500 tons of supplies. In September, C-47's were replaced almost entirely by C-54's having three times the load capacity. Ultimately the U.S. force exceeded 300 aircraft. Britain used both military and civilian aircraft, many smaller than the C-54.

Americans flew from Frankfurt's Rhein-Main Air Base and neighboring Wiesbaden Air Base. Later they operated from Fassberg and Celle in the British zone. Tempelhof was the main U.S. field in West Berlin, while the British used Gatow. Later a field was built at Tegel in the French sector to relieve congestion at Tempelhof.

Coal constituted approximately two thirds of all tonnage airlifted. Food came next. An unofficial operation, called "Little Vittles," began in July 1948. It consisted of aircrew members dropping candy to children at Tempelhof. Operating on a 24-hour schedule with many landings at three-minute intervals, the airlift reached its climax in mid-April 1949 with 1,398 deliveries totaling 12,940 tons in a single day.

The Soviets raised the blockade on May 12, 1949. The airlift continued, however, until reserve stocks in West Berlin were satisfactory. The last airlift C-54 flew from Rhein-Main to Tempelhof on Sept. 30, 1949. Altogether, 2,325,-000 tons of supplies had been airlifted to West Berlin in 277,569 flights.

The cost of the operation was high; operations and support costs amounted to $181,300,000. Although the accident rate was less than half the average of the entire Air Force, 31 Americans were killed in 12 crashes during the airlift.

CHARLES E. LUCAS, *"Air Force News Service"*

BERLIN CONGRESS, bûr-lin' kong'grəs, in 1878, the third great diplomatic congress of the 19th century (after Vienna, 1814–1815, and Paris, 1856). Berlin was unique because it obliged a great power, Russia, to renounce important parts of a treaty it had made after winning a war—in this case with Turkey.

The congress dealt with the Eastern Question, which became acute in 1875–1876 as the Slavic Balkan peoples revolted against Turkish rule. The rebels had the sympathy of the European powers, especially of Russia, where Pan-Slavic sentiment was vigorous. When the Turks refused to accept reform schemes prepared by the six powers, Russia went to war against Turkey in 1877, and was victorious. The war ended in the Russo-Turkish peace treaty of San Stefano on March 3, 1878, which took Bessarabia, Kars, Ardahan, and Batum from Turkey. It also enlarged the territories of Serbia and Montenegro, gave the Dobruja to Rumania, and declared all three of these countries independent of Turkey. Most important, it established a large autonomous Bulgaria touching the Aegean Sea.

San Stefano made Austria fearful of Russian influence on the Balkan Slavs. Austria also objected to the establishment of a large Bulgarian state athwart its path of economic penetration to the Aegean. Britain opposed increased Russian influence near its Mediterranean route. Under Austrian and British pressure, Russia consented to a congress, which German chancellor Bismarck agreed to chair in order to ward off an Austro-Russian conflict that might involve Germany. Britain meanwhile gained Russia's secret agreement on May 30, 1878, to abandon plans for creating a large Bulgarian state and Austria's secret agreement on June 6 to place limits on a smaller Bulgaria. Britain also forced on Turkey on June 4 a secret treaty allowing Britain to administer Cyprus.

The congress, which opened on June 13, concluded with the signing of the treaty on July 13, 1878. The treaty split Bulgaria into three layers. The northern one was to be autonomous; the middle, called "Eastern Rumelia," was to have a special regime; and the Aegean littoral was to be a regular Turkish province. Austria was permitted to occupy Bosnia and Herzegovina, with further right to garrison the sanjak of Novibazar (Novi Pazar) separating Serbia and Montenegro. Most other provisions of San Stefano were confirmed. Greece was promised territorial extension, achieved in 1881.

Austria and Britain were the chief gainers from Berlin. The Turks salvaged something, and Germany maintained the peace that Bismarck sought. Russia, however, was irritated, and none of the Balkan peoples were really satisfied.

RODERIC H. DAVISON
George Washington University

BERLINER, bûr'li-nər, **Emile** (1851–1929), American inventor, who developed a telephone transmitter and a gramophone. Berliner was born in Hanover, Germany, on May 20, 1851. He emigrated to the United States in 1870, studied electricity and acoustics at Cooper Union, and experimented with the telephone. In 1877 he obtained a patent on an improved telephone transmitter. The patent was bought by the Bell Telephone Company, and he became an inspector for the company. In 1887 he received a patent for a gramophone that played a flat-disc record. This patent was purchased by the Victor Talking Machine Company, which was bought by the Radio Corporation of America (RCA) in 1929.

Berliner's other work includes the design of an airplane engine (1908) and the development of acoustic tiles for soundproofing (1925). He died in Washington, D.C., on Aug. 3, 1929. See also PHONOGRAPH; TELEPHONE.

BERLINER ENSEMBLE, ber-lē'nər an-säm'bəl, a theater company in East Berlin, cofounded in 1949 by Bertolt Brecht (q.v.) and his wife, Helene Weigel, and supported by the government of East Germany. It was universally recognized as the most influential theater company in Germany after World War II.

The Berliner Ensemble was conceived shortly after Brecht returned to Germany from the United States in 1947, as a laboratory for Brechtian experiments in theater production. Devoted largely to performances of Brecht's own plays, which were frequently directed by Brecht and his wife, the company soon became famous as the home of "epic theater"—the all-encompassing but ill-defined term for Brecht's antiromantic, often pageantlike productions.

By 1954, when the company moved into permanent headquarters at the Theater am Schiffbauerdamm, the ensemble was lavishly staffed with more than 150 full-time performers and equipped with stage machinery unrivaled elsewhere in Germany. Thereafter the company toured widely in Europe and was acclaimed by important critics in the West as one of the most accomplished ensembles in the world. However, some audiences complained of a slackening of dramatic tension to the point of boredom—a result partly of the company's rejection of theatrical make-believe. Miss Weigel continued as director after Brecht's death in 1956.

Hector Berlioz, French composer (1803–1869).

BERLIOZ, ber'lē-ōz, **Hector** (1803–1869), French composer, whose important innovations influenced almost every subsequent composer.

Early Life and Career. He was born *Louis Hector Berlioz* at La Côte-St.-André on Dec. 11, 1803, the son of a country physician. While still a child, Hector showed his musical capacities as a self-taught performer and composer. His father, who was well educated, indulged the taste, but he hoped his son would become a physician and sent him to Paris in 1821 to study medicine. Hector soon neglected medical school and spent his days studying scores in the Conservatoire library and his nights attending the opera. In 1823 he was accepted as a student by the then-famous opera composer Jean François Lesueur. In 1826, Berlioz registered at the Conservatoire, where his training included the excellent course in counterpoint given by the Czech master, Anton Reicha.

At the Conservatoire, Berlioz wrote exercises and cantatas. Some of the latter (for example, *Cléopâtre*) are still worthy of performance. In 1830, after four trials, he won the coveted Grand Prix de Rome. Before each competition, the head of the institution, Luigi Cherubini, had to certify a student's competence in fugue, harmony, and composition. However, Cherubini was unfriendly to Berlioz, and erroneous statements have been made about Berlioz' "lack of training" or "incomplete mastery of forms."

The fact was that Berlioz was a precocious genius, eager to develop a technique suited to his own powers. As early as 1825 he wrote a mass, which he had performed at his own expense at the Church of St.-Roch. Dissatisfied with it, he destroyed the work. He also wrote the astonishing choral piece, *Huit scènes de Faust,* based on Goethe's play. At Rome he met Felix Mendelssohn, with whom he developed a lifelong friendship, although Berlioz' admiration of the other's music was not returned.

Mature Compositions. Before leaving Paris for Rome, Berlioz put the finishing touches to a large-scale symphonic work, *Symphonie fantastique* (*Episode de la vie d'un artiste*), and had it performed in December 1830. The work was epoch-making, not, as is commonly thought, because of the "program" which accompanied it, but because of the power and novelty of the melody, form, harmony, and orchestration. Franz Liszt became a devoted disciple of the young French master, and Robert Schumann, studying the score from Liszt's piano reduction, introduced Berlioz and his work to musical Germany.

From 1832 to 1848, Berlioz displayed indefatigable energy in the pursuit of a multiple career as composer, music critic, conductor, and traveler. The great works of this period include the symphony with viola, *Harold en Italie* (1834); *Requiem Mass* (1837); the opera *Benvenuto Cellini* (1838); the dramatic symphony *Roméo et Juliette* (1839); *Grande symphonie funèbre et triomphale* (Funeral symphony, 1840); and the dramatic legend *La damnation de Faust* (1846), a recasting of *Huit scènes.*

Meanwhile, Berlioz toured Germany, Russia, and Austria and paid a visit to England. Though his success was occasionally very great with the public, his main impact everywhere was on the younger generation of composers. The revolution of 1848, as well as the cool reception of his *Damnation de Faust* by the Parisians, drove Berlioz to move to England, but he returned to France to complete and produce his great *Te Deum* (1849), which was to be played much later in America on two important occasions—the opening of Carnegie Hall in 1891 and the Montreal celebration of Allied victory in 1945.

After the *Te Deum,* Berlioz, who was then serving as chief music critic for the *Journal des débats,* finished three works (both poems and music) that he had been contemplating almost since the beginning of his career. The first was the Christmas oratorio *L'enfance du Christ* (*The Infant Christ,* 1854), notable for its use of old modes and its quiet "ancient" coloring. The second was the Virgilian two-part music drama, *Les Troyens* (*The Trojans,* 1856–1859), comprising *La prise de Troie* (*The Fall of Troy*) and *Les Troyens à Carthage* (*The Trojans in Carthage*). The third was the exquisite comic opera *Béatrice et Bénédict* (1862), based on Shakespeare's *Much Ado About Nothing.*

Berlioz used his willpower at the expense of his health, and by middle age he had shown signs of illness. After 1848, discouragement at the increasing difficulties of securing a hearing for his music, the death of many persons close to him, and the pressure of financing his own performances undoubtedly hastened his end. He died at Paris on March 8, 1869.

Influence. A pioneer in many fields, Berlioz fully accomplished his task. He left in the dramatic genre a dozen models whose influence on music is not yet exhausted and, indeed, not yet everywhere understood. He created a new and distinctive form of melody and devised the technique for its appropriate development by modifying established forms. In his *Treatise on Orchestration* (1844), he presented the theory and example of an orchestral style from which almost every subsequent composer has borrowed something. Modern French music is especially indebted to him, both directly through Charles François Gounod and Camille Saint-Saëns, who were Berlioz' unofficial pupils, and indirectly through the Russian school, which acknowledged his influence and repaid the debt, with interest, by influencing Claude Debussy.

Berlioz' musical works, excepting *Benvenuto Cellini* and *Les Troyens,* were republished in 20 volumes by Breitkopf and Härtel under the editorship of Felix Weingartner and Charles Malherbe in 1900. This so-called complete edition is far from faithful and must be used with caution. His critical works and letters have been partly collected in French and in German translation. His *Memoirs*, first published posthumously in 1870 and originally translated into English by Rachel and Eleanor Holmes, were reedited by Ernest Newman in 1932. The composer's *Soirées de l'orchestre* was translated by Jacques Barzun as *Evenings With the Orchestra* in 1956.

JACQUES BARZUN
Author of "Berlioz and His Century"

Bibliography

Barzun, Jacques, *Berlioz and His Century: An Introduction to the Age of Romanticism* (New York 1956).

Berlioz, Louis Hector, *Memoirs*, tr. by Rachel and Eleanor Holmes, rev. by Ernest Newman (New York 1932).

Berlioz, Louis Hector, *Evenings With the Orchestra*, tr. and ed. by Jacques Barzun (New York 1956).

Turner, Walter J., *Berlioz, His Life and Work* (London 1934).

Wotton, Tom S., *Berlioz: Four Works* (New York 1929).

Wotton, Tom S., *Hector Berlioz* (New York and London 1935).

For Specialized Study

Boschot, Adolphe, *Hector Berlioz*, 3 vols. (Paris 1906–13; 1-vol. ed., Paris 1919).

Masson, Paul M., *Berlioz* (Paris 1923).

Prod'homme, Jacques Gabriel, *Hector Berlioz, sa vie et ses oeuvres* (Paris 1905).

BERMAN, bûr'mən, **Eugene** (1899–1972), Russian-American painter and stage designer, who was a leader of the "neoromantic" or "neohumanist" movement of the 1930's. This brief movement, which also included Christian Bérard and Pavel Tchelitchew, aimed at defending the human and spiritual content of art against the intellectualization of abstract painting.

Berman was born in St. Petersburg (now Leningrad) on Nov. 4, 1899, and studied art there and in Germany before settling in Paris in 1919. The development of his dreamlike, melancholy style was strongly influenced by surrealism and by the metaphysical painting of Giorgio de Chirico.

In the 1930's he was recognized as an outstanding stage designer. After moving to the United States in 1937, he designed for American ballet companies and for New York's Metropolitan Opera. From 1957 he lived in Rome, where he died on Dec. 14, 1972.

BERMEJO, bār-mā'hō, **Bartolomé,** Spanish painter, who was active in Aragon and Catalonia in the second half of the 15th century. He is also known by a Latin form of his name, *Bartolomeus Rubeus.* He was born in Córdoba sometime before 1470, but very little is known of his early background and training. Between 1474 and 1477 he was active in Aragon, where he is credited with having introduced the technique of oil painting. He died sometime after 1495.

Flemish influence is apparent in Bermejo's earlier works, such as *Santo Domingo de Silos* (1474; Prado, Madrid), which has an architectural background in the manner of North European painting. Later works, including the *Pietà* (1490) in the Barcelona cathedral, show a romantic Italian influence in the use of chiaroscuro and landscape background. Bermejo may have visited Italy, where there is a signed *Virgin With Donor* in the cathedral at Acqui. Other works attributed to him include *Adoration of the Kings* (Capilla Real, Granada), *Santa Engracia* (Gardner Collection, Boston), and *Madonna and Child* (Prado).

BERMUDA, bər-mū'də, is a small group of islands in the Atlantic Ocean, about 700 nautical miles (1296 km) southeast of New York City. The islands constitute a British colony. They have an area of 21 square miles (53 sq km) and a population (1970) of 52,700, more than half of whom are Negroes. The capital is Hamilton. The Bermudas are also called the *Somers Islands.*

Because the warm Gulf Stream of the Atlantic Ocean passes northwest of Bermuda, the islands have a mild and healthy climate, with no wet and dry seasons. Their climate and beauty attract large numbers of tourists. About 400,000 people visit Bermuda each year. Most of them are Americans, who arrive and leave by air.

Physical Features. Bermuda is made up of about 120 limestone islands and islets and many smaller islands set close together, roughly in the shape of a fishhook. The seven main islands are connected by bridges and a causeway, which form a continuous route of 22 miles (19 km). Relatively few of the islands are inhabited. The largest are Main Island, St. George's, St. David's, Somerset, and Ireland. The highest point is about 260 feet (79 meters) above sea level. The islands generally have a terrain of gently undulating hills covered with luxuriant vegetation and surrounded by brilliant blue ocean.

Military Importance. Bermuda is the most important group of islands protecting the North American coast between Newfoundland and the Bahamas, except for parts of the Atlantic coastal plain such as Long Island. The nearest landfall is Cape Hatteras, 640 miles (1,030 km) west of Bermuda. The islands have long been important as a naval base because of their strategic location. They became particularly vital during World War II. In 1941 the United States obtained from Britain a 99-year lease on an airbase and a naval base in Bermuda.

A U.S. satellite-tracking station completed in the early 1960's in Bermuda has played an important part in the launching of manned orbital space flights.

Economy. The tourist industry has been the main support of the colony since 1905, but industry, agriculture, and trade are important sources of income.

The main industries on the islands are ship repairing and the manufacture of concentrated essences, pharmaceutical products, and beauty preparations.

About 4 percent of Bermuda's land is under cultivation. Onions, potatoes, and green vegetables are produced. Subtropical fruits, such as bananas, papaws, oranges, and grapefruit, also are grown. There is considerable egg and milk production. Easter lily bulbs and flowers are exports.

Domestic exports, mainly concentrated essences, bring in between $1½ and $2 million a year, but reexports are valued at about $25 million a year. The principal reexport items are pharmaceuticals and fuels and stores for ships. Bermuda's biggest customers are Britain, the Netherlands, and the United States.

The colony must import a large proportion of its food, clothing, fuel, and other necessities. Most of these supplies come from the United States and Britain. The volume of imports for local use generally exceeds the volume of exports and reexports.

The currency, weights, and measures of Bermuda are British, but U.S. currency is widely circulated. Customs duties provide the bulk of the government's revenue. There are no taxes on income, land, or inheritance.

Transportation. For a long time, carriages and bicycles were the only means of transportation allowed on the islands. The use of automobiles became legal in 1946, but their size and power are restricted. There are no railroads. There is air service to cities in the United States and to Canada, the West Indies, and Europe. Shipping lines run to North America and Europe.

Education. Primary education is free and compulsory. In the 1960's, about 12,000 pupils were enrolled in public and private primary and secondary schools. More than 2,000 of these were attending secondary schools.

Government. A new constitution was introduced in 1968. Under the provisions, Bermuda's administrative head is the governor, who is appointed by the crown. He has special responsibility for external affairs and matters of security. There is a bicameral legislature, which consists of an upper house (the Legislative Council) of 11 members appointed by the governor, some with the advice of the government and opposition leaders, and a lower house (the House of Assembly) of 40 members elected in 2-member constituencies by universal adult franchise. In the general election of May 1968, the United Bermuda party won 30 seats, and its leader, Sir Henry Tucker, was named Bermuda's first government leader.

The governor is assisted by an executive council consisting of the government leader and at least six other members of the legislature. The governor must take the advice of the council in all matters except those that are especially reserved to him.

History. The history of the islands is linked closely with that of the United States. The islands are named after the Spanish sea captain Juan Bermúdez who, by 1515, had sighted them at least twice. The official name of Somers Islands was given them in honor of the British Admiral Sir George Somers, whose ship, the *Sea Venture,* carrying settlers to Virginia, put in to Bermuda in 1609 after being damaged by a hurricane.

At that time the islands were uninhabited. Pigs, set ashore by the Spaniards years earlier, were running wild. These provided food for the shipwrecked passengers of the *Sea Venture.* A species of pigeon, called cahow, was also plentiful, as were wild turtles. Somers built two small vessels on the islands, stocked them with cahows, turtles, live pigs, and dried fish. He landed the passengers and food at Jamestown, Va., in 1610. The food ended a famine caused by an Indian siege.

Reports of Bermuda received by the Virginia Company in England were so glowing that the company promptly had its charter amended to include the islands, naming them Virginiola, and in 1612 dispatched a party of settlers to colonize them. Three years later the Virginia Company sold the new colony to "the Governour and Company of the City of London for the Plantacion of the Somer Islands" for £2,000, and Daniel Tucker was selected from the successful colony in Virginia as its governor. The colony was surveyed; St. George's and St. David's and part of the main island were reserved as company land, and the remainder was divided into eight tribes (parishes). The land in each tribe was laid out in plots for leasing to settlers, who were required to buy supplies from, and sell their produce to, the company.

Order No. 212 in the Laws of the Bermuda Company (1622) provided for the maintenance of a large piece of land in Virginia, which was made over to the Bermuda Company by the Virginia Company because there was less land in the islands than was supposed at the time of the sale. This land, in Chesterfield County, Va., is still known as the Bermuda Hundred.

On Aug. 1, 1620, the second British colonial legislature (the first was that of Virginia) met in the parish church of St. George's, Bermuda, under an ordinance of the Bermuda Company. So began the self-government of the islands.

The land of the colony was rented to the settlers, who gradually became owners by purchase. With this independence, resentment gradually rose against the restrictions on trade imposed by the Bermuda Company. From 1670 on, many complaints and petitions were sent to the crown, finally resulting in the trial of the company in London for "many misdemeanors and misgovernments by them committed." Judgment was given against the company on Nov. 27, 1684, and its charter was revoked. The legislature continued to sit, so that Bermuda claims the continuity of its legislature from Aug. 1, 1620. The crown appointed as its own governor in 1687 the same man who had served as the Bermuda Company's last governor.

The Bermudians had not succeeded in establishing an agricultural industry; the cultivation of tobacco had proved a failure. However, the building of swift ships with "Bermuda rig," which could outsail Spanish and French privateers, enabled the islanders to create a valuable intercolonial trade. Salt ponds for evaporating salt from sea water by the heat of the sun had been built at Turks and other West Indian islands, and several hundred men and a major part of Bermuda's shipping were engaged in this trade. Salt was taken to Newfoundland and Nova Scotia to be exchanged for salt fish. The fish were traded in the West Indies for sugar and rum, which were bartered for barrels of salt beef and pork in the American colonies or for clothing and hardware in England.

In 1649 the Bermudians repudiated the government of Oliver Cromwell and proclaimed Charles II as their king. They reluctantly accepted Cromwell's rule after the conquest of Barbados, but joyfully took a new oath of allegiance to the crown on the Restoration in 1660.

The most difficult period of Bermuda's history was undoubtedly during the American Revolution. Though sympathetic to the principles of the American protest, the islanders remained loyal to the crown. Britain, however, prohibited trade with the American colonies. Since Bermuda subsisted on provisions from the American colonies, this edict brought real suffering to its people and demoralized its whole economy.

The islanders applied to the American Congress for a renewal of trade, but Congress answered that supplies would be sent only in exchange for firearms and ammunition. It was known that a substantial quantity of powder was in the magazine near the government house north of St. George's, and the Continental Army was in dire need of powder. Accordingly, on the night of Aug. 14, 1775, this powder was taken secretly from the magazine by Bermudians sympathetic to the American cause, rolled to Tobacco Bay, and carried in whaleboats to two

Left: The Bermuda ocean front. Towering cumulus clouds roll over a purple sea which changes to turquoise in the shoal water along the beach. Gray coral cliffs are crowned with verdure the year round.

BERMUDA

Below: Bermuda homes, often single-storied, are built of white coral sandstone. Their walls are either limewashed a sparkling white, or colorwashed pink, yellow, blue green, or ochre. The roofs of coral sandstone are regularly limewashed.

Below: A garden of Easter lilies. Bermuda annually exports vast quantities of these beautiful flowers, as well as lily bulbs, to the mainland. New York City is the chief market for Bermuda lilies.

BERMUDA Cycling down quaint Shinbone Alley in St. George, old port town and original capital of Bermuda.

small vessels that had entered the bay by a little-known passage through the reefs and were lying in readiness for the cargo. It was this powder that enabled George Washington to compel the British to evacuate Boston. On Nov. 22, 1775, the Continental Congress resolved to permit exports to Bermuda and on July 24, 1776, the Congress once more allowed Bermuda vessels to trade with American ports. In November 1777, Bermuda ships were exempted from capture by American privateers.

Shipping often has influenced the history and fortunes of Bermuda. The islands' shipbuilding industry received an impetus from the American victory in the Revolutionary War, and by 1789 more than 175 ships were registered at Bermuda. The War of 1812 brought disaster. So many Bermuda ships were taken by American privateers that the island merchants were virtually ruined.

During the American Civil War, St. George's became a center of activity for blockade runners. Cotton, selling in the South at 4 to 6 cents a pound, was bringing 60 cents a pound in England. For a successful run, a ship's captain received $5,000, and chief officers and chief engineers earned $2,500 each. Seamen and firemen made $250 a voyage, and a pilot received $3,750. But after the Civil War, the islands' shipping virtually was eliminated by the competition of large merchantmen. When shipping finally lost its supremacy in Bermuda's economy, agriculture became the islands' mainstay until the development of the tourist industry.

Though predominantly British in custom and tradition, Bermuda has close ties with the United States. These links were reinforced by the establishment of American bases on the islands during World War II and by increased trade between the countries since the war.

The commemoration of a small episode in American history exemplifies the close relations between Bermuda and the United States. The churchyard at St. George's contains a tablet to the memory of Richard Sutherland Dale, a son of one of John Paul Jones' officers. Dale was wounded while serving aboard Stephen Decatur's frigate *President*, which was captured off Long Island on Jan. 15, 1815, by the British frigate *Endymion*. Brought to Bermuda, Dale was nursed in Stennett's Hotel but died of tetanus. He was buried in the graveyard of the church. For many years his grave has been decorated on Memorial Day by the parish rector.

TERRY TUCKER
Author and Editor, Specialist in Bermudiana
SIR STANLEY SPURLING
Former Member of Legislative Council, Bermuda

Bibliography
Beebe, William, *Nonsuch: Land of Water* (New York 1935).
Fodor, Eugene, ed., *Caribbean, Bahamas, and Bermuda* (New York, annually).
Hannau, Hans W., *Bermuda in Full Color* (New York 1970).
Hayward, Walter B., *Bermuda, Past and Present*, 2d rev. ed. (New York 1933).
Henry, Marguerite, *Bermuda in Story and Pictures* (Chicago 1946).
Roberts, Walter A., *Lands of the Inner Sea, the West Indies and Bermuda* (New York 1948).
Strode, Hudson, *Story of Bermuda*, 2d ed. (New York 1946).
Tweedy, Mary J., *Bermuda Holiday*, rev. ed. (New York 1958).
Wilkinson, Henry C., *Bermuda in the Old Empire* (New York 1950).
Wilkinson, Henry C., *The Adventurers of Bermuda*, 2d ed. (New York 1958).
Williams, Ronald J., *Bermudiana* (New York 1946).

BERMUDA GRASS, bər-mū′də, is a low, spreading perennial grass common in the warmer regions of the world. It grows by means of rhizomes (underground stems) and extensive creepers. The upright stems are flat and up to 16 inches (39 cm) tall, each one bearing four to six flowering spikes. The leaves are flat, narrow, and long, with a conspicuous ring of white hairs on part of each leaf sheath. Native to Eurasia and Australia, Bermuda grass was introduced into the United States. It may be raised on lawns, or in fields for hay, but elsewhere it is a weed, called wire grass. Known botanically as *Cynodon dactylon*, Bermuda grass belongs to the family Gramineae.

BERMUDA TRIANGLE, bər-mū′də, or *devil's triangle*, a triangular region encompassing about 140,000 square miles (305,000 sq km) in the Atlantic Ocean with the corners of the triangle roughly at the southern Virginia coast, the Bermuda islands, and the Florida Keys. Between 1945 and 1972 more than 100 vessels and aircraft and more than 1,000 seamen and airmen have disappeared in this region, leaving no trace. In many cases no distress message was received, heightening the mystery. All of the disappearances have been substantiated by U. S. Navy and Coast Guard records. Citing lack of evidence, the Navy has taken no official stand as to whether the disappearances were more than coincidence.

The Library of Congress had made available a bibliography of published material dealing with the Bermuda triangle mystery. This work, the *Bermuda Triangle Bibliography*, was compiled in 1972 by Deborah K. Blouin and Larry Kuscher of the University of Arizona Library.

BERN, bern, is the capital and fourth-largest city of Switzerland. It is also the capital of Bern canton. *Bern* is the German form of the name; the French form is *Berne*.

The canton of Bern, located in the west central part of the country, is the largest in population and the second largest in area among the cantons of Switzerland. In the south is the Bernese Oberland, an alpine region known for its high peaks, glaciers, and beautiful valleys. The central part of the canton comprises the fertile foothills of the Alps and the area surrounding the city of Bern. In the north is the Seeland, or lake region, which includes the area around the Lake of Biel and extends into the Jura. Agriculture, cheese making, cattle raising, watchmaking, and tourism are among the chief means of livelihood in the canton.

The city of Bern is situated 60 miles southwest of Zürich and 80 miles northeast of Geneva. Most of the people are German-speaking Protestants. Bern is one of the most beautiful cities in Switzerland. It has kept much of its medieval appearance, and the snow-covered Alps provide scenic vistas. The city has comparatively little industry, but it is the headquarters of several international organizations, notably the International Telecommunications Union, the Universal Postal Union, and the International Copyright Union.

Places of Interest. The old part of the city is situated in a bend of the Aar River, on a ridge 100 to 150 feet above the stream. High bridges link it with the modern section on the east bank. Most of Bern's buildings are made of local sandstone, which gives the city a uniform appearance.

BERN has retained much of its medieval appearance. Rising above the old section is the *Münster*, the city's Gothic church.

Its distinctive charm comes from its many fountains, towers, arcaded sidewalks, and stately mansions.

Bern's brilliantly colored and finely carved fountains contrast with the severe lines of its old houses. Some of the fountains date from the 1500's. Often they have imaginative themes. The Ogre Fountain, one of the most popular, depicts a fairy tale monster devouring his victims.

The traditional landmark of Bern is the clock tower. In 1250 the tower was the western gate of the city. An astronomic clock with human and animal figures that move was added in 1530. Father Time, a crowing cock, bears, and other figures appear when the hour strikes.

The pride of the city is its Gothic Münster, begun as a cathedral in the early 1400's. The main door has elaborate carvings depicting the Last Judgment. The church also has beautiful stained-glass windows, the finest dating from the 1400's.

The square in front of the town hall is one of the best-preserved medieval plazas in Europe. The hall was begun in the early 1400's and is the seat of the municipal and cantonal governments.

Bern has a number of interesting museums, including one on Alpine climbing and another on the history of weapons. There are also museums of art, natural history, and local history.

Bern's theaters perform opera and classical and modern plays. Evening concerts of vocal and organ music are given in the main church. The medieval play *Everyman* is performed in the church square. But night life in Bern is limited, and the city is regarded as one of the most stolid capitals of Europe.

History. Bern was founded in 1191 by Duke Berchtold V of Zähringen. According to legend the duke built the city in gratitude to heaven for his surviving an attack by bears while he was hunting. *Bären*, the German word for bears, may be the origin of the city's name, but scholars link the name with the Italian city of Verona, where some of Bern's early settlers came from. Nevertheless, the bear is the emblem of the city, and the symbol is encountered everywhere.

Bern was chartered as an imperial city of the Holy Roman Empire by Emperor Frederick II in 1218. It joined the Swiss Confederation in 1353. A fire gutted the city in 1405, and much of the present old town dates from the reconstruction that took place soon afterward. From the 1500's to the early 1800's Bern was dominated by a patrician oligarchy that built many of the city's fine mansions.

Bern became the capital of Switzerland in 1848 and expanded greatly thereafter. A new section of broad avenues and imposing buildings was built to house the government services. In the 1900's the city spread out further into suburbs with modern houses and apartment buildings. Population: (1960) of the city, 163,172; of the canton, 889,523.

BERN, University of, bern, a coeducational institution in Bern, Switzerland. It was founded in 1528 as a school, advanced to the status of an academy in 1805, and was reorganized as a university in 1834 under the control of the canton of Bern. There are faculties of theology, law and economics, medicine, veterinary medicine, philosophy and history, and natural science and over 50 institutes and clinics. The language of instruction is German. Library facilities include the university and city libraries and special departmental libraries. Graduates must pass a state examination before receiving their degrees. Enrollment in the mid-1960's approximated 2,500, including about 300 foreign students.

BERNADETTE, ber-nà-det', **Saint** (1844–1879), the popular name for *St. Marie Bernarde*, a French girl who was instrumental in founding the shrine at Lourdes, France. Born at Lourdes on Jan. 7, 1844, the eldest of six children of François and Louise Soubirous, she was christened Marie Bernarde but was called Bernadette. Her father, a poor miller, could afford little education for her. She was asthmatic but was a cheerful and obedient girl.

On Feb. 11, 1858, while Bernadette was gathering firewood near the rock of Massabielle, the vision of a graceful lady dressed in white and carrying a rosary appeared to her in a grotto. The lady reappeared many times during the following days. It was not until February 25, however, when she instructed Bernadette to "drink and wash in the spring," that the local clergy gave any credence to the story. Before the day when this command was given, only a trickle of muddy water came from the rock; later the spring produced a steady flow of water.

The lady, who said to Bernadette "I am the Immaculate Conception," requested that a chapel be built on the site. After the Roman Catholic authorities were satisfied that Bernadette's visions of the Blessed Virgin Mary were valid, a basilica was built. By the time it was consecrated in 1876, Bernadette had entered the Convent of Notre-Dame at Nevers. She had sought only obscurity from the day of the lady's 18th and final appearance on July 16, 1858. Bernadette became a novice in 1866 and took perpetual vows in 1878. Bernadette always considered herself a mere intermediary. During one of her many interrogations she compared herself to a broom: "Our Lady used me. They have put me back in my corner. I am happy there." She died on April 16, 1879, at the convent in Nevers.

A larger church, dedicated to the Holy Rosary, was built at Lourdes in 1901 to accommodate the many pilgrims who sought cures from the waters of the spring. Many cures have been validated by a medical board that the church maintains there. In 1907, Pope Pius X created the feast of the Appearances of Lourdes, which is celebrated on February 11. Bernadette was beatified in 1925 and canonized in 1933 as St. Marie Bernarde. Her feast day is April 16. See also LOURDES.

BERNADOTTE, bûr-nə-dot', **Count Folke** (1895–1948), Swedish diplomat. He was born in Stockholm, Sweden, on Jan. 2, 1895. A descendant of the Napoleonic marshal Jean Bernadotte, who in 1810 was elected crown prince of Sweden, and in 1818 succeeded to the throne as Charles XIV, Count Bernadotte was also a grandson of King Oscar II of Sweden and a nephew of King Gustavus V. After graduating from the military school of Karlberg, he studied horsemanship at the Strömsholm military riding school and became cavalry officer in the Royal Horse Guards. On Dec. 1, 1928, he married Estelle Romaine Manville, of New York. He represented Sweden in 1933 at the Chicago Century of Progress Exposition, and in 1939–1940 was Swedish commissioner general at the New York World's Fair. At the beginning of World War II, as head of the Sveriges Scoutförbund (the Swedish Boy Scouts), he integrated that organization into Sweden's defense system, training the scouts in antiaircraft work and as medical assistants. His most important war work, however, was as vice chairman of the Swedish Red Cross, supervising the exchange of disabled British and German war prisoners. This work necessitated frequent trips to London and Berlin involving conferences with high officials of both countries.

In the spring of 1945, while working in the Swedish legation's temporary headquarters at Friedrichsruh, Germany, he was summoned by Heinrich Himmler, head of the Gestapo and commander in chief of the German home front. They met at Lübeck, Germany, on April 24. Asserting that Hitler was dying and that he was in authority, Himmler offered the complete surrender of Germany to Britain and the United States, provided Germany was allowed to continue resistance against Russia. The Swedish foreign office transmitted Himmler's offer to Prime Minister Churchill and President Truman. They in turn notified Premier Stalin, advising him at the same time of the British-American decision to accept only an unconditional surrender to the three Allied governments. A translation of the count's book describing his negotiations was published in the United States under the title *The Curtain Falls* (1945).

On May 20, 1948, the five big powers of the United Nations Security Council agreed on the choice of Count Bernadotte as mediator to seek peace in the Arab-Jewish conflict in Palestine. Ten days later he initiated conferences with Arab and Jewish leaders in Palestine and Arab leaders in Cairo, Egypt, and Amman, Jordan. He succeeded in obtaining agreement to a four-week truce commencing June 11. On June 28 he submitted to the Arab League and the Israeli government a peace plan that both sides rejected in part. On July 12 he made a report to the United Nations Security Council, in session in New York, and shortly thereafter returned to Palestine.

On September 17, Count Bernadotte and Col. André P. Serot of the French air force were assassinated in Jerusalem by members of the Stern group, an organization of extreme Zionists who had committed numerous atrocities over a period of years against the British and Arabs. Three days after his death, Count Bernadotte's final report on his peace efforts was published in Paris. It gave the United Nations General Assembly his suggested terms for a peace that was to be imposed by the United Nations, and won the immediate support of the United States and Britain.

Ralph J. Bunche, an American serving as chief United Nations aide to Bernadotte and as personal representative in Jerusalem of United Nations Secretary General Trygve Lie, was appointed Bernadotte's temporary successor.

Bernadotte's book *Instead of Arms* was published in Sweden and the United States shortly after his death.

BERNADOTTE, Jean Baptiste Jules. See CHARLES XIV JOHN.

BERNANOS, ber-nà-nôs', **Georges** (1888–1948), French novelist. He was born in Paris and was educated at the University of Paris and the Institut Catholique. After serving with the French army during World War I, he worked for an insurance company to support his wife and family. Though he began writing in the 1920's, it was not until 1936 that his books and essays brought him the financial independence that enabled him to leave the insurance business.

Although a political conservative, Bernanos was deeply disgusted by fascism and by France's timorous attitude toward Germany during the years before World War II. In 1937 he published *Les grands cimetières sous la lune;* (Eng. tr., *A Diary of My Times,* 1938), a polemical work that dissociated him from the conservative political elements with which he had formerly been aligned. In 1938 he took his family to Brazil, where he lived until 1945, when he returned to France. Finding "no happiness there," he settled in Tunisia. He died at Neuilly, France, on July 5, 1948.

Bernanos' novels include *Un crime* (1935; Eng. tr., *A Crime,* 1936) and *Journal d'un curé de campagne* (1936; Eng. tr., *The Diary of a Country Priest,* 1937). These forceful and violent works have been called battlegrounds for the warring forces of good and evil.

BERNARD, bər-närd, **Saint** (1090–1153), abbot and Doctor of the Church. He is called *St. Bernard of Clairvaux* because he founded the famous Cistercian abbey at Clairvaux in France. His charm, eloquence, and sanctity profoundly influenced church and civil affairs in Europe in the first half of the 12th century.

Life. He was born of noble parents at Fontaines, near Dijon, France. In 1112, when Bernard was 21 years old, he entered the monastery of Cîteaux, taking with him four of his brothers, an uncle, and a group of companions. He took his vows as a monk in May or June of the following year. In June 1115, St. Stephen Harding, abbot of Cîteaux, chose Bernard, with 12 companions, to found a new abbey, and Bernard selected Clairvaux as its site. Probably in August 1115, Bernard was ordained a priest and received the abbatial blessing from William of Champeaux, bishop of Châlons-sur-Marne. Under Bernard's guidance, Clairvaux became one of the centers of the Cistercian order.

In spite of poor health Bernard spent the next 38 years in strenuous activity. His reforming zeal benefited not only the monks of the Cistercian Order but also those in some older Benedictine monasteries. He was also a leader in wider affairs of the church. Between 1128 and 1147 Bernard took part in nine regional councils. At the council of Troyes (1128) he was instrumental in securing ecclesiastical approval for the Knights Templar. His influence was felt in the decisions rendered against Abélard and Arnold of Brescia and in the trial of Gilbert de la Porrée. Bernard's recognition of Innocent II as the lawful pope ended the schism that followed the death of Pope Honorius II in 1130.

Pope Eugene III, one of his former disciples, commissioned Bernard to advocate a crusade. His preaching kindled enthusiasm for the Second Crusade and won the support of Louis VII of France and Conrad III of Germany for the expedition to the Holy Land. The failure of the crusade and the deceit and defection of his secretary, Nicholas of Clairvaux, saddened Bernard's last days. He died at Clairvaux on Aug. 20, 1153.

Bernard was canonized by Pope Alexander III in 1174 and declared a Doctor of the Church by Pius VIII in 1830. His feast is August 20.

Writings. Bernard's works were all written at Clairvaux. Of his 332 sermons, probably the most important are the 86 preached on the *Song of Songs;* these are permeated with his mysticism. The more widely known of his treatises are *On Consideration,* in 5 books, addressed to Eugene III, outlining the duties of a pope; and the *Apology to William of St. Thierry,* a defense of the Cistercians against their detractors and a condemnation of ostentation and laxity at the abbey of Cluny. The *Life of St. Malachy* is a biography of the archbishop of Armagh; it contains no mention of the prophecy of Malachy, which is apocryphal. Of the hymns ascribed to Bernard only two are authentic: one in honor of St. Victor, another in honor of St. Malachy. Only part of St. Bernard's correspondence has come down to us. Of his collected letters, 497 are authentic.

HERMIGILD DRESSLER, O.F.M.
The Catholic University of America

Further Reading: James, Bruno S., *Saint Bernard of Clairvaux* (New York 1957); Webb, Geoffrey, and Adrian, Walker, *St. Bernard of Clairvaux* (Westminster, Md., 1960); Williams, Watkin W., *Saint Bernard of Clairvaux* (Westminster, Md., 1953).

Claude Bernard

(1813-1878)

BERNARD, ber-når', **Claude** (1813–1878), French physiologist, who was a founder of experimental medicine. Bernard is known chiefly for his hypothesis of an integrated *milieu intérieur,* or internal environment, in an organism. He also made important discoveries concerning the role of the pancreas in digestion, the body's ability to build up such complex substances as glycogen, the sympathetic nervous system, and the action of drugs on the body.

Bernard's first important studies were concerned with digestion. He introduced food directly into the upper part of the small intestine and showed that most digestion takes place in the small intestine and not in the stomach, as had been previously thought. He also found that the secretions of the pancreas played an important part in the digestive process by breaking down fat molecules into fatty acids and glycerine.

In 1851, Bernard discovered that the nervous system controlled the dilation and constriction of blood vessels in response to changes in the environment. For example, in cold weather the blood vessels constrict to permit the maximum conservation of heat. This control mechanism illustrated for Bernard an attempt on the part of the body to maintain a constant internal environment despite changes in the external environment. The maintenance of a stable internal balance depended, Bernard believed, on the close interrelation of the various organs of the body—a novel idea in the mid-19th century.

Bernard found other examples to substantiate his theory. In 1856 he discovered a starchlike substance, which he called glycogen, in the liver. He demonstrated that this complex substance was built up by the body from sugar. This was the first example of the body's ability to build up complex substances from simpler substances. He further showed that this glycogen served as a reserve source of sugar for the body and that when the body needs sugar, it can break down the glycogen molecules into sugar molecules that it can use. The buildup or breakdown of glycogen molecules is governed by the state of the body and is directed to the maintenance of a stable blood-sugar level at all times.

Bernard also made important studies on the action of carbon monoxide and curare on the body. He showed that carbon monoxide could take the place of oxygen in combining with hemoglobin and thus cause oxygen starvation. He also showed that the poison curare produced paralysis by acting on the motor nerves at the neuromuscular junction. Bernard's findings provided the first accurate explanations of how drugs acted on the body, and they opened the door to the field of experimental pharmacology.

Life. Claude Bernard was born in St. Julien, France, on July 12, 1813. After his early education in Jesuit colleges, he entered medical school in Paris in 1834 and obtained his degree in 1843. He worked under the physiologist François Magendie, and he learned from him a great respect for the experimental rather than the speculative approach to the study of physiology and medicine.

Bernard held important posts in Paris at the Collège de France, the Sorbonne, and the Museum of Natural History, and he won the Academy of Sciences prize in experimental physiology four times. He was elected Chevalier of the Legion of Honor in 1849 and Commander in 1867. He died on Feb. 10, 1878, and was the first French scientist to be given a state funeral.

Writings. Bernard's best-known book is the *Introduction to the Study of Experimental Medicine* (1865), a scientific and literary classic that is still widely read by students. He also published lectures and numerous scientific papers.

BERNARD, bûr'nərd, **Sir Francis** (1712–1779), English governor in colonial America. He was educated at Oxford and admitted to the bar in 1737. Through influential family connections he was sent as governor to New Jersey in 1758. After two successful years there he was commissioned governor of Massachusetts. His nine-year term in that colony spanned a period of great turmoil, provoked by such measures as the Stamp Act (1765).

Although he was a capable administrator and more sympathetic to the colonists' viewpoints than many other colonial governors, Bernard inevitably clashed with the colonists when he was obliged to enforce unpopular policies of the British government. His *Letters to the Earl of Hillsborough,* published in Boston in 1769, further angered the colonists. The Massachusetts assembly preferred charges against him, and later in 1769 he was recalled to London. The British government eventually dismissed the assembly's charges, and Bernard lived out his later years in retirement in England. He died on June 16, 1779, at Aylesbury. He also wrote *Select Letters on the Trade and Government of America, and the Principles of Law and Polity Applied to the American Colonies* (1774).

BERNARD, ber-nàr', **Jean Jacques** (1888–   ), French dramatist. A son of Tristan Bernard (q.v.), he was born at Enghien-les-Bains on July 30, 1888. He was an exponent of a theatrical movement known as the "school of silence," in which gestures, half-articulated statements, and silent pauses were intended to convey important meanings and to suggest the most secret feelings of the characters. His plays include *Le feu qui reprend mal* (1922), which is in the repertoire of the Comédie Française; *Martine* (1922); *Le printemps des autres* (1924); and *À la recherche des coeurs* (1934).

Bernard also wrote the novel *Marie et le vagabond* (1949) and three books of memoirs, *Le camp de la morte lente* (1945), *Mon père, Tristan Bernard* (1955), and *Mon ami, le théâtre* (1958).

BERNARD, ber-nàr', **Tristan** (1866–1947), French writer. He was born *Paul Bernard* in Besançon on Sept. 7, 1866. He began his writing career as a journalist, contributing chiefly to the *Revue blanche,* but soon turned to the writing of plays and novels. He had three sons—Raymond, a film director; Étienne, a Paris physician; and Jean Jacques, a playwright (see BERNARD, JEAN JACQUES). He died in Paris on Dec. 7, 1947.

Bernard's plays and novels reveal his keen powers of observation and lively sense of the ridiculous. Under his comic genius, however, he concealed a fundamental pessimism. His most popular plays include *L'anglais tel qu'on le parle* (1899), *Le danseur inconnu* (1910), *La volonté de l'homme* (1917), and *Jules, Juliette et Julien* (1929). He collaborated with André Godfernaux on *Triplepatte* (1905). His most successful novels were *Les mémoires d'un jeune homme rangé* (1899) and *Le voyage imprévu* (1928).

BERNARD DE CHARTRES, ber-nàr' də shàr'trə, French writer of the 12th century. A grammarian and philosopher, he taught at Chartres, the most eminent of the cathedral schools of the 12th century, from 1114 to 1119 and was chancellor there from 1119 to 1124.

Bernard was celebrated as the ablest Platonist of his day, teaching that the forms of things are distinct from the exemplary ideas in the divine mind. He wrote two books, now lost. In one of them he endeavored to reconcile Plato and Aristotle, and in the other he supported the doctrine of a providence, seeking to prove that all material beings, because they possess a nature subject to change, must perish.

BERNARD DE VENTADOUR. See PROVENÇAL LITERATURE.

BERNARD OF CLUNY (c. 1100–1156), ber-nàr', klü-nē', was a Benedictine monk and poet, whose profoundly moving satire in verse, *De contemptu mundi* (*On Contempt of the World,* c. 1140), was a major indictment of moral laxity in his day. He is sometimes called *Bernard of Morval* (or *Morlaix*). Details of his life are unknown, although it is certain that he was a monk at the abbey of Cluny, since his work is dedicated to its abbot, Peter the Venerable.

The 3,000 verses of his satire, written in dactylic hexameters, describe the awesomeness of heaven and hell and, with eloquence, delineate man's sins and virtues. Three segments of the poem are used as English hymns: *Jerusalem the Golden; For Thee, O Dear, Dear Country; and The World Is Very Evil.*

BERNARD OF MENTHON, ber-nàr', män-tôn', **Saint** (923–1008), French Catholic priest, who established the Alpine hospices that bear his name. He was born at Menthon, in Savoy. After his ordination to the priesthood, he was named archdeacon of Aosta (966), and for more than 40 years he worked among the people of the Alps. During this period he built a monastery and hospices atop two dangerous and heavily traveled Alpine passes for the succor of travelers. The hostels and the passes—Great and Little St. Bernard—as well as the dogs who aid the hospice guides, all bear his name. Bernard died at Novara, Italy, on May 28 (?), 1008. He was canonized in 1681. His feast day is June 15, and he is honored by Alpinists as their patron.

BERNARDES, bər-når′dēs, **Artur da Silva** (1875–1955), Brazilian lawyer and political leader. He was born at Viçosa, Minas Gerais, Brazil, on Aug. 18, 1875. He received a law degree at the University of São Paulo in 1900 and then practiced law at Viçosa. He became a federal deputy in 1909 and served in the national Senate before his election to the presidency of the state of Minas Gerais in 1918.

In 1922, Bernardes was elected president of Brazil. His term of office coincided with a period of inflation and soaring foreign debt, and his efforts to deal with the situation were frustrated by the army. Despite widespread civil disorders, Bernardes completed his four-year term. In the 1930's he taught Brazilian studies at the University of Lisbon. He died in Rio de Janeiro on March 23, 1955. See also BRAZIL—10. *History*.

BERNARDIN DE SAINT-PIERRE, ber-når-daN′ də saN pyår, **Jacques Henri** (1737–1814), French author, whose painting-like descriptions of sea voyages and tropical settings influenced the writing of René de Chateaubriand. Bernardin was born in Le Havre on Jan. 19, 1737. He worked as an army engineer and took a post in 1768 on the island of Mauritius (Île de France) in the Indian Ocean. When he returned to France he published *Voyage à l'île de France* (1773). In 1795, Bernardin became a lecturer at the École Normale Supérieure and was admitted to the French Institute. He died at Eragny-sur-Oise on Jan. 21, 1814.

His most famous work is the short novel *Paul et Virginie* (1787), which was influenced by the naturalistic philosophy of Jean Jacques Rousseau, a close friend of Bernardin's. The book, a tragic love idyll set on the island of Mauritius, argues man's nobility in a natural environment. It is notable as much for its lush descriptions of tropical surroundings as for its pathos. The same vividness of description is found in Bernardin's philosophical work, *Études de la nature* (1784), which deduces the existence of God from the harmony of natural scenes. Bernardin also wrote the posthumously published *Les harmonies de la nature* (1815), a naïvely anthropomorphic treatise, and the story *La chaumière indienne* (1791).

BERNARDINO OF SIENA, bär-när-dē′nō, syä′nä, **Saint** (1380–1444), Italian Franciscan reformer. He was born in Massa Marittima, near Siena, on Sept. 8, 1380 and was ordained in 1404. He began his missionary career in 1417, and traveled throughout Italy denouncing vice and preaching reform with great zeal and eloquence. For his apostolic journeys he was called the Apostle of Italy, and for his preaching on the Holy Name of Jesus he became known as the Apostle of the Holy Name. He was also instrumental in reconciling the Guelph and Ghibelline political factions.

Bernardino achieved such fame that he was offered three bishoprics, but he declined them. In 1438 he became vicar general of the Italian Observants, a strict Franciscan order. Under his administration, hundreds of monasteries were reorganized and thousands of persons were recruited into the order. He resigned the post in 1442 to resume his missionary work. He died in Aquila, Italy, on May 20, 1444. He was canonized in 1450, and his feast day is May 20.

Further Reading: Origo, Iris, *The World of San Bernardino* (New York 1962).

BERNARDO DEL CARPIO, ber-när′thō thel kär′pyō, was a legendary Spanish hero. The central figure of earlier epic poems that have been lost, he is known through 12th and 13th century prose chronicles. Bernardo reputedly was the son of Don Sancho, count of Saldaña, and Doña Ximena, sister of Alfonso II the Chaste, king of Asturias. The monarch, annoyed at their secret marriage, blinded and imprisoned Sancho, immured Ximena in a convent, but reared Bernardo at court. Despite Bernardo's valiant exploits against the Moors and Franks (by some accounts he helped to defeat the French hero Roland at Roncesvalles) both Alfonso, who died in 842, and his successor, Alfonso III the Great, refused to release Sancho. Forming a league of disaffected Spaniards and Moors, Bernardo defeated Alfonso in battle several times. Alfonso then offered to exchange Sancho for Bernardo's castle of Carpio. Each performed his part—but Bernardo received his father's corpse.

Among the best-known later versions of the epic are those by Juan de la Cueva, Bernardo de Balbuena, and Lope de Vega.

BERNARDSVILLE, bûr′nərdz-vil, is a residential borough in northern New Jersey, in Somerset County, 8 miles (13 km) southwest of Morristown. A crushed-stone plant is the major industrial establishment. In December 1777, the American general Charles Lee was captured by the British at Veal's Tavern in Basking Ridge, 2 miles (3.2 km) to the east. Until 1840, Bernardsville was called Vealtown. Incorporated in 1924, the borough has a mayor-council government. Population: 6,652.

BERNAUER, ber′nou-ər, **Agnes** (died 1435), Bavarian woman celebrated for her beauty. The daughter of a poor citizen, supposedly an Augsburg baker, she was secretly married to Duke Albert of Bavaria. The duke's father, however, wished his son to marry Anne, daughter of the duke of Brunswick. Albert, therefore, was forced to acknowledge his marriage. The father, incensed at his son's misalliance, caused Agnes to be tried for witchcraft. Found guilty before a special tribunal, she was drowned by being thrown into the Danube with her hands tied (Oct. 12, 1435). Albert in revenge took up arms against his father, but the Emperor Sigismund finally reconciled them.

The story was a favorite theme of German poets, the most notable dramatization being *Agnes Bernauer* (1855) by Friedrich Hebbel.

BERNAYS, bər-nāz′, **Edward L.** (1891–   ), American public relations counsel, who is generally credited with having created the concept of public relations as a profession. He was born in Vienna, Austria, on Nov. 22, 1891. The family (his mother was Sigmund Freud's sister Anna) moved to New York City when he was one year old. He was educated in New York public schools and, at his father's request, earned a degree in agriculture (1912) at Cornell University.

In 1919, Bernays and his wife, the former Doris E. Fleischman, founded the first American public relations consulting firm, which served government, industry, and labor organizations. His pioneering lectures at New York University in 1923 and his writings did much to define the field of public relations. He recounted his career in *Biography of an Idea* (1965).

BERNERS, bûr'nərz, **2d Baron** (1467–1533), English political leader and translator. He was born *John Bourchier,* a descendant of Thomas of Woodstock, youngest son of Edward III. From 1495 to 1529 he was a member of Parliament. In 1497 he aided in suppressing the Cornish insurrection. Under Henry VIII he was chancellor of the exchequer (1516) and headed an embassy to Spain (1518). From 1520 until his death he was the English governor of Calais, where he died on March 16, 1533.

Berners is remembered chiefly for his translation of Jean Froissart's *Chronicles* (2 vols., 1523–25). He also translated *The Golden Boke of Marcus Aurelius* (1534), from the French version of Antonio de Guevara's *El relox de principes* (1529), and *The Castell of Love* (1540), from Diego de San Pedro's *Carcel de Amor.*

BERNESE ALPS, bûr'nəz alps, a section of the Alps in southwestern Switzerland. Also called the *Bernese Oberland,* the mountains are located south of Bern and straddle the boundary of the cantons of Bern and Valais. The chain is separated from the Pennine Alps, which it parallels, by the upper Rhône Valley. It includes such peaks as Finsteraarhorn (14,022 feet; 4,274 meters), Aletschhorn (13,774 feet; 4,198 meters), Jungfrau (13,642 feet; 4,158 meters), and Eiger (13,036 feet; 3,973 meters).

Among the numerous popular summer and winter resorts are Interlaken, Lauterbrunnen, Gstaad, Mürren, Kandersteg, and Grindelwald. The Bernese Alps are traversed by the Lötschen Pass, where there is a road tunnel, and by the Col du Pillon, Grimsel, Gemmi, and Jaun passes.

BERNHARD, (1604–1639), bern'härt, duke of Saxe-Weimar, was a German general who fought on the Protestant side in the Thirty Years' War. He was born in Weimar, Thuringia, on Aug. 16, 1604, a son of John, duke of Weimar, and a younger brother of Ernest I the Pious. In the crucial Battle of Lützen (1632) in the Thirty Years' War he commanded the left wing of the Swedish army under King Gustavus Adolphus, at whose death he turned imminent defeat into victory. The Swedes gave him command of the army and granted him Franconia as a duchy. In 1633 he captured Regensburg (Ratisbon) and Straubing, but the following year his impetuosity led him to defeat at Nördlingen. As a consequence of this battle he lost his duchy.

In 1634, Bernhard made an alliance with France and carried on the war in the country adjacent to the Rhine. After winning several battles against the emperor's Catholic forces, he entered Alsace. In 1638 he was again victorious at Rheinfelden and Breisach. He died in Neuenburg, Baden, on July 18, 1639.

BERNHARD (1911–   ), bern'härt, prince of the Netherlands, the German-born prince consort of Queen Juliana. He was born on June 29, 1911, in Jena, the son of Prince Bernhard of Lippe-Biesterfeld. After graduating as doctor of law from Berlin University, he entered the German chemical industry, which he represented in Amsterdam when he became a naturalized Dutch subject in 1936. In the next year he married Queen Wilhelmina's only daughter, Princess Juliana of Orange, heir to the throne of the Netherlands.

When the Germans invaded his adopted coun-

PRINCE BERNHARD, prince consort of the Netherlands, with his wife, Queen Juliana.

try in 1940 during World War II, Bernhard fled with the royal family to England, where he trained as a pilot and engaged actively in the Allied war effort and the liberation of the Netherlands. In 1944 he was appointed supreme commander of the Netherlands army and air force and of the underground resistance. Following the war he helped promote Dutch commerce and industry. His state visits to various Latin American countries and to the United States in the 1950's and 1960's helped increase the Netherlands' business and cultural relations with those areas.

BERNHARDI, bern-här'dē, **Friedrich von** (1849–1930), German general and military author. The son of an able diplomat, Theodor von Bernhardi, and grandson of the philologist August Ferdinand Bernhardi, he was born in St. Petersburg (now Leningrad), Russia, on Nov. 22, 1849. He fought in the Franco-Prussian War and was attached as a military historian to the German general staff in 1898. During World War I he was a commander on the eastern and western fronts and took part in the Battle of Armentières (1918). He died in Kunersdorf, Germany (now Kunowice, Poland), on July 10, 1930.

Bernhardi's name became a byword for Pan-Germanic chauvinism and warmongering, when the English translation of his *Deutschland und der nächste Krieg* (*Germany and the Next War*) appeared in 1912. The Allies later seized upon the book as revealing the cause of World War I. In it Bernhardi declared that Germany had the "right" and the "duty" to make war to achieve the world power that was her due. Predicting the defection of Italy from the Triple Alliance, he warned Germany that it would have to fight Russia, France, and Britain with only the assistance of Austria. He called war a biological necessity, an indispensable regulative element in the life of man, due to the universal struggle for existence, possessions, power, and sovereignty.

BERNHARDT, ber-när', **Sarah** (1844–1923), French actress, whose physical beauty, grace of movement, and magnificent speaking voice made her one of history's most famous stage performers and won her the name of "the Divine Sarah." In contrast to her most famous rival, Eleanora Duse, Bernhardt subscribed to highly theatrical methods. Bernard Shaw's brilliant comparisons of the two actresses in the same roles heavily favored Duse—which has also been history's verdict. However, most critics, French and foreign, praised Bernhardt extravagantly during her lifetime. Audiences flocked to see her, and she enjoyed an almost perennial vogue. She was an excellent showman and exploited her talents to make large sums of money, much of which she lost in building and operating a theater in Paris that she named for herself.

Early Career. She was born *Henriette Rosine Bernard* in Paris on Oct. 22 or 23, 1844. Her mother was a Dutch Jew; almost nothing is known of her father, except that he took her from her maternal grandparents in Amsterdam when she was a girl, had her baptized as a Roman Catholic, and enrolled her in a French convent school. She studied at the Paris Conservatoire from 1858 to 1860 and made her debut at the Comédie Française, in the title role of Jean Baptiste Racine's *Iphigénie en Aulide*, in 1862. She was not well received then or on other occasions during her first few years on the stage.

Sarah Bernhardt's illegitimate son, Maurice Bernhardt, was born on Dec. 22, 1864. The child's father was Henri, prince de Ligne, whom Bernhardt left soon after. In 1866 she transferred from the Comédie to the Odéon, where she first achieved popular success in the elder Alexandre Dumas' *Kean.* Her first critical success came in 1869 in François Coppée's *Le passant.* She triumphed in 1872 as the queen in a revival of Victor Hugo's *Ruy Blas* and, as a result, was engaged for a return to the Comédie in 1873. There she triumphed again in Racine's *Phèdre,* with Mounet-Sully playing opposite her. Her performances in *Adrienne Lecouvreur,* by Gabriel Legouvé and Eugène Scribe, and in *Hernani,* by Hugo, won critical acclaim and were enormously popular. However, she chafed at the restrictions at the Comédie and resigned in 1879—after her success with the company in London assured her future independence.

Edward Jarrett, an American impresario, offered to star her in America and she accepted. Although she had never acted the younger Dumas' *La dame aux camélias,* she chose it for her American debut in 1880. It was a sensation, and it remained her greatest success. (She continued playing it in its entirety until 1914 and did the letter and death scenes in her ninth and last American tour during World War I.)

In 1882, Bernhardt made a popular hit in Victorien Sardou's *Fédora,* the first of several enormously successful romantic vehicles that he wrote for her. In the same year she married Jacques Damala, a Greek actor, but the marriage lasted only one year.

Actress-Manager. In 1893, Bernhardt acquired a theater of her own in Paris, the Théâtre de la Renaissance, which she operated as actress-manager for six years. In addition to Sardou vehicles, she starred in Hermann Sudermann's *Magda* (1895), Edmond Rostand's *La princesse lointaine* (1895), Alfred de Musset's *Lorenzaccio* (1896), and Edmond Rostand's *La samaritaine* (1897).

In 1899 she built the Théâtre Sarah Bernhardt in Paris, and she owned and operated it for the rest of her life. Its opening season witnessed the first of her famous portrayals of Shakespeare's Hamlet. In 1900, Rostand created another "Hamlet" for her in *L'aiglon,* in which she played opposite Coquelin Aîné. Later that year she triumphed as Roxanne in Rostand's *Cyrano de Bergerac.* In 1902 she played the title role in Gabriele d'Annunzio's *Francesca da Rimini* and the title role in a sensational stage adaptation of Alphonse Daudet's novel *Sapho.* She acted Hermione in Racine's *Andromaque* in 1903 and did his *Esther* in 1905, when she also played Mélisande in Maeterlinck's *Pelléas et Mélisande.*

BROWN BROTHERS

Sarah Bernhardt, French actress (1844–1923).

Last Years. In 1905, Bernhardt suffered a knee injury that lamed her for the rest of her life. Her leg was amputated in 1914, but she continued playing until the year before her death, when she last performed a tour de force as a young man in Louis Verneuil's *Daniel.* She died in Paris on March 26, 1923. Her funeral was magnificent, and millions, either in person or by telegrams and letters, mourned her passing.

Bernhardt was a sculptor of considerable talent, and also a writer. Her writing talents were devoted mostly to writing about herself and to "guiding" (and sometimes sharply revising) the work of playwrights who created vehicles for her. She was also a master of publicity. Her several love affairs excited and scandalized her public. However, in spite of both professional and personal shortcomings, she is still generally regarded as France's greatest actress of all time.

GEORGE FREEDLEY
Coauthor of "A History of the Theatre"

Further Reading: Richardson, Joanna, *Sarah Bernhardt* (London 1959); Row, Arthur, *Sarah the Divine* (New York 1957); Verneuil, Louis, *The Fabulous Life of Sarah Bernhardt,* tr. by Ernest Boyd (New York 1942).

BERNI, ber'nē, **Francesco** (c. 1497–1535), Italian satirical poet. He was born in Lamporecchio, Tuscany, of a noble but poor family. He lived a carefree life close to the papal court in Rome before accepting a canonship in Florence about 1533. He died in Florence on May 26, 1535, probably as a result of poisoning by Alessandro de' Medici after Berni refused to assist in the murder of Alessandro's cousin, Ippolito Cardinal de' Medici.

Berni's burlesque and frequently licentious poetry ranks among the best of his time. His light, facile verses, which started a vogue called *maniera bernesca,* range from bitter satire to a refreshing praise of everyday life. His fame rests chiefly on his only long work, a humorous adaptation of Matteo Maria Boiardo's epic, *Orlando innamorato.*

BERNINI, bär-nē′nē, **Giovanni Lorenzo** (1598–1680), Italian architect, sculptor, painter, and designer, who was the outstanding artist in Italy in the 17th century. The Italian baroque style, with its sensuous flow and magnificent pomp, is essentially Bernini's creation. Most of his architectural and sculptural masterpieces are in Rome, but his influence, which was felt for two centuries, spread throughout Europe.

Bernini's genius is most manifest where he was able to combine architecture and sculpture. For example, the Cornaro chapel (1644–1652; Santa Maria della Vittoria, Rome), often considered his greatest achievement, centers on his great polychrome marble and bronze sculpture of the *Ecstasy of St. Teresa.*

Life. Bernini was born in Naples on Dec. 7, 1598, the son of the sculptor Pietro Bernini (1562–1629), who gave him his early training. About 1605 the family moved to Rome. Bernini's first important patron was Scipione Cardinal Borghese, who commissioned most of the sculpture that brought Bernini his first fame. In 1629 Bernini was appointed to succeed Carlo Maderna as chief architect of St. Peter's Basilica in Rome.

King Louis XIV of France called Bernini to Paris in 1665 to work on the design of the east façade of the Louvre palace. When Claude Perrault's plans were accepted instead of his, Bernini returned to Rome, where he remained for the rest of his life. He died there on Nov. 28, 1860.

Works. One of the most prolific artists of all time, Bernini at the height of his career was sometimes involved in more than 100 projects at once, employing hundreds of assistants and craftsmen. His unlimited creativity moved easily from one art form to another. Although best known as a sculptor and architect, he also executed over 200 paintings, and produced hundreds of masterly drawings. He also found time to design costumes, stage machinery, fireworks displays, and other effects for the theater and for public and religious celebrations.

For Cardinal Borghese, Bernini executed some of his greatest sculptures, including *Aeneas, Anchises, and Ascanius* (about 1618), *David* (1623), *The Rape of Proserpina* (1621–1622), and *Apollo and Daphne* (1622–1624), all in the Galleria Borghese, Rome.

His magnificent portrait busts captured the likenesses of many of the greatest men of the age, including Pope Paul V (1621; Galleria Borghese), Pope Gregory XV (1621–1622; Musée Jacquemart-André, Paris), Pope Urban VIII (about 1623; San Lorenzo in Fonte, Rome), Cardinal Borghese (1632; Galleria Borghese), and Louis XIV (1665; Versailles).

As chief architect of St. Peter's, Bernini designed the throne of St. Peter in the apse, the baldachin (canopy) over the papal altar, and the stately colonnades around the elliptical piazza in front of the church. Two of his greatest late masterpieces, the tombs of Popes Urban VIII and Alexander VII, are also in St. Peter's. For the Vatican he designed the Scala Regia (Royal Staircase).

Bernini designed several of Rome's famous fountains, including the Triton Fountain (1632–1637) and the Fountain of the Four Rivers (1648–1651). Between 1658 and 1670 he designed three important churches, San Tommaso da Villanova at Castel Gandolfo, Santa Maria dell'Assunzione at Ariccia, and Sant'Andrea al Quirinale in Rome.

ALINARI—ART REFERENCE BUREAU

BERNINI'S *Apollo and Daphne* (Borghese Museum, Rome).

Bernini Bibliography

Baldinucci, Filippo, *The Life of Bernini* (University Park, Pa., 1965).
Brauer, Heinrich, and Wittkower, Rudolph, *Die Zeichnungen des Giovanni Lorenzo Bernini,* 2 vols. (Berlin 1931).
Fraschetti, Stanislaos, *Il Bernini* (Milan 1900).
Pane, R., *Bernini architetto* (Venice 1953).
Ricci, Corrado, *Il Bernini* (Bologna 1910).
Wittkower, Rudolph, *Gian Lorenzo Bernini: The Sculptor of the Roman Baroque* (London 1955).
Wittkower, Rudolph, ed., *The Sculpture of Bernini* (New York 1955).

BERNIS, ber-nēs′, **François Joachim de Pierre de** (1715–1794), French cardinal, statesman, and poet. He was born in St.-Marcel in Ardèche on May 22, 1715. His poetry, called *bouquets poétiques,* won him a seat in the Académie Française and the nickname of *Babet la Bouquetière* by the time he was 29. His memoirs and his correspondence with Voltaire contain valuable observations on the events of his times.

He later became a favorite of Madame de Pompadour and through her influence became ambassador to Venice in 1752. Returning to Paris in 1755, he negotiated in 1756 the French alliance with Austria. In 1757, during the Seven Years' War (1756–1763) that followed the new alliance, he was made foreign minister. Bernis was forced from office by French military defeats in 1758. He became a cardinal after his resignation and archbishop of Albi in 1764.

In 1769, Bernis came out of retirement to become ambassador to Rome, where he used his position to force Pope Clement XIV to suppress the Jesuits in 1773. His opposition to the religious reforms of the French Revolution caused Bernis to lose his ambassadorship. He died in Rome on Nov. 2, 1794.

BERNOULLI, Ger. ber-nōōl'ē, Fr. ber-nōō-yē', was a Swiss family that included several generations of men who were distinguished mathematicians and scientists. The Bernoulli family fled from Antwerp (now in Belgium) because of religious persecution. After moving to Frankfurt, Germany, they settled in Basel, Switzerland, where Jacques Bernoulli (1598–1634) obtained citizenship in 1622. Nicolas Bernoulli (1623–1708) was the father of Jacques (I) and Jean (I) Bernoulli. Among the important members of the family are the following:

JAKOB or **JACQUES BERNOULLI (I)** (1654–1705) was a Swiss mathematician who promoted the use of calculus and pioneered in the theory of probability. He was born in Basel on Dec. 27, 1654. After starting as a student of theology, he turned to the study of mathematics. He became a professor of mathematics at the University of Basel in 1687. Jacques used calculus to solve a variety of problems, and he coined the term "integral." He also investigated the properties of the catenary and various spiral curves. He wrote two essays in 1691 on integral calculus. In 1698 he published an essay on differential calculus and its applications to geometry.

In *Ars conjectandi,* published posthumously in 1713, Jacques established fundamental principles of the calculus of probabilities. He stated a theorem, now called Bernoulli's theorem, that any assigned degree of accuracy can be obtained by increasing the number of trials, such as drawing colored marbles out of a bowl. This theorem also is called the law of large numbers. In the same work, Jacques described what are now called Bernoulli numbers, and he explained their use. A two-volume edition of his works, entitled *Iacobi Bernoulli Basiliensis opera,* was published in 1744. Jacques died in Basel on Aug. 16, 1705.

JOHANN or **JEAN BERNOULLI (I)** (1667–1748) was a Swiss mathematician and physicist who contributed to the early development of calculus and mechanics. He was born in Basel on July 27, 1667. Jean, the brother of Jacques, studied medicine and mathematics. Like his brother, he made valuable contributions to the development of differential and integral calculus. He was the discoverer of exponential calculus and, with his brother, the co-discoverer of the calculus of variations. Jean used calculus in solving mechanical problems. He corresponded with Gottfried Wilhelm von Leibniz, and he instructed the marquis de l'Hôpital in mathematics during a sojourn in France (1690–1692).

Jean became a professor of mathematics at Groningen (now in the Netherlands) in 1695. In 1697 he solved the brachistochrone problem. On the death of his brother in 1705, he succeeded him as a professor of mathematics at Basel. While there, he worked on the principles of mechanics. His *Opera omnia* was issued in 1742. Jean died in Basel on Jan. 1, 1748.

NIKOLAUS or **NICOLAS BERNOULLI (I)** (1687–1759) was a Swiss mathematician and law scholar, who contributed works on the theory of probability and on infinite series. He was born in Basel on Oct. 10, 1687. A nephew of Jacques (I) and Jean (I), Nikolaus traveled to England, where he met Isaac Newton and Edmund Halley. On the recommendation of Leibniz, Nicolas was appointed a professor of mathematics at Padua in 1716. He returned to Basel in 1722 as a professor of logic. In 1731, he became a professor of law. He died in Basel on Nov. 29, 1759.

NIKOLAUS or **NICOLAS BERNOULLI (II)** (1695–1726) was a Swiss mathematician whose early death cut short a promising career. He was born in Basel on Nov. 4, 1695, the son of Jean (I). He was a friend of the Swiss mathematician Leonhard Euler, who studied under Nikolaus' father. After becoming a professor of jurisprudence in Switzerland, Nicolas was appointed a professor of mathematics at St. Petersburg (now Leningrad) in 1726. He died there on Oct. 8, 1726.

DANIEL BERNOULLI (1700–1782) was a Swiss physicist and mathematician who made contributions to the science of hydrodynamics, the kinetic theory of gases, calculus, and the theory of probability. He was born in Groningen, Netherlands, on Jan. 20, 1700. Daniel, the son of Jean (I) and the brother of Nikolaus (II), taught mathematics in St. Petersburg from 1725 to 1732. He was a professor of anatomy at the University of Basel from 1733. In 1750, he became a professor of physics. During the 1740's, he investigated the vibrations of a bar clamped at one end. Daniel did work in calculus, differential equations, and the theory of probability as applied to games, and he solved a differential equation that now is called Bernoulli's equation.

Daniel's chief work was his book *Hydrodynamica* (1738). In this work, he used the principle of the conservation of energy in solving problems of fluid flow, and he stated the law that now bears his name (see BERNOULLI'S LAW). He also presented one of the first formulations of the kinetic theory of gases. He stated that the gas pressure on the walls of a container could be explained by the rapid to-and-fro motion of a large number of small molecules. Daniel also wrote papers on the tides of the sea and on problems concerning vibrating strings. He won the annual prize of the French Academy 10 times, as did his friend, Leonhard Euler. Daniel died in Basel on March 17, 1782.

JOHANN or **JEAN BERNOULLI (II)** (1710–1790) was a Swiss mathematician. He was born in Basel on May 18, 1710, the son of Jean (I). After being a professor of rhetoric at the University of Basel from 1743 to 1748, he succeeded his father as a professor of mathematics at the university. His conducted research on the theory of heat and light. He died in Basel on July 17, 1790.

JOHANN or **JEAN BERNOULLI (III)** (1744–1807) was a Swiss astronomer and mathematician. He was born in Basel on Nov. 4, 1744, the son of Jean (II). He became an astronomer and a director of mathematical studies in Berlin (then in Prussia). He wrote a treatise on astronomy called *Recueil pour les astronomes* (1772–76). He died in Berlin on July 13, 1807.

JAKOB or **JACQUES BERNOULLI (II)** (1759–1789) was a Swiss mathematician. He was born in Basel on Oct. 17, 1759, the son of Jean (II). He succeeded his uncle Daniel as a professor of mathematics at St. Petersburg. He died there on July 3, 1789.

Bibliography

Bell, Eric T., *Men of Mathematics* (New York 1937).
Muir, Jane, *Of Men and Numbers* (New York 1961).
Newman, James R., ed., *World of Mathematics* (New York 1956).
Turnbull, Herbert W., *Great Mathematicians* (New York 1961).

For Specialized Study

Spiess, Otto, ed., *Der Briefswechsel von Johann Bernoulli* (Basel 1955). This is the first volume of a projected collection of the correspondence and works of the Bernoulli family.

BERNOULLI'S PRINCIPLE, bər-nōō'lēz prin'sə-pəl, is the form that the law of conservation of energy takes when applied to a fluid. The energy of a stationary mass of fluid consists, in general, of its gravitational potential energy and a potential energy that results from the downward "push" of any fluid above it. If the fluid is moving, it also possesses energy of motion, or kinetic energy. Bernoulli's principle states that for nonturbulent (streamline), nonviscous flow, the sum of these three energies does not change. The principle was first stated by the Swiss mathematician Daniel Bernoulli in the 1700's.

Bernoulli's principle is useful in designing fluid conduit systems, aircraft, and boats. Its utility in aerodynamic and boat-design studies results particularly from the quantitative way in which it predicts that fluid pressure is reduced wherever the speed of flow is increased. An airplane wing is designed so that air travels faster over its upper surface than over its lower surface. This difference in speed of flow causes a lower pressure on the upper surface of the wing, according to Bernoulli's principle, and thus results in an upward force, or lift, on the wing.

The principle also explains how a pitcher can curve a baseball toward or away from a batter by spinning the baseball as he releases it. As a result of the spin, the motion of the air relative to the ball's surface will be faster on the side where the spin is in the same direction as the ball's motion than on the opposite side, as shown in the accompanying figure. The difference in the relative motion between the air and the surface of the ball on the two sides results in a pressure difference that causes the ball to swerve in a curved path.

SAMUEL OLANOFF
Dutchess Community College
Poughkeepsie, N.Y.

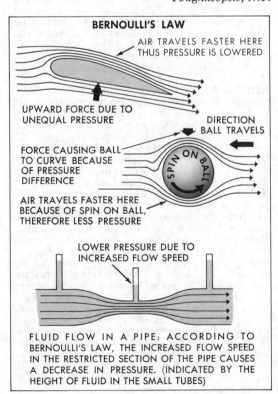

BERNOULLI'S LAW

AIR TRAVELS FASTER HERE THUS PRESSURE IS LOWERED

UPWARD FORCE DUE TO UNEQUAL PRESSURE

DIRECTION BALL TRAVELS

FORCE CAUSING BALL TO CURVE BECAUSE OF PRESSURE DIFFERENCE

SPIN ON BALL

AIR TRAVELS FASTER HERE BECAUSE OF SPIN ON BALL, THEREFORE LESS PRESSURE

LOWER PRESSURE DUE TO INCREASED FLOW SPEED

FLUID FLOW IN A PIPE: ACCORDING TO BERNOULLI'S LAW, THE INCREASED FLOW SPEED IN THE RESTRICTED SECTION OF THE PIPE CAUSES A DECREASE IN PRESSURE. (INDICATED BY THE HEIGHT OF FLUID IN THE SMALL TUBES)

BERNSTEIN, bern'shtīn, **Eduard** (1850–1932), German socialist leader and writer. He was born in Berlin on Jan. 6, 1850. He became a member of the German Social Democratic party (SPD) in 1872 and attained such prominence in its ranks that when Bismarck's antisocialist laws were adopted in 1878, Bernstein was obliged to seek refuge in Switzerland. In 1881 he became editor of the German party's newspaper, *Sozialdemokrat,* prohibited in Germany and published in Zürich (1879–1888) and then in London (1888–1890) after German pressure had brought about Bernstein's expulsion from Switzerland in 1888.

He settled in London, where he studied history and economics and maintained a close relationship with Engels. He was strongly influenced by the Fabians, a group of British socialists whose doctrine of social reform diverged from Marx's doctrine of revolution. Bernstein's revisionist writings of this period had a great effect on the ideological development of the SPD.

Supporting his arguments with statistical evidence, Bernstein contradicted Marx's prophecy that the bourgeoisie would collapse in the near future. He demonstrated that, despite the spread of capitalism, class antagonism had not intensified, the middle class had not disappeared, and the lot of the proletariat had not worsened. Bernstein advised the party to abandon its hopes for imminent revolution and to use peaceful, parliamentary means to effect social reforms. His theories are presented in *Die Voraussetzungen des Sozialismus* (1899; Eng. tr., *Evolutionary Socialism,* 1909).

Upon his return to Germany in 1901, Bernstein joined the passionate debate that his revisionist theory had loosed within the SPD, and he saw his doctrine gain ascendancy in the party before World War I. He was a member of the Reichstag in 1902–1906, 1912–1918, and 1920–1928. Bernstein died in Berlin on Dec. 18, 1932.

C.M. KIMMICH, *Columbia University*

Further Reading: Gay, Peter, *The Dilemma of Democratic Socialism: Eduard Bernstein's Challenge to Marx* (New York 1952; paperback reprint, 1962).

BERNSTEIN, bern-sten', **Henry Léon Gustave Charles** (1876–1953), French playwright. He was born in Paris on June 20, 1876. His forceful earlier plays present human conflicts in terms of suspenseful action; these include *Le voleur* (1907), *Israël* (1908), and *Le secret* (1913). His later plays stress psychological motivations. Although he was an early admirer of Mussolini, Bernstein fled France in World War II and lived in the United States, where he was active against the Vichy government. He returned to France after the war and died in Paris on Nov. 27, 1953.

BERNSTEIN, bûrn'stīn, **Herman** (1876–1935), American journalist. He was born at Neustadt on the German-Russian frontier on Sept. 1, 1876. He emigrated to the United States in 1893. His fluency in German and Russian made him an invaluable European reporter, and he wrote for the New York *Times* between 1908 and 1912. His coverage of the Russian Revolution for the New York *Herald* in 1918–1919 produced his greatest "scoop"—the discovery and publication of secret prewar exchanges between Kaiser William II and Czar Nicholas II.

In the 1920's Bernstein published several books on international affairs. He died at Sheffield, Mass., on Aug. 31, 1935.

Leonard Bernstein, American conductor and composer.

BERNSTEIN, bûrn'stĭn, **Leonard** (1918–   ),
American conductor and composer, who in 1958
became the first American-born music director
of the New York Philharmonic orchestra. Bernstein became distinguished for his spirited and
somewhat romantic conducting style and his
special mastery of contemporary music. His own
compositions often utilize the rhythms of modern
jazz.

Bernstein was born at Lawrence, Mass., on
Aug. 25, 1918. He graduated from Harvard
(1939) and studied music with Fritz Reiner at
the Curtis Institute of Music in Philadelphia. In
1943, after being appointed assistant conductor
of the New York Philharmonic, he suddenly was
called upon to substitute for guest conductor
Bruno Walter. The enthusiastic response of the
critics and public to this performance made his
reputation. The following season three of his
compositions had New York premieres—Symphony No. 1 (*Jeremiah*), the ballet *Fancy Free*,
and the musical *On the Town*. In 1945, Bernstein was appointed conductor of the New York
City Symphony, remaining for three seasons.

Bernstein wrote some of his best-known music
in the 1950's. The musicals *Wonderful Town*
(1953) and *West Side Story* (1957) were long-
run hits, and *Candide* received the New York
Theatre Critics award for 1956. The Serenade
for Violin and String Orchestra with Percussion
(1954) won high critical praise.

In 1957, Bernstein was appointed coconduc-
tor, with Dimitri Mitropoulos, of the New York
Philharmonic, and the following season he became music director. In 1966 he announced his
decision to give up this post in 1969 in order to
concentrate on composing. His televised lecture-
concerts brought a new understanding of serious
music to millions of viewers.

Bernstein's other compositions include *Facsimile* (ballet, 1946), *The Age of Anxiety* (Symphony No. 2, 1949), *La Bonne Cuisine* (song
cycle, 1949), *Trouble in Tahiti* (opera, 1952),
incidental music for *Peter Pan* (1950), the score
for the film *On the Waterfront* (1954), and the
Kaddish Symphony (1963). He is the author of
The Joy of Music (1959) and *Leonard Bernstein's Young People's Concerts for Reading and
Listening* (1962).

BERNSTORFF, bern'shtôrf, a noble German family, several of whose members served Denmark,
Prussia, and Germany in important political and
diplomatic posts.

COUNT JOHANN HARTWIG ERNST VON BERN-
STORFF (1712–1772) was born in Hannover, Germany, on May 13, 1712. He entered the service
of Denmark in 1733 and was ambassador to
Paris in 1744–1750. As foreign minister from
1751 to 1770, he kept Denmark neutral during
the Seven Years' War and negotiated an important treaty (1767) with Russia, exchanging Oldenburg and Delmenhorst for Gottorp, in Holstein. He died in Hamburg on Feb. 18, 1772.

COUNT ANDREAS PETER VON BERNSTORFF (1735–
1797), nephew of the preceding, was born in
Hannover on Aug. 28, 1735. He was Danish foreign minister in 1773–1780 and 1784–1797. His
first act was to complete the territorial exchange
with Russia that had been negotiated by his uncle.
During his second ministry he carried through a
program of liberal reforms, including emancipation of the peasants from serfdom. He died in
Copenhagen on June 21, 1797.

COUNT CHRISTIAN GÜNTHER VON BERNSTORFF
(1769–1835), son of Andreas, was born in Copenhagen in April 3, 1769. After serving as Denmark's ambassador in Berlin and Stockholm, he
became secretary of state for foreign affairs in
1797 and was foreign minister in 1800–1810. In
1818 he entered the service of Prussia as foreign
minister, holding the post until 1832. He died
in Berlin on March 28, 1835.

COUNT JOHANN-HEINRICH VON BERNSTORFF
(1862–1939) was born in London, England, where
his father was Prussian ambassador, on Nov. 14,
1862. He was the grandnephew of Christian von
Bernstorff. After several diplomatic assignments,
he was named German ambassador to the United
States in 1908 and remained there until relations
were severed in 1917. After the war, he entered
the Reichstag as a member of the Democratic
party and was a delegate to the disarmament
conferences of 1929–1931. When the Nazi regime came to power in 1933, he settled in Geneva, Switzerland, and died there on Oct. 6, 1939.

BERNWARD, bern'värt, **Saint** (c. 960–1022),
German cleric noted for his ecclesiastical art
work. His name is also spelled *Berward*. He was
the grandson of Athelbero, count palatine of
Saxony. Bernward studied under Thangmar, director of the cathedral school at Heidelberg, who
later became his biographer. After being ordained at Mainz, he was appointed chaplain at
the imperial court in 987, and the following year
he became the tutor of the boy emperor Otto III.
In 993 he was consecrated bishop of Hildesheim.

Under Bernward's leadership, Hildesheim became a flourishing artistic and literary center.
He is credited with having designed the bronze
doors of the cathedral of Hildesheim, and he may
have planned the basilican abbey church of St.
Michael. The famous jewel-encrusted Bernward
Cross and the Bernward Column, showing scenes
from the life of Christ, are also attributed to him.
Bernward founded a school of copyists and prepared the original manuscripts from which they
worked. He also constructed the fortifications of
Hildesheim. A Benedictine monastery was established by him there, and he became a member
of that order shortly before his death on Nov. 20,
1022. He was canonized in 1193. His feast is
celebrated on November 20.

Beroë

WALTER DAWN

BEROË, ber′ə-wē, is a genus of comb jellyfish (*Ctenophora*) found in all seas. It has a tapered cylindrical shape and is about 4 to 8 inches (10 to 20 cm) long. At the wider end of the body is a large mouth; at the narrower end is a sense organ. The digestive tube (gullet) occupies a large part of the body. The beroë is rose-pink and largely transparent. It is slightly phosphorescent at night.

BERRA, ber′ə, **Yogi** (1925–   ), American baseball player, who won the American League's Most Valuable Player award in 1951, 1954, and 1955, and who was named to the All-Star squad 14 times. He blended greatness with humility in becoming one of baseball's most astute catchers. He was admitted to the Baseball Hall of Fame in 1972.

Lawrence Peter Berra was born in St. Louis, Mo., on May 12, 1925. He entered the Yankee farm system in 1943 and served two years in the U.S. Navy before joining the New York club at the end of the 1946 season. He was the Yankees' regular catcher for 14 seasons and also played in the outfield at times. In 2,116 games, he hit 313 home runs as a catcher (a major league record for catchers) and 45 more as an outfielder.

Berra set a major league record for catchers by playing 148 games without error (1957–1959). He held records for appearing in the most World Series (14) and the most Series games (75), and for making the most Series hits (71). Berra managed the Yankees in 1964. Relieved of that job after his team lost the World Series that year, he coached and later managed the New York Mets of the National League.

BILL BRADDOCK, *New York "Times"*

BERRIEN, ber′ē-ən, **John MacPherson** (1781–1856), American lawyer, public official, and political leader. He was born in Rocky Hill, N.J., on Aug. 23, 1781, was educated privately in New York, and graduated from Princeton University in 1796. He studied law in Savannah, Ga., and practiced briefly in Louisville, Ga., before settling in Savannah. From 1810 to 1821 he was judge of the eastern circuit court of Georgia and in 1822–1823 a state senator. He served in the U.S. Senate as a Democrat from Georgia from 1825 to 1829, when he resigned to accept appointment as attorney general in President Jackson's first cabinet. His disapproval of Jackson's policies led him to resign in 1831, and for the next 10 years he practiced law.

Berrien was elected to the U.S. Senate as a Whig in 1841 but resigned again in 1845. The Georgia legislature, however, elected him to fill the vacancy created by his own resignation, and he remained in Washington until he resigned a third time in 1852.

In the 1840's Berrien advocated moderation on the question of slavery, and in 1848 he successfully opposed an attempt by John C. Calhoun to corral the Southern states into an extremist regional party. In 1850, however, he refused to support Henry Clay's compromise Omnibus Bill, and thereafter he despaired of seeing the Union preserved. He died at Savannah on Jan. 1, 1856.

BERRUGUETE, ber-rōō-gā′tä, **Alonso** (c. 1489–1561), one of the major sculptors of the Spanish Renaissance. His work, polychromed in the Spanish tradition, has a restless agitation and an emotional spirituality that typify the baroque tendencies in Spanish Renaissance art. He was also a painter and an architect.

Berruguete was born at Paredes de Nava, Spain, the son of the court painter Pedro Berruguete, who gave him his early training. From about 1504 to 1517, Alonso studied in Italy, where he knew Michelangelo and may have been apprenticed to him. He also became acquainted with Baccio Bandinelli and other celebrated artists of the late Italian Renaissance. When he returned home, he helped spread the influence of the Italian Renaissance in Spain. In 1523, Berruguete was appointed court painter to Emperor Charles V. A few of his rather uninspired mannerist paintings survive, some at Salamanca and some at Valladolid, where he built himself a house in 1528 after leaving the emperor's service. He died in Toledo in September 1561.

Among Berruguete's major sculptural works are the choir stalls of the Cathedral of Toledo (1539–1548); the carved pieces for the altar of San Benito el Real (1529–1533), now in the museum at Valladolid; and the imposing tomb of Juan Cardinal Tavera at Toledo (1557–1561).

Further Reading: Orueta y Duarte, R. de, *Berruguete y su obra* (Madrid 1917); Gómez Moreno, Manuel, *Golden Age of Spanish Sculpture* (New York 1964).

BERRY, be-rē′ **Duchess de** (1798–1870), wife of Charles Ferdinand de Bourbon, duke de Berry. The eldest daughter of Francis I of Naples, she was born Princess Caroline Ferdinande Louise in Palermo, Italy, on Nov. 5, 1798. Shortly after the assassination of her husband in 1820, she bore his son, the future count de Chambord, the last member of the elder branch of the Bourbons.

After the revolution of 1830 in France, she followed Charles X to England, and then attempted to provoke a counterrevolution. She was arrested at Nantes and imprisoned. Released after the birth of a daughter in May 1833, she retired to Palermo, where she joined Count Ettore Lucchesi-Palli, to whom she had been secretly married. She died at Brunnensee, Switzerland, on April 17, 1870.

The count de Chambord, pretender to the French throne, was called by his partisans Henry V. He died without heirs in 1883.

BERRY, be-rē′, **Duke de** (1340–1416), French prince, who played an important role in French political life during the early part of the Hundred Years' War. He was born *Jean de France*, in Vincennes, on Nov. 3, 1340, the third son of King John II the Good. He became count of Poitiers in 1356 and was made duke of Auvergne and of Berry in 1360. After the Treaty of Brétigny in 1360, he was held hostage in England until 1367. He governed Languedoc in 1380–1388 but was removed when his extortionate taxes caused peasant revolts.

When his nephew, King Charles VI, became insane in 1492, de Berry shared the regency with his relatives the dukes of Burgundy and Orléans. He frequently mediated between the houses of Burgundy and Orléans but in later years he favored the Orléans faction, the Armagnacs.

De Berry was a noted patron of arts and letters. The illuminated book of hours *Très riches heures du duc de Berry* bears his name. He died in Paris on June 15, 1416.

BERRY, be-rē', **Duke de** (1778–1820), French nobleman. He was born *Charles Ferdinand de Bourbon* at Versailles, France, on Jan. 24, 1778. He was the second son of the count d'Artois (afterward King Charles X of France) and Maria Theresa of Savoy. In 1792, during the French Revolution, he fled with his father to Turin, served under him and Condé on the Rhine, and then joined the Russian army. Afterward he lived alternately in England and Scotland, continually planning for the restoration of the Bourbons.

Landing at Cherbourg, in Normandy, on April 13, 1814, he passed through the northern cities of France, winning over soldiers to his cause. When Napoleon returned to France from exile on the island of Elba, King Louis XVIII gave Berry the command of all troops in and around Paris, but he had to retreat. The Battle of Waterloo enabled him to return to Paris.

At the opening of the legislature in Paris, he became president of the fourth bureau, but he soon retired from public life. In 1816 he married Princess Caroline Ferdinande Louise, daughter of King Francis I of Naples. He was assassinated in Paris on Feb. 13, 1820, by a political fanatic named Louis Pierre Louvel and died the next day. The duke left a daughter, Louise Marie Thérèse, and a son, the count de Chambord, born after his death.

BERRY, ber'ē, **Martha McChesney,** (1866–1942), American philanthropist and educator. She was born near Rome, Ga., on Oct. 7, 1866, and was educated at the Edgeworth School in Baltimore, Md. After travels in Europe she decided to devote her time to teaching the impoverished white children of the mountain region where she was born. An elementary school, known as the Mount Berry School, was opened on her Georgia estate in 1902. Berry College was opened in 1926. In the Berry program, students pay for their tuition by part-time work on the school farm or in workshops attached to the schools. The program has enabled thousands of mountain children to earn an education. This pioneer form of work-study plan has been emulated at other places in the United States.

Miss Berry gained many awards, citations, and prizes for her contributions to education. In addition to a Ph.D. earned at the University of Georgia she was granted eight honorary doctorates by other institutions of higher learning. She was a member of the Georgia State Planning Commission and of the Board of Regents of the state university system. She also became well known as a writer and lecturer on the lives of the Southern mountaineers. Miss Berry died in Atlanta on Feb. 27, 1942.

RICHARD E. GROSS, *Stanford University*

BERRY, be-rē', was a province of central France, with Bourges as its capital. Berry (or *Berri*) now forms principally the departments of Indre and Cher.

Under the Romans, Berry was a section of Aquitania Prima. It passed to the Franks in the 6th century, and later was ruled by a line of hereditary counts until 1200 when the French kings gained control. In 1360 it was made a duchy and in 1601 it was annexed by the French crown. It was a province of France until 1789. Berry gave title at various times to French royal princes. The later novels of George Sand give a good picture of Berry.

BERRY, ber'ē, a pulpy and usually edible fruit. It consists of a single ripened ovary whose wall (pericarp) is all or mostly soft and fleshy at maturity. Berries whose entire pericarp is fleshy include the tomato and grape.

A berry with a hard rind, such as a watermelon or a cucumber, is called a *pepo*. A berry with a leathery rind, such as an orange or a lemon, is called a *hesperidium*.

The word "berry" is most commonly used to refer to such common bush fruits as strawberries, blueberries, and cranberries, although these fruits are not classified as berries by botanists. See also FRUIT.

BERRYER, be-rē-yā' **Pierre Antoine** (1790–1868), French lawyer and orator. He was born in Paris, France, on Jan. 4, 1790. The son of Pierre Nicolas Berryer (1757–1841), a well-known specialist in criminal law, Berryer studied law with his father, whom he assisted in the defense of Marshal Michel Ney after the fall of Napoleon in 1815.

Although he supported the legitimist cause, he also defended Bonapartists and liberals, and championed the cause of freedom of the press during the Restoration. He was the only spokesman in the Chamber of Deputies for the Bourbon family after the revolution of 1830. Although he tried vainly to dissuade the duchess de Berry from attempting to place her son, the count de Chambord, on the throne, Berryer was believed to be her accomplice and was arrested (1832) but soon acquitted.

Later he defended Louis Napoleon after the latter's unsuccessful revolt at Boulogne (1840). Elected to the National Assembly in 1848, he continued to uphold the divine right of kings, but stood for liberal principles and for moderation in action. He was elected to the French Academy in 1855. Berryer died in Augerville-la-Rivière, France, on Nov. 29, 1868.

BERRYMAN, ber'ē-mən, **John** (1914–1972), American poet and critic. He was born in McAlester, Okla., on Oct. 25, 1914. He graduated from Columbia College in 1936 and took a B. A. degree at Cambridge University in 1938. After teaching creative writing, poetry, and humanities at other American universities, he joined the faculty of the University of Minnesota in 1954, remaining there until his death, by suicide, on Jan. 7, 1972, in Minneapolis.

Berryman's poetry, usually somber in tone, is collected in such volumes as *Poems* (1942); *The Dispossessed* (1948); *77 Dream Songs* (1964), for which he received the 1965 Pulitzer Prize for poetry; and *Delusions, etc.* (1972). He also wrote *Stephen Crane* (1950), a critical biography.

BERSERK, bər-sûrk′, in Scandinavian legend, one of a group of warriors who in the heat of battle took on the attributes of wild animals. They had superhuman strength and were invulnerable to weapons or fire. They were given this name, which means "bear shirt" or "bare of armor" in Old Norse, because of their practice of wearing bearskins.

According to another account, Berserk was a warrior, the grandson of the eight-handed Starkader (Starkadder) and the beautiful Alfhilde. He and his 12 sons (Berserker), as ferocious as their father, were invincible in battle.

In modern usage, to "go berserk" is to lose oneself in a violent rage bordering on insanity.

BERT, bâr, **Paul** (1833–1886), French physiologist and politician, who studied the effects of gases on living organisms. He was born in Auxerre, France, on Oct. 17, 1833. Educated in engineering, law, and physiology, he taught at Bordeaux and later (1869) at the Sorbonne. He contributed to research on anesthesia and studied the toxic effects of oxygen at high pressure. Bert also was active in politics and served as minister of public instruction briefly in 1881–1882. Shortly after being appointed governor general of Tonkin and Annam (now parts of Vietnam), he died in Hanoi on Nov. 11, 1886. He wrote *La pression barométrique* (1878), an important contribution to aviation medicine.

BERTHELOT, ber-tə-lō′, **Pierre Eugène Marcelin** (1827–1907), French chemist, who was a founder of thermochemistry and a pioneer in organic chemistry. Berthelot was born in Paris on Oct. 27, 1827. He studied chemistry at the Collège de France and wrote a doctoral dissertation on ways to synthesize natural fats. Later, he prepared natural carbon compounds, such as methyl alcohol, ethyl alcohol, methane, benzene, and acetylene, from inorganic sources. Berthelot also prepared compounds of carbon that were not a part of any organism.

Since Friedrich Wöhler's preparation of urea from laboratory chemicals in 1828, chemists had obtained more evidence for the mechanist doctrine that life and life products could be explained by the principles of physics and chemistry. The vitalists, who opposed the mechanists, believed that the presence of living things was required for the formation of organic substances. Berthelot's work continued and strengthened the efforts of chemists who believed in the mechanist view of life.

As a founder of thermochemistry, he introduced the term "exothermic" for chemical reactions that yield heat and the term "endothermic" for chemical reactions that absorb heat. His studies in thermochemistry were in accord with his mechanist point of view, and he held that chemical phenomena can be explained in terms of mechanist principles.

Berthelot was a professor of organic chemistry at the École Supérieure de Pharmacie and at the Collège de France. He was a member of the Academy of Medicine and the Academy of Sciences. His works include *Chimie organique fondée sur la synthèse* (1860); *Sur la force de la poudre et des matières explosives* (1872); *Essai de mécanique chimique fondée sur la thermochimie* (1879); and *Science et philosophie* (1886). He died in Paris on March 18, 1907.

MORRIS GORAN, *Roosevelt University*

BERTHIER, ber-tyä′, **Louis Alexandre** (1753–1815), marshal of France and chief of staff under Napoleon. He was born at Versailles on Feb. 20, 1753. After being educated by his father, he entered the army in 1770. In the American Revolution he served under Rochambeau, rising to the rank of colonel. During the early stages of the French Revolution he fought against the royalists, but he was removed from command in 1793 for being the son of a noble. He reentered the army in 1795 and began serving under Napoleon in the Army of Italy in 1796. In October 1797, Napoleon sent him to Paris to deliver France's treaty with Austria (Treaty of Campo Formio) to the Directory. Berthier entered Rome in 1798 and proclaimed the Roman Republic.

After Napoleon became emperor, Berthier received many honors. He was made marshal in 1804 and prince of Neuchâtel and prince of Wagram in 1809. He was also Napoleon's minister of war from 1800 to 1807. In 1805, Napoleon made him major general of the Grand Army. In this position he was the emperor's closest assistant and played an essential role in French campaigns throughout Europe.

In 1814, after Napoleon was confined on the island of Elba, Berthier joined the forces of King Louis XVIII. Learning of Napoleon's plan to return to France, he retired to Bamberg, Germany. He died at Bamberg, apparently as the result of an accident, on June 1, 1815. Although his death is sometimes attributed to murder or suicide, there is no firm evidence for either. His *Mémoires* was published in 1827.

BERTHIERVILLE, ber′tyä-vēl, is an industrial town in Quebec, on the St. Lawrence River, 45 miles (72 km) northeast of Montreal. Its industries include a tree nursery, a distillery, and factories producing chemicals, small knives, knit goods, wooden boxes, sashes, and doors.

The town was named for Captain Alexandre Berthier, to whom the first estate in the area was granted in 1673. The first Protestant church built in Canada after the British conquest was built here in 1786. Population: 4,080.

BERTHOLET, ber-tô-le′, **Alfred** (1868–1951), Swiss Protestant theologian. He was born at Basel on Nov. 9, 1868. After a brief period as pastor of a Dutch-German church in Leghorn, Italy, he turned to a scholarly career. He held professorships at the universities of Basel, Tübingen, Göttingen, and Berlin, leaving this last post in 1939. During his years in Germany he became a noted Old Testament scholar. After his return to Switzerland in 1939 he lectured at Basel on the history of religions. He died at Münsterlingen on Aug. 24, 1951.

Bertholet's works include a commentary (1897–1902) on the Old Testament books of Leviticus, Deuteronomy, Ezekiel, Ruth, Ezra, and Nehemiah; *Das Geschlecht der Gottheit* (1934), a study of the nature of divinity; and *Über kultische Motivverschiebungen* (1938), a survey of cult beliefs.

Bertholet also compiled a dictionary of religions and prepared a new edition of a famous history of religions by Chantepie de la Saussaye (*Lehrbuch der Religionsgeschichte*, 4th ed., 1925).

FREDERICK C. GRANT
Union Theological Seminary

BERTHOLLET, ber-tô-le', **Claude Louis** (1748–1822), French chemist, who pointed out that a chemical reaction depends partly on the quantities of the reacting substances. Berthollet was born in Talloire, France, on Dec. 9, 1748. He received degrees in medicine at Turin in 1768 and at Paris in 1779. He then turned to chemistry and wrote papers that led to his being named a member of the Academy of Sciences in 1780. Later, he was a professor of chemistry in the higher schools in Paris.

In 1785, Berthollet determined the composition of ammonia. He did research on chlorine and chlorine compounds in 1785–1787 and discovered the bleaching properties of chlorine in 1789. He also showed (1789) that hydrocyanic acid and hydrogen sulfide did not contain oxygen, whereas the view of Antoine Laurent Lavoisier was that all acids contained oxygen. Berthollet, Lavoisier, and others proposed methods for naming chemical compounds, and their work was published as *Méthode de nomenclature chimique* (1787).

After a trip to Egypt with the Napoleonic expedition of 1798, Berthollet explained the part played by mass in chemical changes (1799–1803) and modified the theory of affinity. This work led him to posit the theory that substances combine in indefinite proportions (1803). In a controversy with Joseph Louis Proust, Berthollet argued against the idea that elements combine in definite proportions. Berthollet's works include *Éléments de l'art de la teinture* (1791); *Recherches sur les lois des affinités chimiques* (1801); and *Essai de statique chimique* (1803). He died in Arcueil on Nov. 6, 1822.

Further Reading: Leicester, Henry M., *Historical Background of Chemistry* (New York 1956); Partington, J.R., *A Short History of Chemistry* (New York 1957).

BERTHOUD, ber-tōō', **Ferdinand** (1727–1807), Swiss inventor of marine clocks. He was born in Plancemont, Switzerland, on March 19, 1727. His father had him taught the art of watchmaking, and later sent him to Paris where he lived from 1745. There he made his first marine chronometers, which were used by French navigators. Berthoud died at Goslay, Switzerland, on June 20, 1807.

BERTILLON, ber-tē-yôn', **Alphonse** (1853–1914), French criminologist, who developed a system of identification based on anthropometry, the scientific measurement of the human body (see BERTILLON SYSTEM). He was born in Paris on April 23, 1853, and joined the Paris police department as a clerk in 1878. Later he organized and headed its department of judicial identity. His revolutionary system, including the *portrait parlé*, or "descriptive" sectional photograph, was used in Paris from 1882 and was officially adopted for all of France in 1888. It was widely used in Europe and North America until supplanted in the late 1890's by the fingerprint method of identification. Although he was one of the first users of fingerprints, Bertillon considered this method only supplementary to his own.

Bertillon testified to the guilt of Alfred Dreyfus in both treason trials in this famous case, but in so doing severely damaged his position as an expert on handwriting. Generally, however, his achievements in criminology were favorably recognized by his contemporaries. Bertillon died in Paris on Feb. 13, 1914.

BERTILLON SYSTEM, ber-tē-yôn', a method of identifying criminals developed in 1879 by the French criminologist Alphonse Bertillon (q.v.) and used in almost all countries until about the turn of the century. The system, known also as *bertillonage*, used methods from anthropometry, the scientific measurement of certain bony parts of the body. The system was founded on three basic principles: (1) that precise measurements of certain parts of the body can be easily taken; (2) that these measurements remain constant after maturity; and (3) that no two humans have the same dimensions in all the parts measured. The measurements included length and width of head, length and width of right ear, length of left middle and little fingers, and length of left forearm and foot.

The measurements were classified in terms of small, medium, and large sizes. Index cards were divided into three groups according to length of head. These groups were subdivided into three more groups in terms of small, medium, and large width of head. These classifications were again subdivided according to length of left middle finger and then length of left little finger. These were successively subdivided according to additional measurements, all in terms of small, medium, and large. An individual suspected of crime had his measurements recorded in this fashion, along with a record of any convictions.

An integral part of this system was the *portrait parlé*, or "descriptive portrait." This was a method of sectional photography introduced by Bertillon to revise the prevailing haphazard system of photographing suspects. Front and profile views were taken, as well as views of sections of the face that had distinguishing marks and characteristics. Bertillon emphasized recording the convolutions of the ear as a positive means of identification—a technique similar to the stress on whorls and loops in fingerprint patterns. The descriptive photograph was attached to the measurement card and was referred to when suspects were checked out. The *portrait parlé*, originally devised as a supplement to the system of measurement, became the most important part of the Bertillon system. This aspect of the system is still a vital part of current identification methods.

In addition to its use in criminology, the Bertillon system of measurement and description was used to identify unknown victims of tragedies. The method was employed, for example, after the ship *Drummond Castle* was wrecked on the French coast in 1896. The system was also used by so-called anthropologists in an attempt to prove the superiority of certain races by comparing bodily measurements. Bertillon never intended that his techniques should be so used.

The Bertillon system of measurement is less comprehensive than was originally believed, for the categories he set up were based on data for adult white males and do not necessarily apply to other groups. Moreover, characteristics once held to be positive clues to identification can vary—for example, arthritis or a joint injury might change the length of a finger. Within its limitations, however, the system was remarkably reliable. Moreover, the introduction of technical precision into police methods was a lasting contribution.

Further Reading: Bertillon, Alphonse, *Identification anthropométrique* (Paris 1893); Rhodes, Henry T.F., *Alphonse Bertillon* (New York 1956).

BERTOIA, bâr-toi'ə, **Harry** (1915–   ), American sculptor, whose best-known works are monumental sculptural screens of welded metal, designed for specific architectural settings. A subtle rhythm runs through the abstract pattern of his screens, which are composed of brass plates, open spaces, and metal rods. In smaller pieces, Bertoia explored the possibilities of motion and sound in sculpture.

He was born in San Lorenzo, Italy, on March 10, 1915, and went to the United States in 1930. He attended the Arts and Crafts School in Detroit and the Cranbrook Academy of Art in Bloomfield Hills, Mich. As a designer for Knoll furniture (1950–1954), Bertoia created one of the most successful modern steel-frame chairs.

Among Bertoia's major architectural pieces are those in the Massachusetts Institute of Technology Chapel, Cambridge; General Motors Technical Center, Detroit; and the Dallas Public Library. He did the large bronze *View of the Earth from Space* (1962) for Dulles International Airport, Washington, D.C. He was awarded the gold medal of the American Institute of Architects (1956) and the Graham Foundation award (1957).

BERTRAM OF MINDEN (c. 1345–1414/1415), ber'träm, min'dən, German painter, whose use of gentle rhythms and softly flowing draperies foreshadow the international Gothic style. He was born in Minden, Westphalia, but made his reputation in Hamburg, where by 1367 he was a member of the painters' guild. His workshop attracted many students and helped to make Hamburg an art center. He was a successful and wealthy artist by the time of his death in 1414 or 1415 in Hamburg.

His major work is the Grabow altarpiece (about 1379–1383; Kunsthalle, Hamburg), also called *The Creation, and the Life of the Virgin.* The altarpiece, originally made for St. Peter's Church in Hamburg, consists of 24 panels depicting the creation of the world and the life of the Virgin. Its robust style indicates that Bertram may have seen the work of Theodoric of Prague. The *Passion* altar (about 1379; Landesmuseum, Hannover) is also attributed to Bertram, but the Buxtehude altarpiece (about 1380; Kunsthalle, Hamburg), once thought to be his, is now attributed to a follower.

BERTRAN DE BORN (c. 1140–c. 1215), ber-trän' də bôrn, provençal soldier and troubadour. As the *vicomte de Hautefort,* he was the proprietor of an immense family estate in Aquitaine, of which he secured sole possession by expelling his brother Constantin. He involved himself deeply in wars and politics before retiring to a monk's life at Dalon, near Hautefort, where he died. In the *Inferno,* Dante pictures Bertran as carrying his severed head before him, a fitting punishment for this "sower of schism" between King Henry II of England, Bertran's feudal lord, and Henry's sons, Prince Richard (the Lion-Hearted) and Prince Henry.

Forty-five of Bertran's poems survive. Whether lyrical, satirical, or moral, they mirror the feudal society to which Bertran belonged. He wrote virile love lyrics to several women, including Mathilda, the daughter of Henry II. More characteristic, however, are his *sirventes,* satirical pieces intended to provoke dissension among the nobles of southern France.

BERTRAND, ber-traṅ', **Count Henri Gratien** (1773–1844), French military officer. He was born in Châteauroux on May 28, 1773. Bertrand accompanied Napoleon's expedition to Egypt, later distinguished himself at Austerlitz, and was made Napoleon's adjutant. He was highly praised by Napoleon for the bridges he built across the Danube River before the Battle of Wagram in 1809. Bertrand served in subsequent campaigns and helped save the army after the French defeat at Leipzig in 1813.

He retired with the emperor to Elba in 1814, helped to carry out his return to France in 1815, and finally shared Napoleon's banishment to St. Helena. Bertrand's diary of the years in exile with Napoleon, part of which was translated into English as *Napoleon at St. Helena* (1952), is a frank account of the emperor's character and his life in exile.

On Napoleon's death in 1821, Bertrand returned to France. Although he had been sentenced to death in absentia, the sentence was canceled, and he was allowed to remain in France. In 1831 he was elected to parliament from Châteauroux. With the prince de Joinville, he was sent to St. Helena in 1840 to bring the remains of Napoleon back to France. Bertrand died in Châteauroux on Jan. 31, 1844.

BÉRULLE, bā-rül', **Pierre de** (1575–1629), French cardinal and statesman. He was born near Troyes on Feb. 4, 1575, and ordained to the priesthood in 1599. He introduced the Carmelite Order into France and was its first superior there. In 1611 he founded the French Congregation of the Oratory. This is considered his greatest achievement, because much of the 17th century church reform derived from the work of this community of secular priests. The Oratory established seminaries and improved the quality of preaching and education. Bérulle's spiritual teachings enhanced his stature in the church, and in 1627 he was made a cardinal.

Bérulle also demonstrated unusual ability as a statesman. He obtained the dispensation for the marriage of Henrietta Maria to Charles I of England and accompanied the future queen to England in 1625. A year later his negotiations with Spain over the Valtelline Pass led to the Treaty of Monzón. Cardinal Richelieu strongly opposed Bérulle both for his pro-Spanish policy and for his intransigent anti-Protestantism.

The most noted of Bérulle's many writings is a discourse on the grandeur of Jesus. Bérulle completed a sequel to this work, a life of Jesus, shortly before his death in Paris on Oct. 2, 1629.

BERVIC, ber-vēk', **Charles Clément** (1756–1822), French engraver, who was noted for the accuracy and delicacy of his work. He was born *Jean Guillaume Balvay* in Paris on May 23, 1756. After studying the engraver's art with Jean Baptiste le Prince and Jean Georges Wille, he established his reputation in 1790 with a full-length engraving of Louis XVI in coronation robes, after a painting by Antoine Callet. In 1803 he was elected to the Institut de France. He died in Paris on March 23, 1822.

Bervic worked so slowly that he produced only about 15 plates in his lifetime. All are painstakingly accurate representations of their subjects. After his portrait of Louis XVI, his celebrated engraving of the *Laocoön* is perhaps his best work.

BERWICK, ber'ik, **Duke of** (1670–1734), English nobleman, who attained the rank of marshal of France. He was born *James Fitz-James* at Moulins, France, on Aug. 21, 1670, the illegitimate son of the duke of York (later King James II) and Arabella Churchill, sister of the duke of Marlborough. While in England in 1687, he was made duke of Berwick. After William of Orange landed in England in 1688, Berwick fled to France. He was present at James II's defeat in Ireland at the Battle of the Boyne in 1690.

Following the defeat at the Boyne, Berwick served in the French army. In 1706 he was made marshal of France for his capture of Nice. Sent to help Philip V of Spain in the War of the Spanish Succession in 1707, he won a victory at Almanza that confirmed Philip as king. Berwick was commanding forces on the Rhine during the War of the Polish Succession when he was killed at the siege of Philippsburg on June 12, 1734.

BERWICK, bûr'wik, is a borough in eastern Pennsylvania, in Columbia County. It is situated on the Susquehanna River, 25 miles (40 km) southwest of Wilkes-Barre. Its principal manufactures are steel cars, foundry and machine-shop products, and garments. Berwick was founded in 1786. It is governed by a mayor and council. Population: 12,274.

BERWICK, ber'ik, is a county in the southeastern corner of Scotland, on the border of England. It is bounded on the east by the North Sea. It is known also as *Berwickshire*.

The county has an area of 457 square miles (1,184 sq km). The chief rivers are the Tweed, which forms most of the boundary with England, the Leader Water, the Eye, the Whiteadder Water, and the Blackadder Water. A low, fertile plateau, called the Merse (March), covers the southern two thirds of the county. The land rises in the north to the Lammermuir Hills and in the west to Lauderdale.

Farming is the main economic activity. The Lammermuir district has extensive sheep farms, and the Merse produces grains, potatoes, sheep, and cattle. Other products include stone, woolen goods, lumber, and fish—salmon from the Tweed, and haddock, herring, and shellfish from the sea. The burghs are Duns (the county town), Coldstream, Eyemouth, and Lauder.

Berwick was part of an area annexed to Scotland in 1018. It has many associations with later centuries of border warfare between England and Scotland. Population: (1961) 22,437.

BERWICK-UPON-TWEED, ber'ik, twēd, a municipal borough and seaport in Northumberland, England. It is situated on the north bank of the river Tweed (on the England-Scotland border) near its mouth on the North Sea. It also is called *Berwick-on-Tweed*. It includes the townships of Tweedmouth and Spittal on the south bank of the river and is connected with them by three bridges, one dating from 1624 and another (a railway viaduct of stone) built by Robert Stephenson in 1847–1850. The port exports grain and imports oil and lumber, but it is now relatively unimportant. Industries include a shipyard, chemical plants, and tweed mills. Scenic and historic features nearby attract visitors.

Historically, Berwick was an important border town, long involved in the border wars between England and Scotland. In the early 1100's it was the capital of a district of Scotland known as ·Lothian. It became Scotland's chief seaport and one of its four royal burghs. Beginning in 1147, it changed hands more than a dozen times before being ceded finally to England in 1482. The ramparts now surrounding the town were built originally by Edward I of England when he conquered Berwick in 1302. They were rebuilt under Elizabeth I. Population: (1961) 12,178.

BERWYN, bûr'win, a residential city in northeastern Illinois, in Cook County, 10 miles (16 km) west of downtown Chicago. There are no major industries. It was planned as a residential community in 1891 and received a city charter in 1908. Berwyn has a combined city and town form of government, with a mayor and council and a town board. Population: 52,502.

EMILY POLIVKA, *Berwyn Public Library*

BERYL, ber'əl, is a silicate mineral and the primary source of beryllium, the light metal increasingly in demand for modern technology (see BERYLLIUM). The mineral is best known in its green variety, the gemstone emerald. Other transparent varieties used as gems are the blue-green aquamarine, the pink morganite, the yellow heliodor, and the colorless goshenite. The colors probably result from the presence of impurities, such as chromium in the case of emerald.

The large, prismatic crystals of common beryl are white, yellow, green, or blue, and may be transparent to opaque. The mineral is widely distributed but is seldom found in great abundance. It occurs as crystals, both singly and in groups, or as small irregular masses in granites, primarily pegmatites.

The major sources of common beryl, all of them pegmatite deposits, are found in Brazil, Argentina, Mozambique, and the Malagasy Republic (Madagascar). The Muzo and Chivor mines in Colombia, the Belingwe district in Rhodesia, a region near Sverdlovsk in the Soviet Union, and Stony Point, N.C., in the United States are famous for the occurrence of emeralds.

Composition: $Be_3Al_2Si_6O_{18}$; hardness, 7.5 to 8.0; specific gravity, 2.6 to 2.9; crystal system, hexagonal.

D. VINCENT MANSON
American Museum of Natural History

Beryl crystal from Madagascar

BERYLLIUM, bə-ril'ē-əm, is a lightweight chemical element that exhibits both metallic and nonmetallic properties. Its symbol is Be. It is the first and lightest member of the alkaline earth metals in Group IIa of the periodic table. Its name is derived from beryl, a mineral in which it occurs. The element was discovered in 1797 by Nicolas Louis Vauquelin during an analysis of emerald, a kind of beryl.

Occurrence. Approximately 0.001 percent of the earth's crust consists of beryllium. Beryl, $3BeO \cdot Al_2O_3 \cdot 6SiO_2$, is the most important source of the element. Major deposits are in Brazil, Argentina, Africa, and India. When colored green by the presence of chromium compounds, the mineral is called emerald. When colored blue-green, it is called aquamarine.

Production. Beryllium is produced from beryl by converting the mineral ore to a more reactive compound and then reducing the compound. In this procedure, beryl is sintered with sodium fluoride to form beryllium fluoride, BeF_2, which is then treated with caustic soda to form beryllium hydroxide. Treatment of beryllium hydroxide with hydrochloric or hydrofluoric acid yields beryllium chloride or fluoride. Electrolytic reduction of the molten chloride or reduction of the fluoride with magnesium produces beryllium.

Structure and Properties. The atomic number of beryllium is 4, indicating four protons in its nucleus. Its electron configuration is $1s^2\ 2s^2$, and its oxidation number in compounds is $+2$. Beryllium, which has an atomic weight of 9.0133, is one of the few elements that has only one stable, naturally occurring isotope. Radioactive isotopes of beryllium include Be-7, Be-8, Be-10, and Be-11. The density of beryllium is 1.85 grams per cubic centimeter at 39° F (4° C). Its melting point is 2,341° F (1,283° C), and its boiling point is 5,378° F (2,970° C). The grayish metal crystallizes in the form of a hexagonal close-packed structure. It is hard and brittle and a good conductor of electricity. The element has a great affinity for oxygen, and the formation of a surface oxide film protects it from further oxidation and corrosion. At high temperatures, beryllium is very active.

Uses. In nuclear technology, a mixture of beryllium and radium is used as a source of neutrons. The radium is a continuous source of alpha particles by radioactive decay. When these particles bombard the beryllium, neutrons are produced. The light weight of beryllium makes it useful in neutron-reflector elements, power-control cylinders, and core-moderator elements.

The low atomic weight of beryllium makes it useful for windows of X-ray tubes. The X rays readily pass through it.

Beryllium is used as a structural material in missiles and spacecraft. Its high modulus of elasticity and high elastic limit make it a useful material in inertial guidance systems.

Beryllium-copper alloys are used in high-strength, current-carrying springs, contacts, connectors, fuse clips, and welding electrodes. Beryllium oxide, BeO, the most important compound of beryllium, is useful in ceramics and electronics because it has high thermal conductivity and high electrical resistivity.

Effects on Man. Inhalation of beryllium dust, mist, or vapor results in acute respiratory disease, chronic berylliosis, or dermatitis. In industry, precautions minimize this hazard.

HERBERT LIEBESKIND, *The Cooper Union*

BERZELIUS, bər-zē'lē-əs, **Baron Jöns Jakob** (1779–1848), Swedish chemist, who is regarded by chemical historians as the organizer of the science of chemistry.

Berzelius was born at Väversunda, near Linköping, Sweden, on Aug. 20 or 29, 1779. In his youth, he showed little interest in conventional studies and was saved from failure at the medical school of Uppsala only by a good showing in physics. As a hospital technician he carried on investigations in chemistry in his spare time. The results were so good that he became connected in a gradually increasing degree with the medical college in Stockholm, where he ultimately became a professor.

Early in his career Berzelius turned his attention to combining weights of elements. In the course of this work, he is said to have determined the combining weights of 43 elements by analyzing with his own hands some 2,000 different compounds. In many cases he had to develop his own methods of research. Some of the results, converted to modern formula weights, are surprisingly accurate, considering that his laboratory facilities were extremely limited.

Berzelius is also credited with the discovery of selenium and thorium, and with the isolation of silicon, molybdenum, and several other elements. He did pioneer work in electrolysis, and from these investigations he evolved his dualistic electrolytic theory, in which he stated that all compounds are made up of negatively and positively charged components.

Berzelius was a devoted admirer of Antoine Laurent Lavoisier and a colleague of Joseph Louis Gay-Lussac, John Dalton, Sir Humphry Davy, and many other leaders of science. The great contributions that he made, and his insistence upon sound experimental evidence and the consistency of all theories with the sum of chemical theory, made him one of the outstanding scientists of all time.

Berzelius was admitted to the Swedish Academy of Sciences in 1808 and became permanent secretary of the academy in 1818. He published numerous volumes of the *Jahresbericht,* or annual report of the academy, that covered the progress of chemistry. He also wrote accounts of his own work and an authoritative textbook on chemistry, *Lehrbuch der Chemie* (1813–18). He was made a baron in 1835. Berzelius died in Stockholm on Aug. 7, 1848.

BESANÇON, bə-zän-sôn', a city in France, is the capital of Doubs department. It is situated at the foot of the Jura Mountains, 45 miles (73 km) east of Dijon.

The city is surrounded by hills covered with vineyards. The old city is on a peninsula formed by a meander of the Doubs River, while the modern industrial suburbs are on its right bank.

Besançon is the center of France's clock- and watchmaking industry and has a watchmaking institute. Other products include synthetic textiles, hosiery, leather goods, iron and steel products, lumber, and liquors.

There are remains of several Roman structures, including a triumphal arch, known as the Porte Noir, which is thought to have been built in the 2d century A.D. to celebrate the victories of Emperor Marcus Aurelius. It was partially rebuilt in 1820–1828. There are also a Roman aqueduct, an amphitheater, and a theater.

The Cathedral of St. Jean, built in the 11th

13th centuries, is in Romanesque and Gothic styles. The architecture of the 16th century is represented by the Palais Granvelle and the town hall. The city's outstanding feature is the 17th century citadel, one of the finest examples of the work of the fortifications expert the marquis de Vauban. The citadel, on a hill over 1,200 feet (365 meters) high, was built on the site of an old Roman encampment. With its nearby forts, the citadel was nearly impregnable before modern weapons came into use.

Known as *Visontio* in ancient times, the place was captured by the Romans under Julius Caesar in 58 B.C. In the Middle Ages it was successively part of the kingdoms of Burgundy and Arles. It was made a free imperial city by Emperor Frederick Barbarossa in 1184, and it kept its independence until 1648, when it came under Spanish rule. It was captured by Louis XIV in 1674 and two years later was made the capital of Franche-Comté.

Besançon was the birthplace of the socialist Charles Fourier and the novelist Victor Hugo. Population: (1962) 90,203.

BESANT, bĕz'ənt, **Annie** (1847–1933), English social reformer, theosophist, and Indian independence leader. For more than 60 years she was at the forefront of the liberal movements in behalf of intellectual freedom, women's rights, and individual dignity. She was a woman of great personal beauty, commanding presence, and vast energy. George Bernard Shaw, a longtime friend and associate, regarded her as the greatest woman orator of her time.

Annie Besant (maiden name *Wood*) was born in England on Oct. 1, 1847. Her father died when she was a child, and although he had left his wife and children well provided for, the family's finances were quickly dissipated through inept management by their solicitor. Annie was privately educated by Ellen Marryat, sister of the then-popular writer Frederick Marryat, at Marryat's country estate. A gifted though emotional child, Annie benefited from Miss Marryat's progressive approach to education, which allowed her freedom to pursue her own intellectual interests. As a young woman she was a devout Anglican, and she steeped herself in the Bible and religious literature. In 1867 she married Frank Besant, an Anglican clergyman several years her senior, but could not adjust to his strict conventional standards. Having developed a number of doubts concerning religious dogma, she found herself in constant dispute with her husband, and in 1873 she separated from him.

In 1874 she became associated with Charles Bradlaugh, a professed atheist, and became active in the National Secular Society and free-thought movements. Her writings and lectures made Mrs. Besant a national figure in Britain, and in 1877 she became internationally known as a defendant in a trial involving freedom of the press. She and Bradlaugh had reissued a pamphlet on sex and birth control written some 45 years before by Charles Knowlton, an American physician. With Bradlaugh she stood trial on charges of publishing immoral literature, but both were exonerated by a higher court.

After several years of working for the cause of atheism, Mrs. Besant joined the Fabian Society and contributed one of the seminal articles to the influential collection *Fabian Essays* (1885), edited by Shaw. Some time later Shaw gave her a book to review, *The Secret Doctrine* by Elena Petrovna Blavatsky, which converted her to the religious movement known as theosophy, a synthesis of Oriental and Christian thought that emphasizes the spiritual perfectibility of man. She was president of the Theosophical Society from 1907 until her death.

In 1893, as suddenly as she had made other important decisions in her life, Mrs. Besant went to India, where for the rest of her life she worked for Indian home rule and helped organize the Central Hindu College at Benares (Varanasi) in 1898. A longtime associate of Jawaharlal Nehru, whom she had initiated into the Theosophical Society, she split with him over policies regarding the independence movement, her views being too moderate for Nehru. Annie Besant died at Adyar, Madras, India, on Sept. 20, 1933.

Further Reading: Du Cann, Charles G.L., *Loves of George Bernard Shaw* (New York 1963); Nethercot, Arthur H., *First Five Lives of Annie Besant* (Chicago 1960); Nethercot, Arthur H., *Last Four Lives of Annie Besant* (Chicago 1963).

BESANT, bez'ənt, **Sir Walter** (1836–1901), English author, who is best known for his novels of life in the London slums. He was born in Portsmouth, Hampshire, on Aug. 14, 1836. Educated at King's College, London, and Christ College, Cambridge, he taught from 1861 to 1867 at the Royal College in the British colony of Mauritius. At this time he became interested in French literature and published several scholarly works on the subject, including *Studies in Early French Poetry* (1868), *The French Humourists from the Twelfth to the Nineteenth Century* (1873), and an investigation of the writings of Rabelais (1879). From 1868 to 1886 he served as secretary of the Palestine Exploration Fund, and in 1871 he published, with the Orientalist Edward Palmer, *Jerusalem: The City of Herod and Saladin.* He later edited *The Survey of Western Palestine* (1881–83).

In the 1870's, Besant wrote a number of novels in collaboration with James Rice, including *Ready-Money Mortiboy* (1872), *This Son of Vulcan* (1875), *The Golden Butterfly* (1876), *By Celia's Arbour* (1878), and *The Chaplain of the Fleet* (1879). In 1882 he published *All Sorts and Conditions of Men,* a study of life in the East End slum area of London, which led to the establishment of a famous public center, the People's Palace. In 1884 he wrote what he considered his best work, the novel *Dorothy Forster.* Besant's other novels include *Children of Gibeon* (1886), *The World Went Very Well Then* (1887), *Armorel of Lyonesse* (1890), *The Ivory Gate* (1892), *The Rebel Queen* (1893), *Beyond the Dreams of Avarice* (1895), *The Orange Girl* (1899), and *The Alabaster Box* (1900).

He also wrote biographies of Gaspard de Coligny (1879), Sir Richard Whittington (with Rice, 1881), Edward Henry Palmer (1882), and Captain James Cook (1889). He projected a great survey of London, intended to cover the history of the city from the earliest times, and wrote five volumes of preliminary studies: *London* (1892), *Westminster* (1895), *South London* (1899), *East London* (1901), and *The Thames* (published posthumously, 1902).

Besant did much to promote the interests of writers. He was instrumental in founding the Society of Authors in 1884 and edited the *Author* from 1890 until his death. He was knighted in 1895. Besant died in London on June 9, 1901.

BESNARD, bā-nȧr', **Paul Albert** (1849–1934), French painter, who was one of the last important painters to defend the academic tradition against the onslaught of impressionism and other modern styles. He was born in Paris on June 2, 1849, and attended the École des Beaux-Arts. After winning the Prix de Rome in 1874, he studied in Rome at the Villa Medici.

Besnard first made his reputation as a portrait and landscape painter in London, where he lived from 1879 until 1883, when he returned to Paris. Many of his most important works are murals for public buildings in Paris, including panels for the School of Pharmacy at the University of Paris (1884) and for the Hôtel de Ville (1890) and the Théâtre-Français (1913). He also painted murals for the Peace Palace at The Hague, Netherlands, in 1914. Trips to Spain, Algeria, and India inspired many of his exotic and romantic easel paintings. Besnard headed the Villa Medici from 1913 until 1919, when he became director of the École des Beaux-Arts. He died in Paris on Dec. 4, 1934.

BESSARABIA, bes-ə-rā'bē-ə, is a historical region of southeastern Europe, long disputed between Russia and Rumania. Its 17,000 square miles (44,000 sq km) is bounded by the Dniester (Dnestr) River on the east, the Prut River on the west, and the Danube delta and the Black Sea on the south and southeast. Since 1940 it has been part of the USSR, where most of Bessarabia forms the Moldavian Soviet Socialist Republic. Southern Bessarabia is within the Odessa oblast of the Ukraine.

The terrain, hilly and heavily dissected by stream valleys and gullies, rises to 1,400 feet (425 meters) in the forested Kodry hills of the central part of the region. Precipitation ranges from 20 inches (51 cm) in the north to 12 inches (30 cm) in the south, where the dry Budzhak steppe is periodically threatened by drought.

Bessarabia is a fertile agricultural region, specializing in wine grapes and fruits, with some grains (winter wheat and corn), sugar beets, sunflowers, and tobacco. The region's industry is based primarily on the processing of it farm products. The main cities are Kishinev, Beltsy, Tiraspol, and Izmail.

About two thirds of the population is made up of Moldavians, whose speech is virtually identical with Rumanian. The rest consists of Ukrainians, Russians, Gagauz (a people of Turkic stock), Jews, and Bulgarians.

Early History. The early history of the region is obscure. In the 7th century B.C. the ancient Greek trading city of Miletus in Asia Minor founded a colony on Bessarabia's Black Sea coast on the site of modern Belgorod-Dnestrovsky. The interior was under the control of the nomad Scythians and later the Sarmatians. In the first centuries of the Christian era the region was occupied by the Getae and the Dacians, ancient Thracian peoples who resisted Roman inroads under the emperor Trajan. Remains of Trajan's walls, a series of defensive fortifications across southern Bessarabia, date from this period. After the 4th century, nomads of the Asian steppes —the Goths, the Huns, the Avars and the Hungarians—again swept through the region.

Slavic tribes first appeared in Bessarabia in the 6th century, and Kievan Russia won a tenuous foothold in the region from the 9th to the 13th centuries. After the Mongol invasion of the 13th century, Bessarabia came under the control of the independent principality of Moldavia that arose in the mid-1300's. One of the early Moldavian rulers was a member of Wallachia's Bassarab family, from which the name "Bessarabia" is derived. With the northward expansion of the Ottoman empire in the late 15th and early 16th centuries, Bessarabia came under Turkish rule. The southern Budzhak area became administratively part of the Ottoman empire, while the rest of Bessarabia remained in Moldavia, which accepted Turkish suzerainty.

Russian and Rumanian Rulers. A battleground in the Russian-Turkish wars of the 18th century, Bessarabia passed to Russia in 1812 under the Treaty of Bucharest. After its defeat in the Crimean War, Russia was forced to cede a southern strip of Bessarabia to Moldavia, but regained it in 1878 when Moldavia became part of a newly independent Rumania. After the Bolshevik Revolution in Russia, Rumania seized Bessarabia in 1918 and retained the region until 1940, when the Soviet Union recovered it and made it part of the Moldavian SSR. In World War II, Rumanian forces, allied with the Germans, occupied Bessarabia from 1941 to 1944, but the postwar armistice of 1944 and the Treaty of Paris of 1947 confirmed the incorporation of Bessarabia into the Soviet Union. Population: (1965) 3,000,000.

THEODORE SHABAD
Author of "Geography of the USSR"

BESSARION, bə-sȧr'ē-ən, **Johannes** (1403?– 1472), Byzantine cardinal and humanist. He was born at Trebizond, in Asia Minor, studied at Constantinople, and was ordained in 1423. Under the tutelege of Gemistus Pletho, an ardent Neoplatonist, he developed as a scholar and Platonist in his own right. In 1437 he and Pletho accompanied Emperor John Palaeologus to the Council of Ferrara-Florence. By his learning and tact, Bessarion guided the council to the reunion of the Greek and Latin churches, and in 1439, a long schism ended. Unfortunately the churches were again divided in 1472.

Elevated to cardinal by Eugenius IV in 1439, Bessarion distinguished himself as papal legate and as governor of Bologna. He restored peace in Bologna and rebuilt the university, for which he assembled the outstanding faculty in Europe. He fostered a revival of the Greek classics, both at Bologna and at Rome, and personally translated Zenophon's *Memorabilia* and Aristotle's *Metaphysics*. He died at Ravenna on Nov. 18, 1472. His library, which he willed to Venice, became the nucleus of the library of San Marco.

BESSBOROUGH, bez'brə, **9th Earl of** (1880– 1956), British Commonwealth administrator, who was governor general of Canada from 1931 to 1935. He was born *Vere Brabazon Ponsonby* on Oct. 27, 1880. He graduated from Harrow and Cambridge and entered on a career in law and business in 1903. He was a Conservative member of Parliament in 1910 and from 1913 to 1920, when he succeeded to an earldom. During World War I he served in the army.

In 1931 he became governor general of Canada. During his tenure the Dominion Drama Festivals, annual competitions in amateur theater production, were begun through his initiative. Lord Bessborough returned to his business interests in London in 1935. He died in Hampshire, England, on March 10, 1956.

BESSEL, bes'əl, **Friedrich Wilhelm** (1784–1846), German astronomer, who first measured the distance of a star from the earth. Bessel became the first director of the Königsberg Observatory in Prussia in 1813, and between 1821 and 1833 he measured the positions of some 60,000 stars. He was especially concerned with getting the utmost information from observations. In 1818 he published *Fundamental Astronomiae,* a thorough reduction, or systematization, of Bradley's observations; this was the first rigorous investigation of the effects of instrumental errors on star positions. He followed with *Tabulae Regiomontanae* (1830), in which the "Besselian day numbers" were introduced to facilitate the reduction of observations.

By measuring the changing position of 61 Cygni relative to neighboring stars, Bessel found in 1838 that this star was at a distance of 10 light-years, the first successful distance measurement of a star. In 1844 he demonstrated the nonuniform motions of Sirius and Procyon and deduced that these stars possessed faint companions, later found by direct observation. He worked on the theory of planetary motions, making use of the mathematical functions that bear his name. Like others, Bessel believed the irregular motion of Uranus was due to the attraction of an unknown planet, an explanation shown to be true by the discovery of Neptune six months after his death. His *Astronomische Untersuchungen* (1841–42) contained essays, including a theoretical account of the heliometer (an instrument for measuring the angular separations between celestial bodies), the development of the still-accepted method for calculating solar eclipses, and a study of atmospheric refraction.

Bessel was born at Minden, Prussia, on July 22, 1784. Although self-educated, he made calculations on Halley's comet that came to the attention of Wilhelm Olbers, who recommended him for an assistantship at the Lilienthal Observatory. Bessel won the Lalande prize of the Paris Institut for his calculations on the comet of 1807 and the Berlin Academy prize for his work on the precession of the equinoxes. Elected an associate of almost every academy in Europe, he also received many civil honors. He died at Königsberg on March 17, 1846.

BRIAN G. MARSDEN
Smithsonian Astrophysical Observatory

BESSEMER, bes'ə-mər, **Sir Henry** (1813–1898), English inventor of a low-cost steelmaking process that greatly stimulated the growth of the steel industry. By reducing the cost of manufacture, the Bessemer process made steel available for rails and general engineering work, and this, in turn, accelerated the pace of the Industrial Revolution.

Bessemer was born in Charlton, Herftfordshire, England, on Jan. 19, 1813. He received mechanical training at an early age in the type foundry of his father, a French inventor and engineer, and at 18 went to London, where he began his career as a modeler and designer. His earliest invention, an improved method of stamping deeds, was quickly adopted by the revenue office without compensation to Bessemer. Late in life he brought the matter to the attention of the British government and was then knighted (1879) for his services in that instance.

Bessemer's next invention was a new method of making bronze powder (or gold paint, as it was called), which proved a commercial success. Subsequent inventions included machines for making Utrecht velvet and improved typecasting machinery.

At the time of the Crimean War (1853–1856), he designed a projectile intended to revolve in its flight. But as the cannon of that day were not strong enough to permit its use, he went on experimenting in Paris under the patronage of Louis Napoleon until he had improved the manufacture of cast iron. This, however, did not fully satisfy him, and he continued refining the iron until steel was produced. He took out patents for this invention in 1855 but persevered in experiments until, at his London bronze factory, steel ingots had been manufactured which could be rolled into rails without hammering. When this process had become fully developed the Bessemer Steel Works were built in Sheffield, where a large number of workmen were employed in steel manufacture and many others were trained for similar work in factories all over the world.

On Aug. 13, 1856, Bessemer read before the British Association at Cheltenham a paper entitled *The Manufacture of Malleable Iron and Steel Without Fuel,* which dealt with the invention that made his name famous. This was a new and cheap process of rapidly making steel from pig iron, a process which introduced a revolution in the steelmaking trade. Cheap steel could now be made in vast quantities and be used for many purposes formerly prohibited by high costs. At the Birmingham meeting in 1865 he read a second paper, *On the Manufacture of Cast Steel, Its Progress and Employment as a Substitute for Wrought Iron.*

Bessemer originated a method, still in use, for compressing into a solid block the graphite employed in the manufacture of lead pencils. He also devised a system of rollers for embossing and printing paper, and made improvements in telephones.

Bessemer was president of the Iron and Steel Institute of Great Britain in 1871–1873, and in 1879 became a fellow of the Royal Society. He was an honorary member of many scientific and engineering societies, including the American Society of Mechanical Engineers. Before the latter, in 1896, he presented a paper entitled *The Origin of the Bessemer Process.* He died in London on March 15, 1898.

See also METALLURGY—*Extractive Metallurgy;* STEEL—*Steelmaking Processes* (Bessemer Process); TECHNOLOGY—*The Nineteenth Century.*

BESSEMER, bes'ə-mər, is an industrial city in central Alabama, in Jefferson County, 10 miles (16 km) southwest of Birmingham. It is situated in the great coal and iron region of which Birmingham is the metropolis. Among its industrial products are freight cars, cast iron pipe, explosives, brick and cement, fertilizers, and chemicals.

The site was platted in 1886 and the town was named in honor of Sir Henry Bessemer, English inventor of the Bessemer process of steelmaking. Bessemer was incorporated in 1887. Government is by mayor and council. Population: 33,428.

BESSEMER STEEL PROCESS. See BESSEMER, SIR HENRY; METALLURGY—*Extractive Metallurgy;* STEEL—*Steelmaking Processes* (Bessemer Process); TECHNOLOGY—*The Nineteenth Century* (Steel).

BESSENYEI, be'she-nye-i, **György** (1747–1811), Hungarian dramatist, who has been called the father of modern Hungarian literature. He was born into a noble family in Bercel in northern Hungary. When he was 18, he became a member of the court bodyguards in Vienna. There he came in contact with French literary ideas and began writing in his native Hungarian, a language that had fallen into disuse among the upper classes of Hungary.

In 1772, Bessenyei wrote *The Tragedy of Agis,* which scholars have called the first modern Hungarian tragic drama. His comic plays, the first modern Hungarian examples of that genre, include *The Philosopher* (1777). He also wrote several nondramatic works. He died in Puszta-Kovácsi on Feb. 24, 1811.

BESSIÈRES, be'syâr', **Jean Baptiste** (1768–1813), French marshal. He was born in Prayssac, near Cahors, France, on Aug. 5, 1768. Enlisting in the army in 1791 as a private, he was made a captain after two years. He attracted the attention of Napoleon, who placed him in command of the guards in 1798. He later distinguished himself at the Battle of Marengo. Napoleon made him marshal of France in 1804, and a year later commander of cavalry.

Conspicuous in gallantry at the battles of Austerlitz, Friedland, and Jena, Bessières was made duke of Istria in 1809, and he commanded in Spain in 1811. The following year he covered the French army's retreat from Moscow, saving the lives of many soldiers. He was killed near Lützen, Germany, on May 1, 1813, the day before the Battle of Lützen.

BEST, Charles Herbert (1899–   ), Canadian physiologist, who worked with Frederick G. Banting (q.v.) on the isolation of insulin. Best was born in West Pembroke, Me., on Feb. 27, 1899. He received a B.A. degree from the University of Toronto in 1921 and, while still a medical student, worked with Banting at the University of Toronto. They isolated a watery hormonal extract from the islands of Langerhans in the pancreas. This extract, named "insulin," proved effective in treating diabetes mellitus.

Best received his medical degree in 1925 and continued his studies in various Canadian, American, and European cities. In 1929 he became head of the department of physiology at the University of Toronto.

BESTERMAN, bes'tər-mən, **Theodore Deodatus Nathaniel** (1904–   ), English bibliographer. He was born on Nov. 18, 1904, and was privately educated. Between 1931 and 1938 he served as a lecturer in the London School of Librarianship. From 1942 to 1946 he was joint editor, for the Oxford University Press, of books on bibliography, and in 1944 he founded and edited the *Journal of Documentation.* He lectured extensively in England and the United States on the science of bibliography.

Besterman's *A World Bibliography of Bibliographies* was first published in 1939–1940 in two volumes and revised several times, the 4th edition (1965–66) being expanded to five volumes. His other books include *A Bibliography of Sir James Frazer* (1934), *The Beginnings of Systematic Bibliography* (1935), *British Sources of Reference and Information* (1948), and *Voltaire's Notebooks* (2 vols., 1952).

MEDIEVAL BESTIARY, in St. John's College, Oxford, shows a leopard (*top*) and a lion and family of deer.

BESTIARY, bes'chē-er-ē, an encyclopedic literary form that reached its height of popularity in the 12th to 14th centuries. The bestiary presents a catalog of actual or mythical creatures, describes some of their physical characteristics, and often gives them symbolic meanings. The main source of later bestiaries was the Greek *Physiologus* (*The Naturalist*) of about the 2d century A.D., from which the genre derives its mixture of science and fantasy.

The *Physiologus* entered Western literature in a Latin version in the 4th or 5th century. The Christian fathers allegorized the compilation, enlarging it from the original group of 49 subjects, until in the Middle Ages a bestiary might have more than a hundred separate entries. The bestiary appealed to the medieval mind largely as an image of God's creative power and as evidence of the divine order of all things in the universe.

In the 12th century Philippe de Thaon translated the *Physiologus* into French. With the versified *Bestiaire divin* of Guillaume le Clerc, a 13th century trouvère, the genre reached a peak of moral intensity and literary finish. Medieval bestiaries were frequently enhanced by illustrations.

The bestiary was not always spiritual in meaning; in the *Bestiaire d'amour* (about 1250) Richard de Fournival substituted erotic for Christian allegory. During the Renaissance, scientific skepticism began to undermine the credulity that is the psychological basis of the bestiary. However, the feeling of the genre survives in the fables of such authors as Edward Lear, Lewis Carroll, and James Thurber and in the works of the modern French writers Jules Renard and Guillaume Apollinaire.

ANGUS FLETCHER, *Author of*
"Allegory: The Theory of a Symbolic Mode"

Further Reading: James, Montague R., *Peterborough Psalter and Bestiary* (New York 1921); McCulloch, Florence, *Medieval Latin and French Bestiaries* (Chapel Hill, N.C., 1960); White, Terence H., *The Bestiary* (New York 1954).

BESTUZHEV-RYUMIN, byis-too'zhef ryoo'myin, **Aleksei Petrovich** (1693–1766), Russian chancellor during the reign of Empress Elizabeth (1741–1762), and one of the leading statesmen of Europe in the 18th century. He was born in Moscow on May 22, 1693. Educated in Copenhagen and Berlin, he served under George Ludwig, elector of Hanover (later George I of England), and entered the Russian diplomatic service in 1717. He served in various posts abroad until 1740, when he returned to Russia. In 1741 he became vice chancellor, and at Elizabeth's coronation he was created a count. In 1744 he became grand chancellor of Russia.

From 1741 to 1757, during the period when Russia began to emerge as a European power, Bestuzhev directed Russian foreign policy. In 1743 he had opposed unsuccessfully a Russo-Prussian defensive alliance, but in 1746 he managed to reverse it by concluding a defensive alliance with Austria directed against Prussia. He also concluded important alliances with Denmark (1746), Turkey (1747), and Britain (1747).

By the mid-1750's, Bestuzhev's enemies had succeeded in discrediting him. In 1758 he was arrested, and after an investigation he was banished to his estate at Goretovo. When Catherine II came to power in 1762, he was recalled and made a field marshal. He died on April 21, 1766.

BETA RAYS, bā'tə rāz, are radiation emitted by a naturally radioactive element. Beta rays (β rays) consist of high-speed electrons. Natural radioactive emissions were first separated into their three components about 1900 by Ernest Rutherford, who passed the radiation from a radioactive source through a magnetic field and identified the components as alpha rays (helium nuclei), beta rays, and gamma rays (very penetrating electromagnetic radiation).

SAMUEL OLANOFF, *Bard College*

BETA SIGMA PHI INTERNATIONAL is a non-academic sorority with 250,000 members in 10,000 chapters. Founded in Abilene, Kans., in 1931 by Walter W. Ross, the organization has spread to every state of the United States, to every Canadian province, and to 23 other countries.

The sorority was founded for the social, cultural, and civic enrichment of its members. Donations of approximately $1 million have been made for medical research and treatment and to such institutions as homes for children.

Beta Sigma Phi is not a secret society. The Greek letters of its name represent Life, Learning, and Friendship, which is the organization's motto. Its world headquarters are in Kansas City, Mo., where its monthly magazine, *The Torch*, is published.

WALTER W. ROSS III
*President, International Executive Council
Beta Sigma Phi International*

BETANCOURT, be-tän-koor', **Rómulo** (1908–), Venezuelan political leader and writer. He was born at Guatire, near Caracas, on Feb. 22, 1908. As a student at the University of Caracas in 1928, he was jailed for leftist political activities. In exile from 1928 to 1936, he wrote a searing book about his captivity and, in 1930, briefly joined the Communist party in Costa Rica. Exiled again in 1939, he was permitted to return in 1941 and helped organize the left-wing anti-Communist Democratic Action party.

W.H. HODGE

BETEL NUTS are borne in clusters on the trunk of a palm tree (*Areca catechu*) native to the East Indies.

Following a coup in 1945, Betancourt was made president of a seven-man ruling junta. He launched an energetic program of reform directed toward democratic rule. In 1948 he vacated the presidency in favor of an elected Democratic Action president, but a coup later that year restored reactionary rule. Betancourt was exiled for 10 more years, and his party was outlawed.

Following another coup in 1958, he returned, rapidly revived the party, and campaigned successfully for the presidency. His vigorous and able administration from 1959 to 1964 survived a nearly successful attempt on his life in 1960 and unrelenting harassment from both the left and right. Betancourt initiated well-conceived and continuing programs of land reform, industrial development, education, and democratic government.

BETATRON. See PARTICLE ACCELERATOR—*Types*.

BETEL NUT, bēt'əl nut, the seed of the betel palm (*Areca catechu*), which is chewed as a stimulant throughout southern Asia. The betel nut is about 2 inches (5 cm) long and is mottled brown and gray in color. The ripened seeds are gathered between August and November, boiled in water, cut into slices, and dried in the sun, giving them a dark brown or reddish color. Each dried nut is then wrapped, together with a piece of shell lime, in a leaf of the betel pepper (*Piper betle*) and chewed.

Betel nuts contain the alkaloid arecoline, a mild stimulant that produces a feeling of well-being. They are not habit-forming, but habitual chewing of betel nuts eventually blackens the teeth and may cause them to decay. In some parts of the Orient, betel nuts are used to destroy intestinal worms. Elsewhere, they are used as a dewormer in veterinary medicine.

BETELGEUSE, bē'təl-joōz, is a reddish star in the constellation Orion and the 12th brightest star in the sky. It is a cool red giant, and was the first star to have its diameter measured by an interferometer. Its magnitude ranges from 0.4 to 1.3. The changes in brightness and size are irregular, so it is called an *irregular variable*. If Betelgeuse occupied the sun's place in the solar system, the star when at its greatest extent would envelop the orbit of Mars.

BETHANY, beth′ə-nē, a city in central Oklahoma, is a residential suburb of Oklahoma City. It is on the North Canadian River, in Oklahoma County, 7 miles (11 km) west of the state capital. Settled in 1906 by members of the Nazarene Church, it is the site of Bethany-Nazarene College. It was incorporated in 1931 and adopted city manager government in 1953. Population: 21,785.

BETHANY, beth′ə-nē, was a village in ancient Palestine, at the foot of the Mount of Olives, about 2 miles (3 km) east of Jerusalem. The site, now in Jordan, is occupied by the village of *El Azariyeh*, named in honor of Lazarus, whom Muslims regard as a saint. In the Bible, Bethany is mentioned as the place where Christ raised Lazarus from the dead (John 11:1-44).

BETHE, bā′tə, **Hans Albrecht** (1906–   ), German-born U.S. physicist, who was best known for his work in theoretical nuclear physics, his theories on the origin of solar energy, and his participation in the development of the atomic bomb. Bethe was born in Strasbourg, Alsace-Lorraine, on July 2, 1906. After studying at the universities of Frankfurt and Munich, he taught theoretical physics at Munich and Tübingen from 1930 to 1933. During this period he also worked with Sir Ernest Rutherford and Enrico Fermi. He had to leave Germany in 1933, and for two years he taught in England. He then accepted a position at Cornell University, and became a U.S. citizen in 1941.

Bethe was one of the first to apply quantum mechanics to a number of areas of atomic and nuclear physics. He took a particular interest in the quantum theory of atomic collisions and in the passage of fast-moving particles through matter. In 1938, Bethe published part of the theory that probably brought him his greatest fame—a theory accounting for the source of energy in the sun and the stars. He stated that solar energy comes from a six-step series of thermonuclear reactions, known as the Carbon Cycle because carbon and nitrogen are involved in the process. The end result of the reactions is the fusion of hydrogen nuclei to form helium nuclei. This process was independently suggested at the same time by Carl von Weizsäcker in Germany.

During World War II, Bethe was chief of the theoretical physics division of the Los Alamos Laboratory of the Manhattan Project, which developed the atomic bomb. After the war Bethe took a deep interest in the public implications of nuclear research, writing many articles on the subject. In 1958 he was a scientific adviser at the nuclear test-ban talks in Geneva, and in 1961 he received the Atomic Energy Commission's Enrico Fermi Award for his work in this field. Bethe won the 1967 Nobel Prize in physics for his contributions concerning the energy production of stars.

Further Reading: Edson, Lee, "Scientific Man for all Seasons," *The New York Times Magazine*, pp. 28–29, March 10, 1968.

BETHEL, beth′əl, is a town in southwestern Connecticut, in Fairfield County, 5 miles (8 km) southeast of Danbury. It manufactures chemicals and light industrial products. The town was settled about 1700 and was incorporated in 1855. P.T. Barnum, the famous showman, lived in Bethel. Population: 10,945.

BETHEL, beth′əl, was a city in ancient Palestine, about 11 miles (18 km) north of Jerusalem, and was originally named *Luz*. To the ancient Hebrews the city was a holy place ranking close to Jerusalem in importance. *Bethel*, in Hebrew, means "House of God." At or near the site of its ruins stands the present village of Beitin, in Jordan.

In Biblical history, at the time of Joshua, Bethel was placed under the jurisdiction of the tribe of Benjamin. It was later seized and ruled by Canaan and finally captured by the tribe of Ephraim, in whose control it remained.

Bethel is memorable as the place where Abraham raised an altar (Genesis 12:8). Jacob, too, stopped there to spend a night and, after a vision of angels, commemorated the event by building an altar and giving the place the name of Bethel (Genesis 28:10–22).

BETHEL PARK, beth′əl, is a suburban residential borough in southwestern Pennsylvania, in Allegheny County, 8 miles (13 km) southwest of Pittsburgh. It is situated in a bituminous coal-mining region and has diversified light industry. During the Revolutionary War it was the site of Fort Couch. The first Presbyterian church west of the Allegheny Mountains was founded here in 1776. The community was a center of the Whiskey Rebellion of 1791 against a federal tax on distilled liquors. The borough was incorporated in 1950. Its name was changed from Bethel to Bethel Park in 1960. Government is by borough council and city manager. Population: 34,791.

PAULINE A. GRAHAM
Bethel Park Public Library

BÉTHENCOURT, bā-tän-kōōr′, **Jean de** (1360?–?1425), French navigator and conqueror of the Canary Islands. He was chamberlain to Charles VI of France but was ruined financially during the Hundred Years' War. In an effort to restore his fortunes he invaded the Canary Islands from Spain in 1402. Not having a strong enough force, however, he returned to Spain and obtained additional recruits from Henry III of Castile, who gave him the title of king of the Canary Islands. With his new forces, Béthencourt conquered the islands and converted the greater portion of the inhabitants to Christianity. In 1406 he returned to Normandy, where he remained until his death.

BETHESDA, bə-thez′də, an unincorporated community in central Maryland, is in Montgomery County, 7 miles (11 km) from downtown Washington, D.C., of which it is a residential suburb. The Bethesda voting district of Montgomery County includes the village of Chevy Chase. Bethesda is the home of several private and government sponsored research organizations. Since 1939 it has been the research center of the National Institutes of Health. The Naval Medical Center was established here in 1942. Bethesda became the permanent site of the National Library of Medicine in 1963.

The community developed around the Bethesda Presbyterian Church for which it is named. During the Civil War it was called *Darcy's Store*, after William Darcy, who ran the post office and general store on the toll pike that served the village. Until 1887, wagons and carriages had to pay a 5-cent toll to proceed along this road. Population: 71,621.

BETHLEHEM, famous in the Bible as the City of David and the birthplace of Jesus. Part of the Church of the Nativity can be seen in the left foreground.

BETHLEHEM, beth'li-hem, in Biblical history, was a town in Judah (later Judea), Palestine, about 6 miles (10 km) south of Jerusalem. The name in Hebrew has been construed to mean "House of Bread" or "House of Lehem" (a god). The modern city is situated in Jordan and is known in Arabic as *Beit Lahm.* As the home of David and the birthplace of Jesus, Bethlehem is second only to Jerusalem in sacred interest to Jews and Christians.

The Old Testament and the New Testament contain numerous references to Bethlehem. It was the home of Ruth and the setting of the tender story of love and devotion related in the Book of Ruth. David spent his youth in the hills around Bethlehem and was here anointed by Samuel to be king of Israel (I Samuel 16). The prophet Micah said that a deliverer would come from Bethlehem (Micah 5:1–4). The tomb of Rachel, Jacob's wife, who died giving birth to Benjamin, is north of the city and is venerated by Jews and Muslims. Bethlehem was one of the strongholds fortified by Rehoboam, son of Solomon, to guard the approaches to Jerusalem.

As the birthplace of Jesus, Bethlehem is one of the great Christian shrines. The Gospel of St. Luke tells that Mary and Joseph went to Bethlehem to be enrolled in the census, and it was there that Jesus was born (Luke 2:1-20). The city was leveled by the Roman emperor Hadrian I in 132 A.D. but was revived as a religious shrine by Emperor Constantine the Great and his successors.

Preserved here is the Church of the Nativity, which was built around 326 A.D. by Constantine on the site of the grotto reputed to be the birthplace of Christ. Although some mosaics of this structure remain, the present basilica is primarily the church erected during the reign of Justinian I (526–565). A number of mosaic fragments have survived from additions made to the church by the Crusaders in the 12th century. The basilica, restored in 1671 and again in 1842, contains the Grotto of the Nativity, which is located at the east end of the crypt. It is marked by a silver star bearing the inscription *Hic de Virgine Maria Jesus Christus natus est* (Here of the Virgin Mary Jesus Christ was born). On the south side of the church, a marble-covered niche in the rock is venerated as the site of the manger in which Jesus was cradled after his birth. Also of interest are the tomb and chapel of St. Jerome, who translated the Bible in a nearby grotto. Surrounding the church are monasteries of the Roman Catholic, Greek, and Armenian churches.

Bethlehem came under Muslim control in the 7th century in the time of Umar (Omar) I, but the Church of the Nativity escaped destruction. The Crusaders, under Godfrey of Bouillon, occupied the town in 1099. A year later, on Christmas day, Baldwin I was crowned king of Jerusalem there. Bethlehem became a Roman bishopric in 1110 but, after the town was recaptured by the Muslims in 1187, the bishops resided in Clamecy, France. Briefly restored to Christian control from 1229 to 1244, Bethlehem remained in Turkish control from that time until the end of World War I. Christians were, however, permitted to worship at the shrines of the town. During this period various parts of the town were alternately demolished by the Turks and rebuilt by Christian religious orders. In 1834, Ibrahim Pasha, viceroy of Egypt, destroyed the Muslim section of Bethlehem after an insurrection. Following World War I, Bethlehem was part of the British Palestine mandate, which ended in 1948. During the Arab-Israeli War of 1948–1949, the city was occupied by Jordanian troops. Bethlehem was in the area of Palestine incorporated into Jordan in 1950.

The modern city attracts thousands of pilgrims and visitors because of its religious associations. Its industries cater to the tourist trade, producing religious souvenirs of olive wood and mother-of-pearl, in addition to shellwork and embroidery. It is the commercial center of an agricultural region that produces cereal grains, olives, and wine. Population: (1961) 22,453.

BETHLEHEM, beth'li-hem, a city in eastern Pennsylvania, in Northampton and Lehigh counties, is on the Lehigh River, 46 miles (74 km) north of Philadelphia. With the neighboring cities of Allentown and Easton, Bethlehem forms one of the three most important manufacturing complexes in the state. It is the headquarters of the Bethlehem Steel Corporation and a center for many other industrial firms. Manufactures include foundry products and machine parts; chemical, textile, and food products; and cement, furniture, paint, electrical apparatus, and oil burners. The city also has several research laboratories.

The Bach Choir plays an important part in the cultural life of Bethlehem (see BACH FESTIVAL). Institutions of learning include Lehigh University, with its well-known engineering school; Moravian College (coeducational), which dates from 1742; Moravian Theological Seminary (1807); Moravian Seminary for Girls (at nearby Green Pond); Moravian Preparatory School; and St. Francis Academy. Bethlehem's new city center includes the city hall and the main public library building.

Bethlehem was founded in 1741 by Bishop David Nitschmann and a group of Moravian Brethren who had been exiled from Bohemia and Moravia. Count Nikolaus Ludwig von Zinzendorf, Moravian leader, visited the settlement that Christmas, and as the group assembled in worship it was decided that a fitting name for the new community would be Bethlehem. The traditions of the early Moravians are strong in the community, particularly in music and education. Many early buildings are still standing, among them the Widow's House (1742), the Bell House (1745), and the old Chapel (1751). The Moravian Cemetery, dating from 1742, is annually the scene of an Easter dawn service.

Historic Bethlehem, Inc., is a group that has been organized to restore and preserve some of the old areas and more important landmarks.

During the Revolutionary War, Bethlehem furnished hospital facilities for wounded American soldiers. Events in the community moved slowly until the completion of a canal along the Lehigh River, used for transporting coal. The portion of the city north of the river was incorporated as a borough in 1845, the portion south of the river in 1865; in 1917 the two boroughs incorporated as the present city. Bethlehem's growth as a steel town in the late 19th century brought an influx of European workers, especially from Hungary. Government is by mayor and council. Population: 72,686.

THE BACH CHOIR

Bethlehem is noted for its Bach Choir, which was organized in 1898 to sing the choral works of Johann Sebastian Bach. Members of the choir, numbering more than 160, are Bethlehem area residents who are chosen after tryout performances. They include professional people, clerks, laborers, and housewives. An orchestra and guest artists are invited from New York City and Philadelphia to appear with the choir. On two Fridays and Saturdays in May of each year a Bach Festival is held in the Packer Chapel of Lehigh University. The highlight is traditionally the performances, on the two Saturdays, of Bach's B-Minor Mass.

AMY E. PRESTON, *Bethlehem Public Library*

BETHLEHEM STEEL CORPORATION, one of the largest steelmakers in the United States. It was incorporated in 1904, but the nucleus of the corporation had operated for more than 40 years in Bethlehem, Pa., where the general offices are located. The corporation's main plants are in Bethlehem, Steelton, and Johnstown, all in Pennsylvania; Sparrows Point, Md.; Lackawanna, N.Y.; and Burns Harbor, Ind. There are three plants on the West Coast. The corporation also has eight shipbuilding and ship repair yards on the East, West, and Gulf coasts. It operates coastal, oceangoing, and Great Lakes vessels and several short-line railroads to ship products and to draw raw materials from South America, West Africa, Canada, and from the principal coal, iron, and limestone deposits in the United States.

Bethlehem products include sheet steel; tinplate; pipe for oil, gas, and water lines; rails; tool steel; castings; pig iron; and coal chemicals. Besides ships, it makes freight cars, mine cars, and structural steel.

Rapid ship construction in wartime ranks among Bethlehem's most important achievements. In World War I it constructed more destroyers in its Quincy (Mass.) yards than all other U.S. shipyards combined; in World War II it built 1,127 naval and merchant ships, the greatest number ever turned out by a private builder in a comparable time.

Bethlehem's activities require more than 100,000 employees. Much research on raw materials, refining and finishing techniques, and problems of design is carried out in its 1,000-acre laboratory group at Bethlehem. Annual production typically exceeds 20 million tons (18 million metric tons) of products, valued at $2.5 billion.

The late Charles M. Schwab was the principal founder of the corporation in 1904 and headed its activities until 1939. He was ably assisted by Eugene G. Grace, president of Bethlehem after 1916 and chairman of its board from 1946 to 1957.

COURTNEY ROBERT HALL
Author, "History of American Industrial Science"

BETHLEN, bet'len, **Gábor** (1580–1629), prince of Transylvania and, for a short time, king of Hungary. He was born in 1629 of a prominent Protestant Hungarian family with large estates in Transylvania. As a young man he was sent to the court of Prince Zsigmond (Sigismund) Báthory of Transylvania and served under Zsigmond's son Gábor after Zsigmond lost his title.

At this time Hungary was nominally under the suzerainty of the Holy Roman Empire, but the Ottoman Turks actually controlled the greater part, including Transylvania. Bethlen remained with Gábor Báthory when the latter became prince of Transylvania in 1608, but the two men soon quarreled, and Bethlen fled for safety to the Turks. After Báthory was driven from power and murdered in 1613, the Turks supported Bethlen's candidacy for the title. He was elected by the Transylvanian diet in 1613 and was confirmed by the emperor in 1615.

In the Thirty Years' War, Bethlen sided against Catholic Emperor Ferdinand II. While the emperor was combating a Bohemian revolt, Bethlen led troops into northern Hungary. During negotiations with Ferdinand in 1620, Bethlen was elected king of Hungary. He accepted the title, but then he refused the crown because he knew that the Catholics would not accept a Protestant king.

Negotiations with Ferdinand broke down, and Bethlen entered Austrian territory, laying waste to Moravia. He hemmed in the imperial army and was near victory when the refusal of the Turks to undergo a winter campaign ended his hopes. The approach of imperial troops led by the count of Tilly forced Bethlen to withdraw from Vienna. In a treaty with Ferdinand at the end of 1621, Bethlen renounced the Hungarian crown and received extensive lands and the title of prince of the empire in return.

Despite the peace, Bethlen was still determined to drive the emperor from Hungary, and in 1623 he reentered the war. He met with success in Bohemia, but the defeat of the Protestants in Germany convinced Bethlen that he could not continue the war alone. He made peace with Ferdinand for a second time in 1624.

For the next year Bethlen entertained ideas of driving the Turks out of Hungary, but the emperor's natural reluctance to ally himself with Bethlen ended the plans. In 1625 he married Catherine of Brandenburg, sister of the Protestant elector, and once more entered the Thirty Years' War. Victories by the imperial forces brought a third peace in 1626. Bethlen died at Weissenburg, Germany, on Nov. 15, 1629.

BETHLEN, bet′len, **Count István** (1874–?1947), Hungarian prime minister. The English form of his first name is **Stephen.** He was born at Gérnyeszeg, Transylvania, on Oct. 3, 1874. A member of an old aristocratic family, he was educated in Vienna and at the University of Budapest. In 1901 he was elected to parliament as a Liberal, but he soon joined the national opposition. He was a leader in the counterrevolution in 1919 against the Communist regime of Béla Kun. Two years later he was appointed prime minister by the regent, Miklós Horthy, and held the position until 1931.

Bethlen's aristocratic approach to government was not responsive to the needs of the landless peasants. He tried to hold political and social changes to a minimum. Viewing Hungary's domestic problems in primarily economic terms, he attracted foreign capital as part of his plan to revitalize the country. One of his goals was to reverse the conditions of the Treaty of Trianon, by which Hungary had lost over one half of its territory and population in 1920. He hoped that economic stability and judicious foreign friendships would eventually lead to the reacquisition of some of these areas.

During Bethlen's period of leadership, Hungary achieved a degree of political and economic stability. The prime minister was instrumental in defeating the efforts of the Habsburg contender for the crown, King Charles IV, to regain his throne in 1921. Bethlen negotiated Hungary's admission to the League of Nations and obtained a reconstruction loan from the League. In 1927, Hungary concluded a treaty with Italy that gave Hungary rights to a free port on the Adriatic Sea.

The world economic crisis brought Bethlen's regime to an end in 1931. He warned against Hungary's deepening commitments to the Axis countries before World War II. He evaded the Germans when they invaded Hungary in 1944 but was captured by the Russians and taken to Moscow in 1945. He was reported to have died there in 1947.

BETHMANN-HOLLWEG, bāt′män-hōl′väкн, **Theobald von** (1856–1921), chancellor of Germany. He was born in Hohenfinow, Brandenburg, on Nov. 29, 1856. A lawyer by training, Bethmann was an extremely successful Prussian civil servant and head of the imperial ministry of the interior when he was appointed German chancellor in 1909. Here Bethmann faced two major problems: on the domestic front a critical impasse had been reached because the government had ignored the need for political reforms; in foreign affairs Germany was becoming isolated, and a struggle for the decisive voice in policy had ensued between the civilian government and the military. Moreover, the Kaiser had virtually abdicated the responsibilities of his position.

Bethmann could not meet the demands of his difficult office. He was essentially an administrator, by temperament contemplative and hesitant to act. He was unable to overcome conservative opposition to his attempt at domestic reform, especially of the discriminatory Prussian electoral system. His success in giving greater autonomy to Alsace-Lorraine was offset by his awkwardness in handling the crude militarism of the Zabern (Saverne) incident (1913), a dispute in Alsace between local residents and the army.

In retrospect, it is his role in foreign affairs that is more significant. He saw that the Anglo-French Entente (1904) and the Anglo-Russian Accord (1907) would isolate Germany and that escape from this isolation depended upon its relations with England. Since it was Germany's ambition to expand its fleet that clouded these relations, Bethmann opened negotiations with Britain. However, at the insistence of Alfred von Tirpitz, head of the German navy, he offered concessions only if Britain would pledge strict neutrality in a war involving Germany. Negotiations collapsed in 1912. This meant, in effect, that if a political crisis should arise in Europe, Britain would remain bound to its French and Russian allies.

Role in World War I. In the crisis created by the murder of Archduke Francis Ferdinand on June 28, 1914, Bethmann's role seems ambiguous. He pressed for negotiations between Vienna and St. Petersburg; at the same time, however, he gave Austria-Hungary a free hand by assuring it of Germany's unconditional loyalty. This allowed Vienna to undertake punitive action against Serbia without consulting Berlin.

Modern historical interpretation of Bethmann's motives is divided. Some hold that he manipulated the crisis into war, expecting that military success would solve his domestic problems. Others believe that throughout the crisis the chancellor hoped to preserve peace. He sought to induce Austria to withdraw from its Serbian campaign, but in the meantime Helmuth von Moltke, the German chief of staff, had independently wired his Austrian counterpart and promised military support. At this juncture, Emperor William II failed to assert the civilian government's primacy over the general staff, and the war began. During the war Bethmann's conduct in office compromised him in the eyes of all interested parties. When, in July 1917, Ludendorff and Hindenburg demanded his dismissal, the emperor asked for his resignation. He retired to write his war memoirs, *Betrachtungen zum Weltkriege* (2 vols., 1919–21). Bethmann died in Hohenfinow on Jan. 1, 1921.

C.M. KIMMICH, *Columbia University*

BETHNAL GREEN, beth'nəl, a former metropolitan borough of London, England, is now part of the borough of Tower Hamlets. It is situated north of the Thames River, in the East End, 4 miles (6 km) northeast of Charing Cross. Once noted as a silk-weaving district, it now has a variety of industries and is a workers' residential area. The borough was abolished as of 1965 by the London Government Act of 1963.

BETHPAGE, beth'pāj', is an unincorporated village in southeastern New York on Long Island in Nassau County. The Grumman Aircraft Engineering Corporation, manufacturers of aircraft and space vehicles, is located here.

Bethpage is adjacent to Old Bethpage, also an unincorporated area, which is known for the Old Bethpage Village Restoration, a typical hamlet of the period before the Civil War. Bethpage State Park is between Bethpage and Old Bethpage. Both areas are within, and named for, the Bethpage Purchase, a tract of land bought from the Indians in 1695 by Thomas Powell. Oyster Bay township administers their affairs. Population: Bethpage, 18,555; Old Bethpage, 7,084.

ALONZO GIBBS, *Author of "Bethpage Bygones"*

BETHSAIDA, beth-sā′a-ədə, was a town in ancient Palestine, on the north shore of the Sea of Galilee. The apostles Andrew, Peter, and Philip were born there. On a plain to the east of the town, Christ performed the miracle of feeding some 5,000 persons with five loaves of bread and two fishes (Mark 6:35–45; Luke 9:10–17).

Philip the Tetrarch, king of Ituraea, Batanaea, and Trachonitis (reigned 4 B.C.–34 A.D.), rebuilt the town as his capital and renamed it *Bethsaida Julias*, in honor of Julia, the daughter of Emperor Augustus. The present town of *el-Araj*, in Jordan, stands on the site.

BÉTHUNE, bā-tün', the name of a distinguished family of northeastern France. The family descended from Robert I, seigneur of Béthune.

CONON DE BÉTHUNE (?1150–1219) was a trouvère noted for his epic poems. He became a leader in the Fourth Crusade (1202–1204) and served for a time as governor of Constantinople. His poetry was published by Paulin Pàris in *Le romancero françois* (1833).

MAXIMILIEN DE BÉTHUNE (1560–1641), baron de Rosny and duke de Sully, was one of the chief supporters of Henry IV in his struggle for the throne of France. He was born at Rosny, near Mantes, on Dec. 13, 1560. As a boy he was sent to Henry's court, later serving in the many campaigns that ultimately brought Henry the French throne. He approved Henry's conversion to Catholicism (1593) on political grounds, but he remained a Protestant himself.

Sully was Henry's finance minister from 1597 until the king's death in 1610. In effect prime minister, he stabilized the finances of the strife-torn country, took measures to encourage agriculture, promoted the construction of roads and bridges, and planned a national system of canals. He was created duke de Sully in 1606. His *Mémoires* (1638) provides a valuable, though not always accurate, record of the time. He died in Villebon on Dec. 22, 1641.

ARMAND JOSEPH DE BÉTHUNE (1738–1800), duke de Charost, was noted as an agronomist and philanthropist. He was born in Versailles in 1738. After serving in the army in the Seven Years' War, he retired to his lands and devoted himself to agriculture. He established an agricultural society at Meillant and experimented with new plants and breeds of animals. He also founded charitable institutions.

Although he abolished feudal dues on his estates and wrote against feudal institutions before the French Revolution, he was imprisoned during the Terror in 1793–1794. He died in Paris.

BETHUNE, bə-thūn', **Mary McLeod** (1875–1955), American educator. A child of former Negro slaves, she was born in Mayesville, S.C., on July 10, 1875. After graduating from the Moody Bible Institute, Chicago, in 1895, she taught in Southern mission schools until 1903. In 1904 she founded Daytona Normal and Industrial Institute for Girls, at Daytona Beach, Fla. The institute merged with Cookman Institute in 1923 to form Bethune-Cookman College. She was president of the college until 1942. In 1935 she founded the National Council of Negro Women.

Mary Bethune directed the Division of Negro Affairs of the National Youth Administration from 1936 to 1943, and during World War II served as special assistant to the secretary of war for the selection of officer candidates for the Women's Army Corps. She was also a special adviser to President Roosevelt on minority affairs and a vice president of the National Association for the Advancement of Colored People. She served as a consultant on interracial relations at the San Francisco Conference, which organized the United Nations in 1945.

For her public services, Dr. Bethune received the Spingarn Medal (1935), the Francis A. Drexel Award (1936), the Thomas Jefferson Award (1942), and the Haitian Medal of Honor and Merit (1949). She died in Daytona Beach, Fla., on May 18, 1955.

Further Reading: Holt, Rackham, *Mary McLeod Bethune* (New York 1964); Peare, Catherine Owens, *Mary McLeod Bethune* (New York 1951).

BETJEMAN, bet'jə-mən, **Sir John** (1906–   ), English poet. He was educated at Oxford University and between 1941 and 1943 was the British press attaché in Dublin. In 1944 he worked briefly for the Admiralty and then held an advisory position with the British Council.

His first book of verse was *Ghastly Good Taste* (1933). His other volumes of poetry include *Mount Zion* (1933), *Continual Dew* (1937), *Old Bats in New Belfries* (1940), *Selected Poems* (1948), *A Few Late Crysanthemums* (1954), *Collected Poems* (1959), and the verse autobiography *Summoned by Bells* (1960). Also greatly interested in architecture, Betjeman collaborated on several books in that field, including *Murray's Architectural Guide to Buckinghamshire* (1948) and *English Churches* (1964).

Betjeman's poetry alternates in mood between comic satire and highly polished lyricism. It has been characterized as bearing some resemblance to the work of W.H. Auden, who himself described Betjeman's work as "slick but not streamlined" in the introduction to a volume of Betjeman's verse and prose pieces published in 1947 under the title *Slick but Not Streamlined*. In *Collected Poems*, Betjeman demonstrates his competence as a writer of serious poetry. He was knighted in 1969, and in 1972, after the death of Cecil Day-Lewis, he was appointed poet laureate.

BETROTHAL, bi-trō′thəl, a contract or promise that individuals will marry at a future time. Making a formal betrothal is an ancient social custom. For example, among the Hebrews of Biblical times, betrothals were arranged by the parents or guardians of the couple involved. In ancient Rome also, contracts were made by elders; partners were selected on the basis of equality of social standing, material assets, and religion. In the later Roman empire legislation was enacted limiting marriage choices: Christians and Jews were forbidden to marry one another, and senators and their sons could not legally wed former slaves or actresses. Although from the time of Justinian (483–565) the consent of both contracting parties was required before a betrothal became legally binding, patriarchal directions were rarely questioned. A betrothal was guaranteed by a sum of money, called the *arrha sponsalicia*. If one of the parties broke the contract without showing sufficient cause, the other party was entitled to receive double payment.

From ancient times through the Middle Ages, marriages were traditionally arranged by already established families. Betrothal was the principal legal device for establishing alliances between families. This was particularly so during the Middle Ages, when betrothals were viewed as convenient diplomatic stratagems and infant betrothals were common. Fortunes, estates, and military strength were solidified and great dynasties established through this political expedient. England and Scotland became allied politically by the marriage that Henry VII of England arranged between his daughter Margaret and James IV of Scotland.

Betrothals were sanctified in a church ceremony, and if a promise to marry was unjustly broken, the injured party could claim indemnities in a church court. On the other hand, ecclesiastical dispensations could be granted. The Roman Catholic and Protestant churches no longer accept authority in this matter, and a breach of promise suit is now brought to trial in civil courts.

In Islamic and Eastern cultures, the custom until recent times was for parents to arrange betrothals. Parents with eligible sons made the first move. It was considered a breech of taste for a girl's parents to initiate betrothal proceedings.

The most complex system of patriarchally arranged marriages occurs among the primitive tribes of central Australia. Marriages are frequently arranged before one of the betrothed parties is born: Father X, for example, will betroth his eligible son to Father Y's betrothed infant daughter's first-born daughter—that is, to Y's unborn granddaughter.

In the United States, as in most technologically advanced societies, marriages are rarely arranged. Young people make their own marriage plans, and the engagement, a less formal declaration of intent to marry, has replaced betrothment. Some betrothal customs persist, however, such as giving an engagement ring. An outgrowth of the Roman *arrha sponsalicia* custom, the giving of the ring demonstrates the man's seriousness in promising to wed. During the Middle Ages, also, rings were exchanged by the nobility, but the poorer classes sometimes split a coin in two—each party retaining a half until the marriage was performed.

BETROTHED, The (*I PROMESSI SPOSI*), a historical novel by Alessandro Manzoni. See ITALY —*Literature* (The 19th Century).

BETTENDORF, bet′ən-dôrf, is an industrial city in eastern Iowa, in Scott County. It is situated on the Mississippi River, just east of Davenport. The major manufactures are railroad equipment, oil burners, foundry products, machine tools, aluminum, farm machinery, and dairy products.

Bettendorf's site was first settled in the 1840's. Originally the community was named *Lilienthal* and then *Gilbert Town*. It was little more than a group of market gardeners' shacks until W.P. Bettendorf (1857–1910) brought his railroad equipment plant here in 1902. Renamed in his honor, it was incorporated as a town in 1902 and as a city in 1922. It has a mayor-council government. Population: 22,126.

BETTER BUSINESS BUREAUS are business-supported agencies organized to protect responsible business and consumer interests through voluntary self-regulation. The bureaus handle consumer inquiries and complaints, examine and investigate advertising practices, conduct consumer information programs, and administer industry standards.

Each local Better Business Bureau (BBB) answers inquiries with factual information on business reputation, but neither endorses nor recommends individual businesses. BBB's ask business firms to correct practices that have resulted in justifiable complaints. Should voluntary means fail, BBB's publicize misleading practices, or ultimately may refer them to law enforcement officials. They check advertising in all media for accuracy and, with advertiser and media cooperation, frequently make corrections before release. Consumer information programs provide advance counsel on a variety of buying decisions involving products and services.

Nearly 3,500,000 persons request BBB services annually. Contacts include 2,400,000 inquiries about reputation; 600,000 customer relations services; and 300,000 complaints. There are 131 BBB's throughout the United States and Canada, and in principal cities of Mexico, Puerto Rico, Venezuela, and Israel.

VICTOR H. NYBORG, *President, Association of Better Business Bureaus International, Inc.*

BETTERTON, bet′ər-tən, **Thomas** (1635–1710), English actor and play adapter, who was the foremost actor on the Restoration stage. His performances in Shakespearean and other plays were noted for their intensity and restraint. He created more than 130 roles.

Betterton was born in Westminster, London, in August 1635. His father was a retainer in the royal household, and Thomas was carefully educated until the family's means were exhausted during the English Civil War. He was then apprenticed to a bookseller, John Rhodes, a theater lover, who gave Betterton the opportunity, rare in revolutionary England, of becoming acquainted with theater. When the monarchy was restored in 1660, Rhodes reopened the Cockpit Theatre, where Betterton made his stage debut.

In 1661 the dramatist and poet laureate Sir William Davenant hired Betterton for the Duke's Company, a troupe formed to play in a new theater in Lincoln's Inn Fields. Davenant sent Betterton to Paris to study and adapt methods used to give the French theater its vitality during the period of Molière. Betterton's subsequent innovations in acting style, décor, and the adaptation of older plays, including several of Shakespeare's, exerted a considerable influence on the development of Restoration theater. Betterton emerged as the head of the company, and his performances of Hamlet, Othello, and other Shakespearean roles established him as the troupe's leading tragedian.

In 1671 the Duke's Company moved into a new theater in Dorset Garden, off Fleet Street, where its successes soon undermined the rival King's Men at the Theatre Royal. In 1682 the two troupes were merged under Betterton's direction at the Theatre Royal, which became the undisputed showcase of Restoration drama. In 1695, however, Betterton broke with the theater's sponsors, led a revolt of its principal actors, and reestablished the theater at Lincoln's Inn Fields. They opened with a very successful first production of William Congreve's *Love for Love*, in which Betterton played Alvars, but the theater was not financially successful. Annual benefit performances sustained Betterton toward the end of his life. He died in London on April 28, 1710, and was buried in Westminster Abbey. His wife was the actress Mary Sanderson.

BETTI, bät'tē, **Enrico** (1823–1892), Italian mathematician who contributed to several areas of mathematics and mathematical physics. His research from 1850 to 1862 was chiefly in algebra, especially Galois theory, and in elliptic functions. After 1863 he was attracted to mathematical physics, contributing to studies on capillarity, potential theory, and elasticity (including the "Betti reciprocity theorem"). In 1871 he published a classic memoir on multidimensional spaces in which he laid the basis for topology and developed the properties of the "Betti numbers," which are invariants related to the connectivity of a topological space of any number of dimensions.

Betti was born on October 21, 1823, at Pistoia in Tuscany. He attended the University of Pisa, where he served as professor from 1857 until his death on Aug. 11, 1892.

CARL B. BOYER, *Brooklyn College*

BETTI, bät'tē, **Ugo** (1892–1953), Italian judge and playwright, whose place in the Italian drama of the first half of the 20th century was second only to that of Luigi Pirandello. Betti was born at Camerino, Marche, on Feb. 4, 1892. A lawyer and high court judge by profession, he published three volumes of poetry and two books of short stories before he began to write for the theater. His first play, *La padrona*, was successfully produced in Rome in 1927. From then until his death, in Rome, on June 9, 1953, he wrote an average of a play a year.

Of Betti's 27 plays, 24 were produced in his lifetime, and more than a third were translated and presented in other countries of Europe and in America. The most successful on the American stage was *Il giocatore* (1951), translated by Alfred Drake and Edward Eagle as *The Gambler* and presented in New York in 1952, with Drake in the title role. *Corruzione al palazzo di giustizia* (1949) was produced successfully off-Broadway in 1963 as *Corruption in the Palace of Justice*. Previous productions of two Betti plays in New York were not successful.

Betti frequently uses courtroom settings to dramatize his favorite themes of justice, guilt, and the criminal complicity of innocents. The allegorical devices he employs show the influence of Pirandello. Critics in England and America have charged that Betti's seriousness often verges on pretentiousness and his rhetoric frequently becomes ponderous.

BETTING. See GAMBLING or GAMING.

BETTS, bets, **Samuel Rossiter** (1786–1868), American judge, who was an authority on admiralty law. He was born in Richmond, Mass., on June 8, 1786. Betts was educated at Williams College and established a law practice in Monticello, N.Y. After serving in the War of 1812, he was appointed a judge advocate in New York City, where he first dealt with maritime law cases. He represented a New York district in the U.S. Congress from 1815 to 1817 but declined to run for reelection. From 1823 to 1826, he was a circuit judge of the New York Supreme Court.

Betts was then appointed a U.S. district judge for the southern district of New York and served there for nearly 41 years. The body of his decisions during this period was regarded as a fundamental restatement of maritime law. During the Civil War he helped clarify the laws concerning salvage, slave traffic, blockade, prize, and contraband. Betts died in New Haven, Conn., on Nov. 3, 1868.

BETTY, bet'ē, **William Henry West** (1791–1874), English actor, who was one of the most remarkable child prodigies of the English stage. In the season of 1803–1804, when he was 13, he was the highest-paid actor in London, and the House of Commons adjourned so its members could see his performance of Hamlet.

Betty was born at Shrewsbury on Sept. 13, 1791. He first appeared on stage, using the name "The Young Roscius," at Belfast, Ireland, on Aug. 19, 1803. Conspicuous successes there and at Glasgow and Edinburgh preceded his triumphant debut that winter at Covent Garden, London. For several seasons he eclipsed all the mature performers in London. However, his standing as a player of Shakespeare's tragic heroes rapidly declined, and he was hissed off the stage when he attempted to perform Richard III. He withdrew from the stage on March 26, 1808. After failing on several occasions to make a successful comeback, he lived the rest of his life in almost total obscurity. He died in London on Aug. 24, 1874.

BETULA. See BIRCH.

BETWA RIVER, bät'wä, in central India, rises in the Vindhya Range, in the state of Madhya Pradesh. It flows in a northeasterly direction for about 380 miles (612 km) through the western part of the state to southern Uttar Pradesh where it joins the Jumna River below Kalpi. It is not navigable, but it supplies several irrigation and electrical projects along its course. The Betwa River is dammed at Dukwan village to form the Dukwan Reservoir, an irrigation project.

BEULAH, bū'lə, is a land of heavenly joy in *The Pilgrim's Progress*, by John Bunyan. He describes it as a place where there is nothing that annoys and where all sounds are agreeable.

BEUST, boist, **Count Friedrich Ferdinand von** (1809–1886), Saxon and Austrian statesman. He was born in Dresden, Germany, on Jan. 13, 1809. After serving in the Saxon diplomatic corps, he became, successively, Saxony's minister of foreign affairs (1849), minister of internal affairs (1853), and prime minister (1853). As prime minister, he tried to form a league of the middle German states that would hold the balance of power among the German states. During the Austro-Prussian War of 1866 he allied Saxony with Austria against Prussia.

After Prussia's victory, Beust was forced from office by the Prussian chancellor, Bismarck, but was soon appointed prime minister of Austria by Francis Joseph I. In this post Beust negotiated the Compromise of 1867 with Hungary, establishing the Austro-Hungarian monarchy.

During the period 1866–1870, Beust tried unsuccessfully to arrange an alliance with France and Italy to counter Russia's aggressive Balkan policy and to present an effective combination against the growing strength of Prussia. In the Franco-Prussian War of 1870 he guided Austria-Hungary in a neutral policy, hoping to capitalize on a French victory. Francis Joseph had thought in 1866 that Beust would be able to avenge Austria's defeat by Prussia, but when it became obvious in 1871 that Austria-Hungary could not gain the upper hand over Prussia, Beust was dismissed. He later served as Austrian ambassador to England (1871–1878) and France (1878–1882). Beust died at Castle Altenberg, Austria, on Oct. 24, 1886.

BEVAN, bev′ən, **Aneurin** (1897–1960), British cabinet member and one of the leaders of the British socialist movement. Bevan was born in Tredegar, Monmouthshire, a district on the English-Welsh border, on Nov. 15, 1897. The son of a Welsh coal miner, he entered the mines after leaving school at the age of 13. He soon assumed an active role in the district councils of the British trade union movement, attended the Central Labour College, and in 1926 was named a miners' disputes agent.

In 1928, "Nye" Bevan, as he was popularly called, was elected to the Monmouthshire county council, and the following year he was elected a Labour party member of Parliament, representing the Ebbw Vale constituency. With Sir Stafford Cripps, he led a left-wing Labour faction that vigorously urged socialism at home and alliances against fascism abroad. Bevan and other members of this faction were expelled from the Labour party on March 30, 1939, for advocating a united front of Labourites, Liberals, and Communists, but, following the outbreak of World War II, he was reinstated.

An outspoken critic of the government's war effort, Bevan urged state control of key industries, attacked British policy toward India, early demanded the establishment of a second front in Europe, and denounced Allied policy in North Africa. In 1945, following the Labour party's election victory, he was appointed minister of health in the new government. In this post he pressed vigorously for passage of the National Health Service Act of 1946 and administered the resulting program of tax-supported medical and dental care. He became minister of labor and national service in January 1951, but resigned in April in protest against rearmament. Bevan opposed the party's acceptance of

Aneurin Bevan

(1897–1960)

CAMERA PRESS—PIX

German rearmament and its reliance in foreign affairs on the United States. His opposition led him to resign in 1954 from the party's parliamentary committee, and the following year he was threatened with expulsion from the party because of his continued defiance of Labour's leadership. Thereafter he moderated his criticism, and he was elected treasurer of the party in 1956. He died at Chesham, Buckinghamshire, on July 6, 1960.

Bevan's career is traced in *This Great Journey* (1942), written by his wife, Jennie Lee, whom he married in 1934. She also was a Labour member of parliament.

Further Reading: Brome, Vincent, *Aneurin Bevan* (London 1953); Foot, Michael, *Aneurin Bevan* (New York 1963).

BEVATRON. See PARTICLE ACCELERATOR.

BEVERIDGE, bev′rij, **Albert Jeremiah** (1862–1927), American political leader and historian. He was born in Highland County, Ohio, on Oct. 6, 1862. Beveridge worked his way through Asbury College (now De Pauw University), graduating in 1885, was admitted to the bar, and practiced law in Indianapolis. He was elected to the U.S. Senate as a Republican in 1899 and reelected in 1905.

As a senator, Beveridge supported President Theodore Roosevelt's big navy and conservation programs, pressed for legislation to control child labor, opposed the Payne-Aldrich Tariff Act, and drafted a pioneering meat-inspection law. Because of his association with the Progressive wing of the Republican party, however, he was defeated for reelection in 1910. In 1912 he followed Roosevelt into the Progressive, or Bull Moose, party, delivered the keynote address at its first national convention, and ran unsuccessfully as its candidate for governor of Indiana. He never again held public office, although he later ran twice for the Senate.

As a biographer, Beveridge's major work was *The Life of John Marshall* (4 vols., 1916–19), a monumental study of the history of the Supreme Court and Marshall's influence on it. The work was awarded the Pulitzer prize in 1920. In his last years Beveridge worked on a biography of Lincoln, which was to fill four volumes, but the work was incomplete at his death in Indianapolis, Ind., on April 27, 1927. The first two volumes appeared posthumously as *Abraham Lincoln, 1809–1858* (1928).

Further Reading: Bowers, Claude G., *Beveridge and the Progressive Era* (Boston 1932).

BEVERIDGE, bev'rij, **William Henry** (1879–1963), British economist and social planner, who was the chief architect of Britain's "welfare state" legislation enacted in the 1940's. He was created *1st Baron Beveridge of Tuggal* in 1946.

The son of an official of the Indian civil service, Beveridge was born at Rangpur, Bengal (now in Pakistan), on March 5, 1879. He was educated in England, at Charterhouse and at Balliol College, Oxford, where he graduated in 1902.

Already deeply interested in sociology and economics, he became subwarden of Toynbee Hall, London's famous settlement house, from 1903 until 1905, when he was appointed a member of the Central (Unemployed) Body for London. In 1908 he joined the staff of the Board of Trade to set up a system of labor exchanges, publishing his first important sociological study, *Unemployment: a Problem of Industry* (1909; new ed., 1930). During World War I he organized the rationing system of the Ministry of Food.

Knighted for his services in 1919, Beveridge became director of the London School of Economics and Political Science, a post he continued to hold until 1937, when he returned to Oxford as master (principal) of University College. Besides fulfilling the duties of this latter appointment until 1945, he served from 1934 to 1944 as chairman of the Unemployment Insurance Statutory Committee; undertook for the government several urgent inquiries into labor matters during the early years of World War II; and, notably, in 1941–1942, was chairman of the Inter-Departmental Committee on Social Insurance and Allied Services, which was created to seek means of ending want and preventable disease in Great Britain.

The two-volume report of this body (*Social Insurance and Allied Services,* 1942), popularly known as the Beveridge Plan, was published at a time when the democracies were awakening to the urgent need for concerted postwar planning. The scheme propounded in the report was a social security system for all British citizens, regardless of income, "from the cradle to the grave"; monetary provision was made to cover needs arising from unemployment, ill health, maternity, widowhood, old age, and death. Through the remaining war years and afterward, the merits of the plan were fiercely debated in Parliament and outside, and were considered in other countries.

In 1944, Beveridge was elected to the House of Commons as a Liberal for the Berwick upon Tweed constituency, only to meet defeat the following year at the general election that swept the Labour party into office. He took his seat in the House of Lords in time to make his maiden speech on the National Insurance bill, which embodied his comprehensive scheme of social security. This measure, for which he had been largely responsible, was enacted in 1946 and went into effect in 1948. Among other activities in the postwar years, he gave strong support to the Crusade for World Government.

Among his numerous books are *Full Employment in a Free Society* (1944), *The Price of Peace* (1945), *Voluntary Action* (1948), and *A Defence of Free Learning* (1959). His work, *India Called Them* (1947), includes letters and a biography of his parents; *Power and Influence* (1953) is autobiographical.

BEVERLEY, bev'ər-lē, **Robert** (c. 1673–1722), American historian. He was born in Middlesex County, Va. He was educated in England, and by 1696 had become clerk of the Virginia General Court, clerk of the Council, and clerk of the General Assembly of Virginia. He also was burgess for Jamestown in 1699, 1700–1702, and 1705–1706. While on a visit in England in 1703–1704, Beverley sent home several letters in which he indiscreetly criticized the conduct of certain public affairs. This brought a rebuke from the crown that ended Beverley's political career in Virginia. He retired to Beverley Park, his estate in Virginia, and he presided in the King and Queen County court. He died at Beverley Park in 1722.

Beverley was the author of *The History and Present State of Virginia* (1705; rev. ed., 1722), reprinted in a modern edition by Louis B. Wright in 1947. The first such history by a native Virginian, it is written in a fast-moving, entertaining style, describing from keen observation the government and economic life of the colony.

BEVERLY, bev'ər-lē, is a city in northeastern Massachusetts, in Essex County. It is situated on Massachusetts Bay of the Atlantic Ocean, 18 miles (29 km) north of Boston. Originally a seafaring, agricultural, and commercial town, Beverly is now a residential and manufacturing city. Important products are shoe machinery, electronic metal products, and machinery equipment. There are harbor facilities for shipping and recreation purposes and a municipal airport.

Endicott Junior College, North Shore Community College, and Gordon College and Divinity School are here. Places of interest include the Balch House (built prior to 1636 and believed to be the oldest house in the United States), the Hale House (1694), and the Cabot House (1781), all open to the public. There are beaches at Lyons Park and Independence Park.

The first ship of the American navy, the schooner *Hannah*, was outfitted, armed, equipped, and provisioned at Glover's Wharf in Beverly. Commissioned by Gen. George Washington, it sailed from there on its first cruise, Sept. 5, 1775, and returned two days later with a prize. This important incident, recorded in original documents at the Library of Congress, made Beverly the birthplace of the American navy. The first chemical plant was established in Beverly in 1630 and the first cotton mill in America was set up in 1787. In 1810, America's first Sunday school was organized in the town.

Beverly has been the residence of many famous Americans, including President William Howard Taft, the poet Dr. Oliver Wendell Holmes, Justice Oliver Wendell Holmes, and Henry Cabot Lodge, Jr. Incorporated as a town in 1668 and as a city in 1894, Beverly is governed by a mayor and nine aldermen. Population: 38,348.

BEVERLY HILLS, bev'ər-lē, is a residential city in southwestern California, in Los Angeles County. It comprises an area of 5.7 square miles (14.8 sq km), surrounded by the city of Los Angeles and extending up the slopes of the Santa Monica Mountains. Chiefly a residential center for professional people, it has some light manufacturing, such as electronic equipment production. Beautiful shops and luxurious homes line curving streets and canyons. There are seven parks totaling 54.5 acres (22 hectares) of land. The site, originally an old Spanish land grant known as El Rancho de las Aguas, was given its present name by its subdivider in 1906. It was incorporated in 1914. In 1919, Douglas Fairbanks and Mary Pickford built their home Pickfair here; they were the first of many celebrities of screen, stage, and television whose homes have made the small city famous.

Under California statutes, it is a general law city, governed by five councilmen, one of whom serves as mayor. Under their authority, an administrative officer has coordinated government activities since 1952. Population: 33,416.

MARGARET MONTGOMERY
Beverly Hills Public Library

BEVERLY HILLS, bev′ər-lē, is a residential village in southeastern Michigan, in Oakland County, 12 miles (19 km) northwest of Detroit. Points of interest in the village include Detroit Country Day School, for boys, and Dodge Park, a recreational area of 40 acres (16 hectares). About 1830, settlers from New York and New England began farming the region. In recent years agricultural activity has disappeared. The area was incorporated as Westwood Village in 1958, and the name was changed to Beverly Hills in 1959. Government is by council-manager. Population: 13,598.

BEVIN, bev′in, **Ernest** (1881–1951), British trade union leader and public official, who was minister of labor in World War II and foreign minister in 1945–1951. Born at Winsford, England, on March 9, 1881, he was orphaned at an early age and grew up in Devonshire. He left school at the age of 11 and went to work as a farm boy near Winsford, but two years later he moved to Bristol where he became a drayman.

Bevin's career as a labor leader began in 1905 with his appointment as secretary of the Bristol Right-to-Work Committee. He threw himself into the trade union movement with energy and, in 1910, became national organizer for the Dockers' Union. He pleaded the dock workers' case so eloquently before the Transport Workers' Court of Inquiry (1920) that he won a standard minimum wage for them and national prominence for himself. He went on to his most outstanding achievement as a labor organizer in 1922 when he merged 32 trade unions into the gigantic Transport and General Workers' Union, which he directed as general secretary until 1940. The mightiest trade union leader of his generation,

WIDE WORLD

Ernest Bevin

(1881–1951)

he was the chief planner of the abortive general strike of 1926 and chairman of the general council of the Trades Union Congress (1936–1937).

Minister of Labor. Although long a power behind the scenes in the Labour party, he did not enter active political life until May 1940, when he accepted the post of minister of labor and national service in Winston Churchill's wartime coalition government. A member of the War Cabinet, he wielded the vast powers of his position with ruthless efficiency to mobilize Britain's manpower and industrial resources. He persuaded the workers to accept the voluntary suspension of cherished trade union safeguards, such as those against dilution of skilled labor, which he had spent half his lifetime winning for them. At the same time, however, Bevin raised the living standard of the ordinary wage earner and secured for the working class a place of respect in the community. In this he showed a depth of human understanding that not only enabled him to maintain his popularity with the workers but spurred them on to greater productive effort. A truly great minister of labor, he accomplished a social revolution in the midst of Britain's struggle for national survival.

Foreign Minister. At the close of the war in Europe, he resigned from Churchill's cabinet and, following the victory of the Labour party in the general election of July 1945, served as secretary of state for foreign affairs in the administration of Clement Attlee. One of the most successful of British foreign ministers, he lacked the traditional background of the professional diplomat, but he displayed in the conduct of international affairs the same qualities of courage, patience, resourcefulness, and shrewdness in bargaining that had made him a superb labor negotiator. His one conspicuous failure was on the Palestine question, an issue on which his conviction that Arab friendship was essential to the protection of Britain's vital interests in the Middle East led him to pursue a policy intended to prevent the establishment of Israel.

Against this, however, must be set many achievements, particularly in his strategy of resistance to Soviet imperialism. Assuming the direction of Britain's foreign policy at a time when her strength was exhausted, Bevin was quick to perceive that she must curtail her commitments abroad and that this must be done without creating a power vacuum into which the Soviet Union could advance. Convinced soon after the Potsdam Conference (1945) that Europe's only hope of security lay in American arms, he encouraged the United States to proclaim the Truman Doctrine and enter fully into European defense. He responded eagerly to the Marshall Plan and helped to form the Organization for European Economic Cooperation. A strong advocate of Western unity, he signed the Treaty of Dunkerque with France (1947), enlarged it into the Treaty of Mutual Assistance (1948) to include the Netherlands, Belgium, and Luxembourg (Western European Union), and was one of the prime movers in the establishment of the North Atlantic Treaty Organization.

Bevin resigned as foreign minister in March 1951 because of illness. He died at London on April 14, 1951.

ALLAN M. FRASER
Archivist, Province of Newfoundland

Further Reading: Williams, Francis, *Ernest Bevin, Portrait of a Great Englishman* (London 1952).

BEVIS OF HAMPTON, Sir, bev'is, ham'tən, also known as *Bevis of Southampton*, a medieval romance of a legendary English hero. The oldest extant version is an Anglo-Norman text dated 1230 to 1250. English texts date from the early 14th century. There are also versions in French, Italian, Gaelic, Welsh, Dutch, Norse, Yiddish, Rumanian, and Russian.

Child Bevis escapes a murder plot, but his mother sells him to pagans because he vows revenge against his stepfather, the emperor of Almaine and murderer of his father. Through valorous deeds Bevis wins the favor of the king of Ermyn and his daughter Josian. She agrees to become a Christian and the wife of Bevis, but faces enforced marriage to Ivor of Mombrant while Bevis is in prison. He escapes, recovers his horse, Arondel, and his sword, Morglay. He then rescues Josian, wins the giant Ascapard as squire, and overcomes a number of natural and supernatural enemies. With Josian and Saber, his childhood protector, Bevis reaches England and avenges his father's murder. Now married, he and Josian are forced out of England and are again separated. Rescued by Saber, Josian rejoins Bevis, whose exploits among Christians and heathens have become famous. Bevis kills Ivor, seizes his kingdom, and returns to England for his last great battle, in which he defeats England's King Edgar, winning for his son Miles the hand in marriage of Edgar's daughter. Another son, Guy, now rules Ermyn; and, with Josian and Arondel, Bevis returns to Mombrant, where the three live long, peaceful lives and die together.

Sir Bevis of Hampton illustrates both the weaknesses and strengths of medieval romances. Episodic and overstocked with characters, it derives unity primarily from its hero. Its verse and marvels invite such satire as appears in Chaucer's *Tale of Sir Thopas*. Yet its spontaneity gives a sense of reality to the unrealistic motifs of romances: fights with giants and dragons, famous swords and horses, miracles, defense of the Faith and the distressed. The theme of exile and return sustains motivation. The imperfect hero, devoted heroine, and Hamletlike situation humanize the story. Not the least of its appeals are its poetic passages and its humor.

J.T. McCULLEN, Jr., *Texas Technological College*

BEWICK, bū'ik, **Thomas** (1753–1828), English wood engraver, who began a revival of the art of wood engraving in the 19th century. The "white line" technique that he developed made it possible to achieve more subtle gradations of light and shade than had been accomplished before.

He was born in Ovington Parish, Northumberland, on Aug. 12, 1753, and was apprenticed at the age of 14 to the engraver Ralph Beilby of Newcastle. After a brief visit to London in 1776, Bewick returned to Newcastle and went into partnership with Beilby, who often designed the text areas of the books illustrated by Bewick.

Bewick's early works included illustrations for John Gay's *Fables* (1779) and for an anthology, *Select Fables* (1784). His masterpieces are the *General History of Quadrupeds* (1790) and the *History of British Birds* (2 vols., 1797 and 1804), in which his skill as a naturalist enhances his superb engravings. Bewick's best-known print is the *Chillingham Bull* (1789). His last major work was *Fables of Aesop* (1818). He died at Durham, on Nov. 8, 1828. His *Memoirs* was published in 1862.

LONG-EARED OWL,

THOMAS BEWICK engraving from his books on birds.

John Bewick (1760–1795), Thomas' brother, and *Robert Elliot Bewick* (1788–1849), Thomas' son, were also engravers, but their work is inferior to his.

See also WOOD ENGRAVING AND WOODCUT—*History* (Bewick and the 19th Century Revival).

Further Reading: Hutchinson, Robert, ed., *1800 Woodcuts by Thomas Bewick and His School* (New York 1962); Reynolds, Graham, *Thomas Bewick: a Résumé of His Life and Work* (London 1949); Roscoe, S., *Thomas Bewick: a Bibliography raisonné* (New York 1953); Weekley, Montague, *Thomas Bewick* (New York 1953).

BEXLEY, beks'lē, is a municipal borough in southeastern England. It is situated in Kent, on the Cray River, about 15 miles (24 km) southeast of London. The borough includes Bexley Heath, East Wickham, and Welling. Bexley is mainly a residential suburb of London.

In the 17th century the manor belonged to William Camden, the historian, who bequeathed it to Oxford University for the endowment of a professorship. There are many points of interest. Hall Place is a flint and brick mansion built in the 16th-17th centuries. Part of the Danson Estate (mentioned in historical records as early as 1301) is now a public park. At Bexley Heath is the Red House, where the author and designer, William Morris, lived. The parish church of St. Mary (restored 1883) has early Norman work and a typical Kentish shingled spire. At East Wickham is the disused 12th century Church of St. Michael.

The parish of Bexley was mentioned in a charter of Coenwulf (Kenulph), king of the Mercians, dated 814 A.D. In *Domesday Book* it is referred to as "Bix." Bexley was incorporated as a borough in 1937. Population: (1961) 89,629.

BEXLEY, beks'lē, a city in Ohio, in Franklin County, is a residential community surrounded by, but politically independent of, Columbus, the state capital. Capital University, a coeducational Lutheran institution, is here. A monument at East Broad Street and Drexel Avenue marks the site of Camp Bushnell, used in the Spanish-American War. Bexley was incorporated in 1908 and chartered in 1930. It is governed by a mayor and council. Population: 14,888.

MARY T. ZIMMERMAN, *Bexley Public Library*

BEY, bā, a Turkish title, possibly of Iranian origin, equivalent to "lord" or "sir." It is also transliterated *beg*. The word first appears in the 8th-century Turkic Orkhon inscriptions in its plural form, *begler*, to denote the nobility as opposed to the ruling class and the common people. The title has been assumed by princes of subordinate tribes or communities (such as the rulers of Tunis from 1705 to 1957) to distinguish themselves from their superior "sultans" or "hans." It has also been applied to provincial governors and high-ranking military officers. The use of the word was abolished in Turkey in 1934, but it is still used in speech, following male first names.

J. STEWART-ROBINSON, *University of Michigan*

BEYERS, bā′ərz, **Christiaan Frederik** (1869–1914), South African general. He was born near Stellenbosch, in Cape Province. A lawyer by profession, he enlisted as a private in the Boer army during the South African War (1899–1902) against Great Britain and rose to the rank of assistant commandant general in the Transvaal. In 1906, when the Transvaal was granted self-government by the British, he was elected speaker of the Legislative Assembly, and became commandant general of the federal defense force when the Union of South Africa was established in 1910.

The onset of World War I brought Beyers into conflict with Prime Minister Louis Botha and Gen. Jan Christiaan Smuts, who favored an active campaign against German Southwest Africa. When Botha ordered an invasion of the German colony, Beyers resigned his command and joined Christiaan Rudolph De Wet and Jacobus Hercules De La Rey in an Afrikaner separatist movement. In October 1914 fighting broke out between government forces and the rebels. Beyers and his commandos moved south in hope of joining De Wet in the Orange Free State, but suffered a decisive defeat near Bultfontein on November 17. Beyers escaped but was pursued to the Vaal River, where he drowned on Dec. 8, 1914.

BEYLE, Marie Henri. See STENDHAL.

BEYOND GOOD AND EVIL is a philosophical work by Friedrich Wilhelm Nietzsche (q.v.), first published in 1886 as *Jenseits von Gut und Böse*. In this work Nietzsche began an examination of the structures and purposes of moral systems, which he developed more fully in a later book, *Zur Genealogie der Moral* (1887; Eng. tr., *A Genealogy of Morals*). *Beyond Good and Evil* was to have been the first part of a systematic presentation of Nietzsche's philosophy, and although the project was never carried out, *Beyond Good and Evil* stands as a coherent segment of the philosopher's thought.

In *Beyond Good and Evil*, Nietzsche denies the validity of an absolute and universal moral code and makes a distinction between two primary types of morality, which he calls "master-morality" and "slave-morality." He claims that both types of morality are thoroughly mixed within all highly developed civilizations. While there is a tendency for the upper social classes to operate within the framework of master-morality, and a similar tendency for the lower classes to conduct themselves according to the precepts of the slave-morality, Nietzsche claims that elements of both moralities can exist in the same man.

He describes master-morality as an expression of the virtues that are necessarily found in leaders, such as strength and independence. Slave-morality, on the other hand, regards these qualities as dangerous and instead extols their opposites, such as meekness and humility. Thus, Nietzsche contends, slave-morality tends to encourage mediocrity and dependence on others. Slave-morality is herd-morality and is in direct conflict with master-morality.

BEZALEL, bez′ə-lēl, in the Old Testament, was the son of Uri and a master craftsman from the tribe of Judah. His name means "in the shadow of God"—that is, under God's protection. Together with Aholiab (Oholiab), son of Ahisamach, from the tribe of Dan, he was appointed by Moses to carry out all the gold-, silver-, and brasswork, the stonecutting and woodcarving, the weaving and embroidering of fine linen, and the leatherwork involved in the construction and furnishing of the Tabernacle in the wilderness. Among the sacred objects made by Bezalel was the Ark of the Covenant with cherubim surmounting it, the table, the seven-armed candelabrum, the altars, the ephod, and the breastplate (Exodus 35:30 to 39:43). The ability of Bezalel "to devise skillful works" of decorative art was regarded by the ancient Hebrews as a divinely inspired gift (Exodus 31:1–11). The name "Bezalel" was taken for the School of Arts and Crafts founded in Jerusalem in 1906.

RAPHAEL PATAI, *Theodor Herzl Institute*

BEZANT, bez′ənt, the western European name for a round, flat Byzantine gold coin similar to the Roman solidus. It was in circulation in Europe from about the 6th to the 13th centuries. Silver bezants were in use in England from the 13th to the 15th centuries.

In heraldry, the use of gold disks, called bezants, on coats of arms was introduced by the Crusaders.

In architecture, the bezant is a flat, ornamental disk that is often used in borders and arches.

BEZBORODKO, byez-bō-rôt′kō, **Prince Aleksandr Andreyevich** (1747–1799), Russian diplomat. He was born in Gluchova, Ukraine, on March 25, 1747. He studied at the clerical academy in Kiev, then entered the army and fought in the Russo-Turkish War (1768–1774). In 1775 he became secretary of petitions to Empress Catherine II (the Great). He was sent by her on state business to Copenhagen and on his return presented a report which was substantially a plan for the partition of Turkey between Russia and Austria. In recognition of these services, the government made him postmaster general and plenipotentiary for all negotiations in the foreign office, and he exercised the duties of a secretary of state.

In 1786 Bezborodko became a member of the Senate and was Catherine's mouthpiece in that body. As minister of foreign affairs he concluded with Turkey the Peace of Jassy in January 1792. He was largely instrumental in the third partition of Poland (1795). When Catherine's son, Paul I, ascended the throne (1796), he made Bezborodko a prince of the Russian Empire and soon afterward imperial chancellor, the highest honorary office in Russia. Bezborodko died in St. Petersburg (now Leningrad) on April 17, 1799.

BÈZE, bâz, **Théodore de** (1519–1605), French Protestant theologian. He was also known as *Theodore Beza* and *Théodore de Besze.* Born into a noble family in Vézelay, in the province of Burgundy, France, on June 24, 1519, he was educated at Orléans and later at Bourges under Melchior Wolmar, a German philologist devoted to the Reformation. From 1535 to 1539 he studied law at Orléans, and he began his practice in Paris. He received an interest in the valuable abbey of Froidmond from his uncle and lived on the income of two benefices and on property inherited from a brother.

Familiar from childhood with classical literature, de Bèze was known as a scholar and a Latin poet through his witty *Poemata juvenilia,* an autobiographical work. His habits were somewhat dissipated, but they changed after a secret marriage to Claudine Denosse in 1543. A serious illness confirmed the intention he had formed at Orléans of devoting himself to the Reformed Church, and in 1548 he sacrificed his fortune and went with his wife to Geneva. The following year he became professor of Greek at Lausanne, where he stayed for nearly 10 years. During this time he wrote *Abraham sacrifiant* (*The Sacrifice of Abraham*), a tragicomic drama that was received with great approval. His defense of the burning of Michael Servetus, *De haereticis a civili magistratu puniendis* (*On the Punishment of Heretics by the Civil Magistrate*), was published in 1554. At Lausanne, de Bèze delivered a popular series of lectures on St. Paul's Epistle to the Romans and on I Peter. His work on these lectures served as the basis for his Latin translation of the New Testament, published in 1556 and still reprinted.

Services to the Calvinists. De Bèze was so highly regarded by Swiss Calvinists that he was sent to the German Protestant princes in 1558 to obtain their intercession at the French court for the release of Huguenots imprisoned in Paris. Later that year he went to Geneva as a preacher. He soon became a professor of theology at the Geneva academy and Calvin's most active assistant. He had come to Calvin's attention through several works in which he zealously advocated Calvinistic views. It early became apparent that de Bèze was Calvin's ablest coadjutor and was destined to be his successor.

The Calvinists made much use of de Bèze's talents for negotiation. He was sent to King Anthony of Navarre's court at Nérac to obtain toleration for the Huguenots. He represented the Calvinist viewpoint at the religious conference at Poissy in 1561, where his boldness, presence of mind, and energy won the admiration, although not the conversion, of the French court.

Civil war between the Huguenots and the Catholics in France broke out in 1562, and de Bèze accompanied the prince de Condé during the war as chaplain. After the prince was captured, de Bèze joined Admiral Gaspard de Coligny, leader of the French Huguenot forces.

Successor to Calvin. When a temporary peace was restored in 1563, de Bèze returned to Geneva and resumed his duties as a preacher and a professor, defending Calvinism in many controversies. On the death of Calvin in 1564, de Bèze succeeded him. From this point he was regarded as the leading theologian of the Reformed Swiss Church, and until 1598 he was looked upon as "the true soul of the Geneva Academy." De Bèze presided at the synods of the French Cal-

vinists at La Rochelle in 1571 and at Nîmes in 1572, voicing great opposition to the alteration of clerical discipline. At the religious conference at Montpellier in 1586 he opposed the Lutheran stance of the theologians from Württemberg.

De Bèze's wife died in 1588, and the following year he married Catherine del Plano, the widow of a Geneva citizen. He continued to repel the attacks of his enemies, who were chiefly apostatized Calvinists and Lutherans, and also Jesuits. They spread a rumor in 1597 that he had died and had returned to the Roman Catholic faith before his death. Now 78, de Bèze answered his assailants in a racy, vigorous poem. He also resisted the efforts of St. Francis de Sales to convert him, thus disappointing the hopes of Pope Clement VIII.

Among de Bèze's other works are a brief *Confession of the Christian Faith* and a Latin *Life of Calvin* (1564). The *Ecclesiastical History of the Reformed Churches in France* (1580) has been attributed to him, but some scholars doubt that he wrote it. He also completed Clément Marot's translation of the Psalms into French. His name is associated with the 6th century Greek-Latin Codex D of the Gospels and Acts, which he presented to the University of Cambridge in 1581. De Bèze died in Geneva on Oct. 13, 1605.

FREDERICK C. GRANT
Union Theological Seminary

BÉZIERS, bā-zyā′, a city in southern France, is in Hérault department, on the Orb River and the Canal du Midi, 38 miles (61 km) southwest of Montpellier. It is a commercial center of the wine trade, has large brandy distilleries, and manufactures fertilizer, vineyard equipment, rubber articles, biscuits, and candy.

The city, called *Baeterrae* in ancient times, was a Gallic stronghold and was taken by the Romans in 120 B.C. In the 12th century it was a stronghold of the counts of Carcassonne. In 1209 some 20,000 of its inhabitants were massacred by order of Simon IV de Montfort, leader of the crusade against the Albigenses, because the city had given asylum to some of the fugitives of this sect. It was the birthplace of Pierre Paul de Riquet (1604–1680), builder of the Canal du Midi. Population: (1962) 57,601.

BEZIQUE, bə-zēk′, is the card game that first used *melding* (declaring certain combinations of cards for points) as the principal means of scoring. Of the many variations, *rubicon bezique* is the most popular in the United States.

Bezique is played by two persons with 128 cards: four each of A, K, Q, J, 10, 9, 8, 7 of spades, hearts, diamonds, and clubs. The object is to make the most possible points in one deal.

Each player is dealt nine cards, three at a time; the remainder form the *stock.* Trump suit is set by the first *marriage* (K, Q of the same suit) melded. The nondealer leads by playing any card in his hand. In response, his adversary also may play any card, but the trick is won by the high card of the suit led or by a trump.

The winner of a trick may declare any one meld for points (see scoring below). He then draws the top stock card and leads to the next trick. His adversary then draws. A player can play a card from a meld. If he does, he may reform that meld with another card and score again. Also, the same card may be used in several different melds.

When the stock is down to two cards, melding stops. Then the second player must follow suit on each trick if he can and must win the trick if he can. Taking the last trick counts 50 points. The player with the most points wins and gets a bonus of 500. Each ace and 10 taken in play counts 10 points only when points are needed to avoid a *rubicon* (having less than 1,000 points). If the loser has a rubicon, the winner scores his own points, his adversary's points (including 10 for each ace and 10), and a 1,000-point bonus.

Points for Melds: K, Q of trump, 40; K, Q of any other suit, 20; A, K, Q, J, 10 of trump, 250; A, K, Q, J, 10 of any other suit, 150; any 4 A's, 100; any 4 K's, 80; any 4 Q's, 60; any 4 J's, 40; bezique (♤ Q and ◊ J), 40; double bezique, 500; triple bezique, 1,500; quadruple bezique, 4,500.

FRANK K. PERKINS, *Boston "Herald"*

BEZRUČ, bez′rōōch, **Petr** (1867–1958), Czech poet, who wrote nationalistic verse, primarily in protest of Austrian suppression of the Czechs. His austere but moving style has a universal appeal that gave his poetry a significance that extends far beyond his homeland.

Bezruč was born in Troppau, Austrian Silesia (now Opava, Czechoslovakia), on Sept. 15, 1867, the son of a prominent patriot and philologist. After studying classics for a time at the University of Prague, he entered the postal service in Brünn (now Brno), Moravia. He was imprisoned during World War I for his anti-Austrian views.

Bezruč's reputation rests on a single collection of verse, first published in 1903 as *A Silesian Number.* The collection, renamed *The Silesian Songs* in 1909, was ultimately enlarged to include 88 poems. Bezruč's semifree verse reflects his admiration of Walt Whitman, but it nevertheless is highly original. After World War II the Czech government granted Bezruč a pension as a "national artist." He died in Kostelec, Moravia, on Feb. 17, 1958.

Further Reading: Harkins, William E., *An Anthology of Czech Literature* (New York 1953); Otruba, Mojmir, ed., *Linden Tree: An Anthology of Czech and Slovak Literature* (New York 1962); Selver, Paul, *A Century of Czech and Slovak Poetry* (London 1946).

BHAGALPUR, bäg′əl-pŏŏr, is a city in India, in Bihar state. It is the capital of Bhagalpur district. The city is situated on the Ganges River, 120 miles (190 km) southeast of Patna. Bhagalpur is a road and railroad junction and the trading center for a fertile area in which rice, wheat, corn, barley, oilseeds, and sugarcane are the chief crops. The city has rice and sugar mills, and silk- and wool-weaving factories, and it is a distribution center for hemp narcotics. A silk culture institute and an agricultural research station are located there.

Ancient cave sculptures dating from the reign of the Emperor Asoka (about 274–232 B.C.) are found in the neighborhood, and 5 miles (8 km) west of the city, at Sultanganj, is an early temple of the Gupta period of architecture (about 320–500 A.D.). Population: (1961) 143,850.

BHAGAVAD GĪTĀ, bug′ə-vəd gē′tä, an ancient religious-philosophical treatise of India. Its title means, in Sanskrit, "The Song of the Lord." The *Bhagavad Gītā* consists of about 700 verses, divided into 18 chapters. The earliest date of composition given by Western scholars is the 2d century B.C. One of the three chief canonical books of Hinduism (the others being the Upani-

shads and the *Brahma-sutras*), it has been interpreted by almost every noted Indian philosopher and theologian. The earliest important commentator was Shankara (Śaṅkara), who lived around 800 A.D.

The *Bhagavad Gītā,* a part of the *Mahābhārata* (q.v.), is written as a dialogue between Krishna, the supreme manifestation of the Godhead, and Arjuna, a warrior prince, the third of the Pandava brothers. The Pandavas are at war with their kinsmen the Kauravas, who have deprived them of their ancestral kingdom. On the eve of battle, Arjuna is depressed to think of the impending slaughter of his friends and relatives, and asks Krishna's advice regarding his duty.

The *Bhagavad Gītā* does not give a cut-and-dried system of philosophy or formal theology, but deals with all the major problems thereof, such as the soul, the Absolute God, creation, and perfection. A manual of spiritual discipline, it discusses the path of devotion to the personal God (*bhakti-yoga*), philosophical discrimination (*jñāna-yoga*), right activity (*karma-yoga*), and concentration (*rāja-yoga*). It emphasizes, however, the performance of duty following one's inborn nature (dharma) by those still identified with the body and the world. Such duty must be performed in a detached spirit, the doer surrendering the results to God. Relinquishment of duty is prescribed only for those who have realized the world's unreality. Likewise, motiveless devotion to God is considered easier to practice than contemplation of the Absolute. Perfection is described from both the cosmic and the acosmic standpoint; the perfected soul may maintain difference from or realize identity with the supreme Reality. The universe is a projection of the Godhead, whose lower nature manifests the material bodies and whose higher nature animates them with life. The Godhead is described, from different standpoints, as Pure Being, the personal God, and the Incarnation. The soul is essentially birthless and deathless Spirit but is phenomenalized by the power of *māyā,* or cosmic ignorance. Through knowledge of God, and by His grace, man can liberate himself from the bondage of matter.

SWAMI NIKHILANANDA
Editor and Translator of "The Bhagavad Gītā"

Bibliography
Translations of the *Bhagavad Gītā* include those by Arnold, Sir Edwin (Boston 1885); Edgerton, Franklin (Cambridge, Mass., 1944); Nikhilananda, (Swami) (New York 1944); and Prabhavananda, (Swami), and Isherwood, Christopher (New York 1944).
Ghose, Sir Aurobindo, *Essays on the Gītā* (Calcutta 1926–28).
Vinoba, A. Bhave, *Talks on the Gītā* (New York 1960).

BHAKTPUR, bäkt′pŏŏr, is a city in central Nepal adjoining the capital city of Katmandu. The name is also spelled *Bhadgaon* or *Bhatgaon.* It is a processing center for grains and vegetables of the Nepal Valley. For 200 years prior to the Gurkha conquest in 1769, it was the most important town in the valley. Population: (1961) 33,075.

BHAMO, bə-mô′, is a town in Burma, situated at the head of navigation of the Irrawaddy River. Located near the Chinese border, it has for centuries enjoyed an active trade with China. In World War II, Bhamo was an important station on the Ledo (Stilwell) Road, a supply route for Allied troops in China. Population: (1953) 9,817.

BHARAT, bu′rut, is the Hindi name for India and an alternate official name for the country. The word is derived from the Bharata, a tribe famous in Vedic tradition. Many Hindus still refer to India as *Bharata-Varsha,* the land of the Bharata. They prefer "Bharat" to "India," a name they believe to be of foreign origin.

BHARAVI, bä′rə-vē, was an Indian poet of the 6th century A.D. He is known for his *kāvyas,* or artificial epics. Bharavi's principal poem is the *Kirātārjunīya* (The Story of Kirāta and Arjuna). For many months, Arjuna, one of the heroes of the *Mahābhārata* (q.v.), practiced severe austerities in order to gain invincibility for himself and his family in the coming war. So much energy did he acquire by his self-imposed penance that the world was in danger of being burned up, and the god Siva decided to grant his prayer. Siva chose to appear to his devotee, however, in the likeness of the man-eating forester Kirata, who challenged Arjuna to archery and wrestling contests. Though Arjuna could not overcome Kirata, he, like the Biblical Jacob, won from the disguised god, by combined physical strength and spiritual adoration, the blessing he sought.

RODERICK MARSHALL, *Brooklyn College*

BHARTRIHARI, bur′trē-hu′rē, Indian poet, philosopher, and grammarian of the 7th century A.D. Although he is fabled to have been the brother of King Vikramaditya, who in turn is fabled to have lived in the 1st century B.C., it is more likely that Bhartrihari lived 800 years later. He was the author of the three *satakas,* or centuries of verse—*The Century of Love, The Century of Worldly Wisdom,* and *The Century of the Quiet Heart.*

Bhartrihari's poems give a fascinating picture of a man distracted by passionate love of women. From such experiences he sought refuge in the ragged gown of the monk, but he was constantly driven by restlessness back to the arms of women and the life of the court (he may, indeed, have been of royal stock), for both of which he felt, finally, pure scorn.

Anticipating in a beautiful poem Jaques' seven-ages-of-man speech in *As You Like It,* Bhartrihari seems also to have ended, like Jaques, among forest "convertites."

Oh Mother Earth, Father Wind, Friend Sun, Kinsman Water, Brother Sky, for the last time I clasp my hands in reverence before you. The power of error being destroyed within me by the stainless knowledge and the rich store of good works born of your companionship, I sink into the Supernal Spirit.

Bhartrihari was the first Indian writer to become known in Europe. His poems were translated into German by Abraham Rogerius (1653) and Peter von Bohlen (1833) and into English by Charles H. Tawney (1877), B. Hale Wortham (1866), Paul Elmer More (1898), and Arthur W. Ryder (1910).

RODERICK MARSHALL, *Brooklyn College*

BHASKARA, bäs′kə-rə, was a Hindu astronomer and mathematician who was born in 1114 A.D. He was the sixth successor of Brahmagupta as head of the College of Astronomy at *Ujjain.* Bhaskara wrote the *Siddhāntasiromani* (Crowning Work on the Stellar System), a work on both astronomy and mathematics, in verse with a prose commentary. He was known as *Bhaskara Acarya*—Bhaskara the Learned.

BHATPARA, bät-pä′rä, is a city in India, situated in the state of West Bengal, on the Hooghly River, 21 miles (34 km) north of Calcutta. Once a center of Sanskrit learning, Bhatpara is now an industrial city, with jute and paper industries and rice mills. Population: (1961) 147,630.

BHAVABHUTI, bə-və-boo′tē, was an Indian dramatist who lived about 700 A.D.

Of his three great plays, two, the *Mahāvira-carita* (Early Life of Rama) and the *Uttararā-macarita* (Later Life of Rama), add up to an impressive seven-act dramatization of the story of the hero of the *Rāmāyana;* the other, *Mālatī-mādhava* (Malati and Madhava) is traditionally referred to as the Hindu counterpart of *Romeo and Juliet.* For dramatic vigor and variety of characters, Bhavabhuti is often placed next in rank after Kalidasa, the 5th century Hindu dramatist and lyric poet.

BHAVE, bä′vä, **Acharya Vinoba** (1895–   ), Indian philosopher, who founded the *Bhoodan Yajna* (land-gift) movement for the distribution of land of the wealthy among the poor.

Born in Bagode, Baroda state, India, on Sept. 11, 1895, Bhave early became a disciple of Mohandas K. Gandhi and devoted himself to a life of austerity. Seeking to improve conditions in the villages, he conceived of the *Bhoodan Yajna* idea in 1951 and thereafter toured India appealing for land gifts. Several million acres were donated in this way. To prevent fragmentation of the land, the Indian government encouraged villagers to operate their properties cooperatively. Bhave explained his philosophy in the book *Bhoodan Yajna* (1953).

BHAVNAGAR, bäv′nə-gər, is a city in India and the chief port of Kathiawar peninsula. Situated in Gujarat state, on the west coast of the Gulf of Cambay, the city is 90 miles (155 km) southwest of Ahmadabad. Bhavnagar carries on an active trade in cotton, grain, timber, and handicrafts. Industries include silk and cotton textiles, and the manufacturing of bricks, tiles, and metal products. Two colleges of Gujarat University are located in the city. Founded in 1723, it was the capital of the princely state of Bhavnagar. Population: (1961) 171,039.

BHILS, bēls, a people of west central India. They have dark skins, thick lips, and broad noses, thus resembling Munda-speaking hill peoples. But although they are believed to have formerly spoken a Munda or Dravidian language, they now speak Aryan dialects.

Under Rajput rule the Bhils enjoyed some status, but when the Mahrattas invaded central India in the 18th century, the Bhils became brigands, raiding the plains from strongholds in the hills. Only late in the 19th century were they pacified.

A majority of Bhils have settled in the plains as farm servants, laborers, or village watchmen. These have become Hindus or Muslims. Over 200,000 remain hill dwellers and pagans. They lead a precarious existence, subsisting on wild plant and animal food, and on grain obtained by farm employment at harvest time. These hill pagans abandon their primitive villages whenever illness occurs.

ELIZABETH BACON
Editor, "India: A Sociological Background"

BHIMA, bē'mə, is a hero of Hindu mythology. In the *Mahābhārata,* he is the son of Vayu, the god of the wind, and is the second of the five Pandava brothers. He is depicted as being prodigiously strong and courageous. See also MAHĀBHĀRATA.

BHOJA, bō'jä, was the name of several Rajput kings of India, of whom the following were most noteworthy:

BHOJA (c. 840–885 A.D.) was the fifth king of the Gurjara-Pratihara dynasty of Kanauj, the imperial city in post-Gupta India, situated near Kanpur (Cawnpore). The distribution of his inscriptions establishes that his empire extended from the Sutlej to the Tapti rivers and to modern Bihar.

BHOJA (c. 997–1060 A.D.) was the ninth and most prominent ruler of the Parmar dynasty of Malwa, in west-central India. For a few years he ruled over Kanauj, but his dominions were mostly in Malwa. During his reign, his capital, Dhar, and the city of Ujjain became famous Hindu and Jain centers of learning. Himself a scholar, he wrote poetry and books on astronomy, astrology, and architecture. The mosque at Dhar known as Bhoja Masjid originally was built by him as a Sanskrit college. Bhoja also founded the city of Bhopal and designed an artificial 250-square-mile (648-sq-km) lake there, which is now in disrepair. The poet Ballalla collected his anedotes in *Bhoja Prabhanda.*

BRIJEN K. GUPTA
Brooklyn College

BHOPAL, bō-päl', a city in India, is the capital of the state of Madhya Pradesh and was the capital of the former princely state of Bhopal. The city is situated 360 miles (579 km) south of New Delhi and 410 miles (660 km) northeast of Bombay.

Bhopal and its setting provide one of the most attractive sights in India. From the shore of a lake the city rises in tiers up the side of a sandstone ridge to its summit, 500 feet (152 meters) above the lake. Important buildings include the palace of the former ruling family and the Taj-ul-Masjid, the largest mosque in India.

In the early 1700's, with the decline of Mughul (Mogul) power in the area, Bhopal was established as an independent state by an Afghan chief who had served Mughul Emperor Aurangzeb. It became the second-largest Muslim-ruled princely state of British India. A major industrial installation, Heavy Electricals (India) Ltd., began operations in Bhopal in 1960. Population: (1960) 185,374.

JOEL M. ANDRESS
Central Washington State College

BHUBANESWAR, bōō-və-näsh'wər, is a city in India and the capital of Orissa state. Located 140 miles (225 km) southwest of Calcutta, the city is particularly noteworthy for its magnificent Hindu shrines. Seven thousand tombs once stood here, but today only about 500 remain. Built between the 6th and 12th century, they illustrate every phase of Orissan architecture. The Great Temple, built to the sun god in the 7th century, is considered one of the finest examples of Hindu architecture in India. Every part of the temple's surface is decorated with elaborate carvings. Bhubaneswar is being developed as a model administrative center. Population: (1961) 38,211.

CENTRAL PRESS FROM PICTORIAL PARADE

KING BHUMIBOL AND QUEEN SIRIKIT of Thailand are seen here on a state visit to England in July 1960.

BHUMIBOL ADULYADEJ, pōō'mĭ-pōōn ä-dōō-nyä'dä (1927–   ), king of Thailand. He succeeded to the throne in 1950 as King Rama IX, the ninth ruler of the Chakri dynasty, which was founded in 1782. His name is also spelled *Phumiphon Adundet, Phumiphon Adundadet, Phumiphol Aduldet,* and *Phumipol Aduldet.*

Bhumibol was born on Dec. 5, 1927, in Cambridge, Mass., where his father, Prince Mahidol of Songkhla, earned an M.D. degree from Harvard University in 1928. Prince Mahidol, the younger son of King Chulalongkorn and the brother of Prajadhipok, the last absolute monarch of Siam, died a few months after his return to Thailand, and Bhumibol and his older brother Ananda were sent to live in Switzerland in 1929. When King Prajadhipok abdicated in 1935, Ananda was declared his successor, but the brothers remained in Switzerland, Bhumibol receiving an LL.B. degree from the Gymnase de Lausanne. They returned to Thailand in 1945.

When Ananda was found shot to death under mysterious circumstances on June 9, 1946, Bhumibol was declared successor to the throne. Two months later he left to study law at the University of Lausanne. Returning to Thailand in 1950, he married Princess Sirikit Kitiyakara on April 28. His coronation followed on May 5. He ascended the throne as a constitutional monarch under a temporary constitution.

JAMES R. SHIRLEY, *Northern Illinois University*

BHUT, bōōt, in the mythology of the animistic Dravidians of India, is a ghost, evil spirit, or goblin. Bhuta worship, as it is known in Sanskrit, has existed from the earliest ages, and in later periods the god Shiva (Siva) was recognized as chief of the Bhuta. Hence, Shiva is also called Bhutapati—"Lord of the Bhuta."

The Bhuta are worshiped and propitiated in temples and houses by many non-Aryan tribes in India, under the forms of animals, such as boars, tigers, pigs; of human beings in gaudy dress; or of stones and pyramidal mounds of earth. Blood sacrifices are offered to them in a ceremony performed with wild dances accompanied by tom-toms. A Hindu purificatory rite also is called Bhuta Shuddhi; however, in this context "Bhuta" signifies the four elements.

IN BHUTAN, Lamaist shrines flank the main entrance to Paro, an administrative center. Men waiting to see officials wear the required ceremonial scarves.

BHUTAN, bōō-tän', is a small kingdom in the eastern Himalaya, strategically located between India and China. By treaty it must seek Indian advice on foreign policy and defense. Thimbu (Thimphu) is the capital, but the Development Secretariat is at Paro. Bhutan has an area of about 18,000 square miles (46,620 sq km) and a population (1964) estimated at 750,000.

People. Bhutan's population comprises three ethnic groups. The majority are Bhutias, of Tibetan descent, who call themselves Dukpas or Drukpas ("dragon people"). About one fifth of the people are of Nepali descent, while some small communities in eastern Bhutan appear to be related to the hill tribes of Assam. Bhutia migration to Bhutan was heaviest from the 14th to 17th centuries, but some migrated much more recently. The Nepali settlements, in the southern duar (pass) areas on the Indian border, date mostly from 1910 or later. Nepali migration has been limited, to maintain the population ratio between Nepali and Bhutia communities.

There are four main languages spoken in Bhutan: Dzongka, the official language, in western and northern Bhutan; Bumthangka, a related Tibetan dialect, in central Bhutan; Sarchapkkha in eastern Bhutan; and Nepali in southern Bhutan. These languages are mutually unintelligible, but Dzongka, spoken by the largest number of people, is the main medium of communication.

The Bhutia and the ethnic groups in eastern Bhutan are adherents of the Dukpa sect of Tibetan Buddhism, which was superimposed on the primitive animism, called Bon, in the 16th and 17th centuries. The Hindu Nepalis are outside the official Buddhist religious system.

Land. From the Himalaya, on the northern border, eight mountain ranges running north-south divide the country into series of valleys. Five principal river systems drain the country, all flowing into India and the Brahmaputra (Tsangpo) River. Climate varies with elevation, which drops, often steeply, from the frigid 24,000-foot (7,300-meter) peaks of Kula Kangri and Chomo Lhari on the northern border to the hot and humid jungle areas of the south. Between these extremes lie eight fertile river valleys, with well-irrigated terraced hillsides and extensive forests of oak, beech, and conifers. The fauna includes elephant, rhinoceros, tiger, leopard, and bear.

Economy. The chief crops are rice, corn, wheat, millet, barley, mustard, vegetables, walnuts, oranges, and the spice cardamom. Bhutan's many small farms also raise yaks, cattle, sheep, and pigs, and their small, strong Tangun ponies are valued for mountain transportation. Silver, copper, and iron have long been mined in small quantities for craftsmen. Among other crafts are the weaving of cloth, mats, and baskets; papermaking; and handwork in wood, leather, and metal.

Exports, mostly to India, include foodstuffs, timber, and craft work. The usual surplus of rice used to be sent to Tibet, but this trade was cut off in 1959. India needs the rice, and receives more of it as transportation improves.

Travel in Bhutan was entirely by foot or horse until the completion, after 1962, of several roads connecting both western and eastern Bhutan with India. An east-west road in the central highlands was to be completed in the 1960's. Every family in Bhutan was obligated to contribute labor in the construction of this road system, with India supplying money and technical aid. Indian helicopters are used extensively by officials, and the first airfield has been built at Thimbu. India also assists in the building of small hydroelectric plants and in the exploitation of forest and mineral resources.

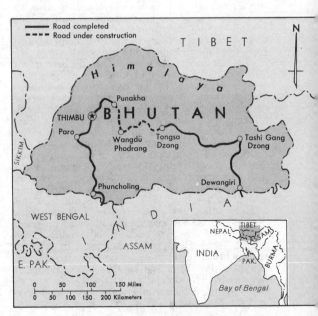

DESMOND DOIG PHOTOS, FROM MAGNUM

PARO, western Bhutan's administrative center, has a strategic position overlooking the fertile Paro Valley.

DESMOND DOIG PHOTOS, FROM MAGNUM

VILLAGE IN CENTRAL BHUTAN may be seen beyond the prayer flags that surround its small monastery.

Government. The first Maharaja (Duk Gyalpo, or "King of the Dukpas") of Bhutan was Ugyen Dorji Wangchuk, who founded the present dynasty in 1907. He was succeeded by his son Jigme Wangchuk in 1927, by his grandson Jigme Dorji Wangchuk in 1952, and by his great-grandson Jigme Singye Wangchuk in 1972.

The king is, in theory, an absolute monarch, who rules with the assistance of a small Advisory Council. Legislation is enacted in consultation with the Tsongdu, a representative assembly that has 130 members, of whom one fourth are nominated by the king and the rest elected by village headmen. The king also appoints all officials, including the governors (ponlops) of the two provinces and the district officers (dzongpons). The only political party, the Bhutan State Congress, is proscribed in Bhutan and has its headquarters in India. The party's leadership is entirely Nepali.

The Bhutan government has a trade agent in Calcutta who handles commercial relations with India and other foreign countries. Political relations with India are conducted through the Indian political officer to Sikkim and Bhutan, who resides at Gangtok, Sikkim. There is also an Indian adviser to the government of Bhutan who advises on both developmental and political matters. An Indian military mission has helped transform the Bhutan militia into a modern army.

Bhutan has often been called a "hermit" or "forbidden" kingdom, and admission of foreigners is still discouraged. To meet the Communist Chinese threat, however, the Bhutan government decided in 1959 to accept Indian aid in modernizing the country's economic system. King Jigme Dorji Wangchuk introduced a number of social reforms, including the freeing of slaves and restriction of Bhutia polyandry and Nepali polygamy. A secular education system outside of the Buddhist monasteries is also being developed, with primary schools scattered throughout Bhutan and a high school in Thimbu. Some Bhutanis attend Indian universities under Indian grants.

Despite evident economic and social progress, political stability was endangered when a high official, Jigme Dorji, was assassinated in 1964 by rival political factions, and when an attempt was made on the life of the king in 1965. Relations between the royal family and the Dorjis, one of the leading noble families, deteriorated badly, and the latter were exiled. The king apparently had firm control of the government, but political dissidence remained.

History. Bhutan's early history is obscure. Around 1630, a refugee Dukpa Lama from Tibet made himself the first Dharma Raja (Shabdung), with both spiritual and temporal powers. He made the Dukpa sect of Tibetan Buddhism the official religion, and appointed a Dev Raja (Duk De-si) and four provincial governors (ponlops) to assist him in the administration. By the 19th century both the Dharma Raja and the Dev Raja were little more than pawns in the struggle for power between the two most powerful ponlops—Tongsa and Paro. With British approval, the Tongsa ponlop, Ugyen Dorji Wangchuk, established a monarchy under his family in 1907.

Despite its isolation, Bhutan has often been beset by its neighbors; yet it has managed to retain internal autonomy. The Tibetans invaded Bhutan several times in the 17th and 18th centuries, but were always successfully resisted. The British invaded Bhutan first in 1772–1773, and again in 1865. The 1910 British-Bhutan treaty granted Bhutan full internal autonomy but obliged it to seek advice on foreign affairs, as did the 1949 treaty with independent India. India restored a strip of territory to Bhutan and raised the annual subsidy to Bhutan from 100,000 to 500,000 rupees ($105,000). Communist China has several times made vague references to a presumed historical sovereignty over Bhutan, and claims certain border areas. This and the destruction of Buddhism in Tibet led the Bhutan government to close the border with Tibet and to seek Indian guarantees concerning the defense of Bhutan.

LEO E. ROSE
University of California, Berkeley

Further Reading: Coelho, V. H., *Sikkim and Bhutan* (Barnes & Noble 1972); Karan, Pradyumna P., *Bhutan: A Physical and Cultural Geography* (Univ. of Ky. Press 1967); Oischak, Blanche, *Bhutan* (Stein and Day 1971); Rahul, Ram, *Modern Bhutan* (Barnes & Noble 1972).

BHUTTO, bōōt′ō, **Zulfikar Ali** (1928–   ), Pakistani public official, was born on Jan. 5, 1928, on his family estates near Larkana in the Sind, now a province of Pakistan. His family was wealthy and distinguished. He earned degrees at the University of California at Berkeley and at Christ Church, Oxford University. He was admitted to the bar in London and returned to Pakistan in 1953 to practice law and teach.

Bhutto became minister of commerce in Ayub Khan's government in 1958. In the next few years he received additional cabinet posts, and in 1962 he became deputy leader of the Muslim League, the majority party. He was formally named foreign minister in 1963 and held that post until Ayub ousted him in 1966, partly for urging an alliance with China even at the cost of losing U. S. support. After forming the Pakistan People's party in 1967, Bhutto was arrested in November 1968 but was released in February 1969. When Yahya Khan became president in March 1969, he called for national elections. Bhutto's party won a majority of the seats allotted to West Pakistan, but the election was voided when East Pakistanis won a majority of the seats.

In December 1971, Bhutto became chief martial law administrator and president. Under the new constitution of 1973, he became prime minister. Thereafter he maintained a tight control over the government until July 5, 1977, when he was removed in a military coup led by the army chief of staff, Gen. Mohammad Zia ul-Haq.

BIAFRA. See NIGERIA.

BIALIK, byä'lik, **Hayim Nachman** (1873–1934), Russian Jewish poet, whose works stimulated the Zionist movement. He was born at Rady, Volhynia, Russia, on Jan. 9, 1873. In 1892 he moved to Odessa, where, in the early 1900's, he founded a Hebrew publishing house, Moriah, and edited the monthly Hebrew magazine *Hashiloah*. He became renowned throughout world Jewry for his Hebrew poetry, and in 1924, when he settled in Tel Aviv, Palestine, he was received as a national hero. He died on July 4, 1934, in Vienna, Austria.

Bialik's poetry, which often employs biblical modes of expression, is both lyrical and exhortative. Describing the lot of the Jews in Russia as "the life of a chained and hungry dog," Bialik attempted to scold his people into rebellion against their treatment. *In the City of Slaughter*, his poem about the Kishinev pogrom of 1903, helped inspire the establishment of Jewish self-defense groups in Russia, which eventually developed into the Haganah (defense force) in Palestine. Others of his poems are *The Dead of the Wilderness*, *The Scroll of Fire*, and *Orphanhood*. His complete poetic works appeared in English translation in 1948.

Bialik also wrote short stories, essays, and children's tales. He edited volumes of ancient and medieval Hebrew legends and verse and translated Shakespeare's *Julius Caesar* and Cervantes' *Don Quixote* into Hebrew.

BIAŁYSTOK, byä-li'stôk, the capital of Białystok province in Poland, is about 105 miles (169 km) northeast of Warsaw. It is the leading manufacturing center of northeastern Poland. The chief industries are textiles and metal-processing.

Founded in 1320, it became part of Prussia in 1795 and passed to Russia in 1807. The Germans captured the city during World War I, and in 1919 it became part of Poland. During World War II it was occupied by the Germans (1939), turned over by them to the Russians (1939), reoccupied by the Germans (1941), and retaken by the Russians (1944). After the war it was returned to Poland (1945). Its industry, heavily damaged during the war, was rebuilt and expanded. Population: (1974) 187,100.

BIANDRATA, Giorgio. See UNITARIANISM.

BIARD, byàr, **Pierre** (c. 1567–1622), French Jesuit missionary. He was born in Grenoble and joined the Jesuit order in 1583. After teaching theology in Lyon for many years, he was sent to French Canada in 1611 to head a Jesuit mission. Biard's letters to his superiors in France, reporting the establishment of a mission at Port Royal, Acadia, in May of that year, are said to be the earliest sent by the Jesuits from Canada.

Biard was successful in converting and caring for many of the Indians, but he was forced to leave Port Royal because of the hostility of the colonists to the Jesuits. A new settlement, Saint Sauveur, was founded near what is now Bar Harbor, Me. In 1613, however, this colony was destroyed by English forces under Samuel Argall, who captured Biard. When the English attacked Port Royal, they took Biard with them and forced him to witness the destruction of the settlement. On his return to France, he was accused of collaborating with the enemy. In his defense, he wrote *Relations de la Nouvelle France* (1616), an account of the Jesuit fathers in New France, in which much of the early history of Canada is found. Acquitted in 1616, he resumed his duties as professor of theology at Lyon, and later served as chaplain in the king's army. He died in Avignon on Nov. 17, 1622, as a result of the privations of military life.

BIARRITZ, byà-rēts', is a town in southwestern France in Basses-Pyrénées department, near the Spanish border. It is on the Bay of Biscay, 4 miles (6.5 km) west of Bayonne. The native population is Basque. Because of its mild climate, fine beaches, and mineral waters, it has been one of the country's most popular resorts for many years. Its most dominant feature is the promenade, which runs along the beach past gambling casinos, mineral baths, and the many hotels.

The town's prosperity as a resort dates from 1838, when exiles from Spain sought facilities similar to the resorts on the Spanish coast of the Bay of Biscay. After 1855, Biarritz was the summer residence of Emperor Napoleon III and Empress Eugénie.

Other famous visitors, including many of the European nobility, helped to give the town an international reputation as a fashionable resort. Population: (1968) 26,985.

BIAS OF PRIENE, bī'əs, prī-ē'nē, was one of the Seven Sages of Greece. Born in Priene, a principal city of Ionia, he lived in the 6th century B.C. He was a practical philosopher who studied the laws of his country and employed his knowledge in the service of his friends, defending them in courts or settling their disputes.

Many of the stories attributed to him are of doubtful authenticity, but a number of his pithy sayings have survived. When the inhabitants of Priene resolved to abandon the city with their property during the Persian invasion, one of the citizens expressed astonishment that Bias was making no preparation. Bias is said to have replied: "I carry all that is mine with me." When the Persians occupied Ionia, he told the inhabitants to migrate to Sardinia and there establish a new city for all Ionians. The maxims attributed to Bias were collected by F.W.A. Mullach and published in 1860 as *Fragmenta Philosophorum Graecorum*.

BIATHLON, bī-ath′lən, is a sport that combines cross-country ski racing with rifle marksmanship. Originating in Sweden as a hunting competition, the sport spread among European infantry troops and led to the initiation of international military ski races in 1908. The modern biathlon, an off-spring of these events, emerged after World War II and made its first Olympic appearance in the 1960 Winter Games at Squaw Valley, Calif.

Standard equipment for the biathlon includes cross-country skis, poles, lightweight ski boots, and bolt-action rifles. The course is 20 kilometers (about 12½ miles) long, marked over terrain that is approximately one third uphill, one third downhill, and one third level. From each of four stations between the 5th and 18th kilometer of the course, the biathlete fires five shots with a nonautomatic rifle at targets at a range of 150 meters (164 yards). He uses a prone firing position on the first range, and then alternates between prone and standing.

The biathlon is both an individual and a team event. Total adjusted time of the three leading members makes up the team score. In the four-man, 7.5-kilometer relay event, a racer must ski a 200-meter penalty loop for each missed target.

The first modern biathlon competition in the United States was held at Camp Hale, Colo., in 1956. National championships are sponsored by the U.S. Modern Pentathlon Association, the U.S. Ski Association, and the National Rifle Association. Civilian as well as military personnel are trained at the U.S. Army's Modern Winter Biathlon Training Center at Ft. Richardson, Alaska, for international competition.

BILL BRADDOCK, *New York "Times"*

BIBAUD, bē-bō′, **Michel** (1782–1857), French-Canadian poet and historian. He was born at Côte-des-Neiges, near Montreal, on Jan. 20, 1782. After graduating from the college at St.-Raphael in 1806, he worked for a number of years as a teacher and a journalist. In 1830 he published a volume of poems entitled *Epîtres, satires, chansons, épigrammes, et pièces de vers,* the first miscellany of poems in the history of French-Canadian literature.

His most important historical work was the three-volume *Histoire du Canada* (vol. 1, 1843; vol. 2, 1844; vol. 3, published posthumously in 1878), the first history of French Canada by a French Canadian. Written from a British point of view, it was poorly received by his compatriots. Bibaud died in Montreal on July 3, 1857.

BIBER, bē′bər, **Heinrich Ignaz Franz von** (1644–1704), German violinist and composer, who was one of the founders of the German school of violin playing. He was born at Wartenberg, Bohemia, on Aug. 12, 1644. He was first employed at the court of Emperor Leopold I at Vienna and subsequently at the Bavarian court, but he lived most of his adult life at Salzburg, where he became *Kappelmeister* in 1684 and was made a noble by the emperor in 1690. He died at Salzburg on May 3, 1704.

Biber was regarded as the greatest German violinist of his time. A virtuoso performer, he was one of the first to employ *scordatura,* a method of tuning the violin slightly off key for virtuosic effect. He was also one of the earliest important composers for the violin in central Europe, which was then dominated by inferior Italian composers. His 16 sonatas for violin and clavier have distinctively personal qualities and a semblance of unity that point toward the much greater instrumental music of the 18th century in Germany. Biber also composed operas, solo sonatas, trios, and other chamber works.

BIBERACH, bē′bər-äкн, is an industrial town in West Germany in the state of Baden-Württemberg, 22 miles (35.5 km) southwest of Ulm. It is situated on the Riss River, at an elevation of about 1,750 feet (535 meters). Its old walls, two towers, and gate give the town a medieval appearance. Biberach manufactures machinery, pharmaceuticals, precision instruments, and textiles. A museum in the town is named after the 18th century poet Christoph Martin Wieland, who was born nearby. He translated Shakespeare's plays into German.

During the Napoleonic Wars, the French twice defeated the Austrians near Biberach. On Oct. 2, 1796, Gen. Jean Victor Moreau was the victor. In May 1800, Saint-Cyr led the French in their second victory here over the Austrians. Population: (1961) 21,524.

BIBIENA, bē-byä′nä, an Italian family of artists and architects of the 17th and 18th centuries. Their name, which they took from the birthplace of the founder of the family, is also spelled *Bibbiena.* Later members of the family devoted themselves to scenic design for the theater and opera and for court functions. Unfortunately, because of the temporary character of the materials used, little of their work of this type has survived, but museums in Vienna, Munich, and elsewhere in Europe have drawings that show its great beauty and originality.

GIOVANNI MARIA GALLI (1625–1665), the founder of the family, was a painter of imagination and skill. He studied under Francesco Albani.

FERDINANDO GALLI BIBIENA (1657–1734), the elder son of Giovanni, was the architect of the Church of Sant'Antonio Abbate (1712–1716) in Parma, but is best known for his scenic designs.

FRANCESCO GALLI BIBIENA (1659–1739), the younger son of Giovanni, assisted his brother in the execution of theatrical designs. He also designed theaters in Nancy, Verona, and Rome.

ALESSANDRO GALLI BIBIENA (1687–?1769), one of three sons of Ferdinando, was an architect and painter at the court of the elector of the Palatinate, in Mannheim, where he built an opera house (destroyed) and a Jesuit church (1733).

GIUSEPPE GALLI BIBIENA (1696–1756), also a son of Ferdinando, was probably the most distinguished member of the family. He was in charge of the organization of court functions and gala entertainments at the courts of Vienna, Munich and Prague. A skilled architect whose work took him all over Europe, he designed the interior of the Markgräfliches Opernhaus (1748), a baroque structure in Bayreuth, Germany.

ANTONIO GALLI BIBIENA (1700–1774), the third son of Ferdinando, was an architect and designer. He was employed at the imperial court in Vienna during most of his working life, but his best works are the Teatro Scientifico (1769) of the Accademia Virgiliana in Mantua and the Teatro Communale (1756) in Bologna.

CARLO GALLI BIBIENA (1728–?1780), the last artist of the family, was the son of Giuseppe. A painter and architect, he was employed in many European courts.

BIBLE

THE KING JAMES VERSION. The page reproduced above is from the famous English translation of 1611.

THE SONCINO BIBLE. The page below is from the first complete Old Testament printed in Hebrew (1488).

BIBLE, bī′bəl, the Jewish and Christian sacred book, or collection of sacred books, often called the *Holy Bible*. It is in two parts, the *Old Testament* and the *New Testament*. The original text of the Old Testament is in the Hebrew language, with a few brief passages in Aramaic; the original of the New Testament is in Greek. The Old Testament is the ancient Hebrew Bible, preserved and treasured through many centuries by the Jews. It is also the first part of the Bible of the Christians, who added to it, in the Greek translation, the books of the New Testament. They also preserved the Jewish books known as the Apocrypha, all but one in Greek.

The Apocrypha is often printed between the Old and New Testaments; but in the Eastern Orthodox Church and the Roman Catholic Church these books are distributed through the Old Testament, more or less chronologically. Most Protestants accept only the 24 books of the Old Testament found in the Hebrew Bible—counting them as 39 when divided up in parts—and the 27 books of the New Testament. But the Eastern Orthodox Church, the Roman Catholic Church, the Anglican Communion, and some others include in their Bibles the 14 books of the Apocrypha, the "Deutero-canonical" books as St. Jerome called them. (See the table of books of the Bible on pages 652–653.)

Almost from the beginning the books of the Bible have been translated into other languages. The earliest translations of the Hebrew Scriptures were into Aramaic, the common language of Jews

THE RHEIMS NEW TESTAMENT was translated for Roman Catholics and was printed at Rheims, France, in 1582.

THE
NEVV TESTAMENT
OF IESVS CHRIST, TRANS-
LATED FAITHFVLLY INTO ENGLISH,
out of the authentical Latin, according to the best cor-
rected copies of the same, diligently conferred vvith
the Greeke and other editions in diuers languages: Vvith
ARGVMENTS of bookes and chapters, ANNOTA-
TIONS, and other necessarie helpes, for the better vnder-
standing of the text, and specially for the discouerie of the
CORRVPTIONS of diuers late translations, and for
cleering the CONTROVERSIES in religion, of these daies:
IN THE ENGLISH COLLEGE OF RHEMES.

Psal. 118.

Da mihi intellectum, & scrutabor legem tuam, & custodiam illam in toto corde meo.

That is,

Giue me vnderstanding, and I vvil searche thy lavv, and vvil keepe it vvith my vvhole hart.

S. Aug. tract. 2. in Epist. Ioan.

Omnia quæ leguntur in Scriptura sanctis, ad insaructionem & salutem nostram intente oportet audire: maxime tamen memoria commendanda sunt, quæ aduersus Hæreticos valent plurimum: quorum insidiæ, infirmiores quosque de negligentiori circumuentos non resinant.

That is,

All things that are readde in holy Scripture, vve must heare vvith great attention, to our instruction and saluation: but chieflie those things specially must be commended to memorie, which make most against Heretikes: whose deceites ceasse not to circumuent and beguile al the vveaker sort and the more neglig. nt persons.

PRINTED AT RHEMES,
by Iohn Fogny.

1582.

CVM PRIVILEGIO.

CONTENTS

OLD TESTAMENT

Section	Page
1. Canon of the Old Testament	649
2. Language of the Old Testament	650
3. Manuscripts and Versions of the Old Testament	655
4. Textual Criticism of the Old Testament	658
5. Growth of the Old Testament Literature	662
6. Old Testament History, Including Archaeology and Chronology	670
7. Religion and Theology of the Old Testament	678
8. History of Old Testament Interpretation	686

NEW TESTAMENT

Section	Page
9. New Testament: Introduction	690
10. Canon of the New Testament	691
11. Languages of the New Testament	694
12. The Text of the New Testament: Textual Criticism, Manuscripts, and Versions	695
13. Growth of the New Testament Literature	699
14. New Testament History, Including Chronology and Archaeology	702
15. Religion and Theology of the New Testament	708
16. History of New Testament Interpretation	713
17. History of the English Bible	716

in Palestine and throughout the Middle East after the Exile in the 6th century B.C. The Torah (first five books of the Old Testament) was translated into Samaritan about 400 B.C. Following the conquests of Alexander the Great, Greek became the common language of the whole eastern Mediterranean area and even of many regions farther east. The Hebrew Scriptures were accordingly translated into Greek at Alexandria from about 250 B.C. onward. Here also were produced the books of the Apocrypha, either by translation from Hebrew or as original writings in Greek. By the time the early Christian writings appeared (about 50–150 A.D.), they were naturally written in Greek, for they arose chiefly in the Greek-speaking Gentile churches.

By 150 A.D. translations of both Old Testament and New Testament books were available in Syriac, Latin, and other languages. There were several versions of the Old Testament in Aramaic. Soon followed the Coptic translation, the Armenian, and many more. As time went on, these translations were revised and made more accurate. Near the end of the 4th century, St. Jerome revised the Old Latin version of the New Testament, beginning with the Gospels, and completed the Latin version of the Old Testament. Thus he produced the "Vulgate" or common Latin version that was used in the West for many centuries and is still standard in the Roman Catholic Church. Around these translations arose a new Christian literature based on their vocabularies and teaching.

Still other local and national groups required translations, partly for missionary purposes. Such were the Gothic, Ethiopic, Slavic, Persian, Arabic, Saxon, and eventually all the emerging languages of the West. In due time came King Alfred's, Ælfric's, and Wycliffe's English translations of parts or all of the Bible, and many others, including Luther's German Bible, Tyndale's and Coverdale's English versions, and the French and Dutch. In fact, the process of Bible translation has never ceased. The Bible has been translated, in whole or in part, into about 1,250 languages and dialects, and millions of copies have been spread abroad. See BIBLE SOCIETY.

The word "Bible" comes from the Greek *biblos* or *bublos*, the inner bark enclosing the pith of the papyrus plant from which paper (*papyrus*) was made in ancient times. The diminutive plural *biblia* (books) was viewed as a singular in Latin, and from this came the modern English word. In the Jewish Bible, the "Books" or the "Writings" (Hebrew *kethubim*) formed only the third part of Holy Scripture.

The Torah, or Pentateuch, or "Law," formed the first part, while the historical and prophetic books, called the "former" and the "latter" prophets, made up the second. But among the Christians the "Writings" (Greek *hai graphai*) or the "Writing" (*hē graphē*) became the title for the Scriptures as a whole; this was the word used for the Greek Old Testament, as a rule, which was the Bible of the earliest Christians. The terms "Bible," "Writings," and "Scriptures" have survived to this day. The word "Testament" was derived from Latin *testamentum*, a translation of the Greek *diathēkē* (meaning "covenant" or "will"). It was in use from the 2d century but was a term more theological than descriptive of the contents of either the Hebrew Scriptures or the Christian.

The main use of the Bible among both Jews and Christians is in public worship. Its influence on prayers and hymns and whole liturgies has been immeasurable. It has enriched and deepened religious thought, literature and language, and even ideals of justice and right in all the nations where it has been read and studied. Even "secular" poetry, oratory, drama, music, and art strongly reflect its influence. The Bible is of the greatest value and importance to Jews and Christians, because to them it is either in part or in whole an inspired collection (the Jews so recognize the Old Testament, the Christians both Old and New Testaments). But the influence of the Bible is by no means limited to Jews and Christians. Its light "has gone out into all the world." It is now viewed as an ethical and religious treasure whose inexhaustible teaching promises to be even more valuable as the hope of a world civilization increases.

This article discusses the content of the Bible and the scholarly study of the Bible under 17 headings. The section titles are listed in the table of contents above. Within sections, cross-references cite the titles of related articles in other parts of the encyclopedia. Each section has its own list of books for further reading.

See also EXODUS, BOOK OF; GENESIS, BOOK OF; KINGS, BOOKS OF (and articles on other books of the Old Testament); ACTS OF THE APOSTLES; MATTHEW, GOSPEL ACCORDING TO; PHILIPPIANS, EPISTLE TO THE; (and articles on other books of the New Testament); ABRAHAM; MOSES; PAUL, SAINT (and articles on other figures in the Old and New Testaments); APOCRYPHA; EXEGESIS; JEWISH HISTORY AND SOCIETY; SCROLLS, THE DEAD SEA; and the Index entry *Bible*.

FREDERICK C. GRANT
Union Theological Seminary

OLD TESTAMENT

1. Canon of the Old Testament

Canon is a Greek word meaning "straight rod," but it came to be particularized to mean a carpenter's measuring rod and then was used figuratively for other standards by which things could be measured. Thus we read of certain literary works that represented the canon of good writing and of certain rules of conduct that were the canon of good behavior. In the New Testament (II Corinthians 10:13–16; Galatians 6:16) the word refers to rules both of right conduct and of right doctrine, and in the literature of the early church it referred to "the rule of faith and practice." Since the rules of both faith and practice, however, are based on Scripture, it was necessary to have some way of deciding which writings circulating in the community were to be regarded as inspired Scripture and which were merely works of piety, so we presently find the word in use for "Canon of Scripture," that is, a measuring rod that will distinguish canonical from uncanonical writings.

Origin of the Idea of Scripture. Although this use of the word *canon* arose among Christians, the idea for which it provided a convenient technical term was much older and is concerned with a problem that will arise in any religion that comes to have a body of writings regarded by the community as normative for its religious life and practice. Such writings are regarded as of special authority, of special sanctity, and as Scripture they take a place apart from other writings. There are religions that have no sacred writings, and there are religions that have writings regarded as more or less sacred but that never have come to be thought of as authoritative Scripture. Wherever this idea of a Scripture develops within a community, however, there inevitably will arise the necessity of some measuring rod that will decide which writings belong to the class of Scripture and which do not.

There was literary activity among the Israelites at a relatively early period. Tribal traditions were written down; collections of community laws were put into fixed form; cultic and ritual prescriptions were recorded; songs of the people and hymns of the shrines were collected; oracles from priestly circles, utterances of divinely inspired prophets, words of wisdom from the mouths of sages and the lips of the wise, and chronicles of court events were gathered and preserved. Not all of this was religious, although much of it did concern the religious life of the community. As national life stabilized and the religious cult developed, literary material of this kind was used cultically and woven into historical narratives telling the story of the community as Yahweh's people. Thus, gradually and doubtless unconsciously, there emerged from this literature certain bodies of material that the community recognized as speaking with unique authority for their religious life. As such, this material was given a deference and treated with a reverence not accorded to other literature in use among them, and thus it took on a sacred character.

The original writers of this material generally would not have realized that what they were writing would one day have this unique place in the life of the community. But from very early times in the Near East it had been recognized that the word of God (or the gods) might come to men expressed through the words of men; and in Israel the community came to recognize cases in which the word of their God spoke to them, with an authority that was normative for their religion, through the prescriptions of the priests, the words of the prophet, the verses of the poet, the maxims of the sage, and the writing of the scribe.

Collections of Hebrew Writings. The earliest formal collections of writings that so expressed the word of the Lord were apparently legal in character. In Deuteronomy 31:9–26; Joshua 24:25, 26; and I Samuel 10:25, we read of leaders laying up documents at shrines; and in II Kings 22, 23, we read that in the reign of Josiah a book of law was discovered in the sanctuary, the reading of which caused great consternation and the initiation of far-reaching reforms to bring the community life into accord with its prescriptions. Again in Nehemiah 8:10, we read that Ezra, on the return from the Exile, brought with him a book of laws that was read before and accepted by the people as normative for their new community life. The prophecies of some of the prophets who spoke in the name of the Lord also were written down, and collections of them began to be formed. Zechariah, for instance, knows of and refers to as authoritative what earlier prophets had said (Zechariah 1:4–6, 7:7); and Daniel (9:2) states what he had observed in the book of an earlier prophet. From Psalm 137 we learn further that the exiles had with them some collections of the "Songs of Zion."

The grandson of Sirach, writing about 130 B.C. in his prologue to Ecclesiasticus, mentions three collections of writings of special authority in use among his people and names them "the Law, the Prophets and the other books." The writer of II Maccabees in the 1st century B.C. knows of a "holy book," the contents of which, including Law, Prophets, and other writings, had been scattered by the war but were gathered up by Judas Maccabaeus (2:13–15; 8:23; 15:9). So the New Testament has references to the Law, the Prophets, and the Psalms, which are authoritative Scripture to which appeal may be made with the words "Is it not written?" (Compare Mark 9:12; 11:17; John 10:34; Acts 17:2; 18:24; 28:23; I Corinthians 14:21; II Timothy 3:15, 16.) This passage in II Timothy gives us the important information that the reason these writings were regarded by the community as authoritative for religion was that they were "inspired" —that is, although they were the words of men spoken or written at a particular time and in view of a local situation, they were nevertheless part of the timeless "word of God," for through them God had spoken to mankind.

But what was the extent of the collection? The Hebrew Old Testament as we have it consists of three groups of writings, labeled Law (Torah), Prophets (Nebiim), and Writings (Kethubim), yet there are references in it to other writings of similar nature that are not now in any of these three groups. (Compare Numbers 21:14, 15; Joshua 10:13; II Samuel 1:18; I Kings 11:41; I Chronicles 29:29; II Chronicles 9:29; 12:15.) The Greek translation of the Jewish Scriptures, known to us as the LXX (see SEPTUAGINT), also contains writings not included in our Hebrew Bible, and the New Testament refers on occasion to such writings as to writings of religious authority (for example, Jude 14; I Corinthians 2:9).

By the end of the 1st century A.D., Josephus in his *Contra Apion* (1, 8) is able to tell us that the authoritative writings are but 22 in number, 5 of them being laws and traditions called the books of Moses, 13 being the books of the prophets who came between Moses and Artaxerxes, and 4 being books of hymns and maxims. Since the days of Artaxerxes, he says, there have been writings, but they are not of like authority because the succession of prophets had ceased. The 22, however, are not merely sacred but are now sacrosanct, for no one ever would dare to add to, subtract from, or change them, but one must abide by them as teachings of God and if necessary die for them.

Only a little later than Josephus is the passage in the Fourth Book of Ezra (14:37–48) that tells the legend of Ezra, who, when the Scriptures had been lost, was specially inspired to reproduce the 24 books at a sitting as well as 70 "reserved" books. The number 24 occurs again in a Baraita (an excluded tradition) of the late 2d century preserved in the Talmud (*Baba bathra* 14b–15a), which counts 5 books of Moses, 8 of Prophets, and 11 of Writings, telling us that the proper order of the Prophets is Joshua, Judges, Samuel, Kings, Jeremiah, Ezekiel, Isaiah and the Twelve; and the proper order of the Writings is Ruth, Psalms, Job, Proverbs, Ecclesiastes, Song of Songs, Lamentations, Daniel, Esther, Ezra (and Nehemiah), Chronicles. These are the books that compose our present Hebrew Bible, and Josephus probably got his 22 by counting Ruth with Judges and Lamentations with Jeremiah. Josephus also seems to have arranged his books according to subject matter in the fashion preferred by the LXX.

Disputed Writings. In the Rabbinic writings there is evidence of some dispute about the inclusion or exclusion of certain books. The Torah (instruction) in its five parts (Pentateuch) was clearly the first collection to have a fixed form. During the 3d century B.C., it was translated into Greek in Egypt, in very much the same form as that in which we now have it, and it was the only group of writings taken over by the Samaritans at their schism in the 2d century B.C. As associated with the name of Moses, these five books were the Law (Malachi 4:4; John 1:17; Acts 13:39). The Prophets consisted of the historical books, known as the "former prophets," and the prophets proper, known as the "latter prophets." The only book among them that was disputed was Ezekiel, which some thought should be "reserved." There was much more dispute over the Writings. The inclusion of Ecclesiastes, Esther, and Song of Songs was strongly disputed, and there were rumbles of disputation over Proverbs and Ruth. Some wanted to include the book of Ben Sira (Ecclesiasticus). The list in the above cited Baraita in *Baba bathra* represents the final judgment of the Rabbis as to the Canon. The books in this list "defile the hands," that is, they are canonical and authoritative (the expression being a survival of a very ancient notion that holy things "infected" whatever touched them, and made ritual cleansing necessary to remove the "infection"); but those not in the list do not so defile the hands and so are not canonical and not authoritative,

although they may be read for edification. A decision on this matter would seem to have been reached at a gathering at Jamnia, about 90 A.D., and this decision probably was not unconnected with the fact of the growing circulation of Christian writings that also were regarded as "inspired" and of religious authority.

The Greek word used to designate the "reserved" writings was *apocrypha*, and this word began to be used for those writings of the Greek Old Testament that were not included in the Hebrew list. Sometimes they were called "deuterocanonical" books. They were a collection with a somewhat indefinite fringe, so that presently the name Apocrypha came to be used for those writings commonly found in most manuscripts, namely I and II Esdras, Tobit, Judith, the Additions to Esther, Wisdom, Ecclesiasticus, Baruch, Epistle of Jeremiah, Susannah, the Song of the Three Holy Children, Bel and the Dragon, the Prayer of Manasseh, I and II Maccabees; while the name *Pseudepigrapha* was used for the books on the fringe, such as Enoch, IV Ezra, Odes and Psalms of Solomon, III and IV Maccabees.

Such Biblical scholars as Origen (died 253) and Jerome (died 420) were aware of and favored the Palestinian limitation of the canon, but in the Greek and Eastern churches the deuterocanonical books have continued in use, and in some cases even books belonging to the Pseudepigrapha, as books of authority. The Roman Catholic Church at the Council of Trent (1546) officially pronounced in favor of the Apocrypha being canonical, a position that is taken also by some Protestant groups; but the Reformed churches as a whole have followed Calvin in limiting the Old Testament to the books of the Hebrew Canon, although their arrangement of them has not followed Jewish custom.

ARTHUR JEFFERY, *Columbia University*

Bibliography

Pfeiffer, Robert H., *Introduction to the Old Testament*, rev. ed. (New York 1948).
Pfeiffer, Robert H., *The Books of the Old Testament* (New York 1965).
Robinson, H. Wheeler, *The Old Testament, Its Making and Meaning* (London 1937).
Ryle, Herbert E., *The Canon of the Old Testament*, 2d ed. (London 1925).
Zeitlin, Solomon, *An Historical Study of the Canonization of the Hebrew Scriptures* (Philadelphia 1933).

For Specialized Study

Bentzen, Aage, *Introduction to the Old Testament*, vol. 1 (Copenhagen 1948).
Bernfeld, Simon, "Bibel: 1. Die Bücher der Bibel," in *Encyclopaedia Judaica*, vol. IV (Berlin 1929).
Budde, Karl, *Der Kanon des Alten Testaments* (Giessen, Germany, 1900).
Buhl, F., *Canon and Text of the Old Testament* (Edinburgh 1892).
Dennefeld, L., *Introduction à l'Ancien Testament* (Paris 1934).
Eissfeldt, O., *Einleitung in das Alte Testament*, 3d ed., (Tübingen, Germany, 1964).
Hölscher, Gustav, *Kanonisch und Apokryph* (Naumburg, Germany, 1905).
Lindblom, J., *Kanon och apokryfer* (Stockholm 1920).
Meyer, R., "Kanonisch und Apokryph," in Gerhard Kittel's *Theologisches Wörterbuch*, vol. 3 (Berlin 1938).
Wildeboer, G., *Die Entstehung des alttestamentlichen Kanons* (Gotha, Germany, 1891).

2. Language of the Old Testament

The books of the Old Testament were written in Hebrew, with the exception of some isolated words or expressions (for instance, the name *Jegar-sahadutha*, "the-heap-of-witness," in Genesis 31:47), one verse (Jeremiah 10:11), and a few chapters (Ezra 4:8 to 6:18; 7:12–26; Daniel 2:4b to 7:28) that were written in Aramaic. Hebrew was the language of Israel and Judah until the Babylonian exile (6th century B.C.), but the postexilic Jews, while preserving Hebrew as a sacred tongue, adopted the Aramaic language, which was then the *lingua franca* of Western Asia. Hebrew and Aramaic belong to the Semitic family, and as such they have practically nothing in common with Greek, Latin, or English, which are members of the Indo-European stock. The Semitic languages are represented by (1) an Eastern group (Assyro-Babylonian, now generally designated as Akkadian); (2) a Southwestern group (Arabic, Ethiopic); and (3) a Northwestern group (Ugaritic, Canaanite or Phoenician, Moabite, Hebrew, Aramaic, Syriac).

The Hebrew Dialects. Inasmuch as the Old Testament is not a homogeneous book but a collection of many documents composed over a period of a thousand years by men of various ethnic backgrounds, Biblical Hebrew is a mixed language both in its origin and in its development. The Old Testament itself acknowledges that Jacob was "a nomad Aramaean" (Deuteronomy 26:5) and that Jerusalem had a foreign ancestry (Ezekiel 16:3, 45). Likewise, tradition represented as aliens a number of the wives and mothers of the famous ancestors (Genesis 24:10 to 25:6; 29:5–35; 41:45), and as maternal influences constitute a predominant factor in linguistic evolution, it is legitimate to induce that Hebrew was not a pure tongue. This conclusion is borne out by a philological study of the Biblical writings themselves. There were various Hebrew dialects closely related to other members of the Northwestern Semitic group, particularly Canaanite and Aramaic.

Biblical Hebrew. In the course of the centuries the documents now preserved in the Old Testament received the stamp of Judean, and later Jewish, editors. In addition, as the manuscripts were copied and recopied in a fixed, canonical form (see section *1. Canon of the Old Testament*), a slow process of standardization took place, with the result that the Hebrew of the Masoretic text (see section *3. Manuscripts and Versions of the Old Testament*) now presents characteristics of uniformity that did not exist when the language originally was spoken and written.

The Hebrew Verb. The essential element of the Hebrew tongue is the verb, from which most of the other parts of speech—nouns, adjectives, adverbs, and even some prepositions—are formed. Only occasionally are verbs derived from nouns. This fact opens up a vista on the mentality of the Biblical writers, for whom actions were more important than states of being. The Hebrews were notably deficient in conceptual thinking, but they succeeded in showing concretely that an intricate and indissoluble relationship exists between religion and ethics. They trusted in a God who acts, creates, judges, condemns, and saves, rather than in a deity that merely exists. They worshiped not a philosophical entity but "the faithful creator" of the cosmos and the ruler of mankind's history. They believed that man's life has a meaning only insofar as it responds to the will of a God who reveals himself in historical events and through the lives of historical figures. Hence the verbs are more important than the nouns.

The Hebrew Voices. In the Hebrew tongue, though to a lesser degree than in some of the other Semitic languages, the verb is extraordinarily versatile. As in the Indo-European languages, it may be used in the familiar voices of active and passive or in their subsidiary variations

of reflexive and reciprocal. It also may be conjugated in a number of other voices, through various transformations of its generally triliteral stem. For example, the simply voiced verb *kabhedh,* "he was heavy," may become *kibbedh,* "he honored," "he glorified" (causative), *kubbadh,* "he was made honorable" (passive-causative), *hikhbidh,* "he made dull and unresponsive" (another causative), *hithkabbedh,* "he made himself numerous" or "he honored himself" (causative-reflexive). Similarly, *halakh,* "he went," may produce *hillekh,* "he tramped" or "he prowled" (intensive), *holikh,* "he led" or "he brought" (causative), *hithhallekh,* "he walked to and fro," "he roamed" or merely "he lived" (intensive-alternative). Likewise, *tsadheq,* "he was righteous," may become *hitsdiq,* "he justified" (declarative), and *hitstaddeq,* "he justified himself" (reflexive-declarative). Again, *nibba,* "he prophesied" (a voice commonly used for the passive, thus suggesting the psychological process of compulsion in prophetic inspiration) may be conjugated as *hithnabbe,* "he was a false prophet," literally, "he acted in an excited manner like a prophet" (intensive-reflexive, which may be called "pretensive"). Thus, although the Hebrew vocabulary may not be as rich as that of Greek or English, the Hebrew verbal system permits a variety of expression.

The Hebrew Tenses. More remarkable still to the Occidental mind is the fact that the Hebrew verb has two main tenses, the so-called "perfect" and "imperfect." These do not correspond unmistakably to the time categories of past, present, or future.

The *perfect* refers to an act or state conceived in its totality as an event, whether it already has occurred or not. Stative verbs in the perfect usually designate a present. For instance, "The God . . . before whom I stand . . ." (I Kings 17:1), or "I wait for the Lord, . . . and in his word do I hope" (Psalm 130:5). Active verbs in the perfect generally correspond to the past. Thus, "God created . . ." (Genesis 1:1), or "What hast thou done?" (Genesis 4:10). However, they also may be used to indicate the present. For example, ". . . I profess this day unto the Lord . . ." (Deuteronomy 26:3). In predictions they refer to a future, but the event that they describe possesses a quality of such certainty that it truly transcends the limitations of time and stands as if it already had taken place: indeed it already is known by God as a realized fact. "For unto us a child is born, unto us a son is given . . ." (Isaiah 9:6). For the Hebrew mind, history is a drama that must be grasped in its oneness. Thus, even a promise that necessarily deals with the future is couched in the perfect tense. ". . . Unto thy seed have I given this land, . . ." (Genesis 15:18).

The *imperfect* designates the incipiency of a process, its coming into being, and its progressive development. It therefore is particularly well suited for indicating the future. However, it also may be used for expressing repetition, duration, or progression in the present and even in the past. For instance, ". . . in his law doth he meditate day and night . . ." (Psalm 1:2), or "Thus did Job continually" (Job 1:5). Both perfect and imperfect may be translated by a past, a present, or a future, depending on the context and on the active or stative qualities of the verb.

Furthermore, there are two secondary tenses, the "consecutive imperfect" (probably similar to the Akkadian "preterit") and the "consecutive

THE BOOKS OF THE BIBLE

HEBREW	GREEK	LATIN	ENGLISH

───────────────── THE OLD TESTAMENT ─────────────────

HEBREW	GREEK	LATIN	ENGLISH
TORAH	**THE SEPTUAGINT**	**THE VULGATE**	**THE KING JAMES VERSION**
Genesis	Genesis	Genesis	Genesis
Exodus	Exodus	Exodus	Exodus
Leviticus	Leviticus	Leviticus	Leviticus
Numbers	Numbers	Numbers	Numbers
Deuteronomy	Deuteronomy	Deuteronomy	Deuteronomy
FORMER PROPHETS			
Joshua	Joshua	Joshua	Joshua
Judges	Judges	Judges	Judges
1-2 Samuel	Ruth	Ruth	Ruth
1-2 Kings	1-2-3-4 Kingdoms	1-2 Samuel	1-2 Samuel
	1-2 Chronicles	1-2 Kings	1-2 Kings
	1 Esdras (apocr.)	1-2 Chronicles	1-2 Chronicles
	2 Esdras (Ezra-Neh.)	1 Esdras (Ezra)	Ezra
		2 Esdras (Nehemiah)	Nehemiah
LATTER PROPHETS		Tobit	
Isaiah	Psalms	Judith	
Jeremiah	(+Odae in Codex A)	Esther (with Greek	Esther (without
Ezekiel	Proverbs	additions in app.)	Greek additions)
The Twelve:	Ecclesiastes		
Hosea	Song of Songs		
Joel	Job	Job	Job
Amos	Wisdom of Solomon	Psalms	Psalms
Obadiah	Wisdom of Sirach	Proverbs	Proverbs
Jonah	(Ecclesiasticus)	Ecclesiastes	Ecclesiastes
Micah	Esther (with addits.)	Song of Songs	Song of Solomon
Nahum	Judith	Wisdom	
Habakkuk	Tobit	Ecclesiasticus	
Zephaniah	1, 4 Maccabees (Cod. S)		
Haggai	1-2-3-4 Macc. (Cod. A)		
Zechariah	(Macc. om. in Cod. B)		
Malachi	Hosea	Isaiah	Isaiah
	Amos	Jeremiah	Jeremiah
THE WRITINGS	Micah	Lamentations	Lamentations
Psalms	Joel	Baruch (with Ep. of	
Proverbs	Obadiah	Jeremiah in app.)	
Job	Jonah	Ezekiel	Ezekiel
	Nahum	Daniel	Daniel
Song of Songs	Habakkuk		
Ruth	Zephaniah	Hosea	Hosea
Lamentations	Haggai	Joel	Joel
Ecclesiastes	Zechariah	Amos	Amos
Esther	Malachi	Obadiah	Obadiah
		Jonah	Jonah
Daniel	Isaiah	Micah	Micah
Ezra-Nehemiah	Jeremiah	Nahum	Nahum
1-2 Chronicles	Baruch	Habakkuk	Habakkuk
	Lamentations	Zephaniah	Zephaniah
	Epistle of Jeremiah	Haggai	Haggai
	Ezekiel	Zechariah	Zechariah
		Malachi	Malachi
	Susanna		
	Daniel (incl. Prayer of	1-2 Maccabees	
	Azariah and Song of		
	the 3 Young Men)		
	Bel and the Dragon		

GREEK	LATIN	ENGLISH
EARLY CHURCH CODICES	THE VULGATE	THE KING JAMES VERSION

ENGLISH — THE KING JAMES VERSION

THE APOCRYPHA

1 Esdras (=Greek	Baruch
1 Esdras, Latin	Epistle of Jeremiah
3 Esdras)	(=Baruch, ch. 6)
2 Esdras (=Latin	The Prayer of Azariah
4 Esdras)	The Song of the Three
Tobit	Young Men
Judith	Susanna
Additions to Esther	Bel and the Dragon
Wisdom of Solomon	(The last 4 are
Ecclesiasticus	additions to Dan.)
(Sirach)	The Prayer of Manasseh
	1-2 Maccabees

Note: The Hebrew Bible does not include the Apocrypha. The Greek and Latin Bibles contain the Apocrypha but locate the books in various places. The English version prints the apocrypha between the Old and New Testaments, as shown by the list at the right.

THE NEW TESTAMENT

GREEK	LATIN	ENGLISH
Matthew	Matthew	Matthew
Mark	Mark	Mark
Luke	Luke	Luke
John	John	John
Acts	Acts	Acts
James	Romans	Romans
1-2 Peter	1-2 Corinthians	1-2 Corinthians
1-2-3 John	Galatians	Galatians
Jude	Ephesians	Ephesians
	Philippians	Philippians
Romans	Colossians	Colossians
1-2 Corinthians	1-2 Thessalonians	1-2 Thessalonians
Galatians	1-2 Timothy	1-2 Timothy
Ephesians	Titus	Titus
Philippians	Philemon	Philemon
Colossians	Hebrews	Hebrews
1-2 Thessalonians		
Hebrews	James	James
1-2 Timothy	1-2 Peter	1-2 Peter
Titus	1-2-3 John	1-2-3 John
Philemon	Jude	Jude
Apocalypse of John	Apocalypse of John	Revelation of John

APPENDIX

The Prayer of Manasseh

3 Esdras

4 Esdras

The order and even the contents of the Septuagint (the Greek Old Testament) vary in different manuscripts and in modern editions. *The Longer Catechism of the Eastern Church* lists the contents of the Eastern Orthodox Bible, but omits the Apocrypha as not found in the Hebrew Canon. Nevertheless, Orthodox theological writers frequently quote it and so do the official documents (for example, The Synod of Jerusalem in 1672). The general tendency in the East has been in the direction of restricting canonicity to those books found in the Jewish Bible (the Hebrew Canon).

But the great 4th and 5th century manuscripts of the Greek Bible, Vaticanus (B), Sinaiticus (S), and Alexandrinus (A), reflect a wide inclusiveness which was characteristic of early church usage rather than canonical definition. Codex Vaticanus contains most of the Greek Old Testament, but omits the Prayer of Manasseh and the Odae (that is, the Old Testament canticles), the Psalms of Solomon, and the Books of Maccabees. Most modern editions of the Septuagint closely follow B in both order (as above) and text. In the New Testament it breaks off in the middle of Hebrews 9:14, though it must once have contained the Pastoral Epistles (1-2 Timothy, Titus), Philemon, and the Apocalypse of John (Revelation). Its arrangement of the New Testament brings the apostolic epistles into what was probably thought to be the apostolic,

or chronological, order. Some modern editions of the New Testament also follow this arrangement.

Codex Sinaiticus contains about a third of the Old Testament, the rest having been lost in transmission, but includes 1 and 4 Maccabees and the entire New Testament, together with the Epistle of Barnabas and part of the *Shepherd* of Hermas.

Codex Alexandrinus contains most of the Old Testament, including the *Odae* following the Psalter, and 1-2-3-4 Maccabees. It also contains most of 1-2 Clement, following the New Testament, and the Table of Contents shows that the Psalms of Solomon were once included at the end.

The numbering of the books of "Esdras" differs widely in the different versions: (1) In the Septuagint, I Esdras is an apocryphal paraphrase of 2 Chronicles 35-36, Ezra, and Nehemiah. II Esdras is a translation of the Hebrew books of Ezra and Nehemiah. (2) In the Vulgate, I Esdras is Ezra, II Esdras is Nehemiah, III Esdras is a translation of the Greek I Esdras, and IV Esdras is a Latin apocalypse (the underlying Greek translation and the original Hebrew have both disappeared). Today it is often called IV Ezra. (3) In the King James Version and later English translations, I Esdras is the Greek I Esdras, which was the Latin III Esdras; II Esdras is the Latin IV Esdras (or IV Ezra).

perfect" (apparently related to the Akkadian "permansive"). There are used respectively in the sequence of storytelling (as if the past were dramatically brought back to present reality) and in the succession of predictive oracles (as if the future were ahead of its time and considered as a realized event). The understanding of these grammatical peculiarities throws a light upon the Biblical apprehension of both past and future as a liturgical present. The cultic act in the Old Testament, especially at the celebration of the festivals, offers the striking feature of summoning at once before the theological imagination of the participants the deity's creative and redeeming acts (Creation, Flood, Call of Abraham, Exodus) and their eschatological fulfillment (the "end" of Creation, the salvation of the Remnant). It may not be a philological accident that the Hebrew tongue is especially well adapted to the formulation of the only theological philosophy of history that was produced by the ancient civilizations. While the Egyptians, the Babylonians, the Phoenicians, and the Greeks made distinctive contributions to art, science, psychology, and philosophy, only the Hebrews interpreted history as an unfragmented whole that has a meaning for all the generations of men and leads them to a goal, which is the perfecting of the universe of man into the Kingdom of God.

Poetic Conciseness. Several aspects of the Hebrew tongue combine to make it an instrument of conciseness that admirably suits poetic diction, particularly in the epic and elegiac styles, confers upon it forcefulness and eloquence without pomposity, and packs the phonetic sounds and rhythms with hard-hitting sense or emotion. There is no clear-cut distinction between the adjective and the noun. Most adjectives are actually nouns that are related to other nouns in appositive or predicate fashion. Nouns also are connected with other nouns through the so-called "construct state." For example, the expression "his holy name" is literally "the-name-of-his-holiness." In addition, the use of the adjective is extremely sparse: not a single one appears in the poetic gem known as Psalm 23. Pronominal suffixes are attached to nouns in order to express origin, material, or possession. The short compound *Eli* means "my God" (Psalm 22:1), literally, "God-of-me." They also may cling to verbs as direct objects: *chonneni,* "have mercy upon me" (Psalm 51:1), literally, "grace-me." The participle (which is an ambiguous verb-noun kind of word) may be used with a definite article or with a pronominal suffix, sometimes with both, and thus may stand for a whole relative clause with its antecedent: *qamay,* "those-that-rose-up-against-me" (Psalm 18:39). The infinitive construct with prepositional prefix and pronominal suffix or nominal object may correspond to a whole subordinate clause of circumstance, consequence, restriction, and so on: *kaharimi qoli,* "as-I-lifted-up my-voice" (Genesis 39:18); *lehakkireni,* "that-thou-shouldest-take-knowledge-of-me"(Ruth 2:10). Other grammatical phenomena, such as the use of apocopation for the jussive and the addition of an ending for the cohortative, make the Hebrew tongue a tool of supple and often subtle formulation. All these morphological and syntactical peculiarities produce such a quality of compactness that the English translation of a given text often requires twice as many words as those of the original. For instance, the two words *abhinu shebbashamayim* are rendered "Our Father

which art in heaven." A line of six words like *weyahweh bhehekhal qodhsho has mippanaw kolhaarets* needs fifteen English words, "The Lord is in his holy temple, let all the earth keep silent before him." (Habakkuk 2:20.)

Symbolic Undertones of Key Words. Biblical Hebrew is essentially a poetic language, not only in its ability "to contract the immensities" of time and life, but also through the forceful strains of thought associations that are emitted by its words. Lexicographical analysis should beware of conclusions obtained through the study of etymology alone. In every tongue, words assume new meanings that cannot be ascertained from a knowledge of their derivation. Nevertheless, as Carlyle said, words "are a seed-grain that cannot die." Many words used in the Old Testament carry with them undertones that create a specific atmosphere and are lost in translation. They cast a spell upon the subliminal consciousness of those who hear or read them and thus possess a virtue of evocation far wider than their literal equivalence in a foreign tongue may convey. Admittedly, the ambiguity of some Hebrew terms represents a linguistic deficiency. For instance, *mishpat* may be rendered by a score of different English words, not all of them synonymous, from "judgment" to "duty," "custom," and even "constitution." Many words of the Old Testament, however, possess in the original a richness of sense and a sharpness of delineation that are lost in foreign renderings, and some among them have acquired a primary importance in the religious vocabulary of Western civilization. Even simple synonyms like *choshekh, tsalmuth,* and *araphel,* which usually are translated by "obscurity," "deep shadow," and "thick darkness," refer to three different kinds of realities. The first applies to darkness in general, such as that of the night, whereas the second usually describes the realm of death without hope. The third, on the contrary, which is originally associated with the storm cloud and its vivifying rain, possesses within itself the potentiality of life and renewal and is connected specifically with the symbol of God's presence in the midst of his people (Exodus 20:18) or in the innermost part of the Jerusalem temple (I Kings 8:12). Likewise, three Hebrew words, *naar, elem,* and *bachur,* are rendered indiscriminately as "youth" or "young man," but the first conveys the idea of immature and shy responsibility (as in Jeremiah 1:6), the second suggests, on the contrary, the lustful vigor of surplus energy (as in I Samuel 17:56), and the third literally means "chosen," thereby suggesting not only the prime of manhood but also the sense of mission and purpose in life (as in I Samuel 9:2).

Even terms designating virtues or moral dispositions connote concrete experiences and even physical sensations. Thus *bissar,* "he announced good news" (hence, "he preached the gospel") stems from *basar,* "flesh," as good tidings thrill the flesh of the listener with the emotion of gladness. Likewise, *emunah,* "faith," is the other facet of *emeth,* "truth," both derived from *amen.* They suggest an attitude of leaning securely on a support that will not fail, always in a context of impending crisis. Another instance is proffered by the idea of "peace," which in Greek or in Latin and therefore in English is related to that of material strength and order. Its Hebrew original, *shalom,* describes the state of what is *shalem,* "whole and healthy." It is not coercive, nor is it directed against a defeated enemy. It is not a negative term designating the cessation of warfare but a positive and dynamic reality that involves completeness, inclusive soundness, solidarity, and coherence, and its aim is social prosperity and welfare. In brief, it offers quite a contrast to the Latin *pax* or even the Greek *eirene*.

Thus, if the vocabulary of the Hebrew language, like its morphology and syntax, makes it inadequate as a channel of analytical, logical, legal, or scientific communication, those losses and limitations are compensated by distinctive advantages, particularly in the realm of theological exposition.

SAMUEL TERRIEN, *Union Theological Seminary*

Bibliography

Barr, James, *The Semantics of Biblical Language* (London 1961).
Barr, James, *Biblical Words for Time* (London 1962).
Moran, W.J., "The Hebrew Language in Its Northwest Semitic Background" in *The Bible and the Ancient Near East*, ed. by G.E. Wright (Garden City, N.Y. 1961).
Rosenthal, F., *A Grammar of Biblical Aramaic* (Wiesbaden, Germany, 1961).

For Specialized Study

Brockelmann, G., *Hebräische Syntax* (Neukirchen, Germany, 1956).
Gertner, M., *Terms of Scriptural Interpretation: A Study in Hebrew Semantics* (London 1962).
Moscati, S., ed., *An Introduction to the Comparative Grammar of the Semitic Languages* (Wiesbaden, Germany, 1964).
Watts, J.W., *A Survey of Syntax in the Hebrew Old Testament* (Grand Rapids, Mich., 1964).

3. Manuscripts and Versions of the Old Testament

As a collection of sacred books the Old Testament has come down in a written text, transmitted from generation to generation by scribes. Doubtless many of the traditions and fragments of early verse embedded in it, and perhaps certain of its laws and prescriptions, were transmitted orally for some time before they were reduced to writing, but the history of the text in the strict sense begins when written documents appear. It is possible that some of the material now in the Old Testament was composed as early as the 11th century B.C. Writing in an alphabetic script was well known in Palestine and Syria at a much earlier date than that, and neighboring peoples long had been accustomed to the use of religious texts in written form, so there is no reason to deny that this material might have been put in writing at that date.

In the Old Testament itself Moses is represented as writing (Exodus 24:4); writing was in use in court circles (II Samuel 11:14; I Kings 21:8; II Kings 10:1; II Chronicles 30:1); and we read of prophets having their messages recorded in written form (Jeremiah 36:4). Most of the early writing from the Near East that has survived is on stone or clay, but we know of writing on metal, bone, wood, cloth, leather, and papyrus. It is most probable that the early forms of our Biblical documents were written in ink with a reed pen on papyrus and in a script not very much different from that seen in the Lachish or the Samaritan ostraca (broken shards of pottery inscribed in ink).

The Work of the Scribes. No autographs of the writings collected in the Old Testament have survived. The texts we possess were transmitted to us by generations of scribes. We have ample evidence of how scribes both wittingly and unwittingly altered the documents they were copying. Unwittingly they would misread (or mishear) words, make mistakes in spelling, divide what ought to have been kept joined and join what ought to have been kept apart, copy words or lines twice, miss words or even passages. Wittingly they would alter things they thought wrong or unseemly and would condense, omit, expand, transpose, insert explanatory matter, and so on. There is no reason to suppose that the documents in our Old Testament, at least in the period before they came to be regarded as sacrosanct, did not suffer from the usual types of scribal corruption.

As certain documents, however, came to be regarded as something apart, something of importance for the religious life of the community, there arose among the Jews, as there arose in similar circumstances among other religious communities, those who devoted themselves in a particular way to the care of such writings. These later were called *Sopherim,* and although this is popularly translated "scribes" (Ezra 7:6, 11, 12; Nehemiah 8:13), they were not merely copyists, but keepers of records, interpreters, and "bookmen" in the widest sense. Theirs was not the authority of those who spoke or wrote "in the name of the Lord," but they assembled the "inspired" writings, arranged, redacted, and guarded them, labored at their interpretation, and transmitted them as sacred books. It was the Sopherim who saw to the changing over of documents written in the old script into the later "square" script of our manuscripts and indeed developed this script into an elegant manuscript hand. They provided the rubrics necessary for some books and the paragraphing needed in others. They attended to matters of orthography and scribal abbreviations, marked sense divisions in the text, and worked out the technical problems of spacing the text in the columns of scrolls. It was by their labors that the text was standardized for transmission, and in that process of standardization, as reverence for Scripture increased, they, from motives of piety, introduced little alterations, safeguarding the divine name, disfiguring the names of heathen deities, replacing indelicate or unseemly expressions by euphemisms, emending passages likely to be misunderstood, and at times modernizing the language. The evidence for all this is in the text as they have transmitted it to us.

The period of the early Sopherim may be considered to have extended from about 500 B.C. to 100 A.D. From the closing of the Palestinian Canon about 100 A.D. to about 500 A.D. is the period of the later Sopherim. Part of the activity associated with the closing of the canon was concerned with the question of a standard exemplar of the text. This would seem to have been settled by the labors of the School of Rabbi Akiba (died 135), so that the activity of the later Sopherim was concerned largely with stereotyping the text.

The Sopherim were succeeded by the *Masoretes,* whose labors extend from about 500 A.D. to the invention of printing. The early text left by the Sopherim was for the most part a purely consonantal text with no pointing for vocalization or accentuation, no punctuation in our sense, and with little more to help the reader than some breaking up of the text into paragraphs. The Masoretes labored to supply the text with these elements that were lacking and in addition compiled a great body of annotations, some statistical, some text-critical, some exegetical, all with the twofold purpose of safeguarding the text and making it fully intelligible to the reader. They standardized a system of verse division, and broke up the text into pericopes of convenient size for liturgical cycles of public reading of the Scriptures. Three systems of vocalization worked out by them are known, a Babylonian, a Palestinian, and a Tiberian, the latter of which is found in most manuscripts and the printed texts. There are also three systems of accentuation. The vocalization consists of little signs written below, within, or above the consonants to indicate correct pronunciation. The accents are another such system of signs to serve three purposes: (1) to be a kind of punctuation, guiding the reader to the relation of part to part within the sentence; (2) to be a guide to the cantillation; and (3) to mark where necessary the correct accentuation of words. The Masoretes also counted words and letters, noted anomalies and peculiarities of the text, recorded variant readings, suggested corrections and emendations, although they no longer dared to introduce them into the text, and drew up rules for the copyists of Biblical manuscripts. There were Schools of Masoretes, but it was the Tiberian School that finally came to dominate textual studies, so that most Hebrew manuscripts of the Old Testament derive from the famous 10th century Tiberian Codices of Ben Asher and Ben Naphtali.

Versions of the Text. Until the discovery in 1947 of the Dead Sea Scrolls and fragments, which possibly may date from the 1st century B.C., our actual manuscript evidence for the text of the Old Testament was relatively late. From the Cairo *Genizah* many Biblical fragments have been recovered, some of them dating from the 7th and even from the 6th century, but our earliest manuscripts containing any considerable amount of text are a very few codices that may be dated to the 9th and 10th centuries. The Cambridge Codex XIII is a complete Old Testament, and may be as early as the middle of the 9th century, and the Cairo Karaite manuscript of the Prophets may be of the late 9th century. The Aleppo Sephardic Codex containing the whole Old Testament dates from early in the 10th century, and the imperfect Pentateuch Codex in the British Museum, Or. 4445, is of about the same date. The St. Petersburg Prophet Codex is dated 916 A.D., and there are six manuscripts in the Firkowitsch Collection at Leningrad that belong to the 10th century. The Codex Urbinus 2, now in the Vatican, which contains the whole Old Testament, also may be of the 10th century. The famous Codex L from Old Cairo and now at Leningrad is dated 1008 and contains the whole Old Testament. From later centuries there is a very great number of manuscripts, but they are of less importance for the text. Hebrew Biblical manuscripts are of two kinds: (1) synagogue Scrolls, written on leather or parchment, and for the most part unpointed; and (2) Codices, written on parchment or paper, and for the most part pointed, although the pointing is not always by the original scribe.

The earliest printed Hebrew Scriptures were portions; for example, the Psalms at Bologna in 1477; the Pentateuch at Bologna, 1482; the Megilloth (the festival scrolls, Song of Songs, Ruth, Lamentations, Ecclesiastes, Esther), Bologna, 1482; the Prophets, Soncino, 1485; the Kethubim, Naples, 1486–1487; the Pentateuch, Faro, 1487. The first complete Hebrew Bible to be printed was issued at Soncino in 1488, the second at Naples in 1492–1493, and the third at Brescia in 1494. This latter was the text that Martin Luther used. The first great Rabbinic Bible was printed by Daniel Bomberg at Venice in 1516–1517, for which the text was prepared by Felix Pratensis. For the second Rabbinic Bible, Venice 1524–1525, the text was prepared and a Masorah compiled by Jacob ben Hayyim (Chayyim). This was a monumental work for its time, but it unfortunately was based on relatively late manuscripts. Its text, however, came to have such authority that it was the basis of practically all subsequent printed editions until Paul Kahle, in editing the text for the third edition of Kittel's *Biblia Hebraica* (Stuttgart 1937), took a Leningrad manuscript as the basic text and attempted to give a purer Ben Asher text. (See section *4. Textual Criticism of the Old Testament.*)

The text of the Old Testament is in Hebrew, save for some passages in Daniel and Ezra, one word in Genesis, a few isolated proper names, and one verse in Jeremiah that are in Aramaic. When the exiles returned from Babylon, they found this Aramaic the dominant language in Palestine, and although Hebrew still continued in use, it had to give way more and more before the popular Aramaic. It is possible that some of the later books in the Old Testament were composed in this Aramaic and only later were translated into the Hebrew form in which we have them. In any case, there came a time when Hebrew was so little understood by the common people who attended services at which the Scripture was read that it was necessary for the Hebrew text to be translated for them into the vernacular Aramaic with which they were familiar. In Nehemiah 8:8 we learn that they read the Law of God distinctly and then gave the sense so that the people might understand the meaning. At first this giving of the sense was somewhat haphazard, either the Reader himself or some instructed person, such as the local schoolmaster, giving a running translation of the passages as they were read. The verb "to translate" is *tirgēm*, so the translator was a *tõrgemān* or *methõrgemān*, and his translation a *targum*. Now from very ancient days in the Near East the interpreter (*tãrgumānu*) had been an important court official, so it is not strange that with the development of the synagogue we find the *tõrgemān* coming to be an official personage beside the Reader and rules being worked out to control his office. One such rule in the Mishna (Megillah 4:4) directs that in the case of the Law the interpretation must be one verse (or clause or sentence, *pesek*) at a time, although in the case of the Prophets the Reader may read three verses before the Interpreter gives the sense. Doubtless at first the giving of the sense was free paraphrase by each individual Interpreter and always oral. A number of factors, however, would work toward the production of "standard" interpretations. It was obviously necessary that certain key words and phrases, particularly in the Law, should not be misinterpreted, and there were advantages in such passages being uniformly rendered. In other cases a literal rendering of passages would be inadvisable, and yet individual caprice in rendering them would be equally inadvisable, so that felicitous renderings would be remembered and generally adopted. On controversial passages it would be wise to adopt some standard rendering that would avoid dangerous issues. In this way, little by little, "fixed" renderings would increase and presently there would be in circulation a number of recognized Targums, and inevitably they would come to be written. There was some disapproval of a written Targum, but the story in the Talmud (Jerusalem Megillah 74d) that tells of this also is clear evidence that written Targums were in use.

No early Aramaic Targums have survived, although it is quite possible that fragments of early material are embedded in later Targums. Save for the books of Daniel and Ezra-Nehemiah, the Rabbinic Bibles print Targums to all the books of the Old Testament. On the Pentateuch we have four Targums: (1) Onkelos, the Babylonian Targum; (2) Yerushalmi I, or the Targum of Pseudo-Jonathan; (3) Yerushalmi II, or the Fragment Targum; and (4) Yerushalmi III, of which only a few fragments survive. On the Prophets we have (1) Jonathan, or the Babylonian Targum to the Prophets; and (2) fragments of a Yerushalmi Targum. To the Hagiographa only late Targums exist: (1) Targums to Psalms, Proverbs and Job; (2) Targums for the five Megilloth; (3) a Targum to Chronicles. These extant Targums often are paraphrastic rather than literal, tend to bring in explanatory and homiletic matter, and in their wording often reflect the theological ideas of later Judaism. They seem to have begun to take their present shape during the 4th and 5th centuries, and they began to drop out of use when Arabic came to oust Aramaic as the vernacular in the lands of the Near East. Only two Targums ever came to have any official standing among the Jews, that of Onkelos on the Pentateuch and that of Jonathan on the Prophets. Both are Babylonian Targums, and neither, as we have them, is the work of a single author but represents compilations of material from various sources worked over to form official Targums. Another Aramaic Targum is that on the Pentateuch in use among the Samaritans and thus called the Samaritan Targum. The Samaritan Pentateuch is in Hebrew, being merely the type of text current among the Samaritans at the time of their separation but written out in Samaritan characters. When their people no longer understood Hebrew, they too needed an interpretation into the local dialect of Aramaic familiar to them. No official redaction of their Targum ever was made, although there are traces of an attempt to fix its text. It began to take form in the early centuries A.D. and was in use until Arabic superseded Aramaic as their vernacular in the 11th century. The researches of Paul Kahle and his students, and especially the discovery at the Vatican Library in 1957 of a complete Targum of the Pentateuch, throw much light on the earliest history of the Targums.

The Greek version of the Old Testament also doubtless began as a Targum in Greek for those communities of Jews living in areas of Greek speech who knew little or no Hebrew. There is evidence that certain portions of the Hebrew Scriptures were circulating in Greek translation in the 3d century B.C. The tradition in the much-discussed *Letter of Aristeas* (about 100 B.C.) indeed makes it clear that at that time there were in circulation a number of Greek versions of the Law that the learned found unsatisfactory, so that an attempt was made to secure official sanction for a new version by a kind of "revision committee." This was the version of the Seventy or the Septuagint (LXX). This version found favor with the Christian Church, which extended the name Septuagint to cover the Greek version of the other parts of the Hebrew Scriptures, along with such other religious writings as Ecclesiasticus (Sirach), I Maccabees, Tobit, and even writings like Wisdom, II Maccabees, and I Esdras, which originally were written in Greek. All our manuscripts of the Septuagint are of Christian origin, as are practically all our papyrus fragments of the Old Testament in Greek. Origen's great *Hexapla* was intended to be a critical revision of this Greek Old Testament, but there were other revisions, notably those by Lucian and by Hesychius. When the work of Rabbi Akiba's School gave a final standard text of the Hebrew Old Testament in the 1st century A.D., this Septuagint in the hands of the Christians was no longer satisfactory to the Jews, and so we find new Greek versions being made from the newly authorized Hebrew text. Such are the versions of Aquila, Symmachus, and Theodotion. Fragments of still other Greek versions also are known.

The Syriac version also would seem to have had its origin in a translation made for the needs of a Jewish community living in the area where this dialect of Eastern Aramaic was in use. It too, however, was taken over by the Christian Church and revised to give the version known as the Peshitta, which from the 5th century onward has been the version in use by both the Jacobites and the Nestorians. Chronicles seems to have been missing from the early Peshitta. Many manuscripts of this version contain books from the Apocrypha and sometimes even from the Pseudepigrapha. Paul of Tella in 616–617 made a slavishly literal translation into Syriac of Origen's *Hexapla*, and portions of this Syro-Hexapla have survived. In 704–705, Jacob of Edessa undertook a revision of the Syriac Bible on the basis of Greek texts. Some portions of this are still extant, as well as portions of a Melkite version made from the Greek in the 6th century and known as the Christian-Palestinian version.

Several Latin versions made from the Greek were in circulation in Italy, Gaul, and North Africa, some of them dating perhaps from the 2d century. The surviving fragments of these generally are lumped together as the Old Latin. Jerome (died 420) attempted to revise this Old Latin from the Greek texts available to him but gave this up in favor of a new translation directly from the Hebrew where the original was in Hebrew, although he used the Greek and tried to preserve familiar Latin renderings. His labors produced the original Vulgate version.

Of the Coptic version we have more or less extensive portions of the Old Testament in all four dialects: the Sahidic, spoken in upper Egypt; the Fayyumic, spoken in the area around the Fayyum; the Akhmimic, spoken to the north of the Thebaid; and the Bohairic, spoken in Lower Egypt toward the Mediterranean. The Sahidic is the oldest, coming from the 4th century, and the Bohairic, from the 7th and 8th centuries, is the youngest. All are made from the Greek, sometimes apparently from the Hesychian recension but sometimes from what may be a pre-Hexaplaric text. The Armenian version of the 4th century is also from the Greek, essentially from Hexaplaric manuscripts, though with some revisions from the Syriac. The Ethiopic, Georgian, Arabic, Slavonic, and Gothic versions are later, and although each of them has an interest of its own, they are too late to be of much importance for the history of the text.

ARTHUR JEFFERY, *Columbia University*

Bibliography

Bentzen, Aage, *Introduction to the Old Testament* (Copenhagen 1948).

Burrows, Millar, ed., *The Dead Sea Scrolls of St. Mark's Monastery*, vol. 1 (New Haven 1950).

Burrows, Millar, *More Light on the Dead Sea Scrolls* (New York 1958).

Driver, G.R., *Semitic Writing* (London 1948).

Grant, Frederick C., *Translating the Bible* (New York 1961).

Pfeiffer, Robert, *Introduction to the Old Testament*, rev. ed. (New York 1948).

Roberts, B.J., *The Old Testament Text and Versions* (Mystic, Conn., 1951).

For Specialized Study

Birkeland, H., *Akzent und Vokalismus im Althebräischen* (Oslo 1940).

Blau, L., *Zur Einführung in die Heilige Schrift* (Budapest-Strassburg 1894).

Geden, A.S., *Outlines of Introduction to the Hebrew Bible* (Edinburgh 1909).

Geden and Kilgour, *Introduction to the Ginsburg Edition of the Hebrew Old Testament* (London 1928).

Kahle, P., *Die hebräischen Handschriften aus der Höhle* (Stuttgart 1951).

Kahle, P., *Masoreten des Ostens* (Leipzig 1913).

Kahle, P., *Masoreten des Westens*, 2 parts (Stuttgart 1927–30).

Kahle, P., *The Cairo Geniza*, 2d ed. (Oxford 1959).

Kenyon, F.G., *The Text of the Greek Bible* (London 1937).

Loisy, A., *Histoire critique du texte et des versions de la Bible* (Amiens, France, 1892).

Nestle, E., *Urtext und Übersetzungen der Bibel* (Leipzig 1897).

Paret, O., *Die Bibel: ihre Überlieferung in Druck und Schrift* (Stuttgart 1949).

Peters, N., *Der Text des Alten Testamentes und seine Geschichte* (Münster, Germany, 1921).

Stummer, F., *Einführung in die lateinische Bibel* (Paderborn, Germany, 1928).

Swete, H.B., *An Introduction to the Old Testament in Greek* (Cambridge, Eng., 1914).

Torczyner, H., in *Encyclopedia Judaica*, vol. 4 (1929).

Vandervorst, H., *Introduction aux textes hébreu et grec de l'Ancien Testament* (Mechelen, Belgium, 1935).

Weir, T.H., *A Short History of the Hebrew Text of the Old Testament* (London 1899).

Zarb, S.M., *Il Testo biblico* (Rome 1939).

4. Textual Criticism of the Old Testament

The purpose of textual criticism is to reconstruct the original text of the Old Testament. It frequently is called *lower criticism,* to distinguish it from *higher criticism,* which deals with questions of authorship, date, source analysis, historical background, and the like.

This type of criticism is not peculiar to Biblical studies. It must be practiced on any piece of literature that we wish to study seriously and that has not come down to us in a copy made by the author's own hand. There is textual criticism, for example, of the plays of Shakespeare. The peculiarities of Old Testament textual criticism arise from the nature of the Hebrew language and the history of the Old Testament text.

The Old Testament is written in Hebrew, with the exception of the following passages, which are in the closely related Aramaic language: Ezra 4:8 to 6:18; 7:12–26; Daniel 2:4b to 7:28; and Jeremiah 10:11, and a few isolated words or expressions in Genesis. In ancient times these languages were written with consonants only, the pronunciation of vowels being preserved only by oral tradition. In time some of the vowels were indicated by the use of certain consonant letters (called *matres lectionis*), and eventually all vowels were marked by these or by vowel points. Certain of the letters of Hebrew and Aramaic are similar, either in appearance or in sound. For example, in the square script that came into use about 200 B.C. the following pairs of letters are very similar in appearance and may easily be confused: D and R, B and K, H and CH, T and CH. Certain letters may be readily confused in sound: there are two K-sounds, three S-sounds, and two T-sounds. In ancient times the words often were not divided in manuscripts, and verses were not separated as they are now. These features of the original languages of the Old Testament have helped to make errors possible in the transmission of its text.

History of the Text. The books of the Old Testament were written between 1000 and 100 B.C., and the canon was closed toward the end of the 1st Christian century (see section *1. Canon of the Old Testament*). Not a single book has come down to the present in its original, autograph form. The earliest manuscripts are those generally known as the Dead Sea Scrolls, which were found in the caves of Wadi Qumran and Wadi Murabbaat and elsewhere in the desert region of Palestine near the Dead Sea. Complete scrolls or fragments have been found of all books of the Old Testament except Esther. Many are from the 1st and 2d centuries B.C. These manuscripts contain several different kinds of Hebrew text. Some are like the Greek Septuagint or the Samaritan Pentateuch, while others are very similar to the Masoretic text, which is discussed below.

The manuscripts found at Wadi Murabbaat are very close to the Masoretic text and are mostly from the 2d century B.C. It is probable, therefore, that a "proto-Masoretic" text was established by the year 100 A.D. This was the result of a process extending over two or three centuries, climaxed by needs that were felt in Judaism as the result of the rise of Christianity and the capture of Jerusalem by the Romans in 70 A.D. Rabbi Akiba may have been the leader in the final stage of this process.

For four centuries after Akiba the textual scholars were the *Sopherim,* the Scribes. While they were concerned mainly with the correct copying of the text, they were students of it as well. In various ways they sought to point out difficulties in the text: by the "extraordinary points" placed above words in fifteen passages, which point out passages that are doubtful in one respect or another; by the eighteen "emendations of the Scribes" (*tiqqune ha-sopherim*), most of which attempt to avoid blasphemy against God; and by the *Sebirin,* which point out "unexpected" forms. The Scribes made subdivisions in the text that eventually became chapters and verses.

It was not until the time of the Masoretes that a really standard text was established. The Masoretes were Biblical scholars who lived in the period between the 6th and 10th centuries A.D. The word *Masorete* means "one who hands down the tradition." These scholars were not scientific critics of the text but men who sought to preserve the best traditions regarding the reading of the text. There were several Masoretic schools, both in Palestine and Babylonia. The Masoretes sought to fix a standard, authoritative text on the basis of the manuscripts available to them, and to provide the text with notations that would be of aid in its study. One of the most important of their activities was to provide the text with complete vowel points. They also provided it with elaborate symbols to aid in the correct reading of the text, partly the equivalent of modern punctuation marks. They furnished in some cases indications of variant readings in two families of manuscripts (the so-called *Kethib-Qere*). The notations that they provided for the margins of the text gave information as to the number of times a given word or form occurred, the number of words in a book, and so on.

THE ISAIAH SCROLL, one of the Dead Sea Scrolls, discovered in 1947. This version of the Book of Isaiah is the oldest complete manuscript of any book of the Old Testament. It is on leather and dates from about 100 B.C.

The Masoretes flourished in several schools over a period of about four centuries. The form of the text made by the school at Tiberias, Palestine, finally won out over other systems. In the 10th century there were in Tiberias two main families of Masoretes—the Ben Asher family and that of Ben Naphtali. Five generations of the Ben Asher family are known, the two most famous members being Moses ben Asher and Aaron ben Moses ben Asher. The Ben Asher text ultimately was accepted as the most authoritative, through a pronouncement of Maimonides in the 12th century.

The Ben Asher text is believed by most modern scholars to be the best text that has survived from ancient times. A manuscript made in 1008 A.D. from a copy by Aaron ben Asher has been preserved in the Public Library of Leningrad (manuscript B 19a). This is the basis of the critical edition of the Hebrew Bible published as the 3d edition of Kittel's *Biblia Hebraica* (1937). Another Ben Asher text, which had been preserved for a long time in a synagogue at Aleppo (Syria), is now in the Hebrew University in Jerusalem. It is being used as the basis of a new critical edition of the Hebrew Bible. For further information on manuscripts, see section 3. *Manuscripts and Versions of the Old Testament.*

Reconstruction of the Original Hebrew Text. It should be obvious from this history of the text that a period of a thousand years or more elapsed between the completion of the latest book of the Old Testament and most of the manuscripts on which modern study is based. During this time the text was repeatedly copied and recopied by hand. When one thinks of the errors that may arise even with the use of modern typewriters and composing machines, it is not difficult to realize why errors arose in this repeated copying by hand. Errors could arise from failure to read a text properly, failure to hear correctly when manuscripts were written from dictation, fatigue, failure to understand what one was writing, and even sheer carelessness. Sometimes material originally written in the margin was incorporated in the text.

It can be proved that errors have slipped into the text by comparison of parts of the Hebrew Bible that give the same material in two places: for example, II Samuel 22 and Psalm 18; or Psalm 14 and Psalm 53; or Isaiah 36 to 39 and II Kings 18:13 to 20:19. More extensive comparison may be made of the material in I-II Chronicles that has been adapted from I-II Samuel and I-II Kings. Small or large differences suggest that one form or the other may be original.

Errors also are obvious to the modern scholar in passages that do not make sense, even when read by one who has a thorough knowledge of Hebrew. The purpose of textual criticism, therefore, is to remove as many errors as possible from the present text and thereby to recover the original text.

A comparison of the available Hebrew manuscripts helps only a little in the recovery of the original text of the Old Testament. Careful studies have shown that the Masoretic manuscripts that have come down to us contain few significant variants. Those that occur are largely differences in orthography or vocalization (and

THE DEAD SEA SCROLLS

(*Below*) An infrared photograph of one of the scrolls is compared with a modern Hebrew text of the same book.

(*Above*) A fragment of the First Book of Samuel—the oldest known Biblical manuscript (3d century B.C.).

(*Left*) A scholar works to reconstruct a section of the Dead Sea Scrolls from the fragments found in caves.

possibly dialects) and seldom give differences in meaning. The task of the Old Testament textual critic is therefore different from that of the New Testament textual critic, who must rely largely upon careful comparison of early Greek manuscripts.

The complete Isaiah scroll among the Dead Sea Scrolls (known as 1QIs*a*) is one of the earliest and best known pre-Masoretic manuscripts. While it very often agrees with the Masoretic text, it offers in a few places readings that appear to be superior to the readings of that text. For example, the Masoretic text of Isaiah 3:24 may be translated as follows:

> Instead of sweet spices there will be rottenness,
>   and instead of a girdle, a rope;
> instead of well-set hair, baldness,
>   and instead of a robe, a girdling of sack-cloth;
>   branding instead of beauty.

The last line of this verse presents two difficulties: it reverses the order of words in the four preceding lines, and it assumes a meaning for the common Hebrew word *ki*, here translated "branding," that it has nowhere else in the Bible. The Dead Sea Scroll of Isaiah contains an additional word to the last line, which makes it possible to render it as follows:

> for instead of beauty (there will be) shame.

In a few instances the Dead Sea Scroll of Isaiah supports the reading of the Septuagint or another ancient version. (Consult the marginal notes to Isaiah in the Revised Standard Version of the Bible, where these readings often are cited.)

In a small number of cases the original text of the Old Testament was altered in very ancient times, before the earliest known manuscripts and versions. For example, in II Samuel the word *Baal* (the name of a non-Hebrew deity) in personal names has been replaced by the word *bosheth,* which means "shame." In Chronicles, however, the original forms have been retained. For example, the name of Saul's son is given as *Ish-bosheth* in II Samuel 2:8, but as *Esh Baal* in I Chronicles 8:33. It is certain that his original name was not one that meant "man of shame," but rather "man of Baal."

Recovery of the original text often requires more than comparison of ancient Hebrew manuscripts and comparison of parts of the Old Testament. The textual critic sometimes must resort to emendation of the received Hebrew text. The purpose of an emendation never should be to "improve" what was written by an ancient author but simply to recover what he actually wrote. Old Testament scholars in the latter part of the 19th century and the first quarter of the 20th very often emended the Hebrew text and frequently seemed to have little respect for the Masoretic text. Scholars now have greater respect for that text and resort to emendation only as a last resort. This heightened respect has come in part from the discovery of the Dead Sea Scrolls, in part from increased knowledge of the history of the text and the recovery of relatively early manuscripts, and in part from careful study of the Semitic languages that are cognate with Hebrew.

Thus the primary concern of the scholar should be to understand and interpret the Masoretic text; if he cannot do that, he may resort to emendation.

Emendations of the Hebrew text may be classified as follows: (1) those that rest on the evidence of an ancient version, such as the Septuagint; (2) those that are based on conjecture without versional support; and (3) emendations that involve both conjecture and occasional evidence.

Several of the ancient versions of the Old Testament were produced before the time of the Masoretes. The most important are the Greek Septuagint, the Aramaic Targums, the Syriac Peshitta, and the Latin Vulgate of St. Jerome (see section 3. *Manuscripts and Versions of the Old Testament*). These versions sometimes differ in details from the Hebrew Bible. It is possible, therefore, that in some instances they represent the original text and the Masoretic text does not.

It is frequently very difficult to decide whether one of these versions or the Masoretic text represents the original reading. It is rash to assume that in every case of difference the Septuagint or another version is more original only because it is older than our Masoretic manuscripts. The scholar must very carefully consider every individual case of variation. For example, in comparing the Septuagint with the Hebrew text, the scholar must exercise great care. He must realize that the various translators of the Septuagint differed in their competence and in the care they took in their work. Sometimes they paraphrased rather than translated literally; sometimes they misunderstood a verse or passage. Corruptions have taken place in the manuscripts of the Septuagint itself, as in the Hebrew text. Nevertheless, even when these and other possibilities have been considered, the Septuagint and other ancient versions sometimes do give sound

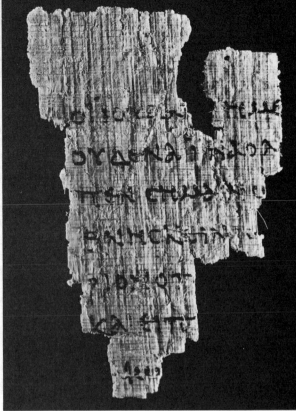

PAPYRUS FRAGMENT of the oldest known copy of the New Testament contains verses from the Gospel of John.

aid in restoring the original Hebrew. The following examples will illustrate their use in textual emendation.

In I Samuel 14:41 a long clause obviously has dropped out of the Masoretic text but has been preserved in the Septuagint and the Vulgate. In the following translation, the words in italics are omitted in the Hebrew:

> And Saul said to the Lord, God of Israel, "*Why hast thou not answered thy servant today? If the guilt be in me or Jonathan my son, O Lord God of Israel, give* Urim; *but if the guilt be in thy people Israel* give Thummim." Jonathan and Saul were taken, and the people escaped.

It is clear that this longer form of the verse is necessary to the sense, and it is easy to see why the Hebrew scribe made the omission. His eye skipped from the word "Israel" near the beginning of the verse to the same word near the end, and he unconsciously omitted all the intervening words. This type of error is known as homoioteleuton. The same error sometimes is made by typists today.

Another kind of error may be illustrated from Psalm 49:11. The first half of the verse in Hebrew may be translated literally: "Their inwardness (*qirbam*) is their homes forever, their dwellingplaces to all generations." This is nonsense, which is not adequately relieved by the King James Version: "Their inward thought *is, that* their houses *shall continue* for ever, *and* their dwellingplaces to all generations," the words in italics not being in the Hebrew at all but inserted in order to attempt to make sense of the verse. Yet, when one turns to the Septuagint, Peshitta, and Targum, one finds that the verse should be read: "Their graves (*qibram*) are their homes forever, their dwellingplaces to all generations." The scribal error was simply that of transposing B and R, so that what was originally written as *qibram* eventually became *qirbam*.

A few suggested emendations of the Masoretic text have been confirmed by the discovery of the Dead Sea Scroll of Isaiah. For example, the Masoretic text of Isaiah 49:24, 25 reads as follows:

Can prey be seized from the mighty,
    or the captives of a *righteous man* be rescued?
For thus says the LORD:
Even the captives of the mighty shall be seized,
    and the prey of the tyrant be rescued;
For I will contend with those who contend with you,
    and your children I will save.

In the second line the italicized term seems strangely out of place. It breaks the poetic parallelism, and one expects on the basis of the reading of the fifth line a word such as "tyrant." That is just the word that is presupposed by the Septuagint, Peshitta, and the Vulgate, and the Hebrew word for "tyrant" occurs in the Dead Sea Scroll. The error probably arose from the fact that in the Hebrew square script the words ʿariṣ ("tyrant") and ṣaddiq ("righteous man") are very similar in appearance.

Emendations that are based wholly on conjecture must be the last resort of the textual critic, yet they are sometimes necessary and sound. They may be suggested out of a knowledge of the types of errors that scribes can make, the forms of the Hebrew letters, and common sense as to the meaning of a passage. One very simple emendation that has commended itself to most modern scholars may be found in Amos 6:12. The first half of the verse reads in Hebrew: "Do horses run on the rock? Does one plow with oxen?" The first rhetorical question implies the answer "no," but the second implies "yes." One naturally expects in the light of the context that both questions imply the same answer. The King James Version attempts to resolve the difficulty by translating, "Will one plow there with oxen," but "there" is not in the Hebrew. A simple solution gives a suitable rendering. The Hebrew word *babeqarim*, "with oxen" can be divided into two Hebrew words, *bebaqar yam*, "with oxen the sea." We thus translate the emended text: "Does one plow the sea with oxen?" The difficulty arose from the fact that in ancient times manuscripts did not always separate words, or in some cases words were wrongly separated.

Sometimes the text may be emended partly on the basis of ancient versions and partly by conjecture. A good example is Proverbs 25:27. Translated literally, the Hebrew seems to say: "It is not good for one to eat much honey; and searching out their glory is glory." The meaning of this is far from apparent. One may attempt to restore the original text by comparing the Septuagint and Targum and adopting their reading at the end of the verse, and then conjecturing that the first word (in Hebrew) of the second half of the verse is the same as the first word in Proverbs 25:17. One then gets the proverbial saying: "It is not good for one to eat much honey; so be sparing of complimentary words."

Textual criticism has made great progress in the attempt to restore the original text of the Old Testament. Much remains to be done, but on the whole the original text of the Old Testament is as well known as that of any other book that has survived from antiquity and probably better known than most.

J. PHILIP HYATT, *Vanderbilt University*

Bibliography

Ap-Thomas, D.R., *A Primer of Old Testament Text Criticism,* rev. ed. (London 1965).

Ginsburg, Christian D., *Introduction to the Masoretico-Critical Edition of the Hebrew Bible* (New York 1966).

Roberts, Bleddyn J., *The Old Testament Text and Versions* (Cardiff, Wales, 1951).

Würtheim, Ernst, *The Text of the Old Testament,* tr. by P.R. Ackroyd (New York 1957).

5. Growth of the Old Testament Literature

The Hebrew Bible consists of three parts: *The Law:* Genesis, Exodus, Leviticus, Numbers, Deuteronomy; (2) *The Prophets:* (A) Former Prophets: Joshua, Judges, Samuel, Kings; (B) Latter Prophets: Isaiah, Jeremiah, Ezekiel, and The Twelve (Minor Prophets); and (3) *The Writings* (Hagiographa): (A) Psalms, Proverbs, Job; (B) Song of Songs, Ruth, Lamentations, Ecclesiastes, Esther; (C) Daniel, Ezra-Nehemiah, Chronicles. As combined and arranged in the Hebrew Bible, these total 24 books.

The three divisions mark successive canonizations: the Law (about 400 B.C.); the Prophets (about 200 B.C.); and the Writings (about 90 A.D.) (see section *1. Canon of the Old Testament*). These books are written in Hebrew, except for a few passages that are in Aramaic (see section *2. Language of the Old Testament*).

The Greek translation of the Hebrew Scriptures, called the Septuagint, arranged the books of the Old Testament as follows, disregarding the three canons of the Hebrew Bible and adding the Apocrypha (which are included in the Latin Vulgate, the official Bible of the Roman Catholic Church) (see also SEPTUAGINT).

(1) *The Pentateuch:* Genesis, Exodus, Leviticus, Numbers, Deuteronomy.

(2) *Historical Books:* Joshua, Judges, Ruth, I-II Kings (that is, I-II Samuel), III-IV Kings (that is, I-II Kings), I-II Chronicles, I or III Esdras (Greek Esdras), II Esdras (Ezra-Nehemiah).

(3) *Poetical and Didactic Books:* Psalms, Proverbs, Ecclesiastes, Song of Songs, Job, Wisdom of Solomon, Ecclesiasticus.

(4) *Stories:* Esther with additions, Judith, Tobit.

(5) *Prophetic Books:* The Twelve, Isaiah, Jeremiah, Ezekiel, Baruch, Lamentations, Epistle of Jeremy, Ezra, Daniel with additions (the Song of the Three Holy Children, Susanna, and Bel and the Dragon).

(6) *Late Histories:* I and II Maccabees; (occasionally also III and IV Maccabees).

The Latin Vulgate adds at the end of the New Testament the Apocalypse of Esdras (II or IV Esdras), which is not preserved in the Greek text from which the Latin was translated, as well as the Prayer of Manasses (included, in some manuscripts, among the Odes or Canticles appended to the Greek Psalter), and Greek (I or III) Esdras.

General Characteristics of Old Testament Literature. The Old Testament was written during the course of more than one millennium, approximately in the period 1200–100 B.C. We can visualize the extent of this period by comparing it with a similar one in English literature (from Beowulf to Tennyson) and in Greek literature (from Homer to the New Testament). The political, cultural, and religious changes among Israelites and Jews during this period (from Moses to the Maccabees) are hardly less revolutionary and far-reaching than in England and Greece: in all three cases the nations passed from a primitive cult to a noble religion and made immense progress in civilization. Such changes naturally are reflected in the three literatures. In Israel, the great political events that left their impact on the literature are: the exodus from Egypt under the leadership of Moses (about 1225 B.C.); the invasion into Canaan (about 1200 B.C.); the united monarchy under Saul, David, and Solomon (about 1025–930); the subsequent monarchy in North Israel (ending with Sargon's capture of Samaria in 722) and in Judah (ending with Nebuchadnezzar's destruction of Jerusalem in 586); and the subjections of the Jews to the Neo-Babylonian (586–538), Persian (538–332), and Hellenistic (332–142) kings; and after their independence under the Hasmonaeans, or Maccabees (142–63), the subjection of Israel to Roman rule (63 B.C.–395 A.D.).

The Hebrew Old Testament represents a small remnant of the literature of Israel and the early Jews; how much valuable Hebrew and Aramaic literature has been irretrievably lost can only be surmised. Biblical scholars were astonished when in 1947 some ancient Hebrew and Aramaic scrolls were discovered in a cave near Ain Feskha on the western shore of the Dead Sea, not far from Jericho. Aside from copies of Biblical books (notably Isaiah), hitherto unknown works were found: *The War between the Children of Light and the Children of Darkness, Hymns of Thanksgiving,* a commentary on Habakkuk, a sectarian *Manual of Discipline,* and presumably the lost *Book of Lamech.* These new writings may well be earlier than 90 A.D., when II or IV Esdras was written.

We may partially envisage the great mass of ancient Hebrew literature that is lost forever by noting, for instance, that only a single poem of Nahum (chapters 2, 3) has accidentally survived, and it is inconceivable that a poet of his genius never wrote anything else; and in the time of Jeremiah there must have been fifty other prophets no less able than Zephaniah or Habakkuk. Aside from the supreme masterpieces of the Bible, it is mere chance that has preserved for the editors of the prophetic canon in 200 B.C. and of the writings in 90 A.D. some of the writings included in the Old Testament. Judith and Tobit probably would have been included with Ruth and Esther if their original Hebrew text had been available in 90 A.D.

The final selection includes the following works: a historical corpus going from the creation of the world (dated 3761 B.C., by the Jews and 4004 B.C. by Bishop James Ussher) to 561 B.C., when Jehoiachin was delivered from his Babylonian prison; it comprised nine volumes (Genesis, Exodus, Leviticus, Numbers, Deuteronomy, Joshua, Judges, Samuel, Kings) and was edited substantially as we have it about 400 B.C., when the first five volumes (ending with the death of Moses) were separated and canonized as the *Torah* (Law) of Moses; the other four volumes became canonical (with additions) two centuries later. About the same time an editor collected all the prophetic writings written from 750 B.C. to 250 B.C. that could be found and published them in a four volume corpus (Isaiah, Jeremiah, Ezekiel, the Twelve). Thus in 200 originated

"The Law and the Prophets." The rest of the Old Testament consists of ten miscellaneous separate works of various dates, classed as follows: Poetical books (Psalms, Proverbs, Job); the five scrolls, each of which is read in the synagogue at one of the five annual festivals (Song of Songs, Ruth, Lamentations, Ecclesiastes, Esther); a prophecy (Daniel); and a history (Chronicles, Ezra, Nehemiah).

The selection was dictated by the religious needs of the Jews and included what was regarded as divinely inspired. Fortunately, however, as in the case of Homer in Greece and of the Rig Veda in India, much brilliant literature from ancient times that had no direct bearing on faith and practice was preserved and eventually was interpreted allegorically. Thus it happens that the Old Testament contains more writings of a purely patriotic or literary character than such sacred books as the New Testament and the Koran, which embody the teachings of the great religious reformers without including earlier national epics and literary masterpieces. Some stories about King David, the Hebrew patriarchs, and Esther—to name but a few examples—the love poetry of the Song of Songs do not belong, strictly speaking, in a Bible but are part of a national lay literature and lack devotional appeal. But as literature the Old Testament is unsurpassed among the various sacred scriptures in brilliance and beauty of style.

The greatest literature in the Old Testament is the earliest. The golden age of Hebrew literature comes to its end with the destruction of Jerusalem in 586 B.C.; its last masterpiece is the poem of Nahum (chapters 2, 3) on the destruction of Nineveh in 612; the decadence begins with Jeremiah and Ezekiel, who fail to attain the brilliance of Amos and Isaiah in the 8th century. The next two centuries may be called the silver age.

It is not without significance that the end of the golden age corresponds more or less with the end of the Judean state under the Davidic dynasty and with the adoption of the prophetic teaching that created Judaism (a reformation of Israel's national religion) in 621 B.C., when "The Book of the Law" of Moses (most of Deuteronomy 5 to 26; 28) was found in the Temple at Jerusalem and was ratified as the divine law of the land (II Kings 23:3). In religion, as in culture in general, the years about 600 B.C. proved to be an epoch-making turning point. A canonical book of Moses, around which the Pentateuch and eventually the whole Bible grew, took the place of the occasional utterances of inspired prophets in presenting God's requirements. Prophecy soon gave way to apocalypse—a Utopian vision of a future divine intervention to glorify the Jews. Even the priesthood, which at first acquired immense prestige, eventually gave way to the rabbinate, as the synagogues took the place of the Temple in the religious life of the Jews. The study of the Law eventually became more vital than the offering of sacrifices (compare Psalm 1). Yahweh, the God of Israel, soon was recognized as the creator of heaven and earth, as the only God in existence. Just about the time that such revolutionary changes were taking place among the Judeans, similar spiritual and religious transformations were occurring elsewhere: philosophy was born in Greece (Thales), India (the *Upanishads*), and China (Lao-tzu and Confucius); Zoroaster and Gautama Buddha reformed the religions of Persia and India, respectively.

The Deuteronomic "Book of the Law" had a profound impact on thought and literature as well as on religion. The Book of Kings (two books in English) was written about 600 B.C. to prove by means of historical examples the truth of the basic Deuteronomic doctrine: the survival of Israel depends on the fulfillment of the terms of the covenant promulgated by Moses. About fifty years later (about 550 B.C.) a second Deuteronomistic editor published the historical records from the creation to 561 B.C. (Genesis-Kings) in a similar spirit, rewriting the Book of Joshua and providing the stories in the Book of Judges with suitable introductions and conclusions, in accordance with his philosophy of history (stated in Judges 2:6 to 3:6). Stories unsuited to his religious teaching (Judges 9: 17–21; II Samuel 9 to 20) were omitted in spite of their superb literary and historical merit (even the Song of Deborah in Judges 5 was omitted). This illustrates the change in literary taste after 600 B.C.: piety prevails over literary excellence. The love for literature of course did not disappear, and these masterpieces not only were preserved but were introduced again into the Bible where we now find them. But the prevailing point of view remained that of the second Deuteronomist; and the author of Chronicles (about 250 B.C.), in his rewriting of the Books of Samuel, omitted entirely its unrivaled prose masterpiece (II Samuel 9, 10), even though he was familiar with it. In fact, nothing illustrates better the changed fashion in literature than a comparison between the most ancient parts of Samuel and I Chronicles. After 600 B.C. and especially after 400 B.C. (when the Pentateuch was canonized), the Jews were concerned with obedience to the divinely inspired Law and disclosed their sense of superiority over the Gentiles based on past achievements (magnified in Chronicles) and future triumphs predicted in apocalyptic oracles. The later parts of the Old Testament clearly illustrate these interests, which did not produce literary masterpieces comparable to those of the golden age before 600 B.C.

TYPES OF LITERATURE IN THE OLD TESTAMENT

Modern scholars have classified Old Testament writings according to their literary genres (*Gattungen* is the German technical term) and have searched for their origin in preliterary oral traditions and in the daily life of the people (or to use the German technical term, in the *Sitz im Leben,* or "place in life"). From this point of view we may classify the Old Testament writings as songs, wisdom, oracles and prayers, narratives, and laws.

Songs. No tribe or people has lacked songs to express the intense feelings of persons, whether love or hatred, joy or sadness. From time immemorial the Hebrews had love songs, whether serenades to the beloved (compare Song of Songs 1:2–4; 2:8–14; 4:8–11) or wedding songs (3:6–11; 6:13 to 7:5; Psalms 45). Riddles were proposed at banquets (Judges 14:14, 18), and a frequent theme of the songs that were sung was, as in Egypt, Greece, and Rome, "Let us eat and drink, for to-morrow we die" (Isaiah 22:13; Wisdom of Solomon 2:6–9; I Corinthians 15:32). Other happy occasions, such as the birth of children, were similarly celebrated in verse. From the blessings of fathers on their sons (Genesis 27:27–29, 39–40) eventually arose the blessings of nations, predicting their achievements (Genesis 9:25–27; 49; Numbers 23, 24; Deuteronomy 33).

Boys' mockeries (II Kings 2:23) were the origin of taunt songs (Isaiah 23:16) and later of sarcastic personifications of nations as immoral women (Isaiah 37:22–29; 47; Ezekiel 16, 23). Likewise the funeral lament (II Samuel 18:33) became first an elegy (II Samuel 1:18–27) and then a dirge over a nation (Amos 5:2; Lamentations 1 to 4).

The Bible preserves two ancient songs about the two basic tribal activities: provision of food and war. They celebrate the digging of a well (Numbers 21:17–18) and the slaying of an enemy in blood revenge (Genesis 4:23–24). From songs like the second of these came eventually the victory song extolling the deity (Exodus 15:21; compare Exodus 15:1–8; Judges 5) or the leader (I Samuel 18:7). Later, numerous Psalms praise the Lord for his achievements in peace and war and extol a king for his triumphs through divine help (Psalm 21); Psalm 110 commemorates Simon Maccabeus on his installation as high priest in 141 B.C., and Psalm 2 celebrates the marriage of Alexander Janneus to Queen Alexandra in 103 B.C. (according to the acrostics in the Hebrew text). These two Psalms and others were interpreted, of course, as prophecies of the coming of the Messiah, in accordance with real Messianic poems (Isaiah 9:2–7; 11:1–9; Micah 4:1–4; 5:2; Zechariah 9:9). Eventually Ecclesiasticus 44 to 49 and Hebrews 11 praised the great religious heroes of the Old Testament.

Wisdom. Popular proverbs are probably as old as songs. Some examples of ancient pithy sayings have been preserved in the Bible: "Let not him that girdeth on his harness boast himself as he that putteth it off" (I Kings 20:11); "What is the chaff to the wheat?" (Jeremiah 23:28); "As is the mother, so is her daughter" (Ezekiel 16:44); "The fathers have eaten sour grapes, and the children's teeth are set on edge" (Jeremiah 31:29; Ezekiel 18:2). Two fables (Judges 9:7–15; II Kings 14:9) ridicule rulers by comparing them to worthless bushes afflicted with megalomania. Nathan's classical parable is preserved in II Samuel 12:14; Isaiah's Song of the Vineyard (Isaiah 5:1–6) is a famous parable in verse; another possible example is the fictitious story told to David by the woman from Tekoa (II Samuel 14:4–7).

From such popular wisdom a special poetic genre developed in Egypt and Mesopotamia and later in Israel. In every one of these cases wisdom was at first purely practical, utilitarian. Knowledge was required for a career in government service, and thus instruction in wisdom was invaluable. Seldom after 586 B.C. could young Judeans hope to attain high positions in the service of Babylonian, Persian, or Hellenistic rulers; nevertheless, some counsels for achieving success in government work still are found in Proverbs. In general, however, the middle class pupils were trained for commercial and agricultural careers; the advice deals chiefly with the acquisition and preservation of wealth, with its best use, with amusements, family life, and friendship (Proverbs, Ecclesiasticus). In harmony however with the general trend in Judaism, this practical counsel becomes more and more pious, until wisdom is identified with the Law of Moses (Ecclesiasticus, Baruch).

An entirely different type of wisdom literature reaches its culmination in the Book of Job. Early philosophical thought grew out of mythological explanations of historical facts. The myths of creation, of the Garden of Eden, of the fight of Yahweh with the dragon of chaos, and of the Tower of Babel explain the origin of the world and of man (constituted of clay and spirit), of man's mortality and misery, of the continued battle in nature between regularity and disorder, and of the variety of languages. On the other hand, legends and sagas explain the subjection of Canaanites and Israelites under the Philistines (Genesis 9:20–27), the volcanic features in the vicinity of the Dead Sea (Genesis 19:24–28), and the rites of the Passover (Exodus 12:21–39). Eventually, the Book of Job attempted to solve a problem that seems destined to baffle forever the ablest thinkers: in view of the presence of evil in the world (notably the misery of the good and the good luck of some evildoers), can God be both omnipotent and just?

Oracles and Prayers. Strictly religious literature consists originally of communications either of the deity to man (oracles) or of man to the deity (prayers). As happened in other types of Hebrew literature, out of oral prophetic oracles developed the written sermon (such as the one attributed to Moses in Deuteronomy 5 to 26; 28) and the apocalyptic revelation; from oral prayers came various types of psalms and hymns.

In ancient Israel the deity communicated with man through dreams, the priestly oracle (*Urim*), and the prophetic inspired speech (I Samuel 28:6). Omens interpreted by professional diviners (such as astrologers) played a secondary role in Israel. From dreams developed the apocalyptic vision (as in Daniel 7). The priestly oracle was based on the interpretation of lots drawn from a sacred box and could only be the answer to a question involving two alternatives, such as "yes or no" or "A or B," that is, the sort of answer obtained by flipping a coin (heads or tails). This oracular procedure played no role in literature and became obsolete in Israel soon after 900 B.C., when prophecy proved much more articulate. In the reign of Ahab (875–853 B.C.), prophets instead of priests gave oracular responses to rulers (I Kings 22:5–28). But it was only with Amos (about 750 B.C.) that the prophetic oracles, in the form of sermons, attained such literary excellence that they began to be preserved in writing for all future generations. The sermon of Moses (Deuteronomy 5 to 26; 28) was written shortly before 621 B.C., under the influence of the prophetic books, and gave rise to the notion of inspired scripture; until then divine revelation had been oral.

Persons in dangers, calamities, and illness appeal for help to their gods. Similarly, nations invoke divine help in war or other trouble. Later than such personal or communal petitions are confessions of sin and songs of thanksgiving (the earliest of which in the Bible is Exodus 15:21). Confessions of sin (like Psalm 51), as in Babylonia, were at first lamentations of individuals seriously ill (Isaiah 38:10–20): these are the sources of national lamentations (Lamentations 1 to 4) and national confessions of sin (Nehemiah 9:6–37; Daniel 9:4–19). The earliest example of a superb literary prayer is found in I Kings 8:23–53 (dated 600 B.C.). About that time the confessions of Jeremiah—outpourings of his agonized

soul before his God—were destined to create in some of the Psalms a mystical sense of communion with God.

Narratives. Thus far we have dealt with three types of poetry. We now come to prose literature, which in most nations comes later than poetry as an art.

In Hebrew literature our modern distinction between fact and fancy, history and story, must be disregarded, for the narratives of Israel's antecedents and history present all gradations from pure fiction (Adam, Noah, and Samson), through legend and saga (Abraham, Isaac, and Jacob), to actual historical writings of the most genuine kind (the biography of David in the old source of the Books of Samuel; the autobiography of Nehemiah). Naturally, the more remote the events are from the narrator, the less historicity can be expected. Except for contemporary historical narratives, imaginary histories of the past, and short stories (Ruth, Jonah, Daniel 1 to 6, Esther), the bulk of Old Testament narrative is based on oral tradition—tales told by storytellers to an audience of shepherds and farmers interested in the plot more than in historicity. Except for Simeon and Levi's unfortunate attack on Shechem (Genesis 34), Israel did not remember anything before Moses, and from Moses to Saul recalled merely events enhancing national pride (Exodus–Judges), describing them with some imaginative details: for instance, the two accounts of the killing of Sisera, the contemporary one (Judges 5:24–27) and a later one (Judges 4:17–21).

Fiction is either primitive philosophy (myth, fable, saga, and legend; see section *Wisdom*) or plain storytelling (fairy tales and short stories). The second type abounds in folkloristic plots (like those of Moses saved in infancy, Exodus 2:1–10; and of Potiphar's wife, Genesis 39:7–20) and discloses vivid Oriental imagination. The stories about Joseph are tales told to an upperclass audience, while those about Samson were enjoyed by shepherds and peasants. Eventually this abundant narrative material was utilized by able literary men in writing the stories in the books from Genesis to Judges. Later some brilliant short stories (Judith, Susanna, Tobit, the Three Youths at the Court of Darius, and others) were written, some with, others without, supernatural features.

Laws. In ancient Israel, civil, religious, and ethical laws were sharply distinguished, as in all ancient civilized nations. Beginning with the Deuteronomic Code found in the Temple in 621 B.C. (Deuteronomy 5 to 26; 28), all three types of law (as may be observed in the Ten Commandments, Deuteronomy 5) are inextricably combined in order to make of Israel a holy nation devoted to Yahweh. It was then that all the laws of Israel came to be regarded as divinely inspired.

But previously, when Israel entered Canaan (about 1200 B.C.), it adopted the civil laws of the country, which now are found, in an Israelitic edition, partly in Exodus 21 to 23 (the Covenant Code) and partly rewritten in scattered sections of Deuteronomy 12 to 26. Like the Code of Hammurabi, king of Babylon (about 1770 B.C.), this code of civil laws has three divisions: Law of Persons, Law of Property, Law of Procedure (in the inverse order in Hammurabi's Code). An ancient ritual decalogue, likewise adopted in Canaan, is preserved in a late edition in Exodus

34 and in a much earlier edition in the Covenant Code (Exodus 23:12a, 15a, 16–17; 22:29b–30a; 23:18–19): the first five laws deal with the religious festivals, and the other five with sacrifices and offerings. This decalogue was utilized by the author of the Deuteronomic Code of 621 B.C., but he deliberately disregarded the ancient code of civil laws except for laws having an ethical implication.

The earliest civil laws are based on custom and have primarily the purpose of preserving the integrity of the tribe or the nation. Religious laws, by prescribing the rites and conduct required by the deity, assured help from the deity in times of danger and thus served the same purpose. Eventually both were joined together with moral and philanthropic prescriptions in the Jewish codes beginning with 621 B.C., so that in Judaism the distinction between ethical and ritual, between criminal and impious, eventually was obliterated in spite of the contrary teaching of Amos and the prophets following him.

The instruction of the priest is called *Torah* (Law); originally it was distinct from legislation based on custom, to which reference was made above. Although most of these prescriptions were derived from immemorial practice (as Leviticus 17 to 26), they might be valid only at individual sanctuaries, rather than for the nation, and were not enforced by the state authorities in the monarchical period. The priests, however, were responsible for collecting and preserving a good part of the Old Testament, and to some extent it is due to them, indirectly, that the whole has been regarded as divine Law (in part through allegorical interpretation).

OLD TESTAMENT LITERATURE OF THE EARLIEST PERIOD (BEFORE 1200 B.C.)

It may be surmised that the Israelites preserved some poems and laws preceding the death of Moses and the invasion of Canaan (about 1200 B.C.).

Poems. The Song of Lamech (Genesis 4:23–24) is addressed to his wives and boasts brutally of his savage excesses in avenging himself: it seems to reflect a Bedouin rather than a Palestinian background. Another desert song extols the digging of a well (Numbers 21:17–18) and may be an early example of a work song. Some of the war songs that are assigned to the time of Moses actually may belong to Israel's nomadic period. The most genuine and most magnificent is the Song of Miriam (Exodus 15:21; expanded several centuries later in Exodus 15:1–18):

> I will sing unto the Lord, for he hath triumphed gloriously: The horse and its rider hath he thrown into the sea.

Everything indicates that this paean of victory was sung antiphonally by the women after Israel safely crossed the Red Sea. An ancient anthology, called *The Book of the Wars of the Lord*, contained a poetic list of localities in Moab that Israel traversed under the leadership of Moses (Numbers 21:14–15, probably a fragment). Another poem (Numbers 21:27–30) laments sarcastically the conquest of Moab and cannot be dated exactly. It is presumably later than the time of Moses, as are the two poems expressing enmity for the Amalekites (Exodus 17:14, 16) and the formulas used when bringing the ark into battle and returning it to its sanctuary (Numbers 10:35–36). Even though these three songs have a nomadic background, they probably

were composed in Canaan two or three centuries after 1200 B.C., in a reminiscent mood.

Laws. Orthodox Jews and many Christians have maintained the traditional views, according to which Moses wrote the whole Pentateuch under divine inspiration. Critical research, however, has proved that the Pentateuch was edited as we have it from 1200 to 400 B.C., utilizing narrative and legal sources of varying dates. Of the various codes embodied in the Pentateuch, the Ten Commandments (Deuteronomy 5:6–21 and Exodus 20:2–17) are attributed by some modern scholars to Moses, except for certain expressions and matters belonging to a later time, clearly unsuited to nomadic conditions. Only one code listing ten capital offenses seems to be ancient Bedouin law of the desert, possibly as early as Moses: the Hebrew text of each of these ten laws is limited to five words, and they all end with the words *moth yumath* (he must be put to death). The following crimes are to be punished with death: murder (Exodus 21:12); smiting father or mother (Exodus 21:15); cursing father or mother (Exodus 21:17); kidnaping (Exodus 21:16); bestiality (Exodus 22:19); necromancy (Leviticus 20:27); blasphemy (Leviticus 24:16); adultery (Leviticus 20:10); incest (Leviticus 20:11 or 20:12); homosexuality (Leviticus 20:13). The other laws in Exodus and Leviticus exhibiting the same formulation are considerably later.

Two other codes seem to have originated about 1200 B.C. or even earlier, but they were adopted by the Israelites from the Canaanites after the settlement in Palestine. A ritual decalogue, found in a late edition with the addition of two additional laws in Exodus 34:17–26, regulated the observance of the Sabbath and of the three annual festivals (five laws: Exodus 23:12a, 15–17) and the presentation of sacrifices and oblations (five laws, Exodus 22:29–30; 23:18–19). The other is an ancient code of civil laws preserved in part in Exodus 21:1 to 22:20 (the bulk of the so-called Covenant Code) and in part in Deuteronomy 15:12–18; 19:16–20; 21:18–21; 22:13–29; 24:1–4, 7; 25:1–3, 5–12. The original code was divided like the Code of Hammurabi into three main parts, but like Roman law it was arranged in the inverse order: (1) Law of Persons (liability [arising from contract and from tort]; the family [inheritance and marriage]); (2) Law of Property (ownership; possession [legal and illegal]); (3) Law of Procedure (false witness; punishment of the offender).

LITERATURE OF THE PERIOD OF THE JUDGES AND OF THE UNITED MONARCHY (ABOUT 1200–950 B.C.)

Poems. The blessing of Noah (Genesis 9:25–27) reflects the early triumphs of the Philistines ("Japheth") over Canaanites ("Ham" or "Canaan") and Israelites ("Shem"), after the Philistines' settlement along the coast soon after 1190 B.C. Israelitic battle and victory hymns are found in Joshua 10:12b–13a; Judges 15:16; I Samuel 18:7. The greatest of them is the superb Song of Deborah (Judges 5; about 1150 B.C.). The riddle of Samson and its solution (Judges 14:14, 18) is earlier than David (about 1000 B.C.), who composed a superb elegy over Saul and Jonathan (II Samuel 1:18–27) and a brief one over Abner (II Samuel 3:33–34). The Blessing of Jacob (Genesis 49) and the earliest oracles of Baalam (Numbers 24:3–9, 15–19) belong to the time of

Solomon (about 950 B.C.). Psalm 24:7–10 may have been sung when Solomon brought the Ark of Shiloh into the newly built Temple of Jerusalem; if so, it is apparently the earliest of the Psalms.

Prose. The masterpiece of Hebrew prose was composed in the time of Solomon, possibly by the priest Ahimaaz, son of Zakok. It is the biography of David contained in the following passages: I Samuel 4:2 to 7:1; 9:1 to 10:16; 10:27b to 11:11; 11:15; 13:2–7a, 15b–18, 23; 14:1–46, 52; 16:14–23; 18:3–9, 20, 22–29a; 19:11–17; 21:1–9; 22:6–23; 23:1, 5–14a; 25:2–44; 26, 27; 29, 30; 28; 31; II Samuel 1 to 5; 21:15–22; 23:8–39; 6; 24; 21:1–14; 9 to 20; I Kings 1; 2:13–46.

It is possible that the early account of mankind's beginning (Genesis 2:5–9, 15–25; 3; 4:1, 17–24; 6:1–4; 9:20–27; 11:1–9) and the legends of Southern Palestine and Transjordania (Genesis 14:1–17, 21–24; 19:1–26, 30–38; 34; 35:5; 35:21–22a; 36:9–39; 38) constituted a separate document dated about 1000–950 B.C.

EPHRAIMITIC (NORTHERN KINGDOM) LITERATURE (950–722 B.C.)

Poetry. The later Oracles of Balaam (Numbers 23:7–10, 18–24) and the Blessing of Moses (Deuteronomy 33) imitate the earlier Balaam oracles and the Blessing of Jacob, respectively, but extol Joseph instead of Judah. For by now North Israel surpassed Judah in power and culture and so continued from the division of the kingdom, at the death of Solomon, to its conquest by Sargon of Assyria in 722 B.C.

Psalm 45 is an *epithalamium* (a nuptial song or poem) written on the occasion of a royal wedding and seems to have been composed for a king of North Israel before 722 B.C.

Narratives. The History of the Kings of Israel, of which some portions have been preserved (I Kings 11:26–28, 40; 12:1–14, 16, 18–20, 25; 20:1–12, 15–21, 23–27, 29–34; 22:1–38; II Kings 3:4–27; 6:24 to 7:20; 9:1 to 10:27; 14:8–14), as well as the stories of Elijah (I Kings 17 to 19; 21), are the prose classics of North Israel. The stories about Elisha (II Kings 2:1 to 8:15; 13:14–21), conversely, do not attain this literary magnificence and were written later, although earlier than 722 B.C.

The so-called Elohistic (E) document of the Pentateuch, running parallel to the J document, was composed presumably by the priests of Bethel about 750 B.C. It is the swan song of North-Israelitic literature. It is best preserved in the Joseph stories, but its masterpiece is the story of the sacrifice of Isaac (Genesis 22:1–13, 19). (These two documents as a rule use two different names for God: *Elohim* in E, *Yahweh* in J. Further, the E Document has been associated with Ephraim, a northern tribe, and J with Judah, the southern tribe.)

Laws. The ten anathemas of Deuteronomy 27: 16–25 (27:15 and 26 are later additions) seem to have originated in the Northern Kingdom in the 9th or 8th century: through them Israel cursed criminals whose malefactions were committed so secretly that only God could punish the evil-doers.

Prophetic Oracles. Amos was a Judean from Tekoa in Judah but preached in the Northern Kingdom, notably at Bethel (Amos 7:10–17) about 750 B.C. He is the first and greatest of the reforming prophets. Soon after him came Hosea, the only Northern Israelite prophet whose book has come down to us. He was active from 745 to 735 B.C. To stress the divine censure of the religious, moral, and political decay of the Northern Kingdom, he gave symbolical names to his children (Hosea 1): Jezreel (Jehu's dynasty would be destroyed as a punishment of his crimes in Jezreel [II Kings 10:11]), Lo-ruhamah (she to whom no mercy is shown), and Lo-ammi (not my people); see Amos 1. By worshiping the Baals of Canaan, Israel had committed adultery against her true spouse, Yahweh; but after a period of seclusion Israel will come to her senses (Hosea 2, 3). Later, however, Hosea seems to have realized that Israel could not mend its ways and would be punished (Hosea 4 to 14).

LITERATURE OF THE KINGDOM OF JUDAH FROM 950 TO 700

Narrative. Next to the biography of David, the J (Yahwistic) document of the Pentateuch and the early parts of Judges are the outstanding prose masterpieces of the Old Testament. The J Document in epic and dramatic style describes the fulfillment of the three divine promises to Abraham (Genesis 12:1–3, 7): "I will make of thee a great nation" (J in Genesis 12 to 33); "in thee shall all families of the earth be blessed" (through Joseph; J in Genesis 37; 39; 41 to 48; 50); "unto thy seed will I give this land" (J from Exodus 2:11 to Judges 1:36). This magnificent pageant of Israel's beginnings, from the call of Abraham to the invasion of Canaan, was written in Jerusalem, probably about 850 B.C.

The early source of the Book of Judges, after chapter 1, which is a late annotated summary of J's account of the invasion in Canaan, consists of the following passages: 3:15–29 (Ehud); 5 (the Song of Deborah); 6 to 8 (in part; Gideon); 9:26–41 (Abimelech); 11–12 (in part; Jephthah); 13 to 16 (Samson); 17, 18 (Micah and the Danites); 19 to 21 (the crusade against the Benjamites). Much of this material may be North Israelitic, like the Song of Deborah.

Prophetic Oracles. The prophet Isaiah of Jerusalem was active during an agitated period of history (about 740–700 B.C.), when Assyria was beginning to conquer western Asia. Following his call (Isaiah 6:1–11), Isaiah reported his part in the Syro-Ephraimitic war (735–734 B.C.) in Isaiah 17:1–11; 7:1 to 8:18. His oracles in chapters 2 to 5 also belong, apparently, to the early period of his ministry; chapter 1 contains oracles from the beginning to the end of his activity. During the last years of the Northern Kingdom (735–722 B.C.), Isaiah inveighed against its upper classes (28:1–4; 5:8, 11, 14, 18–24; 10:1–2) as Amos had done; and he announced the imminence of the divine punishment (9:8–12, 14, 17, 19–21; 10:3–4; 5:25; an oracle inspired by Amos 4:6–12). After the fall of Samaria in 722 B.C., Isaiah denounced Judah (14:28–32; 20:1–6; 18:1–6; 28:7–22; 29:1–5; 30:1–17; 31:1–3) and Shebna, Hezekiah's majordomo (22:15–25). Sennacherib's advance is pictured epically in 5:26–29. During Sennacherib's siege of Jerusalem in 701 B.C., Isaiah's warnings and denunciations did not cease (1:2–9), but later, viewing the ruin of Judah, he wept amidst the celebrations for the deliverance (22:1–14) and denounced Assyria in stirring verse (10:5–9, 13–15).

The Messianic and apocalyptic oracles contained in Isaiah 1 to 39 (1:24–31; 2:2–4 [compare Micah 4:1–4]; 4:2–4; 9:2–7; 11:1 to 12:6; 24 to 27; 32 to 35) and the oracles against foreign nations (13 to 23, except for 22:15–25) belong to the period 550–200 B.C., as does Isaiah 40 to 66.

The prophet Micah of Moresheth near Gath, a younger contemporary of Isaiah, was active under Hezekiah (720–692 B.C.). In contrast with Isaiah, an urban aristocrat, he was, like Amos, a humble peasant (Micah 1:1; Jeremiah 26:17–18), and he announced the coming divine punishment of Samaria and Jerusalem for the exploitation of the lower classes (Micah 1 to 3; the rest of the book is much later).

LITERATURE OF THE 7TH CENTURY

Poetry. The last Judean poetic masterpiece is Nahum's ode celebrating the destruction of Nineveh in 612 B.C. (Nahum 1:11 to 3:19). The poem was composed one or two years before this event.

Narratives. The J and E documents of the Pentateuch were combined about 650 B.C., when parts of the late source of Samuel were written. The first edition of the Books of Kings was published about 600 B.C.

Prophetic Oracles. Jeremiah was active from 626 B.C. to 585 B.C. His book contains his public addresses, his mystical confessions, which inspired many Psalms, his biography, presumably written by his secretary Baruch; and later additions in prose and verse. The prophets Zephaniah and Habakkuk (Habakkuk 1, 2) were his contemporaries. In 621 B.C. the Book of the Law of Moses (most of Deuteronomy 5 to 26, 28), written shortly before, was found in the Temple at Jerusalem (II Kings 22, 23): in reality this book is not a code of laws but a long sermon attributed to Moses. The Ten Commandments (Deuteronomy 5:6–21, and, in a later edition, Exodus 20:2–17) probably were compiled by the author of this book.

Wisdom. The earliest parts of Proverbs (such as Proverbs 25 to 27) probably originated in the 7th century. The Book of Job (omitting Job 1:1 to 2:10; 32 to 37; 40:15 to 41:34; 42:10b–17) is unsurpassed for the magnificence of its poetry and the depth of its thought. The most plausible dates suggested for its composition are within the period 600–400 B.C. Some of the most beautiful Psalms (such as Psalm 104) seem to belong, with Nahum and Job, to the end of the golden period of Hebrew literature (about 600 B.C.).

LITERATURE OF THE 6TH CENTURY

Poetry. Lamentations contains elegies on the destruction of Jerusalem by Nebuchadnezzar in 586. The four dirges in chapters 1 to 4 are alphabetic acrostics: 2 and 4 seem to have been written by eyewitnesses of that catastrophe, 1 and 3 are later. Lamentations 5 is a Psalm: the poet laments the ruin of the Temple and prays for its restoration. Some Psalms and Proverbs were composed in this century.

Narratives. About 550 B.C. the Deuteronomistic editor published the combined JE narratives of the Pentateuch, added Deuteronomy to them, extensively rewrote Joshua, edited Judges, changed little (aside from omissions) in Samuel, and issued a second edition of Kings, bringing its history down to 561 B.C. (he wrote before Cyrus conquered Babylon in 538 B.C.).

Laws. The so-called Holiness Code (H) in Leviticus 17 to 26 is, like the Deuteronomic Code, a sermon of Moses. It embodies 7th century ritual laws (also cited by Ezekiel), civil laws, and moral precepts but presents them all in hortatory form. It usually is dated by scholars about 550 B.C.

Prophetic Oracles. Ezekiel's oracles are dated in his book 592 to 570 B.C. He was exiled to Babylonia in 597, but from 593 to 587 he was active in Jerusalem, returning to Babylonia before the destruction of Jerusalem in 586. Before 587, in Jerusalem, he denounced the people and proclaimed their doom; later, in Babylonia, he comforted the dismayed Exiles. In a different way the unknown author of Isaiah 40 to 55 (known as the Second Isaiah) brought encouragement to the Exiles shortly before 538, when Cyrus conquered Babylon; his enthusiastic verses predict a glorious future. Haggai in 520 B.C. and Zechariah (chapters 1 to 8) in 520–518 exhorted the people to rebuild the Temple in Jerusalem (completed in 516). Micah 6:1 to 7:6 probably was written near the end of the 6th century.

LITERATURE OF THE 5TH CENTURY

Poetry. The latest poems of the Pentateuch are the Song of Moses (Deuteronomy 32), reflecting the depressed state of mind of the Jews during the first half of the 5th century; the paraphrase of the ancient song of Miriam at the Red Sea (Exodus 15:1–18), a little later in date; and the Psalm in which the Blessing of Moses is enclosed (Deuteronomy 33:2–5, 26–29) probably to be dated 450–400 B.C. We do not know how many Psalms and Proverbs were composed in this century.

Narratives. The best historical source of this period is Nehemiah's report of his activity in Jerusalem in 444 B.C. (1, 2; 4:1 to 19) and in 432 (13). The best short story is the Book of Ruth.

Laws. The Priestly Code (P) beginning in Genesis 1 and ending in Joshua 13 to 22 dates from about 450 B.C. It consists partly of a dogmatic Utopian history of the holy Congregation of Israel, from the creation of the world to the distribution of the Land of Canaan to the twelve tribes; and partly of ritual laws (Exodus 25 to 31; all of Leviticus [including earlier codes]; and parts of Numbers). The whole Pentateuch was canonized about 400 B.C.

Prophetic Oracles. Aside from additions to Isaiah 1 to 39 and Jeremiah, we may date in the 5th century III Isaiah (that is, Isaiah 56 to 66), Obadiah, and Malachi.

LITERATURE OF THE 4TH CENTURY

Poetry. Many Psalms and Proverbs, Job 32 to 37, Nahum 1:1–9, Habakkuk 3, I Samuel 2:1–10, and other poems belong to this period.

Narrative. The best known is the Book of Jonah, which many scholars regard as an allegory designed to teach the mission of Israel to all mankind.

Prophetic and Apocalyptic Oracles. Joel and presumably many of the Messianic prophecies found in the books of the prophets originated shortly before or after the conquests of Alexander the Great (334–331 B.C.).

LITERATURE OF THE 3D CENTURY

Poems. Aside from many Psalms and Proverbs, we may date the charming love poetry of the Song of Songs—in its present form—in the 3d century, although some of the poems may be much earlier.

Narratives. The great work of the Chronicler in four volumes (I–II Chronicles, Ezra, Nehemiah) was issued about the middle of the century; it is a doctrinal and imaginative history of the Jewish Congregation, in the spirit of the Priestly Code, from Adam to Nehemiah, omitting the "heretical" Northern Kingdom of Israel.

Apocalyptic Oracles. All four volumes of the Prophets (Isaiah, Jeremiah, Ezekiel and the Twelve) before they were canonized about 200 B.C. were supplemented with revelations of a glorious future for the Jews: Isaiah 24 to 27 and Zechariah 9 to 14 are the best examples of 3d century apocalypses.

LITERATURE OF THE 2D CENTURY

Poetry. Some Psalms (44; 74; 79; 83; and others were written during the Maccabean rebellion (168–141 B.C.). Others are even later: Psalm 110 (having the acrostic "Simeon") celebrates the appointment of Simon Maccabeus as high priest; Psalm 2 (having the acrostic "For Janneus A. and his wife") celebrates the marriage of Alexander Janneus to Queen Alexandra in 103 B.C. The final edition of the Psalter is dated about 100 B.C.

Wisdom. Ecclesiastes—a skeptical essay annotated in a pious vein—belongs probably to the middle of the 2d century, although some date it a century or two earlier.

Narrative. If the Book of Daniel is a unit, it was written in 165 B.C., but some scholars, without compelling reasons, date the narrative chapters (1 to 6) 250 B.C. Esther probably was written about 125 B.C. It often is dated more than a century earlier, but the passionate hostility between Jews and Gentiles in Esther is unknown before 168 B.C.

Apocalypse. The first and greatest real apocalypse or revelation of the events at the end of time is Daniel 7 to 12, dated 165 B.C. Daniel 2:4b to 7:28 is written in Aramaic instead of Hebrew, as is Ezra 4:8 to 6:18; 7:12–26.

THE APOCRYPHA

The books contained in the Greek Bible (called the Septuagint) but lacking in the Hebrew Bible and II or IV Esdras, which is included in the Latin Bible (the Vulgate), are recognized as canonical by the Roman Catholic Church and in part by the Greek Orthodox Church, but not by the Jews (even though they were written by Jews). Roman Catholics call these books "deuterocanonical," while Protestants call them "the Apocrypha." Except for II or IV Esdras (about 90 A.D.), the Apocrypha date from the last two centuries before Christ. The extant Greek text (Latin translated from the Greek for II or IV Esdras) of these books either is the original or a translation from Hebrew or Aramaic: in other words, they are either Palestinian or Alexandrian (Greek) writings. See also APOCRYPHA.

Palestinian Apocrypha Written in Hebrew—Written from 200 to 100 B.C. *Psalms:* Ecclesiasticus 39:12–35; 42:15 to 43:33; 51:1–12 (in the Hebrew text also the liturgy following 51:12); Tobit 13; Judith 16; Baruch 3:9 to 4:4. *Wisdom Literature in Verse:* Ecclesiasticus; Baruch 3:9 to 4:4. *History of the Jews in the Persian Period:* I or III Esdras. *History of the Jews from 332 to*

135 B.C.: I Maccabees. *Fiction:* Judith. *Legends:* Baruch 1:1 to 3:8.

Written from 100 to 1 B.C. *A Penitential Psalm:* The Prayer of Manasses. *History:* A (lost) life of John Hyrcanus (135–104 B.C.) is mentioned in I Maccabees (16:23–24).

Palestinian Apocrypha Written in Aramaic—Written from 200 to 100 B.C. *Fiction:* Tobit; Susanna; Bel and the Dragon; the Additions to Esther (except 11:1; 13:1–7; 16:1–24, which were composed in Greek); the Story of the Three Youths in I or III Esdras 3:1 to 4:63 probably was written in Aramaic long before 200 B.C. and is therefore earlier than I or III Esdras and even earlier than Chronicles. *Legends:* II Maccabees 1:1 to 2:18 (letters written from Palestine to the Jews in Egypt in 123 and 164 B.C., to urge them to observe the Feast of Dedication, celebrating the rededication of the Temple by Judas Maccabeus in 165 or 164 B.C.). *Wisdom:* Tobit 4:3–21; 12:6–10.

Written from 100 to 1 B.C. The Epistle of Jeremy (a tract ridiculing Babylonian idolatry).

Written About 90 A.D. II or IV Esdras 3 to 13 (six apocalyptic visions). Chapter 14 (Esdras restored the 24 books of the Hebrew Bible and 70 esoteric apocalyptic books) and chapters 1, 2 and 15, 16 were later Christian additions.

Alexandrian Apocrypha (written in Greek)—Written Between 100 and 50 B.C. The Wisdom of Solomon is a diatribe or popular address intended to revive the religion of wealthy indifferent Jews (1 to 5), encourage the afflicted pious Jews (10 to 12; 16 to 19), prove to the heathen the truth of Judaism (6 to 9) and the folly of idolatry (13 to 15).

Written Between 75 and 1 B.C. II Maccabees 2:18 to 15:39 is a legendary history of the Jews from 175 to 161 B.C., summarizing the five-volume history of Jason of Cyrene.

THE PSEUDEPIGRAPHA

These are books written by Jews between 200 B.C. and 100 A.D. that have been preserved by Christians in Oriental translations (Ethiopic, Syriac, Armenian, and others) and occasionally in Greek and Latin.

Palestinian Books Written in Hebrew—Written in 200–100 B.C. The Testaments of the Twelve Patriarchs contain legends, moral precepts, and apocalyptic hopes that the twelve patriarchs allegedly uttered to their descendants before their death.

Written about 40 B.C. The Psalms of Solomon.

Written in 1–100 A.D. The (legendary) Lives of the Prophets.

Palestinian Books Written in Aramaic—Written in 200–1 B.C. The Book of Jubilees (a legendary paraphrase of Genesis 1 to Exodus 12); the Testament of Job (legends); the Book of Enoch (mostly apocalypse).

Written in 1–100 A.D. Legends with Christian additions: the Martyrdom of Isaiah, the Paralipomena of Jeremiah, the Life of Adam and Eve (also called the Apocalypse of Moses). Apocalypses: Assumption of Moses, Syriac Baruch, Apocalypse of Abraham.

Alexandrian Books Written in Greek—Written in 200–75 B.C. Jewish propaganda ascribed to Gentiles: The Letter of Aristeas to Philocrates (Pseudo-Aristeas), which gives a legendary account of the translation of the Pentateuch into Greek (about 250 B.C.); Sibylline Oracles 3:97–808.

Written in 75–1 B.C. III Maccabees reports

the divine deliverance of the Egyptian Jews from a death sentence: it is entirely legendary.

Written in 1–100 A.D. IV Maccabees (a philosophical and historical demonstration of the Stoic statement: devout reason is master of the passions). Slavic Enoch and Greek Baruch are apocalypses containing Christian additions.

ROBERT H. PFEIFFER, *Harvard University*

Bibliography

Bentzen, Aage, *Introduction to the Old Testament* (Copenhagen 1948).

Bewer, J.A., *The Literature of the Old Testament in Its Historical Development*, 3d. ed., rev. by E.G. Kraeling (New York 1962).

Charles, R.H., ed., The *Apocrypha and Pseudepigrapha in English* (Oxford 1913).

Eissfeldt, Otto, *The Old Testament, an Introduction* (New York 1965).

Goodspeed, Edgar J., *The Story of the Apocrypha* (Chicago 1939).

Metzger, Bruce M., *An Introduction to the Apocrypha* (New York 1957).

Oesterley, W.O.E., *An Introduction to the Books of the Apocrypha* (London 1935).

Pfeiffer, Robert H., *History of New Testament Times, with an Introduction to the Apocrypha* (New York 1949).

Pfeiffer, Robert H., *Introduction to the Old Testament* (New York 1941).

Torrey, Charles C., *The Apocryphal Literature* (New Haven 1945).

For Specialized Study

Hempel, J., *Die althebräische Literatur und ihr hellenisch-jüdisches Nachleben* (Potsdam 1930).

Leslau, Wolf, *Falasha Anthology*, Yale Judaica Series, vol. 6. (New Haven 1951).

Lods, A., *Histoire de la littérature hébraïque et juive* (Paris 1950).

Schürer, E., *A History of the Jewish People in the Time of Jesus Christ*, 5 vols. (Edinburgh 1885–90).

6. Old Testament History Including Archaeology and Chronology

As late as the middle of the 19th century our knowledge of Old Testament history was limited almost entirely to information supplied by the Old Testament itself. A very little was furnished by the remains of histories of the Orient in Greek, chiefly preserved for us by the Jewish historian Josephus. Then came illustrative finds in Egypt and Assyria, followed by a rapid increase in the recovery of ancient objects and written documents in all the lands surrounding Palestine. At first the finds were scattered and often fragmentary; then, as gaps were filled, they began to form continuous patterns. By 1930 this archaeological material was so well organized and interpreted that it became a major factor in the reconstruction of Israelite history. After 1930 every year saw steady progress toward the goal of understanding the background of Biblical history as fully as possible. Even the six war years (1939 to 1945) showed notable advances both in excavation and in the study of previous results. Independent research by Europeans and Americans had made unexpected gains, which were rapidly consolidated in the postwar years.

ARCHAEOLOGY

For our present purpose archaeological data may be classified roughly as consisting of written and unwritten materials. Since the Old Testament consists of written documents, contemporary inscriptions naturally throw the most direct light on it. However, basic archaeology has become more and more important for reconstruction of cultural history and chronology of historical events, as well as for interpretation of details in our ancient narratives. It is impossible to make a clear separation between basic archaeology and the chronology of culture.

Written Documents. Most important under this heading are the tablets and other inscriptions written in Akkadian (Assyro-Babylonian) and Persian cuneiform characters. Many of the hundreds of thousands of available documents antedate Patriarchal times and hence come only indirectly into the picture for us. However, even such early written texts as these contain a great mass of useful background information. To the Patriarchal Age belong over 5,000 tablets from the early Assyrian merchant colonies that were established in Cappadocia in the 19th and early 18th centuries B.C., more than twice as many from the old Amorite capital of Mari on the Middle Euphrates (late 18th century B.C.), and tens of thousands of Babylonian tablets from the general period of the 1st Dynasty of Babylon (about 1800–1500 B.C.). Closely related to these groups of documents are several thousand tablets from Nuzu (or Nuzi) in southeastern Assyria east of the Tigris, dating from the 15th century B.C., after the end of the Patriarchal Age in the strict sense. The great importance of these bodies of documents lies particularly in the light they shed on the history and culture of the Patriarchs, as well as on the background of the legal institutions of early Israel. From the following period (about 1450–1200 B.C.) come a mass of tablets from Egypt (the Amarna Tablets), Palestine, Syria (especially from Ugarit, Qatna, and Alalakh), and the Hittite capital at Boghazköy in Asia Minor. These documents illuminate the background of the struggle between Canaan and Israel before, during, and after the time of Moses. Assyrian tablets and stone monuments from the period 900–600 B.C. have been unearthed in great abundance since 1843; they enable us to restore the history of Assyria and its relations with Syria-Palestine in exact chronological and military detail. The great library of Ashurbanipal (Sardanapalus) at Nineveh has yielded a wealth of literary documents and official letters; subsequent excavations at other Assyrian capitals, especially at Khorsabad (Dur Sharrukin), Nimrud (Calah), Assur, and Harran, have greatly increased our literary and historical documentation. Babylonian tablets from the Chaldaean and Persian periods (about 625–330 B.C.) provide us with rich material bearing on this period of history, although the annals of Nebuchadnezzar have not been recovered. And finally, we have in the stone and clay records of the kings of Persia (539–330 B.C.) valuable evidence for the political history of the period.

Second in value for our purposes are the Egyptian inscriptions, both hieroglyphic texts on stone and hieratic texts on papyrus and ostraca (shards of pottery inscribed in ink). Here again a very considerable part of our material antedates the Patriarchal Age but is valuable for background purposes. Of special significance for us are the inscribed reliefs of the Middle Kingdom (about 2000–1800 B.C.), which shed great light on the material culture of the early Patriarchal Age. Then there are the so-called Execration Texts, which list scores of places and chieftains in Palestine and southern Syria between 1925 and 1825 B.C., enabling us to distinguish between occupied towns and nomadic tribes. Among literary texts of this period we note especially the story of Sinuhe, now known to give a faithful picture of conditions of life in Syria and Palestine in the 20th century B.C. From the New Kingdom (18th–20th dynasties, about 1570–1150 B.C.) we have inscriptions celebrating the vic-

PHYSICAL MAP OF THE HOLY LAND

Copyright by C. S. HAMMOND & CO., N.Y.

Scale of Miles

0 5 10 20 30 40

Perennial Rivers   Seasonal Rivers and Streams

Elevations in feet.

Modern Arabic names are underlined.

ALTITUDES IN FEET

5000	
3000	
2000	
1000	
500	

Sea   Level

| 600 | −500 |
| | −1000 |

Mediterranean Sea
(The Great Sea)

The coast of the Holy Land is very
regular south of Carmel. Only the
coastal cities of Phoenicia had the
advantage of natural harbors.

The Jordan Valley is
the northern end of the
Great Rift Valley which
extends over 3000 miles to
Lake Nyasa in southern
Africa.

The Dead Sea shore is the
earth's lowest point of land —
1292 feet below sea level. The
maximum depth of the Dead Sea
is 1300 feet below the level of
the shore.

The annual rainfall of the Holy
Land varies from under 5 inches in
the Negeb to over 40 inches in the
mountains of Lebanon.

PHOENICIA

MOUNT LEBANON

Sidon

Damascus

Tyre

Dan

UPPER

GALILEE

BASHAN

Lake Hula
(L. Semechonitis)

Accho

3963

LOWER
GALILEE

Sea of Galilee
(Chinnereth)

Nazareth

Mt. Tabor
1929

H a u r a n

Plain of
Esdraelon or
Jezreel

Hill of
Moreh

Dor

MT. CARMEL

1732

Shihor-libnath

Mt. Gilboa
1630

Beth-shan

Caesarea

Plain of Sharon

SAMARIA

GILEAD

Samaria

Mt. Ebal
3084

El Ghor

Kanah

Shechem

Mt. Gerizim
2890

Jebel Yusha'
3852

EPHRAIM

Joppa

Jabbok R.

Zerqa

Tell Asur
3333

Rabbath-ammon

AMMON

Aijalon

Jericho

Jerusalem

Mt. of Olives
2680

Plain of
Moab

Mt. Nebo
2631

Bethlehem

Sorek

D E S E R T

Dead
(Salt)
Sea

Elah

Plain of Philistia

Shephelah

JUDAEA

3514

Gaza

Hebron

Arnon R. (W. el Mujib)

Gerar

Wilderness of Judah

M O A B

Raphia

Besor

Beer-sheba

Kir-moab

IDUMAEA

River of Egypt

N e g e b

Ascent of
Akrabbim

Wilderness of
Zin

E D O M

MT. SEIR

Arabah

Jebel Helal
2926

Kadesh-barnea

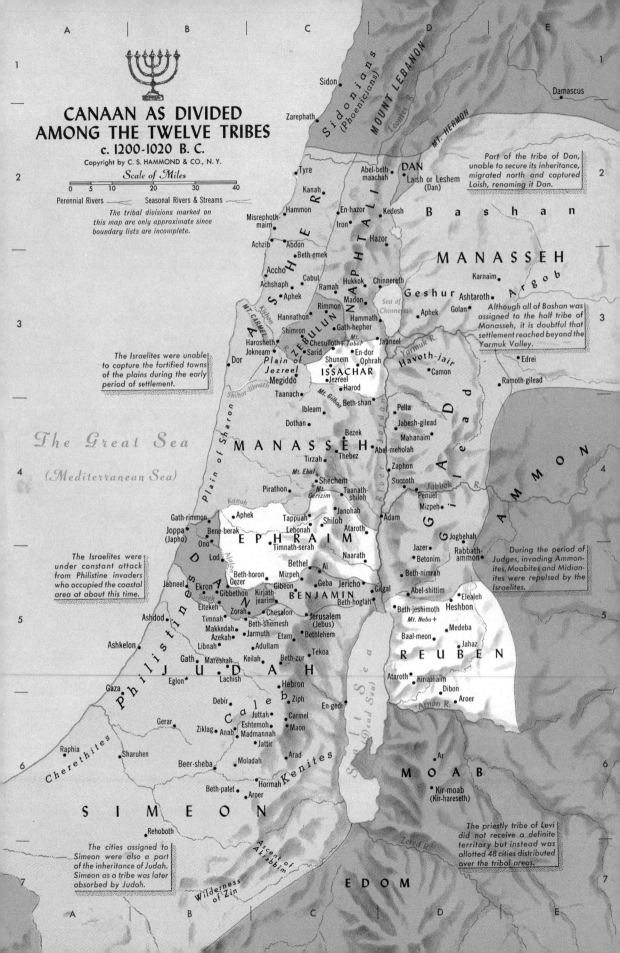

CANAAN AS DIVIDED AMONG THE TWELVE TRIBES
c. 1200-1020 B.C.

Copyright by C. S. HAMMOND & CO., N.Y.

Scale of Miles

0 5 10 20 30 40

Perennial Rivers ——— Seasonal Rivers & Streams

The tribal divisions marked on this map are only approximate since boundary lists are incomplete.

Part of the tribe of Dan, unable to secure its inheritance, migrated north and captured Laish, renaming it Dan.

Although all of Bashan was assigned to the half tribe of Manasseh, it is doubtful that settlement reached beyond the Yarmuk Valley.

The Israelites were unable to capture the fortified towns of the plains during the early period of settlement.

During the period of Judges, invading Ammonites, Moabites and Midianites were repulsed by the Israelites.

The Israelites were under constant attack from Philistine invaders who occupied the coastal area at about this time.

The cities assigned to Simeon were also a part of the inheritance of Judah. Simeon as a tribe was later absorbed by Judah.

The priestly tribe of Levi did not receive a definite territory but instead was allotted 48 cities distributed over the tribal areas.

The Great Sea
(Mediterranean Sea)

DAN

Sidon
Damascus
Zarephath
Sidonians (Phoenicians)
MOUNT LEBANON
Leontes R.
MT. HERMON

Tyre
Abel-beth-maachah
DAN
Laish or Leshem (Dan)
Bashan
MANASSEH

Kanah
En-hazor
Kedesh
Karnaim

Hammon
Iron
Hazor
Geshur
Ashtaroth
Argob

Misrephoth-maim
Achzib
Abdon
Hukkok
Chinnereth
Aphek
Golan

Beth-emek
Ramah
Madon
Sea of Chinnereth

Accho
Cabul
Rimmon
Hammath
Edrei

Achshaph
Aphek
Hannathon
Gath-hepher
Jabneel
Yarmuk R.

Shimron
Chesulloth
Mt. Tabor
Havoth-jair
Ramoth-gilead

Harosheth
Sarid
Shunem
En-dor
Ophrah

Jokneam
Plain of Jezreel
ISSACHAR
Jezreel
Camon

Dor
Megiddo
Harod

Shihor-libnath
Taanach
Mt. Gilboa
Beth-shan

Ibleam
Bezek
Pella

Dothan
Thebez
Jabesh-gilead
Mahanaim

MANASSEH
Abel-meholah

Tirzah
Zaphon

Mt. Ebal
Shechem
Succoth
Jabbok R.

Pirathon
Mt. Gerizim
Taanath-shiloh
Penuel
Mizpeh

Plain of Sharon
Kanah
Janohah
Adam

Gath-rimmon
Aphek
Tappuah
Shiloh
Ataroth

Joppa (Japho)
Bene-berak
Lebonah
Jazer
Betonim
Rabbath-ammon

Ono
Lod
Timnath-serah
EPHRAIM
Naarath
Jogbehah

Bethel
Beth-nimrah

Beth-horon
Mizpeh
Ai
Geba
Jericho

Ekron
Gezer
Gibeon
Jerusalem (Jebus)
Gilgal
Abel-shittim

Jabneel
Gibbethon
Kirjath-jearim
BENJAMIN
Beth-hoglah
Beth-jeshimoth
Elealeh
Heshbon

Eltekeh
Zorah
Chesalon
Mt. Nebo
Medeba

Ashdod
Timnah
Jarmuth
Jerusalem
Bethlehem
Baal-meon
Jahaz

Makkedah
Azekah
Etam
REUBEN

Ashkelon
Libnah
Adullam
Tekoa
Ataroth
Kirialhaim
Dibon

Gath
Mareshah
Keilah
Beth-zur
Aroer

Eglon
Lachish
Hebron
Arnon R.

Gaza
Debir
Ziph
En-gedi

Gerar
Juttah
Carmel
Ar

Raphia
Ziklag
Anab
Eshtemoh
Madmannah
Maon
Kir-moab (Kir-hareseth)

Sharuhen
Jattir
Arad
MOAB

Beer-sheba
Moladah
Kenites

Beth-palet
Hormah
Aroer
Salt Sea (Dead Sea)

SIMEON
Rehoboth
Zered R.

JUDAH
Caleb

Philistines
Cherethites

Ascent of Akrabbim

Wilderness of Zin

EDOM

THE KINGDOMS OF ISRAEL AND JUDAH
c. 925-842 B.C.

Copyright by C. S. HAMMOND & CO., N.Y.

Scale of Miles

0 5 10 20 30 40

Perennial Rivers ....
Seasonal Rivers & Streams ....
Capitals ....
Egyptian & Syrian Attacks ⟶

Elijah took refuge in Zarephath and brought back to life the widow's son.

In the reign of Baasha the cities of northern Israel were raided by the King of Damascus in league with Asa, King of Judah.

Aram waged almost constant war against Israel. The Syrians were held in check by Ahab until his death in battle at Ramoth-gilead.

Elijah challenged the prophets of Baal at Mt. Carmel.

The introduction of Phoenician cults following the marriage of Ahab with Jezebel caused violent reactions in Israel that eventually wiped out the house of Omri.

Samaria, fortress capital of Israel was built by Omri c. 870 B.C.

Moab was ruled as a vassal kingdom during the Omri dynasty. The Dibon stele commemorates the victory of Mesha, King of Moab, over Israel and the return of Moabite independence.

Shishak (Sheshonk), Egyptian Pharaoh, raided the divided kingdoms, plundering Jerusalem c. 925 B.C.

During the reign of Jehosophat Judah regained control over Edom.

The Great Sea
(Mediterranean Sea)

PHOENICIA
MOUNT LEBANON
MT. HERMON
Damascus
Abana R.
Leontes R.

ISRAEL
GESHUR
Bashan
GILEAD
Havoth-jair
AMMON
MOAB
EDOM
JUDAH
PHILISTIA

Sidon
Zarephath
Tyre
Ijon
Abel-beth-maachah
Dan
Kedesh
Hazor
Accho
Cabul
Chinnereth
Sea of Chinnereth
Aphek
Karnaim
Ashtaroth
Edrei
Ramoth-gilead

MT. CARMEL
Kishon R.
Dor
Megiddo
Taanach
Plain of Jezreel
Mt. Tabor
Shunem
Jezreel
Beth-shan
Hammath
Plain of Sharon
Ibleam
Dothan
Jabesh-gilead
Tishbe
Mahanaim
Sochoh
Abel-meholah
Samaria
Mt. Ebal
Tirzah
Shechem
Mt. Gerizim
Penuel
Janohah
Aphek
Shiloh
River Jordan
Jabbok R.
Yarmuk R.
Joppa
Jeshanah
Zemaraim
Bethel
Rabbath-ammon
Lod
Beth-horon
Mizpeh
Geba
Jericho
Jabneel
Gezer
Aijalon
Ramah
Gilgal
Cherith R.
Ekron
Gibbethon
Ashdod
Timnah
Zorah
Jerusalem
Elealeh
Heshbon
Ashkelon
Azekah
Beth-shemesh
Bethlehem
Mt. Nebo
Medeba
Gath
Shoco
Etam
Tekoa
Baal-meon
Jahaz
Libnah
Adullam
Mareshah
Beth-zur
Ataroth
Gaza
Lachish
Hebron
Dibon
Adoraim
Ziph
Aroer
Debir
En-gedi
Arnon R.
Gerar
Salt Sea (Dead Sea)
Ar
Ziklag
Raphia
Kir-moab (Kir-haresheth)
Beer-sheba
Wilderness of Judah
Valley of Salt
Zered R.

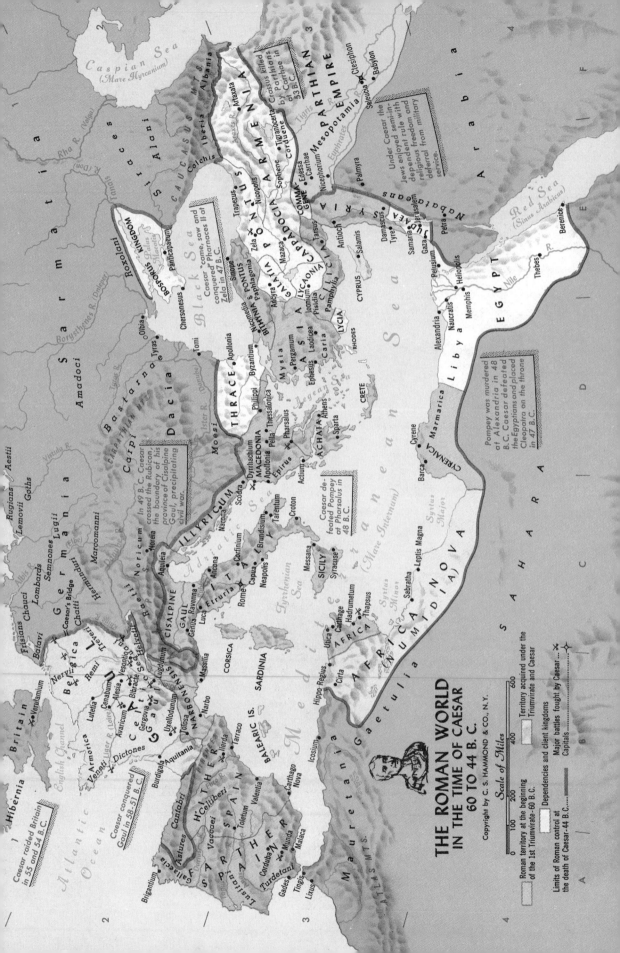

THE ROMAN WORLD
IN THE TIME OF CAESAR
60 TO 44 B.C.

Copyright by C. S. HAMMOND & CO., N.Y.

Scale of Miles

0   100   200   300   400   500   600

Roman territory at the beginning
of the 1st Triumvirate-60 B.C.

Territory acquired under the
Triumvirate and Caesar

Dependencies and client kingdoms

Limits of Roman control at
the death of Caesar-44 B.C.

Major battles fought by Caesar

Capitals:

tories of Pharaoh, often accompanied by lists of conquered places. We also have elaborate series of reliefs, generally with accompanying labels, portraying details of the wars with the Asians and later with the Philistines. Hieratic texts on papyrus and ostraca furnish a mass of supplementary information, thanks to which our knowledge of the background of the Mosaic Age is unusually complete. The fortunes and the cultures of Egypt and its Asian provinces were closely interwoven during these four centuries. Thus almost everything found in Egypt that came from these provinces possesses indirect, if not direct, background value. The following centuries have less to offer. Most significant is the Report of Wenamun, dating from about 1060 B.C. and giving a vivid picture of conditions along the coasts of Palestine and Phoenicia shortly before the Philistine triumph over Israel. A century and a half later comes the Shishak List of towns of Judah, Edom, and Israel taken by that king. The tombs of many Egyptian rulers of the period immediately preceding and following Shishak, discovered at Tanis after 1935, throw light on the history of the period. Later Egyptian records are much less satisfactory for the historian, but they provide a useful chronological skeleton.

The importance of early Northwest Semitic inscriptions (from about 2000 to about 550 B.C.) has been increasing very rapidly since 1930. Earliest in time are probably the still undeciphered inscriptions on copper and stone from Byblos in Phoenicia. Next come the partially deciphered proto-Sinaitic inscriptions from the 15th century B.C., written in the oldest form of our own alphabet yet known. To the next century belong most of the Ugaritic tablets from Ras Shamrah, inscribed in a cuneiform alphabet. These tablets, in a dialect closely related to parent Canaanite and Hebrew, contain a large portion of the lost religious and mythological literature of Canaan before the Israelite conquest of Palestine. We have a very few Canaanite inscriptions in our linear alphabet from Palestine, dating chiefly from the 13th century B.C.; their script passes directly into the oldest known Phoenician, from 10th century Byblos. To the latter century belong virtually all the early inscriptions yet recovered from Phoenicia proper; best known is the inscription on the stone coffin of Akhiram, king of Byblos. Only a few Phoenician inscriptions were known from the four following centuries until the discovery in 1945 of the Karatepe bilinguals (Hittite and Phoenician). The yield of Aramaic and other non-Phoenician inscriptions from Syria has been considerably larger and includes inscriptions of kings of Damascus, Hamath, Arpad, and of several kings of Sham'al, all throwing light on the period of the Divided Monarchy in Israel. Most interesting of all is the Moabite Stone, inscribed by Mesha, king of Moab, about 830 B.C., to celebrate his triumph over Israel. Israelite inscriptions in Biblical Hebrew are still rare, but their number slowly increases; most important are the Gezer Calendar (about 925 B.C.), the Ostraca of Samaria (about 775 B.C.), the Siloam Inscription (about 700 B.C.), and the Lachish Ostraca (about 589 B.C.). Owing to their first hand testimony to script, spelling, and language, they are of great value to Old Testament scholars.

For the postexilic period of Old Testament history we have a wealth of documentation in the Aramaic papyri and ostraca from Egypt, mostly from a Jewish colony on the island of Elephantine at the southern boundary of Egypt proper. Nearly all these documents date from the 5th century B.C. After two major publications in 1906 and 1911 had made a large number of valuable documents available to scholars, a considerable number of new finds were made, including valuable papyri collected by the Brooklyn Museum and two groups of papyri and leather rolls from other parts of Egypt. The amount of available Aramaic material from Egypt alone is several times the total of all other written documents in Northwest Semitic before the Macedonian conquest (330 B.C.).

Although the written material listed above includes practically everything of direct value, there are other groups of inscriptions that are beginning to throw light on Old Testament history: the Hittite hieroglyphic texts from Asia Minor and Syria, and the South Arabian and Proto-Arabic inscriptions from the Arabian Peninsula. The Hittite inscriptions are in the process of being interpreted, following the publication of the Hittite part of the Karatepe bilinguals since 1948; they date chiefly from 1000 to 700 B.C. Both South Arabian and Proto-Arabic inscriptions span most of the last millennium B.C.; the former go back to at least 1000 B.C., and the latter to at least 700 B.C. Thanks to the results of the American Foundation excavations in South Arabia since 1950, it is possible to fix the dates of inscriptions and other cultural remains within narrow limits, after a century of confusion following the decipherment of the South Arabian inscriptions.

Unwritten Sources. Increasing amounts of information on Old Testament history come from archaeological studies of other than written records. The Middle East is unique in the antiquity of its settled cultures, illustrated by many thousands of flat mounds with sloping sides—low truncated cones—that are found from the Balkans to South Arabia and from central Asia to Nubia. The Arabs call a mound of this type a "tell," carrying on a word already used in the Hebrew Bible and familiar to the Babylonians as early as the third millennium. Their characteristic shape is due to the fact that each represents an accumulation of successive layers of human occupation, protected from being washed or blown completely away by the substructures of the fortress or town walls within which they were built. Careful excavation of these mounds yields a whole series of superimposed strata, each with its own distinctive remains. Sometimes a single layer reflects a culture that is not found above or below it in the mound. More often we find that two or more adjacent strata reflect a single cultural period, with little change in civilization between them. There may be gaps of centuries—even of millenniums—in a mound. When all types of artifacts (objects of human manufacture), especially all forms of pottery, belonging to one clearly defined layer are sorted and classified, they may be compared with similar objects from a well-defined stratum in another mound in the same region. In this way, stratigraphy (the science of digging and defining strata) is supplemented by typology (the science of comparing classified objects made by human hand). In combination the two methods yield a relative chronology valid over entire geographical areas and applicable, with appropriate caution, to the whole Middle East. Thanks to the help provided by written documents, it has become possible to date archaeological periods and sub-periods or phases back into the late fourth millennium B.C., with a maximum variation of some two or three centuries. Radiocarbon (carbon isotope 14) dating came into use in 1948 and provided independently determined dates for archaeological materials of organic origin. The radiocarbon dates and the dates worked out by older methods agree strikingly within their respective limits of reliability.

Once dates have been fixed within broad limits by the combination of stratigraphy and typology that we have described, it becomes possible to date assemblages of objects from the same cultural phase within still narrower limits by "sequence dating," a method introduced by Flinders Petrie in 1902. In sequence dating, each type of pottery or other artifact is analyzed with a view to determining its relative place in the evolution of the type in question. For example, a tomb group from the Late Bronze Age (the Mosaic Age) can be assigned to one of a number of different phases within this broad period of some four centuries (16th–12th centuries B.C.) by studying the relative development of each type of object included in the tomb group.

While the value of interpreting the function of all excavated objects may be obvious to the cultural anthropologist, it does not always appear so to the historian. Actually, we cannot understand the way in which any civilization operates until we have recorded or reconstructed every possible phase of its activity. Knowledge of the archaeology of any culture thus becomes part of the necessary equipment of a historian who is working on the period and area in question. This fact has been strangely misunderstood by Biblical historians and is partly responsible for their failure to see Old Testament history as a whole.

CHRONOLOGY

For the exact dating of events in Old Testament history proper we are dependent on the three main bodies of material: Biblical, Egyptian, and Mesopotamian. Biblical writers undertook to provide later generations with detailed chronological information. In exilic and postexilic times they dated events by the years of Babylonian and Persian kings, or by years dependent on Babylonian chronology (for example, Ezekiel). For the Divided Monarchy they furnished elaborate formulas, including as a rule the age of each king at his accession, the year in the reign of his contemporary Israelite (or Judahite) colleague in which he became king, and the length of his reign. There are also valuable synchronisms with foreign rulers, Egyptian, Assyrian, Aramaean, and Phoenician. Our material is much less detailed for the chronology of the United Monarchy (Saul, David, and Solomon) than for subsequent periods, and as we go backward into the period of the Judges and Conquest, it becomes still more vague and more difficult to interpret. Before the Exodus a gap of several centuries is indicated by tradition, before which we come again in Genesis to a period of detailed chronological information of questionable historical utility, since we have no means of knowing either its factual basis or the method of transmission. We shall see below how our external sources enable us to interpret Biblical data.

In Egypt there was a systematic effort to preserve accurate chronological information. Lists of successive dynasties and the kings who constituted them are found in the Turin Papyrus, copied in the 13th century B.C. Unfortunately it is fragmentary, and there no longer can be any doubt that the totals which it gives for the Old Kingdom are too high. The same is also apparently true for the Middle Kingdom, though to a much smaller degree. The Turin Papyrus is not preserved for the New Kingdom. If we had the original text of the Greek history of Egypt prepared by an Egyptian priest named Manetho early in the 3d century B.C., on the basis of hieratic records, we should probably be in a position to fix dates back to the beginning of the New Kingdom (16th century B.C.). Unhappily the recensions that we possess of Manetho all are based on a much later epitome (or perhaps on different epitomes), quoted by Josephus, Eusebius, and Georgius Syncellus (after Julius Africanus), all of which are preserved in mediaeval copies. However, the studies of M.B. Rowton and others have shown that much reliable information still may be gleaned from our garbled fragments of Manetho. There is nothing after 2000 B.C. comparable to the accurate list of yearly events and feasts that was kept in the Old Kingdom, preserved to us in two large fragments known as the Palermo and Cairo stones. Owing to the fact that the Egyptian civil year of 365 days lost about a fourth of a day each year, it diverged further and further from the Julian calendar, until it returned to its starting point just a year after the expiration of a full "Sothic" cycle (1,460 years). Classical writers and Egyptian inscriptions give us enough information to fix the dates at which two Sothic cycles ended or began, and also fix a number of precise dates for the reigns of kings within the cycles. In this way Richard A. Parker has fixed the accession of the 12th Dynasty in the year 1991 B.C. A combination of calendrical, astronomical, and other documentary evidence has established nearly all important Egyptian dates in the second millennium B.C. to within a few years at most. The accession of Ahmose I, founder of the 18th Dynasty, has been set at 1570 B.C., and M.B. Rowton in 1948 fixed the reign of Rameses II, probable pharaoh of the Exodus, at 1290–1223 B.C. Thereafter Egyptian chronology ceases to be exact (with a maximum variation of about 20 years in some periods) until we reach the exact data provided by the inscriptions on mummified Apis bulls, which fix the reign of Tirhakah, the Ethiopian king of Egypt who was Hezekiah's contemporary, to 689–663 B.C.

In Babylonia and Assyria, documentary material is much fuller because of the relative indestructibility of clay tablets, but we lack anything like the Sothic Cycle to control our long-range datings. However, there has been steady progress toward ultimate fixing of dates since the 1850's. Persian, Neo-Bablyonian, and Assyrian dates are established exactly back to the end of the 10th century B.C. by a combination of data. First comes the famous Canon of Ptolemy, which gives names and dates of all Persian and Babylonian kings back to 747 B.C. The first century of this list overlaps the last century of the Assyrian Eponym Lists, which give the names of the officials after whom the years were officially named. In the year 763 B.C. the Eponym List recorded a solar eclipse—and there is exact agreement between a dead reckoning based on the overlap with the Canon of Ptolemy and astronomical calcula-

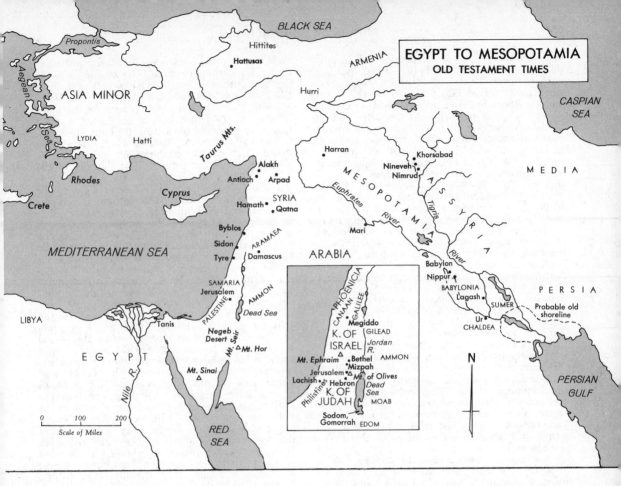

tion of the eclipse in question. This makes it possible to fix the precise year of nearly all recorded synchronisms between kings of Israel and Judah on the one hand and kings of Assyria on the other. When we go back into the second millennium we have many lists of kings and year names; but there remain gaps, uncertainties about the extent of overlaps, and contradictions between our different cuneiform sources. Synchronisms between Assyria and Babylonia and with Egypt and Asia Minor help fix our chronology of Mesopotamia within a decade back to about 1400 B.C. For the Patriarchal Period full agreement has not been attained, but since 1936 it has been brought much closer by the discoveries at Mari, which prove that Hammurabi of Babylonia, Shamshi-Adad of Assyria, and Zimri-Lim of Mari were all contemporary. After 1945 most Assyriologists adopted one of four different views, dating Hammurabi's accession anywhere from 1848 to 1704 B.C.: we thus have a maximum variation of about 150 years for all Mesopotamian dates from 2000 to 1500 B.C. The great majority of scholars hold to intermediate dates between the extremes proposed by A. Goetze and E.F. Weidner.

HISTORY

The Patriarchal Age. Like other peoples with a strong national consciousness, the Israelites carefully preserved the oral traditions of their forefathers. They considered themselves as members of the Hebrew people (Hebrew *Eber, Ibri*), which appears in cuneiform and Egyptian sources from the 18th century B.C. on as *Hapiru* or *Apiru*. They traced their ancestry back to Ur in southern Babylonia and Harran in northwestern Mesopotamia. Discoveries at Mari on the Middle Euphrates after 1935, as well as at many other sites throughout southwestern Asia, show that tribes that shared common proper names and language with the Patriarchal Hebrews swarmed over Syria, Palestine, and Mesopotamia during the first half of the second millennium B.C. and established themselves in these lands as a ruling population. The names Abraham, Jacob, Zebulon, Benjamin, etc., appear as personal names belonging to these "Westerners" (*Amurriyu*, "Amorite," in early Babylonian). Such towns as Harran, Nahor, and Jerusalem, which appear in Genesis, also appear as seats of "Amorite" princes in this period. The traditions of the first eleven chapters of Genesis have close Mesopotamian parallels, but no known parallels in Egyptian, Canaanite, Hittite, or other literature from regions west of Mesopotamia; they must, accordingly, have been brought by the ancestors of Israel from their Mesopotamian home.

The Patriarchs were seminomadic, not fully nomadic; they wandered over the hill country and southland (Negeb) of Palestine with the seasons; they raised flocks of sheep and goats, but they also tilled the soil; they lived in tents, but they buried their dead in caves, like the sedentary Canaanites among whom they lived. Their customary law was closely related to that of contemporary northern Mesopotamia and Syria and differed in important respects from that of later Israel. It is no longer possible to regard the traditions of the Patriarchs in Genesis as being fictional reflections of later Israelite conditions; they are prose paraphrases of much older stories in verse and prose, handed down orally through many centuries before being put into written form. Every year brings striking new verifications of details. However, they were handed down for didactic and pedagogical purposes, and it is impossible to translate them directly into political or tribal history. But whenever we compare them with first-hand narratives of life in Palestine and Syria in those early centuries of the second millennium, we find remarkable similarity in atmosphere. This is just as true of the Egyptian Adventures of Sinuhe, written in the 20th century B.C., as it is of the biography of King Idrimi of Alalakh in northern Syria, composed in the early 15th century B.C.

Just as persistent as the tradition deriving the ancestors of Israel from Mesopotamia is the tradition that they spent generations, perhaps centuries, in Egypt. It is impossible to separate the traditions of Jacob and Joseph in Egypt from the Hyksos Age, during which Northwestern Semites with proper names like those of the Patriarchs invaded Egypt in successive waves and established a Semitic empire, with its center at Tanis in the northeastern Delta. It was precisely around Tanis that the Israelites are said by their own traditions to have been settled from the time of Joseph to that of Moses. Here they established their residence between the end of the 18th and the beginning of the 16th century B.C. Joseph has not yet been discovered on the monuments of the Hyksos Age, which are extremely few and yield scarcely any historical information, but names of other Semitic officials from this period are attested.

The Exodus and Conquest of Canaan. About 1550 B.C. the founder of the New Kingdom, Ahmose I, captured Avaris (Tanis), and began to reconquer Palestine and Syria. The Hyksos capital was destroyed and disappeared from Egyptian records for more than two centuries. Then a family from the district seized power and founded the 19th Dynasty about 1310 B.C. Rebuilding of the old capital began almost immediately, and Rameses II called it by his own name, under which it is mentioned (Exodus 1:11) as one of the cities that the Israelites were forced by their Egyptian masters to build. The figure of Moses towers above all others in the dawn of Israelite history. Bearing a common Egyptian name, Moses belonged to an Egyptianizing family, several of whose personal names were Egyptian (Phinehas, Hophni). Living in a district around the capital of the Ramesside kings, on the frontier of Palestine, such Hebrews as Moses possessed a composite culture, with elements of Hebrew, Egyptian, and Canaanite origin. It was in such a highly complex international situation that one might expect such an advanced religion as the ethical monotheism of Israel to have arisen. This is the consistent picture that is portrayed for us in our Biblical sources, and modern scholars are coming to recognize its sound historical basis. An advanced religion, with such an elevated theology as that of Israel, must have had a great founder, and if the figure of Moses had not been preserved by tradition, it would have to be reconstructed in order to explain the unique phenomenon of Israel's religion and higher culture.

According to Israelite tradition, confirmed more and more by archaeological discoveries, the Israelites escaped from their Egyptian oppressors by crossing the Papyrus Sea (Hebrew, *Yam Suph*) under the leadership of Moses and wandering for a full generation ("forty years") in the deserts south and east of Canaan. The date of the Exodus is still uncertain, but since the Israel Stele of Pharaoh Marniptah places the Israelites in western Palestine before 1219 B.C., a good case may be made for setting it about 1280 B.C., in the early years of Rameses II. Certainly the main phase of the conquest of the Canaanite cities by Israel came in the last decades of the 13th century B.C. The conquest was more gradual than often supposed and was begun while Moses was still alive in Transjordan; it was finished under David, more than two centuries later. In the early phases of the conquest of Canaan proper (western Palestine), associated chiefly with Joshua by Israelite tradition, seminomadic Hebrew tribes and sedentary Canaanites were absorbed in considerable numbers into the Israelite confederacy. Since Israel was a "mixed multitude" even before the Exodus, according to Biblical tradition, its composite character might have disrupted it completely if it had not been for the tradition of unified religious belief and legal practice, which it owed to Moses. During the period of the Judges it was loosely held together by a tribal union around a central sanctuary (Shiloh), resembling in basic structure the Greek amphictyonies of following centuries. The blows of aggressive neighbors, including especially the Philistines (who had settled on the coast of Palestine in the early 12th century B.C.), hammered the Israelite confederacy into a closer union, and the "judges" of the 12th and 11th centuries were replaced by kings. It was no accident that the greatest traditional judge, Samuel, was followed by the first king (about 1020 B.C.).

The United Monarchy (1020–922 B.C.). For a century Israel was held together, except for occasional civil wars, by three kings, Saul (1020–1000 B.C.), David (1000–961 B.C.), and Solomon (961–922 B.C.). Saul does not seem to have controlled his kingdom much more effectively than the stronger judges who had preceded him; nor was he able to hand down his power to his sons. Partly this was due to the fact that Israel's strength was exhausted in fighting the hereditary Philistine foe; partly also it may be blamed on Saul's own defects of personality, which are vividly brought out by tradition.

David was a man of very different qualities, who was able not only to consolidate the Israelite state and to establish an empire but also to transmit his rule through a dynasty that lasted four centuries. We are well informed about David's wars and family relationships but poorly acquainted with details of his organization and administration of the new state. After seven years as king of the southern tribes, with his capital at Hebron, he reunited Israel and soon was forced into a series of wars with his aggressive neighbors. After conquering the Philistines and annexing much of the coastal plain to Israel, he had to repel an Ammonite coalition with the Aramaean states of northern Transjordan and eastern Syria. This war ended with the subjugation of eastern Syria as far north as the border of Hamath on the Orontes. Wars with Edomites, Moabites, and various nomadic tribes ended with Israelite control of all Transjordan as well as the Arabian caravan routes from the frontier of Egypt to the Euphrates. Common hostility to the Philistines and Aramaeans brought a permanent alliance with the South Phoenicians, then organized into a dual monarchy of Tyre and Sidon. This close relation with the rapidly expanding Phoenician commercial state, together with Israelite control of all important caravan routes in North Arabia, led before David's death to a rapid increase in the wealth of the new empire. David undertook to reorganize Israel into less refractory units and carried out an unpopular census in order to form a basis for administrative reforms. It was not until the reign of Solomon, however, that the time-honored tribal divisions actually were replaced by a new pattern of districts, most of which disregarded tribal boundaries. The same pattern of breaking down tribal divisions appears in David's establishment of his capital at Jerusalem, a previously non-Israelite town that did not belong to any of the tribes but was centrally situated with respect to his empire. In order to eliminate the threat of priestly competition, which would have continued to exist if the Tabernacle and Ark had been allowed to remain in another place, he brought the Tabernacle and Ark to Jerusalem, together with the attendant priests, while he seems to have scattered the Levites through Israel.

Solomon's reign continued the Davidic tradition. In order to protect his empire and guard the far-flung commerical activities of the state, he established a powerful standing army, relying for the first time in Israelite history on chariotry. A list of his chariot cities is given, and excavations in one of them (Megiddo) have uncovered well-built stables for at least 450 horses. We are told in some detail about his commercial ventures, which included expeditions carried out jointly with the Phoenicians in the Red Sea and Indian Ocean, and entrepreneur trade with Egypt on the south and Asia Minor on the north. Excavations also have brought to light evidence of extensive copper refining operations at Ezion-geber on the Red Sea. The detailed description of the visit of the queen of Sheba vividly illustrates the rapid growth of the caravan trade with South Arabia, which had to pass through Israelite customs barriers in order to reach the Mediterranean. At that time, as shown by explorations and excavations in South Arabia since 1950, the recently settled people of Sheba (the Greek Sabaeans) were establishing a kind of empire, which rapidly developed caravan trade with the north and reached its culmination about the 8th century B.C. The then rapidly expanding Phoenician commercial empire in the Mediterranean also brought great indirect profit to Israel, since the Phoenicians were dependent on the latter for much of their food and raw materials.

Solomon used the tremendous wealth that poured into his coffers in elaborate construction as well as in maintaining a court of legendary magnificence. His temple and palaces, together with a great many other building operations, known both from the Bible and from excavation, used up his resources and led to unprecedented drafting of the subject peoples and even of free-born Israelites into labor gangs. The combination of heavy levies and conscription led to widespread disaffection, which generated rebellions in the vassal states and sporadic uprisings among the Israelites themselves. It is scarcely surprising, therefore, that Solomon's death became the signal for the revolt of all northern Israel against the house of David (about 922 B.C.).

Israel and Judah (922–721 B.C.). The two new states that emerged from the Solomonic empire were disproportionate in size; the Northern Kingdom was several times as large and as populous as Judah, but the latter inherited much of the wealth of Solomon as well as control of Edom and the southern caravan routes. The Aramaeans and the smaller states in Transjordan broke away from the Northern Kingdom, which thus was deprived of its outside revenues. Lack of a stable dynastic tradition meant that none of the successive strong men in the north was able to establish a permanent dynasty. The dynasty of Omri lasted just over a third of a century, and the dynasty founded by Jehu continued for less than a century. Jeroboam set up new shrines of Yahweh in the north in order to counter the prestige of the Temple of Solomon, but there is no evidence that religious belief and practice differed appreciably in the north and in the south. Intermittent conflict between Judah and Israel weakened both of the rump states, which were further undermined by foreign invasions. About 918 B.C. the founder of the 22d (Bubastite) Dynasty in Egypt, Shishak I, overran Judah, Edom, and Israel, carrying off most of the temple treasure of Jerusalem as tribute. About 877 B.C. the Syrian allies of Asa, king of Judah, invaded Palestine from the north and detached large slices of Israelite territory, including especially northern Transjordan. Israel's territory in eastern Palestine thus was reduced to Gilead.

The best-known phase of Israelite history between Solomon and the Fall of Samaria is the period of Elijah and Elisha, during which the worshipers of Yahweh were engaged in a mortal struggle with the votaries of Baal. The conflict between the sole God of Israel and the head of the Canaanite pantheon had continued for centuries, with alternating victories and defeats on both sides; on the whole it appears that the former had gained ground rather steadily at the expense of the latter. However, Omri's son Ahab was married to the Phoenician princess Jezebel, daughter of Ethbaal, king of Tyre. Jezebel was an ardent votary of Baal Melkart, the chief god of Tyre, whose cult contained orgiastic elements, which were particularly objectionable to pious Israelites. The new contest ended, after a violent struggle, in the triumph of the followers of the prophet Elijah. The dynasty of Omri was destroyed in a drastic blood purge, and we hear no longer of the cult of Melcarth in Israel. Six years later the cult of Baal Melcarth was similarly uprooted in Judah, where it had been introduced by Athaliah, another queen of the Omride line.

The dynasty of Jehu lasted in Israel from 842 to about 745 B.C. The growing power of the Aramaeans of Damascus, checked during Jehu's life by the pressure of the revitalized Assyrian empire, grew rapidly again while the Assyrians were involved in a bitter civil war, followed by exhausting struggles with their neighbors on the north and south. Hazael of Damascus was thus free to continue his feud with Israel, which led to the total destruction of Israelite power about 815 B.C. and the subjugation of Israel to the Aramaeans. In 805 Adadnirari III of Assyria resumed the war against the Aramaeans in Syria, and the latter were reduced in their turn to the status of Assyrian vassals. This turn of the wheel gave Joash of Israel his opportunity to throw off the Aramaean yoke (about 800 B.C.).

Before his death he had succeeded in reducing Judah in its turn to a vassal status, thus setting the stage for the brilliant reign of his son, Jeroboam II (about 786–746 B.C.). Under the latter, northern Israel reached the height of its power as a separate state, expanding in all directions and developing flourishing trade with its neighbors, especially with Phoenicia. This was the age of the first prophets whose words have been handed down to us in collected form: Amos of Judah, who worked in Israel, and Hosea of Israel. These prophets condemned the growing corruption of the civic and religious leaders; they inveighed against the spread of pagan practices and the increasing oppression of the poor. We are not told whether Judah continued to be a vassal of Israel, but it seems probable that this was the case. However, under King Uzziah, Judah increased in strength, and Edom again was reduced to vassalage, while the men of Judah developed the caravan trade of northwestern Arabia. Toward the end of Uzziah's reign, after the death of Jeroboam, Judah became the most influential state in Palestine and was credited by the Assyrian inscriptions with being the chief instigator of resistance to Assyrian arms.

The last quarter century of Israel's independence was characterized by a series of destructive Assyrian invasions, followed by abortive rebellions against the heavy yoke of the conquerors. Egyptian rulers undertook to fish in the troubled waters of Palestine, giving the Israelites specious promises of aid that never materialized. In 742 B.C., Tiglath-pileser III of Assyria took the important North Syrian town of Arpad; in 732 Damascus fell, and the state of Aram came to an end. A year before the Assyrians had stripped Israel of its territory in Gilead, in Galilee, and on the coastal plain, leaving nothing but the hill country of Ephraim and western Manasseh, around the ancient capital, Samaria. The final rebellion began in 724 under Shalmaneser V, and Samaria fell in the first months of 721, after the accession of Sargon II to the Assyrian throne. The captured people of Samaria were exiled to northern Mesopotamia and Media.

Judah (721–582 B.C.). The fall of Samaria left Judah almost alone; nearly all the autonomous states of Syria and Palestine had now been reduced to Assyrian provinces. In 701 B.C., Hezekiah of Judah, who had rebelled against Assyrian oppression, again relying on Egyptian promises, was crushed by Sennacherib's army, and tribute of staggering size was levied against Judah. Jerusalem, however, escaped destruction. Since there are a number of episodes in the longer Biblical account of Sennacherib's invasion that cannot be harmonized with the invasion of 701, such as the reference to Tirhakah as king of Egypt and the account of the destruction of the Assyrian army by pestilence, many scholars hold that there was a second Assyrian invasion toward the end of Hezekiah's reign. The sensational defeat of Sennacherib by the Chaldaeans and Elamites at Khalule in 691 must have had very serious repercussions in the western provinces of Assyria. Furthermore, we have no dated records of Assyrian campaigns from 689, the year in which Tirhakah became pharaoh, to the death of Sennacherib in 681. It is, therefore, only reasonable to suppose that there was a second rebellion of Hezekiah between 689 and 686 and that this was successful for the time being.

The fall of Samaria made a tremendous impression on the people of Judah. Under the guidance of such prophets as Isaiah and Micah, who were favored by Hezekiah, there was a strong reform movement, which eliminated many survivals of older folk religion. It also was pressed into the service of politics, and efforts were made to bring the North Israelites back to the official cult of the Temple of Solomon. Since there was no longer effective competition in the north (except perhaps at Bethel), this missionary activity appears to have been quite successful. However, the reform did not last, and under Hezekiah's successor, Manasseh (about 687–642 B.C.), there was a revival of paganism, said to have extended into the Temple as well as to the royal court. This pagan revival was accompanied by a vogue of astrology and divination—probably derived from contemporary Assyria, as illustrated by the masses of such material found in the library of Ashurbanipal at Nineveh. The Chronicler has preserved a tradition that Manasseh was taken as captive to Babylon (after a rebellion?) and that he was converted to orthodox Yahwism as a result of this experience. In any event, there was a reaction against the paganizing tendencies of Manasseh's reign, and his grandson, Josiah (640–609 B.C.), headed a new reform movement, which seems to have followed the lines of Hezekiah's reform but to have been much more thorough. As a result of the rapid collapse of the Assyrian empire after the death of Ashurbanipal (between 630 and 626), Josiah regained most of the territory of the old Northern Kingdom. In defending his title to it he fell in battle against the Egyptian Necho (609 B.C.) at the ancient city of Megiddo. The reign of Josiah was long remembered as a period of return to the ancient faith of Israel, as a result of which king and people were abundantly blessed by Yahweh. It was to be the last happy period for many generations.

After the conquest of Palestine by Necho, events moved swiftly. Probably in 603 B.C. the armies of the Chaldaean king Nebuchadnezzar overran Judah. Several years later king Jehoiakim revolted, relying like his predecessors on Egyptian promises that proved illusory. In 598–597 the Chaldaean armies devastated Judah and took Jechoiachin, the son and successor of Jehoiakim (who had died meanwhile), into exile in Babylonia, along with several thousand other Judahites. Cuneiform tablets from Babylon describe the rations given periodically to King Jechoiachin and other men of Judah; they are dated 592, after he had been a captive for six years. Since the Chaldaeans still considered Judah as a useful buffer state on the borders of Egypt, Jehoiachin's uncle, Zedekiah, was appointed acting king and regent for his nephew. Before many years had passed, however, a new rebellion broke out, again with Egyptian support; it was better organized than the first and took longer to crush. The Lachish ostraca, discovered by British excavators in 1935 and 1938 at Lachish in the low hill country of Judah, throw a vivid light on conditions during the year or two before the final catastrophe. Finally, in 587 B.C., Jerusalem was stormed and destroyed, together with the Temple of Solomon. But Judah was not yet entirely obliterated; it was put under a native governor, Gedaliah (known from a seal discovered at Lachish to have been royal chamberlain). Gedaliah's new capital was at Mizpah, north of Jerusalem; there he and his followers were murdered in cold blood by a chauvinistic member of the royal family named Ishmael. It is commonly believed that the death of Gedaliah took place only some three months after the fall of Jerusalem, but this seems unlikely for several reasons. In any case, there was a third deportation in the 23d year of Nebuchadnezzar, five years after the fall of Jerusalem, and this presumably was brought about by the rebellious activities of Ishmael and other chauvinists. The year 582 B.C., therefore, stands as the end of organized Jewish life in the land of Judah before the Restoration.

Exile and Restoration. The disasters of the period made a tremendous impression on the spirits of men, as may be seen by perusing the bitter and eloquent words of Jeremiah and Ezekiel. For one thing, the threat of doom, which had been deferred so often, actually had been fulfilled, and the stern warnings of the prophets had become fact. Two centuries or more were to elapse before paganizing tendencies vanished from normative Jewish religious circles—and even then they were to return occasionally, as happened in Jerusalem during the persecution of Antiochus Epiphanes. Yet the work of Jeremiah and Ezekiel was not in vain, and the polytheistic deviations of pre-exilic centuries did not recur, as far as we know, among the Jews of Babylonia and Judah. Conditions of life in these two lands were extremely difficult. Most of the Jewish exiles were settled among the swamps of central Babylonia, where the old irrigation system had fallen into ruins and malaria was endemic. They were settled on old mounds that had long been abandoned, in an area where in summer the temperature rises as high as 120° F in the shade. Judah had been completely devastated by the Chaldaean armies; all towns had been burned, and only the poorest people remained. The contrary view, that most towns either were not really destroyed or were resettled immediately, is completely disproved by archaeological evidence, which is in full agreement with the documentary data of the Bible. Northern Judah was turned over to the Babylonian governor of the province of Samaria to administer, while southern Judah was resettled by Edomite fugitives, forced out of Mount Seir by invading Arab tribes, precursors of the Nabataeans.

So intense was the impression created among the Jews by the fulfillment of prophetic predictions of doom that the predictions of restoration after destruction, which were a usual part of the prophetic pattern, also were taken to heart, and there was a general expectation of such restoration. Although Ezekiel warned against the dangers of this attitude, it remained latent among the descendants of the exiles, now scattered over southwestern Asia and Egypt. The conquest of the Babylonian empire by Cyrus in 539 B.C. fanned the spark into a burning flame, the intensity of which is vividly illustrated by the contemporary prophets, among whom we may mention particularly the author of the last chapters of the Isaiah anthology, as well as Zechariah, Haggai, Obadiah, and Joel. In his very first year, in keeping with the policy enunciated in his own inscriptions, Cyrus promised the Jews that the Temple would be erected again with government aid. It is true that many scholars have denied the authenticity of the Cyrus decree in Ezra 1, but it is so thoroughly in accord with the other evidence now available that this attitude raises much more serious problems than it superficially appears to solve. Actually it would not even be taken seriously if it were not for a persistent tendency since 1896 to reject the authenticity of the memoirs of Ezra and since 1925 to deny the authenticity of Ezekiel. These scholars naturally go on to deny wholly or in large part that there was a complete destruction of Judah, a Babylonian Exile, or a Restoration. Archaeological evidence is wholly opposed to all these extreme views, and we shall not deal with them further here.

The Cyrus decree took time and effort to implement, and we have no indication in our sources of any great progress toward the restoration of the Temple or of the Jewish commonwealth in Palestine until the beginning of the reign of Darius Hystaspis. It was the weakness of Persia, during the spasmodic rebellions that convulsed the empire after the accession of Darius, that called forth a supreme effort on the part of the Jews, who finished the Temple in March 515 B.C., in spite of setbacks of every kind. But the failure of the expected restoration of the Davidic kingdom under a scion of the Davidic house created a general attitude of discouragement and certainly caused a slackening of further efforts.

The Jews Under the Persians and Macedonians. The 5th century B.C. was a period of general tranquillity and prosperity in the Persian empire. The Jews by now had struck new roots in the lands of their Dispersion, as we know from many hundreds of papyri and ostraca belonging to the Jewish colonists at Elephantine on the southern border of Egypt proper, as well as from scores of cuneiform tablets from Nippur in central Babylonia that deal with business transactions in which Jews took part. Owing to confusion in the text of the books of Ezra and Nehemiah, on which we depend for most of our knowledge about Judah and Jerusalem in this period, we are not certain about the order in which Ezra and Nehemiah arrived in Jerusalem. The evidence points increasingly, however, to the priority of Nehemiah and supports the chronology followed by Josephus rather than that preserved in the Hebrew text. If this is correct, Nehemiah, who was an official at the Persian court, came first in 440 B.C. and finished building the wall of Jerusalem in 437. Ezra then came a few years after Nehemiah, who made it possible for Ezra to come to reorganize the Temple cult and establish normative Judaism according to strict Babylonian Jewish ideas. Although it would appear that the two men did not get along well, both played decisive roles in the development of the priestly state of Judah, which thenceforth became the religious center of the Jewish world. We know that there were pronounced religious differences between the paganizing Jews of Egypt and Palestine, on the one hand, and the returned Babylonian Jews, on the other. The paganizing tendencies of the Egyptian Jews probably disappeared with the burning of the Jewish temple at Elephantine and the dissolution of their colonies about 400 B.C. in the course of the successful Egyptian rebellion against the Persians. It probably took longer to get rid of paganizing tendencies among descendants of the old Israelite communities in northern Palestine and Transjordan; they may not have been completely eradicated until after the Maccabean conquest.

We have little information about details of

Jewish life in Palestine between Ezra and Antiochus Epiphanes. We know that Judah continued to be administered largely by Jewish high priests during the last century of the Persian empire and the first century and a half of Macedonian rule. This was also the age when later sectarian movements began to form in protest against overly rigid definitions of orthodoxy. Very little in the Old Testament can safely be attributed to the two centuries following the last historical references in the work of the Chronicler (I and II Chronicles, Ezra, Nehemiah); it was a period of fixing the text and limits of canonical literature rather than of writing new books. However, we may safely attribute such books as Esther, Ecclesiastes, and Daniel to this period, and many scholars would date much more of our Hebrew Bible to it. A number of extant books included in the Apocrypha or counted among the Pseudepigrapha also are to be dated before 168 B.C. During these centuries the political activity of the Jewish people became more and more subordinated to their religious life, which was intensely alive, preparing the field for the rich flowering of the spirit in the last century of the Second Temple.

W.F. ALBRIGHT, *The Johns Hopkins University*

Bibliography

Albright, William F., *Archaeology and the Religion of Israel*, 4th ed. (Baltimore 1956).
Albright, William F., *The Biblical Period from Abraham to Ezra* (New York 1963).
Albright, William F., *From the Stone Age to Christianity* (Baltimore 1957).
Albright, William F., *Archaeology of Palestine* (Baltimore 1960).
Bright, John, *A History of Israel* (Philadelphia 1961).
Noth, Martin, *The History of Israel*, 2d ed. (New York 1960).
Rowley, Harold H., ed., *The Old Testament and Modern Study* (New York and London, 1951).
Wright, G.E., *Biblical Archaeology* (Philadelphia 1957).
Wright, G. Ernest, and Filson, Floyd V., *The Westminster Historical Atlas to the Bible*, rev. ed. (Philadelphia 1956).

For Specialized Study

Kittel, R., *Geschichte des Volkes Israel* (Stuttgart 1923–29).
Olmstead, A.T., *History of Palestine and Syria* (New York 1931).
Robinson, Theodore H., and Oesterley, W.O.E., *A History of Israel* (New York and London 1932).

7. Religion and Theology of the Old Testament

The study of the religious content of the Old Testament is customarily divided into two parts: the history of the religion of Israel, and the theology of the Old Testament. The former undertakes to present chronologically the story of the development of Old Testament religion from its earliest to its latest manifestations; the theology depicts in systematic outline the basic conceptions and presuppositions that to some extent underlie Old Testament faith in all periods of its history.

THE HISTORY OF THE RELIGION OF ISRAEL

Sources. The differences that exist among scholars as to the course of the history of Old Testament religion arise largely from differing estimates as to the date, character, and reliability of the available documentary sources. All the books of the Old Testament contribute in some measure to an understanding of the problem, but certain documents are of crucial importance for particular periods. The early parts of the Pentateuch are the only sources for the Patriarchal and Mosaic periods, but unfortunately for historians of religion, they contain much legendary material and much that evidently reflects the outlook of a later age. Critics of the extreme radical school have been inclined to regard this material as of slight value for the reconstruction of the times with which it purports to deal. The historical books from Joshua to Kings are of prime significance for secular history in the time of the judges and the kings, but give only fragmentary and unsatisfying glimpses of religious ideas and practices, and such evidence as they do give is in constant need of special evaluation.

The best sources for the religion of the late monarchy, and for exilic and early postexilic times, are the various books of the prophets. Although these books contain some mixture of material from later times, they are essentially contemporary and thoroughly reliable records of the thinking of Israel's greatest religious teachers. Recognition of the primary historical value of the prophetic writings frequently has led to an unfortunate depreciation of the older records and to the conclusion that the creative factor in the Old Testament is to be found only in these late books. If that were true, then the origin of Israel's unique religion would have to be sought in the time of the writing prophets (beginning with Amos in the 8th century) rather than in the work of Moses (somewhere in the 14th to the 12th century). It should be noted that there has been a strong reaction against this view in the decades following World War I.

For the postexilic period the chief sources of knowledge (in addition to the later prophetic books and the latest parts of the Pentateuch) are the books of Chronicles, Ezra, and Nehemiah. The evidence of these books is fragmentary at best and of uncertain value, while their interpretation presents more difficult problems than are to be found in any other part of the historical literature. Finally, it may be noted that the Wisdom Literature is evidence for the existence of a philosophical strain in Israel's religion, at least at the late period in which most of it is to be dated. The Psalms, in view of the difficulty of arriving at a commonly accepted date for most of them, are more valuable for Old Testament theology than for the history of the religion of Israel.

Patriarchal Period. According to the most probable interpretation of the evidence, the religion of the Hebrews before the time of Moses was essentially the same as that of other peoples at a similar stage of cultural development. In the Book of Genesis, from which our information about this period is derived, the stories of the patriarchs frequently are made vehicles for the expression of high religious and ethical insights, but evidence as to the actual religion of the Patriarchal Age is to be found in the reminiscences of more primitive religious ideas and practices that constantly appear. Certainly men of this period were not worshipers of a single god. Reference is made to various local gods and *numina* who were objects of veneration (for example, Genesis 16:13; 21:33; 32:29) and also, as Albrecht Alt has pointed out, to tribal gods who were especially connected with ancestral heroes (for example, Genesis 31:42, 53; 49:24). In the present narrative these older gods have of course been identified in every case with Yahweh, the god of the later Hebrews. The religious practices of the patriarchs, who are represented in our sources as seminomads, were directed chiefly toward securing the favor of deity to promote the well-being of their tribes and the fertility of their flocks and herds. As is true among most peoples, sacrifice was the principal religious rite and accompanied every feast at which an animal was slaughtered. By offering to their god part of the meal, he was brought within the communion fellowship of the group, and his benevolence was assured. The principal times of religious observance were those of the lunar calendar, especially the "new moon" and possibly the "Sabbath" (on the supposition that the Sabbath originally was connected with the phases of the moon rather than with a strict seven-day week). The beginning of the new year was marked by the "Passover," when a lamb was slain and certain rites were performed that were designed to ward off harm during the coming season. Circumcision presumably was practiced, although rather as a social rite than as a sign of faith. All these observances persisted into the later religion of the Mosaic age, but in every case their significance was altered.

Mosaic Period. Although there are still scholars of eminence who doubt the historicity of Moses or who at least deny him any significant role in establishing the unique character of Old Testament faith, there is a growing tendency to believe that so vastly important a movement as the rise and growth of Israel's religion demands the existence of a great creative personality to explain it. All attempts to explain the rise of ethical monotheism in Israel on the basis of unilinear evolution from a simple religion of primitive taboos to the incomparable pronouncements of the Hebrew prophets shatter on the rock of the inescapable, but unanswerable, question first asked in the 19th century: "Why is it that Yahweh of Israel became the world-god instead of Chemosh of Moab?" Environmental, social, and ethnic characteristics were the same in Israel as in several surrounding nations, and yet it was only in Israel that anything resembling the high religion of the prophets appeared. All the results of 20th century study of comparative Near Eastern religion and archaeology have tended only to confirm the absolute uniqueness of the religion of the Old Testament. Just as Zoroastrianism, Christianity, and Islam owe their major distinguishing characteristics to the genius of their respective individual founders, so historical probabilities lead us to assume that the unique features that marked off Israel's religion from that of her neighbors also were due to the original impress of a single great personality. Such is the view of the Old Testament itself and despite the inadequacy of the early records, there is no sound reason for denying that this view is substantially correct.

The stories about Moses and his work come down to us through a long period, first of oral tradition and then of complicated literary history. Many of the incidents must be dismissed as legendary, but beneath the incrustation of legend is a solid substratum of fact. Moses' primary achievement was that he led the Hebrew tribes to the worship of one God. This is not to say that Moses taught monotheism in the later philosophical sense of the term. Such a metaphysical abstraction is hardly in accord with the ethos of the Mosaic age. But Moses did induce his people to accept the worship of Yahweh as their sole tribal god, a "jealous god" who would tolerate no other gods "before him." Whatever may be the under-

lying truth about the details of the Exodus, there evidently occurred a series of striking events in which both Moses and his people saw this powerful deity at work delivering them out of slavery in Egypt. Under Moses' guidance, the tribes entered into a compact or "covenant" at a sacred mountain called Sinai or Horeb by which they accepted Yahweh's protection and overlordship and pledged themselves to His sole service and to implicit obedience. With the conclusion of this solemn act the nation of Israel came into existence, and Moses proceeded to organize its life on the basis of laws that he laid down with Yahweh's authority to support him. Around this original nucleus of genuine Mosaic laws, the precise extent of which is no longer recoverable, developed the great body of social and religious legislation that subsequently came to be known as "the Law of Moses." By these acts, Moses founded the nation of Israel and created the framework within which all later developments took place.

Period of the Judges. When the new people of Israel, at this period only an amphictyony or religious confederation of tribes, took possession of Canaan and thus became a nation in the fullest sense of the term, they came into immediate conflict with the ancient inhabitants of the land and with their religious and social traditions. Whereas the basic culture of the Hebrews was nomadic and the inherited forms in which their faith expressed itself were of pastoral origin, the basic culture of Canaan was agricultural. The gods of Canaan were gods of fertility; their worship involved a considerable sexual element designed to ensure the productivity of the land; and their festivals were those of the agricultural calendar.

The conflict with this alien pattern of culture is the keynote of the period of the so-called "judges." While the religion of Moses was maintained and the more repulsive features of the Canaanite cult ultimately were repudiated by the official teachers of Israel, yet the basic tension continued for many generations and Mosaic religion was permanently affected, especially on its cultic side, by the practices and beliefs of the Canaanites. Yahweh, originally a god of the desert and the defender of his people in time of war, became the god of the land of Canaan and the source of the fertility of its soil. The rites of agricultural religion were taken over into the Hebrew cult and adapted to the worship of Yahweh. Agricultural festivals, such as the feast of unleavened bread, seem at times to have supplanted such older nomadic observances as the passover but later were combined with them.

There was, of course, great danger in the process, the danger that Mosaic Yahwism might lose its essential character and become simply another fertility cult like the religion of the Canaanite *baalim*. It was all too possible for Israel to assimilate the unsavory features of the worship of her neighbors and to forget her own heritage. That the pure spirit of Yahwism survived this conflict was largely the work of the great prophets. Their story, however, belongs to a later period of Israel's history. In the time of the judges we see only that the issue was joined and the outcome was still uncertain. The age of the judges was not a creative one. It was rather a period of adjustment to new conditions. Unsettled times and the lack of political unity made impossible any kind of general advance in religious thinking. The general impression made upon the reader by the Book of Judges is rather that of a certain retrogression from the high achievements of the Mosaic age.

Period of the Early Monarchy. The political unification of the tribes under the monarchy of Saul, David, and Solomon gave a new impetus to cultural and religious activity in Israel. The monarchy itself received a religious sanction, and the ruler came to play an important part in the cultus. Although the precise extent to which common Near Eastern ideas of Divine Kingship became acclimated in Israel is uncertain, there can be no doubt that the ancient Hebrew kings were far more significant for religion than our present records would have us believe and that the king was regarded as in some way an important mediator of divine power to his people. The later development of Messianic doctrine is an outgrowth of ideas of sacred kingship that first found root in Israel in the early days of the monarchy. It was a natural result of the increasing wealth and stability of the nation that the cultus came to be surrounded with a splendor that had been unknown to the nomadic period or to the rude age of the judges.

Most important of all movements in this direction, and most enduring in its consequences, was the erection of Solomon's temple. While not originally erected as the sole sanctuary for the land, its magnificence and its status as the shrine of the king and his court gave it an inevitable precedence among the temples of the land, and this predominant position could only increase with the passing years. The need for a central sanctuary as a focus for the religious affections of the nation was an obvious one. Shiloh seems to have played such a role in the time of the judges. After the establishment of the Davidic dynasty in Jerusalem and the building there of Solomon's temple, the shrine of the capital city came more and more to occupy the same position. Although the Jerusalem temple was constructed along the lines of the typical temples of other civilized nations of the ancient Near East, a sense of the continuity of its worship with that of older Hebrew times was assured by the fact that the inner sanctuary ("the holy of holies") enshrined the Ark, the old palladium of nomadic Israel that in former days had accompanied the troops in battle and was a visible symbol of the presence of Yahweh with his people.

The historical records tell us that when the nation broke into two parts after the death of Solomon, a purer form of Mosaic religion was maintained in the Southern Kingdom than in the North. In the Northern Kingdom the older shrines of Bethel and Dan were revitalized to counteract the emotional attraction of the Solomonic temple in Jerusalem, and the use of bull images, symbols of fertility and strength, in the worship of Yahweh was tolerated and even encouraged. Nevertheless there were abundant reserves of religious vitality in the North, which became evident during the 9th century in the struggle between the prophetic party led by Elijah and Elisha and the syncretizing movement represented by Jezebel, Ahab's Tyrian queen, who attempted to give to the worship of Melkart, the god of her own ancestors, equality with the worship of Yahweh. The conflict, bloody and horrible in some of its aspects, resulted in a clear-cut victory for the Yahwistic party. From this time on there could be no real doubt that the essential character of the ancient religion of Israel would be preserved. The new energy released by the prophetic revolution undoubtedly helped to prepare the way for the rise of the "literary" prophets in the following century.

Period of the Prophets. About the middle of the 8th century there began a succession of great religious leaders, the so-called writing prophets, who gave classic expression to the spirit of Mosaic religion. So striking and original was their genius that some have regarded them as the real founders of the Old Testament faith. However, they certainly did not regard themselves as innovators in any sense, and their real function seems rather to have been that of refining the religious concepts inherited from older times and drawing out their logical implications.

To say this is in no sense to depreciate the prophets, since they still must be numbered among the greatest religious teachers the world has known. The vigorous originality of their thought and the incisive brilliance of their language set the stamp of creative genius on them. They are not of course to be thought of primarily as writers and philosophers, but rather as men of speech and action who were intimately and almost exclusively concerned with the living issues of their times. They are called "literary" prophets only because their addresses (or "oracles") have been preserved for us by the industry of their pupils and partisans in the prophetic books of the Old Testament. The theology of the Old Testament is based far more upon the books of the prophets than upon any other part of the Bible, since it was in their teaching that the religion of Israel both found its definitive expression and reached its greatest heights.

While there is, in one sense, an outlook common to all the great prophets, an outlook that sees God meeting man at every crisis of his existence with a command to obey and a promise of help, yet each of the prophets individually had something of special importance to contribute to the total picture. Amos, who addressed his message to the Northern Kingdom shortly before its downfall, was chiefly concerned that his hearers should understand that God's demand is not merely for external conformity to cultic laws nor even for a merely negative personal morality, but for a dynamic spirit of justice that must penetrate every aspect of the social organism. "Let justice roll down as waters, and righteousness as a mighty stream" (Amos 5:24, American Standard Version). This is also the primary emphasis of the southern prophet Micah, whose oracles are preserved in the first three chapters of the book published under his name.

Hosea, the last of the northern prophets, exhibits less interest in social justice and more in God's demand for absolute and unconditional loyalty to Himself. For him God's relationship to His people is to be understood on the analogy of husband and wife (Hosea 2:2–15) or father and son (11:1) rather than of king and subject. God desires "mercy, and not sacrifice; and the knowledge of God more than burnt offerings" (6:6). In Isaiah the distinctive note is that of confident trust in God's protecting care, a message especially appropriate to the situation of the little southern kingdom of Judah in a century marked chiefly by the rapid and violent expansion of the Assyrian Empire. "If ye will not believe," he says, "ye shall not be established" (Isaiah 7:9).

The prophetic succession was interrupted for over half a century by the reactionary policies of King Manasseh under whom syncretistic religion flourished once more and the teaching of the prophets was proscribed; but with the accession of Josiah to the throne it reappeared with renewed vitality, first of all in the work of Zephaniah, who pictured in unforgettable words "the day of wrath" that was about to break over the land, and more notably, in the ministry of Jeremiah, the subtlest and most appealing of the prophets. Jeremiah's contribution to Old Testament theology does not lie in the direction of any special doctrine but rather in his vindication of the right of personal religion. Before his time religious thinking had been largely concerned with the relationship of God to the nation. Jeremiah makes of religion a far more individual affair, and this aspect of his thought culminates in his view of the New Covenant (Jeremiah 31:31–34) that God will establish in the future, by which every man will know God directly without the mediation of a written law or of an official prophetic or priestly class.

Toward the beginning of Jeremiah's career occurred one of the most decisive events of Hebrew religious history, the reformation of Josiah. During this time a book, presumably the core of our present book of Deuteronomy, was found in the temple, in some mysterious manner, and was declared to be the official lawbook of the land. This canonization of Deuteronomy marks the beginning of "the religion of the book," and Deuteronomy itself became the nucleus around which the whole of Holy Scripture eventually was to gather. On the whole, Josiah's reform represented official acceptance of prophetic teaching and the final victory of Yahwism as interpreted by the 8th century prophets. Although Jeremiah must have felt strongly attracted to the purposes of the movement, there is evidence that he was not altogether sympathetic with that aspect of it that tended to reduce the spontaneous religion of prophecy to the cold formality of a written code.

Babylonian Exile. Like all the prophets before him, Jeremiah had foreseen the doom of his people, but unlike his predecessors, he lived to experience it. He went through the horrors of the siege and saw part of the nation taken to Babylonia. Jeremiah did not doubt that in God's providence the nation still had a great future before it, and he foresaw that the hopeful and creative element among the people would not appear in the remnant left in Judah, but rather among those who had gone into exile. His judgment was justified by the event, since it was in Babylonia that those tendencies developed that were to give distinctive character to Judaism, the religion of postexilic Israel. Deprived of land, temple, and sacrifice, the Jews in Babylon soon began to find a center for their religion in new institutions and practices that were independent of the locality of Palestine, particularly the study of the law and the observance of such characteristic rites as circumcision and the Sabbath.

Because the priesthood no longer was capable of discharging its duties in the absence of the temple, a new type of religious functionary came into prominence, the scribe or student of the Law. The beginnings of the synagogue began to appear in the form of meetings in private houses for the purpose of study and prayer. In Ezekiel, the great prophet of the early years of the exile, the spirit of Judaism already is clearly marked, although he is better known to religious history as the one who carried Jeremiah's emphasis on the value of persons to its (perhaps too logical) conclusion and declared the absolute independence of individual men (Ezekiel 18). Living as they did, far from Yahweh's land, near the capital of a great world empire, which was ostensibly the domain of other gods, it was inevitable that the Jews should either lose their faith in Yahweh altogether or else transform and enlarge it. Fortunately the latter took place. It ceased to be possible to think of Yahweh as merely the "god of the land of Israel." If Yahweh's land could be taken by foreigners and His people carried into exile, then either He was no god or else He was the God of the whole earth, the true, although unrecognized, God of the Babylonians as well as of the Hebrews. It was under these circumstances that the Jews achieved a pure and self-conscious monotheism.

It is probably true that monotheism was implicit in the teaching of Moses; it remains a fact, nevertheless, that it became explicit only in the teachings of the great prophet of the latter years of the exile, who, for want of a better name, is called the Second Isaiah (because his oracles are preserved in Isaiah, 40 to 55). In passage after passage he declares the absolute nonexistence of foreign gods and the sole sovereignty of Yahweh (for example, 44:6; 45:21), who is the creator of heaven and earth and the Lord of all that is in them (40:22–26; 42:5). It was also Second Isaiah who, in a series of mysterious passages culminating in chapter 53, propounded the exalted theory that the sufferings of Israel and its prophets were vicarious in nature and were intended in God's providence to bring deliverance to the Gentiles. The writings of this prophet, both in content and form, are the high-water mark of Old Testament thinking about God. The immediate occasion that led to the activity of this remarkable anonymous teacher was the onward march of Cyrus of Persia, which was destined to bring doom to Babylon and new freedom to the Jews. Second Isaiah saw the figure of Yahweh, the God of Israel, marching in the forefront of Cyrus's armies, bringing deliverance to His people.

Postexilic Period. With the end of the Exile, ancient Hebrew religion attained its greatest heights, and Judaism, which was a crystallization of the spirit of Mosaic religion in a fixed and final mold, already was established. The postexilic period is much harder to characterize than the preceding periods. This is partly due to the fact that it was not, on the whole, a creative age, but rather a time for the consolidation of gains and the reinforcement of achieved positions. The unprogressive character of the time no doubt was due in part to the struggle for mere existence that continually confronted the impoverished postexilic community. The little band of Jews living in the neighborhood of Jerusalem was hardly more than a shadow of the nation that once had been there. Merely maintaining their identity, in the face of pressure from hostile neighbors without and faint-hearted adherents within, consumed a large part of the energies that otherwise might have been turned to more constructive pursuits.

The great men of the age, and they must not be denied the title, were not such attractive figures as the prophets of the 8th and 7th centuries.

Rather, they were men of comparatively small interests—such as Haggai and Zechariah, who were concerned largely with the rebuilding of the temple; Malachi, who denounced irreverence in the conduct of the cult; Nehemiah, whose great life work was the reconstruction of Jerusalem's demolished fortifications; and Ezra, who demanded rigid separation between Jews and foreigners and strict obedience to the Code of Law he had brought with him from Babylon (possibly the priestly document of the Pentateuch).

The modern reader is impressed with the comparatively narrow vision of these men, although in fairness he must acknowledge that without them the great spiritual treasures inherited from the age of Moses and the literary prophets would have been lost. And even in this age there were men of larger minds who kept alive the broad and tolerant spirit of the greatest of the older prophets. Such, for example, were the author of the book of Jonah, who sees the Gentiles as having equal importance with the Jews in the eyes of God, and (probably) the author of the charming little book of Ruth. Also to be numbered in this company are the authors of the Wisdom Literature—Job, Ecclesiastes, and much of Proverbs—books in which, whether for good or ill, almost nothing of the exclusive spirit of postexilic Judaism appears. Also many of the Psalms that come from this age breathe a spirit of simple-hearted devotion that owes nothing to consciousness of race or nation.

The new features that emerge in postexilic Judaism are partly the result of an unfolding of the implications of older ideas in the light of new situations and partly the result of the contact with foreign nations, especially Greece and Persia. Such, for example, is the emergence of a new type of literature—Apocalyptic, represented particularly in the book of Daniel—which begins to supplant older prophetic types. The sufferings of the martyrs in the age of the Maccabees provided a situation favorable to the acclimatization and popularity of such a literature as this, which so strongly encouraged fervent belief in the sovereignty of Israel's God and in the ultimate triumph of His kingdom. This same situation also made possible the doctrine of the resurrection of the body as it is found in the book of Daniel (chapter 12) and in the late apocalypse now preserved in Isaiah 24 to 27. In this latest period of Old Testament religious history most of those tendencies of Judaism reflected in the New Testament are already plainly evident.

THEOLOGY OF THE OLD TESTAMENT

It is possible to speak of a theology of the Old Testament because, despite all the modifications Hebrew religion underwent in the various periods described above, the changes were largely matters of detail, while the essential structure of Israel's faith remained unchanged. In this section this basic structure of faith will be described.

Nature of Revelation. The religion of the Old Testament, and of the Bible as a whole, is to be distinguished from most religions by the fact that it declares that God has revealed Himself in certain historical events. Thus it is to be sharply differentiated from all religious systems, ancient or modern, that think of the knowledge of God as being based either upon mere oracular revelations or upon human speculation. To the men of the Old Testament, God had made Himself clearly known to Israel in the series of events through which He delivered them out of bondage in Egypt. The God of Israel was not an impassive absolute whose character was to be discerned by philosophical inquiry or interior meditation; He was a God of action whose nature could be learned only by inference from His acts. This pattern had been set at the beginning of Hebrew history, and it was confidently expected that from time to time God would reveal Himself by further acts of deliverance and judgment. Thus the subjective element was almost entirely eliminated from the Hebrews' approach to God. The Old Testament is entirely free of any attempt to prove that God exists. Such proofs as are adduced by modern philosophical systems, based upon logical probabilities, would have seemed almost blasphemous to men whose convictions as to God's nature and being were founded upon the certainty that in the events of Hebrew history "The Lord hath made bare his holy arm in the eyes of all the nations" (Isaiah 52:10).

Although God's primary revelation thus was believed to be found in His "mighty acts," the men of ancient Israel also conceived that God revealed Himself through the words of great prophets. Actually this was not understood as a different, but rather as a concomitant, mode of revelation. In many cases it required special insight to know just which historical events were revelatory and in precisely what sense they were to be understood. So Moses, acting in the role of a prophet, caused his people to see the redeeming hand of God at work in the events of the Exodus; the prophets of the 8th and 7th centuries taught the people of their day to perceive Him at work inflicting punishment for disobedience through the catastrophes that brought an end to the Hebrew kingdom; while the Second Isaiah and his pupils declared that it was plainly God who had inspired Cyrus and the Persians to conquer Babylonia and set Israel free from its second bondage. Revelation in the Old Testament sense occurs through the conjunction of the inspired event and the inspired person who interprets it.

Election of Israel. The prophet Amos says, "You only have I known of all the families of the earth" (Amos 3:2). This puts in blunt form a conviction that pervades the whole history of Old Testament religion. For His inscrutable purposes God was believed to have chosen Israel as His own people, "a kingdom of priests, and a holy nation" (Exodus 19:6). Historically this belief in Israel's election undoubtedly originated with Moses, but it became so deeply ingrained in the religious consciousness of the Hebrews that later generations read it back into traditions that dealt with their remote origins. They said God had called their most distant ancestor, Abraham, out from Ur of the Chaldees and had promised to make of him a great nation. In the Genesis story, God says to Abraham, "I will bless them that bless thee, and curse him that curseth thee: and in thee shall all the families of the earth be blessed" (Genesis 12:3). Although men in all periods of Hebrew history were agreed as to the fact of election, there was distinct progress in the understanding of its purpose. To early ages, the time of the judges and the early monarchy, it seemed apparent that Yahweh had favored Israel for her own sake and that He was committed to come to her assistance whenever she needed help. The common, unreflective citizen naturally was inclined to think that Yahweh was Israel's god in exactly the same sense in which other gods, such as Chemosh of Moab (Judges 11:23–24), were the national gods of their people.

The refinement of the idea of election was chiefly the work of the literary prophets, who taught that Yahweh's choice of Israel was not irrevocable but was strictly conditioned upon the nation's sincere response to His ethical demands. In the long run the only interpretation of the doctrine of election that was compatible with the prophetic conception of Israel's God was that of Second Isaiah and a few others of the late teachers of Israel for whom it seemed self-evident that Israel had not been chosen for her own sake but that she might be a source of blessing to all the nations of the earth (Isaiah 49:3, 6; 56:6–8; 19:24–25). Thus within the framework of the ancient Hebrew doctrine of election there arose the idea of Israel's redemptive vocation, a conception of inestimable importance in later Judaism and in Christianity.

The Covenant. Since the relationship between Yahweh and Israel was traced to a specific historical act, it was impossible to conceive of it in purely natural terms. For prophetic religion, Yahweh was not Israel's god in the sense in which other gods were the gods of their people. Yahweh was not related to Israel by physical ties, but by a free act of the will in which both had taken part. The initiative had come from Yahweh; He had chosen Israel to be His people. But it was necessary that the people who were chosen should respond and accept Yahweh as their God. By this act of choice, Israel became the people of Yahweh on the basis of a "covenant," a legal relationship that implied mutual privileges and mutual responsibilities. It was Yahweh's duty to be the protector of His people; it was Israel's to keep God's commands and walk in accordance with His laws. The existence of this covenant was the foundation of Hebrew morality and the constant basis of the teaching of the prophets. There always were spiritually obtuse persons who were inclined to think and act as though Yahweh were god of Israel in a purely natural or physical sense and therefore obliged to save her in time of peril, regardless of her moral worth. The prophets insisted that God was under obligation to fulfill His part of the covenant only if Israel fulfilled hers. Since Israel had failed, the earliest of the literary prophets were sure that her doom was fixed, although later prophets modified the absoluteness of this doom by declaring the sufferings of the nation to be merely purgative so that she might be fit to carry out God's will.

While the covenant and the conception that underlay it continued to be a basic and distinctive element in Israel's religion, the more refined thinkers of later times came to feel a certain repugnance toward interpreting it in a legal and contractual sense. The priestly writers of the Pentateuch speak of it as purely a divine ordinance without any suggestion of mutuality between parties. For them the covenant was on God's side a matter of pure grace, while on Israel's side its acceptance was merely an act of moral obedience to a divine imperative. Every suggestion of bargaining was eliminated from the conception, and its apparent exclusiveness was partially modified by the theory of an original and universally binding covenant that God had established with Noah and therefore with the whole human race (Genesis 9:1–17). The greatest refinement of the idea of the covenant is to be found in the teaching of Jeremiah, who foresaw the coming of a time when an entirely spiritual relationship would be established between God and every individual man, written not on tablets of stone but in the human heart (Jeremiah 31:31–34).

The Concept of God. Yahweh's most distinctive attribute in the Old Testament is that of *unity*. The sole authoritative creed of ancient Judaism was that formulated in the 7th century by the disciples of the prophets: "Hear, O Israel, the Lord our God is one Lord" (Deuteronomy 6:4). This asserts unequivocally the unity of God, but the sense in which the term is used requires some elucidation. It cannot be proved that even in this late period of Israel's history such a statement is to be understood as strictly monotheistic; much less can abstract, philosophical monotheism be claimed for Moses. For the Hebrew mind the question as to whether the gods of the pagans had any ontological existence was comparatively irrelevant. This was true at least down to the time of the Babylonian Exile. The Hebrews were not chiefly concerned with the metaphysical question as to how many gods there are but with the moral question as to how many gods one should obey. From the time of Moses onward there was no doubt but that Yahweh was a "jealous" God. He was the sole Lord of Israel and demanded undivided loyalty and absolute obedience from His worshipers. Pure monotheism was not the initial presupposition of Israel's religion but its inevitable end product, the logical outgrowth of Moses' insistence that Yahweh the God of Israel would not share His throne with any other claimant, human or divine. "Thou shalt have no other gods before me" (Exodus 20:3).

Along with God's unity, His *spirituality* was also a basic tenet of Old Testament faith, although it must be noted that we use this word only for want of a better. It does not necessarily imply pure immateriality, nor can it have all the connotations that belong to it in the modern philosophical vocabulary. When used in discussing the theology of the Old Testament, God's spirituality must be understood to mean merely that God was conceived to be so different from everything perceptible or tangible that it was irreverent to represent Him in any kind of visible form. In spite of the general prohibition against the making of images, there seems to have been widespread tolerance in early Israel of certain kinds of figures which were used for superstitious purposes (the "ephod" of Judges 8:27 and the "teraphim" of I Samuel 19:13), but there is no evidence that anyone ever presumed to make an image of Yahweh Himself. The aniconic worship of the national deity was a cardinal principle of Israelite religion from the beginning. The full implications of this were unfolded only in the age of the prophets, when it came to be realized, as is implied in Isaiah 31:1–3, that God is in some sense pure "spirit"—spirit being understood to be the finest and most impalpable form of substance.

The attributes of God in which the Hebrews were most interested were His moral attributes. The first of these was His *righteousness*, a term which meant that Yahweh's character was both absolutely unchanging and that it conformed to the highest moral ideas conceived by man. That the God of Israel is not capricious, as are the gods of the pagans, but is unalterable in His purposes is expressed in classic form in the words, "The Strength of Israel will not lie nor repent: for he is not man, that he should repent" (I Samuel 15:29). That His unchangeable character is wholly beneficent and just is implied by the rhetorical question of Genesis 18:25, "Shall not the Judge of all the earth do right?" and was the solid foundation of the whole structure of Hebrew prophetic thought.

The *holiness* of God, which is so strongly emphasized in the book of Isaiah, includes His righteousness but means more than that. In primitive thinking, such as is exemplified in some of the earlier strata of the Old Testament, "holiness" meant little more than "taboo," and the underlying conception seems to be that of "separateness." This sense of the term never was lost entirely and at every level of Hebrew thought the term "holy" continues to denote the absolute qualitative difference between God and His creation. It meant that an unbridgeable gulf separates God from all merely contingent beings. This excluded every possible tendency toward pantheism. In the thinking of the prophets the concept of holiness was ennobled by extending it from the purely metaphysical to the moral sphere, so that God was conceived of as transcending every other being with respect to His goodness as well as to all His other characteristics. The mysterious holiness of God is well expressed by His distinctive Old Testament name *Yahweh*, which, whatever its original signification, seems to have been interpreted by the Hebrews to mean "He will be what He will be" (that is, His nature is essentially undefinable in human terms).

Basic to the whole idea of deity in the general Semitic world, and therefore in the Old Testament, is the idea of *power*. The underlying root of the common Semitic word for "god" (*'el*) is probably a verb that means "to be strong" (*'ul*). No limit is placed upon the power of Yahweh, and at least in the developed theology of later Israel, He was regarded as the creator and sustainer of all that is (for example, Genesis 1; Psalm 104). Less obvious to the casual reader of the Old Testament is the fact that Yahweh was also a God of *love*. This side of His nature, which needs to be more commonly recognized than it is, receives special emphasis in Hosea (for example, 11:1), Deuteronomy (7:7, 8), Second Isaiah (for example, 49:15), Psalm 103, and the frequently quoted epitome of divine attributes first found in Exodus 34:6, 7.

Other Spiritual Beings. In contrast to many other religions, that of the Old Testament is remarkably reticent with regard to spiritual beings other than the supreme deity. This is no doubt a consequence of the fear of anything that might be suggestive of polytheism. Nevertheless it is apparent that from the earliest times the Hebrews were at least vaguely aware of the existence of creatures in the unseen world. There are references to Yahweh's heavenly court, to "sons of God," to "spirits," and to "angels," although in no case are these beings described as having personal names or fixed characteristics.

The "cherubim" who guarded the ark in the temple and the "seraphim," who appear only in Isaiah 6 are isolated figures that are either the products of non-Israelite influence or survivals from pre-Mosaic times. The elaboration of angelology and demonology that characterized later Jewish and Christian times seems to have been largely the result of contact with Persia and has left traces in only one or two of the latest books of the Old Testament, such as Daniel.

Clearly to be distinguished from angels or spirits in general are the mediatorial powers demanded by an increasing emphasis upon divine transcendence in order to provide some means of contact between Yahweh and His creation. Amongst these are the so-called "Angel of Yahweh" of the early literature (a term that seems to be merely a surrogate for Divinity itself); the "Spirit" or breath of Yahweh, which gives life to all that lives and is partly personified in one or two late passages; and the "Wisdom" of God, which in the 8th chapter of Proverbs is poetically personified as a female figure, existing from all eternity, that stood at God's side in the day of creation.

The Concept of Man. Hebrew psychology was markedly different from Greek psychology in that it regarded man as a unitary being. For the Hebrew, man's body was not the "prison house" of the soul, but man in his essential nature was an animated body. The separate existence of the "soul," or *nephesh,* was inconceivable. The soul was merely the life of the body. This fact had important consequences, as will readily be seen, for Hebrew morality and for the conception of an afterlife. On the more specifically theological side, Man was regarded as the crown of God's creation, made "but little lower than God" (Psalm 8:5, in the Hebrew; consult Revised Standard Version) and bearing God's image in his own being (Genesis 1:27). This high and optimistic concept of humanity, which is to be understood as a description of man's *ideal* nature, was counterbalanced by a conviction, based on observation, that he does not exhibit the moral qualities God intended him to have and is, in fact, more inclined toward evil than toward good.

The pessimistic view of Jeremiah that "the heart is deceitful above all things and desperately wicked" (Jeremiah 17:9) is shared by all the prophets. The story of "the fall" in the opening chapters of Genesis is an attempt to picture vividly the actual state of man and to explain it as the consequence of an act of rebellion against the divine will on the part of man's first ancestor. It is significant that in this story sin is not pictured as the result of a victory of man's physical nature over his spiritual nature, but rather as a voluntary act of rebellion against the personal will of God. The ideal man, according to the Hebrew way of thinking, was not the philosopher whose unruly physical passions were under the strict control of his higher, or spiritual, nature, but rather the devoutly religious man who was completely obedient to God's will. The goal of all religious striving was, therefore, not (as in Greek ascetic thought) to put the "soul" firmly in control of the body but to bring the whole man, body and soul, under the control of the righteous personal will of God. Until that state of perfect obedience was attained, the religious teachers of Israel were sure that life would continue to be marked by pain and tragedy. Only when men "returned" to God and "hearkened to His voice" would they enjoy once more the happiness of which the idyllic life in the Garden of Eden was an attractive symbol.

The Requirements of Religion. The insistence upon obedience as the primary virtue of the devout man necessarily implies that the will of God is known. For men of the Old Testament, that will was perfectly revealed in the traditional Law of Israel, the *Torah*, which in some form or other went back to Moses and the events that accompanied the making of the Covenant at Sinai.

Historically it is clear that the Law underwent considerable development in response to the needs of successive generations and the insights of later religious thinkers. Nevertheless the basic structure did not change, and the essential spirit remained the same. The Law consisted of two parts, Moral and Ceremonial, and of these two there never could be any question but that the moral was primary. While small-minded men might suppose that God was satisfied with minute observances of formal rules covering matters of diet, custom, and worship, the prophets were insistent that God's chief concern was with the weightier concerns of justice, mercy, and a right personal relationship to God and to one's fellow man. "What does the Lord require of thee, but to do justly, and to love mercy, and to walk humbly with thy God?" (Micah 6:8.)

Because of the vehemence with which the prophets proclaimed this principle, it sometimes has been supposed that they repudiated the ceremonial law entirely. This is unlikely, since some of the prophets, notably Ezekiel and Malachi, make the reverent observance of cultic law their specific concern, and the utterances of other prophets in an apparently contrary sense can quite easily be interpreted as homiletic hyperbole. All the legal codes consist of a mixture of both ceremonial and moral laws. The general attitude seems to have been that careful observance of prescribed ceremonies was evidence of a worshiper's intention to do the whole will of God. It was felt that one who was meticulous in obeying regulations indifferent in themselves would be even more meticulous in responding to the demands of the moral law. This did not always prove to be so, but that fact in no way brings discredit upon the high motives that actuated the teachers of the Law in Israel. The place of the Torah in Old Testament religion will not be understood unless it is realized that its entire purpose, both on the moral and the ritual side, was to bring the life of man in every particular, however minute, under the direct rule of God. It is worth noting that the greatest of the moral laws of the Old Testament, "Thou shalt love thy neighbor as thyself" (Leviticus 19:18), is preserved in a book that consists mostly of cultic regulations.

The Rewards of the Good Life. According to the Old Testament, the world in which God placed man originally was "very good" (Genesis 1:31). If man had remained in a state of simple and childlike obedience there would have been no disharmony in his life. Nature would have yielded her fruits without toil; the wild animals would have been his friends and subjects; and if death were to be his lot, it would have come naturally and quietly when he was old and full of years. Because of man's disobedience, the order of nature had become unfriendly; profitable and pleasant work had become burdensome toil; children were born at the price of their mother's agony; and life had turned bitter for all men (Genesis 3:16–19). But even in man's actual state of sin and estrangement from God the intended harmony of life could in some way be realized by those who devoutly endeavored to walk in God's ways.

The supreme goal of life in the Old Testament was "peace" (*shalom*), not in the negative sense that the word suggests to English ears, but in the positive sense that it has in the Semitic languages, in which it means "well-being," "prosperity," a state in which all life's powers work together harmoniously. Such peace is the fruit of a good life. Since the purview of the ancient Hebrews did not include the possibility of a happy life after death, this "peace" was conceived of chiefly in terms of material prosperity —full barns, many children, defeat of enemies, physical health, and long life. Deuteronomy and Proverbs are the books that set forth this conception in classical form.

There came a time in Israel, beginning about the end of the 7th century, when this too-simple outlook had to be modified in view of the obvious inequities of real life, and we find, in such writers as Habakkuk, Jeremiah, and the authors of Job and the 73rd Psalm, a frank recognition that prosperity is not always the lot of the righteous and that the true and lasting rewards of piety are to be found rather in the assurance of God's constant and friendly presence.

The Afterlife. While Hebrew thought in the classical period contained no conception of a happy life after death, it was not possible for the Hebrews or any other ancient people to think in terms of the complete extinction of personal consciousness. The Hebrew view of the persistence of identity in *Sheol* was practically identical with that of the ancient Greeks with regard to *Hades*. In some vague, shadowy way, it was believed, the individual continued to be conscious of himself in the underworld, which was not clearly distinguished from the actual grave, but this was an existence without joy, hope, or satisfaction of any kind. Psalm 88:4–12 conveys the sense of hopeless gloom that surrounded the ancient Hebrew idea of the afterlife. In this respect, of course, the original teachers of Israel had nothing new to offer; these beliefs were simply part of a common cultural heritage that they shared with the Babylonians and other related peoples of the Near East.

The distinctive contribution of the Old Testament lay in its emphatic repudiation of anything suggesting necromancy or the worship of ancestors. The drive of Hebrew religion toward monotheism would not permit the spirits of the dead to usurp any of the reverence that belonged to God alone. There came a tremendous revolution in the attitude of the men of Israel toward the afterlife at the very end of the Old Testament period. As a result of the serious questions that had been raised about the evident injustices of life in the present world, particularly in the case of the Maccabean martyrs who seemingly had suffered heroic and painful deaths to no purpose, there arose a new and confident assurance that God would provide a better life beyond the grave. Persian influence certainly had something to do with the rise of this new and far-reaching doctrine of the resurrection of the dead, but the presuppositions of it are supplied by the religion of Israel itself, for the basic assertion that God is righteous ultimately would have become incredible if men had been able to believe that He allowed the brave and the good to perish without reward and without hope. It is therefore correct to say that the doctrine of resurrection was implicit in the Old Testament doctrine of God and that it was the final but inevitable flower of Israel's faith.

Eschatology. The men of the Old Testament thought of history in linear terms in contrast with most pagans who saw it in purely cyclical terms. For the pagan, history moved in circles that constantly returned to their beginnings. Strangely enough, this pagan view is expressed in Ecclesiastes, a very late Old Testament book that clearly shows the impress of Greek philosophical ideas and declares that "there is no new thing under the sun" and "the thing that hath been, it is that which shall be" (Ecclesiastes 1:9). This book serves only to set in vivid contrast the general Old Testament point of view, according to which history moves forward under God's direction from a definite point in the past to a definite point in the future. History begins with Creation, the Fall of Man, and the Election of Israel. It moves toward some kind of divine consummation in the future.

The precise nature of this consummation varies in detail from book to book and from period to period. Nevertheless, two elements in it seem to be relatively constant. Because of the sin that prevails among men, there will be *judgment*. In early times this usually was conceived of as occurring on the plane of history in the near future and as involving Israel alone. Such is the point of view of the book of Amos. It is not clear that Amos had any eschatology other than an eschatology of doom for Israel. In this respect, however, Amos seems to give us only a partial and one-sided picture that probably is not entirely fair even to his own understanding of things. Certainly later prophets saw that the judgment of Israel could be only a prelude to greater things. Israel must be punished in order to be purified for further service to God.

Beyond the judgment would come *redemption*, which, in the minds of the greatest representatives of Old Testament thought, would include not only Israel but all the nations of the world. Typical expressions of this conception are found in Isaiah 2:1–4 (Micah 4:1–5), 60:1–3, and Zechariah 8:20–23. The apocalyptic writers, who eventually took the place of the prophets, tended more and more to speak in terms of a purely supernatural eschatology, in which the normal forces of historical development had but little importance, but even in these books the essential underlying pattern remained the same. In spite of the differences that appear in various books and periods, it may be said that Hebrew eschatology consistently looked forward to the ultimate establishment of the perfect rule (or "kingdom") of God by means of a series of great final acts in which evil would be judged and condemned and the righteous delivered from their present bondage.

The Messiah. Different eschatological schemes picture God's final judgment and deliverance as being accomplished in a variety of ways. According to one view, it will be God Himself who will establish His kingdom, without the assistance of a mediator of any kind. But in what might be called the classical view, God was to perform His mighty work through a supernatural figure who would appear on the stage of history at the crucial moment. The concept of this divinely chosen deliverer derives ultimately from ancient Near Eastern ideas of kingship, which, as we have previously noted, became more or less naturalized in Israel under the Davidic dynasty. To the world of the ancient Near East the king was a divine or semidivine figure from whom radiated powers that brought prosperity in peace and victory in war. Since these grandiose ideas of kingship constantly were being disappointed by the actual kings of David's line, it was only

natural that they should be transferred to an ideal king of the future, and by the time the monarchy came to an end in 586 B.C., this figure probably already had become a fixed feature of Hebrew eschatological expectation.

In the exilic and postexilic periods, when political independence had ceased, it no longer was possible to put much hope in human political action, and the expectations of Israel came to be centered almost exclusively in the idea that God would intervene shortly in the affairs of the world and set up His eternal rule. Such circumstances provided the necessary setting for the tremendous growth of Messianic ideas that marks the period immediately preceding the beginning of the Christian era. The name *Messiah* means "anointed one" and was anciently one of the titles of the Hebrew king. With the end of the monarchy it was reserved for the ideal king of the future and eventually became a technical term to describe him. This, however, occurred only after the close of the Old Testament period. Literally translated into Greek, the term "Messiah" became *christos* (Christ). This term and the eschatological views associated with it provided a framework into which the New Testament Gospel could be set and a vocabulary with which it could be expressed. In eschatology and Messianism are to be found the links that bind together most closely the Old Testament and the New Testament.

ROBERT C. DENTAN, *General Theological Seminary*

Bibliography

Baab, Otto, *The Theology of the Old Testament* (Nashville, Tenn., 1949).
Heinisch, Paul, *The Theology of the Old Testament* (Collegeville, Minn., 1950).
Jacob, Edmond, *Theology of the Old Testament* (New York 1958).
Kaufmann, Yecheskel, *The Religion of Israel* (Chicago 1960).
Knight, G.A.F., *A Christian Theology of the Old Testament* (Richmond, Va., 1959).
Oesterley, W.O.E., and Robinson, T.H., *Hebrew Religion*, rev. ed. (New York 1937).
Pfeiffer, Robert H., *Religion in the Old Testament* (New York 1961).
Rad, Gerhard von, *Old Testament Theology* (New York 1965).
Ringgren, Helmer, *Israelite Religion* (Philadelphia 1966).

For Specialized Study

Davidson, A.B., *The Theology of the Old Testament* (Edinburgh 1904).
Eichrodt, Walther, *Theologie des Alten Testaments:* vol. 1, *Gott und Volk;* vol. 2, *Gott und Welt;* vol. 3, *Gott und Mensch* (Leipzig 1933–39).
Knudson, Albert, *The Religious Teaching of the Old Testament* (New York 1918).
Köhler, Ludwig, *Theologie des Alten Testaments* (Tübingen 1936).
Marti, Karl, *The Religion of the Old Testament* (London 1910).
Robinson, H. Wheeler, *The Religious Ideas of the Old Testament* (New York 1913).
Sellin, Ernst, *Alttestamentliche Theologie auf religionsgeschichtlicher Grundlage* (Leipzig 1933).
Smith, Henry Preserved, *The Religion of Israel* (Edinburgh 1914).

8. History of Old Testament Interpretation

Like all literature written in an environment and era very different from our own, the Old Testament presents to its readers a serious problem of interpretation, if we are to understand what it says and what it means. Unlike secular literature, however, the Old Testament to Jews and Christians is a special, sacred writing, possessing a unique significance because it reveals the true God, the true nature of man and the world, and the action of God toward, and His will for, man. To those who accept it as such, this literature is thus more than an ancient writing; it is intended by God also to be contemporary testimony. Hence the problem of interpretation includes not merely what the original says but the meaning it has for the religious community at a subsequent time, for interpretation is the bridge between the ancient documents and the later groups that accept them as Scripture.

Jewish Interpretations. Early Jewish interpretation was done under the faith that the Scripture was the very word of God, verbally inspired by Him. In it the will of God for Jewish life was clearly and definitely revealed. The destruction of the Judean state in 587 B.C. had made clear the truth of the prophetic indictment, that the catastrophe was God's judgment upon a people who had violated His will as contained in the Mosaic covenant. Since the consummation of God's Kingdom was delayed, what the Jew must do is to take the 613 precepts of the Mosaic law with intense seriousness and see to it that they are obeyed in every phase of his existence. Consequently, "normative" or Rabbinic Judaism is characterized by its careful and detailed concentration upon the Law in order to explain its meaning and how in detail it is to be applied to a different life situation. There thus arose with the passing centuries a large body of law (*halakoth,* or "regulations for life"), of equal sanctity with the Mosaic law because it was the application of the original to the multitudinous activities of existence.

The attempt to interpret the writings by means of a more theological exegesis (*haggada*) was characterized chiefly by what appears to a modern reader as an extreme verbalism that tends to interpret words and phrases independently of their context and to search for hidden meanings in textual peculiarities and adiaphora. That the same methods we find in the Talmud were used also by the Jewish sectarians is indicated by the Habakkuk Commentary of the Jewish Covenanters. This document, found among the Dead Sea Scrolls in 1947 and dated the 1st century B.C., interprets the prophet as speaking in veiled terms about events of the author's own time and as describing the origin of the sect. The "woes" in Habakkuk 2 are viewed as directed against the "Wicked Priest" who persecuted the "teacher of righteousness" (the sect's founder). To interpret in this way meant that numerous words and textual peculiarities were given a forced and abnormal construction in accordance with the accepted practice of the day.

Hellenistic Judaism, as represented especially by Philo of Alexandria, had been exposed to Greek culture and had come to have a great admiration for Greek philosophy. Since Old Testament Law is God's Word for man's life and since Greek philosophy also contains truth, the two were believed to have some connection. The interpretative clue to this relationship was found in allegory, a method of interpretation that many Greeks, particularly the Stoics, had used to explain the meaning of old myths that intelligent men no longer could take literally. To Philo, therefore, Scripture had a double meaning, the literal and allegorical, corresponding to the duality of body and soul in Greek psychology. When something appears in the text that is without meaning to us or seems unworthy of the Divine Author or is of an unexpected or contradictory nature, then allegory certainly must be used. By such means a large amount of Platonic philosophy was found in the Pentateuch, and the Old Testament was understood in the Greek spirit.

History lost its meaning; eschatology in its Biblical sense was not comprehended; and Old Testament people were interpreted solely as eternal types of moral and spiritual value.

Early Christian Interpretation. The early Christian interpreters of the Bible acknowledged the authority of the Old Testament as Scripture but at the same time held that the Law had been fulfilled in Christ. Except for such general prescriptions as are contained in the Ten Commandments, the Law of the Old Covenant, therefore, was not binding on the Christian. To the writers of the New Testament the most significant thing in the Old Testament is the *activity* of God, rather than the *Law* of God. This activity constituted a redemptive history, the first stage in God's work to usher in His Kingdom on earth. Hence the events and personalities in the Old Testament were considered not as ends in themselves but as pointing beyond themselves to their fulfillment. They were "types" in the sense that they were the foretaste and preparation for God's work in Christ. Thus Christ was interpreted in terms of this redemptive history, not merely as teacher and martyr, but as the new and climactic event in God's activity, one that had ushered in the Kingdom soon to be consummated. While an occasional example of allegory appears in the New Testament, the interpretation is basically nonallegorical; it is instead chiefly typological in the above sense.

During the 2d century A.D. a major problem in Christian circles was that concerning the meaning and significance of the Old Testament in a church now composed almost entirely of Gentiles. To many intellectuals of the day the Old Testament appeared so filled with crudities as to form a most difficult stumbling block. Consequently, the Gnostic movement in its radical form denied the divine origin of the literature. The Creator-god and Lawgiver was thought to be a different God than the Father of Jesus Christ, either a limited being subordinate to the latter or a Satanic power in rebellion against him. This position was rejected as heretical by the church as a whole. Instead, the Law was viewed either as a Christian revelation that the Jews had not understood or else as possessing a temporal validity only, which Christ had set aside.

Nearly all writers used the Old Testament as a book of predictions of Christ and the Kingdom being fulfilled in him. The method used was chiefly that of allegory, learned from Hellenistic Judaism, in which the sense of history was largely lost and the emphasis laid upon hidden meanings. This enabled the interpreter to find the whole Gospel in the Old Testament in such a manner as to obscure the distinction between allegory and typology. The emphasis was thus on the Old Testament as a "field of hidden treasure" (Irenaeus), and this remained the dominant attitude in interpretation for more than a thousand years.

Allegory was an effective weapon in the apologetics of the time, and while it permitted the exegete to interpret the Old Testament in Greek categories, nevertheless the historical meaning still was grasped firmly enough to prevent the complete Hellenization of the Gospel. Thus the Old Testament kept alive the Biblical sense of time in terms of prediction and fulfillment, the concept of the church as transcending history, and the understanding that God was not cosmic law but the One who reveals Himself in what He does (whence the understanding of the person of Jesus).

It was the School of Alexandria during the 3d century that undertook for the first time to expound the meaning of the allegorical method and to justify it. From the Septuagint rendering of Proverbs 22:20–21, Origen concluded that the Scripture has a threefold sense: the bodily or physical, which is the literal sense; the "soul," which is the moral sense; and the spiritual, which is the allegorical-mystical sense. He was most concerned, however, with the first and the third of these, the problem of the letter and the spirit of the writing. There are many things in the Old Testament that no intelligent man can accept in their literal sense: for example, the first three days of creation without the existence of the sun and stars, the anthropomorphisms, many of the legal prescriptions, and so on. In such cases and in many others where there are obscurities or contradictions, he believed that the divine author was speaking either nonsense, which is impossible, or in mystery that the Christian exegete must penetrate as best he can by the comparison of texts, especially where one brings out a spiritual meaning, and by the rule of faith. In this way a Christological interpretation of the Old Testament was possible, whereby exegesis was used not so much to discover truth as to illustrate and expound the faith already received.

The allegorical method was opposed in the church, however, especially by those who were influenced by the more literal interpretation of the synagogue. This was particularly true of the members of the School of Antioch, the most illustrious of whom were Theodore of Mopsuestia and Chrysostom. This school attacked Origen for his refusal to take history seriously and for turning the historical into a world of symbols and hidden mysteries. Scripture has no hidden meaning that only the initiated can comprehend. In prophecy, for example, the prediction is both historical and messianic; but the latter is based on the former. It is not something added to the former but is already implicit in it. Those parts of the Old Testament that are not historical and messianic (that is, the Wisdom literature) represent purely human wisdom that is not authoritative. Indeed, Theodore claimed that they should not be included in the sacred canon.

The School of Antioch, though condemned as heretical in 553 A.D., had a wide influence. It is especially evident in Jerome, in the medieval interest in Jewish exegesis, in St. Thomas Aquinas, and in the Reformation. Yet in the meantime the views of the Alexandrian school were to prevail in the West. The excessive use of allegory in support of heretical tendencies was held in check by the authority of received doctrine. Augustine, for example, held that all interpretation must be controlled by the Scriptural law of love on the one hand and by the rule of faith on the other. The latter was the faith as received and transmitted through the church since apostolic times. Hence the freedom of allegory actually was limited by the church's authoritative tradition, because the interpretation must conform to what the church always has taught.

The Middle Ages. Medieval interpretation followed the same lines, except that toward its end there was an increasing concern for the literal sense of Scripture. The moral and spiritual (allegorical) senses still were adhered to, but in St. Thomas Aquinas, for example, there is an insist-

ence on the primacy of the literal and historical sense as the basis for other meanings. For instance, with regard to the Garden of Eden the church always had been divided as to whether it was actually historical or only to be conceived spiritually. St. Thomas held that everything that the Scripture sets forth as history is to be taken as such, and only on that foundation is spiritual exposition to be built. Insistence on literal interpretation greatly influenced Old Testament study, for it encouraged the study of Hebrew and the production of historical commentaries.

Throughout this period the Old Testament was viewed as an integral part of the one unique revelation of God in history, which culminated and concluded in Christ. The Mosaic law was regarded as a necessary stage in God's preparation of the people for Christ's coming. It was filled with types that Christ reenacted. As law it was fulfilled, not contradicted, by Christ. The permanent element is that found in both Testaments, while the first is the necessary preparation for the New Covenant in Christ. The Old Testament thus was read and interpreted as Christian Scripture, and allegory enabled the interpreters to find the substance of the Gospel within it. Yet it was the Old Testament that prevented the Hellenization of the Gospel, because time and history were seen there to be the arena of God's work and revelation.

The Reformation. Reformation interpretation marked a fresh beginning by the radical reinterpretation of the authority of the church and of the Fathers on the one hand and the forthright rejection of the multiple sense of Scripture on the other. Only one meaning of a text is permissible, and that is the meaning in the mind of the original author as inspired of God. That meaning does not involve a multiple sense, although traditional explanations frequently were given credence in the interpretation of the implications of a text for faith. For Luther and Calvin, theology and exegesis must not be separated pursuits, as they were in the medieval period. The authority of Scripture is supreme, above church and above theology. The latter must be derived from Scripture, which means a fresh study of the text, not simply through the mediation of the Fathers and the Vulgate, but through the intensive study of the original languages. To both these great reformers the unity of the Testaments is to be found in their common revelation of the grace of God and the needed response of faith. The Law was not a natural law through which men were justified by the addition of faith, nor was it a bondage to which the grace of Christ was added as a relief. Instead, it was given to the People of God, who had been brought into being as God's people by grace and faith. It was the guide to life in God's service for God's elect. Through it one could not lift himself to a position where grace was available by faith; both grace and faith were known before the Law was given.

The Post-Reformation Period. In the Protestant orthodoxy of the post-Reformation period the importance of the Old Testament and its link with the New was conceived to lie in the common moral demands found in both Testaments. All study of the Old Testament was directed toward the discovery of God's will for mankind. Generalized principles of universal applicability were found that in a sense were not dissimilar to those found in Catholic natural law. God's demands and promises, His rewards and judgments in the

Old Testament, are, therefore, in many ways as important as the New Testament. Of course, with Calvin one must distinguish between the ceremonial, judicial, and moral laws. The first was fulfilled in Christ and is not binding on the church. The second, dealing with the ordering of Jewish national life, cannot be applied in detail, but it does illustrate important general principles. The moral laws, however, are binding on all and are of timeless significance because they are the righteous demands of the same holy God.

Hence Protestant orthodoxy, not unlike Catholic orthodoxy, approached the interpretation of the Old Testament through the category of law and regarded it as "the schoolmaster" (Galatians 3:24). Through it men saw their impotence and came to hope for salvation. This salvation is revealed in the New Testament through God's act in Christ. The Old Testament is needed, therefore, to show men God's holy will, their impotence, and their hope. To the Law, then, the New Testament has added grace. Such a view lies in a different dimension from that of the great reformers themselves, who saw grace before law in the Old Testament and conceived of the Law as given to the people who had known this grace. To Luther the law was completely abrogated in Christ, whereas Calvin made much of it as the guide to proper life under God. Yet both were agreed that the fundamental unity of the Bible lay in its portrayal of the gracious *acts* of God.

The legalism of the post-Reformation orthodoxy was coupled with a literalism based on the theory of verbal inspiration of the text. Hence every part of Scripture was believed to be of equal validity as the Word of God, with the result that a static view of the literature was obtained, while the newness of the Gospel in relation to the Old Testament was obscured, even as it had been formerly in allegory. New Testament typology, on the other hand, led to an excessive use of it in interpreting the Old Testament so that there arose a Christological exegesis of a kind not radically different from allegory (the angel and the glory of God are actually Christ; their historical meaning is of little concern). Yet in spite of this situation the Reformation began a new day in interpretation, one marked by the intensive study of the original languages, by numerous commentaries and new translations, and in the reformers themselves by a great deal of what subsequently was known as higher criticism. The dynamic view of Scripture that made such criticism possible was stifled in Protestant orthodoxy, but it nevertheless lived on in minority circles. Meanwhile, the Enlightenment and the rise of rationalism brought about an entirely new approach to the Old Testament in the scholarly circles of Protestantism.

The 19th and 20th Centuries. The interpretation of the 19th century was governed by the new views of history. The ideas of progress, development, and evolution were taken over from natural science and applied to history. Geological, anthropological, and archaeological study made it impossible for thinking men to take seriously the Biblical view of the universe and the stories of creation in Genesis. Biblical miracles became suspect because they appeared to conflict with natural law. Significant strides were taken in the recovery of the ancient world, so that the Bible was fitted more securely into its ancient setting. A tremendous amount of work was done in the fields of comparative religion and the literary and historical study of Old Testament literature. The prophets were recovered and seen as significant historical figures in their own right, instead of being used chiefly for their predictive value. The Mosaic authorship of the Pentateuch was given up in leading scholarly circles. Instead the early historical literature was shown to be made up of various literary strata, composed between the 10th and 4th centuries B.C. and fitted together by a complex process of compilation and supplementation. Such views differed so radically from those of the older orthodoxy that it is small wonder the 19th century became a time of heated controversy and, toward the end of it, the time of the famous Anglican and Presbyterian heresy trials in England, Scotland, and the United States. Yet so persuasive was the new approach that no section of the world church, whether Protestant or Catholic, has remained unaffected by its stimulus, while many Jewish scholars have joined its ranks and become leaders in its work.

The idea of progress as applied to the Old Testament meant that the literature was viewed as the gradual human discovery of the Divine. Theologically, it was fitted into the church's faith by the concept of *progressive revelation:* God revealed more of himself through history as the people became ready to comprehend. Like living organisms, Biblical history is to be viewed in terms of seed, growing plant, and fruit or as babe, youth, and mature man. Since little was known then about contemporary religion during the early part of the 2d millennium B.C., the religion of the patriarchal period was conceived as little more than animism, while the remainder of the literature was thought to exhibit a perfect example of religious evolution through polytheism and henotheism to monotheism. Since all information about the Mosaic era is from later sources, this period was devaluated and the prophetic achievement was interpreted as the discovery of "ethical monotheism."

Basic to this interpretative procedure is a concept of emergent value, in which the earliest datable materials are assumed to be the most "primitive" and the later the more "advanced." By this means the Old Testament was joined to the New as childhood and youth are joined to maturity. Yet a result has been a weakening of the hold of the Old Testament on the religious community, because in the proclamation of the Gospel only the most "advanced" stage of the revelation is to be used, in which the values and ideals, so slow in emerging, appear in their purest form. Thus 20th century Protestantism has experienced a revival of the heretical views of 2d century Gnosticism, in which the God of the Old Testament was viewed as inferior and radically different from the God of Jesus Christ.

In the second and third quarters of the 20th century much work has been done in revising 19th century views and in healing the breach in the church between the Old and New Testaments that the developmental concept had unwittingly brought about. In the first place, the phenomenal accumulation of archaeological information about the Biblical world has made it impossible to accept the older evolutionary theory in its simplest form. By patriarchal times the religion of the ancient world had advanced far beyond any such stage as primitive animism to a highly sophisticated polytheism. The study of the structure of this type of religion has led to a new emphasis upon the radical difference between it and the faith of Israel, even in the latter's earliest stages as we know them from datable literature. Hence such development as Israelite religious life reveals must be conceived to have taken place within the framework of this uniqueness; there is no empirical means whereby the evolution of Israelite faith by gradual process from polytheism can be demonstrated.

In the second place, this awareness of the nature of contemporary religion has led to a fresh emphasis on historical revelation as the distinctive note in Israelite faith, rather than upon a supposed prophetic "discovery of ethical monotheism." That is, God is known by what He has done in history. Hence Biblical history differs from secular history in that it is the confessional recital of the acts of God by the worshiping community, something quite unknown in other religions. Israelite "realism" consisted in its attempt to take history seriously as the revelation of the true nature of God and of His purposes in history. In this viewpoint the relation between the two Testaments in the Christian Bible is to be found in the Biblical conception of a special redemptive history (what German scholarship calls *Heilsgeschichte*), in which the redemptive acts of God in salvation and judgment are seen fulfilled and climaxed in Christ, with whom God has established the new community, the new Israel, the church. Such a view allows for the great variety of the Bible and even for differences in viewpoint among writers, while still maintaining an essential unity.

The church is not yet entirely agreed, however, as to precisely what this means for the interpretation of the Old Testament. Christ, it is held, is the clue to the meaning of God's activity in Israel, but what is the meaning of the Christological exegesis of the Old Testament? In certain extreme cases Christological interpretation has resulted in a defense of allegory and typology in a limited and disciplined sense but nevertheless not radically different in method from the usage of the early church. In most of the church's scholarship, Catholic and Protestant, the tendency is to reject allegory almost completely in practice, while the subject of typology is approached with grave misgivings. One method of dealing with the ambiguity involved in "Christological exegesis" has been to insist upon a "Trinitarian interpretation." By means of this term scholars have been able to see Christ as the guide to the meaning of the Old Testament, while avoiding every temptation to read New Testament meaning into Old Testament passages where Christ is not in the mind of the original writers. Yet the Holy Spirit is held still to speak to us authoritatively through the testimony of Israel by confronting us with the true God in all His holy majesty, with His inescapable will, with our sin, God's judgment upon it, and the hope that this faith engenders.

See also section 16. *History of New Testament Interpretation;* and separate article Exegesis.

G. ERNEST WRIGHT
The Divinity School, Harvard University

Bibliography

Albright, William F., *From the Stone Age to Christianity*, 2d ed. (Baltimore 1957).
Dugmore, C.W., ed., *The Interpretation of the Bible* (London 1944).
Grant, Robert M., *A Short History of the Interpretation of the Bible*, rev. ed. (New York 1963).
Richardson, Alan, and Schweitzer, Wolfgang, eds., *Biblical Authority for Today* (Philadelphia 1952).
Smalley, B., *The Study of the Bible in the Middle Ages* (New York and London 1941).

For Specialized Study

Armstrong, G.T., *Die Genesis in der Alten Kirche* (Tübingen, Germany 1962).
Diestel, L., *Geschichte des Alten Testaments in der Christlichen Kirche* (Jena 1869).
Farrar, F.W., *History of Interpretation* (London 1886).
Fullerton, K., *Prophecy and Authority* (New York 1919).
Gilbert, G.H., *Interpretation of the Bible* (New York 1908).
Van Ruler, A.A., *Die Christliche Kirche und das Alte Testament* (Munich 1955).
Westermann, C., ed., *Essays on Old Testament Hermeneutics*, tr. by J.L. Mays (Richmond, 1963).

NEW TESTAMENT

9. New Testament: Introduction

"New Testament" is the name given the collection of 27 sacred writings that supplement the Jewish Scriptures in the Christian Bible: the Jewish Scriptures accordingly are called the Old Testament. The English word "testament" is, however, an inadequate translation of the Greek word *diatheke*, which was meant to convey the idea of a covenant rather than of a document governing inheritance (that is, "last will and testament"). Thus the title of the Revised Standard Version (1946) reads: "The New Covenant commonly called the New Testament of our Lord and Savior Jesus Christ." It is by contrast with—or as an extension of—the idea of the Holy Covenant of God with Israel, presented in the Old Testament, that the term came to be used in the early church (as in St. Paul's Letters, Romans 9:4, Galatians 3:17, and in the Epistle to Hebrews 8:8; 10:16; 12:24). The use of the term as title of a collection of books came later (in the work of Melito of Sardis, in the 2d century) and reflects the conviction that the terms of the New Covenant are explained in these specifically canonical or inspired writings. The New Covenant was viewed not only as the supplement to the Old but also as its real climax: from the beginning of the long course of divine revelation God had intended to proclaim this final and complete "covenant," "new law," or "way of salvation" (Hebrews 1:1–4, John 1:1–18). Hence the Christian Scriptures include both Old and New Testaments: the New does not supplant the Old but completes it.

The earliest Christians, who were Jews, would have been surprised to learn that their Bible (the "Old" Testament) was incomplete. For them the Scriptures included "the Law and the Prophets and the Psalms" (Luke 24:44). But the Christians in the vast worldwide mission field outside Palestine were mostly Gentiles—at least Gentiles were in the majority by the time St. Paul's missionary labors had ended. These earliest Gentile Christians had the Jewish Scriptures in a Greek translation (the so-called Septuagint, usually referred to as the LXX, since it was thought to be the work of the "seventy" scholars chosen to translate the Hebrew Scriptures in the days of Ptolemy II Philadelphus, reigned 285–246 B.C.). This Greek Old Testament already had been supplemented by the so-called Apocrypha (that is, books found in the Greek translation but not in the original Hebrew Bible of Palestine). In the early Christian services of worship, throughout the Greek-speaking Mediterranean world and even as far East as the Euphrates, it was this Greek Bible that was read and expounded—the Bible that had been adopted from the Jewish synagogues of the Western Diaspora (the "Dispersion" or scattering of the Jews in foreign lands). Very naturally this Greek Bible was still further supplemented, as early Christian writings (also in Greek) were read in the church's services of worship. The earliest of these, Paul's Letters, certainly were so read (Colossians 4:15–16). The Gospels probably were intended to be read aloud (Mark 13:14)— in them many modern scholars find traces of adaptation to liturgical use and even to a sequence of seasons in a very early form of the church year. The Apocalypse of John, the last book in the collection, certainly was meant to be read aloud (see the letters to the seven churches in chapters 2 and 3). Hebrews, James, and part of I Peter are thought to be homilies rather than letters. The Pastoral Epistles (I, II Timothy, Titus) are early examples of "church orders" (collections of rules for guidance in ecclesiastical administration and worship). We now recognize more clearly the uses to which the New Testament writings were put; accordingly, we also can understand how the Christian supplement to the Greek Bible grew, became standard, or "canonical," and eventually was regarded as equally inspired.

During the very earliest period the Old Testament provided the Christian standard of doctrine in ethics, in church discipline, and in theology—even various incidents in the life of Christ were thought to be foreshadowed in the Psalms, the Prophets (especially Isaiah 53), and the Law. That is to say, the early Christians studied the Jewish Scriptures diligently to find "testimonies" to Christ, "prophecies" of his coming, and "types" of his life, death, and resurrection (John 5:39, Acts 17:11). That they read into it meanings that were not originally there (compare Matthew 1:23 with Isaiah 7:14 or Matthew 2:15 with Hosea 11:1) never occurred to them; their "exegesis" was pursued in all good faith but was rejected by the Jews, for whom such interpretations were impossible. (See EXEGESIS.) Throughout the New Testament we find traces of the constant use of the Old Testament (that is, the Greek translation of the Jewish Bible). During the period before even the earliest of the Gospels was written, the oral tradition of Jesus' life and teaching was a standard by which the interpretation of the Old Testament was determined; so also was the authoritative doctrine ("teaching") of the apostles found in the Epistles. Paul's letters certainly were authoritative, and they contained much interpretation of the Old Testament, from the new Christian point of view. It is not strange, therefore, that Old Testament phrases as well as ideas occasionally influenced the oral tradition that was being applied to the Jewish scriptures to unlock their "true" (often allegorical) meaning. Since early Christianity, at least in its initial stages, was very strongly apocalyptic in outlook (that is, convinced that the "last times" had arrived) and was concerned with the remaining events that were to precede the "end of the age," it was natural that such books as Ezekiel and Daniel should have exercised great influence on the church's thought and literature;

but the Old Testament influence was paramount in such other areas as moral teaching, the doctrine of Christ's true nature, the organization of the church, and even the orders of the ministry. So powerful was this influence that it continued long after the collection of New Testament writings had become practically fixed (about 180).

The 27 Christian books thus added to the Greek Old Testament comprised four Gospels according to Matthew, Mark, Luke, and John; the Acts of the Apostles (really part 2 of a two-volume work of which part 1 was the Gospel according to Luke); 13 (or 14) Letters attributed to Paul and addressed to Romans, Corinthians (2), Galatians, Ephesians, Philippians, Colossians, Thessalonians (2), Timothy (2), Titus, Philemon, Hebrews (of the authorship of some of these letters the early church was not sure— notably of Hebrews); 7 "Catholic" or "Apostolic" Letters (presumably by the older apostles) addressed to the whole church: the Epistles of James, Peter (2), John (3), Jude; finally the Apocalypse (or Revelation) attributed to John— containing the long and elaborate vision seen by him when he was an exile in the island of Patmos.

Undoubtedly there were other early Christian writings that have not survived; in fact the New Testament itself contains references to such writings (Colossians 4:16c, Luke 1:1–2). Moreover, there were some that served as "sources" on which the surviving books were based (for example, the sources underlying the Gospels). Once incorporated in larger works, these earlier collections of material ceased to be copied and so eventually disappeared. But it is the conviction of most modern scholars that the number of "lost books" of the New Testament is insignificant. The time soon passed when there were still survivors of the first Christian generation who might have added much to the tradition of Jesus' life and teaching (I Corinthians 15:6). Moreover, the early Christian movement, for all its immense vitality, was not primarily or chiefly a literary or a philosophical movement, and its followers were too intent upon the approaching end of the age to be interested in writing for posterity—a posterity that never would exist.

FREDERICK C. GRANT, *Union Theological Seminary*

10. Canon of the New Testament

The term "canon" (Greek, *kanōn*) is applied to the list of books accepted generally throughout the church as inspired and therefore as containing the authoritative statement of Christian doctrine. (The term is applied to both the Old Testament and the New.) "History of the New Testament Canon" means the history of the process by which these inspired or authoritative books gradually were set apart from the rest of early Christian literature and added to the collection of Jewish sacred writings contained in the Greek Old Testament. Originally the word *kanōn* meant a rule, standard, measuring line, or rod; eventually, the classical Greek writings—such as those of Homer, Thucydides, Plato, Pindar, and other great writers—came to be known as models, or standards (*kanōnes*); from this usage it was an easy step to the meaning, "a standard list of books," and then to the standard list of sacred books used by the church.

Early Versions of the New Testament. The contents of the New Testament as we have it today were not fully determined until the 4th century: the first list that tallies exactly with our New Testament is found in the *Festal* (that is, Easter) *Epistle* of St. Athanasius (Epistle 39) dated 367 A.D. But this does not mean that the church had no New Testament until that late date. By the year 200 the contents of our New Testament were quite generally recognized. The main contents, namely the Four Gospels and the Epistles of Paul, were widely accepted. Uncertainty attached to only three or four of the other books now in the canon, and there was some question whether or not to include two or three that eventually were excluded. A glance at the oldest of the surviving canonical lists will make this clear.

The so-called *Muratorian Fragment*, discovered in an 8th century manuscript by L.A. Muratori and published by him in 1740, reflects the usage of the church in Rome about 180 A.D. It is complete, but it obviously began with Matthew and Mark, and it lists our New Testament, with the following exceptions: Hebrews, James, I-II Peter, and III John are lacking; but the Revelation of Peter (which some reject) and the Wisdom of Solomon (from the Old Testament apocrypha) are included; the Epistles to the Laodiceans and Alexandrians are rejected; the Shepherd of Hermas may be read, but not at public worship.

The Clermont List, found in the 6th century Codex Claromontanus of Paul's letters, names the Old Testament books from Genesis to Tobit and then lists the New Testament books, which are the same as ours except that the Gospels are listed as Matthew, John, Mark, Luke (the apostolic authors coming first); then the Letters of Paul, save that Philippians, I-II Thessalonians, and perhaps Hebrews were omitted by oversight; the Epistle of Barnabas, the Shepherd of Hermas, the Acts of Paul, and the Revelation of Peter are included. The list probably embraces the canon as it existed in Egypt (i.e., in Alexandria) about 300 A.D.

The Cheltenham List was discovered by Theodor Mommsen in 1885 in a manuscript at Cheltenham in England. It probably reflects the usage of North Africa about 360 A.D. and contains the Four Gospels, 13 letters of Paul, the Acts of the Apostles, Revelation, three letters of John, and two letters of Peter.

These lists may be compared with the actual contents of the oldest uncial manuscripts, for example, Codex Sinaiticus (5th century, possibly 4th). These manuscripts contained our New Testament, plus the Epistle of Barnabas and the Shepherd of Hermas. Codex Alexandrinus (5th century; its Table of Contents is later) contains the Four Gospels, Acts, seven Catholic epistles, 14 letters of Paul, Revelation, I-II Clement, and the 18 Psalms of Solomon (included as an appendix). Codex Vaticanus (4th century) unfortunately breaks off at Hebrews 9:14, and so we cannot tell what the rest contained.

It is clear that from the end of the 2d century the main contents of our present New Testament were not questioned. It was not by any decree of synod or council that the choice was made; but by the constant test of daily usage these books stood out as uniquely valuable for edification, instruction, and the positive statement of historic Christianity against the speculative vagaries and misinterpretations of the Gnostic and other heretical groups. Only in the case of two major New Testament books was there long delay. Although written in the West,

perhaps in Rome, probably in Italy, the homily known as the Epistle to Hebrews was not accepted in the West for a long time. The reasons for this delay are not clear; perhaps there was too much uncertainty of its authorship, or its theology and exegesis may have seemed too un-Pauline, or its somewhat philosophical outlook may have been uncongenial to the church in the West. But it was accepted in the East, where Philo's Stoicized Platonism and his allegorical exegesis of the Old Testament had been taken over by the church, and where the difficulty of the unknown authorship did not seem so serious. Origen of Alexandria acknowledged that no one knew who its author was ("Only God knows") but insisted that its teaching was consonant with Paul and with the rest of Scripture. It was the East that saved the Epistle to Hebrews for the New Testament canon.

The other major writing that was delayed in its admission to the canon was the Apocalypse (or Revelation) of St. John. In this case it was the East that hesitated. There were many such books in circulation in the East, such as the Revelation of Peter and the apocalyptic books ascribed to Enoch, Baruch, Ezra, and others. The East was perfectly familiar with such writings and did not overrate them. Curiously, it was the West that first admitted the Revelation of John, and it did so on the ground that it contained a preview of future church history, from the time of the seer on Patmos to the end of the age, the Last Judgment, and the future Consummation.

The Process of Establishing the Canon. The process by which the 27 books of the New Testament were selected and authorized for reading in public worship and for private devotional study goes back, undoubtedly, to the 1st century. E.J. Goodspeed advanced the theory that the surviving Pauline letters were first collected soon after the "publication" of the Book of Acts (that is, vol. II of "Luke-Acts"), about 95 A.D., and that the Epistle to the Ephesians was compiled as an encyclical, or "covering letter," to head this collection, being drawn (or paraphrased) from several of the authentic letters. This theory has come to be widely accepted among New Testament scholars. If it is correct, the original nucleus of the New Testament was the Epistles of Paul, to which were added, presently, the so-called "Catholic" epistles, written presumably by other apostles (James, Peter, John, and Jude), and the "Pastoral Epistles," a supplement to the Pauline collection dating from about 100–105 A.D. The Gospels were gathered together into the "fourfold evangel" about 150 A.D. and thus formed another main group of New Testament writings. The whole New Testament, at this early age, was known as the *Euangelion* (Evangel) and the *Apostolos* (Apostle).

It used to be thought that the main influence in the creation of the canon was the attempt of Marcion, about 140 A.D., to collect a group of Christian sacred writings in order to offset and supplant the Old Testament. His views were strongly anti-Jewish and more or less Gnostic; he held that the God of the Jews, the Lawgiver, the Creator of the world, was a subordinate and really evil deity and that Christ had come to earth to reveal the one good God, the "Father" of Jesus Christ, who is superior to the Creator God of the Mosaic Law. In his attempt to weed out all traces of Judaism from the Christian sacred books, Marcion produced a "New Testament" limited to Luke (which he drastically revised to fit his own peculiar views), Galatians (strongly critical of the Law), I-II Corinthians, Romans, I-II Thessalonians, Laodiceans (our Ephesians), Colossians, Philippians, and Philemon. This was the "Evangel" and "Apostle" that Marcion set against the Law and Prophets of the Old Testament.

But it cannot be imagined that, had it not been for Marcion, the Christian church never would have possessed a New Testament. Nor can it be supposed that it was only by reaction against his fantastic anti-Jewish and ultra-Pauline views that the church came to select first a collection of Apostolic Epistles and soon after, a group of Gospels for use in public worship or in private instruction. As we have seen, the Epistles were in use from the time they were written; and doubtless they were copied and recopied and circulated widely throughout the church.

The same holds true of the Gospels. That writers as far apart, theologically and perhaps geographically, as Matthew and Luke both should use the Gospel of Mark and make it the basis of their narrative shows how widespread was the use of that earlier Gospel a generation or more later. Furthermore, as we have seen, the oral tradition of Jesus' life and teaching, His "mighty works," His death and resurrection, was in existence from the very beginning of the church's history. It was not surprising that this tradition should be written down in the Gentile world, and written at the date usually assigned to the writing of the Gospels, that is, after 65 or 70 A.D. But the oral traditions of "the Lord" had long been in use in the church, perhaps even in an early kind of liturgical use, when the first of the evangelists took stylus in hand to write down these traditions in orderly sequence. In other words, the beginnings of the New Testament canon are to be found, not in the struggle with Marcion's views about 140 A.D., but much earlier, in the life and thought, the worship and propaganda, the ministry of edification, and the scriptural exegesis of the primitive church.

The Conflict with Gnosticism. Nevertheless, it is also true that the Marcionite crisis sharpened the issue, hastened the process, and limited the canon more severely than otherwise might have been the case. It became necessary to guard carefully the books already received and to admit none of the current fictions or forgeries that began to appear fairly early in the 2d century. This necessity became even more imperative as soon as the church found itself confronted, and in some areas infiltrated, by Gnosticism. The origin, extent, and precise nature of Gnosticism still is debated among scholars. Some view it as a Christian heresy, pure and simple, an intra-ecclesiastical movement that threatened to transform Christianity into a speculative, mythological, even polytheistic religion of "salvation by knowledge" (gnōsis); others hold it to be a vast worldwide religious movement, earlier than Christianity in its origins, and sweeping into the early church as part of its tidal movement everywhere in the 2d and 3d centuries. To a large extent, the debate is over the name rather than the thing. A type of religious thought similar to, indeed largely identical with, what in the church was called "Gnosticism," can be seen rising and spreading throughout the Hellenistic world from the 2d century B.C. on. It was fundamentally dualistic and set

spirit and matter in complete opposition. Owing much to earlier Orphism, it looked upon the body as the tomb of the soul (sōma, body = sēma, tomb). Owing something likewise to astrology and its fatalistic presuppositions, this type of thought assumed that the soul of man somehow had "fallen" into this realm of matter and so came under the sway of the physical elements: the material universe itself was the creation of the downward-tending passions of once-pure ethereal spirits. Creation itself is evil; birth is evil; the body is evil; procreation is evil; hence marriage is evil—so ran the metaphysics and the ethics of this strange creed.

Salvation from this enslavement to evil, from this dark dungeon of the material world (or the physical body) can come about only through the soul's realization (= knowledge, gnōsis) of its own true nature and heavenly origin. This knowledge is brought to it by the heavenly Redeemer, the Savior, who descends the long scale or ladder letting down into the dungeon and rouses the sleeping soul and bids it rise. There were many other features in this doctrine, which took various forms, some highly intellectual (for example, the systems of Basilides, Valentinus, and Mani), others crass, barbarous, and even immoral. In fact, Gnosticism is not just one philosophy, heresy, or system of thought, but a whole constellation of cults and systems, the major principles of which were dualism, the evil of material existence, salvation by knowledge, and escape from the body. That any such theory should be thought compatible with Christianity seems to us utterly absurd—but that is only because we do not live in the 2d century, and because the church won the victory over Gnosticism.

Had the church (that is, the part of it that professed what later is known as the orthodox faith) succumbed, Christianity probably would have disappeared along with other cults and movements of later antiquity. Instead, a great battle was joined that lasted the better part of two centuries. The battle can be described in terms of three claims and counter-claims.

First, against the claims of "Gnōsis falsely so-called" (I Timothy 6:20), the orthodox believers—that is, the conservatives—appealed to the original faith of the apostles (compare Ephesians 2:20, Jude 3). The so-called "Apostles' Creed," which is basically the old Roman Baptismal Creed of the middle of the 2d century, became the primary affirmation of the church's faith: its clauses were carefully chosen to rule out the Gnostic misinterpretation of Christianity (God is the Creator of heaven and earth; Christ really was born, really suffered, really died, and rose from the dead; the flesh of believers, instead of being abandoned, will be raised and glorified).

Second, against the claim of the Gnostics to possess a secret tradition of true (that is, Gnostic) doctrine derived from the apostles, the orthodox appealed to the "apostolic succession" of the teachers (that is, bishops) in the great Christian centers—Ephesus, Antioch, Alexandria, Jerusalem, Rome. Each bishop was asked to state what his predecessor had taught and what this predecessor had affirmed as the teaching of his predecessors, all the way back to the time of the foundation of the church. In every case the answer was: the faith of the Apostles, the true, that is, orthodox, non-Gnostic doctrine.

Third, against the claim of various Gnostic or semi-Gnostic writers merely to have copied authentic Gospels or Epistles or the Acts of various apostles (for example, the Gospel of Peter, of Mary, or of Thomas; the Acts of Peter, of Paul, or of John), the orthodox appealed to the already recognized collection of apostolic writings, that is, to our gradually emerging New Testament.

All these had been written by apostles or by "apostolic men," the disciples of apostles, and they accordingly set forth the genuine, indisputable doctrine of the church's earliest and most authoritative teachers. Hence the great emphasis upon apostolic authorship, observable to this day in the titles of the New Testament books. Hence also the reinforced tendency to omit from the collection any books not written by apostles or "apostolic men"—books like I-II Clement, the Didache, the Shepherd of Hermas—even though some of them were older than the latest of the "received" books, and contained teaching that was pure, innocuous, and non-Gnostic. Moreover, the traces of early anti-Gnosticism in the New Testament books especially in Colossians, Ephesians, Jude, John, and the Johannine epistles, were a great resource in the struggle against these perverse and antihistorical speculations. The Gospel of John, for example, repeatedly emphasizes the reality of Jesus' human nature: that is, he possessed a real physical body: he wept, he was hungry and thirsty, he was weary and needed rest, he died on a cross, and when he was dead, the soldier's spear brought water and blood from his side (John 19:34); therefore he was no phantom, like the Docetic aeon Christ, who returned to the celestial realm before the first nail was driven through his hands—so that the Roman soldiers really crucified a corpse; nor did he merely "assume" human nature, only to lay it aside once more like a soiled garment—instead, the Logos actually "became" flesh and dwelt among us (John 1:14).

As Adolf Harnack maintained, it was this threefold appeal to the *apostolic faith* as set forth in the creed, the *apostolic succession* of the teachers of this faith, and the *apostolic writings* contained in the New Testament, that formed the church's chief bulwark of defense in the struggle with Gnosticism.

They were like three parallel and successive lines of fortification; and if they seem very conservative, rather than "constructive" or "creative" advances into the realm of religious thought, let us recall that in the nature of the case they could be nothing else. The whole question was one concerned with the true and original nature of Christianity.

Against the kaleidoscopic, phantasmagorian cloudland of unhistorical aeons that were intercalated between the One, the Supreme, the Monad, who is above all being, and the dark, dank muck of matter, here in this bottom-most subcellar of the universe, the only possible appeal that conservative, orthodox Christians could make was to history, tradition, documents, universal consent, and the demonstrable succession of the Church's teachers and their doctrine. No other kind of appeal—certainly not an appeal to reason or philosophy or an appeal to a secret tradition, which the heretics claimed for their own—would impress a 2d or 3d century Christian faced with the pretentious claims of the Gnostics.

FREDERICK C. GRANT
Union Theological Seminary

Bibliography

Grant, Robert M., *The Formation of the New Testament* (London 1965).
Gregory, C.R., *Canon and Text of the New Testament* (New York 1907).
Harnack, Adolf, *The Origin of the New Testament* (New York 1925).
Knox, John, *Marcion and the New Testament* (Chicago 1942).
Moore, E.C., *The New Testament in the Christian Church* (New York 1904).
Souter, Alexander, *Text and Canon of the New Testament* (New York 1913).

11. Languages of the New Testament.

The New Testament is, from beginning to end, a *Greek book*. Although the earliest oral tradition of Jesus' deeds and sayings undoubtedly circulated in Aramaic, which was still the spoken language of Palestine and of some other parts of the Near East (certainly among Jews), it was not long before this oral tradition was translated into the ordinary, everyday Greek spoken everywhere else in the civilized Mediterranean world. (Traces of the original Aramaic tradition survive here and there: for example, in Mark 5:41, 15:34.)

This ordinary, or "common" (*koinē*), Greek was spoken and written by people everywhere, from the borders of Nubia to the market towns in Gaul and the army camps beyond the Danube, from the Strait of Gibraltar to the borders of India. It was basically the Attic dialect of classical and 4th century Greek, together with numerous Ionic and a few Doric forms and spellings, for it was this language that had been carried across the Middle East by Alexander the Great (reigned 336–323) and that soon became the *lingua franca* of the whole Eastern Mediterranean and Near Eastern world ruled by his successors, chiefly the Ptolemies in Egypt and the Seleucids in Syria, Asia Minor, and the whole vast territory eastward to the Indus. In the West, Greek long before had been introduced by colonists in lower Italy, Sicily, Gaul, and Spain and by traders here and there as far as the Atlantic Ocean.

It was a language grown simpler and less varied as the centuries had gone by, and various peoples introduced certain strains from their own vernacular. The ancient optative and subjunctive forms of the verb were used less frequently. The old purposive *hina* had lost much of its force. *Hoti* was scarcely more than a quotation mark. The dual noun and pronoun were almost totally disused. The spelling of many words had been altered, and the meanings of many had changed—usually by the accumulation of additional uses in popular speech.

Furthermore, in some circles, notably among Greek-speaking Jews, who were influenced by their own great familiarity with the Septuagint (LXX), a wholly new and different religious vocabulary had begun to develop. But this was not some special sacred language: Jewish Greek, or LXX Greek, was still a part of the everyday *koinē*. The *koinē* Greek of the Hellenistic age could receive and welcome such additions to its vocabulary, as ancient classical Greek never would have done. Such expressions as "respecter of persons," to "make (show) mercy" to someone, "all flesh" (all human beings), "Christ" (the anointed, the Messiah), "angel" (not "messenger"), "devil" (*diabolos*, not *daimōn*), "anathema," "temptation" (*peirasmos*, trial or testing) are only a few examples of the specialized vocabulary already in process of creation by the Greek-speaking synagoges of the Western Diaspora. To this vocabulary, as also to the LXX itself, the Christian church fell heir.

Thus the New Testament is written in a language that is basically that of the ordinary reader in the 1st century, although its vocabulary includes a number of words with a highly specialized meaning, derived from Jewish religious literature in Greek and chiefly from the Septuagint. Such a term as *Kyrios* (Lord), the Septuagint translation of the divine name YHWH, is a good example. What the early Gentile church did was to take this title and apply it not only to God, as the Jews did, but also to Christ, the "Lord" of the church's faith and worship. Hence in the New Testament, *Kyrios* is used in both senses, and it is sometimes hard to know which is meant (Acts 2:36, 3:19, 13:11).

Another term found in *koinē* Greek and adopted by the early Christians is *Logos* (Word), meaning now not "reckoning," "statement," "narrative," "utterance," "speech," "saying," "reason," but the divine mediator between God and the world (John 1:1–18), or the divine thought or utterance, by which—or by whom—all things hold together (Colossians 1:17); that is, the One who is God's agent in the creation and the continued existence of the universe (Hebrews 1:3). Such a term is not entirely philosophical: its real background, as Rudolf Bultmann has shown, is not Stoicism or Stoicized Platonism so much as it is the theosophical or "mysteriosophical" theorizing of various religious cults and movements found here and there in the ancient Near East. Other terms have a more specifically philosophical connotation, even a more or less Stoic flavor, such as *epithumia* ("desire"). Not that St. Paul or any other apostle was a student of Stoic philosophy; instead, such terms were "in the air" (like the technical terms "evolution," "species," "libido," "repression" today), thanks to several generations of popular street preaching of philosophy, especially by Cynics and Stoics.

But the great and overwhelming mass of illustrative parallels for New Testament Greek come, not from literary sources, but from the sands of Egypt. Here the long-buried rubbish heaps outside ancient towns and villages have preserved through many centuries the dry and unfaded papyrus letters, bills, personal notes and memoranda, legal documents, copies of books, plays, and poems, and countless other flotsam and jetsam of a literate society in possession of cheap writing materials. The realization that these ancient Egyptian papyri are of primary value for the student of the Greek New Testament has been due in large measure to Adolf Deissmann of Berlin. In the university library at Heidelberg one day, it suddenly dawned on him that the Greek papyrus he was reading was in the very language of the New Testament, and from that moment he dedicated himself to the most far-reaching pursuit of this new branch of lexicography.

Thanks to Deissmann, the old notion of a special "Biblical Greek," the "language of the Holy Ghost," has disappeared. We now recognize the Greek of the New Testament for what it really is: rugged, simple, direct *koinē* Greek, with a strong infusion of LXX or Jewish-Greek religious terms (derived from the Diaspora synagogues); with a sprinkling of other terms, chiefly from the realm of popular religious philosophy and ethics; with a wide range of style and diction—all the way from Mark's simple, pedestrian prose with its ubiquitous historic presents ("he goes," "he says"), its monotonous repetition ("immediately" so-and-so happens), and its careless use of impersonal verbs, to the lofty and unsurpassed style of Luke. Paul's style is somewhat intermediate between the two —the vigorous dynamic expression of a powerful personality, who sometimes is so vehement in his utterance that his language breaks down under the burden of his thought; or time allows for writing down only every other step in his advancing logic, so that the reader must fill in for himself the intervening steps between points a-c-e-g-i-k; or his amanuensis was expected (like a good secretary) to smooth out and fill in these gaps but failed to do so—and naturally, since who ever fully understood St. Paul?

It was no high, literary, Atticistic style that Paul or the other New Testament writers aimed at. They aimed only to state clearly and in common terms the message of salvation with which they had been entrusted; and if they ever ventured into philosophical or other literary realms, it was only momentarily and then with a purely practical motive—the furtherance of the Gospel. As practical a book, or collection of books, as the New Testament does not promise much, in advance, in the way of sublimity of style or profundity of speculation: the wonder is, as Professor Ulrich von Wilamowitz-Möllendorff (1848–1931) observed, that the Letters of Paul, for example, have a rightful place in the history of Greek literature. They belong there, not by virtue of the careful cultivation of Hellenistic rhetoric, but by sheer force of genius.

FREDERICK C. GRANT
Union Theological Seminary

Bibliography

Arndt, William F., and Gingrich, F.W., *A Greek-English Lexicon of the New Testament* (Chicago 1957).
Blass, F., and Debrunner, A., *A Greek Grammar of the New Testament*, tr. by R.W. Funk (Chicago 1961).
Deissmann, Gustav Adolf, *Light from the Ancient East*, new ed. (London 1927).
Moulton, James H., *Grammar of New Testament Greek*, 3 vols. (Edinburgh 1906–1963).
Moulton, James H., and Milligan, George, *The Vocabulary of the Greek New Testament* (New York 1930).
Robertson, A.T., *A Grammar of the New Testament in the Light of Historical Research*, 4th ed. (New York 1923).

12. The Text of the New Testament: Textual Criticism, Manuscripts, and Versions

Textual criticism, or the study of the New Testament text, means the study of the exact wording of the New Testament as it appears in Greek manuscripts, in versions (ancient translations into languages other than Greek, such as Latin, Syriac, or Coptic), and in quotations made by the church fathers (the ancient ecclesiastical writers). The purpose of all textual criticism— whether of the New Testament or the Old Testament or any other ancient writing—is to recover as far as possible the precise words of the author. When books were copied by hand, as was the case everywhere before the invention of printing, every manuscript usually repeated whatever errors or alterations had crept into its immediate ancestor, the model from which it was copied. As time passed and as still more copies and copies of copies were made, certain family resemblances became obvious, although it is also true that copies belonging to other families were introduced sometimes into the line. As a result, a "mixed" type of text arose, the errors and peculiarities of which would be perpetuated (unless corrected by some reviser) by the succeeding members of the family. Such phenomena are found in all textual history—whether of secular or sacred books. Accordingly, the task facing the textual critic is to trace corruptions and errors to their beginning in the archetype that first introduced them, and in the case of changes that cannot be classed as corruptions, to find the source of the change and to decide whether it is really a change (from the original) or only a disagreement with other manuscripts or families of manuscripts—in which case perhaps it may belong to the original and it is the other manuscripts that are at fault.

If we possessed all the manuscripts ever made of any writing, from the autograph (the author's original) to the latest copy, it would be a fascinating but relatively easy task to arrange them in sequence and by families. But, alas, we do not have the autographs or any of the very earliest copies. Of the New Testament writings the period of greatest textual change and alteration was the 2d century, but from this century (in the first half) we have only one tiny scrap of papyrus—the Rylands fragment of John. From the 3d century we have only the Chester Beatty fragments. From the 4th century we have *Codex Vaticanus* (B) and *Codex Sinaiticus* (Aleph or, preferably, S). From the 5th century we have *Codex Alexandrinus, Codex Ephraemi rescriptus* (a palimpsest), and the oldest manuscripts of the Old Latin translation of the Gospels (*a, e, ff₂, h, k, n, t*). From the 6th and later centuries we have an increasing quantity of manuscripts: there are, in fact, vastly more manuscripts of the New Testament than of any other ancient book. But the greater number of later manuscripts does not compensate for the lack of manuscripts from the earliest and most ancient period.

Procedure. In this situation the textual critic must proceed with great caution. As expounded by the most eminent textual critics—such as B. F. Westcott, F.J.A. Hort, Kirsopp Lake, J.H. Ropes, Sir Frederic G. Kenyon, Eberhard Nestle, H.J. Vogels, Alexander Souter, C.R. Gregory, Ernst von Dobschütz—certain rules of procedure must be followed faithfully.

First, one must study each manuscript by itself to gain familiarity with its peculiarities and to check its errors of spelling, typical mistakes in copying, and its "family" characteristics, if any are observable.

The second step is to group similar manuscripts by such "family" likenesses as spelling, common omissions, common rearrangements of the order of words, and common additions to the text. Community of error—or peculiarity of reading—certainly implies a common origin. This process must be applied to all available manuscripts. In each case the archetype (or common ancestor) must be identified either with some existing manuscript or hypothetically as "x" or "y" or "z."

As the third step, these archetypes are compared, and a provisional or hypothetical type of text is reconstructed on their basis—the archetype of all the archetypes, presumably identical with the autograph as it left the author's hand. In the case of the New Testament we can work back to four or five main types, as they existed, presumably, at the end of the 3d century. These are (1) the Western type of text, represented by *Codex Bezae* (D) and the Old Latin version (OL, or "it" for Italia); (2) the Caesarean

type, represented by the Koridethi Gospels (Theta), Fam¹³, Fam¹, the Old Georgian version, and the Old Armenian; (3) the Alexandrian (sometimes called Egyptian), represented by *Codex Sinaiticus* (S), *Codex Vaticanus* (B), the Sahidic version, the Bohairic version, *Codex Ephraemi rescriptus* (C), the minuscule numbered 33, the Washington manuscript (W) of the Gospels, and others; (4) the Syrian, represented by the Old Syriac version with two manuscripts, the Sinaitic (sy^s) and the Curetonian (sy^c), the later "authorized version" of the Syriac (the Peshitto), and others; and (5) other types, not yet fully identified. Some scholars distinguish two or three types of Western manuscripts: *D, b, a, ff₂* from Italy and Gaul, *k, W* (in Mark) *e, c* (in Mark and Luke) from Carthage, that is, North Africa. Others distinguish the Italian from the Gallic representatives; but this seems to be an unprofitable overrefinement.

There is still a fourth step. Even after all this involved work of identification, classification, and reconstruction by hypothesis has been finished, the textual critic's labors are not ended. In many cases he must still decide between what seem to be equally good alternative readings, and in some cases he may have to resort to conjectural emendation, because all the manuscripts and their archetypes—whether existing or hypothetical—contain a few primitive errors, which crept into the text at an early copying, perhaps even the earliest. As a rule, the critic must let an author write his own style: if there is a choice between equally good readings, and one of them is demonstrably in the style of the author concerned, that reading must prevail. Again, if there is a choice between two or more good alternative readings, and all are ably supported by manuscript evidence, the reading that most satisfactorily explains the others must be preferred—the others are presumably corruptions of this reading. There used to be much more reliance upon certain other rules, such as "prefer the shorter reading" (as if scribes always amplified) or "prefer the harder reading" (as if a mistake in copying could not produce a hard reading); but it now is recognized that textual criticism is more than application of rules. A good textual critic must possess not only knowledge and skill but also a touch of genius.

Variations. Of the abundant variations and disagreements between manuscripts (John Mill in 1707 estimated them at 30,000) the vast majority are merely errors due to mistaken copying: *dittography* (writing a word or phrase twice); *homoeoteleuton* (similar ending of two successive lines or series of lines, so that the scribe omitted one by oversight); *haplography* (writing a word once when it should be repeated— "Lord" instead of "Lord, Lord"); *itacism* (the substitution of *i* [iota] for other similar sounding letters or dipthongs—like E, Ē, AI, EI, OI, and even ŌI, all of which were pronounced ī in Hellenistic Greek). Another type of error is due to the contraction of certain words: the 14 *nomina sacra,* by some of the later scribes, such as "IS" with a bar over it for "Jesus," "IM" with a bar over it for "Jerusalem," "DD" with a bar over it for "David." A capital example is found in I Timothy 3:16, where "OS" ("who") later was taken for *theta sigma* with a bar above, which stood for *theos* ("God"). Since the new reading suited both the context and also the orthodox doctrine of the church, it got into many of the

THE PIERPONT MORGAN LIBRARY

THE PIERPONT MORGAN LIBRARY

Italian. The first page of Genesis, reproduced above, is from an illuminated Bible printed in Venice in 1471.

French. The page above is from the introduction to the first complete French Bible, printed about 1498.

BIBLES IN FOUR LANGUAGES

Low German. The page below is the opening of Genesis, from a Bible printed in Cologne about 1477.

Persian. Reproduced below is the opening page of the Gospel According to St. Matthew, as translated in 1878.

THE PIERPONT MORGAN LIBRARY

THE BRITISH MUSEUM

later manuscripts—although the majority even of Byzantine manuscripts still preserved the true reading.

Another source of error, or at least of confusion, was the *lectio continua:* the most ancient manuscripts neither separated the words nor used any punctuation. Thus in John 1:3–4 it is difficult to read the following:

ANDWITHOUTHIMWASNOTANYTHING
MADETHATWASMADEINHIMWASLIFE

In the Greek it is equally possible to place a period after "anything made" and then read "That which has been made was life in him" or to place a period after "that was made" and then read "In him was life."

The foregoing are accidental or unintentional alterations. More serious are the intentional changes introduced by scribes and before them by owners of manuscripts, who wished to improve or to correct their text by reference to some other manuscript that they preferred or to some familiar quotation of a text or, especially, to some familiar version, such as the Latin, Syriac, or Coptic. At the same time the influence of harmonies of the Gospels (or of a harmonization taking place in the copyist's own mind) was very marked: the text of one gospel (often it was Matthew) influenced that of another, or a passage in one of Paul's Letters influenced the wording of a similar one in some other epistle. Finally, the work of revisers who worked in the interest of some dogmatic view or other also must be taken into account, although such instances are extremely rare—far more rare than many persons have been led to suppose. A good example is John 1:18, where "the only begotten God" has taken the place of "the only Son" in the Alexandrian (or Hesychian) text and in the quotations by Irenaeus, Clement, and Origen but where the better reading still is preserved in the later Byzantine manuscripts, in the Koridethi Gospels, in the Latin version, and in the Curetonian Syriac. Another is Mark 6:3, where we read "the carpenter, the son of Mary," although Origen (died 254), the greatest Biblical critic of his time, said that he never had seen a manuscript that read "carpenter," but only "the son of the carpenter," as in Matthew and in Luke. It seems not improbable that this was the original reading of Mark.

Apparatus. In a modern edition of the Greek New Testament containing a text-critical apparatus (footnotes giving the variant readings with the chief evidence in their support), various symbols are used for the different authorities. As a rule, p^1, p^2, and so forth refer to papyrus fragments (for example, the Chester Beatty fragments mentioned above); T^1, T^2, and so forth refer to pottery fragments (ostraca; T is for *Tonscherd*); capital letters A, B, C, refer to the uncial manuscripts (written in capital letters); Arabic numbers, 1, 2, 3, refer to minuscule or cursive manuscripts (connected script); italic lower-case letters, *a, b, c,* refer to manuscripts of the Old Latin version; abbreviations are used for reference to other versions (arm for Armenian, sy or syr for Syriac, got for gothic); and similarly, abbreviations are used for church fathers whose quotations are cited (Or for Origen, Hier for Jerome, Ir for Irenaeus). Still other abbreviations and symbols are used, such as T for Tischendorf, H for Hort, among modern editors; and a whole series of symbols for omissions, variations, and additions to the text.

Manuscripts. Among the great uncials the most important are the following:

S (*Sinaiticus*), the 5th (perhaps 4th) century manuscript found by Konstantin von Tischendorf on Mount Sinai in 1844 (now in the British Museum). It is a large quarto, on beautiful thin vellum, with 4 columns to the page and 48 lines to the column. It had several copyists and a series of correctors.

B (*Vaticanus*), a 4th century manuscript in the Vatican Library at Rome. It also is a large quarto but has three columns to the page and 40–44 lines to the column. It probably was written in Alexandria. Some scholars think that both S and B were among the de luxe copies that Constantine ordered (in 333 A.D.) for the churches in his new capital, Constantinople, after the persecution under Diocletian had ended (311), for in the persecution vast quantities of Christian manuscripts had been destroyed.

A (*Alexandrinus*), a 5th or 6th century manuscript in the British Museum. It was presented to King Charles I by Cyril Lucar, the patriarch of Constantinople, but formerly of Alexandria.

C (*Codex Ephraemi Rescriptus*), a 5th century manuscript in the Bibliothèque Nationale in Paris. It is a palimpsest: the New Testament text was scrubbed off, and the manuscript was used again for the writings of St. Ephraim (died 373), the Syrian church father. The original text is barely legible and is difficult to decipher. Only 209 leaves remain.

D (*Codex Bezae*), the great "Western" manuscript of the 5th or 6th century, once owned by the French reformer Théodore de Bèze, who presented it in 1581 to the University of Cambridge. It contains the Gospels and Acts.

W (the Washington manuscript), written in the 4th or 5th century and now in the Freer Collection at the Smithsonian Institution in Washington, D.C. It contains Gospels only.

Theta, the Koridethi Gospels, now at Tiflis, probably was written in the 9th century by a scribe who did not know Greek but copied it as a child might. It is the best example of the Caesarean type of text.

The leading minuscule (cursive) manuscripts are: 1 (12th century, now at Basel), 118 (13th century, at Oxford), 131 (13th century, in the Vatican Library), 209 (14th century, at Venice), 1582 (10th century, at Mount Athos)—these are the leading members of "Family 1" or "Codex 1 and its allies" or the "Lake Group" (as identified by K. Lake), all descended from a common archetype. Another family contains 13, 69, 124, 346, 543, 788, and others, found in various European libraries. This often is called the "Ferrar Group" (as identified by W.H. Ferrar). Independent cursives of great value are 28 (11th century, at Paris); 33 (10th century, at Paris); 565 (9th century, at Leningrad); 700 (11th century, in the British Museum), 579, 1241, 1342, and others.

Versions. Among the versions the Old Latin and Old Syriac are the most important, each presumably having been made about 150 and each somehow related to the other; the two often appear together in support of "Western" readings.

The Old Latin is preserved in a fairly large number of manuscripts, of which *k* and *e* are the most important. *Codex Bobiensis* (*k*, a 4th or 5th century manuscript, at Turin) has a type of text almost identical with that used by St.

Cyprian (died 251). It contains parts of Matthew and Mark. *Codex Palatinus* (*e*, a 5th century manuscript, at Trent) contains most of the Gospels. The Old Latin version was revised by St. Jerome (340?–420) at the request of Pope Damasus I, and his translation is known as the Vulgate (popular) version (vg). In the New Testament he revised the Gospels only slightly, the rest much more thoroughly. The Vulgate remains "the queen of the versions," thanks to Jerome's scholarship and literary skill and to his use of old and good Greek manuscripts. The Gospels were published in 384, the rest in 385 or 386. This version became the standard New Testament text in the Western Church and so remained until the invention of printing.

The Old Syriac version is represented by two important, if fragmentary, manuscripts: (1) the Sinaitic (sy^s), from the 5th century, discovered at Sinai in 1892 by Mrs. A.S. Lewis and her sister Mrs. A.D. Gibson; (2) the Curetonian (sy^c), also a 5th century manuscript, published by William Cureton in 1858. There are a number of later revisions of the Syriac, notably the Peshitto (plain) version dating from the 5th century.

Other ancient versions of major importance are the Sahidic (2d or 3d century), Bohairic, Middle-Egyptian, Ethiopic, Arabic, Armenian, Georgian, and Gothic.

Other Sources. In addition to all these materials there are the quotations from church fathers—Greek, Latin, Syriac, and others—and the lectionaries (books containing the passages chosen from the Bible to read as lections, or lessons, on appointed days). These latter often preserve a type of text much older than the date of the lectionary itself and deserve careful collation and study.

Conclusion. It is obvious that the interpreter of the New Testament must be familiar with a wide range of subjects, not only with the Greek language and its New Testament vocabulary, but also with other ancient languages; with early church history and history of the canon; with the principles and the methods of textual criticism; with the history and the literature, the philosophy and the religious ideas of the ancient world and of early Christianity as a movement within it; with the growth of early Christian literature and theology. Contrary to the popular notion that anyone who can read English can interpret the Bible, it is clear that sound judgment in exegesis requires long training and much experience. This does not mean that no one except scholars ought to read the Bible. But it means that all readers, scholars included, must recognize that accurate knowledge, wide learning, and sound judgment are demanded of the interpreter. The New Testament certainly requires no less skill in its interpretation, but rather more, than is required for any other ancient book or body of literature.

FREDERICK C. GRANT
Union Theological Seminary

Bibliography

Kenyon, Frederic G., *The Story of the Bible* (New York 1937).
Kenyon, Frederic G., *Our Bible and the Ancient Manuscripts*, 5th ed. (London 1958).
Lake, Kirsopp, *The Text of the New Testament*, 6th ed. (London 1928).
Metzger, Bruce M., *The Text of the New Testament* (New York 1964).
Price, I.M., *The Ancestry of Our English Bible*, 2d ed. (New York 1949).
Robertson, Archibald T., *An Introduction to the Textual Criticism of the New Testament* (London 1925).
Robinson, Henry Wheeler, *The Bible in Its Ancient and English Versions* (New York 1940).

For Specialized Study

Vogels, H.J., *Handbuch der Textkritik des Neuen Testaments* 2d ed. (Bonn, Germany, 1955).
Westcott, B.F., and Hort, F.J.A., *The New Testament in the Original Greek*, vol. 2 (Cambridge, Eng., 1881).

13. Growth of the New Testament Literature

There are religions that exist, even for centuries, without a sacred literature. There are religions that exist mainly in their literature, without much in the way of rite or cult. Early Christianity was in neither of these classes but began its written expression early in its career. In the world of Hellenistic culture, where reading and writing were practiced everywhere, this was a natural development, especially after the church crossed the borders of Palestine and began its universal mission in the Graeco-Roman world. In Palestine the sacred book (or books) was the Hebrew Scriptures, studied and expounded by the scribes and translated and explained in the vernacular Aramaic at synagogue services by anyone familiar with Hebrew, who was chosen to do so by the ruler of the synagogue (president of the congregation). There were other books in circulation, aside from the sacred Scriptures; such were some of the apocalypses that have come down to us and also the Hebrew originals of books that now survive only in some other language, such as Greek. But it is very doubtful that these extracanonical books included any early Christian writings, although able scholars have argued that the Jewish Mishnah refers to some of them—the word *gilyōnim*, in Mishnah Yadaim 3:4–5, Tosephta Yadaim 2:13, is understood to mean "gospels." If there ever were any early Christian books in Hebrew or Aramaic, they perished long ago and left no trace upon the Greek New Testament.

Greek Sources. Those parts of the New Testament that possibly may rest upon earlier sources are thoroughly Greek and probably made use of such sources, originally oral, only after they had been translated into Greek. (See section *11. Language of the New Testament.*) Such a source is probably the one used by Matthew and Luke in addition to their use of Mark: it is found in passages where Matthew and Luke are in close agreement, but where their common use of Mark does not explain this agreement (in non-Marcan passages) and where the use of some other common source, written in Greek, is an all but inevitable hypothesis. This second source usually is referred to as Q (for *Quelle*, the German word for "source"), and it probably included the following passages in Luke (compare their parallels in Matthew):

Luke 3: [2b], 3a, 7b–9, 16–17; 4:1b–12; 6:20–49; 7:2, 6b–10, 18b–19, 22–28, 31–35; 9:57b–62; 10:2–16, [17b–20], 21b–24; 11:2–4, [15–8], 9–26, 29b–36, 39b, 42–43, [44], 46–52; 12:2–12, 22–31, 33b–34, 39–40, 42–46, 49–53, [54–56], 57–59; 13:18–21, 24–29, 34–35; 14:11=18:14; 14:16–23, 26–27, 34–35; 15:4–7, [8–10]; 16:13, [16–18]; 17:1–4, 6, 23–24, 26–30, 34–35, 37b; 19:12–13, 15b–26; [22:28–30]. Brackets indicate passages of uncertain source, but probably from Q. (Consult Frederick C. Grant, *The Gospels, Their Origin and Their Growth*, pp. 59ff.)

That this Q source once existed in Aramaic is quite probable, although whether as a body of oral tradition or as a written document it is very difficult to say. In fact, it does not greatly matter. A body of stereotyped oral tradition could be almost as fixed and permanent in form as it would have been if written on parchment or on papyrus. (This was true of the stories about the ancient Palestinian rabbis and their parables and sayings, which were transmitted orally for several generations before being written.) But the probability is that Matthew and Luke knew and used Q in written form and in a Greek translation. Their other sources included M (the material peculiar to Matthew, perhaps an expansion of Q), L (the material peculiar to Luke, perhaps collected by him and added to Q, before he incorporated Mark), the special incidents related in their Infancy or Passion narratives, and other traditions as well. All these no doubt once circulated independently in the Greek-speaking Gentile churches and accordingly either were Greek translations of earlier stereotyped Aramaic traditions or else were freely composed in Greek on the basis of some tradition or other, together with scriptural exegesis or interpretation or the imaginative setting provided by some early Christian teacher, preacher, or evangelist.

Not only Matthew and Luke but probably even Mark (the earliest Gospel) incorporate earlier sources, such as the sequence of events of the day in Capernaum (chapter 1); the collection of controversies in 2:1 to 3:6 and again in 11:27 to 12:40; the collection of parables in chapter 4; the "Little Apocalypse" underlying chapter 13; and above all, the connected series of incidents given in the older form of the Passion narrative embedded in chapters 14 and 15. Other sequences probably already found in the early tradition are 7:1–23 and 8:27 to 10:45. John likewise used earlier sources: the seven great "signs" in chapters 2 to 12, four of them closely resembling the miracle stories in the earlier Synoptic Gospels; the two great farewell discourses, with their closely knit structure of thought; and, in fact, the discourse material as a whole that John incorporates. Much of this material was in poetic form, as the French "Jerusalem Bible" (1955) makes clear.

Sources in Oral Tradition. All these sources underlying the Gospels existed apparently in Greek and were used by the various Gospel writers in their Greek form, version, or recension. Instead of a one-source, a two-source, or even a four-source hypothesis to account for agreements and disagreements between the Gospels, only some form of a multiple source theory will do justice to their actual contents. Moreover, the picture that we form of the earliest Christian literature, to be realistic, must take into account this growing body of traditional literature: an "oral" literature (the term is inevitable) gradually being written, though incompletely, and circulating among the earliest groups of Christians in the great centers of the early church—Caesarea, Antioch, Rome, Ephesus, Alexandria, Corinth, and North Africa. The book of the earliest Christians was the Old Testament; but it was the tradition (at first oral, then written) of the life and teaching of Jesus "the Lord" that provided the clue and key to interpret the Old Testament—with the consequence that the Old Testament often influenced the form, and even occasionally the content, of the early Christian tradition. (See section 9. *New Testament:* Introduction.)

During this early period, while the oral traditions of Jesus' life and teaching, death and resurrection, were in circulation, the use made of them in the church also affected their formulation and transmission. As a rule, it was the church's teachers and preachers who made greatest use of the traditions and to whom we owe the preservation of most of Jesus' sayings and parables. The fact that controversies in which he had engaged still were active in the early church (such as controversies with scribes and Pharisees) led to the appeal to his words and to their preservation. The oldest account of his last days in Jerusalem, the supper, Gethsemane, arrest, trial, condemnation, and crucifixion owed its existence to the intense interest of his followers in this series of events. So, too, did the stories of his resurrection, with their etiological interest, explaining the Christian observance of Sunday rather than Saturday (the Sabbath), the Christian Easter (rather than the Jewish Passover), and providing answers to various questions: What was his appearance like? Why did not everyone see him? Why did he not convince his enemies that he was still alive? How was his resurrection related to his presence in heaven and his coming again? Moreover, the stories of his exorcisms and his healing of the sick were told as evidence of his power over Satan and his hosts and as evidence of the approaching end of the age and the full establishment of the reign of God (Matthew 12:28).

Finally, the "great miracle stories" (as Martin Dibelius called them), the legends of his birth and boyhood, the story of his baptism and divine vocation, his temptation (trial, ordeal, or testing) in the wilderness, his transfiguration on a mountain northeast of Galilee—all these additions to the earliest evangelic tradition (sayings, parables, and the "old stories") clearly were motivated by interests within the church. Christians wanted to know how his career began; how his disciples came to believe in him; how—or whether—his heavenly state of exaltation after the resurrection was anticipated during his earthly life; how his own family, including his mother, understood him; how his career was foreshadowed in the Old Testament and how it compared with the careers or vocations of earlier prophets, saints, and martyrs; how—or whether—his great miracles were superior to those of the Jewish rabbis or the miracle workers and thaumaturgists in the pagan world. All these motives were at work, not so much creating as sifting tradition, reinterpreting and reemphasizing it, amplifying it by means of scriptural analogy or foretype, and embellishing it in the manner of ordinary Jewish Midrash, the imaginative setting and illustration of Scripture provided by the Jewish preachers and teachers.

The study of this phase of the Gospel literature and the endeavor to recover the *form* taken by the tradition during its oral period, before the Gospels or even their underlying sources were committed to writing, is called form criticism. A better translation of the original designation (first used in Germany) would be form history (*Formgeschichte*), for it is not a new and different type of Biblical criticism, a substitute for text or source criticism, but simply a study of the oral tradition lying behind the Gospels and an attempt to reconstruct it as it circulated in its earliest form.

The Epistles. Thus the "literary" activity of the early church goes far back, even though the Gospels were not produced for a generation or more after the church had begun its mission in the Greek-speaking world. Meanwhile the earliest "books" (complete compositions) to be written by Christians were the Epistles, of which the earliest dates from about 49. St. Paul may have written still earlier epistles; if so, they have not survived. The earliest in our New Testament is I Thessalonians. Both I and II Thessalonians deal with the concrete situation that arose in Thessalonica after Paul's departure. The thought of the earliest Christians there (as elsewhere) was centered in the eschatological expectation (the immediate coming of the last judgment and the kingdom of God). Some even had abandoned their occupations and were living in idleness upon the charity of their neighbors. Paul has to tell them, "If anyone will not work, let him not eat" (II Thessalonians 3:10).

The next letter of Paul's that we possess is perhaps the Epistle to Galatians (about 51 or possibly 55 or 56). It deals with the serious problem created in the churches of Galatia (in west central Asia Minor) by the Judaizers. These people probably were not emissaries of the mother church in Jerusalem, although they doubtless claimed to preach the pure teaching of the original Gospel: over and above the response of the Gentile converts to the preaching of Paul and beyond the practices observed in Gentile Christianity, these new Christians were urged to adopt the full observance of the Jewish Law. It was inconceivable to these teachers that full salvation was possible apart from the strict observance of the Mosaic code: had not God Himself given Israel the Law? Paul's letter is the classic statement of the freedom of the Christian from the claims of the Law of Moses and of the principle of guidance by the Holy Spirit (see especially chapter 5).

About 55, Paul wrote a series of letters to the church in Corinth. He was then in Ephesus and was too busily employed there to cross the Aegean Sea and visit Corinth—grave as were the problems of its church. As modern scholars arrange the letters, it seems probable that the series was as follows:

First, a letter from Paul, ordering the exclusion (or excommunication) of an immoral church member. II Corinthians 6:14 to 7:1 may be a fragment of this letter.

Second, a letter from the Corinthians to Paul, asking certain questions, such as about food offered to idols, mixed marriages, the Lord's Supper and the *agapē* ("love feast," or common meal). This letter has not survived.

Third, Paul's reply, our I Corinthians. After writing it, he possibly may have paid the Corinthians a brief visit. But both letter and visit failed of their purpose, for the church's troubles in Corinth continued.

Fourth, a severe letter of rebuke and self-defense, written by Paul in great sorrow and anguish and sent to Corinth by Titus—probably in the spring of 55. II Corinthians 10 to 13 is probably the main part of it. This letter had the desired effect. The church submitted, punished the offending member, and asked for reconciliation with Paul.

Fifth, the letter of reconciliation, written by Paul from Macedonia, probably in the summer of 55. This is our II Corinthians 1 to 9, minus the passage in 6:14 to 7:1.

Read in this order, the correspondence becomes more intelligible, and we can see the tiny church struggling for its life amid the dark, heathenish, immoral, pagan society that surrounded it. We also see the majestic figure of a moral and spiritual giant, St. Paul, and the influence he exerted on these simple, naïve, unruly converts.

Shortly after this, and just before his return to Palestine with an offering for the church in Jerusalem, Paul wrote his Letter to Romans, the most theological of all his letters. Its great theme is the gospel of salvation by faith, apart from works of the Law: "He who is righteous through faith [rather than merely by pious deeds] shall live" (1:17). In chapters 9 to 11 he deals with the relations between church and synagogue, especially the problem posed for Christians by the refusal of most Jews to recognize Jesus as the Messiah. Chapter 7 is the profoundest analysis of the troubled conscience to be found anywhere in the Bible or in all ancient literature, while chapter 8 is a great climactic statement of the victory won by Christians through the new life in Christ—the life in the Spirit.

Paul's purpose in writing these last-named letters (his four main epistles, Galatians, I-II Corinthians, Romans) was wholly practical. Even Romans was meant as a self-introduction to the Christians in Rome, whom he hoped to visit as soon as he had been to Jerusalem and who, he hoped, would help him on his way to Spain for future missionary labors (15:14-33). His later letters, usually now dated between 59 and 62, were similarly practical in purpose.

Philippians is a gracious and grateful letter of thanks for a gift from the Christians in Philippi; it contains the great Christological passage in 2:5-11, the heart of Paul's doctrine about Christ.

Philemon is a note to accompany a runaway slave, who had come in contact with Paul in prison and was being sent home by the apostle as a Christian to his Christian master—one of the most touching notes in all literature.

Colossians, addressed to Christians in Colossae, in western Asia Minor, is an attempt to keep the Christians there from falling into a more or less Gnostic, unhistorical view of Christ.

Ephesians, closely related to it, is probably a cento, or anthology, of Pauline passages put together as a circular epistle (encyclical), perhaps as the covering or introductory letter, when Paul's Letters first were gathered and edited as a collection. (The word "Ephesus" is missing, in 1:1, in the best manuscripts.)

The later epistles, I-II Timothy and Titus (the Pastoral Epistles), now are thought to be not by Paul but by a Paulinist, about 95 to 105. They restate Paul's teaching and practical directions on church administration in terms of the situation that arose at the end of the century.

The Epistle to Hebrews (a homily; consult 5:11; 6:1; 8:1) probably dates from about 95 A.D. and comes from Italy. Its author sought to show that Christ's death superseded the Old Testament sacrifices and that the Law foreshadowed the true and full revelation to come.

I Peter is probably a baptismal homily, expanded into an epistle (also about 95).

Jude is an apocalyptic note of similar date, destined to be expanded (about 150) into II Peter.

The Apocalypse of John, like I Peter, faces the prospect of persecution—in this case the threat of the church's extinction at the hands of insurgent paganism with its cult of Rome and the emperor, under Domitian (reigned 81-96). This cult was rifest in the province of Asia, and it was to seven persecuted (or at least threatened) churches in Asia that the book was addressed (consult the letters in chapters 2, 3). The book was meant to encourage the Christians to remain loyal in spite of persecution.

The letter of James is one of the most practical in the whole New Testament: a series of "wisdom" admonitions, much like the Jewish wisdom books and also like the popular ethical philosophy of the Graeco-Roman world, but Christianized. There is no means of fixing even an approximate date for it.

The Epistles of John belong with the Fourth Gospel: their aim likewise was practical—to counteract the incipient Gnosticism that would turn Christ into a phantom, an unreal, unhistorical aeon, or cosmic power. On Gnosticism, see section 10. Canon of the New Testament.

The Gospels. The Gospel literature represents the crystallization or "precipitation" in writing of the oral tradition about Jesus, his life, teaching, death, and resurrection. For a time this oral tradition sufficed. Then the earliest Gospel sources (such as Q, Mark, L, M, and the Infancy narratives) were recorded gradually, and eventually the finished Gospels were produced. The earliest of these, Mark, comes from Rome, about 68, and was designed to encourage the persecuted Christians under Nero to stand fast and die rather than renounce Christ (see especially 8:34–38; 13:35–37).

A few years later, perhaps about 85–95, Luke wrote his Gospel (based on Mark and Q) and Acts, a two-volume work designed as an apology for Christianity, to show that the new religion was the true Judaism (or "true Israel") and therefore entitled to religious freedom like the Judaism of the Jews and that it was not inimical to law and order. The work was dedicated (presented) to Theophilus (Luke 1:1–4; Acts 1:1–3), perhaps a Roman official.

Later still, perhaps a little later than 100, the Gospel of Matthew was compiled, a didactic, perhaps even a liturgical arrangement of Jesus' deeds and words (based on Mark and Q) in five divisions for use in the church's teaching and worship.

Finally, the Gospel of John was written (about 100–125?) to repudiate and to repel the Gnostic or Docetic interpretation of Christ's life and teaching, which represented him as a divine phantom. Hence John's insistence on the reality of Jesus' human nature. See also section 15. Religion and Theology of the New Testament.

There were certain apocryphal gospels (such as According to the Hebrews, According to Peter), but they are later in date, they add almost nothing to our knowledge of Jesus, and they are often heretical (Gnostic or Docetic).

See also articles on books of the New Testament.

FREDERICK C. GRANT
Union Theological Seminary

Bibliography

Craig, Clarence T., *The Beginning of Christianity* (New York 1943).
Dibelius, Martin, *A Fresh Approach to the New Testament* (New York 1936).
Dibelius, Martin, *From Tradition to Gospel* (New York 1934).
Easton, B.S., *The Gospel Before the Gospels* (New York 1925).
Enslin, Morton S., *Christian Beginnings* (New York 1938).
Goodspeed, Edgar J., *Introduction to the New Testament* (Chicago 1937).
Grant, Frederick C., *The Earliest Gospel* (New York 1943).
Grant, Frederick C., *The Gospels, Their Origin and Their Growth* (New York 1957).
Grant, Frederick C., *Commentary on the New Testament*, 2 vols. (New York 1963).
Grant, Robert M., *Historical Introduction to the New Testament* (London 1963).
Julicher, A., *An Introduction to the New Testament* (London 1904).
McNeile, Alan H., *An Introduction to the Study of the New Testament*, 2d ed. (New York 1953).
Moffat, James, *An Introduction to the Literature of the New Testament*, new ed. (New York 1921).
Scott, Ernest F., *The Literature of the New Testament* (New York 1932).
Streeter, Burnett H., *The Four Gospels* (New York 1925).

14. New Testament History, Including Chronology and Archaeology

A logical place to start the consideration of New Testament history is with chronology. Many well-established dates in Roman and Jewish history make it possible to establish the sequence of events in the early period of Christianity.

CHRONOLOGY

The political framework of New Testament history is clear and definite. Since 63 B.C., when Pompey seized Palestine for the Romans, the life of Palestine had been under Roman control. Jesus was born under the first Roman emperor, Augustus (reigned 27 B.C.–14 A.D.). His public ministry and death occurred under Tiberius (reigned 14–37). The mad craving of Caligula (reigned 37–41) for divine honor may be reflected in the imagery used in Mark 13:14; II Thessalonians 2:4. Under Claudius (reigned 41–54) a disturbance among Jews at Rome, due to disputes concerning the claims made for Jesus, led, about 49 A.D., to an edict expelling all Jews.

It was to Nero (reigned 54–68) that Paul, a Roman citizen, appealed to gain a fair trial when he had reason to fear that the procurator in Palestine would not deal justly with him (Acts 25:11). Nero later used the Christians of Rome as the scapegoat when he himself was blamed for the fire that in 64 largely destroyed the city; he carried out a brutal persecution that resulted in many martyrdoms, although there is no clear evidence that his action brought persecution to Christians in other parts of the empire. Upon his death, Galba, Otho, and Vitellius tried unsuccessfully to gain the throne, but Vespasian, who at Nero's death was busy suppressing the Jewish revolt in Palestine (66–70), won out and ruled for ten years (69–79), to be followed by his son Titus (reigned 79–81).

Under Domitian (reigned 81–96), the demand for emperor worship seems to have been pressed with increased vigor, and Christians, who refused such worship, were persecuted, especially in Asia Minor. Following Nerva (reigned 96–98) came Trajan (reigned 98–117), in whose reign, as we learn from letters of Trajan and Pliny the Younger, the persecution of Christians in Asia Minor continued. Under Hadrian (reigned 117–138) the crushing of a second revolt of the Jews (132–135) showed that the Judaism of Jesus' day, centered in Jerusalem and its Temple, was not to be restored.

The Romans at first governed Palestine through the Herodian family. Herod the Great was puppet king by Roman grant (40–4 B.C.); Jesus was born in the closing years or months of his reign. At Herod's death his kingdom was divided among three sons. Philip became tetrarch of the region northeast of the Sea of Galilee (4 B.C.–34 A.D.). Herod Antipas was made tetrarch of Galilee and Perea (4 B.C.–39 A.D.); most of Jesus' ministry took place in this region. Archelaus became ethnarch of Judea and Samaria (4 B.C.–6 A.D.). When he was deposed for incompetence, a Roman procurator succeeded him.

The fifth such Roman governor was Pontius Pilate (ruled 26–36), who at the request of Jewish leaders condemned Jesus to death. Later, Herod Agrippa I, who at first ruled only the northeast part of Palestine, became king of the entire country (41–44; Acts 12:1, 20–23). His son, Herod Agrippa II (Acts 25:13), seemed to the Romans too young to succeed to the throne. However, he soon was made king of Chalcis, and later he ruled northeast Palestine and parts of Galilee. In 44, Palestine itself again was put under procurators, the fourth and fifth of whom were Felix and Festus. Felix may have been removed as early as 55 or 56, but probably his governorship, under which Paul was arrested at Jerusalem and taken to Caesarea, ran from 52 to 60, and that of Festus, who sent Paul to Rome, from 60 to 62. On Festus' death, and before Albinus succeeded him, hostile Jews at Jerusalem took advantage of the situation to put to death James the brother of Jesus.

The Jewish high priest was the leader of the people. However, the Herodians and later the Romans assumed the right to appoint and remove the high priest. Especially prominent was Annas (6–15), who continued influential after being deposed. Four of his sons, including Ananias (Acts 23:2), held the position and so did a son-in-law, Caiaphas (18–36; John 18:13), who was active in effecting Jesus' death.

The dating of the specific Christian events of the 1st century is rarely exact, but the sequence and approximate date usually can be determined. Jesus was born in the closing part of the reign of Herod the Great; that is, about 6 to 4 B.C. John the Baptist began his brief but influential ministry about 26 to 28 A.D. (Luke 3:1, 2). Jesus' ministry of perhaps a little over two years ended with his death at Passover time in 29 or 30. Paul's conversion was but a few years later, possibly about 34. The famine of Acts 11:28 occurred about 44. An important inscription found at Delphi dates the coming of Gallio to Corinth as proconsul in 51 (or possibly 52). With this as a clue, we may tentatively set the time of Paul's missionary travels: first journey (Acts 13, 14), about 48–49; Apostolic Council at Jerusalem, 49; second journey (Acts 15:36 to 18:22), 49–52; third journey (Acts 18:23 to 21:17), 53–58; arrest in Jerusalem, 58; imprisonment in Caesarea, 58–60; voyage to Rome, 60–61; imprisonment in Rome, 61–63; release (?), 63; execution at Rome after second arrest, 64 or 67. Other dates in early Christian history are: death of James the brother of Jesus, 62; persecution of Christians at Rome, 64; flight of the Jerusalem Christians to Pella at the start of the Jewish revolt, 66; persecution of Christians in Asia Minor, under Domitian (in the latter part of his reign) and Trajan.

HISTORY

Sources of New Testament History. The pagan world took little notice of the rise and early history of the church. Suetonius, in his *Life of Claudius*, probably refers to disputes among Roman Jews over the Christian claims for Jesus.

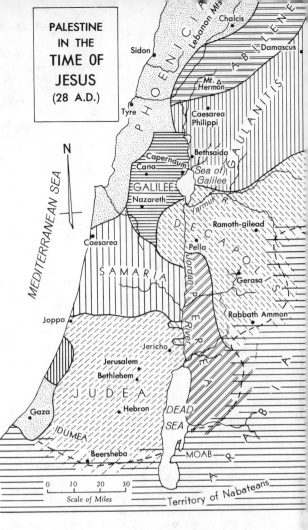

PALESTINE IN THE TIME OF JESUS (28 A.D.)

The report of Nero's persecution of the Christians in 64 is the first explicit reference. Tacitus, writing in the early 2d century, tells of this and refers briefly to Jesus (*Annals*, book 15). The Jews give but little more information. Josephus in his *Antiquities of the Jews* (book 20) tells of the death of James in 62 and of the high regard many Jews had for him; another passage tells more of Jesus (book 18) but the details of the passage in its present form are so Christian in content that it evidently has been revised by later Christian scribes to honor Christ and so cannot be taken as the work of Josephus. The rabbinical literature, written considerably later, attests the historicity, teaching, and miracles of Jesus, and the role of Jewish leaders in his death, but it gives little trustworthy detail. The sources for study of Christian origins, therefore, are almost entirely the New Testament and early Christian writings. Josephus also is invaluable.

The Founder, Jesus Christ. The scene of the rise of Christianity was Palestine. Since it then was included in the eastern portion of the Roman empire, the gospel story could move easily westward into the various provinces of the empire. Life in Palestine was dominantly Jewish. Aramaic was the language most widely spoken, although many residents, including some Jews, used Greek, the common language of the Roman world; in official government circles Latin no doubt found a minor place.

The immediate background of Jesus' ministry

was the prophetic ministry of John the Baptist, who in his wilderness haunts warned his fellow Jews that divine judgment was close at hand, preached the urgent necessity of repentance, and baptized the many who responded. His popular following and his denunciation of Herod Antipas for an offensive divorce and remarriage led Herod to imprison him and later execute him, but the people continued to respect his memory (Mark 11:32), and disciples of John were found years later in such remote places as Ephesus (Acts 18:25; 19:3).

Among those who came to John for baptism was Jesus, born at Bethlehem but raised at Nazareth in Galilee. He heard the call of God in the words of John. When baptized, he became aware that his close filial relation to God called him to fulfill the Jewish hope of a Messiah (this Hebrew word, like the Greek word *christos*, means "anointed"). He soon took up an independent ministry. It was confined to Palestine; rare and brief journeys to nearby Phoenicia and the region of Caesarea Philippi were times of withdrawal and not attempts to extend the area of his public work. It was confined almost entirely to Jews; only on few occasions, in response to urgent appeal, did he turn aside to aid Gentiles; he felt called to win the Jews first to the will and work of God. The main scene of his activity was Galilee; occasional visits to Jerusalem at times of Jewish festivals are reported in the Gospel of John and are doubtless historical, but he worked mainly in the Galilean region, where, with Capernaum as his chief center, he carried on an itinerant ministry on the shores and to the west of the Sea of Galilee.

Jesus' method was to go to the people, especially to the common folk and even the classes most despised, the "tax-collectors and sinners." He taught in the synagogues, by the sea, on the streets and roads, and in the fields—wherever he found a hearing. His central theme was the Kingdom of God (or Kingdom of Heaven, which means the same thing). This phrase meant the rule of God in the hearts, lives, and relations of men. Because of the sin and failure of men, the acceptance of the Kingdom message involved repentance and grateful faith in God; it required taking up a new life of obedience in fellowship with others who were waiting in hope for God to establish His Kingdom, which had begun to come in the work of Jesus. The final establishment of the kingdom was expected to come by the powerful action of God at the end of the age, the coming of which was eagerly expected. Since the loyalty to which Jesus called men included fellowship with him and his other followers, he began to gather disciples. Twelve of these he chose to be his special companions and to be messengers to help him spread his message. The fellowship of his group took on a more definite relation to him when, under Peter's leadership, they recognized him as the expected Messiah, the Christ of Jewish hope; henceforth it was clear that Jesus Christ was central and authoritative in their movement.

Despite his persuasive teaching, kindly healing of the sick, and popular support, official opposition to Jesus grew. The Pharisees and scribes were vigorously hostile. They demanded legal conformity not only to the Mosaic written Law but also to the developed oral tradition that applied it. Jesus' readiness to disregard ceremonial rules and oral tradition to meet human need, his emphasis on the human, the spiritual, the moral, rather than on the legal or ritual, was a challenge to their way of life, and they resisted. At the end of his ministry, Jesus went to Jerusalem to carry his claim to the center of Jewish life and worship. He drove from the Temple the traders who were commercializing and degrading the worship of God. Then the Sadducees, in whose hands was the control of the temple worship, added their opposition to that of the Pharisees. But he still had such popular support that a plotter against his life had to plan a secret arrest. Shortly after Jesus' Last Supper, in which he had interpreted the meaning of his impending death as a benefit for his disciples and a furthering of his cause, he was betrayed at night by Judas, one of the Twelve, and was arrested. After a hearing before Jewish leaders, he was taken to Pontius Pilate, who was induced to execute Jesus on the (false) charge that he was organizing a political revolt against Rome; this was the twisted meaning given to Jesus' acceptance of the title "Christ."

Jesus was executed just outside Jerusalem by Roman soldiers and buried in a nearby tomb. To outsiders this marked the end of his career and movement. But within a few days his followers, scattered at first from the shock of his death, had rallied because they could report that Christ had risen, met with them, and directed them to witness to him and carry forward his work. The Resurrection thus became the foundation of Christian faith, hope, and preaching from that time on. The disciples testified that God had made the risen Christ the Lord of His church.

The Jerusalem Church. It appears that the Eleven (the Twelve minus Judas the traitor) first saw the risen Christ in Galilee. Mark 14:28; 16:7 suggests this, and Matthew 28:10, 16f attests it. But he evidently appeared to his followers in Jerusalem and Judea as well (Luke 24; John 20). The disciples soon rallied at Jerusalem, which became the center of the church in the first generation. On Pentecost (Acts 2) the gift of the Holy Spirit gave them not only buoyant joy but also power for their work and the assurance of divine guidance in it. In these earliest years of the church, Peter was the outstanding leader of the group, speaking, healing, and refusing to be intimidated. Persecution by the religious leaders did not check the rapid growth of the movement, but it increased the hardships and want of the economically unrooted disciples at Jerusalem.

From the first the church included believers who could speak Greek. Two groups emerged in the group of disciples at Jerusalem; the larger spoke Aramaic, and the other used Greek. Neglect in the charitable care of destitute widows of the latter group led the church to appoint the Seven, all of them with Greek names, to care for the interests of this group. Of these Seven, Stephen and Philip were outstanding; it was the vigorous witness of Stephen that led to his seizure by the Jewish authorities, who saw that his teaching would shatter the framework of current Judaism. Upon his martyrdom, the Greek-speaking disciples were scattered, and they became the spearhead of the wider mission of the church.

Among Aramaic-speaking Christians, too, a wider work developed. The travels of Peter through the coast country of Palestine (Acts 9 to 11) involved mainly preaching to Jews in

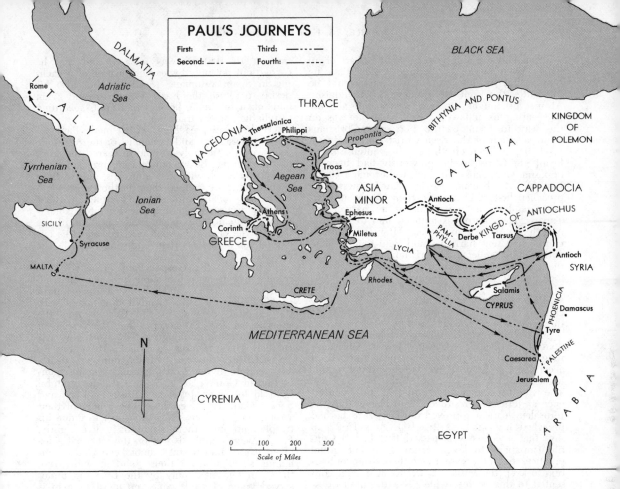

Aramaic, from which the preaching to the Gentile "God-fearer" Cornelius and his household stood apart as a special exception. Christianity was a minor but active phase of the life of Judaism for a few decades; after the death of Stephen, it would appear, the Jewish Christians remaining at Jerusalem were inclined to observe Jewish rites faithfully, to show their loyalty to the ancestral faith. The wide respect for James the brother of Jesus, who by 44 A.D. emerged as the leader of the church at Jerusalem, reflects this legal correctness of such Christians; he was called "James the Righteous." But at the start of the Jewish revolt in 66, the disciples at Jerusalem, acting upon a Christian prophecy or "oracle," as Eusebius reports (*Church History* III. 5:3), fled across the Jordan to the Hellenistic city of Pella and took no part in the defense of Jerusalem against the Romans. This decisively broke the ties of the church with Jerusalem and the Jewish community, and while Jewish Christians continued to exist for several centuries, they were isolated and of little importance for the increasingly Gentile church.

Hellenistic Christianity. As already stated, Greek-speaking Christianity was present at Jerusalem from the earliest days of the church. The persecution following the martyrdom of Stephen scattered these Christians. Philip worked in Samaria and on the coastal plain. Others went to Phoenicia, Cyprus, and Syria. Either then, or more probably earlier, the new faith reached Damascus. Possibly Christianity reached Egypt in the Apostolic Age; this seems inherently likely, and the fact that in Egypt, up the Nile Valley, Christian documents written early in the 2d

century have been found, argues that Christianity had then been in Egypt for decades. Certainly the Gospel reached Rome in the first decade of the church; when Paul wrote to Rome, the church there was of long standing and wide reputation. (Romans 1:8; 15:23). Pilgrims returning from Pentecost (Acts 2:10) could have been the first to bring the Gospel there. At any rate, not many years later an active church was present there, and it was not Peter but unknown Christians who founded it.

It was Greek-speaking Christians driven from Jerusalem after Stephen's martyrdom, however, who began a widespread mission to Gentiles. Some of the refugees went to Antioch in Syria (Acts 11:20). Up to this time the Greek-speaking Christians all had been Jews, or at least Jewish proselytes. At Antioch, Christian witnesses first presented the Gospel directly to Gentiles, without requiring them to become Jewish proselytes as a condition of becoming Christians. The Jerusalem apostles, disturbed by this development, sent Barnabas to investigate. Convinced that the Antioch church was a true Christian church, he became a leader in it. It was he who brought Paul into that church and so opened the way for Paul's wide mission to Gentiles.

The Apostle Paul. A triple heritage made possible Paul's epochal work. He was a Jew by birth and faith, and his Jewish heritage was prominent in his Christian thinking. He was a member of the Greek-speaking Hellenistic world; this prepared him to take the Gospel into any part of the Roman empire. He was a Roman citizen and proud of it (Acts 22:27 ff.); as a result, he had a world outlook.

Paul had the ability to go to the heart of an issue. Even before he became a Christian, he sensed that for Jews to follow Jesus would be to shatter the exclusive framework of Judaism. At first he fought the new movement, actively persecuting its followers. But while he was on the way to Damascus to persecute Christians there, a vision of the risen Christ converted him (Acts 9), and henceforth he was as intense in his loyalty to Christ as he previously had been in opposing Christians. For him, to become a Christian was to become a Christian witness. He preached first at Damascus, then briefly at Jerusalem, and for a longer time at his native city, Tarsus. Then Barnabas induced him to help the church at Antioch in Syria. After the Antioch church had sent Barnabas and Paul to Jerusalem with famine relief for Christians there, it sent them out on a pioneer missionary journey, which took them to Cyprus, Pamphylia, and central Asia Minor (Acts 13, 14). The chief outcome was the startling increase of Gentile members of the church; in city after city they responded to the preaching with eager faith.

The church was on the way to becoming predominantly Gentile. Certain Jewish Christians fought bitterly the practice, begun in Antioch, of accepting Gentiles into the church without requiring circumcision or keeping of the Mosaic Law. The issue became acute at Antioch, and a conference at Jerusalem resulted. Paul claims that the Jerusalem leaders approved the Gospel as he had preached it (Galatians 2:1–10); Acts 15:22–29 says that a decree was passed that bound Gentile Christians to keep certain food and ritual practices but otherwise freed them from obligation to keep the Mosaic Law. Even if Paul consented to this decree, which is a disputed question, he won a major victory at this conference. The Apostles at Jerusalem agreed that Gentiles need not be circumcised and keep the Jewish Law to be true Christians.

This did not end Jewish opposition to Paul. He continued to be denounced and persecuted. But he persisted in a plan to take the Gospel to as much of the empire as possible. His strategy was to seek out the main cities and establish churches there. Visitors to these central cities heard the Gospel and carried it back home. Paul also sent out helpers from such centers into surrounding regions. His travels led him through Asia Minor to Troas, across to Macedonia, down to Greece, and then, after a visit to Palestine and Syria, through Asia Minor to Ephesus, where he made a long stay. In another trip through Macedonia and Greece he sought to strengthen the churches there and complete a collection to take to the poverty-ridden Jerusalem Christians.

When Paul reached Jerusalem, however, the resentment of many Jews at his alleged disloyalty to Judaism caused a riot in the Temple that threatened him with death. Rescued by the Roman guard, which was on duty to prevent such disturbances, he was made a prisoner, taken to Caesarea, and held for two years. Then Festus succeeded Felix. Festus was ready to take Paul back to Jerusalem, to please the Jewish leaders, but Paul, fearing that his life would be sacrificed by Festus for political expediency, appealed to the Roman emperor. On the voyage to Rome his ship was wrecked on the island of Melita (Malta), but he finally reached Rome as a prisoner, and remained in Rome two years. Acts does not say what then happened, but later tradition asserts that he was released and that he carried out not only his earlier purpose of preaching in Spain (Romans 15:23–29) but also his desire to revisit the East. Later, arrested again and taken to Rome, he was martyred, according to reliable ancient tradition.

Widespread preaching, which made Paul the leading missionary and evangelist of the Apostolic Age, was not the only way he furthered the work of the church. By an outstanding use of letters, he kept in touch with new churches, guided their thought and life, helped them in their crises, and built up local leadership. Writing without thought of providing Scripture for later generations, he dealt with each local question in the light of the central Gospel message, and this has earned for his letters their enduring place in the church.

What was the Gospel Paul preached? He stated that it was the same message that all Christians believed and all its leaders taught (I Corinthians 15:11). And it does agree with the essential content of the Gospels and the speeches in Acts. It accepts the Old Testament as Scripture. It announces that God now has fulfilled His promises to Israel. It centers in Jesus Christ; the story of his ministry, death, resurrection, living Lordship, and coming completion of God's plan leads to a call for grateful faith in the risen Jesus as Christ the Lord and Son of God. He saves those who repent of their wrongdoing, and he sends the Spirit to guide his people and give them strength to live rightly. Paul's special emphasis was on the fact that since all men are sinners and cannot keep God's commands so as to earn their standing with Him, they can be saved only by the free and undeserved grace of God. Since no merit of man is involved, none can claim any advantage based on race or class or personal achievement. Hence all men can come to God by the same path of repentance and faith in Christ, who brings to all the free grace of God. This is a universal Gospel. It removes all basis for human pride; entrance into and growth in the Christian life result only from God's working.

The Later Church. For decades after the point at which Acts closes, we possess no clear picture of the development of the church. Even in the period covered by Acts there are many gaps. It was Luke's purpose to describe the spread of the Gospel from Jerusalem to Rome; he did not tell all that he might have told of the spread of the Gospel to other places, nor did he report how the individual churches developed. But once Acts ends, we are left without any connected narrative. However, Christian writings of the 1st and early 2d centuries give us glimpses of what followed, so that we can trace the main lines of development.

The preservation, collection, and wide use of Paul's letters show that his martyr death did not end his influence. Deprived of his voice, his churches fell back upon the reading of his letters. It is not known when they were collected into one group, but since individual churches exchanged his letters during his lifetime (Colossians 4:16), a more extensive exchange and collection probably began immediately after his death. Hebrews was not written by Paul, but later was included wrongly among his letters. The Pastoral Epistles (I Timothy, II Timothy, Titus) may have been expanded into their present form after his death by use of shorter notes from him, to insist on sound teaching, good works, and responsible church leadership. But the other Pauline letters, some of them written from prison, were available at his death to preserve his message and guide churches in life and worship.

In the last third of the 1st century the four Gospels were written. Mark, the earliest, may be dated 65–70, Matthew 85–95, Luke 80–85, and John 90–100; all such dates are tentative. The collection of many brief units of tradition in the Synoptic Gospels (Matthew, Mark, Luke) preserves the memory of what Jesus said and did as it had been repeated and used in the life of the church, where it had proved useful for instruction, worship, problem solving, and guidance in controversy. These Gospels, by thus reflecting the constant earlier use of oral tradition about Jesus, show that he was central in the worship, teaching, and thinking of the Christians during these decades. Matthew shows a stronger Jewish Christian background, Mark a Roman situation, and Luke a Gentile's presentation of the common tradition; but all tell essentially the same story, as it was known, told, and used in the Church. The Gospel of John is unique. It contains much the same basic historical tradition about Jesus that the Synoptics present, but it also draws on fresh sources of information from Palestine and fuses the facts with a reverent interpretation of the significance of Jesus as "the Christ, the Son of God" (John 20:31).

In the later part of the New Testament period the church was often in trouble with the governing authorities. In the earlier years, repeated action by Jewish authorities, first in Palestine and then in Gentile cities, had made difficulties for Christian leaders. Opponents could say not only that Christ the founder of this movement had been executed as a rebel against Rome, but also that Paul had been arrested and finally put to death by the empire as a troublemaker. Such hostility continued. The later instigation of persecution by Jews is suggested by the Book of Revelation (2:9; 3:9) as well as by the middle 2d century *Martyrdom of Polycarp* (13:1).

But the main threat came from the empire. Nero had persecuted the Christians at Rome on false charges of treason, criminal acts, and unworthy lives. This imperial accusation always hung like a shadow over the church.

The more the practice of emperor worship grew, the greater the crisis that lay ahead for the Christians, for they could not reconcile worship of pagan emperors with their faith in "One God, the Father, . . . and one Lord Jesus Christ" (I Corinthians 8:6). This crisis came to a head in Asia Minor, where emperor worship was more vigorously promoted than in Rome itself. The Book of Revelation seems to come from a critical time at the end of the reign of Domitian, when Christians of Asia Minor were threatened with a choice between apostasy or death, and one martyr, Antipas, already could be named (Revelation 2:13). The book was written to nerve the Christians to accept death rather than renounce their Christian faith. I Peter speaks of such a persecution as impending or begun (4:12–19), and Hebrews, perhaps written to Rome or to some other church in Italy, refers to a past persecution and evidently thinks that another one is likely (10:32–39). In I Peter and Hebrews, however, the issue of emperor worship is not clearly present, and these books may come from an earlier date than the Book of Revelation.

All such references to persecution, and the emphatic use that the Synoptic Gospels make of tradition in which Jesus warns his disciples of future ill-treatment, show that these later decades of the 1st century were hard years for faithful Christians, who continually faced the threat of official imperial persecution. Times of relief no doubt occurred, but they were never a permanent release from danger.

The pagan world brought still other dangers. Christian preachers had to use the language and ideas of the world to make their message clear. In this use of terms tied to the first century's pagan heritage lurked the danger that the church itself might adopt pagan ideas and attitudes. Also, new converts not fully alive to the meaning of Christian faith might bring pagan ideas into the church. The ancient world was a ferment of competing philosophies and religions, and the denunciations of false teachers in the New Testament show that not every Christian teacher avoided the danger of surrendering something essential to the world. But for the most part the steadying content of Scripture, the Jewish heritage of monotheism and moral obedience to God, and above all the teaching, example, and work of Jesus himself enabled the church to stay clear of the swirling waters of pagan syncretism.

One persistent danger was the dualism prevalent in much pagan thought. Lacking the Biblical faith in God as creator of a good world, many ancient thinkers held that matter is inherently evil, and one tendency, soon to crystallize as Gnosticism, sought a knowledge that would save from the evil world the soul, the spark of the divine that had become lodged in an evil material body. This view meant that Christ, if actually incarnate in a physical body, had thereby been degraded and could not be the perfect Savior of men; against such a Docetic view the Gospel of John and the Johannine Epistles contend. Such a view also meant that the physical side of life had no place in the religious life of men, and so men would be driven by this view either to an unwholesome, rigid asceticism or to a deplorable laxity of life. Not only Paul, but also the letters Jude and II Peter and the Book of Revelation vigorously oppose these dangers, especially the tendency to be complacent about immoral living. This dualism, this failure to recognize the world as God's creation, this striving to escape from the life of earth and save one's soul by escape to heaven, led to exaggerated individualism and a neglect of the fellowship of the church, and much of the attention of Christian leaders and writers in the later period of the New Testament was directed against such a distortion of the Christian teaching. The tendency in the late books of the New Testament and in some other ancient Christian writings was to insist on authoritative leadership, sound teaching, good works, and wholesome rules of life; this emphasis grew out of the necessity of opposing such false teaching. The task of the church was seen to be that of combining freedom of faith with a clear sense of moral obligation and self-accepted discipline.

ARCHAEOLOGY

Much of the modern interest in New Testament archaeology and geography is misdirected. Attempts to find the exact spot where every event of Jesus' life occurred are persistent but futile. However, substantial progress in recovering the setting of the story has been made. In Palestine, some important sites have been definitely located; for example, Capernaum was at the present Tell Hum, Bethsaida was on the north shore of the Sea of Galilee and slightly east of the entrance of the Jordan into that lake, New Testament Jericho has been found and is being excavated at Tulul Abu el-Alayik, and the ancient outlines of the city of Caesarea on the coast have been traced.

Excavations have thrown light on the Jewish setting of the story. In the 1st century, as Josephus tells us, there was at every gate into the inner temple courts at Jerusalem an inscription warning Gentiles on pain of death to go no farther; two of these ancient inscriptions have been discovered by modern excavations. Elsewhere in the city, a significant inscription in Greek has come to light. It tells that a certain Theodotus had financed the erection of a synagogue and guest rooms for Greek-speaking Jews on pilgrimage to Jerusalem; this illustrates the use of Greek among Jews in the central city of Judaism. Numerous synagogues have been uncovered in recent decades, many in Palestine and some in other countries; while they are later than the 1st century, they help to reconstruct the development of synagogue structure and art. Of special interest are the ruins of a synagogue at Capernaum; however, while this building may have been built on the site of an earlier synagogue in use in Jesus' day, the structure whose ruins now stand there must be dated later than the 1st century. In Corinth an inscription, though fragmentary, seems to read "Synagogue of the Hebrews." If so, it suggests that Aramaic-speaking Jews met there for worship; the date of this inscription, however, is not certain.

Plentiful evidence is available to illustrate the Hellenistic background of the New Testament. Much of it comes from Palestine itself. Excavations at New Testament Jericho, 1st century Samaria, and Herodian Caesarea are examples of the presence of Graeco-Roman influence and culture in the land of Jesus. The Decapolis, ten cities of Hellenistic organization, architecture, and life, all but one of them located east of the Jordan, further illustrate the cultural clash in Palestine between Jewish and Graeco-Roman ways of life. Several Decapolis sites, especially Gerasa (the modern Jerash), have been examined and partly excavated.

Abundant material enables us to reconstruct the setting of 1st century life in the wider Graeco-Roman world. The city plans of many great centers of the empire's life now can be studied. Especially important are Pompeii in Italy and Gerasa in Eastern Palestine. Because, abandoned long ago and not now covered by modern buildings, they offer complete city plans for study. Excavations also have laid bare the main features of ancient Athens, Corinth, Philippi, Ephesus, and other important places. Inscriptions throw light on political situations; for example, an inscription at Thessalonica confirms the correctness of Acts 17:6 when it calls the local rulers of that city "politarchs." They also reflect the general social life and the religious situation. Ephesus especially has yielded numerous such inscriptions. Not only inscriptions, but in particular the papyri, found in large numbers in the dry sands of Egypt, give contemporary examples of the Greek of New Testament times and enable students to relate the Biblical Greek to the common Hellenistic Greek of the surrounding world. The papyri contain numerous documents, including informal letters, that throw light on the personal, social, political, commercial, and religious life of the various classes of people in Egypt.

New Testament study has benefited much from discovery of early manuscripts of the Biblical books. There was very little use of parchment for manuscript material until the 4th century, and until recent decades almost all the manuscripts of New Testament writings dated from the 4th century and later. Excavations in Egypt, and quite rarely discoveries elsewhere, have now brought to light many papyrus copies of these writings. Many date from the 2d and 3d centuries, and although they are fragmentary, they nevertheless suffice to show that the later manuscripts of the New Testament books are trustworthy in every essential respect.

FLOYD V. FILSON
McCormick Theological Seminary

Bibliography

Bornkamm, Günther, *Jesus of Nazareth* (New York 1960).
Cross, Frank M., Jr., *The Ancient Library of Qumran and Modern Biblical Studies* (Garden City, N.Y., 1961).
Filson, Floyd V., *A New Testament History* (Philadelphia 1964).
Finegan, Jack, *Light from the Ancient Past*, 2d ed. (Princeton 1959).
Foakes-Jackson, Frederick J., and Lake, K., *The Beginnings of Christianity*, 5 vols. (London 1920–33).
Goguel, Maurice, *The Life of Jesus* (New York 1958).
Ramsay, William M., *St. Paul the Traveller and the Roman Citizen* (New York 1903).
Schürer, E., *A History of the Jewish People in the Time of Jesus Christ* (Edinburgh 1893).
Weiss, Johannes, *The History of Primitive Christianity*, 2 vols. (New York 1937).
Wright, G. Ernest, *Biblical Archaeology*, new ed. (Philadelphia 1962).
Wright, G. Ernest, and Filson, Floyd V., *Westminster Historical Atlas to the Bible* (Philadelphia 1945).

15. Religion and Theology of the New Testament

The New Testament is the literature the church ultimately selected and canonized out of the first century or more of its history. The religion it reflects developed in Jesus out of the finest flower of the Old Testament prophetic and wisdom tradition, tempered by the poetry and piety of the psalmists, was enriched by his own unique apprehension of God, and was built into the life of a community by men and women who had found in him the way, the truth, and the life. Its theology began with the theological assumptions Jesus had taken over from Judaism, was recast and reinterpreted in the light of the Resurrection, and gradually was "translated out of Semitic into Greek" by many Hellenistic Jewish Christians, of whom Paul is perhaps the only one we can identify positively by name.

When the church came into being as a consequence of the Resurrection faith, Christianity was still a Jewish sect. Within a generation it had become a new religion, no longer recognizing racial limitations, conscious of a worldwide mission, filled with a confident faith, buoyed up by most certain hopes, and creating its own vehicles of thought, forms of worship, and methods of discipline. The following paragraphs undertake to sketch the development of religion and theology during Christianity's most vital and creative years.

THE MESSAGE OF JESUS

The Kingdom of God. According to all sources now incorporated in the Synoptic Gospels, the central theme of the message Jesus proclaimed was the kingdom of God. The variant "heaven" for "God" in Matthew appears to have been due only to a Semitic reticence about the use of the divine name. The Greek word for "kingdom" translates a Semitic original that means "reign" or "rule," and Jesus, therefore, spoke to his followers of the rule of God.

The prophets and many of the psalmists had held that God had always been king; that His purposes make themselves evident in His mighty works; and that the full and effective establishment of His rule on earth would be an event of the last days—the "day of the Lord." During the Persian and Greek periods, however, faith in the manifestation of the kingdom of God within the framework of history was abandoned by many Jews. In a body of literature we call revelation or apocalyptic, they transferred their hopes almost entirely to the future. God must destroy the present evil age and establish the faithful in a new heaven and a new earth.

While Jesus believed that the full realization of God's will would be an event accomplished in the last days, he was far from sharing the deep apocalyptic pessimism about the present. The consummation of God's rule awaits the fulfillment of His mysterious purposes, but He has already taken His great power and begun to reign. The kingdom of God will come "with power" in the last days, but it is already—in germ, at least—in the midst of men.

It is noteworthy that Jesus' concern with the new age of God's rule was only with its religious and ethical implications. When God's kingdom would come, God's will would be done, on earth as it is in heaven. Then all men would gladly recognize His sovereignty and offer Him spontaneous obedience.

God. Like his predecessors in Israel, Jesus never debated the case for belief in God; he simply assumed it. He never argued that God is the Creator of the universe, but he pointed to the lilies that God has clothed in all their beauty. He never discussed God's omnipotence, but he asserted that not a sparrow falls to the ground without the Father's will. He never theorized about divine providence, but he invited men to pray for their daily bread. He never speculated about God's omniscience, but he declared that even the hairs of our heads are numbered.

As for Elijah, Amos, and Isaiah, God for Jesus was the God of uncompromising righteousness. Because He is radical goodness, He cannot tolerate iniquity. There is no shallow sentimentalism in Jesus' thought. Nevertheless, the austerity of the prophetic conception of God is relieved in the gospel by the devout piety of the psalmists. The overtones of Jesus' words are those of God's majesty and justice, but the tones are those of His mercy and His love.

The majesty and the mercy of God, the righteousness and the lovingkindness of God, the justice and the love of God all are summed up by Jesus in the name "Father." Others had used the title before him, but it was he who put the thought of God as Father at the heart of religion. To a great extent all his preaching was an exposition of his distinctive concept. God may be known in many ways, but the thought of Him as Father transcends and crowns them all.

Jesus and the Law of Moses. Jesus reverenced the law as "the commandment of God" but challenged the validity of the scribal tradition. He confirmed the authority of the moral law but questioned the sanctions of ceremonial legislation. He emphasized motive and attitude rather than precept and prescription—a set of the will rather than conformity to a pattern. He even described some commandments in the law as faulty and held that they were superseded by higher principles.

A large part of Jesus' teaching can be paralleled from rabbinical sources. In its totality, however, it was at variance with traditional Jewish legalism. The teaching of the scribes was explanatory and derivative. It was based on the ceremonial legalism of the Old Testament. The gospel was a purified and radical prophetism. Micah, Hosea, Isaiah, and Jeremiah were our Lord's spiritual ancestors.

Jesus' Ethical Teaching. According to Jesus, the qualities that fit a man for the kingdom of God are sincerity, fidelity, humility, and obedience. These already had been highly praised in Hebrew prophecy and Jewish wisdom, but in Jesus' articulation of them they emerge in a singularly radical phrasing.

Radical devotion to God tolerates no vacillation, no half measures, no divided allegiance. It requires utter freedom from all selfishness, covetousness, sensuality, and desire for revenge. It prohibits the lustful passion as well as the adulterous act. It demands absolute truthfulness rather than the mere avoidance of perjury. It forbids retaliation in any form for injustice. It enjoins complete detachment from earthly treasures and anxieties. It call for unreserved commitment of one's whole self to the kingdom of God. It requires an attitude of love that includes God, one's neighbor, and one's enemy.

It is difficult to exaggerate the absolute character of the Gospel ethic. We are to serve God and no other master. We are to eschew all anger rather than content ourselves with inhibiting its fruits. We are to love our enemies as God in His love embraces all men. We are to be perfect as our heavenly Father is perfect.

The complement in the Gospel to this radical ethic of obedience is the message of the love, the mercy, and the forgiveness of God. The God who demands that we be perfect as He is perfect is also the God who is ever ready to renew the fellowship with Himself that is broken by our sin. The God of the Sermon on the Mount is also the God of the parables of the lost sheep, the lost coin, and the lost prodigal son.

Interpretations by the Primitive Church. Various categories of thought were employed by Jesus' followers to interpret his mission: prophet, teacher, herald of eschatological salvation, Son of man, and Messiah. It is difficult to determine whether Jesus himself accepted all these designations and whether, in particular—if he regarded himself as the fulfillment of Jewish messianic hopes—he deliberately recast popular beliefs in the light of the servant of the Lord passages in Deutero-Isaiah.

The picture becomes clearer when the church emerges as the instrument of missionary, didactic, and catechetical Christianity. The speeches in the early chapters of Acts are probably typical primitive sermons and—together with some passages in which Paul specifically declares he is recalling what he had "received," certain "sermonettes" embodied in the Synoptic Gospels, and the Passion narrative in Mark—enable us to reconstruct the outlines of the early Christian *kerygma* (proclamation of the Gospel).

The speech at Pentecost in Acts 2:14–40, supported by other sources, indicates that the primitive Christian preaching included some account of Jesus' ministry (verse 22); some reflection on the meaning of the Crucifixion (verse 23); a proclamation of the resurrection and exaltation of Jesus as Christ and as Lord (verse 24); and a call to repentance associated with a promise of the gift of the Holy Spirit (verse 38). The teaching that Christ would return shortly as God's agent to establish the just in the new age also pervades many of our sources.

While the narrative material in the Synoptic Gospels was preserved and employed in the main to convert unbelievers, to confirm the faithful, and to assist in the ordering of early worship, the large body of teaching matter served catechetical and didactic interests. There is evidence in the letters of Paul as well as in later documents of a primitive *didache* (teaching) complementary to the *kerygma*, based on memories of Jesus' words but also adapting to its use matter drawn from Hellenistic ethical patterns and Jewish wisdom literature.

Although Jesus did not practice baptism, this was the means, probably borrowed from followers of John, by which the church initiated new converts into its fellowship. The Lord's Supper also was celebrated from the beginning as a distinctive Christian rite. It was grounded on reminiscences of Jesus' Last Supper with his disciples but appears early to have taken on sacramental characteristics, possibly influenced in this respect by sacred meals in competing Hellenistic cults. Early Christians thought of themselves as the true Israel and as the fellowship of those who, in obedience to God as He had made Himself known in Christ Jesus, awaited eschatological salvation. Apostles, prophets, teachers, presbyters, bishops, and still other orders came into being at a very early period, but it is not always possible to distinguish their exact functions, and it is clear that different forms of church government flourished in the church for some decades.

PAUL'S CONTRIBUTIONS

Paul's letters were written in almost every instance to meet the practical and pressing problems of newly founded congregations and are not the repository of any highly organized system of thought. Nevertheless, they are characterized by a variety of cardinal ideas.

View of Christ. The risen Christ often is described as the judge and the Savior of the last days, as is the Son of Man of Enoch and of the synoptic tradition. But the title "Christ" has been emptied in large part of its original Jewish content and has come to designate a divine being. Christ has become the object of religious homage and worship and is regularly entitled "Lord." As Lord he has become a redeemer-god after the analogy of gods of Hellenistic mystery cults.

Although Paul attributes the functions of deity to Christ, he is careful to safeguard his inherited monotheism. The Son of God is subordinated to the Father. On several occasions the apostle's speculative interest leads him to speak of Christ as a being already divine in a preexistent state, as in Philippians 2:5–11. In two or three significant passages, such as Colossians 1:15–17, the christological ideas come very close to the Logos category of 2d century apologists.

Paul began his Christian pilgrimage with a profound consciousness of the saving revelation of God in Christ Jesus—a consciousness rooted in his own conversion experience. When Jewish vehicles of thought proved inadequate, he reached out and drew upon Hellenistic categories and thereby significantly enriched the thought forms of Christian faith.

The Redemptive Work of Christ. Paul focused his attention on two great events in the ministry of our Lord—Christ's death and resurrection. By submitting to the Cross and triumphing over it, Christ effected a work of redemption. The believer, by allowing himself to be baptized and by gratefully accepting the grace of God, identifies himself with the experiences of Christ, appropriates the redemption he effected, and becomes a "new creature." He is henceforth "in Christ."

Paul thought of Christ on the Cross as delivering believers from various enemies:

(1) The law was an almost personal power that had held all mankind in bondage. The Redeemer broke its grip and its curse by his vicarious death.

(2) On the Cross, God in Christ triumphed over the hierarchy of demons that control the present age. Their ultimate destruction would not be accomplished until Christ should return as God's vicegerent in the last days, but they took the first step in their downfall when they plotted Christ's crucifixion.

(3) Paul thought of sin as an objective power rooted in what he called "the flesh." The crucifixion of Christ effected its destruction, although the full effects of that victory were not yet evident.

(4) On the Cross death, closely allied with sin, also was overcome. The fact that good Christians continued to die only meant that the complete results of Christ's redemptive work would not be manifest until after his return.

Justification by Faith. According to Paul's understanding of Pharisaic Judaism, God at the bar of judgment would declare to be just only those who had obtained righteousness by obedience to the oral and written tradition of Jewish legalism. As a Jew the apostle had been oppressed by a sense of hopelessness. If salvation were to be achieved only by works of the law, he believed himself to stand condemned. His conversion had brought with it the conviction that God in Christ had opened up a new way of salvation by faith—by the humble and grateful acceptance of the redemptive work effected on the Cross. According to the metaphor the apostle happens to employ, the redeemed man is described as reconciled, adopted, acquitted, freed from debt, or declared just.

The Spirit. By faith a man also acquires a new dynamic—the gift of the Spirit. This is responsible, to be sure, for such abnormal phenomena as "speaking with tongues" but far more for such ordinary ethical virtues of a dedicated Christian life as truth, peace, hope, and love.

The Resurrection and the Future Life. In Paul's day most Jews believed in a future life only because of the doctrine of a physical resurrection—no immortality without a body. For the Greek, on the other hand, the body was the prison house of the soul. The apostle was both a Jew and a Greek. There could be no future life without a resurrection, but the resurrection body would not be the body of this flesh. It would be a spiritual body that has been waiting for us from time eternal in the heavens. Back of such speculation, however, lies the religious conviction that nothing, not even death, can separate us from the love of God in Christ Jesus our Lord (Romans 8:38–39).

IDEAS OF OTHER WRITERS

Mark. Mark appears to have been the earliest Gospel. The author edited a wide range of Jesus' pronouncements, stories of Jesus as a doer of mighty works, narratives of Jesus and his followers and opponents, and accounts of events that revealed our Lord as a divine being. He then wove them into a dramatic sequence around an early version of the Passion.

Mark's Christ is the martyred Messiah. Opposed by Jewish leaders, recognized in his true character first by demons, confessed by Peter, revealed to the eye of faith by an epiphany, and crucified by the Roman procurator, he is known —by the evidence of the empty tomb—to have triumphed over the powers of evil. For a Roman reader threatened with persecution because of his faith there was a ringing summons in the Gospel to take up his cross and follow his martyred Lord. Whoever would lose his life for Christ's sake and the Gospel's would save it (8:34–35).

Matthew. Matthew is a revised and expanded edition of Mark, and most of the new material worked into the framework of the earlier Gospel is didactic. A cycle of birth and infancy narratives is prefixed, a sequence of resurrection narratives is appended, and the Gospel ends with the famous missionary commission.

The prefix and appendix heighten the representation of Christ as a divine being. There is a pronounced interest throughout in the imminence of the end and in Christ's functions as God's vicegerent in the last days. In the Sermon on the Mount our Lord is portrayed as a new lawgiver whose authority now supersedes that of Moses. The church is mentioned twice by name, Jesus is said to have founded it upon Peter, and several of the parables are related to its disciplinary and missionary problems. The arrangement and presentation of Jesus' teaching early made Matthew's Gospel popular as a Christian catechism.

Luke-Acts. Luke-Acts is one work in two volumes. Its author drew upon Mark and on several other sources to depict the miraculous birth, the self-denying ministry, the bitter death and the triumphant resurrection of Jesus Christ. He used Petrine and Pauline tradition to give an account of Christianity's expansion from Jerusalem to the coastal towns of Palestine, to the provinces of the Levant, to eastern Europe, and finally to the imperial capital. He then reworked the whole with the genius of a literary and dramatic artist.

The power of prayer, the work of the Holy Spirit, the role of women, the proper stewardship of wealth, and a marked sympathy for the poor and the outcast in the early Christian community are cardinal interests both of the Gospel and of Acts. The author stresses the universalism of the new faith, represents the church as heir to God's ancient promises to Israel, and protests against any suggestion that Christianity is a politically subversive sect.

Hebrews. The Epistle to the Hebrews was an appeal to second generation Christians, probably at Rome, for a revival of cult loyalty and enthusiasm during a period of incipient conflict with the state. For their encouragement the author undertook in the first place to demonstrate the finality of Christianity as the absolute religion. The new covenant was superior in every respect to the provisional covenant mediated by Moses and was completely adequate to meet the religious needs of men. It had in Christ the eternal high priest who had completely identified himself with those whom he represented, who had offered himself as the only true sacrifice, and who lives forever in the divine presence as the representative of those who believe in him. In the second place, the author set out to rally his readers to a courage worthy of this faith. They were invited to con the roster of heroes and martyrs from the days of Abel and of Enoch to the time of the Maccabees and to fix their eyes upon Jesus, the pioneer and perfecter of their faith. He had tasted the bitterness of death for every man and had been seated at the right hand of the throne of God. In light of his example, readers were urged to cultivate patience and courage and to hold fast their confession.

A sense of the church as a divine community underlies the whole letter. The older Mosaic tabernacle was only a copy and a shadow of the true one in heaven. Christ as the high priest of the new covenant had passed through this greater and more perfect tabernacle and into the heavenly sanctuary. There, with his own blood, he had opened the way to God and had secured eternal redemption for believers. He presides over the cultus, and by virtue of his sacerdotal efficacy Christians are enabled to enter into the holy place. As members of the community of the redeemed they are the ultimate object of God's creative purposes and at one with him who has purified them.

Ephesians. The Epistle to the Ephesians was originally an encyclical addressed "to the faithful in Christ Jesus." Its author made extensive use of Paul's letters, particularly that to the Colossians. Christ is depicted as a heavenly Redeemer, ordained by God to bring hostile and conflicting groups in heaven and on earth into a divine harmony. He has begun this work by the unity he already has effected in the church. The church is his body, conceived in realistic terms with Christians as its several members. It is a supernatural organism in which former heathen have become fellow members with former Jews. The closing chapters exhort readers to walk in a manner worthy of their Christian calling. As members of the body of Christ they are to be knit together by Christ the head, to resist division, to hold to the truth, and to contribute proportionately to the proper growth and upbuilding of the whole.

I Peter. The First Epistle General of Peter was another encyclical. Although the author invoked the authority of Peter, his epistle is permeated with Pauline vocabulary and ideas. He seeks to comfort, encourage, and confirm his readers in their faith during a period of acute persecution. Their afflictions are a test of their steadfastness pending the triumphant return of the Risen Christ. Christ also suffered, a just man for unjust men. To the extent that Christians share their Lord's sufferings, they are to rejoice— that they may rejoice the more when his glory is made manifest. Their trials mark the beginning of a judgment that will be visited in its full force upon the godless. They are to continue to do right and entrust their souls to a faithful Creator.

Chapters 1:4 to 4:11 originally may have been a baptismal discourse to new converts on the significance and obligations of the Christian life and its rewards.

James. The letters of Paul had included brief hortatory passages for the general ethical direction of Christian converts, similar in form and content to popular non-Christian prototypes. Sayings of Jesus, or sayings attributed to him, that had proven useful as norms for the control of individual and community behavior had been assembled and incorporated into the Synoptic Gospels. James is another example of this paraenetic or hortatory literature of early Christianity. In common with its Jewish and Hellenistic models, it lacks any inner unity of thought, and its sayings have only a meager formal sequence. It illustrates the moral precepts felt to be necessary in the church of its day. There is very little in it that can be said to be distinctively Christian. The passage in chapter 2:14–26, where we are told that faith apart from works is dead, reads like an attack on some perversion of the Pauline doctrine of justification by faith.

The Pastoral Letters. Although some of the *personalia* in I-II Timothy and Titus may have been taken from notes left by the great missionary to the Gentiles, the Pastorals as a whole are sub-Pauline. The founder of Christianity in Asia is declared to have anticipated ecclesiastical problems and situations that did not emerge for another half century.

The Pastorals had a twofold purpose:

(1) They were written to oppose heresies that had been gaining a dangerous popularity in certain Christian circles. Christianity is defined as sound belief and sound behavior—orthodoxy and life in accordance with an accepted Christian pattern.

(2) They sought to support with the authority of the great apostle the new ecclesiastical organization that had displaced the primitive ministry. Timothy and Titus are represented as bishops, whose duties Paul describes. Paul is made to call upon the church to render such men respect and obedience.

The Revelation of John. The author of this apocalypse describes himself as John, a servant of God and a brother and companion in distress of Asian Christians. The book opens with seven letters to different churches, together with a covering letter, and then narrates a series of visions. It uses earlier Semitic sources, apocalyptic symbolism, and numerology (666 was probably Domitian as Nero *redivivus*) to convey an esoteric assurance of speedy deliverance from persecutors.

Christianity often is represented in crudely pictorial fashion. Heaven is a place of gold and precious jewels, hell is an abyss of fire and brimstone, and salvation is literal deliverance from oppressors. Christians are now at the mercy of Satan (the dragon) and the Roman empire (the beast rising out of the sea), but Christ soon will appear, Rome will be overthrown, and Satan will be bound for a thousand years. After this messianic interlude the devil will be released, will gather allies, and once more will wage war against Christ. After the final victory Satan and his last adherents will be committed to hell, and Christ and the faithful will live forever in a new Jerusalem.

The Book of Revelation is not distinctively

Christian. Loyalty, patience, purity, and zeal are the virtues praised, and martyrdom is the greatest of good works. God is a heavenly Oriental king, and Satan is a potentate over against Him, each with a retinue of angels. The figure of the historical Jesus has been displaced by the divine warrior Christ, who will triumph in a hard-fought fight.

The apocalypse is written in atrocious Greek; it verges on Zoroastrian dualism, and it is a "tract for hard times." Nevertheless, it abounds in memorable word pictures and is the finest example of its particular genre. It never doubts the ultimate triumph of God, and it is confident that the kingdom of God and of His Christ is the final goal of the historical process.

The Gospel According to St. John. Early in the 2d century some unknown Christian, probably writing in Syria, composed a new Gospel designed to supersede Mark and the Gospel volume of Luke-Acts. His main purpose was to demonstrate that Jesus was the Son of God and to lead men into "life through his name" (John 20:31). Incidentally he wished to combat Gnostic trends, discount claims advanced in favor of John the Baptist as a divine Redeemer, emphasize the independence of Christianity from Judaism, and interpret the Christian message in terms of a Hellenistic rather than a Semitic culture.

The author employed the Logos doctrine in the interests of his christology, a doctrine already adumbrated within the Christian tradition in Paul's letters and in the Letter to the Hebrews. The Logos was the divine agent through whom the world had been created and by whom it is upheld. The Logos had been in the world of men before the Incarnation but had received no recognition or acceptance. At the appropriate time this divine Logos became flesh in Jesus Christ.

Christ came into the world to bring knowledge of God and to give men power to become God's children. He is the way, the truth, and the life. To believe in him is to recognize his divine nature and to enter into a mystical fellowship with him. As bread becomes part of the body when eaten, so Christ as the bread of life must pervade the whole inner being of the believer.

The kingdom of God, the greatest good of primitive Christian preaching, recedes into the background in this Gospel, and its place is taken by the new concept of eternal life. Eternal life is a life higher than the physical; a life made possible by union with Christ and through him with God; a fellowship with God in Christ that transforms the whole man, that begins here and now, and that persists through death to all eternity.

The Fourth Evangelist has passed many other primitive Christian beliefs and traditions through the crucible of his reflection, and a new amalgam has emerged; not a record of the Jesus of history, but a portrait of the Christ of faith; not an account of Jesus' teaching, but an interpretation of the meaning of the church's faith for the believer. In this "chiefest of the Gospels," as Luther described it, "unique, tender and true," the Word of God made flesh, misunderstood and rejected by the Jews, is set forth for the eye of faith in all His glory, full of grace and truth.

I John. First John is a tract warning against doctrinal and moral perils—an attack on some form of Christian Gnosticism or Docetism:

Heretical teachers were denying that Jesus

was the Son of God. The author condemns them as liars and insists that one criterion of true religion is acceptance of the dogma that "Jesus Christ is come in the flesh" (I John 4:2).

False doctrine was associated with false moral standards. False teachers held themselves to be superior to all ethical restraints. The author warns his readers against such antinomianism. Right belief always is associated with right conduct. No one who does not do right is of God, nor is anyone who does not love his brother.

II and III John. Second John urges some Christian community to exclude certain false teachers from its fellowship. Third John protests against the practice of exclusion when it is applied to the author's own emissaries by the leader (possibly bishop) of another congregation.

The elder to whom both letters are ascribed has been identified often with John the Elder, an individual (mentioned by Papias) who was held in high honor by the Church of the early 2d century.

Jude and Second Peter. Jude was a pamphlet addressed "to them that are . . . called"—to all Christians rather than to a specific community. Its purpose was, first, to buttress "the faith which was . . . delivered unto the saints" (orthodoxy), and, second, to warn against teachers who disseminated heretical beliefs and who were guilty of gross immorality. The false doctrine appears to have been some form of Christian Gnosticism, and the letter implies that it had made headway.

Second Peter incorporates most of Jude. Although the author claims to have been an eyewitness of Gospel events, his book demands a 2d century date, and the signature, as in the case of Jude, must have been pseudonymous.

The third chapter of Second Peter makes an interesting plea for a reinterpretation of primitive Christian eschatology. The end of this age is indefinitely postponed on the argument that (3:8) "one day is with the Lord as a thousand years, and a thousand years as one day" (see Psalm 90:4).

Conclusion. There was no sharp break between the religion of Jesus and the best in the religious heritage of contemporary Judaism. Nevertheless, Christianity always has been a theology as well as a religion. It has been the religion of Jesus illuminated and irradiated by God and His saving grace in Jesus himself. "God, who at sundry times and in divers manners spake in time past unto the fathers by the prophets, hath in these last days spoken unto us by his Son" (Hebrews 1:1–2). In various categories of thought, most of them furnished by Hellenistic Judaism, New Testament writers, conscious that they had been called out of darkness into a marvelous light, tried to articulate their overwhelming sense of gratitude. "Thanks be unto God for his unspeakable gift" (II Corinthians 9:15).

S. MacLean Gilmour
Andover Newton Theological Seminary

Bibliography

Barrett, Charles K., *The Gospel According to St. John* (New York 1955).
Beare, Frank W., *The First Epistle of Peter* (New York 1958).
Bultmann, Rudolf, *The Theology of the New Testament*, 2 vols. (New York 1954).
Davies, W.D., *The Setting of the Sermon on the Mount* (New York 1964)
Dodd, Charles H., *The Johannine Epistles* (New York 1946).
Fuller, Reginald H., *The Foundations of New Testament Christology* (New York 1965).

Grant, Frederick C., *An Introduction to New Testament Thought* (New York 1958).
Kümmel, Werner G., *Introduction to the New Testament* (Nashville 1966).
Scott, Ernest F., *The Fourth Gospel* (Edinburgh 1906).
Scott, Ernest F., *The Book of Revelation* (Naperville, Ill., 1949).
Weiss, Johannes, *Earliest Christianity*, 2 vols. (New York 1959).

16. History of New Testament Interpretation

New Testament interpretation includes both exegesis, the historical understanding of a writer's meaning, and interpretation proper, the theological or devotional "divination" of other meanings that the writing is capable of inspiring in the reader's mind. The passage of time and the development of new theological patterns make exegesis difficult and interpretation inevitable. It has been characteristic of Christian theologians to find in various passages or books the keys for the interpretation of their sacred literature and to interpret other passages and books in accordance with these particular keys. See also Exegesis.

The process of reinterpretation begins early in Christianity; when the later evangelists rewrite the Gospel of Mark, their selections of materials to combine with it naturally bring about new pictures of the Christian gospel. This implicit reinterpretation is combined with explicit rewriting of various difficult passages and culminates in the Gospel of John, in which the whole story of Jesus is retold from a new point of view. The reinterpretation of Paul's letters is criticized in II Peter 3:16, where we read of those who are "twisting" Pauline passages as well as the other scriptures.

The Early Interpreters. Early in the 2d century we find Papias of Hierapolis writing a book called *Exegeses of the Dominical Oracles*. These "oracles" may have been sayings of Jesus; more probably, they were Old Testament prophecies related to him. For Papias the Old Testament looks forward to the coming of Christ, but while he knows at least two Gospels, he does not provide interpretation of them. Such interpretation apparently was given first by Marcion of Pontus, who taught at Rome in 137–144 and set forth a "New Testament," consisting of a single gospel (a severely edited form of Luke) and an "apostle" made up of ten Pauline epistles. In Marcion's opinion the Old Testament was to be rejected, while the key to the Gospel and "apostle" was to be provided by Galatians and Romans, especially their more dualistic and anti-Jewish passages. His work is doubly important: (1) he provoked the theologians of the following two centuries to interpret the Bible as a whole, and (2) he was a forerunner of certain later theologians who identified the Bible with Paul and Paul with Romans or Galatians.

Marcion was not alone in interpreting the New Testament in the 2d century. His *Antitheses* set forth the major differences between the Old Testament and the Gospel, but their content was almost purely negative. In the school of Valentinus, an Alexandrian "Gnostic" who also went to Rome, the prologue of the Fourth Gospel was found to contain the various "aeons" of his theosophical system. The first commentary to be written on any New Testament book was by the Valentinian Heracleon (about 170). He finds Johannine thought essentially Valentinian.

In the last quarter of the 2d century the Christian church was confronted with so many problems that not all could be solved. Irenaeus of Lyon wrote against Marcion and the earlier Valentinians, maintaining the unity of the Old and New Testaments and comparing Gnostic exegesis to the work of those who take a mosaic picture of a king and use its pieces to make a picture of a fox. The only legitimate interpretation of the New Testament is the one that treats it as the fulfillment of the Old and is found among the successors of the apostles. While Irenaeus' legalistic view could win ready acceptance among orthodox believers (in fact it strongly influenced later theologians), it was not especially convincing to Gnostics who had "proved" that the New Testament supported their own ideas. Not for a generation did an interpreter arise to meet the church's need of learned interpretation of the New Testament.

This interpreter was Origen of Alexandria (about 185–254). Brought up in the spiritual environment of Philo and Clement, who had applied the allegorical method (see EXEGESIS) to their Bibles, Origen wrote his most important interpretation of the New Testament partly at Alexandria and partly, after his expulsion by the bishop, at Caesarea in Palestine. This is his commentary on the Gospel of John, intended primarily as an orthodox answer to Heracleon. It is a highly allegorical treatise, and at several points it shows the lengths to which Origen was driven both by such Gnostics as Heracleon and by "simple believers." At one point he argues that since the Gospels disagree and there is no reason to regard any one of them as more accurate than the others, we must hold that they contain spiritual truth in what amounts to literal falsehood. Again, he rightly insists that when God is called a Spirit, or Light, or Fire, these terms do not mean that God is corporeal; the divine nature is entirely incorporeal. Elsewhere he claims that Scripture includes many stumbling-blocks in order to lead readers on to higher truths behind and beyond its literal statements. Origen does not mean to deny the historical reality of the incarnation of the Son of God, but his main interest lies not in history but in the eternal order behind history to which God leads His people by a gradual process of education. And since the Old Testament secretly contains the New Testament revelation, the educational process is not genuinely historical. For Origen the whole Bible is a great allegory that only the Spirit-guided interpreter can understand.

Such interpretation naturally encountered opposition. At Antioch there was a school of interpreters whose interests were more severely grammatical and historical; they insisted on the importance of the literal meaning of the text. Thus John Chrysostom and Theodore of Mopsuestia wrote homilies and commentaries on the New Testament that reflect their effort to understand what the apostles and evangelists were trying to say. Chrysostom insisted that allegories should not be sought in the Bible except in passages clearly allegorical. The "letter which kills" (II Corinthians 3:6) is not literal exegesis but the law of Moses. He is interested in questions of date and authorship as well as in the style and thought of such an author as Paul. Similarly, Theodore pays close attention to the language and logic of Paul, to historical facts as well as to theological ideas.

Closely related to the divergent methods of Alexandria and Antioch are differences in theology and philosophy. Thus, in general, Christian Alexandria was Platonist and stressed the suprahistorical divinity of Christ, while Antioch was Aristotelian and emphasized his historical humanity. Similar differences are found in the two environments: at Alexandria, Neoplatonists allegorized the Greek poets; while at Antioch, Jewish teachers expounded literally the Old Testament in both Hebrew and Greek.

A synthesis between allegory and literalism is reflected to a certain extent in the voluminous commentaries of Jerome (340?–420), whose early admiration for Origen, gradually becoming intense dislike, caused him to continue to use Origen's works even as a literalist. Jerome was an exegete rather than an interpreter, and his investigations of Hebrew and Greek have their monument in the Vulgate rather than in any systematic interpretation. On the other hand, his contemporary Augustine studied the New Testament from a more subtly psychological point of view, laying especial stress on the Epistle to the Romans, in which he found much of his own theological system reflected. For Augustine, unlike most Greek exegetes, the New Testament is a book of sin and redemption from sin by grace. Under the influence of his own temperament and of Neoplatonism he saw the Bible subjectively. It reflected the encounter of his soul with God. The Bible, like the world itself, became a mirror of God.

The Middle Ages. The pattern foreshadowed by Augustine became normative for the Middle Ages. Symbolism ran riot, and in medieval homilies and commentaries, as in sculpture, the Bible is an allegory from beginning to end. There were, of course, exceptions. Under Jewish influence several literal explanations of Old and New Testament books were written. But these exceptions, which include some of the interpretation given by Thomas Aquinas, were unusual and looked forward to the future. Some medieval exegetes discovered as many as eight distinct meanings in a single verse. This work of allegorization was made necessary by medieval lack of historical sense as well as by the gradual decline of an archaic Platonic theology. Not until interpretation could be separated from theology was it possible to escape allegorism. Such a divorce was effected by Aquinas.

The ultimate result of Aquinas' work was the freeing of rational theology from the attempt to combine all the insights of Old and New Testaments alike. It became possible to maintain the Catholic faith without trying to prove that every verse of the Bible was in complete harmony with it. In this respect Aquinas looks forward to the exegesis of the Renaissance, the Enlightenment, and after.

The Renaissance and Modern Times. The separation of theology from interpretation brought a sharp reaction, however, in the 16th century. On the one hand, under the influence of the Renaissance, men began to read Greek more frequently and came to recognize the religious value of the New Testament apart from allegory or traditional theology. On the other, critics of a rational theology that had become rationalistic turned back to the Bible in order to remarry it to theology or rather to reinstate it as the sole source of religious knowledge. In Lutheran interpretation we see the attempt, generally speaking, to treat the Bible as the New Testament, the New Testament as Paul, and Paul as Romans and Galatians.

Among Calvinists greater stress was laid on the Old Testament. Calvin's commentaries on the New Testament are full of grammatical and historical exegesis, but it all serves to prove that his theology is that of the Bible itself.

In the late 18th and early 19th centuries, under the influence of advances in classical philology and the study of ancient history, there came a fresh effort to understand the New Testament historically. Not unnaturally this movement, like other living movements, had its excesses. The work of the pioneers, however, retains permanent value. In 1835, Karl Lachmann proved that Mark was prior to the other two "Synoptic" Gospels, Matthew and Luke; in 1859–1862 Konstantin Tischendorf edited a 4th-century manuscript from Sinai and inaugurated modern textual criticism. Historical study of the life of Jesus produced countless new biographies, none of which, unfortunately, was in agreement with the others. Other studies set forth the theory that he never really had lived but was a product of early Christian imagination. The Pauline epistles were microscopically scrutinized, as was the background of Paul's thought in Judaism and Hellenism.

In their enthusiasm for setting the New Testament in its environment, these scholars neglected two facts. In the first place, they were conditioned by their own environment, European liberalism after 1848. They found some sayings of Jesus to be quite "liberal" and interpreted seemingly conflicting sayings as later interpolations; Paul had to be rejected as the corrupter of pure religion. In the second place, they neglected the obvious fact that the New Testament had survived and had possessed religious value for many periods in which its historical meaning had been generally neglected. It was obviously a historical document. Not so obviously, it was more than historical; its meaning transcended history and its authors had been trying to express suprahistorical ideas.

The difficulties of the "liberal" position became plain when stress was laid on Jewish apocalyptic literature, much of it discovered at the end of the 19th century, and it was regarded as the key to the Gospel. Like Paul, Jesus had wrongly proclaimed the imminent end of the world. Two ways out seemed possible. On the one hand, with William Wrede and Adolf Harnack (*What Is Christianity?*) one could hold that the apocalyptic elements in the Gospels and elsewhere were due to early Christians who misunderstood Jesus. On the other, with Albert Schweitzer one could take apocalyptic as the essence of the Gospel and abandon the modern world and the effort to develop a rational or even a Biblical theology. The ensuing conflict between these two views and various modifications of them brought the "liberal" period to an end.

Two ways out of this conflict were opened up at the end of World War I. From the standpoint of the new dialectical theology, Karl Barth wrote a famous commentary on Romans, intended to serve as the starting point for a new Protestant dogmatics. From the standpoint of an increasingly skeptical historical study, three German New Testament critics (Rudolf Bultmann, Martin Dibelius, and K.L. Schmidt) studied the ways in which the tradition about Jesus was handed down in the church and came to the conclusion that to a lesser or greater degree the primitive communities shaped or even created the stories about Jesus and his sayings. No one could say with certainty what Jesus had done or said, beyond the barest essentials. The theological significance of this theory was obvious. In the first place, greater emphasis had to be laid on the meaning of the church as the transmitter of tradition and on the church's faith as contrasted with objective history. In the second place, greater emphasis was to be placed on the common elements of the tradition, often at the expense of its obvious diversity. A strong revival of "Biblical theology" took place, especially in Germany.

In the course of time, however, it became clear that while Biblical theology could effectively undermine theological speculations unrelated to the Bible, it was itself a historical discipline, not a theological one. Only if it did justice to the diversity we have mentioned could it be genuinely historical. In addition, among Bultmann's disciples there arose a new or revived concern for the historical Jesus. The discovery of new documents illuminating the religious background of early Christianity (the Dead Sea Scrolls and the Gnostic documents from Nag Hammadi in Egypt) turned the attention of scholars once more to the historical setting of the 1st century and indicated that the time was not ripe, if it ever would be, for theological synthesis. In the 1960's more attention was being devoted to questions of historical method, in part because of attempts to use electronic computers in New Testament study as in other humanistic fields.

Among Roman Catholics there naturally has been considerable interest in interpretation. Richard Simon (denounced by Bossuet) was one of the first scholars to apply historical criticism to the Bible (in 1689–1704), and the "liberal" school had its counterpart in the Modernist movement, though with significant differences. Four modern papal encyclicals have guided and encouraged Biblical criticism and interpretation: *Providentissimus Deus* (1893), *Pascendi dominici gregis* (1907), *Spiritus Paraclitus* (1920), and *Divino afflante Spiritu* (1943). Theological interpretation can be based only on the literal meaning of a text and must take into account the unanimous consensus of the fathers, where it exists. Attempts in France between 1940 and 1950 to revive the allegorical method have met with vigorous opposition (consult *Humani generis*, 1950). Largely under the influence of the liberalizing tendencies of the Vatican Council, Roman Catholic scholarship in Europe and America has expressed itself in free and vigorous fashion, often in collaboration with non-Catholic movements. In America one may mention especially the significant work of the *Catholic Biblical Quarterly*.

ROBERT M. GRANT
The Divinity School, The University of Chicago

Bibliography

Daniélou, Jean, *The Bible and the Liturgy* (London 1961).
Grant, Robert M., *The Letter and the Spirit* (London 1957).
Grant, Robert M., *A Short History of the Interpretation of the Bible* (New York 1965).
Hanson, Richard P.C., *Allegory and Event* (London 1959).
Lampe, G.W.H., and Woollcombe, K.J., *Essays in Typology* (London 1957).
McCown, C.C., *The Search for the Real Jesus* (New York 1940).
Pelikan, Jaroslav, ed., *Luther the Expositor* (St. Louis 1959).
Robinson, James M., *A New Quest of the Historical Jesus* (Naperville, Ill., 1959).
Smalley, B., *The Study of the Bible in the Middle Ages* (New York 1952).
Smith, H., *Ante-Nicene Exegesis of the Gospels*, 6 vols. (London 1925–29).

17. History of the English Bible

The story of the English Bible is more than a cool and abstract chronicle. The bringing of the whole Scripture to the people in their own familiar speech began amid conditions that called for the unlimited daring of devoted men. Before the Norman Conquest there had been occasional paraphrases in Anglo-Saxon of parts of Scripture; in the centuries following the Conquest, the Miracle and Morality plays gave the common people naïve dramatization of Biblical themes; and by the 14th century, crude primers on the Christian faith contained English versions of such parts of the Bible as the Ten Commandments, the Beatitudes, and the Lord's Prayer. But any idea of making the whole Bible available to the whole people was anathema to the entrenched authorities of church and state.

The language of the church's worship was Latin. The only version of the Scriptures was also in Latin—the Vulgate translation that Jerome had made near the end of the 4th century; and for the common folk a Bible in Latin was hardly different from a Bible that did not exist at all. To the great ecclesiastics of the medieval centuries that seemed indisputably what rightly should be. Pope Innocent III declared in 1199: "The secret mysteries of the faith ought not to be explained to all men in all places, since they cannot be everywhere understood by all men"; and in the century preceding, another pope, Gregory VII, had put the matter still more categorically: "Not without reason has it pleased Almighty God that Holy Scripture should be a secret in certain places, lest, if it were plainly apparent to all men, perchance it would be little esteemed and be subject to disrespect; or it might be falsely understood by those of mediocre learning, and lead to error."

Thus the authorities not only did not desire that the Bible should be put into the language of the people. They also set their faces implacably against what in its bare suggestion seemed to them insubordinate and contumacious. The sacred mysteries of the faith must not be degraded by being put into the language of the vulgar; the submission of the ordinary man to the authority of the priesthood must not be undermined by a new knowledge that could produce pride of opinion, heresy, and rebellion; the sovereignty of the truth as the church proclaimed it must not tolerate an influence that might breed sectarian perversity.

So ecclesiastical conservatism might have reasoned in any case. But by the latter part of the 14th century in England there was another fact that hardened the church's hostility to any general circulation of the Scriptures. It had become linked with social insurrection.

Wycliffe. John Wycliffe, scholar at Oxford and vicar of Lutterworth, denounced the evils of the church: its wealth and greed, its exactions from the poor, the moral corruption in the monasteries, and the spiritual indifference and ignorance among the clergy. Meanwhile, the common people were wretched and embittered. In 1348–49 the Black Death killed a third of the population, and harsh social legislation aggravated the misery that followed. Insurrection broke out in many parts of England, sparked at first by the preaching of John Ball, "the mad priest of Kent," who took as his text:

"When Adam delved and Eve span,
Who was then the gentleman?"

His preaching championed the right of the common people against the rich and powerful, in the name of God and the teachings of the Gospel. Here, to the rulers of church and state, was devastating evidence of the danger in letting the interpretation of the Bible get out of control.

And then the danger was compounded. For in 1382 either John Wycliffe himself or disciples working under his guidance put forth the first complete translation of the Bible into English; and the Lollards, as his followers were called, began to carry this Bible out in preaching and teaching wherever people gathered. Wycliffe died in 1384; but in 1388 there was circulated an improved revision of the Bible that went by his name. What the authorities thought of him and of his work was expressed by Archbishop Arundel in 1412 when, writing to the pope, he called Wycliffe "that wretched and pestilent fellow of damnable memory, . . . the very herald and child of anti-Christ, who crowned his wickedness by translating the Scriptures into the mother tongue." And a provincial council at Oxford early in the 15th century decreed that "no one shall in future translate on his own authority any text of holy scriptures into the English tongue—nor shall any man read this kind of book, booklet or treatise, now recently composed in the time of the said John Wycliffe or later, or any that shall be composed in future, in whole or part, publicly or secretly, under penalty of the greater excommunication."

That prohibition stood throughout the 15th century. But in 1453 the fall of Constantinople dispersed its scholars into the West, and they carried with them a knowledge of Greek language and literature, which the West had almost forgotten. At almost exactly that same time, Gutenberg began the art of printing and thus made possible the spread of the learning of the Renaissance. And in the early 16th century, Luther in Germany and the other reformers on the continent stirred the desire of multitudes to break the restraints of the medieval church and find out for themselves what was in the Bible.

Tyndale. In England, William Tyndale (born about 1492) became at Oxford and Cambridge a well-furnished scholar, both in Hebrew and in Greek. Wycliffe's Bible had been based entirely on the Latin Vulgate and thus was only a translation of a translation. Tyndale had available the whole Old Testament in Hebrew that had been printed in 1488 and the Greek New Testament published by the great scholar Erasmus in 1516. Thus he had new resources; and more important, he had the driving power of the purpose he expressed to one of his contemporaries: "If God spare my lyfe, ere many years I wyl cause a boye that dryveth the plough shall know more of the scripture than thou doest."

In the England of Henry VIII the jealous antagonism to any spread of the Bible among the people was as fixed as it had been in the time of Wycliffe. Tyndale found that there was no room in England for what he was about to undertake. Consequently he went to the Continent, carrying with him his translation of the New Testament, which he had begun secretly in London. He contracted for its printing in 1525 at Cologne; but, followed by spies, he fled to Worms, where publication was resumed of a quarto and then an octavo edition. These New Testaments smuggled into England were seized immediately by the authorities when they could get hold of them and publicly burned at St. Paul's Cross; but these same authorities did not know the ironic fact that the merchant Augustine Packynton, who delivered to the bishop of London most of the copies that he burned, was a friend of Tyndale's, and the good round price he got for the Testaments destroyed went to Tyndale for the printing of more copies.

Meanwhile, Tyndale, besides issuing a revision of his New Testament in 1534 and another in 1535, had started his translation of the Old Testament, and in 1530 and 1531 he published the Pentateuch and the Book of Jonah. He translated also the books from Joshua through II Chronicles, but these he did not live to see in print. Treacherously seized in Antwerp in 1535, he was imprisoned in the castle of Vilvorde, near Brussels; and having been condemned as a heretic, he was strangled and burned at the stake on Oct. 6, 1536. But Tyndale's work could not be brought to an end with his body. Not only was he to be followed by other translators; also his own work, in its integrity, directness and vividness of phrase, was largely incorporated into theirs and sounds as the central note in the language of the English Bible to this day.

Coverdale and Rogers. Of next importance to Tyndale was Miles Coverdale, a priest and friar who had studied at Cambridge and later had become acquainted with Tyndale on the Continent. He did not rank with Tyndale as a scholar and particularly knew little or no Hebrew. He based his work on the Vulgate, Luther's German Bible, a Latin translation by Pagninus, and a Swiss-German Bible published in Zürich, but most of all upon Tyndale. Yet some of his turns of phrase have a felicity and a musical cadence all their own; and his version of the Psalms still is recited in the Anglican and in the American Book of Common Prayer.

When Coverdale published his Bible, presumably at Cologne in 1535—the first printed English Bible containing not just a part of the Old Testament, as in Tyndale's work, but the whole of it—the turbulent religious currents in England had taken a new turn. In his controversy with the papacy, Henry VIII was more interested now in resisting the authority of Rome than he was in maintaining the prohibitions of the church; and therefore, although on the Continent Tyndale was seized as a heretic in 1535, to be executed the next year, Coverdale in 1535 dared to dedicate his translation to Henry and his queen. And more astonishing, in 1537 royal license was given in England not only to Coverdale's Bible, but also to a version published under the pseudonym of Thomas Matthew (who actually was John Rogers, a friend of Tyndale), which included almost entirely the translation of Tyndale for which on the continent he had been burned as a heretic the year before.

It seemed as though antagonism to the Bible made available to the people was dying down. It would flame up again in the reign (1553–1558) of the Roman Catholic Queen Mary, when this same John Rogers who produced "Matthew's Bible" would be executed, and even more conspicuous figures, such as Bishop Hugh Latimer and Bishop Nicholas Ridley and Archbishop Thomas Cranmer, also would go to the stake.

Except for Mary's reign, however, translations continued—though not without surveillance and suspicion, including an act of Parliament prohibiting any unauthorized person from reading the Bible aloud in any public place and forbidding its private reading by all "artificers, apprentices, journeymen, servingmen, yeomen, husbandmen or laborers."

In 1539 appeared a revision of the Matthew Bible by Richard Taverner, the chief distinction of which was that it was the first English version to be printed completely in England itself. In the same year (1539), at the prompting of Archbishop Cranmer, Coverdale brought out the "Great Bible," a version that omitted the controversial prefaces and notes included in earlier translations; and this Bible, "apoynted to the use of the churches," was for nearly 30 years (except in the reign of Mary) the only version that could lawfully be used in England.

The Geneva Bible. In the Counter-Reformation and reaction under Mary, many representatives of the Protestant spirit in England, including Coverdale, took refuge in Geneva. There in 1560 was published the Geneva Bible, based chiefly on Tyndale and the Great Bible, but containing many "most profitable annotations upon all the hard places," which annotations were of a strongly Protestant tone. For that reason the Geneva Bible was highly distasteful to conservatives in England, but it circulated widely and met with intense favor among the people. It was the Geneva Bible that Shakespeare used; and it was the Geneva Bible that shaped the mind of the Puritans of England and New England and in which the meditations of John Bunyan were steeped before he wrote *The Pilgrim's Progress*.

Under the leadership of Archbishop Parker the Church of England set itself to produce a new version to be authorized in place of the Great Bible, which was being crowded out of popular use by the Bible from Geneva. The result was the Bishops' Bible (1568), ordered to be based on the Great Bible but as a matter of fact incorporating many elements of the Geneva Bible that it was meant to replace.

The Douay Bible. Roman Catholic refugees from England, desiring a version that could be used by their preachers in controversy with English Protestantism, translated the Latin Vulgate and added to the English text profuse polemic notes against the Protestant "hereticks." Two former Oxford men, William Allen and George Martin, were the translators; and from the cities in France and Flanders where their work was done, their version is known as the *Rheims-Douai* or *Douai* (in English, *Douay*). The New Testament appeared in 1582, the Old Testament in 1609. Although at the outset the Douay version did not have express official sanction, it became and generally has remained the accepted Bible of English-speaking Roman Catholics.

The King James Version. In England the most influential of all the translations was still to come. At an otherwise almost fruitless conference of clergy held at Hampton Court in 1604, John Reynolds of Corpus Christi College, Oxford, suggested a new revision of the Bible. The suggestion was taken up by James Stuart of Scotland, who had become king of England in 1603, and the revision was ordered. Fifty of the ablest scholars of England were assigned to six companies, meeting two each at Oxford, Cambridge, and Westminster, to work on designated portions of the text, and then as a whole body, and last through a special committee to collate their work for agreement and final review. They were charged to follow the Bishops' Bible with as little alteration as the truth would permit but to take into account also the earlier versions. Though delayed in beginning, the revisers finished their work by 1611, in which year appeared what has been known since as the King James or the Authorized Version, with a laudatory dedication to the king and a most illuminating preface describing the aims of the translators that unhappily is omitted from the usual printings of the Bible.

The King James version by no means won immediate favor. It was resented and opposed on various counts by many who preferred what had grown familiar. But as the clamor of comment died down, it was seen that this translation had brought together into an extraordinary unity and beauty of effect the direct and vital speech of Tyndale and Coverdale, insights from the Geneva Bible, and the translators' own instinctive gift of rich and rhythmic prose. Nor had the Rheims-Douay version been without influence upon them. Its Latinisms, excessive in that version, yet suggested words that gave at certain points a deeper music to what the translator wrote.

In the long span of time since its publication the King James version has colored so incalculably the thought and speech of English peoples, has so affected English literature, and has influenced so much of life that there is no need of enlarging upon its greatness. Except for a few attempts by individuals, most of them superficial, no plan for further revision was set in motion until nearly two and a half centuries after 1611.

Revised Versions. But by that time certain limitations in even so great a work had grown evident. Most important was the fact that the only Greek manuscripts known to the King James translators were relatively late and imperfect. Later, manuscripts far older and more authoritative had been discovered, and there had been immense advance in textual analysis as well as in knowledge of the backgrounds of the Bible, both Hebrew and Greek. Moreover, as the textual basis for the King James version had been superseded, so also had its language grown partly outmoded. It no longer represented the instinctive speech of the living generation. Consequently the Convocation of Canterbury in England in 1870 appointed a committee to undertake a new translation. Out of their work came the English Revised Version of the New Testament in 1881 and that of the Old Testament in 1885. American scholars had been associated with the British Committee as an advisory group; and, continuing their organization after the British committee had dissolved, they published in 1901 the American Revised Version, with changes and amendments beyond those accepted by the British committee.

When the New Testament came out in 1881, there was intense and excited expectation. Tens of thousands of copies were bought in England and America in the first few hours. The scholarly authority and accuracy of the whole work was great, but there was popular disappointment especially in regard to the New Testament, because the meticulous fidelity of the translators to the forms and idioms of the Greek resulted in numberless slight changes that seemed to readers to have no important result except the negative one of destroying the familiar cadence of the King James Bible that they knew.

New Translations. The resurgent interest in bringing the Bible afresh to the contemporary generation prompted translations by scholars, individually or associated in small groups. Among the most influential of these translations since the last years of the 19th century are the version of the four Gospels by Father Francis Aloysius Spencer in 1898, which Cardinal Gibbons in his preface said was an endeavor "to represent Our Lord and the Apostles as speaking . . . in the language they would speak if they lived among us now"; the *Twentieth Century New Testament,* by a group of scholars who wished "to exclude all words and phrases not used in current English"; R.F. Weymouth's *New Testament in Modern Speech;* James Moffatt's *The New Testament* and *The Holy Bible, containing the Old and New Testaments;* and Edgar J. Goodspeed's *The New Testament, An American Translation,* and *The Bible, An American Translation,* which contains Goodspeed's New Testament and the Old Testament translated by J.M. Powis Smith and three associates. From these modern speech versions come many vivid and arresting flashes of meaning that the traditional renderings had left obscure; but their colloquial style for the most part has kept them from general use in public worship.

The Jewish Publication Society issued in 1917 a new translation of the Old Testament that a company of scholars had begun in 1892. Another and more up-to-date translation began to appear in 1962, when volume 1, *The Torah,* was published. Monsignor Ronald A. Knox translated the Vulgate (1945–49) and set forth his aims and method in his engaging *Trials of a Translator.* Another Roman Catholic translation appeared (1941 ff.) under the patronage of the Episcopal Committee of the Confraternity of Christian Doctrine. In 1965 the American *Revised Standard Version* of the Bible (Old and New Testaments and Apocrypha) was authorized by the hierarchy for use by Roman Catholics in the United States and Britain. A very few modifications of the text were made, chiefly the adoption of certain variant readings found in the footnotes.

In recognition of the enrichment of knowledge that had come from newly discovered manuscripts, from archaeology, and from a better understanding of the ancient languages, a committee was formed under the chairmanship of Luther A. Weigle to revise the American Standard edition of the Revised Version of 1901 and make it more adequate for use in both public worship and religious education; at the same time they endeavored to preserve the beauty of style of the King James text as much as possible. The result was the Revised Standard Version (1946–57), published under the auspices of the National Council of the Churches of Christ. In 1961 an entirely new translation, *The New English Bible,* began to appear, the work of British scholars representing the churches of England and Scotland and some of the Free churches, with Charles Harold Dodd as chairman. It aims to use a "timeless" English and is designed, not for public reading in church, but for private perusal, especially by those who rarely hear the Bible read but are interested in it as literature and as a book of religion. Only time can tell how well these two efforts have succeeded and whether they are worthy to stand beside the earlier "authorized" translations (especially the King James Bible of 1611) in the long history of the English Bible, the beginnings of which were not in ordinary labors of translation but in the travail and sufferings of men who died as martyrs for religious liberty and the truth as they saw it.

W. RUSSELL BOWIE, *Virginia Theological Seminary*

EARLY AMERICAN BIBLES

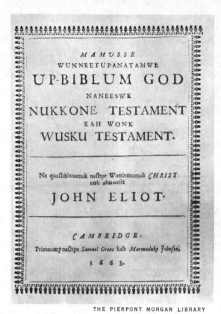

THE PIERPONT MORGAN LIBRARY

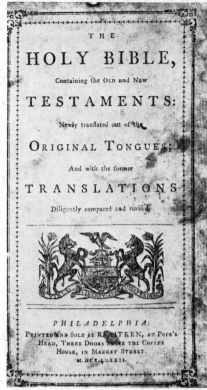

RARE BOOK DIVISION, NEW YORK PUBLIC LIBRARY

(*Left*) The Eliot Bible (1663), first Bible printed in the Western Hemisphere, was translated into an Indian dialect by the missionary John Eliot.

(*Right*) The Aitken Bible (1782), first American Bible printed in English, and the only Bible officially recognized by the U.S. Congress.

(*Left*) *Biblia Hebraica* (1814), the first Hebrew Bible printed in the United States, was published in Philadelphia, Pa.

(*Right*) Mathew Carey's Bible (1790), the first edition of the Rheims-Douay Bible to be printed in the United States.

JEWISH DIVISION, THE NEW YORK PUBLIC LIBARARY

RARE BOOK DIVISION, NEW YORK PUBLIC LIBRARY

Bibliography

Baikie, James, *The Romance of the Bible* (London 1931).
Bruce, Frederick Fyvie, *The English Bible* (New York 1961).
Butterworth, Charles C., *The Literary Lineage of the King James Bible* (Philadelphia 1941).
Colwell, Ernest C., *What Is the Best New Testament?* (Chicago 1952).
Daiches, David, *The King James Version of the English Bible* (Chicago 1941).
Dinsmore, Charles Allen, *The English Bible as Literature* (Boston and New York 1931).
Grant, Frederick C., *Translating the Bible* (New York 1961).

Greenslade, S.L., ed., *Cambridge History of the Bible: The West from the Reformation to the Present Day* (New York 1963).
Kenyon, Frederic George, *Our Bible and the Ancient Manuscripts*, 5th ed. (London 1958).
Knox, Ronald, *The Trials of a Translator* (New York 1949).
Robinson, H. Wheeler, *The Bible in Its Ancient and English Versions* (New York 1940).
Trench, Richard C., *On the Authorized Version of the New Testament* (London 1859).
Weigle, Luther A., *The English New Testament* (New York 1949).
Westcott, Brooke Foss, *History of the English Bible* (London 1905).

BIBLE CHRISTIANS, a Methodist sect formally constituted in England in 1816 under the leadership of William O'Bryan, a Methodist preacher. Originally the members were also called *Bryanites*. They were noted for their devotion to the study and preaching of the Gospel.

The Bible Christians were of the same doctrinal stamp as the Wesleyan Methodist Church, but they separated from it over questions of discipline. They allowed freedom of action to the laity and welcomed women as preachers. The movement spread to Canada in 1831, to the United States in 1846, and to Australia in 1850. In 1907 the Bible Christians joined the Methodist New Connexion and the United Methodist Free Churches to form the United Methodist Church. See also METHODISM.

BIBLE SOCIETY, a local or national organization that makes Christian Scriptures available throughout the world. Besides distributing the Scriptures, Bible societies translate them into foreign languages and revise and publish them.

The Bible society movement was essentially a Protestant enterprise until recent times. Roman Catholics traditionally opposed Bible societies, and during the 19th century, papal encyclicals banned them. This position, however, was changed when Vatican Council II gave tacit approval to Bible society work. In 1966, Pope Paul VI ordered that the possibility of future joint distribution efforts be studied.

Bible societies serve Christian churches in all countries. Their missionary work is particularly extended to those countries dominated by non-Christian faiths. Their work is nonprofit, and where the need arises, Bibles are distributed at less than cost or free. The societies do not comment on or interpret Scripture.

Origins. Sporadic attempts at systematic distribution of Bibles were made from the earliest days of the Protestant Reformation. In 1710 a Bible society was organized in Germany "to provide God's word for the poor at a low price." The modern Bible society movement, however, began in 1804 with the formation in London of the British and Foreign Bible Society, one of many organizations engendered by the evangelic revival led by John and Charles Wesley.

An enormous groundswell of related philanthropic and missionary activity grew from these English beginnings. Local auxiliary societies sprang up all over England and spread to America, where the first Bible society was organized in Philadelphia in December 1808. Bible societies were formed in Connecticut, Massachusetts, New York, and New Jersey in 1809. Within six years, more than 100 auxiliary societies appeared in the United States.

Expansion of the Movement. As the United States grew, local societies could not meet the mounting need for copies of the Scriptures. The American Bible Society was founded in New York in 1816 to coordinate local work. Similar national societies were formed in Finland (1812), Sweden, Denmark, and the Netherlands (1814), Iceland (1815), Norway (1816), and Scotland (1860). The famous Württemberg Society was organized in Stuttgart, Germany, in 1812. Today there are national Bible societies in most parts of the world.

Society work expanded into non-Christian areas chiefly through the outreach of the British, American, and Scottish societies. For example, the American society set up its first foreign agency in Turkey in 1836. Conflicts of activity resulted in adjustments of missionary territory. Overlapping in China in the 1920's became so marked that the British, American, and Scottish groups unified their work for the sake of efficiency. Further consolidation elsewhere paved the way for new national Bible societies to be formed in Japan, Brazil, Korea, India, Pakistan, and Ceylon.

The policy of cooperation and consolidation led to the creation of the United Bible Societies at London in 1946. By the mid-1960's, the original membership of 13 had expanded to 27 full and 8 associate members, with one delegate from each national society or federation of local societies in a particular country. A smaller standing committee served as an interim coordinating body between general meetings.

The Bible societies in the West are self-sustaining and are supported by voluntary gifts from individuals and churches. Societies more recently established in "mission lands" seek additional support from the older societies, especially from the British, American, Scottish, and Dutch.

The United Bible Societies publishes a quarterly bulletin. It also publishes the *Bible Translator*, a quarterly to aid missionaries who are translating and revising the Scriptures. This form of missionary work has been pursued with increasing vigor since World War II.

The headquarters of the United Bible Societies are in London. The American Bible Society offices are in New York City.

Publication of Bibles. Bible societies have published or helped publish the Bible in Braille in 30 languages. The entire Bible has also been put on phonograph records. In the mid-1960's more than 3,000 persons were working on Bible translations. At least one book of the Bible had been completed in more than 1,250 languages and dialects.

The bulk of the publishing is done by the British and American societies. Through their efforts distribution of the Scriptures has increased steadily. In 1947, for example, 14,108,436 Bibles, Testaments, or parts of Testaments were distributed. In 1955 the total reached 25,393,161. In 1964 the American Bible Society alone distributed the following numbers:

	Bibles	Testaments	Portions	Selections
At home:	556,819	1,265,366	4,253,227	19,978,476
Abroad:	1,108,740	1,354,882	16,089,315	9,535,189

The total distributed at home was 26,053,888 and abroad, 28,088,126. The grand total distributed by the American Bible Society at home and abroad amounted to 54,142,014.

Bible Sunday. To stimulate the wider reading of the Bible, what is known as Bible Sunday is observed in almost every country where Bible societies operate. In areas observing the Church of England calendar, the day is set for the second Sunday in Advent, as indicated in the Book of Common Prayer. In the United States and other countries this day is called Universal Bible Sunday and is often celebrated on the second Sunday in December. Services are held emphasizing the need and value of regular Bible reading, and contributions for Bible society work are accepted. Since 1944, the period of special emphasis on Bible study and Bible society work has been extended to include the days from Thanksgiving to Christmas; this observance is called "worldwide Bible reading."

BIBLIA PAUPERUM, bib'lē-ä pou'pə-roŏm, or *Poor Man's Bible,* is the name given to a series of 15th century Dutch and German block books. Of the seven editions published, copies of only five have survived. They vary in length from 40 to 50 pages. Each edition originally bore an individual title (such as *History of Christ in Pictures*). In the 16th century the general title *Poor Man's Bible* came into use, presumably because the books superseded costly illuminated manuscripts and appealed to simple readers.

The illustrations and text for each page were cut on a wood block. In a triptych-like design, the illustrations depicted a scene from the New Testament in a center panel and scenes from the New Testament in each side panel. The pictures have not been attributed to any individual artist. The authorship of the text, which is of 12th or 13th century origin, is also unknown. See also BLOCK BOOK.

BIBLIOGRAPHICAL SOCIETIES, bib-lē-ə-graf'i-kəl sə-sī'ə-tēz, are associations of professional scholars or amateurs interested in collecting information about books. Some promote the study of literature, the art of bookmaking, or book collecting. Others sponsor historical research on books and issue publications containing such research. The memberships of these groups include college and university professors, librarians, teachers, rare-book dealers, and collectors.

Aside from library and literary associations such as the Library Company of Philadelphia (1732), the American Antiquarian Society (1812), and the Century Association (1847), the oldest bibliographical society in the United States is the Grolier Club (1884) of New York City. It was the archetype for the Club of Odd Volumes (founded in Boston in 1886), Rowfant Club Cleveland, 1892), and more recent groups such as the Baltimore Bibliophiles, Caxton Club of Chicago, Pittsburgh Bibliophiles, Roxburghe Club of San Francisco, and Zamorano Club of Los Angeles.

Of the more general societies, the oldest, largest, and most heavily endowed was founded in 1899 as the Bibliographical Society of Chicago; in 1904 it became the Bibliographical Society of America. Among the achievements of this association have been the sponsorship of the 29-volume *Bibliotheca Americana,* begun by Joseph Sabin in 1868 and completed in 1937, and the *Bibliography of American Literature,* which Jacob Blanck started in 1955.

The most scholarly society in the United States is the Bibliographical Society of the University of Virginia (1947), a leader in analytical bibliography, with worldwide membership. More specialized are the Inter-American Bibliographical and Library Association and the Society of Architectural Bibliographers.

Most numerous of all are the "Friends" groups, often the main arteries for private financial support of book collections. Some of the best known are the Friends of the Morgan, Princeton, Clements, John Carter Brown, Newberry, and University of Pennsylvania libraries.

Internationally known groups elsewhere in the Western Hemisphere include the Bibliographical Society of Canada, Sociedad de Bibliófilos Chilenos, Instituto Brasileiro de Bibliografica e Documentação, and Cámara Argentina del Libro.

All these American societies reflect the pattern of their numerous European prototypes.

JOHN COOK WYLLIE, *University of Virginia*

BIBLIOGRAPHY, bib-lē-og'rə-fē, is the name applied to the science, art, or most typical product of the art of recording published material. As a science, bibliography is the organized body of knowledge that treats of books in all aspects, whether as mere physical objects or as vehicles of ideas. As an art, bibliography consists of the techniques for ascertaining, organizing, and presenting information about books. As the typical product of the art, a bibliography is a systematic listing, for a particular purpose, of books that share common characteristics.

As used in this article, the term "books" includes not only books in the narrow sense but also booklike objects, including pamphlets, periodicals, newspapers, and the articles published in them; manuscripts; maps; musical compositions; and even microfacsimiles of published material. The domain of bibliography extends in common usage to all of the foregoing and might logically be held to extend to all forms of recorded information. Indeed, motion pictures and sound recordings would be admitted by many to come within its scope.

The word "bibliography" derives from the Greek *biblios* (book) and *grapho* (to write), and originally denoted the transcribing of books. In the 17th century the word was adapted to mean writing about books. It began to displace such words as *catalogus* and *bibliotheca* in the titles of book listings. Between the 17th and 18th centuries the principal concepts, practices, and varieties of bibliography as it is known today were laid down by a notable succession of bibliographers who were attempting to reduce to order the record of publications that had flooded the world since the invention of printing. Early uses of the term are found in Gabriel Naudé's *Bibliographia Politica* (Paris 1633) and Johann Heinrich Boecler's *Bibliographia Historico-Politico-Philologica* (Germanopoli 1677), which devoted a whole page to Americana. But the term failed to reach Samuel Johnson's dictionary (1755) and did not get into the *Encyclopaedia Britannica* until the 3d edition (1797). An extended discussion of bibliography appeared in the first edition of the *Encyclopedia Americana* (1829).

In its widest meaning, bibliography includes all studies relating to the physical and intellectual aspects of books to the extent that these studies contribute to an understanding of the history of books, of the status of individual works, or of their relationships to other works. Thus, studies of parchment and paper, bindings, xylography and typography, book illustration, the assembly of the parts into volumes, and the facts of authorship, publication, and distribution are all appropriate to bibliography. Similarly, bibliography takes note of the intellectual content of books, not in order to expound or criticize them but to characterize them according to subject matter.

The objectives of bibliography may be pursued by many methods. There are, however, two broad classes that serve to differentiate the main branches of the subject. *Analytic bibliography* uses detailed study in order to discover evidence regarding the facts of authorship, publication, and derivation of text. *Systematic bibliography,* by contrast, depends upon much more general studies in order to produce systematic lists of books.

The word *critical,* applied to bibliography,

has two meanings. Critical bibliography, the science, is equivalent to analytic bibliography—bibliography in the service of textual criticism. A list called a critical bibliography, however, is a bibliography that appraises critically the books it lists.

Similarly, the term *descriptive bibliography* is used to denote the refined methods of description required for analytic bibliography rather than the grosser methods more usually employed in systematic bibliography.

SYSTEMATIC BIBLIOGRAPHY

Systematic bibliography represents bibliography for the most part as art rather than science. Its immediate aim is to identify and describe in a systematic arrangement the books that may be suitable for a particular purpose or that have other common characteristics. Its typical product is called similarly a bibliography. The essential criteria for a bibliography are that it identify the books that it lists with a certainty sufficient for its purpose; that it describe those books in accordance with generally accepted criteria; that the listing be systematized, even if merely through an alphabetical arrangement; that the books so listed possess certain common characteristics; and that the listing be addressed to some recognizable purpose.

Bibliographies are of many types, but certain characteristics can be associated with most of them. Thus, a bibliography may be current or retrospective. The *Cumulative Book Index* (Minneapolis, later New York, 1898–   ), which limits its listings to publications of recent date, is an example of the first, while Joseph Sabin's *Bibliotheca Americana: A Dictionary of Books Relating to America* (29 vols., New York 1868–1936), which has no such restrictions, is an example of the second. Bibliographies may also be comprehensive or selective. The *Cumulative Book Index*, again, attempts to include all publications in the American book trade, while the American Library Association's *Booklist* (Boston, later Chicago, 1905–   ) lists only selections of probable interest to libraries. Bibliographies may or may not be annotated, and annotations, when present, usually determine the purpose and usefulness of the bibliography.

Apart from these varieties, bibliographies may be further considered as belonging to one or the other of the following types:

Enumerative Bibliographies. Enumerative bibliographies, whose primary purpose is to present an inventory, may be contrasted with subject bibliographies, where the primary purpose is content. But enumerative bibliographies can, and often do, provide information about the contents of the books that they inventory. Their principal varieties are as follows:

National Bibliographies. These works record national book production. The American *Cumulative Book Index* and the *English Catalogue* (1868, first volume covering years 1835–1863; a later volume covered 1801 to 1834; now annual) are current national bibliographies. Those historical gaps that they leave may be filled by such retrospective national bibliographies as Charles Evans' *American Bibliography* (13 vols., Chicago, later Worcester, Mass., 1903–1955; in progress), which covers the period 1639 to 1800. The pattern of publication of the national bibliographies varies widely from country to country, and the matter is complicated further by the

fact that some publications record book trade, governmental, and university publications, while others list such things as periodicals, newspapers, music, and maps. The national bibliography of a particular country is, therefore, ordinarily to be sought in a multitude of special publications, and the result is so complicated that it is necessary to consult special guides that list the sources. One such guide is L.-N. Malclès' *Sources du Travail Bibliographique* (2 vols., Geneva 1950–1952).

Catalogs. Many would refuse to apply the name of bibliography to catalogs on the grounds that they reflect merely the sporadic issuances of publishers or acquisitions of libraries. However, to the extent that catalogs fulfill the requirements for bibliographies stated above, it is difficult to see why the name should be withheld from them, especially when it is given to national bibliographies that are even more loosely organized than are catalogs of libraries and book collectors. Indeed, even those who would withhold the title admit that a catalog may become a bibliography if it possesses utility with respect to a particular subject.

Catalogs may in consequence be admitted to represent a type of bibliography, since they fulfill the requirements, but they still have to be differentiated as a type. They are ordinarily lists, inventorial in character, of books of which the common characteristics are not that they have the same author or subject matter (though either or both of these may be true), but that they are issued by a particular publisher or group of publishers, are offered for sale by a particular bookseller, or are owned by a particular library or group of libraries.

Individual American libraries generally maintain their catalogs chiefly on cards, which permit interfiling and withdrawal, but at least two major American libraries—the Library of Congress and the National Library of Medicine—publish their catalogs in book form, reproducing catalog cards for this purpose in reduced facsimile. *The Library of Congress Catalogs* (257 vols., 1942–1955; in progress) currently list books (in the narrow sense) in both author and subject arrangements, as well as music, motion pictures, and sound recordings.

Such catalogs have enormous bibliographic importance for the purpose of identifying and locating books. Other great library catalogs include those of the British Museum and of the Bibliothèque Nationale in Paris.

From the catalog of a single library it is but a step to a union catalog representing the collections of several libraries. The Library of Congress not only maintains the National Union Catalog covering some 12 million cards, which represent the holdings of the principal North American libraries (with special catalogs for books in Hebrew, Chinese, Japanese, and Cyrillic alphabets); but it also publishes in book form the record of those current publications whose acquisition is reported by various libraries. Regional union catalogs exist in Philadelphia, Denver, Seattle, and elsewhere. Among the important national union catalogs manitained abroad are those in London, Bern, The Hague, and Ottawa. The Preussische Staatsbibliothek began publication of a *Deutscher Gesamtkatalog* (vols. 1–4, Berlin 1931–1939), but World War II prevented its completion.

Similar to union catalogs are union lists that

record (usually in book form) the periodicals, newspapers, microfilms, or other materials of a special type held by a group of libraries. These lists help to identify and locate materials and contribute to coordination of acquisition. The best-known example in this country is the *Union List of Serials in Libraries of the United States and Canada,* edited by Winifred Gregory (2d edition, with periodic supplements, New York 1943–).

The principal varieties of catalogs, besides those mentioned, are author, subject, and title catalogs, as well as dictionary and classified catalogs. For the first three, the names indicate the bases of arrangement. Dictionary catalogs interfile entries by author, title, or subject in a single alphabetical arrangement. Classified catalogs, however, arrange the entries according to some particularized scheme of classification. In union catalogs, because of local differences in subject analysis, dictionary catalogs are rarely attempted, though the Cyrillic Union Catalog at the Library of Congress provides one such example.

Other Enumerative Bibliographies. This group includes, of particular note, inventories of rare books. These are important because the books that they list are important. They also include examples of international enumerative bibliography, such as Ludwig Hain's *Repertorium Bibliographicum, . . . ad Annum MD. . . .* (4 vols., Stuttgart 1826–1838) and the *Gesamtkatalog der Wiegendrucke* (vols. 1–8, Leipzig 1925–1940), both of which are devoted to incunabula, Jacques C. Brunet's *Manuel du Libraire et de l'Amateur de Livres* (9 vols., Paris 1860–1880), and *American Book-Prices Current* (New York 1895–), which is an annual record of sales at rare-book auctions.

Subject Bibliographies. These are lists in which both the purpose of compilation and the common characteristics of the listed books are related to the subject matter of their contents. Such lists, like other bibliographies, may be current or retrospective, comprehensive or selective, annotated or not. They may be issued as periodicals or monographs, in book form or on separate cards, and even in the form of film, tape, wire, or punched cards on which the bibliographic information has been coded in some manner to control the operations of a sorting or printing device. They range in importance and comprehensiveness from tools for the work of major disciplines and great industries, like *Chemical Abstracts* (Easton, Pa., 1907–), to brief lists of scattered references on some minute point of interest. They form the great mass of bibliographical writing and are so numerous that special guides are required to identify those suitable for a particular purpose. Such guides are known as bibliographies of bibliographies and are mentioned below.

Indexes. Books are equipped normally with finding-lists of the terms contained in them. By contrast, a bibliographic index was originally, and still often is, a register of books. In current usage the term is applied more particularly to a current and continuing register providing the most meager bibliographic detail and devoid of annotations. Such indexes usually list articles in the periodical literature, for example, the *Industrial Arts Index* (New York 1913–).

Abstracting Services. These services are similar to indexes, except that they are heavily annotated with digests of the listed publications, e.g., *Bio-logical Abstracts* (Philadelphia 1926–). Abstracts are classified as indicative, which merely indicate the scope of the work abstracted, or informative, which fully summarize the content and often make reference to the original writing unnecessary.

Guides to the Literature of a Subject. *Reviews,* in contrast to lists, commonly take the form of discussions or narratives. An example is Nathan Grier Parke's *Guide to the Literature of Mathematics and Physics, Including Related Works on Engineering* (New York 1947). On the other hand, the *Annual Review of Biochemistry* (Stanford, Calif., 1932–) belongs more properly to the class of lists.

Guides to Collections describe the collections of materials available for the support of particular studies. Included among these are the Carnegie Institution's *Guides to Manuscript Materials for the History of the United States* (Washington 1906–1943).

Bio-bibliographies ordinarily record the principal facts in the lives of the authors, along with lists of their publications, such as Claudius Frank Mayer's *Bio-Bibliography of XVI Century Medical Authors* (Washington 1941). But a bio-bibliography can turn interest around and illustrate the life of a man through his comments on the books of other men. This is done in *Catalogue of the Library of Thomas Jefferson,* edited by Emily Millicent Sowerby (Washington 1952–).

Source Lists and Reading Lists. These so frequently occur under the caption "Bibliography" in capital letters that they almost preempt the title for many readers. A bibliography as a source list is merely the list of references appended to a treatise to show the sources used by the author. A bibliography as a reading list is similarly appended to an encyclopedia article or to a chapter in a textbook in order to suggest books for further study or reading that will be helpful for more-detailed study.

Bibliographies of Bibliographies. The reader who has never consulted one of these works can have no conception of the wealth and diversity of information provided by bibliographical writing, or of the varied and complex forms in which such writings occur. Since even bibliographies of bibliographies are numerous, the reader of this article is best served by a minimum of examples from which he can promptly discover others perhaps more peculiar to his interest. Constance M. Winchell's *Guide to Reference Books* (7th ed., Chicago 1951; supplements in progress), though not restricted to bibliographies, will carry the inquirer far in any search for bibliographic information. See also L.-N. Malclès' *Sources du Travail Bibliographique* (2 vols., Geneva 1950–1952), Theodore Besterman's *A World Bibliography of Bibliographies* (3d ed., 4 vols., Geneva 1955–1956), *Index Bibliographicus* (3d ed., 2 vols., edited by Theodore Besterman, Paris 1951–1952), and *Bibliographic Index* (New York 1938–).

Techniques of Systematic Bibliography. It follows from what has been said that systematic bibliography employs various standards of identification, description, and organization. These are described in various manuals, such as Arundell Esdaile's *A Student's Manual of Bibliography* (London 1932), Georg Schneider's *Handbuch der Bibliographie* (3d ed., Leipzig 1926, translated in part by Ralph R. Shaw under the title *Theory* *and History of Bibliography* (New York 1934), and *Bibliographical Procedures & Style* (Washington: Library of Congress, 1954). (See also the article on BOOK.) Bibliographical description as practiced by most libraries is called cataloguing, and is governed by elaborate codes. (See LIBRARIES—*Library Services and Organization: Bibliographic Access*.) In the organization of bibliographies there is great latitude: they may be arranged alphabetically, chronologically, geographically, in accordance with the taxonomy of a science, or on some other principle. The Dewey Decimal Classification (adapted in Europe as the Universal Decimal Classification) has provided a general scheme not only for the arrangement of books but also of bibliographies.

Standardization affects bibliographic work in many other ways—in the arrangement of periodicals, abbreviations of their titles, methods of citing articles contained in them, and transliteration of one alphabet into another. The International Standards Organization is active in this field, but many professional groups issue their own standards, such as "MLA Style Sheet" (*Publications of the Modern Language Association*, April 1951).

ANALYTIC BIBLIOGRAPHY

Analytic bibliography represents bibliography in its scientific aspect. It attempts to organize information, based on or derived from the physical characteristics of books, which will provide evidence regarding their history and especially the history of the texts that they reproduce. Such studies were given great stimulus by the efforts to ascertain, from internal evidence, the facts of publication of the earliest printed books and of the invention and spread of printing. A discussion of these studies is found in Konrad Haebler's *Handbuch der Inkunabelkunde* (Leipzig 1925, translated by L.E. Osborne as *The Study of Incunabula*, New York 1933). Analytic bibliography may also be applied to investigation of problems presented by anonymous and pseudonymous works, spurious imprints, and, more especially, to the study of the derivation of texts (consult Ronald B. McKerrow's *An Introduction to Bibliography for Literary Students*, Oxford 1927).

Because analytic bibliography involves the recognition of variations in books with much greater precision than is required usually by systematic bibliography, its methods of description must be more exacting and are set forth, for example, in Fredson Bowers' *Principles of Bibliographical Description* (Princeton 1949).

A number of publications are devoted to analytical bibliography, such as the *Transactions of the Bibliographical Society* (London 1893– ; from 1920, *The Library*), *Papers* of the Bibliographical Society of America (Chicago, later New York 1906–   ), *Studies in Bibliography* of the Bibliographical Society of the University of Virginia (Charlottesville 1948/49–   ), and the *Gutenberg Jahrbuch* (Mainz 1926–   ).

BIBLIOGRAPHY AND RESEARCH

No discussion of bibliography in its modern applications can neglect to mention its relation to the increasing need for rapid and accurate methods of communicating information; and similarly its relation to the requirement for the rapid and accurate retrieval of information from the enormous accumulations of records on which contemporary civilization depends.

Bibliography, which deals primarily with sources of information but to some extent is involved with the information itself, goes far in meeting such needs but not far enough. (See *Bibliography in an Age of Science*, Urbana, Ill., 1951). It is slow, inexact, expensive and duplicative, and shows enormous gaps in coverage. It is insufficiently selective on the one hand yet insufficiently comprehensive on the other; it is unorganized and lacking a rationalized approach to its task. Many attempts have been made to improve it. The Royal Society spent a fortune between 1900 and 1914 trying to organize the current bibliography of science. The International Institute of Bibliography, founded in 1895 at Brussels and since converted into the International Federation for Documentation (represented in the United States by the American Documentation Institute), has attempted to advance various reforms in the bibliographic arts relating to the communication and retrieval of information. Schemes of bibliographic rationalization, undertaken by the League of Nations through its Institute of Intellectual Cooperation, have been continued since World War II by UNESCO. (Consult the UNESCO–Library of Congress Survey, *Bibliographical Services, Their Present State and Possibilities of Improvement*, Washington 1950.) The search for improvement goes on in many ways—through standardization of the various bibliographical methods and of the materials with which they deal, through the application of new techniques (such as photo-offset printing, punched-card sorting, automatic film-scanning, and electron-computer manipulation. Other improvements have occurred in the development of national and international cooperative arrangements.

VERNER W. CLAPP
Council on Library Resources, Washington, D.C.

Bibliography
Besterman, Theodore, *The Beginnings of Systematic Bibliography*, 2d ed. (London 1936).
Boswell, D.B., *A Text Book on Bibliography* (London 1952).
Bowers, Fredson, *Bibliography and Textual Criticism* (New York 1964).
Mackenzie, Armine D., *Fine Contagion* (Berkeley, Calif., 1958).
Proctor, Robert, *Bibliographical Essays* (New York 1964).
Royal Society of London, *Scientific Information Conference, 1948*, Report and Papers Submitted (London 1948).
Van Hoesen, H.B., and Walter, F.K., *Bibliography, Practical, Enumerative, Historical* (New York 1928).
Willoughby, Edwin E., *Uses of Bibliography* (Hamden, Conn., 1957).

BIBLIOTHÈQUE NATIONALE, bĕb-lyô-tek′ nä-syô-nàl′, the French national library in Paris. Its collections include the libraries of the kings of France, and its beginnings may be traced to Charles V (14th century). Known successively as *Bibliothèque du Roi* and *Bibliothèque Royale*, it was transferred in 1721 to the Palais Mazarin in the Rue de Richelieu, where it has remained ever since. During the French Revolution its name was changed to *Bibliothèque Nationale*, and it became the *Bibliothèque Impériale* during the Empire. The collections of the library are in three departments: books, manuscripts, and prints. There is also a department of medals and antiques. The library increases its collections by purchase, by gifts, and particularly by the required filing by publishers of two copies of all new works.

The Bibliothèque Nationale is not a public library; the applicant for a reader's card must be a university graduate, the author of a literary work, a registered student, or have similar qualifications. The department of medals and antiques and a special reading room are open to the general public. Yearly exhibitions of the library's rarities, bearing on some particular period or writer, are held in the Galerie Mazarine. The Salle des Estampes contains the collection of prints begun by J.B. Colbert. The manuscript department is the treasure house of the Bibliothèque Nationale. See also LIBRARIES—*One Hundred Notable Libraries of the World.*

BICARBONATE, bī-kär′bə-nit, is a salt of carbonic acid that is formed when one of the hydrogen atoms of carbonic acid (H_2CO_3) is replaced by an atom of a metal. Examples of bicarbonates are sodium bicarbonate ($NaHCO_3$), potassium bicarbonate ($KHCO_3$), and calcium bicarbonate ($CaHCO_3$). A carbonate is formed when both of the hydrogen atoms are replaced by atoms of a metal. Sodium carbonate (Na_2CO_3) is an example.

Bicarbonates are formed by the action of excess carbon dioxide (CO_2) on carbonates in solution. For example, sodium bicarbonate is formed by the following reaction: $Na_2CO_3 + CO_2 + H_2O \rightarrow 2NaHCO_3$. Sodium bicarbonate is used as a baking powder and, in medicine, as an antacid.

BICEPS, bī′seps, the principal flexor muscle of the arm. Located on the front of the upper arm, it is the muscle popularly shown as evidence of muscular development. Technically it is called *biceps brachii.* The action of this muscle is to bring the forearm to the upper arm and to turn the inturned hand outward. The biceps consists of two parts at its upper end: the short head, attached to the shoulder bone (scapula) near the shoulder joint, and the long head, attached to the shoulder bone at the shoulder joint. The long head arches over the head of the arm bone (humerus) as a tendon and joins with the short head to form the belly of the muscle. The lower part of the biceps is attached to one of the forearm bones.

BICHAT, bē-shá′, **Marie François Xavier** (1771–1802), French anatomist and physiologist, who was one of the founders of the science of histology. Bichat was the first to show that the organs of the body are made up of tissues, and he identified 21 different kinds of tissues, or "membranes" as he called them. He stated that different organs may be made up of the same basic kinds of tissues, that the tissues carry on vital activities, and that any tissue of an organ can become diseased without the rest of the organ being diseased. Since Bichat was working before microscopes had been perfected, his conclusions were based on his keen naked-eye observations during numerous dissections of human corpses.

Bichat was born in Thoirette, France, on Nov. 11, 1771. He attended the Collège de Nantua and a Jesuit seminary at Lyon. In 1793 he went to Paris and studied surgery under Pierre Desault. Bichat was appointed physician at the Hôtel Dieu in 1800. He died in Paris on July 22, 1802. His major works are *Treatise on Membranes* (1800), *General Anatomy Applied to Physiology and Medicine* (1801), and *Treatise of Descriptive Anatomy* (2 vols., 1801–02).

NEW YORK ZOOLOGICAL SOCIETY

Bichir (*Polypterus retropinnis*)

BICHIR, bich′ər, a genus of freshwater fishes native to western and central Africa. Bichirs have slender elongated bodies with a maximum length of about 28 inches (71 cm). They are generally grayish or greenish above and yellow or white below. Some species have a series of prominent dark vertical markings along their sides. Bichirs have a number of primitive anatomical features, including a spiral valve in the digestive tract and feathery external gills in the newly hatched young. They have functional gills as well as lungs, but die if they are unable to surface for air. They feed at night on small animal life. Bichirs make up the genus *Polypterus*, class Osteichthyes.

BICHLORIDE OF MERCURY. See CORROSIVE SUBLIMATE.

BICKERDYKE, bik′ər-dīk, **Mary Ann** (1817–1901), American nurse. She was born in Knox County, Ohio, on July 19, 1817. Brought up on her maternal grandfather's farm, she studied for four years at Oberlin College, without graduating, and then prepared for nursing in Cincinnati. In 1847 she married Robert Bickerdyke, to whom she bore several children. They moved to Galesburg, Ill., in 1856, and her husband died two years later. With the outbreak of the Civil War she began serving in army hospitals in Cairo, Ill.

During the four years of the war, "Mother" Bickerdyke was present at 19 battles, tending the wounded on the field or in hospitals, directing diet kitchens, resourcefully rounding up supplies, managing army laundries (which she introduced), and in general displaying extraordinary administrative ability and stamina. Zealous in fighting for the enlisted man, she was the bane of incompetent officers, but Generals Ulysses S. Grant and William T. Sherman held her in high esteem. After the war she continued her efforts on behalf of service personnel: as a pension attorney she helped ex-soldiers and nurses obtain pensions, and she took the lead in helping veterans establish homes in the West.

In her later years she operated a hotel in Kansas, did welfare work in Chicago, and was a missionary in New York City. She went to Illinois to help victims of a locust plague, and worked in the United States mint in California. She died at Bunker Hill, Kans., on Nov. 8, 1901. In 1903 the state of Illinois raised a monument in Galesburg to her memory.

Further Reading: Baker, Nina Brown, *Cyclone in Calico* (Boston 1952).

BICUSPID. See TEETH.

ROBERT MOTTAR FROM PHOTO RESEARCHERS

BICYCLES are everyday transport in Europe. Riders crowd a street in Rotterdam, the Netherlands.

BICYCLE, bī′sik-əl, a vehicle of two wheels mounted in tandem on a light metal frame, propelled by the rider through the use of foot pedals and steered by handlebars attached to the front axle. The pedals, mounted below and slightly forward of the saddle on which the driver sits, are attached to a gear and chain mechanism that drives the rear wheel. The bicycle is a vital means of transportation in Europe and heavily populated areas of Asia. In the United States, where it is popular for recreation, about 65 percent of the bicycle users are juveniles.

Early Models. The most succesful early attempt to build a comfortable two-wheeled vehicle was the *Draisine*, a wooden bar with a saddle attached to two medium-sized wheels that the rider propelled by pushing his feet backward against the ground. It was steered by a handle attached to the front axle. The device was constructed about 1816 by Baron Karl von Drais in Karlsruhe, Germany. In England the vehicle was called a *hobbyhorse* or *dandy horse*.

In 1839 a Scots blacksmith, Kirkpatrick Macmillan, attached treadles to long rods connected to cranks on the rear axle, a development that later led to the present chain-and-sprocket drive. Macmillan's model was changed by Gavin Dalzell, another Scot, in 1845. He moved the pedals from under the handlebars to a position under the saddle. He designed handlebars more like

modern ones, changed the slope of the front fork, and used a drop frame to make mounting easier.

Pierre Michaux and his son Ernest created in France about 1861 a vehicle propelled by pedals attached to the front axle. It was called a *velocipede*. It also was dubbed the "boneshaker," because its wooden wheels with iron rims gave a rough ride over cobblestones. Rubber tires that softened some of the jolts were affixed to the boneshaker in 1869. Other models appeared during the 1860's. Pierre Lallement, a mechanic who worked for Michaux, produced one in 1863 and exhibited it at the Paris Exposition in 1865. He migrated to Connecticut and obtained a United States patent for it in November 1866. The name "bicycle" first was used in a patent in 1869.

The velocipede had little speed because the driven wheel (front) turned once with each turn of the pedals. In various later models, the front wheel was made larger, and the rear wheel smaller. This meant that with each turn of the pedals the wheel would cover more ground. To accommodate the rider and make more efficient use of his leg power, the seat was moved to a position over the wheel. When this model, the *ordinary* or *high wheel*, was introduced in 1871, its front wheel had a diameter of 40 to 48 inches (1 to 1.2 meters) and its rear wheel was 16 inches (0.4 meter). Ten years later the average front wheel was 52 inches (1.3 meters). The

BETTMANN ARCHIVE

HIGH-WHEEL BICYCLE for two (left) in 1886. Type for single rider had a large front wheel and a small rear wheel. Primitive bicycle, the Draisine (below) was built about 1820. Rider pushed feet backward on the ground and steered by handle fixed to front axle.

BETTMANN ARCHIVE

726

largest wheel made was 84 inches (2.1 meters). But the practical wheel could be no larger than 60 inches (1.5 meters) because the legs of the average rider could not reach the pedals. The seat was dangerously high for the machine to be used for anything but sport. For general use the public turned to *tricycles*.

The Modern Bicycle. The practical bicycle took form in 1879 with the building of a two-wheeler driven by a chain mechanism attached to the rear wheel. The designer, Harry J. Lawson, adapted a chain to an earlier rope drive on a modified ordinary. He called his machine the *safety bicycle*. James K. Starley, of Coventry, England, produced the prototype of the modern bicycle in 1886. It had two 30-inch (0.76-meter) wheels, their hubs 41 inches (1.04 meters) apart, with the pedals and sprocket mounted between the wheels below the saddle, which was 40 inches (1.02 meters) high. Except for refinements, the bicycle changed little thereafter.

In the late 1960's a bicycle for adults had a standard wheel diameter of 26 inches (0.66 meter). A bicycle for children had wheels of 16 inches (0.41 meter) up. Some machines were geared for 10 speeds. The average had 3 to 5 speeds. Folding machines were common, and a 16-inch wheel model with a high, straight-up steering wheel (called a *high riser*) was a new concept in the mid-1960's.

Accessories. Development of refinements and accessories kept pace with the evolution of the bicycle. Lamps and a crude "break," a leather pad pressed against the side of the wheel by pulling a cord, appeared on the velocipede in the 1860's. The coaster brake, applied to the rear axle by pressing the pedals backward, came with the safety bicycle. Roller bearings used in the velocipede in 1868 became ball bearings to allow free wheeling on the ordinary. The variable speed transmission, used on tricycles, was adapted in 1881. Starley put a bell on his 1887 model Rover. John Dunlop of Ireland made a practical pneumatic tire in 1888. John Palmer of Chicago produced the cotton cord tire in 1892.

Bicycles for Women. The creation of a bicycle for women, which was impossible with the high wheeler, succeeded with the safety bicycle. Models without the bar allowed a woman to ride in long skirts. Partly to accommodate women, the *tandem bicycle*—the "bicycle built for two"—was perfected in 1893.

Popularity. By the 1890's the demand for bicycles for daily use and for recreation had become a craze. Riding clubs conducted outings and tours. Bicycle racing became a great participant and spectator sport. (See CYCLING.)

The bicycle fad died suddenly about 1900. In the United States, bicycles were sold almost entirely for children. But a revival of adult cycling for recreation came after World War II. The Bicycle Institute of America estimated that there was one bicycle to every five or six persons in the United States in the late 1960's.

BILL BRADDOCK
New York "Times"

Bibliography
Bartleet, Horace W., *Bicycle Book* (London 1931).
Bicycle Institute of America, *The Bicycle Story* (New York 1965).
Carter, Frank, *The Boys' Book of Cycles and Motorcycles* (London and New York 1962).
Cycling Press, Inc., *American Bicyclist and Motorcyclist* (New York, monthly).
Grew, W.F., *The Cycle Industry* (New York 1921).
Palmer, Arthur J., *Riding High* (New York 1956).

BIDAULT, bē-dō', **Georges** (1899–   ), French statesman. He was born in Moulins, France, on Nov. 5, 1899. After a brilliant undergraduate career, interrupted by brief service in World War I, he became a history teacher. In the early 1930's he taught in Paris and at the same time became a leader of the Popular Democratic party, helping to found the party's newspaper, *L'Aube*. His trenchant editorials advocated social legislation for the lower classes and warned of the menace of fascism and nazism.

At the outbreak of World War II, Bidault joined the French forces but was soon taken prisoner. After his release in 1941, he joined the French underground, covering his activities by becoming a professor at the University of Lyon. Part of his underground work was editing the clandestine newspaper *Bulletin de la France combattante*. Bidault left his university position and in 1943 became head of the resistance after the death of Jean Moulin, who had united political groups of widely differing beliefs and who had created an underground government called the National Council of the Resistance.

At the liberation of Paris in August 1944, Bidault officially welcomed General de Gaulle on the steps of the Hôtel de Ville. Appointed foreign minister by de Gaulle in September 1944, he immediately began a thorough reorganization of the ministry of foreign affairs and the diplomatic service. Together with de Gaulle, he negotiated and signed economic agreements with Belgium, Luxembourg, and the Netherlands. He also headed the French delegation to the United Nations Conference in San Francisco in 1945. During the negotiations of the Council of Foreign Ministers held at London and Paris between September 1945 and July 1946, prior to the convocation of the Paris Peace Conference, Bidault emerged as the great compromiser.

Bidault's "left of center" party, the Mouvement Républicain Populaire (MRP), was victorious in the June 1946 elections in France, and that same month he was chosen premier of the provisional government. He served as premier until November 1946. In March 1947, during a term as foreign minister that lasted from January 1947 until July 1948, he signed a 50-year Anglo-French defense pact that provided protection against the possible future resurgence of Germany. Bidault was reelected head of the MRP in 1949 and became premier again in October 1949. After his government fell in June 1950, he was not again included in a cabinet until 1952. In January 1953 he resumed the office of foreign minister. After the fall of Laniel's government in June 1954, Bidault held no ministerial posts in the Fourth Republic.

During the 1950's Bidault became increasingly bitter over the loss of the French colonies, particularly in Indochina. In July 1958 he formed the Christian Democracy of France, which demanded the preservation of French rule in Algeria. He opposed de Gaulle's more liberal attitude toward Algeria and denounced his former colleague as a traitor. Bidault's violent opposition to the government during the Algerian crisis finally forced him into exile in 1962. In exile Bidault revived the National Council of Resistance to cooperate with the Secret Army Organization (OAS) against de Gaulle. After Algeria became independent, Bidault went to Brazil, where he worked on his memoirs and taught.

BIDDEFORD, bid'ə-fərd, a trading and manufacturing city in southwestern Maine, in York county, 15 miles (24 km) south of Portland. It is on the Saco River, 6 miles (9.5 km) from the Atlantic Ocean. Biddeford's wholesale and retail trading area is the fifth largest in Maine. During the summer the city is also a trade center for resorts in the White Mountains of New Hampshire and along the Maine coast. Its manufactured products include textiles, textile machinery, lumber products, shoes, boots, plastics, tanned goods, and apparel. Biddeford is the site of St. Francis College, founded in 1953.

The area was visited in 1605 by the French explorer Samuel Champlain, who spent a week observing Indian camps there and made the first map of the region. In 1616 a company of Englishmen, led by Captain Richard Vines, spent a winter surveying the area for development. Vines returned to the site in 1630 to establish the first settlement, which he named Winter Harbour. The export of lumber and salt fish began there in the 1630's. In 1718 the settlement was reorganized as a town and named Biddeford after an English town from which some of the original settlers had come. Abundant waterpower enabled Biddeford to flourish as a mill center, and in 1840 the first Waltham-system cotton mill was established there. Biddeford became a city in 1855. Government is by mayor and council. Population: 19,983.

BIDDLE, bid'əl, **Anthony Joseph Drexel, Jr.** (1896–1961), American diplomat and army officer. He was born in Philadelphia, Pa., on Dec. 17, 1896. Educated at St. Paul's School, Concord, N.H., he engaged in shipping and mining.

Entering a diplomatic career, Biddle was named ambassador to Norway in 1935. He was appointed ambassador to Poland in 1937, and at the outbreak of World War II accompanied the Polish government to London, where he functioned as ambassador to seven governments-in-exile. He left the diplomatic service in 1944, when he was commissioned a lieutenant colonel in the Army (in which he had been a captain in World War I). Promoted to brigadier general in 1951, he served with headquarters of the Allied forces in Europe, as a special assistant to the Army chief of staff. After retiring from active duty in 1955, he was adjutant general of Pennsylvania, with the rank of major general. He was appointed ambassador to Spain in February 1961. Biddle died in Washington, D.C., on Nov. 13, 1961.

BIDDLE, bid'əl, **Clement** (1740–1814), American Revolutionary soldier. He was born at Philadelphia on May 10, 1740. He was a member of his family's importing and exporting firm. Before the Revolutionary War he was active in the cause of the American colonists, and when war broke out in 1775 he helped to form the Quaker Blues, a company of Philadelphia volunteers. In July 1776 he was named deputy quartermaster general of the Pennsylvania and New Jersey militias with the rank of colonel. He fought in the Battle of Trenton, on Dec. 26, 1776, and at General Washington's order he received the swords of the Hessian officers who surrendered. He fought also in the battles of Brandywine, Germantown, and Monmouth, and endured the hard winter of 1777–1778 with the army at Valley Forge, Pa.

Biddle continued as a merchant in Philadelphia after the Revolution, and handled some business affairs for Washington. He was influential in obtaining the passage of the Bill of Rights as a part of the U.S. Constitution to prevent abuse or misconstruction of the federal powers. He was named a judge on the court of common pleas in 1788. When the militia was mobilized to suppress the Whiskey Rebellion in western Pennsylvania in the early 1790's, Biddle was appointed state quartermaster general. President Washington named him U.S. marshal of Pennsylvania in 1789 and he served until 1793. He died at Philadelphia on July 14, 1814.

BIDDLE, bid'əl, **Francis Beverly** (1886–1968), American lawyer, judge, and public official, who was U.S. attorney general in World War II. Biddle was born in Paris on May 9, 1886, and grew up in a prominent Philadelphia family. He attended Groton and graduated from Harvard and Harvard Law School with honors in 1909 and 1911. After serving as private secretary to U.S. Supreme Court Justice Oliver Wendell Holmes in 1911–1912, he became a noted corporation lawyer in Philadelphia and, at various times, was a special U.S. attorney (1922–1926), chairman of the National Labor Relations Board (1934–1935), and counsel for the Tennessee Valley Authority (1938). The social upheavals of the 1930's drew Biddle to the Democratic party and the New Deal, which he described as an effort "to improve social and economic conditions during a depression which was largely caused by the unfettered and cruel play of a free market."

President Franklin D. Roosevelt appointed Biddle judge of the U.S. Court of Appeals in Philadelphia in 1939, U.S. solicitor general in 1940, and U.S. attorney general in 1941. During the war years, Biddle championed civil liberties, especially in respect to the rights of aliens. Following his resignation from the cabinet in 1945, he served on the international war crimes tribunal at Nürnberg, Germany, for a year. In 1951, President Truman appointed him to the Permanent Court of Arbitration at The Hague.

Biddle wrote books and articles on public affairs and international relations, two biographies of Justice Holmes, and two autobiographical volumes, *A Casual Past* (1961) and *In Brief Authority* (1962). He died in Hyannis, Mass., on Oct. 4, 1968.

BIDDLE, bid'əl, **George** (1885–   ), American artist of the realist school. He was born into a prominent family in Philadelphia on Jan. 24, 1885. After attending the Groton School and Harvard College, he went to Paris in 1911 to study art. He served with the U.S. Army in France during World War I, and after the war he spent brief periods in Tahiti, Paris, and Italy before settling permanently in the United States. During the 1930's he was active in the government-sponsored Federal Arts Project.

Biddle described himself as having a strong "social conscience," an attitude that is reflected in most of his painting. His most notable works include a mural depicting the American laborer, in the Department of Justice building in Washington, D.C., and the painting *Tortilla Flat*, in the Whitney Museum of American Art in New York City. He wrote several books, including *An American Artist's Story* (1939).

BIDDLE, bid'əl, **James** (1783–1848), American naval officer. He was born in Philadelphia on Feb. 18, 1783. He entered the Navy in 1800, and in the war against Tripoli he was captured and imprisoned for 19 months.

In the War of 1812, Biddle was a lieutenant on the *Wasp* when she captured the *Frolic* and when the ship was later captured by the *Poictiers*. In 1813 he took command of the *Hornet*, which captured the British brig *Penguin* on March 23, 1815. He was made captain in 1815 and received a gold medal from Congress in reward for his services.

In 1817 he was sent to reoccupy Astoria, Oregon, which had been seized by the British. After negotiations, the British agreed that the United States should repossess the post. Biddle was afterward commissioner to Turkey and China and in 1846 negotiated the first treaty between the United States and China. He also served on the Pacific Coast in the Mexican War. He died in Philadelphia on Oct. 1, 1848.

BIDDLE, bid'əl, **John** (1615–1662), English writer whose *Twelve Arguments* denying the Holy Trinity support his distinction as the father of English Unitarianism. He was born in Wotton-under-Edge, Gloucestershire, and was baptized on Jan. 14, 1615. A graduate of Oxford University, he wrote the *Twelve Arguments* at Gloucester, where he was master of the free school. The manuscript was seized in 1645 and Biddle was briefly imprisoned. In 1647 he published the *Arguments*, which were ordered burned. In defiance of an ordinance imposing death on those who denied the Trinity, he published two anti-Trinitarian tracts in 1648. A plea was instituted in Parliament on his behalf, and although technically under arrest he was allowed to retire to Staffordshire. There he served as a preacher and helped edit an edition of the Septuagint.

A general amnesty restored him to full liberty in 1652, and his followers, called Biddellians, Socinians, or Unitarians, began to hold regular Sunday services. In 1654, Biddle published two catechisms of Unitarian principles and was again arrested. In 1655 he was banished to the Scilly Islands, where he remained until 1658. After his release he returned to London where he was arrested during a private service. He died in prison on Sept. 22, 1662. See also UNITARIANISM.

Further Reading: Wilbur, Earl M., *A History of Unitarianism*, vol. 2 (Boston 1965).

BIDDLE, bid'əl, **Nicholas** (1750–1778), American naval officer. He was born in Philadelphia on Sept. 10, 1750. He enlisted in the British navy in 1770 and in 1773 was aboard a ship on an exploring expedition to the Arctic.

Early in the Revolutionary War he served as captain of the American brig *Andrea Doria*, which cruised the Atlantic Ocean and took a number of valuable British prizes. Commanding the *Randolph* in 1777, he captured a British convoy in the West Indies and escorted the ships to Charleston, S.C. He was blockaded there by a British squadron until February 1778, when he put to sea in the *Randolph*, accompanied by four smaller vessels. On March 7 the *Randolph* engaged the *Yarmouth*, a more powerful British warship. Biddle was wounded but continued in command. His ship was blown up, and he and all but four of his crew of 315 men perished.

THE GRANGER COLLECTION (FROM PAINTING BY REMBRANDT PEALE)

Nicholas Biddle, American financier (1786–1844).

BIDDLE, bid'əl, **Nicholas** (1786–1844), American financier, who as president of the second Bank of the United States bitterly opposed President Andrew Jackson's campaign against it.

The scion of an old and wealthy Quaker family, Biddle was born in Philadelphia on Jan. 8, 1786. He entered the University of Pennsylvania at the age of 10 and later attended the College of New Jersey (now Princeton University), graduating in 1801 at the age of 15. In 1804 he went to France as secretary to the United States minister, Gen. John Armstrong, and two years later became secretary of the legation for James Monroe, minister at London. Biddle returned home in August 1807 to resume his legal studies.

Between 1809 and 1814, except for a short term in the lower house of the Pennsylvania legislature (1810–1811), Biddle gave his attention chiefly to writing. He was an active contributor to Joseph Dennie's literary monthly, the *Port Folio* and became its editor upon Dennie's death early in 1812. From 1810 to 1812 he prepared from the explorers' notes and journals the authorized *History of the Expedition under the Command of Captains Lewis and Clark . . .* (1814), but the pressure of other affairs forced him to turn over to Paul Allen, a journalist, the task of seeing the work through the press.

After serving in the Pennsylvania Senate for a term (1814–1818), Biddle was appointed (1819) by President Monroe as one of the five government directors of the second Bank of the United States, and he was elected its president in 1823. He supported a strong national bank against the state banks, following a conservative policy which antagonized many factions in the country; but the bank flourished under his astute direction. The decision to apply to Congress for a renewal of the bank's charter in 1832, four years before its expiration, was apparently made by him. Jackson vigorously opposed renewal of the charter and won the fight by vetoing the congressional bill for recharter. The Jackson-

Biddle struggle provided one of the most controversial issues of the 1830's, finally engaging as partisans on one side or the other leading political figures of the day.

In March 1836 the institution became a state bank, chartered by Pennsylvania. Soon afterward, the state bank encountered serious difficulties, largely as a result of Biddle's speculative policies. He resigned as president in 1839, although he continued to advise the new directors. In 1841 the bank was forced to close because of bankruptcy. Biddle died at Philadelphia on Feb. 27, 1844.

See also BANK OF THE UNITED STATES.

BIDEFORD, bid'ə-fərd, is a municipal borough in England in northern Devonshire on the coast of the Atlantic Ocean. It is situated on the estuary of the Torridge River, which empties just below Bideford into Barnstaple Bay, also called Bideford Bay. The river is spanned by a bridge with 24 unevenly spaced arches. Bideford, an old market town and an important port in the 16th century is now chiefly a resort center, with varied industries that include boatbuilding and manufacture of leather goods and concrete products.

Sir Richard Grenville, famous naval officer, whose family held the manor of Bideford for centuries, obtained the town's certificate of incorporation in 1574. Nearby is Westward Ho, a seaside resort named for Charles Kingsley's novel *Westward Ho!*, which is set partly in Bideford. Population: (1961) 10,498.

BIDPAI, bid'pī, was the reputed author of a collection of Indian beast fables. The collection was known in the Middle Ages as the *Fables of Bidpai,* and it was mistakenly assumed that Bidpai was the name of the author, whereas it was merely the official title of the narrator, a court scholar. The book, nominally intended to give moral instruction to a prince, became one of the chief sources of fable literature in the world.

BIEDERMEIER-style desk dates from the 19th century.

The Sanskrit original, written probably in the 3d century A.D., has been lost; but another early Sanskrit version called the *Panchatantra* (The Book in Five Parts), and a later abridgement of this, the *Hitopadeśa* (Book of Good Counsel), remain and have long been popular in India.

About 550 A.D. a translation, now lost, of the *Panchatantra* was done in Pahlavi, the literary language of Persia, and from this came a notable version in Arabic (about 750 A.D.) called *Kalilah wa-Dimnah,* by Ibn al-Muqaffa. From the Arabic version translations were made into many languages. A later Persian rendition, *Anwar-i Suhaili,* or *Lights of Canopus,* by Husain Waiz (died 1504 or 1505), was also widely translated. The first English translation, made by Sir Thomas North from an Italian version, was called *The Morall Philosophie of Doni* . . . (1570; reprinted 1888). There is also a modern English version of the *Panchatantra,* translated directly from the Sanskrit by Arthur W. Ryder (1925).

BIDWELL, bid'wəl, **John** (1819–1900), American pioneer and politician. He was born in Chautauqua County, N.Y., on Aug. 5, 1819. He was a leader of the first party of settlers to make the journey overland from the Missouri River to California, in 1841. He worked with John Augustus Sutter at Fort Sutter and in 1844 was naturalized as a Mexican citizen and received a grant of land. He served on the committee that drew up the resolution of independence from Mexico in 1846, and he fought with the U.S. Army in the Mexican War.

Bidwell was the first to find gold on Feather River, and in 1849 he acquired the 22,000-acre (8,910-hectare) Arroyo Chico ranch, north of Sacramento. Devoting the rest of his life to its cultivation, he became the state's most noted agriculturist.

Always interested in public affairs, he was a state senator (1849–1850), a U.S. congressman for one term (1865–1867), an unsuccessful candidate for governor of California in 1867, 1875, and 1890, and the Prohibition party's candidate for president in 1892. He wrote *A Journey to California in 1841* (1842; reprinted 1937). Bidwell died at his ranch on April 4, 1900.

BIEDERMEIER, bē'dər-mī-ər, is a term applied in the 19th century and after to a style of furniture that originated in Germany about 1815. The name was derived from "Papa Biedermeier," a caricatured bourgeois character in a series of comic verses by Ludwig Eichrodt that appeared in the mid-1850's in *Fliegende Blätter,* a humor magazine. The furniture, more comfortable and less expensive than other good furniture, was popular with the German middle class, and when middle-class tastes became identified with the tastes of "Papa Biedermeier," the furniture style acquired its name.

The Biedermeier style combines French Directoire and empire styles but is simpler than Directoire and more graceful than Empire. The Biedermeier period is from 1815 to 1848, but the best Biedermeier designs were created between 1820 and 1830. After 1848, the classic Biedermeier simplicity was gradually replaced by clutter. Carvings of scrolls, swans, griffins, cornucopias, and all kinds of foliage tormented the woodwork, and plush and velvet were substituted for calico and mohair as the standard upholstery fabrics.

BIEL, bēl, **Gabriel** (1425?–1495), German scholastic philosopher. He was born at Speyer. After study at the universities of Heidelberg and Erfurt, he became a noted preacher in the cathedral of Mainz. Later he was appointed superior of the Order of the Brethren of the Common Life. He helped found the University of Tübingen (1477) and in 1484 became its first professor of theology. He died near Tübingen in 1495.

Biel took William of Occam as his master and wrote *Epitome et collectorium ex Occamo,* an exposition on Occam's nominalistic *Quaestiones super IV libros sententiarum,* a commentary on Peter Lombard's *Sententiae.* Book 4 of Biel's work contains an interesting discussion of economics, including the theory of prices. Biel is also noted for a treatise on money, *Tractatus de potestate et utilitate monetarum.* He is sometimes called "the last of the scholastics."

BIEL, Lake of, bēl, in Switzerland, lying mostly in Bern canton. In French the name is *Lac de Bienne,* and in German *Bielersee.* The lake is about 15 square miles (39 sq km) in area, with a maximum depth of 243 feet (74 meters). The main town on its shores is Biel. Canals connect the lake with the Aar River to the northeast and Lake of Neuchatêl to the southwest. The Jura Mountains rise on the western shore.

BIELA, bē′lä, **Baron Wilhelm von** (1782–1856), German astronomer. He was born in Rosslau, Germany, on March 19, 1782. While serving as an officer in the Austrian army, he studied astronomy and in 1826 definitely fixed the orbit of a periodic comet that had been noticed in 1772 and again in 1805. The comet, named *Biela's comet,* split in two in 1846 and was not seen after 1852. The Andromedes, meteors that formerly appeared in showers at regular intervals, are also know as *Bielids* because they are thought to be fragments of Biela's comet. He died in Venice, Italy, on Feb. 18, 1856.

BIELEFELD, bē′lə-felt, is a city in West Germany, in the province of North Rhine–Westphalia, 55 miles (88.5 km) southwest of Hannover. It is the center of the noted Westphalian linen industry, which originated in the 13th century. Other manufactures include machinery and tools, sewing machines, bicycles, pharmaceuticals, and clothing. Sparrenberg Castle, built in the 1200's and restored after 1877, is now a museum. In World War II severe damage was done to the Gothic churches and other buildings in the city. Population: (1961) 174,642.

BIELSKO-BIAŁA, byel′skô-byä′lä, is a city in Poland, 30 miles (48 km) south of Katowice, on the Biała River, near the Czechoslovakian border. The present city was formed in 1950 by the union of Bielsko and Biała Krakowska, two towns on opposite banks of the river.

The area has figured prominently in the woolen industry since the Middle Ages. It came under Austrian rule in 1772 and was returned to Poland in 1919. During World War II, Germany seized its plants, which were largely Jewish-owned. After the war, the area suffered from the loss of raw materials resulting from Soviet annexation of Polish territory. The city produces high-grade woolen textiles. Population: (1964) 81,000.

BIENNIAL, bī-en′ē-əl, a plant that normally requires two years of growth, after starting from seed, to complete its life cycle. During the first year it produces only leaves, which usually grow from a short stem and spread out close to the ground, or form a head, as in the cabbage or celery. The plant develops a thick taproot in which a reserve of food accumulates; beets, carrots, parsnips, and turnips are examples of such plants, in which the food reserve is used by man. During the second year the biennial draws on its stored food to produce a tall stem, with flowers, fruit, and seed.

Under special circumstances favorable to rapid growth, a plant ordinarily a biennial may become an annual by flowering and seeding in its first year; in poor seasons, on the other hand, if plant food is scarce, it may delay its flowering beyond the second year.

Familiar biennials, besides those named, are hollyhock, red clover, pansy, and sweet William.

BIENVILLE, byaN-vēl′, **Sieur de** (1680–1768), French colonial administrator who founded New Orleans, La. He was born *Jean Baptiste le Moyne* at Ville Marie (now Montreal), Canada, on Feb. 23, 1680, one of numerous sons of Charles le Moyne, a French colonist.

Bienville entered the French navy as a midshipman. Under the command of his elder brother Pierre, Sieur d'Iberville, he served at the siege of Pemaquid in Acadia in 1696, in the victorious campaign in Newfoundland in 1696–1697, and in the capture of Fort Nelson on Hudson Bay in 1697.

In 1698, Bienville accompanied d'Iberville's expedition to rediscover the mouth of the Mississippi River, and, in 1701 he became governor of the colony of Louisiana founded at Biloxi by d'Iberville in 1699. Bienville's knowledge of Indian dialects proved invaluable in negotiations with native tribes when he explored the lower Mississippi in 1699 and the Red River in 1700. In 1702 he transferred the colony to Mobile Bay and in 1710 to Mobile, which he founded. The survival of the colony, hard pressed by Indian raids, Spanish hostility, and French neglect, was due mainly to his determined leadership.

In 1712 a monopoly of commercial privileges in Louisiana was granted to a French merchant named Antoine Crozat, and Bienville was superseded as governor by Antoine de la Mothe Cadillac. He was reinstated in 1717, after Crozat sold his interest. As a result of his ability as an administrator, Louisiana expanded rapidly.

Bienville founded New Orleans in 1718 and made it the capital in 1722. He imported Negro slaves and in 1724 promulgated the *Code noir* (Black Code) which, while minutely regulating their lives, was humane compared with other slave laws of the period.

Bienville's defeat by the Natchez Indians led to his dismissal in 1726. Reappointed in 1733 to arrest the colony's decline, he fought indecisive campaigns against the Natchez and their allies, the Chickasaw, and was obliged to sign an unsatisfactory treaty with them in 1740. Resigning his governorship in 1743, he returned to Paris, where he died on March 7, 1768.

ALLAN M. FRASER
Archivist, Province of Newfoundland
Further Reading: Fregault, G., *Le Grand Marquis: Pierre de Rigaud de Vaudreuil et la Louisiane* (Montreal 1952); Oudard, G., *Bienville, le Père de la Louisiane* (Toulouse 1943).

BIERCE, bêrs, **Ambrose Gwinett** (1842–?1914), American journalist and author, who, in his emphasis on the grotesque, anticipated the dark elements found in the work of such later writers as Conrad Aiken, Sherwood Anderson, Nathanael West, and William Faulkner. As a critic and friend, Bierce helped a number of younger writers, among them H.L. Mencken, Edwin Markham, and George Sterling.

Life. Bierce was born in Meigs County, Ohio, on June 24, 1842. After serving as an officer in the Union Army during the Civil War, he went to San Francisco, where he began his journalistic career. He contributed to a number of local papers and magazines, among them the *Overland Monthly* and the *Californian.* He was editor of the *News-Letter* and author of a satirical column of verse and commentary.

After his marriage in 1871, Bierce went to London, where he wrote for *Figaro* and Tom Hood's *Fun.* His first three volumes of sketches were published in London, under the pseudonym "Dod Grile": *Nuggets and Dust* (1872), *The Fiend's Delight* (1872), and *Cobwebs from an Empty Skull* (1874). In 1876 he returned to San Francisco and resumed his journalistic career as editor and columnist until 1886, first on the *Argonaut* and later on the *Wasp.* Then he joined the San Francisco *Examiner* and began a long career as columnist and contributor to the Hearst publications, becoming widely known as the dean of West Coast critics. In 1891 his *Tales of Soldiers and Civilians* was published; *Can Such Things Be?,* a second collection of short stories, appeared in 1893.

In 1900, Bierce moved to Washington, D.C. Still employed by Hearst, he contributed to the New York *Journal,* the San Francisco *Examiner,* and *Cosmopolitan* magazine. In 1906 he published *The Cynic's Word Book* (called *The Devil's Dictionary* in later editions), which collected numerous pessimistic, cynical definitions that had appeared earlier in his various columns. From 1909 to 1912 he edited his *Collected Works.*

Late in 1913, Bierce retired from writing and prepared to travel. He toured the Civil War battlefields and then went to Mexico, where he was attached as an observer to Pancho Villa's army. He was last heard from in late December 1913: "If you hear of my being stood up against a Mexican stone wall and shot to rags please know that I think it a pretty good way to depart this life." He is presumed to have died shortly thereafter.

Bierce's Stories. Bierce's Civil War stories are among his best. Such stories as *Chickamauga, An Occurrence at Owl Creek Bridge,* and *One of the Missing* anticipate the themes and techniques employed later by Stephen Crane in *The Red Badge of Courage* and by Ernest Hemingway. Other stories, such as *Moxan's Master, The Damned Thing,* and *The Death of Halpin Frayser,* deal with the themes and motifs of fear, death, horror, and the supernatural. Bierce has most often been compared to Poe for his use of elements of horror in the short story. He does prefer the outré and unusual, but he adds his own bitter pessimism and cynicism to the Gothic motifs popular in 19th century fiction.

ROBERT A. WIGGINS, *University of California*

Further Reading: Fadiman, Clifton, *The Collected Writings of Ambrose Bierce* (New York 1942); Fatout, Paul, *Ambrose Bierce, The Devil's Lexicographer* (Norman, Okla., 1951); Wiggins, Robert A., *Ambrose Bierce* (Minneapolis 1964); Wilson, Edmund, *Patriotic Gore* (New York 1962).

BIERSTADT, bêr'stat, **Albert** (1830–1902), American landscape painter, who was one of the later members of the Hudson River school of painting (q.v.). The subjects of most of his huge canvases are romantic scenes of the American wilderness, usually in the Rocky Mountains or along the Hudson River valley. His reputation faded after his death but was revived with the mid-20th century interest in the Hudson River school.

Bierstadt was born at Solingen, near Düsseldorf, Germany, on Jan. 7, 1830. His family moved to the United States the following year and settled in New Bedford, Mass., where Albert attended public school. From 1853 to 1857 he studied painting in Düsseldorf under the German romantic landscape painters Andreas Achenbach and Karl Friedrich Lessing. He capped his studies with a trip to Rome and returned to the United States in 1857.

In 1858, Bierstadt joined an expedition surveying a wagon route to the western United States. The impressions of this journey and the sketches he brought back provided the basis for many of his paintings, including *Laramie Peak* (1861), *Lander's Peak, Rocky Mountains* (1863), and *In the Rocky Mountains* (1871). He established a studio at Irvington-on-the-Hudson, N.Y., and added scenes of the Hudson River valley to his output. Later paintings, such as *Storm on the Matterhorn* (1884), were inspired by trips to Europe in 1867, 1878, and 1883. Two of his large canvases, *Discovery of the Hudson* and *Settlement of California,* are in the Capitol at Washington, D. C. He worked in New York City after 1882 and died there on Feb. 18, 1902.

BIG BEN is the name given to the great 13½-ton (12-metric-ton) bell in the clock tower of the British Houses of Parliament in London. It is said to have been named after Sir Benjamin Hall, who was first commissioner of works when it was hung in 1858. The name Big Ben also

BIG BEN sounds every hour on the hour in the impressive clock of the Houses of Parliament in London.

NOEL HABGOOD FROM PHOTO RESEARCHERS

came to be associated with the immense clock (made in 1854 by Frederick Dent, clockmaker to Queen Victoria). The clock entered service on May 31, 1859.

The hours are struck on the bell by a 400-pound (181-kg) hammer, sounding the note of E. The Westminster chimes, a daily feature of the programs of the British Broadcasting Corporation, are played on four smaller bells each quarter hour. The four clock dials are 22½ feet (7 meters) in diameter, and the over-all length of the minute hands is 14 feet (4 meters), including the short extension beyond the center of the clock faces. The clock tower, 320 feet (97.5 meters) high, stands on a 40-foot (12-meter) base. Although the belfry stage and the dials were damaged in 12 direct air attacks on the Houses of Parliament in World War II, the clock maintained its remarkable record for accuracy, striking the hours within 1½ seconds of Greenwich Mean Time.

BIG BEND NATIONAL PARK, a national park in southwestern Texas, along the border of the United States and Mexico. It is named for the great swing of the Rio Grande between the towns of Van Horn on the west and Langtry on the east. Its area is 1,082 square miles (2,801 sq km). It offers spectacular mountain and desert scenery and a variety of unusual geological structures. The Chisos Mountains in the southern part of the park reach a maximum altitude of 7,835 feet (2,388 meters) in Mount Emory. Three scenic canyons—Santa Elena, Boquillas, and Mariscal—are along the course of the Rio Grande. Boquillas is the longest (25 miles, or 40 km) of these famous gorges.

There is a road system within the park, but some points of major interest can be reached only by trail. Campgrounds are available; boating and fishing are permitted. The park was established in 1944. It is administered by the National Park Service.

BIG BERTHA, bûr'thə, was a 420-mm (16.54-inch) German mortar used in World War I. Produced at factories owned by Bertha Krupp, these mortars were employed effectively against Liège, Antwerp, and Verdun. The name is incorrectly applied to three 209.8-mm (8.26-inch) Paris Guns that hit Paris from a distance of 75 miles (120 km) in 1918.

BIG BONE LICK, a salt spring in Boone County, Kentucky, is located 11 miles (17.5 km) south of Burlington. Fossil remains of mastodons and other extinct fauna have been found in the area. These animals presumably gathered at Big Bone Lick to lick the salty earth near the spring.

BIG BROTHER is the embodiment of the state in the British writer George Orwell's novel *1984*, published in 1949. In the novel, which is set in a future totalitarian superstate, Big Brother is not an actual character, although his presence is always felt through the appearance of his picture on television and on countless posters. He rules absolutely but under the guise of benevolence. The term "Big Brother" has been extended to mean any authoritarian political leader.

BIG BROTHERS OF AMERICA, a national organization of hundreds of local member agencies seeking to guide and encourage disadvantaged, alienated boys from poor environments to develop a sense of pride and achievement. Much of the work of the local Big Brother agencies is done among boys who have been brought into children's court or who have shown tendencies toward delinquency. Under the professional supervision of trained social workers, volunteer laymen attempt to create a rapport with these boys through individual relationships based on friendship and understanding.

The Big Brothers concept originated in 1903 in Cincinnati, Ohio, when Irvin F. Westheimer sought to help boys from homes without fathers. The national organization of Big Brothers of America was set up as a coordinating body in 1946 by the 13 then-existing Big Brother associations in the United States and Canada. The purpose of the national body is to interpret to the public the aims and scope of the service. Big Brothers of America organizes new associations, establishes and maintains standards, assists member associations in their local fields, and acts in an advisory capacity to local community councils that want to establish similar agencies.

The first Big Brother organization was established in New York City in 1904, as the Big Brother Movement under the leadership of Ernest K. Coulter. The Big Brother Movement provided summer camps, group work, and health and vocational guidance programs to supplement the individual work performed by the volunteer Big Brothers. The present local agencies, patterned after this initial Big Brother Movement, set up similar programs according to the needs and resources of each community. The work of the individual local agencies is supported by volunteer contributions. The Big Brother agencies cooperate closely with other social agencies, public schools, and institutions, using existing neighborhood resources as fully as possible. In 1957 the Big Brother Movement was absorbed fully into the national organization.

The national organization publishes a quarterly journal called the *Big Brother Bulletin*. Headquarters of the Big Brothers of America are in Philadelphia.

BIG DIPPER, a constellation of the Northern Hemisphere. It is probably the most familiar star group of the hemisphere and one of the easiest to recognize. The Big Dipper is part of the larger constellation Ursa Major (the Big Bear), which was known to the ancient Greeks. It has gained its separate name because of the distinctive dipperlike pattern formed by seven bright stars within the larger constellation.

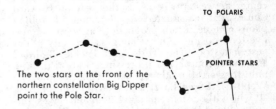

TO POLARIS

POINTER STARS

The two stars at the front of the northern constellation Big Dipper point to the Pole Star.

The two stars forming the front of the dipper are known as the Pointers. They point towards Polaris, the Pole Star, which lies almost directly above the earth's north pole. The Big Dipper is therefore a useful reference constellation for learning to observe the northern heavens.

BIG RAPIDS is an industrial city in west-central Michigan and the seat of Mecosta County. It is situated on the Muskegon River 50 miles (80 km) north of Grand Rapids. The city's principal manufactures are furniture, machinery, tools, and shoes. The surrounding region has many dairy and grain farms. Potatoes and apples also are grown. The city is the seat of Ferris State College, founded in 1884 by Woodbridge N. Ferris as a "school for the masses." Big Rapids was settled in 1856 and named for the rapids in the Muskegon River. It was incorporated as a city in 1869. Government is by council and manager. Population: 11,995.

BIG SANDY RIVER, a river in West Virginia and Kentucky that forms part of the northern boundary between the states. Its length is about 22 miles (35 km). It has two forks, Tug Fork rising in West Virginia and Levisa Fork rising in Kentucky, and flows north to meet the Ohio River near Catlettsburg, Ky.

BIG SIOUX RIVER, sōō, is a stream in South Dakota. It unites with the Missouri about 2 miles (3 km) above Sioux City, Iowa, after a course of 300 miles (483 km). It forms the boundary between South Dakota and Iowa.

BIG SISTERS, INC., The, an agency that was founded in 1908 to provide preventive casework service in New York City for Protestant girls under the age of 16 and Protestant boys under 10, and their parents. Through psychiatric consultation and psychological testing, trained caseworkers work to keep children in their own homes by helping parents understand each child's problems. The caseworkers' aim is to provide relief from immediate problems and better adjustment in the home, school, and community.

Summer camps and weekend recreation activities augment this program. Volunteer Big Sisters, trained and supervised by the staff, provide special activities and often supplement the services of the caseworker.

Offices of The Big Sisters, Inc., are located in the boroughs of Manhattan, Bronx, Brooklyn, and Queens in New York City. Referrals are made to the organization by the family courts in each borough, and by parents, schools, churches, and other agencies. The agency is supported by private contributions and by foundation grants.

MABEL R. THOMAS
Executive Director

BIG SPRING, an industrial city and commercial center in western Texas, is the seat of Howard County. It is situated in a region of rolling plains notable for oil production, agriculture, and livestock raising. Oil refining is the city's biggest industry. The Texas and Pacific Railroad and the chemical, gas processing, and oil drilling industries are the other major civilian employers. Webb Air Force Base, a fighter-interceptor base at which the Air Training Command gives undergraduate pilot training, is nearby. Big Spring has a U.S. Veterans Administration hospital, the Big Spring State Hospital, and four private hospitals. Howard County Junior College is in Big Spring, and the city has a civic theater. Tourist attractions include a rodeo, stock show, rattlesnake roundup, and quarter-horse show. Big Spring State Park has facilities for picnicking.

The first settlement on the site of Big Spring was made in 1881 with the building of a railroad. The city was incorporated in 1907. Its greatest growth came after the discovery of oil in 1928. Government is by council and manager. Population: 28,735.

BIG STONE GAP, a town in southwestern Virginia, in Wise County, 160 miles (267 km) west of Roanoke. Situated in the Cumberland Mountains, it is called the "Gateway to the Jefferson National Forest." Lumber and coal mining are the principal industries. The Southwest Virginia Museum has a permanent exhibit of pioneer arts and crafts. Big Stone Gap was the home of John Fox, Jr., author of *The Trail of the Lonesome Pine* and other popular tales. The town was incorporated as Mineral City in 1888 and adopted its present name in 1890. Government is by council and manager. Population: 4,153.

BIGAMY, big'ə-mē, is the crime of having more than one wife or husband at the same time. Although a distinction is sometimes made between *bigamy* (having two spouses), and *polygamy* (having more than two spouses), the words are frequently used interchangeably. Bigamy, although not a crime at common law, was made a statutory felony in England in 1603. At present, it is a crime throughout the United States and Canada, as well as in England.

Bigamy is committed by the act of marrying while a former valid marriage is still in force, and the former spouse is still alive. In addition to being valid originally, the former marriage must not have been terminated by a valid divorce or annulment. Together with the other necessary elements, the act of engaging in a second or subsequent marriage ceremony is in itself sufficient to constitute bigamy, even without cohabitation or sexual intercourse. Where "common law" marriages (that is, unions not solemnized by a ceremony) are recognized, bigamy may be based on an existing "common law" marriage. If this is the case, or if the bigamous marriage itself is a "common law" one, it may be necessary for the prosecution to show cohabitation to establish the fact of marriage.

The unexplained absence of a former spouse for a specified period of time, varying among different jurisdictions, may be used as a defense in a prosecution for bigamy, even though the first spouse later turns out to be alive. At common law, life was "presumed" to continue for seven years, a period which has been shortened by statutes in some jurisdictions. Some courts also recognize as a defense to a bigamy prosecution a showing of an honest mistake of fact as to the death of a prior spouse.

Even though bigamy is a criminal offense, it is by no means clear in many cases exactly what circumstances may provide a basis for prosecution. In addition to the lack of uniformity in the courts as to the effect of "presumptions" concerning the continuation of life and honest mistakes of fact as to death, there is much legal confusion on the subject of the termination of prior marriages. In the United States, a great deal of the difficulty arises from the existence of the federal system, which leaves each state in part free to make its own determinations as to the legal effect of the divorce decrees of other states, and in part bound by the terms of such decrees.

As a general rule, recognition of divorce granted by another state is required by the "full faith and credit" clause of the U.S. Constitution (Article 4, Section 1). There are a few instances, however, most of them involving "tourist" or "quickie" divorces, where decrees granted by the courts of one state do not have to be accorded recognition by the courts of another state. In *Williams v. North Carolina* (1945), a man and woman domiciled in North Carolina had traveled to Nevada to obtain uncontested "divorces" from their respective spouses. The "divorced" parties then married each other and returned to North Carolina to live as man and wife. On these facts, the U.S. Supreme Court upheld a conviction for bigamous cohabitation in North Carolina, primarily on the ground that the Nevada court had no power to grant divorces, since the persons involved were not really domiciled in Nevada.

RICHARD L. HIRSHBERG, *Attorney at Law*

BIGELOW, big'ə-lō, **John** (1817–1911), American author and diplomat. He was born at Malden, Ulster County, N.Y., on Nov. 25, 1817. After graduating from Union College in 1835, he practiced law briefly. From 1848 to 1860 he was joint owner and editor, with William Cullen Bryant, of the New York *Evening Post*. He was the principal assistant to Republican candidate John C. Frémont in the presidential campaign of 1856. Appointed consul general at Paris in 1861, he wrote articles in the French press to win sympathy for the Union cause. As minister to France from April 1865 to September 1866, he handled with diplomatic skill the difficult problems arising from Napoleon III's efforts to establish an empire in Mexico. He was secretary of state of New York for one term (1875–1877). His remaining years were spent in writing and editing.

While in Paris, Bigelow had discovered the original manuscript of Benjamin Franklin's *Autobiography*, which he edited and printed (1868). He wrote a *Life of Benjamin Franklin* (1874) and edited *The Complete Works of Benjamin Franklin* (10 vols., 1887–88). His other writings include books on Swedenborgianism; *France and the Confederate Navy, 1862–1868* (1888); and *Retrospections of an Active Life*, (5 vols., 1909–13), the last two volumes of which were completed by his son, John. Bigelow died in New York City on Dec. 19, 1911.

BIGELOW, big'ə-lō, **Melville Madison** (1846–1921), American law teacher and author. He was born at Eaton Rapids, Mich., on Aug. 2, 1846. He graduated from the University of Michigan in 1866, took his law degree there two years later, and received his Ph.D. from Harvard in 1879. Bigelow was one of the founders of the Boston University Law School (1872) and taught there for the rest of his life, serving as dean from 1902 until 1911. He died in Boston on May 4, 1921.

Bigelow compiled, edited, or wrote numerous books on legal subjects, many of which became standard texts. He also did important research in early English legal history. His works include *The Law of Estoppel* (1872), *The Law of Fraud* (1877), *Elements of the Law of Torts* (1878), *Elements of Equity* (1879), *Placita Anglo-Normannica* (1879), *History of Procedure in England* (1880), and *Law of Fraud on Its Civil Side* (2 vols., 1888–90).

BIGFOOT is an apelike creature believed by some persons to exist in certain areas of the United States and Canada. It has been called *Sasquatch* by Canadian Indian tribes. Stories about it resemble those of the abominable snowman, or yeti, of Asia.

Hundreds of persons since 1840 have reported sighting such a creature in wooded areas of the Pacific Northwest, California, New Jersey, Pennsylvania, Ohio, Illinois, and British Columbia, and one photographer took a brief movie sequence supposedly showing a bigfoot in northern California in 1967. Tracks measuring up to more than 17 inches (43 cm) long and 7 inches (18 cm) wide, and attributed to bigfoot, have also been found. However, no specimen has ever been captured or photographed clearly.

Bigfoot is generally described as a primate resembling a man or ape, 6 to 8 feet (1.8–2.4 meters) tall, standing erect on two feet, with massive shoulders and a body covered with gray, black, or brown hair. It flees when approached, and generally makes no sound. Although most scientists do not recognize its existence, a few believe that it may be the descendant of an extinct apelike creature, Gigantopithecus, that may have crossed the Bering land bridge from Asia to North America in prehistoric times. Indians of the Pacific Northwest and western Canada for generations have perpetuated legends about *Sasquatch* and similar creatures with other names.

BIGGERS, big'ərz, **Earl Derr** (1884–1933), American writer. He was born at Warren, Ohio, on Aug. 26, 1884. After graduating from Harvard College in 1907, he became a columnist and dramatic critic on the Boston *Traveler*. In 1911 he moved to New York City, where he devoted himself to writing fiction and plays. His *Seven Keys to Baldpate* (1913) was popular as a novel and was also successful as a stage play and as a silent and talking motion picture.

Biggers was best known, however, as the creator of Charlie Chan, a sagacious Chinese detective who quoted ancient maxims of his native land. The first of the "Charlie Chan" books, many of which were made into films, was *The House Without a Key* (1925). This was followed by *The Chinese Parrot* (1926), *Behind That Curtain* (1928), *The Black Camel* (1929), *Charlie Chan Carries On* (1930), and *Keeper of the Keys* (1932). Among Biggers' other works of fiction were *Love Insurance* (1914), *The Agony Column* (1916), and *Fifty Candles* (1926). He died at Pasadena, Calif., on April 5, 1933.

BIGGERS, big'ərz, **John David** (1888–), American glass manufacturer. He was born in St. Louis, Mo., on Dec. 19, 1888. He was educated at the University of Michigan and in 1914 joined the Owens Bottle Company in Toledo, Ohio. In 1926 he resigned the vice presidency of the company to enter the automobile industry, but in 1930 he became president of the Libbey-Owens-Ford Glass Company in Toledo.

In 1941, Biggers went to Washington, D.C., to be director of production in the Office of Production Management, and in August of that year he went to London to expedite lend-lease aid to Britain.

He returned to the presidency of Libbey-Owens-Ford in October 1941 and served until 1953. He was chairman and chief executive officer of the company from 1953 to 1960.

HARRY ENGELS FROM NATIONAL AUDUBON SOCIETY

Rocky Mountain bighorn (*Ovis canadensis*)

BIGHORN, a type of wild mountain sheep of western North America. These sheep range from British Columbia, Canada, to the hills of North Dakota, Nebraska, Colorado, and New Mexico. They are especially numerous near the headwaters of the Yellowstone River.

Anatomy. The common Rocky Mountain bighorn (*Ovis canadensis*) is a strongly built sheep, standing from 14 to 19 inches (35 to 48 cm) tall at the shoulder. The length of the head and body ranges from 4 to 6 feet (1.2 to 1.8 meters); the tail is normally 3 to 6 inches (7 to 15 cm) long. In summer the coat of the bighorn is a tawny yellow, while in winter it may be a grayish brown. Frequently there is a dark line along the spine. The underparts and conspicuous roundish patch on the buttocks are whitish. The face is an ashy color; the muzzle is narrow and the ears pointed. Some males have a fringe of long hair down the front of the neck. The horns of the ram (male) are massive; they sweep around backward in a spiral and may measure 40 to 42 inches (about 1 meter) along the outer curve. The female has slightly curved horns, about an inch (2 or 3 cm) long.

Natural History. Bighorns prefer fairly dry upland and mountain regions and often occupy the rough and precipitous parts of these areas. They find plentiful pasturage between the highest growth of timber and the snow or ice of the summits. Bighorns usually feed during the morning and evening hours and rest during the heat of the day. Their food consists of grass, flowers, young plants, and leaves. During the summer months the sheep, especially the males, wander around in small flocks and often climb to high points or an overhanging ledge from which they can see the approach of any enemy. In winter they descend to lower regions and often stay in mountain gorges. When faced with danger, the bighorns display a high degree of speed, agility, and endurance.

Reproduction. The rams fight for the females during the late fall and early winter. The gestation period for bighorns is from 150 to 180 days. In the spring the female seeks an inaccessible region in which to give birth, producing from one to three young. The young mature in about three years.

Related Sheep. There are two varieties of Rocky Mountain bighorn. One, found in Utah, is a small, pale bighorn known as *Nelson's bighorn;* the other is a large, black bighorn, found in British Columbia, and called *Ston's bighorn.* A species closely related to the Rocky Mountain bighorn is *Dall's sheep,* found in central Alaska. These sheep are white and have moderate-sized horns. There are other related mountain sheep in parts of Europe and Asia. All the mountain sheep belong to the genus *Ovis.*

BIGHORN MOUNTAINS, an outlying range of the Rocky Mountains, extending through the north central part of Wyoming into southern Montana. Its length is about 120 miles (193 km), and its width varies from 30 to 50 miles (48 to 80 km). The mountains are a rugged barrier between the Great Plains on the east and Bighorn Basin on the west, above both of which portions rise 7,000 to 9,000 feet (2,133 to 2,743 meters). The highest summit, Cloud Peak (in Wyoming), is 13,165 feet (4,012 meters) above sea level. Several small glaciers lie in the shadow of the higher peaks, and formerly these ice masses were of considerably greater extent.

The mountains are due to a great uplift in the earth's crust—an arch whose crest has been truncated by erosion, leaving an elevated central area of Archaean granite with flanking ridges of Cambrian, Ordovician, and Carboniferous sandstone and limestone. The central area of granite presents remarkably fine Alpine scenery, and all through the mountains are large running streams teeming with trout. Most of the higher region is heavily forested and is embraced in the Bighorn Forest Reservation. Important oil fields have been developed in the Bighorn Basin.

BIGHORN RIVER, a stream in northern Wyoming and southern Montana, 461 miles (742 km) long. It is formed at Riverton, Wyo., by the junction of the Popo Agie and Wind rivers and flows north between the Absaroka Range on the west and the Bighorn Mountains on the east. The Bighorn River joins the Yellowstone River in Treasure County, Mont. It drains a stockraising region in the Absaroka foothills in addition to the agricultural and oil-producing Bighorn Basin.

BIGLOW PAPERS, big-lō, a masterpiece of humorous, satirical verse by the American poet James Russell Lowell (q.v.). *The Biglow Papers,* first and second series, consist of one prose piece and 19 poems in Yankee dialect, purportedly written by Hosea Biglow, a rustic political philosopher, and edited by his friend, Rev. Homer Wilbur.

The first series was inspired by the author's indignation over the Mexican War. Five "papers" were published in the Boston *Courier,* beginning in June 1846, and four in the *Anti-Slavery Standard,* ending in September 1847. All were anonymous, but when the series was published as a book in 1848, with the name of the author, Lowell became famous. Fourteen years later, urged by his friends and in response to a widespread public demand, he began the second series, the 11 numbers of which were published in the *Atlantic Monthly* between January 1862 and May 1866. The second series deals with slavery, states' rights, the Civil War, and national politics in general.

BIGNONIA, big-nō′nē-ə, is a genus of woody vines whose only species is *Bignonia capreolata.* It is often called the *cross vine* because a cross appears on cross-sectional views of the stem. It is also known as *trumpet flower.*

Bignonia is an evergreen, climbing shrub native to the southeastern United States, where it is found in woods and swamps. It often climbs to 50 feet (15 meters). It has oval-shaped leaves composed of smaller leaflets. Tendrils (slender outgrowths) extend from the leaves and cling to the vine's support. *Bignonia* is frequently grown for the profusion and beauty of its flowers, which are deep orange to reddish on the outside and paler within.

BIGOD, bī′god, **Hugh** (died ?1176), English nobleman. On the death of his elder brother William in 1120, he inherited a vast estate in Essex and Suffolk, including the great castle at Framlingham, granted to his father, Roger Bigod (died 1107), by Henry I. Hugh was created *1st earl of Norfolk* by King Stephen around 1136, in recognition of his services in the struggle against the empress Matilda. Hugh changed sides several times, however, in the ensuing civil wars, and in 1153 supported Henry II's claim to the succession against Stephen's son Eustace. Twenty years later he played a leading role in the unsuccessful revolt against Henry, led by the latter's eldest son.

Roger Bigod (died 1221), Hugh's son, became *2d earl of Norfolk.* He was one of the leaders of the barons' rebellion that obtained the Magna Carta from King John in 1215. Roger's grandson, *Roger Bigod, 4th earl of Norfolk* (died 1270), joined Simon de Montfort's party against Henry III in 1264 and sat in the historic parliament of 1265. The last of the family to hold the title was *Roger Bigod, 5th earl* (1245–1306).

BIGOT, bē-gō′, **François** (1703–?1777), French administrator in Canada. He was born at Bordeaux, France, on Jan. 30, 1703, and trained in law and public administration. Family connections won him favor at court, and in 1739 he was appointed administrator of Cape Breton. Notwithstanding the capitulation of Louisbourg, the capital of his district, in 1745—an event attributed in part to his misappropriation of government arms—he was appointed intendant in French Canada (New France) in 1749. In that capacity he perpetrated large-scale frauds until the capitulation of Montreal to the British in 1760, after which he was imprisoned in France for 11 months, heavily fined, and banished. He died in obscurity in Switzerland.

BIHAR, bē-här′, is one of the 17 states of the Republic of India. Located in northern India, it is bordered on the north by Nepal, on the east by West Bengal, on the south by Orissa and Madhya Pradesh, and on the west by Uttar Pradesh. The area is 67,196 square miles (174,038 sq km). The state capital is Patna (1961 population: 363,700).

The state is made up of two distinct regions. Northern Bihar is a wide plain covering about two fifths of the state. It has most of the state's population. This agricultural region is drained by the Ganges River and several of its tributaries. The chief crops are rice, maize, wheat, and sugarcane. Southern Bihar is a hilly upland, part of the Chota Nagpur plateau, and is noted for

WERNER BISCHOF, FROM MAGNUM

IN BIHAR'S NORTHERN PLAINS, drought can dry up irrigation ditches, causing crop failure and famine.

its mineral production. About 90 percent of India's coal is taken from the Damodar valley fields, and most of the world's mica comes from the Hazaribagh district. Also in this region, at Jamshedpur, is India's largest steel mill, which in 1961 produced over half of India's total output of finished steel.

Annual precipitation ranges from 40 to 60 inches (102 to 152 cm) in different parts of the state, most of it falling during the southwest monsoon season (June through September). The other months are dry. Temperatures occasionally dip to the freezing point in winter and may rise to over 100° F (37° C) in May.

With a population in 1961 of 46,455,610, Bihar is India's second most populous state (after Uttar Pradesh). The average density is 691 persons per square mile (266 per sq km), but in the plains densities of nearly 1,000 (386 per sq km) are found. The population is overwhelmingly rural. The majority are Hindus, but there is a sizable Muslim minority in the towns. In southern Bihar there are nearly 3 million non-Hindu "tribal" people.

Northern Bihar was the setting of early Buddhism and Jainism; Gaya (1961 population: 151,105), especially, has important Buddhist associations. This region, known anciently as Magadha, was the focus of two great dynasties, the Maurya (4th and 3d centuries B.C.) and the Gupta (4th and 5th centuries A.D.), each a center of the Indian civilization of its time.

JOEL M. ANDRESS
Central Washington State College

BIHARI, bē-hä′rē, is a group of dialects of the Indo-Aryan subfamily of Indo-European languages. They are spoken mainly in the state of Bihar, India, and are most closely affiliated with Bengali, Assamese, and Oriya. The dialects fall into three divisions: Maithili, Magahi, and Bhojpuriya. The first two are differentiated from all other Indo-Aryan languages by their complicated system of honorific verb forms.

The literary development of Maithili, beginning in the 14th century or earlier, had as its greatest figure the poet Vidyapati (14th–15th century), who sang of the loves of Krishna and Radha. Imitation of his poems by the Bengalis led to the development of an artificial mixture of Maithili and Bengali, called Braja-buli, in which much lyric poetry was composed in honor of Vishnu. Rabindranath Tagore (1861–1941) also composed poetry in this dialect. Maithili

737

is no longer used as a literary language; in Bihar, it has been replaced by Hindi and Urdu. See also INDIA—9. *Languages.*

BIISK, byē'isk, is a city in western Siberia at the foot of the Altai Mountains in the Altai *krai* of the Russian republic, USSR. Situated on the Biya River, a headstream of the Ob, Biisk is the processing center of a rich agricultural area. Its industries include meat packing, sugar refining (based on the local sugar-beet crop), and dairying. The city is a railhead on a branch of the Trans-Siberian railroad, and the starting point of the Chuya highway leading across the mountains to Mongolia. Founded in 1709 as a Russian military strongpoint, Biisk began to develop in the late 1800's when Russian farmers settled in the area. Population: (1965) 175,000.

THEODORE SHABAD
Author of "Geography of the USSR"

BIJAGÓS ISLANDS, bē-zhə-gôsh', Portuguese-ruled islands in the Atlantic Ocean, just off the west coast of Africa. Known also as the *Bissagos Islands,* they are part of Portuguese Guinea. The group has an area of about 600 square miles (966 km). The largest of the 15 main islands are Orango, Formosa, Caravela, and Roxa. Bolama is the chief town. The people of the Bijagós Islands grow coconuts, rice, and fruit, and raise cattle and pigs. Population: (1960) 9,763.

BIJAPUR, bi-jä'pōōr, is a city in India about 250 miles (402 km) southeast of Bombay. It is the capital of Bijapur district in the state of Mysore. Known in ancient times as Vijayapur (city of victory), it was for centuries the capital of a rich and powerful kingdom. In 1489, Yusif Adil Shah founded an independent Muslim state here, which later became one of the five Muslim kingdoms of the Deccan. Aurangzeb captured the city of 1686, and in the 18th century the Marathas seized it. In 1818 it passed into British hands and was given to the rajah of Satara. Some magnificent specimens of Islamic architecture and sculpture are found in Bijapur. The most notable example of the Mughul (Mogul) style is the Gol Gumbaz, tomb of Sultan Mohammed Adil Shah, built 1626–1656, with its great dome 124 feet (38 meters) in diameter. Equally famous is the fort, completed in 1566, surrounded by a wall 30–50 feet (9–15 meters) high and about six miles (10 km) long. One of the guns, cast in 1549, is said to be the largest piece of brass ordnance in existence. Bijapur is now a trading center for cotton. Chemicals, soap, and iron and copper products are manufactured. Population: (1961) 78,854.

BIJNS, bīns, **Anna** (?1494–1575), Flemish poet. Her last name is also spelled *Byns.* She was born in Antwerp, where she became a teacher and possibly a lay nun. She was an archenemy of reformed theology, particularly Lutheranism, and an ardent advocate of Roman Catholicism in the face of the growing strength of the Reformation in Flanders. Her powerful lyric poetry reflected her views. Called the "Sappho of Brabant," she is generally considered to be the foremost Dutch poet of the 16th century and is often credited with initiating the linguistic transition from Middle to Modern Dutch. Her work was published in three volumes (1528, 1548, 1567). She died in Antwerp on April 10, 1575.

BIKANER, bē'kə-när', a former state in India, was the second-largest princely state of the political agency known as Rajputana. On March 30, 1949, the state of Bikaner, comprising an area of over 23,000 square miles (over 59,570 sq km) was joined to the new state of Rajasthan and split into three districts: Bikaner in the southwest, containing the city of Bikaner, the former capital; Ganganagar in the north; and Churu in the southeast. The people of these districts are overwhelmingly Hindu and speak the Marwari dialect of Rajasthani. The Jats are the largest single group in the population.

The entire area is a plain interspersed by low undulating sandhills. It lies in the northern reaches of the Thar Desert between the Indian state of Punjab and West Pakistan. Rainfall at the city of Bikaner averages 11.5 inches (29.2 cm) annually, falling mainly during the summer. There are no perennial streams. Natural vegetation is sparse and shrubby, with few trees. Agriculture is carried on largely by irrigation, the main irrigated area being in the relatively densely populated Ganganagar district, along the former course of the Ghaggar River, now dry. Pulses, millets, and irrigated wheat are the main crops. Pasturage of sheep, cattle, and camels is also quite important.

The state was founded in the 15th century by Bika, a Rajput of the Rathor clan, who conquered the area from various other Rajput clans, as well as from the Jats and the Muslims. The fort of Bikaner, just north of the city, was built in 1485, and the city itself was begun in 1488. In the 16th century the state of Bikaner fell under the sway of the Mughul (Mogul) empire, though retaining its autonomous Hindu rule. Rai Singh, the first raja of Bikaner, gave the Mughul emperor Akbar valuable military aid in a number of campaigns, and was rewarded with extensive grants of land in Hissar, in southern Punjab. Late in the 17th century the title of maharaja was bestowed upon the ruler.

The turbulent 18th century was marked by a decline in Mughul domination together with constant warfare between the states of Bikaner and Jodhpur, to the south. A revolt of *thakurs,* or feudal chiefs, early in the 19th century caused the maharaja to apply for British protection, which was accorded by a treaty concluded in 1818. British troops thereupon restored order to the state, but final suppression of the *thakurs* was not achieved until the 1880's. The state remained loyal to the British in the Indian (Sepoy) Mutiny of 1857 and was rewarded with additional territory. The famous Bikaner Camel Corps, serving with the British Army, gained distinction in China in 1900 and in the Middle East during World War I.

JOSEPH E. SCHWARTZBERG
University of Minnesota

BIKANER, bē'kə-när', is a city in India, Rajasthan state, about 245 miles (394 km) southwest of Delhi. Founded in 1488, it was the capital of the former princely state of Bikaner until 1949. The city is an important trading center for wool, hides, and building stone, and manufactures a wide variety of handicrafts. The Anup Sanskrit Library, housing one of the world's great collections of Sanskrit manuscripts, is situated here. Population: (1961) 150,500.

JOSEPH E. SCHWARTZBERG
University of Minnesota

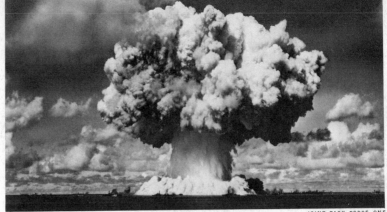

BIKINI ATOLL was the site of the first peacetime atomic bomb test in July 1946. The characteristic mushroom cloud is shown rising from the underwater nuclear explosion.

BIKINI, bə-kē′nē, is the northernmost atoll of the Ralik Chain, which is the westerly chain of the Marshall Islands, a United States-administered United Nations trust territory in the south Pacific Ocean. The atoll consists of coral reefs and more than a score of islands arranged in an irregular oval, forming a lagoon about 12 miles (19 km) wide and over 22 miles (35 km) long. The land area is less than 3 square miles (8 sq km). The atoll, which lies some 225 miles (362 km) northwest of Kwajalein, takes its name from its largest island, Bikini (known before World War II as Escholtz Island). It is best known as the site of Operation Crossroads, a series of two peacetime atomic bomb tests conducted in July 1946 under the direction of Vice Adm. William H.P. Blandy, who commanded a U.S. Army-Navy Joint Task Force. The test necessitated the prior removal from Bikini Island of its native population of 167 Micronesians, who were relocated on other islands in the Marshalls.

On July 1, 1946, a Nagasaki-type, 20-kiloton atomic bomb (the equivalent of 20,000 tons, or 18,000 MT, of TNT) was dropped from a B-29 bomber over an unmanned fleet of 75 Japanese and obsolete American vessels in the lagoon. The bomb was timed to explode above the ocean surface. Damage to the ships was extensive and it was reported that the radiation dosage would have been lethal to any personnel within the blast area. The second test was held on July 25. This time, with nearly 100 vessels in the target area, a 20-kiloton bomb was suspended in the lagoon at a depth of 90 feet (27 meters) and exploded electrically. It raised an enormous column of radioactive water and steam to a height of about a mile. Many ships were sunk and intensive radioactivity was reported in the waters of the lagoon and on the remaining ships. These tests, attended by representatives of the United Nations Atomic Energy Commission and by correspondents from all major nations, reconfirmed the awesome destructive power of the atomic bomb and proved its effectiveness against massed surface naval craft.

BILAC, bi-läk′, **Olavo Braz Martins dos Guimarães** (1865–1918), Brazilian poet. He was born in Rio de Janeiro, on Dec. 16, 1865. When he was only 23 he rose to prominence with the publication of *Poesias* (1888), a volume of poems that climaxed the postromantic development of Brazilian poetry toward Parnassianism. The original edition contained three sections (*Panóplias, Via-láctea,* and *Sarças de fogo*), in which two central qualities stand out: perfection of form in the sonnets of *Via-láctea,* and sensuous subjectivity in the love poems of *Sarças de fogo.*

Poesias was enlarged in the 1902 edition by three new sections (*Alma inquieta, As viagens,* and *O caçador de esmeraldas*). The poem *A alvorada de amor* (*Dawn of Love*) eloquently illustrates Bilac's values. Adam, conscious of life through the human love created by Eve's sin, exalts earth above heaven and man above God. *Tarde* (1919), a final volume appearing shortly after Bilac's death, is characterized by nostalgic reflectiveness and contemplation. Bilac died in Rio de Janeiro on Dec. 28, 1918.

Foremost as poet, Bilac was also a productive journalist, critic, and lecturer. His scope is indicated by *Crônicas e novelas* (1894), *Crítica e fantasia* (1904), and *Conferências literárias* (1906). In collaboration with others he produced such diverse works as a treatise on versification and instructional books for children.

Bilac was devoted to formal perfection; his poems are continually impressive for their correct and graceful versification, exact diction, and logical development. Precisely wrought images involve all the senses. Bilac appealed to cultured tastes, but the polished clarity of his verse enabled the broad public as well to appreciate his rich eloquence and powerful emotional content. His intensely sensuous tone diverges from Parnassian impassivity, but Bilac's subjectivity is unexpectedly compatible with his formal aesthetic principles. For him, emotional and sensory responses, expressed in the varied moods of love, define man's humanity. Bilac feels love is the source of unity and form, but these represent his conscious idea of beauty, and beauty is his supreme goal and final morality. Each value reveals the others through a reciprocal symbolism that gives Bilac's poetry its authentic and enduring appeal.

HENRY J. MAXWELL, *Texas Technological College*

BILBAO, bēl-vä′ō, capital of the province of Vizcaya in Spain, is situated on the Nervión River, 7 miles (11 km) inland from the Bay of Biscay. It is the largest city in the Basque section of northern Spain. Surrounded on three sides by wooded mountains, it has a temperate, humid climate. Five bridges connect the old Basque city on the right bank of the river with the newer, contrasting section on the left.

The exploitation of ores, begun about 1870, has made the production of iron and steel the most important industry and has contributed to the development of Bilbao into one of the main industrial centers of the country. On a smaller scale, the city produces building materials and various consumer goods, particularly fabrics and hats, for home use and export. Bilbao, with its good port facilities and shipyards, is a major shipping center. A large amount of crude oil is exported to British steel mills.

BILBAO'S Plaza de Federico Moyua is the center from which streets radiate through the city's modern section.

The city has many churches, the oldest being Santiago, a Gothic church dating from about the time of the city's founding (1300). Others are San Antonio Abad, Los Santos Juanes, and San Vicente Mártir, all in the Renaissance style. On the outskirts of the city is the 16th century mountaintop shrine of Begoña. The Museo de Bellas Artes has a fine collection of paintings by El Greco, Francisco Goya, and others.

History. Although there are legends that the city occupies the site of the ancient Roman town of Flaviobriga, its modern founder was Diego López de Haro, who established the city on June 15, 1300. On the death of its founder and his widow, the city passed under the protection of the Castilian crown, retaining certain municipal privileges. During the 16th and 17th centuries the merchants' guilds were important in the government of the city. Bilbao's fortunes subsequently declined with those of Spain, and they did not revive until the 19th century, when industrial development began.

Because of its sheltered port facilities, the city was often a prize of war and suffered many sieges. In the 19th century the province of Vizcaya was generally in sympathy with the Carlist pretenders, while Bilbao, the seat of considerable opposition to Don Carlos, was attacked by Carlist forces and was often the center of rebel activities. During the Spanish Civil War, Bilbao was loyal to the republic and, for a brief time (1936–1937), harbored the Basque autonomous government. The city was captured by Gen. Francisco Franco's forces in 1937. Although, by the 1950's, the Basque tongue had been almost completely supplanted by Spanish, an official campaign against its use was much resented and caused a revival of the language in the city. Population: (1960) 293,939.

GREGORY RABASSA, *Columbia University*

BILBO, bil'bō, **Theodore Gilmore** (1877–1947), American politician. He was born in Juniper Grove, Miss., on Oct. 13, 1877. Although his parents were poor, he studied for three years at the University of Nashville, earning his way by working in a series of menial jobs. He entered politics in 1903, after having been licensed as a Baptist preacher, but was unsuccessful as a candidate for circuit clerk of Pearl River County, Miss. He then studied law at Vanderbilt University, became a Mississippi state senator in 1907, and was admitted to the Tennessee bar in 1908.

By this time, Bilbo had acquired demagogic skills which enabled him, despite charges of corruption and abuse of public office, to win popular support. A Democrat, he served as governor of Mississippi in 1916–1920 and 1928–1932 and as United States senator from Mississippi from 1935 to 1947.

Bilbo was a member of the Ku-Klux Klan and became nationally known as an advocate of states' rights and white supremacy. He urged the deportation of all American Negroes to Africa and appealed to his supporters in Mississippi to use any means they could to keep Negroes from the polls. In 1946 he was reelected to the U.S. Senate for a third term but was barred from taking his seat in January 1947 pending the dismissal of charges that he had intimidated Negro voters in his state and that he had accepted favors from war contractors. In the meantime he underwent cancer surgery and died in New Orleans, La., on Aug. 21, 1947.

BILDERDIJK, bil'dər-dĭk, **Willem** (1756–1831), Dutch poet. He was born in Amsterdam on Sept. 7, 1756. In 1782 he received a doctorate of law at Leiden University and became an advocate at the Hague until 1795, when he was forced into exile for refusing allegiance to the Batavian Republic. He returned to the Netherlands in 1806 and became state librarian under the patronage of King Louis Bonaparte. After the restoration to power of the House of Orange in 1815 he expected a professorial appointment at Amsterdam but had to content himself with tutoring and private lecturing. By this time he had become a dominant influence on the intellectual life of his time. Bilderdijk died in Haarlem on Dec. 18, 1831.

Bilderdijk began writing verse at an early age and achieved great popularity as a poet. As a forerunner of Dutch romanticism, he had tremendous influence on writers of the early 19th century, but the great bulk of his voluminous writing is in a neoclassic vein, much of it dull and pedantic. To him the role of the poet was that of a seer; apparently he considered his own poetry, therefore, divinely inspired and above the ordinary and laborious requirements of rewriting and editing.

Although he opposed liberal ideas, Bilderdijk fought against the complacent intellectual and political climate of the day. His work, consequently, created a change of atmosphere that marked the end of the literary apathy characteristic of the Netherlands in the 18th century.

His poetry of ideas is exemplified by *De ziekte der geleerden* (1807; *The Disease of the Learned*). An unfinished epic, *De ondergang der eerste wereld* (*The Destruction of the First World*), was published in 1820. His smaller poems—lyrics and ballads—are among the classics of Dutch literature.

BILE, bīl, is a yellowish orange fluid that is secreted by the liver and aids in the digestion of fats. Bile is produced continuously and is passed from the liver to the gall bladder, where it is stored and concentrated. When food enters the small intestine, the gall bladder contracts, emptying the bile into the duodenum, the upper portion of the small intestine.

The major components of bile are water, bile salts, the pigment bilirubin, and two fatty substances, cholesterol and lecithin. Only the bile salts, however, are important in digestion. When these salts combine with the food mass, they emulsify any fats that are present, breaking up the large fat globules into tiny droplets. This process increases the surface area of the fat globules so that they may be broken down more easily by fat-splitting enzymes.

Bile salts also aid in the absorption of the end products of fat digestion and are important in the absorption of the fat-soluble vitamins, A, D, E, and K. After the bile salts have been used, most of them are reabsorbed and carried back to the liver, where they are used, in turn, to produce more bile.

In addition to its digestive function, bile also plays a role in excretion, ridding the body of bilirubin, the end product of hemoglobin destruction. When bile is secreted into the small intestine, the bilirubin combines with the food mass and is excreted from the body in the feces.

BILFINGER, bil′fing-ər **Georg Bernhard** (1693–1750), German philosopher, mathematician, and political leader. His surname is also spelled *Bülffinger*.

He was born at Bad Cannstatt, Württemberg, on Jan. 23, 1693. After studying theology at Tübingen, he enrolled in 1719 at Halle, where he became a student of the philosopher Christian von Wolff, a follower of Gottfried Wilhelm von Leibniz. In 1721, Bilfinger was appointed professor of philosophy at Halle, and in 1724 he became professor of mathematics there. A year later he lectured at St. Petersburg, Russia, at the invitation of Peter the Great, and he spent the next several years abroad. In 1728 he was awarded the highest prize of the Paris Academy for his dissertation *De causa gravitatis*. He returned to Germany and became professor of theology at Tübingen in 1731.

In 1735, Bilfinger was named privy councillor by Charles Alexander, duke of Württemberg, and two years later he became a member of the regency council. As a statesman, he gained a reputation for his resourcefulness and administrative ability. Bilfinger died at Stuttgart on Feb. 18, 1750.

Bilfinger's most important work was *Dilucidationes philosophicae de Deo, anima humana, mundo et generalibus rerum affectionibus,* published in 1725. It defended but also modified the philosophy of Leibniz and Bilfinger's teacher Wolff. Whereas Leibniz had maintained that nature is made up of units of force, called monads, which are at the same time both physical and spiritual, Bilfinger claimed that monads could be of different types, some spiritual and some physical. He further asserted, in opposition to Wolff and Leibniz, that the term "divine harmony" refers not to the universe but only to the relationship between the body and the soul.

BILHARZIASIS. See SCHISTOSOMIASIS.

BILIRAN ISLAND, bē-lē′rän, is in the central Philippines, in the province of Leyte. It is situated off the northwest coast of Leyte Island, in the Samar Sea. It is about 20 miles long and 12 miles wide (32 by 19 km). The terrain is mountainous, the highest peak reaching 4,230 feet (1,289 meters). Agricultural products include coconuts, rice, and corn. Sulfur is mined; shale oil is found; and a fishing industry has been developed. The chief towns are Caibiran on the east coast, and Naval on the west coast. Population: (1960) 80,130.

BILL OF RIGHTS, a formal constitutional declaration or legislative assertion by which a government both (1) defines fundamental rights and liberties of its citizens and (2) establishes their protection against arbitrary or capricious interference or infringement by the government. Specifically, in Western political tradition, the term is used to signify the Bill of Rights (1689) of England, the Declaration of the Rights of Man and of the Citizen (1789) of France, and in the United States the first 10 amendments to the federal Constitution (1791) and portions of the constitutions of the individual states that establish similar guarantees.

By extension of meaning, bills of rights sometimes are regarded as including the definition and establishment of rights and liberties through tradition or in documents or enactments prior or subsequent to any formal declaration bearing the name. In Great Britain, for example, many of the rights and liberties safeguarded the citizens are not specified in the Bill of Rights of 1689 but are established in common law or defined in the Magna Carta (1215) and the Petition of Right (1628). In the United States, where the protections of its Bill of Rights derive significantly from English sources, the general term "bill of rights" sometimes is construed to include also those additional or strengthened protections asserted throughout the federal Constitution (importantly in the 14th Amendment) and enunciated in constitutional decisions of the federal courts.

Formal bills of rights or their equivalents in legislative enactments—although too often disregarded—have been written by the governments of most nations of the world. In 1948 the Universal Declaration of Human Rights was adopted by the United Nations to serve as a standard of definition of rights among the nations.

Among provisions most commonly found in bills of rights are those asserting the general right to life and liberty; defining specific protections for the freedom of speech, press, and religious expression, the right of petition and of peaceful assembly, the right to equal protection before the law, and the right to public trial; and protections against arbitrary arrest or unreasonable search, against excessive bails or fines, and against cruel or unusual punishment. See also CIVIL RIGHTS AND CIVIL LIBERTIES.

UNITED STATES

In American history and constitutional law the term "Bill of Rights" usually signifies the first 10 amendments to the Constitution of the United States. These amendments, more precisely the first eight of them, specify certain basic freedoms and procedural safeguards of which the individual may not be deprived by governmental power. Taken together, these specified freedoms and pro-

tections are the core of American civil liberty and
provide the constitutional basis for judicial protection of the rights of the individual. Of particular
importance are the provisions of the 1st Amendment (freedoms of religion, speech, press, assembly, and petition); the 4th Amendment (prohibition of unreasonable searches and seizures); the
5th Amendment (prohibitions against double
jeopardy and self-incrimination; no taking of life,
liberty, or property without due process of law;
requirement of fair compensation when private
property is taken for public use); the 6th Amendment (procedural safeguards in criminal prosecutions); and the 8th Amendment (prohibitions
against excessive bail and cruel and unusual punishments). See also CONSTITUTION OF THE
UNITED STATES, where the text of the Constitution, as amended to date, is set out in full.

The Constitution itself, as submitted to the
13 states for ratification in 1787, contained several provisions of major significance for civil liberties—for example, the clauses in Article I, section 9, forbidding bills of attainder, ex post facto
laws, and suspension of the writ of habeas corpus
—but it did not include a catalogue of individual
rights and immunities. The probable explanation
for this omission is that the delegates to the Constitutional Convention did not expect the new
national government to expand its regulatory
activities to any great extent, and therefore
thought that there would be few occasions when
federal power would come into collision with
individual interests and concerns. Liberty-
conscious Americans of the post-Revolutionary
period were, however, unwilling to take the risk
that a powerful national government might some
day move to impair individual liberty.

Indeed, the Bill of Rights tradition was so
strong at this time that by 1789, bills of individual rights had been written into eight state
constitutions. Of these state documents the Virginia Bill of Rights, drafted in large part by
George Mason and adopted in Virginia in 1776,
was the most influential model for what became
the Bill of Rights of the national Constitution.
A Virginian, James Madison, was a principal
draftsman of the first 10 amendments to the Constitution, and use of the Virginia Bill as a drafting model is evident from a comparison of the
two texts concerned.

Throughout the time that the Constitution
was before the state conventions for ratification
(1787–1788), strong concern was expressed in
every state at the absence from that document
of a detailed Bill of Rights. Criticisms were
severe in Virginia and Massachusetts, for example,
and North Carolina went so far as to make its
ratification of the Constitution expressly conditional on the adoption of a Bill of Rights. Historians are agreed generally that the Constitution
might never have been ratified if its proponents
had not given assurance that the proposal of a
bill of individual rights would be an early order
of business at the First Congress convened under
the new Constitution. This pledge was honored,
and the first 10 amendments, which constitute the
Bill of Rights, were submitted together in 1789
and their ratification by the states was completed
on Dec. 15, 1791. The first 10 amendments are,
therefore, virtually contemporaneous with the
Constitution itself.

As originally drafted and ratified, the Bill of
Rights was understood as having effect only as a
limitation on what might be done constitutionally
by the new national government. State, county,
and municipal officers were, of course, subject to
the limitations prescribed by each state's own
constitution, but the Supreme Court early decided (*Barron* v. *Baltimore*, 7 Peters 243, 1833)
that the guarantees of the first 10 amendments
to the Constitution of the United States did not
apply as limitations on the power of the states
and their subordinate local authorities. Suppose,
for example, that a state legislature, at some
time before 1868, had enacted a statute calling
for the censorship of newspapers within the state.
That statute could have been challenged in the
courts as violative of some relevant provision of
the local state constitution, but no question of
federal constitutional law would have been presented. The 1st Amendment's guarantee of freedom of the press, like all the other provisions
of the national Bill of Rights, operated, of its
own force, only to bar restrictive action by the
national government. The states were free, subject only to their own constitutions, to place
such restrictions on civil liberties as their legislatures might see fit to impose.

The original constitutional situation was profoundly changed by the adoption of the 14th
Amendment in 1868. The key clause of that
amendment, in relation to the judicial protection
of civil liberties, reads as follows: "nor shall any
State deprive any person of life, liberty, or property, without due process of law." In a long
series of constitutional decisions, the Supreme
Court has interpreted this clause as a general
limitation on state power, thus making many of
the specific protections of the Bill of Rights as
good against the states as against the national
government. The "incorporation" of the essential
provisions of the first eight amendments into the
due process clause of the 14th is one of the most
important developments in constitutional history.

As the principal steps in the process of incorporation, the Supreme Court has held: (1) that
the essential civic freedoms guaranteed against
unreasonable federal interference by the Bill of
Rights—for example, the free exercise of religion,
freedom of speech, and freedom of the press—
are aspects of the "liberty" specified in the above
quoted clause of the 14th Amendment and so
secured to the individual against state as well
as federal impairment; and (2) that certain of
the procedural safeguards specified in the Bill of
Rights—for example, an accused's right to counsel
in felony prosecutions and the prohibition of
cruel and unusual punishments—are aspects of
the "due process" guaranteed by the 14th Amendment and so secured to accused persons in state,
as well as federal, adjudicative proceedings.

This is not to say that the "due process" of
the 14th Amendment embodies each and every
one of the specific protections recited in the Bill
of Rights. The incorporation of the Bill of Rights
into the 14th Amendment extends only to such of
the safeguards of the first eight amendments as
are "of the very essence of a scheme of ordered
liberty." (Cardozo, J., in *Palko* v. *Connecticut*,
302 U.S. 319, 1937.) As applied by the Supreme
Court, this text excludes from incorporation such
procedural safeguards as the necessity of a grand
jury indictment in prosecutions for crime (5th
Amendment), the right of trial by jury in criminal cases (6th Amendment), and the right of
trial by jury in civil suits at common law (7th
Amendment). But the court affirmed the 5th
Amendment privilege against self-incrimination in

Escobedo v. *Illinois* (1964), on the right to an attorney during police questioning, and in *Miranda* v. *Arizona* (1966), ruling invalid any confession unless the suspect had been warned of his right to be silent and to see a lawyer.

Sharp differences of opinion developed among the members of the Supreme Court since World War II. Justice Hugo L. Black was particularly critical of the selective approach to "incorporation" and urged repeatedly in dissenting opinions that the 14th Amendment be interpreted to make all the specific protections of the Bill of Rights applicable as fully against the states as against the federal government. Although the court has moved in this direction, it is unlikely that it will move all the way; Justice Benjamin Cardozo's "ordered liberty" test seems well established. To this extent the procedural safeguards of the Bill of Rights apply more directly and comprehensively in federal than in state proceedings, and some differences in federal and state practice are therefore to be anticipated. The likelihood that serious differences will exist between federal and state procedures is greatly lessened, however, by the circumstance that almost every state constitution contains in its own bill of rights procedural safeguards substantially coextensive with those specified in the first eight amendments to the Constitution of the United States.

BRITAIN

The English Bill of Rights, enacted by the Convention Parliament on Dec. 16, 1689, is one of the three great landmarks of the English constitutional tradition, the others being Magna Carta (1215) and the Petition of Right (1628). The Bill of Rights was the product of the Glorious Revolution of 1688, whereby the absolutist James II was deposed and replaced with William and Mary; it represents the triumph of Parliament over the crown in the long contest for supremacy that had marked English history.

The Convention Parliament's offer of the English throne to William and Mary had been accompanied by a Declaration of Right, in which certain governmental principles and legal protections were set out as "the true, ancient, and indubitable rights and liberties of the people of this kingdom." In other words, the Declaration of Right stated the conditions on which the invitation to the new sovereigns was being extended. The declaration was accepted by William and Mary on Feb. 19, 1689, and the Bill of Rights was, in effect, a recasting of the declaration into the form of an act of Parliament. Thereafter in English political history, claims to royal prerogative were doomed, and parliamentary supremacy was established as the central principle of the English constitutional tradition.

The specific clauses of the Bill of Rights can be grouped into three broad categories: (1) provisions confirming and safeguarding the institution of parliamentary supremacy, notably those stating that parliaments are to be held frequently, that freedom of speech and debate in Parliament is guaranteed, that there can be no suspension of laws without parliamentary consent, and that parliamentary consent is required for the levying of money or the keeping of a standing army; (2) provisions settling the succession to the crown and restricting the succession to Protestants; and (3) provisions guaranteeing certain individual freedoms and procedural safeguards against impairment by governmental power, for example, the right of petition, prohibitions of excessive bail, and reaffirmation of the right to jury trial.

A century later the English Bill of Rights served as an important source for the first 10 amendments to the Constitution of the United States. Thus, the clause in the English Bill of Rights prohibiting excessive bail and cruel and unusual punishments was taken over, virtually word for word, in the Virginia Bill of Rights of 1776 and ultimately became the 8th Amendment to the Constitution of the United States.

See also DEMOCRACY—*The Development of Modern Democracy;* STATES' RIGHTS.

HARRY WILLMER JONES, *Columbia University*

THE U.S. BILL OF RIGHTS is viewed every year by thousands in the National Archives Building in Washington, D.C.

NATIONAL ARCHIVES

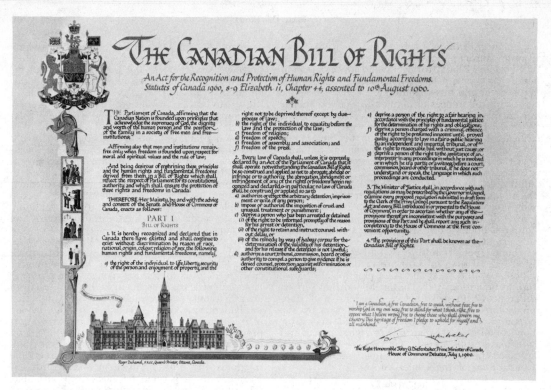

THE CANADIAN BILL OF RIGHTS was signed by Prime Minister John Diefenbaker in 1960.

CANADIAN BILL OF RIGHTS

The Canadian Bill of Rights is a legislative act rather than a formal amendment to the written Canadian constitution (the British North America Act of 1867). It became law in 1960, during the period when John G. Diefenbaker's Conservative government was in power. Since the 1940's, when he was a private member of the House of Commons, Diefenbaker had advocated passage of a bill that would recognize and protect human rights and fundamental freedoms. In 1958, after becoming prime minister, he introduced his bill in the House, but no further action was taken then. In 1960 the bill was reintroduced in slightly modified form. It was passed unanimously by the House on August 4 and by the Senate the next day.

The general purpose of the Canadian Bill of Rights, which consists of a preamble and two parts, is outlined in Section 1 of Part I:

"It is hereby recognized and declared that in Canada there have existed and shall continue to exist without discrimination by reason of race, national origin, colour, religion or sex, the following human rights and fundamental freedoms, namely, (a) the right of the individual to life, liberty, security of the person and enjoyment of property, and the right not to be deprived thereof except by due process of law; (b) the right of the individual to equality before the law and the protection of the law; (c) freedom of religion; (d) freedom of speech; (e) freedom of assembly and association; and (f) freedom of the press." Part II contains a war and emergency clause.

In the years since its passage the bill has proved less effective than many had hoped, and its application has been limited. Because it is federal statutory legislation and not part of the constitution, its provisions extend only to matters coming within the legislative authority of the Canadian Parliament; matters coming under provincial jurisdiction are outside its scope. In addition, although Section 2 of Part I provides that other laws of Canada are to be construed and applied so as not to infringe any of the declared rights and freedoms, courts have been reluctant to accept the bill as an instrument for overriding other federal statutes.

J. CROMWELL YOUNG
Executive Editor, "Encyclopedia Canadiana"

BILLAUD-VARENNE, bē-yō-và-ren', **Jean Nicolas** (1756–1819), French revolutionist. He was born in Rochelle, France, on April 23, 1756. After leaving the Oratorian College in 1785, he went to Paris and became an advocate of the *parlement* (judicial court) there. By 1789 he had subscribed to the principles of the French Revolution, attacking the government in a tract entitled *Despotisme des ministres de la France.* He joined the Jacobin club, a radical revolutionary group, and became a violent antiroyalist. A member of the Commune of Paris (1789–1795), he was elected to the National Convention where he voted for the execution of Louis XVI "within 24 hours" (January 1793).

After contributing to the overthrow of the Girondists, a more conservative faction of the National Convention, in June 1793, Billaud-Varenne became president of the convention. The Jacobins, having gained control, instituted a policy of strong central government, militarism, and terrorism. As a member of the newly formed Committee of Public Safety, Billaud-Varenne was influential and bloodthirsty in carrying out these aims. He supported Maximilien de Robespierre initially against Jacques René Hébert and Georges Jacques Danton, who were suspected of being moderate; later, fearing for his own safety, he turned against Robespierre.

The Thermidorean Reaction—the conservative transition in the government—brought down Robespierre, and also ended the Reign of Terror (1793–1794) with which Billaud-Varenne was associated. He was prosecuted by the National Convention as a terrorist and, in 1795, deported to French Guiana. He later refused a pardon offered by Napoleon Bonaparte. In 1816 he left Guiana and went to Port-au-Prince, Haiti, where he died on June 3, 1819. Apparent forgeries under his name, called *Mémoires de Billaud-Varenne écrites à Port-au-Prince,* were published in Paris in 1821.

Further Reading: Palmer, Robert R., *Twelve Who Ruled: The Year of the Terror in the French Revolution* (Princeton 1959).

BILLERICA, bil-ri′kə, is a residential town in eastern Massachusetts, in Middlesex County. It is situated on the Concord River, 7 miles (2.1 km) south of Lowell and 15 miles (24.1 km) northwest of Boston. Textiles and building materials are manufactured. The town was settled in 1637 and incorporated in 1655. It was once known as *Shawsheen.* Population: 31,648.

BILLETDOUX, bē-ye-dōō′, **François** (1927–), French writer and actor, who wrote political and nonpolitical novels and plays in a style notable for its economy and concentration and its effect of cool, sometimes ironic, objectivity. He was born in Paris on Sept. 7, 1927, attended drama and cinematography schools, and from 1945 was intermittently connected with radio broadcasting as a producer or performer. Meanwhile, he also wrote for the theater, television, and films, and published several novels.

His best-known play, a two-character drama called *Tchin-Tchin,* was produced in Paris in 1959, with Billetdoux appearing in one of the roles. Translated into English, *Tchin-Tchin* had a successful run in New York City in 1962-1963. Billetdoux's other important plays include *Le comportement des époux Bredburry* (1960), a domestic fantasy; *Va donc chez Törpe* (1961), a political satire; and, in collaboration with Eugène Ionesco and Jean Vauthier, *Chemises de nuit* (1962). Among his novels are *Brouillon d'un bourgeois* (1961; Eng. tr., *A Man and His Master,* 1963). His many awards include the Grand Prix du Disque (1957).

BILLETING OF SOLDIERS, bil′-ə-ting, is the compulsory lodging of troops with the inhabitants of cities, towns, or villages. In England, where billeting was popularly resented in the early 17th century, it was declared illegal by the Petition of Right (1628). Although prohibited by law again in 1679, billeting without consent was nonetheless increasingly practiced in England, and the Mutiny Act of 1689 and subsequent statutes authorized it under certain conditions. Billeting was prevalent in Europe during the Napoleonic period of large conscripted armies, but afterward it was considerably reduced by the use of barracks and other arrangements.

The American colonists objected to the billeting of British troops prior to the American Revolution, and the 3d Amendment to the Constitution of the United States provides that "no soldier shall, in time of peace be quartered in any house, without the consent of the Owner, nor in time of war, but in a manner to be prescribed by law."

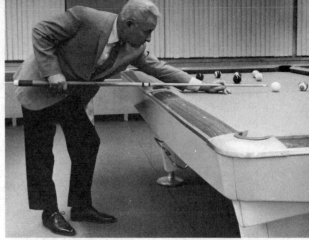

FROM ''WINNING POCKET BILLIARDS'' BY WILLIE MOSCONI (CROWN PUBLISHERS, 1965)

WILLIE MOSCONI, pocket billiards champion, shows perfect stance and cue grip. His head is directly over the cue and on a line with it as he sights the shot.

BILLIARDS, bil′yərdz, is a type of game played with balls and a cue on a rectangular, felt-covered table. In forms of the game played on tables with pockets (pocket billiards), one ball, called the *cue ball,* is used to drive other balls, known as *object balls,* into the pockets. In games played on tables without pockets (carom billiards), the cue ball is made to hit two balls in succession, thereby scoring a *carom.*

GAMES

Pocket Billiards. The form of the game played in pocket billiard championships is called *14.1 continuous.* In this game, 15 object balls, numbered from 1 to 15, are used. These are placed on the table in triangle formation (a triangular wooden form is used for collecting, or *racking,* the balls), with the apex on the foot spot and the triangle base parallel to the foot rail. The object is to complete 150 points, one point being awarded for each ball pocketed. This is a call-shot game; that is, the player announces the ball and pocket he intends to play.

The starting player on the opening, or break, shot must drive two or more object balls to a cushion or cause an object ball to drop into a pocket. This constitutes a legal break. The opponent then takes over and tries to pocket all the balls except one. This is called the *break ball,* which must remain on the table until the pocketed balls are reracked and set in position, with the apex vacant, again at the foot spot. The player then tries to pocket the break ball and carom the cue ball from the break ball into the racked balls. He continues scoring the 14 balls, having them reracked, and breaking until he misses, scratches, or scores the winning point.

In *rotation* the 15 object balls are racked so that the 1-ball is at the apex and placed on the foot spot, the 2-ball is at the left angle of the rack, and the 3-ball at the right. Players must pocket the object balls in numerical order, beginning with the 1-ball. Points are awarded according to the number of the balls, and the player who first reaches 61 points wins.

In *eight ball* the object balls are racked so that the 8-ball is in the center. One player uses balls numbered from 1 to 7; the other, 9 to 15. The first to pocket his allotment, and then pocket the 8-ball, wins.

The game of *American snooker* uses 21 object

Four major types of bridges, or cue supports, are shown in these photos. The *basic bridge* is formed by pressing three fingers against the table. The cue is put through a loop formed by the tips of the forefinger and the thumb. In pocket billiards, the distance between this loop and the cue ball should be about seven inches. To make a vee *bridge*, four fingers rest on the table, and the thumb, turned upward, holds the cue against the top of the hand. In the *rail bridge*, the thumb is tucked under the forefinger, and two fingers and the thumb guide the cue. The *mechanical bridge* is a wooden device used when a hand rest is impractical. Its notches serve as channels for the cue.

BASIC BRIDGE

VEE BRIDGE

MECHANICAL BRIDGE

RAIL BRIDGE

balls. Fifteen are red balls without numbers and score one point each when pocketed; six are colored balls with numbers and score the value of the ball (black, 7; pink, 6; blue, 5; brown, 4; green, 3; yellow, 2). The red balls are racked so that the apex ball is on the foot spot; the numbered balls are spotted according to a designated pattern on the table.

At the start, the first ball to be pocketed must be a red one. As play continues, players alternate between a red and a numbered ball, calling each shot. The numbered balls, however, must be respotted after each pocketing, as long as a red ball remains on the table. Once all red balls are pocketed, the numbered balls must be played in numerical order, from 2 to 7. The winner is the player with the highest score.

Carom Billiards. The most popular of the carom games is *three-cushion billiards*. This game uses three balls: two object balls (red and white) and a cue ball (white, with a black dot). The red ball is placed on the foot spot on the table; the white ball, on the head spot; and the cue ball, on the head string and six inches to the right or left of the white ball.

To begin play, the first player drives his cue ball against the red object ball. Thereafter, in attempts to score a carom (one point), players may strike either the red or the white ball first. In any case, the cue ball must contact at least three cushions before it hits the second object ball. No cushion contact or a number of contacts may be made by the cue ball before it hits the first object ball. The first player to score 50 points wins the game.

In *straight-rail billiards* the cue ball must hit the two object balls in succession, with or without cushion contact. The player who reaches a predetermined number of points first wins.

EQUIPMENT

Tables. Championship billiard tables are twice as long as they are wide and 31 to 32 inches high. Both the carom table and the American snooker table measure 5 by 10 feet over-all; a pocket table measures 4½ by 9 feet. The best tables have beds of slate. All are covered with a felt cloth and have felt-covered cushions.

Most tables have three small spots on which the balls are spotted at the start of various games. One spot is at the exact center; the other two (the *head spot* and the *foot spot*) are in line with the center spot on the table's long axis, each being halfway between the center spot and one of the end cushions. Pocket billiard and snooker tables have six pockets: one at each of the four corners and one at the middle of each side rail. Carom tables do not have pockets.

Balls. Originally all billiard balls were made of ivory. The majority now are of plastic. Pocket billiard balls numbered 1 to 8 are solid colored; those numbered 9 to 15 are striped. The cue ball is always white.

Cues. Cues are made of wood. The butt end, or handle, is generally covered with linen. The long, tapered shaft has a rounded leather tip about ½ inch wide. The spot where the weight of the handle is equal to that of the shaft is the *balance point* of the cue.

BASIC TECHNIQUES

Grip and Stance. In billiards, one hand propels the cue; the other forms a *bridge* to support and guide the cue near its tip. The propelling hand holds the handle lightly, from 3 to 6 inches behind the balance point, with the thumb and first three fingers. The channel through which the propelling hand slides the cue is formed by the fingers of the supporting hand which rests on the table or the rail, depending on the position of the cue ball. The fingers make the cue support, or bridge, essential to aiming. The most-used hand supports are the *basic bridge*, the *rail bridge*, and the *vee bridge*. If shots cannot be reached with any one of these hand bridges, a *mechanical bridge* must be used. (See illustration.)

When facing the shot, a player should place the feet slightly apart, one forward of the other. The body leans from the hips, with the forward knee bent slightly and the head directly over the cue, in a straight line with the shot.

Shots. To make the basic billiard shots— *center, follow, draw,* and *English*—the player must aim for a spot on the cue ball. The center shot, made by hitting the cue ball at dead center, stops the ball after the impact with the object ball. The follow shot, made by striking the ball a cue-tip width above its center to impart overspin, causes the ball to roll forward, or to follow, the object ball. The draw shot, made by striking the ball a cue-tip width below its center, causes the ball to roll backward.

"English" is imparted to the cue ball by striking it off center. This causes it to spin either clockwise or counterclockwise. The cue ball will spin clockwise if it is struck a cue-tip width right of center; this also speeds up the ball. In order to direct it counterclockwise and also slow it below normal speed, it must be struck a cue-tip width left of center.

In carom billiards a target area either on the table or on the rail is used. Players set their sights by one of the 18 small white plastic inlays (called diamonds) on the rail.

Play. To achieve proficiency, a player must learn how to control the speed of the cue ball; how to execute bank shots, frozen rail shots, caroms, and combination shots; and how to plan a sequence of shots to set object balls in position for pocketing. Long shots should be avoided. Sharp angle shots must be surveyed from the intended pocket as well as from the point of impact.

HISTORY

The origin of billiards is obscure. There is reference to the game in Shakespeare's *Antony and Cleopatra* (written about 1607), but the existence of billiards in pre-Christian times has not been substantiated. Some believe that the Knights Templar brought the game to England in the 11th century, on their return from the Crusades. Even the origin of the name is not certain, although it appears to be derived from the French *billard* or *billart* (cue) or *bille* (stick).

The first concrete evidence of the existence of billiards appears in France in the 15th century, during the reign (1461–1483) of Louis XI. In 1571, Charles IX had a billiard table constructed for the court. Its bed was of stone, and it was covered with a cloth that had pockets at each corner. Sometimes later a similar game was played in England at the court of James I (reigned 1603–1625). The first billiard table to appear on the American continent was brought to Florida by Spaniards in 1565.

In 1735 a wooden stick resembling the modern cue replaced the mace which previously had been used to propel the ball. In 1798 a Captain Mingaud, while a political prisoner in France, perfected the game. He was the first player to use a leather cue tip. In the 19th century, Jack Carr, an Englishman, first applied chalk to the cue tip. He also originated the "English" shots. A slate bed replaced the wooden bed about 1825. India rubber cushions supplanted the wooden sides in 1835, and vulcanized rubber cushions became commonplace about 1854.

The first championship game in the United States was held in Detroit in 1859. Since then the game has improved considerably in both method of play and equipment. In the 1930's, billiards lost its popularity, but interest was revived by the 1960's, with well-kept billiard rooms opening their doors to both men and women. Eye-appealing equipment appeared in volume for both commercial and home use. By the mid-1960's, billiards had become a popular family sport, and about 20,000,000 players competed annually in the United States. Tournaments are sanctioned by the Billiard Congress of America, with headquarters in Chicago.

The American Willie Hoppe, until his death in 1959, was regarded as the greatest all-around billiardist. Top carom players were Maurice Vignaux of France and Jacob Schaefer, Sr., Jacob Schaefer, Jr., Welker Cochran, and Harold Worst, all of the United States. Outstanding modern pocket billiard players in the United States include Alfredo DeOro, Ralph Greenleaf, Andrew Ponzi, Erwin Rudolph, Willie Mosconi, Luther Lassiter, and James Caras. George Chenier dominated pocket billiards in Canada.

JOSEPH MARCUS, *New York "Post"*

Bibliography

Billiard Congress of America, *Official Rules Book for All Pocket and Carom Billiard Games,* rev. ed. (Chicago 1966).
Cottingham, Clive, Jr., *The Game of Billiards* (Philadelphia 1964).
Crane, Irving, and Sullivan, George, *The Young Sportsman's Guide to Pocket Billiards* (New York 1964).
Lassiter, Luther, and Sullivan, George, *Billiards for Everyone* (New York 1965).
Mosconi, Willie, *Winning Pocket Billiards* (New York 1965).

GLOSSARY OF BILLIARD TERMS

Ball On.—An object ball that can be shot at in a straight line or driven into a pocket on a combination or a carom shot.
Bank.—A cushion; a *bank shot* is one in which the object ball is driven into the cushion and then into the pocket.
Break Shot.—The opening shot of the game.
Bridge.—The supporting hand's position on the table to guide the cue; also, a cuelike stick with a notched end; used to support the cue.
Called Ball.—The ball a player announces he intends to play.
Combination Shot.—A shot that puts an object ball into a pocket by driving a ball or balls into it.
Carom Shot.—A shot that makes the cue ball bound from one object ball to another.
Cushion.—The cloth-covered ridge bordering the inside rails of the table.
Draw Shot.—A shot that makes the cue ball roll backward after impact.
English.—A stroking technique that influences the action of the cue ball, either before or after it strikes the object ball.
Foot of Table.—The end or short rail that does not bear the name plate of the manufacturer.
Foot Spot.—The spot on the table's long axis midway between the exact center and the foot rail. In pocket billiards the racked ball at the apex of the triangle is centered on this spot.
Frozen.—A term used to indicate that two object balls are touching each other. In a *frozen rail shot* the cue ball hits an object ball that is resting against a cushion.
Head of Table.—The short rail bearing the name plate of the manufacturer.
Head Spot.—The spot on the table's long axis midway between the exact center and the head rail. The game's first ball is shot from behind an imaginary line, called the *head string*, which bisects the head spot and is parallel to the head rail.
High Run.—The highest consecutive series of scored balls in one inning.
Inning.—A turn at the table.
Kiss.—A carom.
Lag.—A procedure followed to determine which player takes the opening shot. Each player drives a ball from the head string to the foot rail. The one whose ball, in its rebound, stops closest to the head rail wins the lag and has the option of refusing to make the break shot.
Miscue.—A faulty contact of the cue against the cue ball.
Pack.—A cluster of balls before or after a break shot.
Rail.—The flat surface of the table, above the bed of the table, from which the cushions slope.
Safety.—A defensive maneuver in which a player drives an object ball against a cushion or into a pocket and relinquishes his turn. A safety usually leaves no set-up for the opponent.
Scratch.—A failure to comply with the rules; also, the pocketing of the cue ball. A scratch may result in a penalty.
Setup.—An easy shot.

BILLINGS, bil'ingz, **John Shaw** (1838–1913), American physician and librarian. He was born in Switzerland County, Ind., on April 12, 1838. After receiving his B.A. degree from Miami University in Oxford, Ohio, and his M.D. from the Medical School of Ohio in Cincinnati, he became a surgeon in the Union Army in 1862 and served with distinction throughout the Civil War. He remained in the Army after the war, and in 1865 was put in charge of the Surgeon General's Library in Washington, D.C. Within eight years he had increased the size of the collection from 600 volumes to over 50,000. In 1880, in collaboration with Dr. Robert Fletcher, he began to publish the monumental *Index Catalogue* of the library, which had run to 16 volumes by 1895, the year he officially retired from military service. Beginning in 1879, Billings and Fletcher also published the *Index Medicus,* a monthly guide to current medical publications. In 1896, Billings was appointed director of the newly formed New York Public Library, where he remained until his death, in New York City, on March 11, 1913.

Billings held many distinctions in the field of medicine, apart from his work as a librarian and bibliographer. He drew up the plans for the organization and construction of the Johns Hopkins University Hospital (1873) and was medical adviser to the trustees. In that capacity he presented several reports on hospital administration and the training of hospital personnel that are regarded as classics in the field. He served as a director of the University of Pennsylvania Hospital (1893–1896), as president of the American Public Health Association (1879), and as vice chairman of the National Board of Health (1878). He supervised the compilation of vital statistics for the United States censuses of 1880 and 1890. He also compiled the *National Medical Dictionary* (1889).

BILLINGS, bil'ingz, **Josh** (1818–1885), American humorist. He was born *Henry Wheeler Shaw* in Lanesboro, Mass., on April 21, 1818. He entered Hamilton College in 1832, but the next year he left school and traveled to the West, where he pursued a number of occupations offered by the primitive frontier life. He returned east in 1858, settling in Poughkeepsie, N.Y., and became an auctioneer. Meanwhile he began contributing humorous articles to a local newspaper under the signature "Josh Billings," but his writing failed to attract much attention until he employed a style of "phonetic" spelling to represent a rustic dialect. In 1863 he began a series of highly successful lectures that consisted of detached bits of homespun philosophy, usually pointing a moral and delivered in an inimitable droll style.

His first book, *Josh Billings, His Sayings* (1865), had an enormous success. Most popular of all his works was *Josh Billings' Farmers' Allminax* (1870), a travesty on the *Old Farmer's Almanac;* it sold over 200,000 copies within two years of its appearance. A new edition of *Josh Billings' Farmers' Allminax* was issued each year until 1880. His other works include *Josh Billings on Ice and Other Things* (1868), *Everybody's Friend* (1874), *Josh Billings, His Works Complete* (1876), *Josh Billings' Trump Kards* (1877), *Old Probability: Perhaps Rain—Perhaps Not* (1879), and *Josh Billings' Spice Box* and *Josh Billings Struggling with Things* (both 1881). He died in Monterey, Calif., on Oct. 14, 1885.

BILLINGS, bil'ingz, **William** (1746–1800), the first professional American composer of music. He was born at Boston on Oct. 7, 1746. He began work as a tanner, but as a young man he abandoned that craft to give his full attention to music. With the few books on music theory available in English he tried to educate himself in the techniques of counterpoint, which he very much preferred to the unison and chordal writing of the anthems then in use in most of the New England churches.

In 1770, Billings published *The New England Psalm Singer,* the first of his six collections of church music. It contained a selection of traditional hymns and a number of his own hymns and "fuguing pieces." The latter were crude imitations of canons, but their liveliness and the novelty of the part writing in them found favor with contemporary choirs. He subsequently published *The Singing Master's Assistant* (1778), *Music in Miniature* (1779), *The Psalm Singer's Amusement* (1781), *The Suffolk Harmony* (1786), and *The Continental Harmony* (1794). Each volume was a varied collection containing several works of his own. Billings died at Boston on Sept. 26, 1800.

After Billings' death his music soon disappeared from the churches. In the 20th century, however, under the aegis of Henry Cowell and other American composers, it enjoyed a modest revival in secular performance.

BILLINGS, bil'ingz, a city in southern Montana, is the seat of Yellowstone County. It is situated on the Yellowstone River, 225 miles (360 km) southeast of Helena. It is a marketing, manufacturing, and shipping center in a vast farming area that produces sugar beets, wheat, vegetables, and livestock. The major industries are oil refining, sugar refining, meat-packing, flour milling, and vegetable canning. Important manufactures include meat and dairy products, farm implements, and electrical equipment.

Billings is the home of Rocky Mountain College, Eastern Montana College, and Yellowstone Museum, where Indian artifacts and mementos of the area's past are exhibited. Nearby is Inscription Cave, which has ancient Indian writing on its walls.

Thirty miles (48 km) south of the city is Plenty Coups State Park, named for the last chief of the Crow Indians, who represented the Indians of the Northwest at the dedication of the Tomb of the Unknown Soldier at Arlington National Cemetery, Va. Custer Battlefield National Monument, 65 miles (105 km) southeast of the city, marks the area where Gen. George A. Custer and his troops were slain by the Sioux and Cheyenne Indians in the Battle of the Little Big Horn on June 25, 1876. About 33 miles (53 km) northeast is Pompey's Pillar, a natural rock shaft 200 feet (61 meters) high. William Clark of the Lewis and Clark expedition climbed this pillar on July 25, 1806, and named it for the son of an Indian guide in the expedition.

Although the region is identified with much of the early history of the West, hostile Indians prevented settlement until after the Sioux War of 1876. Billings was founded in 1882 during the construction of the Northern Pacific Railroad and was named for the line's president, Frederick Billings. Incorporated in 1885, it has a mayor-council government. Population: 61,581.

KATHRYN WRIGHT, *Billings "Gazette"*

BILLINGSGATE, bil'ingz-gāt, is a fish market in London, on the north bank of the Thames River between London Bridge and the Tower of London. It was named from the city gate that once existed nearby. In the 17th century the porters of the fish market were notorious for their coarse, abusive language; hence the word "billingsgate" for such language.

BILLION, bil'yən, a thousand millions, or 1,000,-000,000, according to the system of numeration used in the United States. In Britain, France (since 1948) and Germany, a billion is a million millions, or 1,000,000,000,000, which is called a trillion in the United States. In the British-German-French system, 1,000,000,000 is called a milliard.

BILLITON, bə-lē'ton, is an island in Indonesia, in the Java Sea, off the southeast coast of Sumatra. The Indonesian name for it is *Belitung*. The island is about 43 miles (70 km) wide and 55 miles (90 km) long and has an area of 1,866 square miles (4,834 sq km). The marshy land reaches a height of some 1,670 feet (510 meters) on Mount Tanjem, and the coasts are covered with coral reefs. There are large deposits of tin on Billiton and the adjacent island of Singkep. Tandjungpandan is the chief city and port. Population: (1961) 102,375.

BILLS, Legislative. See Congress of the United States; Legislation.

BILLY BUDD is a novelette by Herman Melville, written shortly before his death in 1891 but not published until 1924, when it helped to promote renewed interest in Melville. Its original title was *Billy Budd, Foretopman.*

Billy Budd is a young English sailor whose sincerity and goodness endear him to his shipmates. Aboard a British man-of-war he incurs the enmity of a jealous petty officer, Claggart. When the latter accuses him falsely of a mutinous conspiracy, Billy, speechless in disbelief, strikes him a fatal blow. Captain Vere, although he believes in the youth's spiritual innocence, is required by regulations to order a court-martial. Billy is tried and found guilty. Billy is hanged, but he lives on in the loving memory of the sailors who knew him. Some critics have called *Billy Budd* the most expert of Melville's stories, surpassing even *Moby-Dick* as a tragedy.

A one-act opera, *Billy Budd,* with a libretto by Salvatore Quasimodo, based on Melville's story, was written by the Italian composer Giorgio Ghedini. It had its premiere in September 1949 in Venice, thus preceding by two years the more celebrated version by British composer Benjamin Britten. Britten's *Billy Budd* is in four acts; its libretto, also based on Melville, is by E.M. Forster and Eric Crozier. This opera, which was first performed in 1951 at Covent Garden, London, tells basically the same story as Melville's novel, but Britten's score, with music that recalls traditional nautical tunes and old sea chanteys, seems to make the sea an additional character, its presence always felt.

Billy Budd, a three-act play, was adapted from Melville's novel by Louis Coxe and Robert Chapman. It focuses on the novel's allegory—the struggle between good as represented by Billy and evil as represented by Claggart. The play was presented on Broadway in 1951.

BILLY THE KID (1859–1881) was an American frontier outlaw. He was born *William H. Bonney* in New York City on Nov 23, 1859. Brought up in Kansas, Colorado, and New Mexico, he is said to have committed his first murder at the age of 12 when he knifed a man for insulting his mother. Four years later he was involved in the robbery and murder of three Indians. By 1877, when he became a cowhand in the Pecos Valley of New Mexico, 12 murders had been charged to his account.

When the Lincoln County (N. Mex.) cattle war erupted in February 1878, the Kid readily accepted the leadership of one of the warring factions and took part in several bloody skirmishes. The climax came on April 1, when he and five companions killed Sheriff James A. Brady and a deputy. In August the Kid spurned an offer of amnesty and embarked on a series of cattle rustlings at the head of a gang of 12, resulting in further killings.

In 1880 a former friend of Billy's, Patrick F. Garrett, became sheriff and launched a campaign to wipe out the Kid's band. Billy eluded capture in a gunfight at Fort Sumner, N. Mex., on Christmas Eve, but a few days later he was taken, along with three companions. Under sentence of death for slaying Brady, he escaped jail in Lincoln on April 28, 1881, killing both his guards. He was finally trapped in a private home in Fort Sumner and shot to death by Garrett on July 15, 1881.

A total of 21 killings is traditionally ascribed to Billy, but there is no reliable evidence for this figure. Because of his youth and extraordinary bravado, a romantic legend grew up around him, and he became the most celebrated outlaw of the old Southwest. The story of his life was first written in 1882 by Garrett.

Bibliography
Adams, Ramon F., *Fitting Death for Billy the Kid* (Norman, Okla., 1960).
Brent, William, *Billy the Kid* (New York 1964).
Burns, Walter Noble, *The Saga of Billy the Kid* (Garden City, N.Y., 1926).
Garrett, Patrick Floyd, *The Authentic Life of Billy the Kid,* new ed. (Norman, Okla., 1954).
Hunt, Frazier, *Tragic Days of Billy the Kid* (New York 1956).
Siringo, Charles A., *History of "Billy the Kid"* (Santa Fe, N.M., 1920).

BILNEY, bil'nē, **Thomas** (c. 1495–1531), English theologian, who was one of the earliest Protestant martyrs. Born in Norfolk, he studied at Trinity Hall, Cambridge, and was ordained a priest in 1519. A gentle man of deep spirituality and devotion to the church, he, like Martin Luther, could not reconcile the fundamentals of Catholicism with an "external" religion of ceremonies, rites, and veneration of saints. His preaching aroused opposition, but he converted some of his colleagues to Reformism. Unlike Luther, Bilney remained orthodox on essential Catholic dogma—the power of the pope and the church, the doctrine of transubstantiation, and the sacrifice of the Mass. Nonetheless, he was arrested for heresy in 1527. Persuaded to recant, he escaped death but was confined in the Tower of London for more than a year.

After his release, he was unable to silence his convictions, which he believed were verified by the teaching of St. Paul, and he began again to preach his views. Although these seem to have differed little from Catholic pronouncements, he was arrested as a relapsed heretic and was burned at the stake in Norwich on Aug. 19, 1531.

BILOXI, bə-lok′sē, is a resort and port city in southeastern Mississippi, in Harrison County, 135 miles (217 km) southeast of Jackson. It is situated on a peninsula between Biloxi Bay and Mississippi Sound, an arm of the Gulf of Mexico. The city is a summer and winter resort. A large fishing fleet operates from the harbor. Canning and shipping of seafood (principally shrimp and oysters) and boatbuilding are major industries. There is a municipal airport.

Biloxi is the site of a 700-acre U.S. Veterans Administration center, which includes a national soldiers' home with general hospital facilities. Keesler Air Force Base is nearby. Places of interest include Beauvoir, the last home of Jefferson Davis, president of the Confederacy.

The first white settlement in the lower Mississippi Valley was made in 1699 by French colonists under the sieur d'Iberville at Old Biloxi (now Ocean Springs), across the bay. The present city was founded in 1719 and served as the capital of the French colony of Louisiana until 1722. It was incorporated as a town in 1838 and as a city in 1896. Government is by commission and council. Population: 48,486.

BILOXI INDIANS, bə-lok′sē, a North American Indian tribe of the Siouan language family, who lived along the lower Pascagoula River (in the present state of Mississippi) in early historic times. "Biloxi" is a corrupt form of an Indian name meaning "first people." While the Biloxi figure importantly in the journals of explorers such as the sieur d'Iberville and Louis Juchereau de St. Denis, their original homeland is uncertain. Their linguistic affiliation indicates a northern origin, since they are the only Siouan-speaking Indians in the midst of the widespread Muskhogean peoples of the South, and their closest relatives are the Mosopelea of Ohio. Early in the 19th century the Biloxi sold their lands and moved to Biloxi Bayou in Texas. Most of them later returned to Louisiana, where their descendants settled near Lecompte, in Rapides Parish. The rest of the Biloxi went to Oklahoma, where their descendants are said to have been assimilated into the Choctaw nation.

FREDERICK J. DOCKSTADER
Museum of the American Indian, New York

BIMELER, bi′mə-lar, **Joseph Michael** (c. 1778–1853), German-American founder of the Separatists of Zoar. Born into a poor family in Württemberg, he educated himself and served for some years as a teacher among a persecuted sect of Pietists. In 1817 he joined a group of Separatists who sailed from Hamburg to the United States, arriving in Philadelphia. Bimeler became the group's spokesman in America.

The new arrivals were befriended by the Quakers, who sold them a 5,500-acre (2,225–hectare) tract in Tuscarawas County, Ohio. There Bimeler and his followers established the village of Zoar, named for the city to which Lot had fled from Sodom and Gomorrah. Zoar flourished as a communistic society under Bimeler's direction. A brewery, mill, textile factory, and foundry made the community self-supporting. After Bimeler's death at Zoar on Aug. 27, 1853, the society venerated him as a saint, but without his leadership the group declined. Communal property was distributed to members in 1898, and soon after it abandoned its communistic way of life the society disintegrated.

BIMETALLISM, bī-met′əl-iz-əm, is the use of either of two metals, such as gold and silver, at a fixed ratio to each other set by law, as the standard of monetary value. In contrast, the use of one metal is known as *monometallism.* Successful operation of bimetallism requires complete interchangeability of the two metals with each other, and with government credit money, at the official ratio. Although bimetallism has been used only as a coinage standard, it could just as well be used as a bullion standard.

Bimetallism is an expression of man's ceaseless, but futile, search for a monetary unit that will not fluctuate in value. Its appeal is based on the simple conclusion of its proponents that a monetary unit based on gold and silver on an interchangeable basis would be more stable than either gold or silver taken alone. Their argument goes like this: An increase in production of silver would lower its value and cause more of it to be used for monetary purposes, which would "cushion" its decline in value. This substitution of silver for gold would release gold from the monetary stock for sale on the open market, which would, in turn, tend to reduce its value. Thus, although both would decline in value, it is maintained that neither would fall as much as either would have fallen if it had been used alone as the monetary metal. In short, bimetallism is an effort to use the principle of Gresham's Law to reduce fluctuations in value through substitution of the cheaper metal (and thus increasing its demand) for the dearer metal (and thus reducing its demand).

Bimetallism does not rest upon any natural ratio; the relationship, or ratio, of the two metals is an arbitrary one fixed by law, and therein lies the great weakness of the idea in practice. Political considerations almost inevitably enter into the fixing of the ratio; and technological developments affecting supply and nonmonetary demand continually press upon the ratio after it is established. These technological developments, in particular, have been of controlling importance, especially in recent years since silver production has been on a byproduct basis. More specifically, the quantity of silver produced in recent years has not been based on cost and demand factors for silver, but upon the demand for nickel, copper, and other metals in the mining of which silver is a byproduct. For example, an increase in the world demand for copper automatically increases the supply of silver, regardless of the demand for it. Obviously, this reduces the utility of silver as a basis of monetary value and thereby deals bimetallism a mortal blow.

Bimetallism, especially under conditions where one of the two metals is a byproduct, is subject to the danger that one of the metals may disappear from the monetary stock. This could happen if political considerations dictated the fixing of a ratio which was out of line with the relative market prices of the metals. Also, it could happen if there were a sudden and sharp change in the value of one of the metals. For example, a sudden increase in the supply of silver through increased production, or through demonetization by some country previously on a silver standard, could decrease the value of silver to the point where only it would be taken to the government to be coined or exchanged for credit money. Under such circumstances, gold would be taken to the market, instead of to the government, and it would be exchanged for the cheap silver, which would be taken to the government for conversion into money. In this fashion, silver would replace gold in the monetary stock.

Then, too, there is always the danger that bimetallism may be fatally undermined by other countries adopting a different mint ratio for the two metals. Depending on which metal the country produces, or other considerations, one metal may be valued more highly by another country, with the result that the metal is attracted to it. Arbitragers hasten to export either monetary metal to any country which overvalues it and, in payment, import the undervalued metal. While it can be argued that such a process is a self-correcting one, the fact is that arbitrary governmental interferences with the movement of trade and the balances of payment have introduced large elements of artificiality which further remove bimetallism from reality.

In bimetallism, the debtor is given the option, by law, as to which metal he will use for repayment. This choice is not offered because the government is trying to favor the debtor, but because the official parity can be maintained in no other way. This fact, that debtors will use the cheaper metal for payments, is advanced as an argument for bimetallism, as the resulting increased demand for the cheaper metal tends to bring its commercial value into line with its legal value and, thus, it is claimed, contributes to the stability of value of both metals.

Bimetallism in the United States. From the earliest days of the republic until comparatively recently, bimetallism was a sensitive political and economic issue in the United States.

Both Alexander Hamilton and Thomas Jefferson urged the establishment of a bimetallic monetary system for the infant republic. Congress, after some delay, followed their counsel by adopting bimetallism as the monetary standard in the act of April 2, 1792. In this act, the gold unit was established at 27 grains, eleven-twelfths fine, and thus contained 24.75 grains of fine (pure) gold, whereas the silver unit was fixed at 416 grains, .8924 fine, and thus contained 371.25 grains of fine silver. Although the act thus established a bimetallic mint ratio of 15:1, in fact the director of the unit made the silver coins .900 fine, which gave them a pure silver content of 374.75, or a true mint ratio of 15.14:1.

After a change in 1803, there was a further change in the official ratio in 1834 to 16:1, to check the outflow of the previously undervalued gold. However, under the new arrangement, silver was as undervalued at the mint as it had previously been overvalued. Gold, therefore, became the only standard money that could be kept in circulation. Silver was exported to points where it would have greater value. Although bimetallism was the national policy from 1834 to 1873, silver (even including fractional silver coins until their reduction to a subsidiary basis by the lowering of their silver content in 1853) practically disappeared from circulation.

In the general revision of the coinage laws in 1873, no mention was made of the silver dollar. Although this was probably only a recognition of the fact that the coin had practically disappeared from circulation, the law has since been referred to by silver protagonists as the "crime of '73." An amended bill, the Bland-Allison Act of 1878, provided that silver dollars should be coined. After that time, there was an active, vocal, and powerful silver bloc in American politics, which obtained much silver legislation. Its crowning achievement was the Silver Purchase Act of 1934, which established as national policy that one fourth of the monetary value of the gold and silver in the monetary stock should ultimately consist of silver. Although much silver was purchased under the act, gold holdings increased even more rapidly, so there was no appreciable progress toward the announced goal. While this policy had some of the aspects of bimetallism, the differentiation between the price of newly mined domestic silver and other silver, the wide variations in the price paid from time to time, and, especially, the restriction of the unlimited purchase of silver at legally fixed prices to newly mined domestic silver, removed it from bimetallism.

In 1965, President Johnson signed legislation authorizing the U.S. Treasury to produce dimes and quarters without silver, and half-dollars with a 40 percent silver content instead of 90 percent. Old silver coins were not withdrawn from circulation. The reason for the new coinage was a shortage of silver caused by a rapid growth in world consumption without a corresponding increase in production.

RAYMOND RODGERS, *Graduate School of Business Administration, New York University*

Further Reading: Bradford, F.A., *Money and Banking*, 6th ed. (New York 1949); Kent, R.P., *Money and Banking*, 4th ed. (New York 1961); Pritchard, L.J., *Money and Banking* (Boston 1964); Studenski, P., and Kroos, H.E., *Financial History of the United States* (New York 1952).

BIMINI ISLANDS, bim′ə-nē, a group of islets in the Straits of Florida, forming the northwest section of the Bahama Islands. The Biminis extend 45 miles in a north-south direction, from North and South Bimini, the largest islets, to South Riding Rock. The largest settlements are Alice Town and Bailey Town on North Bimini. The chief products are sponges, fish, sisal, coconut, and corn.

Legend places Ponce de León's fountain of youth in the Biminis. They have become a tourist resort because of their beautiful setting and excellent fishing, and because they are close to Miami (50 miles to the north) and to Nassau (110 miles to the east). Alice Town has picturesque markets, a fine harbor, and the rare-fish collections of the Lerner Marine Laboratory. Population: (1963) 1,652.

BINARY FORM, bi′nə-rē, is a musical form in which a composition is either divided into two contrasting sections or is based on two principal themes. In the basic binary form, also called the *simple binary*, the first section begins in the tonic or chief key of the piece and ends in a related key, while the second section begins in the related key and works its way back to the original. In the *compound binary*, or sonata, form, a bridge passage unites extended versions of the two sections of the basic form.

The simple binary form was widely used in the dance movements of 17th and 18th century instrumental suites, such as the minuet of Purcell's First Harpsichord Suite. The compound binary form is employed in the music of Karl Philipp Emanuel Bach, Haydn, and Mozart, and is normally the form of the first movement of a Beethoven symphony or sonata.

BINARY NOTATION, bī'nə-rē nō-tā'shən, is a system for representing numbers as the sum of unit multiples of positive or negative integral powers of 2. It is comparable to the decimal system, with 2 replacing 10 as the base. Although binary arithmetic was known for centuries, it was generally considered to be interesting but useless until the development of the modern electronic computer in the mid-20th century. The Hungarian-American mathematician John Von Neumann first recognized that banks of electronic components, capable of representing by their on and off states the ones and zeros in binary numerals, provided not only the most efficient means of storing and manipulating the numbers involved in electronic computations but also the best way to code the instructions in the internally stored programs controlling such computations.

Symbols. Only the symbols 1 and 0 and the binary point are used to represent numbers in the binary system. The principle of position used is analogous to that of the decimal system. For instance, in decimal arithmetic we recognize 101.11 as designating the number whose value is the sum of a hundred (10^2), no tens (10^1), a unit (10^0), a tenth (10^{-1}) and a hundredth (10^{-2}). If we interpret the same configuration of marks, 101.11, as representing a binary number, its value would be the sum of a four (2^2), no twos (2^1), a unit (2^0), a half (2^{-1}) and a fourth (2^{-2}). Since one normally interprets symbols such as 101.11 as a decimal representation, when a binary representation is intended a subscript b or 2 is frequently added to avoid misinterpretation. Thus we write $101.11_b = 5.75$ to indicate that the decimal form of the binary number represented by 101.11 is 5.75.

Operations. One can easily learn to count and do elementary arithmetic using binary notations. Zero and one have the same representation in binary or decimal notation. Two, the binary base, is written 10_b. The next few integers are:

Decimal   3   4   5   6   7   8
Binary 11_b 100_b 101_b 110_b 111_b 1000_b.

Using the fact that $1 + 1 = 10$ as the basis for carrying in addition or borrowing in subtraction, one can quickly develop the techniques for the various binary arithmetic operations. In computations involving special decimal numbers containing only the digits 0 and 1 and no borrowing or carrying, the configuration of symbols displayed in executing the decimal computation may have an equally valid interpretation in binary arithmetic. Thus, the decimal results:

(a)   1,010   (b)   10,011   (c)   1010   (d)   11
     +   101,   − 10,010,   ×   11,   101⟌1111
     1,111   1   1010   101
                                       1010   101
                                     11110   101

have binary interpretations equivalent to the decimal results: (a) $10 + 5 = 15$; (b) $19 - 18 = 1$; (c) $10 \times 3 = 30$; and (d) $15 \div 5 = 3$.

The principle of position for binary representation associates with each binary number $a_0 a_1 \ldots a_n . a_{n+1} a_{n+2} \ldots a_{n+m}$, having $a_0, a_1, a_2, \ldots a_n$ as the $n + 1$ digits occuring on the left of the binary point and $a_{n+1}, a_{n+2} \ldots a_{n+m}$ as the m digits to the right of the binary point, the value of the expansion:

$$\sum_{j=0}^{n+m} a_j \, 2^{n-j}$$

where n is equal to -1 if all digits to the left of the binary point are zero and m is zero if no digits occur to the right of the binary point. The binary digits, 0 and 1, are commonly referred to as *bits*. From the expansion of the value of a binary number it is easily verified that multiplication of a number expressed in binary form by an integral power of two results in a product containing the same bit configuration with the binary point shifted the same number of places to the right or to the left as the magnitude of the positive or negative exponent of two in the multiplier. As in the rules for multiplying decimal numbers by powers of ten, one must place zeros in any vacant positions thus created between the significant bits of the expansion and the relocated binary point. To illustrate, note that 101.11_b multiplied by 1000_b (2^3 in decimal) is $101,110_b$, corresponding to the decimal result $5.75 \times 8 = 46$.

Conversion Between Binary and Decimal Notation. One can obtain the decimal equivalent of a binary number directly by evaluating the expansion of the value in powers of 2. Applying this method in the case of the binary integer 101110_b, we see that its value is $1 \cdot 2^5 + 0 \cdot 2^4 + 1 \cdot 2^3 + 1 \cdot 2^2 + 1 \cdot 2^1 + 0 \cdot 2^0$ or $32 + 8 + 4 + 2 = 46$. However, to apply this method it is first necessary to count the number of bits to determine n in the formula and then to apply the formula very carefully to avoid mistakes. A somewhat simpler method of evaluating a binary integer makes use of synthetic division, in recognition that the successive bits in the expansions represent the coefficients in a polynomial, in x for example, which is to be evaluated for $x = 2$. Applying this method to the example 101110_b:

$$
\begin{array}{c|cccccc|l}
f(x) & 1 & 0 & 1 & 1 & 1 & 0 & \;(x = 2) \\
& & 0 & 2 & 4 & 10 & 22 & 46 \\
\hline
& 1 & 2 & 5 & 11 & 23 & \lfloor 46 & = f(2) = 101110_b.
\end{array}
$$

To convert a decimal integer to binary form, the bits in the number may be obtained in reverse order as the reminders resulting from successive division by 2 until the reduced quotient is zero. To illustrate with 46:

$$46 \div 2 = 23 \text{ with Rem. } 0 = a_5$$
$$23 \div 2 = 11 \text{ with Rem. } 1 = a_4$$
$$11 \div 2 = 5 \text{ with Rem. } 1 = a_3$$
$$5 \div 2 = 2 \text{ with Rem. } 1 = a_2$$
$$2 \div 2 = 1 \text{ with Rem. } 0 = a_1$$
$$1 \div 2 = 0 \text{ with Rem. } 1 = a_0$$

or $46 = a_0 a_1 a_2 a_3 a_4 a_5 = 101110_b$.

Application in Computers. Simple and reliable circuitry has been developed in binary computers to implement computations with binary representations of numbers. Typical operations performed by such circuits include additions of two numbers, or the bit shifts associated with multiplication of binary numbers by powers of two. Multiplication and subtraction are also accomplished internally by combinations of instructions. Present-day computers can accept decimal data, convert it internally to binary, and convert binary results to decimal before printing, so that many casual users employing well-documented libraries of computer programs do not have to become experts in binary arithmetic. Nevertheless, those who develop new programs or improve the existing ones and those who contribute to the design of new computer systems must be thoroughly versed in binary computations.

E.P. MILES, JR.
Computing Center, Florida State University

BINARY STAR, bī'nə-rē, a stellar system composed of two stars circling around a common center of gravity as they travel through space. The distance between the component stars varies widely among binaries, and the two stars in such a system are often physically quite different from one another. Perhaps one fourth of all stars in the sky are binaries or—more rarely—multiple systems of three, four, or more stars.

A small number of binaries can be observed with the naked eye, such as Mizar and Alcor in the handle of the Big Dipper (although through a telescope Mizar itself is revealed as a binary). Several thousand more binaries can be observed on photographs taken through telescopes. A visible double-star system is called a *visual binary.*

However, some stars that appear close together in the sky are actually very far apart and not binary stars at all. These are known as *optical doubles.* Years of observation are sometimes required to determine whether an apparent binary is actually an optical double.

The component stars of many binaries lie too close together or are too distant from the earth for the most powerful telescopes to separate them. Even in a nearby binary one of the stars may be too faint to be observed. Astronomers detect such a binary by studying its spectrum. The orbital motions of the component stars of the binary, known as a *spectroscopic binary,* are revealed by shifts in the lines of its spectrum.

The orbital planes of some binaries are seen edgewise from the earth, so that the two stars periodically eclipse one another. Such an *eclipsing binary* appears to the observer as a variable star—a star with a periodic change in brightness —but is not a true variable. Algol is a well-known example of an eclipsing binary.

See also ASTRONOMY; ASTROPHYSICS; STARS.

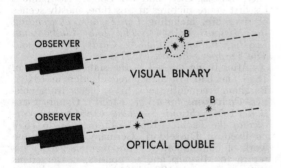

BINARY STARS are two-star systems. (*Above*) Visual binaries are star pairs (A and B) that can be resolved optically. Optical doubles actually are far apart and are not true binaries. (*Below*) Eclipsing binaries are so oriented that, as seen from earth, star B eclipses star A, causing variations in brightness.

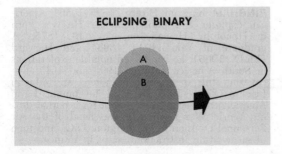

BINCHOIS, baN-shwà', **Gilles** (c. 1400–1460), Flemish composer, whose contribution to the contemporary development of polyphonic music was exceeded only by that of Guillaume Dufay and John Dunstable. He was born at Mons, in Hainaut (now in Belgium), and worked as a musician at the court of Philip the Good of Burgundy. His fame rests chiefly on his unusually expressive secular *chansons,* a complete edition of which was first published in 1957. He died at Soignies, near Mons, on Sept. 20, 1460.

JOHN J. SMITH

Bindweed (*Convolvulus sepium*)

BINDWEED, bīnd'wēd, is a genus of twining annual and perennial herbs that frequently are used as a cover for fences and banks. Many species are pubescent (hairy). The bindweeds constitute the genus *Convolvulus* of the morning glory family, Convolvulaceae. There are many species, widely distributed in temperate and tropical regions.

An important garden species is the dwarf morning glory (*C. tricolor*), a hardy annual. This erect herb has many branches and is covered by dense brownish hairs. Its flowers are blue with yellow throats margined with white. Another important species is *C. arvensis,* a perennial vine. This species has deep roots and is often a persistent weed in cultivated ground. Other noteworthy species include the pink-flowered California rose (*C. japonicus*) and the Rutland beauty (*C. sepium*). These two species are vigorous growers and can be troublesome weeds.

BINET, bē-nā', **Alfred** (1857–1911), French psychologist, who developed the first standard test of intelligence. He was born at Nice on July 11, 1857. In 1871 he went to Paris and began studies that spread into many fields—law, the natural sciences, medicine, and psychology.

As a result of his work with the famous neurologist Jean Charcot, Binet became interested in abnormal psychology, and after a long study he focused on psychology as his primary field. In 1886 and 1887 he published books on hypnotism and subconscious thought, and works on personality and experimental psychology followed. In 1892 he became assistant to the director of the psychological laboratory at the Sorbonne, and in 1894 he was made director, holding this post until his death. While director, he continued to contribute to many fields of psychology, reporting his work in articles and books and in *L'année psychologique,* an annual publication which he founded in 1895.

One of Binet's interests was the investigation

of ways to measure intelligence. He studied both gifted and retarded children and experimented with such factors as body measurements and handwriting as possible gauges of intellectual capacity. His work reached its peak of importance when he was asked to solve a practical problem. In 1904 the French government appointed him to a commission assigned to study ways of setting up special classes for children who were not capable of doing regular schoolwork. Binet, with one of his colleagues, Théodore Simon, developed a test that could be used to classify children according to mental ability.

The first version of the Binet-Simon scale appeared in 1905, and revised forms were issued in 1908 and 1911. This test consisted of questions and problems that, the authors hoped, would measure general intelligence rather than acquired knowledge. Items were graded from those that could be handled by a majority of three-year-olds upward to those suitable for adults. Test items were assigned to age levels by trying them out on numbers of Paris schoolchildren. A child's score, called his "mental age," was based on the number of correct answers.

Binet's own work on the test was ended by his death in Paris on Oct. 18, 1911. However, his pioneering efforts greatly influenced psychologists in other countries, particularly in the United States. Lewis M. Terman, a psychologist at Stanford University, adapted the test for use in the United States, publishing the *Stanford Revision of the Binet-Simon Scale* in 1916. The Stanford-Binet, as it was called, was for many years the most widely used test of its kind in America. See also INTELLIGENCE; MENTAL TESTS.

BING, Sir Rudolf (1902–), Austrian-born opera impresario, who from 1950 to 1972 headed the Metropolitan Opera in New York City. He was born in Vienna on Jan. 9, 1902, the son of an industrialist. He grew up with chamber music at home and a family box at the opera and was so keenly interested in opera that he studied for a professional singing career. His studies were interrupted by World War I and the economic collapse of Austria. Bing then joined a Vienna book concern that also operated a concert agency. He was soon devoting all his time to the concert agency, and in 1927 he went to Berlin to take charge of the opera division of one of the largest theatrical agencies in Germany. In 1928 he became an administrative assistant at the State Theater in Darmstadt, and in 1930 he accepted a similar position at the Charlottenburg Municipal Opera in Berlin.

In 1933, Bing went to England, where the following year he helped found the Glyndebourne Opera Festival, becoming its general manager in 1935. Except for two or three years during World War II, when he managed a London department store, he directed the festival until 1949. He also helped found the Edinburgh International Festival of Music and Drama in 1947.

In 1949, Bing was appointed general manager of the Metropolitan Opera Association of New York, taking office on June 1, 1950. The new Metropolitan Opera House, which took shape under his general direction, opened at Lincoln Center, New York City, on Sept. 16, 1966. Bing, who had become a British subject in 1946, was knighted in 1971. He resigned from the Metropolitan effective in 1972, the year his memoirs, *Five Thousand Nights at the Opera*, were published.

BINGEN, bing'ən, a town in West Germany, in the state of Rhineland-Palatinate, is 17 miles (27 km) west of Mainz, at the junction of the Rhine and Nahe rivers. It has an active river trade, particularly in wine and liquor. Since it is centrally located for trips into the Rhine region, the town has become a tourist center. The castle of Klopp and the Sanctuary of St. Roch are situated on the sites of former Roman buildings. Opposite the town is the Niederwald Denkmal, built to commemorate German victories in the Franco-Prussian War of 1870.

During the Roman era, Bingen was an important fortress. In medieval times the town became known for a legend about Archbishop Hatto. Hatto's cruelty toward his subjects during a famine led to a rebellion and he was forced to take refuge on a rock in the Rhine near Bingen. His place of refuge was called the Mäuseturm (Mouse Tower) because, according to the legend, he was devoured there by mice. Population: (1961) 20,210.

BINGHAM, bing'əm, **George Caleb** (1811–1879), American genre painter, whose works depict small-town political events and riverboat life in 19th century Missouri. He was born in Augusta County, Va., on March 20, 1811. In Missouri, where his family lived after 1819, Bingham met the painter Chester Harding, who encouraged his interest in art. Bingham's first works were primitive portraits painted on trips along the Missouri and Mississippi rivers. He had his first formal training in 1838, when he studied for three months at the Pennsylvania Academy of Art in Philadelphia. From 1840 to 1844 he did portraits of officials in Washington, D.C.

Bingham returned to Missouri in 1844 and thereafter lived for most of his life in Jefferson City, Kansas City, and St. Louis. He painted his first genre pictures at this time, mostly scenes of river life, including *Fur Traders Descending the Missouri* (?1844), *The Jolly Flatboatman* (1846), *Raftsmen Playing Cards* (1847), and *The Trapper's Return* (1851).

After being elected to the state legislature in 1848 (he had lost a disputed election in 1846), Bingham frequently took his subjects from politics—*Canvassing for a Vote* (1851), *County Election* (1852), *Stump Speaking* (1854), and *Verdict of the People* (1854). From 1856 to 1859 he lived in Düsseldorf, Germany, studying the work of contemporary genre painters. After his return to Missouri and to politics, he served as state treasurer (1862–1865) and as adjutant general of Missouri (1875). He died in Kansas City, Mo., on July 7, 1879.

Further Reading: Christ-Janer, Albert William, *George Caleb Bingham of Missouri* (New York 1940); Larkin, Lew, *Bingham, Fighting Artist* (St. Louis 1955); McDermott, John F., *George Caleb Bingham: River Portraitist* (Norman, Okla., 1959).

BINGHAM, bing'əm, **Hiram** (1875–1956), American explorer and public official. He was born in Honolulu, Hawaii, on Nov. 19, 1875. A graduate of Yale (B.A., 1898) and Harvard (Ph.D., 1905), he conducted notable explorations in South America between 1906 and 1915, discovering the Inca cities of Vitcos and Machu Picchu. From 1907 to 1924 he taught Latin American history at Yale, except for a period during World War I when he was head of the Air Personnel Division in Washington, D.C., and then of an aviation instruction center in France.

A Republican, he was lieutenant governor of Connecticut in 1923–1924, and was elected governor in the latter year. He resigned to fill a vacancy in the U.S. Senate, and was reelected to a full term in 1926. He was later chairman of the U.S. Civil Service Commission's Loyalty Review Board (1952–1953). Bingham died in Washington, D.C., on June 6, 1956.

Among his writings are *Journal of an Expedition Across Venezuela and Colombia* (1909), *Across South America* (1911), *Inca Land* (1922), and *Lost City of the Incas* (1948).

Hiram Bingham's father and grandfather were distinguished missionaries and translators. His grandfather, *Hiram Bingham* (1789–1869), was a missionary at Honolulu (1820–1840). With others he devised an alphabet and translated the Bible into Hawaiian. The explorer's father, *Hiram Bingham* (1831–1908), was a missionary at Abaiang in the Gilbert Islands (1857–1864 and 1873–1875). He reduced Gilbertese to writing and translated the Bible into that language.

BINGHAM, bing′əm, **Robert Worth** (1871–1937), American newspaper publisher and diplomat. He was born in Orange County, N.C., on Nov. 8, 1871, and graduated from Bingham School, in Asheville, of which his father was the fourth Bingham family headmaster. He studied at the universities of North Carolina and Virginia and graduated in law from the University of Louisville before beginning practice in Louisville, Ky. Eventually he became a county judge and, briefly in 1907, acting mayor of Louisville.

Bingham, who was married three times and was widowed twice, inherited $5 million from his second wife in 1916. In 1918 he bought control of the nationally known Louisville *Courier-Journal* and Louisville *Times* and, as an active publisher, made them two of the most respected liberal dailies in the United States. He was a personal friend and supporter of President Franklin D. Roosevelt, who appointed him ambassador to Britain in 1933. While holding that office, Bingham died in Baltimore on Dec. 18, 1937. *George Barry Bingham* (1906–   ), his son, succeeded as publisher of the newspapers and also became editor.

BINGHAM, bing′əm, **William** (1752–1804), American merchant, banker, and legislator. He was born in Philadelphia, Pa., on April 8, 1752. He graduated from the University of Pennsylvania in 1768 and served as British consul at St. Pierre, Martinique, from 1770 to 1776, following which he was an agent of the Continental Congress in the West Indies for another four years. His thorough knowledge of the West Indian trade enabled him to amass a great fortune.

Upon his return to Philadelphia he married, in 1780, Anne Willing (1764–1801), the daughter of the wealthy merchant Thomas Willing, a partner of Robert Morris. After Philadelphia became the national capital, their mansion was a social and political center for Federalists, including George Washington. Bingham was a founder, with his father-in-law as president, of the Bank of North America, chartered on Dec. 31, 1781. It was the first bank in the United States. He was also an important landowner, with extensive holdings in Pennsylvania and New York (see BINGHAMTON), and with 2 million acres of timberland in New England. Bingham was a member of the Continental Congress in 1786–1789, of

the Pennsylvania Assembly in 1790–1795, and the United States Senate (from Pennsylvania) in 1795–1801. He died in Bath, England, on Feb. 6, 1804.

BINGHAMTON, bing′əm-tən, is an industrial city in southern New York, situated at the confluence of the Chenango and Susquehanna rivers, near the New York-Pennsylvania line. It is about 75 miles (120 km) south of Syracuse and 165 miles (265 km) northwest of New York City. Binghamton is the seat of Broome County and the metropolis of the community (including Johnson City and Endicott) known as the Triple Cities.

The chief industries in the immediate vicinity are the manufacture of business machines, shoes, aviation training equipment, clothing, dental supplies, furniture, automobile supplies and equipment, electrical and electronic items, wire and metal products, tents and awnings, cosmetics, bricks, metal valves and castings, and books. The principal sources of income in the surrounding areas are dairy products, poultry and poultry products, and lumber and pulp wood. Binghamton is situated on interstate and federal highways and is served by major bus lines as well as by railroads and by scheduled airlines operating from the Broome County airport.

Noteworthy educational institutions include the State University of New York at Binghamton (formerly Harpur College of the State University of New York) and Broome Technical Community College, both situated just outside the city limits. The Binghamton public library system is the central reference unit of a four-county system. Roberson Memorial Center, a museum of art and history, is an important center of creative arts and handicrafts for an 11-county area. The Tri-Cities Opera Workshop has become known throughout the state for its annual productions. Chenango Valley State Park and a ski resort are near the city.

The first organization in the United States formed to work with a county agricultural agent (farm bureau) was established in Binghamton in 1911 as a bureau of the Binghamton Chamber of Commerce. The Broome County Farm Bureau was organized two years later.

The site of the present city was known as Chenango when it was settled in 1787. Later it became Chenango Point and then Binghamton, in honor of William Bingham (q.v.), a Philadelphia merchant who owned much land in the area. Binghamton was incorporated as a village in 1834 and was chartered as a city in 1867. It is governed by a mayor and council. Population: 64,123.

M. CHARLES MILLER, *Binghamton Public Library*

BINGO, bing′gō, is a game of chance played by any number of people using numbered cards and counters. A popular lottery pastime at fairs, carnivals, and fund-raising events, the game appears under many names, including *keno, lotto,* and *beano,* and in several variations.

The object of the standard game is to complete any row of numbers on the card (vertically, horizontally, or diagonally) as the numbers are announced by a banker. He draws the numbers, on tokens, from a box, and an assistant records the numbers on a sheet for checking purposes.

Each player receives one or more bingo cards, with counters, from the banker. The cards are divided into five rows of five squares each; 24 of the squares show numbers between 1 and 75, the center square being unnumbered or "free." All cards have different number combinations. To start the game, each player puts a counter on the center square. Then he puts a counter on each number called that appears on one or more of his cards. When any row is complete, the player calls "Bingo." If several call "bingo" at the same time, duplicate prizes are awarded.

Bingo games usually are conducted by professional promoters, often under the auspices of religious or charitable organizations. The game has been opposed by many as a form of gambling; critics claim that the results can be manipulated, and that only a small part of the profits reaches the sponsoring organizations. In the United States, the game is legalized in some states and banned in others. A number of states permit each community to decide the question of legality for itself.

FRANK K. PERKINS, *Boston "Herald"*

BINH DINH, bin din, a town in South Vietnam, was formerly the capital of the province of Binh Dinh. Located in the central coastal region, the town is 10 miles (16 km) northwest of the port of Qiu Nhon, the present provincial capital. Binh Dinh, on the coastal highway and railroad, is the center of a region producing rice, cotton, sugar, and cinnamon. Mulberry trees are grown for silkworms. The chief industries are the weaving of textile fibers and fish processing. The Vietnamese war, however, disrupted the economy of the region. Binh Dinh province was the scene of heavy fighting between the Vietcong and the South Vietnamese and U.S. forces. Population: (1956 estimate) 18,350.

BINNEY, bin'ē, **Horace** (1780–1875), American lawyer and legal writer, who played an important role in establishing the law of charitable trusts in the United States. Binney was born in Philadelphia on Jan. 4, 1780. He graduated from Harvard in 1797 and, after studying law in Philadelphia for three years, was admitted to the bar there. Following a term in the state legislature from 1806 to 1808, he developed a flourishing practice oriented toward wills and estates. In 1823 he prepared the brief and delivered the winning argument in *Lyle* v. *Richards*, a landmark case that established the common-law foundations of real property law in Pennsylvania. Meanwhile he had published his massive work *Reports of Cases Adjudged in the Supreme Court of Pennsylvania* (6 vols., 1809–14).

Binney was repeatedly recommended for state and U.S. Supreme Court judgeships, but he was regularly bypassed because of his militant federalist views and his outspoken distrust of the two major political parties. He accepted a Whig nomination for the U.S. Congress in 1832 and won election on an anti-Jackson platform. He declined renomination in 1834. His principal role while in Congress, and as a lawyer thereafter, was to oppose President Jackson's campaign against the second Bank of the United States.

In 1844, Binney emerged from semiretirement to make his last and most brilliant appearance in court, in *Vidal et al* v. *Philadelphia et al*. Binney represented the city in an appeal before the U.S. Supreme Court, and Daniel Webster represented the appellants. At issue was the city's right to act as trustee of a bequest of Stephen Girard (q.v.) to establish a school for poor white male orphans (Girard College). The appellants argued that the city could not hold a private trust; the court ruled for the city.

Binney worked in an advisory capacity until 1850, when he turned exclusively to writing. During the Civil War he wrote pamphlets defending President Lincoln's suspension of the writ of habeas corpus. He died in Philadelphia on Aug. 12, 1875.

BINOCULAR, bə-nok'yə-lər, an optical device consisting of two parallel telescopic systems that enable the user to see an enlarged image of a distant object with both eyes. In addition to giving an enlarged view of a distant object, the binocular enhances the stereoscopic perception of depth beyond that of normal vision. This enhancement is aided both by the separation of the axes of the objective lenses and by the magnifying power. The term "binocular" can be applied to any device using the parallel telescope prin-

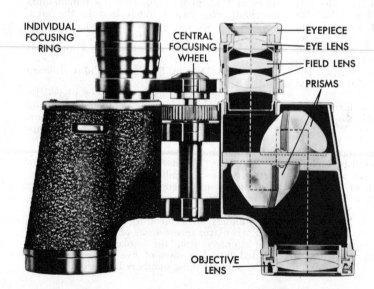

INDIVIDUAL FOCUSING RING

CENTRAL FOCUSING WHEEL

EYEPIECE
EYE LENS
FIELD LENS
PRISMS

OBJECTIVE LENS

BINOCULAR

In the center-focus binocular, shown here, both lens systems can be focused simultaneously once the individual focus ring has been adjusted for the user's eyes. The lenses gather light and magnify, while the prisms turn the image right side up.

BAUSCH & LOMB

ciple, but it is commonly restricted to prism binoculars—instruments that use prisms to erect the image and to shorten the distance between the objective (front) lens and the ocular (rear) lens. Each half of a binocular contains two prisms and at least two lenses.

Binoculars are specified by first giving the magnifying power in diameters and then giving the diameter of the objective lens. Thus, the expression "7 x 50 binocular" tells the user that the instrument has a magnifying power of 7 diameters, a clear objective lens aperture of 50 millimeters, and prisms in the optical path.

The intended use of a binocular determines the appropriate size and power. A large-diameter objective lens provides large light-gathering power, which is useful at low levels of illumination, such as at twilight. Thus a 7 x 50 instrument is eminently suitable for such conditions. For viewing sports events or for bird watching, a 6 x 30 or a 7 x 35 binocular has adequate power and is likely to be relatively lightweight. A fixed, stable mount should be used to support high-power (8 or more) binoculars to prevent shake of the image.

FRANCIS E. WASHER
National Bureau of Standards

BINOMIAL THEOREM, bī-nō′mē-əl thē′ə-rəm, an important theorem in mathematics. A binomial is an expression containing two terms. If x and y are distinct terms and n is any positive integer, then according to the binomial theorem:

$$(x + y)^n = \sum_{j=0}^{n} \binom{n}{j} x^{n-j} y^j \text{ where } \binom{n}{j} = \frac{n!}{j!(n-j)!}$$

and $n!$ is equal to $n(n-1)(n-2)\cdots 3\cdot 2\cdot 1$ for $n \geq 1$ and $0! = 1$ by definition. The binomial coefficients $\binom{n}{j}$ are often written C_j^n because for particular values of n and j they give the number of combinations of n things taken j at a time. They occur frequently in such areas of mathematics as probability, statistics, and combinational analysis. These coefficients for all degrees up to any particular positive integer N may be generated by a method usually attributed to the French mathematician Blaise Pascal, although published as early as the 1300's in China:

$$1$$
$$1\ 1$$
$$1\ 2\ 1$$
$$1\ 3\ 3\ 1$$
$$1\ 4\ 6\ 4\ 1$$
$$\cdots\cdots\cdots\cdots$$
$$1\ N\ \ldots\ N\ 1$$

In this array, called *Pascal's triangle*, 1 occurs as the first and last entry in each row, and all other entries are the sum of the two numbers directly above. See also PASCAL'S TRIANGLE.

By extending the theorem to fractional and negative values of n, Sir Isaac Newton obtained a generalized binomial formula involving infinite series. The convergence properties of these series were examined by N.H. Abel in the early 1800's. Abel showed that for $x < 1$ the series

$$(1 + x)^n = 1 + \frac{nx}{1} + \frac{n(n-1)}{1\cdot 2}x^2 +$$
$$\cdots + \frac{n(n-1)\ldots(n-j+1)}{j!}x^j + \cdots$$

converges. See also SERIES.

E.P. MILES, JR.
Computing Center, Florida State University

BINTAN, bin′tän, in Indonesia, is the largest island of the Riau Archipelago. The name is also spelled *Bintang*. The island, 415 square miles (1,075 sq km) in area, is located in the South China Sea off the southern tip of the Malay Peninsula. Bauxite and tin are mined.

BINTURONG, bin-tōō′rong, a civet cat native to southeastern Asia from the Himalayas to Sumatra and Java. The binturong is from 4 to 6 feet (1.2 to 1.8 meters) long, including the tail, and weighs from 20 to 30 pounds (9 to 13.5 kg). It is covered with long, coarse, grayish black hair and has a prehensile, or grasping, tail. Because it lives in treetops and is nocturnal and shy, the binturong is seldom seen. It feeds mostly on fruits and other vegetation but also eats small animals such as tree frogs. The binturong (*Arctictis binturong*) is in the family Viverridae.

ZOOLOGICAL SOCIETY OF LONDON

Binturong (*Arctictis binturong*)

BINYON, bin′yən, **Laurence** (1869–1943), English art historian and poet, who did much to further Western understanding of Oriental art. He was born *Robert Laurence Binyon*, in Lancaster, England, on Aug. 10, 1869. After attending St. Paul's School in London, he entered Trinity College, Oxford, where he received the Newdigate Prize in 1890 for his poem *Persephone*. He started working for the British Museum's department of prints and drawings in 1895, became assistant director of the section in 1909, and in 1913 was appointed director of the museum's department of Oriental prints and drawings. An acknowledged authority on Oriental art, he gave several lectures abroad, including talks in China and Japan in 1929 and a course at Harvard in 1933. He died in Reading, England, on March 10, 1943.

Binyon's writings on the history of art, mostly concerned with Oriental art, include *Painting in the Far East* (1908), *Court Painters of the Grand Mogul* (1921), *Drawings and Engravings of William Blake* (1922), and *The Spirit of Man in Asian Art* (1935). He also assembled two official British Museum directories: the monumental catalog of English drawings (4 vols., 1898–1904) and the catalog of Japanese woodcuts (1917).

Binyon wrote several volumes of poetry, including *Lyric Poems* (1894), *Odes* (1900), *The New World* (1918), and *North Star and Other Poems* (1941). As a playwright he pioneered in an effort to restore blank verse to the English stage, in dramas that included *Attila* (1907) and *The Young King* (1924).

BIOCHEMISTRY, bī-ō-kem′ə-strē, is the study of chemical processes in living things. Since the 1940's biochemistry has developed more rapidly than all of the other life sciences. Through the use of extremely sensitive analytical tools, high-speed computers, and radioactive tracers, the biochemist has been able to gain an understanding of the mechanisms of cellular reproduction and growth, the utilization of essential nutrients, and above all, the means by which the body regulates these delicate reactions, which distinguish living from nonliving matter.

Despite the dramatic differences in the appearances of living things, the basic chemistry of all organisms is strikingly similar. Even tiny one-celled creatures carry out essentially the same reactions that each cell of a complex organism such as man carries out. This similarity enables the biochemist to find basic information about the chemistry of human beings by studying the chemistry of microorganisms in the laboratory for hundreds of generations in a short period of time.

Classical biochemistry described the chemical components of the cell and separated them into classes such as carbohydrates, amino acids, proteins, nucleic acids, lipids, and minerals. The modern biochemist, however, studies the ways in which these materials change within the cell, while the over-all integrity of the cell—its dynamic equilibrium—is maintained. In order to keep the whole essentially the same even though the parts are constantly changing, living matter requires sensitive regulatory mechanisms that govern both the processes within individual cells and also the interactions among cells that combine to form tissues, organs, and complex individuals.

CHEMICAL COMPONENTS OF BIOLOGICAL SYSTEMS

Water. The most familiar component of cells and by far the most abundant is water. Water constitutes from 65 to 95 percent of the total weight of a cell. This wide range represents differences between types of cells and not fluctuations within any one cell. Any change in the water content of a cell brings about profound biological changes, in many cases extensive enough to result in death.

Proteins. Proteins are important structural molecules, since they form a major part of the architecture of the cell, and they also play key roles in the functioning of the cell.

Protein Structure. Proteins are made up of long chains of amino acid subunits, most of which are manufactured by the cell. An amino acid molecule includes a central carbon atom to which is attached a hydrogen atom, a carboxyl group, and an amino group. The carboxyl group, COOH, consists of a carbon atom, two atoms of oxygen, and an atom of hydrogen; and the amino group, NH_2, consists of a nitrogen atom to which two hydrogen atoms are attached. In addition, each amino acid has a characteristic side group, R, that distinguishes it from other amino acids.

$$\overset{\displaystyle H}{\underset{\displaystyle NH_2}{R-C-COOH}}$$

The amino acids are joined together in long chains of a specific sequence by peptide bonds in which the amino group of one amino acid is attached to the carboxyl group of another. This linking of amino acids forms the *primary structure* of the protein.

One protein differs from another protein in the order in which the amino acids are strung together. While there are many naturally occurring amino acids, it appears that only 20 make up most of the protein in animal tissue. When these amino acids are connected in proper sequence, like the words in a sentence, the protein is a complete functional protein. If, however, even one key amino acid is deleted or changed, the protein is either a different protein or a nonsense protein. One such mistake results in the pathological condition of sickle-cell anemia, a blood disease that is caused by the substitution of one amino acid, valine, for the normal glutamic acid at a single location in the hemoglobin molecule.

In most proteins, part of the chain of amino acids coils into a spiral, or helix. This spiral is referred to as the *secondary structure* of the protein. The protein molecule can also fold and twist over itself, forming a *tertiary structure*. In addition, some proteins are made up of two or more polypeptide chains in a definite orientation to one another. The orientation of these chains is the *quaternary structure* of a protein. An example of the quaternary structure is the structure of hemoglobin (one of the main components of the red blood cell) in which there are four polypeptide chains that fold in a characteristic manner around four porphyrin (metal-free derivative of C_4H_5N) rings.

Both the secondary and tertiary structures of proteins are essential for the preservation of the biological activity of the protein. Two kinds of protein whose activity is known to depend upon their spatial structures are enzymes and anti-

A PEPTIDE LINKAGE (enclosed in dotted line) is formed between amino acids when the carboxyl group (COOH) of one amino acid links up with the amino group (NH_2) of the other. In the process, a hydrogen atom (H) breaks off from the amino group and an OH group breaks off from the carboxyl group, forming a water molecule.

GLYCINE   ALANINE   GLYCYL-ALANINE   WATER

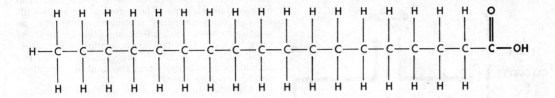

FATTY ACIDS consist of chains of carbon atoms with a carboxyl group at one end. Stearic acid is shown above.

bodies. Both carry out their work by being specific for certain substances. This specificity of enzymes and antibodies is determined by the manner in which their tertiary structures are adapted to fit other molecules. See ANTIBODIES AND ANTIGENS.

If the secondary and tertiary structures of proteins are disorganized, profound changes will occur in the chemical and physical characteristics of the protein. These changes rarely can be reversed. A process such as denaturation is nothing more than the disorganization of these spatial structures of the protein. Heating proteins such as albumin (found in egg white), for example, will produce this disorganization of structure.

Proteins and Function. Some proteins carry out the extraordinary feat of directing the complex changes that go on in the cell. These proteins are the *enzymes*, special molecules that make it easier for a compound to change into a specific and different compound.

Modern biochemists not only are interested in obtaining enzymes in pure form, but also are studying the molecular and atomic composition of individual enzymes to determine how enzymes work. One enzyme, pancreatic ribonuclease, has been studied extensively, and the primary structure, or sequence, of the protein subunits (the amino acids), has been worked out.

Biochemists have discovered that enzyme proteins often are associated with other small nonprotein molecules called *coenzymes*. Without coenzymes, the enzyme cannot function properly. In addition to coenzymes, many enzymes require metals such as calcium, magnesium, iron, or copper as activators.

Lipids. The lipids, or fatty compounds, constitute another major group of cellular components. Unlike the proteins, the various kinds of lipids vary widely in structure and are classed together mainly because all of them are insoluble in water and readily soluble in organic solvents such as chloroform. Lipids include fats and oils, steroids, and phospholipids, as well as more complex materials. Lipids are found abundantly in the cytoplasm of the cell. They also are found in certain specialized structures, particularly the cellular membranes.

Of all the lipids found in animal tissue, neutral fats are the most abundant. Neutral fats (glycerides) consist of glycerol ($C_3H_8O_3$) chemically bonded to fatty acids. The fatty acids are chains of carbon atoms with a carboxyl group at one end. Fatty acids differ from one another both in the length of the carbon chain and in the type of chemical bonding in the chain. Another important group of lipids, the phospholipids, contain nitrogen and phosphorus in addition to car-

bon, hydrogen, and oxygen. Phospholipids are major structural components of cellular membranes.

Carbohydrates. Carbohydrates, particularly the sugars and starches (sugar polymers), are important energy sources for the cell. They also provide the molecular skeleton from which many of the amino acids can be built.

Two very important biological sugars will be discussed more fully later. These are ribose, a five-carbon sugar that is an important constituent of the genetic materials of the cells, and glucose, a six-carbon sugar, from which much of the energy of the cell is derived.

THE CONSERVATION OF LIFE

No cell or complex organism can live isolated from its environment. Every living thing requires, in varying degrees, certain substances from the outside in order to obtain energy, structural components, and growth factors that it is unable to synthesize.

Living things are divided into two groups according to their type of nutrition. Green plants and certain bacteria, for example, require only simple inorganic compounds in the diet since they can obtain energy directly from sunlight and can build all the complex molecules necessary for life from simple compounds. They do this by a process called photosynthesis. Most other organisms, including all of the animal species, lack many of the enzymes necessary to construct all of their substance from simple molecules and therefore these organisms require many complex molecules to be present, preformed, in the diet.

The nutritional requirements of human beings are many. In addition to water, oxygen, and salts, human beings must be provided with energy, essential amino acids, and fatty acids, and a number of accessory food factors that collectively are known as *vitamins*. Chemically, vitamins are a varied group of substances and do not fit into any one group of chemical compounds. Although specific roles for the vitamins in the metabolism of the cell are only just beginning to be understood, vitamins generally are believed to act as coenzymes and are essential factors without which many enzymic reactions cannot occur.

These nutritional requirements are fulfilled by the diet. When foods are ingested, they are acted upon by a series of digestive enzymes that break down the large molecules into simple sugars, amino acids, and fatty acids that can be absorbed into the body. These are transported to the cells where they are used as raw materials for the metabolism of the cell.

Cellular Metabolism. Metabolism in the cell

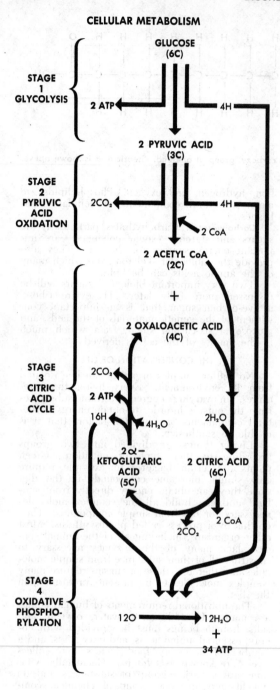

CELLULAR METABOLISM

GLUCOSE
(6C)

STAGE
1
GLYCOLYSIS

2 ATP ← 4H →

2 PYRUVIC ACID
(3C)

STAGE
2
PYRUVIC
ACID
OXIDATION

$2CO_2$ ← 4H →

2 CoA →

2 ACETYL CoA
(2C)

+

2 OXALOACETIC ACID
(4C)

STAGE
3
CITRIC
ACID
CYCLE

$2CO_2$

2 ATP

16H ← $4H_2O$ $2H_2O$ →

2 α-
KETOGLUTARIC
ACID
(5C)

2 CITRIC ACID
(6C)

2 CoA

$2CO_2$

STAGE
4
OXIDATIVE
PHOSPHO-
RYLATION

$12O$ → $12H_2O$

+

34 ATP

THE CELL'S ENERGY-PRODUCING MACHINERY supplies the energy used to manufacture vital cellular compounds. Energy production takes place in the four stages shown above. In the first stage the carbohydrate glucose is broken down into 2 molecules of pyruvic acid, with the production of two molecules of the high-energy compound ATP. In the second stage, pyruvic acid is converted to the highly reactive compound acetyl coenzyme A. Stage three, which is known as the citric acid or Krebs cycle, breaks down acetyl coenzyme A into reduced coenzymes and carbon dioxide; two more molecules of ATP are produced. The final step, oxidation of hydrogen, yields 34 molecules of ATP.

consists of the dual processes of *catabolism* (the chemical breakdown of large molecules into smaller ones that are either reutilized or excreted as waste products) and *anabolism* (the synthesis of complex molecules from simple molecules). The catabolic changes usually are associated with the liberation of energy, while the anabolic reactions usually require energy.

Much of the work done by the cell consists of breaking down molecules to liberate energy for the synthesis of necessary components. Most of this energy comes from the catabolism of carbohydrates and lipids, although proteins can be used as a source of energy. Since cells are unable to use the heat generated from the breakdown of these substances directly, they trap the energy in high energy chemical bonds that are part of the adenosine triphosphate (ATP) molecule. (See ATP.) The ATP molecule is the currency used in most energy transactions in the cell.

Glycolysis. A common method by which carbohydrates are broken down is glycolysis, which occurs in the cytoplasm of the cell. Glycolysis is a fermentation process that does not require oxygen and provides a quick source of energy. In this process, a molecule of the sugar glucose is broken down step by step into two molecules of pyruvic acid. The series of 11 intermediate steps in the process is known as the Embden Meyerhof system. Glycolysis results in a net gain of two molecules of high energy ATP for each molecule of glucose oxidized in the Embden Meyerhof system.

Pyruvic acid then is converted into a highly reactive form of acetic acid called acetyl coenzyme A. This conversion is a complex enzymatic step that requires several B vitamins, magnesium ions, and lipoic acid. The acetyl coenzyme A molecule is the junction point in the metabolism of carbohydrates, amino acids, and lipids, and this molecule represents the route by which each of these substances can be utilized for energy.

Krebs Cycle and Oxidative Phosphorylation. Acetyl coenzyme A feeds into a series of enzymatic reactions known collectively as the Krebs citric acid cycle. This series of reactions, which occurs mainly in the mitochondria, allows the cell to produce far more energy than the glycolysis process. Its total yield of energy for every glucose molecule put into the system is 38 molecules of ATP.

The citric acid cycle breaks down acetyl coenzyme A into carbon dioxide and reduced coenzymes, which are to be used for further oxidation. This oxidative process, called cell respiration, occurs in all cells that require oxygen to live.

The chain of enzymes in which respiration takes place is called the respiratory chain, or the electron-transfer system. In this chain, electrons or hydrogen atoms are transferred from one molecule to another through a chain of reactions that use at least three vitamin-containing coenzymes and a group of molecules known as cytochromes. The last component of the chain is oxygen, which reacts with hydrogen to form water. With this final reaction, the cell successfully harnesses the energy of combustion. The energy released is transferred to adenosine diphosphate molecules, and oxidative phosphorylation adds one more high energy phosphate to form ATP. This energy is now available for powering the synthesis of macromolecules, such as proteins, in the cell.

Control over Metabolism. In a complex organism such as man, there must be some method of regulation so that the liver, for example, can know of another organ's need for more energy or amino acids. Although the complete concept is not at all clear at this time, a picture of the role of *hormones* as regulatory substances at the molecular level is beginning to emerge. Although hormones must directly affect enzymatic reactions, they do so in very indirect ways. This molecular concept of hormone control is very different from the traditional concept of hormones affecting target organs in a general way rather than affecting specific reactions within the target organ.

A concrete illustration of the kind of hormonal control exerted over enzymatic reactions is provided by glucagon, a hormone secreted by the pancreas into the hepatic portal veins. This hormone controls the breakdown of glycogen to increase blood glucose. When glucagon reaches the cell, it stimulates the enzymatic conversion of ATP necessary for the activation of an enzyme needed for glycogen breakdown. The consequent breakdown of glycogen raises the level of blood sugar.

The biochemist is beginning to understand that, in many cases, the products of a reaction can modify its course either by increasing or decreasing the rate of the reaction, or, in some cases, stopping the reaction completely. This kind of control over cellular metabolism is called *feedback inhibition*. It is the kind of rapid, critical control that the cell must maintain in order to keep the proper balance of its internal environment.

THE PERPETUATION OF LIFE

If any one factor had to be chosen to account for the rapid development of the field of biochemistry—so rapid that much of the work done in this area prior to 1960 is considered ancient history—it would have to be the work of one group of biochemists, the molecular biologists. These biochemists, combining theoretical speculation with experimental data, have developed a convincing model that can explain how offspring resemble parents, how liver cells produce identical liver cells, or how bacteria produce identical bacteria.

All the information necessary to determine eye color, to manufacture enzymes, and to determine other genetic traits appears to be coded on long molecules that are found in the nucleus of the cell. Biochemists have started to uncover both the way in which this coded information is transmitted from a cell to its offspring and the way in which the coded information is transformed in a living functioning cell. It even appears that biochemists are well on their way to deciphering the chemical code that these molecules use to transmit their information.

Chromosomes and Nucleic Acids. In the cell, the coded information is found in the genes, or hereditary factors. The genes are found in the chromosomes, which usually are located in the nucleus of the cell. Each gene occupies a fixed locus, or position, on the chromosome and contains the information of a specific biological fact. The hereditary material in different organisms is basically the same and differs only in the nature of the coded information.

When chromosomes are analyzed chemically, regardless of cell origin, two kinds of compounds are found: proteins (already discussed) and nucleic acids. Nucleic acids are made up of either of two sugar molecules (ribose or deoxyribose), an acid (phosphoric acid), and five nitrogen-containing organic bases (adenine, guanine, cytosine, thymine, and uracil). Each sugar commonly is found associated with four of the five bases. Ribose is found with adenine, guanine, cytosine, and uracil, and deoxyribose is found with adenine, guanine, cytosine, and thymine. The combination of one sugar, one base, and phosphoric acid is referred to as a *nucleotide*. Nucleotides are the subunits that constitute the alphabet of the genetic code. It is believed that a combination of three nucleotides, known as a codon or triplet, determines one amino acid in the amino acid sequence of a particular protein. For example, three uracil-containing nucleotides make up the triplet, or codon, that corresponds to the amino acid phenylalanine.

It is the long chains of the deoxyribose nucleotides, the *deoxyribonucleic acid* (DNA) molecule, that contain the coded information necessary for the function and perpetuation of the cell. DNA is reproduced faithfully when the cell divides so that the daughter cells contain exact copies of the parental DNA. This ensures that the daughter cells will be exact copies of the parental cells.

Structure of DNA. A significant clue about the DNA molecule came from Erwin Chargaff's reports of 1950 to 1953. He found that the nucleotides of DNA, represented by the initials of their bases—A, C, G, T—were always found in the surprising ratios of A:C = T:G, and that the amount of A always equaled the amount of T, and the amount of G always equaled the amount of C.

In 1953, James Watson and Francis H.C. Crick used these clues plus the X-ray diffraction data of Maurice H.F. Wilkins to suggest that DNA must not be a single chain but two spiral chains winding around each other. Because of this work, Watson and Crick (along with Wilkins) were awarded the 1962 Nobel Prize in medicine and physiology. They suggested a model in which each chain is made up of nucleotides combined in such a way that the bases protrude perpendicularly toward the long, central axis of the chain. If the geometry of the two chains were just right, an A on one chain would always join with a T on the other, and a C on one chain would always join with a G on the other, thus explaining the ratios that Chargaff uncovered.

As for the duplication, or replication, of the DNA molecule, it was postulated that the two chains unwind, leaving the free bases exposed. Unattached nucleotides in the cell then combine with their complementary bases exposed on the DNA chain. Thus a new nucleotide containing a thymine site combines with an exposed adenine, and a new nucleotide containing a cytosine site binds with the exposed guanine. In this manner, each chain of the DNA reproduces exactly a copy of the other chain to which it originally was paired, and the cell now contains two identical double-stranded DNA molecules. One of these then can be transferred to a daughter cell.

Protein Synthesis. In addition to explaining how information is transmitted from one generation to the next, the model of the double-stranded

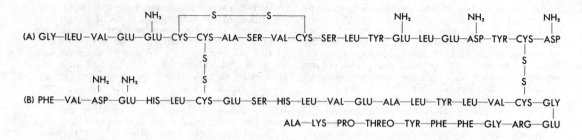

(A) GLY—ILEU—VAL—GLU—GLU—CYS—CYS—ALA—SER—VAL—CYS—SER—LEU—TYR—GLU—LEU—GLU—ASP—TYR—CYS—ASP

(B) PHE—VAL—ASP—GLU—HIS—LEU—CYS—GLU—SER—HIS—LEU—VAL—GLU—ALA—LEU—TYR—LEU—VAL—CYS—GLY

ALA—LYS—PRO—THREO—TYR—PHE—PHE—GLY—ARG—GLU

PROTEINS are large organic molecules consisting of chains of amino acids linked together by disulfide (S—S) bonds. The diagram above shows the *primary structure*—the interconnections between component amino acids—of the simple protein insulin. The diagram below shows both the primary structure and the three-dimensional, pleated-sheet *secondary structure* of a section of another simple protein, silk fibroin. Most proteins are far more complex than the two examples shown here.

AMINO ACID	ABBREVIATION	AMINO ACID	ABBREVIATION
ALANINE	ALA	LEUCINE	LEU
ARGININE	ARG	LYSINE	LYS
ASPARAGINE	ASPN	METHIONINE	MET
ASPARTIC ACID	ASP	PHENYLALANINE	PHE
CYSTEINE	CYS	PROLINE	PRO
GLUTAMIC ACID	GLU	SERINE	SER
GLUTAMINE	GLUN	THREONINE	THR
GLYCINE	GLY	TRYPTOPHAN	TRYP
HISTIDINE	HIS	TYROSINE	TYR
ISOLEUCINE	ILEU	VALINE	VAL

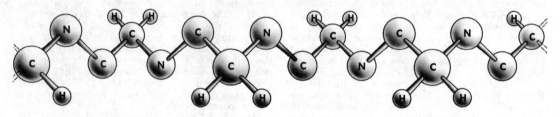

DNA molecule also explains how new proteins are manufactured in the cell. The coded information on the DNA molecule can be read for the purpose of assembling each protein with its unique sequence of amino acids.

This process of protein synthesis also involves ribonucleic acids (RNA), a chain of nucleotides containing ribose and the base uracil in place of thymine. Different types of RNA, each with a specific function, are involved at different steps of the synthetic process.

One type of RNA molecule is formed as a complementary chain to one of the nuclear DNA chains in the same manner as described for DNA replication. In this replication, the DNA molecule is transferring instructions to the RNA molecule for the manufacture of a specific protein. The RNA formed is called messenger RNA (mRNA), or template RNA, since it serves as a pattern for the synthesis of the protein. After it is formed, the mRNA leaves the nucleus and moves to the cytoplasm where it becomes attached to specialized structures of the cell called ribosomes. These structures are the actual site of protein synthesis in the cell. The mRNA carries the information needed for the assembly of a protein chain at this site.

Meanwhile, in the cytoplasm there is another group of smaller RNA molecules known as transfer RNA (tRNA), or soluble RNA (sRNA). Each of these tRNA molecules has a codon site that is specific for a certain amino acid needed for the protein synthesis. They combine with this amino acid (which either has been synthesized by the cell or has entered from the environment), bring it to the ribosome at the complementary codon site on the mRNA. The tRNA with the amino acid attached is bound temporarily at this site, and then the amino acid is attached to the growing protein chain. When the entire sequence of amino acids has been assembled, the newly formed protein detaches from the ribosome site.

The deletion of a base or the exchange of one base for another during the process of replication of DNA is a kind of genetic mutation. When this mutated base sequence is copied during the formation of RNA, a new triplet will be installed at one location on the RNA molecule. The protein formed by the new RNA will then have a different sequence of amino acids from that of the normal protein; or, if the triplet is a nonsense triplet, no protein at all can be formed. A previously discussed example of such a mistake is sickle cell anemia. It is hoped that by a complete deciphering of the genetic code, such diseases can be corrected by rearranging the code defect.

François Jacob and Jacques Monod postulated that, in addition to genes that specify the amino-acid sequence of proteins, there are other genes, known as regulator genes, that determine when to turn the synthesis of a particular protein on or off. The activity of these genes involves interplay of inducer substances and repressor substances that act at various points in the production of proteins to regulate their synthesis as they are required within the cell. Jacob and Monod (along with André Lwoff) were awarded the 1965 Nobel Prize in medicine and physiology.

The current picture of molecular genetics is incomplete, and there are many challenging questions yet to be answered. There are many more types of nucleic acids in the cell than can be accounted for in terms of known functions of nucleic acids. Molecular research is branching out from the studies of heredity and protein synthesis to such topics as the role of RNA in the coding and storage of information in the brain (memory).

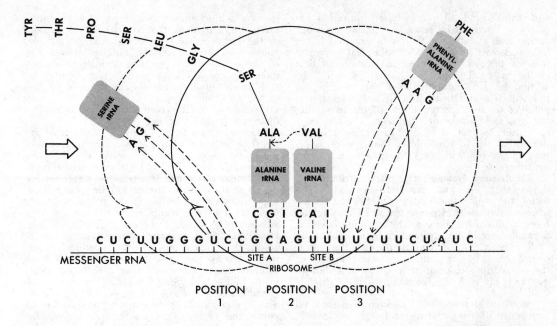

PROTEIN SYNTHESIS occurs at the ribosomes, small particles found within the cell. Instructions for the assembly of a particular protein are carried from the cell nucleus to the ribosome assembly site by messenger RNA (mRNA). Each triplet of nucleotides on the mRNA molecule is a "code word," specifying a particular amino acid. The various amino acids called for by the mRNA triplets are brought to the ribosome assembly site by transfer RNA (tRNA) molecules. As the ribosome moves along the mRNA chain, the nucleotide triplet of each tRNA temporarily attaches itself to a corresponding triplet on the mRNA molecule and transfers its amino acid to the growing peptide chain. In this diagram, serine tRNA, which gave up its amino acid when the ribosome was at position 1, is leaving the ribosome assembly site. Alanine tRNA is in the process of giving up its amino acid, and valine tRNA has just attached to its code site. Phenyl-alanine tRNA is approaching the assembly site and will transfer its amino acid to the peptide chain when the ribosome reaches position 3.

RESEARCH METHODS

Biochemistry has become far too varied for any one laboratory to have all the equipment commonly associated with biochemical research. For example, laboratories that emphasize the analysis of cell composition have instruments and techniques quite different from those used by laboratories interested in determining the chemical mechanism of muscle contraction. There are some research methods and instruments, however, that have widespread use. These include using isotopes to sort molecules and studying protein sequences by means of chromatography. These methods are discussed in this section.

Isotopes. Each element has a characteristic number of electrons encircling its nucleus. The number of electrons determines the chemical properties of the element. Within the nucleus is a corresponding number of protons. Neutrons also are contained in the nucleus; however, their number is not always constant, and several species of atoms of the same element can exist. These species differ only in the number of neutrons in the nucleus. These species, or atomic variations, are called isotopes. Of particular interest to the biochemist are the radioactive isotopes. These isotopes have unstable nuclei that tend to break down and release energy.

Labeling with Radioactive Isotopes. Radioactivity enables the biochemist to identify even a very small amount of one isotope in the presence of a large quantity of another. For example, find-

ing a radioactive carbon atom among a large amount of nonradioactive carbon atoms might be compared to the task of identifying one flashlight in a boxcar full of identical flashlights. If the one flashlight we are trying to locate is lit while the others are not, the task is greatly simplified. The same is true with the carbon atoms. If one of the atoms is radioactive, it is much easier to locate it among the other carbon atoms.

Biochemists use radioactive isotopes to label certain substances they wish to study in the cell. By following the path of the radioactive isotope, they can follow the fate of an atom as it is metabolized by an organism. Much of the knowledge of the intricate changes that occur when food is metabolized by an organism has been obtained in just this way.

Sorting Molecules by Means of Isotopes. Radioactivity is not the only property of isotopes that is important to biochemists. Another characteristic of isotopes—the fact that the different isotopes of an element have different weights—made possible a classic experiment that verified the Watson-Crick hypothesis regarding the way in which DNA replicates itself. In order to describe this experiment, we must first explain the concept of density gradients, which are produced either naturally by the force of gravity or artificially in a centrifuge.

Density Gradient. Some substances tend to distribute their mass unevenly under the influence of gravity. An obvious example is the earth's atmosphere. It has a high density at sea level and thins gradually as higher altitudes are reached. Finally it becomes so thin that it all but disappears. A balloon filled with gas that has a lighter density than the atmosphere at sea level will rise until the density of the air equals that of the gas in the balloon; the balloon will float at that level. Another balloon with a different gas will rise and float at a different level, depending on its density. Thus, in this case, the atmosphere has a density gradient. The tendency of matter to float at a level determined by its density, as the balloons do in the atmosphere, is used in the following experiment with the ultracentrifuge.

The Research Problem. The ultracentrifuge is a device that can spin material very fast. The faster the spin, the higher is the gravitylike force on the material being spun. Increasing the force in this manner causes heavy materials that normally would be suspended in a solution to "fall" toward the circumference of the ultracentrifuge. Materials such as sugar solutions or the salt cesium chloride tend to form a density gradient in such an increased "gravitational" field.

Matthew Meselson and Franklyn W. Stahl used isotopes of nitrogen and the technique of density-gradient centrifugation to demonstrate how DNA reproduces itself and how it is transferred to the daughter cells. The problem that Meselson and Stahl set out to solve was whether during cell division the double-stranded DNA molecule splits into two chains and each chain reconstructs its partner (complementary) chain, or whether the two original DNA chains stay together while an entirely new double-stranded molecule is formed and passed to the next generation.

To carry out their experiment, they grew bacteria in a medium that contained only a heavy isotope of nitrogen, which was to be used as the nitrogen source for the manufacture of new DNA in the bacteria. The DNA isolated from these bacteria floated at a particular level in a cesium chloride gradient, much as the balloon did in the upper atmosphere. Another culture of bacteria was grown in a medium containing only the lighter isotope of nitrogen for its nitrogen source. As would be expected, the DNA isolated from these bacteria floated higher in the gradient than the DNA made with heavy nitrogen.

Meselson and Stahl reasoned that if the bacteria were grown in heavy nitrogen and then placed in a medium containing only light nitrogen, all of the DNA molecules of the next generation would have one heavy and one light chain each if the chains split during replication. On the other hand, if the chains stayed together during replication, half of the DNA molecules of the next generation would have two heavy chains each and the other half would have two light chains each. Thus, when placed in a cesium chloride gradient, the new DNA would give either one band of heavy-light chains floating at a point between those at which the heavy and light DNA's float, or two bands—one for the new light-chain molecules and one for the old heavy-chain molecules.

When the experiment was carried out, Meselson and Stahl found that all of the DNA was concentrated in a single band, floating midway between the light and heavy levels, thus proving that the DNA molecule does in fact split into two chains during replication.

Mapping the Structure of Large Molecules. As the science of biochemistry progresses, it is becoming increasingly evident that the biological activity of the large complex molecules—the macromolecules—is dependent on the unique arrangement of these molecules in space. Although macromolecules are very large as molecules go, they are still much smaller than the limits of resolution of the best microscopes available today. Direct visualization of the conformation of a protein molecule is therefore not possible.

However, techniques now are available for the determination of the atomic structure of proteins, and several proteins have already been analyzed. When the entire atomic structure of the protein is known, the possible distances between atoms and the strength of the bonds holding various atoms together can be calculated, since each atom of the complex macromolecule must adhere to the standard rules of chemical bonding. However, since proteins contain hundreds of atoms, the calculation of all the possible arrangements in space of these atoms, even for a small protein, might very well take a lifetime. However, high-speed computers can perform such calculations in a matter of minutes. In addition, a computer can be programmed not only to calculate the various conformations of macromolecules and print out the answers, but also to display the calculated conformation visually on a screen similar to a television screen. This is only one use to which computers have been applied in the study of biochemical reactions.

Chromatography: Studying Protein Sequences. Most of the present information about amino-acid sequences in proteins and about the composition of lipids in the cell has been provided by chromatographic separation techniques. These techniques take advantage of slight differences in the physical properties of different components in a mixture—for example, the different amino acids from a protein or the different classes of lipids found in a lipid extract. Some methods, such as the gas-liquid chromatograph and the paper chromatograph methods, rely on slight differences in the solubility of the various materials in the mixture. Other methods rely on different adsorption properties or different electrical properties of the various components of a mixture.

A discussion of ion-exchange chromatography will serve to illustrate the concept of chromatography. For this method, a tube is packed with an inert material, such as diatomaceous earth, and then the particles of the packing material are coated with a chemical that has many free negative charges in an acidic solution. The mixture being studied is placed at the top of the column. If the mixture contains amino acids, for example, then some of the amino acids will have positive charges, some will have negative charges, and some will have no charge at all. The amino acids with the most positive charges are held by the negative charges in the column, while the negatively charged amino acids pass easily through the column. Since no two of the amino acids have exactly the same ability to bind with the charged column, they will be separated by the column. Analysis of the separation is carried out by automatic machines. In this way, the amino acid composition of a protein, for example, can be determined.

Other Techniques. Techniques have also been borrowed from other fields. For example, electron and X-ray diffraction equipment, which has been in common use in the field of metallurgy, has been used with much success by Max Perutz and John C. Kendrew (winner of the 1962 Nobel Prize in chemistry) to determine the configuration of myoglobin and hemoglobin.

For the future, it is possible to predict that major discoveries will be made with the *electron probe microanalyzer,* an instrument that is capable of identifying and measuring individual elements within one micron area of tissue. It can, for example, tell how much fluoride or calcium, to name only two elements, is present in the area of one micron of a tooth. Also, *field-ion microscopes* are being developed that theoretically may be able to resolve structures the size of macromolecules and thus permit direct observation of molecular structure.

JUAN NAVIA
Massachusetts Institute of Technology

Bibliography

Asimov, Isaac, *Chemicals of Life* (New York 1962).
Anfinsen, Christian B., *The Molecular Basis of Evolution* (New York 1959).
Barry, John M., *Molecular Biology: Genes and the Chemical Control of Living Cells* (New York 1964).
Bonner, James, *Molecular Biology of Development* (New York 1965).
Broda, Englebert, *Radioactive Isotopes in Biochemistry* (New York 1960).
Budzikiewicz, H., and others, *Structure Elucidation of Natural Products by Mass Spectrometry,* 2 vols. (San Francisco 1964).
Campbell, Peter N., and Grenville, G.D., eds., *Essays in Biochemistry,* vol. 1 (New York 1965).
Glick, David, ed., *Methods of Biochemical Analysis,* 14 vols. (New York 1954–65).
Hartman, Philip E., and Suskind, S.R., *Gene Action* (Englewood Cliffs, N.J., 1965).
Hoffman, K., *Chemistry of Life* (New York 1964).
Ingram, V.M., *The Biosynthesis of Macromolecules* (New York 1965).
Karlson, P., *Introduction to Modern Biochemistry,* 2d ed. (New York 1965).
Neilands, J.B., and Stumpf, P.K., *Outlines of Enzyme Chemistry* (New York 1958).
Pauling, Linus, and Itano, H.A., eds., *Molecular Structure and Biological Specificity* (New York 1961).
Taylor, J.H., ed., *Selected Papers in Molecular Genetics* (New York 1965).
White, Abraham, and others, *Principles of Biochemistry,* 3d ed. (New York 1964).

BIOELECTRICITY, bī-ō-i-lek-tris′ǝ-tē, the electric current found in all biological systems. Bioelectricity consists of a flow of electrons and ions, or charged atoms. Although the phenomenon is commonplace on the cellular level throughout the world of living things, certain fish, such as eels and rays, are highly specialized in their ability to produce electricity.

The special ability of some fish to produce electricity results from their possession of electric organs that are composed mainly of modified muscle tissue. The constituent cells (electroplates) of this modified tissue are disk-shaped and noncontractile. They are stacked in neat rows suggesting battery cells connected in series. Anatomically, the posterior surface of each electroplate is supplied with a motor neuron, whereas the anterior surface is not. During an inactive period the interior of each electroplate is negatively charged, and the two exterior surfaces are positively charged. Because positive and negative charges alternate, no current flows. This condition continues until a nerve impulse reaches the posterior surface of the electroplate via a neuron. Such a nerve impulse triggers a series of complicated chemical reactions, which ultimately produce an electric current by reversing the polarization of the cell.

The production of an electric current depends basically on the presence of two very important chemical molecules: acetylcholine (Ach) and adenosine triphosphate (ATP). The neuron carrying the nerve impulse to the electroplate releases Ach, which is split into separate acetyl and choline fractions. The energy involved in the splitting of Ach is thought to make the posterior membrane of the electroplate more permeable to the inflow of charged sodium atoms (Na^+ ions). This momentarily reverses the polarization of the cell and generates an electric current. After these reactions take place, the ATP is split to form adenosine diphosphate (ADP) and phosphate. The energy released in this splitting reaction is used in recombining the acetyl and choline fractions to form Ach.

Potentials as high as 400 to 550 volts have been measured in the South American electric eel. This voltage is enough to jolt a human severely, to kill other fish, or to light numerous light bulbs.

DAVID A. OTTO, *Stephens College*

BIOGENESIS, Principle of, bī-ō-jen′ǝ-sǝs, the theory that living organisms are produced only by other living organisms; that is, the theory of generation from preexisting life. It is the opposite of *abiogenesis,* or spontaneous generation. See LIFE; SPONTANEOUS GENERATION.

BIOGENETIC LAW. See RECAPITULATION.

BIOGRAPHIA LITERARIA, bī-ō-graf′ē-ǝ lit-ǝ-rär′ē-ǝ, is an essay by Samuel Taylor Coleridge (q.v.), first published in two volumes in 1817. Originally intended as a preface to a volume of Coleridge's poems, explaining and justifying his style and practice in poetry, the *Biographia Literaria* ultimately grew into a project of far greater magnitude. It consists of a description of Coleridge's education, an exposition of his early literary adventures, an extended criticism of William Wordsworth's theory of poetry as presented in the preface to *Lyrical Ballads,* and a statement of Coleridge's philosophical views. Despite its miscellaneous character, the *Biographia Literaria* remains one of Coleridge's few prose works that continue to be read. It is most valuable as the chief vehicle for his very important contributions to critical theory.

In the first part of the work Coleridge is mainly concerned with showing the evolution of his philosophic creed. At first an adherent of the associational psychology of the English philosopher David Hartley, Coleridge gradually discarded this mechanical system in favor of the belief that the mind is an active rather than a passive agent in the apprehension of reality. The discussion involves his definition of the imagination, or "emplastic power," the faculty by which the soul perceives the spiritual unity of the universe. He distinguishes between imagination and fancy, the latter being a merely associative function of the mind.

The later chapters deal with the nature of poetry and with Wordsworth's statement that the language of poetry should be one that is, with due exceptions, taken from the mouths of men in real life, and that there can be no essential difference between the language of prose and of metrical composition. While maintaining a general agreement with Wordsworth's point of view, Coleridge elaborately refutes his principles. A keen and appreciative critique on the qualities of Wordsworth's poetry concludes the work.

BIOGRAPHY, bī-ŏg′rə-fē, may be defined as "the account of an actual life." This description is the only one that will include all versions of biography, for in its long evolution, biography has assumed so many forms that any single definition inevitably excludes important instances. Thus, we must distinguish biography not only in terms of its subject matter but also in terms of its technique and its intention. The myriad forms of biography include catalogs of achievement, literary narratives, and psychological portraits. Each form has been "biography" in the extent to which it purports to deal with the records of an actual life, but each form has been distinct in its authors' strategies and purposes.

The impulse to leave to posterity the record of an impressive life is a natural craving. Commemorative tablets recalling the conquests and reigns of ancient rulers have been found in the archaeological remains of every literate culture, and even nonliterate tribes have left commemorative biographies in the form of hero legends and myths passed down orally from generation to generation. The most ancient literatures contain at least the germ of biography, as witnessed by the demonstrable historicism of many of the personages in Homer's *Iliad* or the "biographies" of the Pentateuch (Noah, Joseph, Moses, and other figures of the Old Testament). The impulse to recall the past, to be aware of one's own tribe and ancestry, is not limited to any epoch, and biography has been one way to satisfy it.

Greece and Rome. The anonymous and eponymous biographies of early cultures evolved into conscious literary form, particularly under Greek humanism of the 5th and 4th centuries B.C. The emphasis on the individuality of the human spirit helped produce the free-standing sculptures of the great artists Polyclitos and Scopas; and as they freed the human figure from the bondage of the entablature, so Greek biographers freed the individual from the frieze of dynastic and mythic ornament. The histories of Herodotus and Thucydides, in their 5th century narratives of the rise and fall of Greek greatness, include biographical portraits in which the personalities stand out from the fabric of the historical details. Several of the 4th century Platonic dialogues, particularly the *Apology, Crito,* and *Phaedo,* with their accounts of the trial, imprisonment, and death of Socrates, transcend philosophic doctrine and project a moving portrait of the philosopher.

Further impetus was given to the production of biography by Greek rhetoricians who, from the 5th century onward, perfected the *encomia,* or admiring recital of the accomplishments of public figures. The 4th century *Rhetoric* of Aristotle placed great emphasis on the understanding of character in rhetorical address, and the *Characters* of his pupil Theophrastus, although they dealt with abstract types rather than real personages, proved to be one of the most enduring influences on the writing of biography. Character studies in the Theophrastan vein were resurrected in 16th century France by Isaac Casaubon and in 17th century England by Joseph Hall, Thomas Overbury, and John Earle. They were adapted to real individuals by the earl of Clarendon, Gilbert Burnet, and John Dryden, and left their imprint on the work of the 20th century American biographer Gamaliel Bradford.

The influence of the classical rhetoricians was a mixed bequest: insofar as it stressed the artistry of the personality sketch, the influence was benign; but insofar as it emphasized character portrayal as part of a didactic intention, the influence was baleful. The biased or argumentative biography has never been completely absent from the literary scene.

Both Greek and Roman antiquity produced noteworthy examples of biography, all of them more or less in the rhetorical tradition. Xenophon's 4th century *Memorabilia* is, in addition to being a biography of Socrates, also a defense of the philosopher; and the collection of brief lives of the Greek philosophers, compiled by Diogenes Laertius in the 2d century A.D., made no pretence to being an objective account. A significant break with the aggressively argumentative biography came with Plutarch (about 46–127 A.D.), deservedly called "the father of biography." In his *Lives of the Noble Grecians and Romans,* a compendium of 44 biographies, he compared a distinguished Greek with a Roman (for example, Alexander with Caesar, as great generals, and Demosthenes with Cicero, as great orators). While Plutarch evidenced obvious likes and dislikes (to be neither a Greek nor a Roman would be, in his view, catastrophic), his biographies have a balance and an anecdotal richness that illuminate the whole personality of his subjects.

Plutarch's contemporary Gaius Suetonius Tranquillus achieved something of Plutarch's fairness and objectivity in his *Lives of the Caesars* but lacked Plutarch's literary skill, while Publius Cornelius Tacitus (about 55–117 A.D.) showed consummate literary skill but little restraint of didactic intention. His *Agricola,* the biography of his father-in-law, who was the conqueror of Britain under Emperor Domitian, is perhaps the finest of Roman biographies, but it is also moralistically intended: the redoubtable Agricola is shown in ironic contrast to the decadent Roman society of Tacitus' time.

Middle Ages and Renaissance. The tradition of biography as an effective moralizing, or didactic, instrument carried over most forcibly into the Middle Ages. The claim of universal leadership once professed by the Roman empire now passed into the custody of the medieval church; and where a historian like Tacitus had used biography as a social and political corrective, medieval church historians used biography as an ethical and spiritual corrective. A proselytizing biography developed, in which the lives of saints and martyrs were held up as exemplars for the people to follow and as demonstrations of God's purposes at work in the world. Amid the profusion of these largely anonymous and didactic biographies a few instances appeared that, if not entirely free of moralistic intention, at least introduced a note of credibility and historicity. The Venerable Bede's *Life of St. Cuthbert* in the 8th century and Eadmer's *Life of Anselm* in the 12th century stand out from the typical hagiography (saints' lives) of the era. But even in the Renaissance, "instructive" biography continued. The 14th century Giovanni Boccaccio adapted the moralism of medieval biography to secular subjects, and his *De casibus virorum illustrium* (Concerning the Downfall of Illustrious Men) used biographic materials to illustrate the pitfalls of worldly pride. A long-lived 16th century gallery of biographies was *The Mirror for Magistrates,* a collection first published in 1555 and added to successively until 1610, at which point it contained 91 moralizing biographies. Sir Thomas More's *History of King Richard III* (1515) was politically motivated—a defense of the Tudor regime accomplished by the character assassination of the previous monarch; and John Foxe's *The Acts and Monuments of the Church,* better known as *The Book of Martyrs* (1563), was a formidable Protestant denunciation of Catholicism under the guise of biographies of English reformers and martyrs during the reign of Mary Tudor.

But while the moralistic tradition continued, the humanism of the Renaissance, like the humanism of Greece in the 5th century B.C., provoked an interest in the individual above and beyond the framework of didacticism. Boccaccio also produced a biography of Dante, in which the great poet emerged as a person and not a type; at the end of the 14th century came Giovanni and Filippo Villani's *Cronaca Universale* (Universal Chronicle), and in 1550, Giorgio Vasari's *Lives of Seventy Most Eminent Painters, Sculptors, and Architects.* In each instance, as in the best of ancient biographies, a sense of distinct and living personalities began to appear. With the Renaissance came republication of the classical biographies: the illustrious French translation of Plutarch by Jacques Amyot (1559) was followed by Sir Thomas North's justly prized English version in 1579; translations of Suetonius and Tacitus came immediately thereafter. The quickening interest in personalities for their own sake as much as for the moral lesson they might point can be seen in the best of 16th century biographies, William Roper's *Life of Thomas More* (1535) and George Cavendish's *Life of Cardinal Wolsey* (1557).

The 17th Century. If the 17th century did not fully realize all the portents of greatness implicit in 16th century biography, it nevertheless expanded the intellectual context favorable to biographical research. The cultural temper of the age was impatient with all authoritarianism of the past, and the appeal to experience and the demand for more precise analytic methods in research was general. Francis Bacon's *Advancement of Learning* (1605) called for further developments in the writing of all history, including biography, and Bacon's assumption that biography is a branch of scholarly history was illuminated by the considerable advances in antiquarianism. Men like Sir Robert Cotton, John Selden, and Thomas Howard, the earl of Arundel—antiquarians and historians extraordinary—were symptomatic of the 17th century pursuit of the past. Their meticulous research and extensive antiquarian collections demonstrated that accuracy and scholarship must accompany such pursuit. The preservation of the whole past became the guide of the historian and the biographer alike. The very word "biography" first began to appear in the 17th century, and it was defined by John Dryden in his introduction to the 1683 English edition of Plutarch.

The emphasis on scrupulous historical research and the presence of gifted literary artists might have been expected to produce paragons of biography. However, as in Roman antiquity, the 17th century produced its share of artful Tacituses and exact Suetoniuses, but rarely a Plutarch. The unfortunate split between art and exactitude was dramatized in the work of two cooperating biographers, Anthony Wood and John Aubrey. Wood prepared for publication (1691) a collection of short lives of distinguished Oxford graduates (*Athenae Oxoniensis*), and he engaged John Aubrey as collaborator. Wood's lives were aggressively honest and reasonably complete; he was a genuine researcher, but truculent and bad-tempered, leaving the impression that he knew his subjects but never understood them. Aubrey, on the other hand, was (in Wood's expression), "maggoty-headed," likely to produce such inconsequential information as the fact that Thomas Hobbes had great trouble in keeping flies off his bald head. But Aubrey's disorganization is compensated for by his own good humor and his sympathy for his subjects. What was needed was a combination of Wood's exactitudes and Aubrey's sensitive comprehension of character.

Something close to such an ideal had been approximated by the most delightful of 17th century biographers Izaak Walton. Beginning with a biography of John Donne in 1640, Walton produced lives of the diplomat Henry Wotton, the philosopher Richard Hooker, the poet George Herbert, and the churchman Robert Sanderson. A man of consummate literary skill, Walton was also a reasonably competent historian; and while modern scholarship has had to correct many of his assertions, his skill as an investigator was not at all contemptible. Walton's *Lives* survive, along with Boswell's *Johnson,* not only as biography but also as a genuine literary classic. He wrote partly in the older hagiographic tradition, and his biographies were evidently thought by him to be memorials to the greatness of his subjects. Consequently, he shaded and highlighted his narratives so that only their best features emerged. In spite of such tactics, real and distinct personalities are reborn in Walton's pages.

The "commemorative biography" was to prove the bane of the 19th century, when it became the most blatant eulogizing of its subject, at the expense of the whole truth. But Walton, two centuries earlier, was too gifted an artist to let his admiration for such men as Donne and Herbert exempt him from his search for the truth of their characters. Much the same must be said for three other fine examples of 17th century commemorative biography: *The Life of William Cavendish* by his wife Margaret (1667); *Memoirs of the Life of Colonel Hutchinson* by his wife Lucy (first printed in 1806); and *The Life of Mrs. Godolphin* by John Evelyn (first printed in 1847). While these biographies were militant defenses of the characters they portrayed, their ulterior motives are not egregious and certainly a long way from the pieties of Victorian biography. All three biographies looked ahead to such successes as Thomas Carlyle's *Life of John Sterling* (1851).

In addition to these prime examples of biography, the 17th century produced a torrent of related literatures: catalogs of historical information interspersed with biographical data (for example, Thomas Fuller's *History of the Worthies of England,* 1622), political histories replete with the lives of those most involved in the events described (the earl of Clarendon's *History of the Rebellion and Civil Wars in England,* begun in 1668, but not printed until 1702), memoirs, journals, and collections of gossip and letters. Man as something to be observed along with other natural phenomena, with unbounded interest and persistent exactness, was an attitude which the 17th century bequeathed to the 18th.

The 18th Century. What lay ahead during the next century had been anticipated in many ways by the 1668 biography of Abraham Cowley by

Thomas Sprat. The poet Cowley had been an admirer of the political theorist and philosopher Thomas Hobbes and the eulogizer of the Royal Society, the chartered organization in England devoted to the advance of experimental science. Sprat was the historian of the Royal Society and a man fervently dedicated to the ideals of the new science. It was inescapable that Sprat's life of Cowley should have the precision, the thoroughness, and the objectivity of the scientific movement in which both biographer and biographee were so involved. The spirit that hovered over the 18th century was contained in the motto of the Royal Society, *Nullius in verba* ("nothing on authority") and the empiricism of the philosopher John Locke. The acuteness of the empirical and scientific method, when added to the 18th century genius for literary narrative (for the 18th century was also an age of great novelists: Samuel Richardson, Henry Fielding, Tobias Smollett, Laurence Sterne), provided the catalyst needed to produce the ideal of all biography: authenticity and complete evidence presented in artistic form to evoke a total personality.

In addition to numerous compendia of brief lives in the Suetonian tradition (for example, Pierre Bayle's *Dictionnaire historique et critique*, 1695–97; Horace Walpole's *Catalogue of the Royal and Noble Authors*, 1758; Samuel Johnson's *Lives of the English Poets*, 1779–81), there were genuine innovations. Roger North, between 1742 and 1744, published lives of his three brothers in which he showed a clear awareness and full documentation of the entire social milieu, thus predicting the massive "Lives and Times" of 19th century biography. Samuel Johnson, in his *Account of the Life of Mr. Richard Savage* (1744), proved beyond cavil the value of intimate knowledge of one's subject.

But it remained for Johnson's friend James Boswell to write what is still the greatest of all biographies in the English language. Indefatigably curious, persistent, uncannily aware of Johnson's complexities, Boswell achieved a nearly total recall of a man and his personality. Boswell frequently toned down Johnson's more earthy comments on men and manners; he knew Johnson personally only in the subject's final years, with the result that the earlier portions of Johnson's life are not nearly so dramatically recreated as the later years. But whatever the few deficiencies of *The Life of Samuel Johnson* (1791), it still remains the apogee of biography.

The 19th Century. The monumental biography, incorporating all conceivable evidence of a man and his times, was not a 19th century creation: William Mason's life of the poet Thomas Gray (1744) was based on exhaustive research, as were Roger North's *Lives of the Norths* and Boswell's *Johnson*. But the massive biography reached a climax in the 19th century. John Gibson Lockhart's *Life of Sir Walter Scott* was issued in 7 volumes (1836–38); Thomas Carlyle's *Frederick the Great* was 13 years in preparation and was published in three enormous installments between 1858 and 1865; David Masson's *Life of Milton in Connection with the History of His Times* occupied 7 volumes published over 35 years (1859–94); James Spedding compiled the 7-volume *Letters and Life of Francis Bacon* (1861). Curiously, the 19th century penchant for colossal biography did not result in completeness: thoroughly competent biographers found the reading public unwilling to accept any

information that they regarded as even slightly scandalous, and the families of eminent personages refused to countenance any divulging of information that might sully the real (or imagined) glorified image of the biographee. Victorian biography was characterized more by its gentility than by its complete revelation of personality.

A change was signaled by James Anthony Froude's *Thomas Carlyle: History of the First Forty Years of His Life* (2 vols., 1882) and *Thomas Carlyle: History of His Life in London* (2 vols., 1884), in which a Boswellian thoroughness, frankness, and intimate knowledge of his subject were offered in place of the panegyrics of much Victorian biography.

The 20th Century. What Froude began, Freud extended. Sigmund Freud's *Leonardo da Vinci* (1910), a psychoanalytic portrait of that artist's basic motivations, initiated a form of biography that undertook to examine not the public and conscious life of a subject but the private and unconscious wellsprings of behavior. Freud's influence on the writing of biography in the 20th century proved to be most potent, as evidenced by such examples as Joseph Wood Krutch's *Edgar Allen Poe* (1926) and Richard Ellmann's *The Identity of Yeats* (1954).

The vogue of biography in the 20th century is perhaps greater than at any other time in history; and while the full account of biography in this era cannot yet be written, major trends may be cited. The first is that established by Freud. Another is that begun by Lytton Strachey's lively and irreverent *Eminent Victorians* (1918), in which four demigods of the Victorian age (Florence Nightingale, Thomas Arnold, General Gordon, and Cardinal Manning) are portrayed as having feet of clay. This procedure of debunking, or presenting a life in satirical terms, constitutes an important trend among modern biographical studies. Emil Ludwig in his *Goethe* (1919), *Bismarck* (1924), and *Napoleon* (1925) formulated the "dramatic" biography, in which the details of the life were rearranged in such a way as to provide an attention-compelling continuity (Catherine Drinker Bowen is perhaps the finest inheritor of this strain). André Maurois presented biography as an exercise in intuition in his *Shelley* (1923) and *Byron* (1930); and while the "life and times" forms have been successfully adapted by Lord David Cecil, the encyclopedic biography of the 19th century has been reinvigorated by the work of Mark Shorer in his study of Sinclair Lewis and by Edward Nehls in his accounts of D.H. Lawrence. Inheritor of a rich variety of traditional kinds of biography and creator of new forms, the 20th century may one day be recorded as another of the great ages of biography.

RICHARD E. HUGHES, *Boston College*

Bibliography

Altick, Richard D., *Lives and Letters: A History of Literary Biography in England and America* (New York 1965).
Carver, George, *Alms for Oblivion* (Milwaukee 1946).
Garraty, John A., *The Nature of Biography* (New York 1957).
Longaker, J. Mark, *English Biography in the 18th Century* (Philadelphia 1931).
Maurois, André, *Aspects of Biography*, tr. by S.C. Roberts (New York 1929).
Nicolson, Harold, *The Development of English Biography* (New York 1928).
Stauffer, Donald A., *The Art of Biography in 18th Century England* (Princeton, N.J., 1941).
Stauffer, Donald A., *English Biography Before 1700* (Princeton, N.J., 1941).

BIOLOGICAL CLOCKS: (*Right*) Two men lived in a cave for a month to see whether their biological clocks could adapt to a simulated 28-hour, six-day week; only one man adapted. (*Above*) Grunions of the California coast swarm onto beaches to spawn at the same time each year; the cycle appears to be timed by a precise internal clock.

BIOLOGICAL CLOCKS are any of various mysterious mechanisms by which living things adjust themselves to periodic changes in their environment. Every organ and even every cell appears to have them. They are remarkably stable, and temperature changes or chemicals that speed or slow ordinary bodily processes do not affect the clocks' accuracy, a most useful attribute. In fact, daily patterns of activity may continue to recur rhythmically when organisms are isolated from periodic daily light or temperature changes. Tidal activity patterns may persist away from ocean tides; and monthly and annual physiological rhythms similarly are able to continue in apparently unvarying environmental conditions.

There are two theories that account for biological clocks. One theory is that the organism inherits a physicochemical timing system that is able independently to generate periods of the same duration as the periodic motions of the earth and moon (days, months, years). The other theory is that when the organism is deprived of obvious environmental variations, such as those in light and temperature, it detects related variations found in such pervasive forces as the earth's magnetic and electric fields.

Human Clocks. In humans the clocks time the daily rhythm of sleep and wakefulness and the nearly monthly rhythm of the menstrual cycles. The timed daily pattern is adjusted to the person's normal schedule. Underlying this rhythm is a host of other timed variations. Body temperature varies from a morning low to an afternoon high. Daily variations occur in blood sugar, circulating corpuscles, kidney excretion, cell-divisions, and secretion of hormones. These and innumerable other variations are each adaptively adjusted to the sleeping-waking cycles.

When humans are deprived of their watches and are screened from all obvious daily variations, their persisting daily patterns systematically drift to progressively earlier or later times of day. The resulting rhythmic periods, now deviating a little from 24 hours, are termed "circadian" (about a day). The tendency for daily variations to become circadian under such conditions occurs widely among living things, but its explanation is still unknown. However, the rate of drift, or observed period, may differ among diverse bodily processes and cause them to get out of step with each other.

Following long east-west airplane trips all the bodily rhythms must be reset to harmonize with the new day-night times. This requires up to a week or two. Since different bodily functions reset at different rates, a temporary desynchronization results, with an associated lowered efficiency in functioning. Not knowing whether the clocks normally depend on subtle terrestrial variations or even whether man or other creatures could survive without biological clocks, one cannot predict the consequences of space travel.

Other Animals. Among other animals, the precisely timed annual return of the swallows to Capistrano, Calif., on the same day each year is well known. Another timed rhythm is the annual breeding of the palolo worms of the South Pacific. Each year at dawn exactly one week after the November full moon, these worms rise to the surface of the water for breeding.

Biological clocks occur throughout the animal kingdom, from single-celled forms to mammals. All the animal clocks seem quite alike. They time cycles, adjusting activities to the day-night cycles or to the ebb and flow of the tides. They also time monthly and annual migratory and reproductive activity.

The animal clock times solar day (24 hours) and lunar day (24.8 hours) periods. Together, these last yield months (29.5 days). It also may time the year, independent of obvious cues. The daily clocks measure relative lengths of day and night (photoperiod) to signal approaching spring or fall. In addition, animals may navigate by celestial bodies, such as the sun and moon, using their clocks to correct for the movements of these bodies across the sky.

Plants. Plants also possess clocks. Some, such as the bean seedling, raise their leaves in the morning and lower them in the evening. Such "sleep movements" clearly do not require daily light changes. Another, the brown alga, *Dictyota*, has a clock-timed monthly reproductive rhythm.

Plants have numerous other clock-timed rhythms. Just as in animals, the rhythms timed by the clocks can be reset or otherwise altered by light or temperature changes. They also may become circadian in varying illumination. Plant rhythms include daily variations in respiration, photosynthetic capacity, and growth rate. Such processes as periodic times of germination and flowering also are regulated by a daily clock regulated by changes in photoperiod. Some of the most striking examples of annual rhythms persisting in constant conditions involve seed germination, plant growth, and respiratory rate.

FRANK A. BROWN JR., *Northwestern University*

BIOLOGICAL WARFARE. See CHEMICAL WARFARE.

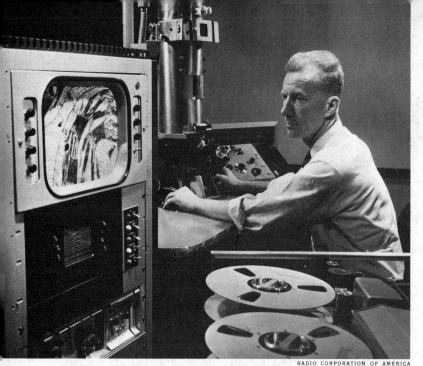

BIOLOGY

ELECTRON MICROSCOPES have done much to push back the frontiers of biology. When coupled with an image-intensification system, as here, the microscope's power is increased by a factor of 10. On the fluorescent screen at left, the structure of an oat-leaf cell is magnified 2,000,000 times.

RADIO CORPORATION OF AMERICA

BIOLOGY, bī-ol'ə-jē, is the study of life in all of its complexities and manifestations. Since life has never been seen to exist outside a cell and the great majority of cells are combined into organisms, biologists have been concerned with research at the cellular and organismic level.

Biology is still in its infancy. The classic scientific questions, in the order of their importance, are "What?" "How?" and "Why?". Biology is far from answering the first, since there are probably well over a million kinds of plants and animals that have not been discovered and described. The answer to the question "How?" is what the majority of contemporary biologists are seeking as they investigate how life works, how cells cooperate in organisms, how organisms continue to exist and change, how organisms exist as a community, and how communities coexist. The question "Why?" is largely unasked and wholly unanswered.

Thus it is impossible to give a simple answer to the question "What is biology?". It is easier to examine what modern biologists are studying and what methods they are using.

─────────────── CONTENTS ───────────────

Section	Page	Section	Page
1. The Scope of Biology	770	3. The Nature of Life	773
2. The Methods of Biological Research	772	4. History of Biology	775

1. The Scope of Biology

Taxonomy. All early biologists were concerned with taxonomy, and many contemporary workers still are. Taxonomy is an endeavor to discover, describe, and arrange in orderly groups all the different kinds of plants and animals that exist. Its major purpose is not the discovery of new forms, but the development of systems of classifications that cast light on relationships and possible ancestries of various organisms.

The major difficulties in developing systems of classifications are the lack of knowledge of existing forms and the ignorance of much of their ancestry. The earliest known fossil-bearing rocks contain many forms, such as trilobites and brach-

iopods, that are as complex as many living animals. Thus the 19th century concept of a family tree of life with a single stem bearing simple branches must be replaced by a diagram of a sort of shrubbery in which numerous stems arise from an indistinct background. The task of the evolutionary taxonomist is complicated by the difficulty of deciding whether two apparently similar forms have derived their similarity from a common ancestor or the selective evolutionary effect of a common environment. Moreover, the determination of valid difference is as difficult as the determination of valid similarity. Many animals and plants once thought to be distinct species have turned out to be merely geographic or even seasonal variations of the same organism.

Biogeography. It is difficult to know whether biogeography lies more in the province of the taxonomist or of the ecologist, whose work is described in the next paragraph. The political boundaries of the world have little relation to the natural boundaries based on the populations of plants and animals. A biogeographer therefore divides the world into zones (corresponding to continents), subzones (corresponding to countries), and so on. These divisions are distinguished from each other by their populations of organisms. Though the zones are in part dependent on similar climate, geographic location also plays a role. For example, the arid regions of the southern parts of America are inhabited by cactuses that are at first sight almost indistinguishable from, but in no way related to, the euphorbids (fleshy, cactuslike plants) inhabiting similar climatic zones of southern Africa. This coincidence is one of the better known examples of "parallel evolution," which often presents grave problems to taxonomists.

Ecology. This science probably has a broader scope than any other branch of contemporary biology. It may be defined as the study of the interaction of organisms with each other and with their environment. But the ecologist is concerned not only with the study of stable aggregations of organisms—like a prairie or forest, which may remain unchanged for thousands of years—but also with the study of their development. Not only does a change in environment produce a change in population, but a population may produce a change in environment. For example, the upthrusting of a new island in an ocean produces a sterile area that is slowly repopulated by plants and animals, but corals can build an island where none existed before. Since ecology comprises the interaction of organisms with each other, it merges almost imperceptibly into *animal behavior* and is thus of direct social significance to man.

Anatomy and Embryology. The variety and distribution of organisms cannot be understood without a knowledge of their structure and development. The study of the structure of organisms is the work of the anatomist, while the study of development is the work of the embryologist. Unfortunately, descriptive anatomy, even of unknown forms, does not yield spectacular results, so that research in this field is progressing slowly. Even experimental anatomy, replete with fascinating problems, is now largely in abeyance.

Embryology is a far more active science than descriptive anatomy is. Most of the structural changes that are involved in the transformation of an egg into an animal or of a seed into a higher plant are known, but the many underlying mechanisms are still a mystery. For example, the egg of many animals, when it divides into two, is establishing the future right and left halves of the adult. If these two halves are mechanically separated, two perfect adults can be produced from a single egg. This separation even occurs naturally, in such forms as the armadillo, which normally bears identical quadruplets derived from a single fertilized egg. It also has been demonstrated that two eggs can be coerced mechanically into producing a single adult. No valid theory has been produced that will explain these remarkable facts. The developing plant presents similar and equally unsolved problems. No explanation, for example, has been put forward to explain why leaves are generated from the growing plant tip in a regular pattern.

Histology and Cytology. The study of structure is by no means confined to that of the whole organism. Histology is the study of the cellular structure of organs, and cytology is the study of the interior of the cell itself. The correlated study of structure and function is carried on actively in both these branches of biology and has yielded extremely interesting results.

It has long been known, for example, that many cells secrete chemicals (hormones) that affect other cells in different parts of the organism. It has been discovered, however, that a single cell may play two very different roles. Some nerve cells, particularly in arthropods, not only originate and transmit impulses but also secrete neurohormones. The water content of insects, for example, is largely controlled by the diffusion of neurohormones along the nerve fiber from one ganglion to another. Hormones secreted by cells are not, of course, confined to animals, but are found also in plants, where the onset of flowering is controlled by the production of a special pigment; the development of this pigment depends on the periodicity and length of the light to which the plant is exposed.

Advances in cytology, aided by the electron microscope (the use of which will be discussed later), have been even more spectacular than

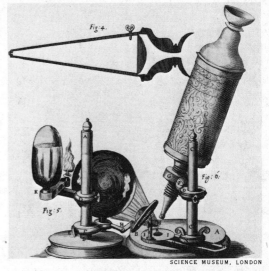

SCIENCE MUSEUM, LONDON

HOOKE'S MICROSCOPE, as shown in his *Micrographia* (1665). Light-producing and condenser apparatus is at left, and a cross section of the microscope is at top.

those in histology. For example, this instrument has disclosed a whole new system, known as the endoplasmic reticulum, within the cell. The endoplasmic reticulum is a network of submicroscopic interconnecting tubules and vesicles, within which lie the minute granular ribosomes involved in the synthesis of protein within the cell. The ribosome receives from the nucleus genetic information for producing the proteins characteristic of the particular organism, and thus maintains the integrity of the organism. However, some ribosomes occur outside the endoplasmic reticulum, and some areas of the endoplasmic reticulum lack ribosomes.

Genetics. Closely linked to cytology is genetics, which has done much to revolutionize the life of contemporary man. The ability to manipulate the heritable characters of domestic plants and animals through cross-breeding has lifted the specter of starvation from vast areas of the world, not only through increased crop yields, but also through the development of strains that flourish in areas where the crop previously could not be grown.

Within the foreseeable future, heritable characteristics may be manipulated chemically and thus make possible the production of completely new forms. These possibilities derive particularly from the elucidation of the structure of the chromosome and of its constituent parts. It has long been known that nucleic acids were localized within the chromosomes in the nucleus and that when the cell divided, these chromosomes normally replicated (reproduced) themselves. Occasional failures in the exact duplication of the chromosomes of sex cells led to variations in the offspring. It is now known that deoxyribonucleic acid (DNA), the constituent of chromosomes, is a spiral structure consisting of relatively few purines and pyramidines (bases such as guanine, adenine, uracil, thymine, and cytosine), often referred to as "building blocks." The order in which these building blocks are placed conveys genetic information to control the heredity of the organism, just as information can be conveyed between persons by Morse code, which is

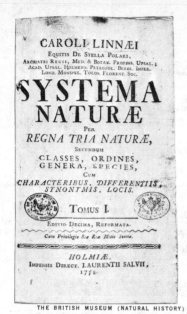

LINNAEUS' *Systema Naturae* provided a system of classification that organized plants and animals logically. The title page of his treatise is shown here.

dependent on the order in which dots and dashes are arranged. It has definitely been shown in bacteria, and rather doubtfully in some higher forms of life, that the insertion of DNA from the cell body of one form into the cell body of another results in the recipient developing the heritable characteristics of the donor. These experiments indicate the possibility of chemical control of animal and plant forms.

Interaction with Other Sciences. It must be emphasized that though all these different varieties of biology properly belong in that discipline, many of them are dependent on chemistry and physics for their application. Partially separated sciences such as *biochemistry* and *biophysics* have developed as a result. They apply the methods developed for the use of one science to the problems of another. Indeed, it is difficult to say that any science can develop apart from any other.

Outmoded Terms. In defining the branches of biology, such terms as botany, zoology, parasitology, protozoology, and the like have not been used because they are obsolescent. A zoologist, technically one who studies animals, and a botanist, technically one who studies plants, are actually engaged in one of the branches of science already discussed, rather than studying the organism for its own sake.

2. The Methods of Biological Research

Biological research can be divided broadly into two approaches: *the study of living organisms* in their entirety and in their parts, and the *study of the life processes* themselves. The two can never be wholly divorced, since the totality of life exists only in an organism; thus the life processes can be studied only in narrowly isolated segments. These divisions are not the same as the old grouping of research into "experimental" and "observational" methods, since experimental techniques can be applied to the study of anatomy, and many chemical approaches to biology are now designed to elucidate fine structures.

Study of Living Organisms. The ecologist, who works entirely with living organisms in their natural state, has a surprising number of modern tools at his disposal. It is commonplace to at-

tach small radio transmitters to such animals as deer and to track their movements with the aid of radio locating equipment. Smaller animals can be tagged with radioactive isotopes to study their movements through restricted areas by the use of directional Geiger counters. Planes and radar equipment are used to track migratory flocks of birds. Bird songs and other methods of communication between animals are recorded with the aid of long-range directional microphones, and the resultant tapes are analyzed with the aid of computers.

The basic tool of the observational biologist is still the microscope. Many new techniques have extended the scope of its usefulness. The use of fluorescent dyes to render structures visible has made possible the use of ultraviolet light without the necessity of photographic recording. Although ultraviolet light is lethal to all forms of life, living forms have been studied successfully with the aid of a flying-spot technique with ultraviolet light that scans each portion of the specimen so rapidly that no damage is done; a total ultraviolet picture can be built up on a device equivalent to a television screen. Probably the most generally useful advance has been the development of phase contrast microscopy. In this method the light waves passing through an object on the stage of a microscope are thrown out of step with those passing around the object. This technique greatly increases the apparent contrast of structures of very similar refractive index so that, for example, a mitochondrion, which cannot be seen by the techniques of ordinary microscopy, stands out sharply in a living cell. Interference microscopy, an extension of this technique, translates the density contrasts into colors, which, used in conjunction with polarized light, permit the measurement of the thickness of thin membranes when viewed from on top.

The limitation in the use of the light microscope has always been the nature of light itself, since it is obviously impossible to examine by its aid structures that are of the same order of magnitude as a light wave. The introduction of the electron microscope, using electron beams 10,000 times shorter in wavelength, has made it possible for the first time to examine submicroscopic structures. The most remarkable of these instruments are capable of bringing sharply into view objects measuring only eight angstrom (1 angstrom = 0.00000001 cm). A magnification of more than a million times is necessary to render such particles visible.

Electron beams can only be transmitted in a high vacuum and will only penetrate very minute structures. Objects to be examined must be completely dry and extremely thin—sections for the electron microscope commonly are cut a millionth of an inch thick. Nonetheless, it has been possible to demonstrate the location of a few molecules of specific enzymes within a minute area of a cell by preparing compounds of metabolites and a heavy metal such as lead, and placing a solution of the compound on an ultrathin section that has been prepared by methods that do not destroy the enzyme. In attacking the metabolite, the enzyme deposits lead on itself and thus appears as a black dot on an electron photomicrograph of the section.

Other localizations of chemicals within the cell have been achieved with the aid of audioradiography. By this technique an organism is fed synthesized metabolites in which an unstable isotope has been substituted for the normal atom. An ultrathin section of the organism is then coated with an ultrafine grain photographic emulsion. Localities in which the unstable isotope has been deposited by the organism will appear on the developed photographic emulsion as black dots.

Study of the Life Processes. Two approaches are used by biologists who study life processes at the molecular level. The first of these is exemplified by the study of metabolic pathways through a cell; an example of the second is the study of isolated portions of the cell in a test tube.

The first technique contributed much to the understanding of the basic process of photosynthesis. It early became apparent that, though carbon dioxide was undoubtedly changed to sugar in a plant cell, it had to pass through a very large number of intermediate reactions to do so. Plants were therefore exposed to an atmosphere of carbon dioxide that had been prepared synthetically from an unstable isotope of carbon. The plants were removed at intervals and killed, thus stopping the process of photosynthesis. Then they were resolved into their constituent components by normal chemical techniques. Each component was examined with a Geiger counter to find out which chemical contained the radioactive carbon. By these means, laborious in the extreme and requiring great technical skill, almost all of the numerous successive steps in photosynthesis were made known. Comparable applications of radioisotope techniques have greatly increased the knowledge of protein synthesis and of many other metabolic processes.

The classic example of the examination of isolated parts of a cell in a test tube was the discovery of the function of the ribosomes. If cells are completely disintegrated, first by fine grinding and then by exposure to ultraviolet vibrations, the ribosomes, which are only about 150 angstroms in diameter, are freed from the endoplasmic reticulum. Since the ribosomes are slightly different in density from any other part of the cell, they may be separated from the pulp into which the cell is reduced by high speed centrifugation and thus secured in relatively pure form. Ribosomes thus isolated were studied in two ways. First, ordinary analytical techniques determined that they were composed of about half ribonucleic acid and half protein. Second, isolated ribosomes in a test tube were used to synthesize protein when "fed" enzymes and the necessary intermediate metabolites. It thus became a logical deduction, confirmed by many subsequent experiments, that the ribosomes were the center of protein synthesis in the cell and that they must receive contributions of nucleic acid that conveyed the genetic information to make sure the proteins peculiar to that particular form were synthesized. The combination of the results from these synthetic and analytic techniques has led to the understanding of how genetic integrity (preserved by the replication of chromosomes) can lead to integrity of form produced by the synthesis of proteins.

3. The Nature of Life

Biologists of all types are dedicated to an attempt to answer the question, "What is life?" Life, at least as it is known on this planet, is based on, or housed in, a water-dispersion of proteins containing carbohydrates, minerals, and a few other substances. Only when such a mixture is derived from another living form can it continue to exhibit the phenomena that we call life.

It is, moreover, remarkable, and so far inexplicable, that both the carbohydrates and the amino acids from which the proteins are built are asymmetrical. Both carbohydrates and amino acids can be synthesized in the laboratory either in right-handed or left-handed forms, and the result of such laboratory synthesis is usually a mixture of equal parts of these. In general, however, all amino acids produced by a living organism are "left-handed" and almost all carbohydrates are "right-handed" molecules. An organism presented with a "wrong-handed" molecule either fails to utilize it, or first converts it by enzyme action to the appropriate "handedness." These curious facts may have some bearing on the origin of life.

Protoplasm—Energy and Enzymes. The jellylike protein, with its other contained constituents, is often referred to as "protoplasm," but protoplasm itself is not living. The life processes in protoplasm consist of an immense number of cyclic, enzymatic reactions by which the protoplasm continually replicates itself. It is this continuous changing of other substances into protoplasm that ultimately distinguishes dead from living matter.

Plants draw minerals and water from the soil and carbon dioxide from the air and turn these inanimate substances into living materials with the aid of energy derived from the sun. Animals are less successful synthesizers; to secure the material and energy necessary to replicate their own substance, they must eat either plants or other animals that have eaten plants. If this process had been going on continuously, the entire surface of the planet would be a pulsating mass of living material. However, the individual life processes terminate in a state known as death, the effect of which is the return of nutrients to the soil after their utilization by living organisms.

The keys to these cyclic processes of replication and death are energy and enzymes. Energy is stored when complex molecules are built up and is liberated when they are broken down. If this process occurs suddenly, the result is known as an explosion. The primary role of the enzymes in living matter is to control the rate at which energy is stored and released. So complex are the processes of life that it has been estimated that several thousand different enzymes are required to maintain the life processes in even the simplest cell, and probably no more than a third of those involved have been identified.

Despite this complexity, the basic mechanism of the liberation of energy in all living forms is the same and depends on a molecule known as adenosine triphosphate (ATP). The last of the chain of the three phosphorus molecules attached to the adenosine is held by what is known as a high-energy bond, which is relatively easily broken by the appropriate enzyme. The energy liberated when this bond is broken can be used to build up a more complex molecule, while, given an adequate supply of nutrients, another enzyme can rebuild the ATP.

A well-known example of energy storage by this method is the Krebs cycle worked out by

POLIO VIRUS particles, viewed with an electron microscope, represent one of the stepping off places in biological research today. Viruses are providing important information about nucleic acids, mutations, and the genetic code, as well as disease.

the biochemist Hans Krebs (q.v.). In this cycle, one molecule of glucose is first turned into glucose phosphate and then enters into a long series of cyclic reactions involving approximately 20 enzymes. At the end of this series, one molecule of glucose yields 38 molecules of ATP, which are available to provide energy in other necessary cyclic reactions. For this reason, sugar is referred to as a "high-energy food" or, more crudely, as a "metabolic fuel."

Proteins and Life. Life could not exist in discrete forms without synthesizing only those specific proteins that are peculiar to itself. The nucleus is composed of chains of deoxyribonucleic acid (DNA), of which the order and arrangement of building blocks are different in every living form. The DNA replicates a series of smaller chains of ribonucleic acid (RNA) in which the building blocks are in the same coded order, and these in their turn control the structure of the synthesized protein.

There are comparatively few protein molecules in a cell, and they are relatively huge compared to other molecules. In the average cell, for example, there are about 18,000 water molecules to each molecule of protein. A reasonable analogy to this situation would be to regard the cell as a city of skyscrapers some 250 feet high and joined by numerous bridges at all levels. Human beings packed solidly between these skyscrapers would then represent the water molecules. If one moderate-sized truck for every 600 persons were added to this mixture, each truck would represent in size and frequency the molecules of carbohydrates. This picture may be brought into even better perspective by considering that about one million small bacteria can be placed on the head of a pin, and that each bacteria contains about 750 million molecules of water. Now consider the fact that many of the smaller proteins are enzymes, and they are engaged in causing constantly fluctuating change in the size and structure of other molecules. With these examples, it is possible to arrive at some concept of the almost incredible complexity in structure and function of even the simplest living forms.

Evolution of Life. The next questions that must be raised is how all this complexity arose and where it all came from. That all life is the same cannot be for one moment doubted. All life is based on proteins, and although each protein is different, each is built up from permutations and combinations of less than a score of amino acids. Exactly the same amino acids occur as the building blocks in bacteria and in the building blocks of human beings. Moreover, all known forms of life not only use ATP for the storage and liberation of energy, but do so with the aid of identical enzymes working on identical substrates in identical manners. Considering the

theoretically vast number of compounds that could potentially be formed and that could potentially carry on similar functions, it is beyond the bounds of coincidence that so few basic materials and processes are found in so many and such varied organisms.

The manner in which life came about is still, however, a field for pure speculation, although almost all contemporary biologists believe that living matter and processes evolved from inanimate ones. In the first place, we live in an orderly universe in which inanimate matter, as we know it on this planet, has steadily evolved from a less complex to a more complex condition. It is relatively certain that the early atmosphere of the cooling planet earth contained large quantities of water vapor, carbon dioxide, ammonia, and methane. It has been established in the laboratory that, when such a mixture is exposed to electrical discharges, amino acids that are identical to those found as the building blocks of the proteins in modern life are synthesized. It seems, therefore, logical to suppose that some similar amino acids would have appeared on the surface of the planet in the normal course of its evolutionary history. It also seems logical to suppose that some of these amino acids would have combined into proteins and that these proteins would have become dispersed in the liquid water then accumulating on the surface of the planet. The time scale of these events should be reckoned in billions, not millions, of years. (Much less than one million days have passed since the birth of Christ.) None of these evolutionary changes, however, produced life. It is only postulated that they produced proteins and thus the basis from which life could develop.

Numerous theories to bridge the gap from proteins to life have been put forward, none of them supported by experimental evidence. The most highly regarded theory is that one of these proteins was an enzyme capable of breaking down other proteins, of resynthesizing them into its own form with the aid of another enzyme that fortunately appeared. Very probably, proteins dispersed in water would tend to aggregate in lumps and the postulated enzyme system or systems could develop in one of these lumps. It is inconceivable that this would happen only once or in one place.

Since all life on earth is of one type, why did only one of the numerous theoretically possible forms of life survive? It has been suggested that this is in some way correlated with the right-handedness and left-handedness of carbohydrates and amino acids—a peculiarity of living matter as we know it. Another postulate is that, since we are dealing with such an immensely long time scale, the first form of life to evolve may have had such a head start on all subsequent ones that it was able to overwhelm and destroy them, just as its complex living descendants today destroy and overwhelm each other.

It is, of course, a necessary part of all these postulates that chlorophyll, or something very like it, must have been among the first of all living substances to emerge. There is certainly little doubt that all of the earliest inhabitants of earth were microscopic green plants. The first animal, in effect, must have been a plant that had lost its chlorophyll but had survived by virtue of a motility which permitted it to become a predator on the energy-storing forms around it.

All of this explanation, except for the fact that plants preceded animals, is pure speculation unsupported by direct observation. However, its fits clearly into the established pattern of the universe, and there is not the slightest doubt that from the time of the appearance of the first known fossil records there has been a steady and continuous evolution of living forms that has led to the present and will continue into the future.

Extraterrestrial Life. There has been much speculation as to whether a similar or even analogous chain of events took place on some other planet. The statistical computations of astronomers lead to the conclusion that there must be many planets in the universe that strongly resemble the earth in their history, structure, and present condition. But if life similar to terrestrial life had been established by evolution on these planets, then of all the possible molecular aggregates something resembling chlorophyll must have occurred, and of all the possible amino acids only the same score must have survived to build into blocks of proteins. Also, of all the conceivable energy storage systems, ATP must have been selected. This piling of improbability on improbability causes most biologists to discount the possibility that anything remotely approaching terrestrial life occurs elsewhere. If, however, life is defined as a form of self-replicating matter without regard to the nature of the replicating processes, it may exist elsewhere.

4. History of Biology

Few sciences have contributed more to the philosophical and physical basis of contemporary society than biology has. The earliest biologists, in the broadest sense of this term, were the agricultural tribes who first began to cultivate plants. From these plants and more than 3,000 generations of their successors have been produced the domestic crops of today. Herdsmen did the same for animals. Major contributions along the road to modern agriculture and stock raising were the 17th century discovery, or at least postulate, of photosynthesis by Stephen Hales and the late 17th century demonstration by Jethro Tull (q.v.) that the cultivation of the soil played a major role in crop yield. In the late 19th century, the Russian Ivan Michurin used the newly discovered principles of genetics to breed plants adapted to new climates and thus laid the basis for worldwide expansion of food production.

The science of taxonomy, which preoccupied early biologists, was in a state of utmost confusion until the late 18th century when Carolus Linnaeus introduced his binomial system of classification in which all organisms are specified by two words. A similar confusion in the unsystematized teaching of biology was brought to an end in the middle 19th century by Thomas Huxley who introduced the concept of teaching by types drawn from each major group of plant and animal, a system that is being replaced by more modern methods.

The major contribution of biology to the philosophical development of man has been brought about through the concept of evolution and genetics. Many early 19th century biologists, such as Chevalier de Lamarck, believed that evolution had probably occurred. It remained, however, for Charles Darwin to bring the idea forward in a logical and acceptable form and to offer a plausible explanation for its manifestation—the survival of those forms best fitted to their environment. This concept that change was a normal part of nature was completely foreign to the social climate in which Darwin lived, and its acceptance did much to bring about true democracy, which is largely dependent on social mobility.

However, the mechanism of evolution remained mysterious until the rediscovery of the genetic principles of Gregor Mendel and their development by Thomas Hunt Morgan and his contemporaries. The next breakthrough in this area was the demonstration by Hermann J. Muller that mutations, previously thought to be of "biological" origin, could be induced by X-rays and other physical causes. The philosophical impact of this discovery, which clearly implied that heredity could be controlled by human manipulation, provided great impetus for the further study of the chromosome. Linus Pauling's demonstration of the structure of the protein molecule and the Watson-Crick demonstration of the structure of the nucleic acids in the chromosomes, revolutionary in the first half of the 20th century, are now the shoreline from which biology is being pushed to new and only dimly perceived horizons.

PETER GRAY, *University of Pittsburgh*

Bibliography

Asimov, Isaac, *The Intelligent Man's Guide to Science*, vol. 2 (New York 1960).
Asimov, Isaac, *Short History of Biology* (New York 1964).
Bates, Marston, and Humphrey, P.S., eds., *Darwin Reader* (New York 1956).
Buchsbaum, Ralph, *Animals Without Backbones* (Chicago 1948).
Gray, Peter, *The Encyclopedia of the Biological Sciences* (New York 1965).
Holt, Rinehart & Winston, Inc., *Modern Biology Series* (New York 1962–63).
Moore, John A., ed., *Biological Science Curriculum Study* (Chicago and New York 1963).
Prentice-Hall, Inc., *Foundation of Modern Biology Series*, 2d ed. (Englewood Cliffs, N.J., 1964).
Reinhold Publishing Corporation, *Selected Topics in Modern Biology* (New York 1964–1967).

For Specialized Study

Ballard, William W., *Comparative Anatomy and Embryology* (New York 1964).
Bates, Marston, *Nature of Natural History* (New York 1962).
Bonner, John T., *Ideas of Biology* (New York 1962).
Bourne, Geoffrey H., ed., *Cytology and Cell Physiology*, 3d ed. (New York 1964).
Loeb, Jacques, *Mechanistic Conception of Life*, ed. by Donald Fleming (Cambridge, Mass., 1964).
Mayr, Ernst, *Methods and Principles of Systematic Zoology* (New York 1953).
Waterman, T.H., and Morowitz, H.J., eds., *Theoretical and Mathematical Biology* (New York 1965).
Watson, James D., *Molecular Biology of the Gene* (New York 1965).
Weisz, Paul B., *Elements of Biology*, 2d ed. (New York 1965).

BIOLOGY, Marine. See MARINE BIOLOGY.

BIOLUMINESCENT fungi are one of the few plants that give off luciferin-produced light. The *Mycena* toadstools at left are photographed in daylight. Those at right are photographed in the dark by their greenish-yellow light.

BIOLUMINESCENCE, bī-ō-lōō-mə-nes′-əns, is the emission of light from living organisms. The color of the light may be blue, bluish green, or green, and it may be produced as a steady glow or in flashes. Unlike the light given off by a flame, bioluminescent light produces very little heat and is sometimes called "cold light."

In bacteria, fungi, and protozoa the value of this light is not clearly understood. However, in fireflies and perhaps in other invertebrates, the pattern of flashing serves as a signal by which members of the same species recognize each other for mating purposes. In deep-sea fish, luminous organs in the head region or inside the mouth act as lures for catching other fish. The luminous secretions produced by squids and some crustaceans serve to hide these animals from their enemies.

Bioluminescence results from the interaction of an enzyme with its substrate. In this chemical reaction, which is usually a form of oxidation, energy is released. This energy excites the substrate molecule, which then gives off light of a characteristic color as it returns to its normal state. The enzymes that act to produce light are called *luciferases,* while the substrates they act upon are known as *luciferins.* The exact chemical nature of many luciferases and luciferins is unknown, but it is known that they differ from one species of organism to the next. Luminous bacteria are known to use riboflavin phosphate in light production, and in the firefly, light is given off by a complex molecule formed from luciferin, luciferase, and the energy-rich compound adenosine triphosphate (ATP). Neither ATP nor riboflavin phosphate are required for light emission by the dinoflagellate *Gonyaulax* or the jellyfish. Instead, the light reaction in *Gonyaulax* requires a high concentration of salt, and the reaction of the jellyfish needs calcium. Diphosphoadenosine is necessary for the light-producing reaction in the sea pansy *Renilla.*

The only land-dwelling or freshwater organisms that can emit light are firefly adults and larvae and certain kinds of worms and fungi. No leafy plants, amphibians, reptiles, birds, or mammals can produce light. In the sea, however, luminous organisms are very common. Most samples of seawater contain enough luminous bacteria so that if a freshly killed fish is allowed to decay, it will develop luminous colonies. In fact, the luminosity of some fish is not due to luciferin and luciferase but is the product of luminous bacteria living in special organs of the fish.

Luminous protozoa include many kinds of dinoflagellates and radiolarians, which emit light in flashes when they are jarred. When dinoflagel-

lates are particularly abundant, whole areas of the sea can be seen to flash when stirred by the passage of fish or boats or by the movements of breaking waves. Jellyfish and sea gooseberries have luminous areas that flash when they are touched. In some marine organisms, such as the crustacean *Cypridina,* the luciferins and luciferases are secreted through separate openings into the surrounding water, where the light-producing reaction occurs.

BEATRICE M. SWEENEY, *Yale University*

Further Reading: Johnson, Frank H., and Haneda, Yata, eds., *Bioluminescence in Progress* (Princeton, N.J., 1966).

BIOME, bī′ōm, in ecology, a natural grouping of plants and animals that extends over a large region of the earth's surface. The general nature and coverage of a biome is determined by such factors as temperature, soil features, rainfall, sunlight conditions, and physical barriers. Each biome is characterized by a particular type of climate, vegetation, and animal life.

There are seven world biomes: tundra, coniferous forest, deciduous forest, grassland, desert, tropical rain forest, and marine. Except for the marine biome they correspond roughly to the main climatic zones of the earth and tend to take the form of belts parallel to the equator. The *tundra* is located in the area of ice and snow surrounding the North Pole and extending to the coniferous forests. It has such organisms as mosses, lichens, musk-oxen, and arctic foxes. The *coniferous forest* extends southward from the margin of the tundra into the temperate areas of Eurasia and North America and has such organisms as pines, firs, moose, deer, and foxes. The *deciduous forest* extends southward from the coniferous forest in the eastern United States and Europe and has oaks, maples, bears, and deer. The *grassland* biome extends from the margins of the deciduous forest through central and western parts of the United States and across central Asia, and also occurs in parts of Argentina, Australia, and South Africa. Grass, hoofed animals, and rodents are common in this biome. The *desert* biome includes the great deserts of Africa, central Asia, and Australia. The vegetation is scattered and highly modified. Cacti, snakes, and rodents are common. The *tropical rain forest* is found near the equator in South America, Africa, India, and Borneo. Lush vegetation supports numerous forms of insects, reptiles, and mammals. The *marine* biome consists of the world's oceans and marine life.

DAVID A. OTTO, *Stephens College*

BIOPHYSICS research uses physical methods to explore biological problems. One valuable technique is the use of radioisotopes as tracers to follow substances in a biological system. This technician is using remote-controlled equipment to handle radioisotopes safely.

BION, bī'ən, Greek philosopher, of the 3d century B.C. He is best known for his *Diatribae*, a satirical work expounding the philosophy of "hedonistic Cynicism," which contended that the life of a Cynic, one who scoffed at all prevailing beliefs and conventions, was a happy and pleasurable one. Only fragments of Bion's works are extant, but it is probable that he was an atheist because he is mentioned in contemporary sources as regarding all questions about the nature of the gods as unimportant.

According to the account of the Greek biographer Diogenes Laërtius, Bion was the slave of a rhetorician who made him his heir. He studied philosophy at Athens, first under Crates of the Cynic school, then with Theodorus, who was called the Atheist. Bion died at Chalcis, in Euboea.

BION, bī'ən, Greek poet, probably of the 2d century B.C., wrote pastoral poetry, of which only fragments are extant. His *Lament for Adonis* is famous as the model for Shelley's *Adonais*. Bion's *Lament* is at times passionate and extravagant, and at times delicate and elegant. All his poetry is similar in style to that of the earlier pastoral poet Theocritus, whom he probably attempted to imitate.

Bion was himself the subject of the *Lament for Bion*, a dirge written in imitation of *Lament for Adonis*, probably by one of Bion's pupils. It indicates that Bion was born in Smyrna (now İzmir, Turkey) but lived most of his life in Sicily, where he died of poisoning.

BIOPHYSICS, bī-ō-fiz'iks, is an area of scientific study in which physical principles, physical methods, and physical instrumentation are used to study living systems or systems related to life. It overlaps broadly with biophysical chemistry, which is more specialized in scope since it is concerned with the physical study of chemically isolated substances found in living organisms.

Advances in Biophysics. Advances in biophysics, like advances in physics, have come about as systems have become available for accurate study. One early branch of biophysics was the geometric optics of the eye. The character of the lens of the eye, the kind of image it makes on the retina, and the ways in which the image can be sharpened are clearly physical problems. Research in this area, which has been proceeding steadily for centuries, has provided vision correction for nearly half of mankind.

In the past, living systems did not reveal many aspects suitable for physical study. A change came about in the middle part of the 20th century with a series of discoveries: the nature of nerve impulses and muscular contraction; the operation of the retina of the eye; the molecular character of genetics; the behavior and composition of viruses; and the operation of plant chloroplast. All these systems are readily studied by physical means. Findings in these areas include the discovery that the eye can detect a single photon, the smallest possible amount of light; the elucidation of the structure of the genetic substance deoxyribonucleic acid (known as DNA); and a start on the symmetry relationships and methods of assembly of viruses.

Division of Biophysics. Roughly speaking, there are three major divisions of present-day biophysics. Perhaps the largest of these is *molecular and cellular biophysics*. This division is concerned with the structure and behavior of the molecular units that have been found to determine the life of the cell. Thus the structure of nucleic acids, of proteins, of lipids, and of polysaccharides—particularly as they are part of the architecture of the cell and form elements of nuclei, ribosomes, membranes, and cell walls—is of major interest to biophysicists.

The methods of study in molecular and cellular biophysics include the electron microscope; the absorption of light (selected as to wavelength); the ultracentrifuge, which subjects objects to greatly enhanced gravity and selects them for size, shape, and density; X-ray diffraction, which reveals regularities and symmetries in structure; as well as the study of the effects of physical stress such as heat and pressure.

Each of these methods is specialized and often involves many research workers. On occasion, the physical agent itself is the subject of study. One such subject is ionizing radiation, which in the form of X rays and gamma rays is either a potential benefit (X-ray diagnosis and cancer treatment) or hazard (radiation-induced leukemia), and so has a large field of biophysics devoted to itself alone.

A second area of biophysical study is *physiological physics*. This is the study of functional organs of a living system. These systems include vision, hearing, sensation in general, nerve action, muscular action, membrane action, and the accumulation of mineral deposits in bone, teeth, and eggs. Workers in these areas use specially designed electrical detection devices—

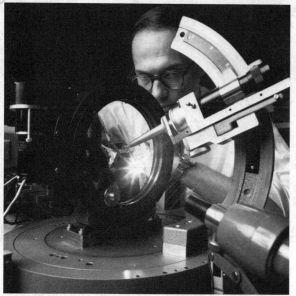

E.I. DU PONT DE NEMOURS & COMPANY

X-RAY pole figure diffractometer is used here to determine the positions of molecules within a substance.

often very elaborate ones. The electron microscope also is used, as well as specialized biochemical detectors.

A third rapidly growing area is *biophysical instrumentation*. As the knowledge of the functioning of living things—from parts of cells to human beings—is developing, so is the need for special instruments.

Thus, while electrocardiographs, used to study the form of the heartbeat, may be familiar to many, they represent only an early version of a whole range of instruments. These include, for example, whole-body radiation counters, which monitor the amount and kind of radioactivity accumulated by an individual; heart pacemakers, which maintain the heart beat when it is necessary to supplement the natural nerve impulses; and automatic amino-acid analyzers, which determine the composition of a protein in a matter of minutes. Background training in electronics is clearly important in this area.

Central to all areas of biophysical work is the use of radioactive isotopes, which are generated in nuclear reactors. Their use has accelerated by decades all these fields of discovery.

Training and Work in Biophysics. Training in biophysics can be obtained at the graduate level in most large universities in the United States, Canada, and the USSR. Undergraduate programs are offered in about 10 percent of the universities and colleges in the United States.

Biophysicists are valued in industries, in universities, and in medical research laboratories. The great majority then work in research laboratories at such institutions, but they are also in demand as administrators.

ERNEST C. POLLARD, *Pennsylvania State University*

Bibliography

First National Biophysical Conference, *Proceedings* (New Haven 1958).
John Wiley & Sons, Inc., *Study Program for Biophysical Science* (New York 1958).
Morowitz, Harold J., *Life and the Biophysical Sciences* (New York 1963).
Setlow, Richard B., and Pollard, Ernest C., *Molecular Biophysics* (Reading, Mass., 1962).
Snell, Fred M., and others, *Biophysical Principles of Structure and Function* (Reading, Mass., 1965).

BIOPSY, bī′op-sē, is the removal of tissue samples from the living body for inspection under the microscope. Microscopic examination of the biopsy specimen often leads to a diagnosis that helps the physician in his therapy.

Biopsy may be performed by direct surgical excision or by aspiration with a special needle. One instance in which the former procedure is used is in the diagnosis of a lump in the female breast. In order to determine whether it is benign or cancerous, the surgeon surgically exposes the lump and excises a small portion. A pathologist does a "frozen section," in which the tissue is hardened chemically and prepared for microscopic examination. The nature of the growth then is determined. If it is benign, a simple excision suffices; if it is malignant, a radical breast operation is performed.

Needle biopsies can be performed on the liver, kidney, and bone marrow without the aid of surgery.

IRVING SOLOMON, M.D.
Mount Sinai Hospital, New York

BIOSPHERE, bī′ə-sfir, the world of living organisms, including the organisms themselves and their physical environment. In includes the thin layer of soil and rocks in which living things are found; the streams, lakes, and oceans inhabited by aquatic plants and animals; and the dense lower layer of the atmosphere. All the organisms in the biosphere are interrelated both to each other and to their environment in the so-called balance of nature, which includes the food web and various cycles such as the nitrogen cycle and the carbon-hydrogen-oxygen cycle.

BIOT, byō, **Jean Baptiste** (1774–1862), French physicist, who investigated polarization of light and properties of electric currents. Biot was born in Paris on April 21, 1774. After attending polytechnic school, he became a professor of physics at the Collège de France in 1800. In 1815, Biot showed that certain liquids, such as sugar solution, rotate the direction of vibration of linearly polarized light. After conducting experiments, Biot and Félix Savart in 1820 formulated the Biot-Savart law, which states that the magnetic flux density near a straight current-carrying conductor is inversely proportional to the distance from the conductor. Biot died in Paris on Feb. 3, 1862. The mineral biotite was named for him.

BIOTIN. See VITAMINS—*Water-Soluble Vitamins* (Vitamin B Complex): Biotin.

BIOTITE, bī′ə-tīt, is a widespread mineral of the mica group (see MICA). It is a silicate of aluminum, iron, potassium, and magnesium, and is sometimes called *magnesia mica;* but the composition varies. The mineral is named for the French physicist J.B. Biot.

Biotite is rarer than the common mica, muscovite. It is distinguished from other micas by its dark color, which ranges from greenish-brown to black. It is therefore sometimes known as *black mica.* A rare form of the mineral found at Vesuvius in Italy is light yellow in color. Crystals of biotite are opaque to translucent and are lustrous. They cleave to form elastic sheets.

Composition: $K(Mg,Fe)_3AlSi_3O_{10}(OH)_2$; hardness, 2.5 to 3.0; specific gravity, 2.8 to 3.4; crystal system, monoclinic.

BIQUADRATIC EQUATIONS, bī-kwod-rat′ik i-kwä′zhənz, in algebra are equations containing but one unknown quantity, of which, in the equation, the highest power is the fourth. An equation of this kind, when complete, is of the form $x^4 + Ax^3 + Bx^2 + Cx + D = O$, where A B C and D denote any known quantities whatever.

See also EQUATION–1. *General Theory of Equations.*

BIRCH, John. See JOHN BIRCH SOCIETY.

BIRCH, bûrch, **Reginald Bathurst** (1856–1943), American illustrator. He was born in London, England, on May 2, 1856. After studying art at the Royal Academy in Munich, Germany, he settled in the United States in 1872. Birch drew illustrations for many popular American magazines, including *Life, St. Nicholas, Harper's,* and *Century,* and for scores of children's books. He died in New York City on June 17, 1943.

Birch is most famous for his pen-and-ink illustrations for Frances Hodgson Burnett's novel *Little Lord Fauntleroy,* first published in 1886. He conceived of Little Lord Fauntleroy as a pretty boy with long blond curls, wearing a black velvet suit with a lace collar. He later referred to his depiction of the golden-haired child as "one of my early crimes for which I am still making expiation." Largely through Birch's drawings, the term "Little Lord Fauntleroy" passed into common usage to refer to a type of children's clothes or to a beautiful but spoiled and rather effeminate small boy.

BIRCH, bûrch, **Samuel** (1813–1885), English Egyptologist. He was born in London, England, on Nov. 3, 1813. Affiliated from 1836 with the British Museum, he served from 1861 as director of its Oriental, medieval, and British collections of antiquities. Birch compiled several catalogs of the museum's treasures, but made his greatest contributions to the study of Egyptian hieroglyphics, deciphering many inscriptions and papyri. He died in his native London on Dec. 27, 1885.

BIRCH, bûrch, **Thomas** (1779–1851), American painter. He was born in London, England, on July 26, 1779, and moved to the United States in 1794 with his father, an engraver. They settled in Philadelphia about 1800 and established the firm of William Birch & Son. Together they designed, engraved, and published pictures of the historic sites of Philadelphia and the surrounding area.

In 1807, Thomas Birch turned his attention to the sea and became noted for his marine paintings. He also painted snow-filled winter landscapes. During the War of 1812 he produced his most famous works—the patriotic canvases depicting American victories at sea. The greatest of these paintings, *The Engagement of the Constitution and the Guerrière,* is at the U.S. Naval Academy, Annapolis, Md. His other paintings of naval battles include *The United States and the Macedonian, The Wasp and the Frolic,* and *The Battle of Lake Erie.*

Birch's other work included designs of coins for the U.S. Mint. In 1816 he contributed designs for the historical pictures on the Naval Monument in Boston. He died in Philadelphia on Jan. 14, 1851.

GORDON H. LORD, FROM MONKMEYER

PAPER BIRCH (*Betula papyrifera*). Inset: White birch leaves and fruit.

HENRY MAYER, FROM NATIONAL AUDUBON SOCIETY

BIRCH, bûrch, a genus of smooth-barked trees and shrubs. Birches are native to the Northern Hemisphere, especially the colder parts, and occur in Europe, India, China, Japan, and Siberia and in North America from the Arctic Circle to Florida and Texas. Dwarf birches grow as far north and (in the Himalaya) as high in altitude as any woody plants.

Description. Birch bark may be white, yellow, brown, or almost black. It is frequently smooth, especially in young trees, and it often has lenticels (small openings) in noticeable horizontal lines. The leaves of a birch are alternate, simple, and toothed.

Birch flowers develop in wormlike catkins of two types, staminate and pistillate. The staminate (male) catkins appear near the ends of the branches in late summer or autumn and elongate the following spring into pendulous structures, thus exposing the brownish bracts (modified leaves). In the axils of the bracts are the minute flowers, each with a pair of 2-lobed stamens (pollen-bearing organs) and a miniature calyx (outer floral envelope). As these flowers sway back and forth, windborne pollen is released into the air. In the temperate zone this happens in April and May, and birch pollen is one of the causes of spring hay fever.

The pistillate (female) catkins are shorter and occur on spurlike branchlets. They are composed of lobed bracts, each of which holds 2 or 3 naked pistillate flowers. The ovaries mature into minute winged nutlets, which are usually scattered in autumn or blown across the snow in winter, stippling it with brown.

Birch Species. Birch trees belong to the genus *Betula* in the hazelnut family, Corylaceae (also known as Betulaceae). There are numerous species in the genus. Some of the species are indistinctly delimited, and there are also many hybrids and subspecies.

There are several important species in North America. Perhaps the best known is the white canoe, or paper, birch (*B. papyrifera*). Usually 60

779

to 80 feet (18 to 24 meters) tall, this tree is found across North America from Labrador and the northern Hudson Bay country to the Yukon River and the Alaskan coast; it extends as far south as New Jersey and the mountains of West Virginia and North Carolina. In autumn the leaves of this tall tree turn pale yellow while the trunk is waxy white.

The gray birch (*B. populifolia*) is a smaller tree, rarely more than 30 feet (9 meters) high. It has white bark with conspicuous black triangles and fluttering, long-pointed leaves that turn a pale gold in the autumn. A rather frail, short-lived tree, it is often seen bending to the ground during storms. It is found on abandoned hillsides and along streams from Nova Scotia to Delaware and Indiana.

Commercially, the most important North American birch is the yellow birch (*B. lutea*). Sometimes 100 feet (30 meters) high, it has shiny yellow aromatic bark and oval leaves. It is abundant throughout the forests of eastern North America, from Newfoundland to Delaware and south along the mountains to Georgia and west to Iowa and Minnesota. It is one of the largest and commercially most valuable deciduous trees of this area.

Another noteworthy North American birch is the cherry birch (*B. lenta*). Also known as the sweet birch, black birch, or mountain mahogany, it grows to about 75 feet (23 meters) and has dark reddish brown bark and slightly heart-shaped leaves. It ranges from Maine to Georgia and Kentucky. When crushed or cut, the twigs and wood smell of wintergreen.

The river, or red, birch (*B. nigra*) has a characteristic spreading trunk, drooping branches, and shaggy, reddish brown to gray bark. It may be over 80 feet (24 meters) high and up to 5 feet (1.5 meters) in diameter. It is found along the banks of streams from Florida and Texas to Kansas, Nebraska, Massachusetts, and New Hampshire. It is, however, mainly a Southern tree, and it is smaller when found in the North.

The European white or silver birch (*B. verrucosa* or *B. pendula*) is widespread throughout Eurasia, from the British Isles through northern continental Europe to Siberia. A very attractive tree, it has snow-white bark, pendant branches, and incised leaves.

Commercial Importance. Birch trees have served varied uses for many centuries. The Indians used the bark for canoes, for coverings for their tepees, and as a material on which to write messages; they used the wood for sleds and snowshoe frames, and the sap as a beverage and syrup. Black birch trees were a source of oil of wintergreen.

European birch trees have a resinous material in the bark that is used in tanning and in the production of scented Russian leather. The wood of these trees is used in making furniture, woodenware, and trinkets. Birch oil and birch tar, also obtained from the European species, have been used as medicine.

In America the three most important species of birch wood are the white, the yellow, and the black. The heartwood varies in color from light to darker brown, and it is often tinged with red. It has fine pores, indistinct rays, and rather inconspicuous growth rings. The wood is of relatively uniform texture. Black birch is somewhat superior to yellow, but both are heavy, hard, and strong. Birch wood takes a good finish and

is used for veneer. It is used for furniture and is made into cabinets, woodenware, spools, and toothpicks. The white and gray birches are used for pulp.

History. The birch tree is an ancient tree. Fossil birches of the Upper Cretaceous period (about 80 million years ago) are found throughout the Northern Hemisphere.

EDWIN B. MATZKE, *Columbia University*

Further Reading: Fenska, Richard, *Complete Modern Tree Experts Guide* (New York 1954); Petrides, George, *Field Guide to the Trees and Shrubs* (Boston 1958); Sargent, Charles S., *Manual of the Trees of North America* (Magnolia, Mass., 1962); Zimmerman, Martin, ed., *Formation of Wood in Forest Trees* (New York 1964).

BIRCH SOCIETY. See JOHN BIRCH SOCIETY.

BIRD, Isabella Lucy. See BISHOP, ISABELLA LUCY.

BIRD, bûrd, **Robert Montgomery** (1806–1854), American playwright and novelist, whose fame was linked with that of the American actor Edwin Forrest. Bird was born in New Castle, Del., on Feb. 5, 1806. He graduated from the medical school of the University of Pennsylvania in 1827 but soon gave up medicine to write for the stage. His blank verse tragedy, *The Gladiator*, a drama of ancient Rome, was first played in New York City in 1831 by Forrest, a close friend of Bird. The play was an immediate success and continued to be performed frequently throughout the 19th century. By 1853 it had had 1,000 performances, the first play in English to achieve this record during its author's lifetime.

Bird's *Oralloossa* was produced in 1832, and *The Broker of Bogota* in 1834. The latter, generally considered Bird's best play, is marked, like *The Gladiator*, by warm, vivid characterization and an expression of strong democratic sympathies.

Unfortunately, Bird never realized adequate financial gain from the success of his plays. The verbal agreements he had with Forrest were not honored, and Forrest would not allow publication of the plays. (They were not published until 1917.)

Bird turned to writing novels, and in this field his artistic success was coupled with material reward. *Calavar; or The Knight of the Conquest* (1834) and *The Infidel; or The Fall of Mexico* (1835) are both set in Mexico at the time of the Spanish conquest. *The Hawks of Hawk-Hollow* (1835)—a convincing picture of declining family fortunes—is the story of a Tory family in Pennsylvania after the close of the American Revolution. *Sheppard Lee* (1836) was a vehicle for Bird's criticism of manners and customs in contemporary America.

Nick of the Woods; or, The Jibbenainosay (1837; new ed., 1966), probably the most popular of Bird's novels, contains the character of the Quaker Nathan Slaughter, who declines to join his Kentucky neighbors to fight the Indians, but works alone in secret to achieve revenge for the Indians' massacre of his family. Bird's Indians are bloodthirsty barbarians, quite different from the noble savages described by James Fenimore Cooper.

In 1840 failing health forced Bird to give up writing. In 1847 he became part owner and literary editor of the Philadelphia *North American*, on which he worked until his death. He died in Philadelphia on Jan. 23, 1854.

BIRD

BIRD, any of a class (Aves) of warm-blooded vertebrate animals with feather-covered bodies. Next to the mammals, birds are the most important group of land-living vertebrates. All birds have feathers, although in some types, particularly those that cannot fly, the normal structure of the feathers may be much modified and be downy, woolly, or strawlike. The forelimbs of birds are modified into wings. The bony part of the tail, except in the very earliest fossil birds, is very short, and the visible tail is composed of feathers only. Teeth are absent except in some fossil forms. As in mammals—the only other group of warm-blooded animals—the circulation is highly perfected so that there is no mixing of arterial and venous blood, but the arrangement of veins and arteries by which this is accomplished is different in the two groups. Birds have keen hearing, although they have no external ears. The sense of sight also is very keen, but the sense of smell is weak or lacking, except in a few vultures and other birds.

(PHOTO OF SOOTY TERN, BY HARVEY FISHER, FROM NATIONAL AUDUBON SOCIETY)

ARCHAEOPTERYX, the oldest known bird, lived about 150 million years ago. More reptile than bird in its skeletal structure, it had teeth, a bony tail, and a reptilelike brain case; its main avian feature was its feathers. A fossil is shown at left and a reconstruction at right.

Evolution. Birds evolved from reptiles and still share so many anatomical characters with them that the biologist Thomas Huxley referred to birds as "glorified reptiles." Some of the carnivorous dinosaurs had a skeleton similar to that of birds in many ways. These dinosaurs ran on the hind legs, and the forelimbs were very small. Birds evolved from some small dinosaur or dinosaur-relative of this general type. The reptilian scales in time became modified into feathers, first perhaps for insulation of a creature that was gradually becoming warm-blooded, but later for use in flight.

Undoubtedly, gliding or parachuting preceded the development of true flight. But we do not know whether the achievement of flight occurred in a ground-living form that flapped its wings to increase its speed of running, as does the rhea today, or whether it occurred in a tree-climbing form that used imperfectly developed wings to aid it in leaping from limb to limb.

The earliest known fossil bird, *Archaeopteryx* (q.v.), known from three specimens, were chicken-sized creatures that inhabited trees. They lived in what is now Bavaria in the Jurassic period, during the middle of the age of reptiles, about 150 million years ago. *Archaeopteryx* had well-developed feathers and is classified as a bird, yet its structure, insofar as it can be made out by the patient research of the paleontologist, was as much that of a reptile as of a bird. The structure of the skull, the small size of the eyes, and the teeth in the jaws are all reptilian. Unlike any living bird, *Archaeopteryx* had a long bony tail. Attached to each of the tail vertebrae was a pair of tail feathers whose impressions are clearly visible in the stone in which the fossil was imbedded. This earliest bird probably was able to glide from branch to branch with the aid of its feathered wings.

No other fossil birds of Jurassic age have been found, but in the following period, the Cretaceous (135 to 70 million years ago), remarkable types existed in central North America, an area which at that time was partly covered by shallow seas. The best known of these Cretaceous birds are *Hesperornis*, a large, flightless diving form, and *Ichthyornis*, a small, flying species. Both were more like birds living today than was *Archaeopteryx*. *Hesperonis*, however, still had reptilelike teeth, which it used for seizing fish.

By the beginning of the Tertiary Period, or age of mammals, approximately 70 million years ago, birds had completed the major part of their evolution. There were, to be sure, many that are no longer in existence, but even they seem to have been basically like present-day birds.

Birds are small and have light skeletons that decompose quickly. Teeth (which because of their hard enamel are the most easily fossilized parts) disappeared early in avian evolution. For such reasons fossil remains of birds are rare and, as a rule, imperfect, and it has not been possible to work out the evolution of birds so fully as that of, for example, mammals or fish. Only in

EARLY BIRD FORMS: (Left) Archaeornis male and female. (Right) Ichthyornis, a small, gull-like flyer.

CLASSIFICATION OF BIRDS

Birds make up the class Aves in the subphylum Vertebrata of the phylum Chordata. The class is divided into the following superorders, of which the first two contain only extinct orders of birds.

PALEOGNATHAE. This group contains only the reptilelike bird of the Jurassic period, *Archaeopteryx*. It is the earliest avian fossil.

ODONTOGNATHAE. This group contains *Hesperornis* and the other toothed birds of the Cretaceous period. Five fossil species have been found in Kansas and Montana. The group probably is an evolutionary offshoot, since no living birds seem to be descendants of the group.

NEOGNATHAE. This group includes all living birds as well as the extinct forms from the more recent geological periods. The Neognathae are divided into two main groups—the Ratitae, which contain only a few large flightless forms and several extinct forms, and the Carinatae, or flying birds.

Ratitae. *Extinct forms* of Ratitae are the moas of New Zealand and the elephant birds of Madagascar. They were the largest of all known birds. Both became extinct before Europeans discovered their habitats. *Living forms* are the rhea of South America, the ostrich of Africa, the kiwi of New Zealand, and the emu and cassowary of the Australian region. These birds no longer have a bony keel on the breastbone for the attachment of flight feathers, and the wings themselves are small and degenerate.

Carinatae. Carinate birds have a breastbone keel. A few have become flightless, and in these the keel may be somewhat reduced, but it is never completely absent as in the ratites. Carinate birds are divided into a number of main orders. The following are the most important:

Tinamous (Tinamiformes). Quail-like birds of tropical America; probably related to the South American rheas.

Fowl-like birds (Galliformes). A large and important worldwide group that includes the domestic chickens and turkeys, pheasants, quail, grouse, and guinea hens.

Penguins (Sphenisciformes). The most highly specialized of living birds adapted for life in the water. The wings are modified into seal-like flippers.

Albatrosses and petrels (Procellariiformes). Seabirds that come to land only during the nesting season.

Loons and grebes (Gaviiformes, Podicipidiformes). Freshwater birds that are expert divers; hence the name "hell-diver" used for the grebes.

Pelicans and related species (Pelecaniformes). Aquatic birds that usually live on fish. Besides the pelicans, the cormorants, anhingas, boobies, and man-o'-war birds belong to this group.

Day-flying birds of prey (Falconiformes). A worldwide group that includes the falcons, hawks, eagles, kites, and buzzards and also the vultures of the New and the Old World, and the African secretary-bird.

Herons, ibises, storks, flamingos (Ciconiiformes). Long-legged wading birds that feed on fish and other aquatic life. Some of the storks feed on carrion.

Waterfowl (Anseriformes). The ducks, geese, and swans, which form an important group because of the value of the domestic species and the large numbers shot for sport and food.

Cranes and relatives (Gruiformes). A diverse group, most members of which inhabit swamps and marshes. The cranes, rails, coots, seriamas, and bustards belong here.

Shorebirds, gulls, terns, auks (Charadriiformes). Another diverse group, most of whose members live in or near the water.

Pigeons, sand-grouse, dodos (Columbiformes). An important group of game birds, which includes the domestic pigeon.

Parrots (Psittaciformes). A well-known, colorful group, chiefly tropical, numbering more than 300 species.

Owls, goatsuckers, swifts (Strigiformes, Caprimulgiformes, Apodiformes). The owls are the nocturnal equivalents of the hawks; the goatsuckers, also nocturnal, feed on insects; the swifts, which pursue flying insects in the air, may be related to the goatsuckers.

Hummingbirds (Trochiliformes). A remarkable group of small, brilliantly colored birds found only in the New World and chiefly in the tropics.

Rollers and allies (Coraciiformes). A diverse group of often brightly colored birds, chiefly tropical, which includes the rollers, kingfishers, hornbills, and bee-eaters. The brilliant trogons and the curious little mousebirds of Africa may be related to this order.

Woodpeckers and allies (Piciformes). In addition to the familiar woodpeckers, this group includes the brilliant, huge-billed toucans of South America, the barbets, and the honey guides of Africa.

Perching birds (Passeriformes). This is the most advanced and successful group of living birds. About 5,000 of the approximately 8,600 species of living birds belong to it. There are two main groups of perching birds: the nonsongbirds (Clamatores) and the true songbirds (Oscines). The latter have certain specializations of the muscles controlling the vocal cords that are not present in other birds. The more primitive group, the nonsongbirds or Clamatores, is found in South America and includes the tyrant flycatchers, the cotingas, manikins, woodhewers, antbirds, and ovenbirds. In the Old World the pittas and the broadbills belong to this group. The true songbirds, or Oscines, are most richly represented in the tropics of the Old World, but there are numerous species in the New World as well. Most songbirds are rather small; the raven is the giant of the group. Typical families are the larks, swallows, thrushes, flycatchers, wrens, orioles, titmice, crows, finches, and many others.

EARLY BIRD FORMS: (*Left*) *Hesperornis*, a large swimming bird. (*Right*) the seven foot-tall *Diatryma*.

AMERICAN MUSEUM OF NATURAL HISTORY

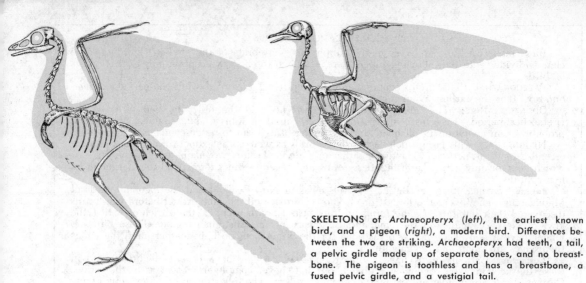

SKELETONS of *Archaeopteryx* (*left*), the earliest known bird, and a pigeon (*right*), a modern bird. Differences between the two are striking. *Archaeopteryx* had teeth, a tail, a pelvic girdle made up of separate bones, and no breastbone. The pigeon is toothless and has a breastbone, a fused pelvic girdle, and a vestigial tail.

a few exceptional cases, such as the giant, flightless moas of New Zealand, do we have ample fossil material of any group of birds.

Classification. The earliest classifications of birds relied upon easily recognized external characters or upon peculiarities of behavior or appearance. All webfooted birds were placed in one group, all seed-eating birds in another, and so on. Following Darwin's publication of his theory of evolution in the middle of the 19th century, classification was placed on a sounder, more scientific basis. Since that time scientists have sought to arrange birds (and other living things) in a way that will best express their blood relationships and lines of descent.

In biological classifications we are trying to express relationships that began millions of years ago, and fossil evidence is never complete enough to work out the details. A further difficulty in the classification of birds is that most of the principal groups or orders became established in the early Tertiary, about 70 million years ago. Since that time relatively few major changes have taken place, although new species, genera, and families of various degrees of distinctness have continued to evolve in large numbers. Birds of similar habits, even though not closely related, often require many adaptive likenesses. Hawks and owls, for example, were for a long time placed together in a group called Raptores, but it is now realized that they are not at all closely allied, even though the members of both groups have similar hooked beaks and sharp claws, used in catching their prey.

The accompanying brief classification outline calls attention to some of the principal groups of birds and indicates their supposed relationship to one another.

Distribution. Birds are found over the entire surface of the globe. They are, of course, limited to land during the nesting season but some of the marine albatrosses, petrels, and penguins usually come to shore only during the nesting season, spending the rest of the year wandering over the remote expanses of the ocean. Almost all the land areas of the globe are occupied by birds; only the Antarctic continent is almost too barren to attract them, although the snowy petrel has been found nesting many miles inland on the mountains of Antarctica. In the north a few species of seabirds, such as the rosy gull, winter to some extent in the Arctic Ocean, searching for the occasional open "leads" of water in the expanse of snow and ice. The great deserts of the world also present something of a challenge to bird life, but some species are especially adapted for life there and can exist in the most inhospitable and driest regions. In general, bird life is most abundant in those parts of the globe that have a warm, moist climate, since it is there that food and cover are most abundant. Many birds that nest in the north migrate to the tropics to spend the winter. In summer, temperate and northern regions may support as rich a population of birds as the tropics. Even in the Arctic there is a great abundance of mosquitoes and other insects during the brief summer, and innumerable shorebirds and waterfowl find ideal feeding and nesting conditions there. Marine life is often more abundant in cool than in warm waters. It is for this reason that one finds immense colonies of seabirds on the islands near Alaska and off the coast of Peru.

As already suggested, the distribution of birds is governed in large measure by the degree to which a given species or family of birds is adapted to a particular environment. One does

WING SKELTON of the bird shows a marked similarity to the skeletal structure of the mammalian forelimb.

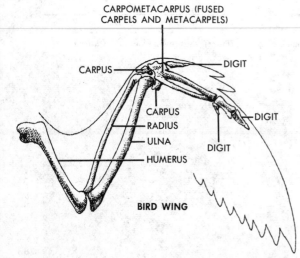

CARPOMETACARPUS (FUSED CARPELS AND METACARPELS)

CARPUS — — DIGIT

CARPUS
— — — DIGIT
RADIUS
ULNA
DIGIT
HUMERUS

BIRD WING

BIRD FLIGHT is powered mainly by the tips of the primary feathers, which serve as propellers. The screech owl (*top*) and falcon shown here are coming in for a landing, with tail feathers extended to brake their flight.

not expect to find penguins in a desert or prairie chickens in a forest. Many species are almost limited to a given type of vegetation; others are restricted by their need for a particular type of nesting area. The peregrine falcon, for example, is cosmopolitan but nests, as a rule, only where suitable cliffs exist near large bodies of water.

The so-called "life zone" concept is an attempt to classify the environmental factors controlling the distribution of birds. As applied to North America, several zones were recognized, including the Hudsonian, Canadian, and Sonoran, each defined by the average summer temperature and each characterized by a different group of birds, plants, and mammals. More recently the tendency has been to minimize the importance of temperature as a direct controlling factor in bird distribution. The type and nature of the vegetation seem more important. Vegetation is strongly affected by temperature, but it is also affected by soil and rainfall. It is more satisfactory to study the distribution of each species of bird in terms of the habitat it prefers. Some species, such as the American robin, are found in a great variety of surroundings, while others are more exacting in the selection of areas that suit their requirements.

The pine warbler of eastern North America is absent from numerous apparently suitable areas of pine forest in the Old World. In such cases the explanation lies in historical factors; a species of bird is often kept by oceans or mountains or unsuitable habitat from reaching regions that would be suitable for it. There are very few native songbirds in the Hawaiian Islands because

FLIGHT ALTITUDES for birds generally are below 3,000 feet, but some birds occasionally attain much higher altitudes. One of the highest-flying birds, the bearded vulture, reaches 25,000 feet. The mallard has been encountered at 21,000 feet, and the evening grosbeak at 12,500 feet. European swifts have been seen at altitudes of 7,000 feet, and whistling swans at 4,000 feet.

HANS DOMMASCH, FROM ANNAN PHOTOS

FOOD OF BIRDS varies widely. This great horned owl clasps the prey it has just killed in its sharp talons.

it is almost impossible for small birds to cross the thousands of miles of ocean separating those islands from the nearest continent. Yet numerous other species, when introduced by man, have found the Hawaiian Islands a congenial home. The same is true, in the United States, of the house sparrow, the starling, and the ring-necked pheasant, all of which were introduced from the Old World.

Flight. As already noted, birds alone, of all living beings, possess feathers. (The structure of feathers is described in the article PLUMAGE.) In most birds feathers do not grow uniformly over the body but are arranged in definite regions or "tracts," whose variations are of some value in classification (see PTERYLOGRAPHY). Not only the feathers but the entire anatomy of birds show an adaptation for flight. The bones of the pelvic or hip region are fused into a single mass, the synsacrum, which includes the sacral vertebrae. The bones corresponding to those of our ankle have become a part of the long bones above and below them. The bones of the foot (carpals) also are fused together. These modifications permit the legs to give a strong upward thrust as the bird takes off in flight and help it withstand the shock of alighting. The bones of the skull are also fused and grown together so that the sutures between them are no longer visible. This fusion strengthens the skull; injury is less likely if the head strikes against twigs or other obstacles in flight. The eyes are large, and in hawks, which sometimes fly very recklessly as they pursue their victims, they are protected by a bony shield.

The long bones of the bird's body are hollow; the hollowed column gives one of the lightest and strongest types of support. These bones are connected with a system of air tubes that connect with the lungs and serve as part of the respiratory system. There are additional air sacs in the body cavity and sometimes just beneath the skin. Birds lack sweat glands and it is probable that this system of air sacs helps to cool the body during the exertion of flight and also ensures a constant supply of fresh air for the lungs.

Anyone who has watched a swift or swallow fly tirelessly hour after hour in hot weather will realize that the avian body is highly efficient. The normal body temperature of most birds is about 105°F (41°C)—in some it is even higher—fitting them for a life of intense activity.

The mechanics and speed of flight vary greatly according to the habits and size of the bird. Soaring flight, of the type seen in hawks, vultures, and storks, is almost restricted to large birds with ample wings. Small birds are buffeted too much by air currents to be successful at this

AN OSPREY (*left*) returns to its nest with a small fish that it has captured to feed its young. The barn owl (*right*), mainly a night hunter, clutches a field mouse in its curved beak.

N.Y. STRAND, FROM ANNAN PHOTOS

RONALD THOMPSON, FROM ANNAN PHOTOS

BIRDS OF NORTH AMERICA

CONTENTS

Perching Birds ....Plates 1-3
Woodpeckers, Kingfishers, and Trogons ....Plate 4
Swifts, Hummingbirds, Nightjars, Owls,
    Cuckoos, Parrots, and Pigeons ....Plate 5
Shorebirds, Gulls, and Alcids ....Plate 6
Cranes and Pheasants ....Plate 7
Vultures, Hawks, Falcons, Ducks,
    Geese, and Swans ....Plate 8
Herons, Storks, and Flamingos ....Plate 9
Pelicans ....Plate 10
Albatrosses, Petrels, Grebes,
    Loons, and Tinamous ....Plate 11

The birds depicted on this and the following plates represent every family of birds that live in North America, and include members of each of the world's 20 orders of living birds. The range of many of these birds extends into South America and the Caribbean, and some are also found elsewhere. The sequence of illustrations begins with the most highly developed order of birds—the perching birds—and ends with a representative of the most primitive order—the tinamou. All of the birds illustrated are males, which are usually more vividly colored than are the females. An indication of the approximate size of the birds is given below the title of each plate.

Illustrations by Gaetano di Palma

PERCHING BIRDS (PASSERIFORMES)

(Approximately 1/4 life size)

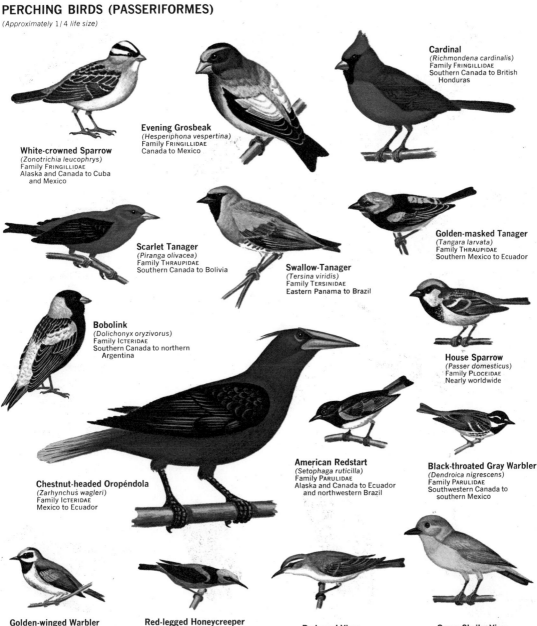

White-crowned Sparrow
(Zonotrichia leucophrys)
Family FRINGILLIDAE
Alaska and Canada to Cuba
and Mexico

Evening Grosbeak
(Hesperiphona vespertina)
Family FRINGILLIDAE
Canada to Mexico

Cardinal
(Richmondena cardinalis)
Family FRINGILLIDAE
Southern Canada to British
Honduras

Scarlet Tanager
(Piranga olivacea)
Family THRAUPIDAE
Southern Canada to Bolivia

Swallow-Tanager
(Tersina viridis)
Family TERSINIDAE
Eastern Panama to Brazil

Golden-masked Tanager
(Tangara larvata)
Family THRAUPIDAE
Southern Mexico to Ecuador

Bobolink
(Dolichonyx oryzivorus)
Family ICTERIDAE
Southern Canada to northern
Argentina

House Sparrow
(Passer domesticus)
Family PLOCEIDAE
Nearly worldwide

Chestnut-headed Oropéndola
(Zarhynchus wagleri)
Family ICTERIDAE
Mexico to Ecuador

American Redstart
(Setophaga ruticilla)
Family PARULIDAE
Alaska and Canada to Ecuador
and northwestern Brazil

Black-throated Gray Warbler
(Dendroica nigrescens)
Family PARULIDAE
Southwestern Canada to
southern Mexico

Golden-winged Warbler
(Vermivora chrysoptera)
Family PARULIDAE
Southeastern Canada to
Colombia and Venezuela

Red-legged Honeycreeper
(Cyanerpes cyaneus)
Family COEREBIDAE
Southern Cuba; southern Mexico
to Bolivia and Brazil

Red-eyed Vireo
(Vireo olivaceus)
Family VIREONIDAE
Canada to Peru and Brazil

Green Shrike-Vireo
(Smaragdolanius pulchellus)
Family VIREOLANIIDAE
Southern Mexico to Colombia

PLATE 1

PERCHING BIRDS (cont'd)

(Approximately 1/4 life size)

Rufous-browed Peppershrike
(Cyclarhis gujanensis)
Family CYCLARHIDAE
Southern Mexico to Argentina
and Uruguay

Common Starling
(Sturnus vulgaris)
Family STURNIDAE
Nearly worldwide

Loggerhead Shrike
(Lanius ludovicianus)
Family LANIIDAE
Southern Canada to Mexico

Palm-Chat
(Dulus dominicus)
Family DULIDAE
Hispaniola

Phainopepla
(Phainopepla nitens)
Family PTILOGONATIDAE
Southwestern U.S. to
southern Mexico

Cedar Waxwing
(Bombycilla cedrorum)
Family BOMBYCILLIDAE
Alaska and Canada to Panama

Wren-Thrush
(Zeledonia coronata)
Family ZELEDONIIDAE
Costa Rica and western Panama

Water Pipit
(Anthus spinoletta)
Family MOTACILLIDAE
Old World; Alaska and Canada
to Guatemala

Blue-gray Gnatcatcher
(Polioptila caerulea)
Family SYLVIIDAE
U.S. to Bahamas and Honduras

Eastern Bluebird
(Sialia sialis)
Family TURDIDAE
Southern Canada to Nicaragua

Short-billed Marsh Wren
(Cistothorus platensis)
Family TROGLODYTIDAE
Southern Canada to Falkland
Islands and Tierra del Fuego

Northern Mockingbird
(Mimus polyglottos)
Family MIMIDAE
Southern Canada to West Indies
and southern Mexico

American Dipper
(Cinclus mexicanus)
Family CINCLIDAE
Alaska and western Canada to
western Panama

Wrentit
(Chamaea fasciatus)
Family CHAMAEIDAE
Oregon to Baja California

Brown Creeper
(Certhia familiaris)
Family CERTHIIDAE
Old World; Alaska and Canada to
Nicaragua

Red-breasted Nuthatch
(Sitta canadensis)
Family SITTIIDAE
Alaska and Canada to southern
U.S.

Tufted Titmouse
(Parus bicolor)
Family PARIDAE
Eastern and southern U.S.

PLATE 2

PERCHING BIRDS (cont'd)

(Approximately 1/4 life size)

Green Jay
(Cyanocorax yncas)
Family CORVIDAE
Southern Texas to Honduras;
Colombia and Venezuela to
Peru and Bolivia

Clark's Nutcracker
(Nucifraga columbiana)
Family CORVIDAE
Western Canada to northwestern
Mexico

Horned Lark
(Eremophila alpestris)
Family ALAUDIDAE
Old World; Alaska and Canada
to southern Mexico; Colombia

Cliff Swallow
(Petrochelidon pyrrhonota)
Family HIRUNDINIDAE
Alaska and Canada to Chile
and Argentina

Sharpbill
(Oxyruncus cristatus)
Family OXYRUNCIDAE
Costa Rica to Brazil and Paraguay

Great Kiskadee
(Pitangus sulphuratus)
Family TYRANNIDAE
Southern Texas to Argentina

Black Phoebe
(Sayornis nigricans)
Family TYRANNIDAE
Southwestern U.S. to
northern Argentina

Royal Flycatcher
(Onychorhynchus coronatus)
Family TYRANNIDAE
Southern Mexico to Bolivia and
Brazil

Red-capped Manakin
(Pipra mentalis)
Family PIPRIDAE
Mexico to Ecuador

Scaled Antpitta
(Grallaria guatimalensis)
Family FORMICARIIDAE
Southern Mexico to Peru and
northern Brazil

Masked Tityra
(Tityra semifasciata)
Family COTINGIDAE
Mexico to Bolivia and northern
Brazil

Pale-throated Tapaculo
(Scytalopus panamensis)
Family RHINOCRYPTIDAE
Eastern Panama to northwestern
Ecuador

Great Antshrike
(Taraba major)
Family FORMICARIIDAE
Southern Mexico to northern
Argentina and Uruguay

Plain Xenops
(Xenops minutus)
Family FURNARIIDAE
Southern Mexico to northeastern
Argentina and Paraguay

Olivaceous Woodcreeper
(Sittasomus griseicapillus)
Family DENDROCOLAPTIDAE
Mexico to northern Argentina

PLATE 3

WOODPECKERS AND ALLIES (PICIFORMES), KINGFISHERS AND ALLIES (CORACIIFORMES), and TROGONS (TROGONIFORMES)

(Approximately 1/5 life size)

Pileated Woodpecker
(Dryocopus pileatus)
Family PICIDAE
Order PICIFORMES
Canada to southern U.S.

Rufous-tailed Jacamar
(Galbula ruficauda)
Family GALBULIDAE
Order PICIFORMES
Southern Mexico to northeastern
Argentina

Red-headed Barbet
(Eubucco bourcierii)
Family CAPITONIDAE
Order PICIFORMES
Costa Rica to northeastern Peru

Red-headed Woodpecker
(Melanerpes erythrocephalus)
Family PICIDAE
Order PICIFORMES
Southern Canada to southern U.S.

Keel-billed Toucan
(Ramphastos sulfuratus)
Family RAMPHASTIDAE
Order PICIFORMES
Southern Mexico to northern Colombia
and northern Venezuela

Jamaican Tody
(Todus todus)
Family TODIDAE
Order CORACIIFORMES
Jamaica

White-necked Puffbird
(Notharchus macrorhynchos)
Family BUCCONIDAE
Order PICIFORMES
Southern Mexico to northeastern
Argentina

Turquoise-browed Motmot
(Eumomota superciliosa)
Family MOMOTIDAE
Order CORACIIFORMES
Mexico to northern Costa Rica

Ringed Kingfisher
(Ceryle torquata)
Family ALCEDINIDAE
Order CORACIIFORMES
Mexico and the Lesser Antilles
to Tierra del Fuego

Bar-tailed Trogon
(Trogon dollaris)
Family TROGONIDAE
Order TROGONIFORMES
Mexico to Bolivia and Brazil

PLATE 4

SWIFTS AND HUMMINGBIRDS (APODIFORMES), NIGHTJARS AND ALLIES (CAPRIMULGIFORMES), OWLS (STRIGIFORMES), CUCKOOS AND ALLIES (CUCULIFORMES), PARROTS AND ALLIES (PSITTACIFORMES), and PIGEONS AND ALLIES (COLUMBIFORMES)

(Approximately 1/5 life size)

Rufous Hummingbird
(Selasphorus rufus)
Family TROCHILIDAE
Order APODIFORMES
Alaska and western Canada
to southern Mexico

White-necked Jacobin
(Florisuga mellivora)
Family TROCHILIDAE
Order APODIFORMES
Southern Mexico to Bolivia
and Brazil

White-throated Swift
(Aeronautes saxatilis)
Family APODIDAE
Order APODIFORMES
Southwestern Canada to
El Salvador

Common Potoo
(Nyctibius griseus)
Family NYCTIBIIDAE
Order CAPRIMULGIFORMES
Southern Mexico to Argentina

Scarlet Macaw
(Ara macao)
Family PSITTACIDAE
Order PSITTACIFORMES
Mexico to Bolivia and Brazil

Whip-poor-will
(Caprimulgus vociferus)
Family CAPRIMULGIDAE
Order CAPRIMULGIFORMES
Southern Canada to Costa Rica

Burrowing Owl
(Speotyto cunicularia)
Family STRIGIDAE
Order STRIGIFORMES
Southwestern Canada to
Tierra del Fuego; Florida;
West Indies

Mangrove Cuckoo
(Coccyzus minor)
Family CUCULIDAE
Order CUCULIFORMES
Southern Florida; West Indies;
Mexico to northern Brazil

Barn Owl
(Tyto alba)
Family TYTONIDAE
Order STRIGIFORMES
Nearly worldwide

White-winged Dove
(Zenaida asiatica)
Family COLUMBIDAE
Order COLUMBIFORMES
Southwestern U.S. to northern
Chile; West Indies

PLATE 5

SHOREBIRDS, GULLS, ALCIDS, AND ALLIES (CHARADRIIFORMES)

(Approximately 1/8 life size)

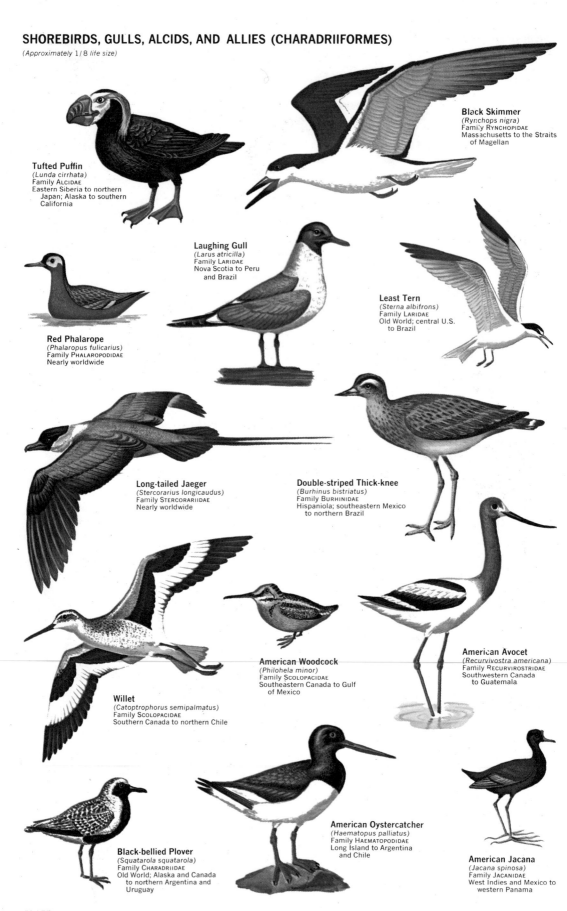

Tufted Puffin
(Lunda cirrhata)
Family ALCIDAE
Eastern Siberia to northern
Japan; Alaska to southern
California

Black Skimmer
(Rynchops nigra)
Family RYNCHOPIDAE
Massachusetts to the Straits
of Magellan

Laughing Gull
(Larus atricilla)
Family LARIDAE
Nova Scotia to Peru
and Brazil

Least Tern
(Sterna albifrons)
Family LARIDAE
Old World; central U.S.
to Brazil

Red Phalarope
(Phalaropus fulicarius)
Family PHALAROPODIDAE
Nearly worldwide

Long-tailed Jaeger
(Stercorarius longicaudus)
Family STERCORARIIDAE
Nearly worldwide

Double-striped Thick-knee
(Burhinus bistriatus)
Family BURHINIDAE
Hispaniola; southeastern Mexico
to northern Brazil

American Woodcock
(Philohela minor)
Family SCOLOPACIDAE
Southeastern Canada to Gulf
of Mexico

American Avocet
(Recurvirostra americana)
Family RECURVIROSTRIDAE
Southwestern Canada
to Guatemala

Willet
(Catoptrophorus semipalmatus)
Family SCOLOPACIDAE
Southern Canada to northern Chile

American Oystercatcher
(Haematopus palliatus)
Family HAEMATOPODIDAE
Long Island to Argentina
and Chile

Black-bellied Plover
(Squatarola squatarola)
Family CHARADRIIDAE
Old World; Alaska and Canada
to northern Argentina and
Uruguay

American Jacana
(Jacana spinosa)
Family JACANIDAE
West Indies and Mexico to
western Panama

PLATE 6

CRANES AND ALLIES (GRUIFORMES) and PHEASANTS AND ALLIES (GALLIFORMES)

(Approximately 1/10 life size)

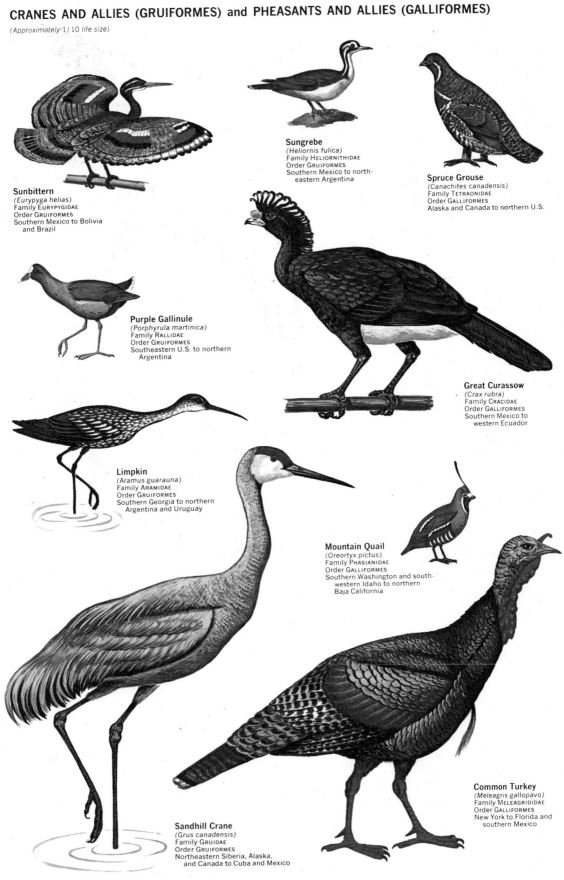

Sunbittern
(Eurypyga helias)
Family EURYPYGIDAE
Order GRUIFORMES
Southern Mexico to Bolivia
and Brazil

Sungrebe
(Heliornis fulica)
Family HELIORNITHIDAE
Order GRUIFORMES
Southern Mexico to north-
eastern Argentina

Spruce Grouse
(Canachites canadensis)
Family TETRAONIDAE
Order GALLIFORMES
Alaska and Canada to northern U.S.

Purple Gallinule
(Porphyrula martinica)
Family RALLIDAE
Order GRUIFORMES
Southeastern U.S. to northern
Argentina

Great Curassow
(Crax rubra)
Family CRACIDAE
Order GALLIFORMES
Southern Mexico to
western Ecuador

Limpkin
(Aramus guarauna)
Family ARAMIDAE
Order GRUIFORMES
Southern Georgia to northern
Argentina and Uruguay

Mountain Quail
(Oreortyx pictus)
Family PHASIANIDAE
Order GALLIFORMES
Southern Washington and south-
western Idaho to northern
Baja California

Common Turkey
(Meleagris gallopavo)
Family MELEAGRIDIDAE
Order GALLIFORMES
New York to Florida and
southern Mexico

Sandhill Crane
(Grus canadensis)
Family GRUIDAE
Order GRUIFORMES
Northeastern Siberia, Alaska,
and Canada to Cuba and Mexico

PLATE 7

VULTURES, HAWKS, AND FALCONS (FALCONIFORMES) and DUCKS, GEESE, AND SWANS (ANSERIFORMES)

(Approximately 1/10 life size)

Osprey
(Pandion haliaetus)
Family PANDIONIDAE
Order FALCONIFORMES
Old World; Alaska and Canada
to northern Argentina and Chile

Swallow-tailed Kite
(Elanoides forficatus)
Family ACCIPITRIDAE
Order FALCONIFORMES
Southeastern U.S. to northern
Argentina

Gyrfalcon
(Falco rusticolus)
Family FALCONIDAE
Order FALCONIFORMES
Old World; Alaska, Canada, and
Greenland to northern U.S.

Goshawk
(Accipiter gentilis)
Family ACCIPITRIDAE
Order FALCONIFORMES
Old World; Alaska and Canada to
mountains of northwestern Mexico

Black Vulture
(Coragyps atratus)
Family CATHARTIDAE
Order FALCONIFORMES
Central U.S. to Argentina
and Chile

Canada Goose
(Branta canadensis)
Family ANATIDAE
Order ANSERIFORMES
Alaska and Canada to central
Mexico and the Gulf States

Whistling Swan
(Cygnus columbianus)
Family ANATIDAE
Order ANSERIFORMES
Alaska and Canada to California
and North Carolina

Harlequin Duck
(Histrionicus histrionicus)
Family ANATIDAE
Order ANSERIFORMES
Eastern Siberia to Japan; Alaska,
Canada, and Greenland to central
California and Long Island

PLATE 8

HERONS, STORKS, AND FLAMINGOS (CICONIIFORMES)

(Approximately 1/9 life size)

Wood Stork
(Mycteria americana)
Family CICONIIDAE
South Carolina to central Argentina
and Uruguay

Boat-billed Heron
(Cochlearius cochlearius)
Family COCHLEARIIDAE
Mexico to Bolivia, Paraguay,
and Brazil

Cattle Egret
(Bubulcus ibis)
Family ARDEIDAE
Old World; U.S. to northern
South America

Glossy Ibis
(Plegadis falcinellus)
Family THRESKIORNITHIDAE
Old World; central U.S. to Chile,
Argentina, and Uruguay

Least Bittern
(Ixobrychus exilis)
Family ARDEIDAE
Northern U.S. to Bolivia,
Paraguay, and Brazil

American Flamingo
(Phoenicopterus ruber)
Family PHOENICOPTERIDAE
West Indies, Yucatan, coast of
northern South America and the
Galapagos Islands

Roseate Spoonbill
(Ajaia ajaja)
Family THRESKIORNITHIDAE
Gulf of Mexico and West Indies to
Argentina and Uruguay

PLATE 9

PELICANS AND ALLIES (PELECANIFORMES)

(Approximately 1/12 life size)

Anhinga
(Anhinga anhinga)
Family ANHINGIDAE
North Carolina to northern
Argentina

Magnificent Frigatebird
(Fregata magnificens)
Family FREGATIDAE
Bahamas; Baja California to
northern Peru and Uruguay

Great Cormorant
(Phalacrocorax carbo)
Family PHALACROCORACIDAE
Old World; Newfoundland to
New Jersey

Brown Booby
(Sula leucogaster)
Family SULIDAE
Old World; West Indies and
Mexico to Colombia and Brazil

Red-billed Tropicbird
(Phaethon aethereus)
Family PHAETHONTIDAE
Old World; Lesser Antilles and Baja
California to Venezuela and Peru

Brown Pelican
(Pelecanus occidentalis)
Family PELECANIDAE
Southern British Columbia and North
Carolina to northern Brazil and Chile

PLATE 10

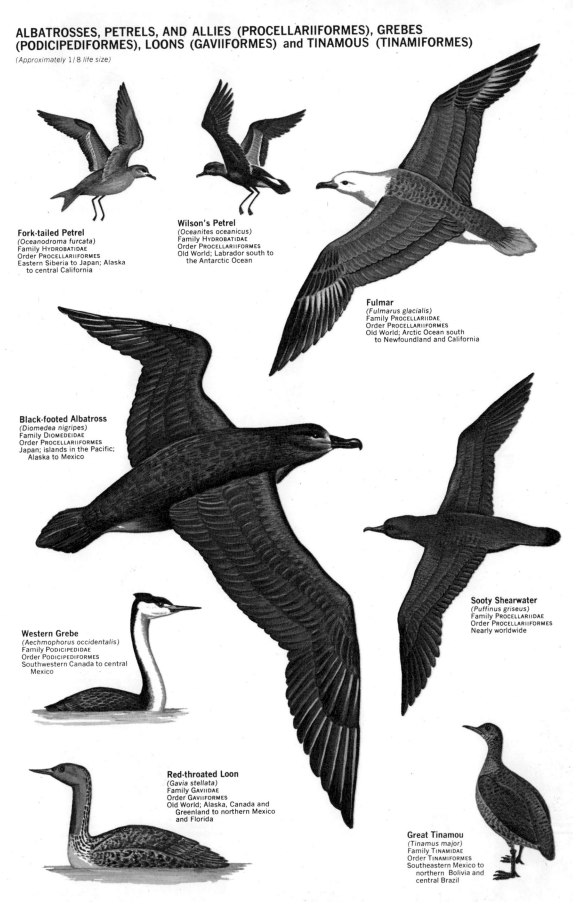

ALBATROSSES, PETRELS, AND ALLIES (PROCELLARIIFORMES), GREBES (PODICIPEDIFORMES), LOONS (GAVIIFORMES) and TINAMOUS (TINAMIFORMES)

(Approximately 1/8 life size)

Fork-tailed Petrel
(Oceanodroma furcata)
Family HYDROBATIDAE
Order PROCELLARIIFORMES
Eastern Siberia to Japan; Alaska
to central California

Wilson's Petrel
(Oceanites oceanicus)
Family HYDROBATIDAE
Order PROCELLARIIFORMES
Old World; Labrador south to
the Antarctic Ocean

Fulmar
(Fulmarus glacialis)
Family PROCELLARIIDAE
Order PROCELLARIIFORMES
Old World; Arctic Ocean south
to Newfoundland and California

Black-footed Albatross
(Diomedea nigripes)
Family DIOMEDEIDAE
Order PROCELLARIIFORMES
Japan; islands in the Pacific;
Alaska to Mexico

Sooty Shearwater
(Puffinus griseus)
Family PROCELLARIIDAE
Order PROCELLARIIFORMES
Nearly worldwide

Western Grebe
(Aechmophorus occidentalis)
Family PODICIPEDIDAE
Order PODICIPEDIFORMES
Southwestern Canada to central
Mexico

Red-throated Loon
(Gavia stellata)
Family GAVIIDAE
Order GAVIIFORMES
Old World; Alaska, Canada and
Greenland to northern Mexico
and Florida

Great Tinamou
(Tinamus major)
Family TINAMIDAE
Order TINAMIFORMES
Southeastern Mexico to
northern Bolivia and
central Brazil

PLATE 11

HANS HANNAU FROM RAPHO GUILLUMETTE

Sulfur-crested Cockatoo *(Cacatua galerita)*
Australia, New Guinea, and the Solomon Islands

T. W. ROTH, H. RUHE FROM PHOTO RESEARCHERS

Violet-crested Touraco
(Gallirex porphyreolophus)
Southeastern Africa

PLATE 12

SOME EXOTIC BIRDS

Common Peafowl *(Pavo cristatus)*
India and Ceylon

ROBERT C. HERMES FROM NATIONAL AUDUBON SOCIETY

Quetzal *(Pharomachrus mocino)*
Central America

P. BERGER FROM NATIONAL AUDUBON SOCIETY

Lesser Bird of Paradise
(Paradisaea minor)
New Guinea and West Indies

Cock-of-the-Rock *(Rupicola peruviana)*
Colombia to Peru

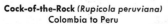

RUSS KINNE FROM PHOTO RESEARCHERS

R. VAN NOSTRAND FROM NATIONAL AUDUBON SOCIETY

WATERBIRDS (*left*) skim the top of the water to pick up small crustacea and other bits of food. (*Right*) The dowitcher's long legs enable it to wade in the water and search for food.

type of flight. The whirring wings of hummingbirds are visible only as a blur. Birds with short, rounded wings usually cannot fly far, but if the flight muscles are powerful, as in grouse or quail, such species are capable of very rapid bursts of speed. Birds of rapid, smooth flight, such as plovers and falcons, have pointed wings of medium length. The golden plover makes nonstop flights of 2,000 miles (3,200 km) over the ocean. Wild ducks and geese also fly strongly for great distances, but their weight is rather great in comparison with their wingspread so that they cannot readily maneuver in the air or dodge obstacles. The most efficient flyers are vultures, which stay aloft for hours with scarcely a flap of the wings by using the ascending air currents.

Now that actual measurements are available, speed of flight has proved to be less than was once claimed. Most small birds travel at rates of only 15 to 30 miles (25 to 50 km) per hour, and even ducks and geese seldom exceed 40 to 60 miles (65 to 95 km) per hour. The peregrine falcon, one of the fastest of all birds, has been clocked at speeds of about 100 miles (160 km) per hour, and there are a few other species, notably some of the larger members of the swift family, that also are capable of such speeds. These figures are for straightaway flight, unassisted by a following wind. When diving, many

birds can attain greater speeds. The golden eagle sometimes plummets earthward from great heights with such velocity that the sound of the air whining through its wing quills is audible for considerable distances.

The upper limit of weight at which flight is possible seems to be about 35 pounds (15 kg). Among the heaviest of flying birds are swans, turkeys, and some of the bustards. These species are exceeded in wingspread by vultures and condors and by the larger albatrosses, whose 11-foot (3-meter) wingspread is the greatest of any bird.

Longevity. Birds live longer in captivity than in the wild. Canaries may live for 12 or 13 years, but small wild birds, as we know from thousands of banding records, seldom reach an age of five or six years. Large birds, with few exceptions, have longer lives than small ones. Eagles, swans, crows, and many other large birds have a potential life span of at least 25 or 30 years. A great horned owl in a zoo lived to be 68 years old, and there are reports of parrots reaching the century mark, although few, if any, of these reports are fully authenticated. The average life of birds is much lower than would be expected from the above figures. There is a tremendous mortality, particularly in the period before and shortly after the young leave the nest.

VULTURES are the scavengers of the bird world. When an animal—like this antelope—dies or is killed, vultures swoop down to clean up the remains.

CAMOUFLAGE helps birds hide from their enemies. The ptarmigan's camouflage is unusual in that it changes with the season. In the summer its feather pattern is streaked (far left), matching the underbrush. In the winter its nearly all-white plumage conceals it in the snow.

Food and Feeding Habits. Birds utilize almost every potential source of food—insects, worms, seeds, fruits, nectar, grass, succulent leaves, fish, and snails. The bill and the feet of birds are variously adapted to aid in the many ways of securing food. Macaws and other large parrots crack nuts and seeds in their powerful bills and then hold them in one foot while extracting the meat with the aid of the tongue. In other species, such as the chicken, hard kernels of grain are swallowed and ground up in the muscular gizzard, by the action of small stones or grit, which the bird swallows. Hawks and owls catch their prey with the aid of their sharp curved claws and then hold it with their feet while rending it with the hooked bill. Loons and cormorants propel themselves swiftly beneath the water in pursuit of fish. Swallows, flycatchers, whippoorwills, and swifts catch insects in the air. The bill of these birds is usually short, and the gape is very wide and surrounded with stiff bristles, which help to enmesh insects. Woodpeckers dig deep into rotten or soft wood in search of the grubs of wood-boring insects, which they extract with their long, barbed tongue. While feeding, they cling to tree trunks with their sharp, curved claws and brace themselves with their tail feathers, which are stiff and

THE WOODCOCK'S CAMOUFLAGE is a mottled plumage that makes it inconspicuous in the twigs and leaves.

pointed. Spoonbills sift through fine mud and silt with the aid of strainerlike projections on the edge of their flat, broad bill. Sunbirds and hummingbirds probe with their needlelike bills in flowers and suck up nectar with their tubular tongues or entrap small insects and spiders with the aid of a brushlike tip on the tongue. These are but a few of the principal feeding adaptations of birds.

Because of their great activity birds consume far more food than might be supposed. This is particularly true of young birds, which grow very rapidly and require large amounts of food. A young owl, for example, has been known to bolt down half a dozen mice at one time, even though the tail of the last victim dangled for a time from the bird's mouth until the rapid process of digestion made room for it.

Many birds, because of their feeding habits, serve man by destroying harmful insects and weed seeds. Flocks of birds often gather in areas where there has been an invasion of insects or rodents and, by consuming great numbers of the invaders, help bring such plagues under control.

Relatively few birds are injurious to man. Blackbirds and crows sometimes rob grainfields; robins and starlings pilfer cherries and other small fruits; some hawks catch poultry and game birds, but most of them also destroy great numbers of harmful rats and mice. Such losses to man usually can be prevented without destroying the birds.

Camouflage, Display, and Courtship. The colors and plumage of birds are extremely varied, and these variations have a relation to behavior. Bright feathers and ornamental plumes serve a function in courtship, but if a bird is too conspicuous it may not be able to avoid its enemies. In many birds the colors blend with the surroundings and thus camouflage the birds from their enemies. Larks and other grassland birds have streaked plumage and are almost invisible as they crouch motionless in the grass or sit on their nests. Perhaps the most remarkable example of camouflage is found in the ptarmigans. These Arctic grouse molt into a pure white plumage in the winter and are then almost invisible against the prevailing snowy landscape. In the summer they acquire a patchwork plumage of black, white, and brown, making them inconspicuous at that season.

In many bird species the males are brilliantly colored, while the females and young are protectively colored. This is the case in such North

A COURTSHIP RITUAL usually precedes mating of birds. The herring gull's ritual consists mainly of pecking and nibbling between the male and female.

ALBATROSS courtship is an elaborate dance with wings spread, accompanied by loud shrieks.

American species as the scarlet tanager and the indigo bunting. So great is the difference between males and females that it is difficult to realize that they belong to the same species. In the two species mentioned and in many others, even the adult male molts into a dull plumage after the breeding season. He does not acquire his bright plumes again until the following spring.

In those species in which only the male is brightly colored, he, as a rule, does not partici-

pate in the duties of incubation or of rearing the young and hence does not jeopardize their safety by attracting enemies to the vicinity of the nest. It must also be remembered that some of the enemies of birds, including most mammals, are, unlike birds, color-blind. Among the most brilliantly colored birds—pheasants, hummingbirds, birds of paradise—and others—one finds many polygamous or promiscuous species. In these, even though more males than females fall victim to predators, the number of males left is sufficient for reproduction.

Birds that possess ornamental plumes display them during courtship. Such displays serve to attract the females and also, in some instances, to drive away other males. The elaborate display of the peacock, in which the stiff wing feathers are audibly rustled to attract attention to the displaying bird, is known to everyone. Cock grouse of several species gather on communal display grounds to strut and perform. They have large, brightly colored sacs on the sides of the head that are inflated with air and then quickly deflated so as to produce a booming noise audible for long distances. The hens come to these display grounds, and their presence leads to much jockeying and fighting among the males. But

ELABORATE PLUMAGE and strutting helps the male sage grouse (right) attract the female for mating.

GANNET pairs show their loyalty to each other during courtship by stretching and crossing their beaks.

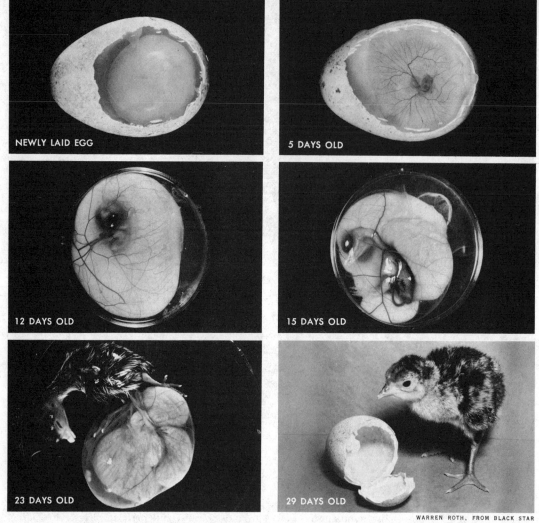

NEWLY LAID EGG

5 DAYS OLD

12 DAYS OLD

15 DAYS OLD

23 DAYS OLD

29 DAYS OLD

DEVELOPMENT OF A TURKEY EMBRYO. The developing embryo first appears as a tiny speck on the yolk's surface. Within a few days both the embryo and its surrounding vessels, which absorb the yolk nutrients, are clearly visible. As the embryo continues to develop, the yolk slowly shrinks and has completely disappeared by the time the bird hatches.

each male is restricted to a small area or territory, which he does not leave and where he does not permit other males to set foot.

The argus pheasant of Borneo carefully clears an area in the jungle so that he can display his long wing plumes without obstruction. Some birds of paradise also make such cleared dancing areas, and the bowerbirds build bowers of twigs in and around which they display themselves and bright objects they bring to the bower. The satin bowerbird of Australia, a blue species with bright blue eyes, decorates its bower with the petals of blue flowers or with any other blue objects it can find. In many species courtship is performed in the air. Male hummingbirds dash through the air to display their iridescent plumage. March hawks perform acrobatics in the air. In species in which the sexes are alike in color, courtship displays often are mutual; for example, albatrosses bow and dance grotesquely as they stand bill to bill.

Displaying birds often call attention to themselves by songs or call notes. Woodpeckers drum with the bill on a dry, resonant branch; snipe produce a whistling sound with their stiff outer tail feathers by diving through the air. In many dull-colored species courtship consists chiefly of the singing of the male. The song serves both to attract a mate and to warn off other males.

Reproduction. The season of reproduction for birds is usually the spring, when food for the young is abundant. Even in the tropics most species nest only once a year, but in equatorial forests this may be at any time of the year. Northern birds that migrate to the tropics to winter do not nest there.

Nests. Birds lay fewer eggs than do oviparous reptiles, but unlike reptiles they incubate them and care for the young after hatching. This increased parental care in birds usually requires a nest to hold the eggs during incubation and the young after hatching. Some reptiles show the first crude beginnings of nest building. Crocodiles and alligators scrape a mass of wet vegetation over their eggs and are said to guard this "nest" until the eggs hatch, although they do not incubate or care for the young. From such crude beginnings have grown the often elaborate nests of birds.

Although most birds build nests, those that lay their eggs on the ground often do not. Many shore birds and terns merely scrape a slight hollow in the sand or grass in which to lay the eggs. The young of such species are usually "nidifu-

FEEDING HUNGRY CHICKS keeps parent birds busy. Here, a male cedar waxwing brings a berry to its waiting young.

gous" or precocial—that is, they are covered with down and follow their mother as soon as they hatch just like chicks or ducklings. In other birds the young remain where hatched for some time, and a substantial nest is usually necessary. The young of such birds are often ugly and naked when hatched, although in hawks and other species they are covered with down. Turkey vultures make no nest, even though their downy young do not leave the cave or hollow where they are hatched for many weeks.

Birds that nest in holes in trees or in the earth often build no nest. Most parrots and owls are examples. Many birds dig a hole in the ground or in a tree in which to lay their eggs. They may or may not make a lining or nest cup in this burrow. Examples are the woodpeckers and many ground-nesting birds—kingfishers, burrowing owls, and others.

REGURGITATED FOOD is hungrily plucked from the parent's bill by two Antarctic ring penguin chicks.

The wood duck and other tree-nesting waterfowl line the nesting cavity with feathers, as do their more numerous relatives that nest on the ground in marshes. In the latter situation the down serves to keep the eggs warm and dry. Eider ducks nest on the bleak, rocky coasts of Norway and Labrador. The mother bird plucks so much down from her own covering to protect her eggs from the inclement weather that the down can be gathered by man and used for blankets or pillows. When the duck leaves her nest, she pulls the down over the eggs to keep them warm and to hide them from enemies.

The earliest known fossil bird, *Archaeopteryx*, was evidently a tree dweller and probably built a nest. All birds that do not now build nests presumably had nest-building ancestors. The most striking "throwback" to a reptilian mode of egg laying is found in the brush turkeys or megapodes of Australia and the South Pacific islands. They bury their eggs in mounds of sand or decaying vegetation which the birds scrape together with their powerful legs and feet. The eggs are not incubated and the young care for themselves as soon as they hatch.

It already is evident that the nest-building habits of birds are easily modified according to

PARTIALLY DIGESTED FOOD is regurgitated by an American egret into the gullet of its hungry young.

A HUMMINGBIRD hovers over its nest as it thrusts food into the gullet of its almost fully grown chick.

conditions and habitats. For this reason nests are not of much help in classifying birds. Most of the American orioles, for example, build elaborate hanging nests, but the cowbird, a closely related member of the same family, builds no nest at all; instead it lays its eggs in the nests of other birds and leaves it to them to hatch and rear the young cowbirds. In other cases the nests of related birds do show a certain uniformity. All swifts have a gluelike saliva that hardens on contact with the air. It is used to glue together the nest materials and to attach the nest itself to a supporting surface. The chimney swift of the United States breaks off dead twigs from trees with its feet and then carries them to the inside of a chimney where they are glued together into a frail platform nest. The edible nest swiftlet of southeastern Asia builds a nest entirely of hardened saliva. (This gelatinous object is melted down by the Chinese and forms the basis of "bird's-nest soup.")

THE HUNGRIEST YOUNG—the one with the loudest cry and longest neck—is fed first by the mother catbird.

Even in families that show considerable variation from species to species in nest-building habits, certain ingrained preferences often are evident. Thus some wrens nest in hollow stubs or in birdhouses, while others, such as the marsh and cactus wrens, build domed nests in grass or bushes. These domed structures provide as secluded a nesting chamber as do holes in trees. Similar tendencies are noticeable among starlings and other birds. The common mynah of India and the too familiar English or house sparrow exhibit adaptability among the members of a single species. Most individuals nest in hollows about buildings or elsewhere, but some build a domed nest in a tree.

In general, variation in nest building among the members of a single species of bird is much less than that found among the species of a family. In a restricted area, such as northeastern United States, well over half of the resident birds build a nest distinctive enough to be recognized even when no eggs or parent birds are present. Yet, birds are inclined to use whatever building material is nearest or most abundant. Baltimore orioles and even robins will use brightly colored yarn if it is available. The chipping sparrow has learned to use horsehair to line its nest and the wood thrush often adds a bit of paper napkin, cellophane, or other man-made material to the fabric of its nest. A downtown New York City pigeon made its nest of paper clips!

When building their nests, most birds work industriously for an hour or two in the morning and again in the late afternoon and rest and feed during the intervening period. In many species both the male and female participate in nest building. Often the female works harder than her mate, and he may limit his activities to bringing nest material for her to shape and fashion. In many species the female builds the nest alone, but there are very few in which the male does so. In certain African weaverbirds the male stakes out a territory, builds a nest, and then seeks a mate. She may add the final lining to the nest. In certain wren species the male suffers from an excess of nest-building zeal. While his mate is safely incubating her eggs in the first nest, he continues to build "dummy" nests or "cock" nests in the vicinity. In some species the male roosts in one of these extra nests; in others the false nests seem to have no function unless perhaps to divert enemies searching for the true nest.

Chickadees and other small birds that winter in the north usually sleep in a tree cavity, sometimes the one in which they nested. Some woodpeckers dig a separate roosting cavity at the approach of winter.

The elaborate structure of many nests is amazing, since birds use only their feet and bill as implements. Moreover, some of the best nest builders, such as the African weaverbirds, have heavy, thick bills adapted for crushing seeds and seemingly unsuited for weaving nests. The red-faced weaver is remarkable because it ties the first shreds of grass to the supporting twigs, using simple knots or half hitches. A related weaverbird builds a nest with both a front and a back exit. Even more remarkable are the Old World tailorbirds. They stitch or sew their grass nests between two large leaves. The leaf is punctured by the sharp bill and the grass is poked through. The tailorbird then wads up or crudely knots the end of the grass to prevent it from slipping back through the leaf.

THE MIGRATORY FLIGHT pattern of Canada geese is a magnificent spectacle. Marshaled in a wedge-shaped formation and honking as they fly, they may reach altitudes of 9,000 feet.

Orioles and their relatives, which build deep hanging nests, first fashion the round opening at or near the top and then gradually extend the nest downward, working from the inside. The penduline titmice of Africa and Asia build a purse-like hanging nest so finely woven of plant down that it immediately resumes its shape after being rolled up in the hand. The entrance of these nests often is covered and protected by a flexible lip that the bird lifts up each time it enters or leaves the nest. At the other extreme are the frail platform nests of doves or herons. These nests are so flimsy that the eggs sometimes are visible through the bottom of the nest.

Many birds cover their nests with bits of leaf or lichen. These are often attached by spider web and serve as camouflage. Among American birds the blue-gray gnatcatcher and the wood pewee build lichen-covered nests that, when completed, look like natural knots or swellings on the limb. Other birds hide their nests among dense twigs or branches. Eagles and hawks can protect their nests from most enemies; they often build a large, conspicuous nest. This may be used and repaired year after year until it attains great size. The nest of the American or bald eagle, the national emblem of the United States, sometimes measures six or eight feet (2 to 2.5 meters) in depth and several feet across. This nest may in time kill the tree in which it is placed, and eventually nest and tree will crash.

Many birds place their nests high in trees or on cliffs where they are safe from enemies. The hanging nests of the American orioles and their relatives are attached to the very ends of thin drooping twigs, so that they are difficult of access. Still other birds place their nests in the vicinity of wasp nests for protection. One of the African weaverbirds places its nest near the occupied nest of a pair of eagles. The eagles do not molest such small birds and their presence keeps away marauding birds and mammals.

As is well known, certain birds are highly sociable and nest in dense colonies. This is particularly true of gulls and other coastal or marshland species. They often place their nests on islands or on cliffs, where they cannot be molested. A further step in community living is found in the sociable weaver of Africa. A large colony of this species builds a huge apartment house nest in a tree. Each of the 30 or more pairs of birds in the colony has an individual nest chamber in the side of this structure. The West Indian palm chat, a relative of the waxwing, also builds a communal nest.

The value of nest building is that greater protection can be given to the eggs. Consequently the risk of their being broken or eaten is reduced, and a greater number in each clutch can be expected to hatch. It is then no longer necessary to lay a large number of eggs to ensure the survival of at least one or two. Also, the more babies there are in the nest, the harder the parents must work to feed them. If there are too many at once, most of them will be underfed and unlikely to survive. So there is a general tendency for birds to lay much smaller clutches than do reptiles, because the reptiles' eggs are comparatively unprotected and liable to damage and the young are not cared for after they hatch.

Eggs. All birds lay hard-shelled eggs, which usually are placed in a nest. Gannets and albatrosses lay only one egg; pigeons, some eagles, and others, two; gulls usually lay three; robins, sandpipers, and many others lay four. As the number of eggs increases, it also becomes more variable. Many small birds lay from three to five eggs per setting, or clutch. If more than one brood is raised per year, as is often the case, the number of eggs in the later clutches may be one or two less. The upper limits in clutch size are found among such birds as quail and coots, which may lay 15 or more eggs. If eggs are taken from the nest during the laying period, most birds continue to lay in an attempt to complete the normal clutch. From this instinct, aided by careful selection, has come the egg-laying feats of the domestic hen, which may lay an egg a day for the better part of her short adult life.

After the eggs are laid they are incubated. In many species only the female incubates; in others both members of a pair take turns on the nest,

MIGRATING FLOCKS stop periodically for food along their flight route. Here a flock of mallards and pintails stop to feed before setting off on the next leg of their journey.

WILFORD L. MILLER, FROM NATIONAL AUDUBON SOCIETY

while in phalaropes and a few other species, the male takes over all the duties of incubating the eggs and caring for the young. The incubation period is as short as 12 days in small songbirds, three weeks in the chicken, about a month in many large water birds, and up to a maximum of two months in the emu. Young birds peck their way through the eggshell with the aid of a little "egg tooth" at the tip of the bill. The egg tooth is then shed.

Young chickens and quail, which are covered with down, usually dry off and leave the nest, never to return, within an hour or two of the time they are hatched. In these and other "precocial" species, as they are called, the parent leads the chicks about, and they instinctively pick up small insects and other bits of food. The parent broods the young to keep them warm at night and during showers. Among many birds the young are helpless and almost or quite naked at birth. In such cases they are fed, brooded, and protected by their parents until they have feathered out and are able to fly. In some hawk species the female guards and feeds the young; the male hunts for the food and brings it to the nest.

The eggs of birds probably were originally white, as are those of reptiles. At present a great variety of markings and many shades of color characterize the eggs of the various species, but brilliant and gaudy colors are absent. Anyone familiar with the birds of a particular region can learn to recognize the eggs of most of the local species. Birds' eggs often match the background closely and so are less apt to be seen by crows or other species that eat eggs. Birds that nest in dark holes in trees—owls, woodpeckers, and others—usually lay white eggs, for in such places the eggs are well concealed from enemies. Pigeons, unlike most birds that have open nests, lay conspicuous white eggs, but one or the other of the parents covers the eggs constantly. Ducks cover their eggs with feathers when they leave the nest.

In polygamous species the male takes no interest in domestic affairs after the time of courtship and mating. Even when both parents participate in the domestic duties, there is often no

great attachment to the mate, and frequent changes occur between broods and from year to year. Among pigeons, swans, and eagles, on the other hand, there is a strong bond, and such species sometimes mate for life.

DEAN AMADON
American Museum of Natural History

Migration. Most birds in the Northern Hemisphere migrate from their nesting regions in the fall to a warmer territory and feeding grounds for the winter months. In the spring they migrate back to their nesting areas. Smaller numbers of Southern Hemisphere birds migrate northward.

Migration may be merely an altitudinal movement, in which the birds descend to a lower altitude for the winter. Birds that migrate in this way include some grouse, nuthatches, and chickadees. Migration may be over short distances, such as that of the bluejay. However, other species travel over long distances to the south or across the Atlantic Ocean or parts of the Pacific. These birds include storks, birds of prey, ducks, geese, swallows, and some songbirds.

Although the exact mechanism of the spring and fall migration impulses is not known, it is believed to involve hormonal factors associated with the sex organs, or gonads. In the spring the gonads grow, and they produce hormones; in the fall they shrink, while their activity falls off. Photo-periodic variations (the seasonal changes in the lengths of night and day) are believed to be an important factor in stimulating the gonadal responses. However, other factors, such as the state of vegetation and the abundance of food, and in some cases the amount of rain, probably contribute to the migratory impulse. Some birds do not migrate unless there is an immediate stimulus, such as the lack of food, or a sudden change in the weather, while others have a strong migratory impulse and depart on a regular schedule.

In migration, the over-all direction of flight is determined by the geographical position of the breeding and winter areas. Among North American birds this direction in autumn is generally south and southeast or southwest; among

European birds, it is south and southwest. Some birds determine this direction by the position of the sun in the daytime and the stars at night, but there still is much to learn about the subjects of navigation and homing.

Some species of birds migrate during the day, others during the night. Pelicans, swallows, storks, birds of prey, and most seed-eating birds migrate during the day. Water birds, American orioles, tanagers, and insect-eating species of the passerines migrate during the night. These species sometimes fly from dusk to dawn, avoiding the danger of landing in unknown territory in the dark. Energy for flying is supplied in part by the unusual amounts of fat, which accumulate in the bodies of these birds before migration.

Although some birds (such as cuckoos, hummingbirds, shrikes, and birds of prey) migrate alone, others (such as wild ducks and geese) migrate in pairs, families, or flocks. Most, however, migrate in flocks, which may include many thousands of birds.

The flock may be a disorderly grouping of its members, or it may be arranged in a specific shape. Rooks fly in an elongated crescent, while Canada geese fly in the well-known wedge-shaped flock. Migratory altitudes range from 200 feet (60 meters) to as much as 29,500 feet (9,000 meters) in the case of geese that migrate over the Himalaya. The height is determined generally by the nature of the terrain and by the weather. However, height above the ground seldom exceeds 3,000 to 4,000 feet (900 to 1200 meters).

Migratory flying speeds also vary. The chipping sparrow flies at a ground speed of 15 mph (25 km), while ducks and geese fly at speeds of 40 to 60 mph (65 to 95 km). Single flights in night migrants are often several hundred miles long. The birds usually accomplish their long journey in a series of stages; they often rest and feed for a few days at some favorite stopping place.

Protection. While traveling in America early in the 19th century, John James Audubon was appalled by the slaughter of wildlife that he observed. In discussing the killing of the great auk, he commented in his journals, "The war of extermination cannot last many years more."

ARTHUR AMBLER, FROM NATIONAL AUDUBON SOCIETY

THE NEARLY EXTINCT nene, or Hawaiian goose, is now being bred in captivity to raise its numbers.

During all the early history of the United States little or no attention was paid to the destruction of birds or other wild animals. Probably the earliest law on the subject was one passed in Massachusetts in 1817, establishing closed seasons for certain mammals and birds shot as game. It was not until many years later that any protection, even in New England, was extended to small birds.

About 1880 it began to be fashionable for women to adorn their hats and other wearing apparel with the feathers of birds, and the whole world was ransacked for fine feathers. To halt the destruction of the birds, societies for bird protection were organized in Britain and on the continent of Europe, and in the United States Audubon societies came into existence and exerted a powerful and permanent influence on the public for the protection of birds (see AUDUBON

THE RAREST BIRD in North America, the ivory-billed woodpecker, is on the verge of extinction.

JAMES TANNER, FROM NATIONAL AUDUBON SOCIETY

ALSO FACING EXTINCTION is the Everglade kite, which eats only one kind of fresh-water snail.

ALLAN D. CRUICKSHANK, FROM NATIONAL AUDUBON SOCIETY

WHOOPING CRANES (*above*), once hunted by sportsmen and driven from nesting areas, are now nearly extinct.

THE CALIFORNIA CONDOR (*right*), now protected by law, inhabits coastal ranges of southern California.

Societies). The result was to discourage the wearing of feather ornaments and restrict the local supply. Laws were passed in most of the states prohibiting the killing of game birds and wildfowl except during limited seasons of the year, or the killing, or destruction of their eggs, of all other birds, with a few exceptions, such as crows and some hawks. With the backing of these laws, it was possible to punish wanton shooting and trapping, to guard breeding colonies of herons (especially the egrets), gulls, terns, and wildfowl, and to carry out plans for educating the young to value birds and other native animals.

In order to complete the reform greater cooperation was needed with foreign efforts directed to the same end. This was seen to be a matter of federal action and resulted in the United States statute of March 4, 1909, known as the Lacey Act. The act prohibited the importa-

tion into the United States of any bird or other animal declared by the secretary of agriculture to be injurious, and forbade common carriers to handle or transport any such animals, or their dead bodies, or parts thereof, or any animals killed in, or shipped from, any state or territory in violation of the laws. This legislation prevented would-be evaders from taking advantage of inequalities between the states concerning open seasons for game.

The differences between state laws covering the shooting seasons for migratory waterfowl brought about conditions that threatened these birds with extinction. Congress took control, first under the McLean Law of 1913 and later through the operation of the Bureau of Biological Survey (now the U.S. Fish and Wildlife Service) in the Department of the Interior. The activities of this unit include the establishment of wildlife refuges throughout the United States and its

MOAS were large wingless ostrich-like birds that inhabited New Zealand. It is believed that they became extinct during the 17th century.

AMERICAN MUSEUM OF NATURAL HISTORY   SMITHSONIAN INSTITUTION   ALFRED GROSS—NATIONAL AUDUBON SOCIETY

THREE SPECIES ERADICATED BY MAN are the dodo (*left*), passenger pigeon (*center*), and heath hen (*right*). The dodo, an inhabitant of the island of Mauritius, was extinct by 1681. The passenger pigeon and heath hen, both of North America, survived until the early 1900's.

possessions. The sites are mainly on submarginal lands not suitable for agricultural purposes and remaining largely in their natural condition. Most of these refuges are on lands controlled solely by the U.S. Fish and Wildlife Service. Large numbers of state, local, and private bird sanctuaries also have been established in the United States.

Bird protectionists in Canada had also been active, but they met with a similar difficulty of differences in provincial laws. Furthermore, action in both the United States and Canada was hampered by the fact that gunners and dealers were shooting and trafficking across the border. It was perceived after the passage of the Migratory Bird Law in 1913 that its full purpose could not be realized in the United States, or forwarded by the Canadians, except by cooperation. This resulted, after much effort, in the formulation of a convention or treaty between the United States and Britain (for Canada) in 1916, unifying the protective laws of both countries. This treaty incorporates the substance of the Migratory Bird Law; provides for closed seasons on migratory game birds; prohibits the killing, capture, or destruction of migratory songbirds, and establishes prohibitory regulations for international commerce in game or other birds.

The destruction of desirable habitats, the increasing use of pesticides, and the tremendous increase in hunting pressure are the greatest threats to bird protection. One of the rarest North American birds is the ivory-billed woodpecker, which may even now be extinct, since no living ivorybills have been observed in recent years. Perhaps the second-rarest species is the whooping crane, with about 30 to 40 survivors on the North American continent. Probably equally as rare or more so is the Everglade kite, a snail-eating hawk restricted to south Florida. The California condor, whose number was estimated at about 40 in 1966, exists primarily in a sanctuary established in the Los Padres National Forest in 1951. Many other rare species, such as the roseate spoonbill, reddish egret, and white pelican, are guarded by wardens of the National Audubon Society and federal conservation agencies.

Interest in the protection of persecuted species of birds, such as hawks, owls, and fish-eating birds, has increased greatly since the 1930's. Most of the states offer protection to all or most of the hawks and owls, and vigorous campaigns are being carried on by Audubon societies, garden clubs, and other groups in an effort to develop public appreciation of the value of predaceous birds. Unfortunately, however, their numbers are declining at an alarming rate, which largely is attributable to senseless and illegal killing. The bald eagle was protected by federal law in the United States in 1940, and in Alaska in 1952. It remains endangered, however, by both vandalistic killing and the widespread use of pesticides.

See also FLIGHT; ORNITHOLOGY; and articles on individual birds, such as ORIOLE; PARROT; SWALLOW; WOODPECKER.

KENNETH D. MORRISON
Mountain Lake Sanctuary

Bibliography

Allen, Arthur A., *Book of Bird Life*, 2d ed. (New York 1961).
Amadon, Dean, *Birds Around the World* (New York 1966).
Armstrong, Edward A., *Bird Display and Behavior*, rev. ed. (New York 1964).
Audubon, John James, *Audubon and His Journals*, ed. by Maria Audubon (New York 1897).
Audubon, John James, *Birds of America*, 7 vols. (New York 1966).
Beebe, William C., *The Bird, Its Form and Function* (New York 1966).
Bent, Arthur C., *Life Histories of North American Birds*, 14 vols. (Washington 1919–48).
Dorst, Jean, *Migration of Birds* (New York 1962).
Fisher, James, and Lockley, R.M., *Sea Birds* (New York 1954).
Gilliard, E. Thomas, *Living Birds of the World* (New York 1958).
Griffin, Donald R., *Bird Migration* (New York 1964).
McLeod, William M., and others, *Avian Anatomy* (Minneapolis 1964).
Marshall, Alexander J., ed., *Biology and Comparative Physiology of Birds*, 2 vols. (New York 1960–61).
Peterson, Roger T., and others, *Field Guide to the Birds of Britain and Europe* (New York 1954).
Reed, Chester A., *North American Bird Eggs*, rev. ed. (New York 1965).
Swinton, William E., *Fossil Birds*, 2d ed. (London 1965).
Tinbergen, Niko, *Bird Life* (New York 1954).
Van Tyne, Josselyn, and Berger, Andrew J., *Fundamentals of Ornithology* (New York 1959).

BIRD CHERRY, a wild cherry tree of North America, classified as *Prunus pennsylvanica*, of the rose family, Rosaceae. It is also called pin, fire, or pigeon cherry. Its small white flower clusters in the spring give way to sour, red fruit. It occurs in thin woodlands of Canada and the northern United States. The name bird cherry also is given in Europe to *P. padus*, the hagberry of Scotland, which resembles the chokecherry.

BIRD LICE are an order of wingless insects that live as parasites, mostly on birds but also on mammals, including dogs, cats, horses, and cattle. They are sometimes called *chewing lice* or *biting lice*. These lice have very flat bodies and are usually less than ⅛ inch (3 mm) long. Their mouthparts are adapted for biting and chewing. The species that are parasitic on birds have two claws on each leg, while the species that are parasitic on mammals have one claw on each leg.

Bird lice feed mostly on feathers, hair, and skin debris, but a few species may bite through the skin or base of the feathers to get blood. Up to 12 generations may develop from eggs in one year. They make up the order Mallophaga.

BIRD OF PARADISE, any of numerous perching birds, usually vividly colored, that live in the trees of the jungles of New Guinea, the Molucca Islands, and northern and western Australia. These birds are best known for their brightly colored, unusual plumes and for their complex courtship behavior.

In the late 19th and early 20th centuries, bird of paradise plumes were used extensively for millinery, and the bird's scalps are still important in the ritual ornamentation of the aboriginal peoples of New Guinea.

Description. Birds of paradise are between 5½ and 40 inches (14–100 cm) long; this overall length includes 24-inch (60-cm) tail feathers in two species. Most birds of paradise have stocky bodies, short, rounded wings, relatively short legs, strong feet adapted for perching, and short, square tails. Their bills may be stout or long and curved.

In most bird of paradise species, the sexes are strikingly different in appearance. The male has elaborate plumes on his head, throat, back, wings, and tail. These plumes, which may be black, green, blue, red, orange, or yellow, become erect during the male's courtship display. They are among the most bizarre of all bird feathers. Some are long and narrow, wirelike, and are twisted at the tips, while others are threadlike, and one species has a series of celluloidlike pennants the whole length of its 24-inch (60-cm) head plumes. In addition to colorful feathers, some males also have brilliant green or yellow coloring on the inside of the mouth. The females of these species are generally dull brown or green. In a few other, rather plain, bird of paradise species, however, the sexes are alike. They are completely black and have only a little blue or green on the throat or head.

Behavior. Birds of paradise are sturdy, active birds, but they are generally not gregarious. Their voices are loud, harsh, and shrill. They usually feed on fruit, berries, seeds, insects, small lizards, and tree frogs.

Courtship. The male begins his courtship display either alone on the forest floor or in a group in trees. The specialized plumes are erected or spread, and the bird moves about so that his iridescent feathers glint. Some courting males assume a horizontal position or hang upside down.

The gaudy plumage and courtship displays not only attract mates but also serve to reduce mating between different species or genera and thus limit wild hybridization. However, mated pairs do not form strong bonds and a large number of wild hybrids are known.

Breeding. The female usually builds a bulky cup-shaped nest of twigs, stems, and leaves on a tree branch, but at least one species is known to nest in a tree cavity. The female then lays one or two pinkish white eggs marked with irregular longitudinal streaks. She generally incubates the eggs and alone cares for the young, although in some of the duller colored species, the male helps to feed the young.

Classification. There are 41 species of birds of paradise, found in two subfamilies: Cnemophilinae and Paradisaeniae in the family Paradiseaidae. Birds of paradise are closely related to the crows and belong to the songbird suborder Oscines of the order Passeriformes.

GEORGE E. WATSON, *Smithsonian Institution*

BIRD-OF-PARADISE FLOWER, the common name of a perennial plant of the genus *Strelitzia* and of the family Strelitziaceae. It is native to southern Africa but is cultivated outdoors in warm climates and in greenhouses by florists. Best known of the five *Strelitzia* species is S. *reginae*, with large, showy, birdlike flowers of bright orange and blue (or yellow in one variety)

JOHN J. SMITH

Bird-of-paradise flower (*Strelitzia reginae*).

standing upright in a long green or purple bract that resembles a boat. The plant grows to about 5 feet (1.5 meters) from a rhizome and has long gray-blue leaves resembling those of the banana. Another species, S. *nicolai*, grows to about 18 feet (5.5 meters) and has blue and gray flowers.

BIRD SANCTUARIES. See BIRD—*Protection;* FISH AND WILDLIFE SERVICE.

BIRD SPIDER, any of the very large tarantulas of the family Theraphosidae, inhabiting tropical jungles, that may sometimes catch and eat small birds. See TARANTULA.

Most of the 400 species, which belong to the family Hippoboscidae (louse flies), have fully developed wings, but in many kinds the delicate membranous rear portion soon breaks off after the young flies have found a new host. The sheep tick is completely wingless.

A great many of the species attack mammals, especially horses, camels, goats, and deer.

Bird ticks are unusual in that the female does not lay eggs. Instead, the larva develops to maturity within the abdomen of the female.

BIRD WOMAN. See SACAGAWEA.

BIRDLIME is a viscous substance used for entangling small birds. In the United States capturing birds by any means is illegal, unless permits are secured. In some other countries, the birdlime method of bird snaring is employed.

Twigs for the purpose are smeared with birdlime, which mats the feathers of birds' wings upon contact and makes flight impossible.

The substance may be prepared in several ways, the commonest of which uses the bark of holly, *Ilex aquifolium.* The bark is boiled in water for several hours, after which the water is strained off and the bark left to ferment for two or three weeks. The substance assumes a mucilaginous form, and after being pounded in a mortar and worked with the hands in water is fit for use. This substance, when prepared, is of a greenish color and very tenacious.

BIRDS, The, a comedy by Aristophanes. It was first performed in Athens in 414 B.C. Critics rank *The Birds* among Aristophanes' masterpieces, commending its imaginative invention and its lyrical charm. But its most enduring interest lies in its pungent satire on political utopianism. This theme may have been suggested by the grandiose dreams of empire connected with the Athenians' ill-fated Sicilian expedition that had sailed to conquer Syracuse several months before the play was produced.

The play tells how two disillusioned Athenians, Peithetaerus (Persuasive) and Euelpides (Hopeful), go to the bird-king Epops to learn if there is a peaceful place in the world where they can settle. When Epops cannot give a positive answer, Peithetaerus proposes that the birds themselves establish a state in the air, walling off heaven from earth. There they would become the rulers of the universe by blocking the rise of scented smoke from the burnt sacrifices of men and thus starving the gods into submission. Epops agrees and summons the chorus of birds, which cooperates in founding Nephelococcygia (Cloudcuckooland).

Ridiculing contemporary mystical philosophies, the chorus tells how the whole universe emerged from a cosmic world-egg, proving that birds were the first of created beings. Several episodes follow in which various human imposters are repulsed in their efforts to join the new commonwealth. Finally, Peithetaerus receives a delegation from Olympus bringing news of the gods' surrender. The action ends with his marriage to Basileia (Sovereignty), a gift from Zeus.

RICHMOND Y. HATHORN
Author of "Handbook of Classical Drama"
Further Reading: Murray, Gilbert, *Aristophanes* (New York 1933); Norwood, Gilbert, *Greek Comedy* (London 1931); Whitman, Cedric, *Aristophanes and the Comic Hero* (Cambridge, Mass., 1964).

BIRD'S-NEST SOUP is an Oriental delicacy made principally from the nests of sea swifts of the genus *Collocalia.* The nests are made of the birds' saliva, which becomes gelatinous and hardens. The whitest nests, produced by the species *Collocalia fuciphaga,* are considered the best for soup. The nests are found chiefly in caves on uninhabited islands of the South China Sea and adjacent bays.

BIRDSEYE, Clarence (1886–1956), American inventor and industrialist, who founded the frozen-food industry. He was born in Brooklyn, N.Y., on Dec. 9, 1886, and attended Amherst College for two years (1908–1910) by working as a field naturalist for the U. S. government, an activity he continued until 1912. He then took part in a fur-trading expedition to Labrador (1912–1916), where he observed that many foodstuffs will keep indefinitely when frozen. In 1917 he returned to New York, determined to turn this information to commercial use.

In seven years of experiments, Birdseye developed a method of reproducing the rapid, dry freezing that occurs in the Arctic, and also hit upon the concept of freezing food in compact, packageable blocks. In 1924, Birdseye and some friends formed a company (later called Birdseye General Foods) that placed packaged frozen fish on the market in 1925. The firm was sold in 1929 to the Postum Company, which assumed the name General Foods Corporation. A millionaire by the early 1930's, Birdseye was able to devote most of his time to invention, and obtained more than 300 patents. In 1949 he perfected anhydrous freezing, which cut normal freezing time from 18 hours to 90 minutes and also reduced preparation times. Birdseye died in New York City on Oct. 7, 1956.

LEONARD M. FANNING
Author of "Fathers of Industries"

BIRDWOOD, William Riddell (1865–1951), British field marshal who commanded the Anzacs (Australian-New Zealand Army Corps) in an unsuccessful Allied attempt in World War I to open the Dardanelles. Born in Kirkee, Bombay presidency, India, on Sept. 13, 1865, he attended the Royal Military College at Sandhurst. After he had served as military secretary to Lord Kitchener in South Africa and India, Kitchener chose him to command the Anzacs, who landed on April 25, 1915, on the Gallipoli Peninsula.

Constantly in the forward lines, Birdwood inspired the valiant Anzac force, which clung precariously to the rocky peninsula for almost eight months. In all, the Turks inflicted 214,000 casualties on the combined British forces on the peninsula. Birdwood then led the withdrawal of all Allied forces without the loss of a man (see WORLD WAR I–11. *Turkish Campaigns*).

Birdwood later commanded the British Fifth Army in the last campaign on the western front in France. He was commander in chief of British forces in India in 1925, when he was promoted to field marshal. In 1938, while he was the master of Peterhouse, Cambridge, he was created 1st Baron Birdwood. He wrote two autobiographical books, *Khaki and Gown* (1941) and *In My Time* (1946).

CHARLES B. MCDONALD
Deputy Chief Historian, Department of the Army

BIRGITTA, Saint. See BRIDGET, SAINT.

BIRKENHEAD, bûr′kən-hed, **1st Earl of** (1872–1930), British lawyer and public official. Ambitious, often intemperate in rhetoric, Birkenhead was equally often conciliatory and constructive away from the glare of publicity. He was born Frederick Edwin Smith, on July 12, 1872, in Birkenhead, England. At Oxford, where he quickly revealed his exceptional forensic skill, he took an honors degree in jurisprudence in 1895. He was called to the bar in 1899 and began a successful practice in Liverpool.

Meanwhile, his political ambitions led him to the public platform and plunged him into the tumultuous conflict over the Irish question. From the beginning he was an Orange sympathizer, and his support for Ulster never wavered, however his tactics might change. In 1906 he was elected to Parliament for the Walton division of Liverpool, representing that constituency for the next 11 years. His maiden speech, on fiscal policy, was a brilliant effort and overnight made him a man to be watched in the Conservative party. He was one of the diehards who resisted to the end the Parliament Act of 1911, which broke the veto power of the House of Lords.

In 1911, by now a privy councillor, he was "galloping" with Sir Edward Carson in supporting Ulster's resistance to the Home Rule Bill. He nevertheless tried behind the scenes to find some accommodation that would protect Ulster while meeting the needs of the parts of Ireland that favored Home Rule. In 1915, Smith became solicitor general, then attorney general, in the coalition government. His appointment as lord chancellor in 1919 was not a popular one, but Baron Birkenhead, as he became in the same year, carried out its duties with good judgment and a temperance quite foreign to his public reputation. He was particularly successful in promoting the huge Law of Property Act (1922), which was concerned with land transfer.

Unlike many of his Conservative colleagues, Birkenhead by the summer of 1921 came around to support Prime Minister Lloyd George's efforts to solve the Irish question by negotiation and consent. With the fall of Lloyd George (1922), Birkenhead left the lord chancellorship and received an earldom. In 1924 he returned to office as secretary of state for India, but it was an uncongenial position, and he retired in 1928 to go into private business. He died in London on Sept. 30, 1930.

HENRY R. WINKLER, *Rutgers University*

Further Reading: Birkenhead, 2d Earl of, *Frederick Edwin Earl of Birkenhead,* rev. ed. (London 1959).

BIRKENHEAD, bûr′ken-hed, a port and industrial center in Cheshire, England, is on the west bank of the Mersey estuary. It is opposite Liverpool, to which it is connected by road and railway tunnels. Birkenhead has an extensive system of docks, amalgamated with the Liverpool system since 1858, and is a major shipbuilding center. Other industries include flour milling, food processing, and engineering.

A shipyard was established here in 1824, but Birkenhead remained a small village until 1847, when opening of the docks stimulated its development. The first iron vessel in England was built here in 1829. The *Alabama,* the famous Confederate commerce raider in the American Civil War, was built in the Birkenhead shipyards. Birkenhead became a county borough in 1888. Population: (1961) 141,813.

GARRETT BIRKHOFF, American mathematician, has made important contributions to the theory of mathematics.

BIRKHOFF, bur′kôf, **Garrett** (1911–   ), American mathematician, who made important contributions to abstract mathematics. Birkhoff was born in Princeton, N. J., on Jan. 10, 1911, the son of the mathematician George David Birkhoff. Garrett received his B. A. from Harvard University in 1932 and was a junior fellow in Harvard's Society of Fellows from 1933 to 1936. He became a member of the Harvard faculty in 1936 and was appointed professor of pure and applied mathematics at the same institution in 1946.

Birkhoff made important studies in the abstract theory of structures, or lattices. In his *Lattice Theory* (1940) and earlier works from about 1934, he defined and developed the idea of a lattice and showed that many mathematical studies could be interpreted as special cases of lattice algebras. Boolean algebra, for example, was shown to be a special type of lattice, as were both projective geometry and affine geometry. In 1940, Birkhoff showed that the abstract function spaces that were developed early in the 20th century could be interpreted as lattices with certain postulates defining a partial ordering of the elements.

Birkhoff also contributed to the introduction of these ideas into mathematical education. With Saunders MacLane, he wrote *A Survey of Modern Algebra* (1941), which became a standard textbook for undergraduates in this field. Other books deal with topics in applied mathematics: *Hydrodynamics* (1950) and *Jets, Wakes, and Cavities* (with E. Zarantonello, 1957).

Birkhoff received honorary degrees from the National University of Mexico in 1958, the University of Lille, France, in 1960, and the Case Institute of Technology in 1964. A member of many scholarly societies, he was elected a vice president of the American Mathematical Society, the American Academy of Arts and Sciences, and the American Philosophical Society. He also served as president of the Society for Industrial and Applied Mathematics.

BIRKHOFF, bûr'kôf, **George David** (1884–1944), American mathematician, who made important contributions to the theory of dynamical systems, such as the solar system. Particularly inspired by the work of the French mathematician Henri Poincaré, he examined the motions of bodies through his work on asymptotic expansions and boundary value problems of linear differential equations. He investigated the general behavior of the paths of moving bodies as solutions of linear equations of the first order, studied the stability and periodicity of orbits, and made essential contributions to the so-called ergodic theories that have developed since 1931. Birkhoff did related studies on closed geodesics on convex surfaces and the three-body problem. He also contributed to the theory of relativity and the 4-color problem and was involved in the application of mathematics to other fields such as art and even ethics.

Birkhoff was born in Overisel, Mich., on March 21, 1884. He studied at the University of Chicago and at Harvard, receiving his Ph. D. from Chicago in 1907. After teaching at the University of Wisconsin and at Princeton, he was professor of mathematics at Harvard from 1912 until his death, on Nov. 12, 1944, at Cambridge.

DIRK STRUIK
Massachusetts Institute of Technology

Further Reading: Birkhoff, George David, *Collected Mathematical Papers* (New York 1950), id., *Aesthetic Measure* (Cambridge, Mass., 1930).

BIRLING, bûrl'ing, is a sport in which contestants perform certain maneuvers while treading on a floating log. Also called *logrolling,* the activity originated among North American lumberjacks about 1840. In its modern form, birling consists of logrolling, log racing or poling, and trick riding.

In logrolling, two opponents (on a single floating log) spin, stop, and reverse the log with their feet, each endeavoring to maneuver the adversary off balance and into the water. Dislodging an opponent is called a fall; two falls out of three constitute a match. In log racing, each contestant, standing upright on a log, uses a long pike pole to guide and propel his log over a measured course. In trick riding, performers display their skills in spectacular and dangerous exhibitions on a log.

I. DONALD BOWDEN

CANADIAN BIRLING CHAMPION Jubiel Wickheim (*right*) keeps his balance in a demonstration of logrolling.

Birling grew out of the hazardous task of working to prevent log jams as cut timber floated downstream to the sawmills with the spring thaw. Lumbermen with hooked poles and hand spikes worked on huge timber rafts, pushing and prying the logs to control their rush in the swift-flowing waters. After the spring drive, rivermen renowned for their daring staged contests, encouraged by high stakes offered by company owners and by the wagers of fellow loggers. Rules were devised in the process, and the first national championship tournament, sponsored by the Lumbermen's Association of America, was held at the Trans-Mississippi Exposition in Omaha, Nebr., in 1898. Since then, tournaments and championships have been held in the United States and Canada from time to time, but the sport's present popularity comes from demonstrations given by professional birlers at fairs and regattas.

HENRY H. ROXBOROUGH
Author of "Great Days in Canadian Sport"